SEP 0 2 2004

P9-BJB-828

OUR
#1
BEST-
SELLER!

2005

Schroeder's
ANTIQUES
Price Guide

Edited by

Sharon & Bob

Huxford

cb

COLLECTOR BOOKS

A Division of Schroeder Publishing Co.

PURCHASED WITH
NEW YORK STATE
CENTRAL LIBRARY
BOOK FUNDS

Geneva Free Library
244 Main St.
Geneva, N. Y. 14456
Tel. 315-789-5303

COLLECTOR BOOKS
P.O. Box 3009
Paducah, Kentucky 42002-3009
www.collectorbooks.com

Copyright © 2005 Schroeder Publishing Co., Inc.

All rights reserved. No part of this book may be reproduced, stored
in any retrieval system, or transmitted in any form, or by any means
including but not limited to electronic, mechanical, photocopy, recording,
or otherwise, without the written consent of the editors and publisher.

The current values in this book should be used only as a guide. They are not intended to set prices, which vary from one section of the country to another. Auction prices as well as dealer prices vary greatly and are affected by condition as well as demand. Neither the editors nor the publisher assumes responsibility for any losses that might be incurred as a result of consulting this guide.

Searching For A Publisher?

We are always looking for people knowledgeable within their fields. If you feel that there is a real need for a book on your collectible subject and have a large comprehensive collection, contact Collector Books.

Introduction

As the editors and staff of *Schroeder's*, our goal is to compile the most useful, comprehensive, and accurate background and pricing information possible. Our guide encompasses nearly five hundred categories, many of which you will not find in other price guides. Our sources are varied; we use auction results and dealer lists, and we consult with national collectors' clubs, recognized authorities, researchers, and appraisers. We have by far the largest advisory board of any similar publication on the market. Each year we add several new advisors and now have over 450 who cover almost all our categories. They go over our computer print-outs line by line, deleting listings that are misleading or too vague to be of merit; they often send background information and photos. We appreciate their assistance very much. Only through their expertise and experience in their special fields are we able to offer with confidence what we feel are useful, accurate evaluations that provide a sound understanding of the dealings in the marketplace today. Correspondence with so large an advisory panel adds months of extra work to an already monumental task, but we feel that to a very large extent this is the foundation that makes *Schroeder's* the success that it has become.

Our Directory, which you will find in the back of the book, lists each contributor by state. These are people who have allowed us to photograph various examples of merchandise from their show booths, sent us pricing information, or in any way have contributed to this year's book. If you happen to be traveling, consult the Directory for shops along your way. We also list clubs who have worked with us and auction houses who have agreed to permit us the use of photographs from their catalogs.

Our advisory board lists only names and home states, so check the Directory for addresses and telephone numbers should you want to correspond with one of our experts. Remember, when you do, *always* enclose a self-addressed, stamped envelope (SASE). Thousands of people buy our guide, and hundreds contact our advisors. The only agreement we have with our advisors is that they edit their categories. They are in no way obligated to answer mail. Some are dealers who do many shows a month. The time they spend at home may be very limited, and they may not be open to contacts. There's no doubt that the reason behind the success of our book is their assistance. We regret seeing them becoming more and more burdened by phone and mail inquiries. We have lost some of our good advisors for this reason, and when we do, the book suffers and consequently, so do our readers. Many of our listed reference sources report that they constantly receive long distance calls (at all hours) that are really valuation requests. If they are registered appraisers, they make their living at providing such information and expect a fee for their service and expertise.

If you find you need more information than *Schroeder's* provides, there are other sources available to you. Go to your local library; check their section on reference books. Museums are public facilities that are willing and able help you establish the origin and possibly even the value of your particular treasure. In today's world of e-commerce, there are many websites you may visit that are full of pertinent, up-to-date information. Check the yellow pages of your phone book. Other cities' phone books are available from either your library or from the telephone company office. Look under the heading Antique Dealers. Those who are qualified appraisers will mention this credit in their advertisement. But remember that if you sell to a dealer, he will expect to buy your merchandise at a price low enough that he will be able to make an appreciable profit when he sells it. Once you decide to contact one of these appraisers, unless you intend to see them directly, you'll need to take photographs. Don't send photos that are under or over exposed, out of focus, or shot against a background that detracts from important details you want to emphasize. It is almost impossible for them to give you a value judgement on items they've not seen when your photos are of poor quality. Shoot the front, top, and the bottom; describe any marks and numbers (or send a pencil rubbing), explain how and when you acquired the article, and give accurate measurements and any further background information that may be helpful.

The auction houses listed in the Directory nearly all have a staff of appraisal experts. If the item you're attempting to research is of the caliber of material they deal with, they can offer extremely accurate evaluations. Of course, most have a fee. Be sure to send them only professional-quality photographs. Tell them if you expect to consign your item to their auction. If you disagree with the value they suggest, you are under no obligation to do so.

Nearly 500 categories are included in our book. We have organized our topics alphabetically, following the most simple logic, usually either by manufacturer or by type of product. If you have difficulty in locating your subject, consult the index. Our guide is unique in that much more space has been allotted to background information than in any other publication of this type. Our readers tell us that these are features they enjoy. To be able to do this, we have adopted a format of one-line listings wherein we describe the items to the fullest extent possible by using several common-sense abbreviations; they will be easy to read and understand if you will first take the time to quickly scan through them.

The Editors

Editorial Staff

Editors
Sharon and Bob Huxford

Research and Editorial Assistants
Loretta Suiters, Michael Drollinger, Donna Newnum, Amanda Drollinger

Layout
Terri Hunter

Scanning
Donna Ballard

Cover Design
Beth Summers

On the front cover: Buckeye Syrup Dispenser, figural ceramic, 8½"x12", EX+, $2,100.00 (photo courtesy Randy Inman Auctions); American Handkerchief Box, blue, Fostoria, $1,500.00 (photo courtesy Gene Florence); Candy Container, pumpkin-head man with hat, 5", $225.00 (photo courtesy Dunbar Gallery); Gustav Stickley Chalet Desk, #505, early narrow form, unsigned, 24"wx17"d x46"h, VG, $3,750.00 (photo courtesy Treadway/Toomey Galleries); Parian Doll, fancy hairdo with molded blue tiara, 24", $1,900.00 (photo courtesy McMasters Harris Auctions); Duffner & Kimberly Ivy Design Table Lamp, "granite" glass on cast bronze base, signed Duffner & Kimberly New York, 17", $17,360.00 (photo courtesy Fontaine's Auctions); Van Briggle Vase, Dos Cabezas under blue and tan matte glaze, incised marks, 1918, 7¾", $3,750.00; South Bend Bait Co. Midget Underwater Minnow, 1920 – 1939, 2½", $35.00 – 50.00 (photo courtesy Dudley and Deanie Murphy).

On the back cover: Rookwood Vase, large double-handled, matt glase with berry and leaf decoration on a purple, blue, and green mottled ground, 1924, 9", $1,100.00.

Listing of Standard Abbreviations

The following is a list of abbreviations that have been used throughout this book in order to provide you with the most detailed descriptions possible in the limited space available. No periods are used after initials or abbreviations. When two dimensions are given, height is noted first. If only one dimension is listed, it will be height, except in the case of bowls, dishes, plates, or platters, when it will be diameter. The standard two-letter state abbreviations apply.

For glassware, if no color is noted, the glass is clear. Hyphenated colors, for example blue-green, olive-amber, etc., describe a single color tone; colors divided by a slash mark indicate two or more colors, i.e. blue/white. Teapots, sugar bowls, and butter dishes are assumed to be 'with cover.' Condition is extremely important in determining market value. Common sense suggests that art pottery, china, and glassware values would be given for examples in pristine, mint condition, while suggested prices for utility wares such as Redware, Mocha, and Blue and White Stoneware, for example, reflect the probability that since such items were subjected to everyday use in the home they may show minor wear (which is acceptable) but no notable damage. Values for other categories reflect the best average condition in which the particular collectible is apt to be offered for sale without the dealer feeling it necessary to mention wear or damage. For instance, advertising items are assumed to be in excellent condition since mint items are scarce enough that when one is offered for sale the dealer will most likely make mention of that fact. The same holds true for toys, banks, coin-operated machines, and the like. A basic rule of thumb is that an item listed as VG (very good) will bring 40% to 60% of its mint price — a first-hand, personal evaluation will enable you to make the final judgement; EX (excellent) is a condition midway between mint and very good, and values would correspond.

AD	after dinner
Am	American
appl	applied
att	attributed to
bbl	barrel
bk	back
bl	blue
blk	black
brn	brown
bulb	bulbous
bsk	bisque
b3m	blown 3-mold
C	century
c	copyright
ca	circa
cb	cardboard
Chpndl	Chippendale
CI	cast iron
compo	composition
cr/sug	creamer and sugar
c/s	cup and saucer
cvd	carved
cvg	carving
dbl	double
decor	decoration
demi	demitasse
dk	dark
Dmn Quilt	Diamond Quilted
drw	drawer
dtd	dated
dvtl	dovetail
emb	embossed, embossing
embr	embroidered
Emp	Empire
eng	engraved, engraving
EPNS	electroplated nickel silver
EX	excellent
Fed	Federal
fr	frame, framed
Fr	French
ft, ftd	foot, feet, footed
G	good
gr	green
grad	graduated
grpt	grain painted
H	high, height
Hplwht	Hepplewhite
hdl, hdld	handle, handled
HP	hand painted
illus	illustration, illustrated by
imp	impressed
ind	individual
int	interior
Invt T'print	Inverted Thumbprint
irid	iridescent
L	length, long
lav	lavender
ldgl	leaded glass
litho	lithograph
lt	light
M	mint
mahog	mahogany
mc	multicolor
MIB	mint in box
MIG	Made in Germany
MIP	mint in package
mk	mark
MOC	mint on card
MOP	mother-of-pearl
mt, mtd	mount, mounted
NE	New England
NM	near mint
NRFB	never removed from box
NP	nickel plated
opal	opalescent
orig	original
o/l	overlay
o/w	otherwise
Pat	patented
pc	piece
ped	pedestal
pk	pink
pnt	paint
porc	porcelain
prof	professional
QA	Queen Anne
re	regarding
rfn	refinished
rnd	round
rpl	replaced
rpr	repaired
rpt	repainted
rstr	restored
rtcl	reticulated
rvpt	reverse painted
s&p	salt and pepper
sgn	signed
SP	silverplated
sq	square
std	standard
str	straight
sz	size
trn	turned, turning
turq	turquoise
uphl	upholstered
VG	very good
Vict	Victorian
vnr	veneer
W	width
wht	white
w/	with
w/o	without
X, Xd	cross, crossed
yel	yellow
(+)	has been reproduced

A B C Plates

Children's plates featuring the alphabet as part of the design were popular from as early as 1820 until after the turn of the century. The earliest English creamware plates were decorated with embossed letters and prim moralistic verses, but the later Staffordshire products were conducive to a more relaxed mealtime atmosphere, often depicting playful animals and riddles or scenes of pleasant leisure-time activities. They were made around the turn of the twentieth century by American potters as well. All featured transfer prints, but color was sometimes brushed on by hand to add interest to the design.

Be sure to inspect these plates carefully for damage, since condition is a key price-assessing factor, and aside from obvious chips and hairlines, even wear can substantially reduce their values. Another problem for collectors is the fact that there are current reproductions of glass and tin plates, particularly the glass plate referred to as Emma (child's face in center) and a tin plate showing children with hoops. These plates are so common as to be worthless as collectibles.

For further information we recommend *ABCs of ABC Ware* by Davida and Irving Shipkowitz (Schiffer Books). Our advisor for this category is Dr. Joan George; she is listed in the Directory under New Jersey.

Ceramic

A, Apple, Ape, Air, mc transfer, unmk, 7".................................185.00
Aesop's Fable, hare & tortoise, mc transfer, unmk, 6½" 175.00
Aesop's Fable, man & boy carrying donkey, bl transfer, unmk, 7" ...135.00
Artist sets up easel, center dmn panel, mc transfer, 8¾" 150.00
Baby Bunting & Her Little Dog, mc transfer, unmk, 7¼" 125.00
Bird & flowers, brn transfer, A Shaw & Son, 7½" 120.00
Boy w/instrument eats bread by fence, brn transfer, unmk, 7½" .120.00
Candle fish, Indian scene, blk transfer, CA & Sons, 6½" 150.00
Child on chair w/puppet, blk transfer, unmk, 6" 125.00
Children skating, mc transfer, unmk, 5½".....................................140.00
Children w/kite, mc transfer, unmk, 6" 145.00
Crusoe on the Raft, mc transfer, RD No 59963 BP Co, 8¼" 175.00
David & Goliath, blk transfer, HC Edmiston, 6" 125.00
Dog, The; mc transfer, unmk, 7¼" 165.00
Dove, mc transfer at left, printed ABCs right, RD No 154, 6½" ...145.00
Family harvesting wheat, mc transfer, unmk, 5" 140.00
Feeding the Donkey, blk transfer, Powell & Bishop, 7" 140.00
Ferret, brn transfer, emb ABC rim, Adams, 7"............................135.00
Flowers That Never Fade, Cheerfulness, blk transfer, Meakin, 5¾" 235.00
Franklin's Proverbs, Little Strokes..., mc transfer, unmk, 6" 165.00
Franklin's Proverbs, Plough Deep..., blk transfer, unmk, 8" 140.00
Girl & ducks, mc transfer, Elsmore & Son, 7" 125.00
Girl w/pups in basket, mc transfer, pk lustre rim, unmk Germany, 7".110.00
Girls (2) w/flowers, mc transfer, unmk, 7"...................................140.00
Horse portrait, blk transfer, W Adams & Co..., 1891, 7¼" 125.00
Humpty Dumpty Sat on a Wall, Wood & Son, later, 7", from $30 to....40.00
Hunters (2) w/dogs (2), brn transfer, CA & Sons, 6½"...............125.00
Kittens (3) taking bath, mc transfer, unmk, 8" 165.00
Lovers in interior scene, mc transfer, emb rim, unmk, 5¾".........140.00
Magpie, red transfer, Edge Malkin, 7¼" 120.00
Mother & daughter in garden, blk transfer, Powell & Bishop, 5¼" 125.00
Nursery Rhymes, Ding Dong Dell, mc transfer, unmk, 8¼" 225.00
Nursery Tales, Whittington & His Cat, RD No 75,500, 8".........225.00
Off w/Him, teeter-totter scene, brn transfer, unmk, 5" 140.00
Oriental Hotel, red transfer, unmk, 5½" 135.00
Rider Rents Horse, center dmn panel, mc transfer, CA & Sons, 7½"..150.00
Soldier tipping hat, blk transfer, JF Wileman, 5" 185.00
Spanish couple dancing, brn transfer, emb rim, unmk, 7" 115.00
Spelling Bee, children in scene, mc transfer, unmk, 5¾" 135.00

Tiger, mc transfer in sq fr, BP Co, 6½" 200.00
Timely Rescue, tiger scene, blk transfer, CA & Sons, 6½".........135.00

Glass

ABCs, numerals, clock face, unmk, 7", from $50 to 60.00
ABCs (emb & pnt) along rim, milk glass, unmk, 7", from $50 to.60.00
Christmas Eve, unmk, 6"..150.00
Diamond center (like snowflake), unmk, 6¼", from $50 to 60.00
Ducks, deep yel, unmk, 6", from $60 to..70.00
Emma (child's face), vaseline, bl or orange, unmk, 8", ea..............30.00
Fan center, scalloped rim, unmk, 6", from $65 to...........................75.00
Months, days, clock face & scalloped ABC rim, unmk, 7" 60.00
Numbers around center, ABC rim, carnival glass, unmk, 7½" 120.00
President Garfield, smooth rim, 6" 150.00

Rabbit, embossed ABC rim, 6", $55.00.

Rooster, smooth rim, unmk, 6", from $65 to 75.00
Sancho Panza & Dapple center, unmk, 6", from $50 to 60.00

Tin

ABCs emb around rim, unmk, 2¾", from $65 to.........................100.00
ABCs emb around rim, unmk, 6¼", from $60 to 95.00
ABCs emb in center sq, unmk, 8", from $80 to 100.00
After Supper Run a Mile, 2-color litho, Kemp...Toronto, 6", up to 200.00
General Tom Thumb, full-length portrait, mc enamel, unmk, 3", up to..300.00
Girls chasing butterflies, mc litho, Made in USA, 6", from $110 to...150.00
Her Majesty Queen Victoria, emb rim, unmk, 8", from $300 to .400.00
Horse emb in center, emb ABC rim, unmk, 5½", from $160 to .200.00
Liberty, emb rim, unmk, 5½", from $110 to................................150.00
Mary Had a Little Lamb, unmk, 7¾", from $130 to 160.00
Simple Simon, Tudor Plate Oneida Community, 6", from $65 to .95.00

Abingdon

From 1934 until 1950, the Abingdon Pottery Co. of Abingdon, Illinois, made a line of art pottery with a white vitrified body decorated with various types of glazes in many lovely colors. Novelties, cookie jars, utility ware, and lamps were made in addition to several lines of simple yet striking art ware. Fern Leaf, introduced in 1937, featured molded vertical feathering. La Fleur, in 1939, consisted of flowerpots and flower-arranger bowls with rows of vertical ribbing. Classic, 1939 – 40, was a line of vases, many with evidence of Chinese influence. Several marks were used, most of which employed the company name. In 1950 the company reverted to the manufacture of sanitary ware that had been their mainstay before the art ware division was formed.

Highly decorated examples and those with black, bronze, or red glaze usually command at least 25% higher prices.

For further information we recommend *Abingdon Pottery Artware 1934 – 1950, Stepchild of the Great Depression*, by Joe Paradis (Schiffer).

#A1, vase, What Not, 3½"	55.00
#P7, jardiniere, La Fleur, 6" dia	20.00
#101, vase, Alpha, 10"	25.00
#113, water jug	90.00
#120, vase, Classic, 10"	25.00
#149, flowerpot, La Fleur, 3"	15.00
#152, flowerpot, La Lleur, 6"	12.50
#154, bowl, La Fleur, Classic, 9"	20.00
#170, vase, Classic, 7"	23.00
#180, vase, Floral, 10"	55.00
#305, bookends, Sea Gull, 6", pr	125.00
#306, ashtray, Abingdon, 8x3"	35.00
#321, bookends, Russian, 6½", pr	175.00
#324, vase, Rope, 6¼"	20.00
#338, bowl, sq w/lid, 4¾"	50.00
#348, box, cigarette; Trix, 3¾x4¾"	40.00
#354, box, Trixtra, 2x3"	20.00
#355, candle holders, Eiffel, pr	75.00
#360, candle holders, Quatrain, sq, 3", pr	40.00
#376F, wall mask, female, 6½"	150.00
#381, vase, Rhythm, 5½"	25.00
#391, vase, Glory, 7½"	40.00
#401, tea tile, Coolie, 5½"	75.00
#412, floor vase, Volute, 15"	55.00
#424, bowl, Fern Leaf, 8½"	75.00
#444D, bookends, Dolphin, 5¾", pr	45.00
#456, ashtray, New Mode, 5¾"	20.00
#457, wall pocket, Ionic, 9"	65.00
#469, vase, Dutch Boy, 8"	50.00
#484, fan vase, 8½"	10.00
#499, bookends, Trojan Head, 7½", pr	175.00
#520, vase, Baden, 9"	25.00
#522, vase, Barre, 9"	20.00
#527, bowl, Hibiscus, 10"	20.00
#539, urn, Regency, 7"	22.00
#550, vase, Fluted, 11"	25.00
#569D, cornucopia, 8" L	22.00
#578, candle holder, Aladdin Lamp, ea	75.00
#598D, vase, Rosette, 7¼"	30.00
#610, bowl, Shell, deep, 9"	42.50
#661, figurine, swan, 3¾"	30.00
#680, shakers, Daisy, 4", pr	15.00
#690D, range set, Daisy, 3-pc	45.00
#702D, string holder, Chinese face, 5½"	165.00
#705, vase, Modern, 8"	20.00
#3801, sculpture, head, 11½"	250.00
Cookie jar, #471, Old Lady, decor, minimum value	250.00
Cookie jar, #495, Fat Boy	250.00
Cookie jar, #549, Hippo, decor, 1942	250.00
Cookie jar, #588, Money Bag	75.00
Cookie jar, #602, Hobby Horse	175.00
Cookie jar, #611, Jack-in-the-Box	270.00
Cookie jar, #622, Miss Muffet	200.00
Cookie jar, #651, Choo Choo (Locomotive)	145.00
Cookie jar, #653, Clock, 1949	100.00
Cookie jar, #663, Humpty Dumpty, decor	200.00
Cookie jar, #664, Pineapple	75.00
Cookie jar, #665, Wigwam	200.00
Cookie jar, #674, Pumpkin, 1949, minimum value	325.00
Cookie jar, #677, Daisy, 1949	45.00
Cookie jar, #678, Windmill, from $200 to	225.00

Cookie jar, #693, Little Girl, from $60 to	75.00
Cookie jar, #694, Bo Peep, from $250 to	275.00
Cookie jar, #695, Mother Goose	275.00
Cookie jar, #696, Three Bears, from $90 to	100.00

Adams, Matthew

In the 1950s a trading post in Alaska contacted Sascha Brastoff to design a line of porcelain with scenes of Eskimos, Alaskan motifs, and animals indigenous to that country. These items were to be sold in Alaska to the tourist trade.

Brastoff selected Matthew Adams, born in April 1915, to design the Alaska series. Pieces from the line he produced have the Sascha B mark on the front; some have a pattern number on the reverse. They did not have the rooster backstamp. (See also the Sascha Brastoff category.)

After the Alaska series was introduced and proved to be successful, Matthew Adams left the employment of Sascha Brastoff (working three years there in all) and opened his own studio. Pieces made in his studio are signed Matthew Adams in script and may have the word Alaska on the front. Mr. Adams's studio is now located in Los Angeles, but at this time, due to his age, he has ceased production. Our advisor for this category is Marty Webster; he is listed in the Directory under Michigan. Feel free to contact Mr. Webster if you have any further information.

Ashtray, Eskimo face, hollow star shape, 13"	75.00
Ashtray, hooded; walrus on blk, 5½"	65.00
Bowl, console; glacier on bl, 12x20"	165.00
Bowl, Grizzly bear on brn, free-form, 6½" L	45.00
Bowl, igloo & dog, #138 boat shape, 9½"	50.00
Bowl, ram on gr, free-form, 7"	55.00
Bowl, seal, oval, 9"	50.00
Bowl, walrus & glacier on brn, free-form, 8"	65.00
Bowl, walrus on yel, w/lid, 7"	75.00
Box, seal on wht, 2¼x6"	50.00
Charger, Eskimo w/harpoon, 16"	135.00
Charger, walrus on dk bl, 17"	150.00
Cigarette lighter, glacier, 6"	30.00
Cigarette lighter, walrus, #183, 6"	25.00
Compote, grizzly bear on brn, tall, 8½" dia	70.00
Cookie jar, Eskimo mother & child on brn, w/lid, 8"	75.00
Cracker jar, Eskimo mother & child on brn, 7"	75.00
Creamer, polar bear on blk, 4¾"	30.00
Creamer & sugar bowl, Eskimo child, #144 & #144a	65.00
Cup & saucer, sled on bl	25.00
Dish, Eskimo child, #099, 2¼x7½" dia	45.00
Ginger jar, seal on brn/wht, w/lid, #095, 6½"	95.00
Humidor, seal on gr, #025, 5¾"	45.00
Jar, Eskimo on ice bl, 6"	30.00
Jar, walrus on lt bl, w/lid, #1492, 7½"	50.00
Mug, husky dog, #112A, 4½x4¾"	45.00
Pitcher, Eskimo, 13"	90.00
Pitcher, grizzly bear, 11", +6 4" tumblers	200.00
Pitcher, walrus, 11½", +6 4½" mugs	255.00
Plate, Eskimo girl, #162, 7½"	50.00
Plate, igloo & Northern Lights, #162, 7½"	36.00
Platter, polar bears (2) on ice, 12x10"	75.00
Pot, walrus, w/lid, 12"	55.00
Shakers, Eskimo child on gray, pr	50.00
Shakers, rams on gr, 4", pr	50.00
Tankard, man on brn, 19", +6 mugs	250.00
Tankard, polar bear on blk, w/lid, 13"	200.00
Teapot, walrus on ice bl, 6½"	75.00

Tile, Eskimo mother & child, 12¾x10½" 125.00
Tile, mountains & glacier on blk, 10x8½" 75.00
Tray, polar bear & iceberg, #910, 13x9¾" 75.00

Trivet, polar bear, 6", $40.00.

Tumbler, cabin 20.00
Vase, Eskimo mother & child on teal, cylindrical, 17" 165.00
Vase, glacier on gray, #143, 5½" 50.00
Vase, mountain & glacier on blk, #114, 12" 80.00
Vase, polar bear on gr, 10" 100.00
Vase, sea lion & seaweed, oval, #128, 8" 95.00
Vase, seal & glacier on brn, free-form, #911, 11" 125.00
Vase, walrus on ice on bl, 10" 110.00

Adams Rose, Early and Late

In the second quarter of the nineteenth century, the Adams and Son Pottery produced a line of hand-painted dinnerware decorated in large, red brush-stroke roses with green leaves on whiteware, which collectors call Adams Rose. Later, G. Jones and Son (and possibly others) made a similar ware with less brilliant colors on a gray-white surface.

Note: Early English dinnerware values have softened considerably due to the influence of the Internet which makes good examples that once were hard to find much more accessible. Unless otherwise noted, our values are for items in mint condition or nearly so; be sure to discount prices for damage.

Bowl, late, mk Imperial Royal, Belgium, 3x5½" 35.00
Coffeepot, late, 3x6¼" 875.00
Creamer, late, 4½" 135.00
Pitcher, water; late, scalloped rim, 8½" 500.00
Pitcher, water; late, 3-color, emb at spout/hdl, 7½" 300.00
Plate, early, scalloped rim, 7½" 150.00
Plate, early, scalloped rim, 10¾", VG 45.00
Plate, late, mk England, 9" 90.00
Plate, stick spatter, mk England, lion & unicorn crest, 7" 65.00
Platter, late, 12", EX...135.00
Teabowl & saucer, early...330.00
Wash bowl & pitcher, early, prof rstr, 12", 4½x13½" 2,100.00

Advertising

The advertising world has always been a fiercely competitive field. In an effort to present their product to the customer, every imaginable gimmick was put into play. Colorful and artfully decorated signs and posters, thermometers, tape measures, fans, hand mirrors, and attractive tin containers (all with catchy slogans, familiar logos, and often-bogus claims) are only a few of the many examples of early advertising memorabilia that are of interest to today's collectors.

Porcelain signs were made as early as 1890 and are highly prized for their artistic portrayal of life as it was then . . . often allowing amusing insights into the tastes, humor, and way of life of a bygone era. As a general rule, older signs are made from a heavier gauge metal. Those with three or more fired-on colors are especially desirable.

Tin containers were used to package consumer goods ranging from crackers and coffee to tobacco and talcum. After 1880 can companies began to decorate their containers by the method of lithography. Though colors were still subdued, intricate designs were used to attract the eye of the consumer. False labeling and unfounded claims were curtailed by the Pure Food and Drug Administration in 1906, and the name of the manufacturer as well as the brand name of the product had to be printed on the label. By 1910 color was rampant with more than a dozen hues printed on the tin or on paper labels. The tins themselves were often designed with a second use in mind, such as canisters, lunch boxes, even toy trains. As a general rule, tobacco-related tins are the most desirable, though personal preference may direct the interest of the collector to peanut butter pails with illustrations of children, or talcum tins with irresistible babies or beautiful ladies. Coffee tins are popular, as are those made to contain a particularly successful or well-known product.

Perhaps the most visual of the early advertising gimmicks were the character logos, the Fairbank Company's Gold Dust Twins, the goose trademark of the Red Goose Shoe Company, Nabisco's ZuZu Clown and Uneeda Kid, the Campbell Kids, the RCA dog Nipper, and Mr. Peanut, to name only a few. Many early examples of these bring high prices on the market today.

Our listings are alphabetized by product name or, in lieu of that information, by word content or other pertinent description. When no condition is indicated, the items listed below are assumed to be in excellent condition, except glass and ceramic items, which are assumed mint. Remember that condition greatly affects value (especially true for tin items). For instance, a sign in excellent or mint condition may bring twice as much as the same one in only very good condition, sometimes even more. On today's market, items in good to very good condition are slow to sell, unless they are extremely rare. Mint (or near-mint) examples are high.

We have several advertising advisors; see specific subheadings. For further information we recommend *General Store Collectibles* by David L. Wilson; *Hake's Price Guide to Character Toys, 3rd Edition*, by Ted Hake; *Advertising Thermometers* by Curtis Merritt; *Collectible Soda Pop* and *Antique & Contemporary Advertising Memorabilia*, both by B.J. Summers; *Encyclopedia of Advertising Tins, Vol. II*, by David Zimmerman; and *Advertising Paperweights* by Richard Holiner and Stuart Kammerman. *Garage Sale and Flea Market Annual* by Sharon and Bob Huxford is another good reference. All of these books are available at your local bookstore or from Collector Books. See also Advertising Dolls; Advertising Cards; Automobilia; Coca-Cola; Banks; Calendars; Cookbooks; Paperweights; Posters; Sewing Items; Thermometers.

Key:
cb — cardboard	sf — self-framed
dc — diecut	tc — tin container
fs — flange sign	ts — tin sign
ps — porcelain sign	

Acme Chocolates, box, paper w/Victorian graphics, 8x11", VG...**55.00**
Admiration Coffee, ps, curved, red/wht/bl, Duncan Coffee Co, 5x5", NM.**330.00**
Alka-Seltzer, dispenser, tin top/chrome base, cobalt bl glass, 15", EX....**400.00**
Anheuser-Busch, display figure, waiter, chalkware, 20", EX **200.00**
Anheuser-Busch, sign, paper, Anheuser Girl, orig wood fr, 39x24", EX..**825.00**
Anheuser-Busch, tray, ornate factory scene, preprohibition, 16x19", NM.**775.00**
Anker-Werke Sewing Machines, sign, paper, lady at machine, 31x21", EX...**225.00**
Arbutus Rolled Oats, cb box, 10-oz, red on yel, 9½", EX+ **115.00**
Arcade, brass paperweight w/emb factory, name & 1885-1927, 3x5", G...**25.00**

Arden, ps, Arden milk boy on red oval w/wht trim, 36x21", VG ...**800.00**

Arrow Collars, display, glass w/wood fr & base, w/collars, 24x15", VG+..**630.00**

Atkins Silver Steel Saws, ts, phrase above handsaw, fr, 10x19", EX....**525.00**

Austin Powder Co, sign, paper, 2 dogs in field, fr, 29x23", VG+.....**465.00**

Baker's Chocolate, poster, girl w/tray, fr, 36x26", NM **300.00**

Bank Note Cigars, sign, dc cb, 2 gents w/5¢ box, fr, 30x23", VG+.....**275.00**

Banner Ox-Blood Shoe Stain Polish, jar, red/wht labels, 1x2½", EX+ ..**150.00**

Bartels Brewing Co, sign, paper, aerial factory scene, fr, 35x46", VG...**2,100.00**

Beech-Nut Chewing Gum, display rack, tin litho, 4-tier, 15x6x7", EX+...**2,000.00**

Beech-Nut Chewing Tobacco, ps, product pack on wht, 9x6", VG....**275.00**

Berry Bros Varnishes, pocket mirror, oval, boy/wagon/dog, NM .**200.00**

Berry Bros Varnishes, pocket mirror, rnd, kids/wagon/dog/steps, NM...**200.00**

Big Boy, kite, Big Boy image on paper, M **100.00**

Blatz Chewing Gum, cb display box w/10 early full packs, 5x8x4", EX ..**900.00**

Blue Bird Handkerchiefs, display box, tin litho, 1920s, 7x12x8", EX+..**450.00**

Borden, game, Elsie the Cow Jr Edition, EXIB.............................**125.00**

Borden, night light, figural Elsie head, rubber-type compo, 9", NM.....**180.00**

Borden Condensed Milk, sign, cb, sleeping baby w/puppy, 15x11", VG+..**450.00**

Boschee's Syrup/Green's August Flower, sign, canvas, fr, 27x35", VG ...**1,100.00**

Brookfield Rye, ts, girl w/bottle, Meek...OH, 33x23", EX **2,750.00**

Brylcreem, ps, For Smart Healthy Hair/product on red, 18x16", VG..**165.00**

Buckeye Harvesting Machines, fan, cb, 4 heart shapes, 6x9", EX .**50.00**

Budweiser, display figure, Bud Man, hard foam, 19", NM............**165.00**

Bull Durham Smoking Tobacco, sign, A Royal Victory, fr, 24x35", EX.**775.00**

Bulldog Tobacco, pocket tin, vertical, dk bl, 4½", EX.................**675.00**

Buster Brown

Buster Brown was the creation of cartoonist Richard Felton Outcault; his comic strip first appeared in the *New York Herald* on May 4, 1902. Since then Buster and his dog Tige (short for Tiger) have adorned sundry commercial products but are probably best known as the trademark for the Brown Shoe Company established early in this century. Today hundreds of Buster Brown premiums, store articles, and advertising items bring substantial prices from many serious collectors.

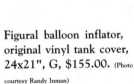
Figural balloon inflator, original vinyl tank cover, 24x21", G, $155.00. (Photo courtesy Randy Inman)

Bank, plastic ball shape w/BB&T busts on top, 1960s, 3½" dia, EX **25.00**

Clicker, tin shoe-sole form w/bl (Blue Ribbon) lettering on yel, VG....**20.00**

Clock, glass w/metal fr, light-up, Pam, 15" dia, EX.....................**925.00**

Display, dc wood BB & Tige figures w/rnd shelves for shoes, 69", VG .**415.00**

Display figure, plastic doll on base, clothed, 34", VG **55.00**

Doll, BB, stuffed cloth, 1974, 14", NM.....................................**40.00**

Hobby horse, wood w/pnt advertising as saddle, rare, 28x36", VG....**300.00**

Kite, 1940s, NM **40.00**

Mask, Bread, paperbrd, BB winking, 8½x11", EX.......................**100.00**

Match holder, BB Bread, litho tin, 7x2", VG+ **475.00**

Painting box, paper on cb, Milton Bradley, 1910, 10½x7", EX..........**50.00**

Shoe box w/Treasure Hunt game on side, 1930s, unused, from $50 to...**75.00**

Sign, dc metal/wood neon, BB/Tige above Shoes, 55x55", VG+ **4,000.00**

Sign, oilcloth, pin-the-bow on Buster game, wood fr, 34x22", VG+.**1,150.00**

Sign, tin, ...Bread/Golden Sheaf Bakery, ts, BB/Tige, 20x29", VG.....**450.00**

Sign, wood, Quality Children's Clothes, 2-sided, 19x43", VG....**125.00**

Buttercup Snuff, door push, emb litho tin, graphics on gr, 9x4", VG+..**100.00**

BVD Union Suits, ts, beveled, man/phrase, 1920s, 13x9", EX **200.00**

Calumet Baking Powder, clock, oak case w/glass front, 39x17", VG **5.00**

Campbell's Soups, Campbell Kids Cooking Set, 1950s, unused, MIB ...**200.00**

Campbell's Soups, kaleidoscope, replica of soup can, 1981, EX.....**40.00**

Canada Dry, door push, emb tin, lg bottle on wht, gr trim, 9x3", NM..**210.00**

Ceresota Flour, jigsaw puzzle, 6 factory views, 1900, 7x9", EX **125.00**

Ceresota Flour, match holder, tin, boy/bbl, ..Prize Bread.., 6", EX+ ...**300.00**

Chicos 5¢ Peanuts, jar, glass w/metal lid & base, 11", VG **130.00**

Cities Services, winterfront, cb, fr, 13x21", EX **50.00**

Clark's Peanut Butter, tc, 1-lb, slip lid, bail hdl, winter scenes, EX....**875.00**

Clark's/Mile-End/ONT/Buttons, cabinet, oak/glass, 4-drw, 15x24", EX....**880.00**

Collin's Honey Scotch Candy, ts, emb, Ten Pieces 5¢/graphics, 7x20", M ...**200.00**

Columbian Fruit...Gum, dc standup, girl w/dogs, 9", EX **385.00**

Continental Cubes, display pocket tin, 7½", EX+.....................**3,700.00**

Continental Cubes, pocket tin, vertical, 5", EX+ **625.00**

Crane's Private Mixture, pocket tin, vertical, gr, crane logo, 4", EX+.**425.00**

Crescent Flour, door push, emb tin, wht on blk, 9½x4", EX+ **300.00**

Crow-Mo-Smokers, lunch pail, oblong, wire hdl, 5x7x5", VG+ ..**425.00**

Crowley's Needles, cabinet, oak/glass, porc knobs, 2-drw, 5x10", EX..**385.00**

Crowley's Needles, cabinet, oak/glass, porc knobs, 6-drw, 12x22", EX .**600.00**

Cudahay's Diamond C Ham, ts, Are the Best, lady, fr, 32x26", EX........**650.00**

Cudahay's Puritan Ham, ts, pkgs ham on red, Ripened, 19x13", G+.....**160.00**

Cunrad Line, tip tray, Aquitania ocean liner, 4½x6½", EX+.......**350.00**

Cunrad Line, ts, Berengaria ocean liner, wood fr, 34x44", EX+ ...**1,540.00**

Dad's Root Beer, ts, pnt, shows lg bottle, 28x10", G+ **155.00**

Dan Patch Cut Plug, pail, oblong, bail hdl w/wood grip, red/yel, VG+...**325.00**

De Laval, thimble, 1910, EX...**475.00**

De Laval Cream Separators, sign, sf tin, lady/child at door, 23" dia ..**3,850.00**

Delaware Rubber Co, sign, paper, Washington crossing river, 26x20", VG ..**165.00**

Derby Tobacco, sign, cb, ad around jockey/horse in emb oval, fr, 27x23" ...**2,300.00**

Diamond Dyes, cabinet, oak/tin, children playing w/balloon, 25", VG...**775.00**

Diamond Dyes, cabinet, oak/tin, children skipping rope, 24", EX.....**1,000.00**

Diamond Dyes, cabinet, oak/tin, lady dying clothes, 30", VG...**1,425.00**

Dilworth's Golden Urn Coffee, tc, sample, screw lid, 2½x2", EX..**150.00**

Dixie Queen Cut Plug, tin canister, girl on ea side, 7½", EX+....**600.00**

Domino Cigarettes, door push, tin litho, America's Best, 14x4", EX+........**100.00**

Dr Daniels' Veterinary Medicines, cabinet, wood/tin, 27", VG ..**1,650.00**

Dr Lesure's Famous Remedies, cabinet, wood/tin, horse head, 27", EX+ ...**5,500.00**

Dr. Pepper

A young pharmacist, Charles C. Alderton, was hired by W.B. Morrison, owner of Morrison's Old Corner Drug Store in Waco, Texas, around 1884. Alderton, an observant sort, noticed that the drugstore's patrons could never quite make up their minds as to which flavor of extract to order. He concocted a formula that combined many flavors, and Dr. Pepper was born. The name was chosen by Morrison in honor of a beautiful young girl with whom he had once been in love. The girl's father, a Virginia doctor by the name of Pepper, had discouraged the relationship due to their youth, but Morrison had never forgotten her. On December 1, 1885, a U.S. patent was issued to the creators of Dr. Pepper. Our advisor for Dr. Pepper is Craig Stifter; he is listed in the Directory under Illinois. See also Soda Fountain Collectibles.

Art plate, girl looking right, holding flowerpot, 1908-12, rare, EX..975.00
Bottle opener, metal, dc lion's head, 3", EX 85.00
Bottle topper, Edith Luce, NM 350.00
Clock, bottle cap, plastic w/metal bl, light-up, 12", dia, EX 70.00
Drinking glass, flared w/etched logo, 1910s, NM......................1,200.00
Menu board, tin chalkboard, bottle/clock/grid logo on yel, 20x18", EX...225.00
Postcard, Free! 6 Bottles of Dr Pepper, red/gr/wht, NM.................15.00
Sign, cb, Madelon Mason w/sign & bottle, 1940s, 19x32", G+ ..100.00
Sign, porc, dc w/stepped bottom & clock graphic, Drink..., 33x53", EX+..1,150.00
Sign, porc, Drink DP/Good for Life!, 1930s-40s, 11x27", EX+ ..275.00
Sign, porc, name in wht stenciled-look on red, wht trim, 8x20", EX..100.00
Sign, porc, 10-2-4/Drink DP, red/wht, 10" dia, NM....................750.00
Stick pin, dc head, 2¼", NM..165.00
Syrup jug, clear glass w/paper label, screw cap, 1958, VG+.........120.00
Thermometer, tin, Hot or Cold/Enjoy..., red/wht, 1950s, 16", EX...200.00

Drake Mercantile Co, crumb scraper, tin litho, kittens, scalloped, EX+...525.00
Durham Tobacco, sign, paper, cyclist w/ads on wheels, fr, 22x17", EX ..450.00
E Robinson's Sons Pilsener Beer, tray, boating scene, 12" dia, EX+ 575.00
Ebbert Wagons, sf ts, In the Shade of the Old Apple Tree, 26x38", G+....825.00
Eberhardt & Ober Brewing Co, sign, factory scene, fr, 36x50", EX .1,320.00
Edgeworth Tobacco, door push, tin litho, pocket tin image, 14x4", EX..170.00
El-Bart Dry Gin, sign, paper, girl on beach, gold fr, 46x33", G ..3,000.00
Eveready Flashlight Batteries, display case, tin, slant front, 16", EX ...475.00
Eversweet Deodorant, tip tray, lady in center, fluted corners, VG+...75.00
Ex-Lax, door push, porc, Get Your Box Now!, bl, 8x4", EX 375.00
Fairway Coffee, tc, 1-lb, key-wind lid, children/steaming cup, 5", EX ..250.00
Fan Tan Gum, tray, oriental scene w/wicker-look rim, 11x14", VG....165.00
Farmers Fire Insurance Co, sign, rvpt, metallic/blk, fr, 33", VG..750.00
Farnam's...Gum, display case, wood/glass/gold letters, 10x1x8", EX ..5,600.00
First Pick Coffee, tc, 1-lb, key-wind lid, 2 yel chicks, 5", EX+ 350.00
Five Roses Flour, door push, porc, wht, 12x4", NM.....................375.00
Forest & Stream Tobacco, pocket tin, vertical, 2 men in canoe, 4", EX+...475.00
Foster Hose Supporters, celluloid, Foster lady on blk, 17x9", EX...425.00
FW Cook Brewing Co, ts, elderly gent w/brew, fr, 30x23", EX....650.00
FW Cough Drops, tin, sq w/rnd slip lid, 8x5x5", EX+ 1,400.00
Genco Razers, display case, tin litho w/glass top, 7x8x15", VG+...300.00
Good Humor Ice Cream, ps, bar & name on wht, 1930s, 18x26", EX+ ..1,200.00
Gorden Dye Hosiery, sign, paper, ladies showing ankles, 27x13", EX..900.00
Green Turtle Cigars, lunch pail, wire hdl, gr, 5x7½x4½", VG+...350.00
Groub's Belle Coffee, tc, 1#, rnd, screw lid, lady's portrait, 6", EX+ 625.00
Guide Pipe & Cigarette Tobacco, pocket tin, vertical, 4", EX 230.00
Gulf Oil Co, pocketknife, inlaid enameled Deco scenes, 3¼", NM....550.00
Hamm's Beer, light-up display building w/slant roof, VG.............150.00
Hartford Fire Insurance, sf ts, oval sepia image of stag, 24x20", EX 110.00
Harvest Maid, sign, paper, maiden w/hand shadowing eyes, fr, 30", EX..225.00
Hasterlik Bros Distillers, ts, The Demand/The Capture, fr, 44x31", VG .7,150.00
Heinz Apple Butter, crock, stoneware/paper label, bail hdl, 8", EX+ ..675.00
Henkle's Flour, pot scraper, litho tin, EX+ 225.00
Hershey's, dispenser, 1¢, pnt steel w/glass front, 18", VG.............440.00

Hires

Charles E. Hires, a drugstore owner in Philadelphia, became interested in natural teas. He began experimenting with roots and herbs and soon developed his own special formula. Hires introduced his product to his own patrons and began selling concentrated syrup to other soda fountains and grocery stores. Samples of his 'root beer' were offered for the public's approval at the 1876 Philadelphia Centennial. Today's collectors are often able to date their advertising items by observing the Hires boy on the logo. From 1891 to 1906, he wore a dress. From 1906 until 1914, he was shown in a bathrobe; and from 1915 until 1926, he was depicted in a dinner jacket. The apostrophe may or may not appear in the Hires name; this seems to have no bearing on dating an item. Our advisor for Hires is Craig Stifter; he is listed in the Directory under Illinois. See also Soda Fountain Collectibles.

Tray, Hires to Your Health..., boy pointing, painted tin, 13", NM, $2,200.00. (Photo courtesy Pettigrew Auctions)

Banner, Enjoy a Hires Float/Only 50¢..., canvas, 32x42", EX 125.00
Bottle carrier, wood w/dvtl corners, Quarter Case, VG+ 30.00
Clock, rnd, glass face, light-up, Drink Hires..., 15", EX...............385.00
Drinking glass, curved top, etched, Enjoy Hires..., NM+ 160.00
Festoon, bottles flanking scrolled banner w/R-J logo, 111x49", EX......400.00
Menu board, tin chalkboard, R-J logo/Ice Cold 5¢ Bottles, 29", NM...350.00
Mug, ceramic, bbl shape w/Hires Boy, Mettlach, 4", EX+ 275.00
Sign, cb, Enjoy... above lady's head on red, fr, 12x9", EX+..........660.00
Sign, cb, The Right Note..., girl at piano, fr, 39x34", VG...........475.00
Sign, paper, emb, hanger, Drink...It Is Pure, gold on red, 6x8", EX....630.00
Sign, sf tin oval, pointing Hires boy/Say Hires, rare, 24x20", VG ...1,750.00
Sign, tin, bottle shape, 1950s, 22", M..200.00
Sign, tin, emb, Enjoy...Healthful Delicious, gold/blk/turq, 10x28", EX 275.00
Sign, tin, emb, Enjoy...It's Always Pure, lady's head, 10x28", EX+ ...475.00
Sign, tin, emb, hanger, Genuine...Served Here, wht on bl, 6x8", VG+ ..660.00
Sign, tin, Say! Drink.../oval portrait on wht, fr, ca 1910, 18x14", NM ...6,820.00
Syrup bottle, rvpt octagonal label, emb knob lid, 13", EX...........825.00
Thermometer, dc tin bottle shape, Genuine Hires..., 1950s, 29", EX+.200.00
Thermometer, tin, Drink Hires, lt bl w/wht stripes, 27", EX+.....325.00
Thermometer, tin bottle shape, Since 1876 label, 29", NM........250.00
Trade card, bust image of lady, Haskell Coffin, 1917, NM+_ 60.00
Trade card, Say Mama I Want Another Glass of..., child, 5x3" ..250.00
Tray, Just What the Doctor Ordered..., ca 1914, 13" dia, G 350.00

Honey Crust Bread, string holder, tin panels, 16x13", VG..........300.00
Humphery's Witch Hazel Oil, mirror w/oak fr, 12x10", G 85.00
Huntly & Palmer's Biscuits, pocket mirror, rnd biscuit shape, 2", EX .110.00
Imperial Club 5cts Cigars, ts, emb, chain hanger, open box, 10x14", EX..150.00
Ingersoll Watches, display case, wood w/slant glass top, 9x10", G+ 520.00
Iroquois Beer/Ale, clock, metal/glass/light-up, logo, 16" dia, EX....525.00
Jas E Pepper Dist'g Go, Born With the Republic 1780, fr, 33x45", EX..5,175.00
Jersey Creme, fs, tin litho, rnd, ...The Perfect Drink 5¢, 6x6", NM 725.00
John Deere, clock, rnd light-up, glass front/metal fr, 15", NM 600.00
Johnson & Johnson Talc, sign, dc cb stringer, baby in bed, 8x14", VG+..575.00
Johnston Harvester Co, sign, paper, The Globe Mower No 8, 20x26", VG ..465.00
Kamm & Schellinger Brewing Co, sign, paper, lion on globe, fr, 37", EX...1,750.00
Kayo Chocolate Drink, decal, Moon Mullins/Kayo, 1940s, NM ...30.00
Kentucky Club Pipe Tobacco, thermometer, pnt metal, 39x8", EX+..200.00
Kis-Me Gum, sign, dc cb, girl fr by pansies, fr, 15x13", G 300.00
La Preferencia Cigar, sign, paper, lady in red, fr, 36x25", EX ...1,550.00
Lakeside Club Bouquet Whiskey, sign, pnt milk glass panel, 19x22" fr...3,300.00

Larkin Soap Co, sign, dc cb standup image of cat w/red bow, 12", EX+ ..**225.00**
Lawrence Barnett Cigar, ps, rnd portrait/text on wht, gold rim, 34x20" ..**2,500.00**
Leisy Brewing Co, tray, ornate factory scene, 14x17", EX+ **775.00**
Levi's, sign, red dc wood w/wht plastic lettering, 45" L, EX...........**55.00**
Lion Brewery/Pilsener Beer, rvpt glass oval w/lion, wood fr, 16", EX ..**250.00**
Little Boy Blue Bluing, dispenser, tin, 1920s, 19x4", NM+ **250.00**

Log Cabin Syrup

Log Cabin Syrup tins have been made since the 1890s in variations of design that can be attributed to specific years of production. Until about 1914, they were made with paper labels. These are quite rare and highly prized by today's collectors. Tins with colored lithographed designs were made after 1914. When General Foods purchased the Towle Company in 1927, the letters 'GF' were added.

A cartoon series, illustrated with a mother flipping pancakes in the cabin window and various children and animals declaring their appreciation of the syrup in voice balloons, was introduced in the 1930s. A frontier village series followed in the late 1940s. A schoolhouse, jail, trading post, doctor's office, blacksmith shop, inn, and private homes were also available. Examples of either series today often command prices of $125.00 to $200.00 and up.

Bank, glass cabin form, rnd metal lid w/slot, 5", NM **45.00**
Blotter, shows cabin & 2 little girls, 3½x6", EX **25.00**
Bottle, 6-sided glass, emb logo, angled hdl, cork stopper, 8", EX ...**16.00**
Spatula, metal w/wooden hdl, 12", EX **10.00**
Spoon, SP w/emb cabin & floral decor, Pat Jan 1883 (?), 6", EX **25.00**
Syrup tin, animal skin on door, 1909-14, label, ½-gal, EX **180.00**
Syrup tin, bear in doorway, 1930s, 5", VG+ **160.00**
Syrup tin, boy in doorway, 1918, paper label, sample, EX **350.00**
Syrup tin, boy in doorway, 1918, paper label, 1-gal, EX **275.00**
Syrup tin, Dr RU Well, 4", EX+ **360.00**
Syrup tin, Frontier Inn, 6", no cap o/w EX...................................**125.00**

Long Distance, pail, rnd/slip lid, bail hdl, paper label, 6", EX+ ...**175.00**
Long's Ox-Heart Chocolates, 2-sided cb disk, We Sell..., 11" VG+ ..**65.00**
Lucky Strike, cb stand-up sign, girl/lg pack on leaf, 18x12", VG......**100.00**
M Hemmingway & Sons, spool cabinet, oak/glass, porc knobs, 6-drw, EX..**600.00**
M Horner's Harmonicas, display box, wood w/paper label, 9x11", G+ ..**220.00**
Mark Rogers Whiskey, sign, 4 gents at table, shadow box fr, 12x14", EX..**415.00**
McCormick Harvesters, sign, paper, King of the Harvest, 16x22", EX..**475.00**
Meadow Gold Ice Cream, ps, 2-sided, Smooth-freeze, bl/wht, 28x29", EX...**175.00**
Mellin's Food for Infants & Invalids, ts, lady at window, fr, 27", VG..**575.00**
Merrick's Spool Cotton, cabinet, oak, ovoid w/glass & mirrors, 24x31" .**3,200.00**
Merry Widow Chewing Gum, sign, cb hanger, 8x6", EX+ **375.00**
Michelin, puzzle, Mr Bib on motorcycle forms figure, MIP.............**55.00**
Michelin, sign, porc, 2-sided, name/Michelin man on bl, 23x17", EX+..**500.00**
Milard's Needles, cabinet, oak/glass, porc knobs, 2-drw, 6x16", EX ...**385.00**
Minute Maid, coloring book, Teddy Snow Crop, Saalfield, 1956, unused ..**45.00**
Monarch Peanut Butter, pail, 2-lb, 1920s Teenie Weenie version, 5", EX...**275.00**

Moxie

The Moxie Company was organized in 1884 by George Archer of Boston, Massachusetts. It was at first touted as a 'nerve food' to improve the appetite, promote restful sleep, and in general to make one 'feel better.' Emphasis was soon shifted, however, to the good taste of the brew, and extensive advertising campaigns rivaling those of such giant competitors as Coca-Cola and Hires resulted in successful marketing through the 1930s. Today the term Moxie has become synonymous with courage and audacity, traits displayed by the company who dared compete with such well-established rivals. Our advisor for Moxie is Craig Stifter; he is listed in the Directory under Illinois.

Toy, auto with horse and rider, lithographed tin, red or blue, 8", EX+, $2,475.00.

Fan, cb, Rocking Horse/Moxie Man, 1922, NM **75.00**
Match holder, dc tin bottle, 7", EX+ **600.00**
Sign, emb tin, phrase in red oval w/gold trim on blk, 19x27", EX+ ...**200.00**
Sign, litho tin, hand-held bottle/Drink... on wht, bl rim, 10x28", EX..**130.00**
Sign, ts, emb, Drink..., wht on red w/gold & blk, 1930s, 6x19", NM+ .**220.00**
Thermometer, tin, red, w/Moxie Man, 1953, 25x10", EX+ **700.00**

Mumm's Extra Rye, sign, cb, lady waiting on train, fr, 29x24", VG **440.00**
Munsingwear, sign, canvas, grandma/2 girls, orig wood fr, 28x36", VG+ ..**630.00**
Munyon's Homeopathic Remedies, cabinet, wood/tin, 24", VG ..**775.00**
Nehi, ts, Curb Service...Sold Here Ice Cold, blk/red/yel, 27x20", EX+..**210.00**
Nestle's Hazelnut Chocolate, display case, metal/glass, 5x19x8", EX+..**500.00**
Nichol Cola, ts, majorette/cap/bottle on yel/brn, 1940s, 12x30", EX+ **85.00**
None Such Mince Meat, clock, orange pumpkin graphics, 10" dia, VG+ ..**1,150.00**
Nova Kola, tray, tin litho, For a Thirsty World, 13x13", EX+.....**375.00**
O! Boy Peanut Butter, tin pail w/bail hdl, 2 kids/seashore, 4", EX+ **650.00**
Oak Motor Suit, pocket mirror, man in suit on red, oval, 2¾", EX ...**240.00**

Old Crow

Old Crow Whiskey items have become popular with collectors primarily because of the dapper crow dressed in a tuxedo, top hat, etc., that was used by the company for promotional purposes during the 1940s through the 1960s. However, there is a vast variety of Old Crow collectibles, some of which carry only the whiskey's name. In the 1970s ceramic decanters shaped like chess pieces were available; these carried nothing more than a paper label and a presentation box to identify them. In 1985, the 150th anniversary of Old Crow, the realistic crow that had been extensively used prior to 1950 re-emerged.

Very little Old Crow memorabilia has been issued since National Distillers Products Corporations, the parent company since 1933, was purchased by Jim Beam Brands in 1987. No reproductions have surfaced, although a few fantasies have been found where the character crow was borrowed for private use. Note that with the increased popularity of Old Crow memorabilia, many items have surfaced, especially the more common ones, thus their values have decreased. Our advisors for Old Crow collectibles are Judith and Robert Walthall; they are listed in the Directory under Alabama.

Ashtray, Bakelite, 3½" dia, NM..**25.00**
Ashtray, ceramic, blk w/Old Crow, etc, 5" dia...........................**35.00**

Bank, wooden bbl, 1985, 6", EX 15.00
Bar light, coach light w/crow figure in center, mk Old Crow, 12", EX..35.00
Bingo card, 100 proof, late 1940s, 7½x8¼" 45.00

Bottle display, glass cylinder with gold plastic crow (shown with bottle), $50.00. (Photo courtesy Judith and Robert Walthall)

Bottle opener, metal bottle shape, 2⅝", NM 25.00
Bottle pourer, plastic figure, sm 5.00
Chess set (32 decanters), ltd ed, empty w/orig boxes & rug 200.00
Cocktail glass, crow stem, safety edge, Libbey, 1970s, from $10 to...15.00
Decanter, figural, Old Crow Distillery Co of Frankfort KY, 13½" ..50.00
Decanter, figural, orange vest, Royal Doulton, w/box, 12½" 125.00
Dice, I Buy, You Buy, crow on 1, ½ set of 2 ....45.00
Dice cup, Bakelite, blk w/yel lettering, felt-lined, NM 100.00
Display, ceramic, 'Broken Leg' mug holds bottle, 5¼", NM 200.00
Doorstop, cut-out 2-D wood crow, 21", EX 125.00
Figure, brass, on rnd ftd base, 11" 85.00
Figure, compo, name emb on base, 1940s, 27½", VG...............450.00
Figure, compo, pnt, 11½x3½", EX, from $75 to 125.00
Figure, plastic, Advertising Novelty & Sign Co, 32", EX 200.00
Figure, plastic, in birdcage, 9" 125.00
Jigger, blk lettering on clear glass, no crow, NM 5.00
Key chain, 2-D figural Old Crow, from $3 to 5.00
Label, paper, gold, shows Hermitage Distillery bbls, ca 1903, 4x4"..25.00
Lighter, 14k gold-plated, Florentine, from $25 to 30.00
Lipstick tissue booklet, Cub Products, 1⅞x3", M, from $15 to 20.00
Money clip, chromed metal, emb disc w/crow on 2" clip, EX........25.00
Phone dialer, hard plastic crow figure, Call For emb on bk, EX 5.00
Pitcher, ceramic, 'Broken Leg' decor, NM 100.00
Pitcher, ceramic, olive gr w/emb crow on reverse, McCoy, 7"......15.00
Pitcher, glass w/metal ring & hdl, 5" 25.00
Plaque, ceramic plate w/appl 4¾" crow, 8", NM 125.00
Pocketknife, pearlized hdls, 2 blades 30.00
Radio, figural, 8-transistor, MIB....................................300.00
Roly-poly, plastic, 9" 95.00
Shot glass, Old Crow & crow fired on in blk 20.00
Sign, plastic bbl form w/crow & The Original Sour Mash, 3x15" 50.00
Stirrer, plastic, full-figure crow on end, from $1 to....................3.00
Thermometer, rnd dial, 1950s, 9x13", EX 150.00
Thermometer, Taste of Greatness, 1960, 5¾x13½", from $75 to...100.00

Old English Tobacco, sign, paper, gent w/pipe, fr, 25x21", VG+.165.00
Old Gold Cigarettes, sign, cb standup, train scene, 31x29", EX+ 1,100.00

Old Mr Boston Fine Liquors, clock shaped like liquor bottle, 22", G+....325.00
Old Seneca Stogies, tc, rnd w/slip lid, 3 for 5¢, 6", EX...............425.00
Oliver Chilled Plows, sf ts, 2 men (1 on horse) at storefront, 32", VG...1,900.00
Orange-Crush, button sign, cb/celluloid, logo on orange, 9" dia, EX...165.00
Orange-Crush, door push, emb litho tin, blk/orange/wht, 12x3", VG+ ..250.00
Orange-Julep, sign, paper litho, couple sharing bottle, fr, 12x8", EX...210.00
Orange-Julep, tray, beach girl, 1920s, 13x19", EX+ 200.00
Orcico Cigars, tc, 2 For 5¢, Indian graphics on wht, 5½x6x4", EX+ ...550.00
Palmer's Root Beer, ps, curved oval, Drink...It's Better, 14x21", EX+...300.00
Peachy Tobacco, pocket tin, vertical, yel, 4⅛", EX+ 150.00
Penzoil Motor Oils, sign, metal, text on blk, wood fr, 14x42", EX..........180.00

Pepsi-Cola

Pepsi-Cola was first served in the early 1890s to customers of Caleb D. Bradham, a young pharmacist who touted his concoction to be medicinal as well as delicious. It was first called 'Brad's Drink' but was renamed Pepsi-Cola in 1898. Various logos have been registered over the years. The familiar oval was first used in the early 1940s. At about the same time, the two 'dots' (indicated in our listings by '=') between the words Pepsi and Cola became one, though more recent items may carry the double-dot logo as well, especially when they're designed to be reminiscent of the old ones. The bottle cap logo came along in 1943 and with variations was used through the early 1960s. Our advisor for Pepsi is Craig Stifter; he is listed in the Directory under Illinois. See also Soda Fountain Collectibles.

Ashtray, chrome bowl w/enameled bottle cap, 1956, 3½" dia, EX+..75.00
Bottle display, dc cb w/bottle, Pepsi & Pete, 1940s, 14x12", EX+ ...350.00
Calendar, 1901, 20", VG 3,200.00
Clock, Be Sociable/Have a Pepsi, light-up, 15¾" sq, EX...............75.00
Clock, Say Pepsi Please/bottle cap, dbl-bubble light-up, 15" dia, EX..625.00
Door push bar, Have a Pepsi flanked by logos on yel, 32", NM...150.00
Lighter, Scripto, plastic w/metal flip top, cap logo, 1950s, EX+ 75.00
Menu board, sf tin chalkboard, modern logo, med bl trim, 1976, 27", G ..30.00
Menu board, tin, Have a Pepsi, yel stripes, 30", NM 135.00
Pull toy, puppy w/hot dog wagon, wood, 10", EX......................250.00
Rack sign, fiberboard, dc, Drink P-C oval on bl/wht stripe, 18x23", EX ..45.00
Sign, cb, half-length J Erbit pinup girl w/bottle on bl, 31x24", VG 250.00
Sign, cb, surfers w/cartons, Board Members...!, 25x36", VG.........40.00
Sign, dc tin bottle, 5¢ dot/octagonal P=C label, 20x8", EX+......675.00
Sign, dc tin bottle cap, Drink P-C/AIR on reverse, 1950s, 14", EX...200.00
Sign, porc, Enjoy Pepsi, bottle cap on yel to tan, 13x29", VG....125.00
Sign, porc, 2-sided, Enjoy P=C 5¢/Hits the Spot, 32x56", EX 700.00
Sign, tin, More Bounce to the Ounce/cap/ribbon, wht, sf, 33x57", EX..300.00
Sign, tin, Say Pepsi Please/bottle/modern cap logo, yel, 46x17", NM.200.00
Sign, tin bottle cap, P-C logo, 37" dia, EX.................................275.00
Syrup dispenser, metal streamline style, Ice Cold P=C 5¢ logo, 23", VG...225.00
Thermometer, dial, Drink P=C Ice Cold, 1951, 12" dia, NM+.1,000.00
Thermometer, tin, More Bounce to the Ounce, wht, 27", VG ...200.00
Toy dispenser/bank, b/o, Linemar, 1950s, 10", unused, EXIB 350.00
Truck, metal, 3-part open bays w/ads, w/carts & cases, Ny-Lint, VGIB...175.00
Truck, Railway Express van, P=C logo, Buddy L, wood, +accessories, MIB..1,700.00
Truck, 1946 Chevy pickup, diecast, Solido, 9½", M, from $15 to.25.00
Vendor, model #27, dome top, 2-pc, med bl, Have a Pepsi, 53", G ...770.00
Vendor, model #27, flat top, lt bl, Say Pepsi Please, 1960s, rstr, 52"..330.00
Whistle, plastic twin bottles, 3x1½", EX..................................20.00

Planters Peanuts

The Planters Peanut Co. was founded in 1906. Mr. Peanut, the dashing peanut man with top hat, spats, monocle, and cane, has represented Planters since 1916. He took on his modern-day appearance after the company was purchased by Standard Brands in November 1960. He remains perhaps the most highly recognized logo of any company in the world. Mr. Peanut has promoted the company's products by appearing in ads; on product packaging; on or as store displays, novelties, and premiums; and even in character at promotional events (thanks to a special Mr. Peanut costume).

Among the favorite items of collectors today are the glass display jars which were sent to retailers nationwide to stimulate 'point-of-sale' trade. They come in a variety of shapes and styles. The first, distributed in the early 1920s, was a large universal candy jar (round covered bowl on a pedestal) with only a narrow paper label affixed at the neck to identify it as 'Planters.' In 1924 an octagonal jar was produced, all eight sides embossed, with Mr. Peanut on the narrow corner panels. On a second octagon jar, only seven sides were embossed, leaving one of the large panels blank to accommodate a paper label.

In late 1929 a fishbowl jar was introduced, and in 1932 a beautiful jar with a blown-out peanut on each of the four corners was issued. The football shape was also made in the 1930s, as were the square jar, the large barrel jar, and the hexagon jar with yellow fired-on designs alternating on each of the six sides. All of these early jars had glass lids which after 1930 had peanut finials.

In 1937 jars with lithographed tin lids were introduced. The first of these was the slant-front streamline jar, which is also found with screened yellow lettering. Next was a squat version, the clipper jar, then the upright rectangular 1940 leap year jar, and last, another upright rectangular jar with a screened, fired-on design similar to the red, white, and blue design on the cellophane 5¢ bags of peanuts of the period. This last jar was issued again after WWII with a plain red tin lid.

In 1959 Planters first used a stock Anchor Hocking one-gallon round jar with a 'customer-special' decoration in red. As the design was not plainly evident when the jar was full, the decoration was modified with a white under-panel. The two jars we've just described are perhaps the rarest of them all due to their limited production. After Standard Brands purchased Planters, they changed the red-on-white panel to show their more modern Mr. Peanut and in 1963 introduced this most plentiful, thus very common, Planters jar. In 1966 the last counter display jar was distributed: the Anchor Hocking jar with a fired-on large four-color design such as that which appeared on peanut bags of the period. Prior to this, a plain jar with a transfer decal in an almost identical but smaller design was used.

Some Planters jars have been reproduced: the octagon jar (with only six of the sides embossed), a small version of the barrel jar, and the four peanut corner jar. Some of the first were made in clear glass with 'Made in Italy' embossed on the bottom, but most have been made in Asia, many in various colors of glass (a dead giveaway) as well as clear, and carrying only small paper stickers, easily removed, identifying the country of origin. At least two reproductions of the Anchor Hocking jar with a four-color design have been made, one circa 1978, the other in 1989. Both, using the stock jar, are difficult to detect, but there are small differences between them and the original that will enable you to make an accurate identification. With the exception of several of the earliest and the Anchor Hocking, all authentic Planters jars have 'Made in USA' embossed on the bottom, and all, without exception, are clear glass. Unfortunately, several paper labels have also been reproduced, no doubt due to the fact that an original label or decal will greatly increase the value of an original jar. Jar prices continue to remain stable in today's market.

In the late 1920s, the first premiums were introduced in the form of story and paint books. Late in the 1930s, the tin nut set (which was still available into the 1960s) was distributed. A wood jointed doll was available from Planters Peanuts stores at that time. Many post-WWII items were made of plastic: banks, salt and pepper shakers, cups, cookie cutters, small cars and trucks, charms, whistles, various pens and mechanical

pencils, and almost any other item imaginable. Since 1981 the company, as a division of Nabisco (NGH) has continued to distribute a wide variety of novelties. In late 2000 NGH was sold to Philip Morris Cos. and Nabisco was combined with its Kraft Foods unit. With the increased popularity of Mr. Peanut memorabilia, more items surface, and the value of common items decrease.

Note that there are many unauthorized Planters/Mr. Peanut items. Although several are reproductions or 'copycats,' most are fantasies and fakes. Our advisors for Planters Planters are Judith and Robert Walthall; they are in the Directory under Alabama.

Key:
cc — common colors	pl — plastic
(green, light blue, red, tan)	pnut — peanut
MrP — Mr. Peanut	

Ashtray, bsk, shell-shape w/3 pnuts behind MrP figure, EX...........**75.00**
Bank, pl, MrP, cc, 1970s, 9", EX...**25.00**
Bank, pl, MrP, yel, Souvenir of Atlantic City decal, 9", 1970s, EX....**250.00**
Bank/vendor, pl, MrP head w/clear hat, 1950s, G........................**300.00**
Box, Salted Cashews, cb w/pnut graphics, held 24 5¢ bags, EX ..**295.00**
Costume, hard pl MrP torso w/arm holes, 47", VG+ **250.00**
Doll, MrP, stuffed cotton, Chase Bag Co, 1967, 21", NM..............**35.00**

Fan, Mr. Peanut driving peanut-shaped car, advertising on back, 1940s, 5¼x8", EX, $225.00 (has been reproduced). (Photo courtesy William Morford)

Figure, MrP, pnt pot metal, 1930s, 7", EXIB.................................**450.00**
Game, paper board, Planters Peanut Party, 1930 premium, NM ..**150.00**
Jar, peanut butter, red paper label, tin lid, 12-oz, 5", VG..............**45.00**
Nodder, MrP on spring, clayware, LEGO, 6½", NM **150.00**
Peanut butter maker, pl MrP figural, Emanee, 12", VG w/box **35.00**
Pencil, mechanical, yel/dk bl, pl MrP at end, 1970s, MIP.............**15.00**
Race car, pl, MrP driving, w/trigger, 1950s, 5¼", EX **350.00**
Sign, dc cb standup, MrP/Petey, ...First in Flavor..., 14", EX **275.00**
Thermometer, pl key w/tassle, 8", M in mailer...........................**800.00**
Tin, Ali D'Italia Peanut Oil, w/graphics, 1930s, 1-gal, G............**200.00**
Tin, Egyptian design, 1919, rare, 2x6" dia, EX.........................**1,000.00**
Tin, Salted Mixed Nuts, key-wind lid, 7-oz, 3", VG **30.00**
Top, Whip-It, MrP label on top, 1940s, 2½", VG **150.00**

Players Cigarettes, call bell w/Players Please ashtray base, 6", G+ ...**150.00**
Players Tobacco, ps, Players Please, w/pack of Navy Cut, 16x45", VG...**450.00**
Pratt's Veterinary Remedies, cabinet, wood/glass front, 30x17x7", VG+ ...**2,200.00**
Princeton Mixture, pocket tin, vertical, paper label, 4½", EX+ ..**400.00**
Queen Quality Brand Shoes, pocket mirror, oval, full image, EX ...**150.00**
Raleigh Cigarettes, sign, cb, lady w/hat over 1 eye, fr, 38x28", EX **465.00**

RCA Victor

Nipper, the RCA Victor trademark, was the creation of Francis Barraud, an English artist. His pet's intense fascination with the music of the phonograph seemed to him a worthy subject for his canvas. Although he failed to find a publishing house who would buy his work, the Gramophone Co. in England saw its potential and adopted Nipper to advertise their product. The painting was later acquired and trademarked in the United States by the Victor Talking Machine Co., which was purchased by RCA in 1929. The trademark is owned today by EMI in England and by General Electric in the U.S. Nipper's image appeared on packages, accessories, ads, brochures, and in three-dimensional form. You may find a life-size statue of him, but all are not old. They have been manufactured for the owner throughout RCA history and are marketed currently by licensees, BMG Inc. and Thomson Consumer Electronics (dba RCA). Except for the years between 1968 and 1976, Nipper has seen active duty, and with his image spruced up only a bit for the present day, the ageless symbol for RCA still listens intently to 'His Master's Voice.' Many of the items have been reproduced in recent years. Exercise care before you buy. The true Nipper collectible is one which has been authorized by either Victor or RCA Victor as an advertising aid. This includes items used in showrooms, billboards, window dressings, and customer give-aways. The showroom items included three-dimensional Nippers first in papier-mâché, later in spun rubber, and finally in plastic. Some were made in chalk. Throughout the years these items were manufactured largely by one company, Old King Cole, but often were marketed through others who added their names to the product. The key to collecting Nipper is to look for those items which were authorized and to overlook those items that were copied or made without permission of the copyright/trademark owner. Some of the newer but unauthorized items, however, are quite good and have become collectible notwithstanding their lack of authenticity.

The recent phenomenon of Internet auctions has played havoc with prices paid for Victor and RCA Victor collectibles. Often prices paid for online sales bear little resemblance to the true value of the item. Reproductions are often sold as old on the Internet and bring prices accordingly. It is common knowledge that auction prices, more often than not, are inflated over sales made through traditional sales outlets. The Internet has exacerbated the situation by focusing a very large number of buyers and sellers through the narrow portal of a modem. The prices here are intended to reflect what one might expect to pay through traditional sales.

Items marked (+) are often reproduced and care should be taken to ascertain age or provenance. Our advisor for RCA Victor is Roger R. Scott; he is listed in the Directory under Oklahoma.

Figure, Nipper, painted papier-mâché, 18", $350.00.

Bank, Nipper figure, flocking over metal, 6", EX+.....................230.00
Clock, RCA Victor Records, w/Nipper 350.00
Figure, Nipper, chalkware, Victor, 4" 40.00
Figure, Nipper, chalkware, 8", EX 60.00
Figure, Nipper, crystal, Fenton, 4"..50.00
Figure, Nipper, papier-mâché, 11"...50.00
Figure, Nipper, papier-mâché, 32", rpt.......................................525.00
Figure, Nipper, papier-mâché, 36"..600.00
Figure, Nipper, plaster, 14½x7½x5", VG (+)............................200.00
Figure, Nipper, plaster (Visco) 100.00
Figure, Nipper, plastic, 36", EX 235.00
Necktie, Nipper, M...20.00
Record brush, Lucite hdl, in faux leather snap case 30.00
Sign, paper, His Master's Voice famous logo on blk, 18x24", EX+ 1,375.00
Thermometer, porc, curved top/bottom, dk bl, RCA Victor Radio, 39", EX ...450.00
Toy truck, RCA Television Service, plastic, Marx, 8½", EXIB ...235.00

Red Goose Shoes

Realizing that his last name was difficult to pronounce, Herman Giesecke, a shoe company owner resolved to give the public a modified, shortened version that would be better suited to the business world. The results suggested the use of the goose trademark with the last two letters, 'ke,' represented by the key that this early goose held in his mouth. Upon observing an employee casually coloring in the goose trademark with a red pencil, Giesecke saw new advertising potential and renamed the company Red Goose Shoes. Although the company has changed hands down through the years, the Red Goose emblem has remained. Collectors of this desirable fowl increase in number yearly, as do prices. Beware of reproductions; new chalkware figures are prevalent.

Clock, light-up, Pam, dtd Nov 1854, 15" dia, NM+....................550.00
Display, figural goose, papier-mâché, red, 11", VG+ 250.00
Display egg layer, plastic goose on cb box, 27x22", G.................200.00
Ring, glow-in-the-dark w/secret compartment & photo, EX.......100.00
Tuck-A-Tub Theatre Play Kit, 1950s premium, complete, unpunched, NM..40.00
Whistle, tin bow-tie shape, wht w/Red Goose logo, 4", EX...........42.00
Whistle, tin goose shape, red, EX 85.00

Remington Firearms Kleanbore Ammunition, sign, cb, woman, fr, 44", G ..440.00
Remington Guns, sign, paper, shotguns/shells fr duck, fr, 21x25", VG ..575.00
Remington UMC, sign, dc cb standup, Let's Go!/dog, fr, 45x36", G..........1,320.00
Richardson's Orangeade, syrup bottle, label under glass, 11", NM...1,700.00
Richmond Maid Baking Powder, tc, 1-lb, key-wind lid, red, 5¼", EX+...100.00
Salada Coffee, ps, shaped like 1-lb key-wind can, 1940s, VG+ 80.00
Sauers Flavoring Extracts, display cabinet, wood/glass, 21x15", VG...875.00
Seal of North Carolina Plug Cut, tc, rnd w/sm slip lid, 6½", EX+ ..375.00

Seven-Up

The Howdy Company of St. Louis, Missouri, was founded in 1920 by Charles L. Grigg. His first creation was an orange drink called Howdy. In the late 1920s Howdy's popularity began to wane, so in 1929 Grigg invented a lemon-lime soda called Seven-Up as an alternative to colas. Grigg's Seven-Up became a widely accepted favorite. Our advisor for this category is Craig Stifter; he is listed in the Directory under Illinois. See also Soda Fountain Collectibles.

Calendar, 1954, bust image of lady in low-cut top, 21", VG+.....120.00
Clock, light-up, 7-Up logo in center, PAM, 15" dia, NM+.........350.00
Clock, plastic 'mod' flower shape w/logo at 7 o'clock, 17", VG 65.00
Clock, sq wood case w/metal dial, We Proudly Serve, 16x16", VG......155.00
Door push bar, porc, Fresh Up w/Seven-Up!, wht, 32", EX+ 225.00

Menu board, tin, hand-held bottle, curved corners, 27½x19½", EX, $180.00.

Sign, cb standup, grocer holding case, dtd 1948, 12x10", M **65.00**
Sign, flange, 2-sided, tin, bubble girl bottle logo, 20x18", EX **650.00**
Sign, tin, emb dc sf oval flanked by fan design & panel below, 44", G...**55.00**
Sign, tin, Fresh Up phrase & logo, dtd 54-3, 18x54", EX............**375.00**
Sign, tin, Get Real Action!/Your Thirst Away, dtd 7-63, 43", NM ...**350.00**

Southern Fruit Julep Co, paperweight/1920s 5-yr calendar, glass, EX ..**325.00**
Squirrel Peanut Butter, tc, wht on orange, 3-lb sz w/pry lid, EX+ ...**425.00**
Squirt, ts, Drink.../Squirt boy on diagonal panel, fr, 36x36", VG **355.00**
Stag Smoking Tobacco, sign, cb, pipe/stag graphics, fr, 42x29", VG+..**650.00**
Sterling Super-Bru, ts, vertical pennant hanger, gr/red trim, 18", EX .**450.00**
Stewart Clipping Machine, sign, cb litho, The Jury, 14x20", EX+ **475.00**
Stroh's Lager Beer, tray, brass, preprohibition, 12" dia, EX+ **1,050.00**
Sultana Peanut Butter, pail, 1-lb, tapering, bail hdl, yel, 4", EX+..**60.00**
Sunny Brook Whiskey, ts, bottle/figure/phrase on gr, 16x12", G ..**300.00**
Sunny South Sweet Chocolate Peanuts, tc, Black lady on bl, 3x8x2", EX..**210.00**
Sure Shot Tobacco, store bin, oblong w/lid, 6½x15x10", EX+ ...**950.00**
Sweet Burley Tobacco, store bin, tin, rnd/sq lid, red on yel, 11", EX+ .**200.00**
Sweet-Orr & Co Pants..., ts, tug-of-war scene, fr, 23x30", VG+ **875.00**
Tennyson 5¢ Cigars, display, tin vertical box on 4-sided base, 8", EX..**400.00**
Tiger Chewing Tobacco, store bin, rare bl version, rnd, 12", VG+ **850.00**
Tobacco Girl Cigars, tc, 50-ct, girl in tobacco leaf, 6", EX+ **3,300.00**
Tootsie Rolls, display rack, litho tin, 3-tier, 1¢/5¢, 13x9x8", EX ..**700.00**
Totem Tobacco, pocket tin, vertical, 3½", VG+ **1,250.00**
Trout-Line Smoking Tobacco, pocket tin, man fishing, gr, 4", EX+...**675.00**
Twenty Mule Team Borax, Woodburning & Project Kit, complete, EXIB...**45.00**
Union Leader, ts, shaped like pocket tin, 15½x10", VG+...........**165.00**
US Ammunition, sf ts, At Bisley England, 22x28", VG...........**1,980.00**
Valentine's Varnish, sign, sf tin/cb, man working on boat, 13x19", EX..**3,400.00**
Van Houten's Cocoa, cb sign, peasant girl w/basket, in 45½x31" fr...**660.00**
Virginia Dare Carbonated Beverages, ts, emb, ...Since 1835, 10x28", G...**165.00**
Wak-Em Up Coffee, pail, 10-lb display sz, bail hdl w/wood grip, EX+..**475.00**
Watkins Products, ps, bold wht lettering on dk bl, wht rim, 8x20", EX..**175.00**
Weideman Boy Brand Three Minute Oat Flakes, box, cb, rnd, 14-oz, EX..**125.00**
Weyman's Cutty Pipe, store bin, tin, sq, gr, rnd slip lid, 14", EX+ ...**1,400.00**
Whip Ready Rolled, pocket tin, vertical, man/horse, gr, 4½", VG+ ..**850.00**
White Manor Pipe Mixture, pocket tin, vertical, 3½", EX+ **210.00**
White Owl Brand Cigars, tc, rnd w/slip lid, rare bl version, 6", EX+..**675.00**
Whiteley Harvesting Machines, sign, paper, vignettes, fr, 34x19", VG..**525.00**
Wilson Whiskey, ts, litho, people milling around coach, fr, 37x50", EX..**4,400.00**
Wonder Bread, ps, name in yel outlined in red on blk, 8½x20", EX ..**375.00**
Wood's First Premium Mowers, sign, paper, 2 images, fr, 23x31", VG.......**685.00**
Wrigley's Gum, dispenser, Chewing Gum 5¢, shows '40s lady, 14x8", G **750.00**
Wrigley's Gum, display, dc tin Wrigley man/4 boxes, 16x14", G..**775.00**
Wrigley's Gum, display box w/20 full Juicy Fruit packs, cb, EX ..**2,500.00**

Wrigley's Gum, match holder, tin, Juicy Fruit, The Man, 5", EX+ **400.00**
Wrigley's Gum, sign, dc cb standup, boy pilot/dog, Spearmint, 32", G+ ..**1,150.00**
Wyandotte Products, ashtray, copper arrowhead shape w/name, 5", EX....**35.00**
Yankee Boy Plug Cut, pocket tin, vertical, brn hair version, 4", EX....**625.00**
Yellow Bonnet Coffee, tc, 1-lb, key-wind lid, red ground, EX+ ..**100.00**
Yellow Bonnet Coffee, tc, 1-lb, key-wind lid, wht ground, scarce, VG+...**325.00**
Zeno Gum, display case, oak, slant glass front/3 shelves, 18x11", EX ..**685.00**

Advertising Cards

Advertising trade cards enjoyed great popularity during the last quarter of the nineteenth century when the chromolithography printing process was refined and put into common use. The purpose of the trade card was to acquaint the public with a business, product, service, or event. Most trade cards range in size from 2" x 3" to 4" x 6"; however, many are found in both smaller and larger sizes.

There are two classifications of trade cards: 'private design' and 'stock.' Private design cards were used by a single company or individual; the images on the cards were designed for only that company. Stock cards were generics that any individual or company could purchase from a printer's inventory. These cards usually had a blank space on the front for the company to overprint with their own name and product information.

Four categories of particular interest to collectors are:

Mechanical — a card which achieves movement through the use of a pull tab, fold-out side, or movable part.

Hold-to-light — a card that reveals its design only when viewed before a strong light.

Diecut — a card in the form of something like a box, a piece of clothing, etc.

Metamorphic — a card that by folding down a flap shows a transformed image, such as a white beard turning black after use of a product.

For a more thorough study of the subject, we recommend *Reflections 1* and *Reflections 2* by Kit Barry; his address can be found in the Directory under Vermont. Values are given for cards in near-mint condition.

American Machine ice cream freezer, Brownie figures & freezer...**45.00**
Arm & Hammer Soda, 8 cherubs & box **25.00**
Austen's Forest Flower Cologne, cherub w/bottle...........................**6.00**
Basset Horhound Troches, bottle diecut w/pills ` **18.00**
Belvidere Shirt Waist, boy in bedroom in front of mirror.............**35.00**
Bixby Royal Polish, Liberty holding shoe w/women of nations **25.00**
Brovinine, Bush's Fluid Food, bull w/2 sheep **25.00**
Brown's Iron Bitters, baby sucking finger, hold-to-light **25.00**
Brown's Iron Bitters, Lily Langtree sitting by milk pail **8.00**
Brown's Iron Bitters, 2 puppies in bbl **6.00**
Burdock Blood Bitters, girl's head in horseshoe **5.00**
Burdock Blood Bitters, Santa holding torch....................................**12.00**
Burdock Blood Bitters, 3 cats in a row sewing.................................**6.00**
Chadwick's Thread, monk sewing...**12.00**
Clarke's Mile-End Thread, boy in sailor suit w/boat........................**6.00**
Collins Bonnet & Hat Bleachery, Manchester NH, man at machine ...**125.00**
Digestine for dyspepsia, boy in cabbage patch..............................**15.00**
Eagle Slate Crayon, pencil & blkboard w/drawings **25.00**
Fairbank Soap, twin Black boys in washtub **55.00**
Fairbank Soap, twin Black boys standing by washtub **55.00**
Ferry Morning Glory Seeds, 5 morning glories................................**20.00**
Ferry Portulaca Seeds, 7 portulacas...**20.00**
Fitch's Tulip Gum, diecut stand-up pug dog holding sign **50.00**
Gilt Edge Shoe Dressing, man & dog in hunting scene **5.00**
Globe Cocktail bitters, bottle & rooster..**25.00**
Goshen Sweeper Co, lady using carpet sweeper **25.00**
Goudy & Kent Biscuits & Confections, 4 girls w/dog at picnic **45.00**

Hammondsport Wine Co, 2 bottles w/6-month calendar 35.00
Horse Head Tobacco, horse head breaking through paper 45.00
Howard's Lotus Flower Cologne, woman w/flowers drinking 8.00
Hoyt's German Cologne, child's head in rose 6.00
Imperial Granum, 10 children eating product 25.00
JP Coats Thread, 2 mice w/spool 6.00
Lone Fisherman Tobacco, fisherman facing right 35.00
Malt Bitters, puzzle w/man's head in smoke cloud 8.00
Malt Bitters, swallows over lily pads 6.00
Malt Bitters, 7 scenes 30.00
Merchant's Gargling Oil, monkey holding bottle 20.00
Miller's Crown Dressing, 3 girls, 'Our Mamas Use' 8.00
Miller's French Blacking, girl w/2 puppies & cat 6.00
Miller's Harness Oil, 3 people in open sleigh w/2 horses 15.00
MK Paine Druggist, 2 babies either side of product display 35.00
Mule Ear Tobacco, Black playing banjo on mule 45.00
Murray & Lanman Florida Water, woman smelling flowers 10.00
Murray & Lanman Florida Water, 5 cherubs pulling bottle in sky ... 15.00
Patent Steam Dishwasher, woman in kitchen w/pan of dishes 35.00
Price's Evening Violet Perfume, girl & butterfly on pansies 15.00

Puck Tobacco, Puck character holding pipe, black and green, $55.00. (Photo courtesy Kit Barry)

Randall Harrow, Warrior Mowing Co, farmer w/2 horses & harrow 35.00
Royal Ham, monkey riding pig backwards 25.00
Royal Ham, shipwreck/castaway scene, 3 men & woman 25.00
Sanitas Wall Covering, 2 boys in tub, dog at side 35.00
Scott's Carbolated Salve, 2 girls by fence 6.00
Sherwin Williams Paint, 4 cherubs w/tree & rainbow 25.00
St Charles Evaporated Cream, court scene w/judge, 14 children .. 35.00
Success Magazine, Nov 1901 cover by JC Leyendecker 35.00
Sulpher Bitters, bird on branch 6.00
Union Web Hammock, woman in hammock, man at side 35.00
US Post Office 100 Year Anniversary, horse mail carrier/train, 2-sided ... 95.00
Vegetable person: corn Indian man 20.00
Vegetable person: cotton ball Black woman 20.00
Vegetable person: onion man 15.00
Vegetable person: pea pod man & woman 20.00
Vegetable person: potato Irishman 15.00
Wanzer Sewing Machine, 2 comic Chinese women at machine ... 25.00
Webb's Stove Polish, woman holding mask in right hand 4.00
Willimantic Thread, boy w/peacock feather hat 6.00
Willimantic Thread, Brooklyn bridge w/many ships 12.00
Willimantic Thread, girl's head in wreath w/2 pansies 5.00
Willimantic Thread, Jumbo in parade, 'Jumbo Must Go' 12.00
Wood's Duchess Coffee, woman w/tray 20.00
Worcester Salt Co, diecut salt bag 20.00
Wrisley Sweet Cream Soap, 2 women washing at basin, cow insert .. 15.00

Advertising Dolls and Figures

Whether your interest in ad dolls is fueled by nostalgia or strictly because of their amusing, often clever advertising impact, there are several points that should be considered before making your purchases. Condition is of utmost importance; never pay book price for dolls in poor condition, whether they are cloth or of another material. Restoring fabric dolls is usually unsatisfactory and involves a good deal of work. Seams must be opened, stuffing removed, the doll washed and dried, and then reassembled. Washing old fabrics may prove to be disastrous. Colors may fade or run, and most stains are totally resistant to washing. It's usually best to leave the fabric doll as it is.

Watch for new dolls as they become available. Save related advertising literature, extra coupons, etc., and keep these along with the doll to further enhance your collection. Old dolls with no marks are sometimes challenging to identify. While some products may use the same familiar trademark figures for a number of years (the Jolly Green Giant, Pillsbury's Poppin' Fresh, and the Keebler Elf, for example) others appear on the market for a short time only and may be difficult to trace. Most libraries have reference books with trademarks and logos that might provide a clue in tracking down your doll's identity. Children see advertising figures on Saturday morning cartoons that are often unfamiliar to adults, or other ad doll collectors may have the information you seek.

Some advertising dolls are still easy to find and relatively inexpensive, ranging in cost from $1.00 to $100.00. The hard plastic and early composition dolls are bringing the higher prices. Advertising dolls are popular with children as well as adults. For a more thorough study of the subject, we recommend *Advertising Dolls With Values* by Myra Yellin Outwater (Schiffer).

AC Man, wht & gr w/AC on chest, gr hat, AC Spark Plugs, 6", EXIB .. 160.00
Allied Van Lines Doll, gr uniform & hat, Lion Uniform Inc, 14", MIB ... 1,200.00
Bazooka Joe, stuffed print cloth, Bazooka Bubble Gum, 1970s, 19", EX+ .. 10.00
Big Boy, PVC, 1990, 3", EX 5.00
Blue Bonnet Sue, stuffed cloth w/yel yarn hair, 1980s, NM 5.00
Breakfast Bear, plush, Aunt Jemima, 13", M 175.00
Burger King, Knickerbocker, 1980, 20", MIB 20.00
Burger King Bear, plush, 4 different, Crayola Christmas, 1986, EX, ea . 10.00
Butterfinger Bear, plush, 1987, 15", M 25.00
Campbell Kid, rag-type boy or girl, 1970s, MIB 75.00
Campbell Kid Cheerleader, vinyl, 1967, 8", EX 75.00
Campbell Kid Paul Revere & Betsy Ross, 1976, 10", M, ea from $45 to .. 65.00
Charlie the Tuna, talker, Star-Kist/Mattel, 1969, 14", NM 50.00
Cheer Girl, plastic w/cloth clothes, Proctor & Gamble, 1960, 10", NM .. 20.00
Chiquita Bananas Girl, stuffed cloth, 16", M 30.00
Chuck-E Cheese, vinyl bank figure, 7", EX 10.00
Corn Girl, yel/gr dress & hat, rooted hair, Green Giant, 1950s, 17", M .. 40.00
Dairy Queen Kid, stuffed cloth, 1974, EX 20.00
Diana, stuffed oilcloth, Aunt Jemima, 1940-50, 8½", EX 150.00
Elsie the Cow, PVC, Borden, 3½", M, from $10 to 20.00
Eskimo Pie Kid, stuffed cloth, 1964-74, 15", EX, from $15 to 20.00
Fig Newtons Girl, plastic, Nabisco, 1980s, 4½", NM 10.00
French Fries Critter, pillow type, McDonald's, 1987, NM+ 10.00
Fruit Stripe Gum Man, bendy, riding motorbike, 1960s, 7½", EX+ .. 75.00
Fry Girl, stuffed cloth, McDonald's, 1987, 4", M 5.00
Gilbert Giddy-Up, stuffed cloth, Hardee's, 1971, EX 25.00
Hamburgler, vinyl & cloth, McDonald's, 1980s, 11", NM 15.00
Harley Hog, Harley-Davidson, 9", M 25.00
Helping Hand, plush, Hamburger Helper, 14", M 10.00
Jolly Green Giant, vinyl, 1970s, 10", EX+ 90.00
Jumbo Peanut Butter Elephant, stuffed cloth, 16", EX+ 525.00
Kiwi Fruit Figures, set of 3, 1985-90, M, ea 10.00
Knorr Soup Boy & Girl, hard plastic/cloth outfits, 1963-64, pr 15.00

Little Debbie, vinyl w/cloth outfit, straw hat, 1980s, 11", NM......**25.00**
Little Sprout, talker, Green Giant, MIP **55.00**
Little Sprout, vinyl, 1970s, 6½", EX **8.00**
Lucky Lymon, vinyl talker, Sprite, 1990s, 7½", M **20.00**
Noid, plush, Dominos Pizza, 1988, 19", MIP **20.00**
Northern Tissue Girl, stuffed/vinyl, rooted hair, 1980s, 15", M.....**10.00**
Pink the Spoon, bendy, Baskin-Robins, 1990s, 5", NM+ **6.00**
Pizza-Pizza Man, plush, Little Caesar's Pizza, 1990, EX **5.00**
Poppin' Fresh, talker, Pillsbury/Mattel, 16", NM **100.00**
Punchy, stuffed cloth, Hawaiian Punch, 20", NM........**90.00**
Raid Bug, plush, 1989, EX+ **25.00**
Sparky the Horse, inflatable, AC Spark Plugs/Ideal, 1960s, 25x15", EX...**100.00**
Tastykake Bakery Doll, stuffed print, 1970s, VG **15.00**
Texaco Cheerleader, 1971, 11", NRFB **20.00**
Toucan Sam, vinyl, Kellogg's Froot Loops, 1984, 5", NMIB **5.00**
Vlasic Stork, plush, 1989, Trudy Toys, 22", NM **20.00**
Wangler Jeans Cowboy, cloth outfit, Ertl, 11½", MIB **50.00**
Wizard of O's, vinyl, Franco American, 1975, 7½", NM **20.00**

Agata

Agata is New England peachblow (the factory called it 'Wild Rose') with an applied metallic stain which produces gold tracery and dark blue mottling. The stain is subject to wear, and the amount of remaining stain greatly affects the value. It is especially valuable (and rare) on satin-finish items when found on peachblow of intense color. Caution! Be sure to use only gentle cleaning methods.

Currently rare types of art glass have been realizing erratic prices at auction; until they stabilize, we can only suggest an average range of values. In the listings that follow, examples are glossy unless noted otherwise. A condition rating of 'EX' indicates that the stain shows a moderate amount of wear. Our advisors for this category are Betty and Clarence Maier; they are listed in the Directory under Pennsylvania. See also Green Opaque.

Vase, four-sided rim, pinched sides, EX color and mottling, 6", $2,000.00.

Bowl, ruffled, spittoon shape, fair stain, 3x5¼" **750.00**
Bowl, sauce; G color & mottling **350.00**
Bowl, spittoon form w/scalloped edge, VG stain/mottling, 2½x5½" ..**1,265.00**
Creamer & sugar bowl, loop hdls, 3x6" **3,750.00**
Cruet, some wear to stain, 6" **865.00**
Finger bowl, EX stain & color, ruffled, 5¼" **1,250.00**
Pitcher, reeded hdl, water sz **2,500.00**
Punch cup, EX bl & amber stain, pk hdl, 2½", from $400 to......**650.00**
Toothpick holder, tricorner, EX mottling, 2⅜" **750.00**
Tumbler, EX stain & mottling, 3¾", from $750 to **1,000.00**
Tumbler, lemonade; EX stain..........**1,750.00**

Tumbler, lemonade; M stain, 5"..........**2,000.00**
Vase, EX gold & bl staining, pinched body, crimped rim, 3½"....**800.00**
Vase, lily; EX mottling, 7¾" **1,250.00**
Vase, lily; in cattail & reed Tufts fr, 11" **1,500.00**
Vase, lily; wear to stain, 9" **435.00**
Vase, much gold tracery, petal top, thin walls, 4½" **800.00**
Vase, satin (rare), EX stain, waisted neck, 3½" **2,815.00**

Akro Agate

The Akro Agate Company operated in West Virginia from 1914 until 1951, and in addition to their famous marbles they made children's dishes, powder jars with Scottie dogs on top, candlesticks, and ashtrays, for instance — in many colors and patterns. Though some of their glassware was made in solid colors, their most popular products were made of the same swirled colors as their marbles. Though many pieces are not marked, you will find some that bear their distinctive logo: a crow flying through the letter 'A' holding an Aggie in its beak and one in each claw. Some novelty items may instead carry one of these trademarks: 'J.V. Co., Inc.,' 'Braun & Corwin,' 'N.Y.C. Vogue Merc Co. U.S.A.,' 'Hamilton Match Co.,' and 'Mexicali Pickwick Cosmetic Corp.'

Color is a very important worth-assessing factor. Some pieces may be common in one color but rare in others. Occasionally an item will have exceptionally good colors, and this would make it more valuable than an example with only average color. When buying either marbles or juvenile tea sets in original boxes, be sure the box contains its original contents.

Note: Recently unearthed original written information has discounted the generally accepted attribution of the Chiquita and J.P. patterns to the Akro company, proving instead that they were made by the Alley Agate Company.

For more information we recommend *The Complete Line of the Akro Agate Co.* by our advisors, Roger and Claudia Hardy (available from them); they are listed in the Directory under West Virginia. Our advisor for miscellaneous Akro Agate is Albert Morin, who is in the Directory under Massachusetts.

Concentric Rib

Creamer, dk gr or wht, 1⁵⁄₁₆" **15.00**
Cup, pk or dk ivory, 1⁵⁄₁₆" **100.00**
Pitcher, dk or med bl, 2⅞" **40.00**
Plate, lt bl, 3¼"..........**18.00**
Plate, purple, 3¼" **45.00**
Saucer, yel, pk or dk ivory, 2¾" **6.00**
Sugar bowl, dk gr or wht, 1⁵⁄₁₆" **15.00**
Teapot, orange, 2⅜" **60.00**
Teapot lid, dk gr, wht or canary yel, 2⁵⁄₁₆" **5.00**
Tumbler, wht, 2" **7.00**

Concentric Ring

Creamer, bl transparent, 1⅜" **65.00**
Creamer, royal bl, 1⁹⁄₁₆" **40.00**
Cup, purple, 1⅜" **75.00**
Cup, purple, 1⁹⁄₁₆" **100.00**
Pitcher, bl transparent, 2⅞" **75.00**
Plate, canary yel, 3⁵⁄₁₆"..........**90.00**
Sugar bowl, bl/wht marbleized, 1⁹⁄₁₆" **125.00**
Sugar bowl, med or royal bl, 1⅜" **20.00**
Teapot, med or royal bl, 2⅜" **65.00**
Teapot lid, bl & wht marbleized, 2¹¹⁄₁₆" **25.00**
Tumbler, bl transparent, 2" **32.00**

Interior Panel

Cereal, dk gr, 16 panels, 3⅜" 30.00
Creamer, oxblood/wht marbleized, 16 panels, 1½" 50.00
Creamer, pk lustre, 18 panels, 1⁵⁄₁₆" 95.00
Creamer, topaz transparent, 18 panels, 1⁵⁄₁₆" 75.00
Cup, orange, 16 panels, 1½" 30.00
Plate, dk gr lustre, 18 panels, 3⁵⁄₁₆" 10.00
Plate, gr transparent, 16 panels, 4¼" 15.00
Plate, gr/wht marbleized, 18 panels, 3⁵⁄₁₆" 18.00
Sugar bowl, canary yel, 18 panels, 1⁵⁄₁₆" 70.00
Teapot, royal bl, 16 panels, 2¾" 80.00
Teapot, royal bl, 18 panels, 2½" 45.00
Teapot lid, topaz transparent, 16 panels, 2¹¹⁄₁₆" 20.00
Tumbler, gr transparent 18.00

Miss America

Boxed set, gr transparent, 17-pc (serves 4) 1,485.00
Boxed set, wht, 8-pc 388.00
Creamer, wht w/decal, 1⁹⁄₁₆" 70.00
Cup, red transparent, 1⁹⁄₁₆" 175.00
Plate, red onyx, 4½" 75.00
Plate, wht, 4½" 28.00
Saucer, gr transparent, 3⅝" 40.00
Sugar bowl, wht w/decal, 1⁹⁄₁₆" 28.00
Sugar bowl lid, red transparent, 2⅝" 130.00
Teapot, red onyx, 2½" 150.00

Octagonal

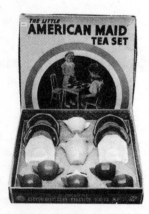

American Maid, opaque, large, 17-piece, MIB, from $265.00 to $440.00. (Photo courtesy Doris Lechler)

Cereal, dk gr wht or ivory, 3⅜" 18.00
Creamer, med or dk bl, open hdl, 1½" 40.00
Creamer, pale bl, open hdl, 1¼" 30.00
Cup, turq or lt bl, 1½" 40.00
Cup, wht or ivory, open hdl, 1¼" 45.00
Pitcher, pale bl, open hdl, 3" 55.00
Sugar bowl, med or dk bl, closed hdls, 1½" 20.00
Sugar bowl, pale, med or dk bl, open hdl, 1¼" 30.00
Teapot, lemon & oxblood, closed hdls, 3⅝" 175.00
Teapot, pale bl, open hdl, 3⅜" 40.00
Teapot, pale bl, open hdl, 3⅝" 70.00
Tumbler, canary yel, apple gr or dk gr, 2" 20.00

Raised Daisy

Creamer, dk ivory, 1⁵⁄₁₆" 125.00
Cup, dk gr, 1⁵⁄₁₆" 40.00

Pitcher/teapot, dk gr, 2⅜" 100.00
Plate, dk turq or dk bl, 3" 28.00
Sugar bowl, lt or dk yel, 1⁵⁄₁₆" 35.00
Teapot, dk turq or dk bl, w/lid, 2½" 75.00
Tumbler, Daisy, lt or dk yel, 2" 25.00
Tumbler, plain, dk ivory, 2" 75.00

Stacked Disc

Creamer, dk gr or wht, 1⁵⁄₁₆" 15.00
Cup, pk or dk ivory, 1⁵⁄₁₆" 100.00
Pitcher, med or dk bl, 2⅞" 90.00
Sugar bowl, dk gr, wht or canary yel, 1⁵⁄₁₆" 15.00
Teapot, lt bl or canary yel, 2⅜" 25.00
Tumbler, pk, dk ivory or canary yel, 2" 10.00

Stacked Disc and Interior Panel

Creamer, bl transparent, 1⅜" 65.00
Cup, orange, 1⅜" 35.00
Pitcher, gr transparent, 2⅞" 50.00
Sugar bowl, med or royal bl, 1⅜" 20.00
Teapot, bl/wht marbleized, 2⅜" 150.00
Tumbler, wht or ivory, 2" 100.00

Stippled Band

Creamer, gr or topaz transparent, 1¼" 85.00
Creamer, gr or topaz transparent, 1½" 28.00
Pitcher, gr transparent, 2⅞" 40.00
Saucer, topaz transparent, 2¾" 6.00
Sugar bowl, gr or topaz transparent, 1½" 50.00
Sugar bowl, gr or topaz transparent, 1¼" 85.00
Teapot lid, gr transparent, 2⅝" 75.00
Tumbler, azure bl, 2⅛" 200.00
Tumbler, gr or topaz transparent, 2⅛" 100.00

Miscellaneous

Ashtray, emb star center w/AA mk 600.00
Ashtray, Hotel Edison, bl 85.00
Ashtray, shell form, 2 to 4 colors, ea from $8 to 25.00
Ashtray, 3-rest w/match slot, any solid color, unmk, 4¾", $30 to...35.00
Basket, 1-hdl, bl marbleized 375.00
Basket, 2-hdl, gr/wht marbleized, 4" 25.00
Candlesticks, Tall Ribbed, gr marbleized, pr.................250.00
Candlesticks, Tall Ribbed, orange, pr 275.00
Flowerpot, #1308 (of #1300 series), 5¼", from $165 to........250.00
Flowerpot, Graduated Dart, marbleized, #308, 6⅜", from $250 to..350.00
Flowerpot, Ribs & Flutes, any color, #305, 3¾", from $25 to....35.00
Flowerpot, Wide Band Top, any color, 4⅜", from $50 to.........65.00
Jardiniere, Ribs & Flutes, sq mouth, solid color, #306CF.......45.00
Planter, Japanese, solid color other than blk, #650, 11¼" ...425.00
Powder jar, Concentric Ring Type 1, solid color, from $45 to....50.00
Powder jar, Ivy, marbleized, #323 ....75.00
Puff box, Colonial Lady, lt bl 100.00
Puff box, Colonial Lady, royal bl............................325.00
Puff box, Scotty Dog, dk gr 400.00
Puff box, Scotty Dog, med bl 125.00
Tray, Victory Safety, 6" 400.00
Vase, Grecian Urn, Niagara Falls, 5-sided ft, 3¼" 35.00
Vase, Hand (holding vase), any color, 3¼", from $20 to 30.00
Vase, Tab-Hdld, solid or marbleized, #317, 6¼", from $65 to....90.00
Vase, Trumpet Type I, emb wheat above decal & 4 emb ribs, rare....750.00

Vivaudou, apothecary jar, pk...95.00
Vivaudou, puff box, factory decor 30.00
Vivaudou, puff box, marbleized..300.00
Vivaudou, shaving mug, blk 45.00

Alamo Pottery

Alamo art pottery (1945 – 1951) was a division of the Alamo Pottery of San Antonio, Texas, which was primarily a maker of sanitary ware (bathroom fixtures). The art pottery division was founded by Jake Rowe, Richard Potter, and Bruce Blunt and produced vitreous china items which have survived the decades without crazing and with the high gloss glazes still gleaming as if new. (Mrs. Potter was a valuable resource in compiling information about Alamo history.)

Rowe, Potter, and Blunt developed glazes, processes, and mold shapes from which came styles and colors that ran the gamut from elegant, classically styled vases to whimsical figurals, and from pale translucent aquas and yellows to bold crayon greens, blues, and yellows. The vast majority of the pieces are monochromatic, and the rare sponge- or spatter-ware pieces are at a premium.

Alamo is usually marked with a mold number (from 701 to 908, and P-2, P-3, and presumably P-1). Many also have an oval Alamo Pottery ink stamp in either black or blue. Bottoms are generally unglazed, although a few pitchers with glazed bottoms exist. Flea bites in the glaze are fairly common and unless excessive are tolerated by most collectors. Crazing and staining are nonexistent, and virtually all interiors are fully glazed. These items were originally intended for the floral trade, and most sold for less than $3.00.

The art pottery division of Alamo closed in 1951 due to high costs of storing and shipping. Rowe, Potter, and Blunt moved to Gilmer, Texas, and founded Gilmer Pottery (see Gilmer listing), which produced many items often mistaken for Alamo.

Bowl, #730, 7½" 35.00
Bowl, console; Delphinium Blue, #775, 3¼x9"........22.50
Novelty, toilet, 4½"..60.00
Pitcher, #760, 4 diagonal sweep indentations, 7½x8½" 40.00
Planter, #771, 3¼x12x7"..34.00
Vase, #702, apricot colored w/blk marbling, 7" 30.00
Vase, #721, 6x4"...15.00
Vase, #746, cornucopia, 7¾"...45.00
Vase, #902-7, yel, ribbed, 7x7" 20.00
Vase, #907, 10"...240.00
Vase, P-3, str sides, vertical ribs, 12½"..........................65.00

Alexandrite

Alexandrite is a type of art glass introduced around the turn of the century by Thomas Webb and Sons of England. It is recognized by its characteristic shading, pale yellow to rose and blue at the edge of the item. Although other companies (Moser, for example) produced glass they called alexandrite, only examples made by Webb possess all the described characteristics and command premium prices. Amount and intensity of blue determines value. Our prices are for items with good average intensity, unless otherwise noted. Our advisors for this category are Betty and Clarence Maier; they are listed in the Directory under Pennsylvania.

Bowl, ruffled rim, 2½x5"...900.00
Finger bowl, Honeycomb, crimped/ruffled, 3¾", +underplate ...2,200.00
Punch cup, 2¾x2¼"..600.00
Toothpick holder, Honeycomb, bulbous w/hexagonal rim, 2½" 2,200.00

Tumbler, Dmn Quilt, 3¾"...975.00
Vase, mushroom shape w/wide flange, EX color, 3½x4½" 1,600.00
Vase, Optic Honeycomb, ovoid with flared ruffled rim, 4¼" ...1,250.00

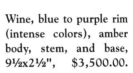
Wine, blue to purple rim (intense colors), amber body, stem, and base, 9½x2½", $3,500.00.
(Photo courtesy Betty and Clarence Maier)

Almanacs

The earliest evidence indicates that almanacs were used as long ago as Ancient Egypt. Throughout the Dark Ages they were circulated in great volume and were referred to by more people than any other book except the Bible. *The Old Farmer's Almanac* first appeared in 1793 and has been issued annually since that time. Usually more of a pamphlet than a book (only a few have hard covers), the almanac provided planting and harvesting information to farmers, weather forecasts for seamen, medical advice, household hints, mathematical tutoring, postal rates, railroad schedules, weights and measures, 'receipts,' and jokes. Before 1800 the information was unscientific and based entirely on astrology and folklore. The first almanac in America was printed in 1639 by William Pierce Mariner; it contained data of this nature. One of the best-known editions, Ben Franklin's *Poor Richard's Almanac*, was introduced in 1732 and continued to be printed for twenty-five years.

By the nineteenth century, merchants saw the advertising potential in a publication so widely distributed, and the advertising almanac evolved. These were distributed free of charge by drugstores and mercantiles and were usually somewhat lacking in information, containing simply a calendar, a few jokes, and a variety of ads for quick remedies and quack cures.

Today their concept and informative, often amusing text make almanacs popular collectibles that may usually be had at reasonable prices. Because they were printed in such large numbers and often saved from year to year, their prices are still low. Most fall within a range of $4.00 to $15.00. Very common examples may be virtually worthless; those printed before 1860 are especially collectible. Quite rare and highly prized are the Kate Greenaway 'Almanacks,' printed in London from 1883 to 1897. These are illustrated with her drawings of children, one for each calendar month.

Unless otherwise noted, our values are for examples in very good condition. See also Kate Greenaway.

Boston Almanac & Business...1872, 400 pgs, hardbk, 5½x3½", VG...60.00
Chicago Daily News Almanac & Yearbook, 1928, hardbk, EX 22.50
Eric Sloane's Almanac & Weather Forecast, 1955, w/dust jacket, EX ..40.00
Farmer's Almanac for 1857, softcover, VG 25.00
Great Western Almanac for 1849, softcover, 34 pgs, VG............450.00
Prairie Farmer's Directory of Farmers & Breeders of IL, 1918, VG...45.00

Richardson's VI & NC Almanac...1865...Confederate States, , 36 pgs, EX **155.00**
Telephone Almanac 1944, Bell & AT&T, 32 pgs, softcover, EX ..**30.00**
Universalist Register & Almanac for 1838, 36 pgs, softcover, VG+ **40.00**
WHIG Almanac & US Register-New York 1848, 64 pgs, softcover, EX...**35.00**
World Almanac & Book of Facts for 1923, 696 pages, hardback, EX...**265.00**
World Almanac & Book of Facts for 1943, w/dust jacket, 8x5", EX...**35.00**

Aluminum

Aluminum, though being the most abundant metal in the earth's crust, always occurs in combination with other elements. Before a practical method for its refinement was developed in the late nineteenth century, articles made of aluminum were very expensive. After the process for commercial smelting was perfected in 1916, it became profitable to adapt the ductile, nontarnishing material to many uses.

By the late '30s, novelties, trays, pitchers, and many other tableware items were being produced. They were often handcrafted with elaborate decoration. Russel Wright designed a line of lovely pieces such as lamps, vases, and desk accessories that are becoming very collectible. Many who crafted the ware marked it with their company logo, and these signed pieces are attracting the most interest. Wendell August Forge (Grove City, PA) is a mark to watch for; this firm was the first to produce hammered aluminum (it is still made there today), and some of their examples are particularly nice. Upwardly mobile market values reflect their popularity with today's collectors. In general, 'spun' aluminum is from the '30s or early '40s, and 'hammered' aluminum is from the '30s to the '60s.

For further information, refer to *Collectible Aluminum, An Identification and Value Guide* (2000 updated values), by Everett Grist, listed in the Directory under Tennessee; *Vintage Bar Ware* by Stephen Visakay; and *Collector's Encyclopedia of Russel Wright* by Ann Kerr. Another excellent reference is *Hammered Aluminum, Hand Wrought Collectibles*, by our advisor, Dannie Woodard, see the Directory for Texas.

Pitcher, Chrysanthemum pattern, Continental Silver, EX, $55.00; Matching tumbler (very rare), from $25.00 to $30.00.

Ashtray, bamboo, single rest, Everlast, 5" dia **30.00**
Basket, acorns/leaves, rolled rim, braided hdls, Continental, 12"..**25.00**
Beverage server, concentric circles, Kromax, 11x5" dia **25.00**
Beverage spoons, Talstirs, anodized, Color Craft, 6 on card **40.00**
Bowl, hammered, serrated rim, 3-loop hdls, Buenilum, 2x12".......**10.00**
Cake stand, shields band/serrated rim/ped ft, Wilson Metal, 8x12" **10.00**
Candy dish, bird-&-grape side hdl on oval, M Bowman, 13" **15.00**
Casserole, bamboo, bamboo finial on lid, no hdls, Everlast, 4x7"..**10.00**
Chocolate pot, mums, hinged lid w/petal finial, Continental, 10"...**85.00**

Coasters, bamboo, set of 4 on ftd trivet, Everlast, 3½" dia **20.00**
Coffeepot, mums, petal finial, Continental, 10"...............................**85.00**
Compote, hammered w/tulip-&-ribbon finial, open ribbon stem, unmk...**15.00**
Creamer & sugar bowl w/tray, dbl loop hdls & finial, Buenilum ...**15.00**
Double boiler, polished w/wood hdl & finial, Pyrex insert, Buenilum......**10.00**
Figurine, goose in flight, ball & socket mt on 'rock,' #145, 10" ..**150.00**
Gravy boat, plain w/serrated lip & base trim, Buenilum, 3x6" dia..**25.00**
Hurricane lamp, grape/leaf, loop hdl, glass chimney, Everlast, 9" ..**20.00**
Ice bucket, hammered, beaded lip, twisted hdl, Buenilum, 6x5" ...**25.00**
Lazy Susan, fruit/flowers, serrated edge, Cromwell, 16" **10.00**
Leaf tray, Bruce Fox, Fox-34, 7¼x10" **125.00**
Matchbox cover, shotgun/flying ducks/clouds, W August Forge....**75.00**
Napkin holder, flower/ribbon, 4-ftd fan shape, serrated, unmk, 6" L....**15.00**
Nut bowl, flower/leaves, ruffled/serrated rim, ped ft, Wilson, 7"....**10.00**
Pitcher, wild rose/hammered, sm ice lip, ear hdl, Continental, 8" ..**40.00**
Plate, dogwood, plain edge, W August Forge, 9".............................**30.00**
Sherbets, anodized bases w/fluted glass inserts, unmk, set of 6 ......**45.00**
Strainer, woven wire basket, red wood hdl, 8"................................**9.00**
Tidbit, mums, crimped edges, 2-tier, Continental, 9¼" **35.00**
Tray, bar; anchor & rope w/sea gulls, Everlast, 9x15"....................**30.00**
Vase, mums, cylindrical w/serrated incurvate rim/ft, Continental, 10"....**85.00**
Wastebasket, emb floral, Everlast, 11x11" dia **60.00**
Water set, anodized, 7" pitcher+6 5" tumblers **75.00**

AMACO, American Art Clay Co.

AMACO is the logo of the American Art Clay Co. Inc., founded in Indianapolis, Indiana, in 1919, by Ted O. Philpot. They produced a line of art pottery from 1931 through 1938. The company is still in business but now produces only supplies, implements, and tools for the ceramic trade.

Values for AMACO have risen sharply, especially those for figurals, items with Art Deco styling, and pieces with uncommon shapes. Our advisors for this category are Suzanne Perrault and David Rago; they are listed in the Directory under New Jersey.

Bust of woman w/braided hair, off-wht, 8x6" **155.00**
Vase, orange/brn/yel/brn swirls, flared rim, 7¼" **25.00**

Amberina

Amberina, one of the earliest types of art glass, was developed in 1883 by Joseph Locke of the New England Glass Company. The trademark was registered by W.L. Libbey, who often signed his name in script within the pontil.

Amberina was made by adding gold powder to the batch, which produced glass in the basic amber hue. Part of the item, usually the top, was simply reheated to develop the characteristic deep red or fuchsia shading. Early amberina was mold blown, but cut and pressed amberina was also produced. The rarest type is plated amberina, made by New England for a short time after 1886. It has been estimated that less than 2,000 pieces were ever produced. Other companies, among them Hobbs and Brockunier, Mt. Washington Glass Company, and Sowerby's Ellison Glassworks of England, made their own versions, being careful to change the name of their product to avoid infringing on Libbey's patent. Prices realized at auction seem to be erratic, to say the least, and dealers appear to be 'testing the waters' with prices that start out very high only to be reduced later if the item does not sell at the original asking price. A lot of amberina glassware is of a more recent vintage — look for evidence of an early production, since the later wares are worth much less than glassware that can be attributed to the older makers. Generic amberina with hand-painted flowers will bring lower prices as well. Our values are taken from auction results and dealer lists, omitting the extremely high and low ends of the range. See also Libbey.

Key:
NE — New England Glass Company

Bowl, deep color, cone shape w/ruffled top, 2½x5½" 150.00
Bowl, deep color, 3x4½" 120.00
Bowl, Dmn Optic, pinched rim, 2x4½" 80.00
Bowl, Dmn Optic, plain rim, 2½x9" 160.00
Bowl, Dmn Quilt, 1½x4¼" 90.00
Bowl, Invt T'print (lt mold), plain rim, 1⅜x4½" 60.00
Canoe, Daisy & Button/Hobbs No 101, 3½x3x8¼" 100.00
Celery vase, Invt T'print, pinched rim, 6½" 300.00
Celery vase, Invt T'print, sq scalloped top, 6½x3½" 350.00
Cordial, lily form, fuchsia rims shade to amber stem/ft, 4½", pr..290.00
Creamer, Invt T'print, amber reeded hdl, 4½" 110.00
Cuspidor, fuchsia shading to amber bowl, flared top, 2½x5¼"....235.00
Finger bowl, deep color, inverted scalloped rim, 2½x5" 175.00
Finger bowl, Dmn Optic (lt mold), waisted, 2¾" 60.00
Goblet, Invt T'print...80.00
Pear, deep red to clear, full stem, 5½" 525.00
Pitcher, alternating rows of flowers & leaves, ruffled rim, 7¼" ...150.00
Pitcher, Dmn Quilt, amber hdl, 5½" 175.00
Pitcher, Hobnail, amber hdl, 7½" 375.00
Pitcher, Honeycomb Optic, clear reeded hdl, ruffled rim, 8".......170.00
Pitcher, Invt Coin Spot, sq mouth, 7" 325.00
Pitcher, Invt T'print, reverse color, 6" 265.00
Pitcher, Invt T'print, tricorner, amber reeded hdl, 8½" 230.00
Pitcher, Invt T'print, 4-corner rim, ogee sides, wear, 7" 150.00
Pitcher, ribbed, amber reeded hdl, ball body, 8" 210.00
Pitcher, sq rim, 4 pinched sides, reeded amber hdl, reverse color, 8"...165.00
Pitcher, Swirled Optic, amber sq hdl, 7" 130.00
Saucer, ice cream; Daisy & Button/Hobbs No 101, 5¾" sq 70.00
Sherbet, Invt T'print, amber stem, 4¼" 90.00
Tumbler, champagne; Ribbed Optic, 4¼" 60.00
Tumbler, Coin Spot, 3¾" 60.00
Tumbler, Dmn Optic, 3¾" 60.00
Tumbler, Invt T'print, EX color, 3¾"..70.00
Tumbler, lemonade; amber reeded hdls, 4" 175.00
Tumbler, ribbed, slightly waisted cylinder, nice color, 4¼"..........115.00
Tumbler, Ribbed Optic, lg, 4½x3" 60.00
Tumbler, Ribbed Optic, 3¾" 70.00
Vase, deep color, bulbous amber bottom, 4-petal top, 4x4" 235.00
Vase, Invt T'print, pinched sides, 6½" 150.00
Vase, lily; ribbed stem, tri-lobe rim, 9" 525.00
Vase, Ribbed Optic, pinched sides, appl rigaree, tricorner, 6" 150.00
Vase, ruffled rim; rstr Meriden #0535 fr, 9½" 550.00
Vase, Swirled Optic, ruffled, 5¾" 60.00

Plated Amberina

Bowl, 5-lobe, paper label, 7½" $7,200.00
Creamer, emb ribs, 2¼x5¼" 3,600.00
Cruet, bulbous, amber hdl, faceted stopper, annealing line, 7"...2,650.00
Punch cup, 2½"...3,000.00
Tumbler, EX shading, 3¾" 1,700.00

American Bisque

The American Bisque Pottery operated in Williamstown, West Virginia, from 1919 to 1982. The company was begun by Mr. B.E. Allen and remained an Allen-family business until its sale in 1982. Figural pottery was produced from approximately 1937 until about the time the pottery closed.

American Bisque pottery is often identified by the 'wedges' or dry-footed cleats on the bottom of the ware. Many designs are unique to the American Bisque Company, such as cookie jars with blackboards and magnets, others with lids that doubled as serving trays, and some with 'action pieces' that show movement. American Bisque pieces are very collectible and are available in a broad variety of color schemes; some items are decorated with 22 – 24k gold. Many items are modeled after highly popular copyrighted characters.

See also Cookie Jars.

Bank, Attitude Papa (pig), no mk, 8½"...70.00
Bank, Bow Pig, pig in yel jacket w/bl bow at neck, USA, 5¼" 30.00
Bank, Chicken Feed, sack w/chicken, no mk, 4½" 25.00
Bank, Fatsy, mk Fatsy USA, 5¾" 80.00
Bank, For Your Rainy Day, 3-D pig aside, no mk, 6¼", from $70 to....75.00
Bank, Snowman (head in top hat), no mk, 6½" 35.00
Cookie jar, Baby Huey, USA, (+), minimum value.....................2,500.00
Cookie jar, Bear, #CJ-701 ....50.00
Cookie jar, Captain, USA, American Bisque..................................125.00
Cookie jar, Chest, #CJ-562, from $150 to 175.00
Cookie jar, Chick, #CJ-702...125.00
Cookie jar, Churn, USA, American Bisque 25.00
Cookie jar, Coach Lamp, USA, American Bisque.........................125.00

Cookie jar, Fawn, unmarked, $100.00.

Cookie jar, Fire Chief, American Bisque......................................125.00
Cookie jar, French Poodle, burgundy, USA American Bisque, from $100 to.......125.00
Cookie jar, Hen w/Chick, mc, USA...150.00
Cookie jar, Herman & Katnip, Harvey Famous Cartoons, c 1960, mk...3,800.00
Cookie jar, Kitten & Beehive, brn/bl on wht (unusual), mk 75.00
Cookie jar, Liberty Bell, USA, American Bisque...........................125.00
Cookie jar, Oaken Water Bucket w/Gourd Dipper, mk, from $100 to..125.00
Cookie jar, Popeye, USA, American Bisque from $550 to..........600.00
Cookie jar, Puppy, #CJ-754 ....60.00
Cookie jar, Rooster, USA, American Bisque...................................95.00
Cookie jar, Rudolph, c RLM, American Bisque (+) 400.00
Cookie jar, Sears Strawberry, Sears Exclusively USA, American Bisque ...40.00
Cookie jar, Teakettle (Martha & George), emb couple on side, gr w/gold...50.00
Cookie jar, Toothache Dog, USA, American Bisque, from $400 to ...425.00
Cookie jar, Yarn Doll, gold trim, no mk 200.00
Planter, Circus Horse, no mk, 7"..30.00
Planter, Dutch girl before lg wooden shoe, no mk, 6" 12.00
Planter, Sailfish, beside free-form opening, 8x10" 50.00
Planter, Southern Bell, dbl-sided; yel hat & wide skirt, 11½" L....35.00

Planter, Whimsical Donkey, pulling cart, no mk, 6½"...................12.00
Planter, Winter couple, embracing, no mk, 7½" 30.00
Planter, Yarn Doll w/Block, no mk, 5¾" 25.00
Vase, Gardenia, flared rim, snail hdls, emb flower w/gold trim, 6" ...20.00

American Encaustic Tiling Co.

A.E. Tile was organized in 1879 in Zanesville, Ohio, for the production of dust-pressed encaustic floor tile. After several important flooring commissions, such as the New York State Capitol in Albany, the company diversified to the production of decorative embossed tiles covered in glossy glazes. The German sculptor Herman Mueller would prove to be their finest modeler, working with glaze chemist Karl Langenbeck. By the late 1920s, A.E. had become one of the largest tile manufacturers in the world, employing over one thousand workers in plants in Ohio, New Jersey, and California. The operation was reorganized by the Schweiker brothers after World War II and would eventually become the American Olean Tile Company. It is now known as Dal-Tile. Our advisors for this category are Suzanne Perrault and David Rago; they are listed in the Directory under New Jersey.

Key:
cs — cuerda seca
Mark 1 — THE AMERICAN ENCAUSTIC TILE CO.
   LIMITED (stamped)
Mark 2 — AETCO L.A. (stamped)
Mark 3 — Large circular mark

Frieze, 4-tile: cattails emb on clear bl, mk 1, fr, 24x6" 920.00
Panel, man (lady), period dress, turq (rare), gilt fr, 18x3", pr, $300 to 500.00
Panel, putto pulling ram on red bsk, H Mueller/mk 1, 6x18" L ..450.00
Paperweight, ram on stepped base, tan/bl crystalline, mk 1, rstr, 6" L ..230.00
Tile, stenciled Arabesques etc, brn gloss on vellum, mk 1, 6", NM ..100.00

American Indian Art

That time when the American Indian was free to practice the crafts and culture that was his heritage has always held a fascination for many. They were a people who appreciated beauty of design and colorful decoration in their furnishings and clothing; and because instruction in their crafts was a routine part of their rearing, they were well accomplished. Several tribes developed areas in which they excelled. The Navajo were weavers and silversmiths, the Zuni, lapidaries. Examples of their craftsmanship are very valuable. Today even the work of contemporary Indian artists — weavers, silversmiths, carvers, and others — is highly collectible. Unless otherwise noted, values are for items with no obvious damage or excessive wear (EX/NM). For a more thorough study we recommend *Arrowheads and Projectile Points*, *Indian Artifacts of the Midwest*, and *Indian Trade Relics*. All of these have been written by our advisor, Lar Hothem; you will find his address in the Directory under Ohio. Other references include *Arrowheads of the Central Great Plains* by Dan Fox; *Field Guide to Flint Arrowheads and Knives* by Lawrence N. Tully and Steven N. Tully; and *Flint Blades and Projectile Points of the North American Indian* by Lawrence N. Tully (all by Collector Books).

Key:
bw — beadwork   p-h — prehistoric
dmn — diamond   s-s — sinew sewn

Apparel and Accessories

Before the white traders brought the Indian women cloth from which to sew their garments and beads to use for decorating them, cloth-

ing was made from skins sewn together with sinew, usually made of animal tendon. Porcupine quills were dyed bright colors and woven into bags and armbands and used to decorate clothing and moccasins. Examples of early quillwork are scarce today and highly collectible.

Early in the nineteenth century, beads were being transported via pony pack trains. These 'pony' beads were irregular shapes of opaque glass imported from Venice. Nearly always blue or white, they were twice as large as the later 'seed' beads. By 1870 translucent beads in many sizes and colors had been made available, and Indian beadwork had become commercialized. Each tribe developed its own distinctive methods and preferred decorations, making it possible for collectors today to determine the origin of many items. Soon after the turn of the century, the craft of beadworking began to diminish.

Belt, Plateau, Pendleton style, mc bw, reattached buckle, 31x3½" 110.00
Cap, Sioux boy's, full geometric bw, 1900s, 2½x6½x5½" 1,500.00
Clout, Chippewa, trade cloth w/bw florals, 1835, 19x18" 110.00
Clout, Santee Sioux, gr trade cloth w/bw/sequins/ribbons, 1890s, 22" .800.00
Cuffs, Sioux, buffalo hide w/bw flags & geometrics, 1890s, 7x5" ..200.00
Dress, Crow, gr trade cloth w/cowry shells & ribbons, 1900, 49" ..375.00
Gauntlets, Plateau, floral bw on buckskin w/fringe, 1920s, 13", EX 145.00
Leggings, Cheyenne child's, bw bars & crosses on wht, 1890s, 11½" ..800.00
Leggings, Comanche lady's, hide w/yel ochre & geometric bw, 19x7" ...900.00
Leggings, Sioux, red trade cloth w/geometric bw strips, 1900s, 29" ..325.00
Leggings, Sioux, s/s buffalo hide strips/bl wool, 1880s, 30" 750.00
Moccasins, Arapaho, ochred buffalo w/bw, 1930s, 10" 200.00
Moccasins, Cheyenne, allover mc bw panels, cloth cuffs, 1920s, 11" .750.00

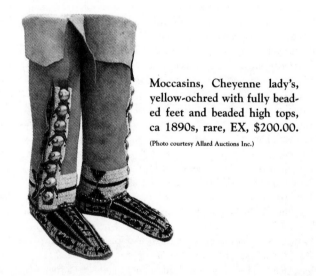

Moccasins, Cheyenne lady's, yellow-ochred with fully beaded feet and beaded high tops, ca 1890s, rare, EX, $200.00.

(Photo courtesy Allard Auctions Inc.)

Moccasins, Cheyenne, mc bw on wht bw ground, cloth cuff, 1890s, 10" ...660.00
Moccasins, Crow, elk-hide high-top, flat bw, ca 1960, 9½".........110.00
Moccasins, Crow man's, full geometric bw, mid-1900s, 10".........350.00
Moccasins, Crow man's, full geometric bw & line bw trim, 1940s, 11" ..400.00
Moccasins, Gros Ventre, high-tops, hide w/full geometric bw, 1920s, 9" ..475.00
Moccasins, N Cree child's, high-tops, moose hide w/bw, 1960s, 8" ..70.00
Moccasins, Osage lady's, flowing foliage bw, hard sole, 1950s, 9½" ..375.00
Moccasins, Plains child's, lazy stitch geometric bw on bl, 1950s, 6" ..375.00
Moccasins, S Plains, tiny bw/silver conchos/fringe, 1900s, 14" H..600.00
Moccasins, Sioux, buffalo hide w/geometric bw, 1890s, 11" 750.00
Moccasins, Sioux, geometric bw on wht, hard soles, 1930s, 11" .425.00
Moccasins, Sioux child's, full 3-color bw, crepe trim, 1900s, 6½" ..485.00
Moccasins, Tlingit, bw on buckskin, ca 1900, 10" 375.00
Pants, Cree boy's, buckskin w/floral bw, fringe, 1940s, 19x12" 130.00
Sash, assumption; Metis, geometric bands, 1930s, 88x9".............275.00
Sash, bw rabbit & Woodlands native designs, fringe, 1920s, 43x1¼" .250.00

Sash, Pueblo, loom-woven fishnet cotton w/aniline dye, 65x7"+fringe .60.00
Shirt & leggings, Kiowa boy's, ochred leather, fringe/bw, 1880s, VG........**21,850.00**
Vest, Metis man's, complex floral bw, button closure, 1890s, 21" L...**635.00**
Vest, Plains, floral/bird bw on trade cloth, ca 1890, 20" L, EX ...**1,100.00**
Vest, Sioux man's, lazy stitch deer/crosses/etc on bl, fringe, 1880s...**3,675.00**

Bags and Cases

The Indians used bags for many purposes, and most display excellent form and workmanship. Of the types listed below, many collectors consider the pipe bag to be the most desirable form. Pipe bags were long, narrow, leather and bead or quillwork creations made to hold tobacco in a compartment at the bottom and the pipe, with the bowl removed from the stem, in the top. Long buckskin fringe was used as trim and complemented the quilled and beaded design to make the bag a masterpiece of Indian art.

Apache, puzzle, lacy borders, dbl faux opening, bw, ca 1900, 10½" ...**400.00**
Blackfoot, medicine, parfleche w/badger paws & geometrics, '30s, 11x6" ..**170.00**
Blackfoot, pipe, ochred antelope hide w/bw, 1880s, 7x30".......**1,100.00**
Cheyenne, tobacco, bw strips, red ticking, 1890s, 29"..............**1,265.00**
Chippewa, bandolier, full bw/Peking glass dangles, 1890s, 17x16"..**325.00**
Chippewa, bandolier, overall floral/berry bw, ca 1880, 46x6¼"....**1,725.00**
Chippewa, bandolier, velvet w/bw & red Stroud trim, 1900s, 46x12"..**1,200.00**
Crow, parfleche, pnt geometrics, 1900s, 4x15x28"........................**700.00**
Kiowa, ration pouch, lazy stitch bw cross on wht, 1880s, 4¼" **635.00**
Nez Perce, belt bag, cornhusk w/geometric panels & flap, 1930s, 6x6"..**400.00**
Nez Perce, cornhusk w/geometrics, floral bw flap, 1930s, 9½x10"...**700.00**
Nez Perce, parfleche, pnt geometrics, 1940s, 2x29x12"............**1,000.00**
Nez Perce, twined cornhusk w/striking geometrics, 1920s, 21x15"..**1,400.00**
Nez Perce, wallet, twined cornhusk/leather w/geometrics, 1970s, 4½" ..**200.00**
Plateau, flat, full bw eagle & Am flag design, 1930s, 14¼x13¼"...**700.00**
Plateau, flat, full bw floral & geometrics, fringe, 1930s, 20x15"..**300.00**
Plateau, flat, full bw w/lg foliate designs, 1930s, 12x9½"..........**325.00**
Plateau, hemp root, drawstring leather top, 1960s, 7x4½" **300.00**
Plateau, parfleche w/pnt geometrics, folded, 1930s, 27x16x4" **900.00**
Shawnee, bandolier, floral seed bw on wool w/silk border, 1850s, 60"...**10,350.00**
Sioux, medicine, s/s bw on ochred antelope hide, w/contents, 1880s, 8" **750.00**
Sioux, strike-a-light, full bw/tin cones, single flap, 1910s, 7x5" ..**800.00**
Sioux, strike-a-light, lazy stitch bw on hard leather, 1900s, 6x5"....**1,200.00**
Sioux, tobacco, mc bw, metal bw trim/feathers/cones, 1890s, 27" ..**2,875.00**

Baskets

In the following listings, examples are coil built unless noted otherwise.

Algonquin, quiver, birch bark w/feathers & moose-hide hdl, 1920s, 27x4" ..**450.00**
Apache, floral w/human/mtn border, early 20th C, 4½x15" **1,380.00**
Apache, intricate geometrics & crosses, 1900s, 5x18".............**1,800.00**
Apache, mc humans/dogs/crosses, ca 1900, 4x13½"..................**2,750.00**
Apache, radiating geometrics, flared sides, 1930s, 9x14" **2,250.00**
Apache, red geometric ferns, EX patina, 1900s, 8½x23" **1,600.00**
Apache, tray, mc star/checkered band/mtns, ca 1910, 4x13½"....**2,250.00**
Apache, tray, squash blossom center w/willow & devil's claw, 9½"......**375.00**
Apache, tus, pitch covered, flared top, orig hdls, 1930s, 11x7"...**275.00**
Chehalis, bands & imbricated gold butterflies, 1940s, 4x7½" **325.00**
Chemehuevi, bowl, flattened star w/radiating steps, 1930s, 3x10"............**800.00**
Chitamacha, purse, thin plaited weave, 1930s, 5x2½" **35.00**
Choctaw, trinket, dbl-neck, plaited, woven hdl, 1920s, 9x12x4"...**275.00**
Hopi, tray, mc butterfly maiden kachinas & rain clouds, 1920s, 11"...**425.00**
Hupa, open weave & traditional banded geometrics, 1940s, 3x4"...**200.00**
Huron, candy, lidded birch bark w/buckskin hdl, 1920s, 6½x7"....**90.00**
Jar, water; Paiute, piñon pitcher, looped shells at neck, 8x7"......**275.00**
Jicarilla, tray, mc squash blossoms & geometrics, 1930s, 2x16"...**200.00**

Karok, fine geometrics & rim designs, 1930s, 3½x5"....................**250.00**
Karok, hat, fine-weave, bands & rhomboid geometrics, 1920s, 3½x6"...**1,200.00**
Karok, rare negative design, ca 1900, 4x5" **1,100.00**
Klamath, concentric mc stepped rectangles, 1930s, 4½x8".........**475.00**
Klamath, str sides, geometrics & yel accents, 1930s, 5x7"...........**200.00**
Maido, traditional rhomboids & ornate checkering, 1910s, 4x8" ..**700.00**
Maidu, geometric snake band, 1920s, 3x10½".............................**550.00**
Mission, bowl, Cahuilla style, radiating stair steps, 2½x8"..........**225.00**
Modoc, soft-weave, mc bands & connecting geometrics, 1920s, 7x13"...**1,200.00**
Navajo, wedding basket, traditional mc, spirit release, 1930, 15" ..**425.00**
Ojibway, quilled birch bark w/bear-design lid, 1940s, 3x6"..........**550.00**
Ojibway, quilled lidded birch bark w/maple leaf design, 1940s, 3x6"......**275.00**
Paiute, sifter, simple contrasting strands, 1920s, 4x10x8" **300.00**
Paiute, tus, pitch & mud covered, orig hdls, 1930s, 11x8" **500.00**
Papago, figures/elongated lozenges, early 20th C, 4⅜x13¼" **260.00**
Papago, tray, open boxed radiating geometrics/blk center, 1940s, 5x16"...**325.00**
Papago, tray, Tohono O'odham, 1950s, 9x12"................................**30.00**
Papago, vessel, continuous polychrome design, 1940s, 6½x7".......**80.00**
Pima, blk center, 2 geometric bands, 1940s, 3x12" **350.00**
Pima, blk wandering geometrics, 1940s, 3x13" **475.00**
Pima, continuous mc snake motif, upright, 1930s, 6½x10' **550.00**
Pima, flared sides, radiating stair steps, 1950s, 4½x13" **350.00**
Pima, geometric radiating serpents, 4x15", VG...........................**475.00**
Pima, ghia (burden basket), jute w/cvd sticks, strap, 1920s, 18x16x3" ..**1,300.00**
Pima, olla, shouldered, intricate geometrics allover, 1920, 14x15" ..**2,500.00**
Pima, reverse radiating stair steps, 1900s, 5x20" **600.00**
Pima, tray, blk center, radiating geometrics, 1920s, 1½x7½" **225.00**
Pima, tray, classic fret design, 1970, 13" **700.00**
Pima, tray, faded geometric blossoms, 1940s, 2x9" **80.00**
Pit River, fine weave, modified quail topknot, 1930s, 4x7".........**450.00**
Pomo, contrasting zigzags, 1930s, mini, ⅜x¼" **70.00**
Salish, storage, 3-color imbricated dmns, orig lid, 1930s, 9x15x9"..**225.00**
Salish, tray, flat weave, butterfly designs, orig hdls, 3½x17" **140.00**
Salishan, twined cedar & bear grass w/bark bottom, 4x5¼"........**215.00**
Washo, fine weave, red & blk stair steps, 1920s, 4x8".................**325.00**
Winnebago, carrying, split ash, vegetal dyes, 1930s, 8x12"............**70.00**
Winnebago, storage, split ash, vegetal dyes, w/lid, 1920s, 6x12½" ..**100.00**

Blades and Points

Relics of this type usually display characteristics of a general area, time period, or a particular location. With study, those made by the Plains Indians are easily discerned from those of the West Coast. Because modern man has imitated the art of the Indian by reproducing these artifacts through modern means, use caution before investing your money in 'too good to be authentic' specimens.

Adena, Burlington flint, early Woodland, IL, 4¼" **150.00**
Adena, dk Upper Mercer flint, OH, early Woodland, 3¼x1⅛" **75.00**
Agate Basin, Crescent Quarry flint, late Paleo, MO, 4¼"...........**800.00**
Ashtabula, gray Flintridge, wide shoulders, late Archaic, 2⅜" **25.00**
Clovis, bl-gray IN hornstone, early Paleo, OH, 2½" **325.00**
Dalton, lt chert, unusually slim, late Paleo, MO, 4½x⅞"............**275.00**
Dalton, slate, serrated edges, late Paleo, MO, 6" **1,750.00**
Dickson, lt Burlington flint, MO, middle Woodland, 3⅞"..........**175.00**
Dovetail, bl KY flint, early Archaic, KY, 2½x1¼"......................**250.00**
Dovetail, gray flint, indented base subtype, early Archaic, 3⅛"....**200.00**
Dovetail, wht chert w/serrated edges, early Archaic, MO, 3½" ..**350.00**
Florence, gray flint, IL, Woodland, 3¾x½", from $100 to **200.00**
Folsom, lt chert w/dk inclusions, late Paleo, MO, 2½x⅞" **800.00**
Graham Cave, Burlington Chert, early Archaic, MO, 4⅜x1½" ..**250.00**
Hardin, Burlington flint, barbed shoulders, early Archaic, IL, 3⅜"...**350.00**
Hardin, gray swirled flint, indented base, early Archaic, IL, 2⅜" ..**125.00**
Hemphill, tan chert, Archaic, IL, 3⅝"...**300.00**

Kampsville, gray striped flint, IL, late Archaic, 2¼" **80.00**
Lost Lake, Bangor chert, well beveled/serrated, early Archaic, 3" ...**450.00**
Mason, Burlington flint, well made, KY, middle Woodland, 3⅞" ..**210.00**
Sedalia, cream to pk chert, late Archaic, IL, 4⅝x1¾" **275.00**
Side-notch, high-grade gray flint w/wht lines, Archaic, 2½" **50.00**
Side-notched, bl Upper Mercer flint, OH, post-middle Woodland, 2" ...**250.00**
Snyders, gray & cream flint, MO, middle Woodland, 4"..........**2,350.00**
Stemmed lance, striped chert w/dk inclusions, late Paleo, OH, 3½" ...**200.00**
Stemmed lanceolate, mottled high-grade Flintridge, late Paleo, 1¾"...**50.00**
Table Rock or Bottleneck, quality flint, late Archaic, 3x1¼" **250.00**
Thebes, bk Upper Mercer, E-notch, resharpened, early Archaic, 2¾" ...**135.00**
Thebes, lt gray Flintridge, early Archaic, IN, 3⅜" **225.00**

Ceremonial Items

Aprons, dance; Plains, floral bw on blanket wool/silk/cotton, 1900s, pr .**200.00**
Aprons, dance; Woodland, seed & cut metal bw on velveteen, 1890s, pr .**600.00**
Blanket, Kiowa, ornate ribbonwork, ca 1920, 70x57"..................**200.00**
Bowl, Haida, cvd/pnt 1-pc feast dish w/lipped rim, 1880s, 5x10x13" ...**3,250.00**
Bowl, wooden w/zoomorphic figures ea side, 1890s, 3x13".......**2,500.00**
Drum, Pueblo, cvd cottonwood w/pnt designs, rawhide beads, 1900s, 7"...**425.00**
Mask, NW Coast, traditional red & blk pnt designs, 1960s, 9"...**250.00**
Moccasins, Arapaho, s/s buffalo hide w/full bw, 19th C, 10½"...**1,700.00**
Moccasins, Blackfoot, blk coloration, bw top vamp, 1890s, 10½"...**1,200.00**
Moccasins, dance; 8-sided bw stars, ca 1900, 10" **900.00**
Moccasins, dance; man's, Sioux, bw geometrics & bands, 1900s, 10".**550.00**
Rattle, dance; Hopi, rawhide w/pnt design & yel ochre, 1930s, 8½"..**250.00**
Rattle, NW Coast, cvd/pnt bird (cedar or alder), 1940s, 3x4x11" **275.00**
Rattle, NW Coast, cvd/pnt bird/stylized zoomorphic figures, 1940s, 13"...**1,000.00**
Rattle, Plains, cloth & rawhide over dowel, dew claw rattlers, 1940s..**70.00**
Rattle, Pueblo, gourd w/cotton-wrapped hdl, pnt head, 1900s, 10½"...**315.00**
Roach, Southern Plains, deer tail/porcupine, early 20th C, 16¼x4"...**260.00**
Shield, wood w/pnt mc zigzags & bands, ca 1900, 18".................**800.00**
Spear, Pueblo, iron barb tip w/pewter inlay & red pigment, 63x1"....**225.00**
Spoon, cvd horn w/bw hdl, ca 1890, 7¼x2½" **230.00**
Spoon, NW Coast, cvd mtn goat horn w/totemic creatures, 1900s, 10¼"...**1,095.00**
Spoon, NW Coast, cvd Shaman figural hdl, 1960s, 13" **225.00**
Spoon, Tlingit, mtn sheep horn w/totemic cvg, 1850s, 13" **1,600.00**
Totem pole, Haida, cvd cedar, Traditional imagery, 1900s, 24"...**1,265.00**
Wand, dance; Plains, beaded/fringed wrapped hdl, 1890s, 18", EX....**550.00**

Dolls

**Nez Perce doll, beaded
buckskin, 1890s, 12",
EX, $1,850.00.**

Apache, cloth, handmade, w/Apache dress, ca 1960, 15x4"..........**50.00**
Cheyenne, s-s buckskin w/buffalo hair, full costume, 20th C...**1,000.00**
Hopi, Kachina, Hoote Ogre, kilt & leather cloak, 1950s, 13".....**200.00**
Hopi, Kachina, Morning Singer, EX detail, 1950s, 7½x2½"......**225.00**
Hopi, Kachina, Sunflower, 1-pc, 1940s, 14x5"............................**225.00**
Seminole, palm frond w/ribbonwork outfit, 1940s, 17x6"............**160.00**
Ute, beaded hide & cloth w/bw features & details, 1900s, 21", EX...**550.00**
Ute, calico-stuffed female w/bw leggings, human hair, 1900s, 11"...**260.00**

Domestics

Blanket, Navajo, eye-dazzler design, wool, 1910, 52x34" **950.00**
Blanket, Osage, silk applications on navy trade cloth, 1900s, 51x54" ...**1,200.00**
Blanket, Plains, silk ribbonwork/metal sequins/fringe, 60x67" **460.00**
Blanket, Rio Grande, striped wearing type, ca 1900, 77x36" **275.00**
Bridle, Plains, lazy-stitch geometric bw, ca 1900, 19x8"..........**1,850.00**
Cradle, denim w/buckskin trim, rawhide wrapped, bw shade, 1950s, 37" ...**90.00**
Cradle, Lakota Sioux, red quillwork/bell trim, 1940s, child sz, 18"....**800.00**
Cradle, Ute, hide-covered wood, yel ochre & geometric bw, 1900s, 41"..**2,000.00**
Scraper, elk horn elbow form, punched/tinted decor, 1850s, 13½"....**700.00**

Jewelry and Adornments

 As early as 500 A.D., Indians in the Southwest drilled turquoise nuggets and strung them on cords made of sinew or braided hair. The Spanish introduced them to coral, and it became a popular item of jewelry; abalone and clam shells were favored by the Coastal Indians. Not until the last half of the nineteenth century did the Indians learn to work with silver. Each tribe developed its own distinctive style and preferred design, which until about 1920 made it possible to determine tribal origin with some degree of accuracy. Since that time, because of modern means of communication and travel, motifs have become less distinct.

 Quality Indian silver jewelry may be antique or contemporary. Age, though certainly to be considered, is not as important a factor as fine workmanship and good stones. Pre-1910 silver will show evidence of hammer marks, and designs are usually simple. Beads have sometimes been shaped from coins. Stones tend to be small; when silver wire was used, it is usually square. To insure your investment, choose a reputable dealer.

Belt, Navajo, sterling o/l buckle w/layered metal belt, 27x1¾" **60.00**
Belt, Navajo, sterling w/lg turq stone in ea of 9 conchos, 37x1¼"..**250.00**
Belt, Navajo, 25 half-dollars & lg buckle tip set w/turq, 1950s, 41" ..**300.00**
Bolo, Navajo, silver & turq, Navajo nation insignia, 1950s, 3¼" ..**315.00**
Bracelet, Navajo, silver Revival cuff style, 1970s, 1⅛" W **100.00**
Bracelet, Navajo, silver w/lg Bisbee turq stone, 1970s, 7x3¾" **170.00**
Bracelet, Navajo, silver w/7 gr-turq stones, 1960s, 8¼x½"..........**120.00**
Bracelet, Navajo, sterling cuff w/turq, stamped design, 1950s, 8¼"..**180.00**
Buckle, silver w/turq inlay teardrop shapes, sgn Jan Navajo, 3½" L...**115.00**
Choker, Plains, glass tube beads w/leather spacers, 1930s, 15" **85.00**
Jaclas, Pueblo, dbl strand natural turq, 1960, 5", pr **70.00**
Necklace, Blackfoot, bear claws & 19th-C tradebeads, 1890s, 24"...**950.00**
Necklace, Navajo, silver, turq & coral squash blossom, 1960s, 31" ..**250.00**
Necklace, Navajo, silver w/3 natural Carlin turqs, sgn DSM, 1960s, 20" ...**140.00**
Necklace, Navajo, 3-row sterling bead squash type w/turq stones, 1970s **300.00**
Necklace, Pueblo, 10-strand coral w/sterling cones & turq, 1970, 24"..**275.00**
Necklace, Pueblo, 10-strand liquid silver w/handmade chain, 1960, 26"..**120.00**
Pendant, Hopi, man-in-the-maze, silver, handmade chain, 1960s, 2⅛" **80.00**

Pipes

 Pipe bowls were usually carved from soft stone, such as catlinite or red pipestone, an argilaceous sedimentary rock composed mainly of hardened clay. Steatite was also used. Some ceremonial pipes were simply styled, while others were intricately designed naturalistic figurals, sometimes in bird or frog forms called effigies. Their stems, made of wood and often covered with leather, were sometimes nearly a yard in length.

Stone pipe, figural bear, elbow form with flared bowl, Northeast Woodlands, 4½", $1,325.00.

Catlinite, ceremonial, tacked/quilled wooden stem, 1890-1910, 8½" L..**1,800.00**
Catlinite, human head effigy, Iroquois, 1700-1800, 2½", $500 to ..**1,000.00**
Catlinite, L-shaped, Sioux, 1890s, 2¾x3¼"..................................**200.00**
Limestone (weathered), disc, short stem, KY, 1¼x1½" **350.00**
Pipestone, obtuse elbow, late p-h, 2¾" **650.00**
Pipestone, platform type, Hopewell, 1¼x1½" **1,000.00**
Pottery, Caddo, Mississippian, 1¾" bowl, 1½x2¾", $150 to **200.00**
Pottery, deer head effigy, Mississippian, 2¾x1½" **125.00**
Pottery, elbow w/incised lines at bowl, late p-h, 1¾"..................**200.00**
Pottery, human effigy, Iroquois, 1600-1750, 3¼x4½"..............**1,200.00**
Pottery, trumpet, Huron-Petun, ca 1590-1650, 3x3", from $700 to...**800.00**
Sandstone, bowl type, fringed bottom w/some eng, 1¼" **225.00**
Sandstone, frog effigy, Mississippian, 2½x2⅞x3" **600.00**
Sandstone, human face, vase shape, Woodland, 2¼", from $375 to..**550.00**
Sandstone, plain w/no keel hole, Mic-mac, 1650-1750, 2¼" **400.00**
Sandstone, rectangular, Mississippian, 2⅛x3" **225.00**
Sandstone, tubular w/peck mks & some polish, KY, 2⅜x3¾" **350.00**
Shell-tempered pottery, elbow w/eng geometrics, ⅝x4½x2¼" **200.00**
Steatite, bighorn sheep effigy, Cherokee, historic, 2⅞" **800.00**
Steatite, elbow, Iroquois, 1700-1800, 2¼"x2", from $300 to **450.00**
Steatite, keel type, well polished, Iroquois, 1600-1700, 2¼" **400.00**
Steatite, snake effigy, Iroquois, 1600-1750, 3x6½", $1,200 to..**2,000.00**
Steatite (blk) T-shaped Plains type, polished, 1700-1800, 3¾x7¾" ..**700.00**
Tomahawk, Plains, forged brass w/cvd/burned hardwood stem, 1890s, 21"...**2,250.00**

Pottery

Indian pottery is nearly always decorated in such a manner as to indicate the tribe that produced it or the pueblo in which it was made. For instance, the designs of Cochiti potters were usually scattered forms from nature or sacred symbols. The Zuni preferred an ornate repetitive decoration of a closer configuration. They often used stylized deer and bird forms, sometimes in dimensional applications.

Acoma, jar, fine-line design, 1930s, 3½x4¼"................................**200.00**
Acoma, jar, ornate blk design on wht, S Garcia, 8x11"...............**250.00**
Acoma, jar, parrot & foliage, orange & blk over buff slip, 6x6" ..**250.00**
Acoma, tile, dbl-headed waterbird, 1920s, 6x6"............................**375.00**
Casa Grande, effigy pot, seated figure w/tooling, red/dk ochre, 8"...**110.00**
Cochiti, blk-banded foliage on red, ca 1920, 4x6" **200.00**
Cochiti, olla, mc foliate designs, 1940s, 8x5½" **130.00**
Hopi, bowl, traditional 2-color decor, ca 1932, 3¾x7½".............**130.00**

Hopi, canteen, mc early-style pnt decor, 1890s, 5x7".............**3,000.00**
Hopi, seed jar, bird/terraces/lines, 2-color, Paqua Naha, 7¼"...**2,000.00**
Mata Ortiz, jar, blkware, curvilinear & checkered design, 5x6" ..**495.00**
Santa Clara, jar, polychrome, unsgn, ca 1970, 3½x4¼" **30.00**
Santo Domingo, chili bowl, buff slip on red w/blk geometrics, 4x7"..**385.00**
Santo Domingo, chili bowl, geometric decor, early 20th C, 4x7½"...**145.00**
Santo Domingo, dough bowl, classic design, 1940s, 10x17" **600.00**
Santo Domingo, dough bowl, deer/cornstalk/yucca designs, 1940s, 14" ..**425.00**
Santo Domingo, olla, blk & wht geometrics on red, ca 1930, 9x9" **800.00**
Tewa, wedding vase, blk-on-blk, dbl-neck, 1930s, 11x8x8".........**200.00**

Pottery, San Ildefonso

The pottery of the San Ildefonso pueblo is especially sought after by collectors today. Under the leadership of Maria Martinez and her husband Julian, experiments began about 1918 which led to the development of the 'black-on-black' design achieved through exacting methods of firing the ware. They discovered that by smothering the fire at a specified temperature, the carbon in the smoke that ensued caused the pottery to blacken. Maria signed her work (often 'Marie') from the late teens to the sixties; she died in 1980. Today examples with her signature may bring prices in the $500.00 to $4,500.00 range.

Bowl, blkware, geometrics, Santana, 1930s, 5x6x6" **600.00**
Jar, blkware, flags & geometrics, shouldered, Marie & Julian, 4½"..**1,265.00**
Jar, blkware, flat/ticked fretwork, Marie, 4½x6" **1,095.00**
Jar, blkware, lightning/clouds/raindrops, J Wo Peen, 3½x4½" **250.00**
Jar, blkware, simple shoulder decor, Marie & Julian, 1940s, 5½x4" ...**850.00**
Olla, blkware, Lupita Martinez, 1980, 8x6"..................................**200.00**
Plate, blkware, long radiating feathers, Marie & Julian, 13", NM....**2,100.00**

Rugs, Navajo

Chimayo, geometrics & line designs, 1950s, 38x18½" **70.00**
Chinle, serrated zigzag bands & stripes, rabbit brush dyes, 79x51"...**110.00**
Coal Mine Mesa, 5-figure Yei w/feathers/raised outline, 1980s, 54x33" ..**650.00**
Crystal, fishhook designs, natural & mc wool, 1950s, 98x38"...**1,200.00**
Crystal, fishooks & crosses w/swastika center, 1935, 54x40" **300.00**
Crystal area, serrated linear dmns, mc on tan, early, 45x75" **770.00**
Crystal Variant, dbl S lozenges/terraces, handspun, 1950s, 77x43"..**1,035.00**
Crystal/Wide Ruins, serrated dmn elements w/dk stripe, 1940s, 92x65" ...**990.00**
Eye-Dazzler, cross inside central lozenge, analine dyes, 1890s, 81x57"...**4,375.00**
Ganado, connected dmns, mc on wht, red selvage, 93x62".........**495.00**
Ganado, lozenge/serrated motif, T border, analine/natural dyes, 88x57".**3,565.00**
Ganado, serrated dmn pattern, red/brn/gray/tan/natural, 73x48"...**925.00**
Ganado Variant, Crystal chain element, dbl lozenges, 1930s, 81x55"...**3,000.00**
Ganado Variant, dbl serrated lozenges, sawtooth border, 1950s, 71x49"...**750.00**
Klagetoh area, sunrise w/terraces & serrated elements, early, 36x65" ..**880.00**
Navajo, rows of dmns, brn/tan/rust on ivory, 64x40", EX............**750.00**
Stepped blocks w/whirling logs, red/natural/tan, dk border, 73x44"...**825.00**
Transitional Eye-Dazzler, stacked pyramids & blk crosses, 84x50" **770.00**
Transitional type, band & dmn pattern, ca 1920, 68x42"............**425.00**
Western Reservation, red/wht/blk box design, 1960s, 58x35" **225.00**
Western Reservation type, stepped terraces, red border, 59x76", VG .**495.00**

Shaped Stone Artifacts

Axe, speckled tan granite, full-groove, PA, 4x3x7" **425.00**
Bannerstone, butterfly form, red & yel quartzite, Archaic, IL, 5"...**2,250.00**
Bannerstone, winged, banded slate, Archaic, IN, 2¾x4¾", $650 to...**800.00**
Boatstone, blk hematite w/red streaks, grooved, Woodland, 4½" ..**850.00**
Gorget, elliptical, banded slate, OH, Adena, 2⅜x4¾"..................**525.00**
Gorget, ridged, banded slate, OH, late Archaic, 4¾" **675.00**
Loafstone, gray hematite w/red patina, OH, Archaic, 1⅛x1x1¾" ...**50.00**

Pendant, banded slate, OH, Woodland, 3½" **400.00**
Pendant, bell shape, banded slate, OH, Woodland, 2x3¾" **350.00**
Pendant, keyhole type, red slate w/blk bands, OH, Adena, 2⅛x4⅛" ..**1,000.00**

Tools

Adz, hardened shale, dbl-groove, Archaic, PA, from $35 to..........**45.00**
Adz, humped, some polish, Archaic, IL, 2¾x5½", from $35 to **50.00**
Axe, banded slate, full-grove, OH, 3¼x1¼x5" **55.00**
Axe, blk hardstone, ½-groove w/raised ridge, IN, 6½x11½" ...**1,300.00**
Axe, brn hardstone w/blk specks, ¾-groove, OH, 4x7"...............**700.00**
Axe, dk granite, ¾-groove, IA, 2¾x1⅝x6¼", from $700 to **900.00**
Axe, gray hardstone, dbl-bitted, 1" groove, 3¼x1½x7½" **650.00**
Axe, hardstone celt, ungrooved, Woodland, AL, 1⅝x3½x8¼" ..**475.00**
Axe, hematite, full-groove, G polish, MO, med-lg **250.00**
Axe, sq bk, brn granite, ¾-groove, polished, MO, 3x2¾x5¾" **525.00**
Celt, hematite, well polished, MO, 2⅛x⅝x4½" **300.00**
Chisel, fire-blackened greenstone, polished, 1x¾x4½" **150.00**
Chisel, greenstone, TN, 1x½x4½" **150.00**
Hammerstone, gray hardstone, ¾-groove, IL, Archaic, 2¼x3⅝" ..**60.00**
Hammerstone, salvaged from axe, ¾-groove, Archaic, 2⅛" **40.00**
Maul, dk hardstone, grooved, IL, Archaic, 8" **165.00**
Pestle, hoof type, mixed hardstone, Archaic, OH, 4" **60.00**
Pestle/maul, dk hardstone, expanded top, polished, OH, 3⅜x6" ...**225.00**
Pestle/maul, wht quartzite, Archaic, OH, 6½", from $325 to......**400.00**
Scraper, Plateau, cvd bone, ca 1910, 13x5x2" **130.00**
Sinew stone, brn granite, MO, Woodland, 1¾x2⅜"......................**50.00**
Ulu (chopper), gr slate, PA, from $175 to....................................**250.00**

Weapons

Arrows, Creek, steel-pointed, sinew wrap w/fletching, 1890s, pr ...**260.00**
Bow, Cherokee, ca 1900, 46½" **715.00**
Bow, Creek, Bois D'Arc, w/sinew string, ca 1900, 43½"............**450.00**
Bow, Mojave, pnt/hand-cvd recurve w/geometric decor, 1900s, 57" ...**375.00**
Bow, Woodlands, ash long bow w/cvg, EX patina, 1920s, 64" **80.00**
Bow case & quiver, Cheyenne, bw panels/trade-cloth trim, 1900s, 38x6"...**1,000.00**
Knife, NW Coast, ivory/argillite, copper blade, 1960s, 21" **120.00**
War club, geode head, bw hafting, gauze-wrapped hdl, 1890s, 17"..**145.00**
War club, Plains, rawhide-wrapped stone head, bw on hdl, 1890s, 18"..**285.00**

Miscellaneous

Canoe, Chippewa, birch bark, cvd spreaders, 1930s, 48x10½x9" ..**600.00**
Horse blanket, S Plains, floral bw stroud & cotton, 1900s, 52x22" **1,265.00**
Peace medal, Louis XVI, silver, dtd 1774, 3" dia..........................**130.00**
Saddle w/stirrups, Cree, padded hide w/bw/tassels, ca 1885, 22" L...**3,565.00**

American Painted Porcelain

The American china-painting movement can be traced back to an extracurricular class attended by art students at the McMicken School of Design in Cincinnati. These students, who were the wives and daughters of the city's financial elite, managed to successfully paint numerous porcelains for display in the Woman's Pavilion of the 1876 United States Centennial Exposition held in Philadelphia — an amazing feat considering the high technical skill required for proficiency, as well as the length of time and multiple firings necessary to finish the ware. From then until 1917 when the United States entered World War I, china painting was a profession as well as a popular amateur pursuit for many people, particularly women. In fact, over 25,000 people were involved in this art form at the turn of the last century.

Collectors and antique dealers have discovered American hand-painted porcelain, and they have become aware of its history, beauty, and potential value. For more information on this subject, *American Painted Porcelain: Collector's Identification & Value Guide*, *Antique Trader's Comprehensive Guide to American Painted Porcelain*, and *Painted Porcelain Jewelry and Buttons: Collector's Identification & Value Guide* by Dorothy Kamm are the culmination of a decade of research; we recommend them highly for further study.

Though American pieces are of high quality and commensurate with their European counterparts, they are much less costly today. Generally, you will pay as little as $20.00 for a 6" plate and less than $75.00 for many other items. Values are based on aesthetic appeal, quality of the workmanship, size, rarity of the piece and of the subject matter, and condition. Age is the least important factor, because most American painted porcelains are not dated. (Factory backstamps are helpful in establishing the approximate time period an item was decorated, but they aren't totally reliable.)

Our advisor for this category is Dorothy Kamm; she is listed in the Directory under Florida.

Bar pin, brass-plated bezel, 1½" W, from $25 to...........................**55.00**
Belt buckle brooch, oval, 1¾x2⅛", from $90 to **175.00**
Bonbon bowl (depending on size), from $18 to **85.00**
Bowl, fruit; from $60 to...**80.00**
Box, 4¾ dia, from $50 to...**75.00**
Brooch, brass-plated bezel, oval, 2x1½", from $55 to **80.00**
Brooch, gold-plated bezel, 1½" dia, from $35 to **55.00**
Brooch/pendant, heart shape, gold-plated bezel, 2x1¾", from $50 to..**85.00**
Cake plate, from $35 to..**75.00**
Candlestick, from $45 to..**125.00**
Celery tray, from $35 to...**75.00**
Condiment set, poppy, tray/shakers/toothpick, 1891-1914, from $45 to ..**55.00**
Cruet, from $60 to..**80.00**
Cuff pin, rectangular, brass-pated bezel, ¼x1⅛", from $12 to **18.00**
Cup & saucer **45.00**
Cup & saucer, bouillon; from $35 to **55.00**
Ewer (depending on size), from $100 to **175.00**
Gravy boat, from $55 to...**75.00**
Handy pin, brass-plated bezel, 1½", from $30 to...........................**45.00**
Hatpin holder, from $88 to **150.00**
Jam jar, from $30 to **75.00**
Jardiniere (depending on size), from $65 to **375.00**
Mug, from $40 to **75.00**
Napkin ring, from $10 to...**35.00**
Pendant, gold-plated bezel, 1" dia, from $50 to...........................**200.00**
Pin tray, from $30 to **50.00**
Pitcher, lemonade; from $175 to..**250.00**
Plate, 6", from $10 to...**35.00**
Plate, 8", from $45 to...**75.00**

Punch or sherbet cup, overglaze paints with burnished gold rim and foot, mother-of-pearl luster interior, signed, Czechoslovakian blank, ca 1920 – 1939, 3⅛", from $25.00 to $35.00.
(Photo courtesy Dorothy Kamm)

Salt cellar, from $20 to **40.00**
Scarf pin, medallion, brass-plated bezel & shank, 1¼" dia, $35 to ...**65.00**
Shakers, pr, from $25 to **40.00**
Shirtwaist button, 1" dia, from $20 to **40.00**
Shirtwaist set, brooch, brass-plated mts, 1¾"+ cuff links, $150 to ...**350.00**
Stein, from $75 to **250.00**
Tea or coffee set, ea set, from $175 to.........................**300.00**
Whiskey set, ears of corn, sgn, Surquist, 1903-17, 8-pc, $300 to ..**400.00**

Amphora

The Amphora Porcelain Works in the Teplitz-Turn area of Bohemia produced Art Nouveau-styled vases and figurines during the latter part of the 1800s through the first few decades of the twentieth century. They marked their wares with various stamps, some incorporating the name and location of the pottery with a crown or a shield. Because Bohemia was part of the Austro-Hungarian empire prior to WWI, some examples are marked Austria; items marked with the Czechoslovakia designation were made after the war. All decoration described in the listings that follow is hand painted unless otherwise indicated.

Our advisor for this category is John Cobabe; he is listed in the Directory under California.

Vase, barnyard scene, fox (figural) climbing to rim, ftd, 9¾" **560.00**
Vase, bird-in-flight band on lt gray, checkered neck band, 11" ...**325.00**
Vase, blackberries/jewels, 3-D gold bear sits on low width, R&K, 23"..**4,000.00**
Vase, butterflies/jewels on twisted form, 9" **900.00**
Vase, cyclamen blooms w/gold, gourd shape w/stem hdls, 8x7" ..**1,900.00**
Vase, geometric mc design w/gold on cream, 4 openings, 4 hdls, 14¼"...**600.00**
Vase, grapes on branch, mc on yel w/gold, urn form, #3170 58, 13"...**350.00**
Vase, kingfisher & water lilies band, hammered ground, bulbous, 12"...**1,700.00**
Vase, lg pk 3-D pheasant on low shoulder, floriform top, #4226, 20", NM..**800.00**
Vase, mc jewels on faux verdigris & bronze, spherical, 3¼" **100.00**
Vase, Nouveau lady/grapes/trees on wht, #529 8, 16", NM **1,300.00**
Vase, oak leaf relief on textured dbl-gourd w/branch hdls, #3517, 7x6"..**3,000.00**
Vase, owl/flowers in wide wht band on brn ground, no mk, 8½"..**170.00**
Vase, pastel floral, ovoid on ochre ped, B509, 7½x3½" **195.00**
Vase, relief trees w/appl pine cones, metallic bronze on rust, 9", NM...**850.00**
Vase, rooks/birches/cottages, blk rim-to-hip hdls, 11", NM.........**475.00**

Vase, stylized cherries and leaves under green matt, two arched buttressed handles, marked, minor nick/bruise, 17x8¾", $920.00. (Photo courtesy David Rago Auctions)

Vase, stylized leaf, tan/gold/brn, dbl-gourd, 11½" **750.00**
Vase, yel w/gr/brn/gold, rtcl/relief design, #12004/56, 12¾" **825.00**

Animal Dishes With Covers

Covered animal dishes have been produced for nearly two centuries and are as varied as their manufacturers. They were made in many types of glass (slag, colored, clear, and milk glass) as well as china and pottery. On bases of nests and baskets, you will find animals and birds of every sort. The most common was the hen.

Some of the smaller versions made by McKee, Indiana Tumbler and Goblet Company, and Westmoreland Specialty Glass of Pittsburgh, Pennsylvania, were sold to food-processing companies who filled them with prepared mustard, baking powder, etc. Occasionally one will be found with the paper label identifying the product and processing company still intact.

Many of the glass versions produced during the latter part of the nineteenth century have been recently reproduced. In the 1960s, the Kemple Glass Company made the rooster, fox, lion, cat, lamb, hen, horse, turkey, duck, dove, and rabbit on split-ribbed or basketweave bases. They were made in amethyst, blue, amber, and milk glass, as well as a variegated slag. Kanawha, L.G. Wright, and Imperial made several as well. It is sometimes necessary to compare items in question to verified examples of older glass in order to recognize reproductions. Reproduction continues today.

For more information, we recommend *Covered Animal Dishes* by Everett Grist, whose address is in the Directory under Tennessee; *Collector's Encyclopedia of Milk Glass* by Betty and Bill Newbound; and *Westmoreland Glass, the Popular Years*, by Lorraine Kovar. In the listings below, when only one dimension is given, it is the greater one, usually length. See also Greentown and other specific companies. For information on modern Westmoreland issues, we recommed *The Garage Sale and Flea Market Annual* (all by Collector Books).

Cat, milk glass, split-rib base, 1 pc mk Mckee, 5½" **275.00**
Chicken, dbl-headed; milk glass, split-rib base, unmk Mckee, 5½" ...**450.00**
Dog, milk glass, wide-rib base, Westmoreland Specialty, 5¼" **50.00**
Duck, Atterbury; wht w/bl head, Pat Apld for, 11" L **650.00**
Duck, clear, wavy base, Challinor Taylor & Co, 8".......................**65.00**
Duck, milk glass, wavy base, Challinor Taylor & Co, 8" **125.00**
Elephant, milk glass, split rib base, unmk McKee, 5½" **1,300.00**
Elephant w/rider, bl opaque, Vallerysthal, 7"...............................**500.00**
Fish, clear frosted, collared base, Central Glass **150.00**
Fox, Ribbed; milk glass, lacy base, Atterbury, no date, 6¼" **100.00**
Hen, bl opaque, wide-rib base, Westmoreland Specialty, 5¼" **85.00**
Hen, milk glass, cattail base, att Couldersport Tile & ...Glass.......**85.00**
Hen, milk glass, red inset eyes, Fenton, 8" **150.00**
Hen, wht w/bl opaque head, lacy base, Atterbury, 6¼" **275.00**
Hen turkey w/chicks, milk glass, split-rib base, unmk McKee, 5½" ...**265.00**
Horse, milk glass, split-rib base, unmk McKee, 5½" **185.00**
Lamb, milk glass, picket base, Westmoreland Specialty................**95.00**
Lamb, milk glass, split-rib base, 1 pc mk McKee, 5½"................**220.00**
Lion, British; milk glass, British Lion on base, 6¼" **195.00**
Lion, Ribbed; milk glass, ribbed base, Atterbury, dtd, 6¼"..........**275.00**
Pekingese dog, milk glass, rectangular base, att Sandwich, 4¼" ...**500.00**
Quail, milk glass, scroll base, unknown maker **85.00**
Rabbit, Atterbury; bl opaque, lg **375.00**
Rabbit, milk glass, split-rib base, unmk McKee, 5½" **175.00**
Rabbit, mule eared; milk glass, picket base, Westmoreland Specialty ...**40.00**
Rabbit emerging from horizontal egg, milk glass, Gillinder **65.00**
Robin, milk glass, ped base, Vallerysthal **75.00**
Robin, milk glass, ped base, Westmoreland repro...........................**60.00**
Rooster, milk glass, lacy base, Westmoreland repro, 6¼"............**110.00**
Rooster, milk glass, wide-rib base, Westmoreland Specialty, 5¼"..**40.00**
Rooster, purple opaque, wide-rib base, Westmoreland Specialty, 5¼".**125.00**
Squirrel, milk glass, split-rib base, 1 pc mk McKee, 5½" **245.00**

Swan, closed-neck; milk glass, Westmoreland Specialty 75.00
Swan, milk glass, split-rib base, both pcs mk Mckee, 5½" 325.00
Turkey, standing, clear, US Glass, lg.................................250.00
Turtle, milk glass, scroll base w/hdls, 7½" 185.00

Appliances, Electric

Antique electric appliances represent a diverse field and are always being sought after by collectors. There were over one hundred different companies manufacturing electric appliances in the first half of the twentieth century; some were making over ten different models under several different names at any given time in all fields: coffeepots, toasters, waffle irons, etc., while others were making only one or two models for extended periods of time. Today collectors and decorators alike are seeking those items to add to a collection or to use as accent pieces in a period kitchen. Refer to *Toasters and Small Kitchen Appliances* published by L-W Book Sales for more information. If you're especially interested in vintage fans, we recommend *Collector's Guide to Electric Fans* by John Witt. (The latter book is published by Collector Books.)

Always check the cord before use and make sure the appliance is in good condition, free of rust and pitting. Unless noted otherwise, our values are for appliances in excellent condition. Prices may vary around the country.

Bread maker, Universal #4, Landers Frary & Clark, crank hdl, EX ..40.00
Broiler, Mirro, avocado, EX...22.50
Broiler oven, Presto, vertical, yel, late 1950s, EX, +booklet 30.00
Can opener, Rival Can-O-Mat, red w/chrome, 1950s, 8" L, EX...45.00
Can opener/knife sharpener, Can-O-Matic, wht w/chrome legs, EX ...48.00
Coffee maker, Cory Nicro Model 468, Bakelite hdl, MIB 85.00
Coffee maker, Sunbeam, chrome w/blk hdl, 12-cup, EX.................35.00
Coffee maker, Universal, cobalt glass lid, bl wood hdls, ca 1934, EX...35.00
Coffee set, Continental aluminum, percolator+cr/sug+tray.........100.00
Coffee urn, Farberware, chrome w/blk hdls, +cr/sug 40.00
Dough mixer, Hamilton Beach, 9-speed, wht, 1970s, MIB............30.00
Egg cooker, Hankscraft Automatic, red & yel, 1950s, 6½x5¾", MIB..35.00
Egg cooker/poacher, Sunbeam EP-4, aluminum & Bakelite, 1960s, NMIB...30.00
Fan, GE Wiz, 4 9" brass blades, 1-speed, 1924, EX........................40.00
Fan, R&M D10-A6-10, 10" blades, Deco-style, oscillator, 1940, EX ...95.00
Fan, Westinghouse Whirlbird, 4 9" blades, ca 1919, EX................25.00
Grill/waffle iron, Dominion, temp gauge in top, 4x14½x8", EX 20.00
Heater, Arvin, Art Deco styling, chrome & tan, EX 70.00
Heater, kerosene; Perfection No 525M, EX....................................75.00
Hot plate, GE Hotpoint, 1-burner, stainless/wht enamel, 4x61" dia 35.00
Kettle, GE Model K51A, chrome, 9x26" dia, NM..........................22.50
Kettle, Russell Hobbs, stainless & wht, 10½" L, NM 40.00
Mixer, Dormeyer #7600, 'Silver Dormy,' chrome & blk, NMIB....70.00
Mixer, GE Powermaster M59/3559, chrome, 2 stainless bowls, 1975, EX...45.00
Mixer, Kitchen Aid, pk, 10-speed, 1950s-60s, EX........................180.00
Mixer, Kitchen Aid 3-C, glass bowl & wire whip, 1950s-60s, EX...70.00
Mixer, Sunbeam Mixmaster #12, yel, 12-speed, 2 bowls, 1957-67, EX...85.00
Mixer/food grinder, Kitchen Aid K5A, Harvest Gold, complete, EX ..95.00
Percolator, GE, chrome w/brn Bakelite, 1950s, lg, EX 55.00
Percolator, GE Hotpoint, chrome w/seashell design, 14-cup, +cr/sug ...60.00
Percolator, Mirro Matic, aluminum, blk hdl, 9-cup, EX................22.50
Percolator, Universal, chrome w/blk hdl, 1940s, 12-cup, EX.........40.00
Popcorn popper, Knapp & Monarch, aluminum w/glass lid, blk hdls, EX ..40.00
Popcorn popper, red & orange enameling, crank hdl at top, EX ...35.00
Skillet, Sunbeam Model VLBT, aluminum w/blk hdls, 1960s, EX...25.00
Toaster, GE T310, chrome w/blk hdls, 2-slot, 7x12", EX...............20.00
Toaster, Gold Seal, chrome, wood ft & hdls, 2-slot, 7x6½x3⅛" ...65.00
Toaster, Manning-Bowman-Meriden #4-26, NP, drop sides, 1920s, EX ..60.00

Toaster, Meridian Home Electrics/M-B Model #60, EX, $60.00. (Photo courtesy Jim Barker)

Toaster, Proctor Electric #1405, NP w/Bakelite hdls, late 1920s, EX ...95.00
Toaster, Superior Electric...MO, chrome w/wood hdls, 2-slot, EX ..97.50
Toaster, Westinghouse Turnover, chrome w/Bakelite hdls, 1930s, EX...30.00
Vacuum cleaner, Electrolux G, 2 tools & 2 extensions, EX...........55.00
Vacuum cleaner, Hoover Constellation #843 canister, EX 60.00
Vacuum cleaner, Royal Electric, hand type, 1960, 15" L, MIB......35.00
Waffle iron, Heat Master, chrome, EX..45.00
Waffle iron, Sunbeam, chrome w/Bakelite hdls, 1940s, MIB 115.00
Waffle iron, Toastmaster, teflon-coated stainless, 1960s, M...........22.50
Waffle/sandwich iron, SuperLectric Model #155, 1940s-50s, M....35.00

Arc-En-Ciel

Named after the French word for 'rainbow,' the Arc-En-Ciel Pottery Company was short lived, operating only from 1903 until 1905. It occupied the old Radford Pottery in Zanesville, Ohio, for the exclusive purpose of producing art wares. Mostly covered in lustered glazes, these were exhibited at the St. Louis Purchase Exhibition of 1904, but to little commercial avail. The lack of demand caused production to be changed to a more utilitarian type of ware. The new Brighton line gave its name to yet another incarnation for the pottery.

One of the original members of the Arc-En-Ciel team, John Lessell, would become art director at the Weller Pottery and introduce his own versions of lustred artware in his LaSa and Lamar lines in the early 1920s. When marked, pieces are stamped with a rainbow-shaped logo containing the name Art-En-Ciel. Our advisors for this category are Suzanne Perrault and David Rago; they are listed in the Directory under New Jersey.

Vase, bl-gray gloss, classic form w/hdls, mk, 9"..............................175.00
Vase, gold-tone w/bust of Lincoln & eagle, mk, 6¾", EX............150.00
Vase, gold-tone w/raised figures, no mk, 7" 150.00
Vase, mottled/textured/dripping gray gloss, bulbous, mk, 10x6" ..540.00

Arequipa

Following the example of the Marblehead sanatorium and pottery, the director of the Arequipa sanatorium turned to the craft of pottery as a curative occupation for his patients. In 1911 Dr. Philip K. Brown asked Frederick Hurten Rhead and his wife Agnes to move to Fairfax, California, to organize such a department. Rhead had by then an impressive resume, having worked at Vance/Avon, Weller, Roseville, Jervis, and University City. The Rheads' stay at Arequipa would be short-lived, and by 1913 they were replaced by Albert Solon, another artist from a renowned pottery family. That same year, the pottery was incorporated as a separate entity from the sanatorium and would greatly expand in the following few years. It distinguished itself with two medals at the Pan-Pacific Exposition in 1915. A third Englishman, Frederick H. Wilde, replaced Solon in 1916, and remained at the helm of the pottery until its closing in 1918.

The finest pieces produced at Arequipa were done during the Rhead years, decorated in squeezebag or slip-trail. Others were embossed with floral patterns and covered in single-color glazes. Early vases are marked with a hand-painted Arequipa in blue on applied white glaze or incised in the clay. Our advisors for this category are Suzanne Perrault and David Rago; they are listed in the Directory under New Jersey.

Bowl, squeezebag heart-like vines, pk/yel/gr, closed rim, 1913, 7" W **4,000.00**
Vase, calyphus, gr matt, shouldered, 7" **3,000.00**
Vase, irises (deeply cvd), olive gr matt, tapered form, rstr, 8" **3,750.00**
Vase, leaves, bl on cream, ovoid, rpr rim chip, 6" **6,500.00**
Vase, mauve matt, bulbous, 4" **600.00**

Argy-Rousseau, G.

Gabriel Argy-Rousseau produced both fine art glass and quality commercial ware in Paris, France, in 1918. He favored Art Nouveau as well as Art Deco and in the '20s produced a line of vases in the Egyptian manner, made popular by the discovery of King Tut's tomb. One of the most important types of glass he made was pate-de-verre. Most of his work is signed. Items listed below are pate-de-verre unless noted otherwise.

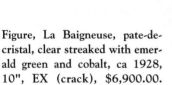

Figure, La Baigneuse, pate-de-cristal, clear streaked with emerald green and cobalt, ca 1928, 10", EX (crack), $6,900.00.

(Photo courtesy Bohnams & Butterfield)

Bowl, berries/vines, red/gr/plum/gray, 2½x3¼" **2,900.00**
Lamp, purple/orange geometric shade; bronze base, 8" **4,400.00**
Night light, purple floral w/in blk V-shape reserve (3X), iron ft, 8"..**7,000.00**
Pendant, floral, purple/gr on clear, 2¼" dia **1,100.00**
Pendant, scarab, orange/red/blk, oval, 2½" **1,500.00**
Tray, berries/leaves, brick red/purple/gray, 1½x3½" **1,000.00**
Vase, amber w/head profiles w/in geometric reserves, 6" **4,250.00**
Vase, anemones, purple/wht/blk w/mc vertical streaks, 5½" **5,300.00**
Vase, chameleon frieze, gr/amethyst/cream, U-shape, #29.07, 6"....**3,750.00**
Vase, thistles/leaves, red/gr/wht, 6x3½" **4,250.00**
Vase, vine/spider/web, blk/maroon/gr/gray, globular, 4½".........**4,500.00**

Art Deco

To the uninformed observer, Art Deco evokes images of chrome and glass, streamlined curves and aerodynamic shapes, mirrored prints of pink flamingos, and statues of slender nudes and greyhound dogs. Though the Deco movement began in 1925 at the Paris International Exposition and lasted to some extent into the 1950s, within that period of time the evolution of fashion and taste continued as it always has, resulting in subtle variations.

The French Deco look was one of opulence — exotic inlaid woods, rich material, lush fur, and leather. Lines tended toward symmetrical curves. American designers adapted the concept to cover every aspect of fashion and home furnishings from small inexpensive picture frames, cigarette lighters, and costume jewelry to high-fashion designer clothing and exquisite massive furniture with squared or circular lines. Vinyl was a popular covering, and chrome-plated brass was used for chairs, cocktail shakers, lamps, and tables. Dinnerware, glassware, theaters, and train stations were designed to reflect the new 'Modernism.'

The Deco movement made itself apparent into the '50s in wrought iron lamps with stepped pink plastic shades and Venetian blinds. The sheer volume of production during those twenty-five years provides collectors today with fine examples of the period that can be bought for as little as $10.00 or $20.00 up to the thousands. Chrome items signed 'Chase' are prized by collectors, and blue glass radios and tables with blue glass tops are high on the list of desirability in many areas.

Those interested in learning more about this subject will want to read *Collector's Guide to Art Deco* by Mary Frank Gaston. (It is published by Collector Books.) See also Bronzes; Chase; Frankart; Jewelry; Lalique; Radios; etc.

Ashtray, chrome sailboat aside bl glass base, FDCo, 5" dia **55.00**
Ashtray, nude stands before open sphere, gr on metal, British Made..**325.00**
Bottle, scent; nude in bath, bottle aloft, Sculptor Products, 1920s...**350.00**
Bust, lady w/angular face, pnt porc, Germany...Marshal Field, 7⅝" ...**300.00**
Candle holder, chrome dancing nude stem, Bakelite/chrome ft, 10½" ..**135.00**
Candle holders, amethyst glass w/faceted stems, unmk, 7", pr.....**135.00**
Candle holders, bl frosted glass, sailboat form, 5½", pr.................**70.00**
Chess set, aluminum, Lossberg/Caldwell, NY, 1934, complete, MIB.......**2,585.00**
Cigarette holder, blk plastic trimmed w/narrow gold bands, 2½"..**25.00**
Cigarette holder, tortoise shell, 4", from $25 to **35.00**
Door hdls, bronze w/brass wash, cylindrical, 33⅜", pr **475.00**
Figurine, cvd agate nude female on block base, 11½" **4,500.00**
Figurine, draped nude w/bowl, gr ceramic, Kent Art Ware, 11"..**165.00**
Figurine, fan dancer seated, spelter w/marble base, France, 12½".**145.00**
Figurine, girl holds fan-shaped skirt wide, chrome/marble, 4½"..**135.00**
Figurine, lady dancer w/skirt held high, pnt porc, Herwig & Co ...**325.00**
Figurine, nude stands w/lg container, bronze, unmk, 9¾" **300.00**
Figurine, recumbent lady w/greyhound, wht plaster, Pecchioli, 25" L ..**300.00**
Figurines, penguins, brass, unmk, 4¼", pr, from $250 to **300.00**
Flatware place setting, stainless steel w/red Bakelite hdls, 4-pc **35.00**
Flower frog, nude in open flower, wht porc, Coronet Germany, 6"..**70.00**
Flower frog, nude w/long veil, wht w/HP details, Coronet, 13½"..**135.00**
Frame, abstract silver design on wide blk border, 10x12", $60 to ..**75.00**
Incense burner, bronze Egyptian-style figure, Art Metal Works, up to...**500.00**
Incense burner, CI w/emb floral on geometric form, Made in France.**175.00**
Incense burner, kneeling Egyptian-like figure, pnt cast metal, France.**400.00**
Lamp, cobalt glass airplane w/chrome wings, chrome base, 13" L......**300.00**
Lamp, conical aluminum shade, Bakelite base, Teague/Polaroid, 13" .**800.00**
Lamp, copper-tone geometrics on stepped base, Armour Bronze Corp..**150.00**
Lamp, wrought-iron foliate base w/7½" alabaster globe shade, 15"..**1,000.00**
Lamp, 3 kneeling nudes support tortoise-glass globe, unmk **750.00**
Lamp, 4 organic stems lift mottled ivory dome shade, bronze/iron, 15"...**900.00**
Medallion, bronze, lady w/flowers, 8-sided, 1½" **175.00**

Medallion, bronze, maiden in headdress, 8-sided, EX patina, 1½" ..**175.00**
Mirror, hexagonal églomisé w/Greek Key designs/vines/berries, 44x36"...**1,500.00**
Panel, Dionysius reclines, lady w/fruit, reverse-etched glass, 31x30"...**400.00**
Perfume vial, dog figural, clear glass, Germany, 1920s, from $110 to...**120.00**
Plant stand, wrought iron tapered form w/spiral base, 25"...........**200.00**
Rug, Egyptian-influenced design in red/blk/tan/gray, Fr, 112x78"...**1,200.00**
Sconces, brass w/emb female, frosted amber shade, 3-light, 56", pr .**5,000.00**
Sculpture, alabaster/bronze, girl kneels/feeds 2 deer, Partlef, 26" L ..**2,100.00**
Sculpture, cat w/arched bk, chiseled granite, 15½" **1,700.00**
Sculpture, VM Pollak, Standing Female Nude, plaster, 1930, 17" ..**600.00**
Silent butler, chrome, emb ribs on lid, rectangular, unmk, 9" L...**45.00**
Torchiere, 3-tiered aluminum 12" shade, chrome/blk enamel pole, 66" ..**400.00**
Tray, faceted rvpt landscape on CI fr, Germonde, 24x10" **300.00**
Vase, berries & branches cvg, brn/gray/tan/bl, Mougin, squat, 6½"...**2,500.00**
Vase, brass w/silver o/l geometrics, George, Fr, 10½"...................**650.00**
Vase, chrome w/ribbed body, flared ft, unmk, 9", pr, from $45 to..**55.00**
Vase, flame design on ftd cylinder, Ditmar Urbach Pottery, 12"...**350.00**
Vase, forest green glass, Zepplin rocket form, 9"............................**60.00**
Vase, lt gr glass w/silver trim on 3 buttressed legs & rim, 9" **95.00**
Vessel, nude panels, gr w/cobalt on brn & gunmetal, Primavera, 16½".**2,100.00**

Art Glass Baskets

Popular novelty and gift items during the Victorian era, these one-of-a-kind works of art were produced in just about any type of art glass in use at that time. They were never marked. Many were not true production pieces but 'whimsies' made by glassworkers to relieve the tedium of the long work day. Some were made as special gifts. The more decorative and imaginative the design, the more valuable the basket. For more information, we recommend *Collector's Encyclopedia of American Art Glass* by John A. Shuman, III (Collector Books).

Note: Prices on art glass baskets have softened due to the influence of the Internet which has made them much more accessible.

Bl opal w/vaseline rim w/wht opal edge, yel HP decor, 6¾x7½" ...**200.00**
Bl satin w/HP Niagara Falls, 2½"..**55.00**
Caramel w/cream swirl, handmade, air bubbles, 12x10x4" **70.00**
Chartreuse, Hobnail, 5x3¼" **100.00**
Cranberry cased, Hobnail, clear hdl, 14x12¼" **160.00**
Cranberry cased w/amber ruffle, hdl & ft, Stevens & Wms, 12½"..**425.00**
Cranberry ruffled rim to wht opal, clear thorn hdl, 8½x8" **300.00**
Custard opaque w/2 appl spatter flowers, amber hdl & leaves, 7¾"..**160.00**
Peachblow, appl amber ft, amber thorn hdl, 6" **175.00**
Rose pk to wht opal, crimped incurvate sides, thorn hdl, 9x8x5"...**500.00**
Rose/yel verticals w/pulled pk waves, clear hdl/ft, Northwood, 12x12".**1,000.00**
Spangle, pk w/mica, ruffled rim, clear hdl, 5x5½" **110.00**
Spangle, yel/wht/gold mica, clear overshot hdl, ca 1915, 5½".......**95.00**
Spatter, mc, wht int, crimped rim, frosted hdl, 8x5½" **235.00**
Spatter, red/pk/gr/yel cased, 16-ruffle, wht loop hdl, emb shells..**195.00**
Spatter, yel/orange/pk cased, 6-lobe petal rim, thorn hdl, 5¾" ...**135.00**
Teal gr w/appl cherries, ruffled base, simple hdl, 10x8".................**85.00**
Vaseline, Dmn Quilt, floriform, pk petal rim, 1890s, 4½x6½"....**400.00**
Vaseline w/appl flower & leaves, clear twist hdl, 6½x4½" **300.00**
Wht opaque w/appl amber leaves/hdl & pk flower, 7½".............**225.00**

Art Nouveau

From the famous 'L'Art Nouveau' shop in the Rue de Provence in Paris, 'New Art' spread across the continent and belatedly arrived in America in time to add its curvilinear elements and asymmetrical ornamentations to the ostentatious remains of the Rococo revival of the 1800s. Nouveau manifested itself in every facet of decorative art. In glassware Tiffany turned the concept into a commercial success that lasted well into the second decade of the twentieth century and created a style that inspired other American glassmakers for decades. Furniture, lamps, bronzes, jewelry, and automobiles were designed within the realm of its dictates. Today's market abounds with lovely examples of Art Nouveau, allowing the collector to choose one or several areas that hold a special interest. Our advisor for this category is Steven Whysel; he is listed in the Directory under Florida. See also Bronzes; Galle; Jewelry; Loetz; Tiffany; Silver; specific manufacturers.

Box, hammered copper w/red & gr stylized flora, Buffalo Studio, 4x8"....**425.00**
Box, wood w/hammered metal lizard & flowers o/l, 3x14½".......**250.00**
Frame, silver swirled openwork, sgn EM&S, 5½" **450.00**
Lamp, table; cast metal, grapes & leaves w/openwork, pyramidal base..**4,250.00**
Lamp, wht metal nude lady, bulbs in 3 flower mts, gold-washed, 34"..**3,100.00**
Marble bust, nude lady draped w/leaves & flowers, 28"...........**6,700.00**
Mirror, cvd fruit trees & mushrooms, att F Zelezny 1902, 18x12"...**900.00**
Powder box, roses on pk w/lg blk butterfly on lid, Fanchon, 2⅞"...**85.00**
Sculpture, bronze snake coiled w/head up, quartz base, 4½" **150.00**
Tapestry, irises, mc on tan, European, 40x37" **1,500.00**
Torchiere, ornate bronze base/slim std, Durand trumpet-form shade, 66" ..**950.00**
Tray, ceramic w/metal hdld fr, enameled lady/irises on red, mk, 20"..**1,300.00**
Tray, cvd mahog, ornate twisted vine hdls, 2¼x28x17"..............**615.00**
Vase, bl/tan/gray crystalline on porc, hdls, Glatigny, 8"..............**500.00**

Vase, bronze with sculpted storks, frogs, beetles, and dragonfly, signed F. Debon, Susse Fres Paris, 16¾x10¼", $6,725.00. (Photo courtesy Fontaine's Auction Gallery)

Vase, cvd band, bl on ivory, Germany, 8½" **400.00**
Vase, deer & foliage, ivory/bl/blk/turq, bulbous, Larchenal, 13"...**1,200.00**
Vase, hand-tooled metal w/9 purple stones, Fr, 1890s, 4" **55.00**
Vase, swirling linear cvg, dk to lt brn matt, Mougin, 14" **800.00**
Wall hanging, bronze, stylized tree, EX patina, oval, sgn WW, 4" W .**150.00**

Arts and Crafts

The Arts and Crafts movement began in England during the last quarter of the nineteenth century, and its influence was soon felt in this country. Among its proponents in America were Elbert Hubbard (see Roycroft) and Gustav Stickley (see Stickley). They rebelled against the mechanized mass production of the Industrial Revolution and against the cumulative influence of hundreds of years of man's changing taste. They subscribed to a theory of purification of style: that designs be geared strictly to necessity. At the same time they sought to elevate these basic ideals to the level of accepted 'art.' Simplicity was their virtue; to their critics, it was a fault.

The type of furniture they promoted was squarely built, usually of heavy oak, and so simple was its appearance that as a result many began to copy the style which became known as 'Mission.' Soon factories had geared production toward making cheap copies of their designs. In 1915 Stickley's own operation failed, a victim of changing styles and tastes. Hubbard lost his life that same year on the ill-fated *Lusitania*. By the end of the decade the style had lost its popularity.

Metalware was produced by numerous crafts people, from experts such as Dirk van Erp and Albert Berry to unknown novices. Metal items or hardware should not be scrubbed or scoured; to do so could remove or damage the rich, dark patina typical of this period. Collectors have become increasingly fussy, rejecting outright pieces with damage or alteration to their original condition (such as refinishing, patina loss, repairs, and replacements). As is true for other categories of antiques and collectibles, premium prices have been paid for objects in mint original and untouched condition. Our advisor for this category is Bruce Austin; he is listed in the Directory under New York. See also Heintz; Jewelry; Limbert; Roycroft; Silver; Stickley; van Erp; specific manufacturers.

Note: When no condition is noted within the description lines, assume that values are given for examples in excellent condition. That is, metal items retain their original patina and wooden items are still in their original finish. Values for examples in conditions other than excellent will be indicated in the descriptions with appropriate condition codes.

Key: h/cp — hammered copper

Armchair, Harden, curved crest, vertical slats, shaped arms, rfn....**175.00**
Armchair, Harden, vertical slats, wavy arms, drop-in seat, 38"...**1,300.00**
Armchair, Shop of the Crafters, inlay bk, reuphl seat, 46".......**2,700.00**
Ashtray, Wm Spratling, silver, cup w/3 rests, ball ft, 2½" **250.00**
Bench, McHugh, high bk, 3 thru tenons per ea curved side, 57x49", VG ..**800.00**
Bookcase, 3 glazed doors, V-brd bk, 61x57", VG **3,000.00**
Bookends, JJB, pierced copper w/gargoyle eating grapes, 3½x5", pr..**225.00**
Bookstand, MI Chair Co, rectangular, slatted sides, 3-shelf, 34x18x14" ...**300.00**
Bowl, ET Hurley, bronze, detailed fish, 5½" **950.00**
Bowl, h/cp, 15", VG **200.00**
Bowl, Jarvie, h/cp, low, 8" W **900.00**
Bowl, Liberty Tudric, h/cp, #0831, 5x7" **150.00**
Bowl, M Zimmerman, h/cp, flared rim, ped ft, 6x13" **1,900.00**
Box, Boston School, h/cp, sq-head rivets, enameled grapes, 2x4¼" ..**2,300.00**
Box, Boston School, h/cp w/enameling, unmk, 2x4½" **475.00**
Box, ET Hurley, bronze w/2 sea horses, hinged, 4½x2" **650.00**
Box, Goberg, hammered metal, Austria, 1½x4½", VG **80.00**
Box, h/cp, emb apple branches on lid, apple finial, unmk, 6½" dia...**70.00**
Box, metal, appl sqs/studs, 4 flaring ft, 6½" W, G **300.00**
Box, wood w/appl h/cp, unmk, 4½x10¼" **350.00**
Box, wood w/cvd leaves & appl jewels, 6x2½" **375.00**
Candlestick, Goberg, metal, elaborate floral center, 5-light, 13½" **375.00**
Candlestick, Jarvie, Beta, bronze, 13", VG **1,000.00**
Candlestick, Jarvie, brass disk bobeche on egg-shaped socket, 10⅞" ..**950.00**
Candlestick, Jesse Preston, bronze, slim stem w/wide base, 14½" ..**950.00**
Candlestick, wrought iron, appl hanging decor at top, 16" **650.00**
Candlesticks, copper/brass, pencil std, 12½", VG, pr **130.00**
Candlesticks, J Preston, bronze, #8, slim std, 13", pr **8,000.00**
Cellerette, Shop o/t Crafters, HP monk, cut-out sides, 63x23", VG ..**1,800.00**
Chair, desk; slant bk, curved open arms, swivel, uphl seat **350.00**
Chair, hall; ornate open cvg to bk/apron, leather bk/seat, 54" **750.00**
Chair, Morris; JM Young, 4-slat adjustable bk, leather uphl, 38" ..**3,175.00**
Chair, side; curved crest over 8 spindles, leather seat, 41½" **600.00**
Chair, side; Old Hickory, spindle bk, split-reed seat, 36", pr **550.00**
Chamberstick, Jarvie, trumpet base, angle hdl, 6", VG **800.00**
Chandelier, Prairie School, flared cone, geometric amber glass, 52x26"...**7,500.00**
Charger, h/cp, rolled rim, 29" dia, VG **650.00**

Child's utensil set, Kalo, hammered sterling, 5" fork+knife+spoon ..**600.00**
China cabinet, sides/2 doors: glazed w/slats, shoe ft, 62x45", VG...**1,800.00**
Clock, Dutch, hammered wrought iron, crimped face w/red-pnt bars, 10"..**700.00**
Clock, Liberty, pewter body, copper face w/MOP inserts, 10"..**5,500.00**
Coal bucket, metal, cylindrical w/appl shield, pad ft, 25x14", VG..**250.00**
Compote, hammered brass, circular design at base, Germany, 6"...**270.00**
Console/server, Ford & Johnson, open ovals w/3 spindles ea side, 36" L....**950.00**
Desk, Lifetime, #8570, slant top over 2 drws, decal, 43x42x19", EX..**2,500.00**
Draperies, daffodils & hollyhocks, mc on gold burlap, 59x27", 4 pr..**825.00**
Figurine, sea horse, bronze, unknown mk, 4" **300.00**
Footstool, rocker ft w/cutouts, narrow leather ft rest, 17x16x13", VG..**425.00**
Frame, emb copper cut to expose etched brass, holds 2 sm photos, 5x7"...**250.00**
Frame, h/cp w/repoussé joined circles pattern, 25½x21¼" **325.00**
Frame, hammered pewter w/leaves & turq inlay jewels, 5" dia....**400.00**
Frame, leather wrap w/red accents at corners, 14" **100.00**
Frame, tooled leather w/emb roses, unmk, 10¼x8"......................**225.00**
Frame, Wm Hutton, hammered silver w/ornate enameling, 5½" ...**1,100.00**
Frame, wood, arched top, shaped base, stylized cvgs, 12x10" **290.00**
Frame, wood w/inlaid ivory & MOP, 13" W **275.00**
Frame, wooden w/h/cp design at bottom, 8½x4" **300.00**
Glider, porch; IN Hickory, orig split reed seat & bk, lg............**3,500.00**
Handbag, embr linen, 10½" W, VG **100.00**
Hinge, Samuel Yellin, wrought iron, pierced cross shape, unmk, 10½"..**225.00**

Humidor, attributed to Benedict, hammered copper, curled brass legs, some cleaning to patina, 7x10x6½", $1,100.00.

Inkwell, Karl Kipp, h/cp, quatrefoil/textured band, 2½x3" sq **300.00**
Jardiniere, Jauchens, h/cp, fluted classical style, 9¾x11½" **700.00**
Lanterns, ldgl stylized floral in 4 panels, brass fr, fixture: 19", pr ..**1,200.00**
Pitcher, C Dressser for Linthorpe, floral/geometrics, mc flambé, 7"...**1,800.00**
Planters, h/cp, bowl on tall riveted stem, mound base, 30x13", pr..**1,100.00**
Plate, h/cp w/enamel decor, mk (?), 7" **110.00**
Rocker, sewing; Rohlfs, 3 leather bands at bk, apron, rfn, 35½"...**700.00**
Rocker, 5 vertical slats to bk/5 ea arm, reuphl spring seat, 36", VG ..**550.00**
Salt & pepper shakers, Lebolt, hammered silver w/appl monogram, 5", pr..**475.00**
Screen, peacock decor in 3 panels in oak fr, ca 1910, 69x32"...**1,400.00**
Settle, even-arm, 13 vertical bk slats, uphl seat/cushions, 70½" ..**1,775.00**
Settle, JM Young, drop-arm, vertical slats, scuffs, 34x82".........**1,400.00**
Stand, magazine; JM Young, 3-shelf, slatted sides, label, 44x22x14"...**1,400.00**
Standish, h/cp, dbl inkwell, monogrammed, 2¾x13¼" **120.00**
Stool, rnd w/inset rush seat, thru tenons, 16x15" dia **200.00**
Table, book; rectangular top, 2 shelves, keyed tenons, 26x26x14" ..**825.00**
Table, dining; Lifetime, Puritan Line, 5-leg, 54" dia+3 leaves...**1,500.00**
Table, drop-leaf; Old Hickory, rnd top over spindle legs, 36" dia ...**800.00**
Table, occasional; rnd top, low median shelf on X stretchers, 29x24"..**765.00**

Table, serving; Lifetime, Puritan Line, 1-drw, label, 36x40x19"...**1,500.00**
Table, trestle; Lifetime, median shelf, keyed tenons, 39x60x36"..**1,750.00**
Tablecloth, bl design on gr linen, 65½x53½", +6 lg napkins......**550.00**
Tablecloth, wool felt w/embr roses & foliate border, 72x68½"....**175.00**
Teapot, WMF, h/brass sphere on base w/burner, 13x9"..............**125.00**
Tray, Liberty Tudric, pewter, stylized branches w/enamel, 12x3½"..**175.00**
Trophy canister, h/cp w/riveted copper o/l, 4 antler ft, 1906, 8½"..**1,175.00**
Vase, C Dresser for Linthorpe, mc flambé, dimpled/ruffled, 4¾"..**400.00**
Vase, C Dresser for Watcombe, Aesthetic Movement pattern, 10x5"...**3,500.00**
Vase, Jarvie, h/cp, invt rim, 4¾"...**1,100.00**
Vase, Jauchens, h/cp, berries/circles/waves, bl-gr patina, 7".........**500.00**
Vase, M Zimmerman, h/cp floriform, 7¼x11½".......................**1,100.00**
Vase, Max Laeuger, stylized fruit trees, 4-color, KTK mk, 9½x8"...**700.00**
Vase, St Lukas, fish in seascape, gr/lav irid, bulbous, 11".........**4,250.00**
Vase, WMF, h/silver pine-cone designs, rectangle, hdls, 4x15"...**850.00**
Vessel, Kalo, hammered sterling, hourglass form, 4½".................**275.00**
Wallpaper, W Crane, peacocks/lilies, ca 1902-11, 20½x41"....**3,750.00**
Wastebasket, paneled octagon w/woven leather jointry at top, 16x13"...**175.00**
Window seat, open ovals w/3 spindles ea slab side, rush seat, 23" W...**750.00**
Woodblock print, AW Dow, floral designs, 6½x7"+mat & oak fr...**500.00**
Woodblock print, AW Dow, houses/trees, in oak fr, 5½x4", EX...**1,100.00**
Woodblock print, C Richert, bridge in autumn, 5x7"+oak fr......**650.00**
Woodblock print, D Babcock, Mt Heloise, 4½x2½"+oak fr.......**400.00**
Woodblock print, F Gearhart, CA coast, mc, w/mat & fr, 11x10", EX.**3,250.00**
Woodblock print, F Gearhart, mtn landscape, 6x4½"+oak fr..**1,900.00**
Woodblock print, Jane Berry Judson, Mt Monadnoch NH, 6x8"+mat & fr..**750.00**
Woodblock print, SR Knox, Torrey Pine #2, 7½x9½"+mat & fr..**750.00**

Austrian Glass

Many examples of fine art glass were produced in Austria during the times of Loetz and Moser that cannot be attributed to any glasshouse in particular, though much of it bears striking similarities to the products of both artists.

Vase, amethyst w/silver-bl irid threading, 6¼".............................**145.00**
Vase, amethyst w/silvered irid threading, 8½"..............................**260.00**
Vase, bl/gr/purple irid w/Nouveau pewter-colored enamel, 5¾", NM...**230.00**
Vase, clear irid w/appl purple grapes & gr leaves, 10½"................**85.00**
Vase, gold irid, corseted, rolled rim, 5¼x6½"............................**285.00**
Vase, gr irid w/threading, dimpled, ruffled, 7".........................**300.00**
Vase, gr w/bl irid, pinched sides & neck, mold blown, 4¾"........**230.00**

Autographs

Autograph collecting, also known as 'philography' or 'love of writing,' used to be a hobby shared by a few thousand dedicated collectors. But in recent years, autograph collecting has become a serious pursuit for more than 2,000,000 collectors worldwide. And in the past decade, more investors are adding rare and valuable autograph portfolios to their traditional investments. One reason for this sudden interest in autograph investing relates to the simple economic law of supply and demand. Rare autographs have a 'fixed' supply, meaning that unlike diamonds, gold, silver, stock certificates, etc., no more are being produced. There are only so many Abraham Lincoln, Marilyn Monroe, and Charles Lindbergh autographs available. In the meantime, it's estimated that more than 20,000 new collectors enter the market each year, thus creating an ever-increasing demand. Hence, the rare autographs generally rise steadily in value each year. Because of this scarcity, a serious collector will pay over $10,000.00 for a photograph signed by both Wilbur and Orville Wright, or as much as $25,000.00, perhaps more, for a handwritten letter of George Washington's.

But by far, the majority of autograph collectors in the country do it for the love of the hobby. A polite letter and self-addressed, stamped envelope sent to a famous person will often bring the desired result. And occasionally one receives not only an autograph but a nice handwritten letter thanking the fan as well!

In terms of value, there are five general types of autographs: 1) mere signatures on an album page or card; 2) signed photographs; 3) signed documents; 4) typed letters signed; and 5) handwritten letters. The signatures are the least valuable, and handwritten letters the most valuable. The reasoning here is simple: with a handwritten letter, not only do you get an autograph but the handwritten message of the person as well. And this content can sometimes increase the value many times over. A handwritten letter of Babe Ruth's thanking a fan for a gift might fetch a few thousand dollars. But if the letter were to mention Ruth's feelings on the day he retired, it could easily sell for $10,000.00 or more.

Today the Internet has become a popular way to buy and sell autographs. A word of warning: Be very careful when buying over the Internet. It is an easy way for unscrupulous forgers to sell their fakes and disappear. Teenagers need to be especially aware that many of the 'signed' photos on the Internet of Sarah Michelle Gellar, Brad Pitt, Katie Holmes, Leonardo DeCaprio, Kate Winslett, and many others are either signed by secretaries or are outright forgeries. Make sure the Internet dealer offers a full money-back guarantee of authenticity and belongs to one of the major autograph organizations. Ask how long the dealer has been in business and for personal references if possible. Remember the old Latin warning, 'caveat emptor,' let the buyer beware.

There are several major autograph collector organizations where members can exchange celebrity addresses or buy, sell, and trade their autographed wares. Philography can be a fun and rewarding hobby. And who knows! In ten or twenty years, those autographs you got for free could be worth a small fortune! Our advisor for autographs is Tim Anderson; he is listed in the Directory under Utah.

Key:
ALS — handwritten letter signed
ANS — handwritten note signed
AQS — autograph quotation signed
DS — document signed
ins — inscription
ISP — inscribed signed photo
LH — Letterhead
LS — signed letter, typed or written by someone else
sig — signature
SP — signed photo

Armstrong, Louis; SP, blk & wht, 8x10".....................................**470.00**
Armstrong, Neil; sig on album pg..**330.00**
Beach Boys, SP of all 5 members, 1960s, 8x10"...........................**475.00**
Bogart, Humphrey; sig on album pg..**800.00**
Buckley, Jeff; sig on 3x4" bar napkin, EX....................................**300.00**
Byrd, Ralph; SP, played Dick Tracy, matted/sepia, 8x10", EX......**150.00**
Calhoun, Rory; sig on album pg..**42.00**
Cantor, Eddie; sig on 2x3½" card..**50.00**
Carter, Jimmy; sgn Thank You card...**75.00**
Cash, Johnny; sig on Carnegie Hall program, 12x9"....................**300.00**
Churchill, Winston; ANS, 7½x4¾"..**750.00**
Cline, Patsy; sig on album card..**260.00**
Clinton, Bill; SP of President & First Lady, color, 8x10".............**255.00**
Cobb, Ty; sig, matted & fr w/Detroit Tigers team photo **410.00**
Cody, William F/Buffalo Bill; dtd 1907, matted & fr w/photo.....**900.00**
Cooper, Gary; sig on album pg, EX..**145.00**
Cooper, Gary; SP, blk & wht, 5½x3½"..**225.00**
Davis, Jefferson; ALS to Secretary of Interior, 1849.................**1,550.00**
Dean, James; sig on 4½x5" album pg...**360.00**
Disney, Walt; on card, matted w/color image.................................**760.00**
Earnhardt, Dale; print, 3 To Get Ready, Sam Bass, 1990 ....**680.00**
Earnhardt, Dale; sig on VIP Press Pass, 1996..............................**250.00**

Edison, Thomas; sig on 2x6" paper **300.00**
Einstein, Albert; sig..**600.00**
Fairbanks, Douglas Jr; sig on album pg, dtd 3/3/61, EX................**45.00**
Ford, Henry; sig, matted **520.00**
Freud, Sigmund; sig, dtd 15/7/27, matted & fr w/photo **1,200.00**

Gable, Clark; two signatures on 1938 hunting license, along with a black and white 12x15" portrait, $2,300.00.

Gerhig, Lou; sig on album pg **390.00**
Ginsberg, Allen; sig on book: Campaign Against Underground Press, EX .**180.00**
Gobel, George; sig on wht card, EX..................................**35.00**
Greene, Lorne; ISP, w/horse..**145.00**
Harrison, George; sig on Revolver album cover, 1960s **290.00**
Harrison, Rex; sig on 3x5" card, dtd 4/12/65, EX................**50.00**
Hayes, Helen; sig on album pg, matted & fr w/photo, EX **40.00**
Hendrix, Jimi; sig on album card **50.00**
Hepburn, Audrey; SP, blk & wht, 5½x3½".....................**285.00**
Hepburn, Katherine; LS, dtd 4/15/87, 6x8", EX...............**195.00**
Hitchock, Alfred; sig on playbill w/self-caricature, 1972 ....**185.00**
Hoover, Herbert; sgn Waldorf-Astoria stationery, 1956.............**125.00**
Hoover, J Edgar; LS, dtd 5/9/63 ....**125.00**
Hope, Bob; sig on 3x5" card, dtd 8/3/67 ....**60.00**
Houdini, Harry; last name only, matted w/blk & wht image.......**610.00**
Jefferson, Thomas; sig, matted w/color image, 11½x8" **2,525.00**
Jefferson, Thomas; sig on OH land grant, dtd 1801, 14x12"....**3,300.00**
Joplin, Janis; sig 4½x5" album pg **600.00**
Kelley, DeForest; ISP, Star Trek scene, 8x10"..................**125.00**
Kennedy, John F; sig, matted & fr w/2 blk & wht photos...........**490.00**
King, Martin Luther Jr; cut sig on 3½x7" paper..........................**230.00**
Laurel, Stan; ALS on Oceana stationery, 1959, w/envelope, EX ...**450.00**
Laurel, Stan; sgn personal stationery, dtd 2/12/59.......................**235.00**
Lee, Brenda; ISP, blk & wht, 8x10" **40.00**
Lee, Robert E; sig, ⅞x3⅜" paper, EX **2,500.00**
Lemmon, Jack; ISP, blk & wht, 8x10" **75.00**
Lennon, John; sig on 4½x3½" card..........................**1,000.00**
Lindbergh, Charles; cut sig, fr & matted w/photo................**340.00**
Lombardo, Guy; ISP, blk & wht, 8x10" **75.00**
Lugosi, Bela; AQS, Best Luck...Dracula, matted & fr w/photo....**430.00**
Madison, James; sig on OH land grant, 1813, 9x14", EX **110.00**
Mancini, Henry; SP, blk & wht, 8x10" **50.00**
Marx, Groucho; LS, personal stationery, dtd 6/9/53 ....**720.00**
McCartney, Paul; sig on album pg **265.00**
McQueen, Steve; To Sam From Steve McQueen, matted & fr w/photo..**425.00**
Miller, Arthur; ALS, response to request, 1972, 1-pg, EX **150.00**
Monroe, Marilyn; ANS, matted w/color image **2,500.00**
Monroe, Marilyn; sig on 4½x6".......................................**1,000.00**

Moorehead, Agnes; ISP, sepia, 8x10" **75.00**
Morrison, Jim; sig on 3x3½" album page, EX.................**610.00**
Mother Teresa, LS, dtd 4/20/92 ....**265.00**
Nelson, Ozzie; sig on pk album card **50.00**
Newman, Paul; sig on personal 3x5" card w/name dtd 8/23/68 ...**150.00**
Nicks, Stevie; sgn 1983 Wild Heart Tour card, 5x7" **520.00**
Nixon, Richard; sgn book, Six Crises, 1962, NM w/dust jacket..**395.00**
O'Brien, Pat; SP, sepia, 5x7".......................................**60.00**
Peck, Gregory; sgn To Kill a Mockingbird video.......................**310.00**
Peppard, George; sig on 3x5" card w/name & dtd 6/19/67 ....**35.00**
Peron, Eva; Argentina's 1st Lady (1919-52), photo sgn on bk, 9x6", EX...**650.00**
Picasso, Pablo; sgn postcard of artwork, 1960, 4x6", EX...........**1,040.00**
Presley, Elvis; sig, matted w/color image **710.00**
Quinn, Anthony; sig on 3x5" card, dtd 1/4/62....................**45.00**
Rachmaninoff, SP, blk & wht, 1934, 8x10"........................**720.00**
Rand, Sally; ISP, bold/in pencil, dtd 1950, 5x7", VG **45.00**
Rawhide, SP of cast...**710.00**
Ritter, John; SP, color 8x10" **320.00**
Rockefeller, Nelson; sig on 3x5" card, dtd 9/4/70....................**55.00**
Romero, Cesar; ISP, blk & wht, 9½x7½"........................**60.00**
Roosevelt, Franklin D; LS, dtd 9/8/32 ....**260.00**
Roosevelt, Theodore; DS, Coast Artillery Corps appointment, 1907....**620.00**
Savalas, Telly; sig on 3x5" card, dtd 7/31/68 ....**40.00**
Seinfeld (cast), SP, color, fr & matted, 8x10".......................**250.00**
Shatner, William; sgn Twilight Zone trading card **325.00**
Skelton, Red; sig on 3x5" card, dtd 8/18/64 ....**40.00**
Steinbeck, John; sgn book, The Moon Is Down, 1942, 1st ed, EX **800.00**
Stewart, Jimmy; ISP, sepia, 5x7"....................................**70.00**
Taylor, Elizabeth; ISP, blk & wht, dtd, 1945, 8x10" **375.00**
Twitty, Conway; sig on album pg **45.00**
Vallee, Rudy; sig on album pg, ca 1950s **35.00**
Vanderbilt, Amy; SP, blk & wht, 8x10"...............................**40.00**
Vaughn, Stevie Ray; sgn publicity photo, 1999.......................**100.00**
Verdi, Giuseppe; matted w/8x10" color image.......................**810.00**
Waller, Fats; ISP, blk & wht, 1930s, 8x10"..........................**220.00**
Wayne, John; AQS blk & wht photo................................**490.00**
Willis, Bruce/Shepherd, Cybill; SP of both, blk & wht, 8x10" ...**300.00**
Wray, Fay; sig on album pg..**55.00**

Automobilia

While some automobilia buffs are primarily concerned with restoring vintage cars, others concentrate on only one area of collecting. For instance, hood ornaments were often quite spectacular. Made of chrome or nickel plate on brass or bronze, they were designed to represent the 'winged maiden' Victory, flying bats, sleek greyhounds, soaring eagles, and a host of other creatures. Today they often bring prices in the $75.00 to $200.00 range. R. Lalique glass ornaments go much higher!

Horns, radios, clocks, gear shift knobs, and key chains with company emblems are other areas of interest. Generally, items pertaining to the classics of the '30s are most in demand. Paper advertising material, manuals, and catalogs in excellent condition are also collectible.

License plate collectors search for the early porcelain-on-cast-iron examples. First year plates (e.g., Massachusetts, 1903; Wisconsin, 1905; Indiana, 1913) are especially valuable. The last of the states to issue regulation plates were South Carolina and Texas in 1917, and Florida in 1918. While many northeastern states had registered hundreds of thousands of vehicles by the 1920s making these plates relatively common, those from the southern and western states of that period are considered rare. Naturally, condition is important. While a pair in mint condition might sell for as much as $100.00 to $125.00, a pair with chipped or otherwise damaged porcelain may sometimes be had for as little as $25.00 to $30.00.

For more information see *Value Guide to Gas Station Memorabilia* by B.J. Summers and Wayne Priddy (Collector Books). Our advisor for this category is Leonard Needham; he is listed in the Directory under California. See also Gas Globes and Panels.

Book, American Automobile, R Stein, Random House 1st printing, EX...**30.00**
Book, Ferrari, Godfrey Eaton, Octopus Books, 1980, w/jacket.........**10.00**
Book, My Days w/the Diesel, C Cummins, Chilton 1st ed, 1967, w/jacket..**160.00**
Book, My Life & Work, H Ford w/S Crowther, Doubleday, 1922 1st ed..**125.00**
Book, Shop Theory, Henry Ford Trade School, 1943, 268-pg, VG..**10.00**
Booket, How To Service Valves in Ford-Built Motors, 1945, 18-pg, G..**10.00**
Booklet, Cadillac, Gentle Art of Motoring, 1948, 12-pg, EX........**12.00**
Brochure, AMC, Pacer, Gremlin, Hornet, Matador, 1977, 36-pg, VG...**14.00**
Brochure, Cadillac, type 53, ca 1916, 32-pg, G **120.00**
Brochure, Chevrolet Station Wagon, 1963, G **8.00**
Brochure, dealer's; Ford V-8, 1933, open: 22¼x10½", VG...........**60.00**
Brochure, Hudson, 1955, open: 21x29½", G.................................**20.00**
Brochure, Lincoln Continental, 1959, 20-pg, 8½x8½", EX **20.00**
Brochure, Mercury, 1949, 12x9", open: 24x18", G........................**25.00**
Brochure, Plymouth Hidden Values, 1954, 28-pg, 8⅜x10", EX.....**30.00**
Brochure, Tucker, 1948, 8½x7½", open: 17x22½", VG..............**165.00**
Catalog, Chevrolet showroom, 1946, 39-pg, 11¼x9", VG..........**275.00**

Clock, Oldsmobile, metal and glass, lights up, Pam, 15½" square, EX, $475.00. (Photo courtesy Collector's Auction Service)

Clock, Pierce-Arrow, 8-day, Waltham, 4 worn pivot points, G-....**45.00**
Decal, AAA, CA State Automobile Assoc, VG **3.00**
Emblem, body; Thunderbird, some pitting to chrome, 1½x9¼", VG ...**80.00**
Emblem, body; Triumph, enameled globe, G.................................**40.00**
Emblem, front fender; Thunderbird, 1959?, 1⅝" dia, EX..............**95.00**
Emblem, hood; Plymouth, minor chrome loss, 1930s?, 1⅞x4⅞", VG...**40.00**
Emblem, hubcap; LaSalle, red enameling, unknown year, 3" dia, G...**30.00**
Emblem, Nat'l Automobile Club, heavy metal w/enameling, 3½x3¾" ..**60.00**
Emblem, radiator; Cadillac, 1920s, 2⅛" dia, EX **150.00**
Emblem, radiator; Chevrolet, pre-1942, enameled logo, 1½x4", G........**30.00**
Emblem, radiator; Chevrolet; bl enamel, unknown year, 3x3", G ..**60.00**
Emblem, radiator; Ford, bl enamel on oval, 1927-30, 1½x2⅞".....**24.00**
Emblem, radiator; Hudson Super Six, triangular, 2½" **120.00**
Emblem, radiator; Hudson 8, worn enamel, triangular, 2½", G.....**40.00**
Emblem, radiator; Nash, 1920s?, 3¼x1⅞", EX **80.00**
Emblem, radiator; Studebaker, enameled tire form, 2⅛" dia, G **40.00**
Emblem, trunk; Cadillac, plastic, ca 1960s?, 4½" dia, G **10.00**
Gauge, tire pressure; Pierce-Arrow, Schrader, 10 to 50 psi, ca 1925 ..**120.00**
Hood latch, Ford, chrome, 1930s, VG..**40.00**
Hubcap, Cadillac, screw-on, worn NP, dent, 1920s, G **20.00**
Hubcap, Dodge Brothers, screw-on, VG..**10.00**
Hubcap, Hupmobile, screw-on, 2 9/16", VG **20.00**
Key holder, Dodge leather boot, 3x2¼", VG.................................**12.00**
Lamp, side; Cadillac, Gray & Davis, 1914, VG **195.00**
Magazine, Antique Automobile, 1931 V-12 Cadillac cover, 1975, EX..**3.00**
Magazine, Automobile Quarterly, Vol 12, No 1, EX **15.00**
Magazine, Honk, Vol 1, No 2, 1953, VG **20.00**
Magazine, Motor Land, CA State Auto Assoc, May 1923, 52-pg, G ..**12.00**
Magazine, Motorcyclist, July 1940, 30-pg, VG **30.00**
Magazine, Rod Builder & Customizer, July 1957, 55-pg, VG **15.00**
Magazine, The Continental, 1965, VG **5.00**
Manual, accessories; Buick, 1966, 7x4¼", 24-pg, G **8.00**
Manual, accessories; General Motors Passenger Car, 1982, 8½x11" ..**8.00**
Manual, owner's; Anglia, 1959, G- **12.00**
Manual, owner's; Buick, red/wht/bl, 1957, 54-pg, 7x4½", EX........**30.00**
Manual, owner's; Buick, 32-pg, 5⅜x8⅜", EX **30.00**
Manual, owner's; Cadillac V-16, 1932, VG **295.00**
Manual, owner's; Chevrolet, 1947, G-..**20.00**
Manual, owner's; Dodge, 1946, 40-pg, VG **25.00**
Manual, owner's; Ford trucks, 1934, 62-pg, EX **55.00**
Manual, owner's; Lincoln, 1956, EX **40.00**
Manual, owner's; Mercury, 1958, NM..**12.00**
Manual, owner's; Model T Ford, 1919, VG **45.00**
Manual, owner's; Opel Kadett, 1965, 24-pg, 5¾x8¼" **10.00**
Manual, owner's; Pontiac, How & When To Buy..., 1941, 36-pg, EX...**20.00**
Manual, owner's; 1968 Ambassador or Marlin, 52-pg, VG **14.00**
Manual, shop; Chevrolet, 1940, 282-pg, G **40.00**
Manual, shop; Dodge Truck (Series R), 1961, VG........................**20.00**
Manual, shop; Ford Thunderbird, 1959, 400-pg, 8½x11", G.........**60.00**
Manual supplement, shop; Chevrolet, 16 sections, 1959-60, 1,068-pg, G ..**40.00**
Pamphlet, Chevrolet Custom Feature Accessories, 1966, NM **8.00**
Parts list, Ford, 1913, G...**120.00**
Pin, mechanic's; Lincoln-Mercury, gold filled, LBG hallmk, 1950s-60s...**30.00**
Postcard, Buick factory photo, dtd 1950, EX **7.00**
Postcard, Jaguar Series 3 V-12 E-type convertible, 1960s, G **7.00**
Postcard, Nash Ambassador, full-color photo, 19549, NM **8.00**
Postcard, 1959 Buick LeSaber 4-door sedan, full color, VG............**7.00**
Ruler, Pontiac, features for 1938 on bk, Indian heads on front, 15" ..**20.00**
Sign, OK Used Cars/Authorized Dealer, 2-sided porc emblem, 46x52", G .**1,200.00**
Tag, tool ID; Pierce-Arrow, Made Especially For..., 2x⅞" **50.00**
Token, General Motors Motorama, shiny metal, 1954, 1¼" dia ...**22.00**
Token/fob, Buick 1903-1953, metal, 1¼" dia, VG **22.00**
Wrench, hub cap; Dodge Brothers, lt rust, G **10.00**
Wrench, open-end; Ford, 11/16" ea end, 5¼" L, VG **15.00**
Wrench, open-end; Pierce Arrow, W in dmn mk, 7/16x½", 6⅞", G......**40.00**
Wrench, open-end/lug; Ford, Moore Drop Forging Co, 11", VG ..**10.00**

Autumn Leaf

In 1933 the Hall China Company designed a line of dinnerware for the Jewel Tea Company, who offered it to their customers as premiums. Although you may hear the ware referred to as 'Jewel Tea,' it was officially named 'Autumn Leaf' in the 1940s. In addition to the dinnerware, frosted Libbey glass tumblers, stemware, and a melmac service with the orange and gold bittersweet pod were available over the years, as were tablecloths, plastic covers for bowls and mixers, and metal items such as cake safes, hot pads, coasters, wastebaskets, and canisters. Even shelf paper and playing cards were made to coordinate. In 1958 the International Silver Company designed silverplated flatware in a pattern called 'Autumn' which was to be used with dishes in the Autumn Leaf pattern. A year later, a line of stainless flatware was introduced. These accessory lines are prized by collectors today.

One of the most fascinating aspects of collecting the Autumn Leaf pattern has been the wonderful discoveries of previously unlisted pieces. Among these items are two different bud-ray lid one-pound butter dishes; most recently a one-pound butter dish in the 'Zephyr' or 'Bingo' style; a miniature set of the 'Casper' salt and pepper shakers; coffee, tea, and sugar canisters; a pair of candlesticks; an experimental condiment jar; and a covered candy dish. All of these china pieces are attributed to the

Hall China Company. Other unusual items have turned up in the accessory lines as well and include a Libbey frosted tumbler in a pilsner shape, a wooden serving bowl, and an apron made from the oilcloth (plastic) material that was used in the 1950s tablecloth. These latter items appear to be professionally done, and we can only speculate as to their origin. Collectors believe that the Hall items were sample pieces that were never meant to be distributed.

Hall discontinued the Autumn Leaf line in 1978. At that time the date was added to the backstamp to mark ware still in stock in the Hall warehouse. A special promotion by Jewel saw the reintroduction of basic dinnerware and serving pieces with the 1978 backstamp. These pieces have made their way into many collections. Additionally, in 1979 Jewel released a line of enamel-clad cookware and a Vellux blanket made by Martex which were decorated with the Autumn Leaf pattern. They continued to offer these items for a few years only, then all distribution of Autumn Leaf items was discontinued.

It should be noted that the Hall China Company has produced several limited edition items for the National Autumn Leaf Collectors Club (NALCC): a New York-style teapot (1984); an Edgewater vase (1987, different than the original shape); candlesticks (1988); a Philadelphia-style teapot, creamer and sugar set (1990); a tea-for-two set and a Solo tea set (1991), a donut jug, and a large oval casserole. Later came the small ball jug, one-cup French teapot, and a set of four chocolate mugs. Other special items over the past few years made for them by Hall China include a sugar packet holder, a chamberstick, and an oyster cocktail. Additional items are scheduled for production. All of these are plainly marked as having been made for the NALCC and are appropriately dated. A few other pieces have been made by Hall as limited editions for an Ohio company, but these are easily identified: the Airflow teapot and the Norris refrigerator pitcher (neither of which was previously decorated with the Autumn Leaf decal), a square-handled beverage mug, and the new-style Irish mug. A production problem with the square-handled mugs halted their production. Additional items available now are a covered onion soup, tall bud vase, china kitchen memo board, and egg drop-style salt and pepper shakers with a mustard pot. They have also issued a deck of playing cards and Libbey tumblers. See *Garage Sale & Flea Market Annual* (Collector Books) for suggested values for club pieces. Our advisor for this category is Gwynne Harrison; she is listed in the Directory under California. For more information we recommend *Collector's Encyclopedia of Hall China, Third Edition*, by Margaret and Kenn Whitmyer.

Tray, glass, 1941 only, $150.00. (Photo courtesy Margaret and Kenn Whitmyer)

Baker, cake; Heatflow clear glass, Mary Dunbar, 1½-qt 85.00
Baker, French, 2-pt 175.00
Baker, French, 3-pt 25.00

Baker, oval, Fort Pitt, 12-oz ind 225.00
Bean pot, 2-hdl, 2¼-qt...250.00
Blanket, Autumn Leaf color, Vellux, full sz.................................175.00
Book, Mary Dunbar Cookbook 30.00
Bottle, Jim Beam, w/stand 130.00
Bowl, cereal; 6", from $8 to..12.00
Bowl, cream soup; hdls 40.00
Bowl, fruit; 5½"...6.00
Bowl, refrigerator; metal w/plastic lids, 3 for 275.00
Bowl, soup; Melmac..20.00
Bowl, vegetable; divided, oval..125.00
Bowl, vegetable; oval, Melmac, from $40 to..................................50.00
Bowl cover set, plastic, 8-pc, 7 assorted covers in pouch.............100.00
Bread box, metal, from $400 to 800.00
Butter dish, 1-lb, bud 'rayed' knob, rare...................................3,000.00
Butter dish, 1-lb, ruffled top, regular...500.00
Butter dish, ¼-lb, ruffled top, regular, from $175 to 250.00
Butter dish, ¼-lb, wings top 1,500.00
Calendar, 1920s to 1930s, from $100 to.......................................200.00
Candle holder, Chamber, club gift, 1991 ....125.00
Candy dish, metal base, from $500 to 600.00
Canister, brn & gold, wht plastic lid...30.00
Canisters, metal, rnd, w/coppertone lid, set of 4, from $600 to ..1,200.00
Canisters, sq, 4-pc set, from $295 to..350.00
Case, carrying; Jewel salesman, from $150 to 300.00
Casserole, Heatflow, Dunbar, clear, w/lid, rnd, 1½-qt, from $50 to ...75.00
Casserole, Royal Glas-Bake, milk wht w/clear glass lid, rnd 90.00
Catalog, Jewel, hardback, from $20 to..50.00
Clock, electric 550.00
Clock, salesman's award 250.00
Coffee dispenser, from $200 to..400.00
Coffee percolator, electric, all china, 4-pc....................................400.00
Coffeepot, Jewel's Best, 30-cup..600.00
Coffeepot, Rayed, 9-cup...45.00
Cookie jar, Big Ear, Zeisel, from $250 to 350.00
Cookie jar, Tootsie, 'Rayed'..310.00
Creamer & sugar bowl, Nautilus...125.00
Creamer & sugar bowl, Rayed, 1930s style 80.00
Cup, custard; Radiance, from $6 to...10.00
Custard cup, Heatflow clear glass, Mary Dunbar, from $40 to.......60.00
Custard cup, Radiance..10.00
Dripper, metal, for 8- or 9-cup coffeepot 35.00
Flatware, SP, ea..35.00
Flatware, stainless steel, ea, from $25 to.......................................30.00
Fondue set, complete, form $200 to..300.00
Fry pan, Mary Dunbar, top stoveware glass 175.00
Gravy boat, w/underplate (pickle dish) 55.00
Hot pad, metal, oval, 10¾", from $12 to...15.00
Hurricane lamps, Douglas, w/metal base, pr, minimum value......500.00
Jug, batter; Sundial (bowl), rare 5,500.00
Loaf pan, Mary Dunbar, from $90 to 125.00
Marmalade, 3-pc, from $100 to...125.00
Mug, conic 65.00
Mustard, 3-pc, from $100 to...120.00
Pickle fork, Jewel Tea 75.00
Pie plate, Heatflow, clear glass, Mary Dunbar, from $45 to 60.00
Place mat, paper, scalloped, set of 8, from $150 to.......................325.00
Plate, salad; Melmac, 7"...20.00
Plate, 6", from $5 to...8.00
Plate, 8", hard to find 18.00
Plate, 9"...12.00
Pressure cooker, Mary Dunbar, metal...225.00
Saucer, regular, Ruffled D 2.50
Shakers, Casper, ruffled, regular, pr...30.00

Shelf liner, paper, 108" roll..**50.00**
Syrup pitcher, club pc, 1995 ....**95.00**
Tablecloth, cotton sailcloth w/gold stripe, 54x72" **140.00**
Teapot, Rayed, long spout, 1935 ....**95.00**
Teapot, Solo, club pc, 1,400 made, 1991 ....**100.00**
Tidbit tray, 3-tier **100.00**
Towel, tea; cotton, 16x33" **60.00**
Toy, Jewel Truck, orange & wht, from $200 to **225.00**
Toy, Jewel Van, brn, Buddy L, from $400 to.........**650.00**
Tray, glass, wood hdl...**140.00**
Tray, metal, oval **100.00**
Tumbler, Libbey, frosted, 9-oz, 3¾".....................**32.00**
Tumbler, Libbey, gold frost etched, flat or ftd, 10-oz, ea **65.00**
Tumbler, Libbey, gold frost etched, flat or ftd, 15-oz, ea **65.00**
Vase, bud; regular decal, 6".................................**350.00**
Warmer, oval, from $150 to **225.00**

Aviation

Aviation buffs are interested in any phase of flying, from early developments with gliders, balloons, airships, and flying machines to more modern innovations. Books, catalogs, photos, patents, lithographs, ad cards, and posters are among the paper ephemera they treasure alongside models of unlikely flying contraptions, propellers and rudders, insignia and equipment from WWI and WWII, and memorabilia from the flights of the Wright Brothers, Lindbergh, Earhart, and the Zeppelins. See also Militaria. Our advisor for this category is John R. Joiner; he is listed in the Directory under Georgia.

Badge, Graf Zeppelin LZ-127, 1929 Weltfahrt, gr/bl on metal, 1", EX..**55.00**
Badge, hat; Eastern Airlines, enameled center, 1940s, 2" dia **385.00**
Badge, hat; National NAL Airlines, enamel on metal, 1¼" dia...**115.00**
Badge, hat; Universal pilot's, wings w/jet center, 2½" W **65.00**
Bag, Aloha Airlines, red on wht cloth, 13x7x14½", EX...............**55.00**
Bag, carry-on; TWA NASA Tours, Airline Textile Mfg Co, 12x12", EX...**50.00**
Bag, National Airlines, Fly Me, 1973, 12x13"................................**48.00**
Bag, Northwest Orient Airlines, red w/wht trim, Bearse, 12x12x5"..**17.50**
Bag, Pan Am, bl nylon w/globe logo, zipper, sq..........................**85.00**
Bag, Pan Am, sky bl canvas w/wht letters, zipper......................**85.00**
Blanket, Allegheny Airlines, gold wool w/brn logo, 48x60", EX...**25.00**
Book, Guide to Commercial Aviation, 1922, 76-pg, VG+ **88.00**
Brochure, TWA, Disneyland map, 1955, open: 15½x8¾" **55.00**
Cap, flight; Pacific Western Airlines, bl w/PWA insignia, EX.......**50.00**
Cap, National Airlines captain's, dk bl w/wht braid **27.50**
Cookbook, Eastern Airlines, Recipes from the Jet Set, 1963, 215-pg, EX ..**15.00**

Cup and saucer, Aeroflot (Russia) china, Soviet-made, 1970s(?), $35.00 for the set. (Photo courtesy Richard Wallin)

Label, Capital Airlines, red & wht, 1950s, 2½x3¾", EX.................**5.00**
Label, luggage; Northwest Airlines, diecut foil plane, 5¼" L, EX...**12.50**
Model, TWA Boeing 707, aluminum, David's Models, 10" wingspan..**265.00**

Pamphlet, National Airlines, 1959 schedule info, EX **20.00**
Pen holder, Alitalia Airlines, red Bakelite dice shape, 1950s, 3" ...**215.00**
Pen set, TWA Disney Moonliner, enameled metal, bl pen ea side, 8"......**45.00**
Photo, Charles Lindbergh w/plane, blk & wht 1927 press release, EX ..**35.00**
Plate, TWA, wht w/red & gold ribbon stripe & logo, Rosenthal, 8½" ..**17.50**
Pocket mirror, Charles Lindbergh portrait, 1927, 2x3", EX.........**215.00**
Scarf, Pan Am flight attendant's, bl/wht striped polyester.............**50.00**
Stainless flatware, American Airlines, AA Stainless, 18-pc set **50.00**
Statuette, Tiki figure, United...Hawaiian Highway, stone-like, 29½" ..**200.00**
Stereoview, Wright airplane in flight at Ft Meyer VA, EX..........**100.00**
Timetable, Fly Mohawk, Now Serving Pittsburgh..........................**65.00**
Timetable, KLM Royal Dutch Airlines, N Am ed, ca 1950, EX....**50.00**
Timetable, TWA & Santa Fe Ry, Transcontinental, ca 1930, EX..**200.00**
Uniform, TWA hostess/stewardess; pale bl, skirt & jacket, ca 1939, EX....**350.00**
Wine glass, TWA Royal Ambassador, etched crystal, ftd.............**35.00**
Wings, Capital pilot's, mc enamel, Blackington hallmk, 3¼" **160.00**
Wings, Eagle Airline pilot's, Sterling hallmk, screw bk, 2¾" W...**80.00**
Wings, Eastern pilot's, embr on cloth, enameled center, 1930s, 4", EX..**165.00**
Wings, IAC pilot's, bl enamel center, screw bk, 2¾" W..............**185.00**
Wings, National Airlines flight attendant's, metal, 2"................**120.00**

Baccarat

The Baccarat Glass company was founded in 1765 near Luneville, France, and continues to this day to produce quality crystal tableware, vases, perfume bottles, and figurines. The firm became famous for the high-quality millefiori and caned paperweights produced there from 1845 until about 1860. Examples of these range from $300.00 to as much as several thousand. Since 1953 they have resumed the production of paperweights on a limited edition basis. Our advisors for this category are Randall Monsen and Rod Baer; their address is listed in the Directory under Virginia. See also Bottles, Commercial Perfume; Paperweights.

Bottle, scent; floral scallops on clear, 1925 Paris Expo, 5¾" **2,200.00**
Bottle, scent; Pinwheel, Rose Tiente, 6x2½" **95.00**
Bottle, wine; Zipper, Rose Tiente, cut paneled neck, 10x5" **235.00**
Bowl, Swirl, Rose Tiente, rolled-over rim, 3x9" **80.00**
Candlestick, Swirl, Rose Tiente, 7⅛"...**190.00**
Candy dish, Bretagne, w/lid, ftd, 5½" **70.00**
Decanter, Massena (Cut), etched mk, 13", MIB...........................**310.00**
Fairy lamp, Pinwheel, Rose Tiente, dome on matching plate, 6"...**250.00**
Figurine, Am Eagle, 7x5", MIB..**175.00**
Figurine, Angel of Peace, etched mk, 6¼", MIB.........................**130.00**
Figurine, bison, 8"..**445.00**
Figurine, bull, 3½x6½"...**215.00**
Figurine, camel, 3½x7"...**220.00**
Figurine, cat, 2⅜x5½x2¼"...**90.00**
Figurine, elephant, 3x3"...**85.00**
Figurine, falcon, 10"...**290.00**
Figurine, female ice skater, 11½"..**160.00**
Figurine, giraffe, 7x2"..**110.00**
Figurine, golfer, 8¾"..**155.00**
Figurine, hippo, 3x6"...**225.00**
Figurine, koala bear in tree, 5x5"...**110.00**
Figurine, lion, 4½x11"...**410.00**
Figurine, lioness w/cub, 4x9½x3½"..**310.00**
Figurine, nude, seated w/head in lap, 4½x3"............................**140.00**
Figurine, owl, 4½x2x2"...**90.00**
Figurine, parrot, gr or purple, 3", ea..**125.00**
Figurine, pelican, 6½x3½"...**90.00**
Figurine, pig, 3x5"...**285.00**
Figurine, polar bear, 4x6½"...**180.00**
Figurine, poodle, 5½x4"...**325.00**

Figurine, porcupine, 3½x5" 85.00
Figurine, snail, 5" 100.00
Figurine, swimming dragon, 4-pc, 12½" 210.00
Glass, brandy; Bacchus, 5¼" 160.00
Glass, highball; Harmonie, 12-oz, 5½", set of 6, MIB....290.00
Goblet, champagne; Angouleme (Plain), 4⅛" 45.00
Goblet, champagne; Aquarelle (yel), fluted, 7⅝" 70.00
Goblet, champagne; Athena (Cut), fluted, 8¼" 90.00
Goblet, claret wine; Angouleme (Plain), 5⅜"....80.00
Goblet, sherbet; Athena (Cut), tall, 5" 80.00
Goblet, water; Angouleme (Plain), 6" 80.00
Goblet, water; Armagnac, 5½" 90.00
Goblet, water; Austerlitz (Cut), 7⅜"....200.00
Goblet, water; Auvergne, 10½-oz, 7⅜", set of 6....1,240.00
Goblet, water; Avignon, 5¾" 80.00
Goblet, water; Biarritz, 6"....90.00
Goblet, water; Bogota (Cut), 7¼" 180.00
Goblet, water; St Remy, 9" 65.00
Jug, whiskey; Buckingham (Cut), w/stopper, 7¾"....240.00
Pitcher, Armagnac, 5⅞" 480.00
Shot glasses, Lulli, 2", set of 6....300.00
Tray, Swirl, Rose Tiente, rectangular, 9x13" L....75.00
Tumbler, Swirl, Rose Tiente, 4¾" 40.00
Vase, Edwige, 21" 1,040.00

Vases, Nouveau floral sprays on pink-flashed oviforms with gilt-metal scrolling mounts, 14⅜", $2,250.00 for the pair.

Badges

The breast badge came into general usage in this country about 1840. Since most are not marked and styles have changed very little to the present day, they are often difficult to date. The most reliable clue is the pin and catch. One of the earliest types, used primarily before the turn of the century, involved a 't-pin' and a 'shell' catch. In a second style, the pin was hinged with a small square of sheet metal, and the clasp was cylindrical. From the late 1800s until about 1940, the pin and clasp were made from one continuous piece of thin metal wire. The same type, with the addition of a flat back plate, was used a little later. There are exceptions to these findings, and other types of clasps were also used. Hallmarks and inscriptions may also help pinpoint an approximate age.

Badges have been made from a variety of materials, usually brass or nickel silver; but even solid silver and gold were used for special orders. They are found in many basic shapes and variations — stars with five to seven points, shields, disks, ovals, and octagonals being most often encountered. Of prime importance to collectors, however, is that the title and/or location appear on the badge. Those with designations of positions no longer existing (City Constable, for example) and names of early western states and towns are most valuable.

Badges are among the most commonly reproduced (and faked) types of antiques on the market. At any flea market, ten fakes can be found for every authentic example. Genuine law badges start at $30.00 to $40.00 for recent examples (1950 – 1970); earlier pieces (1910 – 1930) usually bring $50.00 to $90.00. Pre-1900 badges often sell for more than $100.00. Authentic gold badges are usually priced at a minimum of scrap value (karat, weight, spot price for gold); fine gold badges from before 1900 can sell for $400.00 to $800.00, and a few will bring even more. A fire badge is usually valued at about half the price of a law badge from the same era and material. Our advisor for this category is Gene Matzke; he is listed in the Directory under Wisconsin.

Arkansas State Highway Police, #260, 2x1¾" 510.00
Avalon Police Calif, 6-point star w/wreath & eagle atop, 1⅝" dia...310.00
Burlington Police #10, eagle atop, 3" 130.00
Captain Engine 20 Minneapolis Fire Dept, silver metal, 2¾x2" .185.00
Chicago Police, pie plate center, #36, ca 1910, rpl pin....295.00
Circulation Officer, Quebec Provincial Police, gold w/bl enamel, 1930s..210.00
City of Chicago Police, 1880s, #197, hallmk, EX 675.00
Columbia Exposition, 1893, 6-point star, EX....975.00
Deputy Constable, Alisal Township, #4, 6-point star 415.00
Detective Sergeant, SF Police, 6-point star, bl enamel on sterling, 3" ...810.00
Franklin Park (IL) Fire Dept, eagle atop, leather case, 1960s-70s..165.00
Ithaca NY Sergeant Police, eagle atop, 1930s, 3¼x2¼"....110.00
Kentucky State Police, Detective on eagle atop, 2¾x2½" 295.00
LA Police Consulting Surgeon, bl enamel on gold, ca 1920s......415.00
LAPD, #42, 1900-20s, 2⅝x3", EX....865.00
Meriden Conn Police #157, shield shape, nickel, 19th C, 2½" ..260.00
Military Police, Kearns Utah, #106, shield shape, 1920s....250.00
Naval Land Plane Pilot, German, WWI era 535.00
New Britain Police, hand eng, 1900s, 2¾x2"....210.00
Pilot, wings w/crescent moon & star, Turkish, 2x2¼" 470.00
Police Casper Wyoming, #22, 5-point gold star center on shield, 1920s....235.00
Portland Police #92, plain shield shape, wire pin w/fork-catch...175.00
Press, SF #853, Pass Issued by Chief of Police, 1920s, 2½x2" 240.00
Royal Ordnance Factories FB (Fire Brigade), WWII era....135.00
Special Officer #430 Los Angeles Police, bl on gold, 1930s, 2½x2" 210.00
Winnipeg 26 City Police, sq w/vine border, late 1800s, 1½x2"...110.00

Banks

In general, bank values are established on the auction block and from sales between collectors and dealers, and the driving force that determines the final price is condition. The spread between the price of a bank in excellent condition and the identical model in only good condition continues to widen. In order to be a seasoned collector in the pursuit of wise investments, one must learn to carefully determine overall condition by assessing the amount and strength (depth) of the paint, and by checking for breaks, repairs, and replaced parts; all bear heavily on value. Paint and casting variations are other considerations the collector should become familiar with.

Banks continue to maintain their value. Mechanicals often bring astronomical prices, making it imperative that collectors understand the market. Let's take a look at the price variations possible on an Uncle

Sam mechanical bank. If you find one with considerable paint missing but with some good color showing, the price would be around $1,000.00. If it has repairs or restoration, the value could drop to somewhere near $800.00 or less. Still another example with two thirds of its original paint and no repairs would probably bring $1,800.00. If it had only minor nicks, it could go as high as $3,500.00. Should you find one in 95% paint with no repairs, $5,000.00 or more would not be out of line. After considering all of these factors, remember: the final price is always determined by what a willing buyer and seller agree on for a specific bank.

Mechanical banks are the 'crème de la crème' in the arena of cast-iron toy collecting. They are among the most outstanding products of the Industrial Revolution and are recognized as some of the most successful of the mass-produced products of the nineteenth century. The earliest mechanicals were made of wood or lead. In 1869 John Hall introduced Hall's Excelsior, made of cast iron. It was an immediate success. J. & E. Stevens produced the bank for Hall and as a result soon began to make their own designs. Several companies followed suit, most of which were already in the hardware business. They used newly developed iron-casting techniques to produce these novelty savings devices for the emerging toy market. The social mores and customs of the times, political attitudes, racial and ethnic biases, the excitement of the circus, and humorous everyday events all served as inspiration for the creation of hundreds of banks. Designers made the most of simple mechanics to produce models with captivating actions that served not only to amuse but promote the concept of thrift to the children. The quality and detail of the castings were truly remarkable. The majority of collectible banks were made from 1870 to 1910; however, they continued to be manufactured until the onset of WWII. J. & E. Stevens, Shepard Hardware, and Kyser and Rex were some of the most prolific manufacturers of mechanicals. They made still banks as well.

Still banks are widely collected. Various materials were used in their construction, and each material represents a subfield in still bank collections. No one knows exactly how many different banks were made, but upwards of three thousand have been identified in the various books published on the subject. Cast-iron examples still dominate the market, but lead banks from Europe are growing in value. Tin and early pottery banks are drawing more interest as well. American pottery banks which were primarily collected by Americana collectors are becoming more important in the still bank field.

To increase your knowledge of banks, attend shows and auctions. Direct contact with collectors and knowledgeable dealers is a very good way to develop a feel for prices and quality. It will also help you in gaining the ability to judge condition, and you'll learn to recognize the more desirable banks as well.

Both mechanical and still banks have been reproduced. One way to detect a reproduction is by measuring. The dimensions of a reproduced bank will always be fractionally smaller, since the original bank was cast from a pattern while the reproduction was made from a casting of the original bank. As both values and interest continue to increase, it becomes even more important to educate ourselves to the fullest extent possible. We recommend these books for your library: *The Bank Book* by Norman, *The Dictionary of Still Banks* by Long and Pitman, *The Penny Bank Book* by Moore, *Penny Banks Around the World* by Don Duer, and *Penny Lane* by Davidson, which is considered the most complete reference available. It contains a cross-reference listing of numbers from all other publications on mechanical banks. Other books to consider are *Collector's Guide to Glass Banks* by Charles V. Reynolds, *Ceramic Coin Banks* by Tom Stoddard, and *Collector's Guide to Banks* by Beverly and Jim Mangus which covers modern pottery, porcelain, and composition banks.

All banks are assumed to be complete and original unless noted otherwise in the description. A number of banks are commonly found with a particular repair. When this repair is reflected in our pricing, it

will be so indicated. When traps (typically key lock, as in Uncle Sam) are an integral part of the body of the bank, lack of such results in a severe reduction in the value of the bank. When the trap is underneath the bank (typically a twist trap, as in Eagle and Eaglets), reduction in value is minimal.

To most accurately represent current market values, we have used condition codes in our listings that correspond with guidelines developed by today's bank collectors.

Our advisor for mechanical and still banks is Clive Devenish, who is listed in the Directory under California.

NM — 98% paint	VG — 80% paint
PR (pristine) — 95% paint	G — 70% paint
EX — 90% paint	

Key:

AL — aluminum	NP — nickel-plated
CI — cast iron	RM — Robert McCumber Book:
M — Andy Moore Book:	*Registering Banks*
The Penny Bank Book	SM — Sheet Metal
N — Bill Norman Book:	WM — white metal
The Bank Book	

Advertising

Decker's Iowana (pig), M-603, CI, 2¼", EX	150.00
Eureka gas stove, M-1350, pnt tin, 5¼", EX	60.00
GE refrigerator, M-1331, pnt CI, 4¼", EX	100.00
Kelvinator refrigerater on legs, M-1338 variant, CI, 4⅜", VG	150.00
Mellow furnace, M-1363, pnt CI, 3¾", NM	80.00

Roper Stove, M-1341, cast iron and tin, worn paint, 3¾", $140.00. (Photo courtesy Dunbar Gallery)

Singer electric sewing machine, M-1369, tin/CI, 5⅛", EX	400.00
Zenith radio, M-823, wht metal, 3¾", EX	45.00

Book of Knowledge Banks

Book of Knowledge Banks were produced by John Wright (Pennsylvania) from circa 1950 until 1975. Of the thirty models they made during those years, a few continued to be made in very limited numbers until the late 1980s; these they referred to as the 'Medallion' series. (Today the Medallion banks command the same prices as the earlier Book of Knowledge series.) Each bank was a handcrafted, hand-painted duplicate of an original as was found in the collection of The Book of Knowledge, the first children's encyclopedia in this country. Because the antique banks are often priced out of the range of many of today's collectors, these banks are being sought out as affordable substitutes for their very expensive counterparts. It should also be noted that China has reproduced banks with the Book of Knowledge inscription on them. These copies are flooding the market, causing original Book of Knowledge banks to decline in value. Buyers should take extra caution when investing in Book of Knowledge banks and purchase them through a reputable dealer who offers a satisfaction guarantee as well as a guarantee that the bank is authentic. Our advisor for Book of Knowledge banks is Dan Iannotti; he is listed in the Directory under Michigan.

Artillery Bank, NM..225.00
Butting Buffalo, M...225.00
Cabin, NM..185.00
Cat & Mouse, NM..200.00
Cow (Kicking), NM..250.00
Dentist Bank, EX...175.00
Eagle & Eaglets, M...300.00
Humpty Dumpty, M...195.00
Leap Frog, NM..250.00
Magician, MIB..235.00
Milking Cow, NM...250.00
Organ Bank (Boy & Girl), NM..275.00
Owl (Turns Head), NM...195.00
Paddy & Pig, NM..225.00
Punch & Judy, NM...195.00
Tammany Bank, NMIB..195.00
Teddy & the Bear, NM..200.00
Trick Pony, NM..250.00
US & Spain, M..235.00
World's Fair, mc version, NM..325.00

Mechanical

Jonah and the Whale, N-3490, EX, $5,500.00.

Always Dis 'Spise a Mule (jockey), N-2940, CI, NM...............4,800.00
American Bank (Sewing Machine), N-1050, CI, EX.............15,000.00
Bad Accident, rpl boy behind cactus, N-1150, CI, VG...........1,500.00
Bird on Roof, N-1270, CI, VG...2,000.00
Bulldog Savings (wind-up), N-1440, CI, VG........................4,500.00
Butting Buffalo, N-1570, CI, EX...9,500.00
Cabin Bank, N-1610, CI, VG..600.00
Chandlers Bank, w/orig trap, N-1720, CI & sheet metal, EX.....600.00
Chimpanzee, N-1760, CI, VG...5,800.00
Circus Bank, N-1820, CI, G..6,500.00
Crescent Cash Register, N-2010, NP & CI, EX.....................600.00
Cross-Legged Minstrel, no verse, N-2020, tin, EX................1,750.00
Cross-Legged Minstrel, w/verse, N-2020, tin, EX.................2,250.00
Five Cent Adding (5 cent), N-2410, CI, EX..........................1,600.00
Frog on Rock, N-2520, CI, EX...1,200.00

Gem Bank, N-2570, CI, EX..900.00
Giant in Tower, N-2600, CI, EX......................................10,000.00
Hall's Excelsior, N-2710, CI, VG..400.00
Home Bank, N-2840, tin, EX..300.00
Home Bank (w/Dormers), N-2850, CI, EX...........................4,500.00
Home Bank (w/o Dormers), N-2860, CI, EX.........................3,800.00
Hoop-la, N-2870, CI, VG..2,000.00
Initiating Bank (1st Degree), N-3000, CI, EX.....................17,000.00
Initiating Bank (2nd Degree), N-3010, CI, EX.....................8,800.00
Kick Inn Bank, N-3540, wood, VG.......................................500.00
Leap Frog, N-3590, CI, EX..3,600.00
Lighthouse, N-3620, CI, VG...3,200.00
Lion & 2 Monkeys (rpl top monkey), N-3650, CI, G..............650.00
Magic Bank, N-3730, CI, EX...3,600.00
Mason Bank, N-3800, CI, G..3,500.00
Memorial Money Box (Liberty Bell), N-3810, wood & CI, G....750.00
Milking Cow (for this value MUST be all orig), N-3870, CI, EX....18,000.00
Monkey & Tray (w/orig tray), N-4000, tin, EX......................500.00
Mule Entering Barn, N-3030, CI, EX....................................2,900.00
New Bank (left lever), N-4200, CI, VG.................................1,500.00
Organ, Medium; N-4330, CI, G..600.00
Owl, Slot in Head, N-4370, CI, EX...................................10,000.00
Patronize the Blind Man, N-4460, CI, VG............................5,500.00
Peg-Leg Begger, N-4480, CI, EX..3,600.00
Pump & Bucket, N-4700, CI, EX...2,000.00
Rabbit Standing (lg), N-4810, CI, VG..................................1,800.00
Rabbit Standing (sm), N-4810, CI, VG..................................650.00
Reclining Chinaman, N-4830, CI, VG..................................6,800.00
Safety Locomotive (pnt blk), N-4960, CI, G..........................500.00
Signal Cabin, N-5130, tin, VG...400.00
Smythe X-Ray Bank, N-5140, NPCI, EX...............................3,000.00
Squirrel & Tree Stump, N-5270, CI, VG...............................2,250.00
Treasure Chest Musical, N-5600, WM, EX.............................750.00
US & Spain (rpl mast), N-5800, CI, EX................................4,500.00
US Bank (Building), N-5790, CI, EX..................................12,500.00

Registering

Bean Pot, M-951, CI, 3", EX...250.00
Beehive Registering Savings Bank, CI/NP, 5⅜", EX..............275.00
Bestmaid, tin, 4¾", EX...75.00
Buddy (L) Savings & Recording Bank, SM, 6⁵⁄₁₆", EX..........125.00
Chein Thrifty Elf 'Dime a Day' Register, RM Pg 127, tin, EX.....85.00
Clown & Monkey Daily Dime Bank, RM Pg 225, tin, EX.......75.00
Dandy Self Registering Savings Bank, tin, 4¾", NM..............360.00
Donald Duck Clock Vault, tin, Spanish sayings on drum, EX....140.00
Elves Rolling Coins To Bank Dime Register, RM Pg 126, tin, EX....125.00
Gem Registering, RM Pg 18, CI, 6¹⁄₁₆" L, EX........................1,800.00
Keene Savings Bank, tin, EX..350.00
Keep 'Em Smiling Dime Register, RM Pg 124, tin, EX...........250.00
New York World's Fair Dime Register, RM Pg 129, tin, EX.....75.00
Penny Saver, CI, 5⅛", VG...80.00
Popeye Dime Register (pocket), M-1573, silver pnt on tin, 2½", EX....75.00
Prince Valiant Dime Bank, RM Pg 127, tin, EX.....................85.00
Prudential Registering Savings Bank (10¢), CI/NP, 7¼", EX.....350.00
Snow White Dime Register (pocket), M-1567, tin, 2½" sq, EX....150.00
Uncle Sam, M-1290, sheet steel w/blk & gold, 6¼", EX.........80.00

Still

$100,000 Money Bag, M-1262, CI, 3⅝", EX..........................400.00
Amherst Buffalo, M-556, CI, 5¼", EX...................................475.00
Arcade Steamboat, M-1460, CI, 2⅜" H, EX...........................460.00
Baby in Egg (Black), M-261, lead, 7¼", EX............................450.00

Baseball Player, M-18, CI, 5¾", VG..............................160.00

Baseball Player, M-19, CI, 5¾", NM.........................1,025.00

Battleship Maine, M-1439, CI, 6", EX.........................4,500.00

Bear Stealing Pig, M-693, CI, rpl screw, 5½", G............550.00

Bear w/Honey Pot, M-717, CI, 6½", EX.......................175.00

Begging Rabbit, M-566, CI, 5⅛", EX...........................225.00

Billy Bounce (Give Billy a Penny), M-15, CI, 4¾", VG.............350.00

Blackpool Tower, M-984, CI, partial rpt, rpl screw, 7⅜"............100.00

Boston Bull Terrier, M-421, CI, 5¼", EX.....................200.00

Buffalo, M-560, CI w/gold pnt, 3⅛", EX......................130.00

Bugs Bunny by the Tree, M-278, CI, 5½", EX................125.00

Building w/Eagle Finial, M-1134, CI, 9¾", EX................850.00

Bulldog (seated), M-396, CI, 3⅞", NM........................400.00

Bulldog w/Sailor Cap, M-363, lead, 4⅜", EX.................400.00

Buster Brown and Tige, M-241, gold and red paint, VG, $160.00.

Buster Brown & Tige, M-242 variant, CI, 5½", NM..................850.00

Cadet, M-8, CI, crack at slot, 5¾", VG........................150.00

Camel (kneeling), M-770, CI, 2½", EX.........................750.00

Camel (sm), M-768, CI, sm, 4¾", EX...........................225.00

Campbell Kids, M-163, CI, gold pnt, 3¾", EX................300.00

Captain Kidd, M-38, CI, 5⅝", G...............................130.00

Cat on Tub, M-358, CI, gold pnt, 4⅛", EX....................160.00

Cat on Tub, M-358, CI, 4⅛", EX...............................175.00

Charles Russell, M-247, wht metal, gold pnt, 6¼", EX.........50.00

Charlie McCarthy on Trunk, M-207, compo, 5¼", M............430.00

City Bank w/Chimney, M-1101, CI, old rpt, 6¾".............1,450.00

City Bank w/Teller, M-1097, CI, 5½", NM.....................570.00

Colonial House, M-992, CI, 4", EX.............................125.00

Columbia Bank, M-1070, CI, 5¾", EX..........................560.00

Columbia Tower, M-1118, CI, rpl turnpin, 6⅞", VG............675.00

County Bank, M-1110, CI, 4¼", G..............................160.00

Crosley Radio, M-819, CI, 5⅛", EX............................675.00

Crown Building, M-1225, CI, 5", NM.........................3,000.00

Cupola, M-1146, CI, 4⅛", EX..................................340.00

Dime Bank, M-1183, CI, 4¾", EX..............................125.00

Dog by Ball, M-390, lead/tin, 2⅛", VG........................230.00

Dog on Tub, M-359, CI, 4 1/16", EX...........................175.00

Dolphin, M-33, CI, gold pnt, 4½", EX.........................800.00

Donkey w/Saddle & Reins, M-497 variant, lead, 4", EX.........110.00

Double Decker Bus, M-1490, CI, bl pnt, 2¼", NM............1,025.00

Duck, M-624, CI, 4¾", EX.....................................300.00

Duck on Tub, M-616, CI, 5⅜", EX.............................200.00

Dutch Girl w/Flowers, M-181, CI, 5¼", EX....................110.00

Elephant on Tub, M-483, CI, 5⅜", EX.........................175.00

Elephant on Wheels, M-446, CI, 4⅛", EX......................330.00

Eureka Trust & Savings Safe, CI, 5¾", EX....................425.00

Feed My Sheep (lamb), M-596, lead, gold pnt, 2¾", VG............140.00

Fido, M-417, CI, 5", EX.......................................125.00

Fido on a Pillow, M-443, CI, 7⅜", EX.........................350.00

Flat Iron Building, M-1159, CI, 8¼", EX.....................2,400.00

Flat Iron Building, M-1160, CI, no trap, 5¾", EX.............370.00

Football Player, M-11, CI, 5⅞", EX...........................400.00

Forlorn Dog, M-408, wht metal, 4¾", G.........................75.00

Fortune Ship, M-1457, CI, 4⅛", NM.........................1,600.00

Foxy Grandpa, M-320, CI, 5½", EX............................340.00

Foxy Grandpa, M-320, CI, 5½", G.............................195.00

Frowning Face, M-12, CI, 5⅝", EX...........................1,650.00

General Butler, M-54, CI, 6½", EX...........................3,600.00

General Grant, M-115 variant, CI, Harper, 5⅝", EX..........3,400.00

Globe, M-812, CI, 5", VG.....................................250.00

Globe on Arc, M-789, CI, red pnt, 5¼", EX...................380.00

Globe on Arc, M-789, CI, 5¼", G.............................125.00

Globe Savings Fund, M-1199, CI, 7⅛", EX...................3,000.00

Golliwog, M-85, CI, 6¼", EX..................................500.00

Good-Luck Horseshoe (Buster Brown), M-508, CI, 4¼", EX.....300.00

Graf Zeppelin, M-1428, CI, 1¾" H, EX........................220.00

Grizzly Bear, M-703, lead, pnt worn in bk, 2¾".................100.00

Hansel & Gretel, M-1016, tin, 2¼", EX.......................125.00

Harper Stork Safe, M-651, CI, hdl missing, 5½", EX...........850.00

High Rise, M-1217, CI w/japanning, 5½", EX..................300.00

High Rise, M-1219, CI, 4⅝", EX..............................390.00

High Rise Tiered, M-1215, CI, 5¾", EX.......................350.00

Home Savings, M-1126, CI, 5⅞", EX..........................290.00

Horse on Tub (decorated), M-509, CI, 5¼", VG...............155.00

Horse on Wheels, M-512, CI, 5", EX..........................425.00

Horseshoe Wire Mesh, M-524, CI/tin, G- Arcade label, 3¼", VG...95.00

I Made Chicago Famous (pig), M-629, CI, Harper, 2⅛", EX......220.00

I Made St Louis Famous (mule), M-489, CI, Harper, 4¾", EX...1,950.00

Independence Hall, M-1244, CI, 8⅞", EX......................600.00

Independence Hall Tower, M-1205, CI, 9½", EX..............3,500.00

Iron Master's Cabin, M-1027, CI, 4¼", EX..................3,300.00

Jimmy Durante, M-259, WM, 6¾", EX..........................200.00

Labrador Retriever, M-412, CI, 4½", EX......................270.00

Lindberg w/Goggles, M-125, lead, 5⅞", EX...................225.00

Lindy Bank, M-124, AL, 6½", EX..............................180.00

Lion, M-765, CI, sm, 4", EX..................................100.00

Lion (lg, tail right), M-754, CI, 5¼", EX....................175.00

Lion (sm, tail right), M-755, CI, 4", EX......................75.00

Lion on Tub, M-747, CI, 4⅛", EX.............................150.00

Lion on Wheels, M-760, CI, 4½", EX..........................300.00

Litchfield Cathedral, M-968, CI, 6⅝", EX....................450.00

Main Street Trolley (no people), M-1469, CI, gold pnt, 3", EX..300.00

Maine (battleship), M-1439, CI, 6" H, NM..................4,000.00

Maine (sm battleship), M-1440, CI, 4⅝", EX.................400.00

Mammy w/Hands on Hip, M-176, CI, 5¼", EX..................150.00

Mammy w/Spoon, M-168, CI, 5⅞", EX.........................225.00

Man on Bale of Cotton, M-37, CI, 4⅞", EX..................3,600.00

Mary & Lamb, M-164, CI, 4¾", VG............................700.00

Mary & Lamb, M-164, CI, 4⅜" (ex Moore collection), NM...3,800.00

Metropolitan Safe, CI, 5⅞", NM.............................2,200.00

Mickey Mouse Post Office, tin, cylindrical, 6", NM..........140.00

Middy, M-36, CI, w/clapper, 5¼", G..........................135.00

Model T (2nd version), M-1483, CI, 4", NM................1,050.00

Monkey w/Removable Hat, M-740, brass, 3⅞", EX.............900.00

Mulligan, M-177, CI, 5¾", EX................................160.00

Mutt & Jeff, M-157, CI, gold pnt, 4¼", EX...................150.00

Newfoundland (dog), M-440, CI, 3⅝", EX.....................300.00

Ocean Liner, M-1444, lead, 2¾" H, VG........................140.00

Oregon (battleship), M-1450, CI, rpl guns, 3⅞", G...........230.00

Oregon (battleship), M-1452, CI, rpl turnpin, VG......................**400.00**
Oriental Boy on a Pillow (conversion), M-186, CI, 5½", EX **250.00**
Oriental Camel, M-769, CI, 3¾", G **325.00**
Pass Round the Hat (Derby), M-1381, CI, 1⅝", EX........................**200.00**
Peaceful Bill/Harper Smiling Jim, M-109, CI, 4", EX...............**2,400.00**
Pearl Street Building, M-1096, worn gold overpnt, 4¼" **380.00**
Pet Safe, M-866, CI, 4½", EX...**225.00**
Pig (standing), M-478, CI, 3", EX...**240.00**
Pocahontas Bust, M-226, lead, 3⅛", EX.................................**175.00**
Policeman, M-182, CI, Arcade, 5½", EX................................**1,100.00**
Polish Rooster, M-541, CI, 5½", EX..**1,250.00**
Porky Pig, M-264, CI, 6", EX+..**400.00**
Porky Pig, M-264, CI, 6", VG..**175.00**
Professor Pug Frog, M-311, CI, 3¼", EX................................**330.00**
Puppo, M-416, CI, 4⅞", VG...**155.00**
Quilted Lion, M-758, CI, 3¾", EX...**300.00**
Reindeer, M-376, CI, 6¼", NM..**280.00**
Retriever w/a Pack, M-436, CI, 4¹¹⁄₁₆", EX..........................**150.00**
Rhino, M-721, CI, 2⅝", NM...**1,050.00**
Roller Safe, M-880, CI, 3¹¹⁄₁₆", EX......................................**225.00**
Roof Bank Building, M-1122, CI, 5¼", G...............................**300.00**
Rooster, M-548, CI, 4¾", EX..**130.00**
Rumplestiltskin, M-27, CI, 6", VG...**200.00**
Sailor, M-27, CI, 5¼", G...**85.00**
Sailor, M-28, CI, 5½", G..**125.00**
Sailor, M-29, CI, 5⅝", NM...**800.00**
Santa Claus, Ives, M-56, CI, 7¼", EX.....................................**700.00**
Save & Smile, M-1641, CI, 4¼", EX.......................................**375.00**
Saving Sam, M-158, AL, 5¼", EX..**850.00**
Scottie (standing), M-435, CI, 3¾", VG **140.00**
Scotties (6 in basket), M-427, WM, 4½", EX.............................**75.00**
Seal on Rock, M-732, CI, 3½", EX..**600.00**
Seated Rabbit, M-368, CI, 3⅝", EX..**150.00**
Sharecropper, M-173, CI, 5½", EX..**275.00**
Skyscraper, M-1238, CI, 3¾", EX...**100.00**
Skyscraper, M-1239, CI, 4⅜", EX...**135.00**
Skyscraper (6 posts), M-1241, CI, 6½", EX.............................**300.00**
Songbird on Stump, M-664, CI, 4¾", EX.................................**650.00**
Squirrel w/Nut, M-660, CI, 4⅛", VG.......................................**470.00**
State Bank, M-1078, CI, w/key, 8", NM **1,350.00**
State Bank, M-1083, CI, 4⅛", EX..**250.00**
State Bank, M-1085, CI, 3", EX **300.00**
Stop Sign, M-1479, CI, 4½", G..**220.00**
Tally Ho, M-535, CI, 4½", EX...**275.00**
Tank, M-1436, lead, 3", VG..**725.00**
Tank Bank USA 1918 (lg), M-1435, CI, 3", EX........................**275.00**
Tank Bank USA 1918 (sm), M-1437, CI, 2⅜", EX....................**225.00**
Teddy (Teddy Roosevelt), M-120, CI, 5", EX............................**350.00**
Temple Bar Building, M-1163, CI, 4", EX...............................**600.00**
Tower Bank, M-1208, CI, 9¼", EX...**400.00**
Transvaal Money Box, M-1, CI, recast pipe, 6¼", VG.............**3,200.00**
Triangular Building w/Clock, M-1235, CI, 6", EX **650.00**
Trust Bank, M-154, CI, 7¼", EX..**4,500.00**
Turkey (lg), M-585, CI, 4¼", EX..**450.00**
Turkey (sm), M-587, CI, 3⅜", EX..**150.00**
Two-Faced Black Boy (lg), M-83, CI, EX.................................**300.00**
Two-Faced Black Boy (sm), M-84, CI, 3⅛", EX **200.00**
Two-Faced Devil, M-31, CI, 4¼", EX.......................................**700.00**
US Army/Navy Safe, electroplated CI, 6⅛", EX.....................**1,200.00**
US Mail, M-838, CI, sm, 3⅝", EX..**75.00**
USA Mail Mailbox w/Eagle, M-851, CI, 4⅛", EX......................**75.00**
Watch Me Grow, M-279 variant, tin, 5¾", EX............................**70.00**
Westminster Abbey, M-973, CI, old gold pnt, 6¼" **250.00**
White City Barrel #1, M-908, NP, EX......................................**150.00**

White City Barrel on Cart, M-907, CI, 4", EX **525.00**
Woolworth Building (lg), M-1041, CI, 7⅞", EX........................**300.00**
Woolworth Building (sm), M-1042, CI, 5¾", EX.......................**175.00**
World Time Bank, M-1539, CI, orig paper, 4⅛", EX..................**500.00**
Yellow Cab, M-1493, CI, 4¼", VG..**1,200.00**
Young Negro, M-170, CI, 4½", EX..**250.00**
1882 Villa, M-959, CI, 5⅞", VG..**800.00**
1890 Tower Bank, M-1198, CI, 6⅞", EX................................**1,200.00**
1893 World's Fair Administration Building, M-1072, CI, 6", EX....**650.00**

Barber Shop Collectibles

Even for the stranger in town, the local barber shop was easy to find, its location vividly marked with the traditional red and white striped barber pole that for centuries identified such establishments. As far back as the twelfth century, the barber has had a place in recorded history. At one time he not only groomed the beards and cut the hair of his gentlemen clients but was known as the 'blood-letter' as well, hence the red stripe for blood and the white for the bandages. Many early barbers even pulled teeth! Later, laws were enacted that divided the practices of barbering and surgery.

The Victorian barber shop reflected the charm of that era with fancy barber chairs upholstered in rich wine-colored velvet; rows of bottles made from colored art glass held hair tonics and shaving lotion. Backbars of richly carved oak with beveled mirrors lined the wall behind the barber's station. During the late nineteenth century, the barber pole with a blue stripe added to the standard red and white as a patriotic gesture came into vogue.

Today the barber shop has all but disappeared from the American scene, replaced by modern unisex salons. Collectors search for the barber poles, the fancy chairs, and the tonic bottles of an era gone but not forgotten. Our advisor for this category is Robert Doyle; he is listed in the Directory under New York. See Also Bottles; Razors; Shaving Mugs.

Bowl, shaving; brass, 10½"...**250.00**
Brush, wood hdl, mk Barber Shop Boar Badger, Austria, 5½", EX....**45.00**
Chair, Emil J Paidar, blk leather seat, porc base, 53", EX.........**1,500.00**
Chair, Emil J Paidar, 1930s, child sz, EX orig............................**1,000.00**
Chair, Koken, walnut w/inlay & burl, Congress Pat...1888, 48"..**475.00**
Chair, Melchoir Bros, hydraulic base, 51½", VG+......................**295.00**
Clippers, Boker, Hilton, chrome plated, 1930s, w/instructions......**20.00**
Clippers, Wahl, chrome, eyelet to hang on bk of counter, EX in case ..**17.50**

Globe, Massage Barber Bobbing, painted metal body with two 15" diameter glass lenses, 19½", VG, $250.00. (Photo courtesy Collectors Auction Services)

Jar, comb; Barbicide, glass cylinder w/chrome top, 11x4" dia **20.00**
Jar, comb; King's Barbicide, glass & aluminum, w/lid, 11½"..........**35.00**

Jar, cotton; Dmn Quilt, bl opal, SP lid, 6½" **425.00**
Massager, Oster Stim-U-Lax for Barbers, 1930s, 5¾", EX **50.00**
Mustache curling iron, silver hdl, MOP lever button, ⅜" dia **115.00**
Pole, Koch, pnt wood spiral, 1890-1900, 46x6" dia, VG **850.00**
Pole, red/wht spirals on tapered wood shaft, acorn finial, 19th C, 41"..**750.00**
Pole, red/wht/bl spiral stripes, revolves/lights up, 34x8" **475.00**
Pole, trn wood, red/wht/bl rings, blk wood base, sm, G **400.00**
Razor strop, leather, 19" w/hdl, EX **25.00**
Shaving brush, Ever Ready, clear Lucite w/nylon bristles **10.00**
Shaving brush holder, Bakelite, screw top, 1920s, 3x1½" dia........**18.00**
Shaving soap holder, Bakelite, screw top, 1920s, 3x1½" dia **18.00**
Sign, porc, pole w/Modern Service, half-rnd, Bob White Sign Co, 48"..**175.00**
Tin container, Erasmic Shaving Stick, litho, 1920s, 1½x3½" **55.00**
Tin container, Gibbs Cold Cream, pre-WWII, 3½x2½" dia **75.00**

Barometers

Barometers are instruments designed to measure the weight or pressure of the atmosphere in order to anticipate approaching weather changes. They have a glorious history. Some of the foremost thinkers of the seventeenth century developed the mercury barometer, as the discovery of the natural laws of the universe progressed. Working in 1644 from experiments by Galileo, Evangelista Torrecelli used a glass tube and a jar of mercury to create a vacuum and therefore prove that air has weight. Four years later, Rene Descartes added a paper scale to the top of Torrecelli's mercury tube and created the basic barometer. Blaise Pascal, working with Descartes, used it to determine the heights of mountains; only later was the correlation between changes in air pressure and changes in the weather observed and the term 'weather-glass' applied. Robert Boyle introduced it to England, and Robert Hook modified the form and designed the wheel barometer.

The most common type of barometer is the wheel or banjo, followed by the stick type. Modifications of the plain stick are the marine gimballed type and the laboratory, Kew or Fortin type. Another style is the Admiral Fitzroy of which there are twelve or more variations. The above all have mercury contained either in glass tubing or wood box cisterns.

The aneroid is a variety of barometer that works on atmospheric pressure changes. These come in all sizes ranging from 1" in diameter to 12" or larger. They may be in metal or wood cases. There is also a barograph which records on a graph that rotates around a drum powered by a seven-day clock mechanism. Pocket barometers (altimeters) vary in sizes from 1" in diameter up to 6". One final type of barometer is the symphisometer, a modification of the stick barometer; these were used for a limited time as they were not as accurate as the conventional marine barometer. Our advisor for this category is Bob Elsner; he is listed in the Directory under Florida.

Prices are subject to condition of wood, tube, etc.; number of functions; and whether or not they are signed.

American Stick Barometers

Chas Wilder, Peterboro, NH **1,250.00**
DE Lent, Rochester, NY **1,250.00**
EO Spooner Storm King, Boston, MA.......................................**1,450.00**
FD McKay Jr, Elmira, NY **3,100.00**
Simmons & Sons, Fulton, NY **1,250.00**

English Barometers

Note: The 10" mahogany wheel listed below is marked 'Royal Exchange London Optician to King George IV Prince of Wales.' It may be referenced in Goodison, page 85.

Admiral Fitzory, various kinds, ea from $500 to **3,000.00**
Fortin type (Kew or Laboratory) metal on brd w/milk glass, $750 to....**950.00**
Marine gimballed, sgn Walker, London **4,000.00**
Right angle, sgn John Whitehurst, ca 1790 ....**15,000.00**

Spelzini, London, wheel or banjo with mother-of-pearl inlay, 10" diameter, $1,950.00.
(Photo courtesy Robert Elsner)

Stick, mahog bow-front w/urn-shaped cistern, S Mason, Dublin, 1824-30...**5,000.00**
Stick, rosewood, sgn L Casella, London **1,650.00**
Stick, rosewood w/ivory scale, sgn Adie, dbl vernier, ca 1840 ....**3,200.00**
Symphisometer, sgn Adie...**3,950.00**
Wheel, 6", sgn Stanley, Peterborough **1,500.00**
Wheel, 8", sgn F Molten, Norwich..**1,450.00**
Wheel, 10", mahog, J Smith Royal Exchange...Optician...Prince of Wales.**1,950.00**
Wheel, 10", MOP, sgn Spelzini, London **1,950.00**

Other Types

Aneroid, 4-6" dia in brass case w/half-rnd thermometer, $150 to ...**250.00**
Mahog barograph (recording type), sgn Negretti & Zambra **950.00**
Pocket barometer (altimeter), w/case, from $200 to **300.00**

Barware

Back in the thirties when social soirees were very elegant affairs thanks to the influence of Hollywood in all its glamour and mystique, cocktails were often served up in shakers styled as miniature airplanes, zeppelins, skyscrapers, lady's legs, penguins, roosters, bowling pins, etc. Some were by top designers such as Norman Bel Geddes and Russel Wright. They were made of silver plate, glass, and chrome, often trimmed with colorful Bakelite handles. Today these are hot collectibles, and even the more common Deco-styled chrome cylinders are often priced at $25.00 and up. Ice buckets, trays, and other bar accessories are also included in this area of collecting.

For further information we recommend *Vintage Bar Ware Identification & Value Guide* by Stephen Visakay, our advisor for this category; he is listed in the Directory under New Jersey. See also Bottle Openers.

Bar towel, cloth w/mc printed bar motif.....................................**18.00**
Canope tray, satin chromium over brass, 1935, 4½x6¾"..............**10.00**

Cigarette dispenser, mini bar w/Black bartender, metal/wood, Fr **650.00**
Cocktail cup, Catalin w/chrome stem, mk NUDAWN USA, 6¾x3¼" dia....**27.50**
Cocktail cup, glass insert, mk Farber Bros, Pat, 4¼" **11.00**
Cocktail dish, bar scene w/drink names, 1930s, 8" **90.00**
Cocktail glass, amber w/pierced chrome holder, Farber Bros, 3½" ...**30.00**
Cocktail glass, Catalin w/chrome & Catalin stem, gr, NUDAWN, 5¾" .**10.00**
Cocktail glass, plastic w/colored spring coil stem, 1950s..................**7.00**
Cocktail glass, rooster scenes, ftd, 1930s, 3½x3¼"...........................**8.00**
Cocktail picks, domino tops w/domino holder, plastic, 9-pc, 4½" .**75.00**
Cocktail set, hammered aluminum, shaker/4 cups/rnd tray, TKF, 1930s .**175.00**
Drink muddler, glass **10.00**
Ice bowl w/tongs, chrome, Russel Wright/Chase, 1930s-40s, 7" dia.....**35.00**
Ice bucket, aluminum ball form w/emb penguins, West Bend, 1941, 8" ..**25.00**
Ice bucket, chrome w/porc lining, Bakelite trim, Keystone Ware, 11"....**75.00**
Ice bucket, Ships, wht on cobalt, Hazel Atlas, 4¼x5½"................**55.00**
Ice chopper, cobalt glass w/silk-screened recipes, 1930s, 11½"......**65.00**
Mixer, chrome pitcher w/jade Catalin trim, 1928, 52-oz, 10¾" ..**250.00**
Napkins, orange & brn linen, tuxedoed man & shaker, set of 8 .**130.00**
Pitcher, martini; glass, clear w/brn plastic-wrapped hdl, w/stick, 13" ...**45.00**
Shaker, aluminum, cylindrical, anodized bl, 11¼" **75.00**
Shaker, aluminum, cylindrical w/blk plastic top, 1940s, 12"..........**55.00**
Shaker, chrome, cylindrical, Modernist, Royal Hickman, 1930s, 14"...**450.00**
Shaker, chrome, cylindrical w/horizontal lines, Manning-Bowman, 7½"....**45.00**
Shaker, chrome, Manhattan, vertical ribs, Bel Geddes, 13" **550.00**
Shaker, chrome, orange Catalin trim, Krome Kraft, 12¾".............**80.00**
Shaker, chrome, penguin, hinged beak spout, Napier, 12¼" **600.00**
Shaker, chrome, skyscraper, blk, enamel cap & base, 12¼"...........**60.00**
Shaker, glass, chrome top, mc horizontal stripes, Hazel Atlas, 1930s....**40.00**
Shaker, glass, dumbbell, cobalt, West Virginia Specialty, 13".........**40.00**
Shaker, glass, glass top, orange w/yel spatter, 1930s, 7".................**85.00**
Shaker, glass, gr w/chrome lid, Catalin finial, Cambridge, 13"....**275.00**
Shaker, glass, gr w/eng rooster, SP top, 1926, 10½" **75.00**
Shaker, NP, hammered, Bernard Rice & Sons, 1920s, 13¾" **75.00**
Shaker, NP, hammered & plain, Expressware NY Stamping Co, 17½" ..**300.00**
Shaker, NP, rooster, eng/enameled, Meriden, Pat Jan 11, 1927...**215.00**
Shaker, SP, bell shape, Dunhill, 11"...**90.00**
Shaker, SP, rooster, hammered w/tail hdl, Wallace Bros, 1928, 15"...**1,500.00**
Shaker, sterling, hexagonal, Mexico, 42-oz, 13".........................**300.00**
Shaker, wooden bbl form w/metal insert, chrome top, 9½" **75.00**
Shot jigger, graduated, stemmed, Napier, 4" **85.00**
Shot set, 6 glasses in chrome fr, Farberware, 1935, 5x6" dia..........**85.00**
Stopper, horse head, Heisey, 13½", from $350 to **450.00**
Swizzle sticks, glass, tuxedoed men, 1930s, 7¼", ea **15.00**
Traveling bar, brass/chrome, red stripes, 8-pc, Germany, 1928, 14".....**250.00**
Traveling bar, NP shaker form, 9-pc, mk Germany, ca 1928, 8"....**85.00**
Tray, chrome w/abstract human figure in center, Manning-Bowman, 6½"..**120.00**

Baskets

Basket weaving is a craft as old as ancient history. Baskets have been used to harvest crops, for domestic chores, and to contain the catch of fishermen. Materials at hand were utilized, and baskets from a specific region are often distinguishable simply by analyzing the natural fibers used in their construction. Early Indian baskets were made of corn husks or woven grasses. Willow splint, straw, rope, and paper were also used. Until the invention of the veneering machine in the late 1800s, splint was made by water-soaking a split log until the fibers were softened and flexible. Long strips were pulled out by hand and, while still wet and pliable, woven into baskets in either a cross-hatch or hexagonal weave.

Most handcrafted baskets on the market today were made between 1860 and the early 1900s. Factory baskets with a thick, wide splint cut by machine are of little interest to collectors. The more popular baskets are those designed for a specific purpose, rather than the more common-

ly found utility baskets that had multiple uses. Among the most costly forms are the Nantucket Lighthouse baskets, which were basically copied from those made there for centuries by aboriginal Indians. They were designed in the style of whale-oil barrels and named for the South Shoal Nantucket Lightship where many were made during the last half of the nineteenth century. Cheese baskets (used to separate curds from whey), herb-gathering baskets, and finely woven Shaker miniatures are other highly-prized examples of the basket-weaver's art.

In the listings that follow, assume that each has a center bentwood handle (unless handles of another type are noted) that is not included in the height. Unless another type of material is indicated, assume that each is made of splint. Prices are subjective and hinge on several factors: construction, age, color, and general appearance. Baskets rated very good (VG) will have minor losses and damage.

See also American Indian; Eskimo; Sewing; Shaker.

Birch bark w/hickory splint zigzags & lacing, 14½x14x10" **165.00**
Bushel, concave base, 2-hdl, wrapped rim, 12x23", VG **110.00**
Bushel, sturdy weave, 2-hdl, wrapped ft, 12½x23" dia.................**360.00**
Buttocks, 16-rib, old varnish, 3x5½" **165.00**
Buttocks, 22-rib, wide rim, EX patina, 3½x6¾"..........................**90.00**
Buttocks, 26-rib, wide central band, 7x13½" **100.00**
Buttocks, 32-rib, pnt traces (mc), 2 lift lids, 5x9¼x8¼" **140.00**
Buttocks, 42-rib, old weathered surface, minor losses, 5½x9½"....**110.00**
Cheese, open geometric weave, dry wht pnt, 3¼x8" **195.00**
Gathering, dry/natural, woven ft, 16x17½"...............................**110.00**
Gathering, EX patina, 17"..**220.00**
Gathering, hickory ⅝" splints held by bentwood hoops, 16" **330.00**
Goose feather, w/lid, 2 bentwood hdls, 25" **100.00**
Half buttocks, 10-rib, old weathered patina, 6x5¾" **175.00**
Laundry, dbl hdls, 12x35", VG...**80.00**
Laundry, 2 rim hdls, 13x30½x25" **150.00**
Market, oblong w/red & gr decor, flared oblong shape, 6½x15x11½" **50.00**

Melon, woven wicker, 3¾x5x4", EX, $300.00. (Photo courtesy Collectors Auction Service)

Melon, 26-rib, lt brn patina, 9x12½", VG **110.00**
Melon, 52-rib, tightly woven, 12"..**155.00**
Mini, fine weave, orig red-brn pnt, sq base, w/lid, 2¾x4½" **100.00**
Nantucket, canted sides, walnut base, M Ray label w/verse, 11x15x11"....**1,850.00**
Nantucket, dbl hdls w/brass tacks, 2-tone splint, oval, 4x9½" L .**415.00**
Nantucket, dk splint band at middle, disk base, EX patina, 5x7⅝"..**2,500.00**
Nantucket, faux ivory disks, pegs at hdl, Farnum 1978, 7x8½"...**400.00**
Nantucket, fine weave, wood base, brass tabs at hdls, Boyer, 3x3½" ..**1,550.00**
Nantucket, fine weave, wooden base, brass tabs at hdls, Boyer, 4x5"...**1,450.00**
Nantucket, lt/dk cane, Chadwick Island House 27 EV Seller, 11x12½"....**2,500.00**
Nantucket, swing hdl, oval wood base, 7x14½" **1,500.00**
Nantucket, swing hdl, salmon pnt, copper band rpr to base, 11x15" ...**3,000.00**
Nantucket, swing hdl, trn base, Harrison Gardner, 8½x12" **2,200.00**
Nantucket, swivel hdl, trn disk base, varnish, 6x9½"...............**2,400.00**
Nantucket, trn wooden base, ca 1900, 4¾x10¾" dia **650.00**

Nantucket, wooden base, high sides, EX patina, 10x8⅛"........**2,400.00**
Nantucket, 2 cvd hdls, lt cane on dk wood, mk MPL Seller 25, 12x18"..**3,750.00**
Nantucket purse, wooden base, faux ivory pin, 1982, 7x10¼"....**220.00**
Pnt, deep salmon, w/lid, 5" dia.................................**2,000.00**
Pnt, gr w/bl int, 2 cvd hdls, 5x6¾" dia.........................**1,880.00**
Pnt, lt bl w/pine base, cvd hdl, minor breaks, 17x16x24".....**765.00**
Pnt, mustard w/gr & blk bands, w/lid, 8".........................**500.00**
Pnt, salmon w/brn cotton-lined int, narrow splint, 3x4x5½"..**1,100.00**
Potato stamp, att E Woodland, rectangular w/2 splint hdls, 20" L.....**470.00**
Twisted splint triangles & mc bands, 7¾x9½" dia, EX...............**100.00**
Wall, 3 graduated tiers, terra-cotta pnt, 19th C, 24x11½x6½".....**1,525.00**

Batchelder

Ernest A. Batchelder was a leading exponent of the Arts and Crafts movement in the United States. His influential book, *Design in Theory and Practice*, was originally published in 1910. He is best known, however, for his artistic tiles which he first produced in Pasadena, California, from 1909 to 1916. In 1916 the business was relocated to Los Angeles where it continued until 1932, closing because of the Depression.

In 1938 Batchelder resumed production in Pasadena under the name of 'Kinneola Kiln.' Output of the new pottery consisted of delicately cast bowls and vases in an Oriental style. This business closed in 1951. Tiles carry a die-stamped mark; vases and bowls are hand incised. For more information we recommend *Collector's Encyclopedia of California Pottery, Second Edition*, by Jack Chipman (Collector Books). See also Tiles. Our advisors for this category are Suzanne Perrault and David Rago; they are listed in the directory under New Jersey.

Salesman's sample, plain and decorated tiles mounted in a metal frame, stenciled 24, Batchelder Tiles Los Angeles, 13 1/2 x 12 3/4", $2,100.00. (Photo courtesy David Rago Auctions)

Chest, dk oak fr w/incised daffodil tile in front panel, 14x28x15"..**7,000.00**
Table, 3 2" floral bl-engobe tiles+sm bsk tiles, iron base, 19x19x13"..**1,000.00**
Tile, boy w/dragon & knight toy outside castle, mc mottle, 12", $1,000 to........**1,500.00**
Tile, peacock pr/floral border w/bl engobe, lt wear/sm nicks, 5¾"...**200.00**
Tile, salesman's sample, plain & decorated tile, #124, metal fr 14x14"..**2,100.00**
Vase, brn w/blk runs, Asian influence, swollen form, 5½"..........**500.00**
Vase, multi-tone bl metallic w/separations, swollen, flaw, 5"...**1,000.00**
Vase, multi-tone gr texture, shouldered, 5".....................**400.00**

Battersea

Battersea is a term that refers to enameling on copper or other metal. Though originally produced at Battersea, England, in the mid-eighteenth century, the craft was later practiced throughout the Staffordshire district. Boxes are the most common examples. Some are figurals,

and many bear an inscription. Values are given for examples with only minimal damage, which is normal. Please note that items with printed Bilston labels are new. Our advisor for this category is John Harrigan; he is listed in the Directory under Minnesota

Bottle, scent; Classical Lady musician, glass stopper, 3"............**250.00**
Box, birds, mc in wht reserves on yel, rpr bk, 1⅞".....................**135.00**
Box, motto; 'The Gift is Small...,' wht, 1⅝".............................**525.00**
Box, scrolls/roses, gold/mc on wht, lobed shape, loose lid, 2"......**165.00**
Knob, Dancing Girl (plays triangle), mc, Bilston, 1⅞", pr (1 VG)....**275.00**
Knob, lady & eagle, mc, Bilston, 2", pr...............................**575.00**
Knob, Sacred to Friendship, lady at tomb, mc, Bilston, 1½", pr....**275.00**

Bauer

The Bauer Pottery Company is one of the best known of the California pottery companies, noted for both its artware and its dinnerware. In the past ten years, Bauer has become particularly collectible, and prices have risen accordingly. The pottery actually started in Kentucky in 1885. It moved to Los Angeles in 1910 where it remained in operation until 1962. The company produced several successful dinnerware lines, including La Linda, Monterey, and Brusche Al Fresco. Most popular — and most significant — was the Ringware line introduced in 1932 which preceded Fiesta as a popular solid-color everyday dinnerware. The earliest pieces are unmarked, although to collectors they are unmistakable, partly due to their distinctive glazes which have an almost primitive charm due to their drips, misses, and color variations.

Another dinnerware line favored by collectors is Speckleware, its name derived from the 1950s-era speckled glaze Bauer used on various products, including vases, flowerpots, kitchenware items, and dinnerware. Though not as popular as Ringware, Speckleware holds its value and is usually available at much lower prices than Ring. Keep an eye out for other flowerpots and mixing bowls as well.

Artware by Bauer is not so easy to find now, but it is worth seeking out because of its high values. So-called oil jars sell for upwards of $1,500.00, and Rebekah vases routinely fetch $400.00 or more. Matt Carlton is one of the most desirable designers of handmade ware.

After WWII a flood of foreign imports and loss of key employees drastically curtailed their sales, and the pottery began a steady decline that ended in failure in 1962. Prices listed below reflect the California market. For more information we recommend *Collector's Encyclopedia of Bauer Pottery: Identification & Values* and *The Collector's Encyclopedia of California Pottery, Second Edition*, both by Jack Chipman (Collector Books).

In the lines of Ring and Plain ware, pricing depends to some extent on color. Use the low end of our range of values for light brown, Chinese yellow, orange-red, jade green, red-brown, olive green, light blue, turquoise, and gray; the high-end colors are Delph blue, ivory, dusty burgundy, cobalt, chartreuse, papaya, and burgundy. Black is 50% higher than the high end; to evaluate white, double the high side. Use the low end of the range to evaluate Monterey items in all colors but Monterey blue, burgundy, and white — those are high-end colors. You'll need to double the high end for black in this line as well as Monterey Moderne. An in-depth study of colors may be found in the books referenced above.

Our advisor for this category is Michele Miele; she is listed in the Directory under Montana.

Art Pottery, #200 Hi-Fire and Matt Carlton

Bowl, Half Pumpkin; speckled yel, Tracy Irwin, mk, 10¼"............**85.00**
Bowl, orange red, Matt Carlton, 2½x6" sq....................**150.00**
Bowl, Pumpkin; blk matt w/14k gold, 4x6"...................**90.00**
Flower bowl, turq, deep, Hi-Fire, #211, 6".......................**45.00**

Jar, Carnation, gr #1, 14", minimum value 1,800.00
Jardiniere, gr matt, emb filigree, 10", minimum value 750.00

Pitcher, red-brown, Fred Johnson, Hi-Fire, 11½", minimum value $500.00.

(Photo courtesy Jack Chipman)

Rose bowl, Monterey Blue, Hi-Fire, 4" 5.00
Vase, blk, Fred Johnson, Hi-Fire, #215, 7", minimum value........150.00
Vase, royal bl, emb ribs, flared rim, Matt Carlton, 5¼" 450.00
Vase, royal bl, twist hdls, Matt Carlton, 9½", minimum value ...1,200.00

Brusche Al Fresco and Contempo

Al Fresco, bowl, vegetable; speckled yel, 7½" 24.00
Al Fresco, cup & saucer, Misty Gray, low......................................12.00
Al Fresco, French casserole, Dubonnet, 2-qt................................100.00
Al Fresco, pitcher, Misty Gray, 2-pt..40.00
Al Fresco, shakers, Coffee Brown, jumbo, pr................................30.00
Contempo, bowl, deep soup/cereal; Pumpkin, 5¼" 15.00
Contempo, cup & saucer, Spicy Green..12.00
Contempo, pitcher, Indio Brown, 1-pt 30.00
Contempo, plate, dinner; Spicy Green, 10" 10.00

Cal-Art and Garden Pottery

Bowl, florist's; Brusche Contempo Spicy Green 40.00
Flowerpot, Cal-Art Swirl, gloss gray, drilled, 6"...........................25.00
Flowerpot, Cal-Art Swirl, olive gr, 6" 55.00
Flowerpot, Cal-Art Swirl, turq, 6" 55.00
Flowerpot, Cal-Art Swirl, wht matt, 5" 40.00
Flowerpot, Cal-Art Swirl, yel, 4" 25.00
Flowerpot, Pinnacle, olive gr, 10" 85.00
Jardiniere, Cal-Art Swirl, wht matt, 5"...40.00
Jardiniere, yel Hi-Fire Ring-style, 5"...40.00
Oil jar, speckled bl, 16", minimum value.....................................500.00
Pot, 3-Step, gloss wht, 4"..40.00
Sand jar, speckled wht, 20" 250.00
Spanish pot, speckled gr, 4"...20.00
Spanish pot, turq, 8"...80.00
Swan, blk gloss, Ray Murray, 3x9", minimum value 200.00
Wall pocket, wht matt, Ray Murray, 6½", minimum value 400.00

Gloss Pastel Kitchenware (aka GPK)

Baker, all colors, scarce, 11½x6½"..45.00
Bowl, mixing; #12, all colors 50.00
Casserole, olive gr, 1-qt 45.00

Custard cup, all colors 10.00
Pitcher, all colors, 1½-pt...25.00

Plain Ware

Bowl, salad; 8¼", from $80 to 120.00
Coffee server, w/lid, from $75 to 100.00
Lamp base, 4½", from $300 to 450.00
Mug, handmade, 4", from $100 to 150.00
Pitcher, 12", from $400 to 600.00
Pudding dish, #6, 10¼", from $80 to 120.00
Sugar bowl, from $85 to 125.00

Ring Ware

Bowl, low salad; cobalt, 12", from $125 to 175.00
Bowl, mixing; Double Ring, Delph Blue, #12, EX 150.00
Bowl, punch/salad; ftd, 9", minimum value...............................500.00
Candle holders, 2½", pr, from $150 to 250.00
Cigarette jar, minimum value 750.00
Coffee server, cobalt, open, 8-cup..175.00
Cup, punch; Chinese Yellow 60.00
Custard cup, orange-red...45.00
Platter, oval, gr, 9", from $75 to 100.00
Relish plate, Delph Blue, from $85 to 125.00
Shakers, burgundy, squat, pr 80.00
Sugar bowl, from $75 to 100.00
Teapot, orange-red w/yel lid, 6-cup...95.00

Speckled Kitchenware

Bowl, mixing; wht, #36 ....25.00
Bowl, salad; yel, low, 7" 30.00
Buffet server, brn...45.00
Candle holder, votive, brn 15.00
Casserole, pk, 2½-qt, w/lid & brass-plated fr................................75.00
Pitcher, pk, mk, 1-pt...35.00
Pitcher, yel, Brusche style, 1-pt...35.00

Miscellaneous

Butter plate, cobalt glazed stoneware, Merry Xmas..., 4½".........350.00
Candlestick/bud vase, early stoneware, 8" 300.00
Churn, whtware, no lid, stamped mk on side, 2-gal, 12¾"..........100.00
Olla, redware, 3-gal, 12¾"..85.00
Sand jar, dk gr, stoneware, hand-thrown, 22", minimum value...800.00

Beer Cans

    In the early 1930s one of America's largest can-manufacturing companies approached an East Coast brewery with a novel concept — beer in cans. The brewery decided to take a chance on the idea, and in January 1935, the beer can was born.

    The 'church key' style can opener was invented at the same time, and early flat top cans actually had instructions on how to use it to open a can.

    Canned beer soared in popularity, and breweries scrambled to meet the canning challenge. Since many companies did not have a machine to fill a flat-top can, the cone top was invented. Brewery executives believed its shape would be more acceptable to consumers used to buying bottled beer, and it easily passed through existing bottling machinery. The more compact flat-top can dominated sales, and by the 1950s cone tops were obsolete.

About values: Condition is critical when determining the value of a beer can. Like any collectible, value drops in direct proportion to condition, and off-grade cans are often worth no more than one-half of retail value. Information in our descriptions is given in this specific order: 1) name of brew; 2) company — may be simply repetitive; and 3) city/state or state.

All cone tops with original caps, ca 1950s: White Cap Beer, Two Rivers Brewing, Two Rivers, IA, NM, $125.00; Uchtorff Beer, Uchtorff Brewing, Davenport, IA, EX, $200.00; Bohemian Club Beer, Bohemian Brewing, Boise, ID, EX, $120.00.

Acme Beer, Acme Brg, San Francisco CA, flat top, EX 20.00
Alps Brau, Maier, Los Angeles, flat top, EX 60.00
Ballantine, Bock Ballantine, Newark NJ, pull tab, EX 65.00
Bartels Extra Light, Bartels Brg, Edwardsville PA, flat top, EX 90.00
Berghoff 1887, Berghoff, Fort Wayne IN, cone top, low profile, EX 45.00
Blatz Pilsner, Blatz, Lawrence MI, J Spout, VG+ 90.00
Budweiser, Florida State Semimoles, A-B Brg, St Louis MO, pull tab, M ...45.00
Burger Ale, Burger, Cincinnati OH, flat top, EX 48.00
Canadian Ace, Canadian Ace Brg, Chicago IL, 16-oz flat top, EX+ ..68.00
Carling's Ale, Brg Corp of America, Cleveland OH, cone top, EX 85.00
Dakota, Bismark ND, zip top, NM 45.00
Dart Premium Light Beer, Bavarian Brg, Reading PA, zip tab, EX 65.00
Drewerys Bock, Drewerys, South Bend IN, pull tab, EX 40.00
E&B Special Beer, E&B Brewing, Detroit MI, EX+ 40.00
Ebling Premium Beer, Ebling Brg, New York NY, crowntainer, EX 75.00
Foodtown Beer, Old Dutch Brg, Allentown PA, pull tab, NM 40.00
Fort Schuyler, Fort Schuyler, Utica NY, flat top, EX 45.00
Fort Schuyler Lager, Utica Brg, Utica NY, cone top, EX.............100.00
Goebel Beer, Goebel Brg, Detroit MI, instructional, EX 50.00
Gold Crest 51, Tennessee, Memphis TN, cone top, EX 90.00
Golden Pilsner, Becker, Ogden UT, flat top, EX 45.00
Grand Prize Beer, Gulf Brewing, Houston TX, instructional, EX ..60.00
Hanley's Extra Pale Ale, Hanley Brg, Providence RI, crowntainer, EX ...75.00
Jax Draft, Jackson Brg, New Orleans LA, pull tab, EX 45.00
Krueger Finest Beer, Krieger Brg, Newark NJ, instructional, EX .175.00
Land of Lakes, Pilsen Brg, Chicago IL, flat top, EX+ 23.00
Lebanon Valley Pilsner, Lenanon Valley, Lebanon PA cone top, VG ...85.00
Lone Star Beer, Lone Star Brg, San Francisco CA, flat top, EX 20.00
National Brg, Chesapeake Bay Map, National Brg, Baltimore MD, NM ..175.00
Old Craft, Oconto WI, flat top, EX 32.00
Old Dutch Lager, Maier Brg, Los Angeles CA, flat top, EX 50.00
Old German Beer, Queen City Brg, Cumberland MD, cone top, VG+ ..90.00
Old Reading Beer, Old Reading, Reading PA, cone top, EX.......150.00
Old Shay Beer, Fort Pitt Brg, Pittsburgh PA, crowntainer, EX 100.00
Old Tyme Beer, Maier Brg, Los Angeles CA, flat top, G+ 20.00
Ortlieb's Premium Lager, Ortlieb, Philadephia PA, flat top, VG...15.00

Pabst Blue Ribbon, Pabst Brg, Milwaukee WI, flat top, EX...........64.00
Pickwick Ale, Haffenreffer, Boston MA, cone top, EX.................50.00
Pilsner's Maltcrest Brew, Metropolis Brg, Trenton NJ, flat top, EX 60.00
Rainier Ale, Rainier, San Francisco CA, flat top, EX...................32.00
Royal Bru, Union, New Castle PA, cone top, VG......................135.00
Royal Pilsener, Koller Brg, Chicago IL, J-spot cone top, G+.......120.00
Schlitz Vitamin D, Schlitz, Milwaukee WI, cone top, EX 90.00
Sebewaing Beer, Sebewaing Brg, Sebewaing MI, zip tab................45.00
Sigraa, Reno, Reno NV, cone top, G+...40.00
Stock Ale, Croft Brg, Lacrosse WI, cone top, G..............................62.00
Sunshine Extra, Barbey's Reading PA, cone top, EX 135.00
Tempo Beer, Blatz Brg, Milwaukee WI, flat top, G+.....................21.00
Trophy Beer, Birk Bros Brg, Chicago IL, cone top, EX.................10.00
Utica Club, West End, Utica NY, cone top, EX 185.00
Valley Brew Pale, El Dorado Brg, Stockton CA, cone top, G+.....87.00
White Cap Beer, Two Rivers Brg, Two Rivers WI, cone top, EX...120.00

Bellaire, Marc

Marc Bellaire, originally Donald Edmund Fleischman, was born in Toledo, Ohio, in 1925. He studied at the Toledo Museum of Art under Ernest Spring while employed as a designer for the Libbey Glass Company. During World War II while serving in the Navy, he travelled extensively throughout the Pacific. As a result of this experience, he developed an even broader and enriched sense of design and color.

Marc settled in California in the 1950s where his work attracted the attention of national buyers and agencies who persuaded him to create ceramic lines of his own, employing hand-decorating techniques throughout. He built a studio in Culver City, and there he produced high-quality ceramics, often decorated with ultramodern figures or geometric patterns and executed with a distinctive flair. His most famous line was Mardi Gras, decorated with slim dancers in spattered and striped colors of black, blue, pink, and white. Other major patterns were Jamaica, Balinese, Beachcomber, Friendly Island, Cave Painting, Hawaiian, Bird Isle, Oriental, Jungle Dancer, and Kashmir. Kashmir usually has the name Ingle on the front and Bellaire on the reverse.

It is to be noted that Marc was employed by Sascha Brastoff during the 1950s. Many believe that he was hired for his creative imagination and style.

During the period from 1951 to 1956, Marc was named one of the top ten artware designers by *Giftwares Magazine*. After 1956 he taught and lectured on art, design, and ceramic decorating techniques from coast to coast. Many of his pieces were one of a kind, commissioned throughout the United States.

During the 1970s he set up a studio in Marin County, California, and eventually moved to Palm Springs where he opened his final studio/gallery. There he produced large pieces with a Southwestern style. Mr Bellaire died in 1994. Our advisor for this category is Marty Webster; he is listed in the Directory under Michigan.

Ashtray, Beachcomber, free-form, 13½" 65.00
Ashtray, Bird Isle, blk birds on cream, 8" 85.00
Ashtray, Clown, mc on cream, 7" 65.00
Ashtray, Jamaica, musicians on brn, 10x14"...................................85.00
Ashtray, Mardi Gras, figures on blk, rolled rim, 9" 100.00
Ashtray, Mardi Gras, figures on blk, 14x14".................................125.00
Ashtray, Mardi Gras, figures on blk, 4x8½"....................................35.00
Ashtray, Still Life, matt fruits & leaves, 10x15".............................100.00
Bowl, Fruit - Three Pears, yel & gr 45.00
Bowl, Jungle Dancer, 11½x5½"...150.00
Box, African Figures on lid, 6" 95.00
Box, Beachcomber, low teardrop shape, 12"................................100.00

Box, Cortillian, lady w/bl bird, 13x9" 125.00
Box, Jamaica, man w/guitar, free-form, 6x7" 125.00
Box, Mardi Gras, 10" dia 150.00
Box, Three Geisha Girls, wht & gray, 6" 35.00
Candlestick, Jamaica Man, 10½" 125.00
Charger, Fisherman w/net, 16" 150.00
Charger, Polynesian King & Queen, 15" 200.00
Charger, Stylized Bird on branch, 15" 165.00
Coaster, Mardi Gras, 4½" 15.00
Compote, Cave Painting, 4-ftd, 6x12" 100.00
Compote, Cortillian, 4-ftd, 8x17" 200.00
Cookie jar, Stick People, wood lid, 10" 150.00
Dish, Leaf, gr/wht on gray free-form, 9x15" 55.00
Ewer, Mardi Gras, figures on blk, 18" 400.00
Figurine, Bali, fancy dancer w/headdress, 24" 1,200.00
Figurine, bird w/long neck, 17" 250.00
Figurine, buffalo, brn & cream, 10x10" 260.00
Figurine, bull, 9" 345.00
Figurine, horse, gray/gr/brn, 8x7½" 140.00
Figurine, Jamaica, man playing guitar 300.00
Figurine, Mardi Gras, female seated, 5½" 150.00
Figurine, Mardi Gras, man reclining, very slim, 18" 500.00
Figurine, Mardi Gras, man standing, very slim, 24" 700.00
Figurine, Mardi Gras, man standing, 11½" 235.00
Figurine, Polynesian, man standing, 12" 500.00
Lamp, Mardi Gras, long-neck vase on wood base, 28" ..450.00
Pitcher, Sea Gull, 4½" 50.00
Platter, Fisherman w/net, 16" dia 150.00
Platter, Friendly Island, 10" 135.00
Platter, Hawaiian, 3 figures on orange, 7x13" 55.00
Platter, Mardi Gras, figures on blk, 12x18" 250.00
Platter, Underwater design in sea gr, 16" 100.00
Switch plate, Dancer on blk, B-26, 3x4¾" 150.00
Tray, Beachcomber, low teardrop shape, 12" 75.00
Tray, Black Man dancing, triangle, 8½x17" 75.00
Tray, Cortillian, lady w/bl bird, 13x9" 125.00
Tray, Jungle Dancer, figure on blk/gr, 12" dia 145.00
Vase, Balinese Women, hourglass shape, 8" 100.00
Vase, Black Cats, hourglass shape, 8" 100.00
Vase, Indian on Horseback, Bellaire 89, 10" 150.00
Vase, Mardi Gras, figures on blk, 18" 250.00
Vase, Polynesian Woman, 9" 100.00
Vase, Stick People, irregular beak-like opening, 12" 250.00

Belleek, American

From 1883 until 1930, several American potteries located in New Jersey and Ohio manufactured a type of china similar to the famous Irish Belleek soft-paste porcelain. The American manufacturers identified their porcelain by using 'Belleek' or 'Beleek' in their marks. American Belleek is considered the highest achievement of the American porcelain industry. Production centered around artistic cabinet pieces and luxury tablewares. Many examples emulated Irish shapes and decor with marine themes and other naturalistic styles. While all are highly collectible, some companies' products are rarer than others. The best-known manufacturers are Ott and Brewer, Willets, The Ceramic Art Company (CAC), and Lenox. You will find more detailed information in those specific categories. Our advisor for this category is Mary Frank Gaston.

Key:
AAC — American Art China
CAP — Columbian Art Pottery

Bowl, tiny flowers w/in & w/o, gold rim, AAC, 2½x5" **425.00**
Cream soup & liner, pheasants & fruit w/gold, Gordon Belleek, 8 for ..**185.00**
Cup & saucer, demi; non-factory gold decor on wht, gr mk, 2¼"..**150.00**
Cup & saucer, morning glories, Morgan **175.00**

Demitasse cup, non-factory gold decor, green mark, 2¼", $100.00.
(Photo courtesy Mary Frank Gaston)

Hatpin holder, silver Art Deco decor, obelisk shape, mk, 7" **200.00**
Mug, monk playing violin, CAP, 5", from $35 to **150.00**
Pitcher, grapes & fruit, cylindrical, Belleek, 14" **165.00**
Plate, dainty floral w/gold, scalloped, CAP, 7", from $20 to **75.00**
Plate, mixed floral, bright mc on wht w/gold rim, Coxon, 5¾" ..**115.00**
Salt cellar, sponged gold on scalloped rim & base, AAC, 2½" ...**125.00**
Stein, currants & leaves, red & gr on brn, 5" **250.00**
Teapot, gold-paste decor on dragon shape, red CAP mk, 9" W ..**1,700.00**
Vase, chrysanthemums, mc, sgn, gr mk, 13" **600.00**
Vase, poppies on shoulder, sgn MP, 8" **150.00**

Belleek, Irish

Belleek is a very thin translucent porcelain that takes its name from the village in Ireland where it originated in 1859. The glaze is a creamy ivory color with a pearl-like lustre. The tablewares, baskets, figurines, and vases that have always been made there are being crafted yet today. Shamrock, Tridacna, Echinus, and Thorn are but a few of the many patterns of tableware which have been made during some periods of the pottery's history. Throughout the years, their most popular pattern has been Shamrock.

It is possible to date an example to within twenty to thirty years of crafting by the mark. Pieces with an early stamp often bring prices nearly triple that of a similar but current item. With some variation, the marks have always incorporated the Irish wolfhound, Celtic round tower, harp, and shamrocks. The first three marks (usually in black) were used from 1863 to 1946. A series of green marks identified the pottery's offerings from 1946 until the seventh mark (in gold/brown) was introduced in 1980 (it was discontinued in 1992). The eighth mark was blue and closely resembled the gold mark. It was used from 1993 to 1996. The ninth, tenth, and eleventh marks went back to the simplicity of the first mark with only the registry mark (an R encased in a circle) to distinguish them from the original. The ninth mark, which was used from 1997 to 1999, was blue. A special black version of that mark was introduced for the year 2000 and a Millennium 2000 banner was added. The tenth or Millennium mark was retired at the end of 2000, and the current green mark was introduced as the eleventh mark. Belleek Collector's International Society limited edition pieces are designated with a special mark in red. In the listings below, numbers designated with the prefix 'D' relate to the book *Belleek, The Complete Collector's Guide and Illustrated Reference, Second Edition*, by Richard K. Degenhardt (published by Wallace-Homestead

Book Company, One Chilton Way, Radnor, PA 19098-0230). The numbers designated with the prefix 'B' are current production numbers used by the pottery. Our advisor for this category is Liz Stillwell; she is listed in the Directory under California.

Key:

A — plain (glazed only)	I — 1863 – 1890
B — cob lustre	II — 1891 – 1926
C — hand tinted	III — 1926 – 1946
D — hand painted	IV — 1946 – 1955
E — hand-painted shamrocks	V — 1955 – 1965
F — hand gilted	VI — 1965 – 3/31/1980
G — hand tinted and gilted	VII — 4/1/1980 – 1992
H — hand-painted shamrocks	VIII — 1/4/1993 – 1996
and gilted	IX — 1997 – 1999
J — mother-of-pearl	X — 2000 only
K — hand painted and gilted	XI — 2001 – current
L — bisque and plain	
M — decalcomania	
N — special hand-painted decoration	
T — transfer design	

Further information concerning Periods of Crafting (Baskets):

1 — 1865 – 1890, BELLEEK (three-strand)

2 — 1865 – 1890, BELLEEK CO. FERMANAGH (three-strand)

3 — 1891 – 1920, BELLEEK CO. FERMANAGH IRELAND (three-strand)

4 — 1921 – 1954, BELLEEK CO. FERMANAGH IRELAND (four-strand)

5 — 1955 – 1979, BELLEEK® CO. FERMANAGH IRELAND (four-strand)

6 — 1980 – 1985, BELLEEK® IRELAND (four-strand)

7 — 1985 – 1989, BELLEEK® IRELAND 'ID NUMBER' (four-strand)

8 – 12 — 1990 to present (Refer to *Belleek, The Complete Collector's Guide and Illustrated Reference, 2nd Edition*, Chapter 5.)

Aberdeen Tea Ware Tea & Saucer, D489-II, B	650.00
Bamboo Teapot, D516-I, A, sm	800.00
Belleek Flower Pot, Flowered, D211-III, A, tiny	325.00
Belleek Flower Pot, Flowered, D47-II, A, sm	300.00
Boat Ashtray, D229-VI, B	50.00
Boat Cream, D247-VI, B, sm	75.00
Boat Sugar, D246-VI, B, sm	60.00
Cherub Candelabra, D341-II, B	8,000.00
Cone Tea Ware Dejeuner Set, D437-II, C	4,250.00
Cone Tea Ware Tea & Saucer, D432-II, G	375.00
Daisy Spill, D178-V, E	90.00
Diamond Salt, D293-III, B	60.00
Earthenware Soup Plate, D888-II, T, 10"	250.00
Echinus Tea Ware Egg Cup, D666-IX, B	70.00
Echinus Tea Ware Tea & Saucer, D358-II, N	425.00
Erne Vase, D83-II, C	800.00
Finner Tea Ware Sugar & Cream, D671&2-XI, D	100.00
First Sight of Miss Liberty Plate, D1882-VII, E&M	150.00
Flowered Crate, D268-III, J	450.00
Flying Fish Spill, D168-VI, C	125.00
Frog Vase, D181-II, B, lg	1,100.00
Grass Mug, D214-VI, B	95.00
Grass Tea Ware Honey Pot on Stand, D755-I, D	1,100.00
Harebell Vase, D180-VI, C	80.00
Heart Cup & Saucer, D2085-VII, B	125.00
Institute Cream & Sugar, D1814-VII, F	195.00
Irish Pot Sugar & Cream, D233-III, B, sm	250.00
Island Vase, D88-VI, E	95.00

Ivy Sugar & Cream, D-2411-III, B, sm	175.00
Lace Tea Ware Plate, D806-I, K, 6"	600.00
Lace Tea Ware Plate, no D#-II, G, 10¼"	6,000.00
Lace Tea Ware Tea & Saucer, D799-I, K	1,200.00
Lattice Ashtray, D2092-V, B	50.00
Mask Tea Ware Cream, tall, D1483-III, B, lg	195.00
Mask Tea Ware Hurricane Lamp, D1474-VII, A	210.00
Mask Tea Ware Sandwich Tray, D1492-III, B	400.00
Nautilus Cream, D279-II, A	325.00
Neptune Tea Ware Tea & Saucer, D414-II, G, bl	550.00
Neptune Tea Ware Tea & Saucer, D414-II, G, Robinson Cleaver mk	325.00
Octagon Flower Pot, D219-V, B, med sz	75.00
Panel Vase, D158-V, B	105.00
Pierced Spill, Flowered, D49-III, A, lg	350.00
Pig, D231-V, B, lg	150.00
Plain Heart-Shape Basket, D1284-4, A	525.00

Richard K. Degenhardt Basket, D1696-14, D, 1995, 8", $575.00.

Rock Spill, D161-II, B, sm	275.00
Rose Isle Vase, D1222-III, J	1,200.00
Scroll Sugar & Cream, D242-III, B	450.00
Scroll Tea Ware Tea & Saucer, D502-II, G	600.00
Sea Horse Flower Holder, D130-VI, A	95.00
Shamrock Basket, D109-4, J, sm	700.00
Shamrock Salt, D273-II, E	120.00
Shamrock Tea Ware Moustache & Saucer, D374-II, E	500.00
Shamrock Ware Letter Opener, D2011-VII, E	125.00
Shamrock Ware TV Set, D2017-VII, E	135.00
Single Henshall's Spill, Flowered, D61-III, B	350.00
Straw Basket, D79-III, B	450.00
Sydney Tea Ware Tea & Saucer, D607-XI, G	90.00
Thimble Wild Irish Rose, D2110-VII, D	40.00
Thistle Top Vase, Flowered, D1782-V, D	150.00
Thorn Mug, D217-VI, B	55.00
Toy Shamrock Sugar & Cream, D234-V, E	125.00
Tridacna Tea Ware Kettle, D477-II, A, lg	750.00
Tridacna Tea Ware Milk Jug, D480-IV, B	120.00
Tridacna Tea Ware Teapot, D475-II, N, lg	1,300.00
Tub Salt, D289-III, E, B, lg	250.00
Tulip Vase, D93-I, D, lg	2,700.00
Tyrone Vase, D1791-VII, K	125.00
Victoria Shell, D128-V, B	450.00

Bells

Some areas of interest represented in the study of bells are history, religion, and geography. Since Biblical times, bells have announced morning church services, vespers, deaths, christenings, school hours, fires, and community events. Countries have used them en masse to peal out the good news of Christmas, New Year's, and the endings of World Wars I and II. They've been rung in times of great sorrow, such as the death of Abraham Lincoln.

For further information, we recommend *World of Bells* by Dorothy Malone Anthony (a series of ten books). All have over two hundred colored pictures covering many bell categories. See also Nodders; Schoolhouse Collectibles.

Brass, ball in cast fr, turn side knob to spin bell, 5x5" 185.00
Brass, Colonial lady, Virginia Metalcrafters Hostess Bell..............50.00
Brass, Elizabethan-style lady w/high ruff, ft & legs clacker, 4¼"...135.00
Brass, emb animals birds, 4 saints names along band, 5x4"...........65.00
Brass, lady holding skirt to show shoe, Made in Belgium, 3½" ...110.00
Brass, pyramidal w/unusually long hdl, 1930s.................................20.00
Brass, southern belle w/wide skirt, 3¾x3¼" 30.00
Brass, Texas longhorn bull's head, C Wagner ltd ed, 9x5x4¼"......80.00
Brass, windmill w/rotating blades...28.00
Brass, zoomorphic symbols representing 4 saints, 3⅝x2⅜"............65.00
Brass, 2 ladies in hats standing arm in arm, 2¾" 60.00
Brass w/wood hdl, for tea tray, 4¼x2" 15.00
Brass w/wood hdl, 11x6¾" 150.00
Bronze, lizard/frog/spider relief work, twined serpent hdl, 6".......350.00
Bronze, ornate casting, heavy, 6½x5¼" 85.00
Copper, hand wrought, hammered, unmk, 4" 6.00
Crystal w/pewter bird hdl, Franklin Mint, 1976, 5½" 38.00
Glass, cobalt w/HP floral, glass clapper, Bohemia, 6"....................25.00
Heavy metal, turtle form, gold traces, press head or tail, EX.......185.00

Ormolu, stork and wolf handle (from La Fontaine poem), nodder type, French, 4½", $425.00. (Photo courtesy Dorothy Malone Anthony)

Porc, Cherub Bell 1976, Antonio Borsato, Gorham, 8½" 40.00
Silver w/copper o/l & gr enameling, Chinese symbol design 85.00

Bennington

Although the term has become a generic one for the mottled brown ware produced there, Bennington is not a type of pottery, but rather a town in Vermont where two important potteries were located. The Norton Company, founded in 1793, produced mainly redware and salt-glazed stoneware; only during a brief partnership with Fenton (1845 – 47) was

any Rockingham attempted. The Norton Company endured until 1894, operated by succeeding generations of the Norton family. Fenton organized his own pottery in 1847. There he manufactured not only redware and stoneware, but more artistic types as well — graniteware, scroddled ware, flint enamel, a fine parian, and vast amounts of their famous Rockingham. Though from an esthetic standpoint his work rated highly among the country's finest ceramic achievements, he was economically unsuccessful. His pottery closed in 1858.

It is estimated that only one in five Fenton pieces were marked; and although it has become a common practice to link any fine piece of Rockingham to this area, careful study is vital in order to be able to distinguish Bennington's from the similar wares of many other American and Staffordshire potteries. Although the practice was without the permission of the proprietor, it was nevertheless a common occurrence for a potter to take his molds with him when moving from one pottery to the next, so particularly well-received designs were often reproduced at several locations. Of eight known Fenton marks, four are variations of the '1849' impressed stamp: 'Lyman Fenton Co., Fenton's Enamel Patented 1849, Bennington, Vermont.' These are generally found on examples of Rockingham and flint enamel. A raised, rectangular scroll with 'Fenton's Works, Bennington, Vermont,' was used on early examples of porcelain. From 1852 to 1858, the company operated under the title of the United States Pottery Company. Three marks — the ribbon mark with the initials USP, the oval with a scrollwork border and the name in full, and the plain oval with the name in full — were used during that period.

Among the more sought-after examples are the bird and animal figurines, novelty pitchers, figural bottles, and all of the more finely modeled items. Recumbent deer, cows, standing lions with one forepaw on a ball, and opposing pairs of poodles with baskets in their mouths and 'coleslaw' fur were made in Rockingham, flint enamel, and occasionally in parian. Numbers in the listings below refer to the book *Bennington Pottery and Porcelain* by Barret. Our advisors for Bennington (except for parian and stoneware) are Barbara and Charles Adams; they are listed in the Directory under Massachusetts.

Key: c/s — cobalt on salt glaze

Bank, Uncle Sam, flint enamel, flaw, 4⅜" 300.00
Bank, Uncle Sam, Rockingham, 1849-58, 4¼", EX 250.00
Book flask, Bennington Company C on spine, 1849-58, 7¾".....600.00
Book flask, Bennington Company on spine, flint enamel, rpr, 10½" ..700.00
Book flask, Bennington's Battle, flint enamel, 6"........................850.00
Book flask, Departed Spirits, flint enamel, 7¾x5¾" 750.00
Book flask, Departed Spirits G, flint enamel, rpr, 5¾" 750.00
Book flask, Departed Spirits G, flint enamel, 5⅝" 750.00
Book flask, Indian's Lament, flint enamel, 6", EX......................950.00
Book flask, Kossuth's Life & Suffering, flint enamel, 1849 mk, 6", EX ..950.00
Book flask, Ned Buntline's Bible, flint enamel, 1849 mk, 6" ...2,200.00
Book flask, Ned Buntline's Own, 1849 mk, 6"..........................2,300.00
Book flask, Traveler's Companion, flint enamel, 6" 950.00
Bottle, Coachman, Rockingham, mk, 10½" 1,000.00
Bottle, Toby, Rockingham, 1849 mk, 10½" 765.00
Candlestick, Rockingham, rpr lip, 8"...300.00
Candlesticks, flint enamel, dk & olive gr, 8¼", pr 1,200.00
Coffeepot, flint enamel, bl & orange streaks, w/lid, 13¼", EX..1,500.00
Figure, lion, flint enamel, faces right, coleslaw mane, 7¾x10" ...5,000.00
Foot bath, flint enamel, ribbed, handles, 8¾x20¼" 1,500.00
Inkwell, lion's head, Rockingham, 2x3½" 865.00
Mug, Rockingham, faint mk to base, 4", NM.............................600.00
Pitcher, Cupid & Psyche, wht porc w/bl stipple, leaf hdl, 10½" ...395.00
Pitcher, parian, vining roses, branch hdl, Fenton's Works..., 10" ...275.00
Pitcher, Toby, flint enamel, grapes on hdl, rstr ft, 4¼" 610.00
Pitcher, Toby, Rockingham, grape clusters on hdl, 7" 375.00
Pitcher & bowl, Alternate Rib, flint enamel, prof rpr, 14", 13½" ...1,600.00

Shaving mug, Toby Philpots images in relief, twig hdl, 3½", EX ...150.00
Slop jar, flint enamel, domed lid, rpr, 17¾" 2,000.00
Snuff jar, Toby, flint enamel, 4¼" 600.00
Snuff jar, Toby, Rockingham, firing crack, 4¼" 600.00
Sugar bowl, Alternate Ribs, flint enamel, gr streaks, 7", EX........900.00
Water cooler, Gothic style, flint enamel, bl streaks, 16½", EX.....2,185.00

Stoneware

Preserve jar, #2/floral spray, cobalt on salt glaze, 1880s, 11½", EX, $415.00; Crock, #3/deer, cobalt on salt glaze, restored, ca 1855, 10½", $5,500.00; Jug, #3/peacock on stump, cobalt on salt glaze, ca 1855, 15½", EX, $2,425.00. (Photo courtesy American Pottery Auctions)

Churn, #4/flower spray, E Norton & Co, 17" 150.00
Churn, #6/leaf, c/s, E Norton & Co, rstr, 19" 350.00
Churn, foliage, c/s, E Norton & Co, 17½x8" 500.00
Crock, #2/floral & dog, c/s, L&LP Norton, 11½", EX 360.00
Crock, #4/flower, ochre on salt glaze, L Norton & Son, 1830s, 14", EX...500.00
Crock, #5/thistle (dbl/stylized), c/s, J&E Norton, ca 1855, 13", EX...550.00
Crock, cake; sprig, c/s, E&LP Norton, 7¼x14" dia, NM.............665.00
Crock, feather, c/s, E&LP Norton, chip/stain, 7" 230.00
Jug, #2/flower, c/s, L Norton, stack mks, ca 1830, 14" 660.00
Jug, #2/flower spray, c/s, E&LP Norton, 14", EX 230.00
Jug, bird on branch, c/s, J&E Norton, prof rstr, ca 1855, 12" 800.00
Jug, bird on twig, c/s, J&E Norton, chip, ca 1855, 11" 525.00
Jug, floral, c/s, E Norton & Co, flake, 10¾" 115.00
Jug, leaf, c/s, E&LP Norton, stain, ca 1880, 10½" 190.00
Jug, plume, c/s, J Norton & Co, overall stain, ca 1861, 10½" 200.00

Beswick

In the early 1890s, James Wright Beswick operated a pottery in Longston, England, where he produced fine dinnerware as well as ornamental ceramics. Today's collectors are most interested in the figurines made since 1936 by a later generation Beswick firm, John Beswick, Ltd. They specialize in reproducing accurately detailed bone-china models of authentic breeds of animals. Their Fireside Series includes dogs, cats, elephants, horses, the Huntsman, and an Indian figure, which measure up to 14" in height. The Connoisseur line is modeled after the likenesses of famous racing horses. Beatrix Potter's characters and some of Walt Disney's are charmingly re-created and appeal to children and adults alike. Other items, such as character Tobys, have also been produced. The Beswick name is stamped on each piece. The firm was absorbed by the Doulton group in 1973.

Beatrix Potter, And This Pig Had None, B6 ....85.00

Beatrix Potter, Cottontail, 3B............................45.00
Beatrix Potter, Gentleman Mouse Made a Bow, B6a........200.00
Beatrix Potter, Goody Tiptoes, B3.........................60.00
Beatrix Potter, Hunca Munca (w/cradle & babies), B3.........65.00
Beatrix Potter, Jemima & Foxy Gentleman, B6.............95.00
Beatrix Potter, Jemima Puddleduck Made a Feather Nest, B6.......45.00
Beatrix Potter, Miss Moppet, 3B..........................55.00
Beatrix Potter, Mr Benjamin Bunny & Peter Rabbit, B6.............75.00
Beatrix Potter, Mr Jeremy Fisher, B3.....................65.00
Beatrix Potter, Mrs Rabbit & Peter, B6...................80.00
Beatrix Potter, Mrs Tittlemouse, 3B......................45.00
Beatrix Potter, Peter Ate a Radish, B6 ....65.00
Beatrix Potter, Rebeccah Puddle-Duck, B3 ....40.00
Beatrix Potter, Ribby, 3B.................................65.00
Beatrix Potter, Timmy Tiptoes, B2........................200.00
Beatrix Potter, Tommy Brock, lg eye patch, B3...........65.00
Bird, Barn Owl, #1046, 1940s, 8" 175.00
Bird, Bluebird, #757-3, 4½x4"............................75.00
Bird, Budgie, #1216, 7"..................................400.00
Bird, Goldfinch, ca 1969-95, 3".........................28.00
Bird, Leghorn Cockerel, #1892, 1963-83, 9" 515.00
Bird, Nuthatch, #2413....................................60.00
Bird, Parakeet, on perch, #930, 6".......................125.00
Bird, Pink Legged Partridge, Greddington, #1188-1, 1950-76, 10½"..165.00
Bird, Robin, 2⅜x3¼"......................................40.00
Cow, Aberdeen Angus Calf, #1406A, 3" 575.00
Cow, Aberdeen Angus Calf, #1827A 450.00
Cow, Hereford Calf, brn & wht, #1406B, 3" 275.00
Cow, Sabrina's Sir Richmond, Guernsey bull, 5x8" 215.00
Disney, Alice (Alice in Wonderland)......................185.00
Disney, Mad Hatter, 1974 ....185.00
Disney, Snow White, 2nd version, #1332B.................365.00
Dog, Corgi, brn, stands w/head up, 5½x6½"...............145.00
Dog, Ebonit Av Barbett, wht show poodle, #1294, 5¾", NM 325.00
Dog, English Cocker Spaniel plaque, lg head, #558, 11⅛x10½" 425.00
Dog, Labrador Retriever, yel, 3¼x4".....................32.00
Dog, retriever, Warren Platt, 1993-97, 2½" 45.00
Dog, Scottie, wht, #804..................................24.00
Dog, Sealyham, #302, 1937-67, 6x10".....................215.00
Dog, Springer Spaniel, brn & wht, 3" 35.00
Horse, Grundy, Racehorse of Year 1975, Connoisseur.............250.00
Horse, Indian seated on Shewbald pony, Oswell, ca 1955, 8½"..550.00
Horse, Palomino, 8½x10"..................................145.00
Horse, Percheron, Harnessed Horses Series, #2464, 9¾", NM....425.00
Horse, Welsh Cob, rearing, A Gredington, #1014B, NM 250.00
Horse, Welsh Mountain Pony, gray gloss, 1st version, #1543, 6¼"...185.00
Horse & Jockey, brn gloss, Gredington, #1862, 1963-84, 8" 425.00
Sporting character, It's a Knockout, boxer, #497, 5½"..................65.00
Sporting character, Out for a Duck, cricket player, #895, 5½"......65.00

Bicycles

Bicycles and related ephemera and memorabilia have been collected since the end of the nineteenth century, but for the last twenty years, they have been regarded as bonafide collectibles. Today they are prized not only for their charm and appearance, but for historical impact as well. Many wonderful items are now being offered through live and Internet auctions, rare book sites , etc.

Hobby horse/draisienne bicycles were handmade between during circa 1818 and 1821. If found today, one of these would almost certainly be 'as found.' (Be suspect of any that look to be restored or are brightly painted; it would be very doubtful that it was authentic.)

Bicycle collectors are generally split as specializing in pre- and post-1920. Those specializing in pre-1920 might want only items from the hobby horse era (1816 – 1821), velocipede and manumotive era (1830 – 1872), high-wheel and hard-tired safety era (1873 – 1890), or the pneumatic safety era (post 1890). The development of the Diamond frame-chain drive of the mid-1870s through 1890 had a profound effect on the intricacies and variations which make that era particularly interesting. With the introduction of the pneumatic tire, the field was impacted both socially and technically. From this point, collector interest relates to social, sport, fashion, manufacturing, urbanization, financial, and technical history. Post 1920 collectors tend to be drawn to Art Deco and Aerodynamic design, which forge prices. Many seek not only cycles but signage, prints and posters, watches, medals, photographs, porcelains, toys, and various other types of ephemera and memorabilia. Some prefer to specialize in items relating to military cycling, certain factories, racing, country of origin, type of bike, etc. All radiate from a common interest.

The bicycle has played an important role in the rapid developement of the twentieth century and onwards, impacting the airplane, motorcycle, and automobile, also the manufacture of drawn tubing, differentials, and spoked wheels. It has affected advertising, urbanization, women's lib, and the vote. There are still many treasures to be discovered.

Note: Values in our listings are for lithographs and watercolors that are framed and under glass unless otherwise described. When no condition code is present in the line, assess the item to be at least very good to excellent.

Our advisor for this category is Lorne Shields; he is listed in the Directory under Canada. (Mr. Shields is interested in early cycliana and offers to help evaluate early bicycle-related items.)

Key:
A — as found
Bm — brake mechanism
Bt — balloon tires
C — complete
Fw — front wheels
Ht — hard tires
Ld — lever driven

OC — orignal, complete
Sh — shaft driven
Pd — pedal driven
Pt — pneumatic tires
Rw — rear wheels
R — restored
U — unrestored

Adult's Vehicles

Rudge High Wheel Bicycle, ca 1886, 52", fully restored, $4,500.00. (Photo courtesy Lorne Shields)

Bike, lady's, Pierce Arrow Sd, OC: Fw/Bw/Bt, spring fork/fr, 28", EX....**1,500.00**
Bike, man's, Black Phantom, Bt, Schwinn, 1955, NM orig......**1,000.00**
Bike, man's, hickory fr, wood mudguards/chaincover, OC/needs R, 26"...**4,000.00**
Bike, man's, Huffy Custom Liner Delux, tank/light, 1947, G......**350.00**

Bike, man's, Shelby Supreme Airflow, Bt, tank fr/light, 1938, OC, EX....**4,000.00**
Bike, Western Flyer Super, tank/light/sprung fork, Western Auto, VG....**500.00**
Hobby horse/draisienne, 31" Fw/ft-on-ground propelled, 1820s, OC, R....**15,000.00**
Motobike, man's, Pt, w/tank, Columbia, 1933, A, VG.......**500.00**
Pennyfarthing/Highwheel bike, 50" Fw, Columbia/Pope, 1882, needs parts...**1,650.00**
Pennyfarthing/Highwheel bike, 52" Fw, G&J Chicago, 1887, OC, EX U......**3,000.00**
Roadster, man's, arch bar, Pt, Harley-Davidson, 1920s, OC, A ..**2,500.00**
Safety bike, Ht 30" Rw/28" Fw, unusual fr/sprung fork, Victor/1887, VG..**3,500.00**
Safety bike, man's, Pt (needs tires), Iver Johnson, 1896, OC, A, VG....**400.00**
Tricycle, Columbia 2-track, name plate/lamp, 1885, A, U **15,000.00**
Tricycle, cripper style by Humber (English), 1885, needs parts/U, Fair...**4,000.00**
Tricycle, Rudge Rotary tandem, 1 lg driving+2 side wheels, 1886, R ..**20,000.00**
Velocipede/boneshaker, 39" Fw/35" Fw, buggy-style Rw, Pickering, Bm, VG....**3,000.00**

Children's Vehicles

Fairy style trike, pedal Ld w/tiller, seat w/bkrest, 20" Rw/12" Fw, EX ..**600.00**
Tricycle, metal, 18" spoke Fw/leather saddle, various makes, 1900, EX...**250.00**
Tricycle, wood, hand Ld, 14" Fw/buggy seat, fair orig pnt, needs R, G- ..**1,000.00**
Tricycle, wood, Ld, 14" Fw/buggy seat, 1860, G-pnt, needs rstr, G-....**1,000.00**
Tricycle, wood w/metal parts, Pd, 16" Fw, 1882, orig pnt, G **650.00**
Youth bike, 20" Pt/hammock saddle, Iver Johnson, 1897, OC, VG.......**500.00**

Miscellaneous

Beer glass, Mary Gregory-type bicyclist, Germany, 1900, 8"........**125.00**
Bell, bronze, claw clamp for hi-wheeler w/narrow hdlbar, 1885, working....**350.00**
Bell, CI, snake logo w/glass eyes, dbl-clip clamp, 1900-20, 2¼" dia.....**100.00**
Board game, Century Run, Parker Bros, 1897, OC+box, VG **400.00**
Board game, Cycling Tour, Spear Works/Bavaria, 1896, OC+box, G....**175.00**
Book, American Bicycler, Chas Pratt, 1879, hardbk, VG **150.00**
Book, Fastest...Rider in World, Major Taylor (Afro-Am), 1927, hardbk **20.00**
Book, 10,000 Miles on a Bicycle, K Kron, 1887, hardbk, #d/sgn, VG....**75.00**
Bottle, Cyc-Kola, Clicquot Club Mills MA, Am wheelmen symbols, 1900...**150.00**
Box, Ritchie's Hand Cut Virginia Cigarettes, cyclists, tin, 5" L, VG....**200.00**
Box, tea; tin, 5 litho sporting scenes: cycling/etc, 1900, ftd, 5½"....**300.00**
Broadside, velocipede school w/cyclist image, Chicago/1869, 8x11", NM ..**500.00**
Brooch, lady's figural bike, sterling hallmk, England, 1897, 3"....**200.00**
Button, ad; celluloid, Whitehead & Hoag/1896, many brands, ⅞", $5 to.**60.00**
Button, clothing; metal w/emb lady cyclist, 1920, ½" **10.00**
Calendar, metal fr, pg for ea day or yr, Columbia Co, 1897, 6x3"...**100.00**
Camera, Cycle Poco, Rochester #s 1-7, folding bed plate, bulb, $100 to..**250.00**
Candle lamp, France (no maker's mk), 1900, G...........**75.00**
Carbide/solar lamp, Badger Brass of Kenosha WI, 1910, VG **60.00**
Catalog, AG Spalding for Bicycle Sundries, 1899, lg format, NM.....**150.00**
Catalog, Columbia Bicycle Co, Westfield MA, 1884 ....**150.00**
Catalog, Fenton Bicycle Co, Jamestown NY, 1893, VG **65.00**
Catalog, JN Pierce, Buffalo NY, 1903, VG.................**200.00**
Chocolate mold, man on safety bike, 2-pc, 1900, 13" **200.00**
Cigar cutter, 3-D Pennyfarthing, table model, 1890, 7", VG **350.00**
Clock/automata, bronze Pennyfarthing rider, barometer/thermometer, 16"....**10,000.00**
Clock/barometer, male safety cyclist, England/1896, 7", nonworking/VG........**650.00**
Cup, collapsible; couple on tandem bike, dtd 1897, very common..**15.00**
Cyclometer for hi-wheel bike, Butcher, 1883, Am, VG...........**1,000.00**
Cyclometer for safety bike, New York Standard, enamel dial, 1896, MIB...**200.00**
Fairing pin box, lady velocipede rider, Fr, 1869, 3½"...................**325.00**
Figural flower holder, lady cyclist's accident, bsk, Fr, 1900, 4", NM **125.00**
Figurine, man/lady bicyclists, bsk, Heubach, 1897, 15" **1,500.00**
Hatpin, 3-D sterling bicycle atop 14" steel pin, Victorian, 1896 ..**150.00**
Humidor, Pennyfarthing/tricyclists, bronze top/wood fr, Holland, 1885 ...**1,500.00**
Humidor, velocipedist's accident, figural top, pottery, Fr, 7", VG...........**1,000.00**
Ice cream mold, either male or female, pewter/hinged, 1910, 4½", ea ...**100.00**
Litho, Bearings Magazine, Chas Cox, lady cyclist/Chicago, 1897, 13x18" **300.00**
Litho, Columbia Bicycles, H Sandham, hi-wheelers on hill, 1885, 16x22" ..**1,000.00**

Litho, Iver Johnson Bicycle Factory, Fitchburg MA, 1897, unfr, 24x38" ..**2,000.00**
Lock, brass & steel 17" chain w/orig key, identifiable, 1890, VG....**125.00**
Locket, sterling w/eng Pennyfarthing racer, English, 1880,¾" L...**150.00**
Medal, LAW Meet in Philadelphia, spelter & satin, 1897, VG.....**50.00**
Medal, 1st place, gold/enamel w/eng Pennyfarthing rider, MA, 1888, 4"......**850.00**
Oil lamp, safety bike, bracket mt, Lucas King of Road, 1895-1920, $80...**150.00**
Oil lamp w/font, Pennyfarthing, for Fw hub, Gormuley/Jeffery, 1885, VG...**1,250.00**
Oil painting, Pennyfarthing cyclists, unsgn/EX art, 1885, 14x22", VG...**1,000.00**
Paperweight, safety bicycle, 1920s, 3½" dia, NM...........................**75.00**
Photograph, carte de visite, velocipedist, USA, 1870, 2½x3¾", NM **75.00**
Photograph, couple w/safety bikes in studio, tintype, 2½x3¾" **35.00**
Photograph, uniformed man w/Pennyfarthing+trophy, albumen, 6½x4", M.....**125.00**
Picture fr, NP 3-D moon/lady cyclist, Germany, 1897, w/glass, 11" dia...**350.00**
Pipe, meerschaum, hi-wheel male cyclist, amber stem, 1889, 6", +case ..**650.00**
Pitcher, pressed glass, lady on safety bike, Am, 1900, 10", M ..**1,000.00**
Pitcher, velocipede riders hand-colored transfer, English, 1870, 8½"....**750.00**
Plate, boy w/cap, majolica, 1900, lt crazing, 7" **75.00**
Plate, comic velocipedists, transfer w/mc, English or Fr, 6½", $100 to...**200.00**
Plate, hobby horse rider, soft-paste w/hand-colored transfer, 1820, 7"....**600.00**
Playing cards, bike design, Am Playing Card, 52+joker+box, from $10 to..**35.00**
Pocketknife, cycles on aluminum sides, Germany, 1900, 5½" open, VG..**75.00**
Poster, Am Wheelman, 2-color: Cycling Newspaper on Sale, 1897, 10x17".......**75.00**
Poster, Cleveland Cycles, Nouveau lady w/bike+Am Flag, Cheret, 35x48".....**5,000.00**
Poster, Outing Magazine, cycles/article references, 1896, 12x18"........**100.00**
Poster/book ad: Betsey Jane on Wheels, 1895, 11½x17", M **150.00**
Print, Johnson's Pedestrian Hobby Horse...School, Alken, 1819, 19x15"..**275.00**
Print, Panorama of Chicago, Monarch Cycle Mfrg Co, 1897, fr, 32x13"...**1,000.00**
Sheet music, cycles, bicycle club printed, USA or UK, 1890-1910, $20 to...**60.00**
Sheet music, Velocipede Song & Gallop, Henry Hart, NY, 1896 ...**150.00**
Sign, Iver Johnson, tin w/orig wood fr, 1897, 16x22", VG **650.00**
Sign, Iver Johnson Cycles, litho tin, 1898, company fr, 22x14", VG....**500.00**
Skirt lifter, to pull rider's dress up/away, 1880-1900, 5", $75 to...**150.00**
Statue, lady on safety bicycle, bronzed spelter, Germany, 1900, 8", VG...**500.00**
Statue, racer on Pennyfarthing, bronze, 1885, EX detail/patina, 16", M..**7,500.00**
Stein, cycling couple, porc w/pewter thumb lift, All Heil, 1910, ½-L.....**125.00**
Stein, LAW design, lithophane in base, porc, 1890, ½-liter **500.00**
Stein, 2 racers, HP glass w/pewter thumb lift, Germany, 1895, 1-liter..**350.00**
Stevengraph, Last Lap, hi-wheel bike race, Thos Stevens, 1877, orig mt....**250.00**
Straight razor, safety cycles (various), Germany, 1890-1920s, from $60 to....**100.00**
Thermometer, plaque w/lady cyclist, celsius, Germany, 1900, 8½"......**250.00**
Tie box, celluloid, elves/safety bikes, 1898, top: NM/sides VG, 12" L ...**200.00**
Trade card, various litho bike ads w/men & ladies, 1880-1900, from $5 to....**25.00**
Trade stimulator, 3-D safety bike w/#d wheels, glass case, 5¢, works R **3,500.00**
Trophy, SP w/eng safety bike racer, uninscribed award, 1920, USA, 9" ..**100.00**
Trophy, SP w/3-D Pennyfarthing cyclist, race award, 1884, Meriden, 17"...**3,500.00**
Watch, brass open face, multi-functions for speed & gear, working, 2"..**200.00**
Watch, silver open face w/cyclists on race track, stem wind, 1900, 2"..**200.00**
Watch, silveroid open face, enamel Pennyfarthing, key wind, 1⅞", VG...**350.00**
Watercolor, lady learning to ride bike, Frank Nankiveel, 1899, 13x21"....**500.00**
Whistle, train style/tire activated to pump, NP w/fittings, 1900, 12" ..**250.00**

Big Little Books

The first Big Little Book was published in 1933 and copyrighted in 1932 by the Whitman Publishing Company of Racine, Wisconsin. Its hero was Dick Tracy. The concept was so well accepted that others soon followed Whitman's example; and though the 'Big Little Book' phrase became a trademark of the Whitman Company, the formats of his competitors (Saalfield, Goldsmith, Van Wiseman, Lynn, and World Syndicate) were exact copies. Today's Big Little Book buffs collect them all.

These hand-sized sagas of adventure were illustrated with full-page cartoons on the right-hand page and the story narration on the left. Colorful cardboard covers contained hundreds of pages, usually totaling over

an inch in thickness. Big Little Books originally sold for 10¢ at the dime store; as late as the mid-1950s when the popularity of comic books caused sales to decline, signaling an end to production, their price had risen to a mere 20¢. Their appeal was directed toward the pre-teens who bought, traded, and hoarded Big Little Books. Because so many were stored in attics and closets, many have survived. Among the super heroes are G-Men, Flash Gordon, Tarzan, the Lone Ranger, and Red Ryder; in a lighter vein, you'll find such lovable characters as Blondie and Dagwood, Mickey Mouse, Little Orphan Annie, and Felix the Cat.

In the early to mid-'30s, Whitman published several Big Little Books as advertising premiums for the Coco Malt Company, who packed them in boxes of their cereal. These are highly prized by today's collectors, as are Disney stories and super-hero adventures.

For more information we recommend *Collector's Guide to Children's Books, Volumes 1, 2,* and *3,* by Diane McClure Jones and Rosemary Jones (Collector Books). Our advisor for this category is Ron Donnelly; he is listed in the Directory under Alabama.

Note: At the present time, the market for these books is fairly stable — values for common examples are actually dropping. Only the rare, character-related titles are increasing somewhat.

Jungle Jim and the Vampire Woman, **Whitman #1139, 1937, EX, $45.00.**

Adventures of Huckleberry Finn, Whitman #1422, EX................**30.00**
Alley Oop & Dinny in the Jungles of Moo, Whitman #1473, VG..**25.00**
Andy Panda & Tiny Tim, Whitman #1425, NM **40.00**
Apple Mary & Dennie Fool the Swindlers, Whitman #1130, NM...**35.00**
Believe It or Not by Ripley, Whitman #760, EX...........................**25.00**
Billy the Kid, Whitman, #773, 1935, EX...............................**35.00**
Blondie in Hot Water, Whitman #1410, NM **40.00**
Bringing Up Father, Whitman #1133, NM **60.00**
Buccaneers (TV Show), 1958, EX+...**15.00**
Buck Rogers & the Doom Comet, Whitman #1178, 1935, EX **90.00**
Buck Rogers in the City of Floating Globes, Coco Malt premium, EX..**200.00**
Captain Midnight & the Moon Woman, Whitman #1452, VG ...**45.00**
Charlie Chan of the Honolulu Police, Whitman #1478, 1939, EX...**35.00**
Convoy Patrol, Whitman #1446, NM **20.00**
Cowboy Lingo, Book of Western Facts, Whitman #1457, 1938, EX ...**30.00**
Dick Tracy & the Tiger Lily Gang, Whitman #1460, 1949, VG...**35.00**
Dick Tracy Returns, Whitman #1495, NM **75.00**
Donald Duck Off the Beam, Whitman #1438, EX........................**60.00**
Ella Cinders & the Mysterious House, Whitman #1106, NM.......**50.00**
Felix the Cat, Whitman #1129, 1936, EX....................................**55.00**
Frankenstein Jr, Whitman, 1968, NM **10.00**
Freckles & the Lost Diamond Mine, Whitman #1164, EX...........**35.00**
Gang Busters in Action, Whitman #1451, 1938, NM..................**35.00**
Gene Autry & the Hawk of the Hills, Whitman #1493, NM **50.00**
Goofy in Giant Trouble, Whitman 1968, NM+..........................**10.00**

Green Hornet Strikes, Whitman #1453, VG 60.00
Hal Hardy in The Lost Land of the Giants, Whitman #1413, EX...20.00
In the Name of the Law, Whitman #1155, VG 20.00
Inspector Charlie Chan in Villany on the High Seas, Whitman #1424, EX....35.00
Invisible Scarlet O'Neil Vs the King of the Slums, Whitman #1406, NM....35.00
Jackie Cooper Movie Star of Skippy & Sooky, Whitman #714, NM....45.00
Jane Withers in Keep Smiling, Whitman #1463, EX 30.00
Junior G-Men, Whitman #1442, 1937, EX 30.00
Kayo in The Land of Sunshine, Whitman #1180, EX 35.00
Ken Maynard in Western Justice, Whitman #1430, EX 35.00
Li'l Abner in New York, Whitman #1198, 1936, EX 50.00
Little Women, Whitman #757, EX 40.00
Nancy & Sluggo, Whitman #1400, EX 35.00
Og Son of Fire, Whitman #1115, NM 30.00
Popeye & Queen Olive Oyl, Whitman #1458, EX+ 40.00
Radio Patrol Trailing the Safe Blowers, Whitman #1173, EX 25.00
Return of Tarzan, Whitman #1102, EX+ 65.00
Sir Lancelot, Whitman #1649, NM 10.00
Smokey Stover, Whitman #1413, 1942, EX 35.00
Sombrero Pete, Whitman #1136, VG 20.00
Tarzan Lord of the Jungle, Whitman #1407, NM 60.00
Tarzan the Fearless, Whitman #769, 1934, NM 100.00
Thumper & the Seven Dwarfs, Whitman #1409, EX 60.00
Two-Gun Montana, Whitman #1104, VG 25.00
Wimpy the Hamburger Eater, Whitman #1458, 1938, VG 35.00
Zane Grey's Tex Thorne Comes Out of the West, Whitman #1440, EX....20.00

Bing and Grondahl

In 1853 brothers M.H. and J.H. Bing formed a partnership with Frederick Vilhelm Grondahl in Copenhagen, Denmark. Their early wares were porcelain plaques and figurines designed by the noted sculptor Thorvaldsen of Denmark. Dinnerware production began in 1863, and by 1889 their underglaze color 'Copenhagen Blue' had earned them worldwide acclaim. They are perhaps most famous today for their Christmas plates, the first of which was made in 1895. See also Limited Edition Plates.

Ashtray, Sea Gull, sm, 3½" 10.00
Bonbon, Sea Gull, #222, 6" 42.50
Bowl, cereal/coupe; Ballerina, 6⅝" 22.50
Bowl, coupe soup; Falling Leaves, 8⅛" 20.00
Bowl, oatmeal; Sea Gull, 6⅜" 32.50
Bowl, rimmed soup; Sea Gull, 8½" 35.00
Bowl, serving; Sea Gull, dolphin hdls, 1¼x10½" 65.00
Bowl, serving; Sea Gull, sq, #43 ....100.00
Bowl, vegetable; Blue Traditional, oval, 9½" 120.00
Bowl, vegetable; Falling Leaves, #12B, 9¾" 50.00
Bowl, vegetable; Sea Gull, rnd, 8" 125.00
Cake plate, Blue Traditional, w/hdls, 10⅝" 140.00
Cake plate, Sea Gull, hdls, 10½" 70.00
Cigarette holder, Blue Traditional, 2⅜" 45.00
Cigarette holder, Sea Gull, 2½" 20.00
Coffeepot, Ballerina, #301, 4-cup 175.00
Coffeepot, Cornflower, 6-cup 145.00
Coffeepot, Sea Gull, w/lid, 5-cup, 7¾" 170.00
Creamer, Blue Traditional 70.00
Cup & saucer, Ballerina, #473 ....40.00
Cup & saucer, Blue Traditional, flat 70.00
Cup & saucer, Cornflower 37.50
Cup & saucer, demi; Sea Gull, flat 40.00
Cup & saucer, Falling Leaves, #108 ....20.00
Cup & saucer, Sea Gull, flat 40.00
Figurine, angel, kneeling, arms exended, #BSB5, 1980 ....145.00
Figurine, baby sparrow, #1852 ....60.00
Figurine, bird on branch, #2311 ....60.00
Figurine, Borzoi, Russian wolfhound, brn & wht, #2115, 9x13", NM....125.00
Figurine, boy & girl reading, #1567, 4x3½" 155.00
Figurine, boy w/earache, #2209 ....65.00
Figurine, boy w/puppy, #1747, 6⅝x2½" 95.00
Figurine, Budgie parakeet, #2210, 5¾" 150.00
Figurine, cat, sitting, gray & wht, #1876, 5" 85.00
Figurine, duck, #1537 ....70.00
Figurine, Eskimo w/arms clasped overhead, #2417, 4½" 100.00
Figurine, fisherman, seated w/pipe in hand, #2370, 8¼x5½" 175.00
Figurine, German shepherd dog, seated, 6x8½x4" 115.00
Figurine, girl on bench tying shoe, #2373, 6" 75.00
Figurine, girl seated holding doll, #1526, 1952, 3½" 120.00
Figurine, girl w/cat in basket, #4429, 4x4" 145.00
Figurine, girl w/goat, #2180, 7¾" 135.00
Figurine, girl w/kitten, #1779, 6¾" 95.00
Figurine, girl w/2 calves, #2270, 8⅜x6¾" 265.00
Figurine, goat, #1700 ....110.00
Figurine, Little Hairdresser, #2367 ....145.00
Figurine, milkmaid milking, ca 1905-15, 7½x8" 595.00
Figurine, monkey seated, #1667, 3x2" 175.00
Figurine, mouse w/tail in mouth, #1801F, 1¾" 30.00
Figurine, nude boy w/drape in hand, wht bsk, 19½x9½" 595.00
Figurine, Palace Guard, #2342, 1¾" 240.00
Figurine, perch, #1645 ....145.00
Figurine, polar bear, #1629, 5x7¾" 250.00
Figurine, polar bear cub, #2535, 3¼x6½" 125.00
Figurine, sea gull w/fish in mouth, #1808, 2x6" 75.00
Figurine, sheep dog, #2116, 7⅜x9¼" 400.00
Figurine, spaniel dog w/bird in mouth, brn/wht, #2061, 1988 ....175.00
Figurine, sparrow hawk, shiny muted mc, 11½" 495.00
Figurine, titmouse, tail down, #1635 ....75.00
Gravy boat, Blue Traditional, w/attached underplate, 8" 185.00
Gravy boat, Saxon Flower, #8A, 3¼x8" 35.00
Gravy boat, Sea Gull, attached underplate, 8" 150.00
Plate, dinner; Blue Traditional, 9⅝" 80.00
Plate, dinner; Falling Leaves, 9⅜" 39.00
Plate, dinner; Sea Gull, 9⅝" 50.00
Plate, salad; Blue Traditional, 7½" 40.00
Plate, salad; Cornflower, 8⅛" 20.00
Platter, Blue Traditional, oval, 11" 140.00
Platter, Sea Gull, oval, 11¼" 85.00
Platter, Sea Gull, 13½x9½" 125.00
Platter, Sea Gull, 15¾" L 215.00
Ramekin, Blue Traditional, 3" 60.00
Relish dish, Sea Gull, 7⅛" 30.00
Sugar bowl, Falling Leaves, w/lid, #94, 2½" 32.00
Sugar bowl, Sea Gull, mini 50.00
Teapot, Sea Gull, #92, 4-cup, 4½", from $160 to 185.00
Toothpick holder, Sea Gull, oval, 2½" 20.00
Tureen, soup; Sea Gull, w/lid 225.00
Vase, Sea Gull, 6⅜x5¼" 50.00
Wall pocket, bl & wht plaid design w/holly, 8½x7" 80.00

Binoculars

There are several types of binoculars, and the terminology used to refers to them is not consistent or precise. Generally, 'field glasses' refer to simple Galilean optics, where the lens next to the eye (the ocular) is concave and dished away from the eye. By looking through the large lens (the objective), it is easy to see that the light goes straight through the two lenses. These are lower power, have a very small field of view, and do not work nearly as well as prism binoculars. In a smaller size, they are opera glasses, and their price increases if they are covered with mother-of-pearl (fairly common but very attractive), abalone shell (more colorful), ivory (quite scarce), or other exotic materials. Field glasses are not valuable unless very unusual or by the best makers, such as Zeiss or Leitz. Prism binoculars have the objective lens offset from the eyepiece and give a much better view. This is the standard binocular form, called Porro prisms, and dates from around 1900. Another type of prism binocular is the roof prism, which at first resembles the straight-through field glasses, with two simple cylinders or cones, here containing very small prisms. These can be distinguished by the high quality views they give and by a thin diagonal line that can be seen when looking backwards through the objective. In general, German binoculars are the most desirable, followed by American, English, and finally French, which can be of good quality but are very common unless of unusual configuration. Japanese optics of WWII or before are often of very high quality. 'Made in Occupied Japan' binoculars are very common, but collectors prize those by Nippon Kogaku (Nikon). Some binoculars are center focus (CF), with one central wheel that focuses both sides at once. These are much easier to use but more difficult to seal against dirt and moisture. Individual focus (IF) binoculars are adjusted by rotating each eyepiece and tend to be cleaner inside in older optics. Each type is preferred by different collectors. Very large binoculars are always of great interest. All binoculars are numbered according to their magnifying power and the diameter of the objective in millimeters. Optics of 6 x 30 magnify six times and have 30 millimeter objectives.

Prisms are easily knocked out of alignment, requiring an expensive and difficult repair. If severe, this misalignment is immediately noticeable on use by the double-image scene. Minor damage can be seen by focusing on a small object and slowly moving the binoculars away from the eye, which will cause the images to appear to separate. Overall cleanliness should be checked by looking backwards (through the objective) at a light or the sky, when any film or dirt on the lenses or prisms can easily be seen. Pristine binoculars are worth far more than when dirty or misaligned, and broken or cracked optics lower the value far more. Cases help keep binoculars clean but do not add materially to the value.

As of 2001, any significant changes in value are due to Internet sales. Some of the prices listed here are lower than would be reached at an online auction. Revisions of these values would be inappropriate at this point for these reasons: First, values are fluctuating wildly on the Internet; 'auction fever' is extreme. Second, some common instruments can fetch a high price at an Internet sale, and it is clear that the price will not be supported as more of them are placed at auction. In fact, an overlooked collectible like the binocular will be subject to a great increase in supply as they are retrieved from closets in response to the values people see at an online auction. Third, sellers who have access to these Internet auctions can use them for price guides if they wish, but the values in this listing have to reflect what can be obtained at an average large antique show. The following listings assume a very good overall condition, with generally clean and aligned optics.

Our advisor for this category is Peter Abrahams, who studies and collects binoculars and other optics. Please contact, especially to exchange reference material (SASE required with written questions). Mr. Abrahams is listed in the Directory under Oregon.

Field Glasses

Fernglas 08, German WWI, 6x39, military gr, many makers 50.00
Folding, modern, hinged flat case, oculars outside 10.00
Folding or telescoping, no bbls, old 125.00
Ivory covered, various sm szs & makers 200.00
LeMaire, bl leather/brass, various szs, other Fr same 25.00
Metal, emb hunting scene, various sm szs & makers......................45.00

Pearl covered, various sm szs & makers 90.00
Porc covered, delicate painting, various sm szs & makers............200.00
US Naval Gun Factory Optical Shop 6x30..75.00
Zeiss 'Galan' 2.5x34, modern design look, early 1920s 170.00

Prism Binoculars (Porro)

Barr & Stroud, 7x50, Porro II prisms, IF, WWII 120.00
Bausch & Lomb, 6x30, IF, WWI, Signal Corps..............................50.00
Bausch & Lomb, 7x50, IF, WWII, other makers same 140.00
Bausch & Lomb Zephyr, 7x35 & other, CF...................................160.00
Bausch & Lomb/Zeiss, 8x17, CF, Pat 1897 ....140.00
Crown Optical, 6x30, IF, WWI, filters..50.00
France, various makers & szs, if not unusual 30.00
German WWII 10x80, eyepcs at 45 degrees 500.00
German WWII 6x30, 3-letter code for various makers....................60.00
Goertz Trieder Binocle, various szs, unusual adjustment............110.00
Huet, Paris 7x22, other sm szs, unusual shapes..............................80.00
Leitz 6x30 Dienstglas, IF, good optics 75.00
Leitz 8x30 Binuxit, CF, outstanding optics...................................150.00
M19, US military 7x50, ca 1980...180.00
Nikon 9x35, 7x35, CF, 1950s-70s..140.00
Nippon Kogaku, 7x50, IF, Made in Occupied Japan 150.00
Ross Stepnada, 7x30, CF, wide angle, 1930s 250.00
Ross 6x30, standard British WWI issue 50.00
Sard, 6x42, IF, very wide angle, WWII..900.00
Toko (Tokyo Opt Co) 7x50, IF, Made in Occupied Japan.............45.00
Universal Camera 6x30, IF, WWII, other makers same.................50.00
US Naval Gun Factory Optical Shop 6x30, IF, filters, WWI 70.00
US Naval Gun Factory Optical 10x45, IF, WWI.........................200.00
US Navy, 20x120, various makers, WWII & later 2,200.00
Warner & Swasey (important maker) 8x20, CF, 1902.................200.00
Wollensak 6x30, ca 1940..50.00
Zeiss Deltrintem 8x30, CF, 1930s...95.00
Zeiss DF 95, 6x18, sq shoulder, very early 160.00
Zeiss Starmorbi 12/24/42x60, turret eyepcs, 1920s 2,500.00
Zeiss Teleater 3x13, CF, bl leather 120.00
Zeiss 15x60, CF or IF, various models..700.00
Zeiss 8x40 Delactis, CF or IF, 1930s 230.00

Roof Prism Binoculars

Hensoldt Dialyt, various szs, 1930s-80s 140.00
Hensoldt Universal Dialyt, 6x26, 3.5x26, 1920s..........................120.00
Leitz Trinovid, 7x42 & other, CF, 1960s-80s, EX.......................500.00
Zeiss Dialyt, 8x30, CF, 1960s 400.00

Birdcages

Birdcages can be found in various architectural styles and in a range of materials such as wood, wicker, brass, and gilt metal with ormolu mounts. Those that once belonged to the wealthy are sometimes inlaid with silver or jewels. In the 1800s, it became fashionable to keep birds, and some of the most beautiful examples found today date back to that era. Musical cages that contained automated bird figures became popular; today these command prices of several thousand dollars. In the latter 1800s, wicker styles came into vogue. Collectors still appreciate their graceful lines and find they adapt easily to modern homes.

Wood, lt & dk intersecting cvd segments, ca 1900, 12x10x13" ..175.00
Wood, Oriental cvd cranes, stepped ftd base, ivory spacers, 25"...110.00
Wood & reed fr w/old brn pnt, octagonal dome top, 34x14x9" ..220.00
Wood fr, mc pnt/wire screening, dbl arched doors, 20th C, 31x20x17" ..200.00

Victorian, hardwood with Gothic influence, fine details, on later stand, 41½x33", EX, $2,750.00.

Black Americana

Black memorabilia is without a doubt a field that encompasses the most widely exploited ethnic group in our history. But within this field there are many levels of interest: arts and achievements such as folk music and literature, caricatures in advertising, souvenirs, toys, fine art, and legitimate research into the days of their enslavement and enduring struggle for equality. The list is endless.

In the listings below are some with a derogatory connotation. Thankfully, these are from a bygone era and represent the mores of a culture that existed nearly a century ago. They are included only to convey the fact that they are a part of this growing area of collecting interest. Black Americana catalogs featuring a wide variety of items for sale are available; see the Directory under Clubs, Newsletters, and Catalogs for more information. See also Cookie Jars; Postcards; Posters; Sheet Music.

Our advisor for this category is Judy Posner; she is listed in the Directory under Florida.

Ad page, Aunt Jemima Deviled Ham Pancakes, McCall's, 1962, EX....**18.00**
Ashtray, ceramic head of man w/wide-open mouth/bug eyes, 4", NM ..**55.00**
Ashtray stand, pnt-wood butler figure holding dish, 39", G **100.00**
Bank, tin canister w/litho image of minstrel, prewar, 25", NM ...**185.00**
Bicycle ornament, clamp-on Bike Bobber, eyes blink/wink, 5", MIP ...**35.00**
Book, A Treasury of Steven Foster, Random House, 1st ed, 1946, EX ..**55.00**
Book, Billy Bates, by Blanch Hoke, 1950, soft cover, EX **32.00**
Book, Billy Wiskers in the South, Saalfield, 1917, 1st ed, EX+ ..**135.00**
Book, Booker Washington a Child of Slavery, 1st ed, 1915, VG ..**40.00**
Book, Chloe, 1870, VG..**125.00**
Book, His Eye Is on the Sparrow, by Ethel Waters, 1951, hardbound, EX..**35.00**
Book, Little Black Sambo, H Bannerman, illus by Julian Wehr, 1933, G..**95.00**
Book, On a Slow Train Through Arkansas, by Thos W Jackson, 1908, EX..**35.00**
Book, SNOCers They Probe Down to the CORE, by Bob Washington, 1968, EX..**55.00**
Book, Ten Little Colored Boys, art by EJ Gondor, USA, 1942, diecut, EX...**100.00**
Book, Topsey, diecut/litho image of Topsey, McLoughlin Bros, 1880s, EX ..**120.00**
Book, Well Done Noddy!, by Enid Blyton, hardbound, EX...........**30.00**
Book, What Happened to Squash-Boo, Whitman, 1922, paperback, NM....**75.00**
Bootscraper/shiner, pnt CI Mammy atop, VG..............................**425.00**
Bottle, chocolate milk; head images of 2 children, 1-qt, EX+ **150.00**
Bowl, ceramic, blk child on wht/bl rim, Brownie Downing, 1960s, 6", EX ..**45.00**
Brooch, enameled metal, 2 jazz players, red/blk/silver, 1930s, 2", NM...**80.00**
Candy tin, octagonal w/litho image of Golly/friends on parade, 5", NM..**110.00**

Candy tin, triangular w/litho image of Golly, prewar, 6", EX+ **60.00**
Canister, ceramic figural minstrel seated, mk Sugar, 9½", NM+ ..**120.00**
Cap gun, figural CI w/emb Sambo name, pat date June 1887/90, 5", EX+..**550.00**
Card, birthday; 8-yr old, boy playing banjo, diecut, 1950s, 6x4", EX..**22.00**
Card, greeting; Why Fo' Am I Sendin' Dis?, boy fishing, 1940s, EX....**15.00**
Catalog, Presents Past & Present, Frederick Loeser & Co, 1920s, EX..**65.00**
Clock, CI mammy w/rnd clock face in skirt, moving glass eyes, 12", EX+..**500.00**
Clock, wall; molded pnt compo man's head w/moving tie, 25", NM....**500.00**
Condiment set, nude native & straw hut, Made in Japan, 3x5"..**250.00**
Cookie jar, Aunt Jemima, plastic, F&F **650.00**
Cup, Black boy on wht, Brownie Downing Ceramics, 1960s, 3" dia, EX....**35.00**
Dancing figure, pnt wood w/fuzzy hair, jtd, 1940s, 11", EX...........**85.00**
Dexterity game, child w/watermelon sits on pillow, 1880s, 2" dia, NM ..**300.00**
Diecut minstrel set, emb paper litho, uncut, Germany, 1880s, 3-pc, M ...**50.00**
Doll, celluloid, girl w/pnt eyes, jtd limbs, 10"................................**100.00**
Doll, cowboy, ceramic/Bakelite, cloth outfit/hat, jtd arms, 7", NM.....**120.00**
Doll, Golliwog, stuffed knit yarn, 1950s-60s, 13", EX **40.00**
Doll, I's a Cotton Picker From Luziana, 1950s, 6½", EX **30.00**
Doll, nipple; Mammy w/wht celluloid baby, vintage, rare, 4", EX ...**100.00**
Doll, pickanniny, rag, dress/pinafore/pantaloons/yarn hair, 14", EX..**120.00**
Figurine, Amos, pnt chalkware, 1920s radio premium, 7", EX+..**150.00**
Figurine, boy on hippo, pnt bsk, German, ca 1920, 2x4" **115.00**
Figurine, jockey standing w/trumpet, pnt bsk, 1900s, 13", NM...**150.00**
Figurine, minstrel seated playing accordion, pnt bsk, 1880s, 4", NM..**140.00**
Figurine, native, Windsor McKay Jungle Imp #203, by Irene Nye, 4", EX...**75.00**
Figurine, native on palm-tree base, chenille, Japan, 1950s, 4", EX ..**18.00**
Figurine, pelican eats boy, pnt cast metal, prewar, 3½", NM.......**120.00**
Figurine, Uncle Tom & Eva (mk on base), ceramic, 1880s, 8", NM+ ...**330.00**
Figurine, 3 boys eating watermelon behind fence, pnt chalkware, 1-pc ..**230.00**
Game, Jolly Darkie Target Game, McLoughlin Bros, complete, EX....**400.00**
Game, Jolly Darkie Ten Pins, McLoughlin Bros, complete, EXIB...**550.00**
Game, Piccaninny Bowling Game, cb, roll ball into mouth, 1920s, EX+IB..**285.00**
Game, Snake Eyes, Selchow & Richter, 1940s, NM+IB................**85.00**
Game, Snakes & Ladders, cb, Robertsons premium, unused, MIB...**50.00**
Game, The Chuckler's Game, cb, USA, 1930s, complete, EXIB...**100.00**
Game, Watch on de Rind, cb, shoot ball into mouth, 1930s, NMIB...**400.00**
Humidor, ceramic, sailor seated hugging bbl, Austria, 1880s, 6", NM+..**400.00**
Humidor, terra cotta, boy on log, mc pnt, Austria, 1920s, 7½"..**600.00**
Letter opener, sterling w/Sunny South character finial, 5¼".......**165.00**
Mask, man's face/exaggerated, pnt/coated papier-mâché, 1900s, EX+ ..**150.00**
Match holder, Coon Chicken Inn bellhop bust, pnt copper, rare, 4", EX+...**250.00**
Match holder, litho/stitched diecut leather Mammy's bust, 1900s, 9", NM..**100.00**
Mechanical toy, Be-Bop, litho tin, Marx, 10", EX+....................**250.00**
Mechanical toy, Jigger Bug, tin, Buffalo Toy Works, 1930s, NMIB....**525.00**
Menu, Coon Chicken Inn, diecut cb head of bellhop, M..............**80.00**
Nodder, chef w/arms extended, ceramic, EX **225.00**
Patch, Amos & Andy, Check & Dbl Check, head images, 1930s, 5" dia, EX.....**40.00**
Pincushion, stuffed cloth Mammy holding lg cushion, stitched face, 7"....**80.00**
Plaque, exaggerated native's head, ceramic, Italy, 1930s, 6½".......**65.00**
Pot holder, Mammy, stuffed cotton & wool, embr face, ca 1900, 13x8"....**85.00**
Puzzle, Golly/friends at tea party, England, prewar, 10", unused, MIB.....**75.00**
Puzzle, The Darktown Fire Brigade, cb jigsaw, Parker Bros, 1890s, EXIB..**175.00**
Recipe box, Mammy, yel plastic, Fosta, EX **175.00**
Record, Amos & Andy, 78 rpm, 4 cb records, Monitor, 1947, rare, NM..**50.00**
Record, Porgy & Bess, 78 rpm, set of 2, by Charlie Spivak, 1940s, EX...**35.00**
Sack, Aunt Jemima Hominy Grits, paper w/graphics, 1960s-70s, unused, M ...**22.00**
Shakers, Aunt Jemima & Uncle Mose, plastic, F&F, 3½", pr, EX...**45.00**
Shakers, Aunt Jemima & Uncle Mose, plastic, F&F, 5", pr, EX **75.00**
Shot glass set, pnt/etched comical ethnic scenes, gold rims, set of 4...**65.00**
Stein, ceramic, relief images of drunks w/figural hdl, USA, 1950...**75.00**
Stereo view, children in cotton field, Keystone, 1899, EX............**20.00**
Syrup pitcher, Aunt Jemima, F&F, 5½"..................................**70.00**
Tea set, teapot/creamer/sugar bowl, figural Mammy's heads, ceramic, EX ..**150.00**
Toast rack, ceramic, Golly on motorcycle on ends, Robertsons, 5", EX+...**110.00**

Towel, linen w/embr image of Mammy's holding cake/cat at ft, 1950s, EX ...**35.00**
Toy, hand; tin litho, Clown hits Golly w/hammer, prewar, 5½", NM+ **105.00**
Toy, Little Playette Theatre, 3 Pigs/Sambo stories, 1940s, NMIB ..**235.00**
Toy, Ten Negro Dolls Construction Set, 1950s, unused, M (NM box)..**135.00**
Toy figure, Golliwog, hard rubber, Robertsons premium, prewar, 6", NM .**55.00**
Trivet/Platter, Mammy's head, pnt/glazed redware, Japan, 8", NM **75.00**
Vase, majolica, boy w/fruit in front of floral arrangement, 11", NM+ ..**175.00**
Vase, pottery, female native's head, blk w/gold trim, 1950s, 6", EX ...**30.00**
Watch fob, emb metal, She Was Bred in Old Kentucky, 1907, EX.....**75.00**

Black Cats

Made in Japan during the '50s, these novelty cats may be found bearing the labels of several different importers, all with their own particular characteristics. The best known and most collectible of these cats are from the Shafford line. Even when unmarked, they are easily identified by their red bows, green eyes, and white whiskers, eyeliners, and eyebrows. Relco/Royal Sealy cats are tall and slender, and their bow ties are gold with red dots. Wales is a wonderful line with yellow eyes and gold detailing; Enesco cats have blue eyes, and there are other lines as well. When evaluating your black cats, be sure to inspect their paint and judge them accordingly. Fifty percent paint should relate to 50% of our suggested values, which are given for cats in mint (or nearly mint) paint. Enthusiastic bidding on Internet auctions have resulted in much higher prices on the more hard-to-find items as reflected in our listings.

Our advisor for this category is Sammie Berry; she is listed in the Directory under Florida

Pitcher, squatting cat, pour through mouth, Shafford, rare, 5", $90.00.

Ashtray, flat face, Shafford, hard-to-find sz, 3¾"............................**50.00**
Ashtray, flat face, Shafford, 4¾", from $18 to................................**25.00**
Ashtray, head shape, not Shafford, several variants, ea from $15 to **25.00**
Ashtray, head shape, Shafford, 3", from $25 to **30.00**
Bank, seated, coin slot in top of head, Shafford, from $225 to....**275.00**
Bank, upright, Shafford features, mk Tommy, 2-part, minimum value...**175.00**
Cigarette lighter, Shafford, 5½", from $175 to............................**190.00**
Cigarette lighter, sm cat stands on book by table lamp.................**45.00**
Condiment set, upright, yel eyes, 2 bottles/pr shakers in wire fr....**95.00**
Condiment set, 2 joined heads, J&M bows, spoons, Shafford, 4", $125 to **135.00**
Cookie jar, head form, Shafford, from $80 to.............................**100.00**
Cookie jar, head w/fierce look, yel eyes, brn-blk glaze, red clay, lg.....**250.00**
Creamer, Shafford, from $20 to...**30.00**
Creamer, upraised left paw is spout, yel eyes, gold trim, 6½x6".....**40.00**
Creamer & sugar bowl, head lids are shakers, yel eyes, 5⅜" **50.00**
Cruets, upright, she w/V eyes, he w/O eyes, Shafford, pr, from $60 to....**75.00**
Decanter, long cat w/red fish in mouth as stopper...........................**75.00**

Decanter, upright cat holds bottle w/cork stopper, Shafford, $50 to......**65.00**
Decanter set, upright, yel eyes, 6 plain wines.................................**35.00**
Demitasse pot, tail hdl, bow finial, Shafford, 7½", from $175 to ...**200.00**
Desk caddy, pen forms tail, spring body holds letters, 6½"..............**8.00**
Egg cup, cat face on bowl, ped ft, Shafford, from $50 to...............**75.00**
Grease jar, sm head, Shafford, from $150 to................................**175.00**
Ice bucket, cylinder w/emb yel-eyed cat, 2 szs, ea **75.00**
Measuring cups, 4 szs on wood wall rack w/pnt cat face, Shafford, rare...**450.00**
Mug, cat's head above rim, Shafford, standard, 3½" **50.00**
Mug, cat's head below rim, Shafford, scarce, 3½" **225.00**
Mug, Shafford, hard to find, 4", from $65 to **75.00**
Paperweight, head on stepped chrome base, open mouth, yel eyes, rare ...**75.00**
Pincushion, cushion on bk, tongue measure.................................**25.00**
Pitcher, milk; upright, Shafford, 6" or 6½", ea from $120 to.......**140.00**
Pitcher, squatting cat, pour through mouth, Shafford, rare, 4½"...**75.00**
Pitcher, squatting cat, pour through mouth, Shafford, rare, 5" **90.00**
Pitcher, squatting cat, pour through mouth, Shafford, very rare, 5½" **250.00**
Planter, Shafford, from $35 to..**45.00**
Pot holder caddy, 'teapot' cat, 3 hooks, Shafford, minimum value ...**200.00**
Shaker, long & crouching (shaker ea end), Shafford, 10", from $75 to...**100.00**
Shakers, range; upright, Shafford, 5", pr....................................**35.00**
Shakers, rnd-bodied 'teapot' cats, Shafford, pr **75.00**
Shakers, upright, Shafford, 3¾" (or slightly smaller), pr...............**22.00**
Spice set, triangular, 3 rnd tiers (8 in all), in wood wall mt, rare...**750.00**
Spice set, 4 cat shakers hook onto wireware cat-face rack, Shafford ...**600.00**
Spice set, 6 sq shakers on wood fr, Shafford, from $175 to..........**225.00**
Spice set, 9 pcs in wood fr, yel eyes, Wales, from $85 to **110.00**
Store plaque, Orig Black Cats...Shafford, blk w/red letters & cat, EX....**800.00**
Sugar bowl, Shafford, from $20 to **30.00**
Teapot, ball-shaped body, head lid, Shafford, med szs, ea from $30 to **40.00**
Teapot, ball-shaped body, head lid, Shafford, sm, 4-4½", ea..........**25.00**
Teapot, ball-shaped body, head lid, Shafford, 7", from $50 to **60.00**
Teapot, cat face w/dbl spout, Shafford, scarce, 5", minimum value...**250.00**
Teapot, upright, lift-off head, Shafford, rare, 8", minimum value...**350.00**
Tray, flat face, wicker hdl, Shafford, scarce, from $75 to **100.00**
Utensil rack, flat-bk cat w/3 slots for utensils, cat only, Shafford...**100.00**
Utensil: strainer, dipper or funnel, wood hdls, Shafford, ea.........**100.00**
Wall pocket, 'teapot' cat, Shafford, minimum value....................**185.00**
Wine, emb face, gr eyes, Shafford, sm..**50.00**

Black Glass

Black glass is a type of colored glass that when held to strong light usually appears deep purple, though since each glasshouse had its own formula, tones may vary. It was sometimes etched or given a satin finish; and occasionally it was decorated with silver, gold, enamel, coralene, or any of these in combination. The decoration was done either by the glasshouse or by firms that specialized in decorating glassware. Crystal, jade, colored glass, or milk glass was sometimes used with the black as an accent. Black glass has been made by many companies since the seventeenth century. Contemporary glasshouses produced black glass during the Depression, seldom signing their product. It is still being made today.

To learn more about the subject, we recommend *A Collector's Guide to Black Glass, Books I* and *II*, written by our advisor, Marlena Toohey; she is listed in the Directory under Colorado. Look for her newly updated value guide. See also Tiffin, L.E. Smith, and other specific manufacturers.

Ashtray, lady's, Rosso's Wholesale, ca 1980s, 9" **50.00**
Ashtray, silver o/l, Cambridge, ca 1930s, 5" **20.00**
Bell, Bow & Drape, HP flowers, Fenton, #9266, ca 1990s, 6¾" **35.00**
Bowl, Candlewick w/Black Cosmos decor, Imperial, #400/7F, 1937, 8" ..**250.00**

Bowl, console; Autumn, McKee, 1934, 12x5½" 60.00
Bowl, Doric, Westmoreland, ca 1980s, 12" 68.00
Bowl, rolled rim, HP Copper Rose decor, Fenton, #7523, 1989-91, 3¾" 45.00
Bowl, rose; ftd, Tiffin, #8098, 1924-34, 7¼x5" 52.00
Bowl, Stork & Rushes, beaded band, LG Wright, 1995, 8½" 45.00
Bowl, violet; New Martinsville, 3¾" 10.00
Butter dish, Old Quilt, w/lid, Summit Art, 1993, 7¼" 35.00
Candlesticks, bl satin w/HP flowers & gilt edges, Westmoreland, 3" 40.00
Candlesticks, Garret, bl satin, Paden City, #117, ca 1930s, 8½" ...40.00
Candlesticks, HP w/gold & floral decor, Diamond, 1925-32, 9", pr...45.00
Candy dish, divided, in chrome basket, ca 1920-30s, 8½" 35.00
Compote, #1533, crimped, dolphin hdls & silver decor, ca 1930s, 6" 145.00
Decanter, pewter stopper & decor, ca 1930s, 9½" 95.00
Decanter, unknown maker, 12" 85.00
Ice bucket, Viking, ca 1980s, 6½" 50.00
Plate, Do Si Do, LE Smith, ca 1930s, 8" 12.00
Plate, Mayfair, Fostoria, ca 1930s, 8¼" 20.00
Plate, salad; Dalzell-Viking, #9103, 1990, 8" 34.00
Platter, Mt Pleasant, LE Smith, ca 1930s, 13½" dia......................85.00
Platter, octagonal w/silver decor, Cambridge, ca 1920-40s, 10¼" 65.00
Shakers, ribbed horizontally, Hazel Atlas, ca 1930s, 3½", pr 45.00
Sugar bowl, Dmn Quilt, hdls, Imperial, #414, 1929-32, 3¾".........17.00
Toothpick holder, strawberry pattern, Guernsey, ca 1980s, 2½"....20.00
Tray, lace-edged, hdld, Imperial, ca 1980s, 9" 45.00
Tray, sandwich; hdld, LE Smith, ca 1930s, 10"............................35.00
Vase, bud; slender w/decor, ca 1930s, 10" 35.00
Vase, Diadem, Fostoria, #2430, 1929-33, 8" 45.00

Blown Glass

Blown glass is rather difficult to date; eighteenth and nineteenth century examples vary little as to technique or style. It ranges from the primitive to the sophisticated, but the metallic content of very early glass caused tiny imperfections that are obvious upon examination, and these are often indicative of age.

In America, Stiegel introduced the English technique of using a patterned, part-size mold, a practice which was generally followed by many glasshouses after the Revolution. From 1820 to about 1850, glass was blown into full-size three-part molds. In the listings below, glass is assumed clear unless color is mentioned. Numbers refer to a standard reference book, *American Glass*, by Helen and George McKearin. See also Bottles and specific manufacturers. Our advisor for this category is Mark Vuono; he is listed in the Directory under Connecticut. See also Bottles.

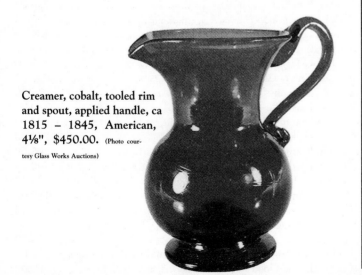

Creamer, cobalt, tooled rim and spout, applied handle, ca 1815 – 1845, American, 4⅛", $450.00. (Photo courtesy Glass Works Auctions)

Bird feeder, clear w/cobalt knob, smooth base, 5⅞" 50.00
Bottle, scent; bright yel-gr, 20 vertical ribs, Am, 1820-40, 3" 700.00
Bowl, apple gr, everted rim, 5½x9¾", EX 850.00
Bowl, dk olive gr, rolled lip, 4⅝x9½" 750.00
Compote, ground top lip, w/lid, 9x8" 140.00
Compote, ruby bowl, clear ft, 1870, 5¾x8" 350.00
Cordial, golden amber, tooled rim, att NE glasshouse, 3⅛"........550.00
Creamer, cobalt, 16 right-swirl ribs, 3" 100.00
Decanter, clear w/gilt Holland scenes, hdls, rigaree, 9¼" 160.00
Fishbowl, aquamarine, bulbous w/flared rim & rnd can ft, 8x9"...350.00
Flask, dk amber, 24 vertical ribs, wear/pot stones, 6¾" 1,265.00
Flask, pocket; bright yel w/lt olive, 20 vertical ribs, Midwest, 7" ...800.00
Fly trap, cranberry red flashing on clear (inside), 3 ft, 6" 350.00
Fly trap, lt gr, 19 vertical ribs, appl lip & ft, 6⅝" 135.00
Jar, bl aqua, 3¾x3¼" 170.00
Jar, Pillar mold, frosted neck, w/lid, 6" 300.00
Jar, utility; med yel-amber, cylindrical w/short can top, 11" 900.00
Pan, golden amber, swirled ribs, folded rim, att OH, 2½x10", EX...110.00
Pan, lt yel, folded rim, sloped sides, att Kent OH, 1½x4⅝", NM ..685.00
Pitcher, aquamarine, appl threading, bulbous, reeded hdl, 6¼" ..850.00
Pitcher, deep aqua, horizontal threads from rim to hdl base, 6", EX....850.00
Rolling pin, dk chocolate-amber, bubbles, 16¼"...........................110.00
Shakers, smoky vaseline, ball top/ovoid body, appl ring, 4", pr ...220.00
Shot glass, fiery wht opal, 6-sided, pontil, 2¼" 100.00
Smoke shade, appl ring, folded rim, 10½" dia 30.00
Vase, hyacinth; med amethyst, 12 vertical ribs, 1870-90, 7" 110.00
Vase, Lily Pad, aqua, ear hdls, threaded neck, 6", NM 330.00
Vase, med forest gr, tooled flared mouth, NE, lt wear, 6" 1,200.00
Vase, peacock bl, 12-flute, trn-over rim, 7½" 9,400.00
Vase, threading at neck, appl 'chain' at waist, strap hdls, 8⅛" 475.00
Wine, eng bird & flowers, twist stem, flat ft, 6" 210.00
Wine, eng bird/flowers/grapes, wht twist runs through stem, 6"...........210.00
Wine, eng name & 1829 marriage date, 4⅛" 50.00

Blown Three-Mold Glass

A popular collectible in the 1920s, 1930s, and 1940s, blown three-mold glass has again gained the attention of many. Produced from approximately 1815 to 1840 in various New York, New England, and Midwestern glasshouses, it was a cheaper alternative to the expensive imported Irish cut glass.

Distinguishing features of blown three-mold glass are the three distinct mold marks and the concave-convex appearance of the glass. For every indentation on the inner surface of the ware, there will be a corresponding protuberance on the outside. Blown three-mold glass is most often clear with the exception of inkwells and a few known decanters. Any colored three-mold glass commands a premium price.

The numbers in the listings that follow refer to the book *American Glass* by George and Helen McKearin. Our advisor for this category is Mark Vuono; he is listed in the Directory under Connecticut.

Bowl, canary yel, Pillar Mold, 12-rib, att Pittsburgh, 5x6½" 700.00
Creamer, dk cobalt, rib & drape pattern, 1825-45, 3⅝" 180.00
Creamer, GIII-26, faint bl tint, appl hdl w/rigaree, 4¼" 575.00
Decanter, GII-7, med olive gr bbl form, flaw, 8⅜"....................2,400.00
Decanter, GII-19, med olive gr, 9⅛" 1,400.00
Decanter, GII-28, lt apple gr, chip, 7⅛" 475.00
Decanter, GIII-16, olive w/trace of amber, 7¼", NM 525.00
Decanter, GIII-16, undersz wheel stopper, 9" 138.00
Decanter, GIII-16, yel olive, cylindrical, pt...............................700.00
Decanter, GIII-19, wheel stopper, 10½"..85.00
Decanter, GV-8, Baroque, hollow stopper, 11" 85.00
Dish, GIII-20, folded rim, 1¼x5"...165.00

Hat, GIII-4, cobalt, tooled inward rolled rim, Sandwich, 2½" 750.00
Pan, GII-16, folded rim, 7" 137.50
Pitcher, bl-gr aquamarine, Lily Pad, NY state, 7½x4½" 6,000.00
Pitcher, GII-18, ribbed hdl, bulbous, mfg flaws, 6½" 475.00
Pitcher, GIV-7, bulbous w/reed hdl, Sandwich, rare form, 7", EX ...600.00
Sugar bowl, GII-18, patterned dome lid, bulbous, 5½" 4,000.00
Tumbler, GIII-8, 2⅞" 195.00

Sugar bowl, GIII-18, clear with faint bluish tint, galleried rim, applied foot knob finial, Sandwich Glassworks, 1820 – 1840, 6½", $2,700.00.

Blue and White Stoneware

'Salt glaze' (slang term) or molded stoneware was most commonly produced in a blue and white coloration, much of which was also decorated with numerous 'in-mold' designs (some 150 plus patterns). It was made by practically every American pottery from the turn of the century until the mid-1930s. Crocks, pitchers, wash sets, rolling pins, and other household wares are only a few of the items that may be found in this type of 'country' pottery, now one of today's popular collectibles.

Logan, Brush-McCoy, Uhl Co., and Burley Winter were among those who produced it, but very few pieces were ever signed. Research and the availability of some manufacturers' sales catalogs has enabled collectors to attribute certain pattern lines to some companies. Naturally condition must be a prime consideration, especially if one is buying for resale; pieces with good, strong color and fully molded patterns bring premium prices. Normal wear and signs of age are to be expected, since this was utility ware and received heavy use in busy households.

In the listings that follow, crocks, salts, and butter holders are assumed to be without lids unless noted otherwise. Items are in near-mint condition unless noted otherwise. Though common pieces seem to have softened to some degree, scarce items and those in outstanding mint condition are stronger than ever. For further information we recommend *Blue and White Stoneware* (1981) by Kathryn McNerny and *Collector's Encyclopedia of Salt Glaze Stoneware* by Terry Taylor and Terry and Kay Lowrance. Terry Taylor is also our advisor for this category; he is listed in the Directory under North Carolina. See also specific manufacturers.

For information on the Blue & White Pottery Club, see the Catalogs, Clubs, and Newsletters section or visit their website at: www.blueandwhitepottery.org.

Bean pot, Wildflower, no lid 178.00
Bowl, Daisy on Lattice, 10¾" 140.00
Bowl, milk; Flying Bird shoulder, 3¾x9½", w/matching lid 1,200.00

Bowl, mixing; Flying Bird, 4x6" 200.00
Bowl, Wedding Ring, 6 szs, $150 ea, or set of 6 for 1,000.00
Bowl, Wildflower (stenciled), 4½x8" 179.00
Bowl (milk crock), Apricot, w/hdl 225.00
Butter crock, Apricot, appl wood & wire hdl, w/lid, 4x7" 275.00
Butter crock, Basketweave & Morning Glory, w/lid, 4x7½" 450.00
Butter crock, Butterfly, orig lid & bail, 6½" 225.00
Butter crock, Cows, appl wood & wire hdl, w/lid, 4½x7¼" 450.00
Butter crock, Daisy & Waffle, 4x8", NM 175.00
Butter crock, Draped Windows, 4½x8" 235.00
Butter crock, Eagle, orig lid & bail, M 1,000.00
Butter crock, Fall Harvest, w/lid, 6" dia. 350.00
Butter crock, Lovebirds, w/lid 5½x6", M 535.00
Butter crock, Peacock, w/lid, 6x6" 600.00
Butter jar, Wildflower, appl wood & wire hdl, 5x7" 275.00
Canister, Basketweave, Cloves, orig lid, 4½" 200.00
Canister, Basketweave, Crackers, w/lid 740.00
Canister, Basketweave, Pepper, orig lid, 4½" 200.00
Canister, Basketweave, Put Your Fist In, orig lid, 7½" 760.00
Canister, Basketweave, Raisins 479.00
Canister, Basketweave, Sugar, orig lid, 7½" 200.00
Canister, Basketweave, Tobacco, orig lid, 7½" 750.00
Canister set, Basketweave, 9-pc 5,000.00
Chamberpot, Peacock, 9¾" 1,250.00
Chamberpot, Wildflower & Fishscale, w/lid 400.00
Coffeepot, Bull's Eye, rim chips, 9¾x3¾" (base) 2,550.00
Coffeepot, Swirl, w/lid & metal base plate 900.00
Cookie jar, Brickers, flat button finial, 8x8" 348.00
Cooler, iced tea;, Blue Band, flat lid, complete, 13x11" 295.00
Cooler, water; Blue Band, orig lid 250.00
Cooler, water; Cupid, brass spigot, patterned lid, 15x12" 700.00
Cooler, water; Polar Bear, Ice Water, w/lid, hairlines, 6-gal, 15¼" ..900.00
Cuspidor, Basketweave & Morning Glory, 5x7½" 150.00
Cuspidor, Flower Panels & Arches, 7x7½" 225.00
Egg storage crock, Barrel Staves, bail hdl, 5½x6" 200.00
Grease jar, Flying Bird, orig lid, 4x4½" 1,000.00
Jardiniere, Tulips, hairline, 7x7⅞" (complete w/stand & crock) 1,625.00
Meat tenderizer, Wildflower, no chips, complete w/wood hdl 500.00
Mug, Basketweave & Flower, 5x3" 150.00
Mug, beer; advertising, Diffused Blue, sqd hdl 150.00
Mug, Flying Bird, 5x3" 130.00
Pie plate, Blue Walled Brick-Edge star-emb base, 10½" 200.00
Pitcher, Acorns, stenciled, 8x6½" 175.00
Pitcher, American Beauty Rose, 10" 450.00
Pitcher, Barrel, +6 mugs 395.00
Pitcher, Blue Band, plain 200.00
Pitcher, Bluebird, 9x7" 450.00
Pitcher, Butterfly, 9x7" 400.00
Pitcher, Cattails, stenciled design, bulbous, 7" 225.00
Pitcher, Cattails, 10" 275.00
Pitcher, Cherry Cluster, 7½" 650.00
Pitcher, Columns & Arches, 8¾x5" 425.00
Pitcher, Daisy Cluster, rare, 7x7" 750.00
Pitcher, Dutch Boy & Girl by Windmill, 9" 200.00
Pitcher, Eagle w/Shield & Arrows, rare, 8" 750.00
Pitcher, Flying Bird, 9" 625.00
Pitcher, Garden Rose, 9" 500.00
Pitcher, Girl & Dog, regular bl, 9" 800.00
Pitcher, Grape & Shield, 8½x5" 150.00
Pitcher, Grape w/Rickrack, any sz 250.00
Pitcher, Grazing Cows, bl, 8" 250.00
Pitcher, Grazing Cows, 6½" 500.00
Pitcher, Indian Boy & Girl (Capt John Smith & Pocahontas), 6" ..300.00
Pitcher, Indian Good Luck (Swastika), 8½" 200.00

Pitcher, Iris, 9" 370.00
Pitcher, Leaping Deer, 8½" 375.00
Pitcher, Leaping Deer in 1 oval, Swan in other (mfg error), 8" ..2,424.00
Pitcher, Lincoln, allover deep bl, 4¾x4¾" 250.00
Pitcher, Lincoln, allover deep bl, 6x4" 300.00
Pitcher, Lincoln, allover deep bl, 7x5" 500.00
Pitcher, Lincoln, allover deep bl, 8x6" 1,000.00
Pitcher, Lovebird, arc bands, deep color, 8½", EX 500.00
Pitcher, Lovebird, pale color, 8½" 300.00
Pitcher, Peacock 1,700.00
Pitcher, Pine Cone, 9½" 1,500.00
Pitcher, Poinsettia, 6½" 275.00
Pitcher, Scroll & Leaf, Compliments of Schroeder Bros..., 8" 898.00
Pitcher, Shield, prof rpr, 8" 200.00
Pitcher, Swan, in oval, deep color, 8½", EX 400.00
Pitcher, Swan, sponged, 8½" 1,548.00
Pitcher, Tulip, 8x4" 325.00
Pitcher, Wild Rose, sponged bands, 9" 500.00
Pitcher, Wildflower/Cosmos, w/advertising 2,100.00

Pitcher, Windmill and Bush, 9", $175.00.

Pitcher, Windmills, 7¼", EX 195.00
Pitcher, Windy City (Fannie Flagg), Robinson Clay, 8½" 450.00
Roaster, Wildflower, domed lid, 8½x12" 225.00
Rolling pin, Blue Band, no advertising, 14x4" 375.00
Rolling pin, orange band w/advertising & dtd 1916 ....756.00
Rolling pin, Swirl, orig wooden hdls, 13" 1,500.00
Rolling pin, Wildflower, plain 375.00
Rolling pin, Wildflower, w/center decor, 15x4½" 650.00
Salt crock, Butterfly, orig lid 350.00
Salt crock, Eagle, w/lid 800.00
Salt crock, Peacock, w/lid 1,000.00
Soap dish, Beaded Rose 135.00
Soap dish, Indian in War Bonnet 250.00
Spice set, Basketweave, 6-pc, w/lids, all M 2,000.00
Toothbrush holder, Bow Tie, stenciled flower 50.00
Vinegar cruet, rare, 4½x3" 375.00
Wash bowl & pitcher, Wildflower & Fishscale 500.00
Washboard, sponge 400.00
Water bottle, Diffused Blue Swirl, stopper w/cork, 10x5½" 800.00

Blue Ridge

Blue Ridge dinnerware was produced by Southern Potteries of Erwin, Tennessee, from the late 1930s until 1956 in twelve basic styles and two thousand different patterns, all of which were hand decorated under the glaze. Vivid colors lit up floral arrangements of seemingly endless variation, fruit of every sort from simple clusters to lush assortments, barnyard fowl, peasant figures, and unpretentious textured patterns. Although it is these dinnerware lines for which they are best known, collectors prize the artist-signed plates from the '40s and the limited line of character jugs made during the '50s most highly. Examples of the French Peasant pattern are valued at double the prices listed below; very simple patterns will bring 25% to 50% less.

Our advisors, Betty and Bill Newbound, have compiled four lovely books, *Blue Ridge Dinnerware, Revised Third Edition*; *The Collector's Encyclopedia of Blue Ridge, Volumes I* and *II*; and *Best of Blue Ridge*, all with beautiful color illustrations and current market values. They are listed in the Directory under North Carolina. For information concerning the National Blue Ridge Newsletter, see the Clubs, Newsletters, and Catalogs section of the Directory.

Ashtray, ind, from $20 to 24.00
Ashtray, Mallard Box shaped, from $65 to 75.00
Ashtray, w/rest (eared), from $20 to 30.00
Bonbon, flat shell, china, from $60 to 75.00
Bowl, hot cereal; from $20 to 25.00
Bowl, mixing; med, from $25 to 30.00
Bowl, soup/cereal; 6", from $20 to 25.00
Bowl, vegetable; oval, 9", from $35 to 40.00
Bowl, vegetable; w/lid, from $60 to 80.00
Box, cigarette; sq, from $85 to 90.00
Box, Mallard Duck, from $650 to 700.00
Box, Rose Step, pearlized, from $85 to 100.00
Box, Seaside, china, from $125 to 150.00
Butter dish, from $35 to 45.00
Cake lifter, from $30 to 35.00
Celery dish, Leaf shape, china, from $45 to 50.00
Coffeepot, ovoid, from $150 to 175.00
Creamer, Charm House, from $70 to 85.00
Creamer, Fifties shape, from $15 to 20.00
Creamer, Waffle shape, from $15 to 18.00
Cup & saucer, Holiday, from $60 to 75.00
Cup & saucer, regular shapes, ea from $20 to 25.00
Demitasse pot, china, from $250 to 300.00
Egg cup, dbl, from $25 to 35.00
Gravy boat, from $25 to 35.00
Jug, character; Daniel Boone, from $450 to 500.00
Jug, syrup; w/lid, from $85 to 95.00
Leftover, w/lid, med, from $50 to 65.00
Mug, child's, from $150 to 175.00
Pitcher, Abby, china, from $175 to 200.00
Pitcher, Antique, china, 5", from $85 to 100.00
Pitcher, Betsy, earthenware, from $120 to 175.00
Pitcher, Clara, china, from $95 to 125.00
Pitcher, Milady, china, from $125 to 185.00
Pitcher, Sculptured Fruit, china, from $75 to 100.00
Pitcher, Spiral, china, 7", from $75 to 100.00
Pitcher, Virginia, china, 4¼", from $175 to 200.00
Plate, dinner; 10½", from $20 to 25.00
Plate, flower/fruit salad; 8½", from $25 to 30.00
Plate, Gold Cabin, artist sgn, from $400 to 450.00
Plate, party; w/cup well & cup, from $35 to 40.00
Plate, Specialty; 11", from $150 to 200.00
Plate, sq, 7", from $12 to 15.00
Plate, Turkey; w/acorns, from $95 to 125.00
Platter, 12½" or 13", ea from $25 to 30.00
Relish dish, Charm House, china, from $175 to 200.00
Relish dish, Loop Handle, china, from $65 to 75.00
Relish dish, t-handle, from $65 to 75.00

Shakers, Blossom Top, pr, from $75 to.............................85.00
Shakers, range; pr, from $40 to 45.00
Sherbet, from $35 to..40.00
Sugar bowl, Colonial, open, sm, from $15 to 20.00
Sugar bowl, Waffle, w/lid, from $20 to 25.00
Tea set, Child's Play, from $400 to..................................450.00
Teapot, ball shape, premium, from $200 to 250.00
Teapot, Colonial, from $95 to...150.00
Teapot, Palisades, from $125 to......................................150.00
Teapot, Skyline, from $110 to...125.00
Tray, demi; Colonial, 5½x7", from $150 to 175.00
Tray, demi; Skyline, 9½x7⅝", from $100 to 150.00
Tumbler, glass, from $15 to 20.00
Tumbler, Invt Baby T'print, 4"..250.00
Vase, boot; 8", from $90 to..95.00
Vase, bud; from $225 to..250.00
Vase, hdld, china, from $95 to..100.00
Vase, ruffle top, china, 9½", from $100 to 125.00
Wall sconce, from $70 to...75.00

Blue Willow

Blue Willow, inspired no doubt by the numerous patterns of the blue and white Nanking imports, has been popular since the late eighteenth century and has been made in as many variations as there were manufacturers. English transfer wares by such notable firms as Allerton and Ridgway are the most sought after and the most expensive. Japanese potters have been producing Willow-patterned dinnerware since the late 1800s, and American manufacturers have followed suit. Although blue is the color most commonly used, mauve and black lines have also been made. For further study we recommend the book *Blue Willow*, with full-color photos and current prices, by Mary Frank Gaston, our advisor for this category. In the following listings, if no manufacturer is noted, the ware is unmarked. See also Buffalo.

Ashtray, Japan, sq, 7½", from $45 to 55.00
Baking dish, Two Temples II, line border, Hall China, Am, 3x8" 30.00
Bank, 3 stacked pigs, Japan, 7"...75.00
Biscuit jar, cane hdl, Two Temples, traditional border, English ...200.00

Biscuit jar, Two Temples II center pattern, Traditional border, cane handle, Adderley, 4½", from $200.00 to $225.00. (Photo courtesy Mary Frank Gaston)

Bone dish, kidney shape, Bourne & Leigh, 6¼", from $45 to 55.00
Bowl, flat soup; Eagle, 8" 12.50
Bowl, lug soup; Homer Laughlin, from $25 to..................30.00

Bowl, Maestricht, 2¾x9⅞" 120.00
Bowl, ped ft, John Tams Ltd, 5x9½", from $150 to 175.00
Bowl, soup; Royal China, 8¼" 15.00
Bowl, vegetable; oval, Japan..35.00
Bowl, vegetable; sq, w/lid, Ridgway's, 1912-27 mk, 10" 250.00
Bowl, vegetable; variant center pattern, pictorial border, 10" 25.00
Bowl, vegetable; Wood's Ware, 10"...................................40.00
Bowl & pitcher, Wedgwood......................................1,200.00
Box, dresser; porc, unmk English, ca 1880s, 2x4", from $175 to...200.00
Butter dish, Royal China, ¼-lb..45.00
Butter pat, Ridgway's, 1912-27 mk, 3¾", 4 for 60.00
Cake stand, Traditional pattern, unmk English, 4x10½",............325.00
Canisters, sq, tin, unmk, set of 4, from $400 to..................500.00
Casserole, Empress, w/lid, Homer Laughlin 75.00
Cheese dish, sq plate w/canted corners, sq lid, Wiltshaw & Robinson ..250.00
Coffeepot, Booths, gold trim, mk Real Old Willow, 8½" 210.00
Condiment shaker, pierced silver lid, Taylor, Tunnicliffe & Co, 2" 50.00
Creamer, Japan...10.00
Creamer, red, Royal China..15.00
Creamer & sugar bowl, w/lid, Steventon & Sons, 3", 4", from $70 to....80.00
Cup, chili; Japan, 3½x4" 50.00
Cup, chili; w/liner plate, Japan 75.00
Cup & saucer, jumbo; Homer Laughlin, from $20 to..........25.00
Cup & saucer, Meakin for Nieman-Marcus, 1970s 30.00
Cup & saucer, Washington Pottery, 3" cup, from $5 to 10.00
Dish, child's, Ridgway, w/lid, 5" 175.00
Egg cup, dbl, 4¼"...30.00
Gravy boat, Homer Laughlin, from $20 to 25.00
Horseradish dish, Doulton, 5½" 65.00
Jug, milk; Homer Laughlin, from $125 to.........................150.00
Lamp, kerosene; ceramic shade, Japan, 11½", from $125 to........150.00
Leaf dish, unmk English, 6" L 175.00
Match safe, slotted cylinder w/saucer base, Shenango China Co, 2" ...80.00
Mug, unmk Japan, 3½", from $10 to 15.00
Mustard pot, bbl shape, 2½", from $65 to 75.00
Pie plate, Royal China, 10" 30.00
Pitcher, Chicago Jug, Doulton, 1907, 3-pt 500.00
Pitcher, milk; Homer Laughlin, 5" 45.00
Pitcher, milk; tankard form, Allerton's, 7", EX 125.00
Pitcher, Traditional center, Wedgwood, 129+ mk, 11¼"............150.00
Plate, Booth's Willow, Meakin for Nieman-Marcus, 1970s, 7" 20.00
Plate, dessert/bread & butter; Japan...................................5.00
Plate, dinner; Imperial, 9¾" 27.00
Plate, dinner; Liner & Carter, 9½" 24.00
Plate, grill; Booth's center pattern, Bow-Knot border, 10¾" 35.00
Plate, salad; red, Jackson China Restaurant Ware 8.00
Plate, salad; red, Wallace China..8.00
Plate, traditional center & border, Charles Meigh & Son, 9¼" 85.00
Platter, Allerton's, 16x12"...275.00
Platter, tab hdls, unmk Royal China, 11¾"........................20.00
Platter, Traditional center, 1912-1927, 15½x12½".....................225.00
Relish tray, Booth's center pattern, Bow-Knot border, Wood & Sons, 9" ...30.00
Salt box, unmk Japan, wall-mt, wood lid, 5" 110.00
Shakers, Royal China, pr...25.00
Spoon rest, dbl rests, Japan, 9", from $40 to 50.00
Sugar bowl, w/lid, Japan..15.00
Sugar bowl, w/lid, Royal China..15.00
Tankard, pewter lid, Burleigh, scroll/flower border, English, 7" ...350.00
Teapot, Allerton's, 6", NM..225.00
Teapot, Two Temples II, butterfly border, Malkin mk: MIE, 3½" ..125.00
Teapot, Well's shape, Homer Laughlin, from $80 to..........100.00
Tumbler, juice; glass, Jeannette, 3½" 12.00
Tumbler, water; glass, Jeannette, 5½" 12.00
Tureen, soup; Traditional center, Ridgway's, 1912-27 mk, 7¾x11"....450.00

Bluebird China

The earliest examples of the pudgy little bluebird in the apple blossoms decal appear in the late 1890s. The craze apparently peaked during the early to mid-1920s and had all but died out by 1930. More than fifty manufacturers, most of whom were located in East Liverpool, Ohio, produced bluebird dinnerware. There are variations on the decal, and several are now accepted as 'bluebird china.' The larger china companies like Homer Laughlin and KT&K experimented with them all. One of the variations depicts larger, more slender bluebirds in flight. The latter variety was made by Knowles Taylor Knowles, W.S. George (Derwood), French Co., Sterling Colonial, and Pope Gosser. The dinnerware was never expensive, and shapes varied from one manufacturer to another. Today, the line produced by Homer Laughlin is valued most highly; it is also the most available. Besides the companies we've already mentioned, you'll find the trademarks of Cleveland; Carrolton; Limoges China of Sebring, Ohio; Salem; Taylor Smith Taylor; and there are others.

Our advisor for this category is Kenna Rosen, author of a new book on this subject (Schiffer); she is listed in the Directory under Texas.

Bone dish, Empress, Homer Laughlin 125.00
Bowl, berry; Cleveland, ind...20.00
Bowl, deep, Derwood, WS George, 4¾" 50.00
Bowl, gravy; Hopewell China, w/saucer 100.00
Bowl, soup; PMC Co, 8" 30.00
Bowl, vegetable; Cleveland, 9¾" 50.00
Butter dish, Carrollton, 6¼" sq..100.00
Butter dish, Empress, Homer Laughlin 200.00
Butter dish, Salem China 150.00
Butter dish, Steubenville, 4½" holder w/in 7" dish....................150.00
Butter dish, Victory, Knowles Taylor Knowles 150.00
Calendar plate, 1921 advertising pc, DE McNicol.......................75.00
Canister set, rnd, unmk, 6½x5", 6 for 300.00
Casserole, Buffalo China, w/lid..150.00
Casserole, Homer Laughlin Empress, w/lid, 8½" dia....................150.00
Casserole, Pope Gosser, w/lid, 10½x10½" 100.00
Casserole, SPI Clinchfield China, w/lid...............................150.00
Casserole, Taylor Smith & Taylor, w/lid, 11x7½" 150.00
Chamber pot, w/lid, unmk, late 1890s..................................250.00
Chocolate cup, ftd, no mk, 3½"...85.00
Covered platter/food warmer, Buffalo Mfg, 19x13" 125.00
Creamer, no mk, 4¼" 25.00
Creamer & sugar bowl, HR Wyllie, w/lid................................125.00
Creamer & sugar bowl, SP Co, w/lid 85.00
Creamer & sugar bowl, TA McNichol, w/lid..............................75.00
Cup, tea; unmk 15.00
Cup & saucer, Owen China, St Louis.....................................40.00
Custard cup, KT&K, 3½"..35.00
Egg cup, Buffalo China, very rare, 2½".................................75.00
Gravy w/attached underplate, Homer Laughlin, 4x9¾" 200.00
Mug, baby's, Cleveland China 100.00
Mug, coffee; unmk, 3½"...60.00
Pitcher, wash; Bennett China 400.00
Pitcher, water; Buffalo Pottery, 7" 100.00
Pitcher, water; Cable, Homer Laughlin 200.00
Pitcher, water; Crown Pottery Co.......................................250.00
Pitcher, water; DE McNicol 150.00
Pitcher, water; Empress, Homer Laughlin................................250.00
Pitcher, water; Knowles Taylor Knowles, w/lid..........................200.00
Pitcher, water; National China 200.00
Plate, baby's, ELP Co China, 7½x7½"....................................150.00
Plate, Cleveland, 9" 25.00
Plate, Knowles Taylor Knowles, 9¾" 40.00

Plate, Steubenville, 9" 40.00
Plate, Wilmer Ware 20.00

Platter, Edwin M. Knowles, 14½x11", $75.00.

Platter, Hopewell China, 13x10" 75.00
Platter, Pope Gosser, 17x13" 100.00
Platter, Thompson Glenwood, 13x10".....................................60.00
Platter, unmk, 9x7" 45.00
Platter, West End Pottery Co, 15½x11" 75.00
Platter, 10 bluebirds, gold trim at rim, DE McNichol, 15¼x11¼" ..100.00
Saucer, Homer Laughlin...15.00
Soap dish, WS George 150.00
Sugar bowl, Illinois China Co, w/lid, 7x6" 50.00
Syrup, Homer Laughlin, 6½" 175.00
Syrup, unmk, 4" 35.00
Tea set, child's, CPCo, 21-pc 400.00
Tea set, child's, Summit China Co....................................1,025.00
Teapot, Carollton 250.00
Teapot, ELP Co, 8½x8½" 250.00
Teapot, Homer Laughlin, from $750 to.................................1,200.00
Teapot, KT&K mk, 3½x7¼" 250.00

Boch Freres

Founded in the early 1840s in La Louviere, Boch Freres Keramis became the foremost producer of art pottery in Belgium. Though primarily they served a localized market, in 1844 they earned worldwide recognition for some of their sculptural works on display at the International Exposition in Paris.

In 1907 Charles Catteau of France was appointed head of the art department. Before that time, the firm had concentrated on developing glazes and perfecting elegant forms. The style they pursued was traditional, favoring the re-creation of established eighteenth-century ceramics. Catteau brought with him to Boch Freres the New Wave (or Art Nouveau) influence in form and decoration. His designs won him international acclaim at the Exhibition d'Art Decoratif in Paris in 1925, and it is for his work that Boch Freres is so highly regarded today. He occasionally signed his work as well as that of others who under his direct supervision carried out his preconceived designs. He was associated with the company until 1950 and lived the remainder of his life in Nice, France, where he died in 1966. The Boch Freres Keramis factory continues to operate today, producing bathroom fixtures and other utilitarian wares. A variety of marks have been used, most incorporating some combination of 'Boch Freres,' 'Keramis,' 'BFK,' or 'Ch Catteau.' A shield topped by a crown and flanked by a 'B' and an 'F' was used as well.

Bowl, wht w/dk gr vertical bands, ped ft, 3x4½" dia...................**70.00**
Box, intersecting floral bands, D704/CT, w/key, 5½x3¾" **265.00**
Vase, birds & foliage (stylized), mc on tan, #960, D1230, 11⅝" ..**1,175.00**
Vase, blossoms/leaves, pk/wht w/blk bands on brn, bulbous, 10" **300.00**
Vase, Deco deer & grasses, bl/blk on ivory, bulbous, 14"...........**3,000.00**
Vase, Deco leaf design, gr on tan, swollen form, 10"....................**550.00**
Vase, floral, gr/brn/ivory on sponged brn, Catteau, 8¾", NM **750.00**
Vase, floral, mc on wht, milk bottle shape 12½" **450.00**
Vase, floral & strapwork on dk brn & ochre, Catteau, 10¼x6"...**1,800.00**
Vase, floral abstracts on wht crackle, ovoid, 7x4½".....................**220.00**
Vase, floral band, mc on cream, Catteau, D1132, 5¾" **350.00**
Vase, floral w/turq & cobalt bands, bulbous, 5¼x3¾" **140.00**
Vase, floral w/yel & blk stripes, slim ovoid, 10¾x5¼"................**415.00**
Vase, flower baskets on wht crackle, bottle form, 8½x4½" **330.00**
Vase, flower bouquet w/gold on gr, #340, 11¾x6½" **385.00**

Vase, flowers and water lily pads on cobalt and white crackle, #39, 9x7", $475.00.

(Photo courtesy Smith and Jones)

Vase, fruit/leaves & ribbons on wht w/bl top, #975/#745, 12".....**900.00**
Vase, geometrics & archways on wht crackle, ovoid, D1210, 12½x7"...**880.00**
Vase, half-moons & blk beads in panels on wht crackle, 11x6½"..**465.00**
Vase, irises w/silver blooms on purple, #446, 6⅛"...................**330.00**
Vase, lg gold starburst florals/gr leaves on tan band, Gres/#902, 10" ...**600.00**
Vase, roses on arbor (yel), w/gold stars on bl, 18½" **1,000.00**
Vase, snake-like swirls & florettes on wht, 9½x6¼".....................**465.00**
Vase, tulips & forget-me-nots on wht crackle, ovoid, #2779, 11x7½"...**600.00**
Vase, veined allover w/leaves, gr/tan, spherical, #906, 5½".........**260.00**
Vase, water lily leaves & flowers w/cobalt on wht crackle, 9x7"...**465.00**

Boehm

Boehm sculptures were the creation of Edward Marshall Boehm, a ceramic artist who coupled his love of the art with his love of nature to produce figurines of birds, animals, and flowers in lovely background settings accurate to the smallest detail. Sculptures of historical figures and those representing the fine arts were also made and along with many of the bird figurines, have established secondary-market values many times their original prices. His first pieces were made in the very early 1950s in Trenton, New Jersey, under the name of Osso Ceramics. Mr. Boehm died in 1969, and the firm has since been managed by his wife. Today known as Edward Marshall Boehm, Inc., the private family-held corporation produces not only porcelain sculptures but collector plates as well. Both limited and non-limited editions of their works have been issued. Examples are marked with various backstamps, all of which have incorporated the Boehm name since 1951.

'Osso Ceramics' in upper case lettering was used in 1950 and 1951. Our advisor for this category is Leon Reimert; he is listed in the Directory under Pennsylvania.

Alec's Red Rose, #300-39, 1980-81, 7x11".................................**365.00**
Am Express Miss Liberty Rose, #F135, 5½" **150.00**
American Eagle, Inaugural; #40185..**750.00**
Angels, boy & girl, #614-05, #613-04, 5", pr...............................**70.00**
Barn Owl, #20...**3,000.00**
Bay Crested Flycatcher, #458..**165.00**
Begonia, #300-41..**950.00**
Black-Headed Grosbeak, #400-03...**795.00**
Blue Magpie, #400-44...**2,800.00**
Bob White Quail, #6..**1,850.00**
Buffalo (Bison), #50022, 1982, 8½x14½".................................**1,050.00**
Bull, Black Angus; #404-01..**1,000.00**
Camel Calf, #400-98, 8x7x4"...**100.00**
Canada Geese, #408, pr, w/base..**950.00**
Cardinals, #415, pr..**3,000.00**
Cheetah Head, gold w/bl nose, #148, 7" **285.00**
Cinderella at the Ball, Cinderella Ballet series, 9" **115.00**
Cygnet, #400-27...**185.00**
Cygnet, #400-46...**245.00**
Cygnet Cygnus Olor, sleeping, #400-13 ....**210.00**
Downy Woodpecker, #427..**850.00**
Fairy Godmother, Cinderella Ballet series, wht, 10" **115.00**
Falcon Head, gold w/bl decor at neck, #80, 1970s, 13¾" **285.00**
First Noel, nativity set, wht bsk, 9-pc..**285.00**
Fledgling Blackburnian Warbler, #478 ....**130.00**
Fledgling Bluebird, #442, 4½" **85.00**
Fledgling Cardinal, #400-57, 4" **80.00**
Fledgling Chickadee, #400-80, 4½" **70.00**
Fledgling Chickadee, #461, open mouth & 1 wing up, 3¼x3½"....**70.00**
Fledgling Goldfinch, #448, 4¼"..**85.00**
Fledgling Robin, #40231...**295.00**
Fledgling Wood Thrush, #444, 4¼" **70.00**
Giant Panda, seated w/bamboo shoot, #40237, 1988, 5x4" **90.00**
Grey Seal, #201-40...**365.00**
Helen Boehm Rose, #F147, 3x5¾"..**70.00**
Hereford Bull, mk, 6x10¼"...**550.00**
Indigo Bunting, #429E..**250.00**
Lapwing, #17...**1,995.00**
Mearn's Quail, #467, pr...**2,150.00**
Mockingbird, #400-52, w/nasturtiums......................................**2,000.00**
Moose, #10094, 18x14"..**1,620.00**
Mourning Doves, #443...**1,000.00**
Nojoqui, baby condor, named for San Diego Zoo condor, #20240, 9½"...**270.00**
Peregrin Falcon, #100-50, outstretched wings **3,750.00**
Peregrine Falcon w/Young, #401-7 ....**2,250.00**
Periwinkle, in open seashell, mk, 3⅝x3⅝"..................................**165.00**
Queen Elizabeth Rose, bronze stem & petal, 3¾x7¼" **120.00**
Rhododendron, #25-15, 3x5x3"...**220.00**
Seal Pup, #36, sgn Helen Boehm, 1980, 2½x5½"..........................**90.00**
Snow Owl, wht w/glass eyes, 9½"..**80.00**
Snuggling Bunnies, #40275, 3½x3"...**85.00**
Sow w/Piglet, #400-88...**265.00**
Sweetheart Rose, #F505, 2001, 3½x5"..**175.00**
Tree Sparrow, #468...**325.00**
Trilafon, wht head w/disecting lines on scalp, 5¼"......................**95.00**
Wedding Rose, #F490..**275.00**
White-Throated Sparrow, #430..**235.00**
Wood Ducks, #16..**2,500.00**
Woodcock, #413, 1954, 10"...**750.00**
Yellow Sapsucker, #400-18..**2,250.00**

Yellow-Throated Warbler, #431, 9½" 310.00
Young & Free, doe w/fawn, #500-14, 12½x13" 1,320.00

American Bald Eagle on a Branch, National Audubon Society, 1989, signed by Helen Boehm, $660.00.

Bohemian Glass

The term 'Bohemian glass' has come to refer to a type of glass developed in Bohemia in the late sixteenth century at the Imperial Court of Rudolf II, the Hapsburg Emperor. The popular artistic pursuit of the day was stone carving, and it naturally followed to transfer familiar procedures to the glassmaking industry. During the next century, a formula was discovered that produced a glass with a fine crystal appearance which lent itself well to deep, intricate engraving, and the art was further advanced.

Although many other kinds of art glass were made there, we are using the term 'Bohemian glass' to indicate glass overlaid or stained with color through which a design is cut or etched. (Unless otherwise described, the items in the listing that follows are of this type.) Red or yellow on clear glass is common, but other colors may also be found. Another type of Bohemian glass involves cutting through and exposing two layers of color in patterns that are often very intricate. Items such as these are sometimes further decorated with enamel and/or gilt work.

Beaker, amber, Rheinstein Castle scene, 1860s, 5" 225.00
Beaker, bl, cameo-cut fawn scene, 1850s, rare, 4½" 1,450.00
Beaker, red, HP duck scene, facets, 1860s, 4" 250.00
Beaker, red & amber, wheel-cut florals, 1930s, 5½" 100.00
Beaker, wht, HP floral, stained/cut panels, 19th C, 5" 250.00
Decanter, red, florals/scrolls, 1930s, 12½", + 6 cordials 175.00
Goblet, amber, stag scenes, 1900s, 6¼" 150.00
Goblet, wine; red, deer & castle, 1900, 5⅛" 40.00
Lustres, gr/milk glass, floral, prisms, 14½", pr 1,200.00
Pokal, amber, horse/dogs/deer, late 1800s, 15", EX 750.00
Powder box, cranberry opaline w/HP foliage & gold, 2¼x4" 350.00
Stein, red, Carlsbad scene, late 1800s, ½-liter 250.00
Stein, red, Steinbad scene, reducer lenses, inlaid lid, ½-liter......400.00
Urn, amber/frost, vintage/stags in forest, w/lid, 24" 800.00
Vase, amber, cut decor, hobnail center band, gold flowers, 10" ...230.00
Vase, cranberry, cut floral/foliage w/gold, 8½" 400.00
Vase, red, X-hatching, HP floral panels, 12" 350.00

Bookends

Though a few were produced before 1880, bookends became a necessary library accessory and a popular commodity after the printing industry was revolutionized by Mergenthaler's invention, the linotype. Books became abundantly available at such affordable prices that almost every home suddenly had need for bookends. They were carved from wood; cast in iron, bronze, or brass; or cut from stone. Chalkware and glass were used as well. Today's collectors may find such designs as ships, animals, flowers, and children. Patriotic themes, art reproductions, and those with Art Nouveau and Art Deco styling provide a basis for a diverse and interesting collection.

Currently, figural cast-iron pieces are in demand, especially examples with good original polychrome paint. This has driven the value of painted cast-iron bookends up considerably.

For further information we recommend *Collector's Guide to Bookends, Identification and Values*, by Louis Kuritzky, our advisor for this category; he is listed in the Directory under Florida. See also Arts and Crafts.

Anchor, gray metal, Dodge, ca 1947, 5¾" 45.00
Angelfish, gray metal on polished stone base, JB Hirsch, ca 1930, 6" ..120.00
Atlas, chalk on polished stone base, JB Hirsch, ca 1940, 7¾" ...135.00
Best Foot Forward, cast gray metal, JB Hirsch, ca 1930, 5" 125.00
Bowling Pins (2)/Ball on Base, CI, mk US&S Duck Pin League/1943-44, 6"..75.00
Cameo Girls, iron, 1926, 4¼" 75.00
Celeste, gray metal, Ronson, ca 1925, 5" 225.00
Chinese Man, gray metal, JB Hirsch, ca 1933, 8¼" 150.00
Chinese Students, gray metal, Ronson #16138, ca 1930, 5¼".......95.00
Companions, gray metal, WB, ca 1929, 7" 195.00
Country Gate, iron, Bradley & Hubbard, ca 1935, 5" 125.00
Cupid & Psyche, in relief, gray metal, X-1 #501, ca 1928, 4½" ..135.00
Dante & Beatrice Books, gray metal, Jennings Brothers, ca 1935, 6"...195.00
Deco Marlin, chrome & bronze, ca 1935, 3¼" 225.00
Elephant at Tree, pnt iron, Judd Co, ca 1925, 4½" 150.00
Fido, gray metal, Bronzart, ca 1925, 6½" 165.00
Flower Basket, pnt iron, Hubley #8, ca 1925, 5¾".......................175.00
Front Door, iron, Bradley & Hubbard, ca 1925, 5¾" 125.00
Gazelle, iron, Hubley, ca 1925 ....125.00
Girl w/Purse, pnt gray metal w/celluloid face, ca 1926, 4¾" 135.00
Golfer, gray metal, Ronson, ca 1930, 6½" 175.00
Great Dane, gray metal, JF Co, ca 1928, 7¾" 125.00
Head Dog, gray metal, Frankart, ca 1928, 6" 175.00
Holy Mother & Child, in relief, iron, Snead Ironworks, 1924, 4¾" ...60.00
Horse Race, gray metal, Nuart, ca 1934, 4¼" 250.00
Ibex Leap, iron, Littco, ca 1920, 5" 125.00
In Pursuit, in relief, gray metal, Ronson, 1924, 4" 110.00
Indian Scout, gray metal, Jennings Brothers, ca 1927, 5" 170.00
King of the Beasts, gray metal, K&O, ca 1934, 5¾" 90.00
Kingfisher, bronze in marble enclosure, ca 1928, 5¾" 195.00
Lady in Red, pnt gray metal, Crescent Metal Works, ca 1932, 9"...275.00
Leaping Greyhounds, gray metal, Ronson #12314, ca 1930, 5½"..195.00
Lily Pad, gray metal, Dodge, ca 1945, 4½" 65.00
Lincoln Profile, in relief, iron, Connecticut Foundry, 1930, 6" 95.00
Mermaids, gray metal on marble base, JB Hirsch, ca 1925, 5".....275.00
Minute Man, gray metal, Jennings Brothers, ca 1930, 9" 175.00
Nouveau Girls, gray metal, Judd, ca 1920, 5" 110.00
Oaken Door, wood w/metal ring, ca 1975 ....15.00
Ocean Voyage, iron, Bradley & Hubbard, ca 1927, 5½"...............70.00
One of Us Was Studying, gray metal, Ronson #12552, 9"...........150.00
Patriotic Eagle, coated chalk, ca 1970, 5"....................................20.00
Perky Pheasant, gray metal on marble base, ca 1932, 6¾" 110.00

Pharaoh, bronze clad, Armor Bronze, L Cudebrod, ca 1926, 7" ..175.00
Pirate Booty, in relief, iron, Hubley, ca 1925, 4¾" 65.00
Pony, iron, Littco, ca 1926, 6" 110.00
President General, in relief, bronze, Hubley #234, ca 1925, 5¼" ...150.00
Ready for Flight, glass, Cambridge Glass, ca 1940, 5½" 160.00
Sailboat, iron, Littco, ca 1929, 7½" 100.00
Silver Scotties, gray metal, Jennings Brothers, ca 1929, 5¼" 125.00
Sleeping Beauty, iron, Niobe, ca 1925, 6¼" 250.00
Swan Design, in relief, gray metal, Ronson #10817, ca 1930, 4¾" ..45.00
Swimmer, gray metal, Dodge, ca 1946, 5¾" 85.00

Tambourine Girl, iron with bronze finish, Gift House, Inc, 1926, 5¼", $110.00. (Photo courtesy Louis Kuritzky)

Thinker, iron, Gift House #D-51, 1928, 5¾" 125.00
This Is a Date?, gray metal, Frankart, ca 1930, 5½" 125.00
Town Crier, gray metal, PM Craftsman, ca 1965, 7¼" 50.00
Tri-berry, copper, Craftsman #269, handmade, ca 1935, 5" 50.00
Tryst, in relief, iron, Hubley #301, ca 1924, 5½" 75.00
Victorian Couple, in relief, iron, Judd #9662, ca 1925, 6" 85.00
Weather-beaten Mariner, gray metal, Ronson, ca 1930, 6" 150.00
Well of Wisdom, iron, Connecticut Foundry, ca 1929, 6" 175.00
Ye Olde Coaching Days, in relief, Jennings Brothers, ca 1924, 4¼" 65.00

Bootjacks and Bootscrapers

Bootjacks were made from metal or wood. Some were fancy figural shapes, others strictly business! Their purpose was to facilitate the otherwise awkward process of removing one's boots. Bootscrapers were handy gadgets that provided an effective way to clean the soles of mud and such. Our advisor for this category is Louis Picek; he is listed in the Directory under Iowa.

Bootjacks

Am Bull Dog, pistol shape, CI, blk pnt, 8", from $75 to...............90.00
Boss emb on shaft, lacy, CI, 15" L...135.00
Bull's head, aluminum, Ricardo, worn pnt.....................................55.00
Cat silhouette, blk-pnt CI, 10½x10"..295.00
Dog, holds U-shaped bone in mouth, CI...25.00
Fish (stylized), cvd wood, worn finish, 22" L..............................115.00
Labrador Retriever, CI, 3x10x4¾"..15.00
Lee Riders advertising, wood w/leather trim, EX............................75.00
Mermaid, hands outstretched above head, CI, 10x4" 22.50
Moose, CI, 11x8"...15.00
Naughty Nellie, nude lady on bk, CI, 9½".....................................27.50
Pistol, CI, emb boars ea side, folding, 9" 275.00
V-shape, ornate CI, VG..48.00

Bootscrapers

Black shoeshine boy atop, CI, oval base, 13", VG.......................140.00
Cat, long tail sticks up, CI, 10x15"...35.00
Cat mtd on oval shallow pan w/foliate rim, CI, 1800s, 12" L ..1,100.00
Dachshund, CI, EX orig pnt, EX..220.00
Dachshund, CI, no pnt, tail forms ring, 20½x7½x7" 185.00
Duck, full body, CI, 14½" L...350.00
Elephant, trunk raised, CI, mtd on wooden base, 9x11"...............30.00
Griffins jtd at wings & tails, CI, marble base, 18".......................880.00
Horseshoe, CI, mtd on rimmed base, 9x11x9"..........................2,500.00
Pointer dog ea end, CI, rust, 13x19x12"......................................765.00
Quatrefoil base, CI, 5½x10½x11"..625.00
Scottie dog, CI, orig pnt, EX..185.00
Scrolled finial (detailed), wrought iron, 21x24"..........................500.00

Borsato, Antonio

Borsato was a remarkable artist/sculptor who produced some of the most intricately modeled and executed figurines ever made. He was born in Italy and at an early age enjoyed modeling wildlife from clay he dug from the river banks near his home. At age eleven, he became an apprentice of Guido Cacciapuotti of Milan, who helped him develop his skills. During the late '20s and '30s, he continued to concentrate on wildlife studies. Because of his resistance to the fascist government, he was interred at Sardinia from 1940 until the end of the war, after which he returned to Milan where he focused his attention on religious subjects. He entered the export market in 1948 and began to design pieces featuring children and more romantic themes. By the 1960s his work had become very popular in this country. His talent for creating lifelike figures has seldom been rivaled. He contributed much of his success to the fact that each of his figures, though built from the same molded pieces, had its own personality, due the unique way he would tilt a head or position an arm. All had eyelashes, fingernails, and defined musculature; and each piece was painted by hand with antiquated colors and signed 'A. Borsato.' He made over six hundred different models, with some of his groups requiring more than one hundred and sixty components and several months of work to reach completion.

Borsato died in 1982. Today, some of his work is displayed in the Vatican Museum as well private collections.

Prices vary according to size and the amount of work involved. Single figures often fetch $1,200.00. Larger pieces, for instance, 'Gypsy Camp' or 'Revelry,' may go from $15,000.00 to as high as $20,000.00. 'Play Gypsy Play' was originally made in the early '30s; a second version followed in the late '40s, and a limited edition was created to mark the thirtieth anniversary of the date he began his work. Though he planned to make thirty of these limited edition groupings, he died after only thirteen had been completed. This version was larger than the first two and has sold on the secondary market for more than $50,000.00. Various pieces were made in two mediums, gres and porcelain, with porcelain being double the cost of gres. In the listings that follow, our suggested values should be regarded as conservative.

Our advisor for this category is Elizabeth Langtree, she is listed in the Directory under California.

Boulevardier, man seated on rustic bench, 6¼x5½" 1,350.00
Canine Casualty, man applies first aid to dog, 9x9".................2,560.00
Child's Prayer, child on lady's lap w/hands folded, 8x6x9½"...1,925.00
Cobbler's Dilemna, man & boy at bench, 10½x7½x8½" 2,900.00
Coffee Counter, 3 figures surrounding coffee urn, 10x9".........4,000.00
Comfort & Love, courting couple, lady & dog in interior, 12x22"...13,600.00
Dog Trainer, man working w/upright poodle, 6x9½"................1,600.00
Elders' Delight, aged couple w/basket of snails, 11x8"..............3,240.00

Elegant Harmony, man at piano, 2nd w/violin, lady beside, 13x15"...**9,600.00**
Fagoters, man w/bundle on bk w/goat & dog, 11½x8½"..........**2,100.00**
Farmer's Twilight, man offers produce to lady, 7x10"................**3,475.00**
Fiddler's Revelry, man seated/playing fiddle, 6x10" **2,140.00**
Grandma's Well, lady/child/goose at well, 10x12" **5,125.00**
Lover's Lane, figures in horse-drawn carriage on base, 11x24"....**8,775.00**
Nomads, 2 figures w/loaded pack horse & sheep on rocky base, 13x22" ...**11,240.00**

Play Gypsy Play, third version, minimum value $50,000.00. (Photo courtesy Elizabeth Langtree)

Psyche & Eros, classical couple on base, 7¾x8" **1,575.00**
Siesta's Price, fruit card, peddler asleep while cash drw is robbed ...**3,200.00**
St George, man on rearing stallion facing dragon, 17¼x11¾" ...**6,625.00**

Boru, Sorcha

Sorcha Boru was the professional name used by California ceramist Claire Stewart. She was a founding member of the Allied Arts Guild of Menlo Park (California) where she maintained a studio from 1932 to 1938. From 1938 until 1955, she operated Sorcha Boru Ceramics, a production studio in San Carlos. Her highly acclaimed output consisted of colorful, slip-decorated figurines, salt and pepper shakers, vases, wall pockets, and flower bowls. Most production work was incised 'S.B.C.' by hand.

Bowl, gr w/pk & bl floral finial, 2½x6", from $50 to **75.00**
Creamer & sugar bowl, wht w/turq bows, open.............................**40.00**
Cup, 3 dinosaur hdls...**75.00**
Novelty, cable car, 3x2¼x5" **30.00**
Shakers, bride & groom, pr **175.00**
Shakers, flower girl & boy, bl w/pk headpc, yel hair, 2½", pr **35.00**
Shakers, King & Queen, 5½", pr **75.00**
Sugar shaker, lady figure, 6" **110.00**
Vase, appl flowers & leaves, 8" **75.00**

Bossons Artware

Bossons closed operations December 1996. The late William Henry Bossons founded the company (formerly located in Congleton, England) in 1944; his son, W. Ray Bossons (deceased 1999) was manager from 1951 until his retirement in 1994. The company was always owned and managed by the Bossons family, who have stored the only remaining molds and patterns. (Many became obsolete and were officially destroyed.)

Now that all Bossons are discontinued, they have become highly collectible. Major Internet search engines have recorded in excess of 700 to 800 Bossons searches each month.

As stock holdings are depleted, some are appreciating at a very fast rate. The last Character Heads produced are shown in the final two-sided colored company leaflet dated October 1, 1996. Included are Nuvolari, No. 243; Sinbad the Sailor, No. 250; Cossack, No. 251; Evzon, No. 248; and The Cook, No. 249. (The Cook was never released into production; only about five examples were ever made.) These last characters are commanding premium prices. For example, many of the Series B heads that originally sold in the US for under $5.00 are now in the $100.00 to $300.00 range. Armenian ($145.00 – $165.00), Lichtensteiner ($145.00 – $150.00), Rumanian ($125.00 – $150.00), and Nigerian Man (see below). The Character Studies or 'masks' have always been the most popular (Dickens and all the Seafarers). Over the past couple of years, Wildlife Collections and many of the the descriptive 'High Relief' plaques (including 'Floral Plaques' and depictions of English life and historical monuments) have become popular as well. Bossons's life-like studies of dogs and cats are coveted by animal enthusiasts. Bossons were exported to nearly forty countries, so collector interest is widespread. Canada and the US were the most important importers, but the U.K., Australia, New Zealand, and South Africa, to mention a few, have become primary havens for collectors wanting to find the rarest specimens. In fact, the extremely rare Paul Kruger was only released in a limited number in South Africa, where he was President. (See photo.)

Major points to remember:

1) Not all will have the name incised under the collar (e.g., Syrian, Smuggler, Tibetan, and Tyrolean, see *Schroeder's* seventeenth edition for pictures).

2) Many character studies in gypsum plaster are produced in England that are not Bossons; to be specific, Legends, Naturecraft, and those incised with only 'Made in England.' Fraser-Art products are Bossons, so are products marked Briar Rose. Osborne Ivorex is not Bossons. Though all rights to Osborne products were purchased by Bossons in 1971, the appearance and coloring were changed and then issued under the Bossons name. (For pictures and technical details about plaster faces that are *not* Bossons, typical trademarks, Bossons Ivorex and Bossons Briar Rose Products, link on the net directly to www.donsbossons.com.)

3) With few exceptions — the Briar Rose Collection, the 6" Shelf Ornaments only carry Bossons stickers — and except for some prototypes and experimental editions, all products carry the incised copyright: Bossons, Congleton, England, World Copyright Reserved,' on the back and in most cases under the collars, along with that particular Bossons specific name. Also very popular today, Fraser-Art ware was invented by Ray Bossons; it was high quality ware with bold design and fine detail, made of hard PVC/Stonite® and colorfully hand painted. Here are a few examples of Fraser-Art with current values: Gazelle, $350.00 to $500.00; Copper Collection of Horatius Cocles, Richard Neville, and Viking head, $200.00 to $300.00 each; and clocks, mirrors, and barometers, $300.00 to $700.00. **Important:** The copyright date is most often a mold date and can help determine value. There are exceptions. (1) A few Character Masks were reissued at a later date, but in very limited quantities; in these cases, their scarcity overshadows their later copyright date. Examples: Chaka, 1962 – 67, $145.00, 1988 reissue, $175.00; Sardinian, 1962 – 69 (blue hat), $145.00, 1989 – 92 reissue (green hat), $185.00; and Nigerian Man, 1962 – 64 (darker coloring), $145.00, 1988 reissue, $185.00. (2) Sometimes incised copyright years do not represent the years of actual production. For instance, Abdhul and Eskimo, though not introduced until 1961 and 1969 respectively, can be found with 1958 copyrights. These are only a couple of examples where the copyright serves to confuse, rather than help determine values.

Though they can be used for authentication, painted initials on the underside are not a critical consideration when determining value. Incised initials, e.g. FW (Fred Wright), AB (Alica Brindley), and WRB

(W. Ray Bossons) are sculptors/modelers and are extremely important in authenticating Bossons and in some cases for evaluation. Prime examples are the rare first edition of the Cheyenne Indian without a red coat. Fred Wright's 'FW' must be incised in two places. 'WRB' (W. Ray Bossons) must be found on all six of the Shakespearean Characters. For the last editions of the Seafarers you will find 'AB' for Alice Brindley. (See Barbarossa, Clipper Captain, Coxwain, Fisherman, Jolly Tar, Bargee, Fisherwoman, and others.) Mold makers' incised initials on the backs of Bossons are extremely important when authenticating Bossons. In the early years (1946 – 50), some plaques and early Character Studies (1957 – 58) were released without the typical copyright, 'W. F. Bossons.' In these cases the only identifying marks are the single letters representing the mold maker. For example, K (Ken Potts), P (George Proudlove), and D (Damen Smith).

Suggestions for evaluating Bossons based on rarity and condition:

A. Attempt to determine the copyright (release) date from under the collar and/or on the back. (See examples above.)

B. Length of production helps determine rarity. With few exceptions, the earlier Character Heads (1958 – 63) and latest (1986 – 98) are found in fewer numbers. Production dates can be found in *Imagical World of Bossons, Vol. 1*, 1946 – 82, and *Vol. II*, 1982 – 94, by Dr. Robert E. Davis. (See advisor's Directory listing for information on this publication.) The final productions from 1994 to 1996 can be viewed in Bossons yearly brochures or by contacting our advisor. Examples in rare color combinations may be valued at 200% to 300% of retail. Included here are the special paintings of popular characters given to members of the International Bossons Collectors Society at yearly meetings from 1988 to 1999. They include Winston Churchill, Pierre, Paddy (1969 edition), Bargee, Smuggler, Fisherman, Boatman, Tyrolean, Jock, and Grenadier (1990 edition).

Condition is a major factor in determining the value of Bossons. If mint and in original colors, a Bossons is worth 100% of its retail value. Premium prices are obtained for only pristine, mint condition Bossons, either factory mint in original boxes or perfectly returned to their original structural and coloring beauty by a professional restoration artist recommended by Bossons.

Beware of fakes and look-alikes; above all, know your dealer. On the Internet, auctions are flooded with plaster 'faces' and figures claiming to be Bossons in mint condition, which are neither mint nor Bossons. (See advisor's directory listing in New Mexico for information on ordering a CD with valuable material relative to this practice.)

See Clubs, Newsletters and Catalogs in the Directory for International Bossons Collectors' Society (IBCS). Our advisor for this category is Dr. Don Hardisty; since 1984 he has been recommended by Bossons to restore their products. He is listed in the Directory under New Mexico. For restoration and purchasing questions, the Do's and Don't's of Bossons repairing, visit his website at www.donsbossons.com.

Seafarers and Dickens Characters

Values are for examples new and in original boxes. Note: Mr. Bumble was released in a very limited number with the coat collar and hat trim in gold leaf as opposed to the more common version with yellow oxide trim. Also, Mr. Micawber can be found in original editions with a black hat instead of the more common gray hat.

Aruj Barbarossa, No 229, 1994-96, from $175 to	215.00
Bargee, No 168, 1988-96, from $145 to	165.00
Betsey Trotwood, reissue, pk collar, 1981-96, from $85 to	125.00
Bill Sikes, No 25, 1964-96, from $85 to	100.00
Blackbeard, No 221, 1994-96, from $175 to	200.00
Boatman, No 45, 1967-96, from $65 to	85.00
Buccaneer, No 61 (1966-96), from $145 to	165.00
Captain Kid, No 141, 1983-96, from $85 to	125.00

Clipper Captain, No 220, 1994-96, from $185 to	250.00
Fagin, No 27, 1964-88, from $125 to	145.00
Fisherman, No 193, 1990-96, from $145 to	165.00
Jolly Tar, No 167, 1988-96, from $145 to	165.00
Lifeboatman, No 31, 1966-96, from $65 to	100.00
Miss Betsey Trotwood, bl collar, 1964-80, from $125 to	165.00
Mr Bumble, No 94, 1970-96, from $100 to	135.00
Mr Micawber, No 22, 1964-96, from $85 to	125.00
Mr Pickwick, No 21, 1964-96, from $85 to	125.00
Mrs Sarah Gamp, No 23, 1964-96, from $85 to	100.00
Old Salt, No 80, 1969-96, from $65 to	100.00

Paul Kruger, rarest of the rare Bossons, Series A, introduced in 1962, one edition of twelve, 8", in original condition, $6,500.00 to $7,900.00.

(From the collection of Dr. Don Hardisty)

Scrooge, No 94, 1981-96, from $145 to	165.00
Sea Captain, No 84, 1972-96, from $125 to	135.00
Sindbad the Sailor, No 250, 1995-96, from $185 to	225.00
Sir Henry Morgan, No 140, bl bow, 1985-96, from $135 to	150.00
Smuggler, No 32, 1964-96, from $65 to	85.00
Tony Weller, No 26, 1964-96, from $85 to	125.00
Uriah Heep, No 28, 1964-88, from $125 to	145.00

Bottle Openers

At the beginning of the nineteenth century, manufacturers began to seal bottles with a metal cap that required a new type of bottle opener. Now the screw cap and the flip top have made bottle openers nearly obsolete. There are many variations, some in combination with other tools. Many openers were used as means of advertising a product. Various materials were used, including silver and brass.

A figural bottle opener is defined as a figure designed for the sole purpose of lifting a bottle cap. The actual opener must be an integral part of the figure itself. A base-plate opener is one where the lifter is a separate metal piece attached to the underside of the figure. The major producers of iron figurals were Wilton Products, John Wright Inc., Gadzik Sales, and L & L Favors. Openers may be free-standing and three dimensional, wall hung or flat. They can be made of cast iron (often painted), brass, bronze, or aluminum.

Numbers within the listings refer to a reference book printed by the FBOC (Figural Bottle Opener Collectors) organization. Those seeking additional information are encouraged to contact FBOC, whose address can be found in the Directory under Clubs, Newsletters, and Catalogs. The items listed are all in excellent original condition unless noted otherwise.

Alligator, F-136, CI, VG **70.00**
Amish boy, F-31, pnt CI, rare, 1953, 4x2" **225.00**
Beer drinker, F-406, CI, Iron Art, from $25 to............................**35.00**
Billy goat, F-74a, aluminum, 2¾x1⅞" **15.00**

Caddy, F-44, painted cast iron, $430.00 (brass, $300.00). (Photo courtesy Charlie Reynolds)

Canadian goose, F-105e, brass-plated CI, Norlin, 2⅛x3¾" **30.00**
Cat, F-95, brass, 2¼x3" **40.00**
Cocker spaniel, F-80, brn & wht pnt CI, EX **80.00**
Donkey, F-60, CI, pnt traces **20.00**
Donkey, F-60a, aluminum, 3½x3¼" **15.00**
Elephant, F-46, CI **35.00**
Fisherman, F-30b, pnt brass, Riverside, 4x2½", EX......................**30.00**
Flamingo, F-120, CI, hollow, Wilton Products, EX, from $100 to...**135.00**
Goat, F-71, CI, tall..**70.00**
Lamppost Drunk, F-1, CI, 4⅛"..**15.00**
Lobster, F-167, CI, EX pnt **32.00**
Monkey, F-89b, aluminum, 2⅝"..**15.00**
Nude native girl kneeling, zinc, 1950s...**25.00**
Parrot, F-108, CI, from $30 to..**40.00**
Pelican, F-129, CI, EX pnt **75.00**
Salted pretzel, F-230 ....**50.00**
Sea horse, F-140, brass, Canada **30.00**
Setter, F-79, CI, EX mc pnt..**80.00**
Squirrel, F-93, brass, 2⅝" **15.00**
Trout, F-159, CI...**120.00**
4-Eyed lady, F-407, CI, wall mt, EX...**130.00**
4-Eyed man, F-413, CI, wall mt, EX, from $40 to **50.00**

Bottles and Flasks

As far back as the first century B.C., the Romans preferred blown glass containers for their pills and potions. Though you're not apt to find many of those, you will find bottles of every size, shape, and color made to hold perfume, ink, medicine, soda, spirits, vinegar, and many other liquids. American business firms preferred glass bottles in which to package their commercial products and used them extensively from the late eighteenth century on. Bitters bottles contained 'medicine' (actually herb-flavored alcohol), and judging from the number of these found today, their contents found favor with many! Because of a heavy tax imposed on the sale of liquor in seventeenth-century England by King George, who hoped to curtail alcohol abuse among his subjects, bottlers simply added 'curative' herbs to their brew and thus avoided taxation. Since gin was taxed in America as well, the practice continued in this country. Scores of brands were sold; among the most popular were Dr. H.S. Flint & Co. Quaker Bitters, Dr. Kaufman's Anti-Cholera Bitters, and Dr. J. Hostetter's Stomach Bitters. Most bitters bottles were made in shades of amber, brown, and aquamarine. Clear glass was used to a lesser extent, as were green tones. Blue, amethyst, red-brown, and milk glass examples are rare. (Please note that color is a strong factor when pricing bottles. For example, an amber Hostetter's bitters sells for $25.00 or less, but a green variant can bring hundreds of dollars. An aqua scroll flask may bring $50.00, but a cobalt blue variation will command over $1,000.00.)

Perfume or scent bottles were produced abroad by companies all over Europe from the late sixteenth century on. Perfume making became such a prolific trade that as a result beautifully decorated bottles were fashionable. In America they were produced in great quantities by Stiegel in 1770 and by Boston and Sandwich in the early nineteenth century. Cologne bottles were first made in about 1830 and toilet-water bottles in the 1880s. Rene Lalique produced fine scent bottles from as early as the turn of the century. The first were one-of-a-kind creations done in the cire perdue method. He later designed bottles for the Coty Perfume Company with a different style for each Coty fragrance.

Spirit flasks from the nineteenth century were blown in specially designed molds with varied motifs including political subjects, railroad trains, and symbolic devices. The most commonly used colors were amber, dark brown, and green.

Pitkin flasks were the creation of the Pitkin Glass Works which operated in East Manchester, Connecticut, from 1783 to 1830. However, other glasshouses in New England and the Midwest copied the Pitkin flask style. All are known as Pitkins.

From the twentieth century, early pop and beer bottles are very collectible as is nearly every extinct commercial container. Dairy bottles are a relatively new area of interest; look for round bottles in good condition with both city and state as well as a nice graphic relating to the farm or the dairy.

Bottles may be dated by the methods used in their production. For instance, a rough pontil indicates a date before 1845. After the bottle was blown, a pontil rod was attached to the bottom, a glob of molten glass acting as the 'glue.' This allowed the glassblower to continue to manipulate the extremely hot bottle until it was finished. From about 1845 until approximately 1860, the molten glass 'glue' was omitted. The rod was simply heated to a temperature high enough to cause it to afix itself to the bottle. When the rod was snapped off, a metallic residue was left on the base of the bottle; this is called an 'iron pontil.' (The presence of a pontil scar thus indicates early manufacture and increases the value of a bottle.) A seam that reaches from base to lip marks a machine-made bottle from after 1903, while an applied or hand-finished lip points to an early mold-blown bottle. The Industrial Revolution saw keen competition between manufacturers, and as a result, scores of patents were issued. Many concentrated on various types of closures; the crown bottle cap, for instance, was patented in 1892. If a manufacturer's name is present, consulting a book on marks may help you date your bottle. For more information we recommend *Bottle Pricing Guide, 3rd Edition*, by Hugh Cleveland.

Among our advisors for this category are Madeleine France (see the Directory under Florida), Mark Vuono (Connecticut), and Monsen and Baer (Virginia). Robert Doyle (New York) advises on barber bottles. Examples in the following listings (most of which have been sold through cataloged auctions), are assumed to be in clear glass unless color is indicated. See also Advertising, various companies; Blown Glass; Blown Three-Mold Glass; California Perfume Company; Czechoslovakia; De Vilbiss; Fire Fighting; Lalique; Steuben; Zanesville Glass.

Key:
am — applied mouth
bbl — barrel
bt — blob top
b3m — blown 3-mold
cm — collared mouth
fl — filigree
fm — flared mouth
gm — ground mouth
gp — graphite pontil
grd — ground pontil

GW — Glass Works
ip — iron pontil
op — open pontil
ps — pontil scar
rm — rolled mouth
sb — smooth base
sl — sloping
sm — sheared mouth
tm — tooled mouth

Barber Bottles

Clear w/mc Property of Lucky Tiger... celluloid label, sb, 7¾" 300.00
Cobalt w/brn & wht geometric decor, tm, ps, 8" 130.00
Cranberry opal w/bl daisies & ferns, melon sides, rm, ps, 7¼" 350.00
Cranberry opal w/wht coral pattern, rm, ps, 8⅛" 325.00
Cranberry opal w/wht swirls to left, rm, 6⅞" 110.00
Deep purple amethyst, emb ribs, wht windmill & Toilet Water, 7¾"..500.00
Deep purple amethyst w/wht girl & Vegederma, rm, ps, 8⅛" 350.00
Emerald gr w/yel & gold Art Nouveau decor, rm, ps, 8⅛" 250.00
Frosted flashed ruby w/mc flowers, rm, ps, 8" 275.00
Grape amethyst w/yel & gold Art Nouveau floral, rm, ps, 7⅞"...200.00

Lime green with gold and enameling, sheared and polished mouth, ca 1885 – 1925, $400.00 for the pair. (Photo courtesy Pacific Glass Auctions)

Milk glass w/blk & gold birds & cattails & Bay Rum, 8¾" 190.00
Milk glass w/mc poppies & Witch Hazel, ps, 9" 200.00
Milk glass w/mc swallow & flower decor & Bay Rum, ps, 9".......170.00
Teal gr w/wht Mary Gregory-style boy, sb, 7¾" 650.00
Turq opal, Hobnail, rm, 7⅛", NM 50.00
Turq opal w/swirls to left, rm, 6¼" 140.00
Turq opal w/wht coral pattern, rm, ps, 8¼" 325.00
Wht opal w/cranberry stripes, rm, sb, 7⅜" 375.00

Bitters Bottles

Bourbon Whiskey copper puce bbl, am, sb, sm chip, 9¼" 275.00
Brown's Celebrated Indian Herb...1868, med amber, Queen, 12⅛" 950.00
Bryant's Stomach, olive gr 8-sided lady's leg, ps, 12½".............2,500.00
Buhrer's Gentian, yel amber, sl cm, sb, stain, 9"...........................60.00
Celebrated Crown...Chevalier...Agents, med amber, sb, 8⅞"......325.00
Clarke's Vegetable Sherry Wine, bl aqua, sl cm, sb, 14"...........1,100.00
Dingen's Napolean Cocktail, med gr, ip, lady's leg drum, 10¼" 10,500.00
Doctor Fisch's...Pat 1866, med golden amber, fish, 11⅞" 300.00

Dr Skinner's Sherry Wine, aqua w/olive striations, am, 8⅝".......300.00
Drake's Plantation...Pat 1862, golden yel, 6-log cabin, 9⅞".....2,200.00
Drake's Plantation...Pat 1862, med apricot puce, 6-log cabin, 10" ..750.00
Drake's Plantation...Pat 1862, med cherry puce, 6-log cabin, 9¾" ..850.00
Greeley's Bourbon, deep amethyst, sb, bbl, 9½" 5,000.00
Greeley's Bourbon, smoky olive topaz, sb, bbl, 9⅜".................1,700.00
Hall's...Established 1842, med amber, bbl, EX label, 9¼" 250.00
Holtzermann's Pat Stomach, med amber, 4-roof log cabin, 9¾", EX.....80.00
Hunki Dori, med amber, sl cm, sb, seed bubbles, 8⅞" 400.00
JW Hutchinson's Tonic, deep olive gr, sl cm, sb, bubbles, 8⅞"......3,250.00
Kelly's Old Cabin...Pat 1863, amber, sl cm, sb, log cabin, 9¼".....2,000.00
Lediard's Celebrated Stomach, emerald gr, dbl cm, ip, 10⅛".......1,800.00
Lediard's Celebrated Stomach, teal gr, am, sb, 10⅛" 1,500.00
National, med amber to yel amber, Pat 1867 on sb, ear of corn, 12⅜"...550.00
Old Homestead Wild Cherry, golden yel amber, sb, cabin, 9⅝".....500.00
Old Sachem & Wigwam Tonic, deep strawberry puce, sb, bbl, 9⅜"......600.00
Old Sachem & Wigwam Tonic, golden yel w/olive tone, sb, bbl, 9¼"...850.00
Reed's..., med golden yel amber, sb, lady's leg, 12½"...................325.00
Russ St Domingo...NY, med yel w/olive tone, sb, 9⅞"................600.00
St Drake's 1860 Plant'n X Pat 1862, deep purple (blk), 10" 2,750.00
St Drake's 1860 Plant'n X Pat 1862, med amber, 4-log cabin, 10⅛".....210.00

Black Glass Bottles

Many early European and American bottles are deep, dark green, or amber in color. Collectors refer to such coloring as black glass. Before held to light, the glass is so dark it appears to be black.

Chestnut flask, med yel olive amber, dbl cm, ps, seed bubbles, 9"...110.00
Magnum, olive amber, am, ps, English, ca 1770-80, 10⅛".......1,200.00
Medicine, deep olive amber, beveled corner panels, ps, 7" 160.00
Pancake onion, opal (bl) olive amber, string mouth, 5½"........2,100.00
Seal: A Von Niessen, opal olive amber w/pressed panels, 8⅛" ...1,100.00
Seal: Class of 1847 W, yel olive amber, Dyottville GW on base, 11"...300.00
Seal: IBB, deep olive amber, ps, dbl cm, 1790-1810, 9¼" 700.00
Seal: IF 1822 Patent, med yel olive, mk ps base, 8¾".................325.00
Seal: IH:M, deep olive amber, am, ps, stain, 9½" 500.00
Seal: John Winn Jr, deep olive amber, mk ps base, 9".................300.00
Seal: Lupton, deep olive amber, dbl cm, sb, b3m, 10¾".............200.00
Seal: Madera, med olive gr w/lt amber tone, dbl cm, ps, 12¼"......200.00
Seal: Rousdon Jubilee 1887, deep olive amber, sl dbl cm, sb, 11¾"...200.00
Seal: 1770 James Oakes Bury, olive amber, am, ps, 1770s, 10¼"...300.00
Snuff, yel deep olive gr, tm, sb, 9⅝" 150.00
Snuff/medicine, olive amber, beveled corners, wide mouth, ps, 5¾"...325.00
Utility, yel amber, fm, op, sm stain, 6" 70.00

Blown Glass Bottles and Flasks

Chestnut flask, deep teal gr, am & hdl, 8⅜" 120.00
Chestnut flask, dk teal gr, appl lip & hdl, 6⅜" 120.00
Chestnut flask, med pk puce w/dk striations, ip, 8½" 650.00
Club bottle, cornflower bl, 24 right-swirl ribs, beehive form, 8", NM....900.00
Flask, sapphire bl w/2 dk striations, 24-rib, sm, Midwest, 7", EX....4,000.00
Pitkin flask, bright yel gr, 16 right-swirl ribs, sm, ps, Midwest, 7"..850.00
Pitkin flask, golden amber, 36 left-swirl ribs, sm, ps, Midwest, 6"...1,100.00
Pitkin flask, med emerald gr, 16 broken right-swirl ribs, ps, 6"....475.00
Pitkin flask, med emerald gr, 30 broken right-swirl ribs, 6⅝"......425.00
Pitkin flask, med to dk sea gr, 32 right-swirl ribs, sm, Midwest, 8" ..800.00
Pitkin flask, sea green, 32 left-swirl ribs, sm, ps, Midwest, 6½"...500.00
Pocket flask, bright med amethyst, 20-rib, sm, ps, att Mantua, 6½"...2,100.00
Pocket flask, bright olive yel, 24-rib, sm, ps, Midwest, 4¾" 1,300.00
Pocket flask, bright yel gr, 14 left-swirl ribs, Midwest, rare sz, 4" ..3,750.00
Pocket flask, bright yel w/lt olive, 20-rib, sm, ps, Midwest, 6½"..800.00
Pocket flask, deep amber, 24 left-swirl ribs, sm, ps, Midwest, 4¾"...750.00

Cologne, Perfume, and Toilet Water Bottles

Atomizer, bl cut to clear, 8 rows of ovals, att Fr, 7" 135.00
Atomizer, bl cut to clear pinwheels, unmk, 5½" 50.00
Atomizer, HP birds on reddish sky, Marfranc...France, tall..........600.00
Blown, lady's hand w/wedding ring, unmk, 5¼" L 35.00
Bright med amethyst, 16 left-swirl ribs, att Pittsburgh, 1820-60, 5"...1,300.00
Canary, corseted/paneled, tm, sb, att Sandwich, 1860-80, 4⅝"....4,750.00
Cobalt (deep), sb, 12-sided, ca 1860-80, 5" 80.00
Crown top, clear glass rollerskate, Salon Palmer, 5" 45.00
Crown top, clown w/flowers, fine HP, #24627, Bavaria, 2¾" 198.00
Crown top, dachshund (comic), red-brn, mk Germany, 3"............75.00
Crown top, lady holding urn, mc, unmk, 3¼" 145.00
Crown top, Pierrette w/arms around bowl, Germany #14937, 3¼" ..165.00
Cut o/l, red/crystal geometric pyramidal form, Saks Fifth Ave, 5½"...165.00
Cut o/l, violet/clear w/silver cap, slightly waisted, 3¼" 660.00

Commercial Perfume Bottles

One of the most popular and growing areas of perfume bottle collecting is what are called 'commercial' perfume bottles. They are called commercial because they were sold with perfume in them — in a sense one pays for the perfume and the bottle is free. Collectors especially value bottles that retain their original label and box, called a perfume presentation. If the bottle is unopened, so much the better. Rare fragrances and those from the 1920s are highly prized. 'Tis a sweet, sweet hobby. Our advisors are Randy Monsen and Rod Baer; they are listed in the Directory under Virginia.

Bourjois, Kobako, frosted snuff bottle form, 2½", red/blk inro box ...385.00
Bourjois, On the Wind set (2, w/orange caps), 3¾" & 1¾", MIB ..77.00
Christian Dior, Poison, metal & glass bracelet, 4" dia, MIB........145.00
Ciro, Chevalier de Nuit, clear w/frosted top, mini replica, 2½"...300.00
Corday, Voiage à Paris, clear horseshoe-like shape, 2¼", MIB 135.00
D'Orsay, Intoxication, clear/pleated, w/gold cap, 2⅛", NMIB.....135.00
E Arden, It's You, clear/frosted hand w/vase, bl enamel, 6¼" ..2,000.00
E Arden, On Dit, frosted w/emb women (2) whispering, 4¼" 110.00
Fabergè, Tigress, clear w/gold label, clear disk top, 3⅛", MIB 65.00

Grenoville, Casanova, glass bottle encased in wood with Casanova graphics, wood overcap, empty, 4", $660.00. (Photo courtesy Monsen and Baer)

H Rubenstein, Gala Performance, clear, dancing lady, 5¾" 275.00
H Rubenstein, Heaven Scent, angel w/metal cap, 2⅜" 80.00
Houbigant, Le Parfum Idèal, clear w/Nouveau gold label, 4¼", +box ...55.00
J Patou, Amour Armour, clear w/gold & bl labels, 3½", +box 440.00
Lenthèric, Miracle, clear rectangle, 2 labels, 2", MIB...................35.00
M Rochas, Femme, wht w/blk lace, long dauber, 2⅝", empty in purse....250.00

Matchabelli, Royal Gardenia, frosted crown, empty, 3⅞" 200.00
Saville, clear w/lady & parasol label, blk cap, 2⅝", empty, +box....45.00
Saville, Mischief, blk w/chrome cap, 1¾", M in dancing couple box...110.00
Worth Dans la Nuit, bl ball, molded moon stopper, empty, 1⅞"...55.00

Dairy Bottles

Alamito Dairy, Omaha Nebraska, covered wagon pyro, cream top, 1-qt..110.00
Anderston Bros & Trojan warrior, bl pyro, rnd, 10-oz....................8.00
Borden's, ruby red w/wht letters, squat, 1-qt 1,750.00
Buena Vista Farms, Pulaski VA, red pyro, 1-qt............................240.00
Carnation, RD Thompson Dairy, Eugene OR, red pyro, cream top, 1-qt....365.00
Cloverleaf Blue Ribbon Farms, Stockton CA, red pyro Mordentop, 1-qt ..25.00
Ferer's Dairy Products, Pocatella ID, red pyro, 1937, 1-qt 160.00
Fountain Dairy Farm, JC Charvat, Hopewell VA, red pyro, 1-pt...215.00
Kane Dairy, Kane PA, orange pyro, 1-qt......................................90.00
KY American Dairy, Hilo, emb words, Hawaiian, 1-pt................315.00
Mt Desert Island Dairies, Barharbour ME, red pyro, 1-qt 235.00
MY Williams Jr, Fort Edward NY Hilltop Farms, cows, maroon pyro, 1-qt....28.00
Nashville Pure Milk Co, amber w/wht pyro, 1-qt 160.00
Neumann Milk Co, Mars Hill IN, clear w/emb letters, 1-qt........160.00
New Ulm Dairy, N Ulm MN, 50th Anniversary of Pearl Harbor, 2-color, sq ..12.00
Onatru Farm, Ridgefield CT, goat on bk, blk pyro, 1-qt............100.00
Party Tonight/You...Cream Top, gr/yel pyro, no location, sq, 1-qt ...14.00
Riggins Inc, Eastern IN's Most Modern Milk Plant, red & yel pyro, 1-qt....300.00
Springport Dairy Farm, blk pyro, Buy War Bonds, rnd, 1-qt 400.00
Thomas Bros Dairy, Frankfort IN, clear w/emb letters, 1-qt........135.00
Waldron's Dairy, Califon NJ, red pyro, rnd, 1-pt..........................15.00

Figural Bottles

Bear, Distrie Mercator Sa/Anvers Belique, sb, tm, 1900, 10" 170.00
Cannon, dk amber w/overall outside frost, sb, tm, bubbles, 9½" ..375.00
Car, Mirabel across hood, deep bl aqua, tm, 3⅞" L 275.00
Cat, clear frosted, rm, sb, 1¾"...40.00
Christmas tree, olive gr, Emb Kyselak at sb, 9½" 60.00
Grant's Tomb, milk glass monument w/pewter bust top, 10".......700.00
Hand holding dagger, turq, Depose at side of base, ps, tm, 11½"...350.00
Joan of Arc, Depose emb on side at base, ps, no stopper, 14" 65.00
Kummel Bear, grape amethyst or milk glass, sb, 11" 100.00
Lemon, Paul Mangiet Will Hand You One, pale aqua, 4¼" L.......80.00
Monkey on bbl pulling hat down, milk glass, sb, 9⅜"..............1,050.00
Policeman, milk glass w/partial gold pnt, ps, tm, 9½" 725.00
Windmill, turq w/mc enameling, hinged top, 1890-1920, 8" 185.00

Flasks

Baltimore/Liberty, GVI-3, clear aqua, sm, ps, pt 350.00
Bent Arm/All Seeing Eye, GIV-43, yel amber, sm, ps, pt 325.00
Clasped Hands/Eagle, GXII-28, med amber, am, sb, chip, pt.........80.00
Clasped Hands/Eagle, GXII-31, amber, am, sb, ½-pt....................170.00
Clasped Hands/Eagle, GXII-43, deep amber, dbl cm, ip, calabash 550.00
Columbia/Eagle, GI-121, aqua, tm, ps, potstone, pt 180.00
Cornucopia/Urn, GII-4, olive gr, sm, op, pt 130.00
Eagle/Cluster of Grapes, GII-55, aqua, tm, ps, crude, qt..............140.00
Eagle/Coffin & Hay, GII-50, pale aqua, tm, ps, ½-pt 120.00
Eagle/Cornucopia, GII-45, aqua, tm, op, ½-pt.............................125.00
Eagle/Eagle, GII-24, moonstone opal, tm, ps, flake, pt.............1,900.00
Eagle/Eagle, GII-26, deep aqua, appl dbl cm, sb, chip, qt............160.00
Eagle/Eagle, GII-31, pale gr aqua, sm, ps, sm stain, qt 160.00
Eagle/Eagle, GII-78, olive yel, tm, ps, qt 375.00
Eagle/Furled Flag, GII-53, aqua, sm, ps, unusual short neck, pt....140.00
Eagle/Furled Flag, GII-54, aqua, tm, ps, pt 170.00
Eagle/Kensington GW, GII-43, aqua, ps, ps, dullness, ½-pt 140.00

Eagle/Willington Glass Co, GII-62, med olive gr, sm, sb, pt 300.00
Ear of Corn/Monument, GVI-4, aqua, am, sb, lt scratches, qt 120.00
Ear of Corn/Monument, GVI-6, aqua, tm, ps, pt 180.00
Fells Schooner/Monument, GVI-2, straw yel w/olive tone, ps, ½-pt ...1,000.00
Franklin/Dyott, GI-96, aqua, tm, ps, lt stain, qt 300.00
Franklin/Franklin, GI-97, aqua, tm, ps, qt 160.00
Hunter/Fisherman, GXIII-4, golden yel amber, sl cm, ip, calabash 400.00
Jenny Lind/Glasshouse, GI-101, aqua, sl cm, ps, calabash 150.00
Jenny Lind/Glasshouse, GI-103, bl aqua, sl cm, op, stain, calabash 60.00
Jenny Lind/Glasshouse, GI-104, bl aqua, am, ps, calabash 130.00
Kossuth/Steam Frigate, GI-112, bl aqua, sl cm, ip, calabash........275.00
Masonic Arch/Eagle, GIV-24, olive amber, sm, ps, ½-pt............300.00
Masonic Arch/Eagle, GIV-27, bl aqua, tm, ps, pt.........................700.00
Masonic Arch/Eagle, GIV-37, aqua, sm, ps, pt............................170.00
Masonic Arch/Masonic Arch, GIV-28, pale bl aqua, tm, ps, ½-pt 325.00
Prospector/Eagle, GXI-11, deep bl aqua, am, ps, pt 170.00
Prospector/Eagle, GXI-15, ice bl, am, sb, pt 450.00
Prospector/Eagle, GXI-25, bl aqua, am, sb, pt 220.00
Schooner/Sunburst, GX-8, aqua, sm, ps, ½-pt 160.00
Scroll, GIX-10a, sapphire bl, sm, op, crack, pt............................450.00
Spring Garden GW/Log Cabin, GXIII-58, yel olive, op, bruise, pt 1,500.00
Stag/Tree, GX-1, aqua, tm, ps, open bubble, pt...........................110.00
Success to Railroad/Horse Pulling Cart, GV-4, yel amber w/olive, pt ..300.00
Summer Tree/Winter Tree, GX-15, ice or cornflower bl, dbl cm, pt...130.00
Sunburst, GVIII-2, deep clear gr, tm, ps, pt 1,100.00
Sunburst, GVIII-3, med yel olive gr, sm, ps, flaw, pt...................450.00
Sunburst, GVIII-25, aqua, sm, ps, ½-pt.......................................275.00
Sunburst, GVIII-27, lt aqua (almost clear), sm, ps, ½-pt 200.00
Sunburst, GVIII-29, deep bl aqua, tm, ps, pt 275.00
Tree/Sheaf of Wheat, GXIII-46, dk cherry puce, dbl cm, ps, calabash...1,000.00
Washington/Adams & Jefferson, GI-14, aqua, sm, ps, pt.............275.00
Washington/Adams & Jefferson, GI-14, med bl gr, tm, ps, pt, NM ..1,800.00
Washington/Eagle, GI-16, aqua, tm, ps, pt.................................450.00
Washington/Eagle, GI-26, deep aqua, tm, ps, qt, NM 250.00
Washington/Jackson, GI-31, med yel amber, sm, ps, pt 250.00

Washington/Jackson, GI-34, medium olive green, tooled mouth, crude with many bubbles, pontil scar, 1825 – 1835, half-pint, $750.00.

Washington/Jackson, GI-34, yel amber, sm, op, ½-pt.................400.00
Washington/Monument, GI-20, gr aqua, tm, ps, haze, pt............240.00
Washington/Monument, GI-21, aqua, sm, ps, wear, qt................125.00
Washington/plain, GI-47, lt to med bl gr, dbl collar, ps, qt 450.00
Washington/Sheaf of Grain, GI-58, bl aqua, sl am, pt....................90.00
Washington/Taylor, GI-24, aqua, tm, ps, pt 170.00
Washington/Taylor, GI-25, bl aqua, tm, ps, qt 140.00
Washington/Taylor, GI-38, med emerald gr, sm, ps, pt............1,700.00
Washington/Taylor, GI-39, deep bl gr, tm, op, qt..........................700.00
Washington/Taylor, GI-39, med bl gr, sm, op, qt 900.00
Washington/Taylor, GI-54, lt to med teal bl, am, ps, flaw, qt......170.00
Washington/Tree, GI-35, aqua, am, ps, calabash 130.00
Washington/Tree, GI-36, aqua, dbl collar, ps, calabash 375.00
Westford/Sheaf of Grain, GXIII-26, olive gr, dbl cm, sb, pt 230.00

Food Bottles and Jars

Peppersauce, cathedral, aqua, dbl cm, open/p, 6-sided, 8¾" 70.00
Peppersauce, cathedral, deep aqua, dbl cm, ip, sq, 8⅜" 70.00
Peppersauce, cathedral, lt emerald gr, dbl cm, sb, 10¼" 90.00
Pickle, bl aquamarine, cathedral panels, rm, sb, 11¾"................275.00
Pickle, bl aquamarine, cylindrical w/5 flutes, 2-pc mold, 10½" ...130.00
Pickle, Stoddard Cloverleaf, red amber, sb, rm, 8¼"...................500.00
Utility, med yel olive, fm, op, crude/bubbles, 5"..........................150.00
Vinegar, This Trade Mark...East Ridge NH, cobalt, tm, sb, 11⅜" ..600.00
Wide mouth, bright olive gr, fm, ps, 9⅜" 160.00

Ink Bottles

Cone, Drape, med cobalt, dbl cm, op, 2½" 4,000.00
Cottage, bl aqua, tm, sb, flakes, 2½" 100.00
Cottage, SI Comp, bl aqua, tm, sb, flake, 2¾" 140.00
Cylinder, Gaylord's Superior...Boston, deep olive gr, ps, 5⅞" ...4,250.00
Cylinder, Hover's Fine...Phila label, yel amber, sm, 2⅝" 450.00
Cylinder, JS Mason Philada, lt bl gr, fm, ps, 4½" 650.00
Cylinder, Stafford's..., med teal bl, tm, pour spout, sb, 10" 110.00
Funnel, lt cobalt, sb, 1¾" 80.00
Geometric, deep olive gr, disc tm, ps, 1⅞x2¼"............................140.00
Harrison's Columbia, aqua, rm, ps, 8-sided, haze, 1⅞"..................80.00
Harrison's Columbia, deep cobalt, rm, ps, 2", EX.........................750.00
Igloo, bird (emb), aqumarine, sm, sb, 1½" 110.00
Teakettle, clear cat figural, gm, sb, 2⅛".......................................300.00
Teakettle, dk powder bl opaque, gm, sb, 2", NM...........................325.00
Teakettle, fiery opal milk glass, sm, sb, 8-sided, 2⅛"...................300.00
Teakettle, milk glass, gm, sb, 2" 100.00
Umbrella, bl gr, rm, op, 8-sided, whittled, 2½"...............................240.00
Umbrella, deep tobacco amber, tm, ps, 8-sided, 2⅜" 160.00
Umbrella, emerald gr, sm, rough op, 8-sided, 2⅝" 210.00
Umbrella, Hover Phila, lt bl gr, rm, ps, 8-sided, 2¼" 700.00
Umbrella, Hover Phila, lt to med bl gr, rm, ps, 12-sided, 1⅞"...1,600.00
Umbrella, James S Mason & Co, bl aqua, rm, ps, 8-sided, 2⅜" ..180.00
Umbrella, SO Dunbar Taunton, bl aqua, rm, 8-sided, crude, 2⅝"............145.00

Medicine Bottles

Brant's Indian Balsam, bl aqua, sl cm, ps, 8-sided, 7⅜" 140.00
C Brinckerhoff's Health...NY, yel olive amber, sl cm, ip, 7¼", EX....700.00
C Heimstreet & Co Troy NY, med cobalt, dbl cm, ps, 8-sided, 7" ..250.00
Carter's Spanish Mixture, yel amber, sl dbl cm, ip, flake, 8"........950.00
Dandelion & Tomato Panacea..., sl cm, ps, whittled, 9"..............750.00
Davis & Miller Druggists, med sapphire bl, disk mouth, ip, 7¾"......3,500.00
Doctor Warren's Cough Mixture, backward S, fm, ps, 4" 375.00
Dr E Blecker's Tonic...Fever, deep bl aqua, sl cm, ps, 6⅞"........1,000.00
Dr Fahnestock's Vermifuge, bl aqua, rm, ps, lt stain, 4" 30.00
Dr Guysott's Compound..., deep brilliant bl gr, sl cm, ip, 9¼" ..3,500.00
Dr JB Henion's Sure Cure for Malaria, cobalt, disk am, sb, 6⅜" 8,500.00
Dr McLane's American Worm Specific, bl aqua, rm, ps, 3⅞" 130.00
Dr Moore's Venereal Antiseptic, med golden amber, 1892 on sb, 8" 375.00
Dr Venable's Vegetable Panokesia, lt ice bl, sl cm, ps, sm stain, 8" .750.00
Dw Wistar's Balsam of Wild Cherry, aqua, fm, ps, 8-sided, 6¼" 170.00
ES Reed's Sons Apothecary, milk glass, sb, orig label, 4⅝" 140.00
From Laboratory of GW Merchant, deep bl aqua w/gr tone, 5¾" ...325.00

Gell's Dalby's Carminative, aqua, tm, ps, milky stain, 3⅞" 160.00
Gleet Seven Day Gonorrhea, cobalt, tm, sb, 4⅞" 600.00
Griswold's Malarian Antidote, bl aqua, am, ps, rectangular, dug, 7" 300.00
Gun Wa's Chinese Remedy...Harmless, bright golden yel amber, 8⅛" ..750.00
GW Merchant Chemist Lockport NY, med bl gr, sl cm, ip, 7"....475.00
GW Merchant Lockport NY, emerald gr, sl cm, ps, 5⅛" 230.00
GW Merchant Lockport NY, med bl gr, sl cm, ps, 5⅛" 150.00
Henshaw & Edmands Druggists, deep bl gr, am, ps, 10⅝" 2,750.00
Jr Nichols & Co Chemists Boston, deep cobalt, tm, sb, 9⅜" 300.00
Lindsey's Blood Searcher, med emerald gr, sl cm, sb, chip, 9¼" ...1,000.00
Log Cabin Extract, med yel amber, 1887 on sb, EX label, 8¼" 425.00
LQC Wishart's Pine Tree...1859, med emerald gr, cm, sb, stain, 9½" 250.00
Mad MJ Goodman's Excelsior Pearl Drops, milk glass, sb, 4⅝" ...100.00
Maguire Druggist St Louis MO, lt apple gr, sl cm, ps, 5¾" 120.00
MB Robert's Vegetable Embrocation, lt bl gr, sl cm, 5⅛" 120.00
Old Dr Townsend's...NY, lt emerald gr, dbl cm, ps, flake, 6½" ..1,600.00
Purcell Ladd & Co Richmond VA, aqua, am, ps, whittled, 9¾" ...1,000.00
Shaker Fluid Extract Valerian, bl aqua, fm, stain, 3⅞" 70.00
Swaim's Panacea Philada, lt to med olive gr, sl cm, ps, bubbles, 8" ...650.00
Swaim's Panacea Philada, med olive gr, sl cm, ps, bubbles, 8" 950.00
USA Hosp Dept, lt cobalt, tm, sb, stain, 3¼" 275.00
USA Hosp Dept, yel olive gr, dbl cm, sb, w/label, 9⅜" 750.00
Wake Up Wake Up, deep olive gr, sl dbl cm, ip, triangular, 11⅞" ...2,500.00
Warner's Safe Cure, red amber, am, sb, 9⅜" 300.00

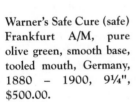

Warner's Safe Cure (safe) Frankfurt A/M, pure olive green, smooth base, tooled mouth, Germany, 1880 – 1900, 9¼", $500.00.

Mineral Water, Beer, and Soda Bottles

B Carter West Chester (in slug plate), med bl gr, am, ip, 7" 500.00
Buffum Pittsburgh, cobalt, sl cm, ip, 7½" 600.00
Buffum...& Lemon Mineral..., med cobalt, sl cm, ip, 10-sided, 7⅞"...850.00
C Cleminshaw...Troy NY, med sapphire bl, am, ip, 7", NM 375.00
City Bottling Works Toledo OH, lt to med sapphire bl, sb, 6⅜" ...400.00
E Roussel Philada..., med cobalt, sl cm, ip, 7½"..........................150.00
Excelsior Ginger Ale 1852..., med amber, bt, sb, 7¼", NM.........250.00
F emb on flattened 10-pin, bl gr, sl cm, op, 8½" 550.00
Fondersmith's Beer, deep root beer amber, cm, sb, 12-sided, 9⅞" ..600.00
Gleason & Cole Pittsbg..., cobalt, sl cm, ip, 10-sided, 7¾" 850.00
Hess Superior..., med cobalt, sl cm, ip, 10-sided, 7⅝".................275.00
Hutchinson Celebrated...Chicago, med cobalt, am, ip, 7¼" 400.00
Improved Mineral, cobalt, bt, ip, 8-sided, 7" 300.00
J Boardman NY, med yel olive gr, sl cm, ip, 7¼" 425.00
J Kennedy Pittsburgh JK, pure yel lime gr, am, ip, 7⅜" 1,200.00
J Steel (in slug plate) Premium, med bl gr, bt, ip, 8-sided, 7⅝"...425.00
J Steel Easton PA (in slug plate), med bl gr, dbl cm, ip, squat, 7" ...300.00
J&A Dearborn NY (in slug plate), med teal bl, sl cm, ip, 6¾"....275.00
J&T Percy (4-point star), med bl gr, bt, ip, 7¼" 450.00
JB Bryant Wilmington, med emerald gr, sl dbl cm, ip, 7", NM ...700.00
JH Magee (in slug plate), med cobalt, dbl cm, ip, crude, 7⅜".....800.00
JT Brown Chemist Boston....Water, med bl gr, bt, sb, torpedo, 8¾" ..250.00
P Conway Bottler, cobalt, bt, ip, lt shoulder wear, 7¼" 100.00
P Stumpf & Co...Richmond VA, golden yel amber, am, sb, 8¼"...230.00
Quinan & Studer 1888 Savannah GA, deep cobalt, tm, sb, 7⅞" ..190.00
Roussel's...Silver Medal 1847..., bl gr, sl cm, ip, 7½", NM 130.00
Saratoga (star) Spring, yel amber, am, sb, seed bubbles, qt, 9⅜" 190.00
Seitz & Bro Easton PA, cobalt, bt, sb, 8-sided, 7¼", NM...........200.00
Steinke & Kornahrens...SC, deep cobalt, sl cm, ip, 8-sided, 8¼" ..400.00
Take & Veile Lager...PA (in slug plate), med bl gr, sb, 7¼" 650.00
TW Gillett New Haven, cobalt, bt, ip, 8-sided, 7⅝", NM..........300.00
Unembossed torpedo, med bl gr, sl cm, sb, 8½" 100.00
Waring Webster & Co...Soda..., deep cobalt, ip, bt, 8-sided, 7⅜" ...300.00
Willis & Ripley Portsmouth, deep sapphire bl, sl cm, ip, 7⅜".....500.00
Wm Hess Jr...Philada, med cobalt, sl cm, ip, 8-sided, 7⅜" 500.00

Poison Bottles

Dmn & Lattice, cobalt, Poison stopper, HBCo on sb, 3¾" 110.00
Gift Flasche (skull & X bones), bright grass gr, sb, 6-sided, 5⅛"...60.00
Gift Flasche (skull & X bones), med yel gr, tm, 100 on sb, 5".......60.00
Lattice & Dmn, cobalt, Poison stopper, HBCo on sb, 4¾" 175.00
Lyon's Powder B&P NY, deep copper puce, rm, op, 4¼" 210.00
Lyon's Powder B&P NY, med olive gr, rm, op, 4⅜" 300.00
Poison Owl Drug Co (owl/mortar/pestle), cobalt, sb, triangular, 6½"...160.00
Poison Owl Drug Co (owl/mortar/pestle), med cobalt, triangular, 5"...90.00
Poison Poison, deep cobalt, CLG...Apl For on sb, 5⅝" 75.00

Sarsaparilla Bottles

Dr Townsend's Comp, aquamarine, sq w/beveled corners, ip, 9½" ..2,000.00
Dr Townsend's...NY, teal, sq w/beveled corners, sb, 9¼" 180.00
Emerson's 50 Cts, bl aqua, WT&CO USA on sb, 9" 80.00
Hall's...JR Gates..., ice bl, tm, sb, 9¼" 50.00
John Bull Extract of...KY, aqua, open pontil, 6½" 250.00
Log Cabin Rochester NY, root beer-amber, sb, am, 80% label, 9"...170.00
Old Dr Townsend's NY, bl-gr, ip, sl cm, flakes, 9½" 325.00
Old Dr Townsend's, ice bl, sq w/beveled corners, ip, 9⅝" 1,300.00

Spirits Bottles

AW Hoffman Claremont...Measure, tm, sb, strap-side ½-pt..........60.00
Bininger's (clock face) Regulator, med amber, ps, clock, 6".........300.00
BM&EA Whitlock...NY, bl aqua, am, op, 8⅛" 1,100.00
Booth & Sedgwick's London, med bl gr, sl cm, ip, 8" 450.00
Distilled in 1848 Old Kentucky, med amber, dbl cm, ps, 8⅛" 300.00
HF&B NY, deep strawberry puce, 6-sided, dbl cm, sb, dullness, 11" ...1,100.00
London (reverse Ns) Jockey Club, deep yel gr, dbl cm, 9¾" 475.00
Louisville Liquor House...Col, tm, sb, coffin flask, 6" 750.00
Mist of the Morning..., amber, sl dbl cm, sb, bbl, 10" 650.00
Turner Bros NY, golden yel amber, sb, bbl, 10" 800.00
Turner Bros NY, root beer amber, sb, bbl, flake, 10" 300.00
Udolpho Wolfe's Schiedam Aromatic, lt gr aqua, dbl cm, ip, 8", EX..160.00
Warranted...RL Christian & Co, strap-sided flask, ½-pt 180.00

Boxes

Boxes have been used by civilized man since ancient Egypt and Rome. Down through the centuries, specifically designed containers have been made from every conceivable material. Precious metals, papier-mâché, Battersea, Oriental lacquer, and wood have held riches from the treasuries of kings, snuff for the fashionable set of the last century, China tea, and countless other commodities. In the following descriptions, when only one dimension is given, it is length. See also Toleware; specific manufacturers.

Apple, cherry w/red wash, sq nails, old split, 5½x11x10" **400.00**
Ballot, walnut, narrow slot in front, arched crest, old rfn, 9x7x10" ...**260.00**
Bentwood, laced seams, pegged posts, old gr pnt, rprs, 7x14" **485.00**
Bible, oak w/floral on bl, wrought hinges, 6x18x15" **990.00**
Bride's, bentwood w/decoupage panel, laced seams, 7x19x13" **800.00**
Bride's, lady's portrait among flowers, laced seams, 6x18x11", VG ..**1,500.00**
Bride's, tulips & stars on blk oval, wire staples at seams, 13x9x5" ...**1,485.00**
Bride's, wooden cylinder w/lapped panels, mc floral, 10x14" dia ..**475.00**
Bride's, worn bl & wht w/red traces, flower panels, 7x16x11" **550.00**
Candle, walnut, high shaped crest w/3 holes, dvtl, 9x13x7" **285.00**
Casket, Regency-style gilt bronze & iron, German mk, ca 1890, 9x6x9" **2,000.00**
Cheese, poplar w/yel wash & old stencil, rpr, 7½x11" **900.00**
Coffer, burl walnut Wm IV w/pewter shield inlay, 5x11x7½" **230.00**
Coffer, burled walnut Geo III, w/lock & key, 4x8x4½" **315.00**
Curly maple w/G figure, wire nails, brass hinges, 4x13x9" **295.00**
Cutlery, mahog Geo III, serpentine front, sloped lid, 15x13x9" ...**1,000.00**
Document, red wash, leather hasp, brass hinges, dvtl, 7x12x6" **385.00**
Dome top, HP roses/etc on salmon pk, rpr, 6x10x6" **195.00**

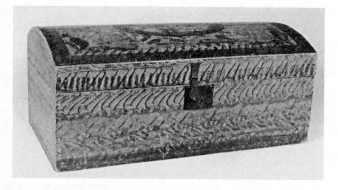

Domed top, putty-colored grain paint on poplar, New England, early nineteenth century, 11½x28x14¼", $1,100.00.

Dough, dvtl pine w/old red wash, sq nails, rprs, 12x28x12½" **330.00**
Dough, red wash, canted sides, appl hdl, dvtl, 11x32x19" **275.00**
Jewelry, walnut w/incised foliage & quail, compartments, 11x11x7" **385.00**
Knife, mahog flame vnr Hplwht w/inlay, 14½x9x10½" **1,045.00**
Knife, mahog vnr English Hplwht, dividers, rprs, 15x10x12" **415.00**
Pantry, bentwood, overlapped w/copper tacks, old pnt, 5½x9¼" **440.00**
Pantry, bentwood, rosemaling on salmon, overlapping seams, 5x7" **330.00**
Pine, blk grpt on red, dvtl, 5⅜x13½x6" **685.00**
Pine, slant lid, spire & ball finial, red & blk pnt, 11x14x8" **1,000.00**
Pine w/pnt landscape, wooden pegs, 6½x13x8½" **415.00**
Pipe, dk pine, sm drw w/iron ring pull in base, ca 1900, 21x10x5" **385.00**
Pipe, mahog, pierced bkboard, lower drw, 19th C, 21x5x5" **600.00**
Pipe, pnt cherry, lower drw, dvtl, brass pull, 15x6x5" **2,350.00**
Storage, staved, wrought iron straps, lock w/key, 1761, 10x14" ...**315.00**
Table, tortoiseshell vnr w/brass mts, dome lid, hdl, 12" L **2,115.00**
Wall, pierced/shaped bk, red wash (worn), 1800s, 9½x14x6½" **500.00**
Wallpaper, mc flowers on blk, similar paper on lid, 2¾x5⅜" **825.00**
Writing, polychromed wood, velvet-covered hinged lid, 19th C, 18" L **1,200.00**
Writing, walnut vnr w/pnt fleur-de-lis, fitted int, 8x12x7" **925.00**

Bradley and Hubbard

The Bradley and Hubbard Mfg. Company was a firm which produced metal accessories for the home. They operated from about 1860 until the early part of this century, and their products reflected both the Arts and Crafts and Art Nouveau influence. Their logo was a device with a triangular arrangement of the company name containing a smaller triangle and an Aladdin lamp. Our advisor is Bruce Austin; he is listed in the Directory under New York.

See also Bookends; Doorstops.

Lamps

Desk, metal o/l shade w/4 nudes, ribbons/garlands, in harp fr, 12" **450.00**
Desk, o/l 6" gr & wht slag shade; Aladdin's lamp base, 12" **1,150.00**
Desk, 10" L o/l shade w/stylized nudes, pivital; ornate base **450.00**
Hanging, 18" pagoda-style shade w/caramel slag panels, 1910s **1,295.00**
Hanging, 5 7" hex paneled shades w/metal leaf o/l, 1910, 16" dia ..**2,500.00**
Hanging, 8" pagoda-style octagonal shade w/caramel slag panels, 18" ...**1,295.00**
Kitchen, milk glass shade w/HP flowers; ornate CI fr, smoke bell ...**375.00**
Table, 14" o/l 4-panel sgn shade w/churches & trees; sqd std ...**1,400.00**
Table, 14" o/l 4-panel shade w/homes & churches; tapered std w/sq ft ...**1,700.00**
Table, 18" rvpt floral shade; oak leaves emb on bronze std, 26" ...**2,300.00**
Table, 20" slag glass dome shade; Celtic knot bronze std, 23" ..**2,700.00**
Table, 22" geometric o/l shade w/ldgl liner, simple std, 34" **1,600.00**
Table, 22" ldgl shade w/geometrics & simple 6-panel o/l, 6-sided std **2,000.00**

Miscellaneous

Andirons, cast brass & iron w/sunburst finials, #9510, 16½" **850.00**
Andirons, hammered iron, sq top, str column, arched legs, 24", VG ..**250.00**
Clock, CI case w/brass trim, 30-hr Terry movement, 1860, 8" **250.00**
Desk set, cast brass, note clip+calendar stand+inkwell+letter holder ...**300.00**
Frame, CI w/gold pnt, ornate florals, mk, 17¼x13⅛" **195.00**
Inkstand, CI w/glass well, Art Nouveau lady motif, #3166, 7½" L ...**165.00**
Pipe tray, old man smoking pipe, #2167, 5x7½" **125.00**
Thermometer, wht metal w/brass coating, Cupid head on base, 11" ..**435.00**

Brass

Brass is an alloy consisting essentially of copper and zinc in variable proportions. It is a medium that has been used for both utilitarian items and objects of artistic merit. Today, with the inflated price of copper and the popular use of plastics, almost anything made of brass is collectible, though right now, at least, there is little interest in items made after 1950. Our advisor, Mary Frank Gaston, has compiled a lovely book, *Antique Brass and Copper*, with full-color photos. See also Candlesticks.

Ash can, lion mask hdls, domed lid w/orb-shaped finial, 19x13" ...**315.00**
Ash pan, sm knobbed hdl, 19th C, 4x21x9¼" **115.00**
Brazier, domed lid, Turkish, 21½x14x12" **750.00**
Brazier, pierced, 32x30" dia **1,495.00**
Buckets, spun brass, mk HW Hayden's Pat...1851, graduated set of 11 ....**1,150.00**
Censer, pierced star motif on lid, 2x7" dia **70.00**
Coffer, dome top, medieval style w/gargoyle clasp, 6x8x5" **195.00**
Colander, dish form w/ring hanger, 19th C, 1½x8" **60.00**
Dipper, stamped fleur-de-lis, 19th C, 17" **175.00**
Fry pan, w/long wood & iron hdl, 1½x11" dia **600.00**
Holder for spit, cylindrical tube w/trn stem, cabriole legs, 11x5" ...**115.00**
Jardiniere, ring hdls w/lion masks, 10½x10¼", pr **150.00**
Kettle, bulbous w/snake spout, early 19th C, 9½" H **600.00**
Kettle, wrought-iron hdl, anchored by iron hoop, 12x18" **575.00**

Kettle stand, pierced top w/eng peacocks, cabriole legs, 8x17x9" ..250.00
Kettle stand, pierced top w/floral medallion, iron bk legs, 14x13x12" ...165.00
Ladle, long hdl, 17¼"...160.00
Pot, bell-metal hdls, heavy, 19th C, 16" dia.............................200.00
Pot, fixed wrought-iron hdl, heavy, 7x13" dia............................175.00
Saucepan, iron rattail hdl, 5x10½" dia.....................................285.00
Skimmer, iron hdl w/heart cutout, 17¾"..................................200.00
Skimmer, 21"...200.00
Spoon mold, 2-part, polished, 10" 145.00
Sundial, chased w/Roman numerals around sun face, 8" 285.00
Teakettle, pumpkin shape w/stem finial, 9¼", w/11" tripod stand...200.00
Tiebacks, cast rosettes & acanthus leaves w/berries, 3¾", 4 for...315.00

Brastoff, Sascha

The son of immigrant parents, Sascha Brastoff was encouraged to develop his artistic talents to the fullest, encouragement that was well taken, as his achievements aptly attest. Though at various times he was a dancer, sculptor, Hollywood costume designer, jeweler, and painter, it is his ceramics that are today becoming highly regarded collectibles.

Sascha began his career in the United States in the late 1940s. In a beautiful studio built for him by his friend and mentor, Winthrop Rockefeller, he designed innovative wares that even then were among the most expensive on the market. All designing was done personally by Brastoff; he also supervised the staff which at the height of production numbered approximately 150. Wares signed with his full signature (not merely backstamped 'Sascha Brastoff') were personally crafted by him and are valued much more highly than those signed 'Sascha B.,' indicating work done under his supervision. Until his death in 1993, he continued his work in Los Angeles, in his latter years producing 'Sascha Holograms,' which were distributed by the Hummelwerk Company.

Though the resin animals signed 'Sascha B.' were neither made nor designed by Brastoff, collectors of these pieces value them highly. After he left the factory in the 1960s, the company retained the use of the name to be used on reissues of earlier pieces or merchandise purchased at trade shows.

In the listings that follow, items are ceramic and signed 'Sascha B.' unless 'full signature' or another medium is indicated. For further information we recommend *The Collector's Encyclopedia of California Pottery, Second Edition*, by Jack Chipman, available from Collector Books or your local bookstore.

Our advisor for this category is Lonnie Wells; she is listed in the Directory under Missouri.

Ashtray, afghan, bl & silver, 5¼x6"..85.00
Ashtray, enameled copper, brn & gold, 10" dia............................60.00
Ashtray, Jewel Bird on blk, rests on 1 side, 5x8¾".......................65.00
Ashtray, mosaic decor, bl/red/brns, 13½" dia 105.00
Ashtray, person in turban & exotic costume, 10½x7¾"................85.00
Bowl, Americana, 5½" 50.00
Bowl, Star Steed, on gray, rolled edge, 10½"..............................110.00
Box, floral, gr w/gold trim on blk, egg shape, 3-ftd, w/lid, #044A, 7"...95.00
Box, Rooftops, pk/turq/blk, w/lid, 6½x5½"................................65.00
Candle holder, Aztec-style mask, gold tones, #S39, 10" 90.00
Candlestick, amber resin, 7¾"...35.00
Cigarette lighter, Star Steed on bl-gr, cylindrical, #L2, 5½"..........75.00
Dish, Eskimo child on gray w/blk edge, 7¼x6" 65.00
Dish, rooster in blk & gold on lt bl, scalloped edge, 8½x8½".......95.00
Figurine, bear, bl resin, 4¼x7¼x3½"......................................365.00
Figurine, horse, on ped ft, textured gold leaf, 10½" 195.00
Figurine, pelican, gr resin 350.00
Jardiniere, Rooftops, scalloped rim, 4¼x5⅝" dia 180.00
Mug, Arabian woman on gray w/purple, mk #070, 5x3" 35.00

Plate, bl bubbles in stream w/gold highlights, metal, 11¾" 38.00
Plate, Golden Gate Bridge on blk w/bl edge, 8⅛" 25.00

Sculpture, horse, textured gold, 16x16", from $595.00 to $795.00.

Tray, Rooftops, irregular shape, 15½" 125.00
Tray, Star Steed, mk F3, 9½x5½"...95.00
Vase, bl/gr/brn/silver bands on wht, 8½x3¾".............................65.00
Vase, Eskimo child's face on wht, ruffled rim, #V9, 4½x4½" 55.00
Vase, gold cryptography on gold & silver, 17¼x3".......................80.00
Vase, Star Steed, on bl, bulbous bottom, 10" 120.00
Vase, Temple Flowers, 10" 150.00

Brayton Laguna

A few short years after Durlin Brayton married Ellen Webster Grieve, his small pottery, which he had opened in 1927, became highly successful. Extensive lines were created and all of them flourished. Hand-turned pieces were done in the early years; today these are the most difficult to find. Durlin Brayton hand incised ashtrays, vases, and dinnerware (plates in assorted sizes, pitchers, cups and saucers, and creamers and sugar bowls). These early items were marked 'Laguna Pottery,' incised on unglazed bases.

Brayton's children's series is highly collected today as is the Walt Disney line. Also popular are the Circus line, Calasia (art pottery decorated with stylized feathers and circles), Webton ware, the Blackamoor series, and the Gay Nineties line. Each seemed to prove more profitable than the lines before it. Both white and pink clays were utilized in production. At its peak, the pottery employed more than 150 people. After World War II when imports began to flood the market, Brayton Laguna was one of the companies that managed to hold their own. By 1968, however, it was necessary to cease production.

For more information on this as well as many other potteries in the state, we recommend *The Collector's Encyclopedia of California Pottery* by Jack Chipman; he is listed in the Directory under California.

Bookends, clown, seated, bks form bookends, 5¾", pr..................75.00
Bowl, wht & yel flowers w/gr leaves on brn, 3x9".......................32.00
Candle holders, Blackamoor, seated w/legs crossed, 4¾", pr 140.00
Chamberstick, orange, tri-cornered rim, w/hdl, early, 3¼"..........165.00
Creamer & sugar bowl, Gingham dog & Calico cat, 6", 6¼"........55.00
Figurine, African drummer, #H25, 10".....................................75.00
Figurine, Anne, seated, 4"..85.00
Figurine, Black dice player 55.00
Figurine, cats, stylized, wht, 4½x5½", pr..................................45.00

Figurine, fawn, brn w/wht spots, Disney, 6" 80.00
Figurine, Figaro, begging, 3½" 100.00
Figurine, Figaro, playing, 3⅜" 100.00

Figurine, Gay 90s Honeymoon, from $100.00 to $125.00.

Figurine, horse, lt brn w/dk brn patch on ea side, 3x4"..................45.00
Figurine, Inger, 7" 50.00
Figurine, lady in gr dress w/wolfhound on ea side, 11"..................60.00
Figurine, lady in lav dress, basket in 1 hand, 8½" 65.00
Figurine, Olga, 7⅛" 50.00
Figurine, panther, snarling, jewelled collar, 20" L, from $175 to ..225.00
Figurine, Pluto, looking up, Disney.....................................130.00
Figurine, purple cow, 6x8⅜"..100.00
Figurine, queen (Alice in Wonderland), 6¾" 140.00
Figurine, red fox, seated, 4x4"...60.00
Figurine, Sambo, bl overalls w/yel hat, 7¾" 140.00
Figurine, stylized bird, blk w/wht trim, twisted neck, #H49, 9½"...140.00
Figurine, swan, turq w/orange beak & feet, 1940 ....25.00
Figurine, Victorian couple, Bedtime, in nightclothes, 3rd of 4, 8¾"...150.00
Figurine, Victorian couple, man seated, 1st in series of 4 ....110.00
Figurine, walrus (Alice in Wonderland), unmk, 7" 110.00
Figurine/flower frog, Pouter Pigeon, ca 1941 ....65.00
Figurine/planter, Blackamoor kneeling, holding gold pot...........125.00
Figurine/planter, peasant woman w/baskets 50.00
Figurines, piano man w/singer, 5¼x6", 8" singer, 3-pc set 500.00
Figurines, Zizi & Fifi, marooon & gr, pr 500.00
Flower holder, elephant, seated, opening on top of head, 5¼" 60.00
Planter, donkey & cart, ceramic cart body, wheels & donkey, wood slats..125.00
Planter, woman's corset shape, bl w/wht trim, 4½x3" 20.00
Plate, bl, handmade, early, 9¾"..70.00
Pot, partridges on blk branches, #V9, w/lid, 4½x4¾" 150.00
Shakers, Black Chef & Mammy, 6½", pr 185.00
Sugar bowl, wht & yel flowers w/gr leaves on brn, 4x4½".............25.00
Teapot, wht & yel flowers w/gr leaves on blk, 6½" 45.00
Vase, sea horse w/bk pocket, 8½"..85.00

Bread Plates and Trays

Bread plates and trays have been produced not only in many types of glass but in metal and pottery as well. Those considered most collectible were made during the last quarter of the nineteenth century from pressed glass with well-detailed embossed designs, many of them portraying a particularly significant historical event. A great number of these plates were sold at the 1876 Philadelphia Centennial Exposition by various glass manufacturers who exhibited their wares on the grounds. Among the themes depicted are the Declaration of Independence, the Constitution, McKinley's memorial 'It Is God's Way,' Remembrance of Three Presidents, the Purchase of Alaska, and various presidential campaigns, to mention only a few.

'L' numbers correspond with a reference book by Lindsey; 'S' refers to a book by Stuart. Our advisor for this category is Darlene Yohe; she is listed in the Directory under Arkansas.

Actress, HMS Pinafore, oval, La Belle, 1880s, 11¼" 100.00
Banner Baking Powder, shield center, 11" 85.00
Beaded Grape...25.00
Bishop, L-201..200.00
Bunker Hill, L-44, 13½x9" 75.00
Canadian, amber, rnd..45.00
Columbia, shield shape, bl, 11½x9½" 165.00
Constitution w/eagle..60.00
Daisy & Button (Hobbs)...25.00
Deer & Pine Tree, apple gr 125.00
Deer & Pine Tree, bl 65.00
Double Hands w/Grapes, milk glass.....................................45.00
Egyptian, Cleopatra center, 13" L 80.00
Flower Pot, We Trust in God 75.00
GAR..265.00
Give Us Our Daily Bread, Dew Drop 65.00
Goddess of Hunt, rectangular, hdls.....................................110.00
Good Luck, dbl horseshoe hdls..120.00
Grant Maple Leaf, Let Us Have Peace, gr................................160.00
Heroes of Bunker Hill..95.00
Jeweled Band (Scalloped Tape)...25.00
Last Supper 40.00
Liberty Bell Signers...95.00
Lotus (Garden of Eden)..45.00
McCormick's Reaper 160.00
Memorial Hall..65.00
Minerva...75.00
National, shield shape, rare..85.00
Old Statehouse Philadelphia Erected 1735, deep bl, 12¼"...........60.00
Panelled Fishbone..35.00
Preparedness, L-481..300.00
Retriever, milk glass..80.00
Rock of Ages, milk glass center, dtd, 8¾" 180.00
Sheraton...45.00
Sheridan Memorial 40.00
Three Graces, Pat dtd 1865...65.00
Three Presidents, In Remembrance, 12½x10" 60.00
US Grant, Patriot & Soldier, sq, 11" 85.00
Washington, First War/First Peace, L-27, 12x8½" 100.00
William J Bryan, milk glass 45.00

Bretby

Bretby art pottery was made by Tooth & Co., at Woodville, near Burton-on-Trent, Derbyshire, from as early in 1884 until well into the twentieth century. Marks containing the 'Made in England' designation indicate twentieth-century examples.

Bowl, gr w/6 vignettes of female profiles, #1967, w/hdls, 8" 45.00
Jardiniere, brn top & bottom w/fishing scene on tan, 7x9"........175.00
Jardiniere, lion's head, brn w/red glass eyes, 12¼" 575.00
Mug, head of King Edward VIII, 1937, E on hdl, 4" 75.00
Vase, brn top & bottom w/Chinese scene in faux ivory, #71511, 5", pr...70.00

Vase, copper colored w/squirrel, dragonfly & leaves, #2023, 10¼" ...**175.00**
Vase, HP bluebird & floral, #2273D, 8" **115.00**
Vase, metallic body w/emb Greco Roman decor, w/hdls, #2421, 7" ..**60.00**
Vase, speckled & oil-spotted metallic brn, #3317E, 8¾" **130.00**
Vase, tree-trunk shape w/lizards on side, #2244, 1930s, 13" **310.00**

Bride's Baskets and Bowls

Victorian brides were showered with gifts, as brides have always been; one of the most popular gift items was the bride's basket. Art glass inserts from both European and American glasshouses, some in lovely transparent hues with dainty enameled florals, others of Peachblow, Vasa Murrhina, satin or cased glass, were cradled in complementary silver-plated holders. While many of these holders were simply engraved or delicately embossed, others (such as those from Pairpoint and Wilcox) were wonderfully ornate, often with figurals of cherubs or animals or birds. The bride's basket was no longer in fashion after the turn of the century.

Watch for 'marriages' of bowls and frames. To warrant the best price, the two pieces should be the original pairing. If you can't be certain of this, at least check to see that the bowl fits snugly into the frame. Beware of later-made bowls (such as Fenton's) in Victorian holders and new frames being produced in Taiwan. In the listings that follow, if no frame is described, the price is for a bowl only.

Apricot cased w/floral, swirl ribs, pinched sides/rim, 9½" **225.00**
Bl cased spangle, ruffled; ornate Southington #120 SP fr, 12½" ...**750.00**
Bl Dmn Quilt MOP; rstr Tufts #1952 fr, 13" **1,250.00**
Bl Herringbone MOP, appl crimped ribbon edge; Reed & Barton fr, 11"....**1,500.00**
Cranberry Invt T'print w/HP floral; rstr Pairpoint #2180 fr, 9" ..**1,500.00**
Cranberry MOP, camphor ruffled rim; Pairpoint cherub fr, 7½x8½" ...**1,500.00**
Cranberry satin, crimped/rolled rim; SP fr w/lady at 1 side **2,000.00**
Cranberry to pk w/silver mica, cased, rope hdl, 8x10" **300.00**
Custard w/HP decor; rstr Meriden Silverplate #01532 fr, 7" **850.00**
Custard w/mc floral; rstr Meriden #01532 7" fr w/filigree & cherub hdl...**850.00**
Gold satin w/birds & floral, clear ruffle, 13"; mk fr......................**495.00**
Maroon to cream cased w/sm flowers, deeply scalloped, 12" **200.00**
Opal w/spaced floral, gently ruffled rim; Pairpoint fr #4732, 9x9"...**350.00**
Peach to vaseline opal, Rib Optic; Adelphi SP fr, 10¾" **950.00**
Pk, ruffled; rstr SP fr w/cherub supporting base, #221, 8½".........**650.00**
Pk cased w/HP floral, ruffled; R&B #4657 fr w/angels..............**1,800.00**
Pk cased w/HP floral; rstr Tufts #231 fr w/hanging cherries, 9" ...**895.00**
Pk satin w/HP floral; rstr Aurora #721 fr, 5¾" **750.00**
Pk spangle Dia Quilt, chartreuse int; ornate Tufts fr **1,850.00**
Rainbow satin, ruffled; Hartford SP fr......................................**1,800.00**
Wht opaline w/allover decor, pk int, 12"; Middletown fr w/fruit hdls....**515.00**
Wht w/red int, sm florals, rim crimed in 4 areas; Wilcox fr #5598, 10"...**350.00**
Yel w/butterscotch int, clear ruffled rim; Meriden SP fr, 9¼"......**400.00**

Bristol Glass

Bristol is a type of semi-opaque opaline glass whose name was derived from the area in England where it was first produced. Similar glass was made in France, Germany, and Italy. In this country, it was made by the New England Glass Company and to a lesser extent by its contemporaries. During the eighteenth and nineteenth centuries, Bristol glass was imported in large amounts and sold cheaply, thereby contributing to the demise of the earlier glasshouses here in America. It is very difficult to distinguish the English Bristol from other opaline types. Style, design, and decoration serve as clues to its origin; but often only those well versed in the field can spot these subtle variations.

Biscuit jar, bl w/daisies & foliage, SP mts, 6¼x4¾" **175.00**
Box, wht w/Cupid in pk floral, hinged lid, 3x5½" dia **295.00**
Mug, wht w/HP eagle/laurel wreath/stars, gold trim, 3¾"...........**470.00**
Pipe, bl, twisted hdl, wht edge at bowl rim, 20" **335.00**
Toilet stand, 3 bottles & powder jar on rstr SP fr w/lg cherub **3,000.00**
Tumbler, wht w/mc branch, 3⅝"..**125.00**
Vase, bird on branch, cylindrical, att Smith Bros, 10½"...............**75.00**
Vase, jack-in-pulpit; gray-gr w/floral, 8½" **58.00**
Vase, pk w/birds in blossoming tree, ftd, 13x7¾", pr **365.00**

Vase, tan with multi-color florals, bulbous with short flared neck, 7", $55.00.

Vase, wht w/bird, nest w/eggs & floral, w/hdls, bulbous bottom, 12" **175.00**
Vase, wht w/cherubs, tapered w/pinched neck, 7¼" **140.00**
Vase, wht w/orange & bl floral, scalloped rim, 10¾x4½"............**115.00**
Vase, wht w/rosebush, baluster w/ped ftd, 10x4¼", pr **150.00**
Vase, yel w/mc floral, tapered cylinder, 13" **75.00**
Wine glass, bl, paneled bowl, stemmed, Georgian, ca 1840, 4" ...**190.00**

British Royalty Commemoratives

Royalty commemoratives have been issued for royal events since Edward VI's 1547 coronation through modern-day occasions, so it's possible to start collecting at any period of history. Many collectors begin with Queen Victoria's reign, collecting examples for each succeeding monarch and continuing through modern events.

Some collectors identify with a particular royal personage and limit their collecting to that era, ie., Queen Elizabeth's life and reign. Other collectors look to the future, expanding their collection to include the heir apparents Prince Charles and his first-born son, Prince William.

Royalty commemorative collecting is often further refined around a particular type of collectible. Nearly any item with room for a portrait and a description has been manufactured as a souvenir. Thus royalty commemoratives are available in glass, ceramic, metal, fabric, plastic, and paper. This wide variety of material lends itself to any pocketbook. The range covers expensive limited edition ceramics to inexpensive souvenir key chains, puzzles, matchbooks, etc.

Many recent royalty headline events have been commemorated in a variety of souvenirs. Buying some of these modern commemoratives at the moderate issue prices could be a good investment. After all, today's events are tomorrow's history.

For further study we recommend *British Royal Commemoratives* by our advisor for this category, Audrey Zeder; she is listed in the Directory under Washington.

Key:
A/S — Andrew/Sarah
ann — anniversary
BD — birthday
C/D — Charles/Diana
chr — christening
com — commemorative
cor — coronation
EPNS — electro-plated nickel
  silver
ILN — Illustrated London News
inscr — inscribed

invest — investiture
jub — jubilee
K/Q — King Queen
LE — limited edition
mem — memorial
Pr — Prince
Prs — Princess
QM — Queen Mother
wed — wedding
Wm — William
vis — visit

Bank, Elizabeth II jub, crown shape, silver-tone, 4x3½"...............45.00
Beaker, Edward VII 1902 King's Dinner, gr, Doulton..................150.00
Beaker, Victoria '87 jub, enamel mc portrait/decor, gold bands, 4"......190.00
Beaker, Victoria 1897 jub, enamel w/portrait, 3¾".......................195.00

Bell, Queen Elizabeth II, ceramic with wooden handle, $40.00.

Book, Victoria 1897, Queen's Resolve, some wear.........................65.00
Booklet, C/D wed, Royal Wedding Official Souvenir, 11x8".........30.00
Booklet, Pr of Wales 1926 Luton visit, 20-pg.............................30.00
Bookmark, Elizabeth II cor, mc portrait/decor on woven silk........25.00
Bottle, Victoria cor, brn crown, beige decor, Imperial Pottery.....750.00
Bowl, Elizabeth II cor, sepia portrait/decor, oval, 1x5x3"...............35.00
Bowl, George VI cor, mc portrait/decor, scalloped rim, 5½".........45.00
Bust, Charles, 1981, wht, Coalport, 5"....................................65.00
Coin, Wm IV 1830, 4 pence, silver groat....................................45.00
Cup & saucer, Edward VII cor, portrait/decor on turq................165.00
Doll, C/D wed, vinyl, Goldberger, 12", MIB.............................195.00
Doll, Pr Philip, vinyl, bl uniform, Nisbit, ca 1950, 8½".............150.00
Egg cup, Elizabeth II '02 jub, blk silhouette, ftd..........................15.00
Egg cup, Geo VI cor, shaded portrait, gold rim, ftd.....................35.00
Egg cup, Geo VI 1937 cor, mc portrait, ftd.................................50.00
Ephemera, Elizabeth II cor coloring book, unused, 14x10½"........50.00
Ephemera, Geo VI 1949 carriage pass to garden party..................26.00
Ephemera, Geo VI 1949, invitation to Buckingham Palace party..45.00
First Day cover, Elizabeth II cor, w/decor envelope.....................20.00
ILN Record No, Elizabeth II jub, bl cover/silver decor, 14x10".....55.00
Jewelry, Elizabeth II cor, crown earrings, MOC..........................25.00
Jewelry, Elizabeth II pin, mc portrait on MOP, 2⅝".....................45.00
Jewelry, Queen Victoria coin, gold bezel w/extended ring.............35.00
Jug, George III, emb portrait, Westerwald, late 18th C.............425.00
Magazine, Elizabeth II cor, ILN, cor week, dbl number, 1953......35.00
Magazine, Hello, Charles/Harry in S Africa, 11/15/97................12.00
Magazine, Telegraph, Remembering Diana, 8/11/98....................15.00

Medal, C/D wed, emb portrait, bronze, Tower Mint, MIB............50.00
Medal, Victoria cor, profile & cor scene, pierced, 2"..................160.00
Medallion, Pr of Wales Open 1887 Jub Exhibit, bronze, 1¾".....125.00
Medallion, Victoria/Albert 1858 vis w/Napoleon, brass, ⅞".........75.00
Miniature, QM 80's plate, mc portrait, purple hat/dress, 2¼".......30.00
Mug, Edward VII, king's profile, Art Deco decor & shape............45.00
Mug, Edward VII cor, mc portrait w/mc enamel, gold rim, 2⅛"..110.00
Mug, Geo V cor, mc portrait in robes, presentation pc...............150.00
Mug, Geo VI cor, mc Coat of Arms, lion hdl, Paragon, 3"...........75.00
Mug, Prs Diana '95 Argentina vis, mc decor, Chown, LE 50......125.00
Mug, Victoria 1897 jub, bl & gray overall transfer, JCN.............195.00
New Testament, Geo VI cor, red cover w/silver seal....................55.00
Newspaper, Gleason's Pictorial 1862, royal coverage inside..........20.00
Novelty, Geo VI crumb pan, emb portrait/decor on brass............75.00
Photograph, Duke of Windsor 1940 radio broadcast, blk/wht, 5x7"..45.00
Pin-bk, Edward VII cor, mc portrait/decor, 1¼"........................245.00
Pitcher, Victoria 1840 wed, mc figure on bl w/copper lustre, 6"..360.00
Pitcher, Victoria 1897 jub, Queen/Prince Edward, Balmoral, 4".270.00
Plaque, Geo VI cor, king/queen/children, tin, 7¼x6"...................45.00
Plate, Edward VII cor, mc portrait, emb/scalloped rim, 8½".......165.00
Plate, Edward VIII '37, mc portrait in cor robe, Royal Winston, 9"..90.00
Plate, Elizabeth II cor, profile, sq w/extended hdls, 10"..............45.00
Plate, George VI cor, mc design w/gold trim, 6½"......................30.00
Plate, Prs Margaret 1930 birth, bird design, Paragon, 7".............120.00
Playing cards, Edward VII cor, mc portrait/decor, full deck..........95.00
Postcard, Elizabeth II '02 jub, queen's portrait & 5 previous monarchs...5.00
Postcard, Prs Margaret '02 mem, mc portrait, doves & rose.............5.00
Postcards, Queen Alexandra on yacht, blk/wht, ca 1905, used.....15.00
Pressed glass, Prs Diana mem plate, portrait, irid, 3½"................30.00
Program, Elizabeth II cor, Church of England Services, 16-pg......20.00
Puzzle, Elizabeth II cor, wood, Valentine, MIB (sealed)................60.00
Spoon, Edward VII 1900s w/Fr President, hallmk.......................80.00
Spoon, Elizabeht II jub, emb portrait, EPNS, set of 6, MIB..........60.00
Spoon, Victoria 1897, emb portrait/design, Sterling hallmk.......150.00
Teapot, Edward VII cor, mc portrait in red uniform, Doulton, 2-cup...210.00
Teapot, Elizabeth II '02 jub, head shape, gold crown, 8"..............95.00
Textile, C/D wed, tea towel, mc portrait, Irish linen....................35.00
Textile, towel, Elizabeth II '02 jub, queen's portrait, mc guards.....10.00
Thimble, Elizabeth II '02 jub, young queen portrait, mc decor........6.00
Tin, Elizabeth II cor, mc portrait, rnd, flat, Daintee, 2x4"............30.00
Tin, Pr of Wales 1930, mc portrait, hinged, Throne's, 4x2½".......65.00
Tin, Pr Wales '33 Morley vis, mc portrait/decor, hinged..............85.00

Broadmoor

In October of 1933, the Broadmoor Art Pottery was formed and space rented at 217 East Pikes Peak Avenue, Colorado Springs, Colorado. Most of the pottery they produced would not be considered elaborate, and only a handful was decorated. Many pieces were signed by P.H. Genter, J.B. Hunt, Eric Hellman, and Cecil Jones. It is reported that this plant closed in 1936, and Genter moved his operations to Denver.

Broadmoor pottery is marked in several ways: a Greek or Egyptian-type label depicting two potters (one at the wheel and one at a tile-pressing machine) and the word Broadmoor; an ink-stamped 'Broadmoor Pottery, Colorado Springs (or Denver), Colorado'; and an incised version of the latter.

The bottoms of all pieces are always white and can be either glazed or unglazed. Glaze colors are turquoise, green, yellow, cobalt blue, light blue, white, pink, pink with blue, maroon red, black, and copper lustre. Both matt and high gloss finishes were used.

The company produced many advertising tiles, novelty items, coasters, ashtrays, and vases for local establishments around Denver and as far away as Wyoming. An Indian head was incised into many of the advertising items, which also often bear a company or a product name. A series of small animals (horses, dogs, elephants, lambs, squirrels, a toucan bird, and a hippo), each about 2" high, are easily recognized by the style of their modeling and glaze treatments, though all are unmarked.

Bookend, Art Deco head, crackle finish, minimum value **165.00**
Bowl, red, incurvate rim, 15" **55.00**
Creamer, squirrel on sq base, brn, stamp, 2" **40.00**
Creamer & sugar bowl, bl matt, 2" **40.00**
Paperweight, Indian head, bl matt, rare................................**65.00**
Paperweight, scarab, ivory, stamp label, 4" **90.00**
Planter, frog figural, red, open mouth **65.00**
Vase, cornucopia; bl to mauve, 6" **50.00**
Vase, Mongol Red, waisted, 8" **75.00**
Vase, pk crackle, side mouth, 10" **250.00**
Vase, red, 3 rim-to-hip hdls, sgn E Hellman, 8" **137.50**

Broadsides

Webster defines a broadside as simply a large sheet of paper printed on one side. During the 1880s, they were the most practical means of mass communication. By the middle of the century, they had become elaborate and lengthy with information, illustrations, portraits, and fancy border designs. Those printed on coated stock are usually worth more.

A Few Rhymes on the Naval Expedition to Port Royal, 1861, 11x5" **55.00**
Alsace-Lorraine, Wilson's speech to congress, 1918, 24x17", EX...**110.00**
Ayer Brass Band Minstrel Show, vignettes, 19th C, 18x4¾" **80.00**
Baseball Stars in Action, Illustrated Current News, 1935, 19x12½"...**110.00**
Boston & Sandwich Glass Co Auction Notice, 1850, 10x8" **215.00**
Buffalo Bill's Wild West, program, ca 1884, 8½x5½" **185.00**
Coon Pizen, Polk/Dallas 1844 National Election, folded, 17½x5½"...**380.00**
Distribution of Vessels...South Atlantic Blockading Squadron, 13x8"...**310.00**
For California!, Good Schooner Civilian, notice of sail, 1850s, 9x8" ...**135.00**
How the War Commenced, Pro-Union Civil War, 1864, 17½x11½"...**490.00**
Iowa Citizen Extra, Capitol of Iowa, 18x6" **185.00**
Lindbergh Kidnapping, $25,000 Reward, handwriting sample, 11x8"...**100.00**
Negro American League Baseball, Satchel Page vignette, 22x14"...**260.00**
Northern Liberties Watchman's Address...1840, fireman's info, rare, G...**100.00**
Pickwick Papers, Charles Dickens play, Theatre Royal, 1837, 11x8"..**210.00**

Report of massacre in Ohio, printed in Boston in 1793, stains and repairs, 22½x60¾", $900.00.

Senate Floor Plan, 31st Congress, seating chart, 1849, 14¾x16½" ...**250.00**
Southern Yankee Doodle, Confederate song sheet, 2-color litho, 9x5"...**185.00**
US Cartridge Co, Self-Cleaning Cartridges Rim Fire-Center Fire, 19x13"...**210.00**
Washington Memorial, linen-bk, copper-eng vignette, 1800, 25x19"..**1,200.00**

Bronzes

Thomas Ball, George Bessell, and Leonard Volk were some of the earliest American sculptors who produced figures in bronze for home decor during the 1840s. Pieces of historical significance were the most popular, but by the 1880s a more fanciful type of artwork took hold. Some of the fine sculptors of the day were Daniel Chester French, Augustus St. Gaudens, and John Quincy Adams Ward. Bronzes reached the height of their popularity at the turn of the century. The American West was portrayed to its fullest by Remington, Russell, James Frazier, Hermon MacNeil, and Solon Borglum. Animals of every species were modeled by A.P. Proctor, Paul Bartlett, and Albert Laellele, to name but a few.

Art Nouveau and Art Deco influenced the medium during the '20s, evidenced by the works of Allen Clark, Harriet Frismuth, E.F. Sanford, and Bessie P. Vonnoh.

Be aware that recasts abound. While often esthetically satisfactory, they are not original and should be priced accordingly. In much the same manner as prints are evaluated, the original castings made under the direction of the artist are the most valuable. Later castings from the original mold are worth less. A recast is not made from the original mold. Instead, a rubber-like substance is applied to the bronze, peeled away, and filled with wax. Then, using the same 'lost wax' procedure as the artist uses on completion of his original wax model, a clay-like substance is formed around the wax figure and the whole fired to vitrify the clay. The wax, of course, melts away, hence the term 'lost wax.' Recast bronzes lose detail and are somewhat smaller than the original due to the shrinkage of the clay mold.

Amatus, Louis; charging lion, 1883, 35x48x14" **10,650.00**
Barye, AL; dog playing w/mouse, 4½x7" at base.........................**450.00**
Bermoud, E; shepherdess & flock, gilt finish, 9" **950.00**
Bormann, Wilhelm; nude child w/cat on shoulder, EX patina, 12½"...**850.00**
Chapin, H; nude w/drape over left side, left hand to head, 29"..**2,500.00**
Chiparus, Russian dancers, gold-pnt & ivory, 22½" **32,315.00**
Christophe, Pierre; Greyhound, patinated, blk plinth, 12¼" **750.00**
Clara, Juan; seated girl plays w/2 cats, 12½" **1,250.00**
Colleoni, B; equestrian in full-body armor, EX patina, 22" **2,235.00**
Cunningham, Mike; Tribute to San Miguel, 2 bulls, 1961, 8".....**650.00**
Dallin, C; Appeal to the Spirit, chief on horseback, 20x19"...**1,200.00**
Descomps, Russian lady dancer, ivory inlay, marble base, 18"..**3,800.00**
Drouot, E; Egyptian woman standing w/harp, 26" **1,624.00**
Du Nouy, Jean; draped lady by cistern w/4 putti, silvered, 1911, 17" ...**7,635.00**
Dullard, Marcu; boy w/frog, pelican at ft, fountain, verdigris, 34"....**5,000.00**
Frampton, George; Enid the Fair (bust), orig dk patina, 1907, 20½"...**6,500.00**
Fremiet, E; Char de Minerve, man & 3-horse chariot, gilt, 25x21"..**7,185.00**
Gaudez, A; gypsy maiden standing on rug, EX patina, 34".......**2,115.00**
Gautier, JL; Mephistopheles, dk brn patina, 1890, 27"............**2,200.00**
Gruzalski, James; Two Feathers, Indian man's head, 28x8" **2,000.00**
Ivanovitch (att); Russian Warrior After Battle, patinated, 25½"..**6,900.00**
Janssen, Ulfert; Walt Whitman (bust), 27"...............................**1,500.00**
Kauba, Carl; Indian chief standing w/carbine, 26x12" **1,000.00**
Kauba, K; Celtic Warrior on Horseback, gilt, 12x14x5½"...........**800.00**
Ladd, crab w/lg open claws, EX patina, 9½x12½x11½" **1,665.00**
Lamarquier, Nature Boy, seated figure, ca 1890-1910, 15¾" **675.00**
Lecourtier, P; Fantasia Arabe, lacks rifle, patinated, 35¼"........**2,400.00**
Leduc, J; Nessus et Dejanire, gilt, marble plinth, 30x32x9" **5,175.00**
Ligueur, soldier w/rifle & sword, 22x7¾" **350.00**

Madrassi, Diane, seated/eyes shielded by right hand, 1890s, 29"..**3,360.00**
Malavolli, F; woman & child on donkey, 17x14" **1,300.00**
Masson, JE; Viking on Horseback...Naked Female, 17½"...........**975.00**
Meit, Conrad (att); Eve, standing nude w/apple in hand, 17th C, 14" ..**3,525.00**
Mene, PJ; Great Dane w/front ft raised, 17th C, 8¼x9¼x3¾" ...**400.00**
Mene, PJ; horse at fence, 11¼x16x5¾" **950.00**
Mene, PJ; Scotch Hunter & Deerhounds, 19th C, 20x13x10"...**1,750.00**
Nelson, A; La Gardeuse Sous, 2-color bust, 20" **1,900.00**
Omerth, Salome, gilt w/ivory inserts, 8"......................................**750.00**
Pautrot, F; rooster about to peck lizard, 17x18x7¾"................**1,795.00**
Pinedo, Emile; Arabe en Marche, walking man, 1870-1905, 24½"..**675.00**
Rose, Adam; Seated Am Bison, dk patina, gr marble base, 8½x15" ...**865.00**
Ruffier, Noell; Bara bust, military attire, late 19th C, 18½" **1,000.00**
Scheaf, C; cape buffalo being attacked by 2 lions, 14½x20"....**4,000.00**
Sciver, Robert M; When I Was a Kid, cowboy on horse, 13x6½" ...**3,500.00**
Silvestre, Paul; female archer, 15½" **650.00**
Stock, Carl; man w/lg hammer over shoulder, marble base, 21"..**900.00**
Sunger, cat prowling, marble base, 13" L................................**850.00**
Unsigned, buffalo, detailed, free-standing, 3½x5½" **450.00**
Unsigned, Classical nude lady w/draped cloth, on base, ca 1900, 44" ..**6,000.00**
Valton, Charles; wounded tiger w/arrows through body, 19" L......**1,000.00**
Vienna, Arab kneeling in prayer, cold pnt, Bergman foundry, 5½" ..**865.00**
Vienna, Arab shoemaker among shoes, cold-pnt, ca 1900, 3"...**1,000.00**
Vienna, boy w/jug on carpet, cold pnt, Bergman foundry, 3⅝"...**1,000.00**
Vienna, elephant rider, cold pnt, inset ivory tusks, 6x7x3⅛"...**1,500.00**
Vienna, Indian warrior on horse, polychrome, Bergman, 6¾x12x5" ...**1,150.00**
Vienna, Persian rug seller, cold pnt, Bergman foundry, 6½x6½x7" ...**2,000.00**
Von Bary-Doussin, Shepherd & His Flock, dk brn patina, 27" L...**2,200.00**
Von Miller, Ferdinand; bird on branch, 5½x5" **550.00**
Wernekinck, S; Nouveau dancing nude, doré finish, marble base, 29"..**2,800.00**
Zach, Bruno; draped nude female on marble base, 17" **7,500.00**

Xavier, Franz; Orientalist Dancer Seated, polychrome, Made in Paris, 23½", $1,000.00. (Photo courtesy Neal Auction Company)

Brouwer

Theophilis A. Brouwer operated a one-man studio on Middle Lane in East Hampton, Long Island, from 1894 until 1903, when he relocated to West Hampton. He threw rather thin vessels of light, porous white clay which he fired at a relatively low temperature. He then glazed them and fired them in an open-flame kiln, where he manipulated them with a technique he later patented as 'flame painting.' This resulted in lustered glazes, mostly in the orange and amber family, with organic, free-form patterns. Because of the type of clay he used and the low firing, the wares are brittle and often found with damage. This deficiency has kept them undervalued in the art pottery market.

Brouwer turned to sculpture around 1911. His pottery often carries the 'whalebone' mark, M-shaped for the Middle Lane Pottery, and reminiscent of the genuine whalebones Brouwer purportedly found on his property. Other pieces are marked 'Flame' or 'Brouwer.' Our advisors for this category are Suzanne Perrault and David Rago; they are listed in the Directory under New Jersey.

Key: fp — fire-painted

Bud vase, fp yel/brn lustre, flared w/squat base, 7x4", EX, $400 to ..**600.00**
Candlestick holder, fp brn lustre, 4 undulating sides, 6".............**300.00**
Vase, fp amber/gr/yel, flat shoulder, 3½x4" **1,035.00**
Vase, fp amber/yel/orange, ribbed, factory drilled, label, 13x9", NM **5,750.00**
Vase, fp yel/orange/purple, 4x5", VG/EX, from $300 to..............**400.00**

Brownies by Palmer Cox

Created by Palmer Cox in 1883, the Brownies charmed children through the pages of books and magazines, as dolls, on their dinnerware, in advertising material, and on souvenirs. Each had his own personality, among them The Dude, The Cadet, The Policeman, and The Chairman. They represented many nations; one national character was Uncle Sam. But the oversized, triangular face with the startled expression, the protruding tummy, and the spindle legs were characteristics of them all. They were inspired by the Scottish legends related to Cox as a child by his parents, who were of English descent. His introduction of the Brownies to the world was accomplished by a poem called *The Brownies Ride*. Books followed in rapid succession, thirteen in the series, all written as well as illustrated by Palmer Cox.

By the late 1890s, the Brownies were active in advertising. They promoted such products as games, coffee, toys, patent medicines, and rubber boots. 'Greenies' were the Brownies' first cousins, created by Cox to charm and to woo through the pages of the advertising almanacs of the G.G. Green Company of New Jersey. The Kodak Brownie camera became so popular and sold in such volume that the term became synonymous with this type of camera. (However, it was not endorsed by Cox. George Eastman named the camera but avoided royalty payment to Palmer Cox by doing his own version of them.)

Since the late 1970s a biography on Palmer Cox has been written, a major rock band had their concert T-shirts adorned with his Brownies, and a reproduction of the Uncle Sam candlestick is known to exist. Because of the resurging interest in Cox's Brownies beware of other possible reproductions. Our advisor for this category is Anne Kier; she is listed in the Directory under Ohio.

Ad, Brownie Rubber Stamps & the Greatest Show on Earth, 10x7", EX...**15.00**
Ashtray, Brownie scene, RS Germany, 1913 ....**95.00**
Book, A Fox Grows Old, 1946, EX...**15.00**
Book, Adventures of a Brownie, Miss Mulock, 1898, EX **80.00**
Book, Another Brownie Book, NY, 1890, 1st ed, w/dust jacket, VG ...**250.00**
Book, Another Brownie Book, 144 pgs, 1967, 9½x6¾", EX.........**15.00**
Book, Brownie Clown of Brownie Town, 1908.............................**235.00**
Book, Brownies & Goblins, Grosset Dunlap, no date, VG...........**45.00**
Book, Brownies & Other Stories, 1918, EX **40.00**
Book, Brownies & Prince Florimel, Century, 1918, VG **95.00**
Book, Brownies & the Farmer, 1902, 8¾x6¾", VG+ **40.00**
Book, Brownies at Home, w/dust cover, 1942, VG **35.00**
Book, Brownies at Home, 144 pgs, Century Co, 1893, VG...........**85.00**
Book, Brownies in Fairyland, Century Co.....................................**45.00**
Book, Comic Yarns in Verse, Prose & Picture, 1898, 7½x5", VG ..**18.00**
Book, Funny Animals, 1 color image, many blk/wht, 1903, 10x7½", VG..**18.00**
Book, Funny Stories About Funny People, 1905, EX....................**35.00**
Book, Little Goody Two Shoes, 1903, EX **40.00**

Book, The Brownies, Their Book, 1897, EX 185.00
Book, Wit & Wisdom, 32 pgs, 1890, 7x4½", VG 15.00
Bottle, soda; emb Brownies, M...30.00
Brownie Portrait Cubes, McLoughlin Bros, c Cox 1892, VG......300.00
Calendar, Brownies, color litho, 1898, EX 225.00
Camera, Eastman-Kodak Brownie 2A, EXIB (not endorsed by Cox)....145.00
Candlestick, Policeman (Bobby), majolica, 7½"..........................300.00
Candy dish, 15 Brownies, ball ft, Tufts SP, 7x5½" 265.00
Cigar box, wood w/Our Brownies emb inner lid label, EX+........185.00
Cigar holder/ashtray, full-figure Brownie, Pairpoint SP 425.00
Comic book, The Brownies, Dell Four-Color, #398, 1952, VG.....20.00
Creamer, Little Boy Blue verse & 4 Brownies, gold trim, china....95.00
Creamer, Scottsman head, majolica, 3¼"....................................100.00
Cup, SP w/9 enameled Brownies, Middletown Plate Co, 3"........235.00
Cup & saucer, demi; comical action Brownies, Ceramic Art Co...110.00
Figure, Chinaman, papier-mâché head, 9", EX 500.00
Figures, papier-mâché w/stick legs, jtd arms, 1900s, 5", EX, 4 for ..1,500.00

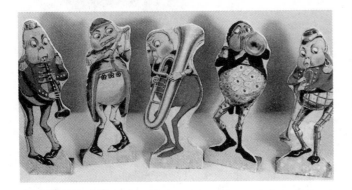

Figures, wooden band members, unmarked, ca 1900, 8", EX, $80.00 for this set of five.

Fruit crate label, harvesting orange juice, 1930s, 10x11", EX........25.00
Humidor, Policeman (Bobby) head figural, majolica, 6".............250.00
Ice cream bag, Cox illus, 5¢ orig value, 1930s, M.........................40.00
Magazine page, Ladies' Home Journal, Cox illus, ca 1890 ....15.00
Match holder, Brownie on striker, majolica 235.00
Needle book, Brownies, 1892 World's Fair, rare 75.00
Nodder, Brownies (3) on donkey, bsk, German, 1890s, 6½x6¼" ..1,950.00
Paper doll, Indian Brownie, Lion Coffee, EX 40.00
Paperweight, Brownie figural, SP..145.00
Pencil box, rolling-pin shape, 15 Brownies in boat......................95.00
Picture, on bank of river, bl ink, fr, 7x5¾", EX............................70.00
Pin box, Brownies running across lid, SP, EX.............................150.00
Pitcher, china, Brownies playing golf on tan, 6" 185.00
Pitcher, china, 2 Brownies on front, 3 on bk, 4½"......................110.00
Plate, porc, mk La Francaise, 7"...85.00
Plate, SP, Brownies on rim, 8½"..95.00
Print, Brownies fishing, matted, 1895, 13½x15½"........................55.00
Print, Brownies toboggan ride, matted, 1895, 13½x15½" 55.00
Rubber stamp, set of 12, NM...100.00
Sheet music, Dance of the Brownies...30.00
Sign, emb Brownies on tin, Howell's Root Beer, EX...................185.00
Sign, orange crate; serving & drinking juice, Brownies Brand, 11x10" 25.00
Stationery, Ten Little Brownies, envelopes/note paper/box, 1930s, G...25.00
Table set, brass, emb Brownies, 3-pc (knife/fork/spoon), no box......85.00
Table set, brass, emb Brownies, 6", in orig box............................95.00
Toy, Movie Top, litho tin w/3 windows, ca 1927, 1⅞x4¾" dia ...150.00
Trade card, Estey Organ Co, playing instruments, 3x5".................15.00
Trade card, Mitchell, Lewis & Stave Co, 3x5", VG.......................30.00

Trade card, Sheriff's Sale Segars, Brownies & product, 5x3" 25.00
Tray, china, 2 fencing Brownies, self hdls, 6¼x4½".....................110.00
Tray, tin, Brownies w/giant dish of ice cream, 13¼x10½", EX....150.00

Brush-McCoy

George Brush began his career in the pottery industry in 1901 working for the J.B. Owens Pottery Co. in Zanesville, Ohio. He left the company in 1907 to go into business for himself, only to have fire completely destroy his pottery less than one year after it was founded. In 1909 he became associated with J.W. McCoy, who had operated a pottery of his own in Roseville, Ohio, since 1899. The two men formed the Brush-McCoy Pottery in 1911, locating their headquarters in Zanesville. After the merger, the company expanded and produced not only staple commercial wares but also fine artware. Lines of the highest quality such as Navarre, Venetian, Oriental, and Sylvan were equal to that of their larger competitors. Because very little of the ware was marked, it is often mistaken for Weller, Roseville, or Peters and Reed.

In 1918 after a fire in Zanesville had destroyed the manufacturing portion of that plant, all production was contained in their Roseville (Ohio) plant #2. A stoneware type of clay was used there, and as a result the artware lines of Jewel, Zuniart, King Tut, Florastone, Jetwood, Krakle-Kraft, and Panelart are so distinctive that they are more easily recognizable. Examples of these lines are unique and very beautiful, also quite rare and highly prized!

After McCoy died, the family withdrew their interests, and in 1925 the name of the firm was changed to The Brush Pottery. The era of hand-decorated art pottery production had passed for the most part, having been almost completely replaced by commercial lines. The Brush-Barnett family retained their interest in the pottery until 1981 when it was purchased by the Dearborn Company.

For more information we recommend *The Collector's Encyclopedia of Brush-McCoy Pottery* by Sharon and Bob Huxford, and *Sanford's Guide to Brush-McCoy Pottery, Books I* and *II*, written by Martha and Steve Sanford, our advisors for this category, and edited by David P. Sanford. They are listed in the Directory under California.

Of all the wares bearing the later Brush script mark, their figural cookie jars are the most collectible, and several have been reproduced. Information on Brush cookie jars (as well as confusing reproductions) can be found in *The Collector's Encyclopedia of Cookie Jars* by Joyce and Fred Roerig; they are listed in the Directory under South Carolina. Beware! Cookie jars marked Brush-McCoy are not authentic.

Cookie Jars

Antique Touring Car...700.00
Boy w/Balloons 800.00
Chick in Nest (+)...400.00
Cinderella Pumpkin, #W32 ....250.00
Circus Horse, gr (+)...950.00
Clown, yel pants...200.00
Clown Bust, #W49 ....300.00
Cookie House, #W31 ....125.00
Covered Wagon, dog finial, #W30, minimum value (+)............550.00
Cow w/Cat on Bk, brn, #W10 (+)...125.00
Cow w/Cat on Bk, purple, minimum value (+) 1,000.00
Davy Crockett, no gold, mk USA (+)......................................300.00
Dog & Basket 250.00
Donkey Cart, ears down, gray, #W33 ....400.00
Donkey Cart, ears up, #W33, minimum value 800.00
Elephant w/Ice Cream Cone (+) 500.00
Elephant w/Monkey on Bk, minimum value...........................5,000.00
Fish, #W52 (+)..500.00

Formal Pig, gold trim, #W7 Brush USA (+) 475.00
Formal Pig, no gold, gr hat & coat (+) 300.00
Gas Lamp, #K1 ....75.00
Granny, pk apron, bl dots on skirt 325.00
Granny, plain skirt, minimum value (+) 400.00
Happy Bunny, wht, #W25 ....225.00
Hen on Basket, unmk 125.00
Hillbilly Frog, minimum value (+) 4,500.00
Humpty Dumpty, w/beany & bow tie (+) 275.00
Humpty Dumpty, w/peaked hat & shoes 225.00
Laughing Hippo, #W27 (+) 750.00
Little Angel (+) 800.00
Little Boy Blue, gold trim, #K25, sm 700.00
Little Boy Blue, no gold, #K24 Brush USA, lg (+) 800.00
Little Girl, #017 (+) 550.00
Little Red Riding Hood, gold trim, mk lg, minimum value (+) ..850.00
Little Red Riding Hood, no gold, #K24 USA, sm 550.00
Night Owl 125.00
Old Clock, #W10 ....150.00
Old Shoe, #W23 (+) 125.00
Panda, #W21 (+) 250.00
Peter, Peter Pumpkin Eater, #W24 ....300.00
Peter Pan, gold trim, lg (+) 800.00
Peter Pan, no gold, sm 550.00
Puppy Police (+) 585.00
Raggedy Ann, #W16 ....475.00
Sitting Pig (+) 400.00
Smiling Bear, #W46 (+) 350.00
Squirrel on Log, #W26 ....100.00
Squirrel w/Top Hat, blk coat & hat 275.00
Squirrel w/Top Hat, gr coat 250.00
Stylized Owl 350.00
Stylized Siamese, #W41 ....450.00
Teddy Bear, ft apart 250.00
Teddy Bear, ft together 200.00
Treasure Chest, #W28 ....170.00

Miscellaneous

Bowl, Mat Green, #01, 1913, 5", from $40 to 60.00
Butter crock, Corn, w/lid, #60, from $300 to 350.00
Casserole, Grape Ware, w/lid, #178, 1913, from $150 to 200.00
Creamer, Corn, #59, 4", from $150 to 175.00
Cuspidor, Frog, #03, 1915, from $185 to 125.00
Jardiniere, Aegean Inlaid, #222, 1914, 10¾", from $300 to 400.00
Jardiniere, Bluebird, #228, 1915, 9", from $450 to 550.00
Jardiniere, Fancy Blended, #202, 1910, 10½", from $150 to 175.00
Jardiniere, Rich Blue, #214, 1917, 6¼", from $175 to 225.00
Jardiniere, Roman Decor, #218, 1914, 8", from $650 to 750.00
Jardiniere, Scenic Egyptian, gr, 1912, 10½", from $400 to 500.00
Jardiniere, Vogue, #213, 1916, 8½", from $250 to 275.00
Jug, Decorated Ivory, #131, 1915, 2-qt, from $150 to 225.00
Jug, Mill, #057, 1912, 4-pt, from $350 to 450.00
Moccasin, Zuniart, 1923, from $750 to 1,000.00
Pitcher, Nurock, #351, 1916, 5-pt, 8½", from $165 to 200.00
Rolling pin, blue & white stoneware, #166, 1913, from $300 to 375.00
Spill vase, Vogue, #046, 1916, 12", from $200 to 225.00
Stein, Corn, #46, 6", from $125 to 150.00
Tankard, Olympia, from $600 to 800.00
Umbrella stand, Liberty, #73, 1912, from $600 to 800.00
Umbrella stand, New Blended Basketweave, #402, 1915, 21", from $450 to 550.00
Vase, Art Vellum, #052, 4", from $125 to 150.00
Vase, bl Onyx, #052, 4", from $100 to 125.00
Vase, Cleo, #042, 11¾", from $750 to 900.00

Vase, Cleo, #044, 1915, 11", from $550 to 650.00
Vase, Jewel, #040, 6", from $450 to 500.00
Vase, Jewel, #042, 9", from $900 to 1,100.00
Vase, Majolica, #0193, 10", from $225 to 250.00
Vase, Panelart, #076, 7", from $1,100 to 1,400.00

Vase, Jewell, 12",
$2,200.00.

Buffalo Pottery

    The founding of the Buffalo Pottery in Buffalo, New York, in 1901, was a direct result of the success achieved by John Larkin through his innovative methods of marketing 'Sweet Home Soap.' Choosing to omit 'middle-man' profits, Larkin preferred to deal directly with the consumer and offered premiums as an enticement for sales. The pottery soon proved a success in its own right and began producing advertising and commemorative items for other companies, as well as commercial tableware. In 1905 they introduced their Blue Willow line after extensive experimentation resulted in the development of the first successful underglaze cobalt achieved by an American company. Between 1905 and 1909, a line of pitchers and jugs were hand decorated in historical, literary, floral, and outdoor themes. Twenty-nine styles are known to have been made.

    Their most famous line was Deldare Ware, the bulk of which was made from 1908 to 1909. It was hand decorated after illustrations by Cecil Aldin. Views of English life were portrayed in detail through unusual use of color against the natural olive green cast of the body. Today the 'Fallowfield Hunt' scenes are more difficult to locate than 'Scenes of Village Life in Ye Olden Days.' A Deldare calendar plate was made in 1910. These are very rare and are highly valued by collectors. The line was revived in 1923 and dropped again in 1925. Every piece was marked 'Made at Ye Buffalo Pottery, Deldare Ware Underglaze.' Most are dated, though date has no bearing on the value. Emerald Deldare was made on the same olive body and on standard Deldare Ware shapes, and featured historical scenes and Art Nouveau decorations. Most pieces are found with a 1911 date stamp. Production was very limited due to the intricate, time-consuming detail. Needless to say, it is very rare and extremely desirable.

    Abino Ware, most of which was made in 1912, also used standard Deldare shapes, but its colors were earthy and the decorations more delicately applied. Sailboats, windmills, and country scenes were favored motifs. These designs were achieved by overpainting transfer prints and were often signed by the artist. The ware is marked 'Abino' in hand-printed block letters. Production was limited; and as a result, examples of this line are scarce today.

Commercial or institutional ware was another of Buffalo Pottery's crowning achievements. In 1917 vitrified china production began, and the firm produced for accounts worldwide. After 1956 all of their wares bore the name Buffalo China. Buffalo China (commercial and institutional ware) is being produced today by Oneida Silver Company.

Our advisor for this category is Lila Shrader; she is listed in the Directory under California.

See also Bluebird China.

Key:
BC — Buffalo China   BS — bottom stamped
BC, Oneida — Buffalo China   SL — side logo
     after 1983   TL — top logo

Abino

Chocolate, cup & saucer; sailing ship scene.................................440.00
Chocolate, cup & saucer; windmill, village scene, boats.............525.00
Chocolate pot, sailing ships at sea, 10"...825.00
Pitcher, boats on rough seas, sgn Harris, octagonal, 7"................995.00

Pitcher, man on path to windmill, village scene and harbor, C. Harris, 10", NM, $1,300.00.

(Photo courtesy Smith and Jones)

Plate, harbor scene w/windmills, sgn E Harris, 9¼"....................358.00
Plate, sailing ship at sea, 8¼"..330.00
Tray, harbor scene w/boats & mtn bkground, sgn R Stuart, 12x9"..2,325.00

Commercial China

Ashtray/matchbox holder, Lil's Tavern/since 1915, 5½" dia..........67.00
Bowl, Roycroft, Ye Olde Ivory Buffalo China, 4"...........................88.00
Butter pat, BCC w/crossed golf tee marker, TL, 1923, 3¼"...........46.00
Butter pat, Mandalay, 1927, 3"..14.00
Butter pat, Plymouth, BC, 2⅞", from $4 to...................................10.00
Butter pat, White Cotton Hotel, BC, TL, 1922, 3¼"....................23.00
Candlestick, Hotel Commodore, w/finger ring, SL & BS.............66.00
Children's ware, bowl, cereal; Mother Goose, 5"............................38.00
Creamer, Mandalay, well-defined spout, hdl, 4"..............................35.00
Creamer, Mory's founded in 1849 (SL), hdl, BC, ca 1930s, 4¼"..42.00
Creamer, SL of Elk descending mtn, hdl, BC, 1923, ind, 2¾"......39.00
Creamer, Yellowstone Park Hotel, YPH SL, no hdl, 2"................136.00
Creamer, York, no hdl, 2", from $8 to...12.00
Cup & saucer, Biltmore Hotel, Los Angeles, gold & blk w/logo...65.00
Cup & saucer, coffee; Red Willow, BC-Oneida era.........................12.00
Cup & saucer, demi; Ahwahnee (Yosemite), blk & brn geometric, BC....55.00
Custard cup, Blue Willow, BC, 1925, 3x3¼".................................36.00
Handle to silver flatware, Biltmore Hotel, gr on ivory, $29 to......65.00

Horseradish pot, Plymouth, w/lid, 2⅞"...35.00
Mug, Mister Donut, SL, BC, from $6 to..10.00
Mustard pot, blk & wht check 2" band, w/lid, BC, 3½"..................26.00
Mustard pot, Plymouth, w/lid, BC, 3¼", from $15 to.....................26.00
Mustard pot, Yellowstone Park Hotel, YPH SL, w/lid, 3¼".........145.00
Plate, Alpine Restaurant in purple script, SL, BC, 9½"..................26.00
Plate, Buffalo Athletic Club, BC, TL, 1926, 9½"...........................24.00
Plate, Country Garden scene, brick red or gr, 11", from $10 to.....22.00
Plate, Fallen Leaf Lodge, CA, 1919, TL, 6¼"................................40.00
Plate, LAAC, Los Angeles Athletic Club, TL, 1926, 9½"..............38.00
Plate, PUC (Pacific Union Club?), harbor & mtn scene, 1927, 8"..46.00
Plate, Steak 'n Shake, TL, BC, 6"..3.00
Plate, stripes, various colors & szs, BC-Oneida era, from $2 to.....12.00
Plate, undulating stripes, various colors & szs, BC-Oneida era, $2 to....12.00
Plate, US Forest Service by BC-Oneida, 9½"..................................11.00
Platter, Ahwahnee (Yosemite), blk & brn geometrics, BC, 1923, 12x9"..125.00
Platter, clipper ship, bl & wht, 1927, 8x6".....................................22.00
Platter, Red Rooster, strutting/holding walking stick, TL, 8x6".....24.00
Platter, Tahoe Tavern, TL & BS, 1926, 8x6"..................................57.00
Platter, USBF w/fisheries' flag, TL, 1927, 12x9"..........................105.00
Relish dish, chicken & chicks scene w/gr stripe, 7x4½".................16.00
Tankard, Fallowfield Hunt, Hunt Supper, mc on ivory, 12".....1,650.00
Teapot, Lenhardt superimposed over lg detailed tree, SL, ind........39.00
Teapot, Roycroft, SL, BC-Oneida era, 4¼"...................................100.00
Tray, pin; Palace Hotel, San Francisco, 1917, 5x3½".....................32.00
Tray, Roycroft, TL, hunter gr & brn on ivory, 10x10"..................330.00
Tray, US Navy, open tab hdls, Captain's Mess w/pennant, 8x5".......46.00
Vase, Roycroft Inn, BC, 1995, 5"...25.00

Deldare

Ashtray/match holder, Fallowfield Hunt, 6" dia...........................700.00
Bowl, cereal; Ye Olden Days, 5½-6½", from $225 to.....................310.00
Bowl, Fallowfield Hunt, Breakfast at Three Pigeons, 5x12".....1,400.00
Bowl, fruit; Emerald, Dr Syntax Reading His Tour, 3¾x9".......1,320.00
Bowl, nut; Emerald, squirrel w/nut, butterfly panel, 8".............1,500.00
Bowl, soup; Ye Village Street, 9", from $135 to............................250.00
Bowl, Yel Olden Days, sgn A Wade, 6¼".......................................195.00
Candlestick, Village Scenes, factory drilled, wired+socket, 8¾"...286.00
Candlestick, Village Scenes, 8¾", from $296 to.............................427.00
Chamberstick, Village Scenes, finger ring+match holder, 5½-6" dia.......990.00
Chop plate, Fallowfield Hunt, The Start, 14".............................1,055.00
Creamer, Fallowfield Hunt, Breaking Cover, 4½"..........................110.00
Creamer & sugar bowl, Village Life in Ye Olden Days, w/lid.......500.00
Cup, punch; Ye Village Street, 3"...440.00
Cup & saucer, chocolate; Emerald, Art Nouveau florals, 5"....1,450.00
Cup & saucer, chocolate; Village Scenes.......................................510.00
Cup & saucer, Fallowfield Hunt scene (uncaptioned), from $145 to...180.00
Cup & saucer, Ye Village Scene..167.00
Hair receiver, Fallowfield Hunt (untitled), 4¾"............................798.00
Humidor, Ye Lion Inn, 8-sided, 7", from $715 to..........................775.00
Inkwell, Emerald, butterflies/arches/dmns, no lid, 2½x2½"........660.00
Mug, Emerald, I Give the Law to That Are Owing..., 2¼".........895.00
Mug, Fallowfield Hunt, Breaking Cover, 3½", from $280 to.......340.00
Mug, Ye Lion Inn, 4½", from $240 to..320.00
Mustard jar, Scenes of Village Life in Ye Olden Days, w/lid, 3¾"....2,100.00
Pitcher, Fallowfield Hunt, Breaking Cover, 6¾"...........................490.00
Pitcher, Fallowfield Hunt, 6"...395.00
Pitcher, Robin Hood on Deldare body, 8¼"..............................1,350.00
Pitcher, To Spare an Old Broken Soldier, 6-sided, 7".................420.00
Plaque, Ye Lion Inn, 12"..488.00
Plate, bread & butter; Ye Olden Days, 6"......................................95.00
Plate, Fallowfield Hunt, The Death, 8¼".......................................155.00
Plate, Fallowfield Hunt, The Start, 9¼", from $150 to.................185.00

Plate, salesman's sample, Hand Painted Deldare...Underglaze, 6¾"..1,155.00
Plate, Ye Olden Times, sgn E Hacker, 9¼", from $144 to 160.00
Plate, Ye Town Crier, sgn Rex, 8½", from $88 to 114.00
Powder dish, Ye Village Street, w/lid, 4¾" dia 375.00
Relish dish, Fallowfield Hunt, The Dash, 12x6½".....................480.00
Saucer, Ye Olden Days, 6" 90.00
Sugar bowl, Fallowfield scenes, untitled, 6-sided, 3½x4"............395.00
Tankard, Great Controversy, 12½" 1,080.00
Tea tile, Fallowfield Hunt, 6¼" dia, from $188 to 310.00
Teapot, Emerald, Dr Syntax Disputing, 5"..................................488.00
Teapot, Fallowfield Hunt, The Start, 4½".....................................465.00
Teapot, Village Life in Ye Olden Days, 4½"................................410.00
Tray, calling card; Emerald, Dr Syntax Robbed..., tab hdls, 7" dia...670.00
Tray, dresser; Dancing Ye Minuet, 12x9".....................................610.00
Tray, pin; Ye Fallowfield Hunt, 6x3½"...610.00
Tray, Pin; Ye Olden Days, 6x3½"...255.00
Vase, Emerald, Am Beauty, butterflies/flowers/pastoral scene, 14"..1,100.00
Vase, fashionable ladies & a gentleman, shouldered, 8½", $920 to ..990.00
Vase, Ye Village Parson/Ye Village Schoolmaster, 8½", from $890 to 940.00

Plaque, Dr. Syntax Sells Grizzle, Streissel, 1911, 13½", NM, $1,000.00.

(Photo courtesy Smith and Jones)

Miscellaneous

In this section all items are marked Buffalo Pottery unless noted. It does not include any commerical (restaurant type) china or items marked Deldare.

Blue Willow, bone dish, crescent shape, dtd 1909, 3½x6½" 58.00
Blue Willow, bowl, rim soup; 8" 48.00
Blue Willow, bowl, vegetable; domed lid, hdls, 11x9½" 166.00
Blue Willow, butter dish, w/dome lid & ice ring, 8¼" dia 98.00
Blue Willow, butter pat, 3¼", from $14 to 42.00
Blue Willow, creamer, bulbous, no collar, 4¼"...........................49.00
Blue Willow, pitcher, recessed hdl, w/lid, dtd 1910, 6¼", $188 to...265.00
Blue Willow, pitcher, rich gold trim, 4¾" 165.00
Blue Willow, platter, 12x9½"...135.00
Blue Willow, underplate for gravy boat, 9x5", from $46 to............65.00
Bowl, lg roses w/gr & pk ground, rich gold, early mk, 10½" 55.00
Butter pat, Bluebird, 3"...48.00
Butter pat, Bonrea, gr-bl ornate scroll border w/rich gold, 3" 10.00
Butter pat, various rose patterns, some w/gold, 3", from $6 to.......21.00
Butter pat, Vienna, cobalt w/rich gold, 3", from $10 to.................25.00
Butter tub, roses w/rich gold, ice ring, BC, 1920............................39.00
Canister, Coffee (sugar/flower/rice/tea/etc), wht w/bl floral, 6¾"...135.00
Chamber pot, pk & yel roses w/gold, hdls, w/lid, 8x10½" 178.00
Chamber set, Tea Rose, pitcher+bowl+pot+soap dish w/lid........325.00
Child's feeding dish, Campbell-like kids, Grace Drayton, 7½"......67.00
Creamer, Geranium, cobalt tones, 3½"..80.00

Creamer, Geranium, mc w/gold, 3½"..44.00
Creamer, Roosevelt Bears, 3" 260.00
Cruet, Oil or Vinegar, pk rose/etc, w/hdl, ceramic stopper, 6¼"....72.00
Cup & saucer, Bluebird 35.00
Cup & saucer, Bonrea, Vienna, bl w/rich gold, from $26 to 35.00
Cup & saucer, Cairo, Tea Rose, Beverly (sm rose patterns), $19 to ..35.00
Cuspidor, Chrysanthemum, 2¾x7½"...90.00
Dinner set, various rose patterns, serves 8 (6-pc settings+8 servers) ..610.00
Egg cup, ivory w/wide gold band, B in script, 3⅞" 46.00
Jug, Cinderella, mc w/much gold, 6½", from $525 to.................685.00
Jug, Dutch, castle & windmill scenes, mc, 6½" 397.00
Jug, Holland, girls knitting, mc on wht, 7", from $360 to 550.00
Jug, Mason, teal gr rosettes w/fishermen & Roman ruins at top, 8¼"...550.00
Jug, Old Mill, bl on ivory w/rich gold, 6¼" 700.00
Medallion, John Larkin cameo on jasperware, wht on dk bl, 7x6"...415.00
Pitcher, Art Nouveau, bl w/rich gold, 8½"...................................710.00
Pitcher, Chrysanthemum (part of toilet set), 11", from $188 to..220.00
Pitcher, Gaudy Willow, brn transfer w/bl, gr & gold, 8" 455.00
Pitcher, Gaudy Willow, brn transfer w/cobalt, gr & gold, 6" 385.00
Pitcher, Gloriana, Nouveau lady w/flowers, bls on wht w/gold, 9¼"..700.00
Pitcher, John Paul Jones, bl on ivory, 9¼" 300.00
Pitcher, sailor, lighthouse on other side, bl transfer, 9" 490.00
Pitcher, wht w/gold, melon shape, 9"..230.00
Plate, Buffalo NY, Bonrea border w/buffalo, cobalt & wht, 7½"....155.00
Plate, Buffalo NY Sesquicentennial, 150th...1982, bl & wht, 9½" ..11.00
Plate, commemorative, Broadwater Natatorium, Helena MT, teal, 7½"...26.00
Plate, commemorative, WCTU, hometown scenes, bl & wht, 9"...250.00
Plate, deer, various species, from RK Beck's studies, 9", from $24 to ..38.00
Plate, Dr Syntax Advertising for a Wife, bl & wht, 14x11" 245.00
Plate, LaFrance, bl & wht florals on edge, 9" 33.00
Plate, Old Hoss (gentle old dog), teal gr, 7¼"..............................80.00
Plate, various stream fish by RK Beck, 9¼", from $19 to 30.00
Platter, Buffalo Hunt, Indians running buffalo, teal gr, 14x12" ...248.00
Platter, Dr Syntax Advertising for a Wife, bl & wht, 11x14"......245.00
Salad set, roses, very early, 10½" bowl+4 4¾" bowls 56.00
Spice jar, bl & wht w/gold, knobbed lid, early mk, 3¾", $45 to....78.00
Teapot, Argyle, bl & wht, orig infusor, chain & wood knob on lid ..188.00
Teapot, Royal Rochester, infusor attached to metal lid, 7½".........98.00
Tray, Geranium, mc, 12x9"..885.00
Vase, Geranium, mc, rose-bowl shape, 3¾".................................125.00

Buggy Steps

The collectors of buggy steps are many. While this is a specialized cagegory, their history is very interesting. First recorded mention is from 2500 B.C. in Mesopotamia (now Iraq). Pilgrims were first to use carts in 1621. George Washington ordered three carriages from England, but shipment was delayed, and after three months at sea, they arrived warped and unusable. Two new carriages were ordered from Philadelphia — thus the building of carriages began in America. The American Carriage Manufactures Association turned the American carriage business into the finest in the world. While the heyday of the buggy is considered to be from 1865 to 1910, this estimation may actually be expanded. There were many types; they ranged from the Conestoga wagon, prairie schooner, and cart to the elegant carriages of the day. Buggy steps played their part in the egress and digress of travelers, from president to child alike. Many different steps were manufactured, registered, and their patents secured. Early manufactures proudly displayed their names upon each step. Some iron steps were handcrafted by the local blacksmith. These bear no mark of origin, and they are highly collectible. Today with the refurbishing and full restoration of old buggies, collectors require correct buggy step replacement. The following is a list of a few of the most sought-after buggy steps. Prices quoted below are only a general guideline. Type and condition must be considered. Our advisor for this category is John Waddell; he is listed in the Directory under Texas.

AB Co	55.00
Abbott Buggy Co	55.00
Beebe Cart	55.00
C&W Co	55.00
Cadillac	70.00
Cole	55.00
Columbia	70.00
Creamer Scott Co	65.00
Dean & Co	75.00
Deere	85.00
Easy	65.00
Eckhart	60.00
Emerson	80.00
Ferguson	55.00
Freeport	60.00
Harper	65.00
Henney Buggy Co	80.00
L Burg Mfg Co	55.00
M&T Co w/elephant	85.00
ML Co	55.00
Moon Bros	80.00
Ney, Canton, Ohio	80.00
Parsons & Goodfellow	55.00
Peerless	55.00
Peru	70.00
Racine W&C Co	65.00
Rambler	70.00
Rockford	70.00
S Frazier & Co	65.00
Sattley, Racine	70.00
Scott Cart	60.00
Selle Co	55.00
Spaulding	75.00
Staver	75.00
Stoughton	55.00
Studebaker	85.00
Thompson	60.00
Tiger	75.00
WO Hesse & Son	70.00
WS Frazier & Co	65.00

Burmese

Burmese glass was patented in 1885 by the Mount Washington Glass Co. It is typically shaded from canary yellow to a rosy salmon color. The yellow is produced by the addition of uranium oxide to the mix. The salmon color comes from the addition of gold salts and is achieved by reheating the object (partially) in the furnace. It is thus called 'heat sensitive' glass. Thomas Webb of England was licensed to produce Burmese and often added more gold, giving an almost fuchsia tinge to the salmon in some cases. They called their glass 'Queen's Burmese,' and this is sometimes etched on the base of the object. This is not to be confused with Mount Washington's 'Queen's Design,' which refers to the design painted on the object. Both companies added decoration to many pieces. Mount Washington-Pairpoint produced some Burmese in the late 1920s and Gundersen and Bryden in the '50s and '70s, but the color and shapes are different.

For more information refer to *Mt. Washington Art Glass* by Betty A. Sisk. Our advisors for this category are Dolli and Wilfred Cohen; they are listed in the Directory under California. In the listings that follow,

examples are assumed to have the satin finish unless noted 'shiny.' See also Lamps, Fairy.

Bowl, finger; Mt WA, shiny, 2¾" H	350.00
Bowl, Mt WA, Dmn Quilt, 2 folded-in sides, appl rim decor, 6½" L	600.00
Bowl, oak leaves/blueberries, flaring rim, 2¾x3½"	375.00
Candlesticks, shiny, 5½", pr	395.00
Celery vase, Mt WA, pinched rim, 6½"	350.00
Cruet, Mt WA, shiny, squat ribbed body, mushroom stopper, 7"	1,250.00
Cruet, Mt WA, 30-rib, 7"	1,250.00
Cup, punch; Mt WA, yel rim/hdl, thin walls, 2¾"	130.00

Epergne, Mt. Washington, two ruffled tiers, silver-plate finial, 12¾" diameter, $1,500.00. (Photo courtesy Neal Auction Company)

Epergne, Webb, flower-form center, 3 sm bud vases in brass fr, 8"	1,950.00
Ginger jar, camel rider/pyramids, w/hdls, 6¾"	3,500.00
Pitcher, dragons & flowers (later decor, EX art), 12½"	1,550.00
Pitcher, tankard; Mt WA, scarce sz, 7½x4"	950.00
Plate, Gundersen, EX color, 9"	275.00
Rose bowl, Mt WA, ribbed, tightly crimped rim thrusts upward, 5x9"	550.00
Rose bowl, Webb, floral/leaf stem in amethyst/gr, incurvate, 3½"	395.00
Rose bowl, Webb, floral/leaves, 6-sided rim, 3½"	395.00
Rose bowl, Webb, lav-bl floral/fall-colored leaves, 3"	325.00
Saucer, shiny	85.00
Sherbet, Pairpoint, 1930s, 3½", +6½" plate	295.00
Toothpick holder, Mt WA, Dmn Quilt, shiny, tricon rim, 2x2½"	595.00
Toothpick holder, Mt WA, lt optic Dmn Quilt, tumbler form w/pinch rim	385.00
Toothpick holder, Mt WA, tricorn rim, 2"	495.00
Toothpick holder, Webb, ball shape w/short neck, 2½"	385.00
Vase, flared/ruffled rim, 4", pr	395.00
Vase, Gundersen, man in balloon flight, stylized flowers, 8"	500.00
Vase, jack-in-pulpit; Mt WA, pie-crust rim, 9"	685.00
Vase, jack-in-pulpit; Mt WA, wild flowers/vines, crimped rim, 14"	1,250.00
Vase, lily; Gundersen, 9½"	365.00
Vase, lily; Mt WA, shiny, EX color, 12¾"	875.00
Vase, lily; Mt WA, 12"	750.00
Vase, lily; Mt WA, 15"	950.00
Vase, lily; Webb, Queen's, mc florals, ormolu base, 9½"	1,200.00
Vase, lily; Webb, sepia vines/leaves, yel berries/red rose, thin, 7"	685.00
Vase, Mt WA, daisies, bulbous w/short can neck, 3x3½"	695.00
Vase, Mt WA, fern leaves, in sgn Dunham holder, 6"	545.00
Vase, Mt WA, floral sprays ea side, urn w/gold hdls/rim/ft, 6"	750.00
Vase, Mt WA, gourd form, 12"	900.00
Vase, Mt WA, Oriental poppy, maroon/yel/gr/gilt, rnd w/stick neck, 11"	2,150.00
Vase, Mt WA, scalloped top, long can neck, squat body, 6½"	500.00
Vase, Mt WA, shiny w/appl Burmese flowers, 4-pinch rim, 5x7", NM	3,500.00
Vase, Pairpoint, petal top, incurvate sides, 1920s, 8½"	450.00

Vase, ruffled top, pale ribbed panels, 5½"......................**600.00**
Vase, Webb, bulbous w/crimped top, circle mk, 3", pr................**350.00**
Vase, Webb, crimped top, bulbous, 3", pr..............**300.00**
Vase, Webb, fuchsia/leaves, squat w/flaring trumpet neck, 3x3"..**400.00**
Vase, Webb, Queen's, stick neck, #1149/4 V48F, 10¾"..............**850.00**
Vase, Webb, tiny bl/coral floral sprigs, bulbous w/trumpet neck, 12"....**935.00**

Butter Molds and Stamps

The art of decorating butter began in Europe during the reign of Charles II. This practice was continued in America by the farmer's wife who sold her homemade butter at the weekly market to earn extra money during hard times. A mold or stamp with a special design, hand carved either by her husband or a local craftsman, not only made her product more attractive but also helped identify it as hers. The pattern became the trademark of Mrs. Smith, and all who saw it knew that this was her butter. It was usually the rule that no two farms used the same mold within a certain area, thus the many variations and patterns available to the collector today. The most valuable are those which have animals, birds, or odd shapes. The most sought-after motifs are the eagle, cow, fish, and rooster. These works of early folk art are quickly disappearing from the market.

Molds

Acorns (2) & leaves divided by twisted rope, 6x4½"..................**135.00**
Beaver, simple cvg, minor damage/stains, 4x3⅜"..........................**400.00**
Cow, farmer w/scythe/stars/Latteria Social, hinged, 3x11x7".......**165.00**
Cow, stylized, rope-twist border, dk patina, 4⅞"..........................**220.00**
Cow (dbl), dvtl corners, 1800s, 6x3" w/7" plunger....................**350.00**

Eagle, EX detail, 4"
diameter, $400.00.

(Photo courtesy James Etrice)

Flowers/cow/farming couple, 5-part, hinged, canted sides, 20½"..**330.00**
Flowers/house/shield, 5-part, hinged, splits, 13x13"....................**155.00**
Flowers/star/house/deer, 5-part, hinged, canted sides, 7½x7½"...**175.00**
Hearts (4) in 2 different designs, EX cvg, lollipop, 4" dia..........**225.00**
Olive branch, scrubbed, 4⅞"..**100.00**
Pineapple in sq, 1⅞"..**200.00**
Pomegranate, case mk Patd Apr 17, 1886, 3¾"..................**135.00**
Sheaf of wheat, dtd Apr 17, 1866, 6½x5"....................**135.00**
Sheaves of wheat (2), dvtl corners, 5x6¼x4" +hdl....................**150.00**
Sheep, scrubbed, age crack, ca 1860s, 3⅞".................................**215.00**
Strawberry, scrubbed, 1¾"..**200.00**
Swan, wings out, EX detail, 1¾"..**330.00**
War bonnet w/feathers, vine border, hdl cracked/edge damage, 2"...**110.00**
8 sqs w/fruit or thistles, hdl missing, 3x5x11".........................**165.00**

Stamps

Beaver w/rope-twist border, EX patina, 3¼" dia..........................**110.00**
Bud & leaves, coggled rim, rpr crack, lollipop, 7½x3¾" dia.......**250.00**
Cow, EX details, threaded hdl, 4⅛" dia....................................**880.00**
Cow & flower, deep cvg, coggled rim, 1-pc hdl, 4¼" dia............**460.00**
Cow's head, rfn, 3" dia..**110.00**
Cow w/fence & tree, EX detail, blk ink traces, 3¼" dia..............**110.00**
Daisy, soft natural finish, 3¾" dia....................................**55.00**
Eagle (stylized), curly maple, lollipop, rfn, 4" dia....................**385.00**
Eagle on laurel branch, coggled rim, 1-pc cvd hdl, 4½" dia........**580.00**
Eagle w/shield & arrows, EX detail, 1-pc cvd hdl, 4⅝" dia..........**200.00**
Eagle w/shield & lg eye, rough surface, 3¾" dia........................**185.00**
Flower & dots, EX patina, 1-pc hdl, 3⅛" dia............................**110.00**
Flower basket (EX/complex), 2-pc hdl w/damage, 3½" dia.........**880.00**
Flowers & buds w/rope-twist borders, worm holes, rpl hdl, 5" dia....**55.00**
Hearts (2) & leaves, EX detail, threaded hdl, 3¼x6"..................**600.00**
Leaves around circumference, scrubbed, 3x2½" dia....................**110.00**
Partridge, delicate cvg, threaded hdl, 4⅛" dia..........................**800.00**
Pineapple, simple cvg, 1-pc hdl, 3½"..................................**140.00**
Pomegranate w/coggled rim, 1-pc cvd hdl, crack/scrubbed, 4½" dia...**195.00**
Quatrefoil leaf, chip cvd, lollipop hdl w/cut-out hole, 3⅝" dia...**715.00**
Rooster & tree, shallow cvg, dk patina/cracks, 3¾" dia..............**220.00**
Rose, EX detail, 1-pc hdl, scrubbed, age cracks, 3¾" dia..........**330.00**
Sheaf of wheat, EX patina, 1-pc hdl, 4½" dia............................**300.00**
Sheaf of wheat, semicircular, scrubbed, threaded hdl, 7" L..........**220.00**
Star flower w/arrow & dmns/flowers & sunrise, dbl-sided lollipop.....**385.00**
Star flower w/ridged edges, lollipop hdl, 9½x4" dia....................**660.00**
Strawberry, simple cvg, scrubbed, 3¼"..................................**110.00**
Swan swimming, incised border, 1-pc cvd hdl, crack/stain, 4⅛" dia...**350.00**
Thistle w/X-hatching, semicircular, threaded hdl, 7" L..............**440.00**
Tulip & other flowers, scrubbed, 1-pc hdl, 3¾" dia....................**165.00**
Tulip in semicircle, EX detail, soft worn finish, threaded hdl, 7" L...**635.00**
Tulip w/flowers & ferns, old rfn, 1-pc hdl, cracks, 5¼" dia..........**165.00**

Buttonhooks

The earliest known written reference to buttonhooks (shoe hooks, glove hooks, or collar buttoners) is dated 1611. They became a necessary implement in the 1850s when tight-fitting high-button shoes became fashionable. Later in the nineteenth century, ladies' button gloves and men's button-on collars and cuffs dictated specific types of buttoners, some with a closed wire loop instead of a hook end. Both shoes and gloves used as many as twenty-four buttons each. Usage began to wane in the late 1920s following a fashion change to low-cut laced shoes and the invention of the zipper. There was a brief resurgence of use following the 1948 movie 'High Button Shoes.' For a simple, needed utilitarian device, buttonhook handles were made from a surprising variety of materials: natural wood, bone, ivory, agate, and mother-of-pearl to plain steel, celluloid, aluminum, iron, lead and pewter, artistic copper, brass, silver, gold, and many other materials, in lengths that varied from under 2" to over 20". Many designs folded or retracted, and buttonhooks were often combined with shoehorns and other useful implements. Stamped steel buttonhooks often came free with the purchase of shoes, gloves, or collars. Material, design, workmanship, condition, and relative scarcity are the primary market value factors. Prices range from $1.00 to over $500.00, with most being in the $10.00 to $100.00 range. Buttonhooks are fairly easy to find, and they are interesting to display.

Our advisor for this category is Richard Mathes; he is listed in the Directory under Ohio. See also The Buttonhook Society listing in the Directory under Clubs, Newsletters, and Catalogs.

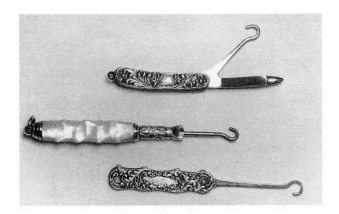

Glove hooks: Sterling, folds, Pat 1886, $50.00; Mother-of-pearl handle, twists out, $90.00; Sterling, folds, $60.00.

Buttonhook/penknife, ivory side plates, man's 50.00
Collar buttoner, stamped steel, advertising, closed end, 3" 20.00
Glove hook, gold-plated, retractable, 3" 90.00
Glove hook, loop end, agate hdl, 2½" 60.00
Shoe hook, colored celluloid hdl, 8" 15.00
Shoe hook, lathe-trn hardwood hdl, dk finish, 8" 15.00
Shoe hook, SP w/blade, repoussé hdl, Pat Jan 5 1892, 5" 40.00
Shoe hook, stamped steel, advertising, 5" 8.00
Shoe hook, sterling, floral & geometrics, 8" 55.00
Shoe hook, sterling, Nouveau lady's face, 6½" 75.00
Shoe hook, sterling, W w/arrow, hammered Florentine decor, mk...55.00
Shoe hook/shoehorn, combination, steel & celluloid, 9" 35.00

Bybee

The Bybee Pottery was founded in 1845 in the small town of Bybee, Kentucky, by the Cornelison family. Their earliest wares were primarily stoneware churns and jars. Today the work is carried on by sixth-generation Cornelison potters who still use the same facilities and production methods to make a more diversified line of pottery. From a fine white clay mined only a few miles from the potting shed itself, the shop produces vases, jugs, dinnerware, and banks in a variety of colors, some of which are shipped to the larger cities to be sold in department stores and specialty shops. The bulk of their wares, however, is sold to the thousands of tourists who are attracted to the pottery each year.

Bowl, gr, incurvate rim, 2¾x8¼" 38.00
Bowl, tan w/brn wash top, stick hdl, sm spout, mk 30.00
Butter dish, yel, dome lid, BB mk, 6½x5¼" 30.00
Canister set, bl, graduated set of 4, NM 80.00
Mug, shaded teal gr, mk Cornelison...Bybee KY, 3¼" 32.50
Pitcher, bl, w/lid, #51, 5½" dia base..38.00
Pitcher, buttermilk; yel, 9¼x9½"..45.00

Cabat

From its inception in New York City around 1940, through various types of clays, designs, and glazes, the Rose Cabat 'Feelie' evolved into present forms and glazes in the late 1950s, after a relocation to Arizona. Rose was aided and encouraged through the years by her husband Erni. Their small 'weed pots' are readily recognizable by their light weight, tiny thin necks, and soft glazes. Pieces are marked with a hand-incised 'Cabat' on the bottom.

Vase, aqua over mustard w/ochre speckles, 8 raised base panels, 7x4" ...**1,760.00**
Vase, aqua w/shimmer & deep mustard streaks, blk toward base, 3x2½" ..**275.00**
Vase, blk drip over bright aqua, frosted cream at neck, 2¾x2⅛" ...**275.00**
Vase, blk satin w/blk matt streaks, 3½x2¼" **220.00**
Vase, brn & yel mottle bands on jade gr, #384, teardrop form, 4x2¼" ..**385.00**
Vase, brn on hunter gr matt, onion form, 2¾x2¼" **220.00**
Vase, brn-speckled chartreuse w/yel streaks, #841, melon form, 4½" ..**990.00**
Vase, Cerulean bl w/brn satin in vertical bands, globular, 3½" ...**350.00**
Vase, Copper Dust on deep brn, 3¾x3½" **330.00**
Vase, emerald gr drip over royal bl gloss, elongated form, 4x1½" ..**300.00**
Vase, forest gr w/taupe streaks & blk spatters, 6x3½"..............**1,200.00**
Vase, geometrics, brn/yel crater glaze, 5" **550.00**
Vase, gr w/blk specks, teardrop w/gourd-shaped mouth, 3¼".......**165.00**
Vase, gray froth on hunter gr w/blk speckles, #841, onion form, 3" ..**350.00**
Vase, gray w/lav hue throughout, deep lav/gr base band, 3½x1½" ...**275.00**
Vase, khaki-gr w/cream drip, patches of brn & ochre, 2¾x2¼" **250.00**
Vase, lime gr w/brn & tan pools, #841, onion form, 3¼x2½" **295.00**
Vase, lt tan w/yel hue under rust streaks & brn speckles, 3x2¼" ...**250.00**
Vase, mocha brn matt w/tan & blk speckles, 3½x2".................**220.00**
Vase, sky bl drip over vivid wht w/gray streaks, onion form, 2¼" ...**300.00**
Vase, speckled khaki gr top, bottom half: coppery w/bl accents, 2x2"..**275.00**
Vase, yel w/tan streaks, gr drip at top, #841, teardrop form, 4¼" ...**330.00**

Calendar Plates

Calendar plates were advertising giveaways most popular from about 1906 until the late 1920s. They were decorated with colorful underglaze decals of lovely ladies, flowers, animals, birds and, of course, the twelve months of the year of their issue. During the 1950s they came into vogue again but never to the extent they were originally. Those with exceptional detailing, or those with scenes of a particular activity are most desirable, so are any from before 1906.

1895, months in center w/floral & swirl border, 8" 270.00
1904, Happy New Year, Cupid & bell, 8" 50.00
1904, months surrounded by berries 65.00
1907, lady drinking from fountain of Roman god Pan 75.00
1907, 4 ladies in vintage clothing, Pownall Hardware, 10" 105.00
1908, lg red rose w/leaves, MC Kittle, Belle Vernon PA, 9"..........40.00
1908, pk rose border 30.00
1909, autumn mountain scene, Sterling China, 9¼" 50.00
1909, cherries & strawberry blossoms, Imperial, 7½" 60.00
1909, cherries in center w/months at border, Imperial China, 7¼" ...30.00
1909, dog's face in center, Evergreen Supply Co, 9½" 85.00
1909, Gibson Girl, scalloped edge, 9¼".......................................70.00
1909, monks drinking wine, 9" 55.00
1909, roses in center w/months around border w/flowers, Wedgwood...50.00
1909, tabby cat, Comp AE Palmer, Dresden China, 8⅜" 45.00
1909, William Jennings Bryan sepia-tone picture, McNicol, 9¼"....90.00
1910, holly berries on 3 sides w/Hauri Bros Grocery ad, 7¼" 45.00
1910, Indian chief, months on headdress feathers, 7½"................65.00
1910, lady center w/seasonal flowers between ea 3 months, 9" 55.00
1910, lady w/horse, months in gr around horseshoe, 8¾" 40.00
1910, magnolias w/holly leaves & berries, Am China Co, 8½" 50.00
1910, man w/kreel stream fishing, 7¼" 40.00
1910, months on pgs of open book, gr ivy & forget-me-nots, 6¾"...40.00
1910, Washington's Old Home at Mt Vernon, 9⅛" 50.00
1911, Abe Lincoln center, 9"..150.00
1911, deer scene in center w/wildlife at rim, Trandle China, 9¾" ...40.00
1911, flying duck center w/months at border w/flowers, 9¼" 35.00
1911, girl w/buggy walks w/boy tooting horn, 8¾" 70.00
1911, ocean scene w/months & roses, emb & scalloped edge, 8¼"...55.00
1911, sea & shoreline w/sm boat on beach, 7⅝" 50.00

1911, violets in center w/time-zone clocks for world cities, Dresden....**45.00**
1911-12, dbl-year, pk ribbons & roses, 8½" **80.00**
1912, airplane/scenic view, fruit/flower border, 8½", EX...............**65.00**
1912, Lincoln, Garfield & McKinley, Am flag, 9¼" **70.00**
1913, lady & cherub at creek's bank w/lady & man reflection **50.00**
1913, Rainbow Falls, Yosemite Valley, 9⅜" **75.00**
1914, deer at stream, 7" **35.00**
1914, Plymouth Rock center w/months at border, mk Carnation ..**35.00**
1914, Washington Capitol, gold scalloped rim, 9⅛" **65.00**
1915, strawberries in center, butterflies between months on border, 8" .**50.00**
1916, yel roses center w/months separated by bluebirds border, 8¼" ..**35.00**
1917, silver vase w/pk roses, 7" **60.00**
1918, American flag, Theodore Goodman Furniture/Carpets..., 8"....**45.00**
1919, WWI airplane/battleships/flags, Peace w/Honor, 8½", EX...**70.00**
1920, US flag in center w/Allied country symbols at edge **65.00**
1923, horseshoe w/outdoor scene center w/months at top, McNicol, 8"....**38.50**
1928, winter scene w/months at border, Columbia Chinaware, 9"....**35.00**
1956, windmill w/gold floral, squarish, 10¼" **15.00**
1963, God Bless This House...1963, brn on wht, Royal Staffordshire, 9"....**30.00**
1967, Fox Terrier head, Walter's Auction Gallery, 9" **27.00**
1973, Bountiful Butterfly theme, Wedgwood **55.00**
1981, horses at border w/1981 center, months between, Wedgwood, 10"...**40.00**
1992, year w/2 birds in center w/fruits around border, Wedgwood ...**55.00**
1998, Woodman, bl & wht, Spode **50.00**

Calendars

Calendars are collected for their colorful prints, often attributed to a well-recognized artist of the period. Advertising calendars from the turn of the century often have a double appeal when representing a company whose tins, signs, store displays, etc., are also collectible. Our advisor for this category is Robert Doyle; he is listed in the Directory under New York. See also Parrish, Maxfield.

1892, Hood's Sarsparilla, 8 kids, complete, 7" dia, NM **70.00**
1894, Hood's Sarsparilla, girl in bl bonnet, diecut, 8¾x5½", EX ...**100.00**
1894, Lampert's Shoes, lady in wht w/rose border, diecut, 10x7", EX....**50.00**

1895, Hood's Sarsaparilla, children as Summer and Winter, unused, 8x7½", EX+, $100.00. (Photo courtesy Past Tyme Pleasures)

1896, Hood's Sarsaparilla, portrait, top only, fr, 14", VG+ **185.00**
1897, Tennessee Centennial, complete, VG **50.00**
1902, Buster/Tige & man/woman in front of estate, fr, 28", EX ..**775.00**
1902, Happy Childhood, complete, 9¾x6½", EX **85.00**
1903, Rapheal Tuck, Dickens characters on ea pg, #5376, 11x6", EX+....**160.00**
1904, De Laval, farm boy & girl by cornfield, fr, 23", VG **160.00**
1905, Christian Herald Bible House, 4 diecuts of girls/birds, fr, 32" **165.00**

1906, ...Joe's Black Magic Stove Polish, complete, 16x9", EX.......**85.00**
1906, lady/purple & wht flowers, diecut, fr, 27", VG **350.00**
1907, Derring Harvesting Machines, boy fishing, complete, 20x14", NM...**200.00**
1907, Hood's Sarsaparilla, Halcyon Days, fr, 21", VG.................**120.00**
1907, Metropolitan Life, 4 rnd portraits from young to old, fr, 32"...**230.00**
1911, Hood's Sarsaparilla, lady w/red roses, fr, 15", G.................**275.00**
1911, US Fidelity & Guaranty Co, portrait of lady, fr, 24", VG+ ..**375.00**
1913, Aztec Mineral Water Co, Indian maiden, fr, 40", VG.......**630.00**
1913, Topeka State Bank, photo, complete, EX **70.00**
1914, Aztec Mineral Water Co, Indian maiden, fr, 30", EX........**770.00**
1916, Jarecki Chemical Co, Ford tractor, complete, 12x10", EX...**55.00**
1916, LL Holden, lady at fence fr by grapes, diecut, fr, 25", EX+ **450.00**
1918, girl w/rabbit w/roses on ea side, diecut, MIG, 20x13¾", EX.....**150.00**
1919, Remington UMC, Canadian geese, Lynn Bouge Hunt, 20x15", VG...**250.00**
1925, Texas A&M, blk leather cover, pictures of school, complete, NM..**60.00**
1927, Oh Susanna, Covered Wagon, R Atkinson Fox, complete, 8x6", NM ..**60.00**
1928, Ford, car image, complete, 4x2½", EX................................**60.00**
1929, Sharpe Bros Milk, lady w/roses, fr, 41", VG **110.00**
1932, IGA Grocer, mother reading to daughter, complete, 17x10", EX....**95.00**
1932, Wyeth cover w/Rembrandt, Hacker & others, Jewish, VG **90.00**
1935, FDR portrait, IGA, complete, 16¾x10", EX.......................**200.00**
1937, Blue Ribbon Brew, Colonial men drinking, complete, 21x12", NM....**65.00**
1939, IGA Grocers, winter scene w/Season's Greetings, 15¾x11", NM+...**75.00**
1939, Rhapsody in Blue, Rolf Armstrong, 20¾x14½", NM **90.00**
1940, Harley-Davidson Motorcycles, tin w/paper pad, 3x6", EX+....**525.00**
1947, Right Number, Sunoco, Marilyn Monroe on phone, 10½x5½", M....**85.00**
1948, NY Central System Trains, trainyard scene, complete, 32x16", EX ..**75.00**
1950, Movie Stars w/horoscopes, complete, EX **45.00**
1950, RC Toasts Best, says Wanda Harris, color litho, 24x12¼", NM....**90.00**
1951, B&B Plumbing & Heating Co, girl hugging cow, fr, 21", NOS...**55.00**
1952, Bikini Bound, R Armstrong, Brown & Bigelow, 33x16", NM+..**300.00**
1953, Golden Dreams, Marilyn Monroe nude, complete, 13x8", M ..**200.00**
1953, Smokey the Bear, Virginia Forest Service, complete, 23x11", M....**60.00**
1957, Kelly Springfield Tires, lady barbecuing, 33", EX+ **110.00**
1958, Playboy Playmate, w/orig sleeve cover, NM+....................**110.00**
1959, Squirt, child Santa w/gifts on chimney, 20⅜x8", VG.........**45.00**
1961, Hennis Freight Lines RR, man reading paper, 33x16", EX+ ..**65.00**
1966, Universal Monsters, Don Post, complete, 21x9", EX...........**60.00**
1973, Americana, Chas Wysocki, themes of nostolgia, EX............**30.00**

California Faience

California Faience was founded in 1913 as 'The Tile Shop' by Chauncey R. Thomas in Berkeley, Calfiornia (recently obtained information has given a new picture of the early days of the company). He was joined by William V. Bragdon in 1915 who became sole owner in 1938. The product line was apparently always marked 'California Faience,' which became the company's legal name in 1924. Production was reduced after 1933, but the firm stayed in business as a studio and factory until it closed in 1959. Products consisted of hand-pressed tiles and slip-cast vases, bowls, flower frogs, and occasional figures. They are notable for high production quality and aesthetic simplicity. Items produced before 1934 were of dark brown or reddish brown clay. After that, tan clay was used. The firm made many of the tiles used at Hearst Castle, San Simeon, California. In the late 1920s, a line was produced in white porcelain marked 'California Porcelain.'

The multicolored art tiles are especially popular with collectors. Generally speaking, matt glazes were in use before 1921; examples are rare, and prices continue to increase. Values for the more common glossy glazed forms, especially the turquoise 'Persian Blue,' have shown no upward movement. Almost all known pieces are marked on the bottom. Occasionally unmarked pieces are seen in a pale creamy clay, probably made from discarded molds after the firm closed. Unmarked tiles are presently being made from original molds by Deer Creek Pottery, Grass Valley, California. They can be distinguished from the old tiles as they are thinner and have a repetition of the raised designs on their backs. Our advisor for this category is Dr. Kirby William Brown; he is listed in the Directory under California. Dr. Brown is currently researching a book on this topic and welcomes input from collectors.

Ashtray, Art Deco dog, blk gloss, porc, 5½" 125.00
Ashtray, Persian Blue gloss, 3" sq...235.00
Bowl, Art Deco incised design, bl gloss, 8½" 250.00
Bowl, blk matt/yel gloss, 10-sided, widely flared, 8" 50.00
Bowl, cream/bl gloss, scalloped & ribbed, 6" 50.00
Bowl, dk bl gloss w/mc cuenca band, Eureka Inn, 4" 625.00
Bowl, Persian Blue gloss, flared rim, 12" 200.00
Bowl, plum/bl gloss, broad ped ft, 11" 75.00
Bowl, red gloss/brn matt varied, oval w/cuenca rim, porc, 13" 275.00
Candle holder, Persian Blue gloss, 4" 40.00
Candle holders, dk bl matt, 7", pr...545.00
Figure, frog for fountain, Persian Blue gloss, sq base, 2½" 615.00
Figure, Madonna of the Flowers, by Hermione, bl gloss, 7" 45.00
Flower frog, ducks (2) side by side, dk bl matt, 6".........................225.00
Flower frog, ducks (2) side by side, Persian Blue gloss, 6" 85.00
Flower frog, yel matt, rnd, 11 holes, 3⅝" 35.00
Jar, Persian Blue gloss, cylindrical, w/lid, 5" 130.00
Jar, Persian Blue gloss, tapered ribbed sides, w/lid, 3½" 310.00
Jar, temple; Persian Blue gloss, w/button lid, 10½" 455.00
Lamp base, orange matt, ribbed, porc, 12" 780.00
Match tray, gr matt, porc, 6" 215.00
Pipe stand, gr-bl matt, for 2 pipes, porc, 5¼" 160.00
Tile, abstract (incised), mc, 5⅜", pr 460.00
Tile, architectural, bl gloss, 3¾", 6 for..135.00
Tile, dove walking (incised), gr matt, 5¾" 340.00
Tile, frigate in circle, mc, 4⅝", in pr copper bookends.............2,605.00
Trivet, birds (3) circling medallion, mc gloss, 5½" dia.............1,400.00
Trivet, bl/wht gloss, hex, entwined vines, 5½"................................460.00
Trivet, California Mission, mc gloss, 5½" dia...................................785.00
Trivet, flower basket, mc gloss, 5½" dia..375.00
Trivet, fruit basket, mc gloss, 5½" dia..405.00
Trivet, fruit basket, mc matt, 5½" dia...1,380.00
Trivet, iris, mc matt, 5½" dia...1,700.00

Trivet, multicolor matt, California Mission, 5½" diameter, $1,400.00.
(Photo courtesy Dr. Kirby Brown)

Trivet, poppies (3), mc gloss, 5½" dia 600.00
Trivet, prancing duck, gr matt, 6" dia..535.00
Trivet, UC Berkeley Campanile, mc matt & gloss, 5½" dia 1,560.00
Trivet, yucca in desert, mc gloss, 5½" dia.......................................350.00
Vase, apple form, Persian Blue gloss, 4"..105.00

Vase, apple form (squat), shaded bl gloss, 2¾"...............................195.00
Vase, cream matt, narrow, ribbed, porc, 8¼".................................365.00
Vase, dk bl matt, lobed melon form, bottom hole, 5" 525.00
Vase, gr crystalline gloss, flared base, porc, 13".........................1,105.00
Vase, gr matt, cylindrical, 4¼"..370.00
Vase, Oriental form, incised lovebirds, red gloss, 6½" 1,035.00
Vase, Oriental form, orange gloss, flared rim, porc, 8½".............130.00
Vase, Oriental form, Persian Blue gloss, flared lip, 8" 140.00
Vase, Pueblo Indian form, gr gloss, 4"...130.00
Vase, Pueblo Indian form, gr matt, 5"...760.00
Vase, volcano form, Persian Blue gloss, 3½"....................................80.00
Vase, yel gloss, cylindrical, 4⅜"..165.00
Wall pocket, woman's head, by Hermione, mc, 6" 25.00

California Perfume Company

D.H. McConnell, Sr., founded the California Perfume Company (C.P. Company; C.P.C.) in 1886 in New York City. He had previously been a salesman for a book company, which he later purchased. His door-to-door sales usually involved the lady of the house, to whom he presented a complimentary bottle of inexpensive perfume. Upon determining his perfume to be more popular than his books, he decided that the manufacture of perfume might be more lucrative. He bottled toiletries under the name 'California Perfume Company' and a line of household products called 'Perfection.' In 1928 the name 'Avon' appeared on the label, and in 1939 the C.P.C. name was entirely removed from the product. The success of the company is attributed to the door-to-door sales approach and 'money back' guarantee offered by his first 'Depot Agent,' Mrs. P.F.E. Albee, known today as the 'Avon Lady.'

The company's containers are quite collectible today, especially the older, hard-to-find items. Advanced collectors seek 'go with' items labeled Goetting & Co., New York; Goetting's; or Savoi Et Cie, Paris. Such examples date from 1871 to 1896. The Goetting Company was purchased by D.H. McConnell; Savoi Et Cie was a line which they imported to sell through department stores. Also of special interest are packaging and advertising with the Ambrosia or Hinze Ambrosia Company label. This was a subsidiary company whose objective seems to have been to produce a line of face creams, etc., for sale through drugstores and other such commercial outlets. They operated in New York from about 1875 until 1954. Because very little is known about these companies and since only a few examples of their product containers and advertising material have been found, market values for such items have not yet been established. Other items sought by the collector include products marked Gertrude Recordon, Marvel Electric Silver Cleaner, Easy Day Automatic Clothes Washer, pre-1915 catalogs, California Perfume Company 1909 and 1910 calendars, and 1916 Calopad Sanitary Napkins.

There are hundreds of local Avon Collector Clubs throughout the world that also have C.P.C. collectors in their membership. If you are interested in joining, locating, or starting a new club, contact the National Association of Avon Collectors, Inc., listed in the Directory under Clubs, Newsletters, and Catalogs. Those wanting a National Newsletter Club or price guides may contact Avon Times, listed in the same section. Inquiries concerning California Perfume Company items and the companies or items mentioned in the previous paragraphs should be directed toward our advisor, Dick Pardini, whose address is given under California. (Please send a large SASE and be sure to request clearly the information you are seeking; not interested in Avons, 'Perfection' marked C.P.C.'s, or Anniversary Keepsakes.) For more information we recommend *Bud Hastin's Avon Collector's Encyclopedia.*

Note: Our values are for items in mint condition. A very rare item or one in super mint condition might go for 10% more. Damage, wear, missing parts, etc., must be considered; items judged to be in only good to very good condition should be priced at up to 50% of listed values, with fair to good at 25% and excellent at 75%. Parts (labels, stoppers, caps, etc.) might be evaluated at 10% of these prices.

Am Ideal Talcum, tin, left profile of lady, 1911, M......................115.00
Baby Powder, tin, CP trademk, 1905, M 120.00
Baby Powder, tin, Eureka trademk, 1898, M 130.00

Baking Powder 'California,' 16 ounce, one pound, or five pound sizes, M, each, $80.00.

(Photo courtesy Dick Pardini)

Bandoline, 1908, 2-oz..100.00
Bay Rum, glass stopper, 126 Chambers St NY, 1898, 16-oz.........215.00
Cut Glass Perfume, stopper, ribbon, 7-sided rnd label, 1915 ....230.00
Daphne perfume, emb glass, flat glass stopper, 1- & 2-oz, 1925, MIB...140.00
Dermol Massage Cream, milk glass, 1923, 1-lb 110.00
Face Lotion, CP trademk, 1908 ....115.00
French Perfumes, 1900s, ¼-oz to 2-oz, ea....................................125.00
Lait Virginal, 1900, 2-oz, MIB 150.00
Lavender Salts, gr w/metal top, glass stopper, 1890s 255.00
Massage Cream, stopper, 1896 ....160.00
Mission Garden Talc set, 2 tins in silk-lined box, 1923, M 235.00
Natoma Rolling Massage Cream, 1914-17, w/booklet & box......260.00
Natoma Rose Perfume, 1-oz w/atomizer, free sample label, 1914, M...210.00
Pyrox Tooth Powder, bl tin, 1925, M....................................80.00
Shampoo Cream, man's face on lid, 1896, 4-oz, M 135.00
Toothwash, brass stopper, 1921, 2-oz 100.00
Trailing Arbutus Cream, tubes, 1925, M 40.00
Traveler's Perfume, metal cover, glass stopper, 1900 ....135.00
Vernafleur Compact, SP, single & dbl, 1928, M............................40.00
Vernafleur Toilet Soap set, 3 bars in box, 1925, M 115.00
Violet Water, glass stopper, Eureka trademk, 1908, 8-oz..............200.00
Witch Hazel, 1896, 8-oz..115.00

Calling Cards, Cases, and Receivers

The practice of announcing one's arrival with a calling card borne by the maid to the mistress of the house was a social grace of the Victorian era. Different messages (condolences, a personal visit, or a good-by) were related by turning down one corner or another. The custom was forgotten by WWI. Fashionable ladies and gents carried their personally engraved cards in elaborate cases made of such materials as embossed silver, mother-of-pearl with intricate inlay, tortoise shell, and ivory. Card receivers held cards left by visitors who called while the mistress was out

or 'not receiving.' Calling cards with fringe, die-cut flaps that cover the name, or an unusual decoration are worth about $3.00 to $4.00, while plain cards usually sell for around $1.00.

Case, cvd ivory, figures in pavillion/flowers, China, 1880s, 4½x3"...350.00
Case, cvd ivory w/floral border & initials, China, 1880s, 4½x3" 750.00
Case, silver, cartouch w/eng/emb eagle/flowers, mk B, 3½x2½" 235.00
Holder, SP, bird perched on rim, #91, rstr 495.00
Holder, SP, Meriden #2049 ....140.00
Holder, SP (rstr) w/etched glass vase, 10½x12½" L 850.00
Holder, SP base w/blk amethyst glass vase, R&B #02353, rstr, 16"...695.00
Holder, SP cherub reaches for etched clear vase, Wilcox #01845 ...850.00
Tray, SP, bird on leaf by glass vase, SH&M #116, rstr..................650.00
Tray, SP, Greenaway girls w/dog, Derby #3537, rstr, 7¼" dia.......550.00

Camark

The Camden Art and Tile Company (commonly known as Camark) of Camden, Arkansas, was organized in the fall of 1926 by Samuel J. 'Jack' Carnes. Using clays from Arkansas, John Lessell, who had been hired as art director by Carnes, produced the initial lustre and iridescent Lessell wares for Camark ('CAM'den, 'ARK'ansas) before his death in December 1926. Before the plant opened in the spring of 1927, Carnes brought John's wife, Jeanne, and stepdaughter Billie to oversee the art department's manufacture of Le-Camark. Production by the Lessell family included variations of J.B. Owens' Soudanese and Opalesce and Weller's Marengo and Lamar. Camark's version of Marengo was called Old English. They also made wares identical to Weller's LaSa. Pieces made by John Lessell back in Ohio were signed 'Lessell,' while those made by Jeanne and Billie in Arkansas during 1927 were signed 'Le-Camark.' By 1928 Camark's production centered on traditional glazes. Drip glazes similar to Muncie Pottery were produced, in particular the green drip over pink. In the 1930s commercial castware with simple glossy and matt finishes became the primary focus and would continue so until Camark closed in the early 1960s. Between the 1960s and 1980s the company operated mainly as a retail store selling existing inventory, but some limited production occurred. In 1986 the company was purchased by the Ashcraft family of Camden, but no pottery has yet been made at the factory.

For further information we recommend *Collector's Encyclopedia of Camark Pottery, Book II*, by David Edwin Gifford. Our advisor for this category is Tony Freyaldenhoven; he is listed in the Directory under Arkansas.

Ball jug, brn stipple, gold ink stamp, 6½", from $180 to 200.00
Basket, orange gr overflow, mk, 6", from $60 to.............................80.00
Basket, wht, emb rings, 1st block letter, 5¾", from $40 to 60.00
Bottle, ear of corn, yel & gr, 1st block letter, 7¾", from $80 to ..100.00
Bowl, Azurite Blue, sm angle hdls, sticker, unmk, 5", from $140 to ..160.00
Box, frosted gr, sticker, 2¼x4¼", from $60 to 80.00
Canoe, bl & wht stipple, 1st block letter, 3¼x11", from $100 to....120.00
Charger, bl & wht stipple, 1st block letter mk, 13¼", from $200 to ..250.00
Flower bowl, yel to bl matt, stamp, 5¼", from $350 to................400.00
Flower frog, rose gr overflow, 1st block letter, ¾x3" dia, $20 to 30.00
Ginger jar, desert scene w/palms, Lessell, sgn LeCamark, 8¾" 800.00
Humidor, brn stipple, 1st block letter, 6½", from $120 to...........140.00
Humidor, rose gr overflow, 1st block letter, 7¼", from $180 to...200.00
Humidor, Sea Green, 6-sided, unmk, 6½", from $120 to 140.00
Lamp base, river scenic, gray-bl, Lessell, 8", from $500 to..........600.00
Paperwight, mirror blk, gold stamp, ¾x3¾", from $60 to...........80.00
Pitcher, Celestial Blue, parrot hdl, ink stamp, 6½", from $160 to...180.00
Pitcher, gr, yel cat hdl, molded mk, #088, 7½", from $80 to.......100.00
Pitcher, waffle batter; deep yel w/bird hdl, gold ink stamp, 4".....100.00

Planter, flower garden & gate, rose gr overflow, 8½x13½x5¼" **350.00**
Planter, orange gr overflow, multiple plant pockets, 8", $160 to...**180.00**
Vase, Autumn glaze, ruffled rim, ftd, 1st block letter, 6", $60 to ...**80.00**
Vase, Aztec Red Mottled, sticker, 8", from $250 to **300.00**
Vase, Azurite Blue, trumpet neck, hdls, 1st block letter, 8".........**120.00**
Vase, Celestial Blue w/blk overflow, flared cylinder, stamp, 10¾"...**300.00**
Vase, Delphinium Blue, hdls, sticker, 7", from $40 to....................**50.00**
Vase, gr crackle, swollen, gold stamp, 12¼", from $700 to **900.00**

Vase, hand-painted iris, 9", from $300.00 to $400.00. (Photo courtesy David Gifford)

Vase, ivory crackle, shouldered, gold stamp, 5¾", from $200 to...**250.00**
Vase, Jeanne Jonquil, LeCamark, gold script mk, 6¼", from $400 to..**500.00**
Vase, mirror blk, Deco style w/integral hdls, unmk, 7¼", $200 to...**250.00**
Vase, Old English Rose, baluster, sgn Lessell, 11", from $800 to ...**1,000.00**
Vase, olive gr w/lt overflow, hdls, sticker, 4½", from $80 to........**100.00**
Vase, orange gr overflow, rim-to-hip hdls, unmk, 7½", $100 to ..**120.00**
Vase, orange matt, emb sea gulls, unmk, 9¼", from $300 to **400.00**
Vase, pine trees, silver lustre, mk LeCamark, 9¾", from $900 to ..**1,100.00**
Vase, rose gr overflow, petal top, ftd, 1st block letter, 8¼" **120.00**
Vase, rust, emb floral, ftd, 1st block letter, 7", from $60 to............**80.00**
Vase, Venetian Jonquil, LeCamark, gold ink stamp, 8", from $800 to ...**900.00**
Vase, Venetian Poppy, LeCamark, unmk, 10", from $500 to.......**600.00**

Cambridge Art Pottery

The Cambridge Art Pottery (not to be confused with the Cambridge Art Tile Works of Covington, Kentucky) was founded in 1901 in Cambridge, Ohio. Charles Upjohn, formerly from the Weller Pottery, was hired as designer and modeler. Cambridge would be known mostly for three artware lines: Terrhea, their variation of Rookwood's Standard Glaze line, underglaze painted with polychrome slips and covered in an amber overglaze; Oakwood, a flambé glaze mix of autumnal colors; and Acorn, a smooth and satiny matt green finish in the Arts and Crafts style. They also produced a commercially successful utilitarian line, Guernsey, named after the county for which Cambridge was the seat. After 1908 only the Guernsey line remained, so in 1909 the pottery name was changed to Guernsey Earthenware. Cambridge pieces are usually stamped with a CAP mark ('AP' within a larger 'C') with the name of the line above or below. Our advisor for this category is Suzanne Perrault; she is listed in the Directory under New Jersey.

Coffeepot, Terrhea, blkbirds on glossy terra cotta, mk, 8½x6" **125.00**
Ewer, Oakwood, amber/gr flambé, squat base, Oakwood/208, 7½" ...**125.00**
Vase, Terrhea, Am Indian portrait, Arthur Williams, rstr at neck, 24" ..**6,500.00**

Vessel, Acorn, matt gr w/lustre, acorn stamp, squat, 3¼x6¾".....**425.00**
Vessel, Terrhea, roses, ftd, 7", EX..**150.00**

Cambridge Art Tile Works

The Cambridge Art Tile Works (not to be confused with the Cambridge Art Pottery of Cambridge, Ohio) initially operated in Cincinnati, Ohio, in 1887. In 1889 they moved to the site where their goods were being manufactured, the Mount Casino Art Tile Company, of Covington, Kentucky. These two companies merged, taking on the title of the Cambridge Tile Manufacturing Company. They employed as modelers Clement Barnhorn and Ferdinand Mersman, both of whom had worked at the Rookwood Pottery. The tiles they produced were in the same style as others made throughout the Ohio Valley at the time: dust-pressed with Classical subjects or floral displays and covered in single-color majolica glazes.

The company expanded several times over the following years, manufacturing mantels, floor tiles, and mosaics. In 1927 they took over the Wheatley Pottery of Cincinnati and organized the Cambridge-Wheatley Corporation to sell tiles made in both locations. During the decades that followed, the company would alter and refine its production regularly to compete with domestic and foreign tile manufacturers. Production ceased in 1986. Cambridge tiles are usually embossed with the company's name on white clay.

Our advisor for this category is Suzanne Perrault; she is listed in the Directory under New Jersey.

Panel, full-length figure, gr, 18x6", from $300 to **500.00**
Tile, child's portrait, burgundy, 6"...**150.00**
Tile, sailing ship scene, mc, 6-panel, sight: 8x12½"+oak fr......**1,150.00**

Cambridge Glass

The Cambridge Glass Company began operations in 1901 in Cambridge, Ohio. Primarily they made crystal dinnerware and well-designed accessory pieces until the 1920s when they introduced the concept of color that was to become so popular on the American dinnerware market. Always maintaining high standards of quality and elegance, they produced many lines that became bestsellers; through the '20s and '30s they were recognized as the largest manufacturer of this type of glassware in the world.

Of the various marks the company used, the 'C in triangle' is the most familiar. Production stopped in 1958. For a more thorough study of the subject, we recommend *Colors in Cambridge Glass* by the National Cambridge Collectors, Inc.; their address may be found in the Directory under Clubs. *Glass Animals* by Dick and Pat Spencer is a wonderful source for an in-depth view of that particular aspect of glass collecting. They are listed in the Directory under Illinois. See also Carnival Glass; Glass Animals.

Apple Blossom, amber, bowl, cereal; 6" **50.00**
Apple Blossom, amber, comport, fruit cocktail; 4" **28.00**
Apple Blossom, amber, ice bucket **145.00**
Apple Blossom, amber, plate, dinner; 9½" **90.00**
Apple Blossom, amber, sherbet, ftd, #3400, 6-oz.........................**22.00**
Apple Blossom, amber, vase, rippled sides, 6" **125.00**
Apple Blossom, crystal, bowl, bonbon; hdls, 5¼" **25.00**
Apple Blossom, crystal, bowl, mayonnaise; w/liner & ladle, 4-ftd....**45.00**
Apple Blossom, crystal, butter dish, 5½".....................................**195.00**
Apple Blossom, crystal, pitcher, ftd, flattened sides, 50-oz **195.00**
Apple Blossom, crystal, platter, 11½" **55.00**
Apple Blossom, crystal, tumbler, ftd, #3135, 5-oz........................**16.00**

Apple Blossom, pk or gr, bowl, fruit; tab hdls 125.00
Apple Blossom, pk or gr, creamer, tall, ftd..............30.00
Apple Blossom, pk or gr, plate, bread/butter; 6" 12.00
Apple Blossom, pk or gr, tray, relish; hdld, 7" 45.00
Apple Blossom, pk or gr, vase, 5"..............145.00
Apple Blossom, pk or gr, water stem, #3130, 8-oz..............45.00
Candlelight, bowl, fancy edge, 4-ftd, #3400/38, 11" 100.00
Candlelight, bowl, ftd, hdls, #3900/28, 11½"..............85.00
Candlelight, comport, cheese; #3900/135, 5" 45.00
Candlelight, plate, salad; #3900/22, 8"..............22.00
Candlelight, relish, 3-part, #3900/126, 12" 675.00
Candlelight, tumbler, juice; ftd, #3111, 5-oz..............30.00
Candlelight, vase, keyhole, ftd, #1238, 12"..............150.00
Caprice, bl or pk, bowl, fruit; crimped, #19, 5"..............95.00
Caprice, bl or pk, candlestick, 2-light, keyhole, #647, 5", ea..............65.00
Caprice, bl or pk, comport, low ft, #130, 6"..............50.00
Caprice, bl or pk, oil, w/stopper, #101, 3-oz..............90.00
Caprice, bl or pk, plate, luncheon; #22, 8½"..............35.00
Caprice, bl or pk, tray, oval, #42, 9"..............50.00
Caprice, bl or pk, vase, ball, #241, 4¼"..............115.00
Caprice, bl or pk, vase, rose bowl; ftd, #235, 6" 150.00
Caprice, crystal, ashtray, shell, 3-ftd, #213, 2¾"..............8.00
Caprice, crystal, cake plate, ftd, #30, 13" 150.00
Caprice, crystal, cigarette box, w/lid, #208, 4½x3½"..............25.00
Caprice, crystal, jelly; hdls, #151, 5"..............15.00
Caprice, crystal, parfait, blown, #300, 5-oz..............95.00
Caprice, crystal, shakers, ball, #91, pr..............45.00
Caprice, crystal, tumbler, tea; blown, #301, 12-oz..............20.00
Chantilly, bowl, celery/relish; 5-part, 12"..............55.00
Chantilly, candlestick, 5", ea..............28.00
Chantilly, cordial, #3600, 1-oz..............60.00
Chantilly, creamer, ind; scalloped edge, #3900..............15.00
Chantilly, ice bucket, w/chrome hdl..............125.00
Chantilly, plate, cake; tab hdls, 13½"..............65.00
Chantilly, shakers, ftd, pr..............40.00
Chantilly, tumbler, juice; ftd, #3779, 5-oz 20.00
Chantilly, vase, flower; high ft, 8"..............55.00
Chantilly, water stem, #3779, 9-oz..............28.00
Cleo, amber, basket, hdls, Decagon, 7"..............30.00
Cleo, amber, bouillon cup, w/saucer, hdls, Decagon..............55.00
Cleo, amber, vase, 5½"..............95.00
Cleo, amber, wine, #3077, 3½"..............95.00
Cleo, bl, bowl, bonbon; hdls, Decagon, 5½"..............60.00
Cleo, bl, creamer, ewer style, 6"..............195.00
Cleo, bl, tumbler, ftd, #3077, 8-oz..............60.00
Cleo, pk or gr, bowl, oval, 11½"..............75.00
Cleo, pk or gr, plate, grill; 9½"..............100.00
Cleo, pk or gr, tray, oval service; Decagon, 12"..............145.00
Daffodil, bonbon, #1181..............30.00
Daffodil, brandy, #1937, ¾-oz..............75.00
Daffodil, comport, ftd, #533, 5½"..............45.00
Daffodil, jug, #3400/140..............275.00
Daffodil, plate, cabaret; #166, 13½" 95.00
Daffodil, relish, 3-part, #214, 10"..............65.00
Daffodil, sherry, #1937, 2-oz..............65.00
Daffodil, tumbler, iced tea; ftd, #3779, 12-oz..............37.50
Daffodil, vase, ftd, #6004, 8"..............110.00
Decagon, bl, bowl, bouillon; w/liner..............15.00
Decagon, bl, bowl, cereal; belled, 6" 30.00
Decagon, bl, cordial, 1-oz..............70.00
Decagon, bl, creamer, scalloped edge 18.00
Decagon, bl, ice tub..............65.00
Decagon, bl, plate, bread/butter; 6¼"..............10.00
Decagon, bl, relish, 6 inserts 165.00

Decagon, bl, tray, pickle; 9"..............40.00
Decagon, pastel colors, bowl, berry; 10" 50.00
Decagon, pastel colors, bowl, cream soup; w/liner..............22.00
Decagon, pastel colors, bowl, relish; 2-part, 11"..............38.00
Decagon, pastel colors, gravy boat, w/hdld liner 100.00
Decagon, pastel colors, ice bucket..............45.00
Decagon, pastel colors, oil, tall, w/hdl & stopper..............70.00
Decagon, pastel colors, plate, salad; 8½"..............15.00
Decagon, pastel colors, tumbler, ftd, 12-oz..............25.00
Diane, basket, hdls, ftd, 6"..............35.00
Diane, bowl, baker; 10"..............60.00
Diane, bowl, relish or pickle; 7"..............35.00
Diane, candelabrum, 2-light, keyhole..............30.00
Diane, candy box, rnd..............95.00
Diane, claret, #1066, 4½-oz..............60.00
Diane, creamer, scroll hdl, #3400..............22.00
Diane, decanter, lg, ftd..............210.00
Diane, goblet, water; #3122, 9-oz..............30.00
Diane, plate, torte; 4-ftd, 13"..............60.00
Diane, shakers, ftd, w/glass tops, pr..............50.00
Diane, tumbler, old-fashioned; w/sham bottom, 7-oz..............55.00
Diane, vase, bud; 10"..............65.00
Elaine, bowl, celery & relish; 5-part, 12"..............75.00
Elaine, bowl, finger; w/liner, #3104..............50.00
Elaine, candlestick, 3-light, 6", ea..............60.00
Elaine, cordial, #1402, 1-oz..............125.00
Elaine, hurricane lamp, candlestick base..............190.00
Elaine, parfait, low stem, #3121, 5-oz..............45.00
Elaine, plate, cake; tab hdls, 13½"..............75.00
Elaine, tumbler, water; ftd, #1402, 9-oz..............25.00
Elaine, vase, ftd, 6"..............75.00
Gloria, crystal, bowl, bonbon; flattened, ftd, 5½" 25.00
Gloria, crystal, bowl, cranberry; 3½"..............40.00
Gloria, crystal, candlestick, 6", ea..............45.00
Gloria, crystal, ice pail, metal hdl w/tongs 75.00
Gloria, crystal, plate, bread/butter; 6"..............12.00
Gloria, crystal, saucer, after dinner; rnd..............12.00
Gloria, crystal, tray, relish; 2-part, center hdl..............30.00
Gloria, crystal, vase, 11"..............145.00
Gloria, crystal, water stem, #3130, 8-oz..............28.00
Gloria, gr, pk or yel, basket, hdls, 6"..............65.00
Gloria, gr, pk or yel, bowl, cereal; rnd, 6" 35.00
Gloria, gr, pk or yel, bowl, cream soup; w/rnd liner..............55.00
Gloria, gr, pk or yel, creamer, ftd 30.00
Gloria, gr, pk or yel, cup, rnd or sq 33.00
Gloria, gr, pk or yel, oil, w/stopper, tall, ftd, w/hdl..............250.00
Gloria, gr, pk or yel, plate, dinner; 9½"..............100.00
Gloria, gr, pk or yel, saucer, AD; sq..............15.00
Gloria, gr, pk or yel, shakers, short, pr..............125.00
Gloria, gr, pk or yel, sherbet, low ft, #3135, 6-oz..............26.00
Gloria, gr, pk or yel, vase, keyhole base, 10"..............160.00
Imperial Hunt Scene, colors, bowl, cereal; 6"..............40.00
Imperial Hunt Scene, colors, creamer, ftd 65.00
Imperial Hunt Scene, colors, ice bucket..............100.00
Imperial Hunt Scene, colors, shakers, pr..............100.00
Imperial Hunt Scene, colors, tumbler, flat, #1402, 15-oz..............35.00
Imperial Hunt Scene, colors, water stem, #3085, 9-oz..............55.00
Imperial Hunt Scene, crystal, candlestick, 3-light, keyhole, ea..............45.00
Imperial Hunt Scene, crystal, ice tub..............65.00
Imperial Hunt Scene, crystal, pitcher, w/lid, #711, 76-oz 195.00
Imperial Hunt Scene, crystal, stem, tomato; #1402, 6-oz..............45.00
Imperial Hunt Scene, crystal, sugar bowl, flat w/lid..............50.00
Marjorie, cocktail, #7606, 3-oz..............25.00
Marjorie, cream, flat, #1917/10..............75.00

Marjorie, jug, #93, 3-pt 155.00
Marjorie, nappie, #4111, 8" 60.00
Marjorie, plate, finger bowl liner; #7606 ....15.00
Marjorie, syrup & lid, #106, 8-oz 150.00
Marjorie, tumbler, ftd, #3750, 10-oz 25.00
Mt Vernon, ashtray, oval, #71, 6x4½" 12.00
Mt Vernon, bonbon, ftd, #10, 7" 12.50
Mt Vernon, bowl, belled, #128, 11½" 30.00
Mt Vernon, bowl, fruit; #6, 5¼" 10.00
Mt Vernon, bowl, ivy ball or rose; ftd, #12, 4½" 27.50
Mt Vernon, bowl, preserve; #76, 6" 12.00
Mt Vernon, box, w/lid, #16, 3" dia 30.00
Mt Vernon, cake stand, ftd, #150, 10½" 35.00
Mt Vernon, comport, belled, #96, 6½" 22.50
Mt Vernon, creamer, ftd, #8 ....10.00
Mt Vernon, decanter, #47, 11-oz 60.00
Mt Vernon, pitcher, #90, 50-oz 90.00
Mt Vernon, relish, 3-part, #200, 11" 25.00
Mt Vernon, sherbet, tall, #2, 6½-oz 10.00
Mt Vernon, stein, #84, 14-oz 30.00
Mt Vernon, vase, squat, #107, 6½" 27.50
No 520 Byzantine, Peach Blo, butter dish 195.00
No 520 Byzantine, Peach Blo or gr, bowl, cream soup 25.00
No 520 Byzantine, Peach Blo or gr, cocktail, #3060, 2½-oz 22.50
No 520 Byzantine, Peach Blo or gr, comport, jelly; #2900 ....35.00
No 520 Byzantine, Peach Blo or gr, plate, sherbet; 6" 10.00
No 520 Byzantine, Peach Blo or gr, saucer, #933 ....7.00
No 520 Byzantine, Peach Blo or gr, tumbler, low ft, #309512-oz ...30.00
No 704 Windows Border, colors, bowl, cereal; 6" 15.00
No 704 Windows Border, colors, bowl, cream soup; hdls, #922 .....20.00
No 704 Windows Border, colors, cafe parfait, #3075, 5½-oz 40.00
No 704 Windows Border, colors, creamer, flat, #137 ....22.50
No 704 Windows Border, colors, cup, demi; #925 ....35.00
No 704 Windows Border, colors, decanter, #0315 ....195.00
No 704 Windows Border, colors, jug, #107 ....150.00
No 704 Windows Border, colors, plate, 13½" 75.00
No 704 Windows Border, colors, tray, center hdl, 10" 45.00
No 704 Windows Border, colors, vase, ftd, #1005, 6½" 100.00
Portia, bowl, cranberry; sq, 3½" 45.00
Portia, bowl, flared, 4-ftd, 10" 50.00
Portia, bowl, pickle or relish; 7" 40.00

Portia, cocktail, fruit/oyster; #3130, 4½" 20.00
Portia, comport, blown, 5⅜" 65.00
Portia, cup, ftd, sq 25.00
Portia, goblet, #3124, 10-oz 28.00
Portia, ice bucket, w/chrome hdl 115.00
Portia, plate, torte; 4-ftd, 13" 65.00
Portia, sugar bowl, ftd, hdls, ball 45.00
Portia, vase, globe; 5" 75.00
Rosalie, amber or crystal, bowl, oval, flanged, 15" 75.00
Rosalie, amber or crystal, candy dish, w/lid, 6" 75.00
Rosalie, amber or crystal, comport, almond; ftd, 6" 30.00
Rosalie, amber or crystal, plate, bread/butter; 6¾" 7.00
Rosalie, amber or crystal, relish, 2-part, 9" 20.00
Rosalie, amber or crystal, tray, center hdl, 11" 20.00
Rosalie, amber or crystal, wafer tray 85.00
Rosalie, amber or cystal, bowl, basket; hdls, 7" 22.00
Rosalie, bl, pk or gr, bowl, bouillon; hdls 15.00
Rosalie, bl, pk or gr, bowl, cranberry; 3½" 50.00
Rosalie, bl, pk or gr, bowl, soup; 8½" 60.00
Rosalie, bl, pk or gr, candlestick, keyhole, 5", ea 45.00
Rosalie, bl, pk or gr, cocktail, #3077, 3½-oz 22.00
Rosalie, bl, pk or gr, creamer, ftd, tall, ewer form 65.00
Rosalie, bl, pk or gr, platter, 12" 100.00
Rosalie, bl, pk or gr, sugar bowl, ftd 20.00
Rosalie, bl, pk or gr, tumbler, ftd, #3077, 2½-oz 45.00
Rosalie, bl, pk or gr, vase, ftd, 5½" 85.00
Rose Point, ashtray, #3500/128, 4½" 60.00
Rose Point, ashtray, sq, #3500/129, 3¼" 60.00
Rose Point, bowl, bonbon; crimped, #3400/203, 6" 100.00
Rose Point, bowl, bonbon; cupped/deep, #3400/204, 3½" 90.00
Rose Point, bowl, cereal; #3400/53, 6" 115.00
Rose Point, bowl, flared, #3400/168, 10½" 85.00
Rose Point, butter dish, rnd, #506 ....195.00
Rose Point, candlestick, Calla Lily, #499, 6½", ea 125.00
Rose Point, cheese dish, #980, 5" 625.00
Rose Point, comport, scalloped edge, #3900/136, 5½" 85.00
Rose Point, creamer, flat, #137 ....150.00
Rose Point, hurricane lamp, candlestick base, #1617 ....300.00
Rose Point, ice pail, #3400/851 ....185.00
Rose Point, oil, ball shape, w/stopper, #3400/96, 2-oz 120.00
Rose Point, pitcher, ice lip, #3400/100, 76-oz 250.00
Rose Point, plate, hdls, #3400/1181, 6" 22.00
Rose Point, plate, service; #3900/167, 14" 80.00
Rose Point, relish, 3-part, 4-ftd, hdls, #3500/64, 10" 75.00
Rose Point, sandwich tray, center hdl, #3400/10, 11" 145.00
Rose Point, tray (sugar/creamer), #3900/37 ....35.00
Rose Point, tumbler, juice; low ft, #3121, 5-oz 40.00
Rose Point, tumbler, str sides, #498, 12-oz 65.00
Rose Point, vase, globe; #3400/102, 5" 110.00
Rose Point, vase, sweet pea; #629 ....350.00
Rose Point, water stem, #3121, 10-oz 42.00
Tally Ho, amber or crystal, bowl, grapefruit; flat rim, 6½" 20.00
Tally Ho, amber or crystal, bowl, salad; flared, 13½" 30.00
Tally Ho, amber or crystal, candelabrum, w/bobeche & prism, 6½" 50.00
Tally Ho, amber or crystal, cup, punch; flat 10.00
Tally Ho, amber or crystal, ice pail, chrome hdl 65.00
Tally Ho, amber or crystal, plate, chop; 14" 35.00
Tally Ho, amber or crystal, tumbler, short, 10-oz 25.00
Tally Ho, amber or crystal, vase, ftd, 12" 95.00
Tally Ho, Carmen or Royal, ashtray, w/center hdl, 4" 27.50
Tally Ho, Carmen or Royal, bowl, belled, 12½" 70.00
Tally Ho, Carmen or Royal, bowl, sauce boat 40.00
Tally Ho, Carmen or Royal, cheese & cracker, hdls, 11½" 90.00
Tally Ho, Carmen or Royal, goblet, oyster cocktail 22.00

Portia, candle holder, double, $40.00.

Portia, candlestick, fleur-de-lis, 2-light, 6", ea 45.00
Portia, candy box, w/lid, rnd 125.00

Tally Ho, Carmen or Royal, ice pail, chrome hdl..................**95.00**
Tally Ho, Carmen or Royal, plate, raised edge, 13½" **60.00**
Tally Ho, Carmen or Royal, sherbet, low ft, 4½-oz..................**20.00**
Tally Ho, Forest Green, ash well, center hdl, 2-pc..................**30.00**
Tally Ho, Forest Green, bowl/pan, 10"..................**45.00**
Tally Ho, Forest Green, comport, low ft, 7" **50.00**
Tally Ho, Forest Green, cookie jar, w/lid, chrome hdls..............**135.00**
Tally Ho, Forest Green, decanter, 34-oz..................**65.00**
Tally Ho, Forest Green, plate, buffet lunch; 18"..................**65.00**
Tally Ho, Forest Green, relish, 3-compartment, hdls, 8"................**30.00**
Tally Ho, Forest Green, stein, rnd bottom, 14-oz..................**35.00**
Tally Ho, Forest Green, sugar bowl, ftd..................**20.00**
Valencia, ashtray, rnd, #3500/124, 3¼"..................**12.00**
Valencia, bowl, cereal; #3500/37, 6"..................**27.50**
Valencia, creamer, #3500/14..................**17.00**
Valencia, decanter, ball shape, #3400/119, 12-oz..................**175.00**
Valencia, goblet, stemmed, ft long bowl, #3500..................**28.00**
Valencia, plate, breakfast; #3500/5, 8½"..................**14.00**
Valencia, saucer, #3500/1..................**3.00**
Valencia, tumbler, #3400/92, 2½-oz..................**25.00**
Wildflower, basket, hdls, ftd, #3400/1182, 6" **35.00**
Wildflower, bowl, celery & relish; #3900/126, 3-part, 12" **55.00**
Wildflower, candlestick, #3400/646, 5", ea..................**45.00**
Wildflower, creamer, #3900/41..................**22.00**
Wildflower, hat, #1704, 5" **295.00**
Wildflower, plate, torte; #3900/167, 14"..................**65.00**
Wildflower, shakers, #3400/77, pr **50.00**
Wildflower, stem, cordial; #3121, 1-oz..................**70.00**
Wildflower, tumbler, juice; #3121, 5-oz **30.00**
Wildflower, vase, keyhole, #1238, ftd, 12" **125.00**

Cameo

The technique of glass carving was perfected 2,000 years ago in ancient Rome and Greece. The most famous ancient example of cameo glass is the Portland Vase, made in Rome around 100 A.D. After glass blowing was developed, glassmakers devised a method of casing several layers of colored glass together, often with a light color over a darker base, to enhance the design. Skilled carvers meticulously worked the fragile glass to produce incredibly detailed classic scenes. In the eighteenth and nineteenth centuries Oriental and Near-Eastern artisans used the technique more extensively. European glassmakers revived the art during the last quarter of the nineteenth century. In France, Galle and Daum produced some of the finest examples of modern times, using as many as five layers of glass to develop their designs, usually scenics or subjects from nature. Hand carving was supplemented by the use of a copper engraving wheel, and acid was used to cut away the layers more quickly.

In England, Thomas Webb and Sons used modern machinery and technology to eliminate many of the problems that plagued early glass carvers. One of Webb's best-known carvers, George Woodall, is credited with producing over four hundred pieces. Woodall was trained in the art by John Northwood, famous for reproducing the Portland Vase in 1876. Cameo glass became very popular during the late 1800s, resulting in a market that demanded more than could be produced, due to the tedious procedures involved. In an effort to produce greater volume, less elaborate pieces with simple floral or geometric designs were made, often entirely acid etched with little or no hand carving. While very little cameo glass was made in this country, a few pieces were produced by James Gillinder, Tiffany, and the Libbey Glass Company. Though some continued to be made on a limited scale into the 1900s (and until about 1920 in France), for the most part, inferior products caused a marked reduction in its manufacture by the turn of the century. Beware of new 'French' cameo glass from Romania and Taiwan. Some of it is very good and may be signed with 'old' signatures. Know your dealer! Our advisor for this category is Don Williams; he is listed in the Directory under Missouri. See also specific manufactures.

English

Biscuit jar, floral branches, wht on red, bulbous, SP mts, 5x6½" ...**2,900.00**
Bottle, lay down; cvd as swan head, wht on yel, 8¾" L +mk case..**6,000.00**
Bottle, lay down; floral, wht on cranberry, in Mappin & Webb case, 10" ...**4,400.00**
Bottle, lay down; floral/butterfly, wht on bl, Gorham top, 10 " L.....**3,200.00**
Bottle, lay down; lily of the valley/butterfly, wht/red/citron, 4" L ...**2,000.00**
Bottle, lay down; palms/butterfly, wht on bl, 8" L **2,000.00**
Bottle, scent; floral branches, wht on bl, ball shape, unmk, 4" ...**2,000.00**
Bottle, scent; floral branches, wht on citron, cylindrical, 2½" **1,100.00**
Bottle, scent; floral/leaves, wht on bl, bell shape, 2½" **750.00**
Bottle, scent; morning glories, wht/amethyst/bl, ball form, 2"...**2,500.00**
Bowl, floral branch, wht on citron, incurvate rim, 2¾"..............**700.00**
Bowl, floral branch/dragonfly, wht/red/citron, incurvate, 1⅝" **1,150.00**
Claret jug, morning glories, wht on bl, silver hdl/neck, 8¾" ...**2,000.00**
Claret jug, mums/leaves, bk: butterfly, wht on red, SP mts, 12" ...**2,400.00**
Lamp base, floral/butterfly, wht on bl, 3 ft, chimney, overall: 8", EX...**575.00**
Letter seal, floral, wht on bl, silver top dtd 1905, 4¼" L, EX **725.00**
Sweetmeat, seashells/aquatic plants, wht/red, SP rim/hdl/top, 5" dia.....**1,600.00**
Vase, lg floral, bk: butterfly, wht/red on citron, 6¼"................**2,200.00**
Vase, oak leaves/acorns, wht on red, 4½" **1,200.00**
Vase, prunus blossoms, red on wht, ovoid w/can neck, unmk, 6½" ...**1,100.00**

French

Vase, Deco floral, gr/wht w/clear ft, D'art Des Cristalleries, 13" ...**525.00**
Vase, floral, grn/wht on frost, Moda, dbl gourd, 11" **365.00**
Vase, floral branches, maroon on orange, bulbous, D'argyl, 9" **465.00**
Vase, flowerheads/leaves, pk/gr on clear, Arsall, 12" **575.00**

Vase, fuchsias and leaves, dark purple on frost, Arsall, 12x6", $1,350.00. (Photo courtesy James Julia Auction Co., Fairfield, Maine)

Vase, grape clusters, brn on yel/brn/orange, Degué, 10"...............**550.00**
Vase, honeysuckle & vines, purple on yel, ovoid, Delatte, 7½"....**425.00**
Vase, iris, purple on cream, Weis, mini, 1¾"..................**120.00**
Vase, leaves/vines/buds, gr on clear, Arsall, 11¾" **575.00**
Vase, roses/foliage, purple/pk on cream/pk/yel, teardrop, Delatte, 8"....**550.00**
Vase, shamrocks on acid-cut floral frosted ground, unmk, 6" **290.00**
Vase, stylized feathers, royal bl on frost, Degué/Made in France, 19"..**2,000.00**
Vase, thistles, gr/amethyst on clear, Gouvenin, 10" **575.00**
Vase, trees/water scenic, Muller, sharply bulbous, 3½" **350.00**

Candle Holders

The earliest type of candlestick, called a pricket, was constructed with a sharp point on which the candle was impaled. The socket type, first used in the sixteenth century, consisted of the socket and a short stem with a wide drip pan and base. These were made from sheets of silver or other metal; not until late in the seventeenth century were candlesticks made by casting. By the 1700s, styles began to vary from the traditional fluted column or baluster form and became more elaborate. A Rococo style with scrolls, shellwork, and naturalistic leaves and flowers came into vogue that afforded the individual silversmith the opportunity to exhibit his skill and artistry. The last half of the eighteenth century brought a return to fluted columns with neoclassic motifs. Because they were made of thin sheet silver, weighted bases were used to add stability. The Rococo styles of the Regency period were heavily encrusted with applied figures and flowers. Candelabra with six to nine branches became popular. By the Victorian era when lamps came into general use, there was less innovation and more adaptation of the earlier styles. For more information we recommend *Glass Candlesticks of the Depression Era* by Gene Florence and *The Glass Candlestick Book, Volume 1, 2,* and *3* by Tom Felt and Elaine and Rich Stoer (Collector Books). See also Silver; Tinware; specific manufacturers.

Bell metal, short stick, saucer base, 17th/18th C, 2¾" **460.00**
Brass, beehive, mk Coronation 1911, registry mk, 12½", pr........**465.00**
Brass, beehive, 10½", pr...**175.00**
Brass, capstan, flared socket, raised rim, 4¾" **745.00**
Brass, capstan, short trn socket w/piercings, early, 4½x4½" **500.00**
Brass, cylinder socket, faceted hub, sq base, 17th C, 6½"...........**600.00**
Brass, disk base, 2", pr...**115.00**
Brass, dome base, Spanish, 17th C, 7½"......................................**600.00**
Brass, eng rings at baluster-trn stem, sq pan, early, 7" **375.00**
Brass, King of Dmns, w/pushup, 12½", pr....................................**175.00**
Brass, octagon base, 18th C, 5½"..**400.00**
Brass, pricket, multi-lobed base, top drip pan, early, 5", pr..........**400.00**
Brass, push-up w/medial ring, low faceted shaft, 9¼" **300.00**
Brass, QA, heavy casting, scalloped, petal sockets, rpr, 8¾", pr..**865.00**
Brass, QA, ornamental ridges, swellings on shaft, 7¼", pr **475.00**
Brass, QA, petal base, baluster stem, EX detail, 7¾", pr **1,750.00**
Brass, QA, scalloped base, 8", VG, pr..**515.00**
Brass, QA, scalloped corners, domed ring, seamed stems, 7", pr...**660.00**
Brass, QA style, raised dome, sq base, 18th C, 6" **300.00**
Brass, spiral trnings, saucer base, Dutch or Spanish, 17th C, 6½" ...**600.00**
Brass, stepped triangular base w/paw ft, 11½" **175.00**
Brass, well formed column on sq base w/4 ft, 6½" **260.00**
Brass, 2 swellings on shaft, faceted ridged base, 1720s, 6⅜" **235.00**
Bronze, trn candle cup, beaded SP plinth, eng decor, 1790s, 10½"...**2,000.00**
Bronze, urn-form cup on tapered std on plinth, Charlex X, 10¼", pr....**1,645.00**
Candelabra, bronze, Fr Aesthetic style, 10-light, late 1800s, 36", pr ..**4,400.00**
Candelabra, bronze, gilt/patinated Louis XV style, 9-light, 30", pr....**4,000.00**
Candelabra, gilt-bronze, lilies, Classical style, 3-light, 35", pr.....**2,250.00**
Candelabra, giltwood Italian Neoclassical, 5-light, 39x42x7", pr....**5,000.00**
Candelabrum, gilt bronze & wht marble Napoleon III, 5-light, 21" **515.00**
Candelabrum, Rose Point #3121, crystal w/encrusted gold, 7½" ...**225.00**
Gilt bronze, Louis XV style, knopped baluster, 19th C, 10½", pr..**2,950.00**
Gilt bronze & champlevé enamel, Barbedienne Foundry, 9", pr..**2,650.00**
Glass candle block, Plantation #1567, crystal, Heisey, 3"...........**110.00**
Glass, clambroth, hexagonal, Sandwich, 8⅜"...............................**325.00**
Glass, Curling Wave, 2-light, unknown mfg, 8"..............................**65.00**
Glass, Duo Leaf #2533, crystal, Fostoria, 2-light, 6¼" **35.00**
Glass, Lotus #1921, crystal, flower base, Westmoreland, 9"..........**45.00**
Glass, Rib & Bead #330, crystal, Canton, 6⅜"...............................**35.00**
Glass, Teardrop, crystal w/red flash, Indiana, 5½".........................**20.00**

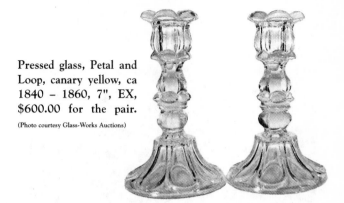

Pressed glass, Petal and Loop, canary yellow, ca 1840 – 1860, 7", EX, $600.00 for the pair.
(Photo courtesy Glass-Works Auctions)

Sconce, brass, 2-socket w/scrolled arms, 20th C, 9½", pr............**120.00**
Sconce, bronze Louis XVI style, 3-light, 22", pr **1,200.00**
Sconce, cut glass Geo III style, 5-light, 25", pr........................**1,000.00**
Sconce, gilt-bronze Emp style, winged goddess, 2-arm, 29", pr......**2,250.00**
Sconce, gilt-bronze Louis XIV style, 2-light, mask center, 15", 4 for...**3,500.00**
Sconce, gilt-bronze Louis XVI style, 6-light, maiden form, 36"..**1,100.00**
Sconce, giltwood/metal compo Louis XVI style, 3-arm, 39", pr..**1,200.00**
Wood, baluster trn w/mustard pnt & smoke decor, 1920, 11", pr ..**185.00**
Wrought iron, spiral w/scrolled lip hangers, pushups, 8", pr........**430.00**

Candlewick

Candlewick crystal was made by the Imperial Glass Corporation, a division of Lenox Inc., Bellaire, Ohio. It was introduced in 1936, and though never marked except for paper labels, it is easily recognized by the beaded crystal rims, stems, and handles inspired by the tufted needlework called candlewicking, practiced by our pioneer women. During its production, more than 741 items were designed and produced. In September 1982 when Imperial closed its doors, thirty-four pieces were still being made.

Identification numbers and mold numbers used by the company help collectors recognize the various styles and shapes. Most of the pieces are from the #400 series, though other series numbers were also used. Stemware was made in eight styles — five from the #400 series made from 1941 to 1962, one from #3400 series made in 1937, another from #3800 series made in 1941, and the eighth style from the #4000 series made in 1947. In the listings that follow, some #400 items lack the mold number because that information was not found in the company files.

A few pieces have been made in color or with a gold wash. At least two lines, Valley Lily and Floral, utilized Candlewick with floral patterns cut into the crystal. These are scarce today. Other rare items include gifts such as the desk calendar made by the company for its employees and customers; the dresser set comprised of a mirror, clock, puff jar, and cologne; and the chip and dip set.

Ashtray, #400/33, rnd, 4" **11.00**
Ashtray, heart, #400/173, 5½" **12.00**
Ashtray, matchbook holder center, #400/60, 6" **150.00**
Bell, #400/179, 4" **85.00**
Bowl, belled, #400/106B, 12" **100.00**
Bowl, belled, #400/63B, 10½" **60.00**
Bowl, centerpiece; flared, #400/13B, 11" **55.00**
Bowl, cottage cheese; #400/85, 6"...**25.00**
Bowl, cream soup; #400/50, 5" **45.00**
Bowl, cupped edge, #400/75F, 10" **45.00**
Bowl, float; #400/92F, 12"...**40.00**
Bowl, hdls, #400/113B, 12" **165.00**
Bowl, mint; hdls, #400/51F, 6" **23.00**

Bowl, sauce; deep, #400/243, 5½" 40.00
Butter dish, rnd, w/lid, #400/144, 5½" 35.00

Cake stand, high foot, 11", $75.00.

Candle holder, 3-toed, #400/207, 4½", ea 100.00
Candle holder, 3-way, beaded base, #400/115, ea 125.00
Candy box, w/lid, #400/259, 7" 165.00
Cigarette box w/4 ashtrays, rectangular, #400/134/6 ......67.50
Coaster, #400/78, 4" 10.00
Cocktail, seafood; bead ft, #400/190 ....90.00
Compote, bead stem, #400/48F, 8" 100.00
Creamer, domed ft, #400/18 ....140.00
Egg cup, beaded ft, #400/19 ....55.00
Finger bowl, #3800 ....35.00
Hurricane lamp, flared/crimped edge globe, #400/152, 3-pc 195.00
Ice tub, #400/63, 5½x8" dia 125.00
Knife, butter; #4000 ....500.00
Marmalade, domed bead ft, w/lid & spoon, #400/8918, 3-pc 100.00
Mustard jar, w/spoon, #400/156 ....40.00
Oil bottle, bead base, #400/166, 6-oz 75.00
Pitcher, #400/24, 80-oz 165.00
Pitcher, low ft, #400/19, 16-oz 250.00
Pitcher, plain, #400/419, 40-oz 50.00
Plate, #400/34, 4½" 8.00
Plate, dinner; #400/10D, 10½" 45.00
Plate, hdls, #400/145D, 12" 45.00
Plate, luncheon; #400/7D, 9" 15.00
Plate, salad; #400/5D, 8" 10.00
Plate, salad; oval, #400/38, 9" 45.00
Plate, triangular, #400/266, 7½" 95.00
Platter, #400/131D, 16" 235.00
Salt dip, #400/19, 2¼" 10.00
Salt spoon, #4000/616, 3" 11.00
Saucer, after dinner; #400/77AD 5.00
Shakers, ftd w/beaded base, #400/190, pr 60.00
Shakers, ind, #400/109, pr 14.00
Snack jar, beaded ft, w/lid, #400/139/1 ....625.00
Stem, claret, #3400, 5-oz 58.00
Stem, cocktail, #400/190, 4-oz 22.00
Stem, sherbet, low, #3800 ....28.00
Stem, wine, #400/190, 5-oz 25.00
Sugar bowl, beaded hdls, #400/30, 6-oz 8.00
Sugar bowl, plain ft, #400/31 ....7.00
Tidbit set, #400/18TB, 3-pc 225.00
Toast set, w/cover, #400/123, 7¾" 350.00
Tray, #400/29, 6½" 18.00

Tray, condiment; #400/148, 5¼x9¼" 45.00
Tray, hdls, #400/113E, 14" 95.00
Tray, lemon; center hdl, #400/221, 5½" 37.50
Tumbler, #3800, 12-oz 37.50
Tumbler, ftd, #3400, 12-oz 20.00
Tumbler, juice; #400/19, 5-oz 12.50
Tumbler, old-fashioned; #400/18, 7-oz 70.00
Vase, #400/198, 6" dia 350.00
Vase, ball, beaded ft, sm neck, #400/25, 4" 65.00
Vase, fan; bead hdl, #400/87F, 8" 35.00
Vase, ftd, #400/193, 10" 250.00

Candy Containers

Figural glass candy containers were first created in 1876 when ingenious candy manufacturers began to use them to package their products. Two of the first containers, the Liberty Bell and Independence Hall, were distributed for our country's centennial celebration. Children found these toys appealing, and an industry was launched that lasted into the mid-1960s.

Figural candy containers include animals, comic characters, guns, telephones, transportation vehicles, household appliances, and many other intriguing designs. The oldest (those made prior to 1920) were usually hand painted and often contained extra metal parts in addition to the metal strip or screw closures. During the 1950s these metal parts were replaced with plastic, a practice that continued until candy containers met their demise in the 1960s. While predominately clear, they are found in nearly all colors of glass including milk glass, green, amber, pink, emerald, cobalt, ruby flashed, and light blue. Usually the color was intentional, but leftover glass was used as well and resulted in unplanned colors. Various examples are found in light or ice blue, and new finds are always being discovered. Production of the glass portion of candy containers was centered around the western Pennsylvania city of Jeannette. Major producers include Westmoreland Glass, West Bros., Victory Glass, J.H. Millstein, J.C. Crosetti, L.E. Smith, Jack Stough, and T.H. Stough. While 90% of all glass candies were made in the Jeannette area, other companies such as Eagle Glass, Play Toy, and Geo. Borgfeldt Co. have a few to their credit as well.

Buyer beware! Many candy containers have been reproduced. Some, including the Camera and the Rabbit Pushing Wheelbarrow, come already painted from distributors. Others may have a slick or oily feel to the touch. The following list may also alert you to possible reproductions.

Amber Pistol, L #144 (first sold full in the 1970s, not listed in E&A)

Auto, D&P #173/E&A #33/L #377

Auto, D&P #163/E&A #60/L #356

Black and White Taxi, D&P #182/L #353 (Silk-screened metal roofs are being reproduced. They are different from originals in that the white section is more silvery in color than the original cream. These closures are put on original bases and often priced for hundreds of dollars. If the top is not original, the value of these candy containers is reduced by 80%.)

Camera, D&P #419/E&A #121/L #238 (Original says 'Pat Apld For' on bottom, reproduction says 'B. Shakman' or is ground off.)

Carpet Sweeper, D&P 296/E&A #133/L #243 (currently being sold with no metal parts)

Carpet Sweeper, E&A #132/L #242 (currently being sold with no metal parts)

Charlie Chaplin, D&P 195/E&A #137/L #83 (Original has 'Geo. Borgfeldt' on base; reproduction comes in pink and blue.)

Chicken on Nest, D&P #10/E&A #149/L #12

Display Case, D&P #422/E&A #177/L #246 (Original should be painted silver and brown.)

Dog, D&P #21/E&A #180/L #24 (clear and cobalt)

Drum Mug, D&P #431/E&A #543/L #255

Happifats on Drum, D&P #199/E&A #208/L #89 (no notches on repro for closure to hook into)

Fire Engine, D&P 258/E&A #213/L #386 (repros in green and blue glass)

Independence Hall, D&P #130/E&A #342/L #76 (Original is rectangular; repro has offset base with red felt-lined closure.)

Jackie Coogan, D&P #202/E&A #345/L #90 (marked inside 'B')

Kewpie, D&P #204/E&A #349/L #91 (Must have Geo. Borgfeldt on base to be original.)

Mailbox, D&P #216/E&A #521/L #254 (repro marked Taiwan)

Mantel Clock, D&P #483/E&A #162/L #114 (originally in ruby flashed, milk glass, clear, and frosted only)

Mule and Waterwagon, D&P #51/E&A #539/L #38 (original marked Jeannette, PA)

Naked Child, E&A 546/L #94

Owl, D&P #52/E&A #566/L #37 (original in clear only, often painted; repro found in clear, blue, green, and pink with a higher threaded base and less detail)

Peter Rabbit, D&P #60/E&A #618/L #55

Piano, D&P #460/E&A #577/L #289 (original in only clear and milk glass, both painted)

Rabbit Pushing Wheelbarrow, D&P #72/E&A #601/L #47 (Eggs are speckled on the repro; solid on the original.)

Rocking Horse, D&P #46/E&A #651/L #58 (original in clear only, repro marked 'Rocky')

Safe, D&P #311/E&A #661/L #268 (original in clear, ruby flashed, and milk glass only)

Santa, D&P 284/E&A #674/L #103 (Original has plastic head; repro [1970s] is all glass and opens at bottom.)

Santa's Boot, D&P #273/E&A #111/L #233

Scottie Dog, D&P #35/E&A #184/L #17 (Repro has a ice-like color and is often slick and oily.)

Station Wagon, D&P #178/E&A #56/L #378

Stough Rabbit, D&P #53/E&A #617/L #54

Uncle Sam's Hat, D&P #428/E&A #303/L #168

Wagon, U.S. Express D&P #530 (Glass is being reproduced without any metal parts.)

Others are possible. If in doubt, do not buy without a guarantee from the dealer and return privilege in writing. Also note that other reproductions are possible.

Our advisor for glass containers is Jeff Bradfield; he is listed in the Directory under Virginia. You may contact him with questions, if you will include an SASE. See Clubs, Newsletters, and Catalogs for the address of the Candy Container Collectors of America. A bimonthly newsletter offers insight into new finds, reproductions, updates, and articles from over four hundred collectors and members, including all authors of books on candy containers. Dues are $25.00 yearly. The club holds an annual convention in June in Lancaster, Pennsylvania, for collectors of candy containers.

'L' numbers used in this guide refer to a standard reference series, *An Album of Candy Containers*, Vols 1 and 2, by Jennie Long. 'E&A' numbers correlate with *The Compleat American Glass Candy Containers Handbook* by Eikelberner and Agadjanian, revised by Adele Bowden. D&P numbers refer to *The Collector's Guide to Candy Containers* by Doug Dezso and Leon and Rose Poirier (Collector Books).

Airplane, P-38 Lightning; Victory Glass, D&P 82/E&A 12/L 326...**225.00**

Amos & Andy, in Auto, Victory Glass, D&P 187/E&A 21/L 77....**500.00**

Baseball Player by Barrel, D&P 190/E&A 77/L 80......................**800.00**

Basket, Hanging; clear or milk glass, D&P 291/E&A 81/L 223.....**40.00**

Betty Lou Toy Town Dairy, cb carrier, D&P 107/E&A 529.........**450.00**

Binoculars, Victor, brass-plated tin fr, no box, D&P 98/E&A 560/L 624....**400.00**

Binoculars, Victor, brass-plated tin fr & box, D&P 98/E&A 560/L 624...**600.00**

Boat, Queen Mary; heavy glass, emb, D&P 103...........................**400.00**

Boat, Uruguay; anchor ea side of bow, D&P 105........................**250.00**

Bottle, Dairy Sweets; w/metal fr, D&P 108/E&A 532/L 501.......**150.00**

Bottle, Dolly's Milk; VG Co, D&P 109/E&A 527/L 66.................**60.00**

Bottle, Seltzer; w/hdl & spout, D&P 112......................................**500.00**

Bureau, slide-on closure, real mirror, D&P 294/E&A 112/L 125...**200.00**

Bus, NY - San Francisco; D&P 154/E&A 118-2/L 346...............**600.00**

Bus, Victory Lines Special, D&P 146/E&A 115/L 347..................**90.00**

Camel, Shriner's; clear or amber glass, sitting, D&P 4..................**40.00**

Cannon, US Defense Field Gun; tin bbl, D&P 387/E&A 128/L 142 ...**350.00**

Car, Boyd; various colors, D&P 159...**25.00**

Car, Coupe - Long Hood w/Tin Wheels; D&P 160/E&A 50/L 357....**175.00**

Car, Hearse #2; open top, D&P 165/E&A 40/L 360....................**140.00**

Car, Little Touring; Stough, D&P 172/E&A 32............................**30.00**

Car, Sedan w/12 Vents; mk VG Co, 90% pnt, D&P 177/E&A 36.....**125.00**

Car, Station Wagon; JH Millstein, D&P 178/E&A 56/L 378 (+)....**40.00**

Car, 4-Door; mk West Bros Co, D&P 168/E&A 41/L 348..........**800.00**

Carpet Sweeper, Baby; wire hdl, D&P 295/E&A 132/L 242 (+).**475.00**

Cash Register, 4 rows of keys, D&P 420/E&A 135/L 244...........**450.00**

Cheery Cholly Clown, cb suit/shoes, compo head, D&P 194/L 530...**300.00**

Chicken on Sagging Basket, D&P 14/E&A 148/L 8.....................**75.00**

Clarinet, red/wht striped tube at top, D&P 448/E&A 316/L 285..**35.00**

Clock, Mantel; stippled w/scrollwork, D&P 482/E&A 164/L 116.....**200.00**

Clock, Milk Glass; Roman #s, 11 o'clock, D&P 483/E&A 162/L 114 (+).....**250.00**

Coach, Angeline - No Couplers; all orig, D&P 519/E&A 168 ...**525.00**

Coal Car - w/Couplers; all orig, D&P 522/E&A 171...................**500.00**

Condiment Set, Rainbow Candy; metal base, D&P 297/E&A 174/L 503...**50.00**

Dirigible, Mu-Mu; Bakelite closure, D&P 90..............................**200.00**

Dog, Bulldog on Rnd Base, Victory Glass, D&P 18/E&A 189/L 15..**60.00**

Dog, Hot Doggie; HE Widmer, D&P 23/E&A 320/L 14..........**1,100.00**

Dog, Little Doggie in the Window; Stough, D&P 30/E&A 178/L 483...**30.00**

Dog, Scottie, looking str ahead, D&P 35/E&A 184/L 17 (+)........**25.00**

Dog w/Umbrella, wide opening, D&P 37/E&A 194-2/L 29 ....**35.00**

Drum Bank, pnt milk glass, emb cannon etc, D&P 289/E&A 195/L 279...**475.00**

Elephant, GOP, orig pnt, D&P 43/E&A 206/L 31.......................**250.00**

Fire Engine, Ladder truck; Victory Glass, D&P 254/E&A 216/L 384...**250.00**

Fire Engine, Lg Boiler; D&P 255/E&A 221.................................**125.00**

Fire Engine, Three Dot USA; D&P 260/E&A 220/L 380..........**100.00**

Flat Iron, snap-on bottom, D&P 306/E&A 344/L 249...............**625.00**

Gas Pump, 23¢ To-Day; D&P 439/E&A 240/L 316...................**375.00**

Gun, Beaded Border Grip; D&P 390/E&A 246............................**20.00**

Gun, Medium w/Hook Grip; screw head in grip, D&P 396/E&A 259...**25.00**

Gun, Stough's Whistling Jim - Str Grip; D&P 402/E&A 249.......**20.00**

Gun, Stough's 1939 Pat Pending, D&P 400/E&A 249 ....**25.00**

Hansel & Gretel Fairy Pups Salt & Pepper, D&P 22/E&A 193/L 23, pr..**90.00**

Helicopter, attached rotor, Stough, D&P 91/E&A 306/L 329......**300.00**

Horn, Musical Clarinet 55, cb tube/tin whistle cap, D&P 451/E&A 316 ..**30.00**

Horn, Stough's 1953; 3 valve buttons, D&P 453/E&A 310/L 283...**40.00**

House w/Chimney, front dormer, D&P 129/E&A 324/L 75........**250.00**

Irish Hat, shamrock on front, D&P 426/E&A 302/L 167 ....**3,000.00**

Jack O'Lantern, Slant Eyes; orig pnt, D&P 265/E&A 349..........**225.00**

Kettle on 3 Feet, horizontal ribs/orig closure, D&P 307/E&A 355/L 251..**45.00**

Lamp, Candlestick Base; waxed paper cup shade, D&P 322/E&A 370/L 559 ..**400.00**

Lamp, Metal Shade; Stough, D&P 335/L 464...............................**50.00**

Lamppost, glass globe/pewter stand, D&P 341/L 553...................**90.00**

Lantern, Beaded #2, pnt clear or milk glass, D&P 348/E&A 405/L 180...**35.00**

Lantern, Dec 20 '04 - Medium; shaker top, D&P 351/E&A 407/L 173...**30.00**

Lantern, Japanese Paper Type; w/candle holder inside, D&P 354/E&A 389.....**425.00**

Lantern, Stough's All Glass; D&P 364/E&A 406 ....**25.00**

Lantern, 16 Hole; D&P 376/E&A 444/L 190 ....**35.00**

Lanterns, Twins on Anchor; hang on metal fr, D&P 370/E&A 385/L 186.....**25.00**

Liberty Bell w/Hanger, gr glass, D&P 95/E&A 85/L 229.............**45.00**

Locomotive, Dbl Window w/Rear Screw Cap; D&P 525...........**200.00**

Locomotive, Mapother's; D&P 499/E&A 494..............................**325.00**

Milk Bottle, German, wire closure at neck, D&P 111.................**100.00**

Mug, Child's; false bottom/base holds candy, D&P 432/E&A 541/L 256 ..**325.00**

Mug, Kiddies' Drinking; Millstein, D&P 433/E&A 540/L 258......**25.00**
Mug, Victory Glass Co; flat-top hdl w/curl at base, D&P 434/E&A 542 .**15.00**
Oil Can, Independence Bell; w/oil-can spout, D&P 435/E&A 556 ....**550.00**
Parlor Car, arched windows, D&P 516/E&A 169 ....**325.00**
Pencil, Baby Jumbo; holds real pencil, D&P 218/E&A 567/L 263 ....**95.00**
Pencil, Kiddies Candy; w/box, D&P 217 ....**50.00**
Phonograph w/Glass Horn, gold pnt trim, D&P 458/E&A 576/L 286 ..**450.00**
Pipe, Germany, cork closure, D&P 437/E&A 585 ....**60.00**
Play Packs, Toy Assortment, Christmas; D&P 469 ....**125.00**
Pumpkin Head Mounted Policeman, no pnt, D&P 269...........**1,300.00**
Rabbit Family, stippled, mk VG Co, D&P 56/E&A 604/L 43...**1,000.00**
Rabbit w/Aluminum Ears, mk Germany/Ges Gesch, D&P 63/L 487...**600.00**
Racer, Stutz Bear Cat; 10-rib radiator, D&P 474/E&A 639 .....**1,250.00**
Racer #12, Victory Glass, D&P 476/E&A 642/L 432 ....**200.00**
Rooster, Crowing; Victory Glass, G pnt, D&P 73/E&A 151.......**350.00**
Santa Claus in Banded Coat, ...3 OZ ADV, G pnt, D&P 277/L 97/E&A 669...**300.00**
Santa Claus Leaving Chimney, Victory Glass, D&P 281/E&A 673/L 102 ...**150.00**
Santa w/Skis, all plastic, D&P 287 ....**20.00**
Soldier, Doughboy; emb helmet/uniform, D&P 209/L 525..........**200.00**
Stop & Go, metal post/blades, D&P 441/E&A 706/L 317 ....**525.00**
Tank, Man in Turret; emb treads, D&P 412/E&A 722/L 437........**45.00**
Tank, 2 Cannons; D&P 413/E&A 723 ....**35.00**
Telephone, Glass Receiver - USA; D&P 226/E&A 736/L 290 .....**70.00**
Telephone, Pay Station; plastic w/glass bottle, D&P 235/E&A 120/L 239...**275.00**
Telephone, Redlich's Bell/Crank; wood receiver, D&P 238/E&A 752/L 294...**350.00**
Telephone, Redlich's Sm Screw Top #2, Pat #, D&P 244/E&A 749/L 296 ...**125.00**
Telephone, Stough's Musical Toy; ringed base, D&P 246/E&A 732/L 310 ...**45.00**
Telephone, Wood Transmitter; D&P 251/E&A 751/L 308 ....**125.00**
Toonerville Trolley, Fontaine Fox, G pnt, D&P 214/E&A 767/L 111...**800.00**
Top, Lg; wood spring-loaded winder; Eagle Glass, D&P 442/E&A 775 .**125.00**
Toy Assortment, Kiddies Candy Filled; 5 toys, D&P 470 ....**650.00**
Uncle Sam by Barrel, slot in closure, 95% pnt, D&P 215/E&A 801/L 112.......**700.00**
Village School House, tin w/insert, D&P 143/E&A 808/L 76J ...**170.00**
Watch, Eagle; w/eagle fob, D&P 486/E&A 823/L 122 ....**450.00**
Watch, Victor; tin face, Pat Aug 12 1913, D&P 487/E&A 824/L 121 ...**1,000.00**
Wheelbarrow, Victory Glass, tin snap-on closure, D&P 531/E&A 832/L 273.....**90.00**
Windmill, Candy Guaranteed; tin blades, D&P 433/E&A 840..**1,000.00**
Windmill, Plastic Bank; D&P 536..**30.00**
Windmill, TG Stough's 1915; D&P 538/E&A 842 ....**375.00**
World Globe, mtd on pewter stand, D&P 445/E&A 860/L 276...**500.00**

Lantern, Pear shaped; pebbled base, ca 1940, 2½", D&P 368/E&A 393, from $25.00 to $35.00. (Photo courtesy Doug Dezso)

Miscellaneous

These types of candy containers are generally figural. Many are

holiday-related. Small sizes are common; larger sizes are in greater demand. Because of eBay's influence, prices have dropped and remain soft. Our prices reflect this trend. Our advisor for this category is Jenny Tarrant; she is listed in the Directory under Missouri. See also Christmas; Easter; Halloween.

Key: pm — papier-mâché

Bulldog, compo, cream w/orange hat, Germany, 4", VG **100.00**
Cat, pm w/gesso, mc pnt, glass eyes, red ribbon, rpt, 6" **190.00**
Cat, seated, pm w/gesso, worn flocking, glass eyes, rpr, 4" **175.00**
Cat in shoe, compo & gesso w/mc pnt, rpr, 4" **150.00**
Doll, bsk open dome head, crepe-paper/cb cylinder body, Germany, 6"..**120.00**
Dove, compo w/gray pnt, pk-pnt metal fr, orange glass eyes, 4½x8" ..**150.00**
Elephant, pm, glass tusks, Germany, ca 1885-1920, 6" L.............**155.00**
English Bobby, pm, EX pnt, Pat No 208063, 12" **160.00**
George Washington, compo, stands on rnd box w/silk flag, Germany, 5"..**195.00**
George Washington bust, bottom plug, compo, 2-3" **95.00**
George Washington bust, bottom plug, compo, 4-6" **150.00**
George Washington w/tree stump, compo, Germany, 3-4" **150.00**
George Washington w/tree stump, compo, Germany, 5-7" **225.00**
Horse, pm, head removes, 4½", VG **85.00**
Pig, pm, gr w/HP features, Made in Germany, 5¼x5½x3" **90.00**
Pig, pm, sleeping, worn/soiled pk flocking, 5⅝" **90.00**
Pigeon, compo w/metal fr, gray/wht/irid purple, 4½x6" **75.00**
Pigeon, compo w/metal fr, yel/red/brn pnt, lt ft wear, 4½x4¾" **75.00**
Rooster, compo w/metal fr, yel/red/brn pnt, lt ft wear, 4½x4¾" ...**120.00**
St Patrick's Day, Irish man bust, w/plug, compo, Germany, 3-4" ..**95.00**
St Patrick's Day, Irish man bust, w/plug, compo, Germany, 5-6" ..**150.00**
St Patrick's Day, Irish man on candy box, compo, Germany, 3½"...**155.00**
St Patrick's Day, pig, flocked gr, plug in tummy, wood legs, 3-5"...**95.00**
St Patrick's Day, pk, pk w/shamrock, compo, Germany, 4-6".........**95.00**
St Patrick's Day, potato, compo, Germany, 3-4" **50.00**
Stag, compo w/metal rack, brn flock, yel glass eyes, Germany, 10", VG..**465.00**
Stork w/baby, spun cotton & paper, lifts leg, Germany, 1930s, 6½" **95.00**
Turkey, compo w/metal ft, head removes, Germany, 5" **150.00**
Turkey, compo w/metal legs, head removes, Germany, 3½"...........**70.00**
Watermelon w/face, molded cb w/celluloid body, Austria, 4¼" ..**125.00**

Canes

Fancy canes and walking sticks were once the mark of a gentleman. Hand-carved examples are collected and admired as folk art from the past. The glass canes that never could have been practical are unique whimseys of the glass-blower's profession. Gadget and container sticks, which were produced in a wide variety, are highly desirable. Character, political, and novelty types are also sought after as are those with handles made of precious metals.

Because our line length is limited, the values we suggest are midrange. Expect to pay as much as 25% more or less than prices listed.

For more information we recommend *American Folk Art Canes, Personal Sculpture*, by George H. Meyer, Sandringham Press, 100 West Long Lake Rd., Suite 100, Bloomfield Hills, MI 48304. Other possible references are *Canes in the United States* by Catherine Dike and *Canes From the 17th – 20th Century* by Jeffrey Snyder. For information concerning the Cane Collectors Club, see the Directory under Clubs, Newsletters, and Catalogs. Our advisor for this category is Bruce Thalberg; he is listed in the Directory under Connecticut.

Bakelite, lady's mirror/comb in vanity hdl, wood shaft, 1920s.....**750.00**
Bakelite bulldog w/glass light-up eyes, batteries in hdl, Austria ..**550.00**
Birch w/ball hdl & ornate silver inlay, Russia, ca 1895 ....**2,000.00**
Bone skull w/bow-tie hdl, ivory ring, ebonized shaft, 1890s **775.00**

Cloisonné floral ball-top hdl, partridgewood shaft, 1900s **900.00**
Damascene egg finial, Macassar ebony shaft, ca 1900 ....**1,800.00**
Ebonized wood tube hdl w/cigarette holder, converts to pipe, ca 1915..**300.00**
Gold knob w/presentation inscription/malacca shaft/horn ferrule, 1850s...**850.00**
Gold-filled hdl w/MOP decor, hardwood shaft w/MOP inlay, 1900s ..**375.00**
Hardwood T-hdl w/telescope & compass, brass mts, 1920s..........**375.00**
Ivory bbl knob w/cvg, horn separators, whalebone shaft, 1850s.......**1,400.00**
Ivory cvd top opens for pen/ink pot/stanhope/seal, ebony shaft.......**1,400.00**
Ivory eagle/cicada & turtle hdl, gold collar, snakewood shaft, 1890s..**1,000.00**
Ivory hdl w/nautical cvg, smooth whalebone shaft w/silver mts, 1840s...**850.00**
Ivory L-shaped lion hdl, segmented ivory shaft w/lion cvgs, ca 1900.....**550.00**
Ivory mtn lion on stump hdl, stepped partridgewood shaft, 1870s..**1,100.00**
Ivory pistol grip w/cvg, silver ferrule, rosewood shaft...................**250.00**
Ivory rabbit head hdl w/glass eyes, rosewood shaft, 1890s **800.00**
Ivory wild boar hdl w/glass eyes, ebony shaft w/ferrule, ca 1885 ....**500.00**
Leather hdl trns to withdraw 26" Toledo sword, malacca shaft, 1900s...**400.00**
Paperweight knob w/mc blossoms, copper ferrule/ebony shaft, 1900s....**800.00**
Rose quartz ball finial w/brass mt, chestnut shaft w/bamboo cvg, 1890s...**350.00**
Rosewood crook hdl w/gold cap, Tiffany & Co 18k, horn ferrule, 1910...**650.00**
Silver duck head w/glass eyes & MOP beak, partridgewood shaft, 1910s **325.00**
Silver fox on stump hdl, blk birch hdl, ornate ferrule, ca 1895 .....**2,000.00**
Silver niello crook hdl, ebony shaft, rpl ferrule, Russia, ca 1910s.....**800.00**
Silver snuff box gadget w/British 1868 hallmk, tropical wood shaft....**900.00**
Sterling crook hdl, tortoise-shell vnr shaft, Am, ca 1885.........**1,300.00**

Sterling L-handle mounted to section of Trans-Atlantic Cable, inscribed and dated 1859, marked Tiffany, $1,850.00; Gold-filled L-handle with foliate engraving, ebonized shaft, dated 1912, $75.00.

Sweet grass over wooden form w/velvet strips, Am Indian, 1900s **350.00**
Telescoping SP hdl unscrews for 1-draw scope, hardwood shaft, 1850s....**1,400.00**
Vegetal ivory, cvd Black man's head w/glass eyes, 1870s..............**850.00**
Whalebone & ivory, clenched fist finial, cvd shaft, 31" **1,850.00**
Wood, cvd L hdl w/stanhope of Last Supper, silver collar, Fr, 1890s ...**600.00**
Wood claw & ball hdl, overall folk cvgs, silver band, 1903........**475.00**
Wood Fr bulldog w/lever under jaw, malacca shaft, 1890s...........**500.00**
Wood terrier hdl w/red tongue, malacca shaft, horn ferrule, 1900s.....**350.00**

Canton

Canton is a blue and white porcelain that was first exported in the 1790s by clipper ships from China to the United States. Importation continued into the 1920s. Canton became very popular along the east coast where the major ports were located. Its popularity was due to several factors: it was readily available, inexpensive, and (due to the fact that it came in many different forms) appealing to homeowners.

The porcelain's blue and white color and simple motif (teahouse, trees, bridge, and a rain-cloud border) have made it a favorite of people who collect early American furniture and accessories. Buyers of Canton should shop at large outdoor shows and up-scale antique shows. Collections are regularly sold at auction and many examples may be found on eBay. Collectors usually prefer a rich, deep tone rather than a lighter blue. Cracks, large chips, and major repairs will substantially affect values. Prices of Canton have escalated sharply over the last twenty years, and rare forms are highly sought after by advanced collectors. Our advisor for this category is Hobart D. Van Deusen; he is listed in the Directory under Connecticut.

Basin, 2¾x9¼" **325.00**
Basket, rtcl, oval, 4⅞x8½", +undertray.....................................**880.00**
Bowl, central design, scalloped rim, 3 flowers on outside, 1½x9"..**440.00**
Bowl, cut-corner, 19th C, chip, 4⅝" +provenance **900.00**
Bowl, panel decor w/in & w/o, sq scalloped top, 4¾x9¼" **260.00**
Bowl, rtcl rim, 3½x8½", +matching 9" underplate.....................**800.00**
Bowl, rtcl rim, 3¼x9¾" L, +10⅞" oval plate.............................**900.00**
Bowl, vegetable; scalloped corners, boar's-head hdls, 3½x6½" ...**400.00**
Candlesticks, trumpet form, 6⅜", pr **1,750.00**
Cider jug, foo dog finial, entwined lapped hdl w/leaf terminals, 7" **950.00**
Cider jug, med & dk bl decor, dome lid w/dog finial, 9" **2,100.00**
Condiment set, 9 dishes in fitted lacquer case (G) w/HP figures, 12" W.....**800.00**
Creamer, bull nose, applied hdl, 3½"......................................**250.00**
Cup & saucer, demitasse; feather-like trees **50.00**
Dish, leaf shape, 7½"...**175.00**
Jar, cylindrical, w/lid, 1⅝x3⅞"..**500.00**
Mug, cylindrical, entwined lapped hdls, 3⅞".............................**500.00**
Mug, twined hdl w/molded berry ends, 4" **550.00**
Pitcher, high hdl w/molded end, 7"...**715.00**
Plate, pinched rim, 10⅛", 6 for...**1,000.00**
Platter, cut corners, 15¾x12¾", NM.......................................**700.00**
Platter, cut corners, 16¾x13½", EX **800.00**
Platter, mid-19th C, 12"..**460.00**
Platter, octagonal, 18½" L...**900.00**
Platter, well & tree; octagonal, 15" **1,000.00**
Sauce boat, scalloped, loop hdl, 1¾x7¾x3¾", pr.......................**500.00**
Shrimp dish, med bl w/2 lg shrimp on hdl, acorn shape **600.00**
Shrimp dish, 19th C, 10⅝"..**585.00**
Sugar bowl, twined hdls w/berry ends, berry finial, 6¼" **300.00**
Tea caddy, hexagonal, 6½"...**700.00**
Teapot, cylindrical, fruit finial, entwined lapped hdl, 5¾" **500.00**
Teapot, dk & med bl boats & pagodas, scrolled ear hdl, prof rstr, 10"..**330.00**
Teapot, fruit finial, twined hdls, 4¾"......................................**500.00**
Teapot, str sides, twined hdl w/berry ends, berry finial, 6", EX....**600.00**
Tureen, boar's-head hdls, stem finial, rpr/glaze chips, 7" H, +tray....**425.00**
Tureen, dk & med bl decor, animal-head hdls, domed lid, 8x13x10" ..**1,875.00**
Vase, Ku-form, rim nicks/hairlines, 13½".............................**1,100.00**
Vase, ovoid w/can neck, intricate lower band decor, 21" **1,400.00**

Capodimonte

The relief style, highly colored and defined porcelain pieces in this listing are commonly called and identified in our current marketplace as Capodimonte. It was King Ferdinand IV, son of King Charles, who opened a factory in Naples in 1771 and began to use the mark of the blue crown N (BCN). When the factory closed in 1834, the Ginori family at Doccia near Florence, Italy, acquired what was left of the factory and continued using its mark. The factory operated until 1896 when it was then combined with Societa Ceramica Richard of Milan which continues today to manufacture fine porcelain pieces marked with a crest and wreaths under a blue crown with R. Capodimonte.

Boxes and steins are highly sought after as they are cross collectibles. Figurines, figure groupings, flowery vases, urns, and the like are also very collectible, but most items on the market today are of recent manufacture. In the past several years, Europeans have been attending U.S. antique shows and auctions in order to purchase Capodimonte items to take back home, since many pieces were destroyed during the two world wars. This has driven up prices of the older ware. Our advisor for this category is James Highfield; he is listed in the Directory under Indiana.

Bell, winged cherubs in mtn landscape, R Capo mk, 4" **25.00**
Box, Greek figures, floral int, oval, BCN, 4x11½x7" **525.00**
Box, hunting scenes, gilt int, BCN over Meissen mk, 1½x2¼x2" ..**135.00**
Box, nude female w/cherubs, BCN France, 3x5½" dia **236.00**
Cake stand, center heraldic crest, BCN, 7x10½" dia **225.00**
Chalice cup, cherubs & Cupids, rnd base, BCN, 7½" **175.00**
Cup & saucer, BCN, imported by Robert Anstead, Los Angeles ..**75.00**
Ewer, dolphins on sq base & under spout, BCN, 8½" **250.00**
Lamp, converted urns, mythological scene, BCN, ¾" w/shade, pr ..**200.00**
Mug, nude female hdl, nymphs & satyrs, BCN, 5½" **200.00**
Musical roundely for cigarettes, 13" H **90.00**
Nut trays, Fr, set of 6 w/holder, 3½x3" **60.00**
Plaque, Marie Antoinette portrait, BCN, 10" dia **72.00**
Scent vase, 3 cherubs surrounding, Meissen mk, 8½x4¾" dia ..**2,500.00**
Snuff box, cherubs, BCN France, oval, 1½x2¾x1¾" **85.00**
Soap dish, BCN Palazzo Reale Napoli, ¾x3½x2½" **50.00**
Stein, battle scene, brass top trim, man & dragon hdl, 13½" **1,950.00**

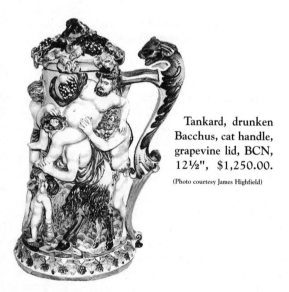

Tankard, drunken Bacchus, cat handle, grapevine lid, BCN, 12½", $1,250.00.

(Photo courtesy James Highfield)

Tea set, tete-a-tete service w/undertray, much gold, BCN **1,600.00**
Urn, Greek female attendants, w/lid, 3¼" sq base, 9" **230.00**
Urn, ram's-head hdls, cherub scenes, sq base, BCN, 7" **275.00**
Wall plate, Roman battle scene w/archers, BCN, 9½" dia **100.00**

Carlton Ware

Carlton Ware was the product of Wiltshaw and Robinson, who operated in the Staffordshire district of England from about 1890. During the 1920s, they produced ornamental ware with enameled and gilded decorations such as flowers and birds, often on a black background. In 1958 the firm was renamed Carlton Ware Ltd. Their trademark was a crown over a circular stamp with 'W & R, Stoke on Trent,' surrounding a swallow. 'Carlton Ware' was sometimes added by hand.

Basket, Flower Basket, #1775, 2¾x4" **75.00**
Basket, Flower Basket, #1810, 3x4" **75.00**

Basket, Foxglove, med gr, 1950s, 6½x10½x7½" **115.00**
Biscuit barrel, floral flow bl, ca 1894-1906, 5¾" **175.00**
Biscuit jar, Iris, cobalt, 9½" **475.00**
Bookends, Walking Ware, polka-dot shoes, 5¼", pr, from $135 to ...**150.00**
Bowl, Apple Blossom, yel, #1665/4, 4¾x8¼" **32.00**
Bowl, Flowers & Basket, yel, 31922/2, 2¾x10¾x8" **59.00**
Bowl, Hazelnut, gr, #2277, 1¾x9½x6½" **40.00**
Bowl, Lettuce (Tomato), oval, 3x12x7½" **48.00**
Bowl, Lobster/Langouste, orange, 3x13x9½" **69.00**
Bowl, Oak Tree, hdls, 2½x11x7" **125.00**
Bowl, Poppy & Daisy, pk, 2x10¼x4¾" **85.00**
Bowl, Rouge Royale, Pagoda, 3 pierced hdls, 3-leg, 10x3" **215.00**
Bowl, salad; Lettuce (Tomato), 3-ftd, 3x9" **47.00**
Bowl, Stork & Bamboo, ca 1925, 4¼x8" **265.00**
Bowl, Swirling Sands, #1926, 2x10½x8½" **75.00**
Bowl, Twin-Tone, burgundy/cream, 2x8½x6" **27.50**
Bowl, Water Lily, 2-lobe, #1750/3, 2½x10½" L **95.00**
Bowl, Wild Rose, #2116/3, 2x9¾x6" **38.00**
Candlestick, Fruit Basket, yel **75.00**
Card holder, Rouge Royale, gold trim, #1210, 3¼x5¼" **85.00**
Cheese plate, Apple Blossom, plain yel colorway, 5x6¼" **38.00**
Coffeepot, Modern Orange, tall cylinder w/emb ribs, 1960s, 12" ..**90.00**
Comport, Flowers & Basket, gr, ftd, 2½x6½x5" **38.00**
Comport, Foxglove, yel, stemmed, 2¼x6x4" **42.00**
Comport, Hazelnut, 2½x12¼x7" **235.00**
Cruet, Wild Rose, #2117 ....**95.00**
Cruet set, Apple Blossom, 2x5x4¼" **100.00**
Cruet set, Red Robin, 2 cruets on 5¾" tray **85.00**
Cruet set, 3 shells (lime gr) on blk tray **100.00**
Cup, Walking Ware, brn shoes, yel check socks, 5x3" **100.00**
Cup & saucer, bl lustre quatrefoil w/gold int, 1930s **58.00**
Cup & saucer, Foxglove **90.00**
Deep dish, Flowers & Basket, yel, 2½x9½x7" **59.00**
Demitasse set, Bleu Royale, 1953, pot+cr/sug+6 c/s **375.00**
Dish, Apple Blossom, gr, #1621, 5x4" **19.00**
Dish, Crocus, 1¾x12x7" **145.00**
Dish, Foxglove, gr, #1870, 9½x6½" **34.00**
Dish, Foxglove, gr, 5x4" **19.00**
Dish, Morning Glory, #2491, 4¼x4" **14.00**
Dish, Rouge Royale, Spider Web, 8½" **112.00**
Egg cruet set, floral, gr, 4 cups+2 shakers+tray **165.00**
Egg cup, chicken w/legs sticking out as lid to cup, 1976, 6½" **120.00**
Egg platter, Lobster/Langouste, orange, 12" **79.00**
Ginger jar, lyre-tail bird ea side & fruit baskets, #2979, 4¾" **105.00**
Ginger jar, Rouge Royale, Oriental scene, 11½x6" **300.00**
Jug, Apple Blossom, yel, #1686/1½, 4½" **90.00**
Jug, Apple Blossom, yel, 3½" **40.00**
Jug, Guinness advertising, Thorens music box base, 4" **1,200.00**
Jug, Hazelnut, cream, 6" **45.00**
Jug, milk; Foxglove, #1385/2, 4", from $65 to **85.00**
Jug, Oak Tree, beige, 31191, 5¼" **150.00**
Jug & saucer, Primula, 2½" H **57.00**
Lamp, sea lion, w/Guinness banner on nose (shade), 14x7" **1,100.00**
Leaf dish, Apple Blossom, #1621, 4½x3¾" **36.00**
Leaf dish, Foxglove, #1876, 1930s-40s, 5x4" **38.00**
Leaf dish, Hydrangea, gr, 2-leaf form, 9x7", from $90 to **110.00**
Leaf dish, Hydrangea, 3-lobe, #3319, 10½x10", from $100 to **120.00**
Leaf dish, Lettuce (Tomato), 1920-76, 5¾x4¼" **34.00**
Leaf dish, Primula, yel, 13x5" **28.00**
Leaf dish, Twin-Tone, lime gr/pale gr wash, 5x4" **18.00**
Leaf plate, Pin-Stripe, teal w/gold veins, #2377, 10½" **40.00**
Mug, turtle figural ft, 5" **130.00**
Nut dish, Foxglove, w/spoon, sm **45.00**
Plate, Buttercup, yel, 9½x8½" **60.00**

Plate, Foxglove, yel, #1883/4, 5¾x5" 25.00
Plate, Lettuce (Tomato), lt gr, #2095/3, 9x5½" 22.00
Plate, Morning Glory, teal, #2496, 10½x9½" 28.00
Platter, Hydrangea, #2210, 13" 285.00
Pot, Woodland, w/lid, 1950s, 3½" 32.00
Sauce boat, Magnolia, 3½x6¾" 115.00
Sauce boat & liner, Morning Glory, teal, 32508, 3½x6" 30.00
Shakers, Sea Shells, 3¾", pr 35.00
Tea set, Windstream, brn/beige, 5" pot+cr+sug+jelly jar+plate+spoon..250.00
Teapot, Foxglove, gr, 5", from $185 to 200.00
Teapot, Magnolia, #2599, 4½x7½" 135.00
Teapot, Primula, 5½" 145.00
Toast rack, Foxglove, yel, 3¼x4x2¼" 125.00
Toast rack, Walking Ware, lg ft w/polka-dot shoes, 5x8" 150.00
Toast rack, Wild Rose, 2-slice, compartment ea end 135.00
Trio, Foxglove, 1925-57, c/s+sm plate 90.00
Triple dish, Lobster/Langouste, orange, 11x11½" 75.00
Vase, Bell, red, 5½" 1,225.00
Vase, Butterflies, pale bl lustre w/gold, stick neck, 7" 250.00
Vase, Hollyhock on gr semi-lustre, #3973, 1930s, 10½" 325.00
Vase, lyre-tail birds & fruit baskets, stick neck, #2959, 8" 105.00
Vase, Rouge Royal, no pattern, 3¼x3½", from $65 to 85.00

Carnival Collectibles

Carnival items from the early part of this century represent the lighter side of an America that was alternately prospering and sophisticated or devastated by war and domestic conflict. But whatever the country's condition, the carnival's thrilling rides and shooting galleries were a sure way of letting it all go by — at least for an evening.

For further information on chalkware figures, we recommend *The Carnival Chalk Prize* by our advisor, Thomas G. Morris, who is listed in the Directory under Oregon.

In the shooting gallery target listings below, items are rated for availability from 1, commonly found, to 10, rarely found (these numbers appear just before the size), and all are made of cast iron. Our advisors for shooting gallery targets are Richard and Valerie Tucker; their address is listed in the Directory under Texas.

Popeye standing with left hand across chest, 1935 – 1950, 13½", $165.00 (also made in 15½" size, valued at $195.00). (Photo courtesy Tom Morris)

Bellhop girl w/hand on hip, 1930s, 14¼" 75.00
Call Me Papa, 1935-45, 14" 15.00
Cat & goldfish bowl (clear glass), 1930-40, 9½" 47.50

Colonial lady standing w/dog, 1935-45, 11¼" 17.50
Dog sitting upright w/flower, 1935-45, 10¾" 30.00
Donald Duck, 1934-50, 14" 70.00
Elephant sitting upright trumpeting, bank, 1955, 12½" 67.50
Girl reading, bust, 1910-25, 12x8½" 65.00
Gorilla standing beating chest, 1940s, 6¼" 15.00
Indian chief on horseback, 1930-50, 11", from $50 to 60.00
Indian chief standing w/arms crossed, 1930-45, 19" 45.00
Lone Ranger, 16" 85.00
Monkey sitting upright scratching head, bank, 1940-50, 12¼" 47.50
Navy WAVE, mk Remember Pearl Harbor, 1944, 13" 65.00
Pancho, 1940s, 11½" 25.00
Paul Revere, 1935-45, 14½" 25.00
Pinocchio standing w/arms down to side, 1940-50, 11½" 95.00
Pirate girl, 1930s, 14¼" 95.00
Porky Pig, 1940-50, 11" 65.00
Shirley Temple holding hem of dress, 1935-40, 10" 49.50
Snake coiled, ashtray, 1940s, 5½" 15.00
Snow White standing w/hands clasped, 1930s, 13½" 95.00
Westward Ho Cowboy, 1945-50, 10" 25.00

Shooting Gallery Targets

Battleship, worn wht pnt, Mangels, 5, 6¼x11⅜", $200 to 300.00
Birds (8) on bar, worn pnt, Mangels, 9, 3½x41½", $700 to 800.00
Bull's-eye w/pop-up duck, old pnt, Quakenbush, 7, 12" dia, $500 to...600.00
Clown, worn red/wht pnt, Mangels, 9, 19x9½"+movable arms, minimum........1,000.00
Clown standing, bull's-eye, mc pnt, Evans or Hoffman, 20 12", minimum.....1,000.00
Dog running, worn wht pnt, Smith or Evans, 6, 6x11", $100 to ..200.00
Duck, detailed feathers, old pnt, Parker, 8, 3¾x5½", $100 to.....200.00
Duck, detailed feathers, worn pnt, Evans, 4, 5½x8½", $100 to ..200.00
Eagle w/wings wide, mc pnt, Smith or Evans, 6, 14¾", $650 to..750.00
Elephant, wht pnt, flakes, 9½" L 250.00
Elephant, worn red pnt, King, 10, 17x19", minimum value 1,000.00
Greyhound, bull's-eye, old patina, Parker, 8, 26" W, minimum ..1,000.00
Indian chief, worn mc pnt, Hoffmann or Smith, 10, 20x15", minimum.....1,000.00
Lion running, old wht pnt, 12½" L 220.00
Monkey standing, worn pnt, 10, 9¾x8½", $300 to 400.00
Mountain goat leaping, worn wht pnt, 8¾" 150.00
Owl, bull's-eye, wht traces, Evans, 6, 10¾x5⅛", $400 to 500.00
Pipe, old patina, Smith, 1, 5⅜x1¾", value less than 50.00
Rabbit running, bull's-eye, old patina, Parker, 8, 12x25x1", minimum..1,000.00
Rabbit standing, worn pnt, Smith or Mueller, 8, 18x10", $900 to..1,000.00
Reindeer (elk), wht pnt (worn/rusty), 7, 10x9", $300 to 400.00
Saber-tooth tiger, old patina, Mangels, 7, 7¾x13", $300 to 400.00
Soldier w/rifle, pnt traces/old patina, Mueller, 5, 9x5", $100 to ..200.00
Squirrel running, old patina, Smith, 4, 5⅛x9¼", $100 to 200.00
Stag running, worn blk pnt, hooves missing, 9½" 220.00
Star spinner, dbl, worn mc pnt, Mangels, 6, 8x2¾", $200 to 300.00
Swan, worn pnt, Mueller, 7, 5¾x5", $100 to 200.00

Carnival Glass

Carnival glass is pressed glass that has been coated with a sodium solution and fired to give it an exterior lustre. First made in America in 1905, it was produced until the late 1920s and had great popularity in the average American household, for unlike the costly art glass produced by Tiffany, carnival glass could be mass produced at a small cost. Colors most found are marigold, green, blue, and purple; but others exist in lesser quantities and include white, clear, red, aqua opalescent, peach opalescent, ice blue, ice green, amber, lavender, and smoke.

Companies mainly responsible for its production in America include the Fenton Art Glass Company, Williamstown, West Virginia;

the Northwood Glass Company, Wheeling, West Virginia; the Imperial Glass Company, Bellaire, Ohio; the Millersburg Glass Company, Millersburg, Ohio; and the Dugan Glass Company (Diamond Glass), Indiana, Pennsylvania. In addition to these major manufacturers, lesser producers included the U.S. Glass Company, the Cambridge Glass Company, the Westmoreland Glass Company, and the McKee Glass Company.

Carnival glass has been highly collectible since the 1950s and has been reproduced for the last twenty-five years. Several national and state collectors' organizations exist, and many fine books are available on old carnival glass, including *The Standard Encyclopedia of Carnival Glass*; *Carnival Glass, The Best of the Best*; *Collector's Companion to Carnival Glass*; and *Standard Encyclopedia of Millersburg Crystal* by Bill Edwards and Mike Carwile; and *Imperial Carnival Glass* by Carl O. Burns.

Acanthus (Imperial), plate, marigold, 10" 165.00
Acorn (Fenton), bowl, amethyst, 6¼-7½" 200.00
Acorn Burrs (Northwood), tumbler, gr, ...95.00
Alternating Dimples, vase, marigold, enameled, 8-sided 70.00
Amaryllis (Dugan), compote, amethyst, deep, rnd, sm 350.00
American (Fostoria), rose bowl, marigold, rare 400.00
Apple Blossom (Diamond), bowl, peach opal, 7½" 100.00
Apple Blossom (Enameled Northwood), tumbler, bl 90.00
Apple Panels (English), sugar bowl, marigold, open 35.00
Arcs (Imperial), compote, amethyst 90.00
Asters, rose bowl, marigold 200.00
Australian Panels (Crystal), creamer, marigold 50.00
Autumn Acorns (Fenton), bowl, amethyst, 8½" 95.00
Aztec (McKee), pitcher, marigold, rare..................................1,300.00
Balloons (Imperial), cake plate, marigold..................................85.00
Band of Roses, tray, marigold 75.00
Banded Diamonds (Crystal), flower set, amethyst, 2 pcs 195.00
Banded Diamonds & Bars, decanter, marigold, complete............200.00
Banded Drape (Fenton), tumbler, bl..50.00
Basketweave & Cable (Westmoreland), sugar bowl, gr, w/lid......100.00

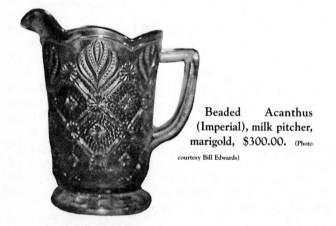

Beaded Acanthus (Imperial), milk pitcher, marigold, $300.00. (Photo courtesy Bill Edwards)

Beaded Block, pitcher, milk; clambroth..75.00
Beaded Bull's Eye (Imperial), vase, squat; marigold, 5½-7½" 85.00
Beaded Panels (Imperial), powder jar, marigold, w/lid...................50.00
Beaded Shell (Dugan), butter dish, amethyst................................150.00
Beaded Stars (Fenton), plate, marigold, 9".................................110.00
Bells & Beads (Dugan), nappy, amethyst.....................................95.00
Big Basketweave (Dugan), basket, amethyst, lg 145.00
Big Fish (Millersburg), bowl, marigold, tri-cornered....................800.00
Blackberry Spray (Fenton), compote, bl..50.00
Blackberry Wreath (Millersburg), bowl, ice cream; gr.................325.00
Blocks & Arches (Crystal), creamer, marigold.............................40.00
Boggy Bayou (Fenton), vase, bl, 6-11".......................................135.00

Border Plants (Dugan), bowl, aqua opal, flat, 8½".....................180.00
Brocaded Acorns (Fostoria), candle holder, ice bl, ea..................85.00
Brocaded Daffodils (Fostoria), plate, cake; ice gr, hdld 85.00
Brocaded Palms (Fostoria), bonbon, ice gr 55.00
Brocaded Poppies (Fostoria), tray, cake; ice gr 150.00
Broken Arches (Imperial), punch bowl, marigold, w/base...........400.00
Bubbles, bowl, marigold, sq, 6"..50.00
Butterflies (Fenton), bonbon, bl...65.00
Butterfly & Berry (Fenton), vase, wht, 6½-9"...........................150.00
Butterfly Bower (Crystal), cake plate, amethyst, stemmed 200.00
Buzz Saw & File, goblet, marigold 175.00
Cameo (Fenton), vase, Celeste Blue, scarce, 11-17" 250.00
Captive Rose (Fenton), compote, gr 100.00
Carolina Dogwood (Westmoreland), bowl, aqua opal, 8½" 450.00
Caroline (Dugan), banana bowl, peach opal..............................125.00
Cartwheel #411 (Heisey), goblet 75.00
Checkerboard (Westmoreland), cruet, clear, rare 750.00
Checkers, ashtray, marigold..40.00
Cherries & Little Flowers (Northwood), pitcher, marigold 175.00
Cherry (aka Hanging Cherries) (Millersburg), spooner, amethyst...175.00
Cherry & Cable (Northwood), bowl, marigold, scarce, 5"............75.00
Cherry Chain (Fenton), bonbon, bl 60.00
Cherry Smash (US Glass), butter dish, marigold 150.00
Chesterfield (Imperial), candy dish, marigold, w/lid, tall............65.00
Circle Scroll (Dugan), tumbler, amethyst, very scarce................425.00
Classic Arts, powder jar, marigold 400.00
Coin Dot (Fenton), bowl, aqua opal, 6-10"...............................150.00
Coin Spot (Dugan), compote, peach opal..................................175.00
Colonial (Imperial), goblet, lemonade; marigold 40.00
Columbine (Fenton), tumbler, gr...55.00
Concave Diamonds (Northwood), pitcher, russet gr, w/lid..........450.00
Concave Flute (Westmoreland), rose bowl, gr 100.00
Concord (Fenton, bowl, amber..400.00
Corinth (Dugan), bowl, peach opal, 9" 125.00
Cosmos (Millersburg), bowl, gr, ruffled, scarce, 6½"..................150.00
Cosmos & Cane (US Glass), tumbler, wht 150.00
Country Kitchen (Millersburg), sugar bowl, amethyst, w/lid.......400.00
Crab Claw/Blaze (Imperial), bowl, gr, 5" 40.00
Crackle (Imperial), candlestick, marigold, 3½", ea....................25.00
Curved Star (Cathedral), rose bowl, bl, scarce...........................400.00
Cut Crystal (US Glass), compote, marigold, 5½".......................110.00
Czechoslovakian, tumbler, marigold 100.00
Daisy & Cane, decanter, marigold, rare.....................................100.00
Daisy & Scroll, decanter, marigold, w/stopper 250.00
Daisy Dear (Dugan), bowl, wht...85.00
Daisy Wreath (Westmoreland), bowl, aqua opal, 8-10"..............300.00
Dandelion (Northwood), tumbler, ice bl....................................135.00
Dewhirst Berry Band, carafe, marigold, 7"................................175.00
Diamond & Daisy Cut (US Glass), vase, marigold, sq, 10".........225.00
Diamond & Rib (Fenton), vase, gr, 7-12" 60.00
Diamond Checkerboard, butter dish, marigold 90.00
Diamond Cut (Crystal), banana bowl, amethyst..........................115.00
Diamond Lace (Imperial), bowl, gr, 5".......................................50.00
Diamond Pinwheel (English), butter dish, marigold 90.00
Diamond Point Columns (Late), pitcher, milk; marigold 50.00
Diamond Point Columns (Late), powder jar, marigold, w/lid........40.00
Diamond Ring (Imperial), bowl, fruit; amethyst, 9½" 90.00
Dianthus (Fenton), tumbler, ice gr...60.00
Dogwood Sprays (Dugan), compote, peach opal........................250.00
Double Daisy (Fenton), pitcher, marigold, bulbous 200.00
Double Dolphin (Fenton), plate, cake; Celeste Blue, center hdl...85.00
Dragon & Lotus (Fenton), bowl, bl, ftd, 9".............................150.00
Drapery Variant (Finland), shot glass, marigold........................225.00
Egyptian Lustre (Dugan), vase, blk aqua 100.00

Elektra, compote, bl, 4½" 65.00
Elks (Fenton), Detroit bowl, amethyst, scarce 800.00
Embroidered Mums (Northwood), bonbon, wht, stemmed......1,000.00
Emu (Crystal), bowl, amethyst, rare, 5" 175.00
Enameled Chrysanthemum, pitcher, bl 195.00
Enameled Freesia, tumbler, marigold 25.00
English Hob & Button, bowl, gr, 7-10" 95.00
Engraved Grapes (Fenton), candy jar, marigold, w/lid 85.00
Estate (Westmoreland), vase, bud; smoke...............................75.00
Etched Deco (Standard), nappy, marigold, hdld 40.00
Fanciful (Dugan), bowl, wht, 8½" 110.00
Fashion (Imperial), cup, punch; amethyst 40.00
Feather & Heart (Millersburg), tumbler, gr, scarce 200.00
Feather Swirl (US Glass), vase, marigold 65.00
Fenton #1502 (Diamond Optic Dolphins), bonbon, aqua.......125.00
Fenton #643, compote, Celeste Blue 70.00
Fenton #847, vase, fan; ice gr 85.00
Fentonia Fruit (Fenton), pitcher, marigold, rare 600.00
Field Flower (Imperial), pitcher, milk; gr, rare 220.00
Field Thistle (US Glass), compote, marigold 150.00
File (Imperial & English), bowl, amethyst, 5" 40.00
Fine Cut & Roses (Northwood), candy dish, ice bl, ftd 325.00
Fine Cut Rings (English), cake stand, marigold, stemmed 175.00
Fine Rib (Fenton), vase, peach opal, 2⅝" 150.00

Fishnet (Dugan), epergne, amethyst, $300.00. (Photo courtesy Carl O. Burns)

Flannel Flower (Crystal), cake stand, amethyst 195.00
Fleur-De-Lis Variant (Millersburg), bowl, gr, flat, 9-10" 250.00
Florabelle, tumbler, ice gr 175.00
Floral & Optic (Imperial), cake plate, red, ftd 550.00
Floral Oval (Higbee), goblet, marigold 75.00
Florentine (Fenton & Northwood), candlesticks, ice gr, lg, pr..125.00
Fluer-De-Lis (Czech), chop plate, marigold, rare, 12" 700.00
Fluffy Peacock (Fenton), tumbler, gr 110.00
Flute (Northwood), sherbet, teal 80.00
Flute & Cane (Imperial), pickle dish, marigold 25.00
Four Flowers (Dugan), plate, peach opal, 6½" 175.00
Freesia (Fenton), tumbler, marigold.....................................35.00
Frosted Block (Imperial), pickle dish, clambroth, hdld, rare 65.00
Gaelic (Indiana Glass), sugar bowl, marigold, w/lid...............85.00
Garden Mums (Fenton), plate, amethyst, regular or handgrip, 7"...450.00
Garden Path Variant (Dugan), bowl, wht, deep rnd, 8-10" 350.00
Georgia Belle (Dugan), compote, peach opal, ftd 140.00
God & Home (Dugan), tumbler, bl, rare...............................175.00
Golden Harvest (US Glass), decanter, amethyst, w/stopper........250.00
Golden Honeycomb, creamer, marigold 25.00
Golden Pineapple & Berries, plate, marigold, 10" 500.00

Gooseberry Spray (US Glass) (Palm Beach ext), bowl, amethyst, 10" ...95.00
Grape & Cable (Fenton), bowl, bl, spatula ft, 7-8" 125.00
Grape & Cable (Northwood), bowl, orange; olive gr, ftd...........350.00
Grape & Cable (Northwood), cologne, ice bl, w/stopper.........550.00
Grape & Cable w/Thumbprint (Northwood), sherbet, gr..........60.00
Grape & Gothic Arches (Northwood), sugar bowl, bl, w/lid......125.00
Grape Star Multi-Star Variant (Millersburg), bowl, ice cream; gr, 10"...150.00
Grape Wreath (Millersburg), bowl, ice cream; amethyst, 10" 275.00
Grapevine Lattice (Dugan), tumbler, bl, rare 165.00
Greek Key (Northwood), tumbler, marigold, rare 110.00
Greengard Furniture (Millersburg), bowl, advertising, amethyst, rare..2,000.00
Ground Cherries, pitcher, bl 125.00
Hawaiian Lei (Higbee), creamer, marigold 75.00
Heart & Vine, bowl, bl, 8½" 85.00
Heart Band Souvenir (McKee), mug, gr, sm 140.00
Hearts & Flowers (Northwood), compote, wht......................185.00
Heavy Diamond (Imperial), vase, smoke 85.00
Heavy Grape (Imperial), bowl, fruit; amber, w/base 400.00
Heavy Iris (Dugan), tumbler whimsey, marigold 350.00
Heavy Vine, powder box, marigold 75.00
Heisey Colonial, tumbler, juice; marigold..............................65.00
Heisey Flute, toothpick holder, marigold 150.00
Heisey Puritan (#341), compote, marigold 75.00
Hex Optic (Honeycomb) (Jeannette, Depression era), bonbon, marigold...20.00
Hobnail (Millersburg), spittoon, amethyst, scarce 625.00
Hobstar & Cut Triangles (English), rose bowl, gr 70.00
Hobstar & Feather (Millersburg), bowl, marigold, heart shaped, 5"...450.00
Hobstar Band, spooner, marigold 65.00
Hobstar Reversed (English), butter dish, bl............................70.00
Holly Sprig (Millersburg), bonbon, gr, 2 shapes, ea 80.00
Holly Whirl (Millersburg), nappy, gr, tri-cornered................110.00
Holly Wreath (Millersburg), bowl, ice-cream; amethyst, 8-9"...........350.00
Honeycomb & Clover (Fenton), compote, gr 60.00
Hoops (Fenton), bowl, marigold, scarce, 8" 50.00
Hyacinth (Dugan), vase, marigold..75.00
Ice Crystals, candlesticks, wht, pr 160.00
Imperial #3939, punch bowl, gr, w/base, scarce 500.00
Imperial #499, sherbet, red...95.00
Imperial Grape, basket, gr 85.00
Imperial Grape, goblet, amethyst 100.00
Imperial Jewels, plate, bl, 7" 80.00
Interior Panels, decanter, marigold 65.00
Interior Swirl, spitton, peach opal 140.00
Inverted Strawberry (Cambridge), bonbon, gr, stemmed w/hdl, very rare ...900.00
Iris (Fenton), goblet, buttermilk; amber 80.00
Isaac Benesch (Millersburg), bowl, advertising, amethyst, 6½" 425.00
Jacobean (Inwald), decanter, marigold 200.00
Jacobean Ranger (Czech & English), pitcher, marigold 325.00
Jasmine & Butterfly (Czech), decanter, marigold 100.00
Jewel (Dugan), bowl, candle; ice gr 175.00
Kangaroo (Australian), bowl, amethyst, 5" 180.00
Keg, toothpick holder, gr 25.00
Laco, oil bottle, marigold, 9¼" 80.00
Lacy Dewdrop (Westmoreland), tumbler, moonstone irid..........175.00
Late Strawberry, tumbler, marigold 75.00
Lattice & Daisy (Dugan), bowl, wht, 5" 100.00
Lattice & Grape (Fenton), pitcher, bl 450.00
Lattice Heart, plate, blk amethyst, 7-8"...............................325.00
Leaf Chain (Fenton), plate, bl, 7½" 150.00
Leaf Rays (Dugan), nappy, amethyst, spade shape..................40.00
Leaf Swirl (Westmoreland), compote, teal 80.00
Leaf Tiers (Fenton), creamer, marigold, ftd 75.00
Lightning Flower (Northwood), bowl, marigold, rare, 5" 100.00
Lily of the Valley (Fenton), tumbler, bl, rare........................225.00

Little Beads, compote, aqua opal, sm.............................85.00
Little Fishes (Fenton), bowl, aqua, flat or ftd, 5½".............200.00
Long Buttress, toothpick holder, marigold.........................200.00
Long Hobstar (Imperial), compote, marigold.....................65.00
Long Thumbprint Variant, compote, gr...........................40.00
Lotus & Grape (Fenton), bonbon, bl.............................85.00

Lotus and Grape (Fenton), bowl, green, flat, 8½", $165.00. (Photo courtesy Bill Edwards)

Lotus & Grape Variant (Fenton), bowl, bl, ftd, 6"..............80.00
Louisa (Westmoreland), candy dish, gr, ftd 65.00
Lustre & Clear (Imperial), butter dish, marigold 65.00
Lustre Rose (Imperial), bowl, fruit; amber, ftd, 11-12".........90.00
Lutz (McKee), mug, marigold, ftd.............................90.00
Magnolia Drape (Fenton), sugar bowl, marigold, w/lid.........75.00
Magnolia Rib (Fenton), butter dish, marigold 125.00
Manhattan (US Glass), decanter, marigold....................250.00
Maple Leaf (Dugan), bowl, bl, stemmed, 4½".................40.00
Massachusetts (US Glass), mug, marigold, rare 150.00
Melon Rib, candy jar, marigold, w/lid.........................30.00
Memphis (Northwood), punch bowl, lime gr, w/base 65.00
Meydam (Leerdam), cake stand, marigold.....................95.00
Milady (Fenton), tumbler, bl 125.00
Miniature Intaglio (Westmoreland), basket, bl opal...........450.00
Miniature Wash Bowl & Pitcher, pitcher, marigold, 2¾".......70.00
Moonprint (Brockwitz), tray, marigold.........................75.00
Morning Glory (Imperial), vase, gr, squat, 4-7" 120.00
Mt Gambier (Crystal), mug, marigold.........................100.00
My Lady, powder jar, marigold, w/lid.........................125.00
Napoli (Italy), decanter, marigold.............................75.00
Near Cut (Northwood), goblet, amethyst, rare.................125.00
Nola (Scandanavian), basket, marigold........................65.00
Northern Star (Fenton), card tray, marigold, 6"...............40.00
Northwood #699, cheese dish, vaseline.......................100.00
Number 2351 (Cambridge), cup, punch; gr, scarce............65.00
Number 270 (Westmoreland), compote, aqua 150.00
Nutmeg Grater, sugar bowl, marigold, open 55.00
O'Hara (Loop), goblet, marigold..............................25.00
Octagon (Imperial), tumbler, gr, ftd..........................80.00
Oklahoma (Mexican), decanter, marigold.....................850.00
Old Fashion, tray, marigold, w/6 tumblers, complete 150.00
Open Edge Basket (Basketweave) (Fenton), bowl, aqua, lg......105.00
Open Rose (Imperial), plate, gr, 9".............................525.00
Optic (Imperial), rose bowl, smoke 100.00
Optic & Buttons (Imperial), goblet, lav 90.00
Optic Flute (Imperial), compote, marigold.....................50.00
Orange Peel (Westmoreland), bowl, dessert; teal, stemmed, scarce...70.00
Orange Tree (Fenton), powder jar, bl, w/lid...................135.00

Orange Tree & Scroll (Fenton), tumbler, bl....................75.00
Orange Tree Orchard (Fenton), pitcher, wht..................425.00
Orchid, pitcher, wht..400.00
Ostrich (Crystal), bowl, amethyst, sm.........................60.00
Oval & Round (Imperial), bowl, amber, sm....................45.00
Palm Beach (US Glass), sugar bowl, lime gr, w/lid...........125.00
Panama (US Glass), spittoon, marigold 750.00
Paneled Dandelion (Fenton), tumbler, bl......................65.00
Paneled Holly (Northwood), bonbon, amethyst, ftd...........90.00
Papini Victoria (Argentina), compote, marigold 250.00
Peach (Northwood), butter dish, wht..........................275.00
Peacock (Millersburg), bowl, ice cream; amethyst, 5" 300.00
Peacock & Grape (Fenton), nut bowl, marigold, ftd, scarce.........55.00
Peacock & Urn (Fenton), compote, wht.......................200.00
Peacock at the Fountain, creamer, ice bl......................250.00
Peacock Tail (Fenton), bonbon, bl, hdls, stemmed or flat.........65.00
Pennsylvania Dutch (Jeannette), tumbler, marigold.............15.00
Persian Garden (Dugan), bowl, fruit; wht, w/base.............400.00
Persian Medallion (Fenton), compote, bl, sm.................225.00
Petal & Fan (Dugan), plate, amethyst, ruffled, 6".............550.00
Petals (Dugan), banana bowl, peach opal 100.00
Pillar & Flute (Imperial), rose bowl, smoke....................80.00
Pineapple (English), compote, bl..............................60.00
Plain (Fenton), bowl, gr, 8¾" 425.00
Plain Jane (Imperial), bowl, ice gr, 4".........................200.00
Plums & Cherries (Northwood), spooner, bl, rare 1,800.00
Pompeian (Dugan), vase, hyacinth; wht 250.00
Pretty Panels (Fenton), pitcher, red, w/lid....................500.00
Primrose (Millersburg), bowl, gr, ruffled, 8¾"................200.00
Prism & Daisy Band (Imperial), compote, marigold 35.00
Propeller (Imperial), vase, marigold, stemmed, rare...........90.00
Question Marks (Dugan), bonbon, ice gr......................300.00
Radiance, shaker, marigold, ea................................55.00
Rainbow (Northwood), bowl, gr, 8"...........................75.00
Ranger (Mexican), perfume, marigold, 5¼"....................150.00
Raspberry (Northwood), gravy boat, amethyst, ftd............135.00
Rays & Ribbons (Millersburg), bowl, gr, tri-cornered.........325.00
Ribbon Tie (Fenton), plate, amethyst, low/ruffled, 9½"........250.00
Ribs (Czechoslovakia), vase, bud; marigold...................60.00
Rising Sun (US Glass), bowl, sauce; marigold, sm.............35.00
Rose Garden (Sweden & German), bowl, bl, 8¼"...............225.00
Rose Show (Northwood), plate, wht, 9½".....................600.00
Round-Up (Dugan), bowl, lav, 8¾"...........................600.00
Royalty (Imperial), bowl, fruit; smoke, w/stand..............100.00
Ruffled Rib, spittoon, marigold, ruffled, rare.................250.00
Rustic (Fenton), vase, amethyst or bl, squat, 6-7½"...........80.00
S-Repeat (Dugan), tumbler, amethyst 125.00
Scale Band (Fenton), plate, marigold, dome base, 7"...........80.00
Scales (Westmoreland), bonbon, bl opal......................200.00
Scroll Embossed (Imperial), bowl, dessert; gr, stemmed........90.00
Seaweed (Millersburg), bowl, ice cream; marigold, rare, 10½"....500.00
Shell (Imperial), bowl, smoke, 7-9"..........................125.00
Shell & Jewel (Westmoreland), creamer, gr, w/lid..............60.00
Sheraton (US Glass), butter dish, pastel marigold.............130.00
Split Diamond, compote, marigold 55.00
Springtime (Northwood), spooner, amethyst 350.00
Stained Rim (Czech), bowl, berry; marigold, ftd, sm...........20.00
Star & File (Imperial), decanter, marigold, w/stopper.........100.00
Star Medallion (Imperial), custard cup, marigold.............20.00
Star Spray (Imperial), bowl, smoke, 7".........................40.00
Starburst (Finland), spittoon, bl.............................175.00
Stippled Rays (Fenton), bonbon, bl...........................45.00
Stork & Rushes (Dugan), mug, aqua 650.00
Strawberry (Northwood), plate, gr, stippled, 9"............1,100.00

Strawberry Wreath (Millersburg), bowl, marigold, tri-cornered, 9½" ..450.00
Summer Days (Dugan), vase, bl, 6" 125.00

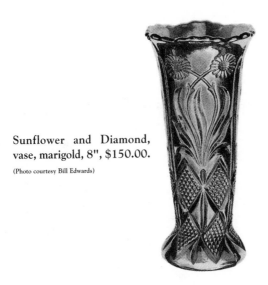

Sunflower and Diamond, vase, marigold, 8", $150.00.

(Photo courtesy Bill Edwards)

Swirl (Imperial), mug, marigold, rare..90.00
Swirl (Northwood), pitcher, gr 700.00
Swirl Variant (Imperial), plate, peach opal, 6-8¼" 65.00
Taffeta Lustre (Fostoria), candlesticks, amethyst, rare, pr............300.00
Thin & Wide Rib (Northwood), vase, ice gr, ruffled.................300.00
Thistle & Thorn (English), bowl, marigold, ftd, 6" 50.00
Thread & Cane (Crystal), salver, amethyst................................175.00
Three Fruits (Northwood), plate, amethyst, stippled, 9" 650.00
Three-In-One (Imperial), rose bowl, marigold, rare 125.00
Tiger Lily (Imperial), tumbler, peach opal...................................225.00
Tree Bark (Imperial), pitcher, amber, open top...........................100.00
Tulip & Cane, compote, marigold 45.00
US #310 (US Glass), mayonnaise set, ice gr 95.00
US Diamond Block (US Glass), compote, peach opal, rare 90.00
Vineyard (Dugan), tumbler, wht..250.00
Vintage (Dugan), perfume, amethyst, w/stopper 600.00
Vintage (Fenton), bonbon, bl 60.00
Vintage (Fenton), whimsey fernery, amethyst.............................425.00
Waffle Block (Imperial), parfait glass, marigold, stemmed............30.00
Wagon Wheel, candy dish, marigold, w/lid, enameled 45.00
Washboard, creamer, marigold, 5½" 45.00
Water Lily (Fenton), bonbon, marigold...40.00
Water Lily & Cattails (Fenton), bowl, berry; bl, lg.......................50.00
Weeping Cherry (Dugan), bowl, amethyst, ftd 130.00
Western Thistle Variant, compote, marigold, sm........................100.00
Whirling Hobstar, pitcher, marigold 200.00
Wide Panel (Northwood), compote, marigold, #645 ....40.00
Wide Rib (Dugan), vase, peach opal, squat, 4-6" 65.00
Wild Berry & Variant, powder jar, bl opal, ftd, w/lid..................425.00
Wild Longanberry (Westmoreland), goblet, peach opal 150.00
Windflower (Dugan), tray, gr, flat...85.00
Wine & Roses (Fenton), goblet, wine; aqua 145.00
Wishbone (Northwood), bowl, wht, ftd, 7½-9"............................400.00
Wishbone & Spades (Dugan), bowl, peach opal, 10" 325.00
Wisteria (Northwood), tumbler, ice gr, rare 525.00
Wreath of Roses (Dugan), nut bowl, marigold...............................70.00
Wreath of Roses (Fenton), bonbon, gr, stemmed 70.00
Wreathed Cherry (Dugan), creamer, amethyst...............................80.00
Zig Zag (Fenton), tumbler, ice gr, decorated.................................75.00
Zip Zip (English), flower frog, marigold...60.00
Zipper Stitch (Czech), bowl, marigold, oval, 10" 125.00

Zipper Variant, sugar bowl, lav, w/lid...50.00
Zippered Heart (Imperial), bowl, amethyst, 5" 65.00

Carousel Figures

For generations of Americans, visions of carousel horses revolving majestically around lively band organs rekindle wonderful childhood experiences. These nostalgic memories are the legacy of the creative talent from a dozen carving shops that created America's carousel art. Skilled craftsmen brought their trade from Europe where American carvers took the carousel animal from a folk art creation to a true art form. The golden age of carousel art lasted from 1880 to 1929.

There are two basic types of American carousels. The largest and most impressive is the 'park style' carousel built for permanent installation in major amusement centers. These were created in Philadelphia by Gustav and William Dentzel, Muller Brothers, and E. Joy Morris who became the Philadelphia Toboggan Company in 1902. A more flamboyant group of carousel animals was carved in Coney Island, New York, by Charles Looff, Marcus Illions, Charles Carmel, and Stein & Goldstein's Artistic Carousel Company. These park-style carousels were typically three, four, and even five rows with forty-five to sixty-eight animals on a platform. Collectors often pay a premium for the carvings by these men. The outside row animals are larger and more ornate and command higher prices. The horses on the inside rows are smaller, less decorated, and of lesser value.

The most popular style of carousel art is the 'country fair style.' These carousels were portable affairs created for mobility. The horses are smaller and less ornate with leg and head positions that allow for stacking and easy loading. These were built primarily for North Tonawanda, New York, near Niagara Falls, by Armitage Herschell Company, Herschell Spillman Company, Spillman Engineering Company, and Allen Herschell. Charles W. Parker was also well known for his portable merry-go-rounds. He was based in Leavenworth, Kansas. Parker and Herschell Spillman both created a few large park-style carousels as well, but they are better known for their portable models.

Horses are by far the most common figure found, but there are two dozen other animals that were created for the carousel platform. Carousel animals, unlike most other antiques, are oftentimes worth more in a restored condition. Figures found with original factory paint are extraordinarily rare and bring premium amounts. Typically, carousel horses are found in garish, poorly applied 'park paint' and are often missing legs or ears. Carousel horses are hollow. They were glued up from several blocks for greater strength and lighter weight. Bass and poplar woods were used extensively.

If you have an antique carousel animal you would like to have identified, send a clear photograph and description along with a LSASE to our advisor, William Manns, who is listed in the Directory under New Mexico. Mr. Manns is the author of *Painted Ponies*, containing many full-color photographs, guides, charts, and directories for the collector.

Key:
IR — inside row	OR — outside row
MR — middle row	PTC — Philadelphia Toboggan Company

Coney Island-Style Horses

Carmel, IR jumper, unrstr 4,800.00
Carmel, MR jumper, unrstr...7,900.00
Carmel, OR jumper w/cherub, rstr..17,000.00
Illions, IR jumper, rstr 5,200.00
Illions, MR stander, rstr 9,200.00
Looff, IR jumper unrstr 3,200.00
Looff, OR jumper, unrstr 14,000.00

Stein & Goldstein, IR jumper, unrstr.....................................4,700.00
Stein & Goldstein, MR jumper, rstr..8,000.00
Stein & Goldstein, OR stander w/bells, unrstr......................18,000.00

European Horses

Anderson, English, unrstr 3,500.00
Bayol, French, unrstr..2,500.00
Heyn, German, unrstr 3,200.00
Hubner, Belgian, unrstr...2,000.00
Savage, English, unrstr..2,500.00

Menagerie Animals (Non-Horses)

Dentzel, bear, unrstr...20,000.00
Dentzel, cat, unrstr...22,000.00
Dentzel, deer, unrstr...16,000.00
Dentzel, lion, unrstr..35,000.00
Dentzel, pig, unrstr...9,500.00
E Joy Morris, deer, unrstr 10,000.00
Herschell Spillman, cat, unrstr..11,000.00
Herschell Spillman, chicken, portable, unrstr..........................5,500.00
Herschell Spillman, dog, portable, unrstr................................6,500.00
Herschell Spillman, frog, unrstr...18,000.00
Looff, camel, unrstr...10,000.00
Looff, goat, rstr...13,500.00
Muller, tiger, rstr...32,000.00

Philadelphia-Style Horses

Dentzel, IR 'topknot' jumper, unrstr.......................................5,500.00
Dentzel, MR jumper, unrstr 7,800.00
Dentzel, OR stander, female cvg on shoulder, rstr.................20,000.00
Dentzel, prancer, rstr..8,000.00
Morris, IR prancer, rstr...4,500.00
Morris, MR stander, unrstr..7,000.00
Morris, OR stander, rstr 17,000.00
Muller, IR jumper, rstr..5,000.00
Muller, MR jumper, rstr 7,500.00
Muller, OR stander, rstr...23,000.00
Muller, OR stander w/military trappings.................................27,000.00
PTC, chariot (bench-like seat), rstr 7,500.00
PTC, IR jumper, rstr 4,000.00
PTC, MR jumper, rstr..8,500.00
PTC, OR stander, armored, rstr 30,000.00
PTC, OR stander, unrstr...19,000.00

Portable Carousel Horses

Allan Herschell, all aluminum, ca 1950....................................500.00
Allan Herschell, half & half, wood & aluminum head 1,300.00
Allan Herschell, IR Indian pony, unrstr..................................2,200.00
Allan Herschell, OR, rstr..3,200.00
Allan Herschell, OR Trojan-style jumper 3,500.00
Armitage Herschell, track-machine jumper..............................2,800.00
Dare, jumper, unrstr 3,000.00
Herschell Spillman, chariot (bench-like seat) 3,800.00
Herschell Spillman, IR jumper, unrstr.....................................2,400.00
Herschell Spillman, MR jumper, unrstr 2,900.00
Herschell Spillman, OR, eagle decor 4,500.00
Herschell Spillman, OR, park machine 10,000.00
Parker, MR jumper, unrstr..4,200.00
Parker, OR jumper, park machine, unrstr.................................6,500.00
Parker, OR jumper, rstr 5,800.00

Parker, carved polychrome and jewelled horse, restored by Fred Lampé in 1986, red seat, 53" long, $4,000.00.

Cartoon Art

Collectors of cartoon art are interested in many forms of original art — animation cels, sports, political or editorial cartoons, syndicated comic strip panels, and caricature. To produce even a short animated cartoon strip, hundreds of original drawings are required, each showing the characters in slightly advancing positions. Called 'cels' because those made prior to the 1950s were made from a celluloid material, collectors often pay hundreds of dollars for a frame from a favorite movie. Prices of Disney cels with backgrounds vary widely. Background paintings, model sheets, storyboards, and preliminary sketches are also collectible — so are comic book drawings executed in India ink and signed by the artist. Daily 'funnies' originals, especially the earlier ones portraying super heroes, and Sunday comic strips, the early as well as the later ones, are collected. Cartoon art has become recognized and valued as a novel yet valid form of contemporary art. In the listings below all cels are untrimmed and full size, unless noted otherwise.

Ad work, Beatles chased by girls, re: cartoon series, 1969, 13x10"..215.00
Cel, Bambi among rabbits, Courvoisier setup, Disney, 1942 ....5,000.00
Cel, Betty Boop singing, HP ltd ed pc, Culhane, oversz: 16x20"...650.00
Cel, broom army on march, Fantasia, Disney, 1940 ....7,500.00
Cel, Bugs Bunny & Elmer Fudd, Bunny Snatchers, 1990............300.00
Cel, Bugs Bunny in bl tails, sgn C Jones, 15x17".........................165.00
Cel, Bugs Bunny/DaffyDuck/Porky Pig in Looney Tunes logo, 1980s...750.00
Cel, Droopy dog, Droopy in bkground, Filmation, 1978..............250.00
Cel, Farscape, Revenging Angel, Season 3, Episode 16, E bkground...185.00
Cel, Fozzie & Miss Piggy, Muppet Babies, Hensen, 1980s 95.00
Cel, Fred Flintstone, angry, Flintstones, Hanna-Barbera 100.00
Cel, Garfield in chair, Resourceful, United Artists, 1978............225.00
Cel, George & Elroy Jetson, Jetsons, Hanna-Barbera 200.00
Cel, Lady & Tramp in alley behind restaurant, Disney, 1955 .....9,500.00
Cel, Muppet baby & lg beetle, production bkground, Hensen, 1980s...45.00
Cel, Pinocchio, printed bkground, Disney, 1940 ....3,500.00
Cel, Smurf boy, production bkground, Hanna-Barbera................100.00
Cel, Winnie the Pooh in nightshirt w/gun, 16x19" 275.00
Cel, Woody Woodpecker playing golf, ltd ed Sericel, Lantz, 1992...80.00
Drawing, Dennis the Menace, ink, Hank Ketcham, 10x12"..........50.00
Drawing, My God, It's Your Mother, newlyweds in car, R Weber, 20x16"..70.00

Cast Iron

In the mid-1800s, the cast-iron industry was raging in the United States. It was recognized as a medium extremely adaptable for uses ranging from ornamental architectural filigree to actual building construction. It could be cast from a mold into any conceivable design that could be reproduced over and over at a relatively small cost. It could be painted to give an entirely versatile appearance. Furniture with openwork designs of grapevines and leaves and intricate lacy scrollwork was cast for gardens as well as inside use. Figural doorstops of every sort, bootjacks, trivets, and a host of other useful and decorative items were made before the 'ferromania' had run its course. For more information, we recommend *Antique Iron* by Kathryn McNerney (Collector Books). See also Kitchen, Cast-Iron Bakers and Kettles; and other specific categories.

Architectural finial, pineapple, weathered pnt, 19th C, 13x11", pr..**470.00**
Bench, fern design, Barbe...Lafayette IN, welded rstr, 30x45½" **220.00**
Bench, heavy foliate casting w/front apron & scrolls, worn wht, 45"..**1,300.00**
Bench, openwork medallions, scrolled arms & ft, EX pnt, 45"....**550.00**
Bench, scrolled panels, openwork seat, Washington Iron Wks, 45"...**230.00**
Bench, vintage designs, old blk pnt, welded rstr, 32x43" **165.00**
Birdhouse, Victorian Gothic style, old mc pnt, 10½x14½x11"....**2,000.00**
Building anchor, star shape, weathered gr pnt, 1810-40, 11¼" ...**560.00**
Eagle, wings wide, gilt traces, on wooden plinth, overall: 8x15¼" ..**825.00**
Eagle, wings wide, mtd on scrolling platform, Am, 19th C, 9x15"..**1,645.00**
Figure, Geo Washington, 2-pc, mk Pat Aug 26 18??, 46½" **6,000.00**
Figure, Tory man, mc attire, sgn GH Greene...MA, pnt touchups, 15"...**825.00**
Fountain, frog on ball, attachment in mouth, no pnt, 9", VG **350.00**
Fountain/urn, geometrics/foliage/scrolls, Abendroth...NY, 63x48"..**5,950.00**
Greyhound, hollow body, EX detail, welded rprs, 21x50" **1,450.00**
Hitching post, horse head, acanthus leaves at base, 13", EX **440.00**
Hitching post, horse head, worn pnt, Marten & Anderson..., 32"..**825.00**
Hitching post, horse head on octagonal base, old pnt, 13"..........**415.00**
Kettle, sugar; 19th C, 79" dia, EX **1,500.00**
Planter, relief scrolls & line, 4-ftd, oval, 8½x19½", pr **400.00**
Rabbit, pnt removed (detailed fur), 12x11" **315.00**
Roaster, tin lid, iron hdl, 8x15½" **175.00**
Urn, classical style w/2 lg hdls, 2-pc, JW Fiske, 41x24" dia **2,300.00**
Urn, hdls, old gr pnt, minor rust, 24x20", EX............................**1,435.00**

Urns on plinths, everted rim with chain pattern, waisted body with floral decor, staff handles, late nineteenth century, 32½", $2,115.00 for the pair. (Photo courtesy Bohnams & Butterfield)

Water sprinkler, alligator form, worn gr pnt, EX **695.00**
Water sprinkler, turtle form, ca 1920s, EX **750.00**

Castor Sets

Castor sets became popular during the early years of the eighteenth century and continued to be used through the late Victorian era. Their purpose was to hold various condiments for table use. The most common type was a circular arrangement with a center handle on a revolving pedestal base that held three, four, five, or six bottles. A few were equipped with a bell for calling the servant. Frames were made of silverplate, glass, or pewter. Though most bottles were of pressed glass, some of the designs were cut, and on rare occasion, colored glass with enameled decorations was used as well. To maintain authenticity and value, castor sets should have matching bottles. Prices listed below are for those with matching bottles and in frames with plating that is in excellent condition (unless noted otherwise). Note: Watch for new frames and bottles in clear, cranberry, cobalt, and vaseline Inverted Thumbprint as well as reproductions of Czechoslovakian cut glass bottles. These have recently been appearing on the market. Our advisors for this category are Barbara and Steve Aaronson; they are listed in the Directory under California.

2-bottle, dmn cut cruets; angel w/torch & dog cutouts in silver fr, 7"....**220.00**
3-bottle, Daisy & Button, SP fr w/toothpick holder finial...........**175.00**
3-bottle, Gothic Arch, orig stoppers, pewter fr **115.00**
3-bottle, rubena, cut dmns, SP fr, 5½x4" **215.00**
4-bottle, Bellflower, single vine, w/pewter fr **400.00**
4-bottle, King's Crown, ruby stain, orig glass stand.....................**350.00**
4-bottle, Log & Star, amber, orig ped-base fr **145.00**
5-bottle, Bristol glass, floral on pk, cherub SP fr, 1890s, 15x5" ...**975.00**
5-bottle, clear, rstr Meriden B #157 fr w/cherub atop hdl............**525.00**
5-bottle, clear/sq, revolves, rstr #2165 fr...................................**650.00**
5-bottle, cut facets/etched leaves, SP fr, 17½" **100.00**
5-bottle, etched amberina, cut amberina stoppers, gilt fr, EX...**2,200.00**
5-bottle, vaseline glass, Meriden #827 SP fr, 13¾" **775.00**
6-bottle, Daisy & Button, ornate rstr Wilcox fr revolves............**375.00**
6-bottle+bud vase, pressed glass, rstr SP #2114 fr, revolves **750.00**
7-bottle, cut crystal, gadrooned/shell border Geo III SP fr **495.00**
7-bottle, cut crystal, lg ped-ft Gleason fr w/doors **1,550.00**

Catalina Island

Catalina Island pottery was made on the island of the same name, which is about twenty-six miles off the coast of Los Angeles. The pottery was started in 1927 at Pebble Beach by Wm. Wrigley, Jr., who was instrumental in developing and using the native clays. Its principal products were brick and tile to be used for construction on the island. Garden pieces were first produced, then vases, bookends, lamps, ashtrays, novelty items, and finally dinnerware. The ware became very popular and was soon being shipped to the mainland as well.

Some of the pottery was hand thrown; some was made in molds. Most pieces are marked Catalina Island or Catalina with a printed incised stamp or handwritten with a pointed tool. Cast items were sometimes marked in the mold, a few have an ink stamp, and a paper label was also used. The most favored colors in tableware and accessories are 1) black (rare), 2) Seafoam and Monterey Brown (uncommon), 3) matt blue and green, 4) Toyon Red (orange), 5) other brights, and 6) pastels with a matt finish.

The color of the clay can help to identify approximately when a piece was made: 1927 to 1932, brown to red (Island) clay (very popular with collectors, tends to increase values); 1931 to 1932, an experimental period with various colors; 1932 to 1937, mainly white clay, though tan to brown clays were also used on occasion.

Items marked Catalina Pottery are listed in Gladding McBean. For further information we recommend *Catalina Island Pottery Collector's Guide* by Steven and Aisha Hoefs, and *The Collector's Encyclopedia of California Pottery, Second Edition,* by Jack Chipman (Collector Books). Our advisor for this category is Steven Hoefs; he is listed in the Directory under Georgia.

Ashtray, cowboy hat form, yel...225.00
Ashtray/match holder, bl, Mexican man taking a siesta, 3½x6x7" ...215.00
Bowl, bl, #710, 3½x13"...75.00
Candelabrum, 3 leaf-form holders, turq, 2½x11" 325.00
Candle holder, Cactus flask form, Descanso Green, 6¼", ea.......900.00
Candlestick, gr, flared base, 3¼", ea 75.00
Carafe, bl, bulbous bottom w/triangular top, wooden hdl, 8½"...265.00
Casserole, bl, single serving, w/lid..425.00

Charger, swans on water, multicolor, #907-65-B, 12½", NM, from $800.00 to $900.00.

Coaster, bl or gr, #501, 4" dia...60.00
Coffee server, gr w/metal hdl, 10½"..500.00
Coffeepot, Deco-style, Catalina Blue, 4½x11"+cr/sug.............1,200.00
Dish, lt gr, fluted w/scalloped edge, oval, 6x14" 120.00
Figurine, cat, blue, 4½" 600.00
Head vase, peasant lady, off-wht, #801, 6½" 75.00
Plaque, stagecoach w/2 drivers, mk Graham #745-65B, 12½" 930.00
Plate, seafoam, fluted w/scalloped edge & turned lip, 8"...............90.00
Plate, Serenade, HP by FM Graham, 12½", from $800 to..........900.00
Plate, Swordfish, red, 14", from $1,200 to.............................1,600.00
Porringer, Mandarin Yellow, 2 tab hdls, 5" 55.00
Shakers, 1 yel, 1 orange, gourd shape, pr.................................70.00
Table top, 6-tile: parrots on branch, mc, 17x21x16", from $5,000 to...6,000.00
Tumbler, turq, honeycomb design at base................................100.00
Vase, aqua, bulbous bottom w/stepped base, hdls, 8" 265.00
Vase, biege, graduated knobs on side, #601, 7⅛" 190.00
Vase, gr, trumpet form, 7¼" 425.00
Vase, yel, fluted, ftd, 8" 260.00
Vase, yel, rnd bottom w/fluted neck, #627, 7½"........................95.00
Vase, yel w/emb birds in tree, cylindrical, 11", from $900 to ...1,200.00

Catalogs

Catalogs are not only intriguing to collect on their own merit, but for the collector with a specific interest, they are often the only remaining source of background information available, and as such they offer a wealth of otherwise unrecorded data. The mail-order industry can be traced as far back as the mid-1800s. Even before Aaron Montgomery Ward began his career in 1872, Laacke and Joys of Wisconsin and the Orvis Company of Vermont, both dealers in sporting goods, had been well established for many years. The E.C. Allen Company sold household necessities and novelties by mail on a broad scale in the 1870s. By the end of the Civil War, sewing machines, garden seed, musical instruments, even medicine, were available from catalogs. In the 1880s Macy's of New York issued a 127-page catalog; Sears and Spiegel followed suit in about 1890. Craft and art supply catalogs were first available about 1880 and covered such varied fields as china painting,

stenciling, wood burning, brass embossing, hair weaving, and shellcraft. Today some collectors confine their interests not only to craft catalogs in general but often to just one subject. There are several factors besides rarity which make a catalog valuable: age, condition, profuse illustrations, how collectible the field is that it deals with, the amount of color used in its printing, its size (format and number of pages), and whether it is a manufacturer's catalog verses a jobber's catalog (the former being the most desirable).

Albany Foundry Co, grey iron castings, 1925, 20+ pgs, G.............63.00
American Type Founders Co, printing supplies, ca 1930, 64 pgs, EX-...51.00
Brodies, Inc, restaurant supplies, ca 1959, 327 pgs, G+ 28.00
Brown, Thompson & Co, bicycles, 1898, 15 pgs, VG 190.00
Butterick Publishing Co, amateur photography, 1899, 86 pgs, G ..21.00
California Perfume Co, 1933, 124 pgs, G+ 130.00
CE Ward & Co, Odd Fellows supplies, 1927, 88 pgs, G+ 68.00
Chicago Flag & Decorating, ca 1925, 72 pgs, G+ 48.00
Clark & Hill Mfg Co, wagons & carriages, 1892, 64 pgs, G........215.00
Cleveland Steel Barrel Co, undtd, 19 pgs, G 21.00
Cutaway Harrow Co, 1895, 32 pgs, G 33.00
Dr Hess & Clark Inc, veterinary supplies, ca 1938, 24 pgs, VG 19.00
Eastern Rubber Co, rubber goods, pre-1900, 16 pgs, G+ 53.00
Edward Parrish & Son, drugs, 1871, 42 pgs, G 79.00
Eli Bridge Co, Ferris wheels & equipment, 1922, 20 pgs, G 50.00
Emerson Piano Co, early 1900s, 24 pgs, G+ 41.00
Ford Motor Co, 1959 Ford station wagon, 1958, 8 pgs, VG 13.00
Franks & Heideke, photography, ca 1953, 10 pgs, G 15.00
Frigidaire Corp, refrigeration & parts, 1929, 34 pgs, G+ 31.00
Harley-Davidson, motorcycle specs & pictures, 1974, 20 pgs, VG...24.00
HB Claplin Co, Oriental rugs & carpets, 1923, 112 pgs, G+ 47.00
Hires Turner Glass Co, store display windows, 1916, 20 pgs, VG...32.00
Home Building Plan Service, 1964, 48 pgs, G+ 19.00
Hudson Motor Car Co, The Hudson Triangle, 1915, 16 pgs, G+ 97.00
Independent Lock Co, ca 1927, 136 pgs, VG+ 43.00
Iowa Jewelers Supply Co, 1968, 76 pgs, VG...............................16.00
Ives Mfg Co, model trains, ca 1920s, 44 pgs, G...........................35.00
James Lees & Sons, home decor, 1947, 32 pgs, VG 12.00
Jell-O Co Inc, recipes, 1926, 24 pgs, G+ 12.00
Joseph Harris Co, Moreton Farm Seeds, 1897, 42 pgs, G 42.00
Ketchum Mfg Co, marking supplies for livestock, ca 1939, 32 pgs, VG...37.00
Lanston Monotype Co, The Monotype Casting Machine, 1908, 172 pgs, VG.....58.00
Levy, Dreyfus & Co, jewelers' supplies, 1882, 50 pgs, VG+...........98.00
Loughlin, Forsyth & Co, school furniture, ca 1894, 20 pgs, G 79.00
Lyons Band Instruments Co, 1941, 48 pgs, VG............................19.00
Middleby-Marshall Oven Co, 1925, 43 pgs, VG+ 66.00
Miller, Stockman Supply Co, western clothing, 1946, 36 pgs, G+...24.00
Mills Brothers, Milbro model kits, ca 1933, 52 pgs, G 32.00
National Cloak & Suit Co, clothing, 1913, 34 pgs, G+ 32.00
Nonotuck Silk Co, sewing, 1910, 15 pgs, VG 83.00
North Bros Mfg Co, Yankee tool book, 1929, 40 pgs, VG 38.00
Paichney Instrument Corp, hospital supplies, 1936, 121 pgs, VG ..77.00
Ray H Bennett Lumber Co, ready-cut homes, ca 1920s, 104 pgs, VG ..47.00
RE Dietz Co, Dietz lanterns, ca 1930, 49 pgs, G 56.00
RH Macy & Co, Fall & Winter clothing, 1910, 450 pgs, G+ 72.00
RH Stearns & Co, clothing, 1907, 48 pgs, G 7.00
Richmond Cedar Works, woodenware, 1935, 16 pgs, VG 34.00
Sargent & Co, builders' hardware, 1887, 183 pgs, VG 189.00
Scanton Bolt & Nut Co, 1908, 72 pgs, VG 27.00
Sears, Roebuck & Co, Fall & Winter, 1972, 1,484 pgs, G+ 34.00
Shakespeare Co, fishing tackle, 1963, 48 pgs, VG+......................26.00
Siegel Cooper Co, alcohol imports, early 1900s, 40 pgs, G 85.00
Sperry & Hutchinson, S&H Green Stamps, 1915, 66 pgs, G+ 38.00
Success Barber & Beauty, supplies, 1952, 72 pgs, G+ 24.00
Vitale Fireworks Mfg, 1938, 4 pgs, G+ 87.00

Washington-Eljer Co, plumbing, 1935, 8 pgs, VG.......................14.00
Westinghouse Electric & Mfg, trolleys & equipment, 1928, 24 pgs, G+ ..126.00
Wilbur H Murray, carriages, 1901, 40 pgs, G- 65.00
William Dixon Inc, tools for metal crafts, 1939, 183 pgs, VG+ 31.00
Wm PB Schmidt Furniture, ca 1900, 17 pgs, G 65.00
World Mfg Co, novelties, 1885, 44 pgs, VG 41.00

Ceramic Art Company

Jonathan Coxon, Sr., and Walter Scott Lenox established the Ceramic Art Company in 1889 in Trenton, New Jersey, where they produced fine belleek porcelain. Both were experienced in its production, having previously worked for Ott and Brewer. They hired artists to hand paint their wares with portraits, scenes, and lovely florals. Today artist-signed examples bring the highest prices. Several marks were used, three of which contain the 'CAC' monogram. A green wreath surrounding the company name in full was used on special-order wares, but these are not often encountered. Coxon eventually left the company, and it was later reorganized under the Lenox name. See also Lenox. Our advisor for this category is Mary Frank Gaston.

Bell, tulip form, silver decor on wht, unmk.................150.00
Bowl, finger; gold leaves & flowers on gr, scalloped rim.............130.00
Bowl, gold florals, pastel sponging, ruffled, 2x4½".................135.00
Cream soup & saucer, wht Irish-style Tridacna form, w/gold, CAC mk...120.00
Creamer, gold floral, hdl & trim, mk, 3¾" 135.00
Cup, chocolate; bl beading & gold on ivory, ped ft.................90.00
Cup, demitasse; gold-paste floral, ring hdl, 2" 100.00
Humidor, lilies, red-orange on orange, ca 1897, 6x5½".................350.00

Ink blotter holder, flowers and butterflies with gold, brown CAC mark, 6", $225.00. (Photo courtesy Mary Frank Gaston)

Inkwell, mums (non-factory) w/gold on wht, sq, CAC mk, 4½" ...200.00
Jug, Rye, brn & gr w/silver o/l, palette mk 200.00
Loving cup, 3 HP roses, 3-hdl, 1889-1906, 7¼x3¾" 150.00
Mug, gr hops, artist sgn, palette mk, 4¾" 75.00
Mug, strawberries, emb hdl & base, palette mk, 6" 95.00
Pitcher, strawberries & leaves w/gold, sgn Lenox, 6" 400.00
Salt cellar, scalloped rim, palette mk 25.00
Stein, monks eating in cellar, copper/sterling lid, mk, ½-liter.....600.00
Tankard, lady in wispy gown w/flower wreath, Heidrich, unmk, 13"..1,200.00
Vase, chrysanthemums, bulbous, sgn, 7½" 725.00
Vase, irises, mc on salmon, 8" 275.00
Vase, shell form w/snail hdls & emb decor, no pnt, 6x7".............300.00
Vase, wht neck w/purple lustre body, gr mk, 3¾".................125.00
Vase, 3 heron reserves, iris on blk at neck, mk, 22".................575.00

Ceramic Arts Studio, Madison

The Ceramic Arts Studio Company began operations sometime prior to the 1940s, but it was about then that Betty Harrington started marketing her goods through this company. Betty Harrington was the designer primarily responsible for creating the line of figurines and knickknacks that has become so popular with collectors. There were two others — Ulli Rebus, who not only designed several of the animals and various other pieces but taught Betty the art of mold-making as well; and Ruth Planter, whose work may have been limited to 'Sonny' and 'Honey.' About 65% of these items are marked, but even unmarked items become easily recognizable after only a brief study of their distinctive styling and glaze colors. At least eight different marks were used, among them the black ink stamp and the incised mark: 'Ceramic Arts Studio, Madison, Wisc.' A paper sticker was used in the early years.

After the 1955 demise of the company in Madison, the owner (Ruben Sand) went to Japan where he continued production under the same name using many of the same molds. After a short time, the old molds were retired, and new and quite different items were produced. Most of the Japan pieces can be found with a Ceramic Arts Studio backstamp. The Japan identification was often on a paper label and can be missing. Japan pieces are never marked Madison, Wisc., but not all Madison pieces are either. Red or blue backstamps are exclusively Japanese.

Another company that also produced figurines operated at about the same time as the Madison studio. It was called Ceramic Art (no 's') Studio; do not confuse the two.

A second and larger building in the C.A.S. complex in Madison was for the exclusive production of metal accessories. The creator and designer of this related line was Zona Liberace, Liberace's stepmother, who was art director for the line of figurines as well. These pieces are rising fast in value and because they weren't marked can sometimes be found at bargain prices. They were so popular that other ceramic companies bought them to complement their own lines, so they may also be found with ceramic figures other than C.A.S.'s.

Our advisor for this category is BA Wellman; his address can be found under Massachusetts. Mr. Wellman encourages collectors to e-mail him with any new information concerning company history and/or production. See also Clubs, Newsletters, and Catalogs.

Ashtray, hippo, 3½" 135.00
Bank, Paisley Pig, 3" 150.00
Bank, Skunky, 4" 195.00
Bell, Winter Bell, 5¼" 90.00
Birdbath, 4½" 125.00
Bowl, Bonita, paisley shape, 3¾" L 75.00
Candle holder, Triad Girl, center, 5" 165.00
Candle holder, Triad Girl, right or left, from $90 to 145.00
Candle holders, Bedtime Boy & Girl, 4¾", pr 225.00
Figurine, Al the Hunter, 6¼" 100.00
Figurine, angel, sleeping girl, 3¼" 85.00
Figurine, Autumn Andy, 5" 90.00
Figurine, Blyth, 6½" 135.00
Figurine, bunny baby, 2¼" 40.00
Figurine, Calico Cat, 3" 45.00
Figurine, Carmen, 7¼" 85.00
Figurine, Chinese Boy & Girl, 3" 50.00
Figurine, chipmunk, 2" 45.00
Figurine, Cinderella & Prince, bl, 6½", pr 225.00
Figurine, Dinky Girl, 2" 45.00
Figurine, Dutch Boy & Girl, 4½", pr, from $50 to 65.00
Figurine, Elsie the Elephant, 5" 95.00
Figurine, fawn, from Indian group, 4¼" 50.00
Figurine, Fire Man, 11¼", from $185 to 200.00

Figurine, frog, singing, 2" 45.00
Figurine, Gay '90s Man, dog at side, 7" 60.00
Figurine, Gingham Dog, 2¾" 45.00
Figurine, Gypsy Man, 6½" 95.00
Figurine, Hansel & Gretel, 1-pc, 3" 100.00
Figurine, imp, recumbent, 3½" 150.00
Figurine, King's Flutist & Lutist Jesters, pr 395.00
Figurine, lion, 5½" 200.00
Figurine, Little Jack Horner #2, 4" 80.00
Figurine, longhorn ox, 3" L 90.00
Figurine, lovebirds, 1-pc, 2¾" 65.00
Figurine, Lucindy, 7" 75.00
Figurine, Mary & lamb w/bow, 6¼" & 4", pr 80.00
Figurine, Mermaid on rock, 4" 165.00
Figurine, Mexican boy w/cactus, 7" 80.00
Figurine, Modern Colt, stylized, 7½" 200.00
Figurine, Mop-Pi & Smi-Li, pr 65.00
Figurine, Mr & Mrs Penguin, 3¾", pr 65.00
Figurine, Our Lady of Fatima 125.00
Figurine, Palomino Colt, 5¾" 90.00
Figurine, panda w/hat 60.00
Figurine, Pekingese, 3" 95.00
Figurine, Polish Boy & Girl, 6½", pr 120.00
Figurine, Promenade Man & Woman, pr 175.00
Figurine, Ralph the Goat, 4" 95.00
Figurine, Sambo, 3½" 365.00
Figurine, shepherd, 8½", from $100 to 135.00
Figurine, Spring Colt, 3½" 125.00
Figurine, Square Dance Boy & Girl, 6½", 6", pr 145.00
Figurine, St Agnes w/lamb, 1-pc 75.00
Figurine, St Francis w/extended arms, 7" 150.00
Figurine, swan, neck up, 6" 110.00
Figurine, Temple Dancer, from $135 to 165.00
Figurine, tom cat, standing, 5", from $90 to 120.00
Figurine, tortoise w/hat, crawling, 2½" L 125.00
Figurine, Wee Scottish Girl, 3" 45.00
Figurine, Winter Willie, 4" 65.00
Head vase, African Man, 8" 325.00
Head vase, Barbie, 7" 195.00
Head vase, Mei-Ling, 5" 150.00
Head vase, Svea & Sven, 6", pr 425.00
Honey pot, w/bee, 4" 150.00
Lamp, Jester Flutist, very scarce 450.00
Lamp, Manchu lantern holder, scarce 396.00
Miniture, teapot, appl swan, open 65.00
Mug, Barbershop Quartet, 3½" 150.00
Pitcher, George Washington & stars, wht on bl 65.00
Pitcher, Pine Cone, mini, 3¾" 65.00
Plaque, Dutch Boy & Girl, dancing, pr 145.00
Plaque, Greg & Grace, 9" & 9½", pr 135.00
Plaque, Jack Be Nimble, 5" 125.00
Plaque, Manchu & Lotus, 8", pr 190.00
Plaque, striped mother fish, 9" 90.00
Plaque, Tragedy Mask, 5", from $80 to 90.00
Razor blade bank, Tony, #319, 4¾" 125.00
Shakers, baby chick in nest, snuggle, pr 50.00
Shakers, bear & cub, snuggle, pr 90.00
Shakers, Black boy & alligator, pr 275.00
Shakers, boy & chair, pr 70.00
Shakers, Calico Cat & Gingham Dog, 3", 2¾", pr 125.00
Shakers, cocks fighting, pr, from $70 to 80.00
Shakers, covered wagon & oxen, ea 3" L, pr 135.00
Shakers, fish on tail, pr 125.00
Shakers, fox & goose, snuggle, 3¼" & 2¼", pr 225.00

Shakers, frog & toadstool, pr, from $75 to 90.00
Shakers, horse's head, pr 95.00
Shakers, kangaroo mother & joey, snuggle, 4¾" & 2½", pr 160.00
Shakers, Oak Spirite & Spring Leaf, pr 85.00
Shakers, Paul Bunyan & tree, pr 200.00
Shakers, Santa Claus & Christmas tree, 2¼", pr 200.00
Shakers, Sooty & Taffy (Scotty dogs), pr 65.00
Shakers, Suzette the Poodle on pillow, snuggle, pr 250.00
Shakers, Wee Pigs, pr 95.00
Shelf sitter, Budgie (bird) 65.00
Shelf sitter, Collie mother, 5" 95.00
Shelf sitter, Dutch Girl, 4½" 35.00
Shelf sitter, girl w/cat, 4¼" 75.00
Shelf sitter, Maurice & Michelle, 7", pr 165.00
Shelf sitter, Persian mother cat, gr eyes, 4¼" 125.00
Shelf sitter, Willy, ball down, 4½" 225.00
Shelf sitter, Winney & Willy, pr 425.00
Shelf sitter, Young Love Couple (kissing boy & girl), 4½", pr 90.00

Sofa for Maurice and Michele, designed by Zona Liberace, 10x3¾", $85.00.

Vase, Flying Ducks, rnd, 2" 95.00
Vase, Wing-Sang & Lu-Tang, wht w/gr trim, vase behind, 7", pr ..95.00

Metal Accessories

Arched window for religious figure, 6½" 95.00
Artist palette w/shelves, left & right, 13" W 125.00
Beanstalk for Jack, rare 185.00
Birdcage w/perch, 14" 125.00
Box, dmn shape, 15½x14" 125.00
Corner spider web for Miss Muffet, flat bk, 4" 165.00
Frame w/shelf, 22" sq 95.00
Garden shelf, for Mary Contrary, 4x12" 125.00
Musical score, flat bk, 14x12" 125.00
Pocket step shelf, w/planter, rnd, 8" 75.00
Pyramid shelf 95.00
Rainbow arch w/shelf, blk, 13½x19x5½" 135.00
Sofa, for Maurice & Michelle 85.00
Star for angel, flat bk 80.00
Triple ring for birds (shelf sitting), 15" 135.00

Chalkware

Items such as animals and birds, figures, banks, toys, and religious ornaments modeled after more expensive Staffordshire wares were often sold door to door. They were made from gypsum or plaster of Paris formed in a mold and then hand painted in oils or watercolors. Their origin is attributed to Italian immigrants. Today regarded as a form of folk art, nineteenth century American pieces bring prices in the hundreds of dollars. Carnival chalkware from this century is also collectible, especially figures that are personality related. For those, see Carnival Collectibles.

Bulldog, blk & wht pnt, tooled fur, rpr, 6½x7½"	**100.00**
Bust of lady w/turban, rnd plinth, EX mc pnt, 7½"	**550.00**
Cat, gray tabby w/yel eyes, orange collar, lt wear, 15½", EX+	**2,650.00**
Cat, mc spots, curled tail, red collar, touchups, 5½"	**550.00**
Cat, recumbent, blk & gray w/pk ears & bl bow, 5½x12", VG	**460.00**

Cat, striped paints with red details, American, nineteenth century, repair, 10", $4,600.00.

(Photo courtesy Skinner, Inc.)

Chicken, bank, mc pnt, minor wear, 5¾"	**365.00**
Dog, amber w/blk details, seated, flaw, 6"	**195.00**
Dog, seated, mc w/much detail, 9½", VG	**275.00**
Dog, seated, wht w/curly tail, blk ears/muzzle, yel eyes, 6", VG	**120.00**
Dove, wht on red & gr berry branch, EX details, 10⅜"	**500.00**
Dove, wht w/yel ft on cherry branch base, 10¼"	**275.00**
Ewe w/lamb, detailed wool, mc details, sm rpr, 6¼"	**165.00**
Fruit & foliage on stand, red-brn w/mc on wht base, 10¾", EX+	**1,700.00**
Fruit & kissing birds on urn, mc, lt wear, 12", EX+	**4,295.00**
Horse, wht w/blk hooves, tan details, 9½"	**415.00**
Parrot, well-detailed feathers, mc pnt, 8¼"	**495.00**
Pigeon, red & gr wings, blk base/beak/ft, molded perch, 6", EX+	**1,265.00**
Poodle, wht w/molded fur, blk tail, gr base, 7"	**300.00**
Poodle w/long legs, molded fur on shoulders & ears, mc details, 6⅞"	**400.00**
Rabbit, yel eyes, orange ears & mouth, gr base, 5½", EX	**475.00**
Reindeer, brn & blk pnt, recumbent, rpr base, 10", EX-	**275.00**
Rooster, free-standing, worn mc pnt, 6¾", pr	**660.00**
Rooster, mc, minor damage, 8¼"	**140.00**
Squirrel, yel-gr & ochre pnt, rstr base, 7¼"	**300.00**

Chase Brass & Copper Company

Chase introduced this logo in 1928. The company was incorporated in 1876 as the Waterbury Manufacturing Company and was located in Waterbury, Connecticut. This location remained Chase's principal fabrication plant, and it was here that the 'Specialties' were made.

In 1900 the company chose the name Chase Companies Inc., in honor of their

founder, Augustus Sabin Chase. The name encompassed Chase's many factories. Only the New York City sales division was called Chase Brass and Copper Co., but from 1936 on, that name was used exclusively.

In 1930 the sales division invited people to visit their new Specialties Sales Showroom in New York City 'where an interesting assortment of decorative and utilitarian pieces in brass and copper in a variety of designs and treatments are offered for your consideration.' Like several other large companies, Chase hired well-known designers such as Walter Von Nessen, Lurelle Guild, the Gerths, Russel Wright, and Dr. A Reimann. Harry Laylon, an in-house designer, created much of the new line.

From 1930 to 1942 Chase offered lamps, smoking accessories, and housewares similar to those Americans were seeing on the Hollywood screen — generally at prices the average person could afford.

Besides chromium, Chase manufactured many products in a variety of finishes, some even in silver plate. Many objects were of polished or satin-finished brass and/or copper; other pieces were chromium plated.

After World War II Chase no longer made the Specialties line. It had represented only a tiny fraction of this huge company's production. Instead they concentrated on a variety of fabricated mill items. Some dedicated Chase collectors even have shower heads, faucet aerators, gutter pipe, and metal samples. Is anyone using Chase window screening?

Chase products are marked either on the item itself or on a screw or rivet. Because Chase sold screws, rivets, nails, etc. (all with their logo), not all items having these Chase-marked components were actually made at Chase. It should also be noted that during the 1930s, China produced good quality chromium copies; so when you're not absolutely positive an item is Chase, buy it because you like it, understanding that its authenticity may be in question. Remember that if a magnet sticks to it, it's not Chase. Brass and copper are not magnetic, and Chase did not use steel.

Prior to 1933 Chase made smoking accessories for the Park Sherman Co. Some are marked 'Park Sherman, Chicago, Illinois, Made of Chase Brass.' Others carry a Park Sherman logo. It is believed that the 'heraldic emblem' was also used during this period. Many items are identical or very similar to Chase-marked pieces. Produced in the 1950s, National Silver's 'Emerald Glo' wares look very similar to Chase pieces, but Chase did not make them. It is very possible that National purchased Chase tooling after the Chase Specialties line was discontinued.

For further study we recommend *Chase Complete, Chase Catalogs 1934 & 1935, 1930s Lighting — Deco & Traditional by Chase*, and *The Chase Era, 1933 and 1942 Catalogs of the Chase Brass & Copper Co.*, all by Donald-Brian Johnson and Leslie Pina (Schiffer); *Art Deco Chrome, The Chase Era*, by Richard Kilbride; and *Art Deco Chrome* by James Linz (Schiffer).

In the listings that follow, examples are polished unless noted satin. A co-advisor for this category is Barbara Endter; she is listed in the Directory under New York. Donna and John Thorpe are our advisors for Chase lighting; they are listed in the Directory under Wisconsin.

Key:
Ge — Gerth   LG — Laurelle Guild
HD — Helen Bishop Dennis   RW — Russel Wright
HL — Harry Layton   VN — designed by Von Nessen

Antelope Ash Receiver, frosted glass w/chrome trim, #881, 4½"	**115.00**
Bomb Flashlight, polished nickel, A Mitchell, 3½" dia, $45 to	**50.00**
Brittany Bell, brass, #13002	**75.00**
Bubble Cigarette Holder, open chrome ball/sq ft, #860, 2¼", $40 to	**50.00**
Bud Holder, 4-Tube; polished copper w/wht plastic collar, Ge, #11230	**45.00**
Butter Dish, chrome w/wht, VN, #17067	**110.00**
Candy Jar, copper or satin copper w/brass knob, VN, #NS316, $150 to	**175.00**
Carefree Set, chrome, 4 cup holders on tray, #8003, from $100 to	**125.00**
Cat Doorstop, Deco, tubular copper w/brass head, emb mk, 8½x4⅞"	**200.00**

Cocktail Canape Server, chrome, #28001 ....185.00
Colonial Bookends, satin or blk nickel or copper, #11248, 5¼" 150.00
Compton Console Bowl, polished brass, HL, #15007 ....125.00
Continental Sugar Bowl, chrome w/blk, VN, #17052 ....25.00
Coronet Coffee Set, pot+cr/sug+tray, #90121, from $600 to.......650.00
Croyden Candelabra, polished brass or satin silver, #17114, pr...125.00
Davy Jones Bookends, brass/walnut/Bakelite, wheel shape, #90142 ..60.00
Dinner Gong, chrome, Ge, #11251, 8½x6¼", from $150 to.......175.00
Diplomat Tray, chrome/blk, VN, #17030, 33" dia........................240.00
Duplex Jelly Dish, chrome w/frosted glass, HL, #90062 ....35.00
Elephant Bookends, polished copper, #17043, VH, from $500 to ...550.00
Federal Plate, satin copper, #09007...75.00
Festivity Tray, chrome, stepped hdls, #09018, 19½x12¼" 150.00
Holiday Cocktail Set, chrome, shaker+4 cocktails+tray, #90064, $100 to..110.00
Ice Bowl, chrome, RW, #28002, w/tongs, 1934, from $80 to.........90.00
Imperial Bowl, chrome w/brushed nickel base, #15003 ....125.00
Informal Tray, copper, #09012..70.00
Jubilee Globe Mustard, copper or chrome w/wht, #90070, 4", from $45 to ...55.00
Jubilee Syrup Jug w/Plate, copper/glass, HL, #26004................60.00
Lamp, Binnacle; wired, 1933-34 Chicago Expo, #25002, from $75 to....100.00
Lamp, Constellation, bronze helmet w/milk glass dome, VN, 8¾x7"...300.00
Lamp, Desk, chrome w/pivoting socket on ribbed O shaft, 13½x12"...50.00
Lamp, Glow, chrome w/blk cone shade, #01001, 8", M..............85.00
Lamps, Colonel & Colonel's lady, red/wht/blk figures, LG, 8¾", pr...300.00
Lazy Boy Smoker's Stand, brass w/compo top, VN, 21½x11"......200.00
Manchu Table Bell, chrome/Catalin, #13006, 1936, from $45 to 50.00
Marionette Ashtray, #304..30.00
Niagara Watering Can, Ge, #05004, 8⅜", from $65 to 75.00
Nut Cracker Big'N Small, copper or brass, HL, #90150, from $45 to ...50.00
Pelican Smokers' Stand, English bronze, VN, #17056, 21½x8¾" ...375.00
Pretzelman Plate, copper, LG, #90038, from $95 to 110.00
Serving Fork & Spoon, chrome w/wht, HL, #90076, pr 45.00
Skyway Shakers, chrome/wht Bakelite, #17095, pr.....................35.00
Snack Server, 3 glass bowls w/chrome lids, in base, #90093, 14½" ..75.00
Spheres Shakers, chrome, RW, #28004, pr 45.00

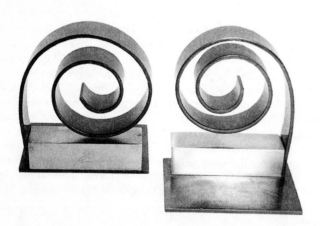

Spiral bookends, black and satin nickel finish, #17018, 1933, from $200.00 to $250.00. (Photo by Dale Endter/courtesy Barbara Endter)

Squirrel Napkin Clip, copper w/wht, HL, #90107 ....70.00
Stratosphere Smoking Stand, chrome, VN, #17076, 1937, from $350 to..400.00
Sugar Shaker, chrome, #90057..50.00
Sunday Morning Waffle Set, chrome, compo hdls, #90059, 4-pc, $200 to...240.00
Sunshine Watering Can, brass/copper, GE, #5003, 5x8½", from $30 to..40.00
Target Tray, chrome/wht, w/hdls, #09023, 12½" 300.00
Tarpon Fish Bowl, amber bronze, HD, #90125, 8" 80.00
Taurex Candlesticks, chrome or copper, VN, #24003, 7", pr, $125 to ..150.00

Tea Ball, chrome/wht, HL, #90118...95.00
Tripod Ashtray, copper & brass, 3-leg, VN, #301.......................45.00
Trophy Vase, chrome, #3005, 9"..75.00
Two-In-Hand Tray, chrome/wht, VN, #17077 ....100.00

Chelsea Dinnerware

Made from about 1830 to 1880 in the Staffordshire district of England, this white dinnerware is decorated with lustre embossings in the grape, thistle, sprig, or fruit and cornucopia patterns. The relief designs vary from lavender to blue, and the body of the ware may be porcelain, ironstone, or earthenware. Because it was not produced in Chelsea as the name would suggest, dealers often prefer to call it 'Grandmother's Ware.' For more information we recommend *Collector's Encyclopedia of English China* by Mary Frank Gaston, our advisor for this category.

Grape, bowl, 8" 35.00
Grape, cake plate, emb ribs, 10" dia, from $25 to 30.00
Grape, cake plate, w/copper lustre, 10" sq, from $25 to 30.00
Grape, coffeepot, stick hdl, 2-cup, 7"......................................75.00
Grape, creamer, 5½"..55.00
Grape, cup & saucer, from $25 to 35.00
Grape, egg cup, 2¼", from $35 to 50.00
Grape, pitcher, milk, 40-oz 60.00
Grape, plate, 6", from $12 to..15.00
Grape, plate, 7"...18.00
Grape, plate, 8", from $22 to..25.00
Grape, plate, 9½"...22.50
Grape, sugar bowl, w/lid 65.00
Grape, teapot, 2-cup..75.00
Grape, teapot, octagonal, 8½", from $125 to 150.00
Grape, teapot, octagonal, 10"..165.00
Grape, waste bowl..40.00
Sprig, cake plate, 9"...40.00
Sprig, cup & saucer..40.00
Sprig, pitcher, milk..60.00
Sprig, plate, dinner..25.00
Sprig, plate, 7"..18.00
Thistle, butter pat..15.00
Thistle, cake plate, 8¾", from $25 to 30.00
Thistle, cup & saucer, from $30 to...35.00
Thistle, plate, 6", from $6 to..8.00
Thistle, plate, 7"..15.00
Thistle, sugar bowl, 8-sided, w/lid, 7½" 45.00

Chelsea Keramic Art Works

In 1866 fifth-generation Scottish potter Alexander Robertson started a pottery in Chelsea, Massachusetts, where his brother Hugh joined him the following year. Their father James left the firm he partnered to help his sons in 1872, teaching them techniques and pressing decorative tiles, an extreme rarity at that early date. Their early production consisted mainly of classical Grecian and Asian shapes in redware and stoneware, several imitating metal vessels. They then betrayed influences from Europe's most important potteries, such as Royal Doulton and Limoges, in underglaze and barbotine or Haviland painting. Hugh's visit to the Philadelphia Centennial Exposition introduced him to the elusive sang-de-boeuf or oxblood glaze featured on Ming porcelain, which he would strive to achieve for well over a decade at tremendous costs.

James passed away in 1880, and Alexander moved to California in 1884, leaving Hugh in charge of the pottery and his oxblood glaze experiments. The time and energy spent doing research were taken away from producing saleable artwares. Out of funds, Hugh closed the pottery in 1889.

Wealthy patrons supported the founding of a new company, the short-lived Chelsea Pottery U.S., where the emphasis became the production of Chinese-inspired crackleware, vases and tableware underglaze-painted in blue with simplified or stylized designs. The commercially viable pottery found a new home in Dedham, Massachusetts, in 1896, whose name it adopted. Hugh died in 1908, and the production of crackleware continued until 1943.

The ware is usually stamped CKAW within a diamond or Chelsea Keramic Art Works/Robertson & Sons. Our advisors for this category are Suzanne Perrault and David Rago; they are listed in the Directory under New Jersey. See also Dedham Pottery.

Pilgrim flask, pilgrim in landscape, glossy teal on olive body, H. Robertson, CKAW, 6¾", EX, $750.00; Medallion, trumpeting post-boy, forest green, Hugh Robertson/James Kelly, 4x4¾", $825.00; Pillow vase, flowers, butterflies, and bees, teal and brown mottle, footed, artist signed, 11x7", $725.00. (Photo courtesy David Rago Auctions)

Ewer, cvd geometrics & scrolls, gr gloss, CKAW, ca 1885, 11¼" ...**1,650.00**
Match/cigarette holder, man's head over sq compartment, Robertson, 6"...**1,200.00**
Plate, Upside Down Dolphin & Baby, CPUS clover mk, 8½" **600.00**
Tile, emb floral, caramel w/gr tones, 1800s, 5¾" sq..................**1,430.00**
Vase, oxblood, shouldered, 9x4"..**3,750.00**
Vase, oxblood w/red streaks/some crystalline, lt pitting, 8¾x4¼"...**3,100.00**

Chicago Crucible

For only a few years during the 1920s, the Chicago (Illinois) Crucible Company made a limited amount of decorative pottery in addition to their regular line of architectural wares. Examples are very scarce today; they carry a variety of marks, all with the company name and location.

Match holder, fireplace; frog figural, blk matt, 5x6x6" **415.00**
Soap dish, pale gr, nude posed face down, 1½x5x8" **360.00**
Vase, mottled green, twisted mushroom form, factory chips, 9" ...**1,500.00**
Vase, spade leaves on twisted stems, curdled med gr matt, 9x6"...**1,600.00**

Children's Books

Children's books, especially those from the Victorian era, are

charming collectibles. Colorful lithographic illustrations that once delighted little boys in long curls and tiny girls in long stockings and lots of ribbons and lace have lost none of their appeal. Some collectors limit themselves to a specific subject, while others may be far more interested in the illustrations. First editions are more valuable than later issues, and condition and rarity are very important factors to consider before making your purchase. For further information we recommend *Collector's Guide to Children's Books, 1850 – 1950*, and *Boys' and Girls' Book Series*, both by Diane McClure Jones and Rosemary Jones; and *Whitman Juvenile Books Reference & Value Guide* by David and Virginia Brown. All are available from Collector Books or your local bookstore.

ABC for the Library, ME Little, Antheneum, hardcover, 1975, EX..**10.00**
Adventures of Isabel, Nash, Trumpet Club Special Ed, 1992, EX...**20.00**
Adventures of S Holmes, Doyle, Whitman, pictorial cover, 1965, EX...**7.50**
Alfred Hitchcock's Daring Detectives, Random House, 1969, 208-pg, EX....**18.00**
Amy's Long Night, Garber, Whitman Tell-A-Tale, 1970, EX **10.00**
Andy Panda's Rescue, Lantz, Whitman, pictorial cover, 1949, EX ...**8.50**
At Daddy's Office, Misch, Knopf, Gibralter Library Binding, 1946, EX...**12.50**
Barbara & 5 Little Purrs, EL Gould, HM Caldwell, cloth cover, 1908 ...**20.00**
Behind Black Brick: Modern, Benedict, HKH Silk Co, 1920, VG..**15.00**
Big Brown Bear, Duplaix, Golden Press, 1944, 1947, 2nd printing, EX..**20.00**
Black Stallion Returns, Farley, Random House, pictorial cover, 1983...**12.50**
Bobbsey Twins, Merry Days Indoors...; Hope, Grosset & Dunlap, 1928, EX **15.00**
Book of Cowboys, Holling, Platt & Munk, cloth hardcover, 1936, EX....**18.50**
Boy Scouts in Blue Ridge, H Carter, AL Burt Co, 1913, VG..........**9.50**
Cat & Fiddle, Jeter, Parents' Magazine Press, 1968, 1st ed, EX **14.50**
Child's Book of Planes, Sinnickson, Caxton Pub, hardcover, 1950s, EX **15.00**
Choctaw Code, Davis, McGrall Hill, hardcover, 1961, EX **15.00**
Christmas Gifts, Cousins, Doubleday, hardcover, 1952 ed, EX......**15.00**
Cinderella, translated/illus by Marcia Brown, c 1954, 27-pg, EX ..**10.00**
Clue of Leaning Chimney, Keene, Grosset & Dunlap, 1967, EX **7.50**
Cowboys, Gorsline, Random House Pictureback, softcover, 1978, EX ...**12.50**
Crocks of Gold, CR Brink, EB Taylor illus, Saalfield, #4110, 1940, EX..**14.50**
Dilly the Dinosaur, Bradman, Weekly Reader Books, 1987, NM.....**9.00**
Dinosaurs, Gibbons, Scholastic, 1993, 1st printing, EX................**47.50**
Dreams of Victory, Conford, Little Brown, 1973, NM w/jacket **20.00**
Emma, Stevenson, Greenwillow Books, 1985, 1st ed, EX w/jacket..**12.50**
First Book of Antarctic, Icenhower, Watts, 1956, 7th printing, EX...**15.00**
First Dog, Jan Brette, Trumpet Club, c 1988, 1992 printing, EX **7.50**
Five Little Peppers Midway, Sidney, Lothrop Lee & Shepard, 1918, EX..**15.00**
Flyaways & Goldilocks, Hardy, Grosset & Dulap, cloth cover, 1925, EX...**15.00**
Four Little Foxes, Woods, Saalfield #4110, 1940, EX **13.50**
Glob, O'Reilly, Viking, hardcover, 1952, NM w/jacket **32.00**
God & World He Made, Walton, Chariot Books/Cook, 1986, 1st printing, NM.....**6.00**
Hans Brinker...Silver Skates..., MM Dodge, Grosset & Dunlap, 1945, VG......**13.50**
Hat Book, L Shortall, Golden Shape Book, #5912, 1965, EX **7.00**
Helen Keller: Story of My Life, Keller, Pendulum Press, 1969, EX ..**12.50**
Hope for Flowers, T Paulus, Paulist Press, 1972, EX **12.50**
Hoppity, M Barrows, Rand McNally Junior Elf #8144, 1967, EX..**10.00**
How a Seed Grows, Jorden, Crowell, Book Club ed, 1960, EX **7.00**
How Six Found Christmas, Hyman, Little Brown, 1969, 1st ed, EX w/jacket..**35.00**
I Am a Bunny, Scarry, Golden Sturdy Book, hardcover, 1963, EX ..**25.00**
I Live in the City ABC, Moore, Whitman Tell-A-Tale Book, 1969, EX..**6.00**
Joyful the Morning, Unwin, David McKay, 1963, 1st ed, NM w/jacket....**15.00**
Kidnapped, Stevenson, Pendulum Press, Elephant Edition, 1959, EX...**12.50**
Lassie Come Home, Knight, Holt-Rinehart-Winston, 1978, 1st print, EX **15.00**
Let's Take a Trip..., Raymond, Whitman, hardcover, 1951, 1st ed, EX..**10.00**
Lewis Carroll: Biography; A Clarke, Schocken Books, 1979, EX w/jacket...**24.50**
Little By Little, Optic, Donohue, pictorial hardcover, ca 1960, EX...**10.00**
Little Elephant, Broderick, Rand McNally Jr Elf #8007, 1959, EX...**9.50**
Little Eskimo Boy, Nigalek, Platt & Munk, 1935, EX....................**15.00**
Little Lost Angel, Heath, Rand McNally Jr Elf #8205, 1953, EX..**10.00**
Little People & Big Fib, Wein, Fisher-Price, Marvel, 1987, NM.....**9.00**

Little Toy Train, Stahlmann, Rand McNally Jr Elf #8031, 1965, VG+ ...8.00
McBroom & Big Wind, Fleischman, WW Norton & Co, 1967, 1st ed, VG ..7.50

Morning Face, Gene Stratton-Porter, Doubleday Page & Co., 1st edition, 1916, EX, $275.00.

My Diary, M O'Brien, Lippincotte, 1947, 1st ed, EX w/jacket 30.00
My Treasury of Fairy Tails, Burnford/Barnham, Zigzag Pub, 1997, M......22.50
Night Before Christmas, Moore, Random House Pictureback, 1975, EX 8.00
Outdoor Chums in the Forest, Capt Q Allen, Goldsmith, 1911, VG...8.50
Pinocchio: Tale of Puppet, C Collodi, MA Donohue, no date, VG..12.00
Puss in Boots, Perrault, Golden Book, 1987, 20-pg, EX 9.50
Rainbow Book of People & Places, Mead, World Pub, 1972 printing, EX........17.50
Robin on the River, Hayes, Little Brown, 1950, 1st ed, EX w/jacket..15.00
Steadfast Tin Soldier, HC Anderson, Little Brown & Co, 1983, 1st ed, EX.....27.50
Strike-Out King, J DeVries, World Pub, 1948, 216-pg, VG.............8.50
Stuck in the Tub!, Van Hulst, Golden Tell-a-Tale Book, 1987, 1st ed, EX ...8.00
Swiss Family Robinson, Wyss, Grosset & Dunlap, 1949, EX.........18.50
Tales From Shakespeare, Lamb, JC Winston, orange cover, 1934, EX..22.50
Tell Me About Heaven, Jones, Rand McNally, 1956, 1st ed, EX w/jacket .30.00
Treasure Island, Stevenson, JC Winston, c Great Britain, 1924, EX....28.50
Tum Tum Jolly Elephant..., Richard Barnum, Barse & Co, 1915, VG...27.50
Who Cried for Pie, V Buffington, Troll Assoc, 1970, EX 18.50
Witches Four, M Broan, Parent's Magazine Press, 1980, EX.........14.00
Yellow Fairy Book, Lang, Grosset & Dunlap, cloth cover, no date, EX..17.50
Yellow River, Margaret Rau, Messner, 1959, 1st ed, EX.................10.00
Zoo That Moved, Micklowitz, Follet, hardcover, 1968, EX w/jacket ...25.00
365 Bedtime Stories, Whitman, pictorial hardcover, 1944, EX.....58.00

Children's Things

Nearly every item devised for adult furnishings has been reduced to child size — furniture, dishes, sporting goods, even some tools. All are very collectible. During the late seventeenth and early eighteenth centuries, miniature china dinnerware sets were made both in China and in England. They were not intended primarily as children's playthings, however, but instead were made to furnish miniature rooms and cabinets that provided a popular diversion for the adults of that period. By the nineteenth century, the emphasis had shifted, and most of the small-scaled dinnerware and tea sets were made for children's play.

Late in the nineteenth century and well into the twentieth, toy pressed glass dishes were made, many in the same patterns. Today these toy dishes often fetch prices in the same range or above those for the 'grown-ups'!

Our advisors for this category are Margaret and Kenn Whitmyer; you will find their address in the Directory under Ohio. See also A B C Plates; Blue Willow; Clothing; Stickley; etc.

China

Bowl, berry; Pastel Blue Rib & Floral, KT&K 6.00
Bowl, Blue Marble, oval, England, 4½" 55.00
Bowl, Blue-Banded Ironstone, 8-sided, Iron Stone, 4" 20.00
Bowl, Myrtle Wreath, oval, JM&S, 5" 27.00
Bowl, soup; Flow Blue Dogwood, Minton, 4⅛" 48.00
Bowl, Twin Flower, flow bl, England, 4¾" 80.00
Canister, Blue Banded, Germany, 3⅝" 34.00
Casserole, Bluebird, Noritake, w/lid, 6" 45.00
Casserole, Gold Floral, England, 5½" 55.00
Casserole, Maiden-Hair Fern, England, 5½" 35.00
Casserole, Twin Flowers, England, 5" 132.00
Comport, Bluebird, Choisy & LeRoi, 4¼" 75.00
Compote, Walley Ironstone, England, 5¾" 400.00
Creamer, Angel w/Shining Star, Germany, 3¾" 37.00
Creamer, Butterfly, Made in Japan, 2¼" 9.00
Creamer, Chinaman (figural), Japan, 2¼" 42.00
Creamer, Daffodil, Southern Potteries, 3" 20.00
Creamer, Dutch Children, Made in Japan 13.00
Creamer, Gaudy Ironstone, England, 2⅜" 48.00
Creamer, Girl w/Pets, Allerton & Sons, 3⅛" 17.00
Creamer, Joseph, Mary & Donkey, Germany, 3" 40.00
Creamer, Kewpies, c Mrs Rose O'Neill Wilson, Bavaria..............65.00
Creamer, Mary Had a Little Lamb, England, 1½" 15.00
Creamer, Old Moss Rose, brn & wht, Am 18.00
Creamer, Roman Chariots, bl & wht, Cauldon, England, 2"........40.00
Creamer, Stick Spatter, Staffordshire, 3⅛" 46.00
Creamer, Tan Lustre & White, England, 3¼" 12.00
Cup, Dr Franklin's Maxims, bl transfer, unmk, 2¼x3", EX.........480.00
Cup, Water Hen, England, 2" 22.00
Cup & saucer, House That Jack Built, Germany, 3⅜" 25.00
Cup & saucer, Mini Floral, mc on wht, England, 2⅛" & 4⅜" 13.00
Cup & saucer, Nursery Rhyme, Germany, 1¾" & 3¾" 18.00
Cup & saucer, Orient, bl & wht, England, 3" 28.00
Cup & saucer, Silhouette Children, Czech, 1⅞" & 3¼" 12.00
Egg whip, Blue Onion, Germany, 4½" 180.00
Gravy boat, Kite Fliers, England, 3¼" 125.00
Ladle, Greek Key, mk RSR (Ridgway, Sparks & Ridgway), 5" 15.00
Mug, blk transfer 'William' in beaded/vine fr, Staffordshire, 1830...220.00
Mug, Blue Willow, Coalport (Made in England), 1⅞" 22.00
Mug, Catherine, brn transfer, 2¾" 250.00
Mug, Football, blk transfer w/mc, 2½" 130.00
Plate, Barnyard Animals, Germany, 5½" 14.00
Plate, Basket, flow bl, England, 5" 20.00
Plate, Basket, Salem China, 6¼" 7.00
Plate, Chauffeur w/Lady, pk lustre 12.00
Plate, Dutch Figures, bl & wht, Japan.........................5.00
Plate, Father Christmas & the Children, Germany, 5" 25.00
Plate, Flowers That Never Fade, children, blk transfer, 5", EX ...180.00
Plate, Friends, Germany 15.00
Plate, Godey Prints, Salem China, 6¼" 5.00
Plate, Holly, Germany, early 1900s 25.00
Plate, Humphrey's Clock, Ridgway's England, 3⅞" 12.00
Plate, Kite Fliers, bl & wht, England, 3½" 48.00
Plate, Myrtle Wreath, JM&S, 3¼" 8.00
Plate, Pink Open Rose, Made in England, 4½" 7.00
Plate, Robinson Crusoe, blk transfer/mc, 1920s, 6", EX.................75.00
Plate, Sunset, Made in Japan, 4¼" 5.00
Plate, Tiger Hunt, bl transfer, emb floral rim, 4¾" 130.00
Platter, Butterfly, England, 6¼" 18.00
Platter, Fancy Loop, England, 6" 30.00
Platter, Humphrey's Clock, Ridgway's England, 8" 47.00
Platter, Myrtle Wreath, JM&S, 5¾" 30.00

Platter, Rosamond, flow bl, Bistro England, 4¼" 60.00
Platter, Spirit of Children, England, 5" 24.00
Rolling pin, Mary had a Little Lamb, 9"..................................195.00
Sugar bowl, Banded Floral, England, w/lid, 4½" 20.00
Sugar bowl, Gaudy Ironstone, England, w/lid, 4" 72.00
Sugar bowl, Godey Prints, Salem China, 2¼"..............................12.00
Sugar bowl, Humphrey's Clock, Ridgway's England....................33.00
Sugar bowl, Playful Cats, Germany, w/lid, 2¾"..........................45.00
Sugar bowl, Standing Pony, gr lustre, Germany, w/lid..................30.00
Sugar bowl, Sunset, Made in Japan, w/lid, 3⅛"..........................13.00
Teacup & saucer, Acorn, England, 2" & 4¾"..............................18.00
Teacup & saucer, Dutch Windmill, Germany, 2¼" & 4⅝" 25.00
Teacup & saucer, Peter Pan, Japan, 1¼" & 3½" 12.00
Teapot, Banded Floral, England, 5½" 40.00
Teapot, Blue Banded, Dimmock & Co, 3¾" 100.00
Teapot, Blue Willow, Made in Japan, 3¾"................................75.00
Teapot, Dutch Children on tan lustre, Made in Japan..................27.00
Teapot, Godey Print, Salem China.......................................55.00
Teapot, May, bulbous, bl & wht, England, 5"............................75.00
Teapot, mc floral, Nippon, 3¼"..27.00
Teapot, Pink Rose, Germany, 6¼" 60.00
Teapot, St Nicholas, Germany, 5½" 200.00
Teapot, Teddy Bear, Germany, 6½" 200.00
Teapot, Water Hen, England, 5¼"..90.00

Tea set, elephant figural serving pieces, orange lustre, red Japan mark, fifteen pieces, serves four, from $280.00 to $380.00. (Photo courtesy Carole Bess White)

Tray, Dimity, gr on cream, England, 4½" dia.............................22.00
Tureen, Athens, England, 3½"..55.00
Tureen, Calico, brn on cream, 3¾".......................................60.00
Tureen stand, Livesley Fern & Floral, England, 5½".....................28.00
Underplate, Blue Marble, England, 5½"..................................50.00
Wash bowl & pitcher, Blue Floral, England 225.00
Waste bowl, By the Mill, brn on wht, Methvin & Sons................40.00
Waste bowl, Gaudy Ironstone, England, 2⅞"............................110.00
Waste bowl, Lady Standing by Urn, 2⅞".................................48.00

Furniture

Examples with no dimensions given are child size unless noted doll size.

Key: ds — doll size

Armchair, crest, 5 spindles, bamboo-trn arms & legs, old bl pnt, 21"...300.00
Armchair, director-style, cvd swan's-head arm terminals, pnt 600.00
Armchair, maple, trn posts, cane seat, 2-slat bk, rfn, 18" 135.00
Armchair, oak Lincolnshire, spindle bk, rush seat, 30" 1,400.00
Armchair, trn legs, scrolled arms, reuphl seat, Vict, 21x11"........225.00
Armchair, walnut, 6 trn spindles, raised pegs, old dk finish, 18"....275.00
Armchair, Windsor style, 4-spindle bk, rnd seat, rprs, 20"..........200.00
Armchair, 2-slat ladderbk, brn pnt over red, rpl tape seat, 10"....200.00
Armchair, 3-slat bk, trn stiles/arms, rush seat, red stain, 25" 865.00
Bed, cherry, chip-cvd, rolled ft/head brds, ball finials, Zoar OH, 43"..2,400.00
Bed, cherry cannon-ball rope type, trn posts, rfn, ds, 14x22" 200.00
Bed, soft wood, vertical spindles, sq rail below & above, ds, 22" L...100.00
Bench, cut-out silhouette ends, old mc pnt, some wear, 12x12x7"...1,265.00
Blanket chest, maple QA, rose-head nails, dvtl drw, 23x27x13"...8,250.00
Bureau, bl w/red & mc pnt birds, ornately cut mirror fr, Pat 1881, 28"..700.00
Chair, bamboo Windsor, 6-spindle bk, shaped seat, old yel, 31" 300.00
Chair, curly maple, 3-slat, splayed legs, rush seat, old rfn, 17" 1,700.00
Chair, ladderbk; pnt pine, trn finials/stiles, rush seat, 1800s, 15"...450.00
Chair, mahog, Chpndl-style wing bk, worn uphl, 1900s, 29" 350.00
Chair, mahog, velvet-uphl seat, English, 22" 360.00
Chair, Windsor birdcage, bamboo trn, shield seat, 1890s, 21" pr....600.00
Chest, cherry Sheraton w/inlay, 5-drw, dbl-tab construction, 20x18x10"....1,980.00
Chest, dk umber feather grpt on mustard, 3-drw, wood pulls, 16x12", EX...200.00
Chest, pine, orig pnt & decoupage, 3-drw, PA, 9½x7x5"...........440.00
Chest, pine, 6-brd, hinged top, old cream pnt, 1800s, 16x29x13"..600.00
Chest, pine w/wht pnt, Am, 19th C, ds, 15⅜x13⅜x7¾"............200.00
Chest, pnt maple Fed, 4-drw, 1825-35, 22x17x11"..................1,850.00
Chest, 6-brd, red pnt, cut-out ft, 1790s, 14x21x9" 1,150.00
Chest over drw, pine, red pnt, hinged top, early 1800s, 19x18x13" ..1,380.00
Cradle, bentwood, 2 wheels, orig pnt w/silver striping, 54".........600.00
Cradle, brn/yel comb pnt w/blk trim, cut-out hdls, 35" L............275.00
Cradle, cherry & poplar, hooded type, old red wash, rpr, 34x43x22"....285.00
Cradle, curly maple, cut-out hdls, dvtl corners, 20x41"..............385.00
Cradle, mahog, flamed vnr hood, mortised rockers, dvtl, 40"......330.00
Cradle, mahog, w/hood, cut-out rockers, scrolled details, 44"..1,100.00
Cradle, mahog Am, Gothic arch hanger, trestle base, 1840s, 48x39x21"....1,435.00
Cradle, pine, hooded type, orig red & blk grpt, dvtl, rprs, 40" 150.00
Cradle, walnut, scroll bk, shaped rockers, rfn, 19th C, 21x39x18"....230.00
Crib, birch, tall slender posts, 4 urn splats ea side, 70" H............220.00
Crib, poplar w/worn blk sponging on yel, old bl int, rprs, 42".....275.00
Crib, walnut Southern w/mosquito net bars & spindles, 1850, 47x35x38"...1,000.00
Cupboard, chip-cvd pine w/dk varnish, dbl doors, 7 dwrs, 21x15"....415.00
Cupboard, oak w/alligatored finish, panel do, dvtl drw, 30x20x12"...375.00
Cupboard, pine w/worn finish, panel door, shelves, 17x13x6" 175.00
Cupboard, step-bk, cherry, cornice, shelves, 2 doors, 1850s, 37x24"...1,725.00
Cupboard, step-bk, walnut, open shelf, 2 drws, dbl do, 27x16x9"...865.00
Cupboard, step-bk; 4-drw on cut-out bracket base, no pnt, 30x19x7" ...700.00
Desk, slant lid, birch & maple QA, compartments, old rfn, 26x28" 2,800.00
Desk, slant lid, gallery, 2 short drw, fitted int, 38x20x22" 1,000.00
Desk, slant lid, 4-drw, w/eagle brasses, rstr, 31x26x15".............5,175.00
Dresser, oak w/serpentine top drw+2, brass pulls, mirror, 26" 600.00
Dry sink, poplar/pine w/old brn pnt, drw, porc pulls, wire nails, 34"..660.00
Highboy, mahog QA style, 5 top drws, 3 in base, early 20th C, 45" ...2,200.00
Highchair, ash/cherry, ring-trn stiles, spindle bk, splint seat, 35"...1,000.00
Highchair, bamboo Windsor, sm medallion in crest, rprs, 36".....500.00
Highchair, blk/red grpt w/gold & red stenciled crest, 3-spindle, 35"...440.00
Highchair, hard & softwood w/pnt traces, spindle bk, 31" 200.00
Highchair, mixed woods w/cane bk & seat, Vict, EX...................250.00
Highchair, trn maple & ash, urn finials, old red wash, 37"..........315.00
Highchair, Windsor, thumb-bk spindles, bamboo legs, old pnt, 34"..400.00
Highchair, Windsor w/bamboo trnings, old blk pnt, PA, 34½"..385.00
Highchair, yew English, 8 trn spindles & supports, 37" 635.00
Mammy's bench w/rockers, 5 cvd spindles, grpt w/floral, 1800s, 14" L..850.00
Potty chair, rabbit-ear style, orig blk pnt w/gold pinstriping, 21"..110.00

Potty chair, walnut cvd Louis XVI style, old rfn, 34".................250.00
Recamier, oak fr, classical style, reuphl, late 19th C, 15x40" 300.00
Rocker, bent elements intertwined, solid splat, plank seat, 1900s...250.00
Rocker, blk pnt w/mc floral crest, red arms, NY, 26½".............220.00
Rocker, Boston type w/orig blk pnt & stenciling, 23"...................80.00
Rocker, brn comb pnt w/HP foliage, w/arms/trn legs, plank seat, 22"...195.00
Rocker, wing-bk, pine w/old red stain, rpl rocker, 25" 200.00
Rocker, 3-slat ladderbk, splint seat, spindle arms, 25½" 220.00
Settee, orig pnt/stencil, spindled bk, plank seat, 1800s, 22x26x9"...3,000.00
Stand, Fed tiger maple, drw, ball ft, early 19th C, 19x17x15"..3,000.00
Table, drop-leaf; pine w/dk finish, trn legs, 22x22x14"+7" leaves....385.00
Table, walnut, 8-sided top w/ornate cvd 4-leg base, 4½x5x5" 375.00
Table, work; birch & pine w/old red wash, 2-brd top, 17x25x16"....330.00
Table, work; tapered/splay legs, mortise/tenon built, 13x15x28" 135.00

Tester bedstead, carved and reeded footposts, complete with fittings, 1830s, doll size, 27x23¾x16¼", EX, $1,450.00.

Glass

Acorn, butter dish, frosted, 4"..350.00
Acorn, creamer, frosted, 3⅜" 250.00
Arched Panel, pitcher, cobalt, 3¾" 150.00
Arched Panel, tumbler, pk, gr or cobalt, Westmoreland, 2", ea.....30.00
Arched Panel, water set, cobalt, 3¾" pitcher+6 2" tumblers.......300.00
Arrowhead & Oval, table set, 4-pc..135.00
Baby Thumbprint, cake stand, 2" 125.00
Baby Thumbprint, compote, flared rim, US Glass 200.00
Banded Portland, pitcher, water; blush...55.00
Beaded Swirl, butter dish, amber or cobalt, Westmoreland, 2⅜"...150.00
Beaded Swirl, spooner, amber or cobalt, Westmoreland, 2¼", ea.....150.00
Beaded Swirl, sugar bowl, amber or cobalt, w/lid, 3¾", ea 125.00
Betty Jane, pie plate, McKee, #97, 4½"..12.00
Betty Jane, ramekin, McKee, #294..6.50
Bucket (Wooden Pail), spooner, Bryce Bros, 2½".......................180.00
Bucket (Wooden Pail), sugar bowl, Bryce Bros, 3¾" 200.00
Button Panel, creamer 50.00
Clear & Diamond Panel, butter dish, gr, 2⅞" 65.00
Clear & Diamond Panel, butter dish, gr, 4" 130.00
Cloud Band, butter dish, milk glass w/pnt decor, Gillinder, 3¾" ...200.00
Colonial, spooner, Cambridge..25.00
Colonial Flute, punch cup, 1⅞"...14.00
Dewdrop, butter dish, bl or amber, 2⅝", ea.................................190.00
Diamond Ridge/D&M No 48, creamer, Duncan & Sons, 2½"......85.00
Doric & Pansy, creamer, pk, 2¾"...35.00
Doyle No 500, tray, bl, 6⅝"..80.00
Dutch Boudoir, bowl, bl opaque, 1⅛"...120.00
Dutch Boudoir, pomade, milk glass, 1½" (+)...............................125.00
Fine Cut Star & Fan, butter dish, Higbee, 2½"..............................35.00

Galloway, pitcher, clear w/gold, 3⅞" 35.00
Galloway, tumbler, blush, US Glass, 2"..20.00
Galloway No 15071, water set, blush, US Glass, 7-pc.................250.00
Hawaiian Lei, spooner..25.00
Hickman, condiment set, complete...45.00
Homespun, plate, 4½"..7.00
Homespun, teapot, pk, w/lid, Jeannette..125.00
Horizontal Threads, butter dish, clear w/ruby stain, 1⅞"............120.00
Kidibake, bread baker, Fry, clear opal, #1928, 5"..........................65.00
Kidibake, casserole, clear opal, w/lid, #1938, 4½"........................85.00
Kittens, banana dish, marigold..185.00
Kittens, cup & saucer, marigold, Fenton, 2⅛" & 4½" 140.00
Lamb, spooner, 2⅛"...110.00
Laurel, sugar bowl, French Ivory, 2⅜"..35.00
Liberty Bell, butter dish, 2¼"..225.00
Lion, cup & saucer, crystal w/frosted head, Gillinder, 1¾" & 3¼"...80.00
Little Tots, creamer, gr, England, 1⅜"..10.00
Mardi Gras, spooner...45.00
Michigan, pitcher, water...40.00
Michigan, stein, crystal w/gold, US Glass, 2⅞"..............................55.00
Moderntone, set, beige/aqua/rose/Sunny Yellow, 16-pc..............220.00
Moderntone, teapot, wht, 3½"..110.00
Nursery Rhyme, bowl, master berry 90.00
Nursery Rhyme, pitcher, US Glass, 4¼" 120.00
Optic, creamer, gr 30.00
Pattee Cross, bowl, berry; US Glass, 1" 12.00
Pennsylvania, creamer, crystal w/gold, US Glass, 2½".................56.00
Pennsylvania, creamer, gr...110.00
Pennsylvania, spooner, gr, US Glass, 2½" 95.00
Pillar, mug...12.00
Puritan, mug..16.00
Rex (Fancy Cut), butter dish, 2⅜" 42.00
Rooster No 140, nappy, King Glass, 3"..140.00
Rose in Snow, mug, appl hdl 35.00
Sawtooth, sugar bowl, w/lid, 4⅞" 50.00
Sawtooth Band No 1225, creamer, Heisey, 2½"............................60.00
Standing Lamb, spooner, frosted...1,100.00
Stippled Diamond, creamer, bl or amber, 2¼", ea.......................100.00
Stippled Vines & Beads, butter dish, 2⅜"...................................110.00
Stippled Vines & Beads, creamer, NM 35.00
Sultan, creamer, chocolate, McKee, 2½" 320.00
Sunny Suzy, casserole, w/lid, Anchor Hocking, 10-oz...................10.00
Sweetheart, creamer, Cambridge, 2¼"..12.00
Tappan, butter dish, 3"..34.00
Thumbelina, punch bowl, w/4 cups 65.00
Tulip & Honeycomb, sugar bowl, w/lid, Federal, 3¾"...................35.00
Twist No 137, butter dish, bl opal, Albany, 5⅜"..........................200.00
Two Band, sugar bowl, w/lid, 3¾" 65.00
Wee Branches, spooner 85.00
Whirligig, punch bowl, US Glass, 4¾"...35.00
Wild Rose, butter dish, milk glass, Greentown, 3½".....................75.00
Wild Rose, punch bowl, milk glass 95.00

Miscellaneous

Buckboard wagon, dk gr pnt w/mc decor, wooden spoke wheels, 48" L, EX...1,750.00
Coaster, spring-board; South Paris #84, orig ft brake, 42" L.....2,300.00
Cooking set, Farberware, Linemar, 1950s, NMIB 275.00
Doll carriage, Ellis type, fancy pnt, orig fenders & canopy, 26x36"...925.00
Ice-cream freezer, Dana-Peerless, wooden bbl w/CI crank, bail hdl, EX ...125.00
Iron, Wolverine, 1950s, electric, MIB 35.00
Noah's ark, pine w/stencil & HP, 36 animals & Noah, rprs, 7x16" ..700.00
Rocking horse, hide-covered w/real horsehair mane & tail, 64", VG...1,050.00
Scale, Kenton, red-pnt CI w/NP balance beam & weights, MIB...550.00

Scale, litho tin w/Felix the Cat motif, 7" L, EX...........................550.00
Sewing basket, wicker, sq w/lid & bottom shelf on 4 legs, 17x9", EX+ ..75.00
Sled, HP mc daisies, oak runners w/iron straps (weak), 1890s, 30" L..475.00
Sled, orig red pnt w/lake scene & mc lines, pnt touchup, 55½" ...385.00
Sled, pnt oak & iron w/stenciling, iron runners, 7x43x12", EX ..880.00

Sled, painted wood with stenciled design, repaired runner, 32", VG, $525.00.

Sleigh, S Paris push type w/orig gr & red pnt, uphl seat, 36" 775.00
Spinning wheel, early, oak, fully functional, 28", EX.................350.00
Stove, Little Chef, Ohio Art, 1950s, NM 100.00
Stroller, metal, shows Mickey Mouse & Betty Boop, 10", VG+..1,800.00
Sweeper, Little Queen, Bissel, tin w/wood hdl, functional, 25½", EX..50.00
Tool set, Ideal, 1960s, diecast metal, 5-pc, MIB.............................15.00
Wagon, doll; mk American Express Co, paper-on-wood, 17" L, G+...350.00
Washing machine, Sunny Suzy, Wolverine, #78W, complete, 12", EXIB ..440.00
Washing set, Sunny Monday, Parker Bros, complete, EXIB 400.00

Chintz

'Chintz' is the generic name for English china with an allover floral transfer design. This eye-catching china is reminiscent of chintz dress fabric. It is colorful, bright, and cheery with its many floral designs and reminds one of an English garden in full bloom. It was produced in England during the first half of this century and stands out among other styles of china. Pattern names often found with the manufacturer's name on the bottom of pieces include Florence, Blue Chintz, English Roses, Delphinium, June Roses, Hazel, Eversham, Royalty, Sweet Pea, Summertime, and Welbeck, among others.

The older patterns tend to be composed of larger flowers, while the later, more popular lines can be quite intricate in design. And while the first collectors preferred the earthenware lines, many are now searching for the bone china dinnerware made by such firms as Shelley. You can concentrate on reassembling a favorite pattern, or you can mix two or more designs together for a charming, eclectic look. Another choice may be to limit your collection to teapots (the stacking ones are especially nice), breakfast sets, or cups and saucers.

Though the Chintz market remains very active, prices for some pieces have been significantly compromised due to their having been reproduced. For further information we recommend *Charlton Book of Chintz, I, II,* and *III,* by Susan Scott. Our advisor is Mary Jane Hastings; she is listed in the Directory under Illinois. See also Shelley.

Anemone, cheese keeper, Lord Nelson 125.00
Apple Blossom, cup & saucer, Diamond, James Kent 45.00
Balmoral, cake plate, pierced hdls, Royal Winton 525.00
Balmoral, tea set, stacking, Royal Winton 1,200.00

Bedale, breakfast set toast rack, Royal Winton 70.00
Bedale, plate, Ascot, Royal Winton, 6" 55.00
Cheadle, cup & saucer, Caughley, Royal Winton, from $115 to....185.00
Cotswold, hot water pot, Albans, Royal Winton, 6x6½" 795.00
Dorset, breakfast set, Royal Winton 500.00
Dorset, plate, Royal Winton, 7" 50.00
DuBarry, creamer, Granville, James Kent, 3¼" 75.00
DuBarry, teapot, Dmn shape, James Kent, 4½x9½" 525.00
Eleanor, coffeepot, Albans, Royal Winton 750.00
Eleanor, plate, pleated rim, Royal Winton, 8"...........................145.00
Eleanor, saucer, Royal Winton 25.00
Eleanor, teapot, Albans, Royal Winton......................................650.00
English Rose, tray, Malta, Royal Winton, 12x6" 385.00
Evesham, milk jug, globe shape, Royal Winton, rstr spout, 3¾"...295.00
Fireglow, breakfast set, Athena, rose-shaped shakers, Royal Winton ..750.00
Fireglow, hot water pot, Sexta, Royal Winton, lg 625.00
Floral Feast, sugar bowl, w/lid, Royal Winton 145.00
Florita, bowl, fluted edge, James Kent, 5" 45.00
Florita, plate, Granville, James Kent, 9" 145.00
Florita, shell bowl, wavy edge, James Kent, 8⅜x6¾"..................120.00
Florita, sweet dish, St Chelsea w/tab hdls, James Kent, 5⅜x4" 65.00
Hazel, bud vase, Clywd shape, Royal Winton 195.00
Hazel, cake plate, Ascot, cut-out hdls, Royal Winton 245.00
Hazel, cup & saucer, Royal Winton 65.00
Hazel, egg cup set, Saville, Royal Winton, 4 cups+tray.............350.00
Hazel, jug, Dutch, Royal Winton, 4" 350.00
Hazel, nut scoop, Royal Winton, 5" 175.00
Hazel, plate, Royal Winton, 9" 65.00
Hazel, shakers, Acme, Royal Winton, pr....................................115.00
Hazel, shell dish, Royal Winton, 5¼x4½" 75.00
Hazel, sugar bowl, Royal Winton 35.00
Heather, bud vase, Lord Nelson, 5" 275.00
Heather, tea set, stacking; Lord Nelson 750.00
Hydrangea, creamer, Granville, James Kent, 3⅛" 65.00
Julia, creamer & sugar bowl, Ascot, Royal Winton 350.00
Julia, cup & saucer, Royal Winton 175.00
Julia, nut dish, cut-out hdl, Royal Winton................................195.00
Julia, nut scoop, Royal Winton, rstr hdl, rare...........................195.00
Julia, plate, Ascot, Royal Winton, 6" 125.00
Julia, plate, Royal Winton, 7" 165.00
June Festival, creamer, red, Royal Winton 50.00
June Festival, cup, red, Royal Winton 20.00
Majestic, butter dish, rectangular, Royal Winton, stain...............265.00
Majestic, cup & saucer, Ascott, Royal Winton, rpr......................75.00
Majestic, cup & saucer, demitasse; can shape, Royal Winton 150.00
Majestic, nut dish, heart-shaped cut-out hdls, Royal Winton, 6⅝" ..335.00
Majestic, plate, Ascot shape, Royal Winton, 7" 165.00
Majestic, plate, Athena, Royal Winton, 6" 125.00
Majestic, serving dish, Marina, 5-section, Royal Winton, 12x10¾" ..295.00
Marguerite, cheese keeper, bl trim, Royal Winton, 7½x6¼".......250.00
Marguerite, jug, Globe shape, Royal Winton, 4½" 115.00
Marguerite, tray, Saville, bl trim, Royal Winton, 10x9¼"...........145.00
Marigold, plate, Granville, James Kent, 9" 55.00
Marina, cake plate, sq w/tab hdls, Lord Nelson, 10⅝x9⅛" 125.00
Marina, stacking teapot set, Lord Nelson...................................495.00
Marina, teapot, Lord Nelson, lg..395.00
Marion, plate, Royal Winton, 7" 175.00
Mauve Chintz, bowl, gr trim, Winterton, 3⅝" 45.00
Mayfair, cup & saucer, Raleigh, Royal Winton 75.00
Mayfair, plate, Royal Winton, 7" 115.00
Nantwich, cup & saucer, Raleigh, Royal Winton 90.00
Old Cottage, breakfast set, Royal Winton..................................500.00
Old Cottage, cheese keeper, Rex, Twin Winton 250.00
Old Cottage, creamer & sugar bowl, Royal Winton, ind.............55.00

Old Cottage, jug, Globe, Royal Winton, 4½" 215.00
Old Cottage, jug, Royal Wonton, 4½" 215.00
Old Cottage, plate, Ascot, Royal Winton, 7¾" 55.00
Old Cottage, platter, Royal Winton, 12x10" 300.00
Pansy, cup & saucer, demi; Lord Nelson 45.00
Pansy, egg cup, Bucket, Crown Ducal 85.00
Pansy, plate, Art Deco, hdld, Crown Ducal, 8" 55.00
Pansy, tray, Lord Nelson, 8¼x5¼" 65.00
Pansy, trio, Lord Nelson 95.00
Peony, mayonnaise bowl & liner, Crown Ducal 135.00
Peony, plate, Crown Ducal, 7" sq 85.00
Peony, teapot, Crown Ducal, 4-cup 435.00
Primula, jug, Crown Ducal, 3¾" 95.00
Primula, oval dish, Crown Ducal, 9¾x8¾" 100.00
Primula, toast rack, 2-slice, Crown Ducal 100.00
Queen Anne, teapot, Athena, Royal Winton, 2-3 cup 300.00
Rapture, sugar bowl, James Kent 45.00
Rosalynde, cup & saucer, demi; James Kent 95.00
Rosalynde, plate, James Kent, 7" 75.00
Rosalynde, plate, James Kent, 8" 90.00
Rosalynde, sugar bowl, James Kent 60.00
Rosalynde, toast rack, 4-slice, James Kent, rare 350.00
Rose Brocade, breakfast teapot, bl, Royal Winton 55.00
Rose DuBarry, creamer for stacking pot, Royal Winton 80.00
Rosetime, honeypot, w/lid & tray, Lord Nelson 175.00
Rosetime, plate, Lord Nelson, 8½" sq 75.00
Royalty, creamer, Vera, Royal Winton 145.00
Royalty, creamer & sugar bowl, Ascot, Royal Winton 275.00
Royalty, plate, Royal Winton, 7" 145.00
Royalty, sugar bowl, Countess, Royal Winton, ind 35.00
Royalty, tennis set, Royal Winton 175.00
Skylark, cheese keeper, Lord Nelson 155.00
Somerset, plate, Ascot, Royal Winton, 6" sq 70.00
Spring, plate, Royal Winton, 8" 115.00
Spring Glory, breakfast set, Countess, Royal Winton 495.00
Stratford, pepper shaker, Fife, Royal Winton 55.00
Summertime, breakfast set, Countess, Royal Winton, NM 650.00
Summertime, jug, Dutch shape, Royal Winton, 3¾" 160.00
Summertime, nut dish, Royal Winton, ind 95.00

Summertime pieces: Hot water pot, Albans shape, $495.00; Coffeepot, Perth shape, $850.00; Teapot, Ascot shape, $650.00; creamer and sugar bowl, $175.00; Coffeepot, Ascot shape, $850.00; Duplicate of hot water pot, $495.00. (Photo courtesy Mary Jane Hastings)

Summertime, tidbit tray, center hdl, Royal Winton, 8" dia 145.00
Sunshine, bud vase, Royal Winton, 3¼" 165.00
Sunshine, compote, allover pattern, Lily, Royal Winton, 3x6" 175.00
Sunshine, cup, Countess, Royal Winton 45.00
Victorian Rose, breakfast toast rack, Royal Winton 115.00
Victorian Rose, nut dish, Ascot, Royal Winton, ind 110.00
Victorian Rose, tray, unusual shape, Royal Winton, 8x5" 295.00
Welbeck, jam jar, Rosebud, rstr lid, Royal Winton 245.00
Welbeck, plate, Ascot, Royal Winton, 6" 180.00
White Crocus, teapot, Albans, Royal Winton, 2-cup 450.00

Chocolate Glass

Jacob Rosenthal developed chocolate glass, a rich shaded opaque brown sometimes referred to as caramel slag, in 1900 at the Indiana Tumbler and Goblet Company of Greentown, Indiana. Later, other companies produced similar ware. Only the latter is listed here. See also Greentown. Our advisors for this category are Jerry and Sandi Garrett; they are listed in the Directory under Indiana.

Bowl, Aldine, oval, w/lid 1,650.00
Bowl, Chrysanthemum Leaf, 7" 550.00
Bowl, sauce; Water Lily & Cattails, Fenton, 4" 140.00
Bowl, Shield w/Daisy & Button, 8⅜" 1,300.00
Bowl, Wild Rose w/Bowknot, 8½" 200.00
Box, Aurora, rectangular, open, 9x5½" 1,500.00
Box, dresser; rectangular, w/lid, 4¼x3½" 450.00
Box, jewel; Venetian, w/lid 400.00
Butter dish, File 2,500.00
Butter dish, Fleur-de-lis 750.00
Butter dish, Geneva 500.00
Butter dish, Wild Rose w/Scrolling, child sz 750.00
Candle holder, griffin 3,250.00
Celery holder, Chrysanthemum Leaf, 6" 900.00
Celery holder, Fleur-de-Lis, 5¾" 325.00
Celery tray, Jubilee, 10" 300.00
Compote, jelly; Chrysanthemum Leaf, 4½" dia 325.00
Compote, jelly; Geneva, McKee 125.00
Compote, jelly; Majestic, McKee 650.00
Compote, Melrose, 7¾" 200.00
Cracker jar, Chrysanthemum Leaf, w/lid 2,500.00
Creamer, Aldine 1,300.00
Creamer, Cattail & Water Lily 475.00
Creamer, Wild Rose w/Bowknot 185.00
Creamer, Wild Rose w/Scrolling, child sz, 2¾", NM 175.00
Dish, Honeycomb, rectangular, Royal Glass, 6¾x4" 400.00
Mug, Serenade, 4¾" 100.00
Mug, Swirl 600.00
Nappy, Navarre, hdld 175.00
Novelty, smoking set, McKee & Bros, 3-pc 1,100.00
Pickle dish, Aurora, violin shape 175.00
Pitcher, milk; Feather 1,500.00
Pitcher, Rose Garland 3,000.00
Shaker, Big Rib 575.00
Shaker, Geneva 375.00
Shaker, Wild Rose w/Bowknot 275.00
Spooner, Fleur-de-Lis 175.00
Sugar bowl, Aldine, w/lid 1,750.00
Syrup, Geneva, metal lid 700.00
Toothpick holder, Chrysanthemum Leaf 800.00
Toothpick holder, Kingfisher 1,000.00
Tray, comb & brush; Venetian, McKee, 8x10" 375.00
Tumbler, File 600.00
Tumbler, Geneva, McKee, 3⅞" 110.00
Tumbler, Uneeda Milk Biscuit, Nat'l Biscuit Co, 5¾" 80.00
Tumbler, Water Lily & Cattails, Fenton, from $300 to 200.00
Tumbler, Wild Rose w/Bowknot 85.00

Vase, #400, Fenton, 6" 600.00
Vase, Beaded Triangle, 6¼" 175.00

Christmas Collectibles

Christmas past... lovely mementos from long ago attest to the ostentatious Victorian celebrations of the season.

St. Nicholas, better known as Santa, has changed much since 300 A.D. when the good Bishop Nicholas showered needy children with gifts and kindness. During the early eighteenth century, Santa was portrayed as the kind gift-giver to well-behaved children and the stern switch-bearing disciplinarian to those who were bad. In 1822 Clement Clark Moore, a New York poet, wrote his famous *Night Before Christmas*, and the Santa he described was jolly and jovial — a lovable old elf who was stern with no one. Early Santas wore robes of yellow, brown, blue, green, red, white, or even purple. But Thomas Nast, who worked as an illustrator for *Harper's Weekly*, was the first to depict Santa in a red suit instead of the traditional robe and to locate him the entire year at the North Pole headquarters.

Today's collectors prize early Santa figures, especially those in robes of fur or mohair or those dressed in an unusual color. Some early examples of Christmas memorabilia are the pre-1870 ornaments from Dresden, Germany. These cardboard figures — angels, gondolas, umbrellas, dirigibles, and countless others — sparkled with gold and silver trim. Late in the 1870s, blown glass ornaments were imported from Germany. There were over 6,000 recorded designs, all painted inside with silvery colors. From 1890 through 1910, blown glass spheres were often decorated with beads, tassels, and tinsel rope.

Christmas lights, made by Sandwich and some of their contemporaries, were either pressed or mold-blown glass shaped into a form similar to a water tumbler. They were filled with water and then hung from the tree by a wire handle; oil floating on the surface of the water served as fuel for the lighted wick.

Kugels are glass ornaments that were made as early as 1820 and as late as 1890. Ball-shaped examples are more common than the fruit and vegetable forms and have been found in sizes ranging from 1" to 14" in diameter. They were made of thick glass with heavy brass caps, in cobalt, green, gold, silver, red, and occasionally in amethyst.

Although experiments involving the use of electric light bulbs for the Christmas tree occurred before 1900, it was 1903 before the first manufactured socket set was marketed. These were very expensive and often proved a safety hazard. In 1921 safety regulations were established, and products were guaranteed safety approved. The early bulbs were smaller replicas of Edison's household bulb. By 1910 G.E. bulbs were rounded with a pointed end, and until 1919 all bulbs were hand blown. The first figural bulbs were made around 1910 in Austria. Japan soon followed, but their product was never of the high quality of the Austrian wares. American manufacturers produced their first machine-made figurals after 1919. Today figural bulbs (especially character-related examples) are very popular collectibles. Bubble lights were popular from about 1945 to 1960 when miniature lights were introduced. These tiny lamps dampened the public's enthusiasm for the bubblers, and manufacturers stopped providing replacement bulbs.

Feather trees were made from 1850 to 1950. All are collectible. Watch for newly manufactured feather trees that have been reintroduced.

For further information concerning Christmas collectibles, we recommend *Pictorial Guide to Christmas Ornaments and Collectibles* by George Johnson, available from Collector Books or your local bookstore.

Note: Values are given for bulbs that are in good paint, with no breaks or cracks, and in working order. Examples termed 'mini' measure no more than 1½". When no condition is mentioned in the description, assume values are for examples in EX/NM condition except paper items; those should be assumed NM/M.

Bulbs

Angel w/crossed arms, clear glass, Europe, 3¼" 200.00
Baby in clown suit, milk glass, Japan, 3¼" 85.00
Ball, milk glass, covered w/holly leaves, Japan, ca 1950, 1¾"........15.00
Ball, milk glass, daisy covered, Japan, ca 1950, 1¾" 25.00
Bear waving, milk glass, ca 1940, Japan, 2¾" 60.00
Bell w/zigzag pattern, milk glass, Japan, 2¼" 15.00
Bird in a birdcage, milk glass, Japan, ca 1935-55, 2" 15.00
Candle, milk glass, squat w/out-of-proportion flame, Japan, 2½"..15.00
Candy cane, milk glass, red & white striped, Japan, 3¼" 60.00
Cat in evening gown, milk glass, Japan, ca 1950, 3"....................175.00
Cat puffed up, milk glass, Japan, ca 1950, 1½"......................65.00
Clown head, milk glass, rnd, Japan, ca 1950, 1¾" 60.00
Crosses on a ball, milk glass, Japan, 1¾" 20.00
Dog in clown outfit, milk glass, Japan, ca 1950, 2¼"......30.00
Elephant sitting on ball, milk glass, Japan, 2¾" 40.00
Frog, milk glass, egg-shaped, Japan, ca 1950, 1½".......110.00
Girl w/muff, milk glass, ca 1950, 2¾" 15.00
Guppy fish, milk glass, fat stomach, Japan, ca 1950, 2¼"...45.00
Howdy Doody, milk glass, Japan, ca 1955, 2" 190.00
Humpty Dumpty, milk glass, Japan, 2¾" 225.00
Indian Princess, clear glass, Japan, 3" 175.00
Jack-O-Lantern, milk glass, dbl-sided, Japan, 1¼" 50.00
Lighthouse, clear glass, Japan, 2" 45.00
Lion w/tennis racket, milk glass, Japan, ca 1935-55, 2¾"....30.00
Little Boy Blue, milk glass, Paramount, Japan, 2½" 25.00
Log Cabin, milk glass, mini, snow-covered, Japan, 1½" ...25.00
Monkey sitting, frosted glass, Foreign, 2" 125.00
Mushroom man, milk glass, Germany, 1½".................30.00
Ocean liner, milk glass, Japan, ca 1950, 2¾" 100.00
Owl in vest & top hat, milk glass, standing, Japan, 2¼" 110.00
Parrot-headed girl, milk glass, hands clasped beneath chin, 2½" ...100.00
Penguin, milk glass, mini, American, ca 1950, 1½"......75.00
Puppy on ball, milk glass, Japan, 2¼" 35.00
Rabbit playing banjo, milk glass, Japan, 2¾"...............25.00
Rooster playing golf, milk glass, Japan, ca 1950, 2¾" 25.00
Santa, milk glass, roly-poly, Japan, 3" 25.00
Santa, milk glass, stepping from sq chimney, Japan, 3" 65.00
Santa on top of house, milk glass, Japan, 2¼" 85.00
Santa w/hands in sleeves, clear glass, ca 1920, 2¾" 125.00
Snail, milk glass, on fat toadstool house, Japan, ca 1935, 3¼" 30.00
Snowman skier, clear glass, Japan, 2¼" 125.00
Snowman w/umbrella, milk glass, Japan, 1950s, 2½" 12.00
Soccer player, milk glass, Japan, ca 1950, 2½" 85.00
Star w/Santa face, milk glass, Japan, ca 1950, 2" 65.00

Candy Containers

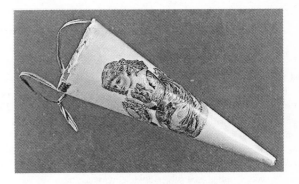

Cornucopia, lithograph on paper, commercially made, large, from $60.00 to $75.00. (Photo courtesy George Johnson)

Apple, emb & mc cb, opens at middle, 2¾", from $70 to **90.00**
Champagne or wine bottle, papier-mâché covered w/netting or label, 3"...**200.00**
Clown's hat, mc paper w/appl Dresden stars, candy bag inside, 3¼" ...**225.00**
Football, oblong w/seams & stitches, opens at middle, 4¼", $70 to ...**80.00**
Heart, red covered cb w/print of angel, 1¾-6", from $45 to **90.00**
Lady's slipper, crepe paper on cb, 2½", from $85 to **115.00**
Mandolin, gold foil on cb, ca 1925, from $75 to........................**100.00**
Peanut, emb & colored realistically, opens at side, 2½", $45 to **55.00**
Suitcase, cb, appl leather straps & metal latch, 4", from $50 to **65.00**
Top hat, fabric over cb, bag inside for candy, 2", from $175 to ...**200.00**
Violin, cb w/litho body & appl neck, 3", from $90 to..................**110.00**

Ornaments

Airplane, free-blown, w/plaster Santa, Blumchen, 7½", from $40 to ...**50.00**
Angel, kneeling, mold-blown, spun glass wings, Germany, 3¼", $90 to....**100.00**
Angel, spun-glass body w/scrap face & wreath, 5¼", from $40 to....**50.00**
Angel in tulip, mold-blown, Germany, 4", from $350 to............**375.00**
Angel w/songbook, scrap w/tinsel, 7", from $30 to **40.00**
Antelope, mold-blown, emb, 2", from $55 to.............................**65.00**
Apple, wax, naturally shaped & pnt, 3½", from $25 to **35.00**
Basket, tin lead, 3-D, covered, oval, Germany, 1950s, 2¼", $15 to...**25.00**
Bear w/bottle, mold-blown, bumpy pattern, 1950s, 2½", $15 to..**20.00**
Bird at nest w/eggs, mold & free-blown, 4", from $90 to.............**110.00**
Bird w/berries & flowers, mold-blown, in wire hoop, 4½", $50 to...**60.00**
Boy head in nightcap, mold-blown, clip-on, Czech, 3", from $100 to..**125.00**
Butterfly, beaded, spread wings, Czech, 3½", from $20 to **30.00**
Cat in shoe, mold-blown, sleeping, Germany, 1980s-90s, 3", from $10 to..**12.00**
Child in manger, mold-blown, wrapped in cloth, 3½", from $15 to...**20.00**
Clown in boot, mold-blown, Germany, 1980s, 3", from $12 to.....**15.00**

**Deep sea diver, 4½",
from $250.00 to
$300.00.** (Photo courtesy
George Johnson)

Dog w/cigar, mold-blown, bow at neck, ca 1915, 4¾", $150 to ..**175.00**
Dove soaring, mold-blown, detailed feathers, 4½", from $50 to....**60.00**
Duck in top hat, free-blown, in flying position, 5", from $30 to ...**40.00**
Dwarf w/pick, mold-blown, long beard, Germany, 2½", from $50 to...**75.00**
Fish, tin lead, flat, 3 faceted jewels, Am, 2¾", from $60 to...........**70.00**
Flamingo, mold & free-blown, Germany, 3", from $20 to..............**25.00**
Flowers & ribbon, Dresden, gold/silver, pnt, Germany, 7½", $100 to...**110.00**
Frog under mushroom, mold & free-blown, wrapped in wire, 4", $125 to...**150.00**
Girl w/tree, scrap w/tinsel, blond w/long dress, Germany, 5", $30 to..**40.00**
Harp w/emb angel, mold-blown, Germany, 1970s, from $10 to.....**15.00**
Heart w/flowers, Dresden, gold/silver, dbl, Germany, 2", from $95 to...**110.00**
Horseshoe, Good Luck, Dresden, gold/silver, flat, 2¾", $75 to **95.00**
Icicle, mold-blown, tubes w/emb lines, 6", from $5 to **10.00**

Little Miss Muffet, mold-blown, emb spider, Germany, 3", from $175 to...**200.00**
Man & woman, kissing, mold-blown, emb oval, 3¼", from $90 to.....**100.00**
Man in the moon, Dresden, gold/silver, flat, 4½", from $100 to ..**125.00**
Mermaid, mold & free-blown, wears sm necklace, 3¾", from $180 to...**190.00**
Mistletoe, scrap w/tinsel, 5½", from $6 to **12.00**
Monkey w/tambourine, cotton & crepe paper, 18¾", from $175 to....**200.00**
Mushroom w/face, mold-blown, squat w/thick stem, 2¾", from $140 to...**175.00**
Owl head, mold-blown, milk glass, lg beak, 3", from $150 to......**175.00**
Parrot, mold-blown w/spun-glass wings, head feathers, 3", from $80 to **90.00**
Pear w/clown face, mold-blown, rnd eyes/triangle nose, 2½", $100 to...**125.00**
Pigeon, mold-blown, yel & blk glass eyes, 4½", from $40 to.........**50.00**
Purse, Dresden, gold/silver, 3-D, Victorian, 3", from $150 to......**175.00**
Rabbit on pine tree, mold-blown, emb, Germany, 2½", $75 to...........**85.00**
Santa head, scrap w/tinsel, face framed w/bl hood, 2½", from $8 to...**12.00**
Santa in frame, Dresden, gold/silver & scrap, flat, 7½", $100 to..**125.00**
Santa on sled, mold & free-blown, 4x3¼", from $175 to............**200.00**
Santa w/girl & lamb, scrap w/tinsel, 6", from $20 to...................**25.00**
Snow angel boy w/roses, scrap, 3½", from $15 to..........................**18.00**
Snowball, spun cotton ball, Germany, 2¾", from $25 to...............**35.00**
Snowboy angel, spun cotton w/scrap face, 3½", from $40 to.........**45.00**
Snowflake, brass, 8-armed, 8 faceted gems, 3¼", from $30 to **35.00**
Snowflake, tin lead, 6-armed w/dangle, lg facets, 5¾", from $70 to ...**80.00**
Songbird w/key, mold-blown, open beak, clip-on, 4¼", from $60 to..**75.00**
Stork w/baby on bk, mold-blown, spun-glass tail, 4½", $200 to..**225.00**
Swan, free-blown, Art Glass, Germany, 3½", from $30 to............**40.00**
Tree, mold-blown, w/emb cottage, 3", from $35 to **45.00**
Umbrella, Dresden, gold/silver, flat, open w/curved hdl, 2", $50 to...**75.00**
Uncle Sam boy, mold-blown, red, wht & bl suit w/top hat, 3", $90 to..**110.00**

Miscellaneous

Bubble light, Paramount, oil, C6 & C7 ....**8.00**
Bubble light, Paramount Kristal Snow Animated Candle, ca 1947-48....**45.00**
Bubble light, Reliance Spark-L-Light, ca 1949-51, C6 ....**8.00**
Bubble light, Renown, tri-color, ca 1957...**12.00**
Bubble light, rocket ship, US...**30.00**
Bubble light, Royal, ca 1948-54...**10.00**
Bubble light, USA Lite, ca 1949-56..**6.00**
Celluloid light, dog, spaniel head, 2"...**70.00**
Celluloid light, pear, 2¼"..**30.00**
Celluloid light, rabbit in jacket, arms at side, 5¾".........................**80.00**
Celluloid light, sailor boy holding parrot, 4"..................................**50.00**
Lamp, Santa w/present, pnt frosted glass, US, 8"...........................**300.00**
Light cover, Dresden glass, basket of fruit, 2¾".............................**75.00**
Light cover, Dresden glass, rose, 2½"...**60.00**
Light cover, Dresden glass, sunburst, ball-shaped, 2¾" **60.00**
Light cover, Kristal Star, metal, Japan, ca 1935, 2¾" **2.00**
Light reflector, cb & foil, 11-pointed star, US, 3¼" **1.00**
Light reflector, Nomalite Star plastic star, 3" **75**
Light reflector, plastic & glitter, wht or tinted, 4" **1.50**
Light reflector, plastic jewel, 12-pointed star or snowflake, 3".........**1.00**
Light reflector, single-layer foil, star or petaled flower, 3½".............**3.00**
Light shade, Gyro, Magic Revolving Shade....................................**8.00**
Light-up, Santa, hard plastic, 1955-60...**20.00**
Light-up, Santa on reindeer, ca 1955, 11" **35.00**
Rudolph Sled Set, Bradford, 1950s, w/orig box, 15".......................**40.00**
Santa, Belsnickle, papier-mâché, thinner shape, w/tree, 1890s, 11"...**750.00**
Santa, Belsnickle, plaster coated, gr coat, no tree, ca 1900, 8"....**500.00**
Santa, Belsnickle, plaster coated, gr coat w/hood & mica, 1890s, 10" ...**700.00**
Santa, Belsnickle, red-trimmed coat w/mica, feather tree, 1890s, 12"...**725.00**
Santa, Belsnickle, wht coat w/mica, feather tree, 1890s, 8½" **500.00**
Santa, cloth stuffed w/straw, red satin clothes, 25" **200.00**
Santa, papier-mâché & plaster, w/lg bag, Germany, 4½"............**150.00**
Stocking, net w/orig toys, ca 1939, 11"...**35.00**

Tree, feather; gr, early 1900s, 36" **265.00**
Tree, feather; gr, 1930s, 26" **210.00**
Tree, feather; gr, 1930s, 38" **315.00**
Tree, feather; lt gr, early 1900s, 22" **195.00**
Tree, feather; wht, 1930s, 25" **185.00**
Tree stand, CI, 3-legged w/tree roots, 45 cm **45.00**
Tree stand, common 3- or 4-legged, rnd pan & ring w/thumb screws, 32" ..**6.00**
Tree stand, metal, standard style, crimped holder, 11" **15.00**
Tree stand, rock-shaped, rotates & plays music, Germany, 12"dia...**600.00**

Tree stand, square with geometric openwork, bronze patina, European, ca 1928, 4¾x13⅜", $250.00. (Photo courtesy Skinner, Inc.)

Tree stand, 4-legs, electrified, North Bros, ca 1920s, 14" **60.00**
Tree top, angel, kneeling, mold & free-blown, hands in prayer, 10" ..**175.00**
Tree top, angel, scrap, wears robe & stands on cloud, 14½" **90.00**
Tree top, angel w/colored wings, GEM, ca 1940-50s, w/orig box, 8" ..**25.00**
Tree top, angel w/flower, mold & free-blown, 1980-90s, 10" **30.00**
Tree top, Angel-Glo w/magic wand, plastic, 1940-50s, 7" **15.00**
Tree top, Santa face, plastic & glass, Germany, 14" **60.00**
Tree top, star, Krystal Star, metal, plastic gem center, 4½" **10.00**

Chrysanthemum Sprig, Blue

This is the blue opaque version of Northwood's popular pattern, Chrysanthemum Sprig. It was made at the turn of the century and is today very rare, as its values indicate. Prices are influenced by the amount of gold remaining on the raised designs. Our advisors for this category are Betty and Clarence Maier; they're listed in the Directory under Pennsylvania. Unless noted otherwise, our values are for examples with excellent to near mint gold.

Bowl, berry; ind, M gold, 2⅝x5x3¾", from $165 to **250.00**
Bowl, master fruit; 10½" W, from $450 to...................................**600.00**
Butter dish **1,250.00**
Butter dish, lt in color..**500.00**
Celery, from $400 to..**550.00**
Compote, jelly **600.00**
Condiment tray, rare, VG gold **750.00**
Creamer, from $350 to **450.00**
Cruet, from $975 to **1,200.00**
Pitcher, water **1,100.00**
Shakers, pr **450.00**
Spooner, from $300 to..**350.00**
Sugar bowl, M gold, w/lid, 7", from $450 to **600.00**
Toothpick holder, 2¾", from $450 to **550.00**
Tumbler, 3¾" **185.00**

Circus Collectibles

The 1890s were the golden age of the circus. Barnum and Bailey's parades transformed mundane city streets into an exotic never-never land inhabited by trumpeting elephants with jeweled gold headgear strutting by to the strains of the calliope that issued from a fine red- and gilt-painted wagon extravagantly decorated with carved wooden animals of every description. It was an exciting experience. Is it any wonder that collectors today treasure the mementos of that golden era? See also Posters.

Key:
B&B — Barnum & Bailey   RB — Ringling Bros.

Banner, Alligator Boy, pnt canvas w/grommets, 35x35", EX **35.00**
Banner, Helium Girl, floating in air, pnt canvas, T Frank, 10" sq ...**525.00**
Banner, Tattooed Girl, painted canvas w/grommets, 35x45" **45.00**
Banner, train; RB B&B, lions, tigers, globe, plastic fr, 72x300", EX **600.00**
Business card, RB, World's Greatest Shows, A Ringling, VG........**15.00**
Cabinet photo, Thin Man from sideshow, ca 1900, EX **50.00**
Coloring book, Clyde Beatty Circus, 16 pgs, 1950-40s, 13½x10", EX...**13.00**
Magazine, B&B 2 Hemispheres Band Wagon, elephant & bears, 52 pgs, EX...**25.00**
Magazine & Daily Review, RB B&B, 1934, 80 pgs, EX **25.00**
Mug, RB B&B, tigers, plastic, 1988, 5x4", M **12.00**
Photo, B&B Circus Car #3 w/circus workers, 1912, 5x7", EX **95.00**
Photo, sepia; lion tamers Clyde & Harriett Beatty, 1938, 8x10", EX...**85.00**
Pillow case, RB B&B, elephant & other circus scenes, EX............**12.50**
Postcard, Harry & Grace, 2 midgets, EX **30.00**
Program, RB B&B, 1919, Circus Colossal, EX **58.00**
Program, RB B&B, 1927, 120 pgs, 10x6¾", NM **60.00**
Program, RB B&B, 1937, clown on cover, 10-pg, 11x8½", EX **40.00**
Program, RB B&B, 1955, lady w/leopard on elephant, VG...........**15.00**
Route book, Great Wallace Shows, 1902, G **95.00**
Shot glass, red & amber w/blk letters, ftd, 2½", EX **10.00**
Songster, Bully Burke cover, Barnum Circus, 1880s, 32-pg, 6½x4"..**195.00**
Thimble, RB B&B Circus World eng, pewter w/plastic insert, EX ..**20.00**
Trade card, Millie-Christine, 2-Headed Lady, EX **105.00**

Cleminson

A hobby turned to enterprise, Cleminson is one of several California potteries whose clever hand-decorated wares are attracting the attention of today's collectors. The Cleminsons started their business at their El Monte home in 1941 and were so successful that eventually they expanded to a modern plant that employed more than 150 workers. They produced not only dinnerware and kitchen items such as cookie jars, canisters, and accessories, but novelty wall vases, small trays, plaques, etc., as well. Though nearly always marked, Cleminson wares are easy to spot as you become familiar with their distinctive glaze colors. Their grayed-down blue and green, berry red, and dusty pink say 'Cleminson' as clearly as their trademark. Unable to compete with foreign imports, the pottery closed in 1963. For more information we recommend *The Collector's Encyclopedia of California Pottery, Second Edition*, by Jack Chipman (Collector Books).

Bowl, Galagray, 4x11x9" **65.00**
Bowl, Gram's on front, roses on brn wreath on lid, 2½" **30.00**
Cleanser shaker, Kate, 6½" **40.00**
Clothes sprinkler bottle, Chinaman, 8½".................................**85.00**
Cookie canister, Galagray...**90.00**
Creamer & sugar bowl, Distlefink.......................................**25.00**
Cup, child's; clown head, hat lid..**80.00**

Cup & saucer, My Old Man w/man sleeping, 5½" dia, 8" dia, $15 to..20.00
Darning egg, lady w/Darn It on front, 5" 50.00
Darning egg, winking sailor, 1 hand behind bk, 5" 100.00
Gravy boat, Distlefink, bird shape, ladle hdl forms tail, 7x7" 45.00
Pie bird, rooster, wht w/dk gr, yel & blk, 4¼", from $45 to 55.00
Pitcher, Distlefink, cylindrical, 5" 30.00
Pitcher, Distlefink, 9½" 45.00
Pitcher, watering can shape, wht w/bl & magenta floral decor, 5" ...35.00
Plaque, Family Tree, child & bunny at bottom, from $60 to 75.00
Razor blade bank, bell w/man shaving, 3½" 25.00
Ring holder, wht & peach dog w/tail in air 30.00
Shakers, Distlefink, lg, pr 35.00
Shakers, Galagray, Deco lady, 6½", pr 52.50
Shakers, Galagray, rhumba couple, dk red trim, 6½", pr...............45.00
String holder, heart shape w/You'll Always Have a Pull w/Me 80.00
Wall plaque, roses & butterflies, scalloped fluted border, 7" dia 40.00

Clewell

Charles Walter Clewell was a metal worker who perfected the technique of plating an entire ceramic vessel with a thin layer of copper or bronze treated with an oxidizing agent to produce a natural deterioration of the surface. Through trial and error, he was able to control the degree of patina achieved. In the early stages, the metal darkened and if allowed to develop further formed a natural turquoise-blue or green corrosion. He worked alone in his small Akron, Ohio, studio from about 1906, buying undecorated pottery from several Ohio firms, among them Weller, Owens, and Cambridge. His work is usually marked. Clewell died in 1965, having never revealed his secret process to others.

Prices for Clewell have advanced rapidly during the past few years along with the Arts and Crafts market in general. Right now, good examples are bringing whatever the traffic will bear.

Cider set, 9½" pitcher and four 4½" mugs, heavy copper overlay, embossed Clewell Coppers, $1,000.00 for the set.

Mug, copper clad, riveted, 4⅜" 135.00
Vase, berries/leaves relief, incurvate/cylindrical, 8" 550.00
Vase, bl-gr patina, bulbous bottom w/slim neck, #364-6, 6½" 440.00
Vase, brn-to-copper patina, mk #362-4-6, 4⅞x3½" 480.00
Vase, dk bronze at shoulder over strong bl-gr patina, #388, 5½x5" ..600.00
Vase, dk patina, minor abrasions, 3½" 250.00
Vase, dk patina to gr at base, minor abrasions, 6" 400.00
Vase, Egyptian man/woman relief, bulbous, 12½" 2,000.00
Vase, EX verdigris & bronze patina, bulbous, #461-29, 7x6" 850.00
Vase, solid dk patina, cylindrical w/angle shouder & sm rim, 13½" ..850.00
Vase, strong bl patina over copper, cylindrical, 10" 900.00

Clews

Brothers Ralph and James Clews were potters who operated in Cobridge in the Staffordshire district from 1817 to 1835. They are best known for their blue and white transfer-printed earthenwares, which included American Views, Moral Maxims, Picturesque Views, and English Views. A series called Three Tours of Dr. Syntax contained thirty-one different scenes with each piece bearing a descriptive title. Another popular series was Pictures of Sir David Wilkie with seven prints. (Though we once thought that the Don Quixote series was made by Clews, new information seems to indicate that it was made instead by Davenport.) Both printed and impressed marks were used, often incorporating the pattern name as well as the pottery. See also Staffordshire, Historical.

Bowl, soup; Chase After a Wolf, ca 1825, 9½" 595.00
Coffeepot, Water Girl, bl transfer, ca 1825, 10½", NM 1,500.00
Cup & saucer, Christmas Eve, Wilkie, dk bl transfer..................230.00
Plate, Coronation, floral, dk bl transfer, 10⅛" 200.00
Plate, Escape of the Mouse, dk bl transfer, 10".........................450.00
Platter, Dr Syntax Gazing, dk bl transfer, sm rstr, 9" 2,000.00
Platter, Genevese, brn transfer, 1818-34 mk, 19¼x16" 600.00
Sugar bowl, Basket & Urn, med bl transfer..................................375.00
Vase, Chameleon Ware, HP geometrics, conical, 5⅜" 140.00
Vase, Chameleon Ware, Lava, bls/grs/wht, Deco style, #252, 4½x4" ...95.00

Cliff, Clarice

Between 1928 and 1935 in Burslem, England, as the director and part owner of Wilkinson and Newport Pottery Companies, Clarice Cliff and her 'paintresses' created a body of hand-painted pottery whose influence is felt to the present time.

The name for the oevre was Bizarre Ware, and the predominant sensibility, style, and appearance was Deco. Almost all pieces are signed. There were over 160 patterns and more than 400 shapes, all of which are illustrated in *A Bizarre Affair — The Life and Work of Clarice Cliff*, published by Harry N. Abrams, Inc., written by Len Griffen and Susan and Louis Meisel.

Note: Non-hand-painted work (transfer printed) was produced after World War II and into the 1950s. Some of the most common names are 'Tonquin' and 'Charlotte.' These items, while attractive and enjoyable to own, have little value in the collector market. Our advisors for this category are Wilfred and Dolli Cohen; they are listed in the Directory under California.

Ashtray, Orange Roof Cottage, 3 rests, 4¾" dia..........................320.00
Biscuit bbl, Celtic Harvest, spherical, 2 hdls, 7" 265.00
Biscuit bbl, Woodland, w/lid & wicker hdl, 6½" 900.00
Bowl, Crocus, sm ped ft, 1¾x4" 215.00
Bowl, Rodanthe, ribbed sides, 2¾x7" 245.00
Bowl, Secrets, 3-ftd, 3½x10" 305.00
Bowl, Viscaria, 1½x6½" 325.00
Cake stand, Curea, ftd, scalloped rim, 4x9½" dia 185.00
Cauldren, Flowers & Squares, 3-ftd, tab hdls, 2⅞" 670.00
Coaster, Diamonds, 3⅝" 200.00
Cocoa pot, Chick, chicken figural, wht w/red mouth & comb, 6½"...510.00
Comport, Inspiration Lily, 7x3" 950.00
Cup & saucer, Applique Lucerne, 2", 4" dia 1,735.00
Cup & saucer, Blue Firs, conical cup w/angled tab hdl.................715.00
Cup & saucer, coffee; Spring Crocus 185.00
Dish, bonbon; Tulips, 5¾" 345.00
Honey pot, Autumn Harvest, bee finial, 3x2½" 465.00
Honey pot, Honeydew, bee finial, conical, 2¾x2¾" dia (at base)....495.00

Honey pot, Sunray, w/lid, 3" 360.00
Jam jar, House & Bridge, 3⅛" 1,100.00
Jam jar, Orange House, 2¾" 1,180.00
Jug, Athens; Crocus, 5" 535.00
Jug, Athens; Secrets, 6-sided, 6" 590.00
Jug, Crocus, 8-sided, 6¾" 450.00
Jug, My Garden, flared rim, 7¾" 395.00
Jug, Perth; Cubist, 5" 695.00
Match/cigarette holder, Secrets, shape #463 ....715.00
Pitcher, hot water; Tree & House, mc on cream, pewter lid, 7" ..765.00
Plate, Blue Japan, 6-sided, 5¾" 655.00
Plate, Coral Firs, sq w/center indent, 8x10½" 750.00
Plate, Idyll, sq, 6½x5" 715.00
Plate, Rhodanthe, sq w/center indent, 9x7½" 450.00
Plate, Triple Star, vivid colors, yel/bright bl predominate, 10", NM ..250.00
Pot, Autumn Crocus, ftd, 3⅜x3⅜" dia.......................250.00
Pot, fern; Broth, 3x4" dia..435.00
Pot, Red Roof, str sides, 3½x3½" 475.00
Shakers, Crocus, flared top & bottom, pr....................210.00
Shakers, Hollyhocks, pk, conical, 3", pr.....................195.00
Sugar sifter, Autumn Crocus, conical, 5½" 780.00
Sugar sifter, Rhodanthe, arched top w/sq sides, 4⅞"....695.00
Teapot, Teepee, Indian spout, totem pole hdl, moose/leaf decor....495.00
Teapot, Tree & House, mc on cream, Fantasque..., 6¾".............825.00
Toast rack, Nasturtium, 4-slice...................................485.00
Tray, Melon, oval, 8½" 595.00
Vase, Pine Grove, spherical, 7x6½"..............................525.00
Vase, Rhodanthe, ribbed, #371, 4½x5½" 420.00
Vase, Umbrellas, 8½" 975.00
Vase, yo-yo; Swirls, 2 opposing conical shapes, 9" 225.00
Wall pocket, Monique, lady's face w/red flowers in hair, 1930s, 7" ...410.00

Clifton

Clifton Art Pottery of Clifton, New Jersey, was organized ca 1903. Until 1911 when they turned to the production of wall and floor tile, they made artware of several varieties. The founders were Fred Tschirner and William A. Long. Long had developed the method for underglaze slip painting that had been used at the Lonhuda Pottery in Steubenville, Ohio, in the 1890s. Crystal Patina, the first artware made by the small company, utilized a fine white body and flowing, blended colors, the earliest a green crystalline. Indian Ware, copied from the pottery of the American Indians, was usually decorated in black geometric designs on red clay. (On the occasions when white was used in addition to the black, the ware was often not as well executed; so even though two-color decoration is very rare, it is normally not as desirable to the collector.) Robin's Egg Blue, pale blue on the white body, and Tirrube, a slip-decorated matt ware, were also produced.

Vase, Indian Ware, Arkansas #216, marked, 5¼", $350.00. (Photo courtesy David Rago Auctions)

Humidor, hammered gunmetal gray w/raspberry & bl cabochons, 5x4" ...200.00
Jardiniere, Indian Ware, buff/brn/blk, 4 Mile Ruin, AZ, 8½x11" ..500.00
Teapot, Indian Ware, geometric decor, #274-42, 5".....................185.00
Teapot, matt gr, flat bottom, w/lid, 8"..50.00
Vase, Crystal Patina, gr, rim-to-shoulder hdls, flaw, 6½x8" 350.00
Vase, Crystal Patina, gr, squat, 2¼x4" 210.00
Vase, Crystal Patina, gr & brn organic shape, 1906, 8" 500.00
Vase, Crystal Patina, yel/buff mottle, 4-sided flared neck, 7" 275.00
Vase, Indian Ware, blk geometrics, #219, 3½x6" 85.00
Vase, Indian Ware, blk/tan/red, sgn Arizona, 7½" W...................200.00
Vase, Indian Ware, geometric shoulder band, collared rim, 4½x6¾"...90.00
Vase, Tirrube, jonquils, yel/wht/gr on brick red, 8x4"..................325.00
Vase, Tirrube, mums, wht/yel on plum, att Haubrich, flaw, 5" 200.00
Vessel, Crystal Patina, gr, hexagonal, 1905, X, 4" dia.................350.00

Clocks

In the early days of our country's history, clock makers were influenced by styles imported from Europe. They copied the European's cabinets and reconstructed their movements — needed materials were in short supply; modifications had to be made. Of necessity was born mainspring motive power and spring clocks. Wooden movements were made on a mass-production basis as early as 1808. Before the middle of the century, brass movements had been developed.

Today's collectors prefer clocks from the eighteenth and nineteenth centuries with pendulum-regulated movements. Bracket clocks made during this period utilized the shorter pendulum improvised in 1658 by Fromentiel, a prominent English clock maker. These smaller square-face clocks usually were made with a dome top fitted with a handle or a decorative finial. The case was usually walnut or ebony and was sometimes decorated with pierced brass mountings. Brackets were often mounted on the wall to accommodate the clock, hence the name. The banjo clock was patented in 1802 by Simon Willard. It derived its descriptive name from its banjo-like shape. A similar but more elaborate style was called the lyre clock.

The first electric novelty clocks were developed in the 1940s. Lux, who was the major producer, had been in business since 1912, making wind-up novelties during the '20s and '30s. Another company, Mastercrafter Novelty Clocks, first obtained a patent to produce these clocks in the late 1940s. Other manufacturers were Keebler, Westclox, and Columbia Time. The cases were made of china, Syroco, wood, and plastic; most were animated and some had pendulettes. Prices vary according to condition and rarity.

Unless noted otherwise, values are given for eight-day time only clocks in excellent condition. Clocks that have been altered, damaged, or have had parts replaced are worth considerably less.

For more information consult *The Standard Antique Clock Value Guide* by Alex Wescot. Our advisor is Bruce A. Austin; he is listed in the Directory under New York.

Key:
br — brass   reg — regulator
dl — dial   rswd — rosewood
esc — escapement   TS — time & strike
mcr — mercury   wt — weight
mvt — movement   vnr — veneer
OG — ogee   2nds — seconds
pnd — pendulum

Calendar Clocks

Ithaca, #3 Vienna, 30-day, rstr dls/rollers, rstr case, 1880, 52", G ..2,450.00
Ithaca, #8 Shelf Library, G- dls, rfn walnut case, 1875, 25", G ...550.00

New Haven, Rutland, dbl dl, rfn oak, 30-day mvt, 1910, 48" **925.00**
Seth Thomas, Parlor #1 shelf, TS 2-wt, rstr/rfn, 1870, 32"..........**650.00**
Seth Thomas, Plymouth Hollow Parlor shelf, TS 2-wt, 1863, VG .**1,550.00**
Seth Thomas, store, oak case, ca 1900, 35".................................**600.00**
Southern Calendar Clock Co #2, rstr dls/rollers, rfn, 1880, 31½"....**800.00**
Welch, Arditi, DJ Gale Pat perpetual, discolored dls, 1885, 27"....**500.00**
Welch, Wagner, dbl dl (w/flaking), early base, 1877, 30", G ...**1,200.00**

Novelty Clocks

Beam Engine, Fr Industrial Series, moon hands, porc dl, 1890, 7½"...**3,200.00**
Blinking Sambo, Lux, minor pnt chips, 1950, 9" **400.00**
Lighthouse, Fr Industrial Series, Reaumer thermometer, 1880, 21½"...**1,900.00**
Lion blinker, Bradley & Hubbard Pat Appl...1858, rpt, 8" **1,600.00**
Mystery, female figure holds pnd in raised hand, Fr, 1890, 23", G....**4,250.00**
Organ grinder & monkey, rpt case, Am, ca 1860, 17½" **1,750.00**
Sambo, blinking eyes, partial rpt, Am, 1860, 16" **1,625.00**
Steam hammer, MM Diette design, pnd moves up & down, 1880, 18" ...**2,500.00**
Topsey, CI, blinking eye, old rpt, G dl & bezel, Am, 1860, 16½"...**1,875.00**
Waterwheel, Fr Industrial Series, barometer/thermometer, rstr, 1880 ..**2,350.00**
Windmill, Fr Industrial Series, w/barometer/thermometers, 1880, 18"..**5,200.00**

Shelf Clocks

Ansonia, Beauty, carriage, 1-day time only, porc dl, 1900, 4¾", EX+...**350.00**
Ansonia, Cute boudoir, porc dl, 1910, 4" **210.00**
Ansonia, Fortuna, bronzed spelter swinging mystery type, 1890, 30"...**4,000.00**
Ansonia, Gem, silvered dl, worn gold, 1910, 4½" **525.00**
Ansonia, Jewel, carriage, time only/silvered dl/cast top, 1900, 4¼"....**450.00**
Ansonia, Mercury figural, gray spelter, 1895, 15", VG **400.00**
Ansonia, Savoy Louis XIV, enameled iron, 1895, 9¾", VG **125.00**
Ansonia, Triumph, rfn case/2 rpl cherubs, 1900, 24½", VG........**500.00**
Birge & Fuller, TS dbl-steeple Wagon Spring, 1845, 27", G rstr....**725.00**
Brewster & Ingrahams, steeple w/orig cones, rprs, 1845, 20" **400.00**
Chelsea, Willard house striking, Mt Vernon tablets, 1930, ¾-sz, 32"...**1,050.00**
Ephraim Downs, pillar & scroll, 30-hr wooden works, 1835, 31½"...**2,400.00**
Evans, Aberdaire, pnt dl, arch top w/river scene, 1840, 13x19".....**800.00**
Forestville, orig ripple beehive, JC Brown dl, old rpr, 1850, 19" ..**1,825.00**

France, Louis XVI style gilt-bronze figure and doves on marble base, two-train half-striking movement, early twentieth century, 16", $1,400.00.

(Photo courtesy Skinner, Inc.)

German, 30-hr musical 'reveille' alarm, walnut, 1910, 12", VG..**230.00**
Gilbert, br & glass crystal reg, open esc, 1910, 9½"......................**350.00**
Gilbert, porc, bl case (stained), TS, 1900, 9½", VG **235.00**
JC Brown, beehive, steel spring mvt, rstr dl, 1850, 19" **300.00**

JC Brown, Ripple Beehive, etched heart tablet, 1845, 19" **1,650.00**
Molgatini a Orleans (on dl), lady & cherub, gilt bronze, 1960, 20"...**4,600.00**
New Haven, Eclipse, TS, alarm, rst dl, rfn, 1910, 25" **130.00**
New Haven, Paris, carriage, time only, br case, 1915, G **80.00**
Seth Thomas, Helmsman, 7-jewel ship's strike mvt, 1935, 8¼"...**325.00**
Seth Thomas, Joker Lever, carriage, time & alarm, 1895, 7" **110.00**
Seth Thomas, Long Alarm, mahog Adamantine case, 1910, 11" ..**150.00**
Seth Thomas, Plymouth Hollow, column, 30-hr, fading dl, 1855, 26"...**180.00**
Seth Thomas, Thomaston, cottage, Plymouth mvt, rfn, 1870, 14"...**230.00**
Sterling Bronze, drum on bks of 2 kneeling men, Chelsea mvt, 1924...**1,500.00**
Terry, Cottage Extra, 30-hr, rswd & walnut, 1868, 13", VG........**125.00**
Waterbury, Companion, carriage, TS, worn gold, 1903, 5¼", VG..**200.00**
Waterbury, Herald, carriage, strike & repeat, rprs, 1905, 7¼".....**300.00**
Welch, steeple, clear tablet, EX dl, 1875, 19", VG **230.00**

Tall Case Clocks

Abel Stowell, cherry Fed w/inlay, br details, 1800s, 19".........**18,400.00**
AH Rowley, Victorian Gothic Revival, golden oak, 19th C, 100"....**4,700.00**
Andrew Millar Edinburgh, fruitwood, arched crest, rstr/rpl, 78" ..**1,000.00**
Ezekiel Reed, Bridgewater, mahog Fed w/inlay, 1790, 92½"...**9,985.00**
Geo Eberman, cherry/mahog, scrolled cornice, pnt dl, rfn, 1820s, 105"...**7,000.00**
J Bowman Strasburg #4, cherry/mahog flame vnr, br works, 91"...**3,575.00**
J Hawthorn Newcastle...Tyne, cherry, dvtl hood, br works, 1816, 93"...**1,925.00**
Jas Black Kirkaldy, mahog Hplwht w/inlay, br works, 88" **2,500.00**
S Hoadley Plymouth, pine w/red/yel grpt & faux inlay, touchups, 83"...**2,475.00**
Simon Willard, mahog Fed w/inlay, br fretwork, 1801, 89½" ...**51,700.00**
Willard, mahog Chpndl w/inlay & br work, Am ship scene in arch...**55,000.00**
Wm Cummens, inlay mahog, fretwork arch w/3 br balls, rfn/rstr, 91"...**16,450.00**

Wall Clocks

A Willard Jr, banjo, mahog Fed, pnt medal dl, pnd, 1820s, 33¼"...**3,525.00**
Ansonia, chisel bottom, flaking dl, vnr chips, 1852, 24"..............**170.00**
Ansonia, Nantucket Belle, eng/silvered dl, steel rod strike, 1920s..**650.00**
Atkins, Ives pat Wagon spring mvt, 30-day, 1855, 25", EX+ ...**2,200.00**
Austria, Late Biedermeier reg, 1-wt, walnut/rswd vnr, 1850, 39"...**2,200.00**
Austria, 3-wt Vienna reg, Grand Sonnerie, walnut, 1860, 54"...**3,100.00**
Benj Morrill, mirror w/releafed fr, wheelbarrow mvt, 1821, 30"...**4,600.00**
Biedermeier, 3-wt Grand Sonnerie, milk glass dl/shell bezel, 1830, 53"...**7,000.00**
Chas Alvah Smith, 8-day wooden works, ash, 1929, 25", G **300.00**
Chauncey Jerome, 8-day TS fusee, rswd, Ives CI holder, 1850s, 22" ...**675.00**
E Howard, #1 banjo reg, rswd grpt, orig pnd, ca 1890, 50" **5,000.00**
E Howard, #12 Reg, pnt metal dl, NP pnd, 1880, 63½" **5,000.00**
E Howard, #2 banjo reg, retouched tablet, rpl pnd, 1858, 44"...**4,500.00**
E Howard, #3 banjo reg, rswd grpt, retouched dl/tablets, 1880, 38"...**4,300.00**
E Howard, #4 banjo reg, rswd grpt, retouched tablet, 1890, 32" ...**2,000.00**
E Howard, #70 reg, oak, prof rfn dl, orig tablet, 1905, 31".......**2,100.00**
E Howard, #70 reg, rpt dl, rfn oak case, 1900, 32", VG **1,500.00**
E Howard, #9 reg, figure-8 for Riggs Bros, walnut, 1890, 37"...**4,500.00**
E Howard, Keyhole, hinged door, rvpt tablets, old rfn, 1870, 50"...**8,500.00**
E Howard, rosewood grpt, metal dl, shaped pnd, banjo, 29"...**2,575.00**
F Kroeber, #43 reg, TS, cut glass/mirror pnd, ca 1875, 43" **2,000.00**
G Bucker, Grand Sonnerie 3-wt reg, dbl-door walnut case, 1880, 50"..**2,100.00**
German, Vienna reg, 2-wt, reeded ½-columns, cast mtn goat, 1875, 51"....**900.00**
German Blk Forest picture fr, 30-hr, 2-wt, repoussé dl, 10x11"...**250.00**
Gustav Becker, Vienna reg, time only, walnut, 43", EX...............**725.00**
Gustav Becker (unsgn), late Biedermeier style, porc dl, 1855, 43", G....**800.00**
JB Hatch, Baltimore banjo, rpt dl/tablets w/gold leaf, rfn, 1860, 33" ..**1,000.00**
Jerome, English rolling pin parlor case, flaking dl, rprs, 1870s, 36"...**300.00**
Kronberger, 2-wt reg in Vienna style, re-ebonized, ca 1875, 42" ...**350.00**
Leopold Mager, 3-wt, grid-iron pnd, porc dl, 1880, 60"...........**2,800.00**
New Haven, Blake short drop, oak w/cvgs, rpl dl/pnd, rfn, 27", G ...**125.00**
New Haven, Waring banjo, TS, flaking tablets, 1930, 37".........**150.00**

New Haven, Willis banjo, mahog, Mt Vernon tablets, 12-day, 17", VG..**125.00**
New Haven, Winsome Westminster chime banjo, flaked tablets, 1929, VG...**175.00**
SB Terry, mini wt-driven OG, wooden dl, cleaned, 1845, 19"..**2,100.00**
Seth Thomas, #2 reg, mahog, prof rpt dl, rstr, ca 1900, 36" **1,375.00**
Seth Thomas, #2 reg, walnut, orig dl w/sm flakes, 1885, 34", VG..**1,350.00**
Seth Thomas, #3 reg, nickel wt, rpr pnd stick, 1890s, 42" **2,000.00**
Seth Thomas, Gallery, 18" dl, 15-day, damascene pnd, 1910, 25½"..**1,750.00**
Seth Thomas, Litchfield, 30-day, mahog, gold-leaf tablets, 1890s, 31"..**1,100.00**
Seth Thomas, 12" Drop Octagon, advertises 5¢ Coca-Cola, 1935, 23½"..**500.00**
Waterbury, Mobile, missing br trim, rstr numerals, 1890s, 57½"'..**1,475.00**
Welch, #11 reg, rfn walnut, 30-day dbl-spring time mvt, 1885, 62"..**2,100.00**
Welch, Drop Octagon #1, rswd, pnt dl, orig hands, 1880s, 24½", VG..**170.00**
Welch, 30-hour, TS/alarm, orig dl/tablet, ca 1865, 18", VG **120.00**
Wm Pratt, mahog banjo w/bracket, handmade mvt, sgn dl, 1840, 38" **2,100.00**

Cloisonné

Cloisonné is defined as 'enamel ware in which the surface decoration is formed by different colors of enamel separated by thin strips of metal.' In the early original process, precious and semi-precious stones were crushed and their colors placed into the thin wire cells (cloisons) in selected artistic designs. Though a French word, cloisonné was first made in tenth-century Egypt. To achieve the orginal result, many processes may be used. There are are also several styles and variations of this art form. Standard cloisonné involves only one style, using opaque enamel within cloison borders. Besides metal, cloisonné is also worked into and on ceramics, glass, gold, porcelain, silver, and wood. Pliqué a jour is a style in which the transparent enamel is used between cloisons that are not anchored to a base material. In wireless cloisonné, the wires (cloisons) are pulled from the workmanship before the enamel is ever fired. Household items, decorative items, and ceremonial pieces made for royalty have been decorated with cloisonné. It has been made for both export and domestic use.

General cloisonné varies in workmanship as well as color, depending on the country of origin. In later years some cloisonné was made in molds, almost by assembly line. Examples of Chinese cloisonné made in the past one hundred years or so seem to have brighter colors, as does the newer Taiwan cloisonné. In most of the Japanese ware, the maker actually studies his subject in nature before transferring his art into cloisonné form.

Cloisonné is a medium that demands careful attention to detail; please consult a professional for restoration. Our advisor for this category is Jeffrey M. Person. Mr. Person has been a collector and dealer for forty years. He is a speaker, writer, and appraiser on the subject of cloisonné. He is listed in the Directory under Florida.

Chinese Porcelain

Ashtray, bl w/wht dragon, 3"..........**15.00**
Astray, bl w/mc birds & flowers, ftd, 5" **30.00**
Bowl, aqua w/mc decor, 12"..........**85.00**
Bowl, center; aqua w/mc carp, 18"..........**400.00**
Bowl, mc w/flowers & birds, 6" **40.00**
Bowl, rice; mc w/blk foo dogs, 4" **30.00**
Box, candy; mc birds, flowers & butterflies, 6"..........**75.00**
Box, card; blk w/deck of cards, ftd, 5" **75.00**
Box, cigarette; mc flowers & birds, other mc decor, 6" **55.00**
Box, cigarette; mc w/wht dragons, 6"..........**70.00**
Box, stamp; blk w/mc geometric cloisons **50.00**
Candelabra, 5-branch, blk w/no decor (cloisons only), 14"..........**325.00**
Candlesticks, bl w/mc flowers, 6", pr **125.00**
Censer, bl w/floral, ftd, 4"..........**95.00**
Charger, aqua w/scene, 18", w/stand **350.00**

Charger, blk w/mc carp, 12"..........**100.00**
Cigarette holder, bl w/mc dragon, 5" **50.00**
Compote, gr w/mc scene & flowers, brass ft, 9" **225.00**
Cup & saucer, blk w/mc flowers, 4" **65.00**
Flowerpot, scene w/floral decor, rstr, 9" **175.00**
Ginger jar, cinnamon w/mc trees & leaves, 8", pr..........**195.00**
Jar, blk w/mc geometrics, 3" **60.00**
Jar, powder; gr w/mc floral, 4"..........**80.00**
Jar, tobacco; blk w/mc scene & horses, 7"..........**175.00**
Jardiniere, blk w/mc scene, 9"..........**275.00**
Mug, bl w/floral, copper hdl, 5" **45.00**
Napkin ring, bl w/dragons **20.00**
Napkin ring, mc flowers **20.00**
Pitcher, cinnamon w/mc floral, 9"..........**65.00**
Plate, blk w/mc floral & scene, wall mount, 6" **60.00**
Saki cup, mc geometrics, 1¼"..........**30.00**
Sculpture, camel, mc, cloisons only in geometric form, 8", pr.....**575.00**
Sculpture, foo dog, aqua, cloisons only in geometric form, 6", pr...**450.00**

Sculpture, man and horse, rug on horse's back lifts off to reveal incense burner, 14x18", $3,000.00. (Photo courtesy Jeff Person)

Shakers, wht w/aqua flowers, 2", pr..........**45.00**
Snuff bottle, yel w/mc floral, 3" **100.00**
Table screen, aqua w/yel bird, mc scenic & floral, teak stand, 16" ..**2,000.00**
Tea caddy, brn w/mc floral, 5" **65.00**
Teapot, bl w/mc floral, 7" **125.00**
Teapot, gr w/mc carp, 4" **65.00**
Toothpick holder, aqua w/mc floral, 2½"..........**30.00**
Toothpick holder, blk w/floral, ftd, 3" **40.00**
Vase, aqua w/mc scene & floral panels, 24", pr..........**950.00**
Vase, aqua w/wht dragons, 6", pr..........**125.00**
Vase, bl w/mc flowers, mini, 1" **25.00**
Vase, bl w/mc foo dogs, 18", pr **750.00**
Vase, blk, cloisons only in geometric form, 9", pr **150.00**
Vase, cinnamon w/mc butterflies, 9", pr..........**225.00**
Vase, gr w/horses in scene, 9"..........**95.00**

Japanese

Ashtray, bl w/mc scene, Inaba, 4" **60.00**
Belt buckle, blk w/2 mc dragons, foil, standard **125.00**
Bowl, blk w/mc floral, scalloped, 8" **215.00**
Bowl, mc flowers & leaves, pliqué a jour, 4" **350.00**
Box, cigarette; bl w/dogwood on lid, Inaba, 6"..........**275.00**
Box, eggplant w/stylized flower, Ando, 4" dia **250.00**
Box, stamp; dk bl w/floral top, standard **125.00**

Candlestick, blk w/wht roses & gr leaves, 6", ea 175.00
Censer, dk bl w/mc floral & foliage, 3-ftd, Inaba, 3½" 250.00
Charger, blk/goldstone w/phoenix bird reserves, scalloped borders, 18" ..850.00
Charger, gr w/mc butterfly & leaves, flower cloisons 275.00
Charger, gray w/mc leaves, eagle soaring above, 24" 2,200.00
Compote, lav w/geometric cloisons, sgn, 9" 325.00
Cup & saucer, demi; blk w/mc geometrics, ho ho & phoenix birds ...150.00
Flowerpot, wht, scenic & floral reserves, brass cloisons, standard, 6" ..210.00
Ginger jar, bl w/foil & mc butterflies, 4" 200.00
Jardiniere, gr foil w/mc patterns, floral border, 6 bronze legs, 12" ..1,400.00
Jewel chest, blk w/silver cloisons, mc scenes, 3-drw, 5" 1,200.00
Napkin ring, yel w/red rose 35.00
Pitcher, blk w/5 flying wht cranes 275.00
Saki cup, blk w/gr bamboo 65.00
Salad bowl, bl w/3 flying wht cranes, 10", +6 6" bowls................650.00
Screen, 4-panel, blk w/mc scenes, silver cloisons, Inaba, 6" 700.00
Shakers, wht w/scattered mc flowers, silver tops, pr.....................75.00
Snuff bottle, blk w/red phoenix bird, 3" 125.00
Snuff bottle, turq w/mc floral, 3" 135.00
Tea caddy, blk w/butterflies & mc leaves, standard, 6" 165.00
Teapot, blk, mc floral borders w/2 medallions, squat, 4" 175.00
Teapot, blk w/ho ho birds & mc florals, +cr/sug, 2 c/s & tray 950.00
Toothpick holder, gr w/red rose & gr leaves 45.00
Vase, bl-gray w/baby chicks in naturalistic colors, 10", pr 2,500.00
Vase, celadon w/mc hydrangea cluster, Ando, spherical, 12" ...1,200.00
Vase, gr foil w/1 red rose, 8" 225.00
Vase, mc geometrics, scalloped rim, standard, 10" 235.00
Vase, pigeon blood w/1 wht hibiscus, 6"......................................185.00
Vase, turq on porc, 2 scenic mc medallions w/mc flowers, 10" 325.00

Clothing and Accessories

The field of collectible, vintage, and antique clothing is often confusing, especially for the novice collector or nonspecialty dealer. Prices vary enormously, depending on where you are — the Midwestern and Southern states still harbor the best deals, sometimes as much as 70% below book value — and the individual article of clothing in question. Prior to 1940 almost all apparel was custom made, therefore each garment is unique in both design and quality of construction. Specialty gowns, i.e. dresses which can be worn by modern-day brides or for special events, fetch the highest prices. Civil War re-enactors have driven up the prices of authentic Civil War apparel. Dresses with intact bustles continue to be rare finds. Young collectors are creating a demand for wearable 1950s – 1970s clothing, although prices in these categories still remain reasonable. A first-time collector needs to do thorough research to understand vintage clothing construction techniques before venturing into this field because of the many reproductions and mismarked items now finding their way onto the market. For example, reproductions of Victorian dresses usually close with a zipper instead of the traditional hooks and eyes. Zippers were not commonly used until after 1935.

For further information we recommend *Collector's Guide to Vintage Fashions* by Kristina Harris (an easy-to-use guide for dating women's clothing); *Vintage Hats and Bonnets, 1770 – 1970*, by Susan Langley; *Ladies' Vintage Accessories* by LaRee Johnson Bruton; and *Antique & Vintage Clothing: A Guide to Dating and Valuation of Women's Clothing, 1850 – 1940*, by our advisor, Diane Snyder-Haug, available from Collector Books or your local bookstore. (Ms. Snyder-Haug is listed in the Directory under Florida.) Vintage denim values are prices realized at Flying Deuce Auctions, who specialize not only in denims but Hawaiian shirts, souvenir jackets, and various other types of vintage clothing. They are listed in the Directory under Auction Houses. Our values are for items of ladies' clothing unless noted 'man's' or 'child's.' Assume them to be in excellent condition unless otherwise described.

Key:
cap/s — cap sleeves
embr — embroidery
hs — hand sewn
l/s — long sleeves
ms — machine sewn
n/s — no sleeves
plt — pleated
s/s — short sleeves

Dress, second day (marriage), yellow silk gauze, short sleeves, ca 1810 – 1820, with provenance, EX, $925.00.

Coat, blk leather, buttons, raglan/s, lined, knee-length, 1970s......50.00
Coat, brn brushed leather, tan fur collar, pockets, 1960s 72.00
Coulottes, red rayon satin, 53" W hems, no pockets, 1950s 30.00
Dress, bias-cut satin, cowel neck, n/s, rhinestone belt buckle, 1930s ..95.00
Dress, bl knit shift, button front, wht collar, s/s, Leslie Fay, 1960s...18.00
Dress, bl sheer rayon, V-neck, ¾ darted/s, decor shoulders, 1930s.....48.00
Dress, bl silk, l/s bodice w/fringe, boned, peplum, full skirt, 1860s ..995.00
Dress, blk crepe, plt V-neck, sequined long skirt, elbow/s, 1940s......70.00
Dress, blk knit, l/s, 3-ruffle skirt, Arpega, 1970s...........................32.00
Dress, blk linen sheath, s/s, tie belt, floral applique, 1950s...........34.00
Dress, blk polished cotton, bias-cut neck, cap/s, rhinestones, 1950s ...35.00
Dress, blk rayon, self collar, dolman s/s, full skirt, 1940s.............60.00
Dress, blk rayon crepe, Mandarin collar, s/s, mid-calf skirt, 1940s....90.00
Dress, blk rayon crepe float w/Chantilly neck & ¾ s, Korell, 1950s.....56.00
Dress, blk silk, sm collar, split-cuff l/s, princess bodice, 1940s.......42.50
Dress, blk velvet, bell/s w/cutwork/scallop, 1960s 55.00
Dress, blk wool, bias-cut bodice, elbow/s, invt-plt skirt, 1940s......80.00
Dress, cotton w/mc floral embr, s/s, yoke bodice, calf length, 1960s ...22.50
Dress, dotted Swiss net over taffeta w/bows, strapless, 1950s.......100.00
Dress, Duchesse satin bodice, 8-gore knit skirt, s/s, 1930s 85.00
Dress, floral polyester, high waist, s/s, full skirt, long, 1960s 32.00
Dress, girl's, cotton print, s/s w/ruffle, piping, hand sewn, 1850s ..185.00
Dress, gr crushed velvet, Emp waist, n/s, mini, 1960s 52.00
Dress, Hawaiian print, n/s, Emp waist, mid-calf length, 1960s........30.00
Dress, Hawaiian print polyester, wide l/s, full length, label, 1960s..38.00
Dress, navy cotton, scoop neck, s/s, sheath skirt, 1950s.................40.00
Dress, navy twill, shawl collar, zipper front, cloth belt, 1950s.......35.00
Dress, navy/wht print, sailor collar w/wht bow, n/s, 1960s.............29.00
Dress, pk Chantilly on satin, cap s/s, sheath w/scalloped hem, 1950s ..48.00
Dress, pk taffeta, V neck, s/s, full-length gathered skirt, 1940s......65.00
Dress, plaid cotton blend, s/s w/cuffs, patch pockets, Sears, 1960s ...18.00
Dress, plaid taffeta, scoop neck, ¾ dolman/s, circle skirt, 1950s 52.00
Dress, princess A-line wrapper type, l/s w/cuffs, lined, 1870s.......200.00
Dress, print polyester, V-neck, Empire waist, l/s, maxi, 1960s.......49.00
Dress, printed cotton (tie-dye effect), s/s, calf-length, 1960s.........25.00
Dress, printed cotton sateen, V-neck sheath w/s/s, 1950s 32.00
Dress, printed moire silk, collar, button front, ¾ s, Tobie, 1950s 32.00
Dress, printed nylon, V-neck, collar, l/s, swing skirt, 1970s 28.00

Dress, printed rayon, dbl-button front, cuffed s/s, rnd collar, 1940s ...**58.00**
Dress, purple crepe wool, scoop-neck sheath w/dolman/s, lined, 1950s **45.00**
Dress, rayon crepe (lined), collar, ¾ s, calf-length skirt, 1950s **32.00**
Dress, rayon shirtwaist, cuffed s/s, rhinestone buttons, 1950s **38.00**
Dress, red linen w/blk collar/cuffs, l/s, plt-front skirt, 1930s **60.00**
Dress, wht cotton w/machine embr, MOP buttons, ca 1906, EX..**215.00**
Dress, wht crinkle cotton, flower applique, s/s, maxi, 1960s..........**49.00**
Dress, wine polyester, sailor collar, l/s, fabric belt, 1960s **38.00**
Dress, wool faille w/knife-plt trim, ¾ s, flared skirt, 1940s **26.00**
Dress, yel & bl striped knit, jewel neck, n/s, A-line mini, 1960s...**20.00**
Dress/robe, wht check cotton w/piping, hand sewn, loose fit, 1850s..**150.00**
Gown, wedding; chantilly lace/net/taffeta, scoop neck, s/s, 1950s...**100.00**
Gown, wedding; Duchesse satin, sm collar/Emp ties/puffy s/s, 1930s.......**175.00**
Gown, wedding; satin w/sheer o/l, floral lace w/pearls, l/s, 1970s..**45.00**
Gown, wedding; taffeta, Sweetheart neck, puff l/s, net/train, 1940s...**350.00**
Jacket, blk soft leather, wedge cut, dolman/s, 1980s......................**46.00**
Jacket, brn suede, 3-button, fringed yoke/hem, 1950s, VG...........**45.00**
Jacket, man's, suede leather, 3-button front, placket pockets, 1960s..**58.00**
Jacket, man's, tan leather, patch pockets, zip-out liner, 1970s.....**100.00**
Jacket, tweed wool w/leather trim, dbl-breasted, car length, 1980s..**44.00**
Jumper, gr wool, ns/, box-plt skirt, lined, 1960s **32.00**
Jumper, houndstooth wool, scoop neck, faux pockets, lined, 1940s...**30.00**
Jumpsuit, bl denim, full-front zipper, pockets, wide legs, s/s, 1960s ..**45.00**
Nightgown, cotton w/bands of tucking & heavy lace, ca 1900, VG..**140.00**
Pants, bl slubbed cotton (lined), capris w/slit at hem, 1960s.........**28.00**
Pants, blk velvet, braided cord buttons, front plt, cuffs, 1950s **45.00**
Pants, cotton/spandex denim, 5-pocket, low-rise bellbottoms, 1980s ..**17.00**
Pants, man's, bl gabardine, plt front, tapered legs, 1950s **30.00**
Pants, man's, blk wool, plt front, slash pockets, cuffs, 1940s..........**48.00**
Pants, man's, brn gabardine, western cut, corner-button pockets, 1950s.**65.00**
Pants, man's, navy gabardine, slant pockets, str legs, 1950s...........**42.00**
Pants, maroon, western style, pearl snap pockets, 1940s...............**150.00**
Pants, polyester dbl-knit, sewn-down creases, 31" bellbottoms, 1970s...**28.00**
Pants, printed cotton capris, button closure, 1950s......................**32.00**
Pants, red stretch denim w/vinyl snake print, flared, Guess, 1980s ..**24.00**
Pants, textured dbl-knit, 23" bellbottoms, 1970s.........................**22.50**
Pantsuit, blk velvet, tunic top w/rhinestones+str-leg pants, 1960s...**36.00**
Pantsuit, brushed denim, l/s shirt w/V-yoke, 24" bellbottoms, 1970s ..**32.00**
Pantsuit, dbl-knit, V-neck cardigan flat-front Bermuda shorts, 1960s..**26.00**
Pantsuit, patterned twill, dbl-breasted l/s jacket+lined pants, 1960s..**35.00**
Pantsuit, printed shiny knit, n/s tank top, bellbottom pants, 1960s ...**30.00**
Peignoir set, sheer nylon, spaghetti-strap gown, s/s robe, 1960s **26.00**
Petticoat & pantelets, cotton w/tucking & heavy lace, 1900s.....**140.00**
Romper, child's, cotton check, wide straps, elastic bk & waist, 1950s ...**40.00**
Shirt, Hawaiian print, pocket, s/s, 1980s **19.50**
Shirt, lt dbl-knit, sequin braid at neck, n/s, 1960s **18.50**
Shirt, man's, blk cotton, western style, l/s, Rustler, 1980s............**24.00**
Shirt, man's, gabardine, chest pocket w/flap, l/s w/cuffs, 1940s ...**125.00**
Shirt, man's, gabardine, l/s, western style w/piping, 1920s...........**225.00**
Shirt, man's, ltweight dbl-knit, l/s, patch pocket, Van Heusen, 1970s...**19.00**
Shirt, man's, red/wht/bl striped polyester, s/s, collar, 1970s...........**25.00**
Shirt, man's, western style, cotton blend, l/s, 1980s **18.00**
Shirt, printed polyester, l/s disco style, Koret of CA, 1970s...........**18.00**
Shirt, printed polyester chiffon, l/s, tapered body, 1970s **20.00**
Shirt, unisex, patchwork print nylon, l/s, pocket, 1960s................**27.50**
Shoes, blk brocade mesh pumps w/bow, 1¾" kitten heels, 1960s ..**36.00**
Shoes, blk elastic lace mules, 1980s, MIB.................................**25.00**
Shoes, blk suede, open-toe sling-bk sandals, 3" heels, 1960s **32.00**
Shoes, blk suede pumps w/grosgrain & bow, 3" Louis heels, 1960s ..**40.00**
Shoes, gold vinyl ankle boots w/bk zipper, 1½" heels, 1970s.........**32.00**
Shoes, man's, brn faux buffalo hide wingtip-style oxfords, 1970s ..**36.00**
Shoes, man's, brn faux crocodile leather loafer w/buckle, 1960s ...**44.00**
Shoes, man's, sea turtle leather moccasin-toe oxford, Mexico, 1950s ..**50.00**

Shoes, red patent leather pumps w/clear swirl toe, 1960s **22.00**
Shoes, taupe leather open-toe sling-bk sandals, 3" heels, 1980s **26.00**
Shorts, Bermuda; plaid cotton, elastic bk, Glenbrooke, 1960s **18.00**
Suit, button-front wool jacket w/dolman/s, plaid plt skirt, 1980s...**38.00**
Suit, popcorn-stitch sweater, n/s shell, knit unlined skirt, 1980s...**48.00**
Suit, printed polyester elbow/s jacket, unlined skirt, 1960s **30.00**
Sweater, acrylic & mohair hand-knit, s/s, 1960s, EX **27.50**
Sweater, acrylic l/s cardigan, rollable cuffs, 1950s **32.00**
Sweater, acrylic w/knitted-in leaping fish, l/s, zipper front, 1960s...**32.00**
Sweater, bl knit, ribbed neck w/short zipper, s/s, ribbed hem, 1950s...**22.00**
Sweater, blk acrylic cardigan w/rabbit fur collar, rhinestones, 1950s..**195.00**
Sweater, blk acrylic n/s shell, button-bk closing, 1950s **18.00**
Sweater, blk mohair cardigan, ¾ s, 1950s......................................**26.00**
Sweater, cashmere (lined) cardigan w/sequins/seed beads, ¾ s, 1950s **225.00**
Sweater, man's, brn wool blend, V-neck cardigan, l/s, 1970s **17.50**
Sweater, pk knit w/emb roses, n/s shell, 1960s **22.00**
Sweater, red/wht striped knit tunic, l/s, roll collar, 1960s.............**12.50**
Sweater, worsted yarn, snowflake pattern yoke, l/s, 1980s **30.00**
Tuxedo, blk wool jersey, peaked lapels w/brocade trim, 1970s.....**100.00**
Tuxedo, man's, blk wool, shawl collar, single-breasted, 1970s **48.00**
Tuxedo, man's, lined wool, notched lapel, dbl-breasted, 1940s ...**160.00**
Tuxedo, man's, navy wool w/satin, shawl collar, single-breasted, 1950s ..**70.00**

Vintage Denim

Bib overalls, Osh Kosh B'Gosh, vest bk, Union Made, dk, 32" waist ..**25.00**
Jacket, Hedlight buckle-bk 1st edition, med color, 1930s-40s, lg, G..**250.00**
Jacket, Hercules, indigo, red tag, med...**85.00**
Jacket, Lee 101-J, red label, 1950s...**150.00**
Jacket, Lee 91-B, indigo, M...**260.00**
Jacket, Levi, blanket-lined 1st edition, full leather patch, dk, 1930s...**700.00**
Jacket, Levi 507 XX 2nd edition, G color, wear/damage, sm.......**220.00**
Jacket, Levi 507 XX 2nd edition, paper patch, XL, NM.............**650.00**
Jeans, Lee 101 Z, med bl, med-lg, EX+......................................**45.00**
Jeans, Levi 501, red lines, #6 underlined, sm, NM.....................**120.00**
Jeans, Levi 501, red lines, med bl w/hege, med, NM **110.00**
Jeans, Levi 501 big E, red lines, dk bl, 32" waist **275.00**
Jeans, Levi 501 XX, leather patch, G color/hege/contrast, lg, EX ...**850.00**
Jeans, Levi 501XX, leather patch, 1-sided red tag, prof rpr, 32" waist....**1,200.00**
Jeans, Levi 503 Z XX, leather patch, 1949, 26" waist................**300.00**
Jeans, Levi 505, big E, med dk, 34" waist, prof rpr....................**100.00**
Jeans, Levi 505, sm e, single-stitched, paper tags, sm, M............**220.00**
Jeans, Levi 701 XX women's, orig flashers, 24" waist.................**225.00**
Overalls, Hercules, indigo denim, w/flashers, 1940s, 34" waist....**425.00**
Shirt, Levi, western style, short horn tag, med, NM **150.00**
Shirt, Sears Roebuck, wht pnt snaps, 1950s, med **60.00**
Work jacket, Dubbleware, 3-pocket, 1930s, med **275.00**
Work jacket, Headlight, 3-pocket, change button, 1930s, med, NM..**900.00**

Cluthra

The name cluthra is derived from the Scottish word 'clutha,' meaning cloudy. Glassware by this name was first produced by J. Couper and Sons, England. Frederick Carder developed cluthra while at the Steuben Glass Works, and similar types of glassware were also made by Durand and Kimball. It is found in both solid and shaded colors and is characterized by a spotty appearance resulting from small air pockets trapped between its two layers. See also specific manufacturers.

Bowl, finger; amethyst, 2⅝x5" dia **285.00**
Bowl, wht w/pk int, no mk, 10"...**100.00**
Plate, opal & amethyst mottle, att Kimball, 4¾".............................**250.00**
Vase, autumnal colors on grey-wht, classic form, Kimball, 8½" ..**625.00**

Vase, brn, gr & yel, mk #K 1812-6, Kimball, 6½" **350.00**
Vase, gr mottle, bulbous w/flared rim, #1986-6K, Kimball, 6" **175.00**

Vase, green with ribs and bubbles, Kimball, #20177-6 Dec 09, 6", $325.00.

Vase, mottled agate colors, oval on bulbed stem, Kimball, 12" ...**250.00**
Vase, orange random splotches, K 54-9 Dec 7, Kimball, 8½"......**250.00**
Vase, orange/brn/opal mottle, tapered, Kimball, 12", pr **600.00**
Vase, orange/wht mottle, charcoal hdls, Kimball, 11"..................**425.00**
Vase, royal bl, spherical, Kimball, 4x4", pr..................................**475.00**
Vase, turq to gr on wht, crystal ft, shouldered, Kimball, 9" **300.00**
Vase, yel & wht in clear, long neck, #1949, Kimball, 16" **350.00**

Coalport

In 1745 in Caughley, England, Squire Brown began a modest business fashioning crude pots and jugs from clay mined in his own fields. Tom Turner, a young potter who had apprenticed his trade at Worcester, was hired in 1772 to plan and oversee the construction of a 'proper' factory. Three years later he bought the business, which he named Caughley Coalport Porcelain Manufactory. Though the dinnerware he produced was meant to be only everyday china, the hand-painted florals, birds, and landscapes used to decorate the ware were done in exquisite detail and in a wide range of colors. In 1780 Turner introduced the Willow pattern which he produced using a newly perfected method of transfer printing. (Wares from the period between 1775 and 1799 are termed 'Caughley' or 'Salopian.') John Rose purchased the Caughley factory from Thomas Turner in 1799, adding that holding to his own pottery which he had built two years before in Coalport. (It is from this point that the pottery's history that the wares are termed 'Coalport.') The porcelain produced there before 1814 was unmarked with very few exceptions. After 1820 some examples were marked with a '2' with an oversize top loop. The term 'Coalbrookdale' refers to a fine type of porcelain decorated in floral bas relief, similar to the work of Dresden.

After 1835 highly decorated ware with rich ground colors imitated the work of Sevres and Chelsea, even going so far as to copy their marks. From about 1895 until the 1920s, the mark in use was 'Coalport' over a crown with 'England A.D. 1750' indicating the date claimed as the founding, not the date of manufacture. From the 1920s until 1945, 'Made in England' over a crown and 'Coalport' below was used. Later the mark was 'Coalport' over a smaller crown with 'Made in England' in a curve below.

Each of the major English porcelain companies excelled in certain areas of manufacture. Coalport produced the finest 'jeweled' porcelain, made by picking up a heavy mixture of slip and color and dropping it onto the surface of the ware. These 'jewels' are perfectly spaced and are often graduated in size with the smaller 'jewels' at the neck or base of the vase. Some ware was decorated with very large 'jewels' resembling black

opals or other polished stones. Such pieces are in demand by the advanced collector.

It is common to find considerable crazing in old Coalport, since the glaze was thinly applied to increase the brilliance of the colors. Many early vases had covers; look for a flat surface that would have supported a lid (just because it is gilded does not mean the vase never had one). Pieces whose lids are missing are worth about 40% less. Most lids had finials which have been broken and restored. You should deduct about 10% for a professional restoration on a finial.

In 1926 the Coalport Company moved to Shelton in Staffordshire and today belongs to a group headed by the Wedgwood Company. See also Indian Tree.

Bowl, Queen Elizabeth Silver Jubilee, 1977 ltd ed, 4½x10"........**265.00**
Cottage, Toll House, 1974-81, 5¼" **200.00**
Cup & saucer, coral petals w/gold, 1948-59, from $100 to **125.00**
Figurine, Doris, yel & gr skirt, 1915-49, 4½" **110.00**
Tray, Hong Kong, 10¼x4"...**325.00**
Urn, floral w/gold lattice, bolted, 1914, 8½", NM.....................**175.00**
Urns, lovers reserves on pk w/gold, late 19th C, 15¾", pr **2,650.00**
Vase, appl flowers, mc on wht, sm hdls, 1830s, 8⅛", pr..............**625.00**
Vase, lady's portrait on ivory & pk, w/lid, 8½" **1,800.00**
Vase, scenic reserve/jewels/gold hdls, shape #166/12, 1900s, 5¾" ...**650.00**

Coca-Cola

J.S. Pemberton, creator of Coca-Cola, originated his world-famous drink in 1886. From its inception the Coca-Cola Company began an incredible advertising campaign which has proven to be one of the most successful promotions in history. The quantity and diversity of advertising material put out by Coca-Cola in the last one hundred years is literally mind-boggling. From the beginning, the company has projected an image of wholesomeness and Americana. Beautiful women in Victorian costumes, teenagers and schoolchildren, blue- and white-collar workers, the men and women of the Armed Forces (even Santa Claus) have appeared in advertisements with a Coke in their hands. Some of the earliest collectibles include trays, syrup dispensers, gum jars, pocket mirrors, and calendars. Many of these items fetch prices in the thousands of dollars. Later examples include radios, signs, lighters, thermometers, playing cards, clocks, and toys — particularly toy trucks.

In 1970 the Coca-Cola Company initialed a multimillion-dollar 'image-refurbishing campaign' which introduced the new 'Dynamic Contour' logo, a twisting white ribbon under the Coca-Cola and Coke trademarks. The new logo often serves as a cut-off point to the purist collector. Newer and very ardent collectors, however, relish the myriad of items marketed since that date, as they often cannot afford the high prices that the vintage pieces command. For more information we recommend *Petretti's Coca-Cola Collectibles Price Guide*; *B.J. Summers' Guide to Coca-Cola, Fourth Edition*, *B.J. Summers' Pocket Guide to Coca-Cola, Fourth Edition*, and *Collectible Soda Pop* by B.J. Summers; also *Coca-Cola Commemorative Bottles, Second Edition*, by Bob and Debra Henrich. You may wish to call our advisor for this category, Craig Stifter, at 630-789-5780; he is listed in the Directory under Illinois.

Key:
CC — Coca-Cola   sf — self-framed
dc — diecut   tm — trademark

Reproductions and Fantasies

Beware of reproductions! Prices are given for the genuine original articles, but the symbol (+) at the end of some of the following lines indicate items that have been reproduced. Warning! The 1924,

1925, and 1935 calendars have been reproduced. They are identical in almost every way; only a professional can tell them apart. These are *very* deceiving! Watch for frauds: genuinely old celluloid items ranging from combs, mirrors, knives, and forks to doorknobs that have been recently etched with a new double-lined trademark. Still another area of concern deals with reproduction and fantasy items. A fantasy item is a novelty made to appear authentic with inscriptions such as 'Tiffany Studios,' 'Trans Pan Expo,' 'World's Fair,' etc. In reality, these items never existed as originals. For instance, don't be fooled by a Coca-Cola cash register; no originals are known to exist! Large mirrors for bars are being reproduced and are often selling for $10.00 to $50.00.

Of the hundreds of reproductions (designated 'R' in the following examples) and fantasies (designated 'F') on the market today, these are the most deceiving.

Belt buckle, no originals thought to exist (F), up to **10.00**
Bottle, dk amber, w/arrows, heavy, narrow spout (R).....................**10.00**
Bottle carrier, wood, yel w/red logo, holds 6 bottles (R)................**10.00**
Clock, Gilbert, regulator, battery-op, ¾-sz, NM+ (R).................**175.00**
Cooler, Glascock Jr, made by Coca-Cola USA (R) **300.00**
Doorknob, glass etched w/tm (F)..**3.00**
Knife, bottle shape, 1970s, many variations (F), ea.....................**5.00**
Knife, fork or spoon w/celluloid hdl, newly etched tm (F).............**5.00**
Letter opener, stamped metal, CC for 5¢ (F)...............................**3.00**
Pocket watch, often old watch w/new face (R) **10.00**
Pocketknife, yel & red, 1933 World's Fair (F) **2.00**
Sign, cb, lady w/fur, dtd 1911, 9x11" (F) **3.00**
Soda fountain glass holder, word 'Drink' on orig (R) **5.00**
Thermometer, bottle form, DONASCO, 17" (R) **10.00**
Trade card, copy of 1905 'Bathtub' foldout, emb 1978 (R)...........**25.00**

The following items have been reproduced and are among the most deceptive of all:
   Pocket mirrors from 1905, 1906, 1908, 1909, 1910, 1911, 1916, and 1920
   Trays from 1899, 1910, 1913, 1914, 1917, 1920, 1923, 1925, 1926, 1934, and 1937
   Tip trays from 1907, 1909, 1910, 1913, 1914, 1917, and 1920
   Knives: many versions of the German brass model
   Cartons: wood versions, yellow with logo
   Calendars: 1924, 1925, and 1935

These items have been marketed:
   Brass thermometer, bottle shape, Taiwan, 24"
   Cast-iron toys (none ever made)
   Cast-iron door pull, bottle shape, made to look old
   Poster, Yes Girl (R)
   Button sign, has one round hole while original has four slots, most have bottle logo, 12", 16", 20" (R)
      Bullet trash receptacles (old cans with decals)
      Paperweight, rectangular, with Pepsin Gum insert
      1930 Bakelite radio, 24" tall, repro is lighter in weight than the original, of poor quality and cheaply made
      1949 cooler radio (reproduced with tape deck)
      Tin bottle sign, 40"
      Fishtail die-cut tin sign, 20" long
      Straw holders (no originals exist)
   Coca-Cola bicycle with cooler, fantasy item: the piece has been totally made-up, no such original exists
   1914 calendar top, reproduction, 11¼x23¾", printed on smooth-finish heavy ivory paper
      Countless trays — most unauthorized (must read 'American Artworks; Coshocton, OH.')

Centennial Items

The Coca-Cola Company celebrated its 100th birthday in 1986, and amidst all the fanfare came many new collectible items, all sporting the 100th-anniversary logo. These items are destined to become an important part of the total Coca-Cola collectible spectrum. The following pieces are among the most popular centennial items.

Bottle, gold-dipped, in velvet sleeve, 6½-oz..................................**75.00**
Bottle, Hutchinson, amber, Root Co, ½-oz, 3 in case................**375.00**
Bottle, International, set of 9 in plexiglas case.........................**400.00**
Bottle, leaded crystal, 100th logo, 6½-oz, MIB **150.00**
Medallion, bronze, 3" dia, w/box **100.00**
Pin set, wood fr, 101 pins **300.00**
Scarf, silk, 30x30" **40.00**
Thermometer, glass cover, 14" dia, M...**35.00**

Coca-Cola Originals

Ashtray, ceramic, rnd w/bottle lighter, 1950s, NM **250.00**
Badge, Bottler's Conference, celluloid/tin, 1930s, 2½x2¾", EX+ ..**125.00**
Bank, dispenser form, red, w/single glass, EX+ **375.00**
Banner, canvas, Drink CC.../bottle graphic, 1910, 16x70", VG+...**4,000.00**
Blotter, party crowd in front of fireplace, Canadian, 1950s, NM+ ...**25.00**
Blotter, Pure & Healthful..., bottles flank oval, 1913, G **15.00**

Blotter, Restores Energy, Strengthens the Nerves, 1906, EX, $225.00.

Bottle carrier, aluminum, 24-bottle, w/ad-on steel hdl, 4x12x17", EX+ ..**150.00**
Bottle carrier, aluminum, 6-pack, wire hdl, 1950s, EX................**175.00**
Bottle carrier, wood, 6-pack, yel/red, cut-out hdl, w/bottles, 1940s ..**155.00**
Bottle opener, flat metal bottle shape, 1950s, NM........................**25.00**
Bowl, ceramic, gr w/emb logos around fluted rim, 1930s, M **550.00**
Calendar, 1905, incomplete, EX+ **7,500.00**
Calendar, 1914, Betty, incomplete, VG **2,400.00**
Calendar, 1919, lady in pk, 40" (in fr), EX **1,650.00**
Calendar, 1925, VG **425.00**
Calendar, 1926, lady seated drinking from glass, 23" (in fr), G...**385.00**
Calendar, 1945, EX+ **375.00**
Calendar, 1945, teenage girls atop ea pg, complete, NM............**210.00**
Calendar, 1957, NM+ **175.00**
Calendar, 1959, Santa w/bottles of Coke, complete, 22x12", VG....**85.00**
Clock, plastic, Drink CC, serrated red-dot decal, 13" sq, EX **200.00**
Clock, Seth Thomas, rnd, Drink CC in Bottles, 1930s, EX.....**1,100.00**
Coin purse, leather triangle shape w/Drink CC in gold, 1908, rare, EX ...**250.00**
Cooler, airline; red w/end opener, top hdl, 13x17", EX **350.00**
Cooler, picnic; aluminum w/red trim, gold-tone hdls, 1960s, EX...**200.00**
Cuff links, bottle form, gold, mk 1/10 10k, ¾", NM, pr.................**50.00**
Decal, Drink CC in Bottles, red, curved corners, 9x15", NM **45.00**
Dispenser, arched top, red, Drink CC on sides, 1930s, NM+...**1,500.00**
Dispenser, salesman's sample, later 3-spigot, Things, 12x19", EX+......**1,500.00**
Display, cb, Friends for Life, fishing boy, Rockwell, 1935, 36", VG..**2,500.00**

Display bottle, plastic, pnt to appear full, metal cap, 1940s, 19", EX..**185.00**
Display bottle, 1923 clear glass bottle, no cap, 20", M **225.00**
Doll, Buddy Lee in uniform w/hat, compo, 1950s, EX+..............**875.00**
Door pull, plastic bottle on metal bracket, 1950s, 8x2", NMIB ..**425.00**
Door push bar, porc, Drink CC panel on wrought-iron bar, EX..**475.00**
Drinking glass, flared, frosted 5¢ arrow logo, lg, G..............**475.00**
Drinking glass, frosted 5¢ arrow logo, sm, NM.................**750.00**
Festoon, Autumn Girl, 5-pc, 1927, NM.................**3,500.00**
Festoon, nautical, 9-pc, 1930s, EX+ **4,700.00**
Festoon, Poppies, 5-pc, 1930s, unused, M (orig envelope).......**1,100.00**
Game, Age Cards, w/orig envelope, 1920s, NM **775.00**
Game, Safety & Danger, 1938, complete, EX+ **100.00**
Ice bucket, waxed cb, striped swag around top, EX+..................**50.00**
Lighter, Blue-Bird musical, by Hadson, 2¼", NMIB.................**200.00**
Lighter, Zippo, Enjoy CC & bell glass on chrome, 1960s, EX.....**310.00**
Menu board, Sprite Boy, red cb inserts behind glass, chrome fr, 13x28" ..**300.00**
Menu board, tin, silhouette girl, 1941, 28x20", EX......................**425.00**
Menu board, tin sf chalkboard, Refresh Yourself, 1930s, VG **325.00**
Paperweight, bottle caps encased in plastic, 4x4½", NMIB.........**50.00**
Pencil holder, ceramic 1896 dispenser form, 1960s, 7", EX **150.00**
Pin-back button, Member Hi-Fi Club, mc, 1950s, EX **20.00**
Playing cards, Airplane Spotter deck, 1940s, unused, NMIB **250.00**
Playing cards, Welcome Friend!, 1958, MIB **150.00**
Pocket mirror, girl w/bottle, 1916, oval, EX **200.00**
Pocket mirror, 1910 Hamilton King girl, EX+ **300.00**
Postcard, CC girl, 1910, NM+.................**775.00**
School kit, Real Pals, 1930s, complete, unopened, VG...............**150.00**
Sign, cash register; red glass panel w/wood base, 1950s, EX **300.00**
Sign, cb, Betty, 1914, 41x26", VG...................**650.00**
Sign, cb, Cool Contrast to a Summer Sun, beach girl, 1941, 48x72", G..**200.00**
Sign, cb, girl seated on diving board w/bottle, 1940s, 28x30", VG ...**200.00**
Sign, cb, Good/Pause, girl on trapeze, fr, 1954, 28x57", EX **375.00**
Sign, cb, Have a Coke, bottle on iceberg, 1944, 20x36", NM.......**30.00**
Sign, cb, Mind Reader, girl reaching for bottle, 1940s, 28x56", VG ...**20.00**
Sign, cb, Pause!, clown & ice skater, 1950s, 27x16", NM+ **2,500.00**
Sign, cb, Refreshed Through 70 Years, 2-sided, 1955, 28x56", EX..**250.00**
Sign, cb, Santa's Helpers, w/2 bottles, 1960s, 32x66", EX **125.00**
Sign, cb, Things Go Better..., girl on phone, fr, 1960s, 27x16", EX..**275.00**
Sign, cb, Things Go Better..., skaters, fr, 1960s, 24x40", EX **200.00**
Sign, cb, Year-Round Answer to Thirst, ice skater on log, 50x30", EX+..**1,100.00**
Sign, cb cutout, couple at sundial, 36x29", EX+......................**4,000.00**
Sign, cb cutout, Drink CC, Lionel Hampton, 1950s, 15x12", NM ..**975.00**
Sign, cb cutout, Stop for a Pause/Go Refreshed, cop, 1937, 32x42", VG...**1,100.00**
Sign, cb standup, Military girl w/bottle, 1940s, 17", EX+ **425.00**
Sign, cb standup, Navy service girl w/bottle, 1943, 18", NM...**1,000.00**
Sign, cb standup, Santa, Greetings From CC, 1948, 14", NM+ ...**350.00**
Sign, cb trolley, Around the Corner..., 1927, 11x21", EX+......**2,600.00**
Sign, cb trolley, Work Refreshed, work whistle, 1940s, 11x21", NM+...**875.00**
Sign, cb trolley, 4 seasons, 1923, 10x20", NM **4,000.00**
Sign, Edgebrite light-up clock (rnd or sq), 1950s, 9x20", EX **700.00**
Sign, Edgebrite motion light-up, Pause, 1950s, 9x20", EX **850.00**
Sign, masonite, Drink CC, girl tipping bottle, 1940s, 12x34", EX+....**250.00**
Sign, neon, CC Classic..., palm tree, 1980s, 28" dia, NM+ **1,500.00**
Sign, neon, CC on red plastic fishtail, 15x28", NM **300.00**
Sign, paper, Treat Yourself Right, man w/bottle, 1920s, 20x12", EX ..**550.00**
Sign, paper, Which?/CC or Goldelle Ginger Ale/lady, 1913, 24x18", EX+...**9,500.00**
Sign, paper, 5¢/Drink CC/5¢, wht on red, wht edge, 1930s, 6x24", EX...**75.00**
Sign, paper cutout, Home Refreshment/25¢ 6-pack, 1940s, 16x22", NM ..**50.00**
Sign, porc, Lunch/Pause Refresh, yel, 2-sided, 1950s, 26x28", EX+ ..**2,000.00**
Sign, porc button, CC lettered over bottle, red, 24" dia, EX+ **550.00**
Sign, porc emblem, Fountain Service w/taps, 1930s, 14x27", EX..**1,500.00**
Sign, rvpt glass light-up on base, Brunoff, 1930s, 14x12", EX+ ..**4,250.00**
Sign, sidewalk, fishtail logo w/menu board, metal fr, 28x20", VG...**125.00**

Sign, tin, ...Enjoy That Refreshing, fishtail/bottle, 53x18", VG+ **300.00**
Sign, tin, bottle on wht, red/yel/gr border, Drink, 1931, 13x5", NM...**400.00**
Sign, tin, Drink CC/D&R, bottle at left, Dasco, 1920s, 11x35", VG..**235.00**
Sign, tin, Drink CC/1915 bottle, wht, beveled, 1920s, 13x26", VG ..**1,400.00**
Sign, tin, Drink.. on red/bottle on wht, gr rim, 1934, 12x36", EX...**235.00**
Sign, tin, Drink/'New' Betty w/bottle, red w/gr sf, 1940s, 12x34", EX+...**825.00**
Sign, tin bottle form, 1930s, 39", G+ **425.00**
Sign, tin button, Drink CC in Bottles, red, 16" dia, EX+...........**475.00**
Sign, tin fishtail, CC in wht on red, 28x60", EX **250.00**
Sign, tin flange, Drink CC, bottle on yel dot, 1940s, 20x24", EX+ ..**550.00**
Sign, tin sf oval, Drink...Carbonated.../bottle, 1903-12, 11x9", VG..**6,050.00**

Sign, tin, Take a Case Home Today, 28x19", NM, $850.00. (Photo courtesy Craig Stifter)

Sign, triangle hanger w/filigree top, tin, 2-sided, 1930s, 23", VG ..**700.00**
Sign, wood, Battleship, K Displays, 8½x25", EX **650.00**
Sign, wood plaque/metal filigree top, 2 glasses, 1930s, 12x9", NM...**675.00**
Syrup jug, paper label w/Coke glass, 1950s, EX **20.00**
Thermometer, dial, metal/glass front, red, Drink...in Bottles, 12", EX...**180.00**
Thermometer, masonite, Thirst Knows No Seasons, 1940s, 17x7", VG...**250.00**
Thermometer, metal cigar shape, Drink CC/Sign of Good Taste, 30x8", VG...**250.00**
Thermometer, tin bottle shape, 1950s, 17", EX **125.00**
Thermometer, tin emb bottle on red panel w/curved ends, 1930s, 16" ..**225.00**
Thermometer, wood, Drink CC/D&R, 1905, 21", EX **500.00**
Tip tray, 1903, VG.................**900.00**
Tip tray, 1909, EX+ **875.00**
Tip tray, 1910, NM+.................**1,540.00**
Tip tray, 1916, EX+ **275.00**
Toy truck, metal, b/o, enclosed bay, yel/wht/red trim, 1960s, EXIB..**260.00**
Toy truck, metal, Dinky #402, red w/wht lettering, 1950s, EXIB...**200.00**
Toy truck, metal, Tonka tanker, yel w/red trim, 1950s, NMIB **200.00**
Toy truck, plastic, Marx, w/6 plastic cases, EX+IB......................**600.00**
Village, stained glass, lights up, 7-pc, Franklin Mint, G **200.00**
Writing tablet, landmarks of the USA, 1960s, EX **10.00**

Trays

All 10½x13½" original serving trays produced from 1910 to 1942 are marked with a date, Made in USA, and the American Artworks Inc., Coshocton, Ohio. All original trays of this format (1910 – 40) had REG TM in the tail of the C. The 1934 Weismuller and O'Sullivan tray has been reproduced at least three times. To be original, it will have a black back and must say 'American Artworks, Coshocton, Ohio.' It was not reproduced by Coca-Cola in the 1950s.

1897, Victorian Lady, 9¼" dia, VG.................**15,000.00**
1901, Hilda Clark, 9¾", VG.................**4,000.00**

1903, Hilda Clark, oval, 18½x15", EX	6,000.00
1905, Lillian Russell, glass or bottle, 10½x13¼", EX	3,500.00
1906, Juanita, glass or bottle, oval, 13¼x10½", EX	2,200.00
1907, Relieves Fatigue, 10½x13¼", NM	4,000.00
1907, Relieves Fatigue, 13½x16½", EX	3,600.00
1908, Topless, Wherever Ginger Ale..., 12¼" dia, NM	11,500.00
1909, St Louis Fair, 10½x13¼", EX	1,800.00
1909, St Louis Fair, 13½x16½", NM	3,000.00
1910, Coca-Cola Girl, Hamilton King, 10½x13¼", EX+	1,200.00
1914, Betty, oval, 12¼x15¼", EX+	400.00
1914, Betty, 10½x13¼", EX+	600.00
1916, Elaine, 8½x19", NM	600.00
1920, Garden Girl, oval, 10½x13¼", EX+	800.00
1921, Autumn Girl, oval, 10½x13¼", EX+	800.00
1922, Summer Girl, 10½x13¼", NM	1,100.00
1923, Flapper Girl, 10½x13¼", NM	500.00
1924, Smiling Girl, brn rim, 10½x13¼", NM	650.00
1924, Smiling Girl, maroon rim, 10½x13¼", EX+	1,050.00
1925, Party, 10½x13¼", NM	650.00
1926, Golfers, 10½x13¼", EX+	800.00
1927, Curbside Service, 10½x13¼", EX	850.00
1928, Bobbed Hair, 10½x13¼", NM	700.00
1929, Girl in Swimsuit w/Glass, 10½x13¼", EX+	450.00
1930, Swimmer, 10½x13¼", EX	425.00
1930, Telephone, 10½x13¼", NM	650.00
1931, Boy w/Sandwich & Dog, 10½x13¼", NM	1,100.00
1932, Girl in Swimsuit on Beach, Hayden, 10½x13¼", EX+	625.00
1933, Francis Dee, 10½x13¼", NM	900.00
1934, Weismuller & O'Sullivan, 10½x13¼", NM	1,200.00
1935, Madge Evans, 10½x13¼", NM	575.00
1936, Hostess, 10½x13¼", NM	675.00

1937, Running Girl, 10½x13¾", NM, $425.00.

1938, Girl in the Afternoon, 10½x13¼", NM	275.00
1939, Springboard Girl, 10½x13¼", NM	375.00
1940, Sailor Girl, 10½x13¼", NM	480.00
1941, Ice Skater, 10½x13¼", NM	450.00
1942, Roadster, 10½x13¼", NM+	500.00
1950s, Girl w/Wind in Hair, screen bkground, 10½x13¼", M	100.00
1950s, Girl w/Wind in Hair, solid bkground, 10½x13¼", NM	225.00
1955, Menu Girl, 10½x13¼", M	65.00
1957, Birdhouse, 10½x13¼", NM	125.00
1957, Rooster, 10½x13¼", NM	175.00
1957, Umbrella Girl, 10½x13¼", M	375.00
1961, Pansy Garden, 10½x13¼", NM	30.00

Vendors

Though interest in Coca-Cola machines of the 1949 – 1959 era rose dramatically over the last decade, values currently seem to have leveled off. The major manufacturers of these curved-top, 5¢ and 10¢ machines were Vendo (V), Vendorlator (VMC), Cavalier (C or CS), and Jacobs. Prices are for machines in excellent or better condition, complete and working. They vary greatly according to geographical location.

Cavalier, model #C27, EX orig	1,200.00
Cavalier, model #C27, M rstr	2,800.00
Cavalier, model #C51, EX orig	1,100.00
Cavalier, model #C51, M rstr	2,000.00
Cavalier, model #CS72, EX orig	1,600.00
Cavalier, model #CS72, M rstr	3,200.00
Jacobs, model #26, EX	1,200.00
Jacobs, model #26, M rstr	2,500.00
Vendo, model #23, EX orig	900.00
Vendo, model #39, EX orig	1,100.00
Vendo, model #39, M, rstr	2,700.00
Vendo, model #44, EX orig	2,700.00
Vendo, model #44, M rstr	3,200.00
Vendo, model #56, EX orig	1,400.00
Vendo, model #56, M rstr	3,000.00
Vendo, model #80, EX orig	600.00
Vendo, model #80, M rstr	1,250.00
Vendo, model #81, EX orig	1,400.00
Vendo, model #81, M rstr	3,200.00
Vendorlator, model #27, EX orig	1,350.00
Vendorlator, model #27, rstr (w/stand)	2,750.00
Vendorlator, model #27A, EX orig	900.00
Vendorlator, model #27A, M rstr	2,000.00
Vendorlator, model #33, EX orig	1,100.00
Vendorlator, model #33, M rstr	2,250.00
Vendorlator, model #44, EX orig	1,250.00
Vendorlator, model #44, M rstr	2,300.00
Vendorlator, model #72, EX orig	1,200.00
Vendorlator, model #72, M rstr	2,100.00

Coffee Grinders

Coffee mills continue to be a popular collectible and interest grows annually as more people discover the beauty of their intricate designs and variety of materials from which they are made. Interest remains high even among seasoned collectors. This is largely due to the fact that there is such a wide variety of makers and models of both US and European mills that no one person could ever assemble a collection that would encompass them all.

Prices remain strong on attractive mills that display well and continue to rise on scarce or rare mills that turn up from time to time. The value of common, incomplete, or damaged mills remains low. The majority of values have gone up; but as more mills enter the market, some prices have come down as supply outstrips demand. There are many nice mills that can be added to a collection for less than $100.00. Mills fall into only a few categories — side mills, wall mills, box mills, and uprights; these can be table, counter, or floor-standing and have any combination of cranks and/or wheels. The last type of mill to appear is the electric. These were first produced in the early 1900s for industrial use. The first electric coffee mill made for home use was not, as many believe, the Kitchen Aid/Hobart of the mid-1930s, but rather a Hamilton-Beach model produced and sold around 1915. These are very scarce and rarely turn up. When they do they are quickly purchased.

In the last few years several large and important collections have come on the market and added to the mill collecting frenzy as they have been dispersed around the country. The Internet continues to play an important role as many never-before-seen mills and scarce items are offered for sale or auction. Mills can be found on the many auction sites and for sale at online malls and shops. As always, buyer beware. There are unknowing or untrustworthy sellers trying to pass off fantasy or reproduction items as authentic old mills. Doing research is key, and there are many fine books on the market that address coffee mills in particular. We recommend joining online collector clubs, website chat rooms, or a collector organization to learn more. (See Association of Coffee Mill Enthusiasts listed under Clubs, Newsletters, and Catalogs in the Directory.) Our advisor for this category is Shane Branchcomb; he is listed in the Directory under Virginia.

American Beauty, canister, CI/tin, orig cup/papers, NM 135.00
American Duplex No 47, electric, working, VG.........................85.00
American Duplex No 50, electric, working, VG 105.00
Arcade, table, w/decal, orig drw, Pat 6, 5, 1884, 1-lb, NM 155.00
Arcade Favorite No 27, side, CI w/orig lid, VG/EX.....................115.00
Arcade Favorite No 30, EX..180.00
Arcade Favorite No 47, wood box, CI hopper, EX 160.00
Arcade Imperial, lap, CI closed hopper, wood box, EX 110.00
Arcade Imperial No 200, lap, CI hopper, w/eagle, Pat 88, 89 .....155.00
Arcade IXL, table, ornate CI hopper, hdl on side, 1-lb, EX 425.00
Arcade Jewel, canister, rectangular glass hopper, w/lid, EX 595.00
Arcade No 147, lap, fancy CI closed hopper, wood box, EX 95.00
Arcade Telephone, canister, CI front, Pat Sept 25, '88, EX 600.00
Arcade Telephone, CI & wood, rnd brass tag, early, EX.............675.00
Bell, canister, similar to Golden Rule, CI & wood, EX 675.00
Blacksmith-made, funnel shape, 2-hdl, wall mt to 2x4", VG 375.00
Bronson-Walton Monitor, table, tin, w/cup, ca 1909, EX..............75.00
Bronson-Walton Silver Lake, canister, glass hopper, EX 700.00
C Ibach stamp on hdl, dvtl walnut, CI hopper, orig drw 165.00
Cannon No 2, table, CI box & drw, brass hopper, EX.................185.00
Caravan, canister, CI works, tin hopper, ca 1910, VG/EX 165.00
Chase & Sanborn, coffee bin...175.00
Coles Mfg No 7, counter, CI, Pat 1887, 16" wheels, 27", EX 900.00
Coles No 00, CI, wall mt w/CI cup, NM 325.00
Crescent, table, wood, top fill, cylinder, 13", EX 115.00
DeVe Holland, lap, copper-plated hopper, decals..........................85.00
Elgin Nat'l, floor, silver hopper, 24" wheels 1,650.00
Elma, counter, CI, closed hopper, 10" single wheel, 17", EX.......175.00
Elma, tin box, EX...175.00
Elma No 0, single wheel, 9¼"..125.00
Elma No 1, CI, single wheel, 11"...155.00
Elma No 2, CI, single wheel, 12½" 145.00
Elma No 3, CI, single wheel, 15½" 160.00

Enterprise, cast iron with wood base and drawer, ca 1910, 18x13", repainted and replaced top, 18x13", $330.00.

Enterprise, counter, CI, eagle on hopper, Pat 1873, 2 wheels......575.00
Enterprise Boss, floor, CI, closed hopper, 1873, 39" wheels......3,250.00
Enterprise No 1, CI, wall mt, w/orig catcher................................125.00
Enterprise No 1, counter, open hopper, hdl, Pat 1873, 11", VG 285.00
Enterprise No 1, counter, orig pnt/decals, side hdl, 1898.............255.00
Enterprise No 2, orig pnt/decal, 2 8¾" wheels, EX...................1,100.00
Enterprise No 3, counter, CI, wood drw, orig pnt/decals, NM 1,200.00
Enterprise No 7, counter, CI, orig pnt, 17" wheel w/eagle, VG 900.00
Enterprise No 9, CI, brass eagle, Pat 1898, 19" wheels, 28", VG.....895.00
Enterprise No 12, counter, w/eagle decals, 2 wheels, Pat 1898......895.00
Enterprise No 12½, orig pnt/decals, 24¾" wheels 1,200.00
Enterprise No 16, floor, CI, orig pnt, CI hopper.......................3,100.00
Euclid No 4, counter, aluminum hopper, 10" wheels, VG...........395.00
Grand Union Tea, table, CI sq base, rnd hopper, mfg Griswold...650.00
Griswold, counter, CI, 2 wheels, Pat 1897, EX........................1,295.00
Hobar No 265, electric, covered hopper 295.00
Husqvrna No 7, Swedish made, single wheel, 16½" 525.00
J Fisher Warranted, lap, dvtl walnut, pewter hopper, unique.......265.00
Japy Freres, ornate woodwork, brass hopper, ftd......................145.00
Juvenile (toy), lap, CI top, wood box, orig drw & decal, EX.......115.00
Landers, Frary & Clark, CI, rnd, sq base, ornate, Pat 1875 ....725.00
Landers, Frary & Clark, lap, fancy CI top, wood box, VG/EX 125.00
Landers, Frary & Clark, table, CI, Pat Feb 14, 1905, EX.............125.00
Landers, Frary & Clark Crown No 20, counter, 8" wheels, EX ...900.00
Landers, Frary & Clark No 24, w/orig mk hopper, NM 155.00
Landers, Frary & Clark No 50, counter, CI, 12" wheels, EX+ 1,100.00
Landers, Frary & Clark Universal No 10, table, tin.......................85.00
Landers, Frary & Clark Universal No 14, table, Pat 1905, VG.....85.00
Logan & Strobridge Franco-American, lap, ornate CI hopper....125.00
Logan & Strobridge Queen, glass canister, CI works, EX 425.00
Mimosa, table mt, CI, open hopper, heavy..................................85.00
Nat'l Specialty, CI, brass hopper, 2 12½" wheels......................1,225.00
Nat'l Specialty, CI, single crank, 12", EX...............................475.00
Nat'l Specialty No 0, table, CI, covered hopper, clamps on........325.00
Nat'l Specialty No 7, CI, 16½" wheels, EX 1,000.00
New Model, lap, CI w/CI drw, bottom open all 4 sides, EX 150.00
None Such, Bronson Co Cleveland OH, table, tin, pnt, EX.......165.00
Olde Thompson, lap, orig drw, EX..65.00
Parker, No 60, side, tin hopper, brass eagle medallion lid..............85.00
Parker, side, CI, front grind adjusts, Pat 1876, on orig brd 75.00
Parker (mk CPCo) No 1350, CI, wall mt, NM.........................85.00
Parker Eagle No 50, side, CI, Pat 1860, EX...............................85.00
Parker No 2, counter, CI, orig decals, 9" wheels, EX 795.00
Parker No 49, side, tin hopper w/brass eagle, tin lid...................110.00
Parker No 340, w/label, tin catcher, 1-lb box, EX......................155.00
Parker No 400 series, lap, split-covered top, ornate....................135.00
Parker No 449, canister, CI, orig lid & catcher, EX....................145.00
Parker No 700, counter, CI, wood drw, 17" wheels, G 885.00
Parker No 3000, drw, eagle on top, 11" wheels, orig...................975.00
Parker No 5005, counter, CI, 12½" wheels, 17", EX 875.00
Parker Victor No 535, table, wood/tin hopper, hdl.......................135.00
Persepolis, table, CI & brass, unique, rare 700.00
Primitive, lap, cherry, brass hopper, handmade/unique, 4x4" 195.00
Primitive, lap, dvtl walnut, wrought iron, brass hopper.............175.00
PS&W Standard No 31, lap, CI open hopper, wood box...........170.00
PS&W Vortex No 40, lap, wood box, CI hopper 195.00
PSW&Co No 6, side, orig CI lid, EX 75.00
Queen (toy), CI hopper & drw front, wood box, label, mini 125.00
Richmond, side, CI, Chatham Conn (2 szs made), EX, ea..........375.00
Royal Blue, Supplee Hdwe Co, CI, tin hopper, EX....................255.00
Russell & Erwin Diamond, CI, bronze finish, EX 475.00
Russell & Erwin No 60, britannia hopper, wood box....................90.00
S&H, counter, CI, w/drw, 19" wheels, 21", VG 950.00
Selsor, Cook & Co, lap, name on hdl, Pat 1859 ....185.00

Silvers No 1, CI, dbl-grind, w/cup, EX **1,000.00**
Standard Cabinet Co, spice cabinet w/mill built in, EX **600.00**
Star, canister, tin w/CI works, Pat 1910, VG **120.00**
Star, floor, brass hopper 2 CI wheels **1,100.00**
Star Model A, floor, 34½" wheels, G **700.00**
Star No 12, CI, brass hopper, 2 wheels, rstr, EX **2,500.00**
Steinfield, canister, CI works, glass jar, orig lid, EX **175.00**
Stuttle, Henry; #2, CI, tin hopper, Pat 2/20/77, EX......................**425.00**
Sun Mfg No 1080, orig lid & drw, 1-lb box, EX/NM....................**125.00**
Sun No 1050 Improved, lap, wood, tin hopper **85.00**
Sun No 94, side, CI, Greenfield OH, VG **75.00**
Swift, drug mill, CI, open hopper, Pat June 30 1874 ....**525.00**
Swift No 12, Lane Brothers, 98" wheel **550.00**
Swift No 13, counter, orig tin drw, red pnt, 12" wheels, 19" **475.00**
Swift No 16, counter, red w/lg decal, 2 wheels............................**795.00**
Tillmann's Hawaiian Coffee, CI, wall mt, EX **250.00**
Universal No 109, blk tin w/gr decal, Pat 1905, NM....................**75.00**
W Cross & Sons, lap, CI w/orig CI drw, brass hopper & pull........**85.00**
Wright, John; CI, red or gr, ca 1968, 2 6¾" wheels, NM **250.00**
Wrightsville Hdwe, CI, eagle pnt on lid, 2 wheels, sm **325.00**
Wrightsville Hdwe Peerless No 200, canister, CI/glass, EX **175.00**

Coin-Operated Machines

Coin-operated machines may be the fastest-growing area of collector interest in today's market. Many machines are bought, restored, and used for home entertainment. Older examples from the turn of the century and those with especially elaborate decoration and innovative features are most desirable.

The www.GameRoomAntiques.com website and *Chicagoland Antique Amusements, Slot Machine, and Jukebox Gazette* are excellent sources of information for those interested in coin-operated machines; see the Clubs, Newsletters, and Catalogs section of the Directory for publishing information. Jackie and Ken Durham are our advisors; they are listed in the Directory under the District of Columbia.

Arcade Machines

Ask Me Another About Love, 1940s, G working.......................**495.00**
Clam Shell Mutoscope, M rstr..**6,850.00**
Exhibit 1¢ Oracle Fortune Teller, countertop, 1920s, EX.........**1,250.00**
Hanson Grip Tester, 15x10½x10½", EX **350.00**
Ingo 5¢ Grip Tester, lights up, battery op, 1950s, 48", EX...........**750.00**
Iron Claw, digger, rpl marque, orig mirror, 1930s, M rstr..........**3,500.00**
Junior Deputy Sheriff Pistol Range, 1940s-50s, EX **1,295.00**
Miniature Steam Shovel, digger, 1930s, M rstr..........................**3,000.00**
Over the Top, wall machine, 1920s, 20", M rstr **875.00**
Poker Ball Flip, Peo-type skill game, 1930s, EX rstr....................**495.00**
Smiley the Clown, skill maze, 1940s, M rstr **800.00**
Wee Gee Penny Drop Fortune Teller, wall machine, 1920s, M rstr ...**975.00**

Jukeboxes

The coin-operated phonograph of the early 1900s paved the way for the jukeboxes of the 1920s. Seeburg was first on the market with an automatic eight-tune phonograph. By the 1930s Wurlitzer was the top name in the industry with dealerships all over the country. As a result of the growing ranks of competitors, the '40s produced the most beautiful machines made. Wurlitzers from this era are probably the most popularly sought-after models on the market today. The model #1015 of 1946 is considered the all-time classic and even in unrestored condition often brings prices in excess of $8,000.00.

AMI Model B, white plastic dome top, 1949, EX with selection of 1950s 78 rpm discs, $3,600.00.

Rockola #447 Console Deluxe console, 1973, EX orig............**1,195.00**
Rockola #456 Console Deluxe, rebuilt amp, 1975...................**1,150.00**
Scopitone Movie, 1950s, rstr **3,995.00**
Seeburg #HF100R, oak vnr, 1954, M rstr.................................**6,250.00**
Seeburg #M100A, zebra wood vnr, 1949-50, M rstr **4,795.00**
Seeburg #M100B, 1950-51, rstr **4,495.00**
Seeburg #Q-160, 1959, rstr **2,950.00**
Seeburg #100A, 100 selections, rstr zebra wood vnr, 1949-50...**4,795.00**
Seeburg #100B, 1950-51, rstr..**4,195.00**
Seeburg #100C, 1952, rstr...**6,450.00**
Seeburg G, rstr **6,995.00**
Seeburg V-200, EX orig..**4,500.00**
Seeburg VL-200, EX orig **4,500.00**
Wurlitzer #1015 Bubbler, plays 78 rpms, prof rstr.................**12,995.00**
Wurlitzer #1050, ca 1946, 59", EX orig....................................**8,815.00**
Wurlitzer #1100, converted to 45 rpms, 1948-49, M rstr **7,995.00**
Wurlitzer #1610, 1962, VG orig..**2,550.00**
Wurlitzer #2600, 1962, EX orig..**2,700.00**
Wurlitzer #2700, 1963, VG orig..**2,550.00**
Wurlitzer #3600 Super Star, rebuilt amp, 1972........................**1,045.00**
Wurlitzer #412, 1936, VG orig..**4,000.00**
Wurlitzer #81, on orig Mae West stand, 1941, VG orig.........**14,000.00**

Pinball Machines

Bally Barrel-o-Fun Bingo, 6-card, 1960, G working....................**900.00**
Bally Carnival Queen Bingo, 1958, G working **1,150.00**
Bally Champion One Ball, 1949, G working **950.00**
Bally Dude Ranch Bingo, 1953, G working **850.00**
Bally Figure Spa Electronic, 1979, G working **1,195.00**
Bally Spy Hunter Electronic, 1984, EX working.......................**1,900.00**
Bally 5¢ Turf King One Ball, 1950, G working........................**1,050.00**
Gottlieb Spin Wheel Electro Mechanical, 1968, G working **700.00**
Gottlieb/Premiere Genesis Electronic, 1986, G working..........**1,495.00**
Gottlieb/Premiere Rock Electronic, 1985, G working..............**1,350.00**
Standard Mfg 1¢ Jockey Club Horse Race, 1933, G working...**2,450.00**
Williams Space Shuttle Electronic, 1984, G working **1,550.00**
Williams Upper Deck Baseball, 1973, G orig............................**2,750.00**

Slot Machines

Bally #1901 Dollar, 3-coin multiplier, 1973, EX orig...............**1,500.00**

Bally #831 Quarter, 3-line fruit, 1968, EX orig 2,500.00
Bally #956 Quarter, 5-coin multiplier, 1974-75, EX orig 2,000.00
Bally 5¢ DeLuxe Draw Bell, console, 1948, M rstr 2,500.00
Dewey Upright, color wheel, early 1900s, EX........................12,000.00
Jennings Electric Tic Tac Toe Challenger, console, 1960s, EX ...2,300.00
Jennings Nevada Club 25¢ Light-Up, 1950s-60s, rstr 3,995.00
Jennings 1¢ Little Duke, gumball side vendor, 1933, EX orig ..4,600.00
Jennings 10¢ Hunting, 1937, M rstr......................................3,500.00
Jennings 25¢ Super Chief, 1937, EX orig..............................3,200.00
Keeney 25¢ Bonus Super Bell Twin, console, 1947, VG orig...2,150.00
Keeney 25¢ Sweet Shawnee, console, Indian motif, 1960s, EX orig...800.00
Keeney 5¢ Black Dragon, console, EX orig.............................1,800.00
Mills 25¢ Bonus, 1949, M rstr 3,500.00
Mills 25¢ Bursting Cherry, 1938-42, M rstr 3,195.00
Mills 25¢ Castle Front, pays $35, 1930s, M rstr......................3,195.00
Mills 25¢ Extra Bell, M rstr 3,200.00
Mills 25¢ Golden Nugget, wht front, M rstr...........................3,200.00
Mills 25¢ Lion Head (aka Wolf's Head), 1932, M rstr 3,200.00
Mills 25¢ War Eagle, 1931, M rstr..3,195.00
Mills 5¢ Skyscraper, 1936, EX orig......................................3,200.00
Mills 5¢ Vest Pocket, 1930s-40s, EX working, minimum value...750.00

Trade Stimulators

Bomb Hit Penny Drop, WWII motif, rstr case, EX working 1,250.00
Cowper Cracker Jack, 1898-1911, EX rstr 4,750.00
Exhibit Supply Little Gypsy, rstr case, 1920s, EX working 1,295.00
Groetchen Punchette, VG orig..975.00

Jennings Favorite 1¢, penny drop, cast aluminum font, oak case and base, 20x14x13", with gum vendor, EX, $2,950.00.

Mills Kounter King, gum dispenser, 1930s, EX orig 650.00
Rockola Radio Wizard, rstr case, 1930s 850.00
Twins Dice, w/gumball vendor, remade award card, rstr case 395.00

Vendors

Vending machines sold a product or a service. They were already in common usage by 1900 selling gum, cigars, matches, and a host of other commodities. Peanut and gumball machines are especially popular today. The most valuable are those with their original finish and decals. Older machines made of cast iron are especially desirable, while those with plastic globes have little collector value. When buying unrestored peanut machines, beware of salt damage.

Advance 1¢, gumball, glass globe, 1920, 12½", M rstr 395.00
Advance 1¢ Big Mouth, peanut/candy, 1920, 16½", M rstr 395.00
Ajax Challenger, hot nuts, 3-globe, 1947, EX working............1,250.00
Atlas 5¢ Bantam Tray, peanut, 1940s, rstr..................................395.00
Columbus Bi-More, 3 Columbus bbl locks, 1930s, M rstr 1,850.00
Columbus 1¢ Model M, gumball/candy, glass globe, 1920s, M rstr..495.00
Columbus 1¢ Model 21, candy/gumball, 1920s, M rstr...............850.00
Femachen 1¢ Radio, hot nuts, aluminum, 1930s, EX working 495.00
Hawkeye, glass globe, bell rings on 10th vend, 1930s, 15", EX ...595.00
Internat'l 1¢ Mutoscope Old Mill, candy/gum/gifts, M rstr......3,995.00
Magna 1¢, multi-side glass globe, lt wear on decal, 1930s, EX orig ..975.00
Mills Automatic Tab, gum, 5-column w/aluminum front, 1936, M rstr..295.00
Northwestern 1¢, peanut, porc base, 1930s, 15", EX 350.00
Play Ball decal, baseball theme gumballs, 1940-50s, 14", M rstr 195.00
Premier 2¢, baseball card/gumball, 1950s, M rstr 650.00
Silver King 1¢, peanut/candy, red, 1940s, 1", M rstr...................295.00
Victor 1¢ Model V, gumball, blk & wht w/glass globe, 1940s, M rstr..195.00
Victor 1¢ Topper, gumball, red/blk w/glass globe, 1940s-50s, M rstr..195.00

Compacts

The use of cosmetics before WWI was looked upon with disdain. After the war women became liberated, entered the work force, and started to use makeup. The compact, a portable container for cosmetics, became a necessity. The basic compact contains a mirror and a powder puff.

Vintage compacts were fashioned in a myriad of shapes, styles, materials, and motifs. They were made of precious metals, fabrics, plastics, and in almost any other conceivable medium. Commemorative, premium, patriotic, figural, Art Deco, plastic, and gadgetry compacts are just a few of the most sought-after types available today. Those that are combined with other accessories (music/compact, watch/compact, cane/compact) are also very much in demand. Vintage compacts are an especially desirable collectible since the workmanship, design, techniques, and materials used in their execution would be very expensive and virtually impossible to duplicate today.

Our advisor, Roselyn Gerson, has written six highly informative books: *Ladies' Compacts of the 19th and 20th Centuries*, *Vintage Vanity Bags and Purses*, *Vintage and Contemporary Purse Accessories*, *Vintage Ladies' Compacts*, *Vintage & Vogue Ladies' Compacts*, and *The Estée Lauder Solid Perfume Compact Collection*. She is listed in the Directory under the state of New York. See Clubs and Newsletters for information concerning the compact collectors' club and their periodical publication, *The Powder Puff*.

Bolster, gold-tone, Dorset Fifth Ave 60.00
Book, gold-tone w/emb grid pattern, polished border, Coty, 1940s ..60.00
Carryall, gold-tone/radiating ribs, ruby bijou, Evans 'Park Lane,' 4" ..200.00
Carryall, MOP w/HP peacock & glitter on lid, Marhill...............200.00
Carryall, Round Towner, blk & lurex damask w/mesh strap, Zell, 4x3"..90.00
Carryall, sq, silvered w/oval cameo, w/chain, DF Briggs 220.00
Cigarette/compact, oblong, plastic w/metal cut-out Scottie, 1940s...110.00
Clamshell, frosted milk glass w/gold-tone trim, Russia, 3"...........250.00
Damascene, Mt Fuji, sq, gold & silver on blk matt, Japan, 1920s 150.00
Envelope, gold-tone, Coty, 1940s...80.00
Fan, gold-tone w/silver-tone o/l, Henriette, 4¾x2" 150.00
Finger-ring chain, rnd, silver-tone w/pnt roses on yel enamel, 1⅞" ..100.00
Half-moon, lt bl-gr enamel, diagonal gold-tone band, Rex, 5x2½" ..100.00
Heart, pk & yel gold-tone puffy basketweave, Evans, ca 1946 ....200.00
Horseshoe, bl leather (no design) 60.00
Mask, polished gold-tone harlequin form, Elizabeth Arden, 3"...175.00
Musical, gold-tone w/applied sheet music of 'Star Dust,' 1920s...125.00
Musical, gold-tone w/musical notes on MOP, Stratton, 3¼x2¾" ..175.00
Necessaire, blk & ivorene Bakelite w/rhinestones, cord/tassle, 1¾" ...450.00
Octagonal, bl champlevé enameled lid w/dancers, Montral, 2" ..200.00

Octagonal, ivory enamel w/oval rhinestone decor, Allwyn, 2½"..**150.00**
Oval, brushed gold-tone w/harlequin mask decor, Dorothy Gray, 4" ..**124.00**
Oval, gold-tone w/mirror inset on red enamel, Rex Fifth Ave **100.00**
Oval, MOP w/faux sapphires & rhinestones, K&K, 1930s-40s......**75.00**
Petit-point, fan shape, gold-tone trim, Elgin Am, 3½x3"............**120.00**
Petit-point, half-moon, gold-tone scalloped rim, 1930s...............**100.00**
Picture hat, silver-tone w/emb ribs, flowers & bow, Dorothy Gray...**150.00**
Pocket-watch style, MOP, Volupte, 1940s-50s.........................**75.00**
Purse, gold-tone, rnd photo under flap, lipstick on chain, Volupte...**160.00**
Rnd, blk matt w/gold silver inlayed floral scene, Amita, 1920s...**125.00**
Rnd, brn pigskin w/running Scottie dog, 3¼" **80.00**
Rnd, gold-tone basketweave, orig pouch, Ritz, 3" **50.00**
Rnd, hammered gold-tone, emb lady, powder sifter, Norida, 1920s...**60.00**
Rnd, sterling w/red, yel, gr, bl & gold swirls, 2¾" **300.00**
Rnd, wht enamel w/red anchor & bl rope decor, Volupte, 2½".....**70.00**
Rnd, wht metal, emb butterfly & floral motif, Jaciel, 2" **65.00**
Rnd gold-tone w/emb polished leaping gazelles & cloud design, 5⅞"..**325.00**
Scalloped, gold-tone w/allover stylized design, Kigu, 3½" **80.00**
Shell, gold-tone w/sm shell & sunray design, Volupte, 3" **65.00**
Souvenir, San Francisco, sq, gold-tone w/engraved points of interest...**45.00**
Sq, gold-tone w/Apres la pluie beau temps, Gloria Vanderbilt, 3¾" ..**225.00**
Sq, gold-tone w/butterfly in spider web, Volupte, 3" **125.00**
Sq, gold-tone w/clear plastic waffle top, Wadsworth, 1930s **125.00**
Sq, gold-tone w/pnt tropical scene on encased Lucite lid **60.00**
Sq, HP enamel Japanese scene on wht ground, 2¾x2½" **75.00**
Sq, Simplicity Printed Pattern 25 Cents, Wadsworth, from $225 to..**400.00**

Sterling and enamel with profile of young woman, $65.00.

Suitcase, brn lizard w/2 carrying hdls, zippered **150.00**
Suitcase, tan leather w/gold-tone trim, Atomette, 3" **120.00**
Sunburst medallion, gold-tone Lucite, Roger & Gallet, 4" dia....**225.00**
Triangular, gr & yel check, Volupte **80.00**
Vanity, acorn w/lipstick in tassel, carrying cord, cvd plastic, 2¼"..**1,000.00**
Vanity, book, Mondaine, floral design on tan leather, 3"..............**80.00**
Vanity, cushion, gold swirl design on red enamel, Lupe, 3" **150.00**
Vanity, keystone, blk silhouette lady on ivory, 3¼" **100.00**
Vanity, oblong, blk Bakelite w/clear & gr rhinestone decor, 4x2¼" ...**475.00**
Vanity, oblong, w/carrying chain, pnt flower basket on gr enamel ..**250.00**
Vanity, octagonal, couple on gr enamel, tube on chain, RAC, 2"...**175.00**
Vanity, pouchette w/pk & gr trim, mirror on outside base, 1920s...**100.00**
Vanity, rnd, bl enamel w/silver-tone mesh trim, Evans, 4" **80.00**
Vanity, rnd, wht metal, Art Deco lady's profile, Woodsworth, 2"...**250.00**
Vanity, saddlebag w/lamé fabric cover, gold-tone & blk trim, 4"....**150.00**
Vanity, triangle, gr Bakelite, silver leaves/rhinestone, cord/tassel...**225.00**
Vanity/Trio-ette, plastic hand-mirror, Plate, from $125 to **250.00**
Watch/compact, trunk shape w/straps, gold-tone, Evans, 1940s..**175.00**

Consolidated Lamp and Glass

The Consolidated Lamp and Glass Company of Coraopolis, Pennsylvania, was incorporated in 1894. For many years their primary business was the manufacture of lighting glass such as oil lamps and shades for both gas and electric lighting. The popular 'Cosmos' line of lamps and tableware was produced from 1894 to 1915. (See also Cosmos.) In 1926 Consolidated introduced their Martele line, a type of 'sculptured' ware closely resembling Lalique glassware of France. (Compare Consolidated's 'Lovebirds' vase with the Lalique 'Perruches' vase.) It is this line of vases, lamps, and tableware which is often mistaken for a very similar type of glassware produced by the Phoenix Glass Company, located nearby in Monaca, Pennsylvania. For example, the so-called Phoenix 'Grasshopper' vases are actually Consolidated's 'Katydid' vases.

Items in the Martele line were produced in blue, pink, green, crystal, white, or custard glass decorated with various fired-on color treatments or a satin finish. For the most part, their colors were distinctively different from those used by Phoenix. Although not foolproof, one of the ways of distinguishing Consolidated's wares from those of Phoenix is that most of the time Consolidated applied color to the raised portion of the design, leaving the background plain, while Phoenix usually applied color to the background, leaving the raised surfaces undecorated. This is particularly true of those pieces in white or custard glass.

In 1928 Consolidated introduced their Ruba Rombic line, which was their Art Deco or Art Moderne line of glassware. It was only produced from 1928 to 1932 and is quite scarce. Today it is highly sought after by both Consolidated and Art Deco collectors.

Consolidated closed its doors for good in 1964. Subsequently a few of the molds passed into the hands of other glass companies that later reproduced certain patterns; one such reissue is the 'Chickadee' vase, found in avocado green, satin-finish custard, or milk glass. Our advisor for this category is Jack D. Wilson, author of *Phoenix and Consolidated Art Glass, 1926 – 1980*; he is listed in the Directory under Arizona.

Bird of Paradise, candy box, purple wash, oval............................**325.00**
Bird of Paradise, vase, gr wash, 10"...**275.00**
Bird of Paradise, vase, sepia wash, fan form, 6" **135.00**
Bittersweet, lamp, reverse ruby stain on crystal..........................**150.00**
Bittersweet, vase, gr cased...**275.00**
Bittersweet, vase, ruby stain on crystal **150.00**
Catalonian, candlestick, rainbow: pk/bl/gr, ea..............................**75.00**
Catalonian, candlestick, yel, ea...**45.00**
Catalonian, vase, bl irid stretch, cased, fan shape.......................**175.00**
Catalonian, vase, Nasturtium, russet (rare color).........................**275.00**
Catalonian, vase, purple wash, pinched, 6" **165.00**
Chickadee, lamp, amber wash w/blk highlighting, 3-way lighting ..**195.00**
Chickadee, vase, gr wash on crystal..**110.00**
Chickadee, vase, sepia wash on crystal......................................**200.00**
Chrysanthemum, case, 3-color highlights on satin milk glass **175.00**
Chrysanthemum, vase, bl on creamy milk glass, 12"....................**115.00**
Cockatoo, bowl, console; bl frosted crystal (rare color), 13" **395.00**
Cockatoo, candlestick, purple wash, ea **165.00**
Cockatoo, vase, yel cased..**425.00**
Con-Cora, cookie jar, violets on milk glass, 6½" **85.00**
Dancing Girls, vase, bl highlights on satin milk glass, 12" **525.00**
Dancing Nymph, goblet, pk frosted...**125.00**
Dancing Nymph, plate, frosted, 8"..**75.00**
Dancing Nymph, tumbler, ftd, gr frosted, 6½" **105.00**
Dancing Nymph, vase, crystal, fan shape....................................**125.00**
Dogwood, lamp, 3-color on satin milk glass **125.00**
Dogwood, vase, bl transparent over wht irid casing (rare color)...**400.00**
Dragon Fly, vase, gold on glossy custard, 7".................................**175.00**
Dragon Fly, vase, reverse bl highlights on satin milk glass..........**135.00**

Fish, tray, reverse ruby-stain highlights on crystal.........................275.00
Fish, tray, yel wash...200.00
Five Fruits, goblet, yel wash 35.00
Five Fruits, plate, sepia wash, 12"...110.00
Five Fruits, tumbler, gr wash, ftd...30.00
Floral, vase, ruby stain on crystal..125.00
Florentine, vase, coffee brn, etched 250.00
Florentine, vase, gr, 7"...155.00
Foxglove, lamp, wht w/lav-bl flowers & gr leaves, orig mts, 10¼" ..145.00
Foxglove, vase, 2-color highlights on satin custard.....................145.00
Hummingbird, compote, yel wash..85.00
Hummingbird, powder jar, amethyst, 3" dia 225.00
Hummingbird, vase, amber wash 75.00
Hummingbird & Orchids, candlestick, purple wash, ea..............115.00
Iris, bowl, console; pk wash, 10¾"..145.00
Iris, candlestick, gr wash, ea 75.00
Iris, jug, transparent gr over wht casing, ½-gal.......................225.00
Iris, mayonnaise bowl, purple wash...40.00
Iris, tumbler, transparent gr over wht casing 90.00
Jonquil, vase, gold highlights on milk glass 110.00
Katydid, ashtray, purple wash, rare..275.00
Katydid, vase, bl on satin milk glass, ovoid 165.00
Line 700, bowl, fruit; bl, 10" 175.00
Line 700, vase, gold highlights on custard, 10" 425.00
Line 700, vase, satin blk (rare color), 6½" 475.00

Line 700, vase, yellow wash with clear, 7x8", $175.00.

Love Birds, banana boat, reverse bl highlights on crystal............450.00
Love Birds, glove box, gr wash, very rare 350.00
Love Birds, vase, pk wash, 10x8"...275.00
Love Birds, vase, ruby stain on crystal, ornate surmount, 11" 450.00
Nuthatch, planter vase, sepia cased..250.00
Olive, bowl, purple wash, 4" 125.00
Olive, lamp, 3-color highlights, very rare................................300.00
Olive, vase, gold highlights on glossy milk glass 125.00
Olive, vase, gr & yel highlighting on satin custard.....................165.00
Pine Cone, vase, reverse rose highlights on glossy custard..........150.00
Pine Cone, vase, ruby-satin highlights on crystal 150.00
Pine Cone, vase, straw opal, 6½" 225.00
Poppy, vase, irid metallic red & gold on glossy custard (rare color)....400.00
Poppy, vase, purple cased (rare color).....................................400.00
Regent Line, vase, aqua over wht opal 125.00
Regent Line, vase, ash-rose pk over wht opal casing, #1174-B, 4½" ..125.00
Ruba Rombic, bonbon, Smoky Topaz, 8" 375.00
Ruba Rombic, bowl, cupped, Smoky Topaz, 8" 1,425.00
Ruba Rombic, nut dish, Jungle Green, very rare.......................275.00
Ruba Rombic, plate, service; Jungle Green, 10".......................275.00

Ruba Rombic, plate, Sunshine (soft yel), 8¼", pr.......................290.00
Ruba Rombic, toilet bottle, Smoky Topaz, 7¾".....................1,200.00
Ruba Rombic, vase, Smoky Topaz, 9½" 2,900.00
Santa Maria, boudoir light, orange & blk 550.00
Santa Maria, cigarette box, crystal..130.00
Screech Owl, vase, sepia wash 250.00
Sea Gull, vase, blk & gold irid highlights on custard gloss, 11" ..850.00
Sea Gull, vase, gr cased, 11"..650.00
Sea Gull, vase, orange highlighting on satin custard 275.00
Spanish Knobs, candlestick, yel, ea...45.00
Spanish Knobs, sundae, yel 30.00
Tropical Fish, vase, French crystal, 9".....................................250.00
Tropical Fish, vase, gr wash on crystal, 9" 300.00
Tropical Fish, vase, rose & bl on milk glass, 9" 300.00
Tropical Fish, vase, straw opal, 9"..480.00

Conta & Boehme

The Conta & Boehme company was in business for 117 years in the quaint town of Poessneck, Germany (Thuringer district). Hand-painted dishes and pipe heads were their main products. However, in 1840, when the owner's two young sons took over the company, production changed drastically from dishes to porcelain items of almost every imaginable type.

For their logo, the brothers chose an arm holding a dagger inside a shield. This mark was either impressed or ink stamped onto the porcelain. Another mark they used is called the 'scissor brand' which looks just like it sounds, a pair of scissors in a blue or green ink stamp. Not all pieces were marked, many were simply given a model number or left completely unmarked.

England and the U.S. were the largest buyers, and as a result the porcelain ended up at fairs, gift shops, and department stores throughout both countries. For more information we recommend *Victorian Trinket Boxes* by Janice and Richard Vogel, and their latest book, *Conta & Boehme Porcelain*, published by the authors.

Conta & Boehme often produced their porcelain items in several different sizes (sometimes as many as nine). The prices below reflect a range to accommodate the different sizes. Values are for items with no chips, cracks, or repairs. Our advisors for this category are Richard and Janice Vogel; they are listed in the Directory under Florida.

Fairings, Figural

Fairings are small, brightly colored nineteenth century hard-paste porcelain objects, largely figural groups and boxes. Most portray amusing if not risque scenes of courting couples, marital woes, and political satire complete with an appropriate caption on the base.

Broken Hoop, #3343 ....275.00
Five O'Clock Tea, #3339...112.00
How Bridget Served the Tomatoes Undressed, #3362, minimum value ...400.00
Looking Down Upon His Luck, #2863................................175.00
O' Do Leave Me a Drop, #3350..200.00
Returning at One O'Clock in the Morning, #2857 ....125.00
Sarah's Young Man, #2874...125.00
Shamming Sick, #3358...150.00
Tea Party, #3365..150.00
Tug of War, #3336...100.00
Walk In Please, #2892...250.00
Which Is Prettiest?, #3366..175.00

Who Is Coming?, #3382 ....**70.00**
Who Said Rats?, #3359 ....**150.00**

Fairings, Trinket Boxes

Dresser, boy & girl on teeter-totter, #2988 ....**150.00**
Dresser, boy in bed putting on his trousers, #3576 ....**175.00**
Dresser, boy sitting on box eating, dog on his bk, #3577 ....**150.00**
Dresser, cats play on dresser top, #3564, from $175 to **225.00**
Dresser, child in bed w/cat on covers, #3566 ....**175.00**
Dresser, dog sitting on pillow, #2959 ....**125.00**
Dresser, girl & doll, #3591, from $150 to **225.00**
Dresser, girl & goose, #3521 ....**225.00**
Dresser, girl in bed putting on socks, #3572 ....**175.00**
Dresser, girl sitting, w/kitten in basket, #3589 ....**90.00**
Dresser, girl w/sheep, #255 ....**125.00**
Dresser, jester sitting on drum, #3505 ....**100.00**
Dresser, Kiss Me Quick, bicyclists on lid, #288 ....**225.00**
Dresser, monkey & drum, #3570 ....**200.00**
Dresser, monkey wearing top hat, #3567 ....**250.00**
Dresser, swans (2) & frog, #3520 ....**50.00**
Lg, boy & girl at checkerboard, #3639, 7x6¼" **450.00**
Vintage, girl in chair, 2 chickens in front, #433 ....**125.00**
Vintage, Mary & her lamb, #255 ....**50.00**
3-spot, checker player w/1 onlooker, #2100 ....**160.00**
3-spot, Sleeping Beauty **175.00**

Figurines

Birds (6 in series), Green Woodpecker, etc, ea, from $50 to **80.00**
Boy w/dog, #1436, from $50 to **75.00**
Cherub carrying cradle under right arm, #1246, from $125 to **150.00**
Figures of the Month (12 in series, Jan - Dec), ea, from $150 to **200.00**
Five Senses (5 in series), Hear, lady playing spinet, ea, from $100 to..**150.00**
Girl/boy pulling cart, #5048, ea, from $125 to **150.00**
Girl/boy pushing pram, #8510, ea, from $125 to **150.00**
Girl/boy riding pony sidesaddle, shield, ea, from $300 to **400.00**
Musical band (6-pc), French horn player, #5321, ea, from $150 to..**200.00**
Musical band (9-pc), monkey players, #2344-#2352, ea, from $150 to ...**200.00**
Paperweight, pig laying on base, #5048, (series of 12), ea, $125 to **150.00**
Swinger, lady on swing, lg, 8½", from $500 to **600.00**
Toy, 3 Little Maids w/bonnet & muff on base, #5558, from $35 to..**75.00**

Nodders

Card Players (4), heads nod, #8587, from $500 to **600.00**
Cat w/glass eyes, head nods, from $250 to **300.00**
Chess players (2), couple at table, heads nod, from $300 to **400.00**
Colonial man standing beside birdcage, bird nods, #8630, from $450 to ...**500.00**
Girl sitting in chair, head nods, from $250 to **300.00**
Man & lady sit cross-legged, head/tongue/hands nod, #5380, $750 to...**950.00**

Piano Babies

Seated, baby w/ball, mini, 3¾", from $50 to **75.00**
Seated, holding cup, #482, from $175 to **275.00**
Seated, holding fruit, #8266, from $175 to **275.00**
Seated, holding sponge, #489, from $175 to **275.00**
Seated, leaning on left hand, waving w/right, #487, from $400 to....**500.00**

Miscellaneous

Candelabra, 3-arm, girl (boy) w/pail (swings), #674, pr, from $400 to ..**500.00**
Candle holders, man (lady), single cup, #8330, pr, from $175 to..**225.00**

Candle holders, owls, #670, pr, from $175 to **225.00**
Cigar holder, Enpassant, couple ready to kiss, #1693, from $175 to ...**250.00**
Cigar holder, frogs dueling, #3013, from $85 to **125.00**
Cigar holder, rooster beside basket & sm pail, #3063, from $125 to..**150.00**
Compote, man (lady) w/sheep, pr, minimum value **500.00**
Condiment, bird between acorn & walnut, #5772, from $85 to..**125.00**
Condiment, clowns, 1 lg & 2 sm, #6241, from $100 to **125.00**
Condiment, dog nodder, pulls cart, basket (shaker) ea side, $100 to ..**150.00**
Humidor, Asian lady's head w/bow, #6050, from $300 to **500.00**
Humidor, dog's head, #2584, from $300 to **500.00**
Humidor, lady in bbl w/grapes, #2552, from $200 to **225.00**
Humidor, man reading newspaper, #2557, from $200 to **275.00**
Humidor, owl, #6009, minimum value **1,000.00**
Ink & pen holder, vanity w/mirror, 2 covered wells, #3259, $100 to..**150.00**
Ink & pen holder box, lg dog & sm cat, leafy base, from $75 to....**125.00**
Inkwell, Erst Beten, lady urges child to pray, dog, from $600 to **700.00**
Lamp, oil; owl w/glass eyes, #5482, from $300 to **400.00**
Match striker, boy (girl), basket/tub, feeding lamb, #4253, ea, $75 to..**125.00**
Match striker, boy (girl), suitcase/satchel, #4204/#4205, ea, $100 to..**150.00**
Match striker, boy (girl) w/hoop, #4192, ea, from $150 to **200.00**
Match striker, boy (girl) w/lg sailboat, ea, from $150 to **200.00**
Match striker, child w/pretzel & dog, #4112, from $100 to **150.00**
Match striker, lg frog on shell base, #1527, from $100 to **150.00**
Matchbox, sailing ship, Bristol to London, #2133, from $150 to..**200.00**
Menu holder, boy sits aside holding covered pot, shield mk, $150 to...**200.00**
Mustard pot, dog in doghouse, #5795, from $100 to **125.00**
Napkin holder, clown lying on stomach w/ring on bk, #5401, $125 to...**150.00**
Pincushion, 3 dolphins support bowl-like cushion holder, unmk, $75 to...**125.00**
Placecard holder, cat on bk, shield mk, from $95 to **125.00**
Placecard holder, child sits w/lg fan, #3482, from $125 to..........**150.00**

Placecard holder, shield ink mark only, from $95.00 to $125.00. (Photo courtesy Janice and Richard Vogel)

Planters, boy (girl) leans on basket in wheelbarrow, #5079, pr, $95 to..**135.00**
Salt cellar, red coral supports seashell, #2423, from $100 to........**125.00**
Salt cellar, wheelbarrow w/spoon, w/ or w/o girl, #1741, from $35 to...**150.00**
Shakers (boy (girl) in rope base, #5108, from $85 to **125.00**
Shoe, boy/girl w/bouquet of flowers inside shoe, #5035, from $125 to...**175.00**
Shoe, w/medallion & ruffles, #2431, pr, from $200 to **300.00**
Toothpick holder, girl (boy) w/half eggshell, shield mk, pr, $85 to..**125.00**
Trinket box, hand holding covered box, #490, from $85 to **125.00**
Vase, boy (girl) sits on books/reads letter, #6688, pr, from $85 to..**125.00**
Vase, boy (girl) stands beside urn on pillar, #1294, pr, from $75 to...**100.00**
Vase, flared, shield mk, #19, from 3" to 8", ea from $5 to.............**45.00**
Vase, Nouveau, lady/child/swan, shield/Saxony mk, lg, pr, $550 to...**1,000.00**
Wall pocket, angels holding cornucopia, shield mk, pr, from $400 to ..**500.00**
Wall relief, mother w/cherub, #7200, pr, from $400 to **500.00**
Watch holder, hand holding watch fr aloft, #2720, from $150 to..**200.00**
Watch holder, horse, #2716, from $150 to **200.00**

Cookbooks

Cookbooks from the nineteenth century, though often hard to find, are a delight to today's collectors both for their quaint formats and printing methods as well as for their outmoded, often humorous views on nutrition. Recipes required a 'pinch' of salt, butter 'the size of an egg' or a 'walnut,' or a 'handful' of flour. Collectors sometimes specialize in cookbooks issued as advertising premiums. Especially desirable are the figurals that were shaped like a jar, a slice of bread, or some other form relative to the product. Others with unique features such as illustrations by well-known artists or references to famous people or places are priced in accordance. Cookbooks written earlier than 1874 are the most valuable and when found command prices as high as $200.00; figurals usually sell in the $10.00 to $15.00 range.

As is true with all other books, if the original dust jacket is present and in nice condition, a cookbook's value goes up by at least $5.00. Right now, books on Italian cooking from before circa 1940 are in demand, and bread baking is important this year. For further information we recommend *A Guide to Collecting Cookbooks* by Col. Bob Allen and *Price Guide to Cookbooks and Recipe Leaflets* by Linda Dickinson. Our advisor for this category is Charlotte Safir; she is listed in the Directory under New York.

Key: CB — cookbook

ABC of Herb & Spice Cookery, Peter Pauper Press, 1957, 61-pg, EX...10.00
All About Home Baking, General Foods, 1933, 1st edition, 144-pg, VG+...15.00
Am Frugal Housewife, Mrs L Child, 1850, 20th edition, hardcover..90.00
Amy Vanderbilt Success Casserole Cookery, C Adams, 1966, hardcover .15.00

Around the World Cook Book, 50th Year Kalamazoo Golden Jubilee, 1951, $10.00.

Art of Creole Cookery, Kaufman & Cooper, Doubleday, 1962, VG w/jacket ..18.00
Art of Fine Baking, P Peck, Galahad NY, 1961, 320-pg, VG+......15.00
Bake-Off Classics III, Pillsbury, 1983, 95-pg 8.00
Baker's Best Chocolate Recipes, Walter Baker & Co, 1932, 60-pg, EX..12.50
Barker's Illustrated Almanac, Farmer's Guide..., 1915, 32-pg 25.00
Bayou CB: Creole Cooking..., TJ Holmes Jr, 1974, 181-pg, EX.....17.50
Best Chocolate & Cocoa Recipes, W Baker & Co, General Foods, 60-pg..15.00
Better Homes & Gardens Cooking w/Whole Grains, Meredith, 1984, G....3.00
Better Homes & Gardens New CB, 1968, hardcover, 400-pg, EX ...15.00
Betty Crocker's Bisquick Party Book, General Mills, 1957, 24-pg...7.50
Betty Crocker's Party Book, Golden Press, 1960, 1st edition, hardcover...5.00
Bond Bread CB, General Baking Co, 1933, 22-pg booklet.............9.00
Boston Cooking School CB, Fannie Merritt Farmer, 1916, 648-pg, VG...25.00
Broce's CB, P Cannon, 1954, 1st edition, hardcover, 400-pg, EX...25.00
CB for Family Camping, W Williams, Golden Press, 1969, 2nd printing..7.00
Ceresota CB, MH Neil, Northwestern Consolidated Milling, 1890s, 32-pg.....30.00
Chinese Stand-Up CB, B Frank, wire-bound, PSI Associates, 1986, 63-pg..8.00
Complete Am CB, Stella Stanard, 1957, revised, hardcover, 512-pg, EX ..20.00
Complete Book of Mexican Cooking, Lamber, M Evans, 1967, 3rd printing...15.00
Complete Book of Mexican, EL Ortiz, M Evans, 1967, 3rd printing.....15.00
Cookies, Gebhard & Albright, Wheat Flour Institute, 1944, 16-pg, EX ...12.50
Country CB: Favorite Farm Recipes Using Bob Evans Sausage, 1950s, EX....6.00

Cow Brand Baking Soda CB, Dwight's Baking Soda, 1916, 33-pg, G...10.00
Creative Cooking w/Cottage Cheese, Am Dairy Assoc, no date, 23-pg, EX.....5.00
Creative Holiday Recipes, Pillsbury, 1982, 93+ pgs, EX...................9.00
Daily Food for Christians, DeWolfe Fiske Co, 1898, hardcover, EX...60.00
Dainty Desserts for Dainty People, Knox Gelatin, 1924, 41-pg.....16.00
Diet for a Small Planet, FM Lappe, Ballantine Books, 1977, 3rd printing...8.00
Dr Miles Candy Book, Miles Medical Co, ca 1910, 32-pg, VG.....12.00
Dr Price CB, Royal Baking Powder, 1929, 41-pg, VG 15.00
Early American CB, O'Connor, Rutledge Book, 1974, 160-pg, EX ..12.00
Electric CB, Portland Railway Light & Power Co, 1910, 82-pg....20.00
Exciting World of Rice Dishes, General Foods, 1959, 20-pg, EX ...10.00
Fabulous Sandwiches CB, D Townsend, Ridge Press, 1965, 160-pg, EX...5.00
Family Save-All, Hannah Mary Peterson, pre-1873, hardcover, EX 95.00
Feasts for All Seasons, De Groot, AA Knopf, 1966, G w/jacket 8.00
Fish 'N' Fowl CB, Editors of McCalls, Advance, 1978, 64-pg, EX ..6.00
Food Processor CB, B Grumes, Ideals, 1971, softcover, G 3.00
Frozen Food CB, JI Simpson/DM Taylor, 1948, 2nd printing, 496-pg, EX...20.00
General Foods Kitchens, 1967, mailer, EX 8.00
Glorious Stew, D Ivens, Harper & Row, 1969, 1st edition, 255-pg, EX...12.50
Gold Medal flower CB, Washburn-Crosby Co, 1904, 70-pg, G- ...12.00
Good Housekeeping's Book of Cookies, Consolidated, 1958, 68-pg, EX...14.00
Graham Kerr CB, Doubleday, 1969, 8th printing, 284-pg, EX 9.00
Great Am Ice Cream Book, Dickson, Atheneum NY, 1972, 2nd printing, EX...15.00
Ground Meat CB, Culinary Arts Institute Chicago, 1972, 68-pg, EX...6.00
Guide to Royal Success in Baking, Royal Baking Powder, 1940, EX...7.00
Happy Times Recipe Book, Calumet, 1934, 23-pg, EX 15.00
High-Calcium Low-Calorie CB, B Marks, Contemporary Books, 1987, EX....4.00
History of Salt, Morton Salt Co, 1951, 22-pg, VG 12.50
Holiday Candy Book, V Pasley, Little Brown, 1952, 7th printing, EX..15.00
How To Use Spices, Watkins Products, 1958, 48-pg, VG................9.00
Howdy Doody CB, Welch Grape Juice, 1952, booklet, EX 25.00
Ida Bailey Allen's Time-Saving CB, Rand McNally, 1940, 192-pg, EX ...12.00
Internat'l CB, MW Heywood, 1929, 2nd printing, hardcover, 383-pg, EX...25.00
Jewish Cookery, LW Leonard, Crown Pub, 1949/1975, 499-pg, EX.....12.50
Ladies' Home Journal Handbook of Holiday Cuisine, 1970, 1st edition..10.00
Mama Never Cooked Like This, Mendelson, St Martin's Press, 1982, 1st ed...12.00
Margaret Rudkin Pepperidge Farm CB, Grosset & Dunlap, 1981, EX...15.00
McCall's Cookie Collection, Advance Publishers, 1974, 64-pg, VG ...10.00
Melting Pot: CB of All Nations, E Beilenson, Peter Pauper Press, 1958...10.00
Mexican Cookery for Am Homes, Gebheardt's Chili Powder, 1949, 47-pg ..12.50
Micro Menus CB, Whirlpool, Meredith Corp, 1982, 192-pg, EX...8.00
My Favorite Honey Recipes, Mrs WT (Ida) Kelly, 1960s, 19-pg, EX...6.00
Old-Fashioned CB, Jan McBride Carlton, Crown Publishers, 1975, EX ..7.50
Our Favorite Recipes 1951, spiral bound, Jr Woman's Club, 136-pg, EX ..12.00
Our New CB & Household Receipts, S Annie Frost, 1883, 454-pg, VG..100.00
PA Dutch CB of Fine Old Recipes, Culinary Arts Press, 1936, EX ..8.00
Perfect Endings, Nestle's Chocolate, metal spiral-bound, 1962, 192-pg..12.00
Peter Hunt's Cape Cod CB, P Hunt, 1957/1962, hardcover, 181-pg, EX ...15.00
Peter Hunt's Cape Cod CB, Gramercy, 1954 & 1962, 181+ pgs, EX 10.00
Pies Men Like Best, Tested Recipe Institute, 1953, 15-pg...............8.50
Pillsbury's Best Butter Cookie CB Vol II, no date, 50-pg, EX 9.00
Pillsbury's 3rd Grand National $100,000, 1952, 1st edition, EX ...15.00
Pure Food CB, Mrs Mary J Lincoln (editor), 1907, 79-pg, VG 25.00
Ransom's Family Receipt Book, D Ransom, orange cover, 1912, 32-pg..12.50
Recipes for Today, Consumer Service Dept, 1943, 39-pg, EX........12.50
Royal Baker & Pastry Cook, 1911, 46-pg, EX 20.00
Rumford Common Sense CB, Wallace, Rumford, ca 1920, 64-pg, VG...10.00
Simple New England Cookery, E Beilenson, Peter Pauper Press, 1962, EX...10.00
Slim Wok Cookery, Ceil Dyer, HP Books Inc, 1986, 1st edition.....4.00
Smorgasbord CB, AO Coombs, AA Wyn NY, 1949, 3rd printing, 240-pg...12.00
Story of Chocolate & Cocoa, 1926, 24-pg booklet, EX 15.00
Taste of Georgia, Newman Jr Service League, Moran, 1981, 5th printing ..9.00
Wolf in Chef's Clothing..., RH Loeb Jr, 1950, hardcover, 123-pg, EX ..20.00
Woman's Day CB of Relishes, 1963, booklet....................................5.00

Cookie Cutters

Early hand-fashioned cookie cutters command stiff prices at country auctions, and the ranks of interested collectors are growing steadily. Especially valuable are the figural cutters; and the more complicated the design, the higher the price. A follow-up of the carved wooden cookie boards, the first cutters were probably made by itinerant tinkers from leftover or recycled pieces of tin. Though most of the eighteenth-century examples are now in museums or collections, it is still possible to find some good cutters from the late 1800s when changes in the manufacture of tin resulted in a thinner, less expensive material. The width of the cutting strip is often a good indicator of age; the wider the strip, the older the cutter. While the very early cutters were 1" to 1½" deep, by the '20s and '30s, many were less than ½" deep. Crude, spotty soldering indicates an older cutter, while a thin line of solder usually tends to suggest a much later manufacture. The shape of the backplate is another clue. Later cutters will have oval, round, or rectangular backs, while on the earlier type the back was cut to follow the lines of the design. Cookie cutters usually vary from 2" to 4" in size, but gingerbread men were often made as tall as 12". Birds, fish, hearts, and tulips are common; simple versions can be purchased for as little as $12.00 to $15.00. The larger figurals, especially those with more imaginative details, often bring $75.00 and up.

Advertising cutters and product premiums (usually plastic) are collectible as well, so are the aluminum cutters with painted wood handles. Hallmark makes cutters in plastic — many of them character related and often priced in the $15.00 to $35.00 range.

The cookie cutters listed here are tin and handmade unless noted otherwise.

Deer, flat back, light rust, 7⅝", $470.00; Reindeer, strap handle, 6⅞", $440.00; Statue of Liberty, flat back, detailed, 9⅝", $2,475.00.

(Photo courtesy Garth's Auctions, Inc.)

Amish man, flat bk, 6¾"	50.00
Axe, flat bk, 1x7x4"	45.00
Betsy McCall, aluminum, McCall Publishing, 1971, 8", EX	38.50
Cat, flat bk, star-patterned vents, 4x3½", EX	35.00
Catholic Celtic Cross, copper, 6½x4½", MIP	25.00
Charlie Brown & Gang, Charlie Lucy, Linus & Snoopy, plastic, 4½"	30.00
Chicken, flat bk, 4x3", EX	25.00
Cookie Cutters, set of 12, metal, Sears Roebuck & Co, M (EX box)	15.00
Cresent moon, Nutbrown Products, 3"	8.50
Deer, running, flat bk, 3⅜x4⅜", VG+	35.00
Donald Duck, plastic, Hallmark, ca 1970s, 4½", MIP	18.00
Eagle, scalloped edge tail & wings, flat bk, 6"	165.00
Gingerbread man, Betty Crocker, red plastic, 3"	15.00
Gingerbread man, flat bk, 9½x6½"	55.00
Girl Scout emblem, mk Drip-O-Lator, aluminum	22.50
Guitar, flat bk, 4¾x1¾"	40.00

Hand w/heart, 5x5½"	18.50
Heart, mk Mason's, 2"	17.50
Heart in hand, 3½x3¼"	90.00
Hobby horse, flat bk, 4½x3¼"	15.00
Horse, pierced bk, no hdl, 4¼x6¼"	100.00
Kansas City Chiefs, football shape, red plastic, 6"	15.00
Man, mk MIG, 5¾"	45.00
Mickey Mouse, bl plastic, Tupperware, #3528-6, 3¾"	15.00
Mickey Mouse, metal w/hdl, 4¼"	15.00
Numbers & Alphabet, plastic, Wilton, 1988, MIP (sealed individually)	35.00
Owl, flat bk, 4½x2½", EX	22.50
Pig, flat bk, 4x7½", EX	170.00
Pig, red plastic, HRM, EX	15.00
Raggedy Ann & Andy, plastic, Bobbs Merrill, 7¾x4¼", pr	15.00
Reddy Kilowatt, plastic, M (EX box)	25.00
Rooster, flat bk, mk HF in circle, 10½x7"	75.00
Rooster, star-pattern vents, 4x4½"	15.00
Santa & Rudolph, red plastic, HRM, pr	15.00
Scottie dog, bl plastic, Transogram, 2½"	30.00
Snoopy on pumpkin, orange plastic, 6½"	45.00
Snowman, aluminum, 5"	8.00
Trick or Treat, bat, cat, jack-o'-lantern, witch, owl & broom, MIB	25.00
Windmill, copper, 4"	10.00
X & O, red plastic, Hallmark, 1983, 3", pr	10.00
3 Little Pigs, tin, pigs (3½"), 1 wolf (4½"), 1940s, EX (VG box)	195.00
3-D Cookie Cutter & Cake Decorating Kit, M (EX box)	10.00

Cookie Jars

The appeal of the cookie jar is universal; folks of all ages, both male and female, love to collect 'em! The early '30s' heavy stoneware jars of a rather nondescript nature quickly gave way to figurals of every type imaginable. Those from the mid to late '30s were often decorated over the glaze with 'cold paint,' but by the early '40s underglaze decorating resulted in cheerful, bright, permanent colors and cookie jars that still have a new look fifty years later.

Stimulated by the high prices commanded by desirable cookie jars, a broad spectrum of 'new' cookie jars are flooding the marketplace in three categories: 1) Manufactures have expanded their lines with exciting new designs specifically geared toward attracting the collector market. 2) Limited editions and artist-designed jars have proliferated. 3) Reproductions, signed and unsigned, have pervaded the market, creating uncertainty among new collectors and inexperienced dealers. One of the most troublesome reproductions is the Little Red Riding Hood jar marked McCoy. Several Brush jars are being reproduced, and because the old molds are being used, these are especially deceptive. In addition to these reproductions, we've also been alerted to watch for cookie jars marked Brush-McCoy made from molds that Brush never used. Remember that none of Brush's cookie jars were marked Brush-McCoy, so any bearing the compound name is fraudulent. For more information on cookie jars and reproductions, we recommend *The Collector's Encyclopedia of Cookie Jars, Books I, II,* and *III,* by Fred and Joyce Roerig; they are listed in the Directory under South Carolina. Another good source is *An Illustrated Value Guide to Cookie Jars* by Ermagene Westfall. Our advisors for this category are Fred and Joyce Roerig; they are listed in the Directory under South Carolina.

The examples listed below were made by companies other than those found elsewhere in this book; see also specific manufacturers.

ABC Bear, Sierra Vista	125.00
Airplane, North Am Ceramics, movable propeller	300.00
Albert Apple, Pitman-Dreitzer & Co, from $90 to	115.00
Alpo Dan the Dog, USA, from $50 to	60.00

Balloon Lady, Pottery Guild, unmk 125.00
Bartender, Pan Am Art...175.00
Beaver Fireman, Sigma..250.00
Big Al, c Disney on bk, from $50 to 75.00
Big Bird, Newcor 45.00
Blanket Couple, A Little Co c 87, 12".......................150.00
Blue Bonnet Sue, Nabisco, from $60 to.....................80.00
Checkered Taxi Sedan, Cavanagh...............................300.00
Chipmunk, Japan, #2863..30.00
Clown, Maurice c Calif USA.......................................175.00
Cookie Factory, Fitz & Floyd c FF 1987, FF Japan label, from $90 to...100.00
Cookieville, Treasure Craft 45.00
Cool Cookie Penguin, Hallmark Card Inc 300.00

Cowardly Lion, Star Jars, from $250.00 to $300.00.

(Photo courtesy Joyce and Fred Roerig)

Disney Channel, Treasure Craft, cylinder, from $80 to.................90.00
Doctor, Doranne of California, CJ-130 ....200.00
Dog Stump, California Originals, #2620 ....35.00
Dorothy & Toto, Star Jars..375.00
Dragon, Doranne of CA, mk USA...............................175.00
Duck w/Yarmulke, Doranne of California (unmk), from $50 to....60.00
Dutch Girl, Delft 55.00
Edmund, A Little Co c 1992, 19".................................125.00
Elephant Sailor Girl, DeForest of California...............100.00
Elephant w/Ball & Glove, Cara Marks for Sigma... ....100.00
Elsie, Pottery Guild, unmk 400.00
Ernie the Keebler Elf, c 1898 Keebler Co, Benjamin Medwin.......80.00
Fat Cat, Sigma...275.00
Fire Truck, California Originals, #841 ....225.00
Fred Flintstone, Vandor c 1989, from $150 to 175.00
Fred Flintstone & Pebbles, Vandor, paper label 325.00
Frog Sitting, bowl/flowers, CA Originals, mk 877 USA, from $40 to...50.00
Garfield on Cookie, Enesco 325.00
Gnome, Holiday Designs...40.00
Goodies Pig, DeForest of CA, ca 1956, from $95 to....110.00
Grandmother w/Child, A Little Co, ltd ed, 1992, 13"...............150.00
Gulden's Mustard, glass, 12¼" 200.00
Harley-Davidson Gas Tank, Taiwan, from $75 to 125.00
Henny (Dandee Hen), DeForest of CA USA 195.00
Herman Munster, Star Jars/Treasure Craft c 1996, from $250 to.....300.00
Hippo, Doranne of California......................................100.00
Hippo Fishing, Japan 45.00
Horse Mechanic, Japan 45.00
Humpty Dumpty, Clay Art, 1991................................125.00
Ice Wagon, Treasure Craft..95.00
Indian Maiden, Wihoa's Limited...1989 Rick Wisecarver, from $175 to..200.00
Italian Couple, A Little Co c 1991...............................150.00
Jack-'O-Lantern w/Bat, Exclusively for Lotus, 1989.................50.00

Jaguar XK-140 Convertible, Appleman, 12 made 1,500.00
Jeep, Doranne of California CJ 115, from $125 to 150.00
Juke Box, Vandor...150.00
King, DeForest of California, 1957, minimum value 450.00
Kooky Klown, c By Newhauser Pat Pending Green Prod Cleveland..125.00
Las Vegas Jackpot Slot Machine, Doranne of CA, mk J 64 c USA ..50.00
Little Red Riding Hood, California Originals, #320 USA 275.00
Mammy (Gone w/the Wind), Enesco, paper label.....................300.00
Marsh Pig w/Apple, Marsh Ceramics, unmk 95.00
Michael Jordan & Bugs Bunny Space Jam, TM & c 1996 WB, from $125 to.....150.00
Mickey Mouse Club House, c Walt Disney Prod, from $100 to ..125.00
Mrs Tiggy-Winkle, Sigma..300.00
Mushrooms, Sierra Vista Ceramics...USA c 1957 ......40.00
Nun, WH Hirsch Mfg Co USA, from $200 to 225.00
Olympic Torch, Warner Bros 95.00
Oscar the Grouch, California Originals, #972 ....100.00
Owl, Whoo's eating 'owl' cookies?, Enesco E-9227, c 1997 ....30.00
Panda, Fitz & Floyd 125.00
Peasant Woman, Department 56 ....125.00
Peter Panda, DCJ-24 c 1985...NAC, from $30 to 50.00
Pickup Truck (4x4), Doranne of California 200.00
Pig Clown, Cara Marks for Sigma..., from $100 to 125.00
Pinocchio, WH Hirsch...USA c 60 on base 190.00
Pirate Bust, Treasure Craft c Made in USA 275.00
Polka-Dot Witch, Fitz & Floyd....................................325.00
Poodle, DeForest of California 75.00
Popcorn Vendor, Sigma, paper label, from $325 to.....................350.00
Potbellied Stove, Treasure Craft 40.00
Queen, Maddux of CA USA c 210, from $100 to........125.00
Raccoon Cookie Can, Japan, unmk.............................35.00
Rag Doll, Sigma..175.00
Rocking Horse, Lane 125.00
Scarecrow Turnabout, CA Originals, 858 on lid & base, from $60 to...75.00
Sheriff, Fitz & Floyd 250.00
Snowman, Doranne of CA, mk J 52 USA 175.00
Soccer Ball, Treasure Craft c Made in USA, from $40 to.............45.00
Stagecoach, Sierra Vista..200.00
Sylvester Head w/Tweety, Applause 95.00
Teapot & Flowers, CA Originals, mk 737, from $25 to.................35.00
Tepee, Wihoa's...Rick Wisecarver...No 1 89...............250.00
The Wistler, New Rose Collection #66 ....125.00
Tommy Pickles (Rugrats), Viacom Created By Klasky/Csupo, 1996...75.00
Train, Sierra Vista 75.00
Transformer, Great Am Housewares 150.00
Upside Down Turtle, CA Originals, 2627 USA on lid & base, from $75 to..100.00
US Soccer Ball, Proctor & Gamble, Friendship Pottery 45.00
Vegetable House, Department 56 1990, from $50 to 60.00
Walt Disney Cookie Bus, c 1961 Walt Disney Prod.................1,000.00
Wonder Woman, California Originals, #847, DC Comics, rare, 14"...600.00
Yellow Cab, California Originals, unmk......................175.00
Yogi Bear, Harry James, c 1990 Hanna-Barbera Prod Inc, from $300 to.....325.00

Cooper, Susie

A twentieth century ceramic designer whose works are now attracting the attention of collectors, Susie Cooper was first affiliated with the A.E. Gray Pottery in Henley, England, in 1922 where she designed in lustres and painted items with her own ideas as well. (Examples of Gray's lustreware is rare and costly.) By 1930 she and her brother-in-law, Jack Beeson, had established a family business. Her pottery soon became a success, and she was subsequently offered space at Crown Works, Burslem. In 1940 she received the honorary title of Royal Designer for Industry, the only such distinction ever awarded by the Royal Society of

Arts solely for pottery design. Miss Cooper received the Order of the British Empire in the New Year's Honors List of 1979. She was the chief designer for the Wedgwood group from 1966 until she resigned in 1972. After 1980 she worked on a freelance basis until her death in July 1995.

Vase, orchids, multi-color on cream, M42, 1932, 5½", $350.00.

Bowl, cereal; Sunflower, coupe shape, 6¼"......................32.00
Bowl, Patricia Rose, oval, 7x9¾"..................................65.00
Bowl, Patricia Rose, 7¾"...60.00
Bowl, salad; Swansea Spray, pk, 2¾x9"........................50.00
Bowl, soup; Dresden Spray, rimmed, 9½"......................45.00
Bowl, soup; Dresden Spray, 7½"..................................35.00
Bowl, soup; Nosegay, 8"..40.00
Bowl, soup; Patricia Rose, 9".......................................58.00
Bowl, soup; Printemps, w/underplate...........................120.00
Bowl, vegetable; Sunflower, w/lid................................135.00
Candle holder, Dresden Spray, 2½x3½" dia, ea.............110.00
Coffee set, Black Fruit, pot+8 c/s................................240.00
Creamer & sugar bowl, Glen Mist, open........................60.00
Cup & saucer, Asterix, cylindrical, 2½".........................45.00
Cup & saucer, demi; Glen Mist, cylindrical, from $25 to.....30.00
Cup & saucer, demi; Nosegay.......................................45.00
Cup & saucer, Dot, 2½"...30.00
Cup & saucer, Dresden Spray, from $60 to....................75.00
Cup & saucer, Red Heraldry, cylindrical........................40.00
Cup & saucer, Sunflower, ftd.......................................45.00
Cup & saucer, Venetia, cylindrical, 2½".........................45.00
Egg coddler, Patricia Rose, 2 lg hdls, 4" dia, from $80 to.....90.00
Jam pot, Highland Grass, w/notched lid........................90.00
Plate, Black Fruit, 9"..25.00
Plate, Corn Poppy, 10½", from $25 to...........................35.00
Plate, Dresden Spray, 6"...12.00
Plate, Dresden Spray, 9"...30.00
Plate, Dresden Spray, 10", from $35 to..........................45.00
Plate, Nosegay, 8"...20.00
Plate, Nosegay, 9"..27.50
Plate, Patricia Rose, 9"...50.00
Plate, Patricia Rose, 10"...55.00
Plate, snack; Sunflower, +matching cup.......................48.00
Plate, Sunflower, 6⅝"..18.00
Plate, Sunflower, 8½"..22.00
Plate, Swansea Spray, pk, 9".......................................25.00
Platter, Glen Mist, 10½", from $70 to............................95.00
Platter, Nosegay, oval, 12", from $100 to.....................120.00
Platter, Swansea Spray, pk, oval, 12"............................45.00
Sauce boat, Dresden Spray, #11411, 6½" L, from $55 to.....62.00
Saucer, Patricia Rose, 5¾"...20.00

Sugar bowl, Glen Mist, open, ftd..................................30.00
Sugar bowl, Patricia Rose, w/lid.................................160.00
Sugar bowl, Scarlet Runner Bean, open, mk E241.........200.00
Teacup, Nosegay..40.00
Teapot, Banded, Kestral shape, #446..........................160.00
Teapot, Glen Mist, 4¾"..145.00
Teapot, Patricia Rose, Kestral shape, 5½", from $240 to.....280.00
Trio (c/s+plate), Sunflower...75.00
Tureen, Patricia Rose, 2 hdls on base, 1 on lid, 5x8¼"......195.00

Coors

The firm that became known as Coors Porcelain Company in 1920 was founded in 1908 by John J. Herold, originally of the Roseville Pottery in Zanesville, Ohio. Though still in business today, they are best known for their artware vases and Rosebud dinnerware produced before 1939.

Coors vases produced before the late '30s were made in a matt finish; by the latter years of the decade, high-gloss glazes were also being used. Nearly fifty shapes were in production, and some of the more common forms were made in three sizes. Typical colors in matt are white, orange, blue, green, yellow, and tan. Yellow, blue, maroon, pink, and green are found in high gloss. All vases are marked with a triangular arrangement of the words 'Coors Colorado Pottery' enclosing the word 'Golden.' You may find vases (usually 6" to 6½") marked with the Colorado State Fair stamp and dated 1939. For such a vase, add $10.00 to the suggested values given below.

Rosebud

Apple baker, w/lid...55.00
Ashtray..175.00
Bean pot, sm..65.00
Bowl, cream soup; 4"..38.00
Bowl, mixing; hdls, 1½-pt..40.00
Bowl, mixing; 3-pt..45.00
Bowl, mixing; 6-pt..45.00
Bowl, oatmeal..35.00
Bowl, pudding; 2-pt, from $35 to...................................40.00
Bowl, pudding; 7-pt...75.00
Cake knife..85.00
Casserole, Fr; 7½"...65.00
Casserole, str sides, 5"..50.00
Casserole, str sides, 8"..65.00
Casserole, w/lid, 9½"...100.00
Cookie jar, Deluxe, rope hdls, w/lid.............................110.00
Cup & saucer..45.00
Dish, oatmeal...25.00
Egg cup...50.00
Honey pot, w/spoon...300.00
Jar, utility; w/lid...85.00
Loaf pan, from $40 to..50.00
Muffin set, w/lid, rare..225.00
Pitcher, water; w/lid..150.00
Plate, cake; 11"...45.00
Plate, dinner; 9¼"...18.00
Plate, 5"...8.00
Plate, 8"...25.00
Platter, 12x9", from $42 to...48.00
Shakers, kitchen; slanted or pillar style, lg, pr...............65.00
Shirred egg dish..35.00
Sugar bowl, w/lid..40.00
Sugar shaker..80.00
Teapot, 2-cup..200.00

Teapot, 6-cup, from $160 to	185.00
Tumbler, ftd	125.00
Water server, cork stopper, 6-cup	120.00

Miscellaneous

Cake knife, Hawthorne, decalcomania	90.00
Cake plate, Floree	55.00
Casserole, Open Window, decalcomania, str sides, w/lid, lg	125.00
Creamer, Mello-Tone or Rockmount	15.00
Figurine, Laughing or Crying Monk, 6", ea	300.00
Gravy boat, Mello-Tone or Rockmount	15.00
Lamp base, bl	200.00
Pie plate, Coorado	55.00
Plate, dinner; Tulip, decalcomania	100.00
Shakers, Coorado, gr, pr	50.00
Teapot, Chrysanthemum, decalcomania	150.00
Tumbler, Mello-Tone or Rockmount	35.00
Vase, Beehive, orange matt, sm rings, 6"	45.00
Vase, Deco style, wht, low hdls, 12"	345.00
Vase, Empire, yel matt, stepped form, 10"	110.00
Vase, Leadville, gr matt, angled hdls, 8"	70.00
Vase, Montrose, bl matt, neck-to-shoulder hdls, 8"	70.00
Vase, Montrose, bl matt, neck-to-shoulder hdls, 12"	125.00
Vase, Trinidad, wht matt w/turq int, 12"	125.00
Water server, Mello-Tone or Rockmount	45.00

Copper

Handcrafted copper was made in America from early in the eighteenth century until about 1850, with the center of its production in Pennsylvania. Examples have been found signed by such notable coppersmiths as Kidd, Buchanan, Babb, Bently, and Harbeson. Of the many utilitarian items made, teakettles are the most desirable. Early examples from the eighteenth century were made with a dovetailed joint which was hammered and smoothed to a uniform thickness. Pots from the nineteenth century were seamed. Coffeepots were made in many shapes and sizes and along with mugs, kettles, warming pans, and measures are easiest to find. Stills ranging in sizes of up to fifty-gallon are popular with collectors today. Mary Frank Gaston has compiled a lovely book, *Antique Brass and Copper,* with many full-color photos and current market values, which we recommend for more information.

Hot water urn, brass finial and spout, scrolled acanthus handles with rings, square base with brass ball feet, 1800 – 1820, 9¾", $1,500.00.

(Photo courtesy Neal Auction Company)

Bowl, waisted stem, circular base, 5x9"	175.00
Candy pan, folded rim, 2 trn brass hdls, 7x20" dia	2,300.00
Cauldron, wrought-iron bail hdl, dvtl seam, w/lid, 14x15"	525.00
Dipper, long hdl, 1½x5" dia	185.00
Fry pan, ram's horn top, tin lined, long iron hdl, 39" L	60.00
Fry pan, wrought-iron hdl, str sides, LFD&H NY, 2x7½" dia	315.00
Funnel, 19th C, 11x10½"	150.00
Hot water urn, orb finial, on conforming underplate, 20x9½"	635.00
Hot water urn, scrolled acanthus hdls, brass finial, 1820s, 19"	1,500.00
Kettle, apple butter; dvtl, wrought-iron hdl, 25"	350.00
Kettle, brass hdl & finial, minor dents, 13½"	110.00
Kettle, molded bottom & hdls, 12", on iron tripod	400.00
Kettle, snake-form spout, early 19th C, 12¼x11"	800.00
Kettle, w/lid, 10x17"	350.00
Kettle, wrought-iron hdls, mid-19th C, 13x17"	925.00
Kettle, wrought-iron hdls, 14x20½"	700.00
Lavabo, chased w/armorial crest, 3x17x12"	600.00
Measures, graduated set of 5, from 3-10"	230.00
Pan, au-bain-Marie, w/lid, Bazar Francais NY, 4x7⅝"	435.00
Pan, fish poaching; ovoid, w/hdl, 19th C, 6x29"	800.00
Pan, poaching; incised Chinese characters on lid, oval, 11x13"	700.00
Pan, poaching; oval, w/lid, 16x14¼"	350.00
Pie pan, w/hanging hook, 10"	200.00
Rush holder, wood base, curled hdl & brass rivet, 10"	115.00
Saucepan, iron hdl, w/lid, late 19th C, 6¾x12¼" dia	575.00
Saucepan, wrought-iron rattail hdl, early, 5x11½" dia	750.00
Teakettle, dvtl, rpl brass knob, sgn D&J Bentley, 15¾"	500.00
Teakettle, gooseneck, dvtl bottom, str sides, domed top, 4¾x4"	300.00
Teakettle, hammered, dvtl bottom seam, riveted spout flap, ind, 4"	110.00
Wash bowl, flared rim, 6x18"	350.00

Copper Lustre

Copper lustre is a term referring to a type of pottery made in Staffordshire after the turn of the nineteenth century. It is finished in a metallic rusty-brown glaze resembling true copper. Pitchers are found in abundance, ranging from simple styles with dull bands of color to those with fancy handles and bands of embossed, polychromed flowers. Bowls are common; goblets, mugs, teapots, and sugar bowls much less so. It's easy to find, but not in good condition. Pieces with hand-painted decoration and those with historical transfers are the most valuable.

Butter pat, cobalt & wht center scene, 4"	45.00
Creamer, bl band w/Gen Jackson Hero of New Orleans portraits, 5¾"	2,200.00
Cup & saucer, House, mini, 1¼"	25.00
Jug, cherub scenes, wht band at top, 1830s, 4½"	75.00
Mug, bl band, 3"	100.00
Pitcher, cottage scene, ca 1820-30, 5"	275.00
Pitcher, deer relief & scrolls, 5⅝"	275.00
Pitcher, mc floral band, scroll hdl, 4⅛"	100.00
Pitcher, pk stripes, 4x6"	60.00
Salt cellar, House band, pk int, ftd	85.00
Sherbet, floral band, 4"	55.00
Vase, floral decor on bl band, English, 1840s, 3½x5"	45.00
Vase, shepherdess w/sheep (purple transfer), hdls, 7"	225.00

Coralene Glass

Coralene is a unique type of art glass easily recognized by the tiny grains of glass that form its decoration. Lacy allover patterns of seaweed, geometrics, and florals were used, as well as solid forms such as fish, plants, and single blossoms. (Seaweed is most commonly found and not as valuable as the other types of decoration.) It was made by several glasshouses both here and abroad. Values are based to a considerable extent on the amount of beading that remains. Our advisors for this category are Betty and Clarence Maier; they are listed in the Directory under Pennsylvania.

Bowl, pk satin w/gold seaweed, Webb, 2⅞x4½" 400.00
Bowl, wht opaque w/yel seaweed, 2x3" 60.00
Cracker jar, rose Dmn Quilt w/yel seaweed, silver mts, 7" 800.00
Tumbler, NE Wild Rose w/seaweed, 4" 500.00
Tumbler, peachblow w/yel seaweed 225.00
Vase, amber w/flower branch, ruffled rim, 4½" 115.00
Vase, champagne color w/seaweed, 3⅝x2¾" 135.00
Vase, cream w/allover orange seaweed, shouldered, 5" 225.00
Vase, fuchsia to pale pk w/yel seaweed, 7¼" 350.00
Vase, peachblow w/seaweed, Webb, 5½" 500.00
Vase, peachblow w/yel seaweed, dbl-branch camphor hdl, 7" 650.00
Vase, pk cased w/yel seaweed, bulbous w/long neck, 9¾" 635.00
Vase, pk satin cased w/yel seaweed, 5x3½", NM 260.00
Vase, wht w/charcoal seaweed, 6" 220.00

Cordey

The Cordey China Company was founded in 1942 in Trenton, New Jersey, by Boleslaw Cybis. The operation was small with less than a dozen workers. They produced figurines, vases, lamps, and similar wares, much of which was marketed through gift shops both nationwide and abroad. Though the earlier wares were made of plaster, Cybis soon developed his own formula for a porcelain composition which he called 'Papka.' Cordey figurines and busts were characterized by old-world charm, Rococo scrolls, delicate floral appliqués, ruffles, and real lace which was dipped in liquefied clay to add dimension to the work.

Although on rare occasions some items were not numbered or signed, the basic figure was cast both with numbers and the Cordey signature. The molded pieces were then individually decorated and each marked with its own impressed identification number as well as a mark to indicate the artist-decorator. Their numbering system began with 200 and in later years progressed into the 8000s. As can best be established, Cordey continued production until sometime in the mid-1950s. Boleslaw Cybis died in 1957, his wife in 1958.

Due to the increased availability of Cordey on the Internet over the last year, values of the more common pieces have fallen off. Our advisor for this category is Sharon A. Payne; she is listed in the Directory under Washington.

Key: ff — full figure

#401A, pincushion, $125.00.
(Photo courtesy Sharon A. Payne)

#313, bust of lady in pk shawl w/flowers exposed, mk MB Cybis, 8½" 60.00
#324, mallards, 14", pr...295.00
#861, wall sconces w/roses, pr..120.00
#1949, bust of lady, drilled for lamp, 7" 80.00
#4034, lady in lt bl dress w/pk roses, matching hat, ff, 8¼" 85.00
#4074, gentleman, lace shirt neck & cuffs, 13"................................125.00
#5002, bust of lady in pk w/roses at base & in hair, 5¾" 45.00
#5005, bust of lady in pk w/bl roses at base & in hair, 6" 60.00
#5009, bust of lady, bl Fedora-style hat, 6" 45.00
#5009, bust of lady in bl bonnet 60.00
#5011, bust of lady in wht w/lg collar, gold rose at base & hair, 6" .45.00
#5020, bust of man in pk w/lg wht curls, 2 roses at base, 6½" 60.00
#5025, bust of lady, 6"..60.00
#5025, bust of lady w/lace shawl, 6" 70.00
#5026, bust of Madonna w/wht shawl, gold at base, 6" 65.00
#5030, bust of lady in bl shawl w/pk roses, lg hat w/bl ribbon, 8" ...70.00
#5034, Raleigh, bust of man, gr shirt, blk vest, 8½" 70.00
#5036, bust of lady in silver gown, bl hat w/pk roses, 8½" 85.00
#5037, bust of lady (¾) in bl dress w/red roses in hair, 9½" 65.00
#5042, Monsieur DuBarry, ff, bl coat, pk pants, 11".....................125.00
#5045, girl w/water jug, 10½"...95.00
#5051, bust of lady in cream dress, bl ribbon at neck, bl hat w/roses ..75.00
#5054, bust of lady (¾) in wht w/roses at base & in hair, 9".........75.00
#5059, bust of Victorian lady, ¾-figure, 9½" 75.00
#5077, woman praying, 13" 90.00
#5084, Madame DuBarry, in bl & pk, ff, 11".................................125.00
#5092, 18th-C man, bl coat, pk breeches, 11" 95.00
#5138, bust of lady w/bl bow on dress & bl Fedora hat, Papka curls, 6"..65.00
Lamp, lady in kimono, 11¼" figure, 24½" overall 90.00
Lamp, Victorian man, 11", 27" to top of porc finial.......................60.00
Lamps, ladies' high-button shoes, appl flowers, brass base, 30", pr...225.00
Lamps, 18th-C couple w/gold, brass base, 19" to top of bulb, pr...100.00
Wall sconces, lady & man, mid-1940s, 4-pc set 250.00

Corkscrews

The history of the corkscrew dates back to the mid-1600s, when wine makers concluded that the best-aged wine was that stored in smaller containers, either stoneware or glass. Since plugs left unsealed were often damaged by rodents, corks were cut off flush with the bottle top and sealed with wax or a metal cover. Removing the cork cleanly with none left to grasp became a problem. The task was found to be relatively simple using the worm on the end of a flintlock gun rod. So the corkscrew evolved. Endless patents have been issued for mechanized models. Handles range from carved wood, ivory, and bone to porcelain and repoussé silver. Exotic materials such as agate, mother-of-pearl, and gold plate were also used on occasion. Celluloid lady's legs are popular.

For further information, we recommend *The Ultimate Corkscrew Book* and *Bull's Pocket Guide to Corkscrews* by Donald Bull, our advisor for this category. He is listed in the Directory under Virginia. In the following descriptions, values are for examples in excellent condition, unless noted otherwise.

Bar mt, mk Champion (1898) 150.00
Clough, wire 2-finger eyeglass type..115.00
Collapsing type, w/brewery advertising..100.00
Dbl-lever, Magic Lever Cork Drawer..115.00
Dbl-lever, Monk Cellarmaster, metal..35.00
Figural, clown, Syroco 450.00
Figural, elephant, cvd wood, wire worm 22.00
Figural, English bulldog, brass, 1930s, 6" 55.00
Figural, fish swallowing worm, cast metal, mk JB............................60.00
Figural, horse head, emb metal w/folding worm 40.00

Figural, owl, brass, 2-finger pull, English 35.00
Figural, parrot, brass, 6¼" 90.00
Figural, teepee, pewter, mk Roux 75.00
Figural, Viking ship, pewter, sail mk Zero 90.00
Figural, woman w/toothache, pnt metal 60.00
Finger pull, 3-finger, leather-wrapped 100.00
Flynut, Valenzia, brass-colored metal, 1943-44 Pat 115.00
Gay '90s, folding legs, red & wht stripes, 2⅝" 175.00
Italian rollover hdl, mk Edwin Jay 30.00
Mermaid waiter's friend, celluloid hdls 600.00
Old Snifter, chrome, turning head, 5¾" 140.00
Pewter, Viking ship form, sail mk Zero 90.00
Picnic, metal w/wood sheath, rare 250.00
Pocket folder, metal, mk So-Ezy Made in USA Pat Pend 50.00
Roundlet, sterling, sliding action 250.00
Scissors, metal, mk GMS No 10983 Germany 325.00
Silver, paneled bar over foliate finial, Jensen/#925S/Denmark, 4⅝" ...300.00
Spoon, SP, Walker & Orr, 1932, American Pat 125.00
Syroco, Scottie dog opener/corkscrew set 200.00
T-hdl, celluloid, ivory color 55.00
T-hdl, chrome, w/closed barrel, mk Italy 35.00
T-hdl, metal, 2-finger grip, mk Jaques Perille 125.00
T-hdl, silver, hammered design 450.00
T-hdl, wood, w/brush, ornate brass-colored barrel, Thomason 650.00
T-hdl, wood, w/spring, Richard Recknagel's 1899 German Pat ...275.00
T-hdl, zigzag, multi-lever, concertina action 60.00
Tip Top, metal fold-up type, Williamson 50.00
Whistle, metal roundlet, parts unscrew to form opener 325.00

Cosmos

Cosmos, sometimes called Stemless Daisy, is a patterned glass tableware produced from 1894 through 1915 by Consolidated Lamp and Glass Company. Relief-molded flowers on a finely crosscut background were painted in soft colors of pink, blue, and yellow. Though nearly all were made of milk glass, a few items may be found in clear glass with the designs painted on. In addition to the tableware, lamps were also made.

Bottle, cologne; orig stopper, rare, from $275 to 300.00
Butter dish, 5x8" 275.00
Creamer 150.00
Lamp, bouquet; kerosene, 24" 575.00
Lamp, bouquet; slender base, rnd globe, all orig, 16" 525.00
Lamp, mini: 8", from $400 to 450.00
Lamp, 10" 450.00
Pickle castor, rstr Toronto #0182 fr, from $700 to 850.00
Pitcher, milk; 5" 250.00

Syrup pitcher, 6", $300.00.

Pitcher, water; 9" 350.00
Shakers, tall, orig lids, pr 175.00
Spooner 125.00
Sugar bowl, open 150.00
Sugar bowl, w/lid 185.00
Sugar shaker 400.00
Tumbler, 3¾" 75.00

Cottageware

You'll find a varied assortment of novelty dinnerware items, all styled as cozy little English cottages or huts with cone-shaped roofs; some may have a waterwheel or a windmill. Marks will vary. English-made Price Brothers or Beswick pieces are valued in the same range as those marked Occupied Japan, while items marked simply Japan are considerably less pricey. Our advisor for this category is Grace Klender; she is listed in the Directory under Ohio. All of the following examples are Price Brothers/Kensington unless noted otherwise.

Bank, dbl slot, 4½x3½x5" 95.00
Bell, minimum value 50.00
Biscuit jar, wicker hdl, Maruhon Ware, Occupied Japan, 6½" 92.50
Bowl, salad 65.00
Butter dish 65.00
Butter dish, cottage int (fireplace), Japan, 6¾x5" 85.00
Butter dish, oval, Burlington Ware, 6" 60.00
Butter dish, rnd, Beswick, England, w/lid, 3½x6", from $75 to ...100.00
Butter pat, emb cottage, rectangular, Occupied Japan 20.00
Chocolate pot 148.00
Condiment set, mustard, 2½" s&p on 5" hdld leaf tray 85.00
Condiment set, mustard pot, s&p, row arrangement, 6" 50.00
Condiment set, mustard pot, s&p, tray, row arrangement, 7¾" ...50.00
Condiment set, 3-part cottage on shaped tray w/appl bush, 4½" ..85.00
Cookie jar, pk/brn/gr, sq, Japan, 8½x5½" 75.00
Cookie jar, windmill, wicker hdl 165.00
Cookie jar/canister, cylindrical, rare sz, 8x3¾" 275.00
Cookie jar/canister, cylindrical, 8½x5" 140.00
Cookie/biscuit jar, Occupied Japan 95.00
Creamer, windmill, Occupied Japan, 2⅝" 30.00
Creamer & sugar bowl, 2½x4½" 50.00
Cup & saucer, chocolate; str-sided cup, 3½x2¾", 5½" 45.00
Cup & saucer, 2½", 4½" 50.00
Demitasse pot 110.00
Dish w/cover, Occupied Japan, sm 40.00
Egg cup set, 4 on 6" sq tray 65.00
Gravy boat & tray, rare 275.00
Grease jar, Occupied Japan, from $25 to 38.00
Hot water pot, Westminster, England, 8½x4" 50.00
Marmalade 45.00
Marmalade & jelly, 2 conjoined houses 85.00
Mug, 3⅞" 55.00
Pin tray, 4" dia 22.00
Pitcher, emb cottage, lg flower on hdl, rare 150.00
Pitcher, tankard; rnd, 7⅞" 138.00
Platter, oval, 11¾x7½" 65.00
Reamer, Japan 65.00
Sugar box, for cubes, 5¾" L 50.00
Tea set, Japan, child's, serves 4 ....165.00
Teapot, Keele Street, w/creamer & sugar 95.00
Teapot, Occupied Japan, 6½" 55.00
Teapot, Ye Olde Fireside, Occupied Japan, 9x5" 85.00
Teapot, 6¼" 55.00
Toast rack, 3-slot, 3½" 75.00

Toast rack, 4-slot, 5½" **85.00**
Tumbler, Occupied Japan, 3½", set of 6 ....**65.00**

Teapots, English and Occupied Japan, 6½", each $55.00.

Coverlets

The Jacquard attachment for hand looms represented a culmination of weaving developments made in France. Introduced to America by the early 1820s, it gave professional weavers the ability to easily create complex patterns with curved lines. Those who could afford the new loom adaptation could now use hole-punched pasteboard cards to weave floral patterns that before could only be achieved with intense labor on a draw-loom.

Before the Jacquard mechanism, most weavers made their coverlets in geometric patterns. Use of indigo-blue and brightly colored wools often livened the twills and overshot patterns available to the small-loom home weaver. Those who had larger multiple-harness looms could produce warm double-woven, twill-block, or summer-and-winter designs.

While the new floral and pictorial patterns' popularity had displaced the geometrics in urban areas, the mid-Atlantic, and the Midwest by the 1840s, even factory production of the Jacquard coverlets was disrupted by cotton and wool shortages during the Civil War. A revived production in the 1870s saw a style change to a center-medallion motif, but a new fad for white 'Marseilles' spreads soon halted sales of Jacquard-woven coverlets. Production of Jacquard carpets continued to the turn of the century.

Rural and frontier weavers continued to make geometric-design coverlets through the nineteenth century, and local craft revivals have continued the tradition through this century. All-cotton overshots were factory produced in Kentucky from the 1940s, and factories and professional weavers made cotton-and-wool overshots during the past decade. Many Jacquard-woven coverlets have dates and names of places and people (often the intended owner — not the weaver) woven into corners or borders.

Note: In the listings that follow, examples are blue and white and in excellent condition unless noted otherwise. When dates are given, they actually appear on the coverlet itself as part of the woven design.

Key: mdl — medallion

Jacquard

Birds/roses/tulips, 4-color, OH/1838, 2-pc, minor rstr, 97x70" **660.00**
Daisy & Star, tree/fence border, dbl weave, NY, ca 1838, 90x79" ..**2,585.00**
Dmn grid w/flowers & birds, red/navy/gr/natural, 2-pc, 1852, 90x73"..**1,265.00**
Floral mdl w/hound's-tooth ground, red/navy/gr/natural, 82x68"...**250.00**
Floral mdl/eagle border, tan/gr/brn/red, Biederwand, 92x70".......**415.00**

Floral mdls, bl/red/mustard/natural, 2-pc, fringe, 84x75" **575.00**
Floral mdls & acanthus leaves, bl/natural, 2-pc, 86x72" **395.00**
Floral/star mdls, bl/red/burgundy/natural, 2-pc, 1850, 86x72" **700.00**
Foliage mdls, dbl borders, sgn/1850, 2-pc, 77x72" **625.00**
Fruit & floral mdls, red/navy/gr/natural, 2-pc, 1855, 88x76" **400.00**
Fruit in urns, Christian & heathen border, OH, 2-pc, 76x66" **950.00**
Mdls (16) & dmns w/basketweave, bl/natural, Jackson/OH, 2-pc, 86x81"..**1,900.00**
Memorial Hall w/in wreath, vine border, 3-color, Pat 1875, 82x76", VG....**400.00**
Pineapple & floral mdl, fringe, 1837, 2-pc, 94x72" **385.00**
Rose mdls/circles/dbl borders, dbl weave, 2-pc, 83x78" **300.00**
Rose mdls/florals/branches, 3-color, dbl weave, 2-pc, 82x74" **400.00**
Rose mdls/flowers/vines, bl/natural, sgn, 1-pc, 88x66" **365.00**
Roses/flowers, eagle corners, 4-color, 1-pc, 1850, 74x74" **400.00**
Star mdl w/grapes & baskets, red/bl/lt gr/wht, 81x67" **200.00**

Overshot

Dmns, bl/red/wht, stains/wear, 2-pc, 84x66" **200.00**
Geometrics, tomato red/brn/wht, 2-pc, wear, 69x61" **225.00**
Grid pattern, red/navy/gr, wavy border, edge wear, 78x72" **275.00**
Optical, fringe 1 end, 2-pc, 74x74" **150.00**
Optical, 2-color, 2-pc, 94x76" **240.00**
Sm blocks, 5 sqs & geometric borders, summer/winter, rebound, 94x74"...**220.00**
Stars w/pine tree border, 4-color, 2-pc, 92x70", VG **220.00**
Sunrise variant, red/wht, 93x69" **300.00**

Cowan

Guy Cowan opened a small pottery near Cleveland, Ohio, in 1913, where he made tile and artware on a small scale from the natural red clay available there. He developed distinctive glazes — necessary, he felt, to cover the dark red body. After the war and a temporary halt in production, Cowan moved his pottery to Rocky River, where he made a commercial line of artware utilizing a highly fired white porcelain. Although he acquiesced to the necessity of mass production, every effort was made to insure a product of highest quality. Fine artists, among them Waylande Gregory, Thelma Frazier, and Viktor Schreckengost, designed pieces which were often produced in limited editions, some of which sell today for prices in the thousands. Most of the ware was marked 'Cowan,' except for the 1930 mass-produced line called 'Lakeware.' Falling under the crunch of the Great Depression, the pottery closed in 1931.

The use of an asterisk (*) in the listing below indicates a nonfactory name that is being provided as a suggested name for the convenience of present-day collectors. One example is the glaze *Original Ivory, which is a high-gloss white that resembles undecorated porcelain. It was used on many of Cowan's lady 'flower figures' (Cowan's more graceful term for what some collectors call frogs).

For more information, we recommend *Cowan Pottery and the Cleveland School* by Mark Bassett and Victoria Naumann. Our prices are for marked examples in mint condition, unless noted otherwise.

Ashtray, Denset, Parchment Green, W Gregory, #925, 5½" **55.00**
Bookends, Boy-Girl, *Orig Ivory, F Wilcox, #519, 6½", pr **375.00**
Bookends, toucan, blk/silver/bronze finish, Jacobson, 5¼", pr **2,800.00**
Bowl, Ambassador, Daffodil, RG Cowan, #B-2, 2¼x11¼x9¼" **50.00**
Bowl, Apple Blossom/Ivory, RG Cowan, #733-B, 4x9½" **60.00**
Bowl, Columbine, #731, 5x16x11", from $75 to **125.00**
Bowl, Logan, Dawn, RG Cowan, #537-A, 2½x7" **50.00**
Bowl, Lohengrin, Azure, #B-11-B, 3¼x13¼x9½", from $55 to **75.00**
Bowl, Nasturtium, #731-X, 4x13x9" **55.00**
Bowl, Pterodactyl, Verbena, A Blazys, #739, 3x15x10" **60.00**
Bowl, Radiant, April/blk, #845-A, 3x10" **80.00**
Bowl, Terpsichore, Hyacinth, W Gregory, #785-A, 9x12½x9" **90.00**

Candelabrum figurine, Swirl Dancer, Special Ivory, #745, 9½" ..**650.00**
Candelabrum flower grid, triple; Ivory, RG Cowan, #761, 8" **50.00**
Candlesticks, Apple Blossom Pink, #734, 4", pr..................**20.00**
Figurine, Flamingo, Oriental Red, W Gregory, #D-2-D, 11" **400.00**
Figurine, Wildwood Stag, Caramel, W Gregory, #926, rstr, 13¼" ...**450.00**
Flower frog, Flamingo, Special Ivory, #D-2-F, 11", EX **275.00**
Flower frog, Scarf Dancer, *Orig Ivory, RG Cowan, #686, 6" **200.00**
Jar, strawberry; April Green, RG Cowan, #SJ-3, 12" **220.00**
Lamp, Foliage, #X-11, 8¾" **130.00**
Lamp, Oriental Red, W Atchley, #L-13, 10"................................**150.00**
Plaque, Atlanta, Oriental Red, W Gregory, #778, 13", from $800 to...**1,000.00**

Plaque, horse and rider among birds, dogs, etc., multicolor on oatmeal colored ground, green scallop border, Viktor Schreckengost, 11½", $1,000.00. (Photo courtesy Skinner, Inc.)

Plate, Oriental Red, #X-10-B, RG Cowan, 11½", from $55 to **65.00**
Plate, Thunderbird, Guave, A Blazys, #750, 15½", from $450 to ..**600.00**
Serving set, Colonial, Special Ivory, #X-24/#X-25/#X-33, cr/sug+tray...**120.00**
Vase, April Green, RG Cowan, #V-2-A, 3½" **45.00**
Vase, Azure, Art Deco hdls, #V-63, 10¾", from $100 to.............**150.00**
Vase, bud; Diamond, Onyx, RG Cowan, #V-871, 6½", from $45 to ..**65.00**
Vase, bud; Sea Horse, Delphinium, #725, 7½" **80.00**
Vase, Copper, #544, 6" **120.00**
Vase, Delphinium, #662, 5¼" **50.00**
Vase, Fawn, RG Cowan, #801, 5", from $70 to...........................**90.00**
Vase, floral (stylized), blk on yel to gr, bulbous, 9" **1,100.00**
Vase, Foliage, #V-853-B, 8¼", from $100 to **125.00**
Vase, Lakeware, Peacock, #V-71, 9" **100.00**
Vase, Larkspur, #590, 7¼" **50.00**
Vase, Larkspur, #635, 9½", from $110 to..................................**130.00**
Vase, Lime, #V-72, 5¼" **60.00**
Vase, Marigold, #732, 10", from $70 to.....................................**85.00**
Vase, Sea Horse, Apple Blossom, #715-X, 5¾" **40.00**
Vase, Sea Horse, Lapis, #715-B, fan form, 8", NM.......................**120.00**
Vase, Snifter, Fawn, RG Cowan, #808, 5½", from $80 to **100.00**
Vase, Terra Cotta, RG Cowan, #V-91, 6¼"..................................**70.00**

Cracker Jack

Kids have been buying Cracker Jack since it was first introduced in the 1890s. By 1912 it was packaged with a free toy inside. Before the first kernel was crunched, eager fingers had retrieved the surprise from the depth of the box — actually no easy task, considering the care required to keep the contents so swiftly displaced from spilling over the side! Though a little older, perhaps, many of those same kids still are looking — just as eagerly — for the Cracker Jack prizes. Point of sale, company collectibles, and the prizes as well have over the years reflected America's changing culture. Grocer sales and incentives from around the turn of the century — paper dolls, postcards, and song books — were often marked Rueckheim Brothers (the inventors of Cracker Jack) or Reliable Confections. Over the years the company made some changes, leaving a

trail of clues that often help collectors date their items. The company's name changed in 1922 from Rueckheim Brothers & Eckstein (who had been made a partner for inventing a method for keeping the caramelized kernels from sticking together) to The Cracker Jack Company. Their Brooklyn office was open from 1914 until it closed in 1923. The first time the sailor Jack logo was used on their packaging was in 1919. The sailor image of a Rueckheim child (with red, white, and blue colors) was introduced by these German immigrants in an attempt to show support for the U.S.A. during the time of heightened patriotism after WW I. For packages and 'point of sale' dating, note that the word 'prize' was used from 1912 to 1925, 'novelty' from 1925 to 1932, and 'toy' from 1933 on.

The first loose-packed prizes were toys made of wood, clay, tin, metal, and lithographed paper (the reason some early prizes are stained). Plastic toys were introduced in 1946. Paper wrapped for safety purposes in 1948, subjects echo the hype of the day — yo-yos, tops, whistles, and sports cards in the simple, peaceful days of our country, propaganda and war toys in the '40s, games in the '50s, and space toys in the '60s. Few of the estimated 15 billion prizes were marked. Advertising items from Angelus Marshmallow and Checkers Confections (cousins of the Cracker Jack family) are also collectible. When no condition is indicated, the items listed below are assumed to be in excellent to mint condition. 'CJ' indicates that the item is marked. Note: An often-asked question concerns the tin Toonerville Trolley called 'CJ.' No data has been found in the factory archives to authenticate this item; it is assumed that the 'CJ' merely refers to its small size. For further information see *Cracker Jack Toys, The Complete, Unofficial Guide for Collectors*, by Larry White. Our advisor for this category is Harriet Joyce; she is listed in the Directory under under Florida. Also look for *The Prize Insider* newsletter listed in the Directory under Clubs, Newsletters, and Catalogs.

Dealer Incentives and Premiums

Badge, pin-bk, celluloid, lady w/CJ label reverse, 1905, 1¼" **100.00**
Blotter, CJ question mk box, yel, 7¾x3¾".................................**185.00**
Book, pocket; riddle/sailor boy/dog on cover, RWB, CJ, 1919.......**30.00**
Book, Uncle Sam Song Book, CJ, 1911, ea.................................**35.00**
Corkscrew/opener, metal plated, CJ/Angelus, 3¾" tube case **85.00**
Jigsaw puzzle, CJ or Checkers, 1 of 4, 7x10", in envelope..............**35.00**
Mask, Halloween; paper, CJ, series, 10" or 12", ea.........................**28.00**
Mirror, oval, Angelus (redhead or blond) on box **89.00**
Pen, ink; w/nib, tin litho bbl, CJ **485.00**
Pencil top clip, metal/celluloid, tube shape w/pkg......................**220.00**
Puzzle, metal, CJ/Checkers, 1 of 15, '34, in envelope, ea..............**14.00**
Tablet, school; CJ, 1929, 8x10"...**195.00**
Thimble, aluminum, CJ Co/Angelus, red pnt, rare, ea **165.00**
Wings, air corps type, silver or blk, stud-bk, CJ, 1930s, 3", ea.......**55.00**

Packaging

Box, popcorn; red scroll border, CJ 'Prize,' 1912-25, ea...............**150.00**
Canister, tin, CJ Candy Corn Crisp, 10-oz....................................**75.00**
Canister, tin, CJ Coconut Corn Crisp, 10-oz **65.00**
CJ Commemorative canister, wht w/red scroll, 1980s, ea **8.00**

Prizes, Cast Metal

Badge, 6-point star, mc CJ Police, silver, 1931, 1¼" **55.00**
Button, stud bk, Xd bats & ball, CJ pitcher/etc series, 1928 ....**130.00**
Coins, Presidents, 31 series, CJ, mk cancelled on bk, 1933, ea **12.00**
Dollhouse items; lantern, mug, candlestick, etc; no mk, ea............**6.50**
Pistol, soft lead, inked, CJ on bbl, early, rare, 2⅛".....................**180.00**
Rocking horse, no rider, 3-D, inked, early, 1⅛" **25.00**
Spinner, early pkg in center, 'More You Eat...,' CJ, rare **295.00**

Prizes, Paper

Book, Animals (or Birds), to color, Makatoy, unmk, 1949, mini...35.00
Book, Birds We Know, CJ, 1928, mini ...105.00
Book, Chaplin flip book, CJ, 1920s, ea ...140.00
Book, Twigg & Sprigg, CJ, 1930, mini ...105.00
Decal, cartoon or nursery rhyme figure, 1947-49, CJ ...12.00
Disguise, ears, red (still in carrier), CJ, 1950, pr...22.00
Disguise, glasses, hinged, w/eyeballs, unmk, 1933...6.00

Finger puppet, C. Cloud design, 1937, four different, each, $30.00. (Photo courtesy Harriet Joyce)

Fortune Teller, boy/dog on film in envelope, CJ, 1920s, 1¾x2½" ..80.00
Game, Midget Auto Race, wheel spins, CJ, 1949, 3⅜" H ...15.00
Game spinner, ...baseball at home, unmk, 1946, 1½" dia ...60.00
Hat, Indian headdress, CJ, 1910-20, 5⅜" H...275.00
Hat, Me for CJ, early, ea...120.00
Magic game book, erasable slate, CJ, series of 13, 1946, ea ...25.00
Movie, Goofy Zoo, trn wheel(s): change animals, unmk, 1939.....25.00
Movie, pull tab for 2nd picture, yel, early, 3", in envelope...125.00
Sand toy pictures, pours for action, series of 14, 1967, ea...65.00
Top, string; Rainbow Spinner, 2-pc, cb, different designs, ea ...45.00
Transfer, iron-on, sport figure or patriotic, unmk, 1939, ea...6.00
Whistle, Blow for More, CJ/Angelus pkgs, 1928, '31 or '33, ea.....45.00
Whistle, Razz Zooka, C Carey Cloud design, CJ, 1949...25.00

Prizes, Plastic

Animals, standup, letter on bk, series of 26, Nosco, 1953, ea...4.00
Baseball players, 3-D, bl or gray team, 1948, 1½", ea...8.00
Disc, emb fish plaque, oval, series of 10, 1956, unmk, ea...14.00
Figure, circus; stands on base, 1 of 12, Nosco, 1951-54...3.00
Fob, alphabet letter w/loop on top, 1 of 26, 1954, 1½"...4.00
Palm puzzle, ball(s) roll into holes, dome or rnd, from 1966...6.00
Palm puzzle, ball(s) roll into holes, sq, CJ, 1920s, ea ...45.00
Ships in a bottle, 6 different, unmk, 1960, ea...6.00
Spinner, tops varied colors, 10 designs, from 1948, ea ...2.50
Toys, take apart/assemble, variety, from '62, unassembled, ea...6.00
WWII Cl Cloud punch-out war vehicles, CJ, series of 10, ea...30.00

Prizes, Tin

Badge, boy & dog diecut, complete w/bend-over tab, CJ ...150.00
Badge, emb/plated CJ officer, 2⅜" or 1⅝", early, ea...110.00
Bank, 3-D book form, red/gr/or blk, CJ Bank, early, 2"...120.00
Brooch or pin, various designs on card, CJ/logo, early, ea ...125.00
Clicker, 'Noisy CJ Snapper,' pear shape, aluminum, 1949 ...14.00
Doll dishes, tin plated, CJ, '31, 1¾", 1⅞", & 2⅛" dia, ea...35.00
Helicopter, yel propeller, wood stick, unmk, 1937, 2⅝" ...27.00
Horse & wagon, litho diecut, CJ & Angelus, 2⅛"...65.00
Horse & wagon, litho diecut, gray/red mks, CJ, 1914-23, 3⅛"....350.00
Pocket watch, silver or gold, CJ as numerals, 1931, 1½" ...30.00
Small box shape; garage litho, unmk, 1⅛" ...60.00
Small box shape: electric stove litho, unmk, 1⅛" ...80.00
Soldier, litho, die-cut standup, officer/private/etc, unmk, ea ...17.00
Spinner, wood stick, Fortune Teller Game, red/wht/bl, CJ, 1½" ...90.00
Spinner, wood stick, 2 Toppers, red/wht/bl, Angelus/Jack, 1½" 85.00
Stand up, oval Am Flag, series of 4, unmk, 1940-49, ea ...18.00
Tall box shape: Frozen Foods locker freezer, '47, unmk, 1¾" ...75.00
Tall box shape: grandfather clock, unmk, 1947, 1¾" ...65.00
Train, engine & tender, litho, CJ Line/512 ...125.00
Train, litho engine only, red, 1941, unmk ...20.00
Train, Lone Eagle Flyer engine, unmk ...60.00
Truck, litho, RWB, CJ/Angelus, 1931, ea...65.00
Wagon shape: Tank Corps No 57, gr & blk, 1941...30.00
Wagon shape: CJ Shows, yel circus wagon, series of 5, ea ...175.00
Wheelbarrow, tin plated, bk leg in place, CJ, 1931, 2½" L ...35.00

Miscellaneous

Ad, Saturday Evening Post, mc, CJ, 1919, 11x14"...18.00
Lunch box, tin emb, CJ, 1970s, 4x7x9"...30.00
Medal, CJ salesman award, brass, 1939, scarce...125.00
Sign, bathing beauty, 5-color cb, CJ, early, 17x22"...460.00
Sign, child on lady's lap reaching for box, mc cb, 1900, 15x11", EX+ ..50.00
Sign, Santa & prizes, mc cb, Angelus, early, lg ...220.00
Sign, Santa & prizes, mc cb, CJ, early, lg ...265.00

Crackle Glass

Though this type of glassware was introduced as early as the 1880s (by the New England Glass Co.), it was made primarily from 1930 until about 1980. It was produced by more than five hundred companies here (by Benko, Rainbow, and Kanawah, among others) and abroad (by such renown companies as Moser, for example), and its name is descriptive. The surface looks as though the glass has been heated then plunged into cold water, thus producing a network of tight cracks. It was made in a variety of colors; among the more expensive today are ruby red, amberina, cobalt, cranberry, and gray. For more information we recommend *Crackle Glass, Identification and Value Guide, Books I* and *II*, and *Crackle Glass from Around the World* (Collector Books) by Stan and Arlene Weitman, our advisors this category; they are listed in the Directory under New York. See also Moser.

Ashtray, dk bl, bowl w/incurvate rim, 3 rests, 7¼"...35.00
Candle holder, apricot (flashed-on like carnival glass), 10½" ...75.00
Candy dish, dk topaz, pan shape w/clear ribbed drop hdl, Hamon, 5½"...100.00
Creamer & sugar bowl, gold, Kanawha, 1957-87, 3½" ...70.00
Cruet, amber, 2-ball stopper, pulled-bk hdl, Rainbow, 6½" ...100.00
Cruet, sea gr, ball stopper, flared w/fluted rim, Pilgrim, 6" ...85.00
Decanter, amber, urn w/teardrop stopper, thick rolled bottom, 9½"...175.00
Dish, gold, flared ruffled rim, Kanawha, 1957-87, 3" ...45.00
Hat, amberina, smooth flat bottom, Kanawha, 1957-87, 2" ...45.00
Pitcher, amberina, bulbous, drop-over hdl, Pilgrim, 1949-69, 3¾"...45.00
Pitcher, amberina, spout pointing up, Kanawha, 1957-87, 13¼" 85.00
Pitcher, amethyst, drop-over hdl, waisted, Pilgrim, 1949-69, 3¼" ..55.00
Pitcher, bl, cylinder/flared fluted rim, drop-over angled hdl, 3½"...50.00
Pitcher, emerald gr, waisted, drop-over hdl, Pilgrim, 1949-69, 4" ...40.00
Pitcher, olive gr, flared rim, drop-over hdl, Pilgrim, 1949-69, 3½"...40.00
Pitcher, ruby, flared/flat bottom, pulled-bk hdl, 1949-69, 4"...45.00
Pitcher, ruby, fluted bottle neck/flared bottom, pulled-bk hdl, 4½"...45.00
Pitcher, ruby, teardrop shape, drop-over hdl, Pilgrim, 1949-69, 3½"...45.00
Vase, amber, bulbous w/trumpet neck, clear ped ft, 1920s, 11½"...150.00
Vase, amberina, bulbouse w/long ruffled bottle neck, Hamon, 7¼"...65.00

Vase, amberina, pinched, Pilgrim, 1949-69, 4"..............................80.00
Vase, amberina, plain urn w/flared neck, tapered bottom, 5½" 85.00
Vase, amberina, slender w/flared scalloped rim, Kanawha, 7¾" 75.00
Vase, bl, bulbous, long neck w/appl serpentine, Pilgrim, 6½"........65.00
Vase, bl, flared top/bottom, applied rigaree, fluted, Pilgrim, 3½"....45.00
Vase, crystal, cylindrical w/flared fluted rim, Bischoff, 5½" 60.00
Vase, crystal, vertically ribbed beaker, Gillinder, 10"..................100.00
Vase, lemon lime, pinched bulbous body/plain bottle neck, Pilgrim, 5"....45.00
Vase, sea gr, bulbous w/fluted bottle neck, 4¼"............................40.00
Vase, topaz, ped ft w/wide ruffled rim, Bischoff, 1942-63, 10¼"..135.00

Cranberry Glass

Cranberry glass is named for its resemblance to the color of cranberry juice. It was made by many companies both here and abroad, becoming popular in America soon after the Civil War. It was made in free-blown ware as well as mold-blown. Today cranberry glass is being reproduced, and it is sometimes difficult to distinguish the old from the new. Ask a reputable dealer if you are unsure.

See also Cruets; Salts; Sugar Shakers; Syrups.

Bowl, applied white opalescent candy ribbon edge, flint, 3¼x8¾", $175.00. (Photo courtesy John A. Shuman III)

Basket, ruffled rim, clear twist hdl 230.00
Bowl, mc floral w/gold, clear scallops, brass ft, 5x6⅜"..................195.00
Box, HP decor, hinged lid, ormolu base, 5" 150.00
Compote, mc floral w/gold berries, clear ped, 4x6⅛"....................135.00
Creamer, ruffled rim, clear hdl, rigaree at neck, shell ft, 4¼"......145.00
Decanter, floral, ribbed, flared rim, hollow stopper, 9¼" 175.00
Epergne, single trumpet, crystal rigaree, 12"................................230.00
Mug, Invt T'print, clear hdl, 4" 110.00
Pitcher, ice bladder, 10x5" 210.00
Pitcher, Invt T'print, bulbous, clear hdl, 7x7", +4 3¾" tumblers ...380.00
Pitcher, Invt T'print, bulbous, 8" 215.00
Plate, 8"..55.00
Sugar bowl, clear ft, clear bubble finial, 6x4"................................110.00
Tumbler, bellflower eng, 1880s, 3¾"..125.00
Vase, Invt T'print, 4¼" 65.00
Vase, tulip form w/opal flutes, bronze base, 12x5"........................450.00
Vase, wht lilies of the valley w/gold leaves, 7½" 135.00
Water set, Ribbed Optic, wht enamel & gold, 8¾" pitcher+6 tumblers...250.00

Crown Devon

Devon and Crown Devon were trade names of S. Fielding and Company, Ltd., an English firm founded after 1879. They produced majolica, earthenware mugs, vases, and kitchenware. In the 1930s they manufactured an excep-

tional line of Art Deco vases that have recently been much in demand.

Basket, lt yel w/floral decor, ribbed int, 5½x7½" 50.00
Biscuit bbl, emb floral w/gold, EPNS hdl/rim/lid, gilded, 3-ftd, 10"..240.00
Bonbon, leaping stag on wht, leaf shape, #5385, 8¾x6¼" 70.00
Bowl, cream w/floral border, ribbed int, 2½x10x8", +matching spoon..40.00
Bowl, floral w/scalloped rim, #X543, 3½x4½", w/orig SP stand..150.00
Bowl, rose; Wick pattern, floral on cream, #6942, 6⅜"...............90.00
Box, cigarette; cobalt w/gold band, slanted sides, #3249, 6x3½x2"..120.00
Box, couple on bicycle on lid, musical, #813582, 3¾x8" 290.00
Box, trinket; Killarney, verse w/horse & cart scene, musical, 5x3x3"..165.00
Cup & saucer, HP partridges, gold int..265.00
Dish, enameled butterflies & flowering/climbing plants, 10½x6¾"....75.00
Dish, roses decor, mk #X543, 1½x5¼", w/orig SP stand 140.00
Dish, Sevres, floral on cream w/pk border, #202739, 15x9½" 65.00
Figurine, Juanita, dancer w/fan, 8" 150.00
Figurine, nude draped from waist down, picking apples, 18" 925.00
Figurine, Pekingese dog head, 5x6½"..155.00
Figurine, Scottie dog, blk w/wht mks, seated, lg head, 5" 65.00
Figurine, wht dog w/1 blk eye & 1 blk ear, red mouth & collar, 5½"...70.00
Figurine, Winston Churchill Bulldog, w/military hat & cigar, 5x6"..910.00
Hatpin holder, Perth, 9 holes, 4¾x2½" dia at rim......................105.00
Honey pot, yel w/honeycomb design, lg blk bee finial, #558, 5x5x4" ..75.00
Jug, Garden Path, 5⅛" 100.00
Jug, King George VI coronation, musical, 8" 440.00
Jug, mc Art Deco design, mk HP by Dorothy Ann........................95.00
Jug, Pegasus on red, scalloped at rim/down hdl, #A550, 7", $110 to..125.00
Jug, Robert Burns, Auld Lang Syne, musical, #804875, 6¾".......320.00
Jug, Sandy Macnab, Scottish thistles, 7½"..................................210.00
Jug, Scottsman w/verse on bk, musical, 9½".................................275.00
Jug, Widdicombe Fair, men w/horse, musical, #802897, 7¼" 325.00
Mug, George VI & Queen Elizabeth coronation, floral hdl, musical, 5"..215.00
Mustache cup, red w/horses, 3½x4¼"..60.00
Mustard pot, wht w/floral, gold hdl & finial on notched lid, 2¾"..100.00
Plate, German Shepherd dog w/landscape bkground, 10¾" 200.00
Plate, roses on vellum, gold scrolls at edge, #X482, 9½" 130.00
Platter, cream w/gr center & border, floral at tab hdls, 12x6½" 75.00
Preserve pot, Garden Path, gr w/mc floral on lid, 4" 60.00
Salad strainer set, Etna, leaf-shaped bowl w/underplate 110.00
Sifter, Hilltop, teepee shape, 5½x3" (dia at base) 75.00
Sugar bowl, Etna, gilt, hdls, open, #578617, 3¼x6½" 75.00
Sugar bowl, Garden Path, gr, hdls, w/lid, 3½x5½" 75.00
Tankard, Daisy Bell lyrics w/couple on tandem bike, 5", from $60 to ..70.00
Tankard, John Peel, #753789, musical, ½-pt.................................130.00
Tankard, John Peel, fox hunting w/verse , #758782, 6½"............100.00
Tankard, Widdicombe Fair, men w/horse/verse, musical, #804874, 6"...165.00
Tankard, 2 men & 1 woman drinking, thistle hdl, musical, #804875, 6" ..85.00
Teapot, Hilltop, doughnut-type hole in center, blk hdl & spout, 7"...85.00
Teapot, Icicles, mk HP by Dorothy Ann, 7".................................95.00
Teapot, roses decor, gold hdl/spout, scalloped base/rim, #X543, 6" ...170.00
Teapot, Tiger Trees, sq body, HP by Dorothy Ann, 4½"...............65.00
Tobacco jar, sailing ship, brass screw-top for lid, 5x5" dia............60.00
Toby jug, Charrington's Beer, 9"..360.00
Vase, cobalt lustre w/emb ocean scene, tulip shape, 9"...............185.00
Vase, Fairy Castle, on maroon, #5351, 9"....................................140.00
Vase, floral design, 2 off-set dbl-loop hdls, 7"..............................110.00
Vase, Geisha girl, Tokio, #0874, 12"...160.00
Vase, Kingfisher on branch w/leaves, gilded hdls, mk #509, 9"...120.00
Vase, Matitta, bl/yel/orange flowers on blk w/gr basketweave, 6½"....95.00
Vase, mc floral on bl, #2103, 5¼"...210.00
Vase, Poppies, 2 blk hdls & base, cylindrical, 8½x2½".................60.00
Vase, Royal York, floral design, scalloped rim, 9"........................150.00
Wall plaque, English Champion Crackley, wire terrier, 6¾x5¾"......240.00

Crown Ducal

The Crown Ducal mark was first used by the A.G. Richardson & Co. pottery of Tunstall, England, in 1925. The items collectors are taking a particular interest in were decorated by Charlotte Rhead, a contemporary of Suzie Cooper and Clarice Cliff, and a member of the esteemed family of English pottery designers and artists.

See also Chintz.

Bowl, Bristol, red transferware, tab hdls, w/lid, #RD762055, 5½x11" 170.00
Bowl, fruit; Orange Tree, ped ft, 5x9" dia......................................225.00
Charger, Ankara, C Rhead, 12½"..175.00
Charger, Art Deco queezebag decor, blk/gold/ivory, C Rhead, 14"....350.00
Charger, bl & tan leaves, C Rhead, 12½"..................................310.00
Charger, Byzantine, #2681, floral decor, Rhead, 10"...................460.00
Charger, floral, mc on gray speckled, C Rhead, Bursley Ware, 14"...350.00
Coffeepot, Bristol, 10"..85.00
Coffeepot, pk roses on wht, gold trim, w/lid, 6¾"......................100.00
Creamer, Orange Tree, 2⅛"..50.00
Creamer & sugar bowl, Colonial Times, pk on wht....................135.00
Dish, meat serving; Edwardian, w/lid, 12x8"............................185.00
Dish, young Princess Elizabeth, mk Snow Glaze, 8¼x5½"............95.00
Figurine, bulldog, Flambé Red, glass eyes, 3x5"........................75.00
Gravy boat, Colonial Times, bl on wht, w/underplate..................50.00
Jug, Ankara #5983, 5½"..150.00
Jug, milk; Orange Tree, 6x4¼" dia (at base)..............................90.00
Jug, Persian Rose, #4040, 8"..150.00
Jug, tulips on wht w/reddish-brn on base, blk rim/hdl, C Rhead, 8"...90.00
Pitcher, squeeze-bag floral on ribbed body, C Rhead, 8x7".........200.00
Plaque, Manchurian Dragon & abstracts, ribbed body, C Rhead, 12"....385.00
Plaque, squeeze-bag floral, C Rhead, 12½"...............................200.00
Plaque, squeeze-bag floral/abstracts, C Rhead, Bursley Ware, 14¼"...220.00
Plate, Bristol, red transferware, scalloped edge, 10"....................40.00
Plate, dinner; Colonial Times, bl on wht.................................32.50
Platter, wht w/bl border & gold rim, oval, ca 1925, 13x16".........130.00
Sugar bowl, Colonial Times, bl on wht, hdls, w/lid....................40.00
Sugar pot, Orange Tree, w/lid, 6", w/spill tray..........................80.00
Teapot, Colonial Times, bl on wht, 7"....................................155.00
Teapot, Orange Tree, 6-cup...330.00
Teapot, pk & orange floral on gr, 5".......................................155.00
Tennis set, Orange Tree, cup w/tray.......................................160.00
Vase, bl & red flowers on gray center w/bl top & bottom, C Rhead, 6"....75.00
Vase, daffodil decor on gr, tapered sides, C Rhead, 10"................60.00
Vase, Egyptian, shouldered w/tapered sides, C Rhead, 9⅝"..........140.00
Vase, Golden Leaves, C Rhead, ribbed body, 8"........................200.00
Vase, Golden Leaves, wht, mk #4921, 8"................................120.00
Vase, Manchurian Dragon/abstracts, C Rhead, Bursley Ware, 7x6", EX....100.00
Vase, squeeze-bag floral band on dk brn, C Rhead, 4½".............500.00

Crown Milano

Crown Milano was a line of decorated milk glass (or opal ware) introduced by the Mt. Washington Glass Co. of New Bedford, Massachussetts, in the early 1890s. It had previously been called Albertine Ware. Some pieces are marked with a 'CM,' and many had paper labels. This ware is usually highly decorated and will most likely have a significant amount of gold painted on it. The shiny pieces were recently discovered to have been called 'Colonial Ware' and have a laurel wreath and a crown. This ware was well received in its day, and outstanding pieces bring high prices on today's market. Advisors for this category are Wilfred and Dolli Cohen; they are listed in the Directory under California.

Biscuit jar, floral, silver-plated top, lid stamped MW 4419/c, 6" to top of finial, $1,250.00. (Photo courtesy John A. Shuman III)

Biscuit jar, allover bamboo on pnt burmese, SP mts, 6" 900.00
Biscuit jar, dandelions on pnt burmese, simple shape, SP mts, 7" ..575.00
Biscuit jar, pansies/other flowers, scrolls around rim, 8" 700.00
Biscuit jar, peonies on wht w/gold, bulbous, mk lid, to top of hdl: 8" ...1,350.00
Biscuit jar, roses/mums/gold by Frederick, bowl shape, w/fixed hdl: 9"..985.00
Box, gold maidenhair fern on gr tint, heart shape, w/lid, 3x6x5"...975.00
Box, jewel; pansy panels on emb scrolls/pincushion lid, 3¼x5¼"...525.00
Bride's basket, gold & orange flowers, sq top, Pairpoint fr, 10x10"...1,600.00
Bride's bowl, floral in ivory, sq/shaped rim; hdld Webster ped fr, 10" ..575.00
Bride's bowl, florals, int: gold scrolls, tricon rim, 9½" 1,250.00
Candlesticks, portrait on wine w/gold, Pairpoint metal base, 8", pr...1,750.00
Cup & saucer, demi; floral vine w/gold on wht, pk-tinted rim, 2", 5"...2,500.00
Ewer, Colonial Ware, floral w/gold, rope hdl, 6½x7½" 835.00
Ewer, farmyard scene cartouche w/gold, rope hdl, #504, 10½" ...2,250.00
Lamp, Colonial Ware, floral/swags/etc w/gilt, ball shade/urn base, 23"..2,950.00
Mustard jar, gold floral on beige, str sides, fancy SP lid/hdl, 4", NM...575.00
Pitcher, gold mums in blown-out reserves, reeded hdl, 8¼"........800.00
Plate, Colonial Ware, floral clusters/gold scrolls on wht, 7"........450.00
Sweetmeat, Colonial Ware, flowers/scrolls on ribbed wht, gilt mts ..485.00
Sweetmeat, Dmn Quilt w/gold oak leaves/jewels, SP lid, branch hdl, 5".....900.00
Sweetmeat, Dmn Quilt w/thistles, SP lid, 5x4¼" 400.00
Sweetmeat, line scrolls/jewels, shadow florals, turtle on lid, 5" dia ...545.00
Syrup, netting, gold on pk, florals, melon ribs, 6"...................1,850.00
Syrup, 6 gilt-lined panels of roses, SP #d mts, 4" 695.00
Vase, cherub w/gold & jewels, #503, sm rstr, 19x8"................1,725.00
Vase, Colonial Ware, floral/gold shadow leaves, V-cut rim, 9"....945.00
Vase, Colonial Ware, mums, gold scrolls border pk areas, petal rim, 5"...375.00
Vase, floral mc w/gold scrolls, tricorner stick form, 8¼"...........1,200.00
Vase, florals/foliage on yel to cream, 4-lobe rim, spherical, 6"...1,350.00
Vase, forget-me-nots, bulbous, 4-fold top, 24 swirled ribs, 6x5¾"....1,350.00
Vase, gold rose branches, rnd w/long trumpet neck, 15x6" 2,275.00
Vase, lg thistles on lt tan w/gold, 12½x5½".........................1,100.00
Vase, Nouveau peonies/buds/etc, 24 swirled ribs, 6x5¾"..........1,250.00
Vase, oak leaves, mc on shaded tan, bulbous, petal top, 5¾"...1,300.00
Vase, pansies on wht w/free-form gold accents, petticoat form, 10½"...750.00
Vase, petit-point iris/scrolls on lt tan, 8-rib, petal top, 4½" 850.00
Vase, thistles, gold on cream to melon, shadow thistles, str sides, 9"...985.00
Vase, wild roses, pk on yel/wht, long neck pulled to 4 points, 9½" ..750.00

Cruets

Cruets, containers made to hold oil or vinegar, are usually bulbous with tall, narrow throats, a handle, and a stopper. During the nineteenth century and for several years after, they were produced in abundance in virtually every type of glassware available. Those listed below are assumed to be with stopper and mint unless noted otherwise.

See also specific manufacturers.

Ada...45.00
Alaska, bl opal...325.00
Amazon...45.00
Amberette..90.00
Arched Ovals..60.00
Argonaut Shell, wht opal.........................350.00
Art...60.00
Beaded Grape/California, gr, 6¾", NM......40.00
Beaded Ovals in Sand, gr opal................225.00
Beatty Honeycomb, wht opal...................175.00
Bethlehem Star...50.00
Bevelled Star...45.00
Bismark Star..50.00
Block & Fan...45.00
Brittanic...55.00
Bryce Ribbon Candy...................................50.00
Bubble Lattice, bl opal.............................175.00
Cathedral..60.00
Cathedral, amber.......................................125.00
Cherry, bl opal..75.00
Chrysanthemum Base Swirl, cranberry opal....500.00
Chrysanthemum Base Swirl, gr opal.......675.00
Chrysanthemum Base Swirl, wht opal....200.00
Consolidated Criss-Cross, wht opal........275.00
Cord Drapery..65.00
Cupid & Venus...175.00
Daisy & Button, bulbous, faceted stopper, 7½"......130.00
Daisy & Fern, gr opal................................175.00
Dakota...100.00
Dewey..65.00
Double Circle/No 231, apple gr, clear stopper, Jefferson.....110.00
Elson Dewdrop #2, wht opal.....................90.00
Everglades, bl opal....................................425.00
Everglades, wht opal.................................325.00
Fandango, 2 szs, from $45 to.....................60.00
Fern, bl opal...225.00
Flower Fan..50.00
Galloway...55.00
Gonderman (Adonis) Swirl, bl opal.......400.00
Hanover...50.00
Hobbs Block..65.00
Honeycomb w/Star.......................................50.00
Indiana..45.00
Intaglio, wht opal.....................................150.00
Invt Coin Spot, Prussian bl w/HP floral, 5"......80.00
Invt Fan & Feather, bl opal.....................500.00
Invt Fan & Feather, pk slag, 6¾"............900.00
Invt T'print, cranberry w/mc & gold floral, cut faceted stopper, 7".....180.00
Invt T'print w/Swirl, rubena, clear hdl, cut stopper, 5¼".........100.00
Ivy Scroll, gr...125.00
King's Block...50.00
Late Thistle, non-flint, 7¼".......................25.00
Leaf & Star...70.00
Masonic...45.00
New Jersey..50.00
Niagara..50.00
Paneled Thistle...60.00
Panelled 44..50.00
Pleated Medallion..40.00
Polka Dot, wht opal..................................250.00
Portland..65.00
Reflecting Fans, bl, panelled stopper, Belmont, 6½"......180.00
Reverse Cruet, vaseline opal...................175.00
Ribbed Opal Lattice, cranberry opal.....500.00

Rising Sun..55.00
S Repeat, gr...175.00
Scroll w/Acanthus, vaseline opal...........375.00
Sextec...50.00
Spanish Lace, wht opal............................200.00
Startec...55.00
Teasel..65.00
Texas, rose stain.......................................250.00
Truncated Cube..65.00
Utopia Optic, gr..150.00
Wheat Sheaf, dbl hdl, scarce......................65.00
Z-Ray, gr w/gold..250.00
Zipper..45.00

Cup Plates, Glass

Before the middle 1850s, it was socially acceptable to pour hot tea into a deep saucer to cool. The tea was sipped from the saucer rather than the cup, which frequently was handleless and too hot to hold. The cup plate served as a coaster for the cup. It is generally agreed that the first examples of pressed glass cup plates were made about 1826 at the Boston and Sandwich Glass Co. in Sandwich, Cape Cod, Massachusetts. Other glassworks in three major areas (New England, Philadelphia, and the Midwest, especially Pittsburgh) quickly followed suit.

Antique glass cup plates range in size from 2⅝" up to 4¼" in diameter. The earliest plates had simple designs inspired by cut glass patterns, but by 1829 they had become more complex. The span from then until about 1845 is known as the 'Lacy Period,' when cup plate designs and pressing techniques were at their peak. To cover pressing imperfections, the backgrounds of the plates were often covered with fine stippling which endowed them with a glittering brilliance called 'laciness.' They were made in a multitude of designs — some purely decorative, others commemorative. Subjects include the American eagle, hearts, sunbursts, log cabins, ships, George Washington, the political candidates Clay and Harrison, plows, beehives, etc. Of all the patterns, the round George Washington plate is the rarest and most valuable — only four are known to exist today.

Authenticity is most important. Collectors must be aware that contemporary plates which have no antique counterparts and fakes modeled after antique patterns have had wide distribution. Condition is also important, though it is the exceptional plate that does not have some rim roughness. More important considerations are scarcity of design and color.

The book *American Glass* by George and Helen McKearin has a section on glass cup plates. The definitive book is *American Glass Cup Plates* by Ruth Webb Lee and James H. Rose. Numbers in the listings that follow refer to the latter. When attempting to evaluate a cup plate, remember that minor rim roughness is normal. See also Staffordshire; Pairpoint.

Note: Most of the values listed below are prices realized at auction for cup plates of exceptional value. The more common varieties generally run from $35.00 to $75.00 in very good condition.

R-69, Rosette, scroll border, cloudy/roughness, 3½".....................175.00
R-81, 8-Heart, sprig border, opal w/gr tint, 3¾", from $425 to....500.00
R-88, concentric circles, potted floral rim design, opal, 3¾", NM....420.00
R-89, Basket w/Fronds, opal, NE, minor rim chips, 3¾"............200.00
R-90, Basket w/Fonds border, concentric ring center, opal, 3¾", NM....190.00
R-95, Shield & Pine Tree, opal, minor rim chips, 3⅝"...................90.00
R-159, stylized flower w/vine border, bull's-eye scalloped rim, EX....415.00
R-210, Rosette in center, vining floral border, Ft Pitt, few chips....825.00
R-211, Rosette, foliate rim, Ft Pitt, several rim chips, 3⅝".........200.00
R-253, Roman Rosette, peacock gr, Midwest, several lg/sm chips, 3½"..265.00
R-262, Scroll w/Lily, quatrefoil/trefoil border, amethyst, 3⅜", EX...500.00

R-277, trefoil center, scrolled leaf border, sapphire, 3⅜", EX **950.00**

R-288, Roman Rosette, cobalt, few chips, 3½" **295.00**

R-315, AE&SR Filley/Importers..., Midwest, 3⅜", G **95.00**

R-400b, Heart, lyre rim, cobalt, few rim chips, 3½" **175.00**

R-440b, Heart, lyre/scrolled leaf border, Sandwich, 3½", EX **150.00**

R-443, Heart & Bull's Eye, Midwest, chip/rim roughness, 3" **150.00**

R-459E, Heart, emerald gr, Sandwich, 3⅜"..............................**440.00**

R-465f, quatrefoil center, heart border, bl-violet, chips/sm cracks ...**325.00**

R-561, Washington Bust, chips/roughness, 3½" **385.00**

R-562, Henry Clay (facing right), trefoil border, several sm chips ..**265.00**

R-565b, Henry Clay, bl, lg rim underfill/several chips, 3½" **120.00**

R-585c, portrait: Ringold/Palo Alto, 2 short cracks/rim chips, 3½"..**585.00**

R-594, Log Cabin, floral border, amber, several sm rim chips, 3¼" ..**300.00**

R-597, Log Cabin w/emb Ft Meigs/Wm H Harrison Tippecanoe (vt), EX **120.00**

R-612, Steamboat, shield & scroll rim, Midwest, roughness, 3½" ..**1,750.00**

R-651a vt, sm Eagle, concentric rings, vine border, opal, 3⅝", EX ..**1,400.00**

R-670b, Eagle, bull's-eye rim, bl, Midwest, several rim chips, 3½" **650.00**

R-671, Eagle & Shield, bull's-eye/point rim, opal, 3½", G **475.00**

R-679, Before & After Marriage, Wedding Day & 3 Weeks After, NM ..**130.00**

R-689, Plough & Foliate, Pittsburgh, numerous rim chips, 3⅜" ...**385.00**

Cups and Saucers

The earliest utensils for drinking were small porcelain and stoneware bowls imported from China by the East Indian Company in the early seventeenth century. European and English tea bowls and saucers, imitating Chinese and Japanese originals, were produced from the early eighteenth century and often decorated with Chinese-type motifs. By about 1810, handles were fitted to the bowl to form the now familiar teacup, and this form became almost universal. Coffee in England and on the continent was often served in a can — a straight-sided cylinder with a handle. After 1820 the coffee can gave way to the more fanciful form of the coffee cup.

An infinite variety of cups and saucers are available for both the new and experienced collector, and they can be found in all price ranges. There is probably no better way to thoroughly know and understand the various ceramic manufacturers than to study cups and saucers. Our advisors for this category, Susan and Jim Harran, have written a series entitled *Collectible Cups and Saucers, Identification and Values, Books I, II*, and *III*, published by Collector Books. Book III contains more than eight hundred full-color photos; it is divided into six collectible eras: cabinet cups, nineteenth and twentieth century dinnerware, English tablewares, miniatures, Japanese tablewares, and art glass cups and saucers. The Harrans are listed in the Directory under New Jersey.

Demitasse cup and saucer, hand-painted flowers, loop handle with spur, Adams Titian Ware, 1896 – 1920s, from $30.00 to $35.00. (Photo courtesy Susan and Jim Harran)

Chocolate, emb harebells & gilt holly leaves & berries, Limoges, 1895...**60.00**

Chocolate, floral on wht, scalloped saucer, Limoges, 1891-1914...**50.00**

Coffee, floral w/cobalt & gold, Ridgway, ca 1825, from $80 to ...**100.00**

Coffee, mc flowers & insects, Lomonosov, 1930s-50s, from $50 to...**60.00**

Coffee, roses/cobalt oak leaves/purple thistle/gilt, Alcock, 1840s **125.00**

Coffee can, daisies, wht on pk, HP, loop hdl, Bodley, 1875+, $50 to..**65.00**

Coffee can, mythological transfer on pk/gold, Austria, 1890-1918....**60.00**

Demi, beaded & hand-gilded decor on gr, Minton, 1891-1901, $100 to..**125.00**

Demi, Cattail, Bute cup w/loop hdl, Lenox, 1950s, from $40 to ...**50.00**

Demi, floral transfer, Osier molded edge, Royal Copenhagen, ca 1950....**35.00**

Demi, floral transfer/gold bands, 16-panel, Limoges, 1920s **45.00**

Demi, florals, paneled/ftd cup, Schumann, 1918-29, from $45 to...**55.00**

Demi, Golden Orchid, artist sgn, Stouffer Co, 1838-46", from $50 to....**60.00**

Demi, metallic gold, ribbed broken-loop hdl, Japan label, 1950s ..**10.00**

Demi, shamrocks HP on emb basketweave, Belleek, 1965-80, $50 to...**60.00**

Demi, silver o/l flowers on wht, angle hdl, Lenox, 1906-24 ....**160.00**

Mini, floral transfer, loop hdl, Foley, 1921-29, from $100 to.......**150.00**

Mini, Rosebud, str-sided cup w/loop hdl, Shelley, 1945-66, $175 to....**200.00**

Snack, forget-me-nots, fan hdl, Limoges, ca 1882-90, from $100 to..**125.00**

Tea, bl bachelor buttons on wht/gold trim, scalloped, Royal Vale, '60s....**35.00**

Tea, blk/pk w/gilt, scalloped/corset-shaped cup, Lenegie, 1950s....**40.00**

Tea, Blue Willow w/gold, Booths Ltd, 1912+, from $40 to...........**50.00**

Tea, cobalt w/butterfly inside cup, Aynsley, 1950s, from $100 to...**125.00**

Tea, courting scenes alternate w/flowers, HP, Dresden, R Klemm, 1900s...**100.00**

Tea, DuBarry Rose, Tuscan China, 1947-60, from $30 to..............**40.00**

Tea, Fence, underglaze bl, Worcester, 1780, from $250 to...........**300.00**

Tea, floral, bl transfer, ft/scalloped cup, Taylor & Kent Ltd, 1939-49...**40.00**

Tea, floral, lav on wht/gilt, scalloped, Rosenthal, 1910, from $40 to..**50.00**

Tea, floral, red transfer, ribbed/zigzag hdl, Royal Standard, 1949+...**40.00**

Tea, floral on cobalt w/hand gilding, Copeland Spode, 1891+, $100 to...**125.00**

Tea, floral transfer, quatrefoil cup w/feathered hdl, Moore Bros, 1891 ...**70.00**

Tea, floral transfer w/cobalt & gold, Paragon, 1957+, from $35 to...**45.00**

Tea, geometric relief, majolica, 8-sided, Choisy-le-Roi, 1870s **125.00**

Tea, geometrics, HP, Adam Titian Ware, 1896-1920s, from $25 to...**35.00**

Tea, gilt floral band, swirled/fluted/ftd, Aynsley, 1950s **45.00**

Tea, gold border on cream, 6-sided, Lenox, 1920s, from $60 to **75.00**

Tea, gold trim on bl lustre, 3-ftd/rtcl saucer, Lefton, 1950s............**35.00**

Tea, Indian, purple w/gold dots, 12-lobed cup, Meissen, 1860-1924..**275.00**

Tea, oriental couple by gazebo, floral trim, London style, 1825-35 ..**95.00**

Tea, rose transfer, 8-flute, Royal Albert, ca 1945+ **35.00**

Tea, roses on lt gr, Old Royal Bone China, 1930-41, from $30 to....**40.00**

Tea, roses transfer w/gold, ftd/ribbed cup, Colclough China Ltd, 1950+ ...**35.00**

Tea, Royal Flute, HP portrait medallion, Dresden, 1887-91, $350 to..**400.00**

Tea, Yule Tide, holly & berries, ftd, Queen Anne, 1859+, from $30 to.....**40.00**

Currier & Ives by Royal

During the 1950s dinnerware decorated with transfer-printed scenes taken from prints by Currier and Ives was manufactured by Royal China and distributed as premiums through A&P stores. Though it was also made in pink and green, blue is by far the easiest to find and the most popular. Pie plates have been found in black and brown, and dinnerware items have been reported in black as well. Occasionally the blue line has been found decorated with a hand-painted pattern. Currier and Ives has long been a very popular collectible at malls and flea markets around the country. Included in our listings are pieces from hostess sets by Royal which should be of great interest to collectors. The 11½" round platter with the 'Rocky Mountains' scene is very rare. This piece does not have tabs but is round like the 12" platter. An interesting note: There are six different (decal/shape) variations of the teapot. Our advisors for this category are Treva Jo and Jack Hamlin; they are listed in the Directory under Ohio.

Ashtray, 5½" **12.00**

Bowl, cereal; tab hdl, 6¼" **45.00**

Bowl, cereal; 6¼" **15.00**

Bowl, dessert; 5½" **5.00**

Bowl, soup; 8" 10.00
Bowl, vegetable, 9" 20.00
Bowl, vegetable; deep, 10" 30.00
Butter dish, Fashionable (Summer) decal............45.00
Butter dish, Road (Winter) decal.................35.00
Casserole, angle hdls 100.00
Casserole, tab hdls, knob turned 90 degrees.......200.00
Clock, 10" plate, bl #s, 2 decals, Charles Denning.......200.00
Creamer, angle hdl..8.00
Creamer, rnd hdl, tall..................................45.00
Cup, angle hdl..4.00
Cup, rnd hdl, flared top................................10.00
Gravy boat, pour spout 20.00
Gravy boat, tab hdls 55.00
Gravy ladle, all wht 45.00
Lamp, candle; w/globe 300.00
Mug, coffee; regular 25.00
Mug, coffee; rnd hdl 35.00
Pie baker, 9 decals, 10" 30.00
Plate, bread; 6½" 5.00
Plate, calendar; 10" 15.00
Plate, chop; Getting Ice, 11½" 35.00
Plate, chop; Rocky Mountains, 11½" 150.00
Plate, chop; 12¼" 30.00
Plate, dinner; 10" 5.00
Plate, luncheon; 9" 20.00
Plate, salad; 7¼" 15.00
Plate, snack; w/cup well, 9" 125.00
Platter, oval, 13" 30.00
Platter, tab hdls, 10½" dia 20.00
Platter, 13" dia 150.00
Saucer, 6⅛" 2.00
Shakers, pr 25.00
Spoon rest plaque, wall hanging 100.00
Sugar bowl, hdld, w/lid 15.00
Sugar bowl, no hdls, flared top, w/lid............45.00
Sugar bowl, no hdls, str sides, w/lid.............30.00
Teapot, 6 different decal & shape variations 125.00
Tray, gravy boat; regular..............................18.00
Tray, gravy boat; wht tabs, 7" plate decal........60.00
Tumbler, iced tea; 12-oz, 5½" 12.00
Tumbler, juice; 5-oz, 3½" 12.00
Tumbler, old fashioned; 7-oz, 3¼" 12.00
Tumbler, water; 8½-oz, 4¾" 12.00

Hostess Set Pieces

Bowl, candy; 7¾" 25.00
Bowl, dip; 4⅜" 25.00
Pie baker, 11" 50.00
Plate, cake; flat, 10" 30.00
Plate, cake; ftd, 10"...................................150.00
Plate, serving; 7" 15.00
Tray, deviled egg 200.00

Custard Glass

As early as the 1880s, custard glass was produced in England. Migrating glassmakers brought the formula for the creamy ivory ware to America. One of them was Harry Northwood, who in 1898 founded his company in Indiana, Pennsylvania, and introduced the glassware to the American market. Soon other companies were producing custard, among them Heisey, Tarentum, Fenton, and McKee. Not only dinner-

ware patterns but souvenir items were made. Today custard is the most expensive of the colored pressed glassware patterns. The formula for producing the luminous glass contains uranium salts which imparts the cream color to the batch and causes it to glow when it is examined under a black light. Our advisors for this category are Wilfred and Dolli Cohen; they are listed in the Directory under California.

Argonaut Shell, creamer and sugar bowl, with lid, gold trim, $390.00.

Argonaut Shell, bowl, master berry; gold & decor, 10½" L.........275.00
Argonaut Shell, bowl, sauce; ftd, gold & decor..............................75.00
Argonaut Shell, butter dish, gold & decor 350.00
Argonaut Shell, butter dish, no gold 300.00
Argonaut Shell, compote, jelly; gold & decor, scarce 165.00
Argonaut Shell, creamer, no gold...110.00
Argonaut Shell, cruet, gold & decor 850.00
Argonaut Shell, pitcher, water; gold & decor 475.00
Argonaut Shell, shakers, gold & decor, pr.................................435.00
Argonaut Shell, spooner, gold & decor 275.00
Argonaut Shell, tumbler, gold & decor 110.00
Bead Swag, bowl, sauce; floral & gold 50.00
Bead Swag, goblet, floral & gold..65.00
Bead Swag, tray, pickle; floral & gold, rare...............................300.00
Bead Swag, wine, floral & gold..60.00
Beaded Circle, bowl, master berry; floral & gold.........................350.00
Beaded Circle, butter dish, floral & gold....................................500.00
Beaded Circle, creamer, floral & gold..180.00
Beaded Circle, pitcher, water; floral & gold 750.00
Beaded Circle, shakers, floral & gold, pr................................1,000.00
Beaded Circle, spooner, floral & gold..200.00
Beaded Circle, tumbler, floral & gold...150.00
Cane Insert, berry set, 7-pc 350.00
Cane Insert, table set, 4-pc 450.00
Cherry & Scales, bowl, master berry; nutmeg stain 145.00
Cherry & Scales, butter dish, nutmeg stain................................250.00
Cherry & Scales, creamer, nutmeg stain 125.00
Cherry & Scales, pitcher, water; nutmeg stain, scarce 350.00
Cherry & Scales, spooner, nutmeg stain, scarce.........................125.00
Cherry & Scales, sugar bowl, w/lid, nutmeg stain, scarce 150.00
Cherry & Scales, tumbler, nutmeg stain, scarce 75.00
Chrysanthemum Sprig, bowl, master berry; gold & decor 300.00
Chrysanthemum Sprig, bowl, master berry; no gold 175.00
Chrysanthemum Sprig, bowl, sauce; ftd, gold & decor..................60.00
Chrysanthemum Sprig, butter dish, gold & decor........................450.00
Chrysanthemum Sprig, celery vase, gold & decor, rare 1,250.00
Chrysanthemum Sprig, compote, jelly; gold & decor 150.00
Chrysanthemum Sprig, compote, jelly; no decor 100.00
Chrysanthemum Sprig, creamer, gold & decor 135.00

Chrysanthemum Sprig, cruet, gold & decor, 6¾" 495.00
Chrysanthemum Sprig, pitcher, water; gold & decor.................485.00
Chrysanthemum Sprig, pitcher, water; no decor.........................350.00
Chrysanthemum Sprig, shakers, gold & decor, pr.......................300.00
Chrysanthemum Sprig, spooner, gold & decor.............................135.00
Chrysanthemum Sprig, spooner, no gold..75.00
Chrysanthemum Sprig, sugar bowl, gold & decor........................250.00
Chrysanthemum Sprig, toothpick holder, gold & decor 295.00
Chrysanthemum Sprig, toothpick holder, no decor......................175.00
Chrysanthemum Sprig, tray, condiment; gold & decor, rare 595.00
Chrysanthemum Sprig, tumbler, gold & decor.................................80.00
Dandelion, mug, nutmeg stain...175.00
Delaware, bowl, sauce; pk stain..65.00
Delaware, creamer, breakfast; pk stain 75.00
Delaware, tray, pin; gr stain...85.00
Delaware, tumbler, pk stain..65.00
Diamond w/Peg, bowl, master berry; roses & gold 225.00
Diamond w/Peg, bowl, sauce; roses & gold....................................50.00
Diamond w/Peg, butter dish, roses & gold....................................275.00
Diamond w/Peg, creamer, ind; no decor 35.00
Diamond w/Peg, creamer, ind; souvenir 50.00
Diamond w/Peg, creamer, roses & gold 85.00
Diamond w/Peg, mug, souvenir 50.00
Diamond w/Peg, napkin ring, roses & gold 125.00
Diamond w/Peg, pitcher, roses & gold, 5½".................................275.00
Diamond w/Peg, sugar bowl, w/lid, roses & gold 175.00
Diamond w/Peg, toothpick holder, roses & gold 175.00
Diamond w/Peg, tumbler, roses & gold 75.00
Diamond w/Peg, water set, souvenir, 7-pc.....................................650.00
Diamond w/Peg, wine, roses & gold 65.00
Diamond w/Peg, wine, souvenir 40.00
Everglades, bowl, master berry; gold & decor...............................295.00
Everglades, bowl, saucer; gold & decor..60.00
Everglades, butter dish, gold & decor 395.00
Everglades, creamer, gold & decor...155.00
Everglades, cruet, EX gold & decor...2,250.00
Everglades, shakers, gold & decor, pr..375.00
Everglades, spooner, gold & decor...160.00
Everglades, sugar bowl, w/lid, gold & decor 235.00
Everglades, tumbler, gold & decor...100.00
Fan, bowl, master berry; good gold 295.00
Fan, bowl, sauce; good gold..60.00
Fan, butter dish, good gold...345.00
Fan, creamer, good gold...110.00
Fan, ice cream set, good gold, 7-pc 500.00
Fan, pitcher, water; good gold..395.00
Fan, spooner, good gold...100.00
Fan, sugar bowl, w/lid, good gold 175.00
Fan, tumbler, good gold..85.00
Fan, water set, good gold, 7-pc...725.00
Fine Cut & Roses, rose bowl, fancy int, nutmeg stain 85.00
Fine Cut & Roses, rose bowl, plain int..69.00
Geneva, bowl, master berry; floral decor, ftd, oval, 9" L............110.00
Geneva, bowl, master berry; floral decor, rnd, 9" 130.00
Geneva, bowl, sauce; floral decor, oval..50.00
Geneva, bowl, sauce; floral decor, rnd...50.00
Geneva, butter dish, floral decor 250.00
Geneva, butter dish, no decor...145.00
Geneva, compote, jelly; floral decor 95.00
Geneva, creamer, floral decor...115.00
Geneva, cruet, floral decor..475.00
Geneva, pitcher, water; floral decor...275.00
Geneva, shakers, floral decor, pr..280.00
Geneva, spooner, floral decor...100.00

Geneva, sugar bowl, open, floral decor...85.00
Geneva, sugar bowl, w/lid, floral decor..175.00
Geneva, syrup, floral decor...500.00
Geneva, toothpick holder, floral w/M gold 375.00
Geneva, tumbler, floral decor...60.00
Georgia Gem, bowl, master berry; good gold 135.00
Georgia Gem, bowl, master berry; gr opaque 115.00
Georgia Gem, butter dish, good gold..200.00
Georgia Gem, celery vase, good gold..145.00
Georgia Gem, creamer, good gold...100.00
Georgia Gem, creamer, no gold 60.00
Georgia Gem, cruet, good gold..295.00
Georgia Gem, mug, good gold..45.00
Georgia Gem, powder jar, w/lid, good gold.....................................80.00
Georgia Gem, shakers, good gold, pr..140.00
Georgia Gem, spooner, souvenir 55.00
Georgia Gem, sugar bowl, w/lid, no gold...95.00
Grape (& Cable), bottle, scent; orig stopper, nutmeg stain.........495.00
Grape (& Cable), bowl, banana; ftd, nutmeg stain.......................350.00
Grape (& Cable), bowl, master berry; flat, nutmeg stain.............200.00
Grape (& Cable), bowl, orange; ftd, flat top, nutmeg stain.........400.00
Grape (& Cable), bowl, orange; ftd, nutmeg stain 500.00
Grape (& Cable), bowl, sauce; nutmeg stain, ftd.............................50.00
Grape (& Cable), butter dish, nutmeg stain 300.00
Grape (& Cable), compote, jelly; open, nutmeg stain...................150.00
Grape (& Cable), compote, nutmeg stain, 4½x8".........................300.00
Grape (& Cable), cracker jar, nutmeg stain....................................850.00
Grape (& Cable), creamer, breakfast; nutmeg stain........................80.00
Grape (& Cable), humidor, bl stain, rare 950.00
Grape (& Cable), nappy, nutmeg stain, rare 60.00
Grape (& Cable), pitcher, water; nutmeg stain 550.00
Grape (& Cable), plate, nutmeg stain, 7"...50.00
Grape (& Cable), plate, nutmeg stain, 8"...65.00
Grape (& Cable), powder jar, nutmeg stain....................................350.00
Grape (& Cable), punch bowl, w/base, nutmeg stain..............1,900.00
Grape (& Cable), spooner, nutmeg stain...155.00
Grape (& Cable), sugar bowl, breakfast; open, nutmeg stain 85.00
Grape (& Cable), sugar bowl, w/lid, nutmeg stain.......................225.00
Grape (& Cable), tray, dresser; nutmeg stain, scarce, lg 375.00
Grape (& Cable), tray, pin; nutmeg stain..150.00
Grape (& Cable), tumbler, nutmeg stain...75.00
Grape & Gothic Arches, bowl, master berry; pearl w/gold..........200.00
Grape & Gothic Arches, bowl, sauce; pearl w/gold, rare 80.00
Grape & Gothic Arches, butter dish, pearl w/gold 235.00
Grape & Gothic Arches, creamer, pearl w/gold, rare....................100.00
Grape & Gothic Arches, favor vase, nutmeg stain 80.00
Grape & Gothic Arches, goblet, pearl w/gold..................................75.00
Grape & Gothic Arches, pitcher, water; pearl w/gold 300.00
Grape & Gothic Arches, spooner, pearl w/gold 85.00
Grape & Gothic Arches, sugar bowl, w/lid, pearl w/gold 135.00
Grape & Gothic Arches, tumbler, pearl w/gold 65.00
Grape Arbor, vase, hat form..90.00
Heart w/Thumbprint, creamer..90.00
Heart w/Thumbprint, lamp, good pnt, scarce, 8".........................450.00
Heart w/Thumbprint, sugar bowl, ind..95.00
Honeycomb, wine..65.00
Horse Medallion, bowl, gr stain, 7"...85.00
Intaglio, bowl, master berry; gold & decor, ftd, 9" 250.00
Intaglio, bowl, sauce; gold & decor...50.00
Intaglio, butter dish, gold & decor...300.00
Intaglio, compote, jelly; gold & decor 125.00
Intaglio, creamer, gold & decor..125.00
Intaglio, pitcher, water; gold & decor..395.00
Intaglio, shakers, gold & decor, pr...250.00

Intaglio, spooner, gold & decor.................................135.00
Intaglio, sugar bowl, w/lid, gold & decor....................180.00
Intaglio, tumbler, gold & decor................................95.00
Inverted Fan & Feather, bowl, master berry; gold & decor..........275.00
Inverted Fan & Feather, bowl, sauce; gold & decor.................75.00
Inverted Fan & Feather, butter dish, gold & decor................400.00
Inverted Fan & Feather, compote, jelly; gold & decor, rare........500.00
Inverted Fan & Feather, creamer, gold & decor....................175.00
Inverted Fan & Feather, cruet, gold & decor, scarce, 6½".......1,100.00
Inverted Fan & Feather, pitcher, water; gold & decor.............700.00
Inverted Fan & Feather, punch cup, gold & decor..................250.00
Inverted Fan & Feather, shakers, gold & decor, pr................750.00
Inverted Fan & Feather, spooner, gold & decor....................165.00
Inverted Fan & Feather, sugar bowl, w/lid, gold & decor..........250.00
Inverted Fan & Feather, tumbler, gold & decor....................115.00
Jackson (Alaska Variant), bowl, master berry; good gold, ftd......150.00
Jackson (Alaska Variant), bowl, sauce; good gold.................50.00
Jackson (Alaska Variant), creamer, good gold....................85.00
Jackson (Alaska Variant), pitcher, water; good gold.............250.00
Jackson (Alaska Variant), pitcher, water; no decor..............175.00
Jackson (Alaska Variant), shakers, good gold, pr................195.00
Jackson (Alaska Variant), tumbler, good gold....................50.00
Louis XV, bowl, master berry; good gold........................250.00
Louis XV, bowl, sauce; good gold, ftd...........................50.00
Louis XV, butter dish, good gold..............................250.00
Louis XV, creamer, good gold...................................85.00
Louis XV, pitcher, water; good gold...........................250.00
Louis XV, spooner, good gold..................................110.00
Louis XV, sugar bowl, w/lid, good gold........................165.00
Louis XV, tumbler, good gold...................................65.00
Maple Leaf, bowl, master berry; gold & decor, scarce..........350.00
Maple Leaf, bowl, sauce; gold & decor, scarce..................50.00
Maple Leaf, butter dish, gold & decor.........................350.00
Maple Leaf, compote, jelly; gold & decor, rare................475.00
Maple Leaf, creamer, gold & decor.............................150.00
Maple Leaf, cruet, gold & decor, rare.......................3,000.00

Maple Leaf, pitcher, gold and decor, $400.00.

Maple Leaf, shakers, gold & decor, very rare, pr............1,500.00
Maple Leaf, spooner, gold & decor.............................175.00
Maple Leaf, sugar bowl, w/lid, gold & decor...................250.00
Maple Leaf, tumbler, gold & decor.............................100.00
Panelled Poppy, lamp shade, nutmeg stain, scarce..............900.00
Peacock & Urn, bowl, ice cream; nutmeg stain, sm...............80.00
Peacock & Urn, bowl, ice cream; nutmeg stain, 10".............350.00
Punty Band, shakers, pr.......................................175.00
Punty Band, spooner, floral decor.............................100.00
Punty Band, tumbler, floral decor, souvenir....................65.00
Ribbed Drape, bowl, sauce; roses & gold........................45.00

Ribbed Drape, butter dish, scalloped, roses & gold............400.00
Ribbed Drape, compote, jelly; roses & gold, rare..............200.00
Ribbed Drape, creamer, roses & gold, scarce...................180.00
Ribbed Drape, cruet, roses & gold, rare.......................700.00
Ribbed Drape, pitcher, water; roses & gold, rare..............365.00
Ribbed Drape, shakers, roses & gold, rare, pr.................400.00
Ribbed Drape, spooner, roses & gold...........................195.00
Ribbed Drape, sugar bowl, w/lid, roses & gold.................250.00
Ribbed Drape, toothpick holder, roses & gold..................475.00
Ribbed Drape, tumbler, roses & gold............................75.00
Ribbed Thumbprint, wine, floral decor..........................80.00
Ring Band, bowl, master berry; roses & gold...................200.00
Ring Band, bowl, sauce; roses & gold...........................50.00
Ring Band, butter dish, roses & gold..........................300.00
Ring Band, compote, jelly; roses & gold, scarce...............195.00
Ring Band, creamer, roses & gold..............................125.00
Ring Band, cruet, roses & gold, scarce........................500.00
Ring Band, cruet, roses decor, clear stopper..................175.00
Ring Band, pitcher, roses & gold, 7½".........................375.00
Ring Band, shakers, roses & gold, pr..........................155.00
Ring Band, spooner, roses & gold..............................125.00
Ring Band, syrup, roses & gold, scarce........................475.00
Ring Band, table set, 4-pc....................................600.00
Ring Band, toothpick holder, roses & gold.....................155.00
Ring Band, tray, condiment; roses & gold......................200.00
Singing Birds, mug, nutmeg stain...............................85.00
Tarentum's Victoria, bowl, master berry; gold & decor.........200.00
Tarentum's Victoria, butter dish, gold & decor, rare..........350.00
Tarentum's Victoria, celery vase, gold & decor, rare..........300.00
Tarentum's Victoria, creamer, gold & decor, scarce............135.00
Tarentum's Victoria, pitcher, water; gold & decor, rare.......375.00
Tarentum's Victoria, spooner, gold & decor....................135.00
Tarentum's Victoria, sugar bowl, w/lid, gold & decor..........175.00
Tarentum's Victoria, tumbler, gold & decor.....................75.00
Vermont, butter dish, bl decor................................195.00
Vermont, toothpick holder, bl decor...........................125.00
Vermont, vase, floral decor, jeweled..........................125.00
Wide Band, bell, roses..195.00
Wild Bouquet, bowl, sauce; gold & decor........................60.00
Wild Bouquet, butter dish, gold & decor, rare.................750.00
Wild Bouquet, creamer, no gold................................145.00
Wild Bouquet, spooner, gold & decor...........................250.00
Wild Bouquet, tumbler, no decor...............................100.00
Winged Scroll, bowl, master berry; gold & decor, 11" L........250.00
Winged Scroll, bowl, sauce; good gold..........................50.00
Winged Scroll, butter dish, good gold.........................235.00
Winged Scroll, butter dish, no decor..........................175.00
Winged Scroll, celery vase, good gold, rare...................400.00
Winged Scroll, cigarette jar, scarce..........................195.00
Winged Scroll, compote, ruffled, rare, 6¾x10¾"................495.00
Winged Scroll, cruet, good gold, clear stopper................400.00
Winged Scroll, hair receiver, good gold.......................135.00
Winged Scroll, pitcher, water; bulbous, good gold.............400.00
Winged Scroll, shakers, bulbous, good gold, rare, pr..........400.00
Winged Scroll, shakers, str sides, good gold, pr..............300.00
Winged Scroll, sugar bowl, w/lid, good gold...................175.00
Winged Scroll, syrup, good gold...............................450.00
Winged Scroll, tumbler, good gold..............................75.00

Cut Glass

The earliest documented evidence of commercial glass cutting in the United States was in 1810; the producers were Bakewell and Page of

Pittsburgh. These first efforts resulted in simple patterns with only a moderate amount of cutting. By the middle of the century, glass cutters began experimenting with a thicker glass which enabled them to use deeper cuttings, though patterns remained much the same. This period is usually referred to as Rich Cut. Using three types of wheels — a flat edge, a mitered edge, and a convex edge — facets, miters, and depressions were combined to produce various designs. In the late 1870s, a curved miter was developed which greatly expanded design potential. Patterns became more elaborate, often covering the entire surface. The Brilliant Period of cut glass covered a span from about 1880 until 1915. Because of the pressure necessary to achieve the deeply cut patterns, only glass containing a high grade of metal could withstand the process. For this reason and the amount of handwork involved, cut glass has always been expensive. Bowls cut with pinwheels may be either foreign or of a newer vintage, beware! Identifiable patterns and signed pieces that are well cut and in excellent condition bring the higher prices on today's market. For more information, we recommend *Evers' Standard Cut Glass Value Guide* (Collector Books). See also Dorflinger; Hawkes; Libbey; Tuthill; Val St. Lambert; other specific manufacturers.

Basket, Eldorado, Pitkins & Brooks, 6", from $425 to **475.00**
Basket, Sunbeam, Pitkins & Brooks, 7½", from $275 to **325.00**
Bell, Premier, JD Bergen, 6", from $200 to....................................**225.00**
Bell, Premier, JD Bergen, 7", from $225 to....................................**275.00**
Bonbon, Dariel, JD Bergen, 5x9", from $110 to............................**130.00**
Bonbon, Delmar, w/lid, Pitkins & Brooks, 10", from $350 to......**375.00**
Bonbon, Halle, Pitkins & Brooks, 6", from $60 to.........................**75.00**
Bonbon/Spoon tray, Madison, 8", from $150 to............................**175.00**
Bottle, catsup; Strawberry/Diamond/Fan, hdl/stopper, 7", from $100 to..**125.00**
Bowl, Adonis, TB Clark & Co, 9", from $200 to............................**225.00**
Bowl, Averbeck, 10", from $200 to...**250.00**
Bowl, Bermuda, JD Bergen, 7", from $65 to **80.00**
Bowl, fruit/berry; Florida, Higgins & Seiter, 9x14", from 250 to **275.00**
Bowl, Genoa, Averbeck, 10" oval, from $300 to............................**350.00**
Bowl, Golf, JD Bergen, 10", from $150 to.....................................**200.00**
Bowl, Lisbon, Higgins & Seiter, 8", from $100 to.........................**125.00**
Bowl, Manhattan, ped ft, TB Clark & Co, 8", from $200 to.......**250.00**
Bowl, Manhattan, ped ft, TB Clark & Co, 9", from $250 to.......**300.00**
Bowl, nut; Sparkle, 3-ftd, Pitkins & Brooks, 6", from $100 to **125.00**
Bowl, salad; Empress, 9", from $200 to...**225.00**
Bowl, salad; Venice, Pitkins & Brooks, 8", from $125 to.............**150.00**
Butter tub & plate, Seaside, JD Bergen, from $250 to **300.00**
Butterette, Canton, Averbeck, 3½", from $25 to...........................**30.00**
Candlestick, Oro, Pitkins & Brooks, 8", from $200 to...............**250.00**
Carafe, Acme, Averbeck, qt, from $200 to.....................................**250.00**
Carafe, Daisy, Averbeck, qt, from $150 to.....................................**200.00**
Carafe, Goldenrod, JD Bergen, qt, from $250 to..........................**300.00**
Carafe, Meteor, JD Bergen, qt, from $150 to...............................**175.00**
Carafe, Newport, JD Bergen, qt, from $150 to.............................**175.00**
Celery dip, hexagonal, Pitkins & Brooks, 1⅞", from $800 to........**10.00**
Celery dish, Cortez, Pitkins & Brooks, 11", from $250 to **300.00**
Celery tray, Dorrance, TB Clark & Co, from $50 to.....................**75.00**
Celery tray, Nordica, TB Clark & Co, from $75 to **100.00**
Celery tray, Ruby, Averbeck, 11¼", from $200 to........................**250.00**
Celery tray, St Cloud, Higgins & Seiter, 4x11½", from $75 to ...**100.00**
Comport, Arcadia, w/lid, JD Bergen, from $350 to......................**400.00**
Comport, Diamond, Averbeck, from $300 to...............................**350.00**
Comport, Glee, Pitkins & Brooks, 8x7½", from $250 to.............**300.00**
Comport, Naples, Averbeck, 9½", from $100 to...........................**150.00**
Comport, Vienna, Averbeck, from $250 to **300.00**
Cordial set, Henrietta, Higgins & Seiter, 8-pc, from $500 to......**750.00**
Cordial set, Premier, JD Bergen, 8-pc, from $750 to................**1,000.00**
Creamer & sugar bowl, Belvedere, Higgins & Seiter, from $75 to ...**100.00**
Creamer & sugar bowl, Halle, ftd, Pitkins & Brooks, from $175 to.....**200.00**

Creamer & sugar bowl, Lady Curzon, Averbeck, from $100 to ...**120.00**
Creamer & sugar bowl, Washington, Higgins & Seiter, from $75 to....**100.00**
Cruet, Aladdin, Pitkins & Brooks, from $200 to **250.00**
Cruet, Florida, Averbeck, 7½", from $85 to...................................**100.00**
Cruet, Prism, JD Bergen, ½-pt, from $75 to..................................**100.00**
Cup, Occident, ftd, Averbeck, from $40 to.....................................**45.00**
Cup, Premier, JD Bergen, from $20 to..**25.00**
Cup, Vienna, Averbeck, from $25 to..**30.00**
Decanter, Glenwood, JD Bergen, 1-qt, from $200 to..................**225.00**
Decanter, Savoy, JD Bergen, 3-pt, from $275 to **325.00**
Glove box, Hiawatha, Pitkins & Brooks, 10½", from $200 to **350.00**
Goblet, Florence, Higgins & Seiter, from $65 to **75.00**
Goblet, Golf, JD Bergen, from $40 to...**50.00**
Goblet, Premier, JD Bergen, from $50 to.......................................**60.00**
Hair receiver, Esther, Pitkins & Brooks, 5", from $200 to **250.00**
Ice tub, Golf, JD Bergen, from $200 to...**250.00**
Ice tub & plate, Coral, TB Clark & Co, from $250 to................**300.00**
Jar, horseradish; Golf, w/stopper, JD Bergen, 6", from $100 to **125.00**
Jewel box, Hiawatha, Pitkins & Brooks, from $175 to **200.00**
Knife rest, ball w/dmn design, Pitkins & Brooks, 6", from $18 to **20.00**
Lamp, Delmar, electric, w/prisms, Pitkins & Brooks, 14", from $850 to ...**1,200.00**
Mustard, Premier, JD Bergen, from $100 to **125.00**
Nappy, Bermuda, JD Bergen, 5", from $45 to...............................**55.00**
Nappy, Desdemona, TB Clark & Co, from $150 to......................**175.00**
Nappy, Jubilee, Higgins & Seiter, 6", from $50 to........................**75.00**
Nappy, Mars, Pitkins & Brooks, 6", from $75 to..........................**100.00**
Pickle dish, Marietta, Averbeck, 8", from $150 to........................**175.00**
Pitcher, claret; Lakeland, Higgins & Seiter, 11", from $250 to ...**300.00**
Pitcher, Georgia, Averbeck, 9¾", from $200 to **250.00**
Pitcher, Maude Adams, Averbeck, 4-pt, from $300 to...............**350.00**
Pitcher, Napoleon, Higgins & Seiter, 1-qt, from $175 to **200.00**
Pitcher, water; Naples, Averbeck, 4-pt, 10½", from $300 to **350.00**
Plate, Lowell, Averbeck, 7", from $70 to..**80.00**
Plate, Vienna, Averbeck, 7", from $100 to.....................................**125.00**
Puff box, Crete, Pitkins & Brooks, from $175 to..........................**200.00**
Punch bowl, Arbutus, TB Clark & Co, 14", from $450 to..........**500.00**
Punch bowl, Beverly, ftd, Pitkins & Brooks, 14", from $900 to ..**1,200.00**
Punch bowl, Comet, ftd, Higgins & Seiter, 15", from $1,200 to ..**1,500.00**
Punch bowl, St James, JD Bergen, 15", from $900 to...............**1,200.00**
Saucer, Bedford, 5", from $70 to...**85.00**
Spoon dish, Baltic, JD Bergen, from $100 to **125.00**
Spoon dish, Rajah, Pitkins & Brooks, from $150 to....................**175.00**
Spoon holder, Ashland, Averbeck, from $125 to..........................**150.00**
Spoon holder, Wheeler, dbl hdld, Higgins & Seiter, from $125 to...**150.00**
Syrup, Oregon, JD Bergen, ½-pt, from $125 to.............................**150.00**

Table lamp, Daisy and Button floral design, 22", **$850.00.** (Photo courtesy Fontaine's Auction Gallery)

Tankard jug, Henry VIII, TB Clark & Co, 1-qt, from $175 to **200.00**
Tray, bread/cake; Madonna, JD Bergen, 11½x7", from $300 to...**350.00**
Tray, comb & brush; Delmar, Pitkins & Brooks, 11", from $300 to..**350.00**
Tray, ice cream; Frisco, JE Bergen, 10½x18", from $600 to **800.00**
Tray, ice cream; Oak Leaf, Pitkins & Brooks, from $500 to.........**600.00**
Tray, ice cream; Webster, Higgins & Seiter, 8½x14", from $350 to ...**400.00**
Tumbler, Coral, TB Clark & Co, from $40 to **45.00**
Tumbler, Florida, Averbeck, from $22 to.......................................**25.00**
Tumbler, Manhattan, TB Clark & Co, from $35 to......................**40.00**
Tumbler, Melba, Averbeck, from $18 to **20.00**
Vase, Naples, Averbeck, 17", from $1,000 to...........................**1,200.00**
Vase, Nevada, JD Bergen, 12", from $300 to.............................**350.00**
Vase, Palmetto, TB Clark & Co, 8", from $125 to **150.00**
Vase, Palmetto, TB Clark & Co, 18", from $400 to **500.00**
Vase, Saratoga, Averbeck, 14", from $750 to.............................**900.00**
Vase, Wallace, JD Bergen, 10", from $400 to.............................**450.00**
Water set, Newport, 8-pc, from $400 to......................................**450.00**
Water set, Ruth, Pitkins & Brooks, 8-pc, from $450 to..............**500.00**
Whiskey set, Colonial, Higgins & Seiter, 8-pc, from $200 to **250.00**
Whiskey set, Glenwood, JD Bergen, 8-pc, from $500 to **750.00**

Cut Overlay Glass

Glassware with one or more overlying colors through which a design has been cut is called 'cut overlay.' It was made both here and abroad. Watch for new imitations.

Bottle, cordial; cranberry/clear, late 1800s, 14x4½".....................**450.00**
Bottle, scent; wht to bl w/gold, matching stopper, 6" **150.00**
Bowl, nappy, red to emerald gr, clear finger loop, 2¼x4⅝" **55.00**
Champagne, cobalt/clear, vintage cutting, faceted bowl, 4" **65.00**
Compote, cobalt/clear, geometrics, appl clear stem, flint, 4½x9"...**275.00**
Decanter, cranberry to clear w/paneled base & sides, 11"............**250.00**
Jug, gr to clear, vintage, panelled stopper w/star & teardrop, 8"..**440.00**
Jug, whiskey; cranberry/clear, orig stopper.................................**785.00**
Mustard pot, wht/clear, cloverleaves, gilt trim, hdl, 4½" **135.00**
Pitcher, caramel/wht/clear, 4¾"..**90.00**
Sweetmeat jar, wht/cobalt/clear, oval/punty cuts w/gold, 14⅝" ..**1,880.00**
Tumbler, red, Invt T'print, 4"..**110.00**

Vase, cobalt to clear, engraved fans and cross-hatched lines with dots border, star-cut base, ca 1925, 6x8", $200.00.

Vase, cobalt/wht/clear, trefoils/loops/rings, baluster, 12", pr.....**1,850.00**
Vase, wht/bl clambroth, ornate gold decor, 19th C, 12", pr.........**700.00**
Wine, cranberry to clear, paneled sides, teardrop stem, 5", pr.....**220.00**
Wine, cranberry/clear, strawberry/dmns/fans, star base, 4½"...........**75.00**

Cut Velvet

Cut Velvet glassware was made during the late 1800s. It is charac-

terized by the effect achieved through the execution of relief-molded patterns, often ribbing or diamond quilting, which allows its white inner casing to show through the outer layer.

Cup, Dmn Quilt, pk **130.00**
Lamp, Dmn Quilt, rose pk, opal glass ball shade, 17" **495.00**
Pitcher, Dmn Quilt, deep sapphire bl, bl reeded hdl, 8¾x6".......**400.00**
Pitcher, Dmn Quilt, rose to wht, ewer form, 11" **425.00**
Rose bowl, Dmn Quilt, 4-lobe top, 3½"......................................**200.00**
Rose bowl, Ribbon (swirled), bl, 4"...**230.00**
Tumbler, yel to wht, rose lining, scarce **130.00**
Vase, Dmn Quilt, dk to lt pk, ruffled 4-lobe top, Mt WA, 4¼x3"...**225.00**
Vase, Dmn Quilt, orange, ruffled/flared top, 9x6"..........�..........**675.00**
Vase, Dmn Quilt, pk, gold coralene, red jewels, 11½"..................**300.00**
Vase, Dmn Quilt, royal bl, squat, 2" rim, 3".................................**200.00**
Vase, Herringbone, pk, bulbous, 11"...**330.00**
Vase, vertical ribs, pk, rnd w/stick neck, 6" **175.00**

Cybis

Boleslaw Cybis was a graduate of the Academy of Fine Arts in Warsaw, Poland, and was well recognized as a fine artist by the time he was commissioned by his government to paint murals in the Polish Pavilion's Hall of Honor at the 1939 World's Fair. Finding themselves stranded in America at the outbreak of WWII, the Cybises founded an artists' studio, first in Astoria, New York, and later in Trenton, New Jersey, where they made fine figurines and plaques with exacting artistry and craftsmanship entailing extensive handwork. The studio still operates today producing exquisite porcelains on a limited edition basis.

Alexander the Elephant, gold trim, #682, 1975, 7½x6½"...........**500.00**
American Bullfrog, #654, 5¾" **325.00**
Baron, turtle w/frog on bk, 1970s, 3x3½".....................................**175.00**
Betty Blue, #479, 1974..**310.00**
Bust, Geo Washington, parian, blk enameled base, 12¾" **250.00**
Carousel goat, gold trim, #362, 1973 ltd ed **1,200.00**
Cheerful Dragon, #4029, 1979, 10"..**160.00**
Circus bear, clown hat & horn, 1975, 6½".................................**125.00**
Cleopatra, bust, gold head/neck-pc, #32, 1989, 9"......................**160.00**
Dapple Gray Foal, 5½x8"..**285.00**
Deermouse in clover, ca 1972, 3½x2½" **150.00**
Doves on rocky ledge, #253, on walnut base, 11x12x6" **415.00**
Duchess of 7 Rosettes, lady bug, 1970s, 2x4x5" **175.00**
Eleanor of Aquitane, #465, 1971, 13½" **820.00**
Enchanted Prince, bullfrog, ca 1973, 6x6" **450.00**
Eros, #477, 1974, 10"...**130.00**
Girl w/bl ribbon in hair holding flowers, #427, 5" **130.00**
Goldilocks & 3 Bears, 1978, 2-pc set...**325.00**
Heidy, Children to Cherish series, #432, 1962-73, 8"..................**495.00**
Lady (waist up) w/roses, #40, wooden base, 11".........................**670.00**
Lady w/bl bonnet (bust), 1940s, #5009, NM...............................**250.00**
Madonna w/bird, ca 1970, 11½" (on base) **575.00**
Madonna w/bluebird, 1956, 12"..**250.00**
Mouse on acorn branch, pre-1980, 5"...**750.00**
Mr Fluffy Tail (squirrel), #630, 8"...**285.00**
Mr Snowball, rabbit, 3¼x4"..**95.00**
Mushroom, Jack-o'-Lantern; mushroom w/butterfly, 1970s **325.00**
Ophelia, #375, 1969, 13" **560.00**
Owl on branch, 1970s, 4½"...**125.00**
Pandora w/box, ca 1979, 5"...**295.00**
Pinto pony, recumbent, #670, 1972-75, 5½x9"...........................**335.00**
Raccoon, #636, 1965, 7x8½"...**215.00**
Red Riding Hood, 1973, 6¼"...**115.00**

Rumples the Clown, #4014, 1979, 7" **210.00**
Sir Henry Escargot, #641, 1968, 3x4" **250.00**
Snow Bunting, Eskimo boy, ca 1972, 10" **350.00**
St Patrick, #2063, early 1950s, 12" **290.00**
Sugar Plum, carousel pony, #319, 12¼" on 12" base **1,200.00**
White Steer, #48, 1965, 12x14x7" **820.00**

Czechoslovakian Collectibles

Czechoslovakia came into being as a country in 1918. Located in the heart of Europe, it was a land with the natural resources necessary to support a glass industry that dated back to the mid-fourteenth century. The glass that was produced there has captured the attention of today's collectors, and for good reason. There are beautiful vases — cased, ruffled, applied with rigaree or silver overlay — fine enough to rival those of the best glasshouses. Czechoslovakian art glass baskets are quite as attractive as Victorian America's, and the elegant cut glass perfumes made in colors as well as crystal are unrivaled. There are also pressed glass perfumes, molded in lovely Deco shapes, of various types of art glass. Some are overlaid with gold filigree set with 'jewels.' Jewelry, lamps, porcelains, and fine art pottery are also included in the field.

More than seventy marks have been recorded, including those in the mold, ink stamped, acid etched, or on a small metal nameplate. The newer marks are incised, stamped 'Royal Dux Made in Czechoslovakia' (see Royal Dux), or printed on a paper label which reads 'Bohemian Glass Made in Czechoslovakia.' (Communist controlled from 1948, Czechoslovakia once again was made a free country in December 1989. Today it no longer exists; after 1993 it was divided to form two countries, the Czech Republic and the Slovak Republic.) For a more thorough study of the subject, we recommend *Made in Czechoslovakia* and *Made in Czechoslovakia, Book 2*, by Ruth A. Forsythe. Other fine books are *Czechoslovakian Perfume Bottles and Boudoir Accessories* by Jacquelyne Y. Jones North, and *Czechoslovakian Pottery* by Bowers, Closser, and Ellis. In the listings that follow, when one dimension is given, it refers to height; decoration is enamel unless noted otherwise. See also Amphora; Erphila.

Candy Baskets

Autumn mottled colors, ruffled, crystal thorn hdl w/str top, 6½" **200.00**
Bl mottle w/yel ruffled rim, jet rope hdl, 7" **220.00**
Blk w/silver mica, bl int, waisted, jet hdl, 8" **350.00**
Gr & red mottled, clear twisted thorn hdl, 6½" **240.00**
Gr varicolored stripes, flared rim, gr hdl, 8" **200.00**
Red & yel mottle, ruffled rim, clear twisted thorn hdl, 7" **220.00**
Red & yel mottle, waisted, clear hdl, 8½" **125.00**
Red solid w/blk trim at petal rim, cylindrical, clear hdl, 6½" **200.00**
Red varicolored, ruffled rim, clear twisted thorn hdl, 5½" **250.00**
Yel w/blk-edged rim, simple clear hdl, 6½" **200.00**

Cased Art Glass

Bowl, mottled autumn colors, amber cased, ftd, 4⅛" **175.00**
Mayonnaise jar, bl varicolored, w/lid, 5½" **175.00**
Stem, wine; orange w/silver exotic bird, clear stem, 3¼" **40.00**
Stem, wine; red w/silver trim, blk stem & ft, 7½" **65.00**
Vase, bl w/cobalt o/l, tapered cylinder, 7" **85.00**
Vase, bud; mottled autumn colors, 8¼" **75.00**
Vase, classical figure in silver & blk on orange, 12" **185.00**
Vase, dk mc mottle, shouldered, 6-sided, 4" **65.00**
Vase, lav/yel/wht mottle, ruffled fan form, 8¼" **200.00**
Vase, mc canes on blk, red band, bulbous w/stemmed ft, 6" **200.00**
Vase, Niagara Falls scene on yel, bottle-neck cylinder w/sm ft, 6¼" ...**75.00**
Vase, red varicolored, flared rim, ftd, 11" **130.00**

Vase, red w/gr aventurine, fan form, 7½" **195.00**
Vase, wht opaque, trumpet neck, bl open ear-shaped hdls, 4¾" **75.00**
Vase, wht opaque w/mc mottle in lower half, swollen cylinder, 8⅛" ..**95.00**
Vase, wht w/rose int, ruffled/pleated rim, 5½" **110.00**
Vase, yel & wht mottle, yel int, trumpet neck w/blk edge, 6¾" ..**130.00**
Vase, yel w/blk floral decor, 3 blk buttress hdls, 3½" **675.00**
Vase, yel w/blk serpentine decor, blk at ruffled rim, 10" **120.00**

Cut Glass Perfume Bottles

Bl, triangular w/3 ft, crystal vine/flower stopper, 8½" **300.00**
Crystal, cut/waisted, oversz lady w/flowers stopper, 10" **595.00**
Crystal, faceted/pyramidal, birds & flower intaglio top, 5¾" **200.00**
Crystal, highly cut, intaglio 3-roses stopper, 6¼" **200.00**
Crystal, highly cut, 4-ftd, faceted top, 6½" **110.00**
Crystal, rectangular w/4 ft, lady intaglio rectangular stopper, 4¾" **330.00**
Crystal w/cutting, hexagonal, nude w/fan stopper, 7¼" **1,000.00**
Crystal w/geometric cutting, blk stopper w/star design, 5" **165.00**
Crystal w/geometric cutting, nude w/jug intaglio stopper, 6¼" ...**350.00**
Crystal w/geometric cutting, tall cut stopper, 6¼" **100.00**
Crystal w/geometric cutting, 3-ftd, figure-8 stopper, 6½" **100.00**
Crystal w/geometric cutting, 4-ftd, cameo stopper, 7¼" **385.00**
Crystal w/overall cutting, stylized flower/butterfly stopper, 8½" **350.00**
Gr w/X-hatching, crystal roses & trellis stopper, 6" **145.00**
Peach w/geometric cutting, matching stopper, 6" **100.00**
Pk, church-window cutting, matching crystal stopper, 6¼" **165.00**
Red to dk red, leaves & berries, button-shape top, 3" **1,875.00**
Rose w/geometric cutting, tiara roses stopper, 6½" **1,200.00**
Yel cut crown form, ornate cut yel stopper, 6¼" **250.00**

Lamps

Boudoir, lady figural, porc, glass flower skirt & bodice, 10¼" ..**1,200.00**
Boudoir, mc mottled satin base & shade, 12½" **80.00**
Chandelier, yel-gr w/alabaster segments, 12 yel-gr arms, 1930s, 23x29" ..**750.00**
Desk, metal base, acid-cut shade, 10" **600.00**
Perfume, enameled florals, 4" **350.00**
Sconce, crystal, 2-arm, prisms, 14½" **300.00**
Shade, mottled colors, globular, cased, 5¾" **150.00**
Shade, mottled colors, globular, cased, 7¼" **200.00**
Student, metal base, acid-cut shade, 21" **1,000.00**
Table, Art Deco geometric base & matching conical shade.....**1,000.00**
Table, basket, bl flowers, crystal beaded base, 8½" **800.00**
Table, basket, mc fruit on bl beaded base, 8" **900.00**
Table, basket, mc nuts & fruit, crystal beaded base, 10¾" **1,200.00**
Table, beaded shade, 7" **110.00**
Table, Deco figure (gold-tone metal) beside crystal paperweight, 9"..**800.00**
Table, dk bl lustre, rpl shade, 13¼" **200.00**
Table, milk glass w/HP decor, kerosene, 12¾" **200.00**
Table, peacock figural, brass w/beaded glass tail/blk onyx base, 12"...**1,400.00**
Table, pnt decor on clear base & globe shade, 8¾" **500.00**

Mold-Blown and Pressed Bottles

Atomizer, gr w/emb Deco maiden among flowers, 4½" **90.00**
Blk crystal & frosted Deco design, simple crystal top, 6½".........**165.00**
Blk w/metal frieze w/red & blk jewels, metal cap, dauber, 2" **285.00**
Crystal w/molded steps, abstract red & blk design, 3¾" **110.00**
Crystal w/2 beaded figures hanging from chain on Bakelite lid, 2½" ..**125.00**
Lav w/gold & jewels, lav flower intaglio stopper, 5½" **660.00**
Lav w/gold metal, pearls & violet stones, clear stopper, 2¾" **550.00**
Metal clad w/goddess cameo & bl stones, 2" **175.00**
Smoky topaz w/emb nude among leaves, floral top, Ingrid, 5⅜" ..**1,045.00**
Yel flat 7-point star-like base, frosted maiden stopper, 7" **995.00**

Opaque, Crystal, Colored Transparent Glass

Bowl, crystal w/Deco floral & yel stripes, 4¼" 90.00
Candy jar, gr w/dk bl ornaments & finial, 6" 275.00
Candy jar, mc geometric enameling, stepped sides, 3¾"..............175.00
Decanter, topaz-tinted w/HP carriage scene by Borokistol, 10¼" ..140.00
Pitcher, cobalt w/mc exotic bird decor, w/lid, 11¼" 350.00
Tumbler, wine; gr w/bubbles & HP riding scene, 4¼"....................55.00
Vase, bl, wide trumpet neck, 7" 100.00
Vase, bl lustre, flared rim & ft, low waist, 5⅞".............................750.00
Vase, crystal w/red & blk overlay, ftd goblet form, 8¼".................200.00
Vase, mauve w/acid etching, ruffled rim w/blk trim, 5⅝" 125.00
Vase, mc mottle, slim neck, 8¼"...85.00
Vase, pk lustre w/blk threading at top, ftd, 9⅜" 475.00
Vase, red & yel varicolored, horizontal ribs, flared ft, 7¼" 110.00
Vase, wht opal, graduated balls form hdls, 8⅝"............................275.00

Pottery and Porcelain

Bowl, Deco floral on blk, wht int, str sides, 3" 75.00
Creamer, cow figural, yel & wht lustre, 6¼" 110.00
Creamer, duck figural, 3¾"...60.00
Flower holder, bird on stump, 5⅜"...40.00
Flower holder, bird perched at side of open log, 3½" 40.00
Napkin ring, girl figural, mc details, 4"...45.00

Pitchers, Goat figural, 18½", $600.00; Bird perched on handle, 10½", $950.00.

Plate, chicks pecking, mc on wht, lustre rim, 6½" 30.00
Shakers, Mexican couple figural, red/wht/yel, 2¾", pr...................30.00
Sprinkling can, floral swag on wht, 4½"..45.00
Teapot, rooster, mc on tan, child sz, 5¼"......................................45.00
Vase, Egyptian chariot scene in relief, mc on brn, head hdls, 8½"....400.00
Vase, Egyptian figures in mc band, gourd shape, 9⅛".................300.00
Vase, HP floral on wht cylinder w/orange rim, 4⅜".....................100.00
Wall pocket, bird perched at base of fan, 5¼"...............................60.00
Wall pocket, bird perched at side of wishing well, 6"....................60.00
Wall pocket, bird perched beside birdhouse, 5½" 60.00

D'Argental

D'Argental cameo glass was produced in France from the 1870s until about 1920 in the Art Nouveau style. Both floral and scenic designs were developed through acid cuttings. Our advisor for this category is Don Williams; he is listed in the Directory under Missouri.

Atomizer, trees & ruins, amethyst on amber, Ovington, 4¾" 360.00
Bowl, floral branches, burgundy on citron, ftd, 3¾x6¼"..............900.00
Box, orchids/moths, lt bl on amethyst, 4x6" 800.00
Candy dish, floral, dk gr on orange, w/lid, 5x7" dia..................1,400.00
Vase, cherry branches, brn/orange on lt gr, full body/bottle neck, 12"..1,300.00

Vase, floral garden, gr/gray on clear, rose top/base, shouldered, 14" ...2,000.00
Vase, lily-of-valley & leaves, wht/gr on brn, classic shape, 5¼"..1,600.00
Vase, orchids, red/maroon on frost, tapering, 13½" 2,400.00
Vase, palm trees/island beyond, purple on amethyst frost, 9¾" ...700.00
Vase, peonies/buds, brn multi on yel/peach/brn frost, shouldered, 12"..2,000.00
Vase, trees/river, fortress beyond, rose on yel, ftd, 14" 1,250.00
Vase, vineyard, orange-amber/brns, classic form, 13½" 1,050.00

Daum Nancy

Daum was an important producer of French cameo glass, operating from the late 1800s until after the turn of the century. They used various techniques — acid cutting, wheel engraving, and handwork — to create beautiful scenic designs and nature subjects in the Art Nouveau manner. Virtually all examples are signed. Daum is still in production, producing many figural items. Our advisor for this category is Don Williams; he is listed in the Directory under Missouri.

Cameo

Bowl, sunset lake scene, dk gr on orange to red, 2¾x5¾"...........800.00
Bowl, 4 lg blossoms, pk/purple/red/yel/gr on clear, 2½x6"........1,800.00
Pitcher, floral, ruby/frost w/gold, silver mts, 4½" 800.00
Vase, berried branch, maroon on peach, club form, 6½" 900.00
Vase, berries/leaves, brn/orange on red/yel/gr mottle frost, ftd, 19"..8,000.00
Vase, berries/leaves, gr/orange on red/yel/gr, bottle form, 13" ..5,500.00
Vase, berries/leaves, purple on bl-gr mottle, elliptical, 12".......2,800.00
Vase, birch trees, cvd/pnt on pk frost, slim, ftd, 7½"................2,300.00
Vase, bleeding hearts/leaves, pk/gr on mottled frost, ftd, 10"..7,500.00
Vase, field flowers at angled shoulder, orange/yel on yel/gr, 10" ...1,750.00
Vase, floral, brn on lt brn & orange mottle, slim, ftd, 9¼" 2,600.00
Vase, floral, cut/pnt pk & gr on yel & frost, ovoid, 3¼" 1,000.00
Vase, floral, purple & gr on yel to rose, slim, 30"....................7,000.00
Vase, floral, purple/yel/rose mottle, slim cylinder, flared ft, 20"...5,500.00
Vase, floral/banner, gr to clear w/gold, block form, 4¾" 550.00
Vase, iris, cut/pnt yel gr on yel to frost, long neck, 5½" 850.00
Vase, iris, cut/pnt yel/gr on yel to frost, flared neck, 3½" 850.00
Vase, junk boats & sunset, brn/mottled yel/orange/gr, cylinder, 7¼" ..2,000.00
Vase, landscape, cut/HP on frost, ftd, 5" 3,500.00
Vase, landscape, red/yel/frosted purple/red, stick neck, 16" 2,800.00
Vase, lily-of-valley, gr on mottled red to wht, bells shape, 5½"..1,700.00
Vase, lily-of-valley, teal on frost & hammered teal, gourd, 5" ..1,500.00
Vase, morning glories, purple/gr on gray, shouldered cylinder, 4"..1,900.00
Vase, mushrooms/pine cones, HP on frost/yel/rose, waisted, 19½" ..16,000.00
Vase, orchids, HP on gr/brn/yel mottle, ftd, slim, 14"..............2,900.00
Vase, spikey flowers/slim leaves, brn on yel mottle, wide body, 8"..1,700.00
Vase, sweet peas, maroon/lt bl, fire polished, globular, 11½" ...3,500.00
Vase, thistles, brn/yel on frosted brn & yel mottle, slim, 16" ..2,600.00
Vase, thistles between trunks, dk brn to red, 11½"..................6,000.00
Vase, tobacco flowers, brn on yel hammered, squat, ftd, 7½" ..2,300.00
Vase, trees, cut/HP on frost to yel, bottle form, 2¼".................700.00
Vase, trees/boats/birds, brn on yel/rose mottle, trumpet form, 20" ..2,600.00
Vase, trees/lake, mocha/gr/mottled orange/yel, cylinder, 9".....4,500.00
Vase, wispy floral/leaves, cut/HP on clear frost, 5"......................350.00
Vase, wisteria, purple on purple mottle to gr, 7" 3,500.00

Enameled Glass

Box, thistles & vines, 3¼" dia 900.00
Vase, boats/birds/windmills, blk on ivory, long slim neck, 3" 475.00
Vase, fuchsia on mottled purple & wht, block form, 4¾" 1,000.00
Vase, tree/water scenic, brn on ivory, bulbous, 1" 425.00

Lamps

Base, cameo foliage, purple on yel, bronze spider, 2-light, 14" **700.00**
Table, cameo acorn/leaves shade/base, purple/frost/gr, 14" **4,500.00**
Table, cameo lilies shade & base, purple on frost to gr, 16½"....**5,000.00**

Lamp, riverside scene with trees and grass in foreground, green and black over turquoise, marked base and ball shade, black metal fittings, 19", $12,000.00.

Miscellaneous

Bowl, male & female nudes becoming tree, pate-de-verre, 14¾" ..**1,000.00**
Candelabrum, tree form w/snail at base, mc pate-de-verre, 2-light, 8" ..**1,400.00**
Owl, pate-de-verre, sage gr, #d, after Demarchi, 20th C, 7¼" **200.00**
Vase, amber w/yel streaks, long stick neck, appl ant, 4¾" **1,300.00**
Vase, gr/purple w/gold foil inclusions, wrought o/l, Majorelle, 9" **2,300.00**
Vase, purple mottle to bl-gray, wrought silver floral mt, 5¾" **415.00**
Vase, red w/foil inclusions, wrought-iron o/l, Majorelle, 9½" ..**2,900.00**

De Vez

De Vez was a type of acid-cut French cameo glass produced by Cristallerie de Pantin in Paris around the turn of the century. Our advisor for this category is Don Williams; he is listed in the Directory under Missouri.

Cameo

Atomizer, rose garden, dk bl on turq, no sprayer, 6" **350.00**
Bowl, cascading foliage w/mtns/island beyond, gr on yel lid, 3½" ...**350.00**
Lamp, Venice scenes/panels on gourd shade/base, bl on wht/yel, 18" **3,600.00**
Lamp base, 4 sailing ships, bl on gr to wht, 24" **1,800.00**
Rose bowl, vintage, maroon/red on citron, 4-crimp rim, 3x4½" **500.00**
Vase, branches/lake/islands/mts, bl frost to gr, 7½x3¾" **1,000.00**
Vase, cherries, farm/tree/lake/mtns beyond, low width, 6", NM..**325.00**
Vase, cottages/mother/child, maroon/fiery amber, ovoid, 6" **865.00**
Vase, fish boat/mtn lake/village, bl on amber sky, 5x5" **850.00**
Vase, island w/distant chalet, florals at bulbous rim on rust, 8"...**700.00**
Vase, Moroccan waterfront, burgundy on vaseline opal, 4½"......**675.00**
Vase, pines/mtns/cabin, violet on yel/bl, swollen cylinder, 8" ..**1,250.00**
Vase, poppies/butterfly, dk persimmon on textured opal, 8" **1,380.00**
Vase, sm deer/trees/snowy hills, maroon on orange, 6½" **650.00**
Vase, trees/water/islands, bl on gr, 3½" **485.00**
Vase, trumpet flowers/leaves, rose/gr citron, cylindrical, 10¼"....**950.00**
Vase, water/trees/island/buildings, blk/salmon on pearl gray, slim, 8" ..**450.00**
Vase, windmills/ships/clouds, brn/orange/frost/yel, 7½" **900.00**
Vase, wisteria, amethyst on frost, 5¾" **160.00**

De Vilbiss

Perfume bottles, atomizers, and dresser accessories marketed by the De Vilbiss Company are appreciated by collectors today for the various types of lovely glassware used in their manufacture as well as for their pleasing shapes. Various companies provided the glass, while De Vilbiss made only the metal tops. They marketed their merchandise not only here but in Paris, England, Canada, and Havana as well. Their marks were acid stamped, ink stamped, in gold script, molded in, or on paper labels. One is no more significant than another. Our advisor for this category is Randy Monsen; he is listed in the Directory under Virginia.

Key:
A — atomizer   B — bulb

Bottles

Aqua, onion body on tall ped/disk base, metal A, new B, tassel, 6" ...**110.00**
Bl enamel w/blk stenciled floral, wider at flat bottom, metal A, 7"....**110.00**
Blk w/gold inclusions, slim/tapering to disk ft, orig AB, 6¾" **165.00**
Chrome w/floral top band, body tapers to disk ft, metal A, 5½"....**110.00**
Clear, sq body/top, chrome A attachment, 2¼", +VG blk leather case....**165.00**
Clear w/etched gold/orange upright points, blk int, tall ft, rpl B, 8" ...**360.00**
Clear w/gold o/l, cut-in bird panel at trumpet bottom, rpl AB, 10" **350.00**
Clear w/gr int, textured gold & blk petal-motif well, tall stem, A, 7"...**365.00**
Clear w/int gr enamel, on Z-form metal fr w/sq base, rpl AB, 6" ...**385.00**
Clear w/orange int, blk enamel leaves/gilt, slim on disk ft, A, 7" ..**275.00**
Clear w/orange int, slim panels w/blk segments/gilt, disk ft, A, +box **770.00**
Clear w/textured gold o/l & triangle windows, shouldered, metal A, 8"...**220.00**
Clear w/yel int & gold bands, waisted body/tall ft, 1 w/A, 7", pr ...**275.00**
Coral w/fancy gold o/l well on tall slim gold stem, orig AB, 9½"...**1,050.00**
Cranberry w/gold scroll band on body & disk ft, 1 w/A, 7½", pr...**1,430.00**
Cranberry w/swirl mold, elongated teardrop on disk ft, 6¼" **285.00**
Frosted w/emb forget-me-nots, cylindrical, A, w/tassel, 5" **175.00**
Gold irid, slim/shouldered top, trumpet bottom, orig AB, 6" **365.00**
Gold irid satin (Quezal's), slim w/flared base, metal A/rpl B, 7½"...**525.00**
Gr, squat/wide body, w/matching disk-top dropper, 2½" **45.00**
Lt bl textured enamel, shouldered/elongated, disk base, 1 w/A, 7", pr ...**330.00**
Lt bl to yel body w/jewel-set gold o/l bottom half & disk ft, A, 7" ..**4,950.00**
Lt gr w/gr enamel int & gold bands, tall stem, A, 6½", +Deco box.....**170.00**
Orange body w/gold abstracts, on tall gold-textured stem, metal A, 8"...**360.00**
Penguin, Lenox porc w/blk felt cape, 4½" **220.00**
Pk, body & lid form cone shape, hardened A, label, 2½"..............**65.00**
Yel, elongated ovoid on ped ft, orig AB, 6¾"..............................**110.00**

Miscellaneous

Ginger jar, amber w/heavy gold pine-needle o/l, A, dome lid, 6"...**330.00**
Perfume lamp, bl balloon shade w/blk band, rtcl gilt base, 5¼" ..**145.00**
Powder jar, clear w/coral pk int & stenciled blk abstracts, 1¾" **75.00**
Powder jar, cvd leaves on radiating leaf panels on mauve w/gold, +tray...**110.00**
Powder jar, orange w/gold/blk enamel money plant, ftd, 4½" dia ...**2,200.00**
Powder jar+A, clear w/blk int+gold bands, clear stem, orig B, 7", +box ..**55.00**
Powder jar+6½" A bottle+11" tray, pk enameled w/blk line trim, NM...**155.00**
Tray, floral vines in gr/blk/orange enamel w/gilt, rectangle, 10" L **365.00**

Decanters

Ceramic whiskey decanters were brought into prominence in 1955 by the James Beam Distilling Company. Few other companies besides Beam produced these decanters during the next ten years or so; however, other companies did eventually follow suit. At its peak in 1975, at least twenty prominent companies and several on a lesser scale made these decanters. Beam stopped making decanters in mid-1992. Now only a couple of companies are still producing these collectibles.

  Liquor dealers have told collectors for years that ceramic decanters are not as valuable, and in some cases worthless, if emptied or if the federal tax stamp has been broken. Nothing is further from the truth. Following are but a few of many reasons you should consider emptying ceramic decanters:

  1) If the thin glaze on the inside ever cracks (and it does in a small percentage of decanters), the contents will push through to the outside. It is then referred to as a 'leaker' and worth a fraction of its original value.

  2) A large number of decanters left full in one area of your house poses a fire hazard.

  3) A burglar, after stealing jewelry and electronics, may make off with some of your decanters just to enjoy the contents. If they are empty, chances are they will not be bothered.

  4) It is illegal in most states for collectors to sell a full decanter without a liquor license.

  Unlike years ago, few collectors now collect all types of decanters. Most now specialize. For example, they may collect trains, cars, owls, Indians, clowns, or any number of different things that have been depicted on or as a decanter. They are finding exceptional quality available at reasonable prices, especially when compared with many other types of collectibles.

  We have tried to list those brands that are the most popular with collectors. Likewise, individual decanters listed are the ones (or representative of the ones) most commonly found. The following listing is but a small fraction of the thousands of decanters that have been produced.

  These decanters come from all over the world. While Jim Beam owned its own china factory in the U.S., some of the others have been imported from Mexico, Taiwan, Japan, and elsewhere. They vary in size from miniatures (approximately two ounce) to gallons. Values range from a few dollars to more than $3,000.00 per decanter.

  Most collectors and dealers define a 'mint' decanter as one with no chips, no cracks, and label intact. A missing federal tax stamp or lack of contents have no bearing on value. All values are given for 'mint' decanters. A 'mini' behind a listing indicates a miniature. All others are fifth or 750 ml unless noted otherwise. Our advisor for this category is Roy Willis; he is listed in the Directory under Kentucky.

Aesthetic Specialties (ASI)

Cadillac, 1903, bl or wht 70.00
Chevrolet, 1914 ......75.00
Golf, Bing Crosby 38th 50.00

Beam

Casino Series, Golden Gate, 1970 ......20.00
Casino Series, Harold's Club Pinwheel 45.00
Casino Series, Reno Horseshoe, Primadonna or Cal-Neva 10.00
Centennial Series, Alaska Purchase 9.00
Centennial Series, Key West 8.00
Centennial Series, Lombard 6.00
Centennial Series, Statue of Liberty, 1975 ......20.00
Executive Series, 1979 Mother of Pearl 16.00
Executive Series, 1981 Royal Filigree 15.00
Executive Series, 1982 American Pitcher 20.00
Executive Series, 1983 Partridge Bell 35.00
Executive Series, 1984 Carolers Bell 25.00
Foreign Series, Australia, Galah Bird 25.00
Foreign Series, Australia, Kangaroo 18.00
Foreign Series, Fuji Islands 8.00
Foreign Series, New Zealand, Kiwi Bird 12.00

Organization Series, Ducks Unlimited #3, 1977, $45.00.

Organization Series, Ducks Unlimited #6, 1980 ......50.00
Organization Series, Ducks Unlimited #7, 1981 ......42.00
Organization Series, Ducks Unlimited #9, 1983 ......65.00
Organization Series, Ducks Unlimited #10, 1984 ......95.00
Organization Series, Elks, 1968 ......6.00
Organization Series, Phi Sigma Kappa 25.00
Organization Series, Shriner, Raja Temple 25.00
Organization Series, VFW 10.00
People Series, Cowboy 20.00
People Series, Emmett Kelly 35.00
People Series, George Washington 20.00
People Series, Martha Washington 14.00
State Series, Delaware 10.00
State Series, Kentucky, blk head stopper 25.00
State Series, Maine 9.00
State Series, Ohio 12.00
Wheel Series, Cable Car, 1968 ......6.00
Wheel Series, Cable Car, 1983 ......60.00
Wheel Series, Corvette, 1954, bl 125.00
Wheel Series, Corvette, 1978, red, yel or wht, ea 80.00
Wheel Series, Crovette, 1955, bronze 125.00
Wheel Series, Ford 1913 Model T, blk or gr, ea 80.00
Wheel Series, Ford 1964 Mustang, blk 140.00
Wheel Series, Ford 1964 Mustang, wht 75.00
Wheel Series, Golf Car 50.00
Wheel Series, Harold's Club Covered Wagon (1974) 40.00
Wheel Series, Mack Fire Engine 140.00
Wheel Series, Train, Caboose, gray 90.00
Wheel Series, Train, Caboose, red 75.00
Wheel Series, Train, Locomotive, Grant 80.00
Wheel Series, Train, Locomotive, JB Turner 135.00
Wheel Series, Train, Passenger Car 55.00
Wheel Series, Train, Tender, Coal for Grant 70.00
Wheel Series, Train, Tender, Wood for General 150.00

Brooks

American Legion, Denver, 1971 ......15.00
Amvets 10.00
Car, Auburn Boat Tail 30.00
Car, 1962 Corvette Mako Shark 35.00
Elk 25.00
Fire Engine 20.00
Indy Racer #21 (1970) 50.00
Keystone Cops 75.00
Man O' War 45.00
Phonograph 25.00

Pistol, Dueling 12.00
Setter w/bird, 1970 ....15.00
Shrine, King Tut Guard................................20.00
Ticker Tape 10.00
Trail Bike..25.00
Train, Iron Horse 12.00
Vermont Skier...12.00
Whale, Killer 22.00

Dant, J.W.

American Legion 10.00
Field Birds, 8 different, ea.............................10.00
Indy 500 ....9.00

Dickel, George

Golf Club (glass)..12.00
Powder Horn, amber, qt 15.00
Powder Horn, dk, ⅘-qt.................................12.00

Famous Firsts

Coffee Mill..35.00
Roulette Wheel..35.00
Scales, Lombardy 30.00
Spirit of St Louis, midi 80.00
Spirit of St Louis, mini 50.00

Hoffman

Big Red Machine 50.00
Cats, 6 different, ea......................................15.00
College Series, Helmet, Auburn 35.00
College Series, Helmet, Missouri 35.00
College Series, Mascot, Nevada Wolfpack 50.00
Mr Lucky Series, Fireman, mini 25.00
Mr Lucky Series, Mr Blacksmith...................40.00
Mr Lucky Series, Mr Blacksmith, mini 15.00
Mr Lucky Series, Mr Policeman.....................50.00
Mr Lucky Series, Mr Policeman, mini 20.00
Race Car, AJ Foyt #2....................................125.00
Wildlife Series, Doe & Fawn.........................50.00

Kontinental

Dentist..35.00
Dockworker...30.00
Innkeeper 28.00
Stephen Foster 28.00
Surveyor..35.00

Lionstone

Backpacker..30.00
Barber...45.00
Barber, mini 20.00
Camp Cook...25.00
Camp Follower..25.00
Canada Goose w/base 55.00
Clown, 6 different, ea...................................45.00
Doctor, Country...22.00
Fisherman...40.00
Football Players...60.00

Johnny Lightning #1 ....100.00
Johnny Lightning #2 ....90.00
Laundryman, Chinese...................................25.00
Meadowlark...25.00
Photographer...60.00
Photographer, mini......................................24.00
Rainmaker, mini 18.00
Riverboat Captain 25.00
Sheepherder...40.00
Telegrapher 25.00
Turbo Car, STP, red......................................60.00

McCormick

Abe Lincoln...40.00
Alexander Graham Bell 30.00
Elvis, 1979, plays Love Me Tender, mini 55.00
Elvis, 1980, plays Can't Help Falling in Love, 750-ml...................90.00
Elvis, 1981, plays Can't Help Falling in Love, mini.....................50.00
Elvis, 1983, Golden Tribute, plays My Way, mini......................150.00
Elvis, 1984, Designer #3 Gold Encore, plays It's Now or Never, 750-ml 300.00
Elvis, 1985, Teddy Bear, plays Let Me Be Your Teddy Bear, 750-ml 650.00
Elvis, 1986, Designer #1 Silver, plays Are You Lonesome Tonight, mini ...190.00

Gunfighter Series, Black Bart, $40.00.

Hank Williams Sr..140.00
Iwo Jima..175.00
Iwo Jima, mini...75.00
Jimmy Durante...75.00
King Arthur's Court Series, King Arthur.........60.00
Marilyn Monroe 600.00
Pony Express..55.00
Robert Peary..35.00
Shrine Dune Buggy.......................................40.00
Telephone Operator......................................65.00

O.B.R.

Engine, General..19.00
Guitar, Music City..18.00
WC Fields, Bank Dick...................................50.00
WC Fields, Top Hat......................................60.00

Old Bardstown

Foster Brooks..28.00
Surface Miner 28.00
Tiger 35.00

Old Commonwealth

Coal Miner #1, w/Shovel 95.00
Coal Miner #1, w/Shovel, mini.......................27.00
Coal Miner #2, w/Pick....................................45.00
Firefighter, Fallen Comrade............................80.00
Firefighter, Fallen Comrade, mini 30.00
Firefighter, Modern Hero #1..........................75.00
Firefighter, Modern Hero #1, mini.................27.00
Forefighter, Nozzleman #2 ....75.00

Old Fitzgerald

Irish, Blarney...12.00
Irish, Leprechaun, Plase God 28.00
Irish, Luck, 1972 ....26.00
Irish, Wish, 1975 ....22.00
Rip Van Winkle..30.00

Ski Country

Barrel Racer 90.00
Barrel Racer, mini...40.00
Birth of Freedom..125.00
Birth of Freedom, 1-gal...............................2,000.00
Bob Cratchit...60.00
Bob Cratchit, mini..34.00
Cardinals, Holiday, 1991, mini........................40.00
Deer, Whitetail...175.00
Ducks Unlimited, Pintail, 1978 ....110.00
Ducks Unlimited, Pintail, 1978, mini.............35.00
Ducks Unlimited, Pintail, 1978, ½-gal...........225.00
Ducks Unlimited, Widgeon, 1979....................70.00
Ducks Unlimited, Widgeon, 1979, 1.75-L........175.00
Eagle, Majestic..300.00
Eagle, Majestic, mini.......................................140.00
Eagle, Majestic, 1-gal...................................1,700.00
Elk..200.00
Indian, Cigar Store...50.00
Indian, Cigar Store, mini 32.00
Indian, North American, set of 6....................260.00
Indian, Southwest Dancers, mini, set of 6........225.00
Jaguar 160.00
Jaguar, mini...50.00
Koala 50.00
Owl, Barred, wall plaque 140.00
Owl, Great Gray 85.00
Owl Great Gray, mini......................................45.00
Pelican 65.00
Pelican, mini...35.00
Pheasant, Standing, mini 60.00
Phoenix Bird...40.00
Ram, Bighorn, mini 35.00
Ruffed Grouse 70.00
Ruffed Grouse, mini..30.00
Skunk Family..65.00
Skunk Family, mini...35.00
Wild Turkey..140.00

Whooping Crane,
$65.00.

Wild Turkey

Series I, #1, #2, #3, or #4, mini, ea 18.00
Series I, #1, 1971 ....225.00
Series I, #2 ....150.00
Series I, #3 or #4, ea.......................................65.00
Series I, #5, #6, or #7, ea................................30.00
Series I, #8 ....45.00
Series I, set of #5, #6, #7 & #8, mini..............175.00
Series II, Lore #1...25.00
Series II, Lore #2...38.00
Series II, Lore #3...45.00
Series II, Lore #4...55.00
Series III, #1, In Flight 120.00
Series III, #1, In Flight, mini..........................50.00
Series III, #2, Turkey & Bobcat 140.00
Series III, #2, Turkey & Bobcat, mini.............60.00
Series III, #3, Fighting Turkeys 150.00
Series III, #3, Fighting Turkeys, mini.............65.00
Series III, #4, Turkey & Eagle 95.00
Series III, #4, Turkey & Eagle, mini...............85.00
Series III, #5, Turkey & Raccoon 95.00
Series III, #5, Turkey & Raccoon, mini...........50.00
Series III, #6, Turkey & Poults, mini..............50.00
Series III, #6, Turkey P Poults........................95.00
Series III, #7, Turkey & Red Fox 100.00
Series III, #7, Turkey & Red Fox, mini...........60.00
Series III, #8, Turkey & Owl...........................100.00
Series III, #8, Turkey & Owl, mini 60.00
Series III, #9, Turkey & Bear Cubs 100.00
Series III, #9, Turkey & Bear Cubs, mini........60.00
Series III, #10, Turkey & Coyote 100.00
Series III, #10, Turkey & Coyote, mini............60.00
Series III, #11, Turkey & Falcon......................100.00
Series III, #11, Turkey & Falcon, mini 60.00
Series III, #12, Turkey & Skunks 125.00
Series III, #12, Turkey & Skunks, mini............65.00

Decoys

American colonists learned the craft of decoy making from the Indians who used them to lure birds out of the sky as an important food source. Early models were carved from wood such as pine, cedar, balsa, etc., and a few were made of canvas or papier-maché. There are two basic types of decoys: water floaters and shorebirds (also called 'stick-ups'). Within each type are many different species, ducks being the most plentiful since they migrated along all four of America's great waterways. Market hunting became big business around 1880, resulting in large-scale commercial production of decoys which continued until about 1910 when such hunting was outlawed by the Migratory Bird Treaty.

Today decoys are one of the most collectible types of American folk art. The most valuable are those carved by such artists as Laing, Crowell, Ward, and Wheeler, to name only a few. Each area, such as Massachusetts, Connecticut, Maine, the Illinois River, and the Delaware River, produces decoys with distinctive regional characteristics. Examples of commercial decoys produced by well-known factories — among them Mason, Stevens, and Dodge — are also prized by collectors. Though mass produced, these nevertheless required a certain amount of hand carving and decorating. Well-carved examples, especially those of rare species, are appreciating rapidly, and those with original paint are more desirable. In the listings that follow, all decoys are solid-bodied unless noted hollow.

Key:
CG — Challenge Grade
DDF — Dodge Decoy Factory
DG — Detroit Grade
MDF — Mason's Decoy Factory
OP — original paint
ORP — old repaint

OWP — original working paint
PDF — Pratt Decoy Factory
PG — Premier Grade
SG — Standard Grade
WDF — Wildfowler Decoy Factory
WOP — worn original paint

Canada goose, George Boyd, tiny touchup on bill tip, minor restoration, tack eyes, EX patina, $7,000.00. (Photo courtesy Decoys Unlimited, Inc.)

Black duck, BJ Schmidt, feather cvg, OP, orig keel & weight **150.00**
Black duck, Frank Schmidt, preening, solid body, OWP, cvd wings...**250.00**
Black duck, Hays Factory, glass eyes, solid body, EX OP, chip.....**300.00**
Black duck, HV Shourds, rusted tack eyes, hollow, WOP, crack....**225.00**
Black duck, John Blair Sr, ORP down to WOP, structurally EX....**5,350.00**
Black duck, Ken Gleason, sleeping, OP, M **1,150.00**
Black duck, MDF, PG, G OP, prof rpr/shot **550.00**
Black duck, MDF, PG, G OP, prof rstr chip, no weight, NM ...**2,000.00**
Black duck, MDF, tack eyes, SG, NM OP, weight removed **825.00**
Black duck, Nathan Cobb Jr, inlet head, WOP, filler cracks, early....**9,000.00**
Black duck, T Fitzpatrick, low head, EX OP, slight separation....**2,150.00**
Black duck, unknown maker, glass eyes, WOP, oversz/weighted, shot....**375.00**
Black duck, W Baldwin, sleeping, branded WCB underside, OP, M..**2,400.00**
Black duck, Ward Bros, preening, raised wing cvg, sgn Lem, 1960, M...**11,950.00**
Black duck, Ward Bros, trn head, ribbed & branded, EX orig.....**125.00**
Black-Bellied Plover, Geo Boyd, NM OP, minor shot scar.......**6,575.00**
Blue-wing Teal drake, O Billiot, sm chip, ca 1935, EX orig.........**425.00**
Blue-wing Teal pr, Geo Frederick, glass eyes, NM OP.............**4,750.00**
Bluebill drake, BJ Schmidt, sleeper, OP w/touchup, orig keel, 1950.....**400.00**
Bluebill drake, Ogdensburg NY area, cvd eyes, inlet head, WOP..**275.00**
Bluebill hen, F Baumgardner, glass eyes, EX OP, orig keel, 1940s..**175.00**

Bluewing Teal pr, Davy Nichols, OP, dtd 1971, M **1,000.00**
Brandt, HV Shourds, OP, minor separation, rstr bill, EX **4,500.00**
Brant, att N 'Rowley' Horner, glass eyes, WOP, lead weight **500.00**
Bufflehead drake, Ken Harris, branded, M **835.00**
Bufflehead pr, Charles Buchanan, detailed feather cvg, OP, M ...**700.00**
Bufflehead pr, RG Kerr, glass eyes, tucked head, OP, 1975, mini, EX ...**500.00**
Canada goose, BJ Schmidt, glass eyes, WOP, hollow w/bottom brd..**3,750.00**
Canada goose, H Conklin, swimming, OP w/lt wear, NM **1,195.00**
Canada goose, H Gibbs, EX OP, legs loose from base, mini **275.00**
Canada goose, J Lincoln, glass eyes, EX OP, classic style, shot....**1,600.00**
Canada goose, RG Kerr, glass eyes, trn head, detailed OP, mini **350.00**
Canvasback drake, Chauncy Wheeler, VG OP w/touchup, 2 wood plugs....**3,350.00**
Canvasback drake, Elmer Crowell, OP, minor flake, mini, NM....**2,000.00**
Canvasback drake, unknown maker, glass eyes, bobtail, ORP.......**40.00**
Canvasback pr, Bob Bolle, trn heads, detailed cvg, 1975, EX orig...**350.00**
Curlew, MDF, glass eyes, curved metal bill, sgn TJ78, EX OP.....**200.00**
Eider drake, Herter Factory, solid body, 1893, EX orig...................**80.00**
Goldeneye drake, MDF, glass eyes, SG, ORP, lead weight...........**175.00**
Goldeneye hen, T Schroeder, Whistler Female on bottom, mini, EX...**1,000.00**
Goldeneye pr, MDF, tack eyes, WOP, cracked filler/checks.........**850.00**
Greenwing Teal pr, Lloyd Johnson, trn heads, detailed cvg, M ..**3,100.00**
Greenwing Teal pr, ML Whipple, OP, 1970s, NM......................**800.00**
King Eider, Elmer Crowell, OP, M..**3,585.00**
Mallard drake, att C Oliver, cypress root w/EX patina, lt wear, 1920s...**1,500.00**
Mallard drake, att Joe Prosperia, tack eyes, EX OP, river style, 1920s...**1,100.00**
Mallard drake, Frank Brogan, OWP, hollow, cracks/wear **60.00**
Mallard drake, JF Mott Sr, sleeping, tack eyes, hollow, WOP **675.00**
Mallard drake, MDF, CG, EX OP (dry), lead weight, cracked filler....**1,850.00**
Mallard hen, Joel Barber, OP, sgn/inscribed, dtd 1943, OP, NM...**10,000.00**
Mallard pr, Elmer Crowell, male standing/she resting, OP, mini, M...**3,585.00**
Merganser drake, R Mitchell, glass eyes, EX OP, lead weight, dings ...**65.00**
Ne Ne goose, BJ Schmidt, glass eyes, EX OP, solid, sm chip....**2,750.00**
Oldsquaw drake, Ben Schmidt, OP, VG structually, NM **2,850.00**
Oldsquaw drake, BJ Schmidt, glass eyes, EX OP, orig keel/weight, rare ..**1,500.00**
Pintail drake, Lloyd Sterling, trn head, balsa w/cvd inset tail, EX OP..**425.00**
Pintail pr, Geo Frederick, glass eyes, cypress root, ca 1960, NM **5,000.00**
Puffin, Geo Boyd, pnt tack eyes, mini, early, EX orig...............**4,000.00**
Red-breasted Merganser drake, Geo Boyd, glass eyes, trn head, EX OP ...**7,750.00**
Redhead drake, att Chris Smith, OP w/touchups, neck crack, ca 1900....**900.00**
Redhead drake, HK Chadwick, glass eyes, EX OP, inlet weight, rare **2,450.00**
Redhead hen, Ken Harris, glass eyes, EX OP, orig keel, sm dents....**275.00**
Sea gull, Ward Bros, working style, sgn/dtd 1965, M................**6,575.00**
Snow goose, Charles Shang Wheeler, OP, minor mars, EX+ **23,900.00**
Snow goose, Ward Bros, OP, sm separation, sgn Lem, dtd 1967 ...**10,755.00**
Willet, MDF, tack eyes, OP, lightly hit by shot, EX..................**1,900.00**
Yellowlegs, New England, tack eyes, OP, orig bill, split tail.........**175.00**
Yellowlegs, unknowm maker, bold cvg, tack eyes, upright mt, WOP ...**300.00**
Yellowlegs, Ward Bros, preening, driftwood base, 1964, M **9,560.00**

Dedham Pottery

Originally founded in Chelsea, Massachusetts, as the Chelsea Keramic Works, the name was changed to Dedham Pottery in 1895 after the firm relocated in Dedham, near Boston, Massachusetts. The ware utilized a gray stoneware body with a crackle glaze and simple cobalt border designs of flowers, birds, and animals. Decorations were brushed on by hand using an ancient Chinese method which suspended the cobalt within the overall glaze. There were thirteen standard patterns, among them Magnolia, Iris, Butterfly, Duck, Polar Bear, and Rabbit, the latter of which was chosen to represent the company on their logo. On the very early pieces, the rabbits face left; decorators soon found the reverse position easier to paint, and the rabbits were turned to the right. (Earlier examples are worth from 10% to 20% more than identical pieces manufactured in later years.) In addition to the standard patterns, other designs were produced for special orders. These and artist-signed pieces are highly valued by collectors today.

Though their primary product was the blue-printed, crackle-glazed dinnerware, two types of artware were also produced: crackle glaze and flambé. Their notable volcanic ware was a type of the latter. The mark is incised and often accompanies the cipher of Hugh Robertson. The firm was operated by succeeding generations of the Robertson family until it closed in 1943. Our advisor for this category is Dale MacLean; he is listed in the Directory under Massachusetts. See also Chelsea Keramic Art Works.

Ashtray, Rabbit, stamped, 1x3¾" dia 300.00
Ashtray, Turkey, stamped/registered, 1x3¾" 475.00
Bacon rasher, Rabbit, stamped/registered/imp, 1½x9¾", NM 475.00
Bowl, Elephant & Baby, #5, stamped, 2x4¼" 600.00
Bowl, Lotus Leaf, paneled, 2½x5" 650.00
Bowl, nappy, Rabbit, stamped, 1¾x6" 375.00
Bowl, Rabbit, #3, stamped, 3¼x7", NM 350.00
Bowl, Rabbit, #6, stamped, 2x4½" 275.00
Bowl, Rabbit, stamped, 1¾x9" 375.00
Butter pat, Star, stamped/1931, 3¼" 495.00
Charger, Rabbit, stamped, 12" 700.00
Coaster, Rabbit, stamped/registered, 3¾" 400.00
Coaster, Striped Iris, stamped, 4" 425.00
Coffeepot, Rabbit, bell-shaped lid, stamped, 8¾x7" 1,300.00
Compote, Rabbit, hdld chalice form, stamped, 3½x6", NM 475.00
Creamer, Duck, stamped, 3x3¼" 425.00
Creamer, Elephant, flat style, stamped, 2¼x5¼" 850.00
Cup & saucer, Butterfly, stamped, 2x5¼", NM 450.00
Cup & saucer, Duck, stamped, 2", 6" 350.00
Cup & saucer, Elephant & Baby, 2¼", 6", NM 675.00
Humidor, Rabbit, stamped, 6½x6¼", NM 1,200.00
Knife rest, Crouching Rabbit figural, 2¾x3¾" 450.00
Marmalade jar, Rabbit, stamped/1931, 5x4½" 500.00
Marmalade jar, Swan, stamped, 5x4¼" 650.00

Mustard jar, Elephant, flat lid with tiny finial, rare, $1,200.00. (Photo courtesy Smith & Jones Inc.)

Olive dish, Rabbit, stamped, 1¾x8" 475.00
Paperweight, Crouching Rabbit figural, stamped/registered, 1½x3" 450.00
Paperweight, frog figural, sgn CD (Charles Davenport), 2⅛" 600.00
Pitcher, Night & Morning, roosters/hens/smiling sun/owl, 5" 600.00
Pitcher, Rabbit, long neck, #5, stamped/registered, rpr, 5¼" 300.00
Pitcher, water; Rabbit, stamped/imp, 8½x7½" 975.00
Plate, Azalea, stamped/registered/imp, 8½", EX 300.00
Plate, Bird in Potted Orange Tree, stamped, 8⅝" 475.00
Plate, Bird in Potted Orange Tree, stamped/imp, 6" 425.00
Plate, Butterfly, stamped, 6¼" 400.00
Plate, Clover, stamped/imp, 10" 1,100.00
Plate, Crab, stamped, 8¼" 265.00

Plate, Day Lily, stamped, 6" 950.00
Plate, Elephant, stamped/1931/imp, 7½" 825.00
Plate, French Mushroom, stamped/imp, 8¼" 525.00
Plate, Grape, Maude Davenport, stamped/imp, 10" 375.00
Plate, Grape, stamped/imp, 8½" 300.00
Plate, Grape, stamped/registered, 9¾" 350.00
Plate, Horse Chestnut, bl ink stamp, 8½" 300.00
Plate, Horse Chestnut, stamped, 6" 250.00
Plate, Horse Chestnut, stamped, 10" 350.00
Plate, Iris, stamped/imp, 6", NM 275.00
Plate, Lobster, registered/imp, 6¼" 475.00
Plate, Lobster & Crab, stamped/imp, 6", pr 1,100.00
Plate, Lunar Moth, stamped/imp, 8¾" 750.00
Plate, Mushroom, Maude Davenport, stamped/imp, 6" 500.00
Plate, Polar Bear, registered/imp, 6¼" 575.00
Plate, Polar Bear, stamped, 9¾" 800.00
Plate, Pond Lily, imp, 10" 400.00
Plate, Pond Lily, stamped/imp, 8½" 300.00
Plate, Pond Lily, stamped/registered/imp, 6" 225.00
Plate, Poppy, stamped, 8½" 700.00
Plate, Rabbit, imp, 8½" 275.00
Plate, Rabbit, Maude Davenport, stamped/imp, 10" 300.00
Plate, Rabbit, stamped, 6" 200.00
Plate, Rabbit, stamped/registered/imp, 7½" 200.00
Plate, Rabbit, stamped/registered/imp, 9½" 275.00
Plate, Rabbit (2-eared), Maude Davenport, stamped/imp, 8½" ...325.00
Plate, Snow Tree, registered/imp, 6⅛" 250.00
Plate, Snow Tree, stamped/registered/imp, 8¼" 300.00
Plate, Snow Tree, 10" 325.00
Plate, Swan, stamped/imp, 8½" 350.00
Plate, Tapestry Lion, stamped/imp, 8½" 1,200.00
Plate, Tufted Duck, imp, 8½" 350.00
Plate, Turkey, stamped, 7⅝" 325.00
Plate, Turkey, stamped/imp, 10" 400.00
Plate, Wild Rose, Hugh Robertson, 9¼" 2,500.00
Platter, fish; Rabbit, stamped, 1¼x12¼" 1,800.00
Shakers, Rabbit, ped ft, stamped, 3¾x2¼", pr 495.00
Star dish, Oriental Poppy, stamped/registered, 1½x7½" 900.00
Stein, Rabbit, Maude Davenport, stamped/imp, 4x5½" 495.00
Sugar bowl, Rabbit, Maude Davenport, w/lid, incised/stamped, 4¾" 400.00
Tea stand, Rabbit, short ped, stamped/imp, 1x6" 400.00
Toothpick holder, boot form, pnt bl lace, stamped, 2½x2" 500.00

Miscellaneous

Vase, frothy chocolate/indigo/gr mottle, bruise, 6x3¾" 800.00
Vase, irid oxblood, sgn Robertson, 7½" 1,500.00
Vase, multi-earth tone in streaky gloss w/wht int, experimental, 8x6" ..1,200.00
Vase, poppies, bl & wht on mottled gr, shouldered, sgn BW, 10"...16,000.00
Vase, red oil spots w/overall irid, swollen form, 6½" 1,000.00
Vase, tan & bl drips on thick brn, shouldered, 7½" 850.00
Vase, thickly textured bl/wht/gr drip on gray, swollen form, 5½"...800.00

Degenhart

The Crystal Art Glass factory in Cambridge, Ohio, opened in 1947 under the private ownership of John and Elizabeth Degenhart. John had previously worked for the Cambridge Glass Company and was well known for his superior paperweights. After his death in 1964, Elizabeth took over management of the factory, hiring several workers from the defunct Cambridge Company, including Zack Boyd. Boyd was responsible for many unique colors, some of which were named for him. From 1964 to 1974, more than twenty-seven different moulds were created, most of them resulting from Elizabeth Degenhart's work and creativity, and over 145 official colors were developed. Elizabeth died in 1978, requesting that the ten moulds she had built while operating the factory were to be turned over to the Degenhart Museum. The remaining moulds were to be held by the Island Mould and Machine Company, who (complying with her request) removed the familiar 'D in heart' trademark. The factory was eventually bought by Zack's son, Bernard Boyd. He also acquired the remaining Degenhart moulds, to which he added his own logo.

In general, slags and opaques should be valued 15% to 20% higher than crystals in color.

Bird w/Cherry Salt, Dark Caramel Slag.................20.00
Bird w/Cherry Salt, Tomato Slag 40.00
Chick Salt, Milk White, 2".....................................20.00
Elephant Head Toothpick Holder, Amethyst.........20.00
Forget-Me-Not Toothpick Holder, Caramel (lt).....20.00
Heart Jewel Box, Crown Tuscan 25.00
Heart Jewel Box, Custard 35.00
Heart Jewel Box, Nile Green 25.00
Heart Jewel Box, Pink 20.00
Hen Covered Dish, Custard, 5"..............................50.00
Hen Covered Dish, Frosted Vaseline (satin) 65.00
Hen Covered Dish, Sapphire, 5"............................30.00
Hen Covered Dish, Taffeta, 5" 60.00
Lamb Covered Dish, Amethyst...............................35.00
Lamb Covered Dish, Opalescent............................40.00
Owl, Amber Dichromatic..40.00
Owl, Bloody Mary #1 ....100.00
Owl, Dark Caramel Slag...75.00
Owl, Desert Sun...30.00
Owl, Jabe's Amber 50.00
Owl, Orchid..30.00
Owl, Ruby Red..55.00
Owl, Shamrock 20.00
Owl, Tiger 30.00
Paperweight, worm & duck on grass, sgn, 3x2¾" 300.00
Pooch, Bittersweet Slag...30.00
Pooch, Buttercup Slag (heavy slag).......................30.00
Pooch, Green Marble 30.00
Priscilla Doll, April Green 80.00
Priscilla Doll, Dark Amethyst 60.00
Robin Covered Dish, Cobalt, 5".............................35.00
Skate Boot (Roller Skate), Crystal 20.00
Skate Boot (Roller Skate), Vaseline 30.00
Texas Creamer & Sugar Bowl, Opalescent.............60.00
Turkey Covered Dish, Amethyst, 5" 40.00

Delft

Old Delftware, made as early as the sixteenth century, was originally a low-fired earthenware coated in a thin opaque tin glaze with painted-on blue or polychrome designs. It was not until the last half of the nineteenth century, however, that the ware became commonly referred to as Delft, acquiring the name from the Dutch village that had become the major center of its production. English, German, and French potters also produced Delft, though with noticeable differences both in shape and decorative theme.

In the early part of the eighteenth century, the German potter, Bottger, developed a formula for porcelain; in England, Wedgwood began producing creamware — both of which were much more durable. Unable to compete, one by one the Delft potteries failed. Soon only one remained. In 1876 De Porcelyne Fles reintroduced Delftware on a hard

white body with blue and white decorative themes reflecting the Dutch countryside, windmills by the sea, and Dutch children. This manufacturer is the most well known of several operating today. Their products are now produced under the Royal Delft label.

For further information we recommend *Discovering Dutch Delftware, Modern Delft and Makkum Pottery*, by Stephen J. Van Hook (Glen Park Press, Alexandria, Virginia). Examples listed here are blue on white unless noted otherwise. See also specific manufacturers. Our advisor is Ralph Jaarsma; he is listed in the Directory under Iowa.

Bowl, Dutch, mc floral w/cobalt borders, 18th C, 5½x10".......**2,200.00**
Bowl, Holland, Oriental scene w/children playing, 5x10"........**1,000.00**
Bowl, punch; English, floral sprays w/gate in bkground, prof rpr, 12"....**975.00**
Chandelier, Holland, floral decor, pewter mts, 6-arm, 20th C, 26" dia..**165.00**
Charger, Dutch, castle landscape, leafy border, 18th C, 13½", EX ...**800.00**
Charger, Dutch, flowers in Oriental pot, late 18th C, 14", EX....**485.00**
Charger, Dutch, 5 flower panels, early, 13" **925.00**
Charger, English, man in landscape, 18th C, 13¼", EX..........**1,725.00**
Charger, English, mc floral, 13¾"................**770.00**
Charger, English, several scenes w/Asian figures in courtyard, 16", G ..**400.00**
Plaque, Dutch, harbor scene w/lg building & ships, 17½x21".....**700.00**

Plaque, Dutch, windmill and water scene, 1900s, 19x14", EX, $1,000.00.
(Photo courtesy Jackson's Auction Gallery)

Tile, Dutch, sea dog, rare, 17th C, 5" sq, G....................115.00
Vase, quintal; flowers & birds, late 1700s, 8½", NM 550.00

Depression Glass

Depression glass is defined by Gene Florence, author of several best-selling books on the subject, as 'the inexpensive glassware made primarily during the Depression era in the colors of amber, green, pink, blue, red, yellow, white, and crystal.' This glass was mass produced, sold through five-and-dime stores and mail-order catalogs, and given away as premiums with gas and food products.

The listings in this book are far from being complete. If you want a more thorough presentation of this fascinating glassware, we recommend *The Collector's Encyclopedia of Depression Glass, Pocket Guide to Depression Glass, Elegant Glassware of the Depression Era, Treasures of Very Rare Depression Glass*, and *Glass Candlesticks of the Depression Years*, all by Gene Florence, whose address is listed in the Directory under Kentucky. See also McKee; New Martinsville.

Key:
AOP — allover pattern   PAT — pattern at top

Adam, ashtray, gr, 4½" 28.00
Adam, bowl, dessert; pk, 4¾" 25.00
Adam, cake plate, pk, ftd, 10" 30.00
Adam, platter, pk, 11¾" 33.00
Adam, tumbler, iced tea; pk or gr, 5½" 65.00
Adam, vase, gr, 7½" 95.00
American Pioneer, bowl, crystal or pk, w/lid, 9¼" ...125.00
American Pioneer, candlesticks, gr, 6½", pr 135.00
American Pioneer, goblet, water; crystal or pk, 8-oz, 6" ...45.00
American Pioneer, pitcher, crystal or pk, w/lid, 5" ...175.00
American Pioneer, plate, gr, hdls, 11½" 40.00
American Pioneer, tumbler, juice; crystal or pk, 5-oz....40.00
American Sweetheart, bowl, berry; cremax, rnd, 9" 50.00
American Sweetheart, bowl, cereal; pk, 6" 17.00
American Sweetheart, bowl, soup; smoke & other trims, 9½"....165.00
American Sweetheart, plate, bread & butter; smoke & other trims, 6" ...22.00
American Sweetheart, plate, salver; pk or monax, 12" 24.00
American Sweetheart, platter, monax, oval, 13" 80.00
American Sweetheart, sherbet, pk, ftd, 3¾" 25.00
American Sweetheart, sugar bowl, red, open, ftd.......165.00
Aunt Polly, candy dish, bl, ftd, hdls 60.00
Aunt Polly, creamer, bl 60.00
Aunt Polly, plate, luncheon; bl, 8" 20.00
Aunt Polly, vase, gr or irid, ftd, 6½" 38.00
Aurora, bowl, cereal; cobalt or pk, 5⅜" 18.50
Aurora, plate, cobalt or pk, 6½" 12.50
Avocado, bowl, salad; pk, 7½" 50.00
Avocado, creamer, crystal, ftd 12.00
Avocado, sugar bowl, gr, ftd 40.00
Beaded Block, bowl, lily; crystal, pk, gr or amber, rnd, 4½" 20.00
Beaded Block, sugar bowl, colors other than crystal, pk, gr or amber...45.00
Beaded Block, vase, bouquet; crystal, pk, gr or amber, 6" 25.00
Block Optic, bowl, berry; gr or pk, lg, 8½" 35.00
Block Optic, ice bucket, gr..45.00
Block Optic, plate, grill; yel, 9" 65.00

Block Optic, sandwich server, pink, center handle, $75.00.

(Photo courtesy Gene Florence)

Block Optic, sherbet, gr, 4¾", 6-oz 18.00
Block Optic, tumbler, pk, ftd, 9-oz..........................17.00
Bowknot, bowl, cereal; gr, 5½" 35.00
Bowknot, tumbler, gr, ftd, 10-oz, 5" 25.00
Cameo, bowl, cereal; yel, 5½" 35.00
Cameo, bowl, cream soup; gr, 4¾" 195.00
Cameo, cake plate, gr, 3-leg, 10" 30.00
Cameo, decanter, gr, w/stopper, frosted, 10" 40.00
Cameo, relish, gr, 3-part, ftd, 7½" 35.00
Cameo, sherbet, pk, molded or blown, 3⅛" 75.00

Cameo, tumbler, juice; pk, ftd, 3-oz........................135.00
Cherry Blossom, bowl, vegetable; gr or Delphite, oval, 9" 50.00
Cherry Blossom, pitcher, pk, PAT, flat, 42-oz, 8"......75.00
Cherry Blossom, plate, dinner; Delphite, 9" 20.00
Cherry Blossom, tray, sandwich; gr, 10½" 33.00
Cherry Blossom, tumbler, pk, PAT, flat, 9-oz, 4¼" ...17.00
Cherryberry, bowl, salad; pk or gr, deep, 6½" 25.00
Cherryberry, butter dish, crystal or irid..................150.00
Cherryberry, comport, crystal or irid, 5¾" 18.00
Cherryberry, plate, sherbet; pk or gr, 6" 12.00
Chinex Classic, bowl, vegetable; decal decor, 9".......25.00
Chinex Classic, butter dish, Brownstone or plain ivory...............55.00
Chinex Classic, plate, sandwich or cake; castle decal, 11½" 28.00
Circle, bowl, gr, 4½" 14.00
Circle, plate, sandwich; gr, 10" 14.00
Circle, tumbler, water; gr, 8-oz, 4" 9.00
Cloverleaf, ashtray, blk, match holder in center, 4" 65.00
Cloverleaf, bowl, cereal; gr, 5" 50.00
Cloverleaf, plate, grill; yel, 10¼" 28.00
Cloverleaf, tumbler, pk, flat, flared, 10-oz, 3¾" 30.00
Colonial, bowl, cream soup; crystal, 4½" 65.00
Colonial, pitcher, gr, 54-oz, 7" 55.00
Colonial, stem, water; gr, 8½-oz, 5¾" 30.00
Colonial, tumbler, lemonade; crystal, 15-oz.............45.00
Colonial, whiskey, pk or gr, 1½-oz, 2½" 16.00
Colonial Block, bowl, pk or gr, 7" 22.00
Colonial Block, pitcher, crystal...............................22.00
Colonial Block, sugar bowl, wht...............................8.00
Colonial Fluted, bowl, cereal; gr, 6" 16.00
Colonial Fluted, creamer, gr 10.00
Colonial Fluted, plate, luncheon; gr, 8" 8.00
Columbia, bowl, low soup; crystal, 8" 25.00
Columbia, plate, bread & butter; pk, 6" 15.00
Coronation, bowl, nappy; Royal Ruby, hdld, 6½" 18.00
Coronation, pitcher, pk, 68-oz, 7¾" 595.00
Coronation, sherbet, gr..85.00
Cube, bowl, dessert; gr, pnt edge, 4½" 9.00
Cube, butter dish, pk 70.00
Cube, creamer, gr, 3⁹⁄₁₆" 14.00
Cube, pitcher, pk, 45-oz, 8¾" 210.00
Diamond Quilted, bowl, cream soup; bl or blk, 4¾" ...25.00
Diamond Quilted, goblet, champagne; pk or gr, 9-oz, 6" 11.00
Diamond Quilted, pitcher, pk or gr, 64-oz 50.00
Diamond Quilted, tumbler, water; pk or gr, 9-oz 9.00
Diamond Quilted, vase, fan; bl or blk, dolphin hdls ...75.00
Diana, ashtray, pk, 3½" 3.50
Diana, bowl, amber, scalloped edge, 12" 20.00
Diana, coaster, pk, 3½" 8.00
Diana, shakers, pk, pr 85.00
Diana, tumbler, crystal, 9-oz, 4⅛" 30.00
Dogwood, bowl, berry; monax & cremax, 8½"...........40.00
Dogwood, bowl, cereal; pk or gr, 5½" 35.00
Dogwood, cake plate, gr, heavy, solid ft, 13" 150.00
Dogwood, sherbet, pk, low ft 35.00
Dogwood, tumbler, pk, molded band 25.00
Doric, bowl, berry; Delphite, lg, 8¼" 150.00
Doric, candy dish, pk or gr, w/lid, 8" 42.00
Doric, plate, salad; gr, 7" 25.00
Doric, tray, gr, hdls, 10" 30.00
Doric, tumbler, pk, ftd, 10-oz, 4" 75.00
Doric & Pansy, bowl, pk or crystal, hdls, 9"............25.00
Doric & Pansy, butter dish, gr or teal 495.00
Doric & Pansy, plate, sherbet; pk or crystal, 6" 7.50
Doric & Pansy, tray, gr or teal, hdls, 10" 38.00

English Hobnail, ahstray, pk or gr, sq, 4½" 25.00
English Hobnail, bonbon, turq or ice bl, hdls, 6½" 40.00
English Hobnail, bowl, nappy; turq or ice bl, rnd, 5" 40.00
English Hobnail, compote, honey; pk or gr, rnd, 5" 25.00
English Hobnail, ice tub, pk or gr, 4" 47.50
English Hobnail, pitcher, pk or gr, rnd, 23-oz 150.00
English Hobnail, plate, turq or ice bl, rnd, 10" 85.00
English Hobnail, stem, sherbet; turq or ice bl, rnd ft, low 12.00
English Hobnail, tumbler, ginger ale; pk or gr, 5-oz 18.00
English Hobnail, vase, pk or gr, flared top, 8½" 135.00
Fire-King Philbe, bowl, salad; pk or gr, 7¼" 80.00
Fire-King Philbe, goblet, crystal, thin, 9-oz, 7¼" 95.00
Fire-King Philbe, plate, grill; bl, 10½" 95.00
Fire-King Philbe, sugar bowl, pk or gr, ftd, 3¾" 135.00
Fire-King Philbe, tumbler, juice; bl, ftd, 3½" 175.00
Floral, bowl, salad; pk or gr, 7½" 32.00
Floral, butter dish, gr 95.00
Floral, plate, dinner; Delphite, 9" 150.00
Floral, tray, gr, sq, closed hdls, 6" 20.00
Floral & Diamond Band, bowl, berry; gr, 4½" 12.00
Floral & Diamond Band, sugar bowl, pk or gr, 5¼" 18.00
Floral & Diamond Band, tumbler, iced tea; pk, 5" 45.00
Florentine No 1, ashtray, crystal or gr, 5½" 22.00
Florentine No 1, bowl, cereal; yel, 6" 30.00
Florentine No 1, comport, cobalt bl, ruffled, 3½" 65.00
Florentine No 1, platter, pk, oval, 11½" 25.00
Florentine No 1, sherbet, crystal or gr, ftd, 3-oz 11.00
Florentine No 1, tumbler, pk, ribbed, 9-oz, 4" 22.00
Florentine No 1, tumbler, water; yel, ftd, 10-oz, 4¾" 24.00
Florentine No 2, bowl, cream soup; yel, 4¾" 22.00
Florentine No 2, coaster, pk, 3¼" 16.00
Florentine No 2, comport, cobalt bl, ruffled, 3½" 65.00
Florentine No 2, tumbler, juice; pk, 5-oz, 3⅜" 12.00
Flower Garden w/Butterflies, bowl, console; blk, w/base, 8½" 150.00
Flower Garden w/Butterflies, candlesticks, amber, 4", pr 42.50
Flower Garden w/Butterflies, creamer, pk, gr, or bl-gr 75.00
Flower Garden w/Butterflies, vase, Dahlia, blk, cupped, 6¼" 155.00
Fortune, bowl, berry; pk or crystal, 4" 10.00
Fortune, candy dish, pk or crystal, w/lid, flat 28.00
Fortune, tumbler, water; pk or crystal, 9-oz, 4" 15.00
Fruits, cup, pk 9.00
Fruits, pitcher, gr, flat bottom, 7" 95.00
Fruits, plate, luncheon; gr or pk, 8" 12.00
Hex Optic, bowl, mixing; pk or gr, 8¼" 20.00
Hex Optic, ice bucket, pk or gr, metal hdl 30.00
Hex Optic, pitcher, pk or gr, sunflower motif in bottom, 32-oz, 5" ..25.00
Hex Optic, platter, pk or gr, rnd, 11" 15.00
Hex Optic, tumbler, pk or gr, 12-oz, 5" 7.00
Hobnail, decanter, crystal, w/stopper, 32-oz 32.00
Hobnail, goblet, milk; crystal, 18-oz 22.00
Hobnail, plate, luncheon; pk, 8½" 7.50
Hobnail, sherbet, pk 5.00
Homespun, bowl, cereal; pk or crystal, closed hdls, 5" 30.00
Homespun, plate, sherbet; pk or crystal, 6" 8.00
Homespun, tumbler, iced tea; pk or crystal, 12½-oz, 5⅜" 35.00
Homespun, tumbler, pk or crystal, str, 7-oz, 3⅞" 24.00
Indiana Custard, bowl, flat soup; French Ivory, 7½" 35.00
Indiana Custard, butter dish, French Ivory 65.00
Indiana Custard, platter, French Ivory, oval, 11½" 40.00
Iris, bowl, berry; crystal, beaded edge, 4½" 45.00
Iris, bowl, salad; irid, ruffled, 11½" 13.00
Iris, creamer, crystal or irid, ftd 13.00
Iris, goblet, cocktail; crystal, 4-oz, 4½" 24.00
Iris, plate, sandwich; irid, 11¾" 30.00

Iris, tumbler, crystal, flat, 4" 150.00
Iris, vase, transparent gr or pk, 9" 225.00
Jubilee, bowl, pk, 3-ftd, 11½" 250.00
Jubilee, cup, yel 14.00
Jubilee, plate, sandwich; pk, hdls, 13½" 85.00
Jubilee, tray, pk, center hdl, 11" 195.00
Laced Edge, bowl, soup; opal, 7" 90.00
Laced Edge, cup, opal 35.00
Laced Edge, mayonnaise, opal, 3-pc 135.00
Laced Edge, plate, salad; opal, 8" 35.00
Laced Edge, tidbit, opal, 2-tier, 8 & 10" plates 110.00
Lake Como, creamer, wht w/bl scenes, ftd 32.50
Lake Como, plate, dinner; wht w/bl scenes, 9¼" 35.00
Laurel, bowl, White Opal or French Ivory, 3-leg, 10½" 40.00
Laurel, candlesticks, White Opal or French Ivory, 4", pr 35.00
Laurel, tumbler, Jade Green or decor rims, flat, 9-oz, 4½" 65.00
Lincoln Inn, bonbon, cobalt bl or red, hdls, sq 15.00
Lincoln Inn, goblet, water; cobalt bl or red 30.00
Lincoln Inn, tumbler, colors other than cobalt bl or red, ftd, 12-oz ...19.00
Lincoln Inn, vase, colors other than cobalt bl or red, ftd, 12" 100.00
Little Jewel, bowl, honey dish; colors, sq, 5½" 15.00
Little Jewel, pickle dish, crystal, 6½" 12.50
Little Jewel, vase, bouquet; colors, 6" 18.00
Lorain, bowl, cereal; yel, 6" 70.00
Lorain, creamer, crystal or gr, ftd 20.00
Lorain, plate, luncheon; crystal or gr, 8⅜" 20.00
Lorain, platter, yel, 11½" 45.00
Madrid, bowl, sauce; bl, 5" 30.00

Madrid, butter dish, amber, $65.00.

Madrid, butter dish, gr 90.00
Madrid, pitcher, pk, sq, 60-oz, 8" 35.00
Madrid, plate, cake; amber, 11¼" dia 22.00
Madrid, platter, gr, oval, 11½" 16.00
Madrid, shakers, amber, ftd, 3½", pr 135.00
Madrid, tumbler, pk, 9-oz, 4¼" 15.00
Manhattan, ashtray, crystal, sq, 4½" 18.00
Manhattan, bowl, berry; pk, hdls, 5⅜" 24.00
Manhattan, comport, crystal, oval 12.00
Manhattan, tumbler, pk, ftd, 10-oz 24.00
Mayfair Federal, bowl, cream soup; amber, 5" 25.00
Mayfair Federal, creamer, crystal, ftd 10.50
Mayfair Federal, plate, grill; gr, 9½" 15.00
Mayfair Federal, platter, amber, oval, 12" 30.00
Mayfair/Open Rose, bowl, cereal; bl, 5½" 55.00
Mayfair/Open Rose, bowl, cream soup; pk, 5" 65.00
Mayfair/Open Rose, cake plate, gr, ftd, 10" 150.00
Mayfair/Open Rose, goblet, water; pk, 9-oz, 5¾" 80.00
Mayfair/Open Rose, plate, luncheon; bl, 8½" 55.00
Mayfair/Open Rose, platter, bl, oval, open hdls, 12" 75.00
Mayfair/Open Rose, platter, grill; yel, hdls, 11½" 125.00

Mayfair/Open Rose, shakers, pk, flat, pr 65.00
Mayfair/Open Rose, sherbet, bl, flat, 2¼" 165.00
Mayfair/Open Rose, tumbler, yel, ftd, 10-oz, 5¼" 225.00
Miss America, bowl, berry; gr, 4½" 15.00
Miss America, bowl, pk, curved in at top, 8" 95.00
Miss America, butter dish, crystal 210.00
Miss America, goblet, wine; Royal Ruby, 3-oz, 3¾" 325.00
Miss America, pitcher, pk, 65-oz, 8" 165.00
Miss America, plate, gr, 6¾" 14.00
Miss America, platter, crystal, oval, 12¼" 15.00
Miss America, tumbler, iced tea; pk, 14-oz, 5¾" 110.00
Moderntone, bowl, cream soup; cobalt, ruffled, 5" 65.00
Moderntone, cheese dish, cobalt, w/metal lid, 7" 395.00
Moderntone, plate, sandwich; amethyst, 10½" 40.00
Moderntone, tumbler, amethyst, 9-oz 30.00
Moondrops, bowl, cream soup; colors other than bl or red, 4¼" ...40.00
Moondrops, creamer, bl or red, regular, 3¾" 16.00
Mt Pleasant, bowl, fruit; amethyst, blk or cobalt, sq, ftd, 9¼" 35.00
Mt Pleasant, candlesticks, pk or gr, 1-light, pr 20.00
Mt Pleasant, mint dish, amethyst, blk or cobalt, center hdl, 6" 25.00
Mt Pleasant, vase, amethyst, black or cobalt, 7¼" 35.00
New Century, bowl, cream soup; gr or crystal, 4¾" 22.00
New Century, pitcher, pk, cobalt or amethyst, w/ or w/o ice lip, 80-oz...42.00
New Century, plate, breakfast; gr or crystal, 7⅛" 10.00
New Century, shakers, gr or pk, pr 40.00
Newport, bowl, berry; cobalt or amethyst, lg, 8¼" 45.00
Newport, creamer, cobalt 16.00
Newport, plate, dinner; cobalt or amethyst, 8¾" 30.00
Newport, platter, amethyst, oval, 11¾" 43.00
No 610 Pyramid, bowl, master berry; pk, 8½" 55.00
No 610 Pyramid, ice tub, crystal 95.00

No. 610 Pyramid, pitcher, pink, $350.00.

No 612 Horseshoe, bowl, cereal; gr, 6½" 30.00
No 612 Horseshoe, platter, yel, oval, 10¾" 35.00
No 616 Vernon, plate, luncheon; crystal, gr or yel, 8" 9.50
No 616 Vernon, sugar bowl, crystal, ftd 11.00
No 616 Vernon, tumbler, gr, ftd, 5" 45.00
No 618 Pineapple & Floral, bowl, salad; amber or red, 7" 10.00
No 618 Pineapple & Floral, creamer, crystal, dmn shape 9.00
No 618 Pineapple & Floral, platter, amber or red, closed hdls, 11" ...18.00
No 618 Pineapple & Floral, tumbler, crystal, 12-oz, 5" 50.00
Normandie, bowl, cereal; pk, 6½" 50.00
Normandie, creamer, irid, ftd 10.00
Normandie, tumbler, water; pk, 9-oz, 4¼" 60.00
Old Cafe, bowl, Royal Ruby, closed hdls, 9" 18.00
Old Cafe, candy dish, crystal or pk, low tab hdls, 8" 14.00
Old Cafe, olive dish, crystal or pk, oblong, 6" 10.00
Old Cafe, sherbet, Royal Ruby, low ft, 3¾" 12.00
Old English, bowl, pk, gr or amber, flat, 4" 22.00
Old English, goblet, pk, gr or amber, 8-oz, 5¾" 35.00
Ovide, bowl, berry; decor wht, lg, 8" 22.50
Ovide, candy dish, gr, w/lid 22.00
Ovide, cup, blk 7.50
Ovide, plate, luncheon; Art Deco, 8" 60.00
Oyster & Pearl, bowl, fruit; wht & fired-on gr or pk, deep, 10½" 25.00
Oyster & Pearl, candle holders, Royal Ruby, 3½", pr 65.00
Oyster & Pearl, relish dish, crystal or pk, oblong, divided, 10½" ..18.00
Parrot, bowl, berry; amber, 5" 23.00
Parrot, butter dish, gr 425.00
Parrot, tumbler, gr, ftd, heavy, 5¾" 195.00
Patrician, bowl, cereal; pk, 6" 25.00
Patrician, pitcher, amber or crystal, molded hdl, 75-oz, 8" 135.00
Patrician, plate, grill; amber or crystal, 10½" 14.00
Patrician, sherbet, gr 14.00
Patrician, tumbler, pk, 9-oz, 4¼" 26.00
Patrick, bowl, fruit; yel, hdls, 9" 145.00
Patrick, goblet, juice; pk, 6-oz, 4¾" 80.00
Patrick, mayonniase, yel, 3-pc 150.00
Patrick, tray, pk, center hdl, 11" 155.00
Pebbled Rim, bowl, vegetable; all colors, ruffled edge, shallow 28.00
Pebbled Rim, plate, bread/butter; all colors, 6" 5.00
Petalware, bowl, berry; crystal, lg, 9" 8.50
Petalware, bowl, cereal; pk, 5¾" 14.00
Petalware, sherbet, red trim or floral, low ft, 4½" 38.00
Petalware, sugar bowl, cremax, monax, florette, or fired-on decor, ftd....10.00
Pillar Optic, mug, amber, gr or pk, 12-oz 32.50
Pillar Optic, pitcher, crystal, w/lip, 80-oz 30.00
Pillar Optic, tumbler, juice; Royal Ruby, 5-oz, 4" 30.00
Primo, bowl, yel or gr, 7¾" 40.00
Primo, cake plate, yel or gr, 3-ftd, 10" 45.00
Primo, sherbet, yel or gr 14.00
Princess, bowl, cereal or oatmeal; gr, pk, topaz or apricot, 5" 40.00
Princess, butter dish, gr 100.00
Princess, relish, topaz or apricot, divided, 4-part, 7½" 100.00
Queen Mary, ashtray, pk, oval, 2x 3¾" 50.00
Queen Mary, bowl, berry; pk, flared, 5" 12.00
Queen Mary, candlesticks, crystal, dbl-branch, 4½", pr 22.00
Queen Mary, comport, crystal, 5¾" 15.00
Queen Mary, plate, sandwich; pk, #450, 12" 25.00
Queen Mary, sherbet, pk, ftd 10.00
Raindrops, bowl, cereal; gr, 6" 12.00
Raindrops, creamer, gr 7.50
Raindrops, tumbler, gr, 14-oz, 5⅜" 14.00
Ribbon, bowl, berry; blk, lg, flared, 8" 40.00
Ribbon, candy dish, gr, w/lid 45.00
Ribbon, sherbet, gr, ftd 10.00
Ring, bowl, soup; w/decor or gr, 7" 14.00
Ring, decanter, crystal, w/stopper 28.00
Ring, plate, sandwich; crystal, 11¼" 7.00
Ring, tumbler, juice; w/decor or gr, ftd, 3½" 10.00
Ring, vase, crystal, 8" 17.50
Rock Crystal, bonbon, colors other than red, scalloped edge, 7½" 35.00
Rock Crystal, bowl, red, center hdl, 8½" 250.00
Rock Crystal, bowl, relish; crystal, 5-part, 12½" 45.00
Rock Crystal, cheese stand, colors other than red, 2¾" 30.00
Rock Crystal, goblet, iced tea; red, low ftd, 11-oz 67.50
Rock Crystal, parfait, crystal, low ft, 3½-oz 25.00
Rock Crystal, sandwich server, colors other than red, center hdl ...40.00
Rock Crystal, tray, crystal, ⅞x5⅜x7⅜" 65.00
Rock Crystal, tumbler, whiskey; red, 2½--oz 50.00
Rosemary, bowl, cream soup; pk, 5" 45.00
Rosemary, creamer, gr, ftd 12.50

Rosemary, platter, amber, oval, 12" **16.00**
Roulette, pitcher, crystal, 65-oz, 8" **30.00**
Roulette, tumbler, water; pk or gr, 9-oz, 4⅛" **28.00**
Round Robin, bowl, berry; gr, 4" **10.00**

Round Robin, cup and saucer, $9.00.

(Photo courtesy Gene Florence)

Round Robin, sherbet, irid...**10.00**
Roxana, bowl, wht, 4½x2⅜"..**20.00**
Roxana, tumbler, yel, 9-oz, 4¼"...**22.00**
Royal Lace, bowl, bl, 3-leg, str edge, 10" **95.00**
Royal Lace, cookie jar, gr, w/lid **100.00**
Royal Lace, plate, grill; crystal, 9⅞"...................................**11.00**
Royal Lace, shakers, pk, pr **65.00**
Royal Lace, tumbler, bl, 5-oz, 3½" **60.00**
S Pattern, bowl, berry; yel, amber or crystal w/trims, lg, 8½" **20.00**
S Pattern, tumbler, crystal, 12-oz, 5" **12.00**
Sandwich, basket, amber or crystal, 10"..............................**33.00**
Sandwich, bowl, console; pk or gr, 11½" **50.00**
Sandwich, bowl, teal or bl, hexagonal, 6".............................**14.00**
Sandwich, creamer, red..**45.00**
Sandwich, pitcher, amber or crystal, 68-oz **22.00**
Sandwich, sherbet, teal or bl, 3¼" **14.00**
Sharon, bowl, cereal; amber, 6"...**22.00**
Sharon, butter dish, pk..**60.00**
Sharon, cake plate, gr, ftd, 11½" **65.00**
Sharon, platter, pk, oval, 12½" **33.00**
Sharon, tumbler, gr, thick, 9-oz, 4⅛"..................................**80.00**
Ships, cocktail shaker, bl & wht **38.00**
Ships, plate, salad; bl & wht, 8"...**30.00**
Ships, tumbler, iced tea; bl & wht, 12-oz.............................**25.00**
Sierra, bowl, vegetable; pk, oval, 9¼" **75.00**
Sierra, platter, gr, oval, 11"..**75.00**
Sierra, tumbler, gr, ftd, 9-oz, 4½" **90.00**
Spiral, bowl, berry; gr, lg, 8"..**12.50**
Spiral, pitcher, gr, bulbous, 54-oz, 7⅝" **40.00**
Spiral, sandwich server, gr, center hdl.................................**25.00**
Spiral, tumbler, water; gr, 9-oz, 5" **10.00**
Starlight, bowl, cereal; pk, closed hdls, 5½" **12.00**
Starlight, plate, dinner; crystal or wht, 9"...........................**7.50**
Strawberry, bowl, berry; pk or gr, 4" **12.00**
Strawberry, compote, crystal or irid, 5¾"............................**18.00**
Strawberry, pitcher, crystal or irid, 7¾"............................**175.00**
Strawberry, tumbler, pk or gr, 8-oz, 3⅝"..............................**40.00**
Sunburst, bowl, berry; crystal, 8½"....................................**18.00**
Sunburst, tray, crystal, oval, sm...**12.00**
Sunflower, cake plate, pk or gr, 3-leg, 10" **15.00**
Sunflower, plate, luncheon; pk, 8".......................................**35.00**
Swirl, bowl, console; ultramarine, ftd, 10½" **30.00**
Swirl, creamer, Delphite, ftd **12.00**
Swirl, tray, Delphite, hdls, 10½"..**27.50**
Swirl, vase, pk, ftd, ruffled, 6½"..**23.00**

Tea Room, bowl, celery; gr, 8¼" **35.00**
Tea Room, creamer, gr or pk, 3¼"......................................**27.50**
Tea Room, ice bucket, gr..**60.00**
Tea Room, shakers, pk, pr **65.00**
Tea Room, vase, gr or pk, ruffled edge, 6½" **110.00**
Thistle, bowl, fruit; gr, lg, 10¼"..**295.00**
Thistle, plate, grill; pk, 10¼" **30.00**
Twisted Optic, bowl, cream soup; bl or canary yel, 4¾" **25.00**
Twisted Optic, candy jar, bl or canary yel, w/lid, flat............**85.00**
Twisted Optic, plate, cracker; bl or canary yel, 9½"..............**30.00**
US Swirl, bowl, berry; pk, lg, 7⅞".......................................**16.00**
US Swirl, butter dish, gr or pk **120.00**
US Swirl, vase, gr, 6½"...**30.00**
Victory, bowl, blk, amber, pk or gr, rolled edge, 11"............**28.00**
Victory, gravy boat, bl, w/platter......................................**350.00**
Victory, sherbet, blk, amber, pk or gr, ftd...........................**13.00**
Vitrock, bowl, vegetable; wht, 9½".......................................**15.00**
Vitrock, plate, soup; wht, 9"...**33.00**
Vitrock, sugar bowl, wht..**6.00**
Waterford, bowl, cereal; crystal, 5½" **19.00**
Waterford, creamer, pk, oval...**12.00**
Waterford, lamp, crystal, spherical base, 4" **26.00**
Waterford, sherbet, crystal, ftd, scalloped base **6.00**
Waterford, tumbler, pk, ftd, 10-oz, 4⅞"...............................**27.00**
Windsor, ashtray, crystal, 5¾"..**13.50**
Windsor, bowl, pk, boat shape, 7x11¾"................................**40.00**
Windsor, cake plate, gr, ftd, 10¾".......................................**28.00**
Windsor, shakers, crystal, pr **20.00**
Windsor, tray, gr, sq, hdls..**12.00**

Desert Sands

As early as the 1850s, the Evans family living in the Ozark Mountains of Missouri produced domestic clay products. Their small pot shop was passed on from one generation to the next. In the 1920s it was moved to North Las Vegas, Nevada, where the name Desert Sands was adopted. Succeeding generations of the family continued to relocate, taking the business with them. From 1937 to 1962 it operated in Boulder City, Nevada; then it was moved to Barstow, California, where it remained until it closed in the late 1970s.

Desert Sands pottery is similar to Mission Ware by Niloak. Various mineral oxides were blended to mimic the naturally occurring sand formations of the American West. A high-gloss glaze was applied to add intensity to the colorful striations that characterize the ware. Not all examples are marked, making it sometimes difficult to attribute. Marked items carry an ink stamp with the Desert Sands designation. Paper labels were also used.

Ashtray, 1¼x6¾" dia..**20.00**
Bowl, incurvate rim, blk int, 2x3½"....................................**30.00**
Bowl, 1¾x7¾"...**25.00**
Bowl, 2½x9"..**65.00**
Candle holders, bulbous top, tapered bottom w/base, 3¾x5" dia, pr...**60.00**
Shakers, bulbous top w/tapered bottom, 3½", pr...................**55.00**
Vase, flared rim, 6½x3"...**35.00**
Vase, tapered neck & bottom, 6"..**35.00**
Vase, 3¼x3¼"..**22.00**

Documents

Although the word 'document' is defined in the general sense as 'anything printed or written, etc., relied upon to record or prove something...,' in the collectibles market, the term is more diversified with broadsides, billheads, checks, invoices, letters and letterheads, land grants, receipts, and waybills some of the most sought after. Some documents in demand are those related to a specific subject such as advertising, mining, railroads, military, politics, banking, slavery, nautical, or legal (deeds, mortgages, etc.). Other collectors look for examples representing a specific period of time such as colonial documents, Revolutionary or Civil War documents, early western documents, or those from a specific region, state, or city.

Aside from supply and demand, there are five major factors which determine the collector-value of a document. These are:

1) Age — Documents from the eastern half of the country can be found that date back to the 1700s or earlier. Most documents sought by collectors usually date from 1700 to 1900. Those with twentieth century dates are still abundant and not in demand unless of special significance or beauty.

2) Region of origin — Depending on age, documents from rural and less-populated areas are harder to find than those from major cities and heavily populated states. The colonization of the West and Midwest did not begin until after 1850, so while an 1870s billhead from New York or Chicago is common, one from Albuquerque or Phoenix is not, since most of the Southwest was still unsettled.

3) Attractiveness — Some documents are plain and unadorned, but collectors prefer colorful, profusely illustrated pieces. Additional artwork and engravings add to the value.

4) Historical content — Unusual or interesting content, such as a letter written by a Civil War soldier giving an eyewitness account of the Battle of Gettysburg or a western territorial billhead listing numerous animal hides purchased from a trapper, will sell for more than one with mundane information.

5) Condition — Through neglect or environmental conditions, over many decades paper articles can become stained, torn, or deteriorated. Heavily damaged or stained documents are generally avoided altogether. Those with minor problems are more acceptable, although their value will decrease anywhere from 20% to 50%, depending upon the extent of damage. Avoid attempting to repair tears with scotch tape — sell 'as is' so that the collector can take proper steps toward restoration.

Foreign documents are plentiful; and though some are very attractive, resale may be difficult. The listings that follow are generalized; prices are variable depending entirely upon the five points noted above. Values here are based upon examples with no major damage. Common grade documents without significant content are found in abundance and generally have little collector value. These usually date from the late 1800s to mid-1900s. It should be noted that the items listed below are examples of those that meet the criteria for having collector value. There is little demand for documents worth less than $5.00. For more information we recommend *Owning Western History* by our advisor Warren Anderson. His address and ordering information may be found in the Directory under Utah.

Key:
illus — illustrated   vgn — vignette

Advertising currency, Let' Er Buck, Pendleton Round Up, 1914, EX ..**110.00**
Bank note, Confederate, 1861, for $20, cherub & lady vgn **30.00**
Bill, UT Territory/Central Pacific RR, 1877, preprinted, 8x10"...**23.00**
Billhead, CA blacksmith, vgn, blk on yel, charges for horseshoes, 1903 ...**20.00**
Billhead, Knudson & Ellsworth...Engineers, NY City, 1889 ....**25.00**
Billhead, Lovin & Withers...Merchandise, AZ Territory, 1907, 7x8"...**12.00**
Certificate of disability, Civil War, preprinted, Union officer, 7x9"...**22.00**
Charges, re: stolen gun, TX, 1907, legal-sz pg, EX **22.00**
Check, KS, 1899, Bank of Fort Scott, blk on wht, 3x8" **11.00**
Check, NM Territory, 1889, issued to Mexican, cut/cancelled, 3x6"..**14.00**
Check, UT, 1898, Becker Brewing & Malting, flag/eagle vgn, 4x9"..**14.00**

Check, Wells Fargo Bank, brn on wht, bold title, 1888, 3x7", EX...**20.00**
Claim, 1868, handwritten by family of dead soldier, 5x8" **20.00**
Claim refusal, Dept of Interior, 1894, no record of evidence, 8x8" ..**12.50**
Complaint, TX, 1907, bootlegging in dry county, legal-sz pg, EX....**23.00**
Death certificate, TX, 1895, train accident, handwritten, sgn **25.00**
Deed, Cripple Creek Mining, 1901, preprinted, 11x17", EX **22.00**
Deed, CT, 1798, tract of land, EX...**15.00**
Deed, sheriff's; OK, 1927, foreclosure of mortgage, legal-sz pg **11.00**
Deposit, Denver Mint, 1909, gold bullion, pre-printed, 5x11" **28.00**
Field notes, CA, 1859, survey of valley, handwritten, 7 legal-sz pgs..**23.00**
Flyer, Appeal to Women of US, 1871, suffrage information, 4-pg...**140.00**
Indenture papers, PA, 1779, vellum, 2 wax seals, 15x26" **27.50**
Insurance policy, Nat'l Fire Ins, CT, 1913, ornate title/vgn, 9x14" ..**16.00**
Invoice, MT, 1903, Butte Ice Co, photo vgn, 3x7" **15.00**
Invoice, TX, 1853, Fort Ewell, re: grain shipment, handwritten, 8x10"...**55.00**
Invoice, Union Civil War, 1864, supplies listed, 8x11", EX **30.00**
Land grant, OR, 1896, proxy sgn by Grover Cleveland w/emb seal ...**40.00**
Land grant, soldier's entitlement to NM land, 1860, EX **135.00**
Land receipt, CA ranch, taxes paid, 1876, ornate printing, 5x10"...**15.00**
Ledger, OH River, 1884-87, steamer captain wharf-charges record...**55.00**
Letter, KS/CO, 1892, handwritten, re: purchase of lumber, 5x8" pg ...**13.00**
Letter, NV, 1897, ordering gloves in Austin TX, 8x10" **20.00**
Letter, Omaha NE, 1870, re: title to land, 8x10" **30.00**
Letter, Pasadena CA, 1921, girl writes of fun time to parents, 9-pg ...**5.00**
Letter, San Francisco, 1854, growth/daily life described, 6-pg, EX ..**250.00**
Letterhead, CO, 1891, Levy & Moore RR Contractors, re: purchase, 5x8" ...**22.00**
Letterhead, CO, 1899, general store, typed mortgage concerns, 7x8"....**12.00**
Letterhead, MT 1892, Manhattan Malting Co, ornate vgn/seal, 8x11"...**18.00**
Letterhead, NE, 1910, Willow Springs Distillery, vgn, re: prices, 7x8" ...**15.00**
Letterhead, NV, 1910, typed, purchase of stock, 1-pg **14.00**
Letterhead, OK, 1910, Osage Bank, Indian vgn, re: warrants, 8x10"...**15.00**
Letterhead, OK Indian Agency in Muskogee, 1912, guardianships, EX...**27.00**
Letterhead, OK Sheriff, 1910, re: summons of man, 8x11"............**17.50**
Letterhead, PA Nat'l Guard, 1895, handwritten inquiry, 8x11" **10.00**
Letterhead, Sacramento CA, 1882, County Treasurer, re: taxes, 6x8" ...**13.00**
Letterhead, Society of Montana Pioneers, 1900, activities, 8x11" ..**18.00**
Letterhead, War Dept Adjutant General's Office, 1869, explains forms ..**20.00**
Letterhead, Wells Fargo, 1915, re: quarantine of livestock, 8x11" pg...**20.00**
Letterhead, WY, 1886, blksmith, horse vgn, acknowledges payment, 5x8" ...**30.00**
Letters, TX, 1911-12, re: land purchase/costs/types/etc, 3 for........**12.00**
Letters, UT, ca 1915, re: family news/illnesses/etc, ea 4-pg, 3 for ..**12.50**
Marriage certificate, PA, 1900, 16x20" in orig silver fr.................**50.00**
Muster roll, N Cumberlandy Co Blues who marched in 1814, 8x12", EX...**35.00**

North Carolina 50¢ note from the Civil War, dated 1864, faded, G, $20.00.

Order, ID Territory, 1887, re: purchase of beer, handwritten pg **25.00**
Pay order, AZ Territory, 1889, preprinted, work as teamster, 3x8" ...**20.00**
Pay order, 1870, pre-printed, service in Army **50.00**
Pay voucher, Civil War officer's pay to Negro servants, preprinted **45.00**

Poster, reward; MO, 1918, escaped convict, $50 reward, 8x9" **25.00**
Promissory note, CA, 1884, Nat'l Bank of Do Mills, preprinted ...**25.00**
Prospectus, CO/AZ mining, 1905, 4x6", 12-pg, EX **25.00**
Receipt, CA Pioneer Assoc, 1877, preprinted, vgn, 3x8", EX **22.00**
Receipt, MT, 1878, preprinted, re: purchase of hay, 3x8" **30.00**
Receipt, 1997, purchase of steer for $19, EX **25.00**
Report, NAACP Legal Defense Fund, 1964, 2-sided, 9x14", EX ..**20.00**
Report, 1808, health inspection of ship, for entering port, EX **10.00**
Satisfaction of mortgage, NE, 1882, 2-party/notarized, legal sz......**12.00**
Sight draft, MT, 1891, issued to Oriental, cut/cancelled, 4x8" **35.00**
Warrant, MT, 1890, Stock Indemnity Fund, horse/bull vgn, 4x9" ...**22.00**
Warrant, treasury; TX, 1864, for $3, EX **25.00**
Will, Buckingham Co/1855, handwritten, lists children/slaves, 8x12"...**100.00**

Dollhouses and Furnishings

Dollhouses were introduced commercially in this country late in the 1700s by Dutch craftsmen who settled in the east. By the mid-1800s, they had become meticulously detailed, divided into separate rooms, and lavishly furnished to reflect the opulence of the day. Originally intended for the amusement of adults of the household, by the late 1800s their status had changed to that of a child's toy. Though many early dollhouses were lovingly hand fashioned for a special little girl, those made commercially by such companies as Bliss and Schoenhut are highly valued.

Furniture and furnishings in the Biedermeier style featuring stenciled Victorian decorations often sell for several hundred dollars each. Other early pieces made of pewter, porcelain, or papier-mâché are also quite valuable. Certainly less expensive but very collectible, nonetheless, is the quality, hallmarked plastic furniture produced during the 1940s by Renwal and Acme, and the 1960s Petite Princess line produced by Ideal. For more information, see *Schroeder's Collectible Toys, Antique to Modern*. Our advisor for this category is Barbara Rosen; she is listed in the Directory under New Jersey. See also Miniatures.

Furnishings

Acme/Thomas, carriage, any color, ea **6.00**
Acme/Thomas, shoofly, dk bl w/yel horse head......**18.00**
Allied/Pyro, bed, red w/wht spread **10.00**
Allied/Pyro, cupboard, corner; aqua......**8.00**
Arcade, bathtub, wht, G pnt......**125.00**
Arcade, bedroom set, 6-pc, gr-pnt CI, EX......**1,430.00**
Ardee, chair, ivory w/brn......**10.00**
Ardee, sofa, ivory w/brn **15.00**
Best, cradle, bl **4.00**
Blue Box, bed, lt brn w/bl spread **5.00**
Blue Box, piano & stool **15.00**
Fisher-Price, kitchen set, #252 ......**15.00**
Fisher-Price, stove/hood unit, yel **5.00**
Fisher-Price, table, kitchen; wht w/red marble top **3.00**
Ideal, birdbath, marbleized ivory **18.00**
Ideal, buffet, dk brn or dk marbleized maroon, ea **10.00**
Ideal, buffet, red......**15.00**
Ideal, china closet, red......**20.00**
Ideal, fireplace, brn......**35.00**
Ideal, sofa, any color, ea......**22.00**
Ideal Petite Princess, bench, vanity; #4502-1 ......**25.00**
Ideal Petite Princess, books & bookends, #4428-9, ea......**5.00**
Ideal Petite Princess, candelabrum, Royal #4439-6 ......**15.00**
Ideal Petite Princess, hamper, #4499-0 ......**25.00**
Ideal Petite Princess, wastebasket, #4501-3 ......**20.00**
Ideal Young Decorator, chair, kitchen; wht **10.00**
Ideal Young Decorator, television, complete **100.00**

Irwin, Garden Set, 5-pc, MOC **75.00**
Jaydon, buffet, reddish brn......**4.00**
Jaydon, sink, bathroom; ivory **10.00**
Marx, iron, hard plastic, wht, ¾" scale **8.00**
Marx, juke box, hard plastic, yel or red, ½" scale, ea......**20.00**
Marx, swimming pool, hard plastic, red, ¾" scale **10.00**
Marx Little Hostess, chair, occasional; yel......**12.00**
Marx Little Hostess, refrigerator, avocado **25.00**
Mattel Littles, sofa......**8.00**
Plasco, buffet, any color, ea **4.00**
Plasco, doll, baby **20.00**
Plasco, tub, any color, ea **4.00**
Reliable, piano & bench, rust **45.00**
Reliable, radio, floor; rust **15.00**
Renwal, broom, metallic bl hdl......**75.00**
Renwal, chair, club; dk bl base **15.00**
Renwal, doll, father, plastic rivets, brn suit **30.00**
Renwal, doll, father; plastic rivets, all tan **25.00**
Renwal, server w/opening drw, brn w/stenciling......**12.00**
Renwal, telephone, red & yel......**22.00**
Renwal, tricycle, yel w/bl & red......**25.00**
Renwal, vanity w/finials & mirror, brn **18.00**
Strombecker, bed, pk, 1940s, ¾" scale **8.00**
Strombecker, clock, lt gr or walnut, ¾" scale, ea **10.00**
Strombecker, tub, any, ¾" scale, ea......**10.00**
Tomy Smaller Homes, armoire, w/hangers......**15.00**
Tomy Smaller Homes, bed, canopy......**15.00**
Tootsietoy, chair, bedroom; bl or pk **7.00**
Tootsietoy, chair, simple bk w/arms, dk brn **8.00**

Tootsietoy, dining room set, table, six chairs, and five other pieces, G in original box, $125.00.

Tootsietoy, lamp, table; bl......**45.00**
Tootsietoy, tea cart, dk brn......**22.00**

Houses, Shops, and Single Rooms

Bliss, Garden House, 1-story, paper on wood, brass trim, 16x15", VG...**1,100.00**
Bliss, Wild Rose Cottage, 1-story, paper on wood, 11x13x9", EX ...**1,320.00**
Christian Hacker, 2-story mansion, 4 rooms/foyer, pnt wood, 27x22", EX **2,420.00**
Converse, 2-story, 2 rooms, wood, red/wht/bl, complete, 18x11x7", EX...**915.00**
Durable Toys & Novelty, General Grocery, tin/cloth awning, 13", VG ...**500.00**
Dutch, 2-story mansion w/6 rooms (1 outdoor), ornate, 1860s, VG+..**6,050.00**
France, Ecole (Schoolroom), paper on wood, complete, 16x22", EX...**1,750.00**
Germany, kitchen, 3-sided, complete w/celluloid doll, 22x19x17", EX...**1,375.00**
Gottschalk, parlor, wood, accessories/5 china dolls, ornate, 15x24x14"...**3,025.00**
Gottschalk, 2-story Victorian, 2 rooms, wood, porch, 28x17", EX+ ..**2,100.00**
Irish, 2-story Georgian, pnt wood/glass windows, 1760-80, 26x18", VG....**8,800.00**
Louvre/France, bedroom, box w/fold-down front, ornate, 17x9", EX....**525.00**
Marx, ABC Nursery, ½" scale, EX **60.00**
Mosher, log cabin, 2-story, paper on wood, deer head, 17x12x10", VG...**500.00**

Schoenhut, 1-room, 'brick' & 'stone' facade, roof opens, 12x14", VG **275.00**
Schoenhut, 2-story Tudor, 4 rooms, electric, complete, 19x18", EX....**935.00**
T Cohn, 2-story, ¾" scale, EX...**75.00**
Tynie Toy, 2-story New England townhouse/garden, electric, 29x49x17" **17,250.00**
Wolverine, Corner Grocery, litho tin, EX **475.00**

Dolls

To learn to invest your money wisely as you enjoy the hobby of doll collecting, you must become aware of defects which may devaluate a doll. In bisque, watch for eye chips, hairline cracks and chips, or breaks on any part of the head. Composition should be clean, not crazed or cracked. Vinyl and plastic should be clean with no pen or crayon marks. Though a quality replacement wig is acceptable for bisque dolls, composition and hard plastics should have their originals in uncut condition. Original clothing is a must except in bisque dolls, since it is unusual to find one in its original costume.

It is important to remember that prices are based on condition and rarity. When no condition is noted, either in the line listing or the subcategory narrative, dolls are assumed to be in excellent condition. In relation to bisque dolls, excellent means having no cracks, chips, or hairlines, being nicely dressed, shoed, wigged, and ready to to be placed into a collection. Some of our values are for dolls that are 'mint in box' or 'never removed from box.' As a general rule, a mint-in-the-box doll is worth twice as much (or there about) as one mint, no box. The same doll, played with and in only good condition, is worth half as much (or even less) than the mint-condition doll. Never-removed-from-box examples sell at a premium; allow an additional 10% to 20% over MIB prices for a doll in this pristine condition.

For a more thorough study of the subject, refer to *Modern Collectible Dolls, Volumes IV* and *V,* by Patsy Moyer; *Doll Values, Antique to Modern, Eighth Edition,* by Barbara DeFeo and Carol Stover; *American Character Dolls* by Judith Izen; *Arranbee Dolls* by Susanne L. DeMillar and Dennis J. Brevik; *Small Dolls of the 40s and 50s* by Carol J. Stover; *Collector's Guide to Horsman Dolls* by Don Jensen; *Encyclopedia of Nancy Ann Storybook Dolls* by Elaine M. Pardee and Jackie Robertson; *The World of Raggedy Ann Collectibles* by Kim Avery; *Collector's Guide to Dolls of the 1960s and 1970s, Volumes I* and *II,* by Cindy Sabulis; *Collector's Encyclopedia of American Composition Dolls, 1900 – 1950,* by Ursula R. Mertz; and *Collector's Guide to Celebrity Dolls,* by David Spurgeon. Several other book are referenced throughout this category. All are published by Collector Books.

Key:
bjtd — ball-jointed
blb — bent limb body
b/o — battery operated
c/m — closed mouth
hh — human hair
hp — hard plastic
jtd — jointed
MIG — Made In Germany
NC — no clothes
o/c/e — open closed eyes
o/c/m — open closed mouth

OC — original clothes
o/m — open mouth
p/e — pierced ears
pwt — paperweight
RpC — replaced clothes
ShHd — shouder head
ShPl — shoulder plate
SkHd — socket head
str — straight
trn — turned

American Character

AC or Petite mk baby, compo/cloth, all orig, 14" **185.00**
Baby, hp head, vinyl body, RpC, 12", EX **60.00**
Bessie the Bashful Bride, Whimsie, stuffed vinyl, 1960, MIB......**225.00**
Bottletot, compo/cloth, crier, sleep eyes, o/m, 1926, OC, 13", EX ...**250.00**
Carol Ann Beery, compo Patsy type, sleep eyes, c/m, OC, 13", EX..**415.00**
Eloise, cloth character, orange yarn hair/crooked smile, 1950s, 15", G....**150.00**

Little Miss Echo, hp/vinyl, talker, RPC, 1964, 30", EX **65.00**
Mary Make Up, vinyl, high-heels, no-grow hair, OC, 1965-66, 11", M...**75.00**
Peggy, compo, jtd, scowling, pnt eyes & hair, 1928, OC, 13", EX **500.00**
Ricky Jr, vinyl 5-pc body, sleep eyes, OC, 1953, 20", M.............**225.00**
Sally, compo ShPl, cloth body, ringlets, OC, 1934, 24", EX........**375.00**
Sally Says, plastic & vinyl, talker, OC, 1965, 19", M **70.00**

Sweet Sue, hard plastic, all original, 17", MIB, $525.00. (Photo courtesy McMasters Harris Auctions)

Sweet Sue Sophisticate Bride, vinyl head, earrings, OC, 19", M ...**250.00**
Tiny Tears, hp & vinyl, 1950-62, OC, 8", M...............................**75.00**
Toodles, hp/vinyl, 1960s, 11", w/wardrobe+accessories, MIB **285.00**
Tressy, Black; vinyl, high-heels, OC, 1960s, 11", minimum value **300.00**

Annalee

Barbara Annalee Davis has been making her dolls since 1950. What began as a hobby, very soon turned into a commercial venture. Her whimsical creations range from tiny angels atop powder puff clouds to funky giant frogs, some 42" in height. In between there are dolls for every occasion (with Christmas being her specialty), all characterized by their unique construction methods (felt over flexible wire framework) and wonderful facial expressions. Naturally, some of the older dolls are the most valuable (though more recent examples are desirable as well, depending on scarcity and demand), and condition, as usual, is very important. To date your doll, look at the tag. If made before 1986, that date is only the copyright date. (Dolls made after 1986 do carry the manufacturing date.) Dolls from the '50s have a long white red-embroidered tag with no date. From 1959 to 1964, that same tag had a date in the upper right-hand corner. From 1965 until 1970, it was folded in half and sewn into the seam. In 1970, a satiny white tag with a date preceded by a copyright symbol in the upper right-hand corner was used. In '75, the tag was a long white cotton strip with a copyright date. This tag was folded over in 1982, making it shorter. Our advisor for Annalee dolls is Jane Holt; she is listed in the Directory under New Hampshire.

Angel on cloud, 1992, 5"..**20.00**
Ballerina on music box, 1991, 7" **40.00**
Be My Honey Bear, phrase & red heart on wht undershirt, 1985-86, 18"....**85.00**
Bear on sled, 1988, 10" **45.00**
Bellhop, assorted colors, 1963, 24" **750.00**
Boy building boat, 1957, 10"..**700.00**
Boy building snowman, 1993, 7"...**30.00**
Boy w/firecracker, red & wht shirt, bl shorts, 1984, 7".................**75.00**
Bunny boy, Easter parade, 1988, 10" **35.00**
Cat, blk, 1991, 12"..**40.00**
Choir boy, red robe, bandage on nose, 1964, 10" **125.00**

Clown, 1980, 10" 45.00
Clown, 1980, 18" 95.00
Clown, 1980, 42" 350.00
Colonial boy & girl mice, he w/flag, she knitting, 1975-76, 7", pr.....125.00
Country Cousins (boy & girl mice), 1970, 7", pr, M 175.00
Dentist mouse, 1984, 7" 35.00
Desert Storm mouse, w/flag & gun, 1991, 7" 50.00
Dracula kid, 1994, 7" 30.00
Duck, in Santa hat, 1987, 5" 20.00
Duck on sled, 1989, 5" 20.00
Elf, pk or yel, 1990, 22" 50.00
Frog aviator, wearing goggles & standing w/flag, 1991, 10" 40.00
Ghost kid, carrying pumpkin, 1987-91, 7" 35.00
Goose, Christmas, 1988, 10" 30.00
Gypsy girl, 1995, 7" 30.00
Hershey kid, dressed in foil-like chocolate kiss, 1994, 7" 50.00
Hockey kid, 1995, 7" 30.00
Horse, brn, w/hearts, 1968, 10" 225.00
Indian boy mouse, 1993, 12" 50.00
Kitten, w/mittens, 1989, 10" 35.00
Lover Boy bear, red vest & wht shirt & shoes, w/heart box, 1996, 10"...45.00
Medicine man w/drum, 1997, 10" 50.00
Monkey, chartreuse, bl or hot pk, 1970, 10" 225.00
Mouse, bowling, 1984, 7" 35.00
Ornament, Be Mine heart, 1985 ....10.00
Reindeer w/flat face, 1966, 36" 375.00
Reindeer w/red nose, 1974, 18" 95.00
Santa, 1986, 48" 350.00
Santa & Mrs Claus, w/cape, 1971, pr 50.00
Santa card holder, various fabrics, 1984, 18" 40.00
Santa on bob-ski, w/sack, 1971, 7" 150.00
Santa's helper, 1993, 10" 35.00
Scarecrow girl, 1994, 12" 55.00
Science Center mouse, w/glass dome, 1989, 7" 150.00
Skunk boy, gr polka-dot vest holding red heart, 1982, 12" 95.00
Spider, 1991, 12" 45.00
Spring Fairy, 1990, 10" 30.00
St Patrick's Day boy dancing & playing accordion, 1996, 7" 35.00
State Trooper, w/glass dome, 1987, 10" 200.00
Sweetheart duck, 1983-84, 5" 30.00
Sweetheart girl mouse, in wht eyelet, w/red heart, 1970s-80s, 7"..20.00
Teacher mouse, 1985, 7" 40.00
Valentine Panda, 1986, 10" 75.00
Windsurfer mouse, Annalee birth date on sail, 1982, 7" 125.00
Witch mouse on broom flying across moon, 1981-85, 7" 50.00
Wizard mouse, 1994, 7" 30.00

Armand Marseille

#225, bsk SkHd, glass eyes, o/m/teeth, jtd compo body, RpC, 19", EX ..4,650.00
#250, domed head, ca 1912, RpC, 15", EX 600.00
#251, SkHd, o/c/m, ca 1912, 13", VG..................................1,100.00
#310, Just Me, bsk SkHd, flirty eyes, c/m, compo body, 1929, 11", VG ...1,300.00
#310, pnt bsk, labeled Vogue outfit, 8", EX 850.00
#341, My Dream Baby, bsk SkHd or flange neck, cloth body, 12", VG ..225.00
#345, Kiddiejoy, bsk SkHd, glass eyes, c/m, RpC, 16", EX...........525.00
#350, glass eyes, c/m, RpC, 14", EX.................................725.00
#350, glass eyes, c/m, RpC, ca 1926, 16", EX.......................2,250.00
#370, o/m, glass eyes, kid body, RpC, 15", EX.......................190.00
#372, Kiddiejoy, ShHd, pnt eyes, o/c/m/teeth, kid body, 18", VG 500.00
#390, compo body, o/m, glass eyes, RpC, 21", EX 450.00
#449, pnt eyes, c/m, RpC, ca 1930, 13", EX............................635.00
#520, domed head, glass eyes, o/m, kid body, RpC, 16", EX.....1,000.00
#570, domed head, c/m, RpC, ca 1910, 12", EX........................1,850.00

#590, sleep eyes, o/c/m, RpC, 1926, 9", EX............................500.00
#630, domed ShHd, pnt/molded hair, pnt intaglio eyes, c/m, 17", VG ...750.00
#700, pnt eyes, c/m, RpC, ca 1920, 12½", EX 1,870.00
#1890, bsk ShHd, glass eyes, o/m/teeth, compo body, RpC, 8", EX ...325.00
#1892, bsk ShHd, kid body, glass eyes, o/m/teeth, RpC, 12", EX ...150.00
#1897, bsk ShHd, glass eyes, o/m/teeth, wig, OC, 16", VG.........135.00
#1901, bsk SkHd, glass eyes, o/m/teeth, kid body, wig, RpC, 26", EX...450.00
Alma, kid body, RpC, 15", EX..200.00
Baby Phyllis, c/m, pnt hair, RpC, 9" 450.00
Rosebud, compo body, 31", VG 775.00

#253, bisque socket head, blue googly eyes, closed smiling mouth, original mohair wig, crude five-piece composition body, nicely replaced clothes, 7", $700.00. (Photo courtesy McMasters Harris Auctions)

Barbie Dolls and Related Dolls

Though the face has changed three times since 1959, Barbie is still as popular today as she was when she was first introduced. Named after the young daughter of the first owner of the Mattel Company, the original Barbie had a white iris but no eye color. These dolls are nearly impossible to find, but there is a myriad of her successors and related collectibles just waiting to be found.

For further information we recommend *The Story of Barbie, Second Edition*, by Kittarah B. Westenhouser; *Barbie, The First Thirty Years*, by Stefanie Deutsch; *Collector's Encyclopedia of Barbie Doll Exclusives and More* by J. Michael Augustyniak; *The Barbie Doll Years* by Patrick C. and Joyce L. Olds. *Barbie Fashion, Vol I, II*, and *III*, by Sarah Sink Eames, gives a complete history of the wardrobes of Barbie, her friends, and her family. *Schroeder's Toys, Antique to Modern*, is another good source for current market values. All these are published by Collector Books.

Allan, 1965, bendable legs, NRFB...............................550.00
Barbie, #1, 1958-59, blond or brunette, MIB, ea from $5,000 to...6,500.00
Barbie, #2, 1959, blond or brunette, MIB, ea from $5,000 to ..6,000.00
Barbie, #3, 1960, blond hair (extra long), orig swimsuit, NM..1,100.00
Barbie, #3, 1960, blond or brunette, orig swimsuit, NM..............950.00
Barbie, #4, 1960, blond or brunette, orig swimsuit, M, ea from $450 to...500.00
Barbie, #5, 1961, red hair, orig swimsuit, NM............................375.00
Barbie, #6, blond, orig swimsuit, EX.................................250.00
Barbie, #6, brunette, MIB, from $525 to 600.00
Barbie, American Girl, 1964, blond, brn or brunette, NRFB, ea ..1,500.00
Barbie, Ballerina Barbie on Tour, 1976, NRFB 125.00
Barbie, Bubble-Cut, 1962, blond or brunette, NRFB, ea............400.00
Barbie, Deluxe Quick Curl, 1976, Jergens, NRFB....................100.00
Barbie, Dramatic New Living, red hair, OC, 1970, NM.............175.00
Barbie, Fabulus Fur, 1986, NRFB 65.00
Barbie, Gold Metal Skater or Skier, 1975, NRFB 75.00
Barbie, Great Shape (Black), 1984, NRFB..............................25.00
Barbie, Kellogg Quick Curl, Kellogg Co, 1974, NRFB 60.00
Barbie, Malibu (Sunset), 1971, NRFB....................................65.00

Barbie, Miss America, Kellogg Co, 1972, NRFB........................175.00
Barbie, Peaches 'n Cream, 1985, MIB 35.00
Barbie, Queen of Hearts, Bob Mackie, 1994, NRFB..................325.00
Barbie, Scottish, Dolls of the World, 1981, NRFB 140.00
Barbie, Standard, brunette, str legs, 1967, NRFB......................600.00
Barbie, Swirl Ponytail, blond or brunette, 1964, NRFB 650.00
Barbie, Ten Speeder, 1973, NRFB..30.00
Casey, Twist 'n Turn, blond or brunette, 1968, NRFB................350.00
Christie, Fashion Photo, 1978, MIB 95.00
Christie, Kissing, 1979, MIB 65.00
Francie, Busy, 1972, NRFB..425.00
Ginger, Growing Up, 1977, MIB 95.00
Ken, Arabian Nights, 1964, NRFB..420.00
Ken, California Dream, 1988, NRFB.......................................30.00
Ken, Hawaiian, 1979, MIB...45.00
Ken, King Arthur, 1964, NRFB..500.00
Ken, pnt blond hair, bendable legs, 1965, NRFB.......................650.00
Ken, Sun Charm, 1989, MIB..25.00
Ken, Walk Lively, 1972, MIB..150.00
Midge, Ski Fun, Toys R Us, 1991, MIB 30.00
PJ, Deluxe Quick Curl, 1976, MIB 65.00
PJ, Malibu, 1978, MIB...55.00
Ricky, orig outfit & shoes, 1965, NM 75.00
Skipper, Deluxe Quick Curl, 1975, NRFB 125.00
Skipper, Growing Up, 1976, MIB 100.00
Skipper, Pepsi Spirit, 1989, NRFB 70.00
Skipper, Western, 1982, NRFB 40.00
Stacy, Twist 'n Turn, blond, 1968, NRFB................................900.00
Tutti, brunette, orig outfit, 1966, NM 85.00
Whitney, Nurse, 1987, NRFB..80.00

Barbie Gifts Sets and Related Accessories

When no condition is indicated, the items listed below are assumed to be mint and in the original box or package (if one was issued). Items in only excellent condition may be worth 40% to 60% less.

Ballerina Barbie on Tour, 1976, MIB.....................................175.00
Barbie Travel in Style, Sears Exclusive, 1968, MIB..................1,500.00
Barbie Wedding Party, 1964, MIB 700.00
Francie & Her Swingin' Separates, Sears Exclusive, 1966, MIB...600.00
Golden Groove Barbie, Sears Exclusive, 1969, NRFB 2,000.00
Happy Birthday Barbie, 1985, NRFB......................................50.00
Loving You Barbie, 1984, MIB...75.00
Malibu Barbie Fashion Combo, 1978, NRFB 80.00
Skipper Party Time, 1964, NRFB 500.00
Superstar Barbie & Ken, 1978, MIB......................................175.00
Talking Barbie Golden Groove Set, Sears Exclusive, 1969, MIB..1,500.00
Tutti & Todd Sundae Treat, 1966, NRFB 500.00

Belton Type

Bru-type face, bsk, o/c/m or c/m, wig, 14", VG 800.00
Bru-type face, EX bsk, o/c/m or c/m, wig, RpC, 18", EX 2,925.00
French-type face, bsk, o/c/m or c/m, wig, 9", VG.......................900.00
French-type face, bsk, o/c/m or c/m, wig, 12", VG 1,500.00
French-type face, bsk, o/c/m or c/m, wig, 16", VG 1,775.00
French-type face, bsk, o/c/m or c/m, wig, 24", VG 2,800.00
French-type face, EX bsk, o/c/m or c/m, wig, RpC, 12", EX.....2,000.00
French-type face, EX bsk, o/c/m or c/m, wig, RpC, 24", EX.....3,700.00
German-type face, bsk, o/c/m or c/m, wig, 18", VG 1,450.00
German-type face, EX bsk, o/c/m or c/m, wig, RpC, 9", EX.....1,100.00
German-type face, EX bsk, o/c/m or c/m, wig, RpC, 23", EX...2,750.00
German-type face, EX bsk, o/c/m or c/m, wig, RpC, 25", EX...3,000.00

Betsy McCall

Am Character, Linda McCall, vinyl, rooted hair, 1959, 36", G 50.00
Am Character, Sunday Best, hp, sleep eyes, 8", MIB..................985.00
Am Character, vinyl, rooted hair, jtd, OC, 1961, 22", NM.........250.00
Am Character, vinyl, rooted hair, jtd, 1961, 22", G.....................30.00
Am Character, vinyl, rooted hair, Patty Playpal type, 1959, 36", NM...325.00
Am Character, vinyl, rooted hair, rnd sleep eyes, 1958, 14", NM...500.00
Horsman, vinyl/hp, sleep eyes, teen type, OC, 1974, 29", NM ...275.00
Horsman, vinyl/hp, sleep eyes, 1961, 12½", G.............................25.00
Rothchild, hp, sleep eyes, pnt lashes, 35th Anniversary, 1986, 8", M....35.00
Uneeda, vinyl, rooted hair, sleep eyes, slim, OC, 1964, 11½", NM....95.00

Boudoir Dolls

Boudoir dolls, often called bed dolls, French dolls, or flapper dolls, were popular from the late teens through the 1940s. The era of the 1920s and 1930s was the golden age of boudoir dolls!

More common boudoir dolls are usually found with composition head, arms, and high-heeled feet. Clothes are nailed on (later ones have stapled-on clothes). Wigs are usually mohair, human hair, or silk floss. Smoking boudoir dolls were made in the late teens and early 1920s. More expensive boudoir dolls were made in France, Italy, and Germany, as well as the U.S. Usually they are all cloth with elaborate sewn or pinned-on costumes and silk, felt, or velvet painted faces. Sizes of boudoir dolls vary, but most are around 30". These dolls were made to adorn a lady's boudoir or sit on a bed. They were not meant as children's playthings! Our advisor for this category is Bonnie Groves; she is listed in the Directory under Texas.

Anita, glass eyes, nude, 1920s, 30", G, minimum value...............150.00
Anita, trn head, all orig, 30", EX, minimum value 425.00
Anita, 1920s, all orig, 30", EX 135.00
Apache male, cloth, all orig, 26", VG......................................225.00
Black child, cloth, all orig, 1930s, 24", VG................................150.00
Blossom, cloth, 1930s, all orig, 30", MIB................................360.00
Blossom, cloth, 1930s, all orig, 30", VG..................................250.00
Bride, all orig, 1940s, 29", VG...125.00
Bucilla kit for making boudoir doll costume, EX, minimum value..125.00
Cloth, Gerling type, 1920s, all orig, 30", VG, from $150 to 300.00
Cloth (possibly Gerling), 1920s, 27", VG.................................275.00
Cloth, Standard quality, OC, ca 1920s, 16", EX 125.00
Cloth, Standard quality, OC, 1920s, 32", EX.............................235.00
Compo, OC, 1915-40, 25", EX...245.00
Compo, OC, 1915-40, 28", EX...375.00
Compo, Standard quality, OC, 1930s, 28", EX 175.00

Cubeb, smoker, all composition, jointed, 1925, 25", EX, from $650.00 to $900.00. (Photo courtesy Bonnie Groves)

Cubeb, smoker, jtd compo, 1925, 25", VG, minimum value **400.00**
Gerbs, cloth, 1920s, Fr, all orig, 25", EX..............................**375.00**
Lenci, Fadette, smoker, 25", VG, minimum value **3,000.00**
Lenci, salon lady, all orig, 25", EX, minimum value **3,000.00**
Lenci, 1915-40, 28-26", EX, ea, minimum value **2,250.00**
Pierrot, felt, all orig, 23", G..**315.00**
Shoes for doll, 3", EX, pr **35.00**
Silk face, bsk arms & legs, Fr, 33", VG, from $300 to.................**600.00**
Smoker, cloth, OC, 1920s, 16", EX......................................**285.00**
Smoker, cloth, OC, 1920s, 25", EX......................................**525.00**
Sterling, all orig, 1930, 27", VG.....................................**185.00**
Sterling, Halloween, all orig, 1930s, 28", G **370.00**
W-K-S, Gypsy, all orig, 25", VG **185.00**

Bru

Bébé Automate (breather/talker), key or lever in torso, RpC, 19", VG ...**4,600.00**
Bébé Brevetè, bsk swivel head ShPl, pwt eyes, c/m, wig, RpC, 14", EX...**13,750.00**
Bébé Gourmand (eater), o/m w/tongue, hinged soles, RpC, 16", VG...**25,000.00**
Bébé Merchant (walker), clockwork mechanism, RpC, 17", VG.....**6,800.00**
Bébé Modele, cvd wooden body, RpC, 19", VG, minimum value....**19,000.00**
Bébé Tetour (nursing), o/m, screw-type key bk of head, RpC, 14", VG ...**7,000.00**
Bru Jne, swivel head, cork pate, pwt eyes, o/c/m/teeth, RpC, 12", EX....**11,500.00**
Bru Jne, swivel head, cork pate, pwt eyes, o/c/m/teeth, wig, RpC, 17"...**17,000.00**
Bru Jne R, bsk swivel head, pwt eyes, o/m/teeth, wig, RPC, 12", EX...**1,400.00**
Bru Jne R, bsk swivel head, pwt eyes, o/m/teeth, wig, RpC, 20", EX...**3,000.00**
Bru Jne R, swivel head, pwt eyes, c/m, wig, RpC, 11", EX **2,500.00**
Bru Jne R, swivel head, pwt eyes, wig, RpC, 19", EX **5,750.00**
Circle Dot Bébé, bsk swivel head, pwt eyes, o/c/m/teeth, RpC, 11", EX...**12,000.00**
Circle Dot Bébé, bsk swivel head, pwt eyes, o/c/m/teeth, wig, 18", VG **13,500.00**
Fashion type, swivel ShHd, c/m smile, wood body, RpC, 16", VG....**4,500.00**
Fashion type, swivel ShPl, c/m smile, kid body/arms, RpC, 13", EX...**3,000.00**
Fashion type, swivel ShPl, c/m smile, kid body/arms, RpC, 21", EX...**5,600.00**
Fashion-type, swivel head, pnt eyes, kid body, wig, RpC, 12", EX...**3,050.00**
Fashion-type, swivel head, pnt eyes, wig, RpC, 15", VG..........**2,500.00**

Celebrity

Andy Gibb, Ideal, 1979, MIB **85.00**
Audrey Hepburn, Breakfast at Tiffany's, Mattel, 1998, 11½", MIB ...**50.00**
Betty Grable, International Doll Co, 1940s, 19", minimum value ..**400.00**
Debbie Boone, Mattel, 1978, 11½", MIB..............................**100.00**

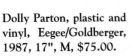

Dolly Parton, plastic and vinyl, Eegee/Goldberger, 1987, 17", M, $75.00.

Dorothy Lamour, print cloth, Film Star Creations, 1940s-50s, 14", NM....**135.00**
Eleanor Roosevelt, Effanbee, 1985, 14", MIB..........................**125.00**
George Burns, in blk tuxedo, Effanbee, 1996, 17", MIB..............**150.00**
Ginger Rogers, World Doll, 1976, MIB................................**100.00**
Groucho Marx, Julius Henry/Effanbee, 1982, 18", MIB..............**150.00**
Harold Lloyd, stuffed cloth, 1920s, 12", EX+........................**100.00**
Humphery Bogart, Casablanca, Effanbee, 1989, 16", MIB..............**30.00**
Ingrid Bergman, Casablanca, Effanbee, 1989, 16", MIB **150.00**
James Dean, in sweater & pants, DSI, 1994, 12", MIB **55.00**
John Wayne, Great Legends, cavalry uniform, Effanbee, 1982, 18", MIB...**150.00**
John Wayne, Great Legends, cowboy outfit, Effanbee, 1981, 17", MIB..**150.00**
Laurel & Hardy, in denim overalls, Goldberger, 1986, 12", MIB, ea ..**55.00**
Leslie Uggams, in lt pk dress, Madame Alexander, 1966, 17", MIB...**350.00**
Liberace, glittery outfit, Effanbee, 1986, 16½", MIB **250.00**
Lucille Ball, in tuxedo & top hat, Effanbee, 1985, 15", MIB **175.00**
Mae West, Great Legends, Effanbee, 1982, 18", MIB **125.00**
Muhammad Ali, Hasbro, 1997, 12", MIB................................**45.00**
Muhammad Ali, Mego, 1976, 9", MOC..................................**150.00**
Patty Duke, Horsman, 1965, rare, 12", MIB...........................**450.00**
Soupy Sales, in yel sweater & red tie, 1960s, 11½", MIB.............**250.00**
WC Fields, stuffed cloth talker, Knickerbocker, 1972, 16", MIB...**75.00**
Willie Nelson, stuffed cloth, Catena Int Inc, 1989, 16", M...........**65.00**

China

Child or boy, short blk or blond hairdo, exposed ears, RpC, 21", EX..**365.00**
French, pnt or glass eyes, cork pate, wig, kid body, RpC, 14", EX..**3,150.00**
Japanese, mk or unmk, blk or blond hair, RpC, 1910-20, 10", EX **125.00**
Kling, mk w/bell & #, RpC, 13", EX...................................**350.00**
KPM, Nymphenburg portrait, ShPl, ca 1901, RpC, 16", VG (auction value)...**1,500.00**
KPM, ShPl, brn hair in bun, 1960s, RpC, 17", EX **4,500.00**
P/e, ornate hairdo, RpC, 17", EX, minimum value **1,550.00**
Queen Victoria, young, RpC, 16", 23", EX **2,500.00**
Sophia Smith, str sausage curls form ridge around head, RpC, 19", EX..**1,325.00**
Swivel neck, flange type, RpC, 13", EX **2,700.00**
1840 style, Covered Wagon, center part w/sausage curls, RpC, 14", EX...**400.00**
1840 style, Covered Wagon, center part w/sausage curls, RpC, 25", EX...**700.00**
1850 style, Alice in Wonderland, snood/headband, RpC, 16", EX...**400.00**
1850 style, bald head, hh or mohair wig, RpC, 12", EX **650.00**
1850 style, Greiner type, glass eyes, various hairdos, RpC, 21", EX...**4,000.00**
1850 style, Greiner type, pnt eyes, various hairdos, RpC, 18", EX, ea...**1,200.00**
1860 style, flat-top blk hair w/center part, side curls, RpC, 10", EX **165.00**
1860 style, flat-top blk hair w/center part, side curls, RpC, 22", EX...**365.00**
1860 style, highbrow w/high forehead & curls, rnd face, RpC, 19", EX...**700.00**
1860 style, Mary Todd Lincoln, blk hair w/gold snood, RpC, 21", EX.....**850.00**
1860 style, w/grape cluster & leaves, RpC, 18", EX..................**2,000.00**
1870 style, Adelina Patti, center part/ringlets, RpC, 14", EX......**325.00**
1870 style, bangs, aka Highland Mary, blk hair, RpC, 19"...........**425.00**
1870 style, Jenny Lind, blk hair in bun or coronet, RpC, 15", VG...**1,150.00**
1880 style, Dolly Madison, blk hair w/ribbon, pnt eyes, RpC, 18", EX...**475.00**
1880 style, overall curls, narrow shoulders, china legs, RpC, 27", EX...**675.00**
1890 style, common or low brow, printed body, RpC, 19", EX....**215.00**
1890 style, jeweled necklace, RpC, 14", VG **240.00**

Cloth

    A cloth doll in very good condition will display light wear and soiling, while one assessed as excellent will be clean and bright.

Alabama Indestructible, baby, 12", EX..................................**1,500.00**
Alabama Indestructible, Black child, 23", EX..........................**6,800.00**
Alabama Indestructible, child, 15", VG **800.00**
Art Fabric Mills, Improved Life Size, printed underwear, 20", EX....**275.00**
Babyland Rag, Black, 1893-1928, 24", EX...............................**800.00**

Babyland Rag, color litho, 1893-1928, 24", EX..................550.00
Babyland Rag, flat pnt face, 16½", VG 450.00
Babyland Rag, molded/pnt faces, 13", VG, ea...............350.00
Beecher, Missionary rag baby, 16", EX 3,450.00
Bing Art, pnt hair, cloth or felt, 15", EX........................650.00
Bing Art, wig, cloth or felt, 16", EX..............................650.00
Chad Valley, Character (Fisherman, Conductor, etc), 18", EX.....775.00
Chad Valley, Character (Pirate, Policeman, etc), glass eyes, 18", EX...1,000.00
Chad Valley, child, glass eyes, 16", EX 725.00
Chad Valley, child, pnt eyes, 18", EX............................625.00
Chad Valley, child, pnt eyes, 9-10", VG 40.00
Chad Valley, Princess Elizabeth, glass eyes, EX.........1,700.00
Chase, baby, fully jtd, RpC, 19", EX..............................700.00
Chase, baby, jtd hips & shoulders only, later, RpC, 15", EX........250.00
Chase, child, molded bobbed hair, fully jtd, 16", EX........1,600.00
Chase, solid dome, simple pnt hair, RpC, 189", EX........625.00
Deans Rag Book Co, lithographed face, RpC, 1905+, 15", EX ...165.00
Drayton, Chocolate Drop, brn w/yarn tufts, printed face, 1923, 14", EX.....550.00
Drayton, Dolly Dingle, printed face, RpC, 1923, 11", EX...........385.00
Fangel, baby, flat face, mitten hands, RpC, 1920-30+, 13"..........425.00
Gund, character, cloth mask face, pnt features, RpC, 19", EX....300.00
Mammy style, pnt or embr features, 1910-20, 16", EX...............285.00
Mammy style, pnt or embr features, 1930s, 15", VG.....................55.00
Mollye, child, mask face, RpC, 13", EX...........................130.00
Mollye, lady, long dress or gown, 16", EX........................175.00
Printed cloth w/printed clothing, cut & sewn, ca 1903, 19", EX ...325.00
Topsy-turvy, 2-heads (1 Black/1 wht), oil pnt, EX 650.00
Wellings, child, glass eyes, RpC, 15", EX 550.00

Effanbee

Bernard Fleischaker and Hugo Baum became business partners in 1910, and after two difficult years of finding toys to buy, they decided to manufacture dolls and toys of their own. The Effanbee trademark is a blending of their names, Eff for Fleischaker and bee for Baum. The company still exists today. For more information we recommend *Collector's Encyclopedia of American Composition Dolls, 1900 – 1950, Volume II*, by Ursula R. Mertz.

Honey, hard plastic, blue sleep eyes, closed mouth, floss hair, original Schiaparelli dress, 18", NM, $450.00. (Photo courtesy McMasters Harris Auctions)

Baby, Black, all compo, pnt face, o/c/m, RpC, 1918+, 6", EX 225.00
Baby Dainty, compo/cloth, RpC, 1912+, 12-14", EX, ea.............245.00
Baby Evelyn, compo/cloth, RpC, ca 1925, 17", EX...................275.00

Baby Lisa Grows Up, hp/vinyl, toddler, 1983, NM in trunk w/wardrobe ...150.00
Barbara Lou, all compo, separated fingers, RpC, 1936-39, 21", EX...900.00
Betty Brite, compo, tousel wig, sleep eyes, OC, 1932, 16", EX....300.00
Bubbles, compo ShHd, o/c/m, sleep eyes, RpC, 1924+, 22", EX....525.00
Coquette/Naughty Marietta, compo/cloth, bow in hair, RpC, 12", EX...400.00
Currier & Ives, hp/vinyl, OC, 12", NM.................................45.00
Dy-Dee Wee, rubber, sleep eyes, drink/wets, OC, 9", EX.............300.00
Grumpty Aunt Dinah, Black, compo w/cloth body, RpC, 14½", EX ..425.00
Gumdrop, vinyl, jtd toddler, sleep eyes, rooted hair, OC, 16", NM....35.00
Historical, jtd compo, hh wig, pnt eyes, OC, 21", EX, minimum value ...1,500.00
Honey Walker, hp walker, OC, 1950s, 14", NM......................350.00
Ice Queen, compo, o/m, skater outfit, 1937+, 17", EX 850.00
Lamkin, compo/cloth, sleep eyes, o/m, crier, compo legs, RpC, 16", EX ..475.00
Mary Ann, compo, o/m, sleep eyes, wig, OC, 1932+, 19", EX 350.00
Patricia (mk)/Ann Shirley, all compo, RpC, 1935-40, 15", EX....550.00
Patsy Baby, compo, pnt or sleep eyes, OC, 1931, 10", EX 350.00
Patsy Joan, compo, OC, 1931, 16", EX..............................550.00
Patsy Mama, compo/cloth, o/m/teeth, swing legs, OC, ca 1926, 29", EX...550.00
Patsy Ruth, ShHd, sleep eyes, cloth body, crier, OC, 1934, 26", EX...1,300.00
Pouting Bess, compo #166 mk head, cork-stuffed body, c/m, RpC, 15", EX ...350.00
Rosemary, compo, OC, 1926, 18", EX..............................350.00
Sister, compo/cloth, pnt eyes, yarn hair, RpC, 1943, 12", EX......175.00
Susie Sunshine, vinyl, fully jtd, rooted hair, sleep eyes, OC, 18", NM ..60.00

Half Dolls

Half dolls were never meant to be objects of play. Most were modeled after the likenesses of lovely ladies, though children and animals were represented as well. Most of the ladies were firmly sewn on to pincushion bases that were beautifully decorated and served as the skirts of their gowns. Other skirts were actually covers for items on milady's dressing table. Some were used as parasol or brush handles or as tops to candy containers or perfume bottles. Most popular from 1900 to about 1930, they will most often be found marked with the country of their origin, usually Bavaria, Germany, France, and Japan. You may also find some fine quality pieces marked Goebel, Dressel and Kester, KPM, and Heubach.

Arms away, china or bsk, bald head w/wig, 6", EX.....................210.00
Arms away, holding item, 4", EX.....................................185.00
Arms away, mk by maker or mold #, 6", EX.............................300.00
Arms away, mk by maker or mold #, 12", EX............................900.00
Arms in, close to figure, bald head w/wig, 4", EX.....................80.00
Arms in, close to figure, bald head w/wig, 6", EX....................115.00
Arms in, decor bodice, necklace, fancy hair or holding article, 3", EX ...135.00
Arms in, hands attached, 5", EX.......................................45.00
Arms in, mk by maker or mold #, 6", EX 155.00
Arms in, papier-mâché or compo, 6", EX................................80.00
Arms in, w/legs, dressed, fancy decor, 7", EX........................400.00
German mk, 4", EX..200.00
German mk, 6", EX..500.00
Japan mk, 3", EX..15.00
Japan mk, 6", EX..50.00
Jtd shoulders, china or bsk, molded hair, 7", EX.....................200.00
Jtd shoulders, solid dome, mohair wig, 6", EX........................400.00
Man or child, 4", EX...120.00
Man or child, 6", EX...160.00

Handwerck, Heinrich

#69, child, bsk SkHd, o/m, sleep eyes, bjtd, wig, RpC, 15" EX 575.00
#79, child, bsk ShHd, c/m, RpC, 15", EX 1,800.00
#79, child, bsk SkHd, o/m, RpC, 13", EX..............................500.00
#89, child, bsk SkHd, o/m, set eyes, wig, RpC, 28", VG 775.00

#99, child, bsk SkHd, sleep eyes, bjtd body, wig, RpC, 15", EX **575.00**
#109, child, bsk ShHd, o/m, kid body, RpC, 14", EX **235.00**
#109, child, bsk SkHd, o/m, RpC, 15", VG **475.00**
#119, child, bsk SkHd, o/m, RpC, 18", EX................................**725.00**
#139, child, bsk SkHd, o/m, RpC, 32", EX **1,350.00**
#199, child, bsk SkHd, o/m, RpC, 22", EX................................**825.00**
No mold #, child, bsk SkHd, o/m, set eyes, bjtd, wig, RpC, 21", EX ...**700.00**

Hertel, Schwab, and Company

#127, child, character face, molded hair/sleep eyes, o/m, RpC, 15", EX **1,350.00**
#130, bsk head, o/c/m/teeth, sleep or pnt eyes, bent-leg, RpC, 9", EX........**325.00**
#130, bsk head, o/m/teeth, pnt eyes, toddler, RpC, 14", EX **600.00**
#131, character face, pnt c/m, RpC, ca 1912, 18", VG, (auction value) ..**1,300.00**
#140, character, laughing o/c/m, glass eyes, RpC, ca 1912, 12", VG **2,550.00**
#142, bsk head, o/m/teeth, pnt eyes, wig, bent legs, RpC, 22" **900.00**
#150, bsk head, o/c/m, sleep eyes, toddler body, RpC, 20", EX **800.00**

Heubach, Ernst

#250, child, o/m, kid body, RpC, 13", EX..................................**250.00**
#251, child, o/m, kid body, RpC, 16", VG **200.00**
#267, baby, SkHd, o/m, glass eyes, 5-pc body, RpC, 14", EX **400.00**
#275, child, ShHd, o/m, kid body, RpC, 27", EX **675.00**
#302, child, o/m, kid body, RpC, 32", EX..................................**900.00**
#320, SkHd, o/m, glass eyes, 5-pc body, wig, RpC, 20", EX.........**550.00**
#338, newborn, solid dome, glass eyes, c/m, cloth body, RpC, 12", EX ...**425.00**
#348, solid dome, glass eyes, c/m, cloth body, RpC, 17", EX **800.00**
#444, baby, Black, RpC, 12", EX **400.00**
#1900, child, o/m, glass eyes, cloth body, Horseshoe mk, RpC, 22", EX.....**415.00**
#1900, child, o/m, glass eyes, kid body, Horseshoe mk, RpC, 12", EX ..**150.00**

Heubach, Gebruder

#5636, character, glass eyes, open mouth with teeth, re-dressed, 15½", $2,100.00. (Photo courtesy McMasters Harris Auctions)

#5689, character, o/m, sunburst mk, RpC, ca 1912, 14", EX....**1,800.00**
#5777, Dolly Dimple, o/m, for Hamburger & Co, RpC, 14", EX....**2,300.00**
#6345, character child, pk-tinted, c/m, RpC, ca 1912, 17", VG....**1,150.00**
#6688, character child, ShHd, molded hair, intaglio eyes, c/m, 10", EX.....**625.00**
#6692, character child, ShHd, intaglio eyes, c/m, RpC, 14", VG ..**650.00**
#7246, SkHd, c/m, RpC, ca 1912, 16", EX **1,300.00**
#7604, character, SkHd, o/c/m, intaglio eyes, RpC, ca 1912, 12", EX ..**725.00**
#7644, character child, pnt eyes, laughing o/c/m, RpC, 17", EX...**1,200.00**
#7847, ShHd, intaglio eyes, smiling c/m/teeth, RpC, 20", VG...**2,100.00**
#7850, Coquette, o/c/m, RpC, 11", EX.....................................**750.00**

#7946, character, pnt eyes, c/m, sq mk, RpC, 7½", EX...............**800.00**
#7972, intaglio eyes, c/m, RpC, 20", EX **2,000.00**
#8221, dome head, intaglio eyes, o/c/m, sq mk, RpC, 14", EX **675.00**
#8316, grinning boy, SkHd, o/c/m/teeth, glass eyes, wig, RpC, 16", EX...**3,400.00**
#9355, o/m, glass eyes, sq mk, RpC, ca 1914, 19", EX..............**1,250.00**

Ideal

Two of Ideal's most collectible lines of dolls are Crissy and Toni. For more information, refer to *Collector's Guide to Ideal Dolls, Second Edition,* by Judith Izen (Collector Books).

Baby, compo w/compo or cloth body, pnt eyes, wig, OC, 1913+, 12", EX ..**100.00**
Baby Crissy, jtd vinyl, auburn rooted grow hair, o/c/e, OC, 24", MIB...**265.00**
Bizzie Lizzie, vinyl, rooted blond hair, o/c/e, power pack, 18", M ..**50.00**
Bonnie Play Pal, vinyl, o/c/e, rooted blond hair, OC, 1959, 24", EX ..**275.00**
Child, compo, pnt eyes, cloth or compo body, OC, 1915+, 13", EX ...**125.00**
Cinderella, compo, flirty eyes, o/m/teeth, hh wig, 1938-39, 13", EX.....**325.00**
Cinderella, compo, flirty eyes, o/m/teeth, OC, 1938-39, 27", EX ..**450.00**
Clarabell, mask face, cloth body, OC, 1954, 16", EX....................**90.00**
Clown Flexy, compo head, wood torso, 1938-42, 13½", EX........**225.00**
Cover Girl, Dana, Black, poseable, jtd hands, OC, 12½", M.........**50.00**
Deanna Durbin, compo, brn sleep eyes, o/m/teeth, OC, 1938-41, 25", EX....**1,100.00**
Dennis the Menace, printed cloth, OC, 1976, 14", M..................**20.00**
Dopey, ventriloquist doll, compo/cloth, OC, 1938, 20", EX........**800.00**
Judy Garland, jtd compo, braids, brn sleep eyes, OC, 13", NM ..**1,000.00**
Kissy, vinyl, rooted hair, o/c/e, press hands for kiss, OC, 22½", M..**155.00**
Liberty Boy (Dough Boy), compo, orig Army uniform, 1918+, 12", EX...**250.00**
Magic Skin Baby, hp head, latex body, o/c/e, pnt hair, OC, 15", EX ..**75.00**
Mama, compo, cloth torso w/crier, wig, OC, 1921+, 20", EX......**300.00**
Snow White, cloth body, mask face, hh wig, 1938, 16", NM......**550.00**
Snow White, jtd compo, pnt hair & eyes, OC, 1938-29, 14½", EX..**200.00**
Sparkle Plenty, hp head, Magic Skin body, yarn hair, OC, 14", EX...**250.00**
Tammy, vinyl/plastic, OC, 1962, 12", NRFB...............................**200.00**
Tara, Black, vinyl, long blk grow hair, o/c/e, OC, 1976, 15½", M .**390.00**
ZuZu Kid, compo/cloth, orig clown costume, 1966-67, 15½", EX ..**450.00**

Jumeau

The Jumeau factory became the best known name for dolls during the 1880s and 1890s. Early dolls were works of art with closed mouths and paperweight eyes. When son Emile Jumeau took over, he patented sleep eyes with eyelids that drooped down over the eyes. This model also had flirty (eyes that move from side to side) eyes and is extremely rare. Over 98% of Jumeau dolls have paperweight eyes. The less-expensive German dolls were the downfall of the French doll manufacturers, and in 1899 the Jumeau company had to combine with several others in an effort to save the French doll industry from German competition.

#1907, some w/Tête Jumeau stamp, o/c/e, o/m, jtd Fr body, RpC, 17", EX ...**2,500.00**
BL Bébé, SkHd, pwt eyes, c/m, jtd compo body, p/e, wig, RpC, 22", EX ...**5,100.00**
Depose E (sz #) J, RpC, 19", EX **5,850.00**
Depose E (sz #) J, RpC, 26", EX **8,000.00**
Depose Jumeau, bsk head, pwt eyes, c/m, p/e, wood body, RpC, 14", EX...**5,000.00**
EJ Bébé, bsk SkHd, pwt eyes, c/m, jtd body, p/e, wig, RpC, 17", EX ...**10,250.00**
EJ w/sz # between, RpC, 17", EX...**6,600.00**
EJ w/sz # between, RpC, 26", EX...**9,000.00**
Fashion type, swivel head, c/m, pwt eyes, p/e, kid body, RpC, 11", EX.....**2,600.00**
Fashion type, wood body, bsk lower arms, RpC, 16", VG **3,800.00**
Jumeau portrait, wood body, RpC, 20", VG..............................**6,300.00**
Portrait, almond eyes, wig, 20", EX **25,000.00**
Tête Jumeau, adult, bsk SkHd, o/m, RpC, 17", EX....................**2,800.00**
Tête Jumeau, child, bsk SkHd, c/m, glass eyes, wig, RpC, 19", EX...**4,650.00**
Tête Jumeau, child, bsk SkHd, c/m, RpC, 12", EX.....................**3,500.00**

Kammer and Reinhardt

#100, character baby, dome head, intaglio eyes, o/c/m, RpC, 20", EX ...**1,100.00**
#109, Elise, pnt eyes, c/m, RpC, ca 1909, 14", EX....................**7,000.00**
#114, Hans or Gretchen, pnt eyes, c/m, RpC, ca 1909, 13", EX ...**3,725.00**
#115, solid dome, pnt hair, sleep eyes, c/m, toddler, RpC, 15", EX .**5,750.00**
#116, Mein Liebling, glass eyes, c/m, RpC, ca 1911, 15", EX ..**4,400.00**
#117N, Mein Neuer Liebling, flirty eyes, o/m, ca 1916, 28", EX...**2,900.00**
#121, o/c/e, o/m, baby body, RpC, ca 1912, 24", EX **1,300.00**
#121, o/c/e, o/m, toddler body, RpC, 14", VG **750.00**
#122, o/c/e, toddler body, RpC, 13", EX...............................**1,100.00**
#127N, domed head (like mold #126), bent-leg baby, RpC, 14", EX...**1,200.00**
#135, o/c/e, o/m, baby body, RpC, ca 1923, 13", EX.................**850.00**
#191, child, dolly face, o/m, o/c/e, jtd body, RpC, 17", EX.........**865.00**
#192, child, dolly face, c/m, o/c/e, RpC, 18", EX....................**2,800.00**
#192, child, dolly face, o/m, o/c/e, jtd child's body, RpC, 9", EX...**1,000.00**
#401, SkHd, glass eyes, o/m, RpC, 19", EX **750.00**
K*R, SkHd, glass eyes, o/m, RpC, 19", EX.................................**750.00**
No mold #, SkHd, glass eyes, o/m, RpC, 12", EX......................**500.00**

Kestner

Johannes D. Kestner made buttons at a lathe in a Waltershausen factory in the early 1800s. When this line of work failed, he used the same lathe to turn doll bodies. Thus the Kestner company began. It was one of the few German manufacturers to make the complete doll. By 1860, with the purchase of a porcelain factory, Kestner made doll heads of china and bisque as well as wax, worked-in-leather, celluloid, and cardboard. In 1895 the Kestner trademark of a crown with streamers was registered in the U.S. and a year later in Germany. Kestner felt the mark was appropriate since he referred to himself as the 'king of German doll-makers.'

#XI or #103, pouty child, c/m, RpC, 20", EX............................**2,600.00**
#108, SkHd, glass eyes, c/m, jtd body, RpC, 16", EX..............**9,000.00**
#128, pouty child, c/m, glass eyes, bjtd body, wig, RpC, 15", EX...**1,000.00**
#129, child, o/m, glass eyes, jtd body, RpC, 15", EX **675.00**
#143, child, o/m, glass eyes, jtd body, RpC, ca 1897, 13", EX ..**1,000.00**
#144, child, bsk SkHd, o/m, glass eyes, bjtd body, RpC, 24", EX.**1,000.00**
#146, child, bsk SkHd, o/m, glass eyes, bjtd body, RpC, 18", EX ...**950.00**
#155, child, o/m, glass eyes, 5-pc or fully jtd body, RpC, 7½", EX ..**925.00**
#171, bsk SkHd, called Daisy, RpC, 18", EX.............................**1,150.00**
#172, Gibson Girl, ShHd, c/m, glass eyes, kid body, RpC, 18", EX..**2,700.00**
#177, character child, SkHd, c/m, glass eyes, jtd body, RpC, 20", EX ..**5,000.00**
#211, character baby, SkHd, glass eyes, o/m, wig, RpC, 12", EX ..**775.00**
#220, character toddler, SkHd, glass eyes, o/m, toddler, RpC, 19", EX..**6,200.00**
#234, character baby, ShHd, o/c/e, o/c/m, RpC, ca 1912, 12", EX....**700.00**
#236, character baby, solid dome, glass eyes, o/m, RpC, 26", EX...**1,650.00**
#247, character baby, SkHd, o/c/e, o/m, RpC, ca 1915, 15", EX..**1,900.00**
#257, SkHd, o/c/e, o/m, RpC, ca 1916, 14", EX..........................**900.00**
#262, character baby, SkHd, glass eyes, o/m, wig, RpC, 18", EX..**1,000.00**
Child, bsk ShHd, o/c/m, plaster pate, kid body, RpC, 1880s, 15", EX....**700.00**
Child, bsk ShHd, o/m, RpC, ca 1892+, 21", EX **500.00**
Child, trn ShHd, c/m, Sz # only, RpC, 1880s, 18", EX...............**850.00**
JDK or unmk baby, solid dome SkHd, glass o/c/e, bent-leg, RpC, 26", EX....**950.00**
Unmk, Baby Jean, solid dome, fat cheeks, RpC, 23", EX.........**2,000.00**

Lenci

Characteristics of Lenci dolls include seamless, steam-molded felt heads, quality clothing, childishly plump bodies, and painted eyes that glance to the side. Fine mohair wigs were used, and the middle and fourth fingers were sewn together. Look for the factory stamp on the foot, though paper labels were also used. The Lenci factory continues today, producing dolls of the same high quality. Values are for dolls in excellent condition — no moth holes, very little fading. Dolls from the 1940s and beyond generally bring the lower prices; add for tags, boxes, and accessories. Mint dolls and rare examples bring higher prices. Dolls in only good condition are worth approximately 25% of one rated excellent.

Baby, pre-1940, 13", EX...**1,500.00**
Baby, pre-1940, 22", EX...**3,200.00**
Celebrity, Jack Dempsy, 18", EX...**35.00**
Character, Bellhop (winking) w/love letter, 11", EX **750.00**
Character, Benedetta, 19", EX..**1,100.00**
Character, Fascist Boy, rare, 14", EX...**1,500.00**
Character, Indian, 17", EX..**3,600.00**
Character, Salome, brn felt, swivel waist, ca 1920, 17", EX.....**3,500.00**
Child, hard face, less ornate costume, 1940s-50s+, 13", EX **400.00**
Child, hard face, less ornate costume, 1940s-50s+, 17", EX **600.00**
Child, soft face, elaborate costume, 1920s-30s, 13", EX............**1,750.00**
Child, soft face, elaborate costume, 1920s-30s, 21", EX............**2,750.00**
Ethnic or Regional, Eugenia, 25", EX...**1,100.00**
Ethnic or Regional, Scottish girl, ca 1930, 14", EX **700.00**
Eye variation, flirty glass eyes, 15", EX.......................................**2,200.00**
Eye variation, flirty glass eyes, 20", EX.......................................**2,800.00**
Eye variation, glass eyes, 16", EX..**1,600.00**
Eye variation, glass eyes, 22", EX..**3,000.00**
Mascot, rare outfit & accessories, 8½", EX **450.00**
Mascot, swing legs, may have loop on neck, 8½", EX **325.00**
Mini, child, 9", EX **400.00**
Mini, Tyrol boy, 9", EX..**375.00**
Modern, ca 1979+, 13", EX..**125.00**
Modern, ca 1979+, 21", EX..**200.00**
Modern, ca 1979+, 26", EX..**260.00**
Smoker, pnt eyes, 28", EX..**2,400.00**

Liddle Kiddles

From 1966 to 1971, Mattel produced Liddle Kiddle dolls ranging in size from ¾" to 4". They were all poseable and had rooted hair that could be restyled. There were various series of the dolls, among them Animiddles, Zoolery Jewelry Kiddles, Extraterrestrials, and Sweet Treats, as well as many accessories. Our advisor for this category is Paris Langford; she is listed in the Directory under Louisiana. Please send SASE for information or contact Paris by e-mail: bbean415@aol.com.

Playhouse Kiddles, five-piece bedroom set, #3848, MIB, $300.00. (Photo courtesy Tamela Storm and Debra Van Dyke)

Animiddle Kiddles, MIP, ea..**75.00**
Aqua Funny Bunny, #3532, MIP..**65.00**
Beach Buggy, #5003, complete, NM **35.00**

Chocolottie's House, #2501, MIP **35.00**
Flower Ring Kiddle, #3741, MIP......................................**50.00**
Heart Ring Kiddle, #3744, MIP **50.00**
Hot Dog Stand, #5002, complete, M **25.00**
Jewelry Kiddles, #3735 & #5166 Teasure Box, M, ea...........**25.00**
Kampy Kiddle, #3753, complete, M **150.00**
Kiddle Kologne, #3705, Sweet Pea, NRFB........................**75.00**
Kiddle Komedy Theatre, #3592, EX **20.00**
King & Queen of Hearts, #3784, MIP................................**150.00**
Lady Crimson, #A3840, NRFB..**75.00**
Laffy Lemon, #3732, MIP...**85.00**
Lenore Limousine, #3743, complete, M **60.00**
Liddle Kiddles Klub, #3301, M..**20.00**
Lois Locket, #3541, complete, M.......................................**50.00**
Lolli-Grape, #3656, complete, M **60.00**
Lolli-Mint, #3658, MIP **75.00**
Lucky Lion, #3635, complete, M..**40.00**
Luvvy Duvvy Kiddle, #3596, MIP......................................**50.00**
Miss Mouse, #3638, MIP..**75.00**
Nappytime Baby, #3818, complete, M................................**45.00**
Pink Funny Bunny, #3532, MIP...**65.00**
Robin Hood & Maid Marion, #3735, MIP.........................**150.00**
Rosemary Roadster, #3642, complete, M.............................**60.00**
Sizzly Friddle, MIP...**300.00**
Snap-Happy Furniture, #5171, MIP...................................**30.00**
Suki Skediddle, #3767, complete, M **25.00**
Tiny Tiger, #3636, MIP...**75.00**
Windy Fliddle, #3514, complete, M....................................**85.00**

Madame Alexander

Beatrice Alexander founded the Alexander Doll Company in 1923 by making an all-cloth, oil-painted face, Alice in Wonderland doll. With the help of her three sisters, the company prospered; and by the late 1950s there were over 600 employees making Madame Alexander dolls. The company still produces these lovely dolls today. For more information, refer to *Madame Alexander Collector's Doll Price Guide* and *Madame Alexander Store Exclusives and Limited Editions*, both by Linda Crowsey, published by Collector Books.

In the listings that follow, values represent dolls in mint to near-mint condition.

Alexander-kin, bend-knee walker, NC, 1956-65, EX face color..**175.00**
Alexander-kin, French braid, cotton dress, 1965 ....**600.00**
Alice in Wonderland, cloth/vinyl, Barbara Jane, 1952, 29", minimum...**700.00**
Anatolia, str legs, #524, 1987 only, 8" **65.00**
Aunt Betsy, cloth/felt, 1930s...**900.00**
Bali, hp, #533, 1993 only, 8" **65.00**
Ballerina, compo, Wendy Ann, 19367, 11-14", ea.......................**425.00**
Belle Brummel, cloth, 1930s **775.00**
Bo Peep, Little; Classic Series, Mary Ann, #1563, 1988-89, 14"..**100.00**
Bonnie, plastic/vinyl toddler, 1964 only, 18".................................**375.00**
Bride, hp, Cissette, tulle gown, short veil, 1957, 10" **375.00**
Butch McGuffey, compo/cloth, 1940-41, 22"................................**275.00**
Cinderella, compo, Princess Elizabeth, Sears Exclusive, 1939, 14"...**500.00**
Clarabell Clown, 1951-53, 19"..**350.00**
Dare, Virginia; compo, Little Betty, 1940-41, 9".........................**450.00**
Dilly Dally Sally, compo, Tiny Betty, 1937-42, 7".......................**325.00**
Elise, hp/vinyl, jtd ankles/knees, ball gown, 1957-64, 16½"........**750.00**
Flora McFlimsey, compo, Little Betty, 1938-41, 9".....................**425.00**
Gibson Girl, hp, eyeshadow, Cissette, 1962, 10", minimum value...**800.00**
Hansel, compo, Tiny Betty, 1935-42, 7".......................................**325.00**
Hyacinth, vinyl toddler, 1953 only, bl dress & bonnet, 9" **150.00**
June Bride, compo, Portrait Series, Wendy Ann, 21", minimum value...**2,500.00**

Lacy Lovelace, cloth/felt, 1930s..**650.00**
Little Southern Boy (or Girl), latex/vinyl, 1950-51, 10", ea **150.00**
Lucinda, plastic/vinyl, Janie, 1969-70, 12", minimum value **525.00**
Mambo, hp, Wendy Ann, #481, 1955 only, 8", minimum value ..**850.00**
Mary Mary, hp, str leg, #451, 1976-87, 8".................................**65.00**
Morocco, hp, Wendy Ann, bend-knee, #762, 1968-70, 8" **90.00**
Nurse, cloth/felt, 1930s, 16"..**675.00**

Pierrot, hard plastic, 1957, 8", MIB, from $400.00 to $600.00. (Photo courtesy McMasters Harris Auctions)

Pocahontas, hp, bend-knee, Wendy Ann, has baby, #721, 1967-70, 8"..**450.00**
Princess Ann, hp, Wendy Ann, #396, 1957 only, 8", minimum value ..**800.00**
Rebecca, compo, Wendy Ann, 1940-41, 21" **1,000.00**
Rozy, plastic/vinyl, Janie, #1130, 1969 only, 12" **375.00**
Simone, hp/vinyl, Jacqueline, 1968 only, 21", in trunk, minimum **2,150.00**
Sound of Music, Louisa, Mary Ann, #1404, 1965-70, 14"...........**275.00**
Sweet Baby, cloth/latex, 1948 only, 28½-20", ea from $50 to.....**100.00**
Truman, Bess; First Ladies Series, Mary Ann, 1989-90, 14" **100.00**
Winnie Walker, hp, Cissy, 1953 only, 15" **325.00**
Withers, Jane; compo, c/m, 1937, 12-13½", ea, minimum.......**1,000.00**

Mattel

For more information refer to *Talking Toys of the 20th Century* by Kathy and Don Lewis. Our values are for examples in near-mint to mint condition.

Baby Beans, vinyl, bean-bag body, 1971-75, 12" **70.00**
Baby First Step, b/o walker, rooted hair, o/c/e, pk dress, 18"........**150.00**
Baby First Step, b/o walker, rooted hair, sleep eyes, talker, OC, 18" ..**300.00**
Baby Pattaburp, vinyl, drinks/burps, OC, 1964-66, 16" **200.00**
Baby Play-a-Lot, poseable, pulls string/switch, OC, 1972-73, 16"...**22.00**
Baby's Hungry, b/o, eyes move/lips chew, OC+bottle, 17".............**30.00**
Baby Secret, vinyl face, stuffed body, 11 phrases, 1966-67, 18".....**75.00**
Baby Tender Love, newborn, realistic skin, OC, 13" **65.00**
Baby Tender Love Brother, realistic skin, OC, 11 /2" **50.00**
Charmin' Chatty, talker, vinyl, 5 disks, OC, 1963-64, 24"..........**300.00**
Chatty Cathy, vinyl/hp, pull-string talker, OC, 1960-63, 20" **350.00**
Drowsy, vinyl head/stuffed body, sleepers, pull-string talker, 15½"..**175.00**
Guardian Goddess, 1979, 11½" **50.00**
Shogun Warrior, plastic, b/o, 23½"..**250.00**
Tiny Chatty Brother, vinyl, OC, 1963-64, 15½" **75.00**
Tippee Toes, b/o, legs move, rides accessory, 1968-70, 17" **80.00**

Papier-Mâché

1820-60s milliner's type, braided bun w/side curls, RpC, 9", EX...**800.00**
1820-60s milliner's type, molded comb, RpC, rare, 16", EX.....**3,300.00**
1820-60s milliner's type, topknot & side curls, RpC, 16", EX..**2,125.00**

1820s-60s milliner's type, center part & sausage curls, RpC, 14", EX..575.00
1835-50 Fr type, solid dome ShHd, glass eyes, pnt hair, RpC, 18", EX...1,750.00
1835-50 Fr type, solid dome ShHd, pnt eyes, pnt blk hair, RpC, 12", EX....750.00
1840s-60s, ShHd, cloth body/wooden limbs, glass eyes, RpC, 24", EX..2,200.00
1844-92, M&S Superior, ShHd, glass eyes, RpC, 12", EX...........500.00
1844-92 M&S Superior, #1020, ShHd, molded hair, pnt eyes, RpC, 22", EX...675.00
1879-1900s, trn ShHd, solid dome, glass eyes, c/m, RpC, 16", EX ...700.00
1879-1900s, washable ShHd, glass eyes, RpC, EX quality, 18", EX ..700.00
1879-1900s, washable ShHd, glass eyes, RpC, G quality, 16", EX 250.00
1920s+, Fr, bright coloring, wig, ethnic OC, 15", EX 300.00
1920s+, German, bright coloring, wig, OC, 15", EX 115.00
1920s+, unmk, bright coloring, wig, OC, 16" 175.00

Parian

Alice in Wonderland, molded headband or comb, RpC, 16", EX 625.00
Countess Dagmar, headband/curls on forehead, unmk, RpC, 21", EX...950.00
Dolly Madison, RpC, 22", EX...1,600.00
Empress Eugenie, headpc/snood, RpC, 25", EX........................750.00
Glass eyes, RpC, 14", EX 2,400.00
Lady, fancy molded hair, glass eyes, p/e, RpC, 20", EX............2,700.00
Lady, fancy molded hair, pnt eyes, p/e, RpC, 22", EX..............1,700.00
Lady, fancy molded hair, swivel neck, glass eyes, RpC, 15", EX ...2,700.00
Lady, simple molded hair w/no decor, RpC, 15", EX...................300.00
Lady, simple molded hair w/no decor, RpC, 25", EX...................525.00
Man or boy, center part, decor shirt & tie, glass eyes, RpC, 16", EX ..2,825.00
Man or boy, center part, decor shirt & tie, pnt eyes, RpC, 17", EX....1,000.00
Mary Todd Lincoln, headband, snood, RpC, 25", EX.................700.00
Molded bodice, fancy trim, RpC, 17", EX 800.00
Molded hair, blond or blk pnt hair, pnt eyes, RpC, 16", EX 2,300.00

Schoenhut

Albert Schoenhut left Germany in 1866 to go to Pennsylvania to work as a repairman for toy pianos. He eventually applied his skills to wooden toys and later designed an all-wood doll which he patented on January 17, 1911. These uniquely jointed dolls were painted with enamels and came with a metal stand. Some of the later dolls had stuffed bodies, voice boxes, and hollow heads. Due to the changing economy and fierce competition, the company closed in the mid-1930s.

#100, girl, no iris outline, RpC, 1911-12, 16", EX...................1,500.00
#101, girl, cvd hair, grin, squinting eyes, RpC, 1911-12, 16", EX ...3,000.00
#101, girl, cvd hair bob, no iris outline, RpC, 1912-23, 14", EX ...2,200.00
#102, girl, cvd braids, RpC, 1911-12, 16", EX 1,500.00
#103, girl, cvd hair, loose ringlets, RpC, 1911-12, 16", EX 3,000.00
#105, girl, short cvd bob w/cvd ribbon, RpC, 1912-23, 14-16", EX...1,900.00
#106, girl, cvd/molded bonnet & short hair, RpC, 1912-16, 19", EX...2,800.00
#107, toddler, elastic strung, RpC, 1924-26, 14", EX..................750.00
#107W, toddler, walker, cloth body w/crier, RpC, 1924-26, 14", EX...600.00
#108, toddler, RpC, 1917-26, 17", EX 850.00
#108W, toddler, walker, elastic strung, RpC, 1924-26, 17", EX...725.00
#203, boy, cvd hair, spring-jtd body, grinning, RpC, 1911-12, 16", EX ...3,000.00
#203, boy, smiling, rnd eyes, no iris outline, RpC, 1911-12, EX ...1,500.00
#206, boy, cvd hair, covered ears, RpC, 1912-16, 19", EX 2,600.00
#301, girl, bob wig, #102 face, RpC, 1911-12, 16", EX 1,500.00
#301, girl, bobbed wig w/bangs, spring-jtd body, RpC, 1911-12, 16", EX...1,500.00
#304, girl, wig in braids, ears stick out, RpC, 1911-12, 16", EX ...1,500.00
#305, girl, wig w/braids, #303 face, RpC, 1911-12, 16", EX 1,500.00
#308, girl, wig w/braids, RpC, 1912-16, 14", EX 800.00
#309, girl, 2 teeth, wig w/long curls, RpC, 1912-13, 16", EX 825.00
#310, girl w/long curl wig, #105 face, RpC, 1912-16, 14-16", EX, ea ...775.00
#314, girl, teeth, wig w/long curls, RpC, 1912-16, 19", EX 725.00
Maggie & Jiggs, cartoon characters, RpC, 7-9", ea 525.00

Max & Moritz, cvd w/pnt hair, cvd shoes, 8", ea 625.00
Rolly-dolly, 9-12", ea..850.00

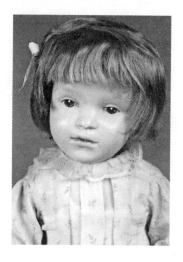

Pouty girl, wooden character head, blue intaglio eyes, mohair wig, spring-jointed wooden body, partially original clothes (some replacements), 18", EX, $900.00. (Photo courtesy McMasters Harris Auctions)

SFBJ

By 1895 Germany was producing dolls at much lower prices than the French dollmakers could, so to save the doll industry, several leading French manufacturers united to form one large company. Bru, Raberry and Delphieu, Pintel and Godshaux, Fleischman and Bodel, Jumeau, and many others united to form the company Society Francaise de Fabrication de Bébés et Jouets (SFBJ).

#226, character, bsk SkHd, glass eyes, c/m, wig, RpC, 20", EX...2,400.00
#234, character, bsk SkHd, o/c/e, compo body, RpC, 18", EX 3,250.00
#237, character, glass eyes, o/c/m, RpC, 16", EX 1,700.00
#239, character, SkHd, glass eyes, wig, Poulbot design, RpC, 1913, 14"..6,000.00
#251, character, SkHd, glass eyes, o/c/m/teeth/tongue, RpC, 15", EX...1,500.00
#301, Bleuette, bsk SkHd, glass eyes, o/m/teeth, wig, RpC, 11⅜", EX 975.00
#301, bsk head, glass eyes, o/m, wig, jtd body, RpC, 24", EX ...1,150.00
#301, bsk SkHd, o/c/e, o/m/teeth, p/e, rpl wig, jtd body, RpC, 28½" 800.00
#301, lady's body, kiss thrower, RpC, 22", EX 1,700.00
#60, Bleuette, bsk SkHd, glass eyes, o/m/teeth, wig, RpC, 10⅝", EX...1,000.00
no #, Jumeau type, o/m, RpC, 20", EX 1,650.00

Shirley Temple

Prices are suggested for dolls complete and in at least near-mint condition. Add up to 25% (depending on her outfit) if mint with box. A played-with doll in only very good condition would be worth only about half of listed values.

Bsk, 6", unlicensed Japanese, OC, NM 250.00
Celluloid, 13", Dutch, metal pate, o/c/e, OC, 1937+, NM..........350.00
Compo, 13", Ideal, jtd body, gr o/c/e, o/m/teeth, mohair wig, OC, NM...750.00
Compo, 18", Ideal, Baby Shirley, jtd body, gr o/c/e, o/m/teeth, OC, EX...1,200.00
Compo, 18", Ideal, Marama, blk yarn hair, grass skirt, OC, EX ..950.00
Compo, 22", jtd body, gr o/c/e, o/m/teeth, mohair wig, OC, 22", NM ..1,200.00
Porc, 16", Danbury Mint, M..90.00
Vinyl, 12", o/c/e, o/c/m/teeth, rooted wig, OC,1957, NM...........350.00
Vinyl, 15", o/c/e, o/m/teeth, mk ST//15, OC, 1958-61, NM 400.00
Vinyl, 35", jtd wrists, mk ST-35-38-2, OC, 1960, NM.............2,100.00
Vinyl, 36", mk Doll Dreams & Love, OC, 1984, NM 250.00

Simon and Halbig

Simon and Halbig was one of the finest German makers to operate during the 1870s into the 1930s. Due to the high quality of the makers, their dolls still command large prices today. During the 1890s a few Simon & Halbig heads were used by a French maker, but these are extremely rare and well marked S&H.

#150, character face, intaglio eyes, c/m, RpC, 1910+, 21", VG 15,500.00
#151, character face, pnt eye, laughing c/m, RpC, ca 1912, 15", EX.....5,000.00
#619, child, sleep eyes, c/m, p/e, jtd body, RpC, ca 1886, 18", EX.....3,700.00
#729, character laughing face, glass eyes, o/c/m, RpC, 1888, 16", EX.....2,550.00
#739, child, glass eyes, o/m, p/e, jtd body, RpC, 15", EX..........2,100.00
#749, character, SkHd, glass eyes, c/m, p/e, RpC, ca 1888, 21", EX....3,100.00
#749, glass eyes, o/m/teeth, p/e, wig, jtd body, RpC, ca 1888, 9", EX 950.00
#852, bsk Oriental, swivel head/glass eyes, c/m, wig, RpC, 5½", EX...1,100.00
#949, glass eyes, c/m, RpC, ca 1888, 16", EX............................2,350.00
#969, smiling o/m, RpC, ca 1887, 19", EX................................7,600.00
#1009, o/c/e, o/m/teeth, p/e, wig, kid body, RpC, ca 1889, 19", EX...525.00
#1019, laughing, o/m, RpC, ca 1890, 14", EX...........................5,700.00
#1039, bsk SkHd, glass eyes, o/m, papier-mâché body, RpC, 17", EX..725.00
#1079, glass eyes, o/m, 5-pc body, RpC, ca 1892, 8", EX.............600.00
#1080, child, ShHd, o/c/e, RpC, 18", EX 575.00
#1109, dolly face, glass eyes, o/m, RpC, ca 1893, 13", EX 750.00
#1159, Gibson girl, glass eyes, o/m, RpC, ca 1894, 20", EX 2,950.00
#1249, Santa, glass eyes, o/m, RpC, ca 1898, 6", EX 650.00
#1250, dolly face, ShHd, RpC, ca 1898, 15", EX 550.00
#1260, ShHd, glass eyes, o/m, kid body, RpC, 19", EX 800.00
#1294, character baby, glass eyes, o/m, RpC, ca 1912, 16", EX ...750.00

#1294, socket head, glass eyes, open mouth with teeth, mohair wig, nicely re-dressed, 8", EX, $750.00. (Photo courtesy McMasters Harris Auctions)

#1469, flapper, glass eyes, c/m, RpC, ca 1920, 15", EX.............3,500.00
#1478, c/m, RpC, ca 1920, 15", EX...9,000.00
#1488, character baby, glass eyes, o/c/m, RpC, ca 1920, 20", EX ..4,500.00
#2428, character baby, glass eyes, o/c/m, RpC, ca 1914, 13", EX ..1,600.00
S&H (no mold #), ShHd, molded hair, RpC, 1870s, 19", EX..1,600.00

Steiner, Jules

Jules Nicholas Steiner established one of the earliest French manufacturing companies (making dishes and clocks) in 1855. He began with mechanical dolls with bisque heads and open mouths with two rows of bamboo teeth; his patents grew to include walking and talking dolls. In 1880 he registered a patent for a doll with sleep eyes. This doll could be put to sleep by turning a rod that operated a wire attached to its eyes.

Bébé, Series A, SkHd, pwt eyes, c/m, jtd body, RpC, 14", EX .6,000.00
Bébé, Series C, SkHd, pwt eyes, c/m, RpC, 34", EX 13,000.00
Bébé le Parisien, bsk SkHd, cb pate, pwt eyes, o/m, wig, RpC, 21", EX..4,100.00
Bébé w/Motschmann body, solid bsk head, glass eyes, c/m, RpC, 14", EX.4,800.00
Kicker/crier, key-wind, glass eyes, o/m/teeth, wig, RpC, 18", EX .2,200.00
Le Petit Parisien, bébé, bsk SkHd, glass eyes, c/m, wig, RpC, 16", EX .4,900.00
Unmk bébé, bsk SkHd, pwt eyes, o/m/teeth, jtd body, RpC, 18", EX ..6,000.00

Vogue

This is the company that made the Ginny doll. Composition was used during the 1940s, but vinyl was the preferred material throughout the decade of the 1950s. An original mint-condition composition Ginny would be worth a minimum of $450.00 on the market today (played-with, about $90.00). The last Ginny came out in 1969. Another Vogue doll that is becoming very collectible is Jill, whose values are steadily climbing. For more information, we recommend *Collector's Encyclopedia of Vogue Dolls, Second Edition*, by Judith Izen and Carol Stover. Our advisor for Jill dolls is Bonnie Groves; she is listed in the Directory under Texas.

Accessory, bed & bedding, VG 36.00
Accessory, closet/wardrobe, 1957, EX..42.00
Accessory, desk & chair, EX..76.00
Accessory, Jill leotard, VG 57.00
Baby Dear, vinyl/cloth, rooted hair, OC, 1959-64, 18", NM 325.00
Baby Too Dear, vinyl toddler, o/m/teeth, OC, 1963-65, 23", NM...350.00
Booklet, Vogue Dolls, 1957, VG..23.00
Crib Crowd baby, o/c/e, caracul wig, curved legs, OC, 8", minimum..650.00
Cynthia, compo, o/c/e, o/m, mohair wig, 5-pc body, OC, 1940s, 13", EX..350.00
Dora Lee, compo, o/c/e, c/m, OC, 11", NM 375.00
Ginnette, vinyl, jtd, pnt eyes, o/m, OC, 1955-56, 8", NM..........250.00
Ginny, Black, hp, OC, 1953-54, 8", EX, minimum value............600.00
Ginny, hp, bent-knee walker, o/c/e, wig, OC, 1957-62, 8", EX ...175.00
Ginny, hp, walker, o/c/e, dynel wig, 7-pc body, OC, 1954-56, EX..225.00
Ginny, hp, walker, OC, carrying 8" doll, 1960, 36", EX 175.00
Ginny, hp walker, o/c/e, strung, dynel wig, OC (common dress), 8", EX..350.00
Ginny, pnt hp, molded hair w/mohair wig, OC, 1948-50, 8", EX..375.00
Ginny, pnt hp, o/c/e, OC, 1953, 8", EX 400.00
Ginny, soft vinyl/hp, walker, o/c/e, rooted hair, OC, 1963-65, 8", NM.50.00
Ginny, vinyl, jtd non-walker, o/c/e, rooted hair, OC, 1977-82, 8", NM .35.00
Ginny, vinyl, Meritus/Hong Kong, OC, 1984-86, 8", NM.............55.00
Ginny, vinyl, nonwalker, o/c/e, rooted hair, OC, 1972-77, 8", NM.50.00
Ginny, vinyl, str leg, o/c/e, rooted hair, OC, 1965-72, 8", NM 50.00
Ginny Baby, vinyl, jtd, o/c/e, rooted hair, drinks/wets, OC, 12", NM..40.00
Jan, vinyl, rooted hair, rigid body, OC, 1958-60, 1963-64, 10½", NM.150.00
Jeff, vinyl, pnt hair, 5-pc body, OC, 1958-60, 11", NM...............100.00
Jennie, compo, o/c/e, o/m, mohair wig, 5-pc body, OC, 1940s, 13", EX..350.00
Jill, hp teenager, bend-knee walker, OC, 1960s, 10½", MIB.......225.00
Jimmy, vinyl, pnt eyes, o/m, OC, 1958, 8", NM..........................60.00
Li'l Imp, vinyl, walker, o/c/e, orange hair, OC, 1959-60, 10½", NM.75.00
Little Miss Ginny, vinyl pre-teen, o/c/e, OC, 1965-71, 12", NM..40.00
Love Me Linda, vinyl, long str hair, OC, 1965, 15", NM 65.00
Miss Ginny, vinyl, jtd arms, 2-pc hp body, swivel waist, 1962, 15", M..45.00
Toddles, compo, pnt/e, mohair wig, jtd body, OC, 8", EX 425.00
Welcome Home Baby Turns Two, vinyl/cloth, OC, 1980, 22", M..200.00

Wax, Poured Wax

Bonnet head, molded cap, RpC, 1860-80, 16", EX 325.00
Over compo, Alice in Wonderland style w/molded headband, RpC, 23", EX.475.00
Over compo, child, glass eyes, inserted hair, RpC, 1860-90, 14", EX..1,000.00
Over compo, man, trn ShHd, molded top hat, set eyes, RpC, 17", VG..1,000.00
Over compo ShHd, child, glass eyes, o/m, later, OC, 11", EX.....225.00

Over compo ShHd, glass eyes, o/m, RpC, later, 23", EX 575.00
Over compo slit ShHd, wire-closure glass eyes, RpC, 1830-60s, 25", EX..2,300.00
Poured, baby, ShHd, pnt features, glass eyes, cloth body, RpC, 17", EX..1,500.00
Poured, child, ShHd, inserted hair/glass eyes, wax limbs, RpC, 13", EX..1,100.00
Poured, infant nurser, trn ShHd, glass eyes, wig, RpC, 26", VG..1,325.00
Poured, lady, ShHd, glass eyes, wig, RpC, 8", EX........................770.00
Poured, 2-faced (laughing/crying), Bartenstein, 1880-90s, RpC, 15", EX.900.00

Door Knockers

Door knockers, those charming precursors of the doorbell, come in an intriguing array of shapes and styles. The very rare ones come from England. Cast-iron examples made in this country were often produced in forms similar to the more familiar doorstop figures. Beware: Many of the brass door knockers being offered on Internet auctions are new.

Wreath, red and green painted cast iron, $350.00; Girl knocking at door, painted cast iron, c 1921, from $300.00 to $400.00. (Photo courtesy Bertoia Auctions)

Alsation Wolf Dog (German shepherd), brass, 5x4", EX...............60.00
Birdhouse, cream w/mc, cream bkplate, CI, Hubley #629, 3⅜x2⅝".......425.00
Birds at birdhouse, CI, floral emb bkplate, 3¾", EX, from $400 to.425.00
Bloodhound's head, brass, English, ca 1940, 3¼x2¼", EX............95.00
Bulldog, brass, unmk, 3" dog on 5" bkplate...................................75.00
Cardinal on wigs, pnt CI, rare, 5x3", m...285.00
Dog, CI, brn, at entrance to cream doghouse, pk dish, brn bkplate, 4x3".......785.00
Dog's head resting on front paws, cvd wood, lifts at nose, 6½" ...250.00
Dragon, tooled wrought iron, w/strike, 6½" 115.00
Flower basket, CI, mk #205, rectangular bk, 1⅞x4" 185.00
Highlander w/bagpipes, brass, mk Made in Great Britain, 6" 85.00
Ivy pot, pnt CI, Hubley #123, EX..160.00
Kewpie, brass, ca 1920, 4¾"...80.00
Liberty bell, CI, ca 1920, 3¼", EX..225.00
Morning glory, gr leaves bkplate, Judd #608, 3¼", EX.................285.00
Parrot, mc pnt on CI, ca 1890, 4½x3", EX 125.00
Pear, pnt CI, flower bkplate, rare, 4¼x3", M 360.00
Rabbit, running, brass, 4"..160.00
Russian eagle, dbl-headed, brass, 12¾x12¼" 105.00
Spider, CI, mc on gray & blk web, mc fly, 3½x1⅞" 750.00
St Thomas w/Canterbury Cathedral above, brass, 4½x2½" 85.00
Woman's head wearing bonnet, CI, Hubley #619, 4¼x3", EX....385.00
Woodpecker, Hubley, CI, ca 1930, 3¾x2⅝", from $135 to.........150.00
Zinnias, pnt CI, mk Pat Pend LVL, rare, 3¾x2½"......................550.00

Doorstops

Although introduced in England in the mid-1800s, cast-iron doorstops were not made to any great extent in this country until after the Civil War. Once called 'door porters,' their function was to keep doors open to provide better ventilation. They have been produced in many shapes and sizes, both dimensional and flat-backed, and in the past few years have become a popular, yet affordable collectible. While cast-iron examples are the most common, brass, wood, and chalk were also used. An average price is in the $100.00 to $200.00 range, though some are valued at more than $400.00. Doorstops retained their usefulness and appeal well into the 1930s.

In some areas of the country, it may be necessary to adjust prices down about 25%. When no condition code is present, items are assumed to be in exceptional original condition, flat-backed unless noted full-figured, and cast iron unless another material is mentioned. To evaluate a doorstop in only very good to excellent paint, deduct at least 35%. Values for examples in poor to good paint drop dramatically.

Key: ff — full figured

Aunt Jemima, all blk, 10½x6½", from $350 to...........................400.00
Begging Boston Terrier, ff, 8¾x5", from $300 to.........................375.00
Boy in Tuxedo, wood wedge, 7¼x4⅜", from $375 to 500.00
Boy w/Hands in Pockets, ff, 10½x3⅝", from $350 to.................425.00
Buddha, sitting, ff, 7x5¾", from $200 to 275.00
Cape Cod Cottage, Hubley #444, 5½x7¾", from $125 to 200.00
Castle, on mountain w/road, 8x5¼", from $350 to.....................425.00
Cat, w/lg bl bow, 14½x7½", from $200 to 250.00
Cottage w/Fence, National Foundry #32, 5¾x8", from $125 to..200.00
Doberman Pinscher, standing, ff, Hubley, 8x8½", from $400 to .550.00
Dolly, girl w/doll, Hubley #45, 9½x5½", from $425 to...............550.00
Donald Duck, w/stop sign, Walt Disney 1971, 8⅜x5¼", from $250 to..325.00
Duck w/Top Hat, wearing bl pants, 7½x4¼", from $275 to........325.00
Ducks, 2 on base, Hubley #291, 8¼x6¼", from $325 to 400.00
El Capitan, marching on base, 7¾x5¼", from $175 to................250.00
Elephant by Palm, wedge, 13¾x10¼", from $275 to..................350.00
Elk, standing on rocks, 11x10", from $175 to 250.00
Fisherman at Wheel, 6¼x6", from $150 to 225.00
French Girl, curtsying, Hubley #23, 9¼x5½", from $250 to.......325.00
Frog, laying flat, Hubley, 1½x7½", from $125 to.........................200.00
Fruit Basket, 9¾x7½", from $275 to 350.00
Gaucho, ff, 18½x7", from $450 to...525.00
Geese, group of 3 marching, Hubley, 8x8", from $375 to 450.00
Girl Holding Bouquet, ff, Albany Foundry Co, 7⅝x4¾", $175 to.250.00
Grapes & Leaves, Albany Foundry, 7¾x6½", from $125 to........200.00
Horse Jumping Fence, Eastern Specialty Co #79, 7⅞x11¾", $400 to....475.00
House w/Woman, Eastern Specialty Mfg Co #50, 5¾x8½", $300 to..500.00
Lambs Under Tree, 7¼x6⅜", from $300 to.................................375.00
Li'l Bo Peep, ruffled dress, w/flowers, 6¾x5", from $225 to.........300.00
Lighthouse, brick, ff, 13½x8", from $150 to................................225.00
Lilies of the Valley, Hubley #189, 10½x7½", from $175 to.........250.00
Little Southern Belle, National Foundry, ff, 6¾x3", $100 to 125.00
Maid of Honor, holding flowers & skirt, Hubley, 8¼x5", from $300 to.375.00
Man w/Cane, 10x4⅞", from $400 to 450.00
Mary Quite Contrary, w/water can & flowers, #1292, 15x8", from $500 to..750.00
Monkey on Barrel, Taylor Cook #3, 1930, 8⅜x4⅞", from $400 to....475.00
Nasturtiums, in striped vase, Hubley #221, 7¼x6½", from $125 to.175.00
Overhead Swinging Golfer, Hubley #238, 10x7", from $500 to..700.00
Owl on Books, Eastern Specialty Mfg Co, 9¼x6½", from $550 to.750.00
Oxen & Wagon, mk c64, 6¼x10¼", from $150 to.......................225.00
Pansy Bowl, Hubley #256, 7x6½", from $125 to.........................175.00
Parrot, on stump, glass eye, National Foundry, 10⅜x6¾", $150 to.200.00
Parrot in Ring, B&H, 13¾x7¼", from $225 to...........................275.00
Peacock by Urn, Hubley #208, 7½x4¼", from $200 to..............275.00
Pelican on Dock, Albany Foundry #113, 8x7¼", from $250 to ..325.00
Police Boy, w/whistle & puppy, 10⅝x7¼", from $550 to 750.00
Rabbit by Fence, Albany Foundry, 6⅞x8⅛", from $375 to 450.00

Rabbit w/Top Hat, Albany Foundry #94, 9⅞x4¾", from $425 to ...**550.00**
Sailor, w/rope & barrel, 11⅜x5", from $450 to **550.00**
Ship, mc sails, National Foundry, 10x12", from $150 to..................**225.00**
Skier, standing w/skies, ff, unmk, 12½x5", from $500 to.............**750.00**
Sleeping Cat, ff, 4½x13", from $750 to **1,000.00**
Squirrel, eating nut, 6x6", from $150 to.......................................**225.00**
Stagecoach, w/driver & 2 horses, 7½x12¼", from $75 to **125.00**
The Patrol, yel coat, w/lantern, 8⅜x3¾", from $225 to.............**300.00**
Tulips, in vase w/bl bow, Hubley, 12¾x6⅞", from $275 to.........**350.00**
Welsh Corgi, tilted head, B&H, 8¼x5⅞", from $200 to...**275.00**
Windmill, w/2 cottages, #6, 9⅞x11½", from $450 to **600.00**
Woman w/Muff, ff, unmk, 9¼x5", from $225 to **275.00**

Boston Terrior With Paw Up, EX original paint, $625.00.

Dorchester Pottery

Taking its name from the town in Massachusetts where it was organized in 1895, the Dorchester Pottery Company made primarily utilitarian wares, though other types of items were made as well. By 1940 a line of decorative pottery was introduced, some of which was painted by hand with scrollwork or themes from nature. The buildings were destroyed by fire in the late 1970s, and the pottery was never rebuilt. In the listings that follow, the decorations described are all in cobalt unless otherwise noted. Our advisor for this category is Dale MacLean; he is listed in the Directory under Massachusetts.

Key:
CAH — Charles A. Hill (noted artist)   IM — in memory of
EHH — Ethel Hill Henderson

Bowl, cereal; scrollwork, CAH/IMEHH, 2x5¾" **100.00**
Bowl, clown, mk CAH/N Ricci, 1⅛x4" **110.00**
Bowl, Pine Cone, hdls, 3½x6" **150.00**
Bowl, whale, CAH/N Ricci, 1⅛x3½" **100.00**
Candle holder, cobalt scrollwork, CAH/Ricci/IMEHH (In memory), 6" dia.**125.00**
Casserole, Colonial Lace (sgraffito), wht on med lb, CAH, 7½" dia.**275.00**
Casserole, Pine Cone, w/lid, CAH, 2¼x4½" **75.00**
Casserole, Pine Cone, w/lid, 5x6½"..**225.00**
Creamer, Strawberry, mk CH **75.00**
Creamer & sugar bowl, Strawberry, Denisons/CAH, 3½", NM ..**150.00**
Cup & saucer, Pear, CAH, 3¼", bl-lined 6¼" saucer **110.00**
Foot warmer, Henderson; metal screw-type cap mk 1912, 11" **75.00**
Mug, Pear, CAH/EHH, 4½" **75.00**
Mug, Sacred Cod, CAH/EHH, 4½" **110.00**
Pitcher, pilgrim w/lg gun, Robert Trotter, 7½", EX.....................**220.00**
Plate, Blueberry, CAH/N Ricci, 10" **195.00**

Sugar bowl, flowers & bands, K Denisons, w/lid, 3x4"................**110.00**
Sugar jar, Polka Dot, Robert Blake, 3½" **100.00**
Syrup pitcher, flowers, w/lid, CAH/N Ricci, 5" **150.00**
Syrup pitcher, stripes/leaves/curvy lines, CAH/N Ricci, 4½" **160.00**

Dorflinger

C. Dorflinger was born in Alsace, France, and came to this country when he was ten years old. When still very young, he obtained a job in a glass factory in New Jersey. As a young man, he started his own glassworks in Brooklyn, New York, opening new factories as profits permitted. During that time he made cut glass articles for many famous people including President and Mrs. Lincoln, for whom he produced a complete service of tableware with the United States Coat of Arms. In 1863 he sold the New York factories because of ill health and moved to his farm near White Mills, Pennsylvania. His health returned, and he started a plant near his home. It was there that he did much of his best work, making use of only the very finest materials. Christian died in 1915, and the plant was closed in 1921 by consent of the family.

Dorflinger glass is rare and often hard to identify. Very few pieces were marked. Many only carried a small paper label which was quickly discarded; these are seldom found today. Identification is more accurately made through a study of the patterns, as colors may vary.

Bowl, banana; Hob Diamond, 3¼x6x11" **105.00**
Bowl, Marlboro, 3½x9" **135.00**
Candy jar, Kalana Poppy, w/lid, 7½x5¼", EX **60.00**
Carafe, Pattern #28, bulbous bottom, 7½" **115.00**
Carafe, Strawberry, Diamond & Fan, bulbous bottom, 8x5½" base dia.**135.00**
Cordial, Hob Diamond, 4⅜" **25.00**
Cruets, oil & vinegar; Hob Diamond, 7" **215.00**
Decanter, Hob Diamond, w/stopper, 11½" **185.00**
Decanter, Marlboro, w/stopper, 8½" **260.00**
Goblet, Hob Diamond, 6¼" **35.00**
Goblet, wine; Split & Oval, cranberry to clear, 5"......................**160.00**
Grapefruit set, Kalana Lily, #155, w/liner **180.00**
Ice cream set, Parisian, 1x7⅜" plates (4), w/1¾x8x14" tray, EX.**365.00**
Pitcher, Hob Diamond, 9⅛" **465.00**
Vase, sweet pea; Kalana Pansy, pinched rim, 4¼" **85.00**

Dragon Ware

Dragon ware is fairly accessible and is still being made today. New dragon ware is distinguishable by the lack of detail in the application of the dragon. In the older pieces, much care is given to the slipwork of the dragon itself, including the eyes, wings, scales, and pearl. The new ware tends to be flat, lacking personality and detail. Many pieces were made for souvenirs and will carry the name of the place or attraction they commemorate.

The color referred to in our descriptions are the primary color found on the piece. This usually tends to be black or gray with splashes of pink and blue. The newer pieces are generally glossier than their older counterparts, except for lusterware items. Older colors tend to be more vibrant, while many of the newer colors are pastels. In addition to the primary colors, splashes of other colors are often found, creating a cloud effect behind the dragon. At this writing, pieces that are older and not the typical black/gray are commanding slightly higher prices and attention than similar pieces in black.

Primary colors are applied in several ways, the most common method being a wide band of color on the top and bottom of each piece. The 'cloud' effect is achieved when the primary color (and often the only color besides those of the dragon) is swirled on, creating a cloud-like backdrop for the dragon. Lustreware items have very shiny, almost pearl-like backgrounds, and solid-color pieces are those completely done in one color except for the dragon, clouds, and pearl.

Many cups have lithophanes depicting the face of a geisha girl. Nude lithophanes can also be found, although they are harder to find. The newer the lithophane, the less detail it seems to have.

Items listed below are unmarked unless noted otherwise. Ranges are given to take into consideration the age and quality of the piece. Examine a piece carefully to determine if it is old or new. The Internet offers various sites for Dragon Ware enthusiasts — www.dragonware.com is especially informative. For information about a collector club, see Clubs, Newsletters, and Catalogs (under Dragon Ware).

Key:
MIJ — Made in Japan   MIOJ — Made in Occupied Japan

Ashtray, bl, 3¾", from $7.50 to......................................**12.50**
Ashtray, gray w/gold, ball form, MIJ, 2½x4", from $40 to **55.00**
Barrel jar, blk w/rattan hdl, 8½", from $75 to **125.00**
Candy dish, blk, w/lid, from $100 to **150.00**
Casserole, blk w/gold hdl, w/lid, MIJ, 9", from $75 to **125.00**
Condiment set, blk, shakers+mustard w/spoon+tray (5 pcs), from $40 to.**75.00**
Creamer & sugar bowl, orange & wht, 3½", from $25 to **40.00**
Cup & saucer, blk cloud, HP Betsons, from $20 to **25.00**
Cup & saucer, coffee; bl, Dianan, from $25 to **45.00**
Cup & saucer, demi; dbl nude lithophane, gray, Nikoniko China, from $75 to....**125.00**
Cup & saucer, demi; google eyes, orange, from $25 to...................**45.00**
Cup & saucer, demi; google eyes, red/blk, Castle mk, from $30 to .**35.00**
Cup & saucer, demi; orange cloud, MIOJ, from $20 to...................**25.00**
Cup & saucer, gr, D China, child sz, from $10 to...........................**20.00**
Divided dish, gray, TT HP MIJ, 8⅛x6", from $75 to...................**125.00**
Dutch shoe, gray, from $20 to...**30.00**
Ginger jar, bl cloud, Lego MIJ, 5", from $35 to...........................**50.00**
Ice bucket, blk, rattan hdl, M over wreath mk, 8", from $75 to..**125.00**
Incense burner, gray, HP MIJ, 3½", from $35 to **45.00**
Mustard jar, gray, w/spoon, 3½", 3-pc, from $15 to.....................**40.00**
Nappy, gray, HP MIJ, 5½" sq, from $20 to **35.00**
Pitcher, yel, MIJ, mini, 2⅞", from $15 to **25.00**
Planter, gray, hanging, HP Japan, 6", from $75 to.......................**125.00**
Planter, orange, w/frog, MIJ, 5½", from $30 to **75.00**
Plate, bl cloud, 7¼", from $20 to..**25.00**
Saki set, bl cloud, geisha in center plate, Kutani, 8-pc, from $150 to .**175.00**
Saki set, bl cloud, Orient China Japan, from $50 to......................**75.00**
Saki set, bl cloud, whistling, kitten on decanter/plate, 8-pc, $125 to..**175.00**
Saki set, wht, whistling, HP Japan, 5-pc, from $75 to **125.00**
Shakers, gray, MIJ, pr, from $10 to..**25.00**
Shakers, gray, unmk, pr, from $10 to...**25.00**
Shakers, pk, Florida souvenir, pr, from $5 to **20.00**
Table lighter, blk, from $50 to..**75.00**
Tea set, demi; gray, HP Nippon bl circle mk, 17-pc, from $225 to..**350.00**
Tea set, demi; gray, MIJ, 24-pc, from $175 to.............................**275.00**
Tea set, demi; wht pearl, Japan, 17-pc, from $75 to......................**125.00**
Tea set, gray, sq, Noritake, pot+cr/sug w/lid, from $75 to **125.00**
Tea/coffee set, gr, lithophane, dragon spout, 23-pc, from $175 to..**250.00**
Tea/coffee set, red/brn, MOIJ, 23-pc, from $275 to.....................**350.00**
Tidbit tray, gray, Nippon, 9x6½", from $100 to **175.00**
Vase, aqua, Deco style, MIJ, 10¼", from $100 to........................**175.00**
Vase, bl w/gold, raised dragon, MIOJ, 2⅜", from $5 to.................**10.00**
Vase, gray, glass eyes, ftd, HP Nippon w/gr wreath, 4⅜", $125 to..**225.00**
Vase, gray, yel or orange, 4¼", set of 3, from $30 to **60.00**
Vase, orange, MIJ, 7½", from $30 to...**75.00**
Vase, orange, 4", from $20 to **50.00**
Vase, yel w/scribble pnt, MIJ, 5", from $15 to **50.00**
Wall pocket, bl, Kutani, 7", from $25 to......................................**75.00**

Wall pocket, bl/orange lustre, Japan flower mk, 7", from $25 to ...**50.00**
Wall pocket, orange, MIJ, 9", from $50 to....................................**75.00**

Dresden

The city of Dresden was a leading cultural center in the seventeenth century and in the eighteenth century became known as the Florence on the Elbe because of its magnificent baroque architecture and its outstanding museums. Artists, poets, musicians, philosophers, and porcelain artists took up residence in Dresden.

In the late nineteenth century, there was a considerable demand among the middle classes for porcelain. This demand was met by Dresden porcelain painters. Between 1855 and 1944, more than two hundred painting studios existed in the city. The studios bought porcelain white ware from manufacturers such as Meissen and Rosenthal for decorating, marketing, and reselling throughout the world. The largest of these studios include Donath & Co., Franziska Hirsch, Richard Klemm, Ambrosius Lamm, Carl Thieme, and Helena Wolfsohn.

Most of the Dresden studios produced work in imitation of Meissen and Royal Vienna. Flower painting enhanced with burnished gold, courting couples, landscapes, and cherubs were used as decorative motifs. As with other hand-painted porcelains, value is dependent upon the quality of the decoration. Sometimes the artwork equaled or even surpassed that of the Meissen factory.

Some of the most loved and eagerly collected of all Dresden porcelains are the beautiful and graceful lace figures. Many of the figures found in the maketplace today were not made in Dresden but in other areas of Germany. For more information, we recommend *Dresden Porcelain Studios* by Jim and Susan Harran, our advisors for this category. They are listed in the Directory under New Jersey.

Basket, mint; appl & HP flowers w/gold, Thieme, 1920s, 2½"......**65.00**
Bell, swirled mold w/flowers & gold, unmk, ca 1900-1930..........**165.00**
Charger, Watteau scene in 2 panels+2 floral panels, R Klemm, 14".**365.00**
Compote, HP courting scene inside, rtcl, much gold, Thieme, 6x8¼"..**365.00**
Crumber, HP flowers & gold, H Wolfsohn, 1886-1900 ....**250.00**
Cup & saucer, coffee; HP flowers on cobalt w/gold, H Wolfsohn, ca 1886...**275.00**
Figurine, ballerina, arms out/lace, Unterweissbach, 1940-62, 4½".**115.00**
Figurine, Charlotte, bsk head/arms, lace/ruffles, crown mk, ca 1900.**225.00**
Figurine, couple having tea w/dog at side, Alboth & Kaiser, 1955-70..**265.00**
Figurine, dancing couple, HP costumes, much lace, crown mk, ca 1900.**325.00**
Figurine, lady curtsying, HP flowers/lace, Von Schierholz, 9¼" ..**325.00**
Figurine, lady in chair, much lace/ruffles, Reiber, 1945-76, 2¼" .**115.00**
Figurine, Spanish dancer, 6-tier ruffled dress, crown mk, ca 1900, 9"..**475.00**
Figurine, terrier, seated/barking, HP, C Thieme, 1930-50s, 5¼" .**135.00**
Figurine, 3 ballerinas, much lace/appl flowers, H Wolfsohn, 1886-1900.**550.00**
Ginger jar, HP flowers w/gold, A Hamann, 1883-1949 ....**275.00**

Lady sitting in chair holding fan, blue ruffled dress, Josef Rieber & Co., Germany, 1945 – 1976, 2¾", from $100.00 to $125.00.

(Photo courtesy Jim and Susan Harran)

Hair receiver, flower garlands w/gold, can form, F Hirsch **135.00**
Leaf dish, gold decor on cobalt, Meissen blank, O Lorenz, 1880s .**65.00**
Mint dish, alternating scenic & flower panels, R Klemm, 3" **55.00**
Plate, gypsy lady's portrait, gr lustre rim, ca 1900, 9" **700.00**
Plate, HP classical lady, gold-paste floral rim, A Lamm, 9¼"......**425.00**
Plate, HP flowers & gold, rtcl rim, F Hirsch, 1901-30, 9¾" **135.00**
Plate, putti playing instruments on cobalt w/gold, A Lamm, 9¾".**425.00**
Shoe, HP floral w/gold, appl yel bow, R Klemm, 1888-1916, 8½" L.**335.00**
Tea set, floral w/gold, angle hdls, F Hirsch, 4" pot+cr/sug w/lid ..**325.00**
Tea strainer, HP flowers w/gold, H Wolfsohn, ca 1886, 5½x4" ...**215.00**
Teacup & saucer, HP flowers w/gold, low cup w/loop hdl, A Lamm..**125.00**
Teacup & saucer, HP scenes & flower panels w/gold, Thieme, mini.**215.00**
Tray, dresser; HP flowers w/gold, scalloped, R Klemm, 10¾x8"..**215.00**
Urn, courting scene reserves w/gold, 3-pc, Donath & Co, 10½"..**450.00**
Urn, floral panels/geometrics/laurel roping, 2-pc, Thieme, 18½".**800.00**
Vase, courting scene reserve on yel, sea horse hdls, R Klemm, 3¼"..**225.00**
Vase, lady's protrait on cobalt w/jewels & gold, hdls, 11½" **2,400.00**
Vase, Louise, lady's portrait on gr w/much gold, mk RK/crown, 6½".**540.00**

Dresser Accessories

Dresser sets, ring trees, figural or satin pincushions, manicure sets — all those lovely items that graced milady's dressing table — were at the same time decorative as well as functional. Today they appeal to collectors for many reasons. The Victorian era is well represented by repoussé silver-backed mirrors and brushes and pincushions that were used to display ornamental pins for the hair, hats, and scarves. The hair receiver — similar to a powder jar but with an opening in the lid — was used to hold long strands of hair retrieved from the comb or brush. These were wound around the finger and tucked in the opening to be used later for hair jewelry and pictures, many of which survive to the present day. (See Hair Weaving.)

Celluloid dresser sets were popular during the late 1800s and early 1900s. Some included manicure tools, pill boxes, and buttonhooks, as well as the basic items. Because celluloid tends to break rather easily, a whole set may be hard to find today. (See also Plastics.) With the current interest in anything Art Deco, sets from the '30s and '40s are especially collectible. These may be made of crystal, Bakelite, or silver, and the original boxes just as lavishly appointed as their contents.

Jewel case, Victorian lady in rose garden reserve on celluloid, 2½x11x8", from $225.00 to $275.00. (Photo courtesy Joan Van Patten and Elmer and Peggy Williams)

Box, bl enamel casket in rstr Forbes #505 SP fr, 4¾" sq **750.00**
Box, handkerchief; celluloid, lady's portrait among flowers, 6" L...**150.00**
Box, handkerchief; celluloid, Little Boy Blue on lid, 5x6¼" sq...**135.00**

Box, nickel silver, velvet lining, Deco style, 3½x6½" **40.00**
Box, pk glass w/gilt metal lid w/ballerina finial, 6½" L...............**235.00**
Box, powder; chrome w/gr enamel, glass insert, mirrored lid, 5½"..**90.00**
Box, repoussé w/cherub fininl, Meriden #1173, 5½x3" dia **325.00**
Case, glove; celluloid, birds on flowering branch on lid, 13" L ...**235.00**
Case, manicure; celluloid, girl's portrait on lid, sgn Brundage, 14".**450.00**
Case, manicure; celluloid, lady's portrait, upright **400.00**
Clock, boudoir; peach glass face, mirrored base, Deco style, 7x6"..**250.00**
Grooming set, man's, sterling, 3 brushes+shoe horn+3 jars+razor hdl..**200.00**
Hair brush, brn plastic, Deco stepped design, from $20 to............**25.00**
Jar, Paul & Virginia pattern, sterling, Foster & Bailey hallmk **750.00**
Mirror, hand; beveled, wht Lucite w/cut-out hdl, from $25 to **35.00**
Mirror, hand; celluloid, appl decor surrounds lady's portrait, 9¾"..**135.00**
Nightlight, EverReady, hammered metal w/chrome bands, 4¼" ...**45.00**
Set, bl satin glass, 2 candle holders+2 boxes+ring tree+12" tray.**135.00**
Set, porc w/silver & bl band, Deco, Czech, pr candle holders+2 boxes..**135.00**
Stand photo album, celluloid, little girl's portrait, 11¾x8½" **400.00**

Dryden

World War II veteran, Jim Dryden founded Dryden Pottery in Ellsworth, Kansas, in 1946. Starting in a Quonset hut, Dryden created molded products which he sold at his father's hardware store in town. Using Kansas clay from the area and volcanic ash as a component, durable glossy glazes were created. Soon Dryden was selling pottery to Macy's of New York and the Fred Harvey Restaurants on the Santa Fe Railroad.

After ten years, six hundred stores stocked Dryden Pottery. However, direct sales to the public from the pottery studio offered the most profit because of increasing competition from Japan and Europe. Using dental tools to make inscriptions, Dryen began to offer pottery with personalized messages and logos. This specialized work was appreciated by customers and is admired by collectors today.

In 1956 the interstate bypassed the pottery and Dryden decided to move to Hot Springs National Park to find a broader and larger tourist base. Again, local clays and quartz for the glazes were used. Later, in order to improve consistency, commercial clay (that fired bone white) and controlled glazes were used. Sometimes overlooked by collectors who favor the famous potteries of the past, Jim Dryden, son Kimbo, and grandsons Zach, Cheyenne, and Arrow, continue to develop new glazes and shapes in the studio in Hot Springs, Arkansas. Glazes comparable to those created by Fulper, Grueby, and Rookwood can be found on pottery for sale there. Dryden was the first to use two different glazes successfully at the same time.

In 2001 The Book Stops Here published the first catalog and history of Dryden pottery. The book shows the evolution of Dryden art pottery from molded ware to unique hand-thrown pieces; the studio illustrations show the durable and colorful glazes that make Dryden special.

Kansas pieces have a golden tan clay base and were made between 1946 and 1956. Arkansas pieces made after 1956 were made from bone white clay. Dryden pottery has a wide range of values. Many collectors are interested in the early pieces while a fast-growing number search for wheel-thrown and hand-decorated pieces made within the past twenty years. One-of-a-kind specialty pieces can exceed $500.00. Our advisor for this category is Ralph Winslow; he is listed in the Directory under Missouri.

Kansas Dryden (1946 – 1956)

Ashtray, souvenir, 5½" sq..**25.00**
Boot, souvenir, 4¾" **21.00**
Candle holders, #42, 4", pr..**24.00**
Creamer & sguar bowl, souvenir, #108 ....**28.00**
Ewer, #715, 11½"...**35.00**

Figurine, buffalo, souvenir, 4¼" 175.00
Figurine, panther, brn 98.00
Figurine, stork, #720, 10" 39.00
Juice set, gr, 7-pc 49.00
Leaf dish, souvenir, 5" 19.00
Mug, blk, bbl form, 3¾" 15.00
Pitcher, blk, 4½" 24.00
Pitcher, souvenir, #94, 6" 21.00
Pitcher, souvenir, #180, 4" 15.00
Planter, donkey, #2 ....27.00
Planter, fish, #7M, 4¾" 35.00
Planter, log, #X, 10" 39.00
Rose bowl, #105, 4¾" 20.00
Shakers, tall, 6¾", pr 25.00
Water set, tankard, #70, +6 #4 tumblers.........................65.00

Arkansas Dryden (1956 to Present)

Basket, metal holder, 5¼" 16.00
Ewer, Arkansas, 11½" 25.00
Face jug, 6" 35.00
Leaf, bl, 9¼" 19.00
Mug, face, Loi 77, wheel thrown...................................18.00
Nude, Long-Hua Xu, 15½" 75.00
Pitcher, pnt, Maj Lis, 10" 34.00
Teapot, JB Buck 25.00
Vase, bl, 8" 15.00
Vase, bud; JB Buck, 6½" 20.00
Vase, fish, HP by Jim Dryden, mini 35.00
Vase, wheel thrown, JK Dryden, 9" 100.00
Vase, wheel thrown, 1979, 4½" 16.00

Duncan and Miller

The firm that became known as the Duncan and Miller Glass Company in 1900 was organized in 1874 in Pittsburgh, Pennsylvania, a partnership between George Duncan, his sons Harry and James, and his son-in-law Augustus Heisey. John Ernest Miller was hired as their designer. He is credited with creating the most famous of all Duncan's glassware lines, Three Face. (See Pattern Glass.) The George Duncan and Sons Glass Company, as it was titled, was only one of eighteen companies that merged in 1891 with U.S. Glass. Soon after the Pittsburgh factory burned in 1892, the association was dissolved, and Heisey left the firm to set up his own factory in Newark, Ohio. Duncan built his new plant in Washington, Pennsylvania, where he continued to make pressed glassware in such notable patterns as Bagware, Amberette, Duncan Flute, Button Arches, and Zippered Slash. The firm was eventually sold to U.S. Glass in Tiffin, Ohio, and unofficially closed in August 1955.

In addition to the early pressed dinnerware patterns, today's Duncan and Miller collectors enjoy searching for opalescent vases in many patterns and colors, frosted 'Satin Tone' glassware, acid-etched designs, and lovely stemware such as the Rock Crystal cuttings. Milk glass was made in limited quantity and is considered a good investment. Ruby glass, Ebony (a lovely opaque black glass popular during the '20s and '30s), and, of course, the glass animal and bird figurines are all highly valued examples of the art of Duncan and Miller.

Expect to pay at least 25% more than values listed for other colors, for ruby and cobalt, as much as 50% more in the Georgian, Pall Mall, and Sandwich lines. Pink, green, and amber Sandwich is worth approximately 30% more than the same items in crystal. Milk glass examples of American Way are valued up to 30% higher than color, 50% higher in Pall Mall. Chartreuse Canterbury is worth 10% to 20% more than crystal. Add approximately 40% to 50% to listed prices for opalescent items.

Etchings, cuttings, and other decorations will increase values by about 50%. For further study we recommend *The Encyclopedia of Duncan Glass* by Gail Krause; she is listed in the Directory under Pennsylvania. Several Duncan and Miller lines are shown in *Elegant Glassware of the Depression Era* by Gene Florence. Also refer to *Glass Animals* by Dick and Pat Spencer; they are both listed under Illinois. See also Glass Animals and Figurines. Our advisor is Roselle Shleifman; she is listed in the Directory under New York.

Canterbury, crystal, ashtray, club; 3" 8.00
Canterbury, crystal, basket, oval, 3½" 25.00
Canterbury, crystal, bowl, finger; 4½x2" 12.00
Canterbury, crystal, bowl, flared, 12x3½" 30.00
Canterbury, crystal, bowl, gardenia; 7½x2¼" 17.50
Canterbury, crystal, bowl, salad; shallow, 15x2¾" 45.00
Canterbury, crystal, candlestick, 3-light, 6", ea 37.50
Canterbury, crystal, creamer, 7-oz, 3¾" 9.00
Canterbury, crystal, decanter, w/stopper, 32-oz, 12" 65.00
Canterbury, crystal, oval, 3½" 15.00
Canterbury, crystal, pitcher, martini; 32-oz, 9¼"...............75.00

Canterbury, crystal, pitcher, 64-ounce, $250.00.
(Photo courtesy Gene Florence)

Canterbury, crystal, plate, cake; hdls, 13½" 35.00
Canterbury, crystal, plate, cracker; hdls, w/ring, 11" 22.00
Canterbury, crystal, relish, 3-part, 3-hdl, 8x1¾" 17.50
Canterbury, crystal, stem, cordial; #5115, 1-oz, 4¼" 28.00
Canterbury, crystal, sugar bowl, ind, 3-oz, 2½" 9.00
Canterbury, crystal, tumbler, ice cream; #5115, ftd, 5-oz, 2½" 10.00
Canterbury, crystal, urn, 4½x4½" 15.00
Canterbury, crystal, vase, cloverleaf; 6½" 35.00
Caribbean, bl, bowl, grapefruit; hdls, ftd, 7¼" 35.00
Caribbean, bl, ice bucket, w/hdl, 6½" 195.00
Caribbean, bl, mayonnaise, hdls, w/liner & spoon, 5¾" 80.00
Caribbean, bl, plate, salad; 7½" 20.00
Caribbean, bl, server, center hdl, 5¾" 45.00
Caribbean, bl, stem, sherbet; ftd, 4¼" 24.00
Caribbean, bl, tumbler, iced tea; ftd, 11-oz, 6½" 60.00
Caribbean, crystal, bowl, vegetable; flared edge, 9¼" 32.50
Caribbean, crystal, candelabrum, 2-light, 4¾" 40.00
Caribbean, crystal, pitcher, water; w/ice lip, 72-oz, 9" 225.00
Caribbean, crystal, plate, torte; 16".............................35.00
Caribbean, crystal, shakers, metal tops, 3", pr 32.00
Caribbean, crystal, teacup 15.00
Caribbean, crystal, vase, bulbous, flared edge, ftd, 7½" 32.50
First Love, crystal, basket, #115, oval, 10x4¼x7" 195.00
First Love, crystal, bowl, flared, #115, 12x3¼"..................60.00
First Love, crystal, candelabrum, 2-light, w/prisms, #30, 6" 60.00

First Love, crystal, candy box, 3-hdl, 3-part, w/lid, #115, 6x3½" ..85.00
First Love, crystal, cheese stand, #111, 3x5¼" 25.00
First Love, crystal, creamer, #115, 7-oz, 3¾" 15.00
First Love, crystal, lamp, hurricane; #115, w/prisms, 15" 175.00
First Love, crystal, nappy, w/bottom star, #25, 5x1" 20.00
First Love, crystal, pitcher, ice lip, #5202, 80-oz, 9" 200.00
First Love, crystal, plate, lemon; hdls, #111, 6" 14.00
First Love, crystal, plate, torte; rolled edge, #111, 12" 40.00
First Love, crystal, relish, 3-hdl, flared, #115, 9x1½" 32.50
First Love, crystal, stem, cordial; #5111½, 1-oz, 3¾" 60.00
First Love, crystal, tray, celery; hdls, #111, 8x2" 17.50
First Love, crystal, urn, sq ft, 5½" 37.50
First Love, crystal, vase, crimped, #115, 5x5" 35.00
Lily of the Valley, crystal, ashtray, 3" 25.00
Lily of the Valley, crystal, candlestick, dbl, ea 55.00
Lily of the Valley, crystal, candy dish, w/lid 85.00
Lily of the Valley, crystal, cheese & cracker dish 75.00
Lily of the Valley, crystal, creamer 25.00
Lily of the Valley, crystal, plate, 8" 30.00
Lily of the Valley, crystal, relish, 3-part 25.00
Lily of the Valley, crystal, stem, water goblet 40.00
Nautical, bl, cigarette jar 75.00
Nautical, bl, comport, 7" 295.00
Nautical, bl, ice bucket 125.00
Nautical, bl, plate, cake; hdls, 6½" 25.00

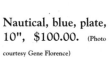

Nautical, blue, plate, 10", $100.00. (Photo courtesy Gene Florence)

Nautical, bl, relish, 2-part, hdls 45.00
Nautical, bl, tumbler, orange juice; ftd 28.00
Nautical, crystal, candy jar, w/lid 295.00
Nautical, crystal, cocktail shaker (fish design) 60.00
Nautical, crystal, marmalade 25.00
Nautical, crystal, plate, 8" 10.00
Nautical, crystal, sugar bowl 15.00
Nautical, crystal, tumbler, water; ftd, 9-oz 15.00
Sandwich, crystal, ashtray, sq, 2¾" 8.00
Sandwich, crystal, bonbon, ftd, w/lid, 7½" 50.00
Sandwich, crystal, bowl, epergne; w/center hole, 12" 100.00
Sandwich, crystal, bowl, fruit; flared edge, 12" 45.00
Sandwich, crystal, bowl, ivy; crimped, ftd, 5" 40.00
Sandwich, crystal, bowl, nappy, 2-part, 5" 12.00
Sandwich, crystal, candelabrum, 1-light, w/bobeche & prisms, 10".85.00
Sandwich, crystal, candlestick, 3-light, 5", ea 50.00
Sandwich, crystal, comport, flared, low ft, 6" 27.50
Sandwich, crystal, epergne, garden; 9" 150.00
Sandwich, crystal, pitcher, metal top, 13-oz 65.00
Sandwich, crystal, plate, cracker; w/ring, 13" 35.00
Sandwich, crystal, plate, deviled egg; 12" 85.00

Sandwich, crystal, relish, 3-part, oblong, 10" 32.50
Sandwich, crystal, stem, sundae; flared rim, 5-oz, 3½" 12.00
Sandwich, crystal, tray, ice cream; rolled edge, 12" 55.00
Sandwich, crystal, tray, mint; rolled edge, w/ring hdl, 7" ..22.00
Sandwich, crystal, tumbler, juice; ftd, 5-oz, 3¾" 12.00
Sandwich, crystal, vase, crimped, ftd, 3" 22.50
Spiral Flutes, amber, gr or pk, bowl, almond; 2" 13.00
Spiral Flutes, amber, gr or pk, bowl, lily pond; 10½" 40.00
Spiral Flutes, amber, gr or pk, comport, 6⅝" 17.50
Spiral Flutes, amber, gr or pk, cup, demi 25.00
Spiral Flutes, amber, gr or pk, ice tub, hdls 75.00
Spiral Flutes, amber, gr or pk, plate, torte; 13⅝" 40.00
Spiral Flutes, amber, gr or pk, relish, oval, 3-pc, 10x7⅜" ..100.00
Spiral Flutes, amber, gr or pk, stem, parfait; 4½-oz, 5⅝" ...17.50
Spiral Flutes, amber, gr or pk, sweetmeat, w/lid, 7½" 100.00
Spiral Flutes, amber, gr or pk, tumbler, ginger ale; 11-oz, 5½"...70.00
Spiral Flutes, amber, gr or pk, vase, 6½" 20.00
Tear Drop, crystal, ashtray, 5" 8.00
Tear Drop, crystal, bonbon, 4-hdl, 6" 12.00
Tear Drop, crystal, bowl, flower; oval, 8x12" 50.00
Tear Drop, crystal, bowl, fruit; flared, 10" 30.00
Tear Drop, crystal, bowl, punch; 2½-gal, 15½" 110.00
Tear Drop, crystal, butter dish, hdls, ¼-lb 25.00
Tear Drop, crystal, candy box, w/lid, 2-part, hdls, 7" 65.00
Tear Drop, crystal, comport, low ft, hdls, 6" 15.00
Tear Drop, crystal, cup, tea; 6-oz 6.00
Tear Drop, crystal, ice bucket, 5½" 85.00
Tear Drop, crystal, mustard jar, w/lid, 4¼" 40.00
Tear Drop, crystal, olive dish, hdls, oval, 4¼" 15.00
Tear Drop, crystal, plate, lazy Susan; 18" 90.00
Tear Drop, crystal, plate, lemon; hdls, 7" 12.50
Tear Drop, crystal, relish, 4-part, 4-hdl, sq, 12" 40.00
Tear Drop, crystal, shakers, 5" 27.50
Tear Drop, crystal, stem, claret; 4-oz, 5½" 20.00
Tear Drop, crystal, sugar bowl, 8-oz 8.00
Tear Drop, crystal, tray, hdls, 8" 12.50
Tear Drop, crystal, tumbler, old-fashioned; flat, 7-oz, 3¼" .12.00
Tear Drop, crystal, vase, fan shape, ftd, 9" 30.00
Terrace, cobalt or red, bowl, finger; #5111 ½, 4¼" 75.00
Terrace, cobalt or red, comport, 3½x4¾" 80.00
Terrace, cobalt or red, plate, cracker; w/ring, hdls, 11" ...110.00
Terrace, cobalt or red, plate, lemon; hdls, 6" 30.00
Terrace, cobalt or red, saucer, sq 12.00
Terrace, cobalt or red, tumbler, water; 9-oz, 4" 40.00
Terrace, cobalt or red, urn, 10½x4½" 350.00
Terrace, crystal or amber, ashtray, sq, 3½" 17.50
Terrace, crystal or amber, bowl, flared rim, ftd, 10x3¾" 55.00
Terrace, crystal or amber, bowl, nappy, hdld, 6x1¾" 22.00
Terrace, crystal or amber, candlestick, 1-light, bobeche/prisms, ea ...75.00
Terrace, crystal or amber, creamer, 10-oz, 3" 18.00
Terrace, crystal or amber, plate, sandwich; hdls, 11" 30.00
Terrace, crystal or amber, stem, ice cream; #5111 ½, 5-oz, 4"...14.00
Terrace, crystal or amber, tray, celery; hdls, 8x2" 17.50

Durand

Durand art glass was made by the Vineland Flint Glass Works of Vineland, New Jersey. Victor Durand Jr. was the sole proprietor. The division called the 'fancy shop' was geared to the production of fine hand-blown art glass in the style of Tiffany and Steuben. Crystal, ambergis, and opal glass were each used as a basis to create such patterns as King Tut, Heart and Vine, Peacock Feather, and Egyptian Crackle. Cased glass was used to produce cut designs. Production of art glass began in 1924 and continued until 1931. Although much of this art glass was unsigned, when it was, it was generally signed within the pontil 'Durand' or 'Durand' written across the top of a large letter V, all in silver script. The numbers that sometimes appear along with the signature indicate the shape and height of the object. Owner Victor Durand employed the owner and several workers from the failed Quezal Art Glass and Decorating Co. This is why early Durand may sometimes look similar to Quezal art glass. In 1926 Durand art glass was awarded a medal of honor at the Sesquicentennial International Exposition in Philadelphia, Pennsylvania. Our advisor for this category is Edward J. Meschi, author of *Durand — The Man and His Glass* (Antique Publications); he is listed in the Directory under New Jersey.

Bowl, finger; ambergris w/gr trim, 2½x5", w/6½" underplate **225.00**
Bowl, hearts & vines, wht on bl irid, 2x4¼" **625.00**
Bowl, peacock feathers, opal/gr on gr over crystal, 4x9½" **825.00**
Bowl, yel lustre, wht-trim ft, bl/wht crisscross bands, 4½x10½"..**1,300.00**
Candlesticks, King Tut, bl on marigold, gold int, 10", pr **2,750.00**
Champagne, Optic Rib, amethyst, 4" **225.00**
Champagne, ruby flashed w/Spanish Yellow stem & ruby ft, 6"..**325.00**
Cocktail, peacock feathers, opal/red on red on crystal, 4½" **375.00**
Compote, gold irid, #V5002, 6x7½" **575.00**
Compote, King Tut, bl w/gold irid int, 6½x6" **825.00**
Compote, Optic Rib, amethyst, #744, 5¼x7" **375.00**
Compote, peacock feathers, opal/gr on clear, ambergris ft, 6" **600.00**
Ginger jar, King Tut, gr on orange gold, 8" **3,900.00**
Goblet, feathers, opal on red over crystal, crystal stem/ft, 6".......**375.00**
Goblet, Optic Rib, bl w/Spanish Yellow stem, ruby ft, 8½" **425.00**
Goblet, peacock feathers, opal/red on red to clear, yel stem/ft, 7" .**375.00**
Jar, feathers, opal/bl on gold, overall threading, 7" **2,400.00**
Lamp base, gold irid w/overall gold threading, 18½x7" **325.00**
Lamp base, Lady Gay Rose, King Tut, opal & pk, 12½" **2,500.00**
Luminare, Moorish Crackle tumbler shade; brass base w/dolphins, 7" ..**725.00**
Plate, Optic Rib, bl, scalloped rim, 11½" **150.00**
Plate, salad; pk w/opal threads, floral & vine cutting, 7½" **190.00**
Shade, bk & wht Moorish Crackle over ambergris, ruffled, 8½" H..**700.00**
Sherbet, feathers, wht on Spanish Yellow w/bl & wht trim, 4" ...**575.00**
Table torchere, Moorish Crackle shade, gr/wht/yel, on iron base, 17" ..**1,250.00**
Torchiere, Egyptian Crackle striated w/gold int, electrified, 12" .**975.00**
Tumbler, iced tea; ambergris w/gr trim, 6" **125.00**
Tumbler, lemonade; Optic Rib, ambergris w/gr trim, 5½" **150.00**
Vase, allover gold threading on orange-gold irid, bl/gold ft, 10", EX ..**500.00**
Vase, ambergris w/wht single-line 'feather,' 3 panels cut w/grapes, 7".**650.00**
Vase, bl irid, cylindrical, #1968-8, ca 1924-31, 8⅛" **725.00**
Vase, bl irid w/bl threading overall, #1710-6, 6½" **825.00**
Vase, bl irid w/gold & silver coils, urn shape, orange int, 9¼".**1,500.00**
Vase, clear w/controlled airtrap, ovoid, #1995, 4x4"....................**275.00**
Vase, cut o/l, red to clear, 9" **2,375.00**
Vase, feathers, gold on gr w/gold lustre int, shouldered/ribbed, 4x5"..**1,600.00**
Vase, feathers, opal & bl on crystal, w/cut florals, 9¾"...............**780.00**
Vase, feathers, opal & red on red to clear, appl ft, 12" **1,375.00**
Vase, feathers, opal on red to clear, #1997-10, 10" **550.00**
Vase, feathers, opal/gold w/gr tips, threading, stick neck, 10" ..**1,050.00**
Vase, feathers, red & wht on ruby, 10" **1,350.00**
Vase, gold irid, onion form w/long stick neck, dimpled side, 15"..**750.00**
Vase, gold irid, vasiform w/flared rim, #1812-8, 8⅝" **440.00**
Vase, gold irid, wide mouth, #V-1968-6, 6" **350.00**
Vase, gold irid w/overall threading, 1812-7, 7½" **800.00**
Vase, gold w/red highlights, flaring neck, 7x4"............................**425.00**
Vase, hearts & vines, opal on bl irid, can neck w/2 rings, 10" .**2,100.00**
Vase, hearts & vines, opal on bl irid, ruffled, #1728, 4⅞" **950.00**
Vase, hearts & vines, silver on cobalt irid, vasiform, 9½" **2,200.00**
Vase, hearts & vines on gold irid, ruffled, 6¾" **1,900.00**
Vase, King Tut, apple gr w/gold swirls, ftd trumpet form, #20120, 12"..**2,000.00**

Vase, King Tut, bl on gold lustre, #1710, 4¼" **1,500.00**
Vase, King Tut, bl-gold irid, V 1716-7, 6¾" **900.00**
Vase, King Tut, gold on gr, 1968, 8" **1,500.00**
Vase, King Tut, gold on opal, gold int, shouldered, 8¾" **1,375.00**
Vase, King Tut, gr on gold irid, plain gold irid int, 1990, 6" **1,035.00**
Vase, King Tut, opal on platinum bl, 6½" **1,000.00**
Vase, King Tut, silver-gold irid on lime gr, orange irid int, 11", NM.**1,100.00**
Vase, King Tut, wht on gold irid, #1937-10, 10" **1,600.00**
Vase, King Tut on rose-pk, shouldered, 7"................................**3,800.00**
Vase, Lady Gay Rose w/irid coils, squat/ftd w/long neck, 12½" ..**4,100.00**
Vase, leaves, gr/gold irid on wht irid, #20120-12, 11½", EX **575.00**
Vase, marigold w/bl irid coil, 10" **950.00**
Vase, Moorish Crackle, gr/wht over ambergris, lustered, 10x10"...**3,000.00**
Vase, peacock feathers, opal w/emerald gr top, 13"...................**1,200.00**
Vase, red crackle over crystal w/lustre, 6"................................**1,900.00**
Vase, red to crystal w/geometric cuttings, 10" **1,650.00**

Easter

In the early 1900s to the 1930s, Germany made the first composition candy containers in the shapes of Easter rabbits, ducks, and chicks. A few were also made of molded cardboard. In the 1940s West Germany made candy containers out of molded cardboard. Many of these had spring necks to give a nodding effect. From the 1930s and into the 1950s, United States manufacturers made Easter candy containers out of egg-carton material (pulp) or pressed cardboard. Ducks and chicks are not as high in demand as rabbits. Rabbits with painted-on clothes or attached fabric clothes bring more than the plain brown or white rabbits. When no condition mentioned in the description, assume that values reflect excellent to near mint condition for all but paper items; those assume to be in near mint to mint condition. Our advisor for this category is Jenny Tarrant; she is listed in the Directory under Missouri.

Note: In the candy container section, measurements given for the rabbit and cart or rabbit and wagon containers indicate the distance to the tip of the rabbits' ears.

Candy Containers

German, rabbit (brown composition) pulling wooden cart, ca 1900 – 1920, 7", $325.00. (Photo courtesy Jenny Tarrant)

German, begging rabbit, brn w/glass eyes, compo, 1900-30s, 5" **95.00**
German, begging rabbit, brn w/glass eyes, compo, 1900-30s, 6"..**125.00**
German, begging rabbit, brn w/glass eyes, compo, 1900-30s, 7"..**150.00**
German, begging rabbit, brn w/glass eyes, compo, 1900-30s, 8"..**175.00**
German, begging rabbit, brn w/glass eyes, compo, 1900-30s, 9"..**250.00**
German, begging rabbit, mohair covered, compo, 1900-30s, 4"..**135.00**
German, begging rabbit, mohair covered, compo, 1900-30s, 5"..**150.00**

German, begging rabbit, mohair covered, compo, 1900-30s, 6" ..**195.00**
German, begging rabbit, mohair covered, compo, 1900-30s, 7" ..**200.00**
German, duck, yel w/glass eyes, compo, 1900-30s, 5" **110.00**
German, duck or chick, pnt-on clothes, compo, 1900-30s, 3-4" .**125.00**
German, duck or chick, pnt-on clothes, compo, 1900-30s, 5" .**145.00**
German, duck or chick, pnt-on clothes, compo, 1900-30s, 6" .**185.00**
German, duck or chick, pnt-on clothes, compo, 1900-30s, 7" ...**200.00**
German, egg, molded cb, 1900-30, 3-7" **45.00**
German, egg, molded cb, 1900-30, 8" **65.00**
German, egg, tin, 1900-10, EX, 2-3" **55.00**
German, rabbit (dressed) in car, compo, 1900-30s, from $250 to ..**325.00**
German, rabbit (dressed) in shoe, compo, 1900-30s, from $250 to.**275.00**
German, rabbit (dressed) on egg, compo, 1900-30s, from $200 to.**250.00**
German, rabbit (dressed) on log, compo, 1900-30s, from $200 to .**250.00**
German, rabbit pulling wood cart, mohair covered, 1900-30s, 4" ..**175.00**
German, rabbit pulling wood cart, mohair covered, 1900-30s, 5"..**225.00**
German, rabbit pulling wood cart, mohair covered, 1900-30s, 6"..**295.00**
German, rabbit pulling wood cart, mohair covered, 1900-30s, 7"..**325.00**
German, rabbit pulling wood wagon, brn compo, 1900-30s, 4"..**150.00**
German, rabbit pulling wood wagon, brn compo, 1900-30s, 5"..**175.00**
German, rabbit pulling wood wagon, brn compo, 1900-30s, 6"..**195.00**
German, rabbit pulling wood wagon, brn compo, 1900-30s, 7"..**225.00**
German, rabbit w/fabric clothes, compo, 1900-30s, 4" **250.00**
German, rabbit w/fabric clothes, compo, 1900-30s, 5" **300.00**
German, rabbit w/fabric clothes, compo, 1900-30s, 6" **325.00**
German, rabbit w/fabric clothes, compo, 1900-30s, 7" **350.00**
German, rabbit w/glass beading, compo, 1900-30s, 6" **150.00**
German, rabbit w/pnt-on clothes, compo, 1900-30s, 4" **150.00**
German, rabbit w/pnt-on clothes, compo, 1900-30s, 5" **200.00**
German, rabbit w/pnt-on clothes, compo, 1900-30s, 6" **225.00**
German, rabbit w/pnt-on clothes, compo, 1900-30s, 7" **250.00**
German, sitting rabbit, brn w/glass eyes, compo, 1900-30s, 5" **95.00**
German, sitting rabbit, brn w/glass eyes, compo, 1900-30s, 6" **110.00**
German, sitting rabbit, brn w/glass eyes, compo, 1900-30s, 7" **125.00**
German, sitting rabbit, mohair covered, compo, 1900-30s, 4" **140.00**
German, sitting rabbit, mohair covered, compo, 1900-30s, 5" **160.00**
German, sitting rabbit, mohair covered, compo, 1900-30s, 6" **175.00**
German, standing rabbit (Ma), pnt-on clothes, molded cb, 10½".**250.00**
German, standing rabbit (Pa), pnt-on clothes, molded cb, 10½".**250.00**
German, walking rabbit, brn w/glass eyes, compo, 1900-30s, 5"..**110.00**
German, walking rabbit, brn w/glass eyes, compo, 1900-30s, 6"..**125.00**
German, walking rabbit, brn w/glass eyes, compo, 1900-30s, 7"..**135.00**
German, walking rabbit, brn w/glass eyes, compo, 1900-30s, 8"..**150.00**
German, walking rabbit, brn w/glass eyes, compo, 1900-30s, 9"..**175.00**
German, walking rabbit, mohair covered, compo, 1900-30s, 4"..**150.00**
German, walking rabbit, mohair covered, compo, 1900-30s, 5"..**185.00**
German, walking rabbit, mohair covered, compo, 1900-30s, 6"..**225.00**
German, walking rabbit, mohair covered, compo, 1900-30s, 7"..**245.00**
German, walking rabbit, wht compo, 1900-30s, 6" **125.00**
German, wht w/pnt on clothes, compo, 1900-30s, 3" **175.00**
US, begging rabbit, pulp, 1940-50, w/base...............................**55.00**
US, sitting rabbit, pulp, brn w/glass eyes, Burk Co, 1930 ....**85.00**
US, sitting rabbit, pulp, no basket, 1940-50 ....**45.00**
US, sitting rabbit next to lg basket, pulp, 1930-50 ....**75.00**
US, sitting rabbit w/basket on bk, pulp, 1940-50 ....**75.00**
W German/US Zone, dressed chick, cb, spring neck, 1940-50......**65.00**
W German/US Zone, dressed rabbit, cb, spring neck, 1940-50.....**80.00**
W German/US Zone, egg, molded cb, 1940-60, 3-8", from $25 to ..**40.00**
W German/US Zone, plain rabbit, cb, spring neck, 1940-50 ....**60.00**

Miscellaneous

Celluloid chick or duck, dressed, 3-5", M.................................**45.00**
Celluloid chick or duck, dressed, 6-8", M **75.00**

Celluloid chicken pulling wagon w/rabbit, M **125.00**
Celluloid rabbit, dressed, 3-5", M...**65.00**
Celluloid rabbit, dressed, 6-8", M...**75.00**
Celluloid rabbit, plain, 3-5", M...**20.00**
Celluloid rabbit, plain, 6-7", M...**30.00**
Celluloid rabbit & chick in swan boat, M..................................**150.00**
Celluloid rabbit driving car, M **150.00**
Celluloid rabbit pulling wagon, M...**125.00**
Celluloid rabbit pushing or pulling cart, lg, M...........................**125.00**
Celluloid rabbit pushing or pulling cart, sm, M..........................**75.00**
Celluloid windup toy, Japan or Occupied Japan, M **150.00**
Cotton batten rabbit w/paper ears, Japan, 1930-50, 2-5".............**30.00**
Cotton batten rabbit w/paper ears, Japan, 1930-50, 6" **45.00**

Egg Cups

Egg cups, one of the fastest growing collectibles, have been traced back to the ruins of Pompeii. They have been made in almost every country and in almost every conceivable material (ceramics, glass, metal, papier-mâché, plastic, wood, ivory, even rubber, and straw). Popular categories include Art Deco, Black memorabilia, chintz, characters/personalities, Golliwoggs, railroadiana, Steamship, Souvenir Ware, etc.

Still being produced today, egg cups appeal to collectors on many levels. Prices can range from quite low to many thousands of dollars. Those made prior to 1840 are scarce and sought after, as are the character/personality egg cups of the 1930s.

For a more thorough study of egg cups we recommend *Egg Cups: An Illustrated History and Price Guide* (Antique Publications) by Brenda Blake, our advisor. You will find her address listed in the Directory under Maine.

Key:
bkt — bucket, a single cup without a foot
dbl — 2-sided with small end for eating egg in shell, large end for mixing egg with toast and butter
fig — figural, an egg cup actually molded into the shape of an animal, bird, car, person, etc.
hoop — hoop, a single open cup with waistline
inst. dbl — large custard cup shape
set — tray or cruet (stand, frame or basket) with 2 to 8 cups
sgl — single, with a foot; goblet shaped

American China/Pottery

Dbl, Autumn, mc fruit basket, Lenox **35.00**
Dbl, Blueberry, Stangl...**25.00**
Dbl, Bride, Cleminson, 1940s **35.00**
Dbl, Brittany, Homer Laughlin **19.00**
Dbl, Chesterton, teal, Harker, 1950s **14.00**
Dbl, Horse, MA Hadley **24.00**
Dbl, Magnolia, Stangl, 1950s **25.00**
Dbl, Pear, gr, MA Hadley **24.00**
Dbl, Poppytrail, Metlox **35.00**
Dbl, Tuxedo, fancy gold rim, Lenox, ca 1930 ....**38.00**
Dbl, woman in apron, Cleminson, 1940s **30.00**
Sgl, Apple, Franciscan...**32.00**
Sgl, Lei Lani, lotus flower, Vernon Kilns, ca 1940, lg **65.00**
Sgl, Valencia, Louise Bauer, Shawnee, 1937.................................**22.00**
Sgl, Vistosa, red, Taylor, Smith & Taylor, ca 1940 ....**50.00**

Characters/Personalities

Bkt, Marilyn Monroe, transfer, 1993, rare **65.00**

Fig, ET..22.00
Fig, Humpty Dumpty on wht wall, Germany 55.00
Fig, Prince William, Spitting Image, 1982 ....125.00
Fig, Princess Di, Spitting Image, 1980s...................100.00
Set, Beatles (4 bkts), blk & wht bust portraits w/names, KSP mk ..275.00
Sgl, Alice in Wonderland, integral saucer, Hammersley.............50.00
Sgl, Batman, recent 16.00
Sgl, Field Marshall Roberts, Boer War General, ca 1903 ....80.00
Sgl, Prince Rainier/Princess Grace of Monaco, wedding, Limoges, 1950s..100.00

English/Staffordshire

Bkt, Cornish kitchen ware, bl bands, TC Green & Co, 1930s......16.00
Bkt, Crocus, Clarice Cliff..125.00
Bkt, Daffodil, Moorcroft..60.00
Bkt, Fantasque Bizarre, Clarice Cliff..........................175.00
Bkt, Orange Tree, Art Deco, Crown Ducal 38.00
Bkt, Polka Dots, bl, Susie Cooper 35.00
Bkt, Primavera, Midwinter 25.00
Dbl, Cornishware, bl bands, TC Green, 1930s...............58.00
Dbl, Dresden Spray, Susie Cooper...............................85.00
Dbl, Friendly Village, Johnson Bros 25.00
Dbl, Fruit Basket, Masons..25.00
Dbl, Madras, flow bl, Royal Doulton, ca 1900 ....110.00
Dbl, Madras, Maddock, ca 1925...............................25.00
Dbl, Marguerite, chintz, Royal Winton 50.00
Dbl, Mr Snowman w/hat, Royal Doulton.....................100.00
Dbl, Old Cottage, chintz, Royal Winton.......................90.00
Dbl, Old Mill Stream, Johnson Bros 2.00
Dbl, Rose Chintz, Johnson Bros.................................20.00
Dbl, side-by-side, brn, Troika 150.00
Dbl, Tea Leaf, Adams, 1970s repro 100.00
Set, Felicia, gr sunflowers, TC Green, 4 bkt cups+sq tray 40.00
Set, Polka Dot, Babbacombe, 4 cups on tray 70.00
Sgl, Bl Dragon, Royal Worcester................................30.00
Sgl, Creamware, Wedgwood, ca 1810........................125.00
Sgl, Mabel Lucie Attwell, Shelley 100.00
Sgl, Orange Tree, Art Deco, Crown Ducal....................60.00
Sgl, Tea Rose, yel, Royal Albert.................................22.00
Sgl, Tower, bl, Spode Copeland, ca 1930.....................25.00

Figurals

Black male (sitting) w/hat, Japana, 1930s 120.00
Black male face, Germany, ca 1912 ....80.00
Chicks, molded, Fanny Farmer, 1930s 25.00
Dog w/blk & wht spots hoisting cup 26.00
Duck, bl, Fanny Farmer, 1930s.................................25.00

Duck pulling egg cart, unmarked Japan, 2", $15.00.

Golly Sailor behind rnd cup, Sailing Club, Silver Crane, 1987-94..40.00
Rabbit pushing wheelbarrow cup, plastic........................20.00
Running legs, Carlton 68.00
Sergeant Chimp, plastic, w/lid 28.00
Steam engine, bl, O'Donaghue's Pottery 18.00
Walking leg w/peg leg, Carlton..................................65.00
Walking legs, gr shoes, Carlton..................................40.00
Whistler, bear, lustre, Foreign 100.00

Foreign

Bkt, Cardinal Tuck, red robe, Goebel, 1960s 175.00
Dbl, geometric gold band, T&V Limoges......................32.00
Dbl, rooster & hen, yel base, T&V Limoges...................60.00
Dbl, Rothschild's Bird, scalloped rim, 1990s................90.00
Dbl, Sheridan, Noritake...32.00
Set, Blue Onion, Meissen, 1890s, 6 cups+stand...........600.00
Set, chicken, ftd, HP bsk, Bing & Grondahl, 1865, 2-tier stand+12 cups..750.00
Set, cup+salt shaker+tray, Limoges.............................28.00
Sgl, Bluebird, Lefton, Japan......................................60.00
Sgl, Celadon, gr leaves, pk enamel flowers, Japan, ca 1910 ....30.00
Sgl, fruit & flowers w/Greek Key border, China............12.00
Sgl, Limpet, Belleek, 3rd gr mk.................................50.00
Sgl, Regina, Gouda, 1920s......................................115.00
Sgl, Saladon, Bavarian style, Hutschenreuther.............22.00
Sgl, wht flower, Goebel, 1985...................................20.00
Sgl, Willow, Japan, recent 6.00

Glass

Dbl, Cape Cod, Imperial 40.00
Dbl, Hobnail, milk glass, Fenton................................55.00
Dbl, Raindrop, amber, hobs, flared rim........................42.00
Dbl, vaseline crackle, ca 1890s.................................82.00
Fig, chicken, bl, Portieux...25.00
Fig, chicken, milk glass, John E Kemple.......................18.00
Fig, face, pk, Mosser, recent 12.00
Fig, rooster, vaseline, Boyd......................................14.00
Sgl, Argus, flint, ca 1850-70.....................................28.00
Sgl, Ashburton, flint, ca 1850-70...............................26.00
Sgl, bottle glass, gr, 2-part mold, ca 1910 ....32.00
Sgl, Cremax, bl to wht 7.50
Sgl, Hobnail, ruby flashed 55.00
Sgl, mercury glass, gold-wash lining, ca 1910 ....68.00
Sgl, Nailsea, pk looping..285.00
Sgl, Smocking, amethyst, Sandwich, 1840s.................275.00

Railroad

Dbl, Meridale, Wabash RR..35.00
Dbl, Traveler, CMStP&P 150.00
Inst dbl, Galatea, CMStP&P.....................................110.00
Inst dbl, Roxbury, KCS Rail OPCO China 25.00
Sgl, Bows & Leaves, Canadian Pacific.........................45.00
Sgl, California Poppy, ATSF.....................................165.00
Sgl, Denver & Rio Grande, recent 14.00
Sgl, Dewitt Clinton, NYC 275.00
Sgl, Mercury, NYC, NY Central RR............................130.00
Sgl, Mimbreno, ATSF..500.00
Sgl, Winged Streamliner, UP, Scammell.......................70.00

Souvenir

Bkt, Berlin Hilton (BH), Rosenthal, 1967 ....19.00

Bkt, British Airways, bl & wht, Royal Doulton 16.00
Dbl, Caesar's Palace, brn logo, 1990s.................................15.00
Dbl, Canadian Royal AF..25.00
Dbl, Coast Guard, 1942...35.00
Dbl, McGill University, maroon seal, 1930s..................35.00
Dbl, US Army Medical Dept, red trim 20.00
Dbl, US Coast & Geodetic Survey.............................100.00
Fig, Harrods' Doorman, Wade, 1990s 30.00
Inst dbl, US Navy Admiral's Mess, ca 1940 ....55.00
Sgl, Crystal Palace London, pk lustreware, Germany, ca 1900 ......40.00
Sgl, Graceland, Japan, 1970s.......................................20.00
Sgl, Soldier's Monument, Gettysburg PA, transfer, Germany, ca 1900 ...40.00

Miscellaneous

Bkt, Melmac, 1950s 6.50
Dbl, Presidential Lines, gr band, maroon bird 40.00
Hoop, Atlantic Transport Line, Wedgwood 135.00
Hoop, horn, ca 1820..80.00
Set, christening, silver, ca 1878, cup+spoon+wooden case.........350.00
Set, christening, SP, cup & spoon, presentation box 75.00
Set, silver, Elkington, Victorian era, 6 cups+spoons 300.00
Set, silver, Walker & Hall, Victorian era, 4 cups+spoons............225.00
Sgl, Bakelite, on 3 prongs, ca 1940s..............................12.00
Sgl, Smiley Face, rubber 10.00
Sgl, traveler's; trn wood, 19th C, 2 cups w/removable bases 70.00
Sgl, wrought iron, ca 1850 ....18.00

Elfinware

Made in Germany from about 1920 until the 1940s, these miniature vases, boxes, salt cellars, and miscellaneous novelty items are characterized by the tiny applied flowers that often cover their entire surface. Pieces with animals and birds are the most valuable, followed by the more interesting examples such as diminutive grand pianos, candle holders, etc. Items covered in 'spinach' (applied green moss) can be valued at 75% to 100% higher than pieces that are not decorated in this manner. See also Salts, Open.

Baby buggy, appl forget-me-nots & moss, 3½x4½" 50.00
Basket, appl flowers, 2" dia...40.00
Boot, lg pk rose w/leaves appl on wht, 1¾x2¾".........28.00
Bootie, appl flowers & spinach, ca 1920-40, 2x3½" 32.00
Box, appl flowers & spinach on lid w/dog's head, mk Germany, 2¼" ...175.00
Box, appl flowers on lid, sm 15.00
Box, Niagara Falls scene, appl flowers on sides, sm........32.00
Candle holders, saucer type, appl flowers, pr................100.00
Lipstick holder, gondola shape w/appl flowers & moss, 9" L..........65.00
Pin dish, appl mc flowers, 3" dia 12.50
Pot, appl flowers & spinach, Germany, 1¾x1¾" 25.00
Salt cellar, appl pk rose amid bl forget-me-nots & much spinach..125.00
Salt cellar, basket form w/appl flowers 15.00
Salt cellar, swan form w/bl appl flowers, 5" L 35.00
Settee, appl flowers, 3x4¼x2"......................................40.00
Shoe, pointed toe, appl flowers & much spinach, 2¼x5¼" 100.00
Vase, appl flowers, angle hdls, 2x2½" 42.00
Vase, appl pk flowers & gr spinach on basketweave, 6¼" 45.00
Vase, oval reserve w/HP bouquet, gr spinach w/bl floral rim, 2½x1"..65.00

Epergnes

Popular during the Victorian era, epergnes were fancy centerpieces often consisting of several tiers of vases (called lilies), candle holders,

dishes, or a combination of components. They were made in all types of art glass, and some were set in ornate plated frames. Our advisors for this category are Barbara and Steven Aaronson; they are listed in the Directory under California.

Amberina w/appl amber serpentine, 3-lily, red ruffled base, 1880s, 14".1,495.00
Amethyst frost to clear, 1-lily; bronze-finish ft, 16x10" 365.00
Bl opaque to milk glass, 4-lily, wht ruffled base, 16x14" 450.00
Clear opal w/cranberry rim, 3-lily, ruffled bowl, 15" 550.00
Cranberry opal to vaseline, 3-lily, 21¾" 1,200.00
Cranberry w/clear swirls on body, 4-lily, 19" 900.00
Cut crystal, tazza base w/central lily, ca 1890...........................1,675.00
Gr overshot bowl w/matching lily; ormolu base, 16½x9½".........325.00

Overshot cranberry shading to clear, ornate silver-plated base with shell-shaped dishes, engraved base, scrolled feet, ca 1850s, $1,300.00.

Pk opal lilies (4); 3-ftd scrolling SP base, 16" 475.00
Pk opaque w/appl threading, 4-lily; mirror base, 13½x10½"....2,400.00
Pk satin irid, 4-lily; SP griffin fr, 16" 4,250.00
Rose o/l w/HP floral, 1-lily, clear ruffle; ormolu fr, 11½" 250.00
SP, 3 floral cups w/glass bowl, Reed & Barton, 1900s, 15x22x9" ..1,150.00
SP wirework fr w/floral work, 7 conical vases, Sheffield, 16x12x16" ..1,035.00
Vaseline opal, 3-lily, ruffled base, 18x12"..................................1,695.00

Erickson

Carl Erickson of Bremen, Ohio, produced hand-formed glassware from 1943 until 1960 in artistic shapes, no two of which were identical. One of the characteristics of his work was the air bubbles that were captured within the glass. Both clear and colored glass were produced. Rather than to risk compromising his high standards by selling the factory, when Erickson retired, the plant was dismantled and sold.

Ashtray, blk, kidney-bean shape, mk Erickson #54, 8x6½" 95.00
Bowl, amber over crystal, paperweight, 8" 65.00
Candlesticks, gr, controlled bubbles, paperweight, tall, pr...........137.50
Candy dish, pk & lav, upturned ends, 3x8" 75.00
Compote, smoke, clear paperweight base, 9¾x7¼" 275.00
Decanter, bl flame at base, teardrop-shaped stopper, flanged lip, 9"..65.00
Pitcher, gr to clear, 9½", +pr old-fashioned tumblers 190.00
Tumbler, dbl old-fashioned; clear to gr, 4x2¾", w/gr muddler 80.00
Vase, crystal over smoke w/controlled spiral bubbles, 15"...........140.00
Vase, gr trumpet neck, clear base w/controlled bubbles, 12" 150.00
Vase, lav w/horizontal rows of bubbles, clear base, 15" 165.00
Vase, smoke, clear paperweight base w/bubbles, 6½" 45.00

Erphila

The Erphila trademark was used by Ebeling and Ruess Co. of Philadelphia between 1886 and the 1950s. The company imported quality porcelain and pottery from Germany, Czechoslovakia, Italy, and France. Pieces more readily found are from Germany and Czechoslovakia. A variety of items can be found and pieces such as figural teapots and larger figurines are moving up in value. There are a variety of marks, but all contain the name Erphila. One of the earlier marks is a green rectangle containing the name Erphila, Germany. In general, Erphila pieces are scarce, not easily found.

Bowl, floral center, sq latticework sides, #9411/3, 2¼x8" sq..........**78.00**
Cake plate, flower decals on wht, late 1800s, 11", +matching server....**130.00**
Creamer, pk draped form w/cat hdl, mk Erphila Fayence..., 5¾"...**80.00**
Figurine, bloodhound dog, brn to blk, head up, 5x7"....................**75.00**
Figurine, bulldog, blk & wht, gr mk, 3½x6" **75.00**
Figurine, child pulling wheelbarrow, 6x5" **55.00**
Figurine, mtn goats, brn & wht, 8"....................................**95.00**
Figurine, pheasants (2) on oval base, MIG, 5½"........................**45.00**
Mug, beer; drinking transfer on wht, ca 1921-37, 4⅛" **40.00**
Pitcher, gr polka-dots & trim on cream, w/lid, ca 1920, EX **65.00**
Pitcher, gr/yel plaid-like pattern, bulbous, 5"......................**35.00**
Pitcher, toucan form, red/wht/blk, 9"................................**275.00**
Plate, Viking ship, flow blue, 1930s, 11".............................**45.00**
Reamer, orange figural, 2-pc, pre-1917, 6" **285.00**
Teapot, cat figural, blk & wht w/red boy, #67008, 8"..................**170.00**
Teapot, dachshund (begging) figural, brn tones, US Zone, #67038 .**175.00**
Teapot, Georgian Leaf, emb pattern, #6679/2, late 1800s..............**75.00**
Teapot, poodle figural, #734, 8¼" **175.00**
Teapot, Princess Rose, 5¼" **65.00**
Vase, bl matt, 6-lobe w/incurvate rim, 3¼x5" **27.50**

Eskimo Artifacts

While ivory carvings made from walrus tusks or whale teeth have been the most emphasized articles of Eskimo art, basketry, and woodworking are other areas in which these Alaskan Indians excel. Their designs are effected through the application of simple yet dramatic lines and almost stark decorative devices. Though not pursued to the extent of American Indian art, the unique work of these northern tribes is beginning to attract the serious attention of today's collectors.

Basket, coiled willow splint w/faded chevrons, w/lid, 8½x8½" ...**550.00**
Basket, coiled willow w/spaced stitches, w/lid, 8x11" **375.00**
Basket, 2-color checkered geometrics, Hooper Bay, 1910s, 10x9"..**275.00**
Boots, sealskin, knee length, ca 1900, EX **375.00**
Carving, bone, man w/inset eyes, EX patina, 5x2½" **145.00**
Carving, ivory, bear w/baby seal, sgn Gambell, 2⅜x3½" on base...**435.00**
Carving, soapstone, man seated, stylized, EX details, 7" **550.00**
Carving, soapstone man w/club (wood w/ivory tips), Thornsen, 1950s, 7"...**265.00**
Carving, stone, Inuit hunter, nice detail, 1980s, 4¼x3x1½".......**295.00**
Cribbage board, cvd walrus tusk, masonic emblems, ca 1900, 11" ..**275.00**
Doll, full sealskin outfit, sewn hide face, 1900s, 18x7" **550.00**
Knife, whale tooth hdl w/scrimshaw cvg, 5½" blade, 10½".........**715.00**
Mask, hand-cvd porous whalebone, flat classic facial form, 1950s ...**60.00**

Face Jugs, Contemporary

The most recognizable form of Southern folk pottery is the face jug. Rich alkaline glazes (lustrous greens and browns) are typical, and occa-

sionally shards of glass are applied to the surface of the ware which during firing melts to produce opalescent 'glass runs' over the alkaline. In some locations clay deposits contain elements that result in areas of fluorescent blue or rutile; another variation is swirled or striped ware, reminiscent of eighteenth-century agateware from Staffordshire. Collector demand for these unique one-of-a-kind jugs is at an all-time high and is still escalating. Choice examples made by Burlon B. Craig and Lanier Meaders sometimes bring over $1,000.00 on the secondary market. If you're interested in learning more about this type of folk pottery, contact the Southern Folk Pottery Collectors Society; their address is in the Directory under Clubs, Newsletters, and Catalogs. Our advisor for this category is Billy Ray Hussey; he is listed in the Directory under North Carolina.

China clay eyes (unglazed), gr w/brn runs, L Meaders, 10½"...**1,300.00**
China clay teeth & eyes, redware w/gr ash glaze, L Meaders, 10"...**1,300.00**
China teeth, clear over brn/cream swirlware, C Lisk, 8½" **150.00**
China teeth, lt clay eyes, dk rust feldspathic, C Brown, 1990, 10½"..**140.00**
China teeth, pop eyes, glossy crushed Coke bottle glass, Craig, 6" ...**500.00**
China teeth, wht/blk eyes, frogskin gloss, Chester Hewell, 11¼"...**100.00**
Devil, redware w/brn ash glaze/bl runs, WA Flowers NC, 9¼"....**100.00**
Dk gr w/wht & blk eyes, 4 pottery teeth, Lanier Meaders, 1978, 9"...**465.00**
Lt clay teeth, rnd eyes w/inserted pupils, orange, Westmoore, 10"..**175.00**
Lt clay teeth/eyes, wavy hair/thick brows, dk rust, Cole Pottery, 15" ..**250.00**
Monkey, weeping, gray-blk w/aqua melts, strap hdl, BR Hussey, 9⅝"...**800.00**
Rock teeth, wht/dk eyes, streaky olive, dbl-face, CJ Meaders II, 11"...**800.00**
Rock teeth, wht/dk glazed eyes, olive gr alkaline, QL Meaders, 10"..**1,700.00**

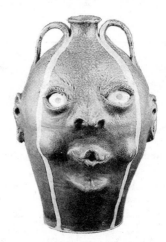

Stoneware, 'Just A Whistlin',' dark brown matt with glass melts, incised BH (Billy Ray Hussey) and titled, ca 1990, 19x12", $1,200.00.
(Photo courtesy David Rago Auctions)

Wht-glaze teeth, defined sculpting, splotchy/drippy mc, BJ Cabe, 9"..**150.00**
Wht-glaze teeth/eyes, cobalt brows/lashes/mustache, Jerry Brown, 17"..**150.00**
2-face, happy/sour expressions, Reggie Meaders 1892-1992, 8¼" ..**550.00**

Fans

The Japanese are said to have invented the fan. From there it went to China, and Portuguese traders took the idea to Europe. Though usually considered milady's accessory, even the gentlemen in seventeenth-century England carried fans! More fashionable than practical, some were of feathers and lovely hand-painted silks with carved ivory or tortoise sticks. Some French fans had peepholes. There are mourning fans, calendar fans, and those with advertising.

Fine antique fans (pre-1900) of ivory or mother-of-pearl are highly desirable. Those from before 1800 often sell for upwards of $1,000.00. Fans are being viewed as works of art, and some are actually signed by known artists. Our advisor for this category is Vicki Flanigan; she is listed in the Directory under Virginia.

Blk silk w/gold sequins in floral pattern, ebony sticks w/inlay, 14" ..**165.00**
Hawaiian souvenir, pnt hula dancer & flowers on wht paper, 7", M ..**30.00**
HP kidskin, adults & children on lawn, ca 1800 ....**1,200.00**
HP silk, farm scene, cvd ivory sticks, ca 1830 ....**500.00**
HP silk, landscape, MOP sticks, ca 1840...................................**450.00**
HP silk landscape, gold decor wood sticks, 13½", EXIB **95.00**
HP silk w/courting scene, sequins/stars, MOP rivet, Fr, 1800s, 8" ...**500.00**
HP silk w/daisies/roses/dragonfly, pierced ebony sticks, 14".........**295.00**
HP silk w/mc daisies, gold decor wood sticks, 14"...........................**85.00**
HP silk w/pansies, ornate pnt wood sticks, 13½", EX **225.00**
HP silk w/Spanish dancer scene, ivory sticks, 8", EX.................**235.00**
HP silk w/violets & butterflies, cvd wooden sticks, 1910s, 14" ...**125.00**
Litho dancing scene on canvas, sandalwood sticks, 1890s, 12"...**125.00**
Ostrich feathers, blk, ca 1890s, 22" open **150.00**
Ostrich feathers, wht, known as Sally Rand, 30x50".................**250.00**
Pierced celluloid, 7⅞", EX..**40.00**

Farm Collectibles

Country living in the nineteenth century entailed plowing, planting, and harvesting; gathering eggs and milking; making soap from lard
rendered on butchering day; and numerous other tasks performed with
primitive tools of which we in the twentieth century have had little first-
hand knowledge. Our advisor for this category is Lar Hothem; his address
is listed in the Directory under Ohio. See also Cast Iron; Lamps,
Lanterns; Woodenware; Wrought Iron.

Bone grinder, FW Mann...Mass USA, CI, crank hdl, 6 cutters, EX...**175.00**
Book, Yearbook of Dept of Agriculture, 1919, NM.......................**20.00**
Check rope tensioner (for corn planter), Farmer's Friend, ca 1875, EX..**85.00**
Corn cutter, leg; Merriam, CI, Pat 1874 & 1892, w/o boot clamp, EX...**90.00**
Corn grinder, spiral-feed to series of knives, wood body, crank hdl ...**85.00**
Corn planter, Macomber (unmk), tin hopper, 2 Pat dates, G **155.00**
Corn sheller, Black Hawk, AH Patch...TN, Pat 1886...1889, EX..**40.00**
Corn sheller, Buch's No 15½, 2-hole, 20" belt pully, EX.............**475.00**
Corn sheller, E Morrison...NH, CI & wood, 1856, 44x19x25"....**175.00**
Corn sheller, Fisher Canton OH, CI, hand-held, pliers-like, 1890s, EX...**495.00**
Corn sheller, Grey Bros, hand-held squeeze type, EX **295.00**
Cow bell, hand forged, 5¾x3¼" **27.50**
Cow bell, sheet metal w/sq iron hdl, iron ball clapper, 7x5½x3"....**37.50**
Cream separator, Am Wonder...NY, stacked cones, Indian decal, EX..**495.00**
Feed grinder, 5½" burs, 12 5-spoke crown flywheel, 28" H, EX ..**125.00**
Feed mill, New Holland #10, 8" mill w/8 plates, worn pnt on box, EX....**200.00**
Feed sack, Bemis, homespun linen, 40½x19½"................................**15.00**
Feed sack, Fagley Seed Co, Archbold OH, Alfalfa, NM................**27.00**
Feed sack, Plainsman Feeds, covered wagon scene on burlap, EX ..**12.50**
Fodder fork, Z&M Randleman....IA, wood lever, Pat 1888, EX **95.00**
Grain carrier, gr-pnt wood w/cvd star, dvtl, sq nails, EX................**45.00**
Grain drill box, Am Harrow Co, CI & wood, Pat 1876 & 1878, 53" L..**750.00**
Grain scoop, tin w/long wood hdl, lt rust, 11"................................**12.50**
Grain shovel, softwood, str front edge, arched hdl, 37x12", VG ...**45.00**
Hames, wrought iron w/leathers, brass balls at ends, 28" **40.00**
Hames, wrought iron w/leathers, USHCo, EX **50.00**
Hay fork, CI, spring-loaded trigger release, #430, 33" **35.00**
Hay rake, all wood, 10-tine, 77" **90.00**
Horse collar, EX leather, rpl straps **75.00**
Implement seat, Avery w/cross ea side, CI, no pnt, 16¾x13¼" ..**465.00**
Implement seat, Frost & Wood #208, CI, old rpt, 16¾x15¼" **80.00**
Implement seat, HP Deuscher, CI, old pnt, 17x13", EX.............**325.00**
Implement seat, Parlin & Orendorff Co Canton IL, CI, no pnt, 16½"...**125.00**
Implement seat, South Bend Chilled Plow, CI, no pnt, 17⅛x15"...**200.00**
Lantern, half-rnd, pnt/pierced, fitted w/candle holder, 14¾" **265.00**
Lantern, tin, ring hdl, pierced air vent, 2 glass panels, 15"..........**265.00**

Lantern, tin w/hinged glass panel, glass chimney, 1850s, 15⅝"...**200.00**
Oxen yoke, wood w/3¾" dia iron ring, dbl, 33", EX **65.00**
Potato grader, Duplex, conveyor type, 10" iron wheels, EX...........**95.00**
Rice measure, wood w/worn turq pnt, flush wood hdl **195.00**
Rope maker, Ideal, Pat 1907, EX **225.00**
Rope maker, 3-strand, primitive, unmk, EX **175.00**

Seed grains scraper, handmade, 1800s, $45.00. (Photo courtesy
Kathryn McNerney)

Trough, CI, keyhole hangers, 1½x9½x2½", EX.............................**25.00**
Wheelbarrow seeder, Crown Mfg...NY, triangular box, 1880s, 14' L.**125.00**
Wheelbarrow seeder, Star Seeder...NY, wood fr, 16" seed box, EX...**95.00**

Fenton

The Fenton Art Glass Company was founded in 1905 by Brothers
Frank L. and John W. Fenton. In the beginning they were strictly a decorating company, but when glassware blanks supplied by other manufacturers became difficult to obtain, the brothers started their own glass
manufactory. This factory remains in operation today; it is located in
Williamstown, West Virginia.

Early Fenton consisted of pattern glass, custard glass, and carnival
glass. During the 1920s and 1930s, Fenton introduced several Depression-era glass patterns, including a popular line called Lincoln Inn, along
with stretch glass and glassware in several popular opaque colors — Chinese Yellow, Mandarin Red, and Mongolian Green among them.

In 1939 Fenton introduced a line of Hobnail glassware after the
suprising success of a Hobnail cologne bottle made for Wrisley Cologne.
Since that time Hobnail has remained a staple in Fenton's glassware line.
In addition to Hobnail, other lines such as Coin Spot, the crested lines,
and Thumbprint have been mainstays of the company, as have their popular opalescent colors such as cranberry, blue, topaz, and plum. Their
milk glass has been very successful as well. Glass baskets in these lines
and colors are widely sought after by collectors and can be found in a
variety of different sizes and shapes.

Today the company is being managed by third- and fourth-genera-
tion family members. Fenton glass continues to be sold in gift shops and
retail stores. Additionally, exclusive pieces are offered on the television
shopping network, QVC. Desirable items for collectors include limited
edition pieces, hand-painted pieces, and family signature pieces. With
the deaths of Bill Fenton (second generation) and Don Fenton (third
generation) in 2003, family signature pieces are expected to become
more desirable to collectors.

For further information we recommend *Fenton Art Glass, 1907 –
1939*, and *Fenton Art Glass Patterns, 1939 – 1980*, by Margaret and Kenn
Whitmyer; *Fenton Glass, The Third Twenty-Five Years*, by William Heacock (with 1998 value guide); and *Fenton Glass: The 1980s Decade* by
Robert E. Eaton, Jr. (1997 values). Additionally, two national collector
clubs, the National Fenton Glass Society (NFGS) and the Fenton Art
Glass Collectors of America (FAGCA) promote the study of Fenton Art
through their respective newsletters, *The Fenton Flyer* and *The Butterfly
Net* (see Clubs, Catalogs, and Newsletters in the Directory). Our advi-

sors for this category are Laurie and Richard Karman; they are listed in the Directory under Illinois. See Also Carnival Glass; Custard Glass; Stretch Glass.

Apple Blossom, cake plate, ftd, #7213, 1960-61, from $125 to ...**165.00**
Apple Blossom, epergne, #7308, 1960-61, 4-pc **300.00**
Apple Tree, vase, blk, crimped or flared, #1561, 10", from $175 to..**200.00**
Apple Tree, vase, Royal Blue, #1561, 1935, 10", from $225 to ...**270.00**
Aqua Crest, basket, #1523, 1941-43, 13", from $300 to **350.00**
Aqua Crest, basket, #36, 1942-43, 6¼", from $85 to **95.00**
Aqua Crest, candle holder, melon rib, #192, ea, from $35 to **40.00**
Aqua Crest, hand vase, #193, 1942, 11", from $250 to **275.00**
Aqua Crest, tidbit, 2-tier, #680, 1950-52, from $75 to **90.00**
Aqua Crest, top hat, #1924, 1942-43, 5", from $40 to **50.00**
Basketweave w/Open Edge, basket, bl opal, crimped, 6", from $35 to...**45.00**
Basketweave w/Open Edge, bonbon, milk glass, 5¾", from $25 to ..**30.00**
Basketweave w/Open Edge, vase, Mandarin Red, flared, 5½", $150 to...**200.00**
Big Cookies, basket, amber, #1681, 1933, 10½", from $100 to ...**125.00**
Big Cookies, basket, Chinese Yellow, #1681, 10½", from $200 to...**250.00**

Big Cookies, macaroon jar, amber, #1681, 1933 – 1934, 7", from $200.00 to $225.00. (Photo courtesy Margaret and Kenn Whitmyer)

Big Cookies, macaroon jar, Flame, #1681, ca 1924, 7", from $400 to ...**500.00**
Black Crest, plate, #7219, 6", from $40 to **55.00**
Black Crest, tidbit, 2-tier, #7294, from $150 to **175.00**
Black Crest, vase, fan; #7356, 6¼", from $80 to **95.00**
Black Rose, vase, #7350, 1953-55, 5", from $65 to **80.00**
Block & Star, basket, milk glass, 1955-56, from $30 to **35.00**
Block & Star, tumbler, milk glass, #5647, 1955-48, 12-oz, $15 to ..**22.00**
Blue Crest, bowl, dbl-crimped, #7321, 1963, 11½", from $85 to...**90.00**
Blue Ridge, bowl, crimped, oval, #1522, ca 1939, 10", from $75 to ..**85.00**
Blue Ridge, top hat, #1921, ca 1939, 10", from $200 to **250.00**
Blue Ridge, vase, flared, #188, ca 1939, 9½", from $110 to **130.00**
Blueberry, vase, gr, #1462, 1933, 10", from $55 to **65.00**
Bubble Optic/Honeycomb, vase, Apple Green, #1350, 1961-62, 5"..**45.00**
Bubble Optic/Honeycomb, vase, pinch; coral, #1358, 1961-61, 8"..**85.00**
Bubble Optic/Honeycomb, vase, powder bl o/l, #1359, 1961-62, 11½" ..**155.00**
Burred Hobnail, cup, child's; milk glass, #489, 1950-52, from $20 to...**25.00**
Butterfly & Berry, bowl, master berry; Rose, 3-ftd, #1124, from $50 to...**60.00**
Cactus, basket, milk glass, #3430, 1959-60, from $25 to **35.00**
Cactus, vase, bud; milk glass, #3450, 1959-65, 8", from $10 to **15.00**
Cactus, vase, swung; topaz opal, #3452, 1959-60, tall, from $200 to...**225.00**
Cameo Opal, bowl, flared, #857, 1929, 11", from $65 to **70.00**
Cameo Opal, comport, rnd, flared, #1533, 1929, 6", from $65 to...**80.00**
Chrysanthemum, bowl, blk, rolled rim, 10½", from $125 to **170.00**
Coin Dot, basket, Fr opal, #1924/1435, 1948-53, 5", from $50 to ..**60.00**
Coin Dot, bottle, bl opal, hdl, #814/1469, 1948-54, 8", from $200 to ..**225.00**
Coin Dot, bottle, cologne; bl opal, #92/1465, 1948-55, from $100 to ..**125.00**
Coin Dot, bottle, cologne; Fr opal, #92/1465, 1948-52, from $70 to ..**90.00**
Coin Dot, bowl, cranberry, #203/1427, 1947-65, 7", from $45 to..**55.00**

Coin Dot, bowl, Honeysuckle, #203, 1948-49, 7", from $50 to.....**65.00**
Coin Dot, candy jar, cranberry, w/lid, #91, 1948-54, from $185 to **200.00**
Coin Dot, creamer, cranberry, hdl, #1924, 1948-57, from $65 to ..**75.00**
Coin Dot, cruet, topaz opal, #1473, 1959-60, from $225 to **250.00**
Coin Dot, jug, bl opal, ice lip, #1353, 1948-55, 70-oz, from $225 to ..**275.00**
Coin Dot, top hat, Lime opal, #1924/1492, 1952-54, from $75 to...**80.00**
Coin Dot, tumbler, Fr opal, bbl, #1353, 1947-52, 10-oz, from $25 to....**30.00**
Coin Dot, vase, bl opal, dbl-crimped, #1934, 1947-50, 7", from $75 to..**85.00**
Coin Dot, vase, bl opal, hdls, #194, 1947-53, 8", from $150 to ..**175.00**
Coin Dot, vase, cranberry, crimped/triangular, 1948-50, 5½", $55 to ..**65.00**
Coin Dot, vase, Honeysuckle, #194, 1948-49, 8", from $65 to......**75.00**
Crystal Crest, candle holder, cornucopia, #951, 1942, ea, from $50 to ...**65.00**
Crystal Crest, vase, triangle, tulip, #1924, 1942, 5", from $30 to ..**35.00**
Daisy & Button, basket, Colonial Amber, oval, #1939, 1965-73 ..**15.00**
Daisy & Button, basket, milk glass, #1934, 1953-55, 4", from $18 to ..**20.00**
Daisy & Button, bell, bl satin, #1966, 1973-80+, from $25 to **35.00**
Daisy & Button, candle holder, Fr opal, 2-light, #1974, 1950s, ea...**45.00**
Daisy & Button, candy box, Colonial Blue, #1980, 1958-71, $40 to...**45.00**
Daisy & Button, hat, milk glass, #1991, 1953-55, from $10 to......**12.00**
Dancing Ladies, bowl, milk glass, #900, 1933, 11", from $130 to ..**150.00**
Dancing Ladies, bowl, Pekin Blue, #900, 1932, 11", from $350 to...**400.00**
Dancing Ladies, vase, Chinese Yellow, #901, 5", from $250 to ...**300.00**
Dancing Ladies, vase, Mongolian Green, #901, 1934, 8", from $400 to...**450.00**
Dancing Ladies, vase, Periwinkle Blue, #901, 1934, 9", from $500 to ..**525.00**
Diamond Lace, basket, Fr opal/Aqua Crest, #1948, 1948-50, scarce, 12"..**300.00**
Diamond Lace, bowl, bl opal, #1948, 1950-54, 9½", from $60 to ..**75.00**
Diamond Lace/Emerald Crest, cake plate, Fr opal, #1948, 1950-52, 14"..**145.00**
Diamond Optic, basket, aquamarine, #1502, 1927, from $30 to **45.00**
Diamond Optic, basket, Jade Green, #1502, 1928, from $35 to **45.00**
Diamond Optic, basket, orange, #1737, 1963-65, 7", from $30 to...**45.00**
Diamond Optic, basket, ruby o/l, #192, 1942-49, 10½", from $125 to...**150.00**
Diamond Optic, candlestick, Mulberry, #192, 1942, ea, from $75 to...**90.00**
Diamond Optic, creamer, aquamarine stretch, #1502, 1920s-30s ..**145.00**
Diamond Optic, creamer, gr, #1502, 1927, from $20 to **25.00**
Diamond Optic, creamer, Rose, #1502, 1927, from $20 to **25.00**
Diamond Optic, cup, ruby, #1502, 1933 ....**20.00**
Diamond Optic, goblet, bridge; Jade Green, #1502, 1928, 11-oz...**25.00**
Diamond Optic, shakers, Rose, #1502, 1928, pr **50.00**
Diamond Optic, vase, aquamarine, flared, #1502, 1927, 8½" **45.00**
Diamond Optic, vase, Colonial Amber, #1751, 1962-65, 7", from $10 to...**15.00**
Diamond Optic, vase, Moonstone, #1502, 1933, 10", from $60 to ..**75.00**
Diamond Optic, vase, Mulberry, crimped, #192, 1942, 9", from $120 to ...**150.00**
Diamond Optic, vase, Orchid, dolphin hdls, #1502, 1927, 5", $35 to...**50.00**
Diamond Optic, vase, ruby o/l, dbl-crimped, #192, 1943-49, 5½" ...**35.00**
Diamond Optic, vase, Tangerine, fan form, #1502, 1927, 8½", $95 to..**110.00**
Diamond Optic, vase, Velva Rose stretch, dolphins, #1502, 6"..**125.00**
Egyptian Mosaic, vase, bl threading, urn form, #3024, 1925, 8½" ..**2,000.00**
Elizabeth, batter set, blk, jug+syrup+tray, from $350 to..............**400.00**
Elizabeth, mint jar, Royal Blue & crystal, from $150 to **165.00**
Elizabeth, sugar bowl, Lilac, 3½", from $45 to **55.00**
Emerald Crest, nut dish, ftd, #690/#7229, 1949-56, from $30 to...**35.00**
Emerald Crest/Beaded Melon, vase, bud; #711, 1950-52, mini, $45 to...**50.00**
Fern, cruet, bl satin, #815/#1863, 1952-54, from $250 to...........**300.00**
Fern, vase, rose satin, #580/#1858, 1952-55, 8", from $100 to **125.00**
Flame Crest, bonbon, #7428, 1963, 8", from $55 to **65.00**
Flower Windows, tumbler, iced tea; ruby, #1720, 1937-38, from $50 to...**55.00**
Georgian, candy jar, amber or crystal, from $25 to **35.00**
Georgian, jug, aquamarine, 54-oz, from $150 to **175.00**
Georgian, plate, compartment; ruby or Royal Blue, 11", from $30 to...**40.00**
Gold Crest, basket, #201, 1943-44, 10", from $95 to.....................**105.00**
Gold Crest, candle holder, #1523, 1943-44, ea, from $25 to **30.00**
Gold Crest, puff box, #192-A, 1943-44, from $40 to **45.00**
Hanging Heart, basket, custard irid, #8939, 1976, from $160 to ..**190.00**
Hanging Heart, tumbler, turq irid, #8940, 1976, 10-oz, from $55 to......**65.00**

Hanging Heart, urn, ftd, #3046, 11", from $1,400 to 1,600.00
Hanging Heart, vase, #3000, 11", from $1,200 to....................1,400.00
Hanging Heart, vase, custard irid, #8958, 1976, 8", from $90 to ..115.00
Historic America, goblet, wine; Fort Dearborne, 1937-40s, 4½"...30.00
Hobnail, basket, Fr opal, #3835, 1949-55, 5½", from $40 to.........50.00
Hobnail, bonbon, milk glass, hdls, #3706, 1969-80+, 8", from $14 to 20.00
Hobnail, bonbon, ruby, #3716, 1972-80+, 8", from $10 to............15.00
Hobnail, bottle, cologne; topaz opal, 1941-44, from $100 to 125.00
Hobnail, bowl, Fr opal, shallow/ftd, #389/3923, 1941-44, 11", $70 to....85.00
Hobnail, butter dish, bl opal, #3977, 1954-55, ¼-lb, from $200 to...250.00
Hobnail, cake plate, crystal, ftd, #3913, from $15 to 20.00
Hobnail, cake plate, turq opaque, #3813, 1955-58, 13", from $45 to.....50.00
Hobnail, candle bowl, Colonial Blue, #3872, 6", ea, from $15 to.....20.00
Hobnail, candle holder, amber, #3974, 1959, from $8 to..............12.00
Hobnail, chip 'n dip, milk glass, #3703, 1958-80, from $45 to......55.00
Hobnail, cigarette lighter, amber, #3692, 1965-71, from $10 to....12.00
Hobnail, comport, bl pastel, #3920, 1954-55, from $35 to............45.00
Hobnail, compote, gr pastel, ftd, #3920, 1954-56, from $25 to.....35.00
Hobnail, creamer & sugar bowl, Fr opal, #3901, 1940-57, $35 to..45.00
Hobnail, cruet, cranberry, #3863, 1941-78, from $95 to.............125.00
Hobnail, decanter, ruby, #3761, 1977-79, from $200 to 250.00
Hobnail, fairy lamp, orange, #3608, 1969-78, from $25 to...........32.00
Hobnail, goblet, water; bl opal, sq, #3846, 1951-54, from $45 to...50.00
Hobnail, goblet, wine; plum opal, #3843, 1961, from $50 to 65.00
Hobnail, jug, gr opal, squat, #389, 1940-41, 32-oz, from $150 to...200.00
Hobnail, jug, milk glass, #3764, 1958-81, 54-oz, from $70 to........85.00
Hobnail, jug, syrup; powder bl o/l, #3762, 1961-62, 12-oz, $30 to ...35.00
Hobnail, lavabo, turq opaque, #3867, 1955-47, from $150 to 200.00
Hobnail, plate, torte; Fr opal, #3817, 1950-55, 16", from $35 to ..50.00
Hobnail, puff box, cranberry, #3885, 1940-57, from $65 to...........80.00
Hobnail, puff box, rose o/l, #389, 1943, from $60 to 80.00
Hobnail, punch cup, milk glass, 8-sided, #3840, 1953-58, from $10 to...15.00
Hobnail, relish, amber, #3822, 1959-60, from $10 to....................15.00
Hobnail, slipper, bl marble, #3995, 1970-74, from $20 to 22.00
Hobnail, slipper, Fr opal, #3995, 1941-46, from $14 to 18.00
Hobnail, toothpick holder, blk, #3795, 1970s, from $10 to...........12.00
Hobnail, tumbler, crystal, ftd, 1940s, 12", from $12 to 14.00
Hobnail, tumbler, iced tea; Fr opal, ftd, #3842, 1940-65, $25 to...28.00
Hobnail, tumbler, topaz opal, ftd, 1941-44, 9-oz, from $35 to.......40.00
Hobnail, vanity set, gr opal, 1940-41, 3-pc, from $350 to...........400.00
Hobnail, vase, Apple Green o/l, #3752, 1960-62, 11", from $80 to ..90.00
Hobnail, vase, bl opal, flared bottle shape, 1941-43, 10", $150 to...185.00
Hobnail, vase, bud; Cameo opal, #3950, 1979-82, 10", from $24 to...30.00
Hobnail, vase, Burmese, #3752, 1971-72, 11", from $150 to.......180.00
Hobnail, vase, coral, #3752, 1961-62, 11", from $125 to............150.00
Hobnail, vase, cranberry, dbl-crimp, #3858, 1941-73, 8", from $85 to...95.00
Hobnail, vase, Fr opal, dbl-crimped, ftd, #3958, 1940-56, 8" 45.00
Hobnail, vase, gr, dbl-crimped, ftd, #3952, 1965-77, 4", from $4 to...6.00
Hobnail, vase, handkerchief; gr opal, #3750, 1960-61, 6", from $35 to..50.00
Hobnail, vase, honey-amber, #3752, 1961-63, 11", from $65 to....85.00
Hobnail, vase, lime gr opal, dbl-crimped, #3858, 1952-54, 8".....125.00
Hobnail, vase, milk glass, 3-toed, #3654, 1963-80, 5", from $10 to...15.00
Hobnail, vase, orchid opal, mid-1940s, 6", from $60 to................85.00
Hobnail, vase, Peachblow, dbl-crimped, #3856, 1952-56, 6", from $30 to..40.00
Hobnail, vase, powder bl o/l, #3752, 1961-62, 11", from $65 to ...85.00
Hobnail, vase, rose pastel, dbl-crimped, #3854, 1954-57, 4½" 18.00
Hobnail, vase, Springtime Green, #3752, 1977-78, 11", from $20 to ..30.00
Hobnail, vase, swung; Colonial Blue, #2652, 1965-78, 24", from $40 to...50.00
Hobnail, vase, Wild Rose, #3858, 1960-63, 8", from $60 to..........70.00
Hobnail/Blue Bell, vase, swung; milk glass, ftd, #3753, 1971-72, 12"...60.00
Hobnail/Holly, basket, milk glass, #3837, 1973-75, 7", from $45 to..55.00
Hobnail/Roses, vase, bud; milk glass, #3950, 1974-76, 10", from $28 to..35.00
Horizon, bowl, amber, #8122, 1959, from #20 to 25.00
Horizon, candle holder, Jamestown Blue, w/insert, #8175, 1959, 5", ea...15.00

Horizon, creamer & sugar bowl, Fr opal, #8101, 1959, from $55 to....65.00
Hyacinth, vase, amber, #180, 1935, from $30 to........................35.00
Ivory Crest, basket, #203, 1940-42, 7", from $45 to....................65.00
Ivory Crest, vase, sq, #1923, 1940-42, 6½", from $30 to 35.00
Jacqueline, vase, pansy; Apple Green o/l, #9150, 1961-62, from $20 to ..30.00
Jacqueline, vase, tulip; bl opaline, #9152, 1960-61, 7", from $65 to ...75.00
Jade Green, bowl, crimped, ftd, #857, 1927, 10", from $40 to.......60.00
Jade Green, candlestick, #249, 6", ea, from $25 to 30.00
Jade Green, vase, fan; #847, 1931, 6", from $30 to 40.00
Lacy Edge, bowl, banana; milk glass, #9024, 1955-59, from $40 to....60.00
Lacy Edge, bowl, bl pastel, #9026, 1954-55, 8", from $30 to.........45.00
Lacy Edge, plate, gr pastel, #9011, 1954-56, 11", from $20 to.......25.00
Lacy Edge, plate, rose pastel, #9011, 1954-55, 11", from $20 to.....25.00
Leaf Tiers, cake plate, Royal Blue, #17990, 1935, 12", from $160 to...180.00
Lilac, flowerpot, w/underplate, #1555, 1933, from $130 to 150.00
Lilac, vase, bottle form, #894 from $150 to................................200.00

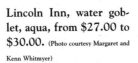
Lincoln Inn, water goblet, aqua, from $27.00 to $30.00. (Photo courtesy Margaret and Kenn Whitmyer)

Mandarin Red, ashtray, #308, from $50 to 60.00
Mandarin Red, macaroon jar, #1684, 1933-35, 6½", from $225 to....275.00
Mandarin Red, vase, flip; #1668, 1933, 8", from $120 to 135.00
Ming, basket, crystal satin, wicker hdl, #1684, 9", from $42 to....50.00
Ming, bowl, gr satin, oval, #1663, 12", from $80 to.....................85.00
Ming, ginger jar, rose satin, w/lid & base, #893, from $200 to....225.00
Mosaic, cologne, #53, from $1,000 to 1,200.00
Mosaic, vase, #3051, 10½", from $1,200 to 1,400.00
Peach Crest, bowl, #722/203, 7", from $35 to 45.00
Peach Crest, bowl, 8-point, #1522/192, 10", from $75 to..............85.00
Peach Crest, rose bowl, #201, 5", from $30 to.............................35.00
Peach Crest, vase, #7459, 1959-62, 9", from $75 to......................85.00
Peach Crest, vase, dbl-crimped, #192, 5", from $25 to 30.00
Peacock, vase, milk glass, flared, 4", from $125 to 150.00
Peacock, vase, Mongolian Green, flared, 10", from $220 to........260.00
Polka Dot, bottle, barber; Jamestown Blue, #2471, 1957-59, $150 to ..185.00
Polka Dot, creamer, ruby o/l, #2461, 1956-59, from $30 to 35.00
Polka Dot, vase, ruby o/l, #2453, 1958-63, 10", from $100 to.....125.00
Priscilla, basket, crystal, 1950-52, 12", from $75 to....................85.00
Priscilla, goblet, water; bl, 1950-52, from $27 to.........................30.00
Pulled Feather, vase, #3020, 12⅝", from $750 to.......................850.00
Pulled Feather, vase, #3034, from $1,100 to 1,200.00
Rib & Holly Sprig, comport, gr, #231, from $20 to.....................25.00
Rib Optic, bowl, gr opal, #1522, 1939, 10", from $60 to 80.00
Rib Optic, cruet, rose satin, #815/#1663, 1952-55, from $250 to ..275.00
Rib Optic, ivy ball & base, cranberry, #1622, 1950s, from $100 to ..150.00
Rib Optic, pitcher, Victoria Topaz stretch w/cobalt hdl, 8¼"......600.00
Rib Optic, vase, pinch; bl satin, #1720/1657, 1952-53, 7½", $75 to ..85.00

Rose, ashtray, Colonial Green, #9271, 1966-70 ....5.00
Rose, comport, Colonial Pink, dbl-crimped, #9223, 1966-69, $12 to ..18.00
Rose, vase, bud; Colonial Amber, #9256, 1968-72, 9", from $10 to ..12.00
Rose, vase, handkerchief; Colonial Blue, #9254, 1968-70, from $18 to ...20.00
Rose Crest, bonbon, dbl-crimped, #36, 1946-48, 5½", from $14 to..18.00
Rose Crest, creamer, #1924, 1947-48, scarce, from $50 to.............60.00
Rose Crest, vase, tulip; #192-A, 1946-48, 9", from $65 to.............80.00
Ruby, bowl, flared, ftd, #857, 1933, 11", from $60 to....................70.00
Silver Crest, basket, #203/#7237, 1943-80+, 7", from $35 to........45.00
Silver Crest, bowl, banana; #7324, 1956-67, from $45 to.............60.00
Silver Crest, candle holder, #7474, 1963-78, 6", ea, from $20 to ..22.00
Silver Crest, comport, dbl-crimped, ftd, #680/#7228, 1949-80, $25 to ...30.00
Silver Crest, jug, #192A, 9", from $45 to 65.00
Silver Crest, top hat, #1924, 5", from $25 to 30.00
Silver Crest, vase, dbl-crimped, sq, melon ribs, #192A, 9", $28 to ...35.00
Silver Crest w/Yellow Rose, basket, #7436, 1969-71, sm, from $45 to ...55.00
Silver Crest/Beaded Melon, jug, #711, 8", from $55 to.................60.00
Silver Crest/Violets in Snow, bonbon, metal hdl, #7498, 1968-78 ..40.00
Silver Crest/Violets in Snow, planter, sq, #8494, from $40 to 50.00
Silver Crest/Violets in Snow, vase, #7458, 1969-72, 11", from $100 to ..145.00
Silver Jamestown, vase, #7350, 1957-59, 5", from $40 to.............50.00
Silver Rose, relish, heart shape, #7333, 1956-58, from $50 to.......60.00
Snowcrest, hurricane lamp, dk gr, #170, #3109, 1951-53, from $90 to..125.00
Snowcrest, top hat, ruby, #1921/#3192, 1951-53, 7", from $200 to ..225.00
Snowcrest, vase, bl, #4516, 1950-51, 8½", from $45 to 55.00
Snowcrest, vase, dk gr, #3005/#3157, 1950-53, 7½", from $80 to ..85.00
Spanish Lace w/Silver Crest, cake plate, #3510, 1962-80+, 11"....45.00
Spiral Optic, bowl, Orchid, flared, #1503, 10", from $30 to..........35.00
Spiral Optic, candle holder, Fr opal, #1523, 1939, ea, from $20 to ..30.00
Spiral Optic, candy box, cameo opal, #3180, 1979-80, from $45 to ...55.00

Spiral Optic, console set, green or gold: #1623 candlesticks, from $20.00 to $22.00 each; console bowl, #1503-A, flared rim, dolphin feet, 10", from $30.00 to $35.00. (Photo courtesy Margaret and Kenn Whitmyer)

Spiral Optic, pitcher, bl opal, #3164, 1979-80, 44-oz, from $100 to ..135.00
Spiral Optic, rose bowl, cranberry, crimped, #201, 1938-40, $45 to..55.00
Spiral Optic, top hat, gr opal, #1922, 1939, 9", from $200 to 225.00
Spiral Optic, top hat, Stiegel Blue, #1924, 1939, 4", from $40 to....50.00
Spiral Optic, tumbler, cranberry, #1353, 1938-40, 12-oz, from $55 to..60.00
Spiral Optic, tumbler, Fr opal, #1353, 1939, 12-oz, from $25 to ...30.00
Spiral Optic, vase, cranberry, #3264, 1956-60, 11½", $150 to 185.00
Spiral Optic, vase, Stiegel Blue, flared, #895, 1939, 10", $200 to ..225.00
Spiral Optic, vase, tulip; topaz opal, #1924, 1940, 4", from $50 to..60.00
Stretch, bowl, Celeste Blue, flared, cupped, #857, 11", from $70 to..85.00
Stretch, bowl, Celeste Blue, shallow, #109, 4¼", from $25 to.......30.00
Stretch, candlestick, Florentine Green, #649, 10", ea 125.00
Stretch, candlestick, Persian Pearl, #549, 8½", ea, from $80 to 85.00
Stretch, candy jar, Velva Rose, #635, ½-lb, from $55 to 60.00
Stretch, cologne, topaz, #56, from $130 to.................................150.00
Stretch, comport, Grecian Gold, cupped, #736, 6½", from $30 to ..35.00
Stretch, plate, sandwich; Celeste Blue, #631, 11½", from $80 to 90.00
Stretch, sherbet, Tangerine, low ft, from $40 to..........................50.00
Stretch, tray, Florentine Green, oval, hdls, #318, 7", from $50 to.....60.00
Stretch, vase, Persian Pearl, #1531, 14", from $130 to 150.00

Stretch, vase, ruby, crimped, dolphins, #1533, 5¼", from $500 to....**600.00**
Swirl, bowl, bl pastel, deep, #7025, 1954-55, 11", from $40 to......**50.00**
Swirl, shakers, rose pastel, #7001, 1954-55, pr, from $35 to **40.00**
Swirl, vanity set, milk glass, #7005, 1954-59, 3-pc, from $65 to ...**85.00**
Swirled Feather, atomizer, gr satin, 1954-55, from $200 to..........**250.00**
Swirled Feather, candy jar, Fr satin, #2083, 1953-55, from $150 to ...**200.00**
Swirled Feather, puff box, bl satin, 1953-55, from $185 to..........**225.00**
Teardrop, cake plate, milk glass, ftd, #6913, 1957-59, from $35 to ..**45.00**
Teardrop, condiment set, Goldenrod, #6909, 1956-57, from $200 to...**225.00**
Thumbprint, ashtray, Colonial Amber, #4469, 1967-70, 6½" **8.00**
Thumbprint, candle holder, Colonial Amber, #4473, 1964-68, 8¼", ea..**10.00**
Thumbprint, chip 'n dip, Colonial Amber, #4404, 1963-67, from $45 to...**50.00**
Thumbprint, jug, Colonial Pink, #4465, 1965-67, 34-oz, from $60 to...**75.00**
Thumbprint, tumbler, Colonial Blue, ftd, #4449, 1966-69, 13-oz...**22.00**
Thumbprint, tumbler, juice; Colonial Amber, #4446, 1965-67, 6-oz ..**8.00**
Thumbprint, vase, Colonial Green, ftd, #4454, 1964-74, 8", $10 to ..**12.00**
Valencia, ashtray, Colonial Blue, #8377, 1969-73, from $8 to.......**10.00**
Valencia, candle holder, Colonial Amber, #8374, 1970-72, ea, $6 to...**8.00**
Valencia, shakers, crystal, #8309, 1970-72, pr, from $10 to...........**12.00**
Valencia, vase bud; Colonial Amber, #8356, 1969-75, sm, from $8 to ...**10.00**
Vasa Murrhina, pitcher, rose w/gr aventurine, #6465, 1965-66 ...**175.00**
Vasa Murrhina, vase, Blue Mist, #6459, 1964-65, 14", from $110 to ..**145.00**
Venetian Red, bonbon, open, cupped, #643, 1925, from $30 to ...**35.00**
Venetian Red, salver, ftd, #647, 1924, 13", from $75 to **95.00**
Violets in Snow/Spanish Lace, candle holder, #3570, 1975-80+, ea..**30.00**
Waffle, basket, milk glass, #6137, 1960-61, from $35 to...............**40.00**
Waffle, candy box, bl opal, #6180, 1960-62, from $85 to **90.00**
Waffle, vase, gr opal, #6152, 1960-61, 4", from $35 to **45.00**
Wild Rose w/Bowknot, vase, Apple Green, #2855, 1961, 5", from $30 to...**35.00**
Wild Rose w/Bowknot, vase, milk glass, #2858, 1961-62, 8", from $30 to ...**40.00**
Wistaria (etch), basket, wicker hdl, #1684, 1937-38, from $70 to ...**85.00**
Wistaria (etch), jug, #1352, 1937-38, from $195 to.....................**225.00**
Wistaria (etch), vase, fan; #857, 1937-38, 8", from $50 to **65.00**
Wisteria (lt purple), candy jar, #736, 1920s, 1-lb, from $75 to......**95.00**
Wisteria (lt purple), pitcher & lid, #220, 1920s, from $350 to....**400.00**
Wisteria (lt purple), tumbler, w/hdl, #222, 1920s, from $45 to **65.00**
Wisteria (lt purple), vase, #251, 1920s, 10", from $45 to..............**60.00**

Fiesta

Fiesta is a line of dinnerware that was originally produced by the Homer Laughlin China Company of Newell, West Virginia, from 1936 until 1973. It was made in eleven different solid colors with over fifty pieces in the assortment. The pattern was developed by Frederick Rhead, an English Stoke-on-Trent potter who was an important contributor to the art-pottery movement in this country during the early part of the century. The design was carried out through the use of a simple band-of-rings device near the rim. Fiesta Red, a strong red-orange glaze color, was made with depleted uranium oxide. It was more expensive to produce than the other colors and sold at higher prices. During the '50s the color assortment was gray, rose, chartreuse, and dark green. These colors are relatively harder to find and along with medium green (new in 1959) command the highest prices.

Fiesta Kitchen Kraft was introduced in 1939; it consisted of seventeen pieces of kitchenware such as pie plates, refrigerator sets, mixing bowls, and covered jars in four popular Fiesta colors.

As a final attempt to adapt production to modern-day techniques and methods, Fiesta was restyled in 1969. Of the original colors, only Fiesta Red remained. This line, called Fiesta Ironstone, was discontinued in 1973.

Two types of marks were used: an ink stamp on machine-jiggered pieces and an indented mark molded into the hollowware pieces.

In 1986 HLC reintroduced a line of Fiesta dinnerware in five colors: black, white, pink, apricot, and cobalt (darker and denser than the original shade). Since then yellow, turquoise, seafoam green, 'country' blue, lilac, persimmon, sapphire blue, chartreuse, gray, juniper, cinnabar, plum, sunflower yellow, shamrock, tangerine, and scarlet have been added.

For more information we recommend *The Collector's Encyclopedia of Fiesta, Harlequin, and Riviera* by Sharon and Bob Huxford, and *Post86 Fiesta* by Richard Racheter, both by Collector Books.

Note: More than ever before, condition is a major price-assessing factor. Unless an item is free from signs of wear, smoothly glazed, and has no distracting manufacturing flaws, it will not bring 'book' price.

Dinnerware

Item	Price
Ashtray, '50s colors	85.00
Ashtray, red, cobalt or ivory	65.00
Ashtray, yel, lt gr or turq	50.00
Bowl, covered onion soup; cobalt or ivory	725.00
Bowl, covered onion soup; red	750.00
Bowl, covered onion soup; turq, minimum value	8,000.00
Bowl, covered onion soup; yel or lt gr	650.00
Bowl, cream soup; '50s colors	75.00
Bowl, cream soup; med gr, minimum value	4,200.00
Bowl, cream soup; red, cobalt or ivory	70.00
Bowl, cream soup; yel, lt gr or turq	45.00
Bowl, dessert; '50s colors, 6"	55.00
Bowl, dessert; med gr, 6"	600.00
Bowl, dessert; red, cobalt or ivory, 6"	50.00
Bowl, dessert; yel, lt gr or turq, 6"	45.00
Bowl, fruit; '50s colors, 4¾"	40.00
Bowl, fruit; '50s colors, 5½"	40.00
Bowl, fruit; med gr, 4¾"	525.00
Bowl, fruit; med gr, 5½"	80.00
Bowl, fruit; red, cobalt, ivory or turq, 11¾"	250.00
Bowl, fruit; red, cobalt or ivory, 4¾"	35.00
Bowl, fruit; red, cobalt or ivory, 5½"	35.00
Bowl, fruit; yel, lt gr or turq, 4¾"	25.00
Bowl, fruit; yel, lt gr or turq, 5½"	28.00
Bowl, fruit; yel or lt gr, 11¾"	195.00
Bowl, ftd salad; red, cobalt, ivory or turq	425.00
Bowl, ftd salad; yel or lt gr	340.00
Bowl, ind salad; med gr, 7½"	120.00
Bowl, ind salad; red, turq or yel, 7½"	90.00
Bowl, nappy; '50s colors, 8½"	60.00
Bowl, nappy; med gr, 8½"	145.00
Bowl, nappy; red, cobalt, ivory or turq, 8½"	52.00
Bowl, nappy; red, cobalt, ivory or turq, 9½"	68.00
Bowl, nappy; yel or lt gr, 8½"	40.00
Bowl, nappy; yel or lt gr, 9½"	45.00
Bowl, Tom & Jerry; ivory w/gold letters	260.00
Bowl, unlisted salad; red, cobalt or ivory	1,200.00
Bowl, unlisted salad; yel	110.00
Candle holders, bulb; red, cobalt, ivory or turq, pr	140.00
Candle holders, bulb; yel or lt gr, pr	110.00
Candle holders, tripod; red, cobalt, ivory or turq, pr	350.00
Candle holders, tripod; yel or lt gr, pr	450.00
Carafe, red, cobalt, ivory or turq	350.00
Carafe, yel or lt gr	240.00
Casserole, '50s colors	300.00
Casserole, French; standard colors other than yel	725.00
Casserole, French; yel	300.00
Casserole, med gr	900.00
Casserole, red, cobalt or ivory	225.00
Casserole, yel, lt gr or turq	165.00
Coffeepot, '50s colors	275.00
Coffeepot, demi; red, cobalt, ivory or turq	550.00
Coffeepot, demi; yel or lt gr	400.00
Coffeepot, red, cobalt or ivory	255.00
Coffeepot, yel, lt gr or turq	195.00
Compote, red, cobalt, ivory or turq, 12"	175.00
Compote, sweets; red, cobalt, ivory or turq	100.00
Compote, sweets; yel or lt gr	80.00
Compote, yel or lt gr, 12"	150.00
Creamer, '50s colors	45.00
Creamer, ind; red	365.00
Creamer, ind; yel	80.00
Creamer, med gr	90.00
Creamer, red, cobalt or ivory	45.00
Creamer, stick hdld, red, cobalt, ivory or turq	70.00
Creamer, stick hdld, yel or turq	48.00
Creamer, yel, lt gr or turq	25.00
Cup, demi; '50s colors	325.00
Cup, demi; red, cobalt or ivory	80.00
Cup, demi; yel, lt gr or turq	70.00
Egg cup, '50s colors	165.00
Egg cup, red, cobalt or ivory	75.00
Egg cup, yel, lt gr or turq	70.00
Lid, for mixing bowl #1-#3, any color, minimum value	800.00
Lid, for mixing bowl #4, any color, minimum value	1,000.00
Marmalade, red, cobalt, ivory or turq	325.00
Marmalade, yel or lt gr	275.00
Mixing bowl, #1, red, cobalt, ivory or turq	245.00
Mixing bowl, #1, yel or lt gr	180.00
Mixing bowl, #2, red, cobalt, ivory or turq	130.00
Mixing bowl, #2, yel or lt gr	115.00
Mixing bowl, #3, red, cobalt, ivory or turq	135.00
Mixing bowl, #3, yel or lt gr	125.00
Mixing bowl, #4, red, cobalt, ivory or turq	160.00
Mixing bowl, #4, yel or lt gr	130.00
Mixing bowl, #5, red, cobalt, ivory or turq	225.00
Mixing bowl, #5, yel or lt gr	175.00
Mixing bowl, #6, red, cobalt, ivory or turq	250.00
Mixing bowl, #6, yel or lt gr	215.00
Mixing bowl, #7, red, cobalt, ivory or turq	475.00
Mixing bowl, #7, yel or lt gr	375.00
Mug, Tom & Jerry; '50s colors	100.00
Mug, Tom & Jerry; ivory w/gold letters	65.00
Mug, Tom & Jerry; red, cobalt or ivory	85.00
Mug, Tom & Jerry; yel, lt gr or turq	60.00
Mustard, red, cobalt, ivory or turq	250.00
Mustard, yel or lt gr	210.00
Pitcher, disk juice; gray, minimum value	3,000.00
Pitcher, disk juice; Harlequin yel	60.00
Pitcher, disk juice; red	550.00
Pitcher, disk juice; yel	45.00
Pitcher, disk water; '50s colors	280.00
Pitcher, disk water; med gr, minimum value	1,000.00
Pitcher, disk water; red, cobalt or ivory	170.00
Pitcher, disk water; yel, lt gr or turq	125.00
Pitcher, ice; red, cobalt, ivory or turq	160.00
Pitcher, ice; yel or lt gr	140.00
Pitcher, jug, 2-pt; '50s colors	175.00
Pitcher, jug, 2-pt; red, cobalt or ivory	110.00
Pitcher, jug, 2-pt; yel, lt gr or turq	88.00
Plate, '50s colors, 6"	9.00
Plate, '50s colors, 7"	13.00
Plate, '50s colors, 9"	30.00
Plate, '50s colors, 10"	55.00

Plate, cake; red, cobalt, ivory or turq 1,000.00
Plate, cake; yel or lt gr 900.00
Plate, calendar; 1954 or 1955, 10" 45.00
Plate, calendar; 1955, 9" 50.00
Plate, chop; '50s colors, 13" 65.00
Plate, chop; '50s colors, 15" 120.00
Plate, chop; med gr, 13" 375.00
Plate, chop; red, cobalt or ivory, 13" 40.00
Plate, chop; red, cobalt or ivory, 15" 70.00
Plate, chop; yel, lt gr or turq, 13" 28.00
Plate, chop; yel, lt gr or turq, 15" 50.00
Plate, compartment; '50s colors, 10½" 75.00
Plate, compartment; red, cobalt or ivory, 10½" 60.00
Plate, compartment; red, cobalt or ivory, 12" 65.00
Plate, compartment; yel, lt gr or turq, 10½" 40.00
Plate, compartment; yel or lt gr, 12" 60.00
Plate, deep; '50s colors 50.00
Plate, deep; med gr 140.00
Plate, deep; red, cobalt or ivory 50.00
Plate, deep; yel, lt gr or turq 38.00
Plate, med gr, 6" 25.00
Plate, med gr, 7" 40.00
Plate, med gr, 9" 50.00
Plate, med gr, 10" 80.00
Plate, red, cobalt or ivory, 6" 7.00
Plate, red, cobalt or ivory, 7" 15.00
Plate, red, cobalt or ivory, 9" 25.00
Plate, red, cobalt or ivory, 10" 50.00
Plate, yel, lt gr or turq, 6" 5.00
Plate, yel, lt gr or turq, 7" 9.00
Plate, yel, lt gr or turq, 9" 16.00
Plate, yel, lt gr or turq, 10" 32.00
Platter, '50s colors 58.00
Platter, med gr 175.00
Platter, red, cobalt or ivory 40.00
Platter, yel, lt gr or turq 32.00
Relish tray, gold decor, complete 250.00
Relish tray base, red, cobalt, ivory or turq 120.00
Relish tray base, yel or lt gr 100.00
Relish tray center insert, red, cobalt, ivory or turq..........................65.00
Relish tray center insert, yel or lt gr...50.00
Relish tray side insert, red, cobalt, ivory or turq.............................68.00
Relish tray side insert, yel or lt gr 50.00
Sauce boat, '50s colors...70.00
Sauce boat, med gr 150.00
Sauce boat, red, cobalt or ivory...65.00
Sauce boat, yel, lt gr or turq 45.00
Saucer, '50s colors..6.00
Saucer, demi; '50s colors..85.00
Saucer, demi; red, cobalt or ivory..22.00
Saucer, demi; yel, lt gr or turq 18.00
Saucer, med gr...25.00
Saucer, orig colors 4.00
Shakers, '50s colors, pr 45.00
Shakers, med gr, pr 150.00
Shakers, red, cobalt or ivory, pr...30.00
Shakers, yel, lt gr or turq, pr...22.00
Sugar bowl, ind; turq 365.00
Sugar bowl, ind; yel 125.00
Sugar bowl, w/lid, '50s colors, 3¼x3½" 85.00
Sugar bowl, w/lid, med gr, 3¼x3½" 225.00
Sugar bowl, w/lid, red, cobalt or ivory, 3¼x3½" 65.00
Sugar bowl, w/lid, yel, lt gr or turq, 3¼x3½" 55.00
Syrup, red, cobalt, ivory or turq 425.00

Syrup, yel or lt gr 375.00
Teacup, '50s colors..38.00
Teacup, med gr...60.00
Teacup, red, cobalt or ivory..32.00
Teacup, yel, lt gr or turq..25.00
Teapot, lg; red, cobalt, ivory or turq 250.00
Teapot, lg; yel or lt gr 210.00
Teapot, med; '50s colors..325.00
Teapot, med; med gr, minimum value 1,200.00
Teapot, med; red, cobalt or ivory..225.00
Teapot, med; yel, lt gr or turq 165.00
Tray, figure-8; cobalt..100.00
Tray, figure-8; turq or yel...400.00
Tray, utility; red, cobalt, ivory or turq 45.00
Tray, utility; yel or lt gr..38.00
Tumbler, juice; chartreuse, or dk gr...600.00
Tumbler, juice; red 60.00
Tumbler, juice; rose 65.00
Tumbler, juice; yel, lt gr or turq...40.00
Tumbler, water; red, cobalt, ivory or turq 65.00
Tumbler, water; yel or lt gr 50.00

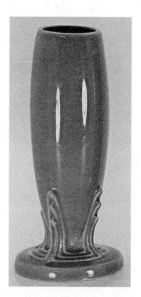

Vase, bud; red, cobalt, ivory, or turquoise, $100.00; yellow or light green, $80.00.

Vase, red, cobalt, ivory or turq, 8" 575.00
Vase, red, cobalt, ivory or turq, 10" 700.00
Vase, red, cobalt, ivory or turq, 12", minimum value.....................900.00
Vase, yel or lt gr, 8" 425.00
Vase, yel or lt gr, 10" 500.00
Vase, yel or lt gr, 12", minimum value..700.00

Kitchen Kraft

Bowl, mixing; lt gr or yel, 6" 72.00
Bowl, mixing; lt gr or yel, 8" 85.00
Bowl, mixing; lt gr or yel, 10" 115.00
Bowl, mixing; red or cobalt, 6"...78.00
Bowl, mixing; red or cobalt, 8"...95.00
Bowl, mixing; red or cobalt, 10"..125.00
Cake plate, lt gr or yel..55.00
Cake plate, red or cobalt 65.00
Cake server, lt gr or yel...145.00
Cake server, red or cobalt..155.00
Casserole, ind; lt gr or yel..150.00
Casserole, ind; red or cobalt...160.00

Casserole, lt gr or yel, 7½" 85.00
Casserole, lt gr or yel, 8½" 105.00
Casserole, red or cobalt, 7½" 90.00
Casserole, red or cobalt, 8½" 115.00
Covered jar, lg; lt gr or yel 250.00
Covered jar, lg; red or cobalt...275.00
Covered jar, med; lt gr or yel 225.00
Covered jar, med; red or cobalt......................................250.00
Covered jar, sm; lt gr or yel 235.00
Covered jar, sm; red or cobalt 250.00
Covered jug, lt gr or yel..280.00
Covered jug, red or cobalt...290.00
Fork, lt gr or yel...125.00
Fork, red or cobalt..135.00
Metal frame for platter 26.00
Pie plate, lt gr or yel, 9" 45.00
Pie plate, lt gr or yel, 10" 45.00
Pie plate, red or cobalt, 9" 48.00
Pie plate, red or cobalt, 10" 52.00
Pie plate, spruce gr 305.00
Platter, lt gr or yel..70.00
Platter, red or cobalt 75.00
Platter, spruce gr 350.00
Shakers, lt gr or yel, pr 90.00
Shakers, red or cobalt, pr 100.00
Spoon, ivory, 12", minimum value...................................500.00
Spoon, lt gr or yel 150.00
Spoon, red or cobalt 165.00
Stacking refrigerator lid, ivory 225.00
Stacking refrigerator lid, lt gr or yel..................................75.00
Stacking refrigerator lid, red or cobalt.............................150.00
Stacking refrigerator unit, ivory 210.00
Stacking refrigerator unit, lt gr or yel 48.00
Stacking refrigerator unit, red or cobalt.............................58.00

Fifties Modern

Postwar furniture design is marked by organic shapes and lighter woods and forms. New materials from war research such as molded plywood and fiberglass were used extensively. For the first time, design was extended to the masses, and the baby-boomer generation grew up surrounded by modern shape and color, the perfect expression of postwar optimism. The top designers in America worked for Herman Miller and Knoll Furniture Company. These include Charles and Ray Eames, George Nelson, and Eero Saarinen.

Unless noted otherwise values are given for furnishings in excellent condition; glassware and ceramic items are assumed to be in mint condition. This information was provided to us by Richard Wright. See also Italian Glass.

Key:
alum — aluminum   plwd — plywood
cntl — cantilevered   ss — stainless steel
fbrg — fiberglass   uphl — upholstered
lcq — lacquered   vnr — veneer
lm — laminated

Armchair, att Thonet, cream piped leather w/tacks, blk wood fr, 34" ..600.00
Armchair, Breuer/Knoll, Wassily, hard leather, chrome fr, 39x31x26"..550.00
Armchair, Eames, Zenith, yel fbrg w/rope edge, X-leg base, 29½"...250.00
Armchair, Eames/Miller, Alum Group, purple channeled uphl, 34"...350.00
Armchair, Eames/Miller, DAW, rope-edged fbrg shell, Venice label..1,100.00
Armchair, Ekstrom, oak & teak w/brn leather uphl, 40x27x25"...1,300.00

Armchair, Mathsson/Dux, Eva, bentwood, webbed seat, 32½"...450.00
Armchair, Wormley/Dunbar, tufted bk, tapered mahog ft, 36", pr ..850.00
Armchair rocker, Eames/Miller, fbrg shell, cat's cradle base 900.00
Armchair rocker, Eames/Miller, RAR, bl fbrg, zinc fr, 26"..........950.00
Armchair rocker, Woodard & Son, oak w/metal bbl fr, vinyl seat...300.00
Armchairs, occasional; Wormley/Dunbar, slim bk, bl uphl, 42", pr, VG...800.00
Armchairs, Weber/Lloyd, uphl seat/bk, tubular chrome fr, 32", 6 for..450.00
Bar cart, Rohde, blk lcq w/tubular chrome fr, 33x33x17½" 950.00
Bed, Watanabe, bench-supported headboard w/4 sliding doors, 31x81x94"...500.00
Bench, Bertoia/Knoll, grooved ash top, steel rod base, 66", VG 650.00
Bench, Nelson/Miller, narrow slats to primavera top, blk legs, 92" ..1,300.00
Bench, Nelson/Miller, wht lm w/blk wool cushion 1 end, ss legs, 76" ..650.00
Bench, Nelson/Miller, wooden slat top, metal legs, 14½x58x18½"...2,950.00
Bench, Nelson/Miller, 3-seat, uphl cushion, chrome legs, 60" L...950.00
Bowl, Stavre Gergor Panis, abstract enamel on copper, 1955, 7" ..90.00
Buffet, Brn Saltman, blond mahog, 4 drws/2 doors, 33x66x24" ..475.00
Buffet, Wormley/Dunbar, 9 rosewood drws, ebonized oak fr, 30x69x18"..1,600.00
Cabinet, china; Rohde/Miller, burlwood & mahog vnr, #3725, 60½"...1,700.00
Cabinet, Nelson/Miller, Thin Edge, graduated drws, 32x67x18½" ..3,500.00
Cabinet, Nelson/Miller, Thin Edge, 3-drw, hairpin legs, 29½x34"...1,115.00
Cabinet, Nelson/Miller, walnut, door beside 5 drws, walnut, 40x40"...2,000.00
Cabinet, Nelson/Miller, walnut, 2-door w/X pulls, blk legs, 40x40", VG ...425.00
Cabinet, Nelson/Miller, walnut vnr, 3-drw/door, chrome pulls, 30x56" ..1,000.00
Cabinet, Wormley/Dunbar, mahog, 2-drw, 2 woven-slat doors, 32x42x18"..1,700.00
Chair, Aalto/Artek, att; webbing (rpl) on molded birch fr, unmk, 39"....350.00
Chair, Bertoia/Knoll, Bird, bl uphl, tubular & wire fr, 37¼" 550.00
Chair, Bertoia/Knoll, Diamond, blk wire, tubular base, vinyl pad, 30" 250.00
Chair, C&R Eames/Miller, LCM, plwd seat/bk, chrome ft, label, 26" ..500.00
Chair, desk; Miller, fbrg, swivel, rollers, 42¾" 265.00
Chair, dining; Wegner, oak, curved crest/cord seat/taper legs, 4 for....600.00
Chair, Eames/Evans, lm plwd, red pnt, 28¾", 4 for 2,000.00
Chair, Eames/Miller, LAX, molded fbrg, tubular steel legs, 26"...175.00
Chair, Eames/Miller, LCW, birch vnr, foil label, 27" 850.00
Chair, Eames/Miller, PKW, birch & steel, 32¾" 825.00
Chair, executive; Maloof, wool uphl seat/bk, oak fr, X base, 50"....11,000.00
Chair, folding; Wegner/Hansen, woven reed bk/seat, 30½" 1,200.00
Chair, Hardoy/Bonet & Kurchan, Butterfly, sling in tubular fr, 36"....425.00
Chair, Hovelskov/Christensen & Larsen, Harp, ash & flag line, 51½"...2,000.00
Chair, Jacobsen/Hansen, Egg, uphl fbgl w/alum base, 42" 2,000.00
Chair, Jacobsen/Hansen, Swan, foam-covered fbrg/alum base, 30", VG 500.00
Chair, LaVerne, Lily, clear Lucite, fuzzy seat pad, 37" 2,700.00
Chair, lounge; Eames/Miller, #670, rosewood plwd/leather, +ottoman, G...1,300.00
Chair, lounge; Eames/Miller, Soft Pad, blk leather/alum, 34" 400.00
Chair, lounge; Kagan, wool uphl, silver drum base, 25x30x27"...900.00
Chair, lounge; Mathsson/Dux, bentwood, canvas & vinyl uphl, +ottoman ...900.00
Chair, lounge; Nakashima, Conoid, walnut w/hickory spindles, web seat ...8,000.00
Chair, lounge; Rapson/Knoll, 1-pc webbed seat/bk, birch fr, 30½", G...1,100.00
Chair, Nelson/Miller, Coconut, red reuphl, 32x41x33"............2,000.00
Chair, office; Eames/Miller, Time-Life, tufted leather, alum base, 35"...250.00
Chair, Risom/Knoll, Scissor, birch fr w/webbed seat & bk, 30", VG...750.00
Chair, rocker; Eames/Miller, RAR, fbrg shell, 27" 1,115.00
Chair, Roma, Safari, knock-down wood fr, leather sling seat, 41"...550.00
Chair, side; Bertoia/Knoll, wht wire, tubular base, vinyl pad, pr...350.00
Chair, slipper; Wormley/Dunbar, stripe uphl, mahog legs, 30x26x21"...1,100.00
Chair, Sperlich/Ironite, Health, pnt steel/wood, 27" 300.00
Chair, stacking; Heany/Treitel-Gratz, alum fr w/canvas seat/bk, 8 for...800.00
Chair, swivel; Eames/Miller, PKW, birch dowel legs, gr uphl, 32½"...380.00
Chairs, dining; Beck/Madsen & Larson, teak w/caned bk/seat, 6 for...600.00
Chairs, dining; Nakashima, spindle bk, saddle seat, 5 side+1 arm ..9,500.00
Chairs, dining; Ponti/Singer & Son, vinyl seat/bk, wood fr, 33", 6 for...2,600.00
Chairs, Eames/Miller, DCW, birch plwd, 29", pr....................600.00
Chairs, Eames/Miller, Eiffel Tower, blk wire fr & brn leather, 4 for ..660.00
Chairs, Jacobsen/Hansen, series 7 #33107, teakwood, 1-pc, 6 for...1,000.00
Chairs, Laverne, Champagne-1, clear Lucite, uphl cushion, ped base, pr....2,000.00

Chairs, Leib/Add Interior Sys, Warren, vinyl uphl/plastic arms, pr...50.00
Chairs, LM van der Rohe/Knoll, Barcelona, brn uphl, 31", pr....1,750.00
Chairs, Max Bill/Horgen Glarus, molded birch plwd bk/seat, 6 for..4,000.00
Chairs, Panton/Miller, molded 1-pc plastic, sgn/1974, 33", pr 600.00
Chairs, Platner/Knoll, bronze wire cone base, seat/bk reuphl, 30", pr..1,600.00
Chairs, stacking; Wegner/Hansen, oak/teak, 3-leg, 28½", 8 for..1,600.00
Chaise, Eames/Miller, rubberized sling seat on cast alum fr, 76"..3,000.00
Chaise, James Mont, pickled oak vnr platform, gr velvet uphl, 112"..4,500.00
Chaise, Morgue/Airborne, Djinn, free-form, pk wool uphl & pillow, 67"...1,200.00
Chandelier, Arteluce, Sputnik, lcq metal & brass, 45x31".......1,400.00
Chest, Nelson/Miller, Thin Edge, rosewood vnr, 3-drw, 33x38x18½".....3,000.00
Chest, Rohde/Miller, rosewood w/ivory lm, 4-drw, 32x45x18"...2,100.00
Chest, Wormley/Dunbar, #4723, Mr, curved front/tambour doors, 36x48"..4,500.00
Chest, Wormley/Dunbar, drw/2 doors, blk w/brass ring pulls, 25x32x15"...950.00
Chest, Wormley/Dunbar, mahog, leather-wrapped base, 5-drw, 32x42x18"...1,000.00
Clock, Nelson/Miller, Asterisk, enameled metal, red/blk hands, 10"...225.00
Clock, Nelson/Miller, Ball, blk balls on 12 brass rods, VG..........400.00
Clock, Nelson/Miller, Starburst, walnut spikes, 18" 60.00
Clock, Nelson/Miller, Sunflower, walnut/birch, wht hands, 30" ..1,900.00
Clock, Nelson/Miller, tall vertical, blk w/wht lines sqs, 20x6"......220.00
Clock, Nelson/Miller, Zoo-Timer, pk elephant w/wht #s, 11x11"..500.00
Credenza, Danish, rosewood vnr, 9 graduated drw, ebonized base, 30x77" 475.00
Credenza, Knoll/Knoll, walnut, 4 sliding doors, leather pulls, rfn, VG...375.00
Daybed, Kjaerholm/Miller, #KC080, steel fr, leather cushion, 75" 6,500.00
Daybed, Nelson/Miller, blond wood w/blk uphl, loose cushions, 75"..2,800.00
Daybed, Nelson/Miller, 2-part uphl cushion, sqd chrome legs, 90" ..1,300.00
Daybed, Wegner/Getama, teak, gr uphl, rear shelf, 30x77x34", VG...1,600.00
Desk, Eames/Miller, ESU D-10-C, plwd/steel/Masonite, 29x40x24½" ..3,500.00
Desk, Nelson/Miller, beige lm top, 2 shallow drw, chrome base, 53"..750.00
Desk, Nelson/Miller, 1 ped, walnut vnr/formica top/tubular base, 60"..850.00
Desk, Watanabe, walnut, 1 ped, 3-drw, dowel legs, 72" 1,700.00
Dinette suite, Platner/Knoll, chrome/marble/uphl, rnd table+4 chairs..2,235.00
Dresser, James Mont, tiger maple vnr, 4 drw, 32x48x18"..........1,300.00
Dresser, Nelson/Miller, walnut, 5-drw, chrome pulls, label, 40x24", VG ..400.00
Dresser, Wormley/Dunbar, walnut, 2 banks of drw, 1 short/1 long, 54" L ..2,400.00
Figure, Waylande Gregory, rooster crowing on post, mc ceramic, 14"..300.00
Flatware, A Michelson, stainless, serves 8, in 12" dia canteen....2,650.00
Headboard, Wormley/Dunbar, ebonized oak, uphl, drop-down arms, 38x81"....1,600.00
Lamp, ceiling; Nelson/Miller, Bubble, spun fiber & steel, 18" dia ...265.00
Lamp, ceiling; Nelson/Miller, Bubble, 1960s, 10x27" dia, VG 400.00
Lamp, ceiling; Panton/Luber, Fun O DM, shells & metal, 27½x21¼"..1,115.00
Lamp, ceiling; Panton/Luber, Fun 12, shell discs & metal, 20x32" dia..1,400.00
Lamp, floor; Kurt Versen, brushed steel & chrome, 16" shade, 45" ..880.00
Lamp, floor; Laurel, mushroom frosted glass shade, chrome base, 56" ..600.00
Lamp, floor; Sarfatti/Arteluce, pnt brass, alabaster base, 82" ...5,275.00
Lamp, Henningsen/Poulsen, Artichoke, copper/wht enamel, 24x32" ..2,500.00
Lamp, Nelson/Miller, Bubble, spun fiber & ss, 14" 140.00
Lamp, Nelson/Miller, Bubble, spun fiber & ss, 21" 300.00
Lamp, table; James Mont, plate-glass base, drum shade, 30½x14½"..1,200.00
Lamp, table; Nakashima, Minguren-style base, orig shade, 30x15"..5,500.00
Lamp, table; Paulin/Phillips, brass Z-form base, enamel blk 12" shade...375.00
Lamp base, Palshus, pottery, horizontal ribs ot bottom, long neck, 16"..150.00
Lounger, Eames/Miller, #670, rosewood/leather, +#671 ottoman ..2,500.00
Lounger, Eames/Miller, Alum Group, dk gr wool uphl, +ottoman 1,000.00
Lounger, Eames/Miller, Alum Group, olive gr wool uphl, 39"..........650.00
Needlepoint hanging, Ackerman, Garden, hand hooked, 1963, 24x36"...825.00
Night stand, James Mont, maple vnr, 3-drw, brass pulls, 24x17x13" ..350.00
Night stand, McCobb, Irwin Collection, mahog/brass/marble, 24x20" sq ..650.00
Night stand, Nakashima, cherry, drw, open shelf, dowel legs, 20" sq ..2,000.00
Ottoman, Nelson/Miller, Coconut, yel Naugahyde, 15½x23x18" ..2,115.00
Plant stand, Salterni, flared metal insert, flower shaft, 43x10"....500.00
Print, Herbet Bayer, Blue Square, image: 14½" sq......................700.00
Rocker, Eames/Miller, molded fbrg, birch runners, 26½".............945.00
Rug, Edward Fields, Shared Harvest, wool, 60x72"....................600.00

Sconce, Arredoluce, 1 dk gr/1 yel metal shade, flexible arms, G...50.00
Sconce, Panton/Luber, pearl shells & metal, 17x11" 380.00
Sconce, Pergay, brushed/polished chrome, 23¼x13" 2,200.00
Screen, C&R Eames/Miller, FSW-6, molded ash plwd, 68x60", VG..3,000.00
Sculpture, Fantoni, 2 horses, brn/bl/ivory, 11x12", EX 375.00
Settee, Hoffman, bentwood, curved bk, leather seat, 45", VG....800.00
Settee, Jacobsen/Hansen, leather uphl, tubular chrome fr, 29x49x29"..1,800.00
Settee, Knoll/Knoll, blk leather, chrome base, armless, 45" 900.00
Settee, Saarinen/Knoll, Womb, uphl fbrg fr, 35½x60x26" 4,400.00
Sideboard, Nakashima, walnut, 2 sliding spindle-front doors, 32x77" ..12,000.00
Silkscreen, Alexander Girard, Environmental Enrichment #3035, 47x46"....700.00
Sofa, Dunbar, 3 seat/3 bk cushions, 6 ebonized legs, 92½".......1,800.00
Sofa, Eames/Miller, Compact, Toostripe uphl, ss/blk enamel fr folds ..1,900.00
Sofa, Jacobsen/Hansen, Swan, taupe wool uphl, alum base, 57" ..3,000.00
Sofa, Kagan, blk wool uphl, walnut base, sloping sides, 107" ..3,250.00
Sofa, Kagan, Cloud, bimorphic, fully uphl, casters, 25x116x42"...11,000.00
Sofa, Kagan, L-shape, velvet uphl, plexiglas base, 88½" 3,000.00
Sofa, Knoll, tube chrome fr w/floating bk rest, worn uphl, 72", VG...700.00
Sofa, Nelson/Miller, gray bouclé on chromed-steel base, armless, 92" ..800.00
Sofa, Nelson/Miller, Marshmallow, 18-cushion, pnt steel fr, 51" ..14,000.00
Sofa, Nelson/Miller, tufted bk, sqd brushed ss fr, 94"................1,900.00
Sofa, Wilkes/Miller, Modular Group, foam over ss & wood, brn uphl, 61"...650.00
Stand, Baughman, walnut lm plwd & tubular alum, 23½x18x16", pr..585.00

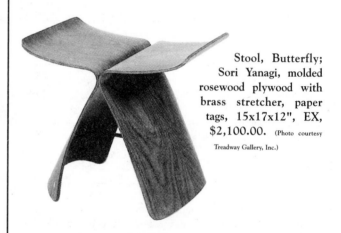

Stool, Butterfly; Sori Yanagi, molded rosewood plywood with brass stretcher, paper tags, 15x17x12", EX, $2,100.00. (Photo courtesy Treadway Gallery, Inc.)

Stool, Eames/Evans, molded plwd, child sz, 8½x11¼" 1,750.00
Stool, Eames/Miller, Time Life, trn wood, 15x13" 1,000.00
Stool, Knoll, 4 blk wire legs, lm top, 18x13" dia, pr 350.00
Stool, Saarinen/Knoll, Tulip, red uphl seat on wht ped base, 16x14"...1,000.00
Table, Aalto/Artek, 28" sq glass top, birch fr, 18" 110.00
Table, cafe; Eames/Miller, marble on tube shaft on 5 alum ft, 36" dia...375.00
Table, cocktail; Frankl, lm cork top, 4 sq cut-out legs, 14x48" dia....1,300.00
Table, coffee; Baughman, walnut, glass & copper inserts, 48" L...3,000.00
Table, coffee; Dunbar, glass top, bronze ribbon-like base, 28x42"...1,200.00
Table, coffee; Knoll/Knoll, rosewood on angular chrome fr, 17x45x23" ...750.00
Table, coffee; McCobb/Winchendon, Platner Group, dk stain, 48" L..125.00
Table, coffee; Platner/Knoll, bronze wire-rod base, 36" glass top....500.00
Table, coffee; TH Robsjohn-Gibbings, walnut, free-form, 21x59x48"...2,950.00
Table, console/dining; Rohde/Miller, Paldao, 2 leaves, 39x36x20" ...750.00
Table, corner; France & Son, teak, V-shaped top shelf, dowel legs, 31"..225.00
Table, dinette; Noguchi/Knoll, wht lm, chrome shaft, metal base ...1,880.00
Table, dining; Hoffmann/Howell, blk top on chrome base, 39x59x34"...500.00
Table, dining; Nakashima/Conoid, walnut, trestle base, 1-plank top ..11,000.00
Table, dining; Nelson/Miller, Oval Soft-Edge #5259, plastic top, 78" 425.00
Table, dining; Noguchi/Knoll, Cyclone, lm top, CI base, 48" dia...1,300.00
Table, dining; Saarinen/Knoll, Tulip, lm top, ped base, 29x96x54"...3,750.00
Table, Eames/Miller, CTW, ebonized dished-out top, 23" dia, VG ...550.00
Table, Eames/Miller, CTW, molded ash plwd dished-out top, 34" dia..900.00

Table, Eames/Miller, LTR, wht lm top, zinc rod base, 10x13x16" ..**250.00**
Table, Eames/Miller, Surfboard, blk lm plwd, wire strut bases, 10x89" **3,500.00**
Table, Katavalos Littell & Kelley/Laverne Orig, dowel top, 17x15x62"..**950.00**
Table, Nelson/Miller, #5451, 17" dia blk birch plwd top, 21", pr ...**500.00**
Table, occasional; Aalto, lower shelf, bentwood legs, 27" dia......**450.00**
Table, occasional; Baughman, walnut w/chrome legs, 14x30x20"..**175.00**
Table, occasional; Wormley/Dunbar, ebonized mahog, 2-shelf, 29" sq..**600.00**
Table, side; Danish, rswd, single drw, tapered legs, 19x18x28" **100.00**
Table, side; Nelson/Miller, blk lm birch plwd top, 21½" **250.00**
Table, side; Shultz/Knoll, 8-part wht enamel top, ped base, 19x16" dia ..**4,000.00**
Tray, Nelson, molded plastic, Boltabest/Made in USA 247, 13¾" ..**2,000.00**
Vanity, P Laszlo, blk lcq & glass, mirror, 52x59", +chair.........**1,525.00**
Vase, Arne Bang, crystalline gr, ribbed, pumpkin form, 5" **250.00**
Vase, Gambone, geometric band, rust on wht, goblet form, 12"...**650.00**
Vase, Heino, blk modernist motif on multitone brn, finger ridges, 3" ..**50.00**
Vase, Heino, wht drips over brn stoneware body, tiny rim, 6x6" ..**125.00**
Vase, Lovera, thick lt bl crater glaze, spherical, 5" **250.00**
Vase, Waylande Gregory, mermaids/fish/bubbles, mc on gray, 15", pr ..**3,800.00**
Wall hanging, Ross Littell, screened print on linen, 12x36", VG **40.00**
Wall unit, McRobb/Calvin, 3 open shelves/4 drw/dbl doors, 84x71x19" **2,250.00**

Finch, Kay

Kay Finch and her husband, Braden, operated a small pottery in Corona Del Mar, California, from 1939 to 1963. The company remained small, employing from twenty to sixty local residents who Kay trained in all but the most requiring tasks, which she herself performed. The company produced animal and bird figurines, most notably dogs, Kay's favorites. Figures of 'Godey' type couples were also made, as were tableware (consisting of breakfast sets) and other artware. Most pieces were marked, but ink stamps often came off during cleaning.

After Kay's husband, Braden, died in 1962, she closed the business. Some of her molds were sold to Freeman-McFarlin of El Monte, California, who soon contracted with Kay for new designs. Though the realism that is so evident in her original works is still strikingly apparent in these later pieces, none of the vibrant pastels or signature curliques are there. Kay Finch died on June 21, 1993.

For further information we recommend *Kay Finch Ceramics, Her Enchanted World* (Schiffer), written by our advisors for this category, Mike Nickel and Cynthia Horvath; they are listed in the Directory under Michigan. *The New Kay Finch Ceramics Identification Guide* (published in 1996), containing many reprints of original catalog pages, is available from Frances Finch Webb; she is listed in the Directory under California. See also Clubs and Newsletters.

Note: Original model numbers are included in the following descriptions — three-digit numbers indicate pre-1946 models. After 1946 they were assigned four-digit numbers, the first two digits representing the year of initial production. Unless otherwise described, our prices are for figurines decorated in multiple colors, not solid glazes.

Ashtray, Bloodhound head, #4773, 6½x6½", from $65 to **75.00**
Ashtray, Swan, #4958, 4½" **50.00**
Bank, Lion, #5921, 8" **400.00**
Brooch, Afghan head, 2x3"..**250.00**
Candlesticks, turkey figures, #5794, 3¾", pr **225.00**
Cookie jar, Cookie Puss, #4614, 11¾", from $2,000 to **2,500.00**
Covered dish, Swan, #4957, 6"...**125.00**
Cup, Kitten Face, Toby, 3"..**100.00**
Cup, Missouri Mule, natural colors, 4¼" **125.00**
Egg box, 9x8"...**175.00**
Figurine, Armour, mare, #474, 12" **650.00**
Figurine, Baby Bunny, #5303, 3½"...**125.00**
Figurine, Banu, Afghan dog (head only), #476, 12" **2,500.00**

Figurine, bull, #6211, 6½"..**300.00**
Figurine, Caress the Colt, #4806, 11"....................................**325.00**
Figurine, Chanticleer, rooster, #129, 11"................................**300.00**
Figurine, Cockatoo, #5401, 15" **750.00**
Figurine, Cocker, cocker spaniel, sitting, #5260, 4½"...............**350.00**

Figurine, Dachshund pup, #5320, 8", $750.00.

Figurine, Dog Show Maltese, #5833, 2½" **500.00**
Figurine, Dog Show Yorkie, #4851 ....**500.00**
Figurine, Donkey Standing, Florentine White, #839, 9½" **300.00**
Figurine, Grumpy, pig, #165, 6x7½" **200.00**
Figurine, Guppy, fish, #173, 2½" **125.00**
Figurine, Hannibal, angry cat, #180, 10½".............................**600.00**
Figurine, Harvey, rabbit w/bow, #4622, 21" **3,500.00**
Figurine, Jezebel, contented cat, #179, 6x9"..........................**200.00**
Figurine, Kneeling Madonna, #4900, 6".................................**100.00**
Figurine, Listening Bunny & Carrots (bunny), #452/#473, 8¼", pr ...**600.00**
Figurine, Mama Quail, #5984, 7"...**425.00**
Figurine, Mehitable, playful cat, #181, 8½".............................**350.00**
Figurine, Mouse, rare, 3" **350.00**
Figurine, Nativity Set, Madonna/Baby/Manger, #4900/#4900a, 3-pc ..**300.00**
Figurine, Pajama Girl, #5002, 5½"..**500.00**
Figurine, Pekinese, #154, 14" L..**400.00**
Figurine, Perky, poodle, #5419, 16".......................................**4,000.00**
Figurine, Pheasant, pk lustre w/gold, rare, #5020, 18" L, pr.........**750.00**
Figurine, Piggy Wiggy, #5408, 1x1½" **125.00**
Figurine, Prancing Lamb, #168, 10½"...................................**475.00**
Figurine, Scandi Boy & Girl, #126 & #127, 5¼", pr **150.00**
Figurine, Seababy, #162, 2½x3½" **175.00**
Figurine, Siamese Cat, #5103, 10"..**375.00**
Figurine, Sitting Angel, #4802, 4½"......................................**180.00**
Figurine, Skunks, #4774/#4775, 4¼", 3", pr **550.00**
Figurine, Squirrel Family, #108A/B/C, 3½" parents, 1¾" baby ...**125.00**
Figurine, Tootsie, #189, 3¾" **35.00**
Figurine, Turkey, #5843, 4½"..**125.00**
Figurine, Windblown Afghan, pewter-like glaze, #5757, 6x6".....**650.00**
Figurine, Yorky Pups, #170 & #171, pr, from $450 to **550.00**
Figurine, 3 Wise Men, mottled tan, #5590/#5591/#5592, 10", set of 3....**350.00**
Moon bottle, #5502, 13"...**175.00**
Plaque, Starfish, #5790, 9"...**250.00**
Shaker, kitchen; Puss, cat, #4616, 6" **350.00**
Shakers, stallion heads, 5", pr..**200.00**
String holder, dog w/bow over left ear, wall mt, 4½x4" **400.00**
Tea tile, Yorkshire Terrier emb, 5½" sq..................................**95.00**
Tumbler, Afghan design (emb), mk Kay & Brayden, 6" **250.00**
Vase, South Sea Girl, #4912, 8¼" **180.00**
Wall pocket, Santa, #5373, 9½"..**375.00**

Findlay Onyx and Floradine

Findlay, Ohio, was the location of the Dalzell, Gilmore, and Leighton Glass Company, one of at least sixteen companies that flourished there between 1886 and 1901. Their most famous ware, Onyx, is very rare. It was produced for only a short time beginning in 1889 due to the heavy losses incurred in the manufacturing process.

Onyx is layered glass, usually found in creamy white with a dainty floral pattern accented with metallic lustre that has been trapped between the two layers. Other colors found on rare occasions include a light amber (with either no lustre or with gilt flowers), light amethyst (or lavender), and rose. Although old tradepaper articles indicate the company originally intended to produce the line in three distinct colors, long-time Onyx collectors report that aside from the white, production was very limited. Other colors of Onyx are very rare, and the few examples that are found tend to support the theory that production of colored Onyx ware remained for the most part in the experimental stage. Even three-layered items have been found (they are extremely rare) decorated with three-color flowers. As a rule of thumb, using white Onyx prices as a basis for evaluation, expect to pay five to ten times more for colored examples.

Floradine is a separate line that was made with the Onyx molds. A single-layer rose satin glassware with white opal flowers, it is usually valued at twice the price of colored Onyx.

Chipping around the rims is very common, and price is determined to a great extent by condition. Our advisors for this category are Betty and Clarence Maier; they are listed in the Directory under Pennsylvania. Unless noted otherwise, our prices are for examples in near-mint condition.

Floradine

Bowl, fluted, squat bulbous base, 4"	950.00
Bowl, low, nick, 5¾"	1,400.00
Celery vase, fluted cylinder neck, bulbous body, 6½"	1,800.00
Celery vase, fluted cylinder neck, bulbous body, 6½", VG/EX	1,000.00
Creamer, bulbous, 4⅝"	950.00
Mustard pot	1,550.00
Spooner, 4¾"	1,285.00
Sugar bowl, bulbous, w/lid, 5½"	1,200.00
Sugar shaker	1,500.00
Syrup pitcher	2,500.00
Toothpick holder, 2½"	1,500.00
Tumbler, bbl shape, 3½"	2,100.00

Onyx

Bowl, wht w/raspberry decor, fluted top, 2½x4½"	2,000.00
Butter dish, wht w/silver decor, 3x6"	1,250.00
Celery vase, wht w/silver decor, 6¾"	485.00
Covered dish, wht w/silver decor, 5½"	1,000.00
Creamer, wht w/silver decor, 4½"	485.00
Lamp, oil; blk opaque base, sm rpr to collar, 7¼"	6,500.00
Mustard, wht w/raspberry decor, hinged metal lid, 3¼"	2,900.00
Mustard, wht w/silver decor, 3½"	800.00
Pitcher, apricot w/orange decor, 4½"	4,200.00
Pitcher, water; wht w/silver decor, 8"	1,200.00
Shaker, wht w/silver decor, minor wear, 2¾", ea	650.00
Shaker, wht w/silver decor, Pat 2/23/1889, 2⅝", ea	800.00
Spooner, raisin w/wht decor, rare color, 4"	2,250.00
Spooner, raisin w/wht decor, 4", VG/EX	1,250.00
Spooner, wht w/orange decor, 4"	1,500.00
Spooner, wht w/silver decor, 4½", VG/EX	250.00
Spooner, wht w/silver decor, 4½x4"	550.00
Sugar bowl, wht w/silver decor, 5½", EX	475.00

Sugar shaker, wht w/silver decor, brass mts, mfg defects, 5½"	335.00
Sugar shaker, wht w/silver decor, sterling cap, 6¼", from $600 to	800.00
Syrup, gr (unusual color) w/silver decor	3,000.00
Syrup, wht w/silver decor, 7¾", from $850 to	1,150.00
Toothpick holder, wht w/silver decor, from $325 to	500.00
Tumbler, wht w/apricot decor, lt line unseen from w/in, bbl	2,300.00
Tumbler, wht w/silver decor, bbl shape, 3½"	450.00
Tumbler, wht w/silver decor, bbl shape, 3½", VG/EX	350.00
Tumbler, wht w/silver decor, thin str sides (rare), 3¾"	1,250.00

Bowl, master berry; white with silver decor, 9" diameter at base, $400.00.

Fire Marks

The earliest American fire marks date back to 1752 when 'The Philadelphia Contributionship for the Insurance of Houses From Loss By Fire' (the official name of this company, who is still in business) used a plaque to identify property they insured. Early fire marks were made of cast iron, sheet brass, lead, copper, tin, and zinc. The insignia of the insurance company appeared on each mark, and they would normally reward the volunteer fire department who managed to be the first on the scene to battle the fire. (Altercations occasionally broke out between firefighting companies vying for the chance to earn the reward!)

Fire marks were first used in Great Britain about 1780 and were more elaborate than U.S. marks. The first English examples were made of lead and carried a policy number. They were used to identify insured property to the fire brigades maintained by the insurance companies. Most copper and brass fire marks are of European origin.

During the latter half of the nineteenth century, municipalities replaced the volunteer fire companies and fire brigades with paid fire departments. No longer was there a need for fire marks, so the companies discontinued their use (though some companies still use fire marks for advertising purposes).

Prices listed are for legitimate fire marks in good to excellent condition. Reproductions are identified when possible. Many fire marks have been and continue to be widely reproduced in cast iron and aluminum. They are sold legitimately as decorator items and collectible reproductions. Fantasy items, on the other hand, are not reproductions, as they depict items that never existed in the first place. They are twentieth century fabrications and never existed in their present form prior to this recent production. They appear in cast iron, aluminum, and other mediums.

Alliance Assurance Co, London, copper, 8x8"	45.00
British, copper on brass, lion & shield, 8" dia	110.00
Eagle, Philadelphia Fireman's Hall, cast brass, 20x16"	115.00
FA, CI, 11¼x7¼"	80.00
Insured Home New York, tin, 5¼x8⅛", VG	80.00
London Assurance Incorporated AD 1720, blk/gold/red, 20x16", in fr	45.00
Mutual Assurance of Phila, gr tree type on wooden shield	100.00

Mutual Assurance of Phila, gr tree type on wooden shield, repro...**15.00**
Ohio Farmers, tin, blk w/gold lettering, 3½x6½" **50.00**
Philadelphia Contributionship (hand in hand), metal on wood shield...**100.00**
Valiant Hose #2, pnt CI, 19th C, fantasy item, 10½" **15.00**

Firefighting Collectibles

Firefighting collectibles have always been a good investment in terms of value appreciation. Many times the market will be temporarily affected by wild price swings caused by the 'supply and demand principle' as related to a small group of aggressive collectors. These collectors will occasionally pay well over market value for a particular item they need or want. Once their desires are satisfied, prices seem to return to their normal range. It has been noticed that during these periods of high prices, many items enter the marketplace that otherwise would remain in collections. This may (it has in the past) cause a price depression (due again to the 'supply and demand principle' of market behavior).

The recent phenomena of Internet buying and selling of firefighting collectibles and antiques has caused wild swings in prices for some fire collectibles. The cause of this is the ability to reach into vast international markets. It appears that this has resulted in a significant escalation in prices paid for select items. The bottom-line items still languish price wise but at least continue to change hands. This marketplace continues to be active, and many outstanding items have appeared recently in the fire antiques and collectibles field. But when all is said and done, the careful purchase of quality, well-documented firefighting items will continue to be an enjoyable hobby and an excellent investment opportunity.

Today there is a large, active group of collectors for fire department antiques (items over 100 years old) and an even larger group seeking related collectibles (those less than 100 years old). Our advisors for this category (except grenades) are H. Thomas and Patricia Laun; they are listed in the Directory under New York. (SASE required.)

Fire grenades preceded the pressurized metal fire extinguishers used today. They were filled with a mixture of chemicals and water and made of glass thin enough to shatter easily when thrown into the flames. Many varieties of colors and shapes were used. Not all grenades contain salt-brine solution, some, such as the Red Comet, contain carbon tetrachloride, a powerful solvent that is also a health hazard and an environmental threat. (It attacks the ozone layer.) It is best to leave any contents inside the glass balls. The source of grenade prices are mainly auction results; current retail values will fluctuate. Our fire grenades advisor is Willy Young; he is listed in the Directory under Nevada.

Air pump, used w/smoke helmet, fitted bellows, brass horn, EX...**200.00**
Alarm, Gamewell, CI, weight driven, working, EX orig, from $375 to...**425.00**
Alarm box, Gamewell, Fire Alarm Station #112, w/inner box & key..**110.00**
Axe, CI w/Comp Weldon Fire Co & advertising, 9½" L..............**90.00**
Axe, Viking style, early, VG **275.00**
Badge, Allentown Fire Department-14-172, steel shield, 2⅛" **60.00**
Badge, Brockton Fire Dept #563, silver, mk Sterling **65.00**
Badge, Captain Enterprise...NY, gold presentation w/bl enamel...**375.00**
Badge, Chief Ticonderoga NY Fire Dept, gold-tone.................**25.00**
Badge, Hubbard Hose 2, gold-tone 2 shape, sm **90.00**
Badge, Montgomery-1-1847, nickel/brass, 2-pc w/cut-out center ..**155.00**
Badge, Pequot Engine Co-6-LFD 30 Yrs, sterling, sm **40.00**
Badge, Steamer Co No 1 Washington NJ, nickel/brass shield, 2⅛" **50.00**
Badge, 1857 Co Defender...PA, hand-drawn ladder wagon, sterling, 2-pc...**250.00**
Bed key **150.00**
Bell, captain's tapper; electromechanical, brass acorn, EX...........**750.00**
Bell, jumper; solid brass, 7" dia **235.00**
Bell, muffin; brass, trn wood hdl, 5½" dia, 12" L **275.00**
Bell, muffin; brass, trn wood w/whalebone separator, 3½", EX....**300.00**

Bell, muffin; brass, trn wooden hdl, 3½" dia, 8½" L............**300.00**
Belt, parade; leather, Ridgefield Park Hose, blk/wht/red, VG **100.00**
Belt, parade; leather w/UNION cutouts, red & wht, VG **80.00**
Bookends, Hartford Fire Ins Co 1810-1935, brass, 5½", pr.......**80.00**
Box, ballot; 2-compartment, hinged lid, blk & wht marbles, EX ..**65.00**
Bracket, apparatus; for Dietz Queen lantern (or similar), EX......**125.00**
Bucket, gr leather w/blk RRB lettering, orig hdl, 12x8", VG **435.00**
Bucket, gr leather w/gold & blk: Fireman's Office No 0, 12x8", VG...**700.00**
Bucket, leather, Cairns, 1960s, EX.........................**80.00**
Bucket, leather, faint gold 2, w/hdl, early, warped.................**110.00**
Bucket, leather, gr pnt w/mustard GT Falls B&M, w/hdl, EX **900.00**
Bucket, leather, mustard pnt w/blk J Rugles, detached hdl, VG..**275.00**
Bucket, leather, pnt scrolls/designs/banner/name, early 1800s, EX...**1,600.00**
Bucket (overhaul), rubber over canvas, blk w/gold #14, VG.......**200.00**
Extinguisher, Badger's Pony..., copper & brass, w/plaque, EX **70.00**
Extinguisher, Boyce, empty w/paper labels, mounting bracket, 12" ..**180.00**
Extinguisher, Carbona, amber glass, 8-sided, w/paper label, EX ..**140.00**
Extinguisher, Phoenix, tin tube, dry powder type, VG **45.00**
Extinguisher, Presto, in bucket..................................**40.00**
Extinguisher, Rex, soda & acid, early, 2½-gal **30.00**
Extinguisher, Security, pony sz **70.00**
Extinguisher, Shur Spray, ceiling mt, empty, 1-gal **40.00**
Extinguisher, Stop Fire, w/gauge & shut-off, VG **15.00**
Gong, Gamewell, 8" brass ball, wooden 21" case, EX.............**2,200.00**
Gong, Gamewell house type, brass, beveled glass on door, ball top, 15" ..**3,450.00**
Gong, Gamewell Moses Crane style w/brass plaque, 10" brass bell, 24"...**2,700.00**
Gong, turtle; Gamewell, polished well, orig key for winding, 10" ...**165.00**
Grenade, C&N-W Ry, clear w/cobalt contents...........................**350.00**

Grenade, Harden's Improved Petal Variant, cobalt blue, smooth base, tooled mouth, pint, 6½", M, $1,650.00.
(Photo courtesy Glassworks Auctions)

Grenade, Harkness, Indigo Blue **550.00**
Grenade, Hayward's Pleated, clear, 1-pt **250.00**
Grenade, Hayward's Pleated, plum amethyst, 1-pt................**750.00**
Grenade, HSN, dk amber..................................**450.00**
Grenade, Kalamazoo, cobalt...........................**750.00**
Grenade, Letson & Honegger's, aqua **2,500.00**
Grenade, PSN, dk amber **750.00**
Helmet, aluminum, high eagle, leather frontispc, EX **275.00**
Helmet, aluminum, Senator style, leather frontispc: CRFD, w/liner, EX ...**110.00**
Helmet, cork, front badge: Fire Service Gloucestershire, w/liner ..**80.00**
Helmet, leather, high eagle, frontispc: Chief BHFD, w/liner.......**475.00**
Helmet, leather, high eagle, frontispc: Riverton Fire Co 1, VG..**350.00**
Helmet, leather, high eagle, metal frontispc: Montgomery 1, 1847, EX..**750.00**
Helmet, leather, high eagle, metal 8" frontispc, Cairns, w/liner, EX...**825.00**
Helmet, leather, high eagle, 32 comb, frontispc: Poughkeepsie, EX......**525.00**
Helmet, leather, lacks frontispc, gold stripe on bk, w/liner.........**175.00**
Helmet, leather, New Yorker, frontispc: Engine-1-CFC, Cairns, VG ...**200.00**

Helmet, leather, wht S Am style jockey, metal frontispc, VG.....**750.00**
Helmet, leather, 64 comb, metal shield, lion frontispc, Olson, EX....**1,400.00**
Hose, riveted leather section, VG..**70.00**
Hose rack, interior; #5, 9x19"...**30.00**
Hose reel, interior; Star Swing Hose...92, 14½" dia, EX...............**30.00**
Hose reel hanger, cast brass, Wisconsin badger head, 20x24", G....**825.00**
Lamp, engine; Cartrwright 2, 6-sided, red glass panels w/decor.....**2,250.00**
Lamp, motion; Insure Before the Fire, burning building, 18x24", EX....**550.00**
Lantern, chief's hand inspection; CT Hamm, NP brass, VG **325.00**
Lantern, Dietz, tubular, Pat date on water shield, slide-off cage, EX....**225.00**
Lantern, Dietz Fire King, Am LaFrance...NY, EX.......................**450.00**
Lantern, Dietz Fire King Dept, NP brass, clear globe, EX...........**250.00**
Lantern, Dietz Fire King Dept, NP brass, Seagrave Co, Pat 07, EX....**550.00**
Lantern, Dietz King Fire Dept, brass/copper gin, red pnt & globe, EX....**120.00**
Lantern, Dietz King Fire Dept, red pnt, clear globe **175.00**
Lantern, Dietz King Fire Dept, red pnt, polished copper, brass hdl **175.00**
Lantern, wrist; Mayflower 1 on clear globe, early, 17½" w/hdl ...**1,000.00**
Nozzle, brass, shut-off valve mk C Callahan's...1885, 5½"..............**35.00**
Nozzle, brass, underwriter's playpipe..**50.00**
Nozzle, brass & copper, flow control by AJ Morse Boston MA, 1917...**110.00**
Nozzle, brass & copper, flow control by Wooster, leather hdl, VG...**125.00**
Nozzle, brass & copper, play pipe, Boston Coupling Co, VG **70.00**
Nozzle, copper & brass, 3-part, 67"...**500.00**
Nozzle, hand pumper; brass, cord wrapped, 52"...........................**575.00**
Nozzle, hand tub; leather-covered pipe, 42" **650.00**
Nozzle, NP brass, 36½"..**200.00**
Pipe, cord covered, 2-hdl playpipe, Powhattan, Underwriter's, 15"...**60.00**
Plate, engine; James Boyd & Bro Inc Philadelphia.......................**110.00**
Portrait, fireman in oval fr, FD 281 Phila, oval 21x16" fr............**165.00**
Rattle, single reed, golden oak w/trn hdl, working, EX.................**80.00**
Rattle, triple reed, wood w/trn wood hdl, 9½" L, working, VG **60.00**
Rattle, watchman's, brass ends, eng NO 6 SG, EX **100.00**
Rattle, watchman's, dbl reed, metal end plate, EX.......................**80.00**
Shirt, red bib style w/lg 11 & silver FD buttons, Klein, VG........**250.00**
Sign, Boston Fire Insurance Co Boston MA, rvpt, 17½x23½", EX...**350.00**
Torch, apparatus, brass w/wood shaft, iron spike, swivel mt, EX...**700.00**
Torch, apparatus, NP/brass, to mt on bk of horse-drawn pc, EX...**125.00**
Torch, parade; brass, mtd on trn wood hdl, VG **70.00**
Torch, parade; nickel/brass, 3"...**45.00**
Transmitter, Gamewell, w/50 brass code wheels, oak case........**2,500.00**
Trophy, 2nd Prize Hose Coupling Contest....1913, silver..............**50.00**
Trumpet, parade; NP brass, red tassel, 17½", EX.........................**625.00**
Trumpet, speaking; presentation, Alert No 2...NJ, silver, 18" **625.00**
Trumpet, speaking; presentation, silver w/eng name/1862, 17", VG..**825.00**
Trumpet, speaking; brass w/gold tassel, dvtl seam, 16", EX..........**500.00**
Trumpet, speaking; solid brass, unusual tassel mts, 20½", EX......**600.00**
Wrench, spanner; American LaFrance Foamite Corp, 11½" L **20.00**

Fireplace Accessories and Implements

In the colonial days of our country, fireplaces provided heat in the winter and were used year round to cook food in the kitchen. The implements that were a necessary part of these functions were varied and have become treasured collectibles, many put to new use in modern homes as decorative accessories. Gypsy pots may hold magazines; copper and brass kettles, newly polished and gleaming, contain dried flowers or green plants. Firebacks, highly ornamental iron panels that once reflected heat and protected masonry walls, are now sometimes used as wall decorations. By Victorian times the cookstove had replaced the kitchen fireplace, and many of these early utensils were already obsolete; but as a source of heat and comfort, the fireplace continued to be used for several more decades. See also Wrought Iron.

Andirons, brass, cannon ball finial, trn stem, ball & claw ft, 28" ..**275.00**
Andirons, brass, dbl-belted lemon finials, penny ft, 1780s, 19"...**765.00**
Andirons, brass, seamed, dbl lemon top, beaded rings, early, 21"...**660.00**
Andirons, brass, trn columns w/urn finials, claw & ball ft, 22"...**165.00**
Andirons, bronze, Deco peacock w/verdigris/old pnt, 32"........**5,600.00**
Andirons, bronze, Geo Washington figural, Am, 19th C, 20¼"...**1,400.00**
Andirons, CI, Boston bull terrier w/glass eyes, Howes, 17⅛" **350.00**
Andirons, CI, owl w/yel & blk glass eyes, twig base, 15"..........**300.00**
Andirons, CI, turkey head finials, acanthus shafts, J Burns, 19"...**1,645.00**
Andirons, wrought iron, cut & flared wings on front, 19"..........**175.00**
Ash pan facade, brass, lunette shape, 19th, C, 4x16x4" **60.00**
Bellows, mc cornucopia w/gold on gr, brass nozzle, rstr leather, 19"...**500.00**
Broom, 2-tone horsehair bristles, stenciled hdl, 29".................**385.00**
Coal bucket, brass helmet shape w/swivel hdl, 19"...................**110.00**
Coal hod, CI, ornate floral/portrait medallion, 1880, 17x12x20"....**850.00**
Coal hod, figured mahog English Regency w/inlay, tin liner, 15x17x13"...**300.00**
Fender, brass, pierced, 9½x42x9"...**865.00**
Fender, brass, 5 cast paw ft w/worn gilt, 8x48x14".....................**250.00**
Fender, brass & wirework, Georgian style, bud finials, 13x36x12"....**550.00**
Fender, brass bottom & top rails w/bun ft, wire body, 12x50x11"..**250.00**
Fender, brass rail over patterned wirework, ca 1800, 10x45".......**350.00**
Fender, brass rim, sm sq wirework grid, wirework scroll decor, 36x43"..**1,800.00**
Fender, brass rim over vertical wirework w/swags, 24x41x15"..**1,175.00**
Fender, brass w/fine eng & piercing, urn finials, English, 58"......**440.00**
Fender, CI w/lion's head ft & geometric piercings, 1900s, 54" **260.00**

Fender, U-shape with rolled brass rim above vertical bars with wire screening, 'S' scroll decoration, early nineteenth century, 12x42", EX, $1,000.00.

Fire basket, CI, 16x19x12" **400.00**
Fire bucket, brass, 12x17x11½"...**60.00**
Fireback, CI, molded scene w/figures, dtd 1742, 2-pc, 25x25" ...**250.00**
Grate, CI Fed-style fr, cement lining, appl rosettes, 25x39x21"..**525.00**
Grille, CI w/fleur-de-lis cartouch, 17x19x12" **260.00**
Hook, wrought iron, 4-prong, sq shaft, w/ring for hanging, 10" **50.00**
Kettle, water; CI, swing hdl, 3-ftd base, 11x13", EX...................**315.00**
Kettle stand, brass front top, w/openwork, wrought legs, 12x15x11"...**200.00**
Mantel, mahog w/griffin & floral cvgs, ca 1880, 54x60", EX ...**3,650.00**
Mantel, pine w/worn pnt, ornate cove-molded cornice, 50x64x6"....**300.00**
Peat bucket, mahog Wm IV, vasiform w/brass liner, 1830s, 16"..**1,950.00**
Peel, wrought iron, ram's horn finial, 6½x42".............................**65.00**
Roaster, chestnut; brass, eng tulip, heart top, rprs, 35" **120.00**
Roaster, wrought iron, high tripod base w/rack, late, 25" **200.00**
Screen, mahog w/ornate needlepoint insert, ca 1900, 40x27" **500.00**
Spit jack, brass, w/rnd CI hnger, J Linwood Warranted, w/key, 12½" ..**165.00**
Stand, kettle; brass & wrought iron, rtcl top, 9⅜x7¾x10¾" **175.00**
Toaster, CI, rotates, scrolled ft, well-formed hdl, 7x12½x15", EX...**200.00**
Toaster, CI w/scrolls among sq ironwork, rotates, ftd base, 6x14x18"....**460.00**
Toaster, wrought iron, 4 arched holders, w/revolving rack, 22".....**55.00**
Tongs, ember/pipe; steel spring type w/formed hands as grabber, 16"..**425.00**
Trammel, wrought iron, twisted shaft, lg & sm hooks, 12" bar, 55"...**40.00**
Wafer iron, CI, E Pluribus Unum w/eagle & shield, 5½" disk, 26"...**575.00**

Fishing Collectibles

Collecting old fishing tackle is becoming more popular every year. Though at first most interest was geared toward old lures and some reels, rods, advertising, and miscellaneous items are quickly gaining ground. Values are given for examples in excellent or better condition and should be used only as a guide. For more information we recommend *19th-Century Fishing Lures* by Arlan Carter; *Fishing Lure Collectibles, Vol. One,* by Dudley Murphy and Rick Edmisten; *Fishing Lure Collectibles, Vol. Two,* by Dudley and Deanie Murphy; *Collector's Encyclopedia of Creek Chub Lures and Collectibles, Second Edition,* by Harold E. Smith, MD; *Commercial Fish Decoys* by Frank R. Baron; *The Heddon Legacy* by Bill Roberts and Rob Pavey; *Captain John's Fishing Tackle Price Guide* by John A. Kolbeck and Russell E. Lewis; and *Modern Fishing Lure Collectibles, Vol. 1* and *2,* by Russel Lewis. All are published by Collector Books. Our advisor for this category is Dave Hoover; he is listed in the Directory under Indiana.

Book, Complete Angler, Izaak Walton, Little Brn & Co, 1867, 445 pgs **40.00**
Book, Where Trout Hide, Kit Clarke, Brentano's, 1889 1st ed, EX **30.00**
Catalog, Creek Chub, 1947, 22-pg, EX **250.00**
Catalog, Heddon Dowagiac Bait Casting Equipment #19, 1922, 9x12"..**880.00**
Creel, reed w/pattern weaving, sliding pin latch, EX **85.00**
Creel, split willow, wire hinges, canvas/leather harness, EX........**110.00**
Creel, Turtle Trade Mk, split rattan w/cvd turtle latch, EX.........**440.00**
Creel, wicker w/canvas & leather harness, sliding peg latch, EX **80.00**
Creel, wide splint w/narrow lashing, center hole, 9½x8x15", EX ..**110.00**
Creel, woven reed w/twisted reed hinges, half-rnd w/harness, EX....**125.00**
Decoy, Boone Bait Co Saucer Dancer, blk & yel stripe, from $25 to ...**35.00**
Decoy, catfish, wood gesso w/wire whiskers/tack eyes, old pnt, 12"..**575.00**
Decoy, fish spearing; Bob's Tying Shop, various colors, 7½", $35 to ...**45.00**
Decoy, fish-spearing; Cy Halverson, red & wht, no scale pattern, MIB..**35.00**
Decoy, fish-spearing; Martin Pestrue Saginaw Bay Spottail, from $35 to...**45.00**
Decoy, Jenkins, various colors, ea from $35 to **50.00**
Gaff, brass & copper, MIE, extends to 36", polished....................**120.00**
Gut cutter, Olsen's, complete, NM **140.00**
Ice saw, commercially made, EX, from $35 to **50.00**
Lure, Creek Chub, Castrola #3100, 3 trebles, 1927-41, 3⅝" **70.00**
Lure, Creek Chub, Gar Minnow #2900, 3 trebles, 1927-53, 5½" ..**300.00**
Lure, Creek Chub, Jointed Pike #3000, 3 trebles, 1931-78, 6" **40.00**
Lure, Creek Chub, Lucky Mouse #3600, 2 trebles, 1931-47, 3"....**85.00**
Lure, Creek Chub, Striker Pikie #6900, 3 trebles, 1950-78, 6¼" ..**60.00**
Lure, Creek Chub, Surface Dingbat #5400, 2 trebles, 1939-55, 1¾" ..**50.00**
Lure, Heddon, Baby Dowagiac #20, tack eyes, 1952, 1½" **27.50**
Lure, Heddon, Basser #8500, pnt eyes, 3 trebles, 1922-50s, 4" **22.50**
Lure, Heddon, Chugger Jr #9250, 2 trebles, 1954, 2¼" **12.50**
Lure, Heddon, Flaptail Jr #7110, glass eyes, 2-pc, 1937, 3"............**32.50**
Lure, Heddon, Go-Deeper Crab #D1900, 2 trebles, 1951, 2½"....**22.50**
Lure, Heddon, Great Vamp #7540, 3 trebles, 1937, 4⅞" **80.00**
Lure, Heddon, King Fish Vamp-Snook #KF9750, 3 trebles, 1934, 4⅛" ...**30.00**
Lure, Heddon, King Spoon #290, red, hidden hook, 1937, 2¾" ...**22.50**
Lure, Heddon, Salmon River-Runt #8850, 2 trebles, 1939, 5" **80.00**
Lure, Heddon, Super Surface #210, flocked finish, 1936, 3⅜" **80.00**
Lure, Paw Paw, Aristocrat Minnow, 2 trebles, 1946, 3¼" **42.50**
Lure, Paw Paw, Baby Popper #1200, 2 trebles, 1960s, 2¼" **15.00**
Lure, Paw Paw, Belly Hook Underwater Minnow, 3 trebles, 1939, 3"..**42.50**
Lure, Paw Paw, Croaker #71, frog skin covering, 2 trebles, 1940 ...**275.00**
Lure, Paw Paw, Feather Tail Minnow #1200, 1 treble, 1940s, 2½"....**42.50**
Lure, Paw Paw, J Jointed Darter #9200, spatter finish, 1960s, 3⅞" **35.00**
Lure, Paw Paw, Old Wounded Minnow #2500, 2 trebles, 1940s, 3½"...**22.50**
Lure, Paw Paw, Pike Caster #6400L, fish shape, 3 trebles, 1940, 5⅛" ..**80.00**
Lure, Paw Paw, Saltwater Bait, Go-Getter body, 2 trebles, 1940....**45.00**
Lure, Paw Paw, Seagram's Lucky 7, crown & 7 w/treble, 1953, 3" ...**17.50**

Lure, Pflueger, Cyclone Spinner #3000, 1959, 1⅛" blade..............**17.50**
Lure, Pflueger, Fan-Tail Squid, celluloid tube w/dressed hook, 1940...**20.00**
Lure, Pflueger, Harp Spinner, dressed treble, 1937, 1¼" blade **12.50**
Lure, Pflueger, Heavy Duty Mustang Minnow #9500, 3 trebles, 1939, 5" **27.50**
Lure, Pflueger, Kidney Pearl Bait #600, hidden treble, 1940, 2" blade...**17.50**
Lure, Pflueger, Live Wire Minnow #9400, 3 trebles, 1931-35, 3¾".....**27.50**
Lure, Pflueger, Mustang Underwater Popping Minnow #8600, 1937, 2½"....**22.50**
Lure, Pflueger, Neverfail Minnow #3100, 5-hook, 1940, 3⅝" **165.00**
Lure, Pflueger, Salamo Spoon #1500, dressed treble, 1948, 4½" ...**12.50**
Lure, Shakespeare, Baby Blitz #6550, 2 trebles, 1942, 2" **24.00**
Lure, Shakespeare, Sardinia #621, 2 trebles, 1936, 3"..................**150.00**
Lure, Shakespeare, Seimming Mouse Jr #6580, 2 trebles, 1940.....**16.00**
Lure, Shakespeare, Spinning Pop-Eye #6375, 1950, 1⅞"...............**22.50**
Lure, Shakespeare, Striped Bass Wobbler, 2 trebles, 1940, 6", $95 to ...**160.00**
Lure, South Bend, Baby Teas-Oreno #939, 2 trebles, 1931-50, 3¼"...**35.00**
Lure, South Bend, Explorer #920, 2 trebles, 1951-52, 3¾".............**12.50**
Lure, South Bend, Jointed Midget Pike-Oreno #2955, 1940s, 2¼" ...**40.00**
Lure, South Bend, King Andy #975, 2 trebles, NP bk strip, 1950s ..**35.00**
Lure, South Bend, Lunge-Oreno #966, 3 trebles, 1932-42, 7¼" **175.00**
Lure, South Bend, Min-Oreno #927, pnt tack eyes, 2 trebles, 1930s ...**25.00**
Lure, South Bend, Panatella #915, 5 trebles, 1916-42, 4¼" **110.00**
Lure, South Bend, Slim-Oreno #912, pnt eyes, 2 trebles, 1933-39 ..**55.00**
Lure, South Bend, Spoon-Oreno #586, polished or pnt, 1932-43 ...**7.50**
Lure, South Bend, Standard Woodpecker #923, 2 trebles, 1912-42, 4½"...**90.00**
Minnow bucket, Air-Fed...Quincy IL, orig gr pnt, air pump on lid, EX...**195.00**
Minnow bucket, copper w/iron hdls, hinged lid, 9½x15x8½" **275.00**
Minnow bucket, Falls City Expert Floating..., galvanized, VG.....**25.00**
Minnow bucket, Falls City Jones & fish decal on front, gr pnt, lg, NM ...**200.00**
Minnow trap, blown lt gr glass w/wire neck, EX **90.00**
Outboard motor, Mercury, electric, gr/gray/chrome, mini, 5½" L ...**330.00**
Reel, Bean's Special Steel Pivot Bearing Casting, 1930s, 2¼" dia **85.00**
Reel, Bear Creek Bait Co, ice shanty, plastic & aluminum, 1956-60, 6"........**50.00**
Reel, Bill Ballan Model 50 Raised Pillar Trout, ⅞x2⅞" dia **415.00**

Reel, Benjamin Thumezy Patents Pending, mechanical thumb brake, free spool canting, VG, $525.00.

Reel, Coxe Coronet 25 Bait Casting, aluminum, EX in case.........**55.00**
Reel, Edw Vom Hofe NY Pat Jan 23 83, Model 360 trout, #3 sz, EX...**6,000.00**
Reel, Endicott Wilson Corp 6/0 Big Game, anti-reverse, 4½" dia...**195.00**
Reel, Farlow Ambassador Salmon, single action, ¾x4" dia, VG ...**85.00**
Reel, Hardy Featherweight Trout, thick silver line guide, VGIB ...**165.00**
Reel, J Vom Hofe...89 Trout, mk SZ 2 Extra Narrow Spool, 2¾" dia..**990.00**
Reel, JC Arsenault...Trout Click, aluminum w/S hdl, 1⅜" dia....**195.00**
Reel, Shakespeare 1740 Free Spool Tournament Model FK, neweled, EX **85.00**
Reel, TH Bate NY Trout, German silver, ca 1860, 1x2½" dia....**1,265.00**
Rod, FE Thomas Special Bait Casting, 2-pc, 2-tip, scarce, VG......**415.00**
Rod, Foster Bros Ashbourne Manifold Trout, 2-pc, 1 tip, 9', VG.....**85.00**
Rod, Gary Howells Custom Made Fly, 2-pc, 2-tip, exotic wood, 8' 9", M ...**770.00**
Rod, Gary Howells Trout, 2-pc, brn w/gold wraps, 8', M in bag...**1,450.00**
Rod, Gillum Dry Fly, 3-pc, 2-tip, Super-Z ferrules, 8', M in bag **3,000.00**
Rod, Hardy Palakona Fly, 2-pc, 1 tip, soiled hdl, 9', VG in case....**330.00**

Rod, Hardy Phantom Hollokona Trout, 2-pc, 1-tip, soiled hdl, 9', EX....**330.00**
Rod, Leonard 2-Handed Salmon, 3-tip, 12', EX in case **85.00**
Rod, Mills Standard, 3-pc, 2-tip, med-slow action, 8', EX in bag ..**550.00**
Rod, Orvis Rocky Mtn, 3-pc, 2-tip, 6½', EX in bag & case **660.00**
Rod, Paul H Young Martha Marie Model, 2-pc, 2-tip, 7½', NM **2,200.00**
Rod, Payne Model 205 Trout, 3-pc, 2-tip, 8½', M in bag.........**1,875.00**
Rod, Ron Kusse Trout, 2-pc, lt bamboo, butternut cap, 1981, 7', M...**1,375.00**
Rod, Thomas & Thomas Individualist Ultra-light, 5' 9", M in bag...**2,865.00**
Rod, Thomas Four Housatonic...Sam Carlson, flamed shaft, 1975, M ..**4,400.00**
Sign, EC Simmons Fine Fishing Tackle, oilcloth, ca 1915, 18x36" ..**250.00**
Spear, eel; thistle shape, from $75 to **100.00**
Spear, eel; tulip shape, from $100 to.................................**150.00**
Spear, Shurkatch, chisel-cut barbs on wire tines, 8" to hdl socket ...**20.00**
Split shot container, celluloid, Abercrombie K& Fitch, sliding cover ..**100.00**
Split shot container, celluloid, Kelso BB, VG **95.00**
Sunfish decoy, sgn GJB, cvd/pnt, tin fins, screw eye line tie, EX...**90.00**
Tackle box, gr leather cover, fitted int, Knickerbocker...Chicago, 16" ..**440.00**
Tackle box, home made, cedar, fitted int, brass hdl, 8½x25", EX......**95.00**
Tackle box, pnt metal, leather-covered hdl, Shakespeare decals, 20" ...**195.00**

Flags of the United States

Over the past few years the popularity of vintage flags has grown dramatically, and prices have risen greatly as a result. The pending restoration of the Fort McHenry Flag (The Star Spangled Banner) has also created greater public interest in flag collecting.

The brevity and imprecise language of the first Flag Act of 1777 allowed great artistic license for America's early flag makers. This resulted in a rich variety of imaginative star formations which coexisted with more conventional row patterns. In 1912 inviolate design standards were established for the new 48-star flag, but the banners of our earlier history continue to survive:

The 'Great Star' pattern — configured from the combined stars of the union, appeared in various star denominations for about 50 years, then gradually disappeared in the post-Civil War years.

The utilitarian 'scatter' pattern — created through the random placement of stars, is traceable to the formative years of our nation and remained a design influence through most of the nineteenth century.

The 'wreath' pattern — first appearing in the form of simple single-wreath formations, eventually evolved into the elegant double- and triple-wreath medallion patterns of the Centennial period.

Acquisition of specific star denominations is also a primary consideration in the collecting process. Pre-Civil War flags of 33 stars or less are very scarce and are typically treated as 'blue chip' items. Civil War-era flags of 34 and 35 stars also stand among the most sought-after denominations. Market demand for 36-, 37-, and 38-star flags is strong but less broad-based, while interest in the unofficial 39-, 40-, 41-, and 42-star examples is largely confined to flag aficionados. The very rare 43 remains in a class by itself and is guaranteed to attract the attention of the serious collector.

Row-patterned flags of 44, 45, and 46 stars still turn up with some frequency and serve as a source of more modestly priced vintage flags. Ordinary 48-star flags flood the flea markets and are priced accordingly, while the short-lived 49 is regarded as a legitimate collectible. Thirteen-star flags, produced over a period of more than 200 years, surface in many forms and must be assessed on a case-by-case basis.

Many flag buffs favor sizes that are manageable for wall display, while others are attracted to the more monumental proportions. Allowances are typically made for the normal wear and tear — it goes with the territory. But severe fabric deterioration and other forms of excessive physical damage are legitimate points of negotiation.

The dollar value of a flag is by no means based upon age alone. The wide price swings in the listing below have been influenced by a variety of determining factors related to age, scarcity, and aesthetic merit. In fact, almost any special feature that stands out as unusual or distinctive is a potential asset. Imprinted flags and inscribed flags; eight-point stars, gold stars, and added stars; extra stripes, missing stripes, tricolor stripes, and war stripes are all part of the pricing equation. And while political and military flags may rank above all others in terms of prestige and price, any flag with a significant and well-documented historical connection has 'star' potential (pardon the pun). Our advisor for this category is Ryan Cooper; he is listed in the Directory under Massachusetts.

13 stars, Dmn pattern, hand sewn, early 1800s, 32x38" **8,365.00**
13 stars, hand/machine sewn, Centennial **850.00**
13 stars, printed glazed muslin, 1880s, 7x11" **300.00**
13 stars, str rows, hand/machine sewn, Civil War era, 40x50" ..**1,800.00**
13 stars, US Naval boat insignia, 1880, 50x96" **750.00**
15 stars, union jack from War of 1812, rare, 35x62" **23,000.00**
15 stars, 15 stripes, all machine sewn, ca 1912, 48x72" **375.00**
16 stars, Great Star, hand sewn, 1850s, 54x78" **9,500.00**
19 stars, 16 orig+3, sewn scrap fabric, 39x66"..........................**7,500.00**
20 stars, oval pattern, ship's flag, 1818, worn, 64x128" **6,500.00**
21 stars, Commissioning pennant, ship 'Herald,' 1819, 50-ft...**8,500.00**
25 stars, oval pattern w/central star, ship's flag, 96x200"..........**6,700.00**
25 stars, row pattern, Civil War, 90x175" **2,200.00**
26 stars, Great Star, embr on sewn silk, 30x43" **8,500.00**
26 stars, Great Star, printed cotton, 12x17"............................**3,885.00**
29 stars, entirely hand sewn, poor condition, 43x68" **4,500.00**
30 stars, gold stars/fringe, silk, delicate, 52x68" **4,500.00**
31 stars, Great Star, hand-sewn silk, 14' **4,000.00**
31 stars, row pattern, hand-stitched bunting, 104x247"..........**2,500.00**
31 stars, Scatter Star pattern, hand sewn, 45x68" **4,480.00**
32 stars, dbl wreath of inset stars, hand sewn, 36x48" **5,200.00**
33 stars, Great Star, hand-sewn muslin, 60x96".......................**5,000.00**
33 stars, hand-/machine-sewn wool bunting, 66x92" **2,250.00**
33 stars, in rows, printed bunting, 28x44", G-...........................**1,200.00**
34 stars, dbl-wreath pattern, printed silk, 18x28" **1,600.00**
34 stars, Great Star, from Albany RR Depot, 116x175"..........**6,500.00**
34 stars, Great Star, printed cotton, 25x39"............................**3,500.00**
34 stars, printed linen, 3 sewn sections, 22x48" **600.00**
34 stars, random pattern, hand sewn, 66x140" **1,600.00**
35 stars, dbl-wreath pattern, printed, sized muslin, 19x28" **1,500.00**
35 stars, recruiting flag, sewn bunting, 50x116"......................**1,800.00**
35 stars, row pattern, hand/machine sewn, 96x180"................**1,500.00**
36 stars, cut-in, in rows, machined stripes, 25x50" **1,000.00**
36 stars, inscribed parade flag, muslin print, 6x9" **350.00**
36 stars, sailing ship's, inscribed & dtd, 75x142"......................**950.00**
37 stars, medallion pattern, printed/sewn muslin, 48x87" **550.00**
37 stars, printed silk, 32x40" **300.00**
37 stars, row pattern, hand-sewn silk, poor, 60x80" **350.00**
37 stars, row pattern, stitched bunting, 30x48" **600.00**
38 stars, medallion-wreath pattern, printed cotton, 12x17" **550.00**
38 stars, printed silk w/ribbon ties, 30x47" **350.00**
38 stars, row pattern, clamp dyed in 3 sections, 60x120" **325.00**
38 stars, row pattern, hand/machine-stitched bunting, 71x116"...**450.00**
38 stars, unique wreath pattern, sewn, 89x134".....................**1,200.00**
38 stars, 1776-1876 pattern, printed linen, 27½x46" **1,800.00**
39 stars, Centennial 'International Flag,' 16x24".......................**275.00**
39 stars, row pattern, all machine-stitched bunting, 40x84" **450.00**
39 stars, row pattern variation, printed silk, 12x24" **200.00**
39 stars (6-5 pattern), printed gauze bunting, 19x34"................**200.00**
40 stars, row pattern, hand-sewn bunting, lg, 98x204" **270.00**
40 stars, row pattern, printed/sewn British import, 55x106".......**250.00**
41 stars (rare), printed cotton sheeting, 15x24".........................**375.00**
42 stars, sewn cotton, from Ft Hamilton NY, 120x177" **275.00**
42 stars, 7-row pattern, printed cotton, 12x17"........................**125.00**

43 stars, machine-sewn bunting, extremely rare, 29x70"..........**1,500.00**
44 stars, machine-sewn cotton bunting, 53x82"..........................**200.00**
44 stars, triple-wreath pattern, printed cotton, 23x26"................**350.00**
45 stars, HP w/sewn stripes, 38x70"..**120.00**
45 stars, machine-sewn cotton bunting, 80x108"..........................**55.00**
45 stars, printed silk w/red ribbon ties, 32x46"............................**45.00**
45 stars, row pattern variant, printed muslin, 9x13" **25.00**
46 stars, machine-sewn wool bunting, 72x138"..............................**60.00**
46 stars, printed silk, GAR Post in gold, 32x45"..........................**350.00**
47 stars, unofficial, sewn bunting, 108x137".............................**350.00**
48 stars, all crocheted, dtd 1941, 20x38"....................................**85.00**
48 stars, machine-sewn cotton bunting, 60x96"............................**50.00**
48 stars, printed cotton w/GAR surprint, 11x16"..........................**40.00**
48 stars, sewn to form 'USA,' unauthorized WWI, 45x69" **300.00**
48 stars, USN Union Jack, machine-sewn wool, 23x33"...............**35.00**
48 stars in gold, sewn WWII casket flag, 58x118" **95.00**

48 stars (incorrect pattern), homemade WWII liberation flag from Liege, Belgium, 68x93", $95.00. (Photo courtesy Robert Banks)

49 stars, embroidered, sewn stripes, 36x60" **45.00**
49 stars, 3 uncut flags, printed cotton sheet, 37x36" **25.00**
50 stars, early prototype 'June 1959,' 52x66"..............................**220.00**
50 stars, hand-knitted coverlet w/fringe, 30x51"..........................**30.00**
51 stars, printed flaglette for DC statehood, 4x6" **15.00**

Florence Ceramics

Figurines marked 'Florence Ceramics' were produced in the '40s and '50s in Pasadena, California. The quality of the ware and the attention given to detail has prompted a growing interest among today's collectors. The names of these lovely ladies, gents, and figural groups are nearly always incised into their bases. The company name is ink stamped. Examples are evaluated by size, rarity, and intricacy of design. For more information we recommend *The Collector's Encyclopedia of California Pottery, Second Edition,* by Jack Chipman; *The Florence Collectibles* by Doug Foland; and *The Complete Book of Florence Ceramics: A Labor of Love* by Sue and Jerry Kline and Margaret Wehrspaun. Our advisor for this category is Jerry Kline; he is listed in the Directory under Vermont.

Adeline, fancy, 8¼" **350.00**
Amelia, 8¼" **275.00**
Ava, flower holder, 10½", from $300 to **325.00**
Baby, flower holder, from $75 to **100.00**
Beth, 7½", from $125 to **150.00**
Blossom Girl, flower holder..**125.00**
Bride, rare, 8¾", from $1,800 to..**2,000.00**
Butch, 5½", from $175 to **200.00**

Caroline, brocade, rare, 15", from $3,000 to **3,500.00**
Catherine, 6¾x7¾"..**700.00**
Charles, 8¾"..**325.00**
Cinderella & Prince Charming, from $3,000 to **3,200.00**
Claudia, 8¼", from $250 to..**275.00**
Darleen, 8¼", from $825 to..**900.00**
David, 7½", from $125 to **140.00**
Deborah, rare, 9¼" **750.00**
Diana, powder box, 6¼", from $500 to **550.00**
Don, prom boy, 9½", from $425 to...**475.00**
Edward, 7"...**450.00**
Eve, 8½", from $375 to **425.00**
Fair Lady, rare, 11½", from $3,250 to.......................................**3,500.00**
Gary, 8½", from $150 to **170.00**
Georgette, 10" **750.00**
Halloween Child, 4", from $600 to...**700.00**
Jim, child, 6¼", from $175 to...**200.00**
Joy, child, 6", from $175 to..**200.00**
Joyce, 9", from $500 to **600.00**
Kiu, 11"...**250.00**
Leading Man, 10½" **475.00**
Lillian, 7¼"...**150.00**
Madonna, 10½", from $500 to..**550.00**
Margo, rare, 8½", from $650 to **700.00**
Mary, seated, 7½", from $650 to **700.00**
Masquerade, rare, 8¼", from $800 to..**900.00**
Nita, 8", from $500 to **550.00**
Pamela, 7¼", from $350 to **400.00**
Patsy, flower holder, 6", from $50 to..**60.00**
Pinkie, 12", from $400 to **450.00**
Rebecca, aqua dress w/violet trim, 7", from $225 to **250.00**
Rebecca, other colors, 7", from $225 to..**250.00**
Sherri, 8½", from $450 to **500.00**
Story Hour w/Boy & Girl, 8", from $1,100 to..........................**1,250.00**
Sue Ellen, 8¼", from $160 to...**175.00**
Summer, 6¼", from $400 to **450.00**
Toy, 9", from $325 to **350.00**
Victor, 9¼", from $275 to **325.00**
Violet, wall pocket, w/gold, 7", from $150 to **160.00**
Virginia, brocade, rare, 15", from $3,000 to.............................**3,500.00**
Yvonne, plain, 8¾", from $425 to **500.00**

Florentine Cameo

Although the appearance may look much like English cameo, the decoration on this type of glass is not wheel cut or acid etched. Instead a type of heavy paste — usually a frosty white — is applied to the surface to create a look very similar to true cameo. It was produced in France as well as England; it is sometimes marked 'Florentine.'

Pitcher, orange w/wht bird & grass, 8", +4 4¾" tumblers............**325.00**
Vase, allover flowers in dotted bands w/fringe below, 12"............**265.00**
Vase, cobalt w/wht daisies & pheasant, 3¾" **55.00**
Vase, sapphire bl w/opaque morning glories, 7¾" **75.00**

Flow Blue

Flow Blue ware was produced by many Staffordshire potters; among the most familiar were Meigh, Podmore and Walker, Samuel Alcock, Ridgway, John Wedge Wood (who often signed his work Wedgewood), and Davenport. It was popular from about 1825 through 1860 and again from 1880 until the turn of the century. The name describes the blurred or flowing affect of the cobalt decoration, achieved through the introduction of a chemical vapor into the kiln. The body of the ware is ironstone, and Oriental motifs were favored. Later issues were on a lighter body and often decorated with gilt. For further information we recommend *The Collector's Encyclopedia of Flow Blue China* by Mary Frank Gaston (Collector Books).

Acorn, soup plate, Furnivals Ltd, 10 " 60.00
Agra, bone dish, F Winkle & Co, 3½x6" 75.00
Alaska, bowl, WH Grindley, oval, 9" 140.00
Albert, plate, Dudson Wilcox & Till Ltd, 7" 40.00
Albion, soup plate, W&E Corn, 10" 65.00
Aldine, bone dish, WH Grindley, 6½" 50.00
Amoy, berry bowl, Davenport, 5½" 80.00
Amoy, pitcher, WE & Co, 6½" 700.00
Amoy, plate, Davenport, 9¼" 150.00
Amoy, sugar bowl, 8-sided, w/lid, Davenport, 6½x8¼x4½".......550.00
Amoy, teapot, Davenport, 9½"...1,200.00
Anemone, sauce bowl, Lockhart & Arthur, ped ft, hdls..............500.00
Arundal, salad bowl, Doulton, silver trim 275.00
Ashburton, demitasse cup, ped base, WH Grindley......................70.00
Ashburton, plate, WH Grindley, 9"..90.00
Aster, vegetable bowl, Upper Hanley Pottery, 10" 160.00
Bay, bowl, Ford & Sons 70.00
Bay, cup, Ford & Sons 50.00
Beatrice, gravy boat, gold trim, John Maddock, 9" L 100.00
Bejapore, ladle, Geo Phillips, 12½" 400.00
Bejapore, platter, Geo Phillips, 18x14" 1,200.00
Bejapore, tureen, Geo Phillips, 12x15" 1,400.00
Belmont, bowl & pitcher, WH Grindley 2,000.00
Bentick, gray boat w/underplate, gold trim, Cauldon, 6¼x8½" L ...300.00
Bentick, platter, Ridgeway, 14x17"..1,000.00
Bentick, tureen, w/lid, polychromed, Cauldon...........................800.00
Bisley, plate, WH Grindley, 9" 85.00
Blue Rose, fruit/dessert bowl, gold trim, WH Grindley, 5" 40.00
Bolingbroke, plate, gold trim, Ridgways, 10" 80.00
Bombay, demitasse cup, Furnival..70.00
Botanical, toothbrush holder, w/lid, Minton................................450.00
Burleigh, sauce tureen, gold trim, Burgess & Leigh, 5x8" 350.00
Burleigh, underplate, gold trim, Burgess & Leigh, 7¾x5¼" 200.00
Burmese, serving dish, gold trim, Rathbone, 13½x9" 500.00
Burslem Berries, gravy boat, ped base, Newport Pottery.............100.00
California, cup, ped base, att Podmore, Walker & Son, 3".........120.00
California, plate, Podmore, Walker & Co, 10" 140.00
California, teapot, att Podmore, Walker & Co, 8½" 1,000.00
Campion, bowl & pitcher set, WH Grindley............................1,800.00
Campion, chamber pot, w/lid..450.00
Canton, demitasse cup, Maddock, 2½" 120.00
Carlton, teapot, John & Geo Alcock, 8½" 800.00
Cashmere, cup & saucer, Ridgway & Morley, 2¼", 5¾" 140.00
Cashmere, plate, Ridgway & Morley, 7"..120.00
Cattle Scenery, bowl, oval, W Adams & Sons, 14x19"............1,000.00
Celestial, pitcher, Ridgway, 7"..800.00
Celestial, platter, canted corners, John Alcock, 7x10"................350.00
Chatsworth, plate, Ford & Sons, 10¼"..90.00
Chatsworth, soap dish, Keeling & Co, 6x9½" L 120.00
Chen Si, plate, 12-sided, JM Mier, 6⅝" 75.00
Cherubs, plate, polychromed center, English, 9" 75.00
Chiswick, plate, scalloped rim, Ridgway, 10"...............................85.00
Chiswick, vegetable bowl, w/lid, gold trim, Ridgway, 8½" 225.00
Chusan, pitcher, ped base, Collinson, 11".................................1,200.00
Chusan, sugar bowl, w/lid, Clementson, 8"..................................800.00
Cimerian, soup plate, Maddock, 11"...160.00
Claremont, plate, gold trim, Johnson Bros, 10".............................85.00

Claremont, vegetable bowl, w/lid, hdls, gold trim, Johnson Bros....325.00
Clarendon, platter, Henry Alcock, plain wht center, 13½x18" 450.00
Clayton, soup bowl, plain wht rim & center, Johnson Bros, 7½"...60.00
Clematis, vase, ped ft, high hdls, ped ft, 8" 450.00
Cleopatra, cake stand, wide ped ft, att E Walley, 2⅝x11¾" 1,000.00
Cleopatra, fruit compote, ped ft, upturned hdls, Walley, 9x13" ..1,200.00
Clive, pitcher, T Rathbone, 8"...450.00
Coburg, cup plate, John Edwards, 4½" 140.00
Coburg, ladle for tureen, gold trim, Barker & Kent, 7" 140.00
Coburg, plate, John Edwards, 8" 130.00
Coburg, platter, scalloped edge, gold trim, B&K, 10½x13".........325.00
Coburg, soup tureen, gold trim, 4¾x7½".......................................275.00
Coburg, underplate for tureen, gold trim, 6x8½"........................175.00
Colonial, platter, Meakin, 17½x14" 300.00
Corey Hill, pitcher, polychromed, gold trim, unmk, 11" 375.00
Countryside, teapot, gold trim, HJ Wood....................................500.00
Crescent, cake plate, WH Grindley, 13¼x14" 160.00
Crescent, gravy boat & underplate, WH Grindley, 4x9" 17,500.00
Crescent, soup plate, gold trim, WH Grindley...............................85.00
Crescent, soup tureen, w/lid, gold trim, WH Grindley, 7x14".....600.00
Crescent, vegetable bowl, gold trim, WH Grindley, 8x10"..........175.00
Crumlin, soup plate, Myott, Son & Co, 9".......................................85.00
Cyprus, bowl, Ridgway, 10½"...160.00
Dahlia, platter, canted corners, EC (Challinor), 8¼x10¾".........325.00
Dahlia, sugar bowl, w/lid, ped ft, hdls, att to Challinor, 7½" 550.00
Daisy, butter pat, Burgess & Leigh 30.00
Delamere, cereal bowl, Alcock, 6½"..50.00
Delamere, cup, gold trim, Alcock, 2½" 60.00

Delft, plate, Mintons, 9", from $80.00 to $90.00. (Photo courtesy Mary Frank Gaston)

Delph, cake plate, ped base, gold trim, unmk, 7½"......................325.00
Delph, cup, ped ft, 3" 120.00
Devon, sugar bowl, w/lid, no hdls, same pattern as made by Meakin, 4"..175.00
Devon, underplate for vegetable bowl, Ford & Sons, 8x10"........275.00
Devon, vegetable bowl, w/lid, hdls, Ford & Sons, 6½x9".............350.00
Doreen, chamber pot, w/lid, hdl, Grindley....................................450.00
Doreen, pitcher & bowl set, hexagonal, Grindley 1,600.00
Doreen, shaving mug, Grindley 175.00
Doreen, soap dish, w/lid, Grindley..300.00
Doreen, toothbrush holder, Grindley..275.00
Doreen, waste jar, w/lid, hexagonal, hdls, Grindley....................750.00
Doric, platter, 15⅝x19¾"...600.00
Douglas, vegetable bowl, w/lid, Ford & Sons, 8x11"...................350.00
Dresden, platter, Johnson Bros, 6x12"...200.00
Dunkeld, bread & butter plate, Breadmore, 7½"............................35.00
Eagle, platter, canted corners, Podmore Walker & Co, 10½x13½"...450.00
Eileen, soup plate, Grindley, 10"...80.00
Excelsior, teapot, ped ft, Thomas Fell 1,000.00

Fairy Villas, individual serving dish, att Adams, 4x5½" 75.00
Fallow Deer, plate, Wedgwood, 10" 150.00
Fallow Deer, serving dish, w/lid, Wedgwood, sq w/curved corners 375.00
Ferrara, cup, no hdl, Wedgwood, 3" 165.00
Ferrara, pitcher, 8 panels, Wedgwood, 6" 165.00
Fibre, plate, Globe (made for Woolworth's), 6" 35.00
Fisherman, pitcher, att Podmore Walker, 5½" 250.00
Fleur De Lis, saucer, Meakin, 6" 25.00
Floral, vegetable bowl, w/lid, T Hughes & Son, oblong 300.00
Florian, platter, Burgess & Leigh, lg oval 500.00
Formosa, platter, Mayer, minor rstr, 13¼x10¼" 300.00
Fulton, plate, Johnson Bros, 10" 90.00
Genevese, plate, Edge, Malkin & Co, 9¼" 150.00
Geraneum, plate, Podmore, Walker & Co, 9½" 140.00
Gironde, berry dish, gold trim, Grindley, 6" 30.00
Gironde, bone dish, leaf shape, gold trim, Grindley 50.00
Gironde, cup & saucer, Grindley, 2" & 6" 90.00
Gladiolius, pitcher, cylindrical, Doulton, 9" 700.00
Grace, plate, plain wht center, Grindley, 9" 70.00
Hague, serving tray, tab hdls, Wedgwood, 8x17½" 500.00
Idris, platter, Grindley, 11½x16" 275.00
Indian, pitcher, 11", EX 350.00
Iris, cheese dish, w/lid, Doulton, 9½x9" 600.00
Iris, cup & saucer, gold trim, Wilkinson 85.00
Ivy, pitcher, unmk (Williams), 8" 550.00
Janette, gravy boat & underplate, Grindley 225.00
Jedo, plate, Doulton, 10" 140.00
Jewel, pitcher, Johnson Bros, lg...350.00
Jewel, pitcher, Johnson Bros, sm..300.00
Kyber, plate, Adams, 10" 145.00
LaBelle, bone dish, Wheeling Pottery, 6⅜x3⅜" 125.00
LaBelle, bowl, oval, Wheeling Pottery, 3¼x11¼x9¼" 300.00
LaBelle, bread tray, Wheeling Pottery, 11x6" 250.00
LaBelle, pitcher, Wheeling Pottery, 7x9½" 600.00
Lancaster, platter, New Wharf Pottery, 9½x7", EX.....................100.00

Lonsdale, gravy boat, gold trim, Samuel Ford & Co., from $80.00 to $100.00. (Photo courtesy Mary Frank Gaston)

Lotus, jardiniere, swirled, gold spattered.......................................600.00
Manilla, plate, Podmore Walker, 7¾" 150.00
Manilla, platter, Podmore Walker, 15¾x12" 900.00
Marguerite, toothbrush holder, gold sponged, H Bros..................275.00
Navarre, saucer, Wedgwood, 6½" 30.00
Nonpareil, platter, Burgess & Leigh, 17¾" L 600.00
Norfolk, cereal/soup bowl, Doulton 85.00
Oakland, butter pat, Maddock & Sons, 2¾x2⅞" 40.00
Onion, plate, Allertons, 8"...85.00
Oregon, vegetable bowl, w/lid, Mayer, 8½x11" sq, EX 575.00
Oyama, pitcher, Doulton, 6½" 500.00

Peach, platter, Johnson Bros, 14x17"...400.00
Pekin, vegetable bowl, scalloped ftd base, w/lid, 6½x12" 350.00
Peking, toothbrush/razor box, unmk, 8x3¼" 300.00
Persian Spray, cake stand, ped ft, gold trim, 3x9" 450.00
Petunia, jardiniere, gold trim, initialed C&H, 6½x8" 550.00
Rhoda Gardens, plate, Hackwood, 9½" 150.00
Rhone, platter, att to Challinor, 15x11" 400.00
Rock, plate, Challinor, 8½" 110.00
Scinde, coffeepot, 8-sided, scroll hdl, Alcock, EX 1,000.00
Scinde, plate, Alcock, 10¼" 150.00
Scinde, plate, Walker, 10½" 140.00
Scinde, soup bowl, Alcock, 9½" 125.00
Scinde, tea bowl & saucer, Alcock, 3", 5¾" 250.00
Shanghae, vegetable bowl, w/lid, 7x12" 450.00
Shapoo, cup plate, T Hughes, 4⅛" 200.00
Swallow, plate, gold trim, Grove & Stark, 10" 85.00
Temple, plate, Podmore Walker, 8¾" 150.00
Temple, plate, Podmore Walker, 9¾" 175.00
Thistle, bowl vase, gold trim/sponging 275.00
Tonquin, platter, Adams & Sons, 13½x10¼", NM 500.00
Tonquin, relish, att to J Heath, 8¾x5" 275.00
Turkey, plate, Cauldon, 10"...150.00
Watteau, plate, courting couple, ca 1895, 9¾", 6 for.................500.00

Flue Covers

When spring housecleaning started and the heating stove was taken down for the warm weather season, the unsightly hole where the stovepipe joined the chimney was hidden with an attractive flue cover. They were made with a colorful litho print behind glass with a chain for hanging. In a 1929 catalog, they were advertised at 16¢ each or six for 80¢. Although scarce today, some scenes were actually reverse painted on the glass itself. The most popular motifs were florals, children, animals, and lovely ladies. Occasionally flue covers were made in sets of three — one served a functional purpose, while the others were added to provide a more attractive wall arrangement. They range in size from 7" to 14", but 9" is the average.

A Sweet Treat, basket w/strawberries, 9½", from $85 to...............95.00
Asian Beauty, oriental women w/flowers in hair, 7", from $70 to..80.00
Autumn, trees w/farm in background, 8¼x6½", from $50 to........60.00
Bear Facts, bear writes on chalkboard, 8½", from $150 to 175.00
Carla in a Cape, girl w/blond curls, 7¾", from $55 to 65.00
Casting the Nets, fishing boats in water, 6x5", from $50 to 60.00
Collecting Firewood, cottage in winter w/man & boy, 8½x7", $50 to....60.00
Daddy's Girls, 2 girls hugging, 9½", from $60 to 70.00
Fun Gathering Twigs, 3 children, 9½", from $80 to......................90.00
Fun on the Pond, boy & girl ice skate, 9½", from $85 to 95.00
Gathering the Greens, boy & girl, 9½", from $85 to.....................95.00
Gift, The; flowers & strawberries in basket, 12", from $75 to 85.00
Grandpa's Story, grandpa reads to sm girl, 11¾", from $90 to.....100.00
Halo of Roses, lady surrounded by roses, 9½", from $85 to 95.00
His Intentions, courting couple in winter, 8½x10½", from $60 to ..70.00
Holding Tiny Teddy, girl in cape holds sm dog, dmn shape, 9x9", $60 to....70.00
In the Garden, 2 cherubs w/arms around ea other, 14", from $90 to..100.00
Lady w/Fan, blk curly hair, 9x9", from $50 to................................60.00
Lariet Lassie, cowgirl w/lasso, 9½", from $90 to.........................100.00
Linda's Fruit, girl in bonnet w/strawberries, 9½", from $75 to.......85.00
Maria w/Roses, girl w/blk curls & lg red bow, 8½", from $85 to....95.00
Moose at the Lake, 7½", from $45 to 55.00
Nursing the Wounded, woman nurses soldier, 6¼x6¼", from $55 to....65.00
Over the Fence, courting couple at wood fence, 9½", from $60 to ...65.00
Painter, The; girl paints cottage scene, 9½", from $90 to............100.00

Peck's Bad Boy, sm boy w/mischievous grin, 9¾", from $75 to......**85.00**
Pink Wild Rose, in red vase, 9¾", from $75 to **85.00**
Playmates, 2 girls, dmn shape, 9x9", from $75 to **85.00**
Ready To Pick, cluster of grapes, 9½", from $75 to.........................**85.00**
Red Riding Hood & the Wolf, 9½", from $90 to..........................**100.00**
Resting w/Storm, lady rests arm on horse, 9¼", from $65 to.........**75.00**
River Town, cottages along river, 8½", from $65 to........................**75.00**
Sir Winston, blk horse, 9½", from $70 to......................................**80.00**
Sophisticated Lady, signed G Putikalery, 9¼", from $90 to.........**100.00**
Storm, The; woman holds blanket over 2 children, 9½", from $85 to ..**95.00**
Storytime, Victorian girl reads book, 9½", from $70 to **80.00**
Student, The; girl in red w/glasses reading, 9½", from $100 to ...**110.00**
Summer Leisure, Victorian lady & girl under umbrella, 9½", $85 to ...**95.00**
Thinking, lady looks out window, 7¾", from $55 to **65.00**
Under the Oak Tree, courting couple in woods, 9¼", from $55 to ..**65.00**
Violet Lady, in yel gown, 7¾", from $50 to **60.00**
Walking Rover, boy walks dog, 4⅝", from $55 to **65.00**
Web, The; lady w/pk gown sits in spider web, 9½", from $85 to...**95.00**
Wintertime, 2 girls dressed in winter attire, 5¾", from $55 to **65.00**
Yellow Daisies, in wht box, 9½", from $85 to **95.00**
Young Master, A; sm boy in wht wig, 7¾", from $50 to **60.00**

Folk Art

That the creative energies of the mind ever spark innovations in functional utilitarian channels as well as toward playful frivolity is well documented in the study of American folk art. While the average early settler rarely had free time to pursue art for its own sake, his creativity exemplified itself in fashioning useful objects carved or otherwise ornamented beyond the scope of pure practicality. After the advent of the Industrial Revolution, the pace of everyday living became more leisurely, and country folk found they had extra time. Not accustomed to sitting idle, many turned to carving, painting, or weaving. Whirligigs, imaginative toys for the children, and whimsies of all types resulted. Though often rather crude, this type of early art represents a segment of our heritage and as such has become valued by collectors.

Values given for drawings, paintings, and theorems are 'in frame' unless noted otherwise. See also Baskets; Decoys; Frakturs; Samplers; Trade Signs; Weather Vanes; Wood Carvings.

Chair, carved and painted, ca 1850s, EX, $690.00.

Birdhouse, CI, Victorian Gothic style, old mc pnt, 10½x14½x11"...**2,000.00**
Drawing on sandpaper, sailboat in moonlight among mtns/etc, 22x27" fr...**355.00**

Family register, calligraphic watercolor/ink on paper, 1876, 12x9"...**300.00**
Family register, watercolor scene & statistics, 1800s, 22x17"...**3,000.00**
Gourd basket, mc floral decor, shaped rim, 19th C, 6¾x7", EX..**230.00**
Painting on velvet, girl w/lamb among trees, sgn, OH, 22x19" 19th C fr....**750.00**
Paper cutout, squirrel/birds/rabbit/tree, S Lindsey, OH, in 16x14" fr ...**515.00**
Paperweight, hand w/sailor's sleeve grips lady's hand, cvd stone, 2x5" ..**1,300.00**
Pipe bowl, man's head, cvd burlwood, Am, 19th C, 2⅞" **475.00**
Plaque, Am Indian chief cvd in relief, sandstone, S Greer, 14x12"....**175.00**
Plaque, chip-cvd eagle w/arrow in high relief, 19th C, 9x16" **825.00**
Plaque, cvd bird on branch among fruit & leaves, 1890s, 12" dia ...**475.00**
Sandstone cvg, Indian maiden w/3 babies, sgn E Reed, 58"...**45,000.00**
Sandstone cvg, mother & child on stump, sgn E Reed, 12½"...**3,450.00**
Sandstone cvg, totem pole, sgn Popeye Reed, 95"....................**3,450.00**
Shelf, cvd man's head below, orig blk pnt, wht at eyes, 8x11x9" ...**975.00**
Shelf, 3-tier, cvd scrolls, dk finish, Am, 19th C, 24x27x6" **750.00**
Sketch on paper, man w/long beard, sgn TW Wood, dtd 1859, 13x11" .**250.00**
Spencerian drawing, dove/flowers/Mother & Father 1909, blk ink, 17x20" **250.00**
Spencerian drawing, elephant w/flat in trunk & ring on tail, 23x30" fr **550.00**
Theorem on velvet, rooster w/tulip, sgn DYE (Ellinger), 8x10"+fr..**1,045.00**
Valentine, 8 folded segments w/pin pricks & watercolors, 1927, 15"..**1,150.00**
Watercolor on paper, basket of fruit w/bird, 1800s, 12x17", EX ...**1,650.00**
Watercolor on paper, bird w/flower & star, mc, in 7½" sq beveled fr....**550.00**
Watercolor on paper, naive lady w/tulip, bird hovers at head, 8x6" fr ..**465.00**
Watercolor on paper, winter farm scene, glued down, sgn, 1890s, 10x8"..**880.00**
Watercolor on velvet, church & willows w/2 figures, 20x16"+fr **2,000.00**
Whirligig, Am Indian in canoe, wood w/mc details, 1920s, 16½" L..**1,600.00**
Whirligig, Indian w/paddles, orig mc pnt, lt wear, 20th C, 11"...**550.00**
Whirligig, 2 men sawing wood, mc pnt wood w/tin, 1950, 33x40"....**230.00**

Fostoria

The Fostoria Glass Company was built in 1887 at Fostoria, Ohio, but by 1891 it had moved to Moundsville, West Virginia. During the next two decades, they produced many lines of pressed patterned tableware and lamps. Their most famous pattern, American, was introduced in 1915 and was produced continuously until 1986 in well over two hundred different pieces. From 1920 to 1925, top artists designed tablewares in colored glass — canary (vaseline), amber, blue, orchid, green, and ebony — in pressed patterns as well as etched designs. By the late '30s, Fostoria was recognized as the largest producer of handmade glassware in the world. The company ceased operations in Moundsville in 1986.

Many items from both the American and Coin Glass lines have been reproduced by Lancaster Colony. In some cases the new glass is superior in quality to the old. Since the 1950s, Indiana Glass has produced a pattern called 'Whitehall' that looks very much like Fostoria's American, though with slight variations. Because Indiana's is not handmade glass, the lines of the 'cube' pattern and the edges of the items are sharp and untapered in comparison to the fire-polished originals. Three-footed pieces lack the 'toe' and instead have a peg-like foot, and the rays on the bottoms of the American examples are narrower than on the Whitehall counterparts. The Home Interiors Company offers several pieces of American look-alikes which were not even produced in the United States. Be sure of your dealer and study the books suggested below to become more familiar with the original line.

Coin Glass reproductions flood the market. Among items you may encounter are an 8" round bowl, 9" oval bowl, 8¼" wedding bowl, 4½" candlesticks, urn with lid, 6¼" candy jar with lid, footed comport, sugar and creamer; there could possibly be others. Colors in production are crystal, green, blue, and red. The red color is very good, but the blue is not the original color, nor is the emerald green. Buyer beware!

For further information see *Elegant Glassware of the Depression Era* by Gene Florence, and *Fostoria Tableware* and *The Fostoria Value Guide* by Milbra Long and Emily Seate. See also Glass Animals and Figurines.

Alexis, crystal, bowl, crushed ice 25.00
Alexis, crystal, bowl, nappy; 5" 15.00
Alexis, crystal, decanter, w/stopper...100.00
Alexis, crystal, pitcher, 32-oz 75.00
Alexis, crystal, stem, cocktail, 3-oz 12.50
Alexis, crystal, tray, celery 25.00
Alexis, crystal, tumbler, iced tea; ftd, 10-oz.............................20.00
Alexis, crystal, vase, sweet pea; ftd, 7" 50.00
Alexis, crystal, water bottle 85.00
American, crystal, basket, w/reed hdl, 7x9"..............................95.00
American, crystal, bottle, cordial; w/stopper, 9-oz, 7¼"............90.00
American, crystal, bottle, water; 44-oz, 9¼" 625.00
American, crystal, bowl, banana split; 9x3½" 550.00
American, crystal, bowl, bonbon; 3-ftd, 6".................................15.00
American, crystal, bowl, cream soup; hdls, 5" 45.00
American, crystal, bowl, fruit; rolled edge, 11½".......................42.50
American, crystal, candy box, w/lid, triangular, 3-part 90.00
American, crystal, comport, jelly; 4½"..15.00
American, crystal, creamer, 9½-oz 12.50
American, crystal, finger bowl, smooth edge, 4½" 40.00
American, crystal, goblet, sundae; #2056, low ft, 6-oz, 3⅛" 9.00
American, crystal, goblet, water; #5056, w/plain bowl, 10-oz, 6⅛" ...18.00
American, crystal, mayonnaise, w/liner & ladle 35.00
American, crystal, mug, beer; 12-oz, 4½" 70.00
American, crystal, oil, 5-oz...35.00
American, crystal, pitcher, w/ice lip, fat, ftd, 3-pt, 6½" 60.00
American, crystal, plate, bread & butter; 6" 12.00
American, crystal, plate, torte; oval, 13½" 50.00
American, crystal, platter, oval, 10½" 40.00
American, crystal, rose bowl, 3½" 20.00
American, crystal, tray, ice cream; oval, 13½"............................185.00
American, crystal, tray, muffin; 2 upturned sides, 10" 30.00
American, crystal, tumbler, old fashioned; #2056, flat, 6-oz, 3⅜"...15.00
American, crystal, tumbler, water; #2056, flat, flared, 8-oz, 4⅛"...15.00
American, crystal, urn, sq, ped ft, 6" 30.00
American, crystal, vase, bud; flared, 6" 18.00
Baroque, crystal, bowl, cream soup 35.00
Baroque, crystal, bowl, jelly; w/lid, 7½".....................................45.00
Baroque, crystal, shakers, pr 60.00
Baroque, crystal, tumbler, juice; 5-oz, 3¾" 15.00
Baroque, crystal, vase, 6½"..50.00
Baroque, yel, candlestick, 3-light, 6", ea 75.00
Baroque, yel, creamer, ftd, 3¾" 20.00
Baroque, yel, sugar bowl, ftd, 3½" 20.00
Brocade Grape, bl, bowl, #2371, oval, rolled edge w/grid frog, 13"...225.00
Brocade Grape, bl, vase, #4100, 8" 125.00
Brocade Grape, gr, candy box, #2331, w/lid, 3-part 145.00
Brocade Grape, gr, comport, #2327, twist stem, 7" 55.00
Brocade Oakleaf, crystal, bonbon, #2375 ....30.00
Brocade Oakleaf, ebony, vase, bulbous, #4103, 3", 4" 75.00
Brocade Oakleaf, gr or rose, candlestick, scroll, #2395, 3", ea.......65.00
Brocade Oakwood, orchid or azure, finger bowl, #869 ....75.00
Brocade Oakwood, orchid or azure, plate, cake; #2375, 10" 125.00
Brocade Oakwood, orchid or azure, whip cream, #2375, scalloped, hdls 55.00
Brocade Palm Leaf, rose or gr, bowl, #2394, 3-toe, flared rim, 12"....150.00
Coin, amber, ashtray, #1372/115, oblong....................................15.00
Coin, amber, ashtray, center coin, 7½" 28.00
Coin, amber, lamp, patio; #1372/466, electric, 16⅝" 175.00
Coin, bl, cigarette box, #1372/374, w/lid, 5¾x4½".....................80.00
Coin, crystal, pitcher, qt 95.00
Coin, gr, jelly, #1372/448 ....35.00
Coin, olive, nappy, #1372/499, w/hdl, 5⅜"................................18.00
Coin, ruby, ashtray, #1372/119, center coin, 7½" 25.00
Coin, ruby, urn, 31372/829, w/lid, ftd, 12¾"..............................100.00

Coin, blue, candy jar, $100.00; wedding bowl with lid, $125.00. (Photo courtesy Milbra Long and Emily Seate)

Colony, crystal, ashtray, rnd, 3"..15.00
Colony, crystal, bowl, cream soup; 5" 60.00
Colony, crystal, bowl, flared, 11"...40.00
Colony, crystal, butter dish, ¼-lb...50.00
Colony, crystal, creamer, 3¾"..9.00
Colony, crystal, pitcher, milk; 16-oz...75.00
Colony, crystal, plate, lemon; 1-hdl, 6½" 12.00
Colony, crystal, platter, 12"...52.50
Colony, crystal, relish dish, 3-part, hdls, 10½"...........................27.50
Colony, crystal, rose bowl, 6"..25.00
Colony, crystal, tumbler, juice; 5-oz, 3⅝"..................................25.00
Colony, crystal, vase, cornucopia; 9"..85.00
Fairfax #2375, amber, ashtray, 5½"..13.00
Fairfax #2375, amber, bowl, lemon; hdls, 9" 10.00
Fairfax #2375, amber, plate, whipped cream..............................8.00
Fairfax #2375, amber, stem, low sherbet, 6-oz, 4¼"....................9.00
Fairfax #2375, amber, vase, 2 styles, 8" 40.00
Fairfax #2375, gr or topaz, baker, oval, 9"..................................30.00
Fairfax #2375, gr or topaz, bowl, cereal; 6"................................15.00
Fairfax #2375, gr or topaz, ice bucket..65.00
Fairfax #2375, gr or topaz, plate, bread; oval, 12".......................27.50
Fairfax #2375, gr or topaz, relish, 3-part, 8½"............................15.00
Fairfax #2375, gr or topaz, shakers, ftd, pr.................................45.00
Fairfax #2375, gr or topaz, tray, center hdl, 11" 30.00
Fairfax #2375, rose, bl or orchid, bonbon...................................12.50
Fairfax #2375, rose, bl or orchid, bouillon, ftd 15.00
Fairfax #2375, rose, bl or orchid, bowl, centerpiece; 15" 55.00
Fairfax #2375, rose, bl or orchid, plate, grill; 10¼"......................40.00
Fairfax #2375, rose, bl or orchid, sauce boat...............................50.00
Fairfax #2375, rose, bl or orchid, whipped cream pail..................75.00
Fuchsia, crystal, candlestick, #2375, 3", ea 35.00
Fuchsia, crystal, stem, parfait; #6004, 5½-oz, 6" 37.50
Fuchsia, wisteria, bowl, #2470, 12"..175.00
Fuchsia, wisteria, comport, #2470, low, 6" 95.00
Fuchsia, wisteria, tumbler, juice; #6004, ftd, 5-oz 45.00
Hermitage, amber, gr or topaz, bottle, oil; #2449, 27-oz.............40.00
Hermitage, amber, gr or topaz, sherbet, #2449, low ft, 7-oz, 3"........8.00
Hermitage, amber, gr or topaz, tray, condiment; #2449, 6½".........12.00
Hermitage, amber, gr or topaz, tumbler, #2449½, 13-oz, 5⅞"........16.00
Hermitage, azure, decanter, #2449, w/stopper, 28-oz.................150.00
Hermitage, azure, pitcher, #2449, 1-pt......................................60.00
Hermitage, azure, relish dish, #2449, 2-part, 6" 15.00
Hermitage, crystal, bowl, salad; #2449½, 7½"..............................8.00
Hermitage, crystal, ice tub, #2449, 6"...17.50

Hermitage, crystal, vase, ftd, 6" 22.00
Hermitage, wisteria, creamer, #2449, ftd 30.00
Hermitage, wisteria, finger bowl, #2449½, 4½" 22.50
Hermitage, wisteria, stem, water goblet, #2449, 9-oz, 5¼" 40.00
June, crystal, bowl, mint; 3-ftd, 4½" 15.00
June, crystal, cheese & cracker set, #2368 or #2375 ....50.00
June, crystal, ice bucket 85.00
June, crystal, platter, 15" 75.00
June, crystal, vase, fan; ftd, 8½" 90.00
June, rose or bl, bowl, cream soup; ftd 60.00
June, rose or bl, bowl, Grecian, 10" 175.00
June, rose or bl, plate, bread/butter; 6" 15.00
June, rose or bl, tumbler, ftd, 2½-oz 100.00
June, topaz, bowl, dessert; lg, hdls 150.00
June, topaz, comport, #2400, 5" 75.00
June, topaz, goblet, water; 10-oz, 8¼" 50.00
June, topaz, tray, center hdl 40.00
Kashmir, bl, bowl, pickle; 8½" 30.00
Kashmir, bl, cup, AD; ftd 55.00
Kashmir, bl, shakers, pr 175.00
Kashmir, bl, stem, cocktail; 3-oz 25.00
Kashmir, bl, sugar bowl, ftd 20.00
Kashmir, bl, vase, 8" 175.00
Kashmir, yel or gr, ashtray 25.00
Kashmir, yel or gr, candlestick, 9½", ea 40.00
Kashmir, yel or gr, plate, luncheon; 9" 9.00
Kashmir, yel or gr, saucer, rnd 5.00
Kashmir, yel or gr, tumbler, water; ftd, 10-oz 22.00
Lafayette, burgundy, cake stand, oval, hdls, 10½" 60.00
Lafayette, burgundy, creamer, ftd, 4¼" 40.00
Lafayette, crystal or amber, bonbon, hdls, 5" 15.00
Lafayette, crystal or amber, vase, rim ft, flared, 7" 45.00
Lafayette, Empire Green, creamer, ftd, 4½" 40.00
Lafayette, Empire Green, sugar bowl, ftd, 3⅝" 40.00
Lafayette, Regal Blue, bowl, baker, oval, 10" 75.00
Lafayette, Regal Blue, plate, torte; 13" 115.00
Lafayette, rose, gr or topaz, bowl, nappy, 8" 40.00
Lafayette, rose, gr or topaz, plate, torte; 13" 50.00
Lafayette, wisteria, bowl, fruit; 5" 22.50
Lafayette, wisteria, tray, lemon; hdls, 5" 40.00
Navarre, crystal, bowl, #2496, flared, 12" 75.00
Navarre, crystal, bowl, sweetmeat; #2496, 6" 32.50
Navarre, crystal, candlestick, #2496, dbl, 4½", ea 42.50
Navarre, crystal, comport, cheese; #2496, 3¼" 37.50
Navarre, crystal, mayonnaise, #2375, 3-pc 75.00
Navarre, crystal, plate, torte; #2496, 16" 135.00
Navarre, crystal, tidbit, #2496, 3-ftd, upturned edge, 8¼" 30.00
Navarre, crystal, tumbler, water; #6106, ftd, 10-oz, 4⅝" 27.50
Navarre, crystal, vase, #4121, 5" 120.00
New Garland, amber or topaz, bonbon, hdls 15.00
New Garland, amber or topaz, bowl, cereal; 6" 12.00
New Garland, amber or topaz, comport, 6" 20.00
New Garland, amber or topaz, platter, 12" 35.00
New Garland, amber or topaz, tumbler, #4120, 5-oz 12.00
New Garland, amber or topaz, vase, 8" 65.00
New Garland, rose, candlestick, 2", ea 20.00
New Garland, rose, plate, cake; hdls, 10" 35.00
New Garland, rose, relish, 4-part 27.50
New Garland, rose, stem, goblet, #6002 ....25.00
New Garland, rose, sugar bowl, ftd 17.50
Pioneer, azure or orchid, comport, 8" 35.00
Pioneer, azure or orchid, relish, 3-part, rnd 17.50
Pioneer, bl, bouillon, flat 14.00
Pioneer, bl, bowl, cream soup; flat 27.50

Pioneer, bl, plate, chop; 12" 32.50
Pioneer, bl, sauce boat, flat 35.00
Pioneer, bl, tumbler, water; ftd 25.00
Pioneer, crystal, amber or gr, ashtray, 3¾" 16.00
Pioneer, crystal, amber or gr, bowl, nappy, 8" 20.00
Pioneer, crystal, amber or gr, plate (for sauce boat), oval 10.00
Pioneer, ebony, cup, ftd 12.50
Pioneer, ebony, egg cup 25.00
Pioneer, ebony, plate, salad; 7" 9.00
Pioneer, rose or topaz, ashtray, lg, deep 22.00
Pioneer, rose or topaz, creamer, ftd 12.00
Pioneer, rose or topaz, relish, 3-part, rnd 12.50
Pioneer, rose or topaz, sugar bowl, ftd 12.00
Rogene, crystal, creamer, #1851, flat 30.00
Rogene, crystal, jug, #2270, 7" 165.00
Rogene, crystal, marmalade, #1968, w/lid 45.00
Rogene, crystal, oyster cocktail, #837, ftd 12.50
Rogene, crystal, plate, w/cut star, 11" 27.50
Rogene, crystal, stem, parfait, #5082, 6-oz 22.50
Rogene, crystal, sugar bowl, #1851, flat 30.00
Rogene, crystal, tumbler, whiskey; #887, 2½-oz 17.50
Rogene, crystal, vase, rolled edge, 8½" 95.00
Royal, amber or gr, ashtray, #2350, 3½" 22.50
Royal, amber or gr, bowl, console; #2329, 13" 30.00
Royal, amber or gr, candy dish, w/lid, ftd, ½-lb 195.00

Royal, amber or green, cologne/powder jar combination, $295.00. (Photo courtesy Gene Florence)

Royal, amber or gr, comport, jelly; #1861½, 6" 25.00
Royal, amber or gr, plate, deep soup/underplate; 8½" 37.50
Royal, amber or gr, tumbler, #869, flat, 5-oz 22.50
Royal, amber or gr, vase, #2292, flared 135.00
Seville, amber, bowl, cereal; #2350, 6½" 18.00
Seville, amber, bowl, console; #2329, rolled edge, 11" 32.00
Seville, amber, bowl, grapefruit; #2315, molded 25.00
Seville, amber, candlestick, #2324, 9", ea 45.00
Seville, amber, plate, dinner; #2350, 10½" 35.00
Seville, amber, tumbler, #5084, ftd, 2-oz 35.00
Seville, gr, bowl, baker, #2350, oval, 9" 30.00
Seville, gr, creamer, #2315½, flat, ftd 15.00
Seville, gr, ice bucket, #2378 ....65.00
Seville, gr, platter, #2350, 10½" 35.00
Seville, gr, stem, cordial, #870 ....70.00
Seville, gr, vase, #2292, 8" 95.00
Sunray, crystal, bonbon, hdld 16.00
Sunray, crystal, bowl, rolled edge, 13" 42.50

Sunray, crystal, ice bucket, w/hdl................................**65.00**
Sunray, crystal, nappy, tri-corner, w/hdl.......................**15.00**
Sunray, crystal, plate, torte; 11".................................**35.00**
Sunray, crystal, tray, oblong, 10½"..............................**40.00**
Sunray, crystal, tumbler, old fashioned; #2510½, 6-oz, 3½".........**14.00**
Sunray, crystal, vase, rose bowl; 5"............................**32.50**
Trojan, rose, relish, #2350, 3-part, rnd, 8¾"..................**55.00**
Trojan, rose, shakers, #2375, ftd, pr.........................**130.00**
Trojan, rose, tray, #2375, center hdl, 11"....................**60.00**
Trojan, rose, tumbler, #5099, ftd, 2½-oz......................**60.00**
Trojan, rose, whipped cream pail, #2378.....................**150.00**
Trojan, topaz, bowl, baker, #2375, 9".........................**75.00**
Trojan, topaz, bowl, cream soup; #2375, ftd..................**35.00**
Trojan, topaz, candlestick, #2375, flared, 3", ea............**25.00**
Trojan, topaz, plate, chop; #2375, 13".........................**70.00**
Versailles, bl, ashtray, #2350...................................**35.00**
Versailles, bl, bowl, bouillon; #2375, ftd......................**40.00**
Versailles, bl, creamer, tea; #2375½...........................**75.00**
Versailles, bl, plate, canape; #2375, 6"........................**40.00**
Versailles, bl, sherbet, #5098/5099, low, 4¼" **25.00**
Versailles, bl, tray, #2375, center hdl, 11"....................**75.00**
Versailles, bl, tumbler, #5098 or #5099, ftd, 12-oz, 6" **40.00**
Versailles, pk or gr, bowl, baker, #2375, 9" **95.00**
Versailles, pk or gr, candlestick, #2395½, scroll, 5", ea **55.00**
Versailles, pk or gr, goblet, water; #5098 or #5099, 10-oz, 8¼" ...**100.00**
Versailles, pk or gr, ice bucket, #2375.......................**90.00**
Versailles, yel, bowl, cereal; #2375, 6½".....................**45.00**
Versailles, yel, cup, AD; #2375 ....**40.00**
Versailles, yel, platter, #2375, 12"..........................**85.00**
Vesper, amber, bowl, bouillon; #2350, ftd....................**22.00**
Vesper, amber, comport, #2327, twisted stem, 7½"...........**40.00**
Vesper, amber, egg cup, #2350.................................**45.00**
Vesper, amber, vase, #2292, 8"...............................**110.00**
Vesper, bl, bowl, #2375, 3-ftd, 12½"........................**125.00**
Vesper, bl, bowl, cereal; #2350, sq or rnd, 6½"...............**50.00**
Vesper, bl, cup, #2350...**40.00**
Vesper, bl, stem, water goblet, #5093 ....**55.00**
Vesper, gr, ashtray, #2350, 4" **25.00**
Vesper, gr, candlestick, #2324, 2", ea **22.00**
Vesper, gr, ice bucket, #2378 ....**85.00**
Vesper, gr, tumbler, #5100, ftd, 2-oz........................**35.00**

Fostoria Glass Specialty Company

The Fostoria Glass Specialty Company was founded in Fostoria, Ohio, in 1899. In 1910 they were purchased by General Electric. The new owners had an interest in developing a high-quality lustre-type art glass able to compete with the very successful glassware produced by Tiffany. They hired Walter Hicks, who had previously worked for Tiffany, to help develop the line they called Iris. Their efforts were extremely successful. The art glass they developed was cased and iridescent, very similar to Steuben's Aurene. Colors included green, tan, white, blue, yellow, and rose. It was made in several patterns, including Heart and Leaf, Leaf and Tendrils, Heart and Spider Webbing, and Lustred Dot. Although the main thrust of their production was lamp shades, vases and bowls were made as well. Iris was made for only four years, since gold was required in its production and manufacturing costs were very high. It was marked with only a paper label, without which identification is sometimes difficult. Look for a pronounced, well-finished pontil that shows the glass layers represented. Most items show a layer of white which Fostoria called Calcite, as did Steuben. Very little has been written on the history of this company, but for more information refer to *The Collector's Encyclopedia of Art Glass* by John Shuman

(Collector Books), and *Fostoria Ohio Glass, Vol II*, by Melvin L. Murray (self published).

Our advisor for this category is Frank W. Ford; he is listed in the Directory under Massachusetts.

Rose bowl, Iris, gold lustre leaves on opal, ovoid.........................**500.00**
Shade, feathers, gr on opal, gold int, ruffled...............................**300.00**
Shade, festoons, gr on opal, 7"...**250.00**

Shade, Iris, gold lustre leaves on opal, 4½", $300.00. (Photo courtesy Frank W. Ford)

Shade, leaves & vines, gr & gold on opal, 4-sided.......................**250.00**
Shade, leaves & vines on pearly wht, gold int, bell form, 4½" ...**300.00**
Shade, opal w/gold zipper over gr pulled decor, 7¼"..................**430.00**
Vase, Iris, gold lustre, pinched-in sides, narrow neck, ftd, 4½" ...**600.00**
Vase, Iris, gold lustre w/gr leaves/vines, sq top, 12" **2,000.00**

Frakturs

Fraktur is a German style of black letter text type. To collectors the fraktur is a type of hand-lettered document used by the people of German descent who settled in the areas of Pennsylvania, New Jersey, Maryland, Virginia, North and South Carolina, Ohio, Kentucky, and Ontario. These documents recorded births and baptisms and were used as bookplates and as certificates of honor. They were elaborately decorated with colorful folk-art borders of hearts, birds, angels, and flowers. Examples by recognized artists and those with an unusual decorative motif bring prices well into the thousands of dollars; in fact, some have sold at major auction houses well in excess of $10,000.00. Frakturs made in the late 1700s after the invention of the printing press provided the writer with a prepared text that he needed only to fill in at his own discretion. The next step in the evolution of machine-printed frakturs combined woodblock-printed decorations along with the text which the 'artist' sometimes enhanced with color. By the mid-1800s, even the coloring was done by machine. The vorschrift was a handwritten example prepared by a fraktur teacher to demonstrate his skill in lettering and decorating. These are often considered to be the finest of frakturs. Those dated before 1820 are most valuable.

The practice of fraktur art began to diminish after 1830 but hung on even to the early years of this century among the Pennsylvania Germans ingrained with such customs. Our advisor for this category is Frederick S. Weiser; he is listed in the Directory under Pennsylvania. (Mr. Weiser has provided our text, but being unable to physically examine the frakturs listed below cannot vouch for their authenticity, age, or condition. When requesting information, please include a self-addressed stamped envelope.) These prices were realized at various reputable auction galleries in the East and Midwest. Unless otherwise noted, values are for examples in excellent condition. Note: Be careful not to confuse frakturs with prints, calligraphy, English-language marriage certificates, Lord's Prayers, etc.

Key:
lp — laid paper   wc — watercolored
pr — printed   wp — wove paper
p/i — pen and ink

Birth Records

P/i/w/c, verse/scallops/flowers/trees, 1769, in 19x16" fr **1,265.00**
P/i/wc/lp, angels/flowers/birds, 1803, in 16x19" fr..................**4,950.00**
P/i/wc/lp, circles/flowers/birds/branches, PA/1907, 13x17"+fr......**2,300.00**
P/i/wc/lp, flowers/circle/text, 1806, 8½x10⅜"..........................**385.00**
Pr/hc, Taufschein, angels/cherubs/fruit, PA, 1814, 17x19"+maple fr.**660.00**
Pr/wc, angels/birds/Bible/etc, PA/1830, in cherry 20x17" fr.........**195.00**
Pr/wc, birds & flowers, 1827, fold lines, in 7¼x7¼" fr................**230.00**
Pr/wc, birds/tulips/etc, Reading/Jungmann & Gruber, 1794, 15x17" fr..**865.00**
Pr/wc, eagle/angels/birds/etc, Lange/PA, 1823, 15x11⅝"+fr........**440.00**
Pr/wc, Lutz & Scheffer, PA/1844, matted & fr: 16½x12½".........**100.00**
Pr/wc/lp, tulips/birds/roses/grape leaves/deer, Baumann/1786, 16x13" ..**385.00**

Miscellaneous

Family record, wc, tree of life/hearts/etc, MA/early 1800s, 14x12"+fr ...**9,200.00**
Family register, p/i/wc, compass stars/sun, 1800s, rprs, 16x10"+fr ..**2,000.00**
Marriage record, wc/lp, tree/hearts/flowers, NH/1817, 17x15"+fr ...**9,775.00**

Frames

Styles in picture frames have changed with the fashion of the day, but those that especially interest today's collectors are the deep shadow boxes made of fine woods such as walnut or cherry, those with Art Nouveau influence, and the oak frames decorated with molded gesso and gilt from the Victorian era.

As is true in general in the antiques and collectibles fields, the influence of online trading is greatly affecting prices. Many items once considered difficult to locate are now readily available on the Internet; as a result, values have declined. Our advisor for this category is Michael Hinton; he is listed in the Directory under Pennsylvania.

Note: Unless another date is given, frames described in the following listings are from the nineteenth century.

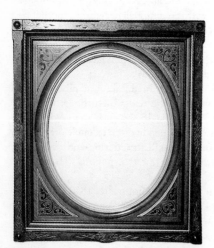

Black walnut and gold leaf, stamped with 1871 patent date, 24x20" oval image size, 34½x30½", $1,150.00. (Photo courtesy Michael Hinton)

Alligator hide covered, easel bk, 6⅜x5¾x1¼" **465.00**
Brushed aluminum, beveled glass, 14x12½" **65.00**
Cast brass, Cupid design, 20x12" **250.00**
Cherry/pine shadowbox w/cvd crest & acanthus leaves, 18x11x2⅛" ..**220.00**
CI, emb floral, 14x8" **85.00**

Cut brass, filigree, Italian, 1700s, 9x7" **595.00**
Cvd stepped sunburst medallions, scalloped aperture, gr pnt, 31x27" ...**440.00**
Giltwood & gesso w/foliate scrolls, shell corners, 1850s, 55x45" ...**635.00**
Giltwood & gesso w/oak leaves, Am, 22¼x26" **330.00**
Grpt red-brn over lt red, 15x12" **220.00**
Mahog veneer, 2⅛" W, 16x18" **50.00**
Pine w/red rosewood grpt, beveled, 12x16" **135.00**
Plaster over wood, oval shadow box, Victorian, 20x17x4" **75.00**
Tiger maple w/appl molding, E Goss Salem MA label, 16x20" ...**560.00**
Walnut, beveled, 2" molding, 17x14" **100.00**
Walnut crisscross, cvd leaves at corners, Victorian, 22x128" **175.00**

Frances Ware

Frances Ware, produced in the 1880s by Hobbs, Brockunier and Company of Wheeling, West Virginia, is a term refering to the decoration or finish used in the production of some of their glassware lines. Hobnail (Dewdrop) is the most commonly found of these lines, though Swirl and on occasion Quartered Block with Stars were also finished with the frosted surface and amber-stained band that defines the Frances Ware indication. Though collectors in general tend to regard examples in crystal with simply an amber-stained band as Frances Ware, according to *Hobbs, Brockunier & Co. Glass* by Nelia and Tom Bredehoft, this is incorrect. The company called this finish 'decorated #7.' To evaluate examples in crystal with amber stain, deduct 10% from the values given below, which are strictly for the frosted finish. Our advisors for this category are Betty and Clarence Maier; they are listed in the Directory under Pennsylvania.

Hobnail, bowl, ftd, berry pontil, 6x10" **150.00**
Hobnail, bowl, nappy, 4½" sq **25.00**
Hobnail, bowl, no flange, 9" sq **85.00**
Hobnail, bowl, oblong, 8" **75.00**
Hobnail, bowl, shell ft, 8" **250.00**
Hobnail, bowl, sq, 7½" **70.00**
Hobnail, bowl, 10" **90.00**
Hobnail, bowl, 2½x5½" **30.00**
Hobnail, bowl, 7½", from $65 to **75.00**
Hobnail, bowl, 8" dia **75.00**
Hobnail, bowl, 8" sq **75.00**
Hobnail, butter dish, from $80 to **120.00**
Hobnail, celery vase **125.00**
Hobnail, chandelier, amber font, brass fr, 14" dia **950.00**
Hobnail, creamer, from $40 to **60.00**
Hobnail, cruet, from $425 to **500.00**
Hobnail, finger bowl, 4", from $25 to **35.00**
Hobnail, molasses can **375.00**
Hobnail, pickle jar..**175.00**
Hobnail, pitcher, milk **175.00**
Hobnail, pitcher, water; sq top, 8½" **195.00**
Hobnail, sauce dish, sq, 4" **28.00**
Hobnail, shakers, very rare, pr **300.00**
Hobnail, sugar bowl, w/lid, from $65 to **80.00**
Hobnail, syrup, pewter lid **375.00**
Hobnail, toothpick holder/toy tumbler.................................**60.00**
Hobnail, tray, cloverleaf, 12", from $90 to **125.00**
Hobnail, tumbler, water...**45.00**
Hobnail, vase, ruffled top..**165.00**
Quartered Block w/Stars, bowl, oval, 10" **65.00**
Quartered Block w/Stars, butter dish **95.00**
Quartered Block w/Stars, goblet **140.00**
Quartered Block w/Stars, sugar bowl, w/lid **75.00**
Swirl, bowl, 4"..**25.00**

Swirl, bowl, 8" 90.00
Swirl, butter dish 95.00
Swirl, celery, ind 35.00
Swirl, cruet, from $250 to 295.00
Swirl, mustard jar, from $90 to 125.00
Swirl, pitcher, water 225.00
Swirl, plate, 6" 30.00
Swirl, shakers, pr 165.00
Swirl, sugar bowl, w/lid 80.00
Swirl, sugar shaker, orig lid 195.00
Swirl, syrup, Pat dtd 295.00
Swirl, toothpick holder 160.00
Swirl, tumbler 45.00

Franciscan

Franciscan is a trade name used by Gladding McBean and Co., founded in northern California in 1875. In 1923 they purchased the Tropico plant in Glendale where they produced sewer pipe, gardenware, and tile. By 1934 the first of their dinnerware lines, El Patio, was produced. It was a plain design made in bright, attractive colors. El Patio Nouveau followed in 1935, glazed in two colors — one tone on the inside, a contrasting hue on the outside. Coronado, a favorite of today's collectors, was introduced in 1936. It was styled with a wide, swirled border and was made in pastels, both satin and glossy. Before 1940 fifteen patterns had been produced. The first hand-decorated lines were introduced in 1937, the ever-popular Apple pattern in 1940, Desert Rose in 1941, and Ivy in 1948. Many other hand-decorated and decaled patterns were produced there from 1934 to 1984.

Dinnerware marks before 1940 include 'GMcB' in an oval, 'F' within a square, or 'Franciscan' with 'Pottery' underneath (which was later changed to 'Ware'). A circular arrangement of 'Franciscan' with 'Made in California USA' in the center was used from 1940 until 1949. At least forty marks were used before 1975; several more were introduced after that. At one time, paper labels were used.

The company merged with Lock Joint Pipe Company in 1963, becoming part of the Interpace Corporation. In July of 1979 Franciscan was purchased by Wedgwood Limited of England, and the Glendale plant closed in October 1984.

Note: Due to limited space, we have used a pricing formula, meant to be only a general guide, not a mechanical ratio on each piece. Rarity varies with pattern, and not all pieces occur in all patterns. Our advisors for this category are Mick and Lorna Chase (Fiesta Plus); they are listed in the Directory under Tennessee. See also Gladding McBean.

Coronado

Both satin (matt) and glossy colors were made including turquoise, coral, celadon, light yellow, ivory, and gray (in satin); and turquoise, coral, apple green, light yellow, white, maroon, and redwood in glossy glazes. High-end values are for maroon, yellow, redwood, and gray. Add 10 – 15% for gloss.

Bowl, casserole; w/lid, from $45 to 90.00
Bowl, cereal; from $10 to 15.00
Bowl, cream soup; w/underplate, from $25 to 40.00
Bowl, fruit; from $6 to 12.00
Bowl, nut cup; from $8 to 12.00
Bowl, onion soup; w/lid, from $25 to 40.00
Bowl, rim soup; from $14 to 25.00
Bowl, salad; lg, from $20 to 35.00
Bowl, serving; oval, 10½", from $20 to 33.00
Bowl, serving; 7½" dia, from $12 to 18.00

Bowl, serving; 8½" dia, from $10 to 17.00
Bowl, sherbet/egg cup; from $10 to 15.00
Butter dish, from $25 to 35.00
Cigarette box, w/lid, from $40 to 75.00
Creamer, from $8 to 12.00
Cup & saucer, demitasse; from $20 to 32.00
Cup & saucer, jumbo 32.00
Demitasse pot, from $100 to 150.00
Fast-stand gravy, from $25 to 35.00
Jam jar, w/lid, from $45 to 60.00
Pitcher, 1½-qt, from $25 to 45.00
Plate, chop; 12½" dia, from $18 to 32.00
Plate, chop; 14" dia, from $20 to 30.00
Plate, crescent hostess; w/cup well, no established value
Plate, crescent salad; lg, no established value
Plate, ind crescent salad; from $22 to 32.00
Plate, 6½", from $5 to 8.00
Plate, 7½", from $7 to 10.00
Plate, 8½", from $8 to 11.00
Plate, 9½", from $10 to 15.00
Plate, 10½", from $12 to 18.00
Platter, oval, 10", from $12 to 20.00
Platter, oval, 13", from $24 to 36.00
Platter, oval, 15½", from $25 to 45.00
Relish dish, oval, from $12 to 25.00
Shakers, pr, from $15 to 30.00
Sugar bowl, w/lid, from $10 to 20.00
Teacup & saucer, from $8 to 12.00
Teapot, from $45 to 75.00
Tumbler, water; no established value
Vase, 8", no established value

Desert Rose

Ashtray, ind 12.00
Ashtray, oval 95.00
Ashtray, sq 195.00
Bell, Danbury Mint 95.00
Bell, dinner 95.00
Bowl, bouillon; w/lid 395.00
Bowl, cereal; 6" 15.00
Bowl, divided vegetable 45.00
Bowl, fruit 7.00
Bowl, mixing; lg 175.00
Bowl, mixing; med 165.00
Bowl, mixing; sm 155.00
Bowl, porringer 175.00
Bowl, rimmed soup 25.00
Bowl, salad; 10" 95.00
Bowl, soup; ftd 32.00
Bowl, vegetable; 8" 32.00
Bowl, vegetable; 9" 40.00
Box, cigarette 95.00
Box, egg 115.00
Box, heart shape 165.00
Box, rnd 165.00
Butter dish 45.00
Candle holders, pr 95.00
Candy dish, oval 225.00
Casserole, 1½-qt 75.00
Casserole, 2½-qt, minimum value 395.00
Coffeepot 75.00
Coffeepot, ind 395.00
Compote, lg 55.00

Compote, low	125.00
Cookie jar	295.00
Creamer, ind	40.00
Creamer, regular	15.00
Cup & saucer, coffee	85.00
Cup & saucer, demitasse	45.00
Cup & saucer, jumbo	45.00
Cup & saucer, tall	35.00
Cup & saucer, tea	15.00
Egg cup	35.00
Ginger jar	225.00
Goblet, ftd	225.00
Gravy boat	30.00
Heart	145.00
Hurricane lamp	325.00
Jam jar	125.00
Long 'n narrow, 15½x7¾"	495.00
Microwave dish, oblong, 1½-qt	225.00
Microwave dish, sq, 1-qt	185.00
Microwave dish, sq, 8"	125.00
Mug, bbl, 12-oz	35.00
Mug, cocoa; 10-oz	95.00
Mug, 7-oz	25.00
Napkin ring	50.00
Piggy bank	295.00
Pitcher, jug	195.00
Pitcher, milk	65.00
Pitcher, syrup	75.00
Pitcher, water; 2½-qt	95.00
Plate, chop; 12"	50.00
Plate, chop; 14"	75.00
Plate, coupe dessert	65.00
Plate, coupe party	125.00
Plate, coupe steak	150.00
Plate, divided; child's	195.00
Plate, grill	95.00
Plate, side salad	35.00
Plate, TV	175.00
Plate, 6½"	6.00
Plate, 8½"	12.00
Plate, 9½"	20.00
Plate, 10½"	18.00
Platter, turkey; 19"	295.00
Platter, 12¾"	35.00
Platter, 14"	45.00
Relish, oval, 10"	25.00
Relish, 3-section	65.00
Shaker & pepper mill, pr	295.00
Shakers, rose bud, pr	15.00
Shakers, tall, pr	45.00
Sherbet	20.00
Soup ladle	75.00
Sugar bowl, open, ind	75.00
Sugar bowl, regular	25.00
Tea canister	225.00
Teapot	125.00
Thimble	75.00
Tidbit tray, 2-tier	125.00
Tile, in fr	50.00
Tile, sq	35.00
Toast cover	195.00
Trivet, fluted, rnd	325.00
Tumbler, juice; 6-oz	45.00
Tumbler, 10-oz	32.00

Tureen, soup; flat bottom	495.00
Tureen, soup; ftd, either style	695.00
Vase, bud	75.00

For other hand-painted patterns, we recommend the following general guide for comparable pieces (based on current values):

Daisy	-20%
October	-20%
Cafe Royal	Same as Desert Rose
Forget-Me-Not	Same as Desert Rose
Meadow Rose	Same as Desert Rose
Strawberry Fair	Same as Desert Rose
Strawberry Time	Same as Desert Rose
Fresh Fruit	Same as Desert Rose
Bountiful	Same as Desert Rose
Desert Rose	Base Line Values
Apple	+10%
Ivy	+20%
Poppy	+50%
Original (small) Fruit	+50%
Wild Flower	200% or more!

Wild Flower, vegetable bowl, 9", $195.00.

There is not an active market in Bouquet, Rosette, or Twilight Rose, as these are scarce, having been produced only a short time. Our estimate would place Bouquet and Rosette in the October range (-20%) and Twilight Rose in the Ivy range (+20%).

There are several Apple items that are so scarce they command higher prices than fit the above formula. The Apple ginger jar is valued at $600.00+, the 4" jug at $195.00+, and any covered box in Apple is at least 50% more than Desert Rose.

Apple Pieces Not Available in Desert Rose

Bowl, batter; minimum value	450.00
Bowl, str sides, lg	55.00
Bowl, str sides, med	45.00
Casserole, stick hdl & lid, ind	65.00
Coaster	65.00
Half-apple baker, from $125 to	195.00
Jam jar, redesigned	425.00
Shaker & pepper mill, wooden top, pr	395.00

El Patio, 1934 – 1954

This line includes a few pieces not offered in Coronado, and the colors differ; but per piece these two patterns are valued about the same.

Franciscan Fine China

The main line of fine china was called Masterpiece. There were at least four marks used during its production from 1941 to 1977. Almost every piece is clearly marked. This china is true porcelain, the body having been fired at a very high temperature. Many years of research and experimentation went into this china before it was marketed. Production was temporarily suspended during the war years. More than 170 patterns and many varying shapes were produced. All are valued about the same with the exception of the Renaissance group, which is 25% higher.

Bowl, vegetable; serving, oval 50.00
Cup...20.00
Plate, bread & butter...18.00
Plate, dinner...30.00
Plate, salad...25.00
Saucer..12.00

Starburst

Ashtray, ind 20.00
Ashtray, oval, lg..50.00
Bonbon/jelly dish..22.00
Bowl, crescent salad..40.00
Bowl, divided, 8"...25.00
Bowl, fruit; ind...13.00
Bowl, salad; ind..25.00
Bowl, soup/cereal..13.00
Bowl, vegetable; 8½"...45.00
Butter dish...45.00
Candlesticks, pr, from $175 to..200.00
Casserole, lg..100.00
Coffeepot..150.00
Creamer..15.00
Cup & saucer...25.00
Gravy boat, from $20 to...30.00

Gravy boat with attached undertray, $40.00; Ladle, $30.00.

Jug, water; 10"..90.00
Mug, sm..60.00
Mug, tall...95.00
Oil cruet...75.00
Pepper mill..150.00
Pitcher, water; 10" 85.00
Pitcher, 7½", from $50 to..75.00
Plate, chop; from $55 to...65.00
Plate, dinner...12.00

Plate, 6"...6.00
Plate, 8"...8.00
Plate, 11"..45.00
Platter, 15"...80.00
Shakers, bullet shape, lg, pr...50.00
Shakers, sm, pr..20.00
Snack/TV tray w/cup rest, 12½", from $75 to.....................100.00
Sugar bowl..25.00
Tumbler, 6-oz, from $40 to...50.00
Vinegar cruet..75.00

Frankart

During the 1920s Frankart, Inc., of New York City, produced a line of accessories that included figural nude lamps, bookends, ashtrays, etc. These white metal composition items were offered in several finishes including verde green, jap black, and gunmetal gray. The company also produced a line of caricatured animals, but the stylized nude figurals have proven to be the most collectible today. With few exceptions, all pieces were marked 'Frankart, Inc.' with a patent number or 'pat. appl. for.' All pieces listed are in very good original condition unless otherwise indicated. Our advisor for this category is Walter Glenn; he is listed in the Directory under Georgia.

Aquarium, 3 kneeling nudes encircle 10" fish bowl, 10½".......**1,050.00**
Ashstand, nude stands atop arch supports tray, 22x6¾" **850.00**
Ashtray, nude dancing, holds tray on hip, box on base, 10"......**750.00**
Ashtray, nude kneels on cushion, holds 3" pottery tray, 6"..........**450.00**
Ashtray, nude stands, 3" ashball on geometric base, 10".............**750.00**
Ashtray, nudes bk to bk hold rack of 4 rnd ashtrays, 8"..............**750.00**
Ashtray, satyr (striding) holds 3" ceramic tray, 8".....................**450.00**
Bookends, nude fan dancer holds books, 10", pr......................**625.00**
Bookends, nude sits atop metal book, 10", pr..........................**550.00**
Bookends, nude sits atop mushrooms, 8", pr **550.00**
Bookends, nudes in headstands support books, 10", pr **600.00**
Candy dish, majorette, 1 knee supports dish, 10" **750.00**
Cigarette box, nudes bk to bk hold 4" rectangular glass box, 9"..**950.00**
Clock, nudes (2) kneel & hold 10" rnd glass clock, 12½" **2,550.00**
Lamp, nude holds rod above, glass panel hangs by rings, 13"....**1,600.00**
Lamp, nude seated, leg extended, 2 cylinders on sides, 8"........**1,575.00**
Lamp, nude silhouettes (standing) against rectangular glass panel, 11" ..**1,050.00**
Lamp, nude stands, arms bk, glass butterfly wings, 10¼" **1,800.00**
Lamp, nude stands atop frost glass panel, light below, 10"...........**950.00**
Lamp, nudes (2) kneel bk to bk, 8" crackle globe between, 9"..**1,450.00**
Smoke set, seated nude, cigarette box on base, tray in ea arm, 9" ...**775.00**
Wall plaque, Diana the Huntress, 8" sq....................................**550.00**
Wall sconce, nude sits on floral framework, 6"..........................**650.00**

Frankoma

The Frank Pottery, founded in Oklahoma in 1933 by John Frank, became known as Frankoma in 1934. The company produced decorative figurals, vases, and such, marking their ware from 1936 to 1938 with a pacing leopard 'Frankoma' mark. These pieces are highly sought. The entire operation was destroyed by fire in 1938, and new molds were cast — some from surviving pieces — and a similar line of production was pursued. The body of the ware was changed in 1955 from a honey tan (called 'Ada clay,' referring to the name of the town near the area where it was dug) to a red brick clay (known as Sapulpa), and this, along with the color of the glazes (over fifty have been used), helps determine the period of production. A Southwestern theme has always been favored in design as well as in color selection.

In 1965 they began to produce a limited-edition series of Christmas plates, followed by a bottle vase series in 1969. Considered very collectible are their political mugs, bicentennial plates, Teenagers of the Bible plates, and the Wildlife series. Their ceramic Christmas cards are also very popular items with today's collectors.

Frankoma celebrated their 50th anniversary in 1983. On September 26 of that same year, Frankoma was again destroyed by fire. Because of a fire-proof wall, master molds of all 1983 production items were saved, allowing plans for rebuilding to begin immediately.

Frankoma filed for Chapter 11 in April 1990, and eventually sold to a Maryland investor in February of 1991, thereby ending the family-ownership era. For a more thorough study of the subject, we recommend *Frankoma Treasures* and *Frankoma and Other Oklahoma Potteries* by Phyllis Bess, our advisor; you will find her address in the Directory under Oklahoma.

Ashtray, cigar; Draft Proof, Prairie Green, #455............................50.00
Ashtray, Elephant, Desert Gold, Ada clay, #459, 1952...............250.00
Ashtray, Fish, Desert Gold, Sapulpa clay, #T7............................15.00
Ashtray, Peach Glow, Sapulpa Clay, #479...................................25.00
Ashtray, Prairie Green, Ada clay, #456.......................................30.00
Baker, Lazybones, Desert Gold, Sapulpa clay, #4V.....................35.00
Bookends, Collie Head, White Sand, Sapulpa clay, #122............200.00
Bookends, Cowboy Boot, Brown Satin, Sapulpa clay, #433..........50.00
Bowl, cereal; Desert Gold, Sapulpa clay, 5"..................................8.00
Bowl, cereal; Plainsman, Desert Gold, Sapulpa clay, #5XL............8.00
Bowl, Clam Shell, dk Coffee w/Flame int, Sapulpa clay, #TI........30.00
Bowl, console; Dogwood, Prairie Green, Sapulpa clay, #200.........35.00
Bowl, vegetable; Plainsman, Desert Gold, sq...............................17.50
Candle holder, Aladdin Lamp, Brown Satin, Sapulpa clay, #309..25.00
Canisters, Desert Gold, Sapulpa clay, #25C/S/T (coffee/sugar/tea)...125.00
Chirstmas card, 1957..70.00
Christmas card, 1944, from $400 to...500.00
Christmas card, 1947-48, from $95 to.......................................115.00
Christmas card, 1949, from $85 to...95.00
Christmas card, 1950-51, from $125 to.....................................150.00
Christmas card, 1952, Donna Frank, from $150 to.....................200.00
Christmas card, 1952, from $125 to..140.00
Christmas card, 1953, from $90 to..110.00
Christmas card, 1954..110.00
Christmas card, 1958-60, ea...65.00
Christmas card, 1969-71, ea...40.00
Christmas card, 1972...35.00
Christmas card, 1973-75, ea...35.00
Christmas card, 1976-82, ea...25.00
Christmas plate, King of Kings, White Sand, 1970.......................20.00
Christmas plate, Seeking the Christ Child, White Sand, 1972.....20.00
Console set, Dogwood/Magnolia, Sapulpa clay, #200 & #300, 3-pc.60.00
Cookie jar, Prairie Green, Sapulpa clay, #25K.............................65.00
Cornucopia, Early Turquoise, Ada clay, low, #57, 1942, 10".........75.00
Creamer, Prairie Green, Ada clay, #897A, 10-oz..........................27.50
Creamer & sugar bowl, Lazybones, Prairie Green, Sapulpa clay, #4A/#4B.45.00
Creamer & sugar bowl, Plainsman, Ada clay, #51/#5B,................35.00
Creamer & sugar bowl, Wagon Wheel, Desert Gold, #94A/#94B...40.00
Cup, tea; Plainsman, dk Brown Satin, 5-oz.................................10.00
Cup, tea; Plainsman, Prairie Green, 5-oz....................................10.00
Easter plate, Jesus Is Not Here..., Oral Roberts Assoc, 1972.........25.00
Jug, Guernsey, Brown Satin, Sapulpa clay, #93, +6 #90C juice cups...125.00
Leaf dish, dk Brown Satin, #226..12.00
Mug, Donkey, Plum, 1983..35.00
Mug, Donkey, yel, 1975...40.00
Mug, Elephant, brn, 1973...40.00
Mug, Elephant, 1968, from $45 to..75.00
Mug, Elephant, 1969, from $40 to..65.00

Mug, Elephant, 1974, from $30 to..40.00
Mug, Elephant or Donkey, 1975-76, from $30 to.........................40.00
Mug, Elephant or Donkey, 1979-90, from $20 to.........................30.00
Mug, Mayan-Aztec, Flame, Sapulpa clay, #7CL.............................6.00
Mug, Mayan-Aztec, Prairie Green, 16-oz, NM..............................20.00
Mug, Plainsman, Desert Gold, Sapulpa clay, w/advertising, #4C..15.00
Mug, Reagan/Bush, celery w/wht int, 1981.................................35.00
Mug, soup; Lazybones, Flame, 11-oz...15.00
Napkin rings, Butterfly, Sapulpa clay, #263, 4 for......................20.00
Pitcher, Ringed, Prairie Green, Sapulpa clay, #26D, +6 #26D tumblers...75.00
Planter, window; Desert Gold, Sapulpa clay, #15.........................20.00
Plaque, Buffalo, Prairie Green, Sapulpa clay, #195......................75.00
Plate, dinner; Wagon Wheel, Prairie Green, 10"..........................22.50
Plate, salad; Wagon Wheel, Desert Gold, 7"...............................10.00
Plate, salad; Westwind, White Sand, 7"..7.50
Ramekin, Desert Gold, w/lid, Sapulpa clay, #97U, 1950-61.........45.00
Sculpture, Collie Head, Desert Gold, walnut base, 1950s...........250.00
Sculpture, Indian Bowl Maker, Prairie Green, Ada clay, #123, $300 to..500.00

Sculpture, Indian Bowl Maker, Prairie Green, Sapulpa clay, 6", $90.00. (If marked 'Taylor,' from $2,500.00 to $3,000.00.)

Sculpture, Pacing Leopard, Prairie Green, Ada clay, #104L, 15" L...725.00
Sculpture, Pony Tail Girl, Desert Gold, Sapulpa clay, #106..........90.00
Sculpture, Swan, Prairie Green, Ada clay, #168, mini................125.00
Sculpture, Trojan Horse, Prairie Green, Ada clay, #162, mini....125.00
Shakers, Oil Derrick, Prairie Green, Ada clay, #49H, pr..............40.00
Stein, Desert Gold, Sapulpa clay, #M2, lg, 18-oz.........................12.50
Teapot, Wagon Wheel, Desert Gold, Ada clay, #94J, 2-cup..........45.00
Teapot, Westwind, Desert Gold, Sapulpa clay, #62, 5-cup, +4 7-oz cups...75.00
Tray, Palm Leaf, Desert Gold, Sapulpa clay, #226.......................85.00
Tumbler, Plainsman, Terra Cotta, 12-oz.......................................7.50
Vase, bud; Draped, Prairie Green, Sapulpa clay, #46..................10.00
Vase, bud; Snail, blk, Ada clay, #31...60.00
Vase, bud; Snail, Flame, Sapulpa clay..30.00
Vase, collector; V-1, from $125 to...150.00
Vase, collector; V-2, 1970, 12", from $80 to.................................90.00
Vase, collector; V-4, 1972...85.00
Vase, collector; V-5, 1973, 13"..85.00
Vase, collector; V-6, from $80 to..90.00
Vase, collector; V-7, 13"..80.00
Vase, collector; V-8, w/stopper, 13"..75.00
Vase, collector; V-9, w/stopper, 13"..65.00
Vase, collector; V-10 & V-11, ea, from $40 to...............................50.00
Vase, collector; V-12, 13"..65.00
Vase, collector; V-14, from $75 to...80.00
Vase, collector; V-15, 13", from $75 to..80.00
Vase, Crocus, Prairie Green, Sapulpa clay, #43...........................30.00
Vase, Fan Shell, Prairie Green, Ada clay, #54.............................45.00
Vase, Mountain Haze, angle hdls, Sapulpa clay, #20...................25.00

Vase, Pansy/Wedding Ring, Turquoise, Sapulpa clay, #200...........**50.00**
Vase, Pillow, Prairie Green, Sapulpa clay, #63................................**30.00**
Vase, Ringed, Desert Gold, Ada Clay, #500, mini **75.00**
Wall pocket, Billiken, Prairie Green, Sapulpa clay, #187 ....**150.00**
Wall pocket, Woodland Moss, Sapulpa clay, #190 ....**95.00**

Fraternal Organizations

Fraternal memorabilia is a vast and varied field. Emblems representing the various organizations have been used to decorate cups, shaving mugs, plates, and glassware. Medals, swords, documents, and other ceremonial paraphernalia from the 1800s and early 1900s are especially prized. Our advisor for Odd Fellows is Greg Spiess; he is listed in the Directory under Illinois. Information on Masonic and Shrine memorabilia has been provided by David Smies, who is listed under Kansas. Assistance concerning Elks collectibles was provided by David Wendel; he is listed in the Directory under Missouri.

Elks

Ashtray, 3 elk's head over BPOE on edge w/3 rests, brass, 4½" dia ..**40.00**
Case, membership paper; SP w/enameled emblem, EX **55.00**
Cigar cutter, mk Sterling, elk's head & clock, 1¾" **75.00**
Cuff links, elk's tooth w/clock emblem, ⅞x½", pr, EX, +orig box ...**185.00**
Flask, elk's tooth shape w/elk's head & clock, ceramic, MIG, 4½" ..**95.00**
Handbook, Ritual ...Order of the Elks, 100 pgs, 1939, EX.............**15.00**
Match safe, elk's head, clock & BPOE, SP w/brass top & bottom, NM...**70.00**
Medal, Elks Club Detroit, 1910, turtle & steamship, Bastion, 5" **65.00**
Medal, Maltese cross w/TFMM in copper w/elk's tooth, 2⅝", EX....**50.00**
Mug, Home of the Elks, Lancaster PA, ceramic, MIG, 3½", EX ...**50.00**
Ring, elk's head on ruby w/2 dmns, 10k gold **100.00**
Watch fob, elk's tooth w/clock & elk's head emblem, 1½x¾" **160.00**
Wristwatch, elk's head, clock & BPOE, Omega, ca 1961, EX **70.00**

Masons

Tumbler, carved horn with multicolor stain, 1800s, 3¾", from $100.00 to $125.00.

Apron, treasurer's, wht cloth w/bl trim, 12½x14½", EX...............**25.00**
Ballot box, dovetailed, ca 1900, w/clay marbles, EX....................**110.00**
Book, Dare We Be Masons, Thomas S Roy, hardbk, 111 pgs, 1966, EX...**8.00**
Book, Frontier Cornerstone-Story of Freemasonry in Ohio, 1980, M.**10.00**
Book, Masonic Manual & Code; 1954, 621 pgs, EX......................**12.00**
Bookends, AF & AM, bronze, 5¼x3¾", pr......................................**30.00**
Bookends, columns w/emblem center, bronze, 4½x4½", pr...........**90.00**
Bracelet, enameled seal on gold-tone metal, EX **15.00**
Brooch, sword shaped, emblem & ruby, sterling, 2¾", M (EX box) ..**12.00**

Cross, KT, gold presentation, 1914, Apollo #16, 2¼x4½", +case ..**200.00**
Light fixture, sq & compass, old..**65.00**
Match holder, aluminum, emblem at top, wall mt, 8½x5½".........**90.00**
Pocket watch, triangular w/emblems, mk Brevet #25265, NM **1,250.00**
Ring, 32nd degree, Scottish Rite, 10k gold, .75 point dmn......**1,700.00**
Sign, Free & Accepted Masons, wht on bl w/gold emblem, 18" dia, EX...**20.00**

Odd Fellows

Ballot box, wood w/43 porc & compo balls, 15x6½", EX..............**95.00**
Banner, red satin w/gold-leaf, hourglass/coffin/Bible etc, EX........**95.00**
Book, History & Manual Illustrated, c 1887, VG **20.00**
Book, Lodge Costumes & Regalia, 1,342 pgs, ca 1900, EX **150.00**
Book, Pocket Companion, Guide to All Matters, ca 1870, VG ...**20.00**
Costume, guard; bl velvet w/insignia w/Xd swords, EX...............**100.00**
Gavel, shepherd's crook shape, brass w/wood hdl, 17", EX **60.00**
Grave marker, wht dove sits on lily, pre-1900, CI, 23" **45.00**
Hat rack, lodge; 3 steer horns w/symbol & FLT, 1922, 24x12x6"...**235.00**
Ice cream mold, 3-link chain shape, pewter, 5¾x2x1½", EX **55.00**
License plate ornament, eye, chain emblem & skull & crossbones, EX...**25.00**
Mug, emblem on bl w/gold hdl & rim, ceramic, mk France, 5½", EX...**30.00**
Pipe bowl, cvd symbols, Made by JC Lare, 1867, 2⅜" H **1,400.00**
Plate, Cambridgeport Mass Hall, 1884-1910, Buffalo Pottery, 7½" ...**40.00**
Postcard, Ilion IL Temple & Post Office, 1954, EX **20.00**
Sign, Odd Fellows w/emblem center, porc, 29½" dia..................**475.00**
Tray, sterling silver, bk mk Imperial Council Session...1932, 9" dia...**40.00**

Shrine

Cane, Smile w/Nile, Seattle, 1936..**75.00**
Goblet, ruby flashed, emblems, St Paul, 1908 ....**75.00**
Tumbler, Steering over Hot Sands to Dallas, 1898 ....**85.00**

French Enameled Ware

In France during the 1880s, it became commonplace to decorate metalware items, decorative as well as utilitarian, with enameling that was often embellished with birds, flowers, and various other devices. The work was done by hand and was often very detailed and intricate.

Bottle, scent; figure scene w/dog, silver parrot finial, ewer form, 3" ..**800.00**
Bowl, classical figures, int/ext decor, silver rim/3-wheeled base, 7"...**1,600.00**
Bowl, maids/cupid panels, winged maid hdl/4 ball ft in silver, 3½"...**840.00**
Bowl, 4 lobes, ea w/courting pr, int/ext decor, winged maid hdls, 7" W...**1,265.00**
Box, jewel; man w/lute & lady, brass frwork, 8-sided, 9x7x4" ..**1,400.00**
Box, man ties ribbon in lady's hair, allover decor, 2½x2x1", EX....**900.00**
Compote, angels/dying maid, int/ext decor, figural hdls, 5x8", VG....**865.00**
Parlor set, cherub musicians, ormolu mts, 2 chairs+table+3" sofa...**1,265.00**
Plaque, portrait disk on floral bkground, ornate gold metal fr, 9x12"...**8,000.00**
Vases, figure in elaborate attire in garden, sgn, ftd, 4¼", pr **425.00**

Fruit Jars

As early as 1829, canning jars were being manufactured for use in the home preservation of foodstuffs. For the past twenty-five years, they have been sought as popular collectibles. At the last estimate, over 4,000 fruit jars and variations were known to exist. Some are very rare, perhaps one-of-a-kind examples known to have survived to the present day. Among the most valuable are the black glass jars, the amber Van Vliet, and the cobalt Millville. These often bring prices in excess of $20,000.00 when they can be found. Aside from condition, values are based on age, rarity, color, and special features. For more information, consult *1,000*

Fruit Jars by Bill Schroeder. Our advisor for this category is John Hathaway; he is listed in the Directory under Maine.

Acme (on shield w/stars & stripes), clear, qt or pt, ea......................**2.00**
Atlas, E-Z Seal, aqua, sq, ½-gal..**2.00**
Atlas, E-Z Seal, aqua, ½-gal..**7.00**
Atlas E-Z Seal, gr, qt...**15.00**
Atlas E-Z Seal, ½-pt...**3.00**
Atlas HA Mason, qt...**1.00**
Atlas Junior Mason, clear, ⅔-pt..**10.00**
Atlas Mason Patent, aqua, qt...**4.00**
Ball (undropped & no underscore) Perfect Mason, qt **2.00**
Ball (3 L loop) Mason Improved, aqua, pt....................................**15.00**
Ball Eclipse, base: Pat 7-14-08, qt..**4.00**
Ball Eclipse, wide mouth, clear, ½-gal.......................................**6.00**
Ball Freezer, 16-oz...**2.00**
Ball Ideal, bl, rnd, ½-gal..**12.00**
Ball Ideal, reverse: Pat'd July 14 1908, ½-pt...............................**10.00**
Ball Ideal, rnd, bl, ½-gal..**12.00**
Ball Ideal, sq, pt...**3.00**
Ball Improved (dropped A), clear, pt...**9.00**
Ball Mason, bl, pt...**2.00**
Ball Perfect Mason, bl, sq, qt..**10.00**
Ball Perfect Mason Made in USA, bl, 8 ribs, qt..............................**25.00**
Ball Sanitary Sure Seal, bl, qt..**5.00**
Beaver (beaver), strong emb, midget...**150.00**
Bernardin (script) Mason (underlined), pt...................................**10.00**
Clark's Peerless, aqua, pt...**6.00**
Corona Jar Made in Canada, pt..**3.00**
Cross Mason's Patent Nov 30th 1858, aqua, ½-gal.............................**15.00**
Crown (crown) Imperial, aqua, qt...**5.00**
Crown Crown (ring crown), aqua, qt...**17.00**
Crown Mason, qt..**2.00**
Daisy, pt...**20.00**
Double Safety, qt..**1.00**
Double Safety (script), clear, ½-pt..**12.00**
Double Seal, clear, qt..**15.00**
Drey Improved Ever Seal, clear, pt...**2.00**
Economy Sealer Patd Sept 15th 1885, aqua, wax sealer w/tin lid, qt...**25.00**
Electric Trade Mark (in circle), aqua, ½-gal **75.00**
Empire (in stippled cross), qt...**5.00**
Eureka (script), base: Eureka Jar Co, ½-pt **40.00**
Gem (CFJCo), aqua, ½-gal..**30.00**
HW Pettitt Westville NJ, aqua, pt..**8.00**
Ideal, The; aqua, midget..**100.00**
Ideal, The; aqua, qt..**25.00**
Kerr Self Sealing Trade Mark Patented Mason, ½-gal **5.00**
King (on banner below crown), pt or qt......................................**10.00**
Knox (K in Keystone) Mason, regular zinc lid, pt.............................**2.00**
Leotric (sm mouth), aqua, qt...**5.00**
Made in Canada Crown (crown), qt..**3.00**
Mason (star) Jar, pt...**1.00**
Mason (underlined), reverse: 1776 Liberty Bell 1976, qt.....................**1.00**
Mason's (Keystone in circle) Patent Nov 30th 1858, aqua, midget....**50.00**
Mason's (Keystone) Patent Nov 30th 1858, aqua, qt.......................**12.00**
Mason's (reversed apostrophe) A Patent Nov 30th 1858, aqua, qt ...**30.00**
Mason's Improved, amber, ½-gal..**175.00**
Mason's Patent, aqua, ½-gal..**10.00**
Mason's Patent Nov 30th 1858, aqua, qt......................................**4.00**
Mason's Patent Nov 30th 1858, base: 2-line cross, aqua, qt **12.00**
Mason's Patent Nov 30th 1858, reverse: hourglass, aqua, qt **15.00**
Mason's 22 Patent Nov 30th 1858, aqua, ½-gal...............................**30.00**
Mason's 6 Patent Nov 30th 1858, aqua, gal **15.00**
Midwest Canadian Made, qt...**14.00**

Mountain Mason, rnd, qt..**22.00**
Mountain Mason, sq, qt...**28.00**
Mrs Chapin's Mayonnaise Boston Mass, pt......................................**6.00**
Perfect Seal Wide Mouth Adjustable, pt..**6.00**
Presto, glass top, qt...**2.00**
Presto, ½-pt..**35.00**
Presto Supreme Mason, ½-gal...**5.00**
Protector, 1 panel recessed, aqua, qt.......................................**50.00**
Putnam (on base), aqua, 7⅜"..**75.00**
Root (looped Os), aqua, qt...**10.00**
Royal (in crown) TM Full Measure Registered, gal **25.00**
Safe Seal (in circle), bl, pt...**5.00**
Sko Queen (in shield), sun-colored amethyst, wide mouth, pt......**10.00**
Tight Seal, reverse: Pat'd July 14 1908, bl, pt..............................**4.00**
TM Lightning, aqua, pt..**4.00**
Trade Mark Banner, clear, wide mouth, ½-pt..................................**75.00**
Trade Mark Lightning, amber, qt...**68.00**
Trademark Banner Registered (in banner), qt................................**10.00**
Trademark Banner Warranted, bl, pt..**7.00**
Trademark Banner WM Warranted, bl, qt..**7.00**
Trademark Keystone Registered, pt or qt......................................**6.00**
Wears (on banner below crown), pt, twin side clamps....................**9.00**

Mason's Patent Nov 30th 1858, deep yellow-olive green, quart, $325.00.

Fry

Henry Fry established his glassworks in 1901 in Rochester, Pennsylvania. There, until 1933 when it was sold to the Libbey Company, he produced glassware of the finest quality. In the early years they produced beautiful cut glass; and when it began to wane in popularity, Fry turned to the manufacture of occasional pieces and oven glassware. He is perhaps most famous for the opalescent pearl art glass called 'Foval.' It was sometimes made with Delft Blue or Jade Green trim in combination. Because it was in production for only a short time in 1926 and 1927, it is hard to find. Our advisor for this category is Ron Damaska; he is listed in the Directory under Pennsylvania. See also Kitchen Collectibles, Glassware.

Baker, pearl ovenware, 9" sq...**30.00**
Bean pot, pearl ovenware, w/lid, 1924, 1-qt...............................**120.00**
Bell, amber, needle etched, 7½"..**45.00**
Bottle, scent; Foval, Delft Blue stopper w/etched flower, 7½".....**385.00**
Bowl, cut, Lyton, sawtooth rim, 4x8"...**80.00**
Bowl, cut stars/fans/X-hatching, notched rim, 3x7", NM **100.00**
Bowl, fruit; cut, Orient, ftd, 9"...**175.00**
Bowl, needle etched, 2-spout, 4½x5⅞" (spout to spout)..............**28.00**
Brown Betty, pearl ovenware, 9", from $55 to..............................**65.00**
Candle holder, blk, wide flat ft, 3", ea....................................**18.00**

Candlesticks, cobalt, clear swirl ball in stem, 5", pr.....................210.00
Casserole, blk w/silver resist, w/lid, pre-1933, 1½-qt in NP fr...215.00
Casserole, pearl ovenware, w/lid, 7" sq, in metal holder, from $85 to ..95.00
Casserole, pearl ovenware, 2-part, shallow, 9" 40.00
Chicken roaster, pearl ovenware, #1946, 14".....................................60.00
Compote, Foval, Delft Blue teardrop stem, 7x6"...........................200.00
Compote, wht w/lt gr stem, 6⅞"..460.00
Cordial, bl w/clear stem, 4½"..55.00
Cup, coffee; pearl ovenware 27.50
Cup, custard; pearl ovenware 16.00
Cup & saucer, Foval, Jade Green hdl, 4 for.....................................325.00
Dish, cut, heart shape, 5¾"..160.00
Goblet, Diamond Optic, azure, 7"...35.00
Jar, jelly/marmalade; Foval, w/hdls & lid, 1924, 9-oz 60.00
Mug, lemonade; Foval, Jade Green hdl...75.00
Percolator, Ovenglass, complete, 10", NM.......................................375.00
Pie plate, pearl ovenware, #1916, 9"..30.00
Pitcher, bl w/bubbles & threaded rim band, 9½", +9" underplate...125.00
Pitcher, Celeste Blue, bubbles/rim threading, bl hdl, 9", +underplate...150.00
Pitcher, Foval, ftd, Delft Blue hdl, 7" 125.00
Pitcher, lemonade; Foval, textured w/gr lid & hdl; +6 hdld tumblers...725.00
Plate, cut, Brighton, 7" sq 245.00
Plate, cut, Flower Basket, 9"...95.00
Plate, sherbet; Rose etch, plain center, 6" 20.00
Platter, fish; eng, 11", from $60 to 65.00
Platter, tree & well; Ovenglass, w/matching SP holder, 16¾x12"....55.00
Relish, cut, Asteroid, oblong, 13"..150.00
Roaster, pearl ovenware, dome lid, 7½x14x10", from $200 to 225.00
Saucer champagne, Rose etch, str sides 20.00
Sherbet, cut, geometric pattern, clear w/8-petal blk base, 2½" 20.00
Sherbet, Foval, Delft Blue stem & ft 120.00
Shirred egg dish, pearl ovenware, 7½" dia, from $30 to 35.00
Snack set, opal, 1930s, 6x9¼" tray+2" cup.......................................57.50
Tea set, Foval w/silver o/l, pot+cr/sug+6 c/s, ca 1920 ....865.00
Teapot, Foval w/Jade Green hdl, spout & finial, EX....................365.00
Tumbler, brilliant cutting, 4x3", 4 for..215.00
Tumbler, iced tea; Japanese Maid etch, cherry blossom hdl, ftd, 5" ...115.00
Tumbler, lemonade; Foval, Jade Green hdl/ft, sterling rim, 5¼"...175.00
Vase, cut, trumpet form, 12x4½", NM...135.00
Vase, Dmn Quilt w/blk glass threading, 9½x7x4¾" 195.00
Vase, Foval, Delft Blue rim & 3 ball ft, dbl-gourd body, 5⅜" 100.00
Vase, jack-in-pulpit; Foval, Delft Blue rim, raised rnd base, 10"...300.00

Fulper

Throughout the nineteenth century the Fulper Pottery in Flemington, New Jersey, produced utilitarian and commercial wares. But it was during the span from 1902 to 1935, the Arts and Crafts period in particular, that the company became prominent producers of beautifully glazed art pottery. Although most pieces were cast rather than hand decorated, the graceful and classical shapes used together with wonderful experimental glaze combinations made each piece a true work of art.

The company also made dolls' heads, Kewpies, figural perfume lamps, and powder boxes. Their lamps with the colored glass inserts are extremely rare and avidly sought by collectors. Examples prized most highly by collectors today are those produced before the devastating fire in 1929 and subsequent takeover by Martin Stangl (see Stangl Pottery).

Several marks were used: a vertical in-line 'Fulper' being the most common in ink or incised, an impressed block horizontal mark, Flemington, Rafco, Prang, and paper labels. Unmarked examples often surface and can be identified by shape and glaze characteristics. Values are determined by size, desirability of glaze, and rarity of form. Our advisor for this category is Douglass White; he is listed in the Directory under Florida.

Bookends, stylized grotesque face, gr/gunmetal, label, 5½x6" 350.00
Bowl, bl/red/cream flambé w/bl/blk/gr int, hdls, low, 8"...............300.00
Bowl, centerpc; hammered metallic gray-blk, squat urn, 3-ftd, 11" ...1,295.00
Bowl, gr matt, invt rim, ftd, pre-1920, 3¾x18¼".........................350.00
Bowl, mirrored bl & gr, low, 4"..150.00
Bowl, Oriental flambé w/crystalline, 3x10¼"................................495.00
Candle holder, bl/blk/yel flambé, integral hdls, 3", ea 250.00
Candlestick, bl crystalline, 3-hdl, 1¼x6", ea.................................150.00
Chamberstick, brn/gr/bl flambé, hooded, 3 geometric glass pcs, 7"..1,800.00
Figurine, cat, metallic dk gr w/cream patches, pre-1920, 9½" L...1,295.00
Lamp, Cafe-Au-Lait, inset geometric glass shade, minor rpr, 21½" 11,000.00
Urn, dripping bl & gr flambé over bl, sq hdls, vertical mk, 9½x8" ..850.00
Urn, frothy mirrored bl-gr, emb upright hdls, 11½x9"...............2,200.00
Urn, Mirror Black, hdld urn, vertical mk, 12¾x7¼"...................700.00
Vase, amber drip on mirror brn, baluster, 13x6½"......................2,000.00
Vase, bl & Copperdust flambé, baluster, drilled, 15½x7¾" 650.00
Vase, bl crystalline, hdls, 8" W...550.00
Vase, bl speckled matt, 4 rim-to-hip hdls, bulbous, 9".............3,000.00
Vase, bl/beige/purple flambé, baluster, 11".....................................375.00
Vase, bl/blk/tan flambé w/4 buttresses, low, 5" dia 400.00

Vase, brown and black drip over blue-green, 11½", $3,300.00.

Vase, brn/tan/bl crystalline on blk/gr gloss, incurvate rim, 5x14"...750.00
Vase, Cafe-Au-Lait, banded geometrics, butressed hdls, 3x6" 325.00
Vase, Cat's Eye flambé, bullet shape, 3-hdl, 7x5".........................400.00
Vase, Cat's-Eye flambé, flared mouth, 7½x5½" 330.00
Vase, Chinese Blue flambé, trumpet form, rpr drill hole, 15x7¾"...500.00
Vase, Cucumber Green (textured), squat urn w/hdls, rstr, 9x9" ..450.00
Vase, Famille Rose, bl/gr/cobalt drip on rose, angle hdls, 11x5"..495.00
Vase, Famille Rose, spherical w/closed-in rim, 6".........................475.00
Vase, Flemington Green, tapered w/4 buttresses, 8¼" 550.00
Vase, Flemington Green flambé, corseted/ruffled, ink mk, 10¼"...950.00
Vase, Flemington Green flambé, cut-out butressed hdls, 11x4½"..900.00
Vase, frothy bl on Famille Rose, squat base w/4 buttresses, 13" 3,500.00
Vase, frothy gunmetal/ivory flambé over mustard, rstr, 12x9"...1,600.00
Vase, gr & brn flambé w/bl crystalline, shouldered, hdls, 10" ..1,100.00
Vase, gr crystalline w/blk charcoaling, melon form, 5½x7".........550.00
Vase, gr/gold/Copperdust crystalline, hdls, 10"............................750.00
Vase, Leopard's Skin crystalline over butter yel, rstr hole, 16"....2,000.00
Vase, Leopard Skin crystalline, bullet shape w/3 hdls at rim, 6½"....375.00
Vase, Leopard Skin crystalline, corseted, hdls, 4½x67" 350.00
Vase, Leopard Skin crystalline, flat shoulder, vertical mk, 7¼x8"...1,000.00
Vase, lt yel flambé on Chinese Blue & brn, baluster, 9¼x6½" ...275.00
Vase, Mirror Black crystalline, angled open hdls, 6½x8".............950.00
Vase, Mirror Black over bl & Famille Rose flambè, collared, 8x7½"...900.00
Vase, Mirror Black to butterscotch, bullet shape, 3-hdl, 6¾x5" ...415.00
Vase, mirrored bl & gr flambé, lizard at neck, ink mk, 8x4½" 450.00
Vase, mirrored gr, bulbous w/cylindrical neck, 8x5¼" 375.00
Vase, multi-tone Mission Brown matt, dbl-gourd w/hdls, 6½x10"..1,000.00

Vase, pk matt under purple crystalline drip w/Mirror Black top, 11"...**1,300.00**
Vase, purple under bl, sm angle hdls, swollen, 7½".......................**350.00**
Vase, red/purple textured matt, ovoid, 9½"................................**450.00**

Furniture

Aside from its obvious utility, furniture has always been a symbol indicating wealth, taste, and social position. Each period of time has wrought distinct changes in style, choice of wood, and techniques — all clues that the expert can use to determine just when an item was made. Regional differences as well as secondary wood choice give us clues as to country and locale. The end of the Civil War brought with it the Industrial Revolution and the capability of producing man-made furniture. With this came the Victorian period and the many revival styles.

Important to the collector (and dealer) is the ability to recognize furniture on a 'good, better, best' approach. Age alone does not equal value. During a recessionary market the 'best' of forms always seem to do well. The 'better' or middle market will show a drop in value, and the 'good' or lower end of the marketplace will suffer the most. Many of this year's values emphasize what has been going on in the marketplace. Auction estimates for part of the year were way off the mark due to unforseen economic factors. The marketplace although recovering still enables astute shoppers to find wonderful buys. Value is based on scarcity, form, and technique, as well as what is fashionable in the marketplace at the time. Some pieces are timeless classics and will always have a place in the antiques marketplace. Others are strictly fashionable at the time, and value is speculative at best.

Still popular and continuing to rise are the mahogany classic copies from the early twentieth century. This includes the styles of Queen Anne, Duncan Phyfe, Chippendale, Sheraton, and Hepplewhite. The English counterparts are also enjoying popularity. Turn-of-the-century European inlaid and carved furniture is still rising in value. Stronger in the marketplace is the 'decorator trade,' who realize this type of furniture is a sound investment and can be refinished (without any loss of value) to suit the client's needs. Upholstered pieces that are 'floor ready' are bringing stronger prices at auction. Frames for sofas, chairs, and benches needing new upholstery and some work are being sold reasonably to eager collectors and dealers. They realize that when the work is completed, they will have a unique, well-made item at a reasonable price.

Items that have sold at auction for at least 25% lower than their normal market values will be designated with (*). Items listed in the lines that are designated with (**) are pieces in the best of form and of museum quality.

Please note: If a piece actually dates to the period of time during which its style originated, we will use the name of the style only. For example: 'Hepplewhite' will indicate an American piece from roughly the late 1700s to 1815. The term 'style' will describe a piece that is far removed from the original time frame. 'Hepplewhite style' refers to examples from the turn of the century. When the term 'repro' is used it will mean that the item in question is less than thirty years old and is being sold on a secondary market. When only one dimension is given for blanket chests, dry sinks, tables, settees, sideboards, and sofas, it is length.

Condition is the most important factor to consider in determining value. It is also important to remember that *where* a piece sells has a definite bearing on the price it will realize, due simply to regional preference. Our advisor for this category is Suzy McLennan Anderson, ISA CAPP, of Heritage Antiques and Anderson Auctions, LLC, whose address is listed in the Directory under New Jersey. (Photo and SASE required; no phone appraisals.) To learn more about furniture, we recommend *Heywood-Wakefield Modern Furniture* by Steve and Roger Rouland; *Antique Oak Furniture* by Conover Hill; *American Oak Furniture, Book II*, and *Victorian Furniture, Our American Heritage, Books I and II*, by Kathryn McNerney; *Collector's Encyclopedia of Wallace Nutting Furniture* by Michael Ivankovich; *Stickley Brothers Furniture* and *Roycroft Furniture and Collectibles* by Larry Koon; *Collector's Guide to Oak Furniture* by Jennifer George; and *Early American Furniture* by John Obbard. See also Art Deco; Art Nouveau; Arts and Crafts; Fifties Modern; Limbert; Nutting, Wallace; Shaker; Stickley.

Key:
* — auction price but 25% under the norm
** — museum quality
: — over (example, 1 do:2 drw)
bj — bootjack
brd — board
cvd, cvg — carved, carving
c&b — claw and ball
do — door
drw — drawer
Emp — Empire
Fed — Federal
Fr — French
ftbd — footboard
G — good
Geo — Georgian
grpt — grainpainted
hdbd — headboard
hdw — hardware
Hplwht — Hepplewhite
mar — marriage
mahog — mahogany
NE — New England
QA — Queen Anne
R/R — Renaissance Revival
rswd — rosewood
trn — turning, turned
uphl — upholstered/upholstery
vnr — veneer
Vict — Victorian
W/M — William and Mary

Armoires, See Also Wardrobes

Burlwood Art Deco, center do w/oval mirror, marquetry bands, 84x54"....**1,500.00**
Cherry Am, cvg/inlay, cornice:dbl do:skirt:cabriole legs, 19th C, 85"....**35,650.00**
Cherry Louis XV style, 2-do, orig int, cabriole legs, 78x55"....**57,500.00**
Cyprus, cvd cornice:3 panel do:ped w/2 drw:molded plinth, 108x85x29"...**1,500.00**
Mahog Am Fed, cornice:dbl do:beehive-trn legs:brass ball ft, 92x61"...**9,200.00**
Mahog Fed, cornice:plain frize:panel do w/center stile, 91x56x20"...**8,625.00**
Mahog Scottish Vict, arched pediment:3 do w/cvg, 88x76x20"...**925.00**
Mahog/satinwood LA Louis XV style, cornice:2 panel do w/inlay, 85"....**23,000.00**
Oak Fr Baroque, checkered pnt decor/ochre sgraffito, 18th C, 75x51"...**8,225.00**
Pine w/grpt & gr marbleized & red accents, Scandinavia, 1810s, 73x62"...**2,300.00**
Rswd Am Rococo, arched pediment:2 do w/mirror:2 drw:ft, 100x66x23"...**3,000.00**
Rswd/burl vnr ornately-cvd breakdown, center mirror, 2-drw, 83x73"....**1,000.00**
Walnut Am, Gothic-arch panel do, ogee bracket ft, ca 1850, 90x51"...**3,450.00**
Walnut Am Gothic, arched ornate pediment, fluted columns, 97x62"...**3,500.00**
Walnut Louis XV, cornice:2 shaped panel do:drw:cabriole legs, 99"...**5,000.00**
Walnut R/R, 3-do, cvd pilasters, base drw, 88x98"...**3,000.00**
Walnut Southern, cornice:dbl panel do:bracket ft, 1830s, 87x47"...**1,725.00**
Walnut Vict, 2 do:2 drw w/grape-cluster hdls, 2-part, 85x54x18"...**1,265.00**

Beds

Burled walnut/figured mahog Late Fed 4-poster, 110x91x72"...**2,500.00**
Cannonball, cypress Am w/old red stain, early 19th C, 45x78x56"...**3,450.00**
Cannonball, maple, rfn, 52x53x73"...............**300.00**
Field, birch/pine Sheraton w/brn wash, arched hdbd, rstr, 65x73x55"...**6,600.00**
Gesso Fr w/HP scenes & Rococo scroll panels, much cvg, 49x80x67"...**715.00**
Half-tester, mahog Am Rococo w/serpentine cvg, scroll brackets, 119"...**18,500.00**
Half-tester walnut/burl walnut R/R, 129x88x72".....................**8,500.00**
Low-post pnt Fed, wht w/gold-leaf stencil, NY, 1830s, 47x54"...**1,150.00**
Mahog Edwardian w/inlay & pnt decor, molded panels, 60x72x65"...**1,725.00**
Mahog Emp w/gilt bronze mts, urn finials, early 19th C, 49x82x43"...**2,650.00**
Mahog Fed, Gothic spires, paneled hdbd & ftbd, 42dx83x58"...**1,380.00**
Rope, birch/pine, trn legs, pegged joints, old red, 34x44x73"...**220.00**
Rope, bird's-eye maple hd & ftbds, 60x55x76"...**1,100.00**
Rope, curly cherry/poplar, urn & ball finials, trn legs, 43x78x52"...**250.00**
Rope, curly maple Co, trn posts, arched hdbd, rfn/rpl, 55x74x52"...**1,450.00**
Rope, peaked hdbd, trn legs, robin's egg bl pnt, 33x70x53"...**300.00**
Sleigh, mahog Charles X, figured scroll crest, 43x67x38"...**750.00**

Sleigh, mahog Louis Philippe w/cvg, ½-rnd crest rail, 40x46 W.**350.00**
Tester, cherry/walnut Am, trn posts, shaped hdbd, spindled ftbd, 91"...**70,000.00**
Tester, curly maple Co Sheraton, high trn posts, paneled hdbd w/crest....**3,575.00**
Tester, mahog Am, ogee fr w/columnar uprights, 1840s, 120x90x69"...**5,000.00**
Tester, mahog LA, stepped/molded fr:pedimented hdbd, 1850s, 104x86x69"...**3,000.00**
Tester, mahog w/ornate cvd posts, Marlborough legs, 84x53x68"......**2,000.00**
Tester, tiger maple/mahog Am, later rails, ca 1825, 98x80x60"..**6,000.00**
Trundle, pine, spindle gallery, 15x80x41"...**515.00**
Walnut/rswd vnr/poplar Vict, medallion hdbd, octagon posts, 98x73"...**2,750.00**
4-poster, walnut Am (LA), bold-trn posts, scrolled hdbd, 1825, 100"....**19,500.00**

Benches

Bucket, pine w/red traces, sq nails, cutouts, 32x39x12"...**550.00**
Bucket, pine/poplar Co, step-bk, 2-shelf, bj ends, rfn, 41x41x15"...**880.00**
Bucket, poplar Co, 2-shelf top w/canted sides:base w/2 do, 45x41x17"...**1,500.00**
Bucket, poplar w/old bl-gray, sq nails, bj cutouts, 39x45x14"......**950.00**
Bucket, poplar w/old red wash, sq nails, arched cutouts, 47x44x12"...**1,100.00**
Bucket, single-brd ends w/shaped top corners, bl-gray pnt, 30x40x16"..**600.00**
Burl walnut Biedermeier style, scrolled sides, paw ft, 38x28x17", pr..**800.00**
Cherry Windsor style, trn legs, thick top, ca 1940, 20x30x16"...**250.00**
Deacon's, mixed woods w/mustard pnt, 17-spindle, scroll arms, 69", pr...**1,200.00**
Fireside, oak/pine w/inset panels, rpl lids, 55x60x19"...**1,550.00**
Fireside, pine Co w/inset panels, trn arm supports, old rfn, 59x56x22"...**1,250.00**
Fireside, pine/mixed woods, mortised seat, bbl bk, rfn, 66x72x20"...**600.00**
Mahog Chpndl style, slip uphl seat:6 sq legs, serpentine arms, 47"..**1,300.00**

Oak bench with arms and splatted back, early 1900s, 37x50x20", $415.00.
(Photo courtesy Robert W. and Harriett Swedberg)

Oak English w/cvg, flower finials, bj cutouts, 48x72x18"...**825.00**
PA decor, plank seat, scrolled arms, 8 trn legs, 35x67x26"...**880.00**
PA decor w/orig copper & silver flower stencil on crest, trn legs, 84"..**1,550.00**
Pine, mortised top:2 slanted braces, sq nails, bl-gr pnt, 19x31x7"...**440.00**
Pine Co, beaded apron, bj cutouts, old brn pnt, 18x81x12"...**150.00**
Pine Co w/splayed legs, scalloped aprons, 8½x60x12½"...**110.00**
Poplar Co, sq nails, old red, C cutouts, scrubbed, 16x27x16"...**275.00**
Settle, arrow-bk, old blk pnt w/gold decor, trn legs, rprs, 36x78x24"...**660.00**
Settle, curly maple/birch, serpentine arms, rush seat w/old pnt, 77"..**1,980.00**
Settle, European, 12 relief-cvd panels, gr wash, rstr, 83"...**660.00**
Settle, mc fruit & flower stenciling, trn legs, arms, 19th C, 73" L...**1,450.00**
Settle, oak English QA, molded crest:5-panel bk, pegged, 73"...**550.00**
Settle, pnt Co, flat top:grooved bk:lift seat:paneled front, 19th C...**2,400.00**
Window, cherry Chpndl style, silk uphl, Southwood, 31x43x18"...**200.00**
Window, mahog Regency style w/inlay, scroll armrests, 38x32x16", pr...**575.00**

Bureaus, See Chests

Blanket Chests, Coffers, Trunks, and Mule Chests

Cherry/poplar Sheraton, high trn legs/ball ft, 28x41x18"...**1,200.00**

Oak English Chpndl style w/mahog inlay, 2 faux drw:5, 36x66"...**2,500.00**
Oak English w/fine cvg, bj cutouts, 2-brd top, rpl hinges, 49" L...**800.00**
Over drws, pine QA, hinged top:2 drws:molded base, brn pnt, 40x37x20"...**1,150.00**
PA decor, 6-brd, dvtl box, molded lift top, 1830s, 23x49x22"..**18,808.00**
Pine Co Chpndl w/old red-brn pnt, dvtl drw, 33x44x20"...**2,530.00**
Pine Co QA w/old red-brn, 2 dvtl drw, 5 false fronts, 41x36x17"...**1,550.00**
Pine w/flame grpt, sq nails, 2-brd top, till, rprs, 41"...**1,875.00**
Pine w/old red, 3-drw, trn pulls, rprs, att Hudson River Valley...**880.00**
Pine w/old red, 6-brd, dvtl, rpl lock/hinges, 18x50x16"...**275.00**
Pine w/orig red, dvtl, 1-brd lid, short trn ft, 17x25x14"...**715.00**
Pine w/orig red, 2 dvtl drw, hinged lid, sq-nail rpr, 39x42x19"...**1,100.00**
Pine w/orig yel/red/blk grpt, cut-out ends/wrought hinges, RI, 24x45"...**2,200.00**
Pine/poplar, blk grpt on red, dvtl, 3-drw, till, 30x50x23"...**825.00**
Pnt tulips on blk reserves on wht, trn pilasters, dvtl, 25x55x23"...**400.00**
Poplar, 3 tombstone panels w/pnt decor, dtd 1817, sm rstr, 18x37x16"...**1,100.00**
Poplar w/OH flame grpt, dvtl case/appl moldings, rprs, 25x45x21"...**880.00**
Poplar w/red grpt & gold stencil, PA, ca 1847, 24½x46x20"...**1,265.00**
Poplar/pine w/orig grpt blk, trn ft, sm rpr, OH, 26x48x19"...**660.00**
Walnut/curly maple Sheraton style, 2-brd lid, 22x41x18"...**275.00**
Walnut/oak Co Chpndl, 2 dvtl drws, bat-wing brasses, 20x51"..**1,550.00**

Bookcases

Breakfront, mahog Geo III style w/cvg, 6 glass do:6 panel, 94x156"...**8,625.00**
Cypress, 2 glazed do:2, shelved int, 20th C, 86x52x14"...**1,265.00**
Fr Provincial, arched cornice:2 scalloped do:2 do, much cvg, 102"...**7,775.00**
Mahog Regency-style, open top:4 drw:apron:Fr ft, 2-pc, 63x49"...**525.00**
Oak, wide cornice w/appl moldings & lion-head cvgs, rfn, Am, 59x44"..**1,165.00**
Oak Am Rococo, cvd central do & scroll glazed do:2 drw & 2 do, 77x93"...**1,600.00**
Revolving, mahog Geo III, 5 grad tiers:drum 2-do base, 72x30"...**15,275.00**
Revolving, mahog Vict, molded top:2 shelves w/dividers, 32x21" sq...**1,600.00**
Walnut Am Rococo, 2-do:2 drw, scroll & shell cvgs, 1840s, 98x67x21"...**5,465.00**
Walnut Dutch bombè, arched pediment w/crest, 2-part, c&b ft, 109x72"...**8,625.00**

Cabinets

Apothecary, blk stain, 48-drw, scalloped bj ends, wire nails, 62x43"..**4,000.00**
China, oak, swell-front glass do, curved glass sides, paw ft, 63x36"...**975.00**
Corner, cherry glaze, cornice:12-pane do:2 panel do, rfn/rprs, 86"...**4,300.00**
Corner, cherry LA, tenoned, iron hinges, Fr legs, 68x42x23"..**5,000.00**
Curio, Fr gilt w/ormolu trim, HP floral, cabriole legs, 20th C, 50x27"..**800.00**
Display, mahog Edwardian, molded cornice, bow-front do, 83x60x14"..**2,300.00**
Hoosier, oak, flour bin & glass sugar can swing out, ca 1910, 89x40"..**1,500.00**
Press, mahog Geo III, 2-part, panel dos:4 drw, 1780s, rprs, 88x50"...**3,300.00**
Rswd/walnut R/R w/inlay, missing gallery, 44x49x21"...**990.00**
Spice, mahog Chpndl style, arched panel do, 7 int drws, 23x17x12"...**990.00**
Vitrine, cherrywood & ebony Biedermeier style, gilt capitals, 76x46"...**3,500.00**
Walnut Fr Baroque, cornice:2 panel do:2 drw:2 panel do, 17th C, 80x57"...**6,450.00**

Candlestands

Birch Chpndl-Hplwht transitional, 8-sided 2-brd top, 27x17x18"...**375.00**
Cherry Chpndl, dish top:urn column:tripod:snake ft, sm rpr, 19" dia.**700.00**
Cherry Chpndl, tripod w/pad ft, rstr/old finish, 28x30"...**465.00**
Cherry Co, tilt-top:trn ped:tripod legs:high pad ft, rfn, 36x27x16"...**2,950.00**
Cherry Co Chpndl, 2-brd top:tripod w/snake ft, rfn/rprs, 37x15x15"...**575.00**
Cherry Fed, tilt-top w/dbl-string inlay:tripod:pad ft, rfn, 38x16x21"...**1,000.00**
Cherry Hplwht w/birdcage on tripod w/medallion ft, rprs, 25" dia...**1,100.00**
Cherry QA, cabriole legs w/padded snake ft, dish top, 28x17" dia...**2,000.00**
Mahog Chpndl, tilt top:tripod w/cabriole legs:snake ft, 27x22" dia...**330.00**
Mahog Chpndl, tilt-top:trn legs w/snake ft, rprs, 20x19" dia...**330.00**
Mahog Chpndl/Hplwht transitional w/1-brd tilt top, rprs, 39x22x16"...**550.00**
Mahog Fed, serpentine tilt-top:tripod:spade ft, 30x18x18¼"...**765.00**
Maple Co Hplwht, spider legs, 1-brd 8-sided top, rpr/rfn...**330.00**

Maple Fed w/much cvg, reeded post, tripod base, old rfn, 36x14x15" ..650.00
Maple/pine/curly maple Co Chpndl, high tripod w/snake ft, rfn/rstr **385.00**
Pine Windsor style, 3 trn legs on column w/threaded top, 20th C, 48" **130.00**

Chairs

Arm, Co QA, grad 4-slat bk, early red, rpl rush seat, 41" **195.00**
Arm, Co QA ladderbk, old worn rpt, splint seat, 44", VG **385.00**
Arm, laminated rswd cvd Rococo, Stanton Hall variant, att Meeks ..**3,200.00**
Arm, mahog Am Gothic, arched crest:rectangular tablet, reuphl, 30" **3,165.00**
Arm, maple/birch Chpndl, mortise & peg, old rush seat, 40" **660.00**
Arm, maple/birch/pine QA style, paper rush seat, 1890s, 43" **550.00**
Arm, mixed hardwood 4-slat ladderbk, rush seat, ball ft, 46½"...**275.00**
Arm, pine Black Forest style w/much cvg, dk rfn, 45" **900.00**
Arm, rswd Am Gothic, arched uhpl bkrest, cvd legs, NY, 38"....**2,875.00**
Arm, walnut bbl, cane seat, 1850s, 30" **1,200.00**
Arm, walnut Louis XVI style w/much cvg, old reuphl, 19th C, 35" **300.00**
Arm, walnut Vict, molded fr w/cvg, new reupl, 43" **195.00**
Arm, walnut Vict w/cvd foliage, new uphl, 43", VG **250.00**
Arm, walnut/burl walnut R/R w/bronze mts, reuphl.................**1,600.00**
Arm, 4-slat ladder-bk, splint seat, orig red traces, 45" **220.00**
Corner, mixed hardwoods, 12 trn spindles, scrolled arms, 29".....**330.00**
Desk, walnut QA style, reclines/swivels, uphl, Hickory Chair Co....**110.00**
Opera, brass tubing w/appl rings, trn finials, uphl seat, 34", pr....**385.00**
Rocker, bentwood hickory w/natural finish, att Amish, 43"........**110.00**
Rocker, benwtood hickory w/red-brn pnt, 5-slat bk, 44" **150.00**
Rocker, Boston, blk:red grpt, red:mustard sponging, 5-spindle, 36"...**165.00**
Rocker arm, bentwood hickory, 6 vertical slats, weathered, 40" **250.00**
Rocker arm, curly maple 4-slat ladderbk, hickory rockers, rfn, 42"....**495.00**
Rocker arm, PA decor w/grapes/acorns/foliage, mc on gr, 41" **550.00**
Rocker arm, 7-spindle bk, woven seat, rprs, Old Hickory, 35" **300.00**
Side, banister bk:rush seat:sausage-trn legs, old blk pnt, 43" **275.00**
Side, birch QA, vase splat/shaped crest, rush seat, att NH, 40" **1,045.00**
Side, cherry/hickory, shaped bk, plank seat, Zoar OH, rfn, 38", pr...**500.00**
Side, cherry/hickory Co QA, vase splat, rush seat, rfn/rpr, 39½"....**385.00**
Side, Co QA, sausage-trn legs, worn rush seat, rprs, 42" **220.00**
Side, Co QA, 4-spindle bk, blk pnt & red lines, rush seat, 36"...**110.00**
Side, curly maple Sheraton, 4-slat bk, rush seat, old rfn, 34½"...**200.00**
Side, European QA style, painted bl foliage on wht, slip seat, pr...**660.00**
Side, mahog Chpndl, pierced splat w/cvg, c&b ft, prof rstr, 37" **2,200.00**
Side, mahog Chpndl-style ribbon-bk, molded front legs, 1900s, 37" **230.00**
Side, mahog Regency, gadroon crest:wavy splat:uphl seat:trn legs, pr...**320.00**
Side, maple Chpndl, crest:pierced splat:slip seat:cabriole legs, 39" ...**1,115.00**
Side, maple Co Chpndl, pierced splat, rush seat, red wash, 39", pr ..**850.00**
Side, pine Moravian, scalloped/pierced bk, pencil-post legs, pr...**220.00**
Side, rswd Vict, bow-front seat, pierced/cvd bk, reuphl/rstr, 37"....**165.00**
Side, walnut QA, front cabriole legs, pad ft, rpl seat, 42"............**935.00**
Slipper, curly maple Co, 4 arched slats:rush seat:trn legs, 42" **220.00**
Slipper, Louis XVI style, bl & olive pnt, reuphl, early 20th C, 32"....**200.00**
Windsor birdcage w/bamboo trn, old red wash, EX rpr, 35" **550.00**
Windsor bow-bk arm, 8-spindle, trn legs, rpr, 45" **350.00**
Windsor bow-bk side, dk stain, 35", 3 for **1,300.00**
Windsor brace-bk continuous arm, 9-spindle, old red:gr, 35"....**2,185.00**
Windsor brace-bk w/scrolled arms, blk rpl/rprs...........................**450.00**
Windsor butterfly birdcage side w/bamboo trn, 34", pr...............**770.00**
Windsor comb-bk arm w/bamboo trns, brn finish, 45".............**1,450.00**
Windsor fan-bk arm, serpentine crest, plank seat, 46"................**475.00**
Windsor fan-bk rocker arm, orig blk pnt w/yel decal, 32" **275.00**
Windsor fan-bk side, 7-spindle, shield-shaped seat, old rfn, 35"...**500.00**
Windsor fan-bk 7-spindle arm, bamboo trn, old brn rpt, 34" **550.00**
Windsor rocker arm, bamboo w/comb crest, old rfn, 39½".........**400.00**
Windsor sack-bk arm, trn legs w/stretcher base, rpl/rstr, 39" **400.00**
Windsor sack-bk arm, 7-spindle, baluster-trn legs, 37½"............**600.00**
Windsor sack-bk arm, 7-spindle, old brn:gr pnt, 35" **2,200.00**

Windsor sack-bk arm, 7-spindle, saddle seat, dk stain, 40".......**2,645.00**
Windsor sack-bk arm w/scalloped hand-holds, rprs/rfn, 35" **650.00**
Windsor side, 5-spindle step-down bk, old gr pnt, 33".................**165.00**
Windsor side, 7-spindle fan-bk, old dry red pnt, rprs, 36" **1,800.00**
Wing, mahog Chpndl, old rfn, reuphl, rprs, 43½" **2,200.00**
Wing, mahog Geo III style, padded bk, uphl loose seat, 44" **350.00**
Wing, mahog Hplwht style, fine uphl, Hickory Chair Co, 46" ...**400.00**
Wing, mahog QA style w/eagle cvg, c&b ft, new reuphl, 20th C, 47" **800.00**
Wing, walnut European QA style, faded velvet uphl, old finish, 41" ..**330.00**
Wing, walnut Jacobean style, Spanish ft, reuphl, 20th C, 49¼" **400.00**
Youth, PA dove & fruit stencil, yel lines on blk, 35x23"..........**1,100.00**

Chair Sets

Dining, mahog Chpndl style, c&b ft/cvd knees, uphl seat, 2 arm+3 side **1,325.00**
Dining, mahog Chpndl-style ribbon-bk, reuphl seat, 1 arm+5 side ...**2,475.00**
Dining, mahog Geo III style, serpentine rail, 2 arm+10 side....**9,000.00**
Dining, mahog Geo III style w/cvg, slip seat, 2 arm+10 side **36,800.00**
Library arm, mahog Geo III-style, caned seat, ca 1900, 34", 4 for...**1,265.00**
Parlor, Louis XVI style, ivory pnt, 2 arm+4 side **1,000.00**
Parlor, rswd Vict, much cvg, velvet reupl, gentleman's+5 side ...**1,750.00**
Side, Co 3-slat ladderbk, old blk pnt, splint seat, 6 for **440.00**
Side, Hitchcock style, 5 dbl-slat bk, blk over red w/stencil, 6 for ..**500.00**
Side, mahog English Chpndl, slip seat, rprs/rfn, 35", 6 for **1,400.00**
Side, mahog Fed shield-bk w/pierced fan, reuphl, 38", 4 for ..**11,000.00**
Side, mahog QA style, flame uphl, handmade repro, ca 1900, 6 for..**1,375.00**
Side, maple Co, 2-slat, rush seats, trn legs, rfn, 12 for **990.00**
Side, plank seats w/early blk rpt w/rose decor, worn, 33", 6 for ...**550.00**
Side, tiger maple Fed, scroll crest/rush seat, yel pnt details, 4 for...**750.00**
Side, walnut Chpndl style, serpentine apron, c&b ft, reuphl, 4 for....**550.00**
Side, Windsor pnt 7-spindle fan-bk, 35", 4 for...........................**950.00**
Windsor, 5-spindle bk w/rabbit ears, blk on red w/stenciling, 6 for ..**1,650.00**
Windsor bow-bk side, 7-spindle, saddle seat, 37", 6 for **2,000.00**

Chests (Antique), See Also Dressers

Mahogany/cherry Federal, four graduated cockbeaded drawers with inlay, flaring French feet, refinished, replaced brasses, 45½x44¼x20", $2,125.00. (Photo courtesy Skinner, Inc.)

Basswood/pine Co w/brn grpt over yel, 3-drw, trn ft, 35x36x17"...**1,550.00**
Birch Chpndl, 5 grad drws w/batwing brasses, NH, 43x41x21" ...**3,000.00**
Birch/mahog flame vnr Sheraton, 4-drw, rope trn, 40x44x19" ...**1,750.00**
Butler's, curly maple/pine/mahog vnr Emp, crest:4 drw, rfn, 51x45x24"...**715.00**

Card, mahog Fed w/inlay, kidney-end top:cuff inlaid ft, rfn, 39x16" ..**4,400.00**
Cherry Chpndl, 3 short:2:5 grad drws, minor rprs, 70x44x23" **23,000.00**
Cherry Chpndl, 4 drw w/old rpl batwing brasses, ogee ft, 39x40x29" ..**6,600.00**
Cherry Chpndl, 4 dvtl drw, rpl batwing brasses, 39x40x29" **2,850.00**
Cherry Chpndl reverse serpentine, 4 grad drw, ogee ft, 32x40x20" ..**2,800.00**
Cherry Fed bow-front, grad drws:shaped bracket base, rfn, 34x38x23" ..**4,400.00**
Cherry Fed bow-front, 4 grad cockbeaded drw, rfn, 38x40x22" ..**3,525.00**
Cherry Fed bow-front, 4 grad cockbeaded drw:bracket ft, 32x36x22" ..**2,100.00**
Cherry Fed w/string inlay, 6 grad drw:skirt:bracket ft, rfn, 38x10x18" ..**6,500.00**
Cherry QA w/much cvg, 2 short:4 grad drw, rfn, 70x39x21" ..**8,800.00**
Cherry/birch/pine NE, 4 grad drw, trn pulls, 36x40x20" **1,750.00**
Cherry/curly maple Co, 7-drw, paneled ends, 49x42x22" **600.00**
Cherry/pine Chpndl, 4 drw, reeded pilasters, att Belden, 38x40x21"..**9,900.00**
Cherry/pine/curly maple Sheraton bow-front, 4-drw, trn legs, sm rpr ..**1,750.00**
Curly maple Chpndl, 2 short:4 grad drw, dvtl ft, rprs, 46x37x19"....**6,875.00**
Curly maple Co, 4 dvtl drw w/beaded edges, maple pulls, rprs, 44x45"..**1,450.00**
Curly maple Co Hplwht, 2-brd top:4 grad drw:Fr ft, 42x39x40" **4,000.00**
Curly maple/cherry Emp, dvtl drw:3 w/2 candle drws, rprs, 57x43" **880.00**
Mahog Chpndl serpentine, 4 grad cockbeaded drw, rfn, 33x35x20" ..**15,275.00**
Mahog English Chpndl, 4-drw, brass trim, old rstr/rprs, 40x47" **2,400.00**
Mahog European w/marquetry inlay, 4-drw, later marble top, 43x51" **770.00**
Mahog Fed bow-front, grad drw w/inlay:serpentine skirt:Fr ft, 36x41" ..**1,750.00**
Mahog Fed bow-front w/inlay, 4 grad drw, old finish, 34x36x22" ..**6,325.00**
Mahog flame vnr/pine/mahog English Hplwht bow-front w/inlay, 42x41" **1,450.00**
Mahog Sheraton bow-front, 4 dvtl drw, high trn legs, 39x40x19" **1,100.00**
Mahog/bird's-eye maple Fed w/string inlay, 4 grad drw, Fr ft, rfn, 39" ..**8,800.00**
Mahog/figured mahog Hplwht, 4 grad drw, eagle brasses, 40x46x23" ..**1,450.00**
Maple Chpndl, 2 short:4 grad long drws, RI, old rfn, 42x36x18"....**1,800.00**
Maple Chpndl, 6 grad thumb-molded drw:bracket base, rfn, 47x41x20" **3,300.00**
Maple/cherry Chpndl, 5 grad drw:bracket base, old rfn/rprs, 44x38x20" **3,800.00**
Oak English Chpndl w/burled vnr, 5-drw, rprs/rpl, 38x39x22" **1,650.00**
Pine Co Sheraton, 4-drw, trn legs w/button ft, rfn, 38x45x19" **550.00**
Pnt/molded pine, 6-brd, cvd front panel, MA, ca 1700, 24x50x19" **4,100.00**
Sugar, cherry Sheraton, dvtl drw, burled panels, KY, rpl/rstr **4,675.00**
Sugar, cherry/poplar, 2-compartment, dvtl, sq nails, rfn, 33x37x19" **1,100.00**
Walnut Chpndl, 4 grad drw, quarter columns, 37x32x20" **30,000.00**
Walnut English Hplwht, 5 dvtl drw w/beading, wood pulls, 44x42" **990.00**
Walnut/pine Chpndl, 8 grad/dvtl drw, dvtl case, rstr/rpl, 45x39x20" ..**3,300.00**
Walnut/poplar Chpndl, 3 short:5 grad dvtl drw, rfn/rstr, 52x41x24" **3,300.00**

Cupboards, See Also Pie Safes

Cherry Fed w/inlay, 2 panel do:2, cvd moldings, 84x46x22" **2,700.00**
Cherry/poplar Co, cornice:9-pane do:2 drw:2 panel do, 78x46x24" ..**2,500.00**
Corner, cherry/poplar Co, 2 6-pane do:2 shelves, cornice/apron, 85x60" **2,500.00**
Corner, curly maple Co, 2 8-pane do:2 panel do, sq nails, 85x50x21" ..**5,000.00**
Corner, mixed woods w/old gr, 2 panel do:shelves:drw, rpr/rpl, 78x48" ..**2,475.00**
Corner, Pine Co, 2 long panel do:1 short, 1890s, 87x47x22" ..**1,265.00**
Corner, poplar Co, dk grpt, 12-pane do:2 panel do, 2-pc, 84x43x19" **4,125.00**
Corner, poplar Co, 12-pane do:2 panel do, 2-pc, 78x46x24" **2,750.00**
Corner, poplar/pine, full-length do w/raised panels, rprs, 79x34x13" **500.00**
Corner, walnut Co, cornice:6-pane do:panel do:apron, 83x38x20" **4,950.00**
Corner, walnut Co, 2 8-pane do:2 flat panel do, old rfn, 82x46" **3,500.00**
Court, oak English, 2 mirrored do:lg w/cvd medallion, 2-part, 77x54" **550.00**
Court, oak English, 7 inset panels w/much cvg, 1649 on case, 57x56x23"..**1,100.00**
Court, oak English w/fine cvg, 3 do:2 drw:2 do, 54x66x23" **935.00**
Hanging, oak English, tombstone panel do, rosehead nails, 45x32x16" ...**550.00**
Hanging, pine Co, raised panel do, 2 int shelves, 25x16x6½", VG..**330.00**
Hanging corner, mahog English, panel do:drw, pnt int, 43x27x14" **225.00**
Hanging corner, pine Norwegian, shelf, scrolls & cvgs, 20th C, 41x21" ..**440.00**
Jelly, cherry/walnut Co, do w/2 inset panels, sq nails, rprs, 67x33" ...**750.00**
Jelly, pine cleaned to old gr, dbl do, removable top, 72x51x22" **2,000.00**
Jelly, pine Co, mortise & peg, red wash, old rstr hinges, 68x39x14"....**1,650.00**
Jelly, pine hutch-bk, panel do in base, rfn/rstr, 49x36x19" **1,375.00**

Jelly, pine/poplar Co, 2 dvtl drw:2 panel do:ball ft, red pnt, 56x45" ...**1,450.00**
Jelly, walnut Co, raised panel do w/beading, OH, rfn, 50x43x16"....**1,000.00**
Jelly, walnut/poplar Co, 2 drw:2 panel do, old rfn, 50x48x19" **1,045.00**
Kitchen, oak Co, paneled, 4-dr, 4-do, 2-pc, 19th C, 82x40x18" ...**925.00**
PA or OH, cornice:2 panel do:2 drw:2 do, old pnt, 2-pc, 82x50x18"...**7,000.00**
Pewter, pine Co, 4-shelf:single lg center do, mc pnt, early, 72x50".....**1,875.00**
Pewter, red-pnt pine, 3 shelf:base w/do by 4 drw, MA, 1790s, 83x70"..**7,500.00**
Pine Co step-bk corner, 9-pane do top:drw:2 panel do, 2-pc, 82"...**1,300.00**
Pine Co 2-part step-bk, raised panel dos, bl traces, 83x55x20" ..**4,300.00**
Pine English, arched opening, raised moldings, rfn, 90x48x25".......**1,200.00**
Pine NE 1-pc step-bk, old red wash, rprs, 70x36x16" **1,500.00**
Pine step-bk, 3-shelf top:panel do, old red pnt, 2-pc, 62x37"......**990.00**
Pnt pine step-bk, 4 open shelves:1-do base, NE, early 1800s, 80x40"....**3,500.00**
Poplar Co, cornice:2 do:shelf & 2 sm drw:3 drw:2 do, red pnt, 86x57"...**12,925.00**
Poplar Co, cornice:2 6-pane do:shelf:3 drw:2 do, old red, 85x49x10"....**9,200.00**
Poplar Co, cornice:4 raised-panel do, old pnt, 19th C, 75x40x16"....**2,800.00**
Poplar Co step-bk, blk on brn grpt, 4-do/shelf, 2-pc, OH, 82x50x20"....**2,750.00**
Poplar Co step-bk, 2-shelf:top:panel do, 1-pc, rfn/rstr, 70x28x19"....**600.00**
Step-bk, 2 6-pane do w/cutouts:2 drw:2 panel do, red pnt, 83x52" ..**6,600.00**
Walnut Co, 2 do:2 drw:2 do, old orange-red & blk pnt, 82"....**2,000.00**
Walnut Co, 2 panel do:shelf:2 do:2 panel do, 2-pc, 85x56x18"..**2,500.00**
Walnut Co, 2 6-pane do:shelf:3 drw:2 panel do, 1-pc, 90x51x21" ...**6,000.00**
Walnut Co step-bk, 2 6-pane do:shelf:2 drw:2 do, 1-pc, OH, 84"....**25,500.00**
Welsh, pine, 3-shelf top:base w/2 drw:4 panel do, rfn, 78x59x25"....**600.00**
Welsh oak/pine, open top:2 drws flanking shelf:2 drw:2 do, 19th C, 77".....**990.00**

Desks

Birch/bird's-eye maple/mahog Fed, slant-lid, cvd/inlay drws, 46x41" ..**1,645.00**
Butler's, mahog Am Late Fed, fold-out top, 38x37x18"............**2,500.00**
Butler's, mahog Fed w/inlay, fitted int:3 drw:Fr ft, 45x45x21" **2,750.00**
Butler's, mahog Late Fed w/flame grain vnr, fitted int, 50x43" ...**1,200.00**
Cherry Chpndl, closed bookcase:drop-lid:4 grad drw, rfn, 90x41"....**7,000.00**
Cherry Chpndl, dvd drw amid 4 compartments:4 short:4 grad drw, 41x36"...**1,880.00**
Cherry Chpndl, slant-lid, fitted int, rfn/rprs, 40x40x19"..........**1,500.00**
Cherry Chpndl, slant-lid, fitted int, rpl brasses/old rfn, 48x36x19" **4,400.00**
Cherry Co Hplwht, slant-lid:4 dvtl drws, old rstr, 47x40x20" **900.00**
Cherry Fed w/bookcase top, fold-out front:3 long drw, 68x40x21" ...**3,800.00**
Cherry/pine Hplwht, slant-lid, fitted int, dvtl, rfn, 43x40x18" **3,200.00**
Cherry/poplar Hplwht, slant-lid w/inlay, rpl brasses/rfn, 44x40x20" **625.00**
Cherry/poplar slant-lid w/chevron inlay base, 4 dvtl drw, rstr, 47x44"...**2,200.00**
Mahog Chpndl, cvd oxbow, slant-lid, grad drw, 44x42x22" **20,000.00**
Mahog Chpndl, oxbow front, relief-cvd drop, dvtl, rstr, 45x43x22" ..**1,870.00**
Mahog Chpndl, slant-lid, 4 dvtl drw, rprs/rpl, 45x34x19" **6,000.00**
Mahog Chpndl w/cvg, slant-lid:4 grad drws:c&b ft, 44x40x19" ...**5,000.00**
Mahog Fed, bookcase top:fall front:4 drw:Fr ft, rfn, 78x39x19" ...**4,400.00**
Mahog Fed w/bookcase top, scroll pediment, old rfn, 80x42x22" ...**4,000.00**
Mahog/hardwoods Chpndl style, leather inserts:5 drw, Hekman repro, 58" ...**825.00**
Mahog/pine English Chpndl-style ped, 9-drw, leather top, 54" ..**1,320.00**
Mahog/rswd vnr Fed, rectangle top:cylinder:2 short:2 long drws, 46"....**2,100.00**
Maple Chpndl, slant lid, fitted int, ogee ft, 1787, 42x36x38"..**13,200.00**
Pnt Chpndl, slant-lid:4 drw:bracket ft, red pnt, 41x36x18" **11,500.00**
Satinwood Geo III style w/polychrome, Carlton House, 1875, 37x42x23".....**8,000.00**
Walnut Chpndl, slant-lid, fitted int, rpl ft/rfn, 44x44x22" **2,475.00**
Walnut Dutch Baroque w/ebony, drop-front, mid-18th C, 42x38x20" ..**6,450.00**
Walnut Italian Baroque w/ebony & marquetry inlay, 17th C, 46x56" ...**14,000.00**
Walnut/poplar/pine Chpndl, slant-lid, dvtl, fitted int, PA, 44x40"....**3,850.00**

Dressers (Machine Age), See Also Chests

Mahog, mirror:2 short:2 long drw, G Baver NY Pat, 52x23"....**1,450.00**
Pine/poplar Sheraton w/flame grpt, 3 dvtl dry, NY, 40x36" **1,550.00**
Walnut Am Rococo w/figure, marble;4 grad drw, EC Peck, 39"...**1,400.00**
Walnut Vict w/figured walnut vnr, 5-drw, marble insert, 78x38" **385.00**

Dry Sinks

Poplar Co, 2 mortise & pegged do, sq nails, scrubbed, 34x64x21" ...**935.00**
Walnut Co w/red brn, single brd ends, 2 panel do, 30x51x22"...**1,375.00**
Walnut/pine, 3-drw:2 panel do, old bl-gr pnt, 37x50x21"...........**2,500.00**

Hall Pieces

Bench, cvd oak-panel bk, open arms, lift seat, ca 1900 ....**500.00**
Bench, mahog Fed style w/claw ft & gadrooning, drw, 46x42x20" ...**1,500.00**
Chair, James II style, trn legs/stretchers, antique uphl, 19th C ...**770.00**
Chair, oak Gothic, pierced arches:cvd apron:spade ft, 1860s, 52" **865.00**
Hall tree, CI Rococo Revival w/blk rpt, umbrella stand, 78" **990.00**
Hall tree, oak w/4 iron hooks & mirror, lift seat, 81x31x16" **500.00**
Hall tree, walnut Am Reform w/mirror, trn pegs, drw, 91x36x11" ...**925.00**
Hall tree bench, golden oak, beveled mirror, 4 hooks, 81x42" **880.00**
Mirror, oak w/rnd corners, 4 dbl hooks ea corner, 1900s, 40x25"............**250.00**
Pier table, blk pnt/gold decal, kidney shape, shelf, 20th C, 32x57x21" ...**110.00**
Pier table, cvd giltwood, stenciled mahog, bronze mts, paw ft, 40x44" ..**10,350.00**
Stand, CI Coalbrookdale, ornate foliage/Welcome banner, 1870s, 88x52" **9,900.00**
Table, blk enamel w/lt gold highlights, blk marble top, 20th C, 60" ...**500.00**
Table, giltwood Italian Neo-Classical, marble top, later pnt, 70"...**11,500.00**
Table, giltwood Louis XVI style, marble top, much cvg, 32x45x22", pr ...**2,500.00**
Table, giltwood Rococo style w/gr marble top, 35x54x19" **550.00**
Table, mahog Regency style w/foliate shell cvg, 20x36x60" **1,150.00**
Table, pnt Louis XVI style w/blk marble top, 20th C, 30x36x19" **415.00**
Table, walnut European cvd Rococo, scrolled legs, 20th C, 33x53x22" ...**770.00**

Highboys

Maple Queen Anne, scroll top with fan carvings, original brasses, 1760 – 1780, refinished, North Shore, 89x40x18", $9,200.00.

(Photo courtesy Skinner, Inc.)

Birch/pine QA, flat top:2 drw:4:5-drw base, old red wash, 2-pc, 71"...**33,000.00**
Cherry Hplwht, 3:2:4 grad drw:Fr ft, old rfn/rprs, 63x39" **6,000.00**
Cherry QA, cornice:5 grad drw:3 sm drw, rfn, 74x39x21" **19,500.00**
Cherry QA, cvd scroll top:3 short:4 grad:base w/1 long:3 drw, 84"..**8,800.00**
Cherry/curly maple Co, cornice:3 short:5 grad drw:ball ft, rprs, 72" ...**4,125.00**
Curly maple QA style, 11 dvtl drws w/cvd fans, modern repro, 70½"...**3,685.00**
Mahog Chpndl style, broken arch:reeded quarter columns:c&b ft, 88"...**1,550.00**
Mahog Chpndl style, 2 short:2:5 drw:4-drw base:c&b ft, 82x41" **1,600.00**

Maple Chpndl, 6 thumb-molded grad drw, rpl/rfn, 54x37x18" ...**1,900.00**
Maple QA, 5 grad drw:3 in base:cabriole legs, rfn, 68x38x22" ...**9,350.00**
Maple QA, 5 grad drw:5-drw base:cabriole legs:pad ft, rfn, 76x42x20"......**9,350.00**
Maple/birch QA, 2 short:4 grad:long:3 short drw, MA, 72x38x21"...**8,000.00**
Maple/curly maple/walnut QA, 8-drw, rstr/rpl, 85x46x24".......**4,400.00**
Oak/burl vnr English QA, 10-drw w/inlay, rstr/rpl, 62x39x19" .**1,875.00**
Walnut burl vnr/tiger maple inlay W&M, 6 trumpet-shaped legs, 68"...**40,000.00**
Walnut Chpndl, 3 short:5 grad drws, rprs, old dk rfn, 55x41x23"....**3,000.00**
Walnut QA, dvtl w/cvd shells, bat-wing brasses, old rfn, 88x42x22"..**14,375.00**
Walnut QA, scrolled cornice:3 short:3 grad drw:6 short drw, 80" ...**8,225.00**
Walnut/pine Co, 3 short:2:4 grad drws, rfn/rprs, 60x40x23" **3,500.00**
Walnut/poplar Chpndl, 3 short:2:4 grad drw, bat-wing brasses, 57" .**3,300.00**

Lowboys

Cherry/chestnut/pine QA, 1:3 short drw, 2-brd top, rfn, 39x36x23" ...**1,750.00**
Curly maple QA, 2 drw flank sm drw, shaped skirt, rstr, 30x25x15"...**1,000.00**
Mahog/oak English Chpndl style, 3-drw, rfn/rpl bat-wing brasses, 29"..**770.00**
Oak English QA, 3 dvtl drw, bat-wing brasses, 37x30x19" **1,000.00**
Walnut/pine W&M, 3 dvtl drw:serpentine X-stretchers, rpr, 30x34x22" ...**5,225.00**

Pie Safes

Cherry/poplar OH, 6 punched tins, removable shelves, trn ft, 46x41x20" **1,495.00**
Pine, 12 pierced tin panels, 2 dvtl drw, old putty pnt, 50x40x18" ...**1,045.00**
Poplar, 12 punched tins w/basket design, rfn, 57x46x19" **1,375.00**
Walnut Co, 2 6-pane do:2 drw:2 panel do, punched tin sides, 83x51x18" ...**3,850.00**
Walnut/butternut Co, 12 punched-star tin panels, rfn, 60x46x16" ...**1,200.00**
Walnut/poplar OH w/horse & rider punched tins, rprs, 65x53x20" .**3,200.00**
Walnut/poplar w/pierced tin, sq nails, bracket ft, 46x38x16" **600.00**

Secretaries

Mahog Emp, 2 1-pane do:2 drw:slant top:3 drw, 2-pc, 73x40", VG ..**1,200.00**
Mahog Fed w/bird's-eye maple drw fronts, ca 1800, 67x38" **8,815.00**
Mahog Hplwht, bookcase top:2-part top:4 drw base, 78x40x19" ..**12,650.00**
Mahog Louis XVI style, drw:fall front:leather top:2 drw:2 do, 57x37" **925.00**
Mahog vnr Hplwht w/satinwood banding, minor rstr, 46x38x21" ..**2,600.00**
Mahog/mahog flame vnr Hplwht 2-pc w/line inlay, old rprs, 57x35" ..**2,500.00**
Pine Geo IV w/bookcase top, 9-pane do:slant top:trn legs, 78" ...**1,495.00**
Rswd vnr Fr-style drop-front w/appl trim, fitted int, 53x27x13"......**660.00**
Walnut/poplar Vict 2-pc cylinder w/rswd vnr panels, 2-do top, 101" **3,575.00**

Settees

Bentwood hickory, splint seat & bk, Old Hickory, 36x47x27" **770.00**
Mahog Am Fed style, foliate scrolled arms, reuphl, 32x27x24", pr...**4,000.00**
Mahog English Hplwht, shield bk:scrolled arms: old uphl, 37x58" **550.00**
Mahog Transitional, oval medallion bk/serpentine base, reuphl, 33x42" **500.00**
Mahog Vict, 4-section, scrolled & padded arms, reuphl, 36x60x45" ...**1,000.00**
Mahog/flame vnr/oak Emp, trn legs, velvet uphl, 35x64x24" **550.00**
Oak w/ornate eagle/head/angel cvgs, red uphl, c&b ft, 42x70x21" ...**1,785.00**
PA decor, shaped crest:3 splats:curved arms:plank seat, 34x78x21" ...**3,750.00**
Pnt Windsor, 4-section crest, gold fruit/leaves on gr, rush seat, 85" ...**3,750.00**
Walnut Italian Rococo, arched bk/shaped arms & seat, reuphl, 48x73"...**5,875.00**

Shelves

Chestnut Co, 3-shelf pierced sides, NE, 19th C, 37x31x8" **300.00**
Etagere, corner; bird's-eye maple Vict, 8 trn supports, 62x32x24" **800.00**
Etagere, mahog English Regency, 3-shelf, 4 trn posts, brass ft, 41x18" ..**2,000.00**
Etagere, mahog Fed, 4-shelf:base w/2 drw:casters, 62x23x18" ..**1,725.00**
Etagere, walnut w/wht marble top, cut fretwork, cvd apron, 84x40" ..**2,245.00**
Faux marble pnt, 4 scroll brackets & cove molding, 1870s, 10x42x7" ..**4,400.00**

Mahog, scrolled crest & finials, 3-shelf, hangs, 37x23x10" **990.00**
Pine Co, blk grpt on red w/yel stripes, 3-shelf, 26x22x6" **440.00**
Pine Co, sq nails, drw w/brass pull, scalloped top, 11x14x6" **500.00**
Pine primitive, 3-shelf w/sq nails, old red rpt, 40x30x9½", VG ..**475.00**
Wall, walnut European 3-tier, trn legs/scroll-cut galleries, 50x39x19" ..**360.00**
Walnut Co, pierced leaves & scrolls, 3 grad shelves, 33x34x9½", VG....**200.00**

Sideboards

Cherry/bird's-eye maple/mahog Sheraton, 3 short:2 drw:4 do, 47x46x21" ..**3,000.00**
Curly maple Sheraton, gallery:3 drw:2 center drw & 2 do, 49x48x20" **10,450.00**
Flame-grain cherry vnr/pine Sheraton bow-front w/inlay, rfn, 79" ...**2,200.00**
Huntboard, pine Southern Co Hplwht, 4 dvtl drw:2 panel do, 42x36x22" **500.00**
Mahog English Hplwht-style bow-front w/inlay, ca 1900, 60"..**1,750.00**
Mahog Fed w/patterned inlay edge, cockbeaded drws, 37x61x23" **7,000.00**
Mahog Geo III style w/inlay, 2 drw & do, spade ft, 38x85x25"...**5,000.00**
Mahog Geo IV style, bksplash:molded top:2 drw & 2 do, 45x84x24"..**1,265.00**
Mahog Late Fed, bow-front, 3 drw:4 do:ball ft, 52x76x28" **3,500.00**
Mahog vnr Fed w/acanthus cvgs, 2-drw, 30x36x21" **3,025.00**
Mahog/crotch mahog vnr English Hplwht style w/flower cvg, 3-pc, 88"..**825.00**
Oak R/R, tooled leather decor, appl details, 40x60x24" **550.00**

Sofas

Beechwood Grecian w/gilt-bronze mts, scrolled arms, reuphl, 33x76" ..**3,000.00**
Cvd Louis XV style, cabriole legs/aprons, old velvet uphl, 78" ...**330.00**
Laminated rswd Rococo w/rose crest, reuphl, att J&M Meeks, 47x66" ..**5,500.00**
Laminated rswd w/Rococo cvg, reuphl, att J&J Meeks, 49x76" **6,000.00**
Mahog Am Fed, tubular crest, acanthus arms, paw ft, reuphl, 32x84" ...**2,500.00**
Mahog Am Rococo w/floral crest, reuphl, 33x76x27" **600.00**
Mahog Chpndl-style camel-bk, molded front legs, rpr, 34x80" ...**275.00**
Mahog Chpndl-style camel-bk, worn uphl, c&b front legs w/cvg, 82"...**300.00**

Mahogany Empire with floral crest and apron, reupholstered, 38x80x27", $1,000.00. (Photo courtesy Fontaine's Auction Gallery)

Mahog Fed, tablet bk w/cvg:foliate arms/paw ft, reuphl, 36x78" ..**2,300.00**
Mahog Fed w/cvg, beveled crest centers, ball ft, NE, 36x88" ...**1,200.00**
Mahog Geo III-style camel-bk w/scrolled arms, old uphl, 84"..**2,300.00**
Mahog Late Fed, arched bkrest w/scrolled arms, scrolled ft, 36x75x23"....**800.00**
Recamier, mahog Fed style, red brocade uphl, saber legs, 81" ..**1,200.00**
Walnut Chpndl style w/cvg, camel-bk, c&b ft, reuphl, 34x77x23"..**1,500.00**
Walnut Vict, medallion bk, serpentine front, old uphl, 40x65" ..**925.00**
Walnut Vict, molded fr w/rose cvgs, reuphl, rprs, 40x77x32" **660.00**

Stands

Basin, mahog Fed, scrolled splashboard:2 sm drw:shelf:drw, MA, 40x20"....**235.00**
Canterbury, mahog Sheraton style, brass casters, dvtl drw, 19x20x14"....**250.00**

Cherry Co Sheraton, dvtl drw w/maple vnr front, trn legs, 28x18x20"...**465.00**
Cherry Emp bow-front, 2-drw w/burl vnr panels, 30x22x22" **880.00**
Cherry/bird's-eye maple Sheraton, dvtl drw, 26x18x18" **400.00**
Cherry/curly maple Sheraton style, dvtl drw, modern repro, 25x17x16" ...**140.00**
Cherry/mahog vnr Sheraton, 2-drw:trn legs w/rope-twist cvgs, 39x20x18"..**440.00**
Cherry/poplar Co Sheraton, 2 dvtl drw, ring-trn legs, ball ft.......**750.00**
Cherry/poplar Sheraton, 1-brd top:2 dvtl drw:trn legs, rfn, 39x18x18"..**715.00**
Curly maple Co Sheraton, dvtl drw, ring-trn legs, rfn, 39x18x18"...**1,045.00**
Curly maple Co Sheraton, dvtl drw:trn legs:ball ft, 29x21x20"...**825.00**
Curly maple Co Sheraton, 1-brd:dvtl drw:trn legs:ball ft, 38x22x18" ..**1,550.00**
Curly maple Co Sheraton, 2-brd top:dvtl drw:trn legs, 37x17" sq...**825.00**
Drop-leaf, curly maple Hplwht style, dvtl drw, sq legs, 30x15x17"...**300.00**
Fern, brass w/marble insert, cabriole legs w/animal-head ft, 30x13"...**85.00**
Fern, mahog Hplwht w/inlay, 2-tier, sq legs, 39x12" dia **200.00**
Fern, walnut Co, 9 pnt platforms on trn support, NY, 1860s, 55x38"..**1,175.00**
Fern, walnut R/R, marble top:molded frieze:3 legs, 29x16" **635.00**
Figured maple/cherry Co Sheraton, dvtl drw, rfn, 39x22x20" **440.00**
Music, walnut R/R, gilt incised/ebonized decor, 45x15" **230.00**
Poplar Co Sheraton, 1-brd top:drw:tapered ft, old red, 27x17" sq **660.00**
Sewing, cherry Sheraton, dvtl drw:ped w/3 saber legs, OH, 39x19x15"...**450.00**
Sewing, rswd, hinged top w/fitted int:ped:tripod:claw ft, 30x19x16" ..**2,875.00**
Walnut Fed, overhang top:drw:4 tapered legs, 39x19x22" **550.00**
Walnut Hplwht, dvtl drw, 1-brd top w/age split, OH, 29x19x15" **990.00**
Work, tiger maple Fed, 2-drw, trn legs w/colonettes, rfn, 37x20x15"....**5,425.00**
Writing, walnut Am, lift top w/fitted int:skirt:trn legs, 38x21x18"...**115.00**

Stools

Footstool, cvd oak w/heart cutouts, worn pnt over early red, sm ...**300.00**
Footstool, leather top, pnt cabriole legs, brass tacks, 13x17x12"...**220.00**
Footstool, pine Co w/slip seat, reshaped aprons, 14x16x12"........**155.00**
Footstool, poplar w/arched cutouts, mortised top, apron, 7x16x6"..**150.00**
Footstool, poplar w/old red-brn wash, sq nails, 8¼x15x9"...........**195.00**
Footstool, walnut serpentine stretcher base & legs, pegged, 12x19x16" ...**300.00**
Footstool, walnut/pine, cyma cutouts on legs, 8x18x6" **100.00**
Gout, mahog Emp, serpentine ends, reuphl, 8x14x13" **330.00**
Piano, mahog Geo IV, ring-trn legs, 20x12" dia..........................**145.00**
Piano, rswd Am Late Fed, padded adjustable seat, 20x15x15" **300.00**
Piano, walnut Italian Grotto style, shell seat: lion-mask fish base **2,650.00**

Tables

Banquet, mahog Regency style, reeded edge:trn peds, 44x144" w/leaves.....**3,750.00**
Banquet, mahog Regency style, 2-ped, brass paw ft, 114"+2 leaves...**3,000.00**
Banquet, mahog Sheraton, 2-part, hinged leaves, rfn/rpr, open: 100"...**4,125.00**
Breakfast, mahog English Sheraton, tilt-top, saber legs, rfn, 53"...**2,850.00**
Breakfast, mahog Fed w/cvg, 2 dws:cvd ped:legs, NY, 32x41x21"...**2,585.00**
Card, mahog Chpndl, serpentine front & beading, 39x30x14" ...**7,650.00**
Card, mahog Fed w/inlay, bowed top:paneled skirts:slim legs, 30x36x18" **21,000.00**
Card, mahog vnr Fed demilune w/fan inlay, att Wm Whitehead, 39x36x18"..**54,625.00**
Card, mahog/bird's-eye maple vnr, elliptical front, Boston, 30x36x17" **3,000.00**
Center, mahog Emp style, bronze mts, 30x29" dia....................**3,000.00**
Center, mahog Fed, marble top:cylinder shaft:tripod:ball ft, 37" dia..**2,250.00**
Center, mahog Portuguese Baroque style w/brass mts, 1850s, 35x60x33".....**16,450.00**
Center, rswd Wm IV, narrow frieze, column:3 lobed ft, 30x48" dia **4,000.00**
Corner, hardwoods Fr w/marquetry inlay, pegged aprons, 30x41x31"...**575.00**
Demilune, pine Co, 3 beaded sq legs, str skirt, old gr pnt, 28x40x20" **460.00**
Dining, mahog Late Fed, 2 D-shaped parts, ea w/drop-leaf, open: 92" ..**1,500.00**
Dressing, cherry QA w/cvg, long:3 short drw:cabriole legs, 34x36" ..**7,650.00**
Dressing, cherry/mahog Fed, shaped bkbrd:2 short:4 grad drws, 40x30"....**800.00**
Dressing, cherry/mahog vnr Sheraton, step-bk, 3 drws:4, 40x39x22"..**1,325.00**
Dressing, cherry/pine/poplar Sheraton style, dvtl drw, 39x38x18" **660.00**
Dressing, decor Co Sheraton, fruit stencil w/gold, drw, 34x34x17" **1,550.00**
Dressing, Fr w/sunburst vnr & band inlay top, drw, 29x18x13" ..**1,650.00**

Dressing, mahog Sheraton style, curly maple vnr drw front, 2-brd top....**495.00**
Dressing, NE, yel w/HP fruit/foliage/borders, 1820s, 38x33" **1,200.00**
Dressing, walnut Chpndl, 2 brd top:4 drw:aprons:Spanish ft, 34x42" ...**770.00**
Dressing, walnut QA w/beading & herringbone band, MA, 30x33x28"..**25,000.00**
Drop-leaf, birch Hplwht, rfn w/orig red traces, 40"+2 12" leaves....**475.00**
Drop-leaf, birch QA, rpl top:cabriole legs:pad ft, rfn, 48"+2 leaves...**600.00**
Drop-leaf, cherry Chpndl style, pegged, 1-brd top/2-brd leaves, 40x31" ...**275.00**
Drop-leaf, cherry Co Sheraton, trn legs, 1-brd, rfn, 39"+2 15" leaves...**300.00**
Drop-leaf, cherry Sheraton, 6 ring-trn legs, rpl top & leaves **440.00**
Drop-leaf, curly maple/cherry Co Sheraton, drw, ball ft, 40"+leaves **935.00**
Drop-leaf, figured vnr Biedermeier style, cvd paw ft, 33+2 9" leaves ..**3,850.00**
Drop-leaf, mahog English Chpndl, 1-brd top, rprs/rfn, 48"+leaves **500.00**
Drop-leaf, mahog Sheraton, trn legs, 1-brd top, 32x20x36"+leaves....**700.00**
Drop-leaf, mahog/flame vnr English cvd, 1-brd top, 37"+2 leaves **715.00**
Drop-leaf, mahog/pine English Chpndl, pegged, rfn, 48"+2 leaves...**900.00**
Drop-leaf, walnut QA, scrolled skirt:trifid ft, rfn/rprs, open: 50" ...**3,525.00**
Drop-leaf sofa, mahog Fed, drws in skirt, rfn, 27x40x28" **3,400.00**
End, 2-tier, marble top w/ormolu: 2-drw, blk pnt, 20th C, 35x29x20" ..**1,500.00**
Game, Fr marquetry, oxbow aprons, brass trim, cabriole legs, 30x32x23"....**1,375.00**
Game, mahog Fed w/inlay at top & legs, Boston, rfn, 39x36x18"...**17,000.00**
Game, Moroccan leather top, bone & wood inlay, 32x30x16", pr **1,800.00**
Gate-leg, maple Baroque, drw, ring-trn legs, 1720-80, 48"+leaves....**19,550.00**
Gate-leg, maple W&M, drop-leaf top, apron w/drw, rfn/rstr, 27x41x48"....**650.00**
Gate-leg, tiger maple/maple, drw, trn ft, rpl pull, old rfn, 45" ..**1,500.00**
Hutch, pine Co, scrubbed 3-brd top, rpl pegs, 38x48x35".........**2,200.00**
Hutch, pine Co w/old rfn, 3-brd top, 29x48x30½" **1,875.00**
Hutch, pine w/old red, cyma cut-out ends, hinged lid, 3-brd top, 63".....**2,900.00**
Hutch, pine/hickory Co, 3-brd scrubbed top, old pegs, 38x49x39"...**1,500.00**
Library, mahog w/burled vnr panels, reeded corners, 30x72x36"....**330.00**
Library, oak Am Gothic, molded top:cornice frieze, scroll ft, 54" **5,750.00**
Library, rswd Wm IV, 2 blind frieze drw, trestle base, 30x51x26"...**2,750.00**
Library, walnut Portuguese, rope cvg, raised panel drws, 19th C, 46"...**6,325.00**
Pembroke, birch/pine Hplwht, dvtl drw, 34"+2 scalloped leaves....**500.00**
Pembroke, Cherry Fed w/inlay, ½-rnd leaves, rfn, 38x37x20¾"..**2,500.00**
Pembroke, cherry Hplwht, drw in apron, prof rstr, 34"+2 11" leaves ..**4,000.00**
Sawbuck, pine, 3-brd top, breadbrd ends, rfn, 28x62x37" **1,250.00**
Sewing, walnut w/cvg, drw, cvd legs w/appl rosettes, brass c&b ft....**660.00**
Sewing drop-leaf, rswd Vict, serpentine top:drw:scrolled legs......**350.00**
Side, Flemish Baroque w/ebony & tortoise-shell inlay, 39x33x22"...**2,645.00**
Side, mahog Geo III, banded top w/inlay, cuffed ft, 34x72x30"...**4,600.00**
Side, mahog Louis XV style, single ped, 30x25" **1,000.00**
Side, rswd Am w/marble top, serpentine front, 1850s, 31x42x16"...**500.00**
Side, walnut Chpndl style, 2-brd top, rfn, ca 1900, 38x30x18"...**165.00**
Tavern, butternut/maple QA, mortise & peg, 2-brd rnd top, 37x28"...**1,300.00**
Tavern, maple Co QA, 2-brd top, pegs & rosehead nails, 27x36" **825.00**
Tavern, maple Co QA, 4-brd top (old), worn ft, old rfn, 24x36x24"..**825.00**
Tavern, maple/pine, Co Hplwht w/old red, scrubbed top, 26x45½" ...**1,980.00**
Tavern, maple/pine Co QA, mortise & peg, old rpl 1-brd top, rfn ..**2,200.00**
Tavern, tiger maple, 2-brd top, drw, EX patina, 28x39x22" **8,000.00**
Tavern, walnut/pine, mortise & peg, dvtl drw, 1-brd top, 32x40x24"...**2,500.00**
Tea, curly maple QA style, scallop:graceful legs:pad ft, 37x29x20" ...**1,045.00**
Tea, mahog Chpndl, tilt-top:tripod:arris pad ft, rfn, 31x28" dia **1,000.00**
Tea, mahog Chpndl tilt-top w/birdcage, snake ft, rprs, 37x32" dia....**440.00**
Tea, mahog cvd Chpndl tilt-top, dish top:tripod:c&b ft w/cvg, 26x25" ..**600.00**
Tilt-top, birch Chpndl, snake ft, att J Short (MA), 28x33x34"......**2,200.00**
Tilt-top, walnut/cherry Chpndl, birdcage, c&b ft, rfn, 37x23x25"...**1,650.00**
Trestle, pine 3-brd top:CI scroll ends w/ivy & fleur-de-lis, 29x95x24"...**275.00**
Wine tasting, hardwood English, mortise & peg/shoe ft, 28x40" dia...**350.00**
Work, ash/pine w/yel & red traces, drw (G-), 3-brd top, 54" **385.00**
Work, birch/butternut Co Sheraton, dvtl drw, 29x30x18" **385.00**
Work, mahog Fed w/cvg, bamboo-trn/reeded legs, old rfn, 28x20x16" ...**2,450.00**
Work, maple Fed, canted corners:drw:bag drw:str skirt, 38x15x21"...**2,875.00**
Work, tiger maple Co, drop-leaf:recessed drw:trn legs, 30x19x21" ...**1,650.00**
Work, walnut/chestnut Co Sheraton, drw, 2-brd top, ball ft, 28" **500.00**

Work, walnut/pine Co Hplwht, dvtl drw, 2-brd top, rfn, 28x38x24" ..**600.00**
3-tier, mahog Wm IV, trn supports/short legs, brass castors, 26x18x18"....**1,495.00**

Wardrobes

Figured walnut vnr Fr breakdown, 2 mirror front:drw, 99x46" **715.00**
Kas, pine/poplar, 2 raised-panel do:2 drw, old mustard pnt, 67"....**880.00**
Kas, polar w/brn grpt, 2 panel do, breakdown type, 1854, 82"...**1,650.00**
Linen press, cherry/flame vnr/poplar Sheraton, 4-drw, att KY, 89x43" ...**5,000.00**
Linen press, cherry/poplar, 2 dvtl drw, 1-pc, rstr, 90x52x18"....**2,000.00**
Linen press, cherry/poplar Co Hplwht, 2-pc, att KY, 92½x42" ..**4,000.00**
Linen press, mahog Wm IV, cornice:2 panel do:6 drw:plinth, 100x60" ..**4,000.00**
OH 1-pc w/orig dk red pnt/overvarnish, dvtl drw base, 80x42x18"....**1,875.00**
Pine Co, later mc floral decor, HR 1802 on cornice, 72x50x22" ...**425.00**
Pine Co w/pnt floral panels, drw in base, dtd 1805, 70x48" **935.00**
Poplar NE, cornice:2 recessed-panel do:drw, red stain 81x58"...**2,000.00**
Walnut Co, cornice: 3-panel dbl do:sq legs, pegged, 84x54x27" ...**1,350.00**

Washstands

Corner, curly maple/bird's-eye vnr Co Sheraton, dvtl drw, rfn, 39x24"...**1,875.00**
Corner, mahog Fed w/ebonized band inlay, 39x30x18" **1,295.00**
Curly maple Co, shelf:dvtl drw, rpl top, golden rfn, 32x19x17" **660.00**
Mahog Late Fed, splashbrd top:drw:shelf:trn legs, 40x19x16" **230.00**
Mahog Sheraton, dvtl gallery, drw in base, att MA, 19x15" **1,450.00**
Mahog Sheraton, ironstone bowl in cutout:shelf:drw, 38x18x15" **550.00**
Maple/poplar Co Sheraton, dvtl drw, trn legs, 36x38x18"..........**300.00**
ME pnt, 1-drw, mustard yel w/blk triangles/fruit/etc, 35x17x17", EX..**925.00**
Pine w/old brn grpt on mustard, dvtl drw, 37x17x14"..................**440.00**
Pnt Co, mustard w/gold & gr stenciling, scroll bksplash:drw, 38x17"..**975.00**
Walnut Late Fed, splashbrd top:drw:shelf, 34x24x17" **175.00**

Miscellaneous

Bed steps, 3-step, pnt cherry & pine, gold stringing, 21x20x18", EX....**1,500.00**
Bedroom suite, bird's-eye maple faux bamboo, Horner NY, 1875, 5-pc......**13,800.00**
Book rack, mahog w/band inlay, acorn cutouts on shaped ends, 9x15x9" **55.00**
Bookmill, mahog English, revolving, egg & dart molded top, 40x21" ..**1,150.00**
Cellarette, oak European, wrought-iron hdls, 10x16x10" **550.00**
Dumbwaiter, mahog Geo III style, 3-tier, urn-form stem, c&b ft ...**775.00**
Parlor suite, walnut Am Rococo, triple-bk sofa+4 side & 2 armchairs, ..**2,550.00**
Pedestal, mahog Fr style, marble:tapered legs w/brass caps, 47x13" sq ...**300.00**
Pew, pine w/orig red & blk pnt, wide brd ends, sq nails, 56" **330.00**
Quilt rack, 3-part folding, dry lime gr over wht, 63x71"..............**660.00**
Server, pine/poplar decor Co Sheraton, 2-drw, shelf, rprs, 36x36x16" ..**550.00**
Shotgun case, dvtl mahog w/brass inlay on lid, English, 18x31x10" **400.00**

Galena

Potteries located in the Galena, Illinois, area made generally plain utility wares with lead glaze and often found in a pumpkin color with some slip decoration or splashes of other colors. These potteries thrived from the early 1830s until sometime around 1860. In the listings that follow, all items are made of red clay unless noted otherwise.

Jar, redware, med gr w/orange spots, slanted shoulders, 8", EX....**250.00**
Jug, dk gr w/burnt orange spots, 8¼", EX **880.00**
Jug, pumpkin color w/3 yel 'balloons,' strap hdl, 10" **5,775.00**

Galle

Emile Galle was one of the most important producers of cameo glass in France. His firm, founded in Nancy in 1874, produced beautiful cameo in the Art Nouveau style during the 1890s, using a variety of techniques. He also produced glassware with enameled decoration, as well as some fine pottery — animal figurines, table services, vases, and other objets d' art. In the mid-1880s he became interested in the various colors and textures of natural woods and as a result began to create furniture which he used as yet another medium for expression of his artistic talent. Marquetry was the primary method Galle used in decorating his furniture, preferring landscapes, Nouveau floral and fruit arrangements, butterflies, squirrels, and other forms from nature. It is for his furniture and his cameo glass that he is best known today. All Galle is signed. Our advisor for this category is Don Williams; he is listed in the Directory under Missouri.

Cameo

Atomizer, floral/broad leaves, amethyst on frost, bell form, 5½" ..**325.00**
Bottle, leaves/seed pods, gr/yel on orange to clear, stopper, 10", NM....**600.00**
Bowl, poppies, orange on clear, 4¾x7" **700.00**
Box, rabbit & trees, purple on clear, egg form, 4" **900.00**
Lamp, palm fronds on dome shade; base w/3-D lion, 2 palm tree supports **21,900.00**
Tumbler, water lilies, amber on lt bl, 4" **650.00**

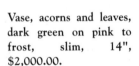
Vase, acorns and leaves, dark green on pink to frost, slim, 14", $2,000.00.

Vase, acorns/oak leaves, gr/brn/blk, Oriental mk, 6¼" **2,900.00**
Vase, bleeding hearts, amethyst on frost, shaped neck/bell body, 5"....**300.00**
Vase, clematis, lav/bl on frost & yel, swollen, ftd, 14½" **4,000.00**
Vase, clematis (EX detail), pk/amethyst on frost, ovoid, 6½" ..**3,200.00**
Vase, ferns, dk gr on lt gr, 3¼" **450.00**
Vase, floral, amethyst on yel, dbl-gourd shape, 4¾"....................**500.00**
Vase, floral, bl/gr on frost, swollen cylinder, 10" **4,750.00**
Vase, floral, purple-brn on yel-orange, shouldered, 2½" **500.00**
Vase, floral, red on yel to frost, bulbous, Oriental mk, 9".........**3,750.00**
Vase, floral, red on yel to frost, shouldered, ftd, 23" **11,000.00**
Vase, floral, red/orange on frost, slim, Oriental mk, 17"...........**3,500.00**
Vase, floral (extensive), lt/dk amethyst on frost, ftd, 3½x3½" **525.00**
Vase, floral (extensive), pk/purple on clear, Oriental mk, 4¾" **2,000.00**
Vase, floral spires/narrow leaves, amethyst on bl/frost, tapered, 6x6" ..**600.00**
Vase, floral/lg leaves, brn on yel, bulbous w/can neck, 4" **550.00**
Vase, grapevines/grapes, umber/amber on rose to frost, shouldered, 8" **425.00**
Vase, irises, lav/brn on frost to yel, slim, ftd, 14" **2,900.00**
Vase, irises, purple on frost to purple, flared ft, 10½" **2,600.00**
Vase, lady slippers landscape, gr to wht mottle, swollen, 6½" ..**2,200.00**
Vase, leaves/berries, brn/red on frost & yel, ftd, 11½" **6,500.00**
Vase, leaves/berries, gr/brn on brn/frost/gr, ftd, 9"....................**4,500.00**

Vase, leaves/buds, purple on lt purple/yel/frost, long tube neck, 7"...**650.00**
Vase, magnolia blossoms, red on yel to frost, bulbous, 12" **7,500.00**
Vase, maple leaves, dk gr on lt gr & yel frost, disk ft, 8"..............**650.00**
Vase, morning glories (EX detail), lt/dk red on yel, ovoid, 12½"..**4,250.00**
Vase, mtns/trees, bl/gr on gr & frost, stick neck, 7" **1,000.00**
Vase, nasturtiums, orange to clear, cylinder neck/globular base, 13" **1,800.00**
Vase, orchids, dk brn on med brn/orange/frost, ftd, 15"...........**4,500.00**
Vase, orchids, dk purple on yel, cone shape, 6½" **500.00**
Vase, peonies, gr on red, baluster, 4¾" **1,800.00**
Vase, sm flower clusters/lg blade leaves, red on yel & frost, 3½" ...**500.00**
Vase, snapdragons, maroon on pk, teardrop form, 6¾" **650.00**
Vase, sweet pea vines, gr to pk, cylinder w/globular base, 11¼"..**950.00**
Vase, trees, dk bl on wht w/bl 'mtns', flattened sphere w/cup neck, 6" **900.00**
Vase, trees (lg), bl/gr on frost, ogee w/short trumpet ft, 6" **850.00**
Vase, trees/lake/bushes, amber/dk gr on frost, conical, 9½"......**2,100.00**
Vase, trees/mtns, brn/purple on frost & yel, cylindrical, 9" **3,000.00**
Vase, Veronica sprigs, lav/gr, waisted cylinder, 19" **2,500.00**
Vase, water lilies (EX detail), amber/gr/teal on apricot frost, 10x4"....**1,600.00**
Vase, woodland/lake/birds, gr tones on frost, banjo form, 7" **1,500.00**

Enameled Glass

Bowl, boy picks fruit on amber, 2 sides fold, 3rd w/petals, unmk, 9"....**345.00**
Bowl, orchids (3), gold on gr, folded petal rim, 1¾x6" **475.00**
Box, thistle on amber, 6"...**900.00**
Cruet, praying mantis & clover on amber, 8" **2,250.00**
Cup, stylized flowers w/gold, 2⅝", pr......................................**150.00**
Decanter, grasshopper/wildflowers, mc w/blk & gold, bulbous, 8½" ...**1,035.00**
Dresser set, floral, amber/wht/turq/gr/gold, 2 bottles+jar+tray.....**800.00**
Rose bowl, floral w/gold on wht to clear gray, 4¾"....................**1,000.00**
Salt cellar, rain scene w/trees, 1x2", NM **2,000.00**
Vase, floral branch, mc w/gold on gr, emb ribs, 15¾"...............**4,600.00**
Vase, leaves/tendrils, mc on amber, sq, 4⅜"............................**700.00**
Vase, orchids, gr/maroon mottle, appl buttons, globular base, 13½"...**2,000.00**

Marquetry, Wood

Box, country scene inlay, mixed woods, 14x8x5", VG **1,950.00**
Nesting tables, various inlay designs, largest: 27x22x15", 4 for **4,750.00**
Table, occasional; 2-tier, foliate design, stretcher shelf, 39x23".....**2,500.00**
Vitrine, flowers, tops/sides/front panel, glass door, 53x24" **6,500.00**

Pottery

Bowl, faience, flowers/shore HP int, foliate shape, gilt rim, 10¼" ...**315.00**
Figurine, cat, yel w/bl & wht hearts, gr glass eyes, 13" **2,900.00**
Pitcher, Fr peasant, J-shape body w/loop hdl, prof rstr spout, 8x6" ...**865.00**
Vase, floral swag, pastels on gray, side festoons, cut rim, ftd, 5"...**700.00**
Vase, grasshopper on gr & brn w/gold, floriform top, 3½"...........**635.00**

Gambling Memorabilia

Gambling memorabilia from the infamous casinos of the West and items that were once used on the 'Floating Palace' riverboats are especially sought after by today's collectors.

Ashtray, Hotel Humboldt, Winnemucca NV, smoke glass w/logo, 40s, EX...**40.00**
Ashtray, Montmartre, Havana Cuba, clear w/card suits on corners, 4x4"...**45.00**
Chip, Deauville Habanam $25, gr w/wht center, 1950s, EX..........**90.00**
Chip, Flamingo Hotel, $1, beige w/blk & red letters, EX.............**170.00**
Chip, Harold's Club $100 For Fun, EX...**30.00**
Chip, Hotel Hacienda Card Room/$25 Non-Negotiable, maroon, 1950s, M **80.00**
Chip, The Dunes, gray w/Sultan center inlay, ca 1955, EX.........**130.00**

Dealer's tie, Primadonna Club, Reno NV in wht on blk, EX **35.00**
Dice, Flamingo Hotel, red w/wht dots, set of 6, MIB (clear w/logo)...**65.00**
Dice, ivory, bbl shaped, late 1800s, EX, pr..**65.00**
Dice, Pan Am Airlines logo, 5 w/leather rolling cup, EX **30.00**
Dice, SS Rex, Long Beach gambling boat, 1930s, VG+, pr...........**45.00**
Gambling device, Hawtin's All-Win, wood & metal, ca 1930s, EX....**325.00**
Game, Chuck-a-Luck, Evans, NP cage/orig dice, late 1800s, 21x18", EX..**1,250.00**
Game, Deluxe Monte Carlo Casino, roulette, craps, etc, 1950s, EXIB....**30.00**
Glass, Tiki; Bally's Casino Reno NV, 7¼"...**8.00**
Keno goose, wooden, late 1800s, EX...**550.00**
Punchboard, Lucky Bucks, Indian graphic, 1940s, 7½x4¾", NM....**22.50**
Punchboard, Rodeo Bucks, 1930s, 9x5", M **35.00**
Punchboard, Round-Up Time, 1940s, 13½x11½", NM.................**35.00**
Roulette wheel, handmade, pnt wood, late 1800s, 16" dia, VG+....**300.00**
Wheel, pnt wood w/gold wash, on stand, 1880s, 53x32½" dia, VG.....**3,200.00**

Roulette wheel, miniature, wooden, missing ball for wheel and accessories, 2x10x5", EX, $475.00. (Photo courtesy Early Americana History Auctions)

Game Calls

Those interested in hunting and fishing collectibles are beginning to take notice of the finer specimens of game calls available on today's market.

Crow, Herter's #309, 1962, EX (VG box).....................................**45.00**
Crow, Lohman's #4, EXIB **15.00**
Crow, PS Olt Crow Call Record, 45 rpm, 1950, VG **25.00**
Crow, PS Olt Model #E-1, EX **25.00**
Crow, PS Olt Model #V-16, 3¼", EX **20.00**
Crow, Ranger, wood, handmade, Sears & Roebuck, EXIP (tube)..**60.00**
Crow, Sears #2193, EXIB...**25.00**
Crow, Tex Wirtz Champion, wood, 1960s, 4¼" **30.00**
Duck, Bill Grant's #782, wood w/brass collar, EX.........................**60.00**
Duck, Charles H Perdew, Pat 11/2/09, cedar w/nickel band, 5¼".....**260.00**
Duck, Deluxe Laminated Olla Banded Dixie Mallard Call, 1973 ....**185.00**
Duck, E Stoper KCMO, 4⅞"..**475.00**
Duck, Faulk's WA-11, wood, paper label, 4½" **20.00**
Duck, Herter's #272, Glodo-Type, NM (VG box) **30.00**
Duck, Iverson #CT-4, mahog w/brass reed, 5¾" **130.00**
Duck, NC Hansen Broadbill Call, EX **85.00**
Duck, PS Olt Model #D-2, Bakelite, EX **60.00**
Duck, PS Olt Model #66, EX..**110.00**
Duck, Scotch #1401, 11", EX (G box) **25.00**
Duck, Thomas Dual Reed #158D, MIP **20.00**
Fox, Jake Frye & Son, wood w/plastic end, EX (VG box) **50.00**
Fox/Coyote, PS Olt #T-20, EXIB...**25.00**
Game, Lohman No 111, wood, EX (VG box) **20.00**
Game, Sure Shot Game Calls, Buck 500, wood w/paper label, VG ..**15.00**
Goose, Faulk's #CH-44, 4⅞", EX (G box)..**20.00**
Goose, Lohamn's #301, 1973, MIB...**25.00**
Hawk, Sta-Dri #602, MIB **65.00**

Johnny Stewart's Electri-Call, 5 calling records, metal, EX.........**110.00**
Predator, fox, wolves & cats, Weems Dual-Tone Wild Call, EXIB....**35.00**
Predator, Herter's, Gludo type, amber reed holder, insert, 1950s, EXIB.....**80.00**
Predator, PS Olt #33, EXIB...**70.00**
Shorebird whistle, brass w/figural bird atop, dtd 1923, VG...........**50.00**
Turkey, Leon's Turkey Caller, diaphragm type, 1950s, EXIB.........**85.00**
Turkey, Lynch Modified World Champion, 1956, w/orig pamphlet **900.00**
Turkey, ML Lynch #102, 1958, VG **90.00**

Gameboards

Gameboards, the handmade ones from the eighteenth and nineteenth century, are collected more for their folk art quality than their relation to games. Excellent examples of these handcrafted 'playthings' sell well into the thousands of dollars; even the simple designs are often expensive. If you are interested in this field, you must study it carefully. The market is always full of 'new' examples. Well-established dealers are often your best sources; they are essential if you do not have the expertise to judge the age of the boards yourself. Our advisor for this category is Louis Picek; he is listed in the Directory under Iowa.

Baseball dart game, cork on plywood w/pnt dmn, ca 1930, 22" sq......**1,400.00**
Checkers, blk/gilt w/yel & blk on oak, 19th C, 19x18"............**1,600.00**
Checkers, cream & gr w/red, dbl-sided, 1890s, 15x18".............**1,725.00**
Checkers, eng glass, geometric borders, sgn/dtd 1869, 19⅜" sq.....**1,000.00**
Checkers, leather-covered pine, 19" sq..**85.00**
Checkers, mc pnt, box w/mitered fr & pull-out drw, 19x25" ..**1,600.00**
Checkers, mc w/geometric border, brass ft, lt wear, 1850s, 14" sq....**4,000.00**
Checkers, red/blk/yel pnt wood, 2 drws, 19th C, 22x28" **1,295.00**
Checkers, red/wht/bl pnt, ca 1876, 19x23¾" **2,300.00**
Checkers, 7-color pnt wood w/appl molding & gold, 19th C, 18" sq **1,650.00**
Checkers/backgammon, mc pnt on single brd, scribed decor, 22x15" ...**2,500.00**
Checkers/backgammon, orig mc pnt, appl breadboard ends, 17x13"...**660.00**
Checkers/backgammon, red/blk/orange/gr on pine, ca 1900, 22" sq....**985.00**
Checkers/Fox & Geese, gr/cream/mustard/red, 1890s, 15" sq...**1,000.00**
Checkers/parcheesi, appl litho flower & animal decals, mc pnt, 16x17" ..**2,500.00**
Checkers/parcheesi, mc pnt w/gold striping, 22" sq **500.00**
Checkers/parcheesi, red/blk/mustard pnt on wood, 1900, 31x19¼" ..**2,300.00**
Checkers/parcheesi, 8-point star/foliage/etc, appl fr, 23x25" **4,000.00**
Chinese checkers, mc pnt wood, ca 1900, 19½", EX..................**920.00**
Fox & Geese, pine, flower shape w/appl tin game-pc holder, 1930s, 9"....**115.00**
Parcheesi, appl fr on star-centered brd w/mc pnt, 1900s, 14" sq.......**1,600.00**
Parcheesi, bucking bronco center, tractor & dogs at corners, 1920s...**2,650.00**
Parcheesi, castle mc decor on pine, ca 1930, 23" sq **2,300.00**
Parcheesi, gray/blk/yel-gr on pine, ca 1900, 22½" sq **800.00**
Parcheesi, mc mosaic-like field, 1890, 19" sq.............................**4,000.00**
Parcheesi, mc pnt, breadboard ends, ca 1880, 18" sq **865.00**
Parcheesi, scribed, mc pnt, Am, ca 1900, 15" sq **1,150.00**
Parcheesi/backgammon, mc pnt on brd, center fold, ca 1900, 18" sq....**1,500.00**

Games

Collectors of antique games are finding it more difficult to find their treasures at shows and flea markets. Most of the action these days seems to be through specialty dealers and auctions. The appreciation of the art on the boards and boxes continues to grow. You see many of the early games proudly displayed as art, and they should be. The period from the 1850s to 1910 continues to draw the most interest. Many of the games of that period were executed by well-known artists and illustrators. The quality of their lithography cannot be matched today. The historical value of games made before 1850 has caused interest in this period to increase. While they may not have the graphic quality of the later period, their insights into the social and moral character of the early nineteenth century are interesting.

Twentieth-century games invoke a nostalgic feeling among collectors who recall looking forward to a game under the Christmas tree each year. They search for examples that bring back those Christmas-morning memories. While the quality of their lithography is certainly less than the early games, the introduction of personalities from the comic strips, radio, and later TV created new interest. Every child wanted a game that featured their favorite character. Monopoly, probably the most famous game ever produced, was introduced during the Great Depression.

For further information, we recommend *Schroeder's Collectible Toys, Antique to Modern*; available from Collector Books.

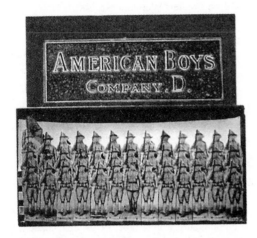

**American Boys Company D., McLaughlin Bros.
WWI era, incomplete, several soldiers missing,
otherwise EX, $100.00.** (Photo courtesy Buffalo Bay)

American Boy Ten Pins Game, McLoughlin Bros, VGIB 250.00
Amusing Game of Kilenny Cats, Parker Bros, 1890, VGIB 400.00
Astro Launch, Ohio Art, 1960s, NMIB...................................35.00
Astro the Wizard From Mars Questions & Answers, Peerless, 1953, EXIB...35.00
Bamboozle, Milton Bradley, 1962, NMIB................................30.00
Baseball Pitching Game, Marx, 1940s, NMIB 225.00
Bash!, Milton Bradley, 1965, NMIB 20.00
Big Game Hunter, Schoenhut, EXIB.....................................275.00
Big Maze, Marx, 1955, MIB..50.00
Candyland, Milton Bradley, 1955, NMIB................................20.00
Catching Mice, McLoughlin Bros, c 1888, VGIB.....................250.00
Challenge the Chief, Ideal, 1973, NMIB................................25.00
Chutes & Ladders, Milton Bradley, 1956, NMIB.....................20.00
Count Down Space Game, Transogram, 1960, NMIB.................20.00
Crazy Clock, Ideal, 1964, NMIB..50.00
Don't Spill the Beans, 1967, EXIB.......................................25.00
Electric Target Game, Marx, 1950s, unused, EXIB 300.00
Fish Pond, McLoughlin Bros, c 1890, VG+ (wood box w/paper litho lid)....110.00
Foot Ball Game (Popular Edition), Parker Bros, VGIB 175.00
Funny Finger, Ideal, 1968, NMIB 15.00
Game of Famous Men, Parker Bros, VGIB..............................50.00
Game of Flags, McLoughlin Bros, VGIB 75.00
Game of Innocence, Parker Bros, 1888, GIB 100.00
Gee-Wiz Horse Race, Wolverine, EX 100.00
Get in the Tub, Hasbro, 1974, unused, NMIB 50.00
Go Back, Milton Bradley, 1968, EXIB...................................15.00
Higgly Piggly, Cadaco, 1953, NMIB 20.00
High Gear, Mattel, 1953, NMIB...40.00
Hippety Hop, Corey, 1940, EXIB..30.00
Historical Dominoes Card Game, EXIB (wood box w/paper litho cover)......225.00

Improved Game of Fish Pond, McLoughlin Bros, 1890, VGIB ...100.00
Intrigue, Milton Bradley, 1955, NMIB...................................40.00
Jerome Park Steeple-Chase, McLoughlin Bros, EXIB................400.00
Jerome Park Steeple-Chase, McLoughlin Bros, VGIB................200.00
Jolly Jungleers, Milton Bradley, VGIB...................................100.00
Last Straw, Schaper, 1966, NMIB..20.00
Let's Drive, 1969, VGIB..20.00
Let's Face It, Hasbro, 1950s, NMIB......................................35.00
Li'l Stinker, Schaper, 1956, NMIB..20.00
Lie Detector/Spy Detector, Mattel, 1960, NMIB 65.00
Literary Salad, Parker Bros, GIB..25.00
Magic Magic Magic Game Set, Remco, 1975, NMIB................30.00
Masquerade Party, Bettye-B, 1955, EXIB..............................40.00
Match Game, 1963, EXIB..50.00
Military Tenpins, Ives, Pat 1885, EXIB.............................1,540.00
Mind Maze, Parker Bros, 1970, NMIB..................................15.00
Monday Morning Coach, James DeHart, 1934, VGIB 85.00
Monopoly Deluxe, Parker Bros, 1964, EXIB...........................35.00
Moving Picture Game, Milton Bradley, EXIB..........................125.00
Mystery Date, Milton Bradley, 1965, NMIB...........................100.00
Mystic Skull - The Game of Voodoo, Ideal, 1964, NMIB 50.00
Neck & Neck, Wolverine, NMIB..200.00
Newport Yacht Race, McLoughlin Bros, GIB 450.00
Office Boy — The Good Old Game, Parker Bros, 1889, VGIB..140.00
Our Country, ca 1884, VGIB..550.00
Park & Shop, Milton Bradley, 1960, NMIB.............................75.00
Parlor Croquet, Bliss, GIB...150.00
Pirate & Traveler, Milton Bradley, 1936, NMIB 20.00
Play Ball! Game & TV Scorer, Colorforms, 1960s, NMIB..........40.00
Play Sheriff, Milton Bradley, 1958, NMIB..............................30.00
Playing Department Store, Milton Bradley, VGIB.....................400.00
Pop the Chutes Target Game, NN Hill, NMIB 225.00
Pop Yer Top! Game of Suspense, Milton Bradley, 1968, EXIB......30.00
Pop-A-Puppet Pinball Game, Marx, 1960s, EX 25.00
Pretty Village, McLoughlin Bros, EXIB..................................110.00
Prisoner of Zelda, Parker Bros, 1896, EXIB...........................125.00
Puzzle Parties, Gilbert, c 1920, EXIB...................................40.00
Rendezvous, Create, 1965, NMIB..25.00
Rocket Race to Saturn, Lido, 1950s, VGIB............................50.00
Roulette Wheel, Marx, NMIB...55.00
Scores 'N Stripes Bagatelle Game, Marx, 1949, NMIB 125.00
Secret Agent, Milton Bradley, 1966, EXIB.............................25.00
Shenanigans, Milton Bradley, 1964, EXIB.............................50.00
Shopping at the Supermarket, Whitman, 1955, NMIB..............20.00
Smack-A-Roo Game Set, Mattel, 1964, EXIB.........................40.00
Snake's Alive Ideal, 1966, NMIB..30.00
Soldiers on Guard, McLoughlin Bros, VGIB............................125.00
Space Pilot, Cadaco-Ellis, 1951, EXIB..................................75.00
Spear's 'Quick Change' Comic Pictures, VGIB........................65.00
Spot Shot Marble Game, Wolverine, 1930s, NM 50.00
Spy Detector, Mattel, 1960, NMIB.......................................75.00
Steeple Chase, JH Singer, GIB...125.00
Steeple Chase, McLoughlin Bros, VGIB.................................200.00
Stop, Milton Bradley, 1950s, NMIB......................................20.00
Submarine Search, Milton Bradley, 1973, EXIB......................40.00
Superstition, Milton Bradley, 1977, NMIB.............................20.00
Tip It, 1965, VGIB...20.00
Touchdown Football Game, Wilder, GIB.................................75.00
Town & Country Traffic, Ranger Steel, 1940s, EXIB................50.00
Town Hall, Milton Bradley, 1939, NMIB................................20.00
Turn Over, Milton Bradley, EXIB..75.00
Uncle Wiggily, Milton Bradley, 1961, NMIB...........................25.00
Voodoo, Schaper, 1967, EXIB..25.00
Which Witch?, Milton Bradley, 1970, NMIB 65.00

Wink Tennis, Transogram, 1956, NMIB.........15.00
Wow Pillow Fight Game, Milton Bradley, 1964, NMIB.........25.00
You Don't Say, Milton Bradley, 1963, EXIB.........20.00
Young America Target, Parker Bros, VGIB.........275.00
Zamboola, Norstar, VGIB.........85.00
Zippy Zepps Air Game, All Fair Toys & Games, VGIB.........500.00

Personalities, Movies, and TV Shows

A-Team, 1984, VGIB.........15.00
Addams Family (Cartoon Series), Milton Bradley, 1974, NMIB..35.00
Adventures of Davy Crockett, Harett-Gilmor, 1955, EXIB.........75.00
Adventures of Lassie, Whiting, 1955, EXIB.........50.00
Adventures of Rin-Tin-Tin, Transogram, 1955, EXIB.........50.00
Adventures of Robin Hood, Bettye-B, 1956, EXIB.........65.00
Adventures of Superman, Milton Bradley, 1942, EXIB.........225.00
Adventures of Tom Sawyer & Huck Finn, Stoll & Edwards, VGIB..125.00
Alien, Kenner, 1979, EXIB.........50.00
Allen Sherman's Camp Grenada, EXIB.........45.00
Alvin & the Chipmunks Acorn Hunt, Hasbro, 1960, EXIB.........35.00
Amazing Spider-Man, Milton Bradley, 1966, EXIB.........50.00
Annette's Secret Passage Games, Parker Bros, 1958, EXIB.........20.00
Around the World in 80 Days, Transogram, 1975, NMIB.........25.00
As the World Turns, Parker Bros, 1966, NMIB.........30.00
Atom Ant Saves the Day, Transogram, 1966, NMIB.........40.00
Babe Ruth's Baseball Game, Milton Bradley, EXIB.........500.00
Babes in Toyland, Parker Bros, 1961, EXIB.........30.00
Barbie's Key to Fame, Mattel, 1963, EXIB.........35.00
Barney Google & Spark Plug Game, Milton Bradley, 1932, VGIB..85.00
Beany & Cecil Ring Toss, Pressman, 1961, EXIB.........50.00
Ben Casey, Transogram, 1961, MIB.........20.00
Beverly Hillbillies, Standard Toycraft, 1963, NMIB.........50.00
Bewitched, T Cohn Inc, 1965, MIB.........85.00
Bobbsey Twins, Milton Bradley, 1957, NMIB.........30.00
Bozo the Clown in Circus Land, Transogram, 1960s, NMIB.........25.00
Brady Bunch, Whitman, 1973, MIB.........100.00
Buccaneers, Transogram, 1957, NMIB.........45.00
Bullwinkle & Rocky Magic Dot Game, Transogram, 1962, NMIB..100.00
Burke's Law, Transogram, 1963, EXIB.........30.00
Candid Camera, Lowell, 1963, NMIB.........45.00
Captain America, Milton Bradley, 1977, NMIB.........20.00
Captain Kangaroo TV Lotto, Ideal, 1961, EXIB.........25.00
Car 54 Where Are You?, Allison, 1963, EXIB.........150.00
Cheyenne, Milton Bradley, 1957, EXIB.........30.00
CHiPs, Ideal, 1981, MIB.........30.00
Combat, Ideal, 1963, NMIB.........30.00
Creature From the Black Lagoon, Hasbro, 1963, EXIB.........250.00
Davy Crockett Radar Action, Ewing, 1955, EXIB.........85.00
Dennis the Menace Baseball Game, MTP, 1960, NMIB.........70.00
Detectives, Transogram, 1961, NMIB.........50.00
Dick Tracy Crime Stopper Game, Ideal, 1963, NMIB.........30.00
Donkey Kong Board Game, 1982, EXIB.........25.00
Dr Kildare, Ideal, 1962, NMIB.........30.00
Dudley Do-Right's Find Snidley Game, Whitman, 1976, NMIB..30.00
Dukes of Hazzard, Ideal, 1981, EXIB.........25.00
Emergency, Milton Bradley, 1973, NMIB.........20.00
Fantastic Voyage, Milton Bradley, 1968, NMIB.........20.00
Felix the Cat Target, Lido, 1960s, EXIB.........25.00
Flintstones, Milton Bradley, 1971, NMIB.........20.00
Flying Nun, Milton Bradley, 1968, NMIB.........30.00
Fugitive, Ideal, 1964, NMIB.........75.00
Gene Autry Bandit Trail Game, Kenton, EXIB.........200.00
Get Smart!, Ideal, 1965, NMIB.........70.00
Gilligan's Island, Game Gems/T Cohn, 1965, EXIB.........225.00

Godzilla, Mattel, 1978, EXIB.........40.00
Gomer Pyle, Transogram, 1964, EXIB.........50.00
Goodbye Mr Chips, Parker Bros, 1969, MIB.........25.00
Groucho Marx TV Quiz, Pressman, 1950s, EXIB.........65.00
Gumby & Poky Playful Trails, 1968, NMIB.........25.00
Gunsmoke, Lowell, 1958, NMIB.........75.00
Hair Bear Bunch, Milton Bradley, 1971, NMIB.........30.00
Hardy Boys Treasure, Parker Bros, 1957, VGIB.........35.00
Hawaiian Eye, Lowell, 1963, EXIB.........85.00
Hector Heathcoate - The Minute-And-A-Half Man, Transogram, 1963, NMIB....100.00
Hopalong Cassidy Target Game, Marx/W Boyd, 1950, EXIB......125.00
Howdy Doody's Own Game, Parker Bros, 1950s, EXIB.........75.00
I Dream of Jeannie, Milton Bradley, 1965, EXIB.........75.00
Ipcress File, Milton Bradley, 1966, unused, NMIB.........40.00
Jack & Jill, Milton Bradley, VGIB.........100.00
James Bond 007 Tarot Game, 1973, NMIB.........75.00
Jan Murray's Treasure Hunt, Gardner, 1950s, NMIB.........15.00
Jetson's Fun Pad, Milton Bradley, 1963, NMIB.........80.00
Jules Verne's Around the World w/Nellie Bly, McLoughlin, 1890, EXIB....200.00
Kojak Stakeout Detective, Milton Bradley, 1975, VGIB.........50.00
Legend of Jesse James, Milton Bradley, 1966, NMIB.........75.00
Little Orphan Annie Game, GIB.........65.00
Lone Ranger Silver Bullets, Whiting, 1956, MIB.........165.00
Lone Ranger Target Game, Marx, 1946, NMIB.........400.00
Lost in Space, Milton Bradley, 1965, NMIB.........75.00
Man From UNCLE Secret Code Wheel Pin Ball Game, Sears/MGM, 1966, EXIB..450.00
McHale's Navy, Transogram, 1962, NMIB.........50.00
Mickey Mouse Circus, Marks Bros, EXIB.........650.00
Mickey Mouse Pop Game, Marks Bros, 1930s, EXIB.........650.00
Mighty Mouse Skill Roll, Pressman/Terrytoons, 1950s, EXIB.....150.00
Mission Impossible, Ideal, 1966, EXIB.........75.00
Nancy & Sluggo Game, 1944, rare, NMIB.........100.00
Nancy Drew Mystery Game, Parker Bros, 1957, NMIB.........100.00

Patty Duke, board game, Milton Bradley, 1963, EXIB, $45.00.
(Photo courtesy June Moon)

Perils of Pauline, Marx, 1964, NMIB.........100.00
Popeye's Game, Parker Bros/KFS, 1948, unused, NMIB.........200.00
Rawhide, Lowell, 1960, EXIB.........125.00
Red Riding Hood, Parker Bros, 1895, VGIB.........150.00
Rifleman, Milton Bradley, 1959, NMIB.........100.00
Rip Van Winkle, Parker Bros, VGIB.........125.00
Scarlett O'Hara One of Her Problems Marble Game, Marietta, 1939, EXIB...75.00
Sea Hunt, Lowell, 1961, EXIB.........75.00
Snoopy & the Red Baron, Milton Bradley, 1970, MIB.........40.00
Star Trek Board Game, 1975, EXIB.........50.00
Surfside 6, Lowell, 1961, unused, MIB.........100.00
Tennesse Tuxedo, Transogram, 1963, EXIB.........135.00
That Girl, Remco, 1969, EXIB.........70.00

Top Cat, Cadaco, 1961, NMIB...**45.00**
Untouchables Target Game, Marx, 1950s, complete, NM **350.00**
Virginian, Transogram, 1962, EXIB..**85.00**
Wanted Dead or Alive, Lowell, 1959, EXIB.............................**85.00**
Wyatt Earp, Transogram, 1958, EXIB.......................................**50.00**
Yogi Bear Score-A-Matic Ball Toss, Transogram, EXIB **65.00**
Zorro, Parker Bros, 1964, EXIB...**45.00**

Garden City Pottery

Founded in 1902 in San Jose, California, by the end of the 1920s this pottery had grown to become the largest in Northern California. During that period production focused on stoneware, sewer pipe, and red clay flowerpots. In the late '30s and '40s, the company produced dinnerware in bright solid colors of yellow, green, blue, orange, cobalt, turquoise, white, and black. Royal Arden Hickman, who would later gain fame for the innovative artware he modeled for the Haeger company, designed not only dinnerware but a line of Art Deco vases and bowls as well. The company endured hard times by adapting to the changing needs of the market and during the '50s concentrated on production of garden products. Foreign imports, however, proved to be too competitive, and the company's pottery production ceased in 1979.

Because none of the colored-glazed products were ever marked, to learn to identify the products of this company, you'll need to refer to *Sanford's Guide to Garden City Pottery* by Jim Pasquali, our advisor for this category, who is listed in the Directory under California. Values apply to items in all colors (except black) and all patterns, unless noted otherwise. Due to relative rarity, 20% should be added for any item found in black.

Bean pot, Deco, w/lid, lg **85.00**
Bean pot, Deco, w/lid, sm...**35.00**
Bowl, batter; solid color, 2-qt...**65.00**
Bowl, mixing; Wide-Ring, solid color, #1 ....**20.00**
Bowl, soup; plain, solid color..**25.00**
Bowl, Succulent, conical, solid color, 9".........................**35.00**
Candle holders, flared ft, solid color, 3", pr **45.00**

Carafe, blue, plain, open, $45.00; Artichoke plate, orange, $45.00. (Photo courtesy Jim Pasquali)

Casserole, narrow or wide rings, solid color, 7", ea.........**35.00**
Cookie jar, Deco style, solid color, 7½" **75.00**
Creamer, Geometric, solid color **15.00**
Creamer & sugar bowl, solid color, w/lid, jumbo.............**65.00**
Flowerpot, dbl rim, solid color, 10" **50.00**
Jardiniere, ribbed, solid color, 10"..................................**45.00**

Mug, chowder; solid color, w/lid **45.00**
Nappy, solid color, #6, lg **35.00**
Pitcher, orange, Deco style, 3⅞".....................................**95.00**
Plate, dinner; solid color, 9"...**20.00**
Ramekin, solid color, 3"..**20.00**
Shakers, Deco 'Rocket,' solid color, 5", pr.......................**55.00**
Teapot, plain, solid color..**95.00**
Tumbler, solid color **20.00**
Tumbler, wide ring, solid color **15.00**
Vase, bud; hand-thrown tumbler shape, solid color, 5" **45.00**
Water cooler, crockery...**75.00**

Gas Globes and Panels

Gas globes and panels, once a common sight, have vanished from the countryside but are being sought by collectors as a unique form of advertising memorabilia. Early globes from the 1920s (some date back to as early as 1912), now referred to as 'one-piece' (Type 4) globes, were made of molded milk glass and were globular in shape. The gas company name was etched or painted on the glass. Few of these were ever produced, and this type is valued very highly by collectors today.

A new type of pump was introduced in the early 1930s; the old 'visible' pumps were replaced by 'electric' models. Globes were changing at the same time. By the mid-teens a three-piece (Type 3) globe consisting of a pair of inserts and a metal body was being produced in both 15" and 16½" sizes. Collectors prefer to call globes that are not one-piece or plastic 'three-piece glass' (Type 2) or 'metal body, glass inserts' (Type 3). Though metal-body globes (Type 3) were most popular in the 1930s, they were common in the 1920s, and some were actually made as early as 1914. Though rare in numbers, their use spans many years. In the 1930s Type 2 and Type 3 globes became the replacements of the one-piece globe. The most recently manufactured gas globes are made with a plastic body that contains two 13½" glass lenses. These were common in the '50s but were actually used as early as 1932. This style is referred to as Type 1 in our listings.

Values here are for examples with both sides in excellent condition: no chips, wear, or other damage.

Note: Standard Crowns with raised letters are one-piece globes that were made in the 1920s; those made in the 1950s (no raised letters), though one-piece, are not regarded as such by today's collectors. Our advisor for this category is Scott Benjamin; he is listed in the Directory under Ohio.

Type 1, Plastic Body, Glass Inserts (Inserts 13½") — 1931 – 1950s

D-X Marine, rare, EX..**1,800.00**
Dixie, plastic band, EX...**250.00**
Fleet-Wing, EX..**500.00**
Kendal Deluxe, Capcolite body w/red pnt, 13½", EX.................**350.00**
Marathon, no runner, EX..**250.00**
Never Nox Ethyl, EX..**600.00**
Phillips 66, EX...**350.00**
Sinclair H-C Gasoline, red & gr on wht, EX **300.00**
Spur, oval body, EX **350.00**
Texaco Diesel Chief, Capcolite body, 13½", EX.................**1,350.00**

Type 2, Glass Frame, Glass Inserts (Inserts 13½") — 1926 – 1940s

Aerio, gr gill ripple body, 13½" dia, EX **10,000.00**
Aladdin Gasoline, 2-lens w/wide body, EX **850.00**
Amoco, gill body, 13½", EX.....................................**500.00**
Barnsdall Be Square Gasoline, 2 lenses in wide body, EX...........**600.00**
Capitol Kerosene Oil Co, EX......................................**600.00**

Esso, EX	325.00
Globe Gasoline, metal base ring, EX	2,000.00
Kan O Tex, gill body, metal base ring, EX	1,250.00
Lion, Knix Knox, metal base, EX	3,000.00
Lion, metal base, EX	1,500.00
Pure, EX	500.00
Sinclair Dino, milk glass, EX	300.00
Sinclair Pennant, EX	1,200.00
Sky Chief, gill body, 13½", EX	650.00
Standard Crown, bl, EX	800.00
Standard Crown, gray, EX	1,500.00
Standard Flame, EX	650.00
United Hi-Test Gasoline, red/wht/bl, EX	450.00
WNAX, w/radio station pictured, EX	5,000.00

Type 3, Metal Frame, Glass Inserts (Inserts 15" or 16½") — 1915 – 1930s

Aero Mobilgas, new metal body, rare, 15", EX	2,800.00
Atlantic Ethyl, 16½", EX	950.00
Blue Anti-Knock Gasoline, Interstate Oil Gas, EX	1,200.00
Farmer's Union High Octane, red/wht/bl, high profile metal body, 15"	1,000.00
General Ethyl, 15" fr, complete, EX	1,500.00
Marathon, low profile metal body, 15", EX	1,500.00
Mobilgas Ethyl, 16½", EX	600.00
Phillips Benzo, low profile metal body, 15", EX	4,000.00
Purol Gasoline, w/arrow, porc body, EX	900.00
Royal Gasoline w/Maine pictured, high profile metal body, 15", EX	2,500.00
Signal, old stoplight, 15", EX	6,000.00
Stanolined Aviation, rare, 16½", EX	5,000.00
Texaco Leaded, glass panels, complete globe, EX	5,000.00
White Star, 15" fr, complete, EX	2,000.00

Type 4, One-Piece Glass Globes, No Inserts, Company Name Etched, Raised, or Enameled — 1912 – 1931

Atlantic, chimney cap, EX	5,000.00
Mobil Gargoyle, gargoyle pictured, oval, EX	2,500.00
Pierce Pennant, etched, EX	3,500.00
Shell, rnd, etched, EX	1,200.00
Super Shell, clam shape, EX	1,800.00
Texaco, etched letters, wide body, EX	3,000.00
Texaco Ethyl, EX	2,200.00
That Good Gulf..., emb, orange & blk letters, EX	1,500.00
White Eagle, blunt nose, 20¾", EX	1,800.00
White Rose, boy pictured, pnt, EX	5,000.00

Gaudy Dutch

Inspired by Oriental Imari wares, Gaudy Dutch was made in England from 1800 to 1820. It was hand decorated on a soft-paste body with rich underglaze blues accented in orange, red, pink, green, and yellow. It differs from Gaudy Welsh in that there is no lustre (except on Water Lily). There are seventeen patterns, some of which are War Bonnet, Grape, Dahlia, Oyster, Urn, Butterfly, Carnation, Single Rose, Double Rose, and Water Lily. Unless otherwise noted, assume that values apply to items in at least near-mint condition and that cups are without handles.

Butterfly, coffeepot, 11"	4,400.00
Butterfly, creamer, lg	1,450.00
Butterfly, pitcher, milk; 4"	910.00
Butterfly, teapot, 5¾"	2,530.00

Butterfly, teapot, 5¾", VG-	1,265.00
Butterfly, toddy plate, rare, 4¼"	825.00
Butterfly, waste bowl	1,400.00
Carnation, plate, EX color, 7¼"	550.00
Carnation, plate, lg yel dot border, 10"	825.00
Carnation, plate, 8"	660.00
Carnation, soup plate, 8½"	770.00
Dahlia, creamer	990.00
Dahlia, tea bowl & saucer	825.00
Double Rose, creamer, helmet shape, shaped hdl, 5"	1,375.00
Double Rose, cup (handleless) & saucer, EX color	360.00
Double Rose, cup & saucer, hdl	180.00
Double Rose, cup plate, 3⅝"	1,350.00
Double Rose, plate, 9¾", VG	330.00
Double Rose, platter, slightly mellowed, 10½"	3,000.00

Double Rose, soup plate, 9¾", $850.00.

(Photo courtesy John A. Shuman III)

Double Rose, sugar bowl	880.00
Double Rose, teapot, rectangular, EX color, 6¼"	3,200.00
Dove, creamer	770.00
Dove, creamer, helmet shape, rare	1,400.00
Dove, cup & saucer	560.00
Dove, plate, 9¾"	880.00
Dove, teapot, EX	880.00
Dove, waste bowl, 3x6¼", EX	365.00
Grape, cup & saucer	515.00
Grape, cup & saucer, rpr/hairline	220.00
Grape, cup plate, 3½"	990.00
Grape, plate, minor pnt loss, 7"	275.00
Grape, plate, stains, 7⅛"	440.00
Grape, plate, 9¾"	660.00
Grape, soup plate, 7"	495.00
Grape, sugar bowl, w/lid, open finial, oval, 5½", EX	660.00
Grape, teapot, prof rstr, 6½x11½"	1,000.00
Leaf, cup & saucer	800.00
Oyster, creamer	1,100.00
Oyster, cup & saucer, EX	800.00
Oyster, teapot	610.00
Oyster, waste bowl, 6¼"	1,200.00
Primrose, tea bowl & saucer	770.00
Single Rose, coffeepot	800.00
Single Rose, creamer	925.00
Single Rose, creamer, 4½x6", VG	135.00
Single Rose, cup & saucer, EX	220.00
Single Rose, cup & saucer, from $350 to	370.00

Single Rose, cup & saucer, VG	140.00
Single Rose, cup plate, 4", from $750 to	950.00
Single Rose, plate, 7¼"	475.00
Single Rose, sugar bowl, oblong shell hdls	825.00
Strawflower, plate, 8½"	900.00
Sunflower, plate, EX colors, 8¼"	4,870.00
Sunflower, plate, 7½"	600.00
Urn, cup & saucer, chip on ea pc	110.00
Urn, plate, soup; 8⅞"	550.00
War Bonnet, cup plate	715.00
War Bonnet, cup plate, flaking/surface wear, 3½"	500.00
War Bonnet, plate, 8"	715.00
War Bonnet, plate, 8¼", EX	415.00
War Bonnet, soup plate, EX color, 8½"	825.00
War Bonnet, toddy bowl, 5¼"	1,040.00
Warbonnet, cup plate, 3½"	1,375.00
Zinnia, plate, deep, 9¾"	1,245.00
Zinnia, plate, 6⅜"	660.00

Gaudy Welsh

Gaudy Welsh was an inexpensive hand-decorated ware made in both England and Wales from 1820 until 1860. It is characterized by its colors — principally blue, orange-rust, and copper lustre — and by its uninhibited patterns. Accent colors may be yellow and green. (Pink lustre may be present, since lustre applied to the white areas appears pink. A copper tone develops from painting lustre onto the dark colors.) The body of the ware may be heavy ironstone (also called Gaudy Ironstone), creamware, earthenware, or porcelain; even style and shapes vary considerably. Patterns, while usually floral, are also sometimes geometric and may have trees and birds. Beware! The Wagon Wheel pattern has been reproduced.

Our advisor for this category is Cheryl Nelson; she is listed in the Directory under Minnesota.

Note: Prices are rising. Each day more collectors enter the field. For the first time British auction houses are picturing and promoting Gaudy Welsh. Demand for Columbine, Grape, Tulip, Oyster, and Wagon Wheel is slow. We should also mention that the Bethedsa pattern is very similar to a Davenport jug pattern. No porcelain Gaudy Welsh was made in Wales.

Aber, lamp feeder/stand, 4"	695.00
Betws-y-Coed, jug, 7"	495.00
Bryn Prystyll, jug, 5"	485.00
Celyn, bowl, 9"	1,000.00
Chinoiserie, mug, 2-hdl, 4"	550.00
Coed Cae, jug, 7"	860.00
Columbine, teapot, 8"	400.00
Crafnant, jug, 6¼"	495.00
Duck, jug, 5½"	725.00
Forget-Me-Not, jug, 6½"	375.00
Fruit, cup & saucer	235.00
Grape, child's mug, 3"	195.00
Grape, coffeepot, 10½"	920.00
Harmony, mug, gr, 5"	650.00
Herald, plate, 7½"	315.00
Jewel, teapot, 8¼"	800.00
Llangennith, mug, 5¾"	685.00
Marigold, jug, 5"	450.00
Morning Glory, platter, 13½"	895.00
Oriental/Coloured Hexagon, mug, 4"	485.00
Oyster, teapot, 8"	300.00
Poinsettia, cup & saucer	245.00

Repoussé, vase, 5½"	615.00
Sahara, plate 7"	375.00
Seaweed, sucrier, 8½"	800.00
Shallow falls, vase, 4½"	595.00

Strawberry, coffeepot, 9⅛", EX, $525.00.

Tal-y-Coed, jug, 6¼"	815.00
Tea House, cup & saucer	265.00
Tricorn, bowl, 6"	415.00
Tulip, teapot, 8"	325.00
Vine, plate, 7½"	295.00
Welsh War Bonnet, cup & saucer	245.00

Geisha Girl

Geisha Girl Porcelain was one of several key Japanese china production efforts aimed at the booming export markets of the U.S., Canada, England, and other parts of Europe. The wares feature colorful, kimono-clad Japanese ladies in scenes of everyday Japanese life surrounded by exquisite flora, fauna, and mountain ranges. Nonetheless, the forms in which the wares were produced reflected the late nineteenth- and early twentieth-century Western dining and decorating preferences: tea and coffee services, vases, dresser sets, children's items, planters, etc.

Over a hundred manufacturers were involved in Geisha Girl production. This accounts for the several hundred different patterns, well over a dozen border colors and styles, and several methods of design execution. Geisha Girl Porcelain was produced in wholly hand-painted versions, but most were hand painted over stencilled outlines. Be wary of Geisha ware executed with decals. Very few decaled examples came out of Japan. Rather, most were Czechoslovakian attempts to hone in on the market. Czech pieces have stamped marks in broad, pseudo-Oriental characters. Items with portraits of Oriental ladies in the bottom of tea or sake cups are *not* Geisha Girl Porcelain, unless the outside surface of the wares are decorated as described above. These lovely faces, formed by varying the thickness of the porcelain body, are called lithophanes and are collectible in their own right.

The height of Geisha Girl production was between 1910 and the mid-1930s. Some post-World War II production has been found marked Occupied Japan. The ware continued in minimal production during the 1960s, but the point of origin of the later pieces was not only Japan but Hong Kong as well. These productions are discerned by the pure whiteness of the porcelain; even, unemotional borders; lack of background washes and gold enameling; and overall sparseness of detail. A new wave of Nippon-marked reproduction Geisha emerged in 1996. If the

Geisha Girl productions of the 1960s – 1980s were overly plain, the mid-1990s repros are overly ornate. Original Geisha Girl porcelain was enhanced by brush strokes of color over a stenciled design; it was never the 'color perfectly within the lines' type of decoration found on current reproductions. Original Geisha Girl porcelain was decorated with color washes; the reproductions are in heavy enamels. The backdrop decoration of the current reproductions feature solid, thick colors, and the patterns feature too much color; period Geisha ware had a high ratio of white space to color. The new pieces also have bright shiny gold in proportions greater than most period Geisha ware. The Nippon marks on the reproductions are wrong. Some of the Geisha ware created during the Nippon era bore the small precise decaled green M-in-Wreath mark, a Noritake registered trademark. The reproduced items feature an irregular facsimile of this mark. Stamped onto the reproductions is an unrealistically large M-in-Wreath mark in shades of green ranging from an almost neon to pine green with a wreath that looks like it has seen better days, as it does not have the perfect roundness of the original mark. Other marks have also been reproduced. Reproductions of mid-sized trays, chunky hatpin holders, an ornate vase, a covered bottle, and a powder jar are among the current reproductions popping up at flea and antique markets.

Many of our descriptions contain references to border colors and treatments. This information is given immediately preceding the mark and/or size. Our advisor for this category is Elyce Litts; she is listed in the Directory under New Jersey.

Basket vase, Bamboo Trellis, gold trim, 8½", pr............................150.00
Biscuit jar, Baskets of Mums, melon ribbed, 3-ftd, red w/gold 49.00
Bonbon dish, Battledore, mum shaped, olive gr............................22.00

Bouillon cup and saucer, Garden Bench J, with lid, multicolor border, $55.00. (Photo courtesy Elyce Litts)

Bowl, berry; Dragonboat, cobalt w/gold, master+6 ind 85.00
Bowl, carp, red w/gold, 6"..18.00
Bowl, Cherry Blossoms, red-orange edge, 7½" 30.00
Bowl, master nut; Basket A, 9-lobe, 3-ftd, dk apple gr, 6" 28.00
Bowl, salad; Garden Bench A, 9-lobed, red, 7¼"..........................25.00
Box, Mother & Daughter, gold trim, 2x5x4".................................32.00
Celery dish, Foreign Garden, bl border....................................45.00
Cocoa pot, Pillar Print, red-brn w/gold, cylindrical 55.00
Cocoa set, Temple B, red/orange w/gold, pot+6 c/s.......................175.00
Cracker jar, Spider puppet, ftd & lobed, cobalt bl w/gold border ..65.00
Creamer, Chinese Coin, Battledore & scenic reserves....................18.00
Creamer, Porch, red-orange, modern.......................................10.00
Creamer & sugar bowl, Kite A, brn w/gold 28.00
Cup & saucer, AD; Basket B, dk apple gr w/gold, str side.............15.00
Cup & saucer, AD; Parasol B: Torii & Parasol, red-orange w/gold...15.00
Cup & saucer, child's, Mother & Son, red 12.00
Cup & saucer, cocoa; Child wearing E-Boshi, cobalt bl-gray wash ..20.00
Cup & saucer, tea; Blue Hoo...14.00
Cup & saucer, tea; Cloud B, red-orange w/yel.............................14.00
Cup & saucer, tea; Origami, cobalt bl w/gold.............................15.00

Cup & saucer, tea; Writing B, bl w/gold.................................15.00
Egg cup, dbl, Child reaching for Butterfly, red w/gold.................13.00
Ewer, Garden Bench H, red w/gold lacing.................................35.00
Hair receiver, Carp A: Watching the Carp, cobalt w/gold.............30.00
Jar, sachet; Fan C, red w/gold, hdls, ftd, 6½"..........................75.00
Jug, Battledore, ribbed & fluted, yel-gr w/gold, 4¼" 25.00
Lemonade set, Bellflower, brn w/trim, pitcher+5 mugs...............125.00
Mint dish, Gardening, 4-lobed, cobalt w/gold..........................13.00
Nappy, Mother & Daughter, lobed, gold lacing, fan-shaped reserves ...30.00
Nappy, Temple A, hand-fluted edge, single hdl, sea gr border.......35.00
Pitcher, Processional, red w/mc geometrics, gold hdl/border, 4½" ..25.00
Plate, Butterfly Dancers, red w/gold, 7" 35.00
Plate, Child's Play, cobalt bl w/gold buds, 6½".........................15.00
Plate, Oni Dance A, swirl-fluted/scalloped, red w/gold lacing, 7¼" ..20.00
Plate, Parasol K: Parasol & Basket, swirled flutes, cobalt w/gold, 7" 22.00
Plate, Wait for Me, floriate shape, red-orange w/gold buds, 8¾"..26.00
Powder jar, Footridge A, red, 3 long legs 28.00
Puff box, Field Laborers, red w/gold.....................................20.00
Ramekin w/saucer, Checkerboard, cobalt bl w/gold 45.00
Relish dish, Paper Carp, fluted edge, cut-out hdls, red.................20.00
Sauce dish, Meeting B, dk apple gr.......................................12.00
Shakers, Dressing, red, pr...12.00
Talcum shaker, Parasol L, red-orange w/yel lacing 28.00
Tea set, River's Edge, gr 3-banded border w/gold, pot+cr/sug+6 c/s ...125.00
Toothbrush holder, Flute, red-orange, 4"................................25.00
Toothpick holder, Circle Dance, cylindrical, red 15.00
Tray, dresser; Garden Bench D, HP gr & red w/gold....................55.00
Vase, Cloud A, cobalt bl w/gold-drip neck & rim, 5½" 30.00

Georgia Art Pottery

In Cartersville, Georgia, in August 1935, W.J. Gordy first fired pottery turned from regional clays. By 1936 he was marking his wares 'Georgia Art Pottery' (GP) or 'Georgia Art Pottery' (GAP) and continued to do so until 1950 when he used a 'Hand Made by WJ Gordy' stamp (HM). There are different configurations of the GAP mark, one being a three-line arrangement, another that is circular and thought to be the earlier of the two. After 1970 his pottery was signed. Known throughout the world for his fine glazes, he won the Georgia Governor's Award in 1983. Examples of his wares are on display in the Smithsonian. His father W.T.B. and brother D.X. are also well-known potters.

Basket, feldspathic sky bl, fluted rim, 2 hdls at sides, 3¼x7⅛".....90.00
Chambersticks, Mountain Gold matt, WJ Gordy, 1970s, 5x6¼", pr.......50.00
Couples set, Mountain Gold, WJ Gordy, 1960s, pitcher+bowl+mugs+cr/sug....350.00
Pansy pot, sky bl gloss, sgn WJG, ca 1935-36, 9¼"......................115.00
Pitcher, cream; Dogwood, mk DX Gordy, 3½x4"............................165.00
Pitcher, turq gloss, rnded top hdl, 1970s, 5⅜"...........................60.00
Vase, chocolate & milk-color swirled colors, egg shape, glazed int, 6"...125.00
Vase, cornucopia; wht, GP mk, 5x5"......................................125.00
Vase, Mountain Gold w/bl int, incurvate neck, 3½" 135.00

German Porcelain

Unless otherwise noted, the porcelain listed in this section is marked simply 'Germany.' Products of other German manufactures are listed in specific categories. See also Pink Paw Bears; Pink Pigs; Elfinware.

Figurine, cockatoo on oval ped, bright mc, ca 1900, 16"............460.00
Figurine, nude w/violin, Gerold Porzellan...West Germany mk, 8¾"...250.00
Figurine, semi-nude child sits & reads, H Dopping, 17⅝"............235.00

Plaque, bound woman floating in water, V Duchesne, 1877, 14¾" **1,500.00**
Plaque, brunette's portrait, sgn E Preiks...L Richter, 11¾"+fr **800.00**
Plaque, draped female among rocks, 5½x4"+brass fr **1,000.00**
Plaque, elderly religious scolar w/manuscript, 9x7"+16¼x14" fr.**700.00**
Plaque, Fatima von Lichel portrait, in red, 7¼x5½"+fr **650.00**
Plaque, Julima von Lichel portrait, much jewelry, 7x5½"+fr.......**700.00**
Plaque, Odalisque, diva's portrait, 6x4"+11¾x10" fr **500.00**
Plaque, Proposal, man on knee before lady, unmk, 8½x7"+fr **350.00**
Vase, Margeurite w/flowers, Wagner, gold/jewels, 10⅛" **2,250.00**

Figurine, lady holding skirt high, painted details, Herwig & Co., 1930s, from $300.00 to $350.00. (Photo courtesy Mary Frank Gaston)

Gladding McBean and Company

This company was established in 1875 in Lincoln, California. They first produced only clay drainage pipes, but in 1883 architectural terra cotta was introduced, which has been used extensively in the United States as well as abroad. Sometime later a line of garden pottery was added. They soon became the leading producers of tile in the country. In 1923 they purchased the Tropico Pottery in Glendale, California, where in addition to tile they also produced huge garden vases. Their line was expanded in 1934 to included artware and dinnerware.

At least fifteen lines of art pottery were developed between 1934 and 1942. For a short time they stamped their wares with the Tropico Pottery mark; but the majority was signed 'GMcB' in an oval. Later the mark was changed to 'Franciscan' with several variations. After 1937 'Catalina Pottery' was used on some lines. (All items marked 'Catalina Pottery' were made in Glendale.) For further information we recommend *The Collector's Encyclopedia of California Pottery, Second Edition*, by Jack Chipman (Collector Books). See also Franciscan Ware. Our advisor for this category is Kathy Eichert; she is listed in the Directory under California.

Ashtray, Nautical Artware, coral shell form, ca 1939, 4x3⅜" **30.00**
Bowl, bl matt, low, Catalina Pottery, 11½" sq...............................**25.00**
Bowl, console; turq, #C204, Catalina Pottery, 3⅞x17¾x11" **40.00**
Bowl, console; wht/turq, Catalina Pottery, 3¼x12¾", NM **35.00**
Bowl, fruit/centerpc; bright orange, ftd, Tropico stamp, 4x10" **35.00**
Bowl, shell form, wht w/coral int, USA, 15" L **75.00**
Carafe, El Patio, lt gr, GMcB in oval mk, 7" **80.00**
Cup & saucer, demi; assorted solid colors, GMB, set of 6..............**75.00**
Dish, Capistrano Ware, celadon, low rectangle, Catalina mk, 12x9" **50.00**
Head vase, ivory gloss w/HP decor, #C801, Dorr Bothwell, 5¾x7" **185.00**
Pitcher, El Patio, Glacial Blue (turq), mk GMB, 9".....................**125.00**
Pitcher, water; pk-tan, Catalina Pottery, 8"...............................**125.00**
Planter, turq & wht, Catalina Pottery, 2¼x10¼x7¼" **28.00**
Platter, bl, Catalina Pottery, 12½" **30.00**
Platter, med gr, Catalina Pottery, 16" **125.00**

Vase, Aurora, fish, cream w/aqua int, C362, California Pottery, 8¼" **365.00**
Vase, Oxblood, flared neck, bulbous body, Catalina Pottery, 6" ..**150.00**
Vase, oxblood w/celadon int & top edge, ftd, GMB USA, 6" **195.00**
Vase, shell form, wht w/turq int, Catalina Pottery, 7¼"................**45.00**
Vase w/Scarf Dancer flower frog, wht, Catalina Pottery, NM......**220.00**
Wall pocket, tropical leaf, lt bl, Catalina Pottery, 8x6" **60.00**

Glass Animals and Figurines

These beautiful glass sculptures have been produced by many major companies in America — in fact, some are still being made today. Heisey, Fostoria, Duncan and Miller, Imperial, Paden City, Tiffin, and Cambridge made the vast majority, but there were many other companies involved on a lesser scale. Very few marked their animals.

As many of the glass companies went out of business, their molds were bought by companies still active, who have used them to produce their own line of animals. While some are easy to recognize, others can be very confusing. For example, Summit Art Glass now owns Cambridge's 6½", 8½", and 10" swan molds. We recommend *Glass Animals and Figural Related Items, Second Edition*, by Dick and Pat Spencer, if you are thinking of starting a collection or wanting to identify and evaluate the glass animals and figural-related items that you already have. Our advisors for this category are listed in the Directory under Illinois.

Cambridge

Bashful Charlotte, flower frog, Dianthus, 6½" **250.00**
Bashful Charlotte, flower frog, gr, 11½" **350.00**
Bashful Charlotte, flower frog, Moonlight Blue satin, 11½", minimum ...**950.00**
Bird, crystal satin, 2¾" L **28.00**
Bird on stump, flower frog, gr, 5¼", minimum value **400.00**
Bridge hound, ebony, 1¼" **50.00**
Draped Lady, flower frog, amber, 8½" **175.00**
Draped Lady, flower frog, Dianthus, 13¼" **250.00**
Draped Lady, flower frog, gr frost, 8½" **150.00**
Draped Lady, flower frog, ivory, oval base, 8½", minimum value.....**1,000.00**
Draped Lady, flower frog, Moonlight Blue, 13¼", minimum value.....**1,000.00**
Eagle, bookend, crystal, 5½x4x4", ea...**80.00**
Mandolin Lady, flower frog, dk amber **400.00**
Owl, lamp, ivory w/brn enamel, ebony base, 13½", minimum value..**1,250.00**
Rose Lady, flower frog, crystal satin, tall base, 9¾" **175.00**
Rose Lady, flower frog, dk amber, tall base, 9¾" **275.00**
Scottie, bookends, crystal, hollow, pr **250.00**
Sea gull, flower block, crystal..**65.00**
Swan, Apple Green, #1 style, 13½"..**850.00**
Swan, Crown Tuscan, 3" **45.00**
Swan, ebony, 3" **65.00**
Swan, ebony, 10½" **300.00**
Swan, emerald, 3" **55.00**
Swan, milk glass, 6½"...**100.00**
Swan, punch bowl (15") & base, crystal, +12 cups **3,000.00**
Turkey, bl, w/lid **700.00**
Turtle, flower holder, ebony **200.00**
Two Kids, flower frog, amber satin, 9¼" **350.00**

Duncan and Miller

Bird of Paradise, crystal **650.00**
Dove, crystal, head down, w/o base, 11½" L **175.00**
Duck, ashtray, red, 7" **375.00**
Mallard duck, cigarette box, crystal, #30, w/lid, 3½x4½".............**60.00**
Swan, candle holder, red, 7", ea..**80.00**
Swan, milk glass w/red neck, 10½"..**400.00**

Swordfish, bl opal, rare...................................500.00
Swordfish, crystal...225.00
Tropical fish, ashtray, pk opal, 3½".................65.00

Fenton

Airedale, Rosalene, 1992 issue for Heisey 75.00
Alley cat, Teal Marigold, 11"...............................125.00
Bunny, lt bl 16.00

Butterfly on stand, blue satin, 1989 souvenir, 7½", $35.00.

Butterfly on stand, Lime Sherbet, 1989 souvenir, 7½" 35.00
Butterfly on stand, ruby carnival, 1989 souvenir, 7½" 40.00
Donkey, custard, HP daisies, 4½"..........................40.00
Filly, Rosalene, head front, 1992 issue for Heisey 125.00
Fish, paperweight, red carnival, ltd ed, 4½"..........65.00
Fish, red w/amberina tail & fins, 2½".....................65.00
Giraffe, Rosalene 100.00
Peacock, bookends, crystal satin, 5¾", pr............300.00
Rabbit, paperweight, Rosalene, 1992 issue for Heisey...................70.00
Turtle, flower block, amethyst, 4" L......................85.00

Fostoria

Bird, candle holder, crystal, 1½", ea 20.00
Cardinal head, Silver Mist, 6½"..........................175.00
Chanticleer, blk, 10¾" 500.00
Deer, bl, sitting or standing, ea 40.00
Deer, milk glass, sitting or standing, ea................40.00
Duck, mama, crystal 35.00
Eagle, bookend, crystal, 7½", ea 100.00
Frog, bl, lemon or olive gr, 1⅞", ea......................30.00
Goldfish, crystal, vertical 150.00
Lady bug, bl, lemon or olive gr, 1¼", ea 30.00
Madonna & Child, Silver Mist, lighted base optional, 13½"......250.00
Pelican, amber, 1987 commemorative 65.00
Polar Bear, crystal, 4⅝".......................................55.00
Rebecca at Well, candle holder, crystal frost, ea 125.00
Seal, topaz, 3⅞" 75.00

Heisey

Airedale, crystal 1,400.00
Bull, crystal, sgn, 4x7½" 2,400.00
Chick, crystal, head down or up, ea.....................100.00
Colt, amber, kicking..650.00
Colt, cobalt, kicking 1,200.00
Colt, crystal, rearing...250.00
Cygnet, baby swan, crystal, 2½" 225.00

Dolphin, candlesticks, crystal, #110, pr 400.00
Duck, ashtray, Marigold....................................400.00
Duck, flower block, Flamingo 200.00
Elephant, amber, lg or med, ea 2,400.00
Elephant, crystal, lg or med, ea 450.00
Filly, crystal, head bkwards.............................1,300.00
Fish, bowl, crystal, 9½"......................................600.00
Flying Mare, crystal 4,000.00
Gazelle, crystal, 10¾".....................................1,400.00
Giraffe, crystal, head bk 275.00
Giraffe, crystal, head to side..............................275.00
Goose, crystal, wings up 100.00
Hen, crystal, 4½"...425.00
Horse head, bookend, crystal, ea........................150.00
Irish setter, ashtray, crystal.................................30.00
Irish setter, ashtray, Flamingo............................45.00
Kingfisher, flower block, Flamingo......................225.00
Mallard, crystal, wings down.............................350.00
Mallard, crystal, wings up..................................200.00
Plug horse, cobalt 1,200.00
Rabbit, paperweight, crystal, 2¾x3¾"................200.00
Ram head, stopper, crystal, 3½"..........................300.00
Rooster, amber, 5⅜"......................................2,500.00
Rooster, crystal, 5½x5".......................................525.00
Rooster, vase, crystal, 6½".................................110.00
Rooster head, cocktail, crystal..............................50.00
Rooster head, cocktail shaker, crystal, 1-qt............85.00
Scotty, crystal..150.00
Show horse, crystal..1,250.00
Sparrow, crystal...120.00
Swan, ind nut, crystal, #1503 ....20.00
Swan, pitcher, crystal...650.00
Tropical fish, crystal, 12"................................2,000.00
Wood duck, crystal, mother...............................600.00
Wood duck, crystal, standing 225.00

Imperial

Airedale, caramel slag 125.00
Airedale, Ultra Blue...100.00
Bulldog-type pup, milk glass, 3½".........................65.00
Chick, milk glass, head down...............................20.00
Clydesdale, Salmon..200.00
Colt, amber, balking...140.00
Colt, caramel slag, balking..................................140.00
Colt, Sunshine Yellow, standing 75.00
Cygnet, caramel slag..40.00
Donkey, caramel slag...55.00
Donkey, Ultra Blue..65.00
Elephant, caramel slag, sm 75.00
Elephant, Meadow Green carnival, #674, med 75.00
Filly, satin, head forward......................................85.00
Fish, candlestick, Sunshine Yellow, 5" 40.00
Flying mare, amber, NI mk, extremely rare.........1,500.00
Giraffe, amber, ALIG mk, extremely rare.............200.00
Mallard, caramel slag, wings down.....................200.00
Mallard, caramel slag, wings up............................40.00
Mallard, lt bl satin, wings down............................35.00
Owl, Hootless; caramel slag..................................50.00
Owl, jar, caramel slag, 6½"...................................85.00
Owl, milk glass..35.00
Piglet, ruby, standing 35.00
Rabbit, paperweight, Horizon Blue, 2¾"..............110.00
Rooster, amber..475.00

Scolding bird, Cathay Crystal 175.00
Scottie, milk glass, 3½" 55.00
Terrier, Parlour Pup, amethyst carnival, 3½" 50.00
Tiger, paperweight, Jade Green, 8" L 100.00
Wood duck, Ultra Blue satin 55.00
Wood duckling, floating, Sunshine Yellow satin 20.00
Wood duckling, standing, Ultra Blue 45.00

L.E. Smith

Camel, crystal 50.00
Elephant, crystal, 1¾" 8.00
Goose Girl, crystal, orig, 6" 25.00
Horse, bookend, amber, rearing, ea 38.00
Horse, bookend, ruby, rearing, ea 50.00
King Fish, aquarium, gr, 7¼x15" 400.00
Rooster, butterscotch slag, ltd ed, #208 ....100.00
Swan, milk glass w/decor, 8½" 35.00
Swan, soap dish, crystal 25.00

New Martinsville

Bear, mama, crystal, 4x6" 175.00
Chick, frosted, 1" 25.00
Gazelle, crystal w/frosted base, leaping, 8¼" 60.00
Nautilus, bookend, crystal frost, 6", ea 35.00
Pig, mama, crystal 300.00
Piglet, crystal, standing 175.00
Rabbit, mama, crystal 350.00
Seal, baby w/ball, crystal 60.00
Seal, candlesticks, crystal, lg, pr 150.00
Ship, bookend, crystal, ea 65.00
Wolfhound, crystal, 7" 80.00
Woodsman, crystal, sq base, 7⅜" 90.00

Paden City

Bunny, cotton-ball dispenser, crystal frost, ears bk 175.00
Bunny, cotton-ball dispenser, pk frost, ears up 250.00

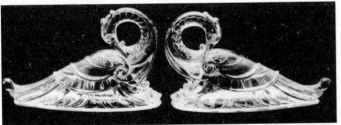

Dragon swans, slightly hollow bases, crystal, 9¾" long, $250.00 each.

Pelican, crystal 650.00
Pheasant, crystal, head bk, 12" 100.00
Pony, crystal, 12" 125.00
Pouter pigeon, bookend, crystal, 6¼", ea 95.00
Rooster, Barnyard; crystal, 8¾" 125.00
Rooster, Chanticleer; crystal, 9½" 125.00
Squirrel on curved log, crystal, 5½" 55.00

Tiffin

Cat, blk satin, raised bumps, #9445, 6¼", minimum value 450.00

Cat, Sassy Suzie, milk glass, minimum value.....................450.00
Fawn, flower floater, Copen Blue......................................450.00
Frog, candle holders, blk satin, pr 225.00
Owl, lamp, cobalt, 1934-29, minimum value...................1,000.00

Viking

Angelfish, amber, 7x7" 100.00
Bird, candy dish, med gr, w/lid, 12" 50.00
Bird, moss gr, tail up, 12" 45.00
Bird, Orchid, 9½" 100.00
Bird, ruby, #1310, 12" 60.00
Dog, orange 50.00
Duck, crystal, standing, Viking's Epic Line, 9" 65.00
Duck, orange, rnd, ftd, 5" 35.00
Duck, vaseline, 5" 60.00
Egret, orange, 12" 50.00
Owl, amber, Viking's Epic Line 30.00
Penguin, crystal, 7" 35.00
Rabbit, amber, 6½" 35.00
Rooster, avocado, Viking's Epic Line 55.00
Swan, bowl, amber, 6" 25.00
Swan, Yellow Mist, paper label, 6" 25.00

Westmoreland

Bird in flight, Amber Marigold, wings out, 5" W 45.00
Butterfly, Blue Mist, 2½" 35.00
Butterfly, crystal, 4½" 45.00
Butterfly, pk, 2½" 25.00
Cardinal, Green Mist..22.00
Pig, amberina 85.00
Pouter pigeon, any color, 2½", ea 25.00
Robin, pk, 5⅛" 25.00
Starfish, candle holders, milk glass, 5", pr 45.00
Turtle, cigarette box, crystal 35.00
Turtle, paperweight, Green Mist, no holes, 4" L 25.00
Wren, red, 2½" 25.00
Wren on perch, lt bl on wht, 2-pc 45.00

Miscellaneous

American Glass Co, horse, crystal, jumping........................60.00
Co-Operative Flint, elephant, pk, tusks rpr, 13" 350.00
Haley, horse, crystal, jumping, 9½" L 65.00
Haley, horse, milk glass, jumping 75.00
Haley, thrush, crystal 40.00
Indiana, pouter pigeon, bookend, crystal frost, ea 35.00
LG Wright, turtle, amber 80.00
Viking for Mirror Images, baby seal, ruby 100.00
Viking for Mirror Images, police dog, ruby 100.00

Glass Knives

Glass knives were manufactured from about 1920 to 1950, with distribution at its greatest in the late '30s and early '40s. Colors generally followed Depression glass dinnerware: crystal, light blue, light green, pink (originally called rose), and more rarely amber, forest green, and white (opal). Many glass knives were hand painted in fruit or flower designs. Knife blades were ground to a sharp edge. Today knives are usually found with blades nicked through years of use and bumping in silverware drawers or reground, which is acceptable to collectors as long as the original knife shape is maintained.

Many glass knives were engraved for gift-giving, personalized with the recipient's name and, on occasion, with a greeting. Originally presented in boxes, most glass knives were accompanied by a paper insert extolling the virtues of the knife and describing its care.

Boxes printed with World's Fair logos are fun to find, though not rare. Butter knives, which are smaller than other glass knives, typically were made in Czechoslovakia and sometimes match the handle patterns of glass salad sets. Knife lengths often vary slightly because the knives were snapped off the molded glass and the end ground during manufacture.

Several styles of knives (i.e. Vitex, Dur-X, Cryst-O-Lite) were manufactured by the thousands and are therefore found more often. Prices have become volatile due to the popularity of online, Internet auctions and the competition that results. Values reflect knives with minimal blade roughness or resharpening.

Aer-Flo, crystal, 7¼", from $30 to 40.00
Aer-Flo, gr, 7½" 70.00
BK Co, gr, 9¼" 60.00
Block, crystal, 8¼", from $15 to..20.00
Block, crystal, 8¼", MIB...30.00
Block, gr, 8¼" 25.00
Candlewick, crystal, 8½", from $400 to 450.00
Cryst-O-Lite, 3-flower hdl, MIB 18.00
Dur-X, 3-leaf, crystal, 8½"...22.00
Dur-X, 3-leaf, pk, 8½", from $35 to 40.00
Dur-X, 5-leaf, gr, lg center..45.00
Dur-X, 5-leaf, pk, 8½", MIB...45.00
Pinwheel, crystal, 8½", from $12 to......................................15.00
Star, crystal, 9½"..12.50
Star, pk, 9¼"...20.00
Steel-ite, crystal, 8½", from $35 to.......................................45.00
Steel-ite, gr, 8½"...75.00
Stonex, amber, 8½"..250.00
Stonex, opal, 8½"...350.00
Vitex (Star & Diamond), crystal...15.00
3-Star, pk or bl, 8½ or 9¼", ea...35.00

Glass Shoes

Little shoes made of glass can be found in hundreds of styles, shapes, and colors. They've been made since the early 1800s by nearly every glasshouse, large and small, in America. To learn more about them, we recommend *Shoes of Glass II* by our advisor Libby Yalom, who is listed in the Directory under Maryland. Numbers in the listings refer to her book. Another reference is *Collectible Glass Shoes, Second Edition*, by Earlene Wheatley, published by Collector Books. See also Degenhart.

#101, blue and white slag, English Sowerby, 1880s, 2½x5⅞", $170.00. (Photo courtesy Libby Yalom)

#10A, slipper, Daisy & Button, frosted bl, 5" 60.00
#131, boot, Daisy & Button, ruby & crystal, 1880s, 4¼" 165.00
#137, boot, w/cuff & spur, purple/bl/wht slag, 3¼x4" 75.00
#147A, boot, high-button w/horizontal ribs, frosted amber, 4¼" ..70.00
#171, high-button, crystal w/gold, 4 buttons, solid heel, 4½"........50.00
#181, boot, alligator or snakeskin pattern, amber 85.00
#207A, bootee, knitted look, clear apple gr, King Glass Co, 3⅝"...70.00
#248B, man's, milk glass w/bl-pnt flowers & gold trim, 3⅞" 70.00
#264B, slipper, clear w/fancy gold-tone metal bow & rim, 5"......135.00
#276, flat bow, crystal w/stippled finish, 4⅜" 30.00
#316, slipper, clear over cobalt w/gold-pnt trim 150.00
#319A, clog, sm knob on bk, clear gr, 8¼".................................90.00
#385, Dutch style, crystal, 3 ridges on vamp, 3 buttons, 7" 50.00
#388, slipper, sunburst design, clear, Sowerby, 7½".....................140.00
#395, boot match holder, flat-sided, wall mt, dk gr......................45.00
#432, Dutch shoe, frosted w/gold-pnt decor 45.00
#495, thimble holder, bl, emb B&R, ca 1890, 4" 130.00
#523, bootee, milk glass, knitted look, pk pnt w/gold, 2¾" 60.00
#555, bottle shoe, upturned toe is bottle neck, clear w/emb decor...65.00
#569A, boot (man's riding type), ruby w/gold & enamel decor, 6⅞" 75.00
#748, high-heel, stylized w/lg flower, teal, Czech, 6x6" 250.00
#761, boot, low cut, bl w/wht coralene effect, gold trim, 7".....1,200.00
#778, high-heeled slipper, pointed toe, ruffled, striped, Venetian, 5"..115.00
#817, tennis shoe, clear, 5⅝" 50.00

Glidden

Genius designer Glidden Parker established Glidden Pottery in 1940 in Alfred, New York, having been schooled at the unrivaled New York State College of Ceramics at Alfred University. Glidden pottery is characterized by a fine stoneware body, innovative forms, outstanding hand-milled glazes, and hand decoration which make the pieces individual works of art. Production consisted of casual dinnerware, artware, and accessories that were distributed internationally.

In 1949 Glidden Pottery became the second ceramic plant in the country to utilize the revolutionary Ram pressing machine. This allowed for increased production and for the most part eliminated the previously used slip-casting method. However, Glidden stoneware continued to reflect the same superb quality of craftsmanship until the factory closed in 1957. Although the majority of form and decorative patterns were Mr. Parker's personal designs, Fong Chow and Sergio Dello Strologo also designed award-winning lines.

Glidden will be found marked on the unglazed underside with a signature that is hand incised, mold impressed, or ink stamped. Interest in this unique stoneware is growing as collectors discover that it embodies the very finest of mid-century high style. Our advisor is David Pierce; he is listed in the Directory under Ohio.

Ashtray, Green Mesa, boat, 18¼"..150.00
Ashtray, Gulfstream Blue, #274 ....60.00
Ashtray, Safex, 10⅝"...20.00
Ashtray, Teardrop, Sage & Sand, #183....................................10.00
Ashtray, Teardrop, Turquoise Matrix, #183 ....8.00
Bean pot, Alfred Stoneware, Saffron, #808 ....75.00
Bean pot, Alfred Stoneware, Saffron, #809 ....135.00
Bowl, cobalt, #27 ....3.00
Bowl, cobalt, #36 ....20.00
Bowl, Pear, #17...130.00
Bowl, Turquoise Matrix, #17 ....10.00
Cache pot, Green Mesa, #4005 ....200.00
Casserole, Charcoal & Rice, Fish, #412 ....140.00
Casserole, Feather, w/lid, #167 ....20.00
Casserole, High Tide, w/lid, #167 ....60.00

Cigarette box, dbl; High Tide, #223 ....115.00
Creamer & sugar bowl, Feather, w/lid, #143 & #144 ....50.00
Creamer & sugar bowl, Flourish, w/lid, #143 & #144 ....60.00
Cup & saucer, Sage & Sand, #441 & #442 ....10.00
Figurine, Turquoise Matrix, Bird 130.00
Planter, cobalt, #89 ....5.00
Planter, Flourish, #88 ....70.00
Plate, 'W,' #33 ....20.00
Plate, Cat & Flowers, #35 ....6.00
Plate, Circus Clown, #35 ....10.00
Plate, Circus Strongman, #35 ....15.00
Plate, Flourish, #33 ....25.00
Plate, grille; Mexican cock, #300 ....30.00
Plate, Lamb & Flowers, #35 ....40.00
Plate, Menagerie, deer, #35 ....10.00
Plate, Mengerie, bull, #35 ....7.00
Plate, Turquoise Matrix, #33 ....6.00
Relish dish, Leaf, Fred Press, #280 ....30.00
Tile, serving; Garden, #606 ....80.00
Tray, candy/nut; Afrikans, w/stand, #200 ....315.00
Tray, candy/nut; Blackfish, w/stand, #200 ....45.00

Tray, serving, 'W' pattern, #29, $35.00. (Photo courtesy David Pierce)

Tumbler, Feather, #1127 ....75.00
Tumbler, Flourish, #1127 ....25.00
Tumbler, Menagerie, tiger, #1127 ....25.00
Tumbler, Turquoise Matrix, underglazed band, #1127 ....18.00
Vase, Early Pink, #52 ....15.00
Vase, Turquoise Matrix, #5 ....10.00
Vase, Turquoise Matrix, #63 ....12.00
Vase, Yellowstone, #6 ....15.00

Goebel

F.W. Goebel founded the F&W Goebel Company in 1871, located in Rodental, West Germany. They manufactured thousands of different decorative and useful items over the years, the most famous of which are the Hummel figurines first produced in 1935 based on the artwork of a Franciscan nun, Sister Maria Innocentia Hummel.

The Goebel trademarks have long been a source of confusion because all Goebel products, including Hummels, of any particular time period bear the same trademark, thus leading many to believe all Goebels are Hummels. Always look for the Hummel signature on actual Hummel figurines (these are listed in a separate section).

There are many other series — some of which are based on artwork of particular artists such as Disney, Charlot Byj, Janet Robson, Harry Holt, Norman Rockwell, M. Spotl, Lore, Huldah, and Schaubach. Miscellaneous useful items include ashtrays, bookends, salt and pepper shakers, banks, pitchers, inkwells, perfume bottles, etc. Figurines include birds, animals, Art Deco pieces, etc. The Friar Tuck monks and the Co-Boy elves are especially popular.

The date of manufacture is determined by the trademark. The incised date found underneath the base on many items is the mold copyright date. Actual date of manufacture may vary as much as twenty years or more from the copyright date.

Most Common Goebel Trademarks and Approximate Dates Used
1.) Crown mark (may be incised, stamped, or both): 1923 – 1950
2.) Full bee (complete bumble bee inside the letter 'V'): 1950 – 1957
3.) Stylized bee (dot with wings inside the letter 'V'): 1957 – 1964
4.) 3-Line (stylized bee with three lines of copyright info to the right of the trademark): 1964 – 1972
5.) Goebel bee (word Goebel with stylized bee mark over the last letter 'e'): 1972 – 1979
6.) Goebel (word Goebel only): 1979 – present

Our advisors for this category are Gale and Wayne Bailey; they are listed in the Directory under Georgia.

Cardinal Tuck (Red Monk)

Calendar holder, complete set of plastic calendar cards, 3¼" 190.00
Creamer & sugar bowl, mk S141/0 & Z37, 3¾", 4" 150.00
Cup, coffee; mk T74/0 ....125.00
Decanter, mk KL92, 10½" 250.00
Egg cup, mk E95/4, 1⅞" 150.00
Figurine, 2¼" 125.00
Match holder, 3" 125.00
Mustard pot, notched lid w/spoon, mk M42/A, 4" 85.00
Sugar bowl, mk M43/B, 1956 ....75.00
Wine stopper, figural monk on top, 3¼" 75.00

Charlot BYJ Redheads and Blonds

Baby Sitter, #66, 5¼x4⅛" 100.00
Bongo Beat, #65, 1970, 4⅞" 115.00
Display plaque, #47, 1966, 4½x6" 100.00
Guess Who?, boy tapping girl on shoulder, #40, 1956, 5" 135.00
Heads or Tails, #73, 1983-86, 5x5½" 115.00
Oops, girl w/3 blk cats, BYJ-3, 4½" 85.00
Plenty of Nothing, BYJ-27, 1958, 4¼" 55.00
Putting on the Dog, BYJ-25, 1958, 5" 70.00
Sea Breezes, girl in beach chair, BYJ-75, 1980, 4¾x2½" 115.00
Trim Lass, #49, 1969-78, 4½x4" 85.00
Young Man's Fancy, boy watching girl read book, BYJ-6, 4½" 115.00

Co-Boy Figurines

Bob the Bookworm, #510, 7" 55.00
Brad the Clock 135.00
Candy the Pastry Chef, Well #523, 1875 ....60.00
Conny the Watchman, Well #520, 1972, 7¼" 50.00
Greg the Gnome, seated on stool w/plate of food, 7" 65.00
Homer - Pretending To Drive, #17555-16, 1982, 6½" 45.00
Kuni the Painter, #515, 7¾" 60.00
Max the Boxer, #17527-003, 1975, 7⅜" 60.00
Merry Co-Boy, display plaque, English version, 5½x7¼" 55.00
Merry Co-Boy, display plaque, German version, 1971 ....115.00
Mike the Jam Maker, 8" 50.00
Monty the Mountain Climber, Well #18, 1979, 8¾" 45.00
Peter the Accordionist, #17541-18, TMK-6, 7" 60.00
Porz the Mushroom Hunter, Well #511, 1970 ....50.00
Sid the Vinter (or Winemaker) 90.00
Tom the Honey Lover, Well #504, 1970 ....45.00
Tommy the Football Player, #17530-13, 5¾x3" 45.00

Utz, #513, 1970, 7⅞"...**50.00**
Walter the Jogger, #17545-14, 1980, 5½"...............................**60.00**
Wim the Sausage Maker **100.00**

Cookie Jars

Cat, TMK-5, from $100 to...**175.00**
Dog, TMK-5, from $100 to...**125.00**
Friar Tuck, K-29, TMK-5 ....**250.00**
Owl, TMK-5, from $70 to...**80.00**
Panda Bear, TMK-5, from $70 to...**80.00**
Parrot, TMK-5, from $70 to..**80.00**
Pig, TMK-5, from $100 to..**125.00**

Friar Tuck (Brown Monk)

Bank, mk SD29, 4½"...**95.00**
Bank, 3 monks surround bbl, mk Western Germany, 1957, 2¾" ...**350.00**
Candy dish, mk ZF43/II, figural monk on side, 3¾x5¼" **70.00**
Cruets, oil & vinegar; 1 w/V on chest other w/O, mk M80, 1960, pr....**130.00**
Decanter, TMK-3, 10½"..**60.00**
Dish, heart shaped w/4⅜" figural monk, mk ZF43/2, 5½x6½" **60.00**
Egg timer, monk stands at well w/timer, mk BK504, 3" **65.00**
Figurine, w/gr hymnal, mk KF60/A, 1960, 4¾"...........................**65.00**
Figurine, 2¼" **55.00**
Goblet, wine; gold-leaf deer & geese on bowl, monk stem **70.00**
Honey pot, w/shoes & notched lid, mk H9...............................**115.00**
Matchbox holder, mk RX111, w/toes, Western Germany, 3", from $85 to....**100.00**
Pitcher, mk S141/111, 8¼"..**80.00**
Pitcher, water; all wht, mk S204, 1961 ....**90.00**
Shakers, 2¼", pr **25.00**
Tea bag holder, mk RF142, 1956, 3x3¾".....................................**75.00**
Thermometer, monk stands at side, mk KF56, 4¼" **80.00**
Vinegar bottle, Fussen on collar, TMK-4, mk M80, 5¼" **70.00**

Shakers

Castle turrets, gray w/cranberry-colored roof, pr **17.50**
Dogs, Pekingese, 1 facing right, 1 left, 2x3", pr.........................**17.50**
Dogs, wht, 1 w/brn ear, other w/blk, 2- & 3-hole, pr **25.00**
Ducks, 1½", pr...**12.50**
Kids, blk robe w/yel cross, 1 w/heart/flower, other w/mug/carrot, pr......**35.00**
Pigs, wht w/gr shamrock decor, pr, on 5x3" wht tray.....................**50.00**
Squirrel & pine cone, on leaf-shaped tray, M36/A, B & C............**65.00**

Miscellaneous

Egg timer, sailor boy & dock post w/timer in middle, TMK-2, 3", EX ..**90.00**
Figurine, bee playing dbl bass, mk KT130/C...............................**145.00**
Figurine, bee playing drum, mk KT130/F...................................**145.00**
Figurine, German shepherd, CH618, dtd 12/76, 7x9"....................**70.00**
Figurine, kingfisher, CV116, TMK-4, 9¾" **150.00**
Figurine, kissing skunks, Disney's Bambi, DIS119, TMK-2, 5x6½"........**285.00**
Figurine, mallard drake, mk CV117, 1970, 10½x13"....................**320.00**
Figurine, owl w/wings Xd in front, brn & wht, 4"........................**350.00**
Figurine, red fox, stalking position, TMK-6, 10" L **225.00**
Figurines, Snow White & 7 Dwarfs, DIS12 & DIS1-7, 1950...........**1,050.00**

Goldscheider

The Goldscheider family operated a pottery in Vienna for many generations before seeking refuge in the United States following Hitler's invasion of their country. They settled in Trenton, New Jersey, in the early 1940s where they established a new corporation and began producing objects of art and tableware items. (No mention was made of the company in the Trenton City Directory after 1950, and it is assumed that by this time the influx of foreign imports had taken its toll.) In 1946 Marcel Goldscheider established a pottery in Staffordshire where he manufactured bone china figures, earthenware, etc., marked with a stamp of his signature. Larger artist-signed examples are the most valuable with the Austrian pieces bringing the higher prices.

A wide variety of marks has been found: 1.) Goldscheider USA Fine China; 2.) Original Goldscheider Fine China; 3.) Goldscheider USA; 4.) Goldscheider-Everlast Corp.; 5.) Goldscheider Everlast Corp. in circle; 6.) Goldscheider Inc. in circle; 7.) Goldcrest Ceramics Corp. in circle; 8.) Goldcrest Fine China; 9.) Goldcrest Fine China USA; 10.) A Goldcrest Creation; and 11.) Created by Goldscheider USA.

Our co-advisors are Randy and Debbie Coe (listed in the Directory under Oregon) and Darrell Thomas (listed under Wisconsin).

American

Beautiful Morning, lady, hands clasped, #272, mk #3, 6½" **65.00**
Bust, lg pk hibiscus in bl/gr hair, EX Deco detail, Baldwin, mk 5, 12"..**350.00**
Busts: Chinese Royalty, gr/yel/orange, gray base, mk 5, 1940s, 6", pr ..**225.00**
Cat, Persian type, EX detail, orange/wht fur, 1950s, 4" L **45.00**
Chinese Wonderland, lady w/swan; man w/turtle, K Waldron, 1940s, pr.**195.00**
Colonial woman, basket w/flowers on head, Peggy P, #812, 9"......**95.00**
Dog, Dachshund, brn w/detailed eyes, 1950s, 9" **55.00**
Dog, Great Dane, blk/wht, EX lifelike qualities, 9½" **75.00**
Dog, Wolfhound, wht w/blk spots, on oval base, #5148, mk #1 ..**160.00**
Juliet (½-body) w/dove on ea hand, gold waist cord, mk #5, '40s, 15"..**150.00**
Lady, hand on head, other holding dress, #257, mk #3, 6¼" **75.00**
Lady, rose in 1 hand, handkerchief in other, #1230, mk #9, 9" ...**125.00**
Lady in winter outfit holds umbrella, #508, mk #11, 11½" **175.00**
Mandarin Dancers, she dancing; he w/drums, K Urbach, '50s, 14", pr.**185.00**
Mare w/colt, #758, mk #5, on 4x8" base, 6¼"..............................**145.00**
Peasant lady, gr/brn dress, w/vegetable basket, grassy base, '40, 10"..**125.00**
Rendezvous, lady lifts dress, bl/gray, #813, mk #9, 8"..................**125.00**
Rendezvous, man holding hat & flowers, #812, mk #9 ....**75.00**
Southern Belle, floral dress/holds hat, #500/mk 5, #500, 10" **150.00**

Austrian

Pierrot and lady, Austria, 1920 – 1953, 15", $325.00. (Photo courtesy Skinner, Inc.)

Bust, bl curls, ebony base, bl/gr/orange/terra cotta, gold mk, 10"..**925.00**
Bust, bl w/wht hair, red lips/cut-out eyes, gold-mk ebony base, WW, 5".**500.00**
Bust, blk w/long lt gray hair, hand w/flower, bl eyes/orange lips, 12" ...**1,250.00**
Diana the Huntress, mc, Latour, rpr, 23¼x19"............................**950.00**
Dolores Del Rio, Egyptian attire, L, #6281, 18"........................**3,220.00**

Lady w/book in lap seated on stool, D, #8006, 9¾"..................**1,520.00**
Mask, Spanish design, pk lace, lg earring on 1 side, yel scarf, 10x6" ...**925.00**
Peasant lady dancing, rpr, 16¼x16¾" **425.00**
Spanish dancer, bl lace w/wht trim, EX detail/color, D/Weiss, 16", EX .**250.00**
Spanish dancer, bl/orange w/gr leaves on face, WW, 8" ..**1,900.00**
Spanish dancer, blk lace/flowers on fan & headdress, EX detail, L, 17"..**1,800.00**
Spanish dancer, kicking, yel w/bl lace, flowered headdress, L/D, 14"..**2,200.00**
Spanish dancer, wht on bl lace, EX detail/color, D/C Weiss, 16", EX...**250.00**

Gonder

Lawton Gonder grew up with clay in his hands and fire in his eyes. Gonder's interest in ceramics was greatly influenced by his parents who worked for Weller and a close family friend and noted ceramic authority, John Herold. In his early teens Gonder launched his ceramic career at the Ohio Pottery Company while working for Herold. He later gained valuable experience at American Encaustic Tile Company, Cherry Art Tile, and the Florence Pottery. Gonder was plant manager at the Florence Pottery until fire destroyed the facility in late 1941.

After years of solid production and management experience, Lawton Gonder established the Gonder Ceramic Art Company, formerly the Peters and Reed plant, in South Zanesville, Ohio. Gonder Ceramic Arts produced quality art pottery with beautiful contemporary designs which included human and animal figures and a complete line of Oriental pottery. Accentuating the beautiful shapes were unique and innovative glazes developed by Gonder such as flambé (flame red with streaks of yellow), 24k gold crackle, antique gold, and Chinese crackle. (These glazes bring premium prices.)

All Gonder is marked with the company name and mold number. They include 'Gonder U.S.A' in block letters, 'Gonder' in script, 'Gonder Original' in script, and 'Gonder Ceramic Art' in block letters. Paper labels were also used. Some of the early Gonder molds closely resemble RumRill designs that had been manufactured at the Florence Pottery; and because some RumRill pieces are found with similar (if not identical) shapes, matching mold numbers, and Gonder glazes, it is speculated that some RumRill was produced at the Gonder plant. In 1946 Gonder started another company which he named Elgee (chosen for his initials LG) where he manufactured lamp bases until a fire in 1954 resulted in his shifting lamp production to the main plant. Operations ceased in 1957.

Ashtray, Trojan Horse on 1 end, turq, #548, 6x6½x4¼" **50.00**
Banana boat, lt gr w/brn overspray, #557, 16" **85.00**
Basket, brn, #L-19, 9x13" **95.00**
Bowl, bl wash over pk, irregular rim, 10½x8" **32.00**
Candle holders, fish, pk or bl, #561, pr.......................................**82.50**
Candle holders, kidney shape, maroon, #520, 2x5½", pr..............**40.00**
Candle holders, snail figural, mk Gonder USA, 4¾", pr **35.00**
Coffeepot, gr w/wht drip, 7" **120.00**
Conch shell, wht crackle, 16" **225.00**
Creamer & sugar bowl, La Gonda, red volcanic glaze, 4" **50.00**
Figurine, Balinese Water Bearer Man & Woman, maroon, 13½", pr..**110.00**
Figurine, goose, 5½" **40.00**
Figurine, panther, brn, #310, 19" **125.00**
Figurine, panther, streaky tan, #217, 5x15" **80.00**
Flower arranger, dk gr, 3-tiered **120.00**
Flower holder, swan figure, golden crackle, #E-44, 5" **25.00**
Ginger jar, bl crackle, #530 ....**72.50**
Jardiniere, gray w/emb floral, pk int, 5½x6½" **50.00**
Lamp base, 2 rearing horses (facing), 13" **75.00**
Pitcher, gr w/wht drip, #917, 8", +8 #909 matching 5" tumblers ...**145.00**
Pitcher, mottled burgundy gloss, w/lid, 8" **115.00**
Pitcher, turq w/brn highlights, wht lines, #801, slanted sides, 8½"..**65.00**

Teapot, gr w/wht drip, 4" **65.00**
TV lamp, ship, 14" **50.00**
Vase, basketweave emb, mustard & brn, 4-sided, #594, 12" ...**135.00**
Vase, cornucopia, bl & brn streaks, pk int, #J-6, 8½x8½" **40.00**
Vase, cornucopia, gr, #691, 8" **35.00**
Vase, fan; bl, #K-15, 10x10" **50.00**
Vase, Flame, #510, 11" **75.00**
Vase, flowing vegetation, yel & gr w/touches of brn, 14½x5x5" ...**82.50**
Vase, gray w/wht sponging, urn shape, #718, 8" **30.00**
Vase, leaf pattern, maroon w/lt brn trim, #599, 15¾" **95.00**
Vase, leaf shape, 2-hdl, #H-77, 8½" **40.00**
Vase, mauve & mustard streaks, ribbon-like design, #594, lg **92.50**
Vase, red-brn on wht, ewer form, #410, 7¾" **35.00**
Vase, shell, maroon, #J-60, 8x11½" **45.00**
Vase, shell, turq, w/starfish decor, #508, 13¼" **60.00**
Vase, streaky brn & tan, sq sides, ftd, #598, 14¾x4½x6" **57.50**
Vase, swan, #802, 9½x5½" **90.00**
Vase, Swirl, gr, bottle neck, waisted, #H-607, 9½", pr.................**135.00**

Goofus Glass

Goofus glass is American-made pressed glass with designs that are either embossed (blown out) or intaglio (cut in). The decorated colors were aerographed or hand applied and not fired on the pieces. The various patterns exemplify the artistry of the turn-of-the-century glass crafters. The primary production dates were ca 1908 to 1918. Goofus was produced by many well-known manufacturers such as Northwood, Indiana, and Dugan.

When no condition is given, our values are for examples in mint original paint. Our advisor for this category is Steve Gillespie of the *Goofus Glass Gazette*; he is listed in the Directory under Missouri. See also Clubs and Newsletters.

Basket, Diamond & Daisy, 6½", EX..**55.00**
Bowl, Butterfly, red & gold, ruffled, 2½x10½", EX+ **65.00**
Bowl, Carnation, La Belle & Roses in the Snow, 5½" sq **12.00**
Bowl, Carnation, La Belle & Roses in the Snow, 9" **15.00**
Bowl, Cherry, red & gold, Dugan, 2¼x10⅛".....................................**65.00**
Bowl, Cherry, ruffled rim, 3¼x10", NM **75.00**
Bowl, Hearts, 7" **45.00**
Bowl, Jeweled Heart, 2x9", NM **45.00**
Bowl, Poppy, red & gold, ftd, 4x9", EX...**60.00**
Bowl, Two Fruits & Olympic Torch, pattern decor, rare, 9" **130.00**
Bread tray, The Last Supper **35.00**
Cake plate, Acorn & Leaf, 12" **30.00**
Cake plate, Wild Flower, crackle glass border, 12" **25.00**
Compote, Butterfly, 6⅞x10¼", EX **70.00**
Compote, Rose, 6" **35.00**
Compote & saucer set, Poppy, crackle glass, 6" **40.00**
Dish, Hearts, rolled rim, 10" **50.00**
Lamp, oil; Grape & Leaf, minor flaking, 13¼" **275.00**
Lamp, oil; Nosegay, #2, EX orig pnt **250.00**
Lamp, oil; Wild Rose, Riverside, finger loop, 15" overall **250.00**
Plate, Butterfly, Dugan, rare, 11"...**80.00**
Plate, Chrysanthemum, frosted ground, 6¼", EX **45.00**
Plate, Hearts, 10" **45.00**
Plate, Lightning Flower, gr, unmk Northwood, 7"..............................**27.00**
Plate, Little Bo Peep, minor gold flaking, 6½" **80.00**
Plate, Poppy, clear, unmk Northwood, 7"...**27.00**
Plate, rose in base amid 8 long-stemmed roses, red/gold, 10¾", EX....**55.00**
Plate, Temple of Music, Pan Am Expo Buffalo NY, 7¼", EX **60.00**
Plate, Wheel & Block, opal, 9½"..**45.00**
Relish plate, Rose, glass hdls, 7"...**50.00**

Shakers, Vintage, dk gr & gold on milk glass, G orig lids, 3¼", pr...**55.00**
Slipper, lg, 7"..**45.00**
Tray, Fruit, 8½" sq **45.00**
Tumbler, Grape, gold on crackle, 4", NM..............................**50.00**
Vase, Basketweave w/Wild Rose, narrow neck & base, 9" **50.00**
Vase, Cabbage Rose, 15" **95.00**
Vase, Magnolia Blossoms, filigree top & bottom, 9½" **75.00**
Vase, peacock, red & gold, 15¼" **100.00**
Vase, Poppy, red flower w/gold leaves, 10"..........................**15.00**
Vase, Poppy, 5"..**15.00**
Vase, Tree Flowers (uncommon), 14½" **95.00**
Vase, Victorian Vase & Rose Buds, 14½" **85.00**

Goss and Crested China

William Henry Goss received his early education at the Government School of Design at Somerset House, London, and as a result of his merit was introduced to Alderman William Copeland, who owned the Copeland Spode Pottery. Under the influence of Copeland from 1852 to 1858, Goss quickly learned the trade and soon became their chief designer. Little is known about this brief association, and in 1858 Goss left to begin his own business. After a short-lived partnership with a Mr. Peake, Goss opened a pottery on John Street, Stoke-on-Trent, but by 1870 he had moved to his business to a location near London Road. This pottery became the famous Falcon Works. Their mark was a spread-wing falcon (goss-hawk) centering a narrow, horizontal bar with 'W.H. Goss' printed below.

Many of the early pieces made by Goss were left unmarked and are difficult to discern from products made by the Copeland factory, but after he had been in business for about fifteen years, all of his wares were marked. Today, unmarked items do not command the prices of the later marked wares.

Adolphus William Henry Goss (Goss's eldest son) joined his father's firm in the 1880s. He introduced cheaper lines, though the more expensive lines continued in production. Shortly after his father's death in 1906, Adolphus retired and left the business to his two younger brothers. The business suffered from problems created by a war economy, and in 1936 Goss assets were held by Cauldon Potteries Ltd. These were eventually taken over by the Coalport Group, who retained the right to use the Goss trademark. Messrs. Ridgeway Potteries bought all the assets in 1954 as well as the right to use the Goss trademark and name. In 1964 the group was known as Allied English Potteries Ltd. (A.E.P.), and in 1971 A.E.P. merged with the Doulton Group.

Aberdeen model of bronze pot, Eastbourne crest **16.00**
Ann Hathaway's cottage, 2½" **145.00**
Chicken Rock lighthouse, Willesden crest, 5" **40.00**
Exeter vase, Exeter crest, 4" **50.00**
Fountains Abbey abbott's cup w/Cinque Port of Rye crest **15.00**
Jersey fish basket, Blackpool crest, 4" **48.00**
Kendal jug, Brighton crest, 3⅜".......................................**15.00**
Lake Village near Glastonbury bowl, City of Exeter crest.............**10.00**
Manx Cottage nightlight, 4¾"..**300.00**
Weymouth vase, Weymouth & Melcombe-Regis crest, 2¼" **35.00**
York Roman ewer, Ipswich crest..**12.00**

Crested China

Arcadia, beer bbl on stand, Inverness crest, 2¼" **10.00**
Arcadia, Blackpool tower, Blackpool crest, 5½" **17.50**
Arcadia, blk cat holding bottle, Wellington New Zealand crest, 2¾"..**110.00**
Arcadia, match holder, Black boy, Weymouth & Melcombe Regis, 4" **315.00**
Arcadia, Welsh harp w/Arms of Barmouth crest, 3¼" **15.00**
Carlton, bust of Edward VII, Hoylake crest, 5¼" **85.00**

Foley China (Shelley), clog, coronation of Edward VII crest **10.00**
Grafton, Welsh hat, Arms of Wales crest, 2"..................................**17.50**
Willow Art, Florence Nightingale statue, Great Yarmouth crest, 5"...**37.50**
Willow Art, Wm Wallace Guardian of Scotland on plinth, Aberdeen crest...**175.00**

Gouda

Gouda is an old Dutch market town in the province of South Holland, famous for producing Gouda cheese. Gouda's ceramics industry had its beginnings in the early sixteenth century and was fueled by the growth in the popularity of smoking tobacco. Initially learning their craft from immigrant potters from England who had settled in the area, the clay pipe makers of Gouda were soon regarded as the best. While some authorities give 1898 (the date the Zuid-Holland factory began operations) as the initial date for the manufacturing of decorative pottery in Gouda, C.W. Moody, author of *Gouda Ceramics* (out of print), indicates the date was ca 1885. Gouda was not the only town in the Netherlands making pottery; Arnhem, Schoonhoven, and Amsterdam also had earthenware factories, but technically the term 'Gouda pottery' refers only to pieces made within the town of Gouda. Today, no Gouda-style factories are active within the city's limits, but in the first quarter of the twentieth century there were several firms producing decorative pottery there — the best known being Zuid, Regina, Zenith, Ivora, and Goedewaagen. At present Royal Goedewagen is making three patterns of limited editions. They are well marked as such.

This information was provided to us by Adela Meadows; she is listed in the Directory under California.

For further information we recommend *The World of Gouda Pottery* by Phyllis T. Ritvo (Front & Center Press, Weston, Massachussets).

Vase, heavy relief artwork, signed JS (att Johannes Stam), Amphora Holland/365/SJS/70, 11", **$770.00**.

(Photo courtesy Smith and Jones)

Bowl, bird on branch, Ivora, Mat 30 pattern, 2½x12"................**550.00**
Bowl, Bonzo pattern, circles/abstract elements/flowers, PZH, 1928, 12"..**465.00**
Bowl, floral & dots, Juliana Ivora, #359, 2½x9¼" **140.00**
Bowl, floral on orange w/cobalt, Anjer, #859, 1922, 4x9" **140.00**
Bowl, shield-like abstracts w/sun rays, Fella, Plazuid, 1929, 4x14" ...**250.00**
Candlestick, Deco florals & dots on sage, Masta, 11½x5", ea.....**140.00**
Candlestick, Holland, grapes, mc on brn, Zaas Princess Ivora, 9¼", ea.**100.00**
Candlestick, Rhodian, rtcl top, wide bobeche, ca 1910, 14½x5½", ea..**275.00**
Chalice, Golota, floral on turq, label/PZH, 1929, 7½x5" **385.00**
Ewer, tulips & star-shaped flowers, Zuid Holland, 9¾x7"...........**550.00**
Humidor, tulips & abstracts, scroll finial, #575, Holland, 7½"....**140.00**
Lamp, oil; abstracts on orange, wall type, Canac, 7½x5" dia **200.00**
Pen tray, bird on branch, Goldene ETE Holland, 1919, 9¾" **385.00**
Pitcher, abstracts/narrow swirled bands on gr, Candia, 6¾x5"......**165.00**
Pitcher, floral, mc on brn, bulbous, Goedewaagen, ca 1925, 8x5"....**140.00**
Pitcher, floral, rope-style bands, Anette, Royal Zuid, 13½x7", NM...**360.00**

Pitcher, Persian-type floral, mc on cream semimatt, Arnhem, 10½" ..**230.00**
Pitcher, Rosalie, floral, gr hdl, Zuid Holland, #5115, 5¾" **195.00**
Pitcher, stylized berries, mc w/cobalt, Holland, 1919, 10½x6½" ...**550.00**
Planter, ship scene on clog form, Zuid Holland, 1904-10, 2¼x5½" **110.00**
Plaque, birds & flowers, Zuid Holland, 1910, 18" **2,500.00**
Plaque, floral, Dolores Koninklyk, Royal Holland, #5041/46, 18" **220.00**
Plaque, Madeleine pattern, floral, PZH, 1930, 9" **220.00**
Pot, pansies & swirls, ftd, w/lid, Plateelfabriek Ivora, 1920s, 4x6" **700.00**
Tazza, mushrooms & grass blades on cobalt, Elma, Holland, 5x6" **195.00**
Tray, Fanny, Deco-style flowers, PZH, 1927, 1x12x8", NM **250.00**
Urn, Virginia, abstracts/triangles, Holland, 1919, 15x8", NM.....**800.00**
Vase, abstract teardrops & lace, Massa, Holland, 1920s, 4¾x5½" **150.00**
Vase, abstracts & dots, flared mouth, Candia, 12x7" **220.00**
Vase, abstracts on cerulean bl w/cobalt, Hollandia, 1921, 13x8" ...**525.00**
Vase, abstracts on dk brn, cylindrical, Rosario, Regina, 8½x5¼" ..**165.00**
Vase, abstracts w/cobalt on gr, dbl-gourd, Alad, Holland, 12x6" ...**330.00**
Vase, abstracts w/gr borders, looped hdls, PZH, 1919, 7x7½" **300.00**
Vase, bursting stars, dmn border, baluster, Astra, 1925, 18x9" **715.00**
Vase, Deco circles & ovals, waisted, Lero, PZH, 1928, 6¾x4" **640.00**
Vase, floral, mc on wht, ovoid w/wide mouth, Holland, 1923, 16½" **220.00**
Vase, floral, yel stripes/cobalt dots, buttress hdls, Holland, 7¾" ..**165.00**
Vase, floral & abstracts on ivory, Majoli, Regina, 5x6" **150.00**
Vase, floral & mc bands, Aurora, Plazuid, 1929, 12½x8½" **385.00**
Vase, floral w/oak leaves on ivory, Averil Royal Plazuid, 10¾" ...**330.00**
Vase, floral w/spiraling petals, Spino, 1924, 7¾x5" **140.00**
Vase, flower trio reserve on indigo, Lino, 1928, 14x5½" **300.00**
Vase, Holland, Nouveau flowers, integral hdls, Regina, 11" **500.00**
Vase, lilies/leafage, allover decor, bulbous w/long slim neck, NB, 13" ..**865.00**
Vase, ovals (mc) & bl waves, Massa, Holland, 1915-20, 5x5½" **140.00**
Vase, poppy & silhouette foliage on magenta, Gambir, Regina, 1920, 11" ..**715.00**
Vase, Rembrandt portrait/Nouveau florals, hdls, PZH, 1908, 8x9", NM ..**825.00**
Vase, stylized lion among swirls, Distel, sgn Arie Boom, 10¼x6" **330.00**
Vase, Tessel, abstract buds/shapes, factory bruise, PZH, 1920, 8x5" **495.00**

Graniteware

Graniteware, made of a variety of metals with enamel coatings, derives its name from its appearance. The speckled, swirled, or mottled effect of the vari-colored enamels may look like granite — but there the resemblance stops. It wasn't especially durable! Expect at least minor chipping if you plan to collect.

Graniteware was featured in 1876 at Phily's Expo. It was mass produced in quantity, and enough of it has survived to make at least the common items easily affordable. Condition, color, shape, and size are important considerations in evaluating an item; cobalt blue and white, green and white, brown and white, and old red and white swirled items are unusual, thus more expensive. Pieces of heavier weight, seam constructed, riveted, and those with wooden handles and tin or matching graniteware lids are usually older. Pieces with matching granite lids demand higher prices than ones with tin lids.

For further study we recommend *The Collector's Encyclopedia of Graniteware, Book II,* by our advisor, Helen Greguire. It is available from the author and Collector Books. For information on how to order, see her listing in the Directory under South Carolina. For the address of the National Graniteware Society, see the section on Clubs, Newsletters, and Catalogs.

Note: Unless noted otherwise, our values are for pieces in mint or near-mint condition; appropriate deductions must be made if damage is present.

Bean pot, solid bl w/wht int, perforated lid, seamless, 7¾" **125.00**
Bowl, bl & wht lg swirl, wht int, blk trim, 2¼x5⅞" **155.00**
Bowl, mixing; apple gr w/tangerine int, 4x7" **25.00**
Bowl, mixing; yel & wht lg swirl w/blk trim, 1950s, 6x12¼" **50.00**
Bowl, vegetable; brn & wht lg swirl, wht int, oval, 1½x7½x9" **295.00**
Bread pan, bl & wht lg mottle, wht int, oblong, 3x4¾x9¾" **345.00**
Bucket, berry; cream w/gr trim, wire bail, seamless, 5x3½", G+..**145.00**
Bucket, blk & wht lg swirl w/blk trim, wooden bail, 7½x7½", G+....**575.00**
Bucket, gray med mottle, riveted ears, wire bail, 5x4¾" **115.00**
Bucket, slop; bl & wht med mottle, blk wooden bail, 9½" **225.00**
Butter dish, wht w/cobalt trim, spun knob, L&G Mfg Co, 4¾" ..**325.00**
Candlestick, solid red w/blk trim, shell-shaped w/finger ring, 1½" **195.00**
Candlestick, solid wht, carrying hdl, sq base, 2" **150.00**
Chamber pot, bl & wht lg mottled, bl trim & hdls, seamless, 8" dia, G+....**135.00**
Coffee biggin, gray lg mottle, seamed body, matching lid, 9¾", NM....**895.00**
Coffee biggin, pk & wht lg swirl, wht int, blk trim, 5¼" dia **625.00**
Coffee biggin, reddish brn & wht lg swirl, wht int, 10½", G+ **595.00**
Coffee boiler, bl & wht lg swirl, blk trim, hdl & knob, 10½x9" **495.00**
Coffee carrier, red & wht lg mottle, wire bail, red trim, 8½", G+ **695.00**
Coffeepot, cream w/gr trim, welded hdl & finial, 7¾x5½" **95.00**
Coffeepot, red & wht lg swirl, blk trim, Bakelite knob, 1950s, 8¾" **275.00**
Coffeepot, solid aqua, wht int, blk trim & hdl, Pyrex, 9" **85.00**
Coffeepot, wht w/blk trim, squatty, 4¾" dia **165.00**
Cream can, brn & wht fine mottle, wooden bail, 8x4¼" **140.00**
Creamer, aqua gr & wht lg swirl, squatty, 4⅝x3⅜" **495.00**
Cup, yel & wht lg mottle w/blk trim, 1960s, 2x3⅛" **45.00**
Cupsidor, wht w/cobalt trim, 2-pc, mk Sweden, 2⅜x8" **95.00**
Custard cup, bl & wht fine mottle, cobalt trim, 4¼" dia **95.00**
Dbl boiler, brn & wht lg swirl, wht int, dk brn trim, 8½" **375.00**
Dbl boiler, cream w/gr trim & hdls, Belle shape, seamless, 6½" **75.00**
Dbl boiler, gray med mottle, wooden bails, L&G Mfg Co, 11¾" G+ ...**115.00**
Dipper, bl & wht lg swirl, cup-shaped, blk trim & hdl, 2⅜x4¼" **250.00**
Dipper, lg mottled gray, seamless, riveted hdl, lg, 2⅝x6⅛" **75.00**
Dustpan, solid red, 13⅜x10½" **265.00**
Egg cup, wht w/gr trim, 2x2" **95.00**
Egg pan, gray lg mottle, riveted hdl, 5-eye, 1¼x12" **275.00**
Fry pan, grayish-lav & wht lg swirl, iron base, 2⅛x10½" **350.00**
Fry pan, red & wht lg swirl, blk trim & hdl, 1¼x7⅞" **185.00**
Fry pan, yel & wht lg mottle, wht int, blk hdl & trim, 1¾" **165.00**
Funnel, bl & wht fine mottle, blk trim, squatty, 4" L **195.00**
Funnel, charcoal gray & wht, w/finger ring & seamed spout, fluted, 6" **120.00**
Funnel, wht w/blk trim & hdl, squatty, 4¾x7½", G+ **45.00**
Grater, bl & wht med mottle, riveted hdl & ft, 13⅜x4⅞" **425.00**
Grater, solid red, flat hdl, 10x3⅝", G+ **125.00**
Kettle, gray lg mottle, flared, wooden bail, 7x15¾" **165.00**
Ladle, sauce; wht w/blk trim & hdl, 9x2½" **40.00**
Ladle, soup; gray sm mottle, riveted hdl, 7¾" L, G+ **75.00**
Ladle, soup; wht w/gr trim & hdl, mk Savory Ware, 14" **30.00**
Measure, aqua gr & wht lg swirl, riveted spout, strap hdl, 4⅞" ...**450.00**
Measure, bl & wht med mottled blk trim, riveted hdl, 7⅜x4", G **175.00**
Milk can, brn & wht lg swirl, seamless w/flat ears & wire bail, 9½" ...**1,095.00**
Milk can, lt bl & wht wavy mottling, blk trim, wire bail, 8¾" ...**1,000.00**
Milk can, wht w/gr trim & hdl, wooden bail, mk Savory Ware, 6¼" **95.00**
Mold, gray med mottle, rolled top edge, 2⅜x5¼x6½", G+ **225.00**
Mold, lion, solid wht, 4½x5⅛" **375.00**
Mold, lobster, solid bl w/wht int, hdls, 3¾x7x10", G+ **165.00**
Mold, melon, solid cobalt w/wht int, tin lid, 7¼x5½" **115.00**
Mold, ribbed style, solid cobalt w/wht int, 2⅞x8¼", G+ **95.00**
Mold, ring, solid yel w/wht int, 2¼x8⅛", G+ **65.00**
Muffin pan, aqua gr & wht lg swirl, wht int, 6-cup, 10⅛" L **950.00**
Muffin pan, gray lg mottle, wire fr, 12-cup, 9½x12½" **235.00**
Mug, aqua gr w/wht int & blk trim, 1960s, 3½x3¾", G+ **20.00**
Mug, bl & wht lg swirl, blk trim, wht int, 3⅛x3⅞" **95.00**
Mug, lt gray & wht lg marbleized, wht int, 4⅛x4", G+ **75.00**
Pail, water; bl & wht lg swirl, blk trim & ears, wooden bail, 10" dia ..**395.00**
Pail, water; solid yel w/blk ears & trim, wooden bail hdl, 9⅜" **55.00**
Pan, pk & wht lg mottle, cobalt trim, wht int, hdls, 8¼" **235.00**

Pan, tart; gray lg mottle, 6" dia, G+ **45.00**
Pitcher, milk; brn & wht med mottle, blk hdl, Onyx Ware, 5½" G+ .. **135.00**
Pitcher, milk; gray lg mottle, squatty, weld hdl, 6⅞x4½" **325.00**
Pitcher, water; bl & wht med swirl w/wht int, 8¾x6½" **595.00**
Pitcher, water; gray lg mottle, weld hdl, 10⅝x7" **295.00**
Pitcher, water; mauve rose w/wht int, blk trim, seamless, 9¼" **135.00**
Pitcher, water; red & wht lg mottle w/wht int, riveted hdl, 9" **595.00**
Platter, red & wht lg swirl, wht int, blk trim, oval, 13x17½" **195.00**
Pudding pan, bl & wht lg swirl, wht int, blk trim, 3¼x9⅝" **195.00**
Pudding pan, blk & wht lg swirl, blk trim, seamless, 3⅛x9¾" **295.00**
Pudding pan, brn & wht mottle w/blk trim, Onyx Enamel Ware, 7¼" ... **20.00**
Pudding pan, red & wht lg swirl w/wht int, bl trim, old, 8½", G+...... **575.00**
Pudding pan, wht w/cobalt bl, eyelet for hanging, 1½x7" **35.00**
Roaster, cream & gr, oval, emb Savory, 8x10⅝x17", G+ **85.00**
Roaster, solid red w/bl trim & hdls, wire insert, 8½x9x14¼" **110.00**
Scoop, solid red, flat bottom, mk Portugal, 5¾" L **175.00**
Scoop, spice; solid red w/gold bands & trim, wht int, 4¼" L **185.00**
Spoon, brn & wht lg swirl, 13⅜x2¼" **195.00**
Strainer, gray lg mottle, 8-sided, 3 spatula-shaped ft, 4x8¼", G+ .. **325.00**
Strainer, tea; gray med mottle, perforated bottom, 4x⅞" **95.00**
Strainer, tea; solid wht, triangular, perforated bottom, 4" **105.00**
Teakettle, blk & wht lg swirl, wht int, Bakelite knob, 9" dia **595.00**
Teakettle, lg & dk gray relish, aluminum spout lid, 4⅝x7⅛", G+ **170.00**
Teakettle, lt gray lg mottle, wooden bail, 6½x8½", G+ **225.00**
Teakettle, red w/blk int, bottom, trim & hdl, seamless, 7½" **100.00**
Teakettle, solid red, wht int, blk trim & hdl, 5¾x6¼" **130.00**
Teapot, bl & wht chicken wire w/wht int, 5¾x4⅝" **165.00**
Teapot, brn & wht lg swirl, wht int, blk trim, 11x7" **750.00**
Teapot, red & wht lg mottle w/wht int & red trim, seamed, old, 8¾" ... **750.00**
Tray, bl & wht lg swirl, wht int, blk trim, oblong, 15⅝" **595.00**
Tumbler, brn & wht lg swirl, wht int, brn trim, 3½x3¼" **575.00**
Wash basin, bl & wht lg spatter, wht int, blk trim, 2⅝x10¼" **145.00**
Wash basin, bl & wht lg swirl, eyelet for hanging, 3⅝x13¾" **225.00**
Wash basin, red & wht lg swirl w/wht int & bl trim, old, 3½x12¼" .. **950.00**
Water carrier, gray med mottle, seamed, riveted hdls, 15¾x10" **1,395.00**

Green Opaque

Introduced in 1887 by the New England Glass Works, this ware is very scarce due to the fact that it was produced for less than one year. It is characterized by its soft green color and a wavy band of gold reserving a mottled blue metallic stain. It is usually found in satin; examples with a shiny finish are extremely rare. Values depend to a large extent on the amount of the gold and stain remaining. Our advisors for this category are Betty and Clarence Maier; they are listed in the Directory under Pennsylvania.

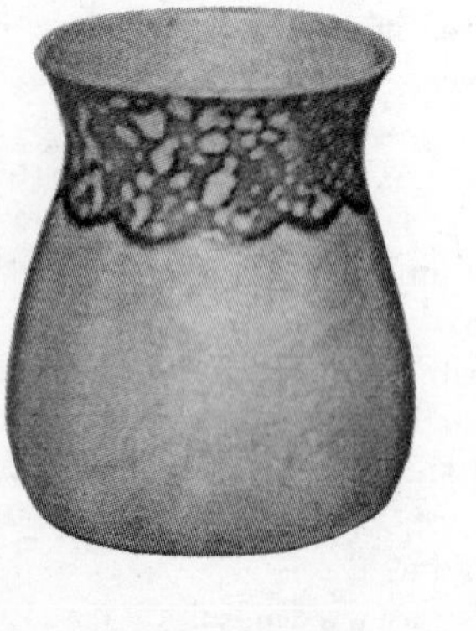

Spooner, EX stain and gold, 4", $925.00. (Photo courtesy James Julia)

Bowl, EX stain & gold, w/lid, 4x6" **1,250.00**
Bowl, EX stain & gold, 3½x8" **995.00**
Bowl, M stain & gold, 4x8" **1,150.00**
Bowl, VG stain & gold, w/lid, 6⅜" **900.00**
Celery vase, worn stain & gold, 6½" **450.00**
Creamer, EX stain & gold **950.00**
Cruet, M stain & gold, orig stopper **1,950.00**
Cruet, VG stain, orig stopper **1,500.00**
Mug, EX stain & gold, 2¼" **500.00**
Mug, M stain & gold, 2½" **700.00**
Punch cup, M stain & gold **750.00**
Punch cup, worn stain & gold, 2½" **225.00**
Shaker, M stain & gold, 2½" **400.00**
Sugar bowl, EX stain & gold **500.00**
Toothpick holder, EX gold **900.00**
Toothpick holder, M gold **1,150.00**
Tumbler, EX stain, 3¾" **475.00**
Tumbler, lemonade; w/hdl, M stain & gold, 5" **950.00**
Tumbler, M stain & gold, 3¾" **600.00**
Tumbler, VG mottling, 3¾" **300.00**
Vase, flared, M stain & gold, 6" **900.00**

Greenaway, Kate

Kate Greenaway was an English artist who lived from 1846 to 1901. She gained worldwide fame as an illustrator of children's books, drawing children clothed in the styles worn by proper English and American boys and girls of the very early 1800s. Her book, *Under the Willow Tree*, published in 1878, was the first of many. Her sketches appeared in leading magazines, and her greeting cards were in great demand. Manufacturers of china, pottery, and metal products copied her characters to decorate children's dishes, tiles, and salt and pepper shakers as well as many other items.

What some collectors/dealers call Kate Greenaway items are not actual Kate Greenaway designs but merely look-alikes. Genuine Kate Greenaway items (metal, paper, cloth, etc.) must bear close resemblance to her drawings in books, magazines, and special collections. Our advisor for this category is James Lewis Lowe; he is listed in the Directory under Pennsylvania. See also Napkin Rings.

Biscuit jar, ceramic, boy w/tinted features, w/lid **165.00**
Book, A Apple Pie, Warne, 1940, w/dust jacket, VG **30.00**
Book, Almanack for 1884, printed by Edmund Evans, EX **135.00**
Book, cloth; A Apple Pie, Saalfield, 1907, EX+ **85.00**
Book, cloth; Greenaway's Babies, Saalfield, 1907, EX+ **85.00**
Book, cloth; Ring-Round-a-Rosy, red cover, Saalfield, 1907, EX+ **100.00**
Book, cloth; Ring-Round-a-Rosy, wht cover, Saalfield, 1907, EX+...... **85.00**
Book, Good-Night Stories for Little Folks, NY & London, no date, EX+ .. **65.00**
Book, Kate Greenaway Pictures, London, Warne, 1st ed, 1921, VG .. **300.00**
Book, Kate Greenaway's Alphabet, London, 1880, EX **190.00**
Book, Kate Greenaway's Book of Games, Routledge, 1st ed, 1889, NM .. **475.00**
Book, Little Ann & Other Poems, by Taylor, VG **50.00**
Book, Marigold Garden, London, 1888, VG **60.00**
Book, Mother Goose, London, later print of 1st ed, VG **150.00**
Book, Pictures & Rhymes for Children, paperbk, McLoughlin, ca 1900 .... **65.00**
Book, Pied Piper of Hamlin, NM **100.00**
Book, Sunshine for Little Children, 1884, EX **80.00**
Book, Under the Window, ca 1900 (no date), mini, 4x5", VG **85.00**
Book, Under the Window, Routledge, 1st ed, orig cloth **165.00**
Bowl, Daisy & Button, amber; Reed & Barton SP fr w/girl & dog **525.00**
Butter pat, children playing transfer, pre-1910 .... **40.00**
Button, Autumn from Almanack, metal silhouette, 1⅛" **40.00**
Button, Christening, metal silhouette, 1" **60.00**
Button, Johnny at Fence Post, metal, ¾" **30.00**
Button, Johnny's Friend, metal, 2" **50.00**
Button, Little Bo Peep, flat or cupped metal, ⅝-¾", from $20 to **25.00**

Button, Little Bo Peep, metal silhouette, scalloped, ¾-1", $20 to ..**30.00**
Button, Miss Pelicoes, metal silhouette, rear or front view, 1¼" ...**40.00**
Button, Pretty Patty & Trumpeter, cupped metal, ⅝" **30.00**
Button, Pretty Patty Sitting on Fence, cupped metal silhouette, ¾" **20.00**
Button, Pretty Patty Sitting on Fence, metal, ¾" **20.00**
Button, Pretty Patty Sitting on Fence, thin metal, felt bk, 1½" ...**30.00**
Button, Ring the Bells Ring, 4 girls in queue, gold on glass, ⅝"....**30.00**
Button, Ring the Bells Ring, 4 girls in queue, gold on glass, ⅞"....**40.00**
Button, Ring the Bells Ring, 4 girls on queue, silver on glass, ⅞".**40.00**
Button, See-Saw from Mother Goose, gold & wht metal, fancy, 1½"...**80.00**
Button, Spring from Almanac, glass, 1".................................**40.00**
Button, Spring from Almanac, metal silhouette, ⅝"...................**30.00**
Button, Spring from Almanac, wht metal on brass, ¾" **40.00**
Button, Summer from Almanac, brass on bl metal, ¾x⅞", from $20 to **25.00**
Button, Summer from Almanac, glass, ¾"..............................**20.00**
Button, Summer from Almanac, metal, sq, ¾" **25.00**
Button, Summer from Almanac, metal silhouette, 1" **25.00**
Button, Winter from Almanac, metal silhouette, ¾x⅞", from $20 to.....**30.00**
Button, 2 Girls Sitting on Rail, metal, ¾" **50.00**
Button, 2 Lazy Loons, wht metal on MOP, ⅝" **50.00**
Calendar, chromolithograph, Routledge, 1884, 7⅜x9½", EX........**60.00**
Card, Christmas; girl in wht w/roses, Tuck, metal stand, 7x8¾"....**100.00**
Cup & saucer, children transfer, pk lustre trim, pre-1910...........**125.00**
Engraving, Harper's Bazaar, Jan 1879, full-pg **25.00**
Figurine, girl (seated) tugs on lg hat, bsk, pre-1910, sm................**75.00**
Hatpin holder, SP, girl figural, Meriden, 4" **125.00**
Inkwell, boy & girl, bronze...**215.00**
Match holder, ornate SP, girl in fancy clothes, Tufts **195.00**
Paperweight, CI, Victorian girl in lg bonnet, pre-1910, 3x2¾"...**110.00**
Pencil holder, pnt porc, pre-1910 ....**100.00**
Pickle castor, bl; SP fr w/2 girls, blown-out florals **455.00**
Plate, ABC, girl in lg hat, Staffordshire, 7" **120.00**
Scarf, children on silk, early, EX **65.00**
Tea set, semi-porc, floral motif, pre-1910, child sz, 3-pc **95.00**
Toothpick holder, SP, girl holds amberina cup, ornate base, 5" ...**785.00**
Toothpick holder, SP, girl stands by Sandwich glass holder w/crane.....**750.00**
Wall pocket, ceramic, 6 girls on open-book form, 6x9x3" **137.00**

Greentown Glass

Greentown glass is a term referring to the product of the Indiana Tumbler and Goblet Company of Greentown, Indiana, ca 1894 to 1903. Their earlier pressed glass patterns were #75 (originally known as #11), a pseudo-cut glass design; #137, Pleat Band; and #200, Austrian. Another line, Dewey, was designed in 1898. Many lovely colors were produced in addition to crystal. Jacob Rosenthal, who was later affiliated with Fenton, developed his famous chocolate glass in 1900. The rich, shaded opaque brown glass was an overnight success. Two new patterns, Leaf Bracket and Cactus, were designed to display the glass to its best advantage, but previously existing molds were also used. In only three years Rosenthal developed yet another important color formula, Golden Agate. The Holly pattern was designed especially for its production. The dolphin covered dish with a fish finial is perhaps the most common and easily recognized piece ever produced. Other animal dishes were also made; all are highly collectible. There have been many repros — not all are marked! The symbol (+) at the end of some of the following lines was used to indicate items that have been reproduced.

Our advisors for this category are Jerry and Sandi Garrett; they are listed in the Directory under Indiana. See the Pattern Glass section for clear pressed glass; only colored items are listed here.

Animal dish, bird w/berry, chocolate (+)................................**1,000.00**
Animal dish, cat on hamper, canary, low **850.00**

Animal dish, cat on hamper, wht opaque, tall **550.00**
Animal dish, dolphin, chocolate, smooth rim.........................**275.00**
Animal dish, dolphin, emerald gr, beaded rim **850.00**
Animal dish, dolphin, teal bl, sawtooth rim (+) **925.00**
Animal dish, fighting cocks, Nile Green **3,000.00**
Animal dish, hen, cobalt...**500.00**
Animal dish, rabbit, wht opaque (+).....................................**225.00**
Animal pitcher, heron, chocolate..**650.00**
Animal pitcher, squirrel, chocolate **550.00**
Austrian, bowl, canary, rectangular, 5¼x8¼" L.......................**250.00**
Austrian, butter dish, canary...**500.00**
Austrian, creamer, chocolate, 4¼"......................................**127.00**
Austrian, pitcher, water; canary..**525.00**
Austrian, sugar bowl, chocolate, w/lid, 2½" dia **150.00**
Brazen Shield, butter dish, bl...**275.00**
Brazen Shield, cake stand, bl, 9⅜".....................................**250.00**
Brazen Shield, goblet, bl..**250.00**
Brazen Shield, relish tray, bl..**125.00**
Brazen Shield, spooner, bl..**130.00**
Cactus, bowl, chocolate, 5¼"..**80.00**
Cactus, compote, chocolate, 5¼".......................................**90.00**
Cactus, cruet, chocolate, w/stopper **135.00**
Cactus, mug, chocolate..**50.00**
Cactus, vase, chocolate, 6"...**550.00**
Cord Drapery, bowl, amber, w/fluted top, 8" **200.00**
Cord Drapery, butter dish, cobalt, 4¾"................................**450.00**
Cord Drapery, compote, cobalt, w/lid, 8½" **375.00**
Cord Drapery, creamer, emerald gr, 4¼"..............................**175.00**
Cord Drapery, sauce bowl, amber, ftd, 3⅞".........................**95.00**
Cord Drapery, tray, water; emerald gr **325.00**
Cupid, butter dish, chocolate...**700.00**
Cupid, creamer, chocolate..**375.00**
Cupid, spooner, Nile Green...**425.00**
Cupid, sugar bowl, wht opaque, w/lid..................................**125.00**
Dewey, creamer, Nile Green, 5"..**375.00**
Dewey, parfait, chocolate, no lid **225.00**
Dewey, pitcher, canary...**175.00**
Dewey, sugar bowl, emerald gr, w/lid, 4" **125.00**
Dewey, tumbler, amber **40.00**
Diamond Prisms, tumbler, chocolate **675.00**
Early Diamond, dish, amber, rectangular, 8x5".......................**225.00**
Early Diamond, dish, cobalt, rectangular, 8x5".......................**275.00**
Early Diamond, pitcher, amber **350.00**
Early Diamond, tumbler, chocolate **225.00**
Greentown Daisy, creamer, chocolate, w/lid **175.00**
Greentown Daisy, sugar bowl, wht opaque, w/lid **80.00**
Herringbone Buttress, bowl, amber, 5¼" **350.00**
Herringbone Buttress, cordial, emerald gr, 3¾"......................**325.00**
Herringbone Buttress, plate, emerald gr, 7¼".........................**350.00**
Herringbone Buttress, vase, emerald gr, 6"............................**225.00**
Holly Amber, bowl, rnd, 7½"...**550.00**
Holly Amber, bowl, 4½" **225.00**
Holly Amber, bowl, 8½"...**700.00**
Holly Amber, butter dish, ped ft...**3,000.00**
Holly Amber, cake stand **3,000.00**
Holly Amber, compote, jelly; w/lid, 4½"...............................**1,350.00**
Holly Amber, compote, low ped base, 4½x4", EX **1,350.00**
Holly Amber, creamer...**750.00**
Holly Amber, mustard pot, open, 3¼"..................................**1,000.00**
Holly Amber, pickle dish, oval w/tab hdls, 8¾" **400.00**
Holly Amber, sauce dish, 4½"...**225.00**
Holly Amber, syrup pitcher, metal lid **2,250.00**
Holly Amber, tray, rnd, 9¼"..**1,500.00**
Holly Amber, tumbler, 4"..**450.00**

Holly Amber, vase, 6" **700.00**
Leaf Bracket, relish dish, chocolate, 8x5" **55.00**
Leaf Bracket, sauce dish, wht opaque **150.00**
Leaf Bracket, tray, celery; chocolate, 11" **70.00**
Leaf Bracket, tumbler, chocolate **40.00**
Mug, deer & oak tree, chocolate **1,750.00**
Mug, dog & child, Nile Green **1,000.00**
Mug, indoor drinking scene, chocolate, 8½" **500.00**
Mug, outdoor drinking scene, Nile Green **125.00**
Novelty, corn vase, amber, 4⅝" **850.00**
Novelty, cuff set, chocolate.................................**2,250.00**
Novelty, Dewey bust, teal bl, w/base **325.00**
Novelty, dustpan, teal bl (+) **135.00**
Novelty, mitted hand, Nile Green **1,250.00**
Novelty, trunk, chocolate.....................................**1,800.00**
Pattern #75, bowl, cobalt, rnd, 6¼" **150.00**
Pattern #75, toothpick holder, emerald gr **65.00**
Pattern #75, tumbler, iced tea; chocolate **450.00**
Pattern #75, vase, emerald gr, 6" **65.00**
Pleat Band, compote, chocolate, plain stem, smooth rim, 4¼"...**125.00**
Pleat Band, wine, canary..**275.00**
Sawtooth, tumbler, chocolate.......................................**65.00**
Scalloped Flange, vase, Nile Green **425.00**
Shuttle, mug, cobalt **425.00**
Shuttle, nappy, chocolate...**190.00**
Teardrop & Tassel, butter dish, cobalt **250.00**
Teardrop & Tassel, compote, Nile Green, 4⅝" **475.00**
Teardrop & Tassel, pitcher, amber **325.00**
Teardrop & Tassel, wine, emerald gr............................**350.00**
Toothpick holder, dog head, frosted bl **375.00**
Toothpick holder, picture frame, teal bl **400.00**
Toothpick holder, sheaf of wheat, Nile Green **750.00**
Toothpick holder, witch head, chocolate (+) **1,500.00**

Grueby

William Henry Grueby joined the firm of the Low Art Tile Works at the age of fifteen and in 1894, after several years of experience in the production of architectural tiles, founded his own plant, the Grueby Faience Company, in Boston, Massachusetts. Grueby began experimenting with the idea of producing art pottery and had soon perfected a fine glaze (soft and without gloss) in shades of blue, gray, yellow, brown, and his most successful, cucumber green. In 1900 his exhibit at the Paris Exposition Universelle won three gold medals.

Grueby pottery was hand thrown and hand decorated in the Arts and Crafts style. Vertically thrust tooled and applied leaves and flower buds were the most common decorative devices. Tiles continued to be an important product, unique (due to the matt glaze decoration) as well as durable. Grueby tiles were often a full inch thick. Many of them were decorated in cuenca, others were impressed and filled with glaze, and some were embossed. Later, when purchased by Pardee, they were decorated in cuerda seca.

Incompatible with the Art Nouveau style, the artware production ceased in 1907, but tile production continued for another decade. The ware is marked in one of several ways: 'Grueby Pottery, Boston, USA'; 'Grueby, Boston, Mass.'; or 'Grueby Faience.' The artware is often artist signed. Our advisors for this category are Suzanne Perrault and David Rago; they are is listed in the Directory under New Jersey.

Key: c — cuenca   cs — cuerda seca

Frieze, 3-tile, water lilies/pads, 3-color, 6x18", EX+.................**6,000.00**
Humidor, ivory/yel/gr, tobacco blossoms, W Post, hairlines, 7½".....**4,000.00**

Lamp, gr swollen lappet-leaf base, 21"; 21½" ldgl shade **23,500.00**
Lamp, gr w/yel 3-petal floral band, 21½"; gr ldgl 22x16" shade **27,500.00**
Paperweight, scarab, olive gr w/dk gr charcoaling, 4" L...............**600.00**
Tile, geometric floral, curdled gr on dk clay, 8¼", EX **935.00**
Tile, horses frieze, ivory on bl & gr, c, rstr, 2-pc, 6x12" **9,135.00**
Tile, puffy trees landscape, mc, cs, 4" **1,850.00**
Tile, rabbit in lettuce, mc, c, burst bubble, 6" **3,600.00**
Tile, ship on curly waves, mc, c/cs, unmk, 8" **9,700.00**
Tile, St George on horsebk slaying dragon, 7-color, c/cs, unmk, 8", NM...**24,500.00**
Tile, St Louis on horsebk mosaic, mtd in orig steel fr: 48x42½"....**21,850.00**
Tile, water lilies, 3-tile frieze, mc, c, 6x8¼" **6,250.00**
Tile, 2 geese & trees, mc, c, 4", NM...................................**1,150.00**
Tile, 2-masted ship in strong waves, 6-color, c/cs, unmk, 8" **9,000.00**
Tile, 3-masted ship/stylized waves, 4-color, c, artist sgn, 6" **2,800.00**
Vase, bl, veined leaves, swollen form w/pinched top, 5½" **2,300.00**
Vase, curdled deep mauve, stacked leaves, M Seaman, Faience mk, 8½"....**4,000.00**
Vase, floor; yel/feathery gr, buds/leaves, drilled, 23x8½" **13,000.00**
Vase, frothy sand, leaves, G Priests, Faience mk, 5x4", NM **1,700.00**
Vase, gr, buds on long stems, cylindrical, sgn, 11½" **6,500.00**
Vase, gr, buds/stems, corseted neck, 7½x5" **2,500.00**
Vase, gr, daffodils (3-color), vasiform, R Erickson, 10¼" **11,150.00**
Vase, gr, jonquils (3), sgn ER, swollen cylinder, ca 1905, 11⅝" **2,585.00**
Vase, gr, leaves, bulbous, nicks, 5¼x4" **1,900.00**
Vase, gr, leaves, ovoid, firing lines, sgn ERF, 10x6" **6,000.00**
Vase, gr, leaves & buds alternate, hexagonal rim, 1904, 7⅜"....**4,115.00**
Vase, gr, low leaves alternate w/stems & buds, long neck, 8" ...**1,600.00**
Vase, gr, overlapped leaves at bulbous bottom, tall can neck, sgn, 7" ...**1,600.00**
Vase, gr, paneled, bulbous bottom, 7½" **1,700.00**
Vase, gr, vertical blade leaves, bulbous w/sm neck, 5½" **2,600.00**
Vase, gr, wide leaves, squat/shouldered, sgn, 8x6" **2,900.00**
Vase, gr, wide upright leaves, sharply bulbous, sgn, 5½"...........**2,000.00**
Vase, gr, 3 rows of sculpted overlapped leaves, sgn, 8½x10"....**3,500.00**
Vase, gr w/heavy curdling, trumpet form, 7x5¼"....................**1,425.00**
Vase, gr w/upright leaves & yel buds, sgn, rpr, 8"...................**3,000.00**
Vase, gr w/wht clay showing through, leaves, Faience mk, 7¼"......**1,500.00**
Vase, gr w/yel slim upright leaves/crocus, ER, 8½", NM **3,000.00**
Vase, gr/wht/bl-gray, crocus buds/leaves, bulbous, 5¼", NM **3,750.00**
Vase, leathery gr, broad leaves, spherical, sgn ERF, 4x4¾", NM **5,000.00**

Vase, leathery green with yellow trefoils on long stems alternating with leaves, Wilhemina Post, EX mold, perfectly fired, #188A, 18", $92,000.00.

(Photo courtesy David Rago Auctions)

Vase, matt brn, unmk, 3¼x3½" **600.00**
Vase, oatmeal matt w/brn veins, caramel int, 3⅛x5½", NM.......**990.00**

Gustavsberg

Gustavsberg Pottery, founded near Stockholm, Sweden, in the late 1700s, manufactured faience, creamware, and porcelain in the English taste until the end of the nineteenth century. During the twentieth century, the factory has produced some inventive modernistic designs, often signed by their artists. Wilhelm Kage (1889 – 1960) is best remembered for Argenta, a stoneware body decorated in silver overlay, introduced in the 1930s. Usually a mottled green, Argenta can also be found in cobalt blue and white. Other lines included Cintra (an exceptionally translucent porcelain), Farsta (copper-glazed ware), and Farstarust (iron oxide geometric overlay). Designer Stig Lindberg's work, which dates from the 1940s through the early 1970s, includes slab-built figures and a full range of tableware. Some pieces of Gustavsberg are dated.

Our advisors for this category are Suzanne Perrault and David Rago; they are listed in the Directory under New Jersey.

**Bowl, blue and amber mottled with impressed rows of petals, designed by Wilhelm Kage, 3¼x11½",
from $400.00 to $600.00.**

(Photo courtesy David Rago Auctions)

Bowl, Argenta, silver o/l, #1094 I, 1½x3⅞" 85.00
Bowl, Farsta, emb stars, red-brn/lt olive/ochre, Kage, 1940, 8⅝" ...1,400.00
Bowl, Farsta, incised decor, yel ochre/brick red, Kage, 1952, 10" 2,295.00
Bowl, Farsta, radiating lines, red & bl, Kage, 1957, low, 8⅜" ..1,070.00
Bowl, Vaga, wht, ruffled rim, 1950s, 2⅞x7" 200.00
Bowl, Verkstad, bl haresfur, Kage, 1950s, 1⅞x7¼" 250.00
Figurine, lion, Africa series, Lisa Larson, 15x16" 535.00
Vase, Argenta, silver circles & crisscross decor, Kage, 5¾x4" 500.00
Vase, Argenta, silver fish, top & bottom rim, flat sides, Kage, 5" ..510.00
Vase, Argenta, silver flower sprigs, 1935, 8x6¾" 230.00
Vase, Argenta, silver geometrics, anchor mk, 1932, 10¼" 650.00
Vase, Argenta, silver geometrics, sq sides, 1948, 11⅜" 1,225.00
Vase, Argenta, silver linear decor, 4-ftd, #A47 R, 1948, 8¾" 445.00
Vase, Argenta, silver mermaid, Kage, #1045, 9x8" dia 2,650.00
Vase, Argenta, silver mermaid & top & bottom rim, 3-ftd, Kage, 8x4" ..800.00
Vase, Argenta, silver nude figures, 1930-50s, 7½" 800.00
Vase, Argenta, silver swordfish/bubbles, pillow form, 7½", EX, $250.....350.00
Vase, bl w/emb linear decor, cylindrical, 1959, 12¼" 2,350.00
Vase, dk gr, bulbous w/sm flared neck, Friberg, 3¾" 360.00
Vase, dk turq w/dk bl & gray sgraffito, Lindberg, sm neck, 2½" ..390.00
Vase, Domino, stoneware, blk on buff, ribbed, Lindberg, 3¾x3½" 250.00
Vase, Farsta, bl, bottle shape, Kage, 1957, 12¼" 1,950.00
Vase, Farsta, bl-gray drip, ftd teardrop, Kage, 1955, 9" 1,900.00
Vase, Farsta, cross-hatched dmns, Kage, 1947, 4⅜" 1,000.00
Vase, Farsta, emb triangles, red-brn & cream, Kage, 1950, 6" ..1,285.00
Vase, Farsta, linear decor, lt olive & brn, Kage, 1959, 11½" 2,500.00
Vase, Farsta, turq drip on brn, emb ribs, Kage, #182, 1945, 5½" 1,100.00
Vase, gr w/yel/wht edging, sq shoulder w/sm opening, Friberg, 3½" 435.00
Vase, linear decor, bl & brn matt, long neck, 7¼" 500.00
Vase, pale bl w/gr/turq overshot, bulbous w/flared neck, Friberg, 4" 290.00

Vase, Vaga, wht, ruffled rim, 1950, 4¾" 200.00
Vase, Vaga, wht, 2-neck, ruffled rims, 1950, 2⅞" 650.00
Vase, Verkstad, bl haresfur, bulbous, Kage, 1950s, 6¾x5¾" 580.00
Vase, Verkstad, bl haresfur, emb ribs, 1950s, 10¼" 500.00
Vase, wht w/silver o/l, Grazia #219 DN, 1945, 8" 215.00
2 pcs, Argenta pen tray, 2½x10", & paper clip, from $150 to 250.00
4 pcs, 3 gr: 7" vase w/fish, box w/birds, dish, +bl vase, from $400 to...500.00
6 pcs, set of 5 lions by L Larsson, +brn bulbous 9" vase...............375.00

Hadley, M.A.

Founded by artist-turned-potter Mary Alice Hadley, this Louisville, Kentucky, company has been producing handmade dinnerware and decorative items since 1940. Their work is painted freehand in a folksy style with barnyard animals, whales, sailing ships, and several other patterns. The palette is predominately blue and green. Each piece is signed with Hadley's first two initials and her last name, and her artwork continues to be the inspiration for modern designs. Among collectors, horses and other farm animals are popular subject matters. Older pieces are generally heavier and, along with the more unusual items, command the higher prices. Our advisor for this category is Lisa Sanders; she is listed in the Directory under Indiana.

Bank, pig figural, bl dots w/bow on top, slot in top, 3x7" 30.00
Bean pot, cow, w/lid, hdls, 8½x8½" dia 42.50
Bell, house, missing clapper, 6¾" 25.00
Bottle, Dish Liquid; cork lid, 7x2⅝" dia 25.00
Bowl, cereal; church, 5½" 25.00
Bowl, dog; My Dog w/bone inside, 2½x8" 38.00
Bowl, fruit; 2½x8" 25.00
Bowl, Kitty; mouse inside, 1¾x4¼" 13.00
Bowl, lighthouse scene inside, 5x8¼" 45.00
Bowl, rearing horse, 3x6¾" 18.00
Bowl, turtle, 5" 12.00
Bowl, vegetable; sailing ship & whale on lid, 4x8" 30.00
Butter dish, boy w/kite & girl w/flowers on lid, 2x6" dia 32.50
Butter dish, fruit bowl decor on lid, 6⅝" dia 27.50
Casserole, cow & pig, The End inside, w/lid, 2-qt, 4½x10½" dia...40.00
Coaster, I Love You, flowers & hearts around border, 4" dia..........9.00
Coaster, Thanksgiving, 4¼" dia 9.00
Cookie jar, Cookie House, 8x8x5" 95.00
Creamer, horse, 3½" 20.00
Cruets, fruit basket, V on 1 stopper & O on other, 6½", pr 25.00
Cup & saucer, lamb on cup w/The End inside 23.50
Dish, serving; house, 11¾x10" 40.00
Gravy boat, pig, The End inside 25.00
Jar, Goodies; Please Fill Me inside, w/lid, 5½x5¾" dia 30.00
Match holder, Please Fill Me Up inside, w/lid, 5x5" dia 42.00
Mirror, Country, beveled, 16x11½" 150.00
Mug, pig, The End inside 15.00
Mug, rearing horse, The End inside, 4⅞x4" 15.00
Mug, sailing ship, Low Tide inside, 5" 18.00
Mug, sailing ship, 4¾" 15.00
Ornament, house figural, 7" 20.00
Ornament, lamb, 2¾x3⅝" 9.00
Pitcher, cream; house, w/lid, 5x3½" 25.00
Pitcher, house, w/ice lip, 7" 40.00
Plaque, rooster, 2 holes for hanging, 4" 9.00
Plate, cat, 7½" 16.00
Plate, cat, 9" 18.00
Plate, dog, 11" 25.00
Plate, farmer boy w/rake, 11" 22.00
Plate, girl under tree w/Morgan underneath, 9" 25.00

Plate, house, 11" 22.00
Plate, pig, 11"..22.00
Plate, sailboat, 11" 22.00
Platter, horse, oval, 13½" 40.00
Platter, snowman, rnd, 13" 40.00
Shakers, cow on 1 w/S on top, pig on other w/P on top, 5⅜", pr..28.50
Shakers, grapes, pear shape, 4¾", pr 20.00
Sugar bowl, farmer's wife, w/lid, 4¼" 18.00
Teapot, house, w/lid, 4-cup, 5¾".........................28.50
Tile, chicken, 6x6"...13.00
Trivet, horse, 6½" dia 17.50
Wall plaque, Welcome, 3¼x12¼"..........................27.50

Hagen-Renaker

Best known for their line of miniature animal figures, Hagen-Renaker was founded in Monrovia, California, in 1946. It is estimated that perhaps as many as eighty different dogs were produced. In addition to the animals, they made replicas of characters from several popular Disney films under license from the Disney Studio. The firm relocated in San Dimas in 1962, where they remain active to the present time. Their wares are sometimes marked with an incised 'HR,' a stamped 'Hagen-Renaker,' part of the name, or paper labels. For more information, we recommend *The Collector's Encyclopedia of California Pottery, Second Edition*, by Jack Chipman; *Charlton Standard Catalog of Hagen-Renaker, Second Edition*; *Disneyana Collector's Guide to Californian Pottery, 1938 – 1960*, by Devin Frick and Tamara Hodge; and *Hagen-Renaker Pottery: Horses and Other Figurines* by Nancy Kelly (Schiffer). Another source of information is Hagen-Renaker Collectors Club (HRCC), listed in the Directory under Clubs, Newsletters, and Catalogs. Our advisor for this category is Tracy Phillips, she is listed in the Directory under Illinois.

Figurine, Abdullah, Arabian horse, Designer's Workshop, B-649, 6" ...265.00
Figurine, Adelaide, donkey, brn matt, 1956, 5½x6".....................75.00
Figurine, Brookside Stella, show pony, Monrovia, ca 1966, 5½" ...300.00
Figurine, Butch, cocker spaniel, bi-color, 1950s, 5".....................75.00
Figurine, Cinco, draft horse, chestnut, #269/HR2003, 5¾"...........85.00
Figurine, Circus Pony, wht w/gray mane & tail, 1980s, 1¾".........50.00
Figurine, Citation, thoroughbred horse, bay matt, 1961-71, 2¾" ..160.00
Figurine, Don Cortez, blk horse, San Marcos, 1982-84, 6½" 135.00
Figurine, Encore, Arabian horse, dapple gray, 1994 ltd ed...........250.00
Figurine, Erin, quarter horse mare, 1983-86 ....210.00
Figurine, Faline, doe, Disney, 1960s, 1⅝", MOC 235.00
Figurine, Faun #2, on column, Fantasia, #5073............................200.00
Figurine, Faun #3, on column, Fantasia, 1950s 475.00
Figurine, Fauna, fairy from Sleeping Beauty, Disney, 1950s, 2¼" .175.00
Figurine, Fez, Arab horse foal, rose-gray, Monrovia, 3"...............215.00
Figurine, Flower, skunk, Disney, lg, 3" 90.00
Figurine, Golden Lady, collie dog, 1955, 6x8" 100.00
Figurine, Harry, donkey, brn matt, 1956, 3½x3½".......................50.00
Figurine, Heather, Morgan mare, brn gloss, 5" 400.00
Figurine, Heidi's Goat, wht w/gold bell, Farnlund, 1980s, 4½" 95.00
Figurine, Hereford Cutting Steer, Designer's Workshop, 3½x6½"..95.00
Figurine, Lady Jane, ewe w/silver bell, Designer's Workshop, 1950s, 4"...160.00
Figurine, Lippet, Morgan stallion, chestnut, B-704, 1962, 6¼"...475.00
Figurine, Mad Hatter, Disney, 2½" 450.00
Figurine, Maleficent, Disney, 2½" 500.00
Figurine, Mama, Persian cat, standing, 1959-60, 1⅞"....................75.00
Figurine, Michael of Peter Pan, Disney, #5062.............................65.00
Figurine, Mischief, wht yearling horse, B-680, Designer's Workshop.......265.00
Figurine, Miss Pepper, chestnut recumbent foal, Monrovia, 1959-71 ...175.00
Figurine, Nubian Goat doe, Designer's Workshop, mid-1980s, 5" 275.00
Figurine, Pancho Villa, chihuahua dog, H-1529, 1956-62, 4¼" 60.00

Figurine, Peg, dog from Lady & Tramp, Disney, #5079............145.00
Figurine, Pegasus, Disney, #5077......................................230.00
Figurine, Prince Phillip, Disney sticker 170.00
Figurine, Si & Am, Siamese cats, Disney, pr.......................250.00
Figurine, Silky Sullivan, thoroughbred horse, B-770, 1962-71....210.00
Figurine, Snow White, Disney, 2¼" 100.00
Figurine, Sun Cortez, mustang horse, rpr, ca 1958, 6" 235.00
Figurine, Teddy Bear, from Peter Pan, Disney, #5062a, ⅝"......50.00
Figurine, Thunder, Morgan horse, palomino, Designer's Workshop, 1950s....250.00
Figurine, Two Bits, quarter horse bay stallion, 1983-86 ......270.00
Figurine, unicorn, turq/wht/gold, Disney, rpr to horn, 3x2½" 300.00
Figurine, vulture on log, Little Horribles, 2x2" 110.00
Figurine, Wendy, Disney sticker, #5066..............................230.00
Figurine, Wrangler, chestnut Shetland pony, B-566, Designer's, 4" ...155.00
Figurine, Zara, buckskin dun horse w/blk mane & tail, rpr, 6½" ...210.00
Figurine, Zilla, Arabian foal, B-645, Designer's Workshop, 7" 275.00
Plaque, barracuda fish fossil, mc on stone-look, 7¾x20" 250.00

Hagenauer

Carl Hagenauer founded his metal workshops in Vienna in 1898. He was joined by his son Karl in 1919. They produced a wide range of stylized sculptural designs in both metal and wood.

Bust, African lady in profile, patinated bronze, 14x10¼" 1,100.00
Candelabrum, NP steel, 4-branch, 20½x10¼" 1,000.00
Coffee/tea set, copper & brass, wood hdls, 2 pots+cr/sug w/lid+tray...1,000.00
Figurine, gazelle leaping, wood, on wood stand w/brass base, 9x12¾"..235.00
Ice bucket, copper w/appl brass trim, riveted hdl, 14¼x8½" ..1,600.00
Mirror, 2 lady's hands (brass) wrapped rectangle, 26x14".........2,600.00
Sculpture, African lady's head in profile, brass/patinated bronze, 7"..275.00
Sculpture, bugle player, brass & cvd/incised wood, 6¾x10¼".....750.00
Sculpture, horse rearing, wood w/brass tail & base, 11¼x9¾x3"...2,000.00
Sculpture, horse's head, olive wood, brass base, 13x14¼x4¼" ..1,700.00
Sculpture, lady's head in profile, polished chrome, 21x17" 6,000.00
Sculpture, man's head in profile, polished chrome, 21x16½" ..5,500.00

Hair Weaving

A rather unusual craft became popular during the mid-1800s. Human hair was used to make jewelry (rings, bracelets, lockets, etc.) by braiding and interlacing fine strands into hollow forms with pearls and beads added for effect. Wreaths were also made, often using hair from deceased family members as well as the living. They were displayed in deep satin-lined frames along with mementoes of the weaver or her departed kin. The fad was abandoned before the turn of the century. The values suggested below are for mint condition examples. Any fraying of the hair greatly lowers value. For further information, we recommend *Collector's Encyclopedia of Hairwork Jewelry* by C. Jeanenne Bell (Collector Books). See also Mourning Collectibles.

Key:
p-w — palette work   t-w — table work

Bracelet, coiling snake w/gold head & tail w/garnet eyes, 1840-80 ..775.00
Bracelet, gold links, p-w on opaline glass, 1850s, 6½", MIB 950.00
Bracelet, t-w hair in 3 weaves, gold mts, 1¼x6¾", VG+ 395.00
Bracelet, t-w hair w/elastic weave, gold bbl clasp, 1850-80s, 3¾x7" ...425.00
Bracelet, t-w in 2 weaves, heart-shaped compartment, gold mts, 1800s ...375.00
Bracelet, t-w in 5 rows, center tube w/monogram, gold mts, 7" ..285.00
Bracelet, 7 rows t-w hair, gold-filled locket clasp w/photo, 1840s..495.00
Brooch, gold w/braided hair under crystal amid seed pearls.........185.00

Brooch, gold-filled w/tintype, revolves to p-w hair, 1860s, 2⅜"..**375.00**
Brooch, p-w, hair flowers/seed pearls in gold oval, 1790-1830s, 1¼"...**750.00**
Brooch, p-w basketweave & t-w border w/gold mts, 1¾x1½", EX..**395.00**
Brooch, p-w braid under beveled grass, enameled jet fr, 1850s, 1⅜"..**295.00**
Brooch, p-w curl/flowers on gold-filled mt, 1½x1" **300.00**
Brooch, p-w hair under crystal gilt brass navette shape, 1790s, 1½" **475.00**
Brooch, p-w willow scene in oval gold mt, 1840s-60s, 1⅞x1½" **425.00**
Brooch, t-w balls & gold acorns, 1860-70s, 1x2⅝" **425.00**
Brooch, t-w oval gold pinwheel w/harp charm dangle, 1850-70s, 1¾" **275.00**
Brooch, t-w tubes form bow in gold-filled mt, 1850-80s, 2¾" L...**300.00**
Brooch, 18k yel gold eagle w/braids of hair, early 1800s...........**1,000.00**
Brooch & earrings, blk t-w hair in gold pinwheel mts, 1850-80s, 2", 1"...**600.00**
Charm drop, gold purse w/t-w hair insert, 1850-80s **350.00**
Earrings, t-w bells w/gutta-percha details & mts, 1850-70s, 1⅝"..**475.00**
Earrings, t-w drops (3) on gold & t-w crescent, 1850-70s, 2¼" ..**550.00**
Earrings, t-w elonged drops w/gold mts, 1840-70s, 2⅝" **425.00**
Medallion, Prince of Wales feathers p-w on milk glass, 1840s, 1" **250.00**
Necklace, t-w balls w/2 wrapped wood balls, gold mts, 1840-60s...**900.00**
Necklace, t-w chain w/gold heart drop, 1850-80s, 14" **595.00**
Necklace, 3 rows of t-w in 2 weaves, gold mts, 1840-60s, 14".....**450.00**
Pendant, gold mt w/t-w hair & pearl, 1850-80, ⅞x1⅜" **275.00**
Pendant/locket, ornate gold-filled mt, hair swirl under glass, 2¾"....**395.00**
Ring, Georgian gold mt w/compartment w/p-w basketweave, sm sq...**525.00**
Ring, gold hollow band w/cutouts revealing t-w insert, 1850-80s..**380.00**
Ring, gold mt w/dbl-hinged book opens for p-w basketweave, 1830s-70s...**695.00**
Ring, t-w band joined by plaque eng Sarah, 1850-80s, ¼" W **200.00**
Ring, t-w braid w/hollow gold mt w/shield, 1840-80, ⅝" W **275.00**
Stick pin, t-w horseshoe w/gold mts, 1840-80..............................**125.00**
Watch chain, t-w chain in 2 weaves, gold-filled mts, 1860-80s, 56"...**225.00**
Watch chain, t-w twisted tubes (2), gold-filled mts, 1830-50, 9"...**150.00**
Watch chain, t-w 2-color horsehair, ca 1860-90, 13" **155.00**

Hall

The Hall China Company of East Liverpool, Ohio, was established in 1903. Their earliest products were whiteware toilet seats, mugs, jugs, etc. By 1920 their restaurant-type dinnerware and cookingware had become so successful that Hall was assured of a solid future. They continue today to be one of the country's largest manufacturers of this type of product.

Hall introduced the first of their famous teapots in 1920; new shapes and colors were added each year until about 1948, making them the largest teapot manufacturer in the world. These and the dinnerware lines of the '30s through the '50s have become popular collectibles. For more thorough study of the subject, we recommend *The Collector's Encyclopedia of Hall China, Third Edition*, by Margaret and Kenn Whitmyer; their address may be found in the Directory under Ohio.

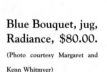

Blue Bouquet, jug, Radiance, $80.00.
(Photo courtesy Margaret and Kenn Whitmyer)

Blue Bouquet, ball jug, #3 ....**150.00**
Blue Bouquet, bowl, flared, 7¾"...**60.00**

Blue Bouquet, bowl, fruit; 5½" **11.00**
Blue Bouquet, bowl, Radiance, 7½"..**25.00**
Blue Bouquet, bowl, str-sided, 9"...**35.00**
Blue Bouquet, bowl, Thick Rim, 8½"...**40.00**
Blue Bouquet, coaster, metal..**15.00**
Blue Bouquet, coffeepot, Five Band..**85.00**
Blue Bouquet, creamer, Boston **28.00**
Blue Bouquet, cup, D-style...**20.00**
Blue Bouquet, custard, Thick Rim..**30.00**
Blue Bouquet, drip jar, Radiance..**200.00**
Blue Bouquet, jug, Medallion, #3...**35.00**
Blue Bouquet, leftover, sq...**170.00**
Blue Bouquet, saucer, D-style..**4.00**
Blue Bouquet, shakers, hdld, pr..**50.00**
Blue Bouquet, sugar bowl, w/lid, Boston **42.00**
Blue Bouquet, tray, metal, rectangular..**60.00**
Cameo Rose, bowl, cereal; E-style, tab hdl, 6¼"...........................**16.00**
Cameo Rose, bowl, vegetable; E-style, rnd, 9"..............................**25.00**
Cameo Rose, cup, E-style...**8.50**
Cameo Rose, plate, E-style, 7¼"...**8.50**
Cameo Rose, platter, E-style, oval, 11¼".....................................**18.00**
Cameo Rose, teapot, E-style, 8-cup...**95.00**
Christmas Tree & Holly, coffee set (pot + cr/sug), E-style...........**340.00**
Christmas Tree & Holly, cup, E-style...**22.00**
Christmas Tree & Holly, plate, E-style, 10"..................................**45.00**
Christmas Tree & Holly, saucer, E-style.......................................**10.00**
Crocus, ball jug, #3...**200.00**
Crocus, bowl, cereal; D-style, 6" **20.00**
Crocus, bowl, D-style, oval..**40.00**
Crocus, bowl, Radiance, 6"...**22.00**
Crocus, bread box, metal...**130.00**
Crocus, cake plate...**42.00**
Crocus, coffeepot, Five Band...**75.00**
Crocus, creamer, Art Deco..**35.00**
Crocus, creamer, Modern..**20.00**
Crocus, drip jar, #1188, open **47.00**
Crocus, leftover, sq..**120.00**
Crocus, mug, flagon style..**90.00**
Crocus, mug, tankard style..**75.00**
Crocus, plate, D-style, 6"...**8.00**
Crocus, plate, D-style, 8¼"..**12.00**
Crocus, platter, D-style, oval, 11¼"...**32.00**
Crocus, shakers, Five Band, pr...**120.00**
Crocus, stack set, Radiance...**350.00**
Crocus, sugar bowl, w/lid, New York **32.00**
Crocus, teapot, Donut..**2,000.00**
Crocus, teapot, Streamline **1,500.00**
Crocus, tidbit, D-style, 3-tier..**85.00**
Gaillardia, bowl, fruit; D-style, 5¼" **8.00**
Gaillardia, casserole, Radiance..**35.00**
Gaillardia, pretzel jar..**150.00**
Gaillardia, teapot, Boston...**195.00**
Game Bird, ball jug, #3 ....**300.00**
Game Bird, casserole, MJ..**85.00**
Game Bird, plate, E-style, 6½"..**11.00**
Game Bird, saucer, E-style..**4.00**
Game Bird, teapot, Windshield..**315.00**
Golden Oak, ball jug, #3..**125.00**
Golden Oak, bowl, cereal; D-style, 6"..**5.00**
Golden Oak, saucer, D-style..**1.50**
Heather Rose, bowl, fruit; 5¼"..**5.00**
Heather Rose, creamer..**10.00**
Heather Rose, gravy boat, w/underplate **32.00**
Heather Rose, teapot, London...**25.00**

Homewood, bowl, fruit; D-style, 5½"................................6.00
Homewood, bowl, Radiance, 6"....................................16.00
Homewood, coffeepot, Terrace....................................75.00
Homewood, shakers, hdls, pr......................................44.00
Mums, bowl, flat soup, D-style, 8½"............................25.00
Mums, bowl, Radiance, 9"..40.00
Mums, bowl, salad; 9"..27.00
Mums, casserole, Radiance..50.00
Mums, creamer, Art Deco..25.00
Mums, cup, D-style..13.00
Mums, custard, Medallion..30.00
Mums, jug, #3, Medallion..55.00
Mums, plate, D-style, 9"..14.00
Mums, shakers, hdls, pr..50.00
Mums, sugar bowl, w/lid, New York..............................35.00
Mums, teapot, Rutherford..250.00
No 488, ball jug, #3..185.00
No 488, bowl, fruit; D-style, 5½"..................................8.50
No 488, bowl, Radiance, 5"..25.00
No 488, bowl, Radiance, 9"..32.00
No 488, butter dish, Zephyr, 1-lb..............................650.00
No 488, casserole, Medallion......................................55.00
No 488, cookie jar, Five Band....................................300.00
No 488, custard, Radiance..25.00
No 488, drip jar, #1188, open......................................45.00
No 488, jug, Medallion..100.00
No 488, jug, Rayed..75.00
No 488, mug, Tom & Jerry..30.00
No 488, plate, D-style, 7"..12.00
No 488, shakers, Medallion, pr....................................94.00
No 488, shirred egg dish..40.00
No 488, sugar bowl, Meltdown, w/lid............................50.00
No 488, water bottle, Zephyr....................................900.00
Orange Poppy, bean pot, #4, New England..................145.00
Orange Poppy, bowl, cereal; C-style, 6"........................25.00
Orange Poppy, bowl, Radiance, 10"..............................50.00
Orange Poppy, cake safe, metal..................................60.00
Orange Poppy, casserole, oval, 8"................................65.00
Orange Poppy, coffeepot, Bellevue, 2-cup..................1,800.00
Orange Poppy, condiment jar, Radiance......................900.00
Orange Poppy, custard, Radiance..................................9.00
Orange Poppy, mustard w/liner..................................145.00
Orange Poppy, plate, C-style, 6"..................................8.00
Orange Poppy, saucer, C-style......................................5.00
Orange Poppy, shakers, Novelty Radiance, pr..............100.00
Orange Poppy, sifter, metal..80.00
Orange Poppy, teapot, Boston....................................250.00
Orange Poppy, teapot, Streamline..............................350.00
Pastel Morning Glory, ball jug, #3..............................210.00
Pastel Morning Glory, bowl, D-style, rnd, 9¼"..............45.00
Pastel Morning Glory, bowl, Radiance, 7½"..................27.00
Pastel Morning Glory, casserole, Medallion..................50.00
Pastel Morning Glory, creamer, New York....................25.00
Pastel Morning Glory, drip jar, #1188, open..................45.00
Pastel Morning Glory, jug, Donut..............................350.00
Pastel Morning Glory, petite marmite..........................65.00
Pastel Morning Glory, platter, D-style, 11¼"................35.00
Pastel Morning Glory, shakers, Teardrop, pr..................44.00
Pastel Morning Glory, tea tile..................................120.00
Pastel Morning Glory, teapot, Aladdin........................700.00
Prairie Grass, bowl, cereal; 6¼"..................................10.00
Prairie Grass, creamer..10.00
Prairie Grass, platter, oval, 11¼"................................22.00
Prairie Grass, sugar bowl, w/lid..................................18.00

Primrose, ashtray, E-style..10.00
Primrose, bowl, flat soup; E-style, 8"..........................12.00
Primrose, creamer, E-style..9.00
Primrose, plate, E-style, 7¼"......................................6.50
Primrose, sugar bowl, w/lid, E-style............................16.00
Red Poppy, baker, French; fluted................................26.00
Red Poppy, bowl, flat soup; D-style, 8½"......................20.00
Red Poppy, bowl, Radiance, 7½"................................22.00
Red Poppy, cake plate..55.00
Red Poppy, canister set, metal, sq, 4-pc......................85.00
Red Poppy, clock, plastic, teapot shape......................135.00
Red Poppy, custard..20.00
Red Poppy, gravy boat, D-style..................................40.00
Red Poppy, jug, milk/syrup; Daniel, 4"........................47.00
Red Poppy, leftover, sq..250.00
Red Poppy, plate, D-style, 9"......................................14.00
Red Poppy, pretzel jar..600.00
Red Poppy, teapot, Aladdin......................................155.00
Red Poppy, tray, metal, rectangular............................50.00
Red Poppy, tumbler, glass, clear..................................40.00
Sear's Arlington, creamer, E-style................................9.00
Sear's Arlington, plate, E-style, 6½"............................3.50
Sear's Fairfax, bowl, vegetable; w/lid, E-style................40.00
Sear's Fairfax, plate, 7¼"..5.50
Sear's Monticello, cup, E-style....................................6.00
Sear's Monticello, plate, E-style, 10"..........................11.00
Sear's Monticello, sugar bowl, w/lid, E-style................18.00
Sear's Mount Vernon, bowl, fruit; 5¼"........................6.00
Sear's Mount Vernon, platter, oval, 15½"....................30.00
Sear's Richmond/Brown-Eyed Susan, bowl, flat soup; 8"......9.00
Sear's Richmond/Brown-Eyed Susan, cup......................6.50
Serenade, bean pot, #4, New England........................145.00
Serenade, bowl, D-style, rnd, 9¼"..............................25.00
Serenade, bowl, fruit; D-style, 5½"..............................5.50
Serenade, bowl, Radiance, 7½"..................................16.00
Serenade, casserole, Radiance....................................40.00
Serenade, creamer, Art Deco......................................22.00
Serenade, fork..125.00
Serenade, platter, D-style, 11¼"................................20.00
Serenade, sugar bowl, w/lid, Modern..........................27.00
Serenade, teapot, New York......................................150.00
Silhouette, bowl, cereal; D-style, 6"............................16.00
Silhouette, bowl, flared, 3⅝"......................................12.00
Silhouette, bowl, Medallion, 7½"................................16.00
Silhouette, casserole, Radiance..................................45.00
Silhouette, coffee dispenser......................................75.00
Silhouette, cup, St Denis..35.00
Silhouette, jug, #2, Medallion....................................22.00
Silhouette, leftover, rectangular..................................55.00
Silhouette, pie baker..30.00
Silhouette, pitcher, crystal, Federal..........................120.00
Silhouette, plate, 8¼"..8.50
Silhouette, pretzel jar..125.00
Silhouette, saucer, D-style..2.50
Silhouette, tea tile, 6"..95.00
Silhouette, wastebasket..65.00
Springtime, ball jug, #3, D-style................................55.00
Springtime, bowl, fruit; D-style, 5½"............................5.50
Springtime, bowl, Thick Rim, 6"................................11.00
Springtime, creamer, E-style......................................27.00
Springtime, custard..14.00
Springtime, gravy boat, D-style..................................25.00
Teapot, Airflow, Citrus, solid color, from $175 to..........225.00
Teapot, Airflow, Indian Red, solid color, from $125 to......150.00

Teapot, Aladdin, Cadet, gold label, from $200 to........................225.00
Teapot, Aladdin, Chinese Red, solid color, from $165 to............180.00
Teapot, Aladdin, Dresden, standard gold, from $100 to 125.00
Teapot, Albany, blk, standard gold, from $50 to 60.00
Teapot, Albany, Mahogany, gold label, from $50 to......................65.00

Teapot, Automobile, Cadet Blue with platinum trim, from $500.00 to $550.00.
(Photo courtesy Margaret and Kenn Whitmyer)

Teapot, Baltimore, bl w/leaf & vine decal, from $200 to.............250.00
Teapot, Baltimore, Marine, standard gold, from $90 to 110.00
Teapot, Basketball, Cadet, solid color, from $400 to....................450.00
Teapot, Birdcage, Warm Yellow, solid color, from $450 to 500.00
Teapot, Boston, Warm Yellow, solid color, from $35 to 40.00
Teapot, Cleveland, Cobalt, solid color, from $90 to 125.00
Teapot, Damascus, bl, from $200 to...250.00
Teapot, Danielle, Maroon, from $185 to 200.00
Teapot, Donut, blk, solid color, from $120 to 150.00
Teapot, Football, Canary, standard gold, from $500 to..................600.00
Teapot, French, turq, 4- to 3-cup, standard gold, from $45 to.......60.00
Teapot, Globe, Camellia, standard gold, from $60 to 75.00
Teapot, Hollywood, Canary, solid color, from $40 to....................50.00
Teapot, Hook Cover, Orchid, solid color, from $250 to 300.00
Teapot, Los Angeles, blk, standard gold, from $45 to 50.00
Teapot, Los Angeles, Monterey, gold label, from $85 to...............95.00
Teapot, Melody, Marine, solid color, from $200 to 240.00
Teapot, Moderne, Ivory, standard gold, from $40 to 45.00
Teapot, Nautilus, Emerald, standard gold, from $260 to..............285.00
Teapot, New York, Canary, solid color, 1- to 4-cup, from $25 to....30.00
Teapot, New York, Rose, 6- to 8-cup, standard gold, from $50 to...55.00
Teapot, Newport, Ivory, solid color, from $30 to...........................35.00
Teapot, Ohio, Stock Green, solid color, from $120 to................140.00
Teapot, Parade, Chinese Red, solid color, from $300 to 350.00
Teapot, Philadelphia, Blue Turquoise w/gold, 5- to 7-cup, from $45 to..50.00
Teapot, Philadelphia, Indian Red, solid color, 10-cup, from $215 to.....230.00
Teapot, Rhythm, Maroon, solid color, from $120 to....................140.00
Teapot, Sani-Grid, Cadet, solid color, from $18 to 20.00
Tulip, bowl, D-style, rnd, 9¼"...35.00
Tulip, bowl, Radiance, 9" 30.00
Tulip, casserole, Radiance...45.00
Tulip, jug, #3, Medallion 85.00
Tulip, platter, D-style, oval, 13¼"...35.00
Tulip, waffle iron, metal 125.00
Wildfire, bowl, fruit; D-style, 5½" 6.00
Wildfire, bowl, Thick Rim, bl parts, 6"......................................22.00
Wildfire, bowl, Thick Rim, 6"...18.00
Wildfire, coffee dispenser, metal 30.00
Wildfire, custard, str-sided..25.00
Wildfire, pie baker 55.00
Wildfire, plate, D-style, 7"...9.50
Yellow Rose, bowl, cereal; D-style, 7½"......................................11.50
Yellow Rose, bowl, Radiance, 7½"..22.00
Yellow Rose, bowl, salad; 9" 27.00
Yellow Rose, coffeepot, Norse...85.00
Yellow Rose, gravy boat, D-style 35.00
Yellow Rose, teapot, New York 200.00

Zeisel Designs, Hallcraft

Century Fern, bowl, soup/cereal; 8" 8.50
Century Fern, gravy boat..30.00
Century Fern, plate, 8" 5.00
Century Garden of Eden, bowl, vegetable; 10½" 25.00
Century Garden of Eden, teapot, 6-cup....................................160.00
Century Sunglow, ashtray...9.00
Century Sunglow, sugar bowl, w/lid...18.00
Tomorrow's Classic Arizona, bowl, coupe soup; 9" 10.00
Tomorrow's Classic Arizona, casserole, 1¼-qt.............................37.00
Tomorrow's Classic Arizona, ladle...22.00
Tomorrow's Classic Arizona, vase 75.00
Tomorrow's Classic Bouquet, bowl, onion soup; w/lid..................45.00
Tomorrow's Classic Bouquet, bowl, salad; lg, 14½" 45.00
Tomorrow's Classic Bouquet, egg cup 60.00
Tomorrow's Classic Buckingham, ashtray 10.00
Tomorrow's Classic Buckingham, candlestick, 8", ea 45.00
Tomorrow's Classic Buckingham, jug, 3-qt.................................47.00
Tomorrow's Classic Buckingham, vinegar bottle 95.00
Tomorrow's Classic Caprice, bowl, fruit; 5¾" 7.00
Tomorrow's Classic Caprice, creamer, AD..................................12.00
Tomorrow's Classic Caprice, platter, 11".....................................13.00
Tomorrow's Classic Dawn, ashtray...10.00
Tomorrow's Classic Dawn, casserole, 2-qt...................................65.00
Tomorrow's Classic Dawn, vase...95.00
Tomorrow's Classic Fantasy, bowl, fruit; 5¾"................................9.00
Tomorrow's Classic Fantasy, egg cup 25.00
Tomorrow's Classic Fantasy, teapot, 6-cup...............................195.00
Tomorrow's Classic Flair, ashtray...10.00
Tomorrow's Classic Flair, plate, 6"...6.00
Tomorrow's Classic Flair, saucer 2.50
Tomorrow's Classic Frost Flowers, bowl, celery; oval 22.00
Tomorrow's Classic Frost Flowers, vase 75.00
Tomorrow's Classic Harlequin, ball jug, #3 ....190.00
Tomorrow's Classic Harlequin, cookie jar, Zeisel-style................300.00
Tomorrow's Classic Harlequin, teapot, Thorley 300.00
Tomorrow's Classic Holiday, ashtray 11.50
Tomorrow's Classic Holiday, candlestick, 8", ea 45.00
Tomorrow's Classic Holiday, ladle...22.00
Tomorrow's Classic Holiday, plate, 11" 9.00
Tomorrow's Classic Lyric, bowl, fruit; 5¾".................................10.00
Tomorrow's Classic Lyric, candlestick, 8", ea..............................40.00
Tomorrow's Classic Lyric, egg cup 55.00
Tomorrow's Classic Lyric, ladle...22.00
Tomorrow's Classic Mulberry, candlestick, 4½", ea.....................32.00
Tomorrow's Classic Mulberry, creamer.......................................14.00
Tomorrow's Classic Mulberry, shakers, pr 32.00
Tomorrow's Classic Peach Blossom, bowl, coupe soup; 9"............11.00
Tomorrow's Classic Peach Blossom, bowl, oval, D-style...............27.00
Tomorrow's Classic Peach Blossom, cup 7.00
Tomorrow's Classic Peach Blossom, platter, 12" 28.00
Tomorrow's Classic Pinecone, ashtray..9.00
Tomorrow's Classic Pinecone, creamer 13.00
Tomorrow's Classic Pinecone, gravy boat 35.00
Tomorrow's Classic Pinecone, plate, E-style, 6"............................4.00
Tomorrow's Classic Pinecone, platter, 17" 38.00
Tomorrow's Classic Satin Black & Hi-White, ashtray 13.00
Tomorrow's Classic Satin Black & Hi-White, ladle......................25.00
Tomorrow's Classic Satin Black & Hi-White, saucer......................2.50
Tomorrow's Classic Spring/Studio 10, butter dish.......................180.00
Tomorrow's Classic Spring/Studio 10, egg cup 45.00
Tomorrow's Classic Spring/Studio 10, marmite, w/lid..................27.00
Tomorrow's Classic Spring/Studio 10, vase.................................75.00

Halloween

Though the origin of Halloween is steeped in pagan rites and super- stitions, today Halloween is strictly a fun time, and Halloween items are fun to collect. Pumpkin-head candy containers of papier-mâché or pressed cardboard, noisemakers, postcards with black cats and witches, costumes, and decorations are only a sampling of the variety available.

Here's how you can determine the origin of your jack-o'-lantern:

American 1940 – 1950s	German 1900 – 1930s

— items are larger	— items are generally small
— made of egg-carton material	— made of cardboard or com- position
— bottom and body are one piece	— always has a cut-out triangular nose; simple, crisscross lines in mouth; blue rings in eyes
	— have attached cardboard bottoms

For further information we recommend *More Halloween Collectibles, Anthropomorphic Vegetables and Fruits of Halloween,* by Pamela E. Apkar- ian-Russell (Schiffer). Other good reference books are *Halloween in America* by Stuart Schneider, and *Halloween Collectables* by Dan and Pauline Campanelli.

Our advisor for this category is Jenny Tarrant; she is listed in the Directory under Missouri. See Clubs, Newsletters, and Catalogs for information concerning the *Trick or Treat Trader,* a quarterly newsletter. Unless noted otherwise, values are for examples in excellent to near mint condition except for paper items, in which case assume the condi- tion to be near mint to mint.

American

Most American items were made during the 1940s and 1950s, though a few date from the 1930s as well. Lanterns are constructed either of flat cardboard or the pressed cardboard pulp used to make the jack-o'- lantern shown on the left.

Jack-o'-lantern, pressed cb pulp w/orig face, 4" 95.00
Jack-o'-lantern, pressed cb pulp w/orig face, 4½" 110.00
Jack-o'-lantern, pressed cb pulp w/orig face, 5" 115.00
Jack-o'-lantern, pressed cb pulp w/orig face, 5½" 125.00
Jack-o'-lantern, pressed cb pulp w/orig face, 6" 130.00
Jack-o'-lantern, pressed cb pulp w/orig face, 6½" 135.00
Jack-o'-lantern, pressed cb pulp w/orig face, 7" 150.00
Jack-o'-lantern, pressed cb pulp w/orig face, 8", minimum value ...175.00
Lantern, cat, pressed cb pulp w/orig face 175.00
Lantern, cat (full body), pressed cb pulp, 7x6½" 350.00
Lantern, cb w/tab sides, any 75.00

Lantern, pumpkin man (full body), pressed cb pulp 350.00
Plastic Halloween car...250.00
Plastic pumpkin stagecoach, witch & cat......................................450.00
Plastic witch holding blk cat w/wobbling head, 7" 150.00
Plastic witch on rocket, upright, 7"...250.00
Plastic witch on rocket, 4"..95.00
Plastic witch on rocket, 5"..250.00
Tin noisemaker, bell style..38.00
Tin noisemaker, can shaker 38.00
Tin noisemaker, clicker..35.00
Tin noisemaker, fry pan style...55.00
Tin noisemaker, horn...55.00
Tin noisemaker, sq spinner 38.00
Tin noisemaker, tambourine, Chein 75.00
Tin noisemaker, tambourine, Kirkoff 95.00
Tin noisemaker, tambourine, Ohio Art, 1930s, 6" dia 75.00

Celluloid (German, Japanese, or American)

Blk cat, plain, M..150.00
Egg-shape house, M...400.00
Long-leg veggie rattle, M...300.00
Owl, plain, M..85.00
Owl on pumpkin, M..175.00
Owl on tree, M...200.00
Pumpkin-face man, M..350.00
Pumpkin-face pirate, M...400.00
Scarecrow, M..175.00
Witch, plain, M..175.00
Witch in auto, M...450.00
Witch in corncob car, M..450.00
Witch pulling cart w/ghost, M 400.00
Witch pulling pumpkin cart w/cat, M 400.00
Witch sitting on pumpkin, M..350.00

German

As a general rule, German Halloween collectibles date from 1900 through the early 1930s. They were made either of composition or mold- ed cardboard, and their values are higher than American-made items. In the listings that follow, all candy containers are made of composition unless noted otherwise.

Candy container, blk cat walking, glass eyes, head removes, 3-4" 225.00
Candy container, blk cat walking, glass eyes, head removes, 5-6" 250.00
Candy container, cat, glass eyes, 4-6" 250.00
Candy container, cat, w/mohair, 5" 350.00
Candy container, cat, 3-5", from $175 to 285.00
Candy container, lemon-head man, pnt compo, 7" 575.00
Candy container, pumpkin-head man (or any vegetable), on box, 3"..175.00
Candy container, pumpkin-head man (or any vegetable), on box, 4" ...185.00
Candy container, pumpkin-head man (or any vegetable), on box, 5" ...225.00
Candy container, pumpkin-head man (or any vegetable), on box, 6" ...275.00
Candy container, witch, pumpkin people, devil, ghost, etc, 3" ...225.00
Candy container, witch, pumpkin people, devil, ghost, etc, 4" ...250.00
Candy container, witch, pumpkin people, devil, ghost, etc, 5" ...275.00
Candy container, witch, pumpkin people, devil, ghost, etc, 6" ...300.00
Candy container, witch or pumpkin man, head removes, 4" 225.00
Candy container, witch or pumpkin man, head removes, 5" 250.00
Candy container, witch or pumpkin man, head removes, 6" 300.00
Candy container, witch or pumpkin man, head removes, 7" 350.00
Diecut, bat, emb cb, from $95 to 125.00
Diecut, cat, emb cb, from $55 to...95.00
Diecut, cat (dressed), emb cb..150.00

Diecut, devil, emb cb, from $95 to 150.00
Diecut, jack-o'-lantern, emb cb...65.00
Diecut, pumpkin man or lady, emb cb, 7½" 125.00
Jack-o'-lantern, compo w/orig insert, 3" 225.00
Jack-o'-lantern, compo w/orig insert, 3½" 250.00
Jack-o'-lantern, compo w/orig insert, 4" 250.00
Jack-o'-lantern, compo w/orig insert, 4½" 275.00
Jack-o'-lantern, compo w/orig isnert, 5" 350.00
Jack-o'-lantern, molded cb w/orig insert, 3" 95.00
Jack-o'-lantern, molded cb w/orig insert, 3½" 100.00
Jack-o'-lantern, molded cb w/orig insert, 4" 125.00
Jack-o'-lantern, molded cb w/orig insert, 4½" 140.00
Jack-o'-lantern, molded cb w/orig insert, 5" 155.00
Jack-o'-lantern, molded cb w/orig insert, 5½" 175.00
Jack-o'-lantern, molded cb w/orig insert, 6" 185.00
Jack-o'-lantern, molded cb w/orig insert, 6½", minimum value ..200.00
Lantern, cat, cb, molded nose, bow under chin, 3-5", from $275 to ...375.00
Lantern, cat, cb, simple rnd style....................................225.00
Lantern (ghost, skull, devil, witch, etc), molded cb, 3-4", minimum..300.00
Lantern (ghost, skull, devil, witch, etc), molded cb, 5"+, minimum...350.00
Lantern (skull, devil, witch, etc), compo, 3", minimum value 375.00
Lantern (skull, devil, witch, etc), compo, 4", minimum value 400.00
Lantern (skull, devil, witch, etc), compo, 5", minimum value 450.00
Noisemaker, cat (3-D) on wood rachet...........................95.00
Noisemaker, cb figure (flat) on rachet 95.00
Noisemaker, db paddle w/diecut face 95.00
Noisemaker, devil (3-D) on wood rachet 95.00
Noisemaker, pumpkin head (3-D) on wood rachet 95.00
Noisemaker, tin frying pan paddle, 5" L 75.00
Noisemaker, tin horn, 3"...75.00
Noisemaker, veggie (3-D) horn (w/pnt face) 125.00
Noisemaker, veggie or fruit (3-D) horn (no face), ea.....65.00
Noisemaker, witch (3-D) on wood rachet 95.00
Noisemaker, wood & paper tambourine 150.00

Hampshire

The Hampshire Pottery Company was established in 1871 in Keene, New Hampshire, by James Scollay Taft. Their earliest products were redware and stoneware utility items such as jugs, churns, crocks, and flowerpots. In 1878 they produced majolica ware which met with such success that they began to experiment with the idea of manufacturing art pottery. By 1883 they had developed a Royal Worcester type of finish which they applied to vases, tea sets, powder boxes, and cookie jars. It was also utilized for souvenir items that were decorated with transfer designs prepared from photographic plates.

Cadmon Robertson, brother-in-law of Taft, joined the company in 1904 and was responsible for developing their famous matt glazes. Colors included shades of green, brown, red, and blue. Early examples were of earthenware, but eventually the body was changed to semiporcelain. Some of his designs were marked with an M in a circle as a tribute to his wife, Emoretta. Robertson died in 1914, leaving a void impossible to fill. Taft sold the business in 1916 to George Morton, who continued to use the matt glazes that Robertson had developed. After a temporary halt in production during WWI, Morton returned to Keene and re-equipped the factory with the machinery needed to manufacture hotel china and floor tile. Because of the expense involved in transporting coal to fire the kilns, Morton found he could not compete with potteries of Ohio and New Jersey who were able to utilize locally available natural gas. He was forced to close the plant in 1923.

Interest is highest in examples with the curdled, two-tone matt glazes, and it is the glaze, not the size or form, that dictates value. The souvenir pieces are not particularly of high quality and tend to be passed over by today's collectors. Our advisors for this category are Suzanne Perrault and David Rago; they are listed in the Directory under New Jersey.

Bowl, cerulean bl w/gray veins, cobalt base, spherical, #149, 6¼" 360.00
Bowl, gr, stylized florals & arches, #19, 2½x5"....................385.00
Clock, mantel; gr matt, Seth Thomas works, 14¾"................1,645.00
Fairy lamp, gr, frosted glass shade (cracked), squat, #140, 2¾" .. 325.00
Lamp base, gr, floral buds, flared ft, 10½x8".......................935.00
Lamp base, gr, pond lily leaves, ped ft, 15½x7"................1,325.00
Lamp base, gr, squat w/gourd-like ribs, 7x11"..................1,295.00
Lamp base, gr, swirled leaves/tall buds, single socket, 14½x8" 850.00
Lamp base, gr, tulips, squat, 6x11½" 1,000.00
Pitcher, feathered bl-gr, squat, 3¼x7"................................200.00
Pitcher, gr, invt cone w/emb hdl, 11½x4" 400.00
Pitcher, gr, melon shape, 4x5"...220.00
Planter/pitcher, gr, 5"...325.00
Stein, cucumber gr, incised Nouveau deisgn, 9x5".............195.00
Tumbler, cerulean bl mottle w/sea gr accents, #17, 5¼x3".........250.00
Umbrella stand, gr, ivy branches on bamboo, flake, unmk, 17½x8" ...1,700.00
Vase, birch leaves emb on gr, tear shape, 3¼", NM..............350.00
Vase, bl mottle, 3-panel w/cobalt at neck, #157, 6¾x3¾" 415.00
Vase, bl w/EX veining, shouldered, 5x6" 375.00
Vase, brn & verdigris, buds & leaves, #33, 7x4", EX 600.00
Vase, cerulean bl mottle w/blk veins, #90, 8¾x5" 600.00
Vase, cerulean bl w/gray veins, stylized waves, kiln pop, #105, 7½" 660.00
Vase, cerulean bl w/sea gr mottle, floral band, #123, 7x5¼" 1,750.00
Vase, cerulean bl w/sea gr mottling & gray veining, #114, 7x4" ...715.00
Vase, cerulean bl w/wht-to-pk mottling, shouldered, 6¼x4" 550.00
Vase, cobalt, long trumpet neck, #107, 9½x6¼" 220.00
Vase, cucumber gr, 3 pinched sections, rtcl mouth, unmk, 3x3"...330.00
Vase, dk bl, mushrooms, low, 6" W.....................................650.00
Vase, feathered bl, leaves & buds, 6½x4" 1,100.00
Vase, feathered bl & gr, row of buds, bulbous, #130, 7¾x7" 1,100.00
Vase, gr, #97, 2¾x4¾" 525.00
Vase, gr, flowers & ferns, 4½x5" 660.00
Vase, gr, foliate repeat at shoulder, ovoid, 7½"....................295.00
Vase, gr, realistic bag form w/cascading ribbon, #12, 11x5½"......880.00
Vase, gr, water lilies & buds, 7⅛x5" 1,425.00
Vase, gr & bl, rim-to-hip hdls, 7", NM................................650.00
Vase, gr w/gray & pk, buds/leaves/stems, trial glaze #, 7" 425.00
Vase, ivory/gr, calla lilies, incurvate rim, 8½" 4,000.00
Vase, khaki gr w/brn & gr streaks, #87351/1/81/M, 5x3¼" 360.00
Vase, lav-mint gr mottle, paneled lower base, #146, 3½x4½", NM...250.00
Vase, mocha brn, oblong panels, #110, 4½x3½" 600.00
Vase, red, 4 broad leaves, trial glaze #, 3½"................................700.00
Vase, red drip, conical, #441/466 & #15, 3¼".............................350.00
Vase, reptilian turq/olive/brn w/raised swirl, squat, 3¼x4" 650.00

Handel

Philip Handel was best known for the art glass lamps he produced at the turn of the century. His work is similar to the Tiffany lamps of the same era. Handel made gas and electric lamps with both leaded glass and reverse-painted shades. Chipped ice shades with a texture similar to overshot glass were also produced. Shades signed by artists such as Bailey, Palme, and Parlow are highly valued.

Teroma lamp shades were created from clear blown glass blanks that were painted on the interior (reverse painted), while Teroma art glass (the decorative vases, humidors, etc. in the Handel Ware line) is painted on the exterior. This type of glassware has a 'chipped ice' effect achieved by sand blasting and coating the surface with fish glue. The piece is kiln fired at 800 degrees F. The contraction of the glue during the cooling process gives the glass a frosted, textured effect. Some shades are sand finished, adding texture and depth.

Both the glassware and chinaware decorated by Handel are rare and command high prices on today's market. Many of Handel's chinaware blanks were supplied by Limoges.

Key: chp — chipped/lightly sanded

Handel Ware

Unless noted china, all items in the following listing are glass. 'HP/rvpt' describes glass that has been painted on both the inside and the outside.

Box, wht & pk roses, sgn Runge, #4058, hinged lid, 4½x5½" **150.00**
Candlestick, windmill scene, sgn Broggi, #4213, 8½", ea............**550.00**
Cigar holder, dog's head on wht opal, orig hdls, 3½"..................**230.00**
Fernery, mums, yel/pk on wht opal, 4x9" **1,750.00**
Humidor, hunting dog on gr, pipe finial, squat, #4060/B, 5" **550.00**
Humidor, yel shading to brn, pipe finial, melon form, #127, 4½" ..**495.00**
Jar, hunting dog w/bird on brn & gr opalware, brass rim, 3½" **400.00**
Pitcher, tankard, palms, gr & gold on ivory, china, 11" **935.00**
Vase, chrysanthemums on dk gr, flared ft, 12"...........................**350.00**
Vase, Teroma, landscape, sgn F Gubisch/#2220, baluster, 8"....**1,115.00**
Vase, Teroma, landscape, sgn F Gubisch/#4209, cylindrical, 9¾"...**1,115.00**
Vase, Teroma, trees/mtns, sgn Broggi, #4210, 8" **920.00**

Lamps

Base, 3 winged lions on rnd ft, fluted column, #953, 25" **3,600.00**
Boudoir, HP 7" windmill scene #5882 shade; mk std, 14"........**4,950.00**
Boudoir, rvpt 10" roses #7176RG shade; bronzed std, 15"........**3,000.00**
Boudoir, rvpt 5" floral #7175 shade; bronze baluster vase std, 15" ...**7,000.00**
Boudoir, rvpt 7" flower basket shade w/HP brn border; simple std, 13" **1,350.00**
Boudoir, rvpt 7" hexagonal shade w/stripes & flowers; std w/emb floral ...**1,100.00**
Boudoir, rvpt 7" jungle bird dome shade; simple bronze std, 13¾"..**2,500.00**
Boudoir, rvpt 7" parrots shade; 6-rib std w/hex ft, 14" **4,300.00**
Boudoir, rvpt 7" stylized floral shade; bronze std.....................**1,125.00**
Boudoir, rvpt 8" parrots shade; bronzed std w/pierced ft...........**9,000.00**
Boudoir, rvpt/chp 7" parakeet shade; bronze std, 14½" **4,125.00**
Boudoir, rvpt/HP 8" scenic shade; tree trunk base....................**2,500.00**
Bridge, rvpt/chp roses #7076 shade; bronze std, 13" **5,500.00**
Desk, etched 10" Mosserine shade; bronze std, 15½" **1,400.00**
Desk, HP/chp 10" cornucopia/scroll shade; bronze swing-arm std, 12" ...**1,100.00**
Desk, ldgl 5x5" cone shade: narrow panels w/half-circle border, adjusts ...**700.00**
Desk, o/l 5½" grape leaves hex shade; harp base w/raised ft, 18" **1,950.00**
Desk, textured 8" caramel to wht opal shade; bronzed std, 16"...**1,500.00**
Floor, chp 14" speckled brn shade; bronze harp std, 58"...........**2,100.00**
Floor, ldgl 24" vintage shade; emb design std w/rnd ft, 65½"...**5,750.00**
Floor, rvpt 10" repeating band on yel shade; bronzed metal std, 51"..**1,600.00**
Hanging, HP 10" perched parrots globe; bronzed hdw **7,500.00**
Hanging, HP 9" birds in flight globe; ceiling mt, 31" overall...**3,650.00**
Hanging, rvpt/chp 10" birds in flight globe; all orig, 38"..........**6,050.00**
Lotus, 5" shade: 2 rows slag petals+bud, curved stem/leaf base, 12"...**1,000.00**
Piano, slag 6½" shade w/metal o/l; curved arm w/weighted std, 8" ..**1,380.00**
Piano/desk, pine needle etch on 8x3" glass shade; shoe-like ft, 11"...**1,850.00**
Shade, gr slag frames cream & wht rectangles, hexagonal, 5¼" H...**600.00**
Table, HP 18" leaf-band ribbed shade; figural water bearer base, 24"...**7,800.00**
Table, HP 18" scenic #7107 conical shade; bronze mk std, ca 1924..**7,150.00**
Table, HP 18" swirl #7499 shade; marblized column std, 26½"..**3,450.00**
Table, HP 18" textured shade, scalloped leaf band; vase std w/rtcl ft,...**4,760.00**
Table, HP/rvpt 14" shade w/red poppy border; simple organic std ...**2,800.00**
Table, HP/rvpt 15" shade w/6 scenes in apron; paneled std w/flared ft..**4,480.00**
Table, ldgl 16" shade w/rows of gr sqs/triangles, red at bottom, 26"...**6,750.00**
Table, ldgl 18" daffodils shade; slim bronze 2-socket std...........**3,575.00**
Table, ldgl 18" 5-panel shade w/geometrics; 3-socket std, 24"..**1,750.00**

Table, ldgl 24" wisteria irregular border shade; trunk std, 27"...**13,500.00**
Table, o/l 12" leaves & berries on slag shade; sq stem/ft, 22" ...**1,000.00**
Table, o/l 16" cutouts/paneled shade; simple std w/dk patina, 22", VG...**2,600.00**
Table, o/l 17" 7-side shade w/detailed scenic border; simple std, EX...**4,000.00**
Table, o/l 18" rose trellis #924457 shade; bronze std, 23", pr **10,350.00**
Table, o/l 18" 6-panel shade; bronzed urn-form std, 22"...........**2,185.00**
Table, o/l 18" 8-panel shade w/leaves; tree trunk std, #5539, 25" ...**3,300.00**
Table, o/l 21" sunset scenic shade; 4-socket baluster base, 25" ...**7,000.00**
Table, Prairie-School design w/slag shade; dbl std, 24x20x14"...**16,000.00**
Table, rvpt 14" floral & ribbon shade; bronze organic std, 20"....**2,500.00**
Table, rvpt 14" goldenrod #6177 conical shade; mk bronze std ...**3,300.00**
Table, rvpt 15" floral shade; blk std w/gold decor, 21"..............**2,300.00**
Table, rvpt 16" dogwood-band #6199 sgn dome shade; bronzed std, 23"..**2,700.00**
Table, rvpt 16" landscape shade; simple bronzed std, 23".........**3,000.00**
Table, rvpt 16" seashore #6814 dome shade; metal baluster std **7,150.00**
Table, rvpt 18" autumn waterway scene #711 shade; bronze std, 24"..........**5,500.00**
Table, rvpt 18" daffodil #7122 shade; bronzed urn std, 23" **6,500.00**
Table, rvpt 18" exotic bird #7125 Palme shade; ornate std, 26½" **25,875.00**
Table, rvpt 18" exotic bird shade; tripod std w/prisms, 23" **13,450.00**
Table, rvpt 18" exotic birds textured shade; paneled vase std w/rtcl ft ..**13,400.00**
Table, rvpt 18" floral dome #1688 shade; bronze std, 23".........**9,500.00**
Table, rvpt 18" floral/butterfly #7227 shade; (3) scroll-leg std....**7,840.00**
Table, rvpt 18" floral/leaf dome shade; vase-shape bronzed base, 24"....**5,500.00**
Table, rvpt 18" landscape #5324 shade; bronze metal std, 23½"......**8,000.00**
Table, rvpt 18" Oriental pheasant shade; polygonal #979664 std, 24"....**16,800.00**
Table, rvpt 18" parrot #7128 shade; 3-leg std on rnd base, 23½"....**21,000.00**
Table, rvpt 18" poppies+2 butterflies flared shade; wide base, sm hdls ...**56,000.00**
Table, rvpt 18" roses #6741 shade; Rookwood base w/emb flowers, 24"....**20,000.00**

Table lamp, reverse-painted 18" shade with roses and butterflies (signed and numbered 5588), three-light scrolled tripod base with fine patina, ca 1919, 23", **$16,500.00.** (Photo courtesy Skinner, Inc.)

Table, rvpt/chp 18" scenic ribbed shade; simple copper-finish std, 23"..**5,600.00**
Table, rvpt/chp 21" #6570 shade w/stylized border; simple rib std, 21"..**6,440.00**

Harker

The Harker Pottery was established in East Liverpool, Ohio, in 1840. Their earliest products were yellow ware and Rockingham produced from local clay. After 1900 whiteware was made from imported materials. The plant eventually grew to be a large manufacturer of dinnerware and kitchenware, employing as many as three hundred people. It closed in 1972 after it was purchased by the Jeannette Glass Company. Perhaps their best-known lines were their Cameo wares, decorated with white silhouettes in a cameo effect on contrasting solid colors. Floral silhouettes are standard, but other designs were also used. Blue and pink are the most often found background hues; a few pieces are found in yellow. For further information we recommend *The Best of Collectible Dinnerware* by Jo Cunningham (Schiffer). Our advisor for this category is Ted Haun; he is listed in the Directory under Indiana.

Advertising plate, boy looking at sign (w/advertising), 8¾" 40.00
Advertising plate, yel roses, 9", from $35 to 45.00
Amy, pitcher, milk; 5-sided, w/lid, 9½" 65.00
Amy, plate, emb edge, 6", from $1 to..5.00
Apples & Nuts, plate, dinner 10.00
Autumn Leaf, plate, 7" 8.00
Bamboo, plate, salad; from $12 to 14.00
Basket of Flowers, bowl, vegetable 15.00
Blue Grapes, pie baker 25.00
Cactus, pie baker 25.00
Cameo Rose, bowl, serving; bl, 8¼", from $18 to 22.00
Cameoware, mug, pk w/circus elephant, 3" 30.00
Charleston (Pink Cocoa), plate, 6"...5.00
Chesterton, plate, dinner; 9¼", from $8 to 12.00
Chesterton, platter, 13½" 22.00
Chesterton (Bermuda Blue), gravy boat 14.00
Country Home, teapot, silver trim..30.00
Countryside, jug, Arches, w/lid, 5¾" 315.00
Currier & Ives, plate, dinner 19.00
Dainty Flower, batter jug, powder bl, w/lid, 8½" 60.00
Dainty Flower, teapot, w/lid, 5½" 35.00
Dogwood, sugar bowl, w/lid 12.00
Donna, cake plate & lifter set 20.00
Gadroon, cake plate, 10½", w/9½" server 45.00
Green Blush, dresser tray, w/pk roses 20.00
Heritance, bowl, 2-part, w/lid 32.00
Heritance, cup & saucer 20.00
Heritance, plate, dinner; 10" 24.00
Intaglio Wheat, bowl, serving; 8¾" 10.00
Intaglio Wheat, cup & saucer 8.00
Ivy, bowl, soup 12.00
Ivy, bowls, nesting; 2-qt, 1½-qt & 1-qt 45.00
Ivy, gravy boat..16.00
Ivy, pitcher, w/lid, 8" 40.00
Ivy, platter, 16" 30.00
Ivy, tidbit tray, 3-tier, 10¼", 7½", 6¼", 13" H 55.00
Laurelton, butter dish 32.00
Laurelton, creamer 20.00
Laurelton, sauce boat, attached underplate 18.00
Lovelace, rolling pin, 15" 45.00
Magnolia, bowl, fruit/dessert; 6" 16.00
Mallow, bowl, 3¼x4¾" 30.00
Mallow, casserole, w/lid, 4x6½" 35.00
Mallow, pie plate, 10" 30.00
Mallow, refrigerator dish, w/lid, 5x4¼" 90.00
Mexican, cup & saucer 35.00
Modern Tulip, jug, Modern Age, w/lid 35.00
Modern Tulip, platter, 13¾"..28.00
Orange Poppy, pie baker, 10", w/matching lifter 50.00
Oriental Poppy, bean pot, ind 12.00
Oriental Poppy, bowl, 4x8½" 35.00
Oriental Poppy, casserole, w/lid, 2½x6½" 35.00
Oriental Poppy, cracker jar, w/lid 50.00
Oriental Poppy, pitcher, Arches, 32-oz 85.00
Pansy, bowl, emb scroll & cable border, 4x8¾"............................40.00
Pate Sur Pate, bowl, serving; w/lid, 10½" 30.00
Pate Sur Pate, platter, 13½" 20.00
Pate Sur Pate, shakers, pr 18.00
Pate Sur Pate, teapot, 5½" 65.00

Petit Fleurs, bowl, soup/cereal 10.00
Petit Fleurs, bowl, vegetable; w/lid, 4x9" 27.00
Petit Point, bowl, batter; 9¾" 60.00
Petit Point, bowl, mixing; 9" 25.00
Petit Point, casserole, tab hdls, w/lid, 8" 35.00
Petit Point, drip jar, w/lid, skyscraper style 28.00
Petit Point, pie baker, 9" 30.00
Petit Point, plate, utility; 11" 22.00
Petit Point, platter, 14" 28.00
Petit Point, water jug, w/lid, 8¼", from $65 to 75.00
Pine Cone, cup 12.00
Pine Cone, plate, salad; 8½" 8.00
Red Apple I, bowl, 1¼x5½" 10.00
Red Apple I, casserole, w/lid, 5½x8½" 40.00
Red Apple I, platter 35.00
Red Apple II, bowl, vegetable; 8½" 30.00
Red Apple II, drip jar, skyscraper style, 3x5x5" 40.00
Red Apple II, plate, serving; sq, 10¾x12" 35.00
Rose, platter, Olympic 14.00
Silhouette, bowl, 9¼" 32.00
Silhouette, pie lifter 24.00
Star-lite, platter, 11¼x9¾" 30.00
Vintage, platter 11.00
White Daisy, plate, salad 10.00

Harlequin

Harlequin dinnerware, produced by the Homer Laughlin China Company of Newell, West Virginia, was introduced in 1938. It was a lightweight ware made in maroon, mauve blue, and spruce green, as well as all the Fiesta colors except ivory (see Fiesta). It was marketed exclusively by the Woolworth stores, who considered it to be their all-time bestseller. For this reason they contracted with Homer Laughlin to reissue Harlequin to commemorate their 100th anniversary in 1979. Although three of the original glazes were used in the reissue, the few serving pieces that were made were restyled, and collectors found the new line to be no threat to their investments.

The Harlequin animals, including a fish, lamb, cat, penguin, duck, and donkey, were made during the early 1940s, also for the dime-store trade. Today these are very desirable to collectors of Homer Laughlin china.

Values are given for the more desirable colors; for turquoise and yellow, you will need to drop down a price point. Unless specifically priced, for medium green, double the values on all items other than flat items and small bowls. *The Collector's Encyclopedia of Fiesta* (Collector Books) by Sharon and Bob Huxford contains a more thorough study of this subject and includes specific pricing for many medium green examples.

Animals, maverick, gold trim, ea 50.00
Animals, non-standard color, ea 325.00
Animals, standard color, ea 195.00
Ashtray, basketweave 40.00
Ashtray, regular 38.00
Ashtray/saucer 55.00
Bowl, '36s 28.00
Bowl, '36s oatmeal 16.00
Bowl, cream soup 25.00
Bowl, cream soup; med gr 900.00
Bowl, fruit; 5½" 8.00
Bowl, ind salad 28.00
Bowl, mixing; Kitchen Kraft, mauve bl, 8" 125.00
Bowl, mixing; Kitchen Kraft, red or lt gr, 6", ea 90.00
Bowl, mixing; Kitchen Kraft, yel, 10" 125.00

Bowl, nappy; 9"	28.00
Bowl, oval baker	27.00
Butter dish, cobalt, ½-lb	300.00
Butter dish, ½-lb	115.00
Candle holders, pr	250.00
Casserole, w/lid	95.00
Creamer, high lip, any color, ea	135.00
Creamer, ind	20.00
Creamer, novelty	28.00
Creamer, regular	14.00
Cup, demitasse	42.00
Cup, lg, any color, ea	185.00
Cup, tea	9.00
Egg cup, dbl	20.00
Egg cup, single	25.00
Marmalade	225.00
Nut dish, basketweave	15.00
Perfume bottle, any color, ea	140.00
Pitcher, service water	75.00
Pitcher, 22-oz jug	50.00
Plate, deep	20.00
Plate, deep; med gr	75.00
Plate, 6"	4.00
Plate, 7"	6.00
Plate, 9"	10.00
Plate, 10"	24.00
Platter, med gr, 11"	175.00
Platter, med gr, 13"	225.00
Platter, 11"	20.00
Platter, 13"	24.00
Relish tray, mixed colors	335.00
Sauce boat	22.00
Saucer	2.00
Saucer, demitasse	18.00
Saucer, demitasse; med gr, minimum value	150.00
Shakers, pr	18.00
Sugar bowl, w/lid	20.00
Sugar bowl, w/lid, med gr, minimum value	100.00
Syrup, red or yel	250.00
Syrup, spruce gr or mauve	340.00
Teapot	90.00
Tumbler	45.00

Hatpin Holders

Most hatpin holders were made from 1860 to 1920 to coincide with the period during which hatpins were popularly in vogue. The taller types were required to house the long hatpins necessary to secure the large hats that were in style from 1890 to 1914. They were usually porcelain, either decorated by hand or by transfer with florals or scenics, although some were clever figurals. Glass examples are rare, and those of slag or carnival glass are especially valuable.

For information concerning the American Hatpin Society, see the Clubs, Newsletters, and Catalogs section of the Directory. Our advisor for this category is Virginia Woodbury; she is listed in the Directory under California. (SASE required.)

Carnival glass, Grape & Cable, purple, 7x2½"	350.00
China, floral decal, on cream w/gold, unmk, 4¾"	95.00
Flow blue, Victorian scenes, Watteau	175.00
Japan, bl & wht export china, windmill scene, 4"	210.00
Limoges, transfer w/HP o/l & gold, 14-hole, 4½"	375.00
LP Limoges, Nouveau lady & peacock, 7-hole, 3⅝", from $250 to	275.00

Nippon, violets reserves w/gold, tapered sq, pre-1921, 4¾"	125.00
Pickard, HP Nouveau floral w/much gold, 4¾"	250.00
Porc, Art Nouveau gold leaf design w/emb swirls, 4x3"	55.00
Porc, HP floral, waisted cylinder, Austrian mk, 1899-1918, 4¼"	125.00
Royal Bayreuth, lily form, yel & gr, unmk, 4½", from $950 to	1,500.00
Royal Doulton, hunt scene, Lambeth & Burslem, 1900s, 4¾", $250 to	350.00
RS Prussia, pk & wht flowers, red mk	225.00
S&V, bsk, lady's portrait reserve, hanging cone form, 6¾", from $275 to	375.00
Volkstedt, gr jasper w/vining fruit, 12-hole, 5⅜x2⅛" sq	250.00
Willow Art China, transfer, souvenir of Jerusalem, 5½"	110.00

British hat stand, Cupid with bow and arrow, A & LL hallmarks, from $285.00 to $315.00. (Photo courtesy Virginia Woodbury)

Hatpins

A hatpin was used to securely fasten a hat to the hair and head of the wearer. Hatpins, measuring from 4" to 12" in length, were worn from approximately 1850 to 1920. During the Art Deco period, hatpins became ornaments rather than the decorative functional jewels that they had been. The hatpin period reached its zenith in 1913 just prior to World War I, which brought about a radical change in women's headdress and fashion. About that time, women began to scorn the bonnet and adopt 'the hat' as a symbol of their equality. The hatpin was made of every natural and manufactured element in a myriad of designs that challenge the imagination. They were contrived to serve every fashion need and complement the milliner's art. Collectors often concentrate on a specific type: hand-painted porcelains, sterling silver, commemoratives, sporting activities, Carnival glass, Art Nouveau and/or Art Deco designs, Victorian Gothics with mounted stones, exquisite rhinestones, engraved and brass-mounted escutcheon heads, gold and gems, or simply primitive types made in the Victorian parlor. Some collectors prefer the long pin-shanks while others select only those on tremblants or nodder-type pin-shanks.

If you are interested in collecting or dealing in hatpins, see the information in the Hatpin Holders introduction concerning a national collectors' club. Our advisor for this category is Virginia Woodbury; she is listed in the Directory under California. (SASE required.)

Brass flower w/4 cabochon sapphires, 8" pin	140.00
Carnival glass, butterfly, gr irid	175.00
Celluloid, Deco accordion pleats, brass mt, 3¼", steel pin	65.00
Celluloid, pierced or cut, Deco 2-mold design, 1920s	125.00
Faux jade, cabochon cut, gilt brass Egyptian style mt	230.00
Gilt mt w/¾" oval aquamarine, ca 1895, on 8" wht pin	200.00
Gilt-brass w/cabochon peacock eye glass center, 1", steel pin	195.00

Mosaic, dbl fr, metallic mt, granular trim, 1870s, 1¼", brass pin ...195.00
Peacock eye glass oval, ⅞", 7½" steel pin 135.00
Plique-a-jour butterfly, bl & gr, 1½" W, 6½" shank 600.00
Silver, scarab w/HP details, Germany, 1½", 10" pin 95.00
Sterling, thistle w/faux topaz stone, English hallmk 275.00

Haviland

The Haviland China Company was organized in 1840 by David Haviland, a New York china importer. His search for a pure white, non-porous porcelain led him to Limoges, France, where natural deposits of suitable clay had already attracted numerous china manufacturers. The fine china he produced there was translucent and meticulously decorated, with each piece fired in an individual sagger.

It has been estimated that as many as 60,000 chinaware patterns were designed, each piece marked with one of several company backstamps. 'H. & Co.' was used until 1890 when a law was enacted making it necessary to include the country of origin. Various marks have been used since that time including 'Haviland, France'; 'Haviland & Co. Limoges'; and 'Decorated by Haviland & Co.' Various associations with family members over the years have resulted in changes in management as well as company name. In 1892 Theodore Haviland left the firm to start his own business. Some of his ware was marked 'Mont Mery.' Later logos included a horseshoe, a shield, and various uses of his initials and name. In 1941 this branch moved to the United States. Wares produced here are marked 'Theodore Haviland, N.Y.' or 'Made In America.'

Though it is their dinnerware lines for which they are most famous, during the 1880s and 1890s they also made exquisite art pottery using a technique of underglaze slip decoration called Barbotine, which had been invented by Ernest Chaplet. In 1885 Haviland bought the formula and hired Chaplet to oversee its production. The technique involved mixing heavy white clay slip with pigments to produce a compound of the same consistency as oil paints. The finished product actually resembled oil paintings of the period, the texture achieved through the application of the heavy medium to the clay body in much the same manner as an artist would apply paint to his canvas. Primarily the body used with this method was a low-fired faience, though they also produced stoneware. For further information we recommend Mary Frank Gaston's *Collector's Encyclopedia of Limoges Porcelain, Third Edition* (the first two editions are out of print), which offers examples and marks of the Haviland Company.

Ashtray, Pigall's Paris, Montmartre advertising, 4½x3" 70.00
Cake stand, dainty bl floral, Marseille form, 2x9" 120.00
Candlestick, Ranson shape, gold trim, 7" 140.00
Chamberstick, rose buds w/rose & cobalt, Marseille shape, 3x5½"....175.00
Chocolate pot, mixed floral w/gold, Henry II form, 8½" 225.00
Coffeepot, wht w/gold trim, scalloped spout, 8" 90.00
Cracker jar, cobalt w/lady & gold trim, Marseille form, 8" 325.00
Creamer & sugar bowl, floral w/emb ribs, Cannele form, 3½", 4" 175.00
Cup & saucer, demitasse; floral w/swirled ribs, 2¼", 4½" 120.00
Egg cup, floral w/gold, ftd, 3" 65.00
Ewer, mouth rinse; roses & daises HP on wht w/gold, 1865-75, 8" 175.00
Footbath, ornate leaf hdls, gold trim, 22x21x13" 800.00
Humidor, elephant figural, ornate bl & gold on wht, ca 1855, 8"..14,000.00
Mayonnaise set, leaf shape w/gold, 6½" bowl+7" plate...............110.00
Pitcher, trees & water scene, gold trim, Ranson shape, 9"...........250.00
Plate, flowers w/wide gold band, F Wallace, gr mk, 8¾" 325.00
Plate, grape clusters around inner border w/gold, Challinor, 9"...325.00
Plate, oyster; 5 shells on bl, Presidential form, Pat 1880, 9" 1,000.00
Plate, salad; floral w/gold & cobalt trim, crescent shape, 10" 125.00
Plate, walnuts & leaves w/gold, Vokral, gr mk, 8½" 300.00
Teapot, penguin figural, sgn Sandoz, 5¾".....................................700.00

Tile, mythological women & children, wht/tan/gray, oval, 17x13"..1,500.00
Vase, cobalt w/gold floral, appl wht bsk floral vine, 14¾"........1,600.00
Vase, roses on ball form, stick neck, sm hdls, non-factory decor, 12"..300.00
Vase, terra cotta, sculpted flowers, mc on brn gloss, 1873-86, 12", pr...1,600.00

Hawkes

Thomas Hawkes established his factory in Corning, New York, in 1880. He developed many beautiful patterns of cut glass, two of which were awarded the Grand Prize at the Paris Exposition in 1889. By the end of the century, his company was renowned for the finest in cut glass production. The company logo was a trefoil form enclosing a hawk in each of the two bottom lobes with a fleur-de-lis in the center. With the exception of some of the very early designs, all Hawkes was signed. (Our values are for signed pieces.)

Bowl, cut, flared scalloped edge, 3¾x10" 230.00
Bowl, cut, hobstars, 3¼x8"..200.00
Bowl, cut, star motif, 3½x8", EX 150.00
Bowl, cut, stars/hobstars/miters, 3¾x8" 200.00
Bowl, finger; cut, hobstars/notches/miters, 1920s, 1x5" 65.00
Candlesticks, floral etch, disk ft, 13¾", pr 765.00
Candy dish, apple gr vaseline, w/lid, 5½" 122.00
Carafe, wine; cut, Holland, fleur-de-lis mk, 7¼x6½" 135.00
Compote, aqua bl w/gold trim, shallow, slim std, disk ft, 6¾x7" ..225.00
Creamer, eng intaglio flowers on gr, ped ft, 1920s, 4x3½"............75.00
Cruet, cut, zippers/hobstars/miters, rayed base, faceted top, 7½" ...310.00
Cruet, floral etch, disk stopper, 7" 150.00
Ferner, cut, Palermo pattern, 3-ftd, 4½x8" dia............................235.00
Jar, apothecary; eng basket/urn/cornucopia/flowers, w/lid, 9½" ...395.00
Plate, cut, Satin Iris, ⅝x8¼" 295.00
Vase, cut, gr, 3-sided cone w/disk foot, 10½" 235.00
Vase, cut, Iris, bucket shape w/silver base, 8½" 725.00
Vase, cut, stick w/disk ft, 17x3½" at base 215.00
Vase, cut bands & wheel-cut flowers, slim, 18" 350.00
Vase, Sweet William; eng fleur-de-lis, 4x4¼" 60.00

Head Vases

Vases modeled as heads of lovely ladies, delightful children, clowns, famous people — even some animals — were once popular as flower containers. Today they represent a growing area of collector interest. Most of them were imported from Japan, although some American potteries produced a few as well.

For more information, we recommend *Head Vases, Identification and Values*, by Kathleen Cole; *Collecting Head Vases* by David Barron; and *The World of Head Vase Planters* by Mike Posgay and Ian Warner.

Our advisor for this category is Larry G. Pogue (L&J Antiques and Collectibles); he is listed in the Directory under Texas.

Baby, blond hair, sideways bonnet, Enesco, 5".............................55.00
Baby, blond in ruffled bonnet, w/bl phone, Enesco #2185, 5" 65.00
Baby, brn hair, bonnet w/lg purple bow, Relpo #K1866, 7"............85.00
Baby, lt brn hair, blanket over head, holding kitten, unmk, 6" 65.00
Baby, ruffled bonnet w/lg wht bow, unmk, 5½" 65.00
Boy, blond, in fireman uniform, Inarco, 5" 75.00
Boy, blond w/bl & wht cap, Relpo #2010, 7" 70.00
Boy, lt brn hair, head bowed & arms folded in prayer, Inarco #E1579, 6"...85.00
Clown, red nose & mouth, gr hat, ruffled collar, Napcoware #3321, 6"......75.00
Clown, wht w/red nose, mouth & cheeks, hat, Inarco #E6730, 5½"...........80.00
Famous People, Charlie Chaplin, blk top hat & jacket, 5½" 65.00
Famous People, Shirley Temple, wht w/yel trim & hat, 6" 75.00

Girl, bl scarf over brn braids, Inarco #2523, 5½" 85.00
Girl, blond, flowered hat, holding fan, winking, unmk, 6" 95.00
Girl, blond braid w/orange cap, Hummel-like, Relpo #K1018B, 8" 225.00
Girl, blond pigtails in Christmas hat, hand up, Napco #CX2707, 6½" 100.00
Girl, blond updo w/bl flower, pk bodice, Inarco #E3157, 5½" 85.00
Girl, blond updo w/hat, both hands up, Enesco, 3" 45.00
Girl, blond updo w/hat, holding umbrella, Velco, 5½" 135.00
Girl, brn hair, yel hat w/gr bow, Inarco #E2520, 6½" 85.00
Girl, brn hair w/lg hat, hands to face, Napcoware #C4556B, 1960, 5" 90.00
Girl, polka-dot scarf, Little Miss Dream #113005, rare, 6" 350.00
Lady, Art Deco, wht w/brn hair, yel hat, pearls, unmk, 7½" 110.00
Lady, blk hair, blk hat w/lg pk bow, pearls, Inarco #E1611, 6¼" ...350.00
Lady, blond, blk bodice w/flowers at shoulder, Napcoware #C6431, 5" ..85.00
Lady, blond, blk hat & bodice, hand to face, Napcoware #C569, 5" 90.00
Lady, blond, flat hat/pk bodice/gloved hands, Lefton's #2705, 6½" 115.00
Lady, blond, gloved hand to face, floral bodice, Napcoware #C6428, 6" ..110.00
Lady, blond, gray hat w/polka-dot bow, Napco #C3959A, 1959, 5½" 85.00
Lady, blond, hat, sleeveless bodice, hands to face, Lefton's #2900, 6" 125.00
Lady, blond, hat/thick lashes/pearls/gloves, Inarco #E241, 6½" ...110.00
Lady, blond curls, ruffled bonnet w/bow & bodice, unmk, 5½" ..175.00
Lady, blond in wht & pk top hat, high collar, unmk, rare, 6" 250.00
Lady, blond updo w/flower/thick lashes/pearls, Inarco #E193/M, 6" 175.00
Lady, brn updo w/bow, gr bodice, pearls, Napcoware #6986, 9" ..475.00
Lady, brn updo w/flower, gloved hands, pearls, unmk, 7" 125.00

Lady, rare, Relpo #K1402, 7", $350.00.

(Photo courtesy Larry G. Pogue)

Lady, short brn hair, blk bodice w/wht collar, Relpo #K1817, 5½" ..95.00
Lady, short brn hair w/flower, floral bodice, Relpo #K936B, 6" 85.00
Lady, wht curls, thick lashes, ruffled collar, hand up, Japan, 5½" ..80.00
Lady, wht w/gold trim, Glamour Girl, 6½" 45.00
Madonna & Child, long lashes, Hull #26, 7" 55.00
Madonna & Child, unmk, 5½" 40.00
Man, wht scarf over blk hair, 1 gold earring, Royal Copley, 7¾" ..65.00
Nun, head bowed & hands in prayer, thick lashes, Napco label, 5½" ...70.00
Teen girl, blk hair, bl bodice w/daisy at shoulder, unmk, 5½" 85.00
Teen girl, blond, hat, brn bodice, Inarco #E5624, 5½" 135.00
Teen girl, blond, pk hat w/bl bow hat, pearls, Rubens #4157, 7" ..325.00
Teen girl, blond curls, pearls, dk eyes, gr bodice, Relpo #2055, 6" ..155.00
Teen girl, blond curls w/bow, blk & wht striped jacket, unmk, 5" 95.00
Teen girl, blond frosted flip, pearls, hand to face, Inarco #E2104, 7" ..350.00
Teen girl, blond ponytail, brn top hat, hand up, unmk, 6½" 85.00
Teen girl, blond ponytails, pearl earrings, Rubens label #4135, 7" 110.00
Teen girl, blond side-swept hair, orange sweater, Inarco #E6211, 5" 95.00
Teen girl, blond side-swept hair, pearls, Inarco #E1539, 1964, 6"..85.00
Teen girl, blond w/blk head band & bodice, Relpo #K1931, 8½" ..425.00
Teen girl, blond w/flowers, blk bodice, Rubens #4136, 5½" 135.00
Teen girl, blond w/yel band, holding blk phone, Inarco #E3548, 5½" ..85.00
Teen girl, brn curls, gr bonnet w/polka-dot bow, unmk, 5¼" 75.00

Teen girl, brn curls w/bow, yel bodice, Rubens label #R4130, 6½"...125.00
Teen girl, brn hair, yel bodice w/wht collar, Napcoware #C8493, 5½"...110.00
Teen girl, brn updo, pearls, ruffled collar, Caffco #E3142, 7" 300.00
Teen girl, coat hood over blond hair, Rubens #4135, 5½" 150.00
Teen girl, orange & wht hat & bodice, pearls, Relpo #2012, 6"...95.00
Teen girl, short blond w/bl cap, bl bodice w/wht scarf, Japan, 5½"...125.00
Teen girl, wht scarf over blond hair, thick lashes, Vcagco, 6" 85.00

Heintz Art Metal Shop

Founded by Otto L. Heintz in Buffalo, New York, ca 1909, the Heintz Art Metal Shop (HAMS) succeeded the Art Crafts Shop (begun in 1903) and featured a new aesthetic. Whereas the Art Craft Shop offered products of hammered copper with applied color enamel and with an altogether somewhat cruder or more primitive and medieval-looking appearance, HAMS presented a refined appearance of applied sterling silver on bronze. Most pieces are stamped with the manufacturer's mark — the letters HAMS conjoined within a diamond, often accompanied by a Aug. 27, 1912, patent date — although paper labels were pasted on the bottom of lamp bases. Original patinas for Heintz pieces include a mottled brown or green (the most desirable), as well as silver and gold (less desirable). Desk sets and smoking accessories are common; lamps appear less frequently. The firm, like many others, closed in 1930, a victim of the Depression. Silver-crest, also located in Buffalo, produced products similar though not nearly as valuable as Heintz. Please note: Cleaning or scrubbing original patinas diminish value. Our advisor for this and related Arts & Crafts subjects is Bruce A. Austin; he is listed in the Directory under New York.

Bookends, poppies, sterling on bronze w/verdris, HAMS stamp, 5"..........250.00
Box, fox hunting scene, silver on bronze, unmk, 2¼x4¾" 465.00
Candlesticks, sterling on bronze, shaped cups, raised rnd ft, 8", pr......425.00
Lamp, boudoir; pussy willows, sterling on bronze, helmet shade, 11"..325.00
Lamp, boudoir; roses, sterling on bronze, silvered base, 11½"........225.00
Lamp, sterling/bronze 9½" helmet shade w/amethyst jewels, 14" ..800.00
Vase, goldenrod, sterling on bronze, med patina, ovoid, 12x6"......400.00

Heisey

A.H. Heisey began his long career at the King Glass Company of Pittsburgh. He later joined the Ripley Glass Company which soon became Geo. Duncan and Sons. After Duncan's death Heisey became half-owner in partnership with his brother-in-law, James Duncan. In 1895 he built his own factory in Newark, Ohio, initiating production in 1896 and continuing until Christmas of 1957. At that time Imperial Glass Corporation bought some of the molds. After 1968 they removed the old 'Diamond H' from any they put into use. In 1985 HCA purchased all of Imperial's Heisey molds with the exception of the Old Williamsburg line.

During their highly successful period of production, Heisey made fine handcrafted tableware with simple, yet graceful designs. Early pieces were not marked. After November 1901 the glassware was marked either with the 'Diamond H' or a paper label. Blown ware is often marked on the stem, never on the bowl or foot.

For more information we recommend *Collector's Encyclopedia of Heisey Glass, 1925 – 1938*, by Neila Bredehoft and *Heisey Glass, 1896 – 1957*, by Neila and Tom Bredehoft.

For information concerning Heisey Collectors of America, see the Clubs, Newsletters, and Catalogs section of the Directory. See also Glass Animals and Figurines.

Charter Oak, crystal, bowl, floral; oak leaf, #116, 11" 50.00
Charter Oak, crystal, comport, low ft, #3362, 6" 45.00

Charter Oak, Flamingo, goblet, high ft, #3362, 8-oz......................35.00
Charter Oak, Flamingo, pitcher, flat, #3362 ....160.00
Charter Oak, Hawthorne, plate, dinner; Acorn & Leaves, #1246, 10½" ...70.00
Charter Oak, Hawthorne, tumbler, flat, #3362, 10-oz 35.00
Charter Oak, marigold, candlestick, Tricorn, 3-light, #129, 5", ea ...150.00
Charter Oak, marigold, cocktail, #3362, 3-oz.........................40.00
Charter Oak, Moongleam, finger bowl, #3362 ....20.00
Charter Oak, Moongleam, plate, luncheon/salad; #1246, 7" 17.50
Chintz, crystal, bowl, cream soup.....................................18.00
Chintz, crystal, comport, oval, 7"...................................40.00
Chintz, crystal, plate, salad; sq, 7" 8.00
Chintz, crystal, sugar bowl, 3 dolphin ft 20.00
Chintz, crystal, tray, sandwich; sq, center hdl, 12" 35.00
Chintz, Sahara, finger bowl, #4107...................................20.00
Chintz, Sahara, mayonnaise, dolphin ft, 5½" 65.00
Chintz, Sahara, parfait, #3389, 5-oz.................................35.00
Chintz, Sahara, tumbler, soda; #3389, 8-oz...........................24.00
Chintz, Sahara, vase, dolphin ft, 9" 185.00
Crystolite, crystal, ashtray/coaster, rnd, 4".........................8.00
Crystolite, crystal, bowl, dessert; 4½" 20.00
Crystolite, crystal, bowl, salad; rnd, 10" 50.00
Crystolite, crystal, cigarette box, w/lid, 4" 35.00
Crystolite, crystal, ladle, punch; glass 35.00
Crystolite, crystal, pitcher, ice; blown, ½-gal 140.00
Crystolite, crystal, plate, torte; 14" 50.00
Crystolite, crystal, tray, leaf relish; 4-part, 9" 40.00
Crystolite, crystal, tumbler, pressed, #5003, 8-oz...................60.00
Crystolite, crystal, vase, short stem, 3" 45.00
Empress, Alexandrite, bowl, frappe; w/center 175.00
Empress, Alexandrite, creamer, ind 210.00
Empress, Alexandrite, plate, bouillon liner 25.00
Empress, Alexandrite, plate, 8".....................................75.00
Empress, Alexandrite, saucer, rnd...................................25.00
Empress, Alexandrite, sugar bowl, dolphin ft, 3-hdl 250.00
Empress, Alexandrite, tray, celery; 10" 150.00
Empress, cobalt, bowl, nappy, dolphin ft, 7½" 300.00
Empress, cobalt, candlestick, dolphin ft, 6", ea 260.00
Empress, cobalt, plate, sq, 7".......................................60.00
Empress, cobalt, plate, sq, 8".......................................80.00
Empress, Flamingo, bonbon, 6" 20.00
Empress, Flamingo, bowl, lemon; oval, w/lid, 6½" 65.00
Empress, Flamingo, comport, sq, 6"...................................70.00
Empress, Flamingo, mayonnaise, ftd, w/ladle, 5½" 85.00
Empress, Flamingo, sherbet, 4-oz.....................................22.00
Empress, Moongleam, bowl, nappy, 4½".................................60.00
Empress, Moongleam, platter, 14" 80.00
Empress, Sahara, bowl, jelly; ftd, hdls, 6" 25.00
Empress, Sahara, bowl, pickle/olive; 2-part, 13" 45.00
Empress, Sahara, ice tub, w/metal hdls 150.00
Empress, Sahara, plate, muffin; uptrn sides, 12" 80.00
Empress, Sahara, tray, buffet relish; 4-part, 16" 75.00
Greek Key, crystal, bowl, banana split; flat, 9"....................45.00
Greek Key, crystal, bowl, nappy, 8"..................................70.00
Greek Key, crystal, cheese & cracker set, 10".......................150.00
Greek Key, crystal, cocktail, 3-oz...................................50.00
Greek Key, crystal, compote, w/lid, 5"..............................130.00
Greek Key, crystal, egg cup, 5-oz...................................80.00
Greek Key, crystal, finger bowl.....................................40.00
Greek Key, crystal, jar, horseradish; lg lid.......................140.00
Greek Key, crystal, jelly; low ft, w/lid, 5".......................110.00
Greek Key, crystal, pitcher, 1-pt..................................130.00
Greek Key, crystal, plate, 6½".......................................35.00
Greek Key, crystal, tray, celery; oval, 12".........................60.00
Greek Key, crystal, tumbler, water; 5½-oz...........................50.00

Ipswich, Alexandrite, goblet, knob in stem, 10-oz 750.00
Ipswich, cobalt, candlestick, 1-light, 6", ea 40.00
Ipswich, crystal, candy jar, w/lid, ¼-lb...........................175.00
Ipswich, crystal, finger bowl, w/underplate 40.00
Ipswich, crystal, oil bottle, ftd, #86 stopper, 2-oz................125.00
Ipswich, gr, candlestick, 1-light, 6", ea 300.00
Ipswich, gr, oyster cocktail, ftd, 4-oz..............................70.00
Ipswich, gr, tumbler, cupped or str rim, flat bottom, 10-oz, ea.....140.00
Ipswich, pk, bowl, floral; ftd, 11" 80.00
Ipswich, pk, plate, sq, 7"...30.00
Ipswich, pk, tumbler, soda; ftd, 12-oz...............................80.00
Ipswich, Sahara, creamer 90.00
Ipswich, Sahara, sherbet, ftd, knob in stem, 4-oz 30.00
Kalonyal, crystal, bowl, crimped, 5".................................35.00
Kalonyal, crystal, cake plate, ftd, 9".............................225.00
Kalonyal, crystal, comport, jelly; deep ft, 5".....................110.00
Kalonyal, crystal, egg cup, 9½-oz...................................75.00
Kalonyal, crystal, mug, 8-oz.......................................175.00
Kalonyal, crystal, plate, 5½".......................................30.00
Kalonyal, crystal, tumbler, 8-oz....................................65.00
Lariat, crystal, ashtray, 4"...15.00
Lariat, crystal, bowl, cream soup; hdls 50.00
Lariat, crystal, bowl, floral or fruit; 12" 40.00
Lariat, crystal, cheese dish, w/lid, 8" 60.00
Lariat, crystal, ice tub 75.00
Lariat, crystal, tumbler, ice tea; blown, ftd, 12-oz.................28.00
Lariat, crystal, vase, swung 135.00
Lariat, crystal, wine, pressed, 3½-oz...............................24.00
Narcissus, crystal, bowl, floral; ftd, #1519, 11"...................65.00
Narcissus, crystal, comport, honey; ftd, #1519, 7".................40.00
Narcissus, crystal, cup, #1519......................................30.00
Narcissus, crystal, goblet, #3408, 9-oz.............................28.00
Narcissus, crystal, vase, rnd, ftd, #1519, 7".......................85.00
New Era, crystal, bottle, rye; w/stopper 120.00
New Era, crystal, bowl, floral; 11".................................35.00
New Era, crystal, cup, AD...62.50
New Era, crystal, goblet, 10-oz.....................................16.00
New Era, crystal, pilsner, 8-oz.....................................27.50
New Era, crystal, plate, bread & butter; 5½x4½"....................15.00
New Era, crystal, saucer, AD..12.50
New Era, crystal, tray, celery; 13".................................30.00
Octagon, crystal, bonbon, #1229, uptrn sides, 6"....................10.00
Octagon, crystal, candlestick, 1-light, 3", ea......................15.00
Octagon, crystal, plate, muffin; #1229, uptrn sides, 10"............15.00
Octagon, crystal, tray, #500, oblong, 6"............................8.00
Octagon, Flamingo, bowl, cream soup; hdls...........................20.00
Octagon, Flamingo, cheese dish, #1229, hdls, 6".....................15.00
Octagon, Flamingo, plate, cream soup liner 5.00
Octagon, Flamingo, platter, oval, 12¾"..............................25.00
Octagon, Hawthorne, bowl, mint; #1229, ftd, 8"......................45.00
Octagon, Hawthorne, mayonnaise, #1229, ftd, 5½".....................55.00
Octagon, Hawthorne, saucer, AD......................................12.00
Octagon, Marigold, basket, #500, 5".................................350.00
Octagon, Marigold, dish, frozen dessert; #500.......................50.00
Octagon, Marigold, tray, variety; #500, 4-part, 12".................350.00
Octagon, Moongleam, bowl, vegetable; 9".............................30.00
Octagon, Moongleam, ice tub, #500...................................80.00
Octagon, Moongleam, sugar bowl, hotel 35.00
Octagon, Sahara, bowl, grapefruit; 6½"..............................22.00
Octagon, Sahara, cup, #1231...20.00
Octagon, Sahara, plate, 10½"..30.00
Old Colony, Sahara, bouillon cup, hdls, ftd 25.00
Old Colony, Sahara, bowl, dessert; oval, hdls, 10"..................50.00
Old Colony, Sahara, bowl, floral; dolphin ft, 11"...................80.00

Old Colony, Sahara, bowl, pickle & olive; 2-part, 13".................24.00
Old Colony, Sahara, comport, oval, ftd, 7"................................80.00
Old Colony, Sahara, decanter, 1-pt 325.00
Old Colony, Sahara, ice tub, dolphin ft...................................115.00
Old Colony, Sahara, plate, cream soup......................................12.00
Old Colony, Sahara, plate, muffin; rnd, hdls, 12" 75.00
Old Colony, Sahara, sherbet, #3380, 6-oz..................................20.00
Old Colony, Sahara, tray, sandwich; center hdl, 12"......................75.00
Old Colony, Sahara, tumbler, soda; #3380, ftd, 8-oz......................18.00
Old Colony, Sahara, vase, ftd, 9"...150.00
Old Sandwich, cobalt, candlestick, 6", ea...............................325.00
Old Sandwich, cobalt, stem, claret; 4-oz.................................150.00
Old Sandwich, cobalt, tumbler, bar; ground bottom, 1½-oz........100.00
Old Sandwich, crystal, beer mug, 12-oz....................................50.00
Old Sandwich, crystal, creamer, oval......................................25.00
Old Sandwich, crystal, pitcher, ice lip, ½-gal...........................100.00
Old Sandwich, crystal, tumbler, iced tea; 12-oz..........................20.00
Old Sandwich, Flamingo, bowl, flower; oval, ftd, 12" 80.00
Old Sandwich, Flamingo, cup...65.00
Old Sandwich, Flamingo, parfait, 4½-oz....................................50.00
Old Sandwich, Flamingo, sundae, 6-oz......................................30.00
Old Sandwich, Flamingo, wine, 2½-oz.......................................45.00
Old Sandwich, Moongleam, bowl, popcorn; ftd, cupped.............135.00
Old Sandwich, Moongleam, decanter, w/#98 stopper, 1-pt 225.00
Old Sandwich, Moongleam, parfait, 4½-oz..................................60.00
Old Sandwich, Moongleam, plate, sq, 8"...................................32.00
Old Sandwich, Sahara, creamer, 14-oz....................................180.00
Old Sandwich, Sahara, finger bowl...60.00
Old Sandwich, Sahara, flower block, #22...................................30.00
Old Sandwich, Sahara, oyster cocktail, 4-oz...............................27.00
Pleat & Panel, crystal, bowl, chow chow; 4"................................6.00
Pleat & Panel, crystal, cheese & cracker set, tray w/compote, 10½"...25.00
Pleat & Panel, crystal, plate, sandwich; 14"..............................15.00
Pleat & Panel, crystal, tray, compartmented spice; 10"...................10.00
Pleat & Panel, Flamingo, bowl, lemon; w/lid, 5"...........................60.00
Pleat & Panel, Flamingo, pitcher, ice lip, 3-pt.........................140.00
Pleat & Panel, Flamingo, plate, bread; 7".................................8.00
Pleat & Panel, Flamingo, vase, 8"...80.00
Pleat & Panel, Moongleam, marmalade, 4¾"..................................35.00

Pleat and Panel, Moongleam, pitcher, three-pint, $165.00.
(Photo courtesy Gene Florence)

Pleat & Panel, Moongleam, platter, oval, 12"..............................47.50
Pleat & Panel, Moongleam, sherbet, ftd, 5-oz..............................12.00
Pleat & Panel, Moongleam, tumbler, tea; ground bottom, 12-oz...30.00
Provincial/Whirlpool, crystal, bowl, gardenia; 13".......................40.00
Provincial/Whirlpool, crystal, bowl, nut/jelly, ind.......................20.00
Provincial/Whirlpool, crystal, coaster, 4"................................15.00
Provincial/Whirlpool, crystal, creamer & sugar bowl w/tray, ind ..80.00
Provincial/Whirlpool, crystal, plate, torte; 14"..........................45.00
Provincial/Whirlpool, crystal, vase, pansy; 4"............................35.00

Provincial/Whirlpool, Limelight Green, bowl, nappy; 4½".................40.00
Provincial/Whirlpool, Limelight Green, creamer, ftd......................95.00
Provincial/Whirlpool, Limelight Green, plate, buffet; 18"...........175.00
Provincial/Whirlpool, Limelight Green, plate, luncheon; 8".........50.00
Provincial/Whirlpool, Limelight Green, tumbler, juice; ftd, 5-oz..60.00
Queen Ann, crystal, bonbon, 6"..12.00
Queen Ann, crystal, bowl, cream soup; w/sq liner.........................25.00
Queen Ann, crystal, bowl, frappe; w/center...............................25.00
Queen Ann, crystal, bowl, lemon; oval, w/lid, 6½".........................45.00
Queen Ann, crystal, bowl, pickle/olive; 2-part, 13".......................20.00
Queen Ann, crystal, candlestick, dolphin ft 6", ea.......................70.00
Queen Ann, crystal, candy dish, w/lid, dolphin ft, 6".....................50.00
Queen Ann, crystal, cup, bouillon; hdls..................................20.00
Queen Ann, crystal, ice tub, w/metal hdls................................60.00
Queen Ann, crystal, plate, hors d'oeuvre; hdls, 13".......................60.00
Queen Ann, crystal, tray, relish; 3-part, 10"............................20.00
Queen Ann, crystal, vase, flared, 8".....................................55.00
Ridgeleigh, crystal, ashtray, rnd, 4"....................................22.00
Ridgeleigh, crystal, bowl, centerpiece; 11"..............................50.00
Ridgeleigh, crystal, bowl, fruit; flared, 10"............................45.00
Ridgeleigh, crystal, bowl, nappy, belled or cupped, 4½"..............20.00
Ridgeleigh, crystal, ice tub, hdls......................................100.00
Ridgeleigh, crystal, marmalade, w/lid....................................90.00
Ridgeleigh, crystal, plate, torte; ftd, 13½".............................45.00
Ridgeleigh, crystal, shakers, pr...45.00
Ridgeleigh, crystal, tray, celery; 12"...................................40.00
Ridgeleigh, crystal, tumbler, juice; blown, 5-oz.........................30.00
Ridgeleigh, crystal, tumbler, soda; blown, 8-oz..........................40.00
Ridgeleigh, crystal, vase, #1469¾, triangular, 8".......................110.00
Ridgeleigh, crystal, vase, #5, scalloped top, ind........................55.00
Saturn, crystal, bitters bottle, w/short tube, blown.....................75.00
Saturn, crystal, bowl, nappy, 5"...15.00
Saturn, crystal, bowl, salad; 11"..40.00
Saturn, crystal, plate, luncheon; 8".....................................10.00
Saturn, crystal, sugar bowl, w/lid, no hdls..............................25.00
Saturn, crystal, tray, tidbit; 2 sides fanned out........................25.00
Saturn, crystal, vase, violet..35.00
Saturn, Zircon or Limelight, ashtray....................................150.00
Saturn, Zircon or Limelight, bowl, whipped cream; 5"....................150.00
Saturn, Zircon or Limelight, parfait, 5-oz..............................110.00
Saturn, Zircon or Limelight, pitcher, w/ice lip, blown, 70-oz......550.00
Saturn, Zircon or Limelight, tumbler, juice; 5-oz........................80.00
Saturn, Zircon or Limelight, vase, flared or str, 8½", ea.............225.00
Stanhope, crystal, bottle, oil; w or w/o rnd knob, 3-oz..............325.00
Stanhope, crystal, bowl, mint; 2-part, hdls, w/ or w/o rnd knobs...35.00
Stanhope, crystal, bowl, salad; 11"......................................90.00
Stanhope, crystal, claret, #4083, 4-oz...................................25.00
Stanhope, crystal, nappy, hdl, w or w/o rnd knob, 4½"................25.00
Stanhope, crystal, plate, torte; rnd, 15"................................45.00
Stanhope, crystal, vase, ball, 7".......................................100.00
Sunburst, crystal, bottle, oil; 2-oz.....................................70.00
Sunburst, crystal, bowl, oblong, 7"......................................35.00
Sunburst, crystal, cake plate, ftd, 9".................................165.00
Sunburst, crystal, finger bowl, 5".......................................25.00
Sunburst, crystal, pitcher, str sides, ½-gal............................175.00
Sunburst, crystal, plate, torte; 13".....................................35.00
Sunburst, crystal, vase, orchid; 6"......................................90.00
Twist, Alexandrite, bowl, nasturtium; rnd, 8"...........................450.00
Twist, Alexandrite, ice bucket..425.00
Twist, crystal, baker, oval, 9"..25.00
Twist, crystal, bowl, nappy, 4"...10.00
Twist, crystal, pitcher, 3-pt..95.00
Twist, crystal, tray, celery; 13"..25.00
Twist, Flamingo, bowl, flower; 9"..40.00

Twist, Flamingo, candlestick, 1-light, 2", ea 40.00
Twist, Flamingo, cup, zigzag hdls...25.00
Twist, Flamingo, plate, utility; 3 ft, 10: 70.00
Twist, Flamingo, sherbet, 2-block stem, 5-oz 18.00
Twist, Marigold, bonbon, hdls, 6" 30.00
Twist, Marigold, cheese dish, hdls, 6" 30.00
Twist, Marigold, ice tub...125.00
Twist, Marigold, platter, 12"..75.00
Twist, Marigold, tray, pickle; ground bottom, 7" 45.00
Twist, Moongleam, bottle, French dressing 110.00
Twist, Moongleam, bowl, flower; rolled edge, 9" 45.00
Twist, Moongleam, comport, tall, 7"...120.00
Twist, Moongleam, tumbler, soda; flat bottom, 5-oz.............................32.00
Twist, Sahara, bowl, flower; oval, 4 ft, 12"....................................85.00
Twist, Sahara, plate, ground bottom, 8" 20.00
Twist, Sahara, shakers, ftd, pr...140.00
Twist, Sahara, tray, celery; 10" 40.00
Victorian, crystal, bottle, oil; 3-oz...65.00
Victorian, crystal, bowl, flower; 10½"..50.00
Victorian, crystal, comport, 3-ball stem, 6" 140.00
Victorian, crystal, decanter & stopper, 32-oz..................................70.00
Victorian, crystal, plate, cracker; 12"...75.00
Victorian, crystal, tray, celery; 12"...40.00
Victorian, crystal, vase, 4" 50.00
Victorian, crystal, wine goblet, 2½-oz...30.00
Waverly, crystal, bowl, lemon; w/lid, oval, 6".................................45.00
Waverly, crystal, box, chocolate; w/lid, 5" 80.00
Waverly, crystal, candle holder, 2-light, flame center, ea.....................65.00
Waverly, crystal, cordial, #5019, 1-oz...60.00
Waverly, crystal, creamer, ftd 25.00
Waverly, crystal, mayonnaise, w/liner & ladle, 5½"............................50.00
Waverly, crystal, plate, sandwich; 14"..35.00
Waverly, crystal, vase, violet; 3½"...60.00
Yeoman, crystal, ashtray, bow tie, hdls, 4" 10.00
Yeoman, crystal, bowl, banana split; ftd..7.00
Yeoman, crystal, platter, oval, 12"...10.00
Yeoman, crystal, salver, low ftd, 10"...15.00
Yeoman, crystal, tray, center hdl, 3-part, 11".................................15.00
Yeoman, Flamingo, bowl, baker, 9" 35.00
Yeoman, Flamingo, bowl, preserve; oval, 6" 12.00
Yeoman, Flamingo, parfait, 5-oz...15.00
Yeoman, Flamingo, plate, grapefruit bowl underliner, 6½" 12.00
Yeoman, Flamingo, syrup, saucer ft, 7-oz.......................................75.00
Yeoman, Flamingo, tumbler, cupped rim, 10-oz...................................15.00
Yeoman, Hawthorne, bowl, bonbon; hdls, 6½".....................................20.00
Yeoman, Hawthorne, gravy boat, w/underliner 50.00
Yeoman, Hawthorne, oil cruet, 2-oz...90.00
Yeoman, Hawthorne, oyster cocktail, ftd, 2¾-oz.................................14.00
Yeoman, Hawthorne, saucer, AD..10.00
Yeoman, Hawthorne, tumbler, tea; 12-oz...30.00
Yeoman, Marigold, bowl, berry; hdls, 8½".......................................50.00
Yeoman, Marigold, bowl, flower; low, 12".......................................55.00
Yeoman, Marigold, plate, cream soup underliner 13.00
Yeoman, Marigold, plate, grapefruit bowl underliner, 6½" 32.00
Yeoman, Marigold, plate, 7" 22.00
Yeoman, Marigold, saucer...10.00
Yeoman, Moongleam, bowl, cream soup; hdls......................................30.00
Yeoman, Moongleam, comport, shallow, high ft, 5"...............................45.00
Yeoman, Moongleam, goblet, 10-oz...25.00
Yeoman, Moongleam, plate, bouillon underliner, 6"..............................10.00
Yeoman, Moongleam, plate, relish; 4-part, 11"..................................32.00
Yeoman, Moongleam, sugar bowl, w/lid...50.00
Yeoman, Sahara, bowl, vegetable; 6"..14.00
Yeoman, Sahara, cup, AD 40.00

Yeoman, Sahara, pitcher, qt 130.00
Yeoman, Sahara, plate, 7"...10.00
Yeoman, Sahara, tray, hors d'oeuvre; w/center lid, 13" 52.00
Yeoman, Sahara, tumbler, whiskey; 2½-oz.......................................25.00

Herend

Herend, Hungary, was the center of a thriving pottery industry as early as the mid-1800s. Decorative items as well as tablewares were made in keeping with the styles of the times. One of the factories located in this area was founded by Moritz Fisher, who often marked his wares with a cojoined MF. Items described in the following listings may be marked simply Herend, indicating the city, or with a manufacturer's backstamp.

Ashtray, Chinese Bouquet Raspberry, scalloped edge, 6" dia.......150.00
Box, Queen Victoria, gold trim, 1939, 3½x5¼x3¾" 170.00
Cache pot, Queen Victoria, hdls, 6x10½" dia.......................350.00
Coffeepot, wht w/birds in branches, #1611/RO, 1940s, 8" 225.00
Creamer & sugar bowl, Market Garden, 6-oz.........................260.00
Cup, Chinese Bouquet Rust, no hdl, gold rim, 1920s, 1¾" 50.00
Cup & saucer, Chinese Bouquet Rust, 8-oz, 6" dia 65.00
Dish, dbl shell; Red Dynasty, 18"................................350.00
Dish, Pommier Chinois, floral on wht, 1939, 3¼x2¾"................80.00
Dish, Rothschild Bird, triangular, rtcl edge, 9½" 265.00
Egg, Chinese Bouquet Rust, gold trim, 3x4½".....................125.00
Figurine, ducks (2), wht w/orange beaks, #5035, 8x15"...........520.00
Figurine, elephant, fishnet, wht w/blk decor, 15" 1,040.00
Figurine, kangaroo w/joey, wht w/bl fishnet, gold trim, #15328, 5¾" 300.00
Figurine, moose, wht w/blk fishnet & gold antlers, #15563, 5½x6" 320.00
Figurine, nude man on 1 knee holding torch, #5797, 9½" 575.00
Figurine, parrot on branch, ##5171 CD-1, 10" 440.00
Figurine, sand dollar, rust fishnet, gold trim, #15594 ....235.00
Figurine, soccer player, kicking ball, #5852, 11x9".............235.00
Figurine, stag, head down, purple fishnet w/gold antlers/hooves, 4x7"...350.00
Figurine, wrestling lion cubs, bl fishnet on wht, 6x5½" 525.00
Leaf dish, Rothschild Bird, gr hdl, 8"...........................120.00
Plate, dessert; Chinese Bouquet Yellow, 7¼"......................35.00
Plate, dinner; Rothschild Bird, #1525/RO, 10¼"...................75.00
Platter, Rothschild Bird, gold trim, oval, 16x11¼"..............320.00
Teapot, Rothschild Bird, rose finial, 4".........................220.00
Tray, Rothschild Bird, rectangular, #427, 18x11½" 340.00
Tureen, Mandarin, lemon finial & appl floral decor at hdls, 8x13" ...460.00
Tureen, Market Garden, lemon finial, 1930s, 4x5" 200.00
Tureen, Rothschild Bird, scalloped, w/lid, 1920s, 4x5" 200.00
Vase, Printemps, floral on wht, flared rim, 10".................250.00
Vase, Queen Victoria, floral on wht, 1950s, 10" 600.00

Heubach

Gebruder Heubach is a German company that has been in operation since the 1800s, producing quality bisque figurines and novelty items. They are perhaps most famous for their doll heads and piano babies, most of which are marked with the circular rising sun device containing an 'H' superimposed over a 'C.' Items with arms and hands positioned away from the body are more valuable, and color of hair and intaglio eyes affect price as well. Our advisor for this category is Grace Ochsner; she is listed in the Directory under Illinois. See also Dolls, Heubach.

Baby girl (nude) on knees, blond hair, 6½" 575.00
Baby in gr bathtub examines ft, 4x5" dia.........................595.00
Baby in wht gown lying on bk playing w/toes, 8" L 695.00
Baby playing w/toes, mk, 9" L....................................725.00

Baby seated, detailed dress, intaglio eyes, 2 teeth, 8½", NM.......550.00
Baby seated in gr bowl, #70, 2¾"...425.00
Baby sits nude w/knees drawn up, laughing, dimples, 9"..............800.00
Baby sits w/well-fed chubby tummy, intaglio eyes, #13, 5" 800.00
Baby standing nude in father's brn shoes, #84, 8" 700.00
Baby stands by cracked egg, ca 1920, 5⅞x6¾x4"....................175.00
Baby w/clenched hands before open eggshell, 5" 495.00
Black boy sits w/ear of corn clutched to chest, 3", from $600 to ..625.00
Boy, semi-nude w/2 fish baskets on bk, 7".................................395.00
Boy & girl fishing, wooden poles, 8½", pr................................475.00
Boy & girl in beaded costumes, intaglio eyes, on base, rprs, 14" 1,000.00
Boy in suit & hat, sitting, 5"...325.00
Boy on sled, opens at waist (candy container), NM 450.00
Boy playing flute standing before open egg, brn cap, 7" 500.00
Boys (2) in oversz bl & wht nightshirt, 5"..................................475.00
Dog on haunches, wht w/tan collar, 9x3⅝" 375.00
Dog w/toothache, scarf around face, gray & wht lustre, 5" L.......375.00
Dutch boy & girl seated flirting, side-glanceing eyes, 10", pr 800.00
Dutch boy & girl standing bk to bk, 7" 400.00
Dutch boy holding cap to head, 6", from $300 to 400.00
Dutch girl gathering oversz Easter egg in apron, #3467, 6" 425.00
Easter bunny child standing beside open egg, sq mk, 6" 400.00
Girl curled up in wicker chair knitting muffler, 7" 525.00
Girl emerging from Easter egg, bobbed hair, side-glancing eyes, 7" ..500.00
Girl holds gr pleated skirt to side, 6¼"....................................395.00
Girl holds pleated skirt high to right, tambourine at ft, 17".....1,200.00
Girl in nightgown curtsying, roses at ft, 11" 475.00
Girl on floor-length gown in dancing pose, rstr, 6" 395.00
Girl sitting on stone wall, holding blanket, 9½" 425.00
Humidor, Indian chief on lid, gr Jasper, 5" 395.00
Lady w/flowing dress, bl scarf, blond hair, #9031, 8", pr 500.00
Oriental lady w/vase, bl kimono & obi, #3944, 8", from $500 to ..600.00
Praying child w/cross on chain around neck, blond, 11" 395.00
Santa sitting on log (candy container), bl intaglio eyes, 1910s, 8x6"..600.00
Vase, lady's profile w/in Nouveau floral reserve on bl, 4½" 415.00
Vase, Nouveau lady w/flowing veils on lav, ca 1884, 7"...............495.00

Hickman, Royal Arden

Born in Willamette, Oregon, Royal A. Hickman was a genius in all aspects of design interpretation. Mr. Hickman's expertise can be seen in the designs of the lovely Heisey figurines, Kosta crystal, Bruce Fox aluminum, Three Crowns aluminum, Vernon Kilns, and Royal Haeger Pottery, as well as handcrafted silver, furniture, and paintings.

Hickman (as a designer), Harvey Hamilton (his son-in-law), and Frank Petty (also as a designer), all worked for Haeger potteries from 1939 through 1944. Hickman and his son-in-law left Haeger, moved to Tennessee in 1944 and started Royal Hickman Industries. Frank Petty left Haeger in 1938 and founded Petty Pottery in Louisiana. He returned to Haeger in 1940 and then joined Hickman and Hamilton in Tennessee.

The Petty glazes are fantastic! Watch for them. Frank Petty has really not received the recognition he truly deserves, as he was an extremely talented artist. Hickman noted this and was the one who started the practice of putting the Petty Glaze sticker on those designs.

Because Mr. Hickman moved around during much of his lifetime (as with all designers), his influence has been felt in all forms of the media. Designs from his independent companies include 'Royal Hickman Pottery and Lamps' (sold through Ceramic Arts Inc., of Chattanooga, Tennessee), 'Royal Hickman's Paris Ware,' 'Royal Hickman — Florida,' and 'California Designed by Royal Hickman.' The following listings will give examples of pieces bearing the various trademarks.

Our advisor for this category is Lanette Clarke; she is listed in the Directory under California. See also Garden City Pottery; Royal Haeger.

Bruce Fox Aluminum

Bowl, leaf shape, stem hdl, 8¾x16¼" 55.00
Candle holders, triple; curved ribbon-like base, 5¾" high end, pr 100.00
Candlesticks, daffodil blossom w/2 leaves, 10⅜x3", pr 110.00
Tray, basketweave w/maple-leaf edging, 8¾x15¾".....................60.00
Tray, charging bull, SP-77, 9x14½"..110.00
Tray, fish form, 22½x7" 85.00
Tray, leaf form, 4 cast ft, long/slender, RH-5, 15½x6" 75.00
Tray, leaf form, 5-lobe w/long stem (hdl), 5-ftd, 9½x11"+stem....80.00
Tray, lobster, sgn Bruce for-RH #73, lg 85.00
Tray, pineapple shape, leaf hdl, 13x6½" 32.00
Tray, wood w/aluminum fr & horse's head in center, 27½x18"......75.00
Tray, 2-acorn, 14½" 45.00

California, Designed by Royal Hickman

Figurine, deer, apple gr w/wht spots, appl eyes, 15" 75.00
Lamp base, flying geese, 17"...250.00
Planter, elephant figural, gr to gray, trunk up, 7x12", NM.............80.00
Vase, fish on wave, brn w/frosty wht, orig label, 9" 157.50

Royal Hickman — Florida

Tray, silver, banana-leaf hdls, 15" L 220.00
Vase, angelfish, #521, 9½" 75.00
Vase, classic ftd shape w/ornate hdls, pk mottle, #342, 12" 145.00
Vase, sailfish figural, gray w/blended mc, 6¼x11½" 45.00
Vase, 3 dolphin figures, 14k gold decor, crown signature label, 13" 300.00

Miscellaneous Signatures

Lamp base, Petty Crystal Glaze, mauve/purple/maroon, unmk, 14½" ...95.00
Tray, 3 heart-shaped leaves, center blossom, SP metal, 3x8½"....167.50
Urn, Petty Crystal Glaze, bl/gr/mauve/cream, ball on sq base, #450, 6"....125.00
Vase, bl mottle, shouldered, Royal Hickman USA, #544, 11½"...165.00
Vase, crystal, sea horse figural, Royal Hickman USA, #468, 8".....75.00
Vase, dk red w/shades of gr, shouldered, USA mk, #202, 7½".....275.00
Vase, Fluted, dusty mauve w/seafoam gr drip, USA mk, 1940, 7"..100.00
Vase, Petty Crystal Glaze, bl & cream mottle, ftd, USA mk, #458, 8" 75.00
Vase, swan form, Petty Crystal Glaze, USA mk, #475, 16⅝" 125.00

Higgins

Contemporary glass artists Frances and Michael Higgins designed high-quality glassware from the late 1940s until his death on February 13, 1999. (Frances continues with her staff.) Their designs were often created by fusing layers of glass together, though sometimes colored ground glass was used to 'paint' the decoration onto the surface. Molds were used, and through a process called 'slumping,' the glass was fired to a very high temperature, causing it to soften and take on the predetermined shape. Their work is ultramodern and is more readily found in metropolitan areas.

The earliest mark was an engraved signature on the bottom of the glass — either 'Frances Stewart Higgins' or 'Michael Higgins' or both, which was dropped in favor of just 'Higgins' with a raised 'Higgins Man.' From approximately 1957 to 1964, the Higgins signature was embossed in gold on the top. After 1964 the signature again appeared on the bottom and was engraved in the glass. Recent items produced at the Higgins studio in Riverside, Illinois, were marked 'Higgins' and for a period of time were dated (example: Higgins 99); but with some exceptions, this is no longer the case. For more information we recommend *Higgins, Adventures in Glass*, by Donald-Brian Johnson and Leslie Pina (Schiffer). Our advisor is Dennis Hopp; he is listed in the Directory under Illinois.

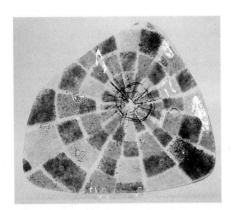

Ashtray, blue, teal, and yellow radiating design with thin black lines, irregular triangular shape, 10½", $130.00.

Ashtray, fish w/lure & hook, mc on smoky gray, 10x7" 125.00
Ashtray, geometrics in bl/gr/gold/blk, 1980s, ½x6¾x4⅞" 148.00
Bowl, geometrics, gr/wht/gold, 3 rnd/3 triangle compartments, 17¾".......265.00
Bowl, wht dandelion puffs w/gold centers between gr veins, 4x12" 195.00
Bowl, 3 daisy-like wht/gold/gr flowers in clear, 3x13½"...............175.00
Box, cigarette; med bl & gr triangles on dk bl, 1960s, 7½x4" 215.00
Candle holder, mc rectangles in red w/blk holder, 1950s, 2¾x5¼"......85.00
Charger, Starburst, wht w/gold threads, 14" sq...........................175.00
Charger, Sunburst, yel & wht on red, 12" 100.00
Charger, wht dandelion puffs on sea green w/gold threads, 12"...175.00
Charger, wht dandelion puffs w/yel centers on gr w/gold streaks, 17" ...210.00
Plate, joined mc scrambled shapes, sgn Shards (title) Higgins, 15⅜" ...465.00
Plate, radiating orange/gray/clear, 8⅜" 100.00
Plate, trees & sun, gr/orange/bl/brn, 7½" 150.00
Screen, Rondelay, 27 mc glass 5½" disks held by brass clips, 1955....3,525.00
Tray, clear/frosted cube-like pattern, 1¼x7x7".............................115.00
Tray, geometrics in rose/purple, bimorphic shape, 10½x9" 175.00
Tray, mc overlapping waves w/lacy gold flowers, 1950s, 14x10"..150.00
Vase, mandarin orange w/gr splotches, flared-out rim, 4x4½".....110.00
Vase, pk/gr/bl drip effect, flared rim, 5" 500.00
Wall vase, mc geometrics, suspended fishtail below, 33" 265.00
Wall vase, mc geometrics w/3 dangles, 37x7"..............................465.00

Historical Glass

Glassware commemorating particularly significant historical events became popular in the late 1800s. Bread trays were the most common form, but plates, mugs, pitchers, and other items were also pressed in clear as well as colored glass. It was sold in vast amounts at the 1876 Philadelphia Centennial Exposition by various manufacturers who exhibited their wares on the grounds. It remained popular well into the twentieth century.

In the listings that follow, L numbers refer to a book by Lindsey, a standard guide used by many collectors. Our advisor for this category is Darlene Yohe; she is listed in the Directory under Arkansas. See also Bread Plates; Pattern Glass.

Ale glass, Centennial...60.00
Bottle, Century of Progress 1833-1933, skyscraper/cabin, 6x6" 38.00
Bottle, Columbus, milk glass, no stopper......................................250.00
Bottle, Granger, L-266 ....110.00
Bottle, Grant's Tomb, milk glass, no stopper 250.00
Bowl, berry; Lindbergh, sm..15.00
Butter dish, Liberty Bell 165.00
Butter dish, Log Cabin 325.00
Celery vase, HMS Pinafore, Actress..170.00
Compote, Actress, Jenny Lind 85.00
Compote, George Peabody..75.00

Cup, Harrison & Morton, bl...235.00
Egg cup, Lincoln Drape 50.00
Goblet, Emblem Centenial, L-61...45.00
Goblet, 3 Presidents, rare 325.00
Hat, Uncle Sam, no pnt, L-110...35.00
Jar, Statue of Liberty, L-530..70.00
Lamp, Emblem, L-62...195.00
Marmalade jar, Log Cabin, w/lid..325.00
Mug, Centennial, waisted..90.00
Mug, McKinley 30.00
Mug, Our Country's Martyrs, Lincoln & Garfield, 2⅝x2¼" 110.00
Mug, Protection & Plenty 50.00
Mug, shaving; Garfield & Lucretia Randolf Garfield, milk glass, 6" ...250.00
Paperweight, Columbian Expo, lady w/upswept hair, US Glass, frosted ...145.00
Paperweight, Shakespeare, frosted, Gillinder 150.00
Pickle dish, E Pluribus Unum...45.00
Pitcher, Garfield Drape, scarce..145.00
Pitcher, Liberty Bell, John Hancock, milk glass 595.00
Pitcher, Lincoln Drape 400.00
Pitcher, Washington Centennial 155.00
Plate, Admiral Dewey, 7" 95.00
Plate, Atlantic City Lighthouse, Egg & Dart border, 5¼" 22.00
Plate, Bryan, flag/eagle/star border, milk glass, L-359................85.00
Plate, Columbus, milk glass, L-7..65.00
Plate, Dewey, clear/frosted, sm..15.00
Plate, flag w/eagles & fleur-de-lis border, milk glass, 7¼", NM 30.00
Plate, For President Winfield D Hancock, 8"...............................110.00
Plate, Grant, Patriot & Soldier, amber, sq, 9½" 50.00
Plate, Indian, milk glass, L-14, 7½"...60.00
Plate, Last Supper 55.00
Plate, Louisiana Purchase Exposition, 7½"................................90.00
Plate, Old State House, L-32...50.00
Plate, Pope Leo, milk glass, L-240..40.00
Plate, Present From the Isle of Man, 10" 60.00
Plate, Texas Campaign, lt bl, 9½" 195.00
Plate, Union, 6½"...60.00
Platter, Carpenter's Hall 65.00
Shot glass, Bryan & McKinney, 1896, NM 130.00
Spill, Lincoln Drape...60.00
Spooner, Liberty Bell...50.00
Spooner, Log Cabin, L-84..115.00
Statuette, Ruth the Gleaner, frosted, 1876 Phila Expo, Gillinder.......175.00
Stein, Centennial 60.00
Sugar bowl, US Grant, Patriot & Soldier....................................25.00
Tumbler, America, L-48 ....35.00
Tumbler, Lincoln Drape...60.00
Tumbler, McKinley, L-337..50.00
Wine, Washington Centennial 65.00

Hobbs, Brockunier & Co.

Hobbs and Brockunier's South Wheeling Glass Works was in operation during the last quarter of the nineteenth century. They are most famous for their peachblow, amberina, Daisy and Button, and Hobnail pattern glass. The mainstay of the operation, however, was druggist items and plain glassware — bowls, mugs, and simple footed pitchers with shell handles.

See also Frances Ware.

Bowl, nappy, Daisy & Button, amberina, sq, 4½" 75.00
Butter dish, Dew Drop, sapphire bl, 5x5" 35.00
Celery vase, Dew Drop, cranberry opal, 7½"..............................230.00
Pitcher, Dew Drop, bl w/bl hdl, No 1, 4½" 200.00
Pitcher, Dew Drop, cranberry opal, clear hdl, No 0, 3⅞"............160.00

Pitcher, Dew Drop, cranberry opal, clear hdl, No 5, 7¾" **600.00**
Pitcher, Dew Drop, rubena verde lt opal w/vaseline hdl, No 0, 4" ...**500.00**
Pitcher, Dew Drop, rubena verde opal, vaseline hdl, No 5, 7¾"....**700.00**
Pitcher, Dew Drop, vaseline plated, appl vaseline hdl, #3, 5½" ..**170.00**
Pitcher, Hobnail, ruby opal, sq mouth, clear hdl, 8" **400.00**
Pitcher, Polka Dot, rubena verde, vaseline hdl, 7½" **475.00**
Pitcher, ring neck, amber-cased deep cobalt w/mica, pinched, 5"..**350.00**
Pitcher, ring neck, clear w/opal cased int & mica, pinched, 5" ...**100.00**
Tumbler, Dew Drop, cranberry opal, 3¾" **70.00**
Tumbler, overshot ruby & opal spatter, 3¾" **100.00**
Water set, Dew Drop, amber, child sz, 4" jug+4 2½" tumblers **400.00**
Water set, Dew Drop, bl, child sz, 4¼" jug +4 2½" tumblers **325.00**

Holt Howard

Novelty ceramics marked Holt Howard were produced in Japan from the 1950s into the 1970s, and these have become quite collectible. They're not only marked, but most are dated as well. There are several lines to reassemble — the rooster, the white cat, figural banks, Christmas angels, and Santas, to name only a few — but the one that most Holt Howard collectors seem to gravitate toward is the pixie line. For more information see *Garage Sale and Flea Market Annual* (Collector Books).

Ashtray, cat on sq plaid base, 4 corner rests, Kozy Kitten, $60 to...**75.00**
Ashtray, starry-eyed Santa...**35.00**
Bank, Coin Kitty Bobbing Head, 5½", from $100 to..................**150.00**
Bell, winking Santa, 1958, 4", from $12 to.............................**15.00**
Bowl, cereal; Rooster, 6" **9.00**
Bud vase, Rooster, figural, from $25 to **30.00**
Butter dish, emb rooster, ¼-lb, from $40 to **50.00**
Candelabra, Winter Green, Santa nestled between branching tree.....**15.00**
Candle holder, NOEL in gr w/Santa inside O, 8¼x1¼x3", ea **25.00**
Candle holder, Santa in convertible, 1959, 3½", ea **25.00**
Candle holders, bride & groom, 4¼", pr.................................**45.00**
Candle holders, elf girls (4) spell out NOEL ea w/candle on head, 3½" ..**60.00**
Candle holders, Santa w/gift bag, candles go in bags, 3½", pr.......**30.00**
Candle holders/bell, 3 Wise Men, 3½", set from $65 to **85.00**
Candle ring, bluebird, 1958, 1¾".......................................**35.00**
Candlesticks, Pixie Ware, pr, from $50 to **65.00**
Chili sauce, Pixie Ware, rare, minimum value **400.00**
Cocktail olives, Pixie Ware, winking gr head finial, from $135 to.....**165.00**
Cocktail onions, Pixie Ware, onion-head finial, from $160 to....**175.00**
Coffee jar, Instant Coffee, attached spoon, Kozy Kitten, from $300 to..**400.00**
Coffeepot, Rooster, electric, from $50 to................................**70.00**
Cookie jar, head form, Kozy Kitten, from $40 to **50.00**
Cookie jar, Rooster, from $100 to.......................................**135.00**
Cottage cheese jar, 2 cats on lid, 4¼x4¼", from $45 to **55.00**
Cup & saucer, Rooster..**15.00**
Face dish, starry-eyed Santa, 6¼x6½" **20.00**
Figurines, pheasants, wings spread, 1958, 3: 10x8", 7x5½", 5½x4" **80.00**
Honey jar, Pixie Ware, very rare, from $400 to **500.00**
Jam & jelly jar, Rooster, from $40 to **50.00**
Ketchup jar, Pixie Ware, orange tomato-like head finial, from $80 to...**110.00**
Lipstick holder, Ponytail Princess, from $50 to **65.00**
Martini shaker, butler (Jeeves), 9", from $175 to **200.00**
Memo minder, full-bodied cat, legs cradle note pad, Kozy Kitten, 7"....**90.00**
Mug, Rooster, 3 szs, ea from $5 to **10.00**
Mug, starry-eyed Santa, str hdl, stackable, from $10 to **15.00**
Mustard jar, Pixie Ware, yel head finial, from $80 to **110.00**
Napkin holder, Rooster **40.00**
Onions jar, Pixie Ware, flat onion-head finial, 1958, from $180 to **200.00**
Pincushion, Rooster, 3¼x4", from $50 to..............................**60.00**
Pitcher, water; Rooster, flaring sides, tail hdl, tall **50.00**

Planter, Santa Express, Santa riding train, 6x7½"....................**45.00**
Platter, Rooster, oval, from $28 to **35.00**
Relish jar, Pixie Ware, male pixie finial, mk 1959 ....**250.00**
Russian dressing bottle, Pixie Ware, from $175 to....................**200.00**
Shakers, cats in wicker baskets, Kozy Kitten, 3", pr, from $30 to ..**35.00**
Shakers, cowboys, 6½", pr..**70.00**
Shakers, ear of corn, 4½", pr..**30.00**
Shakers, Holly Girls, 4", pr...**30.00**
Shakers, Kozy Kitten, 1 w/red collar, 1/bl collar, 1950s, 4¼", pr ...**35.00**
Shakers, Ponytail Princess, pr..**45.00**
Shakers, Rooster, figural, 4½", pr, from $35 to **45.00**
Shakers, Santa holding presents, 2¼", 2¾", pr **15.00**
Shakers, starry-eyed birds, 4", pr......................................**45.00**
Spoon rest, Rooster, figural, from $12 to **15.00**
Tape measure, Kozy Kitten, cat on cushion **85.00**
Tray, Rooster, facing left, from $15 to.................................**20.00**
Wall pocket, Kozy Kitten, cat w/hole in head, 1959, 7½", from $30 to..**40.00**
Wall pocket, mermaid riding a sea horse, 1959, 6¾" **70.00**

Homer Laughlin

The Homer Laughlin China Company of Newell, West Virginia, was founded in 1871. The superior dinnerware they displayed at the Centennial Exposition in Philadelphia in 1876 won the highest award of excellence. From that time to the present, they have continued to produce quality dinnerware and kitchenware, many lines of which are popular collectibles. Most of the dinnerware is marked with the name of the pattern and occasionally with the shape name as well. The 'HLC' trademark is usually followed by a number series, the first two digits of which indicate the year of its manufacture. For further information we recommend *The Collector's Encyclopedia of Fiesta* by Sharon and Bob Huxford; and *The Collector's Encyclopedia of Homer Laughlin China* by Joanne Jasper (both available from Collector Books). Another fine source of information is *Homer Laughlin, A Giant Among Dishes*, by Jo Cunningham (Schiffer). Our advisors for Virginia Rose are Jack and Treva Hamlin; they are listed in the Directory under Ohio.

Our values are base prices, and apply to decaled lines only — not solid color dinnerware. Very desirable patterns on the shapes named in our listings may increase values by as much as 75%. See also Blue Willow; Fiesta; Harlequin; Riviera.

Century

For English Garden or Sun Porch, add from 50% to 75%; Mexican lines are at least double.

Baker, 9", from $14 to...**20.00**
Casserole, w/lid, from $65 to...**85.00**
Cup, coffee; from $10 to..**15.00**
Jug, ⅝-pt, from $55 to...**65.00**
Muffin cover, rare, from $65 to **75.00**
Plate, deep (rim soup); from $10 to.................................**13.00**
Plate, 7", from $5 to...**8.00**
Plate, 9", from $10 to..**13.00**
Teacup, from $6 to...**8.00**

Debutante

For Suntone, add 20%; add 25% for Karol China gold-decorated items.

Bowl, fruit; from $4 to **5.00**
Bowl, onion soup (lug); from $9 to.................................**12.00**
Chop plate, 15", from $16 to...**20.00**

Creamer, from $9 to..12.00
Cup, demitasse; from $4 to...................................6.00
Dish (platter), 11", from $12 to............................14.00
Plate, 6", from $5 to...9.00

Eggshell Georgian

Baker, 10", from $16 to.......................................18.00
Bowl, fruit; 5", from $4 to....................................8.00
Bowl, nappy/salad; from $15 to...........................20.00
Creamer, from $12 to...15.00
Pickle dish, from $6 to..8.00
Plate, 7", from $6 to...10.00

Eggshell Nautilus

Baker, 9", from $14 to...16.00
Bowl, cream soup; from $10 to............................15.00
Bowl, 15", from $16 to...26.00
Egg cup, dbl (Swing); from $12 to.......................16.00
Plate, 9", from $9 to...12.00
Teapot, from $45 to..75.00

Empress

Add 25% for solid colors. See also Bluebird China.

Baker, 8", from $10 to...12.00
Bone dish, from $6 to...8.00
Bowl, 10", from $12 to...16.00
Celery tray, 11", from $20 to...............................25.00
Jug, 24s, 27-oz, from $26 to................................28.00
Ladle, rare, from $18 to.......................................22.00
Oyster tureen, 8", from $45 to............................50.00
Plate, 10", from $9 to..12.00

Marigold

Bowl, deep, 5", from $10 to.................................12.00
Bowl, oatmeal; from $6 to....................................8.00
Butter dish (Jade), from $40 to...........................50.00
Egg cup, dbl; from $14 to.....................................16.00
Pitcher, milk; from $25 to....................................35.00
Plate, 10", from $10 to...12.00

Nautilus

Baker (oval bowl), 9", from $12 to 16.00
Bowl, coupe soup; from $6 to...............................8.00
Bowl, 15½", from $16 to.......................................24.00
Mug, Baltimore coffee; from $15 to......................20.00
Plate, 9", from $8 to...12.00
Sauce boat, from $18 to..22.00

Rhythm

Add 25% for American Provincial.

Bowl, coupe soup; from $8 to...............................10.00
Bowl, 13½", from $14 to.......................................18.00
Cup & saucer, coffee AD; from $14 to 20.00
Plate, 10", from $9 to..12.00
Shakers (Swing), pr, from $15 to.........................18.00
Spoon rest, from $100 to......................................125.00

Swing

Add 30% for Oriental patterns and Mexicali.

Bowl, oatmeal; from $6 to....................................10.00
Butter dish (Jade), from $40 to...........................50.00
Casserole, w/lid, from $35 to...............................45.00
Cup, demitasse; from $10 to.................................18.00
Egg cup, dbl; from $12 to.....................................18.00
Plate, 10", from $10 to...14.00
Sugar bowl, w/lid, from $14 to............................18.00
Tray, utility; from $14 to......................................18.00

Virginia Rose

Use the high end of the price range to evaluate popular patterns such as JJ59 and VR128.

Baker (oval bowl), scarce, 8", from $30 to............35.00
Bread plate, rare, from $20 to..............................25.00
Creamer, from $15 to...20.00
Jug, 5", from $65 to..80.00

Mixing bowl set, from $115.00 to $145.00.

Mug, coffee; from $50 to......................................65.00
Plate, 8", rare, from $15 to..................................18.00
Plate, 10", from $12 to...15.00
Platter, scarce, 10½", from $30 to.......................35.00
Shakers, Kitchen Kraft, scarce, pr, from $160 to...185.00
Shakers, regular, scarce, pr, from $125 to............150.00

Wells

Add 25% for solid colors Sienna Brown, French Rose, or Leaf Green.

Bowl, bouillon; from $10 to 12.00
Cake plate, from $18 to..24.00
Chop plate, from $18 to..24.00
Jug, w/lid, 24s, from $60 to..................................70.00
Plate, 7", from $9 to...12.00
Teacup & saucer, from $9 to.................................14.00

Hoya Crystal Inc.

Hoya Cristal Inc. originated in 1946 in the town of Hoya, Japan. They were manufacturers of fine crystal. Upon learning that General McArthur partook of a glass or two of scotch every evening, Hoya designed a double old-fashioned glass especially for him and presented it to him for his enjoyment during the evening cocktail hour. Today, Hoya Crystal is one of the world's largest and most respected crystal companies. Our advisor for this category is William L. Geary; he is listed in the Directory under Colorado.

Flute, Lily of the Valley, 6-oz, pr	70.00
Martini, Desire, bl, 12-oz	130.00
Martini, Desire, 12-oz	60.00
Sculpture, Equs, 6⅛"	275.00
Sculpture, Hemisphere, 7"	750.00
Sculpture, Moon View, 12"	6,500.00
Sculpture, Origami Crane, 9"	4,000.00
Skeletal clock, 10¼"	475.00
Vase, Hudson, 12"	400.00
Vase, Ice Fall, 10⅛"	1,600.00

Hull

The A.E. Hull Pottery was formed in 1905 in Zanesville, Ohio, and in the early years produced stoneware specialities. They expanded in 1907, adding a second plant and employing over two hundred workers. By 1920 they were manufacturing a full line of stoneware, art pottery with both air-brushed and blended glazes, florist pots, and gardenware. They also produced toilet ware and kitchen items with a white semiporcelain body. Although these continued to be staple products, after the stock market crash of 1929, emphasis was shifted to tile production. By the mid-'30 interest in art pottery production was growing, and over the next fifteen years, several lines of matt pastel floral-decorated patterns were designed, consisting of vases, planters, baskets, ewers, and bowls in various sizes.

The Red Riding Hood cookie jar, patented in 1943, proved so successful that a whole line of figural kitchenware and novelty items was added. They continued to be produced well into the '50s. (See also Little Red Riding Hood.) Through the '40s their floral artware lines flooded the market, due to the restriction of foreign imports. Although best known for their pastel matt-glazed ware, some of the lines were high gloss. Rosella, glossy coral on a pink clay body, was produced for a short time only; and Magnolia, although offered in a matt glaze, was produced in gloss as well.

The plant was destroyed in 1950 by a flood which resulted in a devastating fire when the floodwater caused the kilns to explode. The company rebuilt and equipped their new factory with the most modern machinery. It was soon apparent that the matt glaze could not be duplicated through the more modern processes, however, and soon attention was concentrated on high-gloss artware lines such as Parchment and Pine and Ebb Tide. Figural planters and novelties, piggy banks, and dinnerware were produced in abundance in the late '50s and '60s. By the mid-'70s dinnerware and florist ware were the mainstay of their business. The firm discontinued operations in 1985.

Our advisor, Brenda Roberts, has compiled a lovely book, *The Collector's Encyclopedia of Hull Pottery*, with full-color photos and current values, available from Collector Books.

Special note to Hull collectors: Reproductions are on the market in all categories of Hull pottery — matt florals, Red Riding Hood, and later lines including House 'n Garden dinnerware.

Blossom Flite, basket, #T-2, 6" from $65 to	105.00
Blossom Flite, candle holders, #T-11, 3", pr, from $115 to	165.00
Bow-Knot, console bowl, #B-16, 13½", from $375 to	475.00
Bow-Knot, teapot, #B-20, 6", from $450 to	650.00
Bow-Knot, wall pocket, whisk broom shape, #B-27, 8", from $275 to	325.00
Butterfly, ashtray, #B-7, 7", from $40 to	50.00
Butterfly, lavabo, #B-25 (top)/#B-24 (bottom), 16", from $210 to	260.00
Butterfly, vase, #B-10, 7", from $55 to	85.00
Calla Lily, bowl, #500/32, 10", from $215 to	260.00
Calla Lily, cornucopia, #570/33, 8", from $130 to	160.00
Calla Lily, ewer, #506, 10", from $380 to	480.00

Capri, basket, #48, 12½", from $50 to	75.00
Capri, urn, #50, 9", from $45 to	65.00
Cinderella Kitchenware (Blossom), creamer, #28, 4½", from $45 to	70.00
Cinderella Kitchenware (Blossom), sugar bowl, #25, 4½", from $45 to	70.00
Cinderella Kitchenware (Bouquet), bowl, #20, 7½", from 35 to	50.00
Cinderella Kitchenware (Bouquet), pitcher, #22, 64-oz, from $175 to	230.00
Continental, bud vase, #66, 9½", from $35 to	50.00
Dogwood, basket, #501, 7½", from $350 to	410.00
Dogwood, ewer, #519, 13½", from $800 to	900.00
Dogwood, window box, #508, 10½", from $250 to	310.00
Early Art, pitcher, #27/30, 6½", from $375 to	475.00
Early Art, vase, #26, 8", from $75 to	125.00
Early Utility, flowerpot/saucer, #538, 4", from $45 to	60.00
Early Utility, pitcher, #107/30, 4¾", from $60 to	80.00
Ebb Tide, basket, unmk, 6¼", from $140 to	195.00
Ebb Tide, console bowl, #E-12, 15¾", from $215 to	285.00

Ebb Tide, cornucopia with mermaid at side of shell, E-3, unmarked, from $175.00 to $200.00; vase with fish, E-1, from $50.00 to $75.00.

Ebb Tide, creamer, #E-15, 4", from $95 to	125.00
Ebb Tide, sugar bowl, w/lid, #E-16, 4", from $95 to	125.00
Fantasy, window box, #74, 12½", from $18 to	24.00
Heritageware, mug, #A-8, 3¼", from $8 to	10.00
Heritageware, pitcher, #A-6, 7", from $35 to	45.00
Heritageware, pitcher, #A-7, 4½", from $18 to	25.00
House 'n Garden, bud vase, 9", from $20 to	30.00
House 'n Garden, butter dish, avocado, 7¾", from $20 to	25.00
House 'n Garden, canister set, 6-9", 4-pc, from $375 to	475.00
House 'n Garden, casserole, w/lid, #548, 10", from $40 to	65.00
House 'n Garden, coffeepot, #522, 8-cup, from $40 to	50.00
House 'n Garden, fish tray, 11", from $85 to	120.00
House 'n Garden, mug, #502, 9-oz, from $4 to	6.00
House 'n Garden, plate, 10", from $8 to	12.00
House 'n Garden, shakers, #515/#516, pr, from $14 to	18.00
House 'n Garden, spoon rest, 6¾", from $40 to	55.00
House 'n Garden, steak plate, #541, 11¾", from $20 to	25.00
House 'n Garden, teapot, 5-cup, from $25 to	35.00
Imperial, bucket planter, #94B, 6¼", from $25 to	35.00
Imperial, madonna, #81, 8¼", from $45 to	65.00
Imperial, swan, #81, 10½", from $40 to	60.00
Imperial, urn, gold lustre, #F-88, 5¾", from $50 to	75.00
Iris, ewer, #401, 8", from $175 to	205.00
Iris, ewer, #401, 13½", from $500 to	625.00
Iris, rose bowl, #412, 4", from $120 to	145.00
Iris, rose bowl, #412, 7", from $170 to	220.00
Kitchenware (Crescent), bowl, #B-1, 9½", from $40 to	40.00
Kitchenware (Crescent), casserole, w/lid, #B-2, 10", from $50 to	75.00
Kitchenware (Crescent), cookie jar, #B-9, 9½", from $75 to	105.00

Kitchenware (Floral), grease jar, #43, 5¾", from $40 to **55.00**
Kitchenware (Floral), salad bowl, #49, 10", from $60 to **85.00**
Magnolia, gloss; basket, #H-14, 10½", from $400 to **450.00**
Magnolia, gloss; candle holder, #H-24, 4", ea from $50 to **65.00**
Magnolia, gloss; cornucopia, #H-10, 8½", from $115 to.............**155.00**
Magnolia, gloss; ewer, #H-11, 8½", from $160 to **195.00**
Magnolia, gloss; ewer, #H-19, 13½", from $370 to **465.00**
Magnolia, matt; console bowl, #26, 12", from $200 to **250.00**
Magnolia, matt; creamer, #24, 3¾", from $55 to.......................**80.00**
Magnolia, matt; ewer, #14, 4¾", from $75 to..........................**105.00**
Magnolia, matt; sugar bowl, #25, 3¾", from $55 to **80.00**
Magnolia, matt; vase, open hdls, #21, 12½", from $400 to **500.00**
Mardi Gras/Granada, basket, #65, 8", from $180 to...................**230.00**
Mardi Gras/Granada, planter, #204, 6", from $45 to **65.00**
Mardi Gras/Granada, vase, #48, 9", from $85 to **110.00**
Novelty, dancing girl planter, #955, 7", from $60 to **85.00**
Novelty, duck planter, #104, 9x10½", from $75 to **105.00**
Novelty, flowerpot, #95, 4½", from $15 to **20.00**
Novelty, kitten planter, #61, 7½", from $40 to **55.00**
Novelty, lamb planter, #965, 8", from $40 to **60.00**
Novelty, leaf dish, #85, 13", from $35 to **40.00**
Novelty, lovebirds planter, #93, 6", from $40 to.......................**60.00**
Open Rose (Camellia), console bowl, #116, 12", from $350 to ..**440.00**
Open Rose (Camellia), ewer, #115, 8½", from $280 to.............**315.00**
Open Rose (Camellia), hanging basket, #132, 7", from $260 to....**325.00**
Open Rose (Camellia), vase, #143, 8½", from $200 to **260.00**
Orchid, bookends, #316, 7", pr, from $1,000 to **1,400.00**
Orchid, console bowl, #314, 13", from $375 to.........................**460.00**
Orchid, jardiniere, #317, 4¾", from $155 to.............................**200.00**
Parchment & Pine, cornucopia, #S-2-R, 7¾", from $40 to **70.00**
Parchment & Pine, ewer, #S-7, 14¼", from $195 to **250.00**
Pinecone, vase, #55, 6½", from $175 to **225.00**
Poppy, ewer, #610, 4¾", from $165 to.....................................**215.00**
Poppy, planter, #602, 6½", from $245 to..................................**300.00**
Poppy, wall pocket, #609, 9", from $360 to **460.00**
Regal, planter, #301, 3½", from $10 to **15.00**
Rosella, creamer, #R-3, 5½", from $45 to..................................**65.00**
Rosella, sugar bowl, open, #R-4, 5½", from $45 to **65.00**
Rosella, wall pocket, heart shape, #R-10, 6½", from $160 to......**210.00**
Serenade, ashtray, #S23, 13x10½", from $115 to.......................**155.00**
Serenade, candy dish, #S-3, 8¼", from $155 to **200.00**
Serenade, ewer, #S-2, 6½", from $85 to **125.00**
Sueno Tulip, basket, #102-66, 6", from $300 to **395.00**
Sueno Tulip, jardiniere, #115-33, 7", from $295 to....................**345.00**
Sueno Tulip, vase, #100-33, 10", from $275 to **325.00**
Sun-Glow, basket, #84, 6½", from $95 to **145.00**
Sun-Glow, bell, loop hdl, unmk, 6", from $325 to **450.00**
Sun-Glow, bell, solid hdl, unmk, 6½", from $300 to **375.00**
Sunglow, casserole, w/lid, #51, 7½", from $60 to......................**85.00**
Sunglow, flowerpot, #97, 5½", from $40 to **55.00**
Sunglow, pitcher, #52, 24-oz, from $45 to **65.00**
Thistle, vase, #54, 6½", from $130 to.......................................**150.00**
Tokay/Tuscany, basket, #11, 10½", from $120 to **170.00**
Tokay/Tuscany, ewer, #3, 8", from $80 to **115.00**
Tokay/Tuscany, urn, #5, 5½", from $40 to **60.00**
Tropicana, basket, #55, 12¾", from $700 to.............................**850.00**
Tropicana, vase, #54, 12½", from $450 to **550.00**
Utility, bowl, banded, #E-1-10", from $45 to **65.00**
Utility, jardinere, blended, #546, 3", from $40 to **65.00**
Water Lily, basket, #L-14, 10½", from $400 to **510.00**
Water Lily, console bowl, #L-21, 13½", from $260 to **300.00**
Water Lily, cornucopia, #L-7, 6½", from $115 to.......................**150.00**
Water Lily, jardiniere, #L-23, 5½", from $130 to **170.00**
Water Lily, teapot, #L-18, 6", from $245 to..............................**300.00**

Wildflower, basket, #W-16, 10½", from $375 to....................**425.00**
Wildflower, cornucopia, #W-10, 8½", from $165 to **215.00**
Wildflower, ewer, #W-8, 7½", from $105 to.............................**140.00**
Wildflower, lamp base, #W-17, 12½", from $300 to **350.00**
Wildflower (# series), candle holder, dbl, #68, 4", ea from $175 to..**225.00**
Wildflower (# series), jardinier, #64, 4", from $140 to...............**165.00**
Wildflower (# series), teapot, #72, 8", from $850 to...............**1,150.00**
Woodland, gloss; basket, #W-22, 10½", from $250 to **310.00**
Woodland, gloss; creamer, #W-27, 3½", from $45 to..................**65.00**
Woodland, gloss; ewer, #24, 13½", from $275 to **375.00**
Woodland, gloss; sugar bowl, w/lid, #W-28, 3½", from $45 to **65.00**
Woodland, matt; flowerpot/saucer, #W-11, 5¾", from $245 to ...**315.00**
Woodland, matt; planter, #W-19, 10½", from $175 to **235.00**
Woodland, matt; window box, #W-14, 10", from $175 to...........**235.00**

Hummel

Hummel figurines were created through the artistry of Berta Hummel, a Franciscan nun called Sister M. Innocentia. The first figures were made about 1935 by Franz Goebel of Goebel Art Inc., Rodental, West Germany. Plates, plaques, and candy dishes are also produced, and the older, discontinued editions are highly sought collectibles. Generally speaking, an issue can be dated by the trademark. The first Hummels, from 1935 to 1949, were either incised or stamped with the 'Crown WG' mark. The 'Full Bee in V' mark was employed with minor variations until 1959. At that time the bee was stylized and represented by a solid disk with angled symetrical wings completely contained within the confines of the 'V.' The Three-Line mark, 1964 – 1972, utilized the stylized bee and included a three-line arrangement, 'c by W. Goebel, W. Germany.' Another change in 1972 saw the 'Stylized Bee in V' suspended between the vertical bars of the 'b' and 'l' of a printed 'Goebel, West Germany.' Collectors refer to this mark as the 'Last Bee' or 'Goebel Bee.' The mark in use from 1979 to 1990 omits the 'bee in V.' The New Crown mark, in use from 1991 to 1999 is a small crown with 'WG' initials, a large 'Goebel,' and a small 'Germany,' signifying a united Germany. The current Millennium Mark came into use in the year 2000 and features a large bee. For further study we recommend *Hummel, An Illustrated Handbook and Price Guide*, by Ken Armke; *Hummel Figurines and Plates, A Collector's Identification and Value Guide*, by Carl Luckey; *The No. 1 Price Guide to M.I. Hummel* by Robert L. Miller; and *The Fascinating World of M.I. Hummel* by Goebel. These books are available through your local book dealer. See also Limited Edition Plates.

Key:
CM — Crown Mark	NC — New Crown Mark
cn — closed number	oe — open edition
FB — Full Bee	SB — Stylized Bee
LB — Last Bee	tw — temporarily withdrawn
MB — Missing Bee	3L — Three-Line mark

#II/111, Wayside Harmony, table lamp, CM, 7½" **430.00**
#1, Puppy Love, CM, 5-5¼"...**575.00**
#5, Strolling Along, FB, 4¾-5¾"...**360.00**
#6/I, Sensitive Hunter, CM, 5½-6" **610.00**
#7/II, Merry Wanderer, CM, 9½-10¼" **2,160.00**
#9, Begging His Share, FB, 5¼-6" **360.00**
#11 2/0, Merry Wanderer, 3L, 4¼-4½" **150.00**
#13 2/0, Meditation, SB, 4¼"...**160.00**
#15/0, Hear Ye, Hear Ye, LB, 5-5¼"...**180.00**
#17/2, Congratulations, FB, 7¾-8¼" **3,960.00**
#20, Prayer Before Battle, CM, 4-4½"..**395.00**
#21/I, Heavenly Angel, CM, 6¾-7¼" **575.00**
#23/I, Adoration, SB, 6¼-7" **380.00**

#26/I, Child Jesus, font, CM, 3¼x6" 215.00
#27/3, Joyous News, FB, 4¼x4¾" 720.00
#30/0 A&B, Ba-Bee-Ring, LB, 4¾x5" 185.00
#32/I, Little Gabriel, FB, 5¾-6" 1,080.00
#33, Joyful, ashtray, CM, 3¾x6" 290.00
#34, Singing Lessons, ashtray, FB, 3½-6¼" 215.00
#35, Good Shepherd, font, CM, 2¾x5¾" 290.00
#37, Herald Angels, candle holder, FB, 2¾x4", ea 290.00
#42/0, Good Shepherd, CM, 5¾-6¼" 540.00
#43, March Winds, 3L, 4¾-5½" 150.00
#47/0, Goose Girl, FB, 4¾-5¼" 360.00
#49 3/0, To Market, FB, 4" 215.00
#50/0, Volunteers, CM, 5½-6" 610.00
#51, Village Boy, CM, 8" 650.00
#51/0, Village Boy, FB, 6-6¾" 325.00
#52/0, Going to Grandma's, CM, 4½-5" 575.00
#53, Joyful, CM, 3½-4¼" 250.00
#54, Silent Night, candle holder, LB, 3½x4¾", ea 290.00
#55, Saint George, red saddle, CM, 6¾" 1,800.00
#56/A, Culprits, FB, 6¼-6¾" 430.00
#57/0, Chick Girl, CM, 3½" 395.00
#58/0, Playmates, FB, 4" 235.00
#60 A&B, Farm Boy & Goose Girl, bookends, CM, 4¾", pr......685.00
#62, Happy Pastime, ashtray, CM, 3½x6¼" 325.00
#63, Singing Lessons, CM, 2¾-3" 325.00
#64, Shepherd's Boy, 3L, 5½" 260.00
#66, Farm Boy, CM, 5-5¾" 540.00
#67, Doll Mother, FB, 4¼-4¾" 325.00
#69, Happy Pastime, CM, 3¼-3½" 360.00
#70, Holy Child, SB, 6¾-7½" 250.00
#71, Stormy Weather, 3L, 6-6¼" 450.00
#72, Spring Cheer, SB, 5-5½" 215.00
#73, Little Helper, CM, 4¼-4½" 325.00
#76 A&B, Doll Mother, Prayer Before Battle, bookends, CM, pr 7,200.00
#79, Globe Trotter, SB, 5-5¼" 215.00
#80, Little Scholar, CM, 5¼-5¾" 505.00
#82/II, School Boy, CM, 7½" 865.00
#85/0, Serenade, CM, 4¾-5¼" 290.00
#87, For Father, FB, 5½" 290.00
#88, Heavenly Protection, FB, 9¼" 935.00
#89/I, Little Cellist, FB, 5¼-6¼" 325.00
#92, Merry Wanderer, plaque, CM, 4½x5-5x5½" 325.00
#94, Suprise, CM, 5¾" 575.00
#95, Brother, CM, 5¼-5¾" 435.00
#97, Trumpet Boy, SB, 4½-5¼" 145.00
#98, Sister, CM, 5¾" 430.00
#99, Eventide, FB, 4¼x5" 430.00
#103, Farewell, table lamp, CM, 7½" 5,760.00
#105, Adoration w/Bird, CM, 4¾" 5,040.00
#107, Little Fiddler, plaque w/wood fr, CM, 6x6" 2,160.00
#109/II, Happy Traveler, FB, 7½" 575.00
#110/0, Let's Sing, CM, 3-3¼" 290.00
#112/I, Just Resting, CM, 4¾-5½" 470.00
#113, Heavenly Song, candle holder, FB, 3½x4¾", ea 3,240.00
#118, Little Thirsty, bank, FB, 5-5½" 305.00
#123, Max & Moritz, FB, 5-5½" 325.00
#124/I, Hello, CM, 6¾-7" 575.00
#127, Doctor, CM, 4¾-5¼" 360.00
#128, Baker, SB, 4¾-5" 235.00
#130, Duet, CM, 5-5½" 575.00
#131, Street Singer, SB, 5-5½" 235.00
#132, Star Gazer, CM, 4¾" 505.00
#134, Quartet, plaque, CM, 5½x6¼" 575.00
#135, Soloist, CM, 4½-5" 325.00

#136/V, Friends, CM, 10¾-11" 2,160.00
#138, Tiny Baby in Crib, wall plaque, cn, FB, 2¼x3" 2,160.00
#140, The Mail Is Here, plaque, FB, 4¼x6¾" 325.00
#141/I, Apple Tree Girl, CM, 6-6¾" 540.00
#142, Apple Tree Boy, FB, 6-6⅞" 470.00
#143/I, Boots, SB, 6½-6¾" 325.00
#145, Little Guardian, CM, 3¾-4" 325.00
#146, Angel Dust, font, CM, 3½x4¾" 125.00
#150/I, Happy Days, FB, 6¼-6½" 610.00
#151, Madonna Holding Child, bl, CM, 12½" ...1,440.00
#152/0 A, Umbrella Boy, MB, 4¾" 520.00
#153/0, Auf Wiedersehen, SB, 5½-6" 250.00
#163, Whitsuntide, CM, 6½-7" 720.00
#166, Boy w/Bird, ashtray, CM, 3¼x6" 325.00
#167, Angel w/Bird, font, CM, 3¼x4⅛" 180.00
#168, Standing Boy, wall plaque, FB, 4⅛x5½" 395.00
#169, Bird Duet, FB, 3¾-4" 200.00
#170/I, School Boys, LB, 7¼-7½" 1,150.00
#171, Little Sweeper, CM, 4¼" 325.00
#172/II, Festival Harmony (Mandolin), SB, 10¼-10¾" 470.00
#173/0, Festival Harmony (Flute), SB, 8" 360.00
#174, She Loves Me, She Loves Me Not, CM, 4¼" 430.00
#176, Happy Birthday, CM, 5½" 610.00
#177, School Girls, CM, 9½" 3,240.00
#178, The Photographer, FB, 4¾-5¼" 395.00
#180, Tuneful Goodnight, wall plaque, CM, 5x4¾" 430.00
#182, Good Friends, CM, 4-4¼" 470.00
#183, Forest Shrine, FB, 9" 720.00
#184, Latest News, CM, 5-5¼" 650.00
#186, Sweet Music, SB, 5-5½" 235.00
#187, MI Hummel Plaque (in English), FB, 5½x4" 540.00
#188, Celestrial Musician, FB, 7" 650.00
#190, Old Woman Walking to Market, cn, 6¾" ...10,800.00
#192, Candlelight, candle holder, FB, 6¾-7", ea 575.00
#193, Angel Duet, candle holder, CM, 5", ea 970.00
#194, Watchful Angel, CM, 6¼-6¾" 1,295.00
#195, Barnyard Hero, FB, 5¾-6" 470.00
#197, Be Patient, FB, 6¼" 395.00
#198/I, Home From Market, FB, 5½" 290.00
#199/0, Feeding Time, FB, 4¼-4½" 305.00
#200/0, Little Goat Herder, FB, 4½-4¾" 305.00

#201, Retreat to Safety, crown mark, closed edition, 6", $720.00.

#203 2/0, Signs of Spring, SB, 4" 250.00
#204, Merry Wanderer, CM, 5½-6" 505.00
#207, Heavenly Angel, font, CM, 3x5" 290.00
#209, MI Hummels Dealer's Plaque (in Swedish), FB, 5½x4" 2,880.00
#211, MI Hummels Dealer's Plaque (in English), FB, 5½x4" 14,400.00
#217, Boy w/Toothache, LB, 5¼-5½" 185.00

#218, Birthday Serenade, FB, 5¼" **650.00**

#222, Madonna Plaque (w/metal fr), FB, 4x5" **540.00**

#223, To Market, table lamp, SB, 9½" **470.00**

#224, Wayside Harmony, table lamp, SB, 7½" **325.00**

#226, The Mail Is Here, FB, 4½x6¼" **830.00**

#227, She Loves Me, She Loves Me Not, table lamp, FB, 7½"...**470.00**

#230, Apple Tree Boy, table lamp, FB, 7½" **650.00**

#231, Birthday Serenade, table lamp, FB, 9¾" **1,440.00**

#235, Happy Days, table lamp, FB, 7¾" **650.00**

#238B, Angel w/Accordion, SB, 2-2½" **70.00**

#239B, Girl w/Doll, SB, 3½" **110.00**

#240, Little Drummer, FB, 4-4¼" **235.00**

#246, Holy Family, font, FB, 3⅛x4½" **180.00**

#250 A&B, Little Goat Herder & Feeding Time, bookends, FB, 5½", pr ...**395.00**

#255, Stitch in Time, LB, 6½-6¾" **250.00**

#258, Which Hand?, 3L, 5¼-5½" **190.00**

#260, Large Nativity Set, w/wooden stable, 3L, 16 pcs **4,355.00**

#262, Heavenly Lullaby, 3L, 3½x5" **540.00**

#266, Globe Trotter, annual plate, 1973, LB, 7½" **110.00**

#276, Postman, annual plate, 1983, MB, 7½" **140.00**

#284, Little Goat Herder, annual plate, 1988, 7½" **90.00**

#3/I, Book Worm, 3L, 5½" **325.00**

#304, The Artist, 3L, 5½" **720.00**

#305, The Builder, SB, 5½" **720.00**

#306, Little Bookkeeper, SB, 4¾" **720.00**

III/69, Happy Pastime, box, CM, 6½" **540.00**

Hutschenreuther

The Porcelain Factory C.M. Hutschenreuther operated in Bavaria from 1814 to 1969. After the death of the elder Hutschenreuther in 1845, his son Lorenz took over operations, continuing there until 1857 when he left to establish his own company in the nearby city of Selb. The original manufactory became a joint stock company in 1904, absorbing several other potteries. In 1969 both Hutschenreuther firms merged, and that company still operates in Selb. They have distributing centers in both France and the United States.

Bell, yel-breasted birds on branch, 4" **40.00**

Bowl, rimmed soup; Revere, wht w/platinum trim, 8½" **40.00**

Bowl, vegetable; Richelieu, gold edge, 2¾x10x7¾" **50.00**

Candelabra, 2 cherubs hold up 4 branch-like arms, 10½x18" **150.00**

Candle holder, Cupid on gold ball, branch arm ea side, 7x10"......**65.00**

Figurine, Borzoi dog, early, 9¼x11½" **660.00**

Figurine, dog pulling down deer, 13¾x12x4¾" **525.00**

Figurine, horses, gray w/dk highlights, mk US Zone, 9½x12x5"....**270.00**

Figurine, lady running w/dog, 7x6½" **370.00**

Figurine, Musicians of Bremen, chicken/cat/dog/donkey, 7½" **295.00**

Figurine, nude w/fawn, C Werner, 1916, 12½x9¼" **675.00**

Figurine, polar bear, up on hind legs, #2357/2F, 7¼" **140.00**

Figurine, rabbit seated on hind legs, #2418, 5¾" **150.00**

Figurine, Sunchild, nude w/arms raised, Tutter, 13⅜" **250.00**

Plaque, Hunter's Assistant w/Pheasant, rich color, 15¾" sq **495.00**

Imari

Imari is a generic term which covers a broad family of wares. It was made in more than a dozen Japanese villages, but the name is that of the port from whence it was shipped to Europe. There are several types of Imari. The most common features a design with panels of birds, florals, or people surrounding a central basket of flowers. The colors used in this type are underglaze blue with overglaze red, gold, and green enamels. The

Chinese also made Imari wares which differ from the Japanese type in several ways — the absence of spur marks, a thinner-type body, and a more consistent control of the blue. Imari-type wares were copied on the continent by Meissen and by English potters, among them Worcester, Derby, and Bow. Unless noted otherwise, our values are for Japanese ware.

Bowl, phoenix & brocade patterns, 19th C, 12" **175.00**

Bowl, punch; phoenix & floral roundels, peacock & flower int, 19th C..**1,750.00**

Bowl, Three Friends, flower bud finials, 19th C, 9½", pr **825.00**

Box, scholars viewing scroll, floral border, Koransha, 19th C, 3¾"....**150.00**

Charger, court scene w/gold, brocade borders, 19th C, 22" **1,175.00**

Charger, floral rondel w/flower/bird reserves/bl trellis, 19th C, 25"........**2,000.00**

Charger, floral w/formal floral borders, 13½", pr......................**385.00**

Charger, hawk center, reserves/trellis/emblems, Meiji, 28".......**2,645.00**

Charger, scenic panels (6) surround floral center, 18" **350.00**

Jardiniere, ribbed w/floral molded edge, 19th C, 8x12" **950.00**

Vase, chrysanthemums/dwellings/birds/flowers, gilt bronze mts, 17", pr...**5,875.00**

Vase, phoenixes & dragons, 19th C, 18" **1,050.00**

Vase, women & children reserves alternate w/phoenixes & dragons, 15" ...**1,100.00**

Imperial Glass Company

The Imperial Glass Company was organized in 1901 in Bellaire, Ohio, and started manufacturing glassware in 1904. Their early products were jelly glasses, hotel tumblers, etc., but by 1910 they were making a name for themselves by pressing quantities of carnival glass, the iridescent glassware that was popular during that time. In 1914 NuCut was introduced to imitate cut glass. The line was so popular that it was made in crystal and colors and was reintroduced as Collector's Crystal in the 1950s. From 1916 to 1924 they used the lustre process to make a line called Art Glass, which today some collectors call Imperial Jewels. Free-Hand ware, art glass made entirely by hand using no molds, was made from 1923 to 1924. From 1925 to 1926, they made a less expensive line of art glass called Lead Lustre. These pieces were mold blown and have similar colors and decorations to Free Hand ware.

The company entered bankruptcy in 1931 but was able to continue operations and reorganize as the Imperial Glass Corporation. In 1936 Imperial introduced the Candlewick line, for which it is best known. In the late '30s the Vintage Grape Milk Glass line was added, and in 1951 a major ad campaign was launched, making Imperial one of the leading milk glass manufacturers.

In 1940 Imperial bought the molds and assets of the Central Glass Works of Wheeling, West Virginia; in 1958 they acquired the molds of the Heisey Company, and in 1960 the molds of the Cambridge Glass Company of Cambridge, Ohio. Imperial used these molds, and after 1951 they marked their glassware with an 'I' superimposed over the 'G' trademark. The company was bought by Lenox in 1973; subsequently an 'L' was added to the 'IG' mark. In 1981 Lenox sold Imperial to Arthur Lorch, a private investor (who modified the L by adding a line at the top angled to the left, giving rise to the 'ALIG' mark). He in turn sold the company to Robert F. Stahl, Jr., in 1982. Mr. Stahl filed for Chapter 11 to reorganize, but in mid-1984 liquidation was ordered, and all assets were sold. A few items that had been made in '84 were marked with an 'N' superimposed over the 'I' for 'New Imperial.'

For more information, we recommend *Imperial Glass Encyclopedia, Vols I, II,* and *III,* edited by James Measell; and *Imperial Carnival Glass* by Carl O. Burns.

See also Candlewick; Carnival Glass; Glass Animals and Figurines; Slag Glass; Stretch Glass.

Ashtray, Cape Cod, crystal, #160/134/1, 4" **14.00**

Ashtray, fish, milk glass, 4" **18.00**

Basket, Crocheted Crystal, 9" **45.00**

Basket, ruby slag, 9½" 110.00
Bottle, bitters; Cape Cod, crystal, #160/235, 4-oz 60.00
Bottle, cologne; Cape Cod, crystal, w/stopper, #1601 ....60.00
Bottle, condiment; Cape Cod, crystal, #160/224, 6-oz 65.00
Bottle, cordial; Cape Cod, crystal, #160/256, 18-oz 90.00
Bowl, Atterbury Scroll, milk glass, 3-toed 25.00
Bowl, baked apple; Cape Cod, crystal, #160/53X, 6" 11.00
Bowl, baked apple; Cape Cod, Ritz Blue 25.00
Bowl, Beaded Block, crystal, pk, gr or amber, rnd, flared, 7¼" 30.00
Bowl, Cape Cod, crystal, hdls, #160/145B, 9½" 40.00
Bowl, Cape Cod, crystal, hdls, #160/51F, 6" 33.00
Bowl, console; Cape Cod, crystal, #160/75L, 13" 42.50
Bowl, console; Twisted Optic, amber, 10½" 25.00
Bowl, cream soup; Twisted Optic, bl or yel, 4¾" 25.00
Bowl, Dmn Quilt, blk, crimped, 7" 35.00
Bowl, finger; Cape Cod, crystal, #1602, 4" 12.00
Bowl, Hobnail, purple slag, #641, 8½" 95.00
Bowl, mint; Cape Cod, crystal, hdls, #160/51F, 6" 22.00
Bowl, Monticello, crystal, rnd, 7" 12.50
Bowl, Rose, jade slag, #52c, 8" 65.00
Bowl, Rose, jade slag, #62c, 9" 75.00
Bowl, salad; Crocheted Crystal, 10½" 27.50
Bowl, salad; Twisted Optic, bl or yel, 9¼" 40.00
Bowl, soup; Katy, gr opal, 7" 80.00
Box, dog, purple slag, #822 ....185.00
Box, duck, purple slag, #823 ....185.00
Box, rabbit, purple slag, #157 ....750.00
Butter dish, Cape Cod, crystal, #160/161, ¼-lb 45.00
Butter dish, Fancy Colonial, any color 75.00
Cake salver, Open Lace, milk glass, 12" 25.00
Cake stand, Cape Cod, crystal, #160/103D, 11" 85.00
Cake stand, Cape Cod, crystal, #160/67D, ftd, 10½" 50.00
Candle holder, Cape Cod, crystal, #160/170, 3" 26.50
Candle holder, Cape Cod, crystal, Aladdin style, 4" 150.00
Candle holder, centerpc; Cape Cod, crystal, 6" 95.00
Candle holder, Crocheted Crystal, Narcissus bowl shape 25.00
Candle holder, flower; Cape Cod, #160/45N, 5½", ea 110.00
Candle holder, twin; #160/100, ea 95.00
Candlestick, Free-Hand, heart/vine, wht on clear, bl cup, 10", ea 400.00
Candlestick, Rose, jade slag, 3½", ea 75.00
Candlesticks, Dolphin, caramel slag, #779, 5", pr 65.00
Carafe, wine; Cape Cod, crystal, #160/185, 26-oz 195.00
Celery, Crocheted Crystal, oval, 10" 25.00
Celery, Flute & Cane, crystal, oval, 8½" 25.00
Champagne, Cape Cod, amber, #1602 ....15.00
Cigarette holder, Cape Cod, crystal, ftd, #1602 ....12.50
Claret, Cape Cod, Azalea, #1602 ....20.00
Claret, Cape Cod, crystal, #1602, 5-oz 12.00
Claret, Fancy Colonial, any color, deep, 5-oz 30.00
Coaster, Cape Cod, crystal, flat, #160/1R, 4½" 9.00
Coaster, Cape Cod, crystal, w/spoon rest, #160/76 ....10.00
Cocktail, Cape Cod, crystal, #160b 12.00
Cocktail, Cape Cod, ruby, #160 ....27.00
Comport, Cape Cod, crystal, #160F, 5¼" 27.50
Comport, Cape Cod, crystal, ftd, w/lid, 6" 80.00
Comport, Lace edge, milk glass, 4-toed, 7" 25.00
Cordial, Collector's Crystal, #612 ....14.00
Cordial, Fancy Colonial, pk, #582, 1-oz 50.00
Creamer, Cape Cod, crystal, #160/31, ftd 15.00
Creamer, Crocheted Crystal, ftd 20.00
Cruet, Collector's Crystal, caramel slag, #505 ....50.00
Cup, bouillon; Cape Cod, crystal, #160/250 ....35.00
Cup, coffee; Cape Cod, crystal, #160/37 ....7.00
Cup, punch; Crocheted Crystal, closed hdl 5.00

Cup, punch; Crocheted Crystal, open hdl 7.00
Cup, Reeded, any color 20.00
Decanter, Cape Cod, crystal, #160/163, w/stopper, 30-oz 70.00
Decanter, Grape, Heather, #8 ....55.00
Egg cup, Cape Cod, crystal, #160/225 ....32.50
Egg cup, Grape, milk glass, #1952/225 ....12.00
Goblet, Chroma, Midwest Custard, #123 ....35.00
Goblet, Mt Vernon, crystal, 9-oz 10.00
Goblet, water; Monticello, crystal 15.00
Goblet, wine; Amelia, Rubigold 50.00
Goblet, wine; Atterbury Scroll, milk glass 12.00
Goblet, wine; Crocheted Crystal, 4½-oz, 5½" 25.00
Goblet, wine; Dmn Quilt, pk or gr, 2-oz 12.00
Gravy bowl, Cape Cod, crystal, #160/202, 18-oz 85.00
Ice bucket, Cape Cod, crystal, #160/63, 6½" 195.00
Ice tub, Reeded, any color 55.00
Jar, peanut; Cape Cod, crystal, hdls, w/lid, #160/210, 12-oz 75.00
Jar, pokal; Cape Cod, crystal, #160/128, 11" 85.00
Jelly, Beaded Block, crystal, pk, gr or amber, stemmed/flared, 4½" 25.00
Ladle, marmalade; Cape Cod, crystal, #160/130 ....10.00
Ladle, punch; Cape Cod, crystal 35.00
Lamp, Free-Hand, hanging hearts 1,350.00
Lamp, hurricane; Cape Cod, crystal, #160/79, 2-pc, 5" base 95.00
Lamp, hurricane; Crocheted Crystal, 11" 65.00
Mayonnaise, Monticello, crystal, 3-pc 30.00
Mayonnaise, Open Border, milk glass, #1950/23, 3-pc 25.00
Mayonnaise, Twisted Optic, bl or yel 50.00
Mint dish, Cape Cod, crystal, heart shape, #160/49, 5" 25.00
Muddler, Reeded, any color, 4½" 20.00
Mug, Cape Cod, crystal, #160/188, 12-oz 50.00
Mug, Eagle, Antique Blue 35.00
Nut dish, Cape Cod, crystal, hdls, #160/183, 3" 35.00
Nut dish, Cape Cod, crystal, hdls, #160/184, 4" 30.00
Parfait, Cape Cod, crystal, #1602, 6-oz 12.00
Pickle jar, Mt Vernon, crystal, w/lid 35.00
Pickle tray, Fancy Colonial, any color, oval, 8" 30.00
Pitcher, Atterbury Scroll, milk glass 60.00
Pitcher, Cape Cod, crystal, #160/24, 2-qt 100.00
Pitcher, Cape Cod, crystal, ice lip, #160/239, 2-qt 110.00
Pitcher, Dew Drop, opal, #624, 56-oz 65.00
Pitcher, martini; Cape Cod, crystal, blown, #160/178, 40-oz 225.00
Pitcher, milk; Cape Cod, #160/240, 1-pt 55.00
Pitcher, Windmill, jade slag, satin 150.00
Plate, Beaded Block, yel, sq, 7¾" 30.00
Plate, bread & butter; Cape Cod, #160/1D, 6½" 8.00
Plate, buffet; Twisted Optic, gr, 14" 25.00
Plate, Cape Cod, crystal, #160/3D, 7" 8.00
Plate, Cape Cod, crystal, flat, #160/75D, 14" 50.00
Plate, crescent salad; Cape Cod, crystal, 8" 75.00
Plate, Crocheted Crystal, 17" 40.00
Plate, dinner; Cape Cod, crystal, #160/10D, 10" 37.50
Plate, Flute & Cane, 6" 20.00
Plate, luncheon; Dmn Quilt, bl or blk, 8" 15.00
Plate, Monticello, crystal, rnd, 12" 35.00
Plate, Mt Vernon, crystal, rnd, 8" 10.00
Plate, salad; Katy, bl opal, 8" 32.00
Plate, salad; Laced Edge, opal, 8" 35.00
Plate, salad; Reeded, any color, belled rim, 8" 20.00
Plate, sandwich; Twisted Optic, bl or yel, 10" 20.00
Plate, torte; Cape Cod, crystal, #1608F, 13" 37.50
Platter, Cape Cod, crystal, oval, #160/124D, 13½" 75.00
Puff box, Cape Cod, crystal, #1601, w/lid 50.00
Punch bowl, Crocheted Crystal, 14" 65.00
Relish, Cape Cod, crystal, 3-part, oval, #1602, 11¼" 75.00

Relish, Crocheted Crystal, 3-part, 11½"......................................25.00
Rose bowl, Wide Panel, marigold on milk glass.........................210.00
Shakers, Cape Cod, crystal, sq, #160/109, pr...........................25.00
Shakers, Cape Cod, crystal, stemmed, ftd, #160/243, pr..............40.00
Shakers, Cape Cod, Fern Green, #160/117, pr...........................35.00
Shakers, Monticello, crystal, w/glass tops, pr.........................40.00
Sherbet, Cape Cod, crystal, #1600, 6-oz...............................25.00
Sherbet, Crocheted Crystal, 6-oz, 5".....................................10.00
Sherbet, Dmn Quilt, bl or blk..16.00
Sherbet, Huckabee, pk, ftd...30.00
Sugar bowl, Cape Cod, crystal, ftd, #160/31..........................15.00
Sugar bowl, Fancy Colonial, any color, w/lid..........................30.00
Tidbit, Laced Edge, opal, 2-tier, 8" & 10" plates....................110.00
Tray, pastry; Cape Cod, crystal, center hdl, #160/68D, 11".........85.00
Tumbler, fruit juice; Crocheted Crystal, ftd, 6-oz, 6"................10.00
Tumbler, iced tea; Crocheted Crystal, 12-oz, 7⅛".....................25.00
Tumbler, iced tea; Mt Vernon, crystal, 12-oz..........................12.50
Tumbler, juice; Cape Cod, crystal, #1602, ftd, 6-oz....................6.00
Tumbler, old-fashioned; Cape Cod, crystal, #160, 7-oz..............10.00
Tumbler, water; Atterbury Scroll, milk glass...........................15.00
Tumbler, water; Cape Cod, crytal, 10-oz.................................8.00
Tumbler, water; Fancy Colonial, any color, 10-oz.....................18.00
Tumbler, water; Flute & Cane, crystal, 9-oz............................30.00
Tumbler, water; Katy, gr opal, 9-oz......................................55.00
Vase, bud; Free-Hand, hearts/vines, lt gr on opal, 8½"..............600.00
Vase, Cape Cod, crystal, cylinder, #160/192, 10"....................100.00
Vase, Cape Cod, crystal, ftd, #160/21, 11½"...........................70.00
Vase, Cape Cod, crystal, ftd, #160/22, 6¼"............................35.00
Vase, Crocheted Crystal, 8"...20.00
Vase, Free-Hand, bronze w/waves of bl & orange, waisted shape, 10½"...850.00
Vase, Free-Hand, drag loops, wht on cobalt, 10½"....................850.00
Vase, Free-Hand, hearts/vines, bl irid on opal irid, 8½".............575.00
Vase, Free-Hand, hearts/vines, bl on orange, ruffled, 5x6¾".......600.00
Vase, Free-Hand, hearts/vines, bl on orange irid swollen cylinder, 11"..950.00
Vase, Free-Hand, hearts/vines, gr on wht, orange int, cylindrical, 9"....600.00
Vase, Free-Hand, hearts/vines, lt bl on clear irid, bl rim, 10"...1,100.00
Vase, Free-Hand, leaves, gr on cream w/gold irid, ca 1925, 10½"..950.00
Vase, free-hand, leaves, orange on irid/gold/gr/bl, 5¾"............945.00
Vase, Free-Hand, lg drag loops on orange irid, classic shape, 6"..375.00
Vase, Free-Hand, navy bl w/long trumpet neck, orange irid int, 10"...600.00
Vase, Free-Hand, peach w/orange irid int, #655, 7"..................275.00
Vase, Free-Hand, swags, opal on bl irid, cylindrical, 11½".........550.00
Vase, Free-Hand, swags, orange irid w/bl, shouldered, 6¾".........400.00
Vase, Free-Hand, swirls, mc in cobalt, orange int, stick neck, 9¾"..500.00
Vase, Free-Hand, wht/bl/gray marbleized w/bl int, cylindrical, 9"...500.00
Vase, Nuart, irid aquamarine, shouldered/incurvate, 6¾"...........125.00
Vase, Reeded (Spun), red, 9"..75.00

Imperial Porcelain

The Blue Ridge Mountain Boys were created by cartoonist Paul Webb and translated into three-dimension by the Imperial Porcelain Corporation of Zanesville, Ohio, in 1947. These figurines decorated ashtrays, vases, mugs, bowls, pitchers, planters, and other items. The Mountain Boys series were numbered 92 through 108, each with a different and amusing portrayal of mountain life. Imperial also produced American Folklore miniatures, twenty-three tiny animals one inch or less in size, and the Al Capp Dogpatch series. Because of financial difficulties, the company closed in 1960.

American Folklore Miniatures

Cat, 1½", from $80 to..100.00
Cow, 1¾", from $80 to..100.00

Hound dogs, from $80 to...100.00
Plaque, store ad, Am Folklore Porcelain Miniatures, 4½", $350 to...400.00
Sow, from $80 to..100.00

Blue Ridge Mountain Boys by Paul Webb

Ashtray, #101, man w/jug & snake, from $90 to......................120.00
Ashtray, #103, hillbilly & skunk, from $90 to.........................120.00
Ashtray, #105, baby, hound dog & frog, from $100 to..............135.00
Ashtray, #106, Barrel of Wishes, w/hound, from $85 to............115.00
Ashtray, #92, 2 men by tree stump, for pipes, from $100 to........125.00
Box, cigarette; #98, dog atop, baby at door, sq, from $135 to......165.00
Dealer's sign, Handcrafted Paul Webb Mtn Boys, rare, 9", from $500 to..700.00
Decanter, #100, outhouse, man & bird, from $100 to...............125.00
Decanter, #104, Ma leaning over stump, w/baby & skunk, from $125 to..145.00
Decanter, man, jug, snake, & tree stump, Hispch Inc, 1946, $100 to...125.00
Figurine, #101, man leans against tree trunk, 5", from $100 to...125.00
Figurine, man on hands & knees, 3", from $100 to..................130.00
Figurine, man sitting, 3½", from $120 to...............................145.00
Figurine, man sitting w/chicken on knee, 3", from $100 to.........130.00
Jug, #101, Willie & snake, from $80 to....................................95.00
Mug, #94, Bearing Down, 6", from $80 to................................95.00
Mug, #94, dbl baby hdl, 4¼", from $80 to...............................95.00
Mug, #94, ma hdl, 4¼", from $80 to.......................................95.00
Mug, #94, man w/bl pants hdl, 4¼", from $80 to.......................95.00
Mug, #94, man w/yel beard & red pants hdl, 4¼", from $80 to....95.00
Mug, #99, Target Practice, boy on goat, farmer, 5¾", from $80 to..95.00
Pitcher, lemonade; from $150 to...200.00
Planter, #100, outhouse, man & bird, from $100 to..................125.00
Planter, #105, man w/chicken on knee, washtub, from $100 to..130.00
Planter, #110, man, w/jug & snake, 4½", from $80 to...............95.00
Planter, #81, man drinking from jug, sitting by washtub, from $80 to..95.00
Shakers, Ma & Old Doc, pr, from $85 to.................................115.00

Indian Tree

Indian Tree is a popular dinnerware pattern produced by various potteries since the early 1800s to recent times. Although backgrounds and borders vary, the Oriental theme is carried out with the gnarled, brown branch of a pink-blossomed tree. Among the manufacturers' marks, you may find represented such notable firms as Coalport, S. Hancock and Sons, Soho Pottery, and John Maddock and Sons. See also Johnson Brothers.

Plate, luncheon; Staffordshire, 9", $12.00.

Bonbon, fluted, Coalport, 6¼"...20.00
Bowl, Aynsley, 2¾x8¾" 60.00
Bowl, cream soup; scalloped, Spode.....................................45.00
Bowl, fruit; Johnson Bros, 5"...9.00
Bowl, fruit; Morley, sm...8.00

Bowl, fruit; Spode, 5¼" 28.00
Bowl, Myott, 8" 20.00
Bowl, scalloped, Coalport, 1½x6" 40.00
Bowl, vegetable; John Maddock & Sons, ca 1935, w/lid, 8" dia 55.00
Bowl, vegetable; Noritake, ca 1930s, w/hdls & lid, 10½" 50.00
Butter pat, scalloped, #2/916, 4¼" 18.00
Candy dish, scalloped edge, gr mk, 5¼" L 20.00
Coffee can & saucer, Maddock, 2¼" 18.00
Coffeepot, paneled sides, bud finial, Livesley Powell & Co, EX..330.00
Creamer & sugar bowl, Coalport, bone china mk, late.................40.00
Cup & saucer, AD; Minton...25.00
Cup & saucer, Spode 35.00
Dinner service, Coalport, serves 10+8 serving pieces, 144-pc 750.00
Gravy boat, w/attached underplate, Spode..................145.00
Jar, Sadler, fancy shape, w/lid, 4½" 55.00
Pitcher, Coalport, 4¾" 65.00
Plate, cookie; Coalport, 10½" 55.00
Plate, dessert; ruffled rim, 8".....................................30.00
Plate, dinner; scalloped, Coalport, 10" 40.00
Plate, luncheon; Copeland Spode, 9"..........................35.00
Plate, luncheon; Minton, #5185, 9¼", set of 8 ....100.00
Plate, luncheon; Staffordshire, 9" 12.00
Plate, salad; scalloped, Coalport, 7¾", set of 6...........85.00
Plate, sandwich; closed scroll hdls, Coalport, sq, 10" W.....55.00
Platter, Ashworth, 14½" 90.00
Platter, John Maddock & Son, 14" 35.00
Tazza, scalloped ft, Coalport, 3¼x8" 75.00
Teacup & saucer, cone shape, scalloped, Coalport, gr mk.............32.00
Teapot, Burgess & Lee 60.00
Tray, mc w/gold accents, Coalport, 10¾x8½" 85.00
Tray, octagonal, scalloped rim, Copeland, 8"...............65.00

Inkwells and Inkstands

Receptacles for various writing fluids have been used since ancient times. Through the years they have been made from countless materials — glass, metal, porcelain, pottery, wood, and even papier-mâché. During the eighteenth century, gold or silver inkstands were presented to royalty; the well-known silver inkstand by Philip Syng, Jr., was used for the signing of the Declaration of Independence, and impressive brass inkstands with wells and pounce pots (sanders) were proud possessions of men of letters. When literacy vastly increased in the nineteenth century, the dip pen replaced the quill pen, and inkwells and inkstands were widely used and produced in a broad range of sizes in functional and decorative forms from ornate Victorian to flowing Art Nouveau and stylized Art Deco designs. However, the acceptance of the ballpoint pen literally put inkstands and inkwells 'out of business.' But their historical significance and intriguing diversity of form and styling fascinate today's collectors.

For further information we recommend *Collector's Encyclopedia of Inkwells* by Veldon Badders (Collector Books). See also Bottles, Ink.

Blown in mold, quilted, robin egg bl, hinged brass mt & lid, 3x2½"..700.00
Bronze, child & dog beside doghouse (hinged lid), ca 1900, 6" ..500.00
Bronze, Egyptian gateway, pharoah's head, pen rest, 3x2⅝" 90.00
Cast brass, alligator, porc inserts, Am, ca 1905, 3½x10" 300.00
Cast brass, chestnut leaf & nut w/ladybug, glass insert, 1900s.....250.00
Ceramic, globe w/transfer print, Japan, ca 1900s, 3⅞x3" 125.00
Ceramic, Snoopy stands beside ink bottle, ca 1958, 2½x3¾x4¼" ..45.00
CI, bronzed 4-leaf clover w/lady's head in center, 1910-15, 6" dia 225.00
CI, man pulling rickshaw w/glass insert, neo-Japanese, ca 1890, 5".....200.00
CI, rooster & head on branch, porc cabbage head well, NM pnt.....275.00
CI, stag behind stump, polychrome decor, 1900s, 3¾x2¼x3" 175.00
CI, statue of St Anne, gilded, ca 1900, 5"...................140.00

CI, wheelbarrow, Rococo style, milk glass snail well, Am, 3½x8"....230.00
CI fr w/2 clear revolving 4½" fonts, 1875-95 ....100.00
Copper, emb vines & bird, pen rest, 2 milk glass wells/sponge holder ...110.00
Cut crystal, cane pattern, brass mts, 2" sq 145.00
Cut crystal, trapezoidal w/beveled edge, hinged SP lid, 4¼x3⅝" ..120.00
Gilt bronze w/distressed finish, acanthus decor, 1900s, 3" sq.........95.00
Hand-blown & cut, bl marble pyramid w/pen ledge rest, 2¾x2½" sq....750.00
Metal circus elephant head w/trunk pen holder, monkey finial, 6x4"....400.00
Porc, bellhop w/package, wht & gold, mk Fish/Fulper, ca 1920 ..400.00
Porc, Bob the elf w/bl hat & yel coat, W Germany, #510, 1970, 7" ..275.00
Porc, boy by well & waterfall, German, #1132, ca 1890, 4½x3½" ...280.00
Porc, clown w/pen holder between ft, French, 4¼" 150.00
Porc, dog & child in hair wigs, mk Germany 1959, 2½x3¼".....250.00
Porc, Erphila Ink Girl, Germany, ca 1920, 2¼" sq.......160.00
Porc, gondola shape w/floral decor on wht, Fr, ca 1900, 1¾x7¾" 260.00
Porc, grape & leaf decor on wht w/rust trim, 8-sided, 3⅞x2½"...100.00
Porc, Oriental lady on famille rose, bell shape, ca 1840, 2¼" 190.00
Porc, Pierrot in red w/wht collar, ca 1920, 3¾x3¼" 150.00
Pot metal, dragoon's helmet, dragon finial, porc insert, ca 1885....250.00
Pot metal, Indian chief head, polychromed, Carlsbad Caverns, ca 1905..225.00
Pottery, bird w/young in nest, Staffordshire, late 19th C, 2¾" dia 230.00
Pottery, Blackwood & Co..., lt tan, molded spout, 4½" 80.00
Pottery, boy seated by basket of grapes, mc, Staffordshire............300.00
Pottery, dog, red & wht on bl base, Staffordshire, ca 1860, 4x2½" 300.00
Pottery, Dutch shoe shape w/bl decor on wht, Delft, Holland, 2x4"..120.00
Pottery, lion's head, wht, 2 quill holes, filler hole is mouth, 2⅜" ..50.00
Pottery, man's wigged face w/open mouth, brn, Doulton, ca 1880, 2½" ...250.00
Pottery, swan & egg w/tree trunk, Staffordshire, ca 1860, 3½x2½" 300.00
Pressed glass, Cane, blk Bakelite funnel insert, 1900-10, 2¼" sq 100.00
Pressed glass, Dmn Point & Fan, SP mt & hinged lid, 1900s, 4" dia ...80.00
Pressed glass, Sawtooth w/Bakelite insert, Am, 1900s, 2⅝x3" dia........90.00
Pressed glass, Souvenir of 1,000 Islands 1900, stamped brass stand......50.00
Pressed glass, swirled w/brass collar & lid, att Fr, late 19th C......110.00
Soapstone, dk color, rectangular, Am, 1780s, 2⅛"........................40.00
Threaded glass, brass collar, Am, 1900s, 2¼x2¾" dia....................60.00
Wood, antelope under fir tree, glass well, mk Appenzell, 1900s, 6x3" 190.00

Bronze, greyhound dog chained to fence post, original glass wells and lids, 12" long, $800.00.

(Photo courtesy Jackson's Auctioneers & Appraisers)

Insulators

The telegraph was invented in 1844. The devices developed to hold the electrical transmission wires to the poles were called insulators. The telephone, invented in 1876, intensified their usefulness; and by the turn of the century, thousands of varieties were being produced in pottery, wood, and glass of various colors. Even though it has been rumored that red glass insulators exist, none have ever been authenticated. There are amber-colored insulators that appear to have a red tint to the amber, and those are called red-amber. Many insulators are embossed with patent dates.

Of the more than 3,000 types known to exist, today's collectors evaluate their worth by age, rarity of color and, of course, condition. Aqua and green are the most common colors in glass, dark brown the most common in porcelain. Threadless insulators (for example, CD #701.1) made between 1850 and 1865 bring prices well into the hundreds, sometimes even the thousands, if in mint condition.

In the listings that follow, the CD numbers are from an identification system developed in the late 1960s by N.R. Woodward.

Those seeking additional information about insulators are encouraged to contact Line Jewels NIA #1380 (whose address may be found in the Directory under Clubs, Newsletters, and Catalogs) or attend a club-endorsed show. (For information see Directory under Florida for Jacqueline Linscott Barnes.) In the listings that follow those stating 'no name' have no company identification, but do have embossed numbers, dots, etc. Those stating 'no embossing' are without raised letters, dots, or any other markings. Please note: Our values are for insulators in mint condition.

Key:
* (asterisk) — Canadian
BE — base embossed
CB — corrugated base
CD — Consolidated Design
FDP — flat drip points
RB — rough base
RDP — round drip points
SB — smooth base
SDP — sharp drip points

Threaded Pin-type and Threadless Glass Insulators

CD 102.4, New Eng Tel & Tel Co, BE, aqua............................1,000.00
CD 106, McLaughlin No 9, FDP, lt bl 5.00
CD 110.6, National Insulator Co, BE, lt aqua.......................1,500.00
CD 121, Brookfield, SB, dk orange amber.............................50.00
CD 121, Maydwell-16W, SDP, straw....................................30.00
CD 122.4, Hemingray-E2, SB, lt lemon...............................100.00
CD 130, Cal Elec Works, SB, bl.....................................350.00
CD 133, City Fire Alarm, SB, lt aqua................................75.00
CD 133.1, Homer Brooke's Pat, SB, lt bl.............................40.00
CD 135.5, ERW, SB, lime gr..2,500.00
CD 141.8, Buzby, SB, aqua..20,000.00
CD 143, CNR, SB, aqua..5.00
CD 150, Barclay, SDP, aqua..7,500.00
CD 153, Gayner No 48-400, SDP, aqua.................................10.00
CD 154, CNR, SB, peach...500.00
CD 154, Hemingray-42, RDP, aqua.....................................1.00
CD 154, Maydwell-42/USA, RDP, straw.................................2.00
CD 154.5, Derflingher, RDP, aqua...................................20.00
CD 160, OVGCo, SB, aqua..250.00
CD 160.6, Am Tel & Tel Co, SB, lt yel-gr..........................2,500.00
CD 161, California, SB, purple.....................................30.00
CD 162, BGMCo, SB, lt purple......................................200.00
CD 178, California 303 Santa Ana, RB, purple......................200.00
CD 185.2, BELCo, SB, dk aqua.....................................2,000.00
CD 190 & CD 191, 2-pc/Transposition, SB, milky aqua...............400.00
CD 194 & CD 195, Hemingray-54-A & Hemingray-54-B, purple...150.00
CD 197, Whitall Tatum/No 15, SB, clear..............................2.00
CD 203, Armstrong TW, SB, clear.....................................1.00
CD 213, Hemingray, No 43, RDP, aqua................................10.00
CD 214, Armstrong's No 10, SB, clear................................2.00
CD 217, Armstrong's 51 C3, SB, root beer amber.....................10.00
CD 226, No 115, SB, aqua...30.00
CD 236, Brookfield, SB, dk aqua....................................500.00
CD 238, Hemingray-514, CB, honey amber.............................325.00
CD 239, Kimble, CB, clear..5.00
CD 250, NEGMCo, SB, aqua...1,250.00
CD 252, No 2 Cable, RB, orange amber...............................300.00
CD 253, Knowles Cable, SB, lt aqua.................................40.00

CD 254, No 3 Cable, SB, aqua.......................................30.00
CD 257, Hemingray, No 60, RDP, bl aqua.............................20.00
CD 262, No 2 Columbia, SB, lt bl aqua.............................175.00
CD 267.5, NEGMCo, SB, emerald gr..................................200.00
CD 297, FM Locke Victor NY, RB, dk aqua............................10.00
CD 299.7, Lowex, D-514, SB, lt lemon.............................5,000.00
CD 309.5, Westinghouse Electric & Mfg Co, SB, aqua.........10,000.00
CD 315, Registered Trade Mark, SB, bl.............................125.00
CD 317, Chambers/Pat Aug 14 1877, SB, lt aqua.....................500.00
CD 322, Corning Pyrex, SB, carnival...............................125.00
CD 724, Chester NY, BE, cobalt..................................5,000.00
CD 728.8, Boston Bottle Works, BE, aqua.........................3,000.00
CD 729.4, Mulford & Biddle/83 John St NY, SB, aqua...........1,250.00
CD 734.8* (no emb), SB, olive blk glass...........................300.00
CD 735, Chester NY, SB, aqua......................................600.00
CD 736, NY&ERR, SB, lt gr aqua..................................3,000.00
CD 738, Chester NY (MLOD), SB, root beer amber..............7,500.00
CD 1038, Cutter Pat April 26, 04, SB, aqua........................300.00

Irons

History, geography, art, and cultural diversity are all represented in the collecting of antique pressing irons. The progress of fashion and invention can be traced through the evolution of the pressing iron.

Over seven hundred years ago, implements constructed of stone, bone, wood, glass, and wrought iron were used for pressing fabrics. Early ironing devices were quite primitive in form, and heating techniques included inserting a hot metal slug into a cavity of the iron, adding hot burning coals into a chamber or pan, and placing the iron directly on hot coals or a hot surface.

To the pleasure of today's collectors, some of these early irons, mainly from the period of 1700 to 1850, were decorated by artisans who carved and painted them with regional motifs typical of their natural surroundings and spiritual cultures.

Beginning in the mid-1800s, new cultural demands for fancy wearing apparel initiated a revolution in technology for types of irons and methods to heat them. Typical of this period is the fluter which was essential for producing the ruffles demanded by the nineteenth-century ladies. Hat irons, polishers, and numerous unusual iron forms were also used during this time, and provided a means to produce crimps, curves, curls, and special fabric textures. Irons from this period are characterized by their unique shapes, odd handles, latches, decorations, and even revolving mechanisms.

Also during this time, irons began to be heated by burning liquid and gaseous fuels. Gradually the new technology of the electrically heated iron replaced all other heating methods, except in the more rural areas and undeveloped countries. Even today the Amish communities utilize gasoline fuel irons.

In the listings that follow, prices are given for examples in best possible as-found condition. Damage, repairs, plating, excessive wear, rust, and missing parts can dramatically reduce value. For further information we recommend *Irons by Irons*, *More Irons by Irons*, and *Even More Irons by Irons* by our advisor Dave Irons; his address and information for ordering these books are given in the Directory under Pennsylvania.

Alcohol, German, Matador, w/sun-face trivet, ca 1900, 7½", $200 to....300.00
Alcohol, Manning-Bowman...USA, tank missing, ca 1900, 7¼", $150 to.....200.00
Box, Eclipse Pat...1903 in star, 6¾", from $70 to........................100.00
Box, English, brass w/fancy decor/posts, 1850s, 7½", from $300 to....400.00
Box, European, hinged at bk, ca 1900, 7½", from $50 to..............70.00
Box, European, iron, heat shield, lift-up gate, late 1800s, 7½"...200.00
Box, Fr, man's face on right, mid-1800s, 8", from $500 to..........700.00
Box, Laundry Queen #2, top lifts off, late 1800s, 6¼", $200 to..300.00
Box w/thermometer, Waterman...1889, 7⅛", from $300 to.........500.00

**Charcoal, European, all late 1800s: Jockey head on latch, 5¼";
Bird head on latch, 4⅜"; Lady's head on latch, leather handle,
5", all from $200.00 to $300.00 each.** (Photo courtesy David Irons)

Combination/revolving, Majestic, Pat...Carver...1899, 6¼", $300 to..500.00
Dragon, Pomeroy Peckover...1854, figural chimney, 11", over 750.00
Egg, standing; Fr, ca 1900, 12¾", from $150 to...........................200.00
Flatiron, European, cast, ca 1900, 7", from $10 to 20.00
Flatiron, European, cast horse, late 1800s, 5⅜", minimum value ..700.00
Flatiron, European, cold hdl, early 1900s, 5⅛", from $50 to 70.00
Flatiron, Fr, cast, #2 (anchor), belled-out hdl, 1890s, 7", $50 to...70.00
Flatiron, Pat Sad Iron, cold hdl, ca 1900, 6⅛", from $30 to.........50.00
Flatiron, Wapak #4, cast, ca 1900, 5⅛", from $10 to.....................20.00
Flower, G Molla NY, brass base, iron top, late 1800s, 6¾", $100 to....150.00
Fluter, combination, Little Giant...73, w/board, 5¼", from $300 to....500.00
Fluter, combination/revolving, Pat 1876, 5½", from $500 to 700.00
Fluter, HB Adams Pat Pending, clamp-on, ca 1875, from $200 to...300.00
Fluter, rocker, Pat...1868...1870..., brass plates, 4½", minimum ..500.00
Fluter machine, Perin & Gaff...Nov 20 66 O, decals/pinstripes, up to...300.00
Gas jet, Pat July 4 1893, Sultana Toiley Iron, 4½", from $200 to 300.00
Gasoline, Dmn Iron...Akron OH, Pat Appd...USA, ca 1900, 7½", $50 to...70.00
Gasoline, side tank, early 1900s, 11¼", from $200 to..................250.00
Goffering, dbl; English, wrought, w/heater/tripod, 1600s, 11", minimum...750.00
Goffering, English, brass, Queen Anne tripod, 1850s, 10⅜", $200 to.......300.00
Goffering, European, brass std ornate CI base, mid-1800s, 11", $300 to...500.00
Goffering, European, wrought, sm monkey-tail/tripod, 1800s, 11", up to...700.00
Goffering, single; English, brass base, late 1800s, 4¾", $200 to ..350.00
Hat, McCoys Pat Pd, arched cut-out bottom, late 1800s, 4¾", $100 to...150.00
Hat, Wm Johnson...USA, ca 1900, 9½", from $100 to 150.00
Natural gas, Iwantu Comfort...Strause..., early 1900s, 7½", $70 to 100.00
Natural gas, Uneedit Gas Iron....Pending, early 1900s, 6½", $100 to...150.00
Natural gas, Wright Pat Aug 22 1911, 7", from $70 to...............100.00
Ox tongue, European, acorns at hinges/hdls, early 1800s, 8½" ...350.00
Ox tongue, European, hinged gate, ca 1900, 8", from $100 to 150.00
Pan, Greek, rnd w/high ridges in bottom, ca 1900, 18", $100 to ...150.00
Polisher, GS&Co...8, rnded edges, late 1800s, 5½", from $100 to 150.00
Polisher, Indian emb, dmn grid bottom, late 1800s, 4⅜", $150 to 200.00
Polisher, Pat July 14 63 No 1, egg shaped, 4½", from $150 to 200.00
Polisher, The Goelds, smooth bottom, late 1800s, 4⅛", from $30 to....50.00
Sleeve, Guelph Wap in overlaid letters, late 1800s, 7", from $70 to...100.00
Sleeve, Mt Joy type hdl, late 1800s, 6⅜", from $100 to 150.00
Sleeve, Pat'd June 15 1897 (C in shield), flat toe, 9⅞", $150 to ...200.00
Slug, English, brass w/eng ram & 1884, 6⅛", from $500 to.........700.00
Slug, Scandanavian, HF Skad 1709, eng scorpion top, 5¼", minimum ...750.00
Swan, CI, wht w/bl pinstripes, 2⅛", from $200 to 300.00
Tailor, CI, train form w/smoke as hdl, late 1800s, minimum 700.00
Tailor, Savery & Co Phila, CI, late 1800s, 8", from $70 to 100.00
Tailor, steam, Koenig New Jersey, early 1900s, 11¼", from $70 to......100.00
Tall chimney, E Bless R Drake...1852, vulcan face damper, 6½" 150.00

Ironstone

During the last quarter of the eighteenth century, English potters

began experimenting with a new type of body that contained calcinated flint and a higher china clay content, intent on producing a fine durable whiteware — heavy, yet with a texture that would resemble porcelain. To remove the last trace of yellow, a minute amount of cobalt was added, often resulting in a bluish-white tone. Wm and John Turner of Caughley and Josiah Spode II were the first to manufacture the ware successfully. Others, such as Davenport, Hicks and Meigh, and Ralph and Josiah Wedgwood, followed with their own versions. The latter coined the name 'Pearl' to refer to his product and incorporated the term into his trademark. In 1813 a fourteen-year patent was issued to Charles James Mason, who called his ware Patented Ironstone. Francis Morley, G.L. Asworth, T.J. Mayer, and other Staffordshire potters continued to produce ironstone until the end of the century. While some of these patterns are simple to the extreme, many are decorated with in-mold designs of fruit, grain, and foliage on ribbed or scalloped shapes. In the 1830s transfer-printed designs in blue, mulberry, pink, green, and black became popular; and polychrome versions of Oriental wares were manufactured to compete with the Chinese trade. See also Mason's Ironstone. Our advise for this category comes from Home Place Antiques, whose address is listed in the Directory under Illinois.

Bowl, berry/sauce; Rolling Star, Edwards 30.00
Bowl, soup; Full Ribbed, Pankhurst, 8¾" 32.00
Bowl, vegetable; Tulip Sydenham, T&R Boote, w/lid, 8" 75.00
Chamber pot, Bow & Tassel, ...Burgess & Goddard, 8½x8¼".......85.00
Chamber pot, wicker basket design/acanthus leaves, Meakin 155.00
Coffeepot, Blackberry, Memnon shape, J Meir & Son, 1857, 9½" 130.00
Coffeepot, Grape Octagon, pk lustre accents, Walley, 10" 65.00
Coffeepot, Laurel Wreath, Elsmore & Forster, 11¼" 325.00
Coffeepot, Wheat & Clover, Tomkinson Bros, 10⅝" 245.00
Creamer, octagonal w/paneled sides, Meigh & Son, 5⅛" 85.00
Cup & saucer, Wheat & Clover, Taylor Brothers, ca 1862-71, NM 55.00
Cup plate, Fig, Davenport, 4¼" 55.00
Cup plate, Niagara Falls, Shaw, 3⅞", EX 70.00
Gravy boat, Fig, J Wedgwood, ca 1856.................................110.00
Ladle, sauce; flower on hdl, paneled bowl, unmk.....................65.00
Mustard cup, w/lid, Knowles Taylor & Knowles, ca 1920, 3½" 75.00
Pitcher, Acanthus Leaf, Warranted mk, 10"...........................145.00
Pitcher, bulbous w/emb decor at hdl & spout, J Wedgwood, 8½" 200.00
Pitcher, Cable & Ring, Anthony Shaw & Son, 12½x7¾"..........175.00
Pitcher, Hawthorn's Fern, Wood & Hawthorn, ca 1891, 12¼x8" 185.00
Pitcher, Octagon, TR Boote, 1851, 12"................................120.00
Pitcher, President, J Edwards, 8⅝"...................................155.00
Pitcher, Rhine, Thomas Hughes, 1890s, 6x6" 225.00
Pitcher, simple form, J&G Meakin, 13".................................155.00
Pitcher, Tracery, Johnson & Bros, 11½".................................170.00
Pitcher, Union, TR Boote, 7"...185.00
Pitcher, Wheat, Adams, 1800s, 8¼x8"..................................150.00
Pitcher, Wheat & Hops, paneled sides, Alfred Meakin, 11¾" 120.00
Plate, Lily of the Valley, James Edwards & Son, 10½"................35.00
Plate, Sydenham, T&R Boote, 10½".......................................40.00
Plate, Wheat, Elsmore & Forster, ca 1853-71, 9¾"...................42.00
Platter, De Soto, Thos Hughes, 11⅝x9" 65.00
Platter, emb scrolls & leaves, scalloped border, #639-1, 19x13" 75.00
Platter, oval, Chas Meakin Warranted, 13½x9½" 65.00
Platter, rectangular, LS&S, ca 1870-80, 18x13", NM 65.00
Relish, Ceres, w/rope hdls, Elsmore & Forster.........................78.00
Relish, 3-lobe w/organic hdl, Adams & Sons, 1950s, 12" 65.00
Soup plate, Budded Vine, Meakin, ca 1869, 10¼".....................75.00
Soup plate, Wilkinson, 8"..48.00
Sugar bowl, President, w/lid, John Edwards, ca 1856, 7" 195.00
Sugar bowl, Sydenham, w/lid, T&R Boote, ca 1854, 8x6", NM....75.00
Teapot, Corn & Oats...275.00
Teapot, Full Panel Gothic, octagonal, John Alcock, ca 1848, 8¼".....245.00

Tureen, Gothic, 10-sided, w/lid, Joseph Heath, 7½x9¾x8¼", NM **275.00**
Tureen, sauce; President, John Edwards, 1855, w/lid & ladle **295.00**
Tureen, w/lid & ladle, Maddock & Gater, 6x8" **225.00**
Wash bowl, New York, Clementson, 13½" **165.00**
Wash pitcher, Corn & Oats **175.00**
Waste bowl, Tuscan, unmk, 3⅛x5¼" **80.00**

Patterned Ironstone

Coffeepot, Venus, bl transfer, 8-sided, att Podmore Walker, 8¾", EX....**145.00**
Compote, Shannon, bl transfer, ftd, flared sides, 5½x10¾" **160.00**
Creamer, Garden Scenery, bl transfer, paneled sides, 5½", EX **75.00**
Creamer, Venus, bl transfer, Podmore Walker, prof rpr, 5⅛" **45.00**
Cup & saucer, Geneva, bl transfer, Wedgwood, 2½x4", 5⅞" **50.00**
Custard cup, scenic, bl transfer, paneled sides **70.00**
Plate, Ontario Lake Scenery, bl transfer, Heath, 9¾" **75.00**
Plate, Venus, bl transfer, Wedgwood, 7⅞" **35.00**
Platter, Geneva, bl transfer, Wedgwood, 15⅞x12⅛" **95.00**
Soup plate, Columbia, bl transfer, Wedgwood, 10¾", NM **55.00**
Soup plate, Corinthia, Challinor, 9⅞", EX..................................**65.00**

Italian Glass

Throughout the twentieth century, one of the major glassmaking centers of the world was the island of Murano. From the Stile Liberte work of Artisi Barovier (1890 – 1920s) to the early work of Ettore Sottsass in the 1970s, they excelled in creativity and craftsmanship. The 1920s to 1940s featured the work of glass designers like Ercole Barovier for Barovier and Toso and Vittorio Zecchin, Napoleone Martinuzzi, and Carlo Scarpa for Venini. Many of these pieces are highly prized by collectors.

The 1950s saw a revival of Italy as a world-reknown design center for all of the arts. Glass led the charge with the brightly colored work of Fulvio Bianconi for Venini, Dino Martens for Aureliano Toso, and Ercole Barovier for Barovier and Toso. The best of these pieces are extremely desirable. The '60s and '70s have also seen many innovative designs with work by the Finnish Tapio Wirkkala, the American Thomas Stearns, and many other designers.

Unfortunately, among the great glass, there was a plethora of commercial ashtrays, vases, and figurines produced that, though having some value, do not compare in quality and design to the great glass of Murano.

Venini: The Venini company was founded in 1921 by Paolo Venini, and he led the company until his death in 1959. Major Italian designers worked for the firm, including Vittorio Zecchin, Napoleone Martinuzzi, Carlo Scarpa, and Fulvio Bianconi. After his death, his son-in-law, Ludovico de Santillana, ran the factory and employed designers like Toni Zucchieri, Tapio Wirkkala, and Thomas Stearns. The company is known for creative designs and techniques including Inciso (finely etched lines), Battuto (carved facets), Sommerso (controlled bubbles), Pezzato (patches of fused glass), and Fascie (horizontal colored lines in clear glass). Until the mid-'60s, most pieces were signed with acid-etched 'Venini Murano ITALIA.' In the '60s they started engraving the signatures. The factory still exists.

Barovier: In the late 1920s, Ercole Barovier took over the Artisti Barovier and started designing many different vases. In the 1930s he merged with Ferro Toso and became Barovier and Toso. He designed many different series of glass including the Barbarico (rough, acid-treated brown or deep blue glass), Eugenio (free-blown vases), Efeso, Rotallato, Dorico, Egeo (vases incorporating murrine designs), and Primavera (white etched glass with black bands). He designed until 1974. The company is still in existence. Most pieces were unsigned.

Aureliano Toso: The great glass designer Dino Martens was involved with the company from about 1938 to 1965. It was his work that produced the very desirable Oriente vases. This technique consisted of free-formed patches of green, yellow, blue, purple, black, and white stars and pieces of zanfirico canes fused into brilliantly colored vases and bowls. His El Dorado series was based on the same technique but was not opaque. He also designed pieces with alternating groups of black and white filigrana lines. Pieces are unsigned.

Seguso: Flavio Poli became the artistic director of Seguso in the late 1930s and remained until 1963. He is known for his Corroso (acid-etched glass) and his Valve series (elegant forms of two to three layers of colored glass with a clear glass casing).

Archimede Seguso: In 1946 Archimede Seguso left the Seguso Vetri D'Arte to open a new company and designed many innovative pieces. His Merlatto (thin white filigrana suspended three dimensionally) series is his most famous. The epitome of his work is where a colored glass (yellow or purple) is windowed in the merlotti. His Macchia Ambra Verde is yellow and spots on a gold base encased in clear glass. The A Piume series contained feathers and leaves suspended in glass. Pieces are unsigned.

Alfredo Barbini: Barbini was a designer known for his sculptures of sea subjects and his amorphic-shaped vases with an inner core of red or blue glass with a heavy layer of finely incised outer glass. He worked in the 1950s to the 1960s, and some pieces are signed.

Vistosi: Although this glassworks was started in the 1940s, fame came in the 1960s and 1970s with the birds designed by Allesandro Pianon and the early work of the Memphis school designer, Ettore Sottsass. Pieces may be signed.

AVEM: This company is known for its work in the 1950s and 1960s. The designer, Ansolo Fuga, did work using a solid white glass with inclusions of multicolored murrines.

Cenedese: This is a postwar company led by Gino Cenedese with Alfredo Barbini as designer. When Barbini left, Cenedese took over the design work and also used the free-lanced designs of Fulvio Bianconi. They are known for their figurines and vases with suspended murrines.

Cappellin: Venini's original partner (1921 – 25), Giacomo Cappellin, opened a short-lived company (1925 – 32) that was to become extremely important. His chief designer was the young Carlo Scarpa who was to create many masterpieces in glass both for Cappellin and then Venini.

Ettore Sottsass: Sottass founded the Memphis School of Design in the 1970s. He is an extremely famous modern designer who designed several series of glass for the Vistosi Glass Company. The pieces were created in limited editions, signed and numbered, and each piece was given a name.

Venini Glass

Italia mk bowl, delicate wht spirals, flared, #83, 9" **250.00**
Mezza filigrana ashtray, crystal free-form, 3½x4¾" **35.00**
Murano bird, bl & wht w/crystal comb & base, 21" **350.00**
Murano clown, bright mc, EX details, 8½x5¾" **155.00**
Murano dish, sea gr w/gr aventurine & orange int, shallow, 10" ...**38.00**
Murano duck, cobalt & red cased, orig sticker, 6½" **75.00**
Murano fish, gr cased, amber base, 1960s, 10x12" **180.00**
Murano formia bird, bl & gr cased, 10" **175.00**
Murano handkerchief vase, gr cased, 8" **195.00**
Murano handkerchief vase, mc millefiori canes, 4" **195.00**
Murano horse head, cobalt & crystal, 6" **55.00**
Murano lamps, olive/blk/wht stripes in clear, ball base, 32", pr ..**1,175.00**
Murano lantern-shaped chandelier, amber in metal fr, 21x10"+chain...**385.00**
Murano lemonade set, gr w/wht lacy stripes, 8¼" pitcher+8 tumblers...**590.00**
Murano pear paperweight, yel gr w/dk stem & leaf, 4½" **36.00**
Murano ribbon bowl, red & wht, w/sticker, 4x5" **55.00**
Murano rooster, mc cased, 13x10" **75.00**
Murano sailboat, bl/gr/rose cased, 12½x7⅝" **95.00**
Murano vase, brn w/appl clear prunts & faint irid, 8x6" **925.00**
Murano vase, laced gr satin, bottle neck, 9¼x6" **280.00**
Murano vase, smoky brn w/wht drip lines w/in, 1980s, 13¼x6¼"....**885.00**
Murano vase, wht/purple/red waves w/gold flecks, 1950s, 9¾"....**365.00**

Sommerso floral vase, amethyst/purple/gr layers in clear, 8x7x4" 185.00
Tapio Wirkkala egg vase, clear w/gold leaf, 1¾x2½"+ orig stand.....925.00
Tapio Wirkkala vase, clear w/twist molding/controlled bubbles, 5¼"...225.00
Zanfirico mc latticino bowl, 3x9" 300.00
Zanfirico wht latticino bowl, 9" 169.00

Non-Venini Glass

AVEM compote, clear w/silver specks, appl pk flowers, 1950s, 4x8"...295.00
Barbini duck, amber to orange cased, S-shape, 10" 60.00
Barovier & Toso Black dancing couple, triple cased, mc, 10", 11", pr ...1,200.00
Barovier & Toso bottle, mc vertical stripes, 10½" 1,200.00
Barovier & Toso colonial lady, bl/wht/clear cased w/gold, 10½" ..450.00
Barovier & Toso lamps, bl w/gold accents, 33½x7½", pr.........1,200.00
Barovier & Toso pk bullicante bowl, 1⅝x8½x10" 65.00
Barovier & Toso ribbed jar, bl swirls w/gold dust, 1950s, 7" 325.00
Barovier & Toso vase, striata, purple/yel/gold stripes, 12x12" ..1,300.00
Barovier centerpc bowl, sommerso amberina free-form, 2¼x9¾"..145.00

Barovier, Primavera vase, internal decor, black glass handles, drilled, ca 1930, 12¾", $10,575.00. (Photo courtesy Bonhams & Butterfields)

Cenedese aquarium, glass block w/fish & seaweed, 5" 375.00
Cenedese bowl w/embedded fish, clear & bl, 6" 225.00
Cenedese jester, gold mica in body, wht pompoms, opal collar, 10½"..625.00
Cesare Toso lady figurine, wht opaque to clambroth, 8¾" 195.00
Salviati ringed ice bucket, 7⅝x9⅜"...150.00
Seguso peasant lady w/basket, gr/clear & gold flecks, 1940s, 10"......450.00
Seguso sommerso bowl, emerald gr heart shape w/controlled bubbles, 6"...40.00

Ivory

Ivory has been used and appreciated since Neolithic times. It has been a product of every culture and continent. It is the second most valuable organic material after pearls. Ivory is defined as the dentine portion of mammalian teeth. Commercially the most important ivory comes from elephant and mammoth tusks, walrus tusks, hippo teeth, and sperm whale teeth. The smaller tusks of boar and warthog are often used whole.

Ivory has been used for artistic purposes as a palette for oil paints, as inlay on furniture, and especially as a medium for sculptures. Some are in the round, others in the form of plaques. Ivory also has numerous utilitarian uses such as cups and tankards; combs; handles for knives and medical tools; salt and pepper shakers; chess, domino, and checker pieces; billiard balls; jewelry; shoehorns; snuff boxes; brush pots; and fans.

There are a number of laws domestically and internationally to protect endangered animals including the elephant, walrus, and whale. However ivory taken and used before the various enactment dates is legal within the country in which it is located, and can be shipped internationally with a permit. Ivory from mammoths, hippopotamus, wart hog, and boar is excepted from all bans.

Prices have been stable for the last ten years, rising slightly in the last year. Prices are highest for European, Japanese, and Chinese ivories. Prices are lowest for African and Indian ivories. As with all collectibles, the very best pieces will appreciate most in the years to come. Small, poorly carved pieces will not appreciate to any extent. Our advisor for this category is Robert Weisblut; he is listed in the Directory under Florida.

Bust of Voltaire on marble plinth, France, 19th C, 10"............7,500.00
Children, cvg, Communist Chinese era, 9½" 1,250.00
Fishermen (2) smoking while resting, Tokyo School, early 20th C, 9".....3,500.00
Goddess, multi-armed, w/sitar, Indian, 20th C, 6½"...................125.00
Grouping of gods & children, Chinese, early 20th C, 10" ..2,650.00
Hippo tooth cvg of village scene, Chinese, 1980s, 16" 325.00
Horse-drawn carriage, 20th C, 12" 1,750.00
Lantern, Chinese, late 19th C, 28" 4,500.00
Narwhal tusk shakers, scrimshawed, 2½", pr...........................350.00
Snuff bottle, deep relief, China, 19th C, 5" 1,250.00
Study of rose branch, Japan, early 20th C, 13" 1,750.00
Table screen on stand, Ming Era, 11"...................................2,200.00
Tusk, full, cvd procession of people, African, mid-19th C..........775.00
Vases, set of 2, w/basket, early 19th C, Chinese, 8"...............2,000.00
Village scene, Japanese, ca 1900, 5½"..................................2,000.00
Walrus sailing vessel w/full sails, Eskimo, 1950s, 10" 1,500.00
Woman w/weaving implements, Chinese, early 20th C, 9".........675.00

Jack-in-the-Pulpit Vases

Popular novelties at the turn of the century, jack-in-the-pulpit vases were made in every type of art glass produced. Some were simple, others elaborately appliquéd and enameled. They were shaped to resemble the lily for which they were named.

Gold irid w/threaded design, 8" 325.00
Gold stretch, gold irid stem, bl irid ft, 17½" 460.00
Gr-gold irid flower, swirled/pulled stum, stepped bulb, Radke, 14" 300.00
Vaseline opal w/ribbing; SP ftd base w/'S' hdls, 8", pr 225.00
Vertical latticinio & ribbon mc canes, 7"....................................120.00

Jervis

W.P. Jervis began his career as a potter in 1898. By 1908 he had his own pottery in Oyster Bay, New York. His shapes were graceful; often he decorated his wares with sgraffito designs over which he applied a matt glaze. Many piece were incised 'Jervis' in a vertical arrangement. The pottery closed around 1912.

Bowl, mottled dk gr & burnt orange matt, shouldered, 1908-12, 2¾"...350.00
Vase, bud; floral, gr/wht on gunmetal blk, 4½x3" 550.00
Vase, oval spirals around mid section on dk gr w/blk charcoaling, 5x5" ...330.00

Jewelry

Jewelry as objects of adornment has always been regarded with special affection. Today prices for gems and gemstones crafted into antique and collectible jewelry are based on artistic merit, personal appeal, pure sentimentality, and intrinsic value. In general, diamond prices have gone up more than 20% in the past year, and platinum is becoming popular again, so retail prices are rising. Diamond prices vary greatly depending on cut, color, clarity, etc., and to assess the value of any diamond of more than a carat in weight, you will need to have information about all of these factors. Values given here are for diamond jewelry with a standard commercial grade of diamonds that are most likely to be encountered.

Our advisor for fine jewelry is Rebecca Dodds; her address may be found in the Directory under Florida. Marcia 'Sparkles' Brown is our advisor for costume jewelry and the author of *Unsigned Beauties of Costume Jewelry*; *Signed Beauties of Costume Jewelry, Books 1 and 2*; and *Coro Jewelry* (Collector Books); she is also the host of the videos *Hidden Treasures*. Mrs. Brown is listed in the Directory under Oregon. Other good references are *Collectible Costume Jewelry* by Cherri Simonds; *Costume Jewelry, A Practical Handbook & Value Guide*, and *Collectible Silver Jewelry* by Fred Rezazadeh; *100 Years of Collectible Jewelry*, *Fifty Years of Collectible Fashion Jewelry*, and *Plastic Jewelry of the 20th Century* by Lillian Baker; *Vintage Jewelry for Investment and Casual Wear* by Karen L. Edeen; *Painted Porcelain Jewelry and Buttons* by Dorothy Kamm; *Brilliant Rhinestones* by Ronna Lee Aikens; *Costume Jewelry 101* by Julia C. Carroll; and *Inside the Jewelry Box* by Ann Mitchell Pitman (all available from Collector Books). See also American Painted Porcelain; Hair Weaving.

Key:

B — Bakelite	g-t — gold-tone
C — Catalin	k — karat
ca — cellulose acetate	L — Lucite
cab — cabochon	lm — laminate
clu — celluloid	p — plastic
ct — carat	plat — platinum
dmn — diamond	r — resin
dwt — penny weight	r'stn — rhinestone
Euro — European cut	stn — stone
fl — filigree	t — thermoset
gf — gold filled	tw — total weight
gp — gold plated	wg — white gold
grad — graduated	yg — yellow gold
gw — gold washed	ygf — yellow gold filled

Bar pin, 10k yg fl, 3 lg garnets, 2½".................................225.00
Bracelet, bangle; Geo Jensen, silver fl rope, dainty, pr..................200.00
Bracelet, bangle; Kalo, silver w/spaced incised lines.................265.00
Bracelet, bangle; 14k yg, flower & leaf emb, ⅜" W.................250.00
Bracelet, bangle; 14k yg w/dbl heart ends & 30 sm dmns............250.00
Bracelet, Cartier, 18k yg bangle w/ribbed design, 1.5 oz, MIB.....880.00
Bracelet, cuff; Sam Piaso, 9 semi-precious cab stns.....................850.00
Bracelet, G Jensen, sterling, linked leaves, 7¾"..........................350.00
Bracelet, Napier, sterling silver links w/quilted pattern, 2½" W...300.00
Bracelet, plat, 47 full-cut dmns 2.50ct tw (VS/GHI)..............2,850.00
Bracelet, seed pearls, flexible, 6 rose dmns in clasp.....................425.00
Bracelet, Taxco, silver links of stylized petals.............................425.00
Bracelet, WMF, hand-hammered silver links, 7½".....................300.00
Bracelet, 14k pk gold, Deco style, 1¼" W, 37dwt.......................900.00
Bracelet, 14k wg, rock crystal & dmns .25ct tw..........................550.00
Bracelet, 14k yg w/enameled charm, 30.7 grams, 8" L...............335.00
Bracelet, 14k yg w/30 dmns 1ct tw...525.00
Bracelet & earrings, Kalo, hand-hammered sterling w/leaves & cherries....400.00
Brooch, Carence Crafters, nickeled silver w/etched flowers, 2⅝"...........175.00
Brooch, Carence Crafters, 2 cab coral stns in silver abstract, 1⅜".........650.00
Brooch, Geo Jensen, silver bimorphic form, 1½x1¾"................375.00
Brooch, Geo Jensen, silver stylized deer in oval fr, 1¾x1⅜".......225.00
Brooch, Geo Jensen, silver stylized flower w/3 triangle petals, 1⅝".....400.00
Brooch, James Wooley, silver, Nouveau flowers on rectangle, 2⅝".....440.00
Brooch, Kalo, hand-hammered sterling w/acorns/oak leaves, 2" W....400.00
Brooch, Peer Smed, silver foliage w/3 brass-washed leaves, 1933, 3"....400.00
Brooch, Peer Smed, silver oval w/textured blossom & leaves, 2½".....475.00
Brooch, shell cameo w/marcasites, antique gold rope fr, 1¾x1"..325.00
Brooch, wg w/6 7mm pearls & 30 seed pearls in circle................125.00
Brooch, 14k yg & rose coral, ca 1870, +matching earrings...........375.00
Brooch, 14k yg bow w/2.40ct aquamarine...............................325.00

Brooch, 14k yg Nouveau fl w/.5ct tw dmns & 5 natural pearls...350.00
Brooch, 14k yg w/.40ct dmn & 30 freshwater pearls...................350.00
Brooch/pendant, shell cameo, lady's profile, gold bezel, 1⅝".......450.00
Brooch/pendant, 14k rose gold, pierced lotus design w/2 red stns, 2"........175.00
Charm, 18k yg horseshoe w/coral & turq stones..........................90.00
Cross, 14k yg, 3 grams...55.00
Earrings, Modernist, copper/gold abstracts, 2" L.........................90.00
Earrings, Sam Kramer, sterling abstracts w/dangling elements, 3" W....50.00
Earrings, 14k yg drop style, ea w/1ct+ star ruby sapphires...........285.00
Earrings, 14k yg drop style, Fr hoop closure, 1890-1910.............145.00
Earrings, 14k yg w/1.5ct citrine..75.00
Lapel pin, 14k yg w/7.5ct oval cut amethyst..............................115.00
Locket, ygf, Egyptian princess & snake relief, 1¼".......................55.00
Necklace, Brandt Sterling, enameled scarab on link chain, 12½"......475.00
Necklace, cultured pearls, 1-strand, 48 7.5mm, yg glasp, 15"......450.00
Necklace, cultured pearls, 1-strand, 69 5-5.55mm, yg clasp.........165.00
Necklace, cultured pearls, 1-strand, 98 7mm, wg clasp, 30".......950.00
Necklace, cultured pearls, 2-strand, 20 5-5.5mm, wg clasp, 15"..265.00
Necklace, Taxco, silver stylized wave pattern, 15".....................150.00
Necklace, 14k yg choker styled as snake, 41.5dwt......................850.00
Necklace & earrings, Kalo, hand-hammered sterling w/floral design....1,500.00
Pendant, angel-skin coral cameo, 12k yg ornate fr, 1¼x1"..........350.00

Pendant, plique-a-jour crescent shape with multicolor enamels and half-pearl studs, enclosing a circular disk of similar decor, unmarked German silver, $1,000.00.

Pendant, 18k yg, lady in relief, floral border, dtd 1901...............485.00
Ring, Kalo, hand-hammered sterling w/cvd onyx stn, 1" W........375.00
Ring, Macefeld, 14k yg scarab w/lg bl prong-set stn.....................175.00
Ring, Oakes, 14k yg, multi-sz overlapping flowers w/dmn centers......2,700.00
Ring, palladium & 14k yg, 3 dmns, 1.58 tw............................1,875.00
Ring, plat, .25ct dmn, sm dmns at sides, ca 1935........................375.00
Ring, plat, 5ct aquamarine amid old Euro .25ct tw dmns.........1,325.00
Ring, plat & 14k yg, 2 Euro dmns 1.45ct tw+4 sm dmns tw .15cts..1,425.00
Ring, yg w/2 oval dmns .25ct ea..450.00
Ring, 10k wg leaf shape w/1 .12ct dmn & 12 .0075 melee dmns...125.00
Ring, 10k yg fl w/sm ruby..150.00
Ring, 14k wg, sapphire & sm dmns form flower...........................445.00
Ring, 14k wg fl, carnelian cameo of warrior...............................120.00
Ring, 14k wg w/lg angel-skin coral stn.......................................195.00
Ring, 14k wg w/3 Euro dmns 3.15ct tw (J/SI).......................9,200.00
Ring, 14k yg w/10ct tourmaline & 2 tiers of sm dmns.................265.00
Ring, 14k yg w/7.5mm cultured pearl...75.00
Ring, 18k wg w/.50ct old Euro dmn (GH/VS)........................1,100.00
Ring, 18k yg w/3 calibre-cut & 4 cab sapphires & 6 sm dmns....300.00

Costume Jewelry

Rhinestone jewelry is a very popular field of collecting. Rhinestones are foil-backed, leaded crystal, faceted stones with a sparkle outshining diamonds. Copyrighting jewelry came into effect in 1955. Pieces bearing a copyright mark (post-1955) are considered 'collectibles,' while pieces (with no copyright) made before then are regarded as 'antiques.' Fur clips are two-pronged, used to anchor fur stoles. Dress clips have a spring clasp and are used at the dress neckline. Look for signed and well-made, unmarked pieces for your collections and preserve this American art form. Our advisor for costume jewelry is Marcia Brown (see introductory paragraphs for information on her books and videos).

Bracelet, Eisenberg, dbl-row w/clear chatons, 2-chaton bars between ...110.00
Bracelet, Hobè, faux jade cab w/gp leaves 75.00
Bracelet, Joseff of Hollywood, fuchsia glass stns amid silver chains....280.00
Bracelet, KJ Lane, Good-Luck dragon w/enameling/faux turq/r'stns ...110.00
Bracelet, Renoir, copper 'good health' type 38.00
Bracelet, unsgn, clear hand-set r'stn in single strand.......................18.00
Bracelet, unsgn, elastic w/blk plastic segments w/clear r'stn studs....65.00
Bracelet, unsgn, mc pastel r'stn sqs (5), g-t clasp..........................95.00
Bracelet, unsgn, multi-shaped lav r'stns allover hinged cuff...........75.00
Bracelet, unsgn, pearl & topaz r'stns in single strand 30.00
Bracelet, unsgn, yel cabs amid mc r'stns on japanned finish 35.00
Brooch, Barclay, gp anchor w/gold r'stns & gp rope 65.00
Brooch, Boucher, tropical fish, blk/wht/yel/gold enamel................68.00
Brooch, Boucher, 3 pavé r'stn flowers w/bl moonstone centers 95.00
Brooch, BSK, gp veined leaves w/diamanté pavé center, long, slim......48.00
Brooch, Capri, SP leaf filled w/diamanté r'stns 55.00
Brooch, Doddz, flower w/red r'stn petals & gr navette leaves on stem..50.00
Brooch, Eisenberg, Christmsas tree w/mc r'stns on g-t 85.00
Brooch, Eisenberg, diamanté r'stn ribbon, 3½" 475.00
Brooch, Eisenberg, pavé r'stns in SP Nouveau floral bouquet 275.00
Brooch, Florenza, gold basketweave w/bl baguettes........................80.00
Brooch, Hobè, sterling silver bow w/lav crystal flower center 425.00
Brooch, Hollycraft, butterfly, bl/lav r'stns/pearls/opalene cabs.....125.00
Brooch, Hollycraft, Christmas tree, mc r'stns on gold....................80.00
Brooch, Hollycraft, golden r'stn spray..65.00
Brooch, JJ, gp butterfly w/openwork & enameling.........................35.00
Brooch, JJ, SP striped climbing cat 22.00
Brooch, KJ Lane, pk & bl enameled turtle w/jewel eyes...............110.00
Brooch, Kramer, gold bird w/seed pearl body...............................58.00
Brooch, Lisner, enamel bl flower w/r'stn center & 3 sm pearls......65.00
Brooch, Mazer Bros, enamel peacock w/mc r'stns 225.00
Brooch, Sandor, wht enamel daisy w/gr leaves 62.00
Brooch, Schiaparelli, gold & brn r'stns, 3 drops...........................195.00
Brooch, Star Novelty, clear emerald-cut r'stns form nosegay.......290.00
Brooch, Trifari, faux ruby & diamanté r'stn bouquet 325.00
Brooch, Trifari, gold spider w/clear jelly belly 575.00
Brooch, Trifari, wht enameled owl w/cab eyes 130.00
Brooch, unsgn, bl r'stns w/in gold flower border w/sm r'stn centers 50.00
Brooch, unsgn, chaton r'stn snowflake, very lg...............................55.00
Brooch, unsgn, pk r'stns in gp fr, lg...75.00
Brooch, unsgn, yel enamel ribbon w/gold trim 22.00
Brooch, unsgn Austria, mc r'stn floral nosegay..............................85.00
Brooch, Weiss, gold r'stn sun...85.00
Brooch, Weiss, pale gr & yel Peking glass stns form flowers 85.00
Brooch, Weiss, pk r'stns in gold fr..75.00
Brooch & earrings, Art, aurora borealis & pk navette apples........85.00
Brooch & earrings, Emmons, gp sunbursts w/faux pearls 45.00
Brooch & earrings, Hattie Carnegie, tourmaline crescents 275.00
Brooch & earrings, Judy Lee, silver leaves w/aurora borealis r'stns...48.00
Brooch & earrings, Kramer, blk net over smoky r'stns..................180.00
Brooch & earrings, La Roco, gold & orange snowflake forms 80.00

Brooch & earrings, La Roco, purple/purple/pk/aurora borealis r'stns...145.00
Brooch & earrings, Lisner, gp flowers w/pk aurora borealis r'stns ..68.00
Brooch & earrings, Marvella, gp stars w/pearl centers 54.00
Brooch & earrings, Robert de Mario, faux pearls/r'stns/gold leaves....195.00
Brooch & earrings, Robert Originals, pk pearls/clear & pk r'stns...195.00
Brooch & earrings, S Coventry, enameled dogwood blossoms.......75.00
Brooch & earrings, Schriner, frosted pk/wht cab & pk r'stns.......195.00
Brooch & earrings, Trifari, SP swirling circle, matt & shiny 55.00
Earrings, Robert de Mario, crystal beads/bl balls/pearls/gold flowers 75.00
Earrings, Robert Originals, faux pearls/pk & bl r'stns/bead drops ..90.00
Earrings, unsgn, aurora borealis r'stn cluster 38.00
Earrings, unsgn, clear r'stn studs w/clear drops & honey-colored cabs ...18.00
Earrings, unsgn, gold chandelier w/spirals & crystal bead dangles 35.00
Earrings, unsgn, orange r'stns drip down onto dangle w/3 gr navettes...24.00
Fur clip, Boucher, sapphire bl r'stns on gp 145.00
Fur clip, unsgn, faceted irid r'stns & topaz baguettes spray 300.00
Fur clip & earrings, Mazer Bros, gp w/aquamarine crystals 280.00
Necklace, Castlecliff, Chinese characters on chain, SP, 14".........90.00
Necklace, Christian Dior, lg dk bl crystal in r'stn fr, gp chain.....295.00
Necklace, E Taylor/Avon, gp cross w/gr & ruby cabs/faux pearls.145.00
Necklace, Hattie Carnegie, 20 strands of crystal beads................130.00
Necklace, KJ Lane, enamel & gp elephant pendant w/r'stns.......110.00
Necklace, Les Bernard, 3 strands of metallic pearls.......................65.00
Necklace, Lisner, pk enamel link chains (2) 30.00
Necklace, Miriam Haskell, crystal beads w/silver turban spacers...85.00
Necklace, Monet, gold beads in dbl strand....................................55.00
Necklace, Napier, gp leaves & citrine r'stns, articulated................95.00
Necklace, Sandor, japanned w/diamanté r'stn flowers & baguettes strand.....90.00
Necklace, Tortolani, gp turtle pendant on chain 150.00
Necklace, unsgn, cameo amid row of faux pearls & row of blk beads ...38.00
Necklace, unsgn, dk gr hand-set chaton r'stns................................58.00
Necklace, unsgn, g-t Nouveau leaves w/faux pearl drops...............60.00
Necklace, unsgn, gr & gold beads on short chains on main chain...48.00
Necklace, unsgn, 2 strands of pearls w/pavé r'stn clasp 48.00
Necklace, Venetian beads w/embedded foils/roses/etc, 28".........115.00
Necklace, Weiss, diamanté r'stn bib style.....................................275.00
Necklace & bracelet, Florenza, frosted glass navettes & mc r'stns........150.00
Necklace & bracelet, unsgn, silver-bl beads w/dangling bl chatons.......98.00
Necklace & earrings, glass cabs w/gold veins & topaz r'stns.........115.00
Necklace & earrings, Kramer, aurora borealis r'stns.....................140.00
Necklace & earrings, Miriam Haskell, pk multi-strand bead garlands ...425.00
Necklace & earrings, Schiaparelli, 3-strand, bl & gr beads 190.00
Necklace & earrings, Trifari, 6-strand, gr beads & crystals 80.00
Necklace & earrings, unsgn, silver-tone leaf garland w/bl r'stns....22.00
Necklace & earrings, unsgn, 3-strand aurora borealis beads 95.00
Parure, Trifari, SP leaves form links, 3-pc...................................205.00
Ring, opalene clusters on gp..45.00
Ring, tiger-eye cab w/in clear r'stn circle 45.00
Ring, unsgn, gp dome w/red r'stns...28.00
Ring, unsgn, gp sq filled w/opalene chatons 38.00

Plastic Jewelry

Back comb, clu, intricate cvg, w/rows of r'stns, Art Nouveau, 1925 ...150.00
Belt, clu, 3 8-sided butterscotch sections w/appl blk sqs+others+chain....150.00
Bracelet, B, 5 bk-cvd lt & amber & blk rnd links, 1935.............250.00
Bracelet, bangle; B, tortoise w/inset copper Oriental-motif disks, '50 ...85.00
Bracelet, bangle; Bakelite, butterscotch, cvd, 1935, from $75 to..100.00
Bracelet, bangle; L, teal bl pearlized, 1950s, from $35 to...............45.00
Bracelet, bangle; L, wht w/scattered r'stns, 1935, from $75 to.......85.00
Bracelet, bangle; Lea Stein, ca/lm, red/wht blk w/ellipses, 1960-80 ....250.00
Bracelet, BSK, silver leaves form links w/bl baguette r'stns 45.00
Bracelet, cuff; B, cvd floral openwork, butterscotch, very wide, 1935.......500.00
Bracelet, cuff; clu belt-buckle shape, wht w/red stars & anchor, 1930s..300.00

Bracelet, hinged; p, wht w/aurora borealis r'stns, 1960, from $85 to.**125.00**
Bracelet, t/p cabs, 2 in ea of 5 metal links, Charel, from $45 to...**55.00**
Bracelet, wrap-around; p, tortoise brn fish w/r'stn eyes, 1935 ....**35.00**
Brooch, B, cvd/pnt sombrero w/attached mc glass beads, 1935, rare......**500.00**
Brooch, B, head of horse, metal studs/chain, glass eye, from $250 to.....**350.00**
Brooch, B, lg cvd flower, red, 1953, from $175 to.......................**250.00**
Brooch, B, lg cvd orange frog on brass plate, 1930, from $300 to.....**350.00**
Brooch, B, red heart w/dangling berries, p-covered cord twigs, 1935..**250.00**
Brooch, B, Scottie dog, gr w/pnt features, 1935, from $95 to......**125.00**
Brooch, B oval fr cvd front/bk, molded p cameo center, 1930, lg..**100.00**
Brooch, C, horse head w/metal bridle & glass eye, overdyed, 1937 ....**300.00**
Brooch, C, pear, caramel, cvd w/HP details, 1936-51, from $250 to......**350.00**
Brooch, C, scimitar, caramel w/clear brn cvd hdl, brass chains/studs ..**300.00**
Brooch, Hattie Carnegie, B, rooster, red/blk/yel w/metal accents.....**500.00**
Brooch, Lea Stein, ca/lm fox, built up in layers, 1960-80............**150.00**
Brooch, p, bird in flight, scratched-cvd purple w/r'stn eye, 1935...**65.00**
Brooch, p, lady's hand w/red nails, ring & bracelet, r'stn accents ..**125.00**
Brooch, p, written-out name, 1940, from $15 to.......................**25.00**
Buckle, B, butterscotch disk w/long slim appl gr/orange/brn triangles ...**225.00**
Buckle, B, transparent butterscotch w/cvd-out leaves & r'stns, 1-pc **45.00**
Buckle, B, 2 pcs, pleats/folds radiate from center, butterscotch/blk **100.00**
Buckle, clu, 2 rnded pcs w/1 str side, relief/HP fruit on bl, 1920 ....**135.00**
Buckle, p, 2-D facing elephant forms, amber w/brn marbling, 1935, lg....**75.00**
Comb, clu w/row of r'stns across top, very simple, 1950, from $10 to ...**15.00**
Dress clips, B, deeply cvd flower/leaf shape, 1935, pr....................**75.00**
Earrings, B, flat-cut/triangular drops, yel, 1935, from $55 to **75.00**
Earrings, B red hoop shapes, 1940s, lg, from $45 to **55.00**
Earrings, L, lg red teardrop shapes, 1960, from $35 to **55.00**
Earrings, Lisner, t/p autumn leaves (2 in ea), 1935, from $35 to...**55.00**
Earrings, Missoni (Italian), r, red buttons w/chrome center, 1980 .....**150.00**
Earrings, p, lav/wht flowers w/r'stn center, lg...........................**15.00**
Earrings, p, red, tassel drops, 1940s, from $55 to **65.00**
Earrings, p, red button style w/scattered r'stns, 1935 ....**50.00**
Earrings, p, yel flowers held by r'stn center.............................**14.00**
Eyeglasses, clu, blk w/twisted accents & r'stn flowers, 1950 ....**150.00**
Hat ornament, clu, r, L, & t/p varieties, r'stn accents, 2-pc, ea **30.00**
Necklace, B, beads w/brass bead spacers, 27" **110.00**
Necklace, clu, pk chain w/flower & leaf 'charms,' 3 w/attached beads..**75.00**
Necklace, clu red chain w/various mc fruit & leaf 'charms,' 1935.......**795.00**
Necklace, Encore, L, 3 lg sq beads center sm rnd beads, clear, 1970....**85.00**
Parure, Hobè, p, 3-strand red beads...**135.00**
Ring, B, cvd flower dome, brn marbled, 1935, from $85 to.........**100.00**

Johnson Brothers

A Staffordshire-based company operating since well before the turn of the century, Johnson Brothers has produced many familiar lines of dinnerware, several of which are very collectible. Some of their patterns were made in both blue and pink transfer as well as in polychrome.

Some of their older patterns are still being produced. Among them are Old Britain Castles, Friendly Village, His Magesty, and Rose Chintz. However, the lines are less extensive than they once were.

Values below range from a low base price for patterns that are still in production or less collectible to a high that would apply to very desirable patterns such as Tally Ho, English Chippendale, Wild Turkeys, Strawberry Fair, Historic America, Harvest Fruit, etc. Mid-range lines include Coaching Scenes, Millsteam, Old English Countryside, Rose Bouquet (and there are others). These prices apply only to pieces made before 1990. Look for a crown in the backstamp, which the newer production does not have. Lines currently being produced are being sold in many retail and outlet stores today at prices that are quite different from the ones we suggest. While a complete place setting of Old Britain Castles is normally about $50.00, in some outlets you can purchase it for as little as half price.

For more information on marks, patterns, and pricing, we recommend *Johnson Brothers Dinnerware Pattern Directory and Price Guide* by Mary J. Finegan, who is listed in the Directory under North Carolina.

Bowl, cereal/soup; rnd, sq or lug, ea, from $10 to...........................**15.00**
Bowl, soup; rnd or sq, 7", from $12 to................................**16.00**
Bowl, vegetable; oval, from $30 to upwards of **40.00**
Chop/cake plate, from $50 to...**70.00**
Coffee mug, from $20 to upwards of **25.00**
Coffeepot, from $90 to upwards of................................**100.00**
Covered butter dish, from $50 to.......................................**60.00**
Demitasse set, 2-pc, from $20 to..**24.00**
Egg cup, from $15 to...**20.00**
Pitcher/jug, from $45 to upwards of **55.00**
Plate, dinner; from $14 to **25.00**
Plate, salad; sq or rnd, from $10 to upwards of **18.00**

Friendly Village platter, 13¾x11¼", from $45.00 to $50.00.

Sauce boat/gravy, from $40 to upwards of.....................................**48.00**
Shakers, pr, from $40 to **48.00**
Sugar bowl, open, from $30 to **35.00**
Teacup & saucer, from $15 to **24.00**
Teapot, from $90 to upwards of...**100.00**
Turkey platter, 20½", from $200 to upwards of **300.00**

Josef Originals

Figurines of lovely ladies, charming girls, and whimsical animals marked Josef Originals were designed by Muriel Joseph George of Arcadia, California, from 1945 to 1985. Until 1960 they were produced in California, but costs were high and copies of her work were being made in Japan. To remain competitive, she and her partner, George Good, found a company in Japan to build a factory and produce her designs to her specifications. Muriel retired in 1982; however, Mr. Good continued production of her work and made some design changes on some figurines. The company was sold in late 1985; the name is currently owned by Dakin/Applause, and a limited amount of figurines with the Josef Originals name are being made. Those made during the ownership of Muriel are the most collectible. They can be recognized by these characteristics: The girls have a high-gloss finish, black eyes, and most are signed on the bottom. As of the late 1970s, bisque finish was making its way into the lineup, and by 1980 glossy girls were fairly scarce in the product line. Brown-eyed figurines date from 1982 through 1985. Applause uses a red-brown eye, although they are starting to release 'copies' of early pieces that are signed Josef Originals by Applause or by Dakin. The animals were nearly always done in a matt finish and bore paper labels only. In the mid-1970s they introduced a line of fuzzy flocked-coat animals with glass eyes. Our advisors, Jim and Kaye Whitaker (see the Directory under Washington, no appraisal requests please) have written three books: *Josef Originals, Charming Figurines, Revised Edition; Josef Originals, A Second Look;* and *Josef Originals, Figurines of Muriel Joseph George*. These are all currently available, and each has no repeats of items shown in the other books. Please note: All figurines listed here have black eyes unless specified otherwise. As with many collectibles, values have been negatively impacted to a measurable extent since the advent of the Internet.

Birthday Girls, 1-16, Japan, 7", ea.......................................**25.00**
Birthstone Dolls, Jan to Dec, Japan, very common, 3½", ea **12.00**
Christmas music box angel, Japan, 7" **35.00**
Doll of the Month (tilt head), California, 3¼", ea **35.00**
Elephant, sitting, Japan, 3¾" **15.00**
Engagement, Romance Series, Japan, 8"..................................**75.00**
Hunter, beautiful standing horse, Japan, 6" **25.00**
It's a Wonderful World Series, Japan, 3½", ea........................**25.00**
Kennel Club Series, Poodle, etc, Japan, 4", ea **15.00**
Little Internat'l Series, America, Africa, etc, Japan, 4", ea, $25 to....**35.00**
Louise, White Colonial Days Series (6, varied colors), Japan, 9", ea.....**75.00**
Make Believe series, Japan, 4½", ea..................................**35.00**
Mama Ballerina, California, 7" **55.00**
Mary Ann & Mama, various styles, California, 4" & 7", pr...........**75.00**
Mice, various designs & Christmas, Japan, 2¾", ea **10.00**
Monkeys Mama & Papa, Japan, 3" **15.00**
Music box, Romance Couple, Love Me Tender song, Japan, 6" **55.00**
Nanette, several colors, half doll w/jewels, California, 5½"...........**45.00**
Nurse, Career Girls Series, in yel holding baby, Japan, 5¾" **50.00**
Nursery Rhyme Series, Miss Mary, Jill, etc, Japan, 4", ea.............**35.00**
Pixies, various poses, gr w/red & gold trim, Japan, 2-3¼", ea........**30.00**
Rose Garden Series, brn eyes, 6 different, Japan, 5¼", ea..............**40.00**
Small World Series, Hawaii, Japan, etc, brn eyes, Japan, 4½", ea **25.00**
Story Angel Series, holding star, bubble pipe, etc, Japan, 5½", ea **40.00**
Wee Ching & Wee Ling, boy w/dog, girl w/cat, often copied, California...**45.00**
Wee Folk, various poses, Japan, 4½", ea...............................**15.00**
World Greatest Series, bowler, boxer, hunter, Japan, 4½", ea **15.00**
Zodiac Series, various colors, California, 3½" **25.00**

Judaica

The items listed below are representative of objects used in both the secular and religious life of the Jewish people. They are evident of a culture where silversmiths, painters, engravers, writers, and metal workers were highly gifted and skilled in their art. Most of the treasures shown in recently displayed exhibits of Judaica were confiscated by the Germans during the late 1930s up to 1945; by then eight Jewish synagogues and fifty warehouses had been filled with Hitler's plunder. Judaica is currently available through dealers, from private collections, and the annual auction held in Israel, New York City, and Boston.

Box, vanity; porc w/emb gilt Star of David, ftd, unmk...................**50.00**
Charity container, Hevra Kadisha, blk letters on copper, Boston, 1900s ..**600.00**
Charity container, Russian silver, well form w/domed lid, ca 1895 .....**3,500.00**
Chasma (Hand of Fatima), Middle Eastern metal, old patina, 2⅝" **125.00**
Earrings, Fr gold, Star of David design, 19th C, pr......................**350.00**
Etrog box, German silver, oval w/foliage/scrollwork, inscr lid, 5¾"....**1,000.00**
Etrog box, Russian silver, fruit w/branch finial, 1790s.............**6,000.00**
Hanukkah lamp, Austro-Hungarian silver, peacock form, ca 1900.**10,000.00**
Hanukkah lamp, German silver, scrolled arm, hexagon, early 1900s ..**300.00**
Hanukkah lamp, Israeli, verdrigris patina, mid-20th C **300.00**
Honey pot for Rosh Hashana, Hazorfim 925 silver w/glass, 4⅛" dia ...**150.00**
Kiddush cup, Dutch silver, Hebrew inscription, 1927, 3½".........**800.00**
Kiddush cup, German silver, Remember the Sabbath, early 20th C ..**1,750.00**
Kiddush cup, Russian silver, beaker form w/flared rim, 1860s......**700.00**

Lithograph, Safed village scene, Stematsky, ca 1928, in 38x24½" fr ..**1,200.00**
Menorah, Modernist design, brass, 1920s.....................................**300.00**
Menorah pin, marquise rhinestones & silver enameling, 1½" W..**75.00**
Mezzusah case, Palestine silver, Star of David, pre-1948, 2⅝"....**200.00**
Paperweight, Star of David, Whitefriars, 1978 ltd ed, 3".............**395.00**
Passover plate, Israeli silver, wavy border/oval cartouches, 13" ...**500.00**
Sabbath candlesticks, Russian silver, baroque style, ca 1800, 11⅝", pr..**3,000.00**
Spice box, Polish brass, arched ft, 6-sided, early 1800s, 8" **300.00**
Spice container, Polish silver, tower form, mk 833, late 19th C...**800.00**
Spice tower, German silver w/much filigree, Berlin, late 1800s ..**350.00**
Spoon, Bezalel silver & silver filigree, Jerusalem, early 20th C ...**700.00**
Spoon, SP, Birth of Israel commemorative, baby's face/Israel, 1948....**38.00**

Spice tower, Russian gilt over silver, openwork windows, hinged door, clock with arms above each panel, faceted stem, domed base, early twentieth century, 16", $2,875.00. (Photo courtesy Phillips International Auctioneers and Valuers)

Tankard, London silver, Hebrew inscription, leaf-molded scrolls, 1760s ..**1,500.00**
Tfillin bag, hand-embr blk velvet, ca 1940-50s, 6¼x7⅛"..............**45.00**
Tfillin bag, hand-embr velvet, Bezalel era, 6x8" **75.00**
Torah breastplate, Am Sterling silver, early 20th C.....................**400.00**
Torah curtain, embr velvet w/lion/foliage/Hebrew, Europe, 19th C.......**2,500.00**
Torah finials, Moroccan silver, pointed knop, ca 1900, pr...........**600.00**
Torah mantle, Palestine, hand embr, Bezalel era, pre-1940, 30½" L...**500.00**
Torah pointer, Chas T & Geo Fox, silver/silver gilt, cast foliage **2,250.00**
Torah pointer, Russian silver, Moscow mk, leaf design, 1865, 12½" ...**925.00**
Torah shield, silver gilt, London (mk AT), ca 1937 ....**1,250.00**

Jugtown

The Jugtown Pottery was started about 1920 by Juliana and Jacques Busbee, in Moore County, North Carolina. Ben Owen, a young descendant of a Staffordshire potter, was hired in 1923. He was the master potter, while the Busbees experimented with perfecting glazes and supervising design and modeling. Preferred shapes were those reminiscent of traditional country wares and classic Oriental forms. Glazes were various: natural-clay oranges, buffs, Tobacco-spit Brown, Mirror Black, white, Frog Skin Green, a lovely turquoise called Chinese Blue, and the traditional cobalt-decorated salt glaze. The pottery gained national recognition, and as a result of their success, several other local potteries were established. The pottery closed for a time in the late 1950s due to the ill health of Mrs. Busbee (who had directed the business after her husband died in 1947) but reopened in 1960. Jugtown is still in operation; however, they no longer use their original glaze colors which are now so collectible and the circular mark is slightly smaller than the original.

Bowl, Oxblood & Chinese Blue, low, ftd, 4¼" 200.00
Vase, bud; Chinese Blue, beaker shape, 3½x3½", EX.................225.00
Vase, Chinese Blue, tapered form w/flared lip, 3½" 200.00
Vase, Chinese Blue at top over gray, waisted cylinder, 7" 425.00
Vase, Chinese Blue over dk brn, bulbous, 5½".........................325.00
Vase, Frog Skin, flared rim, bulbous, sm appl hdls, 10".............600.00
Vase, multi-tone brn matt, incised/appl shoulder decor, 7" 425.00

K. P. M. Porcelain

The original KPM wares were produced from 1823 until 1847 by the Konigliche Porzellan Manfaktur, located in Berlin, Germany. Meissen used the same letters on some of their porcelains, as did several others in the area. The mark contains the initials KPM. Watch for items currently being imported from China; they are marked KPM with the eagle but the scepter is not present. Our advisor for this category is Don Williams; he is listed in the Directory under Missouri.

Charger, floral decor w/basketweave border, gold rim, 13" dia 400.00
Cup, chocolate; brunette reclining in boudoir, mid-1800s, ovoid, 5"..475.00
Cup & saucer, cobalt w/HP floral cartouch on wht 145.00
Cup & saucer, turq w/wide gold band, castle scene inside cup ...1,560.00
Figurine, bear, bl, seated, #140/237, 7½".................................400.00
Figurine, boy seated w/basket of grapes, #140/352, 6" 265.00
Figurine, Venus & Cupid w/rtcl basket of grapes, ram at side, 7¼x9"....600.00
Pitcher, syrup; floral on wht w/pk bottom, pewter lid, 4x4¾" 160.00
Plaque, Aurori after Reni, sgn Knoeller, 8x13" in ornate giltwood fr..10,635.00

Plaque, Christ teaching in the temple, signed, 10x15", $7,280.00. (Photo courtesy Jackson's Auctioneers & Appraisers of Fine Art)

Plaque, couple in swing in woodland scene, late 1800s, 15⅜x9⅝"......16,450.00
Plaque, draped beauty among mtn peaks, #237/#158, 8¾x6" ..1,400.00
Plaque, Elder Student, monk sewing beside girl, 9¼x7"+16x14" fr 2,500.00
Plaque, lady feeding birds, 13x7¾".......................................6,500.00
Plaque, Madonna in ¾-profile bust, 10¼"+21x19" gilt fr 1,400.00
Plaque, maid w/ivy crown, gauzy rose robe, Wagner, 11x9"+matt/fr..4,150.00
Plaque, Ruth carrying wheat, FB Dresden, 6x9"+gesso fr 3,000.00
Plaque, Ruth w/sheaf of wheat, R Tittrich, 18x½x11"+25x17" fr...6,000.00
Plaque, seminude in red velvet chair, sgn Piot, 6x8" +gesso fr 2,000.00
Plaque, Spring Time, lady in pasture w/butterfly, #237/258, 21x20"...3,000.00
Plaque, young lady w/flute, oval, 9x6⅝" 2,500.00
Plaque, young people on mountainside, 7½x9⅞".....................3,500.00
Plaque, youth (bust only) w/Turkish scarf, 7¼x4¾" 2,000.00
Plate, floral on wht w/butterfly, pierced edge, #6/60, 9½" 130.00
Tea set, flower bouquet decor, pot+4 c/s.....................................410.00
Umbrella hdl, angel w/wreath & cupid w/bow, cobalt & gold, 5⅞"....315.00

Vase, floral w/gold swags, ca 1900-1920, 13"...........................1,200.00
Vase, wht ovoid urn form w/gilt rim & scrolled hdls, ftd, 38" ..2,500.00

Kayserzinn Pewter

J.P. Kayser Sohn produced pewter decorated with relief-molded Art Nouveau motifs in Germany during the late 1800s and into the twentieth century. Examples are marked with 'Kayserzinn' and the mold number within an elongated oval reserve. Items with three-dimensional animals, insects, birds, etc., are valued much higher than bowls, plates, and trays with simple embossed florals, which are usually priced at $100.00 to about $200.00, depending on size.

Basket, emb floral, Xd hdls w/flower bud finial, 9x11½" 350.00
Bell, cat finial, stylized floral body, 6"......................................600.00
Candlesticks, floral relief, invt trumpet form, #4328, 10", pr 135.00
Inkwell, leaf form w/emb bees, no insert 325.00
Tray, lg fish relief, aquatic life in border, #4325, 24" L 450.00
Tureen, flowers/insects relief on body & lid, ftd, #4121, 10x12"....415.00
Vase, bleeding hearts, 3 pierced openings, rnd shoulders, 9" 200.00
Vase, fox & grapes emb on sides, hdls, EX patina, 12" 900.00

Keeler, Brad

Keeler studied art for a time in the 1930s; later he became a modeler for a Los Angeles firm. By 1939 he was working in his own studio where he created naturalistic studies of birds and animals which were marketed through giftware stores. They were decorated by means of an airbrush and enhanced with hand-painted details. His flamingo figures were particularly popular. In the mid-'40s, he developed a successful line of Chinese Modern housewares glazed in Ming Dragon Blood, a red color he personally developed. Keeler died of a heart attack in 1952, and the pottery closed soon thereafter. For more information, we recommend *The Collector's Encyclopedia of California Pottery, Second Edition,* by Jack Chipman (Collector Books).

Box, Dragon Blood, man at cart etched in lid, 4x5½" 65.00
Candy dish, red rose-like bowl on gr leaf-like ped, 3½x5½" dia ...55.00
Charger, emb fish decor, #141, 11"...150.00
Creamer & sugar bowl w/lid, fish shape, #147 & #148................250.00
Figurine, bird, rose colored, #18, 8¼", from $40 to.......................60.00
Figurine, bird, rose colored, #710, 5", from $30 to 40.00
Figurine, bird on branch, rose colored, #17, 6", from $40 to 60.00
Figurine, blk cat, playing on bk, #779, 3½x7", from $45 to 55.00
Figurine, bluebird, #19, 9½", form $40 to.....................................45.00
Figurine, cardinal, #19, 9½", from $40 to.....................................45.00
Figurine, cockatoo, w/wings up, #30, 10¾", from $80 to 90.00
Figurine, cocker spaniel puppy, sitting up, #748, 4½", from $35 to 40.00
Figurine, fawn, laying down, #879, 3", from $15 to........................25.00
Figurine, flamingo, #1, head up, 12", from $135 to......................165.00
Figurine, flamingo, #3, head down, 7¼", from $75 to...................100.00
Figurine, flamingo, #39, head down, 8½", from $100 to..............125.00
Figurine, hen pheasant, #21, 6½", from $45 to...........................60.00
Figurine, mallard hen, #50, 5x6"..55.00
Figurine, peacock, #703, 13½"...150.00
Figurine, Red Tanager, #27, 5¼", from $35 to...............................45.00
Figurine, rooster, #744, 6¼" 40.00
Figurine, Siamese cat, #798, 7", from $40 to 55.00
Figurine, tabby cat, #923, 8", from $45 to 55.00
Plate, gr leaf shape w/lobster claw, #891, 9x9", from $30 to 38.00
Plate, gr lettuce leaf w/lobster in center, #867, 3-part, 9x12" 80.00
Platter, gr lettuce leaf, lobster centers 2 parts, #698, 17x15" 185.00

Platter, shell shape w/crab, #284, 11¾x10½" **75.00**
Serving dishes, fish shape, #151, 2¼x8", set of 4, from $120 to..**140.00**

Keen Kutter

Keen Kutter was the brand name chosen in 1870 by the Simmons Firm for a line of high-grade tools and cutlery. The trademark was first applied to high-grade axes. A corporation was formed in 1874 called Simmons Hardware Company. In 1922 Winchester merged with Simmons and continued to carry a full line of hardware plus the Winchester brand. The merger terminated in March of 1929 and converted back to the original status of Simmons Hardware Co. It wasn't until July 1, 1940, that Simmons Hardware Co. was purchased by Shapleigh Hardware Company. All Simmons Hardware Co. trademark lines were continued, and the business operated successfully until its closing in 1962. Today the Keen Kutter logo is owned by the Val-Test Company of Chicago, Illinois. For further study we recommend *Collector's Guide to E. C. Simmons Keen Kutter Cutlery Tools*, an illustrated price guide by our advisors for this category, Jerry and Elaine Heuring, available at your favorite bookstore or public library. The Heurings are listed in the Directory under Missouri. See also Knives.

Axe, broad; Bob Taylor Canada pattern, EC Simmons, 12" cutting edge ...**200.00**
Axe, fireman's; lg logo, 12½" **475.00**
Axe box, for 4½-lb hollow bevel axe head, sliding top, 2x9½x6" **175.00**
Bit brace, KBB14, sweep, ratchet, 14" **45.00**
Bits, electrician's or bell hangers; sz 16, 12, 10, 8 or 6, ea.............**12.00**
Book, How To Read a Keen Kutter Square, from $50 to **75.00**
Calendar, tin, pad type w/store name & location, from $75 to ...**125.00**
Calendar, 1929, boy w/gun, dog & sheep, complete, 16½x10", EX....**60.00**
Calendar, 1950, The Future Champion....................................**175.00**
Case, salesman's sample; 15x14x8½" **125.00**
Catalog, Shapleigh, 1957, 30 sections, red leather cover w/hdls **475.00**
Chisel, butt; tanged beveled edge w/rosewood hdls, 3 szs, ea, $50 to **75.00**
Chisel, socket firmer; beveled edge, 4 szs, ea from $10 to..............**20.00**
Clock, plastic, Shapleigh's, 10" dia **350.00**
Corkscrew, 3 styles, ea from $35 to **45.00**
Dental snips, K11D, 7½", from $15 to...**20.00**
Dividers, 67", 7", 8", 10", ea..**45.00**
Drill, electric; KK200,¼"..**50.00**
File, bastard; sq or rnd, 14", ea from $12 to **18.00**
Hammer, ball-pein; EC Simmons, 32-oz.......................................**85.00**
Hammer, bill-poster's; K55 ....**50.00**
Hammer, blacksmith's/riveter's; str-pein, from $100 to **125.00**
Hammer, tack; magnetic...**35.00**
Hatchet, claw; w/label, M **275.00**
Hatchet, EC Simmons flooring; w/nail slot **55.00**
Hatchet, Keen Kutter & Boy Scout logos **100.00**
Hatchet, poll claw; plain **45.00**
Knife, ham slicing; K52, 10" blade, from $20 to **25.00**
Knife, lunch slicer; K33, 8" blade, from $15 to **20.00**
Level, F3-753GK, Shapleigh, non-adjustable, 12", from $50 to **75.00**
Level, KK30, adjustable, brass tip, Pat 12/20/04, 30", from $75 to......**100.00**
Level, K624, CI, 24", from $175 to..**225.00**
Level, mason's; KK25, adjustable, brass button w/logo, from $65 to **95.00**
Marking gauge, wooden, K25 ....**40.00**
Miter box, complete w/saw, from $275 to...................................**350.00**
Pencil, carpenter's; K108, unsharpened **25.00**
Plane, carriage maker's rabbet; KK10, from $200 to **250.00**
Plane, corrugated, mk KK No 5 ....**75.00**
Plane, K31, wooden bottom, 24", from $65 to **85.00**
Plane, scrub; K240, from $150 to..**200.00**

Pliers, combination; K51, center cutters, 10", 8" or 6", ea, $25 to........**35.00**
Pliers, pistol grip; KK7, mk Pat Applied For Shapleigh..., $125 to **175.00**
Pliers, rnd nose, 5¼", from $30 to **40.00**
Pliers, slip joint; K160, from $20 to **30.00**
Plumb bob, hexagonal, 6-oz or 7-oz, ea.....................................**65.00**
Pot fork, K8101, cocobola hdl, from $35 ....**50.00**
Rule, zig-zag; K603, 36" 6-fold, yel enamel, from $175 to **250.00**
Saw, coping; K50, heavy pattern w/logo, from $20 to....................**30.00**
Saw, hack; K188A, adjustable 8-12", from $35 to **45.00**
Saw, hand; EC Simmons #88, fancy flags & writing on 22" blade, $75 to...**125.00**
Saw, 1-man cross-cut; #309, emblem on blade, from $150 to......**200.00**
Saw clamp, folding pattern, 3x12", from $75 to...........................**100.00**
Scissors, embroidery; fancy, 3½", from $35 to **50.00**
Scissors, stork pattern, 4", from $175 to **225.00**
Screwdriver, for sewing machine, from $75 to............................**35.00**
Screwdriver, mk Special, 4", from $40 to....................................**50.00**
Screwdriver, off-set; K7, 6¾", from $65 to **50.00**
Screwdriver, wood hdl w/brass ferrule, 2½-9", ea from $30 to.......**40.00**
Shears, barber's; 7" **15.00**
Shears, mule; 10½", from $20 to...**30.00**
Shipping tape, role, mk Keen Kutter, from $75 to **80.00**
Sign, advertising store & location, tin, 9¾x27¾", from $85 to ..**100.00**
Slaw cutter **45.00**
Square, KF100, EC Simmons, from $25 to **35.00**
Table cutlery set, SP, 6 knives+6 forks, in orig wood box **65.00**
Thermometer, yel border, Shapleigh's, rnd, from -30 to 120 degrees...**325.00**
Trunk lock, w/key **150.00**
Vise, combination pipe swivel base, KC/412, from $225 to...........**275.00**
Wrench, crescent; Shapleigh, 4", from $300 to...........................**350.00**

Kellogg Studio

Stanley Kellogg (1908 – 1972) opened the Kellogg Studio in Petoskey, Michigan, in 1948. It remained in operation until 1976, producing a wide range of both decorative and functional ceramics including dinnerware, vases, and figurines. Most pieces are glazed in rich, solid colors and are marked 'Petoskey' as well as 'S. Kellogg Studio' or 'Kellogg's.' Stanley Kellogg began as a sculptor, and it was while working on an outdoor monument with the great Swedish-American sculptor, Carl Milles, that Stanley suffered the back injury which forced him to turn to studio work. In addition to naturalistic treatments of Michigan wildlife, Kellogg developed some angular, architectural forms in his molded art pottery. Our co-advisors for this category are Walter P. Hogan and Wendy L. Woodworth; they are listed in the Directory under Michigan.

Ashtray, bl, oval, 6" **20.00**
Ashtray, brn, leaf shape w/fish design, 5"...................................**25.00**
Ashtray, gr, sq w/personalized name **20.00**
Bowl, blk, rnd, 8"...**55.00**
Bowl, gr w/wht int, 1" **8.00**
Box, metallic glaze, w/lid, 3x5"...**50.00**
Creamer, brn w/fish, 5"..**40.00**
Dish, teardrop shape, yel w/tiny flower frog insert, 3½" **15.00**
Figurine, Great-Horned Owl on branch, brn & ivory, 7½" **95.00**
Figurine, owl chick, standing, blk, 5" **95.00**
Flower frog vase, gr, spherical, 3¼", w/separate 4" rnd base...........**55.00**
Mug, wht, sq, hdl, 5" **25.00**
Pitcher, bl, curved hdl, 9"..**65.00**
Plate, gr w/flowers & personalized name, 13" **45.00**
Plate/charger, brn w/yel pears, 10"..**45.00**
Vase, bud; bl, 5"...**28.00**
Vase, yel, bulbous w/cylindrical neck & slanted rim, 3"................**35.00**

Kelva

Kelva was a trademark of the C.F. Monroe Company of Meriden, Connecticut; it was produced for only a few years after the turn of the century. It is distinguished from the Wave Crest and Nakara lines by its unique Batik-like background, probably achieved through the use of a cloth or sponge to apply the color. Large florals are hand painted on the opaque milk glass; and ormolu and brass mounts were used for the boxes, vases, and trays. Most pieces are signed. Our advisors for this category are Dolli and Wilfred Cohen; they are listed in the Directory under California.

Biscuit jar, daisies on peach, SP lid/hdl, rare.............................1,250.00
Box, floral, pk on bl, 3x4"...500.00
Box, landscape panels on Crown mold, ormolu mts/ft, med 1,450.00
Box, lilies, wht on pk, 5¾" sq...635.00
Box, roses on bl & cream w/gold, 8" sq.......................................1,150.00
Match holder/ash receiver, floral on gr w/beading, ftd.................500.00
Shakers, floral on gr enamel top, 3", pr..................................850.00
Tray, floral on gr, Crown mold, ormolu collar/hdls, 6" dia..........650.00
Vase, floral on gr, SP ormolu ft, 14".....................................1,500.00
Vase, floral spray on fuchsia, cone shape w/ormolu, 6x2"............650.00
Vase, floral w/gold, 4-ftd metal base, gilt collar, gold hdls, 12"...1,750.00
Vase, lg floral bouquet on gr/pk (shiny), 8x3".............................950.00
Vase, roses w/wht dots on marbled bl, hexagonal, 13"..............1,750.00

Kentucky Derby Glasses

Kentucky Derby glasses are the official souvenir glasses sold at Churchill Downs filled with mint juleps on Derby Day. Many folks from all over the country who attend the Derby take home the souvenir glass, and thus the collecting begins. The first glass (1938) is said to have either been given away as a souvenir or used for drinks among the elite at the Downs. This one, the 1939 glass, two glasses from 1940, the 1940 – 41 aluminum tumbler, the 'Beetleware' tumblers from 1941 to 1944, and the 1945 short, tall, and jigger glasses are the rarest, most sought-after glasses, and they command the highest prices. Some 1974 glasses incorrectly listed the 1971 winner Canonero II as just Canonero; as a result, it became the 'mistake' glass for that year. Also, glasses made by the Federal Glass Company (whose logo, found on the bottom of the glass, is a small shield containing an F) were used for extra glasses for the 100th running in 1974. There is also a 'mistake' and a correct Federal glass, making four to collect for that year. Another mistake glass was produced in 2003 as about 100,000 were made with the 1932 winner Burgoo King listed incorrectly as a Triple Crown winner instead of the 1937 winner of the Triple Crown, War Admiral.

The 1956 glass has four variations. On some 1956 glasses the star which was meant to separate the words 'Kentucky Derby' is missing making only one star instead of two stars. Also, all three horses on the glass were meant to have tails, but on some of the glasses only two have tails. To identify which 1956 glass you have, just count the number of stars and tails.

In order to identify the year of a pre-1969 glass, since it did not appear on the front of the glass prior to then, simply add one year to the last date listed on the back of the glass. This may seem to be a confusing practice, but the current year's glass is produced long before the Derby winner is determined.

The prices on older glasses remain high. These are in high demand, and collectors are finding them extremely hard to locate. Values listed here are for absolutely perfect glasses with bright colors, all printing and gold complete, no flaws of any kind, chipping or any other damage. Any problem reduces the price by at least one-half. Our advisor for this category is Betty Hornback; she is listed in the Directory under Kentucky.

1938..4,000.00
1939..6,500.00
1940, aluminum...1,000.00
1940, French Lick, aluminum...1,000.00
1940, glass tumbler, 2 styles, ea, minimum value.................10,000.00
1941-44, Beetleware, from $2,500 to..................................4,000.00
1945, jigger..1,000.00
1945, regular..1,600.00
1945, tall..450.00
1946-47, clear frosted w/frostom bottom, L in circle, ea.............100.00
1948, clear bottom...225.00
1948, frosted bottom...250.00

1949, He Has Seen Them All, $225.00.

1950..450.00
1951..650.00
1952, Gold Cup..225.00
1953..200.00
1954..225.00
1955..175.00
1956, 1 star, 2 tails...275.00
1956, 1 star, 3 tails...400.00
1956, 2 stars, 2 tails..200.00
1956, 2 stars, 3 tails..250.00
1957, gold & blk on frosted...125.00
1958, Gold Bar..175.00
1958, Iron Leige..225.00
1959-60, ea..100.00
1961..110.00
1962, Churchill Downs, red, gold & blk on clear.....................90.00
1963..70.00
1964, ea...55.00
1965..85.00
1966-68, ea...60.00
1969..65.00
1970..70.00
1971..55.00
1972..55.00
1973..60.00
1974, Federal, regular & mistake, ea...................................200.00
1974, Libbey, mistake, Canonero in 1971 listing on bk...............18.00
1974, regular, Canonero II in 1971 listing on bk.....................16.00
1975..16.00
1976..16.00
1976, plastic..16.00
1977..14.00
1978-79, ea...16.00
1980..22.00
1981-82, ea...15.00

1983-85, ea..12.00
1986 ....14.00
1986 (1985 copy)..20.00
1987-89, ea..12.00
1990-92, ea..10.00
1993-95, ea..9.00
1996-97, ea..8.00
1998-99, ea..6.00
2000-02, ea..5.00
2003 ....4.00
2003, mistake, 1932 incorrectly listed as Derby Triple Crown Winner ...6.00
2004 ....3.50
2005 ....3.00

Keramos

Keramos (Austria) produced a line of decorative items including vases, bowls, masks, and figurines that were imported primarily by the Ebeling & Ruess Co. of Philadelphia from the late 1920s to the 1950s. The figurines they manufactured were of high quality and very detailed, similar to those made by other Austrian firms. Their glazes were very smooth, though today some crazing is present on older pieces.

Most items were marked and numbered, and some bear the name or initials of the artist who designed them. In addition to Ebeling & Ruess (whose trademark includes a crown), other importers' stamps and labels may be found as well. Knight Ceramics employed a shield mark, and many of the vases produced through the 1940s are marked with a swastika; these pieces are turning up with increasing frequency at shops as well as Internet auction sites. Although the workmanship they exhibit is somewhat inferior, the glazes used during this period are excellent and are now attracting much attention among collectors.

Detail is a very important worth-assessing factor. The more detailed the art figures are, the more valuable. Artist-signed pieces are quite scarce. Many artists were employed by both Keramos and Goldscheider. The molds of these two companies are sometimes very similar as well, and unmarked items are often difficult to identify with certainty.

Items listed below are considered to be in excellent, undamaged condition unless otherwise stated. Our advisor for this category is Darrell Thomas; he is listed in the Directory under Wisconsin.

Figurine, boxers, 1 stands/1 sits, Knight Ceramics/ER sticker, '40, pr ...125.00
Figurine, cat, blk/wht tabby, sitting, Austria/E&R, 1950s..............45.00
Figurine, chickadees, Austria, 1950s, ea 3" L, set of 6....................65.00
Figurine, gray poodle, shield mk/Austria, 1950s, 15" L 65.00
Figurine, Madonna holds lamb & Baby, bright mc/EX detail, '40-50s, 12" .85.00
Figurine, nude holds vase on grassy base, Dakon mold, 1930s, 14" ..250.00
Figurine, woman holds basket, flowers/bright mc, Knight Ceramics, 8"..75.00
Mask, lady w/fruit, brn w/orange lips, bl noodle hair, WW mk, '40, 12" ..850.00
Plant holders, gr/gray mottle matt on terra cotta, mk, 1940s, 4 for..45.00
Tea pot, horses/fox hounds, Deco style, Austria/E&R, +sug/cr & 6 c/s .95.00
Vase, floral band, bl/brn on multi-tone gr, shouldered, 13" 600.00
Vase, stylized flowers, ivory/brn/gr on gr to brn, bulbous, 9"........600.00
Vase, weed; orange/gr mottle w/brn streaks, mk/E&R sticker, 1930s, 12"..55.00

Kew Blas

The Union Glass Company was founded in 1854, in Somerville, Massachusetts, an offshoot of the New England Glass Co. in East Cambridge. They made only flint glass — tablewares, lamps, globes, and shades. Kew Blas was a trade name they used for their iridescent, lustered art glass produced there from 1893 until about 1920. The glass was made in imitation of Tiffany and achieved notable success. Some items were decorated

with pulled leaf and feather designs, while others had a monochrome lustre surface. The mark was an engraved 'Kew Blas' in an arching arrangement.

Rose bowl, vertical chains, gr irid/gold on butterscotch, 3½" 950.00
Saucer, gold irid, scalloped, 6¾" 145.00
Tumbler, gold irid, 3½x3" 480.00
Vase, amber w/gold pulled feathers, raised rim, ovoid, 4" 650.00
Vase, creme w/gr & gold pulled feathers, classic shape, 5"..........950.00
Vase, gold irid, emb ribs, scalloped, att, 3⅛" 175.00
Vase, gold irid w/gr pulled feathers, 4-point rim, 10" 950.00
Vase, swirls, irid on gr, 8"..540.00
Vase, trumpet; gold irid, bulbed stem, 12"............................1,175.00

Kindell, Dorothy

Yet another California artist that worked during the prolific years of the 1940s and 1950s, Dorothy Kindell produced a variety of household items and giftware, but today she is best known for her nudes. One of her most popular lines consisted of mugs, a pitcher, salt and pepper shakers, a wall pocket, bowls, a creamer and sugar set, and champagne glasses, featuring a lady in various stages of undress, modeled as handles or stems (on the champagnes). In the set of six mugs, she progresses from wearing her glamorous strapless evening gown to ultimately climbing nude, head-first into the last mug. These are relatively common but always marketable. Except for these and the salt and pepper shakers, the other items from the nude line are scarce and rather pricey. Collectors also vie for her island girls, generally seminude and very sensuous.

Ashtray, Beachcombers, 4 legs extend from under 7" dia hat, $60 to....75.00
Ashtray, Hawaiian hula girl in 7" dia blk ashtray, 4½" 530.00
Champagne glass, nude stem..150.00
Dresser box, Hawaiian girl finial, 5x4x6½" 395.00
Figurine, Carmen, nude w/flowers in hair & legs in air, 9x9"......160.00
Mug, Boy Scout insignia on bark pattern w/axe hdl, 1953, 3½" ...85.00
Mug, clothed-to-nude lady hdl, series of 6, 5¼-6", ea from $35 to........40.00
Shakers, nude hdl, 3", pr, from $45 to 55.00
Shelf sitter, nude w/red turban & red towel on lap, 12", from $175 to ..250.00

King's Rose

King's Rose was made in Staffordshire, England, from about 1820 to 1830. It is closely related to Gaudy Dutch in body type as well as the colors used in its decoration. The pattern consists of a full-blown, orange-red rose with green, pink, and yellow leaves and accents. When the rose is in pink, the ware is often referred to as Queen's Rose.

Cake plate, Queen's Rose, floral rim band, rose in center, 10" 200.00
Coffeepot, dome lid, pearlware, 11¼" 700.00
Cup & saucer, handleless, red rose, vine border..........................245.00
Cup & saucer, Queen's, pearlware, EX 130.00
Pitcher, milk; pearlware, 5⅜"...300.00
Plate, orange stripes on rim, 8¼" 250.00
Plate, pk band w/red stripes, 8⅛"...125.00
Plate, pk border w/emb dmns, 8⅛" 220.00
Plate, plain rim, vining border, #10, 7½", EX 125.00
Plate, Queen's, unmk, 1820-30, 7¼" 125.00
Plate, Rogers, 8½" 135.00
Plate, toddy, Queen's, EX color, 5¼" 115.00
Plate, toddy; 4¾" 275.00
Plate, vine border, red rim band, 9¼"..400.00
Plate, 6¾" 125.00
Plate, 7½" 150.00

Tea bowl & saucer, pearlware, 3¾" & 6⅜" **185.00**
Tea bowl & saucer, Queen's, pk & gr w/mc floral border.............**125.00**
Teapot, Queen's, 6"...**400.00**

Kitchen Collectibles

During the last half of the 1850s, mass-produced kitchen gadgets were patented at an astonishing rate. Most were ingeniously efficient. Apple peelers, egg beaters, cherry pitters, food choppers, and such were only the most common of hundreds of kitchen tools well designed to perform only specific tasks. Today all are very collectible.

For further information we recommend *Kitchen Glassware of the Depression Years; Glass Kitchen Shakers;* and *Anchor Hocking's Fire-King & More, Second Edition,* all by Gene and Cathy Florence; and *Kitchen Antiques, 1790 – 1940,* by Kathryn McNerney. See also Appliances; Butter Molds and Stamps; Cast Iron; Cookbooks; Copper; Glass Knives; Molds; Pie Birds; Primitives; Reamers; String Holders; Tinware; Trivets; Wooden Ware; Wrought Iron.

Key: FW — full writing   TM — trade mark

Cast Kitchen Ware

Be aware that cast-iron counterfeit production is on the increase. Items with phony production numbers, finishes, etc., are being made at this time. Many of these new pieces are the popular miniature cornstick pans. To command the values given below, examples must be free from damage of any kind or excessive wear. Waffle irons must be complete with all three pieces and the handle. The term 'EPU' in the description lines refers to the Erie PA, USA mark. The term 'block mark' refers to the lettering in the large logo that was used ca 1920 until 1940; 'slant logo' refers to the lettering in the large logo ca 1900 to 1920. 'PIN' indicates 'Product Identification Numbers.' Victor was Griswold's first low-budget line (ca 1875). Skillets #5 and #6 are uncommon, while #7, #8, and #9 are easy to find. See also Keen Kutter; Clubs, Newsletters, and Catalogs.

Corn cake pan, Griswold #262, seven-stick, original wrapper, $75.00.

Ashtray, Griswold #770, sq, from $20 to **30.00**
Display rack, Griswold Skillet, Griswold plate, wood rails, $300 to......**350.00**
Dutch oven, Favorite Piqua Ware #7, Stylized TM, from $40 to ..**60.00**
Dutch oven, Favorite Piqua Ware #8, Stylized TM, from $30 to ..**50.00**
Dutch oven, Griswold #6, Tite-Top, Block TMs/FW lid, from $250 to.......**300.00**
Dutch oven, Griswold #8, Early Tite-Top, Block TMs, FW lid, $40 to......**60.00**
Dutch oven, Griswold #8, Tite-Top Baster, Slant/EPU TM, from $50 to......**75.00**
Dutch oven, Griswold #9, Early Tite-Top, Block TMs, FE lid, #40 to.........**60.00**
Dutch oven, Griswold #9, Late Tite-Top, Block TMs, w/trivet, $50 to **80.00**

Dutch oven, Griswold #10, Tite-Top Baster, Slant/EPU TM, from $125 to...**150.00**
Dutch oven lid, Griswold #8, hinged, from $25 to.........................**30.00**
Gem pan, Griswold #3, Slant TM & PIN 942, from $250 to **300.00**
Gem pan, Griswold #11, Fr roll pan, mk MES NO 11, from $30 to **50.00**
Gem pan, Griswold #11, Fr roll pan, mk NES oN (sic) 11, $40 to **60.00**
Gem pan, Griswold #12, Slant/EPU TM, from $300 to **350.00**
Gem pan, Griswold #16, wide band, aluminum, from $500 to **600.00**
Gem pan, Griswold #18, popover, wide hdl, 6 cups, from $50 to **70.00**
Gem pan, Griswold #19, fully mk, 6-cup golf ball, from $250 to **300.00**
Gem pan, Griswold #24, breadstick, PIN 957, from $400 to.......**450.00**
Gem pan, Griswold #240, turk's head, from $230 to **260.00**
Gem pan, Griswold #262, miniature cornstick, 4x8½", from $50 to.....**75.00**
Gem pan, Griswold #273, cornstick, from $15 to **20.00**
Gem pan, Griswold #2700, cornstick, from $275 to **325.00**
Gem pan, Wagner Ware T, cutouts, turk head, 12 cups, from $100 to..**150.00**
Griddle, Griswold #8, Slant/EPU TM, X bar support, hdl, from $20 to......**40.00**
Griddle, Griswold #8, Slant/Erie TM, X reinforcement, hdl, $35 to.....**45.00**
Griddle, Griswold #12 Vapor, mk Erie Gas Griddle, from $275 to......**325.00**
Griddle, Griswold #14 Bailed, Block TM, from $50 to **75.00**
Griddle, Wagner #8, Stylized TM, C#1108, hdl, from $20 to........**30.00**
Griddle, Wapak #8, oval, Early TM, from $50 to..........................**75.00**
Kettle, Wagner, deep fat fryer, w/basket, C#1265, from $50 to......**75.00**
Kettle, Wagner, rimmed pot, mk Wagner, from $75 to................**100.00**
Muffin pan, Filley #1, 14 cups, from $275 to **325.00**
Muffin pan, Filley #4, 8 cups, from $300 to **350.00**
Muffin pan, Filley #6, 11 cups, from $150 to **200.00**
Muffin pan, Filley #10, 11 cups, from $75 to **100.00**
Muffin pan, Griswold #3, mk #3 & #943 only, 11 cups, from $150 to......**175.00**
Muffin pan, Griswold #11, Fr roll, wide band, 12 cups, from $30 to **40.00**
Muffin pan, Griswold #32, Danish cake, fully mk, 7 cups, from $30 to **40.00**
Muffin pan, Griswold #100, heart & star, 5 cups, from $600 to ..**800.00**
Roaster, Griswold #3, oval, Block TMs, w/lid mk Oval Roaster, $475 to **525.00**
Roaster, Griswold #5, oval, Block TMs, mk lid, +trivet, $350 to ..**400.00**
Roaster, Griswold #9, oval, Block TMs, FW lid, $425 to....**475.00**
Roaster, Wagner #7, oval, Stylized TM, incised writing lid, $175 to...**225.00**
Sandwich toaster, Wagner, w/low bailed base, sq, from $125 to..**150.00**
Skillet, breakfast; Cliff Cornell, from $75 to................................**125.00**
Skillet, Griswold #2, Block TM, no heat ring, chrome, from $200 to........**250.00**
Skillet, Griswold #2, Block TM, no heat ring, from $300 to.......**350.00**
Skillet, Griswold #2, Slant/EPU TM, heat ring, from $375 to....**425.00**
Skillet, Griswold #2, Slant/EPU TM, Rau Brothers, from $500 to....**600.00**
Skillet, Griswold #3, Block TM, no heat ring, from $10 to...........**20.00**
Skillet, Griswold #3, Slant/Erie TM, from $30 to **40.00**
Skillet, Griswold #3, Square Fry Skillet, PIN 2103 (+), from $75 to......**125.00**
Skillet, Griswold #4, Block TM, heat ring, from $375 to.............**425.00**
Skillet, Griswold #4, Block TM, no heat ring, from $40 to...........**60.00**
Skillet, Griswold #4, Slant/ERIE TM, NP, from $40 to **60.00**
Skillet, Griswold #5, sm TM, grooved hdl, from $10 to **15.00**
Skillet, Griswold #6, Block TM, heat ring, from $50 to **75.00**
Skillet, Griswold #6, Block TM, no heat ring, from $10 to...........**20.00**
Skillet, Griswold #7, Block TM, heat ring, from $45 to **55.00**
Skillet, Griswold #8, Block TM, no heat ring, from $10 to...........**20.00**
Skillet, Griswold #8, extra deep, Block TM, no heat ring, $50 to........**75.00**
Skillet, Griswold #8, Small TM, extra deep, w/hinge, from $35 to......**45.00**
Skillet, Griswold #8, Spider TM, from $1,100 to **1,400.00**
Skillet, Griswold #8, Victor, fully mk, from $35 to **45.00**
Skillet, Griswold #9, Block TM, heat ring, from $40 to **60.00**
Skillet, Griswold #10, Block TM, heat ring, from $50 to **75.00**
Skillet, Griswold #10, Block TM, no heat ring, from $40 to...........**60.00**
Skillet, Griswold #11, Slant/EPU TM, from $250 to...................**300.00**
Skillet, Griswold #12, Block TM, from $75 to...........................**100.00**
Skillet, Griswold #12, Slant/EPU TM, from $125 to.................**175.00**
Skillet, Griswold #13, Block TM, from $1,400 to **1,600.00**
Skillet, Griswold #13, Slant/EPU TM, from $800 to **1,000.00**

Skillet, Griswold #14, Block TM, chrome, from $100 to **125.00**
Skillet, Griswold #14, Block TM, from $125 to........................**175.00**
Skillet, Griswold #15, oval, from $250 to...............................**300.00**
Skillet, Griswold #55, sq, made on Sidney OH, from $25 to.........**35.00**
Skillet, Griswold Sq Utility , PIN 768, w/iron lid: PIN 769, $275 to...**300.00**
Skillet, Merit #3, from $20 to **30.00**
Skillet, Vollrath #5, from $15 to **24.00**
Skillet, Wagner, Bacon & Egg Breakfast; Stylized TM, from $15 to...**25.00**
Skillet, Wagner #2, Stylized TM, from $50 to.......................**75.00**
Skillet, Wagner #3, Stylized TM, from $5 to.........................**10.00**
Skillet, Wapak #5, Z TM, from $35 to **45.00**
Skillet, Wapak #8, Early TM, from $25 to **35.00**
Skillet, Wapak #9, Tapered TM, from $25 to........................**35.00**
Skillet lid, Griswold #3, high smooth dome, from $150 to..........**200.00**
Skillet lid, Griswold #6, high smooth dome, Block TM, from $50 to.....**75.00**
Skillet lid, Griswold #7, high smooth dome, Block TM, from $40 to.....**60.00**
Skillet lid, Griswold #8, high dome top logo, Block TM, from $30 to.....**40.00**
Skillet lid, Griswold #8, high smooth dome, sm TM, from $20 to **30.00**
Skillet lid, Griswold #8, low, top writing, from $30 to...................**50.00**
Skillet lid, Griswold #10, high smooth dome, Block TM, from $40 to....**60.00**
Skillet lid, Griswold #15, oval, sm TM, P#1013C, from $500 to...**600.00**
Skillet lid, Wapak #9, mk 9 only, recessed basting dots, from $30 to...**50.00**
Teakettle, Griswold #8, Spider TM top, from $400 to.................**500.00**
Trivet, Classic Sad Iron, from $50 to **75.00**
Trivet, Griswold, Family Tree, P#1726, lg/decorative, from $10 to..**20.00**
Trivet, Griswold, Grapes P#1729, lg/decorative, from $10 to **20.00**
Trivet, Griswold #9, Dutch oven, P#207, from $25 to...................**35.00**
Trivet, Old Lace (coffeepot), PIN 1739, lg, from $75 to **125.00**
Trivet, Wagner #9, Dutch oven, aluminum, C#249, from $25 to..**35.00**
Wafer iron, Griswold, side-hdl base, from $300 to.......................**400.00**
Waffle iron, Griswold #2, sq, from $650 to **700.00**
Waffle iron, Griswold #7, finger hinge, low hdl base, from $100 to....**125.00**
Waffle iron, Griswold #8, Fr (3 sets of paddles), finger hinge, up to **800.00**
Waffle iron, Griswold #11, sq, low bailed base, ball hinge, $175 to....**225.00**
Waffle iron, Griswold #19, Heart & Star, low bailed base, $250 to **300.00**
Wax ladle, Griswold, ERIE TM, PIN 964, from $175 to **150.00**

Egg Beaters

Egg beaters are unbeatable. Ranging from hand-helds, rotary-crank, and squeeze power to Archimedes up-and-down models, egg beaters are America's favorite kitchen gadget. A mainstay of any kitchenware collection, in recent years egg beaters have come into their own — nutmeg graters, spatulas, and can openers will have to scramble to catch up! At the turn of the century, everyone in America owned an egg beater. Every household did its own mixing and baking — there were no pre-processed foods. And every inventor thought he/she could make a better beater. Thus American ingenuity produced more than one thousand egg beater patents, dating back to 1856, with several hundred different models being manufactured over the years. As true examples of Americana, egg beaters enjoyed a steady increase in value for quite sometime, though they have leveled off and even decreased in the past few years, due to a proliferation of Internet sales. Some very rare beaters will bring more than $1,000.00, including the cast-iron, rotary crank 'Dodge Race Course egg beater.' But the vast majority stay under $50.00. Just when you think you've seen them all, new ones always turn up, usually at flea markets or garage sales. For further information, we recommend our advisor (author of the definitive book on egg beaters) Don Thornton, who is listed in the Directory under California. (SASE required.)

A over D, dbl-action rachet, Pat Nov 19, 1929, 12¼" **50.00**
A&J, all metal, sm, 9¾"...**5.00**
A&J High Speed Super Center Drive, 11½"............................**5.00**
Aluminum Beauty Pat'd April 20, 1920, rotary crank, 10½" **15.00**

Archimedes type, mk Made in America Pat Pend **65.00**
Ashley Pat May 1, 1860, Archimedes type, 11½"........................**625.00**
Dover, 4-hole wheel, 12½"..**60.00**
Dover Tumbler, pinion gear, 10" **85.00**
Dover...Patd May 6th 1873-1891..., CI rotary crank, 11½" **35.00**
Eagle Precision Tool Co...NY, 1-hand whip, 12½"........................**30.00**
Express, ca 1887, EX **1,200.00**
F/S Dover, CI, Pat May 6th, 1873...Nov 24th 1891 ....**75.00**
Holrick's, Archimedes type **22.00**
Holt's Improved, 10½" **50.00**
Jiffy Whip...Krasbert & Sons Mfg, rotary crank turbine, 11¾"....**25.00**
Lyon, propeller, mk USA **145.00**
One-Hand Whip Pat Pend Eagle Precision..., 12½".....................**40.00**
PD&Co, spring-type dasher, EX...**950.00**
Standard, fold-flat type, Pat June 29 '80 on gear wheel...............**250.00**
Star, April 19, 59 Oct 16, 60, CI rotary crank, 10½" **1,000.00**
T&S No 10 Made in USA, 9¾"...**25.00**
Taplin Pattern Improved April 14, 1903, bl wooden hdl, 11¾"....**25.00**
Vandeusen Egg Whip, CA Chapman...1894, all metal, hand held, 11" ..**15.00**
Whipwell...USA Pat Mch 23 1920..., rotary crank, wood hdl, 11"..**20.00**

Glass

Baking dish, chicken shape, fired-on colors, Glasbake, McKee.....**20.00**
Batter jug, cobalt, McKee, from $150 to **160.00**
Bottle, oil; amber, Cambridge, from $50 to **55.00**
Bottle, water; gr, centered screw-on lid, Hocking, from $30 to **35.00**
Bottle, water; red & fired-on red, McKee, tumbler makes top, $30 to ..**35.00**
Bowl, batter; yel opaque, Hocking, from $110 to........................**125.00**
Bowl, cereal; Fruits, milk glass, Anchor Hocking, 5", from $12.50 to..**15.00**
Bowl, cobalt, Hazel Atlas, 8½", from $45 to **50.00**
Bowl, Delphite, w/metal beater, from $70 to.............................**80.00**
Bowl, Dots, red on custard, McKee, w/spout, 9", from $35 to **40.00**
Bowl, drippings; Ships on red & wht, Hazel Atlas, 8-oz, from $50 to..**55.00**
Bowl, Jade-ite, Jeannette, horizontal rib, 5½", from $45 to...........**50.00**
Bowl, mixing; bl, Hazel Atlas, 6⅝", from $50 to.........................**55.00**
Bowl, mixing; Butter-Print Cinderella, Pyrex, 9¾", from $12 to...**14.00**
Bowl, mixing; gr, Hocking, paneled, 11½", from $55 to...............**60.00**
Bowl, mixing; Hex Optic, pk, flat rim, 9", from $25 to **30.00**
Bowl, mixing; Jade-ite, Hocking, 9", from $22 to **25.00**
Bowl, mixing; Modern Tulip, 3-qt, from $18 to **20.00**
Bowl, pk, Jeannette, 6", from $50 to......................................**60.00**
Bowl, wht w/red trim, 10", from $30 to...................................**35.00**
Butter dish, cobalt, Hazel Atlas, from $300 to **325.00**

Butter dish, Criss Cross, pink, Hazel-Atlas, quarter-pound, from $90.00 to $100.00.

Butter dish, gr, Hocking, from $50 to **55.00**
Butter dish, ultramarine, Jeannette, deep bottom, from $175 to....**195.00**
Canister, caramel, blk lettering, tin lid, 48-oz, from $125 to.......**135.00**
Canister, crystal, w/Taverne scene, lg, from $40 to **45.00**
Canister, gr fired-on color, ribbed, from $35 to **40.00**

Canister, Red Dots on custard, McKee, rnd, 48-oz, from $35 to....**40.00**
Canister, Ships, Hazel Atlas, w/lid, rnd, 48-oz, 5", from $35 to.....**40.00**
Canister, tea; Delphite, 20-oz, from $200 to **225.00**
Casserole, dk amber, oval, w/lid, Cambridge, from $50 to **55.00**
Casserole, fired-on color, stick hdl, Glasbake, McKee, w/lid, ind..**14.00**
Casserole, Peach Blossom, milk glass, Anchor Hocking, 1½-qt **25.00**
Cocktail shaker, gr, Hocking, #151, pinched-in, from $30 to........**35.00**
Cookie jar, blk, LE Smith, from $95 to **110.00**
Cookie jar, pk, Paden City, Party Line #191, from $75 to **85.00**
Cruet, gr, Jeannette, w/correct stopper, from $65 to......................**75.00**
Cup, fired-on red, Glasbake, from $50 to **55.00**
Drawer pulls, blk, ea, from $18 to..**20.00**
Egg cup, amber, Paden City, from $15 to......................................**18.00**
Funnel, Tufglas, from $75 to..**85.00**
Ice bucket, gr clambroth, Fenton, from $60 to..............................**70.00**
Ice bucket, pk, w/Sterling bear, from $50 to.................................**60.00**
Ice tub, Emerald-Glo insert, w/tongs, from $65 to **70.00**
Jug, batter; amber, Paden City #90, from #65 to...........................**75.00**
Ladle, whipped cream; blk, Westmoreland, #1800, from $25 to....**30.00**
Measuring cup, amber, Federal, #2534, w/hdl, from $35 to **40.00**
Measuring cup, Chalaine Blue, 2-spout, from $800 to.................**900.00**
Measuring cup, crystal, McKee Glasbake Scientific, 2-cup, from $40 to **25.00**
Measuring cup, gr, Hocking, 1-cup, from $30 to **35.00**
Measuring cup, gr, Jeannette, tab hdld, from $30 to **35.00**
Measuring cup, Sapphire Blue, Anchor Hocking, 1-cup..............**28.00**
Measuring cup, Seller's, Pat Dec 8, 1925, from $30 to.................**38.00**
Measuring pitcher, custard, McKee, 4-cup, from $50 to...............**55.00**
Measuring pitcher, Delphite Blue, McKee, 4-cup, from $600 to....**650.00**
Measuring pitcher, Jade-ite, Jeannette, 4-cup, from $75 to...........**85.00**
Mug, cobalt, Cambridge, from $50 to...**60.00**
Mug, Jade-ite, Hocking, 7-oz, from $12 to....................................**14.00**
Pitcher, batter; red & fired-on red, w/tray, from $250 to **275.00**
Pitcher, Jade-ite, Hocking, 16-oz, from $200 to **250.00**
Refrigerator dish, fired-on yel, Pyrex, 7x9", from $12.50 to...........**15.00**
Refrigerator dish, pk, rnd, tab hdl, from $40 to **45.00**
Refrigerator dish, yel opaque, 7¼" sq, from $30 to **35.00**
Rolling pin, blown, golden yel-amber, pontil scar, 1820-35, 12¾".....**140.00**
Rolling pin, forest gr, from $150 to...**175.00**
Shaker, blk, ea, from $40 to **45.00**
Shaker, custard w/blk lettering, ea, from $18 to **20.00**
Shaker, nutmeg; Chalaine Blue, from $165 to **185.00**
Shaker, Red Dots on custard, ea, from $25 to **30.00**
Skillet, Jade-ite, 1-spout, from $70 to..**80.00**
Stack set, Skating Dutch, red on wht, Hazel Atlas, 3-pc set **75.00**
Sugar shaker, gr, bullet-shaped w/dots on top, McKee, from $200 to..**225.00**
Tumbler, Jade-ite, Jeannette, #528, 10-oz, from $25 to.................**30.00**

Miscellaneous

Apple peeler, Goodell Co Antrim NH, CI, clamps to table, EX ...**130.00**
Apple peeler, Sinclair Scott, CI, clamps to table, EX **80.00**
Bread box, gr & cream, metal w/glass lid, 1930s-40s, 7¼x16x10½", NM .**60.00**
Bread box, Keramer, red & wht, Deco lettering & latches, 13x13", EX ..**55.00**
Cake carrier, cherries & flowers on cream, metal, 12¼" dia, NM.**40.00**
Cake decorator, cylinder w/screw top, 4 tips, aluminum, 1940s, NM ..**29.00**
Cake knife/pie server, Serrated Stainless...NY, Bakelite hdl, 10", EX..**28.00**
Cake maker, Universal, Landers Frary & Clark, ca 1900, EX........**60.00**
Can opener, CI, 2 triangular blades, eagle surmount, 8x12" on brd, EX .**500.00**
Can opener, Diamond Edge, Shapleigh, Pat Feb 11 1890, EX.......**22.00**
Can opener, Edlund Jr No 5, gr wood hdl, 1940s, 6", EX **10.00**
Can opener, Little Vaughn's Safety Roll Jr, EX..............................**8.00**
Can opener, Maid of Honor, Sears, wall mt, ca 1949, EX.............**15.00**
Can opener, stainless steel w/red Bakelite hdl, 7", EX **23.00**
Canisters, Kromex, blk letters on aluminum, 4-pc set, EX............**40.00**

Carving set, 2-tine fork+spoon, butterscotch Bakelite hdls, pr, EX...**35.00**
Cheese slicer, wht enamel over iron, Tru-Cut, 12", EX **35.00**
Cheese slicer, wire cutter, Bakelite hdl, EX **9.00**
Chopper, crescent steel blade, wooden top w/rnd hdl, 5x7¾", EX .**45.00**
Chopper, curved steel blade, wooden T-hdl, EX............................**17.50**
Chopper, Fedco, turq plastic top over glass jar, 7½", EX **18.00**
Chopper, heavy steel blade, trn wood hdl, 7x6", EX......................**25.00**
Chopper, Landers Frary & Clark, steel blade, wood hdl, EX **17.50**
Chopper, nut; Androck, metal lid on red container w/crank, glass base, EX ..**10.00**
Chopper, steel blade joined to wood hdl by 2 brass screws, EX **20.00**
Chopper/cleaver/can opener, gr wood hdl, Pat Pending, 1900s, 8½", EX...**15.00**
Chopper/slicer, Mouli, 3-ftd, crank hdl, w/5 attachments, EX.......**20.00**
Churn, Dazey #10, beveled edge, 1-qt, EX **750.00**
Churn, Dazey #10, bull's-eye, 1-qt, EX **700.00**
Churn, Dazey #20, EX..**200.00**
Churn, Dazey #30, Pat 1922, EX **225.00**

Churn, Dazey #40,
EX, $150.00.

Churn, Dazey #60, EX...**165.00**
Churn, Dazey #80, EX...**250.00**
Coasters, flower decal on red or blk enamel, 3½", EX, 12 for........**10.00**
Colander, aluminum, hdls, 1930s, 9", EX **20.00**
Cookie cutter, aluminum, rolls to make rnd cookies, ca 1922, 6", G ...**15.00**
Corn cutter, Lee's Orig Corn Cutter & Creamer, stainless, MIB ...**15.00**
Food mill, Foley, metal, center crank w/red wood hdl, 7" dia, M .**12.50**
Fork, Androck, 2-prong, gr wood hdl, 9½", EX...............................**7.50**
Funnel, wht metal w/gold liner & filter holes, 4x6", EX **15.00**
Garnish tool, wavy blade w/red wood hdl, 7", EX **12.00**
Grapefruit cutter, serrated metal pliers form w/gr wood hdls, EX ..**18.00**
Grater, aluminum half-rnd, Forever Arrow...NY, 12½", EX...........**12.50**
Grater, Mouli, hand-crank w/wood hdl, 1940s, 8", EX **50.00**
Grater, nutmeg; CI/tin/wire, 1800s, 7", EX **110.00**
Grater, nutmeg; MTL Co, CI, spring feed on top, crank hdl, 4", EX...**60.00**
Grater, The Edgar, tin w/wood hdl, Pat 1896, EX.........................**35.00**
Grater/shredder, tin, All in One Pat Pending, EX...........................**8.00**
Grease jar, aluminum, w/red-coated hdl/finial, Japan, EX.............**35.00**
Grinder, Griswold #1, CI, clamps to table, EX **35.00**
Grinder, Puriton No 11, CI, clamps to table, 8¼", EX **35.00**
Grinder/mincer, Jaymax, CI w/aluminum top, crank hdl, table clamp, EX....**35.00**
Ice cream freezer, Minute Man Fre-Zee-Zee, EX orig pnt, 2-qt......**65.00**
Ice cream freezer, White Mountain, EX orig pnt, 6-qt...................**65.00**
Ice crusher, Dazy, turq rocket form, 1950s, 10", EX.......................**35.00**
Ice crusher, Swing-A-Way, avocado gr enameling, crank hdl, 1960s, EX..**18.00**
Ice pick, metal, red wood & metal hdl, 8¼", EX **16.00**
Jar lifter, wire w/wood hdls, 4x10", EX **14.00**
Jar opener, Pop Off...Opener, gr wood hdl, EX.............................**15.00**
Knife sharpener, Ekco, 2-wheel, red wood hdl, EX **12.00**

Ladle, Androck, stainless w/Bakelite bullet hdl, EX......................**30.00**
Lemon squeezer, CI, Hot Tin emb on hdl, 4x6", EX....................**10.00**
Meat tenderizer, aluminum cube w/wood hdl, 13" L, EX..............**12.00**
Melon baller, metal w/gr wood hdl, 5½", EX................................**6.00**
Pastry blender, Androck, arched wire w/gr wood hdl, EX **9.00**
Pastry cutter, roller style w/gr wood hdl, 7" L, EX **10.00**
Ricer, CI, mk Pat Pending on hdl, very heavy, 11¾" L, EX **20.00**
Ricer, tin w/red wood hdl, 11" L, NM **15.00**
Rolling pin, aluminum, hdls rotate, 17x2", EX..............................**35.00**
Rolling pin, ravioli; wood, 32 panels, 20", EX..............................**40.00**
Rolling pin, tiger maple, attached hdls, 24x3⅝" dia, EX **60.00**
Rolling pin, wood, Springerle, 20 molds of animals/birds/etc, 16", EX ..**225.00**
Rolling pin, wood (hollow), trn, cylinder opens, 1900s, 8", EX **35.00**
Shelf, heart cutouts & floral applique on cream enamel, 18x13", EX...**35.00**
Sifter, Androck Handi-Sift, tin, cherries on red stripes, 1930s, NM...**48.00**
Sifter, Androck Handi-Sift, tin, pies & cakes on red, EX..............**27.50**
Sifter, Androck Handi-Sift, tin, red flowers on cream, 5½", EX ..**42.50**
Sifter, Androck Handi-Sift, wht w/red hdl, 1940s-50s, EX **20.00**
Sifter, Nesco Royal Jr, tin w/2 gr enamel bands, 4½", EX..............**12.50**
Slicer, Arcadia, iron & wood, ca 1897, 25", EX **12.50**
Slicer, bread; wrought iron & tin w/pnt decor, 19th C, 14", EX....**30.00**
Spoon, A&J, slotted, red & wht wood hdl, 1950s, 12", NM **10.00**
Spoon, ACE Co, stainless steel, Bakelite hdl, 13", VG **12.50**
Spreader/icer, red Bakelite hdl, 11½", EX **14.00**
Sprinkler bottle, cat, marble eyes, ceramic, Am Bisque, M **400.00**
Sprinkler bottle, Chinese man, towel over arm, ceramic, M, from $300 to....**350.00**
Sprinkler bottle, clothespin, HP, ceramic, M, from $250 to........**400.00**
Sprinkler bottle, iron, lady ironing, ceramic, M **95.00**
Sprinkler bottle, Mary Maid, all colors, plastic, Reliance, NM, $25 to..**35.00**
Sprinkler bottle, poodle, gray, pk or wht, ceramic, M, from $200 to **300.00**
Strainer, grease; Foley, turq bl wood hdl, EX **18.00**
Strainer, tea; wire w/wood hdl, EX...**6.00**
Whip, twisted wire coil w/wood hdl, EX **10.00**
Whipper, Speed E Whipper Pat Pend, red top, glass jar, EX..........**15.00**

Knife Rests

Knife rests were used to prevent the tablecloth from becoming soiled by used knives. As the table was cleared after each course, the only utencil allowed to remain was the knife, thus the knife rest was a necessity. Many types have been made in Europe — porcelain, Delft, Majolica, and pottery. European companies made knife rests to match their dinnerware patterns, a practice not pursued by American manufacturers. Research has found only one company, Mackenzie-Childs of New York, who made a pottery knife rest.

Several scholars feel that porcelain knife rests originated in Germany and France; from there, their usage spread to England. Though there were glasshouses in Europe making pressed and cut glass, often blanks were purchased from American companies, cut by European craftsmen, and shipped back to the states. American consumers regarded the European cut glass as superior. When economic woes forced the Europeans to come to the U.S., many brought their motifs and patterns with them. American manufacturers patented many of the designs for their exclusive use, but in some cases as the cutters moved from one company to another, they took their patterns with them.

Knife rests of pressed glass, cut crystal, porcelain, sterling silver, plated silver, wood, ivory, and bone have been collected for many years. Signed knife rests are especially desirable. It was not until the Centennial Exhibition in Philadelphia in 1876 that the brilliant new cut glass rests, deeply faceted and shining like diamonds, appeared in shops by the hundreds. There were sets of twelve, eight or six that came in presentation boxes. Sizes vary from 1¼" to 3¼" for individual knives and from 5" to 6" for carving knives. Glass knife rests were made in many colors such

as purple, blue, green, vaseline, pink, and cranberry. These colors have been made in Europe. It is important to note that prices may vary from one area of the country to another and from dealer to dealer. For further information we recommend our advisor, Beverly Schell Ales; she is listed in the Directory under California.

Bakelite, mottled brn, set of 12, ⅝x3⅝", MIB, from $125 to......**140.00**
China, Meissen, mk X w/sword logo on end, pr..........................**165.00**
China, sea horse, bl & wht, Bing & Grondahl, 1870-90, 3¾" H, lg...**145.00**
Crystal, 6-sided ends w/starburst design, 1¼x3½", set of 12, MIB...**95.00**
Glass, amber, Val St Lambert Belquigue, 1963............................**100.00**
Glass, cut; lapidary ends, Hawkes, 5"..**100.00**
Glass, cut; prisms, Hawkes, 1889 catalog, 3½", from $100 to **150.00**
Glass, cut; rnd shaft, sq ends, Waterford, 2½x7⅛", from $50 to ...**70.00**
Glass, cut; squash form **75.00**
Glass, cut; star pattern on ends w/hexagonal bar, 2x5½" **100.00**
Glass, frog on 1 end, opal, Sabino, 1½x3½" **50.00**
Glass, frosted ends, geometric shape, Lalique, 1½x3¾"................**135.00**
Glass, pressed; clear, Baccarat, 4¾", from $25 to **50.00**
Glass, pressed; frosted baby's head ea end, Baccarat, 4x2" **32.00**
Glass, pressed; Marjorie, plain shaft, Cambridge, 4x2", from $25 to...**30.00**
Glass, pressed; milk glass, mk Imperial, 3½", from $35 to **45.00**
Glass, pressed: gr, Holland, 1½x3½", set of 4................................**75.00**
Ivory on sterling fr, bull-horn shape on sq base, 1½x1⅜", pr......**200.00**
Pearlware, bl & wht, Spode, ca 1820, 4⅛"...................................**125.00**
Porc, flow bl, SP side ft, 3½x1"..**48.00**
Porc, harlequin & clown figurines, Germany, 1920s, 1½x5", pr....**70.00**
Pottery, ducks figural, Goebel, mk K729, ca 1930s, 2¾", pr **90.00**
Pottery, woman & man decor, Quimper, 3", pr, from $80 to **100.00**
Silver, parrot on ea end of bar, 2x4"..**175.00**
SP, greyhounds on ea end of bar, ca 1900, 3¾" **65.00**
SP, grouse figural, mk WMF, 1¼x3¼" **80.00**
SP, lion figural, mk O Gallia, Fr, 1x3¾" **70.00**
SP, monkey on ea end w/bar in mouth, mk WMF, ¾x4½"............**90.00**
SP, polar bear figural, mk WMF 60, 1x3½" **80.00**
SP, Xd tennis rackets on ea end of rod, 1⅜x3" **140.00**
SP wht metal, animal shapes, Rabier, Fr, 1920s, set of 12, MIB.....**200.00**
Transferware, bl floral, Staffordshire, 1830s................................**195.00**

Knives

Knife collecting as a hobby began in earnest during the 1960s when government regulations required for the first time that knife companies mark their products with the country of origin. The few collectors and dealers aware of this change at once began stockpiling the older knives made before this law was enacted. Another impetus to the growing interest in this area came with the Gun Control Act of 1968, which severely restricted gun trading. Frustrated gun dealers transferred their attention to knives. Today there are collectors clubs in many of the states.

The most sought-after pocketknives are those made before WWII. However, as time goes on knives no older than twenty years are collectible if in mint condition. Most collectors prefer knives in 'as found' condition. Do *not* attempt to clean, sharpen, or in any way 'improve' on an old knife.

Please note: Length is measured with blades *closed*. Our values are for knives in used/excellent condition (unless specified 'mint'). Most old knives are usually not encountered in mint condition. Therefore to give a mint price could mislead the novice collector. If a knife has been used, sharpened, or blemished in any way, its value decreases. It is common to find knives made in the 1960s and later in mint condition. Knives made in the 1970s and 1980s may be collectible in mint condition, but not in used condition. Therefore a used knife thirty years old may be be worth no more than a knife for use. For further information refer to *The Stan-*

dard *Knife Collector's Guide; Cattaragus Cutlery Co.;* and *The Big Book of Pocket Knives* by Ron Stewart and Roy Ritchie; *Collector's Guide to E.C. Simmons Keen Kutter Cutlery Tools* by Jerry and Elaine Heuring; and *Sargent's American Premium Guide to Knives and Razors, Identification and Values, 3rd Edition,* by Jim Sargent. Our advisor for this category is Bill Wright, author of *Theatre-Made Military Knives of World War II* (Schiffer). Mr. Wright is listed in the Directory under Indiana.

Key:
alum — aluminum	jack — jacknife
bd — blade	lb — lockback
gen — genuine	pat — pattern
imi — imitation	wb — winterbottom

A Davy & Sons (Sheffield England), 2-bd, Liberty & Union bolster....**700.00**
Aerial Cutlery Co, 2-bd jack, bone hdl, 3⅜" **60.00**
Anheuser-Busch, red & gold emb hdl, w/peephole & picture **250.00**
Barnett Tool Co, bone hdl, bd+punch+pliers **175.00**
Boker, Henrich (German), 1-bd, bone hdl, 4½" **65.00**
Boker (German), 4-bd congress, bone hdl, 4" **125.00**
Boker (USA), 3-bd stockman, imi pearl hdl, 4"............................**40.00**
Boker (USA), 4-bd congress, bone hdl, 3¾" **65.00**
Bulldog Brand (Germany), 3-bd whittler, gen abalone hdl, 5⅛" ...**150.00**
Case, Tested XX, 61093, 1-bd, gr bone hdl, toothpick pat, 5".....**200.00**
Case, Tested XX, 6202½, 2-bd, gen stag hdl, 3⅜" **100.00**
Case, Tested XX, 62031½, 2-bd, gr bone hdl, 3¾" **150.00**
Case, Tested XX, 62100, 2-bd, gr bone hdl, saddlehorn pat, 4⅜" ..**675.00**
Case, Tested XX, 6220, 2-bd, rough blk hdl, peanut pat, 2⅜".....**100.00**
Case, Tested XX, 6392, 3-bd, gr bone hdl, stockman pat, 4" **175.00**
Case, Tested XX, 8383, 2-bd, gen pearl hdl, whittler pat, 3½" ...**500.00**
Case, XX, 2-bd, bone hdl, muskrat pat, 3⅜" **150.00**
Case, XX, 3347hp, 3-bd, yel compo hdl, stockman pat, 3⅜".........**85.00**
Case, XX, 5254, 2-bd, gen stag hdl, trapper pat, 4⅛" **300.00**
Case, XX, 5375, 3-bd, gen red stag hdl, long pull, stockman, 4¼" ..**1,000.00**
Case, XX, 6185, 1-bd, bone hdl, doctor's pat, 3¾" **125.00**
Case, XX, 62009, 1-bd, bone hdl, barlow pat, 3⅜" **70.00**
Case, XX, 6231½, 2-bd, bone hdl, 3¾" **100.00**
Case, XX, 6250, 2-bd, bone hdl, sunfish pat, 4½" **200.00**
Case, XX, 6294, 2-bd, bone hdl, cigar pat, 4¼" **250.00**
Case, XX, 6308, 3-bd, bone hdl, whittler pat, 3¼" **125.00**
Case, XX, 6488, 4-bd, bone hdl, congress pat, 4⅛" **500.00**
Case, XX, 6565sab, 2-bd, bone hdl, folding hunter pat, 5¼" **125.00**
Case, XX USA, 10 dots, 6111½", 1-bd, bone hdl, lb, 4⅜", M **325.00**
Case, XX USA, 52131, 2-bd, gen stag hdl, canoe pat, 3⅜", M ...**350.00**
Case, XX USA, 5354, 2-bd, gen stag hdl, trapper pat, 4⅛", M ...**375.00**
Case Bros, Little Valley NY, 2-bd, wood hdl, 3¼" **100.00**
Case Bros, Little Valley NY, 5321, 3-bd, stag hdl, 3¾" **200.00**
Case Bros, Springville NY, 8250, 2-bd, pearl hdl, sunfish pat ..**3,000.00**
Cattaraugus, D2589, 4-bd, bone hdl, Official Scout Emblem, 3½" ..**200.00**
Cattaraugus, 12839, 1-bd, bone hdl, King of the Woods, 5⅜" **500.00**
Cattaraugus, 22346, 2-bd, wood hdl, jack pat, 3⅜"......................**85.00**
Cattaraugus, 22919, 2-bd, bone hdl, cigar pat, 4¼" **400.00**
Cattaraugus, 3-bd+nail file, gen pearl hdl, lobster gun stock, 3" **150.00**
Cattaraugus, 32145, 3-bd, bone hdl, stockman pat, 3⅜" **200.00**
Challenge Cutlery, 1-bd, bone hdl, lb pat, 4¾" **200.00**
Challenge Cutlery, 3-bd, bone hdl, cattle pat, 3⅜" **125.00**
Diamond Edge, 2-bd, bone hdl, jack, 3⅜" **75.00**
Diamond Edge, 2-bd, pearl celluloid hdl, gun stock, 3" **100.00**
Frost Cutlery Co (Japan), 3-bd, bone hdl, lb whittler, 4" **15.00**
H&B Mfg Co, 3-bd, buffalo horn hdl, whittler, 3⅜" **150.00**
Hammer Brand, NY Knife Co, 2-bd, bone hdl, 3⅜" **85.00**
Hammer Brand, 1-bd, bone hdl, NYK on bolster, lb, 5¼"...........**375.00**
Hammer Brand, 1-bd, tin shell hdl, powder-horn pat, 4¾" **25.00**
Hammer Brand, 2-bd, bone hdl, dog-leg pat, 3¾" **225.00**

Hammer Brand, 2-bd, wood hdl, jack, 3¾" **85.00**
Henckels, JA; 3-bd, bone hdl, whittler pat, 3¼" **65.00**
Henckels, JA; 4-bd, bone hdl, congress pat, 4" **150.00**
Hibbard, Spencer, Bartlett & Co, 2-bd, bone hdl, barlow, 3⅜".....**85.00**
Hibbard, Spencer, Bartlett & Co, 2-bd, bone hdl, dog-leg, 3⅜"....**110.00**
Holley Mfg Co, 1-bd, wood hdl, 5"...**140.00**
Holley Mfg Co, 3-bd, pearl hdl, whittler pat, 3¼"......................**225.00**
Holley Mfg Co, 4-bd, bone hdl, congress pat, 3½" **375.00**
Honk Falls Knife Co, 1-bd, bone hdl, 3" **125.00**
I*XL (Sheffield England), 4-bd, gen stag hdl, congress, 4"..........**350.00**
I*XL (Sheffield), 2-bd, wood hdl, heavy jack, 4" **125.00**
Imperial Knife Co, 2-bd, bone hdl, dog-leg pat, 3⅜" **50.00**
Imperial Knife Co, 2-bd, mc hdl, 3¼" **35.00**
John Primble, Belknap Hdw Co, 3-bd, bone hdl, 4" **75.00**
John Primble, Belknap Hdw Co, 4-bd, bone hdl, 3¾" **85.00**
John Primble, India Steel Works, 2-bd, gen stag hdl, 4¼" **500.00**
John Primble, India Steel Works on bolster, celluloid hdl, 3" **125.00**
Ka-Bar, Union Cutlery, knife & fork, bone hdl, 5¼" **300.00**
Ka-Bar, Union Cutlery, 2-bd, gen stag hdl, dog head, 5¼" **300.00**
Ka-Bar, Union Cutlery, 3-bd, bone hdl, whittler, 3¾" **150.00**
Ka-Bar, 2-bd, gen stag hdl, Old Time Trapper, 4⅛" **85.00**
Ka-Bar, 3-bd, bone hdl, cattle pat, 3⅜" **100.00**

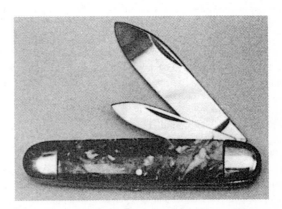

Keen Kutter, Diamond Edge, equal-end jackknife, brown and yellow celluloid handle, 3⅜", $50.00.

Keen Kutter, EC Simmons, 1-bd, bone hdl, lb, 4¼" **200.00**
Keen Kutter, EC Simmons, 1-bd, bone hdl, 3¼" **50.00**
Keen Kutter, EC Simmons, 2-bd, bone hdl, trapper, 3⅜" **250.00**
Keen Kutter, EC Simmons, 2-bd, colorful celluloid hdl, 3⅜" **70.00**
Keen Kutter, EC Simmons, 2-bd, pearl hdl, doctor pat, 3⅜" **250.00**
Keen Kutter, EC Simmons, 2-bd, wood hdl, jack, 3¼" **75.00**
Keen Kutter, EC Simmons, 3-bd, bone hdl, whittler, 3⅜".............**75.00**
Keen Kutter, 1-bd, bone hdl, TX toothpick, 5".............................**125.00**
Keen Kutter, 2-bd, bone hdl, barlow, 3⅜" **75.00**
Keen Kutter, 2-bd, bone hdl, folding hunter, 5¼" **125.00**
LF&C, 2-bd, jigged hard rubber hdl, jack, 3⅜" **75.00**
LF&C, 3-bd, gen pearl hdl, whittler, 3½" **125.00**
Maher & Grosh, 2-bd, bone hdl, jack, 3⅜" **150.00**
Marbles, 1-bd, gen stag hdl, Safety Folding Hunter, lg **700.00**
Marbles, 1-bd, gen stag hdl, Safety Folding Hunter, sm..............**500.00**
Miller Bros, 2-bd, bone hdl, jack, 3½" **100.00**
Miller Bros, 2-bd, screws in bone hdl, 4¼" **500.00**
Miller Bros, 3-bd, gen stag hdl, stockman, 4" **350.00**
Miller Bros, 3-bd, screws in gen pearl hdl, 3⅜" **250.00**
Morley, WH &Sons; 3-bd, bone hdl, whittler, 3¼" **65.00**
MSA Co, Marbles, 2-bd, pearl hdl, sunfish, rare, 4" **3,500.00**
Napanoch Knife Co, X100X, 1-bd, bone hdl, very rare, 5⅜" ..**2,500.00**
Napanoch Knife Co, 2 lg bd, bone hdl, 3⅜".................................**250.00**

Napanoch Knife Co, 4-bd, bone hdl, 3¼"............................**150.00**
Northfield Knife Co, 2-bd, bone hdl, dog-leg pat, 3¾".............**500.00**
Northfield Knife Co, 2-bd, bone hdl, jack, 3⅜"....................**165.00**
Pal, 2-bd, bone hdl, easy-open, 3⅜"................................**85.00**
Pal, 3-bd, bone hdl, jack, 3⅜"....................................**60.00**
Parker, Eagle (Japan), 1-bd, bone hdl, lb, 4½", M.................**25.00**
Parker, Eagle (Japan), 4-bd, gen abalone hdl, congress, 3⅜", M....**100.00**
Queen, #18, 2-bd, wb bone hdl, jack, 3¹¹⁄₁₆".......................**50.00**
Queen, #19, 2-bd, wb bone hdl, trapper, 4⅛"......................**150.00**
Remington, RB43, 2-bd, bone hdl, barlow, 3⅜"......................**75.00**
Remington, R173, 2-bd, bone hdl, teardrop jack, 3¾"..............**150.00**
Remington, R555, 2-bd, candy stripe celluloid hdl, 3¼"...........**125.00**
Remington, R775, 2-bd, red/wht/bl hdl, 3½".......................**185.00**
Remington, R1123, (old) 2-bd, silver bullet on bone hdl, 4½"...**750.00**
Remington, R1153, 2-bd, bone hdl, jack, 4½"......................**250.00**
Remington, R1225, 2-bd, wht compo hdl, 4½".......................**125.00**
Remington, R1306, (old) gen stag hdl, lb, silver bullet, 4⅜"....**600.00**
Remington, R3054, 3-bd, gen pearl hdl, stockman, 4"..............**300.00**
Remington, RS3333, 4-bd, bone hdl, scout shield, 3¾".............**125.00**
Robeson, Shuredge, 2-bd, gen pearl hdl, jack, 3½"................**150.00**
Robeson, Shuredge, 2-bd, strawberry bone hdl, jack, 3¾".........**100.00**
Robeson, Shuredge, 3-bd, bone hdl, stockman, 3⅜"................**125.00**
Rodgers, Jos & Sons, multi-bd, stag hdl, sportsman's............**350.00**
Rodgers, Jos & Sons, 2-bd, gen stag hdl, jack, 3⅜"..............**125.00**
Rodgers, Jos & Sons, 3-bd, bone hdl, stockman, 4"...............**150.00**
Russell, 2-bd, bone hdl, barlow, 3⅜".............................**125.00**
Russell, 2-bd, bone hdl, barlow, 5"..............................**200.00**
Schatt & Morgan (current), 1-bd, w/bone hdl, lb, 5¼", M.........**100.00**
Schatt & Morgan (old), 2-bd, bone hdl, jack, 3⅜"...............**150.00**
Schrade Walden, 2-bd, peach seed bone hdl, 4¼"..................**250.00**
Schrade Walden, 3-bd, peach seed bone hdl, 3⅜"..................**75.00**
Ulster Knife Co, 1-bd, bone hdl, barlow, 5", M..................**200.00**
Ulster Knife Co, 4-bd, imi bone hdl, scout/campers..............**30.00**
Wade & Butcher (Germany), 3-bd, gen stag hdl, whittler..........**125.00**
Wade & Butcher (Sheffield England), 4-bd, gen stag hdl, 4"......**500.00**
Walden Knife Co, 1-bd, bone hdl, toothpick pat, 5".............**200.00**
Wards, 4-bd, bone hdl, cattle pat, 3⅝"..........................**85.00**
Winchester, 1920, (old) 1-bd, bone hdl, 5¼"....................**650.00**
Winchester, 2046, (old) 2-bd, bone hdl, trapper, 3⅜"..........**350.00**
Winchester, 2046, (old) 2-bd), celluloid hdl, jack, 3¾".......**85.00**
Winchester, 2974, (old) 2-bd, bone hdl, dog-leg jack, 3½".....**125.00**
Winchester, 3350, (old) 3-bd, gen pearl hdl, whittler, 3¼"....**125.00**
Winchester, 3960, (old) 3-bd, bone hdl, stockman, 4"..........**275.00**
Winchester, 3971, dtd 89 (1989), 3-bd, bone hdl, whittler.....**75.00**

Sheath Knives

Over the past several years knife collectors have noticed that the availability of quality old pocketknives has steadily decreased. Many collectors have now started looking for sheath knives as an addition to their hobby. In many cases, makers of pocketknives also made quality hunting and sheath knives. Listed below is a small sampling of collectible sheath knives available.

Length is given for overall knife measurement; price includes original sheath and reflects the value of knives in excellent used condition.

Case, (XX) 515-5, stacked leather hdl, 9"........................**35.00**
Case, (XX) 523-5, gen stag hdl, 9¼".............................**85.00**
Case (Bradford PA), bk of tang: Case's Tested XX, 8¼"...........**150.00**
Case (WR & Sons), bone hdl, Bowie knife, 11"....................**400.00**
Case (XX USA), gen stag hdl, Kodiak hunter, 10¾"................**125.00**
Case (XX), V-44, blk Bakelite hdl, WWII, 14½"...................**350.00**
Cattaraugus, gen stag hdl, alum pommel, 10¼"....................**85.00**
Cattaraugus, 225Q, stacked leather hdl, WWII, 10⅜".............**45.00**

I*XL (Sheffield), Bowie knife, ca 1845, 14"..................**2,000.00**
I*XL (Sheffield), leather hdl w/stag, ca 1935, 10".............**100.00**
Ka-Bar, Union Cutlery Co, jigged bone hdl, 9¾".................**150.00**
Ka-Bar, Union Cutlery Co, leather hdl w/stag, 8½"..............**125.00**
Ka-Bar, USMC, stacked leather hdl, WWII, 12¼"..................**100.00**
Keen Kutter, EC Simmons, K1050-6, Bowie knife, 10".............**500.00**
Marbles, Ideal, all gen stag hdl, 10"..........................**275.00**
Marbles, Ideal, stacked leather hdl w/alum, 9".................**100.00**
Marbles, Ideal, stacked leather hdl w/stag, 11⅜"..............**500.00**
Marbles, Woodcraft, stacked leather hdl w/alum, 8¼"...........**125.00**
Randall, Springfield MA, leather hdl, WWII, 13".............**1,750.00**
Randall, stacked leather hdl w/alum, 10¼".....................**300.00**
Remington, RH36, stacked leather hdl w/alum, 10½".............**150.00**
Remington, RH40, stacked leather hdl w/alum, rare, 14½".....**1,500.00**
Remington, RH73, gen stag hdl, 8"..............................**75.00**
Ruana, alum w/elk horn hdl, skinner, current, 7½".............**100.00**
Ruana, RH; alum w/elk horn hdl, ca 1980, 6½"..................**200.00**
Ruana, RH; M stamp, alum w/elk horn hdl, skinner, 9¼".........**275.00**
Winchester, W1050, jigged bone hdl, Bowie knife, 10".........**1,200.00**
Wragg, SC (Sheffield); stag hdl, Bowie knife, 13½"...........**1,500.00**

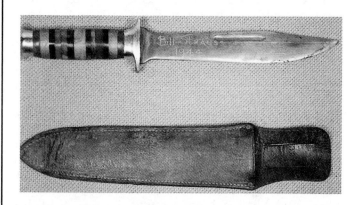

WWII theatre knife (similar knives were made and used during WWII), colorful Bakelite handle, 7¾" blade, EX, $250.00. (Photo courtesy Bill Wright)

WWII, theater knife, mc Bakelite hdl, 12".......................**200.00**
WWII, theater knife, mc hdl, Bowie knife, 12¾".................**125.00**
WWII, theater knife, mc hdl, dagger, 11".......................**150.00**
WWII, theater knife, Plexiglass hdl w/picture, 12".............**175.00**

Kosta

Kosta glassware has been made in Sweden since 1742. Today they are one of that country's leading producers of quality art glass. Two of their most important designers were Elis Bergh (1929 – 1950) and Vicke Lindstrand, artistic director from 1950 to 1973. Lindstrand brought to the company knowledge of important techniques such as Graal, fine figural engraving, Ariel, etc. He influenced new artists to experiment with these techniques and inspired them to create new and innovative designs. Today's collectors are most interested in pieces made during the 1950s and 1960s. Our advisor for this category is Abby Malowanczyk; she is listed in the Directory under Texas.

Bottle, purple w/bl & gr spatters, rnd w/1 flat side, #47267, 7¼"....**500.00**
Bowl, boat shape, med bl opaque cased in clear, LS 618/90, 6½"......**55.00**
Bowl, cameo trefoils inside, clear w/purple int layer, Ehrner, 5x7"..**300.00**
Paperweight, bl swirls in clear w/bubbles, Bergh #90962, 2¾" dia ...**125.00**
Vase, amber cased w/clear, appl ft, LH 1711, 5½"...................**155.00**
Vase, Autumn, mc leaves on clear, Lindstrand/41753, 6"........**1,295.00**

Vase, blk cased in clear w/air bubbles, flattened, LH 1328, 3¼"....**100.00**
Vase, blk-to-purple & wht crisscross, LH1261, 9¼"....................**635.00**
Vase, flattened cylinder, LH 1321/59, 11¼x4" **1,750.00**
Vase, flattened ovoid, Linstrand, LH 1384, 1958-59, 5½x4"......**525.00**
Vase, 6 cameo-cut moths, purple/clear, Boman, 1900, 9" **2,800.00**

Kutani

Kutani, named for the Japanese village where it originated, was first produced in the seventeenth century. The early ware, Ko Kutani, was made for only about thirty years. Several types were produced before 1800, but these are rarely encountered. In the nineteenth century, kilns located in several different villages began to copy the old Kutani wares. This later, more familiar type has large areas of red with gold designs on a white ground decorated with warriors, birds, and flowers in controlled colors of red, gold, and black.

Bowl, exotic bird among branches and flowers, nineteenth century, 14½", $1750.00.

Bowl, red & wht flowers & birds, 5-sided, 3x6" **60.00**
Box, mc floral w/gold, 3 gold ft, 20th C, 2x4¾"..........................**75.00**
Cup, pomegranates & archaic signs...**315.00**
Figurine, woman seated on elephant, late 19th C, 9½" **500.00**
Inkwell, cherry blossoms w/gold, 7x4" **215.00**
Jardiniere, landscapes & brocade patterns w/gold on gr, 19th C, 14"..**475.00**
Teabowl, sunflower w/orange & gr, mk FIJU, 3x5" **110.00**
Vase, pine tree landscape w/2 cranes, sgn Sanyu, 8½".................**210.00**

Labels

Before the advent of the cardboard box, wooden crates were used for transporting products. Paper labels were attached to the crates to identify the contents and the packer. These labels often had colorful lithographed illustrations covering a broad range of subjects. Eventually the cardboard box replaced the crate, and the artwork was imprinted directly onto the carton. Today these paper labels are becoming collectible — not only the art, but also for their advertising appeal. Our advisor for this category is Cerebro; the address is listed in the Directory under Pennsylvania.

Can, Advonda Kidney beans, 2 bowls of beans, EX **15.00**
Can, Blue & Gold Peas, corner store, EX **15.00**
Can, Casserole Oysters, bowl of oysters in cream, M....................**5.00**
Can, Delight Malt Syrup, man w/can, 1929, EX............................**18.00**
Can, Everyday Peas, bowl of peas/pea pod, 1928, EX **12.00**
Can, Fresh Tomatoes, lg tomatoes, 1880s, VG **60.00**
Can, Gaspe Shore Lobster, lobster on coast, Canadian, early, M..**25.00**
Can, Golden Shore Clams, 3 clams/sunset over ocean, EX...........**20.00**
Can, Heart Over Florida Grapefruit, half grapefruit/map of FL, G.**17.00**

Can, Homestead Mushrooms, country home, M **18.00**
Can, La Catalina Peaches, senorita/Barcelona, VG......................**12.00**
Can, Marigold Peaches, peach/flowers on red, 1927, EX.............**14.00**
Can, Monarch Chicken Soup, head of lion, 1922, EX **25.00**
Can, Osseo Early Peas, 2 prospectors/knight on horse, M...........**25.00**
Can, OT Ozark Trail, car on mountain/fruits/vegetables, EX........**40.00**
Can, Penn-Harris, bowls of fruit, map of PA, M..........................**20.00**
Can, Roast Mutton, cowboy on plains after cow, lg, M................**35.00**
Can, Roast Mutton, cowboy on plains after cow, sm, M..............**25.00**
Can, Sun-Lite Prunes, EX..**15.00**
Can, W-G Brand Pineapple, head of Washington, M....................**40.00**
Can, West Shore Peas, bowl of peas/tropical village, EX.............**12.00**
Can, Zig-Zag Malt Syrup, silhouette of castle, 1929, EX **8.00**
Cigar box, inner; Ambassador, oval fr bust flanked by 2 women, EX ...**30.00**
Cigar box, inner; Butterfly, parrot & girl, 1880s, EX **40.00**
Cigar box, inner; Dankbaarheid, Art Nouveau couple on swing, M ...**40.00**
Cigar box, inner; El Unisolo, 2 women/tropics, M **15.00**
Cigar box, inner; Film, silhouette view of people at movies, M....**65.00**
Cigar box, inner; Gran Fabrica de Tabacos, man/crown/coat-of-arms, M ..**10.00**
Cigar box, inner; Havana Inn, old car parked next to inn, M **25.00**
Cigar box, inner; John Hancock, patriot/lg signature, EX.............**35.00**
Cigar box, inner; La Frequensa, Indian maiden next to lion, M...**35.00**
Cigar box, inner; Nell Gwynne, young girl/flowers, EX **40.00**
Cigar box, inner; Piper Heidsieck, woman w/champagne & cigars, M...**100.00**
Cigar box, inner; Riverside, father fishing/wife & child playing, G.....**85.00**
Cigar box, inner; Statesman, eagle/Independence Hall, M **35.00**
Cigar box, inner; The Trotter, spectators rooting for favorite, G...**200.00**
Cigar box, inner; Trakenia, man holding blk stallion, M **50.00**
Cigar box, outer; Al-U-Pa, map of Alaska, AYP Expo, 1909, EX....**35.00**
Cigar box, outer; Anker-Sigaar, Indian, EX **45.00**
Cigar box, outer; Bajazzo, jester looking onto mirror, M **10.00**
Cigar box, outer; Beata, woman/gilded flowers/bl ground, EX **15.00**
Cigar box, outer; Carola, woman w/long braids, M **20.00**
Cigar box, outer; Dick Custer, cowboy holding gun, M................**12.00**
Cigar box, outer; El Dador, woman looking out to sea at ship, M.**30.00**
Cigar box, outer; Hunt's Eliot, cavalier, heavily emb/gilded, M....**45.00**
Cigar box, outer; Motorist, Mercury driving through flames, 1920s, M...**75.00**
Cigar box, outer; Rothkappchen, Red Riding Hood/fox in window, M ..**25.00**
Crate, apple; Best Strike, baseball player, 1920s, M......................**45.00**
Crate, apple; Buckeye Brand, circular w/map of Ohio, 1920s, M..**35.00**
Crate, CA lemon; Honeymoon, Deco castle, bright orange, M **60.00**
Crate, CA lemon; Sea Treat, view of ship through porthole, 1930s, M **20.00**
Crate, CA orange; Bolero, dancing senorita, Lochinvar, EX.........**45.00**
Crate, CA orange; California Sunshine, gold sunburst behind orange, EX...**70.00**
Crate, cranberry; Capital Brand, image of Capital building, M.......**6.00**
Crate, cranberry; Mistletoe Brand, wht berries on red ground, M ...**10.00**
Crate, FL citrus; Cuckoo, sm bird perched on twig, VG **50.00**
Crate, FL citrus; Harvey's Groves, orchards/bay/sailboat, EX **70.00**
Crate, pear; Island Brand, view of Grand Island CA, early, M......**35.00**
Crate, pear; Lake Vista, lake/mountains/trees, EX.......................**100.00**
Crate, TX citrus; Inside Quality, lg Black lady in red scarf, EX.....**20.00**
Crate, TX citrus; Mission's Pride, ½ grapefruit on table, VG........**35.00**
Crate, vegetable, First Flight, military prop plane, M...................**20.00**
Crate, vegetable; Aristocrat, purple ground/gold border, EX.........**15.00**
Crate, yam; Honest John, farmer holding box, M..........................**5.00**
Crate, yam; Peter Piper Potato, boy playing horn/yam, M.............**6.00**

Labino

Dominick Labino was a glass blower who until mid-1985 worked in his studio in Ohio, blowing and sculpting various items which he signed and dated. A ceramic engineer by trade, he was instrumental in developing the heat-resistant tiles used in space flights. His glassmaking shows his versatility in the art. While some of his designs are free-form and futuristic, others are reminiscent of the products of older glasshouses. Because of problems with his health, Mr. Labino became unable to blow glass himself; he died January 10, 1987. Work coming from his studio since mid-1985 has been signed 'Labino Studios, Baker,' indicating ware made by his protegee, E. Baker O'Brien. In addition to her own compositions, she continues to use many of the colors developed by Labino.

Bowl, bl, teal & yel swirl mix, 1971, 3x7¾"	320.00
Bowl, celadon w/pk & yel, 1981, 3x5"	210.00
Bowl, gr w/wide flared rim, 1967, 3x6"	125.00
Bowl, transparent shades of pk, 2x7"	285.00
Candlestick, red w/yel swirls at base w/yel neck	120.00
Cruet, clear to red base, 1981, 6"	200.00
Figurine, dolphin, lt bl, 1979	210.00
Figurine, duck, cinnamon, 1982, 5"	50.00
Figurine, duck, irid bl, 1980, 5¾"	150.00
Figurine, shark, clear, 1980	185.00
Paperweight, aquatic theme on lt bl w/controlled bubbles, 1967, 3½"	340.00
Paperweight, clear w/red & yel floral, 1967, 3"	180.00
Paperweight, cobalt w/yel floral swirls, 1980, 2½"	440.00
Paperweight, vertical latticino bands/twisted mc ribbons, 3¾"	95.00
Pitcher, transparent red, rnd hole forms hdl, 1985	210.00
Sculpture, abstract sommerso w/bubbles & mc veils, 1972, 6x10"	700.00
Sculpture, Emergence, peach, red & yel w/clear peak, dtd 1982, 7½"	4,500.00
Sculpture, flame shape w/internal mc jellyfish, 1971, 7x4½"	800.00
Toothpick holder, clear w/brn loops, 1971, 2¾"	100.00
Vase, bl-gray w/irregular bubbles, mk 1972, 5½x4½"	400.00
Vase, bud; amber w/sculptured air enclosures, 1974, 5"	250.00
Vase, cobalt w/wht decor & textured swirl at base, 1972, 5½"	210.00
Vase, crackle irid w/appl bl medallions, globular, 1968, 4"	350.00
Vase, flared calla lily lip on ped, 1983, 6½"	365.00
Vase, lt bl w/dk bl & wht pulled loops, slender neck, 1969, 12½"	265.00

Vase, light burgundy with lava-like controlled flows, #1400, 1979, 7½", $1,400.00.

Vase, mauve agate swirl, shouldered, flat rim, 1967, 5"	225.00
Vase, multi-tone gr w/emb ribs, 1971, 8"	600.00
Vase, navy bl w/mc swirls & floral decor, 1982, 5"	190.00
Vase, opaque irid purple w/emb ribs, 1991	290.00
Vase, opaque wht w/yel loopings, 1980	415.00
Vase, pulled cobalt & yel cased in clear, dtd 1981, 5½"	965.00
Vase, transparent aubergine w/internal bubbles, spherical, 1967	260.00

Lace, Linens, and Needlework

Two distinct audiences vie for old lace and linens. Collectors seek out exceptional stitchery like philatelists and numismatists seek stamps

or coins — simply to marvel at its beauty, rarity, and ties to history. Collectors judge lace and linens like figure skaters and gymnasts are judged: artist impression is half the score, technical merit the other. How complex and difficult are the stitches and how well are they done? The 'users' see lace and linens as recyclables. They seek pretty wearables or decorative materials. They want fashionable things in mint condition, and have little or no interest in technique. Both groups influence price.

Undiscovered and underpriced are the eighteenth-century masterpieces of lace and needle art in techniques which will never be duplicated. Their beauty is subtle. Amazing stitches often are invisible without magnification. To get the best value in any lace, linen, or textile item, learn to look closely at individual stitches, and study the design and technique. The finest pieces are wonderfully constructed. The stitches are beautiful to look at, and they do a good job of holding the item together.

Key: embr — embroidered

Bedcover, handmade filet lace, scalloped edge, ca 1900, 68x88"	80.00
Bedspread, wht chenille w/yel roses, 1940s, 80x110" +sham	80.00
Biscuit cover, wht linen w/embr ea corner, 1920s	45.00
Bonnet veil, ivory embr net, ca 1890, 23x42"	65.00
Bonnet veil, ivory English Honiton lace, 1890s, 20x56	85.00
Boudoir bag, Torchon lace edge, drawstring top, 1900s, 17x18"	70.00
Boudoir bag, wht linen w/drawstring & lace edging, 1900s, 16" sq	55.00
Breakfast set, embr tray cloth, napkin & tea cosy, 1930s, MIB	75.00
Cheval set, wht linen w/embr & cutwork, 10x8" & 2 6½x5½", 3-pc	60.00
Collar, Brussels lace & Point de Gaz Bertha, 1890s, 66" (outside)	165.00
Collar, cream silk handmade Maltese lace, 1920s, 50" (outside)	195.00
Collar, ecru Irish Youghal lace w/shamrocks/roses/thistles, 1930s	95.00
Collar, hand-crochet wht cotton lace, 1940s, 4x32"	45.00
Collar, ivory Brussels Point De Gaz lace, 1900s, 38" L	185.00
Collar, wht machine-made chemical lace, 1900s, 9x34"	165.00
Crib sheet, wht linen w/mc bunny & flower embr, 1930s, 50x36"	75.00
Cuffs, fine wht cotton handmade lace, 1920s, 5x15", pr	60.00
Curtain, wht Nottingham cotton lace, scalloped edge, 1920s, 118x58"	225.00
Curtains, cotton machine-made lace, 1930s, 48x45", pr	165.00
Curtains, ecru Fr cotton net & lace, ca 1910, 66x34", pr	250.00
Doily, ivory hand-embr Madeira, ca 1930, 5½x10"	25.00
Doily, linen center, 2½" tatted edge, ca 1900, 8" dia	35.00
Doily, linen w/hand-crochet scalloped edge, 1890s, 11½"	35.00
Doily, linen w/Princess lace trim, 1920s, 11", 9", pr	50.00
Doily, linen w/5" scalloped lace edge, ca 1900, 17" dia	45.00
Doily, off-wht Italian needle lace, 1930s, 6" dia, pr	75.00
Doily, wht crochet lace w/stand-up frills, 1930s, 8" dia	35.00
Doily, wht filet lace w/exotic birds, 1930s, 8½x13"	45.00
Doily, wht hand-embr voile, scalloped edge, 1920s, 5½" dia	45.00
Doily, wht tissue linen w/embr monogram, 1890s, 5½" sq, pr	30.00
Hot roll cover, Hot Rolls & floral embr, 1920s	48.00
Lappets, wht English Honiton lace, ca 1885, 5x54", VG	125.00
Mat, wht Duchess lace, 1930s, 9½x14"	50.00
Mat, wht Italian needle lace, ca 1900, 13x8½"	65.00
Napkins, cocktail; linen w/saying, self fringe, 1950s, 8" sq, 11 for	65.00
Napkins, cocktail; wht linen w/mc printed figures, 1960s, 6 for	30.00
Napkins, wht Irish dbl damask linen, 1900s, 22" sq, 11 for	155.00
Napkins, wht linen w/embr & filet lace, 1920s, 22" sq, 12 for	185.00
Napkins, wht linen w/embr corners, 1930s, 22" sq, 12 for	55.00
Napkins, wht linen w/pulled-thread hem, 1920s, 13" sq, 10 for	70.00
Needlepoint picture, allegorical w/ladies & sheep, sgn/1826, 14x19"	1,600.00
Needlepoint tapestry, roses, mc w/dk gr border on burgundy, 49x71"	300.00
Needlework panel, flower urn w/butterfly, silk thread, Fr, 18x15" fr	465.00
Needlework picture, lady at stream w/dog, HP features, 1880s, 12x10"	700.00
Needlework picture, romantic couple landscape, Am, 1806, 17x10", EX	5,275.00
Needlework picture, shepherdess & youth w/sheep, Am, 1800s, 15x13"	5,250.00
Nightdress case, wht linen w/bl ribbon & lace surround, 18x14"	75.00

Pillow cover, wht cotton w/lace o/l & trim, 1920s, 17x25" **65.00**
Pillow shams, wht Egyptian cotton w/corded hem, ca 1940, pr **45.00**
Pillowcase, wht Egyptian cotton w/embr, cloth buttons, 1920s, 30x29" ..**65.00**
Pillowcase, wht w/embr & net lace inserts, 1920s, 15x16"+2" frill..**60.00**
Pillowcases, wht cotton w/embr monogram & tatting, 1920s, 20x31", pr..**70.00**
Pillowcases, wht Egyptian cotton, 1930s, 30x18½", M, 4 for........**90.00**
Pillowcases, wht linen w/bl embr, 1930s, 20x35", pr **65.00**
Pillowcases, wht linen w/cherub cutout cartouch & embr, lace edge, pr..**145.00**
Pillowcases, wht linen w/embr Madeira, 1930s, 36x21", pr...........**70.00**
Place mat, wht Madeira w/embr organdy border, 1930s, 13x19", 8 for **90.00**
Runner, ecru linen w/cutwork embr, 1930s, 15x40" **65.00**
Runner, Irish linen, scalloped embr edge w/cutwork, 1900s, 14x48" ...**50.00**
Runner, Point Plat, ecru bobbin lace w/Phoenix motifs, 104x24"..**1,265.00**
Runner, wht cotton w/mc floral embr, scalloped, 1950s, 14x40"...**35.00**
Runner, wht embr fine voille, ca 1930, 13x32", 13x42", pr...........**65.00**
Runner, wht Irish linen w/crochet grapes, 1920s, 17x54".............**95.00**
Runner, wht Irish linen w/drawn threadwork, 1900s, 18x51" **80.00**
Runner, wht linen, scalloped, cutwork florals, 1930s, 16x42" **65.00**
Runner, wht linen & tape lace w/hand embr, 17x67" **125.00**
Runner, wht linen w/mc Deco-style embr floral ea end, 1930s, 15x40"..**50.00**
Runner, wht linen w/mc hand-embr flowers, 1930s, 12x33" **30.00**
Runner, wht linen w/pulled-thread hem, 1900s, 18x54" **50.00**
Runner, wht Madeira linen w/hand embr, 1930s, 15x30".............**55.00**
Shawl, blk Fr Chantilly lace w/gazebo among flowers, ca 1875, 154"....**725.00**
Shawl, wht handmade Tambour lace stole w/much embr, 1880s, 22x102"..**295.00**
Table center, wht linen w/2" hand lace edge, 1900, 17" dia..........**55.00**
Table topper, ivory linen w/lace inserts, 1920s, 30" sq..................**75.00**
Table topper, wht sheer organdy w/pk embr, 1930s, 32" sq............**65.00**
Tablecloth, Battenburg lace, 1920s, 44" sq....................................**85.00**

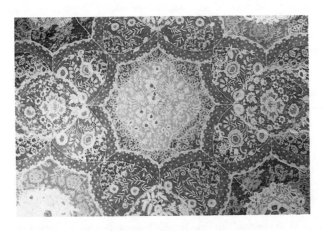

Tablecloth, center of Normandy-work, about 36x45", from $500.00 to $750.00. (Most sought-after examples are a patchwork of nineteenth-century French embroidered and lace cap backs and assorted lace fragments.) (Photo courtesy Lace Merchant)

Tablecloth, ivory linen w/embr & needle lace, 60x98", +6 napkins...**150.00**
Tablecloth, wht dbl damask w/drawn threadwork, 1900s, 42" sq ..**50.00**
Tablecloth, wht Irish linen dbl damask w/monograms, 1890s, 90x174"...**295.00**
Tablecloth, wht Irish linen dbl damask w/pulled thread hem, 69x104"...**85.00**
Tablecloth, wht Irish linen w/embr, 6" lace edge, 1890s, 46" sq....**185.00**
Tablecloth, wht Irish linen w/embr cutwork, 1900s, 50" sq **125.00**
Tablecloth, wht Irish linen w/embr flower bowls, scalloped, 42" sq **95.00**
Tablecloth, wht Irish linen w/scalloped 15" lace edge, 1895, 88" sq...**265.00**
Tablecloth, wht linen w/overall wht embr, 1920s, 50" sq **90.00**
Tablecloth, wht linen w/rnd corners, 1930s, 90x124", +12 20" napkins..**385.00**
Tablecloth, wht organdy w/deer silk applique ea corner, 1930s, 35" sq...**80.00**
Tablecloth, wht sheer organdy & linen, 1920s, 66x104", +12 napkins...**325.00**

Tablecloth, wht tissue linen w/4" lace center, 1920s, 54x78"......**165.00**
Tea cloth, ivory linen w/embr, 1930s, 34" sq, +4 10" napkins.......**70.00**
Tea cloth, wht linen w/printed floral sprays, 1940s, 48" sq............**35.00**
Tea cloth, wht Madeira linen w/pk embr flowers, 1930s, 34" sq .**40.00**
Tea cosy, wht linen w/floral embr, thick padding, 1900s, 11x15"..**55.00**
Topper, gr linen w/wht grapes cutwork, 1940s, 30" sq, +4 napkins..**40.00**
Towel, lemon linen w/Princess lace butterfly 1 end, 1930s, 12x17" ...**40.00**
Towel, wht damask, embr Victorian lady, ca 1930, 16x35" **45.00**
Towel, wht Irish linen w/4" lace ea end, ca 1895, 22x44" **60.00**
Towel, wht linen, 5" geometric lace ea end, 1890s, 23x50", pr...**125.00**
Towel, wht linen, 6" lace ea end w/threaded bl ribbon, 1900s, 22x50" ...**65.00**
Towel, wht linen w/mc embr poodle, 1950s, 13½x19" **48.00**
Towel, wht linen w/wht woven floral design, 3" lace ends, 36x53"..**65.00**
Tray cloth, cotton organdy w/flower basket embr, 1930s, 11x16" **40.00**
Tray cloth, hand-crochet Staff of Life in center, ca 1915, 10x15"....**35.00**
Tray cloth, wht cotton w/3½" lace edge, 1920s, 14x19"...............**50.00**
Tray cloth, wht dbl damask w/drawn threadwork, 1890s, 24x32" .**45.00**
Tray cloth, wht hand embr linen w/3" lace trim, 1885, 20x25" **75.00**
Tray cloth, wht Irish linen w/lace scallops, ca 1900, 18½x26"......**65.00**
Tray cloth, wht linen w/Battenburg edge, 1920s, 13x26" **45.00**
Tray cloth, wht linen w/drawn threadwork & fine embr, 1900s, 14x20"...**30.00**
Tray cloth, wht linen w/embr & applique fruits, 1930s, 11x17"...**46.00**
Tray cloth, wht linen w/hand embr ea end, 4" lace edge, 1900s, 22x27"....**75.00**
Tray cloth, wht linen w/3" handmade floral lace trim, 1900s, 20x26" ..**70.00**
Tray cloth, wht linen w/8" crochet lace edge, 1890s, 28x34"........**80.00**
Tray cloth, wht organdy w/embr flowers, scalloped edge, 1930s, 11x14"....**30.00**
Veil, handmade cotton lace on silk net, 1785-1900 ....**115.00**
Wine mat, linen & Duchesse lace w/monogram, 1900s, 5½" dia, 6 for......**65.00**

Lalique

Having recognized her son's talent at an early age, Rene Lalique's mother apprenticed him at the age of 21 to a famous Paris jeweler. In 1885 he opened his own workshop, and his unique style earned him great notoriety because of his use of natural elements in his designs — horn, ivory, semi-precious stone, pearls, coral, enamel, even plastic or glass.

In 1900 at the Paris Universal Exposition at the age of 40, he achieved the pinnacle of success in the jewelry field. Already having experimented with glass, he decided to focus his artistic talent on that medium. In 1907 after completing seven years of laborious work, Lalique became a master glassmaker and designer of perfume bottles for Francois Coty, a chemist and perfumer, who was also his neighbor in the Place Vendome area in Paris. All in all he created over two hundred fifty perfume bottles for Roger et Gallet, Coty, Worth, Forvil, Guerlain, D'Orsay, Molinard, and many others. In the commercial perfume bottle collecting field, Rene Lalique's are those most desired. Some of his one-of-a-kind experimental models have gone for over $100,000.00 at auction in the last few years.

At the height of production his factories employed over six hundred workers.

Seeking to bring art into every day life, he designed clocks, tableware, stemware, chandeliers, inkwells, bowls, statues, dressing table items, and, of course, vases. Lalique's unique creativity is evident in his designs through his polishing, frosting, and glazing techniques. He became famous for his use of colored glass in shades of blue, red, black, gray, yellow, green, and opalescence. His glass, so popular in the 1920s and 1930s, is still coveted today.

Lalique's son Marc assumed leadership of the company in 1948, after his father's death. His designs are made from full lead crystal, not the demi-crystal Rene worked with. Designs from 1948 on were signed only Lalique, France. The company was later taken over by Marc's daughter, Marie-Claude, and her designs were modern, clear crystal accented with color motifs. The Lalique company was sold in 1995, and Marie-Claude Lalique retired shortly thereafter.

Condition is of extreme importance to a collector. Grinding, polished out chips, and missing perfume bottle stoppers can reduce the value significantly, sometimes by as much as 80%.

Czechoslovakian glassware bearing fradulent Lalique signatures is appearing on all levels of the market. Study and become familiar with the various Lalique designs before paying a high price for a fraudulent piece. Over the past five years Lalique-designed glass has been showing up in a deep purple-gray color. These are clear glass items that have been 'irradiated' to change their appearance. Buyer beware.

Our advisor for this category is John Danis; he is listed in the Directory under Illinois.

Key:
cl/fr — clear and frosted   RL — signed R. Lalique
L — signed Lalique   RLF — signed R. Lalique, France
LF — signed Lalique France

Vase, Sauterelles, grasshoppers, frosted with blue and green patina, R. Lalique France, 1913, 10½", $7,500.00. (In recent years this design has been reproduced and sold with a fake Lalique signature. Buyer beware.)

(Photo courtesy Skinner Inc.)

Ashtray, Soudan, acid cut zigzags, #328, RLF, 1⅞x4⅜x4⅜" **175.00**
Atomizer, Epines, fr, #592, RL/MIF, 3¾" **350.00**
Atomizer, nudes, legs extend to flowing lines, fr, RLF, 9" **360.00**
Bottle, scent; Ambre for D'Orsay, female ea corner, blk, 5¼" **1,500.00**
Bottle, scent; Hélène, classical women, cl/fr w/brn wash, mk, 9" ..**825.00**
Bottle, scent; Parisien, nudes w/garlands, fr, RL, 7¼" **280.00**
Bottle, scent; Sans Adieu, emerald gr column, RL, 4¼" **1,000.00**
Bottle, scent; Teline, fr shell, RL, 3⅞" **1,500.00**
Bowl, Nemours, Eye/floral w/blk center, LF, 10", NM **235.00**
Bowl, Pinsons, finches, cl/fr, LF & paper label, 3⅝x9¼" **300.00**
Bowl, Pissenlit, dandelions, cl/fr, RL, ca 1921, 3½x9¼" **235.00**
Bowl, Volubilis, morning-glories, lt amber, RL, 8½", NM **750.00**
Box, Cleones, beetles/ferns, amber, RLF, 6¾" dia...................**1,500.00**
Box, Grande Cyprins, cl w/opal fish, RL, 2x10" dia................**3,200.00**
Box, Roger, birds & grapevines & 11 polished circles, brn, 5¼" dia ..**2,400.00**
Box, rose-emb bands radiate across top/down sides, fr, L/Paris, 7" L ...**800.00**
Cachet, Rapace, owl, cl/fr, stepped base, France, ca 1931, 2⅞" ..**250.00**
Candlesticks, sq top/ft, rope-trimmed rims, fr/cl, LF, 4¾", EX, pr **100.00**
Champagne, angel figure w/extended wings on bowl, 8", 12 for ...**1,000.00**
Decanter, oval body w/concentric ovals w/emb dotted lines, LF, 10½" **345.00**
Dish, Cielettes, fan-shaped leaves, cl/fr, LF, 14" **500.00**
Luminaire, Gros Poisson Vague (lg fish), bronze base, RLF, 15x15" ...**6,000.00**
Mascot, Coq Nain, rooster, amethyst, RLF, 8".......................**1,500.00**
Mascot, Coq Nain, rooster, cl/fr, RLF, 8" **700.00**
Mascot, Tete De Coq, rooster, cl/fr, LF, 7" **1,100.00**
Sculpture, African bull elephant trumpeting, cl/fr, 6x6" **125.00**
Vase, Acanthus, lt gr stain, #5902, RLF, 11" **2,600.00**
Vase, Archer, cased/fr amber, RL, 10½" **11,500.00**

Vase, Bacchantes, nude, cl/fr, #997, LF, 9⅝"" **500.00**
Vase, Bacchantes, nude, cl/fr, #997, RLF, 1927, 9⅝" **3,000.00**
Vase, Baguette, birds in foliage, cl/fr, LF, 6¾" **265.00**
Vase, Bordure Bluets, cornflower buds, gray, RL, 6¾x6¼" **1,880.00**
Vase, Caudebec, flowers & leaves, cl, #1020, ca 1929, 5¾"........**650.00**
Vase, Ceylan, parakeets & vines, bl wash, faint mk, 9½", EX....**5,500.00**
Vase, Coquilles, overlapping rows of seashells, lt bl/fr, RL, 7½" **1,500.00**
Vase, Domremy, thistles, fr, RLF, ca 1926, 8½" **1,400.00**
Vase, Druides, opal w/bl stain, RL, spherical, 7"......................**1,500.00**
Vase, Fern, bl, spherical, #996, RLF, 7" **2,900.00**
Vase, Mures, fr/lt bl stain, RLF, bulbous, 8¼", NM **1,500.00**
Vase, Orsin/Sea Urchin, lt bl wash, clear flared lip, RLF, 7"....**1,600.00**
Vase, Saint Tropez, berries & foliage, cl opal, RLF, 7⅜"............**600.00**
Vase, Tristan, leaf tips, RLF, ca 1928, 8¼", NM **700.00**

Lamps

The earliest lamps were simple dish containers with a wick that hung over the edge or was supported by a channel or tube. Grease and oil from animal or vegetable sources were the first fuels used. Ancient pottery lamps, crusie, and Betty lamps are examples of these early types. In 1784 Swiss inventor Ami Argand introduced the first major improvement in lamps. His lamp featured a tubular wick and a glass chimney. During the first half of the nineteenth century, whale oil, burning fluid (a highly explosive mixture of turpentine and alcohol), and lard were the most common fuels used in North America. Many lamps were patented for specific use with these fuels.

Kerosene was the first major breakthrough in lighting fuels. It was demonstrated by Canadian geologist Dr. Abraham Gesner in 1846. The discovery and drilling of petroleum in the late 1850s provided an abundant and inexpensive supply of kerosene. It became the main source of light for homes during the balance of the nineteenth century and for remote locations until the 1950s.

Although Thomas A. Edison invented the electric lamp in 1879, it was not until two or three decades later that electric lamps replaced kerosene household lamps. Millions of kerosene lamps were made for every purpose and pocketbook. They ranged in size from tiny night or miniature lamps to tall stand or piano lamps. Hanging varieties for homes commonly had one or two fonts (oil containers), but chandeliers for churches and public buildings often had six or more. Wall or bracket lamps usually had silvered reflectors. Student lamps, parlor lamps (now called Gone-With-the-Wind lamps), and patterned glass lamps were designed to complement the popular furnishing trends of the day. Gaslight, introduced in the early nineteenth century, was used mainly in homes of the wealthy and public places until the early twentieth century. Most fixtures were wall or ceiling mounted, although some table models were also used.

Few of the ordinary early electric lamps have survived. Many lamp manufacturers made the same or similar styles for either kerosene or electricity, sometimes for gas. Top-of-the-line lamps were made by Pairpoint, Tiffany, Bradley and Hubbard, and Handel. See also these specific sections.

When buying lamps that have been converted to electricity, inspect them very carefully for any damage that may have resulted from the alterations; such damage is very common, and when it does occur, the lamp's value may be lessened by as much as 50%. Lamps seem to bring much higher prices in some areas than others, especially the larger cities. Conversely, in rural areas they may bring only half as much as our listed values. One of our advisors for lamps is Carl Heck; he is listed in the Directory under Colorado. Advise for miniature lamps comes from Bob Culver (who is listed in the Directory under Michigan) and Jeff Bradfield (in Virginia) is our advisor for pattern glass lamps. See also Stained Glass.

Key: col — cut overlay

Aladdin Lamps, Electric

From 1908 Aladdin lamps with a mantle became the mainstay of rural America, providing light that compared favorably with the electric light bulb. They were produced by the Mantle Lamp Company of America in over eighteen models and more than one hundred styles. From the 1930s to the 1950s, this company was the leading manufacturer of electric lamps as well. Still in operation today, the company is now known as Aladdin Mantle Lamp Co., located in Clarksville, Tennessee. For those seeking additional information on Aladdin Lamps, we recommend *Aladdin — The Magic Name in Lamps*, *Aladdin Electric Lamps Collector's Manual & Price Guide #4*, and *Aladdin Collector's Manual and Price Guide #21*, all written by our advisor for Aladdins, J. W. Courter; he is listed in the Directory under Kentucky. Mr. Courter has also published a book called *Angle Lamps, Collector's Manual and Price Guide*.

Note: Kerosene lamp values are for lamps with correct burners.

Bed, #832-SS, Whip-o-lite pleated shade, from $275 to.............**375.00**
Bedroom, P-58, ceramic, from $30 to.................................**40.00**
Boudoir, G-153, Moonstone, 1937, from $50 to.....................**60.00**
Boudoir, G-42, Allegro, Alacite, from $40 to......................**50.00**
Bridge, #7092, swing-arm, reflector, from $125 to.................**175.00**
Figurine, G-16, Alacite, lady figure, from $550 to................**650.00**
Floor, #3451, Type B, from $150 to................................**200.00**
Floor, #3625, reflector, candle arms, from $175 to................**250.00**
Floor, #3998, Alacite ring, candle arms, w/night light, from $250 to....**350.00**
Floor, #4597, torchier, from $250 to..............................**300.00**
Floor, #4898C, Circline, fluorescent, trigger ring, from $200 to....**250.00**
Glass Urn, G-379, Alacite, tall ribbed urn w/top, from $250 to....**300.00**
Junior floor (lounge), #1062, candle arms, from $175 to...........**225.00**
Pin-up, G-354, Alacite, from $125 to..............................**150.00**
Table, #785G, Vase, gr, from $200 to..............................**250.00**
Table, G-217, Alacite, from $100 to...............................**110.00**
Table, G-278, Opalique, from $100 to..............................**150.00**
Table, G-296D, Alacite, classic figures, illuminated base, $100 to....**125.00**
Table, G-84, Velvex, from $600 to.................................**700.00**
Table, M-475, ceramic w/blk iron base, from $30 to................**40.00**
Table, MM-7, metal & moonstone, from $200 to......................**250.00**
Table, MT-508, ceramic base, from $300 to.........................**350.00**
Table, P-408, planter, from $75 to................................**100.00**
Table, W-503, wood & ceramic, from $40 to.........................**60.00**
TV, TV-386, creamic, w/planter, from $90 to.......................**110.00**

Aladdin Lamps, Kerosene

Aladdinette candle lamp, glass chimney (2 shapes), ea from $200 to....**250.00**
Caboose, Model 23, aluminum, from $100 to.........................**125.00**
Floor, Model #12, blk & gold, 1928-29, from $200 to...............**350.00**
Floor, Model B, bronze, #1258, 1934-35, from $150 to..............**225.00**
Floor, Model B, satin gold, B-298, 1939-40, from $300 to..........**400.00**
Foreign table, Model #08, London, from $275 to....................**350.00**
Foreign table, Model #12, Sydney, from $75 to.....................**100.00**
Foreign table, Model #21, Greenford England, nickel front, $100 to....**150.00**
Hanging, Model #12, 4-post, w/common paper shade, from $200 to....**250.00**
Hanging, Model #3, w/#203 shade, from $650 to.....................**750.00**
Shade, #201, fancy opal wht glass (Models #1 - #4), from $130 to....**160.00**
Shade, #702, pnt rib (Model B), from $40 to.......................**50.00**
Shade, Aladdinite Parchment, vase or floor, 20-20½" dia, $300 to....**400.00**
Shade, whip-o-lite parchment, table, plain, 14" dia, from $75 to..**150.00**
Shelf, Model #23, Lincoln Drape, clear, no oil fill, from $70 to...**80.00**
Table, Model #10, nickel, from $300 to............................**400.00**
Table, Model #12, Crystal Vase, Orange Venetian Art-Craft, $550 to..**650.00**
Table, Model #21C, Silcrom, S-2100, from $75 to...................**90.00**

Table, Model #23, solid brass, B-2301, from $75 to.....................**90.00**
Table, Model A, Venetian, peach, EX, from $150 to..................**250.00**
Table, Model B, Orientale, Rose Gold, 1935-36, EX, from $225 to..**300.00**
Table, Model B, Vertique, yel Moonstone, B-88, EX, from $600 to..**700.00**
Table, Model B, Victoria, ceramic, w/oil fill, B-25, EX, from $550 to....**700.00**
Table, Model B, Washington Drape, amber crystal, bell, B-49, $275 to....**350.00**
Table, Model B, Washington Drape, gr crystal, filigree, B-51, $125 to..**175.00**
Table, Model B, wht Moonstone, B-85, 1937, from $300 to.......**375.00**
Table, Model C, B-165, aluminum font, no base, from $35 to......**45.00**

Angle Lamps

The Angle Lamp Company of New York City developed a unique type of kerosene lamp that was a vast improvement over those already on the market; they were sold from about 1896 until 1929 and were expensive for their time. Nearly all Angle lamps are hanging lamps and wall lamps. Table models are uncommon. Our Angle lamp advisor is J.W. Courter; he is listed in the Directory under Kentucky. See the narrative for Aladdin Lamps for information concerning popular books Mr. Courter has authored.

Note: Old glass pieces for Angle lamps are scarce to rare; unless noted otherwise, the lamp values that follow are for examples with no glass.

Glass, chimney top, ruby (EX color), petal-top, NM...............**1,000.00**
Glass, chimney top, wht, ribbed, EX...............................**75.00**
Glass, elbow globe, clear, no pattern, EX.........................**75.00**
Glass, elbow globe, clear w/floral bouquet band, EX...............**250.00**
Hanging, #224, nickel, rose floral, no glass, EX..................**1,000.00**
Hanging, #254, 2-burner, rose floral, polished brass, EX..........**1,000.00**
Hanging, #284, antique brass, grape fleur-de-lis, no glass, EX.....**500.00**
Hanging, #352, 3-burner, polished brass, EX.......................**625.00**
Hanging, CW 32 NF, 3-burner, bronze, EX...........................**550.00**
Hanging, dbl, leaf & vine, nickel, EX.............................**400.00**
Hanging, MW 5982, 4-burner, nickel, EX............................**750.00**
Wall, #101, wall cone, tin, pnt, EX...............................**225.00**
Wall, #104, grape pattern, nickel, EX.............................**325.00**
Wall, #185, pinwheel, antique brass, EX...........................**400.00**
Wall, dbl, grape pattern, brass, old glass, EX, from $1,400 to..**1,800.00**
Wall cone, tin, blk pnt, no glass.................................**200.00**

Banquet Lamps

Blue opaline font and stem on double-stepped marble base, nine crystal prisms on brass ring, cut and frosted Oregon shade, #2 Novelty burner, 24", EX, $1,150.00.

Brass w/silver tones, cranberry shade, Patd Mar 19 1895, 19½" **250.00**
Cranberry w/emb ribs, blk stem, wht metal ft, foreign burner, 22", VG ...**400.00**
Pk cased font & stem w/gold, blk-fired base, dbl-wick burner, 19" **350.00**
Pk cased w/cranberry ruffle, brass stem, dbl-wick burner, 18" **400.00**
Poppies emb on red satin, brass fitting, CI base/claw ft, 1890s, 26" **1,200.00**

Chandeliers

Brass, Dutch Baroque style, 8 scrolled candle arms over sphere, 37x41"..**2,350.00**
Brass & glass, Regency style, 6-light w/teardrops/swags, 43x31" **2,000.00**
Bronze, 4-light, tasseled ropes form torch, Art Nouveau style, 40x20" ...**1,500.00**
Bronze w/gilt, Emp style, 12-light, 28x24" **5,500.00**
Bronze w/gilt, prisms, Louis XVI style, 8-light, 34x32" **4,750.00**
Bronze w/gilt, putto holds 2 torches (lights), Louis XVI style, 12x18"..**2,400.00**
Bronze w/gilt, Renaissance Revival style, 16-light, 46x32" **2,500.00**
Bronze w/gilt & patina, Emp style, 12-light, 30x24" **3,500.00**
Bronze w/gilt & patinated metal, Emp style, 6-light, 28x24"..**1,800.00**
Cut glass, 3-tier, 19-light, Louis XV style, 34x34" **2,500.00**
Cut-glass prisms & swags w/gilt-bronze mts, Louis XV style, 46x31" ...**2,900.00**
Gasolier, gilt brass/cut crystal, 4-light, 1850s, 34x43" dia **3,750.00**
Gilt metal & glass, Louis XV style, 24x24" dia **1,100.00**
Gilt metal w/smoky glass prisms, 1-light, Italy, 15x12" dia **400.00**
Pressed glass, 8-light, prisms, Louis XVI style, 48" H **2,100.00**

Decorated Kerosene Lamps

When only one color is given in a two-layer cut overlay lamp description, the second layer is generally clear; in three-layer examples, the second will ususally be white, the third clear. Exceptions will be noted.

Col (2-layer), amethyst, reeded stem, stepped marble, base, 19" ...**1,325.00**
Col (2-layer), bl, quatrefoils, wht opal base, Sandwich, 13" **900.00**
Col (2-layer), cranberry, stepped marble base, Sandwich, 14" **900.00**
Col (2-layer), cranberry, windows/floral, gold-trim milk glass ft, 19"..**800.00**
Col (2-layer), emerald gr, brass stem, marble base, gold trim, 20" ...**3,795.00**
Col (2-layer), pk, reeded brass std, stepped base, Sandwich, 12"....**2,000.00**
Col (2-layer), ruby, ovals/rings, stepped marble base, 11⅜" **700.00**
Col (2-layer), wht, punty cuts, marble base, Sandwich, 15⅞" ...**3,500.00**
Col (2-layer), wht/bl opaque, marble base, Sandwich, 18¼"...**1,300.00**
Col (2-layer), wht/red, brass std, marble base, 19th C, 10" **300.00**
Col (3-layer), bl/wht, ovals, stepped wht opaque base, 13¼" **1,000.00**
Col (3-layer), cranberry/wht, stars/ovals/etc, Sandwich, 11½"...**3,750.00**
Col (3-layer), raspberry/wht, clear font, marble base, 11⅝" **1,300.00**
Col (3-layer), wht/ruby, marble base, Sandwich, 15⅜", pr **8,800.00**
Col (3-layer), wht/turq, trefoil/punty/ovals, wht base, 11⅝" ...**1,000.00**
Wht font w/gold & gr foliage, marble base, 11½" **400.00**

Fairy Lamps

Baby's head, emerald gr frost, pyramid sz, 4½x2⅝" **185.00**
Bl frost w/cut flowers, clear ribbed Clarke cup, 4¾x3⅝" **185.00**
Bl MOP shade, Clarke porc base, on metal bracket w/mirrored base, 6"...**450.00**
Bl satin w/vertical opaque stripes, Clarke cup, 4½x5¼" **450.00**
Burmese, Eden Lite insert, 4-ftd Rogers hdld fr, 9" **525.00**
Burmese, floral spray, in Clarke porc base mk Fairy, 5¾" **700.00**
Burmese, leaves/vines, dome ea side sm bud vase, Clarke cups ..**1,750.00**
Burmese, Tapestry Ware base, Clarke cup, #1439, 6¼x7½" **2,000.00**
English cameo, floral stems, wht on citron, ovoid w/flared shade, 11"..**3,250.00**
Lithophane, children (4 scenes), Clarke cup, 4¼" **1,750.00**
Nailsea, citron w/wht loops, crimped bowl base, Clarke cup, 5x5½" **835.00**
Nailsea, ruby, fluted bowl base, Clarke cup, 5x5½" **1,035.00**
Owl figural, bsk, w/brn & gold pnt, Noritake, 7" **400.00**
Rubena, Dmn Quilt, ruffled, clear Clarke cup, 6¼x3¾" **225.00**
Spatter glass w/clear base, Cricklite Clark's Trademk, S1-250, 4½"....**200.00**

Gone-With-the-Wind Lamps

Banquet, wht shade w/HP cherubs, gilt cherub on base holds font, 34" **150.00**
Checkered shade/bulbous base w/floral, fruit & rondel bands, 22" **2,100.00**
Chrysanthemums on wht opaque ball shade & body, Consolidated, 25½"....**1,800.00**
Gr w/emb leaves & HP florals atop 4 brass ball ft, 27" **500.00**
Milk glass w/bl Delft ball shade/font/bottle std, cast ft, 34" **635.00**

Milk glass with painted floral on multicolor ground with gold, 11½" ball shade (repainted replacement), 31½", $635.00.

Roses on butterscotch to wht 12" ball shade & body, 26½" **325.00**
Roses on wht opaque ball shade & base, Parker, Meriden Conn, 27"...**1,800.00**

Hanging Lamps

Burmese, shiny, swirled cylinder, fancy metal hdw, 9x7", EX **650.00**
Dk to lt pk satin glass pillar-rib str-side shade, brass mts, 10" **575.00**
Milk glass w/transfer, brass fr, prisms, B&H burner, 36"+chain **450.00**
Pk opal bell-shaped shade, clear orig font, brass fr, 14" **250.00**
Wht opaque w/HP dome shade, ornate brass fr, prisms, 48"........**575.00**

Lanterns

Cranberry onion globe w/pierced tin fr, metal font w/burner, 18" **1,295.00**
Fruitwood, tin socket & top, barn type, 11" **230.00**
Glass, 8 bl/gr slag panels in wood fr, sq mt, 20th C, 22x6⅝" **350.00**
Glass onion globe & punched tin, w/burner, 11" **345.00**
Pine w/old natural finish, pegged, insect holes, barn type, 16" ...**220.00**
Skater's, tin w/peacock bl globe, old gold pnt, SAE mk, 6½" **300.00**
Skater's, tin w/pressed cobalt glass globe, 6⅝" **350.00**
Tin, hinged door, conical top, punched design, dents, 14"..........**375.00**
Tin, Paul Revere type, punched starbursts, pnt traces, 15" **275.00**
Tin w/glass panels & wire guard, tin chimney, 21½" **285.00**
Tin, 3 beveled glass panes, dome top, worn pnt, Duntafil Pat, 10"....**415.00**
Tin, 4 glass panels, pierced peaked top, dk patina, 15½" **275.00**
Wood, mortised, 3 glass panes, tin socket, barn type, 12x7x6½" ..**385.00**

Lard Oil/Grease Lamps

Betty, copper w/wrought-iron hanger & wire pick, 4½", +pine stand ...**245.00**
Betty, tin, on tin tidy stand, early 19th C, 14¼" **300.00**
Betty, wrought iron, cast chicken finial, 6½"+hanger **600.00**
Betty, wrought iron, hinged lid, oval, w/wick pick, 4¾x3½x4½" **220.00**

Crusie, dbl; wrought iron, long spike w/hook, 5⅜x4¾" 110.00
Petticoat, japanned tin, acorn font, C hdl, 4¾x3" 160.00
Rush, wrought iron, tripod base, ball finial, 41" 575.00
Rush, wrought iron, tripod base w/snake ft, ball finial, 58" 1,200.00
Rush, wrought iron, tripod w/penny ft/spiral column/counterweight, 15"...275.00
Rush, wrought iron, walnut base, counterweight, 10", pr...........580.00
Rush, wrought iron, wood base, candle socket, 11" 385.00
Rush, wrought iron, wooden base w/worm holes, 13".................165.00
Rush, yew & walnut, domed base, wrought holder/socket, 44" ..1,150.00

Miniature Lamps, Kerosene

Miniature oil lamps were originally called 'night lamps' by their manufacturers. Early examples were very utilitarian in design — some holding only enough oil to burn through the night. When kerosene replaced whale oil in the second half of the nineteenth century, 'mini' lamps became more decorative and started serving other purposes. While mini lamps continue to be produced today, collectors place special value on the lamps of the kerosene era, roughly 1855 to 1910. Four reference books are especially valuable to collectors as they try to identify and value their collections: *Miniature Lamps* by Frank and Ruth Smith, Schiffer Publishing, 1968 (referred to as SI); *Miniature Lamps II* by Ruth Smith, Schiffer Publishing 1982 (SII); *Miniature Victorian Lamps* by Margorie Hulsebus, Schiffer Publishing, 1996; and *Price Guide for Miniature Lamps* by Marjorie Hulsebus, Schiffer Publishing, 1998 (contains 1998 values for all the above books). References in the following listings correlate with each lamp's plate number in these books. Our advisor is Bob Culver; he is listed in the Directory under Michigan.

Sapphire blue with embossed leaves, foreign burner, S-443, 8½", $865.00; Pink satin Pansy ball shade on melon-ribbed base, S-389, 7", $700.00; Medium blue opalescent paneled shade and base with five clear feet, foreign burner, S-514, 7½", EX, $865.00. (Photo courtesy Julia's Auction Company, Fairfield, Maine)

Amberina, ribbed optic, bell shade/mushroom-shaped base, SI-439...600.00
Amethyst, paneled/emb, hornet burner, S1-262, 9" 375.00
Artichoke, milk glass, pk/gr pnt, S1-Figure III, 8" 300.00
Bl, ball shade, cylinder base, new collar, Pet Ratchet burner, 8" ...250.00
Bl cased w/emb swirled ribs, nutmeg burner, S1-421/S1-391, 7½" 390.00
Bl opaque w/ribbed panels, nutmeg burner, S1-310, 8", EX 425.00
Delft, windmills, ball shade, flaring base, SII-267, 8¾"...............750.00
Gr, optic ribs, HP florals, nutmeg burner, S1-470, 7¼"...............400.00
Greek Key, matching chimney shade, SI-166, 8½" 100.00
Leon's Rib/Quarter Dollar Leader Lamp, custard, SI-177, 5¾" ...125.00
Little Jewel, wht w/pk/gr floral & bl borders, SI-196, 7" 300.00
Log Cabin, amber, SI-50, 3⅝" 700.00

Red cased molded ball shade, Pat Feby 27, 1877, S1-167, 7½" ..180.00
Red satin, emb scrolls & shells, SI-397, 8¼" 400.00
Twinkle, amethyst, emb base, ball chimney/shade, SI-432, 7" 275.00
Vaseline, ped base, period burner & chimney, SII-88, 3¼" 80.00
Vertical opal stripes in clear, ball base w/chimney, Feb Y 27 1877, 8" ..70.00
Wht opaque base, clear chimney w/HP flowers & purple stain, SI-219, 9"...150.00
Wht opaque base, clear chimney w/HP flowers/bl stain, SI-219, 9" ...180.00
Wht opaque w/bl stain & HP flowers, umbrella shade, SI-219, 9" ..180.00
Wht opaque w/lime gr trim, swirled/emb red roses, rpl burner, SI-177.....275.00
Wht opaque w/lt brn stain, emb swags/beads, lt pnt loss, SI-183, 8" 180.00
Wht opaque w/mc emb floral & lattice field, ball shade/flared base, 8" ...250.00
Wht opaque w/mc emb floral on swirled net, ball shade/base, SI-195, 7" ..400.00
Wht opaque w/mc floral & bl-pnt ribs, emb lattice/florals, SI-232, 9" 210.00
Wht opaque w/mc shells & floral, rpl shade/ring, SII/p2/TR, 9", EX........120.00
Yel cased, emb rose-petal shade; sq base, nutmeg burner, S1-385, 7"........635.00

Motion Lamps

Animated motion lamps were made as early as 1920 and as late as 1980s. They reached their peak during the 1950s when plastic became widely used. They are characterized by action created by the heat of a light bulb which causes the cylinder to revolve and create the illusion of an animated scene. Some of the better-known manufacturers were Econolite Corp., Scene in Action Corp., and LA Goodman Mfg. Co. As with many collectible items, prices are guided by condition, availability, and collector demand. Collectors should be aware that reproductions of lamps featuring cars, trains, sailing ships, fish, and mill scenes are being made. Values are given for original lamps in mint condition. Any damage or flaws seriously reduce the price. As has been true in many areas of collecting, Internet auctions have affected the prices of motion lamps. Erratic ups and downs in prices realized have resulted in a market that is often unpredictible. Our advisors for motion lamps are Kaye and Jim Whitaker; they are listed in the Directory under Washington.

Annie, Johnson Co, 1981, 15"...25.00
Antique Autos, Econolite, 1957, 11" (+) 100.00
Bar Is Open, Visual Effects Co, 1970, 15" 25.00
Budweiser, Visual Effects Co, 1970, 15" 45.00
Butterflies, Econolite, 1954, 11" (+) 110.00
Coors Beer, wall mt, ca 1960s, 15" 55.00
Elvgrin Pin-Up Girls...375.00
Firefighters, LA Goodman, 1957, 11" 200.00
Fireplace, Potbelly Stove, blk or silver, Econolite, 1958, 11"......125.00
Forest Fire, Econolite, 1955, 11"...95.00
Forest Fire, Rotovue Jr, 1949, 10"..75.00
Forest Fire, Scene in Action, glass/metal, 1931, 10" 100.00
Fountain of Youth, Rotovue Jr, 1950, 10" 90.00
Fresh Water Fish, Econolite, 1950s, 11"....................................110.00
Hamm's Beer, wall mt, picture of coastal area, 1963.....................45.00
Hopalong Cassidy, Econolite (Roto-Vue Jr), 1949, 10" 220.00
Japanese Twilight, Scene in Action, glass/metal, 1931, 13" 100.00
Jet Planes, Econolite, 1950s, 11"..125.00
Merry Go Round, red, yel or bl, Rotovue Jr, 1949, 10" 90.00
Mill Stream, Econolite, 1956, 11" (+) 110.00
Niagara Falls, Econolite, 1955, 11"...95.00
Niagara Falls, Econolite Rainbow, oval, 1960, 11" 110.00
Niagara Falls, Rotovue Jr, 1949, 10"...75.00
Niagara Falls, Scene in Action, glass/metal, 1931, 10" 100.00
Op Art Lamp, Visual Effects, 1970s, 13" (+) 50.00
Reunite Wine, shows wine bottle, 1981, 15" 45.00
Sailboats, Mayflower, etc, Econolite, 1954, 14" (+) 110.00
Seattle World's Fair, Econolite, 1962, 11"...................................155.00
Ship/lighthouse, Scene in Action, 1931, 10"...............................135.00
Snow Scene, Church, Econolite, 1957, 11" 100.00

Steamboats, Econolite, 1957, 11" **95.00**
Trains, Econolite, 1956, 11" (+) **100.00**
Trains, LA Goodman, 1950s, 11" **95.00**
Tropical Fish, Econolite, 1950s, 11" (+) **110.00**
Truck & Bus, Econolite, 1962, 11" **150.00**
7-Up the Uncola, Creative Lighting Co, 1970, 13" **50.00**

Pattern Glass Lamps

The letter/number codes in the following descriptions refer to *Oil Lamps, Books I , II,* and *III,* by Catherine Thuro (book, page, item number or letter). Our advisor for this section is Jeff Bradfield who is listed in the Directory under Virginia.

Acanthus Leaf, clambroth & jade gr w/gold, Sandwich, 13¾" ..**1,000.00**
Aries, ornate hdl, hand lamp, T1-199-h, 5⅜", from $75 to **85.00**
Atterbury Shell 1862, pattern inside, T1-126-c, 8⅛", from $175 to ..**200.00**
Ava, Dmn base, post-1880, T1-263-l, 9¾", from $85 to **95.00**
Beaded Bull's Eye & Leaf, opaline base, T1-93-l, 11⅛", from $150 to ..**200.00**
Bethesda, pattern inside font, T1-148-a, 9½", from $275 to.......**325.00**
Birch Leaf, iron-stem base, T1-173-g, 8⅝", from $90 to.............**120.00**
Blocked Fern, wht opaque base, T1-103-e, 8¾", from $110 to ...**130.00**
Bridges Double Bar Panel, lt gray-amethyst, T1-189-h, 10¼", $80 to **90.00**
Buckle, Sandwich, ca 1870, T1-113-e, 9⅞", from $125 to..........**150.00**
Butterfly & Anchor, T1-271-l, 11⅝" **250.00**
Central Bull's Eye, Central Glass, T1-209-c, 11" **110.00**
Chieftan, figural stem, Atturbury, T1-123-a, 10⅝" **200.00**
Cottage w/Fleur-de-lis, wht opaque base w/gold, T1-121-a, 13", $250 to ..**300.00**
Daisy & Button, Daisy & Button Trumpet stem-base, T1-223-m, 9¼"....**200.00**
Daisy & Button, 1-pc, T1-297-j, 10⅛", from $125 to **150.00**
Dexter, opaque base, T1-168-f, 9⅜", from $150 to......................**175.00**
Diamond Sunburst, 6-scallop base, Bryce, T1-98-c, from $70 to ..**85.00**
Essex, broad rib font, leaded glass base, T1-90-c, 6¼" **75.00**
Eyewinker, Bubble base, T1-249-k, 7⅝" **140.00**
Famous, allover pattern, ca 1898, T1-290-c, 7¾", from $90 to ..**110.00**
Fishscale, Cable Font, Findlay, T1-252-f, 6¼", from $100 to......**110.00**
Gasket Band, T1-97-g, 7¼", from $75 to....................................**100.00**
Gothic Arch, cobalt, hexagonal panels, 7⅜" **1,295.00**
Grape & Festoon, Scalloped Cable base, T1-211-i......................**125.00**
Heart Top Panel, opaque stepped base, T1-167-g, 10⅞", from $150 to....**200.00**
Hobbs Star, clinched-on font, T1-153-g, 8", from $125 to **150.00**
Honeycomb & Cable, iron-stem base, T1-173-l, 10⅛", from $75 to....**90.00**
Laurel, Rib & Roll base, T1-96-c, 8⅝", from $80 to **90.00**
Lowell Loop, hand lamp, T1-273-j, 6¼", from $90 to.................**110.00**
Lynd Single Icicle, opaque base, T1-91-j, 9⅜", from $80 to **90.00**
Macklin, eng decor, opaline base, T1-89-d, 12" **200.00**
Maple Leaf, Chevron stem, Sq Maple Leaf base, T1-221-e, 10½" ..**75.00**
Markham Swirl Band, cranberry/wht spatter, hand lamp, T1-280-H, 10"..**230.00**
Melon, leaded glass, stand lamp, 1860s, T1-88-c, from $80 to....**100.00**
Moon & Star, bl font, amber base, T1-237, 11⅞" **125.00**
Panelled Bull's Eye, T1-92-c, 9¼", from $150 to.........................**175.00**
Panelled Fern, lg & sm scallops on base, T1-101-d, 8¼", $80 to ..**100.00**
Patrician, Centennial base, stand lamp, T1-104-b, 7¾", from $65 to.....**85.00**
Princess Feather, cobalt bl, T1-279-i, 9½" (watch for repros) **475.00**
Prism, gr #40 base, T1-124-b, 9⅝", from $350 to.........................**450.00**
Prism & Loop, Tulip base, T1-143-g, 9¼", from $125 to **175.00**
Rib Banded Panel, 9-panel base, Sandwich, T1-117-e, 8½", $55 to.....**75.00**
Ribbed Loop, 9-panel base, T1-139-k, 8¼", from $75 to **95.00**
Ring Punty, free-blown stem, T1-84-a, 6½", from $140 to **180.00**
Ring Punty, leaded glass base, T1-85-a, 8⅝", from $140 to **180.00**
Ring Punty & Loop, dbl-step marble base, T1-87-c, 10¾", $140 to..**160.00**
Riverside Swag, gold traces, T1-243-d, 8⅞", from $80 to **110.00**
Scalloped Panel, repeated on stem, T1-283-h, 7½", from $75 to **85.00**
Scroll & Rib Band, stepped glass base, T1-203-h, 7⅞", from $80 to **100.00**

Star & Punty, canary yel, hexagonal base, Sandwich, 11⅛" **1,000.00**
Star Oval Panel, stand lamp, T1-99-h, 8½", from $70 to **100.00**
Stippled Daisy & Leaf Band, T1-201-l, 8", from $75 to **100.00**
Triple Peg & Loop, T1-87-h, 9½", from $150 to **175.00**
Tulip, bl, ribbed columnar std, marble base, 10¾".....................**500.00**
Tulip, hand lamp, T1-197-i, 3¼", from $150 to **175.00**
Veronica, opaque Clover Leaf base, T1-151-a, 11¼", from $250 to ...**300.00**
Wave, amber Beaded Bar base, Atterbury, T1-140-e, 9¼", $95 to......**110.00**
Waving Wheat, opaque base, T1-165-k, 10", from $125 to **150.00**
Wheeling Frosted Grape Leaf, T1-157-f, 10", from $150 to........**175.00**
Zipper Loop, carnival, T1-307-a, 8" (many repros) **400.00**

Perfume Lamps

One catalog from the 1950s states that a perfume lamp 'precipitates and absorbs unpleasant tobacco smoke in closed rooms; freshens air in rooms, and is decorative in every home — can be used as a night lamp or television lamp.' An earlier advertisement reads 'an electric lamp that breathes delightful, delicate fragrance as it burns.' Perfume-burner lamps can be traced back to the earliest times of man. There has always been a desire to change, sweeten, or freshen air. Through the centuries the evolution of the perfume-burner lamp has had many changes in outer form, but very little change in function. Many designs of incense burners were used not only for the reasons mentioned here, but also in various ceremonies — as they still are to this day. Later, very fine perfume burners were designed and produced by the best glasshouses in Europe. Other media such as porcelain and metal also were used. It was not until the early part of the twentieth century that electric perfume lamps came into existence. Many lamps made by both American and European firms during the '20s and '30s are eagerly sought by collectors.

From the mid-1930s to the 1970s, there seems to have been an explosion in both the number of designs and manufacturers. This is especially true in Europe. Nearly every conceivable figure has been seen as a perfume lamp. Animals, buildings, fish, houses, jars, Oriental themes, people, and statuary are just a few examples. American import firms have purchased many different designs from Japan. These lamps range from replicas of earlier European pieces to original works. Except for an occasional article or section in reference books, very little has been written on this subject. The information contained in each of these articles generally covers only a specific designer, manufacturer, or country. To date, no formal group or association exists for this area of collecting.

Chinese lantern, mc w/gold dragon top, Goebel W Germany, 7½" ...**175.00**
Indian chief sitting w/bowl, mc, artist sgn, Etling, 7" **415.00**
Lady's head, wht w/red lips & earrings, Leart, 6½" **70.00**
Oriental lady seated, mc w/gold, continental, 7½".......................**350.00**
Pierrot w/violin, wht w/mc details, #10021, 7¾" **415.00**
Polar bear atop globe, mc, #5265, Germany **145.00**
Terrier sitting, pk bow at neck, Germany, 7½" **175.00**
Terrier sitting & begging, brn airbrushing, Germany, 7" **155.00**

Reverse-Painted Lamps

Bellova, 5¾" flowers & shields shade; adjustable bronze std, 15".....**700.00**
Classique, 8" parrots on bell shade; 4-ftd base w/hdls, 14" **2,500.00**
Classique, 16" tropical scene bell shade; blk emb std w/gold, 22"...**3,900.00**
Classique, 18" poppies/butterflies shade; bronzed metal std, 22" ...**3,100.00**
Jefferson, 16" pastoral #2367 shade; bronzed std, 21" **1,600.00**
Jefferson, 18" hollyhocks shade; wood-patina paneled std w/flared ft....**3,360.00**
Jefferson, 18" landscape shade; simple std w/rnd ft, 24" **1,800.00**
MLCo 283, 16" underwater scene shade; gold-pnt fluted base, 23"...**460.00**
Moe Bridges, 18" Greek ruins shade; amphora vase w/hdls on paw-ft base....**3,000.00**
Pittsburgh, 8½x5" scenic desk shade; hdld vase-like gold-tone std **1,350.00**
Pittsburgh, 14" palms scenic shade; floral copper-tone std, 22" **1,150.00**

Pittsburgh, 18" autumn scenic shade; vase-like gold-tone std, 24½"..**2,600.00**
Pittsburgh, 18" Call of the Wild domical shade; owl base, 22" **2,850.00**
Unmk, 18" paneled scenic shade; light-up base w/ornate metal o/l ...**1,450.00**

Moe Bridges, 15" orange and green landscape shade; original base, $1,850.00.

(Photo courtesy Julia's Auction Company, Fairfield, Maine)

Student Lamps, Kerosene

Argand, SP brass, dbl, milk glass shades, dtd 1871, 21x19", EX **800.00**
Berlin, NP brass, cased gr umbrella shade, 1850s, 20⅛".............**325.00**
Cleveland Safety House Argand, wht milk glass shade, 19" **350.00**
Cleveland Safety Library, brass, milk glass globe, 21".................**440.00**
K Brenner, brass w/milk glass shade, 18" **365.00**
Manhattan Brass Co, cased gr umbrella shade, 22½" **135.00**
Miller, brass syphon style, wht shade, cut/frosted font, 21"......**1,150.00**
Post & Co Am Cincinnati, 2 milk glass shades, 24" **2,100.00**
Unmk, brass, dbl, cased gr shades, electrified, 22½x27", pr **400.00**
Unmk, NP brass, cased gr shade, 1-light, 20½", NM **675.00**
Unmk, yel brass, dbl, cased shades, electrified, 27x23", EX **500.00**

TV Lamps

When TV viewing became a popular pastime during the 1940s, TV lamps were developed to provide just the right amount of light — not bright enough to compromise the sharpness of the picture, but just enough to prevent the eyestrain it was feared might result from watching TV in a darkened room. Most were made of ceramic, and many were figurals such as cats, owls, ducks, and the like, or made in the shape of Conestoga wagons, sailing ships, seashells, etc. Some had shades and others were made as planters. Few were marked well enough to identify the maker without some study.

All lamps listed below are ceramic unless otherwise described. See also Maddux; Morton Pottery; Rosemeade; other specific manufacturers.

Accordion, Beachcombers CA, 7x9½" **75.00**
Bluebird pr on foliage, 'pond' in front of them, Lane, 1959, 10x14" **115.00**
Brahma bull's head on base w/Western brands, Kron Hunter, 15"......**185.00**
Brass w/2 flower planters, fiberglass fitted shade, from $95 to.....**110.00**
Bulldogs (2), eyes light up, Williams..., from $120 to **135.00**
Coach, blk w/gold, unmk, from $45 to...**65.00**
Collie dog, sitting, EX detail, pottery w/wht, tan & brn tones, 13"...**165.00**
Covered wagon, pnt plaster, red paper shade, L Pellegrini, $125 to....**140.00**
Deco deer, yel & wht, w/planter base, unmk, from $55 to.................**75.00**
Deco horse head, blk & wht, light inside head, unmk, $75 to **95.00**
Duck, flying, w/planter, brass holder, mini, from $75 to.................**95.00**
Egrets (2), gr, w/planter base, unmk, from $65 to **95.00**

English Setter, wht w/brn spots, on point, gr leafy base, 9x14" **60.00**
Fan, pk paper w/brass center, unmk, from $45 to............................**60.00**
Fish, wht w/glass beads that light up, unmk, from $45 to **60.00**
Foliage, gr, w/planter, Genuine Sheridan...Luminart, $55 to................**70.00**
Gazelle, leaping, gr, w/planter, unmk, from $70 to **90.00**
Greyhound, shiny blk, unmk, from $70 to **95.00**
Horse, prancing, EX detail, 14x11" **110.00**
Horse & colt, brn-toned, planter base, unmk, from $90 to.................**95.00**
Horse heads (2), gr, 2 planters, unmk, from $45 to **55.00**
Jaguar, prowling, pewter, Sarsaparilla Deco, 22" L......................**175.00**
Leopard, brn-toned plaster, unmk, 14", from $200 to.................**250.00**
Leopard, prowling, pottery w/yel glaze, 22" L **170.00**
Mermaid, gr, fiberglass shade, unmk, from $85 to........................**110.00**
Oriental figure, pnt plaster w/gold, Fiberglas shade, unmk, $95 to **110.00**
Oriental's head in fancy headdress, wht, no mk, 15x7"................**200.00**
Panther, upright shade mtd on base, 14" L **115.00**
Pk poodle pr, 1 looking bk at 2nd, Lane, 1956, 16" L, from $150 to....**175.00**
Poodle & bulldog, Kron, 13x12", from $85 to **100.00**
Rooster w/rising sun, bl-gr, unmk, from $125 to **140.00**
Sailfish on waves, planter base, Lane & Co, 1957, 15x16".........**135.00**
Ship, gold pnt pot metal, portholes light up, unmk, $85 to **95.00**
Ship, 3-color, portholes light up, unmk, $65 to **85.00**
Siamese cats (mother & kitten), Kron, 13x10" **95.00**
Siamese cats (mother & 2 babies - 1 playing w/her tail), Lane, 13" ...**125.00**
Swan, wht head & gr wings, w/planter, unmk, from $65 to **90.00**
Tower of Pisa, soapstone, windows light up, from $120 to **130.00**
Tropical leaves (3, upright), pk/teal/wht, Lane, 1955, 13" **95.00**
Victorian lady w/dog, pnt plaster, fiberglass shade, LM Fielack ..**135.00**

Whale Oil/Burning Fluid Lamps

Amethyst Loop font, hex base, Sandwich, 1850s, 7⅞" **825.00**
Canary pressed-glass font, hex socket/columnar shaft, Sandwich, 9⅝"..**825.00**
Canary Star & Punty font, hex base, brass burner, Sandwich, 11"..**1,000.00**
Canary 8-sided font on monument base, Sandwich, 10⅛", VG.......**400.00**
Clambroth & jade gr w/gold, Acanthus Leaf, Sandwich, 13¾"....**1,400.00**
Clambroth font, bl Acanthus Leaf base, Sandwich, 11⅛" **2,000.00**
Clambroth Tulip font, columnar std on stepped base, Sandwich, 11"...**300.00**
Clear Ellipse font, hex base, camphene burner, Sandwich, 11" ..**300.00**
Clear free-flown bulb font on stepped sq base, Sandwich, 1830s, 10" ...**280.00**
Clear 12-flute globe, 3-knop shaft, dome base, Sandwich, 9⅜"..**2,250.00**
Clear 12-flute globe, 3-knop/button shaft, 8" **1,995.00**
Col (3-layer), wht/turq/clear, wht Baroque base w/gold, 11⅝"...**1,000.00**
Emerald 3-Printie Block font, hex base, Sandwich, 7¾" **1,650.00**
Gr font, clambroth Acanthus Leaf base, Sandwich, 11⅜", pr....**1,175.00**
Latticinio bl/wht free-blown font, marble base, Sandwich, 9⅜"..**1,765.00**
Wheel cut, flint glass, 9½", EX...**200.00**
3-color latticinio-stripe font, wht Baroque base, Sandwich, 9⅝"....**1,000.00**

Lang, Anton

Anton Lang (1875 – 1938) was a German studio potter and an actor in the Oberammergau Passion Plays early in the twentieth century. Because he played the role of Christ three times, tourists brought his pottery back to the U.S. in suitcases, which accounts for the prevalence of smaller examples today. As the only son in the family, he took up his father's and grandfather's trade. Following the successful completion of an apprenticeship in his father's workshop in 1891, Lang worked for master potters in Wolfratshausen, Munich, and Stuttgart to better learn his craft. Returning to Oberammergau in 1898, Lang resumed working with his father. The next year the village elders surprised everyone by selecting Lang to play the role of Christ in the 1900 Passion Play. He proved to be a popular choice with the audience and became an international celebrity.

In 1902 Lang married Mathilde Rutz. In that same year, with the help of an assistant and an apprentice, he built his own workshop and a kiln. In the early days Mathilde helped in the pottery as a decorator until Lang could afford to employ girls from the local art school.

During 1923 – 1924 Anton Lang and the other 'Passion Players' toured the U.S. selling their crafts. Lang would occasionally throw pottery when the cast passed through a pottery center such as Cincinnati, where Rookwood was located. The pots thrown at Rookwood are easy to identify as Lang hand signed the side of each piece and they have a 1924 Rookwood mark on the bottom. Lang visited the U.S. only once, and contrary to popular belief, he was never employed by Rookwood. His pottery, marked with his name in script, is fairly scarce and highly valued for its artistic quality.

His son Karl (1903 – 1990) was also a gifted potter. Karl apprenticed with his father and then completed his training at the national ceramic school in Landshut. He took over the day-to-day operations of the pottery while his father was touring America. Over time Karl became the chief designer and was responsible for creating most of the modern pieces and inventing many new glazes. Only pieces bearing a hand-written signature (not a fascimile) are certain to be Anton Lang originals instead of the work of Karl or the Langs' assistants. Anton and Karl also made pieces together; Karl might design a piece and Anton decorate it. In 1925 Karl went to Dresden to study with sculptor Arthur Lange. Under the influence of the famous artist Ernst Barlach, Karl designed his greatest work, the 'Wanderer in the Storm.' This large figure depicts a man dressed in a long coat and hat resisting a violent wind. Between 1925 and 1930, four or five examples of the 'Wanderer' were made in the Lang workshop in Oberammergau. One of the three known examples has only a 'KL' (Karl Lang) mark. The other two are unmarked or the mark is obscured by the glaze. At least one additional 'Wanderer' was produced at a later date, probably after World War II. It is marked with the 'Anton Lang' shop mark, a facsimile of Anton's signature, and is much cruder in appearance than the originals. The later version appears to have been made from a mold taken from one of the originals.

In 1936 Karl Lang was put in charge of the complete operation of the pottery and enlarged and modernized the enterprise. He continued to operate the workshop as the Anton Lang pottery after his father's death in 1938. The pottery is now owned and operated by Karl's daughter, Barbara Lampe, who took over for her father in 1975. The facsimile 'Anton Lang' signature was used until 1995 when the name was changed to Barbara Lampe Pottery. Her mark is an interlocked 'BL' in a circle. Pieces with a facsimile signature and an interlocked 'UL' in a circle were made by Lampe's former husband, Uli Lampe, and date from 1975 to 1982. The 'Anton Lang' mark is not sharp on pieces made in 1975 and later. The brick red clay used in their manufacture can be seen on the bottoms as well as three lighter circular tripod marks. The later pieces are considerably heavier than the earlier work. Our advisor for this category is Clark Miller; he is listed in the Directory under Minnesota.

Bowl, bl w/mc flowers, w/lid, 3¾x4½" 52.00
Bowl, burgundy w/bl flambè, 2¾x9¾" 100.00
Bowl, early abstracts, bl w/mc, indents, real signature, 2¾x3½"...78.00
Bowl, edelweiss flowers, mc, real signature, 3⅞x6⅛" 128.00
Bowl, sage gr, pie-crust edge, 1¾x4"......................................45.00
Candle holder, deep brn w/yel cvd decor, 2¼x4½x2½" 50.00
Candle holder, hearts on body, red on blk, 3x4", ea 60.00
Candlesticks, orange w/turq int, Art Deco style, 5x3½", pr.........50.00
Chamberstick, owls in trees, mc, real signature, 5¼x5¼" 85.00
Cup, gr matt, 3¼x3½" 30.00
Dish, bl w/wht modern decor, 1½x3⅝" 35.00
Figurine, pelican, mc, 9¾"..180.00
Figurine candle holders, griffins, bl on wht, 7x6½", pr 235.00
Jug, bl mat w/emb flowers, 5x4"...46.00
Jug, bl matt w/emb flowers, pewter lid, 6x5½" 185.00

Keystone stereograph, Anton Lang & Henry Ford 56.00
Magazine, Time, Dec 17, 1923, Anton Lang on cover 15.00
Menu/card holder, birds (pr) on basket, mc, 3½x2¾" 32.00
Photo, Anton Lang in pottery, autographed, dtd 1930, 8x10" 48.00
Photo postcard, Anton & Karl Lang in pottery, postmarked 1928..10.00
Photo postcard, Anton Lang & family, ca late 1920s 8.00
Photo postcard, Anton Lang & family, ca 1910............................7.50
Photo postcard, Anton Lang home (Hotel Daheim), 1932...........15.50
Photo postcard, Lang decorating crucifix, ca 1922 ....6.00
Pitcher, lt bl & purple mottle, 8¾x5½" 90.00
Pitcher, yel w/bl flowers, 4½" 48.00
Plaque, Madonna, Della Robbia style, ivory & bl, 10x7¾".........102.00
Plaque/charger, wht slip on brn, 1⅜x11⅝" 33.00
Plate, Lang as Jesus, Rosenthal, 8½" 35.00
Vase, bl w/gr/yel/wht eidelweiss flowers, 4¾" 30.00
Vase, brn & gr, coiled body, incised vertical wavy lines, 7⅝x3⅜"...70.00
Vase, dk bl w/mc flowers, 2¼" 23.50
Vase, early Art Nouveau shape & design, mc, real signature, 9x4½" 150.00
Vase, early stoneware, bl w/gr/brn geometrics, real signature, 6¾".....100.00
Vase, fish in seaweed, mc, real signature, 4¾x6" 270.00
Vase, frog skin, pottery hdl, 8x4½" 14.00
Vase, gr, 2x2" 52.50
Vase, gr feathered matt w/brn int, ovoid w/neck, 5½".................78.00
Vase, St George & dragon, mc, 5½x5½" 190.00
Vase, turq, hdls, real signature, 4x4¾" 76.00
Vase, yel w/lt gr, bl decor, real signature, 3x4" 82.00

Figurine, Wanderer in the Storm, green and blue overflow, first run, no mark, 20", $3,500.00. (Photo courtesy Clark Miller)

Le Verre Francais

Le Verre Francais was produced during the 1920s by Schneider at Epinay-sur-Seine in France. It was a commercial art glass in the cameo style composed of layered glass with the designs engraved by acid. Favored motifs were stylized leaves and flowers or geometric patterns. It was marked with the name in script or with an inlaid filigrane. Our advisor for this category is Don Williams; he is listed in the Directory under Missouri.

Cameo

Atomizer, leaves, orange & brn mottle on yel, brass fittings, 5½" 360.00
Lamp, Deco design, orange/gr mottle on pk, dome shade, 15x7¾"....4,875.00
Lamp, Deco flowers, red on yel mottle, 15x8½" 6,325.00
Vase, 'balls' arranged in circles, pendant drops, red/orange, ftd, 11"...1,350.00
Vase, berries, brn/orange/red on yel, mk Ovington NY, 4x5", NM.....465.00

Vase, facing swans, maroon on orange/yel mottle, ftd, Charder, 10"..**2,750.00**
Vase, floral, maroon on yel mottle to orange, dbl-bulb base, 22" ...**2,800.00**
Vase, floral, orange on yel mottle, mtd as lamp, 9"......................**500.00**
Vase, floral, purple/orange on lt gray, ovoid, 6" **700.00**
Vase, geese & marsh, brn on bl mottle, brn ft & hdls, 13¾"...**3,450.00**
Vase, pendant florals on bell-shaped bottom, long neck, 14" ..**1,000.00**
Vase, roses, pk/gr on rose/frost mottle, flared rim, ftd, 13" **2,600.00**
Vase, stylized plant, orange/brn/gr on clear to orange, ftd, 20"...**2,900.00**

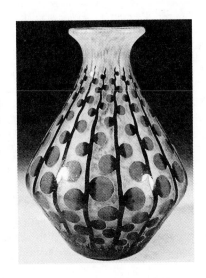

Vase, stylized plants and pods, orange and brown on clear with amber mottling, marked, 12¾", $1,600.00.

Leeds, Leeds Type

The Leeds Pottery was established in 1758 in Yorkshire and under varied management produced fine creamware, often highly reticulated and transfer printed, shiny black-glazed Jackfield wares, polychromed pearlware, and figurines similar to those made in the Staffordshire area. Little of the early ware was marked; after 1775 the impressed 'Leeds Pottery' mark was used. From 1781 to 1820, the name 'Hartley Greens & Co.' was added. The pottery closed in 1898.

Today the term 'Leeds' has become generic and is used to encompass all polychromed pearlware and creamware, wherever its origin. Thus similar wares of other potters (Wood for instance) is often incorrectly called 'Leeds.' Unless a piece is marked or can be definitely attributed to Leeds by confirming the pattern to be authentic, 'Leeds-Type' would be a more accurate nomenclature.

Key:
cw — creamware   pw — pearlware

Bowl, tobacco leaves, rouletted circle band, mc gr/rust, 1820, 5½" **5,000.00**
Creamer, tobacco leaves, 4-color, foliage hdl terminals, rpr, 4"..**5,300.00**
Cup plate, eagle w/Am shield, brn/bl/gold/gr, bl feather edge, 4⅜"..**2,000.00**
Cup plate, peafowl in branch, 5-color, 8-sided, brn feather edge, 4" ..**990.00**
Mug, Greek Key rim band above 5-color marbling, 3¼"............**350.00**
Pepper pot, pineapples, 3-color, 4½", EX......................................**550.00**
Plate, eagle/shield center, brn/bl/mustard w/ochre border, 6"......**700.00**
Plate, peafowl, mc, blue feather edge, 8¾" **1,045.00**
Plate, strawberry, yel, scalloped bl feather edge, sm rpr, 9½" **330.00**
Sugar bowl, mc sprigs in panels, cobalt finial, w/lid, 6½", VG ...**140.00**

Lefton China

The Lefton China Company was the creation of Mr. George Zoltan Lefton who immigrated to the United States from Hungary in 1939. In 1941 he embarked on a new career and began shaping a business that sprang from his passion for collecting fine china and porcelains. Though his funds were very limited, his vision was to develop a source from which to obtain fine porcelains by reviving the postwar Japanese ceramic industry, which dated back to antiquity. As a trailblazer, George Zoltan Lefton soon earned the reputation as 'The China King.'

Counted among the most desirable and sought-after collectibles of today, Lefton items such as Bluebirds, Miss Priss, Angels, all types of dinnerware and tea-related items are eagerly acquired by collectors. As is true with any antique or collectible, prices may vary, dependent on location, condition, and availability. For additional information on the history of Lefton China, its factories, marks, products, and values, readers should consult the *Collector's Encyclopedia of Lefton China, Books I, II, and III,* and *Lefton Price Guide* by our advisor, Loretta DeLozier, who is listed in the Directory under Florida. All are published by Collector Books.

Ashtray, yel leaf dish w/pk butterfly, #1237, from $28 to **32.00**
Ashtray set, 4 trays w/nester, Lilac Chintz, #692, from $18 to......**28.00**
Bank, College Fund graduate girl, #5010, 6¾", from $32 to.........**38.00**
Bank, Love Nest, birds/birdhouse, #7485, 7", from $100 to........**125.00**
Bank, Miss Pimples the pig, #9635, 5½", from $35 to...................**40.00**
Bone dish, Lilac Chintz, #669, from $12 to **15.00**
Bookends, tigers, #6663, pr, from $30 to......................................**40.00**
Bowl, lily of the valley & sponge gold, FTD, #284, from $250 to....**350.00**
Butter dish, Americana, #958, from $55 to...................................**65.00**
Cake plate, Sweet Violets, w/server, #2873, 12¼", from $45 to....**55.00**
Candle holders, Sweet Violets, #2879, 6", pr, from $35 to............**45.00**
Candy box, Americana, #944, 5", from $65 to **75.00**
Candy box, egg shape w/roses/chicks/bow on top, #971, 5", from $12 to...**18.00**
Candy box, White Holly, #6073, from $32 to................................**38.00**
Candy dish, Floral Mood, leaf form, #4669, from $15 to...............**25.00**
Canister set, burlap sacks, 4-pc, #4084, from $110 to **135.00**
Canister set, Sweet Violets, #2875, 4-pc, from $95 to.................**110.00**
Celery dish, Green Holly, #1348, from $35 to **40.00**
Cheese dish, Bluebirds, #437, from $275 to................................**325.00**
Coffeepot, Violet Chintz, #660, from $165 to **185.00**
Compote, Floral Chintz, #8043, 7", from $18 to **22.00**
Cookie jar, elf head, #3969, 8½", from $250 to...........................**350.00**
Cookie jar, mushroom w/caterpillar finial, #130, from $55 to.......**65.00**
Cookie jar, Pear 'n Apple, #4335, from $35 to **45.00**
Cookie jar, pixie baby, #1370, 10½", from $75 to **125.00**
Creamer & sugar bowl, Cuddles, #1449, from $35 to....................**45.00**
Creamer & sugar bowl, Fruit Delight, #3132, from $12 to............**18.00**
Creamer & sugar bowl, Fruits of Italy, #1177, from $18 to............**22.00**
Creamer & sugar bowl, Silver Wheat, #2154, from $20 to **25.00**
Cup & saucer, Blue Paisley, #2339, from $18 to **22.00**
Cup & saucer, gr/wht panels w/pk roses on wht, gold trim, #546, $35 to...**40.00**
Cup & saucer, Pink Cotillion, #3189, from $22 to.......................**28.00**
Cup & saucer, Poinsettia, #4392, from $25 to **35.00**
Egg cup, Lilac Chintz, #698, from $12 to.....................................**18.00**
Figurine, angel boy & girl kneeling/praying, #4565, 4¼", pr, $25 to **30.00**
Figurine, angels w/flowers, bl & wht, #000780, 6½", pr, from $12 to ...**18.00**
Figurine, baby girl w/cup, #3499, 5½", from $75 to......................**85.00**
Figurine, bloomer girl w/parasol, heavy gold trim, #001, from $70 to...**90.00**
Figurine, boy & girl on seesaw, Christopher, #03474, from $25 to ..**35.00**
Figurine, bride & groom honeymoon boat, #990, 6", from $175 to....**200.00**
Figurine, cherub holding bowl w/hands & ft, #435, 5", from $130 to.....**150.00**
Figurine, Chinese lady, wht w/heavy gold, #10600, 8", from $100 to...**150.00**
Figurine, chipmunks on base w/acorn branch, #4753, 11", from $95 to...**125.00**
Figurine, cockatoo, floral base, #1542, 7½", from $85 to **90.00**
Figurine, Heavenly Hobos wedding couple, #04635, from $35 to.**45.00**
Figurine, Kewpie sitting on leaf, #2992, from $28 to.....................**32.00**
Figurine, kissing couple, #10530, 4¼", pr, from $55 to.................**65.00**
Figurine, lady w/parasol, wht/heavy gold, #10289, 10½", $250 to ...**300.00**

Figurine, Marilyn Monroe, #411, from $175 to 225.00
Figurine, Oriental couple, wht/gold/stones, #10008, 5½", pr, $65 to...75.00
Figurine, peacock, #2335, 7¼", from $55 to 65.00
Figurine, rabbit w/pnt tulips, #5469, 3½", from $8 to 10.00
Figurine, raccoon w/baby, #2149, 6", from $75 to....95.00
Figurine, road runners, #3209, 7", pr, from $30 to 40.00
Figurine, robin & baby robin on branch, #8008, 6", from $60 to 70.00
Figurine, Russian lady, #752, 11", from $175 to....225.00
Figurine, Santa & Mrs Claus dancing, #02139, 3½", from $20 to...30.00
Figurine, skunk wearing flower bonnet, #1311, 5½", from $35 to...40.00
Figurine, tabby cat, #6364, 4½", from $22 to....28.00
Figurine, veterinarian w/dog, #1858, 8", from $65 to 75.00
Gravy boat, Americana, #962, from $55 to 65.00
Gravy boat, Pink Clover, #2505, 8½", from $18 to....28.00
Jam jar, Brown Heritage Fruit, w/tray, #2762, from $75 to....95.00
Jam jar, grapes, #4852, 5", from $25 to....30.00
Jam jar, White Christmas, #605, from $30 to 35.00
Leaf dish, Green Holly, #1347, 7½", from $20 to....25.00
Mug, Fruits of Italy, #1209, from $5 to....10.00
Nappy, roses on wht/gold trim, #486, 6¾", from $25 to....30.00
Perfume set, hobnail w/roses, #842, 3-pc, from $75 to 85.00
Pitcher, Bluebirds, #287, 4½", from $75 to 95.00
Pitcher, Misty Rose, #5692, 7", from $95 to 135.00
Pitcher, To a Wild Rose, #2562, from $95 to....125.00
Pitcher & bowl set, Green Heritage, #4172, 5¼", from $55 to.....65.00
Planter, ABC block, #2128, 4", from $8 to 12.00
Planter, blue jay, matt, #573, 7", from $18 to....28.00
Planter, egg urn, Heather Girl, #8213, 3½", from $12 to 18.00
Planter, Garden Daisy, #1511, 8½", from $10 to 15.00
Planter, girl w/basket, #056, 5½", from $65 to....75.00
Planter, hobo clown's head, #4498, 4", from $45 to....55.00
Planter, pilgrim boy & girl w/baskets, #5376, 6¼", pr, from $90 to...100.00
Planter, Santa on reindeer, #1496, 6", from $20 to....30.00

Plaque, Dainty Miss, #6767, 5", from $75.00 to $95.00.
(Photo courtesy Loretta DeLozier)

Plate, Festival, #2621, 9", from $22 to 28.00
Plate, Rose Chintz, #659, 9", from $35 to....40.00
Platter, Pink Clover, #2494, 14" oval, from $55 to....65.00
Punch bowl, Green Holly, #1367, from $50 to 65.00
Relish tray, Fruits of Italy, #1211, 11¼", from $12 to....18.00
Relish tray, White Holly, #6057, 12", from $25 to 30.00
Salt box, Pink Clover, #2497, from $40 to....45.00
Shakers, Christmas candles, #1556, 4", pr, from $18 to....22.00
Shakers, Misty Rose, #5518, pr, from $15 to....18.00
Shakers, Pink Clover, #2586, 3¾", pr, from $40 to 45.00
Shakers, puppies (wht) w/roses, #1726, pr, from $18 to 22.00
Shakers, Santa & Mrs Claus in rocking chairs, #8139, pr, from $22 to.....28.00
Shakers, Violet Chintz, #665, pr, from $25 to....35.00
Sleigh, White Christmas, #1408, from $35 to 45.00
Snack set, Misty Rose, #5691, from $125 to....175.00
Soap dish, Pink Clover, #2504, 7¼", from $8 to 12.00
Tea bag holder, Lilac Chintz, #129, from $10 to....15.00
Teapot, Christmas cardinal, #1655, from $110 to....135.00
Teapot, Elegant Rose, #866, from $55 to 65.00
Teapot, elf's head, #3973, from $175 to 225.00
Teapot, Misty Rose, #5691, from $125 to 175.00
Teapot, Poinsettia, #4388, from $135 to 175.00
Teapot, Vintage Green, heavy gold trim, #6711, from $35 to.......45.00
Tidbit tray, Poinsettia, 2-tiered, #4391, from $52 to....58.00
Tray, Fruits of Italy, 3-part, #1179, from $18 to....22.00
Tray, Violet Chintz, #651, from $30 to....35.00
Vase, Brown Heritage Fruit, #3116, 8¾", from $55 to....75.00
Vase, Green Heritage, 3 different, #4072, 8½", ea, from $55 to ...65.00
Vase, hand-held urn w/fluted rim/flowers, #838, 5½", from $60 to .70.00
Vase, oil-lamp shape, Only a Rose decor, gold trim, #424, from $65 to...75.00
Vase, Rose Chintz, #679, 6¼", from $28 to 32.00
Vase, Violet Chintz, #679, 6¼", from $32 to 38.00
Wall pocket, Miss Priss, #1509, from $125 to....150.00

Legras

Legras and Cie was founded in St. Denis, France, in 1864. Production continued until the 1930s. In addition to their enameled wares, they made cameo art glass decorated with outdoor scenes and florals executed by acid cuttings through two to six layers of glass. Their work is signed 'Legras' in relief and in enamel. Our advisor for this category is Don Williams; he is listed in the Directory under Missouri.

Cameo

Vase, grapes & leaves, amethyst on frost, 7¾"....200.00
Vase, leafy stems, purple multi on etched frost, 11½" 600.00
Vase, leaves & berries, pk to wht mottle, shouldered, 11¼".......515.00
Vase, sm flowers on branches, purple multi on etched frost, 9x8"....700.00
Vase, trees/sailboats, gr on frost, 8", NM....700.00
Vase, vines, brn on olive/lt gr, stick neck, 13¼", NM 780.00
Vase, winter woodland/village in distance, pillow form, 4x5"..1,000.00

Enameled Glass

Rose bowl, trees in winter/bird, crimped/incurvate rim, 4¼"......300.00
Vase, bird & flowers, mc on lt bl, trumpet neck, 10" 150.00
Vase, floral, gr on tan to ivory, HP, invt trumpet form, 7"...........150.00
Vase, floral, mc on yel, trumpet neck, 10" 150.00
Vase, leaves/stems, brn/gr on yellow mottle, ovoid, 7½" 350.00

Lenox

Walter Scott Lenox, former art director at Ott and Brewer, and Jonathan Coxon founded The Ceramic Art Company of Trenton, New Jersey, in 1889. By 1906 Cox had left the company, and to reflect the change in ownership, the name was changed to Lenox Inc. Until 1930 when the production of American-made Belleek came to an end, they continued to produce the same type of high-quality ornamental wares that Lenox and Coxon had learned to master while in the employ of Ott and Brewer. Their superior dinnerware made the company famous, and since 1917 Lenox has been chosen the official White House China. Our advisor for this category is Mary Frank Gaston. See also Ceramic Art Company.

Ashtray, Orleans, sm, 4⅜" 30.00
Baker, Blue Breeze, rectangular, 15⅝"....150.00

Bowl, cereal; Alyssa, 6⅛"..30.00
Bowl, cereal; Columbia, 5⅝"..60.00
Bowl, cereal; Coquette, 5½"..50.00
Bowl, coupe soup; Medley, 7¾".....................................70.00
Bowl, cream soup; Celeste...60.00
Bowl, cream soup; Westbury, flat...................................80.00
Bowl, fruit; Arcadia, 5½"..45.00
Bowl, fruit; Chalet, 5⅝"...40.00
Bowl, fruit; Forever, 5⅝"...60.00
Bowl, pasta; Butler's Pantry, ind, 9⅜"............................15.00
Bowl, rim soup; Cinderella, 8⅜"....................................70.00
Bowl, rim soup; Kelly, 8⅜"..35.00
Bowl, soup; Avon, 8⅜"..50.00
Bowl, soup/pasta; Onyx Frost, 9¼".................................50.00
Bowl, vegetable; Adrienne, oval, 9¾".............................190.00
Bowl, vegetable; Cinderella, gold trim, 9¾".....................200.00
Bowl, vegetable; Colonial, 9½" L....................................130.00
Bowl, vegetable; Columbia, 9¾" L..................................180.00
Bowl, vegetable; Grace, 8½"...70.00
Bowl, vegetable; Lyric, 9¾" L...140.00
Bowl, vegetable; Ming Temple, 9⅝" L............................160.00
Bowl, vegetable; Patricia, 9⅞" L.....................................80.00
Bowl, vegetable; Sabrina, 10" L......................................160.00
Casserole, Blue Breeze, w/lid, ind, 4½"...........................45.00
Cigarette box, Wheat...60.00
Cigarette holder, Chalet 28.00
Coffeepot, Stanford, 4-cup, 7¼".....................................340.00
Creamer, Abigail..80.00
Creamer, Autumn, 1963, 3½"...120.00
Creamer, Brookdale..100.00
Creamer, Buchanan...100.00
Creamer, Celeste, 3½"...80.00
Creamer, Lenox Rose, flat, 3"..80.00
Creamer, Midsummer..80.00
Creamer, Spring Bounty..50.00
Cup, snack; Colonial...40.00
Cup & saucer, Amanda, ftd...50.00
Cup & saucer, Autumn, flat, 2¼".....................................50.00
Cup & saucer, Autumn, striped hdl, ftd, 2⅛".....................55.00
Cup & saucer, bouillon; Coronado, ftd 55.00
Cup & saucer, bouillon; Lenox Rose 40.00
Cup & saucer, bouillon; Washington, ftd..........................50.00
Cup & saucer, Caitlin, ftd...32.00

Dish, purple clematis blossoms with green leaves and gold trim, professional decor, 5" square, $90.00.

(Photo courtesy Mary Frank Gaston)

Gravy boat, Alyssa, w/underplate....................................180.00
Gravy boat, Brookdale, w/attached underplate...................300.00
Gravy boat, Castle Garden, w/underplate..........................240.00
Gravy boat, Columbia, w/underplate 240.00

Gravy boat, Highland Crossing, leaf hdl, w/underplate...............130.00
Gravy boat, Silver Springs, w/underplate.........................200.00
Gravy boat, Summer Wind...50.00
Mug, Butterfly Meadow, 4¼"...10.00
Mug, Hamilton, 3⅝"...20.00
Mug, Monroe, 3⅝"..35.00
Mug, Republic, 3⅝" 50.00
Pepper mill, Jewel...90.00
Pepper mill, Shalimar..75.00
Plate, bread & butter; Arcadia, 6¼"..................................20.00
Plate, bread & butter; Castle Garden, 6⅜".........................28.00
Plate, bread & butter; Colonial, 5¾" or 6¼", ea..................18.00
Plate, bread & butter; Pine, 6⅜".......................................15.00
Plate, bread & butter; Tyler, 6½".......................................20.00
Plate, chop; Autumn, 12⅝"..250.00
Plate, chop; Princess, 12¾"...130.00
Plate, dinner; Abigail, 11"...40.00
Plate, dinner; Buchanan, 10⅝"...40.00
Plate, dinner; Celeste, 10⅜"..35.00
Plate, dinner; Newport, 10½"...80.00
Plate, dinner; Riverwood, 12"..15.00
Plate, luncheon; Aurora, 9"...35.00
Plate, luncheon; Velera, 9"...60.00
Plate, salad; Alaris, 8"..16.00
Plate, salad; Autumn, 8⅜"..35.00
Plate, salad; Constance, 7⅞"...20.00
Plate, salad; Hathaway, 8¼"...50.00
Plate, salad; Solitaire, 8⅛"..15.00
Platter, Alaris, 16" L...140.00
Platter, Avon, 15¾" L...180.00
Platter, Avon, 17⅛" L...240.00
Platter, Castle Garden, 14" L...200.00
Platter, Harvest, 16¼" L..200.00
Platter, Ivory Frost, 13⅝" L...150.00
Platter, Mt Vernon, 16" L..300.00
Platter, Trellis, 16⅞" L..320.00
Platter, Windsong, 13¾" L...240.00
Ramekin, Coronado, w/underplate...................................50.00
Ramekin, Peking, w/underplate..60.00
Saucer, Adrienne 10.00
Saucer, Insignia 25.00
Shaker & pepper mill, Blue Breeze, pr.............................100.00
Shakers, Columbia, 3⅝", pr...125.00
Shakers, Golden Blossom, pr...140.00
Shakers, Potomac, pr..100.00
Sugar bowl, Ascot, w/lid...90.00
Sugar bowl, Coronado, w/lid 100.00
Sugar bowl, Hayworth, w/lid...65.00
Sugar bowl, Laura, w/lid...70.00
Sugar bowl, Moonlight Mood, w/lid.................................120.00
Sugar bowl, Plum Blossoms, w/lid 100.00
Sugar bowl, Sandpiper, w/lid...28.00
Tankard, Indian chief's portrait, cylindrical, 7½".................800.00
Teapot, Alaris, 4-cup, 4⅝"...170.00
Teapot, Caitlin, 4-cup, 5"..190.00
Teapot, Colonial, 3-cup 250.00
Teapot, Hope, 5-cup, 4¾"..220.00
Teapot, Manor, 1961, 4-cup, 4⅞".....................................240.00
Vase, Amanda, 7½"...150.00

Libbey

The New England Glass Company was established in 1818 in

Boston, Massachusetts. In 1892 it became known as the Libbey Glass Company. At Chicago's Columbian Expo in 1893, Libbey set up a ten-pot furnace and made glass souvenirs. The display brought them world-wide fame. Between 1878 and 1918, Libbey made exquisite cut and faceted glass, considered today to be the best from the brilliant period. The company is credited for several innovations — the Owens bottle machine that made mass production possible and the Westlake machine which turned out both electric light bulbs and tumblers automatically. They developed a machine to polish the rims of their tumblers in such a way that chipping was unlikely to occur. Their glassware carried the patented Safedge guarantee. Libbey also made glassware in numerous colors, among them cobalt, ruby, pink, green, and amber. Our advisors for this category are Don and Anne Kier; they are listed in the Directory under Ohio.

Basket, amberina, wide fan-flared rim, tall hdl, 8¼x6x4" **2,695.00**
Basket, cut, Am Brilliant period, 21" **3,500.00**
Bottle, scent; amberina, ovoid, complete, 7½x2½" **1,150.00**
Bowl, Cluthra, pk/crystal, 3¾x11" **395.00**
Bowl, cut, Glenda, 2x9" **550.00**
Bowl, cut, New Brilliant, 1¾x8" **125.00**
Bowl, finger; floral etch **150.00**
Bowl, punch; cut, Spillane, w/base **4,700.00**
Candle holder, clear bowl w/opal camel stem, 5¼" **150.00**
Candlestick, air-twist stem, 8" **225.00**
Candlesticks, cut, Prism, hollow stem, 10x4¾", pr **600.00**
Candy dish, cut, fans in sqs, 1905-10, 7" **95.00**
Carafe, cut, hobstars, fans & mitres **230.00**
Celery, cut, Harvard, 11" **190.00**
Champagne, Patrician (cut), bowl/ft, 6", set of 8 .....**125.00**
Compote, amberina, amber disc ft, label, 3¼x7¾" **650.00**
Compote, eng floral & chain, swirl stem, 6¼x8" **60.00**
Compote, wht opal w/rose swirls, clear stem, 5¾x7¼" **400.00**
Compote, wht opaque w/rose feathers, clear stem & ped, 6x7" ..**400.00**
Creamer & sugar bowl, cut, Colonna **95.00**
Figurine, elephant, blk, circular disc base, att, 4¼" **95.00**
Figurine, elephant, fiery opal, att, 3¾" **95.00**
Goblet, crystal w/appl lily-pad prunts, ped ft, 5" **100.00**
Knife rest, barbell shape w/cut glass ends, ca 1896-1910, 4" **75.00**
Maize, bowl, gr husks on wht opaque, 4x8¾" **275.00**
Maize, butter dish, bl husks on irid **650.00**
Maize, butter dish, bl husks w/gold outlines, 6½x7" **1,000.00**
Maize, butter dish, gr husks on custard **165.00**
Maize, celery vase, gold-tipped gr husks on oyster wht, 6½" **265.00**
Maize, celery vase, gr husks on custard **200.00**
Maize, celery vase, gr leaves on milk glass, ground top, 6¾" **90.00**
Maize, celery vase, lt gold irid on clear, 6⅝" **185.00**
Maize, condiment set, gr husks on custard, 3-pc+tray, metal lids ..**565.00**
Maize, pickle castor, amber stain **595.00**
Maize, pickle castor, gr husks on custard, SP fr **495.00**
Maize, pitcher, gold-yel husks on wht, 8¾x5½" **525.00**
Maize, shakers, bl husks w/gold edge on custard, pr **200.00**
Maize, sugar shaker, gold husks on oyster wht, 5½" **335.00**
Maize, sugar shaker, gold-tipped gr husks on oyster wht, 5½" **485.00**
Maize, syrup, bl husks, gild irid cob, pewter lid, 6" **600.00**
Maize, syrup, gr husks on custard, pewter lid, 7½" **350.00**
Maize, toothpick holder, gr husks w/gold edge on custard **345.00**
Maize, tumbler, bl husks on irid..**135.00**
Maize, tumbler, gr husks on irid..**175.00**
Maize, vase, yel/gold husks on custard, 6½" **210.00**
Plate, cut, Empress, 12" **700.00**
Platter, crystal w/ruby prunts, Nash, 15½" dia.............................**150.00**
Stem, champagne flute; bear, wht opal, 5½" **185.00**
Stem, champagne; squirrel, wht opal, 6" **165.00**

Stem, claret; bear, blk, 5½" **155.00**
Stem, cordial; Embassy, tall **100.00**
Stem, cordial; monkey, wht opal, 5" **145.00**
Stem, cordial; whippet/greyhound, wht opal **175.00**
Stem, goblet; cat, wht opal **200.00**
Stem, goblet; monkey, wht opal, 1930s..**180.00**
Stem, iced-tea; cut, Arctic Rose, 6⅜" **25.00**
Stem, iced-tea; Halifax, 6⅜" **15.00**
Stem, sherbet; squirrel, wht opal, 4" **150.00**
Stem, wine; giraffe, wht opal, 6" **120.00**
Stem, wine; kangaroo, wht opal **230.00**
Stem, wine; monkey, frosted, 5" **85.00**
Sugar bowl, lt bl satin, World's Fair 1893 in gilt, open, 2⅝".......**500.00**
Tray, cut, Regis, 12" **775.00**
Tray, ice cream; cut, Somerset, 12"...**275.00**
Tumbler, juice; cut, Corinthian variant..**70.00**
Vase, amberina, flared top, 4½" **650.00**
Vase, bud; amberina, att, 6" **385.00**
Vase, cut, Brilliant pattern, 4-scallop top, 12x5" **450.00**
Vase, cut, Star & Feather, 16" **1,300.00**
Vase, floral, purple cut to clear, ca 1920, 14".............................**1,300.00**
Vase, floral intaglio, 14x4⅞" **200.00**

Vase, floriform, amberina, strong optic ribs, #9009, 7⅝x3", $1,325.00. (Photo courtesy Julia's Auction Company, Fairfield, MA)

Vase, Optic Dmn, crystal w/bl threading, ca 1932, 8" **300.00**
Water set, cut, geometric floral, 8½" jug+4 3¾" tumblers **625.00**

Lightning Rod Balls

Used as ornaments on lightning rods, the vast majority of these balls were made of glass, but ceramic examples can be found as well. Their average diameter is 4½", but it can vary from 3½" up to 5½". Only a few of the available pattern-and-color combinations are listed here. The most common measure 4½" and are found in sun-colored amethyst and milk glass. Some patterns are being reproduced without marking them as such, and some new patterns are available as well. Collectors are cautioned to look for signs of age (stains) and/or to learn more before investing in a 'rare' lightning rod ball. Our advisor is Rod Krupka, author of a book on this subject. Anyone interested in his book may write to him for more information; he is listed in the directory under Michigan.

Amber, Dodd & Struthers, faint stain, 5¾x5¾" **60.00**
Bl opaque, Round, 4½" **30.00**

Blk amethyst, Plain Round, 4½" **395.00**
Clear, Chestnut, faint staint **60.00**
Cobalt, Dodd & Struthers, 5¾x5¾" **170.00**
Cobalt, Round, 4½" **95.00**
Cobalt mercury, Electra Round, 5x4¾" **500.00**
Gold mercury, Hawkeye, orig tube, aluminum caps, 5¼x4½" **325.00**
Gr opaque, Plain Round, 5¼x5" **95.00**
Gr opaque, Ribbed Grape, 5x4⅜" **130.00**
Milk glass, Chestnut, aluminum caps, 4⅛x3⅞" **30.00**
Milk glass, Electra Cone, bold emb, 5x4½" **40.00**
Milk glass, Maher, sm chips, 5x4½" **225.00**
Milk glass, Mast, copper caps..**75.00**
Milk glass, Round, 4½" **25.00**
Red, Diddie Blitzen, faint stain, 4x3¾" **210.00**
Red, Round, 4½" **100.00**
Red flashed, Pleat-Round, 5x4½" **300.00**
Red flashed, SLRCo, short wide collar (unemb), lt stain **100.00**
Silver mercury, National Round, correct tube, brass caps, 5x4½" **400.00**
Sun-colored amethyst, Moon & Star, 5x4½" **95.00**
Sun-colored amethyst, National Belted, 5¼x4½" **200.00**

Limbert

Charles P. Limbert formed his firm in 1894 in America's furniture capital, Grand Rapids, Michigan, and from 1902 until 1918, produced a line of Arts & Crafts furniture. While his wide-ranging line of furniture is not as uniformly successful as Gustav Stickley, the Limbert pieces that do exhibit design excellence stand among the best of American Arts & Crafts examples. Pieces featuring cutouts, exposed construction elements (e.g., key and tenon), metal and ebonized wood inlays, and asymmmetric forms are among the most desirable. Less desirable are the firm's Outdoor Designs that show exposed metal screws and straight grain, as opposed to quarter-sawn oak boards. His most aesthetically successful forms mimic those of Charles Rennie Mackintosh (Scotland) and, to a lesser extent, Joseph Hoffmann (Austria). Usually signed with a rectangular mark (a paper label, branded in the wood, or a metal tag) showing a man planing wood, and with the words Limbert's Arts Craft Furniture Made in Grand Rapids and Holland. The firm continued to produce furniture until 1944. Currently, only his Arts & Crafts-style furniture holds any interest among collectors.

Please note: Furniture that has been cleaned or refinished is worth less than if its original finish has been retained. Our values are for pieces in excellent original condition unless noted otherwise. Our advisor for this and related Arts & Crafts categories is Bruce A. Austin; he is listed in the Directory under New York.

Key: b — brand

Armchair, #1892, 1 wide bk splat, open arms, cushion seat, b, 39" **235.00**
Armchair, broad bk slat, brn leather seat, 36" **175.00**
Armchair, curved crest & 5 vertical slats, open arms, cushion, 39"...**475.00**
Bookcase, #7218, 10 sqs at top of 1-pane do, copper hdw, 56x28x12"..**1,500.00**
Chair set, T-bk, rpl tacked leather seat, rfn, 27", VG, 6 for.....**2,800.00**
Chair set, 1 vertical bk slat, b, overcoated, 36", 8 for **1,700.00**
China cabinet, #1463, glass front/sides, no mk, 58x32x15", VG ...**1,900.00**
Cricket (footstool), #200½, possible overcoat, b..**300.00**
Magazine stand, #302, 3 open shelves, wide slat in side, 28x28x11", VG...**900.00**
Pedestal, #239, 18" 8-sided top, tapered base w/cutouts & corbels, VG...**2,100.00**
Pedestal, #246, rnd top, 2 rnd shelves, shaped/cut-out supports, 42"....**4,250.00**
Rocker, #842, 5 vertical slats under ea arm, 3 across bk, 32x41x21"....**4,000.00**
Rocker, #982, curved crest over 3 vertical slats, through tenons..**325.00**
Server, #3442, angled top w/3 drw+2 shelves, corbels, rfn, 45" L, VG..**3,750.00**
Sideboard, #460¾, 2 doors between 2 banks of 4 sm drw, lg base drw, VG..**3,000.00**

Sideboard, 2 sm drws over linen drw, mirrored bk, 54x60x21"........**1,700.00**
Table, #148, 30" dia top, wide X stretchers w/sq cutouts, b, VG **3,750.00**
Table, #211, 12x12" sq top, b, 16", VG..**500.00**
Table, #416, oval, flat sides w/cutouts centering shelf, b, 39x45x30" **2,000.00**
Table, console; trestle legs, 3 center slats over stretcher, 72" ...**4,500.00**
Table, dining; #424, 60" dia top, 4 sets of dbl legs, VG **8,000.00**
Table, library, drw w/sq pulls, 8 corbel supports, 1906-18, 42" L ...**825.00**
Table, library; 2-drw, flush top, brass pulls, rfn, 39x48x31" **700.00**
Umbrella stand, #254, tapered panel sides w/sq cutouts, rfn, 27", VG....**1,500.00**

Hall chair, slab back and seat, cut-out designs, original finish, branded, 39x18x21", $2,000.00.

(Photo courtesy Treadway Auction Gallery)

Limited Edition Plates

Current values of some limited edition plates have risen, while many others have fallen. Prices charged by plate dealers in the secondary market vary greatly; we have tried to suggest an average.

Since Goebel Hummel plates have been discontinued, values have started to decline. While those who are trying to complete the series continue to buy them, few seem interested in starting a collection. As for the Danish plates, Royal Copenhagen and Bing and Grondahl, more purchases are for plates that commemorate the birth year of a child or a wedding anniversary than to add to a collection.

Bing and Grondahl

1895, Behind the Frozen Window **6,250.00**
1896, New Moon..**2,300.00**
1897, Christmas Meal of Sparrows..**1,500.00**
1898, Roses & Star **850.00**
1899, Crows Enjoying Christmas **1,800.00**
1900, Church Bells Chiming..**1,000.00**
1901, 3 Wise Men..**450.00**
1902, Gothic Church Interior **375.00**
1903, Expectant Children..**350.00**
1904, View of Copenhagen From Fredericksberg Hill **175.00**
1905, Anxiety of the Coming Christmas Night **175.00**
1906, Sleighing to Church **100.00**
1907, Little Match Girl **135.00**
1908, St Petri Church **100.00**
1909, Yule Tree **105.00**
1910, Old Organist **100.00**
1911, Angels & Shepherds **100.00**
1912, Going to Church..**100.00**

1913, Bringing Home the Tree 100.00
1914, Amalienborg Castle 95.00
1915, Dog on Chain Outside Window 130.00
1916, Prayer of the Sparrows 90.00
1917, Christmas Boat 90.00
1918, Fishing Boat 90.00
1919, Outside the Lighted Window 85.00
1920, Hare in the Snow 85.00
1921, Pigeons 85.00
1922, Star of Bethlehem 85.00
1923, Hermitage 85.00
1924, Lighthouse 90.00
1925, Child's Christmas 90.00
1926, Churchgoers 90.00
1927, Skating Couple 120.00
1928, Eskimos 85.00
1929, Fox Outside Farm 90.00
1930, Tree in Town Hall Square 100.00
1931, Christmas Train 100.00
1932, Lifeboat at Work 100.00
1933, Korsor-Nyborg Ferry 85.00
1934, Church Bell in Tower 85.00
1935, Lillebelt Bridge 85.00
1936, Royal Guard 85.00
1937, Arrival of Christmas Guests 100.00
1938, Lighting the Candles 150.00
1939, Old Lock-Eye, The Sandman 190.00
1940, Delivering Christmas Letters 215.00
1941, Horses Enjoying Meal 225.00
1942, Danish Farm on Christmas Night 190.00
1943, Ribe Cathedral 190.00
1944, Sorgenfri Castle 120.00
1945, Old Water Mill 135.00
1946, Commemoration Cross 115.00
1947, Dybbol Mill 120.00
1948, Watchman 100.00
1949, Landsoldaten 105.00
1950, Kronborg Castle at Elsinore 120.00
1951, Jens Bang 105.00
1952, Old Copenhagen Canals & Thorsvaldsen Museum 110.00
1953, Royal Boat 110.00
1954, Snowman 115.00
1955, Kaulundborg Church 115.00
1956, Christmas in Copenhagen 150.00
1957, Christmas Candles 150.00
1958, Santa Claus 125.00
1959, Christmas Eve 125.00
1960, Village Church 185.00
1961, Winter Harmony 115.00
1962, Winter Night 105.00
1963, Christmas Elf 110.00
1964, Fir Tree & Hare 60.00
1965, Bringing Home the Tree 55.00
1966, Home for Christmas 50.00
1967, Sharing the Joy 50.00
1968, Christmas in Church 45.00
1969, Arrival of Guests 35.00
1970, Pheasants in Snow 30.00
1971, Christmas at Home 30.00
1972, Christmas in Greenland 27.00
1973, Country Christmas 35.00
1974, Christmas in the Village 30.00
1975, The Old Water Mill 25.00
1976, Christmas Welcome 25.00

1977, Copenhagen Christmas 25.00
1978, A Christmas Tale 25.00
1979, White Christmas 35.00
1980, Christmas in the Woods 35.00
1981, Christmas Peace 35.00
1982, The Christmas Tree 40.00
1983, Christmas in Old Town 35.00
1984, Christmas Letter 35.00
1985, Christmas Eve, Farm 35.00
1986, Silent Night 40.00
1987, Snowman's Christmas 45.00
1988, In King's Garden 55.00
1989, Christmas Anchorage 55.00
1990, Changing Guards 55.00
1991, Copenhagen Stock Exchange 75.00
1992, Pastor's Christmas 75.00
1993, Father Christmas in Copenhagen 90.00
1994, Day in Deer Park 85.00
1995, Towers of Copenhagen 85.00
1996, Winter at the Old Mill 85.00
1997, Country Christmas 85.00
1998, Santa the Storyteller 85.00

M. I. Hummel

The last issue for M.I. Hummel annual plates was made in 1995. Values listed here are for plates in mint condition with original boxes.

1971, Heavenly Angel 500.00
1972, Hear Ye, Hear Ye 45.00
1973, Globe Trotter 110.00
1974, Goose Girl 45.00
1975, Ride Into Christmas 45.00
1976, Apple Tree Girl 45.00
1977, Apple Tree Boy 45.00
1978, Happy Pastime 45.00
1979, Singing Lesson 40.00
1980, School Girl 45.00
1981, Umbrella Boy 50.00
1982, Umbrella Girl 70.00
1983, The Postman 140.00
1984, Little Helper 50.00
1985, Chick Girl 50.00
1986, Playmates 90.00
1987, Feeding Time 160.00
1988, Little Goat Herder 90.00
1989, Farm Boy 85.00
1990, Shepherd's Boy 150.00
1991, Just Resting 120.00
1992, Meditation 125.00
1993, Doll Bath 125.00
1994, Doctor 125.00
1995, Come Back Soon 125.00

Royal Copenhagen

1908, Madonna & Child, minimum value 3,500.00
1909, Danish Landscape 265.00
1910, Magi 180.00
1911, Danish Landscape 175.00
1912, Christmas Tree 200.00
1913, Frederik Church Spire 160.00
1914, Holy Spirit Church 170.00
1915, Danish Landscape 190.00

1916, Shepherd at Christmas	130.00
1917, Our Savior Church	110.00
1918, Sheep & Shepherds	110.00
1919, In the Park	110.00
1920, Mary & Child Jesus	105.00
1921, Aabenraa Marketplace	100.00
1922, 3 Singing Angels	100.00
1923, Danish Landscape	100.00
1924, Sailing Ship	140.00
1925, Christianshavn Street Scene	100.00
1926, Christianshavn Canal	90.00
1927, Ship's Boy at Tiller	150.00
1928, Vicar's Family	100.00
1929, Grundtvig Church	100.00
1930, Fishing Boats	155.00
1931, Mother & Child	145.00
1932, Frederiksberg Gardens	145.00
1933, Ferry & Great Belt	190.00
1934, Hermitage Castle	200.00
1935, Kronborg Castle	275.00
1936, Roskilde Cathedral	265.00
1937, Main Street of Copenhagen	300.00
1938, Round Church of Osterlars	425.00
1939, Greenland Pack Ice	550.00
1940, Good Shepherd	595.00
1941, Danish Village Church	475.00
1942, Bell Tower	535.00
1943, Flight Into Egypt	700.00
1944, Danish Village Scene	375.00
1945, Peaceful Scene	625.00
1946, Zealand Village Church	260.00
1947, Good Shepherd	350.00
1948, Nodebo Church	265.00
1949, Our Lady's Cathedral	280.00
1950, Boeslunde Church	335.00
1951, Christmas Angel	500.00
1952, Christmas in Forest	185.00
1953, Frederiksberg Castle	185.00
1954, Amalienborg Palace	185.00
1955, Fano Girl	225.00
1956, Rosenborg Castle	200.00
1957, Good Shepherd	165.00
1958, Sunshine Over Greenland	165.00
1959, Christmas Night	200.00
1960, Stag	165.00
1961, Training Ship	175.00
1962, Little Mermaid	300.00
1963, Hojsager Mill	85.00
1964, Fetching the Tree	85.00
1965, Little Skaters	70.00
1966, Blackbird	60.00
1967, Royal Oak	55.00
1968, Last Umiak	50.00
1969, Old Farmyard	50.00
1970, Christmas Rose & Cat	50.00
1972, In the Desert	35.00
1973, Train Home Bound	40.00
1974, Winter Twilight	45.00
1975, Queens Palace	35.00
1976, Danish Watermill	40.00
1977, Immervad Bridge	35.00
1978, Greenland Scenery	35.00
1979, Choosing Tree	60.00
1980, Bringing Home Tree	45.00

1981, Admiring Tree	50.00
1982, Waiting for Christmas	85.00
1983, Merry Christmas	65.00
1984, Jingle Bells	65.00
1985, Snowman	70.00
1986, Wait for Me	65.00
1987, Winter Birds	70.00
1988, Christmas Eve Copenhagen	90.00
1989, Old Skating Pond	105.00
1990, Christmas in Tivoli	155.00
1991, St Lucia Basilica	100.00
1992, Royal Coach	85.00
1993, Arrival Guests by Train	350.00
1994, Christmas Shopping	95.00
1995, Christmas at Manorhouse	425.00
1996, Lighting Street Lamps	95.00
1997, Roskilde Cathedral	90.00
1998, Welcome Home	190.00

1971, Hare in Winter, $35.00.

Limoges

From the mid-eighteenth century, Limoges was the center of the porcelain industry of France, where at one time more than forty companies utilized the local kaolin to make a superior quality china, much of which was exported to the United States. Various marks were used; some included the name of the American export company (rather than the manufacturer) and 'Limoges.' After 1891 'France' was added. Pieces signed by factory artists are more valuable than those decorated outside the factory by amateurs. The listings below are hand-painted pieces unless noted otherwise.

For a more thorough study of the subject, we recommend you refer to *The Collector's Encyclopedia of Limoges Porcelain, Third Edition* (with beautiful illustrations and current market values), by our advisor, Mary Frank Gaston.

Please note: Limoges porcelain is totally French in origin, but one American china manufacturer, The Limoges China Company, marked its earthenware 'Limoges' to reflect its name. For information concerning this American earthenware, we recommend *American Limoges* by Raymonde Limoges. Both this book and Mrs. Gaston's are available from Collector Books.

Biscuit jar, floral on pale gr w/gold, Bawo & Dotter mk, 7½"	300.00
Box, monkey holding tail figural, Sandoz, 7½", EX	800.00
Cake plate, blackberries w/gold, MR Gray 1900, Pouyat mk, 11½"	350.00
Cake plate, daffodils w/gold, sgn Bay, pierced hdls, Flambeau mk	350.00
Chocolate pot, gold paste floral on wht, Bawo & Dotter, 9"	500.00
Chocolate pot, wide Nouveau band, gold/orange on cobalt, JPL, 11"	525.00
Jardiniere, yel mums w/gold, B&Co mk, 6x6½"	450.00
Leaf dish, flowers & leaves on shaded rust, Mullidy, Bawo & Dotter, 6"	165.00

Pitcher, cider; florals w/gold, T&V mks, 6½" **500.00**
Pitcher, cider; plums & wht flowers w/gold, Guèrin mk, 6½" **425.00**
Pitcher, cider; windmill scenic band w/gold, D&Co mk, 5" ...**275.00**
Plaque, ballet dancers on turq to pk, Camille Faurè, 6x4½" **750.00**
Plaque, cavalier w/pipe, Courdert, Coronet mk, 10½" **450.00**
Plaque, country barn scene, sgn Max, Flambeau mks, 9½" **265.00**
Plaque, daffodils, T&V mk, 13x15½" **2,000.00**
Plaque, nude maiden & angel, ca 1800, 5⅞" in 15⅝x13¾" fr **400.00**
Plaque, pears (1 split open), Coiffe mk, 10" **215.00**
Plaque, sailing scene, sgn Duval, Coronet mk, 10" **350.00**
Plaque, turkey gobbler & hen, Courdert, Coronet mk, 9½" **190.00**
Plate, bird among rocks/flowers, AKCD mk, 9" **200.00**
Plate, blackberries w/gold, sgn Martha, Lanternier mk, 8¾" **185.00**
Plate, cherub transfer w/gold stencil, Redon mks, 8¾" **315.00**
Plate, cherubs in clouds, gold rim, Ahrenfeldt, 9½" **425.00**
Plate, floral border w/gold diapering, Bawo & Dotter, 9½" **60.00**
Plate, game bird, sgn Luc, Blakeman & Henderson, 8½" **215.00**
Plate, lady stands w/flower basket, Le Pic, Coronet mk, 10" **300.00**
Plate, pheasants w/gold, Morseys, Latrille & LS&S mks, 9½" **285.00**
Plate, President Harrison, eagle emblem, corn/star borders, 8⅝" ..**500.00**
Plate, rabbit, sgn Dubois, Laviolette & Flambeau mks, 8½" **115.00**
Plate, roses, gold beadwork, Coiffe mk, 9½" **115.00**
Platter, floral transfer on pale turq, D&Co mk, 14" **300.00**
Platter, turkeys scene, Ahrenfeldt mk, 19½"+12 plates **2,200.00**
Powder jar, mc floral w/gold mts, Guèrin mk, 4½" dia...............**250.00**
Punch bowl, dogwood w/in & w/out, T&V mks, 4½x9"..............**650.00**
Punch bowl, holly w/in & w/out, T&V mks, 4½x9" **650.00**
Punch set, grapes & foliage w/gold, T&V mk, 14" bowl+stand+6 mugs...**1,400.00**
Shaving mug, roses w/gold, T&V/Marshall Field mks, 4" **200.00**
Sugar bowl, brn & rust leaves w/sm bl flowers, w/lid, Bawo & Dotter ..**165.00**
Tankard, mc floral on lav to cream, Janat, Blakeman & Henderson, 14"...**1,300.00**
Tankard, mc pansies w/gold, scalloped hdl, T&V mks, 15½" ...**1,400.00**
Tankard, Nouveau grapes w/gold, Paxton 1905, T&V mk, 15½" **1,000.00**
Tankard, nude lady w/water jug, gold hdl, Pouyat mks, 13" **3,250.00**
Tea set, gold Nouveau chain w/gr leaves, Blakeman & Henderson, 3-pc ...**600.00**
Tray, Nouveau lady's portrait w/emerald-set circlet, ca 1900, 18"..**825.00**
Tray, scattered yel flowers w/gold, Pouyat mks, 10½x8" **225.00**
Vase, cherub on pk w/gold, ftd, hdls, Bawo & Dotter mk, 7" **400.00**
Vase, geometrics, bl/ivory/silver/blk, pewter rim, Camille Fauré, 12" ...**5,000.00**
Vase, poppies on textured mc, Camille Fauré, bulbous, 5"........**1,500.00**
Vase, roses, 3 ornate gold ft, Guèrin mk, 14½" **1,100.00**
Vase, terrace w/flowers, sgn S 1904, Pouyat mk, 13"................**1,300.00**

Lithophanes

Lithophanes are porcelain panels with relief designs of varying degrees of thickness and density. Transmitted light brings out the pattern in graduated shading, lighter where the porcelain is thin and darker in the heavy areas. They were cast from wax models prepared by artists and depict views of life from the 1800s, religious themes, or scenes of historical significance. First made in Berlin about 1803, they were used as lamp shade panels, window plaques, and candle shields. Later steins, mugs, and cups were made with lithophanes in their bases. Japanese wares were sometimes made with dragons or geisha lithophanes. See also Dragon Ware; Steins.

Candle holder, ornate brass, cherub praying, 4 bells, 4½x10½" **900.00**
Panel, Christ as youth among angels, bronze fr, Am, 1856, 19"..**800.00**
Panel, hunter scene, cast metal fr, candle holder behind, mini, 5" **725.00**
Panel, lady w/candle under chin (after Vermeer), wood stand, 9x18" ..**1,500.00**
Panel, maidens, foliate metal fr w/candle holder behind, 1850s, 15" **2,300.00**
Panel, robed lady w/mask, Meissen, brass fr, 1854, 11x8" **1,600.00**
Panel, woman & courtier, foliate fr, candle holder behind, 1850s, 15" **2,600.00**

Fire screen, William Penn's treaty with the Indians, signed GAS, in ornate iron pedestal stand, 1840s, 17x14¼", $1,500.00.

Little Red Riding Hood

Though usually thought of as a product of the Hull Pottery Company, research has shown that a major part of this line was actually made by Regal China. The idea for this popular line of novelties and kitchenware items was developed and patented by Hull, but records show that to a large extent Hull sent their whiteware to Regal to be decorated. Little Red Riding Hood was produced from 1943 until 1957.

For further information we recommend *The Collector's Encyclopedia of Hull Pottery* by our advisor Brenda Roberts, and *The Collector's Encyclopedia of Cookie Jars, Vol. I, II,* and *III,* by Joyce and Fred Roerig. All are published by Collector Books.

Bank, standing, 7", from $900 to **1,350.00**
Butter dish, from $350 to..**400.00**
Canister, cereal **1,375.00**
Canister, coffee, sugar or flour; ea from $600 to **700.00**
Canister, salt **1,100.00**
Canister, tea **700.00**
Casserole, red w/emb wolf, RRH, Grandma & axe man, 11¾", $1,800 to.....**2,500.00**
Cookie jar, closed basket, from $450 to **650.00**
Cookie jar, full skirt, from $750 to..**850.00**
Cookie jar, open basket, from $400 to **500.00**
Cracker jar, unmk, from $600 to **750.00**
Creamer, side pour, from $150 to **225.00**
Creamer, top pour, no tab hdl, from $400 to **425.00**
Creamer, top pour, tab hdl, from $350 to..................................**375.00**
Dresser jar, 8¾", from $450 to **575.00**
Lamp, from $2,000 to **2,650.00**
Match holder, wall hanging, from $800 to................................**850.00**
Mustard jar, w/orig spoon, from $375 to **460.00**
Pitcher, 7", from $450 to...**675.00**
Pitcher, 8", from $550 to...**850.00**
Planter, wall hanging, from $400 to **500.00**
Shakers, Pat design 135889, med sz, pr (+), from $800 to **900.00**
Shakers, 3¼", pr, from $95 to **140.00**
Shakers, 5½", pr, from $180 to **235.00**
String holder, from $1,800 to...**2,500.00**
Sugar bowl, crawling, no lid, from $300 to **450.00**
Sugar bowl, standing, no lid, from $175 to **225.00**
Sugar bowl, w/lid, from $350 to...**425.00**
Sugar bowl lid, minimum value..**175.00**
Teapot, from $400 to..**450.00**
Wolf jar, red base, from $925 to **1,000.00**
Wolf jar, yel base, from $750 to..**850.00**

Liverpool

In the late 1700s Liverpool potters produced a creamy ivory ware, sometimes called Queen's Ware, which they decorated by means of the newly perfected transfer print. Made specifically for the American market, patriotic inscriptions, political portraits, or other States themes were applied in black with colors sometimes added by hand. (Obviously their loyalty to the crown did not inhibit the progress of business!) Before it lost favor in about 1825, other English potters made a similar product. Today Liverpool is a generic term used to refer to all ware of this type.

Bowl, B Franklin/Geo Washington/Am ship, blk transfers, 4x9" **1,265.00**
Cup & saucer, handleless; Washington blk transfer, NM **350.00**
Jug, Brig Adventure of Salem/WA & Lady Liberty, HP transfer, 9 ....**4,675.00**
Jug, Commodore Prebble - Am flag/battle scene, rstr, 8" **2,250.00**
Jug, eagle/E Pluribus Unum/Masonic emblems, blk transfer **2,000.00**
Jug, In God Is Our Trust/farmyard, blk transfer, Herculaneumn, 9"....**800.00**
Jug, Masonic symbols/World Is in Pain..., blk transfer, 11½"...**1,150.00**
Jug, ship Ulysses/Success to Saucy Polly..., blk transfer, 10¾"....**1,150.00**
Jug, Shipwrights Arms/Ship Caroline, blk transfer, HP Am flag, 8", EX..**220.00**
Jug, Success to Trade/Abbas & Abra, blk transfers, 8½" **330.00**
Jug, United for Benefit/Masonic elements, blk w/mc, 11⅜" **1,380.00**
Tureen, figure w/coat-of-arms shields, blk transfer, 9½x12¼" **1,095.00**

Lladro

Lladro porcelains are currently being produced in Labernes Blanques, Spain. Their retired and limited edition figurines are popular collectibles on the secondary market.

A King Is Born, #2198, 12¼", MIB.................**385.00**
Afghan Hound, #1282, retired, 5x5½" **425.00**
Ballet Ovation, #6614, retired, 8", MIB....................**625.00**

Bride and Groom, 1998, MIB, $110.00.

Bust Playing Violin, #5600, 7¾", MIB........................**375.00**
Clown Bust, #5611, 8½"..**420.00**
Clown w/Concertina, #1027, 17⅞"..............................**510.00**
Couple reading on couch w/dog, #5229, 11½", M (EX box) **475.00**
Early Awakening, #2369, 22¾", MIB..............................**560.00**
Embroiderer, #4865, retired, 11".................................**360.00**
Fall Leaves, #1774, retired **425.00**

Flamenco Dancers, #4519, retired, MIB..............**850.00**
German Shepherd w/Pup, #4731G, retired, 7¾"..........**575.00**
Gypsy Woman, #4919, 14½", MIB **450.00**
Happy Swing, #1255, retired, 9½", MIB.................**340.00**
Heavenly Swing, #1739, retired, 10".....................**565.00**
I Love You Truly, #1528, 14¾"..............................**500.00**
Little Pals, #7600, 8¾", from $1,050 to.................**1,350.00**
Little Traveler, #7602, 8½", from $600 to...............**700.00**
Magic of Love, #5771, MIB.................................**960.00**
Mallard Duck, #5288, retired, 4½"........................**420.00**
My Little Sweetie, #6858, 18½", MIB **540.00**
Painful Monkey, #5018, retired, 5½", MIB...............**465.00**
Peter Pan, #7529, Disney, retired, MIB.................**760.00**
Romeo & Juliet, #4750, retired, 17¾" **650.00**
Sad Chimney Sweep, #1253, retired, 18"................**660.00**
Sleigh Ride, #5037, retired **850.00**
Socialite of the '20s, #5283, 14", MIB..................**320.00**
Tennis Players, male & female, #1426 & #1427, retired.............**350.00**
Thai Dancer, #2069M, retired, 16¾"....................**520.00**
Troubadour, #4548, retired, 10¼".........................**345.00**
Wedding Cake, #5587, 13", MIB..........................**540.00**
Woman on Horse, #4516, retired, 17¼", MIB........**575.00**

Lobmeyer

J. and L. Lobmeyer, contemporaries of Moser, worked in Vienna, Austria, during the last quadrant of the 1800s. Most of the work attributed to them is decorated with distinctive enameling; favored motifs are people in eighteenth-century garb. Our advisor for this category is Don Williams; he is listed in the Directory under Missouri.

Beverage set, coats of arms, dtd 1860, pitcher+6 tumblers **1,500.00**
Cordial, pk band, gilt rim on quatrefoil bowl, leaf decor stem, 4⅜" **200.00**
Goblet, mc floral, gold rim/ft borders of U-shaped devices, 5"....**350.00**
Plate, Persian enameling.................................**350.00**
Tumbler, courting couple scene, unsgn, 4½", 5 for.....................**800.00**

Locke Art

By the time he came to America, Joseph Locke had already proven himself many times over as a master glassmaker, having worked in leading English glasshouses for more than seventeen years. Here he joined the New England Glass Company where he invented processes for the manufacture of several types of art glass — amberina, peachblow, pomona, and agata among them. In 1898 he established the Locke Art Glassware Co. in Mt. Oliver, Pittsburgh, Pennsylvania. Locke Art Glass was produced using an acid-etching process by which the most delicate designs were executed on crystal blanks. All examples are signed simply 'Locke Art,' often placed unobtrusively near a leaf or a stem. Some pieces are signed 'Jo Locke,' and some are dated. Most of the work was done by hand. The business continued into the 1920s. For further study we recommend *Locke Art Glass, Guide for Collectors*, by Joseph and Janet Locke, available at your local bookstore.

Our advisor for this category is Richard Haigh; he is listed in the Directory under Virginia.

Cherry dish, Pansy etch, concave ft for pits, flint, 2¾"..............**150.00**
Cup, ice cream; Kalana Poppy etch, ftd **75.00**
Cup, punch; Poppy etch...**95.00**
Pitcher, Orus & Ephialts w/Mars eng w/title panel, amberina, 12"....**875.00**
Pitcher, Vintage Grape etch, corseted, etch hdl, 8½", +6 tumblers....**590.00**

Salt cellar, Vintage, ped ft, 2¼x1¼" 100.00
Sherbet, fruits etch..125.00
Tumbler, brandy; etch flowers & leaves, rare, 3¼" 140.00
Tumbler, Grape & Vine 110.00
Vase, Buds & Poppies, flared rim, 5" 300.00
Vase, Poppy etch, 6x3" 350.00
Vase, Rose etch, flared rim, 6¼" 450.00
Wine, floral etch, dbl-knob stem, rnd ft, 5¾" 125.00

Locks

The earliest type of lock in recorded history was the wooden cross bar used by ancient Egyptians and their contemporaries. The early Romans are credited with making the first key-operated mechanical lock. The ward lock was invented during the Middle Ages by the Etruscans of Northern Italy; the lever tumbler and combination locks followed at various stages of history with varying degrees of effectiveness. In the eighteenth century the first precision lock was constructed. It was a device that utilized a lever-tumbler mechanism. Two of the best-known of the early nineteenth-century American lock manufacturers are Yale and Sargent, and today's collectors value Winchester and Keen Kutter locks very highly. Factors to consider are rarity, condition, and construction. Brass and bronze locks are generally priced higher than those of steel or iron. Our advisor for this section is Joe Tanner; he is listed in the Directory under California.

Key:
bbl — barrel   st — stamped

Brass Lever Tumbler

Ames Sword Co, Perfection st on shackle, 2¾".............65.00
Automatic, emb, flat key, 2⅛" 20.00
Bingham's Best Brand, BBB emb on front, 3¼"............150.00
Chubbs, Patent London, st, 6⅛" 350.00
Cotterill, st High Security key, 5⅛x3⅛" 350.00
Crusader, shield, swords emb on body, 2¾" 45.00
Eagle Lock Co, word Eagle emb on front, scrolled, 3".....60.00
Good Luck, emb, 2¾" 45.00
GW Nock, fancy etch, st, 2⅞" 200.00
JWM, emb, bbl key, 2⅝" 25.00
Mercury, Mercury emb on body, 2¾" 75.00
Motor, Motor emb on body, 3¼" 35.00
Our Very Best, DVB emb on body, 2⅞" 200.00
Roeyonoc, Roeyonoc st on body, 3¼" 30.00
Ruby, Ruby emb in scroll on front, 2¾" 30.00
Siberian, Siberian emb on shackle, 2½" 110.00
Sphinx, sphinx & pharaoh head emb on front, 2¾" 35.00
Tower & Lyon NY, st, 3" 25.00
W Bohannan & Co, SW emb in scroll on front, 2⅜".......30.00
Watch, emb, flat key, 3" 30.00
1898, emb, 2¾" 30.00

Combinations

Chicago Combination Lock Co, st on front, brass, 2¾".......60.00
Corbin Sesamee 4-Dial Brass Lock, st Sesamee, 2¾" 15.00
Junkunc Bros Mfrs, all st on bk, brass, 1⅞" 35.00
Miller Keyless, st, iron, 3¼" 70.00
Number or letter disk, st, 3-disk, brass, 2½" 100.00
Number or letter disk, st, 4-disk, brass, 3½" 170.00
Number or letter disk, st, 4-disk, iron, 4½" 275.00

Permutation Lock Den Co, emb, brass, 3⅝"................600.00
Sorel Limited Canada, st, brass, 3¼".........................200.00
Sutton Lock Co st on body, 3" 200.00
Turman's Keyless, st, brass, 2¼"...............................160.00
Your Own st on body, 3⅞"..400.00

Eight-Lever Type

Blue Chief, st, steel, 4½" 25.00
Excelsior, st, steel, 4¾" 30.00
Mastadon, st, brass, 4½" 30.00
Reese, st, steel, 4¾" 15.00

Iron Lever Tumbler

Airplane, st, 2¾" 60.00
Bear, emb, 2⅝" 25.00
Bull, word Bull emb on front, 2⅝" 30.00
Caesar, emb, 2¾" 15.00
Dragon, word Dragon & dragon emb on front, 2⅞" 25.00
Eagle, 4 dice emb on front, 2¾" 40.00
HC Jones (trick lock), st, 4¼".................................600.00
Jupiter, word Jupiter/star & moon emb on front, 3¼" ...18.00
King Korn, words King Korn emb on body, 2⅞" 40.00
Mars, emb, 2¼" 20.00
Nineteen O Three, 1903 emb on front, 3⅞"..............120.00
Red Chief, words Red Chief emb on body, 3¾"..........150.00
Rugby, football emb on body, 3" 20.00
Star Lock Works, st, 3⅛" 50.00
Unique, word Unique emb on front, 3¼"...................120.00
W Bohannon, Brook NY WB, st, 3¼" 35.00
Woodland, emb, 2⅜" 30.00

Lever Push Key

Aztec, emb 6-Lever, 2⅛" 100.00
California, emb, brass, 2½".......................................300.00
Celtic Cross, emb cross on face, brass, 2¼" 150.00
Cherokee, emb, 6-Lever, iron, 2½"...........................170.00
Columbia, emb Columbia 6-Lever, brass push-key type, 2¼" 35.00
Crescent, 4-Lever, emb, iron, 2" 40.00
Duke, emb 6-Lever, 2⅛" 65.00
Eclipse, 4-Lever, emb, brass, 2½" 20.00
Empire, emb, 6-Lever, brass, 2½" 20.00
Fordloc, emb, iron, 3¼" 50.00
HS&Co, 6-Lever, emb, brass, 2¼" 100.00
Jewett Buffalo, emb, brass, 2¼" 200.00
McIntosh, emb, 6-Lever, iron, 2½"............................150.00
National Lock Co, emb, brass, 2½" 150.00
Nugget, 4-Lever, emb, brass, 2" 50.00
Smith & Egge Mfg Co, Smith & Egge st on front, 3" 75.00
Vulcan, emb, iron, 2¾"..20.00

Logo — Special Made

Anaconda, st, brass, 2⅞"...60.00
City of Boston Dept of Schools, st, brass, 2⅞"............75.00
Conoco, st, brass, 2⅝"..25.00
Delco Products, st, brass..20.00
Hawaiian Elec, st, brass, 3" 30.00
Heart-shape brass lever type st Board Education, bbl key, 3½" 65.00
Lilly, st, brass, 2½"...15.00
Ordinance Dept, st, brass, 2⅞"..................................20.00
Public Service Co, st, brass, 2⅞".................................20.00

Sq Yale-type brass pin tumbler, st Shell Oil Co on body, 3⅛" 25.00
Standard Oil Co, st, brass, 2⅝" 25.00
Texaco, emb, brass, 2¾" 60.00
University of Okla, st, brass, 2⅞" 40.00
USBIR, st, brass, 3¾"..80.00
USMC, st, brass, 2½"..100.00
Zoo, st, iron, 2½" 25.00

Pin-Tumbler Type

Corbin, emb, iron, 2¾" 20.00
Fulton, emb Fulton on body, 2⅝" 30.00
Hope, brass, emb Hope on body, 2½" 20.00
Il-A-Noy, emb Il-A-Noy on body, 2½" 40.00
Rich-Con, emb, iron, 2⅞" 50.00
Sargent, emb, iron, 2¾" 15.00
Segal, iron, emb Segal on shackle, 3¾"....................................30.00
Simmons, emb, iron, 2⅝" 30.00
Yale, brass, emb Yale on body, Made in England on shackle, 3" ...30.00

Scandinavian (Jail House) Type

Backalaphknck (Russian), st, iron, 5" 400.00
Corbin, st, brass, 2½"...50.00
Nrarvck (Russian), st, iron, 4"...250.00
R&E Co, emb, iron, 3¼"..40.00
Star, emb line on bottom, iron, 3¾" 150.00
99 Miller, emb 99, brass, 1¾" 80.00

Six-Lever Type

Eagle, brass, Eagle Six-Lever st on body 18.00
Miller, Six-Lever, st, brass, 3⅞" 20.00
Olympiad Six-Lever, st, iron, 3¾" 25.00
SHCo Simmons Six-Lever, emb, iron, 3⅝" 70.00

Story and Commemorative

Canteen, US emb on lock, lock: canteen shape, 2" 700.00
CI, emb skull/X-bones w/florals, NH Co on bk, 3¼" 200.00
Dan Patch, iron, 1⅞"..125.00
Mail Pouch emb on lock, lock in shape of mail pouch, 3⅛".......225.00
National Hardware Co (NHCo), emb, iron, 2½"........................200.00
National Hardware Co (NHCo), emb SK, iron, 3½"..................600.00
North Pole, brass, 2⅞" 150.00
Russell & Erwin (R&E), emb Aztec figure, iron, 2¼" 200.00
Russell & Erwin (R&E), emb mailbox, iron, 3⅛" 600.00
1901 Pan Am Expo, brass, emb w/buffalo, 2⅝" 450.00

Warded Type

Army, iron pancake ward key, emb letters, 2½"...........................40.00
Cruso Chicken, emb, brass, 2¾"...35.00
G&B, st, brass, 3" 15.00
Hex, iron, sq lock case, emb US on bk, 2⅛" 95.00
Kirby, emb, brass, 2¼" 20.00
Navy, iron pancake ward key, bk: scrolled emb letters, 2½"..........40.00
Red Cross, brass sq case, emb letters, 2" 10.00
Rex, steel case, emb letters, 2⅝" 18.00
Safe, brass sq case, emb letters, 1⅞" 8.00
Sampson, emb, iron, 2½"..20.00
Shapleigh, st, brass, 2"..18.00
Texas, emb, brass, 2½"...50.00
Van Guard, emb, iron, 2⅞"..18.00

Wrought Iron Lever Type (Smokehouse Type)

First and Third: MW&Co., $20.00 each; Center: VR, 3½", $30.00.

DM&Co, bbl key, 4¼" 20.00
R&E, 4½" 40.00
WT Patent, 3¼"..20.00

Loetz

The Loetz Glassworks was established in Klostermule, Austria, in 1840. After Loetz's death the firm was purchased by his grandson, Johann Loetz Witwe. Until WWII the operation continued to produce fine artware, some of which made in the early 1900s bears a striking resemblance to Tiffany's, with whom Loetz was associated at one time. In addition to the iridescent Tiffany-style glass, he also produced threaded glass and some cameo. The majority of Loetz pieces will have a polished pontil. Our advisor for this category is Don Williams; he is listed in the Directory under Missouri.

Biscuit jar, gr w/impressed crackle, bl layers in clear, 7" 115.00
Bowl, gold irid, fold-over rim, 7¾"..100.00
Bowl, gr w/bl oil spots, appl hdls/ft, 4¾x7" 175.00
Bowl vase, gr irid, ball shape w/6 appl gold hdls at top, 9½" dia...475.00
Candlestick, gold irid, flaring drip pan, dbl rings (2X), 15".....1,300.00
Ewer, gold irid oil spots, golden 4-ftd fr w/Northwind panel, 11" 1,800.00
Lamp, dk gr w/oil spots, opal/dk gr trailings, 6" onion shade/harp std...3,600.00
Lamp, gold-plated bronze flower form w/5¼" yel bud shade, 18" 2,500.00
Lamp, shell-shaped shade, SP bronze root-design std, Landry, 14½"...2,700.00
Planter, pig form, much irid, EX detail, 10" L............................900.00
Shade, pulled drapery, bl/platinum on gr to gold, vase shape, 5"...250.00
Vase, agate streaking, gilt/enamel mouth, bottle form, 11" 325.00
Vase, amber craquelle, 2 gr lion-mask medallions, rectangular, 10"....250.00
Vase, amber irid w/bl irid overlay, trefoil rim, 5¼"...................1,250.00
Vase, amber to gold w/lt bl pulls/spots, twisted form, 7¾" 4,500.00
Vase, amber to gr w/red/gr oil spots, bowl-like top, crimped rim, 14"....375.00
Vase, amber w/bl & gold pulled decor, dbl-gourd, 5¼" 1,600.00
Vase, amber w/bl pulled/spotted decor, 4 pinched sides, 6¼" ..1,700.00
Vase, amber w/yel int showing, blk/bl/purple pulls, dbl-gourd, 8"....9,500.00
Vase, bronze color w/silver-bl irid lines, 7¼" 2,530.00
Vase, clear crackle w/2 amber buttresses, flared rim, 8"............750.00
Vase, deep bl w/gr/bl oil spots, 4 indents at waist, 5"..................700.00
Vase, dk maroon to lt gr mottle, 3-fold rim, punched bulb bottom, 8"..350.00
Vase, floriform; amber on gr stem w/hdls, 9¼" 1,000.00
Vase, floriform; gr w/oil spots on lt gr stem/ft, 9½" 450.00
Vase, frog form, gr irid, appl eyes/legs/arms, ribbed, 7"............2,100.00
Vase, gold irid & platinum w/bl pulled swirls, squat, 3½" 600.00
Vase, gold irid w/appl silver & gold irid knobs, 4¾" 2,070.00
Vase, gold irid w/orange oil spots, pinched top, 6½" 460.00
Vase, gold w/gr & bl pulls, swollen neck, 9¾"........................3,750.00

Vase, gold w/platinum pulls & silver tendrils, twisted, 7¼" **4,250.00**
Vase, gr irid w/bl pulled drapes, 3 dimples at bottom, 7½" **550.00**
Vase, gr irid w/brass ormolu dragonfly/etc mts, 10" **300.00**
Vase, gr irid w/lily pad o/l, curved neck widens to cylinder, 13" **765.00**
Vase, gr marbleized w/emb flower garlands, gold & wht enamel, 5¾"..**230.00**
Vase, gr mottle w/wht pulled decor, bulbous bottle form, 5" **400.00**
Vase, gr w/pulled bl & purple drape, 4-lobe top, 10" **500.00**
Vase, gr w/purple irid, appl snake spirals neck, 6" **150.00**
Vase, gr-gold irid w/serpent coiled around body, 13" **650.00**
Vase, gr/bl oil spots on red irid, 4 shoulder indents, 4½" **650.00**
Vase, irid (subdued) w/gold irid pulls, 5" **675.00**
Vase, mc pulled/spotted decor, SP Argenta fr, rectangular, 8¾"..**5,500.00**
Vase, opal irid, gold hooked/appl 'pigtails,' trifold rim, 4¼"........**200.00**
Vase, owl figural, appl beak/eyes/wings, on glass limb, 10½" ...**3,600.00**
Vase, Pampas, amber & purple, pinched, 6" **1,700.00**
Vase, paperweight; cobalt w/bright gr swirls, shouldered, 6"...**1,500.00**
Vase, Phanomen Argus, orange w/platinum & bl, pinched dbl-gourd, 10" ..**2,400.00**
Vase, Phanomen Argus, purple to amber w/bl, ruffled rim, 7" **2,400.00**
Vase, Phanomen Genre, purple w/platinum, shouldered/pinched, 8½" ..**4,750.00**
Vase, purple w/purple/bl/yel waves, dbl-gourd form, 9" **2,800.00**
Vase, random irid o/l, bell shaped, 7"..**5,700.00**
Vase, red/cream/amber pulled decor, dbl-gourd, 5" **1,300.00**
Vase, rose/orange/bl mottle, 2 lion-head ornaments, bulbous, att, 7".....**260.00**
Vase, shaded citron long neck w/gr-purple oil spots to body, 12½" **400.00**
Vase, silver o/l floral at neck, gr/orange mottle, 8" **800.00**
Vase, silver o/l flowers & ribbons on bl irid, 8" **2,280.00**
Vase, silver o/l tree & leaves, pulled spotted mc decor, pinched, 6"...**7,500.00**
Vase, textured gr w/bl irid highlights, twisted, 3-lobe rim, 7" **450.00**
Vase, textured gr w/platinum & purple highlights, shouldered, 6½" ..**325.00**
Vase, Titania, pulled gr & amber paperweight type, bulbous, 6½" ..**2,000.00**
Vase, trumpet; purple irid w/trefoil top, in gilt holder w/putto, 14"....**2,800.00**
Vase, wht w/gold pulls, tapered form, flared ft, 7" **1,500.00**
Vase, yel, bl/gr pulls, silver oil spots, mini, 3¼" **1,300.00**
Vase, yel irid w/pk & wht splotches, twisted/incurvate, sq top, 13"...**750.00**

Lomonosov Porcelain

Founded in Leningrad in 1744, the Lomonosov porcelain factory produced exquisite porcelain miniatures for the Czar and other Russian nobility. One of the first factories of its kind, Lomonosov produced mainly vases and delicate sculptures. In the 1800s Lomonosov became closely involved with the Russian Academy of Fine Arts, a connection which has continued to this day as the company continues to supply the world with these fine artistic treasures. In 1992 the backstamp was changed to read 'Made in Russia,' instead of 'Made in USSR.'

Baikal duck, looking over shoulder, red logo mk, 2½x6" **25.00**
Bears, inkwell, old bl logo mk, 5" **85.00**
Brn bear cubs (2), 1 standing up, 1 seated, red USSR mk, 6", 4½"....**35.00**
Dapple-gray horse, red logo mk, 9x8" **47.50**
Fawn, lt brn w/wht spots, red USSR mk, 4x6¾" **50.00**
Giraffe, baby, seated w/head up, 5⅜x5"..**20.00**
Giraffe, lying down, 12", from $50 to...**70.00**
Giraffe, standing up, USSR mk, 8¼" **65.00**
Hawk, wht w/blk beak & eyes, old bl logo, 1950s, 8"....................**60.00**
Leopard mother, recumbent, red USSR mk, 7"...............................**60.00**
Lion cub, seated, Made in USSR w/red logo, 3¾" **25.00**
Mammoth, red USSR mk, 4½x7"..**90.00**
Mice, wht, bl logo mk, 2x1x1", pr **45.00**
Panda cub, blk & wht, red USSR mk, 3⅜"..**40.00**
Penguin, standing up, red logo mk, 6"..**18.50**
Poodle, brn w/wht underbelly, Made in Russia, 5" **60.00**
Rabbit, wht w/blk features, lt brn nose, 1½x2¼" **17.50**

Rabbit, wht w/gold horn, 1950s, 7"..**140.00**
Rabbits, wht, eating carrot, 3", 4", 4½", 5", set of 4 ....**60.00**
Red fox, stalking, 1¾x8¼" **30.00**
Sailor boy, w/accordion, bl mk, ca 1960s, 5⅛"..............................**47.50**
Tiger cub, Made in USSR, 5x7" **45.00**
Vladimir Lenin, bust, bsk, 1955-60, 7"..**60.00**
White tiger cub, Made in Russia, 5x3"..**17.50**
Young ballerina, seated on gold-banded oval base, bl logo mk, 5x3"...**45.00**

Longwy

The Longwy workshops were founded in 1798 and continue today to produce pottery in the north of France near the Luxembourg-Belgian border under the name 'Sociètè des Faienceries de Longwy et Senelle.' The ware for which they are best known was produced during the Art Deco period, decorated in bold colors and designs. Earlier wares made during the first quarter of the nineteenth century reflected the popularity of Oriental art, cloisonné enamels in particular. Examples are marked 'Longwy,' either impressed or painted under glaze. Our advisors for this category are Suzanne Perrault and David Rago; they are listed in the Directory under New Jersey.

Basket, mc floral on turq, twisted hdl, 6¾x8½x5½" **910.00**
Bowl, red, bl & wht flowers on bl, scalloped edge, 2x8½x11" **225.00**
Charger, 2 birds in branches w/maroon bkground, sgn Gabet, 14½" ...**780.00**
Compote, turq w/wht & red flowers, crackled surface, 4¼x8½" ...**325.00**
Plate, maroon/gr/wht/bl star-shaped flowers on bl, 6".................**100.00**
Vase, wht & pk flowers w/gr leaves & brn branches, 6½x3⅛" dia...**115.00**

Losanti

Mary Louise McLaughlin, who had previously experimented in trying to reproduce Haviland faience in the 1870s and 'American faience' (a method of inlaying color by painting the inside of the mold before the vessel was cast) in the mid-1890s, developed a type of hard-paste porcelain in which the glaze and the body fused together in a single firing. Her efforts met with success in 1900, and she immediately concentrated on glazing and decorating techniques. The ware she perfected was called Losanti (after the early name for Cincinnati), most of which was decorated with Nouveau florals, either carved or modeled. By 1906 she had abanonded her efforts. Examples are marked with several ciphers, one resembling a butterfly, another with the letters MCL superimposed each upon the other, and L. McL in a linear arrangement. Other items were marked Losanti, sometimes in the Oriental manner. Our advisors for this category are Suzanne Perrault and David Rago; they are listed in the Directory under New Jersey.

Vase, blossoms in grain-of-rice technique, white gloss with oxblood flashes, marked Losanti in ink, incised cipher of Mary Louise McLaughlin, 5¾x3½", $25,875.00. (Photo courtesy David Rago Auctions)

Bowl, scrolled wreath cvg, wht on dk bl mottle, sgn/#65, 2¾x4"....**1,250.00**
Trivet, celadon w/emb floral, 6", VG, from $500 to **750.00**
Vase, lilies, wht w/gr on bl/wht mottle, ML McLaughlin, 8".........**15,000.00**
Vase, peacock feathers, beige/oxblood crackle, 4x4", EX, $2,750 to ..**3,750.00**

Lotton

Charles Lotton is a contemporary glass artist. He began blowing glass and developing original designs thirty years ago and now has work on display in many major glass museums and collections, among them the Smithsonian, the Art Institute of Chicago, the Museum of Glass, and the Chrysler Museum. He has become famous for his unique lamps. Every piece is signed and dated. His three sons, David, Daniel, and John, each work in their own studios. All four artists produce distinctive work. They sell their glass at antique shows and in their showroom in Crete, Illinois. For further information read *Lotton Art Glass* by Charles Lotton and Tom O'Conner; see the Directory under Illinois.

Bottle, Floral, Daniel Lotton, 1997, 9½" w/stopper.....................**850.00**
Bowl, Multi Floral, Selenium Red, dbl-layered flowers, 9x16"..**8,000.00**
Bowl, White Opal w/red int, pk flowers & leaves at rim, 8x12"....**2,000.00**
Lamp, Peacock, 1993, 18¼x6¼"..**5,000.00**
Vase, cobalt w/bl/gr/pk irid pulled designs, Daniel...1992, 5"......**325.00**
Vase, emerald gr w/stylized leaves & vines, sgn, 5".....................**225.00**
Vase, gr/purple irid loops on wht, flared rim, set-in base, 1972, 5"....**150.00**
Vase, split leaves on bl irid, 1991, 5"..**175.00**
Vase, Sunset Series Oval, cased flower layers, 12x9"...............**6,250.00**

Lotus Ware

Isaac Knowles and Issac Harvey operated a pottery in East Liverpool, Ohio, in 1853 where they produced both yellow ware and Rockingham. In 1870 Knowles brought Harvey's interests and took as partners John Taylor and Homer Knowles. Their principal product was ironstone china, but Knowles was confident that American potters could produce as fine a ware as the Europeans. To prove his point, he hired Joshua Poole, an artist from the Belleek Works in Ireland. Poole quickly perfected a Belleek-type china, but fire destroyed this portion of the company. Before it could function again, their hotel china business had grown to the point that it required their full attention in order to meet market demands. By 1891 they were able to try again. They developed a bone china, as fine and thin as before, which they called Lotus. Henry Schmidt from the Meissen factory in Germany decorated the ware, often with lacy filigree applications or hand-formed leaves and flowers to which he added further decoration with liquid slip applied by means of a squeeze bag. Due to high production costs resulting from so much of the fragile ware being damaged in firing and because of changes in tastes and styles of decoration, the Lotus Ware line was dropped in 1896. Some of the early ware was marked 'KT&K China'; later marks have a star and a crescent with 'Lotus Ware' added. Non-factory decorated pieces are usually lower in value. Our advisor for this category is Mary Frank Gaston.

Bowl, Columbia, lt/dk pk roses on wht, gr ruffled/gold-beaded top, 4"..**175.00**
Bowl, Columbia, mc roses sgn Milford, filigree disks on sides, 4½"....**400.00**
Bowl, Columbia, rtcl raised medallions ea side, HP florals, gilt, 4".....**225.00**
Bowl, Columbia, shaded pk w/filigree medallions, ruffled/angle rim, 5"...**200.00**
Bowl, Columbia, wild rose branches, pk/gr on wht, gilt beading, 4"........**250.00**
Cracker jar, fishnet/pastel floral panels on wht, 6¾"....................**275.00**
Ewer, Etruscan, floral, pk/yel/gr on gr-gray mottle, 10"...............**600.00**
Ewer, Etruscan, gold filigree & mc beading (heavy at base), 10".....**2,600.00**
Ewer, Tiberian, HP roses w/gold, non-factory decor, 7"............**1,200.00**
Jar, Luxor, rtcl raised medallions/tassels & cords, 4 ft, 7", EX **800.00**

Jug, Globe, daisy band on wht to apricot, gilt-trim twig stem, 5", EX ...**300.00**
Jug, Globe, dk gr over custard w/floral in gilt reserve, twig hdl, 4" **400.00**
Jug, Globe, mc roses, gilt twig hdls, 3¾".....................................**200.00**
Jug, Valenciennes, fishnet, wht on wht, 3¾"................................**150.00**
Jug, Valenciennes, fishnet panels, gr on wht, floral panels/gilt, 4" ...**400.00**
Jug, Valenciennes, gold fishnet, floral inside spout, squat, 3¾" **400.00**
Teapot, Valenciennes, fishnet, wht on wht, +sug/cr...................**525.00**
Tray, shell w/ruffled edge & gilt highlights, HP floral, 8½" L **185.00**
Tray, shell w/ruffled edge/3-branch ft, pk wash w/floral sgn DF, 9"......**265.00**
Vase, body formed of 4 curving arms, intricate HP/gilt on rose, 7¾"..**250.00**
Vase, Cremonian, baluster w/fluted neck, scroll hdls, 6".............**200.00**
Vase, Cremonian, wht w/appl flowers on celadon body, 6¼" ..**1,200.00**
Vase, Egyptian, Victorian ladies' portraits w/gold, 15" **3,500.00**
Vase, Etruscan, HP floral w/gold filigree & hdls, 10" **1,800.00**
Vase, Etruscan, wht ware w/appl florals/beadwork, filigree hdls, 10"..**1,500.00**
Vase, Grecian, mc birds & flowers on wht, gold-lined pk floral top, 6"....**600.00**
Vase, Grecian, pk & lav flowers, gr pate-sur-pate work at neck, 6" **800.00**
Vase, Old Man of Mtn, daffodils on lt gr, sgn Mat 1903, hdls, 8"....**600.00**
Vase, Old Man of Mtn, Venetian, purple violets, gilt, w/hdls, 8".....**800.00**
Vase, Parmian, mold-decorated neck w/1 hdl, 2nd on shoulder, wht, 10"......**200.00**
Vase, Parmian, transfer roses on gr w/gold, integral hdls, 10"..**1,100.00**
Vase, Roman, wht ware, appl flowers & leaves, integral hdls, 10" **2,400.00**
Vase, Roman, wht ware, integral hdls, bulbous base, 10".........**1,000.00**
Vase, Savonian, roses & grapes, dk gr hdls, non-factory decor, 15".....**2,800.00**
Vase, styled as lg lily w/appl stems & leaves, wht, 9"...................**400.00**
Vase, Thebian, dk bl neck/shoulders/ornate hdls, HP mums below, 8" **300.00**
Vase, Thebian, HP flowers w/pk & yel, gold scrolls, hdls, 9"..**1,000.00**
Vase, Tuscan, wht ware, ornate filigree designs & appl flowers, 8½".....**1,800.00**
Vase, Umbrian, appl flowers, wht on lt gr, bulbous w/neck hdls, 8", EX ..**650.00**
Vase, Umbrian, gr neck w/gilt hdls, leaves/berries on body, 8" ...**350.00**

Vase, white with applied, raised, and jeweled designs in gold, white, red, and turquoise, 10¼", from $3,000.00 to $3,500.00.

Lu Ray Pastels

Lu Ray Pastels dinnerware was introduced in the early 1940s by Taylor, Smith, and Taylor of East Liverpool, Ohio. It was offered in assorted colors of Persian Cream, Sharon Pink, Surf Green, Windsor Blue, and Chatham Gray in complete place settings as well as many service pieces. It was a successful line in its day and is once again finding favor with collectors of American dinnerware. Our advisor for this category is Shirley Moore; she is listed in the Directory under Oklahoma.

Bowl, '36s oatmeal..**60.00**
Bowl, coupe soup; flat **18.00**

Bowl, cream soup..70.00
Bowl, fruit; Chatham Gray, 5" 16.00
Bowl, fruit; 5" 6.00
Bowl, lug soup; tab hdld..24.00
Bowl, mixing; 5½"..125.00
Bowl, mixing; 7"...125.00
Bowl, mixing; 8¾"..125.00
Bowl, mixing; 10¼" 150.00
Bowl, salad; any color other than yel 65.00
Bowl, salad; yel..55.00
Bowl, vegetable; oval, 9½"...25.00
Butter dish, any color other than Chatham Gray, w/lid.............50.00
Butter dish, Chatham Gray, rare color, w/lid 90.00
Calendar plates, 8", 9" & 10", ea 40.00
Casserole...140.00
Chocolate cup, AD; str sides 80.00
Chocolate pot, AD; str sides...400.00
Coaster/nut dish 65.00
Coffee cup, AD 20.00
Coffeepot, AD...200.00
Creamer 8.00
Creamer, AD, ind..40.00
Creamer, AD, ind, from chocolate set............................92.00
Egg cup, dbl 30.00
Epergne...125.00
Jug, water; ftd...150.00
Muffin cover..140.00
Muffin cover, w/8" underplate 165.00
Nappy, vegetable; rnd, 8½"...25.00
Pitcher, any color other than yel, bulbous w/flat bottom...........125.00
Pitcher, juice...200.00
Pitcher, yel, bulbous w/flat bottom.................................95.00
Plate, cake 70.00
Plate, Chatham Gray, rare color, 7"................................16.00
Plate, chop; 15" 38.00

Plate, grill; three compartments, $35.00. (Photo courtesy Kathy and Bill Meehan)

Plate, 6" 3.00
Plate, 7" 12.00
Plate, 8" 25.00
Plate, 9" 10.00
Plate, 10" 25.00
Platter, oval, 11½"...20.00
Platter, oval, 13" 24.00
Relish dish, 4-part...125.00
Sauce boat 28.00
Sauce boat, any other color than yel, fixed stand..........35.00
Sauce boat, yel, fixed stand...22.50

Saucer, coffee; AD..8.50
Saucer, coffee/chocolate 30.00
Saucer, cream soup...28.00
Saucer, tea...2.00
Shakers, pr 18.00
Sugar bowl, AD; w/lid, from chocolate set.....................92.00
Sugar bowl, AD; w/lid, ind...40.00
Sugar bowl, w/lid 15.00
Teacup...8.00
Teapot, curved spout, w/lid..125.00
Teapot, flat spout, w/lid..160.00
Tray, pickle 28.00
Tumbler, juice...50.00
Tumbler, water..80.00
Vase, bud 400.00

Lunch Boxes

Early twentieth-century tobacco companies such as Union Leader, Tiger, and Dixie sold their products in square, steel containers with flat, metal carrying handles. These were specifically engineered to be used as lunch boxes when they became empty. (See Advertising, specific companies.) By 1930 oval lunch pails with colorful lithographed decorations on tin were being manufactured to appeal directly to children. These were made by Ohio Art, Decoware, and a few other companies. In 1950 Aladdin Industries produced the first 'real' character lunch box — a Hopalong Cassidy decal-decorated steel container now considered the beginning of the kids' lunch box industry. The other big lunch box manufacturer, American Thermos (later King Seely Thermos Company) brought out its 'blockbuster' Roy Rogers box in 1953, the first fully lithographed steel lunch box and matching bottle. Other companies (ADCO Liberty; Landers, Frary & Clark; Ardee Industries; Okay Industries; Universal; Tindco; Cheinco) also produced character pails. Today's collectors often tend to specialize in those boxes dealing with a particular subject. Western, space, TV series, Disney movies, and cartoon characters are the most popular. There are well over five hundred different lunch boxes available to the astute collector. For further information we recommend *Collector's Guide to Lunch Boxes* by Carole Bess White and L.M. White (Collector Books), and *The Illustrated Encyclopedia of Metal Lunch Boxes* by Allen Woodall and Sean Brickell. In the following listings, lunch boxes are metal unless noted vinyl or plastic, and values include thermoses only when they are mentioned within the descriptions.

As indicated in the lines, our values are for examples in exceptional condition; remember to discount sharply for wear and damage beyond the stated conditions.

A-Team, 1983, VG...20.00
Action Jackson, 1973, w/Thermos, EX 175.00
Annie Oakley & Tagg, 1955, EX....................................250.00
Archies, 1970-71, w/Thermos, EX 100.00
Astronauts, 1969, VG+..50.00
Auto Race, 1967, w/Thermos, EX 75.00
Barbie Lunch Kit, 1962, w/Thermos, vinyl, EX...........300.00
Batman, 1995, vinyl, EX..10.00
Batman & Robin, 1966, w/Thermos, NM 200.00
Battlestar Galactica, 1978, w/Thermos, NM...................45.00
Betsy Clark, 1975, beige, w/Thermos, EX.......................25.00
Beverly Hillbillies, 1963, w/Thermos, NM 150.00
Bond XX Secret Agent, 1966, EX 80.00
Bozo the Clown, 1963, dome top, w/Thermos, NM...................250.00
Brave Eagle, 1957, w/Thermos, NM...............................250.00
Buck Rogers, 1979, EX...28.00

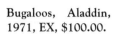

Bugaloos, Aladdin, 1971, EX, $100.00.

Bullwinkle & Rocky, 1962, bl, NM..600.00
Captain Astro, 1966, NM...250.00
Carnival, 1959, EX..350.00
Chavo, 1979, M...100.00
Chuck Wagon, 1958, dome top, w/Thermos, NM....................250.00
Crest Toothpaste, 1980, tubular, w/Thermos, plastic, EX...............50.00
Disney Express, 1979, EX...20.00
Disney School Bus, 1968, dome top, w/Thermos, EX...................85.00
Disney School Bus, 1990, plastic, M (sealed) 35.00
Dr Dolittle, 1967, w/Thermos, EX..95.00
Dudley Do-Right, 1962, bl rim, NM...1,000.00
Dynomutt, 1976, EX...35.00
Fall Guy, 1981, w/Thermos, EX..35.00
Fat Albert, 1973, dome top, plastic, G+...15.00
Flintstones - A Day at the Zoo, Denny's, 1989, plastic, NM.........20.00
Flipper, 1967, EX...100.00
Frontier Days, 1957, VG..100.00
Get Smart, 1966, EX..135.00
Globe-Trotters, 1958, dome top, VG+..175.00
Goofy, 1984, EX+...25.00
Guns of Will Sonnet, 1968, VG...100.00
Hansel & Gretel, 1982, EX..50.00
Hee Haw, 1970, EX..50.00
Huckleberry Hound & Friends, 1961, VG....................................75.00
Incredible Hulk, 1980, dome top, w/Thermos, plastic, EX...........40.00
Indiana Jones & the Temple of Doom, 1984, VG+.......................25.00
Jabberjaw, 1977, plastic, EX...30.00
Johnny Lightning, 1970, VG+...35.00
Jr Deb, 1960, vinyl, EX...100.00
Knight Rider, 1983, EX...20.00
Krofft Supershow, 1976, VG...50.00
Lassie, 1978, VG...35.00
Lawman, 1961, VG..45.00
Lost in Space, reproduction, dome top, M....................................40.00
Lost in Space, 1967, dome top, w/Thermos, EX+.......................385.00
Mardi Gras, 1971, w/Thermos, vinyl, EX...................................100.00
Minnie Mouse, 1988, head form, w/Thermos, plastic, VG+.........25.00
Miss America, 1972, VG+...40.00
Monkees, 1967, vinyl, EX...275.00
Mr Merlin, 1981, VG..25.00
NFL Quarterback, 1964, EX..90.00
Pac Man, 1980, vinyl, EX..30.00
Pathfinder, 1959, VG+...200.00
Pete's Dragon, 1978, EX...35.00
Pit Stop, 1968, EX+...175.00
Popeye, 1979, dome top, plastic, EX...30.00
Robin Hood, 1965, w/Thermos, EX..150.00
Ronald McDonald, 1982, w/bottle, M...55.00

Roy Rogers & Dale Evans, 1957, w/Thermos, EX.......................200.00
Secret Agent T, 1968, VG...50.00
Soupy Sales, 1966, vinyl, NM...300.00
Star Trek: The Motion Picture, 1979, EX+...................................60.00
Star Wars, 1977, characters on band, G...20.00
Superman, 1967, EX...150.00
SWAT, 1975, dome top, w/Thermos, plastic, EX..........................30.00
The Sophisticate, 1970, brunch bag, w/Thermos, vinyl, EX.........50.00
Tic-Tac-Toe, 1970s, vinyl, EX..50.00
Treasure Chest, 1960, dome top, VG+..325.00
Underdog, 1974, NM...1,500.00
Wagon Train, 1964, VG..88.00
Winnie the Pooh, 1990s, w/Thermos, plastic, M...........................25.00
Wonder Woman, 1977, w/Thermos, vinyl, EX............................100.00
Yankee Doodle, 1975, w/Thermos, EX...25.00
Ziggy, 1979, vinyl, EX..50.00

Maddux of California

One of the California-made ceramics now so popular with collectors, Maddux was founded in the late 1930s and during the years that followed produced novelty items, TV lamps, figurines, planters, and tableware accessories.

Ashtray, elephant bust w/tuxedo & top hat, 3-ftd, 1½x7¾x6¼"..25.00
Ashtray, gunmetal gray, triangular, #731, 10½".............................20.00
Bowl, vegetable; wht w/turq lid, swirl decor, #3066B, 4½x7¾"...25.00
Bowl/server, salad; cabbage, 4x12½" dia.......................................20.00
Candy dish, gr, #3211, metal center hdl, 6-part, 2¼x12⅞" dia.....25.00
Chip & dip set, cabbage leaf, 5-part, 14" dia.................................25.00
Figurine, cockatoo on branch, 11"..70.00
Figurine, roadrunner, orange, #9018, 7x16"..................................30.00
Flower frog, turq, #90006, 1966, 1½x6" dia..................................35.00
Planter, blk swan, #150, 11"..35.00
Planter, bluebird, #531, 10½"...22.00
Planter, dbl flamingo, mk Maddux of Calif, 5x6½".......................35.00
Planter, taupe w/emb swans, dtd 1959, 4x9½x3¾".........................35.00
Planter, yel bird w/blk wing-highlights, oval, 9⅛x3".....................20.00
TV lamp, ship, #847, 11x10"...20.00
TV lamp, Siamese cat, sitting on hind paws, 12½", from $125 to......135.00
TV lamp/planter, gr half-moon shape, #3005, w/metal holder, 6x10x8"...15.00
TV lamp/planter, wht swan, #828, 12½", from $25 to..................45.00
Vase, flamingo on ea side, 5", from $50 to.....................................60.00

Magazines

Magazines are collected for their cover prints and for the information pertaining to defunct companies and their products that can be gleaned from the old advertisements. In the listings that follow, items are assumed to be in very good condition unless noted otherwise. For more information, see *Old Magazines* by Richard E. Clear. See also Movie Memorabilia; Parrish, Maxfield.

Key:
M — mint condition, in original wrapper
EX — excellent condition, spine intact, edges of pages clean and straight
VG — very good condition, the average as-found condition

American Heritage, 1970, December, Parrish cover art, NM........40.00
American Magazine, 1909, August, Jack London story, VG+.......40.00
Atlantic Monthly, 1933, November, Wyeth poster, EX................20.00

Avante Garde, 1969, #8, VG 35.00
Baseball Digest, 1951, April, DiMaggio, VG 25.00
Boy's Life, 1969, June, Mickey Mantle, NM 25.00
Collier's, 1912, May 4, Titanic article, VG 35.00
Collier's, 1914, September 12, Leyendecker cover, G 10.00
Collier's, 1945, June, Truman, VG 6.00
Cosmopolitan, 1886, June, Buffalo Bill, EX 25.00
Cosmopolitan, 1955, October, Audrey Hepburn, VG 10.00
Country Gentleman, 1925, September, NC Wyeth cover art, NM 35.00
Ebony, 1967, January, Star Trek cover, NM 5.00
Esquire, 1939, December, Petty art/folder, NM 50.00
Esquire, 1960, November, Lenny Bruce article, EX 6.00
Family Circle, 1939, June 30, Scarlett O'Hara cover, NM 75.00
Family Circle, 1945, January 19, Shirley Temple article, VG+ 16.00
Fortune, 1932, Grand Woods illus, NM 12.00
Good Housekeeping, 1914, August, M 25.00
Ice Capades, 1945, Petty cover art, EX 35.00
Inside Sports, 1980, April, Nolan Ryan, NM 28.00
Ladies' Home Journal, 1927, April, Rose O'Neill Kewpies, NM ..18.00
Life, 1936, December 14, Archbishop Canterbury, EX 42.00
Life, 1936, December 28, Margaret Mitchell article, NM 40.00
Life, 1938, July 11, Rudolph Valentino, EX 40.00
Life, 1938, October 10, Carole Lombard, VG 20.00
Life, 1942, Lana Turner & Clark Gable, EX 35.00
Life, 1942, March 30, Shirley Temple, EX 18.00
Life, 1944, January 10, Bob Hope, EX 20.00
Life, 1944, June 26, Statue of Liberty cover, G 8.00
Life, 1947, November 17, Howard Hughes, EX 15.00
Life, 1949, August 1, Joe DiMaggio, EX 65.00
Life, 1952, April 7, Marilyn Monroe, EX 40.00
Life, 1953, June 8, Roy Campanella, EX 25.00
Life, 1958, December 1, Ricky Nelson, EX 15.00
Life, 1964, August 28, Beatles, EX 40.00
Life, 1964, March 6, Cassius Clay, NM 35.00
Life, 1965, May 7, John Wayne, EX 30.00
Life, 1970, October 23, Muhammad Ali, EX 25.00
Life, 1972, February 25, Liz Taylor at 40, EX 25.00
Life, 1972, June 16, '50s revival news, EX 10.00
Life, 1988, Fall, 150 Years of Photography, NM 6.50
Life, 1991, Fall, Pearl Harbor December 7 1941-1991, NM 6.00
Look, 1939, December 19, 2-pg article & illus of Gone w/the Wind, M ..40.00
Look, 1946, October 15, Ted Williams, NM 75.00
Look, 1963, December 3, JFK & his son, EX 10.00
Look, 1972, May, Vol 1 #5, Jean Harlow article, EX 40.00
Man About Town, 1939, May, EX 28.00
McCall's, 1931, July, NC Wyeth illus, NM 25.00
McCall's, 1951, August, VG 12.00
Modern Photography, 1956, September, Glamour Issue, NM ..12.00
National Geographic, 1915-16, ea 15.00
National Geographic, 1917-24, ea 9.00
National Geographic, 1925-29, ea 8.00
National Geographic, 1930-45, ea 7.00
National Geographic, 1946-55, ea 6.00
National Geographic, 1956-57, ea 5.50
National Geographic, 1968-69, ea 4.50
National Geographic, 1990-present, ea 2.00
Navy Magazine, 1907, November, fleet & maps, NM 18.00
Newsweek, 1953, January 19, Lucille Ball, EX+ 25.00
Newsweek, 1969, September 15, Joe Namath/Jets cover, EX ..55.00
Peek, 1940, July, Betty Grable, NM 15.00
Playboy, 1960, Linda Gamble, NM 25.00
Playboy, 1965, Marylin Monroe tribute, EX 50.00
Popular Magazine, 1909, March, Leyendecker cover art, NM ..70.00
Redbook, 1935, February, William Saroyan story, EX 25.00

Redbook, 1936, June, Tunney & Lewis, NM 10.00
Rolling Stone, 1967, #1, John Lennon, VG 60.00
Rolling Stone, 1971, August 5, Jim Morrison memorial, EX ..62.50
Saturday Evening Post, 1910, October, R Robinson cover art, VG+ 20.00
Saturday Evening Post, 1942, March 14, How To Blockade Japan, EX ..4.00
Saturday Evening Post, 1952, February 16, Rockwell cover art, EX ..30.00
Saturday Evening Post, 1966, July 30, Bob Dylan, EX 12.00
Saturday Evening Post, 1969, January 25, A Miller article, EX 6.00
Sport, 1946, September, Joe DiMaggio, NM 100.00
Sporting News, 1970, March 28, Kareem Jabbar/Bucks, EX ..35.00
Sports Illustrated, 1956, April 23, Billy Martin, NM 28.00
Sports Illustrated, 1962, June 4, Willie Mays/Giants, EX ..60.00
Sports Illustrated, 1979, May 28, Pete Rose, VG 8.00
Sports Illustrated, 1990, 35 Years of Covers, EX 25.00
Time, 1955, Oppenheimer, EX 10.00
Time, 1978, March 6, Cheryl Tiegs cover, EX 7.50
Town & Country, 1948, July, Salvadore Dali, VG 30.00
True Story, 1935, April, Zoe Mozart art cover, EX 30.00
True Story, 1939, December, Bund Love Camp, EX 7.50
TV Guide, 1954, August 21-27, Steve Allen & Jayne Meadows, NM ..63.00
TV Guide, 1957, January 5-11, Arthur Godfrey, NM 32.00
TV Guide, 1959, December 26 - January 1, Loretta Young, NM ..30.00
TV Guide, 1967, November 11-17, Yvette Mimeux, NM ..11.00
TV Guide, 1971, July 3-9, cast of Mod Squad 29.00

TV Guide, 1978, October 28, Mork and Mindy (Pam Dauber and Robin Williams) cover, $9.00.

TV Guide, 1981, August 1-7, Miss Piggy, NM 20.00
Vanity Fair, 1913, September, Babe Ruth, NM+ 80.00
Vogue, 1924, Brissaud cover art, EX 55.00
Woman's Home Companion, 1933, September, Charlie Chaplin, NM ..10.00
Yachtman's Magazine, 1942, May, EX 20.00
Youth's Companion, 1895, October 3, Mark Twain article, EX 40.00

Majolica

Majolica is a type of heavy earthenware, design-molded and decorated in vivid colors with either a lead or tin type of glaze. It reached its height of popularity in the Victorian era; examples from this period are found in only the lead glazes. Nearly every potter of note, both here and abroad, produced large majolica jardinieres, umbrella stands, pitchers with animal themes, leaf shapes, vegetable forms, and nearly any other design from nature that came to mind. Not all, however, marked their ware. Among those who sometimes did were Minton, Wedgwood, Holdcroft, and George Jones in England; Griffin, Smith, and Hill (Etruscan) in Phoenixville, Pennsylvania; and Chesapeake Pottery (Avalon and Clifton) in Baltimore.

Color and condition are both very important worth-assessing factors. Pieces with cobalt, lavender, and turquoise glazes command the highest prices. For further information we recommend *The Collector's Encyclopedia of Majolica* by Mariann Katz-Marks (see Directory, Pennsylvania). Unless another condition is given, the values that follow are for pieces in mint condition. Our advisor for this category is Hardy Hudson; he is listed in the Directory under Florida.

Bank, Indian figural, Continental, 3¾" 200.00
Bank, man w/hat & cigar, 3½" 160.00
Basket, egg; Blackberry, Floral & Leaf, cobalt, bamboo hdl, 11½" L...900.00
Basket, Shell & Seaweed, rope hdl, 8¾" 750.00
Bottle, hobo figural, EX details, 13" 350.00
Bottle, hunting dog figural, Continental, 12½" 1,000.00
Bowl, Basketweave, twig ft, Holdcroft, 9" 250.00
Bowl, centerpc; mermaid hdls, leaf border, Fr, 16x21" 500.00
Bowl, centerpc; mermaids (2) support shell, Minton, 24x40" 15,000.00
Bowl, shell w/dolphin ft, turq, Royal Worcester, 5x5" 800.00
Butter dish, Wheat, cow finial, turq, Geo Jones, 4x7½" 2,300.00
Butter pat, Chrysanthemum, cobalt, Wedgwood 275.00
Butter pat, Geranium, Etruscan 125.00
Butter pat, Pansy, mc, Etruscan...165.00
Butter pat, Pansy, Tenuous, rare 200.00
Butter pat, Pond Lily, gr, Etruscan, NM 125.00
Butter pat, Shell & Seaweed, Etruscan.......................................200.00
Cake stand, Maple Leaves on pk, Etruscan 350.00
Candlestick, elephant w/top hat figural, Continental, 8" 225.00
Cheese keeper, Bird on Branch, cobalt, 9½" 1,000.00
Cheese keeper, Bird on Branch, yel, water lily finial, 7", EX.......600.00

Cheese keeper, Daisy and Fence, cobalt, George Jones, 11", $5,000.00.

(Photo courtesy Mariann Katz-Marks)

Cheese keeper, Primrose, Argenta, Wedgwood, 9½" 550.00
Coffeepot, Shell & Seaweed, crooked spout, Etruscan, 6" 700.00
Compote, Chestnut Leaf, Geo Jones, 5x9¼" 450.00
Compote, mottled shell, 3 dolphin ft, Wedgwood, 9½" 300.00
Creamer, Bird & Iris, cobalt, Etruscan, 3¾" 150.00
Creamer, floral on cobalt, snail hdl & ft, Minton, 5" 2,500.00
Creamer, Leaf & Fern..110.00
Creamer, overlapping shells, EX color, 4½" 200.00
Creamer, Pineapple, 2¾" 175.00
Creamer, Punch & Judy, cobalt accent, Wedgwood....................900.00
Cup & saucer, Bird & Fan, Shorter & Bolton.............................200.00
Cup & saucer, Shell & Swaweed, Etruscan 275.00
Dough box/floor jardiniere, Oak Leaf & Acorn, 13x14½x10", NM ...400.00
Ewer, putti/leaves/flowers in relief, putto hdl, Brownfield, 16½".450.00
Ewer, satyr on cobalt, Minton shape #843, ca 1872, 18" 1,800.00
Figure, Sloth & Mischief, monkey/turtle, turq/cobalt, Copeland, 17" 11,500.00
Fork & spoon, salad; Ocean, Wedgwood Argenta, 11"................250.00
Garden seat, Blackamoor among cattails, Holdcroft, 18" 9,000.00
Garden seat, Corn & wht w/lav ribbons & bow, J Adams, 19" 5,000.00

Garden seat, Nouveau floral, cobalt, 3 flower hdls, G Jones, 19"..5,000.00
Humidor, bear in bl smoking jacket figual, 6¼" 350.00
Humidor, Blackamoor, Old Friends, figure seated on pillow, 7½" 275.00
Humidor, dog w/pipe & red smoking jacket figural, Continental, 6¼".....450.00
Humidor, fox in clown suit figural, 5" 325.00
Humidor, frog on melon figural, 6" 300.00
Humidor, frog playing violin figural, 7" 400.00
Inkwell, frog figural, pond lily top, mc, 3" 550.00
Jardiniere, passion flower, cobalt, lion-head hdls, Minton, 14x18" ..3,000.00
Jardiniere & undertray, Water Lily, gr, Minton, 11½", 19½" ...2,200.00
Jardiniere stand, stork w/fish & cattails, Hugo Lonitz, 35".......8,000.00
Jug, tower w/medieval figures relief, jester finial, Minton 1,200.00
Knife rest, pickle form, Continental, 4½" 100.00
Match holder, basket & oak leaf, wall hanging, Holdcroft, 4½"....300.00
Match striker, Blackamoor lady w/baskets on bridge, 7".............175.00
Match striker, man beside bicycle w/baskets figural, 9" 225.00
Match striker, pug dog w/lg pipe figural, 7"................................350.00
Mug, Blackberry, Clifton, 3½" 80.00
Mug, Nouveau lady & floral, EX color, 3½" 80.00
Oyster plate, Basketweave, 4 turq shells, Minton, rare, 9x7½" ...3,800.00
Oyster plate, cobalt/mottled wells, cracker well, Minton, 1881, 9¾"...1,750.00
Oyster plate, crescent shape w/Oriental decor, 5 wells, 8½" 300.00
Oyster plate, Fan & Insect, 6 wells, Fielding, 9¼" 2,300.00
Oyster plate, fish, 5 cobalt wells, turq center, Minton, rare, 10½"...5,500.00
Oyster plate, fish & seaweed w/gold, Geo Jones, 9" 275.00
Oyster plate, sea life in 5 wells, cobalt, Wedgwood, rare, 9¼"....4,250.00
Oyster plate, 5 fish wells w/turq center, brn seaweed, Minton, 11"..3,000.00
Ped, turq w/Oriental decor open-cut sides, Minton, 31x14½", EX.....3,500.00
Pitcher, Acorn & Leaf, 6¾" 200.00
Pitcher, Asparagus, Fr, 8" 375.00
Pitcher, Bamboo, Banks & Thorley, 7"...180.00
Pitcher, Blackberry, cobalt, 7½"...275.00
Pitcher, dead game, cobalt, Holdcroft, 8¾"................................700.00
Pitcher, Egyptian Lotus, Copeland, 8½" 3,000.00
Pitcher, fish figural, Mafra Caldes Portugal, 10½" 125.00
Pitcher, fish on waves, cobalt, 8¼", EX......................................475.00
Pitcher, Grape & Leaf, Wedgwood, 9"..300.00
Pitcher, Hawthorne, Etruscan, 8"...200.00
Pitcher, Pineapple, 5"...160.00
Pitcher, Pineapple, 8"...250.00
Pitcher, Ram's Head, lav top, 8" 225.00
Pitcher, Stork in Marsh, cobalt, Geo Jones, 6¾" 3,000.00
Pitcher, syrup; Coral & Seaweed, pewter top, Etruscan.............375.00
Pitcher, Water Lily, lav top & hdl, Samuel Lear, 8", EX.............425.00
Pitcher, Water Lily & Iris, Geo Jones, 6" 2,500.00
Pitcher, Wild Rose, butterfly spout, cobalt rim, 7½" 325.00
Pitcher, Wild Rose, Geo Jones, 8¼"...900.00
Plaque, lizard & snake in grass in relief, Portugal Palissy, 6½" 450.00
Plaque, Stork in Rushes, cobalt, cattail hdls, Fr, 13½"................350.00
Plate, Bamboo, Etruscan, 8"...125.00
Plate, Cauliflower, Etruscan, 9"..275.00
Plate, Fish & Cattail on yel, Holdcroft, 8¾"................................300.00
Plate, Fish & Daisy, cobalt, Holdcroft, 8½".................................275.00
Plate, Maple Leaf on Basket, Etruscan, 9" 200.00
Plate, overlapping leaves, dk gr, 8¾"..110.00
Plate, Pineapple, Geo Jones, 8¾"...450.00
Plate, Shell & Seaweed, Etruscan, 8" 250.00
Plate, Strawberry, cobalt, Brownfield, 8¾".................................500.00
Plate, Strawberry & Apple on wht, Etruscan, 9".........................250.00
Plate, Strawberry & Leaf on yel, Wedgwood, 9" 400.00
Platter, Bamboo & Fern, cobalt center, 13½" 300.00
Platter, Corn & Poppy on Basket, Wedgwood, 12¾" 550.00
Platter, Fish & Cattail on turq, 4 cattail ft, Holdcroft, 26" 3,200.00
Platter, fish atop ferns on turq, Wedgwood, 25½" 3,200.00

Salt cellar, conch shell on coral form, Wedgwood, 3¼" **350.00**
Salt cellar, dolphin & shell figural, EX color, 4" **275.00**
Sardine box, fish on lily pads, Victory Pottery.........................**1,500.00**
Sardine box, Pineapple...**450.00**
Sardine box, sardines on cobalt, Minton, 1884 ....**2,100.00**
Sardine box, Scroll & Floral, yel **400.00**
Sauce dish, Butterfly & Floral, 5¾" **140.00**
Saucer, Cauliflower, Etruscan **150.00**
Server, dbl shell w/intertwined dolphin hdl, Geo Jones, 9¾"......**600.00**
Spooner, Dogwood, Holdcroft, 4¾" **200.00**
Teapot, Apple Blossom on turq, Geo Jones **1,000.00**
Teapot, Chinaman figural, cobalt coat, Holdcroft, 7x9½" **4,000.00**
Teapot, lemon form w/mushroom lid, emb leaves, Minton, 4½x7" **8,000.00**
Teapot, rooster figural, mc, Geo Jones, 11" L...........................**8,500.00**
Tile, bird on branch w/cherries, Minton, 8", NM **200.00**
Toothpick holder, Bird & Fan, Argenta, Wedgwood, 1¾" **175.00**
Toothpick holder, eagle figural, 3½" **200.00**
Toothpick holder, rooster w/basket figural, 4¾" **250.00**
Tray, Begonia Leaf, twig hdls, 10½" **200.00**
Tray, Begonia Leaf, 9¼" **160.00**
Tray, dresser; Butterfly & Iris, oval, Geo Jones, 11" **3,000.00**
Tray, fish on leaves in relief on cobalt, Palissy Ware, 13¾" **2,750.00**
Tray, frog on lily pads figural, Continental **150.00**
Tray, Shell & Seaweed, Etruscan **950.00**
Tray, squirrel at side, chestnut leaves on cobalt, 9½"................**400.00**
Tureen, mussel shell form, Minton, 8½" L **900.00**
Vase, golfer figural, Continental, 6"...**100.00**
Vase, Oriental crane & fan, flat sides, 6"...................................**250.00**
Vase, peacock figural, EX detail, Continental, 13" **800.00**
Vase, turq w/snake hdls, lav int, Minton, 23" **2,000.00**

Malachite Glass

Malachite is a type of art glass that exhibits strata-like layerings in shades of green, similar to the mineral in its natural form. Some examples have an acid-etched mark of Moser/Carlsbad, usually on the base. However, it should be noted that in the past thirty years there have been reproductions from Czechoslovakia with a paper label. These are most often encountered.

Bottle, scent; lg Deco nude stopper, flattened hexagon body, Czech, 8"...**150.00**
Bottle, scent; Peacock, clear/frosted floral stopper, Czech, 7½" ..**215.00**
Bottle, scent; woman emerging from flower stopper, Czech, 1930s, 8" ..**100.00**
Box, emb nude, Czech, 1930s, 2¼x3¾" dia **50.00**

Maps and Atlases

Maps are highly collectible, not only for historical value but also for their sometimes elaborate artwork, legendary information, or data that since they were printed has been proven erroneous. There are many types of maps including geographical, military, celestial, road, and railroad. Nineteenth-century maps, particularly of U.S. areas, are increasing in popularity and price. Rarity, area depicted (i.e. Texas is more sought after than North Dakota), and condition are major price factors. World globes as a form of round maps are increasingly sought after. Our advisor for this category is Murray Hudson; he is listed in the Directory under Tennessee.

Key: hc — hand colored

Atlases

Cram's Family World, colored, 1899, 11¾x14¾" book **120.00**
Mitchell's, pre-Civil War (no W VA), missing title pg, ca 1839 ...**150.00**
Rand McNally Commercial...& Marketing Guide, 1953, EX......**100.00**

Maps

Africa, slave coast noted, Colton, NY, 1860, 11½x13½" **75.00**
Am Septentrionalis, hc, D'Anville, 1753, 18½x20½"................**575.00**
Americae Description Nova Impensisn, Seile, London, 1652, 13x16" ..**375.00**
Amerique Septentrionale, Anonymous, Paris, after 1784, 18x23"...**1,250.00**
Canada, Feulle, Paris, 1765, from unidentified atlas, 12x17" **450.00**
Canada & Greenland, hc, Antonio Zatta, 1778, 14½x19½" **50.00**
Canada/West US/Mexico/NE tip of Russia, hc, A Zatta, 1776, 15x20" ..**345.00**
Carte de LA & FL, hc, Rigobert Bonne, Paris, 1770, 15¼x9½"..**1,600.00**
Carte de Louisiane, JB Bourguignon D'Anville, hc, 1752, sight: 21x38"...**1,850.00**
Carte Geographique...de L'Indiana, hc, Fr text, early, 25x32", EX **275.00**
Carte Reduit....Australes, Bellin, Didot, Paris, 1753, 8x11" **1,100.00**
Charte von Nord Am, Gussefeld, Nuremberg, 1787, 19¼x23¼" ..**800.00**
Course of MS River...to Fort Chartres, hc, Sayer, 1775, 46x18"....**2,000.00**
L'Asie (Asia), Desbruslins, Paris, 1744, 5½x7" **125.00**
La Terre Connue...Fut Publie, Paris, ca 19740, 15½x17¼" **450.00**
N America, Geo Grierson, hc w/insets, 18th C, 22½x37¼" ...**4,885.00**
N America, Jefferys, Ballard, London, 1758, rprs, 7¼x9"............**200.00**
Nature of Africa, from atlas, Colton, NY, 1860, 12x10¼" **75.00**
New & Exact...Asia..., T Woodward & A Ward, London, 1744, 14x18"...**450.00**
New Map of N Am, dedicated to Duke of Gloucester, hc, 18th C, 15x20"...**925.00**
Orbis Veteribus Notus, D'Anille, Paris, 1763, 21x30" **500.00**
Reference...LA from Surveys of US, La Tourette, hc, 1847, 55x59"...**3,750.00**
Reise Der Kinder Von Israel...Egypten, Bunging, Hannover, 1581, 10x14"....**1,000.00**

Typus Orbis Terrarum, by Ortelius, colored, minor repairs, 13x19", VG, $10,000.00.

World as Known to Ancients, Seale, ca 1750, 9¾x11¾"............**225.00**
World From Best Authorities, Doolittle, Boston, 1793, 14½" W ..**250.00**

Marblehead

What began as therapy for patients in a sanitarium in Marblehead, Massachusetts, has become recognized as an important part of the Arts and Crafts movement in America. Results of the early experiments under the guidance of Arthur E. Baggs in 1904 met with such success that by 1908 the pottery had been converted to a solely commercial venture. Simple vase shapes were sometimes incised with stylized animal and floral motifs or sailing ships. Some were decorated in low relief; many were plain. Matt glazes in soft yellow, gray, wisteria, rose, tobacco brown, and their most popular, Marblehead blue, were used alone or in combination. They also produced fine tiles decorated with ships, stylized floral or tree motifs, and landscapes. Early examples were lightly incised and matt-painted (these are the most valuable) on 1"-thick bodies. Others, 4" square and thinner, were matt painted with landscapes in indigoes, in the style of Arthur Wesley Dow.

The Marblehead logo is distinctive — a ship with full sail and the letters 'M' and 'P.' The pottery closed in 1936.

Our advisors for this category are Suzanne Perrault and David Rago; they are listed in the Directory under New Jersey. Unless noted otherwise, all items listed below are marked and in the matt glaze.

Bowl, aqua bl drip w/blk spatters on hunter gr, 1½x6" 330.00
Bowl, bl, rnd shoulders, MP cipher, 4¼" 265.00
Bowl, bl mottle, chicory bl int, closed mouth, 3⅛x5½" 330.00
Bowl, caramel w/dk speckles, oatmeal int, sm mouth, 3x5¼" 385.00
Bowl, fruit band, gr/russet on brn/mustard, A Baggs, 1½x4½" ...3,500.00
Mug, stripe, blk on speckled gr, 3½x4"..850.00
Planter, bl, conical w/3 loop hdls, 3¾"...200.00
Tile, basket of flowers, pk/orange/bl on dk brn, 2 glaze chips, 6¼" ...300.00
Tile, basket of fruit/flowers, bright mc on pk, lt abrasion, 4½"...350.00
Tile, tall ship on waves, wht crackle on bl sky, pitting/sm chip, 5" 400.00
Vase, bl, cylinder w/flared base, MP cipher, 12" 700.00
Vase, bl, shouldered, paper label, 9" 900.00
Vase, bl, swollen cylinder, 7½", EX 300.00
Vase, bl & gray w/speckles, floral & berries, Baggs, 8¾x4" ...6,000.00
Vase, bl w/speckles, brn int, baluster w/flared mouth, 6x5½"......600.00
Vase, brn textured, broad shoulders, 4"...400.00
Vase, bud; brn speckled, corseted, 4½x2"......................................425.00
Vase, bud; gray, flaring, rstr rim chip, 4¼x3¼" 115.00
Vase, burgundy/gr/bl, flowers & berries, closed mouth, 3x5¼" ...1,875.00
Vase, caramel w/brn speckles, spherical upper body, 4x5¼" 525.00
Vase, cobalt, baluster, 9x7½"...850.00
Vase, curlicues, gr & blk on indigo, squat, 3½", NM...................850.00
Vase, deep bl, waisted cylinder, 8½" 650.00
Vase, dk olive arches over lt mottled olive, cylindrical, 11¾" 7,000.00
Vase, dragonflies (4), mc on gr speckled, H Tutt, cylindrical, 6", NM.2,500.00
Vase, fan; Persian Blue crackle, 6" 200.00
Vase, floral, bl & gr on pk, sm rim, 6½"..7,000.00
Vase, floral, brn on mottled gr, shouldered tapered cylinder, 8½" 4,500.00
Vase, floral branches, yel/gr on mustard, H Tutt, paper label, 3½" ..3,400.00
Vase, geometric floral band, mc on mottled gray, AE Baggs, 9½"..26,000.00
Vase, geometric top band, gray on speckled lt gray, AE Baggs, rstr, 6"...1,800.00
Vase, golden yel, flared rim, tapered form, 6½" 1,000.00
Vase, gr, rounded sides widen toward bottom, everted rim, 3½"....500.00
Vase, gr, tapered sides, flared rim, 3½" 500.00
Vase, gr, widens at base, 3½" 375.00
Vase, gr/tobacco/teal textured, low, broad, 5"...............................550.00
Vase, grapevine wreath, gr/bl on speckled mustard, HT, rstr, 5x3½" ..1,600.00
Vase, gray w/chickory bl int, spherical upper body, 3¼x4¼".......330.00
Vase, incised leaves, brn on sienna speckled, tear shape, 6½" 6,000.00
Vase, indigo speckled, closed-in rim, burst bubble/bruise, 11½x7" ...800.00
Vase, indigo speckled, paper label, 5¼x5"....................................475.00
Vase, lav, incurvate rim on cylindrical form, 4" 400.00
Vase, lav, ovoid, 5¼", NM 450.00
Vase, lav, waisted cylinder, paper label, 6"...................................550.00
Vase, lav-gray, purple int, short lip, 8½x4¾" 715.00
Vase, lemon trees, yel/gr/brn on mottled gr, 4½" 4,250.00
Vase, organic-design band, gr on yel-gr, cylindrical, 6" 3,250.00
Vase, pk, waisted cylinder, 9" 950.00
Vase, pk speckled, tapered, 6¼"..550.00
Vase, pods on stems repeat at top, cvd/3-color, AE Baggs, 3½x5" ...2,500.00
Vase, sage gr/bl, ovals, 4¾x3½", NM 550.00
Vase, stylized motif, dk gr on speckled indigo, global, 3½x4¾" 2,200.00
Vase, stylized trees, bl on lt bl, H Tutt, slight shoulders, 5½" ..2,900.00

Vase, stylized trees, gr on indigo speckled, cylindrical, 8¼", NM..1,900.00
Vase, stylized trees, mc on mustard, tapered, partial label, 5"...3,250.00
Vase, stylized trees olive gr speckled, H Tutt, tear shape, 6x5" ..2,800.00
Vase, stylized trees/flowers on indigo speckled, H Tutt, 5¼" 2,100.00
Vessel, gray, cylindrical, flared rim, hdl, 8½" 750.00

Vase, stylized floral and geometric decoration in dark olive green on lighter green ground, marked with an impressed MP ship cipher, Hannah Tutt, 8", from $15,000.00 to $20,000.00.

(Photo courtesy David Rago Auctions)

Marbles

Marbles have been popular with children since the mid-1800s. They've been made in many types from a variety of materials. Among some of the first glass items to be produced, the earliest marbles were made from a solid glass rod broken into sections of the proper length which were placed in a tray of sand and charcoal and returned to the fire. As they were reheated, the trays were constantly agitated until the marbles were completely round. Other marbles were made of china, pottery, steel, and natural stones. Below is a listing of the various types, along with a brief description of each.

Agates: stone marbles of many different colors — bands of color alternating with white usually encircle the marble; most are translucent.

Ballot Box: handmade (with pontils), opaque white or black, used in lodge elections.

Bloodstone: green chalcedony with red spots, a type of quartz.

China: with or without glaze, in a variety of hand-painted designs — parallel bands or bull's-eye designs most common.

Clambroth: opaque glass with outer evenly spaced swirls of one or alternating colors.

Clay: one of the most common older types; some are painted while others are not.

Comic Strip: a series of twelve machine-made marbles with faces of comic strip characters, Peltier Glass Factory, Illinois.

Crockery: sometimes referred to as Benningtons; most are either blue or brown, although some are speckled. The clay is shaped into a sphere, then coated with glaze and fired.

End of the Day: single-pontil glass marbles — the colored part often appears as a multicolored blob or mushroom cloud.

Goldstone: clear glass completely filled with copper flakes that have turned gold-colored from the heat of the manufacturing process.

Indian Swirls: usually black glass with a colored swirl appearing on the outside next to the surface, often irregular.

Latticinio Core Swirls: double-pontil marble with an inner area with net-like effects of swirls coming up around the center.

Lutz Type: glass with colored or clear bands alternating with bands which contain copper flecks.

Micas: clear or colored glass with mica flecks which reflect as silver dots when marble is turned. Red is rare.

Onionskin: spiral type which are solidly colored instead of having individual ribbons or threads, multicolored.

Peppermint Swirls: made of white opaque glass with alternating blue and red outer swirls.

Ribbon Core Swirls: double-pontil marble — center shaped like a ribbon with swirls that come up around the middle.

Rose Quartz: stone marble, usually pink in color, often with fractures inside and on outer surface.

Solid Core Swirls: double-pontil marble — middle is solid with swirls coming up around the core.

Steelies: hollow steel spheres marked with a cross where the steel was bent together to form the ball.

Sulfides: generally made of clear glass with figures inside. Rarer types have colored figures or colored glass.

Tiger Eye: stone marble of golden quartz with inclusions of asbestos, dark brown with gold highlights.

Vaseline: machine-made of yellowish-green glass with small bubbles.

Prices listed below are for marbles in near-mint condition unless noted otherwise. When size is not indicated, assume them to be of average size, ½" to 1". Polished marbles have greatly reduced values. (We do not list tinted marbles because there is no way of knowing how much color the tinting has, and intensity of color is an important worth-assessing factor.)

For a more thorough study of the subject, we recommend *Antique and Collectible Marbles, 3rd Edition*; *Machine-Made and Contemporary Marbles, 2nd Edition*; and *Big Book of Marbles, Second Edition*, all by Everett Grist (published by Collector Books); you will find his address in the Directory under Tennessee. Our advisors for this category are Robert and Stan Block; they are listed in the Directory under Connecticut.

Agate, contemporary, carnelian, 1¾" 20.00
Akro Agate, bl slag 1.00
Akro Agate, brick (oxblood swirled w/blk or wht, ⅝-1", from $40 to ...150.00
Akro Agate, corkscrew 2.00
Akro Agate, Cornelian, (orange/wht/oxblood), ⅝-¾", from $15 to 75.00
Akro Agate, egg yoke/oxblood swirls on custard, ⅝"+, NM........150.00
Akro Agate, Popeye corkscrew 25.00
Akro Agate, Popeye corkscrew, red/wht/bl (rare),⅝"..................125.00
Akro Agate, Royal (patched opaque on colored base), ⅝-1", from $2 to ...10.00
Akro Agate, sparkler 45.00
Akro Agate, translucent oxblood swirl, ⅝-¾", from $75 to 250.00
Banded Opaque, gr & wht, 2" 1,200.00
Banded Opaque, gr w/red bands, wht & bl streaks, 1¾", EX.......160.00
Banded Opaque, red & wht, 1¾" 1,200.00
Banded Opaque, red & wht, ¾" 125.00
Banded Transparent Swirl, bl, ¾" 45.00
Banded Transparent Swirl, lt gr, 1¾" 300.00
Bennington, bl, 1¾" 15.00
Bennington, bl, ¾" 1.00
Bennington, brn, 1¾" 15.00
Bennington, fancy, 1¾" 40.00
Bennington, fancy, ¾" 2.00
China, decorated, glazed, apple, 1¾" 750.00
China, decorated, glazed, rose, 1¾" 750.00
China, decorated, glazed, wht w/geometrics, 1¾" 75.00
China, decorated, unglazed, geometrics & flowers, ¾" 125.00
Christensen Agate, Bloodie..80.00
Christensen Agate, clear Cobra, ⅝", NM+ 145.00
Christensen Agate, flame...400.00
Christensen Agate, Guinea...500.00
Christensen Agate, slag...25.00
Christensen Agate, swirl 25.00
Clambroth, opaque, bl & wht, 1¾"..1,500.00
Clambroth, opaque, bl & wht, ¾"..200.00

Clambroth, pk (red)/bl/gr swirls, ⅝", EX.................................130.00
Comic, Andy Gump, M 125.00
Comic, Betty Boop, M 200.00
Comic, Cotes Bakery, advertising 900.00
Comic, Herbie, M...150.00
Comic, Kayo, rare 450.00
Comic, Little Orphan Annie, M 150.00
Comic, Moon Mullins, M 300.00
Comic, set of 12 ....1,500.00
Comic, Skeezix 80.00
Comic, Smitty, M 125.00
End of Day, bl & wht, 1¾" 450.00
Goldstone, ¾" 12.50
Indian Swirl, 1¾" 2,500.00
Indian Swirl Lutz-type, gold flakes, ¾" 1,200.00
Line Crockery, clay, 1¾" 20.00
Lutz type, clear/bl/gold swirls, 1³⁄₁₆" 300.00
Marble King, bumblebee...1.00
Marble King, watermelon...400.00
MF Christensen, bl opaque 250.00
MF Christensen, bl slag 5.00
Mica, bl, ¾" 30.00
Mica, gr, 1¾" 500.00
Millefiori flowers, tight pattern, pontil mk, 1½", EX................575.00
Onionskin, w/mica, 1¾"...1,200.00
Onionskin, w/mica, ¾"..110.00
Onionskin, 16-lobe, unusual, 1¾"..3,000.00
Onionskin, 2 wht panels w/bl streaks & 2 yel w/red streaks, 2¼"...1,125.00
Onionskin, ¾" 80.00

Opaque Indian Swirl, black with orange, yellow, and blue outer bands, two iridescent moons on one black band (largest about ¼" in diameter), 1", $160.00. (Photo courtesy Glass-Works Auctions)

Opaque Swirl, gr, ¾" 40.00
Opaque Swirl, red/yel/bl/wht, pontil mk, 2⅜", EX...................995.00
Opaque Swirl Lutz-type, bl/yel/gr, ¾" 325.00
Peltier Glass, Golden Rebel 500.00
Peltier Glass, National line 25.00
Peltier Glass, NLR Revel, much aventurine, 1¹⁄₁₆", M 200.00
Peltier Glass, Peerless Patch 5.00
Peltier Glass, slag 15.00
Peltier Glass, Superman 150.00
Peppermint Swirl, opaque, red/red/wht/bl, 1¾" 2,000.00
Peppermint Swirl, opaque, red/wht/bl, ¾".................................125.00
Pottery, 1¾" 20.00
Ribbon Core Lutz-type, red, 1¾"...1,500.00
Solid Opaque, gr, 1¾" 300.00
Solid Opaque, ¾"...40.00
Sulfide, angel, full body, w/halo, little detail, 1¾" 750.00
Sulfide, angel face w/wings, 1¾" 1,200.00
Sulfide, baby in basket (Moses in Bullrushes), 1¾" 800.00
Sulfide, bear standing, 1⁵⁄₁₆", VG...145.00
Sulfide, bear cub on all 4s, detailed, 1¼" 100.00
Sulfide, bird, 2" 100.00
Sulfide, boar, 1⅞" 165.00
Sulfide, boy in short pants crawling, 1¾".................................600.00

Sulfide, boy in top hat & dress clothes, gr glass, 1¾" **4,000.00**
Sulfide, buffalo, little detail, 1¾" **300.00**
Sulfide, camel, 1-hump, on grassy mound, 1½" **200.00**
Sulfide, child (girl) w/hammer, EX detail, 1¾" **600.00**
Sulfide, child sitting, 1¾" **600.00**
Sulfide, coin, face ea side, 1¾" **1,500.00**
Sulfide, crane w/fish, 1¾" **250.00**
Sulfide, crucifix, 1¾", M **600.00**
Sulfide, deer, 1¼" **175.00**
Sulfide, dog (Nipper), 1¾", EX **350.00**
Sulfide, dog howling, 1⅜" **140.00**
Sulfide, dog on grass mound, HP/3-color, pontil, 1¼" **3,500.00**
Sulfide, dove, 1⅝" **165.00**
Sulfide, doves (facing pr), EX details, gr glass, 1¾" **5,000.00**
Sulfide, eagle w/closed wings, 1⅞" **200.00**
Sulfide, elephant, head erect, 'bang' tail, 1¾" **300.00**
Sulfide, elephant standing, sea gr glass, 1¾" **400.00**
Sulfide, elephant w/long trunk, 1¼" **140.00**
Sulfide, fish, 1¾" **175.00**
Sulfide, fox, 1½", EX **130.00**
Sulfide, frog leaping, 1¾", EX **165.00**
Sulfide, George Washington, bust, 2⅜" **2,000.00**
Sulfide, girl sitting in chair, bubble around figure, 1⁹⁄₁₆", VG......**260.00**
Sulfide, gnome, 1½", EX **615.00**
Sulfide, hen, 1⅛" **150.00**
Sulfide, horse rearing, 1⅞" **175.00**
Sulfide, horse standing, 2", EX **130.00**
Sulfide, lamb, 1¾" **125.00**
Sulfide, lion standing, male, 1½" **125.00**
Sulfide, man (politician) standing on stump, 1¼", VG..............**450.00**
Sulfide, man seated on potty, 1½", NM..............................**20,000.00**
Sulfide, monkey seated on drum, 1⅜" **200.00**
Sulfide, numeral 1, 1¾" **400.00**
Sulfide, owl, wings spread, detailed feathers, 1¾" **350.00**
Sulfide, owl w/closed wings, 1¾" **150.00**
Sulfide, parrot, 1½", EX **100.00**
Sulfide, peacock, tricolor in clear glass, 1¾"..........................**8,000.00**
Sulfide, peasant boy on stump w/legs crossed, 1½", NM **400.00**
Sulfide, pony trotting through grassy field, EX detail, 1¾"........**200.00**
Sulfide, poodle on hind legs, 1⅛" **100.00**
Sulfide, rabbit crouching, EX detail, 1¾" **250.00**
Sulfide, rabbit running, lg/offset/sm bubble, 1½", M-................**110.00**
Sulfide, razor-bk hog, 1½" **150.00**
Sulfide, rooster, 1¾" **150.00**
Sulfide, sheep, recumbent, 2", EX **88.00**
Sulfide, sheep grazing, 1¼" **150.00**
Sulfide, squirrel standing, 1¾", EX **170.00**
Transitional, Leighton, 1" **1,000.00**
Transitional, oxblood, ¾" **2,500.00**

Marine Collectibles

Vintage tools used on sea-going vessels, lanterns, clocks, and memorabilia of all types are sought out by those who are interested in preserving the romantic genre that revolves around the life of the sea captains, their boats and their crews; ports of call; and the lure of far-away islands. See also Steamship Collectibles; Telescopes; Scrimshaw; Tools.

Beckets, ropework, pr **200.00**
Bell, ship's; brass w/eng Cythelema, 15½" dia, VG..................**775.00**
Billethead, cvd scrolling leaves, unused, 20th C, 20" **675.00**
Binnacle, Castle & Co Hull dry card compass, 7" dia, w/burner housing....**450.00**
Binnacle, lifeboat; copper & brass, w/burner & compass, 10"+hdl **125.00**

Binnacle, yacht; brass w/Orion Marblehead compass, 34" H........**650.00**
Block, single sheave; cvd whalebone, rigged for use, 3¼" L **325.00**
Bodkin, scrimshaw whale tooth, rectangular knob, 3¾"................**50.00**
Book, List of Merchant Vessels of US 1892, complete, EX **100.00**
Chest, bl pnt, ropework beckets, 19x36x19" **400.00**
Chest, camphor wood, dvtl w/brass corners, 20x42x22", VG......**475.00**
Chest, hinged lid, till, dvtl, red/wht/bl/gr pnt, 18x38x19" VG....**635.00**
Chest, leather-covered camphor wood w/brass tacks & hdls, 43" L....**250.00**
Chest, wood w/int flags/figures decor, 19th C, 35x16x16", EX....**325.00**
Chronometer, deck watch; Waltham, 3-section case, rstr............**575.00**
Chronometer, R Roskett Liverpool, mahog case, early 19th C, 6⅝"..**2,650.00**
Chronometer, Wempe-Hamburg, 4½" dial, w/key, EX in mahog case...**700.00**
Clinometer, Elliot Bros..., brass & boxwood, folding, 12", EX in case ...**475.00**
Desk, captain's; portable, brass lift hdl, inlaid top, dvtl, 15x9x7" **150.00**
Desk, captain's; traveling, brass-bound mahog, red felt top, EX ..**400.00**
Drill, hand; brass w/wooden hdl, early 20th C, 15" **60.00**
Fid, scrimshaw whalebone, 8½"..**375.00**
Fishhook, cvd bone, 4" **40.00**
Flare, Internat'l Flare Signal Co...OH, 1951, EX **10.00**
Flare gun, Internat'l Flare Signal...OH, brass & steel, VG **100.00**
Flare gun, RF Sedgley....Philadelphia, 37mm, EX......................**100.00**
Harpoon, Cole, iron, mid-1800s, 37", EX................................**600.00**
Harpoon, iron toggle, orig rough state, 7½"................................**40.00**
Inclinometer, brass, anchor w/heart cutout in center, 9½x11½" ...**175.00**
Indicator, ship's course; wooden, 3 0-9 segments, 17½" L........**425.00**
Knife, whaler's; spear-point blade, whale-tooth hdl, 11", +sheath....**475.00**
Lamp, bulk head; brass, w/carrying hdl, EX..............................**450.00**
Lamp, copper/brass, w/burner, rstr/polished, 20"+hdl, pr **575.00**
Lamp, galvanized tin w/360-degree clear ribbed lens, 20", VG ...**125.00**
Lamp, salon; brass, gimbal mechanism at top, EX......................**950.00**
Lamp, table; brass, Dead Whale of Stove Boat (emb motto), EX..**160.00**
Lantern, signal; Admiralty...Portable..., brass, 1945, 6" dia, VG....**90.00**
Lantern, signal; brass, 13½"+wooden hdl, EX..........................**575.00**
Lantern, signal; copper & brass, shutters, vented top, 17", VG...**110.00**
Lantern, signal; hand held, galvanized, bull's-eye lens, 9", VG **50.00**
Light, life buoy, Water Light Res Q Lite...MD, copper, 9", EX....**225.00**
Log, T Walker Pat Harpoon...London, brass w/porc dial, cased ..**425.00**
Mallet, ship calking; oak & maple, oversz **80.00**
Model, Ictineo Catalunya 1862 (submarine), 25", EX................**450.00**
Model, Maine lobster boat, bl/wht, detailed, 26" L....................**100.00**
Model, Titanic lifeboat, completely fitted, well made, 31" **125.00**
Model, yacht, half-hull, Herreshoff, detailed, 1870s, 20x72"......**250.00**
Model, 2-masted sailing ship w/4 guns, in 18x27x10" case +mahog stand..**300.00**
Octant, WF Cannon London, ebony/ivory/brass, 12", EX in case....**375.00**
Porthole, brass, 19" dia, VG..**225.00**
Print, CSS Alabama, color, Ficklin 86, 18x24"+mat & fr...........**100.00**
Print, Northern Whale Fishery, after Huggins painting, 1829, 26x24" **650.00**
Propeller, brass, 23" dia, polished..**150.00**
Protractor, JM Kleman..., brass, 13½", EX in fitted case.............**225.00**
Quadrant, JP Cutts...Sheffield, ebony/ivory/brass, dbl-T style, 1820s....**700.00**
Register, Schooner Frankonia, sgn by captain, 1965, 18½x14½"..**90.00**
Scraper, rosewood w/ivory base plate, 12" **150.00**
Sextant, Heather London, brass w/silver scales, ca 1790s, 12x12", EX..**850.00**
Sextant, Michael Rupp...NY, brass w/silver scales, EX in case **700.00**
Sextant, Spencer Browning & Rust London, brass w/silver scales, 1800s..**200.00**
Spear, eel; iron, curved hooks, long wooden handle, 98" overall...**100.00**
Spear, eel; smithy-made iron, 5 spiny tines, 22½x5½", EX **345.00**
Spear, eel; wrought iron, 9-tine, VG..**70.00**
Spotlight, General Electric, brass, 1940s, 15" front glass, 28" **375.00**
Taffrail log, steel armored tail-block, JE Hand & Sons, M in case....**325.00**
Timer, sand glass, old red & blk pnt, 6½".................................**615.00**
Wheel, mahog, outer ring: 56½" dia, EX **950.00**
Wheel, mahog w/brass rings, 6 spokes w/35" between ea spoke, EX ...**525.00**
Wheel, walnut, 8 trn spokes & hdls, worn varnish, 44" dia **600.00**

Markham Pottery

This small business evolved from the hobbies pursued by Herman Markham, who enjoyed using clay from his own property (in Ann Arbor, Michigan) to fashion the planters and pots he used for cultivating flowers. By 1905 he went into the ceramics business with his son Kenneth, moving to National City, California, in 1913. They were most famous for their glazes, many of which were veined and rough textured. Their ware was marked with an incised script signature. By 1921 operations had ceased.

Vase, brn mottled, tapered bulbous form, #3140, 6" **1,000.00**
Vase, gr/orange matt, 2 buttressed hdls, ovoid, 7¼x7½" **600.00**

Martin Bros.

The Martin Bros. were studio potters who worked from 1873 until 1914, first at Fulham and later at London and Southall. There were four brothers, each of whom excelled in their particular area. Robert, known as Wallace, was an experienced stonecarver. He modeled a series of grotesque bird and animal figural caricatures. Walter was the potter, responsible for throwing the larger vases on the wheel, firing the kiln, and mixing the clay. Edwin, an artist of stature, preferred more naturalistic forms of decoration. His work was often incised or had relief designs of seaweed, florals, fish, and birds. The fourth brother, Charles, was their business manager. Their work was incised with their names, place of production, and letters and numbers indicating month and year.

Though figural jars continue to command the higher prices, decorated vases and bowls have increased a great deal in value. Our advisors for this category are Suzanne Perrault and David Rago; they are listed in the Directory under New Jersey.

Bowl, snails pnt/cvd on textured ground, ftd, 4-sided, 2¾" **1,000.00**
Bread plate, floral on cream, detailed cvg, mk RW/A3, 1x6" **525.00**
Condiment set, floral cvg, bl/brn, SP mts, shaker+mustard pot, ea 3"...**1,000.00**
Jug, floral cvd on gray, 9" **540.00**
Jug, 2-face, brn/blk mottle, rstr rim chip, 8¼x7½", $1,750 to **2,250.00**
Match holder, head: lady in bonnet, red bsk/bl engobe, wall mt, 5 dia ...**1,100.00**
Pitcher, yel quatrefoils/brn leaves cvd on gray, 9¾x6", EX, $600 to **900.00**
Vase, birds/foliage, brn on tan/brn mottle, flared rim, 2¾".........**500.00**
Vase, creatures, bl on beige w/brn ribs, mk Martin London, 2½"........**525.00**
Vase, floral, mc on textured brn, bulbous/incised collar, 1889, 8½" ..**1,200.00**
Vase, floral relief, bl on brn, mk CR/RX 1874, 4¼x2½" dia **470.00**
Vase, floral stem cvg, yel/bl/gr on brn & ivory, hdls, 8¾x4"........**750.00**
Vase, grotesque face on overlapping fans, bulbous w/flat bk, 8x4½"..**4,250.00**
Vase, lines, bl cvd on wht, 4 full-height buttresses, 10½", NM ..**1,400.00**
Vase, sea creatures, cvd pnt, gr/br/rust/ivory on ivory, 4-sided, 9" **1,500.00**
Vassel, grotesque bird, bl/brn/wht w/mustard beak, wood base, 9¼" ..**12,000.00**

Mary Gregory

Mary Gregory glass, for reasons that remain obscure, is the namesake of a Boston and Sandwich Glass Company employee who worked for the company for only two years in the mid-1800s. Although no evidence actually exists to indicate that glass of this type was even produced there, the fine colored or crystal ware decorated with figures of children in white enamel is commonly referred to as Mary Gregory. The glass, in fact, originated in Europe and was imported into this country where it was copied by several eastern glasshouses. It was popular from the mid-1800s until the turn of the century. It is generally accepted that examples with all-white figures were made in the U.S.A., while gold-trimmed items and those with children having tinted faces or a small amount of

color on their clothing are European. Though amethyst is rare, examples in cranberry command the higher prices. Blue ranks next; and green, amber, and clear items are worth the least. Watch for new glass decorated with screen-printed children and a minimum of hand painting. The screen effect is easily detected with a magnifying glass.

Barber bottle, bl w/boy in woods, 7½"...**215.00**
Bottle, scent; amethyst, child w/balloon, ball stopper, 3½".........**175.00**
Bottle, scent; cranberry, boy w/butterflies, brass cap, 4⅜" **540.00**
Bottle, scent; gr, girl in woods, missing stopper, 9¾" **90.00**
Carafe, vaseline, girl w/flower basket, 12-sided neck (subtle), 8"...**100.00**
Decanter, clear, lady, gold ft/rim/stopper/etc, 14" **80.00**
Dresser box, amber, girl pointing, hinged lid, 1¼x2½" dia, EX ..**220.00**
Pitcher, bl, Invt T'print, child w/flower, 8" **250.00**
Pitcher, clear, deer in winter scene, ruffled rim, 9", +6 4" glasses ..**125.00**
Pitcher, gr, lady feeding birds, w/floral, fluted rim & sides, 9" **200.00**
Pitcher, vaseline, man w/stein, appl hdl, ruffled rim w/gold, 9"...**280.00**
Shot glass, boy in winter scene, mk Muriel World's Fair 1893, 2½"....**115.00**
Tumbler, amber, boy in floral scene, subtle 8-sided shape, 4" **30.00**
Tumbler, clear, children w/enamel faces, 3½" **50.00**
Vase, bl, boy blowing horn in woods, flared ruffled rim, 8" **250.00**
Vase, bl, boy w/floral, scalloped, 5½" **160.00**
Vase, cranberry, Diana the Huntress, gold trim, 12½" **350.00**
Vase, cranberry, girl on butterfly, 6½x4¼", on 3-ftd metal base..**225.00**
Vase, cranberry, girl w/flowers, cylinder, ca 1870, 6¾" **175.00**
Vase, lt amber, girl & trees, bk: flowers, 6¾x3" **225.00**
Vase, sapphire bl, girl, 8"...**250.00**
Vases, cranberry, 1 w/boy, 1/girl, both in woods, crystal stem, 7", pr ...**470.00**

Mason's Ironstone

In 1813 Charles J. Mason was granted a patent for a process said to 'improve the quality of English porcelain.' The new type of ware was in fact ironstone which Mason decorated with colorful florals and scenics, some of which reflected the Oriental taste. Although his business failed for a short time in the late 1840s, Mason re-established himself and continued to produce dinnerware, tea services, and ornamental pieces until about 1852, at which time the pottery was sold to Francis Morley. Ten years later, Geo. L. and Taylor Ashworth became owners. Both Morley and the Ashworths not only used Mason's molds and patterns but often his mark as well. Because the quality and the workmanship of the later wares do not compare with Mason's earlier product, collectors should take care to distinguish one from the other. Consult a good book on marks to be sure. The Wedgwood Company now owns the rights to the Mason patterns and is reproducing Vista. Note: Blue Vista is generally valued at 15% to 20% above prices for pink/red.

Bowl, Colored Pheasants, octagonal, 1840s, 4¼x8½"+underplate......**250.00**
Bowl, nesting; Vista, red, octagonal, 1925-30 mk, 3¼x6½"........**125.00**
Bowl, serving; Vista, red, 1920-30 mk, 3¼x9¼" **70.00**
Bowl, soup; Willow, flow blue, ca 1840, 10½" **125.00**
Chamber pot, Pagoda, mc, serpent hdl, ca 1840, 5¾x10¼"........**225.00**
Creamer, Vista, red, 1925-30 mk, 3½"..**60.00**
Cup plate, English scene, red, ca 1813, 4¾" **100.00**
Dish, Japan, mc, scalloped, emb leaf hdls, ca 1818, 9½" L..........**300.00**
Dish, Orange Leaf, mc, shell form w/gold o/l, 1813-25, 9½" L....**275.00**
Dish, Orange leaf, mc w/emb swags & gold o/l, 1813-25, 11⅛" L....**325.00**
Dish, Oriental Pheasants, mc, ca 1818, 9½x8", EX **250.00**
Dish, Spray, mc, feather & scroll hdl w/gilt o/l, 1840s, 10⅛" L...**200.00**
Jug, Bandana, mc, ca 1840, 4¾x3½", NM **250.00**
Jug, Chinese Landscape, bl, ca 1891, 5" **200.00**
Jug, Colored Pheasants, mc, cobalt/gold serpent hdl, 1840s, 4½"..**275.00**
Jug, Double Landscape, mc, hexagonal, ca 1840, 4¾" **450.00**

Jug, Dragon, gr & blk on wht, gr serpent hdl, ca 1900, 5¼" **300.00**
Jug, Japan, mc, octagonal, branch hdl, ca 1818, 5¼x5" **375.00**
Jug, Landscape Scroll, mc, mask hdl, ca 1835, 6¼" **425.00**
Jug, Scale, red, serpent hdl, ca 1840 mk, 6½x5¾" **300.00**
Jug, Vista, red, octagonal, serpent hdl, late 1900s, 6½" **425.00**
Mug, Japan, mc, ca 1818, 4⅛x5½", NM **275.00**
Plate, dinner; Vista, red, 1925-50 mk, 10¾", 3 for......................**100.00**
Plate, Nang Po, mc, ca 1813, 8" **225.00**
Plate, Orange Leaf, mc w/gold o/l, paneled border, 1813-25, 8½" **150.00**
Plate, Rich Ruby, mc on wht, scalloped rim, ca 1840, 10½" **300.00**
Plate, Vista, brn, 1890-1900 mk, 7¾" **25.00**
Plate, Water Lily, gold o/l throughout, scalloped, 1813-25, 8½"....**600.00**
Plate, Water Lily, gold o/l throughout, 1813-25, 6⅛" **375.00**
Platter, Rich Ruby, mc, scalloped rim, ca 1840, 15¼x12" **325.00**
Platter, Vista, red, late 1900s, mk, rpr, 15x12¼" **175.00**
Trivet, Vista, red, 1925-30 mk, 6x6" **150.00**
Tureen, Rich Ruby, mc, w/lid, ca 1840, 11x13½", +13" undertray, NM...**900.00**
Vase, Colored Pheasants, mc, sq w/bulbous midsection, 1840s, 7x3⅛".....**175.00**
Vase, Flying Birds, mc, sq w/bulbous midsection, 1840s, mini, 4½" **80.00**
Vase, Japan, mc, gilt mask hdls, att, ca 1818-style & pattern, 9⅜"....**400.00**
Wash bowl & pitcher, Persiana, mc, child sz, 3¾", 4¼" dia........**500.00**
Waste bowl, Vista, red, 1925-30 mk, 2¼x4" **80.00**

Massier

Clement Massier was a French artist-potter who in 1881 established a workshop at Golfe Juan, France, where he experimented with metallic lustre glazes. (One of his pupils was Jacques Sicardo, who brought the knowledge he had gained through his association with Massier to the Weller Pottery Company in Zanesville, Ohio.) The lustre lines developed by Massier incorporated nature themes with allover decorations of foliage or flowers on shapes modeled in the Art Nouveau style. The ware was usually incised with the Massier name, his initials, or the location of the pottery. Massier died in 1917.

Our advisors for this category are Suzanne Perault and David Rago; they are listed in the Directory under New Jersey.

Jardiniere, foliate vertical bands on teal gloss, 12½" **300.00**
Tile, detailed landscape, mc w/overall irid, att, in 3x4½" fr.....**1,300.00**

Vase, berries and vines on lavender with gold, double-bulbed body, pinched lower portion, 9⅝", $1,750.00.

(Photo courtesy Skinner, Inc.)

Vase, fleur-de-lis on gr & purple lustre, baluster, rstr, 4x3" **250.00**
Vase, floral on irid, mini, 4" **600.00**
Vase, molded serpents (3) at lip, gr irid metallic, 6¾" **1,000.00**
Vase, multi-tone brn decor shoulder w/yel & tan drip, 4½" **200.00**
Vase, red & wht w/charcoal accents, swollen form, 5½" **250.00**

Match Holders

John Walker, an English chemist, invented the match more than one hundred years ago, quite by accident. Walker was working with a mixture of potash and antimony, hoping to make a combustible that could be used to fire guns. The mixture adhered to the end of the wooden stick he had used for stirring. As he tried to remove it by scraping the stick on the stone floor, it burst into flames. The invention of the match was only a step away! From that time to the present, match holders have been made in amusing figural forms as well as simple utilitarian styles and in a wide range of materials. Both table-top and wall-hanging models were made — all designed to keep matches conveniently at hand. The prices in this category are very volatile due to increased interest in this field and the fact that so many can be classified as a cross or dual collectible.

Caution: As prices for originals continue to climb, so do the number of reproductions. Know your dealer. Our advisor for this category is Ron Damaska; he is listed in the Directory under Pennsylvania. See also Advertising.

Black Forest, cvd bear w/glass eyes, attached striker & tray, 3" ...**165.00**
Bronze, devil figural, holds glass crown, Fr, 19th C, 8½x7¼" **450.00**
CI, grapes & scrollwork, 19th C, 9x5¼" **225.00**
CI, Indian maiden, worn orig pnt, Pat Appd For, 4¾" **165.00**
CI, mechanical bbl depresses to push up match, 1864 pat, 6x2¼" ...**100.00**
CI, Ulysses S Grant portrait from 1872 campaign, 6" (+)...........**315.00**
CI, woodpecker on base, Charles Kitschelt Pat, 6" overall..........**300.00**
Cobalt glass, laughing man, dtd June 13 '76, 4", EX...................**100.00**
Milk glass, skull figural, ca 1870s, 2⅜x3⅝x2⅜" **125.00**
NP CI, Anchor Stoves ad, worn finish, 6x4" **165.00**
NP CI, frog figural, Pointer Stoves...Ind, worn finish **135.00**
Tin, Adriance Farm Machinery, Shonk litho, 4⅞x3⅜" **110.00**
Trn maple w/tin lid, Am, ca 1880, 5¾x2½" dia **115.00**

Match Safes

Before the invention of the safety match in 1855, matches were carried in small pocket-sized containers because they ignited so easily. Aptly called match safes, these containers were used extensively until about 1920, when cigarette lighters became widely available. Some incorporated added features (hidden compartments, cigar cutters, etc.), some were figural, and others were used by retail companies as advertising giveaways. They were made from every type of material, but silver-plated styles abound. Both the advertising and common silver-plated cases generally fall in the $50.00 to $100.00 price range.

Beware of reproductions and fakes; there are many currently on the market. Know your dealer. Our advisor for this category is Ron Damaska; he is listed in the Directory under Pennsylvania. See also Advertising.

NP brass, Edward VII head form, hinged, Pat 1212 SB, 2x1¾" ..**415.00**
Silver, Indian chief figural, monogram, Unger, 2¼x1⅞" **525.00**
Silver, skull form, English, ca 1880..**300.00**
Silver, 4-leaf clover, ca 1900, 800 hallmk, 1⅞" **225.00**
SP & agate, Vesta, 2¼x1" **140.00**
SP w/brass int, John Deere, ca 1890s, 2⅜x1¾" **325.00**
Sterling, HP lesbian couple in boat, Vesta, 2¼x1½"...............**1,550.00**
Sterling, mermaid emb, eng scrolls, hinged lid, 2⅜x1½" **195.00**
18k gold, risqué enameling, Fr, 1800s, 2x1⅜" **1,150.00**

Mauchline Ware

Mauchline ware is the generic name for small, well-made, and useful wooden souvenirs and giftware from Mauchline, Scotland, and nearby locations. It was made from the early nineteenth century into the 1930s. Snuff boxes were among the earliest items, and tea caddies soon followed. From the 1830s on, needlework, stationery, domestic, and cosmetic items were made by the thousands. Today, needlework items are the most plentiful and range from boxes of all sizes made to hold supplies to tiny bodkins and buttons. Napkin rings, egg cups, vases, and bowls are just a few of the domestic items available.

The wood most commonly used in the production of Mauchline ware was sycamore. Finishes vary. Early items were hand decorated with colored paints or pen and ink. By the 1850s, perhaps even earlier, transfer ware was produced, decorated with views associated with the place of purchase. These souvenir items were avidly bought by travelers for themselves as well as for gifts. Major exhibitions and royal occasions were also represented on transferware. An alternative decorating process was initiated during the mid-1860s whereby actual photos replaced the transfers. Because they were finished with multiple layers of varnish, many examples found today are still in excellent condition.

Tartan ware's distinctive decoration was originally hand painted directly on the wood with inks, but in the 1840s machine-made paper in authentic Tartan designs became available. Except for the smallest items, each piece was stamped with the Tartan name. The Tartan decoration was applied to virtually the entire range of Mauchline ware, and because it was favored by Queen Victoria, it became widely popular. Collectors still value Tartan ware above other types of decoration, with transferware being their second choice. Other types of Mauchline decorations include Fern ware and Black Lacquer with floral or transfer decorations.

When cleaning any Mauchline item, extreme care should be used to avoid damaging the finish! Mauchline ware has been reproduced for at least twenty-five years, especially some of the more popular pieces and finishes. Collectors should study the older items for comparison and to learn about the decorating and manufacturing processes.

Bible, Prince Charlie pattern, gilt edges, hand-tinted maps, 7x5", G ...145.00
Box, dome top; Pevensy Castle, 3¼" L 65.00
Box, Dundee Harbour, Royal Arch, Australia, w/lock, 1¾x3¼x2¼"....65.00
Box, Taylor Hall Racine College WI, 1¾x3½x2¼", EX 190.00
Egg cup, Ryde Pier, bk: Bonchurch Pond, 3" 85.00
Glasses case, fernware, layers of ferns/sprayed-on colors, 6" L 325.00
Inkwell stand, Ballmena Castle, heart shaped w/glass ink pot, 3x5x5" ..395.00
Letter holder, 2 scenes: Newport RI, 1½x4¼x5½" 165.00
Master salt, New Brighton Pier, 3" dia bowl on ped ft.................125.00
Match holder, Lodges Burley, 3¾x2⅞x1¾" 160.00
Needle case, Chateau de la Montagne St Honore les Bains FR, silk int ..100.00
Page turner, Eastern Telegraph Co, maps, company banner, etc, 13" L, G ..185.00
Picture album, Redesdale Hall Moreton in Marsh, photo mat pgs, 4x5x1"...125.00
Pincushion, Popping Stone Gilsland, 3-lobed, 2¼", EX..............100.00
Plaque, Centenary of Sir Walter Scott, commemoration, wood fr, 9½" ...190.00
Snuff box, pointer dogs/birds flying, tin lined, 2⅝" L, EX...........180.00
Teapot, Pensarn in North Wales, ring hdl, str spout, 2x3¼" 695.00
Thermometer, Bonchurch Road Isle of Wight+3 others, obelisk form, 6"...100.00
Thimble, children at play, M 150.00
Thimble box, Stonehaven on lid, silver Chas Horne Dorcas thimble w/in....345.00
Thread box, Queen Victoria 1887 Jubilee, 4¼x2¼x1½", EX 165.00
Thread winder, Rob Roy mk on tartan plaid, X w/shaped terminals, 2¼" .395.00
Tumbler, General View, Sidmouth, 2nd scene on bk, 2¾" 85.00

McCoy

The third generation McCoy potter in the Roseville, Ohio, area was Nelson, who with the aid of his father, J.W., established the Nelson McCoy Sanitary Stoneware Company in 1910. They manufactured churns, jars, jugs, poultry fountains, and foot warmers. By 1925 they had expanded their wares to include majolica jardinieres and pedestals,

umbrella stands, and cuspidors, and an embossed line of vases and small jardinieres in a blended brown and green matt glaze. From the late '20s through the mid-'40s, a utilitarian stoneware was produced, some of which was glazed in the soft blue and white so popular with collectors today. They also used a dark brown mahogany color and a medium to dark green, both in a high gloss. In 1933 the firm became known as the Nelson McCoy Pottery Company. They expanded their facilities in 1940 and began to make the novelty artware, cookie jars, and dinnerware that today are synonymous with 'McCoy.' More than two hundred cookie jars of every theme and description were produced.

More than a dozen different marks have been used by the company; nearly all incorporate the name 'McCoy,' although some of the older items were marked 'NM USA.' For further information consult *The Collector's Encyclopedia of McCoy Pottery* by Sharon and Bob Huxford; *McCoy Pottery Collector's Reference & Value Guide, Vol. I, II and III*, by Margaret Hanson, Craig Nissen, and Bob Hanson; and *McCoy Pottery Wall Pockets and Decorations* by Craig Nissen (all published by Collector Books). Also available is *Sanfords Guide to McCoy Pottery* by Martha and Steve Sanford (Mr. Sanford is listed in the Directory under California.)

Alert! Stimulated by the high prices commanded by desirable cookie jars, a broad spectrum of 'new' cookie jars have flooded the marketplace in three categories: 1) Manufacturers have expanded their lines with exciting new designs to attract the collector market. 2) Limited editions and artist-designed jars have proliferated. 3) Reproductions, signed and unsigned, have pervaded the market, creating uncertainty among new collectors and inexperienced dealers. After McCoy closed its doors in the late 1980s, an entrepreneur in Tennessee tried (and succeeded for nearly a decade) to adopt the McCoy Pottery name and mark. This company reproduced old McCoy designs as well as some classic designs of other defunct American potteries, signing their wares 'McCoy' with a mark which very closely approximated the old McCoy mark. Legal action finally put a stop to this practice, though since then this company has used other fraudulent marks as well: Brush-McCoy (the compound name was never used on Brush cookie jars) and B.J. Hull.

Note: Still under pressure from Internet exposure and the effects of a slow economy, the cookie jar market remains soft. High-end cookie jars are often slow to sell.

Our advisor for McCoy cookie jars is Judy Posner; she is listed in the Directory under Florida.

Cookie Jars

Clown Bust, has been reproduced, $75.00.

Apollo Age, minimum value 1,000.00
Apple, 1950-64 ....50.00
Apples on Basketweave 70.00
Asparagus 50.00

Bananas..125.00
Barrel, Cookies sign on lid 75.00
Basket of Eggs 40.00
Bear, cookie in vest, no 'Cookies' 85.00
Black Kettle, w/immovable bail, HP flowers 40.00
Blue Willow Pitcher 75.00
Bugs Bunny 125.00
Burlap Bag, red bird on lid 50.00
Chairman of the Board (+) 550.00
Chef Head...150.00
Chipmunk 125.00
Christmas Tree...800.00
Circus Horse, blk 250.00
Clyde Dog...200.00
Coalby Cat 300.00
Coca-Cola Jug 85.00
Coffee Grinder 45.00
Colonial Fireplace 85.00
Cookie Bank, 1961 ....125.00
Cookie Boy 225.00
Cookie Jug, dbl loop 35.00
Cookie Jug, w/cork stopper, brn & wht 40.00
Cookie Log, squirrel finial 45.00
Cookie Pot, 1964 ....40.00
Cookstove, blk or wht 35.00
Corn, row of standing ears, yel or wht, 1977 ....85.00
Corn, single ear 175.00
Covered Wagon 95.00
Cylinder, w/red flowers 45.00
Dalmatians in Rocking Chair (+)....................200.00
Dog in Doghouse, from $225 to 150.00
Drum, red...90.00
Dutch Boy 65.00
Dutch Girl, boy on reverse, rare 250.00
Dutch Treat Barn 50.00
Early American Chest (Chiffoniere) 85.00
Elephant...150.00
Elephant w/Split Trunk, rare, minimum value ...200.00
Flowerpot, plastic flower on top......................500.00
Football Boy (+) 150.00
Forbidden Fruit 90.00
Freddy Gleep (+), minimum value 500.00
Frog on Stump 75.00
Fruit in Bushel Basket......................................85.00
Globe 275.00
Granny..120.00
Happy Face 80.00
Hillbilly Bear, rare, minimum value (+)..........900.00
Hobby Horse, brn underglaze (+) 150.00
Honey Bear, rustic glaze...................................80.00
Hot Air Balloon..40.00
Indian, brn (+) 350.00
Jack-O'-Lantern...500.00
Kangaroo, bl...300.00
Keebler Tree House..70.00
Kissing Penguins..100.00
Kittens (2) on Low Basket 600.00
Koala Bear 85.00
Lamb on Basketweave 90.00
Leprechaun, minimum value (+).................1,800.00
Little Clown..75.00
Mac Dog..95.00
Mammy w/Cauliflower, G pnt, minimum value (+)...1,100.00
Modern..65.00

Mother Goose...125.00
Mr & Mrs Owl..90.00
Nursery, decal of Humpty Dumpty, from $70 to......80.00
Orange...55.00
Pear, 1952...85.00
Penguin, yel or aqua..150.00
Picnic Basket...75.00
Pine Cones on Basketweave 70.00
Pineapple, Modern 90.00
Popeye, cylinder...150.00
Puppy, w/sign 85.00
Raggedy Ann...110.00
Rooster, wht, 1970-1974..................................60.00
Round w/HP Leaves 40.00
Snoopy on Doghouse (+), mk United Features Syndicate...........200.00
Spaniel in Doghouse, bird finial 250.00
Strawberry, 1955-57 ....65.00
Teapot, 1972 ....60.00
Tepee, slat top...350.00
Thinking Puppy, #0272 ....40.00
Timmy Tortoise...45.00
Touring Car...100.00
Traffic Light 50.00
Tulip on Flowerpot 100.00
Turkey, gr, rare color..300.00
Upside Down Bear, panda 50.00
WC Fields..200.00
Woodsy Owl..200.00
Yellow Mouse (head)..45.00

Miscellaneous

Ashtray, Feb 20 Space Capsule, from $40 to 50.00
Basket planter, Floraline, wht, #561L, 7x7½", from $25 to 35.00
Bowl, console; Butterfly, yel, 7½x11", from $90 to.....................130.00
Canisters, Bamboo, 1974, set of 3, from $75 to............................100.00
Centerpiece, antelope on blk or gr base, 1955, 12" W, from $350 to..450.00
Creamer, Mediterranean Line, 1980, from $12 to.......................15.00
Deviled egg plate, chicken shape, yel, 1973, from $20 to.............30.00
Fernery, bl w/emb leaves & verries, rectangular, 4x7", $45 to.......60.00
Flower holder, Hands of Friendship, various colors, 4x3", $60 to ..150.00
Flowerpot, wavy lines emb on gr, w/saucer, 1960s, 4-6", ea from $25 to ..40.00
Jar, oil; burgundy mottle, stoneware, unmk, 1920s-30s, 25", $400 to..500.00
Jar, porch; leaves & berries on blended matt, 14", from $1,200 to...1,500.00
Jar, pretzel; gr w/emb Pretzels in dmn shape, hdld keg form, $90 to....110.00
Jardiniere, brn onyx, emb rim pattern, 1920s-30s, 7", from $60 to ..60.00
Jardiniere, gr onyx, unmk, 1930s-40s, 6", from $35 to 40.00
Jardiniere, Vesta, emb broken lines, ftd, ca 1962, 10", from $35 to......45.00
Jardiniere & ped, Basketweave, gr or wht, 8½", 12½".................250.00
Jardiniere & ped, emb rings, blended glaze, 10½", 18½", $450 to....550.00
Matchbox holder, wht w/bl speckles, mk, 1970s, 5¾x3¼" 40.00
Mug, gr w/emb grapes & leaves reserve, shield mk, 5", from $20 to ...30.00
Mug, Similac for Ross Coffee, yel or gr, from $10 to......................20.00
Pitcher, cobalt ball form, 7", from $85 to 125.00
Pitcher, fish figural, gr/brn blended, 1949, 7", from $650 to........800.00
Pitcher, pig figural, made in many colors, 1940s, 5", from $500 to..600.00
Planter, Artisan Line, wht, mk, 1965, 7½", from $35 to 45.00
Planter, caterpillar figural, wht, Model 416L, 13½" L, from $30 to....45.00
Planter, dragonflies emb on pastel pk, 1940s, 3½", from $35 to....45.00
Planter, Dutch shoe, tulip laying on top (most common), 7½", $30 to...60.00
Planter, frog beside open lotus flower, wht, from $15 to 20.00
Planter, goose w/cart, gr or bl, 1940s, 4¾x8", from $35 to 45.00
Planter, Happy Face, 1970s-80s, from $25 to 35.00
Planter, lamb, blk gloss, early 1940s, 4½x6x3", from $50 to.........60.00

Planter, leaves emb on gr, mk, 1950s, 7" L, from $35 to **45.00**
Planter, Plow Boy, gr, ca 1955, 7x8", from $125 to **150.00**
Planter, snowman, wht w/blk or red decor, 1940s, 6x4", from $60 to....**75.00**
Planter, wheelbarrow w/rooster, yel & blk, 1955, 7x10½", $100 to **125.00**
Planter, 4-lobe top, 4 sm buttress ft, bl or red, 3½", from $30 to...**40.00**
Planting dish, Capri, bl w/pk int, 1950-60s, 14½", from $40 to....**50.00**
Stein, Schlitz Malt Liquor, #6020, 1973, from $25 to....................**35.00**
Tea set, Pine Cone, bl (unusual color), 1940s-50s, 3-pc, $100 to ..**125.00**
Tumbler, gr, emb rings, flared, stoneware, 1920s-30s, 5", from $40 to ...**50.00**
Vase, Antique Rose, waisted cone form, 10", from $40 to **45.00**
Vase, berries & leaves, 2-color on lt yel, unmk, bulbous, 8", from $70 to ...**85.00**
Vase, bud; Vesta, yel w/trim, unmk, 1963, 8", from $20 to **25.00**
Vase, Butterfly, aqua, hdls, 10", from $125 to................................**200.00**
Vase, cat figural, blk, gray or wht, ca 1960, 14", from $200 to **250.00**
Vase, Floraline Fineforms, dk mauve, unmk, #0488FF, 12½x9", $50 to...**75.00**
Vase, goblet form, Floraline, gr, 6½", from $15 to.........................**25.00**
Vase, gr w/emb lappet V-shapes, mk V2, 1920s, 7½", from $60 to ..**80.00**
Vase, gr w/scrolling ft, 1959, 14", from $75 to.............................**100.00**
Vase, Hyacinth, pk, bl or lav, 1950, 8", from $100 to **125.00**
Vase, Ivy, hand decorated, 1955, 9", from $200 to.......................**300.00**
Vase, peacock emb on gr, hdls, 1948, 8", from $50 to....................**60.00**
Vase, Ribbed, emb vertical ribs, gr or wht, 1950s, 14", from $75 to.....**90.00**
Vase, Ribbed Pedestal, dk gr, #407, 6½x3¾", from $15 to **20.00**
Vase, Sunburst gold, ornate low hdls, 6½", from $40 to **50.00**
Vase, Sunflower, solid glaze, 1950s, 9", from $40 to.....................**60.00**
Vase, wht waisted cylinder w/low hdls & emb rings, 1940s, 10", $85 to...**110.00**
Vase, yel w/low gold hdls, 1950s, 9", from $85 to **120.00**
Wall pocket, bananas, yel on gr leaves, 1950s, 7x6", from $125 to....**150.00**
Wall pocket, clown, red cold pnt, 1940s, 8", from $100 to..........**150.00**
Wall pocket, flower, common glaze, late 1940s, 6", from $35 to ...**50.00**
Wall pocket, leaves w/berries, mk, 1940s, very rare, 9" **1,000.00**
Wall pocket, umbrella, gr, mk, 1950s, 8¾", from $90 to **100.00**

McCoy, J. W.

The J.W. McCoy Pottery Company was incorporated in 1899. It operated under that name in Roseville, Ohio, until 1911 when McCoy entered into a partnership with George Brush, forming the Brush-McCoy Company. During the early years, McCoy produced kitchenware, majolica jardinieres and pedestals, umbrella stands, and cuspidors. By 1903 they had begun to experiment in the field of art pottery and, though never involved to the extent of some of their contemporaries, nevertheless produced several art lines of merit.

The company rebuilt in 1904 after being destroyed by fire, and other artware was designed. Loy-Nel Art and Renaissance were standard brown lines, hand decorated under the glaze with colored slip. Shapes and artwork were usually simple but effective. Olympia and Rosewood were relief-molded brown-glaze lines decorated in natural colors with wreaths of leaves and berries or simple floral sprays. Although much of this ware was not marked, you will find examples with the die-stamped 'Loy-Nel Art, McCoy,' or an incised line identification.

Corn Line, mug, unmk, from $50 to **70.00**
Corn Line, tankard, unmk, 1910, from $300 to **350.00**
Liberty Bell, umbrella stand, Cusick, unmk, 1910, 23", from $800 to **900.00**
Loy-Nel-Art, jardiniere, floral, 1905, 6", from $250 to................**300.00**
Loy-Nel-Art, jardiniere, Halley's Comet, mk, 1910, 4", from $350 to...**400.00**
Loy-Nel-Art, vase, waisted, no hdls, 1905, 8", from $200 to.......**250.00**
Marble Ware, jardiniere & ped, unmk, 1910, 39", from $700 to ...**800.00**
Mt Pelee, ewer, from $1,000 to..**1,200.00**
Olympia, oil lamp, early 1900s, from $125 to **200.00**
Olympia, pretzel bowl, unmk, 1905, from $400 to......................**500.00**
Olympia, vase, rim-to-hip hdls, 1905, 5", from $250 to.............**350.00**

Rosewood, ewer, cylinder neck, 1905, 10", from $350 to **450.00**
Rosewood, vase, #10, 1904, 9", from $125 to...............................**200.00**
Rosewood, vase, trumpet neck, unmk, pre-1903, 9", from $200 to...**250.00**

McKee

McKee Glass was founded in 1853 in Pittsburgh, Pennsylvania. Among their early products were tableware of both the flint and non-flint varieties. In 1888 the company relocated to avail themselves of a source of natural gas, thereby founding the town of Jeannette, Pennsylvania. One of their most famous colored dinnerware lines, Rock Crystal, was manufactured in the 1920s. Production during the '30s and '40s included colored opaque dinnerware, Sunkist reamers, and 'bottoms up' cocktail tumblers as well as a line of black glass vases, bowls, and novelty items. All are popular items with today's collectors, but watch for reproductions. The mark of an authentic 'bottoms up' tumbler is the patent number 77725 embossed beneath the feet. The company was purchased in 1916 by Jeannette Glass, under which name it continues to operate. See also Animal Dishes with Covers; Carnival Glass; Depression Glass; Kitchen Collectibles; Reamers.

Ashtray, cowboy hat, Delphite Blue, 5½"..**33.00**
Bottoms Up, tumbler, butterscotch opal, from $60 to....................**75.00**
Bottoms Up, tumbler, caramel opal **125.00**
Bottoms Up, tumbler, custard...**60.00**
Bottoms Up, tumbler, Jade-ite, from $85 to **120.00**
Bowl, console; Jade-ite, 9-petal bowl on ped ft, emb Dmn Quilt...**275.00**
Bowl, Gladiator, emerald gr, 3½x5"..**47.00**
Carafe, milk glass w/blk neck, dome glass stopper.......................**15.00**
Comport, amethyst, rolled rim, 6x8"..**55.00**
Compote, Rotec, 6½x7"...**30.00**
Decanter, blk amethyst w/silver o/l, Rye, 9⅜x4¾" **145.00**
Pin tray, milk glass hand form, 4¾x2"..**8.00**
Punch bowl, Aztec, +base & 12 cups w/metal holders, MIB.......**135.00**
Punch bowl, pleated sides, w/stand, 11¾x13¼", +12 cups & hangers...**400.00**
Punch mug, Tom & Jerry, clambroth, 3½x4" **28.00**
Punch mug, Tom & Jerry, wht w/blk trim.....................................**32.00**
Relish, Rotec, crystal, 3-compartment, 7½" dia............................**22.00**
Shaker, Roman Arch, blk amethyst, 4½" **25.00**
Straw hat, clear, 4½"...**25.00**

Tambour mantel clock, vaseline, 14" long, $450.00.

Teapot, pastel rings, Glasbake **35.00**
Toothpick holder, Peek-a-Boo, ca 1904 ....**56.00**
Wine, Rainbow pattern, stemmed...**22.00**

Medical Collectibles

The field of medical-related items encompasses a wide area from the primitive bleeding bowl to the X-ray machines of the early 1900s. Other closely related collectibles include apothecary and dental items. Many tools that were originally intended for the pharmacist found their way to the doctor's office, and dentists often used surgical tools when no suitable dental instrument was available. A trend in the late 1800s toward self-medication brought a whole new wave of home-care manuals and 'patent' medical machines for home use. Commonly referred to as 'quack' medical gimmicks, these machines were usually ineffective and occasionally dangerous. Our advisor for this category is Jim Calison; he is listed in the Directory under New York.

Apothecary jar, clear glass w/pnt Pot Bitart label, 1889, 9½"........**40.00**
Apothecary jar, milk glass, Adeps Suil label, 7x4" dia..................**60.00**
Apothecary set, JP Wellman Apothecary & Herbalist, 8-pc.........**20.00**
Bleeder, brass, 2⅛", M in wooden case mk Be Careful................**185.00**
Bone saw, Pilling-Phila, NP brass hdl, steel blade, 11½x2¾"........**65.00**
Book, Dr Pancoast's Ladies Medical Guide, many illustrations, 1875......**20.00**
Book, Managing Diabetic Patients, H John MD, 1927, EX...........**70.00**
Book, Oral Surgery, SV Mead, CV Mosby Co, 1946, 3rd edition, EX..**75.00**
Book, Our Babies, Dr Herman Bundesen, softcover, 1928, 7½x10"......**10.00**
Book, Primer in Physiology, EH Straling, Dutton, 1904, 128-pg, EX....**50.00**
Book, Radiographic Atlas of Skeletal Development, 1955, 1st edition...**40.00**
Book, The Practical Orthodontist, hardcover, AG Meire, 1911, 62-pg...**10.00**
Box, doctor's; pnt decor on pine, rope hdls, 19th C, 15x14x18"....**1,100.00**
Cabinet, First Aid, Bauer & Black #8, complete contents, 1920s, 18x15"..**100.00**
Carrying case, faux leather, 3 trays, Gerstner & Sons OH, 9x16x15".........**350.00**
Clamp, stainless steel, unmk, vintage, 10"..**21.00**
Conversation tube, Vulcanite ear pc & bell, silk-covered tube, 1890s.**235.00**
Ear trumpet, faux tortoiseshell, London Dome style, mk Frost, 4½"......**425.00**
Ear trumpet, faux tortoiseshell, Sonar type, mk Depose, 5x4½"....**550.00**
Exam chair, blk vinyl & tubular steel, headrest, 1940s, EX.........**175.00**
Eye cup, clear, Glasco, 2¼"..**15.00**
Eye cup, emerald gr, Opthalmic Optabs Glass on base...................**22.50**
Eye cup, midnight bl, OpTrex, M in EX box.................................**35.00**
Forceps, stainless, Geo C Frye, 15"...**32.50**
Hearing aid, Acousticon Model A-310, resembles transistor radio, MIB....**45.00**
Hearing aid, Sonotone 1010, resembles transistor radio, 1950s, MIB.....**90.00**
Invalid feeder, porc w/bl & yel florals, H&J mk, 6x2½"................**40.00**
Invalid feeder, Red Cross on porc w/gold, 6½x2½".......................**25.00**
Lamp, vaporizer, Vapo-cresolene, 6⅜", NMIB..........................**200.00**
Quack device, Violet Ray, 2 11" glass wands, MIB w/instructions...**95.00**
Quack device, Violette, Bleadon-Dun, 1920s, NMIB....................**75.00**
Stethoscope, cone-shaped head, Y-shaped metal center, EX..........**40.00**
Syringe, clear glass w/cobalt plunger, 5¾", EX...............................**35.00**
Syringe, glass w/stainless steel tip, Fortuna Optima, 50cc, 1960s, MIB....**25.00**
Syringe, rectal; Rexall Defender, soft rubber bulb, 1950s, MIB.....**40.00**
Teneculum, folding, hand-forged hook, 1860s, 4¾" (open)...........**55.00**
Water bottle/syringe combination, Davol Paris, M in Deco box...**50.00**

Meissen

The Royal Saxon Porcelain Works was established in 1710 in Meissen, Saxony. Under the direction of Johann Frederick Bottger, who in 1708 had developed the formula for the first true porcelain body, fine ceramic figurines with exquisite detail and tableware of the highest quality were produced. Although every effort was made to insure the secrecy of Bottger's discovery, others soon began to copy his ware, and in 1731 Meissen adopted the famous crossed swords trademark to identify their own work. The term 'Dresden ware' is often used to refer to Meissen porcelain, since Bottger's discovery and first potting efforts were in nearby Dresden. See also Onion Pattern.

Bottle, appl flowers, pillow form, tassels in corners, 3½", VG.....**200.00**
Clock, rococo body w/flowers & putti, 18½"............................**2,750.00**

Dish, birds, butterflies & vegetables, gold trim & hdl, Xd swords...**320.00**
Figurine, Archangel Michael defeating dragon, #L113, Xd swords, 8½"..**900.00**
Figurine, boy drinking from cup, dog at ft, Hentschel, #W110, 6½".....**1,940.00**
Figurine, boy riding toy pull horse, Hentschel, ca 1905, 6½"..**1,900.00**
Figurine, boy w/roses, Xd swords, 5"..**325.00**
Figurine, cherub sits on fireplace grinding coffee, Xd swords, 5¼"...**445.00**
Figurine, cherub sits on fireplace stirring bowl, Xd swords, 4¼"....**430.00**
Figurine, cherub w/purple ribbon, floral & gilt, Xd swords, 14".**2,010.00**
Figurine, cherub w/sheaves of wheat, Xd swords, 5⅜".................**450.00**
Figurine, child w/puppy, Hentschel, ca 1905, 6¼"....................**1,800.00**
Figurine, child working in garden, Xd swords, 4⅞".....................**400.00**
Figurine, cook at fireplace, Xd swords, 5⅜".................................**650.00**
Figurine, Cris de Paris, Xd swords, 6⅜"......................................**940.00**
Figurine, eagle, wht w/dagger & sceptor, crown on head, Xd swords, 20"....**2,110.00**
Figurine, elephant w/African rider, Xd swords, 9x10½"...........**2,775.00**
Figurine, female shepherd w/dog & sheep, Xd swords, 11½".......**990.00**
Figurine, girl w/doll & carriage, Hentschel, ca 1905, 5"............**1,200.00**
Figurine, gr & yel parrot on tree-form base, Xd swords, 8½".......**815.00**
Figurine, Greek female archer w/dog, Xd swords, 7¾".................**700.00**
Figurine, lady at piano w/man w/violin, 2 children, Xd swords, 8⅞"..**1,720.00**
Figurine, lady on stool feeds bird in cage, Xd swords, 6x4x3¼"..**810.00**
Figurine, Laughing Mandarin bust, Xd swords, rpr, 23½".........**4,275.00**
Figurine, man & dog sit w/lady w/grape basket, Xd swords, 5x7½"....**1,900.00**
Figurine, man holding sickle at side, Xd swords, 4½".................**500.00**
Figurine, Monkey Band, drummer, Xd swords, 5¾".....................**600.00**
Figurine, putto, 7"...**1,200.00**
Figurine, seated musician drinking w/goat in arms, Xd swords, 5¾"...**620.00**
Figurine, 2 women & 2 children, floral relief, Xd swords, rst, 13"....**1,920.00**
Figurine, 6 figures around tree, Xd swords, 19½".....................**1,410.00**
Plaque, Hope of a Mother, Xd swords, #383, 9⅝x7⅛".............**3,075.00**
Plate, cobalt & gold leaf-shaped decor, Xd swords, 9½"..............**310.00**
Plate, gilt floral relief on bl, Xd swords, 11"................................**240.00**
Plate, 2 ladies sit by creek w/cupid, cobalt & gold border, 11½".....**1,290.00**
Platter, birds, butterflies & vegetables, Xd swords, 2x12x10".......**385.00**
Platter, floral, purple/blk/bl on wht, oval w/gold edge, mk, 19x14".....**275.00**
Sugar bowl, floral w/strawberry finial, appl gr stem hdls, Xd swords...**415.00**
Tea set, Snowball, Xd swords, teapot+underplate+2 c/s...........**2,010.00**
Teapot, turq w/gold decor & finial, dragon-head spout, Xd swords, 8"..**465.00**
Thimble, hunting scene, Rideinger, Xd swords inside, MIB........**665.00**
Urn, battle scene allegorical, Zeus on eagle finial, 19th C, 26"..**4,115.00**
Urn, classical figures & flowers, putti hdls, ped ft, w/lid, 30", pr..**4,600.00**
Urn, Egg & Dart band, cobalt w/gold, gold serpent hdls, 18¾"..**1,875.00**
Urn, floral relief w/sm cherub at base, rtcl lid, bl mk, 28½"....**3,010.00**
Vase, florals on cobalt w/gold, coiled snake hdls, ca 1900, 15¼".,..**1,175.00**
Vase, 18th-C figures in cartouch on cobalt, flared cylinder, 16", pr....**4,750.00**

Mercury Glass

Silvered glass, commonly called mercury glass, was a major scientific achievement of the nineteenth century. It was developed by the glass industry, who was searching for an inexpensive substitute for silver. Though very fragile, it was lightweight and would not tarnish. Mercury glass was made with two thin layers, either blown with a double wall or joined in sections, with the space between the walls of the vessel filled with a silvering compound, the perfecting of which involved much experimentation. Colored glass was also silvered. Green, blue, and amber were favored. Occasionally, colors were achieved using clear glass by adding certain chemicals to the compound. Besides hollow ware items, flat surfaces were silvered as well, through a process whereby small facets were cut on the underneath side, then treated with the silvering compound. Sometimes mercury glass was decorated by engraving; it was also hand painted. Besides decorative items such as vases and candlesticks, for instance, utilitarian items — doorknobs, curtain tiebacks, and reflectors for lamps — were also popular. Silvered Christmas ornaments were produced in large quantities.

Condition is an issue, though opinions are divided. While some prefer their acquisitions to be in mint condition, others accept items with flaked silvering. Watch for reproductions marked Made in China. In the listings that follow, all examples are silver unless noted another color.

Bird, wire clip at ft, 4½x1", 4 for 45.00
Bottle, liquor; crest on front, 57 on bottom, cork stopper, 11x3".....18.00
Bottle, scent; spherical, w/dauber, 2½x2" dia...............................30.00
Bottle, stick neck, 4½" 45.00
Candlestick, baluster, ca 1860-75, 9", pr 200.00
Curtain tieback, 4x4" 60.00
Deer, hand blown, 4x3x1½"..95.00
Lamp, table; urn form, 1950s era, 22x8"..................................235.00
Salt cellar, HP floral on ftd egg form, 1850s, 3⅛x2" 110.00
Vase, gr w/raised pattern, sq sides, 9¾x4".................................185.00
Vase, HP floral, 10½" 60.00
Vase, HP floral, 14x4"...200.00

Merrimac

Founded in 1897 in Newburyport, Massachusetts, the Merrimac Pottery Company primarily produced gardenware. In 1901, however, they introduced a line of artware that is now attracting the interest of collectors. Marked examples carry an impressed die stamp or a paper label, each with the firm name and the outline of a sturgeon, the definition of the Indian word Merrimac. Our advisors for this category are Suzanne Perrault and David Rago; they are listed in the Directory under New Jersey.

Umbrella stand, leathery matt green with tooled and applied leaves, paper label, 22¾x8½", EX, $3,750.00.

Humidor, EX frothy semi-matt gr mottle, 3 sm hdls, 6½x5½", VG 925.00
Vase, cucumber gr w/slight metallic tone, strong finger ridges, 15x11"..3,300.00
Vase, feathered gr matt, bulbous w/shaped bottle neck & hdls, 6¾x6".....800.00
Vase, gr lustre, caramel int, spherical, kiln pop, 3½x4½"............825.00
Vase, gr matt dripping over yel, slightly waisted, 7¾" 1,500.00
Vase, gr w/brn specks, caramel int, ovoid w/flared rim, 11½x5"....2,300.00
Vase, leathery matt gr, shouldered w/hdls, flakes, 4¼x4"............250.00

Metlox

Metlox Potteries was founded in 1927 in Manhattan Beach, California. Before 1934 when they began producing the ceramic housewares for which they have become famous, they made ceramic and neon outdoor advertising signs. The company went out of business in 1989.

Well-known sculptor Carl Romanelli designed artware in the late 1930s and early 1940s (and again briefly in the 1950s). His work is especially sought after today.

Some Provincial dinnerware lines can be confusing. There are two 'rooster' lines, Red Rooster (red, orange, and brown) and California Provincial (dark green and burgundy); and there are three 'homestead' lines, Colonial Heritage (red, orange, and brown like the Red Rooster pieces), Homestead Provincial (dark green and burgundy like California Provincial), and Provincial Blue (blue and white). For further information we recommend *Collector's Encyclopedia of Metlox Potteries, Second Edition*, by our advisor Carl Gibbs, Jr.; he is listed in the Directory under Texas.

Cookie Jars

Apple, Golden Delicious, 9½", from $150 to..............................175.00
Barrel, cookie lid, 11", from $100 to.......................................125.00
Barrel, red apple lid (aka Apple Barrel), 3¾-qt, 11", from $65 to....75.00
Barrel, squirrel & nuts lid, 11", $100 to...................................110.00
Basket, basket lid, wht, from $35 to..45.00
Basket, fruit lid (natural colors), wht, from $40 to.......................50.00
Bear, Beau, from $60 to..75.00
Bear, Circus, from $400 to...450.00
Bear, Panda, w/lollipop, from $400 to......................................450.00
Bear, Panda (w/o lollipop), from $80 to....................................100.00
Bear, Sombrero/Pancho, from $125 to......................................150.00
Bear, Teddy, w/red heart, from $200 to....................................250.00
Bear, Teddy, wht, 3-qt, from $40 to...45.00
Bear, Uncle Sam, minimum value..950.00
Beaver, Bucky, from $125 to...150.00
Calf, Ferdinand, minimum value...900.00
Candy Girl, 9", from $275 to...300.00
Chicken, Mother Hen, wht, from $100 to..................................125.00
Cookie Boy, 9", from $275 to..300.00
Cow, Purple, pk flowers/butterfly, yel bell, from $425 to.............450.00
Debutante, minimum value...400.00
Dog, Bassett, from $325 to...350.00
Dog, Fido, cream, from $150 to...175.00
Duck, Puddles, yel or wht raincoat, from $75 to.........................100.00
Dutch Girl, minimum value...350.00
Egg Basket, from $175 to...200.00
Grape, from $200 to..250.00
Hen, bl, from $250 to..300.00
Hippo, Bubbles, yel & gr, minimum value 350.00
Humpty Dumpty, seated w/ft, from $250 to 275.00
Kangaroo, 11¼", minimum value...1,000.00
Lighthouse, from $275 to...300.00
Lion, yel, 2-qt, from $150 to...175.00
Loveland, from $65 to...75.00
Mammy Cook, yel, from $425 to...450.00
Merry Go Round, from $250 to...275.00
Miller's Sack, from $50 to..75.00
Mother Goose, from $225 to...250.00
Mouse, Chef Pierre, from $75 to..100.00
Mouse Mobile, bsk, from $75 to..100.00
Mushroom Cottage, from $225 to..250.00
Orange, 3½-qt, from $90 to..100.00
Pear, from $125 to..150.00
Pelican, Salty, from $200 to..225.00
Pig, Little Piggy, bsk or plain wht, 3-qt, ea from $90 to...............100.00
Pig, Slenderella, from $125 to...150.00
Pineapple, 3¾-qt, from $75 to..100.00
Pinecone, squirrel on lid, glazed, 11", from $100 to....................125.00

Pretty Anne, 2½-qt, from $175 to................................200.00
Pumpkin, stem on lid, from $150 to.............................175.00
Rabbit, Easter Bunny, solid chocolate, minimum value.........350.00
Raccoon, Cookie Bandit, bsk, from $125 to.....................150.00
Raccoon, Cookie Bandit, glazed, from $175 to..................200.00
Rag Doll, girl, from $175 to..................................200.00
Rex-Tyrannosaurus Rex, French Blue or yel, ea from $150 to.....175.00
Santa Head, from $350 to......................................375.00
Schoolhouse (The Little Country Schoolhouse), 11", minimum value....400.00
Strawberry, 3½-qt, 9½", from $85 to............................95.00
Stump, owls on lid, glazed, from $100 to......................125.00
Whale, wht, from $300 to......................................350.00
Woodpecker on Acorn, 3-qt, from $375 to.......................400.00

Dinnerware

California Apple, bowl, salad; 11¼", from $65 to...............70.00
California Apple, butter dish, from $45 to.....................50.00
California Apple, cup, 6-oz, from $10 to.......................11.00
California Apple, mug, 7-oz, from $23 to.......................25.00
California Apple, platter, oval, 13", from $35 to..............40.00
California Apple, saucer, 6", from $3.50 to.....................4.00
California Fruit, bowl, vegetable; 9", from $32 to.............36.00
California Fruit, celery dish, from $32 to.....................36.00
California Fruit, coaster, 3¾", from $18 to....................20.00
California Fruit, cream soup, from $23 to......................25.00
California Fruit, egg cup, from $28 to.........................30.00
California Fruit, plate, salad; 8", from $10 to................12.00
California Golden Blossom, butter dish, from $70 to............75.00
California Golden Blossom, creamer, from $32 to................35.00
California Golden Blossom, jam & jelly, from $60 to............65.00
California Golden Blossom, plate, chop; from $75 to............85.00
California Golden Blossom, plate, salad; from $12 to...........14.00
California Golden Blossom, shakers, salt or pepper, ea from $15 to...16.00
California Provincial, bowl, cereal; 7¼", from $20 to..........22.00
California Provincial, plate, luncheon; 9", from $28 to........30.00
California Provincial, salad fork & spoon set, from $75 to.....80.00
California Provincial, sugar bowl, w/lid, 8-oz, from $35 to....38.00
California Spatterware, bowl, cereal; 6½", from $10 to.........11.00
California Spatterware, butter dish, from $30 to...............32.00
California Spatterware, creamer, 11-oz, from $16 to............18.00
California Spatterware, plate, dinner; 10½", from $9 to........10.00
California Spatterware, platter, 14½", from $25 to.............28.00
Camellia, bowl, fruit; 6⅛", from $12 to........................15.00
Camellia, cup, from $9 to......................................10.00
Camellia, plate, dinner; 10", from $12 to......................15.00
Camellia, plate, luncheon; 9", from $10 to.....................12.00
Camellia, saucer, from $3 to....................................4.00
Camellia, shakers, ea, from $12 to.............................14.00
Central Park, celery dish, from $32 to.........................35.00
Central Park, fruit dish, from $12 to..........................14.00
Central Park, lug soup, from $18 to............................20.00
Central Park, rim soup, from $16 to............................18.00
Chantilly Blue, bowl, cereal; from $13 to......................14.00
Chantilly Blue, cup, from $9 to................................10.00
Chantilly Blue, plate, dinner; from $12 to.....................13.00
Chantilly Blue, platter, oval, lg, from $40 to.................45.00
Chantilly Blue, saucer, from $3 to..............................4.00
Colonial Heritage, ashtray, 10", from $30 to...................35.00
Colonial Heritage, bowl, salad; from $75 to....................80.00
Colonial Heritage, canister, tea; w/lid, from $45 to...........50.00
Colonial Heritage, cup, decorated or red, from $10 to..........11.00
Colonial Heritage, platter, oval, lg, from $45 to..............50.00
Golden Fruit, ashtray, 4½", from $14 to........................16.00

Golden Fruit, coaster, 3¾", from $16 to........................18.00
Golden Fruit, cup, 7-oz, from $9 to............................10.00
Golden Fruit, pitcher, 1½-pt, from $35 to......................40.00
Golden Fruit, plate, salad; 7½", from $9 to....................10.00
Golden Fruit, saucer, 6¼", from $3 to...........................4.00
Grape Arbor, bowl, cereal; 7⅜", from $14 to....................16.00
Grape Arbor, plate, bread & butter; 6⅜", from $9 to............10.00
Grape Arbor, salad fork & spoon set, from $55 to...............60.00
Happy Time, bowl, soup; 8", from $28 to........................30.00
Happy Time, bread server, 9½", from $75 to.....................80.00
Happy Time, egg cup, from $40 to...............................45.00
Happy Time, gravy, 1-pt, from $45 to...........................50.00
Happy Time, plate, dinner; 10", from $18 to....................20.00
Happy Time, platter, oval, 13½", from $55 to...................60.00
Homestead Provincial, ashtray, 8¼", from $28 to................30.00
Homestead Provincial, bowl, vegetable; divided rectangle, 12", $65 to....70.00
Homestead Provincial, candle holder, ea from $55 to............60.00
Homestead Provincial, lug soup, 5", from $32 to................35.00
Homestead Provincial, plate, salad; 7½", from $14 to...........15.00
Indian Summer, celery dish, from $32 to........................35.00
Indian Summer, cup, from $9 to.................................10.00
Indian Summer, plate, dinner; from $11 to......................12.00
Indian Summer, saucer, from $2 to...............................3.00
Indian Summer, tumbler, from $28 to............................30.00
Jamestown, bowl, cereal; from $11 to...........................12.00
Jamestown, egg cup, from $20 to................................22.00
Jamestown, pitcher, lg, from $60 to............................65.00
Jamestown, plate, dinner; from $11 to..........................12.00
Jamestown, plate, salad; from $8 to.............................9.00
Jamestown, sauce boat, from $45 to.............................50.00
Jamestown, soup tureen, w/lid, from $275 to...................300.00
Jamestown, tray, 3-tier, from $70 to...........................80.00
Provincial Blue, bowl, cereal; 7¼", from $20 to................22.00
Provincial Blue, canister, coffee; w/lid, from $75 to..........80.00
Provincial Blue, canister, sugar; w/lid, from $85 to...........90.00
Provincial Blue, creamer, 6-oz, from $30 to....................32.00
Provincial Blue, cruet, oil; w/lid, 7-oz, from $42 to..........45.00
Provincial Blue, plate, bread & butter; 6⅜", from $10 to.......11.00
Provincial Blue, platter, 13½" oval, from $55 to...............60.00
Provincial Rose, bowl, vegetable; rnd, med, from $40 to........45.00
Provincial Rose, bread server, from $55 to.....................60.00
Provincial Rose, mug, 8-oz, from $18 to........................20.00
Provincial Rose, plate, bread & butter; from $7 to..............8.00
Provincial Rose, salad fork & spoon set, from $50 to...........55.00
Red Rooster, pitcher, 1-qt, from $55 to........................65.00
Red Rooster, plate, luncheon; 9", from $22 to..................25.00
Red Rooster, plate, salad; 7½", from $10 to....................12.00
Rooster Bleu, butter dish, from $50 to.........................55.00
Rooster Bleu, creamer, 6-oz, from $20 to.......................22.00
Rooster Bleu, plate, dinner; 10½", from $12 to.................13.00
Rooster Bleu, sugar bowl, w/lid, 8-oz, from $22 to.............25.00
Rooster Bleu, teapot, w/lid, 6-cup, from $90 to...............100.00
Sculptured Daisy, casserole, w/lid, 1½-qt, from $85 to.........90.00
Sculptured Daisy, plate, dinner; 10½", from $12 to.............13.00
Sculptured Daisy, plate, salad; 7½", from $9 to................10.00
Sculptured Daisy, shakers, salt or pepper; ea from $12 to......13.00
Sculptured Daisy, tumbler, 11-oz, from $32 to..................35.00
Shoreline, bowl, salad; from $75 to............................75.00
Shoreline, bowl, vegetable; from $35 to........................40.00
Shoreline, pitcher, from $65 to................................70.00
Shoreline, plate, bread & butter, from $8 to....................9.00
Vernon Antiqua, baker, oval, 12⅛", from $45 to.................50.00
Vernon Antiqua, platter, oval, 9⅝", from $35 to................40.00
Vintage Pink, bowl, salad; 12⅛", from $70 to...................75.00

Vintage Pink, coffeepot, w/lid, 8-cup, from $90 to 100.00
Vintage Pink, creamer, 10-oz, from $25 to 28.00
Vintage Pink, mug, 8-oz, from $22 to 25.00
Vintage Pink, plate, dinner; 10½", from $14 to 15.00
Woodland Gold, bowl, salad; 11", from $65 to............................70.00
Woodland Gold, lug soup, 6¾", from $20 to..............................22.00
Woodland Gold, pitcher, 1½-pt, from $40 to.............................45.00

Disney Figurines

Alice in Wonderland, from $350 to 400.00
Bambi, jumbo, from $1,000 to...1,500.00
Cinderella (formal), from $400 to 450.00
Cinderella (peasant), from $450 to 500.00
Donald Duck, José or Panchito (Caballeros), ea from $325 to....350.00
Donald Duck w/guitar, from $275 to 300.00
Dwarf (Snow White), any, from $200 to...............................250.00
Figaro, mini, 1¼", from $175 to.......................................225.00
Figaro (Pinocchio), any position, from $175 to 225.00
Hippo (Fantasia), from $325 to 400.00
Jiminy Cricket, from $550 to 600.00
Jock (Lady & the Tramp), miniature, 1¾", from $200 to...........250.00
Mamma Mouse (Cinderella), from $175 to............................200.00
Owl (Bambi), from $175 to 200.00
Prince Charming, from $350 to 400.00
Scamp Pup (Lady & the Tramp), mini, ¾", from $200 to...........250.00
Snow White, #220, from $425 to 500.00
Three Little Pigs, miniature, 1¼", ea from $150 to 200.00
Tinker Bell, from $450 to 500.00
Unicorn (Fantasia), from $250 to......................................325.00
White Rabbit (Alice in Wonderland), from $250 to..................275.00

Miniatures

Alligator, 9", from $150 to 200.00
Caterpillar, from $100 to..140.00
Chimpanzee sitting, 3½", from $100 to................................140.00
Elephant sitting, 3¾", from $125 to 175.00
Fawn, 5½", from $50 to 80.00
Giraffe, 5¾", from $100 to 140.00
Goose, 5", from $40 to 60.00
Jack/Donkey, 3", ea from $50 to..80.00
Penguin, 3", from $40 to 60.00
Turtle standing, from $175 to 225.00

Nostalgia Line

Reminiscent of the late nineteenth and early twentieth centuries, the Nostalgia line contained models of locomotives, gramophones, early autos, stagecoaches, and baby carriages. There were also wagons and carts pulled by horses or donkeys, sometimes with separate drivers and passengers. The line was produced from the late 1940s through the 1960s.

American Royal Horse, colt, prone, 4¼x3", from $90 to 100.00
Cadillac, from $75 to..85.00
Dobbin, 11x9", from $150 to 160.00
Locomotive, from $60 to 65.00
Mail Wagon, from $70 to 80.00
Mary Jane, from $65 to 70.00
Old Cannon, from $50 to 55.00
Pony Cart, from $55 to 60.00
Train set, 3-pc, from $150 to 165.00
Vanderbilt Sleigh, 9", from $65 to 70.00

Poppets

From the mid-'60s through the mid-'70s, Metlox produced a line of 'Poppets,' eighty-eight in all, representing characters ranging from royalty and professionals to a Salvation Army group. They came with a name tag; some had paper labels, others backstamps.

Alaskan Girl, 5", from $40 to...50.00
Arnie, w/4" bowl, from $60 to...70.00
Betsy, goose girl, 8½", from $60 to....................................70.00
Cigar Store Indian, 8¾", from $55 to.................................65.00
Elizabeth (Queen), from $45 to.......................................55.00
Jackie, choir boy #3, from $45 to.....................................55.00
Kitty, sm girl, 6⅝", from $40 to.......................................50.00
Louisa, girl w/muff, 8½", from $45 to................................55.00
Mother Nature, 6¾", from $60 to.....................................70.00
Ronnie, choir boy #2, from $45 to....................................55.00
Zelda, choral lady #2, 7⅝", from $75 to 85.00

Romanelli Artware

Bookends, 7", pr, from $275 to..325.00
Bud vase, Indian woman, 7", minimum value........................500.00
Fan vase, 13½", from $425 to 500.00

Flower holder, Dancing Girl, #1806, 10", from $250.00 to $275.00.

(Photo courtesy Carl Gibbs, Jr.)

Flower holder, Ubangi, 8", from $250 to 275.00
Incense burner, Confucius, 6", from $275 to 325.00
Mug, Pearl Harbor, from $100 to 125.00
Vase, Tropical Fish, 8½", from $75 to..................................90.00
Wall plaque, Prancing Horse, 15", from $325 to........................375.00

Mettlach

In 1836 Nicholas Villeroy and Eugene Francis Boch, both of whom were already involved in the potting industry, formed a partnership and established a stoneware factory in an old restored abbey in Mettlach, Germany. Decorative stoneware with in-mold relief was their specialty, steins in particular. Through constant experimentation, they developed innovative methods of decoration. One process, called chromolith, involved inlaying colorful mosaic designs into the body of the ware. Later underglaze printing from copper plates was used. Their stoneware was of high quality, and their steins won many medals at the St. Louis Expo and early world's fairs. Most examples are marked with an incised castle and the name 'Mettlach.' The numbering system indicates size, date, stock number, and decorator. Production was halted by a fire in 1921; the factory was not rebuilt.

Key:
L — liter   PUG — print under glaze
POG — print over glaze   tl — thumb lift

#485, stein, relief: musical scene, parian, inlaid lid, .5L 375.00
#1108, plaque, etch/HP: castle w/floral & bird, 17" 1,150.00
#1211, basket, etch/glazed: repeating design, SP lid, 4" 185.00
#1221, stein, mosaic: repeating design, inlaid lid, 1.5L.............865.00
#1294, plaque, threading/glazed: floral, 17½", EX 350.00
#1455, stein, glazed relief: repeating design, inlaid lid, 1.4L........460.00
#1471, stein, etch: musicians, inlaid lid, Warth, .5L...................450.00
#1526, stein, HP: student society, eagle tl, 1912, 2L...................660.00
#1526, stein, PUG: fox w/duck transfer, fox pewter lid, .5L 375.00
#1526/1078, stein, PUG: cavalier, sgn Schlitt, .5L...................220.00
#1666, vase, etch/glazed: repeating design, 3-ftd, 5½" 400.00
#1742, stein, etch: Gottingen, 2 students, inlaid lid, Warth, .5L...660.00
#1786, stein, etch/glazed: St Florian, dragon hdl, pewter lid, .5L ..625.00
#1818, stein, etch/relief: man drinking at bbl, pewter lid, 6.2L ..1,500.00
#1861, stein, etch/PUG: Kaiser Frederick, SP lid, .5L...............275.00
#1888, punch bowl, relief: Prussian eagle, orig lid, 6L 800.00
#1890, stein, etch/PUG: Wilhelm I, Wilhelm II, Frederick III, .5L.......660.00
#1909, stein, PUG: Schonblick custom transfer, pewter lid, .4L, NM...250.00
#1915, stein, etch/PUG: Colner Dom Cathedral in Koln, .5L ...1,950.00
#1932, stein, etch: cavaliers toasting, inlaid lid, Warth, .5L........400.00
#1947, stein, etch: man seated in vines, inlaid lid, .5L................380.00
#1998, stein, etch: Trumpeter of Sackingen, castle lid, .5L 465.00
#2001B, stein, etch/relief: medicine, inlaid lid, 5.L, NM.............435.00
#2001F, stein, etch/relief: architecture, inlaid lid, .5L, NM 400.00
#2018, stein, pug dog character, inlaid lid, .5L.........................735.00
#2024, stein, etch/glazed: Berlin, inlaid lid, .5L 835.00
#2036, stein, owl character, inlaid lid (rpr), .5L........................350.00
#2078, plaque, etch: military Ulan, Stocke, 15" 1,150.00
#2082, stein, etch: Wm Tell shooting, inlaid lid, .5L 1,000.00
#2089, stein, etch: Story of Schlaraffenland, inlaid lid, Schlitt, .5L....635.00
#2093, stein, etch/glazed: cards, inlaid lid, .5L 925.00
#2100, stein, etch: Germans meeting Romans, Schlitt, .5L 925.00
#2150, pokal, relief: drinking scenes, castle lid, 23" 775.00
#2178/956, stein, PUG: dwarfs pull bbl, pewter lid, 2.5L, NM ...375.00
#2204, stein, etch/relief: Prussian eagle, inlaid lid, .5L 515.00
#2231, stein, etch: cavaliers drinking, inlaid lid, .5L 415.00
#2277, stein, etch: Burn Nurnberg, inlaid lid, .5L 435.00
#2282, stein, etch: man caught in cellar, inlaid lid, .5L...............485.00
#2299, vase, etch/relief: young girls, 11½" 460.00
#2327/1302, beaker, PUG: Am eagle/flag/monuments, .25L.......350.00
#2327/427, beaker, PUG: Brandenburger Tor, .3L 215.00
#2328, vase, etch: ladies & cherubs, Etruscan, 13½" 485.00
#2402, stein, etch: Siegfried, inlaid lid, .5L................................715.00
#2435, vase, etch: Nouveau floral, 4" 635.00
#2441, stein, etch: man playing dice, barmaid tl, Quidemus, .5L ..485.00
#2462, vase, etch: Art Nouveau, sculpted body, 5x7".................800.00
#2486, pitcher, etch: swan, Eckmann, 8" 1,380.00
#2531, stein, etch: man drinks in house, barmaid tl, .5L 575.00
#2580, stein, etch: Die Kannenburg, festive scene, Schlitt, .5L ..800.00
#2585, stein, etch/relief: Munich child on globe, inlaid lid, .5L....475.00
#2599, stein, etch: festival scenes, inlaid lid, Quidenus, 1L.........750.00
#2684, beer tap, etch: drinking scene at castle, 25".................1,850.00
#2706/6113, vase, man smoking while reading, Rookwood, 12½"....600.00
#2706/6114, vase, lady playing violin, Rookwood, 12½" 1,095.00
#2748, plaque, HP/relief: castle on hilltop, 12½x18", EX 450.00
#2776, stein, etch: man in cellar, inlaid lid, .5L..........................665.00
#2785, stein, man playing bagpipe, pewter lid, Rookwood, 2.2L ...700.00
#2976, vase, etch: Art Nouveau, rare gr, 14½" 835.00
#3005, stein, etch: man stands w/beer glass, pewter lid, Ringer, .5L...500.00
#3043, stein, etch/glazed: Munchen, inlaid lid, .5L 1,725.00

#3142, stein, etch: Ober Bayern, inlaid lid, .5L 460.00
#3143, stein, etch: Tirol, eagle inlaid lid, .5L............................865.00
#3144, stein, etch: Schwarzwald, inlaid lid, Quidenus, .5L 950.00
#3173, stein, etch: man & lady, inlaid lid, Hohlwein, .5L...........925.00
#3177, stein, cameo: hunting scenes, inlaid lid, Stahl, 2.2L 2,185.00
#3249, stein, etch: hikers at table, inlaid lid, .5L.......................430.00
#3250, stein, etch: people eating, inlaid lid, barmaid tl, .5L........515.00
#3264, vase, cameo: lady w/dog, Stahl, 7½"...............................295.00
#3327, beaker, etch: cavalier serenades lady, .3L........................375.00

Microscopes

The microscope has taken on many forms during its 250-year evolutionary period. The current collectors' market primarily includes examples from England, surplus items from institutions, and continental beginner and intermediate forms which sold through Sears Roebuck & Company and other retailers of technical instruments. Earlier examples have brass main tubes which are unpainted. Later, more common examples are all black with brass or silver knobs and horseshoe-shaped bases. Early and more complex forms are the most valuable; these always had hardwood cases to house the delicate instruments and their accessories. Instruments were never polished during use, and those that have been polished to use as decorator pieces are of little interest to most avid collectors.

Bausch & Lomb, 3 objectives, many accessories, 1930s, MIB 175.00
E Leitz, brass, 3-power turret, 4 eyepcs, 13¾", EX in case 515.00
Lionel-Portre Microcraft Lab-Master #22050, 1960, complete set, MIB ..110.00
Seibert, brass, monocular, ca 1876, 12", EXIB 1,500.00
Seibert Wetzlar, brass, compound platform, accessories, NM 700.00
Spencer CENCO USA, eyepc mk B&L Opt Co USA, dbl turret, portable, 11" 175.00
Taxco 1200X, filter lens wheel, w/slides & covers, early, EX in case ..95.00
Watson & Sons, 2 lenses, revolving turret, 1931, EX 675.00
Watson & Sons Kima, monocular, 1949, 14", MIB w/booklet 215.00

Midwestern Glass

As early as 1814, blown glass was made in Ohio. By 1835 glasshouses in Michigan were producing similar pattern-molded types that have long been highly regarded by collectors. During the latter part of the nineteenth century, all six of the states of the Northwest Territory were mass producing the pressed-glass tableware patterns that were then in vogue. Various types of art glass were produced in the area until after the turn of the century. Items listed here are attributed to the Midwest by certain physical characteristics known to be indigenous to that part of the country. See also Findlay Onyx; Greentown Glass; Libbey; Zanesville Glass. Our advisor for this category is Mark Vuono; he is listed in the Directory under Connecticut.

Bottle, aqua, 22 swirled ribs, flared lip, 5" 550.00
Bottle, club; bl aqua, 16 vertical ribs, stain, 8"............................160.00
Bottle, club; bl aqua, 23 right-swirl ribs, 8⅛".............................190.00
Bottle, golden yel amber, 14 swirled ribs, globular, 8⅜" 900.00
Bottle, med amber, globular, pontil scar, 8⅛".............................500.00
Bottle, med amber, 24 broken swirled ribs, globular, appl hdl, 6⅝"..23,000.00
Flask, chestnut; lt gr, 16 vertical melon ribs, flared lip, 5¾" 275.00
Flask, med pk-amethyst, 16 molded ribs, 7¾".............................300.00
Flask, pitkin; med gr w/yel tone, 16 broken right-swirl ribs, 6" ...700.00
Pan, golden yel amber, 16 ribs, folded rim, wear, 5½" dia........6,000.00

Militaria

Because of the wide and varied scope of items available to collectors of militaria, most tend to concentrate mainly on the area or areas that interest them most or that they can afford to buy. Some items represent a major investment and because of their value have been reproduced. Extreme caution should be used when purchasing Nazi items. Every badge, medal, cap, uniform, dagger, and sword that Nazi Germany issued is being reproduced today. Some repros are crude and easily identified as fakes, while others are very well done and difficult to recognize as reproductions. Purchases from WWII veterans are usually your safest buys. Reputable dealers or collectors will normally offer a money-back guarantee on Nazi items purchased from them. There are a number of excellent Third Reich reference books available in bookstores at very reasonable prices. Study them to avoid losing a much larger sum spent on a reproduction. Our advisor for this category is Ron L. Willis; he is listed in the Directory under Florida.

Key: insg — insignia

Imperial German

Badge, wound; brass base metal w/poor blk finish, G.....................25.00
Book, Ran an den Feind, Waldener, 1915, EX 22.50
Booklet, Vaterlands Lieder, patriotic songs, 1914, rpr.....................25.00
Buckle, Prussian enlisted, gray metal, brn leather tab dtd 1916, EX 27.50
Buckle, Prussian enlisted, nickel inset on brass, Gott Mit Uns, EX 35.00
Cover, spike helmet; enlisted, field gray cotton, worn 75.00
Dress tunic, dk bl wool twill, red color, Swedish pattern, EX 80.00
Drum hanger, Prussian Army bandsman's, brass eagle w/swivel, EX 35.00
Epaulettes, Prussian, red wool w/blk/silver lace/brass crescents, pr.....135.00
Field glasses, Army, gray eyepcs, G optics, blk finish, EX 35.00
Helmet, spike; Baden Artillery enlisted, ball spike finial, 1915, EX....700.00
Helmet, spike; Bavarian enlisted, pressed felt, frontispiece, EX ..800.00
Helmet, spike; Wurttemburg Ersatz, thin metal body, frontispiece, EX ...700.00
Identification disk, Infantryman, 1916 pattern, gray metal, EX ..100.00
Locket, blk 1914 Iron Cross & laurel wreath on silver 35.00
Manual, Der Einjahrig Freiwillige der Infanterie, Dilthen, 1915, EX....35.00
Manual, Dienstunterricht Fur Verkehrstruppen, 1918, EX 45.00
Medal, Prussian Life Saving, silver, w/ribbon, EX 155.00
Postcard, Bismarck commemorative, portrait, Nat'l colored border, EX....20.00
Shoulderboards, Bavarian Technical officer, silver on red wool, pr..35.00

Third Reich

Badge, Navy Artillery Mechanic Specialty, yel embr on bl wool ..25.00
Badge, Navy Submarine Combat, gray metal, solid bk 190.00
Badge, SA Sports for Wounded Personnel, bronzed metal, narrow sword...425.00
Badge, 1935 Party Day, bronzed metal..25.00
Book, Blitzkreig, Deighton, 1980, EX..27.50
Booklet, Official German-French Army Language, pocket sz........25.00
Bookplate, EX Libris, eagle/swastika, 1938, EX 25.00
Bread bag, Army, olive khaki canvas w/brn leather, VG 27.50
Cap, side; Army Eastern, field gray cotton w/bl piping, dtd 1944...300.00

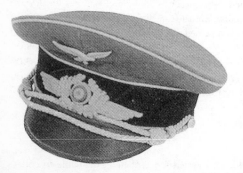

Cap, Luftwaffe officer's, peaked style with yellow piping, aluminum eagle, and cockade, VG, $400.00. (Photo courtesy Julia's Auction Co., Fairfield, Maine)

Collar tabs, Aserbeidshanian Foreign Volunteer, pr.....................60.00
Dagger, Army, Eickhorn, NP furniture, compo grip, w/scabbard....250.00
Dagger, Luftwaffe Model 2, SMF mk, gray metal, celluloid grip, EX...200.00
Goggles, Army Ski, metal eye covers, brn leather binding, EX 25.00
Guide, German Army Uniforms & Insignia 1933-35, Davis, c 1977, EX...35.00
Hat, visor; Luftwaffe Flak Artillery, wht cotton crown, EX 500.00
Hat, visor; Veteran Assoc, blk wool, silk brocade band, EX 50.00
Helmet, Army M42 style, field gray, unrolled edge, EX...............135.00
Helmet, Beichswehr Model 1916, worn pnt, VG...........................70.00
Helmet, flight; Luftwaffe, leather, sheepskin liner, EX................150.00
Helmet, Police, eagle/shield, liner, EX blk finish 110.00
Insignia, cap; Army Mtn Troop Edelweiss, gilt & subdued silver ..25.00
Knife, Army close combat; metal cross guard, wooden grips, EX ..75.00
Lanyard, Army Marksmanship, braided silver bullion, w/badge 45.00
Manual, Oertzenscher Taschenkalender, Army officer's, EX........45.00
Manual, 1931 Flotten Kalender, chart of navies, EX 25.00
Membership pin, Veterans Assoc, pierced silver w/swastika/sword/wreath 25.00
Photograph, Luftwaffe press, Army soldiers digging in mud 20.00
Propaganda leaflet, Sucker You Believed It..., for Am troops 40.00
Publication, Der Weltkrieg, Pixberg, youth propaganda, 1930s, EX ...25.00
Scope, sighting; Field Artillery, rubber eyepc, gray finish, EX.....400.00
Shoulderboards, Army Paymaster Overlieutenant, wht/dk gr wool....25.00
Stickpin, Maltese cross, blk on wht enamel shield, 1930s era 25.00
Stickpin, NSBO Membership, blk hammer highlights, EX 25.00
Teaspoon, hdl mk w/Luftwaffe eagle 20.00

Japanese

Art, linen w/HP Oriental lady's portrait, WWII Occupation era, 16" sq..100.00
Art, parachute silk, lady w/flute & cherry blossoms, 1950s, 38x27"....300.00
Badge, pilot's wings, embr silver & yel on bl wool, WWII era 60.00
Bank note, $10 denomination, WWII Philippine occupation, EX ..20.00
Bank notes, WWII occupation, rupees & shillings, lot of 5 ....25.00
Bayonet, Arisaka, hooked quillon, shaped grips & pommel, WWII era....75.00
Bayonet, Arisaka type 30, Toyada Automatic Loom Wks, WWII era, EX ...100.00
Booklet, identity; character inscription, WWII era, EX 25.00
Bowl, blk lacquer w/silver Army star & red border, WWII era......50.00
Bowl, mess; Army, wht porc w/gr star, WWII era.........................35.00
Dagger, age blemishes, WWII era, 12½", w/resting scabbard 145.00
Flag, Navy Vice Admiral, red & wht cotton, rising sun, WWII, 102x62"....715.00
Flag, red ball on wht silk, WWII, 36x25", EX 35.00
Goggles, pilot's, aluminum fr, velvet padding, WWII era, G.......200.00
Helmet cover, Army, khaki canvas w/yel 5-pointed star, WWII era, EX..125.00
Medal, Red Cross, silver w/ribbon, WWII era..............................20.00
Rifle grenade, hollow charge fitted w/finned tail stabilizer, WWII era...175.00
Tray, blk lacquer papier-mâché w/rising sun flag, WWII era, 6¾" sq.....80.00
Tray, blk lacquer w/cherry blossoms & rising sun, WWII era, 8½" sq....125.00

Russian/Soviet

Amulet, silver, eagle on gold oak leaf, Imperial Era, ca 1900, EX..450.00
Badge, KGB Border Guard officer, gr/red on gilt metal, 1979, EX ...25.00
Badge, Naval Aviator's wings, red enamel on gilt, 1980s...............25.00
Book, identification, bl cover w/gilt, unissued, EX........................20.00
Calendar book, English language propaganda, WWII era, 1945, EX...25.00
Cannon, brass model of Peter the Great's, ca 1890, 9x7x5", EX....300.00
Cap, side; Marine enlisted, blk wool w/red enamel star insg, 1990..25.00
Dagger, dbl-sided blade, eng star/hammer/sickle, Kremlin motif, 1957..150.00
Hat, Army, gray wool w/fur flaps & visor, ca 1980, EX.................50.00
Hat, Navy enlisted, blk wool w/gilt/enameled star, 1980s.............40.00
Hat, Navy enlisted, blk wool w/red star & gilt ship tally, 1980 ....45.00
Hat, Papakha, Army, gray fur w/gold/enamel officer's star insg...55.00
Hat, visor; Air Force officer, bl w/gold wreath/cord, 1980s..........50.00
Hat, visor; Naval Forces officer, blk twill w/gold wreath, 1980s....65.00

Hat, visor; Security Forces officer, gray twill w/red piping, 1980s..**55.00**

Helmet, Army, NM gr finish, fabric liner, leather strap, 1960s......**40.00**

Helmet, Ballistic, titanium w/nylon cover, ca 1991, NM **600.00**

Helmet, Tank Crew, padded blk cotton w/fleece lining, complete, soiled ..**35.00**

Medal, Campaign (against Sweden), silver, Czar's portrait, 1711, EX....**725.00**

Medal, Liberation of Prague, gilt bronze, w/ribbon, WWII era......**40.00**

Medal, 20th Anniversary of WWII, bimetal, w/ribbon, EX...........**20.00**

Medallion, Czar Nicholas II commemorative, bronze, emb portrait, EX **30.00**

Medallion, War of 1812 commemorative, bronze, dtd 1834........**150.00**

Medallion, 1000 Yr commemorative, bronze, Alexander II, EX....**35.00**

Painting, Joseph Stalin, oil on canvas, sgn/dtd 1954, 25½x22" ..**700.00**

Ring, silver w/eagle, bl enamel field w/silver border, ca 1910, EX **275.00**

Wall hanging, Lenin on red wool w/patriotic borders, 1987, 51x35" ..**90.00**

United States

Badge, AAF Senior, cloth wings, wht embr on khaki wool, unissued WWII...**20.00**

Badge, Air Force Good Conduct, bronze, w/ribbon, mini, NM.....**10.00**

Badge, Army Military Police, silvered eagle & shield, Vietnam War era....**35.00**

Badge, Expert Infantryman, bl enamel on sterling, EX **20.00**

Badge, Expert Qualification Rifle, bars, Sterling hallmk, EX **10.00**

Badge, Marine Rifle Sharpshooter, silvered metal, Korean War era, EX ...**35.00**

Belt, cartridge; Cavalry NY Militia, webbed, sword clip, 1890s, EX....**285.00**

Belt ensemble, Army officer, brn leather, brass fittings, dtd 1923, EX...**35.00**

Book, Civil War in Song & Story, F Moore, emb cover, 1889, G....**20.00**

Book, Employment of Tanks w/Infantry, US War Dept, 1944, EX...**32.50**

Boots, Cavalry, brn leather w/pull-on tabs, WWI era, pr, EX **95.00**

Breeches, Army, mtn pattern, khaki cotton, 1920s era, EX...........**25.00**

Canteen, Civil War 1858 model, orig wool cover, tin spout, 10" ..**3,575.00**

Canteen, Confederate Civil War era, cedar wood w/steel bands, 8" dia..**1,650.00**

Canteen, wood drum w/pnt finish, War of 1812 era, 7" dia, EX....**785.00**

Cap, overseas; Army enlisted; dk khaki wool twill, WWII, EX.....**15.00**

Cap, overseas; Artillery enlisted, khaki w/red piping, 1920s pattern....**25.00**

Cap, side; Army Infantry enlisted, folding, khaki wool, WWII, EX.....**25.00**

Cartoon book, Komic Kartoons, Life in the Army, Poley, WWI era, rare ..**35.00**

Coat, Indian War officer, blk bear fur, dbl-breasted, 1880s, EX...**550.00**

Coat, trench; Army officer, khaki twill, dbl-breasted, WWII era, EX...**35.00**

Epaulettes, Infantry enlisted, 1851 pattern, wht wool, pr, EX **115.00**

Epaulettes, Military Captain, gold braid & crescent, ca 1870, pr, EX....**425.00**

Flight suit, AAF, heated, 1-pc coverall, khaki twill, WWII era, EX....**135.00**

Gas mask, Army, khaki canvas, flap closure, WWI era, EX...........**35.00**

Hat, visor; Model 1910, khaki wool, bronze eagle buttons, WWI, EX..**65.00**

Helmet, Army, camo, felt padding, WWI, EX.............................**65.00**

Helmet, coast artillery, camo, insg/liner, British made, WWI, rare, EX...**185.00**

Helmet, field artillery; khaki finish, insg/liner, WWI era, EX **170.00**

Helmet, jet pilot; wht w/chartreuse traces, Korean War era, EX ...**95.00**

Helmet, Shako, blk leather w/brass trim, eagle insg, EX..............**465.00**

Insignia, cap; Tank Corps officer, bronze, WWI era, sm, scarce **50.00**

Insignia, hat; Artillery, gilt brass, Xd cannons, ca 1902, EX..........**25.00**

Insignia, shoulder; Artillery Pioneer, red Xd axes on bl, 1880s, EX....**25.00**

Leaflet, dropped on German forces, safe conduct/etc, WWII era, VG.....**20.00**

Life belt, Army & Navy, inflatable rubberized cotton, 1944, EX...**25.00**

Manual, US Army, Interior Guard Duty, 1914, EX.......................**22.00**

Map, escape; AAF, silk, Japan/S China sea, WWII era, EX...........**25.00**

Medal, American Defense, bronze, w/ribbon, WWII era, EX........**15.00**

Medal, NY Nat'l Guard, gilt cross/Xd rifles/wreath, Indian War era **75.00**

Medal, Selective Service, bronze w/eagle, ribbon bar, M in case...**20.00**

Medal, Veteran Assoc, bronze, Spanish-American era, frayed ribbon...**25.00**

Medal, Vietnam Service, bronze, w/worn ribbon, VG **10.00**

Model, Army amphibious landing vehicle, wood w/khaki pnt, 1945, 15"..**45.00**

Overcoat, Aero officer, khaki wool, dbl-breasted, WWI era, EX...**185.00**

Saddle cloth, Marine Corps officer, khaki canvas, WWI era, EX ..**575.00**

Sash, Civil War Union officer, red silk, fringed tassels, EX **355.00**

Sleeping bag, Army, khaki cotton, down filled, WWII era, EX.....**30.00**

Snare drum, Civil War era, eagle/flags/etc, 14" dia, EX............**1,150.00**

Statue, Gen Eisenhower, gold-pnt plaster, WWII era, 5¼" **50.00**

Straps, shoulder; Army Medical Captain, embr on blk wool, 1960s, EX........**10.00**

Tunic, Army M1017, 4-pocket, khaki wool, WWI era, G **25.00**

Tunic, Navy, khaki cotton, roll collar, gold buttons, WWII era, EX **35.00**

Uniform, field artillery; khaki wool, bronze buttons, WWI era, EX....**150.00**

Miscellaneous

Austria, knife, trench; str crossguard, wood hdl, WWI era, w/scabbard....**125.00**

Austria, medal, Eritrea Campaign, bronze, w/ribbon, ca 1896, EX ..**35.00**

Austria, model, Howitzer, Austrian Skoda Works, WWI era, 10" L...**300.00**

Belgium, cap, side; khaki wool, dk bl braid, red band, folds, WWI **50.00**

Belgium, medal, Order of Industry & Agriculture, bronze, WWII era ..**20.00**

Britain, badge, lapel; Air Raid Protection, sterling, WWII era......**20.00**

Britain, badge, RAF Pilot's wings, khaki w/brn wreath on bl, WWII....**50.00**

Britain, book, British Battles & Medals, Gordon, 1979, EX..........**25.00**

Britain, hat, visor; RAF, bl-gray wool w/blk lacquered visor, 1962, NM ..**25.00**

Britain, helmet, Army, VG khaki finish, liner, WWI era, EX **125.00**

Britain, helmet; combat; brn camo net over khaki pnt, WWII, G ..**45.00**

Britain, knife bayonet, blued, steel grips, Falklands War era, EX ..**40.00**

Britain, medal, Victory, bronze w/Royal Navy sailor's name, WWI era ...**20.00**

Britain, plaque, bronze, Montgomery emb, lists WWII battles, 4½"....**80.00**

China, badge, pilot's wings, gilt/bl/wht enamel, WWII era, EX ..**200.00**

China, postcard, photo of prisoners in neck stocks, 1920s.............**20.00**

East Germany, helmet, Army, camo cover, w/liner & chin strap, EX ..**25.00**

France, bayonet, Model 1874, wood grips, brass pomel, EX w/scabbard ..**45.00**

France, helmet, Dragoon, brass w/emb eagle, plume, 1840s-50s, EX **865.00**

France, helmet, poor bl finish, no badge, w/top comb, WWI relic ..**10.00**

France, statue, Hussar equestrian bugling, pnt porc, 1950s, 14¼"......**600.00**

France, watercolor, biplane fight scene, Prejelan, 1916, 18x13" fr ..**600.00**

Hungary, medal, Service, bronze, Pro Deo et Patria 1914-18, w/ribbon...**20.00**

Italy, helmet, combat; EX field-gray finish, w/liner & strap, WWII era ...**85.00**

Italy, helmet, G field gray, Fascist insg, torn liner, WWII era........**55.00**

Italy, sleeve shield, Fascist Youth, gray metal device, WWII era ...**32.00**

Poland, hat, visor; khaki wool w/mohair band, 1980s, NM **40.00**

Portugal, helmet, steel M1940, EX gray finish, w/liner & strap, EX.....**70.00**

Serbia, cigarette case, silver, dbl-headed eagle, WWI era, EX.....**130.00**

Spain, bayonet, M1893 Mauser, German manufacture, w/scabbard....**50.00**

Swiss, map scarf, Switzerland, edelweiss border, 25x23"..................**25.00**

Vietnam, medal, Soldier of Honor, Viet Cong 3rd class, gilt/enamel **40.00**

Milk Glass

Milk glass is the current collector's name for milk-white opaque glass. The early glassmaker's term was Opal Ware. Originally attempted in England in the eighteenth century with the intention of imitating china, milk glass was not commercially successful until the mid-1800s. Pieces produced in the U.S.A., England, and France during the 1870 – 1900 period are highly prized for their intricate detail and fiery, opalescent edges.

For further information we recommend *Collector's Encyclopedia of Milk Glass, An Identification & Value Guide,* by Betty and Bill Newbound. (CE numbers in our listings refer to this publication.) Another highly recommended book is *The Milk Glass Book* by Frank Chiarenza and James Slater. The newest reference, published in 2001, is *Milk Glass Imperial Glass Corporation* by Myrna and Bob Garrison. Our advisor for this category is Rod Dockery; he is listed in the Directory under Texas. See also Animal Dishes with Covers; Bread Plates; Historical Glass; Westmoreland.

Key:

B — Belknap	G — Garrison
CE — Newbound	MGB — Milk Glass Book
F — Ferson	

Ashtrays, Trivet set, Imperial, G-1950/450 Pg 131, from $40 to ...**45.00**
Basket, Lace Edge, Imperial, CE-408, 8¾" L, $35 to **40.00**
Bottle, cologne; Hobnail, bulbous, ball stopper, CE-4, 6½", $12 to ...**15.00**
Bottle, Joan of Arc figure, mk Jeanne D'Arc De Pose, F-523, $450 to ..**500.00**
Bowl, emb scroll, serrated rim, Imperial, 1955-60, CE-30, 8½".....**22.00**
Bowl, rib & scroll, w/lid, 4-ftd, Vallerysthal, CE-44, 6½x4½" ...**35.00**
Bowl, seashell w/scalloped rim, 3-ftd, Cambridge, CE-28, 3x4¾"....**50.00**
Box, collar; emb bow at base, convex dome lid, HP florals, CE-46, 8"...**85.00**
Box, dresser; scrolls/HP roses, gold trim, Dithridge, CE-35, $55 to..**65.00**
Butter dish, Beaded Drape/HP florals, Heisey, CE-312, 5½x7½" dia **55.00**
Cake stand, pnt florals/rings, Challinor-Taylor, 1885-93, CE-107, 6"..**35.00**
Candlestick, flared skirt form w/rope hdl, gold trim, CE-64, ea $30 to **35.00**
Candlestick, maple leaf w/finger ring, enameled, CE-68, ea from $40 to....**45.00**
Candlestick, Scroll & Lace, 4-ftd/beaded rim, CE-63, 4½", ea $30 to.....**35.00**
Candy dish, plain w/HP roses on lid, CE-45, 6½" dia, from $25 to..........**30.00**
Clock, draped cherubs on either side, satin, CE-433, 4¼x6½"...**300.00**
Compote, emb grape, scalloped rim, octagonal, Anchor-Hocking, CE-29...**12.00**
Compote, emb grape, scalloped rim & tall ped ft, LE Smith, CE-92 ..**40.00**
Compote, swirled, serrated rim, bl, Vallerysthal-Porteiux, CE-85 ....**35.00**
Cookie jar, Con-cora, tufted, HP leaves/gold, Consolidated, CE-182, 9"..**75.00**
Covered dish, Baby Moses, cattail base, unknown maker, B-160, 6¼"..**250.00**
Creamer, sunflowers on panels, CE-299, 4½", from $30 to **35.00**
Creamer & sugar bowl, emb maple leaf decor, Westmoreland, CE-310, pr ...**30.00**
Decanter, wine; emb grapes, Imperial, G-1950/163, Pg 92 ....**45.00**
Dish, heart; open hearts form rim, Westmoreland, CE-23, 3¾"...**15.00**
Dish, leaf; emb detail, Fenton, CE-339, 11½x10½", from $20 to...**25.00**
Epergne, ribs & scallops, single horn, Vallerysthal/Porteiux, CE-106...**125.00**
Figurine, Chubby Dog, emb neck bow, 5", CE-191, from $35 to ...**40.00**
Figurine, deer standing, Fostoria, CE-195, 4¾" **50.00**
Figurine, rabbit, sitting, solid glass, Mosser Glass, CE-198, 6".......**25.00**
Figurine, swan, open back, pnt bill, LE Smith, 1930s, CE-204, 9"..**40.00**
Goblet, Jewel & Dewdrop, Kemple, CE-218, 6"...........................**22.00**
Humidor, Three Guardsmen (Bulldogs)/pipe, brass lid, CE-181, 6¼"..**350.00**
Jar, cylindrical tufted pattern, lid w/cube finial, CE-59, 8" **35.00**
Jar, fruit; owl form, metal lid w/emb MG eagle on top, F-510, 6½"...**135.00**
Jar, honey; beehive form, 4-ftd, Vallerysthal, CE-55, 5½", $100 to ..**125.00**
Jar, marmalade; pineapple form, w/ladle, Imperial, CE-190, 5¾" ..**40.00**
Jar, strawberry form, red pnt, gr stem, CE-55, 3¾".........................**20.00**
Lamp, chimney; dbl ball globes, crosshatch/HP flowers, CE-236, 7½"..**125.00**
Lamp, chimney; scrolling/crosshatching/emb flowers on ftd base, CE-235..**115.00**
Paperweight, Queen Victoria Bust, MGB-54, 3½" **250.00**
Pitcher, 3 birds on branch/gold trim, bulbous, CE-320, $125 to **150.00**
Planter, emb grape & leaf, oblong, scalloped rim, Fire-King, CE-360 .....**7.00**
Planter, oblong/ftd, emb Old King Cole scene, Sowerby, CE-361.......**125.00**
Plaque, HP roses/raised scrolled gold trim, coupe, CE-259, 10", $25 to ...**30.00**
Plate, H-Circle border, colonial decal, Kemple, CE-263, 7⅝", $20 to ...**25.00**
Plate, lacy heart border, various fish decals, Kemple, CE-262, 6½".......**22.00**
Plate, Pennsylvania Turnpike, MGB-203, 8¼" **100.00**
Plate, scroll & waffle border, plain, McKee, 1800s, CE-258, 7¼" **18.00**
Shakers, wht fleur-de-lis on bl, bulbous, CE-288, 2½", pr, $20 to....**25.00**
Spooner, sunflowers on panels, tapered/flared base, CE-299, 4½" ...**35.00**
Tray, dresser; wagon wheel/scroll/floral rim, gold trim, CE-351, 7x10"...**25.00**
Tray, pin; butterfly form w/gold trim, CE-344, 4½x3½" **12.00**
Vase, hand holding horn shape w/fluted rim, bead trim, CE-375, $45 to..**50.00**
Vase, Regent, HP flowers, ball w/ruffled neck, Consolidated, CE-390 .....**40.00**
Vase, tri-panel, 3-ftd, scalloped rim, bead trim, US Glass, CE-377, 9" **20.00**

Millefiori

Millefiori was a type of art glass produced during the 1800s. Literally the term means 'thousand flowers,' an accurate description of its appearance. Canes, fused bundles of multicolored glass threads such as are often used in paperweights were cut into small cross sections,

arranged in the desired pattern, refired, and shaped into articles such as cruets, lamps, and novelty items. It is still being produced, and many examples found on the market today are fairly recent in manufacture. See also Paperweights.

Boudoir lamp, multicolor, glass base and shade, 13", $300.00.

Bowl, mc flower canes cased in clear, 5-ruffle top, 4x9¾"...........**175.00**
Inkwell/paperweight, red/wht/bl, 6¼", EX.................................**180.00**
Pitcher, mc canes, cased satin int, appl hdl, bulbous, 6½" **275.00**
Salt cellar, mc flower canes in clear, ruffled rim........................**100.00**
Vase, mc flower canes, twisted ruffled rim, hdls, 1890s-1910, 4½" **245.00**

Miniature Portraits

Miniature works of art vary considerably in value depending on many criteria: as with any art form, those that are signed by or can be attributed to a well-known artist may command prices well into the thousands of dollars. Collectors find paintings of identifiable subjects especially interesting, as are those with props, such as a child with a vintage toy or a teddy bear or a soldier in uniform with his weapon at his side. Even if none of these factors come to bear, an example exhibiting fine details and skillful workmanship may bring an exceptional price. Of course, condition is important, and ornate or unusual frames also add value.

Note: When no medium is described, assume the work to be watercolor on ivory; if no signature is mentioned, assume them to be unsigned.

Boy in bl jacket w/banner below, watercolor on paper, 4x3⅛"+fr.....**475.00**
Couple in fine wht attire w/red touches, 6x8"..............................**460.00**
Gentleman, fine attire & detail, 5x4½" **200.00**
Gentleman, oval brass mt, wood fr, 2½x2", VG **175.00**
Gentleman, 2½x2" in leather case **475.00**
Gentleman in wht wig, brn coat w/neck scarf, identified, 5x4½"+fr ..**385.00**
Geo Washington, sgn Sarah Goodridge, 6⅞"+fr **1,850.00**
Geo Washington in dk bl, sgn Gainsborough, 5½" ivory fr.........**300.00**
Girl in pk w/dog, sgn Romney, 4¾" oval brass fr **375.00**
John Barry, sgn H Frost, ca 1830, 5¾"+fr **1,150.00**
Lady, lace bonnet/pearls, 5x4½"+fr **385.00**
Lady, much detail, identified, 5x4½"+fr......................................**475.00**
Lady in bl w/fur collar & much jewelry, 1871, 4¼x4" **300.00**
Lady in wht w/wht wig, sgn Cosway, 3½" brass locket **275.00**
Lady in wht wig w/gold pendant, 5⅝" fr **255.00**
Lady Liberty, watercolor on porc, in 5¼" orig fr.........................**220.00**
Lady w/pearls & flowers in hair, sgn Carriera, in 4¼" fr.............**400.00**

Louis XVI in landscape, 6" cvd ivory fr 260.00
Man's profile, watercolor on paper, matted in 5x5" frame 200.00
Man w/curly hair, 3¼x2⅞" 300.00
Man w/sideburns & cape, in ornate 9" fr...425.00
Medieval lady w/pearls, castle beyond, sgn, 4⅝" fr 230.00
Officer, identified, EX details, on paper, ca 1830s, 5¾x4¾".........440.00
Oliver Cromwell, enamel on copper, after Cooper, 4" ebony fr 350.00
Thomas Sumter, sgn Sarah Goodridge, 6⅜"+fr 1,950.00
Youthful man in military coat, on milk glass, 3½" in cloth case....330.00

Miniatures

There is some confusion as to what should be included in a listing of miniature collectibles. Some feel the only true miniature is the salesman's sample; other collectors consider certain small-scale children's toys to be appropriately referred to as miniatures, while yet others believe a miniature to be any small-scale item that gives evidence to the craftsmanship of its creator. For salesman's samples, see specific category; other types are listed below. See also Dollhouses and Furnishings; Children's Things.

Band box, dk bl & gr scrolled wallpaper, 2¼x3½" 525.00
Blanket chest, pine Chpndl style, dvtl, 20th C, 10x17x9" 165.00
Blanket chest, walnut/pine/poplar, dvtl, rfn/rstr, 14x18x11½" 880.00
Box, domed top, pine w/orig mc flowers on wht, 2⅝x4¼x2½" ..440.00
Bucket, staved tin bands, wire bail, old mustard pnt, 4½x5½" ...385.00
Bureau, pnt pine, bow-front, 2 short/2 long drws, 12x11x6¾" 525.00
Chest, cherry Emp style, 4-drw, trn ft, rfn, 17x16x10"................715.00
Chest, flame grain mahog Hplwht bow-front w/inlay, 20th C, 11x11x7"....550.00
Chest, grpt pine & poplar, 3 short over 1 long drw, rpl knobs, 10x9x5"....250.00
Chest, pine, 6 dvtl drw, rpl brass pulls, old rfn, 15x18x9½" 415.00
Chest, pine Country w/old red-brn, 3-drw, cut nails, 9x12x7" 450.00
Chest, pine w/old dk pnt, 5 grad drws, rprs, 20x14x10"...............990.00
Chest, pine/poplar w/oak crest, 3 drws, 13x12x7" 275.00
Cupboard, cherry step-bk, 2-door base, JD Parker 78, 16x15x5" 220.00
Cupboard, pine w/gold striping on red, drw in base, 20x13x8" ...465.00
Totem pole, bear/whale/eagle, folky pnt, 16".................................245.00

Minton

Thomas Minton established his firm in 1793 at Stoke on Trent and within a few years began producing earthenware with blue-printed patterns similar to the ware he had learned to decorate while employed by the Caughley Porcelain Factory. The Willow pattern was one of his most popular. Neither this nor the porcelain made from 1798 to 1805 was marked (except for an occasional number series), making identification often impossible.

After 1805 until about 1816, fine tea services, beehive-shaped honey pots, trays, etc., were hand decorated with florals, landscapes, Imari-type designs, and neoclassic devices. These were often marked with crossed 'Ls.' It was Minton that invented the acid gold process of decorating (1863), which is now used by a number of different companies. From 1816 until 1823, no porcelain was made. Through the 1820s and 1830s, the ornamental wares with colorful decoration of applied fruits and florals and figurines in both bisque and enamel were usually left unmarked. As a result, they have been erroneously attributed to other potters. Some of the ware that was marked bears a deliberate imitation of Meissen's crossed swords. From the late 1820s through the 1840s, Minton made a molded stoneware line (mugs, jugs, teapots, etc.) with florals or figures in high relief. These were marked with an embossed scroll with an 'M' in the bottom curve. Fine parian ware was made in the late 1840s, and in the 1850s Minton experimented with and perfected a line of quality majolica which they produced from 1860 until it was discontinued in 1908. Their slogan was 'Majolica for the Millions,'

and for it they gained widespread recognition. Leadership of the firm was assumed by Minton's son Herbert sometime around the middle of the nineteenth century. Working hand in hand with Leon Arnoux, who was both a chemist and an artist, he managed to secure the company's financial future through constant, successful experimentation with both materials and decorating methods. During the Victorian era, M.L. Solon decorated pieces in the pate-sur-pate style, often signing his work; these examples are considered to be the finest of their type. After 1862 all wares were marked 'Minton' or 'Mintons,' with an impressed year cipher.

Many collectors today reassemble the lovely dinnerware patterns that have been made by Minton. Perhaps one of their most popular lines was Minton Rose, introduced in 1854. The company itself once counted forty-seven versions of this pattern being made by other potteries around the world. In addition to less expensive copies, elaborate hand-enameled pieces were also made by Aynsley, Crown Staffordshire, and Paragon China. Solando Ware (1937) and Byzantine Range (1938) were designed by John Wadsworth. Minton ceased all earthenware production in 1939.

See also Majolica.

Bowl, Bombay, 4x12"..135.00
Bowl, fruit; Bellameade, bl floral, set of 8....................................190.00
Bowl, Jasmine, floral decor, w/lid, 9" 280.00
Bowl, Minton Rose, scalloped edge, 2x9½".................................160.00
Bowl, salad; Riverton, #K227, 4¼x10⅛"....................................450.00
Bowl, serving; Minton Rose, oval, 2¾x7x10¼".........................145.00
Bowl, vegetable; Jasmine, oval, 10¾"...125.00
Coffeepot, St James, 9"...215.00
Coffeepot, Stanwood..100.00
Compote, Faisan, brn, 3⅝x9⅛"...115.00
Compote, 2 cherubs w/2 birds, bl bowl atop, #930, ca 1867, 6½x11"....3,120.00
Creamer & sugar bowl, Jasmine...165.00
Cup & saucer, Henley, set of 6...160.00
Cup & saucer, Marlow..25.00
Dinner service, Lothian, transfer w/ivy border, serves 12, 69-pc....500.00
Figurine, Temperance allegorical lady, parian, ca 1874, 20¾" 825.00
Flask, pilgrim, Oriental butterflies on bl, C Dresser, 6x5½".....2,600.00
Gravy boat, St James, w/underplate, 8½" 110.00
Pitcher, Cockatrice, pk, 4¾"...155.00
Pitcher, Genevese, brn & wht, att, ca 1822-36, 11½".................700.00
Pitcher, syrup; Cockatrice, metal lid, 5".......................................210.00
Place setting, Jasmine, dinner, salad, bread & butter plate & c/s...145.00
Plate, cake; Bellemeade, tab hdls, 10½" 120.00
Plate, dinner; Genevese, 10", set of 4...120.00
Plate, dinner; Minton Rose, 10¼", set of 4, from $150 to...........175.00
Plate, dinner; Stanwood, 10½"...60.00
Plate, Faisan, 7¾", set of 5...145.00
Plate, Henley, 9", set of 6 ....95.00
Plate, Marlow, globe bkstamp, 10⅝", set of 6.............................125.00
Plate, Oriental peony/prunus on bl medallion w/gold, 1874, 9"..600.00
Plate, Penrose, platinum rim, 10½"..170.00
Plate, Porcelain Ball, ivory, 10½"...120.00
Platter, Bellemeade, platinum trim, oval, 12x16"........................175.00
Platter, Jasmine, oval, 10½x13½"...125.00
Platter, Minton Rose, sq, 9x9"..100.00
Platter, Stanwood, oval, globe bkstamp, #735350, 13" 195.00
Shakers, Ancestral, twist body, 3", pr 95.00
Sugar bowl, Cockatrice, pk, w/lid, globe bkstamp, 4x5¼"..........200.00
Teapot, Ancestral, floral decor, gold trim, 6" 120.00
Teapot, Consort, wht w/bl & gold decor, 7"..................................370.00
Tile, King Lear VIII, 6x6" 120.00
Tile, lady in woods picking flowers, sgn W Wise, 6x6" 220.00
Tile, Theroman God Air, bl, 8x8"...225.00
Tile, Winter on Sounding Skates, 6x6" 310.00
Vase, floral, wht/yel/bl on purple, swollen form w/hdls, 9" 450.00

Mirrors

The first mirrors were made in England in the thirteenth century of very thin glass backed with lead. Reverse-painted glass mirrors were made in this country as early as the late 1700s and remained popular throughout the next century. The simple hand-painted panel was separated from the mirrored section by a narrow slat, and the frame was either the dark-finished Federal style or the more elegant, often-gilded Sheraton.

Mirrors changed with the style of other furnishings; but whatever type you purchase, as long as the glass sections remain solid, even broken or flaking mirrors are more valued than replaced glass. Careful resilvering is acceptable if excessive deterioration has taken place. In the listings that follow, items are from the nineteenth century unless noted otherwise. The term 'style' (example: Federal style) is used to indicate a mirror reminiscent of but made well after the period indicated. Obviously these retro styles will be valued much lower than their original counterparts. As with most other items in antiques and collectibles, the influence of online trading is greatly affecting prices. Many items once considered difficult to locate are now readily available on the Internet. Our advisor for this category is Michael Hinton; he is listed in the Directory under Pennsylvania.

Key:
Chpndl — Chippendale QA — Queen Anne
Emp — Empire   Vict — Victorian
Fed — Federal   vnr — veneer

Cheval, gold Rococo style w/beveled glass, ca 1875, 77x42x27" **2,250.00**
Cheval, mahog Fed style, mutton legs w/brass paw caps, 80" **770.00**
Dutch courting, pine w/emb brass facing, ca 1900, 24x14" **110.00**
Flemish Baroque-style repoussé w/tortoise shell inlay, 36x23" **4,400.00**
Fruitwood w/inlay, molded w/pierced arching crown, 46x26" ..**1,900.00**
Gentleman's dressing, mahog, trn/cvd uprights, 4-drw, 24x23x8½" **700.00**
Gilt Fed, cvd eagle finial, rvpt neoclassical scene, 1815, 66x32" ..**3,400.00**
Gilt Fed, eagle surmounts plinth, leaf pendants, 48x29" **2,700.00**
Gilt Fed, extended pediment w/spherules, rvpt scene, rstr, 35x16"..**1,115.00**
Gilt Fed, molded columns, rvpt fishing scene, att MA, 38x13"..**1,045.00**
Gilt gesso Fed, molded cornice, rvp Lady Liberty scene, 27x13".........**700.00**
Gilt gesso floral scrollwork ea side eagle crest, 1900, 52x25" **825.00**
Gilt gesso Rococo shells & scrolls, old crazing, 33x23¼".............**100.00**
Giltwood Napoleon III, chaneled/finger molded, 1860s, 44x32", pr ..**2,000.00**
Giltwood Regency, cvd crest w/acanthus leaves/flowers, 50x34" **4,700.00**
Giltwood Regency convex w/eagle finial, candle branches, 50x40"..**12,365.00**
Giltwood Regency style, eagle finial, acanthus pendant, 43x23"...**750.00**
Giltwood Regency style, floral vines & angel wings, 1890s, 81x50"..**8,800.00**
Giltwood/ebonized Regency, convex, eagle cest, 56x45" **11,500.00**
Gold-pnt pine Emp, stepped cornice/shell crest, 2-part, 38x19"....**575.00**
Mahog & gilt gesso Chpndl, pierced crest, late 18th C, 28x17"....**650.00**
Mahog & gilt gesso Chpndl, scrolled fr, 1800s, 39x20" **1,295.00**
Mahog & giltwood Geo III in Chpndl taste, 1750-90, 48x22"..**2,300.00**
Mahog Chpndl, conch shell inlay, 36½"..................................**1,035.00**
Mahog Chpndl, gilt phoenix in pierced crest, 29x16".............**1,650.00**
Mahog Chpndl, scalloped crest, scrolled-ear base, regilded, 20x12"....**330.00**
Mahog Chpndl, scalloped crest & base w/gilt shell, 44x24".....**1,650.00**
Mahog Chpndl, scrolled crest & base, rpl ears, 39x20" **285.00**
Mahog Chpndl, scrolled crest/pendant, Philadelphia, 1800s, 52x27" **945.00**
Mahog Chpndl, scrolls & arched crest, minor silver loss, 34x13"...**1,200.00**
Mahog Chpndl style, gold-pnt eagle on crest, 20th-C copy, 44x22"....**375.00**
Mahog Fed, eagle & E Pluribus Unum, rvpt eagle & stars panel, 39x20"..**385.00**
Mahog Fed, reeded corner blocks, twist pilasters, rvpt houses, 32x16" ..**360.00**
Mahog Hplwht, flame urn decor (rstr), 38x14" **1,045.00**
Mahog parcel-gilt Chpndl, rfn/regilded, 37x19"..........................**585.00**
Mahog QA, 2-part, gilt gesso liner, scalloped crest, 48x17" **1,100.00**

Mahog vnr Chpndl, phoenix crest, scroll ears, rstr, 37x20"....**2,300.00**
Mahog vnr QA, pierced phoenix crest, rfn, 39x21"....................**880.00**
Mahog/giltwood Am Fed, ogee-molded fr, 30x21" **750.00**
Over-mantel, gilt & gesso Neoclassical, lion's heads, rstr, 24x54"....**1,750.00**
Over-mantel, giltwood Am Fed w/ebonized reeded rabbet, 32x60" **2,300.00**
Over-mantel, giltwood Geo III style, C-scrolls/foliage, 53x51"...**7,650.00**
Pier, giltwood am Renaissance w/blossom fretwork, 122x40"....**5,125.00**
Pier, giltwood Geo III style, architectural form, 55x43x6" **635.00**
Pine Chpndl style, alligatored mahog brn rfn, rprs, 18x12".........**100.00**
Pine Rococo style, shell crest, floral pendant chains, 61x61" ..**1,225.00**

Pine with worn gilt, carved and gessoed detail, Philadelphia Hepplewhite, 60x26", VG, $8,525.00. (Photo courtesy Garth's Auctions)

Shaving, mahog Hplwht style w/inlay, 3-drw base, ca 1900, 33x24x10" ..**250.00**
Silver, emb cherub/dolphin/foliage/scrolls, easel-bk, 17x13" **1,150.00**
Walnut & gilt gesso Chpndl w/scrollings, 21x15"........................**440.00**
Walnut Chpndl, scrolled ears/crest, scallops, 21x13" **825.00**
Walnut Italian Rococo, ornate crest w/cvd acanthus leaves, 46x31" ...**3,000.00**
Walnut parcel-gilt Chpndl, scrolled, late 18th C, 43x22" **550.00**
Walnut QA, scrolled crest, molded frame, rpl glass, 15x8" **5,875.00**
Walnut QA, scrolled crest atop molded fr, rfn, 28x14"................**950.00**
Walnut QA, scrolled vnr crest, 18th C, 14x8"..............................**585.00**
Walnut vnr QA, figured Scalloped/scrolled crest, old rfn, 28x15".**750.00**
Walnut vnr QA, gilt floral device at crest, 39x16"...................**2,200.00**
Walnut/pine Chpndl w/gilt gesso liner, crest rstr, 15x10"............**200.00**

Mocha

Mochaware is utilitarian pottery made principally in England (and to a lesser extent in France) between 1780 and 1840 on the then prevalent creamware and pearlware bodies. Initially, only those pieces decorated in the seaweed pattern were called 'Mocha,' while geometrically decorated pieces were referred to as 'Banded Creamware.' Other types of decorations were called 'Dipped Ware.' During the last forty to fifty years the term 'Mocha' has been applied to the entire realm of 'Industrialized Slipware' — pottery decorated by the turner on his lathe using coggle wheels and slip cups.

Mocha was made in numerous patterns — Tree, Seaweed or Dandelion, Rope (also called Worm or Loop), Cat's-eye, Tobacco Leaf, Lollypop or Balloon, Marbled, Marbled and Combed, Twig, Geometric or Checkered, Banded, and slip decorations of rings, dots, flags, tulips, wavy lines, etc. It came into its own as a collectible in the latter half of the 1940s and has become increasingly popular as more and more people are exposed to the rich colorings and artistic appeal of its varied forms of abstract decoration. (Please note: Values hinge to a great extent on vivid coloration, intricacy of patterns, and unusual features.)

The collector should take care not to confuse the early pearlware and creamware Mocha with the later kitchen yellow ware, graniteware, and ironstone sporting mocha-type decoration that was produced in America by such potters as J. Vodrey, George S. Harker, Edwin Bennett, and John Bell. This type was also produced in Scotland and Wales and was marketed well into the twentieth century.

Our values are prices realized at auction, where nearly every example was in exceptional condition. Unless a repair, damage, or another rating is included in the description, assume the item to be in NM condition.

Bowl, balloons, wht on orange, brn rim, 2-tone brn stripes, 3x6"...7,000.00
Bowl, brn & ochre tortoise-shell slip w/gr florettes, 2½x4½"..1,400.00
Bowl, earthworm, blk on tan band, blk rim w/wht wavy line, 6¼"..2,100.00
Bowl, earthworm, 4-color on bl & dk brands, London shape, 7¼", VG...260.00
Bowl, gr diapering, olive/rust/blk bands, London shape, 1810, 10"..1,150.00
Bowl, mc marble w/tooled gr rim, lt wear, 2¼x5"......................1,550.00
Bowl, seaweed, blk on brn w/gr & cream rouletted bands, 7⅛"...350.00
Bowl, seaweed, blk on burnt umber band w/gr tooled band, 3x6¼", VG...325.00
Bowl, seaweed, cobalt & gr on marbling w/3-color bands, 7⅛"..1,115.00
Bowl, seaweed, 5-color, scrolled shell hdls, w/lid, 4⅞"...............880.00
Bowl, seaweed on brn band, gold & brn stripes, 3x5⅝"...............500.00
Bowl, wavy lines, wht on blk w/bl & blk bands, London shape, 6½"..1,115.00
Can & saucer, ochre/gr/brn/brn marbling w/brn bands, Fr, 1820s, 5"..400.00
Canister, seaweed, cafe-au-lait w/brn stripes, conical lid, 4½"....2,100.00
Coffeepot, red slip w/blk bands & dendritic decor, w/lid, rstr, 12"..3,100.00
Coffeepot, trees, brn on buff w/brn bands, ftd baluster, 10¾"..1,100.00
Creamer, cat's eyes, 3-color on gray bands, leaf hdl, 4½", EX.....990.00
Creamer, earthworm, speckled brn band & bl stripes, sm rpr, 4"...220.00
Creamer, tooled mc stripes, leaf hdl, wear/flakes, 4"................1,540.00
Jar, bl dendritic decor on wht band w/bl bands, 5⅜x6"..............700.00
Jug, cat's eyes & twigs, bl & dk brn wide & narrow bands, 8¾".....2,000.00
Jug, fans, mc on 3-color bands, baluster, 1910s, 9½"...............50,000.00
Jug, geometric pattern on rust/blk, 1790s, chips, 6½"...............3,750.00
Jug, seaweed, dk brn on ochre w/rouletted gr bands/2 bl bands, 9"..2,115.00
Jug, taupe & blk alternating bands, baluster form, 8⅝"...........1,650.00
Mug, blk/brn bands combed vertically, ca 1790, 6¼"...............3,335.00
Mug, blk/rust/bl repeat pattern, wht ft & hdl, ca 1800, 6".......3,450.00
Mug, brn/blk bands w/trn geometrics on 2 wht fields, qt, 5¾"...1,000.00
Mug, cat's eyes (sm), 4-color narrow & wide bands, 6⅛", EX..1,100.00
Mug, circles, mc on on blk, yel & gray bands, 4¾"..................3,000.00
Mug, geometric wht pattern on brn w/caramel bands, 6".........2,500.00
Mug, marbleized brn & gr-tan, tapered sides, 3¾".....................85.00
Mug, marbleized mc w/dk brn edges, leaf hdl, 4⅞", EX............2,450.00
Mug, seaweed, bl on wht marble w/lt bl & ochre bands, 5¾"..1,115.00
Mug, seaweed on brn band w/blk stripes, flakes, 3½".................770.00
Mug, twigs & waves, 3-colored w/bl & blk bands, 1-pt, 4⅞"......2,000.00
Mustard, seaweed, blk on orange bands, blk & brn stripes, 4"....1,550.00
Pepper pot, blk checked middle, gr band, lt brn stripes, 4", EX..1,350.00
Pepper pot, blk circles on tan band, blk stripes, 4½"..............1,045.00
Pepper pot, cat's eyes, lt bl w/mc stripes, 4½"......................2,750.00
Pepper pot, cat's eyes, rust/blk/wht on gray, cobalt crown, 4¾", VG....1,400.00
Pepper pot, earthworm & 3-color balls, bl top, rpr, 4½"..........3,850.00
Pepper pot, feathers, mc, gr band at shoulder, mc stripes, 4"....2,750.00
Pepper pot, geometrics, repeating blk/brn on wht, baluster, rstr, 5"...1,400.00
Pepper pot, lt bl & blk stripes, flat top, flaw, 4"...................800.00
Pepper pot, seaweed, 3-color w/dk brn band & bl stripes, 4½", EX...1,650.00
Pepper pot, tooled brn/gr/orange bands, flakes, 4⅛"..............1,450.00
Pitcher, bl bands w/wht & lt gr bands, flared ft, stain, 5¾".........115.00
Pitcher, bl/brick/brn/gr bands, tooled vertical designs, 5⅛"......3,750.00
Pitcher, earthworm, 3-color band on med bl, 1914 on base, 7¼"..275.00
Pitcher, earthworm, 3-color on tan band w/brn stripes, 4¾".......500.00
Pitcher, feathered mc marbling, tooled gr rim, 5⅝"...............3,200.00

Pitcher, gray & white marbleized, flake, 4¾"......................250.00
Pitcher, seaweed, brn on orange, gr tooled bands, brn stripes, 7"....1,045.00
Pitcher, wide bl bands w/wht stripes, flared ft, chip, 7½"............145.00
Pitcher, 4 fans (or tobacco leaves?) on ochre, bbl form, 5¼"...3,000.00
Porringer, gr/ochre bands, 3 mc dipped fans, 1820s, 3⅜"........6,325.00
Punch bowl, rouletted checkered band above mc marbling, 9"..2,415.00
Salt cellar, cat's eyes, mc on orange-sand w/blk stripes, 2x3⅛"...2,100.00
Salt cellar, earthworm, 4-color w/orange band & dk brn stripes, 2x3"..1,925.00
Tankard, seaweed, brn on orange w/blk stripes, pewter lid, 5"..1,350.00
Tea caddy, blk dendritic decor on ochre, 5⅜".....................2,950.00
Tumbler, mc feathered marbling, gr tooled rim, 2½"...............3,500.00
Waste bowl, earthworm, gr on wht w/slate bl bands, stain, 3⅜x6½"..110.00
Waste bowl, earthworm, 3-color band on gray, 2¾x4¾"............300.00

Molds

Food molds have become popular as collectibles — not only for their value as antiques, but because they also revive childhood memories of elaborate ice cream Santas with candy trim or barley sugar figurals adorning a Christmas tree. Ice cream molds were made of pewter and came in a wide variety of shapes and styles. Chocolate molds were made in fewer shapes but were more detailed. They were usually made of tin or copper, then nickel-plated to keep them from tarnishing or rusting as well as for sanitary reasons. Hard candy molds were usually metal, although primitive maple sugar molds (usually simple hearts, rabbits, and other animals) were carved from wood. Cake molds were made of cast iron or cast aluminum and were most common in the shape of a lamb, a rabbit, or Santa Claus. Our advisors for this category are Dale and Jean Van Kuren; they are listed in the Directory under New York.

Chocolate Molds

Basket, 2-pc, Arnold Kalmeijer, Den Haag, #16142, 4½".............45.00
Bear w/bow tie, 2-pc, att Laurosch #4106, 5½".....................390.00
Boxer (child), 2-pc, Anton Reiche #17126, 4½".......................70.00
Briar pipe, 2-pc, #10196, 4½"L...65.00
Bunny riding rabbit w/basket over shoulder, 2-pc, German, #4082, 6"..240.00
Camel, 2-pc, #56, 3½x4¼"...45.00
Circus elephant, 2-pc, Anton Reiche, Dresden, #8302, 5⅛".......160.00
Clown, 2-pc, German, 7¼x3½"...70.00
Doves (2), 2-pc, 7x11"...45.00
Duck, swimming, 2-pc, Sommett, 5".....................................40.00
Easter bunny riding dog w/eggs coming out of basket, 7¼".........120.00
Easter bunny w/basket, Anton Reiche, 13½".............................870.00
Egg, 2-pc, French, 10x7"...60.00
Fish, 2-pc, iron, Belgium, #16482, 11⅞"................................50.00
Gnome, 3-pc, Van Emden, MIG, 3"...85.00
Hansel & Gretel w/witch in cottage, 2-pc, German, 6½x8½"......80.00
Hershey's, 16 sections, all mk Hershey's, 5x9".........................45.00
Indian on rearing horse, 2-pc, 6"...60.00
Jack-o-lantern, 2-pc, Anton Reiche #21836S, 2½x3¼"...............55.00
Lion, 2-pc, #10, 4⅛"...45.00
Mother w/child in arms, 2-pc, Letang #4244, 6x5"..................280.00
Partridge, 2-pc, 11"..160.00
Pelican, 2-pc, #13070, 4⅝x6"..120.00
Pig, 2-pc, tin, 6"..55.00
Rabbit, seated w/egg at ft, 3-pc clamp-form base, 7"...............25.00
Rabbit pulling wagon, 2-pc, Belgium, 2⅝x4⅞".........................90.00
Rabbit riding rooster, 2-pc, German, #443, 5½"......................160.00
Rabbit sits on milestone w/basket on bk, German, 13½"............135.00
Rabbit w/rifle over stump, 2-pc, Letang, 5".............................50.00
Rabbits (2) playing leapfrog, 2-pc, Made in USA, #4797, 3½".....60.00
Rooster, 2-pc, Anton Reiche #5916, 8".................................100.00

Santa Claus, 2-pc, #3618, 10" 580.00
Santa climbing in chimney, 2-pc, 5¾x6¼" 175.00
Santa riding pig, 2-pc, German, #5539, 3¾" 440.00
Santa's boot, 2-pc, #18, 5" 45.00
Scottie dog, 2-pc, Holland, #15556, 4⅜" 65.00

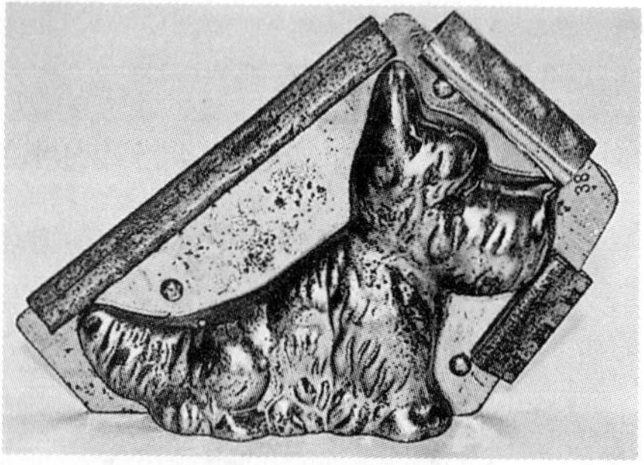

Scottie dog, two-piece, with clips, #383, 5x5½x1½", $100.00. (Photo courtesy Candace Sten Davis and Patricia J. Baum)

Shrimp (3), 2-pc, Sommett, 3⅝" 135.00
Snowman w/ broom, 2-pc, #15957, 7x4" 65.00
Sportsman winner, 2-pc, Anton Reiche #17123, 4⅝" 75.00
Squirrel eating nut, 2-pc, 8¼x6¾" 195.00
Toddler w/teddy bear, 2-pc, French, 3x2x1" 65.00
Violin, 2-pc, Anton Reiche #14916, 7½" 75.00

Ice Cream Molds

Airplane, 1132 E&Co, 5x4½" 85.00
Automobile, #1143 E&Co, 5" 45.00
Battleship, #1069 E&Co, 2½x7" 80.00
Bride w/bouquet of flowers, #1148 E&Co, 4½" 55.00
Butterfly, #181, 5" 100.00
Cannon, #1072 E&Co, 3x5½" 65.00
Donkey, #630, 4¾x4¾" 90.00
Eagle, wings spread, #655 E&Co, 4½x5½" 50.00
Fireman holding trumpet, 5¼" 125.00
Frontiersman, #496, 5¾x3" 75.00
Grape cluster, #580, 5" 80.00
Hearts aflame w/Love on banner, #300 S&Co, 4¾" 70.00
Jack-o-lantern, w/witch's hat, #642, 4x3¼" 310.00
Lighthouse, #565 S&Co, 4½" 110.00
Pear, CC, 8" 160.00
Poinsettia, #1144 E&Co, 5¼" 95.00
Prairie dog, #675 E&Co 130.00
Pumpkin, #1157 E&Co, 3" dia 75.00
Rabbit in Easter egg truck, #1091 E&Co NY, 3½" 185.00
Rooster, #645 E&Co 75.00
Santa w/bag of toys, #194 E&Co, 3-pt, 11x6" 725.00
Skull, #1010 E&Co NY, 4" 225.00
Snowman, Bruningmeyer, Holland, 3⅜" 60.00
Squirrel, 4x4¼" 145.00
Suckling piglet, #678 E&Co, 2½x5" 95.00
Swan, #630 E&Co NY, 4x3" 90.00
Turkey, 2-pc, #6 E&Co NY, 8" 760.00
Valentine card, Valentine & arrow through heart, S&Co, 3½x4" ...140.00
Whale, #602 S&Co, 5" L 110.00
Witch on broom w/crescent moon on end, #640 & K (Krauss), 5½x4" ...375.00
Wreath, #1146 E&Co, 5¾x4¾" 125.00
Zepplin, #1140 E&Co, 6¼" L 140.00

Maple Sugar Molds

Elephant, dog & goat, cvd hardwood, early 1900s, 3½x12", pr 70.00
Fish (4), cvd walnut, lollipop style, 19th C, 2½x13¾" 55.00
Floral & bee designs, cvd wood, 5x10" 36.00
Flower designs (4), cvd wood, EX patina & detail, 11¼x2½" 55.00
Fluted sides, cvd hardwood, 1800s, 7¾x3¾x1¾" 125.00
Heart, cvd maple, 8½x4¼x1¼" 150.00
Heart, cvd wood, 2-part, pins missing, 6x4½" 250.00
Heart w/face, cvd wood, in orig tin case, 1800s, 5½" 300.00
Hearts (2, swirling), cvd wood, EX patina, 13x4¼x2" 200.00
House w/cvd-in windows & doors, separate sides & roof, 5½" 110.00
Rooster, cvd hardwood, 2-pc, early 1800s, 7¾x5¼" 195.00
Sq sections (9), cvd hardwood, 33x5¼" 80.00

Miscellaneous

Aluminum, fish, copper-colored, 5½-cup, 11" 9.00
CI, 3 squirrels seated eating nuts, #155, 2¾x7" 195.00
Copper, emb fruit basket, 20th C, 10" L 140.00
Copper, lobed body w/star center, 5½x10" dia 600.00
Copper, tube, English, 19th C, 6" dia 175.00
Copper, tube, Germany, late 1800s, 4x8" dia 240.00
Copper/tin, grapes emb, oval, English, 19th C 300.00
Stoneware, salt glaze, rnd w/scallop design inside, 10⅞" 140.00
Tin, chicken, 3-part, Germany, 9" 200.00
Tin, heart w/punched flower design, 3 ft, rpr, 3⅛x4½" 385.00
Tin, lion, fluted/scalloped edge, mk 2 Pints, 4¾x7" 150.00
Tin/copper, fruit, 6½" dia 120.00

Monmouth

The Monmouth Pottery Company was established in 1892 in Monmouth, Illinois. It was touted as the largest pottery in the world. Their primary products were utilitarian: stoneware crocks, churns, jugs, water coolers, etc. — in salt glaze, Bristol, spongeware, and Albany brown. In 1906 they were absorbed by a conglomerate called the Western Stoneware Company. Monmouth Pottery Co. became their #1 plant and until 1930 continued to produce stoneware marked with the Western Stoneware Company's maple leaf logo. Items marked 'Monmouth Pottery Co.' were made before 1906. Western Stoneware Co. introduced a line of artware in 1926. The name chosen for the artware was Monmouth Pottery. Some stamps and paper labels add ILL to the name.

Bowl, batter; lt gr, 4¾x8" dia 85.00
Bowl, gr, incised leaf & flower decor, 4½x8½" 110.00
Bowl, salt glazed, brn int, base mk, 2-gal 200.00
Bowl/planter, Aztec, mk base, 2¼x6½" 40.00
Bowls, nesting; tan w/gr band at top & gr int, 6", 8" & 10" 27.50
Casserole, bird-shaped lid, wht w/bl swirl decor, 7½x8¾" 125.00
Churn, #3, cobalt on salt glaze, 3-gal, 13" 250.00
Churn, #4, cobalt on salt glaze, 16½" 250.00
Churn, #5, cobalt on salt glaze, 5-gal 325.00
Churn, Bristol, Maple Leaf mk, 2-gal 250.00
Churn, cobalt on salt glaze, 6-gal 400.00
Churn, salt glaze, mini, 4" 1,200.00
Churn, 2 Men in a Crock stencil, 5-gal 1,000.00
Cooler, ice water; bl & wht spongeware, mini 1,000.00
Cooler, ice water; bl & wht spongeware, w/lid & spigot, 8-gal ...1,500.00
Cow & calf, brn, mk Monmouth Pottery Co 3,000.00
Crock, Bristol, Albany slip int, 4-gal 85.00
Crock, Bristol, Maple Leaf emblem, 2½x3¼" dia 25.00
Crock, Bristol, Maple Leaf mk, 2-gal 75.00
Crock, Bristol, mini, 2½" 600.00
Crock, Bristol, 10-gal 100.00
Crock, Bristol, 20-gal 100.00

Crock, Bristol, 60-gal **1,500.00**
Crock, Bristol Monmouth Pottery Co, bl stencil, 1-qt **250.00**
Crock, early dull Bristol w/cobalt stencil..........................**300.00**
Crock, salt glaze, Albany slip int, 3-gal **95.00**
Crock, salt glaze, hand decor, base mk, 2-gal **250.00**
Crock, salt glaze, unmk, 2-gal **60.00**
Crock, stencil, bl on dk brn Albany slip, 3-gal **300.00**
Crock, stencil, bl on dk brn Albany slip, 6-gal **600.00**
Crock, 2 Men in a Crock stencil, 10-gal **500.00**
Dog, Monmouth Pottery Co, mk, Albany slip.........................**5,000.00**
Hen on nest, bl & wht spongeware..................................**1,200.00**
Jug, Bristol, bl stencil (early rectangle), 5-gal **250.00**
Jug, Bristol, Maple Leaf mk, 5-gal.................................**200.00**
Jug, Bristol w/Albany slip top, mini, 2½"..........................**500.00**
Letterhead, 1898 letter **45.00**
Pig, Bristol, Monmouth Pottery Co..................................**1,500.00**
Pig, brn, mk Monmouth Pottery Co...................................**1,000.00**
Pitcher, gr, ring decor, mk Monmouth USA, 5½" **30.00**
Snuff or preserve jar, wax seal.....................................**350.00**
Tobacco jar, monk, brn Albany slip.................................**300.00**
Vase, bl, emb leaf & foliage decor, unmk, 12" **110.00**
Vase, bl matt, incised shoulder band, 16x10" **495.00**
Vase, blk, rings at waist, flared neck, 18½" **90.00**
Vase, gr, Art Deco style w/long side hdls, 3 lg rings at base, 7" **30.00**

Mont Joye

Mont Joye was a type of acid-cut French cameo glass produced by Cristallerie de Pantin in Paris around the turn of the century. It is accented by enamels. Our advisor for this category is Don Williams; he is listed in the Directory under Missouri.

Bowl, chestnuts on branches, 3-color on icy ground w/gold, 8" ..**525.00**
Rose bowl, violets & leaves on gr, 4¾x5½" **300.00**
Vase, cattails on bl, gold-washed cvd gr leaves on lav to fuchsia, 14" ..**1,100.00**
Vase, floral, yel/gold/gr on brn chipped ice ground, slim/ftd, 9½" **665.00**
Vase, flowers/spider web w/spider, bronze-gr/brn on frost, 9½"....**375.00**
Vase, irises, gold on frost, cylindrical w/flaring base, 15" **800.00**
Vase, lily of the valley etched on lt yel, sq, elongated, 5¾" **200.00**

Moon and Star

Moon and Star was originally produced in the 1880s by John Adams & Company of Pittsburgh. In the 1960s Joseph Weishar of Wheeling, West Virginia, owner of the Island Mould & Machine Company, reproduced some of the original molds and incorporated the pattern into approximately forty new and different items. Two of the largest distributors of this line were L.E. Smith of Mt. Pleasant, Pennsylvania, who pressed their own glass, and L.G. Wright of New Martinsville, West Virginia, who had theirs pressed by Fostoria, Fenton, and Westmoreland. Both companies carried a large and varied assortment of shapes and colors. Several other companies were involved in its manufacture as well, especially of the smaller items.

Over the years the glassware has been pressed in amberina (yellow shading to orange- or ruby-red), green, amber, crystal, light blue, and ruby. Pieces in ruby and light blue are most collectible and harder to find than the other colors, which seem to be abundant. Purple, pink, cobalt, amethyst, tan slag, and light green and blue opalescent were made, too, but on a lesser scale.

In 1992 the Weishar company introduced a new color, teal green, which was followed in 1993 with sapphire blue opalescent, and in 1994 with cranberry ice. These items (and those being made today) carried

the Weishar mark and were made primarily for collectors. Currently the company is producing water sets, salt and pepper shakers, creamers and sugars, spoon holders, and various relish trays in Delphite and Delphite carnival, Crown Tuscan and Crown Tuscan carnival, Colonial Blue, Millennium Rose (pink), and various other colors such as amethyst and cobalt on a more limited basis. Miniature water sets have been made in more than thirty colors, the newest being amethyst slag and amethyst slag carnival. Unless another color is noted, our values are given for vintage glassware in ruby and light blue. For amberina, green, and amber, deduct 20%.

Ashtray, 6-sided, moons at rim, star on base, 8½"..................**20.00**
Banana boat, scalloped rim, allover pattern, 12"....................**40.00**
Basket, scalloped rim, solid hdl, allover pattern, 9", from $50 to ..**60.00**
Bowl, ftd, crimped rim, allover pattern, 7½"........................**35.00**
Cake plate, low collared base, allover pattern, 13" dia, from $50 to **60.00**
Candle holder, bowl-style w/ring hdl, allover pattern, 2x5½", ea **14.00**
Candle holder, flared/scalloped ft, allover pattern, 6", pr, $30 to ..**40.00**
Cheese dish, patterned base, clear plain lid, 9½".................**60.00**
Compote, scalloped rim, allover pattern, 5x6½"....................**20.00**
Decanter, bulbous, allover pattern, patterned stopper, 32-oz, 12"..**75.00**
Goblet, wine; plain rim & ft, 4½"....................................**9.00**
Jardiniere, allover pattern, patterned lid, 7¼", minimum value **65.00**
Lamp, miniature, gr..**135.00**
Lamp, miniature, red, from $175 to................................**200.00**
Nappy, crimped rim, allover pattern, 2¾x6", from $12 to **15.00**
Pitcher, water; str sides w/patterned body, plain ft, ice lip, 7½" **70.00**
Plate, patterned body & center, smooth rim, 8" **30.00**
Shakers, allover pattern, metal lids, 4x2", pr.....................**25.00**
Soap dish, oval, allover pattern, 2x6" **9.00**
Syrup, allover pattern, metal lid, 4½x3½" **65.00**
Toothpick holder, scalloped rim, sm flat ft, allover pattern.............**9.00**
Tumbler, iced tea; no pattern at rim or on disk ft, 11-oz, 5" **18.00**
Tumbler, juice; no pattern at rim or on disk ft, 5-oz, 3½" **12.00**

Moorcroft

William Moorcroft began to work for MacIntyre Potteries in 1897. At first he was the chief designer but very soon took over their newly created Art Pottery department. His first important design was the Aurelian Ware, part transfer and part hand painted. Very shortly thereafter, around the turn of the century, he developed his famous Florian Ware, with heavy slip, done in mostly blue and white. Since the early 1900s there has been a succession of designs, most of them very characteristic of the company. Moorcroft left MacIntyre in 1913 and went out on his own. He had already well established his name, having won prizes and gold medals at the St. Louis World's Fair as well as in Paris. In 1929 Queen Mary, who had been collecting his pottery, made him 'Potter to the Queen,' and the pottery was so stamped up until 1949. William Moorcroft died in 1945, and his son Walter ran the company until recent years. The factory is still in existence. They now produce different designs but continue to use the characteristic slipwork. Moorcroft pottery was sold abroad in Canada, the United States, Australia, and Europe as well as in specialty areas such as the island of Bermuda.

Moorcroft went through a 'Japanese' stage in the early teens with his lovely lustre glazes, Oriental shapes and decorations. During the mid-teens he began to produce his most popular Pomegranate Ware, and Wisteria (often called 'Fruit'). Around that time he also designed the popular Pansy line as well as Leaves and Grapes. Soon he introduced a beautiful landscape series called variously Hazeldine, Moonlit Blue, Eventide, and Dawn. These wonderful designs along with Claremont (Mushrooms) seem to be the most sought after by collectors today. It would be possible to add many other designs to this list.

During the 1920s and 1930s, Moorcroft became very interested in highly fired Flambé (red) glazes. These could only be achieved through a very difficult procedure which he himself perfected in secret. He later passed the knowledge on to his son.

Dating of this pottery is done by knowledge of the designs, shapes, signatures, and marks on the bottom of each piece; an experienced person can usually narrow it down to a short time frame. Prices escalated for this 'rediscovered' pottery in the late 1980s but have now leveled off. This is true mainly of the pre-1935 designs of William Moorcroft, as it is items from that era that attract the most collector interest. Prices in the listings below are for pieces in mint condition unless noted otherwise; no reproductions are listed here. Advisors for this category are Wilfred and Dolli Cohen; they are listed in the Directory under California.

Bonbonnier, rose garland, pk/gold on wht, w/lid & lg hdls, 7" ...**1,500.00**
Bowl, Hibiscus, mc on bl-gr, w/lid, MIE, 3½x5¾" **200.00**
Lamp, leaves & grapes, mc on flambé, urn form, 1928-34, 23½" ...**2,250.00**
Mug, Coronation of King George V, MacIntyre, ca 1911, 3⅝" ...**195.00**
Vase, Alhambra, gilted, baluster, MacIntyre, 11⅞" **1,250.00**
Vase, Claremont, mushrooms, gr/brn on gr, 6" **3,300.00**
Vase, Eventide, mtns & treees, shouldered, flared ft, 6½" **2,500.00**
Vase, fish on wht, ovoid, WM, 1930, 9½" **2,700.00**
Vase, Florian Ware, bl cornflowers on wht, 11", pr **1,995.00**
Vase, Florian Ware, Iris, shouldered cylinder, 12" **2,950.00**
Vase, Hibiscis, mc on bl, bulbous, MIE, mid-20th C, 8¼" **235.00**
Vase, hills/trees/clouds on red, MIE, 8¼" **1,950.00**
Vase, Leaves & Grapes, mc on bl-gr, flared rim, 1928-35, 4¼" **265.00**

Vase, Leaves and Grapes on rust to cobalt, wide shoulder, WM, ca 1930, 17", $1,950.00. (Photo courtesy Skinner, Inc.)

Vase, Lion's Den, rampant lion on cobalt, ltd edition, 9¾" **300.00**
Vase, MacIntyre landscape, flared cylinder, 12½" **6,000.00**
Vase, Moonlit Blue, landscape, bls/grs, bulbous, 4" **1,500.00**
Vase, Moonlit Blue, landscape, bls/grs, tapered cylinder, 19" ...**8,950.00**
Vase, Moonlit Blue, landscape, bulbous, 8½" **3,750.00**
Vase, orchids, mc on bl-gr, bulbous, 1945-49, 6¾" **265.00**
Vase, Pansy, mc on bl, ovoid, MIE, 10" **585.00**
Vase, polar bear, S Tuffin, ltd ed, 1988, 6" **1,390.00**
Vase, Pomegranate, celadon gr hdls, 3⅛x3½" **630.00**
Vase, Pomegranate on tan, 15¾" **2,500.00**
Vase, poppies on wht, curved hdls, MacIntyre, 8" **1,950.00**
Vase, rose garland, WM MacIntyre, 1906, 7½" **2,850.00**
Vase, waving corn on wht, 2-hdl, 8" **875.00**

Morgantown Glass

Incorporated in 1899, the Morgantown Glass Works experienced many name changes over the years. Today 'Morgantown Glass' is a

generic term used to identify all glass produced there. Purchased by Fostoria in 1965, the factory was permanently closed in 1971.

Golf Ball is the most recognized design with crosshatched bumps equally distributed along the stem (very similar to Cambridge #1066, identified with alternating lines of dimples between rows of crosshatching). Color identification is difficult and much information is provided by Gene Florence in his book *Stemware Identification*. For further information we also recommend *Elegant Glassware of the Depression Era, Tenth Edition*, by Gene Florence (both are published by Collector Books).

Golf Ball, colors other than Steigel gr, bell **60.00**
Golf Ball, colors other than Steigel gr, compote, 7½x10" **375.00**
Golf Ball, colors other than Steigel gr, schooner, 32-oz, 8½" **195.00**
Golf Ball, colors other than Steigel gr, stem, cordial; 3½" **40.00**
Golf Ball, colors other than Steigel gr, urn, 6½" **65.00**
Golf Ball, Steigel Gr, Spanish Red or Ritz Bl, stem, parfait, 4¼" ..**85.00**
Golf Ball, Steigel Gr, Spanish Red or Ritz Bl, tumbler, juice; ftd, 5"..**28.00**
Queen Louise, crystal w/pk, finger bowl, ftd..............................**200.00**
Queen Louise, crystal w/pk, plate, finger bowl liner; 6" **125.00**
Queen Louise, crystal w/pk, plate, salad **150.00**
Queen Louise, crystal w/pk, stem, cocktail; 3-oz **350.00**
Queen Louise, crystal w/pk, stem, parfait; 7-oz **395.00**
Queen Louise, crystal w/pk, stem, sherbet; 5½-oz **300.00**
Queen Louise, crystal w/pk, stem, water; 9-oz **385.00**
Queen Louise, crystal w/pk, stem, wine; 2½-oz **350.00**
Sunrise Medallion, bl, cup **100.00**
Sunrise Medallion, bl, finger bowl, ftd...**85.00**
Sunrise Medallion, bl, pitcher..**595.00**
Sunrise Medallion, bl, plate, sherbet; 5⅞" **12.50**
Sunrise Medallion, bl, plate, 8⅜"..**30.00**
Sunrise Medallion, bl, stem, cocktail; 6⅛" **55.00**
Sunrise Medallion, bl, stem, wine; 2½-oz **85.00**
Sunrise Medallion, bl, tumbler, ftd, 5-oz, 4¼" **50.00**
Sunrise Medallion, crystal, parfait, 5-oz **55.00**
Sunrise Medallion, crystal, plate, salad; 7½" **12.50**
Sunrise Medallion, crystal, sugar bowl **25.00**
Sunrise Medallion, crystal, tumbler, flat **25.00**
Sunrise Medallion, crystal, tumbler, ftd, 5-oz, 4¼" **45.00**
Sunrise Medallion, crystal, tumbler, ftd, 9-oz, 4¾" **20.00**
Sunrise Medallion, crystal, vase, bud; slender, 10" **65.00**
Sunrise Medallion, gr or pk, parfait, 5-oz **80.00**
Sunrise Medallion, gr or pk, stem, wine; 2½-oz **55.00**
Sunrise Medallion, gr or pk, sugar bowl......................................**250.00**
Sunrise Medallion, gr or pk, vase, bud; 10" **295.00**
Tinkerbell, azure or gr, finger bowl, ftd.......................................**100.00**
Tinkerbell, azure or gr, night bottle set, 4-pc..............................**600.00**
Tinkerbell, azure or gr, plain top, ftd, #36 Uranus, 10" **350.00**
Tinkerbell, azure or gr, stem, cocktail; 3 ½-oz **125.00**
Tinkerbell, azure or gr, stem, cordial; 1½-oz...............................**175.00**
Tinkerbell, azure or gr, stem, goblet; 9-oz **150.00**
Tinkerbell, azure or gr, stem, wine; 2½-oz **135.00**

Mortars and Pestles

Mortars are bowl-shaped vessels used for centuries for the purpose of grinding drugs to a powder or grain into meal. The masher or grinding device is called a pestle.

Bronze, incised trns, ftd, EX patina, 4½x5¼"................................**95.00**
Burl, ftd, 5x6", +trn 8½"x2½" dumbell-shaped pestle **140.00**
Burl w/G figure, EX patina, 5¼x5½"+trn wood pestle **220.00**
Hardstone, 19th C, 7x13", +2 wood-hdld pestles **635.00**
Hardwood, old bl pnt, trn, center wear, EX patina, 7¼", +pestle ..**600.00**

Marble, 9½x11" 400.00
Wooden, trn, ftd, 5x4½" 20.00

Mortens Studio

Oscar Mortens was already established as a fine sculptural artist when he left his native Sweden to take up residency in Arizona. During the 1940s he developed a line of detailed animal figures which were distributed through the Mortens Studios, a firm he co-founded with Gunnar Thelin. Thelin hired and trained artists to produce Mortens's line, which he called Royal Designs. More than two hundred dogs were modeled and over one hundred horses. Cats and wild animals such as elephants, panthers, deer, and elk were made, but on a much smaller scale. Bookends with sculptured dog heads were shown in their catalogs, and collectors report finding wall plaques on rare occasions. The material they used was a plaster-type composition with wires embedded to support the weight. Examples were marked 'Copyright by the Mortens Studio,' either in ink or decal. Watch for flaking, cracks, and separations. Crazing seems to be present in some degree in many examples. When no condition is indicated, the items listed below are assumed to be in near-mint condition, allowing for minor crazing.

Bay pup, recumbent, unclipped ears, 5½" L 65.00
Boxer, ready to pounce, 1¾x4" 80.00
Boxer, recumbent w/head up, 2¼x5½", from $45 to....................55.00
Chihuahua head, plaque, Mortens 3-D Head Studios, 5½x6", $120 to ..140.00
Chow Chow, red, standing, 5½" 110.00
Cocker Spaniel, recumbent w/head up, 3x6½" 50.00
Collie, recumbent w/head up, 2½x3⅝" 50.00
English Bulldog, standing, 3½x6", from $65 to 75.00
English Setter, gold foil label, mini 55.00
English Springer Spaniel, standing, 5½x7" 70.00
Fox Terrier, seated, begging, 3" 45.00
Great Dane puppy, seated, 3½" 60.00
Kerry Blue Terrier, decal, 4¾x6" 140.00
Palomino horse, running, 5½x7¼" 95.00
Pekingese, standing, 3x4½" 60.00
Saint Bernard, standing, 6¾" 60.00
Springer Spaniel, 5x7½" 115.00
Wire-Haired Terrier, standing, 5¼x6½" 60.00

Morton Pottery

Six potteries operated in Morton, Illinois, at various times from 1877 to 1976. Each traced its origin to six brothers who immigrated to America to avoid military service in Germany. The Rapp brothers established their first pottery near clay deposits on the south side of town where they made field tile and bricks. Within a few years, they branched out to include utility wares such as jugs, bowls, jars, pitchers, etc. During the ninety-nine years of pottery operations in Morton, the original factory was expanded by some of the sons and nephews of the Rapps. Other family members started their own potteries where artware, gift-store items, and special-order goods were produced. The Cliftwood Art Pottery and the Morton Pottery Company had showrooms in Chicago and New York City during the 1930s. All of Morton's potteries were relatively short-lived operations with the Morton Pottery Company being the last to shut down on September 8, 1976. For a more thorough study of the subject, we recommend *Morton's Potteries: 99 Years, Vols. I and II,* by Doris and Burdell Hall; their address can be found in the Directory under Illinois.

Morton Pottery Works — Morton Earthenware Co. (1877 – 1917)

Baker, deep yel ware, 8" dia..50.00

Bank, acorn shape, cobalt, 3¼"...65.00
Bowl, mixing; brn, Rockingham, 4½"....................................25.00
Chamber pot, yel ware, w/lid, 10" dia.................................90.00
Crock, brn Rockingham, mk, 2-gal.....................................60.00
Cuspidor, brn, 7"..50.00
Cuspidor, cobalt, 7" dia 55.00
Jardiniere, brn, Rockingham, 7"..40.00
Marble, brn, Rockingham, 4¼"..35.00
Marble, gr, 3"...25.00
Milk jug, brn, Rockingham, 1-pt...55.00
Milk jug, cobalt, fancy appl hdl, #36s, 1-pt 50.00
Mug, coffee; yel ware w/wht slip lines, 1-pt.........................85.00
Pie baker, yel ware, 7"...75.00
Rice nappy, plain, yel ware, 13" 85.00
Teapot, acorn shape, brn Rockingham, 3 ¾ to 4 cup..................90.00
Teapot, Rebecca at the Well, brn Rockingham, 8½-pt 150.00

Cliftwood Art Potteries, Inc. (1920 – 1940)

Beer set, chocolate drip, bbl-shape pitcher+6 mugs.....................225.00
Bookends, lion & lioness on Herbage Green bases, 4¼x6¼", pr...150.00
Bowl, deep bulb, bl/gray, 6"...24.00
Bowl, sq, gr/yel drip over wht, w/lid, 6".................................50.00
Candlesticks, blk semi-lustre, 7", pr 50.00
Card holder, elephant w/side pockets, cobalt, 5¾x4x5" 90.00
Creamer, cow figural, tail forms hdl, chocolate drip, 3¼x6½" 125.00
Figurine, cat, reclining, brn drip, 4½".....................................45.00
Figurine, cat, reclining, brn drip, 8½".....................................60.00
Figurine, mini bear, brn, 3x1¾" 14.00
Figurine, Police dog, chocolate drip, 5x8½" 80.00
Flower frog, disc, bl/wht drip, 5" 18.00
Flower frog, frog, pk, 5½" 35.00
Flower frog, turtle, bl/mulberry drip, 5½" 30.00
Jug, wine; brn drip, w/music box in base, 9½" 150.00
Shakers, stove top, yel/gr drip over wht, 5", pr.........................30.00
Vase, peacock feather w/twig hdls, matt turq, 15½"...................55.00
Vase, tree trunk w/3 open limbs at top, Herbage Green, 9"..........70.00
Wall pocket, bl & mulberry, cone shape, #123, 6x2¾"................55.00
Wall pocket, Herbage Green, tree trunk shape, 8x3"..................70.00

Midwest Potteries, Inc. (1940 – 1944)

Cow creamer, brn drip w/yel hdl, 5" 24.00
Figurine, Afghan hound, wht w/gold decor, 7" 45.00
Figurine, cockatoo, yel w/gr drip, on ped, 6" 24.00
Figurine, deer, wht w/gold decor, 8-point antlers, 12" 50.00
Figurine, Irish Setter, natural colors, 5".................................35.00
Figurine, pony, yel w/gold decor, 3½" 24.00
Figurine, sunfish on seaweed base, yel/brn spray, 10½"..............40.00
Figurine, tiger, yel w/brn stripes, 6x10" 40.00
Miniature, lion, brn drip, 2½x1¾"..14.00
Pitcher, duck figural w/cattail hdl, brn/gray spray, 10" 40.00
Planter, bird & nest, bl, 6½x3½"...24.00
Planter, Calico cat, bl/yel spatter, 8".....................................20.00
Planter, deer, recumbent, brn spray, 6½x5½".........................18.00
Planter, elephant, bl/yel drip, 5½x6¾"..................................20.00
Planter, fox, brn, 5¾x7" 18.00
Wall mask, African female, ebony/gold, 15 neck rings, 8¼x5" 40.00
Wall mask, man's head caricature, Classical Greek style, wht, 5x4½" ..35.00
Wall mask, man's head caricature, short hair, winking, yel, 5x3¼" 30.00

Morton Pottery Company (1922 – 1976)

Ashtray, hexagon, bl, Dirksen, 3¾" 30.00

Ashtray, ovoid, w/appl pheasant 24.00
Ashtray, teardrop, Rival Crock Pot, 6" 12.00
Bank, acorn, brn 35.00
Bank, church, brn, 3½x4x2" 24.00
Bank, hen, blk/wht 40.00
Bank, kitten reclining, gray, 4x6" 25.00
Bank, log cabin school, brn 30.00
Bank, pig, wall hanger, bl 30.00
Bowl, mixing; Pilgrim Pottery line, bl, nested set of 6 ....150.00
Bowl, mold, heart shape w/dogwood cluster in bottom, brn 50.00
Christmas planter, Santa's boot, red/wht, #676 ....24.00
Cookie jar, Clown, straw hat lid 75.00
Cookie jar, Panda, head is lid 95.00
Creamer/sugar bowl, hen & rooster, wht w/brushed blk, red cold pnt...45.00
Easter planter, hen w/bonnet, yel/bl, 4¾" 20.00
Employee service pin, bronze w/diamond, 25 yrs 70.00
Employee service pin, bronze w/emerald, 15 yrs 40.00
Figurine, cat, recumbent, wht/gray spray, 9x5½" 20.00
Figurine, fawn, brn spray, 7x5x2" 15.00
Figurine, hound dog, wht/brn/blk, #583, 3¼x4½" 15.00
Figurine, kangaroo, pk, mini, 2¼" 10.00
Figurine, political; donkey, gray, mk Kennedy, 2¼x2¼" 40.00
Figurine, Scottish terrier, wht/brn spray, 7½x7" 15.00
Grass grower, Christmas tree 15.00
Grass grower, Jake 24.00
Grass grower, Jolly Jim 20.00
Grass grower, sailor 30.00
Lamp, teddy bear 45.00
Pie bird, duckling, bl/pk/wht, 5½" 45.00
Pie bird, yel/gr/red brushed decor, 5" 40.00
Pitcher, no drip type, hand decor w/gold & enamels 50.00
Stein, beer; bbl shape, Happy Days Are Here Again, brn, 5" 30.00
Stein, beer; Parrot on Lattice, brn Rockingham, 5" 20.00
TV lamp, horse head, brn, 18" 45.00

American Art Potteries (1947 – 1963)

Vase, ruffled tulip shape, pink and mauve, 9", $35.00. (Photo courtesy Doris and Burdell Hall)

Bowl, flat leaf shape, gr, #351, 1½x7" 15.00
Candlestick, donut shape, gr, #140, w/3 cups, 6x7½" 40.00
Doll parts, head/arms/legs, 3", 5-pc 65.00
Figurine, Afghan hounds, blk, 15", pr 55.00
Figurine, deer w/antlers leaping, brn/gr/wht spray, #502, 11½" 55.00
Figurine, horse rearing, brn/gr spray, #501, 11½" 30.00
Figurine, Poland China hog, wht w/gray spots, gr base, 5½x7½"...50.00
Figurine, rooster, gray/blk spray, #305, 8" 24.00
Figurine, wild horse, brn spray, #504, 11½" 40.00
Night light, wall mt, brn/wht spray, rare, 6x3x3¼" 50.00

Planter, baby buggy, wht, decor, 5½x7" 20.00
Planter, deer reclining by stump, gr/brn spray 24.00
Planter, elephant trumpeting, wht, 7½x2½" 30.00
Planter, pig, blk w/wht stripe 30.00
Planter, squirrel sitting, brn, #311, 6½x6" 20.00
Planter, Teddy bear on 3 building blocks, wht/pk/bl, 12x4x4".......30.00
Tray, butterfly shape, pk w/mauve spray, #135G, 1x7x6¼" 25.00
TV lamp, conch shell, tan w/gr spray, 6½" 30.00
Vase, bulbous w/molded flowers, brn w/yel spray, 12¾" 50.00
Vase, cowboy boot, gray/pk, #312, 5½" 20.00
Vase, deer w/fawn, brn spray, #322, 7½" 35.00
Vase, ewer form, pk, 14" 20.00
Vase, mauve/gray, 6-sided, #214, 12" 24.00

Moser

Ludwig Moser began his career as a struggling glass artist, catering to the rich who visited the famous Austrian health spas. His talent and popularity grew and in 1857 the first of his three studios opened in Karlsbad, Czechoslovakia. The styles developed there were entirely his own; no copies of other artists have ever been found. Some of his original designs include grapes with trailing vines, acorns and oak leaves, and richly enameled, deeply cut or carved floral pieces. Sometimes jewels were applied to the glass as well. Moser's animal scenes reflect his careful attention to detail. Famed for his birds in flight, he also designed stalking tigers and large, detailed elephants, all created in fine enameling.

Moser died in 1916, but the business was continued by his two sons who had been personally and carefully trained by their father. The Moser company bought the Meyr's Neffe Glassworks in 1922 and continued to produce quality glassware.

When identifying Moser, look for great clarity in the glass; deeply carved, continuous engravings; perfect coloration; finely applied enameling (often covered with thin gold leaf); and well-polished pontils. Our advisor for this category is Don Williams; he is listed in the Directory under Missouri. Items described below are enameled unless noted otherwise. If no color is mentioned in the line, the glass is clear.

Finger bowl & underplate, amber, jeweled flowers, gilt, pr 310.00
Goblet, allover gold encrustation & prunts, 8" 300.00
Goblet, cranberry, appl acorns/gold prunts, enamel branches, 7½".....800.00
Goblet, cranberry bowl w/HP & gilt, clear stem, gold-banded ft, 6"...100.00
Jar, cranberry w/HP floral & gold, hinged lid, metal ft, 4½" 150.00
Loving cup, cranberry, gold panels/mc florals, 3 clear hdls, 5" 150.00
Pokal, mc florals & sapphire rigaree, stepped base, 11¾" 350.00
Rose bowl, amber w/faceted jewels & gold, 5¼" 650.00
Vase, amber, ribbed, band of warriors, rnd ped ft, 8" 250.00
Vase, amber w/9 cut-bk giraffes/trees, sgn HH, 7x5½" 650.00
Vase, appl/HP gr fish & coral, 8¼" 350.00
Vase, clear to amethyst w/cvd & gilt floral & dragonfly, 7"..........600.00
Vase, clear to aquamarine, intaglio floral/gilt, 2½" 275.00
Vase, cobalt, gold-leaf Greek figures/lines, 11" 265.00
Vase, cobalt w/amber rigaree & ft, cut/gilt florals, 6x4½" 265.00
Vase, cranberry w/allover gold decor, 12½" 650.00
Vase, dk bl rim/base cut to clear, clear band w/cut floral, 10" 325.00
Vase, dk gr, cvd/gilded trees & deer, paneled cylinder, 12½" 265.00
Vase, gold panels/mc floral, trumpet form; mk silver hdld base, 11", EX...200.00
Vase, lt gr, long sq neck w/zipper corners, gold panels/mc floral, 13" ...235.00
Vase, red, mc enamel florals on gold border, pilsener form, 8", EX 120.00

Moss Rose

Moss Rose was a favorite dinnerware pattern of many Staffordshire and American potters of the mid-1800s. In America the Wheeling Pottery of West Virginia produced the ware in large quantities, and it became one of their bestsellers, remaining popular well into the '90s. The pattern was colored by hand; this type is designated 'old' in our listings to distinguish it from the more modern Moss Rose design of the twentieth century, which we've also included. It's not hard to distinguish between the two. The later ware you'll recognize immediately, since the pattern is applied by decalcomania on stark white backgrounds. It has been made in Japan to a large extent, but companies in Germany and Bavaria have produced it as well. Today, there is more interest in the twentieth-century items than in the older ware. In the listings that follow, when no manufacturer is given, assume that item to have been made in twentieth-century Japan.

Ashtray, sm...**6.00**
Bowl, centerpc; gold trim, pierced rim, Rosenthal, 1½x7½" **35.00**
Bowl, sauce...**6.00**
Bowl, soup; Pompadour, Rosenthal, US Zone **42.00**
Bowl, vegetable; w/lid & hdls, John Moses...NJ, old, ca 1895-1904..**40.00**
Bud vase, 3½" **15.00**
Butter pat, 3¼" **5.00**
Candle holders, cornucopia form, 1940s, 3¼x3¼", pr **55.00**
Candle holders, cornucopia style, gold trim, 4", pr **35.00**
Candy dish, fluted, w/lid **22.00**
Chocolate pot **23.00**
Cigarette lighter, gold trim, lg **15.00**
Coffeepot, Pompadour, Rosenthal, 11" **150.00**
Cottage cheese dish **15.00**
Creamer, lg **15.00**
Creamer & sugar bowl, w/lid, gold trim, unmk, 1940s, pr............**35.00**
Cup & saucer, demitasse; Japan..**8.00**
Cup & saucer, Royal Albert **22.50**
Cup & saucer, Ucagco, ftd **10.00**
Dresser box, gold trim, 3x4½x2½" **20.00**
Egg cup **9.00**
Mirror on stand, Japan..**15.00**
Mustache cup, gold trim, Haviland, old, from $225 to **275.00**
Nut dish w/4 nut cups..**35.00**
Pin dish, gold trim, 6¼"..**24.00**
Plate, bread & butter; Johann Haviland, 6¼" **12.00**
Plate, dinner; Johann Haviland Bavaria, 10", from $10 to **15.00**
Plate, salad **6.50**
Plate, 12-sided, Limoges, 9¼" **30.00**
Platter, Pompadour, Rosenthal, 13" **70.00**
Platter, Ucagco, rare, 12", from $65 to **85.00**
Smoke set, flat tray w/4 ashtrays & lighter **40.00**
Soap dish, w/lid & drainer, gold trim, Haviland, old, 5x4", from $175 to..**200.00**
Tea set, stacking; creamer & sugar bowl set atop teapot **30.00**
Tidbit, 2-tier, Japan..**20.00**
Tray, Pompadour, Rosenthal, 13x10" **65.00**
Trays, butterfly shape, stacking set of 4...**15.00**
Tureen, w/lid, Pompadour, Rosenthal, 7¼x12" **110.00**

Mother-of-Pearl Glass

Mother-of-Pearl glass was a type of mold-blown satin art glass popular during the last half of the nineteenth century. A patent for its manufacture was issued in 1886 to Frederick S. Shirley, and one of the companies who produced it was the Mt. Washington Glass Company of New Bedford, Massachusetts. Another was the English firm of Stevens and Williams. Its delicate patterns were developed by blowing the gather into a mold with inside projections that left an intaglio design on the surface of the glass, then sealing the first layer with a second, trapping air in the recesses. Most common are the Diamond Quilted, Raindrop, and

Herringbone patterns. It was made in several soft colors, the most rare and valuable is rainbow — a blend of rose, light blue, yellow, and white. Occasionally it may be decorated with coralene, enameling, or gilt. Watch for twentieth-century reproductions, especially in the Diamond Quilted pattern. Our advisors for this category are Betty and Clarence Maier; they are listed in the Directory under Pennsylvania. See also Coralene; Stevens and Williams.

Bottle, Peacock Eye, bl, silver leaf-emb cover, ball shape, 3¼" ...**650.00**
Bottle, scent; Teardrop, pk, swirled half-rnd form, hinged lid, 2½".**325.00**
Bowl, Dmn Quilt, rainbow, crystal rigaree rim/open ft (losses), 6x6"..**900.00**
Creamer, Dmn Quilt, rainbow, ruffled top, camphor hdl, 2¾", NM...**550.00**
Ewer, Dmn Quilt, citron to pearl, camphor hdl (NM), 6½" **150.00**
Lamp base, Dmn Quilt, sapphire bl, 7¼" **150.00**
Pitcher, Dmn Quilt, rainbow, long cylinder neck, spherical body, 13"...**600.00**
Pitcher, Dmn Quilt, yel, frosted reeded hdl, 7¼" **375.00**
Rose bowl, Dmn Quilt, bl to pearl, pinched rim, 4¼x4⅝" **350.00**
Rose bowl, Dmn Quilt, rainbow, incurvate/scalloped rim, 3¾" ...**275.00**
Rose bowl, Dmn Quilt, rainbow, ruffled, mk Pat, 2¾", +7" undertray..**3,350.00**
Spooner, Dmn Quilt, rainbow, crimped top, 4¾" **650.00**
Toothpick holder, Dmn Quilt, gold-amber to pearl, 4-lobe rim, 3"....**300.00**
Toothpick holder, Dmn Quilt, med bl to pearl, 4-lobe rim, 2¾" ...**375.00**
Tumbler, Dmn Quilt, bl, 3¾"...**75.00**
Tumbler, Dmn Quilt, dk red to pearl, 3¾" **250.00**
Tumbler, Dmn Quilt, rainbow, sq mouth, 3¾" **575.00**
Tumbler, Dmn Quilt, rainbow, vertical stripes, 3½" **400.00**
Tumbler, Dmn Quilt, yel, 3⅞" **120.00**
Tumbler, Dmn Quilt, yel w/floral, 3¾" **150.00**
Tumblers, Dmn Quilt, rainbow, bright mc floral, 3½", set of 4...**2,250.00**
Vase, Dmn Quilt, apricot, ruffled, 10½", NM **200.00**
Vase, Dmn Quilt, lt bl to pearl w/camphor spiral at neck, 7" **175.00**
Vase, Dmn Quilt, Prussian bl, lg crimped cup-like top, Mt WA, 9"....**225.00**
Vase, Dmn Quilt, rose, ornate gold decor, att Webb, bulbous, 7" ..**250.00**
Vase, Dmn Quilt, yel, gourd form, 2 appl rustic hdls, 7", NM **90.00**
Vase, Federzeichnung, brn w/overall gold tracery, bottle form, 13"..**1,600.00**
Vase, Federzeichnung, 4-lobe top, Pat #9159, 7x4½" **2,500.00**
Vase, Raindrop, bl, trifold top, bulbous body, 7½" **275.00**
Vase, Raindrop, rainbow, long neck, dimpled body, 13", pr.........**500.00**
Vase, Raindrop, rainbow w/bird & floral allover front, 10½", pr **1,300.00**

Mourning Collectibles

During the eighteenth and early nineteenth centuries, ladies made needlework pictures, samplers, painting on ivory plaques, watercolor drawings, etc., to commemorate the death of a loved one. Elements contained in nearly all examples are the tomb, mourners, a weeping willow tree, and data relating to the deceased. Often plaits of hair were included. Today these are recognized and valued as a valid form of folk art.

Cut paper, 2 doves/woven heart on open hand w/woven lock of hair, 5x3"...**1,400.00**
Needlework, lg willow/lady by monument w/lg urn atop, church, 17x16" ..**2,200.00**
Needlework, willow overhangs 2 monuments/house, sgn, 22x19", VG....**3,000.00**
Needlework, willows/tombstones/etc, silk, 1830s, 21x21", EX....**4,375.00**
Ring, gold w/oval pc of ivory cvd w/urn, willow, etc, name/1793, EX.......**440.00**
Watercolor & ink on paper, lady by monument, 1828, 18x29" gilt fr ..**3,450.00**
Watercolor & pencil on paper, girl w/rose beside bush, 1840s, 5x7" **750.00**
Watercolor on paper, monument/children/flowers, 14½x18½" ...**550.00**

Movie Memorabilia

Movie memorabilia covers a broad range of collectibles, from books and magazines dealing with the industry in general to the various promotional materials which were distributed to arouse interest in a particular film. Many collectors specialize in a specific area — posters, pressbooks, stills, lobby cards, or souvenir programs (also referred to as premiere booklets). In the listings below a one-sheet poster measures approximately 27" x 41", three-sheet: 41" x 81", and six-sheet: 81" x 81". Window cards measure 14" x 22". Values are for examples in near mint condition unless noted otherwise. Our advisor for this category is Robert Doyle; he is listed in the Directory under New York. See also Autographs; Cartoon Art; Magazines; Paper Dolls; Personalities; Rock 'n Roll Memorabilia; Sheet Music.

Insert card, Animal Farm, George Orwell, 1955, NM+ 100.00
Insert card, Born Yesterday, J Holliday/W Holden/B Crawford, VG+ ... 75.00
Insert card, Clash at Midnight, M Monroe/B Stanwyck/R Ryan, 1952, EX ... 100.00
Insert card, Country Girl, G Kelly/W Holden/B Crosby, 1954, VG+ 50.00
Insert card, Desert Fury, B Lancaster w/others, 1947, VG+ 100.00
Insert card, Gypsy, N Wood/K Malden/R Russell, 1962, VG+ 55.00
Insert card, Happy Go Lucky, D Powell/B Hutton/others, 1943, EX+ 65.00
Insert card, Our Man in Havana, A Guinness/N Coward, 1960, EX 35.00
Insert card, Ring of Fire, M Spillane, 1954, EX 50.00
Insert card, Treat 'Em Rough, Eddie Albert, 1941, EX+ 50.00
Lobby card, College Holiday, Martha Raye, VG+ 75.00
Lobby card, Left Hand of God, H Bogart/G Tiereny, 1955, VG 20.00
Lobby card, Rancho Notorious, Marlene Dietrich, 1952, VG+ 20.00
Lobby card, Voice in the Night, Tim McCoy, 1934, EX 50.00
Lobby card set, Black Sunday, Barbara Steel, 1961, EX 100.00
Lobby card set, Great American Pastime, T Ewell/A Francis, 1956, VG+ .. 45.00
Lobby card set, Kill the Umpire, William Bendix, 1950, rare, VG .. 100.00
Lobby card set, Manchurian Candidate, F Sinatra/L Harvey, 1962, EX ... 75.00
Lobby card set, Othello, Laurence Olivier, 1966, NM 40.00
Lobby card set, Prisoner of War, Ronald Reagan, 1954, VG-EX ... 100.00
Lobby card set, Pushover, Kim Novak/Fred MacMurray, 1954, VG 50.00
Lobby card set, Rock Around the World, Tommy Steele, 1957, EX 50.00
Lobby card set, The Spy Who Loved Me, Bob Peak artwork, 1977, NM... 50.00
Poster, Aristocats, Disney, 1971, 1-sheet, EX 125.00
Poster, Beach Blanket Bingo, Avalon/Funicello, 1965, 60x40", VG... 100.00
Poster, Beast w/a Million Eyes, 1955, 1-sheet, EX......................... 450.00
Poster, Black Sunday, Barbara Steele, 1961, 40x30", EX 150.00
Poster, Bonnie Parker Story, Dorothy Provine, 1958, ½-sheet, VG+.... 50.00
Poster, Broken Arrow, James Stewart, 1950, 1-sheet, EX 500.00
Poster, Call Northside 777, James Stewart, 1948, 1-sheet, EX 300.00
Poster, Dead Reckoning, Bogart/Liz Scott, 1955 reissue, ½-sheet, EX ..50.00
Poster, Dive Bomber, Errol Flynn/Fred MacMurray, 1941, rstr 450.00
Poster, Elmer Gantry, Lancaster/G Simmons, 1960, 6-sheet, M..125.00
Poster, Fantastic Voyage, Raquel Welch, 1966, 3-sheet, VG 65.00
Poster, Forbidden Adventure, gorilla/jungle women, 1940s, 1-sheet, G+ ...50.00
Poster, Forbidden Planet, W Pigeon/others, 1956, 1-sheet, rare, rstr 1,500.00

Poster, Fuller Brush Man, Red Skelton, 1948, 6-sheet, rare, VG+ 100.00
Poster, Godzilla King of the Monsters, Raymond Burr, 1956, 1-sheet, EX ..2,250.00
Poster, Going My Way, Bing Crosby, 1944, VG..........................150.00
Poster, Goldfinger, Sean Connery, 1964, 1-sheet, EX 650.00
Poster, Harvey, James Stewart, 1950, 1-sheet, EX....................1,000.00
Poster, Hawaii, Julie Andrews/Max Von Sydow, 1966, 1-sheet, NM ...35.00
Poster, Hondo, John Wayne, 1953, ½-sheet, G+ 350.00
Poster, How To Steal a Million, A Hepburn/O'Toole, 1966, 3-sheet, NM..175.00
Poster, Hush...Sweet Charlotte, Davis/deHaviland/Cotton, 1965, 40x27"..750.00
Poster, If You Knew Susie, Eddie Cantor/Joan Davis, 1947, 3-sheet, VG+.....100.00
Poster, Judgment at Nuremberg, profiles of cast, 1961, 40x30", EX..100.00
Poster, King Solomon's Mines, Kerr/Granger, 1962 reissue, 1-sheet, EX.....50.00
Poster, Lady Sings the Blues, Diana Ross, 1972, 1-sheet, EX.........40.00
Poster, Love Me Tender, Elvis playing guitar, 1956, 1-sheet, EX.500.00
Poster, Madam, Sophia Loren, 1962, 1-sheet, EX+ 50.00
Poster, Magic Town, James Stewart/Jane Wyman, 1947, 3-sheet, VG+ ...100.00
Poster, Malcom X, documentary, 1972, 1-sheet, NM...................100.00
Poster, Mame, Lucille Ball, 1974, 1-sheet, NM...............................35.00
Poster, Miracle Worker, Patty Duke/Anne Bancroft, 1962, ½-sheet, VG...50.00
Poster, Munsters Go Home, Munster cast, 1966, 2-sheet, VG+..150.00
Poster, Murder on the Orient Express, Amsel artwork, 1974, 1-sheet, EX ...50.00
Poster, No Time for Love, C Cobert/F McMurry, 1943, 1-sheet, VG....76.00
Poster, Painted Hills, Lassie, 1-sheet, 1951, VG+ 50.00
Poster, Remember Pearl Harbor, Don Barry, 1943, 1-sheet, rare, VG+...150.00
Poster, Rings on Her Fingers, G Tierney/H Fonda, 1942, 1-sheet, EX...250.00
Poster, Rock Around the Clock, Bill Haley/others, 1956, ½-sheet, G+..150.00
Poster, Rumba, Caroll Lombard/George Raft, 1935, ½-sheet, G+ 650.00
Poster, Saturday Night Fever, John Travolta, 1977, 1-sheet, VG+......100.00
Poster, Showdown, W Boyd as Hopalong Cassidy, 1940, 1-sheet, EX ...650.00
Poster, Slattery's Hurricane, V Lake/R Widmark, 1949, ½-sheet, VG ..65.00
Poster, Suddenly Last Summer, Taylor/Hepburn/Clift, 1960, 3-sheet, EX ...200.00
Poster, Summer Storm, Linda Darnell/G Sanders, 1944, 1-sheet, EX ..250.00
Poster, The Sisters, B Davis/E Flynn, 1938, 1-sheet, rare 400.00
Poster, Torn Cutain, Paul Newman/Julie Andrews, 1966, 3-sheet, EX+ ..150.00
Poster, Untamed, P Morison/R Milland/A Tamiroff, 1940, 1-sheet, VG+ ..200.00
Poster, Watch on the Rhine, Betty Davis/Paul Lukas, 1943, 1-sheet, EX ..450.00
Poster, Where the Boys Are, C Francis/G Hamilton, 1961, 1-sheet, EX 50.00
Poster, Yellow Rolls Royce, I Bergman/R Harrison, 1965, 1-sheet, EX 75.00
Poster, You're My Everything, Dan Dailey/Ann Baxter, 1949, 1-sheet, EX ...50.00
Poster, Zulu, Michael Cane, 1963, rare, 40x30", EX....................100.00
Pressbook, Black Raven, George Zucco, 1943 ....45.00
Souvenir book, On a Clear Day, B Streisand, EX 15.00
Title card, Black Widow, G Rogers/G Tierney/G Raft, 1954, EX ..25.00
Title card, Sands of Iwo Jima, John Wayne, 1950, VG+ 200.00
Window card, Carousel, Shirley Jones/Gordon MacRae, 1956, VG+..50.00
Window card, China, Alan Ladd/Loretta Young, 1943, VG..........75.00
Window card, Daddy Long Legs, Fred Astaire/Leslie Caron, 1955, VG+...50.00
Window card, Desiree, M Brando/J Simmons/M Overon, 1954, VG+...70.00
Window card, Dragnet, Jack Webb, 1954, VG+ 65.00
Window card, Giant, E Taylor/J Dean/R Hudson, 1956, rare, VG+ ..175.00
Window card, Gone w/the Wind, Gable/Leigh, 1968 reissue, M ..65.00
Window card, I'm No Angel, Mae West/Cary Grant, 1933, rare, EX ..750.00
Window card, Psycho, Anthony Perkins/Janet Leigh, 1960, G+ ...150.00
Window card, Ten Commandments, artwork of Moses w/tablet, 1923, rstr...650.00
Window card, The World Changes, Paul Muni, 1933, VG.........250.00

Poster, From Russia With Love, Sean Connery, Italian, United Artists, 1963, 55x39", NM, $450.00.

Mt. Washington

The Mt. Washington Glass Works was founded in 1837 in South Boston, Massachusetts, but moved to New Bedford in 1869 after purchasing the facilities of the New Bedford Glass Company. Frederick S. Shirley became associated with the firm in 1874. Two years later the company reorganized and became known as the Mt. Washington Glass

Company. In 1894 it merged with the Pairpoint Manufacturing Company, a small Brittania works nearby, but continued to conduct business under its own title until after the turn of the century. The combined plants were equipped with the most modern and varied machinery available and boasted a working force with experience and expertise rival to none in the art of blowing and cutting glass. In addition to their fine cut glass, they are recognized as the first American company to make cameo glass, an effect they achieved through acid-cutting methods. In 1885 Shirley was issued a patent to make Burmese, pale yellow glassware tinged with a delicate pink blush. Another patent issued in 1886 allowed them the rights to produce Rose Amber, or amberina, a transparent ware shading from ruby to amber. Pearl Satin Ware and Peachblow, so named for its resemblance to a rosy peach skin, were patented the same year. One of their most famous lines, Crown Milano, was introduced in 1893. It was an opal glass either free blown or pattern molded, tinted a delicate color and decorated with enameling and gilt. Royal Flemish was patented in 1894 and is considered the rarest of the Mt. Washington art glass lines. It was decorated with raised, gold-enameled lines dividing the surface of the ware in much the same way as lead lines divide a stained glass window. The sections were filled in with one or several transparent colors and further decorated in gold enamel with florals, foliage, beading, and medallions.

For more information, *Mt. Washington Art Glass* by Betty B. Sisk is available from Collector Books. Our advisors for this category are Betty and Clarence Maier; they are listed in the Directory under Pennsylvania. See also Amberina; Cranberry; Salt Shakers; Burmese; Crown Milano; Mother-of-Pearl; Royal Flemish; etc.

Bowl, floral cameo cvg, crimped rim w/griffins, Pairpoint stag fr, 10"...**1,750.00**
Bowl vase, mums on lt bl to opaque wht, ribbed, 2½x3⅜" **350.00**
Cracker jar, poppies/gilt on lt gr/wht pnt opal; Pairpoint lid, 6x8x6"..**950.00**
Fernery, mums/gold on lt gray tracery, 8" dia **1,000.00**
Goblet, Rose Amber, amberina...**250.00**
Nappy, pond lilies, gold/gr on clear, w/hdl, 2x6" **375.00**
Plate, Butterfly & Daisy, 8" **200.00**
Salt, chick head, daisies, yel/wht on opal, 2¾" **600.00**
Shakers, bluerina, Hartford SP fr, pr...**400.00**
Shakers, egg form HP decor, orig caps, in SP fr, pr **450.00**
Shakers, tomato form w/HP decor, orig caps, pr, from $60 to........**80.00**
Sugar shaker, floral below lid, melon ribbed, 3¼" dia..................**115.00**
Sugar shaker, violets/leaves on shaded gr, egg shape, 4½" **385.00**
Tankard, spider mums/gold traceries on clear, 8x6".....................**895.00**
Toothpick holder, floral on melon-rib body, beaded top, 2¼".....**275.00**
Vase, Lava, appl hdls, 4½x5" **2,500.00**
Vase, Napoli, chicks in the rain, 8¾"...**1,400.00**

Mulberry China

Mulberry china was made by many of the Staffordshire area potters from about 1830 until the 1850s. It is a transfer-printed earthenware or ironstone named for the color of its decorations, a purplish-brown resembling the juice of the mulberry. Some pieces may have faded out over the years and today look almost gray with only a hint of purple. (Transfer printing was done in many colors; technically only those in the mauve tones are 'mulberry'; color variations have little effect on value.) Some of the patterns (Corean, Jeddo, Pelew, and Formosa, for instance) were also produced in Flow Blue ware. Others seem to have been used exclusively with the mulberry color. Our advisor for this category is Mary Frank Gaston.

Abbey, pitcher, 8-sided, 7¼" **265.00**
Beauties of China, undertray, Mellor Venables, 10x7¼" **150.00**
Blantyre, platter, Meigh & Son, 21½x17"....................................**300.00**
Bochara, bowl, vegetable; w/lid, Edwards **375.00**

Bochara, plate, Edwards, 10½"..**125.00**
Bochara, plate, 12-sided, Edwards, 9" **95.00**
Canova, sauce tureen, w/lid & 8x6¼" undertray, Mayer **600.00**
Castle Scenery, sugar bowl, w/lid, Furnival **275.00**
Corea, teabowl & saucer **120.00**
Corean, bowl, soup; Podmore Walker, 9¾" dia, from $100 to.....**125.00**
Corean, compote, 9x11"...**325.00**
Corean, plate, Podmore Walker, 8"..**80.00**
Corean, plate, Podmore Walker, 9¾"...**100.00**
Corean, plate, 8"..**80.00**
Corean, posset cup, Podmore Walker, 3".....................................**125.00**
Corean, sauce tureen, ftd, Podmore Walker, 7½x7", +8½" tray **450.00**
Corinthia, soup plate, Challinor, 9⅞", EX.....................................**65.00**
Cypress, plate, 12-sided, Davenport, 9", from $100 to.................**125.00**
Flora, tea bowl & saucer..**110.00**
Foliage, plate, 12-sided, 10¼", from $70 to **80.00**
Fruit Basket, plate, 10½"..**90.00**
Gondola, plate, Davenport, 7¼"...**70.00**
Hong, plate, 12-sided, T Walker, 9", from $100 to **125.00**
Japonica, creamer, unmk, 5¼x6½"..**175.00**
Jeddo, bowl, sauce..**45.00**
Jeddo, bowl, soup; Adams & Sons **125.00**
Jeddo, bowl, vegetable; Adams, 6x7"...**200.00**
Jeddo, plate, Adams, 7½"..**75.00**
Jeddo, plate, Adams, 9¼"..**120.00**
Lucerne, plate, JW Pankhurst, 9½", from $70 to **80.00**
Marble, pitcher, 8"..**325.00**
Marble, platter, 17½x14"..**450.00**
Moss Rose, plate, unmk, 10"..**70.00**
Nankin, creamer, Davenport..**225.00**
Ning-Po, plate, Hall, 9½"...**110.00**
Nonpariel, pitcher, Mayer, 7½"...**595.00**
Oriental, teapot, Ridgway, 7¾"...**695.00**
Panama, plate, 7¼"..**35.00**
Park Scenery, plate, Wallace, 9¼"...**110.00**
Pelew, mitten relish, Challinor, from $100 to **125.00**
Pelew, plate, Challinor, 8½"..**90.00**
Pelew, plate, Challinor, 10⅞", EX...**120.00**
Pelew, saucer plate, 4¼"...**55.00**
Peruvian, platter, Wedgwood, 18x14⅛".......................................**400.00**
Peruvian, sauce tureen & underplate, Wedgwood, 7½x7¼", 8½" **400.00**
Rhone Scenery, plate, Mayer, 9¼"..**95.00**
Rhone Scenery, platter, 13½"...**175.00**
Rose, plate, Edward Challinor, 10", from $75 to **85.00**
Rose, platter, TF&Co, 11x8½"..**125.00**
Royal Festoon, tea bowl & saucer, 2⅜x3½", 5½"..........................**125.00**
Rubens, plate, Wood, 8½"...**50.00**
Sardinia, platter, Hall, 15¼x12¼"..**375.00**
Shapoo, plate, T&R Boote, 9⅜"..**85.00**
Singan, plate, 10-sided, T Goodfellow, 10", from $100 to...........**125.00**
Temple, cup, no hdl, Podmore Walker & Co, from $75 to..........**100.00**
Tivoli, bowl, vegetable; ftd, w/lid, Meigh, 8¾x11" **350.00**
Tuscan Rose, plate, scalloped, Ridgway, 10½"..............................**100.00**
Udina, pitcher, Clementson, 5", from $75 to................................**100.00**
Venus, plate, Podmore Walker, 8¾" **75.00**
Vincennes, bowl, vegetable; w/lid..**395.00**
Vincennes, plate, Alcock, 9½"...**90.00**
Vincennes, plate, Alcock, 10½" **110.00**
Washington Vase, cup plate, Podmore Walker, 4¼", NM **75.00**
Washington Vase, plate, Podmore Walker, 9"...............................**100.00**
Washington Vase, platter, Podmore Walker, 15¾x12¼".............**375.00**
Washington Vase, sugar bowl, w/lid, Podmore Walker, 8¼" **250.00**
Washington Vase, tea bowl & saucer, Wedgwood........................**120.00**
Washington Vase, teapot, 8-sided, Podmore Walker, 9½x8½" ...**425.00**

Wreath, sugar bowl, cockscomb hdls, att Furnival, 8¾" 325.00
Wreath, teapot, cockscomb hdl, unmk Furnival, 10½" 400.00

Muller Freres

Henri Muller established a factory in 1900 at Croismare, France. He produced fine cameo art glass decorated with florals, birds, and insects in the Art Nouveau style. The work was accomplished by acid engraving and hand finishing. Usual marks were 'Muller,' 'Muller Croismare,' or 'Croismare, Nancy.' In 1910 Henri and his brother Deseri formed a glassworks at Luneville. The cameo art glass made there was nearly all produced by acid cuttings of up to four layers with motifs similar to those favored at Croismare. A good range of colors was used, and some later pieces were gold flecked. Handles and decorative devices were sometimes applied by hand. In addition to the cameo glass, they also produced an acid-finished glass of bold mottled colors in the Deco style. Examples were signed 'Muller Freres' or 'Luneville.' Our advisor for this category is Don Williams; he is listed in the Directory under Missouri.

Cameo

Lamp, berries and branches, purple to yellow-amber with autumnal enamels, 12" dome shade, signed base, 19½", $8,625.00.

Bottle, scent; floral, apricot on frost, fp, 3¼" 400.00
Lamp, trees/lake on flared shade/vasiform base, iron disk ft, 15" ...2,200.00
Vase, birds on leafy branches, gr mottle & amethyst, 7½" 1,750.00
Vase, butterflies among leafy stems, yel to amethyst w/gold, 14½" ..6,500.00
Vase, floral, bl/peach, slim, ftd, 12½" 1,700.00
Vase, floral (EX detail), orange on yel, slim, ftd, 7½" 3,250.00
Vase, flowers & leaves, red on frost to gr & mottled yel, 5¾" 800.00
Vase, lady slipper floral, wine on opal, 5¼" 1,150.00
Vase, leaves/insects, Fluorogravure, fall colors, 6¼" 2,000.00
Vase, peonies, gr/frost, bulbus w/stick neck, 13½" 1,100.00
Vase, roses, pk/gr on pk to frost, cylindrical, 10½" 2,500.00

Miscellaneous

Basket, Chapelle iron fr w/scrollwork & appl leafage, +bowl, 18" L...1,500.00
Chandelier, frosted/mc mottled dome w/3 floriform shades, 28" dia...1,300.00
Chandelier, mc internal decor, CI filigree fr, 2-arm w/6" shades 2,000.00
Sconce, tomato/amber/bl mottle, in vintage CI mt: 21", pr 1,950.00
Vase, bl/wht mottle w/sm areas of pk/gr/brn, early 20th C, 9" 400.00

Muncie

The Muncie Pottery was established in Muncie, Indiana, by Charles

O. Grafton; it operated there from 1922 until about 1935. The pottery they produced is made of a heavier clay than most of its contemporaries; the styles are sturdy and simple. Early glazes were bright and colorful. In fact, Muncie was advertised as the 'rainbow pottery.' Later most of the ware was finished in a matt glaze. The more collectible examples are those modeled after Consolidated Glass vases — sculptured with love-birds, grasshoppers, and goldfish. Their line of Art Deco-style vases bear a remarkable resemblance to the Consolidated Glass Company's Ruba Rombic line. Vases, candlesticks, bookends, ashtrays, bowls, lamp bases, and luncheon sets were made. A line of garden pottery was manufactured for a short time. Items were frequently impressed with MUNCIE in block letters. Letters such as A, K, E, or D and the numbers 1, 2, 3, 4, or 5 often found scratched into the base are finishers' marks. For more information, we recommend *Collector's Encyclopedia of Muncie Pottery* by Jon Rans and Mark Eckelman (Collector Books).

Bowl, bl peachskin, shape #159, unmk, 11" 450.00
Ewer, blk gloss, shape #136, mk Muncie - 1, 12" 125.00
Lamp, Dancing Nudes, gr matt, shape #U33, 28½" overall.........500.00
Pitcher, orange peel gloss, shape #U21, mk 2A, 7" 200.00
Vase, bl drip on peach-skin gloss, hdls, shape #427, mk A, 7" 200.00
Vase, gr drip on pumpkin, #460 shape, mk #5A, 12" 350.00
Vase, gr gloss drip on wht, shape #137, mk #1, 11" 350.00
Vase, matt gr over rose, waisted, #215, E-4, 12" 275.00
Vase, Rhombic, triangular panels jut from sides, mint gr/lav, 4x5" 495.00
Vase, Rombic, wht drip on bl, shape #300, mk A, 8" 700.00
Wall pocket, gr airbrushed over rose, shape #266, mk 3E, 9" 300.00

Musical Instruments

The field of automatic musical instruments covers many different categories ranging from watches and tiny seals concealing fine early musical movements to huge organs and orchestrions which weigh many hundreds of pounds and are equivalent to small orchestras. Music boxes, first made in the early nineteenth century by Swiss watchmakers, were produced in both disc and cylinder models. The latter type employs a cylinder with tiny pins that lift the teeth in the comb of the music box (producing a sound much like many individual tuning forks), and music results. The value of a cylinder music box depends on the length and diameter of the cylinder, the date of its manufacture, the number of tunes it plays (four or six is usually better than ten or twelve), whether it has multiple cylinders, if it has extra instruments (like bells, an organ, or drum), and its manufacturer. Nicole Freres, Henri Capt, LeCoultre, and Bremond are among the most highly regarded, and the larger boxes made by Mermod Freres are also popular. Examples with multiple cylinders, extra instruments (such as bells or an organ section), and those in particularly ornate cabinets or with matching tables bring significantly higher prices. Early cylinder boxes were wound with a separate key which was inserted on the left side of the case. These early examples are known as 'keywind' boxes and bring a premium. While smaller cylinder boxes are still being made, the larger ones (over 10" cylinders) typically date from before 1900. Disc music boxes were introduced about 1890 but were replaced by the phonograph only twenty-five years later. However, during that time hundreds of thousands were made. Their great advantage was in playing inexpensive interchangeable discs, a factor that remains an attraction for today's collector as well. Among the most popular disc boxes are those made by Regina (USA), Polyphon, Mira, Stella, and Symphonion. Relative values are determined by the size of the discs they play, whether they have single or double combs, if they are upright or table models, and how ornate their cases are. Especially valuable are those that play multiple discs at the same time or are incorporated into tall case clocks.

Player pianos were made in a wide variety of styles. Early varieties consisted of a mechanism which pushed up to a piano and played on the keyboard by means of felt-tipped fingers. These use sixty-five note rolls. Later models have the playing mechanism built in, and most use eighty-eight note rolls. Upright pump player pianos have little value in unrestored condition because the cost of restoration is so high. 'Reproducing' pianos, especially the 'grand' format, can be quite valuable, depending on the make, the size, the condition, and the ornateness of the case; however the market for 'reproducing' grand pianos has been very weak in recent years. 'Reproducing' grand pianos have very sophisticated mechanisms and are much more realistic in the reproduction of piano music. They were made in relatively limited quantities. Better manufacturers include Steinway and Mason & Hamlin. Popular roll mechanism makers include AMPICO, Duo-Art, and Welte.

Coin-operated pianos (Orchestrions) were used commercially and typically incorporate extra instruments in addition to the piano action. These can be very large and complex, incorporating drums, cymbals, xylophones, bells, and dozens of pipes. Both American and European coin pianos are very popular, especially the larger and more complex models made by Wurlitzer, Seeburg, Cremona, Weber, Welte, Hupfeld, and many others. These companies also made automatically playing violins (Mills Violin Virtuoso, Hupfeld), banjos (Encore), and harps (Whitlock); these are quite valuable.

Collecting player organettes is a fun endeavor. Roller organs, organettes, player organs, grind organs, hand organs — whatever the name — are a fascinating group of music makers. Some used wooden barrels or cobs to operate the valves, or metal and cardboard discs or paper strips, paper rolls, metal donuts, or metal strips. They usually played from fourteen to twenty keys or notes. Some were pressure operated or vacuum type. Their heyday lasted from the 1870s to the turn of the century. Most were reed organs, but a few had pipes. Many were made in either America or Germany. They lost favor with the advent of the phonograph, as did the music box. Some music boxes were built with little player organs in them. Any player organette in good working condition with some music and in their original finish should be worth from $200.00 to $600.00, depending on the model. Generally the more keying it has and the larger and fancier the case, the more desirable it is. Rarity plays a part too. There are a handfull of individuals who make new music rolls for these player organs. Some machines are very rare, and music for them is nearly impossible to find. For further information on player organs we recommend *Encyclopedia of Automatic Musical Instruments* by Bowers.

Unless noted, prices given are for instruments in fine condition, playing properly, with cabinets or cases in well-preserved or refinished condition. In all instances, unrestored instruments sell for much less, as do those with broken or missing parts, damaged cases, and the like. On the other hand, particularly superb examples in especially ornate case designs and those that have been particularly well kept will often command more. Our advisor for mechanical instruments is Martin Roenigk; he is listed in the Directory under Arkansas.

Key:
c — cylinder   d — disc

Mechanical

Accordion, Hobfauer, 20-key, automatic play, not antique, M.**3,900.00**
Box, Bremond, 20" c, 10-tune, alternating tops, G **4,200.00**
Box, Jean Ballan Haller, 7 interchangeable 14" c, EX orig w/c case..**6,500.00**
Box, Kalliope, 17 14" d, single c, burled case, table model **2,600.00**
Box, Lochmann, 17" d, 8 bells, table model, EX, +10 d...........**7,500.00**
Box, Mermod Freres, Ideal Sublime...Piccolo, 6 18" c, cvd case, EX....**11,500.00**
Box, Mira, 18½" d, console w/decal case, rstr........................**11,000.00**
Box, organ; Bremond, w/chiming clock, 14" c, 23-note, M rstr..**7,000.00**
Box, Otto Capital Model B, golden oak, 8 5¼" cuffs, matching base ..**5,000.00**
Box, Paillard Sublime Harmonie Tremolo Zither, 17" c, dbl spring, EX..**3,700.00**

Box, Polyphon, 15½" d, coin-op, 23x34", EX..........................**3,200.00**
Box, Polyphon, 17½" d, 12 saucer bells, inlay case **7,250.00**
Box, Polyphon, 22½" d, 16 bar bells, ornate base/gallery, upright.....**10,000.00**
Box, Regina, 12½" d, dk oak case, ca 1897, rstr, +10 d............**2,800.00**
Box, Regina, 12½" d, short bed plate, dbl c, mahog case, VG+...**3,200.00**
Box, Regina, 15½" d, dbl comb, zither attachment, 1880s, 21" L....**3,800.00**
Box, Regina, 15½" d, inlaid case w/paper label of children, EX...**4,200.00**
Box, Regina, 15½" d, mahog bow-front, auto changer, EX....**18,000.00**
Box, Regina, 27" d, single auto changer, walnut case, EX rstr..**21,000.00**
Box, Regina style 28, cupola top, 20¾" d, M......................**7,500.00**
Box, Stella, 17¼" d, dbl comb, mahog table model, G **4,000.00**
Box, Swiss, rosewood w/mahog & mc inlay, 12" c, 12-tune, 24" L, EX...**1,400.00**
Box, Symphonion, 11⅞" d, dbl comb, mahog table model **2,600.00**
Box, Symphonion, 13¾" d, walnut vnr, 22" case, German **2,700.00**
Box, Symphonion, 15" d, dbl comb, 10 saucer bells, rstr vnr, +25 d ..**6,500.00**
Box, Symphonion, 19¾" d, gallery top, storage base **7,000.00**
Calliope, National, 53-note, w/exterior blower, EX orig **7,900.00**
Harp, Wurlitzer B, ca 1980s repro, M **22,000.00**
Nickelodeon, Peerless #44, rfn oak case, M rstr, +20 rolls **10,500.00**
Nickelodeon, Seeburg A, w/xylophone, rstr **4,500.00**
Nickelodeon, Western Electric B, oak case, art glass, 1925, 62"..**5,000.00**
Orchestrelle, Aeolian V, oak, EX orig **2,000.00**
Orchestrelle, Aeolian Y, mahog, 58-note, M rstr, +12 rolls ...**12,000.00**
Orchestrelle, Wilcox & White Angelus push-up player, rstr, +12 rolls **1,000.00**
Orchestrion, Coinola C-2, EX..**27,000.00**
Orchestrion, Western Electric, 10-tune, G roll, 1920s, rstr......**7,500.00**
Organ, band; Wurlitzer #146-B, single roll fr, rstr **18,000.00**
Organ, band; Wurlitzer #148 Military, natural oak case, EX, +148 rolls....**17,000.00**
Organ, bbl; Bacigalupo, 38-key, 90 pipes, G **6,600.00**
Organ, Grand Roller, 15" roller cob, 32-note **4,000.00**
Organ, military band; Artisan A-1, 1920s, 76", G- **16,000.00**
Organ, monkey; Frati 'Clarion, 46-key, 129 pipes, 1880s, w/cart, rstr ...**11,000.00**
Organ, monkey; Gavioli Uniflute, 25-key, rstr **5,000.00**
Organ, paper roll; Improved Celestina, EX stencils, EX, +1 roll....**800.00**
Organ, street; Josef Riemer, 45-key, 60-pipe, 8-tune bbl, 1890s, rstr.....**5,000.00**
Organ, street; Pell, 3-figure, 48-key, w/cart, rstr **11,000.00**
Piano, baby grand; Baldwin Welte, mahog case, 38x61x56", EX....**2,000.00**
Piano, baby grand; Marshall & Wendel Ampico B, M rstr **12,000.00**
Piano, Cremona A, 25¢ play, takes O rolls (10-tune), ca 1920 ..**2,900.00**
Piano, grand; Knabe Ampico, art case, 68", EX orig **9,500.00**
Piano, grand; Marshall & Wendall Ampico, 60", EX orig........**1,800.00**
Piano, grand; Steinway Duo-Art, Florentine-style case, rstr ..**37,500.00**
Piano, grand; Steinway Louis XV Duo-Art, ca 1924, M rstr..**29,800.00**
Piano, grand; Welte-Mignon, Louis XV style, 1919, 72", M rstr ...**13,950.00**
Piano, upright; Chickering Ampico, EX orig.........................**1,500.00**
Piano, upright; Duo-Art, ft pump, walnut, 1922, EX orig **1,250.00**
Piano, upright; Welte, M rstr...**4,000.00**
Piano, upright; Wurlitzer IX, ldgl front, 5¢ play, 1915 ....**4,650.00**
Pianolin, N Tonawanda, 2 ranks of pipes/art glass, oak cabinet, EX....**12,500.00**
Violano, Mills Virtuoso, single violin & piano, oak, G..........**24,000.00**

Non-Mechanical

Accordion, Hohner Atlantic IV, 41 keys/120 buttons/4 reeds, M in case....**675.00**
Bagpipe, Lawrie, nickel silver ferrules/ivory mts, ca 1920, NM ..**1,850.00**
Banjo, Gibson RB 250 Mastertone, 5-string, NM in case **1,550.00**
Banjo/mandolin (banjolin), August Pollman, 5-string, NM........**675.00**
Bass, Antonius Stradivarius copy (Czech), blond, DeJacques bridge, NM ..**995.00**
Bass, Fender Jazz, rosewood w/pearl inserts, Sunburst, 1969, M..**1,550.00**
Clarinet, Buffet Crampon #308K1 G#, wood w/nickel silver keys, rstr **800.00**
Clarinet, Con Pan Am, rosewood, ca 1949, NM **425.00**
Drum, H Riley & Sons, red/blk/gilt w/rope binders, 19th C, 30½" dia....**260.00**
Drum, snare; Ludwig & Ludwig, blk dmn finish, orig head, NM...**700.00**
Drum set, Gretsch, 1940s, 4-pc, bass+floor tom+mtd tom+snare, EX...**1,200.00**

Drum set, Slingerland, wht satin flame, 1970s, 6-pc, NM 850.00
Euphonium, CG Conn, 4-valve, ca 1920s, EX.............................575.00
Flugelhorn, Couesnon, 2-tone lacquer, nickel pipes, NM in case 1,225.00
Flute, Geo W Haynes NY, silver metal, 27", NM in wooden case.....650.00
Flute, Lebret, Boehm system w/C ft, SP, NM in orig case............795.00
Guitar, Fender Stratocaster, all orig, 1975, NM........................1,850.00
Guitar, Gibson L4-C Archtop, acoustical, sunburst, 1949, NM....2,100.00
Guitar, Gurian Cutaway sz 3, ebony fretboard, rosewood cutaway, NM...1,950.00
Guitar, Martin Model 00-18, steel string acoustic, 1965, NM....1,800.00
Guitar, steel, Fender #6041, 30", EX in case 500.00
Mandolin, Gibson H-1, pearloid dot inlay, Pat July 4 1911, NM in case 1,400.00
Mandolin, Gibson Junior A, Snakehead Peghead, VG 1,150.00
Mandolin, Gibson Style A-4, pearl inlay & Boy Scout emblem, NM ..1,875.00
Marimba, Leedy Ludwig, 2½-octave, rosewood keys, EX, +mallets 650.00
Melodion, Liscomb & Dearborn, hinged lid, trn legs, 30x46x23" ...1,600.00
Piano, baby grand; Crown, dk wood, ca 1930s, EX w/bench....1,000.00
Piano, grand; Pleyel, Louis XVI-style parquetry w/gilt banding, 62" L ..4,000.00
Piano, grand; Steinway & Son, Louis XV style, walnut, 39x60x59"....2,950.00
Piano, grand; Steinway & Sons Model A, ebonized, cvd legs, 40x74x56" ..6,000.00
Piano, Pacific-Pasadena, Arts & Crafts, paneled, 57x68", VG ..2,000.00
Piccolo, Haynes D Flat, 1929, NM in case.................................600.00
Saxophone, Beuscher Aristocrat Baritone, str bell, pearl pads, EX 575.00
Saxophone, CG Conn C Melody Tenor, M gold wash & SP, NM overall.....975.00
Saxophone, CG Conn Naked Lady 10M Tenor, Belmonte mouthpc, 1930s, NM ...1,350.00
Saxophone, Conn Chu Berry Alto, orig NP, rolled tone holes, 1920s, NM....425.00
Saxophone, Conn Liberty Baritone, ca 1914, VG working 1,000.00
Saxophone, Conn Transitional Naked Lady Alto, mid-1930s, rstr.......1,100.00
Saxophone, Conn 6M Alto, underslung neck, 1965, NM in case 750.00
Saxophone, King Saxello Soprano, MOP on keys, EX patina, NM in case..1,600.00
Saxophone, LeBlanc Tenor, gold-tone, MOP buttons, 1950s, NM in case...1,200.00
Saxophone, Martin Silver C Soprano, gold-washed bell, ca 1923, NM...1,750.00
Vibraphone, Trixon, metal keys, EX, +2 prs mallets 925.00
Violin, August Gemunder Excelsior, spruce top, 23", EX w/Tourte bow ..550.00

Mustache Cups

Mustache cups were popular items during the late Victorian period, designed specifically for the man with the mustache! They were made in silver plate as well as china and ironstone. Decorations ranged from simple transfers to elaborately applied and gilded florals. To properly position the 'mustache bar,' special cups were designed for the 'lefties.' These are the rare ones! Our advisor for this category is Robert Doyle; he is listed in the Directory under New York.

Barbershop quartet transfer, gold trim, Japan, 4" 24.00
Currier & Ives-like winter country scene, unmk, 3½x4" 12.50
Floral, lav & gr on wht, bone china, Bavaria, #3817 ....65.00
Floral, wht on gr w/much gold trim, ftd, w/saucer 75.00

Floral, white with peach handle, triangular, 3", $145.00.

Floral swags on wht, Nippon, 2½x3½"...50.00
Flower garlands on wht lustre w/gold trim, 3x3½".........................24.00

Flower w/gold trim, unknown mk, 2½x3" 35.00
Grapes & leaves, Bavaria, early 1900s, 2½x4", +6½" saucer.........85.00
Pk swirling flowers w/gold, 3½" 65.00
Race of the Century, race park scene..12.50
Roses w/gold, RM Bavaria, 1920s, NM...60.00
Viking emb on milk glass, Pat Shaving Mug...1867....................350.00

Nailsea

Nailsea is a term referring to clear or colored glass decorated in contrasting spatters, swirls, or loops. These are usually white but may also be pink, red, or blue. It was first produced in Nailsea, England, during the late 1700s but was made in other parts of Britain and Scotland as well. During the mid-1800s a similar type of glass was produced in this country. Originally used for decorative novelties only, by that time tumblers and other practical items were being made from Nailsea-type glass.

Bottle, bellows; wht w/red & bl loopings, rigaree, hdls, 11¾" 460.00
Flask, clear w/wht loopings, canteen form, ca 1860, 6½" 100.00
Flask, red & wht swirls, 7½x3¾x1½"..230.00
Flask, red & yel over milk glass, 12 swirled ribs, 7"......................200.00
Flask, violet w/wht spirals, pontil scar, 1870-90, 7" 150.00
Flask, wht w/combed pk loopings, 1860s, 8"...............................165.00
Pitcher, lt turq opaque w/raspberry loopings, att Atterbury, 12"..650.00
Salt cellar, cranberry w/rigaree, in SP 3-ftd base 225.00

Nakara

Nakara was a line of decorated opaque milk glass produced by the C.F. Monroe Company of Meriden, Connecticut, for a few years after the turn of the century. It differs from their Wave Crest line in several ways. The shapes were simpler; pastel colors were deeper and covered more of the surface; more beading was present; flowers were larger; and large transfer prints of figures, Victorian ladies, cherubs, etc., were used as well. Ormolu and brass collars and mounts complemented these opulent pieces. Most items were signed; however, this is not important since the ware was never reproduced. Our advisors for this category are Dolli and Wilfred R. Cohen; their address is listed in the Directory under California.

Ashtray, floral on gr, 3 gilt-metal rests, 6" dia 300.00
Bonbon tray, Dmn Swirl, geometric scrolling/beading on bl 550.00
Box, blown-out pansy on bl, 3¼" dia 950.00
Box, cherubs on mauve, 6" dia..750.00
Box, courting couple reserve on peach, 6" dia............................1,150.00
Box, daisies on bright pk, beaded center, 4x6x4" 575.00
Box, Greenaway figures at picnic on bl, beading, 4x6"...............975.00
Box, iris on gr stems on creamy beige, 6" dia 650.00
Box, lady's portrait in reverse on bl w/wht enamel, 5" dia...........900.00
Box, peach/yel panels alternate, wht dots between, hexagonal, 3¼x3".450.00
Box, robin's egg bl w/tan accents & wht beading, hexagonal, 4"..515.00
Box, roses on pale bl, metal base, 3x3¾" dia..................................750.00
Box, Spindrift, floral, pk/wht on bl to yel, emb scrolls, 8" dia..1,950.00
Box, violets on yel, 3¾" dia 350.00
Box, 18th-C courting couple on peach (scarce color), 6" dia......950.00
Card holder, floral on gr, rectangular...650.00
Cracker jar, floral on rose w/gold, gold metal hdl & lid..............895.00
Dresser tray, daisies, pk/wht on gr, ormolu hdls, 6" dia 495.00
Hair reciever, children's tea party, lacy decor, dmn shape............585.00
Humidor, Cigars & flowers on bl 775.00
Humidor, Tobacco, frog reading paper on bl, metal lid, 6¾" ...1,950.00
Jardinier, pk floral on gr, gold rim...750.00
Match holder, tiny beaded flowers on gr, ormolu rim, 2" dia........550.00

Mirror tray, floral, pastel int, 3¾" dia...**695.00**
Smoke set, floral on gr, cigar holder+2 ash bowls+match holder on fr.**800.00**
Sweetmeat, fall leaves on bl, shaped body, metal lid/hdl, 5½" W.**475.00**
Vase, floral, stick neck, 8"..**995.00**

Napkin Rings

Napkin rings became popular during the late 1800s. They were made from various materials. Among the most popular and collectible today are the large group of varied silver-plated figurals made by American manu-facturers. Recently the larger figurals in excellent condition have appre-ciated considerably. Only those with a blackened finish, corrosion, or broken and/or missing parts have maintained their earlier price levels. When no condition is indicated, the items listed below are assumed to be all original and in very good to excellent condition. Check very careful-ly for missing parts, solder repairs, marriages, and reproductions.

A timely warning: Inexperienced buyers should be aware of excel-lent reproductions on the market, especially the wheeled pieces and cherubs. However, these do not have the fine detail and patina of the originals and tend to have a more consistent, soft pewter-like finish. These are appearing at the large, quality shows at top prices, being shown along with authentic antique merchandise. Beware!

Key:
R&B — Reed & Barton
SH&M — Simpson, Hall & Miller

American eagle w/ring atop open wings, Meriden B #203, rstr...**850.00**
Badminton girl leaning on ring on flat rectangular base, R&B #1455..**500.00**
Bear on base beside scrolled holder, Hamilton #127, from $200 to.**350.00**
Bird w/long tail on stem beside ring, Meriden Britannia #202, $200 to ..**350.00**
Bud vase among flowers/pods/leaves, Webster #168, old rstr.......**550.00**
Bull by bright-cut holder on fancy base, Knickerbocker #1250, $200 to.**350.00**
Butterfly atop ring on fancy scroll-ftd base, unmk......................**200.00**
Cat w/arched bk on ring before dog, Meriden #275, rstr.............**775.00**
Cherub before ring, Pairpoint #52, rstr......................................**650.00**
Cherub by ring holds torch-like bud vase, R&B #1285................**950.00**
Cherub looks into mirror (bud vase), Rockford #178, rstr...........**850.00**
Cherub on ring holds reins on stag, Toronto, rstr.....................**1,500.00**
Cherub w/flute on scroll beside ring & sm vase, Rogers & Bros, minimum..**500.00**
Chicken beside rake, Webster #172, rstr.....................................**650.00**
Child stands, faces begging dog, cylindrical ring behind, Meriden, 3"..**435.00**
Cockatoo on ball before ring on plain raised base, Pairpoint #8, under..**200.00**
Conquistador beside ring, Toronto #1137, rstr.........................**1,500.00**
Cow beside milk bucket-shaped holder, Meriden SP #268, from $200 to..**350.00**
Cow by sheaf-of-wheat ring, earth-like base, Meriden #01538, rstr .**850.00**

Dachshund holds ring on back, unmarked, 3", $895.00.

Deer w/long horns on carpet-like base, Toronto #1205, rstr........**850.00**
Dog in harness pulling holder on wheels, SH&M #033, from $350 to..**500.00**

Dog seated on base w/ring holder in mouth, SH&M #14............**500.00**
Dog w/paw up beside bbl-shaped holder, Rockford SP #125, from $200 to.**350.00**
Donkey wearing saddle by plain holder, unmk, from $200 to......**350.00**
Elephant-head hdls on ring, ped base, JW Tufts #1567 ....**350.00**
Elves balance ring atop fretwork on base, R&B #1326, minimum..**500.00**
Fans (2) w/ornate eng on oval vase, Bridgeport #207..................**275.00**
Fr w/ring holds pk-cased bud vase w/gold rim, Roger Smith #219, rstr..**1,100.00**
Frog leaping w/ring on bk, leafy base, Southington #35 ....**350.00**
Goat strides away from holder, Meriden Britannia #195, from $200 to ..**350.00**
Grapes & leaves support ring, Standard #730, rstr......................**375.00**
Grapes draped over bbl ring on ped base, Standard #733............**350.00**
Greenaway baby pushing ring on base, Middletown #25.............**500.00**
Greenaway boy in sailor atop ring, SH&M, from $200 to...........**350.00**
Greenaway boy lies on rectangular base, Tufts #1617.................**995.00**
Greenaway boy w/bat & ball, unmk, rstr **1,100.00**
Greenaway girl atop wooden fence that forms holder, unmk **250.00**
Greenaway girl sitting in branches, unmk, rstr **1,250.00**
Heron holding leaf on oval base, R&B #1126 ....**850.00**
Lizard w/ring on bk, Meriden #202..**350.00**
Lyre atop ring, unmk, rstr..**395.00**
Mastiff-like dog before ring, R&B #1185, rstr..........................**1,700.00**
Miner stands w/pick by Death Valley CA souvenir ring..............**475.00**
Owl (pepper) sits on sq emb holder, unmk, from $200 to...........**350.00**
Owl on leaf before ring, stamped #, rstr...................................**395.00**
Pan prancing beside ring, Pairpoint #82, rstr **950.00**
Peacock on decorative oval base, Schrade, rstr...........................**650.00**
Rabbit w/front ft on holder, unmk, from $200 to......................**350.00**
Reindeer pulling child atop ring on base, SH&M #18 ....**500.00**
Squirrel climing detailed branch, R&B #1150, rstr....................**550.00**
Squirrel on rectangular base, Southington #43, rstr...................**375.00**
Squirrel w/nut facing away from ring, SH&M #09 ....**300.00**
Squirrel w/ring on its bk, unmk SP, EX orig **650.00**
Tennis rackets w/ball resting on strings, MB Co #310, rstr.........**550.00**
Turtle pulling book-shaped ring on wheels, (Derby) #317, rstr ...**995.00**
Turtle w/ring on bk, Pairpoint #51 ....**500.00**

Nash

A. Douglas Nash founded the Corona Art Glass Company in Long Island, New York. He produced tableware, vases, flasks, etc. using delicate artis-tic shapes and forms. After 1933 he worked for the Libbey Glass Company.

Candlesticks, Chintz, Blood Red w/gray, ball stem, 4", pr **775.00**
Candlesticks, Chintz, orange & clear w/clear ft, 3¾", pr.............**200.00**
Lamp, 8" gold irid shade; sgn/#708 gold dorè std, 16", NM......**3,250.00**
Plate, Chintz, orchid & chartreuse spirals, 6½" **230.00**
Vase, amber irid, flared lip, #544, 4½"......................................**625.00**
Vase, gold irid w/emb flowers on stems (low), #549, 5¾"............**950.00**

Natzler, Gertrude and Otto

The Natzlers came to the United States from Vienna in the late 1930s. They settled in Los Angeles where they continued their work in ceramics, for which they were already internationally recognized. Gertrude created the forms; Otto formulated a variety of interesting glazes, among them volcanic, crystalline, and lustre. Our advisor for this category is Abby Malowanczyk; she is listed in the Directory under Texas.

Bowl, beige semimatt, folded rim, sm nick, 2½x8" **550.00**
Bowl, gr-bl w/dk brn clay showing through, short ped ft, 5" **1,300.00**
Bowl, gray & amber microcrystalline, hemispherical, 3½x6"...**1,000.00**
Bowl, lt bl w/bl specks, sm ped ft, 7" **1,100.00**

Bowl, multi-tone gray reduction glaze w/fissures, low, wide, 11" ..4,000.00
Bowl, sang reduction glaze w/slight irid, 3¼" 1,500.00
Bowl, taupe hare's fur, str sides, sm rpr, 3½x7" 500.00
Bowl, volcanic blk, ca 1956, 4x8" 4,995.00
Bowl, volcanic yel & brn, ca 1946, 9¾" 4,400.00
Vase, gray lava w/yel overflow, tapered form, ca 1939-40, 6" ...5,000.00
Vase, gunmetal crystalline, tapered cylinder, ca 1940-50, 7" 3,000.00
Vase, Maritosa reduction glaze w/melt fissures, bottle form, 10" .5,000.00
Vase, orange uranium crystalline, bottle neck, str sides, 7¼x5" ..4,500.00
Vase, Pompeian Earth (cream/tan lava), bulbous, 1939, 8" 4,000.00
Vase, thick textured red clay body, lt gr int, 2½" 2,000.00
Vessel, volcanic indigo/ivory/brn, str walls, L762, 4x4½" 3,750.00

Naughties and Bathing Beauties

These daring all-bisque figurines were made in various poses, usually in one piece, in German and U.S. factories during the 1920s. Admired
for their fine details, these figures were often nude but were also made
with molded-on clothing or dressed in bathing costumes. Items below are
all in excellent undamaged condition.

For further information we recommend *Doll Values, Antique to Modern*,
by Barbara DeFeo and Carol Stover (Collector Books). Our advisors for this
category are Don and Anne Kier; they are listed in the Directory under Ohio.

Action figure, w/wig, 7" 650.00
Action figure, 5" 450.00
Action figure, 7½" 650.00
Elderly woman in suit w/legs crossed, rare, 5¼" 1,400.00
Glass eyes, 5" 400.00
Glass eyes, 6" 650.00
Japan mk, 3" 55.00
Japan mk, 5-6", ea 95.00
Japan mk, 9" 140.00
Painted eyes, 3" 165.00
Painted eyes, 6" 325.00
Swivel neck, 5" 625.00
Swivel neck, 6" 700.00
With animal, 5½" 1,200.00
2 molded together, 4½-5½", ea 1,600.00

New Geneva

In the early years of the nineteenth century, several potteries flourished in the Greensboro, Pennsylvania, area. They produced utilitarian
stoneware items as well as tile and novelties for many decades. All failed
well before the turn of the century.

Flowerpot, dk brn w/flourish at unglazed tan center band, #4, 5½" .250.00
Jar, bl bands/tooling, HP strawberries, stencil: New Geneva, 9½"..2,750.00
Pitcher, floral on tanware, int: dk brn matt, 6⅝", EX.................440.00
Pitcher, unglazed tan w/dk brn glossy floral, tooled shoulder, 6" .770.00

New Martinsville

The New Martinsville Glass Company took its name from the town
in West Virginia where it began operations in 1901. In the beginning
years pressed tablewares were made in crystal as well as colored and
opalescent glass. Considered an innovator, the company was known for
their imaginative applications of the medium in creating lamps made
entirely of glass, vanity sets, figural decanters, and models of animals and
birds. In 1944 the company was purchased by Viking Glass, who contin-

ued to use many of the old molds, the animals molds included. They
marked their wares 'Viking' or 'Rainbow Art.' Viking recently ceased
operations and has been purchased by Kenneth Dalzell, president of the
Fostoria Company. They, too, are making the bird and animal models.
Although at first they were not marked, future productions will be
marked with an acid stamp. Dalzell/Viking animals are in the $50.00 to
$60.00 range. Values for cobalt and red items are two to three times
higher than for the same item in clear. See also Depression Glass; Glass
Animals and Figurines.

Addie, blk, cobalt, jade or red, bowl, vegetable; lg flared rim........45.00
Addie, blk, cobalt, jade or red, mayonnaise, 5" 25.00
Addie, blk, cobalt, jade or red, sherbet, ftd 15.00
Addie, blk, cobalt, jade or red, tumbler, juice; ftd, 6-oz 15.00
Addie, crystal or pk, creamer, ftd...10.00
Addie, crystal or pk, tray, sandwich; hdls 25.00
Addie, crystal or pk, tumbler, water; ftd, 9-oz.................................15.00
Janice, bl or red, basket, 9x6½" 145.00
Janice, bl or red, bowl, hdls, crimped, 6" 35.00
Janice, bl or red, bowl, oval, 11" 75.00
Janice, bl or red, bowl, salad; scalloped top, 12"............................90.00
Janice, bl or red, candlestick, 1-light, 5½x5", ea.............................50.00
Janice, bl or red, jar, jam; w/lid, 6" 50.00
Janice, bl or red, pitcher, berry cream; 15-oz 150.00
Janice, bl or red, plate, cheese; 11" 50.00
Janice, bl or red, plate, rolled edge, ftd, 14"...................................85.00
Janice, bl or red, tray, for creamer/sugar; oval, hdls 25.00
Janice, bl or red, vase, ivy; 3½x4" 50.00
Janice, crystal, bonbon, hdls, 4¾x7" 20.00
Janice, crystal, bowl, cupped, ftd, 11" 45.00
Janice, crystal, bowl, flower; w/8 crimps, 5½" 22.00
Janice, crystal, bowl, fruit; ruffled top, 12"....................................50.00
Janice, crystal, creamer, 6-oz 14.00
Janice, crystal, ice tub, ftd, 6" 115.00
Janice, crystal, mayonnaise, hdls, 6" 18.00
Janice, crystal, plate, cheese; 11"...22.50
Janice, crystal, plate, torte; rolled edge, 15"..................................50.00
Janice, crystal, sugar bowl, tall 17.00
Janice, crystal, vase, flared, 3-toed, 8" 50.00
Lions, blk, cup..35.00
Lions, blk, plate, 12"...40.00
Lions, blk, saucer...10.00
Lions, crystal, candle holder, #37, ea 25.00
Lions, crystal, creamer, #37 ....15.00
Lions, crystal, sugar bowl, #37 ....15.00
Lions, pk or gr, candy dish, w/lid..60.00
Lions, pk or gr, plate, 8" 20.00
Lions, pk or gr, sugar bowl, #34 ....25.00
Meadow Wreath, crystal, bowl, celery; oval, #42/26, 10" 35.00
Meadow Wreath, crystal, bowl, comport; #4218/26, 10" 40.00
Meadow Wreath, crystal, bowl, flat, flared, #4213/26, 12" 47.50
Meadow Wreath, crystal, cup, punch; tab hdls, #42/26..................9.00
Meadow Wreath, crystal, plate, 11"...35.00
Meadow Wreath, crystal, salver, ftd, #42/26, 12" 45.00
Meadow Wreath, crystal, vase, flared, #42/26, 10" 50.00
Moondrops, colors other than red or bl, bowl, console; rnd, 3-ftd, 12" .45.00
Moondrops, colors other than red or bl, bowl, cream soup; 4¼" ...40.00
Moondrops, colors other than red or bl, bowl, pickle; 7½" 20.00
Moondrops, colors other than red or bl, candlesticks, ruffled, pr, 5"...25.00
Moondrops, colors other than red or bl, goblet, wine; 4-oz, 4"......13.00
Moondrops, colors other than red or bl, gravy boat......................100.00
Moondrops, colors other than red or bl, plate, sandwich; rnd, 14" ..23.00
Moondrops, colors other than red or bl, sherbet, 4½" 16.00
Moondrops, colors other than red or bl, tumbler, w/hdl, 9-oz, 4⅞"....18.00

Moondrops, red or bl, ashtray...**30.00**
Moondrops, red or bl, bowl, berry; 5¼" **25.00**
Moondrops, red or bl, bowl, ftd, concave top, 8⅜" **45.00**
Moondrops, red or bl, bowl, soup; 6¾" **90.00**
Moondrops, red or bl, candy dish, ruffled, 8"................................**40.00**
Moondrops, red or bl, comport, 11½"....................................**95.00**
Moondrops, red or bl, decanter, sm, 7¾".............................**70.00**
Moondrops, red or bl, goblet, water; metal stem, 9-oz, 6¼".........**23.00**
Moondrops, red or bl, mug, 12-oz, 5⅛".................................**40.00**
Moondrops, red or bl, pitcher, lg, w/lip, 50-oz, 8" **195.00**
Moondrops, red or bl, plate, sherbet; 6⅛".................................**8.00**
Moondrops, red or bl, platter, oval, 12" **50.00**
Moondrops, red or bl, sugar bowl, 3½" **16.00**
Moondrops, red or bl, tumbler, juice; ftd, 3-oz, 3¼"...................**20.00**
Moondrops, red or bl, vase, rocket-style, 9¼".........................**250.00**
Radiance, amber, bowl, bonbon; w/lid, 6" **55.00**
Radiance, amber, bowl, nut; hdls, 5"...................................**10.00**
Radiance, amber, butter dish...**210.00**
Radiance, amber, decanter, w/stopper & hdl...........................**125.00**
Radiance, amber, pitcher, 64-oz **175.00**
Radiance, amber, plate, luncheon; 8"..................................**10.00**
Radiance, amber, sugar bowl **15.00**
Radiance, amber, vase, flared or crimped, 10" **75.00**
Radiance, Ice Blue or red, bowl, flared, 12"............................**65.00**
Radiance, Ice Blue or red, bowl, punch; 9" **250.00**
Radiance, Ice Blue or red, bowl, relish; 2-part, 7"....................**35.00**
Radiance, Ice Blue or red, candlesticks, 2-light, pr.....................**195.00**
Radiance, Ice Blue or red, comport, 6"..................................**35.00**
Radiance, Ice Blue or red, goblet, cordial; 1-oz **35.00**
Radiance, Ice Blue or red, shakers, pr...................................**95.00**
Radiance, Ice Blue or red, tray, oval **45.00**
Top Notch (Sunburst), any color, creamer **25.00**
Top Notch (Sunburst), any color, cup **20.00**
Top Notch (Sunburst), any color, plate, luncheon......................**18.00**
Top Notch (Sunburst), any color, saucer **8.00**
Top Notch (Sunburst), any color, sugar bowl..............................**25.00**

Newcomb

The Newcomb College of New Orleans, Louisiana, established a pottery in 1895 to provide the students with first-hand experience in the fields of art and ceramics. Using locally dug clays — red and buff in the early years, white-burning by the turn of the century — potters were employed to throw the ware which the ladies of the college decorated. From 1897 until about 1910, the ware they produced was finished in a high glaze and was usually surface painted. After 1905 some carving was done as well. On today's market, even a small piece of carved high glaze ware generally brings a minimum of $4,000.00. The letter 'Q' that is sometimes found in the mark indicates a pre-1906 production (high glaze). After 1912 a matt glaze was favored; these pieces are always carved. Soft blues and greens were used almost exclusively, and decorative themes were chosen to reflect the beauty of the South. The year 1930 marked the end of the matt-glaze period and the art-pottery era.

Various marks used by the pottery include an 'N' within a 'C,' sometimes with 'HB' added to indicate a 'hand-built' piece. The potter often incised his initials into the ware, and the artists were encouraged to sign their work. Among the most well-known artists were Sadie Irvine, Henrietta Bailey, and Fannie Simpson.

Newcomb pottery is evaluated to a large extent by era (early, transitional, or matt), decoration, size, and condition. In the following descriptions, unless noted otherwise, all decoration is carved and painted on matt glaze. The term 'transitional' defines

a period of two to three years (ca 1910 to 1912) between earlier and later work, and signifies changes to the glazes, colors, and style of decoration. Our advisors for this category are Suzanne Perrault and David Rago; they are listed in the Directory under New Jersey.

Key: hg — high glaze

Bowl, bl w/gr banded rim, squat, L Funkhouser, 1926, 4½" **1,725.00**
Bowl, bud wreath on shoulder, corseted, S Irvine, 1921, 1¾x3¾" ..**1,500.00**
Bowl, floral band, AF Simpson, 1917, 2x6½"............................**1,200.00**
Bowl, floral band, wht w/teal on bl, AF Simpson, #277, 1¾x7¾" ...**1,325.00**
Bowl, floral shoulder, H Bailey, 6x7½"....................................**2,500.00**
Bowl, trillium border, S Irvine, low, 1919, 2¼x7½" **950.00**
Candlestick, peacock feathers, H Bailey, rstr, 6½"....................**500.00**
Chamberstick, 2 flowers on trumpet base w/hdl, S Irvine, 3½" ..**1,100.00**
Charger, hg, Newcomb chapel/trees, M Sheerer, ca 1900, 10¾"..**16,000.00**

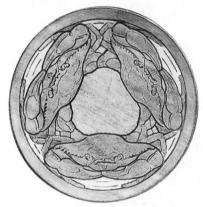

Charger, three blue crabs on blue, Sabrina Wells, 1904, 13", NM, $25,000.00. (Photo courtesy David Rago Auctions)

Match holder, poplar trees, unknown artist, 1907, 2x3"..............**300.00**
Pitcher, honeysuckle, pk/yel/gr on rose to bl, AF Simpson, 6".**3,500.00**
Pitcher, irises & foliage, IB Keep/J Meyer, II 73 Q, 8".............**7,185.00**
Pitcher, trees/sky/water/sailboats, S Irvine, #JM14, 4½"...........**4,750.00**
Plaque, moon/moss/oaks/cottage, 1922, MC/MI/63, rstr bubbles, 10x6"+fr ..**18,400.00**
Plate, hg, mistletoe border, 4-color M Morel #CL98, 9½" **3,750.00**
Tile, moss/trees, bl/gr, S Irvine, #SW5, 5½" dia **3,000.00**
Vase, bud; crocuses, AF Simpson, corseted, 1921, 6¼x2¾".....**2,000.00**
Vase, bud; moss/oaks/moon, S Irvine, #212, 5x2½".................**2,000.00**
Vase, cherries on branch, H Bailey, ovoid, #326, 7x3", NM **1,900.00**
Vase, crocuses, AF Simpson, Transitional, 1912, 8¼x3¾".......**4,750.00**
Vase, daffodils w/yel centers, S Irvine, bulbous, 5" **2,100.00**
Vase, daisies, AF Simpson, squat, shallow lines, 4¼x7½" **950.00**
Vase, Espanol pattern, AF Simpson, 1928, 7x4".....................**5,000.00**
Vase, Espanol pattern, S Irvine, bulbous, 1927, 5¼x2¾".........**2,200.00**
Vase, floral, pk/gr on bl, shouldered, H Bailey/RK 23, 6" **3,000.00**
Vase, floral (EX art), AF Simpson, #FB117, 6½"....................**5,500.00**
Vase, floral band, wht/gr on bl, S Irvine, 1925, 7¼x3¾" **1,900.00**
Vase, floral geometric, bl/gr/matt, C Charlaron, 4¾"..............**1,300.00**
Vase, flowers on leafy stems, mc, sgn RM, #237, ca 1912, 5¼".**1,400.00**
Vase, hg, freesia blossoms, M de Hoa LeBlanc, trumpet form, 1904, 10"..**5,000.00**
Vase, hg, leaves w/4 pendant buds (4X), 4-color H Bailey, 8½", EX ..**12,500.00**
Vase, hg, oaks, K Wright/J Meyer, AM 73/Q, 4⅝x5¾"..........**18,500.00**
Vase, hg, oaks, Marie de Hoa LeBlanc, 11¼" **42,300.00**
Vase, hg, stylized flowers, C Richardson, cylindrical, ca 1906, 7½" ..**8,000.00**
Vase, hg, trillium on long stems, M de Hoa LeBlanc, 1906, 8½x4" ...**9,500.00**
Vase, irises, SB Levy, cylindrical, ca 1905, rstr, 10½x4" **4,500.00**
Vase, irises & leaves, AF Simpson, bulbous, 1923, label, 8x5".**3,250.00**
Vase, jonquils, C Littlejohn, Transitional, bulbous, 6¾x8½"...**5,000.00**
Vase, lemons & leaves on multi-tone bl, sgn, slim, 1906, 12¾"....**15,000.00**

Vase, lotus flower band, bl/gr/ivory, L Nicholson, #BK30, 4" ...**4,000.00**
Vase, magnolia blossoms, S Irvine, Transitional, 1914, 5x8½", NM ...**1,500.00**
Vase, moon/moss/oaks, A Arbo, closed-in rim, 1931, 6x4¼" ...**3,000.00**
Vase, moon/moss/oaks, A Arbo, 1930s, 5x4" **3,000.00**
Vase, moon/moss/oaks, AF Simpson, 1928, 5¼x3" **3,750.00**
Vase, moon/moss/oaks, H Bailey, 1915, ovoid, 6" **2,585.00**
Vase, moon/moss/oaks, S Irvine, bulbous, 1932, 6¼x6" **5,000.00**
Vase, moon/moss/oaks, S Irvine, squat, 1933, 4x5" **3,000.00**
Vase, moon/moss/oaks, S Irvine, Transitional, 1908, 7x4" **3,750.00**
Vase, moon/moss/oaks, S Irvine, Transitional, 1919, 8¼x3¾" .**6,000.00**
Vase, moon/moss/oaks, S Irvine, 7½" **4,250.00**
Vase, moon/moss/oaks/hills, AF Simpson, bulbous, 1926, 8¼" .**9,500.00**
Vase, moon/moss/pines, S Irvine, MD24/Orens Bayue, rpr, 5¼" .**880.00**
Vase, moon/moss/trees, H Bailey, B24, ca 1910-20, 4¾" **3,450.00**
Vase, moon/palms, mc, AF Simpson, baluster, 9½" **17,625.00**
Vase, morning-glory wreath, H Bailey, ovoid, 1926, 6x3½" **2,300.00**
Vase, moss gr w/gunmetal splatters, baluster, E Rogers, 10x9" .**3,450.00**
Vase, moss/oaks, AF Simpson, #JL12, 10" **12,000.00**
Vase, moss/oaks, AF Simpson, rnd shoulders, #JL62, 10" **18,000.00**
Vase, moss/oaks (EX art), H Bailey, bulbous, 1930, label, 5¼x4¼" ..**2,900.00**
Vase, moss/oaks/vermillion sky, S Irvine, bulbous, 1930, 6x3" .**3,500.00**
Vase, mums, AF Simpson/J Meyer, FJ5, 9" **8,500.00**
Vase, pine boughs & cones, H Bailey, NC/HB/SR15/184, 1930, 8¼" .**7,500.00**
Vase, roses, wht on bl, H Bailey, 1926, 4¾x4¾" **1,800.00**
Vase, royal palm trees, purple & pk, AF Simpson, bulbous, 1929, 5¼" .**5,000.00**
Vase, swamp lilies, bl/gr, E Urquhart, #R98, early, 6½" **6,500.00**
Vase, thistle blossoms & foliage, gourd form, CC60 W, 8⅝" .**12,650.00**
Vase, tobacco leaves & wht blossoms, S Irvine, 1925, 4¾x4¾" ..**2,600.00**
Vase, trees, gr/bl, H Bailey, #ES15, experimental, 6½" **3,500.00**
Vase, trumpet blossoms/leaves in band, AF Simpson, 1926, 5¼x4¾" ..**650.00**

Newspapers

People do not collect newspapers simply because they are old. Age has absolutely nothing to do with value — it does not hold true that the older the newspaper, the higher the value. Instead, most of the value is determined by the historic event content. In most cases, the more important to American history the event is, the higher the value. In over two hundred years of American history, perhaps as many as 98% of all newspapers ever published do not contain news of a significant historic event. Newspapers not having news of major events in history are called 'atmosphere.' Atmosphere papers have little collector value. (See price guide below.)

To learn more about the hobby of collecting old and historic newspapers, be sure to visit the mega-websight on the Internet at www.history buff.com/. The e-mail address for the NCSA is help@historybuff.com/. See Newspaper Collector's Society of America in Clubs, Newsletters, and Catalogs for more information.

1800-1820, Atmosphere editions, from $5 to **10.00**
1821-1859, Atmosphere editions, from $4 to **8.00**
1836, Texas declares independence, from $60 to **85.00**
1845, Annexation of Texas, from $35 to **45.00**
1846, Start of Mexican War, from $25 to **35.00**
1846-1847, Major battles of Mexican War, from $25 to **30.00**
1847, End of Mexican War, from $30 to **40.00**
1860, Lincoln elected 1st term, from $115 to **225.00**
1861, Lincoln's inaugural address, from $140 to **275.00**
1861-1865, Atmosphere editions: Confederate titles, from $110 to.**165.00**
1861-1865, Atmosphere editions: Union titles, from $8 to **15.00**
1861-1865, Civil War major battle, Confederate report, $225 to ..**350.00**
1861-1865, Civil War major battle, Union 1st report, $60 to.....**120.00**
1862, Emancipation Proclamation, from $85 to **225.00**

1863, Gettysburg Address, from $165 to **380.00**
1865, April 29 edition of Frank Leslie's, from $175 to **225.00**
1865, April 29 edition of Harper's Weekly, from $150 to **200.00**
1865, Capture & death of J Wilkes Booth, from $85 to **165.00**
1865, Fall of Richmond, from $85 to..**275.00**
1865, NY Herald, Apr 15 (Beware: reprints abound), from $600 to..**900.00**
1865, Titles other than NY Herald, Apr 15, from $125 to **375.00**
1866-1900, Atmosphere editions, from $3 to **5.00**
1876, Custer's Last Stand, later reports, from $30 to....................**80.00**
1876, Custer's Last Stand, 1st reports, from $100 to **250.00**
1881, Billy the Kid killed, from $130 to **350.00**
1881, Garfield assassinated, from $60 to **115.00**
1881, Gunfight at OK Corral, from $175 to **400.00**
1882, Jesse James killed, later report, from $60 to.......................**120.00**
1882, Jesse James killed, 1st report, from $165 to **385.00**
1898, Sinking of Maine, from $25 to...**70.00**
1901, McKinley assassinated, from $45 to...................................**100.00**
1903, Wright Brother's flight, from $200 to **500.00**
1906, San Francisco earthquake, other titles, from $25 to............**50.00**
1906, San Francisco earthquake, San Francisco title, from $300 to ..**500.00**
1912, Sinking of Titanic, later reports, from $25 to **50.00**
1912, Sinking of Titanic, 1st reports, from $100 to **250.00**
1915, Sinking of Lusitania, later reports, from $25 to...................**65.00**
1915, Sinking of Lusitania, 1st reports, from $40 to **125.00**
1927, Babe Ruth hits 60th home run, from $50 to **125.00**
1927, Lindbergh arrives in Paris, 1st reports, from $65 to **125.00**
1929, St Valentine's Day Massacre, from $100 to **225.00**
1929, Stock market crash, from $75 to **180.00**
1931, Al Capone found guilty, from $40 to **80.00**
1931, Jack 'Legs' Diamond killed, from $30 to **45.00**
1933, Machine Gun Kelley captured, from $25 to **45.00**
1934, Baby Face Nelson killed, from $30 to **60.00**
1934, Bonnie & Clyde killed, from $125 to **250.00**
1934, Dillinger killed, from $100 to **250.00**
1934, Pretty Boy Floyd killed, from $25 to **45.00**
1937, Hindenburg explodes, from $75 to **150.00**
1939-45, WWII major battles, from $20 to **50.00**
1941, Honolulu Star-Bulletin, Dec 7, 1st extra (+), from $300 to ..**600.00**
1941, Other titles, Dec 7, w/Pearl Harbor news, from $30 to........**60.00**
1945, Hitler dead, from $35 to **50.00**
1948, Chicago Daily Tribune, Nov 3, Dewey Defeats Truman, from $500 to..**800.00**
1953, Truce signed to end Korean War, from $25 to.....................**35.00**
1960, JFK elected, from $10 to..**25.00**
1961, Alan Shephard 1st astronaut in space, from $15 to **30.00**
1961, Bay of Pigs, from $20 to **50.00**
1961, Roger Maris hits 61st home run, from $20 to......................**40.00**
1963, JFK assassination, Nov 22, Dallas title, from $70 to **100.00**
1963, JFK assassination, Nov 22, titles other than Dallas, from $3 to ..**8.00**
1967, Super Bowl I, from $15 to **30.00**
1968, Assassination of Martin Luther King, from $15 to...............**25.00**
1968, Assassination of Robert Kennedy, from $5 to......................**20.00**
1969, Moon landing, from $5 to **20.00**
1974, Nixon resigns, from $15 to..**20.00**

Nicodemus

Chester R. Nicodemus was born near Barberton, Ohio, August 17, 1901. He started Pennsylvania State University in 1920, where he studied engineering. Chester got a share of a large paper route, a job that enabled him to attend Cleveland Art School where he studied under Herman Matzen, sculptor, and Frank Wilcox, anatomy illustrator, graduating in 1925. That fall Chester was hired to begin a sculpture department at the Dayton Art Institute.

Nicodemus moved from Dayton to Columbus, Ohio, in 1930 and started teaching at the Columbus Art School. During this time he made vases and commissioned sculptures, water fountains, and limestone and wood carvings. In 1941 Chester left the field of teaching to pursue pottery making full time, using local red clay containing a large amount of iron. Known for its durability, he called the ware Ferro-Stone. He made teapots and other utility wares, but these goods lost favor, so he started producing animal and bird sculptures, nativity sets, and Christmas ornaments, some bearing Chester's and Florine's names as personalized cards for his customers and friends. Chester died in 1990.

His glaze colors were turquoise or aqua, ivory, green mottle, pink pussy willow, and golden yellow. The glaze was applied so that the color of the warm red clay would show through, adding an extra dimension to each piece. His name is usually incised in the clay in an arch, but paper labels were also used. For more information, we recommend *Sanford Guide to Nicodemus, His Pottery and His Art*, by James Riebel.

Dish, Ohio State University Columbus, brn wash, 4½" **65.00**
Figurine, bluebird, realistic colors w/red-clay breast, 3¼" **90.00**
Figurine, cocker spaniel, gr mottled gloss, #18, Ferro-Stone label, 5"..**275.00**
Figurine, robin, 4¾x5½" **115.00**
Figurine, sleeping kitten, feathery turq gloss, #133, 3" L **275.00**
Figurine, St Francis, w/birds, #209, 13¾" **420.00**
Figurine, wren, speckled matt, #580, Ferro-Stone label, 2¼" **80.00**
Figurine, young robin, brn w/red-clay breast, Ferro-Stone label, 3"..**60.00**
Flower frog, duck figural, brn & yel mottled, 6½" **265.00**

Flower holder, kneeling girl, curdled blue, 6¾", $250.00.

Ornament, Santa's head, sgn, ca 1938, 2½x2" **165.00**
Pitcher, mottled gr, flared rim, loop hdl, #87, 12-oz, w/lid, 4" **90.00**
Plaque, Chester Nicodemus Golden Age Hobby Show Award, 8-sided, 5"..**210.00**
Vase, brn w/diagonal swirls, 6x5" **125.00**

Niloak

During the latter part of the 1800s, there were many small utilitarian potteries in Benton, Arkansas. By 1900 only the Hyten Brothers Pottery remained. Charles Hyten, a second generation potter, took control of the family business around 1902. Shortly thereafter he renamed it the Eagle Pottery Company. In 1909 Hyten and former Rookwood potter Arthur Dovey began experimentation on a new swirl pottery. Dovey had previously worked for the Ouachita Pottery Company of Hot Springs and produced a swirl pottery there as early as 1906. In March 1910, the Eagle Pottery Company introduced Niloak — kaolin spelled backwards.

In 1911 Benton businessmen formed the Niloak Pottery Corporation. Niloak, connected to the Arts and Crafts Movement and known as 'mission' ware, had a national representative in New York by 1913. Niloak's production centered on art pottery characterized by accidental, swirling patterns of natural and artificially colored clays. Many companies through the years have produced swirl pottery, yet none achieved the technical and aesthetic qualities of Niloak. Hyten received a patent in 1928 for the swirl technique. Although most examples have an interior glaze, some early Mission Ware pieces have an exterior glaze as well; these are extremely rare.

In 1923 Hyten's company found itself facing bankruptcy. Hardy L. Winburn, Jr., along with other Little Rock businessmen, raised the necessary capital and were able to provide the kind of leadership needed to make the business profitable once again. Both lines (Eagle and Hywood) were renamed 'Niloak' in 1937 to capitalize on this well-known name. The pottery continued in production until 1947 when it was converted to the Winburn Tile Company, which exists to this day in Little Rock.

Be careful not to confuse the swirl production of the Evans Pottery of Missouri with Niloak. The significant difference is the dark brown matt interior glaze of Evans pottery.

For further information we recommend *Collector's Encyclopedia of Niloak Pottery* by David Edwin Gifford (Collector Books). Our advisor for this category is Lila Shrader; she is listed in the Directory under California. All items listed below bear the Niloak mark unless noted otherwise.

Key:
H — Hywood   NI — Niloak (impressed) mark
N — N mark   NL — Niloak (in low relief) mark
NB — Niloak (block letters) mark

Mission Ware

Ashtray, rolled rim, 3 rests, 5½" dia **197.00**
Ashtray, 1st art mk, 1¾x4¾" dia, from $100 to...........................**125.00**
Bean pot, w/lid, 2nd art mk, 7¼", from $800 to......................**1,000.00**
Bowl, fruit; mk Patent Pend'g, 4½" dia, from $125 to.................**185.00**
Bowl, fruit; 1st art mk, 4x9", from $400 to...................................**500.00**
Bowl, mixing bowl shape, 5x11"..**400.00**
Bowl (pot?) rolled collar, NI, 3½x4"..**72.00**
Candlestick, flared base, paper label, 10" **220.00**
Candlestick, slim neck, no collar, 1st art mk, 9", from $175 to...**200.00**
Carafe w/tumbler (tumble-up), NI, 9" **525.00**
Chamberstick, finger ring, cupped base, 5½" **210.00**
Cigarette jar, str sides, lid, 4½x3" dia **255.00**
Cigarette jar, w/lid, 3¾x4½" dia, from $275 to.........................**350.00**
Compote, ped ft, w/lid, unmk, 5¾x6" dia **697.00**
Inkwell, mk Patent Pend'g, 2½" dia, from $250 to **350.00**
Jar, canister-like, str sides, flared rim, nobbed lid, NI, 3½".........**265.00**
Jar, potpourri; pierced lid, NI, 4½"...**328.00**
Jardiniere, flared rim, 1st art mk, 7", from $350 to **450.00**
Jug, w/hdl, NI & paper label, 5½"...**630.00**
Lamp base, flared base, NI, 9½x3¼"+hardware fittings **510.00**
Match holder, flared base, 1st art mk, 2½"................................**105.00**
Pitcher, mk Patent Pend'g, 10½", from $1,000 to **1,200.00**
Pitcher, NI, 1-qt, 9¼"...**875.00**
Pitcher, ruffled top flows into spout & elongated hdl, NI, 10½".**895.00**
Planter, cone shape, NI, 10x10" (6" dia base).............................**660.00**
Plate, luncheon; 1st art mk, 8¾", from $300 to **420.00**
Postcard, linen, Home of Niloak Pottery, showroom photo, 1930s.**125.00**
Powder jar, knob finial, 2nd art mk, 3x5"................................**385.00**
Punch bowl, 2" ped ft, 13" **1,410.00**
Punch cup, NI, 2½"..**110.00**
Shot glass, NI, 2½", from $40 to..**90.00**
Tankard, NI & paper label, 10¼"..**1,075.00**
Tankard, str sides, slightly flared base, 1st art mk, 13½" **1,250.00**
Tumbler, conical w/outward sloping sides, flared base, NI, 4" **165.00**

Tumbler, 1-groove motif at base, mk Patent Pend'g, 4¼" **225.00**
Urn, 4-color swirls, factory bubble, 23½x12" **7,000.00**
Vase, bl/red/ivory/brn swirl, ogee sides, 10" **550.00**
Vase, bowling ball shape, no collar, NI, 10x10" **585.00**
Vase, bowling ball shape w/½" collar, NI, 6½" **198.00**
Vase, brn & tan tones, flared rim, mk Patent Pend'g, 8" **475.00**
Vase, bud; flared base, 1st art mk, 7½" **100.00**
Vase, bulbous, long slim neck w/flared rim, NI, 10½" **315.00**
Vase, cache pot shape, NI, 6½x6" **250.00**
Vase, candy cane effect, 1st art mk, 7½", from $200 to **300.00**
Vase, coffee cup shape, sticker, mini, 1½" **300.00**
Vase, corseted w/high shoulders & flared 4" rim, NI, 11" **395.00**
Vase, cylindrical w/ball-like lower third, NI, 12½" **275.00**
Vase, fan shape, 2nd art mk, 7¼", from $350 to **400.00**
Vase, high shoulders, 10" **240.00**
Vase, orange/tan/brn, high shoulders w/rolled collar, NI, 6¼" **105.00**
Vase, slim w/narrow hdls from rim to ⅔ down, NI, 13½" **2,325.00**
Vase, squat, w/neck, mk Pat Pend'g, 3½x5½" **235.00**
Vase, teardrop w/wide flared collar, 1st art mk, 10" **245.00**
Vase, violet, pyramidal w/collared neck, 1st art mk, 3¼" **265.00**
Wall pocket, flared rim, 6x4" **300.00**
Water bottle, bulbous w/'grip' neck, 1st art mk, 8½" **480.00**
Whiskey jug, w/stopper, 1st art mk, 7¾", from $460 to **700.00**

Miscellaneous

Ashtray, advertising; Crow-Burlingame, NB, 3x5½" **55.00**
Ashtray, bl/tan/rust, 3 rests, NI, 1x5½" dia **125.00**
Basket, bl & tan matt, 1st Hywood by Niloak, 6½", from $75 to .**95.00**
Basket, vertical hdl, woven appearance, N, 3½" **42.00**
Bottle, water; pottery stopper, sticker, 7¾", from $100 to **125.00**
Bowl, Peacock Blue II, incised H, 3¾", from $35 to **55.00**
Canoe & frog, Ozark Blue, unmk w/paper label, 3½x11" **66.00**
Churn, bl stripes, w/lid, Eagle Pottery #4, early 1900s, 16" **188.00**
Creamer, Ozark Dawn II, 1st Hywood by Niloak, 4¼", from $35 to.**50.00**
Cup & saucer, Ozark Blue, Peterson petal design, from $75 to ...**100.00**
Figurine, cannon, Ozark Dawn (mauve & bl), 3½" **58.00**
Figurine, Trojan horse, wht matt, NB, 8¼" **230.00**
Head vase, w/hat, burgundy matt, 7¾" **95.00**
Jug, brn, w/hdl, incised mk, 4½" **80.00**
Jug, Spears vinegar jar w/Deco dècor & corked stopper, NB, 7" ..**165.00**
Pitcher, Arkansas 1 side/eagle USA on reverse, NB, 7" **110.00**
Pitcher, deep maroon matt, melon ribs, N, 8¼" **155.00**
Pitcher, Kansas & sheaves on 1 side/hawk on reverse, 7" **160.00**
Pitcher, Memphis steamboat scene on side, NB, 7½" **192.00**
Pitcher, Ozark Dawn, bowling ball shape, ice lip spout, NB, 7" ...**55.00**
Planter, camel, recumbent, wht matt w/brn cold-pnt trim............**47.00**
Planter, Colonial lady in full skirt kneels & holds basket, NB, 5½"..**90.00**
Planter, fox resting, bushy tail bk over body, Ozark Dawn, 4½" L..**29.00**
Planter, kangaroo w/brn boxing gloves, camel color, NB, 5" **38.00**
Planter, parrot perched on side of pleated bowl, wht matt w/HP details..**40.00**
Planter, squirrel w/upright/extended bushy tail, 6" **20.00**
Planter, wooden shoe design, high-gloss, 5x3½" **20.00**
Plate, deep maroon matt, decorative rim, NB, 10½" **110.00**
Plate, dinner; Ozark Blue, NB, 10", from $75 to..........................**100.00**
Shakers, S & P shapes, matt, 2¼", pr **36.00**
Shakers, various other shapes, 2-2½", pr, from $15 to **35.00**
Sugar bowl, gr & tan matt, w/lid, 1st Hywood by Niloak, 4", $50 to.**75.00**
Teapot, Aladdin-like, matt, N, 6", from $54 to **66.00**
Vase, bl (solid), 1st art mk, 12¼", from $600 to **800.00**
Vase, cornucopia form, Ozark Blue, 2nd Hywood by Niloak, 7", $50 to..**75.00**
Vase, Deco style w/accordion pleats, Ozark Dawn, incised H, 7½"..**55.00**
Vase, gr & tan matt, incised H, 2¾-3", ea from $12 to..................**25.00**
Vase, ivory, hand thrown, 1st Hywood by Niloak, 9½", from $55 to .**95.00**

Vase, maroon, hdls, 1st Hywood by Niloak, 6½", from $50 to **75.00**
Vase, Ozark Dawn II, fan shape, Niloak sticker, 7", from $45 to ...**75.00**
Vase, Ozark Dawn II, sq rim, Potteries sticker, 5½", from $20 to..**48.00**
Vase, Pearled Green, hdl, Hywood Art Pottery, 6½", from $75 to..**150.00**
Vase, Pearled Green, hdls, Stoin glaze, Hywood Art Pottery, 5⅛" .**650.00**
Vase, Sea Green, Hywood Art Pottery, 9", from $450 to **550.00**
Vase, wht (solid), flared rim, 1st art mk, 6¼", from $200 to **250.00**
Vase, wing-like hdls, matt, Incised H, 7¼" **36.00**

Strawberry jar, brown, 7¼", $35.00. (Photo courtesy David Edwin Gifford)

Nippon

Nippon generally refers to Japanese wares made during the period from 1891 to 1921, although the Nippon mark was also used to a limited extent on later wares (accompanied by 'Japan'). Nippon, meaning Japan, identified the country of origin to comply with American importation restrictions. After 1921 'Japan' was the acceptable alternative. The term does not imply a specific type of product and may be found on items other than porcelains. For further information we recommend *The Collector's Encyclopedia of Nippon Porcelain* (there are seven in the series) by our advisor, Joan Van Patten; you will find her address in the Directory under New York. In the following listings, items are assumed hand painted unless noted otherwise. Numbers included in the descriptions refer to these specific marks:

Key:
#1 — China E-OH
#2 — M in Wreath
#3 — Cherry Blossom
#4 — Double T Diamond in Circle
#5 — Rising Sun
#6 — Royal Kinran
#7 — Maple Leaf
#8 — Royal Nippon, Nishiki
#9 — Royal Moriye Nippon

Ashtray, Sitting Bull portrait, 3-rest, #2, 5½" **500.00**
Basket vase, gold on cobalt, #2, 7¾" **725.00**
Basket vase, moriage geese on lt bl, integral hdl, unmk, 8½" **700.00**
Bookends, horses in relief, brn tones, #2, 6", pr......................**3,000.00**
Bowl, floral reserves, 8 scallops, #7, 7½" **160.00**
Bowl, floral w/ornate gold rim, 3-leg, 6-sided, #2, 7¼" **145.00**
Bowl, peanuts & leaves emb, smooth rim, #2, 7" **165.00**
Bowl, roses on wht, tub hdls, #2, 7½" **250.00**
Box, cigarette; Indian portrait on brn, #2, 4¼" **475.00**
Box, powder; floral band on wht w/gold, #2, 5½" **70.00**
Box, trinket; floral on wht heart shape, #2, sm **80.00**
Cake plate, floral, pk on wht w/gold, hdls, HP mk, 10½" **115.00**
Cake plate, floral band w/gold, crown mk, 10½" **100.00**
Celery tray, floral reserves on cobalt w/gold, #7, 13¼" L............**450.00**
Chocolate set, mums, pk on wht w/gold, pot+8 c/s....................**925.00**

Coffeepot, river scenic, earth tones, stick hdl, #7, 6" 150.00
Condensed milk container, gold o/l on wht, #7 ....175.00
Cookie jar, gold floral on wht, w/underplate, RC mk, 8" 425.00
Cracker jar, floral on wht w/gold, #2, 9½" w/hdls......................250.00
Demitasse set, pk & gold band on wht, #5, 6" pot+4 c/s+12" tray ..350.00
Egg cup, sampan in sunset scene, #5, 2½" 65.00
Ewer, Madame Lebrun reserve on gr w/gold, #7, 12" 1,800.00
Ewer, moriage flowers, ornate hdl, conical, unmk, 7½" 375.00
Ewer, purple flowers, inv't cone form, #6, 9½"............................225.00
Hair receiver, river scenic, 4-ftd, #2, 3" dia 65.00
Humidor, fox hunt scenic band on gr, #7, 6½" 925.00
Humidor, lady chasing geese, 8-sided, #2, 8" 950.00
Humidor, playing cards on brn, #2, 7" 800.00
Humidor, scattered playing cards on bl, 6-sided, #2, 6½" 600.00
Humidor, 4 scenic reserves on sq Deco-motif body, #2, 5" 450.00
Inkwell, Deco florals on bl, #2, 4" W 275.00
Lamp, flowers w/gold beads, candlestick, #7, 13" 365.00
Letter holder, floral on cream, #2, 4½x6" 200.00
Loving cup, Wedgwood-style scenic, sm gold hdls, #2, 7¾"........550.00
Matchbox holder, gold on wht, rectangular, wall mt, #2, 4½" 140.00
Pitcher, roses on wht w/gold, 6-sided, RC mk, 7" 275.00
Plaque, birds on flowering branch, #2, 10" 325.00
Plaque, cockatoo on perch, #2, 10" 700.00
Plaque, lady's portrait, coralene border, US Pat mk, 11" 4,500.00
Plaque, squirrel emb, #2, 10½" 900.00
Plaque, windmill scenic, gr #2, 10" 275.00
Platter, lobster & fruit, gr & gold border, #2, 16" 850.00
Punch bowl, mc grapes, ftd, hdls, #2, 12¾x13" 1,100.00
Relish, river scene, 2-compartment, #7, 7½" L 150.00
Shaving mug, Indian reserve, ring hdl, #2, 3¾" 325.00
Sugar bowl, floral band on cream, hdls, w/lid, #2, 6½" dia............80.00
Sugar shaker, roses on cobalt w/gold, #7, 4¼" 250.00
Tankard, coralene floral on shaded gr, unmk, 12"....................2,500.00
Tea set, boy in sailor suit holds gun, child sz, 15-pc....................300.00
Tea set, Oriental decor w/gold, Pat mk, 5" pot+cr/sug+4 c/s 400.00
Tea set, palms scenic w/gold, #7, 5" pot+cr/sug w/lid..................300.00
Trivet, Black man stands w/camel, 8-sided, #2, 7" 250.00
Urn, floral reserves on gr w/gold, uptrn hdls, w/lid, #7, 10" 450.00
Urn, man on camel w/gold, ornate hdls, #2, 38" 13,500.00
Vase, Anna Potocka portrait reserve on gold & wht, hdls, #7, 7½".1,500.00
Vase, classical ladies reserve on wht w/gold & pk, cylinder, #7, 16".3,500.00
Vase, floral on wht w/gold, ornate/integral hdls, #7, 7½" 350.00
Vase, floral relief, mc on bl, bottle neck, #7, 9½" 850.00
Vase, floral reserve on cobalt w/gold o/l, slim, #7, 18"............2,500.00
Vase, harbor w/lg ships, intricate borders, gilt, 2-part, 25" 11,200.00
Vase, lady w/flowers in vase reserve on cobalt & gold, #7, 7¾" ..1,700.00
Vase, lilies on brn, gold hdls, #2, 9¾" 350.00
Vase, man on camel scene, 3 elephant-head hdls, #2, 6" 500.00
Vase, moriage dragon, creature hdls, #7, 9½" 750.00
Vase, moriage trees & hdls, bulbous, sm mouth, #7, 9" 565.00
Vase, mtn scenic on cobalt w/gold, ring hdls, #7, 13½" 3,000.00
Vase, orchid reserve band on cobalt w/gold o/l, hdls, #7, 9"........700.00
Vase, Oriental floral on wht w/gr & gold, sm hdls, #2, 18" 800.00
Vase, pastoral scene w/cobalt & gold, bottle neck, #7, 9"...........600.00
Vase, rider's silhouette at sunset, hdls, Imperial mk, 12"............900.00
Vase, rose tapestry, gold hdls, bottle neck, #7, 7¾" 1,300.00
Vase, roses on brn w/gold, #7, 12"..600.00
Vase, sampan scenic, tall ft, angular hdls, #2, 6" 150.00
Vase, sunset scenic band, gold hdls, bottle neck, #2, 10½" 375.00
Vase, swan scene w/moriage grapes & leaves, gr hdls, #7, 9½"....625.00
Vase, Wedgwood, cream on bl, rim-to-hip hdls, gr #2, 8"...........800.00
Vase, windmill scene, angle hdls w/rings, ftd, #2, 14"...............1,000.00
Vase, woodland scene, wht w/moriage, shouldered, #2, 9" 500.00
Wine jug, river scene in earth tones, #7, 11" 1,250.00

Nodders

So called because of the nodding action of their heads and hands, nodders originated in China where they were used in temple rituals to represent deity. At first they were made of brass and were actually a type of bell; when these bells were rung, the heads of the figures would nod. In the eighteenth century, the idea was adopted by Meissen and by French manufacturers who produced not only china nodders but bisque as well. Most nodders are individual; couples are unusual. The idea remained popular until the end of the nineteenth century and was used during the Victorian era by toy manufacturers.

Black boy smoking cigar, standing on ashtray, Made in Austria, 4½" .115.00
Boy on surfboard w/wave behind him, Japan, 1960s-70s, 5¾".......85.00
Bulldog, papier-mâché, Fr, 11x20"...1,000.00
Canadian Mountie, spring neck, MIJ, 5¼".....................................35.00
Cat, orange w/pearl necklace, flocked papier-mâché, Japan, 7¾" .50.00
Charlie Brown, papier-machè, Lego, 1959 ....120.00
Chinese man riding on monkey, head & legs nod, 5x6"..............600.00
Chinese man w/monkey on shoulder (both nod), drum on knee, 5" ..175.00
Ching Chow, Oriental man w/long ponytail braid, German, bsk, 3¾"...110.00
Cockatoo, pnt porc, glass eyes, Germany, 1900s, 6⅝" 375.00
Coin Kitty, blk & wht, lg pk bow, body is bank, Japan, 5" 140.00
Denny Dimwit (Winnie Winkle comic strip), compo, 1948, 10" ..450.00
Donkey, straw hat, gold collar, bushy tail, flocked plastic, Japan, 6"...30.00
Drunk w/2 pk elephants, I Can't Be All Bad, They Like Me, Japan .28.00
Elephant w/Indian boy rider, bsk, 1900s, 4¾" 100.00
Hula dancer, grass skirt, stamped Japan, 9" 215.00
Lady w/fruit basket holding banana, mk #2080, 7" 110.00
Miss Six Flags, red & wht striped uniform, papier-mâché, Japan, 7"..110.00
Mr Peanut, ceramic w/plastic cane, 6¾" 150.00
Navy football player, bl shirt, gold helmet, 6" 95.00
Orange puppy & blk bear on swing, Japan, 3½" 35.00
President Clinton, wearing boxing gloves, ca 1994, 9" 12.00
Roy Rogers, compo, in western outfit, Japan, 1962, 6⅝".............145.00
Santa, holds sign: Hope Your Holidays Are Happy Days, German, 7¾" .50.00
Schroeder (Peanuts), Lego, 1960s, 6" 135.00
Scotsman w/handlebar mustache, papier-mâché 18.00
St Patrick's Day Men, 2 dressed in gr clothes, MIJ, 3¼", pr 215.00
Topo Gigio, ceramic, Rossini Co, 1970s, 7" 115.00
Winnie Winkle, bsk, mk Branner Germany, 3½" 95.00

Nordic Art Glass

Finnish and Swedish glass has recently started to develop a following, probably stemming from the revitalization of interest in forms from the 1950s. (The name Nordic is used here because of the inclusion of Finnish glass — the term Scandinavian does not refer to this country.) Included here are Flygsfors, Hadeland, Holmegaard, Iittala, Maleras, Motzfeldt, Nuutajarvi, and Strombergshyttan.

Our suggested prices are 'fair market values, developed after researching the Nordic secondary markets, the current retail prices on items still being produced, and American auction houses and antique stores.

Our advisor for this category is William L. Geary; he is listed in the Directory under Colorado.

Flygsfors Glass Works, Sweden

Flygsfors Glass Works was established in 1888 and continued in production until 1979 when the Orrefors Glass Group, which had acquired this entity, ceased operations.

Flygsfors is well known for art glass designed by Paul Kedelv, who joined the firm in 1949 with a contract to design light fittings, a specialty of the company.

Their 'Coquille' series, which utilizes a unique overlay technique combining opaque, bright colors, and 'Flamingo' have become very desirable on today's secondary market. Other internationally known artists/designers include Prince Sigvard Bernadotte and the Finnish designer Helene Tynell.

Bowl, Coquille, cranberry & wht, oblong w/flared ends, Kedelv, 11" .195.00
Bowl, Coquille, pk w/cobalt to clear o/l, pinched, Kedelv, 5x3"....75.00
Lamp, gr w/clear o/l, tall stem, flared base, 11" 285.00
Vase, bull & sun motif, mold-blown, rectangular, Bernt, 8" 55.00
Vase, Coquille, bl/red, flared wings, Kedelv, 10¼" 190.00
Vase, Coquille, maroon/gr, flared wings, Kedelv, 13" 265.00
Vase, Flamingo, teardrop w/woven gr/brn/wht threads, Kedelv, 10½" ..245.00

Hadeland Glassverk, Norway

Glass has been produced at this glass works since 1765. From the beginning, their main product was bottles. Since the 1850s they have made small items — drinking glasses, vases, bowls, jugs, etc. — and for the last forty years, figurines, souvenirs, and objects of art.

Important designers include Willy Johansson, Arne John Jutrem, Inger Magnus, Severin Brorby, and Gro Sommerfelt.

Bowl, pk w/blk rim & ft, I Magnus, #10747, 8" 225.00
Bowl, presentation; clear w/eng cranes & stylized leaves, 8x11⅝".150.00
Plate, clear w/brn & bl, A Jon Jutrem, #10814, 23½" 295.00
Plate, opal w/amber center, textured underside, Gro Sommerfelt, 9½" ..65.00
Sculpture, polar bear, cast technique, 4¾" 45.00
Vase, bud; pk underlay, gr speckled base w/wht & blk threads, 6½"...65.00
Vase, cranberry teardrop form, W Johansson, 11½" 50.00

Holmegaard Glassvaerk, Denmark

This company was founded in 1825. Because of a shortage of wood in Denmark, it became necessary for them to use peat, the only material available for fuel.

Their first full-time designers were hired after 1923. Orla Juul Nielson was the first. He was followed in 1925 by Jacob Band, an architect. Per Lukin became the chief designer in 1941. His production and art glass incorporates a simple yet complex series of designs. They continue to be popular among collectors of Scandinavian glass.

During 1965 the company merged with Kastrup and became Kastrup Holmegaard AS; a merger with Royal Copenhagen followed in 1975.

Bowl, wht w/orange o/l, flattened form, Michael Bang, 2x7" 25.00
Jar, gr, sq w/short neck, Per Luken, 6½x5⅞" 35.00
Vase, Flame, gr w/clear o/l, Per Luken, 9⅛x3½" 100.00
Vase, wht opal w/purple lines/2 musical notes, cylinder, Luken, 6¾"..50.00
Vase, wht w/ornate o/l, flared body w/short neck, O Bauer, 4¾x6" .65.00

Iittala Glass Works, Finland

This glass works was founded in 1881; it was originally staffed by Swedish workers who produced glassware of very high quality. In 1917 Ahiststrom OY bought and merged Iittala with Karhula Glass works. After 1945 Karhula's production was limited to container glass. In 1946 Tapio Wirkkala, the internationally known artist/designer, became Iittala's chief designer. Timo Sarpeneva joined him in 1950. Jointly they successfully spearheaded the promotion of Finnish glass in the international markets, winning many international awards for their designs. Today, Oiva Toikka leads the design team.

Sculpture, Dancing Leaves, clear w/paste-on bkground, Sundstrom, 9"...40.00
Sculpture, Dog Listens to Rain, Marko Salo, 8¼" L 275.00
Sculpture, Raven (bird), O Toikka, 4¼x6½" 350.00
Vase, Aalto Flower, clear, 4 forms, Alvar Aalto........................1,575.00
Vase, Claritas, blk/opal/clear, Timo Sarpaneva, 10¼" 1,000.00
Vase, Kantarelli, Tapio Wirkkala, 8"..825.00
Vase, Marcel, ltd ed, Timo Sarpaneva, 11¾" 1,000.00
Vase, Orkidea, clear crystal, T Sarpaneva, in production since 1953 ..325.00

Maleras Glass Works, Sweden

The first glass works at Maleras was founded in 1890. The city of Maleras was an important railway junction in Smaland, the Kingdom of Crystal, where articles from many of the glasshouses were shipped to the Swedish cities of Stockholm, Goteborg, and Malmo.

During the 1940s the company built a reputation throughout Sweden as one of the leading manufacturers of lead crystal. In 1975 the company joined the Royal Krona Group. Six years later, under the leadership of Mats Jonasson, the glass blowers and members of the community bought the factory from the existing management.

During the last twenty years, the company has produced first-class crystal sculptures of wildlife, which are sold around the world. Mats Jonasson is the master designer, and his wildlife images and engraving techniques are superb. Two other designers, artists Erika Hoglund and Lars Goran Tinback, are also important elements in this company's success.

Sculpture, Agitator, ltd ed, Mats Jonasson 3,200.00
Sculpture, Bears, clear, ltd ed, Mats Jonasson 2,100.00
Sculpture, Feather Dreamer, female form, red/crystal, Hoglund, 14½"..55.00
Sculpture, Owl, clear, ltd ed, Mats Jonasson, 13" 2,100.00
Sculpture, Plura, Erika Hoglund, 9¼" 875.00
Sculpture, Sharks, clear, Mats Jonasson, 7¼" 190.00
Vase, Navarra, red underlay teardrop w/blk pulled-up neck, Tinback...265.00
Vase, Twister, red/wht/bl, Klas-Goran Tinback 490.00

Benny Motzfeldt, Norwegian Glass Artist

Benny Motzfeldt, a graduate of the Arts and Crafts School of Oslo, Norway, started her career in glass in 1954 by responding to an ad for a designer of engraving and decoration at Christiania Glassmagasin and Hadeland Glassverk. After several years at Hadeland, she joined the Plus organization and managed their glass studio in Frederikstad. She is acknowledged as one of the leading exponents of Norwegian art glass and is recognized internationally. She challenged the rather sober Norwegian glass designs with a strong desire to try new ways, using vigorous forms and opaque colors embedded with silver nitrate patterns.

Bottle, clear w/wht shards, short neck, sgn, 6" 65.00
Bowl, bl & gr w/bubbled glass applications w/wht & blk shards, 3x5".95.00
Bowl, orange w/int bubbles, sgn, 9¾x6⅛" 75.00
Vase, wht underlay w/gold frit bands & vertical lines, 7¼x4¼"..100.00
Vase, yel w/orange band at rim & bottom, ftd, sgn, 7x7" 100.00

Nuutajarvi Glass Works, Finland

Bowl, dk gray-bl bowl in flower shape, Jaako Neimi, 1¾" 75.00
Bowl, pk heart shape, Kan Franck, 4"...65.00
Goblet, yel cup on wht stem & ft, Kaj Franck, 8½" 185.00
Vase, amber underlay, bubbles surround, rnd, Gunnel Nyman, 4" ..775.00
Vase, clear w/purple circle, apple form w/short neck, S Hopea, 3½"..295.00
Vase, Kupla, bl to clear base w/low turq bubble, Saara Hopea, 7" ...350.00
Vase, Serpentine, clear w/wht winding glass ribbon, G Nyman, 18¼" ..2,950.00

Strombergshyttan, Sweden

The original factory, Lindefors, was founded in 1876. Although the factory was modernized in the 1920s, it closed in 1931. In 1933 Edvard Stromberg bought the factory; Gerda Stromberg designed for the company until 1942. In 1945 the factory was purchased by Stromberg's son Eric and his wife Asta. She designed for them until 1976. Edvard worked with Eric, who was a chemist, and together they developed a new color of glass with a distinctive bluish-silver hue which became the factory's speciality.

Gunnar Nylund, famous for his copper wheel-engraved forms, was at the glass works from 1952 until 1975.

After a renovation in 1962, the factory suffered a serious fire and due to economic conditions was sold to Orrefors Glass Works; it operated under that title until it closed in 1979.

Sculpture, girl & deer w/trees, cast crystal, 7x6" 65.00
Vase, bl-silver teardrop w/eng girl & flying bird, Nylund, 10".....225.00
Vase, dk gray, B963, Stromberg, 14½" 110.00
Vase, gray w/circles of air, Ariel technique, B943, Stromberg, 5"...210.00

Noritake

The Noritake Company was first registered in 1904 as Nippon Gomei Kaisha. In 1917 the name became Nippon Toki Kabushiki Toki. The 'M in wreath' mark is that of the Morimura Brothers, distributors with offices in New York. It was used until 1941. The 'tree crest' mark is the crest of the Morimura family.

The Noritake Company has produced fine porcelain dinnerware sets and occasional pieces decorated in the delicate manner for which the Japanese are noted. (Two dinnerware patterns are featured below, and a general range is suggested for others.)

Authority Joan Van Patten has compiled a lovely book, *The Collector's Encyclopedia of Noritake*, with many full-color photos and current prices; you will find her address in the Directory under New York. In the following listings, examples are hand painted unless noted otherwise. Numbers refer to these specific marks:

Key:
#1 — Komaru   #3 — N in Wreath
#2 — M in Wreath

Azalea

The Azalea pattern was produced exclusively for the Larkin Company, who gave the lovely ware away as premiums to club members and their home agents. From 1916 through the 1930s, Larkin distributed fine china which was decorated in pink azaleas on white with gold tracing along edges and handles. Early in the '30s, six pieces of crystal hand painted with the same design were offered: candle holders, a compote, a tray with handles, a scalloped fruit bowl, a cheese and cracker set, and a cake plate. All in all, seventy different pieces of Azalea were produced. Some, such as the fifteen-piece child's set, bulbous vase, china ashtray, and the pancake jug, are quite rare. One of the earliest marks was the Noritake 'M in wreath' with variations. Later the ware was marked 'Noritake, Azalea, Hand Painted, Japan.' Our advisor for Azalea is Linda Williams; she is listed in the Directory under Massachusetts.

Basket, mint; Dolly Varden, #193 ....165.00
Bonbon, #184, 6¼" 60.00
Bowl, #12, 10" 42.50
Bowl, candy/grapefruit; #185 ....210.00
Bowl, cream soup; #363 ....210.00

Bowl, deep, #310...68.00
Bowl, fruit; #9, 5¼" 12.00
Bowl, fruit; scalloped, glass..95.00
Bowl, fruit; shell form, #188, 7¾" 385.00
Bowl, oatmeal; #55, 5½" 28.00
Bowl, soup; #19, 7⅛" 28.00
Bowl, vegetable; divided, #439, 9½" 295.00
Bowl, vegetable; oval, #101, 10½" 60.00
Bowl, vegetable; oval, #172, 9¼" 58.00
Butter chip, #312, 3¼" 120.00
Butter tub, w/insert, #54 ....48.00
Cake plate, #10, 9¾" 40.00
Candle holders, glass, 3½", pr 100.00
Candy jar, w/lid, #313 ....750.00
Casserole, gold finial, w/lid, #372 ....475.00
Casserole, w/lid, #16 ....95.00
Celery tray, #444, closed hdls, 10" 295.00
Celery/roll tray, #99, 12" 55.00
Cheese/butter dish, #314 ....150.00
Cheese/cracker, glass..110.00
Child's set, #253, 15-pc...2,500.00
Coffeepot, AD; #182 ....695.00
Compote, #170 ....98.00
Compote, glass...95.00
Condiment set, #14, 5-pc 65.00
Creamer & sugar bowl, #7 ....45.00
Creamer & sugar bowl, AD; open, #123, from $125 to 140.00
Creamer & sugar bowl, gold finial, #401 ....155.00
Creamer & sugar bowl, scalloped, ind, #449 ....395.00
Creamer & sugar shaker, berry; #122................................150.00

Cruet, #190, $210.00.

(Photo courtesy Linda Williams)

Cup & saucer, #2 ....15.00
Cup & saucer, AD; #183 ....195.00
Cup & saucer, bouillon; #124, 3½"......................................28.00
Egg cup, #120...45.00
Gravy boat, #40 ....40.00
Jam jar set, #125, 4-pc 155.00
Mayonnaise set, scalloped, #453, 3-pc 525.00
Mustard jar, #191, 3-pc...38.00
Olive dish, #194..30.00
Pickle/lemon set, #121...24.50
Pitcher, milk jug; #100, 1-qt 195.00
Plate, #4, 7½" 10.00
Plate, bread & butter; #8, 6½" 10.00
Plate, breakfast/luncheon; #98 ....22.00
Plate, dinner; #13, 9¾" 22.00
Plate, grill; 3-compartment, #38, 10¼" 195.00
Plate, salad, 7⅝" sq..75.00

Plate, scalloped sq, salesman's sample 950.00
Plate, tea; #4, 7½" 10.00
Platter, #17, 14" 60.00
Platter, #56, 12" 58.00
Platter, cold meat/bacon; #311, 10¼" 175.00
Platter, turkey; #186, 16" 495.00
Refreshment set, #39, 2-pc 48.00
Relish, #194, 7⅛" 65.00
Relish, oval, #18, 8½" 20.00
Relish, 2-part, #171 ....45.00
Relish, 2-part, loop hdl, #450 ....390.00
Relish, 4-section, #119, rare, 10" 160.00
Saucer, fruit; #9, 5¼" 10.00
Shakers, bell form, #11, pr.......................................30.00
Shakers, bulbous, #89, pr...42.00
Shakers, ind, #126, pr..32.00
Spoon holder, #189, 8" 120.00
Syrup, #97, w/underplate & lid 110.00
Tea tile 40.00
Teapot, #15 ....110.00
Teapot, gold finial, #400 ....495.00
Toothpick holder, #192 ....120.00
Vase, bulbous, #452 ....1,800.00
Vase, fan form, ftd, #187 ....185.00
Whipped cream/mayonnaise set, #3, 3-pc 38.50

Tree in the Meadow

Another of their dinnerware lines has become a favorite of many collectors. Tree in the Meadow is a scenic hand-painted pattern which features a thatched cottage in a meadow with a lake in the foreground. The version accepted by most collectors will have a tree behind the cottage and will not have a swan or a bridge. The colors resemble a golden sunset on a fall day with shades of orange, gold, and rust. This line was made during the 1920s and 1930s and seems today to be in good supply. A fairly large dinnerware set with several unusual serving pieces can be readily assembled. Our advisor for Tree in the Meadow is Linda Williams; she is listed in the Directory under Massachusetts.

Basket, Dolly Varden...125.00
Bowl, cream soup; 2-hdl 75.00
Bowl, fruit; shell form, #210......................................285.00
Bowl, oatmeal 25.00
Bowl, oval, 9½" 48.00
Bowl, oval, 10½" 58.00
Bowl, soup 38.00
Bowl, vegetable; 9" 35.00
Butter pat 25.00
Butter tub, open, w/drainer 35.00
Cake plate, open hdl 35.00
Candy dish, octagonal, w/lid, 5½" 425.00
Celery dish 35.00
Cheese dish 95.00
Coffeepot, demitasse..250.00
Compote 95.00
Condiment set, 5-pc 45.00
Creamer & sugar bowl, berry 125.00
Creamer & sugar bowl, demitasse 125.00
Cruets, vinegar & oil; cojoined, #319.............................275.00
Cup & saucer, breakfast 18.00
Cup & saucer, demitasse...48.00
Egg cup..30.00
Gravy boat 50.00
Jam jar/dish, cherries on lid, 4-pc 125.00

Lemon dish 15.00
Mayonnaise set, 3-pc 48.00
Plate, dinner; 9¾" 120.00
Plate, salad; 8" 12.00
Plate, 6½" 8.00
Plate, 7⅝" sq, rare 95.00
Platter, 10" 125.00
Platter, 11¾x9" 58.00
Platter, 13¾x10¼" 65.00
Relish, divided 35.00
Snack set (cup & tray), 2-pc 60.00
Teapot 95.00

Miscellaneous

Ashtray, cigarette & matches on brn, 4 rests, #2, 4¼" sq 90.00
Ashtray, Deco-style lady smoking, #2, 1¾" 200.00
Ashtray, flowers on shaded cream, 4 rests, #2, 5¾" 50.00
Ashtray, harlequin figure seated at side, mc lustre, #2, 5".......675.00
Ashtray, Indian chief's portrait, 3 rests, #2, 5½" 150.00
Ashtray, pipe sits on club shape, #2, 5¼" 140.00
Basket vase, gold o/l on cobalt, mk, 8¾" 350.00
Basket vase, red w/floral int, gold hdl, #2, 5½" 140.00
Bowl, floral rim w/cobalt on wht, gold hdls, #2, 8" 70.00
Bowl, gold-lined floral, orange lustre rim, hdls, mk, 9½" 50.00
Bowl, nappy, floral on wht w/gold, 1 pierced gold hdl, #2, 6½" 45.00
Bowl, parrot on branch, blk rim, #2, 10" 85.00
Bowl, river scenic on yel, gold hdls, #2, 7" 60.00
Bowl, river scenic w/windmill, hdls, #2, 7" 65.00
Bowl, salad; yel w/various vegetables on wht int, #2, 9¾"..........125.00
Bowl, sauce; floral w/exotic bird & tan lustre, #2, 4½", +ladle ...50.00
Cake plate, exotic birds, pk border w/gold, #2, 8¼" 70.00
Candlesticks, floral on bl mottle w/cobalt & gold, sq ft, #2, 9", pr..260.00
Candlesticks, floral/exotic bird reserve on lustre, #2, 9¼", pr ..240.00
Candy dish, river scenic, 8 scallops, center hdl, #2, 7½" 50.00
Candy jar, scenic reserve on lustre, w/lid, #2, 6½" 225.00
Celery set, celery on shaded brn, hdls, #2, 12", +6 3¾" salts 140.00
Chamberstick, floral band on orange lustre, #2, 4¾" 100.00
Chocolate set, exotic bird w/gold, #2, 8¾" pot+6 c/s 350.00
Cigarette holder, floral on bell shape, bird finial, #2, 5" 250.00
Compote, 3 ladies form standard that supports bowl, #2, 7" 1,800.00
Condensed milk container, Deco floral w/gold, #2, 5¼", +tray...160.00
Demitasse set, Deco floral w/red band, #2, pot+tray+cr/sug+6 c/s...300.00
Demitasse set, floral on wht w/orange lustre, pot+tray+cr/sug+6 c/s..300.00
Dresser set, bl band on wht w/gold decor, #2, 12½" tray +6 pcs .260.00
Dresser tray, scenic reserves in gold band on burgundy, mk, 13" L..120.00
Egg cup, fruit compote & gold on wht, #2, 3½" 45.00
Ferner, red leaves & blk berries, triangle w/3 posts, #2, 6" 160.00
Game set, deer in forest, geometric border, #2, 16" platter+8 plates .2,000.00
Honey jar, hive shape w/appl bees, #2, 5½" 180.00
Humidor, couple smoking, yel band, gr #2, 6¾" 850.00
Humidor, geometric floral on bl, pipe finial, #2, 3¾" 200.00
Humidor, horse w/in horseshoe in relief, brn tones, #2, 7" 700.00
Humidor, lion killing python in relief on red, #2, 6¾" 900.00
Lemon dish, blossoms & leaves on yel, oval, #2, 6½" 40.00
Mantel set, ornate Deco florals w/gold, #2, 9" bowl+2 9" candlesticks .425.00
Match holder, horses' heads on brn bell shape, #2, 3½" 200.00
Mug, river scenic, #2, 3¼" 80.00
Mustard jar, floral, bl on wht w/gold, #2, 3½", +undertray 40.00
Napkin ring, roses, mc on wht, #2, 2¼" 45.00
Nut dish, nuts in relief, silver trim, #2, 8" L 100.00
Plaque, elk in relief, brn tones, #2, 10½" 600.00
Plate, sandwich; river scenic, center hdl, #2, 8" 65.00
Playing card holder, horse's head on lustre, ftd, #2, 3¾" 175.00

Potpourri jar, floral on bl, bud finial, #2, 6½" **130.00**
Punch bowl, sunset scene w/gold & cobalt, scroll hdls/ft, #2, 14" W ..**950.00**
Punch set, peacock reserve w/gold on pk, #2, 9x16" bowl+8 cups ..**1,200.00**
Snack set, floral on cream w/yel border, #2, cup+7½" tray............**65.00**
Sugar bowl, parrots on red, gold hdls, w/lid, #2, 3¼" **35.00**
Syrup, Deco-style floral on wht w/gold, #2, 4½", +undertray.........**75.00**
Tea set, floral on blk w/gold, #2, 6" pot+cr/sug **165.00**
Tea set, river scenic w/ornate gold, mk, 6¾" pot+cr/sug+6 c/s **525.00**
Tray, horses' heads emerging from trees, hdls, #2, 12" L **125.00**
Trinket box, lady w/whippet, ftd, gold finial, #2, 3" H **350.00**
Trinket dish, desert scene, earth tones, center hdl, mk, 2¼".........**25.00**
Vase, bird by tree trunk, mc lustres, #2, 5⅛"................................**375.00**
Vase, cottage by lake scene, sm angle hdls, #2, 6¼" **140.00**
Vase, Deco-style florals, 4 integral hdls, #2, 7¼", pr.................**275.00**
Vase, geometric band on orange lustre, waisted, #2, 8¾" **145.00**
Vase, leaping gazelles on blk w/flowers, hdls, #2, 10"................**350.00**
Vase, swan scenic w/cobalt & gold, hdls, mk, 7½", pr................**350.00**
Wall pocket, musician w/wide ruffled collar on lustre, #2, 6"......**350.00**

Various Dinnerware Patterns, ca. 1933 to Present

So many lines of dinnerware have been produced by the Noritake company that to list them all would require a volume in itself. In fact, just such a book is available — *The Collector's Encyclopedia of Early Noritake* by Aimee Neff Alden (Collector Books). And while many patterns had specific names, others did not, so you'll probably need the photographs the book contains to help you identify your pattern. Outlined below is a general guide for the more common pieces and patterns. The high side of the range will represent lines from about 1933 until the mid-'60s (including those marked 'Occupied Japan'), while the lower side should be used to evaluate lines made after that period.

Bowl, berry; ind, from $8 to **12.00**
Bowl, soup; 7½", from $12 to..**16.00**
Bowl, vegetable; rnd or oval, ca 1945 to present, from $28 to.......**38.00**
Butter dish, 3-pc, ca 1933-64, from $40 to **50.00**
Creamer, from $18 to..**28.00**
Cup & saucer, demi; from $12 to.......................................**17.50**
Gravy boat, from $35 to **45.00**
Pickle or relish dish, from $18 to **28.00**
Plate, bread & butter; from $8 to......................................**12.00**
Plate, dinner; from $15 to..**30.00**
Plate, luncheon; from $10 to..**18.00**
Plate, salad; from $10 to..**15.00**
Platter, 12", from $25 to...**40.00**
Platter, 16" (or larger), from $40 to **60.00**
Shakers, pr, from $15 to...**25.00**
Sugar bowl, w/lid, from $18 to **30.00**
Tea & toast set (sm cup & tray), from $18 to **28.00**
Teapot, demi pot, chocolate pot, or coffeepot, ea, from $45 to **60.00**

Norse

The Norse Pottery was established in 1903 in Edgerton, Wisconsin, by Thorwald Sampson and Louis Ipson. A year later it was purchased by A.W. Wheelock and moved to Rockford, Illinois. The ware they produced was inspired by ancient bronze vessels of the Norsemen. Designs were often incised into the red clay body. Dragon handles and feet were favored decorative devices, and they achieved a semblance of patina through the application of metallic glazes. The ware was marked with model numbers and a stylized 'N' containing a vertical arrangement of the remaining letters of the name. Production ceased after 1913. Our advisor for this category is John Danis; he is listed in the Directory under Illinois.

Bowl, geometric bands, bronze colored, #16, 4x6" **225.00**
Bowl, incised waves, 3-ftd, #55, 2½x4½" **200.00**
Candlestick, cvd tree motif on cylinder shaft, dome ft/hdl, 5½", NM ...**550.00**
Jardiniere, serpent hdls, 3-ftd, #70, 4x6" **500.00**
Jug, sea horses in verdigris on blk metallic, w/stopper, 1903-13, 7" .**900.00**
Mug, incised decor, blk w/bronze wash, #51, 5" **250.00**

Pitcher, incised geometric decor and lines, Viking's face as spout, #53, 10", $1,750.00.

Vase, bronze patina, gargoyle hdls & ft, emb snake decor, 4x7½" ...**475.00**
Vase, geometrics, gold wash, #13, 9½x8" **250.00**
Vase, groups of dots/elongations, gr on blk, #11, 5½x7½" **500.00**
Vase, lg lizard on side, gold wash, #25, 12" **2,000.00**
Wall pocket, dmn shape w/lizards, #72, very rare, 11"..............**2,500.00**

North Dakota School of Mines

The School of Mines of the University of North Dakota was established in 1890, but due to a lack of funding it was not until 1898 that Earle J. Babcock was appointed as director, and efforts were made to produce ware from the native clay he had discovered several years earlier. The first pieces were made by firms in the East from the clay Babcock sent them. Some of the ware was decorated by the manufacturer; some was shipped back to North Dakota to be decorated by native artists. By 1909 students at the University of North Dakota were producing utilitarian items such as tile, brick, shingles, etc. in conjunction with a ceramic course offered through the chemistry department. By 1910 a ceramic department had been established, supervised by Margaret Kelly Cable. Under her leadership, fine artware was produced. Native flowers, grains, buffalo, cowboys, and other subjects indigenous to the state were incorporated into the decorations. Some pieces have an Art Nouveau — Art Deco style easily attributed to her association with Frederick H. Rhead, with whom she studied in 1911. During the '20s the pottery was marketed on a limited scale through gift and jewelry stores in the state. From 1927 until 1949 when Miss Cable announced her retirement, a more widespread distribution was maintained with sales branching out into other states. The ware was marked in cobalt with the official seal — 'Made at School of Mines, N.D. Clay, University of North Dakota, Grand Forks, N.D.' in a circle. Very early ware was sometimes marked 'U.N.D.' in cobalt by hand. Our advisor for this category is William M. Bilsland III; he is listed in the Directory under Iowa.

Ashtray, Old Faithful, geyser image on ¼-circle base, mk Sather #13 ..**280.00**
Bowl, bl w/triangles & circles, June Marks 1945, UND seal, 2x3½" ..**55.00**
Bowl, blk, incurvate rim, 2x8½"..**100.00**
Bowl, fruit band, McCosh, flared, 1949, 1½x9¼"........................**175.00**
Bowl, fruits in polychrome on cream, 1949, 1½x9¼"..................**210.00**
Bowl, radiating pattern, gr on oxblood, 1958, 9" **250.00**
Bowl, Russian Olive pattern, Clark, bl-gray/ivory, low, 1942, 7½"...**375.00**
Bowl, wht w/bl floral border, M Cable #1133, 1934, 1¾x7⅞" **280.00**

Bowl, wine colored, shouldered, 3½"..............................270.00
Bowl vase, Prairie Roses on pk, F Huckfield, 2½x3¾", NM 300.00
Carafe, turq, Sioux Calendar motif, Mattson 199, 7½"..............675.00
Jar, birds & pine bows on yel gloss, Marie T, 9½x6"...................700.00
Medallion, buffalo in relief on turq, 2" dia..........................225.00
Paperweight, bl w/3-link chain & 'R,' Rebekah Assemblies, 3½" dia .120.00
Plate, emb fruit center w/lt & dk bl band border, 8¼" 105.00
Tile panel, Hispano-Moresque, M Cable, set of 4 tiles, 6x6".......160.00
Trivet, orange-brn triangular shapes on cobalt, 6¼" dia..............250.00
Trivet, Snowflake, gunmetal & dk gr, Julia Mattson, 5" dia 200.00
Trivet, 5-petal flower, ivory/gr/blk, #402/#4, 5¾" dia, NM..........325.00
Vase, birds cvg, gr matt, E Velch, tapered cylinder, 5½"..............700.00
Vase, blkbirds/suns on brick red, Schroeder, bentonite clay, 3½" .450.00
Vase, caramel shades, incurvate rim, Brown-Kuck-745, 6½".......200.00
Vase, covered wagons (scarce pattern), gr tones/matt, squat, 3¼" ..650.00
Vase, cowboy ropes horse cvg, brn recesses on gr tones, JM, rpr, 7".950.00
Vase, cream, bbl shape, 3½".....................................155.00
Vase, daffodils, 2-tone brn matt, McCosh, cylindrical, 1948, 8".1,500.00
Vase, Delft-type tulips on ivory (glaze test), 1953, mini, 2x3½" .275.00
Vase, floral, bl on indigo, Huckfield, 5x3"......................800.00
Vase, floral, leaves at base, gr/brn, ca 1920-30, 7½", from $600 to...800.00
Vase, leaves on curving stems, yel, ca 1920-30, bulbous, 6", $550 to..650.00
Vase, pine trees, multi-tone gr matt, Huck, 9¼" 6,000.00
Vase, Prairie Rose, oxblood, M Cable, 8½x5½".....................950.00
Vase, sgraffito sheaves of wheat on bl, Cooley, #830, 9¼x5" ...2,500.00
Vase, Sunrise on Prairie, cowboy/oxen, 4-color cvg, Huckfield, 6x5".1,000.00
Vase, tulips, lt & dk brn, shouldered cylinder, #45, 2/47, 8" 2,000.00

North State

In 1924 the North State Pottery of Sanford, North Carolina, began small-scale production, the result of the extreme fondness Mrs. Rebecca Copper had for potting. With the help of her husband Henry and the abundance of suitable local clay, the pottery flourished and became well known for lovely shapes and beautiful glazes. They shared the knowledge they gained from their glaze experiments with the ceramic engineering department of North Carolina University, and during summer vacation they often employed some of the university students. Salt-glazed stoneware was produced in the early years but was quickly abandoned in favor of Henry's vibrant glazes. Colors of copper red, Chinese Red, moss green, and turquoise blue were used alone and combination, producing bands of blending colors. Some swirl ware was made as well. The pottery was in business for thirty-five years; most of its ware was sold in gift and craft shops throughout North Carolina. Items in the following descriptions are earthenware unless noted stoneware within the line.

Bowl, bl, side pour w/stick hdl, 3½x6" (w/hdl) 58.00
Bowl, gr, 1939 stamp, 4¼x5"......................................125.00
Ewer, red/bl/beige drip, mk/label, 13½" 130.00
Flower frog, gr jug form w/openings along hip, 4" 70.00
Honey jar, cream w/gr-brn swirl, Grecian urn form w/hdl, 6" 25.00
Pitcher, Rebekah, bl matt over glossy blk-brn, 1930s, 13"..........300.00
Vase, chrome red gloss, sloping shoulder, W Owens, 1930s, 8¼"...200.00
Vase, glossy blackened gr variations, 1925-26, 5½" 350.00
Vase, rust-gr/bright gr/ivory drips on aqua, W Owens, 1930s, 5½" ..225.00

Northwood

The Northwood Company was founded in 1896 in Indiana, Pennsylvania, by Harry Northwood, whose father, John, was the art director for Stevens and Williams, an English glassworks. Northwood joined the National Glass Company in 1899 but in 1901 again became an independent contractor and formed the Harry Northwood Glass Company of Wheeling, West Virginia. He marketed his first carnival glass in 1908, and it became his most popular product. His company was also famous for its custard, goofus, and pressed glass. Northwood died in 1923, and the company closed. See also Carnival; Custard; Goofus; Opalescent; Pattern Glass.

Berry set, Regency/Leaf Medallion, gr w/gold, 1 lg+4 sm, from $330 to..380.00
Bowl, berry; Peach, ruby stain & gold................................75.00
Bowl, Chinese Coral, blk ped ft, late, 4½x9¾"......................70.00
Bowl, fruit; Southern Gardens, cobalt w/gold, 10"..................325.00
Bowl, Mosaic Hobnail, ruffled edge, 8", from $145 to 160.00
Butter dish, #12, gr w/gold 175.00
Butter dish, #31/Belladonna, bl w/gold & enamel flowers...........175.00
Butter dish, Cherry & Cable, clear, 6½", from $90 to 110.00
Butter dish, Regal, gr w/gold trim, from $125 to...................150.00
Butter dish, Regent/Leaf Medallion, gr w/gold, from $345 to......395.00
Butter dish, Teardrop Flower, gr w/gold 185.00
Comport, sweets; Ribbons & Overlapping Squares, gr w/gold.....150.00
Compote, jelly; Regent/Leaf Medallion, amethyst w/gold 150.00
Cracker jar, Cherry & Cable, clear w/ruby stain & gold, from $110 to..130.00
Creamer, Regent/Leaf Medallion, cobalt w/EX gold, 4½", from $70 to.90.00
Creamer, Regent/Leaf Medallion, emerald gr w/gold, 5", from $80 to...90.00
Creamer & sugar bowl, Mikado, frosted w/mc floral, from $145 to.165.00
Creamer & sugar bowl, Teardrop Flower, amethyst w/gold, from $200 to..235.00
Cruet, Leaf Umbrella, cranberry w/clear hdl & (orig) stopper, $700 to ..750.00
Cruet, Royal Ivy, rubena, 6½", from $400 to 450.00
Pickle castor, opal-cased red spatter w/mica, Leaf Mold; Empire SP fr...600.00
Pitcher, Apple Blossom, milk glass w/emb swirl lattice & HP floral, 8" ..100.00
Pitcher, Atlas, clear w/wine & gold trim, water sz 125.00
Pitcher, bl w/HP flowers, water sz, from $130 to 185.00
Pitcher, Dandelion, bl w/gold, tall, slender, water sz, from $350 to.400.00
Pitcher, Grape & Gothic Arches, clear w/ruby stain & gold, water sz...85.00
Pitcher, Oriental Poppy, gr w/gold, tankard form, from $300 to..350.00
Pitcher, Panelled Holly, gr w/gold, from $245 to..................295.00
Pitcher, Peach, gr w/gold, water sz, from $200 to 245.00
Pitcher, Posies & Pods, clear w/ruby stain & gold, 8", from $125 to ...150.00
Pitcher, Regent/Leaf Medallion, gr w/gold, water sz, from $400 to...450.00
Pitcher, Ribbed Pillar, pk/wht spatter in clear, 9" 175.00
Pitcher, Scroll w/Acanthus, gr w/gold, water sz....................170.00
Sauce dish, Royal Oak, rubena, sm.................................75.00
Shakers, Leaf Umbrella, cranberry, 3", pr, from $185 to 235.00
Shakers, Regent/Leaf Medallion, cobalt w/gold, pr, from $350 to..395.00
Sugar shaker, Netted Oak, wht opaque w/decor, 4" 150.00
Sugar shaker, Quilted Phlox, bl, 12-panel 200.00
Sugar shaker, Quilted Phlox, gr cased.............................175.00
Sugar shaker, Quilted Phlox, wht opaque w/bl flowers & gold neck ...100.00
Sugar shaker, Royal Ivy, frosted rainbow craquelle, from $500 to.600.00
Sugar shaker, Royal Ivy, frosted w/amber stain, NM................1,200.00
Sugar shaker, Royal Ivy, rubena, from $165 to 195.00
Sugar shaker, Wide Waist, wht opaque w/bl floral 100.00
Sugar shaker, 9-Panel, gr, 4½" 125.00
Syrup pitcher, Flat Flower, milk glass............................85.00
Toothpick holder, Leaf Umbrella, bl...............................240.00
Toothpick holder, Scroll w/Acanthus, bl w/gold, from $175 to......250.00
Tumbler, Dandelion, bl w/gold, 4¼", from $40 to 55.00
Tumbler, Leaf Umbrella, cranberry, 3¾"............................70.00
Tumbler, Memphis, gr w/gold 40.00
Tumbler, Oriental Poppy, bl w/gold, 4"............................90.00
Tumbler, Panelled Holly, gr w/gold, 4¼", from $65 to 75.00
Tumbler, Posies & Pods, gr w/gold.................................45.00
Tumbler, Regent/Leaf Medallion, amethyst w/gold, 4", from $45 to..60.00
Tumbler, Regent/Leaf Medallion, cobalt w/gold, 4", from $55 to ..85.00
Tumbler, Regent/Leaf Medallion, gr w/gold, 4", from $45 to.........60.00
Tumbler, Royal Ivy, rubena, 3⅞"...................................70.00

Tumbler, Royal Oak, rubena, 3¾", from $75 to **90.00**
Tumbler, Scroll w/Acanthus, gr w/gold & enamel, 3⅞"................**35.00**
Tumbler, Teardrop Flower, amethyst w/gold, 4".......................**45.00**
Tumbler, Threaded Swirl, rubena, 3¾"..**110.00**
Vase, red/multi pulled diagonal swirls on opal, camphor hdls, 8¾"..**850.00**
Water set, Leaf Umbrella, bl satin, pitcher+4 tumblers................**785.00**

Nutcrackers

The nutcracker, though a strictly functional tool, is a good example of one to which man has applied ingenuity, imagination, and engineering skills. Though all were designed to accomplish the same end, hundreds of types exist in almost every material sturdy enough to withstand sufficient pressure to crack the nut. Figurals are popular collectibles, as are those with unusual design and construction. Patented examples are also desirable. Our advisor for this category is Susan Otto; she is listed in the Directory under Ohio. For more information, we recommend *Nutcrackers* by Robert Mills.

Anri man w/blk derby hat, 1925 sticker **167.00**
Barley twist hdls, pliers type, CI w/dk patina, 6"............................**10.00**
Bearded elf w/hat stands w/hands in pockets, CI, 10".................**150.00**
Court jester, brass, 1930s, 7½" **25.00**
Crocodile, brass, hinged jaws, 6½", EX **15.00**
Crocodile, CI, tail lifts, old bronze patina, 19th C, 15½" L **70.00**
Dog, CI, tail hdl, Harper Supply...Chicago, 1950s **35.00**
Dog striding, bronze, on ornate base...**250.00**
Elephant, bronze, burnished copper patina, Victorian, 6½" **112.00**
Lady's legs, brass w/sea gr pnt, 4¾" **10.00**
Lady's legs & buttocks, brass, EX patina, 4¾" **10.00**
Lion's head w/crown, copper on brass, ca 1930, 5½" **15.00**
Man stands in nightcap w/hands in pockets, cvd wood, Black Forest, 8" ...**195.00**
Monkey, cvd wood, Black Forest, 7½".......................................**125.00**
Shakespeare w/open book/Ann Hathaway's Cottage emb, brass, 1900s, 5"..**15.00**
Ship, 3-masted, brass, made in England..**35.00**
SP, Deco pliers type, 1940s, 5½" **8.00**
Squirrel, brass, pull down on tail...**50.00**
Squirrel, CI, 4½", attached to 9" wood-look bowl **47.50**
Squirrel, cvd wood w/blk eyes, Black Forest, 19th C, EX **195.00**
Trusty Servant figure/Winchester Coat of Arms, brass, Peerage, 5½"....**20.00**
Uncle Sam, pnt wood/metal, Steinbach #670, West Germany, 14¾".**135.00**

Nutting, Wallace

Wallace Nutting (1861 – 1941) was America's most famous photographer of the early twentieth century. A retired minister, Nutting took more than 50,000 pictures, keeping 10,000 of his best and destroying the rest. His popular and bestselling scenes included exterior scenes (apple blossoms, country lanes, orchards, calm streams, and rural American countrysides), interior scenes (usually featuring a colonial woman working near a hearth), and foreign scenes (typically thatch-roofed cottages). His poorest selling pictures, which have become today's rarest and most highly collectible, are classified as miscellaneous unusual scenes and include categories not mentioned above: animals, architecturals, children, florals, men, seascapes, and snow scenes. Process prints are 1930s machine-produced reprints of twelve of Nutting's most popular pictures. These have minimal value and can be detected by using a magnifying glass.

Nutting sold literally millions of his hand-colored platinotype pictures between 1900 and his death in 1941. He started in Southbury, Connecticut, and later moved his business to Framingham, Massachusetts. The peak of Wallace Nutting picture production was 1915 – 25. During this period Nutting employed nearly two hundred people, includ-

ing colorists, darkroom staff, salesmen, and assorted office personnel. Wallace Nutting pictures proved to be a huge commercial success and scarcely an American household was without one by 1925.

While attempting to seek out the finest and best early American furniture as props for his colonial interior scenes, Nutting became an expert in early American antiques. He published nearly twenty books in his lifetime, including his 10-volume State Beautiful series and various other books on furniture, photography, clocks, stools, chairs, settles, settees, tables, stands, desks, mirrors, beds, chests of drawers, cabinet pieces, and treenware. He made furniture as well, which he clearly marked with a distinctive paper label that was glued directly onto the piece, or a block or script signature brand which was literally branded into the furniture.

The overall synergy of the Wallace Nutting name — on pictures, books, and furniture — has made anything 'Wallace Nutting' quite collectible.

Our advisor for this category is Michael Ivankovich, author of many books on Nutting: *The Collector's Guide to Wallace Nutting Pictures, The Alphabetical and Numerical Index to Wallace Nutting Pictures, The Collector's Guide to Wallace Nutting Furniture, The Guide to Wallace Nutting Furniture, The Collector's Value Guide to Popular Early 20th Century Prints, The Guide to Wallace Nutting-Like Photographers of the Early 20th Century,* and *The Hand-Painted Pictures of Charles Henry Sawyer.* Mr. Ivankovich is also expert in Bessie Pease Gutmann, Maxfield Parrish, and R. Atkinson Fox and has written *Collector's Value Guide to Early 20th Century American Prints,* containing a wealth of information on their work. Mr. Ivanovich is listed in the Directory Pennsylvania.

Prices below are for pictures in good to excellent condition. Mat stains or blemishes, poor picture color, or frame damage can decrease value significantly.

Wallace Nutting Pictures

Annapolis Garden...**1,250.00**
Canopied Road...**100.00**
Cluster of Zinnias..**650.00**
Eames House **1,250.00**
Fruit Luncheon **130.00**
Garden of Poe Shrine **1,500.00**
Guardian Mother **2,800.00**
Hope **115.00**
Hope **115.00**
Justifiable Vanity **150.00**
Little Rose of Ireland **1,900.00**
Memory of Childhood...**160.00**
Nuttinghame Nook **210.00**
Returning from a Walk..**140.00**
Rug Pattern...**255.00**
Shady Cove..**290.00**
Venice Afar **1,200.00**
Village Mill..**1,300.00**
Water Tracery **60.00**
Where Grandma Was Wed **190.00**
Yellow Lilies..**1,300.00**

Wallace Nutting Books

Clock Book **75.00**
Connecticut Beautiful **35.00**
Furniture of the Pilgrim Century **100.00**
Ireland Beautiful **50.00**
Maine Beautiful **35.00**
New York Beautiful...**45.00**
Photographic Art Secrets **200.00**
Virginia Beautiful..**50.00**
Wallace Nutting Biography..**100.00**

England Beautiful, first edition, with cardboard sleeve, 1928, $55.00.

Wallace Nutting Furniture

Armchair, child's, #211	2,700.00
Bed, mahog, #823-B	2,600.00
Butterfly table, maple, #623	1,900.00
Candlestand, 3-leg, #17	1,125.00
Comb-back armchair, #415	1,500.00
Jacobean stool, #171	750.00
Maple crane bracket table, script brand, #619	685.00
Mirror, 3-feather, #761	625.00
Queen Anne table, walnut, #697	6,000.00
Stand, 4-leg, #653	500.00
Trestle table, pine top, #614	550.00
Windsor continuous-arm chair, #401	550.00
Windsor rocking chair, #477	700.00
Windsor side chair, #301	525.00
Windsor side chair, #326	600.00
Windsor side chair, fan bk, #310	750.00
Windsor tenon arm chair, #422	1,500.00
Windsor writing arm chair, #730	5,100.00
Windsor 4-leg stool, #145	150.00
Winged settle, pine, #416	3,700.00

Major Wallace Nutting-Like Photographers

Although Wallace Nutting was widely recognized as the country's leading producer of hand-colored photographs during the early twentieth century, he was by no means the only photographer selling this style of picture. Throughout the country literally hundreds of regional photographers were selling hand-colored photographs from their home regions or travels. The subject matters of these photographers was very comparable to Nutting's, including interior, exterior, foreign, and miscellaneous unusual scenes. The key determinants of value include the collectability of the particular photographer, subject matter, condition, and size. Keep in mind that only the rarest pictures in the best condition will bring top prices. Discoloration and/or damage to the picture or matting can reduce value significantly.

Several photographers operated large businesses, and although not as large or well known as Wallace Nutting, they sold a substantial volume of pictures which can still be readily found today. The vast majority of their work was photographed in their home regions and sold primarily to local residents or visiting tourists. It should come as little surprise that three of the major Wallace Nutting-like photographers — David Davidson, Fred Thompson, and the Sawyer Art Co. — each had ties to Wallace Nutting.

David Davidson: Second to Nutting in overall production, Davidson worked primarily in the Rhode Island and Southern Massachusetts area. While a student at Brown University around 1900, Davidson learned the art of hand-colored photography from Wallace Nutting, who happened to be the minister at Davidson's church. After Nutting moved

to Southbury in 1905, Davidson graduated from Brown and started a successful photography business in Providence, Rhode Island, which he operated until his death in 1967.

Sawyer: A father and son team, Charles H. Sawyer and Harold B. Sawyer, operated the very successful Sawyer Art Company from 1903 into the 1970s. Beginning in Maine, the Sawyer Art Company moved to Concord, New Hampshire, in 1920 to be nearer their primary market of New Hampshire's White Mountains. Charles H. Sawyer briefly worked for Nutting in 1902 – 03 while living in southern Maine. Sawyer's production volume ranks #3 behind Wallace Nutting and David Davidson.

Fred Thompson: Frederick H. Thompson and Frederick M. Thompson were another father and son team that operated the Thompson Art Company (TACO) from 1908 to 1923, working primarily in the Portland, Maine, area. We know that Thompson and Nutting had collaborated because Thompson widely marketed an interior scene he had taken in Nutting's Southbury home. The production volume of the Thompson Art Company ranks #4 behind Nutting, Davidson, and Sawyer.

Bicknell, Ammonoosuc Path	80.00
Bicknell, Overhanging Birches	75.00
Bicknell, Springtime in the Meadow	60.00
Davidson, Bridal Aisle	40.00
Davidson, Four Friends	120.00
Davidson, Her House in Order	55.00
Haynes, Great Falls, Yellowstone	40.00
Haynes, Yellowstone Park Bears	210.00
Sawyer, Bridge of Flowers	90.00
Sawyer, February Morning	160.00
Sawyer, Morning Over Squam Lake	150.00
Sawyer, Old Man of the Mountains	270.00
Sawyer, Old Spanish Mission, San Juan Capistrano	150.00
Sawyer, Swiss Village, Lake Mohonk	280.00
Thompson, Golden Trail	75.00
Thompson, Grandmother's Garden	70.00
Thompson, Pin Tray w/US Flag	160.00
Thompson, The Roller	130.00

Minor Wallace Nutting-Like Photographers

Hundreds of other smaller local and regional photographers attempted to market hand-colored pictures comparable to Nutting's during the 1900 – 30s time period. Although quite attractive, most were not as appealing to the general public as Wallace Nutting pictures. However, as the price of Wallace Nutting pictures has escalated, the work of these lesser-known Wallace Nutting-like photographers have become increasingly collectible.

A partial listing of some of these minor Wallace Nutting-like photographers include Babcock; J.C. Bicknell; Blair; Ralph Blood (Portland, Maine); Bragg; Brehmer; Brooks; Burrowes; Busch; Carlock; Pedro Cacciola; Croft; Currier; Depue Bros; Derek; Dowly; Eddy; May Farini (hand-colored colonial lithographs); Geo. Forest; Gandara; Gardner (Nantucket, Bermuda, Florida); Gibson; Gideon; Gunn; Bessie Pease Gutmann (hand-colored colonial lithographs); Edward Guy; Harris; C Hazen; Knoffe; Haynes (Yellowstone Park); Margaret Hennesey; Charles Higgins; Hodges; Homer; Krabel; Kattleman; La Bushe; Lake; Lamson (Portland, Maine); M. Lightstrum; Machering; Rossiler Mackinae; Merrill; Meyers; William Moehring; Moran; Murrey; Lyman Nelson; J. Robinson Neville (New England); Patterson; Owen Perry; Phelps; Phinney; Reynolds; F. Robbins; Royce; Fred'k Scheetz (Phila...Pennsylvania); Shelton; Standley (Colorado); Stott; Summers; Esther Svenson; Florence Thompson; Thomas Thompson; M.A. Trott; Sanford Tull; Underhill; Villar; Ward; Wilmot; Edith Wilson; and Wright.

A very general breakdown of prices for works by these minor Wallace Nutting-like photographers would be as follows: larger pictures, greater than 14" x 17", from $75.00 to over $200.00; medium pictures, from 11" x 14" to 14" x 17", from $50.00 to $200.00; smaller pictures, 5" x 7" to 10" x 12", from $10.00 to $75.00.

The same pricing guidelines that apply to Wallace Nutting pictures typically apply to Wallace Nutting-like pictures.

1.) Exterior scenes are the most common.

2.) Some photographers sold colonial interior scenes as well.

3.) Subject, matter, condition, and size are all important determinants of value.

Burrowes, Addie M Lawrence	80.00
Cacciola, Blossomed Hills	105.00
Carlock, Lincoln Memorial	40.00
Coffin, Westcliff, Nantucket	160.00
Gardiner, Arch Rock, Mackinac	140.00
Gardiner, North Shore Drive, Mackinac	100.00
Gardiner, Where Still Waters Flow	180.00
Gibson, Green Pastures	90.00
Gibson, Old Apple Tree	30.00
Harris, Ft Ticonderoga NY	90.00
Harris, Oldest House in US, St Augustine FL	50.00
Higgins, Apple Blossom Lane	110.00
Higgins, Moonlight Sail	130.00
Higgins, Old Farmhouse	90.00
Lamson, Moonlight	60.00
Lamson, Willow Road	40.00
Neville, Old Mill Pond	40.00
Standley, Big Thompson Canon, Colorado	80.00
Standley, Garden of the Gods, Colorado	100.00
Standley, Pike's Peak	110.00
Villar, All in the Garden Fair	130.00
Villar, Candlelight	160.00

Occupied Japan

Items marked 'Occupied Japan' were produced during the period from the end of World War II until April 18, 1952, when the occupation ended. By no means was all of the ware exported during that time marked 'Occupied Japan'; some was marked 'Japan' or 'Made In Japan.' It is thought that because of the natural resentment felt by the Japanese toward the occupation, only a fraction of these wares carried the 'Occupied' mark. Even though you may find identical 'Japan'-marked items, because of its limited use, only those with the 'Occupied Japan' mark are being collected to any great extent. Values vary considerably, based on the quality of workmanship. Generally, bisque figures command much higher prices than porcelain, since on the whole they are of a finer quality.

For those wanting more information, we recommend *Occupied Japan Collectibles* by Gene Florence; he is listed in the Directory under Kentucky. Our advisor for this category is Florence Archambault; she is listed in the Directory under Rhode Island. She represents the Occupied Japan Club, whose mailing address may be found in the Directory under Clubs, Newsletters, and Catalogs. All items described in the following listings are common ceramic pieces unless noted otherwise.

Ashtray, baseball glove, metal	15.00
Bank, elephant trumpeting, wht w/floral decor	35.00
Bell, chef w/rolling pin, 3"	35.00
Bell, Dutch girl figure in orange lustre skirt, sm	20.00
Book, printed in Occupied Japan, from $25 to	30.00
Bookends, penguins, 4", pr	25.00
Bowl, oval w/open lattice work, floral center, gold trim	15.00
Box, piano form, silver-tone metal w/red velvet liner	25.00
Butter dish, basket-weave, holds stick butter	20.00

Candle holders, Colonial figure seated between 2 flower cups, 4", pr	55.00
Candy dish, 3-part w/hdl, metal	20.00
Cigarette box, pagoda scene	30.00
Cigarette box, wht w/bl floral decor, Rossetti, Chicago	20.00
Clock, birdcage design, metal, working, from $175 to	200.00
Coasters, set of 8 in rnd box, papier-mâché	35.00
Cookie jar, cottage shape	75.00
Crumb pan, metal, emb NY scene, from $10 to	15.00
Cup & saucer, cottage scene, lustre	15.00
Cup & saucer, demitasse; wht w/yel & red roses, gold trim, Chata China	12.00
Cup & saucer, wht w/chintz-like floral decor, Merit	20.00
Cup & saucer, wht w/vining floral decor, Merit	20.00
Doll, baby in snowsuit, celluloid w/pnt detail, from $45 to	55.00
Doll, Kewpie, celluloid, 2¾"	20.00
Egg cup, plain wht w/gold middle & rim band	12.50
Figurine, angelic trio in robes playing instruments, 5¾", ea	30.00
Figurine, ballerina in net dress, 5¾"	40.00
Figurine, Black musicians, 2¾", any of set of 5, ea	20.00
Figurine, boy playing mandolin, 5"	15.00
Figurine, bride & groom on base, bsk, 6⅛"	50.00
Figurine, cat w/tail up over arched back	6.00
Figurine, coach (yel) led by 2 wht horses, 3"	10.00
Figurine, Colonial man & lady in fancy attire, gold trim, 7½", pr	60.00
Figurine, cowboy w/rope, 6½"	20.00
Figurine, dog beside lamp, 2"	8.00
Figurine, dog sitting upright w/pipe & hat, 3½"	12.50
Figurine, Dutch peasant couple, detailed pnt, 8¼", pr	75.00
Figurine, fisher boy w/basket & pole, Ucagco, 7"	40.00
Figurine, girl w/teddy bear in basket, 5⅜"	25.00
Figurine, Hummel-type boy & girl standing under umbrella on base, 6"	45.00
Figurine, Indian maiden standing, 4¼"	15.00
Figurine, lady holding skirt wide to curtsy, 4¼"	15.00
Figurine, lion roaring, celluloid	15.00
Figurine, man in turban, 6"	20.00
Figurine, man playing mandolin for lady on base, 4¾"	20.00
Figurine, Mexican on donkey, 8¼"	30.00
Figurine, news boy, long stride, 5½"	20.00
Figurine, Oriental lady in skirt w/basket on head, gold trim, 8"	30.00
Figurine, Pacific island girl in grass skirt, 4"	20.00
Figurine, pastoral couple before fences on bases, bsk, 8", pr	125.00
Figurine, villain in blk w/captive lady, bl mk, 7½"	65.00
Fish dish, brn/bl glossy glaze	12.50
Incense burner, elephant, wht w/gold trim, 2½"	20.00
Incense burner, Oriental figure, 4¼"	20.00
Jewelry box, silver-tone metal, emb scrolls, ftd, 3½x4½"	20.00
Lamp, bulbous bottle form w/hdls, wht w/appl roses, gold decor, 8½"	40.00
Lamp, Oriental boy seated on books reading, detailed pnt glaze	40.00
Leaf dish, wht w/mc fruit decal in center, gold trim	17.50
Match holder, coal hod, wht w/Colonial couple scene, gold trim	15.00
Mug, elephant w/trunk forming hdl, brn, 4¾"	20.00
Music box, geisha dancer, 4-drw, 12x5"	175.00
Pencil holder, dog figure	10.00
Pie bird, Mammy, high gloss, from $125 to	150.00
Pitcher, chicken form, wht w/red, blk & brn accents	25.00
Planter, cucumber form	10.00
Planter, Cupid on sled, bsk, 5"	45.00
Planter, duck in bonnet, wht w/floral decor	15.00
Planter, elf w/tulip pot	20.00
Planter, girl w/mandolin standing next to basket, 3⅝"	10.00
Planter, heart w/angel playing accordion, 3⅝"	12.00
Planter, lady standing beside lg open flower, bsk, Paulux, 6"	75.00
Planter, oblong box w/emb pnt leaves around scalloped rim w/gold trim	10.00
Planter, stuffed dog form, wht w/roses decor & pk neck bow, 5¾"	12.50
Plate, painter's palette shape w/castle scene, artist sgn	15.00

Plate, wht w/plums or cherries decal, openwork rim, Ucagco China, ea..**25.00**
Relish dish, 2-part wht beehive w/lg bee finial.................................**20.00**
Salt box, wooden lid, Ucagco, 5x5"...**50.00**
Shakers, Dutch windmill form, bl & wht, pr, from $20 to............**25.00**
Shakers, frogs on a tray, gr, 3-pc, from $20 to...............................**25.00**
Shakers, hobnail, glass, bulbous, metal lids, pr, from $18 to.........**20.00**
Shakers, penguin form, metal, pr...**20.00**
Shelf sitter/planter, Oriental lady...**20.00**
Shell dish, deeply fluted, wht w/floral & heavy gold trim, 4" **5.00**
Tea set, child's sz, 13-pc 4-place setting...**65.00**
Tea set, child's sz, 26-pc 6 place settings.....................................**125.00**
Teapot, ribbed stoneware ball shape w/bamboo hdl **30.00**
Teapot, windmill form **50.00**
Toby pitcher, man holding 2 mugs, 5" **40.00**
Tray, papier-mâché, rectangular w/floral & filigree design **18.00**
Tray, 3-part w/lobster in center **40.00**
Vases, cornucopias, silver-tone metal, 8", pr...................................**35.00**
Wall plaques, Colonial couple/trees/grass emb on ovals, bsk, pr....**50.00**
Wall pocket, peacock on branch decor..**30.00**

Ohr, George

George Ohr established his pottery in the 1880s in Biloxi, Missis-sippi. The first pottery burned down and was subsequently rebuilt. Ohr, among other things, was a master of the wheel. This mastery enabled him to create unique forms of unbelievable thinness, verging at times on Abstraction and looking far ahead toward many art movements of the twentieth century. In addition to Abstraction, by studying Ohr, one can discover elements of Expressionism, Fauvism (the wild use of color often seemingly at odds with the piece being glazed), and Dada (meaning shock the bourgeoisie). An Ohr piece may be rooted in the functional form of a teapot, but following his manipulation it becomes a sculpture for which the functional form serves only as a take-off point for the fin-ished piece. Ohr was also a master of glazes. Highly esteemed are his vol-canic and gunmetal glazes. He was not well received in his day and sold few pieces of his art pottery — a van Gogh-like tale. Ohr decorated his pieces with snakes and lizards and sometimes with asymmetrical handles. He believed that like all things on earth, no two things should be alike. This dictum was applied to his pottery making. He signed his pieces either in impressed letters or florid script. In the early 1900s Ohr ceased making pottery and became a motorcycle dealer and ultimately sold automobiles. His pottery was stored away to be rediscovered many years later. Ohr died in 1918. Our advisors for this cateogry are Suzanne Per-rault and David Rago; they are listed in the Directory under New Jersey.

Bank, unglazed pear shape, 3⅜"...**965.00**
Bowl, dk volcanic brn, ruffled/crimped/folded, 3x4¾", EX.........**825.00**
Bowl, sponged burnt orange/gunmetal lustre, cupped/folded rim, 5½" .**3,250.00**
Candlestick, speckled brn, saucer base, 1½x4¾" **700.00**
Chamberpot, brn speckled on yel, w/contents, stilt pull, 2½x3¾" .**1,600.00**
Coffeepot, mirrored gr mottle, snake spout, 6x6¼" **9,500.00**
Creamer, khaki gr w/brn speckles, loop hdl, 2⅞x3½", NM.........**715.00**
Dish, brn mottle, waisted low form w/lid, 4x4⅜" **1,150.00**
Inkwell, donkey's head, gunmetal, firing line, 2¾x5¼" **1,300.00**
Jug, pale bsk, short neck, looped hdl, Expo Clay '04, mini..........**715.00**
Jug, puzzle; brn, stepped hdl, 2 mks, 6½x5" **8,000.00**
Mug, bright gunmetal, flared rim, ear hdl, 5x4½", NM............**2,000.00**
Mug, chartreuse w/gunmetal & gr streaks, orange int, flared, 4¾" .**1,650.00**
Mug, rose/gr/bl mottle, ear hdl, 1896, 4½" **3,750.00**
Pitcher, blk volcanic, folded rim, pinched spout/cut-out hdl, 4x5¼".**4,250.00**
Pitcher, marbleized bsk, pinched hdl/folded rim, script mk, 5x6½"..**3,500.00**
Teapot, brn/gr/gunmetal marbled, ear-shaped hdl, snake spout, 5¼" .**5,500.00**
Vase, beige bsk, 1 pinched side, nicks/chips, script mk, 3x6½" **2,000.00**

Vase, blk gunmetal matt, pinched body, 3½"............................**2,700.00**
Vase, brn w/splotches on red clay, tortured/crimped, 4" **1,900.00**
Vase, brn/gunmetal, shaped sqd top angled over similar base, 3½" W .**1,600.00**
Vase, bsk, wide body w/bottle neck, appl ear hdls, 4x5" **800.00**
Vase, bud; gr & gunmetal mottle, bulbous, flared rim, 4¼x2¾".**2,000.00**
Vase, bud; gunmetal, corseted, 5x2¼".......................................**1,200.00**
Vase, charcoal & gunmetal, waisted cylinder w/swollen top/bottom, 3".**1,200.00**
Vase, cobalt, pinched floriform, 3¾x3¼".................................**4,000.00**
Vase, cobalt to pk gloss, twisted body, 5x3½" **6,500.00**
Vase, crackled gr matt, spherical, firing line, 3x4½"....................**850.00**
Vase, dk brn bsk, tortured/crimped, incised Biloxi, 4" **3,000.00**
Vase, gr & gunmetal, incised sailboats, folded rim, 6¾x5"....**4,000.00**
Vase, gr & gunmetal brn flambé on wht clay, bulbous top/base, 3¾" .**1,600.00**
Vase, gr & gunmetal gray, tortured/crimped, 5" **3,500.00**
Vase, gr & gunmetal w/exposed clay, tortured/crimped, ftd, 2¾".**2,600.00**
Vase, gr & gunmetal-speckled amber, twisted body, torn rim, 5x4½".**4,000.00**
Vase, gr-specked amber, twisted body, collar neck, 6¾x4¼" **5,500.00**
Vase, gr/indigo sponging on marbleized clay, bulbous, rpr, 4x5" ..**950.00**
Vase, gunmetal, gourd w/crimped/folded rim, 4"......................**1,725.00**
Vase, gunmetal brn, floppy hat form, 3x5½"...........................**3,200.00**
Vase, gunmetal gray, dimpled/scalloped rim, squat, 3½x4½", NM .**2,000.00**
Vase, gunmetal gray, twisted/tortured form w/cutouts, 5" **3,000.00**
Vase, mc flambè, bulbous w/ruffled rim, ca 1897, 4¾x4½"....**10,000.00**
Vase, mc mottle, cvd band, bulbous/lobed, 5x4½" **8,500.00**
Vase, red & brn clay, bulbous, folded rim, firing line, 3¾x4"...**1,200.00**
Vase, red/gr/bl mottle, dbl-gourd, 4½" **4,000.00**
Vase, speckled brn gloss, flared rim, twisted body, 4x3¼" **5,000.00**
Vase, speckled gr-bl flambè, ruffled band/notched rim, rstr, 5x6".**4,000.00**
Vase, sponged gunmetal spots on mahogany, ovoid, chip, 3½" .**1,900.00**
Vase, umber/mahogany/gr mottle on brn, baluster, unmk, 7½x4".**4,000.00**
Vase, yel/gr mottle, shouldered/squat, 2½x4½" **1,495.00**
Vessel, brn & gunmetal, crimped form w/open hdl, 3½".........**3,000.00**
Vessel, gummetal, star-shaped folded rim, twisted body, rpr, 3¼x4".**2,200.00**
Vessel, gunmetal brn, cupped rim, 4¼x4¼".............................**1,400.00**
Vessel, twisted/tortured tan bsk w/blk veins, hdl, 5" **700.00**
Vessel, unglazed, low form w/narrow neck, loop hdls, 4x4¼" ..**1,265.00**

Old Ivory

Old Ivory dinnerware was produced from 1882 to 1920 by Herman Ohme, of Lower Salzbrunn in Silesia. The patterns are referred to by the numbers stamped on the bottom of many items. (Some early patterns are marked Old Ivory and are not numbered, but the vast majority bears the tiny blue fleur-de-lis/crown mark with Silesia or Germany beneath. Handwritten numbers signify something other than pattern.) Patterns #16 and #84 are the easiest to find and come in a wide variety of table items. Values are about the same for both patterns. Other floral designs include pink, yellow, and orange roses; holly; and lavender flowers — all on the same soft ivory background. Our price ranges are intended to rep-resent a nationwide average, though you may have to pay a little more in some areas. Minor damage and gold wear can lower these prices by as much as 25%. Holly pieces command from 50% to 100% more than those listed below. Novice collectors should be aware of copycat versions from the turn of the century that are much heavier and of a coarser mate-rial. They are marked 'Old Ivory' without the blue trademark. They are not included in this listing.

Another area gaining in popularity is the vases from Ohme usually featuring portraits of Edwardian children. There are a few other forms with portraits, and these are very pricey, with 4" to 5" vases going in the range of $450.00 to $600.00, and 8" and 9" vases about $800.00 to $1,200.00.

Prices realized on the Internet for Old Ivory now rival RS Prussia. With so many collectors now buying on eBay, prices for common pat-terns have dropped while the rare patterns and pieces have skyrocketed in price. As prices have risen, many collections have come on the market, resulting in a drop in the prices of common pieces. It should be noted that the same items with differing pattern numbers bring widely differing prices. For further information we recommend *Collector's Encyclopedia of Old Ivory China, The Mystery Explored*, by Alma Hillman (our advisor), David Goldschmitt, and Adam Szynkiewicz. Ms. Hillman is listed in the Directory under Maine.

Group of pattern #44, Florette blank: Cracker jar, from $500.00 to $700.00; Charger, from $300.00 to $400.00; Shakers, from $175.00 to $250.00 for the pair; Demitasse pot, from $500.00 to $700.00; Chocolate pot, from $500.00 to $700.00. (Photo courtesy Alma Hillman)

Basket, #134, oblong, 8", from $300 to 425.00
Bowl, berry; #7, 5", from $25...45.00
Bowl, porringer; #39, 6¼", from $800 to...................................1,000.00
Bowl, vegetable; #15, oval, 9½", from $125 to 185.00
Bowl, vegetable; #84, rnd, w/lid, 10½", from $900 to 1,200.00
Butter dish, w/insert, #16, 7½", from $700 to 900.00
Cake plate, #122, open hdls, 10" or 11", ea from $175 to 275.00
Candy dish, #84, bow-tie shape, 8", from $125 to 225.00
Charger, #82, Empire, 13", from $500 to.....................................800.00
Chocolate pot, #75, 9½", from $500 to..600.00
Compote, 9", from $600 to 1,000.00
Creamer, #16 or #84, 3½", from $40 to 50.00
Cup & saucer, cider; #16, 3", from $250 to 350.00
Cup & saucer, tea; #63, Clarion, from $185 to 300.00
Dish, #200, 3-lobed, 8½", from $100 to 175.00
Egg cup, #84, 2½", from $400 to 500.00
Gravy boat, #16, 8½", from $800 to...1,000.00
Jam jar, #200, 3½", from $200 to 300.00
Plate, coupe; #82, 6¼", from $75 to 95.00
Plate, dessert; #113, 7½", from $95 to 195.00
Plate, luncheon; #10, 8½", from $95 to 150.00
Platter, #15, 13½", from $200 to 300.00
Platter, #34, 28", from $1,000 to 1,500.00
Platter, fish; 23", from $1,200 to...1,800.00
Powder jar, w/lid, from $300 to...500.00
Shakers, #75, 2¾", pr, from $100 to 150.00
Sugar bowl, service; 6", from $175 to 350.00
Teapot, #200, 8½", from $400 to..600.00
Vase, many szs, from $400 to 1,200.00

Clear-Glazed Hotelware by Hermann Ohme

Because of climbing values for Old Ivory, interest is growing for the clear-glazed pieces by Ohme, which are still reasonable, though escalat-

ing in price. It was produced between 1882 and 1928 in Niedersalzbrunn, Selesia, Germany (now Western Poland). The body of the ware was white, and many of the Old Ivory patterns and shapes were utilized. It is often marked with the blue fleur-de-lis stamp. In comparison, while an Old Ivory open-handled cake plate might sell for $125.00 to $145.00, a comparable clear-glazed example might go for $45.00 to $55.00 with the same mark

Coffeepot, #84, Deco variant, from $1,200 to 1,500.00
Cracker jar, #7, Triomphe blank, from $700 to.........................1,000.00
Cracker jar, #84, Empire blank, from $450 to 550.00
Creamer & sugar bowl, #118, Rivoli blank, from $225 to 375.00
Cup & saucer, chowder; #U22, Eglantine blank, 3¾", from $300 to.400.00
Cup & saucer, coffee; #84, Empire blank, from $40 to...................60.00
Cup & saucer, demi; #5, Elysee blank, 1⅞", from $200 to 300.00
Cup & saucer, tea; #123, Alice blank, 3", from $75 to 100.00
Pickle dish, #U30, Alice blank, 8½", from $20 to 30.00
Plate, dinner; #16, Clarion blank, 9½", from $200 to 300.00
Plate, dinner; #62, Florette blank, 9½", from $400 to 500.00
Toothpick holder, #15, Clairon blank, from $295 to 350.00
Tray, dresser; #76, Louis XVI blank, from $400 to 600.00

Old Paris

Old Paris porcelains were made from the mid-eighteenth century until about 1900. Seldom marked, the term refers to the area of manufacture rather than a specific company. In general, the ware was of high quality, characterized by classic shapes, colorful decoration, and gold application.

Coffeepot, birds & flowering branch in blk & gold, 10½" 460.00
Compote, flowers & stripes w/gold, scroll ft, 1830-45, 10" 400.00
Figurine, lion w/open mouth & curled tail, bl cross/arrow mk, 7x9" .230.00
Platter, armorial eagles, claret/wht/gold border, 1860s, 18x12" ...460.00
Pots de creme set, 12 lidded cups & 2-tier 12" stand, floral w/gold..3,225.00
Urn, landscape reserve on cream w/much gold, hdls, no lid, 12", EX, pr..2,350.00
Vase, Greek scene, mc on blk matt, rust hdls w/profile disks, 15", pr..3,800.00

Old Sleepy Eye

Old Sleepy Eye was a Sioux Indian chief who was born in Minnesota in 1780. His name was used for the name of a town as well as a flour mill. In 1903 the Sleepy Eye Milling Company of Sleepy Eye, Minnesota, contracted the Weir Pottery Company of Monmouth, Illinois, to make steins, vases, salt crocks, and butter tubs which the company gave away to their customers. A bust profile of the old Indian and his name decorated each piece of the blue and gray stoneware. In addition to these four items, the Minnesota Stoneware Company of Red Wing made a mug with a verse which is very scarce today.

In 1906 Weir Pottery merged with six others to form the Western Stoneware Company in Monmouth. They produced a line of blue and white ware using a lighter body, but these pieces were never given as flour premiums. This line consisted of pitchers (five sizes), steins, mugs, sugar bowls, vases, trivets, and mustache cups. These pieces turn up only rarely in other colors and are highly prized by advanced collectors. Advertising items such as trade cards, pillow tops, thermometers, paperweights, letter openers, postcards, cookbooks, and thimbles are considered very valuable. The original ware was made sporadically until 1937. Brown steins and mugs were produced in 1952. Our advisor for this category is Jim Martin; he is listed in the Directory under Illinois.

Barrel, flour; orig paper label, 1920s...1,000.00

Barrel, grapevine-effect banding...**2,500.00**
Barrel, oak w/brass bands **3,000.00**
Barrel label, Chief Strong Bakers..., 16", EX+........................**150.00**
Barrel label, mk Chief/Strong Bakers, image in center, 16", NM...**175.00**
Blanket, horse; w/logo, EX...**1,000.00**
Butter crock, Flemish bl & gray..**650.00**
Cabinet, bread display; Old Sleepy Eye etched in glass **950.00**
Calendar, 1904, NM...**375.00**
Cookbook, Indian on cover, Sleepy Eye Milling Co, 4¾x4"........**200.00**
Cookbook, loaf of bread shape, NM **120.00**
Coupon, for ordering cookbook **200.00**
Dough scraper, tin/wood, To Be Sure, EX................................**300.00**
Fan, diecut image of Old Sleepy Eye, EX+..............................**200.00**
Flour sack, cloth, mc Indian, red letters **345.00**
Flour sack, paper, Indian in blk, blk lettering, NM...................**125.00**
Hot plate/trivet, bl & wht **3,000.00**
Ink blotter..**125.00**
Letter opener, bronze...**500.00**
Match holder, pnt...**800.00**
Match holder, wht..**850.00**
Mug, bl & gray, 4¼"..**300.00**
Mug, bl & wht, 4¼"..**150.00**
Mug, verse, Red Wing, EX..**1,200.00**
Paperweight, bronzed company trademk **300.00**
Pillow cover, Sleepy Eye & tribe meet President Monroe **350.00**
Pillow cover, trademk center w/various scenes, 22", NM **800.00**
Pin-bk button, Indian, rnd face..**250.00**
Pitcher, #1, 4"..**200.00**
Pitcher, #2..**250.00**
Pitcher, #3..**275.00**
Pitcher, #3, w/bl rim...**1,000.00**
Pitcher, #4..**300.00**
Pitcher, #5..**350.00**
Pitcher, bl & gray, 5"...**300.00**
Pitcher, bl on cream, 8", M **220.00**
Pitcher, brn on yel, Sesquicentennial, 1981, from $100 to..........**125.00**
Pitcher, standing Indian, good color...**1,100.00**
Postcard, colorful trademk, 1904 Expo Winner **185.00**
Ruler, wooden, 15"...**700.00**
Salt crock, Flemish bl & gray, 4x6½".......................................**600.00**
Sheet music, in fr...**200.00**
Sign, emb tin litho, ...Flour & Cereal Products, profile, rstr, 28x19".**760.00**
Sign, self-fr tin, Old Sleepy Eye Flour, 20x24".........................**3,000.00**
Sign, sf tin, portrait w/multiple scenes around border, 24x20", G ..**2,300.00**
Sign, tin litho die-cut Indian, ...Flour & Cereals, 13½"............**1,650.00**
Spoon, demitasse; emb roses in bowl, Unity SP **60.00**
Spoon, Indian-head hdl..**70.00**
Stein, bl & wht, 7¾"..**600.00**
Stein, Board of Directors, all yrs, 40-oz **265.00**
Stein, Board of Directors, 1969, 22-oz.....................................**350.00**
Stein, brn, 1952, 22-oz...**200.00**
Stein, brn & wht...**1,000.00**
Stein, brn & yel, Western Stoneware mk **1,000.00**
Stein, chestnut, 40-oz, 1952..**200.00**
Stein, cobalt..**800.00**
Stein, Flemish, bl on gray..**500.00**
Stein, ltd edition, 1979-84, ea **125.00**
Sugar bowl, bl & wht, 3"..**500.00**
Thermometer, front rpl **600.00**
Vase, cattails, all cobalt..**700.00**
Vase, cattails, bl & wht, good color, 9".....................................**500.00**
Vase, cattails, brn on yel, rare color **1,000.00**
Vase, cattails, gr & wht, rare..**1,500.00**
Vase, Indian & cattails, Flemish, 8½".......................................**270.00**

O'Neill, Rose

Rose O'Neill's Kewpies were introduced in 1909 when they were used to conclude a story in the December issue of *Ladies' Home Journal.* They were an immediate success, and soon Kewpie dolls were being produced worldwide. German manufacturers were among the earliest and also used the Kewpie motif to decorate chinaware as well as other items. The Kewpie is still popular today and can be found on products ranging from Christmas cards and cake ornaments to fabrics, wallpaper, and metal items.

For further information we recommend *Doll Values, Antique to Modern,* by Barbara DeFeo and Carol Stover (Collector Books). In the following listings, 'sgn' indicates that the item is signed Rose O'Neill. Values are for examples in excellent condition with no chips. The copyright symbol, ©, is also a good mark on items. Unsigned items can be of interest to collectors; many are authentic and collectible, some are too small to sign.

Our advisors for this category are Don and Anne Kier; they are listed in the Directory under Ohio.

Book, Jello-Girl, Rose O'Neill, 1916, EX **40.00**
Book, Loves of Edwy, leather cover, 432 pgs, 1904, VG.............**850.00**
Book, They Wanted Jell-O, recipes, 1908, 4½x4½", VG............**40.00**
Boutonniere, bsk Kewpie, lapel stud on bk, 2" **65.00**
Bowl, Kewpies playing, mk Germany, Royal Rudolstadt, 1⅝x6"...**85.00**
Candy container, bsk, Kewpie, 4" **500.00**
Candy container, bsk Kewpie finial, jtd arms, German, 1930s, 5¼"..**400.00**
Cup & saucer, Kewpies on wht w/pk-tint edges, Germany...........**65.00**
Dish, 2 Kewpies inside w/Baby on border, mk Czechloslovakia, 5½"..**155.00**
Dresser box, bsk, Kewpie on lid, 4½", EX..................................**165.00**
Inkwell, bsk, w/writer Kewpie, 4½" **500.00**
Kewpie, bsk, action figure, Aviator, 8½" **850.00**
Kewpie, bsk, action figure, Cowboy, #7863 on ft, 1960s, 6x4" **215.00**
Kewpie, bsk, action figure, Cowboy, Germany, 10", EX/NM.......**800.00**
Kewpie, bsk, action figure, crawler, eye shut/ft up, #487SJ/76, 2½"...**130.00**
Kewpie, bsk, action figure, Farmer, Germany, 6½", EX/NM........**900.00**
Kewpie, bsk, action figure, Fireman, #7863 on ft, 1960s, 6x4" **185.00**
Kewpie, bsk, action figure, Governor, seated in chair.................**325.00**
Kewpie, bsk, action figure, Jester in wht hat, 4½", minimum value ..**850.00**
Kewpie, bsk, action figure, kneeling, 4"....................................**750.00**
Kewpie, bsk, action figure, mandolin player in chair, Germany, 4", EX.**925.00**
Kewpie, bsk, action figure, Minister, 5", EX **250.00**
Kewpie, bsk, action figure, reading book, 3¾" **440.00**
Kewpie, bsk, action figure, Sailor, USN on hat, 4½".................**300.00**
Kewpie, bsk, action figure, Santa hat/hands on hips, Jesco, 4", MIB..**60.00**
Kewpie, bsk, action figure, seated, elbows on knees, 4½"...........**155.00**
Kewpie, bsk, action figure, seated, holds roses, Germany, 2¾x1¼"..**320.00**
Kewpie, bsk, action figure, seated w/blk cat in lap, 2¾".............**310.00**
Kewpie, bsk, action figure, seated w/blk cat in lap, 3¼".............**600.00**
Kewpie, bsk, action figure, seated w/chick, Germany, 2", EX/NM..**600.00**
Kewpie, bsk, action figure, seated w/turkey at ft, 2½" **425.00**
Kewpie, bsk, action figure, Soldier w/helmet, Germany, 4½", EX/NM..**600.00**
Kewpie, bsk, action figure, Thinker, 4-5", EX, ea.......................**275.00**
Kewpie, bsk, action figure, Traveler, w/umbrella & suitcase, 3½".**240.00**
Kewpie, bsk, action figure, w/birthday cake, mk 1991, 4¼" **95.00**
Kewpie, bsk, action figure, writer w/pen in hand, Germany, 2"...**360.00**
Kewpie, bsk, arms folded, Germany, 6"......................................**575.00**
Kewpie, bsk, Black Hottentot, Germany, 5", EX/NM.................**625.00**
Kewpie, bsk, Huggers, Germany, 3½", EX/NM..........................**165.00**
Kewpie, bsk, immobile, bl wings, pnt hair, Germany, 2", NM.....**110.00**
Kewpie, bsk, immobile, bl wings, pnt hair, Germany, 6", EX......**300.00**
Kewpie, bsk, jtd shoulders, Germany, 4½", EX/NM....................**150.00**
Kewpie, bsk, jtd shoulders, Germany, 6½", NM (EX box) **520.00**
Kewpie, bsk, jtd shoulders, Germany, 7".....................................**350.00**

Kewpie, bsk, jtd shoulders, Germany, 8½" **400.00**

Kewpie, bsk, jtd shoulders, Germany, 10", EX/NM......................**625.00**

Kewpie, bsk, jtd shoulders, molded clothing, Germany, 6", EX/NM .**330.00**

Kewpie, bsk, jtd shoulders, molded clothing, 8" **375.00**

Kewpie, bsk, jtd shoulders & hips, Germany, 5" **550.00**

Kewpie, bsk, nude holding drawstring bag, #4882, 4½" **1,195.00**

Kewpie, bsk, on tummy, heart sticker, 4" **550.00**

Kewpie, cast steel on sq base, 5½" **55.00**

Kewpie, celluloid, Bride & Groom, 4", EX, ea **40.00**

Kewpie, celluloid, jtd arms, heart label, 8" **50.00**

Kewpie, cloth, Richard Krueger Cuddle Kewpie, w/tag, 12"........**325.00**

Kewpie, compo, jtd shoulders, Jesco, 1966, 24", EXIB................**295.00**

Kewpie, compo, jtd shoulders, rnd bl base, 13" **325.00**

Kewpie, compo, jts shoulders, Hottentot, heart decal, ca 1946, 11".**575.00**

Kewpie, compo, Scootles, orig romper/shoes, Cameo Dolls Co, 1925, 15"..**400.00**

Kewpie, compo, 1920s, 13" **200.00**

Kewpie, Doodle Dog, bsk, blk & wht w/bl wings, 6" **1,530.00**

Kewpie, hard plastic, ca 1950, 8½", MIB **385.00**

Kewpie, hard plastic, sleep eyes, 5-pc body w/starfish hands, 14", NM..**300.00**

Kewpie, soft rubber, Cameo, 9½" **45.00**

Kewpie, vinyl, molded in 1 pc, 9" **25.00**

Kewpie, vinyl, Ragsy, by Cameo, 1950s, 8" **60.00**

Kewpie Doodle Dog, blk & wht w/bl wings, 3"........................**2,200.00**

Lamp, Kewpie (4½") on lamppost, 8" **575.00**

Napkin ring, Kewpie beside ring, sterling, P&B, 2½x1½" dia **210.00**

Newspaper clipping, Kewpie Korner, 1 Black & 1 wht Kewpie w/verse, EX...**50.00**

Newspaper comic, Tom, Dick & Harry Meet the Kewpies, full pg, 1918..**40.00**

Paper dolls, Ragsy & Ritzy, ca 1912, 12" dolls, VG........................**75.00**

Perfume bottle, seated Kewpie, #31 Germany, 2¼" **180.00**

Pin box, bsk, Kewpie in bed, 2¾x3" **550.00**

Pitcher, jasperware, Kewpies playing, Germany, 4¼" **245.00**

Plate, Happy Days Are Here Again, Cameo 1981, 8¼" **25.00**

Plate, Kewpies on bl & gr, Royal Rudolstadt, 7" **75.00**

Plate, 2 Kewpies w/holly, 2 sm tab hdls, 5" **170.00**

Plate, 3 Kewpies in center w/3 on border, Bavarian, 5⅛" **105.00**

Soap figure, Kewpie, RO Wilson, 1917, 4" **110.00**

Talcum container, Kewpie, celluloid, jtd shoulders, c O'Neill, Japan..**285.00**

Tea set, Kewpies, Rose O'Neill Kewpie Germany, 6", pot+cr/sug.**425.00**

Trinket box, jasperware w/3 Kewpies on ea side, 4 on lid, 3¼" ...**130.00**

Vase, Kewpie sits in gr wicker chair w/hole in bk, 3¼" **490.00**

Vase, Kewpie soldier stands at base of tree, 6½" **335.00**

Onion Pattern

The familiar pattern known to collectors as Onion acquired its name through a case of mistaken identity. Designed in the early 1700s by Johann Haroldt of the Meissen factory in Germany, the pattern was a mixture of earlier Oriental designs. One of its components was a stylized peach, which was mistaken for an onion; as a result, the pattern became known by that name. Usually found in blue, an occasional piece may also be found in pink and red. The pattern is commonly associated with Meissen, but it has been reproduced by many others including Villeroy and Boch and Royal Copenhagen.

Many marks have been used, some of them fraudulent Meissen marks. Study a marks book to become more familiar with them. In our listings, 'Xd swords' indicates first-quality old Meissen ware. Meissen in an oval over a star was a mark of C. Teichert Stove and Porcelain Factory of Meissen; it was used from 1882 until about 1930. Items marked simply Meissen were produced by the State's Porcelain Manufactory VEB after 1972. The crossed swords indication was sometimes added. Today's market abounds with quality reproductions.

Blue Danube is a modern line of Onion-patterned dinnerware produced in Japan and distributed by Lipper International of Wallingford,

Connecticut. At least one hundred items are available in porcelain; it is sold in most large stores with china departments.

Bowl, cereal; Blue Danube, banner mk, 6", from $10 to **15.00**

Bowl, fruit; Xd swords, 5½" **25.00**

Bowl, salad; Xd swords, 4x10¾"........................**240.00**

Bowl, serving; Xd swords, 2⅛x9¾"........................**140.00**

Bowl, vegetable; Blue Danube, oval, 2x7¾x10", from $30 to........**45.00**

Bowl, vegetable; Xd swords, w/lid, 6x9" L **175.00**

Bowl, waste; Xd swords, 3x6" **75.00**

Candle snuffer, Xd swords, 3⅛" **145.00**

Casserole, Blue Danube, w/lid, 4½x8½", 6" spoon, 8x6" underplate.**100.00**

Casserole, Blue Danube, w/lid, 4½x8½" dia, from $65 to **75.00**

Chamberstick, Xd swords, 4¼x5½" dia........................**85.00**

Cheese tray, hole for hanging, Xd swords, ⅜x6⅜x10½", $140 to..**155.00**

Collander, 3-ftd, Xd swords, 7¾" dia........................**200.00**

Compote, emb basketweave pattern, Xd swords, 8x9½"........**320.00**

Compote, Xd swords, 5½x5¾", from $70 to **80.00**

Creamer, Xd swords, lg, 5¾", from $90 to **115.00**

Creamer, 3 tree-bark ft, Xd swords, #36, 4¾" **165.00**

Cutting board, Blue Danube, hole for hanging, 10x5¾"...............**55.00**

Dish, Blue Danube, rtcl, twist hdls, oval, 1⅜x7¾"........................**60.00**

Dish, Blue Danube, triangular, 1¾x9½", from $40 to........................**60.00**

Dish, dbl-shell shape, Xd swords, 4x9x11" **210.00**

Dish, leaf shape, hdls, Xd swords, 2x7x8½" **140.00**

Dish, leaf shape, Xd swords, 4x5" **90.00**

Dish, scalloped edge, Meissen, 1½x7x12", from $85 to **100.00**

Dish, souffle; unmk, 3½x9" **65.00**

Dish, Xd swords, sq, 1½x9x9" **175.00**

Fork & spoon, salad; Xd swords, twig-like hdls, pr........................**145.00**

Gravy boat, Blue Danube, 7x5½", 8½" attached underplate, $50 to.**65.00**

Gravy boat, scalloped rim, w/attached underplate, Hutschenreuther.**80.00**

Gravy boat, Xd swords, 6¾x9½" **200.00**

Jar, Oatmeal on wht band, w/lid, 7½" **75.00**

Knife, master butter; 8½", from $50 to **70.00**

Meat tenderizer, pottery head w/wooden hdl, 10½", from $60 to..**75.00**

Mug, Coffee on wht band, no mk **20.00**

Mustard pot, attached underplate, Xd swords, 4¼x6¼" **175.00**

Pitcher, Blue Danube, 6", from $40 to **50.00**

Pitcher, Dynasty; Blue Danube, 8" **100.00**

Pitcher, juice; Juice in center, Xd swords, 7½", from $125 to......**145.00**

Plate, Blue Danube, sq w/open hdls, 8½x10" **55.00**

Plate, rtcl edge, #321, 8¼", from $65 to........................**80.00**

Plate, rtcl edge, Meissen, 1¼x9", from $70 to........................**80.00**

Plate, rtcl edge, Meissen, 7⅞", from $50 to........................**60.00**

Plate, scalloped, Xd swords, 3⅛"........................**30.00**

Plate, scalloped, Xd swords, 9½", from $60 to........................**75.00**

Plate, Xd swords, 7" **40.00**

Plate, Xd swords, 8" **45.00**

Plate, Xd swords, 10¼", from $70 to **90.00**

Platter, Blue Danube, oval, 12", from $40 to **50.00**

Platter, Blue Danube, oval, 14", from $60 to **70.00**

Platter, Xd swords, 1¾x10¾" dia **150.00**

Platter, Xd swords, 2x12" dia........................**185.00**

Platter, Xd swords, oval, 9x6¼"........................**85.00**

Platter, Xd swords, oval, 13½x10"........................**165.00**

Platter, Xd swords, oval, 16x11¾"........................**195.00**

Platter/drainer, Xd swords, oval, 17x10¾"........................**260.00**

Salt box, Salt on front, Germany, wooden lid, 6" dia **125.00**

Shaker, Xd swords, screw-on lid, 3½x1½", ea........................**80.00**

Slipper, Xd swords, 2½x6½", from $110 to........................**125.00**

Spoon, serving; 9½"........................**55.00**

Sprinkler can, Sprinkler in center, Xd swords, 6", from $110 to .**130.00**

Sugar bowl, w/lid, Xd swords, 3½x5"........................**140.00**

Teapot, Blue Danube, w/lid, 6½x10", from $70 to 80.00
Teapot, Xd swords, 8" 225.00
Teapot, Xd swords/Germany, 10¾", +cr/sug, from $450 to.........475.00
Tidbit tray, 3-tiered, Xd swords, 14", 11", 6" 210.00
Toothpick holder, Xd swords, 3⅝" 75.00
Tray, serving; Xd swords, 16x16¼" 695.00
Trivet, Xd swords, 6⅛" dia 65.00
Tureen, soup; Blue Danube, w/lid, 10¼x6x12", +13x9½" underplate.225.00

Opalescent Glass

First made in England in 1870, opalescent glass became popular in America around the turn of the century. Its name comes from the milky-white opalescent trim that defines the lines of the pattern. It was produced in table sets, novelties, toothpick holders, vases, and lamps. Note that American-made sugar bowls have lids; sugar bowls of British origin are considered to be complete without lids. For further information we recommend *The Standard Encyclopedia of Opalescent Glass* by Bill Edwards and Mike Carwile (Collector Books).

Christmas Snowflake, tumbler, white, $95.00.

(Photo courtesy Bill Edwards)

Abalone, bowl, gr 35.00
Acorn Burrs (& Bark), bowl, sauce; wht 50.00
Ala-bock, candy dish, vaseline or canary 100.00
Alaska, bowl, master; bl 175.00
Alaska, shakers, emerald, pr 250.00
Albany Reverse Swirl, bottle, water; wht 115.00
Arabian Nights, pitcher, wht 200.00
Argonaut Shell (Nautilus), bowl, sauce; bl 65.00
Argonaut Shell (Nautilus), compote, jelly; vaseline or canary 90.00
Ascot, biscuit jar, bl 175.00
Astro, bowl, gr 40.00
Band & Rib (Threaded Optic), rose bowl, wht 30.00
Barbells, vase, gr 50.00
Basketweave (Open Edge), nappy, bl 50.00
Beaded Block, sugar bowl, wht 75.00
Beaded Cable, rose bowl, gr, ftd 60.00
Beaded Fleur de Lis, compote, wht 45.00
Beaded Moon & Stars, banana bowl, bl, stemmed 85.00
Beaded Stars & Swag, plate, advertising; bl 525.00
Beatty Honeycomb, creamer, wht 40.00
Beatty Honeycomb, mug, bl 55.00
Beatty Rib, bowl, master; bl 55.00
Beatty Rib, tumbler, wht 30.00
Beatty Swirl, celery vase, bl 75.00
Beatty Swirl, spooner, wht 60.00
Beaumont Stripe, pitcher, vaseline or canary 350.00
Blackberry, bonbon, amethyst 55.00
Blown Drapery, vase, gr 100.00

Blown Twist, tumbler, cranberry 95.00
Brideshead, butter dish, bl 100.00
Bubble Lattice, toothpick holder, wht 200.00
Bulbous Base Coinspot, syrup, wht 110.00
Buttons & Braids, bowl, cranberry 85.00
Cane & Diamond Swirl, tray, vaseline or canary, stemmed 70.00
Cane Rings, creamer, bl 60.00
Casbah, compote, wht 75.00
Cherry, goblet, bl 75.00
Chippendale, plate, vaseline or canary, 6¼" 95.00
Chrysanthemum Base Swirl, cruet, wht 200.00
Chrysanthemum Base Swirl, spooner, bl 100.00
Circled Scroll, creamer, gr 275.00
Coinspot (includes variants, prices averaged), toothpick holder, gr ..150.00
Colonial Stairsteps, sugar bowl, bl 100.00
Compass, rose bowl, wht 90.00
Consolidated Criss-Cross, shaker, gr or cranberry, ea 100.00
Contessa, basket, bl 60.00
Coral Reef, bottle, bitters; wht 125.00
Coronation, pitcher, bl, vaseline or canary 200.00
Crown Jewels, platter, bl 110.00
Daffodils, lamp, hand; gr 300.00
Daisy & Fern, butter dish, cranberry 300.00
Daisy & Fern, vase, wht 100.00
Daisy & Plume, rose bowl, bl, ftd 45.00
Daisy in Criss-Cross, pitcher, bl 300.00
Daisy May (Leaf Rays), nappy/bonbon, gr 45.00
Diamond & Daisy (Caroline), basket, bl 100.00
Diamond Maple Leaf, bowl, gr, hdls 70.00
Diamond Spearhead, butter dish, wht 175.00
Diamond Spearhead, carafe, water; vaseline or canary 300.00
Diamond Wave, pitcher, cranberry, w/lid 175.00
Diamonds, tumbler, cranberry 70.00
Dolly Madison, creamer, bl 75.00
Dolphin & Herons, tray, novelty; wht, ftd 95.00
Double Greek Key, tray, pickle; bl 150.00
Dragon Lady (Dugan's Diamond Compass), rose bowl, wht 90.00
Drapery, Northwood's, spooner, wht 70.00
Duchess, butter dish, vaseline or canary 275.00
Dugan Peach Intaglio, compote, wht 100.00
Dugan's #1013 (Wide Rib), plate, gr 80.00
Dugan Strawberry Intaglio, bowl, fruit; wht, stemmed 65.00
Elipse & Diamond, tumbler, cranberry 115.00
Elson Dewdrop, sugar bowl, wht, w/lid 60.00
Elson Dewdrop #2, bowl, sauce; wht 15.00
English Ripple, tumbler, bl, vaseline or canary 80.00
Everglades, shakers, bl, pr 150.00
Fan, creamer, gr 75.00
Fancy Fantails, rose bowl, vaseline or canary 45.00
Fenton #220 (Stripe), tumbler, gr, w/hdl 35.00
Fenton #370, nappy, amber 55.00
Fern, cruet, bl or wht 225.00
Field Flowers, compote, vaseline or canary, 2 szs, ea 250.00
Fish-in-the-Sea, vase, wht, scarce 195.00
Flora, butter dish, bl 300.00
Fluted Bars & Beads, rose bowl, gr 65.00
Fluted Scrolls (Klondyke), epergne, bl, sm 100.00
Four Pillars, vase, gr 70.00
Frosted Leaf & Basketweave, creamer, vaseline or canary 135.00
Gonerman (Adonis) Hob, cruet, amber 425.00
Gonerman (Adonis) Swirl, spooner, amber 125.00
Grape & Cable, bonbon, vaseline or canary 90.00
Grape & Cable w/Thumbprints, bowl, gr 175.00
Greely (Hobbs), finger bowl, bl 225.00

Harrow, cordial, bl, vaseline or canary, stemmed............35.00
Hearts & Flowers, compote, wht............80.00
Herringbone, tumbler, cranberry............150.00
Hobnail (Hobbs), barber bottle, bl............150.00
Hobnail & Paneled Thumbprint, pitcher, wht............150.00
Hobnail 4-Footed, spooner, cobalt............100.00
Hobnail-in-Square (Vesta), butter dish, wht............200.00
Honeycomb (Blown), cracker jar, wht............250.00
Honeycomb & Clover, bowl, master; gr............75.00
Idyll, spooner, wht............75.00
Inside Ribbing, celery vase, vaseline or cranberry............60.00
Intaglio, compote, jelly; bl............60.00
Intaglio, pitcher, bl............250.00
Intaglio (Dugan), nappy, wht, 6"-9"............45.00
Interior Swirl, rose bowl, bl............100.00
Inverted Fan & Feather, creamer, bl............225.00
Inverted Fan & Feather, sugar bowl, wht............150.00
Jackson, powder jar, gr............80.00
Jewel & Fan, bowl, banana; bl............125.00
Jewel & Flower, creamer, vaseline or canary............95.00
Jewel & Flower, pitcher, wht............190.00
Jewelled Heart, bowl, sauce; bl............30.00
Jewelled Heart, toothpick holder, wht............200.00
Jewels & Drapery, vase, aqua............75.00
Keyhole, rose bowl, bl or gr............100.00
Lady Caroline, basket, bl, vaseline or canary............60.00
Lady Chippendale, compote, cobalt, tall............100.00
Late Coinspot, pitcher, gr............75.00
Lattice Medallions, rose bowl, wht............50.00
Leaf & Beads, bowl, bl, ftd or dome............60.00
Leaf Mold, sugar bowl, cranberry............300.00
Linking Rings, tray, vaseline or canary............90.00
Lords & Ladies, celery boat (in wire basket), bl............100.00
Lustre Flute, butter dish, wht............200.00
Many Loops, bowl, gr, deep rnd............55.00
Maple Leaf, compote, jelly; bl or gr............65.00
Mavis Swirl, barber bottle, wht............85.00
Melon Swirl, pitcher, bl............275.00
National Swirl, tumbler, bl or gr............50.00
Northwood Block, celery vase, vaseline or canary............55.00
Old Man Winter, basket, bl, lg ftd............95.00
Opal Loops, flask, wht............195.00
Opal Open (Beaded Panels), ring bowl, gr, hdls............90.00
Opal Spiral, sugar bowl, bl............90.00
Over-All Hob, spooner, bl............100.00
Overlapping Leaves (Leaf Tiers), plate, wht, ftd............195.00
Palisades (Lined Lattice), bowl, novelty; gr............50.00
Palm Beach, creamer, vaseline or canary............95.00
Panelled Flowers, nut cup, bl, ftd............85.00
Panelled Holly, butter dish, wht............325.00
Panelled Sprig, shakers, wht, pr............125.00
Pearl Flowers, rose bowl, gr, ftd............80.00
Piasa Bird, plate, wht, ftd............75.00
Picket, planter, bl............75.00
Pineapple & Fan (Heisey), creamer, vaseline or canary............325.00
Poinsettia, bowl, fruit; gr, 2 sizes............110.00
Polka Dot, tumbler, bl............60.00
Popsicle Sticks, shake, wht............35.00
Prince William, basket, bl, vaseline or canary, 6½"............300.00
Princess Diana, compote, bl, metal base............75.00
Pump & Trough, pump, wht............100.00
Queen's Spill, vase, spill; bl, 4"............60.00
Quilted Wide Stripe, finger bowl, cranberry............70.00
Reflecting Diamonds, bowl, bl............60.00

Regal (Northwood's), pitcher, wht............150.00
Reverse Swirl, bottle, water; wht............100.00
Reverse Swirl, custard cup, cranberry............150.00
Ribbed (Opal) Lattice, tumbler, cranberry............150.00
Ribbed Pillar, bowl, berry; cranberry, lg............95.00
Ribbed Spiral, bowl, bl, ruffled............55.00
Ribbed Spiral, vase, vaseline or canary, squat, 4"-7"............75.00
Ribbon Swirl, spittoon, gr............125.00
Richelieu, compote, jelly; bl............75.00
Ring Handle, ring tray, gr............95.00
Roulette, bowl, novelty; wht............30.00
Ruffles & Rings, nut bowl, gr............45.00
Ruffles & Rings w/Daisy Band, bowl, wht, ftd............35.00
S-Repeat, tumbler, bl............65.00
Salmon, bowl, wht, fish-shaped............200.00
Scottish Moor, cracker jar, bl............350.00
Scroll w/Acanthus, cruet, vaseline or canary............300.00
Seaweed, creamer, cranberry............225.00
Seaweed, spooner, bl............125.00
Shell (Beaded Shell), bowl, sauce; gr............65.00
Shell & Dots, rose bowl, wht............35.00
Smooth Rib, bowl, wht, on metal stand............100.00
Snowflake, lamp, oil; bl............325.00
Somerset, pitcher, juice; vaseline or canary, 5½"............90.00
Spanish Lace, bottle, water; vaseline or canary............325.00
Spanish Lace, finger bowl, bl............75.00
Spatter, vase, orange, 9"............100.00
Speckled Stripe, shakers, wht, pr............190.00
Spool, compote, bl or gr............50.00
Squirrel & Acorn, vase, bl............190.00
Stars & Stripes, barber bottle, cranberry............300.00
Stippled Scroll & Prism, goblet, gr, 5"............30.00
Stripe, toothpick holder, bl............250.00
Stripe (Wide), cruet, wht............175.00
Sunburst-on-Shield (Diadem), creamer, bl............100.00
Swag w/Brackets, butter dish, wht............125.00
Swag w/Brackets, spooner, gr............110.00
Swirl, custard cup, cranberry............75.00
Swirl, mustard jar, gr............110.00
Target Swirl, tumbler, cranberry............95.00
Thousand Eye, celery vase, wht............100.00
Threaded Grape, banana boat, bl............225.00
Three Fruits & Meander, bowl, wht, ftd............80.00
Tokyo, compote, jelly; wht............30.00
Tree of Life, shaker, bl, ea............100.00
Tree of Love, plate, wht, 2 szs, rare............135.00
Twigs, vase, vaseline or cranberry, panelled, 7"............85.00
Twist (Miniatures), sugar bowl, vaseline or canary............150.00
Twister, plate, bl............100.00
Victoria & Albert, butter dish, wht............110.00
Vulcan, creamer, bl............65.00
War of Roses, compote, bl, w/metal stand............150.00
Waterlily & Cattails, bonbon, amethyst............85.00
Waterlily & Cattails, relish, gr, hdls............65.00
Wild Bouquet, spooner, gr............85.00
Wild Grape, compote, wht............40.00
Wild Rose, bowl, banana; amethyst............80.00
William & Mary, cake plate, bl, stemmed............150.00
Windows (Plain), barber bottle, cranberry............325.00
Windows (Swirled), mustard jar, wht............55.00
Windows (Swirled), tumbler, bl............85.00
Windsor Stripe, vase, cranberry............125.00
Wishbone & Drapery, plate, gr............60.00
Wreath & Shell, bowl, master; vaseline or canary............125.00

Wreath & Shell, salt dip, wht 85.00
Wreathed Grape & Cable, bowl, orange; wht, ftd, very rare 350.00
Zipper & Loops, vase, bl, ftd 65.00

Opaline

A type of semiopaque opal glass, opaline was made in white as well as pastel shades and is often enameled. It is similar in appearance to English bristol glass, though its enamel or gilt decorative devices tend to exhibit a French influence.

Bottle, scent; cranberry w/gold o/l, lady's portrait stopper 395.00
Bottle, scent; turq w/HP scene, gilt-brass mts & fr 295.00
Goblet, pk opaque w/fiery opal stem & ft, 7" 100.00
Jewel casket, turq egg w/ormolu fr & ft, ca 1850.........................495.00
Jewel casket, wht egg w/HP decor, gold ormolu fr, ftd, hinged lid..495.00
Jewel casket, wht w/HP floral & jewels, hinged lid, 3½x4½x3½" .695.00
Pin tray, wht, oval w/swirl hdls, sm..15.00
Rose bowl, wht w/HP floral, emb fern leaves form panels, 3" 58.00
Vase, turq w/HP floral, ftd, 10½", pr 195.00
Vase, wht w/HP flowers, gourd form, 12" 195.00

Optical Items

Collectors of Americana are beginning to appreciate the charm of antique optical items, and those involved in the related trade find them particularly fascinating. Anyone, however, can appreciate the evolution of technology apparent when viewing a collection of old eye wear and at the same time admire the primitive ingenuity involved in their construction.

Eyeglasses, blonde faux tortoiseshell, rnd lenses, NM 110.00
Eyeglasses, cat eyes, appl decor at outer point, EX......................165.00
Eyeglasses, cat eyes, blk & wht twist design, 1950s 80.00
Eyeglasses, cat eyes, blk plastic, child sz...75.00
Eyeglasses, cat eyes, blk plastic w/rhinestones & cvg, EX 265.00
Eyeglasses, gold plated w/emb floral design, mk 10k, folding, NM..135.00
Eyeglasses, gold-tone wire, sm rnd lenses, late 1800s, EX 185.00
Eyeglasses, silver-colored wire, 1930s style, EX 175.00
Eyeglasses, silver-tone Granny style, early 1900s, EX...................175.00
Eyeglasses, silver-tone wire, octagonal lenses, Bausch & Lomb, 1930s..180.00
Eyeglasses, tortoiseshell w/silver accent at bridge, early 1900s, EX..285.00
Lorgnette, Art Nouveau, sterling silver 225.00
Lorgnette, MOP, JB Watson Optician Edinburgh, NM in velvet pouch.195.00
Magnifying glass, herringbone pattern bone hdl w/cvd cats, 3x7".75.00
Magnifying glass, swings out of case, figural owl on top, 3" 40.00
Opera glasses, abalone at rims, mk Henry Kahn/Lemaire Paris, EX.210.00
Opera glasses, leather wrapped, mk Vendome Paris, VG 35.00
Opera glasses, MOP allover including hdl, Lemaire...Paris, EX...175.00

Orientalia

The art of the Orient is an area of collecting currently enjoying strong collector interest, not only in those examples that are truly 'antique' but in the twentieth-century items as well. Because of the many aspects involved in a study of Orientalia, we can only try through brief comments to acquaint the reader with some of the more readily available examples. We suggest you refer to specialized reference sources for more detailed information. See also specific categories.

Key:
Ch — Chinese   hdwd — hardwood

cvg — carving   Jp — Japan
drw — drawer   Ko — Korean
Dy — Dynasty   lcq — lacquer
E — export   mdl — medallion
FR — Famille Rose   rswd — rosewood
FV — Famille Verte   tkwd — teakwood
gb — guard border

Blanc de Chine

Figure, Kuan Yan seated, Ch, 19th C, 8" 355.00
Figures, man & woman w/2 children, EX details, mk China, tallest: 12" .275.00

Blue and White Porcelain

Beaker vase, floral & lappet pattern, Kangxi, 17¾" 4,115.00
Bottle, sake; flower sprigs, Arita ware, 19th C, 15"......................250.00
Charger, dragon w/sages/bamboo border, Jp, 19th C, 20" 950.00
Charger, shishi (lg), Arita ware, 19th C, 23"..............................1,400.00
Garden seat, drum form w/Canton-style decor, Ch, 19th C.....1,500.00
Jar, egrets & prunus on cracked ice ground, Arita ware, 1890s, 23".1,875.00
Jar, foliage & lotus lappets, baluster, Vietnam, ca 1500, 8" 2,350.00
Jar, Hundred Antiques reserves, floral borders, Ch, 19th C, 12".200.00
Jar, lion dogs among clouds, globular, Vietnam, ca 1500, 4⅞".1,295.00
Jardiniere, dragons chasing flaming jewels, 18th C, 14½", pr..3,250.00
Planter & tray, cranes, Arita ware, late 19th C, 9" 350.00
Umbrella holder, bl & wht, flowering tree/bird, 20th C, 24" 195.00
Vase, E, elephant figural, Ch, ca 1800, 7"................................1,000.00
Vase, Hawthorn pattern, trumpet form, Ch, 19th C, 14" 355.00
Vase, Ku form w/peonies & foliage, Ch, 19th C, 16"...................325.00

Bronze

Figure, Avalokiteshvara on lotus plinth, gilt, Tibet, 17th C, 14".3,000.00
Figure, Buddha standing, gilt lcq, Thailand, 19th C, 3¾"........2,585.00
Figure, geese, old dk patina w/red on heads, unmk, 12x15", pr...575.00
Figure, Shakyamuni seated on serpent king, gilt lcq, 19th C, 44".7,000.00
Figure, Tara seated on lotus branch, gilt, Sin-Tibet, 19th C, 7" .2,000.00
Mirror, cast animals & birds in circles, 5⅜" dia 200.00
Vase, flared bowl on intricate wave design base, Usubata, 19th C, 15"..1,100.00

Celadon

Garden seat, clouds & peonies on trellis, Longquan, Ming Dy, 14"..600.00
Ginger jar, bl decor: 3 figures/deer, on trn mahog stand, 11", VG .400.00
Jar, underglaze bl & red fruit, oviform, 18th C, 5" 550.00
Stand, leafy scrolls & silhouettes, rtcl, Ming Dy, 10⅝", EX 600.00
Vase, gray gr w/crackle, gold foliage, Jp, 1890s, 15½" 125.00

Furniture

Armchair, cvd bats/serpents & dragons, cabriole legs, 20th C, pr..200.00
Armchair, elm w/red-brn pnt, floral cvgs, rprs, 39", pr 195.00
Armchair, rswd w/MOP inlay bk, ornate cvg, 1900s, 40", pr.......325.00
Bed, blk lcq w/mushroom finials, pierced cvgs, 20th C, 45x76x42".220.00
Cabinet, HP figures/butterflies on blk, moon brasses, 19th C, 59x42" .800.00
Chest, Asian wood w/bronze hdw, low form, 2-drw, Jp, 22x42x18"..1,000.00
Chest, dowry; blk lcq w/lg russet chrysanthemums, Meiji, 63x33x31".4,115.00
Cupboard, red & blk pnt w/gold decor, 2-door, Ch, 19th C, 49x36x18"..350.00
Desk, partner's; dragon & scroll cvgs, appl beading, 20th C, 31x60x43".550.00
Hibachi, cvd tree form lined w/hammered copper, Jp, 20x18".1,200.00
Money chest, yew or walnut, hinged drop front, iron hinges, 32"..230.00
Press, red lcq w/old gold decor, 2-door, Ch, 70x52x24"............1,000.00
Screen, ebonized, 2-panel w/relief-cvd stone decor, 68x53" 485.00

Screen, wood/bamboo w/cut-out decor, 4-fold, Jp, 48x52" **400.00**

Screen, 18 figures on brn lcq w/gold, 6-panel, 20th C, 76x90" ...**825.00**

Screen, 38 figures in HP scenes w/pagodas/etc, 4-part, 72x83" ...**600.00**

Server, elm, dvtl drws, mortised top, Ch, 30x83x20" **525.00**

Sofa, Ch Chpndl style, mahog fr w/piercings, 20th C, 74" **660.00**

Table, altar; hdwd, incised dragons/key border, 32x72x18" **700.00**

Table, breakfast; elm, pierced geometrics, mortised, 33x38x38" ..**300.00**

Table, coffee; elm w/paneled sides, 2 dvtl drw w/cvg, rstr, 47x30" sq ...**110.00**

Table, console; hdwd pierced frieze w/flowers/etc, Ch, 1890s, 56" **700.00**

Table, work; E, gilt lcq, lyre supports, claw ft, 1830s, 37x25x18" **1,600.00**

Table, hand-carved rosewood with lion and bat decor, rouge marble insert, China, nineteenth century, 36", $400.00.

Hardstones

Celadon Nephrite, censer, rtcl leaves, dome lid, 18th C, 6½" .**8,225.00**

Coral, figure of Kuan Yin & attendant, salmon pk, Ch, 1800s, 7" .**345.00**

Gr Nephrite, pheasant cocks, twin tail feathers, Ch, 15", pr ...**2,500.00**

Jade, bird, celadon w/bright areas, fitted stand, 1900, 8", pr **690.00**

Jade, ewer, Kuang form, spinach gr, tao-tieh masks/dragon hdls, 12x13" .**800.00**

Jade, mountain w/scholar & attendant, celadon w/brn mks, 1800s, 4" .**575.00**

Jade, ritual ax, gr calcified, Neolithic period, 5½" **300.00**

Jade, ritual disk, gray-gr, patterned Yuan type, Chou period, 2¼" ..**120.00**

Jade, ritual pc, cicada form, gray-gr, 1111-751 BC, 2¼" **765.00**

Jade, scabbard drag, gray-gr w/brn mks, 206 BC-220 AD, 1½x1¾" .**120.00**

Jade, seal, foo dog on lid, bright gr w/emerald mks, 1910, 2½" ...**250.00**

Jade, seal, gray w/brn mks, ca 475-221 BC, 1½" **115.00**

Jade, vase, buffalo form w/relief dragons, gray-gr w/dk mottle, 10x8" ..**285.00**

Jade, vase w/lid, olive gr w/cvd tao-tieh masks, Ch, 1800s, 5¼" .**115.00**

Marble, Buddha head, N Qi Dy, losses, 12½" **11,750.00**

Rock crystal, elephant, transparent, 1890s, 4" **115.00**

Rock crystal, figure on Guarnyn, EX details, ca 1900, 16" **8,800.00**

Serpentine, Kwan Yin in flowing robe by flowers, 10¾" **200.00**

Spinach Nephrite, bowls, thin w/flared rim, 8", pr **3,500.00**

Spinach Nephrite, plaques, dragons/clouds/pearl, Qing Dy, 11", pr .**1,750.00**

Wht Nephrite, plaque, sparrow/duck/grasses, rtcl oval, Ming Dy, 4" ..**2,350.00**

Wht Nephrite, vase, phoenix birds, loop hdls, 19th C, 7" **11,750.00**

Inro

Blk & gilt lcq, 1-case, old lady chasing bull, 19th C, 2½" **2,000.00**

Blk lcq, 4-case, cvd fan medallions w/natural-color birds/flowers, 4" .**430.00**

Blk lcq w/maki-e in silver & gold (boatmen), Koryu saku/seal, 3" .**1,600.00**

Blk/cinnabar lcq, 4-case, scholars in mtn landscape, 1800s, 2¼" .**545.00**

Gilt & blk lcq, 4-case, landscape, Yamada Taigyro, 1800s, 3½" ..**7,000.00**

Gilt lcq, 3-case, sumi-e style boat scene, 19th C, 2⅝" **950.00**

Gilt lcq, 5-case, dragon & waves, Shorinsai, Meiji, 3½" **2,950.00**

Ivory, 4-case, dragons chasing in clouds, unsgn, 19th C, 2¾" .**2,000.00**

Metal, 4-case, shojo drinking/bk: sage by reeds, Kajikawa saku, 3½" .**3,500.00**

Lacquer

Lacquerware is found in several colors, but the one most likely to be encountered is cinnabar. It is often intricately carved, sometimes involving hundreds of layers built one at a time on a metal or wooden base. Later pieces remain red, while older examples tend to darken.

Box, blk & gilt w/scrolls, rounded corners, Meiji, 7⅞" L **1,175.00**

Box, fan-shape maki-e panels w/figures, Jp, 19th C, 8½" L **325.00**

Box, incense; cinnabar cvd w/flowers, Ch, 18th C, 2½" dia **325.00**

Box, ornate floral w/silver inlay, 1½x7" **550.00**

Box, stationery, blk & gilt w/florals, Meiji, 6x10x8" **3,800.00**

Figurine, dancer, cinnabar & blk, Han style, 15½" **175.00**

Vase, cinnabar w/cvd birds/flowers/etc, baluster, 20th C, 30", pr .**1,525.00**

Netsukes

A netsuke is a miniature Japanese carving made with two holes called the Himitoshi, either channeled or within the carved design. As kimonos (the outer garment of the time) had no pockets, the Japanese man hung his pipe, tobacco pouch, or other daily necessities from his waist sash. The most highly valued accessory was a nest of little drawers called an Inro, in which they carried snuff or sometimes opium. The netsuke was the toggle that secured them. Although most are of ivory, others were made of bone, wood, metal, porcelain, or semiprecious stones. Some were inlaid or lacquered. They are found in many forms — figurals the most common, mythological beasts the most desirable. They range in size from 1" up to 3", which was the maximum size allowed by law. Many netsukes represented the owner's profession, religion, or hobbies. Scenes from the daily life of Japan at that time were often depicted in the tiny carvings. The more detailed the carving, the greater the value.

Careful study is required to recognize the quality of the netsuke. Many have been made in Hong Kong in recent years; and even though some are very well carved, these are considered copies and avoided by the serious collector. There are many books that will help you learn to recognize quality netsukes, and most reputable dealers are glad to assist you. Use your magnifying glass to check for repairs. In the listings that follow, netsukes are ivory unless noted otherwise; 'stain' indicates a color wash.

Boy & kitten asleep at study table, wooden, 1800s **485.00**

Boy saves another from drowning in a sake jar, boxwood, Shoraku, 1800s .**485.00**

Buddha at Nara, Keiun, 1913, +box, int: Keiun saku w/artist's seal ...**975.00**

Candy maker stirring pot of sweets, 1800s **345.00**

Daikoku & Jurojin carrying bag of wealth, Tamamitsu, 1800s.....**400.00**

Dancer ringing bells, boxwood, Hijitsu, 19th C, 1⅝" **1,525.00**

Daruma stretching his arm, staghorn, 1800s **345.00**

Dbl mask, wooden, Chika Sanjin, 20th C.....................................**175.00**

Dragon boat w/Daikoku & Hoi-tei, MOP plaque sgn Gyokuzan, 1890s .**115.00**

Fish in state of decomposition, boxwood, 19th C, 2⅜" **585.00**

Foreigner w/drum, dressed in long gown & tall hat, amber patina, 1800s ..**1,265.00**

Frog caught by crab sitting on lotus pad, wooden, 1700s, 2" **635.00**

Goddess, seated w/fan, 1800s **690.00**

Kappa in lotus pond, boxwood, 1800s **375.00**

Karako, boxwood, w/bib of dyed ivory, gold flowers/horn inlay, 1800s .**345.00**

Mask, corpulent man, wooden, Deme to, 1800s **175.00**

Mask, monkey's face, wooden, 1800s, 2" **230.00**

Mask, wood, Deme Shokei, 1700s **230.00**

Monkey in robe w/tobacco pouch, dk stain, Meigyokosai, 1½" .**2,650.00**

Okame, standing/holding gourds, 1800s **230.00**

Oni drumming gong, holding rosary, pigment traces, 1800s........**345.00**
Oriental man dancing w/fan inside persimmon section, yel patina, 1800s.**345.00**
Ox, recumbent, rope harness, dk stain, Tomotada School, 2¼"**.2,950.00**
Quail w/inlaid eyes on millet stalks, Okatomo, 1⅝"...............**1,765.00**
Sage on bk of sishi, EX patina & stain, 18th C, 1¾"...................**880.00**
Sennin w/dbl gourd, 1700s, 3¾"...**920.00**
Sishi mask, hinged jaw, wood, Minko, 19th C, 1½", EX..........**2,950.00**
Tiger, sgn, 1800s **690.00**
Woman w/sake cup, 1800s **345.00**
Young woman, Ryoichi Yosuichi, 1800s **175.00**

Porcelain

Chinese export ware was designed to appeal to Western tastes and was often made to order. During the eighteenth century, vast amounts were shipped to Europe and on westward. Much of this fine porcelain consisted of dinnerware lines that were given specific pattern names. Rose Mandarin, Fitzhugh, Armorial, Rose Medallion, and Canton are but a few of the more familiar.

Basin, E, FR, birds & domestic scenes, C, 19th C, 16"................**485.00**
Basket, chestnut; E, FR, gilt hdls, Ch, 4½x6½" +undertray........**525.00**
Bough pots, E, FR, sq sides, stepped ft, Ch, 19th, C, 9", pr......**6,500.00**
Bowl, E, FR, domestic scenes, Ch, 11½"..................................**350.00**
Bowl, E, FR, ladies & children in garden, Ch, 1800s, 11"...........**700.00**
Bowl, E, shields w/rampant lions/flowers, cobalt/gold, Ch, 10⅜"**.375.00**
Bowl, punch; E, FV, dragons & warriors, Ch, 19th C, 23½" **4,400.00**
Bowl, punch; E, Mandarin palette, figures in garden, Ch, 18th C, 13"**.3,525.00**
Bowl, punch; E, Mandarin scenes w/rococo reserves, Ch, 18th C, 11"**.535.00**
Bowl, vegetable; E, armorial crest, mc w/gold, Ch, 19th C, 5x10x8"**..200.00**
Charger, dragon panels amid geometric floral, 2-tone bl on wht, 16"**.145.00**
Figure, Lan Tsai Ho w/flower basket, Ch, early 20th C, 16"........**175.00**
Ginger jar, Famille Noir, birds & flowers, Ch, 19th C, 14x13" ...**950.00**
Ginger jar, phoenix & peonies on pk, Ch, late 19th C, 9"..........**235.00**
Incense holder, FR flower borders, rtcl turq body, Ch, 19th C, 8" L..**500.00**
Jar, E, FR, pheasants & prunus, ovoid, gilt-bronze mts, 26"..........**1,700.00**
Jar, FV, birds & flowers, rouge-de-fer borders, baluster, 19th C, 16"**.765.00**
Jar, FV, birds/trees/etc on fishscale ground, Ch, 18th C, 13", EX ...**350.00**
Jar, FV, Hundred Antiques, Ch, 19th C, 17' **585.00**
Jug, cider; E, armorial w/foo dog finial, cobalt & gold, Ch, 1800s, 9"**..700.00**
Pitcher, E, Am shield & flower sprigs, mc w/gold, Ch, 19th C, 4"**.350.00**
Plate, E, family crest & shield w/banner/flowers/etc, Ch, 11" **650.00**
Plate, E, Gr/Brn Fitzhugh, center quatrefoil design, prof rpr, 9⅝"**.1,980.00**
Plate, E, Green Fitzhugh, butterfly border, 9¾"........................**550.00**
Plate, E, Orange Fitzhugh, butterfly border, 9¾", EX **935.00**
Plate, E, Orange Fitzhugh, Ch, 19th C, 17"................................**2,585.00**
Plate, E, Orange Fitzhugh, 10", pr...**515.00**
Plate, E, Rose Fitzhugh, butterfly border, 9¾" **1,600.00**
Plate, E, US Eagle w/shield & banner, Ch, 19th C, 9½".............**285.00**
Plate, soup; E, floral reserves on dk bl, made for Persian market, 9"**.235.00**
Platter, E, armorial crest w/bl & gold, Ch, ca 1800, 18¾x16¾" ..**400.00**
Platter, E, Blue Fitzhugh, oval, Ch, 19th C, 20⅛" **880.00**
Platter, E, Cabbage pattern, oval, Ch, 19th C, 19"...................**3,000.00**
Platter, E, flowers/fruit/butterflies, sepia w/gold, Ch, 18¾".........**560.00**
Posset pot, E, brn flower conucopia & flowers w/gold, fruit finial, 6"**..165.00**
Screen, FR, figures in palace garden, Ch, 19th C, 21"................**765.00**
Stand, E, FV, 6-lobe w/flower branch & sea life panels, 9½".......**500.00**
Temple jar, FR, butterflies/bamboo/flowers, inv't pear form, 46"...**1,175.00**
Tureen, E, Blue Fitzhugh, strap hdls, flower finial, 10½x14", NM..**1,000.00**
Tureen & underdish, E, Tobacco Leaf, flowers & birds, Ch, 18th, C, 15"**.15,275.00**
Turene, FR, cranes/geese/ducks/flowers, w/lid, late 1700s, 14"**.2,115.00**
Urn, FV, gilt-metal mts, Ch, 10", pr...**600.00**
Vase, E, floral & figural bands, scalloped baluster, Ch, 15⅝", pr**.2,500.00**
Vase, E, FR, courtiers/flowers/etc, baluster, 19th C, 24¾"........**2,115.00**

Vase, E, FR, phoenix/flowers/floral reserves, gilt mts, Ch, 24" **.2,000.00**
Vase, FR, butterflies/peaches/lotus, long neck, ca 1900, 16⅛"**.1,765.00**
Vase, FR, women in palace scene, Ch, 19th C, 24" **350.00**
Vase, FV, warriors in combat before city, Ch, 19th C, 17"...........**700.00**

Pottery

Bowl, globular alms-bowl shape w/incising, Tang Dy, 7¾", NM.**3,225.00**
Ewer, parrot head in relief, phoenix reserves, cobalt/amber, Tang, 13".**14,000.00**
Figurine, God of War, mc decor, China, Ming Dy, 15" **1,295.00**
Flask, pilgrim; flambè w/gr/bl/red/stripes, Ch, 1890s, 5½"..........**175.00**
Vase, mottled red on brn clay, bulbous, Jp, 7" **260.00**

Rugs

The 'Oriental' or Eastern rug market has enjoyed a renewal of interest as collectors have become aware of the fact that some of the semi-antique rugs (those sixty to one hundred years old) may be had at a price within the range of the average buyer. Unless noted otherwise, values are for rugs in excellent condition.

Belouchistan, mc overall design on brn, 46x111" **715.00**
Caucasian, geometrics w/in 3 borders, med bl/ivory/multi, 24x24", VG **.350.00**
Caucasian, ivory & midnight bl borders on lime gr, 58x88"........**300.00**
Caucasian mat, dmn panels w/Persian motif, mc, 32x30", VG **.1,100.00**
Hamadan, column of palmette motifs flanked by leaves, 74x40", VG...**500.00**
Hamadan, dk bl border, blk spandrels/bl mdls on pk-red, 51x73"**.330.00**
Hamadan, mc elements on dk bl abrash ground, dtd 1914, 38x151"**.500.00**
Heriz, lg central mdl, red/bl/cream, semi-antique, 139x102", EX.**1,300.00**
Heriz, rosette mdl, bls/rose/red/gold on red w/ivory spandrels, 48x34"**.470.00**
Mahal Sarouk, open floral on salmon, midnight bl border, 80x51"**..500.00**
Mashad, mc spandrels on dk red w/wide bl border, 116x154" **825.00**
Mashad, mc spandrels on red w/dk purple-bl & bl borders, 114x150"**..715.00**
Najafabad, tan & bl spandrels on red, midnight bl border, 112x148"**.600.00**
NW Persian, Herati, red/rose/bl/gold/ivory on dk bl, 36x160", VG..**3,800.00**
NW Persian, ivory & med bl borders w/rust ground, 38x180" **.1,000.00**
NW Persian, plum border, midnight bl ground, 54x78" **750.00**
Persian, floral on plum, free-form borders w/dk bl, 78x114"........**990.00**
Persian, lg sqs w/mc rows of hooked designs, semi-antique, 123x55", VG..**475.00**
Persian Bakhtiari, gray border, dk bl spandrels on red, 82x120"**..825.00**
Sarouk, midnight bl border & abrash burgundy ground, 106x138"**..1,875.00**
Sarouk, wide red borders & camel ground, fringe, 118x170" ...**3,000.00**
Sarouk, 5 borders w/central mdl, navy/red/multi, 22x27", VG....**450.00**
Shiraz, dk bl & burnt orange borders on dk red, 59x143" **415.00**
Sirjan, ivory border, bl mdls, mc openwork on red, 51x76".........**385.00**

Snuff Bottles

The Chinese were introduced to snuff in the seventeenth century, and their carved and painted snuff bottles typify their exquisite taste and workmanship. These small bottles, seldom measuring over 2½", were made of amber, jade, ivory, and cinnabar; tiny spoons were often attached to their stoppers. By the eighteenth century, some were being made of porcelain, others were of glass with delicate interior designs tediously reverse painted with minuscule brushes sometimes containing a single hair. Copper and brass were used but to no great extent.

Agate, caramel color, cvd as dbl-gourd w/foliage, 19th C, 2".........**400.00**
Agate, rvpt children, well hollowed, coral glass stopper, 1900s, 3" .**115.00**
Amber, dbl form cvd w/prunus plants, coral/jade stoppers, 1¾x2"**..400.00**
Amber, honey-colored/swirled, deeply hollowed, 1800s, 2¾" **115.00**
Celadon jade, basket form, well hollowed, 1700s, 2¼"...............**800.00**
Gray-wht jade w/gr veins, cvd as gourd w/foliage, 19th 2" **400.00**
Hornbill, floral scrolling across surface, 2" **350.00**

Ivory, cvd as squirrel w/bunch of grapes, 1800s, 2" L **230.00**
Ivory, cvd flowers in high relief, rectangular, 19th C, 2¾" **300.00**
Ivory, cvd in rnd as little boy w/attributes of immortals, 1890s, 4" .**345.00**
Porc, lotus plant shape, gr, 1890s, 2¾" **115.00**
Porc, relief decor w/mc enamel, 1890s, 3" **115.00**
Rose quartz, cvd birds/flowers, European bronze mts, 1900s, 4" **115.00**
Wht jade w/enameled silver mts, 19th C, 2½" **350.00**
Wht nephrite cvd as squirrel, coral stopper, 18th C, 2⅝" **2,250.00**

Textiles

Panel, embr phoenix/symbols on silk w/brocade borders, 18th C, 32" sq.**1,000.00**
Panels, red silk w/embr dragons, late Ming Dy, 42x18", pr........**2,115.00**
Robe, bl silk w/gold dragons & flaming pearls, 19th C, 57½"..**1,300.00**
Robe, chain stitch, midnight bl w/flower embr, Ch, 19th C **400.00**
Robe, peacocks & flowers on blk silk, Ch, 19th C, EX **450.00**
Robe, priest's; gold brocade on silk w/embr floral, Jp, 19th C, 73".**500.00**
Robe, priest's; gold brocade on silk w/pomegranates, Jp, 19th C, 74".**500.00**
Robe, red silk w/embr dragons & scrolls, brocade sleeves, 19th C .**4,700.00**
Robe, russet velvet w/embr flowering branches, 44"..................**4,000.00**
Saddle blanket, tigers & flaming bushes, mc wool, Tibet, 1870s, 52".**3,500.00**

Woodblock Prints, Japanese

Framed prints are of less value than those not framed, since it is impossible to inspect their condition or determine whether or not they have borders or have been trimmed.

Ferryboat at Onmayagashi, Kutsushika Hokusai, 12¼x15¼" **195.00**
Snowfall at Kambara, Hiroshige, matted in 12x15" fr **385.00**
Sudden Rain Storm at Atake, Hiroshige, matted in 15x12" fr **500.00**
Sudden Shower at Shono, Hiroshige, matted in 12x15" fr..........**400.00**

Miscellaneous

Basket, woven bamboo, ring hdls, Hanakago, 20th C, 12½" **240.00**
Basket, woven bamboo, slim, appl hdl, Hanakago, 20th C, 18½"...**425.00**
Basket, woven reeds, tree-root hdl, copper insert, Hanakago, 19½".**1,000.00**
Bust, male divinity, CI w/pnt traces, Ch, Ming period, 10" **6,500.00**
Cvg, dancer w/bells, wood w/ivory insets, mc, Meiji, 3" **415.00**
Cvg, Ganesha (elephant god) dancing, stone, India, ca 1100, 19½".**2,000.00**
Cvg, rat on mushroom, ivory, inlaid eyes, stain, ca 1800, 3"....**4,115.00**
Flower vessel, burnished/lcq natural burlwood w/cvg, Khaki, 13½".**260.00**
Libation cup, cvd rhino horn w/grapevines & squirrels, 1700s, 6", EX..**7,000.00**
Planter, wood panels tied w/leather knots, branch hdl, Jp, 10x5½".**150.00**
Sake container, stained gourd w/blk persimmon stopper, Jp, 19th C, 8"..**300.00**
Shrine, Kannon w/child, mc w/gold, eng gilt-copper mts, Jp, 1800s, 15".**1,295.00**
Vase, silver w/mixed metal inlay birds & wheat, Meiji, 9¾", pr.**2,350.00**

Orrefors

Orrefors Glassworks was founded in 1898 in the Swedish province of Smaaland. Utilizing the expertise of designers such as Simon Gate, Edward Hald, Vicke Lindstrand, and Edwin Ohrstrom, it produced art glass of the highest quality. Various techniques were used in achieving the decoration. Some were wheel engraved; others were blown through a unique process that formed controlled bubbles or air pockets resulting in unusual patterns and shapes. Our advisor for this category is Abby Malowanczyk; she is listed in the Directory under Texas.

Bowl, Ariel, blk w/wht shapes, Arienly 408P/Ingebord Lundin, 5¼" H..**700.00**
Bowl, smoke, 6 panels w/semi-nude dancers, P Gabe 937.1927 R Bayer, 9".**500.00**
Bowl, smoke w/cvd carps/bubbles, E Hald, 32HE127, 1932, 7¼".**300.00**

Sculpture, cat, Orrefors Expo 213-72 O Alberius, 9x3½"............**300.00**
Vase, clear w/int bl globs, cylinder w/flared top, 8¾"....................**35.00**
Vase, Deco nude etch, N 3210 B7AR, 9½x4½"............................**250.00**
Vase, dk bl cylinder w/thick walls, Expo pm 185-60/Sven Palmquist, 9".**325.00**
Vase, fish among seaweed (int decor), ovoid, 5½"........................**400.00**
Vase, Graal, 305N Edw Hald, 6¼x6" **525.00**
Vase, Kraka, bl w/bubbles & bl threading, Palmquist, 13½"........**655.00**
Vase, Mayflower, Johansson, w/sticker, 8½x4¾"..........................**145.00**
Vase, nude & 2 birds in flight eng, Palmquist 2327RB 5, 6x10¾".**225.00**
Vase, Ravenna, med bl w/wht-lined bl circles, Nr 2317/Sven Palmquist.**6,200.00**
Vase, stylized nude intaglio, S Gate 1911 ASRR, bulbous, 5".....**650.00**

Ott and Brewer

The partnership of Ott and Brewer began in 1865 in Trenton, New Jersey. By 1876 they were making decorated graniteware, parian, and 'ivory porcelain' — similar to Irish belleek though not as fine and of different composition. In 1883, however, experiments toward that end had reached a successful conclusion, and a true belleek body was introduced. It came to be regarded as the finest china ever produced by an American firm. The ware was decorated by various means such as hand painting, transfer printing, gilding, and lustre glazing. The company closed in 1893, one of many that failed during that depression. In the listings below, the ware is belleek unless noted otherwise. Our advisor for this category is Mary Frank Gaston.

Basket, pk flowers w/gold, cactus-shaped hdl w/appl tulips **1,200.00**
Bowl, cream soup; gold floral, gold twig hdls, 2½x3"....................**50.00**
Creamer & sugar bowl, pk flowers w/gold leaves, 3", 2x3½".......**150.00**
Creamer & sugar bowl, thistles/butterflies w/gold, w/lid, 1883-93 .**250.00**
Cup & saucer, bouillon; eggshell, pk int w/gilt, 2½", 6" dia........**165.00**
Cup & saucer, demi; wht shell w/yel int & gold rim....................**135.00**
Cup & saucer, ivory w/pk int, gold rim & hdl decor....................**130.00**
Pitcher, daisies, gold on wht, branch hdl, red mk, 10½x6" **900.00**
Pitcher, gold leaves on wht, twig hdl, 6⅜", EX............................**250.00**
Teapot, HP poppies w/gold, bark top & branch hdl, 8½"............**900.00**

Urn, gold leaves and vines on cream, bulbous body with reticulated four-footed base with gold seashells, crown and sword mark, 19x10", $14,500.00.

Vase, duck & dandelions, gold on coral, rtcl hdls, 10¼x7"......**3,000.00**
Vase, gold-paste leaves & butterfly, uptrn hdls, 5½"....................**700.00**

Overbeck

The Overbeck Studio was established in 1911 in Cambridge City, Indiana, by four Overbeck sisters. It survived until the last sister died in 1955. Early wares were often decorated with carved designs of stylized animals, birds, or florals with the designs colored to contrast with the background. Others had tooled designs filled in with various colors for a mosaic effect. After 1937, Mary Frances, the last remaining sister, favored handmade figurines with somewhat bizarre features in fanciful combinations of color. Overbeck ware is signed 'OBK,' frequently with the designer's and potter's initials under the stylized 'OBK.'

Figurine, frog (comical), gr & brn w/checked bk, 3" L **500.00**
Figurine, golfer (somewhat comical), purple/gr/wht, 4" **950.00**
Figurine, goose (comical), wht w/yel beak & oversz ft, 5½" **700.00**
Oil on board, brn bird on morning-glory vine, 7½x9½"+oak fr .**850.00**
Oil on board, nuthatches on tree trunk, 9½x7½"+oak fr **1,000.00**
Oil on board, 2 brn birds on wire fence, 9¼x7¼"+oak fr **1,600.00**
Oil on board, 5 ruby-crowned kinglets on branches, 7¼x9½"+fr.**1,600.00**
Vase, floral, mc modernistic/geometric style, sgn EH, 10"......**15,000.00**
Vase, floral panels (3), purple/brn on gray to gr, flared rim, 7½" .**6,000.00**

Overlay Glass

Art glass having layers of more than one type or color of glass is sometimes called overlay or cased glass. Very often glassware of this type has applied decorations such as fruit, flowers, leaves, or ruffles (rigaree), such as is commonly identified with Stevens and Williams. See also Stevens and Williams.

Biscuit jar, lav-pk w/HP decor, SP trim, 6⅝x4¾" **185.00**
Bowl, pk on wht w/appl 3-color floral/leaves/ft, 5½" H..............**635.00**
Pitcher, orange, ruffled top, reeded hdl, 7¼x4¾" **165.00**
Rose bowl, bl, HP morning glories, frosted ft, 5x4½" **145.00**
Vase, red, HP florals, cut scallops w/gold, gold hdls, 8½" **175.00**
Vase, yel, tomato red int, sq top, 4¼x3½".......................................**70.00**

Overshot

Overshot glass originated in sixteenth century Venice, and the ability to make this ware eventually spread to Bohemia, Spain, and elsewhere in Europe. Sometime prior to 1800, the production of this glass seems to have stopped.

The Englishman Apsley Pellatt, owner of the Falcon Glass Works, is credited with reviving this decorative technique around 1845 – 1850. He acknowledged the origin of this technique by calling his product 'Venetian Frosted Glass' or 'Anglo-Venetian Glass.' Later it would be called by other names, such as Frosted Glassware, Ice Glass, or Craquelle Glass.

It is important to understand the difference between crackle glass and overshot glass. All crackle is not overshot, and all overshot is not crackle. However, most overshot is also crackle glass. Two different processes or steps were involved in making this glassware.

Crackle glass was produced by dipping a partially blown gob of hot glass in cold water. The sudden temperature change caused fissures or cracks in the glass surface. The gob was then lightly reheated and blown into its full shape. The blowing process enlarged the spaces between fissures to create a labyrinth of channels in varying widths. When cooled in the annealing lehr, the surface of the finished object had a crackled or cracked-ice effect.

Overshot glass was made by rolling a partially inflated gob of hot glass on finely ground shards of glass that had been placed on a steel plate called a marver. The gob was then lightly reheated to remove the sharp edges of the ground glass and blown to its final shape. Most overshot pieces were immersed in cold water before application of the ground glass, and such glassware can be considered both crackle and overshot.

Sometimes an object was blown to full size before being rolled over the glass shards. As Barlow and Kaiser explained in *The Glass Industry in Sandwich, Vol. 4*, page 104, 'The ground particles adhered uniformly over the entire surface of the piece, showing no roadways, because the glass was not stretched after the particles had been applied. Overshot glass produced by this second method is much sharper to the touch.'

Overshot glass produced by the first method — with the 'roadways' — has been mistaken for the Tree of Life pattern. However, this pattern is pressed glass, whereas overshot is either free blown or mold blown.

Overshot pieces could be further embellished, requiring a third decorative technique at the furnace, such as the application of vaseline glass designs or fine threads of glass that were picked up and fused to the object. The latter decorative style, called Peloton, was patented in 1880 by Wilhelm Kralik in Bohemia.

Boston & Sandwich, Reading Artistic Glass Works, and Hobbs Brockunier were among the companies that manufactured overshot in the United States. Such products were quite utilitarian — vases, decanters, cruets, bowls, water pitchers with ice bladders, lights, lamps, and other shapes. Colored overshot was produced at Sandwich, but research has shown that the applied ground glass was always crystal. Czechoslovakia is known to have made overshot with colored ground glass. Many such pieces are acid stamped 'Czechoslovakia.' Undamaged, mint condition overshot is extremely hard to find and expensive.

Our advisors for this category are Stan and Arlene Weitman; they are listed in the Directory under New York.

Basket, clear, appl rope hdls, 6½x10½" L **425.00**
Bottle, scent; clear w/3 bl reeded ft, 8¾".......................................**200.00**
Bowl, clear w/red snake on lid, 2½x4¼" **750.00**

Bowl, sterling silver-mounted lid with cherries and leaves, 1880s, 2½x4¼", with 7" bowl, very rare, $850.00. (Photo courtesy Stan and Arlene Weitman)

Compote, clear, tall ft, 7¼x6¾" **475.00**
Goblet, blown, clear w/gold rim, 6" **20.00**
Pitcher, bl, bulbous body, bl hdl, 7¼" **525.00**
Pitcher, champagne; cranberry, clear hdl & rigaree, ice bladder, 12".**500.00**
Pitcher, clear, twisted rope hdl, Sandwich, 1870-87, 13½"...**1,100.00**
Pitcher, cranberry to clear, bulbous body, clear hdl, 5¼".............**525.00**
Pitcher, cranberry to clear, clear reeded hdl, Sandwich, 9" **995.00**
Pitcher, cranberry to clear, cylindrical, low hdl, 7" **750.00**
Pitcher, lemonade; clear, emb swirl, twist hdl, 9", +6 tumblers...**650.00**
Pitcher, tankard; clear, cylindrical, appl rigaree at opening, 10¼" .**950.00**
Pitcher, wine; wht, slim elegant form w/clear ft, 11½" **875.00**
Plate, cranberry w/gold, 8¾", NM, 6 for.......................................**100.00**
Rose bowl, amethyst, crystal thorn legs, 5x4½" **425.00**
Vase, clear w/appl vaseline flower, sq sides, vaseline ft, 12" **1,000.00**

Owen, Ben

Ben Owen worked at the Jugtown Pottery of North Carolina from 1923 until it temporarily closed in 1959. He continued in the business in his own Plank Road Pottery, stamping his ware 'Ben Owen, Master Potter,' with many forms made by Lester Fanell Craven in the late 1960s. His pottery closed in 1972. He died in 1983 at the age of 81.

The pottery was reopened in 1981 under the supervision of Benjamin Wade Owen II. One of the principal potters was David Garner who worked there until about 1985. This pottery is still in operation today with Ben II as the main potter.

Bowl, rice; Mirror Black, Ben, 2x5" **100.00**
Candlesticks, wht cupped bobeches, Craven, 12½", pr **375.00**
Jug, salt glaze, bulbous, Ben Owen III 87 mk, 4¼" **70.00**
Jug, Tobacco-Spit Brown, 2 incised lines at shoulder, 4¼" **90.00**
Pitcher, buttermilk; Frogskin Green, 1960s, 8⅞" **250.00**
Pitcher, salt glaze w/cobalt decor, ca 1980s, 7½" **80.00**
Pot, cobalt on salt glaze, BW Owen II, early 1980s, 5" **70.00**
Vase, Chinese Blue curdled w/wht, 7" **235.00**

Owens Pottery

J.B. Owens founded his company in Zanesville, Ohio, in 1891, and until 1907, when the company decided to exert most of its energies in the area of tile production, made several quality lines of art pottery. His first line, Utopian, was a standard brown ware with underglaze slip decoration of nature studies, animals, and portraits. A similar line, Lotus, utilized lighter background colors. Henri Deux, introduced in 1900, featured incised Art Nouveau forms inlaid with color. In time, the Brush McCoy Pottery acquired many of Owens' molds and reproduced a line similar to Henri Deux, which they called Navarre. (Owens pieces were usually marked Henri Deux and have a heavier body and coarser feel to the glaze than similar McCoy pieces.) Other important lines were Opalesce, Rustic, Feroza, Cyrano, and Mission, examples of which are rare today. The factory burned in 1928, and the company closed shortly thereafter. Values vary according to the quality of the artwork and subject matter. Examples signed by the artist bring higher prices than those that are not signed. For further information we recommend *Owens Pottery Unearthed* by Kristy and Rick McKibben and Jeanette and Marvin Stofft. Mrs. Stofft is listed in the Directory under Indiana.

Bronze Opalesce, vase, pansies (slip), twisted, #102, 5x4" **440.00**
Matt Green, vase, geometric design at top, 4 buttress ft, 9" **550.00**
Matt Green, vase, geometrics, sm hdls, #1157, 7¾x6½" **385.00**
Matt Utopian, jug, leaves & sprig of flowers on brn, 6" **350.00**
Utopian, cat portrait, stick neck, #1077, 16½x6½" **3,100.00**
Utopian, mugs, cherries, 5¼x4¾", 4 for.....................................**150.00**
Utopian, vase, floral, #1044, 9¼" **300.00**
Utopian, vase, floral, #944, 5x4½" **125.00**
Utopian, vase, floral, 4-sided/twisted, #102, 5x4" **150.00**
Utopian, vase, floral (EX art), #266, 5½"...................................**195.00**
Utopian, vase, floral w/leaves, pillow form, 4¼x5½"...................**125.00**
Utopian, vase, leaves, bottle shape, #1010, 10½x5½"................**360.00**
Utopian, vase, wild roses, #013, 11½" **275.00**
Utopian, vase, wild roses, TS (Tot Steel), pillow form, #1051, 5x6" .**250.00**

Paden City

Paden City Glass Mfg. Co. was founded in 1916 in Paden City, West Virginia. It made both mold-blown and pressed wares and is most remembered today for its handmade wares in bright colors with fanciful etchings. A great deal of Paden City's business was in supplying decorating companies and fitters with glass; therefore, Paden City never marked their glass with a trademark of any kind, and the company's advertisements were limited to trade publications, rather than retail. In 1948 the management of the company opened a second plant to make utilitarian, machine-made wares such as tumblers and ashtrays, but the move was ill-advised due to a glut of similar wares already on the market. The company remained in operation until 1951 when it permanently closed the doors of both factories as a result of the losses incurred by Plant No. 2. (To clear up an often-repeated misunderstanding, dealers and collectors alike should keep in mind that The Paden City Glass Mfg. Co. had absolutely no connection with the Paden City Pottery Company, other than their identical locale.)

Today Paden City is best known for its numerous acid-etched wares that featured birds, but other ornate etchings were also produced — some of which are well documented in print, while others have yet to be documented in publications that are widely available. Peacock and Rose and Cupid are two of the most commonly found etched patterns. Currently, collectors especially seek out examples of Paden City's most detailed etching, Orchid, and its most appealing etching, Cupid. However, pieces bearing undocumented etchings or documented etchings on shapes and/or colors on which that etching has not previously been seen are fetching the highest prices from advanced collectors. Pieces in the company's plainer pressed dinnerware lines, however, have remained affordable, even though some patterns are quite scarce.

Below is a list of Paden City's colors. Names in capital letters indicate original factory color names where known, followed by a description of the color.

Amber — several shades
Blue — early 1920s color, medium shade, not cobalt
Cheriglo — pink
Copen, Neptune, Ceylon — various shades of light blue
Crystal — clear
Ebony — black
Emeraldglo — thinner dark green, not as deep as Forest Green
Forest Green — dark green
Green — various shades, from yellowish to electric green
Mulberry — amethyst
Opal — white (milk glass)
Primrose — amber with reddish tint (rare)
Rose — dark pink (rare)
Royal or Ritz Blue — cobalt
Ruby — red
Topaz — yellow

Collectors seeking more information on Paden City would do well to consult the following: *Paden City, The Color Company*, by Jerry Barnett (out of print, privately published, 1979); *Colored Glassware of the Depression Era 2* by Hazel Marie Weatherman (Glassbooks, 1974); *Price Trends to Colored Glassware of the Depression Era 2* by Hazel Marie Weatherman (Glassbooks, Editions in 1977, 1979, and 1981). Also available are *Encyclopedia of Paden City Glass* by Carrie and Jerry Domitz (Collector Books); *Paden City Company Catalog Reprints from the 1920s* (Antique Publications, 2000) and *Paden City Glassware* by Paul and Debora Torsiello and Tom and Arlene Stillman (Schiffer, 2002). There is also a quarterly newsletter currently being published by the Paden City Glass Collectors Guild; this group is listed the Directory under Clubs, Newsletters, and Catalogs. Our advisor for this category is Michael Krumme; he is listed in the Directory under California. If no color is listed, the item is crystal.

Ardith (etched), cake salver, yel or blk, low ft, from $75 to..........**85.00**
Ardith (etched), candy box, yel or blk, sq **150.00**
Ardith (etched), comport, yel or blk, from $75 to.........................**95.00**
Ardith (etched), mayonnaise set, yel or blk, 3-pc........................**150.00**
Ardith (etched), tumbler, pk, blown..**75.00**
Black Forest (etched), bowl, console; amber, 11" **75.00**

Black Forest (etched), candle holders, pk or gr, mushroom style, pr.**125.00**
Black Forest (etched), candy dish, blk, ftd **150.00**
Black Forest (etched), creamer & sugar bowl, blk, from $85 to **95.00**
Black Forest (etched), cup & saucer, red, 3 styles, ea **150.00**
Black Forest (etched), ice tub, pk or gr, tab hdls..........................**125.00**
Black Forest (etched), sugar bowl, blk, 2 styles, ea.........................**60.00**
Black Forest (etched), tray, pk or gr, hdls, from $65 to **75.00**
Crow's Foot Round, candle holders, ruby or cobalt, triple, pr **150.00**
Crow's Foot Round, candle holders, single, pr...............................**65.00**
Crow's Foot Round, plate, cracker; amber, amethyst or pk, 11" **22.50**
Crow's Foot Round, plate, dinner; blk or bl, sm, 9¼" **40.00**
Crow's Foot Round, plate, ruby, 8", from $10 to **12.00**
Crow's Foot Round, tray, amber, center hdl...................................**50.00**
Crow's Foot Square, bowl, cream soup; ruby **20.00**
Crow's Foot Square, bowl, red, blk or bl, ftd, 10" **75.00**
Crow's Foot Square, candlestick, blk or bl, 5¾", ea **30.00**
Crow's Foot Square, candy dish, yel, sq **125.00**
Crow's Foot Square, cup & saucer, ruby, from $15 to....................**20.00**
Crow's Foot Square, vase, amber, wht or crystal, cupped, 10¼" **45.00**
Crow's Foot Square, vase, ruby, cupped, 10".................................**110.00**
Cupid (etched), candy dish, pk or gr, ftd.......................................**275.00**
Cupid (etched), comport, pk or gr..**150.00**
Cupid (etched), creamer, gr or pk, ftd, 5"......................................**150.00**
Cupid (etched), ice bucket, pk or gr, metal bail..............................**195.00**
Cupid (etched), plate, gr or pk, 10½" **150.00**
Cupid (etched), tray, center hdl **125.00**
Cupid (etched), water bottle (w/tumbler), gr or pk **500.00**
Delilah Bird (etched), candle holders, pk, keyhole style, pr........**150.00**
Delilah Bird (etched), creamer, all colors, flat, 2¾"......................**95.00**
Delilah Bird (etched), server, all colors, center hdl.......................**75.00**
Delilah Bird (etched), vase, blk, cylindrical, 9" **250.00**
Gazebo (etched), candlestick, crystal, 5¼", ea **45.00**
Gazebo (etched), server, bl, center hdl, 11" **75.00**
Gazebo (etched), tray, center hdl **45.00**
Gazebo (etched), vase, bulbous, 10"...**75.00**
Gothic Garden (etched), bowl, console; yel or blk, flat rim, $65 to...**75.00**
Gothic Garden (etched), cake plate, all colors, ftd, 10½" **75.00**
Gothic Garden (etched), comport, pk or gr, from $85 to **95.00**
Gothic Garden (etched), tray, pk or gr, hdls, from $75 to **85.00**
Gothic Garden (etched), vase, all colors, 6½"................................**125.00**
Largo, cake plate, colors, ped **75.00**
Largo, cheese & cracker set, ruby...**85.00**
Largo, creamer, colors, ftd **45.00**
Largo, creamer & sugar bowl, lt bl or ruby, from $50 to................**65.00**
Largo, cup & saucer, ruby...**35.00**
Largo, tray, crystal, tab hdls...**20.00**
Lela Bird (etched), comport, pk or gr, ftd, lg.................................**125.00**
Lela Bird (etched), mayonnaise bowl, pk or gr..............................**85.00**
Lela Bird (etched), vase, blk w/gold etching, bulbous, 12"...........**225.00**
Maya, comport, ruby, tall **95.00**
Maya, tray, lt bl, center hdl **50.00**
Nora Bird (etched), tumbler, gr, blown, 5", from $75 to..............**100.00**
Orchid (etched), cake stand, red, blk or cobalt, sq, 2" H **58.00**
Orchid (etched), tray, gr, center hdl...**100.00**
Orchid (etched), vase, red, flared, #412, 10"..................................**480.00**
Party Line, bowl, console; lt bl, rolled edge...................................**50.00**
Party Line, cocktail shaker, gr..**125.00**
Party Line, pitcher, pk, w/lid..**95.00**
Party Line, stem, champagne, pk or gr...**15.00**
Party Line, stem, tulip sundae, pk or gr **25.00**
Peacock & Rose (etched), bowl, all colors, flat, 8½"....................**125.00**
Peacock & Rose (etched), candy dish, pk or gr, ftd **225.00**
Peacock & Rose (etched), creamer & sugar bowl (no peacock), pk or gr..**200.00**
Peacock & Rose (etched), pitcher, all colors, 5" **265.00**

Peacock & Rose (etched), tray, pk or gr, center hdl **95.00**
Penny Line, bowl, serving; cobalt, hdls **55.00**
Penny Line, creamer & sugar bowl, red...**25.00**
Penny Line, decanter, ruby...**85.00**
Penny Line, sherbet, forest gr, low **15.00**
Penny Line, tray, amethyst, center hdl..**45.00**
Spring Orchard (etched), cocktail shaker **150.00**
Spring Orchard (etched), stem, cocktail, hourglass shape **20.00**
Spring Orchard (etched), stem, cordial **25.00**
Spring Orchard (etched), tumbler, whiskey....................................**20.00**
Utopia (etched), relish dish, 3-part **45.00**
Utopia (etched), vase, bulbous, 10"..**125.00**
Utopia (etched), vase, rectangular, gr, 8" **210.00**

Pairpoint

The Pairpoint Manufacturing Company was built in 1880 in New Bedford, Massachusetts. It was primarily a metalworks whose chief product was coffin fittings. Next door, the Mt. Washington Glassworks made quality glasswares of many varieties. (See Mt. Washington for more information concerning their artware lines.) By 1894 it became apparent to both companies that a merger would be to their best interest.

From the late 1890s until the 1930s, lamps and lamp accessories were an important part of Pairpoint's production. There were three main types of shades, all of which were blown: puffy — blown-out reverse-painted shades (usually floral designs); ribbed — also reverse painted; and scenic — reverse painted with scenes of land or seascapes (usually executed on smooth surfaces, although ribbed scenics may be found occasionally). Cut glass lamps and those with metal overlay panels were also made. Scenic shades were sometimes artist signed. Every shade was stamped on the lower inside or outside edge with 1) The Pairpoint Corp., 2) Patent Pending, 3) Patented July 9, 1907, or 4) Patent Applied For. Bases were made of bronze, copper, brass, silver, or wood and are always signed. (In our listings all information before the semicolon pertains specifically to the shade.)

Because they produced only fancy, handmade artware, the company's sales lagged seriously during the Depression, and as time and tastes changed, their style of product was less in demand. As a result, they never fully recovered; consequently part of the buildings and equipment was sold in 1938. The company reorganized in 1939 under the direction of Robert Gundersen and again specialized in quality hand-blown glassware. Isaac Babbit regained possession of the silver departments, and together they established Gundersen Glassworks, Inc. After WWII, because of a sharp decline in sales, it again became necessary to reorganize. The Gundersen-Pairpoint Glassworks was formed, and the old line of cut, engraved artware was reintroduced. The company moved to East Wareham, Massachusetts, in 1957. But business continued to suffer, and the firm closed only one year later. In 1970, however, new facilities were constructed in Sagamore under the direction of Robert Bryden, sales manager for the company since the 1950s.

In 1974 the company began to produce lead glass cup plates which were made on commission as fund-raisers for various churches and organizations. These are signed with a 'P' in diamond and are becoming quite collectible. See also Burmese; Napkin Rings.

Glass

Bottle, scent; clear w/Rosaria stripes & lg flower-form stopper, 7" .**185.00**
Bottle, scent; clear w/Rosaria swirls, tall pointed swirl stopper, 8" .**110.00**
Box, dresser; roses/gold scrolls on swirl-emb lt bl, 7½" dia **785.00**
Castor set, cut, 5 bottles w/fern-like leaves, SP fr revolves, 17" ..**365.00**
Compote, vintage intaglio on lime gr, crystal bubble ball stem, 7x8"..**125.00**
Humidor, monk on brn, bk: pipe, cigar finial on metal lid, 6¼x5"...**400.00**

Pitcher, cut, Butterfly & Daisy, 10"...325.00
Tumbler, Tavern glass w/whale, 5¼x3¾" 175.00
Vase, flip; Tavern glass w/floral, 8x6"..275.00
Vase, Rosaria to clear, bubble-ball connector, sq ft, 13½", EX 350.00
Vase, ruby urn form w/trn-down top, clear bubble stem & M hdls, 10".230.00

Lamps

Puffy 5" lilac/butterfly shade; tree-trunk base, rare 3,400.00
Puffy 6½" 4-color rose shade; sgn B3079 std, 6½" 4,000.00
Puffy 8" Papillon butterfly/roses sgn shade; sgn gilded std.........5,000.00
Puffy 8" Stratford shade w/mc roses; sgn base ....2,800.00.
Puffy 9" roses/butterfly (4X) lobed shade; gold-wash tree trunk std ...3,080.00
Puffy 9" shade, ribbed at top, floral repeats at bottom; C3064 std....2,800.00
Puffy 10" lilac/butterfly shade w/lobed bottom; leafy B3083 std..21,280.00
Puffy 10" pk/yel roses shade, highly flared bottom; gold-wash std, 15"..2,800.00
Puffy 12" grapes open-top shade; sq ftd B3010 base, 19"........10,500.00
Puffy 12" poppy shade; brass std w/repoussé floral bands........30,500.00
Puffy 13" poppy shade; organic #3093 std, 20" 17,250.00
Puffy 14" floral roundels (4X) shade w/closed-in top; #30361/2 std..19,600.00
Puffy 16" begonia Pat 1901 shade; tree-trunk bronzed std, 25" .46,000.00
Rvpt 13" floral & hummingbirds Devonshire shade; gold-tone std, 22"..9,250.00

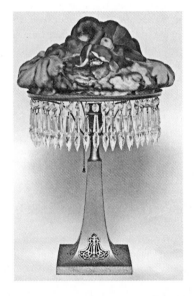

Reverse-painted 14" poppies shade; bronzed metal base in original gold patina with cutouts and prisms, 20", $23,000.00.

Rvpt 15" Allah 4-panel shade; 4-arm hexagonal emb std......11,200.00
Rvpt 15" Lansdowne dome shade; gilt-metal std, 22"..............4,400.00
Rvpt 15" pastoral scenic shade; gold-wash #3070 std, 23"........3,000.00
Rvpt 16" Venetian harbor Chesterfield shade; sq-ftd B3020 mk base, 22".7,500.00
Rvpt 17" farm scene shade sgn Fisher (EX); lobed/flared D3059 std.2,500.00
Rvpt 17" scenic Exeter shade; ornate silvered std, 21" 2,875.00
Rvpt 17½" tropical/exotic birds Exeter shade sgn Frederick; mk std.7,800.00
Rvpt 18" castles & horsebk-rider scene shade; urn-form #D30151/2 std..2,300.00
Rvpt 18" floral-band textured helmet shade; 2-hdl vase std #30151/2..2,100.00
Rvpt 18" Italian garden Berkeley shade; gourd-like gunmetal std, 22"...2,585.00
Rvpt 18" sea gulls/sailing ships shade; matching rvpt std 7,875.00
Rvpt 20" seascape/sea gulls sgn shade; glass base pnt to match, 24".12,000.00
Shade only, puffy 5½" floral/butterfly shade w/gold work/str bottom...2,070.00

Pairpoint Limoges

Limoges china blanks were imported from France in strict accordance with Pairpoint specifications. They were decorated by Pairpoint in designs that ranged from simple to elaborate florals and scenics. Called

Crown Pairpoint French China in old Pairpoint and Mt. Washington catalogs, these are easily identified. Look for the Pairpoint name over a crown with 'Limoges' below. You may also find similar ware marked 'Pairpoint Minton.' Our advisors for this category are Betty and Clarence Maier; they are listed in the Directory under Pennsylvania.

Compote, appl Dresden-like flowers on wht, floral-wrapped stem, 8x5".230.00
Compote, mc floral on cream w/gold, ftd, 6x10", from $550 to ..650.00
Ewer, poppies, yel/rose/gr on pnt brn & gray, #2020/520, 16x8" .975.00
Ferner, mc floral on cream, scrollwork, much gold, from $1,200 to .1,400.00
Plate, sailboat in harbor, L Tripp, fuchsia-tinted rim, 7⅜" 385.00
Vase, girl's portrait on red, gold scrolls/flowers, 14" 485.00
Vase, Venetian scene reserve/bk: sailing vessel on maroon, hdls, 15"..950.00

Paper Dolls

No one knows quite how or when paper dolls originated. One belief is that they began in Europe as 'pantins' (jumping jacks). During the nineteenth century, most paper dolls portrayed famous dancers and opera stars such as Fanny Elssler and Jenny Lind. In the late 1800s, the Raphael Tuck Publishers of England produced many series of beautiful paper dolls. Retail companies used paper dolls as advertisements to further the sale of their products. Around the turn of the century, many popular women's magazines began featuring a page of paper dolls.

Most familiar to today's collectors are the books with dolls on cardboard covers and clothes on the inside pages. These made their appearance in the late 1920s and early 1930s. The most collectible (and the most valuable) are those representing celebrities, movie stars, and comic-strip characters of the '30s and '40s.

When no condition is indicated, the dolls listed below are assumed to be in mint, uncut, original condition. Cut sets will be worth about half price if all dolls and outfits are included and pieces are in very good condition. If dolls were produced in die-cut form, these prices reflect such a set in mint condition with all costumes and accessories.

For further information we recommend *Tomart's Price Guide to Lowe and Whitman Paper Dolls*, and *Tomart's Price Guide to Saalfield and Merrill Paper Dolls*, all by Mary Young, our advisor for this category; she is listed in the Directory under Ohio. We also recommend *Schroeder's Collectible Toys, Antique to Modern*, and *Paper Dolls of the 1960s, 1970s, and 1980s* by Carol Nichols (Collector Books).

Archie's Girls, Lowe #2764, 1964..50.00
Ava Gardner, Whitman #965, 1949 ....175.00
Baby Show, Lowe #1021, 1940 ....100.00
Badgett Quadruplets, Saalfield #2348, 1941.................................150.00
Betty Grable, Whitman #989, 1941...300.00
Blue Feather Indian, Lowe #1044, 1944 ....65.00
Career Girls, Lowe #1045, 1942..75.00
Cinderella Steps Out, Lowe #1242, 1948 ....75.00
Cradle Tots, Merrill #3455, 1945, from $65 to.................................90.00
Debbie Reynolds, Whitman #1955, 1955.......................................150.00
Dinah Shore, Whitman #977, 1943, from $175 to 225.00
Dionne Quints, Whitman #998, 1935..125.00
Dude Ranch, Lowe #1026, 1943 ....40.00
Elizabeth Taylor, Whitman #968, 1949 ....175.00
Evelyn Rudie, Saalfield #4425, 1958 ....60.00
Faye Emerson, Saalfield #2722, 1952..100.00
Flossy Fair & Peter Fair, Whitman #981, 1933 ....75.00
Gabby Hayes, Lowe #4171, 1954...75.00
Gene Autry, Merrill #3482, 1940 ....125.00
Gisele MacKenzie, Saalfield #4421, 1957......................................100.00
Glenn Miller - Marion Hutton, Lowe #1041, 1942 ....400.00
Goldilocks & the Three Bears, Lowe #2561, 1955 ....35.00

Hedy Lamar, Saalfield #1538, 1951 ....125.00
Hollywood Personalities, Lowe #1049, 1941 ....400.00
Honeymooners, Lowe #2560, 1956 ....350.00
Jane Withers, Whitman #989, 1940 ....160.00
Julie Andrews, Saalfield #4424, 1958 ....100.00
Lana Turner, Whitman #964, 1947 ....250.00
Little Women, Lowe #1030, 1941 ....75.00
Mary Martin, Saalfield #287, 1943 ....125.00
My Fair Lady, Ottenheimer #2961, 1965 ....50.00
National Velvet, Whitman #1948, 1962 ....75.00
Oklahoma!, Whitman #1954, 1956 ....150.00
Playhouse Kiddles, Whitman #1954, 1971 ....40.00
Pollyanna, Whitman #995, 1941 ....100.00
Robin Hood & Maid Marian, Saalfield #2748, 1956 ....75.00
Rock Hudson, Whitman #2087, 1957 ....80.00
Rosemary Clooney, Lowe #2569, 1956 ....175.00
Sally & Dick, Bob & Jane, Lowe #1023, 1940 ....60.00
Shirley Temple, Saalfield #1715, 1935 ....200.00
Sonja Henie, Merrill #3418, 1941 ....250.00
Teen Shop, Saalfield, #2701, 1948 ....25.00
Walt Disney's Pinocchio, Whitman #935, 1939 ....300.00
Walter Lantz Cartoon Stars, Saalfield #1344, 1963 ....30.00
Winnie the Pooh, Whitman #947, 1935 ....100.00

Paperweights

Glass paperweight collecting has grown in intensity over the past ten to fifteen years. Many glass artists in the marketplace today are creating beautiful examples that generally sell for less than $100.00. There are hundreds of artisans in the U.S. and factories in China, Italy, and Scotland who produce these 'gift range' paperweights.

Astute collectors are beginning to piece together collections of the old Chinese paperweights that were imported into this country during the 1930s. These were basically unrefined imitations of the lovely and unique French weights of the mid-1800s. When viewed some seventy years later, however, one can appreciate the beauty and craftsmanship these weights exhibit. Other types gaining in popularity are antique motto weights and frit weights, as well as English bottle glass, especially those with sulfide inclusions. With the demise of Perthshire Paperweights of Scotland, collectors began scrambling for their high-end 'annual collection' and Christmas paperweights. Currently interest is strong in advertising paperweights due to their relatively low cost and accessibility. Collectors who are not constrained by budget concerns search for antique French paperweights from the classic period (1845 – 1860), the wonderful English or American weights from the 1850s, or the high quality contemporary weights of master glass artists.

Baccarat, St. Louis, Clichy, Pantin, and St. Mande (names synonymous with classic French paperweights) as well as some American factories stopped making paperweights between the 1880s and 1910 due to a decline in their popularity. In the 1950s Baccarat and St. Louis revived paperweight production and continue today to make lines of high quality, limited production weights. In the 1960s many glass studios began to spring up due to the development of smaller glass furnaces, thereby allowing more freedom for the individual glassmaker to design and fabricate a piece of glass from the fire to the annealing kiln. Such success stories are evident in the creative glass produced by Lundberg Studios, Orient & Flume, and Lotton Studios, to name only a few.

Many factors determine value, particularly of antique weights, and auction-realized prices of contemporary weights usually differ from issue price. Even if two paperweights seem to be identical, their values may not be. Size, faceting, fancy cuts on the base, the inclusion of a seemingly innocuous piece of frit, or a tear in a lampworked leaf can affect cost. And, of course, supply and demand affect prices as well, as do Internet auctions. Antique paperweights have steadily increased in value as has the work of many now deceased glass artists (i.e., Paul Ysart, Joe St. Clair, Charles Kaziun, Del Tarsitano, and Ray Banford).

The dimension given at the end of the line is diameter. Prices are for weights in perfect or near-perfect condition unless otherwise noted. Our advisors for this category are Betty and Larry Schwab, The Paperweight Shoppe; they are listed in the Directory under Illinois. See Clubs, Newsletters, and Catalogs in the Directory for the Paperweight Collector's Associations, Inc., with chapters in many states. They offer assistance to collectors at all levels.

Key:

con — concentric	jsp — jasper
(d) — deceased	latt — latticinio
fct — facets, faceted	mill — millefiori
gar — garland	o/l — overlay
grd — ground	sil — silhouette

Baccarat, Antique

Clematis & leaves on stem, star-cut base, 1845-50, 3" 950.00
Close packed mill canes w/assorted complex canes, 2½" 1,800.00
Floral gar, mc mill canes in cinquefoil design, 3" 650.00
Macedoine w/cobalt wht whorl cane amid twists & mc latt, 3" .1,400.00
Pansy & bud on stem, star-cut base, 1845-55, 3⅛" 600.00
Scattered complex mill w/pk rose cane on wht upset muslin, 2¾".2,750.00
Spaced mill complex canes w/central rose on cobalt, 2⅝" 3,750.00
Yel pompon & 2 red buds w/gr leaves w/in mill gar, 1-5 fct, 2¾" ...3,900.00
5 pk clematis buds on vine w/gr leaves on clear, 1-6 fct, 3" 2,250.00

Baccarat, Modern

Dwight D Eisenhower sulfide, ltd ed 350.00
Lime gr canes w/alternate mc canes forming rings, 1977, 3⅜" 450.00
Sir Winston Churchill sulfide, ltd ed 800.00
Wht con canes/12 Zodiac canes on carpet grd, 1972, 3⅛" 600.00

Banford, Bob and Ray (deceased)

Bee over red flower & 2 buds on azure bl grd, fct, 3¼" 800.00
Dueling snakes (2), 1 spotted/2nd striped, sandy grd, 3³⁄₁₆" 850.00
7 different flowers w/buds on dmn-cut base, 2 bees, 4", from $2,000 to...2,200.00

Caithness

Dragonfly/water lilies/pool, star-cut base, fct, ltd ed, 3⅛" 800.00
Emerald cactus w/chartreuse bloom, chisel fct, 3½", from $300 to...400.00
Flamingos among pond & cattails on aqua, window fct, 2½", $250 to..350.00
Rapture, red rose, pineapple cutting, gr o/l on top, 4¾", $800 to..1,000.00
Water lilies in fct dome flashed w/bl & emerald, window fct, 3⅛" ..450.00

Clichy, Antique

Central pk/gr rose amid spaced complex canes on clear, 1¾" ..1,200.00
Checquer, pk/gr rose amid 20 complex canes, wht latt sections, 2½" .4,000.00
Gr trefoil gar loops around 7 complex canes on clear grd, 2⅜" 2,500.00
Mc close-packed mill canes in gr & wht basket, 1850s, 2⅝" ...1,650.00
Pansies w/bud & 6 leaves, 2½", from $2,000 to 2,400.00
Stylized flower w/complex con cane center on wht latt cushion, 2¾" 18,000.00

Kaziun, Charles

Pansy w/bl & brn on wht petals, yel-gr grd, gold bee mk, 2¼" 750.00
Red rose & red bud on gr stem w/leaves, wht upset muslin, 2¼".1,800.00

Red upright rose & gr leaves in clear, ftd base, 2⅝" 2,400.00
Yel spider lily on sparkled turq grd, sgn, ped ft, 1¾" 400.00

Lundberg Studios

Cupid's Messenger, pk/wht flowers on pk muslin w/mc canes 500.00
Dk red rose on clear cobalt, Proto (experimental), 1999, 2⅞"....300.00
Wht crane w/bamboo on irid yel grd, 3¾" 400.00

New England Glass, Antique

Crown, 3 colors w/alternate latt twists, 2¼" 1,200.00
Flat bouquet amid 3 florets w/leaves, 1850-80, 2⅛"....................175.00
Pears/cherries w/leaves on wht latt basket, 19th C, 2½" 350.00
Poinsettia & 5 leaves on wht latt swirl, ca 1869, 2¾"..............1,000.00

Perthshire

Close packed mc mill canes w/twists & latt, 1989, 3¼" 700.00
Con mill mc canes, 3"...100.00
Flower amid flower spray, dbl-swirl wht latt, amethyst o/l, fct, 3"..700.00
Horse & rider w/in mill gars on dk red grd, 1979, 3⅛"...............425.00
Lav lampwork flower, clear grid-cut grd, 1-8 fct, 1973, 2¼"........250.00
Millennium, mill & lampwork, 1/6 fcts, ltd 1999 ed, 3⅛"..........325.00
Panda w/bamboo on gr dome w/bl flash o/l, 1/16 fcts, 1992, 3⅜".500.00
Shepherd & lamb w/wht stars on blk w/in mill gar, top fct, 1982, 3"..400.00

Patterned millefiori, 3", $125.00. (Photo courtesy Betty and Larry Schwab)

Rosenfeld, Ken

Fiesta, 4 ears of corn/12 chili peppers, 1992, 3⅜" 500.00
Flowering cacti (2) on sandy grd w/rocks, 1993, 3½" 600.00
Mixed bouquet on blk grd, 2002, 3½" 750.00
Pk camellia, yel flower & bl flower cluster, 2½" 300.00
Red maple leaves on branch on bl opaque, 3⅜" 600.00

Sandwich Glass

Poinsettia on stem w/leaves, 1870-87, 2⅞" 500.00
Poinsettia on stem w/3 leaves, dbl-swirl wht latt grd, 1870s, 3⅜".1,400.00
Weedflower, mc flower w/3 leaves, 1870s, 2⅞" 650.00

Stankard, Paul

Ant on yel gourd among flowers & roots, 2002, 3" 3,500.00
Pickerelweed flowers & buds/berries/leaves, 3⅝"....................3,500.00
Wht flower w/leafy stem/roots, bl opaque grd, 1971, 2¼", $1,200 to..1,500.00

Tarsitano, Debbie

Abstract form w/lampwork floral bouquet, 3½"....................2,800.00

Dahlia w/pk center & gr leaves, clear ruby, 2¾".......................1,200.00
Pk & wht flowers w/gr leaves on brn branch in clear, 3⅛" 1,600.00
Purple 17-petal flower & 3 knotweed sprays in clear, 2¾".......1,000.00

Whitefriars

Christmas, angel cane ring & mc mill gar, 1-5 fct, 1975, 3⅛" 750.00
Christmas, 3 wisemen following star, 1-5 fct, 3⅜" 750.00
Con mill w/allover geometric fcts, 1975, 3⅛".............................395.00
Con mill w/yel & wht flower cane, 1-5 fct, 1970, 3" 350.00
Red/wht/bl mill canes, 1-5 fct, 20th C, 3".................................295.00

Miscellaneous

Deacons, J; red flowers (2) w/leaves on latt cushion, 11 fct, 3½".350.00
Donofrio, J; boy playing marbles w/dog beside, sandy grd, 2002, 3⅜"..1,200.00
Ebelhare, D; mc complex canes in gr & wht stave basket, 2"......300.00
Labino, bl & yel swirling ribbons in amber veil, 1972, 2¼" 450.00
Labino, yel upright tulip on clear, 1973, 2⅝"..............................550.00
Manson, Wm; water lilies/beetles/leaves/fish, 2001, 3½" 500.00
McDougal, P; bl lampwork flower, mc twists, wht latt ribbons, 1⅞"..125.00
McDougal, P; close-packed mc canes on clear, 3" 350.00
Millville, red rose & 3 leaves, ped base, 1905-12, 3½", $5,000 to..6,000.00
Millville, yel water lily & leaves, fct top, 1905-12, 3½"...........1,500.00
Orient & Flume, irid surface-design floral, 1970s, 3", from $300 to .400.00
Smith, Gordon; mermaid among shells & rocks, 3¼" 2,000.00
St Louis, bouquet w/leaves, 19-fct top, 8-fct sides, 1850s, 2".......600.00
St Louis, rose bouquet on wht, 1-6 fcts, 1976, 3⅜" 550.00
Strathearn, close-packed mill canes on gr grd, 3", from $125 to...150.00
Trabucco, V; blueberry bouquet on wht latt grd, 3⅜" 950.00
Trabucco, V; wht unicorn among flowers, fct, 4" 1,500.00
Ysart, P; dbl clematis, bl & wht jsp grd, 3".................................850.00
Ysart, P; spaced con mill w/3 rings, blk grd, 3"..........................500.00

Papier-Mâché

The art of papier-mâché was mainly European. It originated in Paris around the middle of the eighteenth century and became popular in America during Victorian times. Small items such as boxes, trays, inkwells, frames, etc., as well as extensive ceiling moldings and larger articles of furniture were made. The process involved building layer upon layer of paper soaked in glue, then coaxed into shape over a wood or wire form. When dry it was painted or decorated with gilt or inlays. Inexpensive twentieth-century 'notions' were machine processed and mold pressed. See also Christmas; Candy Containers.

Bank, pug dog form, realistic modeling, curled tail, red collar, 13" H..2,115.00
Case, 2 sides: lady's portrait; 2 sides: cloth accordion, 3x4⅜" 220.00
Crumber, gilt flowers on blk lcq, w/curved brush, 11" 175.00
Lap desk, Scottish castle scene, MOP inlay, 3x11", EX 300.00
Nodder, goose, wht w/orange, lt wear, 4½" L 55.00
Table, temple scene top w/MOP/gold details/blk lcq, 1850s, 38x25" dia.3,750.00
Tray, floral & scrolls on blk lcq, 1840s, 19½x24½" 315.00
Tray, floral & stenciling on blk, mk Clay King St..., 31x23" 715.00
Tray, floral on blk lcq, style of Jennens & Bettridge, 25x32"+stand...1,600.00
Tray, serpentine form lined w/gilt, 1850s, 25x31" on later stand.635.00

Parian Ware

Parian is hard-paste unglazed porcelain made to resemble marble. First made in the mid-1800s by Staffordshire potters, it was soon after produced in the United States by the U.S. Pottery at Bennington, Vermont. Busts and statuary were favored, but plaques, vases, mugs, and pitchers were also made.

Bust, Alexandra, M Thornycroft, Copeland, ca 1868, 15" **440.00**
Bust, classical female, highly detailed, unmk, 11", NM **140.00**
Bust, Lord Burton, mk H&L (Hewitt & Leadbeater), dtd 1909, 8½" ..**200.00**
Bust, Lord Byron, Copeland, ca 1870, 24" **1,750.00**
Chastity, demure lady, J Durham, Copeland, ca 1865, 25" **880.00**
Conquering Jealousy, woman w/2 dogs, HF Libby, 1878, 14x7" ..**925.00**
Draped female w/putti at her ft, ca 1875, 20¼", NM **1,875.00**
Gladiator dying, Bates, Brown-Westhead & Moore, 8½" **700.00**
Nude lady in shackles, Copeland, 18½" **725.00**
Nude nymph seated w/deer & fawn, CB Birch, 1860s, 9" **1,525.00**
Sunshine, lady shielding eyes, Copeland, 1858, 19½" **750.00**
Young England's Sister, girl w/book & pencil, Copeland, 16" **235.00**
3 fauns hold grapes w/rnd openwork basket above, 11" **400.00**

Parrish, Maxfield

Maxfield Parrish (1870 – 1966), with his unique abilities in architecture, illustrations, and landscapes, was the most prolific artist during 'the golden years of illustrators.' He produced art for more than one hundred magazines, painted girls on rocks for the Edison-Mazda division of General Electric, and landscapes for Brown & Bigelow. His most recognized work was 'Daybreak' that was published in 1923 by House of Art and sold nearly two million prints. Parrish began early training with his father who was a recognized artist, studied architecture at Dartmouth, and became an active participant in the Cornish artist colony in New Hampshire where he resided. Due to his increasing popularity, reproductions are now being marketed.

In our listings, values for prints apply to those that are in their original frames (or very nice and appropriate replacement frames) unless noted otherwise. For further information we recommend *Collector's Value Guide to Early 20th Century American Prints* by Michael Ivankovich. Bobby Babcock, our advisor for this category, is listed in the Directory under Texas.

Key: BB — Brown & Bigelow   EM — Edison-Mazda

Ad, Saturday Evening Post, EM Lamps, full sheet, 1924 ....**85.00**
Ad poster, Ferry Seeds, Jack & the Beanstalk, 1923, cropped, 19"..**2,500.00**
Blotter, Lamp Seller of Bagdad, EM, 1922, 5¾x3¼" **90.00**
Book, Early Years, Skeeter's, 1973...**300.00**
Book, Knave of Hearts, spiral-bound, 1925, EX **900.00**
Book, Mother Goose on Prose, by L Frank Baum, 1st ed, 1897, EX..**1,400.00**
Book, Tanglewood Tales, 1st edition, 1910, EX **225.00**
Bookplate, Villa Bella, Italian Villas & Their Gardens, new matt & fr.**25.00**
Calendar, Ecstasy, 1930, complete, 19x8½", EX.........................**2,700.00**
Calendar, Lampseller of Bagdad, 1923, complete, 37½x18", EX..**2,900.00**
Calendar, Old Glen Mill, 1954, 21½x16½", EX..........................**200.00**
Calendar, Spirit of the Night, 1919, EM, complete, 19x9½" ...**4,500.00**
Calendar, Sunlit Valley, 1951, B&B, complete, 33x16", NM+ ...**285.00**
Calendar, Sunrise, 1933, complete, 19x8½", EX.........................**400.00**
Calendar, Vicobello, 1934, complete, rare, 7x4⅞" **450.00**
Calendar, Waterfall, 1931, EM, complete, 36x17", NM...........**2,500.00**
Calendar top, Golden Hour, 1929, 14½x22⅝", EX.....................**800.00**
Calendar top, Prometheus, 1920, 14⅜x23¾", EX **2,000.00**
Calendar top, Venetian Lamplighter, 1924, 14⅛x23⅝", EX....**1,500.00**
Chocolate box, Crane, textured cb w/Rubaiyat image insert, 11x7x1", EX ..**650.00**
Greeting card, winter landscape, B&B **75.00**
Magazine cover, A Man of Letters, Life, Jan 5, 1922 ....**150.00**
Magazine cover, Balloon Man, Collier's, Dec 12-26, 1908 ....**125.00**
Magazine cover, Boar's Head, Collier's, Dec 16, 1905.................**125.00**

Magazine insert, Pandora's Box, 1908, 9x11" **85.00**
Menu, Broadmoor Hotel, 1920s, 11x15" **200.00**
Menu, Broadmoor Hotel, 1950-60, 10x14" **125.00**
Playing cards, Dawn, EM, MIB..**300.00**
Playing cards, Waterfall, 1931, complete, w/box..........................**175.00**
Postcard, Pied Piper, 7x7" foldout, 1915......................................**175.00**
Postcard, The Billboard/A Blot on Nature..., 3½x5⅝".................**150.00**
Poster, Century Magazine, 1902, 14x20".................................**1,900.00**
Poster, New Hampshire, Winter, 1939, 24x29".........................**850.00**
Print, Autumn, 1905, 10x12" **250.00**
Print, Canyon, 1924, 6x10" **225.00**
Print, Canyon, 1924, 12x15" **325.00**
Print, Circe's Palace, 1908, 9x11" **250.00**
Print, Cleopatra, 1917, 24½x28" **2,300.00**

Print, Cleopatra, House of Art, 30x34" with frame, $2,300.00. (Photo courtesy William Morford)

Print, Daybreak, 1922, 6x10" **175.00**
Print, Dinkey Bird, 1905, 11x16"..**275.00**
Print, Dream Gardens, brochure for Curtis Publishing, 1915, 4x6¼" ..**70.00**
Print, Errant Pan, 1910, 11x9" **350.00**
Print, Evening Shadows, B&B, 1940, 13x17½" **400.00**
Print, Eventide, B&B, 1944, 13¾x9½" **175.00**
Print, Fisherman & Genie, 1906, orig label, 9x11", NM.............**250.00**
Print, Garden of Allah, House of Art, 1918, 15x30" **600.00**
Print, Hilltop, House of Art, 1927, 12x20" **600.00**
Print, Hilltop, 1917, cvd fr, 18x30" **715.00**
Print, Lantern Bearers, Dodge Publishing, 1910, 9½x11½" **450.00**
Print, Light of Welcome, Executive printing, 1945, 9x12"..........**300.00**
Print, Lute Players, 1924, 10x18" **350.00**
Print, Morning, 1926, 12x15" **350.00**
Print, Page, 1928, 10x12" **175.00**
Print, Pied Piper, 6¾x21" **1,200.00**
Print, Polly Put the Kettle On, Jell-O, 1923, 10x14"...................**100.00**
Print, Prince, 1928, 10x12" **185.00**
Print, Queen Gulnare, 1907, 9x11" **250.00**
Print, Romance, 1925, 12x24"...**2,000.00**
Print, Rubaiyat, CA Crane, Cleveland, 1917, 8x31"................**1,200.00**
Print, Stars, House of Art, 1927, 10x6" **350.00**
Print, The Prince (The Knave), 1928, 12x10" **300.00**
Print, Valley of Enchantment, B&B, 1946, 14x22" **310.00**
Print, Waterfall, 1931, 8x10" (cropped), EX **400.00**
Print, Wild Geese, 1924, 12x15" **325.00**
Print, Winter Twilight, Executive print, 1941, 9x12" **350.00**
Triptych, Daybreak flanked by Stars & Hilltop, fr, 12x32", EX ..**1,500.00**

Pate-De-Verre

Simply translated, pate-de-verre means paste of glass. In the manufacturing process, lead glass is first ground, then mixed with sodium silicate solution to form a paste which can be molded and refired. Some of the most prominent artisans to use this procedure were Almaric Walter, Daum, Argy-Rouseau, and Decorchemont. See also specific manufacturers.

Bowl, male & female nudes becoming tree, Daum, 14¾"............550.00
Figurine, seated female w/drape about her, Despret, 5½" 2,100.00
Vase, incised/raised decor, aqua/bl mottle, Decorchemont, 2" .1,800.00

Pate-Sur-Pate

Pate-sur-pate, literally paste-on paste, is a technique whereby relief decorations are built up on a ceramic body by layering several applications of slip, one on the other, until the desired result is achieved. Usually only two colors are used, and the value of a piece is greatly enhanced as more color is added.

Charger, maidens in woods, Schenk, Geo Jones, 1880s, 12" 1,265.00
Medallion, cherub, wht on bl, Fr, 19th C, 3⅜x2⅜" 315.00
Plaque, female & putti, wht/bl, 19th C, 5¾x7½"+gilt fr.............525.00
Plate, cherub cartouch, pierced rim w/gold, Minton, 1856, 9½", pr..4,895.00
Stein, cavalier & older man at table, child w/boot on lid, .5L.1,100.00
Vase, bee/butterfly/cactus, plum w/gold stars, Mintons, 5¼", EX..375.00
Vase, cherubs in flight among foliage on brn, 1880s, unmk, 6", pr..865.00
Vase, standing female, bl w/gold trim, 7½" 325.00

Pattern Glass

Pattern glass was the first mass-produced fancy tableware in America and was much prized by our ancestors. From the 1840s to the Civil War, it contained a high lead content and is known as 'flint glass.' It is exceptionally clear and resonant. Later glass was made with soda lime and is known as non-flint. By the 1890s pattern glass was produced in great volume in thousands of patterns, and colored glass came into vogue. Today the highest prices are often paid for these later patterns flashed with rose, amber, canary, and vaseline; stained ruby; or made in colors of cobalt, green, yellow, amethyst, etc. Demand for pattern glass declined by 1915, and glass fanciers were collecting it by 1930. No other field of antiques offers more diversity in patterns, prices, or pieces than this unique and historical glass that represents the Victorian era in America.

Our advisor for this category is Darlene Yohe; she is listed in the Directory under Arkansas. For a more thorough study on the subject, we recommend *Field Guide to Pattern Glass* by Mollie Helen McCain; *Standard Encyclopedia of Pressed Glass, 1860 – 1930, Identification & Values*, by Bill Edwards and Mike Carwile; and *Much More Early American Pattern Glass* by Alice Hulett Metz. All are available from Collector Books. See also Bread Plates; Cruets; Historical Glass; Salt and Pepper Shakers; Salts, Open; Sugar Shakers; Syrups; specific manufacturers such as Northwood.

Note: Values are given for open sugar bowls and compotes unless noted 'w/lid.'

Acorn, egg cup...20.00
Acorn, sugar bowl..40.00
Acorn Band, bowl..30.00
Acorn Band, compote, open 25.00
Acorn Band, pitcher...85.00
Actress, celery vase, actress head...145.00
Actress, jam jar..140.00
Ada, cruet...45.00
Ada, shakers, pr..40.00
Admiral Dewey, See Dewey; See Also Greentown Dewey
Adonis, berry bowl, vaseline, lg 65.00
Adonis, jelly compote..30.00
Adonis, tumbler, vaseline 25.00

Alabama, bowl, 8" 50.00
Alabama, compote, w/lid...55.00
Alaska, cruet...185.00
Almond, wine decanter..65.00
Amazon, banana stand...50.00
Amazon, compote, w/lid, 4"-6", ea..30.00
Amberette, bowl, oval, 5"-8", ea from $45 to.........................75.00
Amberette, finger bowl..45.00
Amberette, See Also Klondike
Amboy, berry bowl, sm 15.00
Amboy, goblet...35.00
American Beauty, butter dish..55.00
American Beauty, sugar bowl 25.00
American Beauty, tumbler..20.00
Angular, butter dish..65.00
Angular, pitcher..85.00
Arcadia Lace, candy dish, w/lid..35.00
Arcadia Lace, jelly compote...25.00
Arch & Forget-Me-Not Bands, creamer..................................25.00
Arch & Forget-Me-Not Bands, jam jar....................................30.00
Arched Fleur-de-Lis, relish 15.00
Arched Fleur-de-Lis, shaker, ea...20.00
Arched Grape, cake stand..40.00
Arched Grape, wine...20.00
Arched Ovals, goblet...30.00
Arched Ovals, syrup..55.00
Argent, bread plate, 9x13"...45.00
Argent, cake stand..45.00
Argus (Thumbprint), ale glass..50.00
Argus (Thumbprint), salt dip, ind 10.00
Arrowhead-in-Oval, berry bowl, sm..20.00
Arrowhead-in-Oval, punch bowl...125.00
Art, banana stand...70.00
Art, biscuit jar, ruby stained...175.00
Art, goblet..40.00
Artichoke, bobeche...40.00
Artichoke, oil lamp..275.00
Ashman, bread tray...30.00
Ashman, pickle jar..35.00
Ashman, pitcher..75.00
Aurora, decanter...75.00
Austrian, creamer, child's 25.00
Austrian, nappy, w/lid...35.00
Aztec, berry bowl, ruby stained, lg 60.00
Aztec, wine...20.00
Baby Face, butter dish...275.00
Balder, See Pennsylvania
Ball & Swirl, candlestick, ruby stained, ea 30.00
Ball & Swirl, plate, 6"...25.00
Baltimore Pear, sauce bowl..10.00
Banded Buckle, compote, open..35.00
Banded Diamond Point, goblet..35.00
Banded Diamond Point, spooner 20.00
Banded Fleur-de-Lis, egg cup..30.00
Banded Raindrops, spooner, amber..30.00
Banded Raindrops, sugar bowl...30.00
Bar & Block, wine...15.00
Barley, cordial..25.00
Barley, relish...25.00
Barrel Huber, See Huber
Basketweave, egg cup, amber, from $20 to 35.00
Basketweave, saucer..15.00
Bead & Scroll, pitcher...80.00
Bead & Scroll, toothpick holder...30.00

Beaded Diamond, creamer...20.00
Beaded Diamond, pitcher...75.00
Beaded Grape, cake stand 35.00
Beaded Grape, sugar bowl 30.00
Beaded Grape Medallion, castor set, complete 165.00
Beaded Grape Medallion, master salt 30.00

Beaded Oval

Beaded Tulip, champagne...25.00
Beaded Tulip, ice cream dish...20.00
Beaded Tulip, water tray..25.00
Bearded Head, See Viking
Beaumont's Columbia, celery tray..20.00
Beaumont's Columbia, syrup, ruby stained 100.00
Bellflower, butter dish, amber, from $20 to...............................40.00
Bellflower, cordial, milk glass 25.00
Bellflower, plate, amber 30.00
Berlin, bowl, 7" 30.00
Berlin, sugar bowl 50.00
Bethlehem Star, relish 15.00
Bevelled Diamond & Star, celery vase, ruby stained...................70.00
Bevelled Diamond & Star, goblet...40.00
Bird & Strawberry, cake stand...75.00
Bird & Strawberry, tumbler 50.00
Blackberry (Hobb's), pitcher..125.00
Blackberry (Hobb's), tumbler, milk glass 50.00
Bleeding Heart, mug 35.00
Bleeding Heart, plate..30.00
Block & Circle, mug..35.00
Blooms & Blossoms (Mikado), cruet.......................................165.00
Blooms & Blossoms (Mikado), tumbler.....................................35.00
Blue Jay, See Cardinal Bird
Bow Tie, goblet...55.00
Bow Tie, milk pitcher, 2 szs, ea from $45 to 70.00
Brazen Shield, tumbler 20.00
Britannic, banana stand, ruby stained 110.00
Britannic, shaker, ruby stained..90.00
Broken Column, celery vase...30.00
Broken Column, custard cup..15.00
Broken Pillar & Reed, bonbon..15.00
Broken Pillar & Reed, celery vase..25.00
Bryce Hobnail, butter dish, ruby stained 75.00
Bryce Hobnail, wine, ruby stained...30.00
Buckle w/Star, cologne bottle...50.00
Buckle w/Star, honey dish 20.00
Bull's-Eye Band, See Reverse Torpedo
Bull's-Eye in Heart, See Heart w/Thumbprint
Bulls-Eye & Fan, cake stand...55.00
Bulls-Eye & Fan, wine..20.00
Button Arches, bowl, ruby stained..45.00
Button Arches, wine..25.00
Button Arches, wine, ruby stained..35.00

California, See Beaded Grape
Cambridge #2351, olive, hdl 25.00
Canadian, jam jar 65.00
Canadian, milk pitcher..75.00
Cane, bowl, amber, oval..50.00
Cane, finger bowl, vaseline...30.00
Cane, tray..25.00
Cane, tumbler...20.00
Cannonball Pinwheel, berry bowl, sm 15.00
Cannonball Pinwheel, plate, sq, 6" 20.00
Cardinal, tumbler..25.00
Cardinal Bird, tumbler..25.00
Carnation (New Martinsville), tumbler, ruby stained..................25.00
Cathedral, bowl, 7"-8", ea 45.00
Cathedral, spooner, vaseline...55.00
Centennial, See Liberty Bell
Chain, butter dish...45.00
Chandelier, bowl, eng..145.00
Chandelier, sugar shaker 130.00
Cherry & Cable, pitcher..100.00
Cherry & Fig, berry bowl, lg..55.00
Cherry & Fig, pitcher..110.00
Chippendale, relish...20.00
Chrysanthemum Leaf, butter dish..55.00
Clear Ribbon, bread tray...45.00
Clear Ribbon, tumbler..25.00
Clio, plate, 7"-10", ea 35.00
Coin, See US Coin
Colorado, cheese dish, ftd 20.00
Colorado, toothpick holder..40.00
Columned Thumbprints, berry bowl, sm 10.00
Columned Thumbprints, syrup 60.00
Compact, See Snail
Connecticut, basket...35.00
Connecticut, biscuit jar...30.00
Connecticut, water bottle..35.00
Cord Drapery, compote, open, 8½" 35.00
Cord Drapery, water tray 25.00
Cornucopia, creamer...25.00
Cosmos, condiment set...95.00
Cosmos, tray, various, ea from $20 to 45.00
Cottage, claret..15.00
Croesus, creamer...40.00
Croesus, jelly compote...35.00
Croesus, tray...25.00
Crow's Foot, See Yale
Crown Jewels, See Chandelier
Crystal Queen, sugar bowl..40.00
Crystal Wedding, banana bowl, scarce 110.00
Crystal Wedding, claret...25.00
Cube w/Fan, See Pineapple & Fan
Cupid & Venus, goblet...90.00
Currant, bowl, 7"...25.00
Currier & Ives, creamer...35.00
Cut Block (Heisey), celery vase...30.00
Cut Block (Heisey), cruet, ruby stained 125.00
Cut Log, goblet...35.00
Dahlia (Portland), bowl, oval..25.00
Dahlia (Portland), compote, w/lid..60.00
Daisy & Button (Hobbs), bread plate..25.00
Daisy & Button (Hobbs), finger bowl..25.00
Daisy & Button (Hobbs), wall pocket, amber.............................125.00
Daisy & Button w/Crossbars, cordial 15.00
Daisy & Button w/Crossbars, cruet...45.00

Daisy & Button w/Thumbprint, spooner	35.00
Daisy & Button w/Thumbprint, sugar bowl, amber	55.00
Daisy & Plume, bowl, ftd, scarce	55.00
Daisy & Scroll, pitcher	65.00
Daisy-in-Square, pickle tray	15.00
Dakota, cake basket, w/metal hdl, rare	225.00
Dakota, cruet set, ruby stained	1,000.00
Dart, goblet	50.00
Deer & Dog, compote, w/lid, low, 7"-8", ea	150.00
Deer & Oak Tree, creamer	90.00
Deer & Pine Tree, sugar bowl	85.00
Delaware, fruit bowl, ruby stained	55.00
Delaware, finger bowl	20.00
Dew & Raindrop, sauce bowl	10.00
Dew & Raindrop, wine	15.00
Dewey, mug	40.00
Dewey, parfait glass, chocolate	165.00
Dewey, pitcher, rare	250.00
Dewey, See Also Greentown, Dewey	
Diagonal Band, cake stand	45.00
Diagonal Band, relish, amber	35.00
Diamond, vase	25.00
Diamond Lattice, relish, club shape	35.00
Diamond Medallion, See Grand	
Diamond Point Loop, celery vase, vaseline	35.00
Diamond Point Loop, plate, sq	25.00
Diamond Quilted, cordial	15.00
Diamond Thumbprint, honey dish	35.00
Diamond Thumbprint, sweetmeat jar, w/lid	95.00
Diamond w/Peg, tumbler	20.00
Doric, See Feather	
Double Pinwheel, pickle dish	20.00
Double Ribbon, egg cup	20.00
Double Ribbon, tumbler	25.00
Doyle's Shell, mug	30.00
Early Excelsior, champagne	55.00
Early Excelsior, pickle jar, w/lid	50.00
Egg in Sand, water tray	35.00
Elephant, See Jumbo	
Emerald Green Herringbone, See Florida	
Empress, berry bowl, lg	45.00
Empress, toothpick holder	60.00
English Colonial, sauce bowl	10.00
Esther, creamer, ruby stained	80.00
Esther, jelly compote, ruby stained	60.00
Eyewinker, compote, w/lid, 7"-9", ea	45.00
Eyewinker, milk pitcher	70.00
Falling Leaves, tumbler	20.00
Fancy Loop, celery vase	20.00
Fancy Loop, sugar bowl	30.00
Fandango, butter dish	65.00
Fandango, finger bowl	20.00
Fashion, butter dish, sm	40.00
Fashion, nappy	25.00
Feather, cordial, amber stained	165.00
Feather, relish, amber stained	75.00
File, bowl, shallow, 8½"	25.00
Fine Cut & Block, creamer	50.00
Fine Cut & Block, cordial	25.00
Fine Cut & Block, pitcher, amber	80.00
Fine Cut & Block, relish	15.00
Finecut & Panel, bread tray, vaseline	45.00
Finecut & Panel, sugar bowl, vaseline	55.00
Fishscale, bowl, w/lid, 6"-7", ea	40.00
Fishscale, condiment tray	35.00
Florida, butter dish	50.00
Florida, goblet	45.00
Florida, pitcher	65.00
Florida, sugar bowl, amber	55.00
Flower & Panel, butter dish, amber	80.00
Flower Pot, creamer	30.00
Flower Pot, goblet	45.00
Flute, punch bowl	100.00
Flute & Cane, celery vase	25.00
Framed Jewel, tumbler, ruby stained	30.00
Fringed Drape, butter dish	65.00
Frosted Chicken, bowl, w/lid, low	80.00
Frosted Chicken, goblet	65.00
Frosted Leaf, champagne	180.00
Frosted Leaf, wine	130.00
Galloway (Virginia), basket	85.00
Galloway (Virginia), goblet, Maiden's Blush	125.00
Galloway (Virginia), punch cup, Maiden's Blush	40.00
Garfield Drape, cake stand	45.00
Garfield Drape, relish	25.00
Gem, See Nailhead	
Giant Bulls-Eye, compote	45.00
Good Luck, See Horseshoe	
Grand, cordial	15.00
Grape & Festoon, cordial	20.00
Grape & Festoon, egg cup	25.00
Grape w/o Vine, pitcher	110.00
Grasshopper, compote, 7"-8½", ea from $55 to	75.00
Grasshopper (deduct 50% if no insect is present)	
Hand, celery vase	25.00
Hand, pitcher	150.00
Hanover, cheese dish, w/lid	85.00
Hanover, puff box	55.00
Harp, double relish, scarce	150.00
Hartley, bread plate	30.00
Hartley, compote, w/lid, 7"-8", ea	50.00
Hartley, sugar bowl, amber	45.00
Heart Band, butter dish, ruby stained	80.00
Heart Stem, berry bowl, lg	75.00
Heart w/Thumbprint, hair receiver	30.00
Heavy Finecut (#800), claret, amber	30.00
Heisey's #150, pitcher	150.00
Heisey's Old Sandwich, cup, amber	15.00
Heisey's Old Sandwich, pilsner, amber	25.00
Heisey's Old Sandwich, wine, pk	25.00
Henrietta, celery tray	25.00
Hickman, banana stand	60.00
Hidalgo, finger bowl	15.00
Hobbs Block, cruet, amber stained	100.00
Hobbs Block, water bottle	40.00
Hobbs Dewdrop, bitters bottle, vaseline	95.00
Hobbs Polka Dot, celery vase	25.00
Hobbs Polka Dot, tumbler, rubena	60.00
Hobnail, creamer	25.00
Hobstar, fruit bowl, 10½"	35.00
Hobstar, wine	20.00
Hobstar & Feather, ice cream bowl, lg	60.00
Holly Amber, See Greentown, Holly Amber	
Hops & Barley, See Wheat & Barley	
Horseshoe, relish	20.00
Huber, compote	35.00
Hummingbird, cheese plate, amber	55.00
Hummingbird, pitcher	95.00

Hummingbird, water tray, amber 145.00
Idaho, See Snail
Illinois, basket 40.00
Illinois, ice cream bowl 25.00
Illinois, water jug, squatty 55.00
Indiana, catsup bottle 40.00
Indiana, ice tub 45.00
Inside Ribbing, berry bowl, sm 10.00
Inside Ribbing, toothpick holder, vaseline 55.00
Inverted Feather, cake stand 45.00
Inverted Feather, water bottle 65.00
Inverted Fern, egg cup, 2 styles, ea 45.00
Iowa, cake stand, rose flash 65.00
Iris w/Meander, See Opalescent Glass
Jacob's Ladder, bowl, oblong, from $20 to 30.00
Jacob's Ladder, master salt 25.00
Jersey Swirl, candlestick, ea 30.00
Jersey Swirl, plate, 10"-12", ea 30.00
Jewel & Dewdrop, mug, 3½" 35.00
Job's Tears, See Art
Jumbo, creamer 275.00
Kentucky, goblet 30.00
King's Crown, butter dish 55.00
King's Crown, castor bottle, ruby stained 75.00
King's Crown, plate 20.00
Klondike, champagne 135.00
Klondike, tray, amber stained 225.00
Kokomo, bowl, berry; lg 35.00
Kokomo, jam jar 25.00
Ladder w/Diamonds, celery vase 20.00
Ladder w/Diamonds, sugar bowl 30.00
Lattice, egg cup 15.00
Leaf, See Maple Leaf
Leaf & Dart, bowl, ftd 25.00
Leaf & Dart, relish tray 20.00
Leaf & Star, banana boat 40.00
Leaf & Star, custard cup 10.00
Leaf Bracket, See Greentown, Leaf Bracket
Leaf Medallion, See Northwood, Leaf Medallion
Liberty Bell, pickle dish 50.00
Lily of the Valley, egg cup 30.00
Lion w/Cable, sugar bowl 60.00
Locket on Chain, butter dish, ruby stained 95.00
Locket on Chain, tumbler, ruby stained 65.00
Log Cabin, sauce bowl 85.00
Loop & Jewel, tumbler, milk glass 30.00
Loop & Swirl, creamer 25.00
Magic, See Rosette
Manhattan, cake stand 45.00
Manhattan, plate, 5" 20.00
Maple Leaf, butter dish, amber 75.00
Maple Leaf, cup plate, amber 25.00
Maple Leaf, goblet 55.00
Mardi Gras, banana bowl 50.00
Mardi Gras, egg cup 25.00
Maryland, celery vase 25.00
Maryland, cup 10.00
Massachusetts, punch cup 17.50
Medallion, compote, w/lid 50.00
Medallion Sunburst, tumbler 15.00
Minerva, plate, 8"-9", ea from $25 to 45.00
Minnesota, compote, rnd or sq 40.00
Minnesota, mug 25.00
Moon & Star, egg cup, ruby stained 65.00

Moon & Star, goblet 20.00
Moon & Star, salt dip 15.00
Nail, carafe 40.00
Nail, finger bowl 15.00
Nail, pitcher 95.00
Nailhead, dinner plate 25.00
New England Pineapple, egg cup 45.00
New Hampshire, mug, 2 szs, ea from $20 to 35.00
New Hampshire, relish tray 20.00
New Jersey, gas shade 40.00
Niagara, compote 30.00
Niagara, syrup 55.00
O'Hara's Diamond, cake stand 65.00
O'Hara's Diamond, tumbler, ruby stained 50.00
Oaken Bucket, See Wooden Pail
Ohio Star, punch bowl, w/base 750.00
Omero, berry bowl, sm 10.00
Omero, nappy 20.00
One Hundred & One, goblet 50.00
One-O-One, see One Hundred & One
Oregon, cake stand, 6"-10", ea from $25 to 45.00
Oregon, mug 25.00
Palm Beach, spooner 25.00
Panelled Cane, butter dish 45.00
Panelled Cane, relish 15.00
Panelled Forget-Me-Not, berry bowl, sm 10.00
Panelled Forget-Me-Not, jam jar, amber 60.00
Pavonia, master salt, ruby stained 50.00
Pavonia, mug 30.00
Peerless, cordial 20.00
Peerless, olive dish, hdld 25.00
Pennsylvania, biscuit jar 75.00
Pennsylvania, tankard 135.00
Pennsylvania, water bottle 65.00
Pert, compote, open, amethyst, from $35 to 60.00
Pert, mustard, w/lid 35.00
Petal & Loop, candlesticks, vaseline, pr 90.00
Petal & Loop, plate 30.00
Pineapple & Fan (Heisey), custard cup 10.00
Pineapple & Fan (Heisey), spooner 20.00
Pleat & Panel, bowl, w/lid 45.00
Pleat & Panel, sauce bowl, ftd 10.00
Pleat & Panel, shakers, pr 30.00
Prayer Rug, See Horseshoe
Pressed Diamond, berry bowl, amber, lg 35.00
Pressed Diamond, cake stand, vaseline 80.00
Primrose (Canton), bowl, flat 15.00
Primrose (Canton), milk pitcher 55.00
Priscilla, banana stand 50.00
Priscilla, pickle dish 15.00
Prism, decanter 40.00
Queen, cake stand, amber 60.00
Queen, compote, w/lid, amber 75.00
Raindrop, ABC plate, amber 40.00
Raindrop, cup & saucer 35.00
Raindrop, syrup 65.00
Red Block, cup 35.00
Red Top, See Button Arches
Reverse Torpedo, cake stand 40.00
Rexford, butter dish 65.00
Rexford, pitcher 90.00
Rexford, tumbler 20.00
Ribbed Palm, champagne 100.00
Ribbed Palm, pitcher 245.00

Ribbon, cheese dish...110.00
Robin Hood, sugar bowl...30.00
Roman Key, custard cup...15.00
Romeo, See Block & Fan
Rose, cologne bottle..55.00
Rose in Snow, bowl, open, 8-9"..............................30.00
Rose in Snow, pitcher, amber................................165.00
Rose in Snow, sweetmeat, w/lid...............................85.00
Rose Sprig, celery vase..40.00
Rose Sprig, plate, 6"-10", ea from $30 to................40.00
Rosette, fish relish...35.00
Rosette Band, butter dish.......................................75.00
Rosette Band, sugar bowl..30.00
Royal Crystal, cracker jar..65.00
Royal Crystal, tumbler..20.00
Royal Ivy, See Northwood
Royal Oak, See Northwood
Ruby Thumbprint, See King's Crown
S-Repeat, decanter...100.00
S-Repeat, jelly compote..35.00
Sawtooth, carafe..55.00
Sawtooth, spill holder...20.00
Sawtooth Band, See Amazon
Scalloped Daisy Red Top, See Button Arches
Scalloped Skirt, creamer...25.00
Scalloped Skirt, pickle dish....................................15.00
Scalloped Swirl, goblet...40.00
Scalloped Swirl, vase, ruby stained.......................40.00
Scroll w/Flowers, creamer or spooner....................20.00
Sequoia, butter pat..10.00
Sequoia, pitcher..85.00
Sequoia, wine..10.00
Sheaf & Block, wine..15.00
Shell & Tassel, fruit plate.......................................40.00
Sheraton, butter dish, amber..................................65.00
Shuttle, custard cup..10.00
Snail, cake basket, 10"..100.00
Snail, custard cup..35.00
Snow Flake, bread plate..15.00
Snow Flake, compote, sm..30.00

Southern Ivy

Spirea Band, compote, w/lid....................................55.00
Spirea Band, relish..20.00
Spirea Band, tumbler...20.00
Star & File, bowl, 7"..20.00
Star & File, rose bowl...50.00
Star Medallion, pitcher...85.00
Star Rosetted, bread plate, amber...........................40.00
Star Rosetted, plate, amber.....................................30.00
States, relish..25.00
Stippled Chain, cake stand......................................35.00
Stippled Chain, pickle tray.....................................25.00

Stippled Chain, tumbler..20.00
Sunbeam, berry bowl, sm..20.00
Sunbeam, sauce bowl...15.00
Sunbeam, sugar bowl...30.00
Sunburst, butter dish...55.00
Sunk Daisy, carafe...35.00
Sunken Primrose, lamp, ruby stained.....................95.00
Sunken Primrose, pitcher......................................100.00
Swan w/Mesh, butter dish, vaseline......................250.00
Swan w/Mesh, goblet, vaseline..............................150.00
Swirl & Ball, celery vase...20.00
Sydney, celery vase..35.00
Teardrop, candlestick, ea...25.00
Teardrop, goblet...50.00
Teardrop & Tassel, relish...36.00
Teasel, compote..40.00
Teasel, spooner...25.00
Texas, creamer, from $20 to.....................................95.00
Texas, relish tray..15.00
Texas, spooner, ruby stained..................................200.00
Theatrical, See Actress
Thousand Eye, ABC plate.......................................45.00
Thousand Eye, egg cup, amber................................60.00
Thousand Eye, salt dip, ind....................................40.00
Three Face, biscuit jar...350.00
Three Face, cordial..110.00
Three Face, jam jar..250.00
Three Face, sugar bowl..140.00
Thumbprint, See Argus
Thumbprint, See Dakota
Thumbprint Band, See Dakota
Thunderbird, See Hummingbird
Togo, berry bowl, sm...10.00
Togo, compote, vaseline..40.00
Tokyo, compote, vaseline..40.00
Tokyo, pitcher..75.00
Tokyo, vase, vaseline...35.00
Torpedo, cake stand...35.00
Torpedo, finger bowl...25.00
Torpedo, salt dip, ind..15.00
Tulip, celery vase...25.00
Tulip, sugar bowl...25.00
Twin Snowshoes, wine..10.00
Two Panel, butter dish, amber................................70.00
Two Panel, goblet...40.00
Two Panel, mug..30.00
US Coin, berry bowl, frosted, 7"...........................250.00
US Coin, champagne, frosted, flared rim..............750.00
US Coin, compote, w/lid, 10½x7".........................635.00
US Coin, goblet, frosted...425.00
US Coin, sugar bowl, frosted, w/lid......................400.00
US Coin, toothpick holder, 3"................................285.00
Valencia Waffle, butter dish, amber........................75.00
Valencia Waffle, water tray......................................30.00
Venice, pickle jar...25.00
Venice, spooner, amber..25.00
Venus, pitcher..125.00
Viking, apothecary jar...75.00
Viking, cup, ftd...25.00
Viking, pitcher...145.00
Waffle & Fine Cut, tumbler.....................................15.00
Washington (Early), ale glass................................125.00
Washington (Early), lamp......................................150.00
Wedding Ring, butter dish......................................65.00

Wellington, berry bowl, lg..30.00
Wellington, goblet, ruby stained..45.00
Wheat & Barley, cake stand, amber..45.00
Wheat & Barley, goblet, amber...50.00
Wheat & Barley, mug, vaseline...35.00
Wildflower, bowl, 6½"...20.00
Wildflower, cake stand..40.00
Wildflower, relish, amber...20.00
Willow Oak, milk pitcher...65.00
Willow Oak, waste bowl...25.00
Winged Scroll, bonbon..20.00
Winged Scroll, syrup..85.00
Wisconsin, cruet..125.00
Wisconsin, sherbet cup...10.00
Wooden Pail, tumbler..60.00
Wyoming, compote, open..35.00
Wyoming, tumbler...60.00
X-Ray, tray, cloverleaf...45.00
Yale, cake stand..20.00
Yale, pitcher..85.00
Yale, relish, oval...15.00
Zipper, creamer...25.00
Zipper Slash, cup..10.00
Zipper Slash, wine..10.00
Zippered Heart, butter dish..75.00
Zippered Heart, jelly compote..30.00

Paul Revere Pottery

The Saturday Evening Girls was a group of young immigrant girls headed by philanthropist Mrs. James Storrow who started meeting with them in the Boston library in 1899 for lectures, music, and dancing. Mrs. Storrow provided them with a kiln in 1906. Finding the facilities too small, they soon relocated. Because their new quarters were near the historical Old North Church, they chose the name Paul Revere Pottery. Their supervisor was Edith Brown. With very little training, the girls produced only simple ware. Until 1915 the pottery operated at a deficit, then a new building with four kilns was constructed on Nottingham Road. Vases, miniature jugs, children's tea sets, tiles, dinnerware, and lamps were produced, usually in soft matt glazes often decorated with incised, hand-painted designs from nature. Examples in a dark high gloss may also be found on occasion.

Several marks were used: 'P.R.P.'; 'S.E.G.'; or the circular device, 'Boston, Paul Revere Pottery' with the horse and rider.

The pottery continued to operate; and even though it sold well, the high production costs of the handmade ware caused the pottery to fail in 1946.

Our advisors for this category are Suzanne Perrault and David Rago; they are listed in the Directory under New Jersey.

Bowl, bl w/wht int rim, SEG/3-19/SG, 2½x8¼"......................295.00
Bowl, cereal; floral band, ivory on bl-gray, SEG, 2¼x5½"..........550.00
Bowl, daffodils, mc on gr grass & bl, SEG/4-19/SG, 8½".........3,000.00
Bowl, flowers & buds on yel & bl bands, SEG 7-18, 2½x8⅜".3,500.00
Bowl, flying goose over lake & hillside on yel, SEG/3-24/FL, 1½x5"...1,200.00
Bowl, jonquils on gr w/bl sky, closed-in rim, low, 8¼"............1,000.00
Bowl, landscape reserve, cobalt & teal bands, stamped logo, 5x11¼".715.00
Bowl, lotus blossoms, mc on yel, low, EM/6/1, 8½"...................400.00
Bowl, Midnight Ride, rider on horse, PRP/12-37/LS, 3x7".........415.00
Bowl, nasturtiums, gold/gr on bl/gr, SEG/1-17/AM, 3 lines to rim, 9"...2,850.00
Bowl, rabbit in field, imp logo/11-23/LS, rstr rim, 2½x5½"........385.00
Bowl, squirrel on branch on lav-gray, PRP/12-34, 1½x4¾".........385.00
Bowl, swan scene, Mary Her Bowl, PRP/6-34, 1½x5¾"..............880.00
Bowl, teal gr satin, flared rim, SEG/11-22/EG, 3x7½".................250.00

Bowl, water lilies band on ivory, S Gelner, w/lid, SEG, 1913, 5½"..800.00
Creamer, ducks on bl band, SEG/3-2-15, bruise, 3¼x3½"..........715.00
Cup, hen & chick, mc on cream, SEG, 1½"................................650.00
Inkwell, fishing boats/scenic, SEG/11-13/FL, w/o liner/lid, 1½x4x3"..925.00
Mug, rabbit in field, mc sky, PRP/1-34/FL, 3¾x4¾".................550.00
Mug, trees landscape/verse, sgn, SG 1912, 4"........................3,750.00
Pitcher, milk; gr leaves/bl bands on wht, 3½", NM...................350.00
Pitcher, milk; trees band on bl & beige, SEG/3-13-14/JG..........400.00
Pitcher, rabbit in field reserve on bl, illegible mk, 4½", NM......825.00
Plate, duck in central reserve, yel bands, SEG/11-21/LB, 6¼"....525.00
Plate, flowers & Her Plate Markie, SEG/2-23/FL, 7⅝"...............235.00
Plate, lotus blossoms on wht & bl, SEG/4-14/RM, 7½"..............475.00
Plate, lotus blossoms on yel, FL/SEG 7-14, 8¼".......................585.00
Plate, rabbit in gr field, PRP/TE/1-39, 7½"...............................770.00
Plate, stylized flower band, ...Her Plate, SEG/5-20/FL, 7½".......235.00
Plate, swans & flowers in yel band, SEG/1-13/TB, 6¼"..........1,045.00
Plate, trees & sm houses band, SEG/7/14/FL, 6¼"....................950.00
Plate, wht border w/blk ring & bl center, SEG 3-21 EG, 6⅜"....200.00
Trivet, trees/river/mtns in medallion on lt brn, PRP label, 5½" dia...485.00
Tumbler, lotus blossoms band, bl & wht, 4", NM.......................275.00
Vase, daffodils & leaves, yel/gr/blk on bl/gr mottle, 9"............4,000.00
Vase, glossy steel bl, rolled mouth, SEG/11-21/EG, 9¾x5", NM..275.00
Vase, turq & bl glossy drip, ovoid, 4½".....................................265.00
Vase, yel matt, ovoid, incurvate rim, 1924, 8½".....................1,050.00

Peachblow

Peachblow, made to imitate the colors of the Chinese Peachbloom porcelain, was made by several glasshouses in the late 1800s. Among them were New England Glass, Mt. Washington, Webb, and Hobbs, Brockunier and Company (Wheeling). Its pink shading was achieved through action of the heat on the gold content of the glass. While New England's peachblow shades from deep crimson to white, Mt. Washington's tends to shade from pink to blue-gray. Many pieces were enameled and gilded. While by far the majority of the pieces made by New England had a satin (acid) finish, they made shiny peachblow as well. Wheeling glass, on the other hand, is rarely found in satin. In the 1950s Gundersen-Pairpoint Glassworks initiated the reproduction of Mt. Washington peachblow, using an exact duplication of the original formula. Though of recent manufacture, this glass is very collectible. Our advisors for this category are Betty and Clarence Maier; they are listed in the Directory under Pennsylvania.

Creamer, Mt WA, 4¼"...2,700.00
Creamer, Wheeling, amber hdl, 4", from $750 to........................825.00
Creamer, Wheeling, 3¼"...600.00
Cruet, Wheeling, amber reeded hdl, 6¾", from $1,200 to.......1,450.00
Darner, NE Glass, shiny, 6"...200.00
Finger bowl, Wheeling, 2¾x4¾"..425.00
Jar, Webb, floral sprigs, etched brass lid, 5"...............................225.00
Pear whimsey, NE Glass, stem intact, from $100 to....................150.00
Pitcher, NE Glass, appl shell hdl, crimped top, EX color, 6"....1,100.00
Pitcher, Wheeling, amber hdl, 7¼"...1,450.00
Pitcher, Wheeling, intense color, amber hdl, 5⅜".......................950.00
Pitcher, Wheeling, sq mouth, amber hdl, opaque int, 7".........2,000.00
Pitcher, Wheeling, sq mouth, 4"...900.00
Tumbler, Gundersen, satin, EX shading, 4".................................225.00
Tumbler, Mt WA, satin, floral/gilt, 3¾"...................................2,000.00
Tumbler, Mt WA, satin, 3¾"...1,950.00
Tumbler, NE Glass, 3¾"..450.00
Tumbler, Wheeling, 3¾"..300.00
Vase, Morgan; Wheeling, repro griffin holder, 10"......................850.00
Vase, Morgan; Wheeling, satin, orig amber griffin holder, 10".4,000.00
Vase, Morgan; Wheeling, 7"...900.00

Vase, Mt. Washington, crimped tricorner top, three applied shell feet, berry prunt, 6¾", $4,500.00. (Photo courtesy John A. Shuman III)

Vase, Mt WA, gourd form, 8" 2,400.00
Vase, NE Glass, lily form, 8" 725.00
Vase, Webb, bird & gilt floral decor, 6¼" 275.00
Vase, Webb, bl jay on pine branch, gilt, bulbous w/long neck, 14" ..450.00
Vase, Webb, gold florals & ferns w/butterfly, ovoid, 7", pr 250.00
Vase, Webb, gold flowering vines & 2 insects, bulbous, 4⅛" 560.00
Vase, Webb, gold/silver leaves, can neck, 5¾", pr 550.00
Vase, Webb, Matsu No Ke, ovoid w/frosted hdls & ft, 9" 400.00
Vase, Webb, pale flowers, wht 'bull's horn' hdls, neck ring, 6" 225.00
Vase, Webb, shiny, gold florals, pillow form, 9½" 200.00
Vase, Wheeling, dbl gourd, 7" 3,000.00
Vase, Wheeling, Drape, crimped top, wht int, 10" 700.00
Vase, Wheeling, satin, appl rigaree at stick neck, 8" 2,450.00
Vase, Wheeling, sq mouth, bulbous body, 3¾" 700.00
Vase, Wheeling, stick neck, 8½", from $800 to 900.00
Vase, Wheeling, stick neck, 11" 1,175.00
Vase, Wheeling, stick neck/elongated body, shape #14, 9" 1,200.00
Vase, Wheeling, 7½" 750.00

Peloton

Peloton glass was first made by Wilhelm Kralik in Bohemia in 1880. This unusual art glass was produced by rolling colored threads onto the transparent or opaque glass gather as it was removed from the furnace. Usually more than one color of threading was used, and some items were further decorated with enameling. It was made with both shiny and acid finishes.

Biscuit jar, bl w/mc strings, SP lid w/flowers & bird in flight, 7". 500.00
Bowl, wht cased, mc strings, 4-crimp, 3¾x3½" 300.00
Bowl, wht w/mc strings, ribbed, 3 clear ft, 6-pinch rim, 6x7" 325.00
Pitcher, water; yel w/mc strings, reeded hdl 675.00
Rose bowl, lav, ribbed, crystal pulled ft, 3" H 185.00
Vase, bud; pk to wht w/mc strings, pinched sides, 5½", pr 275.00
Vase, crystal cased, mc strings, ribbed, 3-fold rim, 5" 300.00
Vase, wht, pastel strings, ribbed tumbler bottom, ruffled rim, 4¾" ...400.00
Vase, wht w/mc strings, tricorner, 4x4¾" 295.00

Pennsbury

Established in the 1950s in Morrisville, Pennsylvania, by Henry Below, the Pennsbury Pottery produced dinnerware and novelty items, much of which was sold in gift shops along the Pennsylvania Turnpike. Henry and his wife, Lee, worked for years at the Stangl Pottery before striking out on their own. Lee and her daughter were the artists responsible for many of the early pieces, the bird figures among them. Pennsbury pottery was hand painted, some in blue on white, some in

multicolor on caramel. Pennsylvania Dutch motifs, Amish couples, and barbershop singers were among their most popular decorative themes. Sgraffito (hand incising), was used extensively. The company marked their wares 'Pennsbury Pottery' or 'Pennsbury Pottery, Morrisville, PA.'

In October of 1969 the company closed. Contents of the pottery were sold in December of the following year, and in April of 1971, the buildings burned to the ground. Items marked Pennsbury Glenview or Stumar Pottery (or these marks in combination) were made by Glenview after 1969. Pieces manufactured after 1976 were made by the Pennington Pottery. Several of the old molds still exist, and the original Pennsbury Caramel process is still being used on novelty items, some of which are produced by Lewis Brothers, New Jersey. Production of Pennsbury dinnerware was not resumed after the closing. Our advisor for this category is Shirley Graff; she is listed in the Directory under Ohio. Note: Prices may be higher in some areas of the country — particularly on the East Coast, the southern states, and Texas. Values for examples in the Rooster patterns apply to both black and red variations.

Ashtray, Amish, 5 dia...25.00
Ashtray, Pennsbury Inn, 8" dia 45.00
Ashtray, Summerset, 1804-1954, 5" dia 30.00
Bank, Hershey Kiss, brn, 4" 20.00
Bank, jug, pig decor, cork top, 7" 55.00
Bowl, Dutch Talk, 9" 90.00
Bowl, pretzel; Eagle, 12x8" 85.00
Butter dish, Folk Art, 5x4" 35.00
Candle holders, Rooster, 4", pr 85.00
Candy dish, Hex, heart shaped, 6x6" 35.00
Casserole, Black Rooster, w/lid, 10¼x8¼" 100.00
Coaster, Doylestown Trust Co, 1896-1958, 5" dia 25.00
Coaster, Gay Ninety, 5" dia 35.00
Coaster, Quartet, face of Olson, 5" dia 30.00
Coffeepot, Hex, 6-cup, hearts in design, 8½" 40.00
Coffeepot, Red Rooster, 2-cup, 6" 55.00
Compote, w/holly decor, 5" 25.00
Cookie jar, Harvest, w/lid, 8" 160.00
Cookie jar, Red Barn 225.00
Desk basket, Lafayette, train decor, 4" 60.00
Desk basket, National Exchange Club, 5" 40.00
Display sign, bird atop, 4½x5" 175.00
Dresser tray, tulips w/pastel shades, sgn ET (Ester Titus), 7¼x4" ..35.00
Figurine, Bluebird, #103, 4" 150.00
Figurine, Bluejay, #108, 10½" 400.00
Figurine, Chickadee, #111, 3½" 120.00
Figurine, duckling pr, 6½" 295.00
Figurine, hen & rooster, multicolored, pr 550.00
Figurine, Slick-Chick, 5½" 50.00
Lamp, Barber Shop Quartet, w/hdw, 7½" 75.00
Mug, beer; Barber Shop Quartet 25.00
Mug, beer; Fisherman, 5" 50.00
Mug, beverage; Red Rooster, 5" 20.00
Mug, coffee; Amish, 3¼" 28.00
Mug, coffee; Gay Ninety, 3¼" 35.00
Mug, coffee; Quartet, face of Olson, Schultz or Luigi, 3¼", ea 20.00
Mug, coffee; Red Barn, 3¼" 35.00
Mug, coffee; Red Rooster 25.00
Mug, Irish coffee; horse decor w/gold trim...................40.00
Pitcher, Delft Toleware, 5" 55.00
Pitcher, Folk Art, mini, 2½" 30.00
Pitcher, Folk Art (later called Brown Dowry), 5" 50.00
Pitcher, Tulip, 4" 40.00
Pitcher, wht w/horse, gold trim, 1-qt 80.00
Pitcher, Yellow Daisy, ca 1959, 4" 32.00
Plaque, Baltimore & Ohio RR Veterans, Phili 1955, 7½x5½" 50.00
Plaque, Camden & Amboy RR, John Bull, 1831, 11x8" 55.00

Plaque, Fisherman, 5" dia..28.00
Plaque, Greater Lower Bucks County Week June 7-13, 1953, 8" dia ..45.00
Plaque, Mercury Dime, 8" dia 65.00
Plaque, Mother Serving Pie, 6" dia..............................35.00
Plaque, Real Stinker, verse w/skunk, 6" dia...................65.00
Plaque, ship; The Bark, Charles W Morgan, 11x8"..........110.00
Plaque, Swallow the Insult, 6" dia...............................25.00
Plaque, The Flying Cloud, dtd 1851, 9½x7" 110.00
Plaque, Toleware, brn, 5x7"..40.00
Plaque, Walking to Homestead, 6" dia 40.00
Plate, Amish Reading Bible, no primary colors, 9" 75.00
Plate, Blue Dowry, 10"..35.00
Plate, Boy & Girl, no primary colors, 11"......................45.00
Plate, Boy & Girl, w/primary colors, 11" 95.00
Plate, bread; Give Us This Day Our Daily Bread, 8" 40.00
Plate, Eagle, 8"...50.00
Plate, Harvest, 8"...40.00
Plate, Pea Hen over heart, 11" 85.00
Plate, pie; Red Rooster, 9"..40.00
Plate, Red Rooster, 10"...35.00
Shakers, pitcher shaped, Amish man & woman, pr, from $30 to ..45.00
Snack set, Red Rooster, tray & cup, from $20 to 25.00
Sugar bowl, Green Rooster, w/lid...................................30.00
Tray, Black Rooster, 7½x5" 30.00
Tray, Church of the Redeemer, Longport NJ, 1908-1958, 8" dia ..50.00
Tray, cigarette; Eagle, 7½x5" 40.00
Tray, Fidelity Mutual Life, 75th Anniversary, plum colored, 7x6"..40.00
Tray, Laurel Ridge, famous old landmark, 8½x5¼"..........40.00
Tray, tulips, tree shape, 14½x11½".................................30.00
Wall pocket, bellows shape w/eagle in high relief, 10"......50.00
Wall pocket, sailboat w/brn border, cut corners, 6½" sq.....65.00

Pens and Pencils

The first metallic writing pen was patented in 1809, and soon machine-produced pens with steel nibs gradually began replacing the quill. The first fountain pen was invented in 1830, but due to the fact that the ink flow was not consistent (though leakage was), they were not manufactured commercially until the 1880s. The first successful commercial producers were Waterman in 1884 and Parker with the Lucky Curve in 1888.

The self-filling pen of the early 1900s featured the soft, interior sack which filled with ink as the metal bar on the outside of the pen was raised and lowered. Variations of the filling mechanisms were tried until 1932 when Parker introduced the Vacumatic, a sackless pen with an internal pump.

Prices below are for pens in near mint or better condition which have been professionally restored to full operating capacity. For unrestored as-found pens, approximagely one third should be deducted from the values below.

For more information we recommend *Fountain Pens, Past & Present*, by Paul Erano (Collector Books). Our advisor for this category is Gary Lehrer; he is listed in the Directory under Connecticut. For those interested in purchasing pens through catalogs, both our advisor, Mr. Lehrer, and Pen Fanciers (whose address can be found in the Directory under Clubs, Newsletters, and Catalogs) publish extensive catalogs.

Key:

AF — aeromatic filler	HR — hard rubber
BF — button filler	LF — lever filler
CF — capillary filler	NPT — nickel-plated trim
CPT — chrome-plated trim	PF — plunger filler
ED — eyedropper filler	PIF — piston filler
GF — gold-filled	PKF — push knob filler
GFT — gold-filled trim	TD — touchdown filler
GPT — gold-plated trim	VF — vacumatic filler

Fountain Pens

Aiken Lambert, 1900, #2, ED, GF Gopheresque (rare), med, NM .600.00
C Stewart, 1938, #15, LF, gr pearl, NPT, NM 75.00
C Stewart, 1951, #27, LF, silver candystripe, GFT, NM 175.00
C Stewart, 1951, #55, LF, gr marble, GFT, NM 150.00
C Stewart, 1952, #27, LF, Tiger's Eye, GFT, NM 250.00
C Stewart, 1955, #55, LF, bl marble, GFT, NM 200.00
C Stewart, 1955, #58, LF, gr pearl web, GFT, NM......................185.00
C Stewart, 1956, #74, twist fill, red herringbone, fretwork band, NM...200.00
C Stewart, 1956, #76, LF, gr herringtone, GFT, NM 200.00
C Stewart, 1956, #85, LF, bl pearl w/gold veins, GFT, NM 150.00
Carters, 1928, #6 sz INX, LF, Ivory Pearltex, GFT, NM 500.00
Carters, 1928, #7 sz INX, LF, bl pearl, GFT, NM 600.00
Carters, 1928, #7 sz INX, LF, coral, GFT, NM 825.00
Chilton, 1924, #6, sleeve fill, blk, GFT, NM 300.00
Conklin, 1918, #20, CF, blk chased HR, GFT, NM 175.00
Conklin, 1918, #40, crescent fill, blk chased HR, GFT, NM 250.00
Conklin, 1927, #2, LF, wht w/blk veins (rare), GFT, NM 300.00
Conklin, 1927, Endura Large, LF, blk, GFT, NM.......................400.00
Conklin, 1927, Endura Large, LF, sapphire bl, GFT, NM 650.00
Conklin, 1927, Endura Oversz, blk HR, long cap/section, GFT, NM...700.00
Conklin, 1927, Endura Standard, LF, Cardinal, GFT, NM..........225.00
Conklin, 1930, Endura Symetric Oversz, LF, blk/bronze, GFT, NM ..350.00
Conklin, 1932, Nozac, PF, gr pearl w/blk stripe, GFT, NM 300.00
Crocker, 1910, #2, blow filler, GF, NM 375.00
Crocker, 1932, #2, hatchet fill, blk chased HR, GFT, NM..........150.00
Dunn, 1921, #2, pump fill, ring top, blk chased HR, GFT, NM..100.00
Eclipse, 1931, #2, LF, Mandarin Yellow w/jade ends, GFT, NM 75.00
Esterbrook, 1949, LJ Pen, LF, red, NM 30.00
Esterbrook, 1949, SJ Pen, LF, red, NM 20.00
Esterbrook, 1950, Pastel Pen, LF, wht, NM 75.00
Esterbrook, 1950, Relief #12, LF, tiger's eye web, GFT, NM........275.00
Leboeuf, 1928, #4, sleeve fill, ring top, gr pearltex, GFT, NM ...250.00
Leboeuf, 1932, #8, sleeve fill, ring top, gr pearltex, GFT, NM 250.00
Mabie Todd, 1925, #44 Eternal, LF, blk, NM.............................100.00
Mabie Todd, 1925, #44 Eternal, LF, jade, NM............................175.00
Mabie Todd, 1938, Blackbird Bulb, gr & gold spiral, GFT, NM..175.00
Mabie Todd, 1939, #4, LF, silver pearl snakeskin, NM 175.00
Mabie Todd, 1947, Swan #3240, LF, dk gr, GFT, NM.................95.00
Montblanc, 1927, #1266, PIF, chrome plate fluted, NM 200.00
Montblanc, 1935, #20, blk, GFT, NM..600.00
Montblanc, 1935, #20, Coral Red, GFT, NM 500.00
Montblanc, 1935, #25, blk, GFT, NM..600.00
Montblanc, 1935, #25, Coral Red, GFT, NM 750.00
Montblanc, 1935, #30, blk, GFT, NM..800.00
Montblanc, 1935, #30, Coral Red, GFT, NM 850.00
Montblanc, 1937, #134, blk w/long window, NM.......................450.00
Montblanc, 1937, #333½, PIF, blk, GFT, NM 375.00
Montblanc, 1939, #139, PIF, blk, GFT & silver trim, NM.......2,000.00
Montblanc, 1941, #25 Masterpiece, PIF, 12-sided brn marble, GFT, NM .1,250.00
Montblanc, 1947, #136, PIF, blk, GFT, NM...............................650.00
Montblanc, 1950, #146, PIF, gr stripe, GFT, NM 1,250.00
Montblanc, 1950, #246, PIF, blk, GFT, short window, NM.........450.00
Montblanc, 1950, #642N, silver striped, brushed chrome cap w/GFT, NM ...800.00
Montblanc, 1952, #142, PIF, blk, GFT, flat feed/telescoping filler, NM..300.00
Montblanc, 1955, #124, PF, GF, fluted, M 250.00
Montblanc, 1955, #82, PIF, GF pinstripe, M.............................275.00
Moore, 1925, L-96, LF, dk bl, GFT, NM....................................400.00
Moore, 1925, L-96, LF, maroon/burgundy, GFT, NM 500.00
Moore, 1941, #2, LF, gr pearl web, GFT, NM.............................125.00
Moore, 1946, Fingertip, LF, dk gr, GFT, M................................200.00
Parker, 1918, Black Giant, ED, blk HR, NP clip, NM 1,500.00
Parker, 1921, Duofold Jr, BF, red HR, bandless cap, NM............500.00

Parker, 1921, Duofold Sr, BF, red HR, bandless cap, MIB 1,400.00
Parker, 1928, Duofold Sr, BF, Mandarin Yel, GFT, NM............1,500.00
Parker, 1930, Duofold Special, BF, red, GFT, EX 250.00
Parker, 1932, BF, blk, bendless, NM...75.00
Parker, 1932, Thrift Time, BF, gray marble, GFT, NM 200.00
Parker, 1935, Victory, BF, bl marble, GFT, NM.........................300.00
Parker, 1937, Vacumatic Oversz, blk, GFT, NM 350.00
Parker, 1937, Vacumatic Oversz, brn banded, GFT, NM.............400.00
Parker, 1937, Vacumatic Oversz, gr banded, GFT, NM...............450.00
Parker, 1937, Vacumatic Oversz, gray banded, NPT, NM............350.00
Parker, 1937, Vacumatic Oversz, red banded, GFT, NM.............550.00
Parker, 1937, Vacumatic Slender, red laminated, GFT, NM........125.00
Parker, 1939, Duofold Jr, BF, silver geometric, NPT, NM...........125.00
Parker, 1945, Vacumatic Major, silver laminated, NPT, dbl jeweled, EX..150.00
Parker, 1946, #51, AF, forest gr, brushed lustraloy cap, M 100.00
Parker, 1946, NS (new style) Duofold, gray, NPT, NM 300.00
Parker, 1948, #51, AF, Buckskin, GF cap w/pinstripe & plain panels, NM...125.00
Parker, 1948, #51, AF, plum, GF cap, NM 150.00
Parker, 1950, #51 Mark II, AF, rare later version, NM 125.00
Parker, 1951, #51, AF, plum, brushed lustraloy cap, NM............125.00
Parker, 1957, #61, wick fill, blk, 2-tone silver cap, NM.................75.00
Parker, 1960, #45, cartridge/converter, bronzed/anodized, M 100.00
Parker, 1965, #75, sterling silver crosshatch (flat ends), NM 150.00
Parker, 1965, #75 Spanish Treasure LE, sterling silver crosshatch, MIB..1,300.00
Parker, 1970, #65 Titanium Ball (ballpoint) Pen, M 300.00
Parker, 1970, #75 Titanium, M 700.00
Parker, 1970, T-1 (Titanium), M 750.00
Parker, 1975, #75, sterling silver crosshatch (dimpled ends), NM ..100.00
Parker (Valentine), 1935, #2, BF, burgundy pearl web, GFT, rare, NM .150.00
Pelikan, 1937, #100N, gr pearl, GFT, NM 300.00
Pelikan, 1937, #100N, tortoise w/matching cap/derby, Palladium nib, NM..850.00
Pelikan, 1937, #100N, tortoise w/red cap, NM 900.00
Pelikan, 1938, #100N, gr pearl, chased GF band/clip, NM 325.00
Pelikan, 1938, IBIS, PIF, blk, GFT, NM 175.00
Pelikan, 1950, #400, PIF, brn stripe, GFT, NM 185.00
Pelikan, 1950, #400, PIF, gr stripe, GFT, NM 175.00
Pelikan, 1950, #400, PIF, gr V stripe, gr turning knob/section, NM ..450.00
Salz, 1920, Peter Pan, LF, dk red w/blk veins, GFT, NM 110.00
Salz, 1925, Peter Pan, LF, blk HR, GFT, rare longer length, NM..70.00
Salz, 1925, Peter Pan, LF, tan/brn Bakelite, GFT, NM.................75.00
Sheaffer, 1930, Lifetime Balance Lg, brn stripe, LF, GFT, NM....300.00
Sheaffer, 1930, Lifetime Balance Lg, LF, Carmine Red stripe, GFT, NM .600.00
Sheaffer, 1930, Lifetime Balance Lg, LF, ebonized pearl, GFT, NM .500.00
Sheaffer, 1930, Lifetime Balance Lg, LF, gr stripe, GFT, NM 350.00
Sheaffer, 1930, Lifetime Balance Lg, LF, Roseglow stripe, GFT, NM ..900.00
Sheaffer, 1936, Feather Touch #8 Lg Balance, PF, gray marble, NM...450.00
Sheaffer, 1937, Standard Sz Lifetime Balance, LF, blk, GFT, NM..75.00
Sheaffer, 1942, Lifetime Triumph, PF, silver laminated, NPT, EX.75.00
Sheaffer, 1950, Triumph Snorkel, GFM, NM.............................150.00
Sheaffer, 1952, Clipper Snorkel, sage gr, chrome cap w/GFT, MIB.150.00
Sheaffer, 1954, Valiant Snorkel, burgundy, NM...........................30.00
Sheaffer, 1954, Valiant Snorkel, pk, NM....................................75.00
Sheaffer, 1958, Lady Skripsert, gold-plated, jeweled ring, EX........35.00
Sheaffer, 1959, PFM I, blk, blk cap, CPT, NM............................150.00
Sheaffer, 1959, PFM II, blk, chrome cap, NM 175.00
Sheaffer, 1959, PFM II, burgundy, stainless steel cap, GFT, NM.200.00
Sheaffer, 1959, PFM III, blk, blk cap, GFT, NM.........................200.00
Sheaffer, 1959, PFM III, gray (rare), GFT, NM..........................375.00
Sheaffer, 1959, PFM III Demonstrator, transparent, GFT, blk shell, NM.800.00
Sheaffer, 1959, PFM IV, blk, GF cap, GFT, NM 300.00
Sheaffer, 1959, PFM V, blk, polished chrome cap, GFT, NM......325.00
Soennecken, 1952, III Extra, PIF, gr herringbone, NM 600.00
Soennecken, 1952, III Superior, PIF, golden weave, NM 400.00
Soennecken, 1952, 222 Extra, PIF, blk...................................250.00

Soennecken, 1952, 222 Superior, PIF, silver lizard, NM..............300.00
Wahl Eversharp, 1920, #0, LF, GF pinstripe, NM 55.00
Wahl Eversharp, 1927, Gold Seal, LF, rosewood, NM 350.00
Wahl Eversharp, 1929, #2, LF, rosewood, GFT, NM...................150.00
Wahl Eversharp, 1929, Equipoised, LF, blk & pearl, GFT, NM...350.00
Wahl Eversharp, 1929, Oversz Deco Band, LF, blk, GFT, NM....450.00
Wahl Eversharp, 1929, Oversz Deco Band, LF, Lapis, GFT, NM.650.00
Wahl Eversharp, 1929, Oversz Deco Band, LF, woodgrain, GFT, NM...450.00
Wahl Eversharp, 1934, #2 Doric, LF, Ice (blk w/pearl veins), NPT, NM.300.00
Wahl Eversharp, 1942, Skyline Jr, LF, blk Moderne stripe, GFT, NM...100.00
Wahl Eversharp, 1951, Symphony, LF, blk, GFT, M w/orig label ..65.00
Waterman, 1910, #18S Safety, ED, blk HR, rare, M 2,600.00
Waterman, 1915, #14, ED, blk chased HR, stanhope cap, NM..1,895.00
Waterman, 1915, #52, LF, blk chased HR, NPT, NM.................100.00

Waterman, 1915, #453, sterling silver filigree overlay, $350.00. (Photo courtesy Paul Erano)

Waterman, 1920, #52½V, LF, Cardinal HR, GFT, NM 200.00
Waterman, 1920, #055½ LEC, LF, GF Gothic, eng, NM...........325.00
Waterman, 1924, #54, LF, blk HR, GFT, NM............................110.00
Waterman, 1924, #452, LF, sterling Gothic, NM........................350.00
Waterman, 1925, #58, LF, blk HR, GFT, NM............................875.00
Waterman, 1925, #0552½, ED, Secretary in GF filigree, NM.....500.00
Waterman, 1926, #5, LF, red ripple w/red band, GFT, NM+.......275.00
Waterman, 1927, #7, LF, red ripple, pk band, 1st yr model, NM ...400.00
Waterman, 1929, Patrician, LF, blk HR, GFT, NM 850.00
Waterman, 1929, Patrician, LF, moss agate 900.00
Waterman, 1929, Patrician, LF, Nacre (blk & pearl), GFT, M color.1,750.00
Waterman, 1929, Patrician, LF, Onyx (red cream), GFT, M color ..1,500.00
Waterman, 1930, #94, LF, bl & cream, NPT, NM.......................225.00
Waterman, 1930, #94, LF, brn & cream (mahog), GFT, NM 225.00
Waterman, 1930, #94, LF, red ripple HP, GFT, NM 400.00
Waterman, 1940, #2 Model 513, LF (England), GFT, NM 125.00
Waterman, 1941, 100 Yr, blk, smooth cap/bbl, GFT, NM...........300.00

Mechanical Pencils

Anonymous, rifle shape, cocking mechanism, eng: Rin Tin Tin, NM.75.00
Autopoint, 1945, 2-color (blk/bl), w/clip, M.................................15.00
Conklin, 1929, Symetric, gr marble, GFT, no clip, EX 40.00
Cross/Tiffany, 1990, sterling silver pinstripe, clip: Tiffany, MIB ..100.00
Eversharp, 1940, blk snakeskin-pattern leather cover, GFT, NM.100.00
Montblanc, 1924, #6, octagonal, blk HR, eng bbl, rare, lg, NM.900.00
Montblanc, 1930, #92 Repeater, blk HR, NPT, NM 125.00
Montblanc, 1939, #392 Repeater, blk HR, NM 80.00
Parker, 1929, Duofold Jr, jade, GFT, NM 50.00
Parker, 1929, Duofold Jr, Mandarin Yel, GFT, NM.....................150.00
Parker, 1930, Duofold Vest Pocket, burgundy, GFT, w/opener taper, NM..150.00
Parker, 1948, Duofold Repeater, gray, GFT, worn imprint, NM ..150.00
Sheaffer, 1925, Balance, deep jade, GFT, NM+ 50.00
Sheaffer, 1925, Balance, gr marble, GFT, NM+ 40.00
Sheaffer, 1959, PFM III, blk, GFT, M w/orig decal 125.00
Wahl Eversharp, 1929, Oversz Deco Band, blk & pearl, GFT, NM .125.00
Wahl Eversharp, 1939, Coronet, blk w/smooth GF cap, NM 50.00
Wahl Eversharp, 1948, Coronet, bronze pearl, chrome cap w/blk, NM .70.00
Waterman, 1925, blk HR, GFT, M..150.00
Waterman, 1928, #52½ V, olive ripple, GFT, NM.......................85.00

Sets

C Stewart, 1951, #27, LF, lav pearl web, GFT, +#37 pencil, NM.**225.00**
C Stewart, 1952, #14, LF, bl pearl, GFT, MIB.................................**60.00**
Montblanc, 1972, #1266, PIF, sterling, fluted, 18k wht gold nib, M..**400.00**
Parker, 1937, Depression, BF, red pearl, GFT, matching blind caps, NM..**175.00**
Parker, 1940, Vacuum Jr, gr/bronze/blk stripes, GFT, NM **125.00**
Parker, 1957, #61, GF, alternating pinstripes & panels, M **200.00**
Sheaffer, 1925, #2-25 Tall, LF, blk plastic, GFT, NM..................**100.00**
Sheaffer, 1936, Junior, LF, gray marble, NPT, NM **75.00**
Sheaffer, 1952, Clipper Triumph Snorkel, bright red, chrome caps, MIB.**175.00**
Sheaffer, 1958, Lady Skripsert, GF filigree & bl, MIB **45.00**
Sheaffer, 1959, PFM III, blk, GFT, MIB..................................**325.00**
Wahl Eversharp, #4, GF w/chased wave pattern, NM **175.00**
Waterman, 1925, #52, LF, red ripple, GFT, NM **250.00**

Personalities, Fact and Fiction

One of the largest and most popular areas of collecting today is character-related memorabilia. Everyone has favorites, whether they be comic-strip personalities or true-life heroes. The earliest comic strip dealt with the adventures of the Yellow Kid, the smiling, bald-headed Oriental boy always in a nightshirt. He was introduced in 1895, a product of the imagination of Richard Fenton Outcault. Today, though very hard to come by, items relating to the Yellow Kid bring premium prices.

Though her 1923 introduction was unobtrusively made through only one newspaper, New York's *Daily News*, Little Orphan Annie, the vacant-eyed redhead in the inevitable red dress, was quickly adopted by hordes of readers nationwide, and before the demise of her creator, Harold Gray, in 1968, she had starred in her own radio show. She made two feature films, and in 1977 'Annie' was launched on Broadway.

Other early comic figures were Moon Mullins, created in 1923 by Frank Willard; Buck Rogers by Philip Nowlan in 1928; and Betty Boop, the round-faced, innocent-eyed, chubby-cheeked Boop-Boop-a-Doop girl of the early 1930s. Bimbo was her dog and KoKo her clown friend.

Popeye made his debut in 1929 as the spinach-eating sailor with the spindly-limbed girlfriend, Olive Oyl, in the comic strip *Thimble Theatre*, created by Elzie Segar. He became a film star in 1933 and had his own radio show that during 1936 played three times a week on CBS. He obligingly modeled for scores of toys, dolls, and figurines, and especially those from the '30s are very collectible.

Tarzan, created around 1930 by Edgar Rice Burroughs, and Captain Midnight, by Robert Burtt and Willfred G. Moore, are popular heroes with today's collectors. During the days of radio, Sky King of the Flying Crown Ranch (also created by Burtt and Moore) thrilled boys and girls of the mid-1940s. Hopalong Cassidy, Red Rider, Tom Mix, and the Lone Ranger were only a few of the other 'good guys' always on the side of law and order.

But of all the fictional heroes and comic characters collected today, probably the best loved and most well known is Mickey Mouse. Created in the late 1920s by Walt Disney, Micky (as his name was first spelled) became an instant success with his film debut, 'Steamboat Willie.' His popularity was parlayed through wind-up toys, watches, figurines, cookie jars, puppets, clothing, and numerous other products. Items from the 1930s are usually copyrighted 'Walt Disney Enterprises'; thereafter, 'Walt Disney Productions' was used.

For more information we recommend *Schroeder's Collectible Toys, Antique to Modern*, by Sharon and Bob Huxford. *Cartoon Toys & Collectibles* by David Longest; *Collector's Guide to TV Toys & Memorabilia, Second Edition*, by Greg Davis and Bill Morgan; *Roy Rogers and Dale Evans Toys and Memorabilia* by P. Allan Coyle; *Collector's Guide to Celebrity Dolls* by David Spurgeon; *Star Wars Super Collector's Wish Book* by Geoffrey T. Carlton; *McDonald's Collectibles* by Gary Henriques and

Audre Duvall; and *G-Men and FBI Toys and Collectibles* by Harry and Jody Whitworth are other great publications. All are available from Collector Books. See also Autographs; Banks; Big Little Books; Children's Books; Comic Books; Cookie Jars; Dolls; Games; Lunch Boxes; Movie Memorabilia; Paper Dolls; Pin-Back Buttons; Posters; Puzzles; Rock 'N Roll Memorabilia; Toys.

Alice in Wonderland, record player, Bakelite, 1940s, VG...........**175.00**
Amos 'N Andy, figures, bsk, Japan, prewar, 8", 7", EX, pr **575.00**
Amos 'N Andy, sparkler, diecut litho tin head w/cigar, Germany, 4", NM..**425.00**
Andy Panda, bank, pnt compo figure, Crown Toy, 1939, 5x3", EX.**85.00**
Andy Panda, paint book, Whitman, 1944, few pgs colored, EX....**38.00**
Atom Ant, Play Fun Set, Whitman, 1966, NMIB......................**50.00**
Baba Looey, bank, vinyl w/plastic head, Knickerbocker, 1960s, 9", EX.**35.00**
Baba Looey, doll, plush w/vinyl head, Knickerbocker, 1959, EX+.**50.00**
Banana Splits, guitar, Snorky Elephant, 1960s, 10", EX **25.00**
Barney Google & Spark Plug, pull toy, litho tin, Nifty, 1920s, 8", VG..**1,700.00**
Batman, coin set, Transogram, 1966, MIP (sealed).....................**35.00**
Batman, Colorforms Cartoon Kit, 1966, EXIB..........................**40.00**
Batman, Give-A-Show Bat-Projector, Chad Valley/NPPI, 1966, NMIB .**575.00**
Batman, Sparkle Paints, Kenner, 1966, EXIB............................**75.00**
Batman, troll doll, felt outfit, Uneeda Wishnik, 1966, 3", NM **35.00**
Beany & Cecil, bank, Cecil's head, molded plastic, NM **35.00**
Beany & Cecil, doctor kit, Transogram, EX **35.00**
Beany & Cecil, jack-in-the-box, Mattel, 1961, M......................**250.00**
Betty Boop, doll, jtd wood & compo, pnt hair/costume/shoes, 13", EX..**2,475.00**
Betty Boop, doll quilt, cloth, Fleischer, 1930s, 13x18", EX **135.00**
Betty Boop, figure, bsk, playing fiddle, Japan, 1930s, 3½", NM ..**125.00**
Betty Boop, tambourine, litho tin, 1930s, 6" dia, EX..................**150.00**
Beverly Hillbillies, Colorforms, foyer scene, 1963, NMIB..........**100.00**
Big Bad Wolf, figure, bsk, Japan, 1930s, 3½", NM.....................**100.00**
Bionic Woman, Play Doh Action Playset, Kenner, 1977, MIB **20.00**
Bionic Woman, wallet, pk or bl w/image, Faberge, 1976, MIP......**20.00**
Birdman, figure, vinyl, Hanna-Barbera/Japan, 11", NM **250.00**
Brady Bunch, banjo, Larami, 1973, 15", MIP.............................**65.00**
Brady Bunch, Fishin' Fun Set, Larami, 1973, MOC **30.00**
Buck Rogers, crayon/school box, Am Pencil Co #119, 1930s, 5x2½", EX.**125.00**
Buck Rogers, roller skates, metal streamline style, Marx, VG+, pr.**2,850.00**
Bugs Bunny, Colorforms Cartoon Kit, EXIB **100.00**
Bugs Bunny, doll, Bugs as Davy Crockett, 195s, EX....................**325.00**
Bugs Bunny, jack-in-the-box, Mattel, 1960s, NM+ **75.00**
Bugs Bunny, squeak toy, soft rubber, 1930s, EX.........................**175.00**
Captain America, Flashmite, Jane X, 1976, MOC.........................**75.00**
Captain Kangaroo, doll, Mattel, 1967, MIB................................**150.00**
Captain Kangaroo, squeak toy, vinyl figure, 1950s, 8", MIB.........**65.00**
Captain Kangaroo, TV Eras-O-Board Set, Hasbro, 1956, MIB **30.00**
Captain Marvel, wristwatch, Fawcett, 1948, EXIB **700.00**
Charlie McCarthy, figure, Fun-E-Flex, 1930s, 5½", NM+...........**250.00**
Charlie McCarthy, hand puppet, pnt compo head w/cloth body, 1930s, VG.**75.00**
Charlie's Angels, wallet, vinyl w/circular image of stars, 1977, MOC..**35.00**
CHiPs, bicycle siren, 1977, EX **25.00**
CHiPs, Colorforms Playset, 1981, unused, MIB **45.00**
CHiPs, Wind 'N Watch Speedster, Buddy L, 1981, MOC (sealed) .**25.00**
Cisco Kid, gloves & scarf set, Legend of the..., leather, NMIB....**250.00**
Creature From the Black Lagoon, plastic/jtd arms, 1960s, 13", NM+ ..**200.00**
Dale Evans, hat, felt/...Queen of the West band, Lancaster Hat Co, NM+.**100.00**
Dale Evans, outfit, blk & red denim jacket & pants, EX..............**125.00**
Daniel Boone, figure, pnt plaster/vinyl head/fur cap, 1960s, 6", NM..**75.00**
Daniel Boone, View-Master reels, #B-479, MIP.........................**22.00**
Davy Crockett, book bag, cloth/plastic saddle bag w/fringe, unused, M..**250.00**
Davy Crockett, lamp, rotating cylinder, Econolite, 11", NM **275.00**
Davy Crockett, tent, canvas, Empire Mfg Co, 1950s, NM **125.00**
Dean Martin, hand puppet, vinyl head w/cloth body, 1950s, NM.**25.00**
Dennis the Menace, lamp, Dennis/dog, plaster, Hall Syndicate, 1967, NM.**150.00**

Dennis the Menace, Mischief Kit, Hasbro, 1955, NMIB 50.00
Dick Tracy, Handcuffs for Junior, 1940s, NMOC 85.00
Dick Tracy, Jr Detective Kit, Golden Press, 1962, NM, from $40 to.50.00
Don Winslow, magic slate & storybook, Strathmore, 1953, EX 40.00
Donald Duck, Dress Buttons, plastic, set of 3, EXOC..................100.00
Donald Duck, jack-in-the-box, cb/celluloid figure, prewar, 3½", NM.500.00
Donald Duck, pull toy, rowboat, wood, Chad Valley, 1948, 12", EX .300.00
Donald Duck, sweeper, wood litho, Ohio Art/WDE, EX.............125.00
Dr Dolittle, Animal Fist Faces, EXIB..40.00
Dr Dolittle, bank, Dr w/monkey & dog at ft, plastic, NM 50.00
Dr Dolittle, medical playset, Hasbro, NM 75.00
Dr Dolittle, Stitch-A-Story, Hasbro, NMIP 25.00
Dr Seuss, doll, Horton, talker, Mattel, 1970, EX+ 125.00
Dr Seuss, Grow Chart, Cat in the Hat, 1977, MIP (sealed) 20.00
Dracula, doll, cloth outfit, Lincoln Toys, 1975, 8", NM 375.00
Elmer Fudd, pull toy, as fire chief, wood, Brice Toys, 1940s, 9", NM...200.00
ET, Presto Magix Rub-Down Transfer Game (Halloween), MIP...10.00
Family Affair, doll, Buffy/Mrs Beasley, talker, 1960s, rare, 36", MIB..800.00
Family Affair, makeup & hairstyling set, Buffy, Amsco, 1970s, EX ..50.00
Felix the Cat, figure, bsk, Germany, 1½", NM............................350.00
Felix the Cat, figure, wood, Schoenhut, 4", VG+ 125.00
Felix the Cat, figure, wood, Schoenhut, 8", EX 225.00
Felix the Cat, pull toy, litho tin, Felix/2 mice, Nifty, EX.............450.00
Felix the Cat, pull toy, pnt wood, Felix in race car, 12", VG+ 375.00
Felix the Cat, scale, litho tin w/2 bowls on oblong base, 7" L, EX...1,430.00
Flash Gordon, goggles/belt/wrist compass, Esquire Novelty, 1951, NMOC ..200.00
Flash Gordon, puzzles, fr-tray, set of 3, Milton Bradley, 1951, EXIB...65.00
Flash Gordon, wrist compass, FG Inc, 1950s, EX+ 65.00
Flintstones, bank, Pebbles, plastic, Transogram, 1960s, EX 45.00
Flintstones, figure, any character, bendy, Just Toys, MOC, ea 10.00
Flintstones, wallet, vinyl w/image of Dino, Estelle, 1964, unused, NM+ .50.00
Flipper, magic slate, Lowe, 1960s, EX+.....................................25.00
Flipper, wristwatch, glow-in-the-dark, ITF/MGM, M 125.00
G-Man, Police Set, Pressman, EXIB..250.00
Gene Autry, billfold, leather, zippered, Aristocrat, 1950s, VGIB..75.00
Gene Autry, record player, plastic, Flying A decal, Columbia, 13", VG ...250.00
Gilligan's Island (cartoon), figure set, 3-pc, Playskool, 1977, NM ..20.00
Goofy, figure, Weebles, 1973, EX..15.00
Green Hornet, figure, bendy, Lakeside Toys, 1966, 6", MOC 175.00
Green Hornet, masks, set of 2 mk Green Hornet/Kato, 1966, NMOC...225.00
Green Hornet, Stardust Touch of Velvet Art By Numbers, MIB (sealed) .110.00
Green Hornet, View-Master reels, #B-488, MIP 65.00
Gremlins, doll, Gizmo, plush, Quiron, 1984, 14", MIB 150.00
Groucho Marx, Groucho Goggles, Eldon Mfg, 1955, VG (VG card)..150.00
Gulliver's Travels, drum, litho tin, Chein, 3½x6" dia, VG+ 75.00
Gulliver's Travels, plate/mug set, pnt china/gold trim, 1939, EX.125.00
Gumby & Pokey, figure, Gumby seated, windup, 1966, 4", NM....25.00
Gumby & Pokey, stick horse, VG 65.00
Happy Days, belt, Fonz/Gang, Paramount, 1981, unused, M 15.00
Happy Days, wallet, Larami, 1981, MIP 20.00
Hector Heathcote, Colorforms, 1964, EXIB...............................40.00
Henry, figure, bsk, Carl Anderson, 1930s, 7", EX+ 130.00
Hopalong Cassidy, Crayon & Stencil Set, Transogram, 1950, unused, NMIB ..200.00
Hopalong Cassidy, doll, rubber head/outfit/guns/holster, 21", NM..300.00
Hopalong Cassidy, puzzle, jigsaw, Milton Bradley #4025, 1950s, NMIB..125.00
Hopalong Cassidy, TV set, plastic, Automatic Toy, 5x5", EXIB..250.00
Howdy Doody, barrette, Clarabell w/legs crossed, plastic, 1950s, EX..75.00
Howdy Doody, bubble pipe, Howdy, Lido, 1950s, 4", EX+ 175.00
Howdy Doody, canister, Cookie-Go-Round, tin, Luce Mfg, 1950s, 8", EX ..100.00
Howdy Doody, embroidery kit, Summer Fall-Winter Spring, 1950s, VGIB ..50.00
Howdy Doody, lamp base, plastic, Nor East Nauticals, 6½", EX.165.00
Howdy Doody, wall light, Howdy/Santa, plastic, Royal Electric, EX 100.00
I Dream of Jeannie, knitting & embroidery kit, Harmony, 1975, MOC.30.00
I Dream of Jeannie, magic slate, Rand McNally, 1975, M 30.00

Incredible Hulk, Crazy Foam, 1979, w/contents, EX.....................25.00
Jack Benny, TV Bank Safe, hard plastic, 1960s, 5x4", EX+ 80.00
Jackie Coogan, stick pin doll, pipe cleaner style/litho head, '20s, EX ..40.00
James Bond 007, Attaché Case, Multiple, complete, NMIB....1,050.00
James Bond 007, Code-O-Matic Secret Coding/Decoding Machine, NMIB..300.00
Jerry Mahoney, key chain, plastic head w/moving eyes & mouth, EXOC..60.00
Jetsons, slate & chalk set, 1960s, unused, MIB 100.00
Jiminy Cricket, figure, compo, cloth vest/jacket/hat, jtd, 10", VG...160.00
Joan Palooka, doll, Ideal, 1952, 14", EX...................................135.00
Joe Carioca, pencil sharpener, Plastic Novelties, 1940s, 1", EX 50.00
John Travolta, View-Master reels, #K-79, MIP (sealed).................15.00
Kayo, doll, papier-mâché, talking mouth, Williard, 13", EX........140.00
Kayo, figure, jtd/pnt wood, Jaymar, 1938, M 125.00
Kermit the Frog, bank, as pirate w/chest, vinyl, 1989, 10", VG+ ..20.00
King Kong, Colorforms Panoramic Playset, 1976, EXIB...............25.00
King Kong, Jungle Set, Multiple, 1967, complete, NMIB 250.00
King Kong, puzzle, jigsaw, Giant, 1976, MIB.............................45.00
Land of the Giants, Colorforms, 1968, NMIB............................60.00
Land of the Lost, Direction Finder, Larami, 1975, MOC 40.00
Lassie, figure, plastic, name emb on her bk, 1950s, 9", EX+ 20.00
Laurel & Hardy, figures, cb, jtd, string activated, 1950s, EX, pr 50.00
Little Bo Peep, puzzle, jigsaw, Milton Bradley, 7½x13", VGIB....100.00
Little Lulu, doll, stuffed, cowboy outfit, 16", VG 275.00
Little Orphan Annie & Sandy, figures, celluloid, Japan, prewar, 5", NM.125.00
Little Red Riding Hood, tea set, tin, 9-pc, Ohio Art, 1920s-30s, EX+.350.00
Lone Ranger, binoculars, plastic, Harrison, EX+IB.....................135.00
Lone Ranger, tote bag, name/Hi-Yo Silver/head image on red vinyl, EX..175.00
Lost in Space, helmet & gun set, Remco, 1966, NMIB 1,250.00
Magilla Gorilla, doll, plush, Ideal, 1960s, 18½", NM+................100.00
Mammy/Pappy Yokum, dolls, vinyl/cloth outfits, 1950s, 13¼", NM, ea ..200.00
Man From UNCLE, hand puppet, Illya Kuryakin, vinyl, Gilbert, 1960s, NM..175.00
Man From UNCLE, Headquarters Transmitter, battery-op, NMIB..375.00
Man From UNCLE, Thrush Buster Car, EXIB.............................275.00
Marvel Super Heroes, Sparkle Paint Set, Kenner, 1967, MIB (sealed)..400.00
Marvel Super Heroes, stickers, 49-pc set w/cards, Topps, 1976, EX-NM .50.00
Maverick, Eras-O-Picture Book, Hasbro, 1958, complete, EX 40.00
Mary Hartline, doll, Super Circus, Ideal, 1950s, 7", EX+ 65.00
Mary Marvel, pocket watch, rnd chrome case, Fawcett, 1948, VG..125.00

Mickey Mouse, Jazz Drummer, lithographed tin, Walt Disney, lever action, 6½", NM, $6,500.00.

Mickey Mouse, lamp, chalkware, Mickey in chair, shade, 1930s, 13", EX..1,900.00
Mickey Mouse, Magic Movie Palette, cb litho, WDE, 1930s, 8x5", EX..125.00
Mickey Mouse, pillow cover, Vogue Needlecraft, 1930s, 17x15", EX+ 65.00

Mickey Mouse, toy chest/child's seat, wood/cb/cloth, 1930s, 36" L, EX .350.00

Mickey Mouse, tray, porc, c Walt Disney, Made in Japan, 6" **35.00**

Mighty Mouse, doll, rubber w/cloth cape, 1955, 10", EX..............**75.00**

Mighty Mouse, doll, stuffed cloth, Ideal, 1950s, 14", EX+.............**75.00**

Minnie Mouse, tin, triangular, Minnie admiring flowers on yel, 5", EX ..**200.00**

Mister Magoo, drinking glass, various, Polomar Jelly, ea from $25 to....**35.00**

Moon Mullins, figure, bsk, 1930s, 7½", G............................**125.00**

Mork & Mindy, Figurine Painting Set, Milton Bradley, 1979, unused, MOC..**20.00**

Mork & Mindy, scrapbook, The Official..., Wallaby, 1979, unused, M ..**25.00**

Mother Goose, tea set, litho tin, 9-pc, Ohio Art, 1930s, NM.....**300.00**

Mr Ed, coloring book, Whitman #1135, 1963, uncolored, NM.....**65.00**

Mr Magoo, doll, Ideal, 1970, 12", EXIB..............................**50.00**

Mr T, transfer set, 1984, MIB (sealed) **50.00**

Munsters, dolls, any character, Presents, 1980s, 11" to 13", MIB, ea..**65.00**

Mutt & Jeff, mask, Mutt, diecut cb litho, Einson-Freeman, 1933, VG+..**35.00**

New Zoo Revue, Stamp Set, Imperial, 1973, MOC, from $30 to..**40.00**

Odd Job (Goldfinger), hand puppet, vinyl, AC Gilbert, 1965, MIB.**200.00**

Odd Job (Goldfinger), hand puppet, vinyl, Ideal, 1960s, EX+ **150.00**

Our Gang, booklet, How To Roller Skate, 1932, 3½x6½", VG+ .**75.00**

Peanuts, autograph doll, Snoopy, Determined, 1971, 11", unused, MIP ..**35.00**

Peanuts, bank, Linus as baseball catcher, rare, 7", NM.............**125.00**

Peanuts, Camp Kamp Play Set, Child Guidance, 1970s, EXIB **75.00**

Peanuts, doll, Snoopy as Rock Star, plush, Ideal, 1977, 14", VG+..**125.00**

Peanuts, hairbrush, Charlie Brown, vinyl, 1971, 6", VG+.............**10.00**

Peanuts, Mattel-O-Phone, 1968, MIB................................**125.00**

Peanuts, playset, Snoopy Astronaut, Knickerbocker, 1969, EXIB .**75.00**

Peanuts, View-Master reels, Snoopy & the Red Baron, #B-544, MIP ...**12.00**

Peter Pan, song book, 16 pgs, b/w illus, WD Music Co, 1955, 12x9", EX.**30.00**

Peter Rabbit, doll, straw-stuffed, mk Quaddy Pat Jan 30 1917, 17", G..**1,785.00**

Pinocchio, doll, wood/compo, jtd/pnt detail/cloth hat, Ideal, 20", VG+..**525.00**

Pinocchio, Picture Puzzle Set, set of 2, Whitman, 1939, EXIB......**50.00**

Pixie & Dixie, magic slate, 1960, EX................................**25.00**

Pluto, lantern, tin figure w/globe belly, battery, Linemar, 7", NMIB.**450.00**

Pogo, Pogomobile, 22 different characters, Simon & Shuster, 1954, EX..**150.00**

Popeye, bank, Popeye Knockout Bank, tin, Straits Mfg, 1935, EX **475.00**

Popeye, doll, Brutus, vinyl w/cloth outfit, orig tag, 13", M...........**25.00**

Popeye, doll, Popeye, compo (hollow), red/bl, 15", VG+.............**100.00**

Popeye, doll, Wimpy, rubber, Schavoir Rubber Co, 1935, NM ...**275.00**

Popeye, figure set, Popeye & Olive Oyl, chalkware, 15", EX, pr.**150.00**

Popeye, lantern, tin figure, globe belly, battery, 7", NMIB **450.00**

Popeye, soap-on-a-rope, Popeye Head, Lester Gaba Design, EX+IB...**100.00**

Porky Pig, bank, bsk figure, 1930s, EX............................**175.00**

Porky Pig, lamp base, pnt plaster figure, early, EX **200.00**

Quick Draw McGraw, pencil sharpener, pnt ceramic figure, 1960s, 2", NM...**20.00**

Raggedy Andy, bank, Play Pal, 1974, 11", EX+......................**25.00**

Raggedy Andy, doll, Georgene, 1930s-40s, 13", NM **250.00**

Raggedy Andy, planter, papier-mâché, 1974, 8", EX **25.00**

Raggedy Ann, Colorforms Play Kitchen, 1975, MIB **25.00**

Raggedy Ann, doll, musical, Knickerbocker, 15", EX+ **50.00**

Red Ryder, gloves, Playmates, cloth, Wells Lamont Corp & SS, 1950s, NM .**30.00**

Rin-Tin-Tin, program, Boston Garden Rodeo, 32 pgs, Oct 19, 1956, NM+...**55.00**

Road Runner, doll, Mighty Star, 13", EX+ **20.00**

Rocky & Friends, doll, Bullwinkle, plush, Ideal, 1960, 20", NM...**75.00**

Rocky & Friends, doll, Rocky, plush, 1982, 13", VG+...................**20.00**

Rocky & Friends, Signal Flasher, Bullwinkle, plastic, 1970s, MOC..**25.00**

Rootie Kazootie, magic set, 1950s, NMIB **125.00**

Roy Rogers, archery set, Ben Pearson, scarce, 37", unused, NMOC..**185.00**

Roy Rogers, Ball Pen, Tuckersharpe Prod, MOC......................**165.00**

Roy Rogers, Flash Camera, plastic, H George, complete, NMIB ...**325.00**

Roy Rogers, horseshoe set, Ohio Art, MIB **125.00**

Roy Rogers, paint book, Whitman, 1948, 15x11", neatly pnt, VG..**30.00**

Roy Rogers, View-Master reels, #475, MIP.........................**26.00**

Ruff & Reddy, Karbon Kopee Kit, Wonder Art, 1960, EXIB.........**75.00**

Scrappy, bank, book shape, Columbia, 1930s, 3", EX+ **75.00**

Scrappy, doll, compo/cloth outfit, Columbia Studios, 1935, 14", VG.**200.00**

Sesame Street, figure set, PVC, Applause, 1993, 8-pc, M..............**20.00**

Simpsons, Bart figure, bendable, w/slingshot, Presents, 9", MIP....**16.00**

Simpsons, doll, any character, rag-type, Dandee, 11", NM, ea **18.00**

Simpsons, Fun Dough Model Maker, MIB................................**45.00**

Simpsons, Trace 'N Color Drawing Set, Toymax, NMIB.............**85.00**

Six Million Dollar Man, fan club kit, 1970s, NM **85.00**

Smurfs, Smurf Amaze-ing Action Maze, EX...........................**20.00**

Snow White, doll set, dwarfs, compo, Knickerbocker, 9", EX, 8-pc..**935.00**

Speedy Gonzales, doll, Goofy Grams, Dakin, 1971, 9", EX+.........**30.00**

Spider-Man, doll, stuffed talker, Mego, 1974, 28", M...............**50.00**

Spider-Man, skydiving parachute, Ahi, 1973, MOC **35.00**

Spider-Man, squirt gun, plastic head figure, 1974, EX **25.00**

Superman, Crayon-By-Numbers Set, Transogram, 1954, EXIB...**100.00**

Superman, figure, Justice League, plastic, Ideal, 1966, 3", EX+ **75.00**

Superman, figure, pnt wood/compo bead style, w/cape, Ideal, 13", EX.**2,600.00**

Superman, puzzle, jigsaw, Saalfield #1505, EXIB....................**300.00**

Superman, scrapbook, Saalfield #178, 1940, scarce, 11x14", EX.**110.00**

Superman, wallet, Superman in flight, Croyden, 1950s, EXIB....**175.00**

Sylvester the Cat, squeak toy, soft rubber, 1930s, EX..................**150.00**

Three Little Pigs, hand puppets, compo heads/cloth bodies, EXIB, set..**250.00**

Three Stooges, dolls, any character, Presents, 1988, 14", M, ea **65.00**

Tom & Jerry, dolls, cloth/linen faces, 1940s, 17", 7½", VG+, pr.**150.00**

Tom & Jerry, guitar, character design, musical, Mattel, 1960s, M..**150.00**

Tom Corbett, flashlight, rocketship form, NM.........................**250.00**

Tom Corbett, Molding/Coloring Set, Model-Craft, unused, EXIB..**100.00**

Tonto, soap, figural, Castile/Kerk Guild, EXIB.......................**50.00**

Topo Gigio, doll, vinyl/jtd arms/realistic hair, 1963, 12", EX **50.00**

Tweety Bird, lantern, tin, battery-op, Amico, 1950s, 5½", EX **85.00**

Umbriago (Jimmy Durante's pal), hand puppet, 1940s, NM+ (VG+ box) ..**75.00**

Waltons, playset, Farmhouse, complete, Amsco, 1975, MIB.........**75.00**

Welcome Back Kotter, record case, Komack/Walper, 1976, EX **90.00**

Wild Bill Hickok, puzzle, jigsaw, Built-Rite, 1955, NMIB **30.00**

Wild Bill Hickok, toothbrush holder, metal holsters, Tek, 1955, NMOC ..**80.00**

Winnie the Pooh, doll, Chatter Chum, 1976, EX+ **100.00**

Woody Woodpecker, hand puppet, talker, Mattel, 1960s, NM......**75.00**

Woody Woodpecker, kazoo, red plastic, cereal premium, 1958, 6½", EX..**35.00**

Yogi Bear, bubble pipe, plastic figure, 1965, MIP (sealed) **35.00**

Yogi Bear, guitar, Yogi Bear Ge-Tar, Mattel, 1960s, EX...............**75.00**

Yogi Bear, Paint 'Em Pals Paint-By-Number Set, 1970s, complete, EXIB...**30.00**

Zorro, accessory set, mask/whip/lariat/ring, Shimmel, M (24" L card)....**150.00**

Zorro, Target Shoot, Lido/WDP, MIB................................**225.00**

Peters and Reed

    John Peters and Adam Reed founded their pottery in Zanesville, Ohio, just before the turn of the century, using the local red clay to produce a variety of wares. Moss Aztec, introduced about 1912, has an unglazed exterior with designs molded in high relief and the recesses highlighted with a green wash. Only the interior is glazed to hold water. Pereco (named for Peters, Reed, and Company) is glazed in semi-matt blue, maroon, cream, and other colors. Orange was also used very early, but such examples are rare. Shapes are simple with in-mold decoration sometimes borrowed from the Moss Aztec line. Wilse Blue is a line of high-gloss medium blue with dark specks on simple shapes. Landsun, characterized by its soft matt multicolor or blue and gray combinations, is decorated either by dripping or by hand brushing in an effect sometimes called Flame or Herringbone. Chromal, in much the same colors as Landsun, may be decorated with a realistic scenic, or the swirling application of colors may merely suggest one. Vivid, realistic Chromal scenics command much higher prices than weak, poorly drawn examples. (Brush-McCoy made a very similar line called Chromart. Neither will be marked; and due to the lack of documented background material available, it may be impossible make a positive identification. Collectors nearly always attribute this type of decoration to Peters and Reed.) Shadow Ware is usually a glossy, multi-color drip over a harmonious base color but occasionally seen in overall matt glaze. When the base is black, the effect is often iridescent.

Several other lines were produced, including Mirror Black, Persian, Egyptian, Florentine, Marbleized, etc., and an unidentified line which collectors call Mottled-Marbleized Colors. In this high-gloss line, the red clay body often shows through the splashed-on multicolors. At one time, the brown high-glaze artware line with 'sprigged' decoration was attributed to Peters and Reed. However, this line has recently been re-attributed to Weller pottery by the Sanfords in their latest book on Peters and Reed pottery. This conclusion was drawn due to the overwhelming number of shapes proven to be Weller molds. Since the decoration was cut out and applied, however, it is possible that Peters and Reed or yet another Zanesville company simply contracted for the Weller greenware and added their own decoration and finishes.

In 1922 the company became known as the Zane Pottery. Peters and Reed retired, and Harry McClelland became president. Charles Chilcote designed new lines, and production of many of the old lines continued. The body of the ware after 1922 was light in color. Marks include the impressed logo or ink stamp 'Zaneware' in a rectangle.

Bowl, Landsun, 3x7" dia, w/matching flower frog 75.00
Bowl, matt gr, floral relief, 2¾x6¾" 95.00
Bowl, Moss Aztec, dragonfly, brn glazed int, 2x7½" 80.00
Bowl, Moss Aztec, sgn Ferrell, 3x9" 125.00
Ginger jar, Shadow Ware, gr-to-blk w/blk/gr/bl irid, w/lid, #773, 8"..150.00
Vase, bud; Landsun, 6x2¾" 85.00
Vase, Florentine, flared rim, 5⅛" 85.00
Vase, Landsun, bulbous bottom w/flared rim, 5" 130.00
Vase, matt gr, daffodil in relief, 10" 145.00
Vase, matt gr, ivy vines in relief, flared rim & ft, 10x5" 130.00
Vase, Moss Aztec, Egyptian decor, cylindrical, 7¾" 95.00
Vase, Moss Aztec, floral relief, 6x6½" 95.00
Vase, Pereco, 3¼x6½" dia 45.00
Vase, Shadow Ware, drip glaze, #773-7, 7" 150.00
Vase, Wilse Blue, shouldered, 6½" 65.00

Pewabic

The Pewabic Pottery was formally established in Detroit, Michigan, in 1907 by Mary Chase Perry Stratton and Horace James Caulkins. The two had worked together since 1903, firing their ware in a small kiln Caulkins had designed especially for use by the dental trade. Always a small operation which relied upon basic equipment and the skill of the workers, they took pride in being commissioned for several important architectural tile installations.

Some of the early artware was glazed a simple matt green; occasionally other colors were added, sometimes in combination, one over the other in a drip effect. Later Stratton developed a lustrous crystalline glaze. (Today's values are determined to a great extent by the artistic merit of the glaze.) The body of the ware was highly fired and extremely hard. Shapes were basic, and decorative modeling, if used at all, was in low relief. Mary Stratton kept the pottery open until her death in 1961. In 1968 it was purchased and reopened by Michigan State University; it is still producing today. Several marks were used over the years: a triangle with 'Revelation Pottery' (for a short time only); 'Pewabic' with five maple leaves; and the impressed circle mark. Our advisors for this category are Suzanne Perrault and David Rago; they are listed in the Directory under New Jersey.

Bowl, blk/bl/gr metallic, 7½" 200.00
Candle holder, bl crystalline matt, tall stem, wavy base, 4", ea...200.00

Vase, bl, ovoid, 3½" 150.00
Vase, bl lustre, squat w/flared rim, short ft, label/stamp, 4¼x4"..375.00
Vase, bl/gr/silver irid drip w/texture, flared rim, 6" 850.00
Vase, blk & bl volcanic lustre, 3x4½" 425.00
Vase, blk matt crystalline, cvd geometrics/panels, 9½x5", $6,000 to...7,000.00

Vase, brilliant pulled cobalt and turquoise lustre, baluster, 9¾x6½", $5,000.00. (Photo courtesy David Rago Auctions)

Vase, cobalt/bl/purple volcanic lustre, bulbous, 9¼x5¾" 1,700.00
Vase, deep bl gloss over lt bsk bottom, swollen mid-section, 3½" ...260.00
Vase, gr matt w/appl Nouveau floral stems, gourd form, 6¼x4½".4,250.00
Vase, irid silver-gray over thick bl matt, bulbous, 3½" 400.00
Vase, lt cvg, metallic gr/yel/caramel, shouldered cylinder, 4" 200.00
Vase, mottled gray-gr w/irid, thick walled, can neck, 8" 500.00
Vase, mottled purple/maroon/bl, experimental, shouldered, 3⅜" .700.00
Vase, silver/bl/taupe intermingled irid, wide cone shape, 3"........225.00
Vase, tones of bl irid & silver, thrown/shouldered, 7" 500.00

Pewter

Pewter is a metal alloy of tin, copper, very small parts of bismuth and/or antimony, and sometimes lead. Very little American pewter contained lead, however, because much of the ware was designed to be used as tableware, and makers were aware that the use of lead could result in poisoning. (Pieces that do contain lead are usually darker in color and heavier than those that have no lead.) Most of the fine examples of American pewter date from 1700 to the 1840s. Many pieces were melted down and recast into bullets during the American Revolution in 1775; this accounts to some extent why examples from this period are quite difficult to find. The pieces that did survive may include buttons, buckles, and writing equipment as well as the tableware we generally think of.

After the Revolution makers began using antimony as the major alloy with the tin in an effort to regain the popularity of pewter, which glassware and china was beginning to replace in the home. The resulting product, known as britannia, had a lustrous silver-like appearance and was far more durable. While closely related, britannia is a collectible in its own right and should not be confused with pewter.

Key: tm — touch mark

Basin, Amos Treadway Jr tm, minor pitting, 9" 1,265.00
Basin, Joseph Danforth partial tm, battering/splits, 2x8" 200.00
Basin, Samuel Danforth partial eagle tm, 6½" 300.00
Basin, Samuel Danforth partial eagle tm, hammered booge, 8" ..300.00
Basin, TDB under eagle tm, 7¼" 700.00
Basin, Thomas Danforth III eagle tm, 1⅞x8⅛" 235.00

Basin, Townsen & Compton tm, hammered booge & tooled rim, 2x8" .165.00
Beaker, Boardman & Hart NY tm, str sides, flared rims, 1830s, 5⅛"...415.00
Bowl, partial London tm, hammered booge, tooled rim, pitting, 18"..440.00
Bowl, soup; 2 Thomas Danforth Boardman eagle tms, 9¾" 275.00
Candlesticks, Homan & Co (att), 7⅞", near-matched pr............275.00
Chalice, TG flower & crown tm, trn baluster stem, 7⅞" 465.00
Charger, Ash & Hutton tm, normal wear, 16⅝"..........................235.00
Charger, Blakslee Barns tm, battering, 1½x13⅛" 550.00
Charger, Danforth rampant lion tm, wear/split, 13¼" 550.00
Charger, John Hoskyn tm, single reeded, 1750s, 18⅜"...............400.00
Charger, Reutlinger angel tm, raised tooled line, 14" 350.00
Charger, Richard Austin tm, knife mks, 13½" 660.00
Charger, Richard Austin tm, rim split/rstr, 15" 500.00
Charger, Townsend & Compton London tm, dents, 15¾"..........440.00
Coffee/teapot, Israel Trask tm, lighthouse form w/eng bands, 11¾" ..1,035.00
Coffeepot, Calder tm, lighthouse w/scroll hdl, paneled spout, 11", VG...495.00
Coffeepot, F Porter tm, tooled body, wooden wafer finial, 11¾".440.00
Coffeepot, HB Ward tm, lighthouse w/scrolled hdl, 11¼" 660.00
Coffeepot, I Trask tm, lighthouse w/eng band, domed lid, 13" 660.00
Coffeepot, IC Lewis tm, lighthouse form, scroll hdl, 11", VG.....330.00
Coffeepot, Richardson tm, dbl bulb, minor dent/pitting, 11" 230.00
Coffeepot, Roswell Gleason tm, baluster w/hinged lid, S spout, 13" ...200.00
Coffeepot, Sheldon & Feltman tm, lighthouse, ear hdl, 12¼", EX..260.00
Coffeepot, unmk Am, relief-trn rings on body, domed lid, 12" ...300.00
Deep dish, Thomas D Boardman tms, old dk surface, 13" 415.00
Deep dish, Townsend & Compton partial tm, hammered booge, 14½"..385.00
Dish, Gershom Jones tm, rim split, deep, 11⅝" 550.00
Dish, T Boardman tm (2), single reeded, deep, 11⅛".................635.00
Flagon, Boardman & Co tm, 3-wafer finial, split, 8½"............1,100.00
Flagon, communion; Trask tm, G form, SP exterior, dent, 10⅝"..495.00
Flagon, unidentified German mk, knopped cylinder, ca 1855, 10", VG..235.00
Inkwell, unmk, 3 raised rings on body, no insert, 3¾x8¾"..........110.00
Lamp, oil; at Roswell Gleason, dbl bull's-eye, 8½" 800.00
Lamp, oil; unmk, pan base w/appl finger loop, dbl brass burner, 7½"..165.00
Loving cup, unmk English, 3 dbl curved hdls, ca 1850, 6½".......230.00
Measures, Yates & Birch tm, 1¾-6", graduated set of 7..............865.00
Mug, Grimes & Son tm, str sides, eng front, 1805-32, 6"...........175.00
Pitcher, unmk, bulbous w/scroll hdl, pierced guard/filter at spout, 7"....110.00
Plate, Jacob Whitmore partial tm, 7⅞" 330.00
Plate, Samuel Danforth partial tm, polished, 7⅞" 165.00
Plate, Samuel Pierce tm, lt scratches, 8" 600.00
Plate, T Danforth Philada tm, sm dents, 7¾" 330.00
Plate, Thomas Badger tm, inscr owner's initials, 8" 250.00
Porringer, att New England, crown hdl mk IG, minor battering, 4" dia..220.00
Porringer, Hamlin Providence tm, pierced flowered hdl, rpr, 5¼" ..550.00
Porringer, openwork Lee-type hdl w/linen mk inside, 5½x6¾" ..220.00
Porringer, unmk, raised floral design on hdl, dents, mini, 2¼"....165.00
Syrup, Savage Midd Ct tm, scroll hdl, dents, 6" 330.00
Tankard, Boardman & Co NY tm, scrolled ear hdl, dome lid, 8"..1,850.00
Tankard, Sir Geo Alderson tm, curved hdl, open thumbpc, 6" ...345.00
Tankard, unmk English, tulip shape, dome lid, qt, 9" 1,150.00
Tankard, WR faint tm, simple form w/scroll hdl, old rpr, 6" 140.00
Taster, unmk English, Old English hdl w/wedge bracket, 2½" dia...230.00
Tea set, Armitages & Standish tm, 9¼" pot+4" cr/sug 300.00
Teapot, Ashbil Griswold partial tm, pear shape, sm damage, 7"..250.00
Teapot, B&P (Bush & Perkins) tm, pear shape, wood hdl, sm rpr, 6⅝"..865.00
Teapot, Boardman & Co eagle tm, dbl-bulbed form, domed lid, 11⅝"..420.00
Teapot, Calder tm, blk cast-metal knop, scroll hdl, 8¾" 415.00
Teapot, G Richardson tm, scroll hdl, wooden wafer final, 9½"...330.00
Teapot, IC Lewis tm, cast hdl w/acanthus-leaf ends, 8¼"...........175.00
Teapot, J Danforth No 14 tm, domed lid w/wafer finial, rpr, 8" ..440.00
Teapot, Josiah Danforth tm, wide central band, ornate hdl, rpr, 6⅝" ..250.00
Teapot, Luther Boardman Warranted tm, hinged domed lid, 7¾" ...265.00
Teapot, partial European tms, pear shape, wood wafer finial, 7", VG..165.00
Teapot, R Gleason tm, scroll hdl, 9⅛" 275.00
Teapot, Smith & Co, tm, blk pnt on hdl cover, rpr, 7¾" 115.00
Teapot, Thomas Danforth Boardman tm, pear shape w/ornate hdl, 7"..385.00

Pfaltzgraff

Pfaltzgraff has operated in Pennsylvania since the early 1800s making redware at first, then stoneware crocks and jugs, yellow ware and spongeware in the 1920s, artware and kitchenware in the 1930s, and stoneware kitchen items through the 1940s. To collectors, they're best known for their Gourmet Royal (circa 1950s), a high-gloss dinnerware line of solid brown with frothy white drip glaze around the rims, and their giftware line called Muggsy, comic-character mugs, ashtrays, bottle stoppers, children's dishes, pretzel jars, cookie jars, etc. It was designed in the late 1940s and continued in production until 1960. The older versions have protruding features, while the features of later examples were simply painted on.

Their popular Village line, an almond-glazed pattern with a brown-stenciled folk-art tulip design, was discontinued a few years ago, and is today very collectible. Yorktown and Folk Art are manufactured on a very limited basis, so discontinued items in those lines are attracting much interest as well. (In general, use Village prices to help you evaluate those two lines.) For more information on their dinnerware, we recommend *The Flea Market Trader* and *The Garage Sale and Flea Market Annual*, both by Collector Books. Our advisor for the Muggsy line is Judy Posner; she is listed in the Directory under Florida.

Gourmet Royale, baker, #321, oval, 7½", from $8 to....................10.00
Gourmet Royale, bean pot, #11-1, 1-qt, from $10 to....................12.00
Gourmet Royale, bean pot, #11-3, 3-qt 25.00
Gourmet Royale, bean pot, #30, w/lip, lg, from $30 to.................40.00
Gourmet Royale, bowl, #241, oval, 7x10", from $10 to................12.00
Gourmet Royale, bowl, mixing; 6", from $8 to.............................10.00
Gourmet Royale, bowl, salad; tapered sides, 10", from $10 to 14.00
Gourmet Royale, bowl, spaghetti; #219, shallow, 14", from $15 to..20.00
Gourmet Royale, bowl, vegetable; #341, divided 10.00
Gourmet Royale, canister set, 4-pc 60.00
Gourmet Royale, casserole, hen on nest, 2-qt, from $50 to 60.00
Gourmet Royale, casserole, stick hdl, 3-qt, from $15 to 20.00
Gourmet Royale, coffee server, on metal warmer, from $20 to......25.00
Gourmet Royale, creamer, #382, from $4 to....................................5.00
Gourmet Royale, cup & saucer, demi 18.00
Gourmet Royale, gravy boat, w/stick hdl, 2-spout, from $8 to.......12.00
Gourmet Royale, jug, #386, ice lip, from $25 to 32.00
Gourmet Royale, ladle, sm, from $12 to 15.00
Gourmet Royale, mug, #391, 12-oz, from $5 to...............................7.00
Gourmet Royale, pie plate, #7016, 9½", from $10 to 12.00
Gourmet Royale, plate, salad; 6¾", from $1 to................................2.00
Gourmet Royale, platter, #337, 16", from $18 to 20.00
Gourmet Royale, roaster, #325, oval, 14", from $15 to 20.00
Gourmet Royale, scoop, any sz, from $8 to....................................12.00
Gourmet Royale, sugar bowl, from $4 to 6.00
Gourmet Royale, tray, 3-part, 15½" L...25.00
Heritage, butter dish, #002-028...6.00
Heritage, cup & saucer, #002-002, 9-oz 3.00
Village, baker, #024, oval, 10¼", from $7 to 9.00
Village, baker, #237, sq, tab hdls, 9", from $9 to 12.00
Village, baker, #240, oval, 7¾", from $6 to 8.00
Village, beverage server, #490, from $18 to 22.00
Village, bowl, butter; w/spout & hdl, 8", from $22 to 28.00
Village, bowl, fruit; #008, 5" 3.00
Village, bowl, mixing; #453, 1-qt, 2-25, & 3-qt, 3-pc set, $45 to ..50.00
Village, bowl, rim soup; #012, 8½" 6.00
Village, bowl, soup/cereal; #009, 6"...4.00

Village, bowl, vegetable; #011, 8¾" 12.00
Village, bread tray, 12" 15.00
Village, butter bowl, w/spout & hdl, 8", from $22 to 28.00
Village, butter dish, #028 ....8.00
Village, casserole, w/lid, #315, 2-qt, from $18 to............22.00
Village, coffeepot, lighthouse shape, 48-oz, from $20 to ...25.00
Village, cookie jar, #540, 3-qt, from $15 to 20.00
Village, cup & saucer, #001 & #002....................................3.50
Village, flowerpot, 4½", from $12 to..................................15.00
Village, gravy boat, #443, w/saucer, 16-oz, from $10 to......12.00
Village, onion soup crock, #295, stick hdl, sm, from $5 to 7.00
Village, ped mug, #90F, 10-oz 3.50
Village, pitcher, #416, 2-qt, from $20 to...........................25.00
Village, plate, dinner; #004, 10¼", from $3 to 4.00
Village, platter, #016, 14", from $12 to.............................18.00
Village, quiche, 9" 16.00
Village, soup tureen, #160, w/lid & ladle, 3½-qt, from $40 to 45.00
Village, table light, #620, clear chimney, candle-holder base, $12 to...14.00

Muggsy Line

Bottle stopper, head, ball shape...85.00
Cigarette server..95.00
Clothes sprinkler bottle, Myrtle, wht, from $250 to 295.00
Clothes sprinkler bottle, Myrtle, Black, from $275 to 375.00
Cookie jar, character face, minimum value 250.00
Mug, Black action figure 125.00
Mug, character face, ea 38.00
Shot mug, character face, ea from $40 to 50.00
Tumbler..60.00
Utility jar, Handy Hardy, hat w/short bill as flat lid.........150.00

Phoenix Bird

Blue and white Phoenix Bird china has been produced by various Japanese potteries from the early 1900s. With slight variations the design features the Japanese bird of paradise and scroll-like vines of Kara-Kusa, or Chinese grass. Although some of their earlier ware is unmarked, the majority is marked in some fashion. More than 125 different stamps have been reported, with 'Made in Japan' the one most often found. Coming in second is Morimura's wreath and/or crossed stems (both having the letter 'M' within). The cloverleaf with 'Japan' below very often indicates an item having a high-quality transfer-printed design. Among the many categories in the Phoenix Bird pattern are several shapes; therefore (for identification purposes), each has been given a number, i.e. #1, #2, etc. Newer items, if marked at all, carry a paper label. Compared to the older ware, the coloring of the new is whiter and the blue more harsh; the design is sparse with more ground area showing. Although collectors buy later pieces, the older is, of course, more highly prized and valued.

The Flying Turkey is a pattern very similar to Phoenix Bird. Though there are several differences, the phoenix bird's head is facing back or to the right, while the turkey is facing forward. Values are given for this line as well.

Given that there is more 'supply' than 'demand' right now (thanks to eBay), collectors have been able to buy at very low prices. With their collections complete or nearly so, except for the unusual pieces, they buy very little. Older collectors are downsizing or giving up their collections for various reasons. Because of this, the more common items have fallen in value.

For further information we recommend *Phoenix Bird Chinaware, Books I – V*, written and privately published by our advisor, Joan Oates; her address is in the Directory under Michigan. Join Phoenix Bird Collectors of America (PBCA) and receive the *Phoenix Bird Discoveries* newsletter, an informative publication that will further your appreciation of this chinaware. See Clubs, Newsletters, and Catalogs for ordering information.

Bouillon, hdls...8.00
Bouillon & saucer...10.00
Bowl, cereal, 6¼" 10.00
Bowl, mayonnaise; border outside...65.00
Bowl, soup plate; 9½"...20.00
Bowl, soup; 7¼"..15.00
Bread tray...65.00
Butter pat...10.00
Celery tray..75.00
Chocolate pot...85.00
Cracker jar, w/lid, #1 ....85.00
Cup, custard; 2¾x3" 8.00
Cup & saucer, common style (no inside border) 5.00
Gravy boat & underplate, #4 ....55.00
Plate, dinner; 9¾"...25.00
Plate, luncheon; 8½" 12.00
Platter, oval, 10" 20.00
Platter, 17"...90.00
Sugar bowl, w/lid, #6 ....22.00
Sugar bowl, w/lid, #11 ....20.00
Teapot, steam hole in lid, rnd & fat, common 35.00
Teapot & warmer, post-1970...45.00
Tile, rnd...25.00
Tureen, w/lid, rnd or oval, lg..65.00

Phoenix Glass

Founded in 1880 in Monaca, Pennsylvania, the Phoenix Glass Company became one of the country's foremost manufacturers of lighting glass by the early 1900s. They also produced a wide variety of utilitarian and decorative glassware, including art glass by Joseph Webb, colored cut glass, Gone-With-the-Wind style oil lamps, hotel and barware, and pharmaceutical glassware. Today, however, collectors are primarily interested in the Sculptured Artware produced in the 1930s and 1940s. These beautiful pressed and mold-blown pieces are most often found in white milk glass or crystal with various color treatments or a satin finish.

Phoenix did not mark their Sculptured Artware line on the glass; instead, a silver and black (earliest) or gold and black (later) foil label in the shape of the mythical phoenix bird was used.

Quite often glassware made by the Consolidated Lamp and Glass Company of nearby Coraopolis, Pennsylvania, is mistaken for Phoenix's Sculptured Artware. Though the style of the glass is very similar, one distinguishing characteristic is that perhaps 80% of the time Phoenix applied color to the background leaving the raised design plain in contrast, while Consolidated generally applied color to the raised design and left the background plain. Also, for the most part, the patterns and colors used by Phoenix were distinctively different from those used by Consolidated.

In 1970 Phoenix Glass became a division of Anchor Hocking which in turn was acquired by the Newell Group in 1987. Phoenix has the distinction of being one of the oldest continuously operating glass factories in the United States. For more information refer to *Phoenix and Consolidated Art Glass, 1926 – 1980*, written by our advisor, Jack D. Wilson, who is listed in the Directory under Arizona. See also Consolidated Glass.

Bachelor Button, vase, tan w/brn shadow on flowers, rare, 6".....300.00
Blackberry, compote, pk decor on milk glass.........................145.00
Blackberry, wine glass, irid 145.00
Bluebell, vase, beige on milk glass, silver label, 7½"...........175.00
Bluebell, vase, lt pk w/pearlized design, 7" 125.00
Bluebell, vase, rose w/pearlized design, 7" 125.00
Cosmos, vase, bl on milk glass, 7½" 200.00
Cosmos, vase, gr on milk glass, 7½" 165.00
Cosmos, vase, slate bl shadow, 7½" 185.00

Daisy, vase, bl over milk glass, 9x9"................................450.00
Daisy, vase, bl w/frost flowers, 9"................................325.00
Daisy, vase, tan on frost, 9x9"................................325.00
Dancing Girls, vase, frosted nudes on orange, 12"......................575.00
Dancing Girls, vase, med bl over milk glass, 12"....................650.00
Dancing Girls, vase, red pearlized, 12".................................625.00
Diving Girl, banana boat, orange w/frosted design......................425.00
Diving Girl, bowl, bl on milk glass, 14"...............................375.00
Fern, vase, reverse decor pk & gr on wht (strong colors), 7".......280.00
Fern, vase, slate gray pearlized, 7"...................................155.00
Freesia, vase, bl & frosted, 8".......................................295.00
Freesia, vase, yel-tan w/frosted design, fan shape, 8"................195.00
Jewel, vase, bl pearlized, 4¾"...125.00
Jonquil, tray, bl & frosted, 14"......................................300.00
Lacy Dewdrop, pitcher, gray highlights on milk glass...............175.00
Lily, bowl, console; gr wash w/frosted design.........................425.00
Lily, vase, aqua wash, 3-crimp, 9"....................................225.00
Lily, vase, yel wash, 3-crimp, 9".....................................295.00
Line 700, vase, Reuben Blue (extemely rare color), 7"...............525.00
Madonna, vase, brn shadow, 10"...275.00
Madonna, vase, lt bl on milk glass, 10"................................200.00
Madonna, vase, salmon pearlized, 10"...................................230.00
Moon & Stars, fruit holder, heavy caramel irid........................250.00
Philodendron, vase, brn shadow, 11½"..................................200.00
Philodendron, vase, gray w/frosted design, 11½".......................175.00
Phlox, candy dish, bl frosted..200.00
Phlox, candy dish, bl shadow, w/lid....................................200.00
Phlox, cigarette box, deep burgundy pearlized, w/lid..................180.00
Reuben Line of Screech Owls, vase, bl, orig label.....................275.00
Star Flower, vase, bl & milk glass, 7"................................145.00
Thistle, umbrella vase, Florist Green (rare color), 18", NM........495.00
Thistle, vase, lime gr pearlized, 18".................................525.00
Thistle, vase, med gr pearlized, 18"..................................550.00
Tiger Lily, bowl, amethyst frosted, 11½"..............................425.00
Tiger Lily, bowl, pk frosted, 11½"....................................375.00

Wild Geese, pillow vase, white on blue, 9x12", $240.00.

Wild Geese, vase, bl-gray w/frosted design, 9"........................200.00
Wild Geese, vase, lime gr pearlized, 9x12"............................225.00
Wild Rose, vase, brn shadow, 10½".....................................175.00
Zodiac, vase, deep rose over milk glass, 10½".........................950.00
Zodiac, vase, wht frosted, 10½".......................................650.00

Phonographs

The phonograph, invented by Thomas Edison in 1877, was the first practical instrument for recording and reproducing sound. Sound wave vibrations were recorded on a tinfoil-covered cylinder and played back with a needle that ran along the grooves made from the recording, thus reproducing the sound. Very little changed to this art of record making until 1885, when the first replayable and removable wax cylinders were developed by the American Graphophone Company. These records were made from 1885 until 1894 and are rare today. Edison began to offer musically recorded wax cylinders in 1889. They continued to be made until 1902. Today they are known as brown wax records. Black wax cylinders were offered in 1902, and the earlier brown wax cylinders were discontinued. These wax two-minute records were sold until 1912. From 1912 until 1929, only four-minute celluloid blue amberol record cylinders were made. The first disc records and disc machines were offered by the inventor Berliner in 1894. They were sold in America until 1900, when the Victor company took over. In the 1890s all machines played 7" diameter disc records; the 10" size was developed in 1901. By the early 1900s there existed many disc and cylinder phonograph companies, all offering their improvements. Among them were Berliner, Columbia, Zonophone, United States Phono, Wizard, Vitaphone, Amet, and others.

All Victor I's through VI's originally came with a choice of either brass bell, morning-glory, or wooden horns. Wood horns are the most valuable, adding $1,000.00 (or more) to the machine. Spring models were produced until 1929 (and even later). After 1929 most were electric (though some electric-motor models were produced as early as 1910). Unless another condition is noted, prices are for complete, original phonographs in at least fine to excellent condition. Note: Edison coin-operated cylinder players start at $7,000.00 and may go up to $20,000.00 each. All outside-horn Victor phonographs are worth at least $1,000.00 or more, if in excellent original condition. Machines that are complete, still retaining all their original parts, and with the original finish still in good condition are the most sought after, but those that have been carefully restored with their original finishes, decals, etc., are bringing high prices as well.

Key:
cyl — cylinder   NP — nickel plated
mg — morning glory   rpd — reproducer

Amberola VII, cyl, oak table-top.......................................450.00
Amberola 50, cyl, oak table-top, EX....................................275.00
Aretino, disc, orig gr mg horn, 3" center spindle.....................750.00
Bing Kiddyphone, disc, Bing rpd, cone horn, circular base.........250.00
Brunswick Queen Anne, console style, rpr motor, working........350.00
Busy Bee, disc, red mg horn..325.00
Cameraphone, disc, orig rpd, tortoise-shell resonator, oak.........550.00
Cheney Talking Machine, disc, walnut, floor model.................450.00
Chevy, mahog, floor model..200.00
Columbia AA, cyl, eagle rpd, blk horn, oak...........................1,000.00
Columbia AD, cyl, D rpd, brass bell horn..............................500.00
Columbia AH, disc, Columbia rpd, brass bell horn, no decal..1,000.00
Columbia AU, disc, from $450 to.......................................600.00
Columbia BF, cyl, 6" mandrel..600.00
Columbia BG, cyl, chrome bedplate, brass bell horn, mahog...1,650.00
Columbia BI Sterling, disc, Columbia rpd, oak horn..............2,250.00
Columbia BKT (New leader), cyl, Columbia rpd, maroon mg horn.2,400.00
Columbia Eagle B, cyl, nickel horn....................................425.00
Columbia Graphophone AB, w/concert cyls & salon mandrel, rpl horn.2,250.00
Columbia Graphophone BE, cyl, lyre rpd, orig brass bell horn...600.00
Columbia Graphophone K, red & gold, disc, w/brass bell horn...1,150.00
Columbia Q, cyl, w/case, nickel horn..................................375.00
Columbia Q, cyl, 2-min, rstr, rpd, EX japanning/label, rpl horn.675.00
Columbia Regent Desk, disc, Columbia rpd, inside horn, mahog..400.00
Columbia 20th Century BC, cyl, 54" brass horn, floor model crane.1,600.00
Edison Amberola VI, cyl, mahog case...................................325.00
Edison Amberola 30, cyl, Dmn C rpd, inside horn, oak..............375.00
Edison Amberola 75, cyl, mahog floor model...........................550.00
Edison Business C, table model...175.00

Edison Concert C, cyl, R pd, 30" brass bell, floor stand, M 2,500.00
Edison Dmn Disc A-100, DD rpd, inside horn, Moderne golden oak.350.00
Edison Dmn Disc A-100, oak floor model...................................200.00
Edison Dmn Disc C-19, floor model...250.00
Edison Dmn Disc C-150, oak floor model..................................275.00
Edison Fireside A, cyl, Dmn B rpd, oak Music Master horn 2,250.00
Edison Fireside A, cyl, K rpd, maroon horn/crane...................1,000.00
Edison Fireside B, cyl, cygnet horn, rare rpd, VG....................1,700.00
Edison Gem D Maroon, cyl, K rpd, 20" maroon horn..............1,800.00
Edison Home, cyl, 2-4 min, C rpd, brass bell horn 375.00
Edison Home A, cyl, C rpd, 14" blk/brass horn 500.00
Edison Home E, 2-4 min, O rpd, Edison Cygnet horn................950.00
Edison Home Suitcase, banner top, C rpd, 2-min, sm horn 650.00
Edison Opera, mahog case & Music Master Horn...................6,750.00
Edison Standard, cyl, 2-min, C rpd...375.00
Edison Standard, cyl, 2-4 min, C rpd, earphones......................475.00
Edison Standard, cyl, 2-4 min, Dmn B rpd.................................500.00
Edison Standard A Suitcase, Automatic rpd, rstr NP 750.00
Edison Standard D, cyl, K rpd, blk cygnet horn 1,000.00
Edison Standard Flat Top, cyl, VG..600.00
Edison Triumph, cyl, 2-4 min, C rpd, 3-spring motor, lg mg horn....900.00
Jeannette, disc, keywind, child's..65.00
Klingsor, disc, Klingsor rpd, inside horn, ldgl doors...............2,000.00
Melodograph, disc, CI, G..175.00
Peter Pan Graphophone, folding, leather-covered box, VG........110.00
Puck Lyre, cyl, floating, rpd, red mg horn 400.00
Silvertone, disc, oak table-top 150.00
Standard AA, rstr analyzing rpd, blk japanned base.................1,350.00
Standard Talking Machine X2, bl horn, 1906, VG......................450.00
Standard X, disc, lg mg horn..500.00
Thorens Excalda, disc, Excalda rpd, internal horn, camera type.265.00
Victor I, disc, brass bell horn 1,150.00
Victor I, disc, Exhibition rpd, repro brass bell, oak case...........1,000.00
Victor II, disc, Exhibition rpd, brass bell horn.......................1,200.00
Victor II, disc, Exhibition rpd, oak horn & case......................2,500.00
Victor II, humpback, disc, lg brass bell horn..........................1,500.00
Victor M, disc, brass bell horn..1,500.00
Victor P, disc, brass bell horn...1,200.00
Victor R, disc, blk horn..900.00
Victor R Royal, disc, Exhibition rpd, 9½" brass bell, oak........1,000.00
Victor V, disc, Exhibition soundbox, XL mg horn, NM rstr.....2,650.00
Victor V disc, quartersawn oak case, 24" blk & gold mg horn .3,795.00
Victor VV-XIA, disc, mahog table-top 275.00
Victor VV-215, console, disc...200.00
Victor Z, disc, Exhibition rpd, brass bell horn........................1,400.00
Vitaphone, disc, w/horn, minimum value 1,000.00
Zonophone, disc, front mt w/horn, from $1,000 to 3,000.00
Zonophone, disc, rear mt, oak, red petal horn.......................1,050.00
Zonophone Royal Grand, disc, lg NP horn..............................2,200.00

Photographica

Photographic collectibles include not only the cameras and equipment used to 'freeze' special moments in time but also the photographic images produced by a great variety of processes that have evolved since the daguerrean era of the mid-1800s. For the most part, good quality images have either maintained or increased in value. Poor quality examples (regardless of rarity) are not selling well. Interest in cameras and stereo equipment is down, and dealers report that average-priced items that were moving well are often completely overlooked. Though rare items always have a market, collectors seem to be buying only if they are bargain priced.

Our advisor for this category is John Hess; he is listed in the Directory under Massachusetts.

Albumens

These prints were very common during the nineteenth century. The term comes from the emulsion of silver salts and albumen that was used to coat the paper they were printed on.

Carlisle Indian Industry School class group, Chaote, 6¾x9".......125.00
NE str scene w/post office & store, 6x8½", VG 95.00
Palm trees, lg grouping, G Lekegian, 8x10¾" 27.50
Sphinx & pyramids, Bonfils, 9x11", mtd on brd 125.00
Ute man, seated studio pose, ca 1904, 7x5" 100.00
71st NY Am Guard enlisted soldier stands w/rifle, ca 1868, EX....70.00

Ambrotypes

An ambrotype is a type of photograph produced by an early wet-plate process whereby a faint negative image on glass is seen as positive when held against a dark background.

Half plate, man w/open book sits among 7 young ladies, EX in case..185.00
4th plate, couple w/2 daughters, 2 cats & pup, VG+.............350.00
4th plate, storefront w/sign & boy, VG+, +full case 200.00
4th plate, 2 sm boys (2 seated), EX in case........................95.00
6th plate, boy seated w/dog on floor, VG, +full case...............140.00
6th plate, boy w/swollen blk eye, wide-brim hat, EX in case.........65.00
6th plate, Civil War Union artilleryman in shell jacket, EX in case..48.00
6th plate, girl on rocking horse, HP details, VG in broken case ...85.00
9th plate, Civil War Union soldier, seated, thoughtful look, EX....50.00
9th plate, Gen George McClellan, bust, EX in case 265.00

Cabinet Photos

When the popularity of carte de visites began to wane in the 1880s, a new fascination developed for the cabinet card, a larger version measuring about 4½x6½". These photos were produced by a variety of methods. They remained popular until the turn of the century.

Boy on hobby horse, wide-brim straw hat, EX................65.00
Butcher in wht apron stands w/knife & hone, 6x4", VG+ 55.00
Chester A Arthur, Sarony, ca 1881, VG 30.00
Identified soldier (wht beard) stands w/musket, 1890s, EX...........40.00
Lady in blk w/jeweled brooch, 1890s, 4x6"............................10.00
Lumber men chopping huge redwood tree, VG 55.00
Man driving mule-pulled milk cart in CA, wht mt, VG................35.00
Man w/no legs seated in chair, fine clothes, EX 55.00
Middle-aged married couple, identified, 1880s.........................12.50
OH executions, 26 sm portraits of men w/details of crimes, 1907...165.00
Pawnee brave w/much jewelry/sash/apron/bw fringed leggings, 1889, EX ..150.00
Scranton PA police officer, stands in full uniform, EX.................65.00
Sisters (2) in fancy dresses beside Great Dane, 1890s, EX.............55.00
Wild west performer in full regalia, wht mt, G 200.00
Youthful man in suit w/mustache, ca 1890s.................................8.00

Cameras

Collectible high-quality cameras have become harder to find. Most of the pre-1900 examples will be found in the large format view cameras or studio camera types. There are quite a few of these that can be found in well-worn condition, but there is a large difference in value between an average-wear item and an excellent or mint-condition camera. It is rare indeed to find one of these early cameras in mint condition.

The types of cameras are generally classified as follows: large format, medium format, early folding and box types, 35 mm single-lens-reflex (SLR), 35mm rangefinders, twin-lens reflex (TLR), miniature or subminiature, novelty, and even a few others. Collectors may specialize in a type, a style, a time period, or even in high-quality examples of the same camera.

In the 1900 to 1940 period, large quantities of various makes of box cameras and folding bellows type cameras were produced by many manufacturers, and the popular 35mm camera was introduced in the 1930s. Most have low values because they were made in vast numbers, but mint-condition cameras are prized by collectors. In the 1930 to 1955 period, the 35mm rangefinders and the SLR's and TLR's became the cameras of choice. The most prized of these are the early German or Japanese rangefinders such as the Leica, Canon, or Nikon. Earlier, German optics were favored, but after WWII, Japanese cameras and optics rivaled and/or even exceeded the quality of many German optics.

Now there are thousands of different cameras to choose from, and collectors have many options when selecting categories. Quality is the major factor; values vary widely between an average-wear working camera and one in mint condition, or one still in the original box and unused. This brief list suggests average prices for good working cameras with average wear. The same camera in mint condition will be valued much higher, while one with excessive wear (scratches, dents, corrosion, poor optics, nonworking meters or rangefinders) may have little value.

Buying, selling, and trading of old and late vintage cameras on the Internet, both in direct transactions and via e-mail auctions, have affected the number of cameras that are available to collectors. As a result, values have fluctuated as well. Large numbers of old, mass-produced box cameras and folding cameras have been offered; many are in poor condition and have been put up for sale by persons who know nothing about quality. So in general, prices have dropped, and it is an excellent buyers' market at the present, except for the mint quality offerings. Many common models in poor to average condition can be bought for $1.00 to $10.00. The collector is advised to purchase only quality cameras that will enhance his collection.

Note: To date, no appreciable collectors' market has developed for most old movie cameras or projectors. The Polaroid type of camera has little value, although a few models are gaining in popularity among collectors, and values are expected to increase. Note that many fakes and copies have been made of several of the classic cameras such as the German Leica, and caution is advised in purchasing one of these cameras at a price too good to be true. Consult a specialist on high-priced classics if good reference material is not available. Our advisor for this category is Gene Cataldo; he is listed in the Directory under Alabama (e-mail: genecams@aol.com). SASE required for information by mail.

Agfa, Billy, 1930s...15.00
Agfa, box type, 1930-50, from $5 to.................................20.00
Agfa, Isolette..20.00
Agfa, Karat-35, 1940..35.00
Agfa, Optima, 1960s, from $15 to....................................35.00
Ahahiflex 1, 1st Japanese SLR...500.00
Aires, 35III, 1958...35.00
Alpha, Standard, 1946-52, Swiss..................................1,500.00
Ansco, Cadet..5.00
Ansco, Folding, Nr 1 to Nr 10, ea from $5 to.................30.00
Ansco, Memar, 1954-58..20.00
Ansco, Memo, 1927 type...100.00
Ansco, Speedex, Standard, 1950..15.00
Ansco, Super Speedex, 3.5 lens, 1953-58........................150.00
Argoflex, Seventy-five, TLR, 1949-58.................................7.00
Argus A2F, 1940, from $10 to..20.00
Argus C3, Black Brick type, 1940-50..................................8.00
Argus C4, 2.8 lens w/flash..30.00
Asahi Pentax, Original, 1957...200.00
Baldi, by Balda-Werk, 1930s..30.00
Bell & Howell Dial 35..40.00
Bell & Howell Foton, 1948, from $500 to........................700.00

Bolsey B2...20.00
Braun Paxette I, 1952..30.00
Burke & James, Cub, 1914...20.00
Canon A-1, from $100 to..130.00
Canon AE-1, from $40 to...80.00
Canon AE-1P, from $70 to...125.00
Canon F-1...225.00
Canon IIB, 1949-53..250.00
Canon III...250.00
Canon IV SB, rangefinder w/50/fl.8 lens, 1952-55, from $250 to..400.00
Canon J, 1939-44, from $4,000 to..................................5,000.00
Canon L-1, 1956-57..400.00
Canon P, 1958-61, from $250 to.......................................350.00

Canon P MVC-0015, from $200.00 to $350.00. (Photo courtesy C.E. Cataldo)

Canon Rangefinder IIF, ca 1954, from $200 to...............350.00
Canon S-II, 1947-49...375.00
Canon S-11, Seiki-Kogaku, 1946-47, from $600 to........800.00
Canon T-50, from $40 to..65.00
Canon TL, from $40 to...60.00
Canon TX...40.00
Canon VT, 1956-57, from $250 to.....................................300.00
Canon 7, 1961-64, from $300 to.......................................450.00
Canonet QL1, from $25 to..40.00
Ciroflex TLR, 1940s...30.00
Compass Camera, 1938, from $1,000 to........................1,300.00
Conley, 4x5 Folding Plate, 1905, from $90 to.................140.00
Contessa 35, 1950-55, from $100 to.................................150.00
Contex II or III, 1936, from $200 to.................................400.00
Detrola Model D, Detroit Corp, 1938-40...........................20.00
Eastman Folding Brownie Six-20...12.00
Eastman Kodak Baby Brownie, Bakelite.............................10.00
Eastman Kodak Bantam, Art Deco, 1935-38......................35.00
Eastman Kodak Medalist, 1941-48, from $140 to............175.00
Eastman Kodak Retina II..60.00
Eastman Kodak Retina IIa..80.00
Eastman Kodak Retina IIIc, from $125 to.........................180.00
Eastman Kodak Retina IIIC, from $250 to........................375.00
Eastman Kodak Retinette, various models, ea from $20 to....50.00
Eastman Kodak Signet 35...20.00
Eastman Kodak Signet 80...50.00
Eastman Kodak 35, 1940-51..25.00
Eastman Premo, many models exist, ea from $30 to.......200.00
Eastman View Camera, early 1900s, from $100 to..........200.00
Edinex, by Wirgen..30.00
Exakta II, 1949-50, from $100 to......................................130.00
Exakta VX, 195, from $75 to..85.00
FED 1, USSR, postwar, from $35 to....................................50.00
FED 1, USSR, prewar, from $70 to....................................120.00
Fujica AX-3...80.00
Fujica AX-5...125.00
Fujica ST-701..60.00

Graflex Pacemaker Crown Graphic, various szs, ea from $80 to .**150.00**
Graflex Speed Graphic, various szs, ea from $100 to **200.00**
Hasselblad 1000F, 1952-57, from $350 to.....................................**550.00**
Herbert-George, Donald Duck, 1946.......................................**35.00**
Kodak No 2 Folding Pocket Brownie, 1904-07 ....**25.00**
Konica Autoreflex TC, various models, ea from $40 to................**70.00**
Konica FS-1..**60.00**
Konica III Rangefinder, 1956-59, from $90 to **110.00**
Kowa H, 1963-67...**25.00**
Leica II, 1963-67, from $250 to...**400.00**
Leica IID, 1932-38, from $250 to **400.00**
Leica IIIF, 1950-56, from $300 to **400.00**
Leica M3, 1954-56, from $500 to...**1,000.00**
Mamiya-Sekor 500TL, 1966..**20.00**
Mamiyaflex TLR, 1951, from $100 to **150.00**
Mercury Model II CX, 1945..**35.00**
Minolta Autocord, TLR..**100.00**
Minolta HiMatic Series, various models, ea from $10 to.........**25.00**
Minolta SR-7...**50.00**
Minolta SRT-101, from $40 to..**65.00**
Minolta SRT-202, from $50 to..**90.00**
Minolta X-700, from $100 to...**135.00**
Minolta XD-11, 1977..**140.00**
Minolta XG-1, ZG7, EX-9, XG-A, ea from $35 to **80.00**
Minolta 16, mini, various models, ea from $15 to.....................**30.00**
Minolta 35, early rangefinder models, 1947-50, ea from $250 to...**400.00**
Minox B, spy camera **125.00**
Miranda Automex II, 1963 ....**70.00**
Nikkormat (Nikon), various models, ea from $70 to...............**150.00**
Nikon EM, from $45 to..**75.00**
Nikon F, various finders & meters, ea from $150 to................**275.00**
Nikon FG...**115.00**
Nikon FM..**150.00**
Nikon S Rangefinder, 1951-54, from $350 to **700.00**
Nikon S2 Rangefinder, 1954-58, from $300 to **500.00**
Nikon S3 Rangefinder, 1958-60, from $500 to **1,200.00**
Olympus OM-1...**120.00**
Olympus OM-10...**60.00**
Olympus Pen EE, compact half-fr **35.00**
Olympus Pen F, compact half-fr SLR, from $150 to................**200.00**
Pax M3, 1957...**30.00**
Pentax K-1000, from $70 to..**90.00**
Pentax ME, from $50 to...**75.00**
Pentax Spotmatic, many models, ea from $40 to.....................**130.00**
Petri FT, FT-1000, FT-EE & similar models, ea **70.00**
Petri-7, 1961..**20.00**
Plaubel-Makina II, 1933-39..**200.00**
Polaroid, most models, ea from $5 to.......................................**10.00**
Polaroid SX-70...**35.00**
Polaroid 110, 110A, 110B, ea from $25 to................................**40.00**
Polaroid 180, 185, 190, 195, ea from $100 to **250.00**
Praktica FX, 1952-57...**30.00**
Praktica Super TL..**50.00**
Realist Stereo, 3.5 lens...**100.00**
Regula, King, fixed lens, various models, ea **25.00**
Regula, King, interchangable lens, various models, ea.............**75.00**
Ricoh Diacord 1, TLR, built-in meter, 1958 ....**75.00**
Ricoh Singlex, 1965, from $50 to..**80.00**
Rollei 35, mini, Singapore, from $100 to................................**175.00**
Rollei 35, mini Germany, 1966-70, from $175 to **275.00**
Rolleicord II, 1936-50, from $70 to **90.00**
Rolleiflex Automat, 1937 model **125.00**
Rolleiflex SL35M, 1978, from $75 to **100.00**
Rolleiflex 3.5E **300.00**

Samoca 35, 1950s...**25.00**
Sereco 4x5, Folding Plate, Sears, 1901, from $90 to..............**135.00**
Spartus Press Flash, 1939-50 ....**10.00**
Taron 35, 1955...**25.00**
Tessina, mini, from $300 to...**500.00**
Topcon Super D, 1963-74 ....**125.00**
Topcon Uni...**35.00**
Tower 45, Sears, w/Nikkor lens...**200.00**
Tower 50, Sears, w/Cassar lens...**20.00**
Univex-A, Univ Camera Co, 1933 ....**25.00**
Voightlander Bessa, various folding models, 1931-49, ea from $15 to...**35.00**
Voightlander Bessa, w/rangefinder, 1936 ....**140.00**
Voightlander Vitessa L, 1954, from $150 to **200.00**
Voightlander Vitessa T, 1957 ....**200.00**
Voightlander Vito II, 1950 ....**40.00**
Yashica A, TLR **40.00**
Yashica Electro-35, 1966..**25.00**
Yashica FX-70..**60.00**
Yashicamat 124G, TLR, from $150 to......................................**230.00**
Zeiss Baldur Box Tengor, Frontar lens, 1935, from $35 to..........**150.00**
Zeiss Ikokn Nettar, Folding Roll Film, various szs, ea from $20 to...**35.00**
Zeiss Ikon Juwell, 1927-39 ....**500.00**
Zeiss Ikon Super Ikonta B, 1937-56..**150.00**
Zenit A, USSR, from $20 to...**35.00**
Zorki, USSR, 1950-56, from $20 to...**40.00**
Zorki-4, USSR, Rangefinder, 1956-73......................................**50.00**

Carte De Visites

Among the many types of images collectible today are carte de visites, known as CDVs, which are 2¼" x 4" portraits printed on paper and produced in quantity. The CDV fad of the 1800s enticed the famous and the unknown alike to pose for these cards, which were circulated among the public to the extent that they became known as 'publics.' Note: A common portrait CDV is worth only about 50¢ unless it carries a revenue stamp on the back; those that do are valued at about $2.00 each.

Am Indians (3) in studio setting w/hand-tinting, ca 1875, EX **95.00**
Baby on pillow w/legs exposed, ca 1880s **12.50**
Bearded lady, Anthony, VG...**50.00**
Boy stands beside lg drum, early wht mt, no ID, EX **55.00**
Bust of man in suit, mutton-chop sideburns, Godkein...Neb, 1886 ..**12.00**
Carollton OH street scene, Gould & Baxter, ca 1870, VG **35.00**
Gentleman w/full beard, JE Scanlin, 1870s **13.00**
Lumbermen (2/well dressed) stand w/axes, no ID, VG.............**45.00**
Married couple w/sm boy, fine attire, San Francisco, 1880s...........**12.50**
Middle-aged lady w/sunken eyes, blk dress, 1870s.................**11.00**
Mr Charles Decker, 19 Yrs, 31", 45-lbs, VG..............................**35.00**
Native Am ship's pilot at wheel, Montreal, VG+ **125.00**
Niagara Falls, wide-angle winter scene, gold trim **45.00**
Youth seated in uniform-type suit & laced boots, 1880s **9.00**

Daguerreotypes

Among the many processes used to produce photographic images are the daguerreotypes (made on a plate of chemically treated silver-plated copper) — the most-valued examples being the 'whole' plate which measures 6½" x 8½". Other sizes include the 'half' plate, measuring 4½" x 5½", the 'quarter' plate at 3¼" x 4¼", the 'sixth' plate at 2¾" x 3¼", the 'ninth' at 2" x 2½", and the 'sixteenth' at 1⅜" x 1⅝". (Sizes may vary slightly, and some may have been altered by the photographer.)

Half-plate, 4 men w/sluice box & gold pans, rare, EX.............**9,200.00**
4th plate, church in New England, attached stables, EX in half case ...**365.00**

4th plate, portly man in vest coat, gold stickpin, 1850s, EX..........**70.00**
6th plate, Labrador retriever portrait, EX in full case **385.00**
6th plate, lady in Shaker-like bonnet, ca 1860s, EX in case **75.00**
6th plate, mother & baby girl, pk tinted, +full case.....................**100.00**
6th plate, postmortem of sm child wrapped in blanket, EX in case..**270.00**
6th plate, well-dressed mother w/sm boy holding apple, EX in full case ...**145.00**
6th plate, 2 boys hold hands, ea seated w/toy, +full case **225.00**
9th plate, Victorian lady seated w/hands in lap, EX in case...........**60.00**

Photos

Billiard parlor street scene w/men & women out front, 1900s, VG..**110.00**
Cedar shake mill scene w/people seated on shakes, D Kinsey, 13x11"...**155.00**
Fr Revolution scenes, photogravure, 9½x12¾"..............................**60.00**
Glacier Park, Bear Grass Logan Pass Hwy, tinted, McKay, 13½x12½"...**80.00**
Nude lady on couch wearing long necklace, 1920s era, 5½x3½"..**75.00**
Pottery Maker, Roland W Reed, Indian, color, 9x13", VG **450.00**
Race scene w/many types of motorcycles, 1910s-20s, 2¾x4⅝", EX...**75.00**
SS Arrow commuter ship (Lake Erie), 7x8½".............................**60.00**
Up the Cutbank, Roland W Reed, mtns/teepees, color, 9x13" ..**425.00**
Ute Chief Yo-Yo-Witz (Buckskin Charlie) w/2 sons, ca 1900, 10x8"..**145.00**
WWI hazing scene w/sailors in chains, blk/wht, 3¾x4¾"...........**265.00**

Stereoscopic Views

Stereo cards are photos made to be viewed through a device called a stereoscope. The glass stereo plates of the mid-1800s and photo prints produced in the darkroom are among the most valuable. In evaluating stereo views, the subject, date, and condition are all-important. Some views were printed over a thirty- to forty-year period; 'first generation' prices are far higher than later copies, made on cheap card stock with reprints or lithographs, rather than actual original photographs.

It is relatively easy to date an American stereo view by the color of the mount that was used, the style of the corners, etc. From about 1854 until the early 1860s, cards were either white, cream-colored, or glossy gray; shades of yellow and a dull gray followed. While the dull gray was used for a very short time, the yellow tones continued in use until the late 1860s. Red, green, violet, or blue cards are from the period between 1865 until about 1870. Until the late 1870s, corners were square; after that they were rounded off to prevent damage. Right now, quality stereo views are at a premium.

Cole Mine #8, miners at entrance, Kleckner, #164, 1860s, EX **55.00**
French Maid, CH White, 12-card series, ca 1902, EX complete ...**80.00**
Genessee Valley Stone Quary, Woodward #825, EX.....................**28.00**
Girl w/dog, PF Weil, NY, VG **10.00**
Jackson Iron Furnace, Brubaker #149, VG-................................**60.00**
Logging scene w/oxen in CA, RK Bovine, VG **28.00**
Los Angeles business buildings, TE Stanton, ca 1880, EX.............**95.00**
Maple Sugaring in VT, Anthony #193, VG **40.00**
Pittsburgh Lights Up for Edison, Keystone #32412, EX.................**35.00**
Prospectors on Allenkaket River, orange mt, #1366, EX **40.00**
Rock miners w/power drills in Butte MT, ca 1908 (early), VG+...**40.00**
Santa w/toys before fireplace, #284, ca 1861, VG+.......................**75.00**
Smoky View of OH River..., Keystone #23099, EX.......................**15.00**
Train Crossing Main Street, NH, close view, JC Kelly, VG...........**95.00**
Turkey at Nelson Ledges OH, WA Faze #47 & #48, pr **30.00**
Victoria Bridge construction workers in early stages, 1858, VG....**85.00**
Wagon scene in Pittsburgh PA, Underwood & Underwood, 1903 ..**20.00**
Wood Street, Pittsburgh PA, Union View #500, VG.....................**40.00**

Tintypes

Tintypes, contemporaries of ambrotypes, were produced on japanned iron and were not as easily damaged.

Full plate, Union officer with fancy hilt sword, $450.00.

(Photo courtesy Early American Historic Auctions)

Half plate, boy & girl w/sm cart pulled by goat, EX, +full case ...**150.00**
4th plate, couple in canoe, lg lake & mtn scene, Bar Harbor, EX.**80.00**
4th plate, man stands beside lg high-wheeler bicycle, EX **110.00**
4th plate, postmortem baby in christening gown on couch, EX..**175.00**
4th plate, postmortem scene of man laid on board, EX **275.00**
6th plate, baseball player w/hat, VG- **225.00**
6th plate, girl w/dog sleeping w/head in her lap, EX, +full case ..**135.00**
6th plate, hunter w/dog, shotguns/pouches, EX **115.00**
6th plate, identified TX Cavalry Confederate soldier, EX in case..**545.00**
6th plate, man holding lg Colt revolver, EX in copper fr/holder.**195.00**
6th plate, man on high-wheeler bicycle, EX, +full case...............**220.00**
6th plate, Union inlisted infantry man w/overcoat & Hardee hat, EX..**100.00**
6th plate, Union soldier w/sword & pistol, seated, EX **350.00**
6th plate, 4 NY firemen in uniforms & helmets, EX **215.00**

Union Cases

From the mid-1850s until about 1880, cases designed to house these early images were produced from a material known as thermoplastic, a man-made material with an appearance much like gutta percha. Its innovator was Samuel Peck, who used shellac and wood fibers to create a composition he called Union. Peck was part owner of the Scoville Company, makers of both papier-mâché and molded leather cases, and he used the company's existing dies to create his new line. Other companies (among them A.P. Critchlow & Company; Littlefield, Parsons & Company; and Holmes, Booth, & Hayden) soon duplicated his material and produced their own designs. Today's collectors may refer to cases made of this material as 'thermoplastic,' 'composition,' or 'hard cases,' but the term most often used is 'Union.' It is incorrect to refer to them as gutta percha cases.

Sizes may vary somewhat, but generally a 'whole' plate case measures 7" x 9⅛" to the outside edges, a 'half' plate 4⅞" x 6", a 'quarter' plate 3¾" x 4¾", a 'sixth' 3⅛" x 3⅝", a 'ninth' 2⅜" x 2⅞", and a 'sixteenth' 1¾" x 2". Clifford and Michele Krainik and Carl Walvoord have written a book, *Union Cases*, which we recommend for further study. Another source of information is *Nineteenth Century Photographic Cases and Wall Frames* by Paul Berg. Values are for examples in excellent condition unless noted otherwise.

Half plate, Geometrics, K-16, NM **275.00**
Half plate, WA Monument, K-4, couple ambrotype....................**450.00**
4th plate, Parting of Hafed & Hinda, K-35, VG.........................**200.00**
4th plate, Roger deCoverly & Gypsies Fortune, K-30 ....**125.00**
6th plate, Crossed Cannons & Liberty Cap, K-112, NM **200.00**
6th plate, Fireman Saving Child, K-118 ....**150.00**
6th plate, Geometrics/Scrolls, holds 2, Littlefield-Parsons, K-267 ....**90.00**
6th plate, Union & Constitution, K-373 ....**100.00**
9th plate, American Gothic, K-374..**50.00**
9th plate, Chess Players, R-41 variant, NM **90.00**
9th plate, Geometrics/Scrolls, Littlefield-Parsons, K-478 ....**50.00**

9th plate, Scroll, Constitution & Laws, R-76, G 125.00
9th plate (dbl), Children w/Toys, R-29 ....135.00
16th plate, Scroll, w/lady ambrotype, VG 45.00

Piano Babies

A familiar sight in Victorian parlors, piano babies languished atop shawl-covered pianos in a variety of poses: crawling, sitting, on their tummies, or on their backs playing with their toes. Some babies were nude, and some wore gowns. Sizes ranged from about 3" up to 12". The most famous manufacturer of these bisque darlings was the Heubach Brothers of Germany, who nearly always marked their product; see Heubach for listings. Watch for reproductions. These guidelines are excerpted from one of a series of informative doll books by Patsy Moyer, published by Collector Books. Values are for examples in excellent condition. See also Conta and Boehm.

Blk, bsk, 4", EX quality...475.00
Blk, bsk, 4", med quality, unmk 550.00
Blk, bsk, 5", EX quality...550.00
Blk, bsk, 8", EX quality...600.00
Blk, bsk, 8", med quality...400.00
Blk, bsk, 9", EX quality...465.00
Blk, bsk, 12", EX quality...600.00
Blk, bsk, 12", med quality...510.00
Blk, bsk, 14", EX quality...900.00
Blk, bsk, 16", EX quality...925.00
Blk, bsk, 16", med quality...950.00
Bsk, may not have pnt finish on bk, unmk, 4", med quality........310.00
Bsk, may not have pnt finish on bk, unmk, 8", med quality........275.00
Bsk, may not have pnt finish on bk, unmk, 12", med quality......350.00
Bsk, molded hair, unjtd, molded-on clothes, 4", EX quality 600.00
Bsk, molded hair, unjtd, molded-on clothes, 4", med quality 450.00
Bsk, molded hair, unjtd, molded-on clothes, 6", EX quality 675.00
Bsk, molded hair, unjtd, molded-on clothes, 8", EX quality 895.00
Bsk, molded hair, unjtd, molded-on clothes, 8", med quality 565.00
Bsk, molded hair, unjtd, molded-on clothes, 9", EX quality 700.00
Bsk, molded hair, unjtd, molded-on clothes, 12", EX quality 975.00
Bsk, molded hair, unjtd, molded-on clothes, 16", EX quality....1,125.00
Bsk, w/animal/pot/flowers/etc, 4", EX quality 525.00
Bsk, w/animal/pot/flowers/etc, 5", EX quality 565.00
Bsk, w/animal/pot/flowers/etc, 8", EX quality 595.00
Bsk, w/animal/pot/flowers/etc, 10", EX quality 625.00
Bsk, w/animal/pot/flowers/etc, 12", EX quality 800.00
Bsk, w/animal/pot/flowers/etc, 16", EX quality, minimum value ..1,125.00

Picasso Art Pottery

Pablo Picasso created some distinctive pottery during the 1940s, marking the ware with his signature.

Plate, abstract face, cobalt/wht on gr, cobalt border, #46, 10"..1,500.00
Sculpture, abstract figure in profile, ivory, Madoura ltd ed, 11½"..2,700.00
Vessel, lady's head figural, blk on wht semi-matt, 11¼x8¼" 3,500.00

Pickard

Founded in 1895 in Chicago, Illinois, the Pickard China Company was originally a decorating studio, importing china blanks from European manufacturers. Some of these early pieces bear the name of those companies as well as Pickard's. Trained artists decorated the wares with hand-painted studies of fruit, florals, birds, and scenics and often signed their work. In 1915 Pickard introduced a line of 24k gold over a dainty floral-etched ground design. In the 1930s they began to experiment with the idea of making their own ware and by 1938 had succeeded in developing a formula for fine translucent china. Since 1976 they have issued an annual limited edition Christmas plate. They are now located in Antioch, Illinois.

The company has used various marks. The earliest (1893 – 1894) was a double-circle mark, 'Edgerton Hand Painted' with 'Pickard' in the center. Variations of the double-circle mark (with 'Hand Painted China' replacing the Edgerton designation) were employed until 1915, each differing enough that collectors can usually pinpoint the date of manufacture within five years. Later marks included the crown mark, 'Pickard' on a gold maple leaf, and the current mark, the lion and shield. Work signed by Challinor, Marker, and Yeschek is especially valued by today's collectors. For further information we recommend *Collector's Encyclopedia of Pickard China* by Alan B. Reed, available from Collector Books.

Key: AOG — allover gold

Bonbon, Metallic Grapes, leaf shape, 1930-38, Bavaria blank, 7" 165.00
Bonbon, shell form, AOG ext/cream int, 1938-present, Pickard blank, 5" ..40.00
Bowl, Amaryllis & Etched Gold, Beutlich, 1905-10, Limoges blank, 10"..425.00
Bowl, Fisher Pansies & Raised Gold, Charlotte shape, 1905-10, 8" ..235.00
Bowl, Iris & Raised Gold w/Lustre, scalloped/ftd, 1903-05, 11"..575.00
Bowl, punch; Aura Mosaic, Corinthian shape, 1910-12, 10x10½" .3,400.00
Bowl, roses w/gold over-pnt whiplashes, Motsfelt, 1903-05, 6½" .100.00
Bowl, Yellow Iris Conventional, Beutlich, 1905-10, C&G blank, 9"..200.00
Butter tub, Encrusted Gold, 1912-22, Z&S Co Bavaria blank, 3-pc .130.00
Candlesticks, Iris Conventional, 1893-1903, Limoges blank, 8¾", pr.500.00
Candy dish, Crab Apple Blossoms, Leach, 1903-05, Haviland blank, 7" .90.00
Charger, floral sprays on wht, sgn J Sym, gold border, 1906-14...300.00
Charger, Leon Poppies, sgn Leon, 1903-05, JPL France blank, 13"..345.00
Chocolate pot, Raised Gold Daisy, 1905-10, 10¾" 300.00
Cigarette tray, Rose & Daisy, 2-compartment, w/pheasant finial, 6½" ..150.00
Compote, Lilum Ornatum, sgn Yeschek, ftd, 1912-18, 6¼" 275.00
Compote, poppies on glass w/gold, sgn Ross (Roessler, Carl), 1916-17"..225.00
Creamer & sugar bowl, Cyclamen, sgn RH, T&V Limoges blank ...200.00
Creamer & sugar bowl, Tomascheko Poppy Border, 1905-10, Limoges blank..200.00
Cruet, Crocus Conventional, 1903-05, 6¾" 350.00
Cup & saucer, demi; floral w/gold border, 1910-12, T&V Limoges blank....150.00
Cup & saucer, Iris Linear, sgn Lind, 1910-12 ....300.00
Cup & saucer, raspberries w/gold vines, 1903-05, crown over VB blank ..150.00
Cup & saucer, violets w/mc leaves, Sinclair, 1903-05, Limoges blank ...180.00
Ewer, floral, sgn Lind, gold hdl, 10", NM 550.00
Flower frog, Scarf Dancer, overall gold, 1930-38, Germany, 6"..225.00
Ginger jar, oval panel w/flowers on mottled bl, 1925-39, 12" 600.00
Hatpin holder, irises, Beutlich, 1905-10, 5" 300.00
Jam jar, Deserted Garden, J Nessy, 1912-18, hdls/lid 320.00
Jardiniere, lily pads on gold border, Schoner, 1905-10, 5x5".......325.00
Jug, Dorique, orange tree panels, 1903-05, T&V Limoges blank, 7¾" .425.00
Mayonnaise, Rose & Daisy AOG, flower form, w/ladle, 1930-38, Japan, 6".150.00
Mug, cherry spray w/gold, Bietler, 1903-05, Limoges blank, 6" ...375.00
Pin tray, flowers, Beutlich, 1905-10, 5¾" 30.00
Pitcher, berries & blossoms on maroon band, Michel, 1898-1903 mk, 5"..550.00
Pitcher, Dorique, Iris Conventional, 1898-1903, T&V Limoges blank, 7" .550.00
Pitcher, grapes on yel to maroon, 1903-05, AKD France blank, 8" ...425.00
Pitcher, lemonade; peaches on gr w/gold, 1903-05, CAC blank, 8" ..450.00
Pitcher, Rean Pink Mums, 1903-05, Limoges blank, 5¼" 300.00
Pitcher, 6-sided, bluebells on wht w/gold, 1910-12, 8¼" 500.00
Plate, Apple Blossom Bower, scalloped, 1903-05, Haviland blank, 8¾" .185.00
Plate, Butterfly, 1903-05, Limoges blank, 8¼" 235.00
Plate, chop; Autumn Border, sgn EF, 1903-05, CA France blank, 12½" ..275.00
Plate, Clover Blossoms & Honey Bee, 1903-05, AKD blank, 8¾" ..225.00
Plate, grape clusters on gold border, Challinor, 1903-05, 8¾".....165.00

Plate, Nasturtium Conventional, 1898-1903, AKD France blank, 8⅝"...**200.00**
Plate, poppies on cream, Challinor, 1903, Haviland blank, 8½" ...**200.00**
Plate, Tulip Moderne, sgn, 1898-1903, T&V Limoges blank, 8"...**200.00**
Platter, Cornflower & Royal Blue, Yeschek, 1905-10, 14x10".....**275.00**
Platter, mc grapes w/etched gold, 1905-10, T&V blank, 12¼" ...**300.00**
Shakers, currants w/allover gilt, sgn Osbourne, 3½", pr...............**55.00**
Sugar shaker, pansies on cream w/gold, 1905-10, 4¼" **135.00**
Tankard, Metallic Grapes, Hessler, 1903-05, 15" **1,100.00**
Tea set, Rose Garland Rococo, pot+cr/sug, 1898-1903, Germany blank, 6"...**600.00**
Trivet, Aura Argenta Linear, 1905-10, 6½" **75.00**
Vase, Arrow Root on gr lustre, cylindrical, 1905-10, 10¼" **350.00**
Vase, Calla Lily, sgn Marker, shouldered, 1905-10, 11" **525.00**
Vase, crab apples on gr, slim pierced rim, gold ft, 1905-10, 9½" .**300.00**
Vase, Japanese lady w/comb, cylindrical, 1903-05, Willets blank, 12" .**1,950.00**
Vase, Narcissus on dk gr, Post, 1903-05, #3660 blank, 8" **400.00**
Vase, Praying Muhammadan, Farrington, 1903-05, Bavaria blank, 13½"..**2,750.00**
Vase, St Bernard dog on shaded brn, teardrop shape, sgn, 1898-1903, 8"..**3,000.00**

Pickle Castors

Affluent Victorian homes seemed to have something for every purpose, and a pickle castor was not only an item of beauty but of practicality. American Victorian pickle castors can be found in old catalogs dating from the 1860s through the early 1900s. (Those featured in catalogs after 1900 were made by silver manufacturers that were not part of the International Silver Company which was formed in 1898 — for instance, Reed and Barton, Tufts, Pairpoint, and Benedict.)

Catalogs featured large selections to choose from, ranging from simple to ornate. Inserts could be clear or colored, pattern glass or art glass, molded or blown. Many of these molds and design were made by more than one company as they merged or as personnel took their designs with them from employer to employer. It is common to see the same insert in a variety of different frames and with different lids as viewed in these old catalogs.

Pickle castors are being reproduced today. Frames are being imported from Taiwan. New enameling is being applied to old jars; and new or old tumblers, vases, or spooners are sometimes used as jars in old original frames. The biggest giveaway in this latter scenario is that the replacement insert does not fit properly in the old frame. A good thing to remember is that old glass is not perfect glass.

In the listings below, the description prior to the semicolon refers to the jar (insert), and the remainder of the line describes the frame. Unless noted 'rstr' (restored), the silver plate is assumed to be in very good original condition. When tongs are present, they will be will be indicated. Glass jars are assumed to be in near-mint condition.

Our advisor for this category is Barbara Aaronson; she is listed in the Directory under California.

Key:
B — Brittania
R&B — Reed and Barton
SH&M — Simpson, Hall and Miller

Amber, Daisy & Button; SP floral openwork fr, +tongs...............**250.00**
Amber, dbl-pressed; SH&M SP fr, 12", +fork **475.00**
Amber, Heavy Paneled Finecut; SP fr, 11½", +fork & tongs **350.00**
Amberina, Invt T'print w/HP; rstr Empire Mfg Co fr, 10½"...**1,800.00**
Amberina, Invt T'print; rstr FB Rogers #419 fr, 10½"..............**1,500.00**
Amberina, Melon Rib/Invt T'print; rstr Wilcox #4662 fr, 12¼"...**2,000.00**
Bl, Cone, pug dog finial; rstr Rockford #630 fr, 12", EX **795.00**
Bl, Finecut; rstr Derby #112 fr w/pickles, 10¾"...........................**850.00**
Bl, Hobnail; rstr Rogers Smith #156 fr, 11".................................**850.00**
Bl, Invt T'print w/floral; rstr Meriden B #223 fr w/birds, 11¾"...**850.00**
Bl, Invt T'print w/floral; rstr Toronto #0212 fr, 11½" **850.00**
Bl, paneled w/floral; rstr Barbour #122 fr, 10½"........................**725.00**

Bl w/floral; rstr #23 fr w/ornate repoussé base, 12" **895.00**
Bl w/floral; rstr #263 fr, 10", EX+...**850.00**
Clear, Cupid & Venus, glass lid; Pairpoint gold-plated fr, 13", +tongs...**250.00**
Clear, emb Indians & buffalos; rstr R&B #0101 fr, 12¾"............**875.00**
Clear, Lorraine, Fostoria; rstr FB Rogers #499 fr, 10" **650.00**
Clear, paneled w/etched leaves; rstr LB #741 fan & flower fr, 11½"..**250.00**
Clear, paneled; rstr Meriden B #11 fr, 10¾"...............................**250.00**
Clear pressed floral insert; SP Victorian fr, w/tongs **225.00**
Clear pressed stork designs; ornate SP fr w/S-scroll hdl...............**135.00**
Clear, Sunken Daisy; rstr #64 fr **650.00**
Clear & frosted w/etched leaves; rstr SH&M #85 fr w/cherubs, 10½"...**850.00**
Clear etched, pheasant lid finial; rstr Wilcox #4610 fr, 10½" **595.00**
Clear frost w/floral; rstr Crescent #38 fr, 11" **950.00**
Clear Swirl; rstr #0181 fr w/filigree bird & leaves, 10½", EX+.....**250.00**
Clear w/emb birds; rstr R&B #1260 fr, 14", rpl fork **495.00**
Clear w/emb flowers; rstr R&B #1550 fr, 10½"...........................**325.00**
Clear w/etched decor; rstr Wm Rogers #480 fr, 10½"..................**550.00**
Clear w/etched panels, hinged lid; rstr Derby #125 fr, 15" **675.00**
Clear w/floral; rstr Poole #165 fr, 9" **650.00**
Cobalt lantern form; rstr SP fr, 10¼" **950.00**

Cranberry, Hobnail; marked silver-plated holder, $750.00; Cranberry, Inverted Thumbprint, with hand-painted floral; Homan frame, $650.00.

Cranberry, Invt T'print w/HP; rstr Meriden B #250 fr, 10" **775.00**
Cranberry, Invt T'print w/mc floral; Aurora SP fr, 11½"............**450.00**
Cranberry, Invt T'print w/mc floral; Rogers Smith & Co SP fr, +fork...**350.00**
Cranberry, Invt T'print; rstr Middletown #146 fr, 11½" **895.00**
Cranberry, Invt T'print; rstr SP fr, 10½" **550.00**
Cranberry, Mary Gregory boy; Meriden B #304 fr, 9¾" **1,500.00**
Cranberry (shaded), Ribbed Optic; SP fr, 12½".........................**550.00**
Cranberry Opal Swirl; ornate fr, 10½", +tongs...........................**300.00**
Cranberry w/coralene flowers; rstr Aurora #698 fr **695.00**
Cranberry w/daisies & scrolls, SP lid; mk Tufts fr **800.00**
Cranberry w/floral; Meriden B #97 fr **650.00**
Cranberry w/floral; rstr Adelphi #100 fr, 10½" **695.00**
Cranberry w/floral; rstr Derby #115 fr, 12¼"..............................**795.00**
Cranberry w/floral; rstr Derby #117 fr w/fans & butterfly, 11½" .**850.00**
Cranberry w/floral; rstr Derby #119 fr w/owl/fans/leaves, 12" **895.00**
Cranberry w/floral; rstr Meriden B #223 fr w/bird, 11¼"............**895.00**
Cranberry w/floral; rstr Meriden B #1394 fr w/cherubs...............**795.00**
Cranberry w/floral; rstr Tufts #2356 fr w/elephant's heads, 8" **850.00**
Cranberry w/floral: rstr Barbour #2319 fr w/pickle, 11¼", +tongs...**875.00**
Cranberry w/paneled sprigs; rstr Queen City #13018 fr, 10¼" **775.00**
Cranberry w/wht floral; Tufts SP fr, 14", +tongs **650.00**
Gr, Daisy & Button; rstr Meriden B #222 fr, 12½" **595.00**
Milk glass, Apple Blossom, pk & gr decor; SP fr, 10½", +tongs..**425.00**
Pigeon blood, paneled lantern; Crescent #4 fr **750.00**
Pigeon blood, Ribbed Optic; Lexington SP fr, 10", +fork...........**375.00**
Pk, MOP Dmn Quilt w/HP, butterfly finial; rstr Adelphi #18 fr, 12"..**2,400.00**
Purple slag; rstr Tufts #2361 fr w/pickles, 12" **1,100.00**
Rose & yel spatter, Leaf Mold; rstr Wm Rogers #452 fr, 10½"....**950.00**

Rubena w/floral; rstr #0666 SP fr.........................**775.00**
Ruby w/floral; Aurora #635 fr, EX, +fork **750.00**
Sapphire bl w/floral; Tufts SP fr..........................**525.00**
Vaseline, Hobnail; rstr Poole #157 fr, 11¼" **1,100.00**
Vaseline speckled, Reverse Swirl; rstr Wm Rogers #418 fr, 11¼" ..**950.00**
Wht satin w/sm florals, spherical; Benedict #574 oval fr.............**375.00**

Pie Birds

A pie bird or pie funnel (pie vent) is generally made of pottery, glazed inside and out. Most are 3" to 5" in height with arches at the base to allow steam to enter. The steam is then released through an exit hole at the top.

The English pie funnel was as tall as the special baking dish was deep and held the crust even with the dish's rim, thereby lifting the crust above the filling so it would stay crisp and firm. These dishes came in several different sizes, which accounts for the variances in the heights of the pie birds.

The first deviations from the basic funnels were produced in the mid-1930s to late 1940s: the Clarice Cliff (signed Midwinter or Newport) pie bird (reg. no. on white base) and the signed Nutbrown elephant. Shortly thereafter (1940s – 1960s), figures of bakers and colorful birds were created for additional visual baking fun. From the 1980s to present, many novelty pie vents have been added to the market for the enjoyment of both the baker and collector. These have been made by commercial (including Far East importers) and local enterprises in Canada, England, and the United States. A new category for the 1990s includes an array of holiday-related pie vents. Basic tip: Older pie vents were air-brushed, not hand-painted.

Incense burners (i.e., elephants and Oriental people), one-hole pepper shakers, dated brass toy bird whistle, egg timers (missing glass timer), and ring holders (i.e., elephant with clover on his tummy) should not be mistaken for pie vents.

Bear in gr jacket, w/hat & shoes, England, 4½"..............**55.00**
Bird, bl & wht on wht base, Royal Worcester, 2-pc, from $75 to..**90.00**
Bird, thin neck, Scotland, 1972, 4¼", from $75 to.......................**90.00**
Bird, wht w/pk & bl on bl base, Shawnee for Pillsbury, 5½".........**55.00**
Bird on nest, Artesian Galleries, copyright mk, 1950s, from $300 to...**350.00**
Bird w/gold beak, floral transfers on wht body, 4½", from $175 to...**200.00**
Bird w/2 heads, yel, Barn Pottery, England, 1985, from $65 to......**75.00**
Black chef, shiny blk & wht, 3¼"..**55.00**
Black clown holding pie, emb England on pants, 4½"..................**45.00**
Blackbird, wht head, teardrop eyes, Australia, from $40 to..........**60.00**
Bluebird on gr stand w/wht bib, Josef, from $195 to....................**210.00**
Bugs Bunny, made in California, 4"..**27.00**
Bumble bee, mc, California, 5"..**35.00**
Chef w/bl coat, wht hat, 1930-40s..**160.00**
Crow, blk, Made in England, 1950s-60s, 4¼"................................**55.00**
Cutie Pie, Josef (or Lorrie Design), hen in bonnet, from $125 to..**150.00**
Duck, long neck, maroon (hot rose), 5"..**75.00**
Eagle, mk Sunglow, golden color, from $75 to..............................**85.00**
Elephant, mk Nutbrown Pie Funnel MIE..., 3½"..........................**95.00**
Elephant on drum, solid pk base, mk CCC, from $325 to...........**350.00**
Fox in jacket, cap & tie, mc, emb England, 4"..............................**45.00**
Funnel, aluminum, England..**25.00**
Funnel, blk man steals pie from lady w/rolling pin, England, 3½" ...**65.00**
Funnel, Grimwade Perfection, 1909, from $90 to........................**110.00**
Funnel, pagoda, Gourmet Pie Cup, Reg No 69793......................**75.00**
Funnel, wheat stalk, brn, from $150 to..**175.00**
Gobbler's Mountain, Arkansas, solid colors, few made, 1994-95, $75 to....**125.00**
Half-bird, blk w/scalloped or triangular bottom, from $75 to......**100.00**
Lady badger w/bonnet & apron, mc, England, 3½".....................**55.00**
Mushroom, wht w/red dots, grass on stem, Susie Cooper, from $75 to...**80.00**
Patches, rose, yel, turq on wing, Morton, common, 5", from $25 to ..**30.00**

Pie Boy, gr sombreros on outfit, from $350 to............................**400.00**
Pie Duckling, bl, pk or yel, American Pottery Co, 5", from $55 to...**65.00**
Porky Pig, bl jacket, left arm out, 4¼"..**35.00**
Servex Chef, Australia, 1938, from $150 to..................................**165.00**
Welsh dragon, bronze, Creigiau Pottery, from $300 to **325.00**
Welsh lady, Cymru, from $75 to..**95.00**
3-fruits series, peach, apple & cherries, Japan, 2½", ea, $350 to .**400.00**

Pierce, Howard

William Manker, a well-known ceramist, hired Howard Pierce to work for him in 1938. After three years, Pierce opened a small studio of his own in LaVerne, California. Not wanting to compete with Manker, Pierce began designing miniature animal figures, some of which he made into jewelry. Today, his pewter brooches, depending on the type of animal portrayed, sell for as much as $275.00. Howard married, and he and his wife Ellen (Van Voorhis) opened a small studio in Claremont, California. In the early years, he used polyurethane to create animal figures — mostly roadrunners on bases, either standing or running; or birds on small, flat bases. Pierce quickly discovered that he was allergic to the material, so a very limited number of polyurethane pieces were ever produced; today these are highly collectible.

The materials used by Pierce during his long career were varied, probably to satisfy his curiosity and showcase his many talents. He experimentd with a Jasperware-type body, bronze, concrete, gold leaf, porcelain, Mt. St. Helens ash, and others. By November 1992, Pierce's health had continued to worsen, and he and Ellen destroyed all the molds they had created over the years. After that they produced smaller versions of earlier porcelain wares, and they developed a few new items as well.

Pierce died on February 28, 1994. Much of his work quickly appreciated in vlaue, and items not seen before appeared on the market.

For further information we recommend *Collector's Encyclopedia of Howard Pierce Porcelain* by our advisor, Darlene Hurst Dommel; she is listed in the Directory under Minnesota.

Bowl, blk w/bl drip, mk Pierce 1991, 4x6¼".................................**125.00**
Bowl, maroon w/gold int, unmk, 4x8½"..**125.00**
Creamer & sugar bowl, maroon w/wht drip, mk #1XS, open, 2".**100.00**
Cup, coffee; wht w/blk nudes motif, mk HP, 3", minimum value...**200.00**
Dish, tan, triangular, 8"...**80.00**
Figurine, arch w/Madonna & Child inside, blk ink stamp, 12 3¼" ..**175.00**
Figurine, bison, gray w/dk mane & head, unmk, 9"......................**175.00**
Figurine, bison, wht, blk ink stamp, 2½x3½"...............................**75.00**
Figurine, blk cat pr, mk Pierce 1965, 4"..**150.00**
Figurine, dachshund, blk ink stamp, 3¼x10"................................**100.00**
Figurine, dinosaur, off-wht, mk 1991, 5½x4½"..............................**100.00**
Figurine, dolphin riding wave, brn & blk w/orange highlights, 6x9"...**200.00**
Figurine, gazelle, brn, #100P, 11¼x4"...**125.00**
Figurine, giraffe, gold, unmk, rare, 14", minimum value..............**250.00**
Figurine, girl w/dog, cream w/brn highlights, blk ink stamp, 4½" .**75.00**
Figurine, horse, brn w/tan flying mane, blk ink stamp, 8½x7½".**150.00**
Figurine, monk, wht bsk, 9", minimum value................................**200.00**
Figurine, pelican, cream w/blk highlights, blk ink stamp, 7½"......**85.00**
Figurine, pigeon, wht w/blk highlights, blk ink stamp, 5¾"..........**75.00**
Figurine, raccoon, sgn Pierce 1991, 3¼x8½"...............................**100.00**
Figurine, rattlesnake, W shape, brn, 3x6"....................................**100.00**
Figurine, robin, blk w/orange breast, blk ink stamp, 4½x3½".......**75.00**
Figurine, skunk, blk w/wht bk, blk ink stamp, 5x6"......................**100.00**
Figurine, St Francis of Assisi w/lamb, wht, 5½", minimum value ..**300.00**
Figurine, tiger, stalking, blk ink stamp, 2x12", minimum value ..**300.00**
Figurine, 2 wht quail in tree, blk ink stamp, 9x3¼".....................**100.00**
Figurines, baby ducks, 1 head up, 1 head bk, unmk, 2½x3¼", pr..**35.00**
Figurines, seals, blk, mother (6x5½") & baby (2½x3¼")...........**125.00**

Flower arranger, St Francis of Assisi w/birds, unmk, 11½x6½"...**150.00**
Planter, bl w/pale bl border & 4 wht deer, 2½x9¾" **125.00**
Planter, gr w/wht deer nestled at side, #80P, 2½x10"....................**100.00**
Teapot, shepherd w/sheep in bl circle w/pale bl border, 6", +cr/sug..**200.00**
Vase, gr cornucopia shape w/wht fish insert, 8x7".........................**125.00**
Vase, gr w/girl walking dog insert, 6¼x5¼" **100.00**
Vase, wht w/blk etched nudes motif, unmk, 7", minimum value.**300.00**

Pietra-Dura

From the Italian Renaissance period, Pietra-Dura is a type of mosaic work used for plaques, table tops, frames, etc., that includes pieces of gemstones, mother-of-pearl, and the like.

Box, bird on flowering limb, Romanelli label, 6x4x2½", VG.................**400.00**
Plaque, rose & violets, mtd as hinged cover on fr, 3¼x2¼" **300.00**

Pigeon Blood

Pigeon blood glass, produced in the late 1800s, may be distinguished from other dark red glass by its distinctive orange tint.

Ewer, ornate gold floral, bird & butterfly, att Webb, 8" **200.00**
Lamp, oil; conical shade w/gold floral, repeated on font, 2-part, 8" .**625.00**
Tumbler, Hairpin, 3⅝x2¾" **45.00**
Water set, Bulging Loops, 9" pitcher w/clear hdl+6 tumblers......**550.00**

Pigeon Forge

Douglas J. Ferguson and Ernest Wilson started their small pottery in Pigeon Forge, Tennessee, in 1946. Using red-brown and gray locally dug clay and glazes which they themselves formulate, bowls, vases, and sculptures are produced there. Their primary target is the tourist trade. Note: 'PFP' in the listings indicates a 'Pigeon Forge Pottery' mark.

Bowl, bl w/dogwood floral, incurvate rim, PFP, 3x5½" **45.00**
Creamer & sugar bowl, wht w/brn drip, w/sugar lid, 2½", 3".........**30.00**
Creamer & sugar bowl, wht w/Lady's Slipper orchids, PFP............**40.00**
Ewer, wht w/brn drip glaze at top, Douglas Ferguson, 11".............**55.00**
Figurine, bear, brn, seated, resting on front paws, D Ferguson, 6¾" ..**85.00**
Figurine, bird, gray w/brn beak, PFP, 3¼" **85.00**
Figurine, bluejay, D Ferguson 1977/CC, 4¼x8½" **130.00**
Figurine, chipmunk, standing on hind legs, PFP D Ferguson, 4" ...**45.00**
Figurine, eagle, wht head w/lt brn feathers, on rock, Ferguson, 8¼" ...**165.00**
Figurine, Great Horned Owl, volcanic glaze, D Ferguson, 9" **135.00**
Figurine, mother bear on bk w/cub on her belly, brn, PFP, 4¼" **80.00**
Figurine, rabbit, tan, brn specks, 5x6"..**60.00**
Figurines, mother bear (sgn D Gerguson) & 2 cubs, blk, 4x6", 2½x4".**155.00**
Figurines, mother owl w/2 babies, wht & brn, sgn DF, 4½", 3", 2" .**90.00**
Mug, gray w/gr pine tree, PFP **35.00**
Plaque, owl decor, tan w/brn mks, D Ferguson, 12x6" top, 8" bottom...**85.00**
Tile, owl center, D Ferguson, 5½x5½" **65.00**
Vase, blk & wht specks, cylindrical neck, rough texture, 6"..........**65.00**
Vase, turq flambè on brn, trumpet neck, E Wilson, 4"..................**85.00**
Vase, wedding; dbl neck w/1 hdl above, blk w/wht specks, PFP, 8"..**45.00**

Pilkington

Founded in 1892 in Manchester, England, the Pilkington pottery experimented in wonderful lustre glazes that were so successful that when they were displayed at exhibition in 1904, they were met with critical acclaim. They soon attracted some of the best ceramic technicians and designers of the day who decorated the lustre ground with flowers, animals, and trees; some pieces were more elaborate with scenes of sailing ships and knights on horseback. Each artist signed his work with his personal monogram. Most pieces were dated and carried the company mark as well. After 1913 the company became known as Royal Lancastrian.

Their Lapis Ware line was introduced in the late 1920s, featuring intermingling tones of color under a matt glaze. Some pieces were very simply decorated while others were painted with designs of stylized leafage, scrolls, swirls, and stripes. The line continued into the '30s. Other pieces of this period were molded and carved with animals, leaves, etc., some of which were reminiscent of their earlier wares.

The company closed in 1938 but reopened in 1948. During this period their mark was a simple P within the outline of a petaled flower shape.

Paperweight, scarab form, lt bl matt, #2383, ca 1910, 3¾" **120.00**
Vase, deep red w/bl drips, depressions at shoulder, 11" **500.00**
Vase, emb foliage on gr matt w/brn flecks, ca 1910, 6¾x7½" **350.00**
Vase, emerald gr, rolled rim on vasiform body, #2089, 13⅜"....**1,000.00**
Vase, gr streaks on orange w/red crystalline, 1914-35, 9x5".........**200.00**
Vase, vertical leaves, gold-stone glaze, shouldered, 7"..................**550.00**

Pillin

Polia Pillin was born in Poland in 1909. She came to the U.S. as a teenager and showed an interest and talent for art, which she studied in Chicago. She married William Pillin, who was a poet and potter. They ultimately combined their talents and produced her very distinctive pottery from the 1950s to the mid-1980s. She died in 1993.

Polia Pillin won many prizes for her work, which is always signed Pillin with the loop of the 'P' over the full name. Some undecorated pieces are signed W&P, to indicate her husband's collaboration.

Her work is prized for its art, not for the shape of her pots, which for the most part are simple vases, dishes, bowl, and boxes. Wall plaques are rare. She pictured women with hair reminiscent of halos, girls, an occasional boy, horses, birds, and fish. After viewing a few of her pieces, her style is unmistakable. Some of her early work is very much like that of Picasso.

Her pieces are somewhat difficult to find, as all the work was done without outside help, and therefore limited in quantity. In the last few years, more and more people have become interested in her work, resulting in escalating prices. Our advisors for this category are Dolli and Wilfred Cohen; they are listed in the Directory under California.

Bowl, stylized horses, mc on mauve, 7⅛" **750.00**
Bowl, 2 women on brn, 6½x7½" **950.00**
Box, lady in wht robe, child in pk leotards, blk shirt, 5½x4"......**595.00**
Compote, frieze of lady's face on lt marigold w/turq wash, 5x6"..**650.00**
Dish, young girl, free-form, ca 1955, low, 5x4½" **495.00**
Dish, 2 full-length women, eliptical form, 17½" **2,100.00**
Goblet, bust portrait of lady, bl/gr/tan on brn, 9"........................**750.00**
Jug, blistered yel/brn gloss, 7¾x5½" **275.00**
Pendant, female portrait on marigold, 3¼x2½".............................**500.00**
Pendant, 4 songbirds, 3" H..**650.00**
Plaque, 5 dancers against gr wall, 15½" L **2,750.00**
Plate, lady w/chicken & birds, mc on bl, 8½"...............................**800.00**
Plate, lady w/3 birds, mc on bl, 10½" **1,400.00**
Tray, ballerinas, 3 in leotards/1 center front in wht tutu on bl, 9x9"...**950.00**
Tray, 2 women & bird, oval, 8½" L **925.00**
Vase, abstract fish (numerous), mc on bl, stick neck, 6"..............**600.00**
Vase, avocado gr over lt seaweed gr, onion base, can neck, 6½".**250.00**
Vase, birds, bulbous body, flared neck, ca 1955, 4¾" **350.00**
Vase, bust of lady/lg blk cat, U-form, 3½x2½".............................**665.00**

Vase, cat/rooster, trees/female dancers on marigold, 4½x3¾" **750.00**
Vase, chicken/horse/woman, bulbous w/stick neck, 8"................**800.00**
Vase, fish (9) on pastel sea, 6½x6"................................**495.00**
Vase, horse, dancer & lady w/violin, mc, ftd, 7x5" **700.00**
Vase, horses, charcoal/ochre on blk & gray mottled, 7x5", NM..**475.00**
Vase, horses (4), bulbous, 4"..**400.00**
Vase, ladies, mc on bl, rectangular, 9", NM..............................**850.00**
Vase, ladies (3) standing, cylindrical, blk metal base, 14⅛".....**1,115.00**
Vase, lady, various pastel-colored sqs as bkground, 6x4½"..........**625.00**
Vase, lady & birds/lady w/horse, bottle shape, 6½x2½" **550.00**
Vase, lady holding bird, 2nd bird beside; bk: lady, 6¾"...............**550.00**
Vase, lady/horse/goose on brn, 6¼x5", NM...............................**550.00**

Pin-Back Buttons

Buttons produced up to the early 1920s were made of a celluloid covering held in place by a ring (or collet) to the back of which a pin was secured. Manufacturers used these 'cellos' to advertise their products. Many were of exceptional quality in both color and design. Many buttons were produced in sets featuring a variety of subjects. These were given away by tobacco, chewing gum, and candy manufacturers, who often packed them with their product as premiums. Usually the name of the button maker or the product manufacturer was printed on a paper placed in the back of the button. Often these 'back papers' are still in place today. Much of the time the button maker's name was printed on the button's perimeter, and sometimes the copyright was added. Beginning in the 1920s, a large number of buttons were lithographed on tin; these are referred to as tin 'lithos.' Nearly all pin-back buttons are collected today for their advertising appeal or graphic design. There are countless categories to base a collection on.

The following listings contain non-political buttons representative of the many varieties you may find.

Values are for pin-backs in near-mint condition, unless noted otherwise. Our advisor for this category is Michael J. McQuillen; he is listed in the Directory under Indiana.

AF of L, Local 788, AA of Ser & MCE of A, 3-color, 1940, ¾".....**5.50**
AMACO Join the American Party, Am Gas, mc litho **15.00**
Annie Oakley Day, portrait, 1946, 1¼"+red & yel ribbon, EX ...**100.00**
Babe Ruth Champions, blk & wht, Parisian Novelty Co, M.........**50.00**
Batman logo, blk on wht, 2¼"..**6.00**
Brotherhood of RR Trainmen, mc, 1", EX................................**8.00**
Buick, letters on red, stylized shape, #302, NM.........................**40.00**
Clean-Up Week, Dutch girl cleaning, 1⅛", VG **10.00**

Donald Duck Jackets, Norwich Knitting Company, G, $100.00. (Photo courtesy David Longest & Michael Stern)

Dupont Infallible Shotgun Smokeless Powder, tin litho, 1", EX+ .**55.00**
Emmy, Kellogg's Pep pin, 1947, ¾"......................................**8.00**
Florida Vocal Association, cello, red/wht, 1950, EX **12.00**
Hamid's Million Dollar Pier, cello covered, 1930s?, 1½" **95.00**

Helen Keller & Annie Sullivan, sepia portrait, ⅞", EX **100.00**
Howdy Doody, blk/wht/red, NBC, 1960s, 3" **30.00**
I'm a Donut Dunker, man w/donut & coffee, cello, ⅞", EX **8.00**
Jeepster, red letters on silver-tone w/blk border, rectangular..........**12.50**
Maxwell in script letters, silver-tone & blk................................**15.00**
Merry Christmas Happy New Year, Santa mc portrait, ca 1910, 1¼" ..**32.00**
Mickey Mouse, cloth on metal, discolored, ⅞", EX **30.00**
PA State Sabbath School on wht Keystone image, tin litho, ⅞" **8.00**
Railway Car Men of America, blk & wht, 1953, 1", EX **7.00**
Rickenbacker Auto, M...**25.00**
Rin Tin Tin, blk & wht portrait, ¾", EX **10.00**
Roy Rogers & Trigger, w/red/wht bl ribbon, ca 1940s, EX **23.00**
Santa reading book: Good Girls/Good Boys, Smith Bridgman Co, 1¼" .**25.00**
Say No, Boone Hospital Center...Columbia, ca 1959, 1¾" **2.50**
Shirley Temple Fan Club, blk & wht portrait, 1940s, 1¼" **30.00**
Shoot Peters Shells, red shell, cello, ca 1901-10, ⅞" **35.00**
Sonja Henie, 1937 Twentieth Century-Fox...USA, cello, 1¼", EX...**30.00**
Teamsters Chauffeurs & Helpers 627, red/wht/blk, ca 1936, sm, EX ..**10.00**
Tokio Cigarettes, Blind I Can't See You, bl on wht, 1900s, ¾", EX...**36.00**
Tom & Jerry Sunbeam, red/wht/gray/blk, 1950s, 1¼" **23.00**
Tom Mix Decoder, Sheriff Mike Shaw, NO on bk, VG **18.00**
University of Notre Dame, bl & yel, 1¾", w/ribbon **10.00**
Vote for Red Lion the Motorist's Choice, Vitachrome, EX............**25.00**
War Savings Society, Ben Franklin portrait, mc, 1917, ⅝", EX......**15.00**
Watch the Leader, comical man, Geraghty...Chicago, ¾", EX **20.00**
Welcome Lindy & plane, red/wht/bl litho, 1¼", EX.....................**35.00**
Willies-Overland Auto, Bastian Bros...NY, WWI era, 1½", EX **40.00**

Pine Ridge

In the mid-1930s, the Bureau of Indian Affairs and the Work Progress Administration offered the Native Americans living on the Pine Ridge Indian Reservation in South Dakota a class in pottery making. Originally, Margaret Cable (director of the University of North Dakota ceramics department) was the instructor and Bruce Doyle was director. By the early 1950s, pottery production at the school was abandoned. In 1955 the equipment was purchased by Ella Irving, a student who had been highly involved with the class since the late 1930s. From then until it closed in the 1980s, Ella virtually ran the pot shop by herself.

The clay used in Pine Ridge pottery was red and the decoration reminiscent of early Indian pottery and beadwork designs. A variety of marks and labels were used. For more information we recommend *Collector's Encyclopedia of the Dakota Potteries* by our advisor, Darlene Hurst Dommel (Collector Books); she is listed in the Directory under Minnesota.

Basket, hanging; cream-colored geometrics on red, Woody, 5x7½" ..**300.00**
Bowl, cream-colored geometric on red, N Firethunder, 2x10" **350.00**
Bowl, deep bl gloss, Ramona W Knee, 2¾x4"...............................**75.00**
Jardiniere, flowing bl-gray on red, Cottier, mk Sioux Indian, 9¾" W .**500.00**
Vase, brn gloss, shouldered w/flared rim, SD-8 mk, 3½"...............**50.00**
Vase, coiled design, brn, SD-8 & bl seal, 3" **75.00**
Vase, cream-colored geometric decor on red, Cottier, 4".............**150.00**
Vase, gr gloss, bulbous w/stick neck, Woody, 9¼" **85.00**
Vase, gr gloss, flared rim, Talbot, 7" **75.00**
Vase, incised geometrics on speckled brn gloss, Cottier, 2¼x5½" ..**275.00**
Vase, sgraffito cream-colored geometrics on red, Cottier, 7¼x5"..**400.00**

Pink Paw Bears

These charming figural pieces are very similar to the Pink Pigs described in the following category. They were made in Germany during the same time frame. The cabbage green is identical; the bears themselves are whitish-gray with pink foot pads. You'll find some that are unmarked while others are marked 'Germany' or 'Made in Germany.' In theory, the unmarked bears are the oldest, made prior to 1890 when the McKinley Tariff Act required imports to be marked with the country of origin. Those marked 'Made In' were probably produced after the revision of the Act in 1914.

Our advisor for this category is Mary 'Tootsie' Hamburg; she is listed in the Directory under Illinois.

1 by bean pot	135.00
1 by graphophone	150.00
1 by honey pot	145.00
1 by top hat	125.00
1 in front of basket	135.00
1 in roadster (car identical to pk pig car)	225.00
1 on binoculars	175.00
1 peaking out of basket	135.00
1 sitting in wicker chair	150.00
2 in hot air balloon	175.00
2 in purse	165.00
2 in roadster	225.00
2 on pin dish	175.00
2 on pin dish w/bag of coins	145.00
2 peering in floor mirror	150.00
2 sitting by mushroom	135.00
2 standing in wash tub	150.00
3 in roadster	250.00
3 on pin dish	160.00

Pink Pigs

Pink Pigs on cabbage green were made in Germany around the turn of the century. They were sold as souvenirs in train depots, amusement parks, and gift shops. 'Action pigs' (those involved in some amusing activity) are the most valuable, and prices increase with the number of pigs. Though a similar type of figurine was made in white bisque, most serious collectors prefer only the pink ones. They are marked in two ways: 'Germany' in incised letters, and a black ink stamp 'Made in Germany' in a circle. The unmarked pigs are the oldest, made prior to 1890 when the McKinley Tariff Act required imports to be marked with the country of origin. Those marked 'Made In' were probably produced after the revision of the Act in 1914.

At this time three reproduction pieces have been found: a pig by an outhouse, one playing the piano, and one poking out of a large purse. These not difficult to spot because they are found in a rougher poor quality porcelain with darker green. Our advisor for this category is Mary 'Tootsie' Hamburg; she is listed in the Directory under Illinois.

1 at trough, gold trim, 4½", NM	80.00
1 beside lg pot emb Boston Baked Beans, match holder, 4" W	135.00
1 beside shoe	115.00
1 beside stump, camera around neck, toothpick holder	185.00
1 beside wastebasket	95.00
1 coming through gr fence, post at sides, open for flowers	125.00
1 driving touring car	185.00
1 holding binoculars w/case in bk, toothpick holder, 3" W	125.00
1 holding cup by fence	140.00
1 in case looking through binoculars	165.00
1 in Japanese submarine, Japan imp on both sides	125.00
1 on cushion chair w/fringe, 3"	195.00
1 on keg playing piano	225.00
1 pushing head through wooden gate	115.00
1 putting letter in mailbox	125.00

1 riding train, 4½"	225.00
1 sitting on log, mk Germany	135.00
1 standing in front of cracked open egg	135.00
1 w/basketweave cradle, gold trim, 3½" W	140.00
1 w/devil pulling on hose	200.00
1 w/hind leg held by lobster, 4½" W, EX	140.00
1 wearing chef's costume, holds frypan, w/basket	150.00
2, mother in tub gives baby a bottle, lamb looks on, 4x3½"	175.00
2, mother looks at baby in cradle, Hush-a-Bye-Baby..., old MIG mk	185.00
2, 1 at telephone booth, 1 inside, 4½"	165.00
2 at pump, bank, Good Old Annual, 3¾"	170.00
2 at pump & trough, 3¼" W	180.00
2 behind trough, unmk	95.00
2 coming out of woven basket, 3" W, EX	115.00
2 dancing, in top hat, tux & cane	175.00
2 in bed, Good Night on footboard, 4x3x2½"	145.00
2 in carriage	175.00
2 in purse	115.00
2 on basket, head raising lid, plaque on front	145.00
2 on cotton bale, 1 peers from hole, 1 over top	175.00
2 on seesaw on top of pouch bank	175.00
2 sitting at table playing card game 'Hearts'	225.00
2 under toadstool	125.00
2 w/accordion camera, tray, 4½" W	150.00
3, 1 on lg slipper playing banjo, 2 dancing on side	195.00
3 at trough, 4½" L	150.00
3 sm pigs behind oval trough, mk, 2¾x2½x1¾"	115.00
3 w/carriage, mother & 2 babies, Germany	195.00

Pisgah Forest

The Pisgah Forest Pottery was established in 1920 near Mount Pisgah in Arden, North Carolina, by Walter B. Stephen, who had worked in previous years at other locations in the state — Nonconnah and Skyland (the latter from 1913 until 1916). Stephen, who was born in the mountain region near Asheville, was known for his work in the Southern tradition. He produced skillfully executed wares exhibiting an amazing variety of techniques. He operated his business with only two helpers. Recognized today as his most outstanding accomplishment, his Cameo line was decorated by hand in the pate-sur-pate style (similar to Wedgwood Jasper) in such designs as Fiddler and Dog, Spinning Wheel, Covered Wagon, Buffalo Hunt, Mountain Cabin, Square Dancers, Indian Campfire, and Plowman. Stephen is known for other types of wares as well. His crystalline glaze is highly regarded by today's collectors.

At least nine different stamps mark his wares, several of which contain the outline of the potter at the wheel and 'Pisgah Forest.' Cameo is sometimes marked with a circle containing the line name and 'Long Pine, Arden, NC.' Two other marks may be more difficult to recognize: 1) a circle containing the outline of a pine tree, 'N.C.' to the left of the trunk and 'Pine Tree' on the other side; and 2) the letter 'P' with short uprights in the middle of the top and lower curves. Stephen died in 1961, but the work was continued by his associates. Our advisor for this category is R.J. Sayers; he is listed in the Directory under North Carolina.

Bowl, deer hunter cameo on olive, rose int, Stephen, 1957, 5⅝"	400.00
Creamer & sugar bowl, Cameo, wagon	600.00
Jug, aubergine wine, porc clay, 1951, 5"	40.00
Pitcher, turq crackle, rose int w/turq o/l, ca 1950, 5¾"	70.00
Tea set, Cameo, dancers & musicians, wht on Wedgwood bl, 4-pc	950.00
Vase, aqua gloss, slightly bulbous, 1927-28, 9⅛"	250.00
Vase, Cameo, Indian on horse/camp scene, olive on gr crackle, 8x6"	900.00
Vase, Cameo, wagon train/2 men on horse, lt gr/ivory, Stephen, 5x6"	450.00
Vase, cobalt, slightly bulbous, ca 1926-28, 6⅛"	275.00

Vase, crystalline, wht w/vertical gray streaks, shouldered, 6".......**180.00**
Vase, Ku, aubergine wine, waisted cylinder, Stephen, 1949, 7½" .**145.00**
Vase, mint crystalline on gr opaque, rose int, ca 1943, 6¾" **425.00**
Vase, purple, flared swollen form, Stephen, 9" **250.00**
Vase, Tobacco Spit Red, 1934, 9" **250.00**
Vase, wht w/wht crystalline, ovoid, ca 1939, 11" **400.00**

Pittsburgh Glass

As early as 1797, utility window glass and hollow ware were being produced in the Pittsburgh area. Coal had been found in abundance, and it was there that it was first used instead of wood to fuel the glass furnaces. Because of this, as many as 150 glass companies operated there at one time. However, most failed due to the economically disastrous effects of the War of 1812. By the mid-1850s those that remained were producing a wide range of flint glass items including pattern-molded and free-blown glass, cut and engraved wares, and pressed tableware patterns. Our advisor for this category is Mark Vuono; he is listed in the Directory under Connecticut.

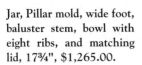

Jar, Pillar mold, wide foot, baluster stem, bowl with eight ribs, and matching lid, 17¾", $1,265.00.

Bowl, strawberry dmns & fan cuttings w/panels below, 4½x8¼"..**330.00**
Celery vase, paneled base w/cut dmns & fans, scalloped rim, 7¾" H .**260.00**
Compote, strawberry dmn & fan cuttings, sawtooth rim, 7½x9¾"..**440.00**
Decanter, cobalt, bulbous w/ribs, appl ring, flared rim, 7½" **110.00**
Syruper, Pillar mold, SP lid, annealing fracture, 10" **165.00**

Plastics

Plastic was invented in 1868. Since then, many types have been developed, each with unique characteristics and uses. Among the earliest, those most familiar to us today are celluloid and French ivory; they were commonly used to make toiletry articles. In the early years of the century, buttons were fashioned from Casein plastics, which could be made in a wide variety of colors and easily laminated and carved. The plastic jewelry that is so popular today had its heyday in the 1930s. The material used for its production was phenol formaldehyde. Two of the more recognizable tradenames for cast phenolics are Bakelite and Catalin. Buckles, buttons, radio and clock cases, cutlery handles, desk sets, and novelties were also made from this type of plastic. Vinyl and Lucite, acrylic resins, were used during the period between the two World Wars. There were many applications for vinyl, which is still commonly used. Lucite items that are particularly interesting to today's collectors are purses and jewelry.

Today's collectors have adopted the term Bakelite to encompass any type of phenoic resin. There are two methods of testing used to identify genuine

Bakelite: 1) using a cotton swab and Semichrome or 409, clean an inconspicuous area — oxidation on any color will tint the cotton ivory or light yellow; 2) hold the edge of item under very hot running water for at least twenty seconds; if it's genuine, it will smell like varnish or paint remover.

For more information we recommend *Celluloid Treasures of the Victorian Era* by Joan Van Patten and Elmer and Peggy Williams; and *Celluloid, Collector's Reference and Value Guide*, by Keith Lauer and Julie Robinson. All are published by Collector Books. See also Jewelry; Purses.

Bakelite/Catalin

Ashtray, marbleized lt gr, sq, 4½"..**30.00**
Bowl, red w/blk marbling, 2¼x8"..**45.00**
Buttons, card of 6, Scottie dog, fruit or cvd floral shapes..............**28.00**
Carving set, wood/Catalin hdls, Sheffield, MIB..............................**25.00**
Chopsticks, ivory, pr **5.00**
Cigarette holder, long, mc or w/rhinestones...................................**25.00**
Clock, Sessions, electric alarm, scalloped case, 4¼" dia **60.00**
Corn holder, Kob Knobs, dmn shape or lathe trn, 8 +box............**50.00**
Crib toy, bracelet, cylinders, discs & spheres on bead chain, EX...**45.00**
Crib toy, doll, blk body w/yel ball-hands & gr ball-ft, 7", EX......**150.00**
Dice, ivory or red, 2½", pr...**15.00**
Dominoes, ivory or blk, full set, w/wood box **40.00**
Flatware, boxed set: butterscotch/apple-juice, Englishtown, for 6, EX....**200.00**
Fruit knives & hdld holder, butterscotch/brn swirl w/yel accent, 6 for..**90.00**
Gavel, lathe trn, red, blk & ivory **35.00**
Inkwell, amber, Carvacraft Great Britian, single well **90.00**
Knife set & hdld holder, amber w/banded ivory tips, 6½", 6 for..**75.00**
Letter opener, blk & amber stripes, Deco design............................**20.00**
Memo pad, amber, Carvacraft Great Britain **55.00**
Nail brush, amber, octagon, Masso, 2" dia **9.00**
Napkin ring, animal or bird, no inlaid eye or ball on head, $60 to.**85.00**
Napkin ring, Mickey Mouse or Donald Duck shape w/decal, from $135 to..**170.00**
Napkin rings, amber swirl, set of 8...**30.00**
Napkin rings, ea a different color, 2" band, set of 6, +orig box......**40.00**
Pencil sharpener, airplane, gr, USA Army decals, 2⅞"..................**40.00**
Pencil sharpener, Alice in Wonderland decal on red, EX..............**35.00**
Pencil sharpener, Baby Hep decal, 1½" dia **55.00**
Pencil sharpener, Charlie McCarthy decal on red, figural, 1¾x1¼" ..**68.00**
Pencil sharpener, Donald Duck decal, EX **75.00**
Pencil sharpener, Joe Carrioca decal on gr swirl, 6-sided, 1½" dia ...**65.00**
Pencil sharpener, Mickey Mouse decal on red, 8-sided metal fr, 1¼" ..**135.00**
Pencil sharpener, Mickey Mouse decal on yel, 1930s, EX.............**85.00**
Pencil sharpener, orange, no decal, ¾x1" **8.00**
Pencil sharpener, Pluto decal on red, 1" dia **45.00**
Pencil sharpener, Popeye decal on red, figural................................**45.00**
Pencil sharpener, red mottle w/scalloped edge, no decal, 1⅛" dia.**30.00**
Pencil sharpener, Trylon & Perisphere, 1939 World's Fair.............**50.00**
Pencil sharpener, We Can Will Must Win, 1⅛" L **75.00**
Picture frame, amber & red Deco design, 6x7"...............................**45.00**
Pipe, amber & gr, bowl lined w/clay **30.00**
Poker chip rack, butterscotch, 4½x4x7½", w/8 stacks of chips, EX...**365.00**
Poker set, brn case w/screw-off lid & 190 mc chips, Count-Rite, EX ...**600.00**
Radio, Addison #5, lt gr w/maroon trim, EX **1,650.00**
Radio, Addison A2A, maroon & butterscotch, EX.................**1,250.00**
Radio, Bendix #526, bright gr swirl w/blk/wht/bl, non-working, EX...**800.00**
Radio, Bendix #526, gr swirl, 11" L, EX **550.00**
Radio, Crosley D-10GN, gr, VG...**210.00**
Radio, Crosley D-25 Dashboard, wht Bakelite, w/clock, NM......**240.00**
Radio, Crosley G-1456, butterscotch w/tortoise grill, rstr, M...**3,400.00**
Radio, Dewald A-502, butterscotch/orange, VG **500.00**
Radio, EKCo RS-3, brn Bakelite, EX **760.00**
Radio, Emerson #400, gr w/red louvres & wht inserts, 1942, VG+ ...**2,040.00**
Radio, Emerson #400 Aristocrat, brn w/yel marbling, rstr works, EX+.**1,450.00**

Radio, Fada #1000 Bullet, butterscotch, ca 1945, non-working, EX+ ..1,150.00
Radio, Fada #1000 Bullet, butterscotch (faded), VG 700.00
Radio, Fada #1000 Bullet, maroon/butterscotch, 1940s, EX 1,200.00
Radio, Fada #1000 Bullet, wht w/red trim, 1945, EX 1,700.00
Radio, Fada #115, butterscotch w/red trim, orig, EX 1,350.00
Radio, Fada #652, butterscotch w/clear swirl, 7x6x11" L, NM....700.00
Radio, Fada #652, maroon/butterscotch, NM 750.00
Radio, Fada #700 (Cloud), lime gr, EX..685.00
Radio, Firestone Air Chief S-7426-1, wht, 1939, VG 240.00
Radio, Fisk Radiolette, dk brn w/wht trim, 13x12x9", EX...........800.00
Radio, General Electric L-622 Jewel Box, red marbleized, EX .1,350.00
Radio, General Television #591, butterscotch w/wht trim, 6x9", NM.3,350.00
Radio, Globe, maroon, 1938, working, VG 1,450.00
Radio, Globe, yel w/tortoise vertical-bar grill, EX rstr.............2,200.00
Radio, Motorola #51-C, butterscotch marbled, 6x4x9" L, EX .1,450.00
Radio, RCA Nipper, swirled butterscotch w/red dial, EX.........2,050.00
Radio, RCA Nipper #9TX, gr marbled w/brn/red/wht/etc, 4x5x9", NM...4,200.00
Radio, RCA Victor, red w/tan swirls, 3-knob, 15" L, EX.............800.00
Radio, RCA Victor X-44, gr/wht marbled, 6x10", NM 450.00
Radio, Sentinel #195-ULTO, brn, 5 tubes, push button, ca 1939, EX...290.00
Radio, Sentinel #284, red/yel, NM..1,100.00
Radio, Sentinel #284-NA, dk butterscotch marbled/yel grill, EX..750.00
Radio, Sentinel #284-NI, butterscotch, 1945, VG 600.00
Radio, Sonora Coronet, orange/dk red, 6x5x9", VG 2,100.00
Radio, Truetone Boomerang D-2018, ivory, EX 340.00
Ring box, yel, 2 columns in front, Made in USA/Pat #, 1½x2⅞".20.00
Ring case, open-top style, amber, red or blk, Deco design 90.00
Roulette wheel, mc Catalin chips, wood pack, w/box, 1930s 200.00
Salad servers, chrome w/red, gr or amber hdls, pr 12.00
Shakers, butterscotch, 'Y' top w/'S' in 1 side, 'P' in other, 3" 20.00
Shakers, butterscotch, columnar w/flare at base, 3½", pr..............40.00
Shakers, butterscotch marbled w/silver checkerboard motif, 1⅝", pr ..85.00
Shakers, caramel/brn swirl bottoms/tops, ea w/1 flat side, 1⅝", pr ...55.00
Shakers, figure of Oriental w/pans ea end of shoulder pole, Rohac, 5" ..125.00
Shakers, gr, bbl shape on flat/ftd 4" L stand, Japan, pr.................125.00
Shakers, gr/butterscotch, mushroom shape, 1¾", pr 165.00
Shakers, gr/yel marbelized, ball shape, NM, 1½", pr.....................50.00
Shakers, red apple w/metal leaves & stem, 2½", pr.......................70.00
Shakers, red marbleized, ball shape, 1⅜", pr 100.00
Shakers, red or butterscotch, pr fits bk to bk on 1¾" rnd tray.......85.00
Shakers, various colors, W Germany, miniature, ½", set of 4......100.00
Shakers, wine/yel, 3-pc barbell, shaker ea end, 4⅛" L 125.00
Shakers, 1 butterscotch w/gr lid, other reversed, 3-tier, 2", pr.....175.00
Spatula, stainless w/red, gr or amber hdl..6.00
Steering wheel knob, amber w/inlaid Scottie dog on wht, 1⅞" .180.00
Swizzle stick, amber or red, baseball shape......................................5.00
Swizzle stick, butterscotch, star finial, 5¼".....................................30.00
Swizzle sticks, assorted styles/colors in case styled as a bar, VG...300.00
Table lighter, nude, pnt figure on bronze base, Dunhill...............165.00
Toast rack, gr/orange, 3" rings, 6½" L, NM 800.00
Writing set, blk, amber or gr marble, Deco, 5-pc, orig box..........175.00

Celluloid

Box, pale peach w/floral decals, velvet lined, 3-part 25.00
Brush & comb set, pk & bl floral, dots & lines, from $10 to.........12.00
Clock, mantel; ivory, marked Ivaleur USA, 6½x4¼", EX............150.00
Compact, w/beveled mirror, 3-tassel wrist cord w/lipsticks, 2" dia ..350.00
Fingernail set, buffer/powder holder, outlined in blk...................12.00
Jewelry box, piano shape, from $35 to 50.00
Pencil sharpener, Black bride, 2¼", from $75 to 85.00
Perfume-bottle holder, holds 3, 3½x2" dia 85.00
Photo album, floral w/Victorian girl vignette, 1890s, 10x8", EX.185.00
Rattle, Santa Claus figural, stamped USA, 3½" 270.00

Sewing tape, Indian figural, tape in base, 3", EX 310.00
Soap box, yel w/floral decor, rectangular, from $6 to......................8.00
Tape measure, cat's head, tongue as pull, 1½", EX.......................290.00
Tape measure, figural chicken w/chick on bk, 1½x1½", EX.......120.00
Tape measure, Porky Pig figural, playing violin, EX....................290.00
Toy, Santa driving train w/wreaths, wht w/red decor, 2½x5½", NM...**200.00**

Playing Cards

Playing cards can be an enjoyable way to trace the course of history. Knowledge of the art, literature, and politics of an era can be gleaned from a study of its playing cards. When royalty lost favor with the people, kings and queens were replaced by common people. During the periods of war, generals, officers, and soldiers were favored. In the United States, early examples had portraits of Washington and Adams as opposed to kings, Indian chiefs instead of jacks, and goddesses for queens.

Tarot cards were used in Europe during the 1300s as a game of chance, but in the eighteenth century they were used to predict the future and were regarded with great reverence.

The backs of cards were of no particular consequence until the 1890s. The marble design used by the French during the late 1800s and the colored wood-cut patterns of the Italians in the nineteenth century are among the first attempts at decoration. Later the English used cards printed with portraits of royalty. Eventually cards were decorated with a broad range of subjects from reproductions of fine art to advertising.

Although playing cards are now popular collectibles, prices are still relatively low. Complete decks of cards printed earlier than the first postage stamp can still be purchased for less than $100.00. In the listings that follow, decks are without boxes unless the box is specifically mentioned. Information concerning the American Antique Deck Collectors Club, 52 Plus Joker, may be found in the Directory under Clubs, Newsletters, and Catalogs.

Key:
AC — ad card	SC — score card
C — complete	std — standard
cts — courts	ws — wide scenic
J — joker	XC — extra card

Advertising

Alexandre Tailoring, Deco building, 1940s, 52+J, EXIB................**24.00**
Badger Tractor Parts...WI, Remembrance, Redi-Slip finish, 52, EXIB ..**22.00**
Camel Presents the Hard Pack, USPC, Printed in Canada, M, sealed...**8.00**
Cir-Q-Lar, rnd w/geometric designs, Waddington 741-945, MIB..**46.00**
Cobb's...Fine Foods..., red (or bl) & gold on wht, 1950s, dbl deck, EX...**25.00**
Independence Safety Match, Independence Hall in Phila on bks, EXIB...**50.00**
Marlboro man, on red or blk, dbl deck, MIB.................................**18.00**
McHenry State Bank Est 1906, 52+J, MIB......................................**7.00**
Mobil Oil, red Pegasus before moon in bl sky, 52+J, EXIB.............**22.00**
Nat'l Gasoline Corp, Remembrance, Brown & Bigelow, 52+2J, EXIB...**10.00**
Park Drive Cigarettes, gold & red on wht, 1930s-40s, EXIB **20.00**
Reddy Kilowatt, face on power plug, USPC, 52+4J+XC, MIB......**48.00**
Virginia Slims, You've Come a Long Way Baby, male jester J, EXIB...**15.00**

Souvenir

California, M Reider, 1907, 52+J+XC+booklet, MIB...................**65.00**
Gillette, Golden Horseshoe Club 1959, dbl deck, MIB, sealed...**145.00**
Great Southwest, F Harvey, aces show lookout, 1910, 52+J+map, EXIB..**95.00**
Jeffersons' silhouettes & info on Monticello, bridge deck, MIB **29.00**
NY City, USPC, Liberty bks, oval views, 52 of 52+J, VG, G box.**20.00**
Ocean to Ocean, Goodall, 1905, 52+J+XC, NM............................**15.00**

Rocky Mountain Souvenir..Tom Jones, c 1899, 52+2J, EXIB **224.00**
US Capital bks, linen, 10¢ tax stamp, MIB..................................**15.00**

Transportation

Air New Zealand, Goofy in spaceship bks, EXIB **20.00**
American Airlines, red & bl As with bl eagle, MIB, sealed **12.50**
Delta Airlines, New York, scenic bks, M, sealed **15.00**
Farrell Lines...Africa, shipping scene bks, ca 1960s, dbl deck, EXIB..**39.00**
Happy Families, ships & histories on bks, Austria, 1970s, 27 in case.**20.00**
Monarch, Shaw Savill ocean liner built in 1930s, 52+J, EX, no box.**30.00**
Port Line Shipping, ship scene bks, MIB..................................**25.00**
Quantas, red dmn shapes on wht, 1960s-70s, EXIB **20.00**
SAS Airline, wht on bl, MIB, sealed **5.00**
Sitmar Line on red (or bl), ca 1970s, dbl deck, MIB, sealed..........**35.00**
Union Steam Ship Shipping Line, TEV Maori ship portrait bks, 52, EXIB..**35.00**
Western Airlines, Ws in grid, red & wht, MIB **15.00**

Miscellaneous

Brunette w/dogs in bicycle basket, Congress, 104+2J, EXIB..........**28.00**
Cowgirl on horse, Pera Crowell, dbl deck, NMIB..................**12.00**
Daughters of Penelope (fraternal group), 52+J, EXIB **9.00**
Deco-style fruit bks, 104+2J, M, sealed......................................**15.00**
Florentine (fleur-de-lis) design, 52+4J, MIB................................**35.00**
Flying geese, Congress, 104 cards (no J), boxed set, G **15.00**
Hole In One bks, quotes on cards, 1975, EXIB **8.00**
HW Longfellow & RW Emerson homes on bks, Congress, 104+2J, EX+.**22.00**
Irish setter/spaniel bks, Whitman, dbl deck, NM in plastic box....**12.00**
King Arthur, Ferd-Piatnik & Sons, dbl deck, MIB........................**32.00**
Kittens w/flowers in paws on gr, Whitman No 8150, mini, EXIB.**12.00**
Ladies in Christmas evening gowns, Congress, dbl deck, NMIB...**10.00**
Lohengrin & Carmen bks, Hallmark, sgn Hans Van, dbl deck, MIB..**6.00**
Non-Violent Politically-Correct War, specially mk cards, MIB.....**10.00**
Nude beauties bks, Novelties Mfg, 1950s, 52+2J, NMIB................**20.00**
On Leash/On Promenade, flappers w/dogs, Congress, 1920s, dbl deck, NM...**38.00**
Poker Sympathy, dogs playing cards, Coolidge, GIB......................**27.00**
Rockwell, Summer/Spring, boy & girl scenes, dbl deck, M, sealed ..**18.00**
Scottie dog wht silhouette on blk ground w/wht dots, Gibson, NMIB.**30.00**
Silver & wht vines on maroon, Congress, dbl deck, EXIB **12.00**
Spaniel dog bks, Hoyle Stancraft, mini, 52+2J, NMIB..................**12.00**
Vegetable wreath on pk or yel, dbl deck, 104+J+bridge SC, NMIB...**12.00**
Vintage car in oval on red or bl, Duratone...ARRCo, dbl deck, MIB..**15.00**
Virgo Zodiac sign on bl bk, 52+J+XC, EXIB................................**12.50**

Political

Many of the most valuable political items are those from any period which relate to a political figure whose term was especially significant or marked by an important event or one whose personality was particularly colorful. Posters, ribbons, badges, photographs, and pin-back buttons are but a few examples of the items popular with collectors of political memorabilia.

Political campaign pin-back buttons were first mass produced and widely distributed in 1896 for the president-to-be William McKinley and for the first of three unsuccessful attempts by William Jennings Bryan. Pin-back buttons have been used during each presidential campaign ever since and are collected by many people. Some of the scarcest are those used in the presidential campaigns of John W. Davis in 1924 and James Cox in 1920.

Contributions to this category were made by Michael J. McQuillen, monthly columnist of *Political Parade*, which appears in *AntiqueWeek* newspapers; he is listed in the Directory under Indiana. Our advisor for this category is Paul J. Longo; he is listed under Massachusetts. See also Autographs; Broadsides; Historical Glass; Watch Fobs.

Arm band/sash, Woman Suffrage Party, stenciled ribbon, 19½x4", G.**1,450.00**
Badge, People's Party, brass shield w/emb letters/stars/bars, ¾" W.**165.00**
Bandana, Progressive - Roosevelt 1912 Battle Flag, red, 20" sq, EX.**150.00**
Bust, McKinley, blk-pnt plaster, 18½" on trn wooden base..........**75.00**
Campaign ballot, Hancock/English portraits, 1880, 6⅛x10⅛", VG...**75.00**
Campaign book, Facts To Fight w/for Wallace & New Party, 1948, 70-pg...**25.00**

Fan, first eleven American presidents in hand-tinted lithograph portraits, pierced ivory ribs, gilt decoration, VG, **$3,400.00.**

Flyer, Roosevelt/Truman/Downey, 4-pg, 1944, VG **50.00**
Hat, campaign; gray-bl cotton w/13 appl stars, 19th C, 8".......**1,400.00**
Leaflet, Debs for President, 4-pg, 1900, 5½x8", EX **60.00**
License plate attachment, Willkie...Hope of Our Country, 6½x11", EX ..**60.00**
LP record, The First Family (Kennedy), satire, 1962, VG **15.00**
March On Washington, hand in peace sign, mc, 1969, 25x18", EX ..**75.00**
Medal, commemorative, LA Troops under Maj Gen Z Taylor, silver.**5,000.00**
Oil painting, McCarthy for President, MB Edelson, 46x54", EX..**585.00**
Pass, People's Party Nat'l Convention, card stock, 1896, 3x6", EX..**150.00**
Postcard, Eisenhower photo & text, blk/wht, EX............................**15.00**
Postcard, image of ballot sending voters to Progressive line, 1912, EX..**120.00**
Postcard, real photo of women in suffrage parade, 1913, EX.......**250.00**
Postcard, Taft in public address photo, VG **15.00**
Poster, Back Ike's Team, red/bl on wht, 1946, 44x28", VG............**55.00**
Poster, Huey Long for FDR, heavy card stock, 1932, 17x11", EX..**500.00**
Poster, McGovern '72, silkscreened dove & peace symbol, 20x26", VG..**50.00**
Poster, Nixon & Agnew as cartoon bikers, blk & wht, 22x34", EX **100.00**
Poster, One World, McGovern/Shriver, sgn Burkhardt, 24½x18", EX..**35.00**
Poster, Smith/Robinson 1928 jugate, brn/wht, 25x19", VG **75.00**
Poster, Truman/Barkley photos, red/wht/bl, 1948, 27x20", EX **50.00**
Poster, Vice President Spiro Agnew dressed as Hippie, 30x21", VG ..**30.00**
Poster, Vote for JFK & LBJ, bl/red on wht, 1960, 44x28", EX **75.00**
Poster, Vote for Stevenson & Kefauver, red/wht/bl, 1956, 42x28", EX...**90.00**
Ribbon, Delegate, Cleveland, red w/brass hanger, 1936, 4½", EX.**85.00**
Ribbon, Freemont, Free Soil...Speech, Free Press, bl silk, 1856, EX..**165.00**
Ribbon, Ike & Dick They're for You, gold on bl, 1952, 6", EX **45.00**
Ribbon, National Convention People's Party, 1892 On to Washington, EX..**90.00**
Ribbon, People's Party Nat'l Convention Exec Committee, 1896, 9".**300.00**
Ribbon, Taft/Sherman jugate, red/wht/bl/blk, 5", EX....................**85.00**
Silk, Business Men's Garfield & Arthur Parade, 1880, 6½" **200.00**
Silk, Charles B Matthews for Governor, People's Party, 5½", VG ...**100.00**
Stick pin, Ulysses S Grant portrait in brass fr, 1868, orig pin......**190.00**
Textile, Wm Henry Harrison on wht charger+sm vignettes, in 38x28" fr..**1,850.00**
Ticket, Raise Less Corn & More Hall, ME Lease speech, 1894, 4½" L..**75.00**
Valentine, Love Me Love My Vote, suffragette, Clapsaddle, VG .**125.00**

Pin-back Buttons

All the Way w/Adlai, flasher, 2½"..**15.00**
Bella Abzug profile silhouette wearing hat, bl/wht, cello, 1¾"......**10.00**

Dewey, bl lettering on wht, 1" 5.00
Draft Eisenhower for President, portrait, red/wht/bl, 1¼" 25.00
Eisenhower Press Party, red on wht, 3⅛", VG+ 15.00
Equal Suffrage & 6 stars, bl on gold, ¾", EX+ 110.00
For Free Spain, map & raised fist, red/wht/bl, cello, ¾" dia, EX ...35.00
Ford For President, blk/wht portrait, red letters on wht, 1¼" 4.00
Franklin D Roosevelt a Gallant Leader, blk & wht portrait, ⅞" ...15.00
Goldwater, America's Choice, portrait, red/wht/bl, 1" 12.00
Goldwater, bl letters on wht arrow on red bkground, 1" 4.00
HHH, green letters on wht w/bl border, 1¼" 3.00
Hoosiers for Perot '92, red/wht/bl, 2¼" 2.00
Humphrey for Senator, red/wht/bl cello, 1954, 2¼", EX 42.00
I Like Ike & Dick above 3 stars, red/wht/bl, ⅞" 5.00
Jimmy Carter portrait on wht, 1976, 1½" 4.00
John Kennedy, blk/wht portrait, 3" 16.00
Johnson & Humphrey, wht letters on bl, blk/wht portraits, ⅞" 6.00
Keep Hope Alive, Jesse Jackson portrait & rainbow, mc, 1¾" 4.00
Let OH Women Vote, blk/charcoal on cream (scarce) cello, ¾", EX..990.00
Macbird, LBJ cartoon caricature, red on blk, 1½", VG+ 200.00
McGovern, red letters on red & yel stripes, 1972, 1½"...................4.00
McGovern 72, portrait, blk/wht/red, 3" 5.00
McKinley/Hobart jugate w/portraits, brn/wht cello, 1896, EX.......18.00
Mondale Ferraro, star & suggestion of flag, red/wht/bl, 1984, 1¾"..5.00
Nixon Drinks Ripple, bl on pk, cello, 1½" 10.00
On the Right Track w/Jack, red/wht/bl, 1¾", EX.........................38.00
Oscar W Underwood for President 1912, portrait, brn-tone cello, 1¾"..80.00
Peace Now, red/wht/bl/yel cello, ca 1969, 1½", EX.....................35.00
SNCC One Man One Vote, bl & wht cello, 1½", EX......................50.00
Stevenson, wht letters on red, blk/wht portrait, 1" 6.00
Stevenson Vote Democratic, portrait, 9", VG...............................75.00
Students for Dukakis '88, red/wht/bl/blk, 1¾" 3.00
Taft portrait, Whitehead & Hoag, 1908, 1¼", EX 55.00
Undecided, Nixon & Kennedy portraits on wht, 3½", EX.............35.00
Victory 1896 WJ Bryan, portrait, red/wht/blk cello, ⅞", VG+ 18.00
Vote Johnson, color portrait, flasher, 2½" 8.00
Vote Republican, Ike & Nixon (portraits), 3½", EX 22.00
Votes for Women, lav/cream/gr cello, Torsch & France Co, ¾"..425.00
Wallace for President Stand Up for America, portrait, red/wht/bl, 3" ...3.00
We Want Debs, red on cream, cello, Pilgrim Specialty, 1920, 1"...915.00
Willkie & McNary, red/wht/bl, ⅞" 5.00
WIN (Whip Inflation Now, Ford slogan), wht on red, 1¼" 2.00
Young Americans for Freedom, red/wht/bl/blk, 1960s, ⅞", EX........8.00
Zapata: Viva La Causa, bl on wht, cello, 1½", EX 15.00

Pomona

Pomona glass was patented in 1885 by the New England Glass Works. Its characteristics are an etched background of crystal lead glass often decorated with simple designs painted with metallic stains of amber or blue. The etching was first achieved by hand cutting through an acid resist. This method, called first ground, resulted in an uneven feather-like frost effect. Later, to cut production costs, the hand-cut process was discontinued in favor of an acid bath which effected an even frosting. This method is called second ground. Our advisors for this category are Betty and Clarence Maier; they are listed in the Directory under Pennsylvania.

Bowl, 1st ground, cylindrical, 3x4½" 275.00
Carafe, 2nd ground, cornflowers (wear), 9" 690.00
Celery vase, 2nd ground, gold on tightly crimped top, appl ft, 6½" ..200.00
Cruet, 2nd ground, cornflowers, w/clear stopper, 6½" 400.00
Finger bowl, 2nd ground, blueberries, crimped, 5", +underplate .485.00
Finger bowl, 2nd ground, cornflowers, 5¼" 185.00
Pickle castor, 2nd ground, cornflowers, rstr Meriden fr, 11¾" .1,800.00

Pitcher, 1st ground, cornflowers, sq top, 6¼" 550.00
Pitcher, 2nd ground, cornflowers, 5¾" 300.00
Punch cup, 2nd ground, cornflowers 110.00
Sugar bowl, 2nd ground, cornflowers, open, 2½x5½" 285.00
Toothpick holder, 2nd ground, gold-stained rigaree collar 425.00
Tumbler, 1st ground, cornflowers, 3⅝" 180.00
Tumbler, 2nd ground, no decor, 3⅝" 30.00
Vase, lily; 2nd ground, Optic Rib w/Dmn Quilt mouth, 10" 385.00

Porcelier

The Porcelier Manufacturing Company, originally in East Liverpool, Ohio, started business in the late 1920s and moved to Greensburg, Pennsylvania, in the early 1930s. The company flourished until the late 1940s and finally closed its doors in 1954.

They produced an endless line of vitrified porcelain products including electric appliances, coffee makers, and light fixtures. These products were sold in many stores under a variety of names and carried over ten different types of marks and labels.

The prices below are for items in excellent condition with no chips, cracks, or excessive wear. For more information, we recommend *Collector's Guide to Porcelier China* by our advisor for this category, Susan E. (Grindberg) Lynn. If you have any questions or information regarding Porcelier, you may contact Mrs. Lynn; she is listed in the Directory under Nevada. (Queries require SASE.)

Bean pot, ind; Basketweave Cameo 12.00
Beer set, Ringed (solid), 7-pc, from $185 to..............................260.00
Boiler, Oriental Deco, 6-cup or 8-cup, ea 65.00
Boiler, Spring, 6-cup, no pan..30.00
Canisters, Country Life, ea..35.00
Casserole, Basketweave Cameo, w/lid, 8½"...............................85.00
Ceiling fixture, single, rnd basketweave w/emb pnt flower stems..40.00
Coffeepot, Beehive Floral Spray, 6-cup.....................................35.00
Coffeepot, Colonial Silhouette, 6-cup, dbl................................75.00
Coffeepot, French Dip #566, 6-cup, decorated or undecorated 35.00
Coffeepot, French Drip; Cameo Silhouette, 6-cup.......................45.00
Coffeepot, Scalloped Wild Flowers, 6-cup.................................45.00
Coffeepot, Serv-All Line, platinum..35.00
Creamer & sugar bowl, Golden Fuchsia Platinum, ea..................20.00
Creamer & sugar bowl, Nautical, ea 35.00
Creamer & sugar bowl, Scalloped Wild Flowers, ea....................15.00
Decanter, Quilted Floral Cameo 40.00
Lamp, table; Antique Rose...45.00
Mug, pheasant, sailfish, dog or horse head, gold trim, ea.............40.00
Percolator, Antique Rose Deco..65.00
Percolator, Cattail 140.00
Percolator, Leaf & Shadow, short hdl.......................................85.00
Percolator, Scalloped Wild Flowers 110.00
Pitcher, batter; Barock-Colonial, ivory, red or bl, #2014 ....70.00
Pitcher, batter; Serv-All Line, gold or red/blk.............................40.00
Pitcher, hexagonal form, Field Flowers or Flower Pot, ea 55.00
Pretzel jar, Barock-Colonial, gold..95.00
Sandwich grill, Scalloped Wild Flowers, from $300 to 375.00
Shakers, #3020, any, ea...15.00
Teapot, Daisy Teardrop, gold trim, 4-cup 110.00
Teapot, Dogwood II, 4-cup, blk...55.00
Toaster, Scalloped Wild Flowers, from $900 to......................1,100.00
Toaster, Serv-All Line, gold or red/blk, #3002, from $1,000 to...1,200.00
Urn, Reversed Field Flowers Hostess or Platinum, ea 225.00
Urn, Silhouette Hostess..95.00
Waffle iron, Silhouette, from $185 to......................................225.00
Wall sconce, floral decal, w/fluted shade 47.00

Postcards

Postcards are often very difficult to evaluate, since so many factors must be considered — for instance the subject matter or the field of interest they represent. For example, a 1905 postcard of the White House in Washington D.C. may seem like a desirable card, but thousands were produced and sold to tourists who visited there, thus the market is saturated with this card, and there are few collectors to buy it. Value: less than $1.00. However, a particular view of small town of which only five hundred were printed could sell for far more, provided you find someone interested in the subject matter pictured on that card. Take as an example a view of the courthouse in Hillsville, Virginia. This card would appeal to those focusing on that locality or county as well as courthouse collectors. Value: $3.00.

The ability of the subject to withstand time is also a key factor when evaluating postcards. Again using the courthouse as an example, one built in 1900 and still standing in the 1950s has been photographed for fifty years, from possibly a hundred different angles. Compare that with one built in 1900 and replaced in 1908 due to a fire, and you can see how much more desirable a view of the latter would be. But only a specialist would be aware of the differences between these two examples.

Postcard dealers can very easily build up stocks numbering in the hundred thousands. Greeting and holiday cards are common and represent another area of collecting that appeals to an entirely different following than the view card. These types of cards range from heavily embossed designs to floral greetings and, of course, include the ever popular Santa Claus card. These were very popular from about 1900 until the 1920s, when postcard communication was the equivalent of today's quick phone call or e-mail. Because of the vast number of them printed, many have little if any value to a collector. For instance, a 1909 Easter card with tiny images or a common floral card of the same vintage, though almost one hundred years old, are virtually worthless. It's the cards with appeal and zest that command the higher prices. One with a beautiful Victorian woman in period clothing, her image filling up the entire card, could easily be worth $3.00 and up. Holiday cards designed for Easter, Valentine's Day, Thanksgiving, and Christmas are much more common than those for New Year's, St. Patrick's Day, the 4th of July, and Halloween. Generally, then, they're worthless; but depending on the artist, graphics, desirability, and eye appeal, this may not always be true. The signature of a famous artist will add significant value — conversely, an unknown artist's signature adds none.

In summary, the best way to evaluate your cards is to have a knowledgeable dealer look at them. For a list of dealers, send a SASE to the International Federation of Postcard Dealers, P.O. Box 1765, Manassas, VA 20108. Do not expect a dealer to price cards from a list or written description as this is not possible. For individual questions or evaluation by **photocopy (front and back)**, you may contact our advisor, Jeff Bradfield, 90 Main St., Dayton, VA 22821. You must include a SASE for a reply.

For more information we recommend *Collector's Guide to Postcards* by Jane Wood and *Vintage Postcards for the Holidays* by Robert and Claudette Reed (Collector Books).

Posters

Advertising posters by such French artists as Cheret and Toulouse-Lautrec were used as early as the mid-1800s. Color lithography spurred their popularity. Circus posters by the Strobridge Lithograph Co. are considered to be the finest in their field, though Gibson and Co. Litho, Erie Litho, and Enquirer Job Printing Co. printed fine examples as well. Posters by noted artists such as Mucha, Parrish, and Hohlwein bring high prices. Other considerations are good color, interesting subject matter and, of course, condition. The WWII posters listed below are among the

more expensive examples; 70% of those on the market bring less than $65.00. Values are for examples in excellent to near mint condition unless noted otherwise. See also Movie Memorabilia; Rock 'N Roll.

Advertising

Cycles Soleil, officer in blue in leisurely pursuit of poachers (on inferior bicycles), 49x35¾", EX, $1,150.00.

Johnnie Walker, Golf Open, 1987, 23x15½" 145.00
My Goodness My Guinness, soldiers, ca 1948, 11¾x8¼" 200.00
My Name Is Chambelle Peach Champagne, couple at car, 1955, 35x25"...250.00
Pawnee Bill's Buffalo Ranch Wild West Show, bright colors, 56x21", G ..90.00
Persian Export, lady at table w/lg bottle, ca 1935, 126x47" 1,200.00
Sanders Veal, calf at milk bucket, ca 1950, 31x23½" 400.00
Smith & Wesson, Last Stand, 1902, 14¾x14" 850.00
Third Annual Automobile Show, lady in open car, 1903, 42x32"...1,100.00

Circus

Key:
B&B — Barnum and Bailey   RB — Ringling Brothers

Arthur Bros, Buy War Bonds at bottom, EX 25.00
B&B, clown bowing & tipping hat, 24x33", EX 150.00
B&B, Freak Show people shown, 1960, EX................................ 20.00
B&B, tiger acts, 1915, 17x24", EX 1,000.00
Blackpool Tower Circus, clowns & acts listed, 1967, 40x24", EX .95.00
Century Bros Circus 41st Annual Tour, 1920s, VG+..................... 55.00
Clyde Beatty-Cole Bros, Captain Astronaut, 1960s, 28x21", EX .210.00
Clyde Beatty-Cole Bros, shows animals in ship, 1950s, 29x27", EX...140.00
Cole Bros, elephants, 1940s, 36x41", EX.................................. 175.00
Cooper Bros, clown face, Donaldson Litho Co, 1930s, 28x20", EX ..500.00
Cristini Bros, riding troupe, 1940s, 36½x21" 110.00
Cronin, lady rider on rearing horse behind big top, 1956s, 56x40", EX..115.00
Gentry Bros, Miss Hilton, horsebk rider, 1930s, 41x28", EX....... 185.00
Great Sells-Floto Circus, clown & circus acts, 1920s, 21x28", VG..465.00
Hamid Morton, horsebk rider w/clown, 1930s, 41x28", EX......... 215.00
King Bros & Cristini Combined Circus, parade scene, 1930s, 28x40", EX...270.00
RB B&B, clown on elephant's trunk, 28x29", EX 50.00
RB B&B, hippos in water, 1944, EX 40.00
RB B&B, inside big top scene, 1940s, 23½x41¾", EX 220.00
RB B&B, juggler, 1950s, 33½x20½", EX 215.00
RB B&B, leopard face, 1948, 42x28", EX.................................. 80.00
RB B&B, monkey act, Lawson Wood artwork, 1940s, 28x30", EX..135.00
RB B&B, rhino, 28x29", EX.. 35.00
RB B&B, 200 Years, elephant, unknown artist, ca 1975, 40x28"...175.00
Robbins Bros Circus, parade scene, 1940s, 27¾x41", EX 280.00
Russel Bros 3-Ring, circus scene, 1941, 36½x41", EX 160.00
Russel Bros 3-Ring, high wire artist, 1930s, 36x20", VG+ 165.00

Magic

Alexander, The Man Who Knows, red litho, ca 1920s, 28x40"..**350.00**
Carter the Great, Cheating the Gallows, 1926, 107x82", NM....**510.00**
Carter the Great, Modern Princess of Delphi, Otis Litho, 76x40"..**765.00**
Love Moods, Lili St Cyr, burlesque, 3-color, 1940s, 41x28" **200.00**
Nostradamus Jr, Argentina, ca 1940s, 29x43" **245.00**
Professor Alba, stands w/skeleton, linen bk, Spanish, 1959, 76x27".**495.00**

Theatrical

Chicago, Broadway Properties Ltd, 1977, 22x14", fr, NM **85.00**
Mary Martin as Peter Pan, Artcraft Litho, 1954, fr, 23x14½" **660.00**
Rose Marie, musical comedy, ca 1930, 78x40" **900.00**
Shakespeare, blk poodle center, Pean, ca 1899, 32x24" **1,600.00**
Zeigfield Follies, couple on street, Bacci, ca 1946, 20x15" **1,200.00**

Travel

Austria Invites You, lady by sea, Binder, 1930s, 37½x24½" **950.00**
Brion, polo player & lady golfer, 1937, 39x27", EX **295.00**
Brussels 7th Official Fair, Toussaint, ca 1926, 39x25½" **900.00**
East Coast, coast view, F Mason, N Eastern Ry/London, 1930s, 40x51"...**950.00**
Fly TWA, Greece, statue, Almabrotier, ca 1960, 40x25¼" **600.00**
Germany Wants To See You, building, Friese, 1930s, 30x20" **350.00**
Germany Wants To See You, lady w/flowers, Plessen, 1930s, 37x24", EX...**225.00**
Germany Wants To See You, Von Axster, 1930s, 29x19¾" **550.00**
Grace Line, map of Americas w/routes & liner, 1937, 42x38", EX.**450.00**
Holiday in Austria, cable car, Binder, 1930s, 37½x24½" **950.00**
Ireland Great Southern Rys, lake scene, Till, ca 1930, 30x40" ...**1,800.00**
Jamaica Calling You!, lady w/fruit basket, 1930s, 17x18", EX...**265.00**
Lido All the Way, Italian Line, Deco passengers, 1937, 36x24", NM..**700.00**
Lincolnshire, See Britain by Train, Steel, 1960, 40x25" **850.00**
Mediteranean Cruises, White Star Line, sphinx, unknown, 1930s, 26x14".**800.00**
Mexico, Mt Paricutin erupting, 1940s, 37x27", EX **600.00**
North Coast Limited in Montana Rockies, locomotive, 1930s, 40x30", EX..**385.00**
Paris, Arch de Triomphe, Falcucci, 1930s, 39x24", EX..................**295.00**
Polska, hunter w/wild cat, Norblin, 1930s, 39x24¾" **1,700.00**
South Devon, coast view, Newbould, 1930s, 40x50", NM **1,175.00**
Stratford Upon Avon, See Britain by Rail, Niecal, ca 1955, 40x25".**850.00**
World's Greatest Military Tatoo at Aldershot, Jones, 1930s, 30x20".**400.00**
Yankee Clippers Sail Again, Pan Am Airways, 1938-39, 25x20", EX.**295.00**
Zurich, atlas/man, unknown artist, ca 1960, 39x25½"..................**300.00**

War

WWI, Beat Back the Hun w/Liberty Bonds, Strothman, ca 1915, 30x20"...**450.00**
WWI, Before Sunset By...Bond, Statue of Liberty, DeLand, 1917, 30x20"..**440.00**
WWI, For Home & Country Victory Liberty Loan, soldier w/family, 30x20"..**440.00**
WWI, Join the Air Service & Serve in France, Verreel, 1917, 42x25", EX..**1,100.00**
WWI, My Daddy Bought Me a...Bond, girl w/red bow, 38¾x28¼"......**220.00**
WWI, Nat'l War Gardens, farmer w/vegetables, Enright, 30x23", EX.**200.00**
WWI, Our Daddy Is Fighting at the Front for You, children, 30x20" ..**330.00**
WWI, Remember the Flag, Buy US Savings Bonds, ca 1917, 30x20".**350.00**
WWI, Statue of Liberty before globe & flags, M Morgan, 40x30", EX..**1,150.00**
WWI, United War Work Campaign, girl w/biplane in hand, 40x30" ..**1,700.00**
WWI, United We Serve, tan letters w/red/wht/bl borders, 30x20", EX ..**55.00**
WWI, YMCA Workers Lend Your..., Gil Spear, 27¼x20", VG ..**110.00**
WWII, Back the Attack! Buy War Bonds, wht on gray, 20x28", NM..**65.00**
WWII, Beware of VD Don't Fraternize, bl/wht, 17x11", VG **70.00**
WWII, Give 'Em Both Barrels, 2 men w/machine guns, ca 1941, 15x20".**900.00**
WWII, I Want You FDR...Finish the Job!, Flagg, 1944, 26x22", rprs...**300.00**
WWII, Remember Me? I Was At Bataan, wht/brn, 28x21", VG+ .**50.00**
WWII, USA Bonds...Boy Scouts of Am..., Leyendecker, 30x20", EX..**220.00**

Pot Lids

Pot lids were pottery covers for containers that were used for hair dressing, potted meats, etc. The most common were decorated with colorful transfer prints under the glaze in a variety of themes, animal and scenic. The first and probably the largest company to manufacture these lids was F. & R. Pratt of Fenton, Staffordshire, established in the early 1800s. The name or initials of Jesse Austin, their designer, may sometimes be found on exceptional designs. Although few pot lids were made after the 1880s, the firm continued into the twentieth century.

American pot lids are very rare. Most have been dug up by collectors searching through sites of early gold rush mining towns in California.

In the following listings, all lids are transfer printed; the color(s) mentioned describe the transfer. Minor rim chips are expected and normally do not detract from listed values. When no condition is given, assume that the value is based on an example in such condition.

American

Bazin's Ambrosial Shaving Cream X Bazin, purple, 3¾", EX **200.00**
Burdell's Tooth Powder, San Francisco, mc, 3", NM....................**525.00**
Cold Cream of Roses...Newport, red, 2½", +pot...........................**150.00**
Dr Boutmar's Celebrated...San Francisco, mc, 3¼" **1,500.00**
Genuine Bear's Grease HP Wakelee...San Francisco, mc, 3", EX ..**700.00**
Improved Shaving Paste...Philadelphia, blk, 2⅝" **325.00**
Perfumers HP & WC Taylor...WA Crossing Delaware, blk, 3¾", EX.**200.00**
Saponaceous, E Phalon...Perfumer NY, girl/desk, blk, G **180.00**
Vinola...Shaving Soap for Sensitive Skins, brn, 3¼" **200.00**
Wright's Shaving Compound, man/mirror, blk, 4¼" **650.00**

English

Allied Generals, mc Pratt, 5", EX..**145.00**
Bear Pit, figures view bear, mc, ca late 1820s, EX **120.00**
Dog guarding baby in cradle, mc, 2½", +base **120.00**
Dr Ziemer's Toothpaste, Alexandra portrait, 3½", EX **300.00**
Fishermen at Sea, mc, 4¼", +base **110.00**
On Guard, man sleeping at guard shack, mc, 4⅛", NM **110.00**
Poultry Woman, lady dressing chicken, mc, Pratt, 4¼", +fr........**100.00**
Residence of Anne Hathaway...Shottery Nr Stratford, mc, 4" **100.00**
Salifrice...Tooth Paste W Martindale...London, blk/wht, 4x2½" ...**215.00**
Shakespeare's House Henley St..., mc, 4¼", +base **80.00**
Strasburg, village scene, mc, 4¾"...**145.00**
The Outs, man & bear seeking lodgings, 3", EX+.......................**550.00**
War, downed horse, mc, Pratt, 4", EX **130.00**
Waterfall, scene, mc, 4", EX...**100.00**
Woods Areca Nut Toothpaste, blk/wht, NM................................**30.00**

Powder Horns and Shot Flasks

Though powder horns had already been in use for hundreds of years, collectors usually focus on those made after the expansion of the United States westward in the very early 1800s. While some are basic and very simple, others were scrimshawed and highly polished. Especially nice carvings can quickly escalate the value of a horn that has survived intact to as high as $1,000.00 or more. Those with detailed maps, historical scenes, etc., bring even higher prices.

Metal flasks were introduced in the 1830s; by the middle of the century they were produced in quantity and at prices low enough that they became a viable alternative to the powder horn. Today's collector regards the smaller flasks as the more desirable and valuable, and those made for specific companies bring premium prices.

Flask, brass, Amelesk & Cap Co #8, emb game, VG **70.00**
Flask, brass, Ames, fouled anchor over USN ea side, EX+ **9,025.00**
Flask, brass, Batty, star & sunburst in oval, dtd 1848, G..............**150.00**
Flask, brass, Oak Leaf, G&JW Hawksley, 8", EX **100.00**
Flask, copper, eagle atop bugle & US, graduated spout, ca 1830.**400.00**
Flask, copper, emb horns & Public Property, VG.........................**200.00**
Flask, copper, unmk, 10", VG **100.00**
Flask, Hawksley, fluted bag shape, minor dents, 11" **135.00**
Flask, leather over brass, Sykes' Patent, 8", VG **35.00**
Horn, British coat of arms eng, ca 1812, 15"................................**660.00**
Horn, church/bird/ship/British crown eng, 1780s, 13½" **1,100.00**
Horn, fort/fox/animals/soldiers/name eng, 12" **1,100.00**
Horn, hunting scene eng (detailed), 1805, 12"........................**1,400.00**
Horn, lion & unicorn/owls/dbl-headed eagle eng, maple plug, 13" ..**990.00**
Horn, man shooting deer/buildings/dbl-headed eagle eng, 1760, 14½".**1,450.00**
Horn, old patina w/pnt robin & blk bird, brass spout, plug, 9" ...**165.00**
Horn, scenes & NE US locations eng, 11", VG...........................**450.00**
Horn, ship/buildings/flowers eng, name/1767, inscr plug, 13"..**1,500.00**

Pratt

Prattware has become a generic reference for a type of relief-mold-ed earthenware with polychrome decoration. Scenic motifs with figures were popular; sometimes captions were added. Jugs are most common, but teapots, tableware, even figurines were made. The term 'Pratt' refers to Wm. Pratt of Lane Delph, who is credited with making the first examples of this type, though similar wares were made later by other Staffordshire potters. Pot lids and other transfer wares marked Pratt were made in Fenton, Staffordshire, by F. & R. Pratt & Co. (See Pot Lids.)

Figurine, boy in red coat & yel knickers w/birds in nest, 7" **275.00**
Figurine, lioness, ochre & brn, 1790-1810, 3x4"...........................**450.00**
Figurine, Winter allegory, mc w/orange fur robe, rpr, 8¾"...........**110.00**
Pitcher, children in heart reserves, 5"..**375.00**
Pitcher, man drinking at table, 2nd smoking near horse, mc, 6".**495.00**
Pitcher, sailor's farewell & arrival, emb acanthus leaves, mc, 7" .**495.00**
Pitcher, tavern scenes, feather motif at spout/hdl, 9", VG **2,750.00**
Plate, Sebastopol, harbor scene w/camel & cart, mc, 9½"...........**100.00**
Teapot, classical motif, 1810-20s, sm rpr **295.00**

Precious Moments®

Known as 'America's Hummels,' Precious Moments® are a line of well-known collectibles created by Samuel J. Butcher and produced by Enesco, Inc. These pieces have endeared themselves to many because of the inspirational messages they portray. Over 300,000 club members have joined the national club since 1982.

The collection is twenty-six years old as of 2004. Each piece is produced with a different mark each year. This mark, not the date, is usually the link to the value of the piece. Most mold changes result in increased values, and when a piece is retired or suspended, its price increases as well. Items listed below are assumed to be in mint condition with the original box. For more information see *The Official Precious Moments® Collector's Guide to Figurines* by John and Malinda Bomm.

#E1372G, Jesus Loves Me, triangle mk, 1981...................................**50.00**
#E1374B, Praise the Lord Anyhow, triangle mk, 1981 ....**65.00**
#E1375B, Prayer Changes Things, hourglass mk, 1982 ....**100.00**
#E2345, May Your Christmas Be Cozy, hourglass mk, 1982...........**60.00**
#E2374, Bundle of Joy, hourglass mk, 1982 ....**80.00**
#E2821, You Have Touched So Many Hearts, fish mk, 1983 ....**50.00**
#E3117, Walking By Faith, hourglass mk, 1982 ....**60.00**

#E4723, Peace Amid the Storm, no mk, pre-1981.......................**80.00**
#E5200, Bear Ye One Another's Burdens, no mk, pre-1981 ....**80.00**

E7166, The Lord Bless You and Keep You, fish mark, $25.00.

#E9253, The End Is in Sight, hourglass mk, 1982..........................**60.00**
#E9258, We Are God's Workmanship, hourglass mk, 1982...........**40.00**
#E9261, Seek Ye the Lord, fish mk, 1983 ....**35.00**
#E9274, Taste & See That the Lord Is Good, fish mk, 1983 ....**45.00**
#E9285, If God Be For Us, Who Can Be Against Us?, fish mk, 1983...**70.00**
#PM841, God's Ray of Mercy, cross mk, 1984................................**40.00**
#PM842, Trust in the Lord, cross mk, 1984.....................................**50.00**
#PM861, Grandma's Prayer, olive branch mk, 1986 ....**50.00**
#PM862, I'm Following Jesus, olive branch mk, 1986 ....**50.00**
#102229, Worship the Lord, dove mk, 1985 ....**35.00**
#12149, Part of Me Wants To Be Good, cross mk, 1984 ....**65.00**
#12262, I Get a Bang Out of You, dove mk, 1985 ....**50.00**
#12459, Waddle I Do Without You?, dove mk, 1985.....................**80.00**

Primitives

Like the mouse that ate the grindstone, so has collectible interest in primitives increased, a little bit at a time, until demand is taking bites instead of nibbles into their availability. Although the term 'primitives' once referred to those survival essentials contrived by our American settlers, it has recently been expanded to include objects needed or desired by succeeding generations — items representing the cabin-'n-corn-patch existence as well as examples of life on larger farms and in towns. Through popular usage, it also respectfully covers what are actually 'country collectibles.'

From the 1600s into the latter 1800s, factories employed carvers, blacksmiths, and other artisans whose handwork contributed to turning out quality items. When buying, 'touchmarks,' a company's name and/or location and maker's or owner's initials, are exciting discoveries.

Primitives are uniquely individual. Following identical forms, results more often than not show typically personal ideas. Using this as a guide (combined with circumstances of age, condition, desire to own, etc.) should lead to a reasonably accurate evaluation. For items not listed, consult comparable examples. Authority Kathryn McNerney has compiled several lovely books on primitives and related topics: *Primitives, Our American Heritage; Blue and White Stoneware;* and *Antique Tools, Our American Heritage.* See also Butter Molds and Stamps; Boxes; Copper; Farm Collectibles; Fireplace Implements; Kitchen Collectibles; Molds; Tinware; Weaving; Woodenware; and Wrought Iron.

Barrel, oak & pine w/20 belted staves, old red, w/lid, 23x16" ..**1,750.00**
Barrel, oak w/gr pnt, staved, 39¼x18" dia at top **965.00**
Barrel, old brn pnt, staved, sq-head nails, sgn JB Grafton, 24"....**110.00**
Bedwarmer, brass pan w/eng sunburst, grpt trn hdl, 42" **300.00**

Bedwarmer, brass w/eng sunburst, copper rivets, trn walnut hdl, 42".250.00
Bedwarmer, brass w/eng tulips & leaves, trn birch hdl, 42" 235.00
Bedwarmer, copper, eng/pierced, trn apple wood hdl, 18th C, 46"..260.00
Bedwarmer, copper w/faint floral eng, trn hdl, 42½" 110.00
Bedwarmer, copper w/tooled birds/flowers/etc, trn hdl, 45" L......220.00
Bedwarmer, copper w/tooled floral, wood hdl, 12x45" 165.00
Bellows, rosemaling over mc on red w/gr edge, worn leather, 19"..500.00
Bucket, kerosene; brass faucet at base, wire bbl hdl, old pnt, 14"..85.00
Bucket, staved, grpt w/name in reserve, cvd wood hdl on bail, 9x8"...300.00
Bucket, sugar; bentwood wooden staves, slanted sides, 7x6" 415.00
Bucket, sugar; staved, copper tacks, salmon under dk gr, 12x11½" ..360.00
Bucket, sugar; staved, iron tacks, w/lid, old rfn, 9⅜x10¼" 165.00
Bucket, sugar; staved, old dk gr pnt, swing hdl, 10x12½" 360.00
Bucket, sugar; staved, old red wash, iron tacks, w/lid, 17" w/hdl.385.00
Bucket, sugar; staved, orig red wash, wht int, rprs, 9½x12¾" 115.00
Bucket, sugar; staved, salmon pnt over older gray, 12", VG 150.00
Bucket, sugar; staved, 1-finger bentwood bands, w/lid, 14½x15½"..440.00
Bucket, 2 iron bands w/iron tacks & copper staples, old gray pnt, 7"..525.00
Candle mold, pewter, 12-tube, dvtl pine case, 20x20x9" 935.00
Candle mold, pewter, 12-tube, walnut fr, 15x21x8" 1,375.00
Candle mold, pewter, 18-tube, poplar fr, sq nails, 14x21x7"........990.00
Candle mold, tin, 6-tube, conical ft, ear hdls, rprs, 12" 275.00
Candle mold, tin, 8-tube, curved ft, ear hdl, 11" 145.00
Candle mold, tin, 36-tube, cherry fr w/dk patina, 14x24x16"..1,550.00
Candle mold, tin, 50-tube, old dents, needs rpr, 11x15x7"..........220.00
Cheese mold, pegged staved bands, orig red pnt, 8½x14¼" 195.00
Churn, blk/red grpt w/wht scrolls, stencil 1858 label, w/lid, 34".450.00
Churn, staved, old red stain, piggin-type hdl, trn top, 36" 385.00
Cookie board, figures on horsebk (4), insect holes, 16x3½" 165.00
Cookie board, flowers & vines in heart, cherry wood, 8⅜x6½"..150.00
Cookie board, incised hearts, 4 stars w/OAG, att PA, 4¾x2¾"..165.00
Cookie board, king 1 side/queen on bk, split, 40x9x1¾" 440.00
Cookie board, 5 images, EX patina, worm holes, 24x3¾" 110.00
Cutlery tray, red wash, flared w/central divider & cut-out hdl, 14" L ...140.00
Cutlery tray, 3-color pnt, heart hdl, central date: 1873, 17" L....440.00
Footwarmer, tin panels w/punched hearts, red-stain wood fr, 6x9x8"..150.00
Footwarmer, tin w/punched hearts, wooden fr, bail hdl, 5¾x9x7½"...195.00
Keg, staved w/iron hoops, wrought-iron swing hdl, 10⅜"............350.00
Kraut cutter, curly maple, dvtl hopper w/pierced hdl, 42x12" 715.00
Kraut cutter, pine w/EX patina & red traces, worn, 19x7¾" 110.00
Kraut cutter, walnut w/EX patina, rnd crest over hanging hole, 25x7".21,500.00
Lamp oil filler, glass, teardrop shape, stopper w/acorn final, 5" ...850.00
Mitten stretchers, wooden, mid-19th C, 6¼x2¾" 100.00
Peel, curly maple, 1-pc w/short hdl, 27x15" dia 550.00
Quilt rack, birch, mortised, shaped shoe ft, rfn, 34x27½" 85.00
Quilt rack, cherry, H-shaped base, mortised posts, 33x33x14" 110.00
Quilt rack, mortised, dk gray-gr pnt, 3-part, 78½x48" 200.00
Rack, herb drying; pine w/old gray pnt, mortised, 3-part, 55x28"..200.00
Rack, herb; wire nails, old dry bl rpt, 48x36" 220.00
Sieve, bentwood, overlapping seam w/wire nails, mesh screen, 5x15"...150.00
Smoothing board, chip-cvd linear designs & medallions, 1801, 23" L.385.00
Smoothing board, dk bl w/red tulips, cvd horse hdl, 5x27" 195.00
Smoothing board, gr pnt w/red/wht trim, cvd horse hdl, 4x27"..160.00
Smoothing board, wormy chestnut w/rope-twist edge & vining tulips, 30"..300.00
Spice box, walnut, 6 units behind drw, 2 more under lift top, 9x11x6" .660.00
Stand, candle drying; maple/ash, red wash, X base w/4 arms, 20".375.00
Stocking stretchers, ca 1860s, 12", pr 80.00

Prints

The term 'print' may be defined today as almost any image printed on paper by any available method. Examples of collectible old 'prints' are Norman Rockwell magazine covers and Maxfield Parrish posters and calendars. 'Original print' refers to one achieved through the efforts of the artist or under his direct supervision. A 'reproduction' is a print produced by an accomplished print maker who reproduces another artist's print or original work. Thorough study is required on the part of the collector to recognize and appreciate the many variable factors to be considered in evaluating a print. Prices vary from one area of the country to another and are dependent upon new findings regarding the scarcity or abundance of prints as such information may arise. Although each collector of old prints may have their own varying criteria by which to judge condition, for those who deal only rarely in this area or newer collectors, a few guidelines may prove helpful. Staining, though unquestionably detrimental, is nearly always present in some degree and should be weighed against the rarity of the print. Professional cleaning should improve its appearance and at the same time help preserve it. Avoid tears that affect the image; minor margin tears are another matter, especially if the print is a rare one. Moderate 'foxing' (brown spots caused by mold or the fermentation of the rag content of old paper) and light stains from the old frames are not serious unless present in excess. Margin trimming was a common practice; but look for at least ½" to 1½" margins, depending on print size.

When no condition is indicated, the items listed below are assumed to be in very good to excellent condition. See also Nutting, Wallace; Parrish, Maxfield. See also *Collector's Value Guide to Early 20th Century American Prints* by Michael Ivankovich.

Audubon, John J.

Audubon is the best known of American and European wildlife artists. His first series of prints, 'Birds of America,' was produced by Robert Havell of London. They were printed on Whitman watermarked paper bearing dates of 1826 to 1838. The Octavo Edition of the same series was printed in seven editions, the first by J.T. Bowen under Audubon's direction. There were seven volumes of text and prints, each 10" x 7", the first five bearing the J.J. Audubon and J.B. Chevalier mark, the last two, J.J. Audubon. They were produced from 1840 through 1844. The second and other editions were printed up to 1871. The Bien Edition prints were full size, made under the direction of Audubon's sons in the late 1850s. Due to the onset of the Civil War, only 105 plates were finished. These are considered to be the most valuable of the reprints of the 'Birds of America Series.'

In 1971 the complete set was reprinted by Johnson Reprint Corp. of New York and Theaturm Orbis Terrarum of Amsterdam. Examples of the latter bear the watermark G. Schut and Zonen. In 1985 a second reprint was done by Abbeville Press for the National Audubon Society.

Although Audubon is best known for his portrayal of birds, one of his less-familiar series, 'Vivaparous Quadrupeds of North America,' portrayed various species of animals. Assembled in corroboration with John Bachman from 1839 until 1851, these prints are 28" x 22" in size. Several octavo editions were published in the 1850s.

Am Marsh Shrew, #25/Plate 125, Bowen Imperial, sheet: 21½x27½".460.00
Annulated Marmot Squirrel, #16, Bowen Imperial, sheet: 21⅛x27⅛"..150.00
Black Vulture, #13-1/Plate 3, Bien, 1860, sheet: 25⅛x38⅞" 375.00
Brewer's Shrew Mole, #15, Bowen Imperial, 1844, sheet: 21x27½".285.00
Bridled Weasel, Male; #12, Bowen Imperial, sight: 19¾x26¼" ..345.00
Camas Rat, #29/Plate 142, Bien Imperial, 1848, sheet: 2½x27½" 230.00
Canada Pouched Rat, #9/Plate 44, Bowen Imperial, sheet: 21⅜x27⅝"..230.00
Cat Squirrel, #4/Plate 17, Bowen Imperial, sheet: 27¼x21½" 315.00
Collier Squirrel, #21/Plate 104, Bowen Imperial, sheet: 27¼x21¾".460.00
Common Star-Nosed Mole, #24, Bowen Imperial, sheet: 21x27⅝".230.00
Douglass's Spermophile, Bowen Imperial, 1844, sight: 20½x26¾"....285.00
Ferruginous Thrush, Plate 141, Bien, 1860, sight: 36x25"........1,150.00
Fish Crow, #10-2, Plate 226, Bien, 1860, sight: 38¼x25"...........800.00
Florida Rat, #1/Plate 4, Bowen Imperial, 1842, sheet: 21½x27¼".315.00

Glossy Ibis, #13-3/Plate 358, Bien, 1860, sheet: 25x38¾" **1,500.00**

Large Tailed Spermophile, #28, Bowen Imperial, sheet: 21⅝x27⅜" .**260.00**

Lewis Marmot, #22/Plate 107, Bowen Imperial, sheet: 21⅝x27⅜" ...**230.00**

Little Am Brown Weasel, #13, Bowen Imperial, sheet: 21¼x27⅝" ..**575.00**

Little Chief Hare, Bowen, 1846, 21⅜x38⅜" in 29x36" fr...........**600.00**

Little Nimble Weasel, #28/Plate 140, Bowen Imperial, sheet: 21x27½".**460.00**

Long-Eared Owl, #77/Plate 383, Havell, 1837, sheet: 38x25¼" ..**2,000.00**

Night Hawk, #7-3/Plate 43, Bien, 1860, sheet: 39⅛x25¼".........**925.00**

Night Heron, #9/1/Plate 363, Bien, 1860, sheet: 26x39" **1,150.00**

Parry's Marmot Squirrel, #2, Bowen Imperial, sheet: 21½x27⅝" .**230.00**

Pigeon Hawk, #13-3/Plate 21, Bien, 1860, sheet: 39x25¼" **635.00**

Pouched Jerba Mouse, #26, Bowen Imperial, sheet: 21½x27⅛" .**115.00**

Red-necked Grebe, Havell, #60/Plate 298, 1836, sight: 16½x22¼" .**1,600.00**

Richardson's Spermophile, #10, Bowen Imperial, sight: 20¾x26¾".**250.00**

Rose-breasted Grosbeak, #3-3/Plate 205, Bien, 1860, sheet: 39⅛x25¼" ..**575.00**

Rusty Grackle, #7/4/Plate 222, Bien, 1860, sheet: 39x25⅛" **515.00**

Says Least Shrew, 314/Plate 70, Bowen Imperial, sheet: 21⅛x27½" .**160.00**

Tawny Weasel, #30/Plate 148, Bowen Imperial, sheet: 21x27⅛" .**350.00**

Tell-Tale Godwit or Snipe, Havel, 1836, dbl elephant folio, +fr .**2,200.00**

White-Fronted Goose, #14/Plate 380, Bien, sheet: 26¾x33⅛".**1,150.00**

Currier and Ives

Nathaniel Currier was in business by himself until the late 1850s when he formed a partnership with James Merrit Ives. Currier is given credit for being the first to use the medium to portray newsworthy subjects, and the Currier and Ives views of nineteenth-century American culture are familiar to us all. In the following listings, 'C' numbers correspond with a standard reference book by Conningham. Values are given for prints in very good condition; all are colored unless indicated black and white. Unless noted 'NC' (Nathaniel Currier), all prints are published by Currier and Ives. Our advisors for this category are John and Barbara Rudisill (Rudisill's Alt Print Haus); they are listed in the Directory under Maryland. See their Directory listing for information regarding a new Gallery website.

Abigail, NC, 1846, C-9, sm folio **95.00**

Admiral Porter's Fleet...Vicksburg April 16 1863, 1863, C-51, sm folio .**425.00**

Alnwick Castle, Scotland; undtd, C-87, med folio **175.00**

American Country Life, October Afternoon, NC, 1855, C-122, lg folio.**2,500.00**

American Country Life, Pleasures of Winter, NC, 1855, C-123, lg folio .**2,800.00**

American Farm Scenes No 3, NC, 1853, C-133, lg folio **3,800.00**

American Fireman, Always Ready, 1858, C-152, med folio.....**1,600.00**

American Fireman, Facing Enemy, 1858, C-153, med folio.....**1,600.00**

American Game, 1866, C-163, lg folio **900.00**

American Homestead, Summer, 1868, C-171, sm folio...............**450.00**

American Winter Sports, Deer Shooting..., NC, 1855, C-209, lg folio.**7,500.00**

Arguing the Point, NC, 1855, C-265, lg folio **5,000.00**

Battle of the Wilderness, undtd, C-436, sm folio **300.00**

Bear Hunting, Close Quarters (summer), undtd, C-447, sm folio..**850.00**

Beautiful Blonde, undtd, C-452, med folio.................................**125.00**

Black-Eyed Beauty, undtd, C-549, sm folio **90.00**

Blue Fishing, undtd, C-578, sm folio.......................................**1,200.00**

Bound Down the River, 1870, C-627, sm folio.........................**1,800.00**

Butt of the Jokers, 1879, C-758, sm folio **200.00**

Cares of a Family, NC, 1856, C-814, lg folio **4,000.00**

Celebrated Mare Flora Temple..., NC, 1860, C-892, lg folio ...**1,850.00**

Celebrated Trotting Mare Lady Thorn, 1866, C-918, lg folio..**1,500.00**

Chicky's Dinner, undtd, C-1029, sm folio **175.00**

City of New Orleans, undtd, C-1100, sm folio...........................**900.00**

Clipper Ship Great Republican, NC, 1853, C-1146, lg folio ...**3,000.00**

Clipper Ship in a Hurricane, 1855, C-1154, med folio **2,300.00**

Clipper Ship Three Brothers 2972 Tons, 1875, C-1169, lg folio.**2,800.00**

Cozzen's Dock, West Point, undtd, C-1277, med folio **800.00**

Darktown Yacht Club, Hard...Breeze, 1885, C-1439, sm folio **275.00**

Death of Gen Z Taylor, 1850, NC, C-1485, sm folio...................**200.00**

Deer Shooting in the Northern Woods, undtd, C-1539, sm folio..**700.00**

Dude Belle, 1883, C-1634, sm folio..**250.00**

Easter Flowers, 1869, C-1655, sm folio......................................**50.00**

Edward & Swiveller, 1882, C-1670, sm folio **3,000.00**

Family Pets, NC, undtd, C-1840, sm folio.................................**125.00**

Farmer's Home-Autumn, 1864, C-1889, lg folio....................**2,600.00**

Fiend of the Road, 1881, C-1945, lg folio................................**1,500.00**

First Ride, NC, 1849, C-1987, sm folio **150.00**

Flora Temple, NC, 1853, C-2015, lg folio................................**1,900.00**

Flora Temple & Lancet, NC, 1856, C-2018, lg folio **1,900.00**

Four Seasons of Life, Middle Ages; 1868, C-2097, lg folio.......**1,500.00**

Gem of the Atlantic, NC, 1849, C-2228, sm folio......................**750.00**

Gen Shields at the Battle..., 1862, C-2294, sm folio..................**225.00**

Gen Z Taylor Rough & Ready, NC, 1846, C-2330, sm folio.......**125.00**

Girl I Love, 1870, C-2376, sm folio..**85.00**

Got the Drop on Him, 1881, C-2455, sm folio **275.00**

Great Fire at Boston, 1872, C-2614, sm folio.............................**425.00**

Great St Louis Bridge Across Mississippi..., undtd, C-2648, sm folio ..**825.00**

Hero & Flora Temple, NC, 1856, C-2800, lg folio **2,000.00**

High Bridge at Harlem NY, NC, 1849, C-2811, sm folio **500.00**

Home of Evangeline, 1864, C-2863, lg folio...........................**1,000.00**

Home of the Deer, undtd, C-2867, med folio **550.00**

Home on the Mississippi, 1871, C-2876, sm folio **700.00**

Home to Thanksgiving, 1867, C-2882, lg folio **16,000.00**

Homeward Bound, NC, 1845, C-2885, sm folio **750.00**

Hues of Autumn on Racquet River, undtd, C-2982, sm folio **300.00**

In Northern Wilds, Trapping Beaver, undtd, C-3073, sm folio ...**550.00**

Inviting Dish, 1870, C-3124, sm folio.......................................**200.00**

Lady Suffolk & Lady Moscow, NC, 1850, C-3390, lg folio **1,800.00**

Lakeside Home, 1869, C-3423, med folio **400.00**

Life in the Woods, Returning, 1860, C-3513, lg folio **3,800.00**

Life of a Fireman...Muscle, 1861, C-3517, lg folio...................**3,000.00**

Life of a Sportsman, Coming Into Camp, 1872, C-3524, sm folio..**500.00**

Lincoln Family, 1867, C-3546, sm folio....................................**100.00**

Little Mary & Lamb, 1877, C-3670, sm folio.............................**175.00**

Little Snowbird, undtd, C-3719, sm folio..................................**250.00**

Loss of Steamboat Swallow, NC, 1845, C-3779, sm folio..........**500.00**

Maggie, undtd, C-3864, sm folio..**95.00**

Maiden Rock, Mississippi River, undtd, C-3891, sm folio **525.00**

Maple Sugaring Early Spring in Northern Woods, 1872, C-3975, sm folio.**1,500.00**

Mother's Pet, NC, undtd, C-4237, sm folio...............................**100.00**

Mother's Wing, 1866, C-4239, med folio **275.00**

Mt Washington & White Mountains..., 1860, C-4242, lg folio .**3,000.00**

My Little White Kittens Playing Dominoes, undtd, C-4336, sm folio .**190.00**

New Suspension Bridge, Niagara Falls, undtd, C-4432, sm folio.**360.00**

Old Mill in Summer, undtd, C-4571, sm folio **325.00**

Old Oaken Bucket, 1864, C-4576, lg folio **1,600.00**

On the Owago, undtd, C-4608, sm folio....................................**225.00**

Partridge Shooting, 1870, C-4718, sm folio **450.00**

Pigeon Shooting, Playing the Decoy, 1862, C-4780, lg folio ...**3,200.00**

Preparing for Market, NC, 1856, C-4872, lg folio **3,500.00**

Pride of the Garden, 1873, C-4914, sm folio **200.00**

Quail Shooting, NC, 1852, C-4989, lg folio............................**3,200.00**

Queen of Beauty, undtd, C-4997, sm folio..................................**90.00**

Racquet River Adirondacks, undtd, C-5049, sm folio **350.00**

Road, Winter, NC, 1853, C-5171, lg folio...............................**53,000.00**

Roadside Mill, 1870, C-5175, sm folio......................................**350.00**

Rysdyk's Hambletonian, 1876, C-5273, lg folio **2,500.00**

See-Saw, undtd, C-5457, med folio **350.00**

Silver Cascade, White Mountains, undtd, C-5521, sm folio **325.00**

Sluice Gate, undtd, C-5564, very sm folio **450.00**

Sperm Whale in a Furry, NC, 1852, C-5648, sm folio **1,500.00**

Spring, NC, 1849, C-5671, sm folio..**250.00**

Steam Ship Bothnia, undtd, C-5750, sm folio 350.00
Steamship Spain of the Nat'l Line, undtd, C-5794, sm folio.......350.00
Summer Ramble, undtd, C-5874, med folio 400.00
Sunrise at Lake Saranac, 1860, C-5895, lg folio 2,800.00
Sylvan Lake, undtd, C-5939, sm folio 250.00
Tacony & Mac, NC, 1853, C-5943, lg folio............................2,000.00
Tomb of Kosciusko, West Point, undtd, C-6103, sm folio 125.00
Trolling for Bluefish, NC, 1866, C-6158, lg folio 12,000.00
Trot for the Gate Money, 1869, C-6161, lg folio......................1,500.00
Valley Forge VA, undtd, C-6355, sm folio 325.00
Velocipede, 1869, C-6365, sm folio.......................................1,600.00
Village Blacksmith, 1864, C-6462, lg folio.............................2,800.00
Virginia Water Windsor Park, undtd, C-6475, sm folio...............150.00
Washington, NC, undtd, C-6539, sm 200.00
Water Jump at Jerome Park, undtd, C-6564, sm folio..................465.00
Whale Fishery Laying On, NC, 1852, C-6626, sm folio 1,650.00
Wild Duck Shooting, Good Day's Sport, NC, 1854, C-6670, lg folio ..6,500.00
Winter Evening, NC, 1854, C-6734, med folio........................2,400.00
Winter Morning, Feeding the Chickens, 1863, C-6741, lg folio .6,700.00
Zachary Taylor, Nation's..., NC, 1847, C-6874, sm folio 175.00

Fox, R. Atkinson

A Canadian who worked as an artist in the 1880s, R. Atkinson Fox moved to New York about ten years later, where his original oils were widely sold at auction and through exhibitions. Today he is best known, however, for his prints, published by as many as twenty print makers. More than thirty examples of his work appeared on Brown and Bigelow calendars, and it was used in many other forms of advertising as well. Though he was an accomplished artist able to interpret any subject well, he is today best known for his landscapes. Fox died in 1935. Our advisor for Fox prints is Pat Gibson whose address is listed in the Directory under California.

An Old Fashioned Garden, #12, 18x30" 325.00
Buffalo Hunt, #209, 7x10" 160.00
Dreamland, #41, 11½x7¾", in vintage fr 90.00
Fountain of Love, #3 15½x9½", in vintage fr 120.00
Garden of Love, #42, 10x18" 105.00
Garden Realm, #82, 10x20" 110.00
Glorious Vista, #6, 17¾x13¾", in vintage fr................................120.00
In Moonlight Blue, #232, 8x6" in vintage fr 175.00
Love's Paradise, #13, 11¾x19½", in vintage fr 150.00
Monarchs of the Prairie, #460, 8x12" 165.00
Nature's Beauty, #16, 10x20" 120.00
Nature's Treasures, #91, 18x30" 250.00
Oriental Dreams, #575, 11½x8½", in vintage fr..........................130.00
Poppies, #45, 18x30" 280.00

Gutmann, Bessie Pease (1876 – 1960)

Delicately tinted prints of appealing children sometimes accompanied by their pets, sometimes asleep, often captured at some childhood activity are typical of the work of this artist; she painted lovely ladies as well and was a successful illustrator of children's books. Her career spanned the five decades of the 1900s, and she recorded over eight hundred published artworks. Our advisor for this category is Dr. Victor J.W. Christie; he is listed in the Directory under Pennsylvania.

Aeroplane, The; #266/#695, 14x21" 800.00
Always, #774, 14x21" 2,100.00
American Girl, The; #220, 13x18"..500.00
An Anxious Moment, #714, 14x21" 650.00
Annunciation, #705, 14x21" 900.00
Awakening, #664, 14x21" 125.00

Baby's First Christmas, #158 ....500.00
Bedtime Story, The; #712, 14x21"...750.00
Betty, #787, 14x21" 250.00
Blossom Time, #654, 14x21" 800.00
Blue Bird, The; #265/#666, 14x21" 650.00
Butterfly, The; #632, 14x18" 210.00
CQD, #149, 9x12"...450.00
Call to Arms, A; #806, 14x21" 700.00
Caught Napping, #153, 9x12"..2,000.00
Chip of the Old Block, #728, 14x21" 600.00
Chuckles, #799, 11x14" 150.00
Chums, #665, 14x21" 350.00
Contentment, #781 ....90.00
Cupid, After All My Trouble, #608, 16x20" 800.00
Cupid's Reflection, #602, 14x21"...800.00
Daddy's Coming, #644, 14x21" 495.00
Divine Fire, The; #722, 14x21" 550.00
Double Blessing, A; #643, 14x21" 500.00
Feeling, #19, 6x9"...250.00
Friendly Enemies, #215, 11x14" 155.00
Goldilocks, #771, 14x21" 1,100.00
Good Morning, #801, 14x21" 250.00
Guest's Candle, The; #651, 14x21" 500.00
Hearing, #22, 6x9" 250.00
Home Builders, #233/#655, 14x21" 185.00
In Arcady, #701, 14x21" 700.00
In Disgrace, #792, 14x21" 200.00
In Slumberland, #786, 14x21" 120.00
Kitty's Breakfast, #805, 14x21" 350.00
Knit Two - Purl Two, #657, 14x21" 850.00
Little Bit of Heaven, A; #650, 14x21"...125.00
Little Bo Peep, #200, 11x14" 150.00
Little Mother, #803, 14x21" 450.00
Lorelei, #645, 14x21" 1,700.00
Love's Harmony, #791, 14x21" 400.00
Madonna, The; #674, 14x21"...2,100.00
May We Come In, #808, 14x21" 385.00
Message of the Roses, The; #641, 14x21" 400.00
Mighty Like A Rose, #642, 14x21" 200.00
Mischief Brewing, #152, 9x12"...2,000.00

The Mothering Heart, #351, 14x21", $700.00.

(Photo courtesy Dr. Victor Christie)

My Honey, #756, 14x21" 1,200.00
New Pet, The; #709, 14x21" 800.00
Nitey Nite, #826, 14x21" 175.00
Now I Lay Me, #620, 14x21"...1,800.00
On Dreamland's Border, #692, 14x21" 155.00
On the Up & Up, #796, 14x21" 190.00

Our Alarm Clock, #150, 9x12".................................250.00
Perfect Peace, #809, 14x21"..................................300.00
Popularity (Has Its Disadvantages), #825, 14x21".....150.00
Priceless Necklace, A; #744, 14x21" 1,200.00
Rosebud, #780, 14x21"...320.00
Seeing, #122, 11x14"..250.00
Smile Worth While, A; #180, 9x12"......................800.00
Snowbird, #177, 14x21"..650.00
Sunkissed, #818, 14x21".......................................125.00
Symphony, #702, 14x21".......................................650.00
Tabby, #172, 9x12"..600.00
Taps, #815, 14x21"..550.00
Television, #821, 14x21".......................................110.00
Thank You, God, #822, 14x21".............................175.00
To Love & To Cherish, #615, 14x21".....................285.00
Tom, Tom the Piper's Son, #219, 11x14"...............175.00
Touching, #210, 11x14"...150.00
Verdict: Love for Life, The; #113, 9x12"................550.00
Watchful Waiting, #697, 14x21"............................700.00
Who's Sleepy, #816, 14x21"...................................260.00
Winged Aureole, The; #700, 14x21"......................500.00
Wood Magic, #703, 14x21"....................................750.00

Icart, Louis

Louis Icart (1888 – 1950) was a Parisian artist best known for his boudoir etchings in the '20s and '30s. In the '80s prices soared, primarily due to Japanese buying. The market began to readjust in 1990, and most etchings now sell at retail between $1,400.00 and $2,500.00. Value is determined by popularity and condition, more than by rarity. Original frames and matting are not important, as most collectors want the etchings restored to their original condition and protected with acid-free mats.

Beware of the following repro and knock-off items: 1. Pseudo engravings on white plastic with the Icart 'signature.' 2. Any bronzes with the Icart signature. 3. Most watercolors, especially if they look similar in subject matter to a popular etching. 4. Lithographs where the dot-matrix printing is visible under magnification. Some even have phony embossed seals or rubber stamp markings. Items listed below are in excellent condition unless noted otherwise. Our advisor is William Holland, author of *Louis Icart: The Complete Etchings* and *The Collectible Maxfield Parrish*; he is listed in the Directory under Pennsylvania.

Belle Rose, 1933, 16x21", M.............................2,200.00
Blossom Time, #213, 1926, 14X18".....................2,000.00
Coursing II, 1929, 15¼x25¼" 3,575.00
Faust, 1928, 21¼x13¾", VG 1,450.00
Guest, 1941, 17x11"..3,750.00
Hydrangeas, 1929, 16¾x21½"..............................1,650.00
Lady of the Camelias, 1927, 16¾x20½", VG+........1,450.00
Lampshade, 1948, 15x19" 1,100.00
Le Lis, lady & lilies, 1934, 27¾x18¾"+fr 3,250.00
Lovers, 1930s, 20½x13½", EX..............................1,950.00
Miss California, 1927, 21x16¾", VG 3,600.00
On the Champs Elyees, 1938, 15½x22¼", VG 2,750.00
Pink Alcove, 1929, 10½x13" oval, in 17¾x19⅝" fr ...1,250.00
Puff of Smoke, 1922, 19¼x13½"..........................1,950.00
Smoke, seminude w/cigarette, ca 1926, 19½x14¼"...2,200.00
Spanish Comb, 1922, 18x14¾", VG......................1,450.00
Springtime Vision, 1914, 11¼x18½".....................1,400.00
Sweet Caress, 1926, 22¼x16¼" in vintage gold fr ...1,800.00
Venus, 1928, 13¾x19"...1,950.00
Werther, lady by garden wall, 1928, 21x14"..........2,000.00
Wounded Dove, 1929, 20¼x16¾", VG...................1,450.00

Kurz and Allison

Louis Kurz founded the Chicago Lithograph Company in 1833. Among his most notable works were a series of thirty-six Civil War scenes and one hundred illustrations of Chicago architecture. His company was destroyed in the Great Fire of 1871, and in 1880 Kurz formed a partnership with Alexander Allison, an engraver. Until both retired in 1903, they produced hundreds of lithographs in color as well as black and white. Unless noted otherwise, values are for prints in excellent condition.

Battle of Atlanta & Death of...McPherson, 1888, 21x28"..........600.00
Battle of Champion Hills, MI, Rear Attack by Gen Logan, 17½x25"...500.00
Battle of Cold Harbor, 1888, 20x26"+fr 600.00
Great Conemaugh-Valley Disaster, Flood & Fire at Johnstown PA ..750.00
Wm Penn's Treaty With Indians, 1621, 17½x25".....................450.00

McKenney and Hall

Chou-Ca-Pe, an Otto Second Chief; JT Bowen, 1855, 10¼x6¾" ..200.00
Kai-Pol-E-Quah, White Nosed Fox; Greenough, 1838, 17½x11¾".250.00
Ma-Has-Kah, An Ioway Chief; Rice & Hart, 1858, 10½x6½" ...175.00
Ma-Has-Kah, Rice & Clark, ca 1837-44, 20x14".....................875.00
Mistippee, Greenough, 1937-44, 20x14" 725.00
No-Way-Ke-Sug-Ga, An Otoe; Rice & Hart, 1858, 10½x6½"...185.00
Paddy-Carr, Creek Interpreter; Rice & Clark, 1838, 20x14".......625.00
Pow-A-Sheek, A Fox Chief; JT Bowen, 1855, 10¼x6¾" 245.00
Shingaba W'Ossin, Rice & Clark, ca 1837-44, 20x14" 700.00
Wa-Na-Ta, Grand Chief of Sioux; JT Bowen, 1855, 10¼x6¾" ..275.00
War Dance of Sauks & Foxes, Greenough, 1838, 13¾x19⅞" 525.00

Yard Longs

Values for yard-long prints are given for examples in near mint condition, full length, nicely framed, and with the original glass. To learn more about this popular area of collector interest, we recommend *Those Wonderful Yard-Long Prints and More*, *More Wonderful Yard-Long Prints, Book 2*, and *Yard-Long Prints, Book 3*, by our advisors Bill and June Keagy and Charles and Joan Rhoden. They are listed in the Directory under Indiana and Illinois respectively. A word of caution: Watch for reproductions; know your dealer.

A Happy Family, 9 monkeys playing, Jos Hoover & Son, #1037...450.00
A Yard of Cherries, sgn Guy Bedford, c 1906.........................275.00
American Girl, Pabst, 1914 ....500.00
Assorted Fruit, Jos Hoover & Son, c 1897 ....275.00
Barbara, sgn C Allan Gilbert, ca 1912 ....350.00
Beauty Among the Roses, Bowles Live Stock Commission, 1912...500.00
Beauty Gained Is Love Retained, Pompeian, 1925 ....475.00
Bridal Favors, Mary E Hart 300.00
Euthymol Girl, The; c 1907 ....500.00
Hope, Union Pacific Tea Co, c 1898......................................550.00
Indian Girl, Schlitz Malt Extract, c 1909 ....500.00
La France Roses, Paul DeLongpre, adv Spiehler's Perfumes, c 1903 ..350.00
Our White House Queen for 1911, ad for White House Shoes ..525.00
Priscilla, Schlitz Malt Extract, c 1910 ....500.00
Rose Girl, Pabst Malt Extract, c 1909 ....500.00
Selz Good Shoes, lady in blk holding rose, 1918 ....500.00
Walk-over Shoe Co, girl in cowgirl outfit................................500.00
White & Purple Lilacs, Paul DeLongpre 350.00
Yard of Tulips, Paul DeLongpre...350.00

Purinton

With its bold colors and unusual shapes, Purinton Pottery is much admired by today's dinnerware collectors. In 1939 Bernard Purinton purchased the East Liverpool Pottery in Wellsville, Ohio, and re-named it the Purinton Pottery Company. One of its earliest lines was Peasant Ware, featuring simple shapes and bold, colorful patterns. It was designed by William H. Blair, who also designed what have become the company's most recognized lines, Apple and Intaglio. The company was extremely successful, and by 1941 it became necessary to build a new plant, which they located in Shippenville, Pennsylvania. Blair left Purinton to open his own pottery (Blair Ceramics), leaving his sister Dorothy Purinton (Bernard's wife) to assume the role of designer. Though never a paid employee, Dorothy painted many one-of-a-kind special-occasion items that are highly sought after by today's collectors who are willing to pay premium prices to get them. These usually carry Dorothy's signature.

Apple was Purinton's signature pattern; it was produced throughout the entire life of the pottery. Another top-selling pattern designed by Dorothy Purinton was Pennsylvania Dutch, featuring hearts and tulips. Other long-term patterns include the Plaids and the Intaglios. While several other patterns were developed, they were short-lived. One of the most elusive patterns, Palm Tree, was sold only through a souvenir store in Florida owned by one of the Purinton's sons.

In addition to dinnerware, Purinton also produced a line of floral ware, including planters for NAPCO. They did contract work for Esmond Industries and RUBEL, who were both distributors in New York. They made the Howdy Doody cookie jar and bank for Taylor, Smith & Taylor; both items are highly collectible.

The pottery was sold to Taylor, Smith & Taylor in 1958 and closed in 1959 due to heavy competition from foreign imports.

Most items are not marked, but collectors find their unusual shapes easy to identify. A small number of items were ink stamped 'Purinton Slip-ware.' Some of the early Wellsville pieces were hand signed 'Purinton Pottery,' and several have emerged carrying the signature 'Wm. H. Blair' or simply 'Blair.' Blair's pieces command a premium price.

Our advisor for this category is Joe McManus; he is listed in the Directory under Pennsylvania. Mr. McManus is also the editor of *Purinton News and Views*, see Clubs, Newsletters, and Catalogs for information.

Apple, ashtray, center hdl, 5½" 40.00
Apple, bottles, oil & vinegar; 1-pt, 9½", pr.........................95.00
Apple, bowl, fruit; plain border, 12" 45.00
Apple, bowl, vegetable; divided, 10½" 35.00
Apple, bowl, vegetable; open, 8½" 30.00
Apple, butter dish, 6½"..150.00
Apple, coffeepot, 8-cup, 8"...90.00
Apple, honey jug, 6¼"..150.00
Apple, planter, rum jug shape, 6½".....................................55.00
Apple, platter, meat; 12"...55.00
Apple, shakers, stacking; 2¼", pr..95.00
Apple, tumbler, 12-oz, 5"..20.00
Blue Pansy, basket planter, 6¼"..65.00
Chartreuse, bowl, vegetable; open, 8½" 30.00
Chartreuse, juice mug, 6-oz, 2½".......................................25.00
Chartreuse, wall pocket, 3½"...50.00
Crescent Flower, coaster, 3½" dia.......................................75.00
Crescent Flower, jug, Dutch; 2-pt, 5¾"...............................75.00
Daisy, canister, any, cobalt trim, 9", ea 75.00
Dorothy Purinton sgn Blessing plate, 12", minimum value 650.00
Dorothy Purinton sgn Fruit plate, 12", minimum value..............650.00
Fruit, canister, wooden lid, 7½" 65.00
Fruit, coffeepot, 8-cup, 8"...65.00
Fruit, coffeepot, 8-cup, 11"...85.00
Fruit, creamer & sugar bowl, 2"..30.00
Fruit, plate, lap; 8½"...30.00
Fruit, relish, 3-part, pottery hdl, 10" 55.00
Fruit, shakers, range style, red trim, 4", pr 40.00

Fruit, tumbler, 12-oz, 5"...20.00
Fuchsia, jug, Kent; 1-pt, 4½"..35.00
Half-Blossom, planter, rum jug shape, 6½".........................25.00
Heather Plaid, creamer, 3"..20.00
Heather Plaid, grease jar, 5½"..60.00
Heather Plaid, shakers, Pour 'n Shake, 4¼", pr...................60.00
Intaglio, butter dish, 6½"..35.00
Intaglio, cookie jar, oval, 9½"..75.00
Intaglio, gravy pitcher, TS&T mold, 3¾" 65.00
Intaglio, jam & jelly dish, 5½"..25.00
Intaglio, jug, 5-pt, 8"..75.00
Intaglio, mug, beer; 16-oz, 4¾"..25.00
Intaglio, tea & toast set (cup & lap plate), 2½" & 8½" 25.00
Intaglio, teapot, 6-cup, 6½"...45.00
Intaglio, tidbit, 2-tier, metal hdl, 10"..................................25.00
Ivy-Red Blossom, biscuit jar, w/lid, 8".................................45.00
Ivy-Red Blossom, cornucopia vase, 6".................................25.00
Ivy-Red Blossom, pitcher, 2-pt, 6¼"...................................25.00
Ivy-Red Blossom, shakers, jug style, 2½", pr........................20.00
Ivy-Yellow Blossom, cornucopia vase, 6".............................25.00
Ivy-Yellow Blossom, creamer, 3½".......................................15.00
Leaves, jardiniere, 5"...25.00
Maywood, baker, 7"...25.00
Maywood, cup & saucer, 2½" & 5½"...................................15.00
Maywood, roll tray, 11"..20.00
Maywood, teapot, 6-cup, 6½"...45.00
Ming Tree, canister, variation on orig pattern, 7½".............65.00
Ming Tree, chop plate, 12"...125.00
Ming Tree, cup & saucer..30.00
Ming Tree, planter, 5"...25.00
Morning Glory, honey jug, 6¼"..50.00
Mountain Rose, bean pot, 4½"..65.00
Mountain Rose, decanter, 5"..45.00
Mountain Rose, jug, Kent; 1-pt, 4½"...................................45.00
Mountain Rose, wall pocket, 3½"...65.00
Normandy Plaid, beer mug, 16-oz , 4¾"..............................40.00
Normandy Plaid, bowl, fruit; 12"..35.00
Normandy Plaid, bowl, vegetable; open, 8½".......................20.00
Normandy Plaid, cookie jar, oval, 9½".................................60.00
Normandy Plaid, grease jar, w/lid, 5½"................................60.00
Normandy Plaid, mug, Kent; 1-pt, 4½"...............................30.00
Palm Tree, basket planter, 6¼"..100.00
Palm Tree, mug, beer; 16-oz, 4¾".....................................150.00
Palm Tree, plate, dinner; 9¾"...125.00
Palm Tree, vase, 5"..75.00
Peasant Garden, pitcher, Rubel mold, 5".............................150.00
Peasant Garden, plate, breakfast; 8½".................................100.00
Peasant Garden, plate, chop; 12"..150.00
Peasant Lady, candle holder, sgn, William Blair, minimum value ..500.00
Pennsylvania Dutch, baker, 7"..45.00
Pennsylvania Dutch, platter, meat; 12" 85.00
Petals, bowl, fruit; 12"...95.00
Petals, coffeepot, 8-cup, 8"..75.00
Petals, jug, 5-pt, 8"...85.00
Petals, teapot, 8-cup, 8"...75.00
Pineapple, pickle dish, unusual sponged edge, 6" dia 35.00
Provencial Fruit, bowl, cereal; 5¼".......................................10.00
Provencial Fruit, bowl, fruit; 12"...95.00
Provencial Fruit, grease jar, 5"..30.00
Saraband, bowl, fruit; 12"..25.00
Saraband, bowl, range; w/lid, 5½".......................................20.00
Saraband, cookie jar; oval, w/lid, 9½".................................100.00
Saraband, plate, dinner; 9¾"..10.00
Saraband, plate, salad; 6¾"..8.00

Saraband, teapot, 6-cup, 6½" **25.00**
Seafoam, shakers, 3", pr **55.00**
Tea Rose, bowl, vegetable; open, 8½" **40.00**
Tea Rose, platter, meat; 12" **50.00**
Tionesta Park, shakers, range style, souvenir, 4", pr **175.00**
Turquoise, cup, 2¼x4" dia **55.00**
Turquoise, plate, dinner; 9¾" **35.00**
Windflower, jardiniere, 5" **30.00**
Woodflowers, pitcher, 6½" **65.00**
Woodflowers, relish tray, 8" **45.00**

Purses

Purses from the early 1800s are often decorated with small, brightly colored glass beads. Cut steel beads were popular in the 1840s and remained stylish until about 1930. Purses made of woven mesh date back to the 1820s. Chain-link mesh came into usage in the 1890s, followed by the enamel mesh bags carried by the flappers in the 1920s. Purses are divided into several categories by (a) construction techniques — whether beaded, embroidered, or a type of needlework; (b) material — fabric or metal; and (c) design and style. Condition is very important. Watch for dry, brittle leather or fragile material. For those interested in learning more, we recommend *More Beautiful Purses* and *Combs and Purses* by Evelyn Haertigi of Carmel, California; and *Purse Masterpieces* by Lynell Schwartz.

Key: W&D — Whiting & Davis

Beaded, amber/steel/brn crochet, cast jeweled fr, chain hdl, 7x7" ..**160.00**
Beaded, blk/gold crochet, SP filigree fr, ca 1900, 5¾x6⅛" **90.00**
Beaded, clear & gray crochet, plated cast metal fr, 7x8½" **120.00**
Beaded, floral basket & ribbon, jeweled brass fr, fringed, 6x11" ..**575.00**
Beaded, mc cottage scene w/lake, metal fr, 8½x6½" **100.00**
Beaded, mc fleur-de-lis, amber cabochons in fr, Fr, 7x5" **350.00**
Beaded, mc flower garden, enameled & jeweled fr, 7x11" **575.00**
Beaded, mc geometrics, foliate brass fr, fringed, 7x11" **500.00**
Beaded, Nouveau flowers on clear, fringed, jeweled fr, 6½x10⅛" ..**180.00**
Beaded, orange, ribbed, SP fr, 6¾x8" **135.00**
Beaded, peacock & roses, ornate SP fr, 8x12" **400.00**
Beaded, robin on bl, lg Bakelite fr, 7x12" **350.00**
Beaded, roses on blk, mc fringe, SP fr, 7x11" **350.00**
Beaded, saddle style w/mc floral motif, fringed, Fr, 7½x14" **400.00**
Beaded, teal & gold paisley, plain brass fr, fringed, 11x6" **525.00**
Celluloid, gold color w/embedded stones & pnt motif, rigid arched hdl.**900.00**
Embroidery, floral decor on burlap material, basket-weave/floral fr.**800.00**
Leather, tooled bird motif, arched Bakelite hdl/clasp, 8x9" **275.00**
Leather, tooled geometrics, metal fr, strap hdl, Jemco, 9x7½" **85.00**
Lucite, blk w/gold confetti, clear cvd top w/brass clasp, 3½x6¾" ..**225.00**
Lucite, vanity type w/mirrored lid, Lili-Staly, 4x7x5" **325.00**
Lucite, wht marbleized box shape w/envelope closure, Elgine, 4" ..**350.00**
Mesh, dragon decor, zigzag fringe, W&D fr **165.00**
Mesh, enameled butterfly, 3-point fringe, emb sq Mandalian fr, 7" .**525.00**
Mesh, enameled cockatoo, 7-point bottom, emb W&D fr, chain hdl, 7"..**750.00**
Mesh, enameled floral/Mandalain fr, fringed bottom, chain hdl, 10" ..**800.00**
Mesh, enameled floral/Mandalain fr, 3-point fringe, chain hdl, 5x9" ..**750.00**
Mesh, enameled geometrics, flared points, gilded openwork W&D fr, 9" .**425.00**
Mesh, enameled geometrics, fringed, Mandalian emb fr, chain hdl, 9"..**650.00**
Mesh, enameled poinsettia/Mandalian fr, drops on zigzag point, 8½" .**750.00**
Mesh, exotic bird on branch, ornate W&D fr, 7x4" **165.00**
Mesh, gold-tone w/gate fr, jeweled lid, chatelaine hook, 2x4" **85.00**
Mesh, landscape, metal fr, fringed, Germany, 10x7" **145.00**
Mesh, plain, tassel on point, W&D fr, cental adjustable strap, 9"...**450.00**
Mesh, red w/zigzag bottom, stylized red W&D fr, 7½x5½" **125.00**
Mesh, rose decor, gold-tone W&D fr & chain hdl, 5x6" **400.00**

Mesh, silver, sq w/emb fr & drops along bottom, chain hdl, 6x6"...**175.00**
Needlepoint, oblong w/grape harvest scene, enameled fr, 6x8" ...**700.00**
Needlepoint, rose decor, jeweled/filigree encrusted fr, chain hdl, 10".**400.00**
Petit point, bird motif, jeweled/filigree scalloped fr, 7x9½" **800.00**
Petit point, dance-type w/floral motif, plain fr w/filigree clasp, 7" .**500.00**
Silk, blk pouch/hdl, arched celluloid fr in blk/wht diamanté, 8".**400.00**
Silk, pouch w/ivory-finished celluloid fr & intricate linked-chain hdl .**750.00**
Tapestry, Aubusson w/courting couple/landscape, jeweled filigree fr ...**875.00**
Tapestry, courting couple on blk, gilt fr w/plunger top, chain hdl, 8" .**850.00**
Tapestry, dance-type w/classical girl on blk, jeweled/enameled fr, 9" .**550.00**
Velvet, flower-basket motif, sq jeweled fr/clasp, 6x9" **475.00**
Velvet, pouch w/gold-stitched leaf decor, faux pearls, crown fr, 7x9" ..**400.00**

Puzzles

'Jigsaw' puzzles have been around almost as long as games. The first examples were handcrafted from wood, and they are extremely difficult to find. Most of the early examples featured moral subjects just as the board games did. By the 1890s jigsaw puzzles had become a major form of home entertainment. During the Depression years jigsaw puzzles were set up on card tables in almost every home. The early wood examples are the most valuable.

Cube puzzles, or blocks, were often made by the same companies as the board games. Again, early examples display the finest quality lithography. While all subjects are collectible, some (such as Santa blocks) often command prices higher than games from the same period. In the miscellaneous subcategory below, all listing are for jigsaw puzzles (that are complete) unless noted otherwise.

Personalities, Movies, and TV Shows

Aristocats, fr-tray, 1970s-80s, MIP **15.00**
Beetle Bailey, jigsaw, Jay, 1960s, NMIB **15.00**
Blondie (Dagwood's in Trouble), jigsaw, Jaymar, 1960s...............**15.00**
Bobbsey Twins, fr-tray, 1958, EX **20.00**
Broken Arrow, jigsaw, Built-Rite, 1958, NMIB **30.00**
Buffalo Bill Jr, fr-tray, Built-Rite, 1956, NM+ **10.00**
Casey at Bat, jigsaw, 1960s, EXIB **15.00**
Charlie's Angels in Action, jigsaw, 1977, EXIB **35.00**
Cheyenne, jigsaw, Milton Bradley, 1957, set of 3, EXIB **40.00**
Combat, jigsaw, Jaymar, 1966, MIB (sealed) **18.00**
Daniel Boone (The Shawnees Attack), jigsaw, Jaymar, 1961, NMIB..**20.00**
Dark Shadows, jigsaw, MIB **75.00**
Disney Movie Classics (Bambi), jigsaw, Jaymar #105, 100 pcs, EXIB..**10.00**
Donald Duck (Hornet's Nest), fr-tray, 1985, 2-sided, EX.............**10.00**
Flash Gordon, fr-tray, Milton Bradley, 1951, set of 3, EXIB **65.00**
Flintstones (Bedrock Postal Service), jigsaw, 1975, EXIB............**15.00**
Flip the Frog, fr-tray, Saalfield, 1932, 1 from set of 4, rare, EX+ .**110.00**
Gunsmoke, jigsaw, Whitman, 1950s, Matt drawing gun, 63 pcs, NMIB..**30.00**
Hey Diddle Diddle the Cat & the Fiddle, fr-tray, 1957, EX...........**15.00**
Hopalong Cassidy, jigsaw, Milton Bradley #4025, 1950s, NMIB.**125.00**
Impossibles (fight scene), fr-tray, Whitman, 1967, EX+ **25.00**
James Bond 007/Goldfinger, jigsaw, Milton Bradley, 1965, NMIB..**60.00**
King Kong, jigsaw, Giant, 1976, MIB **45.00**
Land of the Lost, jigsaw, Whitman #4609, 1975, NMIB **20.00**
Laverne & Shirley, jigsaw, HG Toys, 1976, 3 different, unused, MIB, ea.**15.00**
Linus the Lion Hearted, fr-tray, Whitman, 1966, EX....................**25.00**
Little Bo Peep Puzzle Box, Milton Bradley, 7½x13", VGIB **100.00**
Marlin Perkins' Wild Kingdom (Sparrow Hawk), jigsaw, 1971, VGIB.**15.00**
Mickey Mouse Club (Jimmy singing/members), fr-tray, Whitman, 1956, EX.**40.00**
Mod Squad, jigsaw, Milton Bradley #4089, 1969, EXIB...............**30.00**
Monkees (On Stage), jigsaw, Fairchild, 1967, NMIB....................**50.00**
Monkees (Speed Boat), Fairchild, 1967, NMIB **50.00**
Munsters (family in lab), jigsaw, Whitman, 1965, VG+ **40.00**

Patty Duke, jigsaw, Jr Jigsaw/Whitman, 1963, 100 pcs, EX...........30.00
Peter Pan, fr-tray, Whitman, 1952, EX+......................................30.00
Pinocchio Picture Puzzles Set, Whitman, 1939, set of 2, EXIB.....50.00
Pitfall Harry, jigsaw, Playskool, 1983, EXIB.................................20.00
Punky Bruster, jigsaw, 1984, EXIB...20.00
Rin-Tin-Tin (Rusty holding pups), jigsaw, Jaymar, 1957, NMIB...25.00
Robin Hood, fr-tray, Built Rite, 1950s, set of 3, EX+.....................40.00
Rootie Kazootie, fr-tray, EE Fairchild, 1950s, set of 3, VGIB.........30.00
Shotgun Slade, jigsaw, Milton Bradley, 1960, NMIB....................30.00
Sky Hawks, fr-tray, Whitman, 1970, NM+..................................20.00
Super Six, jigsaw, Whitman, 1969, NMIB...................................30.00
Superman (rescuing Lois & Jimmy on sub), jigsaw, Whitman, 1965, NMIB..30.00
Superman Man the Man of Tomorrow, jigsaw, Saalfield #1505, EXIB...300.00
Sword in the Stone, fr-tray, Whitman #4456, 1963, G+..............10.00
Tennessee Tuxedo, jigsaw, Fairchild, 1971, NMIB.......................40.00
Top Cat, fr-tray, Whitman, NM...25.00
Wacky Races, fr-tray, Whitman, 1969, EX..................................25.00
Welcome Back Kotter, jigsaw, HG Toys, 1976, various, unused, MIB, ea.20.00
Wild Bill Hickok, jigsaw, Built-Rite, 1955, NMIB.......................30.00
Wizard of Oz, fr-tray, 1988, photo image, EX.............................15.00

Miscellaneous

Am Homestead-Autumn, Currier & Ives, 1960s, plywood, 181 pcs, EXIB...35.00
Beach Snipe Shooting, Currier & Ives, 1980, plywood, 177 pcs, EXIB....35.00
Betsy Ross Presenting Flag, Parker Bros/Pastime, 1933, 546 pcs, EXIB..240.00
Birth of Old Glory, Madmar/Interlox, 1930s, 210 pcs, EXIB.........50.00
Canal in Venice, Parker Bros/Pastime, 1931, 303 pcs, VGIB......100.00
Chieftain's Daughter, Leisure Hour, 1909, 363 pcs, EXIB...........150.00

City of Worcester paddle wheeler, picture puzzle, McLoughlin, ca 1889, complete, EX, with original box, $990.00.

Dreamland, R Atkins Fox, 1930s, 486 pcs, EX (rpl box).............200.00
Eastern Getaway (Mediterranean), Malcom/Jones, 1930s, 600 pcs, EXIB.125.00
Flower Market in Holland, 1930s, 646 pcs, EX (rpl box)............125.00
Golden Memories, N Briganti, 1930s, 162 pcs, EX (rpl box)........35.00
Harbor of Venice, Milton Bradley/Perfection, 1908-11, 108 pcs, EXIB.30.00
Irish Setters (family), Osthaus/Jigwood Co, 1930s, 330 pcs, EXIB.80.00
Joy of Spring, H Clements/Parker Bros/Pastime, 1922, 118 pcs, EXIB.50.00
King of the Desert (lion), 1920s, 288 pcs, EXIB........................80.00
Last Change In (coaching), P Bros/Pastime, 1931-33, 1,012 pcs, EXIB..450.00
Lovely Summertime, Detroit Gask, 1930s, 200 pcs, VGIB............70.00
Moonlight Night in Sunny Spain, P Bros/Pastime, 1930s, 525 pcs, EXIB.225.00
Noon Hour (farming), El Ramsdell/P Bros/Pastime, 1910s, 111 pcs, EXIB.45.00
Outward Bound, FJ Aldredge/GS Wesby Jr, 1910-20, 423 pcs, EXIB.120.00
Peacham Vermont (winter), R Chesley, 1950s, 485 pcs, EXIB......95.00
Peep at the Circus, McLoughlin Bros, 1887, VGIB.....................175.00
Red Rock Canyon (wagon train), 1940s, 650 pcs. EX (rpl box).200.00
Restful Moments, Parker Bros/Pastime, 1920-30, EX (rpl box)...300.00
Sparkling Raiment (parade), Par Co, 1940-50, 860 pcs, EXIB..1,000.00
Taj Mahal, Chad Valley, 1930s, 525 pcs, VG (rpl box)..............110.00
Village Road Paved w/Pearl, Thompson (?), 1930s, EXIB............65.00
Winter on the Spreewald, 1910, 631 pcs, EXIB.........................300.00

Pyrography

Pyrography, also known as wood burning, Flemish art, or poker work, is the art of burning designs into wood or leather and has been practiced over the centuries in many countries.

In the late 1800s pyrography became the hot new hobby for thousands of Americans who burned designs inspired by the popular artists of the day including Mucha, Gibson, Fisher, and Corbett. Thousands of wooden boxes, wall plaques, novelties, and pieces of furniture that they purchased from local general stores or from mail-order catalogs were burned and painted. These pieces were manufactured by companies such as The Flemish Art Company of New York and Thayer & Chandler of Chicago, who printed the designs on wood for the pyrographers to burn.

This Victorian fad developed into a new form of artistic expression as the individually burned and painted pieces reflected the personality of the pyrographers. The more adventurous started to burn between the lines and developed a style of 'allover burning' that today is known as pyromania. Others not only created their own designs but even made the pieces to be decorated. Both these developments are particularly valued today as true examples of American folk art.

By the 1930s its popularity had declined. Like Mission furniture, it was neglected by generations of collectors and dealers. The recent appreciation of Victoriana, the Arts and Crafts Movement, the American West and the popularity of turn-of-the-century graphic art has rekindled interest in pyrography which embraces all these styles.

An informative book, *The Burning Passion — Antique and Collectible Pyrography*, by Carole and Richard Smyth, our advisors for this category, is currently available from the authors; they are listed in the Directory under New York.

Key: hb — hand burned

Bedroom set, hb/pnt, Wm Rogers/Forusville PA, 1905-07, 3-pc.4,000.00
Book rack, hb/pnt girl w/book, 5¾" W, extends to 15¾" L.........150.00
Box, flatware; factory burned/pnt poinsettias, Rogers, 9x11x5"...195.00
Box, floral decor, stamped design, 14½" sq.................................40.00
Box, lady w/flowing hair, Flemish Art Co, 1909, 11¼x4¼".........120.00
Box, Miller Bros Steel Pens, 1900, stamped to look hb, 7" L, +contents.45.00
Catalog, Thayer-Chandler, Chicago, 1904, 92 pgs, 12 in full color...27.00
Chair-table, hb/pnt poinsettias, Rest-Ye... on chair bk, EX.........950.00
Checker/backgammon brd, red & gr decor/glass bead insets, 30x15"..1,550.00
Chest, blanket; hb/pnt swans/lady's head/flowers/etc, ca 1890....850.00
Chest, medicine; hb/pnt Nouveau lady & vines, wall mt...........450.00
Coat hanger, hb/pnt poppies & leaves, Mother Dearest...............80.00
Cue holder, hb pool-hall scene, folk art, unique.........................650.00
Egg cup, hb/pnt, pr..60.00
Etching set, Snow White, Disney/Marks, 1938, electric pen, complete..175.00
Footstool, hb/pnt allover w/owl/branches/leaves.........................125.00
Frame, hb/pnt cherries, standing type, 7½x6", EX.......................85.00
Frame, hb/pnt chrysanthemums, Thayer-Chandler, 10½x8", EX..85.00
Frame, hb/pnt flower garland, Thayer-Chandler, 8" dia................85.00
Frame, owls in tree, 2 Is Company, 2 oval cutouts.....................145.00
Gameboard, hb/pnt ea side/edges, Flemish Art, 15" sq (open)....200.00
Humdior, trees & landscape on lid, gold & bl pnt on pine, 3x9x6"..295.00
Knife rack, hb Lizzie Borden w/axe, 5 hooks below, rare.............550.00
Magazine stand, 4-shelf, burned/pnt florals, Thayer-Chandler, 48".800.00
Mirror, hand; hb/pnt lady's head w/flowing hair, 13¼x6¾".........180.00
Nut bowl, hb/pnt squirrel on branch, Flemish Art Co #816, 5"....65.00
Panel, basswood, burned/pnt orange, Thayer-Chandler, 16x30".465.00
Panel, hb after painting: To the Feast, minor gold, 9x34"...........500.00
Pedestal, hb/pnt Nouveau flowers & vines, 45".........................400.00
Plaque, cvd/burned/pnt strawberry basket, 3-ply, 12" dia.............70.00
Plaque, girl bathing puppies, #854, 14½".................................125.00

Plaque, hb orange cat w/bow, paper 1912 calendar, 5¾" dia **50.00**
Plaque, Nouveau lady w/cherries, 19½" **150.00**
Plaque, Oddfellows, hb I O O F in center, early 1900s, 16x10"....**87.00**
Plaque, Victorian couple, Parting by a Wall & flowers...............**145.00**
Ribbon holder, hb/pnt Sunbonnet babies (3), 5x12" **160.00**
Screen, birds & foliage, mc pnt, 3-part, 63x73" **400.00**
Spoon holder, geometric florals, wall hanging, 1915, 10x8" **45.00**
Tie rack, factory stamp, HP soldier/nurse/sailor, WWI motto **125.00**

Quezal

The Quezal Art Glass and Decorating Company of Brooklyn, New York, was founded in 1901 by Martin Bach. A former Tiffany employee, Bach's glass closely resembled that of his former employer. Most pieces were signed 'Quezal,' a name taken from a Central American bird. After Bach's death in 1920, his son-in-law, Conrad Vohlsing, continued to produce a Quezal-type glass in Elmhurst, New York, which he marked 'Lustre Art Glass.' Examples listed here are signed unless noted otherwise.

Bottle, scent; gold irid, 4 ribbed corners, hexagon stopper, 7½" .**700.00**
Bowl, feathers, silver-bl irid on brn irid, 6" **2,300.00**
Compote, apricot w/gold irid int, 4½"...................................**800.00**
Compote, gold irid, wide ped ft, 2¼x5½" **275.00**
Dish, gold irid, ruffled rim, paper label, +6" saucer **425.00**
Lamp, 6 gold irid lily shades w/wave decor, bronze waisted base, 15" .**6,325.00**
Sconces, gold ribbed 2½x2½" lilies (2) on blk matt mts, pr **2,500.00**
Shade, wht w/gr loops, gold irid border, 5½"................................**350.00**
Vase, bl irid, flared rim, ovoid, 7" **650.00**
Vase, bl irid, flared rim, urn form, paper label, 7⅞" **880.00**
Vase, feathers, gr & ivory w/gold, bronze ft w/snakes, 17"........**7,500.00**
Vase, feathers, gr/gold/wht, gold int, #161, 5"............................**2,000.00**
Vase, floriform; feathers, gr irid int, #162, 7" **4,000.00**
Vase, floriform; wht w/gr & gold feathers, gold int, #182, 5" ...**3,450.00**
Vase, gold irid, 4 pinched sides, flared rim, 2¾" **325.00**
Vase, gr & gold swirled & hooked decor, paper label, 6".........**1,035.00**
Vase, jack-in-pulpit; feathers, gr/gold/wht on gold irid, #663, 8½" .**6,000.00**
Vase, jack-in-pulpit; gold irid, stretched rim, #565, 6¾" **1,295.00**
Vase, King Tut, gold irid w/gr & bl swirls, 10" **1,550.00**

Quilts

Quilts, while made of necessity, nevertheless represent an art form which expresses the character and the personality of the designer. During the seventeenth and eighteenth centuries, quilts were considered a necessary part of a bride's hope chest; the traditional number required to be properly endowed for marriage was a 'baker's dozen'! American colonial quilts reflect the English and French taste of our ancestors. They would include the classifications known as Lindsey-Woolsey and the central medallion appliqué quilts fashioned from imported copper-plate printed fabrics.

By 1829 spare time was slightly more available, so women gathered in quilting bees. This not only was a way of sharing the work but also gave them the opportunity to show off their best handiwork. The hand-dyed and pieced quilts emerged, and they are now known as sampler, album, and friendship quilts. By 1845 American printed fabric was available.

In 1793 Eli Whitney developed the cotton gin; as a result, textile production in America became industrialized. Soon inexpensive fabrics were readily available, and ladies were able to choose from colorful prints and solids to add contrast to their work. Both pieced and appliquéd work became popular.

Pieced quilts were considered utilitarian, while appliquéd quilts were shown with pride of accomplishment at the fair or used when itinerant preachers traveled through and stayed for a visit. Today many collectors prize pieced quilts and their intricate geometric patterns above all other

types. Many of these designs were given names: Daisy and Oak Leaf, Grandmother's Flower Garden, Log Cabin, and Ocean Wave are only a few. Appliquéd quilts involved stitching one piece — carefully cut into a specific form such as a leaf, a flower, or a stylized device — onto either a large one-piece ground fabric or an individual block. Often the background fabric was quilted in a decorative pattern such as a wreath or medallions.

Amish women scorned printed calicos as 'worldly' and instead used colorful blocks set with black fabrics to produce a stunning pieced effect. To show their reverence for God, the Amish would often include a 'superstition' block which represented the 'imperfection' of Man!

One of the most valuable quilts in existence is the Baltimore album quilt. Made between 1840 and 1860 only three hundred or so still exist today. They have been known to fetch over $100,000.00 at prominent auction houses in New York City. Usually each block features elaborate appliqué work such as a basket of flowers, patriotic flags and eagles, the Oddfellow's heart in hand, etc. The border can be sawtooth, meandering, or swags and tassels.

During the Victorian period, the crazy quilt emerged. This style became the most popular quilt ever in terms of sheer numbers produced. The crazy quilt was formed by random pieces put together following no organized lines and was usually embellished by elaborate embroidery stitches. Fabrics of choice were brocades, silks, and velvets.

Another type of quilting, highly prized and rare today, is trapunto. These quilts were made by first stitching the outline of the design onto a solid sheet of fabric which was backed with a second having a much looser weave. White was often favored, but color was sometimes used for accent. The design (grapes, flowers, leaves, etc.) was padded through openings made by separating the loose weave of the underneath fabric; a backing was added and the three layers quilted as one.

Besides condition, value is judged on intricacy of pattern, color effect, and craftsmanship. Examine the stitching. Quality quilts have from ten to twelve stitches to the inch. A stitch is defined as any time a needle pierces through the fabric. So you may see five threads but ten stitches have been used. In the listings that follow, examples rated excellent have minor defects, otherwise assume them to be free of any damage, soil, or wear. Values given here are auction results; retail may be somewhat higher.

For more information we recommend *Vintage Quilts, Identifying, Collecting, Dating, Preserving, and Valuing* by Bobbie Aug, Sharon Newman, and Gerald Roy and *Antique Quilts & Textiles* by Bobbie Aug and Gerald Roy (Collector Books).

Key:
hs — hand sewn, sewing   mp — machine pieced
hq — hand quilted, quilting   ms — machine sewn

Amish

Central dmn & 2 wide borders, hs, hq tulips, 20th C, 86" sq......**715.00**
Fan, red/bl/purple/blk on bl, gold thread, 68x78".........................**415.00**
Love Ring, bl/gr/blk/brn/wht, brn bk, sm splits, 88x84"...............**275.00**
Rainbow stripes & diagonal border, hs, 20th C, 78x83" **475.00**
Sawtooth dmn & border, red on ivory, hs, feather hq, 20th C, 102" sq ..**475.00**
T-Square, bl on red blocks w/brn bars, feather hq, 72x86" **770.00**
Trip Around the World, bl/brn/purple/gr/gray/pk, 1900s, 82x84", EX .**935.00**
9-Patch, mc calicos, brn print bk, PA, 74x83", EX **525.00**

Appliquéd

Baskets, calico prints on yel ground, hs, princess feather hq, 72" sq.**440.00**
Carolina Lily, mc on wht dmn blocks, hq, 57x56".......................**500.00**
Central Star w/Am eagle in corners, calicos/wht, PA, hq, 81x87".**660.00**
Eagles (5), yel/bl/wht on wht cotton, bl binding, ltweight, 78x75"...**195.00**
Flower baskets (12), dbl sawtooth border, feather hq, 72x90" **525.00**
Flower medallions, mc on wht, dmn hq, sgn/1850, 87" sq **1,200.00**
Flower medallions, mc on wht w/bud border, feather hq, 88x75".**800.00**
Flowers in red pots, mc on wht, red/wht borders, 86x88", EX **200.00**

Friendship, 20 panels w/flowers/trees/etc, mc on wht, 1855, 90x77" .2,850.00
Friendship, 36 hs blocks w/embr on wht, 1850s, w/1930s binding, NM..1,850.00
Friendship type, 48 mc sqs on red cotton grid, 1858, 86x65½".4,115.00
Holly & flower medallions, gr/red/pk/yel calico, hs, 81" sq.........550.00
Pomegranates, red/gold w/tan vines on wht, feather hq, 70" sq ..450.00
Poppy medallions & border, red/tan/wht, hs, fine hq, 79x82"..1,045.00
Red calico sqs w/red or gray leaves ea corner, fine hq, 100" sq....495.00
Scenes of Childhood, embr captions, 3 sqs w/theme depicted, pets, 1975..30,500.00
Sunflowers & oak leaf medallions, mc on wht, EX hq, 86x88" ...600.00
Tulip medallions, red/gr on wht, fine hq, 35½x36½" 385.00
Tulips, mc on wht w/teal edge, feather hq, OH, 1870, 82x66", EX.770.00
Tulips & flowers w/central medallion, dmn/scalloped hq, 80x96".415.00
Tulips on wht sqs w/navy calico, gr border w/goldenrod, hs, 67x82"..825.00
Union: flag center, spreadwing eagle ea corner, red/wht/bl, 1915, 75".10,000.00
Variable Star (8-point), mc on wht w/gr sawtooth border, 78x80"..300.00
4-petal flowers, pks & grs on wht, ornate hq, pk binding, 92x76" .200.00

Mennonite

Brn sqs w/dmn grid, floral print bk, lt wear, 82" sq 330.00
Concentric sqs, various fabrics & colors, stains, 68x86" 110.00

Pieced

Bear Paw, red calico on wht w/bl grid w/sm red blocks, 87x86" ..375.00
Birds in Flight, mc on red calico, 65x72" 465.00
Birds in Flight, 19th-C prints, paisley bk, few stains, 67x74" 650.00
Bow Tie variant, calicos/prints, hs, wide border, 100" sq............660.00
Broken Glass variant, gr/red/bright yel on wht, OH, 1897, 81x82"..600.00
Broken Star, med rainbow colors, princess feather hq, 75" sq 750.00
Checkerboard, dk gr & wht, fine princess feather hq, 86x87"......550.00
Chinese Coin, mc w/red & orange calico blocks, 89x76"............200.00
Courthouse Sq, 5 11" sqs in mc prints on wht, mc borders, 98x94", EX.750.00
Crazy, mixed materials/colors, mc threads, applique/embr, 68" sq.440.00
Crazy, multiple dk fabrics, silk stitches, embr name, 68x76" 110.00
Crazy, silk & velvet w/much embr & pnt motifs, 1885, 64" sq..1,300.00
Crosses & Losses, mc prints/red/gr, striped bk, fine hq, 68x70"...250.00
Dbl Irish Chain, mc cottons on wht, Am, 20th C, 84x91" 585.00
Dbl Pyramid variant on wht blocks, mc calicos, 73x84"..............200.00
Dmns & Bars, burgundy/bl/wht, hs except for binding, 82x58" ..110.00
Drunkard's Path, bl calico on wht, hs, princess feather hq, 70x90".440.00
Feathered Star & vining flower border, mc on wht, hs, 92x92", EX.715.00
Flower Basket, calicos on wht, yel sawtooth border w/gr, hs, sm.935.00
Flowers (stylized), mc calicos, sawtooth border, stains, 84x98" ...235.00
Geometrics, mc prints on pk cotton, fine hq, 78" sq 275.00
Hills of Vermont, red calico & wht, hs, stains, 42x57"................525.00
Irish Chain, gr & red calico on wht, fine hq, lt stain, 79x81".....600.00
Leaf Medallions, red on wht, hs, princess feather hq, 58x92" 260.00
Log Cabin in Sunshine & Shadow, bl/tans/reds, hs, 68x79", EX.495.00
Log Cabin w/Str Furrows, gingham & prints w/red, 68x82", EX.500.00
Lone Star, red/yel/gr/bl prints on bl, fine hq, ca 1900, 86" sq......475.00
Lone Star, 5-color dmns form star, hs & hq, 60x70", EX.............495.00
Mariner's Compass, 32-point rnd stars, gr/red/pk/gold, 82x78", EX.865.00
Octagonal medallions, mc on wht, bl binding, feather hq, 67x86".635.00
Odd Fellows Patch, gr/orange calico, princess feather hq, 90x76", VG.500.00
PA Shoo-Fly, red & brn calicos w/wht, minor stains, 74x84"......285.00
Pine Tree, mc prints, 3-part border, hs/feather hq, 76x66" 400.00
Pineapple variant, pk/yel calico w/red center on gr, 80x69" 350.00
Pinwheel blocks, red & navy w/mc flower border, EX hq, 96x82".600.00
Postage Stamp in concentric dmns w/sawtooth border, mc, 98x78"..1,000.00
Sqs & dmn chains on wht w/red, hs, spoked-wheel hq, 66x82" ..750.00
Star medallions & dmn bands, trapunto roses, 76x90", EX......2,475.00
Star medallions(16), red/bl/wht, scrolled feather borders, hs, 84x95".1,375.00
Stars (touching), mc prints on red & bl, chintz border, sgn, 80x76".800.00

Stars (20) navy/red on wht, quilted grid, OH, 67x84"................660.00
Stars (36), mc calicos w/red blocks, stains, PA, 76x75" 425.00
State of OH w/counties & surrounding areas, mc, hs/hq, sgn, 72x76", M..2,750.00
Stepped sqs, prints on dk bl ground, hs, lt wear, 64x79".............315.00
Sun & Shade, red & wht, hs, hq, stains, 78x91".........................230.00
Trip Around The World, mc blocks on bl-gray, fine hq, 82" sq...200.00
16 sqs w/embr characters/animals in red grid, ca 1900, 84x96", EX.470.00
9-Patch variant, wht/navy calico, bl gingham sawtooth border, 82" sq..550.00
9-Patch w/inset dmns, 19th-C prints, dtd 1894, 80x83", VG......300.00

Quimper

Quimper pottery bears the name of the Breton town in northwestern France where it has been made for over three hundred years. Production began in 1690 when Jean-Baptiste Bousquet settled into a small workshop in the suburbs of Quimper, at Locmaria. There he began to make the hand-painted, tin enamel-glazed earthenware which we know today as faience. By the last quarter of the nineteenth century, there were three factories working concurrently: Porquier, de la Hubaudiere (the Grand Maison), and Henriot. All three houses produced similar wares which were decorated with scenes from the everyday life of the peasant folk of the region. Their respective marks are an AP or a P with an intersecting B (similar to a clover), an HB, and an HR (which became HenRiot after litigation in 1922).

The most desirable pieces were produced during the last quarter of the nineteenth century through the first quarter of the twentieth century. These are considered to be artistically superior to the examples made after World War I and II with the exception of the Odetta line, which is now experiencing a renaissance among collectors here and abroad.

Most of what was made was faience, but there was also a history of utilitarian gres ware (stoneware) having been produced there. In 1922 the Grande Maison HB revitalized this ware and introduced the line called Odetta, examples of which seemed to embody the bold spirit of the Art Deco style. The companion faience pieces of this period and genre are classified as Modern Movement examples and frequently bear the name of the artist who designed the mold. These artist-signed examples are dramatically increasing in value.

Currently there are two factories still producing Quimper pottery. La Societe Nouvelle des Faienceries de Quimper is owned by Sarah and Paul Jenessens along with a group of American investors. Their mark is a stamped HB-Henriot logo. The other, La Faiencerie d'art Breton, is operated by the direct descendents of the HB and Henriot families. Their pieces are marked with an interlocked F and A conjoined with an inverted B. Other marks include HQF which is the Henriot Quimper France mark and HBQ, the HB Quimper mark. If you care to learn more about Quimper, we recommend *Quimper Pottery: A French Folk Art Faience* by Sandra V. Bondhus, our advisor for this category, whose address can be found in the Directory under Connecticut.

Bannette, wedding scene w/decor riche, HBQ, 10¼x8" 350.00
Bottle, liquor; Breton man figural, HenRiot...France, 11" 180.00
Bowl, rooster strutting, a la touch garland, att AP, 4x11¼" 450.00
Box, demi-fantasie lady & geometrics, HenRiot, 4" dia 160.00
Box, half-moon form w/seated lady on lid, decor riche, HQ 22, 2x5".225.00
Calotte, faience populaire, goemetric lattice, 19th C, stapled rpr, 9".100.00
Charger, Breton musician, decor riche, HBQ, 13½"....................325.00
Coffeepot, Breton smoking pipe/Crest of Brittany, HBQ (HB lid), 9" .275.00
Coupe, bride & groom in meadow, yel trim, HB, 6¾", NM........400.00
Cruet, demi-fantasie lady w/basket, bluets, HRQ, 3½", from $50 to.75.00
Egg cup holder, swan w/6 cygnet egg cups, HQ 71 F, 8x15½"..1,500.00
Figurine, Chann, lady holding towel, pointed coif, HQ 136, 3¼"..85.00
Figurine, Colaik, man w/walking stick, HQF 197, 3¼" 85.00
Figurine, Fanchik, man in red sailor's cap, HQF 191, 5½" 220.00

Figurine, Le Trois Commeres (3 Gossips), HenRiot, Nicot, 10x9½", NM.275.00
Figurine, man w/lantern dressed as coachman, HenRiot, 5½" 180.00
Figurine, Marik, lady w/folded umbrella, HQ 156, 3¼", NM 85.00
Figurine, Mary holding Christ Child, HQ, 4", NM 240.00
Figurine, St Anne w/child (Mary) nestled, HQ, 3¼" 65.00
Figurine, Village Breton couple, HenRiot...JES (Sevellec), 3" 350.00
Inkwell, bagpiper & nosegays/lattice, cut corners, HBQ, 3½" sq..250.00
Inkwell, dbl; sunken center, flowers & butterflies, unmk, 6¼", EX.230.00
Inkwell, demi-fantasie lady & bluets, attached underdish, 4½" dia..220.00
Inkwell, heart shape w/fleur-de-lis & ermine tails, HB, 4" NM...380.00
Inkwell, man playing bagpipes, decor riche, HRQ, 4" 240.00
Inkwell, 6-pointed star w/demi-fantasie lady spinning, HQF, 3½".275.00
Jardiniere, bagpipe form, Breton boy/girl, HBQ in grass, museum quality ..2,300.00
Jardiniere, Breton man w/flower/Coat of Arms, hdls, M 268, 4x6¾" .110.00
Knife rest, sailor relaxing figural, HenRiot...CH Maillard, 4" 175.00
Lamp base, Modern Movement, lady w/basket on shoulder, HenRiot, 9½" .500.00
Match holder, bellows form, peasant man & bluets, HB, 4"........165.00
Match holder/bud vase, Traditional man/lattice, HQ, free-standing, 5"..130.00
Meloniere, Breton musicians/Crest of Quimper, decor riche, HQ, 12½"..425.00
Pipe, Breton man w/pipe, HBQ, from $175 to 250.00
Pitcher, Grecian ewer form, dancing couple, decor riche, HQ 103, 17"..750.00
Plate, asparagus; Breton man & cottage/asparagus spear, HBQ, 8¾".425.00
Plate, couple dancing, acanthus border, decor riche, HQ, 10" 280.00
Plate, courting couple & trees, acorn border, HBQ-R mk, 8¾" ..500.00
Plate, demi-fantasie Breton flutist, HQF95, 9¼", EX 100.00
Plate, geometrics, HQ82F, 9¼" 110.00
Plate, lady knitting, purple coif, Avergne, HB, 9", NM...............180.00
Plate, Laitere de Quimpere, lady on knoll, 1st Period PB, 8¾".2,000.00
Plate, Marchands de Pommes de Carantec, 1st Peroid PB, 8¾" .2,000.00
Plate, motto: Le dieu de eythere...mystere, a la touche petals, HBQ, 7"..100.00
Plate, Roscoff, 2 men look out to sea, 1st Period PB, 8¾" 1,250.00
Platter, biniou form w/couple dancing/Crest of Brittany, HRQ, 11¾"..375.00
Salt shaker, Bigoudienne lady's head form, Gallard, HQ, 3" 110.00
Sugar bowl, a la touche flower garland, w/lid, HRQ, 5x5"............60.00
Teapot, peasant couple, bluets, HRQ, 7x9", NM, from $200 to..250.00
Vase, Broderie Breton, lady & Celtic patterns, hdls, HBQ, 8½".400.00
Vase, bud; high-button shoe w/Souvenir Noirmoutier, att AP, 3¼".200.00
Vase, couple dancing/Crest of Quimper, decor riche, HRQ, 8½"..450.00
Vase, couple dancing/musicians/Crest of Brittany, hdls, HRQ, 13½"..500.00
Vase, fleur-de-lis form w/demi-fantasie man, HQ 71 F, 10¼" 450.00
Vase, partially open donut w/dragon hdls, decor riche, HRQ, 9", NM.1,250.00
Vase, solifleur; Bretonne lady/mc butterfly in flight, HBQ, 6½".170.00
Vase, spill; bagpipe w/demi-fantasie lady/flower basket, HRQ, 6".300.00
Wall pocket, bagpipe w/demi-fantasie pattern, HRQ, 11"...........350.00
Wall pocket, cone w/lady & fleur-de-lis, 1st Period PB, 5½"......950.00
Wall pocket, envelope w/Breton man & bluets, HRQ, 4x4½"....425.00
Wall pocket, parasol w/courting couple, decor riche, HRQ, 12½", EX..500.00

Radford, Albert

Pottery associated with Albert Radford (1882 – 1904) can be categorized by three periods of production. Pottery produced in Tiffin, Ohio (1896 – 1899), consists of bone china (no marked examples known) and high-quality jasperware with applied Wedgwood-like cameos. Tiffin jasperware is often impressed 'Radford Jasper' in small block letters. At Zanesville, Ohio, Radford jasperware was marked only with an incised, two-digit shape number, and the cameos were not applied but rather formed within the mold and filled with a white slip. Zanesville Radford ware was produced for only a few months before the Radford pottery was acquired by the Arc-en-Ciel company in 1903. Production in Zanesville was handled by Radford's father, Edward (1840 – 1910), who remained in Zanesville after Albert moved to Clarksburg, West Virginia, where the Radford Pottery Co. was completed shortly

before Albert's death in 1904. Jasperware was not produced in Clarksburg, and the molds appear to have been left in Zanesville, where some were subsequently used by the Arc-en-Ciel pottery. The Clarksburg, West Virginia, pottery produced a standard glaze, slip-decorated ware, Ruko; Thera and Velvety, matt glazed ware often signed by Albert Haubrich, Alice Bloomer, and other artists; and Radura, a semimatt green glaze developed by Albert Radford's son, Edward. The Clarksburg plant closed in 1912.

Our advisor for this category is James L. Murphy; he is listed in the Directory under Ohio. For pottery marked E. Radford, see Radford, Edward.

Jasper

Bowl, muses & vintage, fluted rim, imp mk, 5½" 295.00
Box, figure w/cornucopia on lid, 5⅝" 600.00
Ewer, grapes/raspberries, Old Man Winter hdl, #17, 9" 350.00
Letter holder, lady w/bow & target, bark trim, #61 ....500.00
Mug, vintage, gray, #25, 5" 165.00
Pitcher, tankard, vintage, lt bl, #26, 12" 250.00
Vase, bust of Washington, bk: eagle, bark trim, #12, 7" 265.00
Vase, cherubs & lion, #15, 6½" 325.00
Vase, cherubs on flying eagles, #23, 9½" 475.00
Vase, girl running, deep bl, flat-sided/twisted, #53, 3½" 100.00
Vase, Gladstone bust ea side, twisted form, 3" 125.00
Vase, lady kneeling w/bird, gray, #24, 10½x4½" 250.00
Vase, lady w/dog, #22, 10x6" 250.00
Vase, lady w/wildflowers, bk: grapes, #59, 4" 165.00

Miscellaneous

Candle holder, Ruko, floral, sgn/mk, rare, 7" 125.00
Jardiniere, Ruko, floral, scalloped, 8½", NM 370.00
Vase, Radura, 4-hdl, scalloped rim, 10"...................................400.00
Vase, Ruko, floral, 15" 325.00
Vase, Thera, floral, mc on gr, #1453, 12½".............................700.00
Vase, Thera, nasturtium, A Haubrich, ovoid, 13½", NM 900.00
Vase, Velvety, mums, mc on gr, sgn, bottle form, 10¼x3"..........550.00

Radford, Edward

Pottery marked 'E. Radford, Burslem,' or 'E. Radford, England,' includes a variety of earthenware designed by Edward Radford (1883 – 1968), first for H.J. Wood and later for himself in Burslem (production ending in 1948). A variety of floral patterns, cottage or tavern scenes, and Art Deco motifs distinguish this ware. His father, Edward Thomas Radford, worked at the Pilkington Tile and Pottery Co. in Manchester, England, and appears to have been a brother of Albert Radford. Items in the following listings are hand painted unless noted otherwise.

Bowl, posy; lilac crocus on pale gr, 3" opening, 2½x8½" 125.00
Ginger jar, red, yel & bl floral on yel w/lt gr sponging, 6".............85.00
Jam pot, pk & bl foxglove on wht, #37QAF, 3¾" 65.00
Jug, red & bl floral on lt yel, #71ECI, 5" 90.00
Pitcher, bl, yel & red floral on lt bl, #258M, 11¼x3¼" 100.00
Plate, Indian Tree, sgn E Radford England, mk 17/V8, oval, 12x7½" .50.00
Teapot, fruit on wht, mk DG 55.00
Tureen, fish on wht w/lemon-slice hdls, #1194, 13" 60.00
Vase, bl trees & floral on yel, gr & cream, 4½" 140.00
Vase, Lemon Tree (JO), #267, 5¾"..170.00
Vase, purple floral on 1 side w/pk on other, #11AC, 7" 165.00
Vase, tree & landscape, mk #125 PF/F, 4x3¾"...........................110.00
Vase, wht w/red & yel flowers, mk E Radford England #1129, 9" .75.00

Radios

Vintage radios are very collectible. There were thousands of styles and types produced, the most popular of which today are the breadboard and the cathedral. Consoles are usually considered less marketable, since their size makes them hard to display and store. For those wishing to learn more about the subject, we recommend *Collector's Guide to Antique Radios, Fifth Edition,* by John Slusser and the staff of *Radio Daze* (Collector Books.)

Unless otherwise noted in the descriptions, values are given for working radios in near mint to mint condition. Our advisor for this category is Dr. E.E. Taylor; he is listed in the Directory under Indiana. See also Plastics.

Key:
BC — broadcast	R/P — radio-phonograph
LW — long wave	s/r — slide rule
pb — push button	SW — short wave
phono — phonograph	tbl/m — table model

Admiral, 4204-B6, tbl/m, wood, s/r, cloth grille, BC, SW, 1941 ...**70.00**
Admiral, 5Z, plastic/chrome, 2 grille bars, BC, 5 tubes, AC.......**100.00**
Air Castle, 6050, wood, slanted s/r, R/P, 5 tubes, BC, AC, 1949 .**30.00**
Airline, 62-437, movie dial, wood, cloth grille, BC, SW, 1936.....**90.00**
American Bosch, tbl/m, rectangular, center window dial, BC, AC, 1928 .**150.00**
Arvin, 6640, walnut w/cloth grille, sq dial, BC, AC/DC, 1948 ....**60.00**
Bendix, 516A, plastic, s/r, vertical louvers, BC, AC/DC, 1946.....**70.00**
Coronado, 686, wood w/cloth grille, BC, SW, AC, 1935.............**80.00**
Crosley, 56TY, tbl/m, s/r, 2 knobs, BC, AC/DC, 1948 ....**60.00**
Delco, 608, tbl/m, wood, multi-band s/r, 4 knobs, BC, SW, AC, 1949.**50.00**
Emerson, BJ-210, tbl/m, wood, airplane dial, BC, AC/DC, 1938 .**70.00**
Emerson, 357A, portable, hdl, 2 knobs, BC, AC/DC/battery, 1940 .**30.00**
Fada, 1470C, tombstone, rnd dial, cloth grille, BC, SW, AC, 1934..**120.00**
GE, A-85, console, wood w/cloth grille, pointer dial, BC/SW, AC, 1936.**130.00**

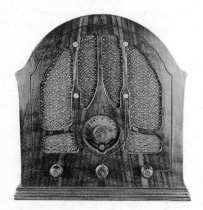

General Electric, K-43-C, cathedral, low wooden case, center front dial, cloth grille with cutouts, 1933, $175.00. (Photo courtesy Sue and Marty Bunis)

GE, YRB-60-2, tbl/m, plastic w/flocked grille, BC, AC/DC, 1948.**45.00**
GE, 42, Musaphonic, console-R/P, s/r, 9 pb, BC/SW/FM/FM1, AC, 1948 ..**80.00**
GE, 42, tbl/m, blk plastic, BC, AC/DC, 1952................................**30.00**
Kadette, 87, tbl/m, wood, rnd dial, BC/SW, AC, 1936 ....**50.00**
Majestic, 130, console, walnut w/cloth grille, lowboy, BC, AC, 1930 .**120.00**
Motorola, 54L3, portable, plastic w/metal grille, BC, fold-down hdl...**30.00**
Motorola, 59T-4, tbl/m, wood w/cloth grille, 4 pb, BC, AC, 1938.**70.00**
Motorola, 6F11, console-R/P (pull-out), ½-rnd dial, BC, AC, 1950 .**50.00**
Olympic, 6-504L, tbl/m-R/P, rnd dial, BC, AC, 1946 ....**25.00**
Philco, PT-4, Transitone, tbl/m, plastic, s/r, BC, AC/DC, 1941....**40.00**
Philco, 37-33, console, wood w/cloth grille, BC, battery, 1937...**100.00**
Philco, 38L, console, wood w/cloth grille, BC/SW, battery, 1933..**140.00**
Philco, 40-145, tbl/m, wood w/cloth grille, s/r, BC/SW, AC, 1940..**70.00**

Philco, 42-380, console, walnut, slanted s/r, 9 pb, BC/SW, AC, 1942 .**100.00**
Philco, 50-1727, console/R/P (pull-out), s/r, pb, BC/FM, AC, 1950..**70.00**
Radiola, 61-3, tbl/m, wood, slanted s/r, BC, AC/DC, 1947...........**40.00**
RCA, HF-8, console, wood, inner dial & tuning eye, BC/SW, AC, 1938..**150.00**
RCA, T-64, tbl/m, 2-tone wood w/cloth grille, s/r, BC/SW, AC, 1940 ..**70.00**
RCA, 16T2, tbl/m, wood, s/r, BC/SW, AC, 1940 ....**60.00**
RCA, 4QB, tbl/m, plastic, slanted dial, BC/SW, battery, 1940 .....**35.00**
RCA, 8V111, console-R/P, wood, tilt-out s/r, BC/FM, AC, 1949.**70.00**
RCA, 94BP66, portable, front dial, BC, battery, 1940 ....**30.00**
Sentinel, 247P, portable, inner dial, hdl, BC, AC/DC/battery, 1942 .**40.00**
Silvertone, 1670, console, wood w/cloth grille, 6 legged, BC, AC, 1933 .**100.00**
Silvertone, 7116, console-R/P, tilt-out s/r, BC/FM, AC, 1947 ......**70.00**
Sparton, 6A66, metal, rectangular dial, 3 knobs, 1948 ....**60.00**
Truetone, D-2237A, tbl/m, plastic w/cloth grille, ftd, BC, AC/DC, 1952 ..**30.00**

Novelty Radios

Annie w/Sandy, 1980s, red & wht plastic, AM, MIB....................**75.00**
Bozo the Clown, 1970s, head & shoulders form, AM, EX.............**50.00**
Bumble Lion Wuzzle, AM, EX..**35.00**
Charlie Tuna, 1970s, w/clamp for handlebars, AM, EX................**65.00**
Donald Duck, head form, speaker in bk, AM, VG **30.00**
Fonz Jukebox, AM, G..**20.00**
Hamburger Helper's Helping Hand, lg wht hand w/face, NM.......**75.00**
McDonald's Big Mac, GE, AM, EX..**60.00**
Mickey Mouse, stuffed figure w/red shorts & yel ft, NM **25.00**
Mr T, 1980s, photo front as BA Baracus, EX..............................**60.00**
Nestlè Crunch Candy Bar, strap hdl, EX+.................................**60.00**
Pinball Wizard, Astra, 1980s, AM, MIB **175.00**
Pound Puppy, 1980s, dog atop AM radio, EX **20.00**
Raid Bug, 1980s, figural clock-radio, NM **200.00**
R2-D2 Robot, Kenner, figural, AM, MIB **150.00**
Smurf, 1980s, head form, EX **50.00**
Snoopy & Woodstock Doghouse, Determined, 1970s, NM **50.00**
Sonic Radio Man, Janex/Marvel, '70s, wristwatch style, AM, EX..**70.00**

Transistor Radios

Post-World War II baby boomers, now in their fifties, are rediscovering prized possessions of youth, their pocket radios. The transistor wonders, born with rock 'n roll, were at the vanguard of miniaturization and futuristic design in the decade which followed their introduction to Christmas shoppers in 1954. The tiny receiving sets launched the growth of Texas Instruments and shortly to follow abroad, Sony and other Japanese giants.

The most desirable sets include the 1954 four-transistor Regency TR-1 and colorful early Sony and Toshiba models. Certain pre-1960 models by Hoffman and Admiral represented the earliest practical use of solar technology and are also highly valued. To avoid high tariffs, scores of two-transistor sets, boys' radios, were imported from Japan with names like Pet and Charmy. Many early inexpensive transistor sets could be heard only with an earphone. The smallest sets are known as shirt-pocket models while those slightly larger are called coat-pockets. Early collectible transistor radios all have civil defense triangle markings at 640 and 1240 on the frequency dial and nine or fewer transistors. Very few desirable sets were made after 1963. Model numbers are most commonly found inside. Our advisor for this category is Mike Brooks; he is listed in the Directory under California and welcomes questions. (Please include a SASE.)

Admiral, Y2461 Galaxy, horizontal, blk leather, 10 transistors, 1963 .**20.00**
Airline, GEN-1202B, horizontal, M/W logo, 1962.......................**35.00**
Airline, GEN-1207A, horizontal, 8 transistors, AM, 1961 ....**30.00**
Arvin, 62R19, vertical, crown logo, AM, 1962 ....**15.00**
Bulova, 670, vertical, plastic, 6 transistors, rhinestone decor, AM ..**65.00**
Bulova, 685, vertical, swing hdl, 4 transistors, AM, 1962 ....**65.00**

Channel Master, 6518A, horizontal, 2 antennas, 14 transistors....**30.00**
Columbia, 400R, vertical, red, 4 transistors, AM, 1960 ....**55.00**
Crosley, JM-8BK, Enchantment, book shape, 2 transistors, 1956..**150.00**
Dewald, K-544A, horizontal, leather, 4 transistors, AM, 1957 .....**65.00**
Emerson, 844, horizontal, 6 transistors, G clef logo, AM, 1956....**45.00**
GE, P815A, horizontal, 7 transistors, AM, 1961 ....**25.00**
Global, GR711, vertical, 6 transistors, AM, Japan, 1961............**100.00**
Graetz, 40H Flirt, vertical, 6 transistors, AM, 1966 ....**45.00**
Holiday, ST-600, horizontal, 6 transistors, AM, Japan **45.00**
Kent, TR-605, vertical, 6 transistors, AM, 1965 ....**15.00**
Lincoln, TR-3422, horizontal, 14 transistors, AM/FM, 1963........**25.00**
Magnavox, AW-24, horizontal, 7 tranistors, s/r, AM, 1960s..........**25.00**
Motorola, X47E, vertical, 7 transistors, AM, 1962 ....**25.00**
Motorola, X48E, horizontal, leather, 7 transistors, AM, 1962.......**15.00**
Motorola, 7X25W, Power 9, vertical, 7 transistors, AM, 1959......**40.00**
Panasonic, T-11 Tiny-Tote, vertical, AM.....................................**50.00**
Raleigh, 805, vertical, 8 transistors, AM, 1965............................**25.00**
Raytheon, T-100 Series, AM, USA, 1956 ....**250.00**
RCA, 1-BT-24, Transicharg Super, horizontal, 6 transistors, 1958 ..**45.00**
Realtone, TR-1887, vertical, 8 transistors, AM, 1965...................**15.00**
Realtone, Tr-870, 6 transistors, AM, Japan, 1959........................**125.00**
Regency, TR-1, blk, vertical, 1st transistor radio, US, 1954 ....**300.00**
Sony, TR-72, horizontal, wood, 7 transistors, Japan, AM, 1956.**300.00**
Summit, S109, vertical, 10 transistors, Ryukyu, AM **30.00**
Toshiba, TR-193, vertical, 6 transistors, AM, Japan, 1958 ....**230.00**
Truetone, DC3270, horizontal, 9 transistors, USA, AM **40.00**
Vista, G-1050, horizontal, 10 transistors, AM/FM, 1964...............**20.00**
Zenith, Royal 130, vertical, AM...**35.00**

Railroadiana

Collecting railroad-related memorabilia has become one of America's most popular hobbies. The range of collectible items available is almost endless; not surprising, considering the fact that more than 185 different railroad lines are represented. Some collectors prefer to specialize in only one railroad, while others attempt to collect at least one item from every railway line known to have existed. For the advanced collector, there is the challenge of locating rarities from short-lived railroads; for the novice, there are abundant keys, buttons, and passes. Among the most popular specializations are dining-car collectibles — flatware, glassware, dinnerware, etc., in a wide variety of patterns and styles. Railroad blankets are also collectible. Most common are Pullman blankets. The early ones had a cross-stitch pattern; these were followed by one in a solid cinnamon color; both are marked clearly with the Pullman name. In the 1920s, Pullman put out a blue blanket marked Pullman, specifically for ethnic use. There is one in the Sacramento railroad museum. Other railroads had their own 'marked' blankets that are even more desirable, such as the Soo line, the Chessie, and one marked Pheasant (which was a private car on the Milwaukee Line that was reserved to carry special parties for hunting trips).

Another name among railroad dining collectors is Fred Harvey. From 1893 until after WWII, Fred Harvey masterminded all the dining halls and dining cars on the Santa Fe Railroad System from Chicago to the west coast. (A little known fact, he also had dining facilities on the Frisco railroad.) He had his famous Harvey girls, as portrayed by Judy Garland, and a lot of personal dining china, silver, and linens marked with his 'FH.'

Berth keys have become scarce and expensive as more and more collectors purchase private rail cars. This is also true of 'window lifters,' specially designed pry bars made of wood used to ram the windows open in the old wood coaches. Most recently Otto Mears (of Silverton, Colorado, railroad fame) 1893 silver filigree railroad passes have surfaced. They are very scarce; made to the individual with possibly only one hundred issued. These are appraised at $12,000.00 and have recently sold for near $11,000.00.

As is true in most collecting fields, scarcity and condition determine value. There is more interest in some railway lines than in others; generally speaking, it is greater in the region serviced by the particular railroad. American collectors prefer American-made products and items with ties to American railroads. For example, English switch lanterns, though of superior quality, usually sell at lower prices, as does memorabilia from Canadian railways such as Canadian Pacific or Canadian National.

Reproductions abound in railroadiana collectibles — from dinnerware and glassware to lanterns, keys, badges, belt buckles, timetables, and much more. Railroad police badge replicas have glutted the market. They are professionally made and only the expert is able to differentiate the replica from the original. Reproduced hand-executed, reverse-painted glass signs have been abundant throughout the country, most of them read 'Santa Fe,' but some say 'Whites Only.' Lately markets in the East have been inundated with Baltimore & Ohio reproductions: menus, glass water carafes, demitasse sets in the George Washington theme, and more. Beware! Also railroad drumheads are coming out of collections. A drumhead is a large (approximately 24" diameter) glass sign in a metal case. They were used on the back end of all railroad observation cars to advertise a special train or a presidential foray, etc. They're now beginning to surface, and a good one like the Flying Crow from the Kansas City Southern Railroad will go for $2,500.00, as will many others. When items of this value come out, the counterfeiters are right there. It is important to 'Know Thy Dealer.' For a more thorough study, we recommend *Railroad Collectibles, Fourth Revised Edition*, by Stanley L. Baker. The values noted for most of our dinnerware, glassware, linen, silverplate, and timetables are actual selling prices. However, because prices are so volatile, the best pricing sources are often monthly or quarterly 'For Sale' lists. Two you may find helpful may be ordered from Golden Spike, P.O. Box 422, Williamsville, NY 14221, and Grandpa's Depot, 6720 E. Mississippi Ave., Unit B, Denver, CO 80224. Our co-advisors for this category are Lila Shrader (See Directory, California) and John White (Grandpa's Depot, see Colorado).

Key:
BL — bottom logo   SL — side logo
BS — bottom stamped   SM — side mark
FBS — full back stamp   TL — top logo
NBS — no back stamp   TM — top mark

Dinnerware

Many railroads designed their own china for use in their dining cars or company-owned hotels or stations. Some railroads chose to use stock patterns to which they added their name or logo; others used the same stock patterns without the added identification. A momentary warning: The railroad dinnerware market has fallen considerably, only the rare and scarce items are saleable; otherwise don't speculate in dining china. For more information, we recommend *Restaurant China, Volumes 1* and *2*, by Barbara J. Conroy (Collector Books).

Ashtray, ATSF, California Poppy, NBS, 5" dia **195.00**
Ashtray, C&O, Geo Washington, 3x7" **110.00**
Ashtray, M&StL, Peoria Gateway Line, TL, 5½" **89.00**
Au gratin, CP, Empress, tab hdls, NBS, 8" dia **24.00**
Bowl, cereal; SP, Prairie Mtn Wildflowers, BS, 6" **82.00**
Bowl, cereal/chile; ATSF, CA Poppy, BS, Bauscher, 3x6¾" on ⅜" ped.**288.00**
Bowl, cereal/chile; ATSF, CA Poppy, NBS, 3x6¾" on ⅜" ped ...**120.00**
Bowl, fruit; ATSF, Bleeding Blue, TM, 5½" **148.00**
Bowl, fruit; MStP&SStM, Logan, BS, 5½".................................**260.00**
Bowl, salad; ATSF, Mimbreno, BS, 3x8¼" **455.00**
Bowl, soup; SP, Sunset, flat, TM & BS, 8¾" **145.00**

Butter pat, ATSF, California Poppy, BS, from $105 to 160.00
Butter pat, ATSF, Mimbreno, BM, 3⅜", from $110 to............130.00
Butter pat, CMStP&P, Peacock, NBS 97.00
Butter pat, CRI&P, Golden State, TL, NBS, 3½" 248.00
Butter pat, FL East Coast, St Johns, BS, 3½" 388.00
Butter pat, UP, Winged Streamliner, NBS 55.00
Chocolate pot, ATSF, California Poppy, NBS, 5½", from $128 to ..144.00
Compote, Uintah, Mesa, ped ft, TL, NBS 750.00
Creamer, ATSF, Mimbreno, BS, ind, 2¼" 465.00
Creamer, B&O, Centenary, Scammell, BS, 3¾" 330.00
Creamer, CN, Tower Inn, Niagara Falls, hdl, SL, ind 178.00
Creamer, MKT, Bluebonnet, BM, ind, 3¼" 430.00
Creamer, Pullman, Indian Tree, no hdl, SL, NBS, ind 46.00
Cup, bouillon; GN, Glory of the West, BS, 3¾" 180.00
Cup & saucer, ATSF, California Poppy, NBS 96.00
Cup & saucer, demi; CMStP&P, Traveler, saucer BS 110.00
Cup & saucer, demi; NP, Northwest, NBS......................250.00
Cup & saucer, demi; Wabash, Banner, NBS....................490.00
Cup & saucer, GN, Glory of the West, both BS................640.00
Cup & saucer, MP, Eagle, saucer BS..........................117.00
Egg cup, CM&StP, Traveler, NBS, 2½x1⅞" 150.00
Gravy boat, GM&O, Rose, SL, 6" 310.00
Ice cream shell, Lake Tahoe Ry, Tahoe Tavern, TM, 4½"..........430.00
Plate, B&A, Berkshire, TL & BS, 10" 445.00

Plate, Baltimore and Ohio, Harper's Ferry, blue transfer, 10½" $50.00.

Plate, D&RGW, Prospector, TL, 10" 107.00
Plate, GN, Manitoba, TL, NBS, 7⅞"............................93.00
Plate, GN, Spokane, NBS, 8½"..................................35.00
Plate, IL Central, Pirate, NBS, 9¾" 200.00
Plate, NP, Yellowstone, TL, NBS, 7¼" 128.00
Plate, service; IL Central, Pirate Alley, BM, 11" 1,135.00
Plate, service; Seaboard Air Line, Old Bay Line, TM, BM, 10⅝" ..150.00
Platter, B&M, Minuteman, TM, 9½x6½" 525.00
Platter, GN, Glory of the West, NBS, 9½x5¾" 145.00
Platter, NP, Monad, TL, 9¾x8"..............................140.00
Platter, SP, Prairie Mtn Wildflowers, oval, BS, 9x8½" 258.00
Relish dish, GN, Oriental, NBS, 9¾"..........................230.00
Sauce boat, GN, Hill, NBS, SL, 3½x6" 250.00
Sherbet, D&RGW, Prospector, ped ft, 2½x3¾" 130.00
Sugar bowl, CMStP&P, Calatea, w/lid, NBS....................235.00
Teapot, ATSF, Mimbreno, FBS................................530.00
Teapot, B&O, Centenary, BM, Shenango 110.00
Vase, CN, Toronto, SL deep red on tan body, 9"..............130.00

Glass

Ashtray, ATSF, Turquoise Room, Super Chief, 3¼x4½"............52.00
Ashtray, PRR, enamel Keystone logo, 6" sq....................17.00
Bottle, ATSF Chemical Dept emb, narrow neck 47.00
Bottle, medicine; emb MKT Employees Hosp Assn Sedalia MO, 3⅝".54.00

Bottle, milk; Missouri Pacific buzz saw logo, emb, 1-qt 72.00
Bottle, milk; PRR, buzz saw logo, ½-pt 30.00
Bottle, oil; SP logo emb+label: Return Bottle to Stationary Store, 5" ..30.00
Bottle, StL&SF, SL, ½-pt, from $28 to 34.00
Carafe, CPR, acid etch Tremblant Ry logo, appl rings, 7½" 128.00
Champagne, ATSF, cut banner: Santa Fe, 3½" 166.00
Champagne, ATSF, SL acid etched Santa Fe, Heisey, 4", from $200 to .260.00
Cocktail, ATSF, SL acid etched script Santa Fe, 4½" 53.00
Cocktail, GN w/interlocking GN monogram, 4¼" 90.00
Cordial, B&O w/Capitol Dome logo+B&O, 3⅞"..................65.00
Cruet, ATSF, WL etched Banner design, no stopper, 5" 1,425.00
Cruet, NYC, Commodore Hotel, orig stopper, acid etched SL, 5" .128.00
Decanter, MKT etched SL, narrow neck, flat base, orig stopper, 8½"..685.00
Hi-ball, CI&L (Monon), enamel circle logo, flared base, 5¼" 78.00
Martini pitcher, UP, pyro UP shield SL, 5¼"..................22.00
Martini set, UP, 5¼" pitcher+2x2¼" roly poly glasses+stirrer.......48.00
Old-fashioned, PRR, enamel train scene & capitol, NY, 4½".......23.00
Pilsner, CRI&P, etched Rock Island logo, 7" 66.00
Pitcher, CMStP&P in BS SP fr w/removable lid, unmk glass 193.00
Shot glass, UP, wht enamel UPRR 1-oz, 2½" 54.00
Swizzle stick, ATSF, plastic w/chief's head+Santa Fe - The Chief Way ..2.00
Swizzle stick, C of NJ, hollow w/CNJ & distiller's ad, 4¾" 36.00
Tumbler, Chicago, Milwaukee, St Paul & Pacific box logo, etch, 4¾" .126.00
Tumbler, Cincinnati, Atlantic & Columbus RR, CAC emb bottom, 4⅝"..23.00
Tumbler, CMStP&P, Milwaukee Road, pyro of Hiawatha engine, 5" .34.00
Tumbler, IC, frosted dmn logo, 5", from $8 to 38.00
Tumbler, juice; ATSF, Santa Fe enamel & script, 3¾" 13.00
Tumbler, juice; B&O in blk enamel Garrett logo, 5"............15.00
Tumbler, juice; Great Northern, GN intertwined wht pyro, 4¼" .42.00
Tumbler, NYC, 50th Anniversary 20th C Limited, 5¼" 22.00
Tumbler, WM, pyro logo, 6½"..................................52.00
Wine, CMStP&P, Milwaukee's box logo in wht enamel, 3⅞" 192.00
Wine, IL Central, pyro IC Dmn SL, 4½"........................17.00
Wine, stem; CN, etched logo w/pinstripes, 4½" 68.00

Keys

Switch keys are brass with hollow barrels and round heads with holes for attaching to a key ring. They were used to unlock the padlocks on track-side switches when the course of the tracks had to be changed. (Switches were padlocked to prevent them from being thrown by accident or vandals, a situation that could result in a train wreck.) A car key used to open padlocks on freight cars and the like is very similar to the switch key, except the bit is straighter instead of being specifically curved for a particular railroad and its accompanying switch locks. A second type of 'car' key was used for door locks on passenger cars, Pullmans, etc.; this type was usually of brass, but instead of having a hollow barrel, they were shaped like an old-fashioned hotel door key. In order for a key to be collectible, the head must be marked with a name, initials, or a railroad identification, with 'switch' generally designated by 'S' and 'car' by 'C' markings. Railroad, patina 'not polished,' and the presence of a manufacturer's mark other than Adlake all have a positive affect on pricing and collectibility.

A new precedent was set in 1995 when a Denver and South Park car key went at a Missouri auction for $2,500.00. The key was marked DSP&P (an early Colorado road that stopped running in 1898); it was brass and had a hollow barrel and straight bit. Switch keys that only recently brought $15.00 to $17.00 are now bringing $35.00.

Caboose, unmk, Adlake, solid long bbl, 3¾" 8.00
Signal, NPSI, 36 hollow bbl, 2"..............................28.00
Switch, C&S, Adlake #4910 ....85.00
Switch, DTRR, Adlake..22.00
Switch, NW, Slaymaker, #44037 ....40.00

Switch, PCRR, Adlake, unused..........15.00

Lamps

Coach, Adams & Westlake, brass/bronze, 2 armitures, oil burner, 21"..1,480.00
Hand, GTW on side, steel/brass, 4 lenses, 12", VG..........85.00
Inspector's, Wabash, Dietz Acme, unmk globe, rpt, EX 815.00
Vertical, Adlake, red & clear lenses, steel, worn pnt, sm 50.00
Wall candle, Adams & Westlake 1907P, older style w/drilled top ...60.00

Lanterns

Before 1920 kerosene brakemen's lanterns were made with tall globes, usually 5⅜" high. These are most desirable to collectors and are usually found at the top of the price scale. Short globes from 1921 through 1940 normally measure 3½" in height, except for those manufactured by Dietz, which are 4" tall. (Soon thereafter, battery brakemen's lanterns came into widespread usage; these are not highly regarded by collectors and are generally not railroad marked.)

All lanterns should be marked with the name or initials of the railroad — look on the top, the top apron, or the bell base (if it has one). Globes may be found in these colors (listed in order of popularity): clear, red, amber, aqua, cobalt, and two-color. Any lantern's value is enhanced if it has a colored globe.

Key: A&W — Adams and Westlake

A&W, C&O, short etched globe, Pat dates..........65.00
A&W Adams, Santa Fe, clear 5½" globe, bell-bottom, 1909.....200.00
A&W Adlake Reliable, CCC&StL, clear 5⅜" globe, wire-ring base ..175.00
Adlake, switch stand, red & bl glass lenses, 12"+6" bail 178.00
Armspear, DM&NRy, clear 5½" globe, twist-off bottom w/pot, 1895...225.00
Armspear Mfg Co, switch stand, gr & yel lenses, 16"..........260.00
B&O, Kelly Lamp Co, TL on rim, single wire fr, bell-bottom .1,030.00
ET Wright & Co, GTR, clear 5½" globe, wire-ring base 145.00
Frisco System coonskin logo emb on globe & fr, bell-bottom..1,600.00
Keystone, PRR, etched 5" red globe, wire-ring base, oil pot, EX..445.00
Santa Fe Rte on lid brim & emb on globe, A&W 2,435.00

Linens and Uniforms

Over the years the many railroad companies took great pride in their dining car table presentation. In the very early years of railroad dining car service, the linens used at the tables were of the finest quality white damask. Most railroads would add their company's logo, name, initials, or even a spectacular scene that would be woven into the cloth (white on white). These patterns were not evident unless the fabric was held at a particular angle to the light. The dining car staff's attire generally consisted of heavily starched blinding white jackets with shiny buttons.

In later years, post-World War II, color began to be used for table linens. Florida railroads created some delightfully colorful items for the table as well as for headrests. The passenger train crew, the conductor, and the brakemen, were generally attired in black suits, white shirts, and black ties. Their head gear generally bore a badge denoting their position. These items have all become quite collectible. Sadly, however, replicas of badges and pins have been produced as well as 'fantasy' items (items that do not replicate an older item but are meant to mislead or deceive).

Key: w/w — white on white

Blanket, Amtrak, logo, polyester, 60x50", M in orig plastic bag ...16.00
Blanket, NYNH&H in lt bl on med bl wool, 72x40"..........126.00
Coat, conductor's; PRR, Keystone lapel patches+PRR buttons, 1940s ..98.00

Coat & vest, SAL lapel patches & buttons, 1940s 88.00
Hat, brakeman's; Santa Fe, blk wool w/bl & wht enamel logo badge..175.00
Hat, conductor's; CMStP&P, blk wool w/enamel logo & badge, gold braid...135.00
Headrest cover, Erie-Lackawanna stitched in red on wht cotton, 18x14"..22.00
Headrest cover, GN & mc Monad logo on wht huck, 17x14" 22.00
Headrest cover, Wabash in bl script on wht huck, envelope type, 22x14"...15.00
Napkin, Burlington Rte rectangular box logo, w/w, 22" sq..........36.00
Napkin, Wht Pass & Yukon circular logo w/center flag, w/w, 20" sq .32.00
Shoe bags, Burlington Rte logo/Zephyr Freight Service, drawstrings, pr..22.00
Suit, UP, Blackford, Portland OR mfg, 1940s, jacket+pants+vest.128.00
Tablecloth, CRI&P, w/w logo w/oak leaves edge, unused, 54x36" ...68.00
Tablecloth, NP, w/w, Yellowstone Park Line Monad center, 53" sq .52.00
Tablecloth, SAL, w/w w/Through the Heart of The South logo, 52x47"..56.00
Towel, hand; GN on red center stripe, wht huck, 26x15"..........22.00
Towel, hand; Pullman, bl center stripe w/date on wht, 23x16", $9 to.23.00
Towel, hand; SOO, bl center stripe w/SOO Lines on wht huck, 26x15"..22.00
Uniform, PRR, pants, vest coat w/full patches & all buttons, wool ..288.00

Locks

Brass switch locks (pre-1920) were made in two styles: heart-shaped and Keen Kutter style. Values for the heart-shaped locks are determined to a great extent by the railroad they represent and just how its name appears on the lock. Most in demand are locks with large embossed letters; if the letters are small and incised, demand for that lock is minimal. For instance, one from the Union Pacific line (even with heavily embossed letters) may go for only $45.00, while the same from the D&RG railroad could go easily sell for $250.00. Old Keen Kutter styles (brass with a 'pointy' base) from Colorado & Southern and Denver & Rio Grande could range from $600.00 to $1,200.00.

Steel switch locks (circa 1920 on) with the initials of the railroad incised in small letters — for example BN, L&H, and PRR — are usually valued at $20.00 to $28.00.

Unless otherwise noted, all switch locks described below are made of brass and are heart shaped.

Signal, ATSF on bottom edge, eagle Lock Co...USA on shackle .35.00
Signal, GNRY on front, RACO on side, w/hex wrench-type key.30.00
Switch, B&MRR on shackle bk, Wilson Bohannon on shackle front..85.00
Switch, B&O, BS, w/key & chain..........44.00
Switch, NP Switch & Pat # on bk, Adlake on key drop, steel......18.00
Switch, NY&P, W Bohannan, BS, Pat 1879, w/chain..........63.00
Switch, Virginian Ry, emb TL, M&S Mfg..........1,590.00
Water service, D&RG, F-S Hdw Co, w/key..........150.00

Silver-Plated Flatware

Fork, dinner; NP, Winthrop, Gorham, TM, 7½" 33.00
Fork, dinner; SAL, Cromwell, Internat'l, TM, 7½"..........28.00
Fork, pickle; NYC, Commonwealth, Internat'l, BS, 5¾" 56.00
Fork, seafood, GN, Astoria, Wallace, TM, 5½" 50.00
Fork, seafood; CMStP&P, Broadway, Internat'l, BS, 5¾" 22.00
Fork, seafood; N&W, Troy, Gorham, TM, 6½" 125.00
Ice tongs, SP, SL, Victor Silver Co, 8¼" 105.00
Iced-tea spoon, GM&O Broadway, Internat'l, 7½" 40.00
Iced-tea spoon, N&W, Holland, TL, Gorham, 7¾" 52.00
Knife, butter; MP, Empire, BM, Internat'l, 7⅛" 22.00
Knife, dinner; PRR, Kings, w/full shell & stainless blade, Adams.22.00
Knife, dinner; SRR, DeSoto, BM, Reed & Barton, 9½" 19.00
Knife, luncheon; CRR of NJ, Cromwell, Meriden, 7⅜"..........38.00
Spoon, bar; CP, Windsor, Rogers, TL, 8" 35.00
Spoon, condiment; CP, Windsor, Elkington, TM 34.00
Spoon, condiment; NYC, Century, Internat'l, TM, 4¼"..........36.00
Spoon, demi; SPLA&SL, Modern Art, Reed & Barton, TL, 4" .120.00

Spoon, soup; GN, Hutton, rnd bowl, Internat'l, TL, 6" **43.00**
Sugar tongs, CMStP&P, Sm, Internat'l, 4" **180.00**
Sugar tongs, NP, Embassy, Monad SL, BS, Reed & Barton **45.00**
Tablespoon, CRI&P, Belmont, TM: RI, BM: Rock Island Lines ...**34.00**
Tea strainer, SP, TM w/Daylight logo on hdl, Reed & Barton, 4¼"..**265.00**
Teaspoon, Grand Trunk Pacific, Windsor, TL, Elkington, 5¾".....**17.00**
Teaspoon, Gulf Coast Lines, Waverly, BM, Internat'l, 5¾" **26.00**
Teaspoon, N&W, Holland, TL, Gorham, 5⅞".................................**52.00**

Silver-Plated Hollow Ware

Bowl, ATSF, SM, BS, Internat'l, 4¾" **135.00**
Bread tray, NP, oval, BM, Internat'l, 10½x4¾" **80.00**
Butter icer, C&A, BS, Reed & Barton, 2-pc, 2¾"+tab hdls **388.00**
Butter pat, CRI&P, BS, Gorham, 3¼" **22.00**
Chocolate pot, GN, hinged lid, SL, BS, Internat'l, 5½" **135.00**
Coffeepot, Rio Grande, Curecanti logo SM, hinged lid, 12-oz ...**200.00**
Coffeepot, SP, hinged lid, SM+ball & wing finial, Internat'l, 6½"..**85.00**
Condiment holder, SP, sugar+pr shakers, w/hdl, BM, 11" W **790.00**
Creamer, IC, hinged lid, Internat'l or Reed & Barton, BS, 7-oz..**86.00**
Crumber & scraper, GNR, intertwined TL, BS, 9" W **370.00**
Frame for finger bowl, PRR, rtcl sides, BM w/Keystone logo, 4" W ..**188.00**
Hot food cover, Dearboard Coast Line, SL, 6½" W **90.00**
Ice bucket, Grand Trunk Pacific SL, Toronto SP Co, 8" **172.00**
Menu holder, CMStP&P, The Milwaukee Road SL, Internat'l ..**240.00**
Mustard fr, DL&W, w/hinged lid & clear glass insert, BS **368.00**
Mustard jar, CP, hinged lid, no glass liner, TM, Elkington, 3½"..**48.00**
Server, Wabash, w/lid, BS, Internat'l, ind, 4x7½" L (hdl to hdl) ..**162.00**
Shakers, MP, fr (BS) & lids (SL), Internat'l, pr..........................**180.00**
Sugar bowl, C&A, hdls, w/lid, BS, 4x7" **280.00**
Sugar bowl, NP, hdls, open, YPL SL, 4½" **80.00**
Syrup, UP, hinged lid, attached tray, BM, Reed & Barton, 6".....**85.00**
Teapot, ACL, hinged lid, SL, Rogers Silver, 4" **120.00**
Teapot, FEC - The Breakers, on swivel stand, SL, Internat'l, 12"..**195.00**
Teapot, MStP&SStM, hinged lid, elegant hdl, BS, 5" **195.00**
Teapot, Southern RR, hinged lid, SM, Reed & Barton, ind, 4"..**235.00**
Teapot fr, L&N, hinged lid, Hall teapot insert, BS.....................**312.00**
Tray, MKT, BM, Wallace, 6" dia..**140.00**
Tray, T&P Eagle TL, rectangular, BS, Internat'l, 7x10½"...........**115.00**
Vase, CPR, wide flared top rim, SM, Elkington, 7" **157.00**

Miscellaneous

Timetables and railroad travel brochures continue to gain in popularity and offer the collector vast information about the glory days of railroading. Annual passes continue to be favored over trip and one-time passes. Their value is contingent upon the specific railroad, its length of run, and the appearance of the pass itself. Many were tiny works of art enhanced with fancy calligraphy and decorated with unique vignettes.

Pocket calendars are popular as well as railroad playing cards. Pins, badges, and uniform buttons bearing the name or logo of a railroad are also sought after. The novice needs to be cautious about signs (metal as well as cardboard) and belt buckles. Reproductions flourish in these areas.

Advertising, C&O, Chessie As We Found Her, orig envelope, 1937, 12x14".**36.00**
Air horn, locomotive, Nathan, 3-chime trumpets, 2, 3 & 4 ....**495.00**
Annual reports (5), GM&O, 1962-65 ....**160.00**
Atlas, 1899 World RR, Rand McNally, 166-pg, 14x21", G+ **185.00**
Badge, breast; Conrail, Police Captain, gold-tone star, Blackinton .**114.00**
Badge, breast; NYC, Police Sergeant, Hanson Co, nickel w/locomotive .**325.00**
Badge, breast; US Post Office Mail...Dept, silver-tone, from $68 to...**146.00**
Badge, cap; B&Me Agent, gold finish, curved top, 3⅝"................**75.00**

Badge, cap; CMStPRy, Baggageman in blk enamel on silver-tone .**180.00**
Badge, cap; MCRR/NYC, Telegraph Operator in bl enamel on nickel..**297.00**
Badge, cap; Southern Ry, Flagman (in script) in blk enamel on nickel..**32.00**
Badge, hat; Penn Central Conductor, anodized brass, dome top...**45.00**
Baggage tags, Fonda, Johnstown & Gloversville RR, brass, matched set..**200.00**
Bell, locomotive; UP, brass, w/clapper/yoke/cradle/arm, TM, 24" ..**1,835.00**
Blotter, BN, Zephyr, 6x3½" **26.00**
Book, Central of GA & Connecting..., Prince, hardbk, 1976, no jacket..**275.00**
Book, Iron Horses of Santa Fe Trail, Worley, 1965, 612-pg, $160 to....**175.00**
Book, Locomotive Dictionary, Simmons & Boardman, 1916, 991-pg .**450.00**
Book, Poor's Manual, hardbk, maps/ads/info, 1890, 1,300+ pgs..**218.00**
Book, RRs of Hawaii, Narrow & Std Gauge, 1979 ....**75.00**
Book, Ry Engineering & Maintenance Cyclopedia, 1926...........**195.00**
Book, US House of Representatives Explorations...MS to Pacific, 1855 ..**300.00**
Booklet, Chicago N Shore Ry Line of Skokie Valley..., 1920s, 32-pg ..**230.00**
Booklet, Fred Harvey, Doing the Grand Canyon, 1922, 20-pg, EX ...**35.00**
Booklet, GN, Montana history, agriculture/maps/photos, 1925, 8½x11" ..**34.00**
Booklet, SP, Inside Track/Southern CA, 1907, 24-pg, 5x7" **26.00**
Box, FL East Coast emb on top, metal, compartments, 5x10x7" ..**80.00**
Broadside, TX Short Line, PTT, St Louis to San Antonio, 1878, 21x7"..**228.00**
Brochure, ATSF, Mesa Verde Nat'l Park, system map, 2-color, 1923, NM...**18.00**
Brochure, Pacific, Hiking Trails, 1920s **66.00**
Brochure, UP, Western Wonderlands, 1930s, 24-pg, 9x6" **25.00**
Builder's plate, B&O, Baldwin Locomotive Works, brass, 1922, 11¾" L...**750.00**
Builder's plate, NP, Schenectady Locomotive Works, brass, 1898, 7x13" ..**1,300.00**
Button, AC&SRR Shore Fast Line, silver, flat, sm.........................**4.50**
Button, Concord & Montreal RR, brass convex style, Waterbury, 1890s.**35.00**
Button, MP, brass flat style, AG Meier & Co on bk, 1920s, lg........**8.00**
Button, UP Ry Service, brass, Waterbury, lg **8.00**
Calendar, Burlington Rte, NB Zephyr illus, 1949, 25½x18".......**124.00**
Calendar, C&NW, freighter by lakeside, 1946, complete, wall hanging.**190.00**
Calendar, Chesapeake RR, Chessie w/kittens in bed, 1946, 24x15", NM+.**80.00**
Calendar, Chesapeake RR, porter at bed/Chessie at ft, 1948, 23x14", EX ...**65.00**
Calendar, GN, Indian Chief, W Reiss, 1943, 22x16", NM **55.00**
Calendar, pocket; PRR, plastic, 1950s, from $7 to........................**16.00**
Calendar, PRR, Giant Conquerors of Space & Time, 1931, 30x29", EX.**700.00**
Calendar, PRR, Grif Teller illus, 1941, complete w/tear sheet, wall mt .**332.00**
Calendar, PRR, Grif Teller illus, 1949, complete, wall hanging....**50.00**
Calendar, Sante Fe, flowers, die-cut corners, 1892, 4½x3½", NM.**90.00**
Calender, GN, 12 monthly cardstock sheets, Indian portraits, 1928, NM.**480.00**
Can, oil; C&NW, coffeepot shape, spout dome font, side grip hdl..**35.00**
Cigar box, PRR, Horseshoe Curve, Crooks, wood, color label, EX .**60.00**
Clock, Santa Fe TM dial, S Thomas, rosewood, short drop, 8-day .**1,150.00**
First-aid kit, UP, metal w/logo on front, fully stocked **38.00**
Hat, conductor's; CMStP&P, blk wool, enamel & brass badge, cording.**200.00**
Hat, station agent's; BAR, blk wool, badge, cording, side buttons..**228.00**
Inkwell, NP, lg 'baked potato,' hinged lid w/inserts, SL, 5½x3¼" ..**675.00**
Jacket, Amtrak CA Capitol Corridor safety award......................**178.00**
Jug, Pullman Co, deodorizer, ceramic, ½-gal, 9½" **26.00**
Magazine, employee; B&O, October 1952, 48-pg, 8½x11"...........**32.00**
Magazine, employee; UP, Multnomah Falls cover, 1931, 64-pg, 11x8½".**22.00**
Magazines, Trains, 1948, 12 unbound issues **17.50**
Matches, Seaboard, 1950s, unused full book **3.00**
Medallion, CPR, commemorating 100 yrs, bronze, 2¾"................**28.00**
Menu, ATSF Monument Valley, CW Love cover, 1951...................**22.00**
Menu, ATSF/Fred Harvey, Am Legion Drum Corps Convention, 1946, 5x7" .**25.00**
Menu, CA Zephyr, cardstock, breakfast, 1960s, 6x9" **90.00**
Menu, Monon Rte, Hoosier Dinner, heavy cardstock, 6-pg, 1930s, 6x10" ..**40.00**
Mirror, GN, frosted Rocky silhouette, bevel edges, 14x28".........**980.00**
Oiler, MKT raised on front, long spout, no stop flow lever, 26½" ...**55.00**
Painting, oil; T&P, Texas Troubador, Ted Rose, 1992, 22x30"..**4,895.00**
Paperweight, GN w/Rocky silhouette, glass, red/bl/wht, domed, 3" dia..**145.00**
Pass, Astoria & Columbia River RR, cardstock, 1909.................**280.00**
Pass, CS+PM&ORR, countersigned by issuant, 1912 ....**25.00**

Pass, CSS&SB, cardstock, 1933 ....**47.00**
Pass, Everett & Monte Cristo Ry, annual/exchange, graphics, cardstock...**295.00**
Pass, Rio Grande Southern, Silver San Juan Scenic Line, 1895, EX....**825.00**
Pass, Silverton, silver figural w/enamel Rainbow Rte, Hartwell, 1890..**11,335.00**
Pass, Vidalia RR, 1911, VG **15.00**
Pen, ballpoint; MP w/buzz saw logo in blk on wht bbl, 5¼" **11.00**
Pencil, mechanical; ATSF, marbleized pearl bbl w/SF logo **11.00**
Pencil, mechanical; UP Road of Streamliners, marbleized pearl bbl..**10.00**
Pin, Bessemer RR, 20 Yr Service, 10k gold, screw-bk, ½x½" **127.00**
Pin, lapel; Rock Island, screw-type mt on bk **10.00**
Pin, SCL, 25 Yr Service, ⅝" dia...**27.00**
Pin-bk button, BRRT Twenty-Fifth Anniv 174, 1883-1908, rare .**55.00**
Playing cards, GN, 52+2+Chief Two Guns joker, slipcase, very early..**400.00**
Playing cards, NP w/Monad logo, 2 bridge decks, in sealed slipcase ..**60.00**
Playing cards, NYC, view of Niagara falls, 52+2+Joker, slipcase...**30.00**
Postcard, B&M Depot, Omaha NB, blk & wht photo, postmk 1901..**17.00**
Postcard, Doland SD RR yards & depot, NM..............................**12.00**
Postcard, Las Vegas NV RR yards, blk & wht photo, 1920s-30s...**54.00**
Postcard, Mt Lowe, High Above the Clouds, 1907 ....**3.00**
Print, T&P, Victorian lady in Indian dress, perhaps 1900s calendar, fr..**585.00**
Receipt, Eastern Express Co, for $73, dtd Dec 12, 1866................**10.00**
RR logos, mini; Post cereal premiums (28), ca 1954-56, from $125 to..**165.00**
Ruler, BAR, It's a Good Rule To Play Safely, wood, 6" **12.00**
Scarf, souvenir, Chessie, silk, Glentex, 22" sq...........................**33.00**
Sign, ATSF, porc w/bl & wht Santa Fe logo, 4 grommets, 36" sq ..**1,635.00**
Sign, E Broad Top RR, Mt Union, gold on blk, brackets, 24x84"..**1,500.00**
Sign, PRR/Truc Train, porc w/Keystone logo, 55" dia **625.00**
Stock holder's report, Atlanta & West Point, 1957.....................**19.00**
Stool, conductor's step; ATSF, TM emb, Morton, 10".................**300.00**
Telegraph key, Vibroples, 6½" bug, orig case **78.00**
Textbooks, Steam Locomotive, Internat'l, 1923-35, 22 volumes .**300.00**
Timetable, employee; N&W, Scioto Division, #19, 1939..............**29.00**
Timetable, employee; SP, Coast Division, #152, 1944....................**86.00**
Timetable, employee; SP, Rio Grande Division, #31, 1945 ....**42.00**
Timetable, employee; WP, Western Division, #31, 1945...............**12.00**
Timetable, public; D&RG system including RGS, LV&Tonopah..., 1908...**48.00**
Timetable, public; KC/Clay County/St Joseph, cardstock, 1913, 5½"..**200.00**
Timetable, public; N&W, 1916, 30-pg, folds down to 3⅞x8½" **29.00**
Timetable, public; Virginian Ry, 1949, 4-pg....................................**40.00**
Torch, PRR, CI cone shape, screw-on spout, Dayton...Iron Co, 5x3½"..**55.00**
Trunk, Fred Harvey, wood w/metal loops, 14x29x17½", VG..**2,000.00**
Wax sealer, Jefferson/Madison/Indianapolis, brass w/wood hdl, 3½"..**1,235.00**
Whistle, Am Steam Gauge Co, Pat Oct 14.84 June 16.85, brass, 100 lbs.**145.00**
Whistle, steam; CMStP&P (SL) for 2-6-6-2 mallet #64 (SL), 6-chime, 24".**2,500.00**
Whistle, steam; Lunkenheimer, brass, 11½x3½" dia...................**224.00**

Razors

As straight razors gain in popularity, prices of those razors also increase. This carries with it a lure of investment possibilities which can encourage the novice or speculator to make purchases that may later prove to be unwise. We recommend that before investing serious money in razors, you become familiar with the elements which make a razor valuable. As with other collectibles, there are specific traits which are desirable and which have a major impact on price.

The following information is based on the second edition of *The Standard Guide to Razors* by Roy Ritchie and Ron Stewart (available from R&C Books, Box 2421, Hazard, KY 41702, $9.95 +$2.50 S&H). It describes the elements most likely to influence a razor's collector value and their system of calculating that value. (Their book is a valuable reference guide to both the casual and serious collector of razors.)

There are four major factors which determine a razor's collector value. These are the brand and country of origin, the handle material,

the artwork found on the handles or blades, and the condition of the razor. Ritchie and Stewart freely admit that there are other factors that may come into play with some collectors, but these are the major players in determining value. They have devised a system of evaluation which is based on these four factors.

The most important factor is the value placed on the brand and country of origin. This is the price of a common razor made by (or for) a particular company. It has plain handles, probably made of plastic, no artwork, and is in collectible condition. It is the beginning value. Hundreds (thousands?) of these values are provided in the 'Listings of Companies and Base Values' chapter in the book.

The second category is that of handle material. This covers a wide range of materials, from fiber on the low end to ivory on the high end. The collector needs to be able to identify the different handle materials when he sees them. This often takes some practice, since there are some very good plastics that can mimic ivory quite successfully. Also, the difference between genuine celluloid and plastic can become significant when determining value. A detailed chart of these values is supplied in the book. The listing below can be used as a general guide.

The third category is the most subjective. Nevertheless, it is an extremely important factor in determining value. This category is artwork, which can include everything from logo art to carving and sculpture. It may range from highly ornate to tastefully correct. Blade etching as well as handle artistry are to be considered. Perhaps what some call the 'gotta have it' or the 'neatness' factors properly fall into this category. You must accurately determine the artistic merits of your razor when you evaluate it relative to this factor. Again, the book we referenced earlier provides a more complete listing of considerations than is used here.

Finally, the condition is factored in. The book's scales run from 'parts' (10% +/-) to 'Good' (150% +/-). Average (100% +/-) is classified as 'Collectible.' See chart D for details concerning condition guidelines for evaluation.

Samplings from charts:

Chart A: Companies and Base Values:

Abercrombie & Finch, NY **14.00**
Aerial, USA **25.00**
Boker, Henri & Co, Germany **14.00**
Brick, F; England **12.00**
Case Mfg Co, Spring Valley NY **50.00**
Chores, James; England...**13.00**
Dahlqres, CW; Sweden **14.00**
Diane, Japan **10.00**
Electric Co, NY..**15.00**
Faultless, Germany...**100.00**
Fox Cutlery, Germany..**11.00**
Fredericks (Celebrated Cutlery), England.........................**13.00**
Gilbert Bros, England...**12.00**
Griffon XX, Germany..**11.00**
Henckels, Germany..**15.00**
Holly Mfg Co, CT...**30.00**
International Cutlery Co NY/Germany **11.00**
IXL, England...**15.00**
Jay, John; NY..**12.00**
KaBar, Union Cut Co, USA...**30.00**
Kanner, J; Germany...**11.00**
Kern, R&W; Canada/England..**12.00**
LeCocltre, Jacque; Switzerland...**12.00**
Levering Razor Co, NY/Germany.......................................**18.00**
McIntosh & Heather, OH..**12.00**
Merit Import Co, Germany..**11.00**
Monthoote, England **12.00**

National Cut Co, OH..15.00
Oxford Razor Co, Germany 10.00
Palmer Brothers, Savannah, GA 25.00
Primble, John; Indian Steel Works, Louisville KY.....25.00
Queen City NY 30.00
Querelle, A; Paris France..................................12.00
Quigley, Germany 12.00
Radford, Joseph & Sons; England......................12.00
Rattler Razor Co, Germany 10.00
Robeson Cut Co, USA 30.00
Salamander Works, Germany 11.00
Soderein, Ekilstuna Sweden..............................12.00
Taylor, LM; Cincinnati OH 15.00
Tower Brand, Germany.....................................16.00
Ulmer, Germany...12.00
US Barber Supply, TX.......................................12.00
Vinnegut Hdw Co, IN.......................................11.00
Vogel, Ed; PA 10.00
Wade & Butcher, England.................................20.00
Weis, JH; Supply House, Louisville KY...............17.00
Yankee Cutlery Co, Germany.............................12.00
Yazbek, Lahod; OH 11.00
Zacour Bros, Germany......................................11.00
Zepp, Germany...12.00

Chart B, as described below, is an abbreviated version of the handle materials list in *The Standard Guide to Razors*. It is an essential category in the use of the appraisal system developed by the authors.

Ivory	550%
Tortoise Shell	500%
Pearl	400%
Stag	400%
Bone	300%
Celluloid	250%
Composition	150%
Plastic	100%

Chart C deals with the artistic value of the razor. As pointed out earlier, this is a very subjective area. It takes study to determine what is good and what is not. Taste can also play a significant role in determining the value placed on the artistic merit of a razor. The range is from superior to nonexistent. Categories generally are divided as follows:

Exceptional	650%
Superior	550%
Good	400%
Average	300%
Minimal	200%
Plain	100%
Nonexistant	0%

Chart D is also very subjective. It determines the condition of the razor. You must judge accurately if the appraisal system is to work for you.

Good   150%

Does not have to be factory mint to fall within this category. However, there can be no visible flaws if it is to be calculated at 150%.

Collectible   100%

May have some flaws that do not greatly detract from the artwork or finish.

Parts   10%

Unrepairable, valuable as salvageable parts.

Razors may fall within any of these categories, ie. collectible + 112%.

Now to determine the value of your razor, multiply A times B, then multiply A times C. Add your two answers and multiply this sum times D. The answer you get is your collector value. See the example below.

(a) Brand and Origin Base Value	(b) Handle Material % Value	(c) Artwork % Value	(d) Condition % Value	(e) Collector Value
Cosmo Mfg. Co Germany **$9.00**	Celluloid 9 x 300%= **$27.00**	Peacock design 9 x 350%= $31.50 **$32.00**	Slight stain Good- **140%**	$27+32= $59 x 140%= $82.60 **$83.00**

Reamers

The reamer market is very active right now, and prices are escalating rapidly. They have been made in hundreds of styles and colors and by as many manufacturers. Their purpose is to extract the juices from lemons, oranges, and grapefruits. The largest producer of glass reamers was McKee, who pressed their products from many types of glass — custard; Delphite and Chalaine Blue; opaque white; Skokie Green; black; caramel and white opalescent; Seville Yellow; and transparent pink, green, and clear. Among these, the black and the caramel opalescents are the most valuable.

The Fry Glass Company also made reamers that are today very collectible. The Hazel Atlas Crisscross orange reamer in pink is valued at $300.00 to $325.00 or more — the same in blue, $350.00. Hocking produced a light blue orange reamer and, in the same soft hue, a two-piece reamer and measuring cup combination. Both are considered rare and very valuable with currently quoted estimates at $1,000.00 and up for the former and $1,800.00 and up for the latter. In addition to the colors mentioned, red glass examples — transparent or slag — are rare and costly. Prices vary greatly according to color and rarity. The same reamer in crystal may be worth three times as much in a more desirable color.

Among the most valuable ceramic reamers are those made by American potteries. The Spongeband reamer by Red Wing is valued in excess of $500.00; Coorsite reamers with gold or silver trim are worth $300.00 and up. Figurals are popular — Mickey Mouse and John Bull may bring $600.00 to $1,000.00. Others range from $55.00 to $350.00. Fine china one- and two-piece reamers are also very desirable and command very respectable prices.

A word about reproductions: A series of limited edition reamers is being made by Edna Barnes of Uniontown, Ohio. These are all marked with a 'B' in a circle. Other reproductions have been made from old molds. The most important of these are Anchor Hocking two-piece two-cup measure and top, Gillespie one-cup measure with reamer top, Westmoreland with flattened handle, Westmoreland four-cup measure embossed with orange and lemons, Duboe (hand-held darning egg), and Easley's Diamonds one-piece.

For more information concerning reamers and reproductions, contact the National Reamer Collectors Association (see Clubs, Newsletters, and Catalogs). Be sure to include an SASE when requesting information.

Ceramic

Black face & hands, red coat & bl pants, 4¾", from $500 to **600.00**
Bucket, 2-pc, bl & wht w/pagoda image, rattan hdl, from $75 to..**100.00**
Camel kneeling, beige lustre w/lt gr top, 4¼", from 200 to **250.00**
Clown, brn body & hat, bl button & collar, 6", from $100 to **125.00**
Clown in tuxedo, 2-pc, 5½", from $125 to **150.00**
Clown's face, 2-pc, mc on wht w/wide red smile & red nose, Japan, 4"...**75.00**
Clown's head in saucer, gr/wht, Goebel, Germany, 5" dia, from $200 to..**250.00**
Clown sitting cross-legged, gr w/wht ruffled coat & hat, Germany, 5" ..**300.00**

Cottage, yel w/orange & gr trim, Carlton Ware (England), 4" ...**125.00**
Cup, 2-pc, yel & wht spatter design, Stangl, 6¼", from $50 to.....**75.00**
Duck figure, orange & gr on wht pearlized body **110.00**
Elephant, wht w/mc blanket, mk Newbach, 5¾", from $115 to .**150.00**
Lady's head, blk hair, gr lustre ruffled saucer, 3¾", from $275 to ...**350.00**
Lemon, 2-pc, yel w/gr leaves, gold trim, Japan, 4", from $65 to....**85.00**
Lemon, 2-pc, yel w/gr leaves, wht top, Germany, 3¼" **70.00**
Mexican taking siesta, 2-pc, mc, Japan, 4¾", from $175 to **200.00**
Orange for Baby, 2-pc, bl flowers, Goebel, 3½" **135.00**
Pear, 3-pc, wht w/blk, leaves on top, outlined, mk Japan, from $55 to ..**75.00**
Pitcher, 2-pc, blk w/gold wheat, 8" **45.00**
Pitcher, 2-pc, cream w/red & blk cattails, Universal Cambridge, 9".**185.00**
Plaid, 2-pc, gr & wht, Japan, 2¼"...**80.00**
Saucer, cream, tan & maroon w/bl trim, England, 3¼" dia.........**100.00**
Swan figure, 2-pc, cream w/rose flowers & gr base, Japan, 4¼" **75.00**
Teapot, 2-pc, wht w/yel & maroon flowers, Nippon, 3¼" **90.00**
Teapot, 2-pc, yel, tan & wht, England/Shelly, 3½" **125.00**

Glass

Argentina, gr, from $125 to..**150.00**
ASCO, crystal, Good Morning Orange Juice, from $25 to **30.00**
Cambridge, crystal, ftd, sm, from $22 to **25.00**
Cambridge, crystal, sm tab, from $18 to......................................**20.00**
Cambridge, pk (lt), from $200 to **225.00**
Federal, gr, ribbed, seed dam, tab hdl, from $25 to **28.00**
Federal, gr, tab hdl, from $25 to **28.00**
Federal, pk, ribbed, looped hdl, from $40 to **45.00**
Fenton, crystal, elephant decorated base, 2-pc, from $110 to **125.00**
Fry, emerald gr, str sides, from $35 to **38.00**
Fry, gr (lt), str sides, from $35 to **38.00**
Fry, pearl (wht opalescent), str sides, from $35 to.......................**40.00**
Hazel-Atlas, crystal, Crisscross, from $20 to **25.00**
Hazel-Atlas, crystal, tab hdl, lg, from $15 to **18.00**
Hazel-Atlas, gr, Crisscross, tab hdl **45.00**
Hazel-Atlas, gr, 4-cup pitcher set, mk A&J, from $45 to **50.00**
Hazel-Atlas, pk, 2-cup pitcher set, from $150 to **160.00**

Hazel Atlas, two-cup pitcher and reamer sets: Yellow, from $350.00 to $375.00; Cobalt, from $295.00 to $325.00 (has been reproduced).

(Photo courtesy Gene Florence)

Indiana Glass, gr, 6-sided cone, vertical hdl, from $85 to **95.00**
Jenkins, frosted crystal, 2-pc, from $50 to **55.00**
Jennyware, pk, from $125 to...**135.00**
McKee, crystal, Glasbake, from $65 to...**75.00**
McKee, Jadite, 6", from $50 to **55.00**
McKee, opaque dk gr, mk Sunkist Pat 68764 Made in USA, from $40 to ..**55.00**
Sunkist, Apple Green, from $50 to **55.00**
Sunkist, Chalaine Blue (dk), from $125 to...................................**155.00**
Valencia, gr, emb letters, from $225 to **275.00**
Valencia, milk glass, emb letters, from $120 to...........................**150.00**
Westmoreland, crystal, 2-pc, from $65 to **70.00**
Westmoreland, pk w/decor, 2-pc, from $200 to **225.00**

Records

Records of interest to collectors are often not the million-selling hits by 'superstars.' Very few records by Bing Crosby, for example, are of any more than nominal value, and those that are valuable usually don't even have his name on the label! Collectors today are most interested in records that were made in limited quantities, early works of a performer who later became famous, and those issued in special series or aimed at a limited market. Vintage records are judged desirable by their recorded content as well; those that lack the quality of music that makes a record collectible will always be 'junk' records in spite of their age, scarcity, or the obsolescence of their technology.

Records are usually graded visually rather than aurally, since it is seldom if ever possible to first play the records you buy at shows, by mail, at flea markets, etc. Condition is one of the most important determinants of value. For example, a nearly mint-condition Elvis Presley 45 of 'Milk Cow Blues' (Sun 215) has a potential value of over $1,500.00. A small sticker on the label could cut its value in half; noticeable wear could reduce its value by 80% (eighty percent). A mint record must show no evidence of use (record jackets, in the case of EPs and LPs, must be equally choice). Excellent condition denotes a record showing only slight signs of use with no audible defects. A very good record has noticeable wear but still plays well. Records of lesser grades may be unsaleable, unless very scarce and/or highly sought-after.

While the value of most 78s does not depend upon their being in appropriate sleeves (although a sleeveless existence certainly contributes to damage and deterioration!), this is not the case with most EPs (extended play 45s) and LPs (long-playing 33⅓ rpm albums), which must have their jackets (cardboard sleeves), in nice condition, free of disfiguring damage, such as writing, stickers, or tape. Often, common and minimally valued 45s might be collectible if they are in appropriate 'picture sleeves' (special sleeves that depict the artist/group or other fanciful or symbolic graphic and identify the song titles, record label, and number), e.g. many common records by Elvis Presley, The Beatles, and The Beach Boys.

Promotional copies (DJ copies) supplied to radio stations often have labels different in designs and/or colors from their commercially issued counterparts. Labels usually bear a designation 'Not for Sale,' 'Audition Copy,' 'Sample Copy,' or the like. Records may be pressed of translucent vinyl; while most promos are not particularly collectible, those by certain 'hot' artists, such as Elvis Presley, The Beach Boys, and The Beatles are usually premium disks.

Many of the most desirable and valuable 45s have been 'bootlegged' (counterfeited). For example, there are probably more fake Elvis Presley *Sun* records in circulation than authentic copies — certainly in higher grades! Collectors should be alert for these often deceptive counterfeits.

Our advisor for this category is L.R. Docks, author of *American Premium Record Guide*, which lists 60,000 records by over 7,000 artists in its sixth edition. He is listed in the Directory under Texas. In the listings that follow, prices are suggested for records that are in excellent condition; worn or abused records may be worth only a small fraction of the values quoted and may not be saleable at all. EPs and LPs are priced 'with jacket.'

Blues, Rhythm and Blues, Rock 'N Roll, Rockabilly

Adams, Charles; Black Land Blues, Columbia 21524, 45 rpm **10.00**
Audrey, Dear Elvis, Plus 104, 45 rpm **15.00**
Beatles, Meet the Beatles, Capitol SXA 2047, 33⅓ rpm, 7".......**150.00**
Beatles, Please Please Me, Vee Jay 498, 45 rpm............................**120.00**
Big Four, Outa Time, Moon 306, 45 rpm **15.00**
Blues Rockers, Trouble in My Home, Aristocrat 407, 78 rpm.......**25.00**

Boston, Bobby; Lazy Daisy, Starwin 7001, 45 rpm 12.00

Buckeyes, Since I Fell for You, De Luxe 6110, 45 rpm 30.00

Capris, It Was Moonglow, Gotham 7306, 45 rpm 40.00

Carl, Steve; Curfew, Meteor 5046, 45 rpm.................................40.00

Chantels, I Love You So, End 1020, 78 rpm 15.00

Classmates, Pretty Little Pet, Marquee 102, 45 rpm 8.00

Clay, Joe; Duck Tail, Vik 0211, 45 rpm.....................................30.00

Contours, Funny, Motown 1012, 45 rpm 15.00

Cruisers, The Moon Is Yours, Finch 353, 45 rpm 20.00

Darby, Teddy; What Am I To Do?, Paramount 12907, 78 rpm ...300.00

Davis, Gene; Facts of Life, Challenge 59091, 45 rpm.....................10.00

Denson, Lee; High School Bop, Kent 306, 45 rpm 30.00

Doss, Bob; Somebody's Knocking, Starday 265, 45 rpm 40.00

Eagles, Such a Fool, Mercury 70464, 45 rpm 12.00

Ervin, Odie; Note Pinned to My Bed, Big Town 111, 45 rpm.......20.00

Esquires, Mission Bells, Meridian, 45 rpm....................................20.00

Ferris & the Wheels, Chop, Chop, Bambi 801, 45 rpm................8.00

Five Swans, Little Girl of My Dreams, Music City 795, 45 rpm ...20.00

Four Jokers, Written in the Stars, Sue 703, 45 rpm 10.00

Freeman, Bobby; Do You Wanna Dance, Jubilee 1086, LP 40.00

Gavin, Tony; It's Never Seven or Eleven, Sims 165, 45 rpm 10.00

Green, Bobby; Little Heart Attacks, Pak 4429/4430, 45 rpm 75.00

Green, Lil; Why Don't You Do Right, Groove 5004, 45 rpm 10.00

Hamilton, George IV; If I Don't Know, ABC Paramount 9765, 78 rpm ..15.00

Heartbreakers, Why Don't I, RCA Victor 4662, 45 rpm...............75.00

Honeycutt, Glen; I'll Be Around, Sun 265, 45 rpm 10.00

Hooker, John Lee; High Priced Woman, Chess 1505, 45 rpm 100.00

Ingram, Benny; Jello Sal, Bandera 1302, 45 rpm 15.00

Jeffery, Wally; Oh Yeah, Do-Re-Mi 1402, 45 rpm.......................50.00

Johnson, Louise; On the Wall, Paramount 13008, 78 rpm...........250.00

Kennedy, Tina; Sister Flat Top, Capitol 840, 45 rpm 20.00

Lam, Tommy; Speed Limit, Nabor 103, 45 rpm............................30.00

Lewis, Smiley; Down the Road, Imperial 5268, 45 rpm 30.00

Lick, Slick & Slide, I Got Drunk, Savoy 1150, 45 rpm.................30.00

Lonesome Drifter, Eager Boy, K 5812, 45 rpm.............................175.00

Maiden, Sidney; Everything Is Wrong, Flash 101, 45 rpm............25.00

McCrory, Jim; Parking Lot, Key 5803, 45 rpm.............................30.00

McDaniels, Gene; In Times Like This, Liberty 3146, LP 20.00

Miller, Carl; Rhythm Guitar, Lu 503, 45 rpm..............................40.00

Morris, Bob; Party Time, Cascade 5907, 45 rpm.........................10.00

Octaves, Mambo Carolyn, Val 1001, 45 rpm 12.00

Pat & Dee, Gee Whiz, Dixie 2006, 45 rpm 25.00

Peacheroos, Be-Bop Baby, Excello 2044, 45 rpm.......................100.00

Poore, Bobby; Heartbreak of Love, Beta 1003, 45 rpm................12.00

Presley, Elvis; Let's Play House, RCA Victor 6383, 78 rpm...........40.00

Presley, Elvis; Shake Rattle & Roll, RCA Victor 6642, 45 rpm....20.00

Presley, Elvis; Shake Rattle & Roll, RCA Victor 6642, 78 rpm....50.00

Rebels, Wild Weekend, Marlee 009, 45 rpm.................................15.00

Robbins, Mel; Save It, Argo 5340, 45 rpm 20.00

Royals, Moonrise, Federal 12088, 45 rpm....................................300.00

Russ, Irvin; Crazy Alligator, Felco 201, 45 rpm...........................60.00

Sequins, Don't Fall in Love, Red Robin 140, 45 rpm...................50.00

Smith, Henry; Good Rocking Mama, Dot 1220, 45 rpm...............40.00

Starlarks, Fountain of Love, Ember 1013, 45 rpm.......................30.00

Sycamores, I'll Be Waiting, Groove 0121, 45 rpm........................75.00

Tennessee Drifters, Corrina Corinna, Dot 1187, 45 rpm...............50.00

Thayer, Frank; Evening Shadows, Outlaw 1, 45 rpm 20.00

Tucker, Billy Joe; Boogie Woogie Bill, Maha 103, 45 rpm...........40.00

Uniques, Tell the Angels, End 1012, 45 rpm 20.00

Vernon, Ray; Evil Angel, Rumble 11349, 45 rpm........................12.00

Ward, Willie; I'm a Madman, Fee-Bee 233, 45 rpm 20.00

Williams, Bernie; Don't Tease Me, Imperial 5360, 45 rpm............10.00

Williams, Hank; Memorial Album, MGM 202, LP, 10" 50.00

Woody, Don; Not I, Arco 4623, 45 rpm.......................................20.00

Country and Western

Baker, Buddy; Box Car Blues, Victor 21589, 78 rpm 15.00

Boggs, Dock; Hard Luck Blues, Vocalion 5144, 78 rpm 60.00

Burnette, Smilie; Mama Don't Like Music, various labels, 78 rpm..12.00

Buster & Jack, Guitar Duet Blues, Victor 23257, 78 rpm.............100.00

Chumbler Family, Jacob's Ladder, Columbia 15481-D, 78 rpm.....12.00

Denmon, Morgan; Drunkard's Dream, Okeh 45327, 78 rpm 12.00

Dixie Crackers, The Old Bell Cow, Paramount 3151, 78 rpm 30.00

Dodds, Johnny; Railroad Boomer, Okeh 45471, 78 rpm 100.00

Green's String Band, Gray Eagle, Champion 16249, 78 rpm.........20.00

Harris, Earl; Fighting Marine, Okeh 45566, 78 rpm 8.00

Horton, Johnny; Candy Jones, Abbott 100, 78 rpm.....................12.00

Horton, Johnny; Plaid & Calico, Abbott 102, 78 rpm 12.00

Jones Brothers, Little Green Valley, Melotone 12179, 78 rpm........8.00

Kutter, Don; Two Little Orphans, Challenge 326, 78 rpm 10.00

Lonesome Cowgirl, Livin' in the Moutains, Superior 2631, 78 rpm ..50.00

Mack, Billy; Play My Boogie, Imperial 8174, 78 rpm 10.00

McKinney Brothers, Old Uncle Joe, Champion 16830, 78 rpm ...15.00

Meridian Hustlers, Queen City Square Dance, Paramount 3173, 78 rpm..60.00

Mr & Mrs Baker, Newmarket Wreck, Victor 20863, 78 rpm 20.00

Oak Mountain Four, Medley, Champion 15874, 78 rpm..............10.00

Owens, EB; Sweet Carlyle, Columbia 15414-D, 78 rpm 20.00

Poindexter, Doug; Now She Cares No More, Sun 202, 78 rpm 40.00

Regan, Walter; Moundsville Prisoner, Superior 2585, 78 rpm 40.00

Scott, Jimmie; Rocky Road, Star Talent 781, 78 rpm...................10.00

Scotty the Drifter, Gooseberry Pie, Decca 5296, 78 rpm..............10.00

Steen, Joe; Railroad Jack, Champion 16258, 78 rpm....................15.00

Turner, Cal; Only a Tramp, Champion 15587, 78 rpm.................18.00

Webber, Sam; My Ozark Mountain Home, Superior 2822, 78 rpm..50.00

White, Reuben; Old Sefus Brown, Challenge 336, 78 rpm............10.00

Jazz, Dance Bands, Personalities

Alabama Creole Band, Choo Choo, Claxtonla 40397, 78 rpm 15.00

Arkansas Trio, Boil Weevil Blues, Edison 51373, 78 rpm 10.00

Banner Dance Orchestra, Bugle Call Rag, Banner 1229, 78 rpm..10.00

Bargy, Roy; Rufenreddy, Victor 19320, 78 rpm 15.00

Boots & His Buddies, The Sad, Bluebird 7236, 78 rpm................15.00

Calloway, Cab & Orchestra; That Man Is Here Again, Variety 501, 78 rpm ..10.00

Calloway, Ermine; Do Something, Edison 52570, 78 rpm.............20.00

Cellar Boys, Barrel House Stomp, Vocalion 1503, 78 rpm...........200.00

Cotton Pickers, Hot Heels, Cameo 9207, 78 rpm 15.00

Detroiters, Dream Dream Dream, Romeo 500, 78 rpm..................5.00

Dixie Stompers, Dynomite, Harmony 209-H, 78 rpm 15.00

Emperors, Go, Joe, Go, Harmony 383-H, 78 rpm........................15.00

Fuller, Bob; I Ain't Got Nobody, Brunswick 7006, 78 rpm 30.00

Goodman, Benny; Not That I Care, Columbia 2542-D, 78 rpm ..25.00

Gray, Jane; Miss Annabelle Lee, Harmony 464-H, 78 rpm 10.00

Harmaniac Five, Harmaniac Blues, Puritan 11476, 78 rpm..........50.00

High Hatters, Low Down Rhythm, Victor 22041, 78 rpm.............8.00

Howell, Bert; Bye Bye Florence, Victor 21062, 78 rpm................30.00

Howell, Burt; You're Driving Me Crazy, Paramount 13063, 78 rpm .50.00

Jazz Masters, Bees Knees, Black Swan 2109, 78 rpm...................20.00

Kay, Dolly; Hot Lips, Columbia A3758, 78 rpm..........................10.00

Langford, Frances; Moon Song, Bluebird 5016, 78 rpm...............12.00

Little Aces, Four or Five Times, Okeh 41136, 78 rpm.................25.00

Louisianna Five, Slow & Easy, Columbia A2949, 78 rpm.............8.00

Marvin, Johnny; Memphis Blues, Edison 51709, 78 rpm 15.00

Mercer, Johnny; The Bathtub Ran Over Again, Decca 142, 78 rpm..15.00

Moonlight Revelers, Alabama Shuffle, Grey Gull 1775, 78 rpm..50.00

New Orleans Owls, Eccentric, Columbia 943-D, 78 rpm..............30.00

Original Indiana Five, Sugar, Banner 6008, 78 rpm 12.00

Original Memphis Five, Farewell Blues, Perfect 14104, 78 rpm....12.00

Pendleton, Andy; Thinking of You, Victor 23389, 78 rpm 75.00
Powell's Jazz Monarchs, Laughing Blues, Okeh 8333, 78 rpn......100.00
Rhythm Aces, Jazz Battle, Brunswick 4244, 78 rpm...................100.00
Rubinoff, Dave; Fiddlin' the Fiddle, Perfect 14483, 78 rpm.........10.00
Sepia Serenaders, Ridiculous Blues, Bluebird 5770, 78 rpm.........20.00
Simms, Howard; Pensacola Joe, Harmograph 841, 78 rpm............50.00
Texas Ten, Charleston, Regal 9835, 78 rpm....................................10.00
Underwood, Sugar; Dew Drop Alley Stomp, Victor 21538, 78 rpm...100.00
Vicksburg Ten, Clarinet Marmalade, Champion 15477, 78 rpm...75.00
Volunteer Fireman, In Your Green Hat, Brunswick 3045, 78 rpm ..8.00
Wally Spencer's Georgians, Rubber Heels, Champion 15307, 78 rpm .90.00
We Three, Plenty Off Center, Perfect 14673, 78 rpm 30.00
Williams, Mary Lou; Isabelle, Decca 1021, 78 rpm.......................12.00
Young, Margaret; Stingo Stungo, Brunswick 2475, 78 rpm 8.00

Red Wing

The Red Wing Stoneware Company, founded in 1878, took its name from its location in Red Wing, Minnesota. In 1906 the name was changed to the Red Wing Union Stoneware Company after a merger with several of the other local potteries. For the most part they produced utilitarian wares such as flowerpots, crocks, and jugs. Their early 1930s catalogs offered a line of art pottery vases in colored glazes, some of which featured handles modeled after swan's necks, snakes, or female nudes. Other examples were quite simple, often with classic styling. After the addition of their dinnerware lines in 1935, 'Stoneware' was dropped from the name, and the company became known as Red Wing Potteries, Inc. They closed in 1967. Each piece is stamped with the potters' initials and the year of production.

For further study we recommend *Red Wing Stoneware, An Identification and Value Guide,* and *Red Wing Collectibles* by Dan DePasquale, Gail Peck, and Larry Peterson; and *Red Wing Art Pottery, Book II,* and *Collector's Encyclopedia of Red Wing Art Pottery* by B.L. Dollen (listed in the Directory under Iowa). All are published by Collector Books. Another good reference is *Red Wing Art Pottery* by Ray Reiss (privately published).

Commercial Art Ware and Miscellaneous

Bowl, cloverleaf, orange/gr, #1412, 8" 32.00
Bowl, gloss fleck Nile Blue, leaf shaped, #1407, 12¾"...................35.00
Bowl, gloss fleck yel, rectangular, ftd, #M1603, 10" 38.00
Bowl, gloss fleck Zephyr Pink, ribbed, rectangular, 12" 54.00
Bowl, gloss forest gr/yel, rectangular, #1333, 13½x8" 30.00
Bowl, Ribbon, gloss cinnamon, #M1486, 10¾" 28.00
Bowl, semi-matt wht, rectangular, #5019, 9" 38.00
Bowl, semi-matt wht/gr, sq ftd, #815, 9"..46.00
Bowl, shell shape, gloss burnt orange/tan, #B2015, 12" 32.00
Bowl, star shape, gloss yel/gray, #1370, 7" 30.00
Candleholders, teardrop, gloss orange/gr, 4½", pr..........................26.00
Candleholders, 2-arm, gloss yel, #B1410, 6", pr.............................40.00
Console set, gloss cinnamon, pr 5" candle holders+12" bowl........68.00
Planter, gloss fleck bl/wht, ftd, silver wing label, 6" 47.00
Planter, lamb, matt bl, silver wing label, 6½"...............................145.00
Vase, bamboo motif, semi-matt wht/gr, 8".....................................42.00
Vase, bud; gloss fleck bl/Colonial Buff, #434, 8¼".........................30.00
Vase, gloss gray/coral, tapering sides, #B1397, 7" 40.00
Vase, gloss maroon/gray, trophy shape, #871, 7½" 58.00
Vase, gloss yel/gray, fan shape, 5½", from $38 to 46.00
Vase, semi-matt gr/wht, fancy leaf hdls 46.00
Vase, semi-matt wht/gr, leaf form, ftd, #M1439, 6".......................54.00
Vase, shell shape, semi-matt orange/wht, #1295, 7" 48.00
Wall pocket, cornucopia, gloss Nile Blue/Colonial Buff, 6" 90.00
Wall pocket, funnel shaped, semi-matt gr, #M1630, 10"............110.00
Wall pocket, sconce, semi-matt wht/pk, #1254, 7" 85.00

Cookie Jars

Be aware that there is a very good reproduction of the King of Tarts. Except for the fact that the new jars are slightly smaller, they are sometime difficult to distinguish from the old.

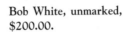

Bob White, unmarked, $200.00.

Carousel, unmk 350.00
Crock, wht..80.00
Dutch Girl (Katrina), yel w/brn trim 175.00
Friar Tuck, cream w/brn, mk..175.00
Friar Tuck, gr, mk..175.00
Friar Tuck, yel, unmk 150.00
Grapes, cobalt or dk purple, ea...275.00
Grapes, gr 135.00
Jack Frost, short, unmk 250.00
Jack Frost, tall, unmk 300.00
King of Tarts, mc, mk (+) 325.00
King of Tarts, wht, unmk 200.00
Kint of Tarts, pk w/bl & blk trim, mk 300.00
Peasant design, emb/pnt figures on aqua....................................110.00
Peasant design, emb/pnt figures on brn.......................................120.00
Pierre (chef), bl, brn or pi, unmk, ea...150.00
Pineapple, yel 135.00

Dinnerware

Dinnerware lines were added in 1935, and today collectors scramble to rebuild extensive table services. Although interest is obvious, right now the market is so volatile, it is often difficult to establish a price scale with any degree of accuracy. Asking prices may vary from $50.00 to $200.00 on some items, which indicates instability and a collector market trying to find its way. (One guide currently on the market, for instance, lists Midnight Rose dinner plates at $15.00 to $20.00, while another terms them 'rare,' and values them at $145.00 each.) Sellers seem to be unfamiliar with pattern names and proper identification of the various pieces that each line consists of. There were many hand-decorated lines; among the most popular are Bob White, Tropicana, and Round-up. But there are other patterns that are just as attractive and deserving of attention. The Dollen books previously referenced both have dinnerware sections, and Ray Reiss has published a book called *Red Wing Dinnerware, Price and Identification Guide,* which shows nearly one hundred patterns on its back cover alone.

Town and Country, designed by Eva Zeisel, was made for only one year in the late 1940s. Today many collectors regard Zeisel as one of the most gifted designers of that era and actively seek examples of her work. Town and Country was a versatile line, adaptable to both informal and semiformal use. It is characterized by irregular, often eccentric shapes, and handles of pitchers and serving pieces are usually extensions of the rim. Bowls and platters are free-form comma shapes or appear tilted, with one side slightly higher than the other. Although the ware is unmarked, it is recognizable by its distinctive shapes and glazes. White (often used to complement interiors of bowls and cups), though an original color, is actually more rare than Bronze (metallic brown, also called gunmetal), which enjoys favored status; Gray is unusual. Other colors include Rust, Dusk Blue, Sand, Chartreuse, Peach, and Forest Green. Pieces have also shown up in Mulberry and Ming Green and are considered quite rare. (These are Red Wing Quartelle colors!) Note: Eva Zeisel recently gave permission to reissue a few select pieces of Town and Country; these are being made by World of Ceramics. In 1996 salt and pepper shakers were reproduced in new colors not resembling Red Wing colors. In 1997 the mixing bowl and syrup were reissued. All new pieces are stamped EZ96 or EZ97 and are visibly different from the old, as far as glaze, pottery base, and weight.

Charles Alexander (who is listed in the Directory under Indiana) advises us on the Town and Country market. Our advisor for the remainder of this category is Brenda Dollen; she is listed in the Directory under Minnesota.

Bob White, bowl, divided vegetable....................................40.00
Bob White, bowl, 1½x5½"...10.00
Bob White, hors d'oeuvres, bird form................................70.00
Bob White, pitcher, 12"..32.00
Bob White, platter, oval, 13"..65.00
Bob White, shakers, bird form, sm, pr...............................28.00
Bob White, shakers, hourglass form, 6", pr.......................22.00
Bob White, water jug, 11¾"..50.00
Brittany, creamer, 4"...35.00
Chevron, plate, 8"..12.50
Fondoso, creamer, 4"...17.50
Lute Song, plate, dinner; 10½", from $25 to 30.00
Magnolia, casserole, stick hdl, w/lid 50.00
Magnolia, cup & saucer..17.50
Magnolia, plate, dinner; 10½"...20.00
Plain, creamer & sugar bowl..35.00
Plain, mug, 4¾", from $25 to...35.00
Random Harvest, bowl, serving; 9x8"...............................35.00
Random Harvest, creamer...26.00
Random Harvest, cup & saucer...15.00
Random Harvest, plate, dinner; 10¾x10"..........................20.00
Random Harvest, sugar bowl, w/lid 30.00
Reed, pitcher, syrup; 5⅞"..32.50
Reed, plate, 9¾"...12.50
Reed, teapot, 5¼"...70.00
Round-Up, bowl, fruit; lg..45.00
Round-Up, cup..25.00
Round-Up, plate, dinner 20.00
Smart Set, creamer 26.00
Smart Set, sugar bowl, w/lid...30.00
Tampico, coffee cup..8.00
Tampico, plate, dinner; 10½"..29.00
Tampico, teacup & saucer...24.00
Tip Toe, bowl, divided vegetable 35.00
Town & Country, bean pot, Rust, w/lid, minimum value 400.00
Town & Country, bowl, mixing; 9"....................................90.00
Town & Country, bowl, salad; 13".....................................95.00
Town & Country, bowl, soup...27.50
Town & Country, bowl, 5"...15.00
Town & Country, coaster...18.00
Town & Country, creamer, Sand.......................................35.00
Town & Country, cup & saucer, tea...................................27.50
Town & Country, lazy susan, mixed colors, complete w/stand....250.00
Town & Country, mug, coffee..75.00
Town & Country, mustard jar, w/lid..................................125.00
Town & Country, pitcher, 2-pt...95.00

Town & Country, pitcher, 3-pt...100.00
Town & Country, plate, Forest Green, 10½" 35.00
Town & Country, platter, 11x7½"......................................55.00
Town & Country, platter, 15x11½".....................................70.00
Town & Country, shakers, Shmoo shape, mixed colors, pr 95.00
Town & Country, sugar bowl, Peach, w/lid.........................55.00
Town & Country, syrup..95.00
Village Green, bowl, salad; 12"...40.00
Village Green, casserole, fondue..67.50

Stoneware

Key:
c/s — cobalt on stoneware   RW — Red Wing
MN — Minnesota   RWUS — Red Wing Union
NS — North Star   Stoneware

Bean pot, Albany slip, str sides, MN, 1-gal, from $90 to............120.00
Bean pot, bailed; Albany slip & wht, RW, ½-gal, from $75 to......95.00
Bowl, Greek Key, bl & wht, 6-10", ea from $125 to...................175.00
Bowl, mc spatter, smooth sides w/3 emb lines, RW, $300 to 350.00
Bowl, shoulder; Albany slip, RW, 1-qt, from $50 to 75.00
Chamber pot, wht, orig lid, RW, from $125 to 150.00
Churn, #4/leaf, c/s, RW, 4-gal, from $1,900 to 2,300.00
Churn, molded seam; #3/leaf, MN, 3-gal, from $1,600 to........1,900.00
Cooler, #4/2 leaves, c/s, 4-gal, RW, from $6,000 to 8,000.00
Cooler, #6/butterfly, c/s, RW, 6-gal......................................4,000.00
Crock, #4/dbl P (aka rib cage), c/s, MN, 4-gal, from $700 to 800.00
Crock, #10/birch leaves (dbl set), c/s, RW oval, 10-gal, $1,300 to.1,600.00
Crock, #15/red wing, c/s, oval mk, 15-gal, from $125 to............150.00
Crock, #25/birch leaves, c/s, MN, 25-gal, from $3,000 to........4,000.00
Crock, #30/butterfly, c/s, RW, from $8,000 to 10,000.00
Crock, #40/leaves, c/s, unmk, 40-gal......................................1,200.00
Crock, butter; salt glaze, RW, 10-lb, from $60 to 80.00
Jar, butter; Albany slip, RW, low, 5-lb, from $50 to 60.00
Jar, pantry; wht w/cobalt stripes & red wing, 5-lb, from $500 to ...600.00
Jar, snuff/preserve; Albany slip, MN, 2-gal, from $150 to...........175.00
Jar, snuff/preserve; Albany slip, RW, 2-gal, from $150 to 175.00
Jar, wax sealer; Albany slip, NS, 1-gal.....................................325.00
Jug, bailed; wht, wide mouth, MN, 1-gal, from $125 to..............150.00
Jug, beehive; #5, Albany slip, RW, from $1,000 to...................1,200.00
Jug, beehive; #5/elephant ear leaves, c/s, Union oval, from $3,000 to ..3,500.00
Jug, common, Albany slip, cone top, MN, 1-qt............................125.00
Jug, common, Albany slip, molded bottom seam, NS, 1-gal, from $175 to..200.00
Jug, common, Albany slip, various neck styles, MN, ½-gal, $65 to..95.00
Jug, fancy, Albany slip top, bl band on wht, MN, 1-pt, $1,300 to..1,500.00
Jug, fancy, Albany slip top w/wht, RW, 2-gal, from $175 to........225.00
Jug, fancy, wht w/brn ball top, MN, ⅛-pt.................................225.00
Jug, molded seam, Albany slip, RW, ½-gal...............................125.00
Jug, molded seam, Albany slip, stylized bird in RW mk, 2-gal, $150 to .175.00
Jug, molded seam, wht, wide mouth, MN, 1-gal 85.00
Jug, shoulder; Albany slip, cone top, RW, 2-gal, from $750 to....850.00
Jug, shoulder; Albany slip/wht w/red wings, 2-gal, from $500 to ...600.00
Jug, shoulder; brn & salt glaze, ball top, RW, 1-gal, from $150 to..170.00
Jug, shoulder; brn & salt glaze, dome top, MN, 1-gal 125.00
Jug, shoulder; brn & salt glaze, funnel top, MN, 1-gal, from $75 to ...100.00
Jug, shoulder; brn & salt glaze, funnel top, MN, 2-gal, $125 to..150.00
Jug, shoulder; brn & salt glaze, wide mouth, NS, 1-gal 500.00
Jug, shoulder; wht, funnel top, MN, 2-gal, from $60 to................90.00
Jug, shoulder; wht, std top, NM, 2-gal, from $60 to.....................90.00
Jug, shoulder; wht, std top, RW, 1-qt.......................................125.00
Jug, shoulder; wht, std top, RW, ½-gal, from $45 to 65.00
Jug, shouldered syrup; wht, MN, ½-gal, from $55 to 75.00
Jug, threshing; #5/red wing, c/s, RW oval, from $1,700 to........2,200.00

Pitcher, dk gr w/emb rim, MN, sm, from $400 to **450.00**
Pitcher, mustard; salt glaze, MN **100.00**
Pitcher & bowl, Lily, lt bl & wht, RW, from $1,200 to **1,400.00**
Spittoon, German style, 2 bands, c/s, MN, from $900 to.........**1,000.00**
Spittoon, salt glaze, no decor, unmk, from $400 to **450.00**
Spittoon, wht w/bl sponging, waisted, unmk **650.00**

Redware

The term redware refers to a type of simple earthenware produced by the Colonists as early as the 1600s. The red clay used in its production was abundant throughout the country, and during the eighteenth and nineteenth centuries redware was made in great quantities. Intended for utilitarian purposes such as everyday tableware or use in the dairy, redware was simple in design and decoration. Glazes of various colors were used, and a liquid clay referred to as 'slip' was sometimes applied in patterns such as zigzag lines, daisies, or stars. Plates often have a 'coggled' edge, similar to the way a pie is crimped or jagged, which is done with a special tool. In the following listings, EX (excellent condition) indicates only minor damage. Our advisor for this category is Barbara Rosen; she is listed in the Directory under New Jersey.

Bank, dresser shape, 2 drw over 3 w/appl rosettes, 6¾x7x4", EX...**250.00**
Basket, tan w/burnt umber spots, JH Bell...KY...1879, 6x6½x4¼"...**3,650.00**

Bird whistle, modeled and wheel-thrown with clear lead glaze, $925.00. (Photo courtesy Aston Americana Auctioneers & Appraisers)

Bowl, brn w/blk dots on int, canted sides, raised rim, 2¾x8", EX.**82.50**
Bowl, dk brn resembling tortoise shell, 2x7" NM **330.00**
Bowl, lg manganese daubs, stabilized crow's ft, 3x8"..................**385.00**
Bowl, manganese X amid 4 daubs, 1½x6¾" **475.00**
Bowl, milk; mustard-colored splotches, sloped sides, 3¾x15⅝"..**300.00**
Bowl, starflower in dk brn, chip, 1¼x4½" **355.00**
Bowl, unglazed ext w/orange-brn int w/mica flecks, 1⅝x3¾".....**210.00**
Charger, Jackson & squiggles in yel slip, coggled rim, 1830s, 14".**3,850.00**
Charger, W in yel slip, coggled rim, chips, 12¼" **2,750.00**
Charger, wavy latticework in yel slip, coggled rim, 13¼", EX.**4,250.00**
Charger, 3-line bird's claw yel slip, coggled rim, chips, 13¼" ..**1,750.00**
Charger, 4-line yel slip, coggled rim, 2½x13⅜" **1,200.00**
Charger, 6 daubs of yel slip, coggled rim, 12" **660.00**
Colander, orange w/gr mottling, ftd, 4½x11¼", EX **400.00**
Creamer, appl rose & doves, rosette at hdl, att A Beecher, 4¾".**715.00**
Crock, apple butter; mottling & lg brn runs, flakes, 4⅜" **165.00**
Crock, brn splotches, domed lid w/incised bands, wide mouth, 11" ...**350.00**
Cup, brn w/manganese splotches, pouring spout, incised lines, 2¼"...**240.00**
Dish, pumpkin w/brn daubs (like leopard spots), 1½x6¼" **430.00**
Dish, red-brn int, 1¾x8" **55.00**
Doorstop, orig red & wht pnt w/dk gold stripes, hollow, 6x6½", EX.**360.00**
Figure, dog seated, dk brn, molded w/hand detail in face, 6" **165.00**
Flask, dk brn spots at sides, ring under lip, 6⅜".........................**365.00**

Flowerpot, mottled tan & lt brn, coggled edges, attached saucer, 6"...**330.00**
Flowerpot, unglazed, A Wilcox West Bloomfield, 1850s, 6¼", EX..**110.00**
Jar, brn daubs, ovoid w/raised rim, att PA, 4½x4" **200.00**
Jar, brn daubs, str sides, 8¼x5" **350.00**
Jar, butter; brn-gr mottle, att NY state, ca 1830, 6" **275.00**
Jar, dk brn mottle, incised ring, strap hdl, 6x5¼" **440.00**
Jar, incised ovoid, red-brn, closely mismatched lid, 9", EX **165.00**
Jar, manganese splotches, ovoid, flared rim, chips, 6x4¾" **365.00**
Jar, preserve; burnt orange w/peppering, chips, ca 1840, 8" **165.00**
Jar, red-brn w/blk sponging, w/lid, 8½", EX **775.00**
Jar, storage; brn irid, John Bell, 5¼x4½" **350.00**
Jar, storage; orange-brn w/manganese splotches, cylindrical, 10x6½"..**180.00**
Jug, blk sponging & runs on brn, 9¼"...**330.00**
Jug, brushed dk brn lines at shoulder, ovoid, 5¼"......................**990.00**
Jug, dk brn daubs, ovoid w/strap hdl, flakes, 7½".......................**550.00**
Jug, harvest; med brn splotches, incised spout, 9¼", EX **550.00**
Jug, red-brn, ovoid w/raised ft, strap hdl, 11¾" **350.00**
Jug, unusual metallic-like glaze, squat, 6"....................................**330.00**
Loaf pan, Lafayette in yel script, coggled rim, flakes/wear, 9x14" .**3,300.00**
Loaf pan, Martha in dk brn on metallic speckles, coggled rim, 10½"..**2,100.00**
Loaf pan, wavy script Ls in yel slip on red-brn, coggled rim, 2x16x11"..**3,650.00**
Loaf pan, 2-line yel slip crisscrosses on brn, 14¾" L **825.00**
Loaf pan, 3-line yel slip bird claw designs, coggled rim, 13¾" L..**1,875.00**
Measuring pitcher, dk brn mottled rim, 2⅞x5½" **525.00**
Mold, orange-brn, fluted sides, 1¼x5½" **100.00**
Mold, Turk's head, brn peppered alkaline, att Wilcox, 1840s, 10½"..**50.00**
Mold, Turk's head, orange w/brn sponging, att PA, 2¼x8¾", EX.**55.00**
Mold, Turk's head, orange w/dk brn splotches, minion flakes, 6½"..**80.00**
Mold, Turk's head, red & brn mottle, ca 1850, 3x9½", EX **45.00**
Mug, brick red, cylindrical, att NY, ca 1860, 10", EX **100.00**
Mug, yel runs w/in & w/out, att Shenandoah, 4¼" **715.00**
Pie plate, all yel slip, sgraffito curlicues/dots around feather, 13"..**15,125.00**
Pie plate, crossed snowshoe & dots in yel slip, coggled rim, 8½" .**5,600.00**
Pie plate, dbl S in gr & brn slip, coggled rim, 6¾" **2,100.00**
Pie plate, lg stylized tulip in yel slip, 1790, 10", VG **1,750.00**
Pie plate, lines in gr & dk brn, coggled rim, att Drys, 8" **4,125.00**
Pie plate, Mary's Dish in yel slip, coggled rim, 9¼", EX **1,550.00**
Pie plate, overall grid design & wavy lines in yel, blisters, 9"..**1,650.00**
Pie plate, pinwheel-like design in dk gr, coggled rim, 8¼"..........**935.00**
Pie plate, random yel slip dots, coggled rim, lt wear, 9⅛" **300.00**
Pie plate, tulip in gr & brn slip, coggled rim, PA, 8"................**8,000.00**
Pie plate, wavy flag-like design in yel slip, possible rpr, 9¾".......**660.00**
Pie plate, wavy intersecting lines in brn & yel slip, PA, 7" **2,500.00**
Pie plate, 3-line yel slip, coggled rim, flake, 10½" **1,500.00**
Pie plate, 3-line yel slip, coggled rim, flakes, 6¾" **220.00**
Pie plate, 4-leaf clover in yel slip, coggled rim, 9¼" **1,650.00**
Pitcher, blk speckles & dk brn splotches, 6¼" **660.00**
Pitcher, brn splotches, strap hdl, w/lid, ea 1800, 7" **650.00**
Pitcher, dk brn sponging, tooled lines, w/lid, 7x6¼", EX............**635.00**
Pitcher, emb ribs in panels, mask spouts, brn daubs, rpr, 7¾" **220.00**
Pitcher, gr alkaline, bottom half unglazed, thin walls, 1850s, 7"...**45.00**
Pitcher, milk; red-brn w/wht splotches, H Swopes, 8¾" **1,200.00**
Pitcher, red w/dk brn splotches, squat w/gallery rim, appl hdl, 6" ...**165.00**
Pitcher, sgraffito Am eagle/shield, mottled glaze, att Medinger, 7".**1,950.00**
Pitcher, yel & gr daubs, wide rim, appl hdl, 7", EX **660.00**
Plate, ABC, fanciful writing, coggled, 10", VG..........................**2,200.00**
Plate, wavy lines & feathers in yel slip, flaw, 8½" **1,450.00**
Plate, X w/in circle & wavy line in yel slip on dk brick red, 9"..**1,850.00**
Plate, 2-line yel slip waves (3X)+2 more slip devices, coggled, 10"...**700.00**
Plate, 3-line yel slip waves (3X), 10½", EX **940.00**
Plate, 3-line yel slip waves (4X), coggled, 11", VG **825.00**
Porringer, dk brn flowing from rim, emb ribs at shoulder, MA, 2½x4"..**1,725.00**
Pot, mottled brn, 2 molded hdls, w/lid, 10x13" **200.00**
Spittoon, brn mottle, funnel-shaped center, John Bell, 4x7⅝"...**500.00**

Regal China

Located in Antioch, Illinois, the Regal China Company open for business in 1938. Products of interest to collectors are James Beam decanters, cookie jars, salt and pepper shakers, and similar novelty items. The company closed its doors sometime in 1993. The Old MacDonald Farm series listed below is especially collectible, so are the salt and pepper shakers.

Note: Where applicable, prices are based on excellent gold trim. (Gold trim must be 90% intact or deductions should be made for wear.) See also Decanters.

Our advisor for this category is Judy Posner; she is listed in the Directory under Florida.

Cookie Jars

Cat, from $340 to	385.00
Churn Boy	250.00
Clown, gr collar, from $650 to	675.00
Davy Crockett, from $450 to	600.00
Diaper Pin Pig, from $450 to	540.00
Dutch Girl, from $600 to	655.00
Dutch Girl, peach trim	720.00
FiFi Poodle, from $600 to	655.00
Fisherman, from $650 to	720.00
French Chef, from $350 to	405.00
Goldilocks (+)	340.00
Harpo Marx	1,080.00
Hobby Horse, from $250 to	270.00
Hubert Lion, from $720 to	855.00
Humpty Dumpty, red, from $275 to	250.00
Little Miss Muffet, from $315 to	350.00
Majorette, from $350 to	400.00
Oriental Lady w/Baskets, from $585 to	630.00
Peek-a-Boo (+), from $1,350 to	1,440.00
Quaker Oats	115.00
Three Bears	175.00
Toby Cookies, unmk, from $675 to	700.00
Tulip, from $200 to	225.00
Uncle Mistletoe	765.00

Old McDonald's Farm

Butter dish, cow's head	175.00
Canister, flour, cereal, coffee; med	275.00
Canister, pretzels, peanuts, popcorn, chips, tidbits; lg	250.00
Canister, salt, sugar, tea; med	150.00
Canister, soap, cookies; lg, ea, from $350 to	425.00
Cookie barn	200.00
Creamer, rooster, from $110 to	125.00
Grease jar, pig	175.00
Pitcher, milk	300.00
Shakers, boy & girl, pr	65.00
Shakers, churn, gold trim, pr	95.00
Shakers, feed sack w/sheep, pr	150.00
Spice jar, assorted lids, sm, ea, from $125 to	150.00
Sugar bowl, hen	95.00
Teapot, duck's head	225.00

Shakers

A Nod to Abe, 3-pc nodder, from $300 to	350.00
Bendel, bears, wht w/pk & brn trim, pr, from $125 to	150.00
Bendel, bunnies, wht w/blk & pk trim, pr, from $125 to	150.00
Bendel, kissing pigs, gray w/pk trim, lg, pr, from $350 to	375.00
Bendel, love bugs, burgundy, lg, pr, from $150 to	185.00
Bendel, love bugs, gr, sm, pr	65.00
Cat, sitting w/eyes closed, wht w/hat & gold bow, pr	225.00
Clown, pr	250.00
Dutch Girl, pr, from $200 to	225.00
FiFi, pr	350.00
Fish, mk C Miller, 1-pc	55.00
French Chef, wht w/gold trim, pr, from $250 to	350.00
Humpty Dumpty, pr	75.00
Peek-a-boo, red dots, lg, pr (+), from $450 to	500.00
Peek-a-boo, red dots, sm, pr, from $250 to	275.00
Peek-a-boo, wht solid, sm, pr	200.00
Pig, pk, mk C Miller, 1-pc	95.00
Tulip, pr	50.00
Van Tellingen, bears, brn, pr, from $25 to	28.00
Van Tellingen, boy & dog, Black, pr	95.00
Van Tellingen, boy & dog, wht, pr	75.00
Van Tellingen, bunnies, solid colors, pr, from $28	32.00
Van Tellingen, ducks, pr	38.00
Van Tellingen, Dutch boy & girl, from $45 to	50.00
Van Tellingen, Mary & lamb, pr	60.00
Van Tellingen, sailor & mermaid, pr, from $225 to	225.00

Relief-Molded Jugs

Early relief-molded pitchers (ca 1830s – 40s) were made in two-piece molds into which sheets of clay were pressed. The relief decoration was deep and well defined, usually of animal or human subjects. Most of these pitchers were designed with a flaring lip and substantial footing. Gradually styles changed, and by the 1860s the rim had become flatter and the foot less pronounced. The relief decoration was not as deep, and foliage became a common design. By the turn of the century, many other types of pitchers had been introduced, and the market for these early styles began to wane.

Watch for recent reproductions; these have been made by the slip-casting method. Unlike relief-molded ware which is relatively smooth inside, slip-cast pitchers will have interior indentations that follow the irregularities of the relief decoration. Values below are for pieces in excellent condition. Our advisor for this category is Kathy Hughes; she is listed in the Directory under North Carolina.

Key: Reg — Registered

Apostle, wht, Meigh, 1842, 9⅞"	565.00
Argos, gr, Brownfield, Apr 29, 1864, 8"	175.00
Barley, gr, Dudson, April 25, 1891, 8"	175.00
Bundle of Faggots, drabware, metal lid, Ridgway, Reg Oct 1, 1835, 8"	250.00
Cain & Abel, tan stoneware, Edward Walley, ca 1850, 10"	325.00
Chelsea Pensioners, wht stoneware, unknown, ca 1845	350.00
Cupid at Play, buff & tan, Turner, ca 1800, 9½"	750.00
Dancers, George of Longton, Reg April 21, 1852, 6"	250.00
Diana, gr stoneware, Edward Walley, Reg June 21, 1850, 10"	425.00
Diston Family Instruments, bl smear/gilt, Alcock, 1840s, 7"	700.00
Gleaner, Edward Walley, Reg Nov 11, 1858, 10¾"	550.00
Good Samaritan, buff & tan, Jones & Walley, 1841, 8"	400.00
Hops, Herbert Minton & Co, wht parian, Reg May 14, 1847, 8¼"	900.00
Idle Apprentices, wht & bl, unknown, 1840, 7"	250.00
Ivy, creamer w/mc enameled trim, S Alcock, 5½"	625.00
Julius Caesar, gray, appl laurel wreath, Meigh, 1839, 8¼"	450.00
Love & War, purple on wht parian, Samuel Alcock, ca 1845, 7¾"	500.00
Mermaid & Cupid, Minton, gr & wht parian, ca 1911, 6"	750.00
Naomi & Daughter-in-law, lav on parian, Alcock, 1847, 8¾"	450.00
Now I'm Grandpa, unknown, ca 1850, 8½"	450.00

Pan, buff, w/lid, Ridgway, 1830s, 7¼" 275.00
Peel & Cobden, yel earthenware, unknown, ca 1846 ....250.00
Princess Charlotte/Prince Leopold, minor rstr, 6" 275.00
Robert Burns, Machin & Potts, cream & wht, Reg June 20, 1834, 6¼" ..500.00
Rose, parian, unmk, ca 1850, 6½"...............................175.00
Shakespeare, wht on purple parian, Samuel Alcock, ca 1850, 6" ..700.00
Sir Walter Scott commemorative, gray-gr, Minton, 8" 350.00
Slavery scenes, Ridgway & Abington, 1855, 7⅞", minimum value ..1,100.00
Stag, gray-gr, Enoch & Edward Wood, ca 1840, 9¼" 350.00
Swans, w/lid, Ridgway & Abington, ca 1850, 8" 300.00
Tam-O'-Shanter, glazed bl, Ridgway, 1835, 8¼".....................295.00
Toho, Masons, drabware stoneware, ca 1845, 6½".....................750.00
Tulip, wht stoneware, Dudson, ca 1860, 8".........................250.00
Two Drivers, parian, Minton, ca 1850, 7½"..........................700.00
Victoria Regina, Sanford Pottery, July 6, 1860, 9¾"....................750.00
Vintage, The; WT Copeland, ca 1845, 6½" 400.00
Youth & Old Age, gray-gr, Copeland-Garret, ca 1845, 8¾" 300.00

Restraints

Since the beginning of time, many things from animals to treasures have been held in bondage by hemp, bamboo, chests, chains, shackles, and other constructed devices. Many of these devices were used to hold captives who awaited further torture, as if the restraint wasn't torturous enough. The study and collecting of restraints enables one to learn much about the advancement of civilization in the country or region from which they originated. Such devices at various times in history were made of very heavy metals — so heavy that the wearer could scarcely move about. It has only been in the last sixty years that vast improvements have been made in design and construction that afford the captive some degree of comfort. Our advisor for this category is Joseph Tanner; he is listed in the Directory under California.

Key:
bbl — barrel	lc — lock case
d-lb — double lock button	NST — non-swing through
K — key	ST — swing through
Kd — keyed	stp — stamped

Foreign Handcuffs

Deutshce Polizei, ST, middle hinge, folds, takes bbl-bit K 80.00
East German, heavy steel, NP single lg hinge, NST, bbl key 120.00
English, Chubb Arrest, steel, ST, multi-bit solid K 250.00
French Revolved, oval, ST, takes 2 Ks: bbl & pin tumbler 170.00
German, 3-lb steel set, 2⅝" thick, center chain, bbl K 175.00
German Clejuso, sq lc, adjusts/NST, d-lb on side, bbl K.............100.00
German Darby, adjusts, well finished, NST, sm 120.00
Hiatt, English Darby, like US CW Darby, stp Hiatt & #d.............75.00
Hiatt English non-adjust screw K Darby style, uses screw K 120.00
Italian, stp New Police, modern Peerless type, ST, sm bbl K 35.00
Russian modern ST, blued bbl key, unmk, crude...........................80.00
Spanish, stp Alcyon/Star, modern Peerless type, ST, sm bbl K 40.00

Foreign Leg Shackles

East German, aluminum, lg hinge, cable amid 4 cuffs, bbl key ...100.00
Hiatt English combo manacles, handcuff/leg irons w/chain........325.00
Hiatt Plug leg irons, same K-ing as Plug-8 cuffs, w/chain............400.00

U.S. Handcuffs

Adams, teardrop lc, bbl Kd, NST, usually not stp.......................300.00

American Munitions, modern/rnd, sm bbl Kd, ST bow, stp..........45.00
Bean Giant, sideways figure-8, solid center, lc, dbl-bit K............550.00
Cavenay, looks like Marlin Daley but w/screw K, NST................180.00
Civil War padlocking type, various designs w/loop for lock........225.00
Flash Action Manacle, like Bean Giant w/ST, K-way center......400.00
Flexibles, steel segmented bows, NST Darby type, screw K 300.00
H&R Super, ST, shaft-hinge connector takes hollow titted K....150.00
Judd, NST, used rnd/internally triangular K, stp Mattatuck........150.00
Marlin Daley, NST, bottle-neck form, neck stp, dbl-titted K......300.00
Palmer, 2" steel bands, 2 K-ways (top & center), NST stp 400.00
Peerless, ST, takes sm bbl K, stp Mfg'ered by S&W Co 75.00
Phelps, NST, twist chain between cuffs, Tower look-alike..........400.00
Providence Tool Co, stp, NST, Darby screw K style...................350.00
Romer, NST, takes flat K, resembles padlock, stp Romer Co......300.00
Strauss, ST, takes lg solid bitted K, stp Strauss Eng Co 120.00
Tower bar cuffs, cuffs separate by 10-12" steel bar 300.00
Tower Detective Pinkerton, NST, sq lc, bbl-bitted K, no stp......165.00
Tower-Bean, NST, sm rnd lc, takes tiny bbl-bitted K, stp 130.00
Walden 'Lady Cuff,' NST, takes sm bbl K, lightweight, stp.........400.00

U.S. Leg Shackles

Forged iron ankle cuffs and link chain, both marked No. 8, illegible manufacturer mark, patent dates (latest 1882), EX, no key, $135.00.

Civil War or prison ball & chain, padlocking or rivet type 500.00
H&R Supers, as handcuffs 650.00
Judd, as handcuffs...155.00
Peerless Big Guy, modern ST, bbl key 60.00
Strauss, as handcuffs...200.00
Tower ball & chain, leg iron w/chain & 6-lb to 50-lb ball..........500.00
Tower Detective, as handcuffs...200.00

Various Other Restraining Devices

African slave Darby-style leg shackles, heavy/hand forged..........220.00
Argus iron claw, twist T to open & close 60.00
English figure-8 nipper, claws open by lifting top lock tab............80.00
German nipper, twist hdl opens/closes cuff, stp Germany/etc 75.00
Jay Pee, thumb cuffs, mk solid body, bbl K..................................15.00
Korean, hand hinged model, blk, bbl key......................................70.00
New Model Russian, chain bbl key, blued 125.00
Phillips nipper, claw, flip lever on top to open..............................90.00
Tower Lyon, thumb cuffs, solid body, NST, dbl-bit center K.......300.00

Reverse Painting on Glass

Verre eglomise is the technique of painting on the underside of glass. Dating back to the early 1700s, this art became popular in the nineteenth century when German immigrants chose historical figures and beautiful women as subjects for their reverse glass paintings. Advertising mirrors of this type came into vogue at the turn of the century.

Dutch landscape w/windmill, flakes, fr, 15x23" 110.00
George & Martha Washington, orig fr, 22x20", pr..................2,400.00
Lady in red dress w/lace collar, yel gloves & flowers, 9½x6½" fr..440.00
Sinking of Titanic w/rafts in water, dark, 16x20", EX 150.00
Vase of flowers, minor flaking, gilt fr, 10x8"..........................11.00

Rhead

Associated with many companies during his career — Weller, Vance Avon, Arequipa, A.E. Tile, and finally Homer Laughlin China — Fredrick Herten Rhead organized his own pottery in Santa Barbara, California, ca 1913. Admittedly more of a designer than a potter, Rhead hired help to turn the pieces on the wheel but did most of the decorating himself. The process he favored most involved sgraffito designs inlaid with enameling. Egyptian and Art Nouveau influences were evidenced in much of his work. The ware he produced there was often marked with a logo incorporating the potter at the wheel and 'Santa Barbara.'

Candlesticks, geometric inlay in white and royal blue, marked Rhead Santa Barbara, 6", NM, $1,300.00 for the pair.

Vase, dk gr w/exposed brn clay, mk w/potter at wheel, 7" 1,900.00
Vase, med/lt gr matt w/brn exposed, Santa Barbara #28/#50, 4"...1,500.00
Vase, multi-brn w/cvd mtns & trees, tapered form, 9" 8,000.00

Richard

Richard, who at one time worked for Galle, made cameo art glass in France during the 1920s. His work was often multilayered and acid cut with florals and scenics in lovely colors. The ware was marked with his name in relief. Our advisor for this category is Don Williams; he is listed in the Directory under Missouri.

Cameo

Vase, berry vines, purple on orange mottle, spherical, 4" 250.00
Vase, butterflies & cherries, mc on citron, 9½" 750.00
Vase, farm bldgs/ladies/trees/lake/mtns, brn on yel to orange, 14" ...1,500.00
Vase, floral vines, brn on maize yel, teardrop form, 9" 300.00
Vase, flowers & butterfly, blk on orange, 4"..................................150.00
Vase, flowers & insects, brn on orange, 8" 600.00
Vase, pine cones & branches, brn on orange, 1920s, 8½"..........880.00

Rie, Lucie

Lucie Rie was born in 1902. She moved to London in 1938 and shared her studio with Hans Coper from 1946 to 1958. Her ceramics look modern; however they are based on shapes from many world cultures dating back to Roman times. Lucie Rie is best known for the use of metallic

oxides in her clay and glazes. She specializes in the hand throwing of thin porcelain bowls, which is a very difficult process. Her works are in the world's best museums. All of her ceramics are impressed with a seal mark on the bottom, a cojoined 'L & R' within a rectangular reserve.

Bowl, textured oatmeal, ftd, 2x5" 600.00
Cup & saucer, sgraffito design, L Rie/H Coper, 2¾", 5¼" 1,050.00
Cup & saucer, tea; wht tin-glaze, w/blk trim, conical shape 720.00
Dish, semi-irid brn w/wht bottom, ¾x5½" dia 370.00
Pourer, blk w/wht int, pulled lip & hdl, ca 1950s, mk, 3" 930.00
Shakers, dk brn matt, flared cone, ca 1950, pr.......................750.00

Riviera

Riviera was a line of dinnerware introduced by the Homer Laughlin China Company in 1938. It was sold exclusively by the Murphy Company through their nationwide chain of dime stores. Riviera was unmarked, lightweight, and inexpensive. It was discontinued sometime prior to 1950. Colors are mauve blue, red, yellow, light green, and ivory. On rare occasions, dark blue pieces are found, but this was not a standard color. For further information we recommend *The Collector's Encyclopedia of Fiesta* by Sharon and Bob Huxford, available from Collector Books.

Batter set, complete 290.00
Bowl, baker; 9" 25.00
Bowl, fruit; 5½" 12.00
Bowl, nappy; 7¼" 25.00
Bowl, oatmeal; 6" 38.00
Butter dish, cobalt, ½-lb..300.00
Butter dish, cobalt, ¼-lb..250.00
Butter dish, colors other than cobalt, turq or ivory, ¼-lb...........135.00
Butter dish, colors other than cobalt, ½-lb...........................120.00
Butter dish, ivory, ¼-lb..175.00
Butter dish, turq, ¼-lb...290.00
Casserole...110.00
Creamer...11.00
Jug, w/lid...130.00
Pitcher, juice; mauve bl 210.00
Pitcher, juice; yel..120.00
Plate, deep 22.00
Plate, 6" 7.00
Plate, 7" 35.00
Plate, 7" 10.00
Plate, 9" 16.00
Plate, 10" 55.00
Platter, closed hdls, 11¼"..24.00
Platter, 11½" 22.00
Platter, 15" 55.00
Sauce boat 22.00
Saucer..4.00
Shakers, pr..18.00
Sugar bowl, w/lid..18.00
Syrup, w/lid..160.00
Teacup...8.00
Teapot...155.00
Tumbler, hdl 70.00
Tumbler, juice 52.00

Robertson

Fred H. Robertson, clay expert for the Los Angeles Pressed Brick Company and son of Alexander Robertson of the Roblin Pottery, experimented with crystalline glazes as early as 1906. In 1934 Fred and his son George established their own works in Los Angeles, but by 1943 they had moved operations to Hollywood. Though most of their early wares were turned by hand, some were also molded in low relief. Fine crackle glazes and crystallines were developed. Their ware was marked with 'Robertson,' 'F.H.R.,' or 'R.,' with the particular location of manufacture noted. The small pottery closed in 1952. Our advisors for this category are Suzanne Perrault and David Rago; they are listed in the Directory under New Jersey.

Vase, bl crystalline crackle, bulbous, 4" 90.00
Vase, feathered gr matt, bulbous, rim rstr, 4½" 200.00
Vase, ivory crackle, bulbous bottom w/cylindrical neck, mk, 9½" ..165.00
Vase, pk crystalline crackle, tapered, 3¼" 90.00
Vase, pk to ivory to bl, tapered cylinder, 6¼" 150.00
Vase, yel crackle, bulbous bottom w/cylindrical neck, 3½" 45.00

Robineau

After short-term training in ceramics in 1903, Adelaide Robineau (with the help of her husband Samuel) built a small pottery studio at her home in Syracuse, New York. She was adept in mixing the clay and throwing the ware, which she often decorated by incising designs into the unfired clay. Samuel developed many of the glazes and took charge of the firing process. In 1910 she joined the staff of the American Women's League Pottery at St. Louis, where she designed the famous Scarab Vase. After this pottery failed, she served on the faculty of Syracuse University. In the 1920s she worked under the name of Threshold Pottery. She was also the founder and publisher of Keramic Studio magazine. Her work was and is today highly acclaimed for the standards of excellence to which she aspired. Our advisors for this category are Suzanne Perrault and David Rago; they are listed in the Directory under New Jersey.

Jar, mossy green flambé with bronze geomteric floral, spherical, with lid, marked AR/44/1920, 4½x4½", NM, $13,000.00. (Photo courtesy David Rago Auctions)

Vase, bl/brn/tan drip, gourd form, 1919, 5" 2,500.00
Vase, dk oxblood petals on lighter ground, AR, 3¾x3¼" 3,500.00
Vase, gr/bl/pk drip, stick neck, 1921, 7" 11,000.00
Vase, irises, celadon/oxblood w/crackled base, 4-hdl, 1920, 4x4" ..3,500.00
Vase, pale yel crackle, teardrop, obscured date, 2¼" 850.00
Vase, robin's egg bl w/wht straps, bottle neck, 1921, 4¼x3½" 1,430.00

Robj

Robj was the name of a retail store that operated in Paris for only a few years, from about 1925 to 1931. Robj solicited designs from the best French artisans of the period to produce decorative objects for the home. These were executed mostly in porcelain but there were glass and earthenware pieces as well. The most well known are the figural bottles which were particularly popular in the United States. However, Robj also promoted tea

sets, perfume lamps, chess sets, ashtrays, bookends, humidors, powder jars, cigarette boxes, figurines, lamps, and milk pitchers. Robj objects tend to be whimsical, and all embody the Art Deco style. Items listed below are ceramic unless noted otherwise. Our advisors for this category are Randall Monsen and Rod Baer; their address is listed in the Directory under Virginia.

Ashtray, wht w/seated figure on side in bl w/gold cone on head, 5x5"..1,800.00
Atomizer, 4 Seasons, glass, eng gilt top, ca 1925, 6" 600.00
Bookends, leaping greyhounds, wht, #44, 5x6½" 450.00
Bookends, Pirogue Indienne, Indians in canoe, wht porc, faint mk ..325.00
Bottle, figural Dutch boy w/gr dbl-breasted jacket, 10½" 520.00
Decanter, General De Brigade, 10¾" 2,660.00
Decanter, lady in wht w/basket of flowers in hand, gold trim, 10¼"..1,500.00
Decanter, monk in brn w/cream hat, 10½" 435.00
Decanter, Scottsman w/blk & wht plaid kilt & blk hat, 10¾" ...700.00
Incense burner, Oriental girl in wht on knees w/pot in front, 7⅛" ..340.00
Inkwell, female genie, mc, 5¼" 180.00
Lamp base, Greek man (woman) w/gilt on wht, mk, 11", pr 460.00
Perfume lamp, Deco-style couple, perfume in her pocket, rpr, 8½"..275.00
Perfume lamp, Oriental man sits on platform, sm lid missing, 8¼"..550.00
Powder jar, lady in tiered gown, yel/blk, mk, 5½x5⅜" 375.00

Rock 'N Roll Memorabilia

Memorabilia from the early days of rock 'n roll recalls an era that many of us experienced firsthand; these listings are offered to demonstrate the many and various aspects of this area of collecting. Beware of reproductions! Many are so well done even a knowledgeable collector will sometimes be fooled.

Our advisor for Elvis memorabilia is Rosalind Cranor, author of *Elvis Collectibles* and *Best of Elvis Collectibles* (Overmountain Press); she is listed in the Directory under Virginia. The remainder is under the advisement of Bob Gottuso, author of Beatles, KISS and Monkees sections in *Garage Sale Gold II* by Tomart; see Pennsylvania. See also Decanters.

Alice Cooper, press kit, Love It To Death album, rare, EX 485.00
Alice Cooper, press kit, School's Out Tour, 1972, NM 365.00
Beatles, assignment book, Select-o-Pak, 1964, M....................250.00
Beatles, banner, Hallmark stamps promo, 3x18", VG+ 50.00
Beatles, belt buckle, metal w/photo under plastic, EX..............40.00
Beatles, binder, vinyl 3-ring, wht, NM..............................125.00
Beatles, book, Lennon Remembers, hardbk, 1971, NM 30.00
Beatles, book, Letters to the..., 1964, EX 25.00
Beatles, brunch bag, bl vinyl w/zippered top, 8" 500.00
Beatles, calender, portraits in doorway, 1964, M 175.00
Beatles, candy dish, Paul, pottery w/gilt edge, UK 160.00
Beatles, card, Fan Club Member, 1964...............................39.00
Beatles, clutch purse, cloth w/leather strap & allover pictures ...240.00
Beatles, collector's stamps, 1964 Hallmark Edition, 5 for.........10.00
Beatles, concert book, 1964, USA, 12x12" 40.00
Beatles, doll, vinyl, John or George w/instrument, Remco, 4", ea ..125.00
Beatles, dolls, blow-up, set of 4, EX...............................150.00
Beatles, eyeglasses case, John, facsimile signature, England..........75.00
Beatles, halloween mask, John Lennon................................125.00
Beatles, handbag, wht cloth w/brass hdl, Dame, w/original tag, 1964, M...600.00
Beatles, magazine, Life, Paul & Linda on cover, 1971, NM 20.00
Beatles, money clip, apple cutout, Apple Records, M 275.00
Beatles, nodder, plastic, 1964, set of 4, VG........................55.00
Beatles, Paint by Number set, 1 portrait, US, 1964, MIB........1,200.00
Beatles, pins, Yellow Submarine, HP brass, 8 for 50.00
Beatles, pop-up book, Yellow Submarine, NM..........................45.00
Beatles, record sleeve, Can't Buy Me Love, rare, M 525.00
Beatles, sheet music, I Want To Hold Your Hand, 1968 ....20.00

Beatles, sunglasses, blk plastic, Bachman Bros, 1964, M 250.00
Beatles, thimble, Fenton, baked-on image, 1990s, EX...................15.00
Beatles, tie-tac set, NEMS, 1964, MOC (watch for repros) 75.00
Beatles, wallet, vinyl w/photos & all extras, by SPP, VG+..........100.00
Bee Gees, book, Legend/Illustrated Story of; 160 pgs, softcover, NM ...20.00
Bee Gees, concert T-shirt, 1979 Fever American Tour, EX...........40.00
Bee Gees, Fan Club Package, 1979, EX 45.00
Black Sabbath, litho poster, Miami Beach Convention Hall, 1978, 20x14" ..45.00
Black Sabbath, T-shirt, Heaven & Hell Tour, 1980, VG+ 50.00
Black Sabbath, T-shirt, 1983 World Tour, VG...............................40.00
Black Sabbath, tour program, European, 1975, 12 pgs, 12x8¼", M ..100.00
Black Sabbath, tour program, N Am, M, from $50 to.................75.00
Bob Marley & the Wailers, tour poster, Germany, 1980, 33x24", M ...85.00
Bobby Sherman, lunch box, photo & hearts, wht plastic hdl, 1972, NM+..145.00
Boy George & Culture Club, book, Maria David, Greenwich House, 1984, M ...20.00
Brenda Lee, paper doll, heavy cb, Merry Mfg, 1964, MIP...........160.00
Brenda Lee, tour book, Japan 1975, 14x10", EX+ 60.00
Bruce Springsteen, concert poster, Fenway Park 2003, M...........100.00
Creedence Clearwater Revival, poster, Fillmore West, 1969, 21x14", EX ...100.00
Crosby, Stills, Nash & Young, concert poster, 1970, 27x14", NM..100.00
Dave Clark 5, button, I Love the Dave Clark 5, 1960s, 3½" dia, NM ..25.00
Dave Clark 5, dolls, vinyl, Remco, 1964, 4½", set of 5, NM 325.00
David Bowie, An Evening With; flyer/invitational, 1969, 19x9½", EX .335.00
David Bowie, T-shirt, 1978 American Tour, NM 110.00
David Cassidy, pennant, image in heart w/Darling David, 1970s, 15", EX..65.00
David Cassidy, 3-ring binder, photo in front & bk, 1972, EX 40.00
Doors, concert handbill, Cheetah Club (CA), 1960s, 5½x8½", EX...300.00
Doors, concert poster, Sam Houston Coliseum, late 1960s, 11x8½", EX.350.00
Doors, concert ticket, LA Forum, 1968, unused, NM 165.00
Eagles, concert ticket, Budokan Tokyo, 1976, EX.......................30.00
Eagles, program, Farewell I Tour, M 45.00
Elton John, tour program, Rock of the Westies, 1975, M.............30.00
Elvis, calendar, RCA, heavy stock, 1963, 11x11", NM 175.00
Elvis, cookie jar, 1968 Comeback, Vandor, MIB...........................75.00
Elvis, decanter, McCormick, 1978, Elvis bust, no music box, 750 ml ...75.00
Elvis, decanter, McCormick, 1983, Elvis Gold Mini, plays My Way, 50 ml.125.00
Elvis, doll, '68 Comeback, Hasbro, 1993, MIB 30.00
Elvis, doll, gold suit, Gemmy, EPE, plays Blue Christmas, 19", MIB..65.00
Elvis, doll, Phoenix Elvis, vinyl, World Doll Co, 21", MIB...........90.00
Elvis, handkerchief, w/guitar on wht, 1956, M 500.00
Elvis, lobby card, Jailhouse Rock, 1956, 11x14", VG+..................75.00
Elvis, lobby card, Wild in the Country, 1961, 14x17", EX 55.00
Elvis, McCormick, decanter, 1983, Sgt Elvis, plays GI Blues, 750 ml ..295.00
Elvis, overnight case, brn or bl, EPE, 1956, EX 650.00
Elvis, photo folio tour book, 1957, 12-pg, 8x10", NM 175.00
Elvis, pin-bk, Don't Be Cruel, red/wht/blk, ⅞", M 30.00
Elvis, plate, Heartbreak Hotel, Delphi, 1992, MIB.......................35.00
Elvis, postage stamps, full sheet of 29¢ stamps (40 total), M 55.00
Elvis, record, For LP Fans Only, Victor 1990, 1959, EX..............130.00
Elvis, sheet music, Hound Dog, M 55.00
Elvis, ticket, Alabama & Mississippi Fair & Dairy Show, 1956, EX .80.00

Grace Jones, concert poster, Austin City Coliseum, 6/24/90, 17x11", M..65.00
Grateful Dead, concert poster, Old Cheese Factory, 1966, 11x8½", NM...285.00
Grateful Dead, concert poster, Syracuse NY, 1977, 23x17", NM...500.00
Grateful Dead, concert poster, Winterland, 1978, NM 160.00
Grateful Dead, cookie jar, tour bus, Vandor, 1998, 8½x12", MIB..100.00
Hollies, concert poster, Sioux Falls Arena, 23x13", NM 60.00
Jim Morrison, book, Lords & New Creatures, poetry, 1970, EX....80.00
Johnny Cash, concert poster, Fillmore 9/26/94, 19x13", NM 210.00
KISS, Army Kit, complete, 1st edition, 1975, M.........................200.00
KISS, belt buckle, chrome letters KISS, NM...............................140.00
KISS, concert poster, 4-scene composite, 1970s, 24x35", M 20.00
KISS, doll, Gene Simmons, Mego, 1978, 14", EX+.......................95.00
KISS, ink pen, Peter, 1970s, MOC...200.00
KISS, patch, silver KISS on blk, 1970s, 4x2", M 12.00
KISS, press kit, Creatures of the Night Tour, 1982, NM 60.00
KISS, puffy sticker set, Rocksticks, 1979, M, 4 for 200.00
KISS, tour book, Destroyer Tour, 1976, EX 120.00
KISS, tour program, 10th Anniversary, EX.................................140.00
KISS, transistor radio, color logo & group photo, 1977, MIB.....200.00
KISS, Your Face Makeup Kit, 1970s, VG+.................................300.00
MC Hammer, fanny pack, Hammer Time, Bustin' Productions, 1991, M..20.00
Michael Jackson, shoes, Billie Jean style, LA Gear, MIB 95.00
Monkees, charm bracelet, 4-color portrait charms, Raybert, 1967, M....50.00
Monkees, puzzles, jigsaw, Speed Boat/On Stage, Fairchild, NMIB, ea....50.00
REO Speedwagon, concert poster, Hawaii, prof laminated, 30x18", NM ...80.00
Rick Nelson, concert poster, blk/wht, 1970, M 200.00
Rock & Roll Hall of Fame Induction Dinner, 1998, 12x8¼", EX ...155.00
Rolling Stones, banner, red w/bl print, 1975 tour, 68x42", VG+..50.00
Rolling Stones, bomber jacket, Steel Wheels Tour 1989, NM ...140.00
Rolling Stones, guest pass, No Security Tour, 1999, laminated, M..35.00
Rolling Stones, movie flyer, Gimme Shelter, 1970, 5½x7½", EX.80.00
Rolling Stones, poster, Aberdeen, Scotland's Capitol Cinema, 1964, EX..1,500.00
Rolling Stones, stand-up, for Some Girls album, cb, 1978, 19x11", EX ..60.00
Rolling Stones, T-shirt, New Barbarians, 1979, EX.....................215.00
Rolling Stones, tour program, 1978, EX.......................................20.00
Rolling Stones, 9" balloons, MIP...55.00
Simon & Garfunkel, concert poster, Philharmonic Hall NY, 1967, EX...100.00
Teen Idols Tour 1998, Davy Jones/Peter Noone/Bobby Sherman, 26 pgs, EX...10.00
Vanilla Fudge, concert flyer, New Year's Day, 1969, M.................30.00
Vanilla Ice, Rap Game, International Games, 1991, MIB 100.00
Yardbirds & Doors, concert poster, 1967, 21½x14½", NM.........190.00

Rockingham

In the early part of the nineteenth century, American potters began
to prefer brown- and buff-burning clays over red because of their durability. The glaze favored by many was Rockingham, which varied from a
dark brown mottle to a sponged effect sometimes called tortoise shell. It
consisted in part of manganese and various metallic salts and was used by
many potters until well into the twentieth century. Over the past two
years, demand and prices have risen sharply, especially in the East. See
also Bennington.

Bank, 2-story cottage w/chimney, sm flakes, 6" 195.00
Bowl, column design, 3¾x11½", EX 45.00
Bowl, sm pings, 5x11"...100.00
Coffeepot, mini, 4½"...550.00
Colander, emb base, ftd/pierced, 3½x8", EX...............................350.00
Creamer, male profile in flower reserve, 4½" 120.00
Cuspidor, shell pattern, 3⅜x7¼"..125.00
Custard cup, 2½", 4 for..70.00
Donut flask, fruit vines & man w/tankard, dk brn, 8½" dia........450.00
Doorknobs, set of 4..35.00

Elvis, wallet, cream,
red, or turquoise vinyl,
EP Enterprises, 1956,
EX, from $575.00 to
$600.00. (Photo courtesy Ros-
alind Cranor)

Figure, dog, seated on base, EX molded details, 10¾" 550.00
Figure, dogs seated, wavy fur, amber & dk brn, 5⅝", 6¼", pr 450.00
Figure, lion reclining, amber w/runs, EX detail, 5¾x9½x4" 800.00
Figure, spaniel, molded details, free-standing front legs, 10x7½"...450.00
Figure, spaniel on base, 10¼", EX 550.00
Flask, fish form, 10¾" 500.00
Inkwell, girl w/hat reclining on tree stump, 5" L 395.00
Jar, Gothic Arch, domed lid, sm rpr, 9x8" 660.00
Mug, strap hdl, flared rim, 3½" 120.00
Mug, strap hdl, 3¾" 120.00
Nappy, emb ribbed ft, 3x10½" 150.00
Pie plate, 9¾" 135.00

Pitcher, dead game, rebuilt handle, 9½", $325.00.

Pitcher, dog figural, open mouth spout, 8⅝".........................165.00
Pitcher, eagle w/shield/stars/cannon/banner, unmk, 9x10" 1,035.00
Pitcher, hound hdl, 9", VG...435.00
Pitcher, hunt scenes & grapevines, hound hdl, OH, 7⅛" 800.00
Pitcher, peacock & palm trees (repeating), 8", EX 125.00
Platter, 12½x9½"...250.00
Soap dish, 1¾x6½" dia..110.00

Rockwell, Norman

Norman Rockwell began his career in 1911 at the age of seventeen doing illustrations for a children's book entitled *Tell Me Why Stories*. Within a few years he had produced the *Saturday Evening Post* cover that made him one of America's most beloved artists. Though not well accepted by the professional critics of his day who did not consider his work to be art but 'merely' commercial illustration, Rockwell's popularity grew to the extent that today there is an overwhelming abundance of examples of his work or those related to the theme of one of his illustrations.

The figurines described below were issued by the Rockwell Museum and Museum Collections Inc. (formerly Rockwell Museum). For Rockwell listings by Gorham see the 2002 edition of *Schroeder's Antiques Price Guide*. Our advisor for this category is Barb Putratz; she is listed in the Directory under Minnesota.

A Tough One, 1983 ....95.00
Adventures Between Adventures, 1972.............................300.00
Antique Dealer, 1983...195.00
At the Vets, Gorham Miniature, 1981................................55.00
At the Vets, 1974..110.00
Baby Sitter, Gorham Miniature, 1987................................90.00
Batter Up, Gorham Miniature, 1984.................................76.00
Beguiling Buttercup, 1977 ....115.00
Best Friends, Gorham Miniature, 1986...............................45.00
Blasting Out, 1983...95.00

Boy & His Dog, 4 seasons set, complete 1,200.00
Boy Meets His Dog, Gorham Miniature, 1981 ....110.00
Canine Solo, 1982 ....100.00
Captain, 1974..115.00
Careful Aim, Gorham Miniature, 1984...............................80.00
Careful Aim, 1981 ....300.00
Checking Good Deeds, 1982, 3½" 25.00
Choosing Up, 1978...175.00
Christmas Goose (Ltd ed of 7,500) 150.00
Closed for Business, 1980 ....240.00
Coal Seasons Coming, 1980 ....240.00
Confrontation, Gorham Miniature, 1988 ....90.00
Cool Aid, 1979 ....260.00
Country Pedlar, 1985 ....100.00
Dad's Boy, 4 seasons set, complete 1,050.00
Day Dreamers, 1975 ....175.00
Day in the Life of a Boy I, 1980 ....115.00
Day in the Life of a Boy III, 1982 ....120.00
Day in the Life of a Girl II, 1981 ....115.00
Diary, Gorham Miniature, 1988 ....95.00
Disastrous Daring, 1976 ....275.00
Downhill Daring, Gorham Miniature, 1981 ....80.00
Downhill Daring, 1973 ....250.00
Drum for Tommy, ltd ed of 7,500, 1986...........................100.00
Expert Salesman, ltd of 1,500, 1983...............................225.00
Final Speech, 1984..100.00
First Annual Visit, 1980 ....185.00
Fishing, Gorham Miniature, 1984 ....80.00
Flying High, 1973...250.00
Football Season, Gorham Miniature, 1986 ....70.00
Four Ages of Love, 4 seasons set, complete........................900.00
Gaily Sharing Vintage Times, 1977.................................130.00
Gay Blades, Gorham Miniature, 1981 ....75.00
Ghostly Gourds, 1977 ....300.00
God Rest Ye Merry Gentlemen, 1976...............................1,400.00
Goin' Fishing, Gorham Miniature, 1984.............................70.00
Going on Sixteen, 4 seasons set, complete 750.00
Grand Pals, 4 seasons set, complete 1,050.00
Grandpa & Me, 4 seasons set, complete 700.00
Helping Hand, 4 seasons set, complete 950.00
Home for the Holidays, 1988 ....140.00
Horse Trader, 1985 ....100.00
In His Spirit, Gorham Miniature, 1984.............................70.00
In His Spirit, 1981 ....250.00
Jolly Coachman, Gorham Miniature, 1984...........................45.00
Lazy Days, 1982...100.00
Life w/Father, 4 seasons set, complete 380.00
Little Angel, Gorham Miniature, 1986 ....70.00
Marriage License, Gorham Miniature 85.00
Marriage License, 1976, 6¼" 310.00
Me & My Pal, 4 seasons set, complete...........................1,100.00
Missed, 1978..245.00
Morning Walk, Gorham Miniature, 1986 ....75.00
New Arrival, Gorham Miniature, 1985...............................50.00
New Year Look, 1979..260.00
No Swimming, 1974..160.00
Oh Yeah, 1978..245.00
Old Sign Painter, Gorham Miniature, 1986..........................90.00
Old Sign Painter, ltd ed of 7,500, 1984...........................120.00
Pensive Pals, 1975..175.00
Pilgrimage, 1978..190.00
Pride of Parenthood, 1972...300.00
Prom Dress, Gorham Miniature, 1987..............................90.00
Puppet Maker, 1985...195.00

Runaway, 1978 ....105.00
Santa's Friend, ltd ed of 7,500, 1985 ....150.00
Santa's Friend, 1983, 3½" 25.00
Season's Greetings, Gorham Miniature, 1986......60.00
Serenade, 1983...170.00
Shared Success, 1984 ....100.00
Shoulder Ride, Gorham Miniature, 1986...........65.00
Snow Sculpture, Gorham Miniature, 1981 ....80.00
Soaring Spirits, 1977......................................250.00
Springtime, Gorham Miniature, 1987 ....85.00
Summer Vacation, pewter, 1980.......................105.00
Sweet Serenade, Gorham Miniature, 1981 ....60.00
Sweet Serenade, 1978.....................................190.00
Sweet Song So Young, 1974 ....225.00
Tackled, 1976..110.00
To Love & To Cherish, Gorham Miniature, 1985.......50.00
Traveling Salesman (ltd ed of 1,500, issued at $175), 1981 ....210.00
Triple Self Portrait, 1980, 10½" 500.00
Trout Dinner, Gorham Miniature, 1983...............80.00
Weighing In, 1974 ....150.00
Welcome Mat, Gorham Miniature, 1986............90.00
Winter, Bringing Home the Tree, pewter, 1980.........105.00
Young Man's Fancy, Gorham Miniature, 1981 ....75.00
Young Man's Fancy, 1976................................275.00
Yuletide Reckoning, ltd ed of 7,500, 1984 ......100.00
Yuletide Reckoning, 1981, 3½" 25.00

Rogers, John

John Rogers (1829 – 1904) was a machinist from Manchester, New Hampshire, who turned his hobby of sculpting into a financially successful venture. From the originals he meticulously fashioned of red clay, he had bronze master molds made from which plaster copies were cast. He specialized in five different categories: theatrical, Shakespeare, Civil War, everyday life, and horses. His large detailed groupings portrayed the life and times of the period between 1859 and 1892. In the following listings, examples are assumed to be in very good to excellent condition. Our advisor for this category is George Humphrey; he is listed in the Directory under Maryland.

Balcony 1,500.00
Bath...2,000.00
Bubbles...2,000.00
Bushwacker..2,000.00
Charity Patient...650.00
Checkers Up at the Farm, 1865, 20½x17½x12" 575.00
Chess...1,200.00
Council of War 1,100.00
Country Post Office 750.00
Courtship in Sleepy Hollow, Pat date 550.00
Fairy's Whisper, 1881......................................1,400.00
Faust & Marguerite, Leaving the Garden 1,200.00
Favored Scholar, 21x16x11".............................425.00
Fetching the Doctor...750.00
Fighting Bob, 1889 ....1,100.00
First Ride 725.00
Frolic at the Old Homestead, 1887, 22½" 800.00
Going for the Cows..450.00
Home Guard...800.00
Madam, Your Mother Craves a Word With You.......700.00
Mail Day 2,000.00
Matter of Opinion..600.00
Neighboring Pews 475.00

One More Shot..550.00
Parting Promise (older man) 475.00
Parting Promise (young man)..............................475.00
Peddler at the Fair...800.00
Photographer, 1878, 18¾".................................4,000.00
Picket Guard..750.00
Referee...800.00
Rip Van Winkle - At Home 325.00
Rip Van Winkle on the Mountain 425.00
Shaughraun & Tatters.......................................700.00
Slave Auction...2,000.00
Speak for Yourself John.....................................500.00
Taking the Oath & Drawing Rations, sgn, 23" 525.00
Tap on the Window 525.00
Village Schoolmaster 850.00
Washington..1,250.00
Watch on the Santa Maria..................................1,000.00
Weighing the Baby, 20½"..................................600.00
Wounded Scout, ca 1864...................................750.00

Rookwood

The Rookwood Pottery Company was established in 1879 in Cincinnati, Ohio. Its founder was Maria Longworth Nichols daughter of a wealthy family who provided the backing necessary to make such an enterprise possible. Ms. Nichols hired competent ceramic artisans and artists of note, who through constant experimentation developed many lines of superior art pottery. While in her employ, Laura Fry invented the airbrush-blending process for which she was issued a patent in 1884. From this, several lines were designed that utilized blended backgrounds. One of their earlier lines, Standard, was a brown ware decorated with underglaze slip-painted nature studies, animals, portraits, etc. Iris and Sea Green were introduced in 1894 and Vellum, a transparent matt-glaze line, in 1904. Other lines followed: Ombroso in 1910 and Soft Porcelain in 1915. Many of the early artware lines were signed by the artist. Soon after the turn of the twentieth century, Rookwood manufactured 'production' pieces that relied mainly on molded designs and forms rather than freehand decoration for their esthetic appeal. The Depression brought on financial difficulties from which the pottery never recovered. Though it continued to operate, the quality of the ware deteriorated, and the pottery was forced to close in 1967.

Unmarked Rookwood is only rarely encountered. Many marks may be found, but the most familiar is the reverse 'RP' monogram. First used in 1886, a flame point was added above it for each succeeding year until 1900. After that a Roman numeral added below indicated the year of manufacture. Impressed letters that related to the type of clay utilized for the body were also used — G for ginger, O for olive, R for red, S for sage green, W for white, and Y for yellow. Artware must be judged on an individual basis. Quality of the artwork is a prime factor to consider. Portraits, animals, and birds are worth more than florals; and pieces signed by a particularly renowned artist are highly prized.

For more information we recommend *Rookwood Pottery, Over Ten Years of Auction Results, 1990 – 2002,* by Treadway Gallery, Inc. of Cincinnati, Ohio; and *Rookwood Pottery* by Nick and Marilyn Nicholson and Jim Thomas.

Our advisors for this category are Suzanne Perrault and David Rago; they are listed in the Directory under New Jersey.

Black Opal

Vase, fishscale band/geometric brush-dragged floral, S Sax, 5½" ..2,500.00
Vase, lotus blossoms, H Wilcox, drilled, ca 1920s, 7⅞", EX 1,500.00
Vase, wht dahlia repeats, H Wilcox, #6080, 1928, rpr, 13".......3,000.00

Cameo

Coffeepot, daffodil, AM Valentien, #843/W, 1891, 9" **800.00**
Pitcher, wild rose, #456W, 1888, 4½" **300.00**
Pitcher, wild roses, AM Valentien, #522/W, 1890, 7" **600.00**

Iris

Vase, apple blossoms, C Baker, #30E, 1904, rpr, 8" **375.00**
Vase, blueberry branches, Clara C Lindeman, #906E, 1906, 4" ...**1,295.00**
Vase, cherry blossom branches, wht on lav, L Epply, 1911, Xd, 8½"..**850.00**
Vase, goldenrod (EX art), R Fechheimer, #940C, 1903, 11"....**7,250.00**
Vase, holly berries & leaves, S Sax, #922D, 1904, 7", NM **550.00**
Vase, hyacinth, S Sax, #907, 1900, 8¼x3" **1,700.00**
Vase, irises, tan-lined/bl stems on cream, 1897, provenance, 11" ..**10,500.00**
Vase, jonquils at gr neck, wht body, M Nourse, #861, 1899, 6" ..**800.00**
Vase, lg barn swallows on branch, bl tones, Shirayamadani, rprs, 15" ...**5,500.00**
Vase, lg yel orchid, S Sax, #904C/W, 1906, 9⅜" **2,500.00**
Vase, lotus flowers, M Nourse, #900B, 1901, 9½", NM **1,300.00**
Vase, pansies on gray to lav, E Diers, #822, 1901, bottle neck, 9" ..**600.00**
Vase, parrot tulips, R Fechheimer, #892B, 1903, Xd, 10¼x5¼"..**1,400.00**
Vase, parrot tulips, yel on wht to gr, S Sax, #786D, 1899, 8" ..**1,600.00**
Vase, peonies (EX art), S Sax, #905C, 1906, 9½" **7,500.00**
Vase, thistle blooms on lt bl, C Schmidt, #654, 1900, 5¼x4" .**1,100.00**
Vase, thistles, L Asbury, #907E, 1904, 8¼", NM **475.00**
Vase, trees/mtns/lake, C Schmidt, #1658, 1912, rpr, 14½" **3,900.00**
Vase, tulips & buds, R Fechheimer, #939D, W, 1904, 7⅛x3½"...**1,650.00**
Vase, Virginia Creeper cascades on blk to gr to wht, S Sax, 1908, 9" ...**3,200.00**
Vase, wild roses, E Lincoln, #915E/W, 1904, 5x3½" **1,100.00**

Limoges

Humidor, spiders and bats on mottled ground, Maria Longworth Nichols, 1882, double lid, 6x6", $2,200.00.

(Photo courtesy David Rago Auctions)

Jug, swallow/Oriental grasses/gilt, M Rettig, #60R, 1884, 4¾" ...**400.00**
Vase, birds/trees, urn shape, unknown artist, 1883, 12" **1,100.00**
Vase, bud; blk birds in flight/Oriental grasses, M Rettig, 1883, 4½" .**415.00**

Matt

Note: Both incised matt and painted matt are listed here. Incised matt descriptions are indicated by the term 'cvd' within the line; all others are hand-painted matt ware.

Bowl, abstracts, cobalt/teal, brn relief bands, WE Hentschel, 6" ...**465.00**
Ewer, leaves & berries, S Coyne, #6008E, 1928, 10¼"...............**850.00**
Vase, abstracts, cobalt/wine/gr on turq, CS Todd, #890E, 1921, 3⅝"..**500.00**
Vase, cherry blossom devices w/ivory centers on bl, E Wilcox, 8x5" ..**660.00**
Vase, cvd dogwood at base, brn/bls, CS Todd, #1278F, 1913, 7", NM..**850.00**
Vase, cvd floral neck band, bulbous body, CS Todd, #161, 1918, 13x8"..**1,900.00**
Vase, cvd floral shoulder, WE Hentschel, #909, 1904, 9½x5"..**1,200.00**

Vase, cvd mc leaves, M McDonald, #925A, 1924, 15½" **1,700.00**
Vase, cvd mc stylized flowers in 3 panels, W Hentschel, 1914, 8", EX ..**850.00**
Vase, cvd pendant florals, subtle dk mc, CS Todd, #857, 1915, 16" .**2,700.00**
Vase, cvd poppy pods, R Fechheimer, dk bl/gr on frothy brn, 7x3", EX .**490.00**
Vase, cvd vertical leaves & seeds, maroon to gr, #2001, 6x5", EX ...**200.00**
Vase, daffodils, blk-lined on lav to gr, Shirayamadani, 1937, 7½" .**1,500.00**
Vase, Deco floral on lt gr, W Rhem, #2193, 1927, U-form, 4⅞"..**650.00**
Vase, dogwood neck band on gr to yel, M McDonald, #314E, 1928, 5½" .**900.00**
Vase, floral, S Coyne, #2722, 1924, 6¼".....................................**375.00**
Vase, floral (repeating/stylized), CS Todd, #534C, 1921, 8" **1,800.00**
Vase, floral abstracts, mc on pk to moss, L Abel, #2441, 1928, 14"...**3,000.00**
Vase, floral band on mint gr, C Klinger, #295E, 1925, 7"...........**600.00**
Vase, impressionistic floral band on pk, K Jones, 1930, ovoid, 6" .**650.00**
Vase, leaf abstracts, gr on crackled rose to gold-tan, E Lincoln, 7" ..**800.00**
Vase, leaves/berries, cobalt on bl, CJ McLaughlin, #2782, 10x6" .**1,100.00**
Vase, lotus, lav/gr, S Coyne, #1369F, 1929, 6" **950.00**
Vase, magnolia/bud (lg), wine on lt gr, E Lincoln, #1269C, 1926, 11x6"..**2,300.00**
Vase, orchids, pk on bl to gr, Shirayamadani, #6869, 1945, 9" .**2,400.00**
Vase, peacock feathers, E Lincoln, bottle shape, #806B, 1920, 12x5"..**1,700.00**
Vase, peacock feathers (EX art), CS Todd, #1064, 1915, 3½x3½"..**1,500.00**
Vase, poppies, CS Todd, #161, 1914, 14x8" **1,800.00**
Vase, poppies in arching devices, maroon/dk gr/purple, E Lincoln, 9x4" ...**1,200.00**
Vase, roses (lg/realistic) around shoulder, H Wilcox, 1902, 8⅜"..**14,500.00**
Vase, tulips, red/wht/gr on bl, JW Pullman, #6195C, 1930, 9½" ...**210.00**

Porcelain

Figure, Jewel, cat, ochre gloss, L Abel, 1946, 6½x5" **400.00**
Ginger jar, cherry blossoms, S Coyne, #1321E, 1923, 4x3½" **950.00**
Ginger jar, hydrangea & butterfly, HE Wilcox, #47C, 1920, 6"..**770.00**
Potpourri jar, French Red, spiders webs/flowers, S Sax, 1917, 6" ..**2,900.00**
Vase, cherry blossom branch on bl to blush, ET Hurley, #915E, 1920, 6"...**600.00**
Vase, cvd/pnt geometric rim band on cobalt, W Hentschel, 1915, 13", EX...**4,100.00**
Vase, Deco animals, E Barrett, #2193, 1944, 4½" **950.00**
Vase, floral swags, yel on bright lime, A Conant, #890E, 1917, 3½"...**1,000.00**
Vase, heads of 5 llamas on bright gr, J Jensen, Special shape, 5½" ...**2,800.00**
Vase, Islamic floral, bl on wht, W Hentschel, #2240, 1921, 6½" ...**900.00**
Vase, Jewel, floral branches, A Conant, #1873, 1928, 5¼x3¾" ...**2,000.00**
Vase, Jewel, fuchsias, H Wilcox, #6276F, 1931, 5" **800.00**
Vase, Jewel, orchids, L Epply (?), 1946, 5½" **500.00**
Vase, Jewel, peonies, K Ley, #6204C, 1946, 7½" **900.00**
Vase, Jewel, Renaissance-style flowers, A Conant, #900C, 1922, 8½"..**2,400.00**
Vase, Jewel, violets, Shirayamadani, #6622, 1937, 4½x3¼"....**1,600.00**
Vase, lg poinsettias, Anniversary int, Shirayamadani, 1918, 12" ..**8,000.00**
Vase, pendant floral branches on rose, S Sax, #551, 1920, 6⅝" ...**1,900.00**
Vase, Persian/geometric band atop pk body, bl int, A Conant, 1917, 6"...**1,000.00**
Vase, sm birds/flowers, pk/bl/tan on wht to bl, A Conant, 1920, 14"....**5,000.00**
Vase, trillium on caramel, Shirayamadani, Special shape, 1934, 6½"....**2,100.00**
Vase, Venice harbor lined w/ships, C Schmidt, 1922, 9½", M ...**14,000.00**
Vase, wild roses, ET Hurley, #2825A, 1925, 16½" **2,600.00**
Vase, 4 nudes/floral, br/ivory/brn, Anniversary glaze int, rpr, 9½"...**14,500.00**

Sea Green

Vase, floral (cobalt-lined), S Coyne, 1929, 8¾x5½" **1,200.00**
Vase, 3 geese in flight before full moon, AR Valentien, 1896, 10", EX...**4,300.00**

Standard

Atomizer, holly leaves, CW, 1895, orig hdw, 6½x3" **440.00**
Bowl, floral, Wm Purcell, 5-hdld, #232, 1885, 4x6½"...............**250.00**
Bowl, lion's portrait, M Daly, #5, 1885, 2½x12¼" **2,750.00**
Candle holder, holly leaves/berries, integral hdl, C Steinle, 1901, 3" ...**275.00**
Cup & saucer, floral, sgn, #414, 1899, 2⅛" H, NM....................**350.00**

Ewer, pansies, A Valentien, #4988, 1891, 5½" **750.00**
Ewer, 5-petal flowers, S Toohey, #101D, 1888, 6¼x4" **550.00**
Ewer, 8 barn swallows (EX art), AR Valentien, #611X/L, 1896, 12½" ..**5,000.00**
Jar, Light, elf sits on stump, S Markland, +lid, #622, 1893, 3x5", EX...**630.00**
Jug, beagle dog, ET Hurley, #747C, 1900, 7½", NM................**2,400.00**
Jug, Chief White Man Kiowa, C Baker, #512B, 1899, w/stopper, 9½" ...**9,250.00**
Jug, ears of corn, L Asbury, #512A, 1900, 10½" **1,400.00**
Pitcher, autumn leaves, A Sprague, #412, 1891, 9¼x6½" **660.00**
Pitcher, orchids, AM Valentien, #496b, 1899, 11¾"...................**880.00**
Pitcher, wisteria, P Peters-Baurer, #193, 1894, 3½" **375.00**
Tankard, cherries, S Toohey, #564, 1898, 10" **950.00**
Teapot, floral, C Schmidt, 1898, 5"...**900.00**
Vase, autumn leaves, L Van Briggle, #734DD, 1900, 7x3¼".......**660.00**
Vase, blk-eyed susans, S Coyne, #932 E, 1902, 7½x3¼".............**660.00**
Vase, chrysanthemums, E Noonan, #935D, 1904, 7¾x4¼"........**465.00**
Vase, clover blossoms, C Lindeman, #922D, 1902, 7x3½", EX ..**460.00**
Vase, daffodils, S Coyne, #925D, 1903, 8"...............................**950.00**
Vase, daisies, E Noonan, #950E, 1905, 7x3¼".........................**770.00**
Vase, daisies & buds (EX art), E Felton, #902, 1903, 7x5" **1,750.00**
Vase, day lilies, AR Valentien, #30AS, 1887, 18x6½" **4,500.00**
Vase, day lilies, G Young, #729B, 1899, Xd, 16", NM **2,200.00**
Vase, English ivy, 3-ftd, J Zettle, #571W, 1893, 7½"...............**750.00**
Vase, fern leaves (Light Standard), E Lincoln, 1893, 5¼x3¼" ...**880.00**
Vase, Japanese quince, L Asbury, #905D, 1903, 7½"..................**750.00**
Vase, Light, magnolias, #313, 1889, 5¾x8" **1,000.00**
Vase, Light, sm 5-petal flowers tooled on sage, AMB, 13x5" **700.00**
Vase, lily of valley, LE Lindeman, #907, 1906, 8½x3¼" **775.00**
Vase, narcissus, E Felton, #535, 1890, 7x3¾" **475.00**
Vase, poppies, C Steinle, #817, 1900, 8x3½".............................**550.00**
Vase, poppies, G Hall, #935D, 1904, 7⅜".................................**700.00**
Vase, tulips, L Van Briggle, #922D, 1903, 6¾", NM **500.00**
Vase, water lilies, L Asbury, #906B, 1901, 7" **800.00**
Vase, wild rose spray, E Lincoln, #868, 1901, 9x5" **550.00**
Vase, yel roses, ML Perkins, ribbed/sqd lower body, rope hdls, 8"..**550.00**

Vellum

Bowl vase, cherry blossom branch on bl/lav, ET Hurley, 1928, 4x6" ..**975.00**
Plaque, Birches, ET Hurley, title & flame mk labels, 14x9" ..**12,500.00**
Plaque, Birches & Lake, ET Hurley, title label, orig fr, 12x9" .**9,700.00**
Plaque, Grey Day, K Van Horn, 1917, title label, orig fr, 9x5" ...**3,250.00**
Plaque, Morning Hour, Venetian sailboats, C Schmidt, 11½x9½"+fr..**6,500.00**
Plaque, Over the Hills, L Epply, 1914, orig fr, sight: 7½x4¾" ..**2,300.00**
Plaque, trees/rocky shore/mtns, L Asbury, 1925, 9½x4¾" **5,750.00**
Plaque, winding road/split rail fence, C Schmidt, 1915, 9x7", +fr .**4,400.00**
Plaque, wooded landscape, ET Hurley, 1912, 7½x5½"+orig fr..**4,250.00**
Vase, apple blossoms, K Van Home, #1655F, 1911, 6½" **550.00**
Vase, arrowroot blossoms, C Schmidt, #922B, 1914, 11x5¾" ..**2,100.00**
Vase, berries, pk on bl to wht, F Rothenbush, #256E, 1928, 6¾"..**700.00**
Vase, berries/leaves on bl to pk, K Curry, #950E, 1916, 7⅝", NM..**350.00**
Vase, cherry blossom branches on wht to bl, ET Hurley, #938D, 1911, 7".**550.00**
Vase, cherry blossoms & leaves, S Coyne, #943D, 1905, 8x4½" ..**1,650.00**
Vase, cherry blossoms in wht band, gr body, #924, E Lincoln, 6x3"..**665.00**
Vase, cherry branch at shoulder on pk, ET Hurley, #922E, 1923, 6"..**900.00**
Vase, crocus & leaves, K Shirayamadani, S, 1934, Xd, 5¼x4" ...**1,400.00**
Vase, cvd/pnt teasel band, gr on bl, L Asbury, #1369C, 1909, 11", NM...**950.00**
Vase, daisies, MG Denzler, #1278F, 1914, 7½" **500.00**
Vase, daisy groups, blk-lined on bl to gr, L Asbury, #1930, 1925, 7"..**1,200.00**
Vase, dogwood branch, L Epply, #900, 1908, 7x3½" **650.00**
Vase, floral, pk & gr, low on ivory body, E Lincoln, 50th Anniv mk, 9"..**1,100.00**
Vase, floral band, H McDonald, #904D, 1917, 9x4" **990.00**
Vase, grapes & vines, dk bl on lt gr, E Noonan, #950E, 1907, 7", NM.**800.00**
Vase, harbor scene, E Diers, #1858D, 1908, 8¾x4½" **2,975.00**
Vase, harbor w/several boats, S Coyne, #907E/V, 1910, 9"..........**220.00**

Vase, lake & trees, #1357, F Rothenbusch, 1909, 9x4¼" **1,650.00**
Vase, lake & trees, C Schmidt, #907B, 1918, 17½", NM........**4,500.00**
Vase, lg crocuses, bl/gr on bl to ivory, ET Hurley, 1929, 15", NM ...**3,100.00**
Vase, lily pads/aquatic tendrils, gr to cream, Shirayamadani, 1907, 9"..**4,900.00**
Vase, long-stemmed irises, yel/gr on bl to gr, pk int, Diers, 1929, 9"..**4,700.00**
Vase, mistletoe, H Lyons, #918E, 1913, 6".................................**700.00**
Vase, mistletoe on wht, S Sax, #907F, 1905, 7⅜" **1,700.00**
Vase, pendant berries/leaves on bl, pk int, L Asbury, #2885, 1926, 8"..**2,100.00**
Vase, poppies & daisies, Ed Diers, ovoid, 6x3¾" **450.00**
Vase, roses, C Steinle, #2048, 1912, 7x3¼" **750.00**
Vase, simple floral shoulder band on pk, P Conant, 1916, 7⅝", NM ...**500.00**
Vase, snowy landscape, S Coyne, 1917, rstr drilling, 9¼x3¾" ...**2,400.00**
Vase, sunflowers & blk seeds, E Diers, #915, 1921, 5x3½" **1,100.00**
Vase, sunset scene, F Rothenbusch, #952F, 1911, 6¼", NM **600.00**
Vase, tree scenic (EX art), F Rothenbush, #904B, 1920, 14½" .**4,200.00**
Vase, trees/sm flying birds, Shirayamadani, ca 1912, rpr drilling, 13"..**5,500.00**
Vase, wild rose band, flared pk rim, gr body, E Diers, 1918, 10", NM..**375.00**
Vase, wild roses, blk-outlined on dk bl to gray, L Asbury, 1921, 14"..**2,500.00**
Vase, wild roses on bl to wht, F Rothenbusch, #927E, 1927, 6" ..**1,300.00**
Vase, wisteria berries at flared top, S Sax, #1357C, 1915, Xd, 11"..**950.00**
Vase, 3 lg barn swallows, C Schmidt, #941D, 1905, hairline, 8½".**2,300.00**
Vase, 3 rose reserves on shaded brn/bl, Shirayamadani, 1910, 8¾" ..**1,600.00**

Wax Matt

Bowl, floral, red on mustard, L Abel, #2757, 1924, 2¼x7¼" **650.00**
Lamp base, floral w/leafy clusters, E Lincoln, #2900, 1933, 9½x6"..**1,550.00**

Vase, abstract flowers in jewel tones on vermillion, Sallie Coyne, #2785, 1927, 13¼x5½", $2,075.00.

(Photo courtesy David Rago Auctions)

Vase, chrysanthemum, E Lincoln, #2790, 1927, 12x5½".........**2,400.00**
Vase, floral, E Lincoln, #2246, 1925, rpr, 14¾x9½" **1,500.00**
Vase, floral, mc on purple, Wm Hentschel, #1780, 1921, 6½x5¾"..**950.00**
Vase, floral (stylized), sgn EM, #1358, 1925, 7¼x3¾" **880.00**
Vase, floral (stylized) at base, bl/rose, E Barrett, #2065, 1924, 8" ..**700.00**
Vase, floral on yel, E Barrett, w/hdls, #2784, 1924, 10x8" **2,800.00**
Vase, flowers/roosters, gray/wht, E Barrett, #2190, 1943, 6" ...**1,200.00**
Vase, palm trees/stone fence, bl on ivory crackle, Holtkamp, 8"..**1,400.00**
Vase, poppies & buds, E Lincoln, #1918, 1927, 9x5½"...........**1,550.00**
Vase, roses on bl to pk, E Lincoln, #2785, X, 1929, 13½x5" **900.00**
Vase, slip-trailed fish on rose, J Jensen, #6148, 1944, 5½", NM..**1,100.00**
Vase, tulips on bl mottle, sgn EM, #1780 X, 1925, 7x6".........**1,100.00**
Vase, vines/florals at shoulder on yel, IF, #1356f, 1925, 6x3" **825.00**
Vase, 5 female faces, brn/cream/yel, E Barrett, Special shape, 5⅜"..**3,800.00**

Miscellaneous

Bookend, #6259, 1931, sunfish pr, celadon gloss, 6", single **1,000.00**
Bookend, #6261, 1931, seated elephant, ivory matt, 5¼", EX, single ..**375.00**
Bookends, #2182/P, 1925, owl on book, bl gloss, 5" **300.00**
Bookends, #2446, 1940, girl on bench, ivory matt, 5⅜", EX **325.00**
Bookends, #2642, 1922, seal on ice floe, aventurine, 6x7½"...**3,400.00**
Bookends, #6158, 1930, Indian head, mottled orange matt, rpr, 5¾" ...**3,600.00**
Bookends, #6417, 1933, turkey on sq base, coromandel, 5½", EX...**2,700.00**
Bookends, #7115, 1953, sleeping man, Bengal Brn, 7¾x5½"...**2,600.00**
Bowl, #0354, 1923, 3-hdl, aqua matt, 3" **150.00**
Bowl, #1800, 1915, butterflies, dk gr w/charcoal drip, aqua int, 3x5"...**330.00**
Bowl, #2106B, yel matt, low, 11½" **100.00**
Bowl, #6132, 1950, Violet Gray, blossom form, 3½x7½".............**170.00**
Bowl, #6424, 1951, turq matt, blossom form, 2⅞x8", NM...........**80.00**
Bust, #1849, 1913, young boy, gray/bl Ombroso matt, 10½" ...**1,000.00**
Candlesticks, #2464, 1920, dolphin-head base, twist stem, 12", pr ...**600.00**
Chalice, 1906, advertising National Convention, Roman bust, 5¾" ...**385.00**
Creamer & sugar bowl, #547, 1944, celadon gloss, 3¼" **90.00**
Figurine, #6484, 1965, seated polar bear, L Abel, striated bl, 6½"...**1,000.00**
Figurine, #6501, 1958, seated monkey, Wine Madder, L Abel....**275.00**
Figurine, #6899, 1948, Madonna & Child, wht gloss, 7¼".........**250.00**
Fountain mask, Faience, grotesque face fr w/grapevines, mc, 14", EX...**2,900.00**
Inkwell, #2022, 1921, maple leaves on gr over bl, w/lid, 2¾x4½"..**365.00**
Jug, #1113, 1905, gr w/thin brn appl to upper portion, zigzags, 6" ...**325.00**
Paperweight, #2797, 1927, elephant on base, wht matt, mfg flaw, 3⅜" ..**250.00**
Paperweight, #5490, 1954, seated baby elephant, lime gloss, 3¾" ...**170.00**
Paperweight, #6030, 1936, rooster on sq base, ivory matt, 5¼"...**350.00**
Paperweight, #6084, 1965, seated monkey, orange gloss, foil label, 4" ..**250.00**
Pin tray, 1929, Ve Ri Tas, Harvard Clubs Meeting, 2¾", EX......**325.00**
Pitcher, #259, 1926, dk gr matt, triangular mouth, 4¼x5¼" **275.00**
Stein, #1071, 1904, trailing abstracts on dk gr, 5½"....................**325.00**
Tile, Faience, Southern Bell w/parasol, 3⅞", +new fr **350.00**
Tile, trees along riverbank, 5-color, Arts & Crafts oak fr, 12" .**2,500.00**
Tile, 2 tall ships, brn/tan on gr & bl, RP/#417/G352, dmn shape, 8" **1,000.00**
Tile bksplash, gr tree/amber ribbon, tan ground, dk bl diagonal, 43x31....**3,800.00**
Tile frieze, cottage scene, 6-color, 3-tile set, new fr, 12x40", EX...**10,000.00**
Trivet, #1794, 1927, rook/trellis bkground, 3-color, 5¾", EX **800.00**
Trivet, #6774, 1940, man in medieval garb w/falcon, turq gloss, 5¾"...**325.00**
Trivet, 1927, indigo rook/Oriental trellis, flame mk, 5¾" **800.00**
Vase, #1358D, 1913, geometrics, bl matt, 8½" **750.00**
Vase, #1825, 1904, paneled ovoid, yel on bl/lime, 5x3" **275.00**
Vase, #1825, 1923, lt bl matt, dmn accented panels, 5" **160.00**
Vase, #1899, 1917, pine cones on shaded dk bl, 6½x3" **425.00**
Vase, #2000, 1922, rose matt, 6x6½"..**140.00**
Vase, #2091, 1922, lg simple upright leaves, slightly incurvate, 6" ..**140.00**
Vase, #2112, 1928, gr mottle on rose matt, 6¼x3"......................**165.00**
Vase, #2122, 1926, half-moons on sharp shoulder, rose speckled, 7" ..**200.00**
Vase, #2135, 1925, mauve mottle on mint gr, twisted panels, 6" .**300.00**
Vase, #2210, 1928, Deco berries & lace emb on honey matt, 7¼" ...**300.00**
Vase, #2354, 1919, artichoke leaves on yel matt, spherical, 5", NM.**300.00**
Vase, #2402, 1921, peacock feathers relief, mint on rose matt, 6¼" .**195.00**
Vase, #2589, 1930, floral branches on pk matt, 5x4½" **165.00**
Vase, #2724, 1944, Design Crystal, floral, M McDonald, 5½", NM .**350.00**
Vase, #2863, 1926, swirls on bl matt, 6x7" **360.00**
Vase, #2897, 1925, curled abstracts, boomerang shoulder band, 9x4"...**365.00**
Vase, #2913, 1929, Deco floral band, lt bl crystalline matt, 6" ...**160.00**
Vase, #2971, 1928, overlapping leaves, lt bl matt, 3¼" **170.00**
Vase, #459E, 1911, geometrics/panels, gr w/maroon wash, 4½"..**425.00**
Vase, #53EZ, 1904, Z-Line, gr matt, Indian style, bulbous, 3½" .**375.00**
Vase, #581C, 1911, Greek Key band over narrow panels, brn matt, 14" ...**3,100.00**
Vase, #6148, 1930, Nubian Black, yel int, 5⅝" **150.00**
Vase, #6194D, 1930, coromandel w/copper crystals, 6" **400.00**
Vase, #6316, 1932, pk/bl flambé drip over brn, 3¾"....................**425.00**

Vase, #6410, 1932, Glaze Effect, oatmeal crystalline/tan/purple, 5" ..**250.00**
Vase, #6468, 1935, 4-sided w/fruit over lattice in ea panel, wht, 6" .**90.00**
Vase, #6644, 1949, pk gloss, 6½"..**70.00**
Vase, #6644, 1950, turq drip over Violet Gray, 6⅝" **140.00**
Vase, #6644E, 1945, Design Crystal, violets, J Jensen, 6", pr...**1,500.00**
Vase, #6762, 1946, Mexicans on burrows emb on yel gloss, 5½" ..**70.00**
Vase, #938D, 1904, dk gr matt, coiled rickrack motif, 5½".........**425.00**
Wall pocket, #2941, 1928, rows of chevrons, pk matt, 7½"........**170.00**

Rorstrand

The Rorstrand Pottery was established in Sweden in 1726 and is today Sweden's oldest existing pottery. The earliest ware, now mostly displayed in Swedish museums, was much like old Delft. Later types were hard-paste porcelains that were enameled and decorated in a peasant style. Contemporary pieces are often described as Swedish Modern. Rorstrand is also famous for their Christmas plates.

Bowl, Aro, bl/brn flambè, oval w/rim raised on opposing sides, 6½"..**225.00**
Bowl, brn & blk mottle, ovoid, porc, G Nylund, AXK, 6x11" ...**150.00**
Box, Picnic, HP food items, bl/gr/red on wht, ca 1940s, 6" L **135.00**
Figurine, penguin, Gunnar Nylund, 1950s, 6½" **85.00**
Plate, My Garden, vertical row of fish, bl/wine on wht, 10½", 8 for...**150.00**
Teapot, Mon Amie, wht w/rows of bl Xs, ca 1950s **365.00**
Vase, brn haresfur to gr, stoneware, Gunnar Nylund, 3-crown mk, 6" ..**165.00**
Vase, dk bl semi-matt mottle, stoneware, Gunnar Nylund, 4x2½"..**295.00**
Vase, gr/brn mottle, stoneware, Gunnar Nylund, ewer form, 7"....**85.00**
Vase, gray/brn/ivory matt, cylinder w/narrow neck, cvd ribs, 6½" ..**200.00**
Vase, rich burgundy shades, cylindrical, bottle neck, B296, 9¾" ...**880.00**
Vase, violet w/bl hue, 4 buttressed hdls, 9¾x6" **465.00**

Rose Mandarin

Similar in design to Rose Medallion, this Chinese Export porcelain features the pattern of a robed mandarin, often separated by florals, ladies, genre scenes, or butterflies in polychrome enamels. It is sometimes trimmed in gold. Elaborate in decoration, this pattern was popular from the late 1700s until the early 1840s.

Bowl, oval, lt wear, 11" **450.00**
Coffeepot, 19th C, 10" **1,500.00**
Cup & saucer, spur hdls, 19th C **285.00**
Dish, rtcl borders, 19th C, 8x9½", NM.......................................**400.00**
Plate, gold borders, 19th C, 10", pr...**650.00**
Platter, 19th C, 16", NM..**1,100.00**
Punch bowl, 19th C, 11", NM..**1,000.00**
Sauce boat, intertwined hdl, 19th C, 8¼"...................................**300.00**
Vase, appl dragons & foo dogs, 19th C, 25" **2,500.00**
Vase, bottle form, 19th C, 15"..**765.00**
Vase, floral gilt borders, hdls, 1850s, 18" **1,115.00**
Vase, hexagonal, gilt dragon hdls, 19th C, 12" **950.00**

Rose Medallion

Rose Medallion is one of the patterns of Chinese export porcelain produced from before 1850 until the second decade of the twentieth century. It is decorated in rose colors with panels of florals, birds, and butterflies that form reserves containing Chinese figures. Pre-1850 ware is unmarked and is characterized by quality workmanship and gold trim. From about 1850 until circa 1860, the kilns in Canton did not operate, and no Rose Medallion was made. Post-1860 examples (still unmarked) can often be recognized by the poor quality of the gold trim or its absence. In the 1890s the ware was often marked 'China'; 'Made in China' was used from 1910 through the 1930s.

Basin, nineteenth century, 4⅞x16½", $1,200.00. (Photo courtesy Skinner, Inc.)

Bowl, shallow, scalloped rim, 2¼x10¼" 470.00
Bowl, soup; w/hdls, lid & underplate 135.00
Bowl, sq, 9x9" 295.00
Bowl, vegetable; rectangular, w/lid, 19th C, 8" 295.00
Bowl, w/gilt, 4x9" 315.00
Bowl, 15" 1,340.00
Brush box, oblong, divided interior, 19th C, 3x4x7½", pr 440.00
Brushpot, 4⅜x2¾" dia 125.00
Butter dish, 4-panel lid, 7¼" dia 165.00
Candle holders, late 19th C, 7½", EX, pr 250.00
Chamber pot, w/hdl & lid, 7½x9" dia 350.00
Charger, 19th C, 13½", from $500 to 700.00
Gravy boat, dbl-spouted, late 19th C, 8" L 235.00
Leaf dish, 7" 125.00
Leaf dish, 8⅜x6¼" 150.00
Moon flask, bat-shaped hdls, 19th C, 16" 2,800.00
Mug, gold rim & details, leaf-twined hdl, EX 150.00
Mustard pot, gold floral finial, 3x6" 315.00
Plate, deep, mid-19th C, 10", 12 for 1,350.00
Plate, late 19th C, 12" 260.00
Plate, 4 panels w/center scene, 9¾" 90.00
Plate, 8-sided, 5⅝" 55.00
Platter, oval, 12x9¼", from $200 to 300.00
Punch bowl, 19th C, 14" 1,750.00
Punch bowl, 19th C, 6⅜x15½" 2,000.00
Punch bowl, 5x11¾" 615.00
Teapot, rnd body, 8" (spout-to-hdl) 250.00
Umbrella stand, cylindrical, 24½x9¼" 2,115.00
Vase, foo dog finial, 19th C, 11" 385.00
Vase, foo dog handles, kylin decor at shoulders, 10⅛", pr 600.00
Vase, gold deer-head hdls, 14" 370.00
Vase, gold trim, lion's-head hdls w/rings, 9" 350.00
Wash bowl & pitcher, late 19th C, 13", 15" dia, EX 500.00
Water bottle, 19th C, 13¼" 825.00

Roselane

William and Georgia Fields began Roselane Pottery in their home in 1938. They moved several times over the years, but when William died in 1973, Georgia sold Roselane to Prather Engineering Corporation and the operation moved to Long Beach where it remained until its final closing in 1977.

Roselane had various lines that included several different glazes and treatments. Chinese-Modern is not as popular as some of Roselane's other products. Certain pieces of Chinese-Modern are plentiful and do not bring high values. In the mid-1940s until the early 1950s, Aqua Marine was a buffet serving line with pieces such as large, deep bowls and trays created in a sgraffito technique. The fish or snowflakes motifs are in demand today. The Sparkler series, created in the 1950s, was also a popular product line for the company. The airbrush-decorated semi-porcelain animals fascinate collectors even though there are some reproductions on the market. Originally they had rhinestone eyes, but the later ones had plastic. Aside from the Sparklers, the deer and deer groups on single bases are sought after as well. Their muted glazes and lifelike appearances have many collectors trying to amass them all. William 'Doc' Fields created beautiful animals on walnut bases, generally finished in high-gloss white glaze. Because they never were good sellers, they were soon discontinued. Today collectors avidly look for items from this line, and prices reflect demand.

Bowl, aqua w/blk sqs, #12, 5x11" 50.00
Bowl, Fish, aqua, #25, 14" 50.00
Bowl, Fish, aqua, 4 peg ft, #30, 12¼x6⅜x3¼" 40.00
Bowl, salad; Fish, aqua, #25, 2¾x12¾", +matching fork & spoon ..70.00
Carafe, Fish, pk, blk lid, #34, 8" 80.00
Dresser box, gray sides w/vertical lines, maroon lid, #S3, 6¼" 27.50
Figurine, angelfish, Sparkler, 4½", from $20 to 25.00
Figurine, Asian female w/lg headpc, pale gr, 8" 22.50
Figurine, bulldog puppy, bl eyes, seated, Sparkler, 1¾" 12.00
Figurine, cat, head trn right, tail & paws tucked under body, Sparkler ...25.00
Figurine, cocker spaniel, Sparkler, 4½", from $15 to 20.00
Figurine, deer w/antlers, standing, jeweled collar, Sparkler, 4½" ..28.00
Figurine, elephant, Sparkler, 6" 30.00
Figurine, giraffe, reclining, olive gr, 7⅜" 25.00
Figurine, kangaroo mother & 2 babies, Sparkler 50.00
Figurine, pheasant, Sparkler, 4¾" 20.00
Figurine, roadrunner, 4x8½" 35.00
Figurine, Siamese, looking str ahead, jeweled collar, Sparkler, 7" .50.00
Figurine, squirrel, Sparkler, 1¾" 30.00
Figurines, deer, 1 w/head down, 1/w head up, 6⅛", 8", pr, $30 to .40.00
Figurines, gazelle, wht gloss, 16", pr 225.00
Figurines, quail, male & female, 6", 5", pr.........................20.00
Shakers, giraffe heads, gr, 10", pr 27.50
Vase, pale bl w/maroon int, sq, flared rim, 8¼" 35.00

Rosemeade

Rosemeade was the name chosen by Wahpeton Pottery Company of Wahpeton, North Dakota, to represent their product. The founders of the company were Laura A. Taylor and R.J. Hughes, who organized the firm in 1940. It is most noted for small bird and animal figurals, either in high gloss or a Van Briggle-like matt glaze. The ware was marked 'Rosemeade' with an ink stamp or carried a 'Prairie Rose' sticker. The pottery closed in 1961. Our advisor for this category is Bryce L. Farnsworth; he is listed in the Directory under North Dakota. For more information we recommend *Collector's Encyclopedia of Rosemeade Pottery* by Darlene Hurst Dommel (Collector Books).

Ashtray, w/squatting mallard figure, 7", from $450 to 500.00
Ashtray, yel w/Hereford bull figure, triangular, 6¼", minimum ..400.00
Bank, fish, tail in air, 3x4¼", from $300 to 350.00
Basket, wht w/rose hdl, 5x5¼", from $100 to 125.00
Bowl, bronze, ruffled edge, 3x5¼", from $50 to 75.00
Candle holder, Egyptian boat, blk or bl, 3x4¾", ea, from $50 to ..75.00
Cotton dispenser, rabbit, 4¾x2½", from $150 to 200.00
Covered bowl, hen on basket, 5½x5½", from $500 to 600.00
Creamer & sugar bowl, twisted hdls, from $200 to 225.00

Figurine, bluebill drake, miniature, 1x1¾", from $200 to 250.00
Figurine, cock pheasant, 9¼x14", from $250 to 300.00
Figurine, dolphin, 2½", from $75 to..100.00
Figurine, fawn, gr w/brn markings, 3¾x3", from $150 to 175.00
Figurine, gopher w/nut, 1½x2", from $50 to 75.00
Figurine, hen pheasant, 4x11½", from $350 to...........................400.00
Figurine, howling coyote, 4½x3⅞", from $250 to 300.00
Figurine, jackrabbit, solid, 3¼x1¾", from $250 to 300.00
Figurine, wht cat, bl base (lunch hour), 4¾x4½", minimum ..1,000.00
Hors d'oeuvres, turkey, 6x6½", from $150 to.............................200.00
Novelty, cowboy boot, mini, 2x1¾", from $200 to.....................300.00
Pin, mountain goat, on base, 2", minimum value....................1,000.00
Pin, prairie rose, 2½", minimum value 1,000.00
Planter, cock pheasant, 3¾x9¼", minimum value 500.00
Planter, lamb, on knees, 6x6½", from $300 to...........................350.00
Planter, rooster, flat, 7½x5", minimum value 300.00
Planter, wooden shoe, floral design, 2¾x5¼", from $85 to.........100.00
Plaque, Minnesota Centennial, 4½x3¾", from $75 to...............100.00
Shakers, bald eagles, wht, 2¾", pr, from $350 to........................400.00
Shakers, bobwhite quail, 2¼x1½", pr, from $50 to 75.00
Shakers, cock pheasants striding, 4x4½", from $125 to 150.00
Shakers, cow & bull, 1¾", pr, from $150 to...............................200.00
Shakers, coyote pups, 3¼x2½", pr, from $300 to 350.00
Shakers, ducks, wht, comic, 2x3", pr, from $75 to......................100.00
Shakers, mallard ducks, 1x1¾", from $150 to.............................175.00
Shakers, northern pike, 1¼x5", pr, minimum value....................500.00
Shakers, potato, 1⅝x2½", w/4¾" tray, from $800 to 1,000.00
Shakers, sailboat, 3½x3¾", pr, minimum value...........................400.00
Shakers, skunk w/tail up, 3", pr 50.00
Shakers, swans, 2", pr, from $75 to...100.00
Shakers, Trojan Seed Corn, 4½", from $450 to...........................500.00
Shakers, Viking ships, rare, 1½x3½", pr, from $400 to 450.00
Shakers, wheat shock, 3¾", pr, from $125 to..............................150.00
Shakers, windmills, plastic fans w/metal fasteners, 3½", pr.........175.00
Spoon rest, tulip, 5", from $80 to 100.00
Spoon rest, turkey gobbler, rare, 5½", minimum value 500.00
String holder, wht kitten in lime gr stocking, rare, 7", minimum value..850.00
Tea bell, flamingo on mud nest, 3¼", from $250 to 300.00
Tea bell, peacock, 5½", from $250 to...300.00
Tea bell, tulip, 3¾", from $125 to 150.00
Tile, pheasant decal, 6x6", from $75 to.......................................125.00
Tile, walleye decal, 6x6", from $100 to 150.00
Tray, Indiana shaped, 5¼", from $100 to 125.00
Vase, fluted, hand-thrown, 3¾", from $50 to..................................75.00
Vase, sq sides w/flared neck, 9", from $100 to............................150.00
Wall plaque, pheasant decal, 6", from $75 to 125.00
Wall pocket, crescent moon, 4¼", from $50 to 75.00
Wall pocket, maid in crescent moon, 6½", minimum value 500.00
Wall pocket, wht kitten in bl stockings, rare, 6½", minimum value...850.00
Watering can, rabbit motif, open spout, 4½", from $75 to 100.00

Rosenthal

In 1879 Phillip Rosenthal established the Rosenthal Porcelain Factory in Selb, Bavaria. Its earliest products were figurines and fine tablewares. The company has continued to operate to the present decade, manufacturing limited edition plates. Our advisor for this category is Raphael Wise; he is listed in the Directory under Florida.

Bowl, floral on wht, 3 ibex mask mts, 6½x9" 250.00
Bowl, grapes, gilded hdls, 2x12¼x6½"..110.00
Bowl, Nouveau floral, ped ft, earthenware, 4¼x7¼".....................450.00
Bowl, roses & leaves, scalloped edge, ca 1900, 2¼x10¼" 185.00
Box, man w/telescope on lid, nude inside, w/lid, 1¾x6x4¾"......110.00
Box, Teheran, red & gr floral on wht, 4-ftd, w/lid, 2⅞x4⅜" dia.220.00
Bust, Beethoven, #1728, 4⅝" 270.00
Cup, commemorative; WWI, wht & gold, ca 1915.....................250.00
Cup & saucer, Dragon on gr, Classic Rose Collection, w/sm underplate..100.00
Cup & saucer, nasturtiums, sgn Schelink, eggshell, 8-sided, 1905 .1,600.00
Figurine, Ariande, nude in bl shorts fixing hair, #K346, 6".........350.00

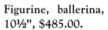

Figurine, ballerina, 10½", $485.00.

Figurine, ballerina, arms raised, Grouau, #1667/1, 12¼".............325.00
Figurine, blk poodle, standing on hind legs, mk Heidenreich, #5155, 8"...375.00
Figurine, borzoi, lying down w/head up, Valentin, 4¾x11".........200.00
Figurine, borzoi, lying on side w/head up, 3½x6" 135.00
Figurine, butterfly, shades of bl, 2x3¼" 95.00
Figurine, cat, ivory matt porc, #5193, 7½" 150.00
Figurine, circus elephant on barrel, Diller #335, 3" 135.00
Figurine, cocker spaniel puppy, Karner #1247, 6"........................200.00
Figurine, dachshund, brn, 3x6½" 115.00
Figurine, Empire Dancer, #206/7, 7¼" 170.00
Figurine, greyhound, seated, #21, 6"..420.00
Figurine, Hunting Horn Player, #K197, Himmelstoss, 7½".........285.00
Figurine, man w/accordion, #1656, 10x9x9" 225.00
Figurine, moose, lying down w/head up, removable antlers, mk, 14x24"...965.00
Figurine, Morrish servant, in lt bl & yel, w/fruit basket, #863, 7" .260.00
Figurine, Morrish servant, in yel, gr & purple, Koch, #684.........260.00
Figurine, nude bent down on 1 knee drinking, Wenck, 6⅝x6" ..425.00
Figurine, nude boy on knees w/lamb, Himmelstoss, 5¾" 340.00
Figurine, pike (fish), silver, Obermaier #634, 14½".....................365.00
Figurine, Prayer Dancer, seminude, #961-2, 9¾"..........................245.00
Figurine, rabbit up on hind legs, #724, 3" 195.00
Figurine, schnauzer, seated, #125, 4¼" 95.00
Figurine, Siamese kitten, 5" L...115.00
Figurine, snake charmer, seminude, 7¾"......................................120.00
Figurine, spaniel, walking w/head trn, Diller, 4⅜x9"..................420.00
Figurine, Wirehaired Griffin Pointer, Karner, 4¾x9" 420.00
Figurine, 2 chickens feeding, rnd base, 5x4" 100.00
Figurine, 2 Princesses, girl & swan, #537, 5½" 275.00
Ginger jar, pk floral w/silver o/l, 12¾".....................................1,450.00
Plate, Old Dutch, 3 women w/sailboat in bkground, bl & wht, 12"..110.00
Platter, lady w/flower basket on gold, Winblad, 12½x9½" 150.00
Vase, Indra, orange bird & palm trees on wht, K Wendler, 6½".455.00
Vase, irises (detailed/ornate), earthenware, ca 1907-10, 8¼x4"..550.00
Vase, poppies on ivory, eggshell porc, 5"...................................1,600.00
Vase, stylized tulips/leaves, yel/gr on cobalt gloss, narrow neck, 13"..635.00
Vase, Versace, Medusa Blue, 10¼x6" dia 115.00
Vase, wht porc, ribbed organic form, Freyer, 4½" 75.00
Vase, wht porc organic form w/beading at neck, Wirhala design, 5" W..325.00
Vase, wht porc w/emb ribs, M Freyer, studio line, 3½"..................75.00
Vase, 4 purple irises on blk, 8"...115.00

Roseville

The Roseville Pottery Company was established in 1892 by George F. Young in Roseville, Ohio. Finding their facilities inadequate, the company moved to Zanesville in 1898, erected a new building, and installed the most modern equipment available. By 1900 Young felt ready to enter into the stiffly competitive art pottery market. Roseville's first art line was called Rozane. Similar to Rookwood's Standard, Rozane featured dark blended backgrounds with slip-painted underglaze artwork of nature studies, portraits, birds, and animals. Azurean, developed in 1902, was a blue and white underglaze art line on a blue blended background. Egypto (1904) featured a matt glaze in a soft shade of old green and was modeled in low relief after examples of ancient Egyptian pottery. Mongol (1904) was a high-gloss oxblood red line after the fashion of the Chinese Sang de Boeuf. Mara (1904), an iridescent lustre line of magenta and rose with intricate patterns developed on the surface or in low relief, successfully duplicated Sicardo's work. These early lines were followed by many others of highest quality: Fudjiyama and Woodland (1905 – 06) reflected an Oriental theme; Crystalis (1906) was covered with beautiful frost-like crystals. Della Robbia, their most famous line (introduced in 1906), was decorated with designs ranging from florals, animals, and birds to scenes of Viking warriors and Roman gladiators. These designs were worked in sgraffito with slip-painted details. Very limited but of great importance to collectors today, Rozane Olympic (1905) was decorated with scenes of Greek mythology on a red ground. Pauleo (1914) was the last of the artware lines. It was varied — over two hundred glazes were recorded — and some pieces were further decorated by hand, usually with florals.

During the second decade of the twentieth century until the plant closed forty years later, new lines were continually added. Some of the more popular of the middle-period lines were Donatello, 1915; Futura, 1928; Pine Cone, 1931; and Blackberry, 1933. The floral lines of the later years have become highly collectible. Pottery from every era of Roseville production — even its utility ware — attest to an unwavering dedication to quality and artistic merit.

Examples of the art pottery lines present the greatest challenge to evaluate. Scarcity is a prime consideration. The quality of artwork varied from one artist to another. Some pieces show fine detail and good color, and naturally this influences their values. Studies of animals and portraits bring higher prices than the floral designs. An artist's signature often increases the value of any item, especially if the artist is one who is well recognized.

The market is literally flooded with imposter Roseville that is coming into the country from China. An experienced eye can easily detect these fakes, but to a novice collector, they may pass for old Roseville. Study the marks. If the 'USA' is missing or appears only faintly, the piece is most definitely a reproduction. Also watch for lines with a mark that is not correct for its time frame; for example, Luffa with the script mark, and Woodland with the round Rozane stamp from the 1917 line.

For further information consult the newly revised *Collector's Encyclopedia of Roseville Pottery, Volume 1* and *Volume 2*, by Sharon and Bob Huxford and Mike Nickel (Collector Books). Other books on the subject include *Collector's Compendium of Roseville Pottery, Volumes I, II*, and *III*, by R.B. Monsen (see Directory, Virginia); and *Roseville in All Its Splendor With Price Guide* by Jack and Nancy Bomm (self-published). Our advisor for this category is Mike Nickel; he is listed in the Directory under Michigan.

Apple Blossom, bowl, #326-6, pk or gr, 2½x6½", from $150 to .**175.00**
Apple Blossom, vase, #392-15, bl, hdls, 15½", from $900 to...**1,000.00**
Apple Blossom, window box, #368-8, bl, 2½x10½", from $200 to..**225.00**
Apple Blossom, window box, #368-8, pk or gr, 2½x10½", $175 to.**200.00**
Artwood, planter, #1055-9, 7x9½", from $85 to..........................**95.00**
Artwood, vase, #1057-8, 8", from $85 to **95.00**
Aztec, vase, floral, waisted, 9", from $400 to **500.00**
Azurean, mug, floral, #4, from $400 to **450.00**

Azurean, vase, floral, #4, Leffler, 7½", from $650 to **750.00**
Baneda, center bowl, #233, gr, hdls, 3½x10", from $600 to........**700.00**
Baneda, center bowl, #233, pk, hdls, 3½x10", from $375 to.......**425.00**
Baneda, vase, #596, gr, hdls, 9", from $1,500 to.....................**1,750.00**
Baneda, vase, #596, pk, hdls, 9", from $1,000 to.....................**1,250.00**
Bittersweet, basket, #809-8, 8½", from $200 to.........................**250.00**
Bittersweet, candlesticks, #851-3, 3", pr, from $150 to.............**175.00**
Bittersweet, dbl vase, #858, 4", from $150 to..........................**175.00**
Bittersweet, planter, #827-8, 11½", from $150 to.....................**175.00**
Blackberry, basket, from $1,100 to...**1,300.00**
Blackberry, jardiniere, 4" H, from $350 to **400.00**

Blackberry, jardiniere and pedestal, 9¼x12", 19½x12½", from $3,500.00 to $4,000.00.

(Photo courtesy Cincinnati Art Galleries)

Bleeding Heart, candlesticks, #1139-4½, bl, 5", pr, from $275 to ..**325.00**
Bleeding Heart, center bowl/frog, #384-14/#40, pk or gr, from $225 to..**275.00**
Bleeding Heart, plate, #381-10, bl, 10½", from $200 to **225.00**
Bleeding Heart, plate, #381-10, gr or pk, 10½", from $150 to....**175.00**
Bushberry, dbl bud vase, #158-4½, orange, 4½", from $125 to...**150.00**
Bushberry, hanging basket, gr, 7", from $400 to.........................**450.00**
Bushberry, hanging basket, orange, 7", from $375 to..................**425.00**
Bushberry, window box, #383-6, gr, 6½", from $125 to.............**150.00**
Cameo II, dbl bud vase, 4x7½", from $350 to **400.00**
Cameo II, jardiniere, 8" H, from $450 to **550.00**
Cameo II, jardiniere, 9" H, from $650 to **750.00**
Capri, bowl, #527-7, 7", from $20 to.......................................**30.00**
Capri, planter, #558, 7", from $85 to.......................................**95.00**
Carnelian I, center bowl, 5x12½", from $125 to.......................**150.00**
Carnelian I, pillow vase, 5", from $90 to.................................**100.00**
Carnelian I, wall pocket, 8", from $250 to **300.00**
Carnelian II, basket, 4x10", from $225 to................................**275.00**
Carnelian II, vase, squatty/trumpet neck, hdls, 10", from $225 to..**275.00**
Carnelian II, vase, 3-ring neck, shaped hdls, 8", from $225 to ...**275.00**
Clemana, bowl, #281, bl, 4½x6½", from $250 to.....................**275.00**
Clemana, bowl, #281, gr, 4½x6½", from $225 to.....................**250.00**
Clemana, vase, #112, tan, 7½", from $300 to............................**350.00**
Clemana, vase, #756, bl, bulbous w/hdls, 9½", from $550 to......**600.00**
Clemana, vase, #758, tan, hdls, 8½", from $500 to.....................**550.00**
Clematis, candle holders, #1158-2, bl, 2½", pr, from $110 to.....**130.00**
Clematis, flowerpot/saucer, #668-5, gr or brn, 5½", from $150 to ..**175.00**
Columbine, cornucopia, #149-6, bl or tan, 5½", from $150 to....**175.00**
Columbine, hanging basket, pk, 8½", from $375 to...................**425.00**
Columbine, vase, #17-7, pk, hdls, 7½", from $225 to **275.00**
Corinthian, bowl, 3" H, from $75 to **95.00**
Corinthian, jardiniere, 7" H, from $175 to...............................**200.00**
Corinthian, wall pocket, 8", from $275 to **325.00**
Cosmos, hanging basket, #361, bl, 7", from $400 to.................**425.00**

Cosmos, hanging basket, #361, tan, 7", from $300 to 350.00
Cosmos, vase, #134-4, gr, hdls, 4", from $150 to 175.00
Cosmos, vase, #956-12, tan, hdls, 12½", from $500 to 550.00
Creamware, cake plate, rose band/bull's-eye center, 10", from $250 to .275.00
Creamware, cuspidor, elegant floral & gold design, 10", from $450 to..500.00
Cremona, urn, 4", from $150 to 175.00
Cremona, vase, 12", from $350 to 400.00
Dahlrose, hanging basket, #343, 7½", from $250 to................300.00
Dahlrose, pillow vase, #419, 5x7", from $250 to 275.00
Dahlrose, vase, #364, 6", from $200 to 250.00
Dawn, bowl, #318-14, gr, 16", from #225 to 250.00
Dawn, bowl, #318-14, pk or yel, 16", from $275 to 325.00
Dawn, ewer, #834-16, pk or yel, 16", from $800 to 900.00
Dogwood I, dbl bud vase, 8", from $175 to 200.00
Dogwood I, tub, w/hdls, 4x7", from $150 to 175.00
Dogwood II, bowl, 2½" H, from $125 to 150.00
Dogwood II, jardiniere, 8", from $250 to 300.00
Donatello, candlestick, 6½", ea from $175 to 225.00
Donatello, dbl bud vase, gate type, 5", from $125 to 150.00
Donatello, plate, 8", from $450 to 500.00
Donatello, powder jar, 2x5", from $450 to 550.00
Dutch, pin tray, 4", from $65 to 75.00
Dutch, plate, incurvate rim, 11", from $100 to...........................125.00
Earlam, bowl, #218, hdls, 3x11½", from $400 to.......................450.00
Earlam, vase, #522, 9", from $800 to..900.00
Falline, center bowl, #244, bl, hdls, 11", from $500 to..............600.00
Falline, vase, #647, bl, hdls, 7½", from $1,000 to 1,250.00
Falline, vase, #653, tan, hdls, 12½", from $1,000 to 1,100.00
Ferella, bowl/frog, #211, tan, 5", from $700 to 800.00
Ferella, candlesticks, #1078, red, pr, from $1,000 to 10,100.00
Ferella, candlesticks, #1078, tan, 4½", pr, from $700 to 800.00
Ferella, vase, #505, red, hdls, 6", from $1,200 to.....................1,300.00
Ferella, vase, #505, tan, hdls, 6", from $700 to 800.00
Florane, bowl, 5", from $125 to 150.00
Florane, bud vase, 7", from $30 to..35.00
Florane, planter, 10", from $45 to 50.00
Florane, vase, 12½", from $300 to..350.00
Florentine, compote, 10" dia, from $125 to 150.00
Florentine, hanging basket, 9" dia, from $275 to.......................325.00
Florentine, jardiniere, 8" H, from $200 to.................................250.00
Foxglove, cornucopia, #166-6, gr/pk, 6", from $200 to.............225.00
Foxglove, hanging basket, #466, pk, 6½", from $300 to 350.00
Foxglove, vase, #47-8, bl, hdls, 8½", from $250 to...................300.00
Foxglove, vase, #53-14, bl, 14", from $450 to...........................500.00
Freesia, basket, #390-7, tangerine, 7", from $225 to....................250.00
Freesia, bowl, #465-8, gr, hdls, 11", from $175 to........................200.00
Freesia, window box, #1392-8, gr, 10½", from $200 to 225.00
Fuchsia, candlesticks, #1132, brn/tan, 2", pr, from $125 to.........150.00
Fuchsia, center bowl, #351-10, gr, 3½x12½", from $225 to........275.00
Fuchsia, frog, #37, gr, from $225 to 250.00
Fuchsia, vase, #893-6, bl, hdls, 6", from $250 to 300.00
Futura, center bowl, #187, 3½" H, from $450 to.......................550.00
Futura, frog, #187, from $100 to 125.00
Futura, pillow vase, #81, 5x6", from $350 to 450.00
Futura, vase, fan form, #82, 6", from $550 to.............................650.00
Gardenia, hanging basket, #661, 6", from $300 to 350.00
Gardenia, vase, #689-14, hdls, 14", from $375 to.......................425.00
Gardenia, window box, #658-8, 3x8½", from $100 to 125.00
Holland, powder jar, w/lid, 3", from $150 to...............................175.00
Holland, tankard, #2, 9½", from $250 to 300.00
Imperial I, basket, #7, 9", from $250 to 300.00
Imperial I, basket, 11", from $300 to 350.00
Imperial I, compote, 6½", from $225 to.....................................275.00
Imperial II, bowl, U-form, 4½", from $300 to 400.00

Imperial II, vase, #473 (in red crayon), 8", from $1,500 to......1,750.00
Iris, basket, #355-10, bl, 9½", from $475 to................................550.00
Iris, basket, #355-10, pk or tan, 9½", from $425 to....................475.00
Iris, center bowl, #361-8, bl, hdls, 3x10", from $200 to 225.00
Iris, center bowl, #361-8, pk or tan, hdls, 3x10", from $175 to...200.00
Ivory II, ewer, #941-10, 10½", from $75 to................................95.00
Ivory II, vase, #274-6, 6½", from $75 to 95.00
Ixia, center bowl, #330-7, 3½x10½", from $150 to.....................175.00
Ixia, hanging basket, 7", from $250 to 300.00
Jonquil, bowl, #523, 3", from $200 to 225.00
Jonquil, jardiniere, #621, 4" H, from $250 to.............................275.00
Jonquil, vase, #529, hdls, 8", from $500 to 600.00
Juvenile, bowl, chicks, 4½", from $150 to..................................200.00
Juvenile, creamer, chicks, 3", from $350 to................................400.00
Juvenile, cup & saucer, rabbit, 2" & 5", from $250 to................300.00
Juvenile, custard, goose, 2½", from $600 to...............................650.00
Juvenile, mug, bear, 3½", from $900 to 1,000.00
Juvenile, mug, fat puppy, 3½", from $600 to.............................700.00
Juvenile, pudding dish, chicks, 3½", from $275 to.....................300.00
Juvenile, teapot, goose, 4", from $1,500 to...............................1,700.00
La Rose, jardiniere, 6½", from $150 to 175.00
La Rose, wall pocket, 9", from $300 to 350.00
Laurel, bowl, #252, gold, 3½", from $250 to..............................300.00
Laurel, bowl, #252, gr, 3½", from $350 to..................................400.00
Laurel, bowl, #252, russet, 3½", from $300 to............................350.00
Laurel, vase, #674, russet, 9½", from $500 to 600.00
Luffa, jardiniere, #631, 7" H, from $350 to.................................400.00
Luffa, vase, #683, hdls, 6", from $350 to....................................400.00
Luffa, vase, hdls, ftd, 15½", from $2,000 to.............................2,500.00
Lustre, candlestick, 10", ea from $100 to 125.00
Lustre, vase, 12", from $250 to..275.00
Magnolia, ashtray, #28, brn or gr, 7", from $100 to 125.00
Magnolia, planter, #388-6, brn or gr, 8½", from $85 to..............95.00
Magnolia, vase, #91-8, brn or gr, hdls, 8", from $125 to 150.00
Mara, vase, average glaze, #13, 5½", from $2,500 to................3,000.00
Mara, vase, exceptional glaze, 13", from $1,750 to 2,000.00
Mayfair, bowl, #1119-9, 10", from $60 to...................................70.00
Mayfair, planter, #1113-8, 3½x8½", from $70 to........................85.00
Ming Tree, ashtray, #599, 6", from $75 to...................................85.00
Ming Tree, bowl, #526-9, 4x11½", from $95 to..........................110.00
Ming Tree, vase, #585-14, 14½", from $400 to...........................450.00
Mock Orange, planter, #931-8, 3½x9", from $125 to 150.00
Mock Orange, vase, #973-8, hdls, 8½", from $150 to.................175.00
Moderne, compote, #295, 5", from $250 to................................275.00
Moderne, vase, #796-8, 8½", from $250 to.................................300.00
Mongol, vase, bowl shape w/flared rim, 2½", from $400 to 500.00
Mongol, vase, long trumpet neck w/squatty bottom, 16", from $2,000 to .2,500.00
Montacello, basket, bl, 6½", from $900 to 1,000.00
Morning Glory, basket, #340, gr, 10½", from $1,300 to...........1,500.00
Morning Glory, basket, #340, ivory, 10½", from $800 to...........900.00
Morning Glory, candlesticks, #1102, ivory, 5", pr, from $400 to.500.00
Morning Glory, center bowl, #270, gr, 4½x11½", from $475 to.550.00
Moss, bowl vase, #290, bl, from $300 to 350.00
Moss, bowl vase, #290, pk/gr or orange/gr, 6", ea from $350 to...400.00
Moss, pillow vase, #781, bl, 8", from $300 to 350.00
Mostique, bowl, hdls, 9", from $450 to 500.00
Mostique, compote, 7", from $350 to 375.00
Mostique, vase, 10", from $550 to..650.00
Olympic, pitcher, Ulysses at the Table of Circe, 7", from $3,000 to ..3,500.00
Orian, candle holder, #1108, tan, 4½", pr, from $300 to 350.00
Orian, candle holder, #1108, yel, 4½", pr, from $350 to 400.00
Orian, compote, #272, red, 4½x10½", from $300 to 325.00
Orian, vase, #733, turq, hdls, from $200 to................................225.00
Orian, vase, #742, tan, hdls, 12½", from $450 to........................500.00

Pauleo, bowl, floral, squatty, 3-ftd, 3", from $1,000 to 1,200.00
Pauleo, vase, broken glaze, #340, 19", from $1,500 to 2,000.00

Pauleo, vase, floral on lavender luster, unmarked, 13½x8½", $1,870.00. (Photo courtesy Smith and Jones)

Peony, basket, #379-12, 11", from $250 to......................275.00
Peony, conch shell, #436, 9½", from $110 to 135.00
Peony, mug, #2-3½, 3½", from $100 to 125.00
Persian, hanging basket, geometric floral/leaves, 9", from $500 to...600.00
Pine Cone, basket, #353-11, brn, from $500 to 550.00
Pine Cone, bowl, #457-7, gr, hdls, from $150 to 175.00
Pine Cone, dbl tray, #462, bl, 13", from $750 to 850.00
Pine Cone, pitcher, #708-9, gr, from $400 to 450.00
Pine Cone, planter, #124, gr, from $150 to................175.00
Poppy, bowl, #336-10, gray/gr, 12", from $225 to 250.00
Poppy, ewer, #880-18, gray/gr, 18½", from $750 to 850.00
Poppy, ewer, #880-18, pk, 18½", from $850 to 950.00
Poppy, vase, #872-9, gray/gr, hdls, 9", from $300 to 325.00
Poppy, vase, #872-9, pk, hdls, 9", from $450 to 500.00
Primrose, vase, #760-6, bl or pk, hdls, 7", from $175 to.............200.00
Primrose, vase, #760-6, tan, hdls, from $150 to.........................175.00
Raymor, divided vegetable bowl, #165, 13", from $55 to 65.00
Raymor, gravy boat, #190, 9½", from $30 to 35.00
Raymor, water pitcher, #180, 10", from $100 to 150.00
Rosecraft Blended, jardiniere, 4" H, from $90 to........................110.00
Rosecraft Blended, vase, 12½", from $150 to 175.00
Rosecraft Hexagon, bowl, bl, hdls, 7½", from $375 to................400.00
Rosecraft Hexagon, bowl, brn, hdls, 7½", from $175 to..............200.00
Rosecraft Hexagon, vase, glossy bl, rare, 5", from $425 to 525.00
Rosecraft Panel, bowl vase, brn, 4" H, from $200 to....................225.00
Rosecraft Panel, bowl vase, gr, 4" H, from $250 to.....................275.00
Rosecraft Panel, covered jar, brn, from $550 to..........................600.00
Rosecraft Panel, covered jar, gr, 10", from $750 to.....................850.00
Rosecraft Panel, window box, brn, 6x12", from $450 to 500.00
Rosecraft Vintage, jardiniere, 9" H, from $400 to 450.00
Rosecraft Vintage, vase, 12", from $550 to 650.00
Rosecraft Vintage, window box, 6x11½", from $550 to 650.00
Rozane, candlestick, floral, J Imlay, 9", from $275 to.................350.00
Rozane, ewer, #950, floral, 7½", from $175 to...........................200.00
Rozane, pillow vase, portrait of dog, 8½", from $2,500 to 3,000.00
Rozane, tankard, J Lamay, 16", from $600 to 700.00
Rozane, vase, floral, #872, 5½", from $200 to 225.00
Rozane Light, mug, cherries, Pillsbury, 5", from $350 to.............400.00
Rozane Light, tankard, grapes, J Imlay, 11½", from $700 to 800.00
Rozane Light, vase, floral, H Pillsbury, 8½", from $500 to..........600.00
Rozane Light, vase, leaves, W Myers, 11½", from $750 to 850.00
Rozane Light, vase, spider mums, M Timberlake, 15", from $3,500 to..4,000.00
Rozane 1917, bowl, w/hdls, ftd, 5", from $175 to 200.00
Rozane 1917, bowl, 4½", from $125 to......................................150.00

Rozane 1917, compote, 8", from $150 to 175.00
Russco, dbl bud vase, 8½", from $125 to 150.00
Russco, vase, heavy crystals, ftd trumpet form, 7", from $175 to ...200.00
Silhouette, box, #740, w/lid, 4½", from $150 to 175.00
Silhouette, vase, #780-6, 6", from $90 to.................................110.00
Snowberry, basket, #1BK-12, gr, 12½", from $275 to.................325.00
Snowberry, pillow vase, #1FH-6, bl or pk, 6½", from $150 to 175.00
Snowberry, tray, #1BL-12, bl or pk, 14", from $250 to 275.00
Snowberry, tray, #1BL-12, gr, 14", from $200 to.........................225.00
Sunflower, center bowl, hdls, 3x12½", from $1,000 to 1,200.00
Sunflower, vase, #486, 5", from $900 to 1,000.00
Teasel, #887-10, lt bl or tan, 10", from $175 to 200.00
Teasel, vase, #887-10, dk bl or rust, 10", from $450 to...............500.00
Thorn Apple, double bud vase, #119, 5½", from $175 to...........225.00
Thorn Apple, vase, #816-8, hdls, 8½", from $250 to 300.00
Thorn Apple, vase, #820-9, hdls, 9½", from $275 to 325.00
Thorn Apple, vase, #822-10, hdls, 10½", from $300 to..............350.00
Topeo, center bowl, red, 3x11½", from $100 to 125.00
Topeo, dbl candlesticks, bl, 5", pr, from $550 to.......................600.00
Topeo, vase, bl, 9", from $600 to 700.00
Topeo, vase, red, 9", from $325 to 375.00
Tourmaline, bowl, shallow, 8", from $75 to 100.00
Tourmaline, vase, hexagonal, 10", from $250 to.........................275.00
Tourmaline, vase, urn form, hdls, ftd, 8", from $150 to 175.00
Tuscany, vase, gray/lt bl, 4", from $75 to..................................100.00
Tuscany, vase, gray/lt bl, 12", from $225 to...............................250.00
Tuscany, vase, pk, 4", from $100 to 125.00
Tuscany, vase, pk, 12", from $300 to...350.00
Velmoss, bowl, #266, gr, 3x11", from $175 to............................225.00
Velmoss, vase, #721, bl, hdls, 12½", from $500 to 550.00
Velmoss, vase, #721, gr, hdls, 12½", from $400 to......................450.00
Velmoss Scroll, vase, 5", from $150 to 175.00
Velmoss Scroll, vase, 12", from $450 to 500.00
Vista, basket, 9½", from $900 to..1,000.00
Vista, vase, #134-18, 18", from $1,750 to 2,000.00
Water Lily, candlesticks, #1155-4½, bl, 5", pr, from $200 to 225.00
Water Lily, frog, #48, brn w/gr, 4½", from $140 to....................165.00
Water Lily, hanging basket, #468, bl, 9", from $350 to 375.00
Water Lily, hanging basket, #468, rose w/gr, 9", from $375 to 425.00
White Rose, candlesticks, #1142-4½, 4½", pr, from $125 to......150.00
White Rose, console bowl/frog, #393-12/#41, hdls, from $150 to .200.00
White Rose, dbl bud vase, #148, 4½", from $85 to 95.00
White Rose, vase, #991-12, hdls, 12½", from $250 to 300.00
Wincraft, cornucopia, #221-8, 9x5", from $150 to 175.00
Wincraft, ewer, #218-18, 19", from $650 to...............................750.00
Windsor, basket, #330, bl, 4½", from $1,100 to 1,200.00
Windsor, center bowl, rust, 3½x10½", from $350 to 400.00
Wisteria, bowl vase, #632, tan, 5", from $350 to 450.00
Wisteria, vase, #682, bl, 10", from $1,750 to..........................2,000.00
Wisteria, vase, #682, tan, 10", from, $850 to 900.00
Woodland, vase, irises, 15", from $3,000 to............................3,500.00
Zephyr Lily, pillow vase, #206-7, bl, 7", from $225 to.................275.00
Zephyr Lily, tray, brn, 14½", from $225 to................................250.00

Rowland and Marsellus

Though the impressive back stamp seems to suggest otherwise, Rowland and Marsellus were not Staffordshire potters but American importers who commissioned various English companies to supply them with the transfer-printed crockery and historical ware that had been a popular import commodity since the early 1800s. Plates (both flat and with a rolled edge), cups and saucers, pitchers, and platters were sold as souvenirs from 1890 through the 1930s. Though other importers —

Bawo & Dotter, and A. C. Bosselman & Co., both of New York City — commissioned the manufacture of similar souvenir items, by far the largest volume carries the R. & M. mark, and Rowland and Marcellus has become a generic term that covers all twentieth-century souvenir china of this type. Their mark may be in full or 'R. & M.' in a diamond. Though primarily made with blue transfers on white, other colors may occasionally be found as well.

Note: Show prices may be as much as 25% higher than our values, which are based on eBay sales. Our advisors for this category are Angi and David Ringering; they are listed in the Directory under Oregon.

Key:
r/e — rolled edge   v/o — view of
s/o — souvenir of

Bowl, English castle, floral border, 8½"	25.00
Bowl, English Countryside, 8½"	25.00
Creamer, Plymouth, mk as Burbank	45.00
Cup, Philadelphia, s/o	35.00
Cup & saucer, Alaska-Yukon-Pacific Expo, 1909	120.00
Cup & saucer, Chicago, s/o	85.00
Cup & saucer, Lemox MA, s/o	75.00
Cup & saucer, Niagara Falls NY, s/o	65.00
Pitcher, Declaration of Independence, 7x7½"	350.00
Pitcher, Plymouth Rock, various scenes, 6½"	250.00
Plate, American Poets, 7 portraits, v/o, 10"	50.00
Plate, Asbury Park, r/e, s/o, 10"	85.00
Plate, Atlantic City, s/o, 9"	78.00
Plate, Battle of Lake Erie, fruit & flower border	50.00
Plate, Bunker Hill Monument, Ye Old Historical Pottery, 9"	35.00
Plate, Charles Dickens, London scenes, r/e, 10"	55.00
Plate, Countess Grosvenor & Sir Thomas Laurence, 10¼"	150.00
Plate, coupe; Denver v/o, 10"	60.00
Plate, coupe; Tucson AZ, 5 scenes, v/o, 6"	40.00
Plate, East Hampton, v/o, 10"	65.00
Plate, Historical Philadelphia, 6 scenes	45.00
Plate, Longfellow, 10"	70.00
Plate, Lookout Mountain TN, r/e, s/o, 10"	70.00
Plate, Mayflower Coat of Arms, 1909, gold edge, 7"	30.00
Plate, New York & Brooklyn Bridge, s/o, r/e, 10"	75.00
Plate, New York City, Statue of Liberty, r/e, v/o, 10"	70.00
Plate, Plymouth MA, 10"	50.00
Plate, Priscilla & John Adams, 10"	50.00
Plate, Richfield Springs NY, 10"	60.00
Plate, Ride of Paul Revere, scalloped edge, r/o, 9¾"	50.00
Plate, Teddy Roosevelt, r/e, 10"	95.00
Plate, The Elm at Cambridge MA, 10"	50.00
Plate, Thomas Jefferson, 6 v/o 1904 St Louis World's Fair, r/e, 10"	100.00
Plate, Vassar College, 6 scenes at border, 10"	85.00
Tumbler, Ashville, mc, s/o	95.00
Tumbler, Ottawa Canada	85.00
Tumbler, Thousand Islands, v/o	85.00

Royal Bayreuth

Founded in 1794 in Tettau, Bavaria, the Royal Bayreuth firm originally manufactured fine dinnerware of superior quality. Their figural items, produced from before the turn of the nineteenth century until the onset of WWI, are highly sought after by today's collectors. Perhaps the most abundantly produced and easily recognized of these are the tomato and lobster pieces. Fruits, flowers, people, animals, birds, and vegetables shapes were also made. Aside from figural items, pitchers, toothpick holders, cups and saucers, humidors, and the like were decorated in flo-

rals and scenic motifs. Some, such as the very popular Rose Tapestry line, utilized a cloth-like tapestry background. Transfer prints were used as well. Two of the most popular are Sunbonnet Babies and Nursery Rhymes (in particular, those decorated with the complete verse).

Caution: Many pieces were not marked; some were marked 'Deponiert' or 'Registered' only. While marked pieces are the most valued, unmarked items are still very worthwhile. Our advisors for this category are Judy White from California, Dee Hooks from Illinois, and Harold Brandenburg from Kansas; they are listed in the Directory under their home states.

Figurals

Ashtray, Devil & Cards, bl mk, 2½x4¼"	300.00
Ashtray, Devil & Cards, mk US Zone in gr, 4x6¼"	235.00
Ashtray, eagle, bl mk, 2x5½"	275.00
Ashtray, elk's head, bl mk, 6x4½"	125.00
Ashtray, Santa, red, bl mk, 1¾x4¾"	1,500.00
Bowl, celery; elk (2 heads), bl mk, 12" L	450.00
Bowl, salad; lobster, bl mk, 3x8"	395.00
Bowl, tomato, bl mk, 4x8"	95.00
Bowl, tomato, w/lid, gr mk, 3½"	100.00
Candy dish, ponsettias, bl mk, 4½x8"	275.00
Cup & saucer, cabbage leaf w/lobster hdl, bl mk	195.00
Inkwell, elk's head, gr mk, 3½x5"	525.00
Match holder, clown, wall hanging, bl mk, 5"	395.00
Match holder, Santa, red, striker on bk, bl mk, 4"	2,250.00
Match safe, Devil & Cards, wall mt, bl mk, 5x4"	395.00
Mug, Devil & Cards, bl mk, 4¾"	305.00
Pitcher, apple, red, bl mk, cream sz, 3¾"	250.00
Pitcher, bear, lt brn & gray, bl mk, 4½"	1,100.00
Pitcher, blk cat, tail hdl, bl mk, milk sz, 5½"	375.00
Pitcher, bull's head, gray, bl mk, cream sz, 3¾"	125.00
Pitcher, butterfly (open winged), bl mk, cream sz, 3¾"	300.00
Pitcher, chamois stirrup, bl mk, cream sz, 4¾"	595.00
Pitcher, chrysanthemum, bl mk, cream sz, 3¾"	400.00
Pitcher, clown, yel, bl mk, cream sz, 3¾"	475.00
Pitcher, coachman, bl mk, milk sz, 5"	295.00
Pitcher, conch shell, bl mk, cream sz, 2¾"	70.00
Pitcher, cow, unmk, cream sz, 3"	150.00
Pitcher, dachschund, bl mk, milk sz, 5"	550.00
Pitcher, Devil & Cards, bl mk, milk sz, 5"	325.00
Pitcher, Devil & Cards, bl mk, water sz, 7"	650.00
Pitcher, duck, mk Registered, cream sz, 3⅞"	150.00
Pitcher, fox stirrup, red & gray, bl mk, cream sz, 4"	3,200.00
Pitcher, frog, brn, bl mk, cream sz, 2½x5", from $295 to	345.00
Pitcher, girl w/pitcher on hip, bl dress, bl mk, cream sz, 4"	450.00
Pitcher, grape cluster, wht, unmk, cream sz, 3¾"	125.00
Pitcher, iris, gr hdl, unmk, milk sz, 5⅜"	1,550.00
Pitcher, iris, gr leaf hdl, bl mk, cream sz, 4½"	795.00
Pitcher, ladybug, 'cut-out eyes,' red & blk, bl mk, milk sz, 4¾"	1,750.00
Pitcher, lobster, bl mk, cream sz, 4¼"	125.00
Pitcher, lobster, bl mk, water sz, 6¾", from $475 to	545.00
Pitcher, lobster on shell, unmk, cream sz, 3", from $95 to	135.00
Pitcher, monkey, bl mk, cream sz, 4"	395.00
Pitcher, Old Man of the Mountain, gr mk, cream sz, 3¾"	125.00
Pitcher, owl, bl mk, cream sz, 4¾"	350.00
Pitcher, pansy, purple, bl mk, cream sz, 4"	250.00
Pitcher, pear, raised flower mk, cream sz, 4½"	450.00
Pitcher, poodle, wht, bl mk, 4½"	250.00
Pitcher, rabbit, unmk, cream sz, 4¾"	4,000.00
Pitcher, rooster, mc, bl mk, cream sz, 4⅜"	400.00
Pitcher, Santa, red, bl mk, milk sz, 5"	2,750.00
Pitcher, shell w/sea horse hdl, unmk, cream sz	110.00

Pitcher, snake, brn & cream, bl mk, cream sz, 3¾" 750.00
Pitcher, spikey shell, pearl lustre, bl mk, cream sz, 4½" 125.00
Pitcher, spikey shell, water sz, 5½" 495.00
Pitcher, strawberry, bl mk, cream sz, 4" 225.00
Pitcher, sunflower, Deponiert, cream sz, 4½" 750.00
Pitcher, tomato, bl mk, cream sz, 3" 110.00
Pitcher, tomato, leaf hdl, bl mk, water sz, 6¼" 425.00
Pitcher, turtle, bl mk, cream sz, 2½" 595.00
Pitcher, turtle, lt brn, bl mk, rare, lemonade sz, 4½" 12,000.00
Plate, tomato, bl mk w/Deponiert, 6" 85.00
Shakers, coachman, red, unmk, pr 600.00
Shakers, grape cluster, purple, gr mk, 3½", pr 150.00
Shakers, tomato, bl mk, 2½", pr 55.00
Sugar bowl, lobster, w/lid, bl mk, 4½" 195.00
Sugar bowl, pineapple, w/lid, bl mk, 5" 450.00
Sugar bowl, poppy, w/lid, unmk, 3" 175.00
Sugar bowl, strawberry, w/leaf finial, 3⅞" 110.00
Tea strainer, pansy, magenta, unmk, 5½" L 575.00
Toothpick holder, spikey shell, pearl lustre, 3-ftd, 3", from $150 to 200.00
Wall pocket, grape cluster, several colors, 9x5½" 275.00

Nursery Rhymes

Bell, Jack & Beanstalk, w/rhyme, w/clapper, bl mk 350.00
Box, Jack & Jill, clam shape, bl mk, w/lid................................250.00
Candlestick, Jack & Jill, w/verse, ring hdl, bl mk, ea 235.00
Candy dish, Jack & the Beanstalk, spade shape, bl mk, 4¾x4½" .85.00
Candy dish, Little Jack Horner, heart shape, bl mk, 4½" 110.00
Coffeepot, Jack & Jill, bl mk 365.00
Dutch shoe, Little Bo Peep, bl mk 375.00
Mug, Jack & the Beanstalk, w/verse, bl mk, lg 250.00
Nappy, Jack & Jill, bl mk, 1½x3½x5½" 100.00
Pitcher, Jack & the Beanstalk, bl mk, water sz 350.00
Pitcher, Little Jack Horner, bl mk, 3½" 175.00
Plate, Jack & Jill, bl mk, 6" 125.00
Plate, Little Bo Peep, bl mk, 6½" 125.00
Plate, Little Bo Peep, bl mk, 7½" 125.00
Plate, Ring Around the Rosies, no verse, bl mk, 6" 125.00
Sugar bowl, Little Boy Blue, no verse, bl mk 215.00
Vase, Babes in Woods, bl mk, 4" 250.00
Vase, Jack & Jill, 2 lg hdls w/gold trim, bl mk 175.00

Scenics and Action Portraits

Bowl, hunting scene, flared & ruffled, 3-ftd, bl mk, 2½x5" 65.00
Bowl, 2 musicians, 3 ftd, gold trim, bl mk, 2x5" 65.00
Candy dish, boy w/donkeys, club shape, bl mk, 4½" 95.00
Chamberstick, Dutch girl in countryside, bl mk, 2x5" 75.00
Creamer, polar bear on bl & brn, unmk, 5" 600.00
Creamer & sugar bowl, girl in lg hat & fur muff, gold trim, bl mk ..125.00
Humidor, sheep on mountain, bl mk, 6¼" 295.00
Jug, dogs chase moose into river, bl mk, 6¼", from $130 to 150.00
Jug, goats in mountains, bl mk, 4¾", from $60 to 85.00
Loving cup, Dutch children at river, 3 gold hdls, bl mk, 3¼" 50.00
Match striker, brn w/wht Roman lady, geometric band in center, 2½"...95.00
Mug, cows in pasture, 3-hdl, bl mk, 3⅜" 150.00
Nut dish, donkeys, w/hdl, bl mk, 2¼x4x9¾" 100.00
Pitcher, cattle in pasture, bl mk, 4" 95.00
Pitcher, cattle in pasture, gr mk, cream sz, 3½" 85.00
Pitcher, horses in pasture, bl mk, cream sz 185.00
Pitcher, hunter w/dog in landscape w/flying birds, bl mk, water sz, 6"..295.00
Pitcher, lobster on conch shell, unmk, 3" 135.00
Pitcher, 2 men (1 on donkey) in desert, 5½" 150.00
Plate, Brittany girls by seashore, bl mk, 7½" 120.00

Powder box, courting scene on lid, bl mk, #20, 2½x3⅞" 95.00
Shakers, lady w/geese, gold rim, unmk, 3", pr 90.00
Teapot, hunting scene, bl mk, 4¼x7" 110.00
Toothpick holder, sheep on mountain, unmk, 2¾" 125.00
Toothpick holder, woman w/horse, unmk 175.00
Tray, vanity; Fr courting couple, bl mk, 8¼x11¼" 150.00
Vase, floral, lion's head hdls & lion's paw ft, bl mk, 5"...............135.00
Vase, hummingbirds, unmk, 6½" 350.00
Vase, hunting scene, bk: sailboat, hdls, bl mk, 5" 85.00
Vase, lady w/hand to forehead in gold vignette, bl mk, 4½" 145.00
Vase, pheasant, flared & ruffled rim, 3¾" 175.00
Vase, roses on wht, bl mk, 7" 125.00
Vase, tavern scene in gold vignette, bl mk, 5¼" 110.00
Vase, toasting cavalier, hdls, bl mk, 6½x7½" 85.00

Sunbonnet Babies

Ashtray, scrubbing, dmn shape, bl mk, 5⅝" 255.00
Bonbon, heart shape, bl mk 350.00
Candlestick, washing, bl mk, 4⅛x2⅞", ea 235.00
Candlesticks, bl mk, 4¼", pr 695.00
Candy dish, ironing, heart shape, bl mk 315.00
Candy dish, sewing, spade shape, bl mk 315.00
Chamberstick, cleaning, bl mk, 5½x4½" 325.00
Cheese dish, ironing, 2-pc, unmk (always), mini, 1½x3"............650.00

Coffeepot, cleaning, stick handle, blue mark, miniature, 5¾", $700.00.

Coffeepot, ironing, w/lid, bl mk, 6¼"....................................450.00
Pitcher, cleaning, bl mk, cream sz, 3¼" 225.00
Pitcher, ironing, bl mk, 3½" 225.00
Planter, fishing, low gold hdls, no insert, bl mk, 2¾x3½" 275.00
Plate, ltd ed, 7 scenes, 13" 250.00
Plates, set of 7 (1 for ea day), later edition, bl mk, 7" 350.00
Relish dish, cleaning, bl mk, oval, 4x7¾" 275.00
Sugar bowl, washing, w/lid, bl mk 350.00
Toothpick holder, sewing, 3-ftd, pie-crust edge, unmk, 2½" 500.00

Tapestries

Basket, Japanese chrysanthemum (rare), bl mk, 7" 2,000.00
Cracker jar, Rose Tapestry, appl china hdls, gilt trim, 5½" 700.00
Cracker jar, sheep scenic, bl mk, 6½x4¾" 800.00
Hair receiver, Rose Tapestry, bl mk, 4¼" dia 225.00
Hatpin holder, Rose Tapestry, ftd, bl mk, 4⅜" 275.00
Hatpin holder, Rose Tapestry, open bottom, unmk, 4½" 175.00
Humidor, 3 cows scenic, bl mk, 6½".................................1,000.00
Lady's shoe, Rose Tapestry, bl mk, 2½x4½", from $300 to..........350.00
Pin box, courting scene on lid, bl mk, 4½x2½" 250.00
Pin dish, Rose Tapestry, leaf shape, bl mk, 4¾" 150.00

Pitcher, Rose Tapestry, bl mk, cream sz, 4" 150.00
Pitcher, Rose Tapestry, corset shaped, bl mk, 4¾" 225.00
Pitcher, Rose Tapestry, gold rim, bl mk, cream sz, 3¼" 150.00
Shakers, Rose Tapestry, bl mk, 3¼", pr 275.00
Shoe, Rose Tapestry, pk, blk mk, 4½" L..................................400.00
Tray, dresser; Rose Tapestry, bl mk, 11¼x8", from $275 to 325.00
Vase, Rose Tapestry, bl mk, 5" 170.00
Vase, tavern scene, 2 gold hdls at shoulder, bl mk, 4⅝" 150.00

Royal Bonn

Royal Bonn is a fine-paste porcelain, ornately decorated with scenes, portraits, or florals. The factory was established in the mid-1800s in Bonn, Germany; however, most pieces found today are from the latter part of the century.

Ewer, tapestry decor on rnd bottom w/lg ornate hdl & neck, 18½"..1,250.00
Vase, blond maiden in yel dress/outdoor scene, #2528 imp, 9½".275.00
Vase, couples ea side, sm gold ring-hdls, long slender neck, 10".250.00
Vase, lady w/long hair, purple & gold floral relief, Volk, hdls, 8".540.00
Vase, lg irises w/squeeze-bag detail on HP 3-color ground, #1430, 7x6"...415.00
Vase, lg yel & purple floral, ornate hdls & rim, 12" 200.00
Vase, roses & river scene, sgn O Leifs, ovoid, 9½", pr................150.00
Vase, roses w/gold on tapered vasiform w/openwork base, 12⅜".300.00
Vase, thistles, gold neck/hdls/base/traceries, ped ft, 11" 150.00

Royal Copenhagen

The Royal Copenhagen Manufactory was established in Denmark in about 1775 by Frantz Henrich Muller. When bankruptcy threatened in 1779, the Crown took charge. The fine dinnerware and objects of art produced after that time carry the familiar logo, the crown over three wavy lines. For further information we recommend *Royal Copenhagen Porcelain, Animals and Figurines*, by Robert J. Heritage (Schiffer). See also Limited Edition Plates.

Ashtray, Blue Fluted, plain, #2185, 3½" 18.00
Bowl, cream soup; Blue Fluted, half lace, w/lid, #746....................55.00
Bowl, rim soup; Blue Fluted, plain, #169, 8" 65.00
Bowl, rim soup; Flora Danica, 8¾" 750.00
Bowl, salad; Blue Fluted, plain, #311, 8" 135.00
Bowl, salad; Flora Danica, triangular, 11¼x10½" 1,550.00
Bowl, vegetable; Blue Fluted, half lace, #512, 8½"......................135.00
Candlestick, Blue Fluted, full lace, 2-arm, #1169, ea 1,550.00
Charger, Flora Danica, 13" 1,250.00
Clock, 2 adults & 1 child, gilt dial, Zenity, ca 1900-20, 9½" ..1,550.00
Coffeepot, Blue Fluted, full lace, #1202, 6-cup, 9" 485.00
Coffeepot, Blue Fluted, full lace, sm, 2-cup 335.00
Coffeepot, Blue Fluted, plain, 6⅞" 245.00
Creamer, Blue Fluted, half lace, #523, 4¾"..................................85.00
Creamer, Blue Fluted, plain, #2305, 2½" 59.00
Cup & saucer, Blue Fluted, half lace, #765, 2½" 75.00
Cup & saucer, Flora Danica, flat 495.00
Figurine, Amager Girl, #12412, 5¼"..435.00
Figurine, boy & calf, #772, 6½" 400.00
Figurine, boy w/umbrellas, #1129, 6¾"......................................375.00
Figurine, cat, gray & wht tabby w/gr eyes, #109, 5x10½" 425.00
Figurine, cat, wht, #667, 7¾" 800.00
Figurine, Fanoe girl, Martin-Hansen, #12413, ca 1922, 5½" 475.00
Figurine, girl w/goats, #694, 9" 295.00
Figurine, Granny, #784, 8"..435.00
Figurine, Harvest Group, peasant couple, #1352, 17x11" 345.00

Figurine, Henrik & Elise, courting couple, #2049, 17"...............585.00
Figurine, horse, gray, #1362, 8x12½" 385.00
Figurine, knight on horse, sits on post (nodder/rocker), 7½x7"..335.00
Figurine, lioness, #804, 6x12" 265.00
Figurine, mermaid on rock, #4431, 8¾" 245.00
Figurine, mother & child, #3457, 8½" 325.00
Figurine, Nathan the Wise, #1413, 13¾" 475.00
Figurine, Pan w/crow, #2113, 6¾" 400.00
Figurine, Pan w/owl, 6x3½" 400.00
Figurine, Pan w/squirrel, #456, 1902, 8" 365.00
Figurine, Pan wrestling bear, #648, 6½x6" 300.00
Figurine, Pekingese pup, #448, 4¾" 425.00
Figurine, Percheron in harness (for cart), Bonnesen, 11½x13" ..635.00
Figurine, polar bear, standing, #502, 13" 265.00
Figurine, Sandman, #1129, 7" 300.00
Figurine, Sealand Girl, sitting w/flowers, #12418, 4"..................600.00
Figurine, Slesvig Girl, Martin-Hansen, #12417, ca 1923, 4".......475.00

Figurines, Amager girl knitting, #1314, $200.00; Pan playing with a rabbit, #439, $285.00.

Pickle dish, Blue Fluted, plain, #144, 9"..60.00
Plate, bread & butter; Blue Fluted, half lace, #575, 6", 6 for 235.00
Plate, cake; Blue Fluted, full lace, #1018, 8"..............................275.00
Plate, cake; Blue Fluted, plain, hexagonal, #2195, 8¾" 200.00
Plate, dinner; Blue Fluted, full lace, #1084, 10" 125.00
Plate, dinner; Blue Fluted, half lace, 10".....................................85.00
Plate, dinner; Blue Fluted, plain, 10" 75.00
Plate, game; Flora Danica, winter hare, ca 1923-35, 10", NM 375.00
Plate, luncheon; Blue Fluted, half lace, 8¾", 6 for 385.00
Plate, luncheon; Flora Danica, early mk, 8⅝", from $725 to 775.00
Platter, Blue Fluted, half lace, #628, 13" 215.00
Sauce boat, Flora Danica, 5¾x9¼x6½"..925.00
Sugar bowl, Blue Fluted, full lace, #112 ....135.00
Sugar bowl, Flora Danica, w/lid, #3624, w/lid, mini................1,200.00
Tureen, Flora Danica, w/lid, #3562 ....9,000.00
Vase, brn & gr crystalline, gourd shape, 1920, 6", NM................75.00
Vase, HP floral, cherub hdls & finial, ca 1890-1900, 17"............835.00
Vase, owls emb in band, deep oxblood, Mogenson, 7x7" 350.00
Vase, pansies (6 lg) on shaded bl, globular, #900, 5¼" 335.00
Vase, school of fish among cattails on speckled wht, bulbous, 12¾"...440.00
Vase, tree, sun & deer, brn & gr tones, Salto, cylinder, 1941, 6¼"..1,275.00

Royal Copley

Royal Copley is a decorative type of pottery made by the Spaulding China Company in Sebring, Ohio, from 1942 to 1957. They also produced two other major lines — Royal Windsor and Spaulding. Royal Copley was primarily marketed through five-and-ten cent stores; Royal Windsor and Spaulding were sold through department stores, gift shops, and jobbers. Items trimmed in gold are worth 25% to 50% more than the same item with no gold trim.

For more information we recommend *Collector's Guide to Royal Copley Plus Royal Windsor & Spaulding, Books I* and *II*, by our advisor for this category, Joe Devine; he is listed in the Directory under Iowa.

Ashtray, pk w/brn edge, odd shaped, 6x9"	15.00
Bank, pig, wht shirt w/red stripes, 7½"	65.00
Bank, teddy bear, blk & wht, 7½"	90.00
Bowl, bird perched on side, 4"	20.00
Creamer, leaf hdls	35.00
Figurine, blk cat w/pk neckerchief, 8"	90.00
Figurine, bluebird, 5"	45.00
Figurine, Hunt's Swallow variants, bl, 8", pr, from $125 to	150.00
Figurine, kingfisher, 5", from $45 to	50.00
Figurine, lark, 5"	15.00
Figurine, nuthatch, 4½"	18.00
Figurine, titmouse, 8", from $25 to	30.00
Figurine, vireo, 4½"	14.00
Figurine, wren, 3½", from $20 to	24.00
Pitcher, Floral Beauty, yel flowers on beige over blk, 8"	60.00
Planter, angel, sm, 6¼"	48.00
Planter, Bamboo, oval, 5¾"	15.00
Planter, barefoot boy, 7½"	45.00
Planter, bear in basket, 8"	75.00
Planter, Big Blossoms, yel on gr, 3"	15.00
Planter, Blackamoor Prince head, 8", from $40 to	45.00
Planter, boy on bamboo bale sits beside bigger bale, 7½"	65.00
Planter, boy w/bucket, 6¼"	25.00
Planter, coach, rose colored, 3¼"	25.00

Planter, dog beside mailbox, from $35.00 to $45.00.

Planter, dogwood w/verse, Home Is Where the Heart Is, 4½"	30.00
Planter, Harmony, leaves in relief, 6½", from $40 to	45.00
Planter, Hildegard, rose & ivory, 2½x7¼"	20.00
Planter, hummingbird on flower, bl, 5¼"	60.00
Planter, Laura's Twigs, 5"	20.00
Planter, lt bl w/pk lining, boat shape w/bird tracks, 3¼"	18.00
Planter, nuthatch, yel, 5½"	20.00
Planter, Oriental boy w/arms around lg vase, 4¾", from $12 to	20.00
Planter, poodles, resting, 6½"	75.00
Planter, Riddle, oval, 4"	15.00
Planter, Siamese cats (2), 8"	125.00
Razor blade receptacle, barber pole, 6¼"	75.00
Vase, Carol's Corsage, 7", from $18 to	20.00
Vase, emb stylized leaf, 8¼"	15.00
Vase, fish shape, tan w/red striped fins, rare, 6"	125.00
Vase, Joyce decal, tab hdls, 4"	15.00
Window box, Harmony, 4½"	20.00

Royal Crown Derby

The Royal Crown Derby company can trace its origin back to 1848.

It first operated under the name of Locker & Co. but by 1859 had become Stevenson, Sharp & Co. Several changes in ownership occurred until 1866 when it became known as the Sampson Hancock Co. The Derby Crown Porcelain Co. Ltd. was formed in 1876, and these companies soon merged. In 1890 they were appointed as a manufacturer for the Queen and began using the name Royal Crown Derby.

In the early years, considerable 'Japan ware' decorated in Imari style, using red, blue, and gold in Oriental patterns was popular. The company excelled in their ability to use gold in the decoration, and some of the best flower painters of all time were employed. Nice vases or plaques signed by any of these artists will bring thousands of dollars: Gregory, Mosley, Rouse, Gresley, and D'esir'e Leroy. If you find a signed piece and are not sure of its value, if at all possible, it would be best to have it appraised by someone very knowledgeable regarding current market values.

As is usual among most other English factories, nearly all of the vases produced by Royal Crown Derby came with covers. If they are missing, deduct 40% to 45%. There are several well illustrated books available from antiques booksellers to help you learn to identify this ware. The back stamps used after 1891 will date every piece except dinnerware. The company is still in business, producing outstanding dinnerware and Imari-decorated figures and serving pieces. They also produce custom (one only) sets of table service for the wealthy of the world.

Bowl, cream soup; Imari, #2451, 1915, 7", +underplate	485.00
Bowl, cream soup; Imari, #2451, 1981-82	165.00
Bowl, fruit; Old Imari, #1128, ftd, 4x8½"	850.00
Bowl, fruit; Old Imari, #1128, octagonal, 4x8"	700.00
Bowl, muffin; Imari, #2451, 1915, w/dome lid, 5x8¾"	450.00
Bowl, Old Imari, #1128, w/hdls, 12½" W, w/lid	750.00
Bowl, Old Imari, #1128/MMI, oval, 2x10¼"	325.00
Bowl, rim soup; Blue Mikado, gold trim, 8"	65.00
Bowl, vegetable; Blue Mikado, oval, 10⅛"	200.00
Coffee set, Old Imari, #128, 3" pot, sug/cr, c/s, 7¾" oval tray	700.00
Cup & saucer, Blue Mikado, flat	40.00
Cup & saucer, Old Imari, #1128, 1920, 1¾", 5¾" dia	145.00
Dish, Imari, #2451, 1920, shaped oval, 1¼x5x7"	245.00
Dish, Old Imari, #1128, 1925, shaped dmn form, 9" L	650.00
Dish, serving; Imari, #2451/11, ftd, 11x8½"	650.00
Figurine, Russian Cat, Imari, bone china, 1988, 8½"	560.00
Gravy boat, Old Imari, #1128, 8" L, +8¼" underplate	400.00
Paperweight, fox figural, bl/purple/wht	615.00
Paperweight, ram, bl & gold fleece w/cobalt face, floral base, MIB	625.00
Pitcher, milk; Imari, #2451, 1915, 3¾"	175.00
Pitcher, Old Imari, #1128, str sides, 1985, mini, 1½x2½"	125.00
Plate, bread & butter; Blue Mikado, scalloped, 6¼"	14.00
Plate, dinner; Blue Mikado, 10⅜"	70.00
Plate, dinner; Imari, #1128, 1978, gold rim, 10½"	150.00
Plate, Gadroon, bird decor w/3 bird scenes & gold border, #3592, 9"	925.00
Plate, luncheon; Imari, #2451, 1900s, 8"	100.00
Platter, Imari, #383, 1911, hdls, 14x16"	450.00
Platter, Old Imari, #1128/MMI, oval, 14"	400.00
Shakers, Blue Mikdao, smooth or pointed top, pr	80.00
Sugar bowl, Old Imari, #1128, 1960, w/ear hdls, 3½x6"	275.00
Sugar box, Old Imari, #1128, bombè shape, gilt finial, 4¼"	700.00
Teapot, Blue Mikado, 6-cup, 5½"	360.00
Teapot, Imari, #8310, gold trim, 5x9"	350.00
Teapot, Old Imari, #1128, 1900, 5x10"	365.00
Tray, Old Imari, #1128, shaped oval, 9x13" L	700.00
Tureen, soup; Imari, #2451, ftd, 6½x8x8"	500.00
Tureen, soup; Old Imari, #1128, w/lid & 2-hdl underplate	665.00
Vase, Old Imari, #1128, 1924, 4½"	365.00
Vases, Imari, #876, bulbous w/cup neck & ½-scroll hdls, 1985, 7", pr	650.00
Watering can, Imari, #6299, 3x2x3½"	350.00

Royal Doulton, Doulton

The range of wares produced by the Doulton Company since its inception in 1815 has been vast and varied. The earliest wares produced in the tiny pottery in Lambeth, England, were salt-glazed pitchers, plain and fancy figural bottles, etc. — all utility-type stoneware geared to the practical needs of everyday living. The original partners, John Doulton and John Watts, saw the potential for success in the manufacture of drain and sewage pipes and during the 1840s concentrated on these highly lucrative types of commercial wares. Watts retired from the company in 1854, and Doulton began experimenting with a more decorative product line. As time went by, many glazes and decorative effects were developed, among them Faience, Impasto, Silicon, Carrara, Marqueterie, Chine, and Rouge Flambé. Tiles and architectural terra cotta were an important part of their manufacture. Late in the nineteenth century at the original Lambeth location, fine artware was decorated by such notable artists as Hannah and Arthur Barlow, George Tinworth, and J.H. McLennan. Stoneware vases with incised animal drawings, gracefully shaped urns with painted scenes, and cleverly modeled figurines rivaled the best of any competitor.

In 1882 a second factory was built in Burslem which continues even yet to produce the famous figurines, character jugs, series ware, and table services so popular with collectors today. Their Kingsware line, made from 1899 to 1946, featured flasks and flagons with drinking scenes, usually on a brown-glazed ground. Some were limited editions, while others were commemorative and advertising items. The Gibson Girl series, twenty-four plates in all, was introduced in 1901. It was drawn by Charles Dana Gibson and is recognized by its blue and white borders and central illustrations, each scene depicting a humorous or poignant episode in the life of 'The Widow and Her Friends.' Dickensware, produced from 1911 through the early 1940s, featured illustrations by Charles Dickens with many of his famous characters. The Robin Hood series was introduced in 1914; the Shakespeare series #1, portraying scenes from the Bard's plays, was made from 1914 until World War II. The Shakespeare series #2 ran from 1906 until 1974 and was decorated with featured characters. Nursery Rhymes was a series that was first produced in earthenware in 1930 and later in bone china. In 1933 a line of decorated children's ware, the Bunnykin series, was introduced; it continues to be made to the present day. About 150 'bunny' scenes have been devised, the earliest and most desirable being those signed by the artist Barbara Vernon. Most pieces range in value from $60.00 to $120.00.

Factors contributing to the value of a figurine are age, demand, color, and detail. Those with a limited production run and those signed by the artist or marked 'Potted' (indicating a pre-1939 origin) are also more valuable. After 1920 wares were marked with a lion — with or without a crown — over a circular 'Royal Doulton.'

Animals and Birds

Ashtead Applause, Collie, HN1057, 7½x10½" 550.00
Biddee of Ifield, Pekingese champion, HN1012, 1931-85, 3" 125.00
Bloodhound, HN2021 ....140.00
Bulldog, HN1045, lg 665.00
Cocker spaniel, HN1036, 1931-85, 5¼" 135.00
Cocker spaniel, HN1037, 3½" 225.00
Cocker spaniel in basket, HN2585, 1941-85, 2"......................100.00
Dog running w/ball, maroon ball, HN1097, 1934-85, 2" 125.00
Drake, standing, #137, med 200.00
Elephant, trunk up, HN2644, 5½"...230.00
Green-Wing Teal, HN3520..200.00
Hare, crouching, WK37..195.00
King of Corgis, HN2558, 1941-58, 5"....................................425.00
Kitten, licking bk paw, HN2580..140.00

Persian cat, model #690, 1930-85, 5"....................................125.00
Shrewd Saint, dachshund champion, HN1128, 1937-85, 4".......185.00
Siamese cat, HN2655 ....150.00
Tawny owl on plinth, #156A..365.00
Terrier, HN1022B, 8x10"..325.00
Warlord of Mazelaine, Boxer dog champion, brn & wht, HN2643, 6½"...200.00

Bunnykins

Autumn Days, DB5...365.00
Bedtime, DB55, brn teddy 45.00
Boy Skater, DB152 ....65.00
Boy Skater, DB187 ....150.00
Bridesmaid, DB173 ....55.00
Cheerleader, DB142 ....235.00
Choir Singer, DB233...75.00
Clean Sweep, DB6...85.00
Cowboy, DB201 ....165.00
Drummer, DB26 ....110.00
Family Photograph, DB1..125.00
Father, DB154..75.00
Gardener, DB156..45.00
Good Night, DB157..45.00
Harry, DB73...75.00
Indian, DB202..175.00
Irishman, DB178...195.00
Judge, DB188...75.00
Mr Bunnykins at Easter Parade, DB18 ....85.00
Nurse, DB74A 295.00
Partners in Collecting, DB151 ....165.00
Sailor, DB166...60.00
Santa, dB17..85.00
Schoolmaster, DB60..65.00
Sleepytime, DB15 ....55.00
Sleigh Ride, DB81...175.00
Tally Ho, DB12...115.00
Tourist, DB190...75.00
Uncle Sam, DB175..250.00
Wizard, DB168 ....325.00

Character Jugs

'Ard of 'Earring, D6591, 1964-67, sm....................................915.00
'Arriet, D6208, 1947-60, lg...150.00
'Arriet, D6236, 1947-60, sm 90.00
'Arriet, D6250, 1947-60, mini 65.00
Ann Boleyn, D6644, 1975-90, lg...120.00
Anne of Cleves, D6754, 1987-90, mini 120.00
Auld Mac, D5823, 1940-86, lg...70.00
Bacchus, D6521, 1960-91, mini..55.00
Beefeater, D6236, 1946-53, lg...130.00
Beefeater, D6251, 1946-53, mini, from $55 to.........................70.00
Betsy Trotwood, D6685, tiny 60.00
Blacksmith, D6585, 1963-83, mini..45.00
Captain Ahab, D6500, 1959-84, lg..100.00
Captain Ahab, D6522, 1960-84, mini......................................60.00
Captain Henry Morgan, D6467, 1958-82, lg 95.00
Captain Hook, D6597, 1965-71, lg..465.00
Captain Hook, D6605, 1965-71, mini....................................340.00
Cardinal, D5614, 1936-60, lg..125.00
Catherine Howard, D6692, 1984-89, sm................................175.00
Cavalier, D6114, 1950-60, lg...110.00
Cavalier, D6173, 1941-60, sm...40.00
Clown - Brown Hair, D5610, 1937-42, rare, lg 4,000.00

Custer & Sitting Bull, D6712, brn eyes, lg 250.00
Dick Turpin, D6528, horse hdl, 1960-81, lg 150.00
Drake, D6115, 1940-60, lg...125.00
Farmer John, D5789, ca 1950, sm...50.00
Fat Boy, D5840, odd sz...300.00
Fat Boy, D6142, 1940-60, tiny...65.00
Fireman, D6697, 1983-91, lg...140.00
Fortune Teller, D6503, 1959-67, sm, from $325 to.............375.00
Fortune Teller, D6523, 1960-67, mini, from $315 to..........330.00
Gaoler, D6584, 1963-83, mini..50.00
Gardener, D6638, 1973-78, mini...85.00
Gladiator, D6556, mini...350.00
Guardsman, D6568, 1963-83, lg...110.00
Gunsmith, D6573, 1963-83, lg...100.00
Izaak Walton, D6604, 1953-82, lg..90.00
John Peel, D6130, 1940-60, mini...80.00
Johnny Appleseed, D6372, shaded rim, 1953-69, lg............315.00
Lawyer, D6504, sm...65.00
London Bobby, D6762, 1987, sm...160.00
Lumberjack, D6613, 1967-82, sm...40.00
Merlin, D6529, 1960-98, lg..70.00
Mikado, The; D6501, 1959-69, lg...585.00
Mikado, The; D6507, 1959-69, sm...300.00
Mikado, The; D6525, 1960-69, mini, from $375 to 400.00
Mine Host, D6513, 1960-82, mini..55.00
Mr Micawber, D5839, 1948-60, sm..70.00

Neptune, D6552, miniature, $70.00.

Old Charley, D6046, ca 1941, mini..40.00
Old Charley, D6791, 1987, sm...175.00
Oscar Wilde, D7146, 2000 Jug of the Year, 6¾".................230.00
Paddy, D5768, 1937-60, sm...50.00
Parson Brown, D5529, ca 1950, sm...55.00
Pearly Girl, D6208, lg..1,000.00
Pied Piper, D6403, 1954-81, lg..145.00
Postman, D6801, 1988, sm...230.00
Punch & Judy Man, D6593, 1964-69, mini............................360.00
Regency Beau, D6559, 1962-67, lg......................................1,150.00
Romeo, D6670, 1983-89, lg..85.00
Sairey Gamp, D5451, 1935-86, lg..65.00
Sam Johnson, D6296, 1950-60, sm...160.00
Sam Weller, D6140, ca 1950, mini...50.00
Sergeant Buzfuz, D5838, ca 1950, sm......................................90.00
Simon the Cellarer, D5616, 1936-60, sm..................................60.00
Simple Simon, D6374, 1953-60, lg...500.00
Smuggler, D6619, sm..75.00
St George, D6618, earthenware, 1968-75, lg..........................295.00
St George, D6621, 1968-75, sm..180.00
Tam O'Shanter, D6636, 1973-80, sm..75.00
Tony Weller, D5531, 1936-60, lg..160.00
Tony Weller, D6044, 1939-60, mini..45.00

Town Crier, D6537, 1960-73, sm..120.00
Ugly Duchess, D6599, 1965-73, lg...595.00
Veteran Motorist, D6641, 1973-83, mini..................................75.00
Viking, D6502, 1959-75, sm...140.00
Wild Bill Hickock, D6736, 1985-89, mid sz 120.00

Figurines

A Penny's Worth, HN2408 ....175.00
Afternoon Tea, HN1747...600.00
Aileen, HN1664 ....1,000.00
Amy, HN3316...525.00
And One For You, HN2970 ....175.00
Angela, HN3419...315.00
Anthea, HN1527...775.00
Apple Maid, HN2160..250.00
Auctioneer, HN2988...550.00
Ballad Seller, HN2766..275.00
Ballerina, HN2116, 1st version...360.00
Balloon Lady, HN1315..225.00
Balloon Lady, HN2935..295.00
Balloon Man, HN1954, from $300 to......................................350.00
Bedtime Story, HN2059 ....375.00
Belle o' the Ball, HN1997...395.00
Biddy Penny Farthing, HN1843 ....255.00
Blacksmith, HN2782...225.00
Blossom, HN1667..1,590.00
Blue Beard, HN2105, 2nd version..535.00
Boudoir, HN2542..295.00
Bride, HN1600..700.00
Bride, HN2166..275.00
Broken Lance, HN2041...320.00
Calumet, HN1689, Noke...1,100.00
Camille, HN1736...950.00
Captain, HN2260..310.00
Carmen, HN2545..275.00
Carpet Seller, HN1464, from $300 to......................................350.00
Carrie, HN2800...255.00
Charley's Aunt, HN24...350.00
Child Study, HN603B...235.00
Christine, HN1840...1,200.00
Christmas Parcels, HN2851..250.00
Christmas Time, HN2110, from $350 to 400.00
Cissie, HN1809...175.00
Clemency, HN1634...520.00
Coralie, HN2307..125.00
Craftsman, HN2284...345.00
Daffy Down Dilly, HN1712 ....320.00
Darling, HN1985, 2nd version 80.00
Day Dreams, HN1732, from $700 to.......................................750.00
Detective, HN2359..300.00
Dinky Do, HN1678...65.00
Doctor, HN2858, from $250 to 300.00
Doreen, HN1389..1,020.00
Duke of Wellington, HN3432, limited edition 1,450.00
Eleanor, HN4463...220.00
Emma, HN2834, from $325 to...375.00
Fair Lady, HN2193..225.00
Faith, HN3082...200.00
Falstaff, HN2054...160.00
Fat Boy, HN1893 ....325.00
Father Christmas, HN3399...265.00
Favorite, HN2249..220.00
Fiddler, HN2171 ....450.00

Fleur, HN2368...260.00
Flower Seller's Children, HN1342 ....700.00
Fortune Teller, HN2159...........................650.00
Forty Winks, HN1974 ....325.00
Friar Tuck, HN2143................................350.00
Genevieve, HN1962, from $250 to...........300.00
Genie, HN2989..240.00
Giselle, HN2139 ....240.00
Grandma, HN2052...................................275.00
Greta, HN1485, from $350 to...................400.00
Gwynneth, HN1980.................................395.00
Harriet, HN3794......................................225.00
Hornpipe, HN2161..................................365.00
Hostess of Williamsburg, HN2209 ....210.00
In the Stocks, HN2163 ....1,195.00
Invitation, HN2170.................................225.00
Irene, HN1621, from $350 to...................400.00
Isadora, HN2938.....................................275.00
Ivy, HN1768..275.00
Jack Point, HN2080 ....1,600.00
Jacqueline, HN2000................................285.00
Jacqueline, HN2001................................495.00
Jane, HN1990 ....320.00
Jane Eyre, HN3842.................................400.00
Janice, HN2165, from $350 to.................425.00
Jester, HN1702..520.00
Jovial Monk, HN2144, from $225 to 275.00
Julia, HN2706...175.00
June, HN1691, from $650 to....................700.00
Katrina, HN2327.....................................285.00
Lady April, HN1958................................395.00
Lady Betty, HN1967, from $350 to..........400.00
Lady Charmian, HN1949 ....275.00
Laura, HN3136..275.00
Lavinia, HN1955.....................................140.00
Leisure Hour, HN2055.............................520.00
Lobster Man, HN2317.............................200.00
Lorna, HN2311..225.00
Lorna, HN2311, from $210 to..................225.00
Lydia, HN1908..195.00
Margery, HN1413 ....375.00
Margot, HN1636......................................500.00
Marguerite, HN1928, from $450 to..........500.00
Mask Seller, HN2103..............................325.00
Maureen, HN1770...................................500.00
Mendicant, HN1365................................325.00
Mermaid, HN9717...................................320.00
Miss Muffet, HN1936, from $185 to 225.00
Monica, HN1467......................................190.00
Moor, The; HN1366..............................1,800.00
Mr Micawber, HN557..............................300.00
Ninette, HN2379.....................................285.00
Noelle, HN2179.......................................450.00
Old Balloon Seller, HN1315 ....300.00
Old King Cole, HN2217...........................215.00
Omar Khayyam, HN2247.........................200.00
Orange Lady, HN1759.............................280.00
Orange Vendor, HN1966..........................665.00
Paisley Shawl, HN1392...........................425.00
Paisley Shawl, HN1987...........................350.00
Partners, HN3119....................................275.00
Pearly Boy, HN2767 ....220.00
Penelope, HN1901...................................390.00
Pensive Moments, HN2704......................260.00

Philippine Dancer, HN2439....................425.00
Phyllis, HN1420......................................320.00
Pied Piper, HN2102, from $235 to...........285.00
Potter, HN1493..525.00
Potter, HN1493, from $535 to..................585.00
Premiere, HN2343...................................350.00
Pretty Polly, HN2768..............................200.00
Pride & Joy, HN2945...............................350.00
Prized Possessions, HN2942....................550.00
Professor, HN2281..................................200.00
Promenade, HN2076.............................1,340.00
Punch & Judy Man, HN2765....................350.00
Puppetmaker, HN2253.............................550.00
Queen Elizabeth I, HN3099 ....350.00
Red Red Rose, HN3994...........................225.00
Reflections, HN3073...............................185.00
Reverie, HN2306.....................................275.00
Roseanna, HN1921, from $550 to............600.00
Rosebud, HN1983, from $325 to..............375.00
Royal Governor's Cook, HN2233 ....650.00
Sabbath Morn, HN1982...........................295.00
Santa Claus, HN2725..............................400.00
Secret Thoughts, HN2382........................225.00
Sir Walter Raleigh, HN2015....................260.00
Skater, HN2117.......................................450.00
Sleep, HN 424...620.00
Solitude, HN2810....................................300.00
Song of the Sea, HN2729........................255.00
Sonia, HN11692......................................675.00
Spanish Flamenco Dancer, HN2831 ....850.00
Spring, HN2085.......................................440.00
Spring Flowers, HN1807..........................320.00
Springtime, HN3033, from $275 to..........300.00
Stayed at Home, HN2207........................250.00
Summer, HN2086, from $325 to..............375.00
Suzette, HN2026......................................420.00
Sweet & Twenty, HN1298, 1st version.....400.00
Thank You, HN2732................................200.00
Thanks Doc, HN2731...............................240.00
Tom, HN2864..225.00
Tootles, HN1680......................................195.00
Uncle Ned, HN2094, from $300 to 350.00
Veronica, HN1517...................................395.00
Victoria, HN2471....................................350.00
Vivienne, HN2073...................................325.00
Wayfarer, HN2362...................................250.00
Willy-Won't-He, HN1561.........................350.00
Young Master, HN2872............................275.00

Flambé

Unless another color is noted, all flambé in the listing that follows is red.

Character jug, Aladdin's Genie, bl, 1994, 7½"............550.00
Character jug, Aladdin's Genie, D6971 ....385.00
Compote, Sung, trees/deer/leafy bands, EX color, Noke/#936, 9" .5,250.00
Figurine, Airedale (dog), 5½x5".......................825.00
Figurine, dragon, red mottle w/bl & yel, late 20th C, 7½" 825.00
Figurine, drake, resting, #112, 2".....................100.00
Figurine, elephant, wht w/bl highlights, 5"........265.00
Figurine, Emperor penguin, #84.......................160.00
Figurine, fox, seated, 1912-46, 3"....................350.00
Figurine, fox, stalking, #29A, 2¾x12½"............625.00
Figurine, Geisha, #3229, 9½"...........................215.00

Figurine, Images of Fire, 2 birds, red & blk, 17" 640.00
Figurine, lop-eared rabbit, seated, wht w/bl highlights...............140.00
Figurine, penguin, standing, 6", from $175 to............................225.00
Figurine, Seated Carpet Seller, HN3277, mc, 7½" 320.00
Jug, Confucious, D7003, 1995, 7¾" 415.00
Plate, Palm Tree, Fred Moore, bl scene on wht 90.00
Vase, cottage in wooded lot w/flowers, Woodcut, bottle shape, 16"..450.00
Vase, farmers & team of horses, Woodcut #1613, 6" 170.00
Vase, horned cattle, squat bottom w/slender neck, 5¼" 170.00
Vase, male figure/sheep, Woodcut, sm neck/wide tapered body, 5⅜"...250.00
Vase, mallard drake, Sung, Noke/FM, ovoid w/flared neck, 6⅜" ...1,800.00
Vase, Persian merchant/pots on deep bl, D-4524, bulbous, 7½" 1,000.00
Vase, shouldered w/short can neck, F Moore, 5⅝" 375.00
Vase, St Marks Square, #11, bl scene on wht, 3¾"....................185.00
Vase, Sung, red/bl/br/wht mottle, flared rim on ovoid, 6¾" 375.00
Vase, Veined, bulbous w/sm neck, #1616, 9" 600.00
Vase, Veined #1614, red over blk, 6" 110.00

Series Ware

Bowl, Richmond Castle, D4643, 10½x8" 115.00
Candlestick, Shakespeare, Romeo, flat top & bottom, 6½", ea 45.00
Charger, Jackdaw of Rheims, D2532, 12½" 135.00
Creamer, Dickens, Fagin, 3x2x5" 130.00
Creamer, Dickens, Mr Pickwick, 3x5" 130.00
Cup & saucer, Pied Piper, Kingsware 100.00
Cup & saucer, Tea for One, coaching scene, cup mk #3804 ....90.00
Dish, Countryside, The Village, 1¾x6½" 55.00
Figurine, Dickens, Fagin, 4" 150.00
Jug, Dickens, Pickwick Papers, D5756, sq body, 5⅝" 175.00
Jug, Dickens, Sam Weller, 2½" 225.00
Jug, Robin Hood, Under the Greenwood Tree, 7¼" 185.00
Plate, Dickens, Bill Sykes, D6327, retired 1960 ....125.00
Plate, Dickens, Bust of Charles Dickens, 10¼" 125.00
Plate, Dog Series, English Setter, #6313, 10¼" 115.00
Plate, Dog Series, Pointer, D5769 ....100.00
Plate, English Castles & Cathedrals, 10½", 9 for 650.00
Plate, Gaffers, man in wht coat w/tall blk hat, D4210, 9½" 115.00
Plate, Gibson Girl, Miss Babbles...Morning Paper..., 10½" 150.00
Plate, Gibson Girl, Quiet Dinner w/Dr Bottles..., 10½" 150.00
Plate, Gibson Girl, She Becomes a Trained Nurse, 10½" 150.00
Plate, Gibson Girl, She Goes to the Fancy Dress Ball, 10½"......135.00
Plate, Gibson Girl, Widow & Her Friends, #10, 10½"...............165.00
Plate, Home Waters, D6434, 8¼" 35.00
Plate, Hunting Man, D6282, 10½" dia 50.00
Plate, Jock of the Bushveld, 4 men & dog around fire, D5464, 10" ...80.00
Plate, Parson, D6280, 10⅛"...65.00
Plate, Professionals, Admiral, #1045, 10½" 85.00
Plate, Professionals, Doctor, D5906, retired 1948.....................150.00
Plate, Professionals, Falconer, D3756 ....95.00
Plate, Shakespeare, Bust of Shakespeare, 10¼" 125.00
Plate, Shakespeare, Hamlet, D3596, sq, 7¾" 85.00
Plate, Shakespeare, Katherine, 10¼" 165.00
Plate, Shakespeare, Portia, 10" 95.00
Plate, Shakespeare, Shylock, D3596, 10¼" 155.00
Sugar bowl, Dickens, Mr Pickwick, open, 3½x6½x3½" 130.00
Tankard, Cavaliers, D1719, #7119A, 5½" 45.00
Vase, Blue Children, 3 girls outdoors, 8x8½" 675.00
Vase, Falstaff w/forest bkground, flared bottom, #7013, 2¼x2½" .50.00
Wash set, Aubrey pattern, Babes in Woods, 5-pc......................1,750.00

Miscellaneous

Ashtray, mc bird on bl stump, stoneware, 4½" 415.00

Bottle, Doulton's Thermette Bed Warmer, stoneware, #5347420..105.00
Ewer, lt brn w/dk maroon top & hdl, stoneware, Slater #5237 RH, 6½"..65.00
Flagon, lt brn w/floral border, dk top, stoneware, #1319, 2¾" 55.00
Jar, appl vines & lace band around neck, w/lid, Silicone, 6x5"...135.00
Jardiniere, leaves, wht on brn, stoneware, Lambeth, 1890s, 9¾"...475.00
Jug, blade-like panels w/cvd leaves & beads, appl face, Silicone, 8" ...165.00
Jug, Special Highland Whiskey (sic), sailing ship, Greenlees Bros, 7".2,100.00
Pin dish, dragonfly on bl pool, stoneware, 5¾" 130.00
Pitcher, brn w/relief deer & tavern scenes, stoneware, Lambeth, 6½"...100.00
Pitcher, motto; He Who Buys...; stoneware, dtd 1947, 6½" 85.00
Pitcher, rows of beading w/diagonals, tankard form, Silicone, 4x5".110.00
Vase, cattle/donkey/bull frieze cvg, Hannah Barlow, #4790, 9¾"..800.00
Vase, Chinè, cobalt w/wide foliage border, #7583, Slater's Pat, 6", pr..90.00
Vase, deer frieze cvg, appl rosettes, Hannah Barlow/1877, 14"...2,300.00
Vase, floral & grapes, stoneware, #7941, 5½" 160.00
Vase, leaf border, brn over gray, hdls, stoneware, Lambeth, #9991, 4"..75.00
Vase, Natural Foliage Ware, autumn leaves, lion/crown mk/#6787, 12"..300.00
Vase, Nouveau floral tan reserve on bl, dbl gourd, stoneware, 8", pr..750.00
Vase, rows of floral arches, Silicone, 6x3", pr 200.00

Royal Dux

The Duxer Porzellan Manufactur was established by E. Eichler in 1860. Located in what is now Duchcov, Czechoslovakia, the area was known as Dux, Bohemia, until WWI. The war brought about changes in both the style of the ware as well as the mark. Prewar pieces were modeled in the Art Nouveau or Greek Classical manner and marked with 'Bohemia' and a pink triangle containing the letter 'E.' They were usually matt glazed in green, brown, and gold. Better pieces were made of porcelain, while the larger items were of pottery. After the war the ware was marked with the small pink triangle but without the Bohemia designation; 'Made in Czechoslovakia' was added. The style became Art Deco, with cobalt blue a dominant color.

Vases, mid-Eastern couple beside palms, late nineteenth century, 36", EX, $1,250.00 for the pair.

Bowl, entwined iris blossom & cattail, nymph & putto at side, 14" .825.00
Bowl, lady kneeling over shell bowl, #598, 10½x7x12½"...........525.00
Centerpc, 2 inverted shells centered by draped nymph on base, 17"..650.00
Centerpc, 2 seminude ladies mounting conch shell, waves at base, 18"..1,300.00
Dish, couple stands on shell w/fence in bk, 11¾" 720.00
Figurine, cockatoo, wht w/red & yel feathers, #402/214, 15½"..140.00
Figurine, female drying ft on rocky craig, early 1900s, 18½" ...1,000.00
Figurine, flamenco dancer, #158/58, 24" 490.00
Figurine, lady in bl shirt & pants w/hand to mouth, #334/14.....500.00
Figurine, lady in lt purple w/1 hand holding dress, #1987/210, 13".125.00
Figurine, lady on rock w/2 wht birds, all on shell, #2105, 9" 440.00
Figurine, nude bather, #2942/1, 11½x4x4½" 610.00
Figurine, nude on plinth, #711, 8¾" 175.00
Figurine, nude playing banjo on blk & wht stool, 14¼".........1,025.00

Figurine, Oriental dancer, man in wht w/gold & red, #3809, 9".525.00
Figurine, parrot on perch, #24500/210, 13½"...........................125.00
Figurine, pheasant, #315/28/32, 12½".....................................200.00
Figurine, seminude w/long drape, arms outstretched, #3251, 12½".560.00
Figurine, shepherd w/staff, shepherdess w/instrument, 22"..........825.00
Figurine, Water Carrier, dressed in gr, #974/5, 12".....................300.00
Vase, 3-D maid sits on edge of well/fills water jug, 17"............**1,350.00**

Royal Flemish

Royal Flemish was introduced in the late 1880s and was patented in 1894 by the Mt. Washington Glass Company. Transparent glass was enameled with one or several colors and the surface divided by a network of raised lines suggesting leaded glasswork. Some pieces were further decorated with enameled florals, birds, or Roman coins. Our advisors for this category are Betty and Clarence Maier; they are listed in the Directory under Pennsylvania.

Bottle, cologne; 3 butterflies, ornate purple/gold bands, 5½x5" ..**6,100.00**
Cracker jar, Guba duck, 9½" to top of bail................................**3,750.00**
Cracker jar, rose/gold leaves/scrolls, ovoid; ornate metal mts, 10x6"..**2,750.00**
Cracker jar, sections w/mc flowers, emb lid mk MW, heart-shape hdl, 7" .**1,600.00**
Cracker jar, thistles, sq, Pairpoint lid w/rpr hdl, 11" overall **900.00**
Ewer, lad spears winged creature, much gold, rnd body, 11" **6,500.00**
Ewer, ornate floral w/gold on frost, sgn FR, rope hdl, #566, 13¾" .**3,300.00**
Ewer, panels/medallions w/mums & gilt, metal top, 12x5½"......**7,500.00**
Ewer, 8 gold-floral panels & 16 medallions, 12x5½" **8,500.00**
Lamp, banquet; thistles, gold-lined lav & amber, no shade, 25"..**1,900.00**
Pickle castor, pansies w/gold on wht satin; Tufts SP fr, 10½" ..**2,900.00**
Tumbler, scrolls, pk on wht, gold wild roses, 4¼"......................**2,200.00**
Vase, Garden of Allah, gold discs w/birds & symbols, 13¾"....**5,750.00**
Vase, snow geese/gold sun & stars, 14½x5" **8,450.00**
Vase, winged griffin, bk: dragon, on geometric panels, bulbous, 10" .**4,200.00**
Vase, 3 gold coins, 1 w/griffin, squat w/distended decorated neck, 11" ...**2,750.00**

Royal Haeger, Haeger

In 1871 David Henry Haeger, a young son of German immigrants, purchased a brick factory at Dundee, Illinois. David's bricks rebuilt Chicago after their great fire in 1871. Many generations of the Haeger family have been associated with the ceramic industry, that his descendants have pursued to the present time. Haeger progressed to include artware in their production as early as 1914. That was only the beginning. In the '30s they began to make a line of commercial dinnerware that was marketed through Marshall Fields. Not long after, Haeger's artware was successful enough that a second plant in Macomb, Illinois, was built.

Royal Haeger was their premium line beginning in 1938 and continuing into modern-day production. The chief designer in the '40s was Royal Arden Hickman, a talented artist and sculptor who also worked in mediums other than pottery. For Haeger he designed a line of wonderfully stylized animals, birds, high-style vases, and human figures, all with extremely fine details. His designs are highly regarded by collectors today.

Paper labels have been used throughout Haeger's production. Some items from the teens, '20s and '30s will be found with 'Haeger' in a diamond shape in-mold script mark. Items with 'RG' (Royal Garden) are part of their Flower-Ware line (also called Regular Haeger or Genuine Haeger). Haeger has produced a premium line (Royal Haeger) as well as a regular line for many years, it just has changed names over the years.

Collectors need to be aware that a certain glaze can bring two to three times more than others. Items that have Royal Hickman in the mold mark or on the label are usually higher valued than without his mark. The current collector trend has leaned more towards the mid-cen-

tury modern styled pieces of artware. The most desired items are those done by glaze designers Helmut Bruchman and Alrun Osterberg Guest (presently employed by Haeger). These items are from the late '60s into the very early '80s.

For those wanting to learn more about this pottery, we recommend *Haeger Potteries Through the Years* by our advisor for this category, David Dilley (L-W Books); he is listed in the Directory under Indiana.

#47, Bowl, Chartreuse, 2½x13¼"...15.00
#128, Ashtray, Gold Tweed, 13x8x2½"...10.00
#243, Twisted stem candle holder, Peach Agate, 7½", ea............40.00
#257, Vase w/relief design, Briar Agate, 9¼" 15.00
#329-H, Pheasant bowl, Gold Tweed, 21¼" L.............................40.00
#342, Bowl, hexagonal, ped ft, Lilac, 6x7"...................................15.00
#345-S, Bowl, scalloped/indented, Lilac, 5x4".............................20.00
#364-H, Lily bowl, yel-orange w/dk tips, 16¼" L.......................30.00
#373-H, Bowl, Madarin Orange, 15" L...20.00
#450, Urn bowl, Gold Tweed, 6x4⅜"...15.00
#489, Sculpted vase, Cotton White & Turquoise, 14" 50.00
#616, Teddy bear planter, Chartreuse, 4¾"...................................15.00
#759, Bowl, dk purple w/lt bl & wht, 6½".....................................30.00
#834, Planter, octagonal, Peasant Red/White, 8½" dia 8.00
#863, Diamond Pattern bowl, tan/wht, 2¾x9¾"............................8.00
#878-H, Bud serving tray, Mandarin Orange, 14" L 25.00
#889, Lighter, ribbed, Mandarin Orange, 5" 15.00
#3003, Compote, Cotton White & Turquoise, 12" L 15.00
#3068, Triple candle holder dish, brn w/wht accents, 12" dia.......45.00
#3318, Colonial girl planter, Chartreuse, 9" 20.00
#3622, Bookends, Chartreuse, 7x4¾x5" 35.00
#3961, Square dish, bl w/blk specks, 2½x8x8" 8.00
#4233-X, Vase, Brown Earth Graphic Wrap, 11".........................30.00
#8170, Candy box w/rooster lid, Roman Bronze, 3x5x9" 75.00
#8172, Bowl planter, Roman Bronze, 6½x8¾"..............................75.00
#8183-X, Pitcher vase, orange/yel w/dk spots, 12¼"......................15.00
#8296, Toe Tapper, Bennington Brown Foam, 9¼", from $50 to..65.00
R-112, Leaf-Edges bowl, Green Agate, 2½x13½" L 75.00
R-224, Daisy bowl, Chartreuse, 2x11¾"..40.00
R-277, Spiral Plume dish, Peach Agate, 7" L 20.00
R-284, Trout vase, Mauve Agate, 7x9" L 60.00
R-290, Cut-out 'V' bowl, Mauve Agate, 10¼" 75.00
R-297, Shell dish, Chartreuse & Silver Spray, 14" L....................30.00
R-298, Cornucopia vase, Boco White on pk, 11" L......................60.00
R-303, Laurel Wreath Bow vase, Mauve Agate, 12x7¾" 75.00
R-304, Fish candle holder, Mauve Agate, 4¼" 60.00
R-320, Elm Leaf vase, Mauve Agate, 12"......................................30.00
R-321, Shell vase, ftd, Chartreuse & white, 7¾"............................25.00
R-333, Bowl, lilac, 16¼" L..20.00
R-352, Bowl, ftd rectangle, Black Mistique, 14½" L 60.00
R-370, Dutch Cup bowl, Green Agate, 18½" L 40.00
R-371, Whirling bowl, bl, 12¾" L...25.00
R-421, Bowl w/fruit clusters, ftd, 7x14½" L 50.00
R-433, Triple Plume candle holder, Mauve Agate, 11" L.............25.00
R-455, Bow vase, wht w/bl bow, 14" 75.00
R-457, Triple leaf dish w/bird finial, Mauve Agate, 8½".............50.00
R-459, Triple shell candy dish w/fish finial, bl, 8½" L.................50.00
R-460, Leaf bowl, lt gr, 5x12" L...50.00
R-475, Calla Lily bookends, amber, 4½"..75.00
R-476, Beaded bowl, Chartreuse & Silver Spray, 15" L...............25.00
R-481, Seashell on ftd vase, Silver Spray & Chartreuse................75.00
R-484, Garden bowl, Chartreuse & Ebony, 13½" L 15.00
R-525, Tulip planter (dbl), Mallow on wht, 9¾" L.......................75.00
R-527, Pillow vase, Chartreuse & Silver Spray, 7¼".....................25.00
R-575, Rose of Sharon basket, Chartreuse/red flowers, 7" dia.......75.00
R-579, Block candle holder (dbl tier), Green Briar, 2x2".............20.00

R-614, Scroll bowl, Green Agate, 14½" L....................................100.00
R-657, Gonolier planter, Green Agate, 19" L................................75.00
R-967, Starfish bowl, Pearl Gray Drip, 14½" L...........................60.00
R-1195, Abstract Fish bowl, lt pk/wht spots, 14½" L...................25.00
R-1446, Basket planter, Turquoise Blue, 9x6½" dia....................15.00
R-1462, Wheelbarrow planter, Briar Agate, 9½" L 15.00
R-1729, Compote, fluted, beige/gold (rough), 9"......................20.00
R-1746, Boat-shaped candle holders, Lilac, 6" L, pr....................20.00
R-1752-W, Eccentric vase, Cotton White & Turquoise, 16¾".....40.00
S-0552, 'S' bowl, mk Studio Haeger, 14¼" L...............................10.00

Royal Rudolstadt

The hard-paste porcelain that has come to be known as Royal Rudolstadt was produced in Thuringia, Germany, in the early eighteenth century. Various names and marks have been associated with this pottery. One of the earliest was a hay-fork symbol associated with Johann Frederich von Schwarzburg-Rudolstadt, one of the founders. Variations, some that included an 'R,' were also used. In 1854 Earnst Bohne produced wares that were marked with an anchor and the letters 'EB.' Examples commonly found today were made during the late 1800s and early twentieth century. These are usually marked with an 'RW' within a shield under a crown and the words 'Crown Rudolstadt.' Items marked 'Germany' were made after 1890.

Biscuit jar, pk/yel roses on wht, gold bow finial, swirled body, 7"..400.00
Bowl, cherub in chariot drawn by winged lion, C-scroll base, 11½".350.00
Bowl, wht roses w/gr leaves, 2¼x9½"...135.00
Cake plate, pk roses w/gr leaves & vines, gold trim, 8½"..............90.00
Celery dish, wht roses w/gr leaves, gold trim, 4x8½"....................50.00
Cup & saucer, pk roses w/gr leaves, gold trim..............................65.00
Plate, apples & roses border, gold trim, 8½"................................50.00
Reamer, pk buds w/gr leaves on wht, gold trim, 2-pc, 3½x4¼"..140.00
Vase, birds & flowers, urn shape, sm gold hdls, ca 1905, 8"........140.00
Vase, L'Amour Desarme, nymph & putto, globular, hdls, 10½"..850.00
Vase, swirled w/florals on wht, gold ft/hdls, bulbous, ca 1905, 6x5"..70.00
Vase, 2 Chinese boys hold horn-shape vase, cream, 4½x7"..........70.00

Royal Vienna

In 1719 Claude Innocentius de Paquier established a hard-paste porcelain factory in Vienna where he made highly ornamental wares similar to the type produced at Meissen. Early wares were usually unmarked; but after 1744 when the factory was purchased by the Empress, the Austrian shield (often called 'beehive') was stamped on under the glaze. In the following listings, values are for hand-painted items unless noted otherwise. Decal-decorated items would be considerably lower.

Note: There is a new resurgence of interest in this fine porcelain, but an influx of Japanese reproductions on the market has affected values on genuine old Royal Vienna. Buyer beware! On new items the beehive mark is over the glaze, the weight of the porcelain is heavier, and the decoration is obviously decaled. Our advisor for this category is Madeleine France; she is listed in the Directory under Florida.

Bowl, couple/maid/child in garden reserve on cobalt/wht w/gilt, 12x10"...400.00
Charger, Armors Triumph scene, geometric borders, 1860s, 13¼"..1,400.00
Clock, mantel; putti on dome & in reserves on sq base, bronze mts, 17"...3,000.00
Cracker jar, pk roses w/sm purple flowers on wht, 6½x9"..........645.00
Cup & saucer, Fatima portrait on cobalt, early 1900s, 4½", 5"...220.00
Figurine, Blackamoor w/butterfly, #1522, 3¼"...........................700.00
Figurine, lady on bench w/book, man at shoulder, 1900s, 10¾".265.00
Figurine, Lippizan stallion w/trainer, #1833, 12x10½"................775.00

Plate, Lady Scheffield portrait, Wagner, beehive mk, 10"........1,125.00
Plate, nude lovers by water's edge, ornate gold border, Wagner, 9½".1,300.00
Plate, Waldesflustern, lady sits, cherub on shoulder, Wagner, 9½"..475.00
Tureen, neoclassical figures on pk & bl, fruit & foliage, 15"....1,900.00
Urn, allegorical scenes after Le Monier w/gold, w/lid, 39".......4,750.00
Urn, philosophers & warriors on cobalt w/gold, sgn Jackl, 12¼"...660.00
Vase, Countess Litta, wht & lt purple w/gold, 7¼".................1,275.00
Vase, lady w/Cupid over shoulder, mc w/gold, 10½"...............1,900.00
Vase, Madame Le Brun, bulbous w/flared scalloped rim, gold hdls, 7"..1,200.00

Vase, portrait of lady on gilt-decorated cobalt, lion ring handles, 11", $850.00.

Roycroft

Near the turn of the twentieth century, Elbert Hubbard established the Roycroft Printing Shop in East Aurora, New York. Named in honor of two seventeenth-century printer-bookbinders, the print shop was just the beginning of a community called Roycroft, which came to be known worldwide. Hubbard became a popular personality of the early 1900s, known for his talents in a variety of areas from writing and lecturing to manufacturing. The Roycroft community became a meeting place for people of various capabilities and included shops for the production of furniture, copper, leather items, and a multitude of other wares which were marked with the Roycroft symbol, an 'R' within a circle below a double-barred cross. Hubbard lost his life on the Lusitania in 1915; production at the community continued until the Depression.

Interest is strong in the field of Arts and Crafts in general and in Roycroft items in particular. Copper items are evaluated to a large extent by the condition and type of the original patina. The most desirable patina is either the dark or medium brown; brass-wash, gunmetal, and silver-wash patinas follow in desirability. The acid-etched patina and the smooth (unhammered) surfaced Roycroft pieces are later (after 1925) developments and tend not to be attractive to collectors. Furniture was manufactured in oak, mahogany, bird's-eye maple, and occasionally walnut or ash; collectors prefer oak. Books with Levant binding, tooled leather covers, Japan vellum, or hand illumining are especially collectible; suede cover and parchment paper books are of less interest to collectors as they are fairly common. In the listings that follow, values reflect the worth of items in excellent original condition unless noted to the contrary. For more information see *Roycroft Furniture and Collectibles* by Larry Koon. Our advisor for this category is Bruce Austin; he is listed in the Directory under New York.

Key: h/cp — hammered copper

Ashtray, h/cp riveted to tooled/weighted leather strap, 2¼x14"..275.00
Bed, vertical slats, Macmurdo ft, mk, 49x55x80"....................4,000.00

Book, Friendship, Henry Thoreau, Levant binding, 1903 ....**400.00**
Book, guest; tooled red leather cover, blank pgs, 6½x8½" **120.00**
Book, Ruskin & Turner, sgn E Hubbard, c Putman, 1895 ....**150.00**
Bookcase, #84, 1 door/low drw, script name/orb at top, rfn, 74x39" ...**12,000.00**
Bookends, h/cp, rectangular w/sm emb owl medallions, 4x6½" ..**250.00**
Bookends, h/cp, rectangular w/tooling framing appl medallion, 5x4¼" ..**195.00**
Bookends, h/cp, upright flatiron shape, tooled/gr device at curled tip ...**425.00**
Bookends, hammered-on brass patina, cutouts, mk, 8½" **170.00**
Bookends, inverted U fr w/riveted-on flaring bk panel, very heavy, 5" .**275.00**
Bowl, h/cp, low/squat/sharp shoulder, new patina, 3x11" **950.00**
Bowl, salad; brn high gloss, ceramic, 12", +8 ind **350.00**
Bowl, silver-washed h/cp, lt wear, 3¾x10" **425.00**
Box, jewelry; tooled leather w/birds, suede lined, 8¼" L **4,000.00**
Calender, desk; h/cp, dome shape, top w/3 tooled flowers, 5½x3½" ..**250.00**
Candelabrum, h/cp, pencil std w/low twist, 3-arm, lt wear, 20" ..**600.00**
Candelabrum, h/cp, 6 bobeches, curled twisted base, 13¾x13½" .**600.00**
Candlesticks, h/cp, tulip form top, tooled base, 13½", pr **2,500.00**
Candlesticks, h/cp, twist stem, disk ft, 13", pr **1,000.00**
Candlesticks, h/cp, 4-sided ft, 12", pr **1,800.00**
Chair, side; 4 vertical slats, rpl leather seat, Macmurdo ft, 38" ...**1,300.00**
Chamberstick, h/cp, flared base & bobeche, 3½x4½" **375.00**
Chandelier, heavy wrought iron, 5 shades, 25x19½" dia **6,500.00**
Chiffonier, mahog, 2 half drws, 4 grad long drws, 52x41x24", EX ...**3,750.00**
Compote, acid-etched copper, dk patina, 4½x11¼" **125.00**
Desk organizer, h/cp w/brass wash, 5" dia, VG..........**110.00**
Dresser, mahog, 5-drw, copper pulls, Macmurdo ft, 36x54x26" ...**950.00**
Dresser, 4-drw, integrated mirror, Macmurdo ft, 61½x43½" **7,500.00**
Frame, oak, holds 6 images, orb mk, 11x36½" **2,000.00**
Humidor, brass-washed, wood-grain pattern, 4-sided, hdls, 9" **425.00**
Humidor, h/cp, Trillum, EX recent patina, 5½"..........**600.00**
Inkwell, h/cp, sharply shouldered, ftd, dome lid w/ball finial, 3" ...**165.00**
Jug, brn high gloss, ceramic, 6¾"..........**20.00**
Lamp, brass-washed h/cp, gr/lav ldgl shade, Hunter, 23½" **16,000.00**
Letter holder/perpetual calendar, copper, acid-etch border, 3½x5x2" ...**100.00**
Letter opener, h/cp, slender blade widens to rnded terminal, 7".**145.00**
Letter rack & pen tray, h/cp, appl medallions, VG..........**210.00**
Menu, hand-colored by Dard Hunter, 7x5½", EX **100.00**
Plate, sq designs in border, Roycroft emblem top center, Buffalo, 9" L..**350.00**
Rocker, open arms, 5 vertical bk slats, rpl leather seat, 36" **1,500.00**
Stand, Little Journeys, oak, keyed tenons, 26x26x14"..........**600.00**
Stand, magazine; mahog, 3-shelf, canted sides, arched top, 38x18x16"..**2,600.00**
Stand, waiter's; folding X w/chain link, from Roycroft Inn, brn pnt ..**850.00**
Table, dressing; integrated mirror, 1-drw, Macmurdo ft, mk, 56x39"..**6,500.00**
Table, library; #072, deep apron, lower stretchers, rstr finish, 74" ...**4,000.00**
Telephone, h/cp & blk Bakelite, candlestick, all orig, 12".......**2,500.00**
Tray, h/cp, hexagonal, hdls, heavy verdigris center, 10" dia **150.00**
Vase, American Beauty, h/cp, 21½"..........**2,500.00**
Vase, American Beauty, orb mk, 6¾" **1,350.00**
Vase, h/cp, flared cylinder, 10½"..........**1,600.00**
Vase, h/cp, squat, 4½"..........**450.00**
Vase, NP h/cp, geometric band at top, 5" **950.00**
Walking stick, oak w/burned-in logo, 6-sided copper cap, 1903, cleaned ..**265.00**
Wall sconces, h/cp w/brass wash, 12½", pr **700.00**

Rozenburg

Some of the most innovative and original Art Nouveau ceramics were created by the Rozenburg factory at the Hague in The Netherlands between 1883 and 1914, when production ceased. (Several of their better painters continued to work in Gouda, which accounts for some pieces being similar to Gouda.) Rozenburg also made highly prized eggshell ware, so called because of its very thin walls; this is eagerly sought after by collectors. T.A.C. Colenbrander was their artistic leader, with Samuel

Schelink and J. Kok designing many of the eggshell pieces. The company was liquidated in 1917. Most pieces carry a date code. Our advisor for this category is Ralph Jaarsma; he is listed in the Directory under Iowa.

Bowl, 3-leaf clovers, ribbed neck, earthenware, 1904, rpr, 4¼x7" .**250.00**
Cup, yel Nouveau flowers on wht, octagonal, 2¼"..........**425.00**
Cup & saucer, nasturtiums, sgn Schelink, eggshell, octagonal, 1905 ..**1,600.00**
Jar, stylized rooster/floral reserves, much decor, rpr lid, 13".........**490.00**
Pitcher, exotic birds, brn/ochre on terra cotta, 7"..........**325.00**
Vase, exotic florals, earthenware, ca 1899, rpr, 15½x6½"..........**440.00**
Vase, floral, baluster shape, earthenware, pnt mk, 1893, 15" **300.00**
Vase, hyacinths on brn, wide shoulder, #374, 8⅝" **500.00**
Vase, irises, sqd bottle form, sgn Schelink, eggshell, 1901, 10"...**1,800.00**
Vase, irises (ornate artwork), earthenware, ca 1907-10, 8¼x4"..**550.00**
Vase, robin on berry branch, sgn, slim neck, ca 1900-02, 8¾x4"..**1,200.00**
Vase, robin on branch, sgn H, ca 1900-02, 8¾x4" **360.00**

Rubena

Rubena glass was made by several firms in the late 1800s. It is a blown art glass that shades from clear to red. See also Art Glass Baskets; Cruets; Sugar Shakers; Salts; specific manufacturers.

Bottle, scent; cut body, faceted stopper, 5⅜" **145.00**
Celery vase, bird & floral, ornate SP holder, 8"..........**750.00**
Celery vase, Hobnail, red top w/opal hobs, 6½" **1,100.00**
Ice bucket, HP design, SP bail hdl **125.00**
Pitcher, Concentric Diamonds, clear hdl, 8" **275.00**
Rose bowl, ca 1880, 4"..........**250.00**
Vase, birds & foliage, gilt trim, 1890s, 12½"..........**165.00**
Vase, gilt spider mums, cylindrical, 9¾"..........**145.00**

Rubena Verde

Rubena Verde glass was introduced in the late 1800s by Hobbs, Brockunier, and Company of Wheeling, West Virginia. Its transparent colors shade from red to green. See also Art Glass Baskets; Cruets; Sugar Shakers; Salts. For more information we recommend *Hobbs, Brockunier and Co. Glass* by Neila and Tom Bredehoft.

Bowl, allover floral, appl rigaree, 11½" L..........**265.00**
Cheese dish, Invt T'print cover, Daisy & Button tray, 5x7" **200.00**
Cruet, Invt T'print, teepee shape, Hobbs Brockunier, 7" **550.00**
Pitcher, Invt T'print, rope twist hdl/collar, Hobbs Brockunier, 7½" ..**300.00**
Pitcher, water; Invt T'print, vaseline hdl, 7½" **345.00**
Vase, dragonflies/wild flowers, ribbed, crimped rim, 7x5"..........**180.00**
Wine, Invt T'print, 4¼" **150.00**

Ruby Glass

Produced for over one hundred years by every glasshouse of note in this country, ruby glass has been used to create decorative items such as one might find in gift shops, utilitarian bottles and kitchenware, figurines, and dinnerware lines such as were popular in the Depression era. For further information and study, we recommend *Ruby Glass of the 20th Century* by our advisor, Naomi Over; she is listed in the Directory under Colorado.

Banana boat, English Hobnail, Westmoreland, 1980, 6¾x9½" **75.00**
Basket, Bambu, rare, Imperial, ca 1960-72, 9¾" **125.00**
Basket, Hobnail, Fenton, #3837, ca 1985-86, 7"..........**30.00**
Basket, Invt Thistle, crystal hdl, Mosser, 1980, 5½"..........**30.00**

Basket, metal hdls & decor, Westmoreland, 5" 20.00
Bell, Butterfly, ruby carnival, Fenton, 1998, 7" 30.00
Bowl, Bambu, Imperial, ca 1960-72, 11" 65.00
Bowl, Hobnail, fluted, Viking 22.00
Bowl, Paneled Grape, lg, fluted, Mosser, 1981, 11½" 30.00
Bowl, 4 legs, silver o/l, Paden City, ca 1920-51, 9¼" 95.00
Butter dish, Sawtooth, Westmoreland, 1980, 6½" 140.00
Candle holder, Ring Stem, 1-light, Cambridge, ca 1949-53, 5", ea.65.00
Candlesticks, Dmn T'print, crimped base, Viking, 1986, 5", pr.65.00
Candy dish, Caprice, Cambridge, ftd, 1936, 5¾" 15.00
Candy dish, Moon & Star, pedestal, w/lid, LG Wright, ca 1970s, 7¼"..30.00
Chocolate box, Maple Leaf, Westmoreland, 1989, 6½" 50.00
Covered dish, chicken on oval 2-hdld basket, Westmoreland, 1983-84, 4"..10.00
Creamer, Argus, Fostoria, 1967, 6-oz 30.00
Decanter, Cape Cod, w/stopper, Avon, ca 1977-80, 16-oz, 10" 20.00
Decanter, w/crystal stopper, LG Wright, ca 1970s, 12" 80.00
Ice bucket, Plymouth, #1620, Fenton, 1933, 5¾" dia 125.00
Nut dish, Scroll & Eye, ruby carnival, ped ft, Fenton, 1980, 5"....45.00
Pie server, Cape Cod, ruby hdl, Avon, ca 1981-84, 8" 15.00
Pitcher, Cape Cod, Avon, 1984, 40-oz 50.00
Pitcher, English Hobnail, ftd w/sm lip, Westmoreland, 1982, 38-oz..150.00
Plate, American, Fostoria, ca 1980, 14" 75.00
Plate, Butterfly Delight, #8319, Fenton, 1995, 9" 65.00
Plate, Diamond, Imperial, ca 1920-30, 8" 15.00
Plate, Doric, lace-edged, Westmoreland, 1981, 12½" 165.00
Plate, Epic, Viking, 17" 55.00
Plate, Fleur-de-Lis, Viking, 1984, 7¼" 35.00
Plate, heart-shaped, pnt Snowflowers, Westmoreland, 1983-84, 8"..45.00
Plate, luncheon; Cape Cod, Avon, 1980, 7½" 8.00
Plate, Pineapple, flashed florals, Indiana, 1970, 8" 15.00
Platter, Cape Cod, Avon, 1986, 13" 60.00
Powder box, lady cover, Mosser, 1980, 5½" 20.00
Rose bowl, Maple Leaf, Westmoreland, 1989, 4½" 30.00
Shakers, Cape Cod, Avon, mk May 1978, 4¼", pr 20.00
Shakers, LG Wright, ca 1970s, 3½", pr 40.00
Sherbet, crystal stem w/knop, Cambridge, ca 1949-53, 7-oz 20.00
Sugar bowl, Eyewinker, LG Wright, ca 1960s, 3¾" 18.00
Sugar bowl, Popeye & Olive, hdls, #994, Paden City, 1932, 3" ..20.00
Toothpick holder, English Hobnail, Westmoreland, 1980, 2½" 25.00
Tray, Regina, Paden City, #210, 1936, 13¼x7¾" 40.00
Tumbler, Invt Thistle, Mosser, 1980, 8-oz, 4" 10.00
Tumbler, oranges & leaves, ruby carnival, Fenton, 1997, 8-oz 25.00
Tumbler, Swirl, Cambridge, ca 1949-53, 12-oz 35.00
Vase, plain w/ruffled top, Blenko, 1980, 10½" 25.00
Vase, sweet potato; Line #1330, Cambridge, 1932, 5" 60.00
Wine, Argus, Fostoria, 1967, 4-oz 25.00
Wine, crystal stem, Paden City, 1932, 2-oz 25.00

Ruby-Stained Glass

Ruby-flashed or ruby-stained glass was made through the application of a thin layer of color over clear. It was used in the manufacture of some early pressed tableware from the Victorian era well into the twentieth century. These items were often engraved on the spot with the date, location, and buyer's name.

Celery dish, Sunk Honeycomb 42.50
Creamer, Box-in-Box, Mother...Atlantic City, 1895, 6⅜" ...120.00
Creamer, eng name & 1904 ....40.00
Creamer, Gettysburg 1863 in silver letters, 2¾" 30.00
Creamer, Ruby T'print, Atlantic City, 1911, 3⅛" 40.00
Mug, 8-panel, eng name & 1904, 1¾x1¼" 40.00
Punch cup, Masonic Temple 1893, 2¾" 25.00

Shaker, salt; Bead Swag, eng/dtd 1908, 2⅞" 50.00
Sugar shaker, Chandelier, 4¾" 250.00
Tankard, Pavonia, eng foliage, 11¾", NM 300.00
Toothpick holder, Grenade, Heisey....1896 in wht, 2¼x1⅝" 50.00
Tumbler, Art Navo w/gold, Co-operative Flint Glass, 4" 45.00
Tumbler, Millard, eng, 3¾" 50.00
Tumbler, Nearcut Daisy, gold decor, 4", NM 60.00
Tumbler, Skilton 20.00

Rugs

Hooked rugs are treasured today for their folk-art appeal. Rug making was a craft that was introduced to this country in about 1830 and flourished its best in the New England states. The prime consideration to consider when evaluating one of these rugs is not age but artistic appeal. Scenes with animals, buildings, and people; patriotic designs; or whimsical themes are preferred. Those with finely conceived designs, great imagination, interesting color use, etc., demand higher prices. Of course, condition is also a factor. Marked examples bearing the stamps of 'Frost and Co.,' 'Abenakee,' 'C.R.,' and 'Ouia' are highly prized. See also Orientalia, Rugs.

Cala lilies w/gray leaves in pot on blk w/pk border, 39x22" 135.00
Concentric rectangles, 5-color, minor edge damage, 26x44" 110.00
Cottage scene w/trees & birds, dtd 1940, 26x48", VG 150.00
Deer in medallion, oak leaf borders, mc on brn w/blk border, 32x57" .220.00
Dmn pattern, 5-color, rebound on 3 sides, 23½x87" 165.00
Dog in leafy landscape, lg robin on branch, scroll border, rprs, 39" L.1,295.00
Elephant in oval, mc w/red & gr borders, 22x36" 275.00
Fisherman asleep under tree in detailed landscape, mc, 25x36" .220.00
Fishscales, 6-color, edge damage, 24x39½" 165.00
Fishscales on tan w/alternating red & gr dmns, gray border, 32x60"...145.00
Floral center & corners, mc on tan w/patterned brn border, 36x52" ..200.00
Flower basket among scrolls, mc, minor rstr, 28x43" 220.00
Flowers & leaves, mc on variegated tan, 24x39½" 140.00
Geometric Deco design, mc on tan & lt pk, stains, 31x65" 165.00
Grenfell, Flying Canada Goose, goose at tree tops, 7½x9¼" 600.00
Grenfell, Seal Hunt, hunter w/harpoon & seal, 17x11½" 765.00
Latticework w/flowers & leaves, red & brn border, old rstr, 72x51"..385.00
Lion among roses, mc on gr, stitched to 23x38" fr 220.00
Mc broken stripes w/multiple borders, cloth binding, 48x74" 220.00
Medallions w/in sq blocks, bright mc, 36x56" 195.00

Mill building with paddlewheel in landscape, naturalistic tones, late nineteenth century, 22x36", EX+, $925.00. (Photo courtesy Skinner, Inc.)

Partridge pr w/in landscape, wool/cotton, 1800s, 32x46", VG....800.00
Peacock w/tail wide, mc, brn/orange/blk borders, oval, 16x27½"..300.00
Pinwheels (7), 5 muted colors on brn, minor rstrs, 26x52" 385.00

Rooster crowing, mc, before rising sun & flowering tree, 19x34" **330.00**
Rooster on hill among flowers, mc on blk, sgn, 20th C, 33x27", EX..**1,100.00**
Roosters crowing, mc on gray w/vine border, 33x44" **1,850.00**
Roses on wht, mc scrolling porder, EHC 1896, 28¼x37"............**110.00**
Shadow-design sqs, brn/tan/lt bl/navy/blk, 20x40" **330.00**
Swan w/yel bill on bl w/lt bl & gr, 22½x35¼" **200.00**
10-point star, mc on med bl, blk scalloped border, 40x25".........**770.00**
5 horses of various colors w/tree on striped ground, 35x20"........**825.00**

RumRill

George Rumrill designed and marketed his pottery designs from 1933 until his death in 1942. During this period of time, four different companies produced his work. Today the most popular designs are those made by the Red Wing Stoneware Company from 1933 until 1936 and Red Wing Potteries from 1936 until early 1938. Some of these lines include Trumpet Flower, Classic, Manhattan, and Athena, the Nudes.

For a period of months in 1938, Shawnee took over the production of RumRill pottery. This relationship ended abruptly, and the Florence Pottery took over and produced his wares until the plant burned down. The final producer was Gonder. Pieces from each individual pottery are easily recognized by their designs, glazes, and/or signatures. It is interesting to note that the same designs were produced by all three companies. They may be marked RumRill or with the name of the specific company that made them. You will find information on RumRill in *Collector's Encyclopedia of Red Wing Art Pottery, Books I* and *II*, by B.L. and R.L. Dollen (Collector Books). Our advisors for this category are Wendy and Leo Frese; they are listed in the Directory under Texas.

Ball jug, bl crackle, orig cork, #50, 7"...**65.00**
Bowl, centerpc; creamy wht S shape w/grape clusters, #612..........**70.00**
Figurine, seal w/bowl on nose, ca 1933, 12" (including bowl) **250.00**
Head vase, lady's head, sea green, #7, 11½", EX............................**80.00**
Pitcher, orange w/blk specks, #52, 9" **165.00**
Pitcher, Scarlett & Bay, #184 ....**100.00**
Planter, Wishing Well, gr & brn, 9⅜"..**60.00**
Vase, bl, emb swirling ribs, T-1, 18" **200.00**
Vase, bl, hdls, #670, 4"..**175.00**
Vase, bl w/speckles, lg trumpet neck, ftd, #535, 13" **85.00**
Vase, elephant hdls, gr w/orange int, 6½".....................................**150.00**
Vase, gr, trumpet neck, bulbous body, sticker, 4¼" **110.00**
Vase, gr opal matt, uptrn hdls, #504, 7½" **60.00**
Vase, Grecian, bl, hdls, 8½" **85.00**
Vase, Grecian, wht, hdls, #506, 7¼" **75.00**
Vase, Manhattan, Dutch Blue, w/label, #314................................**72.50**
Vase, marigold w/wht int, swan hdls, #444, 4½x5½" **95.00**
Vase, orange mottle, bulbous, hdls, #302, 5½"...............................**60.00**
Vase, Scarlett & Bay, bulbous, #207, NM **75.00**
Vase, Scarlett & Bay, integral hdls, #261/934, 7½x8½"..............**200.00**
Vase, Triple Swan, blended gr, 1930s, 4½x7½" **250.00**
Vase, wht w/gr int, flared rim, integral hdls, #638, 5⅜" **100.00**

Ruskin

This English pottery operated near Birmingham from 1889 until 1935. Its founder was W. Howson Taylor, and it was named in honor of the renowned author and critic, John Ruskin. The earliest marks were 'Taylor' in block letters and the initials 'WHT,' the smaller W and H superimposed over the larger T. Later marks included the Ruskin name.

Candlesticks, purple, flared bottom w/step neck, 1908, 6½", pr .**210.00**
Vase, bl & gr flambé, tall flaring neck, 5½".................................**425.00**

Vase, bl to yel to burnt orange, 1933, 9½"...................................**160.00**
Vase, crystalline bl & gr w/flecks, 3" **135.00**
Vase, lav lustre, shouldered baluster, 7½" **300.00**
Vase, mc drip over bl, bulbous, 6½" **400.00**
Vase, metallic orange luster, 1916, 8x4¼" **160.00**
Vase, purple/red/gr crystalline, shouldered, 4" **1,000.00**

Russel Wright Dinnerware

Russel Wright, one of America's foremost industrial designers, also designed several lines of ceramic dinnerware, glassware, and aluminum ware that are now highly sought-after collectibles. His most popular dinnerware then and with today's collectors, American Modern, was manufactured by the Steubenville Pottery Company from 1939 until 1959. It was produced in a variety of solid colors in assortments chosen to stay attune with the times. Casual (his first line sturdy enough to be guaranteed against breakage for ten years from date of purchase) is relatively easy to find today — simply because it has held up so well. During the years of its production, the Casual line was constantly being restyled, some items as many as five times. Early examples were heavily mottled, while later pieces were smoothly glazed and sometimes patterned. The ware was marked with Wright's signature and 'China by Iroquois.' It was marketed in fine department stores throughout the country. After 1950 the line was marked 'Iroquois China by Russel Wright.' For those wanting to learn more about the subject, we recommend *The Collector's Encyclopedia of Russel Wright, Third Edition*, by Ann Kerr.

American Modern

To calculate values for American Modern, at the least, double the low values listed for these colors: Canteloupe, Glacier Blue, Bean Brown, and White. Chartreuse is represented by the low end of our range; Cedar, Black Chutney, and Seafoam by the high end; and Coral and Gray near the middle.

Bowl, baker, from $40 to..**50.00**
Bowl, vegetable; divided, from $135 to......................................**150.00**
Butter dish, from $200 to..**250.00**
Coffepot, 8", from $250 to..**275.00**
Creamer, from $15 to **20.00**
Ice box jar, from $250 to...**275.00**
Plate, salad; 8", from $18 to..**20.00**
Ramekin, from $300 to **325.00**
Saucer, demitasse; from $25 to **30.00**
Sugar bowl, stacking, from $15 to **18.00**

Glass

Morgantown Modern is most popular in Seafoam, Coral, and Chartreuse. In the Flair line, colors other than crystal and pink are rare and expensive. Seafoam is hard to find in Pinch; Canteloupe is scarce so double the prices for that color, and Ruby Flair is very rare.

Appleman Warming trays, rnd or oblong, sm or lg, ea from $100 to..**125.00**
Bartlett-Collins Eclipse, hi-ball, 5", from $20 to............................**25.00**
Bartlett-Collins Eclipse, tumbler, cocktail; 3", from $15 to...........**20.00**
Imperial Flair, tumbler, juice; 6-oz, from $45 to **50.00**
Imperial Flair, tumbler, water; 11-oz, from $50 to.........................**65.00**
Imperial Pinch, tumbler, iced tea; 14-oz, from $30 to...................**35.00**
Imperial Twist, tumbler, juice; rare, from $35 to...........................**50.00**
Old Morgantown, chilling bowl, 12-oz, 3", from $150 to..............**175.00**
Old Morgantown/Modern, goblet, 11-oz, 4½", from $35 to..........**40.00**
Old Morgantown/Modern, pilsner, 7", from $140 to **160.00**
Snow Glass, bowl, fruit/sherbet; from $55 to **75.00**

Snow Glass, saucer, from $65 to **75.00**
Theme Formal Glass, tumbler, wine; 6-oz, 7", from $150 to **200.00**

Highlight

Bowl, soup/cereal; 2 sizes, ea from $30 to **35.00**
Bowl, vegetable; oval, from $65 to **75.00**
Creamer, from $40 to **55.00**
Dish, salad or vegetable; rnd, ea from $100 to **150.00**
Plate, bread & butter; from $12 to **15.00**
Platter, oval, sm, from $50 to **75.00**

Iroquois Casual

To price Sugar White, Charcoal, and Oyster, use the high end of the pricing range. Avocado Yellow, Nutmeg Brown, and Ripe Apricot fall to the low side. Canteloupe commands premium prices, and even more valuable are Brick Red and Aqua.

Bowl, cereal; 5", from $12 to **15.00**
Bowl, fruit; 9½-oz, 5½", from $12 to **14.00**
Bowl, soup; 11½-oz, from $20 to **25.00**
Carafe, wine/coffee; from $200 to **225.00**
Coffeepot, AD; w/lid, from $100 to **125.00**
Cup & saucer, coffee; from $18 to **22.00**
Gravy stand, from $15 to **20.00**
Pitcher, redesigned, from $175 to **200.00**
Plate, luncheon; 9½", from $10 to **12.00**
Teapot, restyled, from $200 to **225.00**

Spun Aluminum

Russel Wright's aluminum ware may not have been especially well accepted in its day — it tended to damage easily and seems to have had only limited market appeal — but today's collectors feel quite differently about it, as is apparent in the suggested values noted in the following listings.

Bowl, from $75 to **95.00**
Casserole, from $150 to **200.00**
Coffee set, percolator+cr/sug, wooden finials, 9", 3¾", 3" **1,300.00**
Cooking item, from $150 to **200.00**
Gravy boat, from $150 to **200.00**
Muddler, from $75 to **100.00**
Pitcher, sherry; from $250 to **275.00**
Pitcher, w/rnd hdl, from $175 to **225.00**
Sandwich humidor, from $150 to **175.00**
Tea set, from $500 to **700.00**
Torchere, trumpet shade w/wooden knob switch, unmk, 64¾" ..**275.00**
Wastebasket, from $125 to **150.00**

Sterling

Ashtray, from $75 to **100.00**
Creamer, ind, 1-oz, from $12 to **15.00**
Pitcher, water; 2-qt, from $125 to **150.00**
Plate, dinner; 10¼", from $10 to **15.00**
Platter, oval, 13⅝", from $30 to **32.00**
Sugar bowl, 10-oz, from $22 to **25.00**

Miscellaneous

Chase, pitcher, beer; Devonshire, #90025, from $225 to **250.00**
Chase, tray, bl glass, for corn set, #9014, from $165 to **175.00**

Country Garden, ladle, from $125 to **175.00**
Country Garden, pitcher, 2-cup, from $250 to **300.00**
Everlast Gold Aluminite, bowl, from $125 to **150.00**
Everlast Gold Aluminite, sugar bowl, from $65 to **75.00**
Ideal Adult Kitchen Ware, bowl, salad; from $20 to **25.00**
Ideal Adult Kitchen Ware, jug, water; lg, from $50 to **75.00**
Knowles Esquire, bowl, soup/cereal; 6¼", from $16 to **18.00**

Knowles Esquire, pitcher, two-quart, from $150.00 to $200.00.

Knowles Esquire, plate, dinner; 10¾", from $15 to **18.00**
Knowles Esquire, shakers, ea from $15 to **20.00**
Meladur, bowl, cereal; from $10 to **12.00**
Meladur, bowl, soup; 12-oz, from $10 to **15.00**
Meladur, plate, dinner; 9", from $10 to **12.00**
Oceana, relish, 1-hdl, from $500 to **600.00**
Oceana, salad fork & spoon, from $275 to **350.00**
Pinch cutlery, butter spreader, from $100 to **110.00**
Pinch cutlery, fork or spoon, ea from $75 to **85.00**
Pinch cutlery, ice tea spoon, from $100 to **125.00**
Theme Formal, coffeepot, from $600 to **650.00**
Theme Formal Lacquerware, plates, ea from $125 to **150.00**
Theme Informal, bowl, soup; from $75 to **100.00**
Vase, apricot mottle w/blk int, teardrop opening, bulbous, Bauer, 9"..**800.00**
White Clover, creamer, Clover decor, from $25 to **35.00**
White Clover, pitcher, Clover decor, 1-qt, from $100 to **150.00**
White Clover, plate, chop; Clover decor, 11", from $40 to..........**50.00**

Russian Art

Before the Revolution in 1917, many jewelers and craftsmen created exquisite marvels of their arts, distinctive in the extravagant detail of their enamel work, jeweled inlays, and use of precious metals. These treasures aptly symbolized the glitter and the romance of the glorious days under the reign of the Tsars of Imperial Russia. The most famous of these master jewelers was Carl Fabergé (1852 – 1920), goldsmith to the Romanovs. Following the tradition of his father, he took over the Faberge workshop in 1870. Eventually Faberge employed more than five hundred assistants and set up workshops in Moscow, Kiev, and London as well as in St. Petersburg. His specialties were enamel work, clockwork automated figures, carved animal and human figures of precious or semi-precious stones, cigarette cases, small boxes, scent flasks, and his best-known creations, the Imperial Easter Eggs — each of an entirely different design. By the turn of the century, his influence had spread to other countries, and his work was revered by royalty and the very wealthy. The onset of the war marked the end of the era. Very little of his work remains on the market, and items that are available are very expensive. But several of his contemporaries were goldsmiths whose work can be equally enchanting. Among them are Klingert, Ovchinnikov, Smirnov, Ruckert, Loriye, Cheryatov, Kuzmichev, Nevalainen,

Adler, Sbitnev, Third Artel, Wakewa, Holmstrom, Britzin, Wigstrom, Orlov, Nichols, and Plincke. Most of them produced excellent pieces similar to those made by Fabergé between 1880 and 1910.

Perhaps the most important bronze Russian artist was Eugenie Alexandrovich Lanceray (1847 – 1887). From 1875 until 1887, he modeled many equestrian groups of falconers and soldiers ranging in height from about 20" to 30". Some of them bear the Chopin foundry mark; they are presently worth from $4,000.00 up. Other excellent artists were Schmidt Felling (nineteenth century), who specialized in mounted figures of cossacks wearing military uniforms, and Nicholas Leiberich (late nineteenth century), who also specialized in equestrian groups. Most of the pieces made by the above artists were signed and had the foundry mark (Chopin, Woerffel, etc.).

Russian porcelain is another field where Imperial connections have undoubtedly added to the interest of collectors and museums worldwide. The most important factories were Imperial Russian Porcelain, St. Petersburg (or Petrograd or Leningrad, 1744 – 1917); Gardner, Moscow (1765 – 1872); Kuznetsoff, St. Petersburg and Moscow (1800 – 1900); Korniloff, St. Petersburg (1800 – 1900); and Babunin, St. Petersburg (1800 – 1900).

Cigarette case, champlevè designs ea side, mk 84, 2⅝x3¾" **220.00**
Frame, silver-mtd nephrite, H Wigstrom Moscow, 1908-17, 5¼x4½" ..**3,000.00**
Icon, Death of the Virgin, mc w/gold on wooden panel, 5⅝x7⅛" **220.00**
Icon, Elevation of Cross, 16th-C style, rare theme, 19th C, 12½x10"...**750.00**
Icon, Entry Into Jerusalem, EX detail, old style, 10th C, 12x10"...**600.00**
Icon, Jesus, some silver & gold, appl halo, hallmk, 8x7" **330.00**
Icon, Kazan Mother of God, gilt incised ground, ornate border, 12x10"....**575.00**
Icon, Lord Almighty, allover eng silver-gilt, Moscow/1890, 10½x9" ..**400.00**
Icon, Not by Hands Made Image, gilt ground, 1890s, 14x12"...**925.00**
Icon, St Margaret, silver halo, hands & cross, 8½x10", EX **940.00**
Icon, St Nicholas, embr silk thread, seed pearls/beads, 20th C, 11x13" .**300.00**
Icon, St Nicholas, ornate borders & bkground, 1880s, 14x12"...**460.00**
Icon, Virgin & Child, w/silver & gold wash, detailed, 1891, 12x9" ..**275.00**
Jardiniere, patinated/gilt bronze Graces, malachite base, 19th C, 16".**4,300.00**
Oil on panel, religious figure w/halo & Jesus in clouds, 7xk6"....**110.00**
Tongs, silver w/ornate enameling, mk 84 in oval hallmk, 5½" ...**750.00**
Troika, sled w/riders & 3 horses, bronze, Fabr DF Woerffel, 10"..**1,485.00**

Sabino

Sabino art glass was produced by Marius-Ernest Sabino in France during the 1920s and 1930s. It was made in opalescent, frosted, and colored glass and was designed to reflect the Art Deco style of that era. In 1960, using molds he modeled by hand, Sabino once again began to produce art glass using a special formula he himself developed that was characterized by a golden opalescence. Although the family continued to produce glassware for export after his death in 1971, they were never able to duplicate Sabino's formula.

Bottle, globular w/lappet leaves, 5¼" **130.00**
Bottle, scent; La Ronde Fleurie, 6" **155.00**
Bowl, Deco-style florals, 3-ftd, 3¼x11¾" **265.00**
Bowl, open shell, 7x4¼"...**55.00**
Box, 3 mermaids w/interlocking hands, opal, 6½" **385.00**
Figurine, butterfly, open wings, #B47, 3x2" **48.00**
Figurine, Capelan, fish, #A42, 2x2"...**40.00**
Figurine, cat, sitting w/head up, 3¼"..**90.00**
Figurine, cherub, #A67, 2x1", from $50 to **75.00**
Figurine, dove, head up, #A63, 2x2"..**88.00**
Figurine, Ecureuil, squirrel, 3" **50.00**
Figurine, Eglefin, fish..**95.00**
Figurine, elephant, #A64, 2½x1"..**40.00**

Figurine, Envolee, birds, #B57, 5½x2" **345.00**
Figurine, Hesitation, draped nude, 8½" **575.00**
Figurine, hunter w/rabbit & bird...**67.00**
Figurine, L'Egyptienne, Egyptian female............................**130.00**
Figurine, lovebirds, 3¾x5x2", from $500 to......................**575.00**
Figurine, nude holds wide flowing cape behind her, 9½"...**1,300.00**
Figurine, Oiseau Sautilliant, hopping bird, #A29, 2x2".......**40.00**
Figurine, rabbit, #A54, 2x1"...**40.00**
Figurine, Reveile, draped nude, 8"....................................**400.00**
Figurine, 3 promenading elephants w/trunks raised, 12x14"....**1,500.00**
Knife rest, bee, 3⅝x1x1¼"..**70.00**
Knife rest, poodle..**60.00**
Snail shell **150.00**
Vase, Abondance, 7" **800.00**
Vase, Carangues, fish, 5" **220.00**
Vase, chevrons, frosted, ovoid, 12", NM **230.00**
Vase, stylized birds & geometrics, clear frosted cylinder, 8⅝" **120.00**

Bottle, scent; draped nudes and flower garlands, red and gold paper label, 6⅛", $225.00. (Photo courtesy Monsen & Baer)

Salesman's Samples and Patent Models

Salesman's samples and patent models are often mistaken for toys or homemade folk art pieces. They are instead actual working models made by very skilled craftsmen who worked as model makers. Patent models were made until the early 1900s. After that, the patent office no longer required a model to grant a patent. The name of the inventor or the model maker and the date it was built is sometimes noted on the patent model. Salesman's samples were occasionally made by model makers, but often they were assembled by an employee of the company. These usually carried advertising messages to boost the sale of the product. Though they are still in use today, the most desirable examples date from the 1800s to about 1945.

Many small stoves are incorrectly termed a 'salesman's sample'; remember that no matter how detailed one may be, it must be considered a toy unless accompanied by a carrying case, the indisputable mark of a salesman's sample.

Baseball home plate, Seamless Rubber Co, emb lettering, 4x4", EX .**180.00**
Bathtub, SM Co, wht porc, ftd, 3x4x8", EX................................**250.00**
Bedsprings, metal, 1x7x5", VG **50.00**
Boxing gloves, Goldsmith & Sons, red leather, w/case, 5", EX ...**350.00**
Carrying case, Wear-Ever Aluminum Specialties ad inside lid, 25", G..**35.00**
Clothes wringer, Abner Riggs, 8x11", VG...................................**250.00**
Draw shave, metal w/orig wooden hdls, 8", G+ **250.00**

Garage door, National Mfg Co, Model No 2, wood/metal, 15x33", VG.**150.00**
Garage door, National Mfg Co, Model No 55, wood/metal, 10x12", Fair.**80.00**
Garage door, National Mfg Co, Model No 806, wood/metal, 18x30", G+..**250.00**
Grater, mahog & CI, feed-lot type, Pat Appl For, EX.................**995.00**
Hand pump, figural CI, 7½", G **50.00**
Hay fork, wrought iron w/wooden pulley, 11¼x9¾" **150.00**
Ice cream freezer, Shepard's Lightning, wood hand crank, 7", G.**225.00**
Piano, Mason & Hamlin, shows internal workings, 14x17", VG .**165.00**
Piano stool, child's, wood w/adjustable screw top, 10", VG.........**220.00**
Safe, Meilink, finished interior, maker's decal & hdl, 14x10", EX .**1,320.00**
Safe door, Corless Safe Co, 25x14", EX+ **7,150.00**
Scale, 1¢ floor model, 1915, 14x5", VG+ **2,420.00**
Showcase, Excelsior Showcase Works, oak/glass/NP trim, 17x12x12", EX+..**6,820.00**
Sickle mower, metal, very early intricate working model, G....**1,760.00**
Sofa, Empire, slip seat w/orig uphl, 7x14x4", EX **2,000.00**
Stand, tiger maple Hplwht, 1 drw, 11x10¼x9", EX.................**1,000.00**
Table, tea; mahog, pie-crust top, 19th C, 16½x9¾" **800.00**
Tire upsetter (shrinker), Pat Oct 14 1879, 6x8x8", EX **1,450.00**
Toilet, ceramic bowl w/2-part seat (no lid), Artison Silent, 7x14"...**825.00**
Trunk, saleman's; bl metal w/Taylor Trunk Works ID badge, 7x19", EX .**825.00**
Wash boiler, Freidley...Ill, Pat Oct 12 1878, EX **1,795.00**
Washing machine, mahog, swing feature, inside agitators, EX.**2,995.00**
Washing machine, 1940s Whirlpool ringer washer, 24", EX **330.00**
Window, promoting Numetal Weather Strips, wood w/decal, 16x9", VG+..**120.00**

Salt Shakers

John Mason invented the screw-top salt shaker in 1858. Today's Victorian salt shaker collectors have a wide range of interests, and their collections usually reflect their preference. There are many possible variables on which to base a collection. You may prefer shakers made of clear pattern glass, art glass, specific types of glass (custard, ruby stain, Burmese, opaque, chocolate), or glass of a particular color (cranberry, green, blue, or amber, for instance). Some collectors search for examples made by only one maker (in particular Mt. Washington, Dithridge, Northwood, Hobbs Brockunier, and C. F. Monroe.) Others may stick to decorated shakers, undecorated examples, or any combination thereof that captures their fancy. If you would like to learn more about Victorian glass salt shakers, we recommend *The World of Salt Shakers, Second* and *Third Editions*, by Mildred and Ralph Lechner; and *Early American Pattern Glass* by Reilly and Jenks.

Unless noted otherwise, values are for examples in excellent condition with near mint decorations (when applicable). Unless 'pr' is specified, the value is for a single shaker. Our advisors for this category are Carla and Doug Hales; they are listed in the Directory under Florida.

Victorian Glass

Amberette, amber satin, Duncan, 1885, 2¾" **80.00**
Atterbury Twin, wht opaque Cryolite, Pat 1873, Atterbury, 3⅛".**175.00**
Babe Ruth figural, red & gold pnt, 1924-32, 5" **790.00**
Bale, bl w/HP flowers, Pairpoint, 1894-1900, 2⅜" **200.00**
Barrel, Inv't Honeycomb, amber w/flowers, New England, 1884, 3¼"...**155.00**
Beaded Dahlia, deep red, 2¾", pr **160.00**
Beaded Dahlia, pk cased, 2½", pr...**19.00**
Beaded Panels, Six; bl opaque, Dithridge & Co, 1897-1903, 2⅝"..**37.00**
Broken Column w/Red Dots, ruby stain, Columbia, 1893, 2⅞"...**150.00**
Chrysanthemum Leaf, chocolate opaque, Indiana, 1901-03, 2⅝"...**325.00**
Corn, custard opaque, Dithridge & Co, 1894-1901, 3⅛" **90.00**
Delaware (4-petal flower), rose flashed w/gold, ca 1899, 2⅝" **125.00**
Diamond & Sunburst Vt, ruby stain, US Glass, 1892, 2¾"..........**70.00**
Diamond Base Lower half, emerald w/HP flowers, 1901-07, 3¼"..**60.00**
Double Leaf, purple variegated opaque, ca 1895-1901, 3⅝"........**110.00**

Eagle's Forget-Me-Not, wht opaque opal, ca 1901, 2⅜" **32.00**
Eye Winker, Danzell Gilmroe & Leighton, 1889-95, 3" (+).........**36.00**
Fence, 18 vertical ribs, clear bl homogeneous, 1891-1901, 2⅞" **35.00**
Flower & Pleat, clear & frosted, ruby stain, ca 1892-93, 3⅛"........**56.00**
Flower Band, pigeon blood satin, Lancaster, 1901-02, 2⅝" **180.00**
Georgia Gem, opaque custard w/HP floral, Tarentum, 1900-40, 2½"...**115.00**
Gibson Girl, milk glass cylinder w/HP image, Kokomo, 1904, 3⅜".**65.00**
Hobnail in Square, crystal & wht opal, Aetna, ca 1887, 2⅞" **72.00**
Ice Cube, opaque w/HP flowers, 1896-1904, 2⅛x1⅞" **45.00**
Jeweled Moon & Star, amber stain, bl HP star, ca 1896, 3"...........**50.00**
Liberty Bell, blown/pressed, hdld lid, Central Glass, 1875-77, 2¼" .**145.00**

Lobe Four, pink and white floral with gold, Crown Milano, $225.00 for the pair.

Melon, 9-Rib; cranberry, ca 1895-1900, 1⅞" **220.00**
Net & Scroll, opaque gr, Dithridge & Co, 1894-1900, 2⅞" **55.00**
Opal Coin Spot, cranberry opal, Hobbs Brockunier, 1888-91, 3⅝"............**190.00**
Paneled, 4-sided, tapered, clear dk bl, 2-pc metal top, 1891-1900, 4".**50.00**
Paneled Teardrop, gr opaque cased, 1905-08, 3⅛" **125.00**
Pear, opaque w/HP flowers, Mt WA(?), 1897-1903, 2¾", pr **225.00**
Reverse Swirl, cranberry opal, orig screw-on lid, 2½" **95.00**
Rhea-D (Protruding Panels), wht opaque opal, ca 1898-1900, 2¾"..**45.00**
Rib & Scroll, lime gr opaque, Consolidated, 1904-05, 3" **70.00**
Ribbed Opal Lattice, cranberry, 3⅛", pr....................................**180.00**
Ribbed Optic, cranberry, 2½", pr **70.00**
Seaweed, wht opal, Hobbs Brockunier, 1890-91, 3"......................**85.00**
Star of Bethlehem (Nearcut Star), ruby stain, ca 1909, 2⅞" **72.00**
Sunset, pk opaque, Dithridge & Co, 1894-97, 2⅞" **75.00**
Swirl, Spiral; clear cranberry, 1888-94, 3" **105.00**
Texas, US Glass, ca 1900, 2¾"..**65.00**
Tripod w/Diamond Band, clear canary yel vaseline, 1904-10, 3½" ..**130.00**
Twisted Cane, opaque bl, 1895-1905, 2⅝" **60.00**
Venetian Diamond, Ring Neck; cranberry, 3¼", pr **90.00**
Wide Diagonal Swirl, bl opaque, ca 1894-96, 2⅜".......................**55.00**
Zippered Borders, ruby-stained thin glass, 1898-1903, 3½" **80.00**

Novelty Advertising

Those interested in novelty shakers will enjoy *Salt and Pepper Shakers, Volumes I, II, III,* and *IV,* by Helene Guarnaccia; and *Florence's Big Book of Salt and Pepper Shakers* by Gene Florence. All are available at your local library or from Collector Books. Note: 'Mini' shakers are no taller than 2". Instead of having a cork, the user was directed to 'use tape to cover hole.' Our advisor for novelty salt shakers is Judy Posner; she is listed in the Directory under Pennsylvania. See also Regal; Rosemeade; Occupied Japan; Shawnee; other specific manufacturers.

Anthracite Bit Co, rotary bit, rotating blades, plastic, 1959, 3", pr..**125.00**
Ballantine Ale, beer can, cb w/metal lid, 2⅜", pr in carrypack **19.00**
Big Boy & dbl cheeseburger, ceramic, 1995 Ltd edition EBR, 4½", pr...**49.00**
Blatz Beer, amber glass bottle, metal tops, 3", pr **26.00**
Calvert Daiquiri, bottles, mk Bottled for Am Airlines, 4¼", pr **24.00**
Carling Black Label Beer, bottle, glass, 4", MIB, pr **28.00**

Chicken of the Sea, fish, aqua, yel, pottery, 2x2⅞", pr **24.00**
Conoco Gas, pump, plastic, decal, 2¾", MIB, pr **95.00**
Drive-In Restraunt, camel, shakers in humps, hard plastic, 3-pc set...**29.00**
Fingerhut truck (cab & trailer), ceramic, 1¾x3¾", 2-pc set **29.00**
General Electric, refrigerator, milk glass, 1940s, 3¼", pr **60.00**
Goetz Country Club Beer, bottle w/decal, 4½", pr........................**35.00**
Greyhound bus, ceramic, Japan, 1960s, 1½x3¼", pr.....................**45.00**
Heinz Ketchup bottle, label, c JS NY Made in Hong Kong, 4¼", pr..**22.00**
Homepride Flour Fred, hard plastic figural, 4¼", pr......................**55.00**
Humble Esso Gas Pump, plastic w/decal label, 2¾", pr..................**39.00**
Jones Dairy, milk bottle w/decal, metal lid, 3½", pr......................**75.00**
Kellogg's, Snap & Pop, porc, w/corks, Japan, 2½", NM, pr **49.00**
KFC Colonel Sanders, wht plastic, blk base on pepper, 4⅜", pr ...**65.00**
Koehler Beer, amber bottle, foil label, 4", pr.................................**28.00**
Lennox Furnace Co, Lennie Lennos, pottery, 1950, 5", pr **125.00**
Magic Chef, chef on milk glass, plastic lid, 1940s, 3½", pr...........**55.00**
Mars Candy, M&M figural man, plastic, Mars Inc c 1991, 3¾", pr .**28.00**
Mason Ball jar, clear glass w/metal lid, 2⅞", pr.............................**24.00**
McWilliams Wine, monk figural, ceramic, Japan, 3½", pr..............**95.00**
Nugget Sam Casino, Nugget Sam, 3¾", pr....................................**75.00**
Old Dr Brown, clear soda bottle w/fired-on label, 4¼", pr **45.00**
Old Erie Beverage Soda, gr glass bottle, metal top, 6", pr..............**35.00**
Old Gunther Beer, amber bottle, foil label, metal lid, 4", pr.........**28.00**
Peerles Beer, Gnome-like character, Hartland Plastic, 1950s, 5", pr...**95.00**
Pure Oil Co, pump, plastic, 2¾", pr **135.00**
Quaker Oats, mill building, wht pottery, Japan, 3½", pr...............**35.00**
Quaker State Motor Oil, cb can, 1940s-50s, 1½", pr **39.00**
Rice a Roni, cable car, pottery, 1970s, 2 pcs form car **32.00**
Sealtest Milk, clear bottle, decals, metal top, 3¼", pr...................**29.00**
Sympathetic Ear Restaraunt, anthropomorphic ears, plastic, 1965, pr...**75.00**
Tee-Eff Tastee Freeze Ice Cream, Tee & Eff figures, Japan, 3¾", pr...**35.00**
Texaco, Bergey & Gehman Fuel Oil, milk glass, 3¼", pr..............**55.00**
Tuborg & Carlsberg Beer, bottle, glass, 2½", pr on wooden stand.**29.00**
Vess Soda, clear & gr glass bottle, decal, plastic top, pr................**45.00**
Westinghouse, washer & dryer, gr plastic, 3½", pr........................**16.00**
White Satin Gin, gr glass bottle, metal top, paper label, 4¾", pr..**24.00**
Woodsy Owl, pottery, 1960s-70s, 4¼", pr....................................**125.00**

Novelty Animals, Fish, and Birds

Bear w/coonskin hat, ceramic, Iowa souvenir label, 1950s, 3¾", pr.**24.00**
Bear w/navy hat, 2nd w/life preserver, ceramic, unmk, 1940s, pr ..**65.00**
Bug musician w/fiddle (or guitar), ceramic, Japan, 1950s, 3", pr ...**22.00**
Bull, lifelike, Victoria Ceramics...Japan, 1950s, 2x4", pr..............**19.00**
Cat & bee on ball, mc ceramic, Japan, 1950s, 3", pr......................**22.00**
Cat & mouse, realistic, mc ceramic, unmk USA, cat: 1¾x3¼", pr..**28.00**
Cat musician & drum (2nd shaker), mc ceramic, Japan, 1950s, 4½", pr.**22.00**
Circus elephant w/hat, realistic, cold pnt, unmk Japan, 4½", pr ...**24.00**
Cow & moon, ceramic, unmk USA, 1950s, 3½", pr.......................**28.00**
Deer w/bell around neck, mc pottery, Japan, 1950s, 4", pr.............**19.00**
Dinosaur, gr or pk, ceramic, c FF (Fitz & Floyd), 4¼", pr............**24.00**
Dinosaur (Dino type) on base, unmk Japan, 1960s-70s, 3⅜", pr ...**39.00**
Dog, brn dots, blk ears, slim, ceramic, Japan, 1950s, 6¾", pr **18.00**
Dog boy (girl) w/ping-pong paddle, ceramic, Japan, 1950s, 2¾", pr.**19.00**
Dog w/hat, begging, mc ceramic, Japan, 1950s, 4", pr..................**22.00**
Donkey laughing, wearing hat, ceramic, Japan, 1950s, 3⅜", pr.....**22.00**
Donosaur, spikey bk, ceramic, 1950s, 2⅜", pr **55.00**
Eagle (patriotic), mc chalkware, Denver souvenir, 2⅝", pr...........**35.00**
Farmer pig, mc ceramic, Enesco label, 5", pr................................**24.00**
Fish & creel, mc ceramic, unmk, 1950s, 2", pr.............................**18.00**
Flamingo, mc pottery, Kenmar Japan foil label, 4¼", pr...............**29.00**
Gingham dog & cat, ceramic, mc quilted motif, 1950s, 4½", pr ...**29.00**
Giraffe w/interlocking neck, mc ceramic, Artmark Japan, 4¾", pr.**65.00**
Goose & golden egg, ceramic, Vallona Star, goose: 5½", pr **45.00**

Halloween cat & skull, mc ceramic, red Japan mk, 2⅜", pr **49.00**
Hen & rooster, ceramic, wht w/red, shiny, unmk, 19540s, 3¾".....**22.00**
Iguanodon dinosaur, necks entwine, ceramic, Japan, 1950s, 4½", pr..**95.00**
Ladybug leaf-head anthropomorphic creature, ceramic, Japan, 3½", pr..**28.00**
Lamb w/glasses, mc details, ceramic, Japan, 1950s, 4½", pr..........**35.00**
Lion w/monocle, mc ceramic, c MS, Japan mk, 1950s, 4⅝", pr ...**39.00**
Mice w/sunglasses kissing, mc ceramic, Canada souvenir, Japan, pr.**26.00**
Mouse baseball player, mc ceramic, unmk Japan, 1950s, 3¼", pr..**59.00**
Oriole male & female, pottery, Napco, 1950s, 2½", pr **24.00**
Penguin, blk & wht, hard plastic, 1950s, 3½", pr **22.00**
Puppy w/big sad eyes in garbage can, mc ceramic, Japan, 5⅝", pr.**35.00**
Puppy w/bow tie, mc pottery, Sunsco Japan label, 1950s, 5¼", pr.**28.00**
Purple cow, 1 w/horns, 2nd w/halo, ceramic, Japan, 1950s **24.00**
Rabbit & cabbage, mc ceramic, Parkcraft, 4", pr...........................**25.00**
Red-head woodpecker, mc pottery, realistic, Japan, 1950s, 3¼", pr..**22.00**
Rooster & hen, glass w/pottery head, Made in Czechoslovakia, 3", pr.**29.00**
Rooster w/head up (2nd w/head down), bone china, Japan, 2⅝", pr.**19.00**
Scottie dog, mc porc, Germany, 1930s-40s, 2½", pr......................**28.00**
Teddy bear dressed up, stacking pr, ceramic, Japan, 4½" **18.00**
Tortoise & hare, mc ceramic, unmk USA, 1950s, 3¾", pr **35.00**
Tropical bird, mc ceramic, red Germany mk, 1930s, 3½", pr **28.00**
Turkey, mc ceramic, red Japan mk, 1950s, 2¾", pr.......................**18.00**
Tweety & Sylvester, ceramic, Warner Bros, Taiwan, cat: 4½", pr...**29.00**
Wolves dressed up, lustreware, Germany, 3½", pr..........................**75.00**

Miscellaneous Novelties

Ariel, Little Mermaid, ceramic, C Disney China, 5¼", pr.............**29.00**
Babar Elephant & girlfriend dressed up, ceramic, unmk, 3½", pr..**55.00**
Babar Elephant, mc ceramic, stacking figure, Japan, 1950s, 4⅞" ..**69.00**
Bahama Policeman, mc ceramic, 1960s, 4½", pr...........................**28.00**
Baseball batter & catcher, comic, ceramic, Japan, 1940s-50s, 4", pr...**85.00**
Basket of clothes & iron, ceramic, OH souvenir, Japan, 1960s, pr .**24.00**
Betsy Ross & Paul Revere, mc ceramic, Japan label, 1960s, 4½", pr.**28.00**
Bible & gavel, ceramic, unmk, 1950s, 1½", 4", pr.........................**19.00**
Billy Sykes & Capt Cuttle, ceramic, Artone stamp, England, 2½", pr..**39.00**
Bimbo (Betty Boop's dog), ceramic, USA, 1930s, 2½", pr **95.00**
Bonzo, cobalt ceramic, unmk, 1930s, 3", pr.................................**38.00**
Boxing glove, Souvenir of Reading Fair, ceramic, 1950s, 3", pr **19.00**
Boy in spacesuit, ceramic, Japan, 1950s, 3¾", pr..........................**39.00**
Charlie Chaplin shoes & hat, ceramic, unmk, 1940s, 1½", 4", pr.**29.00**
Chip 'n Dale, ceramic, NE Disney China, 3⅜", pr **39.00**
Choir boy in red (or blk), ceramic, Japan, 1950s, 4¾", pr.............**22.00**
Cinderella's slipper on pillow, mc ceramic, 2⅞x3", stacking pr **28.00**
Clown musician, HP ceramic, Japan, 1930s, 3½", pr.....................**29.00**
Daisy Duck & grocery bag, ceramic, A Good Company..., Disney, pr .**39.00**
Doc & Bashful dwarfs, ceramic, Foreign, 1930s, 2⅞", pr **85.00**
Donald & Daisy Duck, ceramic, NE Disney mk, 4½", pr **45.00**
Donald as miner in coal car (2nd shaker), ceramic, Disney, 4", pr .**39.00**
Donald Duck, mc ceramic, Dan Brechner, WD-32, Japan, 1961, 4⅞", pr..**95.00**
Eisenhower Lock (2-pc), St Lawrence Seaway, Japan, 1⅜x4⅞x2½" ..**29.00**
Eskimo & igloo, mc ceramic, red Japan mk, 1950s, 4½", pr **32.00**
Flying saucer, red & wht ceramic, 1950s, 1½x2½" dia, pr.............**49.00**
Goldilocks, mc ceramic, Relco label, 1950s, 4¼", pr **35.00**
Golf bag & ball, ceramic, unmk Am, 1950s, pr.............................**19.00**
Headless nude woman, breasts are shakers, ceramic, 3-pc..............**35.00**
Horace Horsecollar & girlfriend, ceramic, NE Disney China, 4½", pr ...**39.00**
Humpty Dumpty on wall (2nd shaker), mc ceramic, unmk USA, 5½", pr..**89.00**
Hunter w/gun & wht rabbit, mc ceramic, unmk, 1950s, he: 3½", pr..**22.00**
Indian boy & girl, mc ceramic, Japan, 1960s, 4⅜", pr **22.00**
Jimmy Carter peanut w/smile, ceramic, Made in Japan, 3½", pr ...**34.00**
Jock (Scottie from Lady & Tramp), ceramic, Disney, 1950s, 3x3", pr..**55.00**
Jogger in running suit w/hat pulled down, Enesco, 1978, 4½", pr..**35.00**
John Alden & Priscilla, mc ceramic, gr Japan mk, 1960s, 4¾", pr.**24.00**

Kate Greenaway boy & girl, heavy pottery, mk FF 77, 4⅜", pr **95.00**
Lady w/rolling pin & man in doghouse, Vallona Star, 3½", pr......**95.00**
Lion tamer w/whip & lion, ceramic, Japan mk, 1950s, 4" **26.00**
Lyndon Johnson portrait on wht ceramic, 3⅜", pr.........................**19.00**
Mammy & Pappy Yokum, ceramic, #2611, Al Capp, Japan, 4¼", pr..**110.00**
Man & lady, naughty plug-in set, ceramic, Japan, #7395, 1950s, pr..**175.00**
Maple leaf anthropomorphic people, ceramic, Regal Convention, 1992, pr.**95.00**
Martian in spaceship (2nd shaker), ceramic, Vallona Star, pr.....**100.00**
McGuffy's Reader & school bell, ceramic, 1950s, pr.....................**24.00**
Mexican man & cart, fruit shakers fit in cart, ceramic, Japan, 3-pc.**23.00**
Mickey sorcerer & broom, ceramic, c Disney Malaysia, 3½", pr ...**35.00**
Miss Muffet & spider, ceramic, Poinsettia Studio, 2½", pr **85.00**
Money sack on safe, ceramic, unmk, 1950s, 2½", 2¼", pr.............**16.00**
Moon man & rocket ship, ceramic, Enesco, 1950s, 4¼", pr..........**59.00**
Moon Mullins, glass w/plastic hat lid, Japan, 3", pr **55.00**
Old King Cole on throne (2nd shaker), HP Royal Japan, 1950s-50s, pr.**39.00**
Old Mother Hubbard & dog, ceramic, Poinsettia Studio, 3½"......**85.00**
Oswald & Homer, ceramic, Lantz, Napco Japan #1C3635, 1958, 4", pr.**135.00**
Pebbles & Bamm-Bamm, ceramic, Harry James, 4", pr..................**49.00**
Pinocchio, glazed bsk, Disney, Japan, 5", pr..............................**125.00**
Pipe on pipe holder, ceramic, Trevewood, 1950s, 2x3¾", pr **19.00**
Pirate & treasure chest, ceramic, unmk, 1950s, he: 3½", pr **22.00**
Pixie & Dixie mice, ceramic, Made in Japan label, 3¼", pr...........**55.00**
Pixie & lily, ceramic, unmk USA, att Elbee Art, 1950s, 3", pr **22.00**
Pixie head, ceramic, Japan, #6981, 3¼", pr.................................**29.00**
Pluto, ceramic, cold pnt, Disney, 1940s, 3¼", pr..........................**39.00**
Pluto & doghouse, ceramic, A Good Co...Applause, 3¼", pr........**39.00**
Popeye & Olive Oyl, ceramic, HP, unmk, 1960s-70s, 6¼", pr.......**95.00**
Queen of Hearts & jester, ceramic, Japan 6440, 4⅜", pr **45.00**
Robin Hood on rock (2nd shaker), Japan, 1950s, 5⅝", pr.............**29.00**
Royal Canadian Mounted Policeman, ceramic, Japan, 4¼", pr.....**29.00**
Rudolf the Red-Nose Reindeer, ceramic, #4370, 3", pr.................**28.00**
Santa head w/tassel on hat, ceramic, Japan, 1950s, 3", pr.............**24.00**
Santa in chimney & Christmas tree, ceramic, Japan, 3½", pr.......**22.00**
Shmoo, Al Capp creature, chalk-like, late 1940s, 3½", pr **225.00**
Shoemaker & elf, majolica type, gr Japan mk, 4", pr **32.00**
Silly Symphony Pig, ceramic, unauthorized Disney, Japan, 1930s, 4", pr ..**59.00**
Skull, chalk-like, ca 1940s, 1⅝", pr **24.00**
Snake charmer & snake, ceramic, red Japan mk, 1950s, pr **22.00**
Snoopy on doghouse, stacking, ceramic, Benjamin & Medwin, 1994, pr..**35.00**
Snow White kissing Dopey (2nd shaker), ceramic, Disney, 4", pr.**39.00**
Space Needle building, metal, K 534 Made in Japan, 2½x5"+tray.**39.00**
Spinning wheel & stool, ceramic, unmk USA, 1950s, wheel: 3¾", pr..**18.00**
SS Love Boat, ceramic, Enesco, 1979, 1⅝x3", pr...........................**29.00**
Statue of Liberty, ceramic, 5 & Dime Co..., c 1992, 5⅜", pr.........**28.00**
Street sweeper & cart (2nd shaker), unmk, 4⅜", 2", pr.................**19.00**
Sylvester cat, ceramic, c Warner Bros Inc, 1970s, 4¼", pr **89.00**
Tom Sawyer & fence, ceramic, unmk, 3", pr **45.00**
Victrola phonograph, ceramic, Napco Originals by Giftcraft, 1950s, pr..**24.00**
White Rabbit (Alice in Wonderland) stacking pr, ceramic, Japan, 4"..**85.00**
Wizard of Oz, ceramic, Clay Art, 3½", pr.....................................**29.00**
Woody & Winnie Woodpecker, ceramic, W Lantz 1990, pr **49.00**
Worm in apple, brn & gr ceramic, unmk, 1950s, pr.......................**19.00**
Yenems Cigarette pack & matches, ceramic, unmk, 1950s, 2⅞", pr .**24.00**
Yosemite Sam, mc ceramic, Warner Bros, Lego label, 1960s, 4", pr.**95.00**
Ziggy & dog, mc ceramic, Universal Press, 1979, Ziggy: 3¼", pr..**45.00**
3 Little Pigs, ceramic, NECC Disney, 3⅜", pr.............................**39.00**

Salts, Open

Before salt became refined, processed, and free-flowing as we know it today, it was necessary to serve it in a salt cellar. An innovation of the early 1800s, the master salt was placed by the host and passed from per-son to person. Smaller individual salts were a part of each place setting. A small silver spoon was used to sprinkle it onto the food.

If you would like to learn more about the subject of salts, we recommend *5,000 Open Salts*, written by William Heacock and Patricia Johnson, with many full-color illustrations and current values.

Our advisor for this category is Chris Christensen; he is listed in the Directory under California. In the listings below, the numbers refer to the Johnson and Heacock book and *Pressed Glass Salt Dishes* by L.W. and D.B. Neal. Lines with 'repro' within the description reflect values for reproduced salts.

Key:
EPNS — electroplated nickel silver   HM — hallmarked

Animals, Figurals, and Novelties

Bandmaster's cap, US Glass, H&J-3738 ....**90.00**
Chickens, dbl, milk glass, sgn, Vallerystahl, H&J-4447 ....**55.00**
Duck, heavy crystal, European, H&J-4677 ....**45.00**

Frog with cart pulling snail shell and lady-bug, pewter-colored metal, Smith #459, 2", $50.00.

Horseshoe, 'Good Luck', H&J-3742, master **100.00**
Wagon, clear, ca 1890, H&J-3739 ....**55.00**

Art Glass

Cranberry, ruffled rigaree, tulip top, SP holder **135.00**
Daum, enameled windmill scenic, sgn, H&J-10.........................**995.00**
Mt WA, shiny, unsgn, H&J-46 ....**175.00**
Steuben, Calcite, ped ft, H&J-34 ....**275.00**
Tiffany, ruffled top edge, sgn, H&J-32 ....**225.00**

China and Porcelain

Austria, HP, rnd, sgn, H&J-1272, ind...**15.00**
Belleek, HP, ruffled top, rnd, mk, H&J-1310...............................**35.00**
Belleek, star shaped, 3rd blk mk..**75.00**
Celery salt, HP, oval platter...**15.00**
Dresden, attached flowers, H&J-1689, ind **45.00**
Elfinware, heavy decor, Germany, H&J-1689, ind **45.00**
Elfinware, Japan, H&J-1222...**10.00**
Elfinware, swan, Germany, ornate, H&J-1039 ....**35.00**
Haviland, H&J-1613 ....**35.00**
Japan, HP, H&J-1443, ind..**20.00**
Meissen, sq, H&J-1595, ind **60.00**
Nippon, HP floral tub, H&J-1454, ind..**20.00**
Royal Bayreuth, figural claw, H&J-1667, ind **35.00**
Satsuma, ca 1940-60, H&J-1931, ind..**25.00**

Cut Glass

Buzz Star, H&J-3127...**15.00**
Canoe shape, cane cutting, 3" L **55.00**
Clear, ped ft, mk Libbey **65.00**

Cranberry, etched, ped ft, ca 1890, H&J-123 ....85.00
Daisy & Button, rnd tub, H&J-2853 ....25.00
Diamond Points, gr to clear, ped ft 95.00
Hawkes, cut lower section, top eng, rnd, sgn, H&J-3083 ....55.00
Heart, club, spade, dmn, H&J-3033 to H&J-3034, 4 for 195.00
Zippered, H&J-3088 to H&J-3089, ea..........................15.00

Doubles

Automobile, pressed glass, mk Pontieux, H&J-3764 ....100.00
French, cobalt pressed glass, H&J-2086......................65.00
German, HP porc, H&J-1150 ....45.00
KPM, figural, porc, ca 1860, H&J-1155 to H&J-1156, ea 295.00
Meissen, porc, w/hdl, H&J-1169.............................125.00
Quimper, porc, sgn, old, H&J-1129 ....175.00

Lacy Glass

American, non-flint, ca 1920-40, repro, VG 45.00
Avon, H&J-3506, repro.......................................10.00
Barlow/Kaiser 1107, Stippled Bull's Eye, opal, rim chips, 6¾" 175.00
Barlow/Kaiser 1443, Beaded Strawberry Dmn, opal, 3¼", EX 350.00
Barlow/Kaiser 1457, Shell Foliate, amber, 3" L, VG 500.00
Barlow/Kaiser 1472, octagonal invt waffle, amethyst, 1x3x2½", G..440.00
French, amber, non-flint, H&J-1771, ca 1920-40, repro, VG........65.00
Metro Museum of Art, vaseline, bl, etc, MMA, repro, VG 20.00
NE Glass Co Boston, flower basket, fiery opal, 2⅞" 415.00
Neal BB-1, Basket of Flowers/Birdbath, wht opaque, chips, 1⅞" ...120.00
Neal BF-1d, Basket of Flowers, gr-bl, Sandwich, losses, 2⅛" 120.00
Neal BS-3a, Beaded Scroll, violet-bl, Sandwich, minor chips, 2".700.00
Neal BT-4d, Boat, cobalt, 1⅝".................................700.00
Neal BT-5, Lafayette Boat, med bl.............................950.00
Neal CN-1a, Crown, wht opal, Sandwich, chips, 2¼" 150.00
Neal CN-1a variant, Flower Basket, 3⅛".....................200.00
Neal CN-1b, Crown, cobalt, Sandwich, rpr/chips, 3¼" 175.00
Neal CN-1b, wht opal, Sandwich, 2¼".......................765.00
Neal CT-1, Chariot, silvery opaque bl, EX.....................750.00
Neal DI-4, dbl, cobalt, 3"......................................825.00
Neal EE-1a, Eagle, Sandwich, 1825-50, 1⅞", pr 100.00
Neal EE-3, Eagle, 3¼"...250.00
Neal EE-6, Eagle, minor edge roughness, 1⅝"...................200.00
Neal GA-4a, Gothic Arch, bl opaque w/wht striations, 1⅝" 525.00
Neal LE-1, Lyre, dk bl opaque, 1⅞" 1,880.00
Neal MV-1b, Beaded Scroll, cobalt, Mt Vernon, chips, 1¾".......235.00
Neal MVI, aqua w/milky wht streak, 2¾", EX 220.00
Neal OG-4, Pittsburgh area 100.00
Neal OL-11, citron, NM 300.00
Neal OO-1a, amber, octagonal, oblong, 1⅝" 500.00
Neal OO-15, amber, 2¾"......................................465.00
Neal OP-14, emerald gr, oval, ftd, 3".........................715.00
Neal OP-20, EX 75.00
Neal OP-4, cobalt, chip 400.00
Neal PO-4, Peacock Eye, bl opaque w/wht striations, 1½" 1,400.00
Neal RP-17, deep sapphire, ftd, 3"............................770.00
Neal RP-3, silvery lt bl opaque, rnd ped, 2" 1,880.00
Neal SC-5, Scroll, med bl, Sandwich, chips, 1⅞"...............470.00
Neal SD-11, Strawberry Dmn, wht opal, Sandwich, roughness, 1¾"..265.00
Neal SD-14, dk purple-bl, 2⅞" 440.00
Neal SD-16, Strawberry Dmn, cobalt, Sandwich, chips, 2".........200.00
Neal SD-9, Strawberry Dmn, gray-bl, Sandwich, chips, 2"..........175.00
Neal SI-1A, gr-bl, Sandwich, 1⅝"............................650.00
Neal SL-1, Shell, red amethyst, roughness, 1¾"...............1,000.00
Neal SL-1a, lt amber, 3".......................................575.00
Neal SL-18, Shell, scroll ped, Sandwich, sm crack, 2⅝"..........2,820.00

Neal SL-4, Shell, dk amber, Pittsburgh area, 1¾".................585.00
Neal SN-1b, cobalt, 3"...440.00
Neal SN-3a, 3¼"...415.00
Neal WN-1a, Wagon, very rare, 3".............................770.00

Pressed Pattern Glass, Clear

Daisy & Button, LG Wright, H&J-875 to H&J-876, repro, ind, ea..8.00
English Hobnail, H&J-2680, ind 10.00
Euchre, H&J-3018 to H&J-3021, ind, ea 12.00
Faceted, H&J-2906-H..7.50
Heisey, Fancy Loop, H&J-2674, ind 25.00
Horseshoe, H&J-3741, ind.....................................30.00
Liberty Bell 1776-1876, H&J-2689, ind 65.00
Plain Band, Heisey, H&J-2560..................................22.00
Roman Key, H&J-3582, flint, master...........................55.00
Sawtooth Circle, H&J-3540......................................30.00
Serrated Rib & Fine Cut, H&J-2535, ind 10.00
Snail, H&J-2656, ind..20.00
Tree of Life, 'Salt', H&J-3582, master.........................85.00
Washington, H&J-2504, ind....................................27.00
Washington Centennial, H&J-2518, ind........................20.00

Silverplate

Clear glass liner, H&J-3918, Victorian 75.00
Dog pulling open salt, mk Hall & Elton, Walkinford, CT 375.00
English, David Hannel, ca 1754, sm dents, pr...................350.00
Fluted, ped ft, H&J-4022.......................................35.00
Heart shaped, rim decor 25.00
Rnd bowl w/kangaroo, EPNS, Australia, H&J-4305, VG............40.00
Shell w/dolphin legs, H&J-4278, VG 25.00
Tulip on leaf, Am, H&J-4155, VG 30.00
Victorian holder, clear liner, hdl, H&J-3918, EX................95.00
Wolf-like dogs w/ bowl on bk, Meriden, H&J-4322, VG 150.00

Sterling

Austria-Hungary, cut/flashed bowl, sterling ped, H&J-106..........250.00
Austria-Hungary, wht opal cut-bk bowl, sterling ped, H&J-138 .175.00
Chinese, mini house w/shaker set, H&J-4743 ....225.00
French, ornate, HM, matching spoon, H&J-3937, ind...............125.00
German, basket, ped ft, HM 800, H&J-4228 ....110.00
German, swan, HM 800, matching spoon, H&J-4299, ca 1890 ....95.00
Russian, chair, HM, dtd, H&J-4737 ....500.00
Steiff, chased, w/pepper, H&J-4385, 1918......................175.00
Tiffany, fish, matching spoon, H&J-4324.......................150.00
Viking, HP, HM, matching spoon, H&J-2002 to H&J-2005, ea .125.00

Samplers

American samplers were made as early as the colonial days; even earlier examples from seventeenth-century England still exist today. Changes in style and design are evident down through the years. Verses were not added until the late seventeenth century. By the eighteenth century, samplers were used not only for sewing experience but also as an educational tool. Young ladies, who often signed and dated their work, embroidered numbers and letters of the alphabet and practiced fancy stitches as well. Fruits and flowers were added for borders; birds, animals, and Adam and Eve became popular subjects. Later houses and other buildings were included. By the nineteenth century, the American Eagle and the little red schoolhouse had made their appearances.

Many factors bear on value: design and workmanship, strength of color, the presence of a signature and/or a date (both being preferred over only one or the other, and earlier is better), and, of course, condition.

ABC panels/pious verse/house/flowers, linen, 1842, 17½x17¼"..**1,875.00**
ABCs/berries/birds/Adam & Eve/verse, homespun, 1823, 19x15" fr..**935.00**
ABCs/berries/verse, linen, sgn/1787, 15x12" blk pnt fr............**1,650.00**
ABCs/Bible verse, homespun, OH/1814, 8½x9" in mahog vnr fr.**625.00**
ABCs/Bible verse/Tree of Knowledge w/serpent, sgn/1794, 14x14", G.**650.00**
ABCs/floral/vines, sgn/1826, 12x15" fr.................................**525.00**
ABCs/flowers/baskets/verse, sgn/1766, rpl 13x11½" fr.............**1,500.00**
ABCs/house/verse, homespun, sgn/1795, 12x8" in curly maple fr..**1,870.00**
ABCs/pines/country estate/couple, linen, sgn/1807, 16x12"+fr.**1,155.00**
ABCs/plants/animals/crowns/strawberries, sgn/1799, 19x15" orig fr....**2,475.00**
ABCs/plants/verses/vines, linen, sgn/1830, 15x17"+fr.............**1,500.00**
ABCs/stylized flowers, sgn/1796, in 13½x10" fr.........................**865.00**
Adam & Eve/boat/sailors/animals, linen, 1804, 19x24" fr........**2,000.00**
Adam & Eve/lengthy verse/Tree of Knowledge, sgn/1792, 16x12", G...**765.00**
Birds/flower branches/flowerpots, linen, 20x17"+gilt fr **770.00**
Church/birds/lady & child/animals/verse, linen, 12x15"+fr **1,045.00**
Couple w/dog & bird/flowers/verse, sgn, in orig 14x11" fr **1,200.00**
Crosses resembling weave of different fabrics, sgn/1805, 13" sq fr.**1,750.00**
Flower & fruit baskets/vines, gr/brn floss on natural, 1828, 20x16" fr.**550.00**
Flowers/birds/peacocks/prayer, silk thread, sgn/1754, 16x11" fr.**1,325.00**
House among trees/flowers/crowns/verse, linen, 1839, 15½x13".**1,650.00**
Letters (unusual)/verse, linen, sgn/1700, 12x7"+rpl fr.............**1,500.00**
Man w/sheep by house, strawberries below, sgn/1851, 20x15" fr.**900.00**
Rose of Sharon verse/strawberries/flowers/etc, linen, 1814, 19x16" fr.**1,300.00**
Shepherd/shepherdess/angels/etc, linen, sgn, 18x12"+rpl fr **440.00**
Verse/lady/potted flowers/birds/etc, sgn/1835, 17x17", G **1,400.00**
Verses (2)/birds/flowers/figures, linen, 1790, 14½x12"+fr **1,750.00**
10 Commandments/Lord's Prayer, florals/etc, sgn/1735, 17x11".**1,650.00**

Sandwich Glass

The Boston and Sandwich Glass Company was founded in 1825 by Deming Jarves in Sandwich, Massachusetts. Their first products were blown and molded, but eventually they perfected a method for pressing glass that led to the manufacture of the 'lacy' glass which they made until about 1840. Up until the closing of the factory in 1888, they made a wide variety of not only flint pattern glass but also beauty fancy glass such as cut, overlay, overshot, opalescent, and etched. Today colored Sandwich commands the highest prices, but it all is becoming increasingly rare and expensive.

Our advisor for this category is Elizabeth Simpson; she is listed in the Directory under Maine. See also Cup Plates; Salts, Open; Trevaise; other specific types of glass.

Bowl, Dmn Quilt, folded rim, 1¾x8½", NM **390.00**
Candlestick, Acanthus Leaf, bl & clambroth, crack, 10⅞" **250.00**
Candlestick, apple gr, petal socket, sq dbl-step base, 9⅛" **550.00**
Candlestick, bl, petal socket, columnar shaft, stepped base, 9" ...**350.00**
Candlestick, cobalt, hexagonal, 9¼", EX **235.00**
Candlestick, Eye, appl hdl, saucer base, 3¼x6⅜", VG **700.00**
Candlestick, Petal & Loop, bl & clambroth, 1840-60, 7" **880.00**
Candlestick, red-purple, 7⅛" **440.00**
Candlesticks, Acanthus Leaf, bl socket, hex base, 11", EX, pr.**1,500.00**
Candlesticks, Acanthus Leaf, bl socket, wht hex base, 9½", VG, pr .**1,000.00**
Candlesticks, amethyst, hex socket on flaring rnd-loop base, 7", pr.**4,100.00**
Candlesticks, canary, rnd bases w/loop design, petal socket, 7", pr..**385.00**
Candlesticks, cobalt, hex base, 9⅛", pr **530.00**
Candlesticks, Dolphin, bl petal socket/wht 2-step base, 9½", VG, pr.**1,500.00**
Candlesticks, Dolphin, hex socket, 1-step base, 6¾", EX, pr **765.00**
Candlesticks, lacy, #1 socket, waterfall base, 7", pr, VG..........**1,400.00**
Candlesticks, Loop, clambroth, petal socket/rnd base, 7", VG, pr..**600.00**

Candlesticks, Petal & Loop, sapphire bl, 1840-60, 6¾", pr.........**650.00**
Candlesticks, sapphire bl, petal socket, hex base, 7⅜", pr........**1,650.00**
Celery vase, dbl-ring Bull's Eye/Sunburst, appl ft, 7x5", NM ...**1,200.00**
Compote, amethyst, 16 open slats, 32-point rim, hex ft, 8x9", NM.**14,100.00**
Compote/ftd nappy, lacy, Shield & Pine Tree, 4x6", EX..............**600.00**
Compote/ftd nappy, lacy, Tulip & Acanthus Leaf, Plume ft, 5x10", EX.**1,800.00**
Decanter, cobalt, pressed 8-flute (no ring), 10½", VG.............**1,000.00**
Decanter, Dmn Sunburst, Dmn Quilt stopper, 5¼" **700.00**
Decanter, Shell & Rib, bl, 9⅜"...**4,500.00**
Decanter, Shell & Rib, bl, 11½", EX **4,200.00**
Dish, lacy, Cornucopia & Shield, scrolls in base, scalloped, 8" L, VG..**300.00**
Dish, lacy, Eagle w/13 stars, octagonal, 7", VG **500.00**
Dish, lacy, Hairpin, scalloped, 6¾x8¾", EX **590.00**
Dish, lacy, Leaf & Gothic Arch, edge chips, 6x8" L **250.00**
Dish, lacy, Princess Feather & Dmn, gr, 4¾".............................**325.00**
Dish, lacy, Roman Rosette, amethyst, 5¼", VG..........................**325.00**
Dish, lacy, Waffle/Crossed Peacock Eye, Strawberry center, 10" L, EX.**245.00**
Dish, lacy, Waffle/Crossed Peacock Eye, Strawberry center, 11" L, EX.**300.00**
Dish, Sunburst & Dmn Quilt, 1⅛x5⅝" **120.00**
Hat, cobalt, blown, ca 1825-35, lt wear.......................................**600.00**
Hat, Dmn Quilt, folded rim, 2½x2½" **700.00**

Honey dish with tray, lacy, Gothic, minor damage, $700.00.

Lamp, hand; Star & Punty, appl hdl, 4½" **265.00**
Lamp, whale oil; bl, acorn font, stepped pressed base, 6" **5,750.00**
Lamp, whale oil; clambroth, bl font w/acanthus leaves, 12"........**385.00**
Molasses can, Ribbed Rosette, appl hdl, tin lid, 7" **475.00**
Mustard pot, lacy, Peacock Eye, 2", +lid & underplate, VG........**675.00**
Nappy, lacy, Stippled Bull's Eye, opal, 5¾", EX..........................**265.00**
Nappy, lacy, Tulip & Acanthus Leaf, bl, 5½", VG.......................**300.00**
Nappy, lacy, Tulip & Acanthus Leaf, opal, 6¼", NM **400.00**
Pitcher, Arch & Fern, emb Xs under hdl, folded rim, decanter mold, 7"..**700.00**
Pitcher, Dmn Quilt, 7x5"...**1,650.00**
Pitcher, Sunburst-in-Square, blown 3-mold, folded rim, 7".......**1,500.00**
Plate, lacy, Roman Rosette, amber, 6", NM **700.00**
Plate, lacy, Thistle & Drape, gr tint, 7", VG **110.00**
Plate, lacy, Thistle & Drape, lt amethyst, 7", VG.......................**385.00**
Plate, lacy, Union Ship of State, 8-sided, 6½", EX...................**1,400.00**
Punch bowl, Dmn Quilt, appl Dmn Sunburst ft (imperfect), 7½x8½".**5,300.00**
Salt cellar, Sunburst, cobalt, flared rim, 1¾"..............................**675.00**
Toy candlestick, cobalt, 1¾"..**600.00**
Toy dish, lacy, Dmn & Scroll, amber, ⅝x3" L, EX......................**700.00**
Toy ewer & basin, cobalt, paneled, 2¼", 3⅛" dia, EX.............**1,200.00**
Toy iron, dk emerald gr, ⅞x1⅜", NM **700.00**
Toy iron, olive gr, ⅞x1⅜", NM **1,550.00**
Toy spoon holder, bl, hexagonal, 1¾x1½", EX............................**600.00**
Toy tureen, lacy, fan/scroll/rosette, cobalt, w/lid, 2x2¾", VG..**1,150.00**
Tray, USF Constitution (ship), rectangular, 5½x7", EX..........**7,300.00**
Tumbler, Dmn Quilt, blown 3-mold, 4¾" **300.00**
Tumbler, tavern; Plume, pontil crack, 3½x3"..............................**180.00**
Tumbler, tavern; ribbed, blown 3-mold, 3½x2⅞" **235.00**

Vase, Elongated Loop, gr, bisecting lines/hex base, 4¾", EX **900.00**
Vase, gr-yel, gauffered rim, hex base, 1840-60, 11½" **350.00**
Vase, Loop, yel, gauffered rim, hex std, rnd base, 10", pr.............**600.00**
Vase, Pillar Mold, canary, cut punties, rnd base, 12", pr...........**7,650.00**
Vase, Tulip, amethyst, scalloped rim, 8-sided base, 10" **1,500.00**
Vase, Tulip, dk amethyst, scalloped rim, 8-sided base, 9¾" **3,000.00**
Vase, Tulip, emerald gr, scalloped rim, 8-sided base, 10¼" **300.00**
Vase, Twisted Loop, cobalt, gauffered rim/8-side std/sq base, 11", EX..**2,500.00**
Vase, 4-Printie Block, emerald gr, hex base/gauffered rim, 12", NM, pr.**7,100.00**
Window pane, lacy, dmn scroll & fan, 8x10", VG **2,300.00**

Santa Barbara Ceramic Design

Established in 1976 by current director Raymond Markow (after three years of refining his decorative process), Santa Barbara Ceramic Design arose less auspiciously than the 'Ohio' potteries — no financial backing and no machinery beyond that available to ancient potters: wheel, kiln, brushes, and paint.

The company produced intricate, colorful, hand-painted flora and fauna designs on traditional pottery forms, primarily vases and table lamps. Although artistically aligned with turn-of-the-century art potteries, the techniques used were unique and developed within the studio.

Vibrant glaze stains with wax emulsion were applied by brush over a graduated multicolor background, then enanced by elaborate sgraffito detailing on petals and leaves. In the early 1980s, a white stoneware body was incorporated to further brighten the color palette, and during the last few years sgraffito was replaced by detailing with a fine brush.

Early pieces were thrown. Mid-1980 saw a transition to casting, except for experimental or custom pieces. Artists were encouraged to be creative and often given individual gallery exhibitions. Custom orders were welcomed, and experimentation occurred regularly; the resulting pieces are the most rare and seldom appear today. Limited production lines evolved, including the Collector Series that featured an elaborate ornamental border designed to enhance the primary design. The Artist's Collection was a numbered series of pieces by senior artists, usually combining flora and fauna.

The company's approach to bold colors and surface decoration influenced many contemporary potters and inspired imitation in both pottery and glass during the craft renaissance of the 1970s and 1980s. Several artists successfully made use of the studio's designs and techniques after leaving. Authentic pieces bear the artist's initials, date and 'SBCD' marked in black stain and, if thrown, the potter's inscription.

Markow employed as many as three potters and twelve decorators at a given time. The ware was marketed through craft festivals and wholesale distribution to art and craft galleries nationwide. An estimated 100,000 art pottery pieces were made before a transition in the late 1980s to silk-screened household and garden items, which remain in production today.

Though less than thirty years old, Santa Barbara Ceramic Design's secondary market has seen upwards of one thousand pieces change hands; these are often viewed as bargains compared to their Rookwood and Weller Hudson counterparts. For artist/potter marks visit the craft cafe at johnguthrie.com. Our advisor is John Guthrie; he is listed in the Directory under South Carolin.

Bowl, #5107, birds, Alvaro Suman, 1979, 10".............................**135.00**
Bud vase, bearded iris, Margie Gilson, 1983, 6" **200.00**
Bud vase, rose, Laurie Linn, 1983, 6"..**55.00**
Goblet, #C, Dutch iris, Kat Korcoran, 1979, 7½".........................**75.00**
Goblet, #C, poppy, Shannon Sargent, 1979, 7½".........................**75.00**
Lamp, #5117, iris, Itoko Takeuchi, 1983, 9".................................**325.00**
Lamp, #5117, orchid, Anne Collinson, 1981, 10½" **130.00**
Lamp, #5117, orchid, Itoko Takeuchi, 1984, 10½" **170.00**

Lamp, #5117, poppy, Shannon Sargent, 1980, 10½" **200.00**
Lamp, #5118, iris, Itoko Takeuchi, 1984, 11"...............................**225.00**
Lamp, #5118, iris, unsgn, ca 1984, 11" **195.00**
Lamp, #5119, bouquet, Itoko Takeuchi, 1984, 15½".....................**595.00**
Lamp, #5119, fuchsia, Shannon Sargent, 1980, 13½" **250.00**
Lamp, #5119, iris/gladiola, Laurie Linn Ball, 1982, 15½"...........**495.00**
Lamp, #5119g, bouquet, Laurie Linn, 1982, 17" **495.00**
Lamp, #5130, lily of the valley, Itoko Takeuchi, 1984, 7" **128.00**
Lamp, #5130, poppy, Laurie Linn Ball, 1986, 7", from $125 to...**165.00**
Lamp, #7105, columbine, Margaret Gilson, 1984, 17" **445.00**
Lamp, #7105, iris, Dorie Knight-Hutchinson, 1984, 17" **335.00**
Lamp, #7115, poppy, Laurie Linn Ball, 1986, 16" **395.00**
Lamp, #7125, calla lily, Itoko Takeuchi, 1984, 18" **375.00**
Lamp, #7125, tulip, Itoko Takeuchi, 1988, 18".............................**300.00**
Lamps, #7101, apple blossom, Gary Ba-Han, 1984, 13", pr.........**650.00**
Oil lamp, #1102, iris, Alvaro Suman, 1980, 6½" **75.00**
Oil lamp, #1102, poppies, Ray, 1976, 6½".....................................**50.00**
Pitcher, #5106, hibiscus, Christine Adcock, 1980, 8½" **160.00**
Pitcher, #5106, trumpet lily, Alison Atwill, 1981, 10½" **230.00**
Plate, #5114, day lily, Margie Gilson, 1981, 7" **145.00**
Plate, #5114, iris, Michelle Foster, 1981, 7" **90.00**
Plate, #5114, Pegasus, Shannon Sargent, 1980, 7"......................**80.00**
Plate, #5114, sweet pea, Michelle Foster, 1982, 7", from $80 to .**130.00**
Plate, #5114, tulip, Eleyña Dhyansky, 1980, 7" **145.00**
Teapot, #5109, lily, Anne Fitch, 1982, 8" **425.00**
Vase, #5101, abstract, John Guthrie, 1984, 7"...............................**80.00**
Vase, #5101, carnation, Margie Gilson, 1982, 7" **145.00**
Vase, #5101, experimental, Itoki Takeuchi, 1984, 7" **80.00**
Vase, #5101, iris, Christine Adcock, 1980, 6½"............................**150.00**
Vase, #5101, morning glory, Laurie Linn, 1982, 6½".....................**155.00**
Vase, #5101, tiger lily, Gary Ba-Han, 1983, 6½" **175.00**
Vase, #5101r, night blossom, Itoko Takeuchi, 1984, 6" **130.00**
Vase, #5102, daffodil, Laurie Cosca, 1982, 9" **125.00**
Vase, #5102, trumpet lily, Laurie Cosca, 1980, 9" **125.00**
Vase, #5102, wisteria, Shannon Sargent, 1985, 9" **125.00**
Vase, #5103, day lily, Mary Favero, 1981, 8" **270.00**
Vase, #5103, experimental, Laurie Linn Ball, 1985, 8" **100.00**
Vase, #5103, orchid, Allison Atwill, 1981, 8½" **280.00**
Vase, #5103, orchid, Mary Favero, 1981, 8" **250.00**
Vase, #5103, watercolor, Itoko Takeuchi, 1986, 8" **125.00**
Vase, #5103cs, poppy, Laurie Cosca, 1982, 9" **250.00**
Vase, #5104, daffodil, Margaret Gilson, 1984, 14" **225.00**
Vase, #5119, morning glory, Laurie Linn Ball, 1986, 15½" **295.00**
Vase, #5133, iris, Shannon Sargene, 1984, 20"........................**1,500.00**
Vase, #6112, fuchsia/bird, Dorie Knight-Hutchinson, 1984, 10".**425.00**
Vase, #7116, hibiscus, Laurie Linn Ball, 1984, 12" **400.00**
Vase, #7116, iris, Dorie Knight, 1981, 12" **280.00**
Vase, #7116, orchid, unsgn, ca 1981, 12" **300.00**
Vase, #7116cs, bouquet, Itoko Takeuchi, 1986, 12" **325.00**
Vase, #7116cs, carnation, Michelle Foster, 1982, 12" **445.00**
Vase, #7116cs, morning glory, Mary Favero, 1982, 12"................**300.00**
Vase, #7116ss, tiger/tiger lily, Shannon Sargent, 1984, 12" **650.00**

Sarreguemines

Sarreguemines, France, is the location of Utzschneider and Company, founded about 1800, producers of majolica, transfer-printed dinnerware, figurines, and novelties which are usually marked 'Sarreguemines.' In 1836, under the management of Alexandre de Geiger, son-in-law of Utzschneider, the company became affiliated with Villeroy and Boch. During the 1850s and 1860s, two new facilities with modern steam-fired machinery were erected. Alexandre's son Paul was the next to guide the company, and under his leadership two more factories were built — one at Digoin and the other at Vitry le Francois. After his death in 1931, the company split but was consolidated again after the War under the name of Sarreguemines - Digoin - Vitry le Francois. Items marked St. Clement were made during the period from 1979 to 1982, indicating the group who owned the company for that span of time. Today the company is known as Sarreguemines - Batiment.

Bowl, grapes & leaves, mk Majolica Sarreguemines, 3x12" **95.00**
Cup & saucer, orange (cup) on leaves (5⅛" saucer)....................**225.00**
Face bottle, sailor, 3½", from $135 to..**150.00**
Face jug, blk hat w/bl band, pale complexion, slight smile, 6½".**250.00**
Face jug, Chamberlain, 6", from $395 to.....................................**450.00**
Face jug, clown, 6½", from $600 to **700.00**
Face jug, Englishman, #3210, 7¾", from $200 to.......................**235.00**
Face jug, John Bull, #3257, 7½", from $250 to...........................**325.00**
Face jug, Jolly Fellow, #3181, 8¾", from $335 to.......................**395.00**
Face jug, Jolly Fellow, 5½", from $150 to **195.00**
Face jug, man w/toothache, 7", from $450 to **525.00**
Face jug, plaid headband, blk hair/mustache/goatee, 6"..............**250.00**
Face jug, plaid headband, blk hair/mustache/goatee, 9"..............**395.00**
Face jug, Puck, gr hat, ca 1890-1915, 7"......................................**150.00**
Face jug, The Judge, 7½", from $210 to **265.00**
Face jug, Uncle Sam, from $750 to **850.00**
Jar, bear figural, EX detail & color, 4½", NM **350.00**
Pitcher, pig figural, #3318, 9¼", from $200 to............................**250.00**
Pitcher, rooster in top coat w/cane, brn tones, 9¼" **395.00**
Plate, grapes & leaves in relief, early 20th C, 7¾" **150.00**
Plate, plums & leaves, early 20th C, 7¾"....................................**150.00**
Plate, Russian equestrian scene, 8"...**125.00**
Soap dish, Louis XV, pre-1915, w/lid, 3½x5⅝x4" **85.00**
Toby pitcher, Judy, #3430, 12", from $450 to **550.00**
Vase, appl lizards on cobalt, stick neck, rpr, 19th C, 8½", pr...**1,000.00**
Vase, morning glories/butterflies w/gold, ovoid, 17" **2,000.00**
Vase, Nouveau irises & violets w/leaves, #3088, ca 1890, 15" .**2,200.00**
Vase, Nouveau trees, ivory/purple/brn/gold on purple to bl, 16".**750.00**
Wash bowl & pitcher, Shell, early 20th C, 16¾" dia, 24"...........**700.00**

Satin Glass

Satin glass is simply glassware with a velvety matt finish achieved through the application of an acid bath. This procedure has been used by many companies since the twentieth century, both here and abroad, on many types of colored and art glass. See also Mother-of-Pearl; Webb.

Bowl, red, Bead & Drape, 3¾x9"..**175.00**
Celery vase, pk w/HP floral, Tufts #2457 fr, 8" **1,100.00**
Cracker jar, pk, HP florals & scrolls, SP trim, 7½x5½"..............**265.00**
Ewer, apricot to wht w/HP birds & flowers, thorn hdl, 10", NM..**200.00**
Rose bowl, bl, HP floral, 8-crimp, 3¼x4⅜" **145.00**
Rose bowl, pk/gr loopings alternate, camphor ft, berry pontil, 5".**175.00**
Tumbler, citron to wht, HP floral branches, 3¾".........................**120.00**
Vase, chartreuse gr o/l, ruffled fan form, HP florals, 5½x3".......**145.00**
Vase, daisies on bl to wht, clear ruffled top, 5"............................**60.00**

Satsuma

Satsuma is a type of fine cream crackle-glaze pottery or earthenware made in Japan as early as the seventeenth century. The earliest wares, made at the original kiln in the Satsuma province, were enameled with only simple florals. By the late eighteenth century, a floral brocade (or nishikide design) was favored, and similar wares were being made at other kilns under the direction of the Lord of Satsuma. In the early part

of the nineteenth century, a diaper pattern was added to the florals. Gold and silver enamels were used for accents by the latter years of the century. During the 1850s, as the quality of goods made for export to the Western world increased and the style of decoration began to evolve toward becoming more appealing to the Westerners, human forms such as Arhats, Kannon, geisha girls, and samurai warriors were added. Today the most valuable pieces are those marked 'Kinkozan,' 'Shuzan,' 'Ryuzan,' and 'Kozan.' The genuine Satsuma 'mon' or mark is a cross within a circle — usually in gold on the body or lid, or in red on the base of the ware. Character marks may be included.

Caution: Much of what is termed 'Satsuma' comes from the Showa Period (1926 to the present); it is not true Satsuma but a simulated type, a cheaper pottery with heavy enamel. Collectors need to be aware that much of the of the 'Satsuma' today is really Satsuma style and should not carry the values of true Satsuma. Our advisor for this category is Clarence Bodine; he is listed in the Directory under Pennsylvania.

Bowl, wisteria w/gold w/in & w/out, sgn, ca 1900, 3¾x6½" **500.00**
Box, children on drum form, Meiji, 1½" dia **450.00**
Ginger jar, Deco-style mc leaves, lid missing, 1930s, 5" **125.00**
Jar, fans, w/4 lugs resembling metalwork, Meiji, 9½"..................**765.00**
Jar, money bag form w/4 lg gilt tassels, rakans/scholars, 22" **300.00**

Palace urn, figural scene in central panels, 40", $3,000.00. (Photo courtesy Neal Auction Company)

Plate, Oriental figures in scene, early 20th C, 7¼" **38.00**
Teapot, Oriental couples in garden, Royal Satsuma, early 1900s, 9¼"..**390.00**
Teapot, scholars in garden, chrysanthemum finial, 19th C, 6" **350.00**
Vase, birds & snow, bl/wht/blk w/gold, globular, 12" **300.00**
Vase, butterfly & bird, classic form, ca 1920s, 7½" **145.00**
Vase, floral, globular, 19th C, 5" **885.00**
Vase, Hundred Arhats, Meiji, 11x11" **2,700.00**
Vase, Hundred Rakans, hexagonal, ca 1900, 4" **250.00**
Vase, Hundred Rakans, hexagonal, ca 1900, 10", pr...................**900.00**
Vase, Hundred Rakans & brocade, 4-lobe, tripod ft, Meiji, 7x6" .**525.00**
Vase, immortals, appl dragon, teardrop form, ca 1880-1900, 6x3½"...**1,800.00**
Vase, Jurojin & Nikko shrine, ca 1900, 6¼" **385.00**
Vase, musicians/shrine/landscape reserves, Meiji, 3".................**2,500.00**
Vase, Oriental figures, bottle neck, sm hdls, 19th C, 8¼", pr......**300.00**
Vase, roundels w/children & sages, floral borders, 19th C, 6" **400.00**
Wall pocket, dragon w/bl eyes, long pk tongue, Nikoriko, 7½".....**75.00**

Scales

In today's world of pre-measured and pre-packaged goods, it is difficult to imagine the days when such products as sugar, flour, soap, and candy first had to be weighed by the grocer. The variety of scales used at the turn of the century was highly diverse; at the Philadelphia Exposition in 1876, one company alone displayed over three hundred different weighing devices. Among those found today, brass, cast-iron, and plastic models are the most common. Fancy postal scales in decorative wood, silver, marble, bronze, and mosaic are also to be found.

A word of caution on the values listed: These values range from a low for those items in fair to good condition to the upper values for items in excellent condition. Naturally, items in mint condition could command even higher prices, and they often do. Also, these are retail prices that suggest what a collector will pay for the object. When you sell to a dealer, expect to get much less. The values noted are averages taken from various auction and other catalogs in the possession of the society members. Among these, but not limited to, are the following: Joel L. Malter & Co., Inc., Encino, CA; *Auktion Alt Technic*, Auction Team, Koln, Germany.

For those seeking additional information concerning antique scales we recommend *Scales, A Collector's Guide*, by Bill and Jan Berning (Schiffer). You are also encouraged to contact the International Society of Antique Scale Collectors, whose address can be found in the Directory under Clubs, Newsletters, and Catalogs. Visit the club website at www.isasc.org.

Key:
ap — arrow pointer	h — hanging
bal — balance	hcp — hanging counterpoise
bm — base metal	hh — hand held
br — brass	l+ — label with foreign coin values
Brit — British	lb w/i — labeled box with instructions
Can — Canadian	lph — letter plate or holder
Col — Colonial	pend — pendulum
CW — Civil War	PP — Patent Pending
cwt — counterweight	st — sterling
Engl — English	tt — torsion type
eq — equal arm	ua — unequal arm
Euro — European	wt — weight
FIS — Fairbanks Infallible Scale Co.	

Analytical (Scientific)

Am, eq, mahog w/br & ivory, late 1800s, 14x16x8", $200 to......**400.00**

Assay

Am, eq, mahog box w/br & ivory, plaque/drw, 1890s, $400 to.**1,000.00**

Coin: Equal Arm Balance, American

Blk japanned metal, eagle on lid, late 19th C, $300 to **400.00**
Col, oak 6-part box, Col moneys, Boston, 1720-75, $800 to ...**1,800.00**
Post Col to CW, oak 6-part box, l+, 1843, $400 to..................**1,000.00**

Coin: Equal Arm Balance, English

Charles I, wooden box w/11 Brit wts, 1640s, $900 to...............**1,500.00**
1-pc wood box, rnd wts, label, Freeman, 1760s, $250 to............**450.00**
6-pc oak box, coin wts label, Thos Harrison, 1750s, $200 to......**450.00**

Coin: Equal Arm Balance, French

Solid wood box, 12 sq wts, J Reyne, Bourdeau, 1694, $400 to.**1,000.00**
Solid wood box w/recesses, 5 sq wts, A Gardes, 1800s, $250 to..**800.00**
1-pc oval box, nested/fractional wts, label, 18th C, $250 to **400.00**
1-pc oval box, no wts, label of Fr/Euro coins, 18th C, $150 to ...**250.00**
1-pc walnut box, nested wts, Charpentier label, 1810, $275 to...**675.00**

Coin: Equal Arm Balance, Miscellaneous

Amsterdam, 1-pc box, 32 sq wts, label, late 1600s, $850 to.....**2,500.00**
Cologne, full set of wts & full label, late 1600s, $1,200 to.......**2,800.00**
German, wood box, 13+ wts beneath main wts, label, 1795, $650 to ..**900.00**

Counterfeit Coin Detectors, American

Allender Pat, lb w/i, cwt, Nov 22, 1855, 8½", $350 to **650.00**
Allender PP, rocker, labeled box, cwt, 1850s, 8½", $450 to **750.00**
Allender PP, rocker, no box or cwt, 1850s, 8½", $250 to **375.00**
Allender PP, space for $3 gold pc, lb w/i, cwt, 1855, #350 to......**750.00**
Allender PP, space for $3 gold pc, no box or cwt, 1855, $275 to..**375.00**
Allender Warranted, rocker, no box or cwt, 1850s, 8½", $350 to..**475.00**
Maranville Pat Coin Detector by CE Staples, Mass, from $600 to..**800.00**
McNally-Harrison Pat 1882, rocker, cwt, JT McNally, $275 to ..**500.00**
McNally-Harrison Pat 1882, rocker, cwt & box, FIS, $400 to **750.00**
McNally-Harrison...1882, rocker, CI base, no cwt/box, $250 to .**400.00**
Thompson, Z-formed rocker, Berrian Mfg, 1877 Pat, $175 to.....**350.00**

Counterfeit Coin Detectors, Dutch

Rocker, Ellinckhuysen, br, +copy of 1829 Patent, $700 to.......**1,000.00**

Counterfeit Coin Detectors, English

Folding, Guinea, self-rising, labeled box, 1850s, $175 to.............**225.00**
Folding, Guinea, self-rising, wood box/label, ca 1890s, $125 to..**175.00**
Folding, Guinea, self-rising, wooden box, pre-1800, $175 to **275.00**
Rocker, simple, no maker's name or cb, end-cap box, $85 to......**125.00**
Rocker, w/maker's name & cb, end-cap box, $120 to **150.00**

Egg Scales/Graders, 1930s – 1940s

Acme Egg Grade, Specialty Mfg St Paul MN, aluminum, from $30 to ..**50.00**
Brower Mfg Save All, sheet steel (cheaply made), Steelyard bal, $50 to..**75.00**
Jiffy Way, Minneapolis MN, steel w/mc bands, pend bal, common, $30 to..**50.00**
Oakes Mft Tipton IN, pend bal, sheet steel, adjustable stop, $30 to ..**50.00**
Reliable, rocker bal, all br, wooden base, 2½x13¾", $75 to........**100.00**
Unique..., Specialty Mfg, sheet steel/aluminum, pend bal, $30 to..**50.00**

Postal

In the listings below an asterisk (*) was used to indicate that any one of several manufacturers' or brand names might be found on that particular set of scales. Some of the American-made pieces could be marked Pelouze, Lorraine, Hanson, Kingsbury, Fairbanks, Troemner, IDL, Newman, Accurate, Ideal, B-T, Marvel, Reliance, Howe, Landers-Frary-Clark, Chatillon, Triner, American Bank Service, or Weiss. European/U.S.-made scales marked with an asterisk (*) could be marked Salter, Peerless, Pelouze, Sturgis, L.F.&C., Alderman, G. Little, or S&D. English-made scales with the asterisk (*) could be marked Josh. & Edmd. Ratcliff, R.W. Winfield, S. Mordan, STS (Samuel Turner, Sr.), W.&T. Avery, Parnall & Sons, S&P, or H.B. Wright. There may be other manufacturers as well.

Brit/Can Bal, eq, br or CI on base, *, 4"-15", $100 to **750.00**
Engl Bal, eq/Roberval, gilt or st, on stand, *, 3"-8", $500 to....**2,500.00**
Engl Bal, eq/Roberval, plain to ornate, *, 3"-8", $100 to **2,500.00**
Engl Spring, candlestick, br or st, *, 3½"-15", $100 to................**500.00**
Engl Spring, CI, br or NP fr, Salter, ozs/lbs, 7"-10", $25 to..........**200.00**
Engl Steelyard, ua, 1- or 2-beam, h lph, *, 4"-15", $100 to......**1,500.00**
Euro pend, gravity, br, CI or NP fr on base, oz/grams, $75 to **350.00**
Euro pend, gravity, 2-arm, bm, br or NP, *, 6"-9", $50 to **300.00**
Euro/US Spring, br or NP, pence/etc, h or hh, *, 4"-17", $10 to.**100.00**

US Pend, gravity, metal, pnt face, ap, hcp, sm, $20 to 100.00
US Spring, pnt base metal, *, 2½"-8", $10 to 80.00
US Spring, pnt bm, *, mtd on inkstand, 2½"-8", $75 to.............250.00
US Spring, pnt bm, rnd glass-covered face, *, 8"-10", $25 to......100.00
US Spring, SP, oblong base, *, 2½"-8", $100 to..........................200.00
US Spring, st, oblong base, *, 2½"-8", $200 to...........................500.00
US Steelyard, ua, CI, *, 5"-13" beam, 4½"-12" base, $25 to.......100.00

Schafer and Vater

Established in 1890 by Gustav Schafer and Gunther Vater in the Thuringia region of southwest Germany, by 1913 this firm employed over two hundred workers. The original factory burned in 1918 but was restarted and production continued until WWII. In 1972 the East German government took possession of the building and destroyed all of the molds and the records that were left.

You will find pieces with the impressed mark of a nine-point star with a script 'R' inside the star. On rare occasions you will find this mark in blue ink under glaze. The items are sometimes marked with a four-digit design number and a two-digit artist mark. In addition or instead, pieces may have 'Made in Germany' or in the case of the Kewpies, 'Rose O'Neill copyright.' The company also manufactured items for sale under store names, and those would not have the impressed mark.

Schafer and Vater used various types of clays. Items made of hard-paste porcelain, soft-paste porcelain, jasper, bisque, and majolica can be found. The glazed bisque pieces may be multicolored or have an applied colored slip wash that highlights the intricate details of the modeling. Gold accents were used as well as spots of high-gloss color called jewels. Metallic glazes are coveted. You can find the jasper in green, blue, pink, lavender, and white. New collectors gravitate toward the pink and lavender shades.

Since Schafer and Vater made such a multitude of items, collectors have to compete with many cross-over collections. These include shaving mugs, hatpin holders, match holders, figurines, figural pitchers, Kewpies, tea sets, bottles, naughties, etc.

Reproduction alert: In addition to the crudely made Japanese copies, some English firms are beginning to make figural reproductions. These seem to be well marked and easy to spot. Our advisor for this category is Joanne M. Koehn; she is listed in the Directory under Minnesota.

Ashtray, Mr Pickwick holding wine glass on front, 6x4" 50.00
Ashtray, Pon My Soul, old man snoring, 1940s, 3x4¼".................55.00

Bottle, Pan hugging smiling moon, blue, marked, 11½", $475.00. (Photo courtesy Joanne M. Koehn)

Box, couple embracing, gr jasper, heart shape, early 1900s, 3¼" ...80.00
Box, googly-eyed girl w/dog on lid, ca 1920, 3½x1¾"...................140.00
Box, lady turtle, open lid to see lady's behind, 2x4".......................50.00
Candy container, Pig 'n Whistle, pk w/intaglio eyes, 1920s........137.50
Cup, Mad Hatter on hdl, 3⅜"..80.00
Figurine, Don't Tell Anyone, boy whispers to girl w/googly eyes, 4" .160.00
Figurine, Dutch boy w/googly eyes, seated, ca 1920, 3¾x3x2" 80.00
Figurine, lady in purple dress & matching hat w/feathers, 3½"...120.00
Figurine, lady seated holding rooster, 3½x4"...............................235.00
Figurine, nude lady in bathtub, 3½x5½x2½" 310.00
Flask, A Wee Scotch, baby w/bottle mk Old Whiskey, brn tones..135.00
Flask, Castle Walk, couple dancing, 6"..525.00
Flask, What a Night, man in overcoat w/finger extended, 5⅛" ..185.00
Flask, Your Health/Drinkometer, man's face on brn, 5¾"............105.00
Hair receiver, gr & wht jasper w/jewels & gold trim....................195.00
Hatpin holder, Oriental lady seated w/legs Xd, holes in hat, 4⅜"..295.00
Humidor, jester's face, pointed hat forms lid, ca 1910, 6" 280.00
Incense burner, Nouveau lady smoking, ca 1910, 3½" 220.00
Jar, lady cameos, bl jasper, early 1900s, 4½x3⅝"...........................75.00
Match holder, Monkey Man, We Are Two! on front, 3½"..........190.00
Match holder, pug dog w/bee on tail, ca 1915, 3x3⅝".................140.00
Match holder/striker, boy in bl coat w/dog in gr plaid 80.00
Mug, elk in relief, orange & brn tones, 1920s, 3¼" 85.00
Nipper (flask), Indian Chief's head, 4⅞x3" 595.00
Nodder, And Dad Said, Be a Man, boy in derby hat w/cigar, 4" .245.00
Nodder, Baby Snookums, on hands & knees, 3¼x3¼" 170.00
Pitcher, chinaman holding pitcher w/umbrella on bk, 3½".........125.00
Pitcher, goat in red coat, 5½" 210.00
Pitcher, Indian chief w/axe in head, 5¼x4¾"..............................300.00
Pitcher, Little Red Riding Hood, shades of bl, 5"...........................90.00
Pitcher, wht tree trunk form w/seed pods, gr branch hdl, 3¼" 75.00
Plaque, lady on swing pushed by 2 cherubs, lav jasper, ca 1910, 5"..60.00
Powder jar, lady seated w/legs crossed on pillow, 5¼x4¼" dia 265.00
Rose bowl, wht cherubs on bl band/ram's head hdls, #5660, 3¼x4¾"....230.00
Shaving mug, lady w/long blonde flowing hair, 3½" + matching brush.510.00
Toby jug, President Taft, Souvenir of Washington on front, 5"...295.00
Toothpick/match holder, On the Bust, man w/bust of lady, 4" 95.00
Trinket pot, googly-eyed baby clings to side, 3½x4" 87.50
Vase, shepherd & flock in relief, ewer form, 5" 50.00

Scheier

The Scheiers began their ceramics careers in the late 1930s and soon thereafter began to teach their craft at the University of New Hampshire. After WWII they cooperated with the Puerto Rican government in establishing a native ceramic industry, an involvement which would continue to influence their designs. In the '50s they retired and moved to Mexico; they currently reside in Arizona.

Bowl, cvd verticals intersect tan lines exposing brn bsk, 3x6" 440.00
Bowl, dbl-circle abstracts spattered in tan/mahog on brn gloss, 9".525.00
Bowl, fish w/in lg fish repeats, Cerulean bl w/brn, 4x5½" 880.00
Bowl, mauve on tan matt, chocolate brn int, sm ft, 5½x5".........415.00
Bowl, mocha brn w/chocolate brn flambè inner rim, flared, 3¼x9" ..330.00
Bowl, taupe/ivory flambe, lg U form on sm raised ft, 4x5", NM..250.00
Tapestry, Man in Fish, ivory & dk brn, 1964, rare, 90x35" 2,400.00
Vase, sgraffito band w/figures on brn matt, ca 1960, 14¼x11¾"...2,115.00

Schlegelmilch Porcelain

For information about Schlegelmilch Porcelain, see Mary Frank Gaston's book, *R. S. Prussia Popular Lines*, which addresses R. S. Prussia molds and decorations and contains full-color illustrations and current values. Mold numbers appearing in some of the listings refer to this book. Assume that all items described below are marked unless noted otherwise.

Key:
  BM — blue mark   SM — steeple mark
  GM — green mark   RM — red mark

E.S. Germany

Fine chinaware marked 'E.S. Germany' or 'E.S. Prov. Saxe' was produced by the E.S. Schlegelmilch factory in Suhl in the Thuringia region of Prussia from sometime after 1861 until about 1925.

R.S. Germany

In 1869 Reinhold Schlegelmilch began to manufacture porcelain in Suhl in the German province of Thuringia. In 1894 he established another factory in Tillowitz in upper Silesia. Both areas were rich in resources necessary for the production of hard-paste porcelain. Wares marked with the name 'Tillowitz' and the accompanying 'R.S. Germany' phrase are attributed to Reinhold. The most common mark is a wreath and star in a solid color under the glaze. Items marked 'R.S. Germany' are usually more simply decorated than R.S. Prussia. Some reflect the Art Deco trend of the 1920s. Certain hand-painted floral decorations and themes such as 'Sheepherder,' 'Man With Horses,' and 'Cottage' are especially valued by collectors — those with a high-gloss finish or on Art Deco shapes in particular. Not all hand-painted items were painted at the factory. Those with an artist's signature but no 'Hand Painted' mark indicate that the blank was decorated outside the factory.

Basket, roses w/gold, non-factory decor, 4" 140.00
Bowl, berry; floral w/gold, scalloped rim, 5" 15.00
Bowl, berry; roses & rose garlands form border w/gold, 5½" 18.00
Bowl, gr, Lettuce mold variant, 2½x4¼", w/6" sq leaf underplate...165.00
Bowl, lt & dk pk roses, 3 knob ft, 2⅜x7½" 75.00
Bowl, pk & wht roses, semi-rolled rim, hdls, 9x4½" 90.00
Bowl, Summer Season portrait on wht satin, Iris mold, hdls, 13"..2,000.00
Bowl, wht wild roses, smooth rim, 10"..50.00
Bowl, yel & gr marbled pearl lustre, pierced hdls, 6½x5½"...........15.00
Cake plate, Dogwood & Pine, dk gr border, 10" 70.00
Cake plate, mc roses, Iris mold variant, 11" 275.00
Cake plate, mums, Carnation mold, 10½" 200.00
Cake plate, pk orchids on shaded brn, 10" 70.00
Cake plate, wild roses w/gold on pale gray, 10" 90.00
Celery dish, yel-tinted roses, 14x6½" 55.00
Celery tray, Cottage scene I (thatched roof), 12¾x5¾" 250.00
Chocolate pot, poppies on shaded tan, glossy, ind, 7¼" 140.00
Chocolate set, flowers on wht w/gold stenciling, 9½" pot+2 c/s.450.00
Creamer, yel daffodils on pearl lustre, 4½" 45.00
Creamer & sugar bowl, Lettuce mold, pearl lustre, w/lid, 2¾", 5"...200.00
Creamer & sugar bowl, pk poppies w/gold, w/lid, 3¼", 4¼"........125.00
Cup & saucer, demitasse; lilies on gr to beige, red mk, 1½" H......45.00
Cup & saucer, demitasse; wht flowers, wide gold border, 3" 60.00
Ewer, wht poppies, 5½" 125.00
Hatpin holder, poppies, 4½" 90.00
Jam jar, roses w/shadow flowers, w/lid & underplate....................120.00
Mustard pot, wht tulips, 3⅛"; w/4¼" wht ladle 125.00
Pitcher, cider; yel & wht tulips, glossy, 5x10" 140.00
Plate, apple blossoms, sgn Lenbach, 8" 50.00
Plate, chop; poppies on shaded orange, pierced hdls, 7¼"............65.00
Plate, lg wht daisies, smooth rim, pierced hdls, 9¾" 85.00
Plate, Lily of the Valley, w/lg gold leaves, smooth rim, 6⅜" 35.00
Plate, orange poppies, irid finish at base of plate, 12¼"................35.00
Plate, pk & wht irises w/gold, 6½"...25.00
Plate, wht lilies w/inner bl border & gold stenciling, 8¼" 40.00
Relish, poppy & sm bl flowers, pierced hdls, 8½x4" 70.00
Sugar bowl, wht roses on gr to brn, w/lid, angle hdls, 4⅝" 45.00

Syrup pitcher, yel roses w/gold tapestry design at top, 3½" 160.00
Toothbrush holder, pk rose on bl-gr tinged ground, 4¼" 150.00
Tray, gold stenciled flowers & leaves, gold hdls, 8½x4¼" 90.00
Tray, mc peonies, pierced work on sides, rectangular, 8x4⅛".....120.00
Vase, Peace Bringing Plenty, allegorical figures, red at top, 13"..2,000.00
Vase, peonies & snowballs, gold uptrn hdls, RS Suhl mold #3, 8¼" ...300.00

R.S. Poland

'R.S. Poland' is a mark attributed to Reinhold Schlegelmilch's factory in Tillowitz, Silesia. It was in use for a few years after 1945.

Coffee set, gold spatter & marbling, pot+6 c/s+cr/sug w/lid 400.00
Cup, chocolate; Dogwood & Pine on irid, RSP mold #509a, 3" ...80.00
Ewer, Night Watch after Rembrandt, RSP mold #900, 6¼"........600.00
Ewer, Windmill scenic, RSG mold, 5½" 500.00
Vase, Chinese pheasants, bottle neck, RS Suhl mold #15, 9" ..1,000.00
Vase, lilac clematis, globular, 5⅞" 175.00
Vase, orange-tinted roses w/gold at top, sloped shoulders, 7½" ...175.00
Vase, pastoral scene w/gold & cobalt, hdls, RS Suhl mold #3, 8½"...1,600.00
Vase, peach roses on shaded brn, Nouveau hdls, RSP mold #956, 12".600.00
Vase, Reapers, 2 ladies in long dresses, salesman's sample, 5¼" ..500.00
Vase, Sheepherder, ornate gold hdls, 6"..500.00

R.S. Prussia

Art porcelain bearing the mark 'R.S. Prussia' was manufactured by Reinhold Schlegelmilch in the early 1900s in a Germanic area known until the end of WWI as Prussia. The vast array of mold shapes in combination with a wide variety of decorations is the basis for R.S. Prussia's appeal. Themes can be categorized as figural (usually based on a famous artist's work), birds, florals, portraits, scenics, and animals.

Cake plate, floral transfer on cobalt with gold, integral handles, $1,650.00. (Photo courtesy Michael Sessman)

Berry set, Cottage, Castle & Mill scenes, 10" bowl+2 5½" bowls.1,200.00
Bowl, center; pk roses w/in & w/out, mold #278, 10" 400.00
Bowl, floral w/gold, open hdls, oblong, red mk, 12"......................75.00
Bowl, gr to brn leafy sprays on satin, mold #154, 9¾"................250.00
Bowl, irises on cobalt w/gold, mold #25b, 4x9½x7½" 550.00
Bowl, magnolias on shaded bl, mold #28, 15" 700.00
Bowl, mc roses, gold border, mold #30, unmk, 2½x7¼" 300.00
Bowl, Mill scene, gold scrolls, red mk, 7½" L.............................225.00
Bowl, pk roses & 1 wht rose w/dk gr border, Iris mold, 10½" 400.00
Bowl, rose garlands around inner border, ftd, mold #218, 6" 140.00
Bowl, roses, emb flowers at rim, red mk, 9¾"..............................150.00
Bowl, Roses & Snowballs, opal jewels, cobalt/gold border, 6½"..350.00
Bowl, Snowbird on satin, pearlized dome shapes, mold #113, 10¾"..300.00
Bowl, swans (2) on satin, mold #203, 10" 425.00
Butter dish, dk & lt pk carnations, mold #108 (base)................700.00
Cake plate, Countess Potocka, gold flower border, unmk, 9½".1,400.00
Cake plate, Fruit IV (mixed fruit) on yel to brn, mold #182, 10".350.00
Cake plate, mc roses, bl dome shapes, mold #78, 11" 300.00

Cake plate, mc roses, gr-tinted irises at rim, mold #25, 10¾" 300.00
Celery dish, carnations w/gold, gr border w/shadow flowers, 13x6¼"..275.00
Celery dish, wht plumes & 1 flower, cobalt/wht/gold, unmk, 12½" .500.00
Chocolate pot, roses on satin pearl-button finish, mold #536, 10" ..500.00
Chocolate pot, Surreal Dogwood, mold #501, 11" 325.00
Chocolate set, Swans on Lake, satin finish, 11" pot+2 c/s 900.00
Coffeepot, Lily of the Valley & pk poppies, mold #584, 9½"...600.00
Cracker jar, pk roses, gold emb carnations, mold #526, 5x9" ...400.00
Creamer & sugar bowl, Swans on Lake, w/lid, mold #452, 5", 4".350.00
Cup & saucer, mustache; roses on wht, mold #560, 2½" H.........300.00
Demitasse pot, hummingbirds on cream to brn, mold #540, mk, 9½" .3,000.00
Ewer, lady in flowing gown holds flowers, gold trim, RM, 9" ...1,150.00
Gravy boat, sm roses & tulips w/gr & gold trim, mold #82, +undertray..225.00
Leaf dish, orange & wht poppies on irid & satin, mold #10b, 9"..300.00
Mustard pot, Swans w/Evergreens, mold #508, unmk, 3½" 400.00
Pitcher, cider; Lilies w/Dogwood, mold #554, 6¼" 400.00
Pitcher, wht roses on pearl lustre, Nouveau shape, 12"...............300.00
Plate, floral, fern-like border, hdls, red mk, 11" 160.00
Plate, lady's portrait in wht gown w/leaves & gold, mk, 8½"...1,250.00
Plate, Mill scene, pk roses & sm buds w/gold, mold #25, 9½".....700.00
Plate, Spring allegorical on purple Tiffany finish w/gold, 9" 2,000.00
Relish, German court figures portraits (4) & roses, red mk, 9¾"...650.00
Relish, Hanging Basket, pierced hdls, mold #155, 12x6".............200.00
Relish, magnolias w/1 closed blossom, pierced hdls, 9½x4¾"......200.00
Relish, swan scene w/gold, beaded rim, red mk, 8" L...................165.00
Shell dish, mc flowers w/gold, mold #20, 7¼".............................225.00
Syrup pitcher & underplate, gr leaves w/gold, mold #481, 4½" ..300.00
Tankard, Fall allegorical portrait, mold #526, 13½" 3,500.00
Tankard, Hanging Basket, mold #582, unmk, 13"........................700.00
Tankard, Madame LeBrun portrait, rose finish, mold #517, unmk, 15" .1,800.00
Tankard, Pheasant w/Evergreens, gold trim, mold #569, 12¼"..1,000.00
Tankard, wht flowers, gold-lined on cobalt, mold #525, 13" 1,000.00
Tea set, roses w/gold, red mk, 3-pc...100.00
Teapot, mc flower clusters, mold #506, 5¾".................................325.00
Toothpick holder, roses w/gold, hdls, mold #609 ....300.00
Tray, dresser; wht tulips on shaded bl w/gold, hdls, 11½x5" 175.00
Tray, Sitting Basket, shadow flowers/medallions on lustre, 11¾x7" .225.00
Vase, Melon Boy, gold trim, hdls, red mk, 7" 500.00

R.S. Suhl

Porcelains marked with this designation are attributed to Reinhold Schlegelmilch's Suhl factory.

R.S. Tillowitz

R.S. Tillowitz-marked porcelains are attributed to Reinhold Schlegelmilch's factory in Tillowitz, Silesia.

Bowl, berry; exotic birds & flowers, 3"..18.00
Bowl, mc flowers w/gold tapestry designs, hdls, 6¾" 55.00
Butter dish, China Blau, bl Oriental decor on wht, 3¾x6⅝".......600.00
Cake plate, pears & grapes, bl mk, 10⅞".......................................100.00
Cake plate, red poinsettias, 10"...80.00
Celery tray, Streurosen (sprinkled roses), ribbed rim, 13½" L 50.00
Coffee set, floral on cream, pot+cr/sug 275.00
Coffeepot, China Blau, bl Oriental scene on wht, 8¾" 275.00
Cracker jar, lav flowers along central gold border, BS Rodgers, w/lid....140.00
Cup & saucer, wht flowers w/yel centers, 1¾" H.............................60.00
Egg cups, wht w/gold, ribbed body, 2¼", 4 on matching tray 175.00
Ginger jar, cobalt & wht floral w/gold trim, gr mk, 9"..................350.00
Lemon dish, coral fuchsias & lg gr leaves, hdl, 6½".........................40.00
Plate, chop; yel-tinted roses on shaded brn, smooth rim, 11" 65.00
Relish, Lily of the Valley, tan border, gold trim, 8x3¾" 45.00

Sugar bowl, lg wht flowers w/gold, w/lid, 3¾" 45.00
Vase, lg pk & sm orange flowers, shouldered, unmk, 6¼" 100.00
Vase, pk & yel roses, salesman's sample, 4⅜"...............................275.00

Schneider

The Schneider Glass Company was founded in 1914 at Epinay-sur-seine, France. They made many types of art glass, some of which sandwiched designs between layers. Other decorative devices were appliqué and carved work. These were marked 'Charder' or 'Schneider.' During the '20s commercial artware was produced with Deco motifs cut by acid through two or three layers and signed 'LeVerre Francais' in script or with a section of inlaid filigrane. Our advisor for this category is Don Williams; he is listed in the Directory under Missouri. See also Le Verre Francais.

Bowl, bl & yel mottle, shouldered, domed lid, 3¾x6¾".............325.00
Bowl, cluthra, pk to wht, 4½"..210.00
Bowl, yel/amber/brn/bl mottle, squat, flared rim, 5⅜x12" 475.00
Compote, gr w/trapped bubbles, blk ftd base, flared rim, 3¼x8".300.00

Compote, mottled yellow with blue rim, bulbed stem, mottled amethyst disk foot, ca 1925, 5x8", $750.00.

Compote, rust w/amethyst neck, raspberry ft, 8¼" 650.00
Compote, yel to clear mottle on bl ped, 7x10½" 200.00
Lamp, orange & red swirl bell shades (2), wrought-iron base, 6" .850.00
Vase, cameo floral/lattice stems, amethyst on lav/yel mottle, rnd, 5" ..800.00
Vase, Deco cameo floral, pk transparent on texture, 3¾x5"........600.00
Vase, etched leaf band at shoulder, 2 appl florals on smoky topaz, 14" ..980.00
Vase, mc blown-out body in metal fr w/starburst design, 15¾" .2,750.00
Vase, orange mottle w/brn ft & swirled lower body, 13¼"...........780.00
Vase, pk mottle to dk red w/appl dk red flower, ftd, 15½" 6,000.00
Vase, red/orange/yel vertical stripes, bulbed neck, ftd, 10" 765.00
Vase, yel/orange spatter on clear, ftd trumpet form, 6½" 85.00

Schoolhouse Collectibles

Schoolhouse collectibles bring to mind memories of a bygone era when the teacher rang her bell to call the youngsters to class in a one-room schoolhouse where often both the 'hickory stick' and an apple occupied a prominent position on her desk. Our advisor for this category is Kenn Norris; he is listed in the Directory under Texas.

Annual, San Francisco Polytechnic, softcover, 1917, 92-pg, EX 7.50
Atlas, Goode's School, Rand McNalley, 1946 edition, 286-pg, EX..15.00
Badge, AAA School Safety Patrol patrolman's, 2⅝x2" 60.00
Bag, grained leather, buckle strap, pockets, 11x17x4", EX............24.00
Band jacket, bl wool w/brass buttons, shoulder braid, EX............125.00
Beanie cap, school insignia embr on wool, ca 1936, 6" dia...........15.00
Bell, brass, wooden hdl, EX patina, 8¼x5"...................................75.00
Bell, Ding Dong School...Nat'l Broadcasting, blk wood hdl, EX...55.00

Book, Child's World, 2nd reader, Browne/Withers/Tage, 1917, EX .25.00
Book, Dick & Jane, Good Times w/Our Friends, 1954, EX **225.00**
Book, Dick & Jane, Guess Who, Jr Primer/2-pg teacher section, 1951, EX..**155.00**
Book, Dick & Jane, More Stories, 1935, 2nd printing, VG+ **85.00**
Book, Dick & Jane, New Fun w/Dick & Jane, hardcover, 1956, M .**225.00**
Book, Dick & Jane, Open the Gate, 1959, 158-pg, M **50.00**
Book, Dick & Jane, Our Big Book, teacher's aid, 1951, oversz, VG+ .**575.00**
Book, Dick & Jane, Our New Friends, 1956 edition, rare, EX **185.00**
Book, Dick & Jane, We Come & Go, 1946-47, EX.....................**250.00**
Book, Dick & Jane, We Work & Play, 1946-47, EX+ **250.00**
Book, Elson-Gray Basic Reader, Book Four, Thorton Burgess, 1936, EX...**20.00**
Book, Fight for Freedom 1750-83, N Farr, Rodondo illus, 1976, EX..**15.00**
Book, McMillan Dictionary for Children, 1976 revised edition, EX..**7.00**
Book, Mission of Teacher, SW Fisher, Albany, 1863, w/jacket......**35.00**
Book, Mitchell's School Geography, 1851, 3rd revised edition, EX...**100.00**
Book, Montreith's 1868 Manual of Geography, 38 states, EX........**24.00**
Book, New Music Horizons #6, Silver Burdett, 1953 reprint, EX....**8.00**
Book, Normal First Reader, Raub, 1878, G- **45.00**
Book, Robinson's Progressive Intellectual Arithmetic, 1874, EX ..**10.00**
Book, School History of US, Revised, Cowperthwait, 1869, VG..**25.00**
Book, Town & Country, Sheldon Reading Series, 1961, 224-pg, EX..**10.00**
Chair, desk; laminated wood w/steel fr, 17" **25.00**
Chair, oak, 2-slat bk, solid seat, 29"...**25.00**
Chalkboard, Quartet Mfg...IL, in 36x48" wood fr w/ledge...........**235.00**
Class ring, Richmond VA, 10k yel gold, 1956.................................**60.00**
Commencement program, held in opera house, 1913, 4½x5½", EX..**10.00**
Copybook, 32 pgs of penmanship exercises, NY, 1938, EX...........**95.00**
Desk, master's; gallery/hinged lid/fitted int, orig pnt, 48x38x26"..**1,500.00**
Desk, pine, single shelf, sq nails, hole for inkwell, 30x42x18" ...**635.00**
Desk, wood, slanted hinged top, dvtl construction, 1800s, 32x24x19"..**185.00**
Desk, Wooten, leather top, right pedestal, 1870s, EX **5,000.00**
Eraser box, wooden w/paper labels, 3¾x6¼x3¼", EX **15.00**
Globe, Crouchley's New Terrestrial, mahog stand, 1850s, 39" H.**8,225.00**
Globe, Geo III Celestial, B Martin, in oak stand, ca 1850s, 17" H.**4,115.00**
Globe, Loring's Celestial, table model w/trn-leg fr, 1841, 18½"...**3,165.00**
Globe, Loring's Terrestrial, Gilman Jaslin, revised 1846, 18" ...**1,850.00**
Globe, Philips Terrestrial #4502, bronze arm, 9" dia, 17", EX **500.00**
Globe, Terrestrial, Weber Costello...Chicago, 14" on stand **60.00**
Graduation hat tassle, royal bl w/gold-tone metal mt, 1960, 8½" ...**8.00**
Letter jacket, bl wool w/leather sleeves, EX **100.00**
Letter sweater, bl wool w/dbl letter, 1969, EX **25.00**
Map, pull-down type of world, Denoyer's, 1947, 67x92", EX.........**65.00**
Paddle, softwood, cvd scrolls & initials, ca 1900, 13" L................**45.00**
Paper cutter, Ideal School Supply, EX...**42.50**
Paperweight, Am Assoc of...Administrators, 139th Conference, 1947, EX..**39.00**
Phrase cards, Dick & Jane Unit Card Set, EX in 4¼x9¼x12¼" box..**110.00**
Pin, school name on front w/book/ink bottle/quill design, ½" **25.00**
Pin, stamped metal badge, School Safety Committee, 1½" **8.00**
Pin, sword form w/school emblem & ruby, mk Sterling, 2¾" **22.50**
Plaque, bronze basketball player, 1934 regional award, 17x11" **65.00**
Postcard, Ft Wayne high school photo, 1908, EX **6.00**
Postcard, photo of children & faculty before brick building, 1900s.**5.00**
Postcard, photo of Springfield MO State Normal School, 1910, EX..**4.00**
Textbook, Wonder Book of Knowledge, HC Hill, 1940, 600-pg, EX....**15.00**
Yearbook, Jamaica NY, 1943, 65-pg, EX...**20.00**

Pencil Boxes

Among the most common of school-related collectibles are the many classes of pencil boxes. Generally from the period of the 1870s to the 1940s, these boxes were made in hundreds of different styles. Materials included tin, wood (thin frame and solid hardwood), and leather; fabric and plastics were later used. Most pencil boxes were in a basic, rectangular configuration, though rare examples were made to resemble other objects such as rolling pins, ball bats, nightsticks, etc. They may still be found at reasonable prices, even though collectors have recently taken a keen interest in them. All boxes listed below are in very good to near-mint condition. Our advisors for pencil boxes are Sue and Lar Hothem, authors of *School Collectibles of the Past;* they are listed in the Directory under Ohio.

Advertising, AW Faber Castell, Scales of Justice on metal............**12.00**
Eagle Pencil Co, railroad image on dk gr, pushbutton latch, 8", EX.**58.00**
Exotic woods inlay w/MOP accents, souvenir, 19th C, EX **395.00**
Ltweight wood w/HP Oriental flowers, dvtl corners, 9½x3x2½" ..**20.00**
Papier-mâché w/HP roses & gold leaves, EX **15.00**
Presidents of US, terms in office, Sterling mfg, 1960, EX.............**18.00**
Pyrographic bluebirds & poinsettias w/HP details, 9x4½x1¼" **65.00**
Spanky & Our Gang, red emb Our Gang School Box, 1930s, EX ...**75.00**
Wood w/decal roses, sliding lid, 1930s, 9¼x2" **35.00**

Schoop, Hedi

In the 1940s and 1950s, one of the most talented artists working in California was Hedi Schoop. Her business ended in 1958 when a fire destroyed her operation. It was at that time that she decided to do freelance work for other companies such as Cleminson Clay. Schoop was probably the most imitated artist of the time, and she answered some of those imitators by successfully suing them. Some imitators were Kim Ward, Ynez, and Yona. Schoop was diversified in her creations, making items such as shapely women, bulky-looking women and children with fat arms and legs, TV lamps, and animals as well as planters and bowls. Schoop used many different marks including the stamped or incised Schoop signature and also a hard-to-find sticker. 'Hollywood, Cal.' or 'California' were occasionally used in conjunction with the Hedi Schoop name. For further information we recommend *The Encyclopedia of California Pottery, Second Edition*, by Jack Chipman; he is listed in the Directory under California.

Candle holder, Madonna praying, gr dress w/brn decor, 11¼" **85.00**
Cigarette holder/ashtray, duck figural, head holder, body tray, 5½"...**30.00**
Figurine, lady in bl dress w/floral, lg hat, holding basket, 11"........**75.00**
Figurine, lady in blk & gold billowing dress held at sides, 9".........**80.00**
Figurine, lady in gr, windblown scarf, holds 2 blk baskets, 12½"...**85.00**
Figurine, lady in gr & wht w/pk headscarf, 3 pockets in dress, 12½"..**85.00**
Figurine, lady in pale pk dress w/pk bow, orchid flower holder, 9¼" ..**65.00**
Figurine, lady in pk w/floral trim reading book w/2 vases behind, 9"..**60.00**
Figurine, lady in wht dress w/gr trim, holding bowl on shoulder, 11" .**70.00**
Figurine, lady w/hands on hips dancing, hole in bk, 9½" **80.00**
Figurine, Marguerita, in wht w/basket on head, hole in dress, 12½" ..**95.00**
Figurine, Oriental man w/blk & wht shirt & wht pants, lg hat, 12½" .**60.00**
Figurine, rooster, gr & brn, 13", from $100 to............................**125.00**
Figurine, Tyrolean girl holds dress out as planter, 11" **80.00**
Figurines, Fr peasant couple w/baskets in red & gr, 12½", 13", pr...**150.00**
Figurines, Oriental couple in rose tops/blk pants, w/baskets, 12", pr.**145.00**
Planter, circus horse, pk & wht w/gr saddle, 9¾" **75.00**
Tray, butterfly, rose colored w/gold trim...**40.00**
Vase, Colonial man's face on 1 side w/lady's on other, 8" **55.00**
Vase, Oriental man on 1 side w/lady on other, 10¼"......................**90.00**

Schramberg

The Schramberg factory was founded in the early nineteenth century in Schramberg Wurttemberg, Germany. The pieces most commonly seen are those made by Schramberger Majolika Fabrik (SMF) dating from 1912 until 1989.

Some pieces are stamped with the pattern name (i.e. Gobelin) and the number of the painter who executed it. The imprinted number identifies the shape. Marks may also include these names: Wheelock, Black Forest, and Mepoco.

Perhaps the most popular examples with collectors are those from the Gobelin line. Such pieces have a gray background with as many as ten other colors used to create that design. For example, Gobelin 3 pieces will be painted with green and orange leaves and yellow eyes along with other colors specific to that design.

Little is known of the designers who worked for Schramberg; however, Eva Zeisel was employed at the factory for nearly two years starting in the fall of 1928. Her duties included design, production, and merchandising. Our advisors for this category are Ralph Winslow who is listed in the Directory under Missouri and Ann Burton who is listed under Michigan.

Box, w/lid, Gobelin 2, 2½x4"...**85.00**
Cake plate, wht lily-of-valley, 12½", +6 7½" plates......................**45.00**
Clock, bl/rose/wht, Garmisch, 13x6".....................................**50.00**
Creamer & sugar bowl, Black Forest chalet...............................**40.00**
Food warmer, child's; cat & bird, w/hdl, 8½x3"..........................**25.00**
Planter, floral, 4½x4x9"..**45.00**
Teapot, Black Forest chalet, 8"...**50.00**
Vase, cream, geometric pattern & hdls, att Eva Zeisel, 8½"......**280.00**
Vase, Gobelin 4, 7"...**60.00**
Vase, Gobelin 7, 8"..**165.00**
Vase, gray/bl/red rosette, 5½"..**30.00**
Wall pockets, blk/yel, Mignon, 4½", pr..................................**26.00**

Scouting Collectibles

Boy Scouts

Scouting was founded in England in 1907 by a retired Major General, Lord Robert Baden-Powell. Its purpose is the same today as it was then — to help develop physically strong, mentally alert boys and to teach them basic fundamentals of survival and leadership. The movement soon spread to the United States, and in 1910 a Chicago publisher, William Boyce, set out to establish Scouting in America. The first World Scout Jamboree was held in 1911 in England. Baden-Powell was honored as the Chief Scout of the World. In 1926 he was awarded the Silver Buffalo Award in the United States. He was knighted in 1929 for distinguished military service and for his Scouting efforts. Baden-Powell died in 1941. For more information you may contact our advisor, R.J. Sayers, author of *Guide to Scouting Collectibles*, whose address (and ordering information regarding his book) may be found in the Directory under North Carolina. (Correspondence other than book orders requires SASE please.)

Axe, Senior Official; mk Waghn, 6¼x4" head on 18" hdl, EX **80.00**
Belt buckle, silvered metal w/emblem in center, 1950s, 1½x3".....**60.00**
Book, BS Year; Stories of Brave Boys & Fearless Men, 1934, EX..**12.00**
Book, Farm Home & Its Planning, Merit Badge Series, 1942, EX...**5.00**
Book, Rocks & Minerals, Merit Badge Series, 59 pgs, 1937, EX ...**22.00**
Book, Scout Trail 1910-1962, history of Scouts in Rhode Island, EX..**40.00**
Book, Seamanship, Merit Badge Series, 60 pgs, 1932, VG+..........**35.00**
Bookends, cast aluminum emblem w/pnt crest, EX, pr..................**90.00**
Booklet, Bugle Calls, 20 pgs, 1929, softcover, 9x4", VG+.............**12.00**
Bugle, brass, Rexcraft, VG+..**60.00**
Calendar, Scout climbing tree, Brown & Bigelow, 1931, complete, NM.**55.00**
Camera, Memo; Official BS, Afga, 1929, VG+ w/EX leather case .**150.00**
Card, gum; Handy Fireplace, #21 Camp Life Series, Goudey, 1933, EX+..**22.00**
Chess set, metal figures of Scouts, missing board o/w complete, EX .**265.00**
Compass, #1075 Bar Needle; Bakelite case, Taylor Instruments, EXIB.**35.00**
Compass, logo at North point, tin, 1½x3" dia, EX **35.00**

Corkscrew, Practic Boy/BS, 2-arm style, 8", EX **215.00**
First-aid kit, Johnson & Johnson, 1942, unused, 6x4x2", EX **15.00**
Game, BS Progress; Parker Bros, 1924, EX (VG box) **110.00**
Handbook, BSA, 4th printing, 1912, VG **375.00**
Handbook, For Scoutmasters, 1st edition, 1919, VG **90.00**
Handbook, Order of the Arrow, 72 pgs, 1950, 8x5", EX...............**40.00**
Hat, ranger style, 1944, wool, leather chin strap, EX....................**40.00**
Knife, fixed-blade; Western/BSA on blade, leather sheath, 8¾", NM+.**120.00**
Manual, Air Scout; 442 pgs, 1942, EX......................................**30.00**
Manual, Woodslore Survival...Philmont..., 88 pgs, 1940s, EX.......**45.00**
Medal, BS Explorer Silver I; mk sterling, NM (NM presentation box).**1,200.00**
Medal, First Aid; Scouts w/dog on medallion, bl ribbon, M (orig case)...**115.00**
Medal, 1st Place; for Signaling, gold, 1931, EX (orig case) **220.00**
Neckerchief, Safety Monitors, 1939 World's Fair, EX.................**400.00**
Neckerchief, 14th World Jamboree, Sarek Greece, bl & wht, M.**460.00**
Patch, Cuban, Scouts of Cuba Siempre Listo, 2¾" dia, EX.........**115.00**
Patch, flap; Order of the Arrow, Lakota Chapter Lodge 11, NM .**165.00**
Patch, Knot Professional Training, blk knot on wht w/blk border, EX..**15.00**
Patch, Order of the Arrow, LA Nat'l Conference, 1952, 2¾" sq, VG..**70.00**
Patch, Participant Badge, 1957 World Jamboree, 2⅜" dia, EX ...**110.00**
Patch, Pioneer Valley/Eastern States Expo '31, Indian Chief center, VG .**285.00**
Patch, 1929 World Jamboree, emblem w/arrow through center, VG+..**295.00**
Patch, 1935 World Jamboree, Washington DC, 8-point star, 3" dia, EX.**245.00**
Patch, 1940 Nat'l Jamboree Staff, emblem in gold wreath, NM....**95.00**
Pin, lapel; Nat'l Executive Board, enameled emblem, ca 1910, NM..**1,550.00**
Poster, Australian BS Law, shows camp, pre-WWI, 15¾x12½", EX..**50.00**

Poster, On to the Jamboree 1937, Scout in uniform before tents at Washington Monument, 41¾x26¾", EX, $250.00.

Poster, Statue of Liberty, Scout w/sword, 1940s, 20x30", EX.......**110.00**
Shovel/pick, mk Vaughan, mk Be Prepared BS mk, 27" **65.00**
Slides, glass; 1920s Jamboree photos, Eastman Lantern Slides, 26, EXIB.**220.00**
Souvenir stamp sheet, Republic of Cyprus, BS 50th (in country), NM.**45.00**
Whistle/compass, mk Emca Regd BS England, 3⅜", VG+............**45.00**

Girl Scouts

Collecting Girl Scout memorabilia is a hobby that is growing nationwide. When Sir Baden-Powell founded the Boy Scout movement in England, it proved to be too attractive and too well adapted to youth to limit its great opportunities to boys alone. The sister organization, known in England as the Girl Guides, quickly followed and was equally successful. Mrs. Juliette Low, an American visitor to England and a personal friend of the father of Scouting, realized the tremendous future of the movement for her own country, and with the active and friendly cooperation of the Baden-Powells, she founded the Girl Guides in America, enrolling the first patrols in Savannah, Georgia, in March 1912. In 1915 National Headquarters were established in Washington, D.C., and the name was changed to Girl Scouts. The first National Convention was held in 1914. Each succeeding year has shown growth and increased enthusiasm in this steadily growing army of girls and young women who are learning in the happiest ways to combine patriotism, outdoor activities of every kind, skill in every branch of domestic science, and high standards of community service. Today there are over 400,000 Girl Scouts and more than 22,000 leaders. Mr. Sayers is also our Girl Scout advisor.

Book, GS in Glacier Park, Lillian Roy, 1928, w/dust jacket, EX ...**90.00**
Book, GS in the Magic City, Lillian Roy, hardcover, 1927, VG ...**15.00**
Book, GS in the Redwoods, Lillian Roy, 1926, w/dust jacket, EX.**15.00**
Camera, Offical Brownie Scouts, Herbert George Co, 1958, EXIB.**55.00**
Catalog, equipment; 1926, 31 pgs, 9x6¾", VG+ **115.00**
Catalog, equipment; 1936, 10x7½", EX **40.00**
Charm, Membership; US Seal w/GS, ½x½", EX **45.00**
Charm bracelet, emblem in center w/4 on ea side, enameled, EX.**85.00**
Cookie cutter, GS shape, flat bk, 8½x4x1", oxidized o/w EX......**150.00**
Handbag, gr w/gold emblem, vinyl, 1960s, 13x10", EX.................**30.00**
Handbook, 154 pgs, 1914, VG...**85.00**
Hatchet, plumb; emblem on head, 1949-53, 13", EX **115.00**
Lunch box, tin, tan on brn, 4x7x5", EX **75.00**
Manual, Mariner Scout; 126 pgs, softcover, 1948, VG **45.00**
Marbles, gr & yel, Scout on card, Made in USA, M (EX cb header).**45.00**
Medal, GS US Treasury War Service; Scout w/emblem, bar w/medallion, EX..**415.00**
Pin, Brownie Scout figure, pnt plastic, ca 1944, 2", EX **50.00**
Pin, Eaglet, eagle w/G & S above wings, gold-tone metal, 1⅛", EX .**510.00**
Pin, emblem, 3 stars w/4 stripes, 1920-23, gold-tone metal, EX **80.00**
Pin, Mariners, Leaders, gold anchor w/emblem center, EX............**45.00**
Pin, Wing Scout, trefoil w/wings, metal, EX **210.00**
Plaque, Brownie Law, ca 1927, VG...**60.00**
Plate, emblem center, pewter, scalloped edge, 10¼", EX **65.00**
Plate, GS Law, gold figures & border, 8", NM+ **35.00**
Pocketknife, gr plastic w/gold emblem, 4-blade, Kutmaster, '40s, EXIB..**45.00**
Print, Scouts Forever, girls in winter, Moss, 1990, 10x10", M **75.00**

Scrimshaw

The most desirable examples of the art of scrimshaw can be traced back to the first half of the nineteenth century to the heyday of the whaling industry. Some voyages lasted for several years, and conditions on board were often dismal. Sailors filled the long hours by using the tools of their trade to engrave whale teeth and make boxes, pie crimpers (jagging wheels), etc., from the bone and teeth of captured whales. Eskimos also made scrimshaw, sometimes borrowing designs from the sailors who traded with them.

Beware of fraudulent pieces; fakery is prevalent in this field. Many carved teeth are of recent synthetic manufacture (examples engraved with information such as ship's or captain's names, dates, places, etc., should be treated with extreme caution) and have no antique or collectible value. A listing of most of these plastic items has been published by the Kendall Institute at the New Bedford Whaling Museum in New Bedford, Massachusetts. If you're in doubt or a novice collector, it's best to deal with reputable people who guarantee the items they sell. Our advisor for this category is John Rinaldi; he is listed in the Directory under Maine. See also Powder Horns.

Bodkin, whale tooth, trn, rectangular knob, 3¾"............................**50.00**
Busk, cherub/flowers/bouquet/sailing ships, 1880s, 13¼" L **275.00**
Busk, eagle/flags/ship/women/dbl heart, 12½" **1,265.00**
Busk, 4 panels w/dbl heart/pinwheel/wreath/etc, 12"....................**575.00**
Jagging wheel, whalebone w/flared piercing element, 5⅝" **175.00**
Tooth, lady playing piano, red stain on dress, 6¼" **765.00**
Tooth, officer in full dress uniform & regal lady, EX cvg, 6¼" **990.00**

Tooth (front and back shown), sperm whale, Victorian lady and American sailing ship with single pennant, bird flying overhead, 9", $6,250.00. (Photo courtesy Maritime Auctions)

Tooth, stars over eagle & Am shield, flowers, red stain, 4⅝" **470.00**
Tooth, 3-mast ship w/Am flag, sgn BMB 1883, 5¾" **1,045.00**

Sebastians

Prescott W. Baston first produced Sebastian Miniatures in 1938 in his home in Arlington, Massachusetts. In 1946 Baston bought a small shoe factory in Marblehead, Massachusetts, and produced his figurines there for the next thirty years. Over the years Baston sculpted and produced more than seven hundred fifty different pieces, many of which have been sold nationwide through gift shops. Baston and The Lance Corporation of Hudson, Massachusetts, consolidated the line in 1976 and actively promoted Sebastians nationally. Many of Baston's commercial designs, private commissions, and even some open line pieces have become very collectible. Aftermarket price is determined by three factors: 1) current or out of production status, 2) labels, and 3) condition. Copyright dates are of no particular significance with regard to value.

Mr. Baston died in 1984, and his son Prescott 'Woody' Baston, Jr. continued the tradition by taking over the designing. To date Woody has sculpted over two hundred fifty pieces of his own. After numerous changes in the company that held manufacturing and distribution rights for Sebastians, Woody and his wife Margery are now sculpting and painting Sebastian Miniatures out of their home in Massachusetts. Sebastians are the only collectible line that is produced from design to finished product by the artist. Our advisor for this category is Jim Waite; he is listed in the Directory under Illinois.

Adams Academy w/steeple..**150.00**
Aunt Polly, #7330, 2¾"...**25.00**
Bob Crachit & Tiny Tim **30.00**
Boy & Pelican, bl label, MIB **35.00**
Boy Scout, plaque..**200.00**
Building Days (girl or boy), ea **40.00**
Captain John Parker, 4" **135.00**
Christoper Columbus, pewter **500.00**
Clown, 3"..**45.00**
Dame Van Winkle, club pc **40.00**
Daniel & Mrs Boone, #21 & #22, Arlington era, 2¾", pr...........**100.00**
Davy Crockett **200.00**
Eskimo holding fish or bottle **500.00**
Ezra, #8054, man w/axe stands by stump **30.00**
Family Picnic **50.00**
Family Reading Aloud, #7345 ....**45.00**
Fisherman, #714, 3¼" **25.00**
Fisherman's Wife **95.00**
George Washington w/Cannon, 3⅜"..**30.00**

Icahbod Crane, #7347 ....30.00
Jimmy Fund (schoolboy) 45.00
John F Kennedy, 2⅜" 30.00
Johnny Appleseed, 3¾" 40.00
Judge Pyncheon 120.00
Judge Thatcher, #7338, 3" 39.00
Kids Love Jell-o, mk PW Baston 1955 ....310.00
Long Arm of the Law 40.00
Majorette 450.00
Mayflower, #7333, 3⅞" 35.00
Mr & Mrs Daniel Boone, #SML-21, SML #22 ....200.00
Nativity, music box 750.00
Old Put Takes a Licking 250.00
Pilgrims 35.00
Pope John XXII 450.00
Sailing Days Girl 35.00
Salem Savings Bank, pen holder, mk PW Baston 1958, 4" 185.00
Sidewalk Days, boy & girl skaters, #360, #8113, pr 30.00
Sitzmark 175.00
Skipping Rope 30.00
Snowy Days (girl or boy), ea 40.00
Soldier's Farewell 35.00
Speak for It 30.00
St Joan of Arc 225.00
Tom Bowline Ashore, 3⅛" 30.00
Trick or Treat 55.00
Uncle Sam, #7344, 4⅛" 20.00
Weaver, #7337, 2¼" 30.00
Weighing the Baby, c 1941 ....350.00
Will Rogers, 2¾" 40.00
Yankee Sea Captain, #132 ....35.00
50th Anniversary plaque 75.00

Sevres

Fine-quality porcelains have been made in Sevres, France, since the early 1700s. Rich ground colors were often hand painted with portraits, scenics, and florals. Some pieces were decorated with transfer prints and decalcomania; many were embellished with heavy gold. These wares are the most respected of all French porcelains. Their style and designs have been widely copied, and some of the items listed below are Sevres-type wares.

Urns, classical scenes with jewels, foliate swags, female mask handles, pineapple finial, trumpet foot, late nineteenth century, 12", $2,800.00 for the pair. (Photo courtesy Skinner, Inc.)

Candle holder, floral reserves, spiraled std w/gilt bronze mts, 12" ..235.00
Cup & saucer, floral w/gold, ca 1860s, bulbous, 7½" 150.00
Cup & saucer, Loetia Bonapart portrait, ca 1806-10, 2½", 5½" .1,000.00
Figurine, Spanish dancer (lady) w/rose in mouth, gold trim, 14x9x7" .1,500.00

Ice bucket/wine cooler, flower swags w/gold, shell-shape hdls, 6¾" .500.00
Plaque, Laure Levy, girl w/basket on wharf, sgn, ca 1880s, 15x13"...1,500.00
Plate, courting couple, floral/gold decor on bl rim, ca 1900, 9½" ..175.00
Plate, Louis XIV, gold trim, dtd 1847, 9" 375.00
Plate, Princess Caroline Murat/Duc de Reichstadt w/gold, 10", pr..550.00
Tea caddy, floral reserves on bl, bronze butterfly finial, 5½" 350.00
Teapot, Josephine portrait, bk: mansion, gold trim, 8" 1,295.00
Urn, couple reserve, cobalt/gold, bronze mts, w/lid, 1928-40, 30", pr ..4,700.00
Urn, floral on blk, scroll hdls, 19th C, 11", pr 1,500.00
Urn, Louis XVI style, bacchante masks/goat hooves, tassels, 12", pr ..1,880.00

Sewer Tile

Whimsies, advertising novelties, and other ornamental items were sometimes made in potteries where the primary product was simply tile.

Bear bottle, dk brn matt, carries watch & bag, 6¼" 155.00
Birdhouse, wire hanger, wooden base, 7¼" 315.00
Cat, seated, hand-tooled fur, translucent brn, 7⅝", EX 525.00
Dog, head up, curly coat w/tooling, open front legs, 10" 1,150.00
Horse, hand molded, no details except for ears, shiny brn, 10" L..65.00
Lion, hand tooled w/full mane & smile, unglazed, 7x10x5¼" 255.00
Lion, molded w/much hand-done detail, 7½x13½x9"................600.00
Lion, reclining on base, dk brn pnt, sgn/dtd 42, 5x8½"..............110.00
Pedestal, molded lions' heads & leaves, chocolate brn, 28" 330.00
Piggy bank, brn glaze, EX detail, chip, 9½"...............................440.00
Planter, tree trunk w/3 open branches, tooling, red-brn, 38x14" dia..300.00
Squirrel, incised detail & lg ears, shiny glaze, 11" 165.00
Squirrel eating nut, mini, 1⅜" 85.00
Vase resembling tree w/dbl hdls, OH, 11x5¾" 95.00

Sewing Items

Sewing collectibles continue to intrigue collectors, and fine nineteenth-century and earlier pieces are commanding higher prices due to increased demand and scarcity. Complete needlework boxes and chatelaines in original condition are rare, but even incomplete examples can be considered prime additions to any collection, as long as they meet certain criteria: boxes should contain fittings of the period; the chains of the chatelaine should be intact and contemporary with the style; and the individual holders should be original and match the brooch. As nineteenth-century items become harder to find, new trends in collecting develop. Needle books, many of which were decorated with horses, children, beautiful ladies, etc., have become very popular. Some were giveaways printed with advertisements of products and businesses. Even early pins are collectible; the first ones were made in two parts with the round head attached separately. Pin disks, pin cubes, and other pin holders also make interesting additions to a sewing collection.

Tape measures are very popular — especially Victorian figurals. These command premium prices. Early wooden examples of transferware and Tunbridge ware have gained in popularity, as have figurals of vegetable ivory, celluloid, and other early plastics. From the twentieth century, tatting shuttles made of plastics, bone, brass, sterling, and wood decorated with Art Nouveau, Art Deco, and more modern designs are in demand — so are darning eggs, stilettos, and thimbles. Because of the decline in the popularity of needlework after the 1920s (due to increased production of machine-made items), novelty items were made in an attempt to regain consumer interest, and many collectors today also find these appealing.

Watch for reproductions. Sterling thimbles are being made in Holland and the U.S. and are available in many Victorian-era designs. But the originals are usually plainly marked, either in the inside apex or outside on the band. Avoid testing gold and silver thimbles for content; this often destroys the inside marks. Instead, research the manufacturer's mark; this will often denote the material as well. Even though the reproductions are well finished, they do not have manufacturers' marks. Many thimbles are being made specifically for the collectible market; reproductions of porcelain thimbles are also found. Prices should reflect the age and availability of these thimbles. Our advisor for this category is Kathy Goldsworthy; she is listed in the Directory under Washington. We also recommend *Sewing Tools & Trinkets* by Helen Lester Thompson, and *Antique & Collectible Thimbles and Accessories* by Averie Mathes.

Bobbin, lace maker's; trn & cvd bone w/colored stain, weighted bangle ..**165.00**
Bodkin, silver, Simons, early 1900s, lg..**35.00**
Book, New World of Crewel, L Perrone, 1975, EX **18.00**
Book, Sewing w/o Pins, R Oblander, softcover, 1977, EX................**5.00**
Book, Simplicity Sewing Hints for Beginners..., 1947, EX **15.00**
Booklet, Star Book of Tatting Designs No 2, Am Thread Co, 1935, EX ..**15.00**
Box, button; wood w/ivy pattern top, Mauchline style, 1890s, 2½"..**65.00**
Box, cherry vnr w/banded wood inlay, dvtl drw, cushion top, 3x5x3".**300.00**
Box, covered in fine needlework w/seed pearls, 17th C, 14x10x7" ..**5,500.00**
Box, decoupage, hinged lid, pen/ink details, brass ft, 5½x11x8".**1,000.00**
Box, mahog vnr w/string inlay, trn ball ft, rprs, 6x5x3" **220.00**
Box, natural pine, slide lid, compartments, tape loom, 6x15x15", EX..**1,485.00**
Box, papier-mâché w/HP florals & MOP inlay, 19th C, lg...........**595.00**
Box, rosewood, curved front, English, 6x11¾x8¾", EX...............**475.00**
Box, walnut w/line inlay & English scenic medallion, fitted int, 12"..**300.00**
Button, blk Bakelite Scottie dog, lg, from $18 to...........................**25.00**
Button, blk glass elephant in brass fr, self-shank, lg **60.00**
Button, blk glass w/emb King Harold portrait, old, lg...................**38.00**
Button, brass w/cut-steel rim, Little Red Hen emb, lg **35.00**
Button, clear glass w/pnt bk, 1-pc w/shank, pre-WWII, sm **4.00**
Button, colored glass w/Deco styling, 1930s, med to lg, ea from $4 to .**6.00**
Button, fabric covered, thread bk, pad shank, 1870-1910, from $3 to..**7.00**
Button, jelly-belly animal w/gold or silver metal, 5 for................**100.00**
Button, pearl crescent moon shape, late 1930s-1950s, sm.................**3.00**
Button, thin celluloid disk w/brass loop shank & plate, lg.............**10.00**
Buttonhole attachment, Grist, w/booklet & templates, MIB, from $7 to .**12.00**
Caddy, Lehnware, orig decor, compartmented base, 3-tier, 13" ...**990.00**
Chest, walnut, 4-drw, dvtl, rstr base, OH, 25x18x13"..................**550.00**
Clamp, CI, screws down, ca 1860s, 4" **115.00**
Crochet hook, MOP hdl, 4", from $20 to.......................................**40.00**
Darner, blk enameled wood egg w/sterling hdl, 4½" **65.00**
Darner, blown glass, bl, 5x2¼x1⅝" **45.00**
Darner, wood, natural color, 6½", EX..**10.00**
Kit, brass, 8-sided tube w/Nouveau decor, ca 1900, lipstick sz.....**110.00**
Measure, brass, drum form, 1½x2" dia, EX..................................**120.00**
Measure, metal case w/woven-silk picture of terrier, 1930s, 1¾"..**125.00**
Measure, Observation Tower Hot Springs..., pushbutton, EX........**26.00**
Measure, owl, emb bronze, Germany, 1940s, 1½" dia **25.00**
Measure, poodle w/plush fur & glass eyes, Japan, 3¾"................**125.00**
Measure, wooden spool w/HP game bird scene, steel tape, 1960s, NM ..**65.00**
Measure/pincushion, seamstress lady, Pull My Nose tag, Japan **10.00**
Needle book, Reliance, parents w/2 children, Japan, complete, NM...**12.00**
Needle book, rocket cover, Made in Japan, 1940s, NM **9.00**
Needle book, Sweetheart, lady sewing, 5¼x3⅜", NM **5.00**
Needle case, Army & Navy, Silver Steer/Seasoned in Oil, NM **6.00**
Needle case, ivory umbrella type w/bodkin & punch, EX **165.00**
Needle case, umbrella shape, wood w/yel glass pinheads, EX **155.00**
Pincushion, bsk, bird on branch beside nest (cushion), pnt, Germany......**65.00**
Pincushion, celluloid & cloth, Lyn White, 3" **12.00**
Pincushion, celluloid loop & bking on cushion, leather strap, EX .**33.00**
Pincushion, ceramic, cat w/mc details, Japan, 3" **20.00**
Pincushion, ceramic, circus dog, yel lustre, Japan **18.00**
Pincushion, ceramic, lady w/cart, mc, cushion in cart, Japan........**12.50**
Pincushion, ceramic, rabbit w/open bk, appl flowers, 1950s, EX ...**15.00**

Pincushion, ceramic, Scottie playing tuba, mc, Japan, EX............**10.00**
Pincushion, ceramic, zebra, blk/wht, Japan, 1930s, Ex..................**17.50**
Pincushion, CI base w/mini urn on 4 ft, red cushion top, 3¾x4".**165.00**
Pincushion, Mauchline ware, dbl-ended, ca 1880, 1½" L **125.00**
Pincushion, metal, cat w/tail curled in front, ca 1900, EX **295.00**
Pincushion, plastic, high-heel shoe, 2¾"..**9.00**
Pincushion, porc, German shepherd on velvet pillow, 1930s **110.00**
Pincushion, pottery, clown w/ball, red & wht, 1930s, 5½x3½"".....**49.00**
Pincushion, red velvet globe in brass fr, 1940s, 5" **16.00**
Pincushion, red velvet oblong top on clamp base w/mirror, 7¼"..**110.00**
Pincushion, silver base w/2½x4" dia cushion, opens for smalls ...**120.00**
Pincushion, velvet pear, early 1800s, wear, 4¼" **120.00**
Pincushion, wooden turtle w/tapestry-covered shell, EX **14.00**
Pincushion/thread holder, wooden rocker w/uphl seat & bk **16.00**
Pinking shears, Weiss, w/1956 pamphlet, MIB..............................**20.00**
Scissors, steel, gold-tone stork figural, 1900s, 4¾", NM **55.00**
Scissors, steel, stork figural, Victorian era, 4" **37.50**
Sewing bird, brass, clamps to table, Pat Feb 15 1853, EX............**140.00**
Sewing bird, brass, clamps to table, w/bird scissors & cushion **265.00**
Sewing bird, brass, clamps to table, 2 corduroy cushions, NM **265.00**
Shears, tailor's; mk Heinische, Pat 1859 Newark NJ, 15", G.........**80.00**
Skirt marker, Orco Products, ruler in gray metal base, MIB **20.00**
Tatting shuttle, Bates & Son advertising, 1950s, 3" **25.00**
Tatting shuttle, bone, 3 pcs held by brass pins, 1890s, 3x¾x¼"....**55.00**
Tatting shuttle, ivory celluloid, Trade Gloria Mark, 2⅝" **30.00**
Tatting shuttle, yel-brn celluloid, 1930s-30s, 3x¾"........................**60.00**
Thimble, bone china, flowers & gold border, Royal Doulton, 1x⅞"..**30.00**
Thimble, china, bluebird on branch, Queen's Fine Bone China, 1⅛" ..**15.00**
Thimble, china, Peace, WWI Armistice, England, ca 1918 ....**75.00**
Thimble, silver, Egg & Dart decor, Sterling, ⅞x⅝" **25.00**
Thimble, silver, emb daisies, mk Sterling, ¾x⅝" **32.00**
Thimble, silver, emb floral panels w/ribs, unmk, ⅞x¾" **45.00**
Thimble, walrus ivory, hand-cvd rings, 1960s, ⅞" **85.00**
Thimble, 14k gold, eng panels, Simons **145.00**
Thimble holder/sewing kit, aluminum, Lydia E Pinkham, w/contents ..**35.00**
Thread winder, bone snowflake form, 19th C, 1⅜" dia, EX **50.00**

Sewing Machines

The fact that Thomas Saint, an English cabinetmaker, invented the first sewing machine in 1790 was unknown until 1874 when Newton Wilson, an English sewing machine manufacturer and patentee, chanced upon the drawings included in a patent specification describing methods of making boots and shoes. By the middle of the nineteenth century, several patents were granted to American inventors, among them Isaac M. Singer, whose machine used a treadle. These machines were ruggedly built, usually of cast iron. By the 1860s and 1870s, the sewing machine had become a popular commodity, and the ironwork became more detailed and ornate.

Though rare machines are costly, many of the old oak treadle machines (especially these brands: Davis, Home, Household, National, New Home, Singer, Weed, Wheeler & Wilson, and Willcox & Gibbs) have only nominal value. Machines manufactured after 1875 are generally very common as most were mass produced. Values for these later sewing machines range from $50.00 to $100.00.

Our advisor for this category is Peter Frei; he is listed in the Directory under Massachusetts. In the listings that follow, unless noted otherwise, values are suggested for machines in excellent working order.

Bel Air, ft-operated, 1930s, EX in solid wood cabinet **60.00**
Bradbury #1, hand-crank, late 1800s, EX in case **425.00**
Child's, Betsy Ross, electric, 1950s, EX in red snakeskin case **80.00**
Child's, Faultless, iron/steel, floral decor, early 1900s, 8x9", EX..**255.00**

Child's, Fischer, tin litho, hand-crank, sliding drw, 1920s, 3".......**165.00**
Child's, Gateway Rotar Model N-8, orig red, lt rust, EX **75.00**
Child's, KAYanEE Sew Master 733T, pk metal, 1940s, 5⅞x8¼", EX.**75.00**
Child's, Little Comfort Improved, Smith & Egge, 1897, EX **175.00**
Child's, Montgomery Wards, lock stitch, plastic base, battery, EX...**35.00**
Child's, plastic, crystal/pk/wht, battery powered, 7½x10x4"..........**45.00**
Child's, Renwall #89, red/bl/yel plastic treadle type, EX...............**49.00**
Child's, Singer Touch & Sew, 1967, NM w/instructions & box **66.00**
Child's, Stitchwell, PA Dutch graphics, table clamp, 6x7", EX...**200.00**
Child's, tin, eagle mk w/Made in Germany, 5x5x2", EX..............**185.00**
Frisby, hand-crank, England, ca 1850s, 9x18", EX in case **195.00**
Frister & Rossman, Egyptian sphinx decor, hand-crank, 1927, NM..**250.00**
Frister & Rossman K Series, hand-crank, early 1900s, EX...........**250.00**
Garanteret Fra Johan Hammer..., CI, manual hand-crank, 13x14x10", VG.**220.00**
Hengstenberg, high-arm, hand-crank, EX in case **450.00**
Jones Electric Serial #2640, EX in case **165.00**
Max Gristner, hand-crank, high-arm, pre-1900, EX **300.00**

**Shaw & Clark, Monitor, M,
$600.00.** (Photo courtesy Peter Frei)

Singer, blk japanning w/gold decals, 1940s, EX in case **125.00**
Singer Model #15, blk w/gold decal, ca 1954, EX in case **50.00**
Singer 12, hand-crank, late 1800s, EX in case **425.00**
Singer 221 Featherweight, EX in case **525.00**
Singer 221 Featherweight, gold graphics, NM **375.00**
Singer 221-1 Featherweight, ca 1952, EX w/many extras in case...**500.00**
Wilcox & Gibbs Automatic Noiseless, vintage decor, EX in mahog case....**300.00**

Shaker Items

The Shaker community was founded in America in 1776 at Niskeyuna, New York, by a small group of English 'Shaking Quakers.' The name referred to a group dance which was part of their religious rites. Their leader was Mother Ann Lee. By 1815 their membership had grown to more than one thousand in eighteen communities as far west as Indiana and Kentucky. But in less than a decade, their numbers began to decline until today only a handful remain. Their furniture is prized for its originality, simplicity, workmanship, and practicality. Few pieces were signed. Some were carefully finished to enhance the natural wood; a few were painted.

Although other methods were used earlier, most Shaker boxes were of oval construction with overlapping 'fingers' at the seams to prevent buckling as the wood aged. Boxes with original paint fetch triple the price of an unpainted box; number of fingers and overall size should also be considered.

Although the Shakers were responsible for weaving a great number of baskets, their methods are not easily distinguishable from those of their outside neighbors, and it is nearly impossible without first-hand knowledge to positively attribute a specific example to their manufacture. They were involved in various commercial efforts other than wood-

working — among them sheep and dairy farming, sawmilling, and pipe and brick making. They were the first to raise crops specifically for seed and to market their product commercially. They perfected a method to recycle paper and were able to produce wrinkle-free fabrics. Our advisor for this category is Nancy Winston; she is listed in the Directory under New Hampshire. Standard two-letter state abbreviations have been used throughout the following listings.

Key:
CB — Canterbury   ML — Mt. Lebanon
EF — Enfield   SDL — Sabbathday Lake
NL — New Lebanon   WV — Watervliet

Basket, fine weave, sq base, rnd rim, gr band, att, 5x11x11".......**100.00**
Basket, laundry; woven splint w/cvd bentwood hdls, ML, 14x17½" ..**350.00**
Basket, woven splint w/ash hdl, SDL, 13x15x11½"....................**325.00**
Bed, infirmary; hickory, trn posts, orig red, G- splint top, 81" L.**1,000.00**
Bench, kneeling, pine w/old brn wash, 3 legs w/arched cutouts, 6x76x7"..**415.00**
Bottle holder, trn central post, cross arm w/cutouts, EF, 18x15x4"..**440.00**
Box, handmade, pasteboard, hinged dome-top lid, paper covered, 4" L.**2,000.00**
Box, maple/poplar/pine, 4-finger, EX patina, splits, 4x10x7".......**415.00**
Box, roll-top writing; fitted int, EF, 1890s, 3¼x8½x5"............**1,495.00**
Box, sewing; woven poplar w/sweetgrass stripe, 20th C, 2¼" sq .**345.00**
Box, storage; quarter-sawn oak, 6-brd, att T Fisher, EF, 1882, 14" L.**750.00**
Box, 2-finger, old red traces, sm rpr, 2⅛x5⅞" **375.00**
Box, 2-finger, yel pnt, EF, 19th C, 1¼x3¾" **3,000.00**
Box, 3-finger, copper tacks, NL, 1850, 3½x9x6"........................**550.00**
Box, 3-finger, copper tacks, old red & mustard layers, 2½x6x4" .**580.00**
Box, 3-finger, copper tacks, 3x7½x5" **440.00**
Box, 3-finger, pumpkin-colored pnt, 5x11x8" **1,035.00**
Box, 3-finger w/copper tacks, old varnish, 2x6⅜" **300.00**
Box, 4 cut fingers on 1 side & 1 on lid, natural, 6x13½x9¼"..**1,265.00**
Box, 4-finger, copper & iron tacks, 3¾x10¼x7¼" **450.00**
Box, 4-finger, copper tacks, Cook Family on base, 4⅜x11¼" ..**2,000.00**
Brush, corner; horsehair, tapered, CB..**125.00**
Caddy, sewing; mahog/pine, 2-tier, trn finials, drw, cushion top, NE..**275.00**
Candlestand, cherry, 1-brd top, spider legs, rpr, att KY, 27¾" **770.00**
Carrier, bottle; wood & wire, swing hdls, ML, 1890s, 3½x13½x12" ...**865.00**
Carrier, knife; maple, hand dvtl, CB **450.00**
Carrier, 2-finger, maple, copper tacks, arched hdl, splits, 7x13x10"...**165.00**
Carrier, 3-finger, copper & brass tacks, dry natural, 3x5x8" **330.00**
Carrier, 4-finger, copper tacks, brass pins, rpr, 4x11" **385.00**
Carrier, 4-finger, copper tacks, swivel hdl, MA, 3¼x9¼x6".......**275.00**
Chair, low-bk, cloth tape seat, ML, ca 1900, 25".......................**500.00**
Chair, side; #6, 4 arched slats, rpl tape seat, OH, 39".................**300.00**
Chair, side; 3 arched slats, rfn maple, rpl tape seat, 40"...............**220.00**
Chair, side; 3 arched slats, tape seat, old gr pnt, KY, 38¾"..........**400.00**
Chair, side; 3-slat bk, dbl rungs, rpl tape seat, OH, 38½"............**400.00**
Chair, side; 3-slat bk, dbl rungs, splint seat, KY, 39"...................**400.00**
Chair, side; 3-slat ladder-bk w/egg finials, tape seat, att CT, 40".**165.00**
Chair, weaver's; 3 graduated slats, pnt traces, splint seat, 43" ..**1,250.00**
Clothes hanger, yel pnt wood, bow shape, EF, late 1800s, 18¼" L.**375.00**
Colander, tin cone w/2 ribbed hdls, att, 5¾x11" **250.00**
Cupboard, pine w/orig gray, sq base/4-door, 3 center drws, 83x28x11"..**1,650.00**
Dipper, cvd wood, finely shaped hdl, 1850s, 2¾x6¼x4¼" dia....**750.00**
Dry sink, walnut/poplar/pine, single-brd ends, rstr/rpt, OH, 32x38"..**935.00**
Engraving, lady watching a Shaker dance, C Gilbert, in 7x9½" fr...**385.00**
Feather duster, trn hdl, held by red ribbon, SDL, 6¾x5¾" **865.00**
Flax beater, maple, old dk patina, age splits, 24½" **225.00**
Footstool, dk stain, ML, ca 1900, 6⅛x11¾x11" **350.00**
Footstool, hickory/maple, later tape seat, 15¼x15x13" **330.00**
Footstool, pine, curved cutouts ea end, slant top, 8½x14x9½" ...**200.00**
Funnel, 2 wooden staves, tapered spout, cut nails, gr pnt, att, 9" dia..**500.00**
Glove form w/finger, maple, CB **295.00**

Letter, handwritten business response, NY, 1927, 1-pg, 15x12½"..**475.00**
Periodical, The Shaker, NY, January 1871, 1st issue, Vol 1, EX..**175.00**
Photo, identified sister in rocking chair, 1885, 13½x10½" **625.00**
Pincushion, scallop shell w/red top, SDL, late 19th C, 2¾"........**225.00**
Pincushion, woven splint fr w/bl velvet top, SDL, 2¾" dia.........**400.00**
Press, walnut/poplar, 2 panel doors/2 dvtl drw, att Union Village, 89"..**3,850.00**
Rocker, #3, maple, 3 arched slats/shawl bar, orig varnish, tape seat .**750.00**
Rocker, #3, woven cloth tape seat, NY, early 20th C, 38"...........**975.00**
Rocker, #4, shawl bar, 3 arched slats, tape seat, ML, 33½" **500.00**
Rocker, #4 side, 3-slat bk, bl/red tape seat, ML, 35" **500.00**
Rocker, arm; #3, tape seat, old finish, 33½" **200.00**
Rocker, arm; #3, woven cloth tape seat, ML, 34" **300.00**
Rocker, arm; #6, old brn w/red traces, rush seat, 42" **360.00**
Rocker, arm; #7, shawl bar, 3-slat bk, tape seat, ML, 40" **935.00**
Rocker, arm; #7, 4 arched slats, orig tape seat, sm rpr, 41" **525.00**
Rocker, arm; birch/hickory, 2-slat bk, att, child sz, 21½" **250.00**
Rocker, arm; hickory/maple, 4-slat ladder-bk, tape seat, KY, 45"..**300.00**
Rocker, arm; maple w/rpl bl & wht tape seat/bk, 20th C, 37".....**385.00**
Rocker, arm; 3 arched slats, trn legs, old blk pnt, NE, 44" **765.00**
Rocker, arm; 4-slat bk, dbl rungs, woven seat, OH, 43"..............**350.00**
Rocker, sewing; 3 arched slats, tape seat, old varnish, 34x16".....**715.00**
Secretary, butler's; cherry/poplar, 4 dvtl drw, rstr, att NY, 95x43"...**3,200.00**
Sewing basket, woven poplar, 8-sided, ca 1900, 2¼x6x3¾"........**200.00**
Sewing basket, 3-finger, copper tacks, silk lining, 3¼x9¼".........**250.00**
Sewing basket/carrier, 4-finger, copper tacks/brass pins, CB, 9" L ..**1,100.00**
Spool, maple, CB, 3", from $65 to **95.00**
Stand, cherry, rnd top w/tripod base, old rfn, ML, 25x17" dia .**3,450.00**

Stove, iron with lift lid, canted corners on cabriole legs, wrought penny feet, MA, ca 1800, 26x22x23", EX, $4,675.00.

Table, work; pine 4-brd top, drw, bottle legs, EF, 30x54x33"....**1,100.00**
Table, work; birch/pine, red wash, pegged, dvtl drw, att, 42" ...**1,980.00**
Washstand, walnut/poplar, drw, 2 panel doors, OH, 31½x23½x16"..**400.00**

Shaving Mugs

Between 1865 and 1920, owning a personalized shaving mug was the order of the day, and the 'occupationals' were the most prestigious. The majority of men having occupational mugs would often frequent the barber shop several times a week, where their mugs were clearly visible for all to see in the barber's rack. As a matter of fact, this display was in many ways the index of the individual town or neighborhood.

During the first twenty years, blank mugs were almost entirely imported from France, Germany, and Austria and were hand painted in this country. Later on, some china was produced by local companies. It

is noteworthy that American vitreous china is inferior to the imported Limoges and is subject to extreme crazing.

Artists employed by the American barber supply companies were for the most part extremely talented and capable of executing any design the owner required, depicting his occupation, fraternal affiliation, or preferred sport. When the mug was completed, the name and the gold trim were always added in varying degrees, depending on the price paid by the customer. This price was determined by the barber who added his markup to that of the barber-supply company. As mentioned above, the popularity of the occupational shaving mug diminished with the advent of World War I and the introduction by Gillette of the safety razor. Later followed the blue laws forcing barber shops to close on Sundays, thereby eliminating the political and social discussions for which they were so well noted.

Occupational shaving mugs are the most sought after of the group which would also include those with sport affiliations. Fraternal mugs, although desirable, do not command the same price as the occupationals. Occasionally, you will find the owner's occupation together with his fraternal affiliation. This combination could add anywhere between 25% to 50% to the price, which is dependent on the execution of the painting, rarity of the subject, and detail. Some subjects can be done very simply; others can be done in extreme detail, commanding substantially higher prices. It is fair to say, however, that the rarity of the occupation will dictate the price. Mugs with heavily worn gold lose between 20% and 30% of their value immediately. This would not apply to the gold trim around the rim, but to the loss of the name itself. Our advisor for this category is Burton Handelsman; he is listed in the Directory under New York.

Decorative, couple on road w/cottage & windmill beyond, 3⅝" ...**90.00**
Decorative, man on horse at bridge w/cottage beyond, Austria, EX..**70.00**
Decorative, roses allover, yel wrap, Austria, 3½" **50.00**
Decorative, winter cottage scene, blk wrap, Koken, 4"................**200.00**
Decorative, 2 cottage scenes, gr wrap, T&V Limoges.................**100.00**
Fraternal, Shriners, Egyptian head/emblem, Haviland..................**90.00**
Occupational, anvil & hammer amid roses w/gold, 4" **100.00**
Occupational, artist's palette, T&V Limoges, 3⅝" **200.00**
Occupational, barbershop scene (detailed), Limoges, 3⅝".......**1,600.00**
Occupational, baseball player & Xd baseball bats, Germany ...**2,400.00**
Occupational, bedroom furniture, dealer's name, 3⅞"..............**1,500.00**
Occupational, caboose w/CRI&PRR, #12138 on side, D&Co, 3⅞" .**550.00**
Occupational, hand at telegraph key, T&V France, 3½" **600.00**
Occupational, handwriting, Feld China Co, dtd 1930.................**140.00**
Occupational, hen & 12 chicks, P Germany, 3⅝" **700.00**
Occupational, horse-drawn hearse, name removed, 3⅞".............**200.00**
Occupational, horse-drawn Milk wagon, WG&Co Limoges, 3¾", EX .**175.00**
Occupational, lady in military-type jacket, T&V France, 3⅝" ...**950.00**
Occupational, lady's high-button shoe/horseshoe & clover, 1905 ...**700.00**
Occupational, livery stable scene, EX detail, 3⅝".......................**475.00**
Occupational, man driving horse-drawn Omnibus Line bus, H&Co..**2,500.00**
Occupational, man in touring car, gr wrap, Royal China Internat'l .**550.00**
Occupational, men working w/steam tractor-driven bailer, 3⅞" .**2,500.00**
Occupational, miner w/pick axe & mtns, 3⅝" **1,600.00**
Occupational, mortar & pestle, yel wrap, 3½" **180.00**
Occupational, sailing schooner, much gold, T&V Limoges **2,000.00**
Occupational, Singer sewing machine, 3¾"................................**550.00**
Occupational, steam fire engine & 2 horses, T&V Limoges, 3⅝" ..**850.00**
Occupational, steer's head & butcher's tools, 3½" **70.00**
Occupational, tailor fitting male customer, 3⅝" **900.00**
Occupational, tug boat, EX detail, ca 1890s................................**800.00**
Occupational/decorative, horse track scene, Limoges/Koken, 3⅞" ..**300.00**
Patriotic, eagle w/wings wide/mc flowers, 3¾" **120.00**
Patriotic, eagle w/Xd Irish & Am flags, France, 3½" **200.00**
Sportsman, hunter & 2 dogs, rpr, 3¾"..**300.00**

Sportsman, man & dog in boat w/ducks, blk wrap, Limoges, 3¾" .230.00

Shawnee

The Shawnee Pottery Company operated in Zanesville, Ohio, from 1937 to 1961. They produced inexpensive novelty ware (vases, flowerpots, and figurines) as well as a very successful line of figural cookie jars, creamers, and salt and pepper shakers.

They also produced three dinnerware lines, the first of which, Valencia, was designed by Louise Bauer in 1937 for Sears & Roebuck. A starter set was given away with the purchase of one of their refrigerators. Second and most popular was the Corn line. The original design was called White Corn. In 1946 the line was expanded and the color changed to a more natural yellow hue. It was marketed under the name Corn King, and it was produced from 1946 to 1954. Then the colors were changed again. Kernels became a lighter yellow and shucks a darker green. This variation was called Corn Queen. Their third dinnerware line, produced after 1954, was called Lobsterware. It was made in either black, brown, or gray; lobsters were usually applied to serving pieces and accessory items.

For further study we recommend these books: *The Collector's Guide to Shawnee Pottery* by Janice and Duane Vanderbilt, who are listed in the Directory under Indiana; and *Shawnee Pottery*, by our advisors for this category, Jim and Bev Mangus; they are listed in Ohio.

Cookie Jars

Basketweave, decal, mk USA, 7½" 150.00
Cottage, mk USA 6, 6¾", minimum value.............................1,500.00
Drum Major, mk USA 10, 10"...............................600.00
Dutch Boy (Jack), dbl striped pants, mk USA...........................600.00
Dutch Boy (Jack), gold & decals, mk USA................................475.00
Dutch Boy (Jack), yel pants & patches, gold, mk USA..............550.00
Dutch Girl (Jill), bl skirt, gold & decals, mk USA.....................375.00
Dutch Girl (Jill), gold & decals, mk USA 375.00
Dutch Girl (Jill), tulip, mk USA...............................275.00
Fruit Basket, mk Shawnee 84, 8"...............................250.00
Great Northern Girl, dk gr, mk Great Northern USA 1026.......500.00
Great Northern Girl, wht, mk Great Northern USA 1026........475.00
Jack, striped pants, mk USA..............................200.00
Jo Jo the Clown, mk Shawnee 12, 9½" 500.00
Jumbo the Elephant, cold pnt, red or bl bow tie, mk USA 250.00
Little Chef, mc, mk USA, 8½"...............................175.00
Little Chef, yel, mk USA.............................200.00
Muggsy, mk Muggsy USA or USA, 11¾".................1,100.00
Owl, mk USA, 11½".............................175.00
Pennsylvania Dutch Jug, mk USA, 8¼"...........................300.00
Sailor Boy (Jack Tar), gold, blk hair, mk USA, 12".................1,150.00
Sailor Boy (Jack Tar), gold & decals, blond hair, mk USA, 12" .1,400.00
Smiley the Pig, bl neckerchief, blk ft, mk USA.........................200.00
Smiley the Pig, clover bud, mk Pat Smiley USA.......................650.00
Smiley the Pig, roses, gold & decals, mk USA...........................700.00
Smiley the Pig, shamrock, mk USA 450.00
Winnie the Pig, bl collar, mk USA 425.00
Winnie the Pig, peach collar, gold, mk USA....................1,100.00
Winnie the Pig, shamrock, mk USA...........................425.00

Corn Line

Bowl, mixing; King, mk Shawnee 8, 8" 45.00
Bowl, mixing; Queen, mk Shawnee 8, 8" 35.00
Bowl, soup/cereal; King or Queen, mk Shawnee 94.................50.00
Butter dish, King or Queen, w/lid, mk Shawnee 72 ....55.00

Casserole, King, mk Shawnee 74, lg 40.00
Casserole, Queen, mk Shawnee 74, lg...........................50.00
Cookie jar, King or Queen, mk Shawnee 66, 10¼" 350.00
Creamer, King, mk Shawnee 70...........................28.00
Creamer, Queen, mk Shawnee 70.............................26.00
Cup, King, mk 90 ....32.00
Cup, Queen, mk 90 ....30.00
Fruit dish, King or Queen, mk Shawnee 92, 6" 45.00
Mug, King or Queen, mk Shawnee 69, 8-oz...........................50.00
Plate, King or Queen, mk Shawnee 68, 10" 40.00
Plate, salad; King, mk Shawnee 93, 8"...........................40.00
Plate, salad; Queen, mk Shawnee 93, 8".............................35.00
Platter, King or Queen, mk Shawnee 96, 12"...........................55.00
Polly Ann's popcorn set, King Corn 200.00
Relish tray, King, mk Shawnee 79 ....40.00
Saucer, King or Queen, mk 91 ....18.00
Shakers, King or Queen, lg, 5¼", pr 40.00
Shakers, King or Queen, sm, 3¼", pr...........................28.00
Teapot, King or Queen, mk Shawnee 65, 10-oz...........................175.00
Teapot, King or Queen, mk Shawnee 75, 30-oz...........................85.00
Town & Country snack set, King 225.00

Kitchenware

Bowl, batter; Snowflake............................25.00
Canister, Dutch decal, mk USA, 2-qt.............................50.00
Canister, fruit decal, mk USA, 2-qt...........................55.00
Canister, Snowflake, 2-qt.............................55.00
Creamer, fern decor, 9-oz...........................45.00
Creamer, Pennsylvania Dutch, heart & flowers decor, mk USA 10..60.00
Creamer, tulip, mk USA 80.00
Grease jar, Laurel Wreath, w/lid, mk USA...........................30.00
Grease jar, Snowflake, 3½" 45.00
Pitcher, ball jug; fruit, mk Shawnee 80, 48-oz...........................80.00
Pitcher, Bo Peep, gold, mk Shawnee USA 47, 30-oz...........................175.00
Pitcher, Boy Blue, gold, mk Shawnee 46, 20-oz...........................200.00
Pitcher, fern decor, 1½-pt...........................70.00

Pitcher, Smiley the Pig, embossed clover bud, marked Pat. Smiley USA, $175.00. (Photo courtesy Janice and Duane Vanderbilt)

Shakers, Boy Blue & Bo Peep, gold, sm, pr 55.00
Shakers, Chanticleer, gold & decor, lg, pr...........................180.00
Shakers, cottage, sm, pr............................375.00
Shakers, Dutch Kids, bl & gold, lg, pr 75.00
Shakers, Farmer Pigs, gold, sm, pr...........................110.00
Shakers, Jack & Jill, lg, pr...........................55.00
Shakers, Jumbo the Elephant, sm, pr...........................100.00
Shakers, Laurel Wreath, lg, pr...........................30.00
Shakers, milk cans, gold, sm, pr...........................125.00
Shakers, Muggsy, gold, sm, pr...........................200.00
Shakers, Muggsy, sm, pr...........................60.00
Shakers, owls, gold, sm, pr...........................80.00

Shakers, Smiley, gr neckerchief, pr	125.00
Shakers, Smiley & Winnie, heart decor, lg, pr	175.00
Shakers, Smiley & Winnie, peach neckerchief, gold, sm, pr	65.00
Shakers, Swiss Kids, gold, lg, pr	65.00
Shakers, watering cans, sm, pr	26.00
Shakers, wheelbarrows, gold, sm, pr	110.00
Sugar bowl, clover bud, mk USA	55.00
Sugar bowl, Flower & Fern, open	25.00
Teapot, clover bud, mk USA, 7-cup	75.00
Teapot, Criss Cross, mk USA, 5-cup	35.00
Teapot, Drape, mk USA, 4-cup	35.00
Teapot, fern decor, 6-cup	85.00
Teapot, Flower & Fern, 6-cup	45.00
Teapot, Granny Ann, plain, mk Patented Granny Ann USA, 7-cup	175.00
Teapot, horseshoe design, mk USA, 8-cup	45.00

Lobsterware

Baker, open, mk 915, 5"	40.00
Batter bowl, hdl, mk 928	50.00
Bean pot, mk Kenwood USA 925, 40-oz	775.00
Butter dish, mk Kenwood 927	110.00
Casserole, French; wht w/lobster finial, mk 904, 2-qt	85.00
Covered relish, mk Kenwood USA 926	50.00
Mug, mk Kenwood 911, 8-oz	85.00
Pin, lobster shape	75.00
Spoon holder, dbl, mk USA 935, 8½"	250.00
Sugar bowl, w/lid, mk 907	26.00

Valencia

Bud vase	20.00
Carafe, w/lid	55.00
Coffeepot, regular, w/lid	50.00
Covered dish, 8"	40.00
Egg cup	20.00
Fork	45.00
Jug, 2-pt	30.00
Nappie, 8½"	22.00
Pie server	55.00
Pitcher, ice	35.00
Plate, chop; 13"	27.00
Plate, 6½"	12.00
Plate, 10¾"	14.00
Relish tray	135.00
Teacup & saucer	22.00
Tray, utility	22.00

Miscellaneous

Bonbon, rectangular, mk USA 352, mc, 5"	10.00
Figurine, dog, unmk, 6½"	30.00
Figurine, Muggsy, gold, mk USA, 5½"	85.00
Jardiniere, mk USA 4055, 5"	12.00
Planter, birds on driftwood, mk Shawnee 502	50.00
Planter, country boy at low stump, cold pnt, mk USA 532	24.00
Planter, dog in boat, mk Shawnee 736	35.00
Planter, dove & planting dish, gold, mk Shawnee 2025	45.00
Planter, giraffe's head, mk Shawnee USA 841	65.00
Planter, girl & mandolin, mk USA 576	24.00
Planter, girl w/umbrella, mk USA 560	28.00
Planter, globe, gold, mk Shawnee USA	55.00
Planter, kitten, mk USA 723	35.00
Planter, old mill, gold, mk Shawnee 769	35.00

Planter, panda & cradle, mk Shawnee USA 2031	32.00
Planter, pony, mk Kenwood 1509	65.00
Planter, rabbit & cabbage, mk USA	10.00
Planter, swan & elf, mk Kenwood 2030	50.00
Planter, train caboose, mk USA 553	55.00
Planter, train engine, mk USA 550	55.00
Vase, butterfly, mk USA 680, 6"	16.00
Vase, emb flowers, mk USA 1268	24.00
Vase, leaf; gold, mk Shawnee 823, 9"	45.00
Vase, wheat, mk USA 1208, 3½"	18.00
Wall pocket, red feather, unmk	45.00
Wall pocket, Scottie dog, unmk	70.00

Shearwater

Since 1928 generations of the Peter, Walter, and James McConnell Anderson families have been producing figurines and artwares in their studio at Ocean Springs, Mississippi. Their work is difficult to date. Figures from the '20s and '30s won critical acclaim and have continued to be made to the present time. Early marks include a die-stamped 'Shearwater' in a dime-sized circle, a similar ink stamp, and a half-circle mark. Any older item may still be ordered in the same glazes as it was originally produced, so many pieces on the market today may be relatively new. However, the older marks are not currently in use. Currently produced Blacks and pirates figurines are marked with a hand-incised 'Shearwater' and/or a cipher formed with an 'S' whose bottom curve doubles as the top loop of a 'P' formed by the addition of an upright placed below and to the left of the S. Many are dated, '93, for example. These figures are generally valued at $35.00 to $50.00 and are available at the pottery or by mail order. New decorated and carved pieces are very expensive, starting at $400.00 to $500.00 for a 6" pot.

Vase, turquoise, bottle neck, 7½", $75.00.

Candle holder, bl-gr gloss, #97, 2", ea	90.00
Creamer, lt bl, bulbous, 3½x4"	50.00
Figurine, Black man on donkey, 6¾x7"	80.00
Figurine, dancing pirate, 6½"	55.00
Figurine, football player, kicking position, 11x8"	40.00
Flower holder, Black man in overalls holding bag open, 4", NM	140.00
Jar, sea-gr runs on brn, sgn JA, flat finial, 6"	350.00
Mug, gr matt, bird hdl, 4"	120.00
Plate, dk bl, mk '92, 1½x9"	25.00
Soap dish, duck figural, mk 1998, 2x6"	30.00
Teapot, brn w/wht wash, w/lid, 4⅞", EX	95.00
Vase, bl crystalline gloss, rnd shoulders, 1930s, 6"	325.00
Vase, brn to gr vellum-like glaze, ovoid, 7x5"	275.00
Vase, textured w/raised metallic blk sections on aqua gloss, 5¾"	425.00
Vase, turq drip on gunmetal, flared cylinder, 11x 4¾" (at base)	135.00

Sheet Music

Sheet music is often collected more for its colorful lithographed covers, rather than for the music itself. Transportation songs (which have pictures or illustrations of trains, ships, and planes), ragtime and blues, comic characters (especially Disney), sports, political, and expositions are eagerly sought after. Much of the sheet music on the market today is valued at under $5.00; some of the better examples are listed here. For more information refer to *Sheet Music Reference and Price Guide, Second Edition*, by Anna Marie Guiheen and Marie-Reine A. Pafik. Values are given for examples in excellent to near-mint condition unless otherwise noted.

After All, James M Reilly & Arthur Gillespie, 1913 ....12.00
Arizona March, Smith & ET Paull......................................35.00
Bees-Wax Rag, Harry J Lincoln, 1911 ....25.00
Bible Tells Me So, Dale Evans, 1945 ....160.00
Bill Bailey Won't You Please Come Home?, Hughie Cannan, 1902..35.00
Carnival King, Ralph K Elicker & ET Paull, 1911 ....35.00
Cement Mixer (Put-Ti, Put-Ti), Slim Gaillard & Lee Ricks, 1946 .5.00
Cow Cow Boogie, Don Raye, Gene De Paul & Benny Carter, 1942 .15.00
Diane, Erno Rapee & Lew Pollack, 1927 ....16.00
Dixie Coon Brigade, Walter E Petry, 1898 ....35.00
Dixie Dimples, James Scott, 1918.....................................15.00
Ebb Tide, Leo Robin & Ralph Rainger, 1937 ....5.00
Entertainer's Rag, Jay Roberts, 1912 ....20.00
Every Chicken Likes Style, Goulart....................................15.00
Felicity Rag, Scott Joplin & Scott Hayden, 1911 ....50.00
Fellow Needs a Girl, Rodgers & Hammerstein, 1951 ....10.00
Flight of the Airship, H Zeiler 35.00
Gallant Hero, Chas A Curtis, 1920 ....16.00
Gold Dust Twins, Nat Johnson, 1913 ....25.00
Golden Girl of My Dreams, Geo Spink, 1927..........................10.00
Hawaiian Smiles, Ballard MacDonald & Mary Earl, 1919.............15.00
Hey Jude, John Lennon & Paul McCartney, 1968.....................25.00
High Flyer, JC Reed, 1904..15.00
I Believe, Ervin Drake, Irvin Graham & Al Stillman, 1952............7.00
If I Thought You Wouldn't Tell, Irving Berlin, 1909 ....12.00
In the Mood, Razaf & Garland, 1936 ....10.00
In the Mood (Glenn Miller Story), Razaf & Garland, 1954 ....120.00
Jiminy Cricket (Pinocchio Movie), Harline & Washington, 1940 ..10.00
Jockey Hat & Feather, Julia Brodwig, 1860............................50.00
John Henry Blues, WC Handy, 1922 ....10.00
Jolly Boys in Gray, Alfred Roth, 1903 ....20.00
Kentucky Blues, Clarence Gaskill, 1921................................10.00
Laddie Boy, Will D Cobb & Gus Edwards, 1907 ....10.00
Land of Dreams, Anita Owne, 1919 ....15.00
Lazy River, Carrie Jacobs Bond, 1923 ....15.00
Let's Take a Ride on the Jitney Bus, McConnell, 1915................20.00
Love in Bloom, Leo Robin & Ralph Rainger, 1934 ....16.00
Man on the Flying Trapeze, Walter O'Keefe, 1934 ....34.00
Melody of Love, H Engelmann, 1903 ....10.00
Moon River, Johnny Mercer & Henry Mancini, 1961..................14.00
Moxie Fox Trot Song, Dennis J Shae & Eddie Fitzgerald, 1930 ....55.00
My Heart's Tonight in Texas, Roden & Witt, 1900 ....20.00
Newport Belles, Ascher, 1901 ....10.00
Nothin' But Love, Alsop & Carrie Jacobs Bond, 1912 ....15.00
Now I Lay Me Down To Sleep, C Arthur Pfeiffer, 1918.............20.00
O'Brannigan Fusilters, Joe Flynn, 1889 ....16.00
Oasis, Harold G Frost & F Henri Klickmann, 1919....................5.00
Over the Rainbow, EY Harburg & Harold Arlen, 1939.............40.00
Paper Doll, Johnny S Black, 1943.....................................10.00
Poor Me, Olin Finney & Bert Adams, 1921............................40.00

Put Me Off at Buffalo, Harry & John Dillon, 1895.....................20.00
Rags to Riches, Richard Alder & Jerry Ross, 1953.....................12.00
Rainbow, Alfred Bryan & Percy Wenrich, 1908 ....35.00
Real Slow Rag, Scott Joplin, 1903 ....50.00
Rippling Waters, Wm T Pierson, 1908................................10.00
Seminola, King & Warren, 1925 ....25.00
Skids Are Out Tonight, Ed Harrington & David Braham, 1879 or 1880, ea..15.00
Sleepy Song, Carrie Jacobs Bond, 1912 ....15.00
Statue of Liberty Is Smiling, Jack Mahoney & Halsey K Mohr, 1918..20.00
Taxi, Harry D Keer & Mel B Kaufman, 1919..........................25.00
Ten Little Fingers & Ten Little Toes, Pease/White Shuster/Nelson, 1921..12.00
That Red Cross Girl of Mine, Ed C Cannon, 1917 ....25.00
They're on Their Way to Mexico, Irving Berlin, 1915 ....16.00
Three Coins in the Fountain, Sammy Cahn & Jule Styne, 1954 ....8.00

Together, G.G. DeSylva, Lew Brown, and Ray Henderson, from a movie of the same title, movie stars on cover, $15.00. (Photo courtesy Anna Marie Guiheen and Marie-Reine A. Pafik)

Under the Yum Yum Tree, Andrew Sterling & Harry Von Tilzer, 1910..6.00
Underneath the Cotton Moon, Sam M Lewis & Geo W Meyer, 1913..15.00
Unlucky in Love, Irving Berlin, 1924..................................10.00
Very Thought of You, Ray Nobel, 1934...............................9.00
Voice of the Violet, Chauncey Olcott, 1902 ....15.00
Voyage to the Bottom of the Sea (Movie), Faith, 1961 ....8.00
Wabash Moon, Dave Dreyer, Morton Downey & Billy McKenney, 1931..10.00
War Babies, Al Jolson, 1916..15.00
Watching the Clock, Whitman, 1930 ....10.00
X Marks the Spot, Willie Hartzell & Walter Kranz, 1940...............3.00
Yankee Doodle Boy, George M Cohan, 1904 ....25.00
Yellow Rose of Texas, Don George, 1955 ....3.00
You Can't Fool Me No More, Nathan Bevins, 1900.....................30.00
Yukaloo, Van Brunt, 1917 ....10.00
Zana Zaranda, Mort Greene & Harry Revel, 1942......................5.00
Zip-A-Dee-Doo-Dah, Allie Wrubel & Ray Gilbert, 1946 ....15.00
Zoma, ES Litchfield, 1920..5.00

Shell-Work Collectibles

Not long after the natural beauty of the shell was discovered, man began to use them for decorative purposes of many types. Shells were used to decorate clothing and household items as well as jewelry, personal gifts, and souvenirs. Remains of shell necklaces have been found that date to a time prior to the great flood!

During Victorian times shell work became a hobby for the middle class. Shell-work jewelry became popular at that time, but very little has survived due to its delicate nature. Examples of love tokens, souvenirs, and whimsies from that era are listed below. For further information we recommend *Neptune's Treasures, A Study and Value Guide*, available from our advisors, Carole and Richard Smyth (see their listing in the Directory under New York for ordering information).

Box, amoire shape w/mirrored door & 3 inside shelves, 9¼x7½x4"..**220.00**
Box, cushion top, fancy shell borders & sides, from $175 to **250.00**
Box, doghouse w/bsk dog peering out, litho paper, English, Vict, EX.**400.00**
Box, Elizabethan lady chromolitho on lid, 3½x10½x7½"...........**220.00**
Box, shoe shape, litho scene at heel, English Vict, EX **385.00**
Dollhouse, garden of shells, 1930s Am folk art, VG.................**1,200.00**
Framed picture, chromolitho under flat glass, from $150 to **500.00**
Handbag, rectangular w/woven hdl, overall decor, souvenir, $150 to..**400.00**
Inkwell/letter holder, 3 lg shells, pnt ship, Fr Vict, EX **185.00**
Love token, anchor shape (symbol of dependability), Vict **350.00**
Miniature chest, overall decor, ftd, Made in England, from $150 to...**250.00**
Necklace, feather/shell, on animal sinew, Am Indian, late 1800s, G..**385.00**
Pin holder, decor front, bk: love message, pins around edge, $50 to..**100.00**
Pincushion, heart shape, 1-sided litho, pins at edge, Vict, EX **185.00**
Plaque, World's Fair litho beneath convex lens on star shape, 9½".**165.00**
Roundel, litho scene under glass w/layered shells, from $125 to.**300.00**
Shadow box, house scene, papier-mâché/wire/grasses, English Vict..**7,000.00**
Symbol of faith, mini shrine, etc, ea, from $50 to.......................**250.00**
TV lamp, 3 conch shells w/2 flamingos, 1950s, EX.......................**45.00**

Shelley

In 1872 Joseph Shelley became partners with James Wileman, owner of Foley China Works, thus creating Wileman & Co. in Stoke-on-Trent. Twelve years later James Wileman withdrew from the company, though the firm continued to use his name until 1925 when it became known as Shelley Potteries, Ltd. Like many successful nineteenth-century English potteries, this firm continued to produce useful household wares as well as dinnerware of considerable note. In 1896 the beautiful Dainty White shape was introduced, and it is regarded by many as synonymous with the name Shelley. In addition to the original Dainty (six-flute) design, other lovely shapes were produced: Ludlow (fourteen-flute), Oleander (petal shape), Stratford (twelve-flute), Queen Anne (with eight angular panels), Ripon (with its distinctive pedestal), and the 1930s shapes of Vogue, Eve, and Regent.

Though often overlooked, striking earthenware was produced under the direction of Frederick Rhead and later Walter Slater and his son Eric. Many notable artists contributed their talents in designing unusual, attractive wares: Rowland Morris, Mabel Lucie Attwell, and Hilda Cowham, to name but a few.

In 1966 Allied English Potteries acquired control of the Shelley Company, and by 1967 the last of the exquisite Shelley China had been produced to honor remaining overseas orders. In 1971 Allied English Potteries merged with the Doulton group.

It had to happen: Shelley forgeries! Chris Davenport, author of *Shelley Pottery, The Later Years*, reports seeing Mocha-shape cups and saucers with the Shelley mark. However, on close examination it is evident that the mark has been applied to previously unmarked wares too poorly done to have ever left the Shelley Pottery. This Shelley mark can actually be 'felt,' as the refiring is not done at the correct temperature to allow it to be fully incorporated into the glaze. (Beware! These items are often seen on Internet auction sites.)

Some Shelley patterns (Dainty Blue, Bridal Rose, Blue Rock) have been seen on Royal Albert and Queensware pieces. These companies are part of the Royal Doulton Group.

Note: Measurements for objects with lids are measured to the top of the finial unless stated otherwise. Be aware that Rose Spray and Bridal Rose are the same pattern. Our advisor for this category is Lila Shrader; she is listed in the Directory under California.

Key:
MLA — Mabel Lucie Attwell   Trio — Cup, saucer, and 8" plate
QA — Queen Anne shape   unless stated otherwise

RPFMN — Rose, Pansy,   W — Wileman, pre-1910
   Forget-Me-Not

Beaker, crested w/2 lions, finely ribbed horn w/o hdl, 4" **23.00**
Biscuit jar, Blue Pansy, chrome hdl, 6¾".....................................**230.00**
Bowl, Dragon & Butterfly w/gold, 8½"..**115.00**
Bowl, fruit; Dainty Blue, sm, 5¼" **55.00**
Bowl, orange/gr/gray/yel drip, 3½x8½"...**86.00**
Butter dish, Melody Chintz, 5x6¾"...**300.00**
Butter pat, Campanula, Dainty shape, #13886, 3⅞".........................**95.00**
Butter pat, Pansy, Dainty shape, #13671, 3⅞"..............................**110.00**
Butter pat, Shamrock, Dainty shape, #14114, 3⅞" **67.00**
Butter pat, Thistle, 3¼"..**34.00**
Cake plate, Imari-like, ped ft, W, 3¼x8½" **138.00**
Candlestick, Art Deco HP stylized fruit, blk looping 'hdls,' 7", ea..**185.00**
Candy dish, Bluebells, Dainty shape, tab hdls, 5⅞" sq....................**30.00**
Candy dish, Dainty Blue, tab hdls, 5⅞"..**55.00**
Children's ware, cup, MLA, BooBoo riding on puppy, 3" **80.00**
Children's ware, horn (tall mug w/hdl), MLA, boy & girl sailing..**165.00**
Coffeepot, Bridal Rose, Dainty shape, #13545, 7½".....................**215.00**
Coffeepot, Georgian, Henley shape, #13360, 7"..........................**195.00**
Coffeepot, Rock Garden, Henley shape, #13454, 7" **400.00**
Coffeepot, Wildflower, Dainty shape, #13668, 6" **210.00**
Coffeepot, Yellow Wild Rose, Warwick shape, 7"..........................**52.00**
Compote, Melody Chintz, ped ft, 2½x5½" **535.00**
Creamer, Dainty Blue, mini, 1½" **265.00**
Creamer & sugar bowl, Dainty Blue, w/lid.................................**235.00**
Creamer & sugar bowl, Dainty Mauve, open, +oval tray **255.00**
Creamer & sugar bowl, Dainty Pink, open.................................**145.00**
Creamer & sugar bowl, Woodland, Cambridge shape, #13348......**40.00**
Cup & saucer, Begonia, Dainty shape, #13427, from $42 to **60.00**
Cup & saucer, Blue Rock, Westminster shape, mini....................**275.00**
Cup & saucer, bright yel int & hdl, blk ext & saucer, QA shape.**110.00**
Cup & saucer, Chrysanthemum, Dainty shape................................**82.00**
Cup & saucer, Dainty White w/bright yel polka-dots, #13748....**310.00**
Cup & saucer, Dainty Yellow, from $240 to **295.00**
Cup & saucer, Green Crystals, Westminster shape, #13918, mini.**200.00**
Cup & saucer, Maytime (inside), Oleander shape, gold ft...........**148.00**
Cup & saucer, mustache; Edmonton, Alberta scene **65.00**
Cup & saucer, Rock Garden, Richmond shape, #13454...............**64.00**
Cup & saucer, Stock (inside), pastel exterior, ftd Oleander shape..**75.00**
Cup & saucer, Stocks, Canterbury shape, #13548, mini..............**170.00**
Cup & saucer, Summer Glory, Ripon shape **78.00**
Cup & saucer, unnamed pattern, Canterbury shape, #13579/p, mini.**440.00**
Dinner set, Serenity, 6-pc place set, serves 12+major serving pcs.**685.00**
Egg cup, Dainty Blue, 2½"...**76.00**
Ewer, Persian style, dk mauve, w/hdl & lid, Late Foley, 9" **46.00**
Figurine, MLA, blue fairy (BooBoo) hugging mushroom, 3".......**395.00**
Figurine, MLA, smiling gr pixie riding lg dog, 3".........................**495.00**
Food mold, armadillo shape, W, 4x10x7"...................................**138.00**
Gravy boat & liner, Blue Rock, Regency, Rosebud, Dainty shape, up to..**145.00**
Horn (tall mug w/hdl), Lily of the Valley, Dainty shape, 4", $22 to...**77.00**
Hot water pot, Dainty Blue, w/lid, 8½" **335.00**
Jug, golfing theme, bulbous w/hdl, earthenware, 5¾" **360.00**
Plate, bread & butter; Old Sevres, 5¾" **35.00**
Plate, dinner; Dubarry, Duchess or Georgian, 10½", from $28 to .**45.00**
Plate, various scenes (not Dainty shape), 10½", from $32 to........**65.00**
Platter, Bridal Rose, Dainty shape, #13545, 16¾x13½" **325.00**
Platter, Dainty Pink, #051/P, 13x10½", from $160 to...................**225.00**
Powder jar, Bridal Rose, w/lid, solid color finial, squat, 3"............**85.00**
Reamer, MLA sgn, dots, strainer at base of spout, 7½" spout to hdl .**585.00**
Relish, Melody Chintz, 3-part, tab hdls, 10½"...............................**110.00**
Shakers, Dainty Blue, pear shape, 3¼", pr **210.00**
Sugar bowl, Blue Iris, QA shape, open, 2⅝".................................**65.00**

Tea & toast set, RPFMN, Dainty shape w/indent & cup, 8¼" **75.00**
Teapot, Blue Iris, Richmond shape, #14008, 6¼" **148.00**
Teapot, Harebell, Oleander shape, #13590, 5¼", from $285 to ..**325.00**
Teapot, Heather, Cambridge shape, #0187, 5" **140.00**
Teapot, Heavenly Pink, Dainty shape, #14075/p, 5½" **685.00**
Teapot, Rambler Rose, Dainty shape, #13671, 4-cup, 5" **215.00**
Teapot, Rosebud, Dainty shape, 6-cup, 6" **385.00**
Teapot, Violets, Dainty shape, #13821, 6¼" **285.00**
Tray, Rock Garden, tab hdls, 14x5¼" **145.00**
Tray, Strawberry, Dainty shape, tab hdls, 14x5¼" **110.00**
Trio, bl & wht, Alexandra shape, W, 6" plate, from $85 to **110.00**
Trio, Blue Rock, Dainty shape, #13591, from $110 to **125.00**
Trio, Blue Rock, Henley shape, #13591, 6" plate **66.00**
Trio, Countryside Chintz, Richmond shape, #13690, 6" plate **215.00**
Trio, Flowers of Gold, Dainty shape, #14187 ....**100.00**
Trio, Pansy (lg), Dainty shape, #13823 ....**145.00**
Trio, Stocks, Dainty shape **125.00**
Trio, Sunray, Vogue shape, #11742, 7" plate **450.00**
Trio, Woodland, Richmond shape, #13348, 7" plate **85.00**
Vase, blk matt w/enamel pk roses & gr leaves, 8½" **34.00**
Vase, Blue Dragon décor, Late Foley, 8½x2¾" **185.00**
Vase, Intarsio, Rhead Arts & Crafts decor, bulbous, W, 8¾" **550.00**
Vase, Oriental-like gr enamel on blk print, lustre, 5½" **55.00**

Shenandoah

The Shenandoah Valley, extending from Virginia to Pennsylvania is well known for the fine pottery made there from the early 1800s until the turn of the century. It is characterized by bright, clear glazes in a variety of colors or in combination. Many small potteries were involved. Items marked 'Bell' indicate one of the larger companies.

Bowl, milk; brushed bl lines, raised rim, hdls, 4¾x10½" **330.00**
Flowerpot, mottled cream/orange/brn, attached saucer, att, 5x5½" .**275.00**
Whistle, bird on tree trunk, redware w/cream & running brn, att, 9".**330.00**

Silhouettes

Silhouette portraits were made by positioning the subject between a bright light and a sheet of white drawing paper. The resulting shadow was then traced and cut out, the paper mounted over a contrasting color and framed. The hollow-cut process was simplified by an invention called the Physiognotrace, a device that allowed tracing and cutting to be done in one operation. Experienced silhouette artists could do full-length figures, scenics, ships, or trains freehand. Some of the most famous of these artists were Charles Peale Polk, Charles Wilson Peale, William Bache, Doyle, Edouart, Chamberlain, Brown, and William King. Though not often seen, some silhouettes were completely painted or executed in wax. Examples listed here are hollow-cut unless another type is described and assumed to be in excellent condition unless noted otherwise.

Key:
c/p — cut and pasted   lp — laid paper
fl — full length   p — profile
hc — hand colored   wc — water color

Bald man w/top hat, fl, c/p, ink details, matted 15x11" fr **635.00**
Boy stands w/whip, fl, c/p, identified, Edouart/1837, 11x9" fr..**1,850.00**
Boy w/book, fl, c/p, ink details & tree, 1845, 10x8" fr................**990.00**
Boy wearing cap w/sm dog, fl, Edouart/1840, 11⅜x9⅜" fr **3,000.00**

Child in long dress & pantaloons, fl, c/p, 9x7" gilt fr **825.00**
Couple, fl, c/p, sgn WH Brown 1847, pr in 11x7½" gilt frs **3,300.00**
Drummer boy w/tasseled cap, fl, c/p, Edouart/1840, 9x7½" fr..**2,200.00**

Family group with mother and three children, black ink with gold details, 12¾x18⅝", in bird's-eye maple frame with repainted gold liner. (Photo courtesy Garth's Auctions)

French lady (matronly), fl, identified, 1851, 14x12" **200.00**
Girl w/flower basket, fl, c/p, Edouart/1840, 9¾x8" fr **3,650.00**
Lady, p, c/p, wc dress on paper, Am, 19th C, 3¼x2½"+fr **475.00**
Lady holding book wearing lace fichu, p, c/p, wc details, 4⅜x3"+fr.**400.00**
Lady w/hair up, p, c/p, Todd's Pat label, 6¾x5¼" fr.................**300.00**
Lady w/ornate hairdo w/feathers & comb, p, 5¾x4¾" fr **440.00**
Man, fl, c/p, lp, pencil/ink seascape, Edouart, 8x11" fr **925.00**
Man, p, c/p, ink details, 5¾" oval fr **220.00**
Man, p, gold ink details, identified, 1833, 4¾x4⅛" ebony fr **285.00**
Man, p, inked details, 8x7" molded walnut fr **330.00**
Man (identified), fl, c/p, HP bkground on lp, Edouart, 16x12" fr ..**990.00**
Man & wife w/pets, fl, c/p, gilt details, ca 1830, pr in 12x9½" frs.**1,800.00**
Man in waistcoat, fl, c/p, ink & gold details, 18x10" fr **220.00**
Man reading book, fl, Eduoart/1840, modern 14x10" fr **1,100.00**
Man w/scarf & ruffled shirt, p, c/p, chalk details, 5½x4¾" fr......**275.00**
Man w/telescope & walking stick, fl, c/p, Goddard/1834, 9x6" fr .**1,430.00**

Silver

Coin Silver

During colonial times in America, the average household could not afford items made of silver, but those fortunate enough to have accumulations of silver coins (900 parts silver/100 parts alloy) took them to the local silversmith who melted them down and made the desired household article as requested. These pieces bore the owner's monogram and often the maker's mark, but the words 'Coin Silver' did not come into use until 1830. By 1860 the standard was raised to 925 parts silver/75 parts alloy and the word 'Sterling' was added. Coin silver came to an end about 1900.

Adolphe Himmel, presentation water pitcher, repoussé foliage, 13" .**9,200.00**
B Wenman, spoon, bright cut w/coffin ends, NY, ca 1800, 9", pr ..**110.00**
Baldwin Gardiner NY, water pitcher, 13½" **5,500.00**
Eoff & Howell NY, teapot, elliptical, 1805-07, 7½" **925.00**
Eoff & Shepherd NY, waste bowl, fluted w/everted rim, 1850s, 14-t-oz ..**575.00**
Forks, Jean Noel Delarue New Orleans, initials, 7⅞", 5 for **975.00**
Gale & Hayden NY, cup, eng panels/presentation, 1846, 3½" ...**1,725.00**
Gorham, cup, plain w/molded rim, scrolled hdl, script eng, 1848-65, 4" ..**230.00**
Isaac Reed & Son Phila, sugar tongs, fiddle hdl w/shell grips, pr..**260.00**
J Conning Mobile, spoon, dessert; script initials **160.00**
Jacob Hurd, salver, shaped rim, trumpet-form base, 1702-58, 7" .**800.00**
Jonathan Otis, cream jug, pear shape, S-scroll hdl, 1723-91, 3¼"..**1,495.00**
Julep cup, Asa Blanchard...KY, cylindrical, 1830s, 3¼" **3,795.00**
Lewis & Smith, tea set, bulbous w/gadrooning, 1810s, 3-pc, 54-t-oz ..**2,875.00**
Louis Muh New Oreans, tablespoon, uptrn hdl w/wavy shoulder, 8 for ..**635.00**
McDannold, julep cup, KY, 19th C, dents, 3⅞" **1,200.00**

R&W Wilson Phila, tureen, lion mask hdls, domed lid, 1825-50, 41-t-oz ..**2,500.00**
Rasch & Co, salver, gadrooning, scrollwork, paw ft, 1850s, 25-t-oz .**2,500.00**
Unmk, creamer, gadrooned rim, monogram, ball ft, dtd 1869, 5½" ..**835.00**
Wm Gale & Son NY, bowl, centerpc; eng scrolls/flowers, 5x15x10" ..**2,185.00**

Flatware

Silver flatware is being collected today either to replace missing pieces of heirloom sets or in lieu of buying new patterns, by those who admire and appreciate the style and quality of the older ware. Prices vary from dealer to dealer; some pieces are harder to find and are therefore more expensive. Items such as olive spoons, cream ladles, lemon forks, etc., once thought a necessary part of a silver service, may today be slow to sell; as a result, dealers may price them low and make up the difference on items that sell more readily. Many factors enter into evaluation. Popular patterns may be high due to demand though easily found, while scarce patterns may be passed over by collectors who find them difficult to reassemble. If pieces are monogrammed, deduct 20% (for rare, ornate patterns) to 30% (for common, plain pieces). Place settings generally come in three sizes: dinner, place, and luncheon, with the dinner size generally more expensive. In general, dinner knives are 9½" long, place knives, 9" to 9⅛", and luncheon knives, 8¾" to 8⅞". Dinner forks measure 7⅜" to 7½", place forks, 7¼" to 7⅜", and luncheon forks, 6⅞" to 7⅛". Our advisor for this category is Rick Spencer; he is listed in the Directory under Utah.

American Victorian, Lunt, butter pick 24.00
American Victorian, Lunt, butter spreader, hollow hdl 18.50
American Victorian, Lunt, luncheon fork 18.00
American Victorian, Lunt, place soup spoon 27.50
Belle Meade, Lunt, olive spoon..30.00
Belle Meade, Lunt, place fork 29.50
Belle Meade, Lunt, place knife, modern 33.00
Belle Meade, Lunt, sugar spoon 27.50
Blossom Time, International, cheese scoop 23.00
Blossom Time, International, cream soup spoon 16.00
Blossom Time, International, olive fork 17.50
Blossom Time, International, teaspoon 11.00
Camellia, Gorham, butter spreader, flat hdl 10.00
Camellia, Gorham, cream soup spoon 15.50
Camellia, Gorham, dinner fork 33.00
Camellia, Gorham, mint jelly serving spoon 22.00
Camellia, Gorham, pate server...33.00
Camellia, Gorham, youth knife 18.50
Chantilly, Gorham, cream soup spoon..29.00
Chantilly, Gorham, gumbo spoon 40.00
Chantilly, Gorham, lunch knife, Fr blade.....................................21.00
Chantilly, Gorham, mustard ladle 32.00
Chantilly, Gorham, oval soup/dessert spoon................................29.00
Chantilly, Gorham, sugar spoon 29.00
Chantilly, Gorham, 4-pc dinner, modern blade 102.00
Chapel Bells, Alvin, luncheon fork 19.00
Chapel Bells, Alvin, salad fork..16.00
Chapel Bells, Alvin, salad set 165.00
Chateau Rose, Alvin, butter spreader, hollow handle...................18.00
Chateau Rose, Alvin, cheese scoop 26.00
Chateau Rose, Alvin, cocktail fork...20.00
Chateau Rose, Alvin, luncheon fork 20.00
Chateau Rose, Alvin, 4-pc luncheon setting, Fr blade 72.50
Chippendale, Towle, bar knife, hollow hdl...................................27.50
Chippendale, Towle, cream soup spoon..24.00
Chippendale, Towle, dinner fork 44.00
Crown Baroque, Gorham, cheese serving knife............................25.00
Crown Baroque, Gorham, serving fork 82.00

Crown Baroque, Gorham, sugar spoon 32.00
El Grandee, Towle, dinner fork...45.00
El Grandee, Towle, place fork 34.00
El Grandee, Towle, place soup spoon..33.00
El Grandee, Towle, serving fork 67.50
El Grandee, Towle, steak carving knife 37.50
Enchanting Orchid, Wesrmoreland, relish scoop 25.00
Enchanting Orchid, Westmoreland, cream soup spoon 22.00
Enchanting Orchid, Westmoreland, gravy ladle............................39.00
Enchanting Orchid, Westmoreland, place soup spoon...................29.00
English Gadroon, Gorham, butter spreader, flat hdl 12.50
English Gadroon, Gorham, cocktail fork.......................................19.00
English Gadroon, Gorham, gravy ladle..55.00
English Gadroon, Gorham, iced beverage teaspoon.......................22.00
English Gadroon, Gorham, luncheon fork 22.00
English Gadroon, Gorham, olive spoon...33.00
Etruscan, Gorham, cocktail fork 14.00
Etruscan, Gorham, dinner fork..42.00
Etruscan, Gorham, fruit spoon 20.00
Etruscan, Gorham, gravy ladle...57.50
Etruscan, Gorham, sugar spoon 17.50
Florentine, Reed & Barton, butter spreader, hollow hdl...............27.50
Florentine, Reed & Barton, pie or cake serving knife....................34.00
Florentine, Reed & Barton, place soup spoon 34.00
Francis I, Reed & Barton, bouillon soup spoon.............................33.00
Francis I, Reed & Barton, cracker scoop 144.00
Francis I, Reed & Barton, luncheon fork.......................................33.00
Francis I, Reed & Barton, stuffing spoon.......................................270.00
Francis I, Reed & Barton, table serving spoon 55.00
George & Martha, Westmoreland, cocktail fork 14.50
George & Martha, Westmoreland, lunch knife, Fr blade..............17.50
George & Martha, Westmoreland, olive spoon..............................27.50
George & Martha, Westmoreland, sugar spoon..............................34.00
George & Martha, Westmoreland, teaspoon 10.00
George & Martha, Westmoreland, 2-pronged roast beef fork........34.00
Grand Duchess, Towle, dinner fork 60.00
Grand Duchess, Towle, fruit spoon 30.00
Grand Duchess, Towle, serving fork...72.00
Grande Baroque, Wallace, fish knife, hollow hdl..........................45.00
Grande Baroque, Wallace, ice tongs 180.00
Grande Baroque, Wallace, mustard ladle 35.00
Grande Baroque, Wallace, place fork...32.00
Grande Baroque, Wallace, place soup spoon 35.00
Grande Baroque, Wallace, table serving spoon 60.00
Heiress, Oneida, cream soup spoon...16.00
Heiress, Oneida, fruit spoon 19.00
Heiress, Oneida, place knife, modern blade 16.50
Heiress, Oneida, sugar spoon...14.50
Joan of Arc, International, baked potato serving fork.....................37.50
Joan of Arc, International, pie or cake serving knife 32.00
Joan of Arc, International, place soup spoon 30.00
Joan of Arc, International, serving fork...44.00
Joan of Arc, International, small meat fork....................................18.00
Lady Hilton, Westmoreland, gumbo soup spoon...........................21.00
Lady Hilton, Westmoreland, relish scoop......................................23.00
Lady Hilton, Westmoreland, salad fork..17.50
Lady Hilton, Westmoreland, serving fork.......................................40.00
Love Disarmed, Reed & Barton, asparagus serving fork.............223.00
Love Disarmed, Reed & Barton, tablespoon 90.00
Love Disarmed, Reed & Barton, 4-pc dinner setting....................280.00
Lyric, Gorham, cocktail fork 16.00
Lyric, Gorham, dinner fork..33.00
Lyric, Gorham, lemon serving fork 22.00
Lyric, Gorham, luncheon fork...17.50

Lyric, Gorham, serving fork...**42.00**
Meadow Rose, Wallace, butter spreader, hollow hdl.....................**17.50**
Meadow Rose, Wallace, cheese scoop......................................**27.00**
Meadow Rose, Wallace, cocktail fork......................................**16.50**
Meadow Rose, Wallace, olive spoon..**33.00**
Meadow Rose, Wallace, sugar spoon.......................................**19.00**
Rambler Rose, Towle, dinner fork...**27.50**
Rambler Rose, Towle, gravy ladle..**40.00**
Rambler Rose, Towle, luncheon fork.......................................**20.00**
Rambler Rose, Towle, olive fork...**18.50**
Rambler Rose, Towle, steak carving set...................................**55.00**
Rhythm, Wallace, iced beverage teaspoon................................**22.00**
Rhythm, Wallace, luncheon knife, Fr blade...............................**17.50**
Rhythm, Wallace, salad fork..**22.00**
Rose Point, Wallace, butter spreader, Fr hdl..............................**13.50**
Rose Point, Wallace, cheese scoop...**29.00**
Rose Point, Wallace, luncheon fork..**22.00**
Rose Point, Wallace, pate knife..**34.00**
Rose Point, Wallace, table serving spoon..................................**55.00**
Royal Danish, International, cream soup spoon............................**27.50**
Royal Danish, International, luncheon fork................................**24.00**
Royal Danish, International, sugar spoon..................................**17.50**
Royal Danish, International, teaspoon.....................................**14.50**
Savannah, Reed & Barton, fruit spoon.....................................**32.00**
Savannah, Reed & Barton, place soup spoon..............................**27.50**
Savannah, Reed & Barton, salad set......................................**174.00**
Savannah, Reed & Barton, wedding cake knife............................**42.00**
Spanish Lace, Wallace, butter spreader, hollow hdl.......................**13.00**
Spanish Lace, Wallace, ice cream spoon/fork..............................**20.00**
Spanish Lace, Wallace, pasta server.......................................**31.00**
Spanish Lace, Wallace, place soup spoon..................................**25.00**
Steiff Rose, Kirk Steiff, gumbo soup spoon................................**33.00**
Steiff Rose, Kirk Steiff, luncheon fork.....................................**22.00**
Steiff Rose, Kirk Steiff, salad fork...**33.00**
Steiff Rose, Kirk Steiff, table serving spoon...............................**49.00**
Strasbourg, Gorham, cocktail fork...**22.00**
Strasbourg, Gorham, dinner knife, modern hdl...........................**37.50**
Strasbourg, Gorham, gravy ladle...**66.00**
Strasbourg, Gorham, steak carving fork...................................**29.00**
Strasbourg, Gorham, sugar spoon...**27.50**
Tara, Reed & Barton, bonbon/candy dish spoon..........................**24.50**
Tara, Reed & Barton, mint jelly serving spoon............................**23.00**
Tara, Reed & Barton, salad fork..**31.00**
Tara, Reed & Barton, steak carving set....................................**57.50**
Waltz of Spring, Wallace, relish scoop.....................................**29.00**
Waltz of Spring, Wallace, salad fork.......................................**33.00**
William & Mary, Lunt, cream soup spoon.................................**25.00**
William & Mary, Lunt, luncheon fork......................................**18.50**
William & Mary, Lunt, place soup spoon..................................**30.00**
William & Mary, Lunt, stuffing spoon....................................**245.00**
William & Mary, Lunt, sugar spoon.......................................**14.00**
Young Love, Oneida, place soup spoon.....................................**18.00**
Young Love, Oneida, sugar spoon..**14.50**
Young Love, Oneida, 4-pc place setting...................................**60.00**
18th Century, Reed & Barton, place fork..................................**24.00**
18th Century, Reed & Barton, serving fork................................**66.00**
18th Century, Reed & Barton, sugar spoon................................**29.00**
18th Century, Reed & Barton, teaspoon...................................**21.00**
18th Century, Reed & Barton, youth fork..................................**23.00**

Hollow Ware

Until the middle of the nineteenth century, the silverware produced in America was custom made on order of the buyer directly from the silversmith. With the rise of industrialization, factories sprung up that manufactured silverware for retailers who often added their trademark to the ware. Silver ore was mined in abundance, and demand spurred production. Changes in style occurred at the whim of fashion. Repoussé decoration (relief work) became popular about 1885, reflecting the ostentatious preference of the Victorian era. Later in the century, Greek, Etruscan, and several classic styles found favor. Today the Art Deco styles of this century are very popular with collectors.

In the listings that follow, manufacturer's name or trademark is noted first; in lieu of that information, listings are by country or item. Weight is given in troy ounces. See also Tiffany, Silver.

Key: t-oz — troy ounce

Wm. Cripps, London, coffeepot, George II, pear form with chased foliage, 1747 – 1748, 10", 29 troy ounces, $2,000.00.

Arthur Stone, tea/coffee set, 1909-37, 6-pc, 115 gross t-oz......**4,125.00**
Arthur Stone/HA Taylor, bowl, ftd, 1908-37, 4⅛x9½", 25.5-t-oz..**600.00**
Ball, Tomkins & Black, ewer, baluster, vine repoussé, 1854, 28-t-oz..**1,115.00**
Ball Black & Co, NY; milk jug, repoussé floral, 6", 12-t-oz.........**260.00**
Birmingham, salver, pie-crust edge, floral eng, 8" dia, 7.2-t-oz....**300.00**
Black, Starr & Frost, bowl, pierced chrysanthemums, 12½", 30-t-oz..**1,500.00**
Black, Starr & Frost, candlesticks, bows/draping, beaded borders, 7", pr.**575.00**
Black, Starr & Frost, casters, 8½", 16-t-oz, pr.............................**400.00**
Caldwell & Co, water pitcher, plain w/ornate hdl, 1880, 8", EX...**375.00**
Celini Craft, compote, lobed, rnd ft, ca 1930, 10½", 30-t-oz......**765.00**
Continental, cow creamer, hinged lid, #925, 2x6".....................**375.00**
Continental, cream pitcher, helmet, strap hdl, appl decor, 7-t-oz...**330.00**
Continental, tureen w/lid & underplate, bombé, 20", 220-t-oz..**7,000.00**
De Matteo, tray, w/appl blossom hdls, 15" L.............................**150.00**
Dominick & Haff, tea/coffee service, 2 pots+bowl+sug+2 cr, 144-t-oz....**2,400.00**
Dominick & Haff, tea/coffee set, 2 pots+cr/sug+tray, 116-t-oz..**1,400.00**
Dominick & Haff, tray, Virginia, 1912, 14" dia...........................**350.00**
Edward Jay (English), tray, ribbed rim, 3 paw ft, Geo III, 1796, 6"..**275.00**
FE Boyden, creamer & sugar bowl, hammered, D hdls, 10-t-oz...**500.00**
Galmer, water goblets, repoussè, 7", 86-t-oz for set of 8..........**1,300.00**
Geo C Erickson, tea set, ivory finial, pot+cr/sug, 33-t-oz...........**700.00**
Geo Jensen, compote, cut-out rim, ftd, 5½x8"...........................**435.00**
Geo Jensen, compote, Johan Rhode design #243, 5x7¼".......**1,500.00**
Geo Jensen, tea service, post 1945, pot+cr/sug+tray, 54-t-oz......**3,300.00**
Georg Jensen, pitcher, Johan Rhode design #432C, 11¼".......**5,000.00**
Gorham, bonbon dishes, emb thistles at rim, 5⅜", pr................**115.00**
Gorham, covered vegetable bowl, reeded rim, 1912, 24-t-oz......**300.00**
Gorham, gravy boat, chased florals, C-scroll hdl, 1899, 4½x7½".**300.00**
Gorham, soup tureen, hdls, monogram, button ft, 14½" L..**450.00**
Gorham, tea set, 8-sided urn forms, 5-pc, 68-t-oz......................**675.00**
Gorham, tea/coffee service, 2 pots+cr/sug+waste bowl+kettle on stand..**5,500.00**
Gorham, water pitcher, Martele, 9", 40-t-oz.............................**15,000.00**

Gorham, water pitcher, reeded band, monogram, 1912, 10⅜", 26-t-oz..**700.00**
Hamilton & Diesinger, coffee/tea set, ca 1895-99, 7-pc, 396-t-oz ..**8,350.00**
Henry Vincent, London; milk pitcher, urn form w/strap hdl, 1800, 4"..**200.00**
Howard & Co, urns, rtcl/repoussé, cobalt glass liners, 1890, 17", pr..**3,640.00**
International, fruit bowl, Royal Danish, scroll hdls, 24-t-oz.......**315.00**
James T Wooley, tea caddy, shouldered, ftd, 4¾", 7-t-oz **500.00**
John Schofield, London; tea caddy, paneled corners/crest, 6-t-oz .**1,265.00**
John Williams, Dublin; gravy boat, Irish Georgian, 1770s, 10½-t-oz..**1,045.00**
Kalo, bowl, hammered floriform, rolled rim, 20th C, 1⅞x7⅛" ...**400.00**
Kalo, compote, hammered floriform, monogram, 1929, 7x9" **900.00**
Kalo, pitcher, hammered, monogram, bulbous, 6½x8½"..........**1,800.00**
Kalo, tea/coffee set, 2 pots+pitcher+cr/sug+18" tray **8,500.00**
Kirk, teakettle, Nouveau style, mask hdls, heating element, 77-t-oz..**3,750.00**
London, mustard pot, hinged lid, strap hdl, ribbed in middle, 1811 ..**250.00**
London hallmk for 1759, pitcher, Geo II, pear form, 4", 3-t-oz...**325.00**
P Bruckmann & Son, tea set, tooled florals, gourd forms, 3-pc, 1925 .**800.00**
Paul Stoor, teapot, Geo III, repoussé rococo, 1814, 7", 23-t-oz .**1,600.00**
Randahl, baby cup, hammered, #218, 1911-30s, 3½-t-oz **175.00**
Reed & Barton, compote, Francis I, 4¾x8", 13-t-oz.............**1,000.00**
Reed & Barton, lady's flask, cherub/florals, hinged lid, 5½".......**525.00**
Samuel Kirk, hot milk jug, repoussé decor, 1845, 7¼", 12-t-oz ...**560.00**
Shreve, bowl, hammered, appl shaped border, 12" W.............**150.00**
Shreve, Crump & Low; bowl, 8", 12½-t-oz.....................**150.00**
Spaulding, fruit bowl, rtcl rim/foliate scroll border, rnd ft, 10½"....**200.00**
Spratling, vessel, flattened ft, angular spout, 5½" **800.00**
Steiff, coffee set, Rose, pot+cr/sug+tray, 103-t-oz **2,400.00**
Towle, water pitcher, Louis XIV, 10", 24-t-oz...................**550.00**
VanBergh, candelabra, 5-arm, rtcl/chased florals, #1457, 20x20", pr..**2,000.00**
Watson & Co, pitcher, emb florals/scrolls, ped base, 11", 28-t-oz..**935.00**
Wm B Kerr & Co, child's porringer, ca 1900, 6-t-oz.............**230.00**
Wm Comyns, London, trumpet vase, repoussé floral, 1892, 14", pr..**1,850.00**
WMF, bowl, centerpiece, hammered w/rtcl oval base, hdls, 14" L ...**1,900.00**

Silver Overlay

The silver overlay glass made since the 1880s was decorated with a cut-out pattern of sterling silver applied to the surface of the ware.

Bottle, scent; cobalt w/leafy o/l, orig stopper, 9¼" **595.00**
Bowl, gr w/daffodil patterned o/l, 3-ftd, 3¼x5" **135.00**
Decanter, clear w/grapevine o/l, petticoat shape, 9x7" **635.00**
Decanter, cobalt w/floral o/l, matching stopper, +6 matching cordials...**385.00**
Decanter, gr, flowers/vines/leaves, silver-wrapped hdl, Gorham, 11" ...**900.00**
Honey jar, clear, floral o/l, mk Rockwell **130.00**

Perfume bottle, abstract scrolls on emerald green, signed Sterling Silver Deposit and numbered, 6x4", $600.00; Bowl, floral on emerald green, marked 999/1000 Fine with Alvin mark, 4½x5", $725.00.

Pitcher, ruby, allover grapes/vines/leaves, eng cartouch dtd 1899, 9" ..**1,900.00**
Vase, blk amethyst, Baroque o/l on 2 sides, 10¼" **250.00**
Vase, gr, Nouveau o/l, mk Gorham, 16" **670.00**
Vase, gr irid stretch glass w/urn & scroll o/l, fan shape, 6x7½" ...**615.00**
Vase, red cased, floral o/l, stylized rim, 10¼"............**550.00**
Vase, red w/floral o/l, bottle form, 3½"................**230.00**

Silverplate

Silverplated flatware is becoming the focus of attention for many of today's collectors. Demand is strong for early, ornate patterns, and prices have continued to rise steadily over the past five years. Our values are based on pieces in excellent or restored/resilvered condition. Serving pieces are priced to reflect the values of examples in complete original condition, with knives retaining their original blades. If pieces are monogrammed, deduct from 20% (for rare, ornate patterns) to 30% (for common, plain pieces). Our advisor for this category is Rick Spencer; he is listed in the Directory under Utah. For more information we recommend *The Standard Encyclopedia of American Silverplate* by Frances M. Bones and Lee Roy Fisher and *Silverplated Flatware, Revised Fourth Edition*, by Tere Hagan. See also Railroadiana, Silverplate.

Flatware

Adoration, 1847 Rogers, gravy ladle **7.00**
Adoration, 1847 Rogers, luncheon fork................**7.00**
Adoration, 1847 Rogers, teaspoon...................**5.00**
Ambassador, 1847 Rogers, dinner fork................**10.00**
Ambassador, 1847 Rogers, lunch knife, Fr blade **9.00**
Ambassador, 1847 Rogers, place soup spoon **6.00**
Anniversary Rose, International, place fork **4.00**
Anniversary Rose, International, table serving spoon.........**8.00**
Anniversary Rose, International, teaspoon..............**5.00**
Baroque Rose, Oneida, place fork **6.00**
Baroque Rose, Oneida, place knife, modern blade **7.50**
Baroque Rose, Oneida, place soup spoon **6.00**
Baroque Rose, Oneida, teaspoon...................**5.00**
Brittany Rose, Rogers, place fork **5.00**
Brittany Rose, Rogers, place knife, modern **6.00**
Brittany Rose, Rogers, serving fork **7.00**
Buckingham, Wallace, dinner knife, Fr hdl..............**10.00**
Buckingham, Wallace, iced beverage teaspoon **7.00**
Buckingham, Wallace, place knife, modern hdl **9.00**
Cavalier, Gorham, cream soup spoon.................**6.00**
Cavalier, Gorham, luncheon fork...................**6.00**
Cavalier, Gorham, luncheon knife, Fr blade **7.00**
Cavalier, Gorham, master butter server, flat hdl...........**6.00**
Century, Holmes & Edwards, luncheon knife, Fr blade **6.00**
Century, Holmes & Edwards, mint jelly serving spoon.........**10.00**
Century, Holmes & Edwards, salad fork **6.00**
Chapel, Reed & Barton, pierced tablespoon **18.00**
Chapel, Reed & Barton, place knife, modern blade..........**12.00**
Classic Bead, Wallace, place soup spoon **8.00**
Classic Bead, Wallace, serving fork.................**9.00**
Classic Bead, Wallace, sugar spoon.................**8.00**
Coronation, Oneida, grill fork....................**5.00**
Coronation, Oneida, salad fork **7.00**
Coronation, Oneida, sugar spoon **6.00**
Coronation, Oneida, 4-pc luncheon setting, Fr blade..........**18.00**
Cottage Rose, Reed & Barton, salad fork **9.00**
Cottage Rose, Reed & Barton, sugar spoon **11.00**
Cottage Rose, Reed & Barton, table serving spoon **10.00**
Cottage Rose, Reed & Barton, teaspoon **6.00**
Danish Princess, Holmes & Edwards, grill knife............**5.00**
Danish Princess, Holmes & Edwards, luncheon fork..........**5.00**
Danish Princess, Holmes & Edwards, mint jelly serving spoon **6.00**
Danish Princess, Holmes & Edwards, sugar spoon...........**5.00**
Dresden Rose, Reed & Barton, gravy ladle..............**12.00**
Dresden Rose, Reed & Barton, serving fork **12.00**
Dresden Rose, Reed & Barton, sugar spoon **10.00**

Emperor, Reed & Barton, place knife, modern hdl 9.00
Emperor, Reed & Barton, place spoon 9.00
Emperor, Reed & Barton, tablespoon 13.50
Emperor, Reed & Barton, teaspoon 5.00
Eternally Yours, 1847 Rogers, cream soup spoon 8.00
Eternally Yours, 1847 Rogers, grill fork 7.00
Eternally Yours, 1847 Rogers, oval soup/dessert spoon 6.00
Eternally Yours, 1847 Rogers, place soup spoon 7.00
Eternally Yours, 1847 Rogers, salad fork 7.00
Eternally Yours, 1847 Rogers, table serving spoon 12.50
Eternally Yours, 1847 Rogers, teaspoon 4.00
Evening Star, Community, luncheon knife, modern 7.00
Evening Star, Community, salad fork 6.00
Evening Star, Community, sugar spoon 5.00
Fairhill, Oneida, cream soup spoon 3.00
Fairhill, Oneida, table serving spoon 5.00
Flower Song, Gorham, master butter server, flat hdl 8.00
Flower Song, Gorham, place knife, modern 9.00
Flower Song, Gorham, salad fork 8.00
Flower Song, Gorham, table serving spoon 10.00
Guild, International, grill fork 6.00
Guild, International, place knife, modern 12.50
Guild, International, sugar spoon 6.00
King Cedric, Oneida, ice cream spoon/fork 6.00
King Cedric, Oneida, luncheon fork 6.50
King Cedric, Oneida, sugar spoon 6.00
Lady Hamilton, Community, grill knife 6.50
Lady Hamilton, Community, 4-pc dinner setting, modern blade ..18.00
Loraine, Oneida, pie or cake serving knife 7.50
Loraine, Oneida, place knife, modern blade 3.50
Loraine, Oneida, salad fork 3.50
Loraine, Oneida, sugar spoon 3.50
Love Lace, 1847 Rogers, grill knife 7.50
Love Lace, 1847 Rogers, luncheon fork 4.50
Love Lace, 1847 Rogers, luncheon knife, Fr blade 6.50
Love Lace, 1847 Rogers, sugar spoon 5.50
Majestic, Rogers, cocktail fork 5.00
Majestic, Rogers, grill knife 6.00
Majestic, Rogers, place soup spoon 4.50
Majestic, Rogers, sugar spoon 4.50
Morning Star, Community, cracker scoop 120.00
Morning Star, Community, cream soup 8.00
Morning Star, Community, grill fork 8.00
Morning Star, Community, luncheon knife, modern 10.00
Old Dominion, Gorham, place knife, modern 8.00
Old Dominion, Gorham, sugar spoon 6.00
Old Dominion, Gorham, teaspoon 4.00
Parthenon, Reed & Barton, cocktail fork 3.50
Parthenon, Reed & Barton, place knife 10.00
Parthenon, Reed & Barton, place soup spoon 8.00
Parthenon, Reed & Barton, sugar spoon 8.00
Patrician, Oneida, dinner fork 8.00
Patrician, Oneida, salad fork 7.00
Patrician, Oneida, serving fork 10.00
Patrician, Oneida, sugar spoon 9.00
Queen Bess, 1924, Oneida, cream soup spoon 6.00
Queen Bess, 1924, Oneida, place fork 6.00
Queen Bess, 1924, Oneida, sugar spoon 6.00
Queen Bess, 1924, Oneida, teaspoon 4.00
Remembrance, 1847 Rogers, gumbo soup spoon 9.50
Remembrance, 1847 Rogers, luncheon fork 7.00
Remembrance, 1847 Rogers, place spoon 8.00
Remembrance, 1847 Rogers, sugar spoon 8.00
Remembrance, 1847 Rogers, table serving spoon 12.50

Romance, Holmes & Edwards, berry serving spoon 12.50
Romance, Holmes & Edwards, gumbo soup spoon 6.00
Romance, Holmes & Edwards, luncheon knife, modern blade 6.00
Romance, Holmes & Edwards, salad fork 6.00
Rosemary, Rogers, berry serving spoon 11.00
Rosemary, Rogers, place knife, modern 6.00
Rosemary, Rogers, salad fork 5.00
Spring Garden, Holmes & Edwards, salad fork 5.00
Spring Garden, Holmes & Edwards, table serving spoon 10.00
Spring Garden, Holmes & Edwards, teaspoon 4.00
Valley Rose, Oneida, gravy ladle 8.00
Valley Rose, Oneida, luncheon fork 5.00
Valley Rose, Oneida, place soup spoon 6.00
Valley Rose, Oneida, salad fork 5.00

Hollow Ware

Baby cup, emb Greenaway children at play, Queen City Silver, rstr .250.00
Biscuit bbl, floral medallions, rtcl base, Elkington, 19th C, 17" ..300.00
Butter dish, chain on fr lifts top, Hartford #800, rstr, 15" 895.00
Butter dish, emb glass insert, revolves, Reed & Barton #1030 ....695.00
Butter dish, fr w/lid hanger & knife, Pairpoint #512, rstr, 13½" .550.00
Candelabra, 5-light, scrolling arms, Elkington, 1882 17¾", pr..1,600.00
Candlesticks, Dickens' character figural, Reed & Barton, rstr, 12", pr.1,900.00
Candlesticks, in Adam style, sq base, urn socket, English, 11½", pr..600.00
Candlesticks, orig bobeches, sq base/scroll corners, English, 10", pr.550.00
Carafe, ornate, orig glass liner, heavy, Derby #162, rstr, 9" 295.00
Cigarette box, Black, Starr & Gorham, 9¼" 275.00
Coffeepot, repoussé florals/chased geometrics, Reed & Barton, 22"...110.00
Entree dish, w/lid & warming stand w/dolphins, Elkington, 7x11x8".400.00
Kettle on stand, Dominick & Haff, 8", 18-t-oz 3,750.00
Meat dome, eng crest, beaded edge, fluted, English, 19th C, 9x14x11" ..385.00
Pitcher, quadruple plate, dbl-walled, lady figural hdl, Wilcox, 13" .300.00
Spoon holder, cornucopia shape, Middletown, rstr, 5x6" 275.00
Spooner w/attached bell, Wilcox #1430, rstr 495.00
Spooner, dbl; unmk, rstr 295.00
Sugar holder w/clear Tree of Life insert, Meriden #1757 ....375.00
Tea urn, plain, globular w/ring hdls, heating elements, Gorham, 15" .500.00
Tureen, 4 lion mask ft, revolves, Elkington, 1882, 7x12" 635.00
Tureen, breakfast; revolving top, James Dixon & Sons, 7x14" 300.00
Vase, repoussé floral festoons & scrolls, unmk, 17¾" 285.00

Sheffield

Dinner plates, Georgian, crested, scalloped border with wreath motif, 1820 – 1830, 10", set of twelve, $1,265.00.

Bacon dish, curved rectangle w/gadrooning, fruitwood hdl, 13½" ..115.00
Cake basket, swirl/fluted sides, scrolls/flower heads, 1830s, 10x13" ...75.00

Candelabra, acanthus chased scrollwork columns, 1830s, 20x18", pr ...**2,100.00**
Candlesticks, columnar form, ca 1904, weighted, 7½", pr...........**500.00**
Candlesticks, incised rings, urn sockets, bobeches, 10¾", pr.......**220.00**
Candlesticks, telescoping, reeded stem, Morton's Pat, 1840s, 8", pr ..**515.00**
Condiment set, 2 salts+2 castors+mustard, cobalt liners, 6-t-oz..**175.00**
Inkstand, cast & chased foliage, 2 cut glass wells, 1855 mk, 9" ..**2,200.00**
Pitcher, emb medallions & scrolled foliage, 1857 mk, 7¼" **660.00**
Salt cellars, ftd rectangle w/gadrooned borders, 1¾x3¾x3", pr...**260.00**
Salt cellars, King's Pattern, eng crests, 1820s, master, pr **260.00**
Tankard, domed lid & scroll thumbpc, curved hdl, 8" **110.00**
Tea set, Regency style w/gadrooned rims, 5¾", pot+cr/sug, ca 1800..**450.00**
Wine cooler, urn w/dbl floral hdls, eng coat of arms, 9½" **440.00**

Sitzendorf

The Sitzendorf factory began operations in East Germany in the mid-1800s, adopting the name of the city as the name of their company. They produced fine porcelain groups, figurines, etc., in much the same style and quality as Meissen and the Dresden factories. Much of their ware was marked with a crown over the letter 'S' and a horizontal line with two slash marks.

Candelabra, 2 angels in flower bed at base, 3-arm, 20", pr.......**1,400.00**
Clock, porc, pierced scrolls, flowers & seated figures, 20" **900.00**
Figurine, dachshund, wht, 20th C, 4½x9½" **140.00**
Figurine, lady beside man seeking her hand, mc details, 7x6x3"..**4,750.00**
Figurine, man holds bagpipes & goat, 7½x3½" **695.00**
Figurine, parrot on flowered perch, fine mc, 12½" **350.00**
Lady w/flowers in apron, lamb at ft, ca 1879, 6½" **460.00**
Lamp, colonial couple w/decalcomania florals, 10" base.............**120.00**
Pin dish, reclining monkey figural, HP details, #24407, 5¼" L...**110.00**
Pin tray, Pierrot figural, seated w/knees up, 1920s style **130.00**
Vase, cornucopia form w/cherub holding flowers at side, 1860-80, 11" ...**800.00**

Skookum Dolls

Representing real Indians of various tribes, stern-faced Skookum dolls were designed by Mary McAboy of Missoula, Montana, in the early 1900s. The earliest of McAboy's creations were made with air-dried apple faces that bore a resemblance to the neighboring Chinook Indian tribe. The name Skookum is derived from the Chinook/Siwash term for large or excellent (aka Bully Good) and appears as part of the oval paper labels often attached to the feet of the dolls.

In 1913 McAboy applied for a patent that described her dolls in three styles: a female doll, a female doll with a baby, and a male doll. In 1916 George Borgman and Co. partnered with McAboy, registered the Skookum trademark, and manufactured these dolls which were distributed by the Arrow Novelty Co. of New York and the HH Tammen Co. of Denver. The Skookum (Apple) Packers Association of Washington state produced similar 'friendly faced' dolls as did Louis Ambery for the National Fruit exchange.

The dried apple faces of the first dolls were replaced by those made of a composition material. Plastic faces were introduced in the 1940s, and these continued to be used until production ended in 1959. Skookum dolls were produced in a variety of styles, with the most collectible having stern, lined faces with small painted eyes glancing to the right, colorful Indian blankets pulled tightly across the straw- or paper-filled body to form hidden arms, felt pants or skirts over wooden legs, and wooden feet covered with decorated felt suede or masking tape.

Skookums were produced in sizes ranging from a 2" souvenir mailer with a cardboard address tag to 36" novelty and advertising dolls. Collectors highly prize 21" to 26" dolls as well as dolls that glance to their left. Felt or suede feet predate the less desirable brown plastic feet of the late 1940s and 1950s. Unless noted otherwise, our values are for skookums in excellent condition. Our advisor for this category is Glen Rairigh; he is listed in the Directory under Michigan.

Baby, looks left, cradle brd, beaded body/head covering, 10½" .**1,100.00**
Baby, mc blanket, leather headband w/pnt decor, 4" **30.00**
Baby, wrapped in mc blanket, feather in headband, 3½x3".........**200.00**
Baby mailer, 1½¢ postcard attached, feather ribbon binding, 4".**100.00**
Baby mailer, 1½¢ postcard attached, rattan binding, 4" **105.00**
Baby/child in loop basket, blanket wrap, necklace, 14".............**200.00**
Baby/child in loop blanket, blanket wrap, unbraided hair, 12"....**225.00**
Boy, brn ft w/pnt decor, Bully Good label, 6½" **100.00**
Boy, brn suede ft w/decor, headband, 10" **150.00**
Boy, mc blanket, felt pants, brn plastic fr w/mk, wood beads, 9½" .**85.00**
Boy, mc blanket, felt pants, leather shoes, 6½", VG....................**50.00**
Chief, w/headdress, paper shoes w/decor, 12½"..........................**250.00**
Family, chief & female w/baby, clothes match, 15" & 14" **600.00**
Family, man w/exposed right arm, 13½", female w/baby, 12½" ...**900.00**
Family, w/blanket/clothes/beads, 35", 33", w/10" baby in arms..**5,900.00**
Female w/baby, floral skirt, glass bead necklace, 11½"................**300.00**
Female w/baby, w/blanket, necklace, feather in hair, 16", G **145.00**
Female w/baby, w/blanket, purple felt ft/skirt, necklace, 11½"....**200.00**
Female w/baby, w/blanket, worn paper ft, 12½", VG...................**150.00**
Girl, cotton-wrapped legs, pnt suede ft covers, Bully Good, 6½" .**100.00**
Girl, w/blanket, felt skirt, decor felt ft, bandana, 10"....................**85.00**
Girl, w/blanket/skirt, leather shoes, feather, label, 6½" **125.00**
Mailer, baby in bl & yel cotton, Grand Canyon, 10-1-52.............**25.00**
Mailer, baby in patterned cotton on yel db **25.00**
Mailer, baby in red bandana on yel cb.......................................**55.00**
Male, w/blanket, feather in headband, loose hair, felt shoes, 14", VG .**115.00**

Slag Glass

Slag glass is a marbleized opaque glassware made by several companies from about 1870 until the turn of the century. It is usually found in purple or caramel (see Chocolate Glass), though other colors were also made. Pink is rare and very expensive. It was revived in recent years by several American glassmakers, L.E. Smith, Westmoreland, and Imperial among them.

The listings below reflect values for items with excellent color. Our advisor for this category is Sharon Thoerner; she is listed in the Directory under California.

Blue, Marquis & Marchioness of Lorne, butter dish, Henry Greener ...**685.00**
Blue, powder jar, flower form, 2½x4"..**25.00**
Caramel, bookends, Scottie dog, Imperial, 6½x5", pr..................**300.00**
Caramel, bowl, ftd, Imperial, 4½x8½" **45.00**
Caramel, candlesticks, dolphins, #779, Imperial, 5", pr **65.00**
Caramel, candy jar, owl figural, Imperial, 6½" **85.00**
Caramel, cigarette holder, ftd, 3⅞x2½" sq **45.00**
Caramel, compote, eagle finial, Imperial, 9½" **85.00**
Caramel, jar, beehive form w/7 bees, Imperial, 5¼x3¾" **60.00**
Caramel, Octagon, toothpick holder, #505, Imperial.....................**25.00**
Caramel, Pansy, nappy w/hdl, Imperial, 5" **35.00**
Caramel, trivet, ornate rayed design, ¾x7½" dia..........................**45.00**
Green, ashtray or pipe holder, bird, Westmoreland.......................**35.00**
Green, bell, Imperial, 5¾"...**65.00**
Green, Open Rose, bowl, ruffled/pleated rim, Imperial, 3¼x9¼" .**55.00**
Green, Paneled Grape/#1881, canister, ftd, w/lid, Westmoreland 10" ..**175.00**
Green, toothpick holder, owl, Westmoreland, 3", from $25 to.......**30.00**
Jade, Rose, bowl, #52C, Imperial, 8"...**65.00**
Jade, Rose, candlestick, Imperial, 3½", ea **75.00**

Orange, bowl, flared rim, 3¼x9½"...45.00
Orange, console set, 5½x7¼" ftd bowl+ 2 8¼" candlesticks...85.00
Pink, Invt Fan & Feather, bowl, berry; 6½"...1,000.00
Pink, Invt Fan & Feather, bowl, fruit; 5x9"...750.00
Pink, Invt Fan & Feather, butter dish, 6" dia...1,500.00
Pink, Invt Fan & Feather, creamer...500.00
Pink, Invt Fan & Feather, cruet, all orig...900.00
Pink, Invt Fan & Feather, jelly comport, 5"...600.00
Pink, Invt Fan & Feather, pitcher, 8"...2,500.00
Pink, Invt Fan & Feather, punch cup, from $285 to...315.00
Pink, Invt Fan & Feather, sauce dish, scalloped rim, 4-ftd, 2½x4"...200.00
Pink, Invt Fan & Feather, shakers, rare, pr...1,200.00
Pink, Invt Fan & Feather, spooner...475.00
Pink, Invt Fan & Feather, sugar bowl, w/lid...1,000.00
Pink, Invt Fan & Feather, toothpick holder, flat...500.00
Pink, Invt Fan & Feather, toothpick holder, ftd, 2⅜"...1,500.00
Pink, Invt Fan & Feather, tumbler...235.00
Purple, bell, Imperial, #720, ca 1850, 6"...55.00
Purple, box, duck (#823) or dog (#822), Imperial, ea...185.00
Purple, butterfly, Westmoreland, lg...50.00
Purple, cardinal, solid, Westmoreland...35.00

Purple, celery vase, paneled sides, 8x4", $85.00.

Purple, Cherry, goblet, LG Wright, 6½"...45.00
Purple, Colonial, ashtray, Westmoreland...30.00
Purple, compote, scalloped, ftd, Greener, 5⅜x5¾"...85.00
Purple, creamer & sugar bowl, rose in flowerpot emb, Imperial, 3"...85.00
Purple, Dmn Star, cruet, Imperial, 7"...45.00
Purple, Hobnail, bowl, #641, Imperial, 8½"...95.00
Purple, jar, peacock head emb, Sowberby's Ellison Glass Works, 2½"...90.00
Purple, Jewel, celery vase, ca 1890, 8x4¼"...85.00
Purple, Old Quilt/#500, butter/cheese dish, rnd, Westmoreland...75.00
Purple, Old Quilt/#500, water pitcher, 3-pt, +6 9-oz tumblers...280.00
Purple, Orange Tree & Leaf, rose bowl, Fenton, 4x6"...95.00
Purple, owl on 2 stacked books, Westmoreland, 3½"...40.00
Purple, Paneled Grape/#1881, butter/cheese dish, rnd, Westmoreland, 7"...75.00
Purple, Pansy/#757, basket, split hdl, Westmoreland...35.00
Purple, pitcher, windmill/cottage/fisherman, Imperial, #340, 6½"...50.00
Purple, toothpick holder, Sowerby, 1880s...125.00
Ruby, ashtray, heart shape, #294, Imperial, 4½"...25.00
Ruby, basket, Imperial, #300, ca 1969-74, 9½"...55.00
Ruby, Open Rose, bowl, Imperial, 3¼x9"...45.00
Ruby, salt cellar, #61, 4-ftd, Imperial...20.00
Ruby, Windmill, pitcher, satin finish, Imperial, 6¾"...55.00

Smith Bros.

Alfred and Harry Smith founded their glassmaking firm in New Bedford, Massachusetts. They had been formerly associated with the Mt. Washington Glass Works, working there from 1871 to 1875 to aid in establishing a decorating department. Smith glass is valued for its excellent enameled decoration on satin or opalescent glass. Pieces were often marked with a lion in a red shield. Our advisors for this category are Betty and Clarence Maier; they are listed in the Directory under Pennsylvania.

Bowl, acorns & leaves on wht, ribbed, blk rim, 4x8½"...575.00
Bowl, moss rose, mc on beige, melon ribs, 4x9"...675.00
Cracker jar, daisies/ferns on lt yel, bbl shape, 4¾"...250.00
Cracker jar, ivy/gold on cream, melon ribs, 7" dia...975.00
Cracker jar, simple floral, gold/tan on cream w/diagonal ribs, sq, 7"...285.00
Creamer, sunflowers & period figure in oval, gold on opal, 3½"...195.00
Creamer & sugar bowl, sunflower/man's portrait on wht w/gold, 3½"...400.00
Creamer & sugar bowl, violets on bl to beige, SP tops, 4", 3¾"...750.00
Humidor, pansies, bl on cream, melon-rib lid, 6½x4"...850.00
Powder jar, allover daisies, melon ribs, 2¾x3¾"...250.00
Powder jar, melon ribs, EX floral decor, beadwork, red mk, 3½x5"...325.00
Shaker, egg form, Columbian Exhibition 1893 in gold...125.00
Sugar shaker, floral on bl wash, SP lid w/dragonflies, #715...385.00
Sugar shaker, floral/vines on opal to pk, egg shape, 4¼"...225.00
Sugar shaker, wild roses on wht, pillar ribs, SP lid (fair), 5¾"...495.00
Sweetmeat, pansies w/raised gold, rampant lion mk...585.00
Toothpick holder, pk w/wht floral panels, 5-scallop top, squat, 2"...350.00
Toothpick holder, wild roses on wht, pillar ribs, 2¼"...250.00
Vase, clematis on lt pk, gold-beaded top, 8x4½"...785.00
Vase, daisy garland on cream, 3 dimpled sides, 4¾"...445.00
Vase, Easter lilies w/gold on crystal, 4-lobe rim, 10x5¼"...375.00
Vase, gold-lined bl wisteria/shadows on cream, emb crown-like top, 9"...1,100.00
Vase, pond lilies, mc on pk, flaring at base, 7", pr...375.00
Vase, wild roses on dk to lt to dk gr, ovoid pillow form, 9¾"...795.00
Vase, wisteria on pnt burmese w/gold, swirled, 7x4½"...1,100.00
Vase, World's Fair 1893/goldenrod & bl flowers on wht opal, 6"...275.00

Snow Babies

During the last quarter of the nineteenth century, snow babies — little figures in pebbly white snowsuits — originated in Germany. They were originally made of sugar candy and were often used as decorations for Christmas cakes. Later on they were made of marzipan, a confection of crushed almonds, sugar, and egg whites. Eventually porcelain manufacturers began making them in bisque. They were popular until WWII. These tiny bisque figures range in size from 1" up to 7" tall. Quality German pieces bring very respectable prices on the market today. Beware of reproductions. Our advisor for this category is Linda Vines; she is listed in the Directory under California.

Baby crawling, pointed hood, very early face, Germany, 5"...350.00
Baby inside igloo, Santa on top, Germany, 2"...165.00
Baby inside igloo, Santa on top, Japan, 2"...75.00
Baby playing musical instrument, Germany, 2"...125.00
Baby standing on lg snowball, Japan, 2½"...50.00
Baby w/seal & red ball, Germany, 2"...150.00
Bear playing w/colorful ball, Germany, 1"...75.00
Child, no-snow boy or girl pushing lg snowball, Germany, 2"...110.00
Child on skates, snow hat & sweater, pastel pants, Germany, 2"...125.00
Penguins (3) walking down brick wall, Germany, 2½"...90.00
Pixies (2) sitting on hobby horse, wood stick legs, Germany, 2"...145.00
Santa atop gray elephant, Germany, 2½"...175.00
Santa driving yel car, toys in bk, Germany, 2"...165.00
Santa in boat beside snow-topped lighthouse, Germany, 3"...165.00
Santa in yel sailboat, Germany, 2"...125.00
Santa riding on snow bear, Germany, 2½"...175.00
Santa sitting on wht swing, Germany, 3"...125.00

Snow bear astride yel sled, comic eyes, Germany, 2" 125.00
Snow dog, rabbit or cat, Germany, 1", ea 50.00

Snuff Boxes

As early as the seventeenth century, the Chinese began using snuff. By the early nineteenth century, the practice had spread to Europe and America. It was used by both the gentlemen and the ladies alike, and expensive snuff boxes and bottles were the earmark of the genteel. Some were of silver or gold set with precious stones or pearls, while others contained music boxes. In the following listings, when one dimension is noted, it is length. See also Orientalia, Snuff Bottles.

Apple shape, enamel on copper, ca 1800, 1⅝" 350.00
Floral/geometrics on porc, Limoges..100.00
Lemon shape, yel enamel on copper, hinged lid, ca 1800, 2½" .1,050.00
Man offers lady rose on scenic lid, enamel on copper, 1⅝x3¾x3" .2,585.00
Silver/gilt, tooled w/oak leaf & acorn border relief, C Reid, 1788, 3" ..575.00

Soap Hollow Furniture

In the Mennonite community of Soap Hollow, Pennsylvania, the women made and sold soap; the men made handcrafted furniture. Rare today, this furniture was stenciled, grain painted, and beautifully decorated with inlaid escutcheons. These pieces are becoming very sought after. When well kept, they are very distinctive and beautiful. Values are for items in excellent condition unless otherwise noted. Our advisor for this category is Anita Levi; she is listed in the Directory under Pennsylvania.

Blanket chest, feathers on mustard & brn, MB/1897 ....1,400.00
Blanket chest, grpt w/blk lid, fruit/florals w/gold, 1882 ....2,900.00
Blanket chest, maroon & gold stencil, rod escutcheon, 1856 ..2,000.00
Blanket chest, poplar, orig red pnt w/blk/gold, att, 22x42" 3,850.00
Blanket chest, poplar, red wash/gr rpt, dtd 1855, 20x50" top, att, G .600.00
Blanket chest, red w/floral stencils, rpl hinges, FJ/1892, VG ...3,800.00
Blanket chest, red/blk, no decor, MT/1848, 2-drw, 49x29x21, EX .6,400.00
Blanket chest, red/gr pnt w/yel stripes/stencil, SH, 1868, 24x49".19,250.00
Blanket chest, rose decals, blk & brn grpt, LK/1890 ....5,000.00
Chest, blanket; red & blk, gold stencil, CW/1874, 25x18x45"...6,700.00
Chest, blanket; red & blk, gold stencil, MH/1871, 25x15x10", VG..6,200.00
Chest, 4 lg/3 sm drws, stencil, enamel pulls, sgn, 1883, EX+ ...5,400.00
Chest, 6-drw, brn w/mustard & decals, blk top & sides, Sala...1,900.00

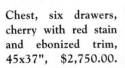

Chest, six drawers, cherry with red stain and ebonized trim, 45x37", $2,750.00.

(Photo courtesy Garth's Auctions)

Chest, 6-drw, no pnt or decor, EX wood, G 475.00

Chest, 7-drw, foliate stenciling, 1851, 55x41" 1,350.00
Chest, 7-drw, grpt w/blk, gold stencil, MH 1887, 47½x39½"..14,500.00
Chest, 7-drw, maroon w/blk top & sides, rpt, CKM/1879, G 550.00
Cradle, gilt stencils, mustard trim, maroon grpt 1,100.00
Cupboard, corner; maroon w/blk, stencil, 1856....................11,500.00
Cupboard, Dutch; 4 doors/2 drws, stencil/old rpt, 1875, 84x65"..8,000.00
Cupboard, poplar w/orig red & gr pnt/striping/stencil, 2-pc, 87x64"..35,200.00
Cupboard, step-bk; 3 glass doors/2 solid, 3-drw, no decor, 87½x64"..20,000.00
Cupboard, top only, 2 glass doors, no decor, 40x42x13"..........3,500.00
Dresser, Emp style, columns on 3 drws, HF/1874....................2,200.00
Frame, cross pcs, gr/yel striping, 15½x19¾" 1,000.00
Frame, gilt edges, stenciled, blk..1,050.00
Rope bed, cherry, red & brn finish, rare...................................2,300.00
Stand, bedside; rpt mustard brn 400.00

Soapstone

Soapstone is a soft talc in rock form with a smooth, greasy feel from whence comes its name. (It is also called Soo Chow Jade.) It is composed basically of talc, chlorite, and magnetite. In colonial times it was extracted from out-croppings in large sections with hand saws, carted by oxen to mills, and fashioned into useful domestic articles such as footwarmers, cooking utensils, inkwells, etc. During the early 1800s, it was used to make heating stoves and kitchen sinks. Most familiar today are the carved vases, bookends, and boxes made in China during the Victorian era. For further information we recommend *Collector's Digest of Soapstone* by L-W Book Sales. Our advisor for this category is Clarence Bodine; he is listed in the Directory under Pennsylvania.

Bookends, cvd floral sprays on rectangular shape, 7", pr.............125.00
Bookends, garden planter w/trailing vine, China, pr 70.00
Figurine, Am Indian warrior beside horse, 12½x9x6" 600.00
Figurine, fisherman w/pole & fish, early 1900s, 10½x7¾x3½" ...435.00
Figurine, foo dog/pups/ball on plinth w/cvd immortals, 19th C, 8x3"..450.00
Figurine, Kuan Yin (goddess of mercy) holding scroll, 17" 350.00
Figurine, Oriental lady w/tropical birds, early 19th C, 20" 275.00
Incense burner, dragon-head lid, ornate cvg, 3-leg base, 11½"......85.00
Snuff box, bird finial, teakwood base, 1890s, 4" dia....................225.00
Vase, dbl; detailed flower & foliage at center, 4⅞x9½x1⅝" 110.00
Vase, dogs (2) fight over food at side, late 19th C, 4¼x6x2¾" 85.00
Vase, mythical animals battle lower figure, ca 1870, 9x7x5¼"....150.00

Soda Fountain Collectibles

The first soda water sales in the United States occurred in the very late 1790s in New York and New Haven, Connecticut. By the 1830s soda water was being sold in drug stores as a medicinal item, especially the effervescent mineral waters from various springs around the country. By this time the first flavored soda water appeared at an apothecary shop in Philadelphia.

The 1830s also saw the first manufacturer (John Matthews) of devices to make soda water. The first marble soda fountain made its appearance in 1857 as a combination ice shaver and flavor-dispensing apparatus. By the 1870s the soda fountain was an established feature of the neighborhood drug store.

The fountains of this period were large, elaborate marble devices with druggists competing with each other for business by having fountains decorated with choice marbles, statues, mirrors, water fountains, and gas lamps.

In 1903 the fountain completed its last major evolution with the introduction of the 'front' counter service we know today. (The soda clerk faced the customer when drawing soda.)

By this time ice cream was a standard feature being served as sundaes, ice cream sodas, and milk shakes. Syrup dispensers were just being introduced as 'point-of-sale' devices to sell various flavorings from many different companies. Straws were commonplace, especially those made from paper. Fancy and unusual ice cream dippers were in daily use, and they continued to evolve, reaching their pinnacle with the introduction of the heart-shaped dipper in 1927.

This American business has provided collectors today with an almost endless supply of interesting and different articles of commerce. One can collect dippers, syrup dispensers, glassware, straw dispensers, milk shakers, advertising, and trade catalogs. (Note: The presence of a 'correct' pump enhances the value of a syrup dispenser by 25%.)

Collectors need to be made aware of decorating pieces that are actually fantasy items: copper ice cream cones, a large copper ice cream dipper, and a copper ice cream soda glass. These items have no resale value. Our advisors for this category are Joyce and Harold Screen; they are listed in the Directory under Maryland. See also Advertising; Coca-Cola.

Straw holders: San-I-Straw, paneled clear glass with mechanical top, 12x4", $300.00; Frosted glass with painted flowers and leaves, 9x4", $800.00. (Photo courtesy Pettigrew Auction Company)

Banana split dishes, milk glass, set of 4, 4x9" 100.00
Bowl, Bardwell's Root Bear, Whites Utica(?), 1900, 20", +tall pitcher..7,500.00
Candy jar, glass, cylinder w/ped ft, dmn-pattern lid, 18x4" dia, VG....460.00
Canister, Borden's Malted Milk, aluminum, w/lid, ca 1940-50....100.00
Catalog, soda fountain supplies, Liquid Carbonic, mc, 1902, 150-pg, EX.900.00
Cone dispenser, metal, Turnball...TN...Pats Pending, 30x8x9", G...150.00
Cone holder, Crisp Cone Cabinet Co, glass w/warming light, 18" .450.00
Cone holder, glass jar w/metal lid & insert, 14x6" dia, VG+ 465.00
Cone holder, plastic cylinder w/metal lid, insert & ped base, 39", EX..550.00
Container, Runkel's Chocolate, soda fountain pictured, 1885, 5-lb, VG.500.00
Container, Snow Sprinkles, sundae graphics, 1937, 10-lb, EX+ 55.00
Cookie jar, glass, 3-pc stacking w/lid, 19" overall 135.00
Dipper, AJ Daniel, parachute shape, wood hdl, Pat 1910, 12", EX ..5,250.00
Dipper, banana split; Gilchrist #32 ....525.00
Dipper, Bonny Prod Co NY, aluminum w/stainless gears, yel plastic hdl..10.00
Dipper, Clipper Disher/Geer Mfg, lg sz 6, 10" L..........................300.00
Dipper, Dover Clipper #20, 11", EX 200.00
Dipper, Ergo Ice Cream 160.00
Dipper, Fisher Cold Dog, German, silver, wood hdl, Canada, 19½".925.00
Dipper, Gilchrist #31, rnd bowl, brass lever, 8", NM+..................65.00
Dipper, Gilchrist #33, conical, sz #6, 10½", EX 150.00
Dipper, Hamilton Beach, sz 8 to 20 ....20.00
Dipper, IcyPi Scoop, Automatic Cone Co, 10", NMIB 450.00
Dipper, Kingery, NP brass, wood hdl, 11" 50.00
Dipper, Mosteller #78..160.00
Dipper, Prince Castle...Pat Pend, sq, EX 200.00
Dipper, sandwich; ICYPI, 10", EX 125.00

Dipper, saucer-shaped bowl, wood hdl, 1932, 10", EX..............1,650.00
Dispenser, Birchola, ceramic ball, 14", EX+.............................2,200.00
Dispenser, Buckeye Root Beer, brn ceramic tree stump, 16", VG.520.00
Dispenser, Buckeye Root Beer, brn ceramic urn, rpl pump, 16", EX.880.00
Dispenser, Buckeye Root Beer, red metal/chrome box, 12x15", VG ..75.00
Dispenser, Buckeye Root Beer, wht ceramic urn, 12", EX+......2,100.00
Dispenser, Cardinal Cherry, ceramic, ca 1910, 9", VG.............5,700.00
Dispenser, Cherry Chic, emb ceramic ball form, no pump, 10", VG+.6,000.00
Dispenser, Chocolate/Hot Fudge/Butterscotch, metal, 13", EX 55.00
Dispenser, Dr Swett's, ceramic stump w/silhouette logo, 14", VG ..4,000.00
Dispenser, Ford's Cherry Phosphate, tall glass, marble base, 1895, EX.3,500.00
Dispenser, Grape Julep, ceramic ball form, bl/wht, VG............1,800.00
Dispenser, GrapeKola, wht ceramic urn w/lid & decor, 21", VG..2,000.00
Dispenser, Grapine/Orangnector 5¢, dbl glass on metal base, 28x16", EX.2,850.00
Dispenser, Green's Muscadine, 1920s, 13" dia, EX.....................110.00
Dispenser, Hires, ceramic hourglass, all orig, w/pump, 14", VG+ .775.00
Dispenser, Hires, milk glass globe/spigot on marble base, 34", VG..5,830.00
Dispenser, Hires Little Boy urn, Mettlach 45,000.00
Dispenser, Howel's Orange Julep, pnt steel/ceramic, 24x15" dia, EX ..700.00
Dispenser, iced tea; glass w/wht lettering, lemon finial, 20 ", EX..165.00
Dispenser, Jersey Cream, wht ceramic urn, gold trim, EX 2,500.00
Dispenser, Johnson's Hot Fudge, w/lid & ladle..........................225.00
Dispenser, Lash's Grapefruit, textured glass globe, 12", NM........200.00
Dispenser, Liberty Root Beer, wooden bbl, 1920s, 27", EX+ 300.00
Dispenser, Magnus Root Beer, ceramic keg, gold trim, 15", EX+ ..1,500.00
Dispenser, Mission Orange, lt gr glass, rubber top, amethyst base, EX..250.00
Dispenser, Orange Julip, ceramic orange on ped base, w/pump, 14", EX..2,500.00
Dispenser, Orange-Crush, ribbed glass, aluminum base, porc top, EX..350.00
Dispenser, Rochester Root Beer, glass pitcher dispenser w/2 mugs, VG+ ...275.00
Dispenser, Ver-ba, wht ceramic urn, w/base, 15", G 1,980.00
Dispenser, Vigoral, ceramic urn on base, +25 matching cups G+..1,980.00
Dispenser, Vola, ceramic urn on base, emb decor, 17", VG......2,000.00
Dispenser, Ward's Lemon-Crush, ceramic lemon, 1920s, no pump o/w EX ..2,000.00
Dispenser, Ward's Orange-Crush, ceramic orange, rpl pump, 14", EX .2,000.00
Dispenser, Wine-Dip 5 Cent, glass bbl on earthenware base, 19", VG..200.00
Dispenser, Zipp's 5¢ Cherri-o, wht ceramic keg, 1910s, 14", EX ..3,000.00
Festoon, Hendler's Chocolate Ice Cream, #128, 9-pc, NM+.......165.00
Flavor board, chrome/glass, slots above Enjoy Our Fountain..., 26", VG ..575.00
Flavor board, Klover Ice Cream, diecut cb, 21x10", EX 450.00
Flavor board, Meadow Gold Ice Cream, rvpt, w/flavor strips 500.00
Fountain glass, Cherry Smash, w/side logo, extremely rare.........800.00
Fountain glass, Green River, flared, etched, 4" 100.00
Fountain glass, Nesbitt's 30.00
Fountain glass, Orange-Crush, flared, etched, waisted, 5½"........225.00
Fountain glass, Seven-Up, gr, sq logo 30.00
Fountain glass, Zipp's Cherri-O, flared, etched, waisted, 5½" 250.00
Ice-cream dishes, glass, 3-leaf clover shape, ped ft, set of 6, 3"....100.00
Jar, Borden's Malted Milk, glass w/emb letters, 6½x4½" 500.00
Jar, Borden's Malted Milk, glass w/metal lid & wht label, 8", EX ..600.00
Jar, Bovox Bouillon, Whites Utica, w/lid 800.00
Jar, National Dairy Malted Milk, aluminum, EX 120.00
Menu board, Hood's Ice Cream, metal 400.00
Mixer, Horlick's Dumore Malted Milk, porc base, NM 1,800.00
Mixer, milk shake; Hamilton Beach, wht porc, light-up, 20", EX..450.00
Mixer, milk shake; Hires, hand cranked or mechanical, w/lid, 13", EX.4,250.00
Mixer, milk shake; Horlick's Dumore, w/lighted base..............1,000.00
Mixer, milk shake; Kwikmix, hand crank, wood base, 10", EX ...450.00
Mixer, milk shake; mechanical, clamp-on counter-edge style ..3,000.00
Mixer, milk shake; Oster, gr porc, 19", EX 100.00
Mixer, milk shake; The Aerator..300.00
Mug, hot soda; Bovox, monk, brn..25.00
Sign, Fountain Menu/We Serve Chapell's Ice Cream, celluloid, 7x5", NM ...350.00
Sign, Ice Cream/Sundaes, glass, silver on bl, rstr, 26x7" fr 550.00
Sign, Royal Purple Grape Juice, mc bottle & lamp, tin, oval......750.00

Sign, 2-sided mc porc w/12 light holes, ...Ice Cream, 38x72", G..2,860.00
Soda fountain magazine, 1906 ....350.00
Soda fountain magazine, 1912 ....250.00
Soda fountain magazine, 1925 ....150.00
Soda fountain magazine, 1935...75.00
Straw holder, Benedict, glass, 10-panel sides, metal lifter, 10" 65.00
Straw holder, glass w/flared base, metal top & insert, 12", EX 325.00
Straw holder, glass w/Greek key bands top/bottom, open, G.......250.00
Straw holder, Manhattan pattern glass, gold top/bottom, 11", EX..700.00
Straw holder, Sani Straw, clear glass w/metal lid, 1917, 11½" 250.00
Sundae dish, stainless, Lily Tulip Cup Corp NY, 3¼", 6 for 30.00
Syrup bottle, Cherry Smash, w/cap, 1905-10, VG+.....................450.00
Syrup bottle, Grapefruitola label, dtd 1912, 12" 300.00
Syrup bottle, Orange Julep, metal jigger cap, 13", VG 400.00
Table & stools, rnd oak top w/wrought-iron base, 2 matching stools, VG...500.00
Tray, Cherry Blossom Soda, shows bottle, rectangular, EX 200.00
Tray, Hoffman's Ice Cream, girl on blk, red border, 15x11", VG.400.00
Tumbler holder, Tuft's Artic Soda, ornate metal, w/matching glass..400.00

Spangle Glass

Spangle glass, also known as Vasa Murrhina, is cased art glass characterized by the metallic flakes embedded in its top or outer layer. It was made both abroad and in the United States during the latter years of the nineteenth century, and it was reproduced in the 1960s by the Fenton Art Glass Company.

Vasa Murrhina was a New England distributor who sold glassware of this type manufactured by a Dr. Flower of Sandwich, Massachusetts. Flower had purchased the defunct Cape Cod Glassworks in 1885 and used the facilities to operate his own company. Since none of the ware was marked, it is very difficult to attribute specific examples to his manufacture. See also Art Glass Baskets; Fenton.

Basket, red/pk/gr/yel, wht int, ruffled, clear loop hdl 240.00
Creamer, cranberry w/pigeon blood & silver mica, wht lining, clear hdl....150.00
Jar, cobalt w/silver mica, wht beaded enamel, ftd, 7x4" 50.00
Pitcher, rainbow cased w/silver mica, ruffled rim, 4½x3½" 155.00
Rose bowl, mc spatter w/silver mica, scalloped top, ca 1920, 4½" ...75.00
Syrup, pk mottle w/gold flakes, pewter top, clear hdl, 6½" 240.00
Tumbler, rainbow satin w/mica, colors appl in 'panels,' 3¾" 650.00
Vase, mc, ruffled rim, ribbed sides, 7x5¾" 55.00
Vase, mc, wht int, ruffled rim, waisted neck, 6½x4", pr 650.00
Vase, mc spatter w/silver mica, flattened bottle form, w/hdls, 11"...100.00
Vase, mc swirls w/mica, wht int, ruffled rim, trumpet neck, 8½x5"..115.00
Vase, vertical mc bands w/silver mica, ruffled, 7½" 200.00

Spatter Glass

Spatter glass, characterized by its multicolor 'spatters,' has been made from the late nineteenth century to the present by American glass houses as well as those abroad. Although it was once thought to have been made entirely by workers at the 'end of the day' from bits and pieces of leftover scrap, it is now known that it was a standard line of production. See also Art Glass Baskets.

Basket, bl, ruffled rim, sapphire rope hdl, 7".................................90.00
Celery vase, bl & wht; rstr Pairpoint #1820 fr 550.00
Pitcher, bl & wht, clear reeded hdl, 7¾".....................................160.00
Pitcher, blood red & opal, tricorner, clear reeded hdl, 7¾".........130.00
Pitcher, ribbed swirl, cased mc, reeded clear hdl, 7½" 150.00
Tumbler, red & wht, 3¾" 45.00
Water set, cranberry & opal, 8½" pitcher+6 tumblers.................350.00

Spatterware

Spatterware is a general term referring to a type of decoration used by English potters as early as the late 1700s. Using a brush or a stick, brightly colored paint was dabbed onto the soft-paste earthenware items, achieving a spattered effect which was often used as a border. Because much of this type of ware was made for export to the United States, some of the subjects in the central design — the schoolhouse and the eagle patterns, for instance — reflect American tastes. Yellow, green, and black spatterware is scarce and highly valued by collectors.

In the descriptions that follow, the color listed after the item indicates the color of the spatter. The central design is identified next, and the color description that follows that refers to the design. When no condition code is present, assume that the item is undamaged and has only very light wear.

Note: These are actual prices realized at a major Midwest auction house over the course of the past year.

Bowl, rainbow, vertical red/bl/gr stripes, 3½x6¾".......................825.00
Bowl, vegetable; rainbow, octagonal, ftd, lid w/shell finial, 8x10" .2,200.00
Bowl, vegetable; rainbow, tulip, red & bl, octagonal, 2x8½x6".2,500.00
Creamer, bl, fort, gray/brn/gr, 4" 250.00
Creamer, bl, pineapple, red & gr, minor rpr, 3⅜" 3,100.00
Creamer, rainbow, purple & bl w/red Adam's Rose, 3¾", VG.....275.00
Creamer, rainbow, red/bl/gr horizontal stripes, 3¾" 880.00
Creamer, red, peafowl on branch, red/gr/dk bl, leaf hdl, 4" 525.00
Creamer, yel, peafowl, red/yel/slate bl on gr branch, 3½" 4,125.00
Cup plate, bl, boy & girl blowing bubbles blk transfer, 3½".......250.00
Cup plate, bl, fort, 4-color, 12-sided, 4¼", EX 500.00
Cup plate, bl, rose, red/gr, 4⅛" 415.00
Cup plate, purple, lady swinging bl transfer, 3½".......................220.00
Cup plate, rainbow, gr w/lt red striped border, bull's-eye center, 4" ..385.00
Cup plate, red, peafowl, red/gr/bl on gr spatter branch, 4" 465.00
Cup plate, yel, cockscomb, red/gr, paneled rim, 4⅛" 1,540.00
Mug, bl, strawberries, pk, hairline, 2⅞" 415.00
Mug, rainbow, purple & bl stripes, leaf-molded hdl terminals, 2¾"...935.00
Mush cup & saucer, stick spatter, flow bl w/red & gr designs, EX..300.00
Mustard jar, purple, holly berries, red & gr, leaf hdl, w/lid, 3"..1,450.00
Pitcher, bl, parrot, red & gr, stain, 6⅛" 3,400.00
Pitcher, rainbow, purple & blk, molded fan under spout, rstr, 6½"...935.00
Pitcher, rainbow, red/bl vertical stripes, paneled hexagon, 6½" ..495.00
Pitcher, rainbow, 5-color, red on inside rim & scroll hdl, 7⅜".7,150.00
Pitcher, yel, tulip, red & gr, flakes/rpt, 6⅜" 4,675.00
Plate, bl, American eagle & shield, bl, 7" 415.00
Plate, bl, fort, 4-color, paneled edge, 9½" 1,100.00
Plate, bl, peafowl, red/yel/bl, molded feather edge, 8½" 700.00
Plate, bl, peafowl, red/yel/bl, rim chip, 8½" 200.00
Plate, bl, peafowl, red/yel/gr, on bl spatter field, 11", VG...........220.00
Plate, bl, tulip, bl/gr/brn, 8"..165.00
Plate, bl, tulip, red/wht/bl, 12-sided, 9⅛" 465.00
Plate, purple, lg rooster/grass, maroon/dk bl/gr, 8½", EX 700.00
Plate, purple, rose, red/gr, flakes, 8¼" 110.00
Plate, rainbow, bull's eye, hairline/flake, 8¼" 935.00
Plate, rainbow, bull's eye, purple & blk, 8¼" 1,325.00
Plate, rainbow, paneled border, 8½"..2,650.00
Plate, rainbow, red & bl w/red star center, paneled, 10" 275.00
Plate, rainbow, red/bl/yel border, chip, 8¾"............................1,300.00
Plate, rainbow, unusual stripes, sm rpr, 9½"...........................5,225.00
Plate, rainbow, 5-color rayed design, scalloped, prof rstr, 8¼" .1,265.00
Plate, rainbow, 5-color rayed design, scalloped, 9¼"................7,000.00
Plate, red, peafowl, bl/gr/dk red, allover pattern, Adams, 9½", EX....425.00
Plate, red, peafowl, gr/yel/bl, 7½" 360.00
Plate, red, peafowl, 4-color, propeller mk, flake, 8½" 415.00

Plate, red, primrose, purple & gr, 8¼" **135.00**
Plate, red, rose, red/gr, wear, 9¼" **135.00**
Plate, red, star, red/gr/bl w/red sunburst border, 9½", EX............**375.00**

Plate, red and blue leaves with blue flower heads and red and green stars in center, border of black rabbits, green flowers, and green toads on yellow ground with black grasses, cut sponge, 1800 – 1850s, 9¼", EX, $350.00.

Plate, red & yel bull's eye, 8¼" **6,875.00**
Plate, soup; red & bl bull's eye, thistle, red & gr, rpr, 10½" **7,425.00**
Plate, stick spatter, red & gr rose, bl & red leaf borders, 8" **110.00**
Plate, yel, thistle, red & gr, molded feather edge, 9½" **4,250.00**
Plate, yel, thistle, red & gr, stain, 8⅜" **1,500.00**
Plate, yel, thistle, red & gr, 9¾" **3,950.00**
Plate, yel, tulip, red & gr, hairline, 8" **2,400.00**
Platter, bl, peafowl, 3-color, 15½x12" **2,100.00**
Platter, rainbow, tulip, 3-color, octagonal, 12½x9½", EX **4,600.00**
Saucer, red, schoolhouse, brn/gr/bl, 4¼" **495.00**
Sugar bowl, bl, fort, 3-color, w/lid, 4" **375.00**
Sugar bowl, bl, parrot, red & gr, w/close-match lid, 7¼" **220.00**
Sugar bowl, bl, peafowl, 3-color, shell hdls, w/lid, 4¾x5", EX.....**415.00**
Sugar bowl, bl, peafowl, 3-color, 8-sided, mismatched lid, 8¼"...**200.00**
Sugar bowl, bl, roses, red/gr, w/lid, rpr, 5½x5" **275.00**
Sugar bowl, bl, trees & buildings, 4-color, 5⅜" **500.00**
Sugar bowl, bl, tulip, 3-color, w/lid, 5⅛x4⅞", EX...................**950.00**
Sugar bowl, rainbow, red/gr/bl vertical stripes, bull's-eye lid **2,200.00**
Sugar bowl, rainbow, thistle, red & gr, w/lid, rpr, 5¼x4¾" **3,750.00**
Sugar bowl, yel, tulips, red/gr, molded hdl, prof rstr, 6½" **1,045.00**
Tea bowl & saucer, bl, dahlia, red/bl/gr, hairlines **220.00**
Tea bowl & saucer, bl, peafowl, 3-color, mini **300.00**
Tea bowl & saucer, gr, flowers & leaves, red & gr, 2¾", 6"............**80.00**
Tea bowl & saucer, gr, peafowl, purple/gr/red, sm stain................**440.00**
Tea bowl & saucer, gr, peafowl, red/yel/bl, EX..........................**195.00**
Tea bowl & saucer, gr w/brn, schoolhouse, red **2,750.00**
Tea bowl & saucer, purple, dove, mc, prof rpr..........................**450.00**
Tea bowl & saucer, purple, dove, 3-color **2,750.00**
Tea bowl & saucer, purple, rooster, 3-color, rpr.......................**440.00**
Tea bowl & saucer, rainbow, concentric circles of red/bl/gr, Adams, EX...**250.00**
Tea bowl & saucer, red, bull's eye, yel................................**880.00**
Tea bowl & saucer, red, peafowl, gr/lt bl/yel.........................**415.00**
Tea bowl & saucer, red, peafowl, 4-color, EX **360.00**
Tea bowl & saucer, stick spatter, bl & red stars, gr & blk flowers, pr...**140.00**
Tea bowl & saucer, yel, morning glory, 3-color, hairline..............**990.00**
Tea bowl & saucer, yel, thistle, red & gr **1,925.00**
Tea bowl & saucer, yel, tulip, red & gr...............................**3,200.00**
Teabowl & saucer, gr, schoolhouse, red & dk brn, stains..........**1,875.00**
Teabowl & saucer, rainbow, purple & bl stripes w/bull's-eye center...**550.00**
Teabowl & saucer, red, peafowl, 3-color...............................**925.00**
Teabowl & saucer, red/bl, buds, mc, lt wear **350.00**
Teabowl & saucer, red/gr thumbprint, peafowl, 3-color, prof rpr.**925.00**
Teapot, bl, peafowl, gr/ochre/pk, arches on shoulder, rstr finial...**990.00**
Teapot, rainbow, red & bl, mismatched lid, rpr, 9¼" **385.00**

Teapot, rainbow, red & bl, molded arches, rpr, 9¼"...................**550.00**
Teapot, rainbow, red & yel vertical stripes, matching lid, 5½"..**2,425.00**
Wash bowl, rainbow, bl & purple w/bull's eye center, chip, 4x12½" .**1,450.00**
Waste bowl, gr, peafowl, 3-color, rpr, 3x5½" **220.00**
Waste bowl, gr, peafowl, 4-color, 2½x4½" **770.00**

Spelter

Spelter items are cast from commercial zinc and coated with a metallic patina. The result is a product very similar to bronze in appearance, yet much less expensive

Bookends, Deco nude leaning bk, silver wash, 1920s, 5x6x2½", pr...**125.00**
Bookends, pixie girl, ivorine face, marble base, JB Hirsch, 1927, pr..**275.00**
Bust, lady in bonnet, Von Der Straeten, 11" **175.00**
Figurine, Agriculture, man w/grain sack & torch, Milliot, 41"....**225.00**
Figurine, Deco dancing lady, cold pnt details, 1920s-30s, 9¾"....**250.00**
Figurine, dogs (2) on blk & wht marble base, sgn Carvin, 1900s, 18x24"...**685.00**
Figurine, Nouveau lady w/harp, griffins at corners, claw ft, 18x8x6".**375.00**
Figurine, pheasant & babies, blk onyx base, Deco style, 8x16" ...**175.00**
Figurine, railroad worker laying track, 15" **675.00**
Figurines, Don Juan & Don Caesar, ea on base, 19th C, 22", pr..**800.00**
Inkwell, eagle w/wings wide, head lifts for pot, ca 1880, 6x6½" .**295.00**
Inkwell, Eiffel tower form, 1950s, 5x5".....................................**125.00**
Inkwell, owl standing beside stump, porc insert, 1890, 3¾" **495.00**

Spode-Copeland

The following is a short cronological history of the Spode company:
1733: Josiah Spode I is born on the 23rd of March at Lane Delph, Staffordshire.
1740: Spode is put to work in a pottery factory.
1754: Spode, now a fully proficient journeyman/potter, works for Turner and Banks in Stoke-on-Trent.
1755: Josiah Spode II is born.
1761: Spode I acquires a factory in Shelton where he makes cream-colored and blue-painted earthenware.
1770: This is the year adopted as the date Spode I founded the business.
1784: Spode I masters the art and techniques of transfer printing in blue under the glaze on earthenware.
1796: This year marks the earliest known record of Spode selling porcelain dinnerware.
1800: Spode II produces the first bone china.
1806: Spode is appointed potter to the royal family; this continues past 1983.
1813: Spode produces the first stone china.
1821: Spode introduces Feldspar Porcelain, a variety of bone china.
1833: William Taylor Copeland acquires the Spode factory from the Spode family and becomes partners with Garrett until 1847.
1870: System of impressing date marks on the backs of the dinnerware begins.
1925: Robert Copeland is born. (He presently resides in England.)
1976: The Company merges with Worcester Royal Porcelain Company and forms Royal Worcester Spode Limited.
1986: The Spode Society is established.
1989: The holding company for Spode becomes the Porcelain and Fine China Companies Limited.

The price quotes listed in these three categories of Spode are for twentieth-century pre-1965 dinnerware in pristine condition — no cracks, chips, crazing, or stains. Minor knife cuts do not constitute damage unless extreme.

The patterns in the first group are the most common and popular earthenware lines. The second group contains the rarer and higher priced pattern; they are both earthenware and stoneware. Bone china patterns comprise the third group.

Our advisor for this category is Don Haase; he is listed in the Directory under Washington.

First Group:

Ann Hathaway, Billingsley Rose, Buttercup, Byron, Camilla Pink, Chelsea Wicker, Chinese Rose, Christmas Tree (green), Cowslip, Fairy Dell, Fleur de Lis (blue/brown), Florence, Gadroon, Gainsborough, Hazel Dell, Indian Tree, Jewel, Moss Rose, Old Salem, Raeburn, Reynolds, Romney, Rosalie, Rose Brier, Rosebud Chintz, Tower Blue, Valencia, Wickerdale, Wickerdell, Wickerlane

Bowl, cereal; 6½"	32.00
Bowl, fruit; 5¼"	28.00
Bowl, waste; 6"	35.00
Coffeepot, 8-cup	265.00
Creamer, lg	75.00
Creamer, sm	65.00
Cup & saucer, demitasse	45.00
Cup & saucer, low/tall	39.00
Plate, bread & butter; 6¼"	28.00
Plate, butter pat	28.00
Plate, salad; 7½"	32.00

Plates, luncheon; Gainsborough, earliest manufacture 1953, $35.00 each. (Photo courtesy Don Haase)

Platter, oval, 13"	140.00
Platter, oval, 15"	160.00
Platter, oval, 17"	180.00
Sauce boat, w/liner	145.00
Soup, cream; w/liner	55.00
Soup, rim, 7½"	35.00
Soup, rim, 8½"	45.00
Sugar bowl, w/lid, lg	75.00
Sugar bowl, w/lid, sm	65.00
Teapot, 8-cup	265.00
Vegetable, oval, 9-10"	155.00
Vegetable, oval, 10-11"	165.00
Vegetable, sq, 8"	145.00
Vegetable, sq, 9"	155.00
Vegetable, w/lid	265.00

Second Group:

Aster, Butchart, Camilla Blue, Christmas Tree (magenta), Italian, Mayflower, Herring Hunt (green/magenta), Patricia, Tower Blue and Pink, Wildflower (blue/red), Delhi, Fitzhugh (blue/red/green), Gloucester (blue/red), Ruins (blue/pink/brown), Tradewinds (blue/red).

Bowl, cereal; 6¼"	39.00
Bowl, fruit; 5½"	35.00
Bowl, waste; 6"	45.00
Coffeepot, 8-cup	375.00
Creamer, lg	95.00
Creamer, sm	85.00
Cup & saucer, demitasse	55.00
Cup & saucer, low/high	65.00
Plate, bread & butter; 6¼"	35.00
Plate, butter pat	35.00
Plate, chop; rnd, 13"	295.00
Plate, dinner; 10½"	65.00
Plate, luncheon; rnd, 8-9"	49.00
Plate, luncheon; sq, 8½"	65.00
Plate, salad; 7½"	39.00
Platter, oval, 13"	165.00
Platter, oval, 15"	180.00
Platter, oval, 17"	225.00
Sauce boat, w/liner	185.00
Soup, rim, 7½"	45.00
Soup, rim, 8½"	55.00
Sugar bowl, w/lid, lg	95.00
Sugar bowl, w/lid, sm	85.00
Teapot, 8-cup	395.00
Vegetable, oval, 9-10"	175.00
Vegetable, oval, 10-11"	195.00
Vegetable, sq, 8"	165.00
Vegetable, sq, 9"	185.00
Vegetable, w/lid	395.00

Third Group:

Billingsley Rose Savoy, Bridal Rose, Carolyn, Chelsea Garden, Christine, Claudia, Colonel, Dimity, Dresden Rose Savoy, Fleur de Lis (gray/red/blue), Geisha (blue/pink/white), Irene, Maritime Rose, Primrose (pink), Shanghi, Savoy.

Bowl, cereal; 6¼"	45.00
Bowl, fruit; 5½"	42.00
Bowl, waste; 6"	55.00
Coffeepot, 8-cup	445.00
Creamer, lg	120.00
Creamer, sm	110.00
Cup & saucer, demitasse	65.00
Cup & saucer, low/tall	75.00
Plate, bread & butter; 6¼"	45.00
Plate, butter pat	39.00
Plate, chop; rnd, 13"	315.00
Plate, dessert; 8"	55.00
Plate, dinner; 10½"	69.00
Plate, luncheon; rnd, 9"	59.00
Plate, luncheon; sq, 8½"	69.00
Plate, salad; 7½"	49.00
Platter, oval, 13"	195.00
Platter, oval, 15"	225.00
Platter, oval, 17"	295.00
Sauce boat, w/liner	145.00
Soup, cream; w/liner	145.00
Soup, rim, 7½"	65.00
Soup, rim, 8½"	75.00
Sugar bowl, w/lid, lg	120.00
Sugar bowl, w/lid, sm	115.00
Teapot, 8-cup	445.00
Vegetable, oval, 9-10"	215.00

Vegetable, oval, 10-11" **235.00**
Vegetable, sq, 8" **245.00**
Vegetable, sq, 9" **275.00**
Vegetable, w/lid **425.00**

Spongeware

Spongeware is a type of factory-made earthenware that was popular during the last quarter of the nineteenth century and into the first quarter of the twentieth century. It was decorated by dabbing color onto the drying ware with a sponge, leaving a splotched design at random or in simple patterns. Sometimes a solid band of color was added. The vessel was then covered with a clear glaze and fired at a high temperature. Blue on white is the most preferred combination, but green on ivory, orange on white, or those colors in combination may also occasionally be found. As with most pottery, rare forms and condition are major factors in establishing value. Spongeware is still being made today, so beware of newer examples. For further information we recommend *Collector's Encyclopedia of Salt Glaze Stoneware* by Terry Taylor, our advisor for this category, and Terry and Kay Lowrance, available from Collector Books.

Our values are for undamaged examples, unless a specific condition code is given within the description.

Baker, gr/cream, close pattern, Am, 1880s, 3½x11" **170.00**
Bank, gr/brn, pig figural, pierced eyes, 3½x6" **200.00**
Bowl, bl/brn/wht, It Pays To Mix...Osage IA, emb ribs, 8" **100.00**
Bowl, bl/wht, pattern sponging, 3x9½", from $75 to **125.00**
Bowl, bl/wht, scalloped edge, 1½x9" **175.00**
Bowl, bl/wht w/2 bl bands, stain, 6¼x14", EX **100.00**
Bowl, mixing; bl/brn, patterned sponging, molded collar, 2¾x5¼"..**150.00**
Bowl, mixing; bl/wht, molded arched panels, 6x13", EX **300.00**
Bowl, mixing; bl/wht, wht band w/bl band ea side, flared, 3¾x8", NM..**220.00**
Butter crock, bl/wht, Village Farm Dairy stencil, 4x5½", $125 to..**150.00**
Chamber pot, bl/wht, close sponging, child sz, 4½x7½", $250 to..**275.00**
Chamber pot, bl/wht w/bl/wht rings on lid, 10x10½", from $250 to...**275.00**
Cookie jar, bl/wht, ftd ball shape, orig lid, 9" **245.00**
Cooler, bl/wht, orig brass spigot, rpl lid, 3-gal, 10", NM..............**500.00**
Crock, milk; bl/wht, 5 sm ft, bail hdl, 5x10", from $300 to.........**425.00**
Cup & saucer, mush; bl/wht, patterned sponging, saucer: 8½"....**195.00**
Cuspidor, bl/wht w/bl band at rim & center, ca 1900, 5" **150.00**
Grandma's Syrup Jug, bl/wht, w/bail, smallest sz......................**1,200.00**
Jardiniere, bl/wht, emb foliage scrolls, worn gold, 9x10½" **250.00**
Mug, bl/wht, emb lady's face, bk: man's face, spurred hdl, 5x3½"..**200.00**
Mug, lt bl/wht, heavy stoneware, 5¼", NM **165.00**
Pitcher, bl/wht, bl-edged wht horizontal bands, ovoid, 9" **575.00**
Pitcher, bl/wht, child & dog in oval ea side, 9", NM...................**875.00**
Pitcher, bl/wht, cylindrical w/bl accent bands at bottom, 6" **165.00**
Pitcher, bl/wht, emb leaping deer, 8x5½" **2,200.00**
Pitcher, bl/wht, pattern sponging, bulbous, 12"...........................**395.00**
Pitcher, bl/wht, ring-style sponging, str flaring sides, 9", VG **330.00**
Pitcher, bl/wht, swollen at waist, angle hdl, 7¾x7½", EX...........**300.00**
Pitcher, bl/wht (EX color), cylindrical w/bulged-out bottom, 9x7", EX ..**495.00**
Pitcher, bl/wht repeating pattern, Old Fashioned Garden Rose, 9"..**900.00**
Pitcher, brn/bl on cream, 11", EX **200.00**
Pitcher, hot water; bl/wht w/bl bands, 7", from $225 to **300.00**
Plate, bl/wht, patterned sponging, scalloped rim, 8¾"................**195.00**
Plate, bl/wht, patterned sponging, 9", 4 for **225.00**
Plate, bl/wht, 7", NM **110.00**
Plate, gr/red/wht, 8¼" **175.00**
Platter, bl/wht, patterned sponging, rectangular, 13¾x10⅛".......**250.00**
Platter, bl/wht, 13½" **375.00**
Salt box, Salt stenciled in rickrack reserve, wood lid, wall mt, 6x6"..**550.00**
Soap dish, bl/wht w/bl bands, 5x3½" **125.00**

Soap dish, red/bl on wht, 3½x4⅝" **175.00**
Sugar bowl, gr/wht w/red trim, rpr, 5x5"..................................**250.00**
Tray, bl/wht, pattern sponging, wreath hdls, 10" **55.00**
Tray, bl/wht, patterned sponging w/gold spatter, scroll rim, 10" ..**100.00**
Umbrella stand, bl/wht w/bl bands at top & bottom, OH........**1,200.00**
Vase, bl/wht, emb ribbon, 7½", EX...**110.00**
Wash bowl & pitcher, bl/gr/wht w/bl band, 8", 4x12", from $400 to ..**425.00**
Washboard **400.00**

Spoons

Souvenir spoons have been popular remembrances since the 1890s. The early hand-wrought examples of the silversmith's art are especially sought and appreciated for their fine craftsmanship. Commemorative, personality-related, advertising, and those with Indian busts or floral designs are only a few of the many types of collectible spoons. In the following listings, spoons are sorted by city, character, or occasion. For further information we recommend *Collectible Souvenir Spoons, Book I* and *Book II*, by Wayne Bednersh (Collector Books).

Key:
B — bowl	gw — gold washed
emb — embossed	H — handle
eng — engraved	HR — handle reverse
ff — full figure	

Alaska, transfer print enamel finial, sterling, demi, from $5 to **15.00**
Bitter Root (& flower) Hamilton MT eng in B; Lunt, from $30 to ..**50.00**
Blanket weaver emb in B; Am Indian figural H; Hirsch & Oppenheimer .**85.00**
Bronco rider finial, Hirsch & Oppenheimer, from $30 to.............**50.00**
Brooklyn Bridge eng in B; Waverly pattern, Wallace, ca 1892, $35 to ..**70.00**
Buffalo NY on H; buffalo finial; plain B; Durgin, from $30 to.......**45.00**
California on H; bear finial, plain B; Shiebler, from $75 to **125.00**
Carnegie Library Chanute KS eng in B; simple H; Manchester/Baker ...**45.00**
Cemetery Gate Vicksburg eng in B; Shepard, from $30 to...........**60.00**
Chanute KS & oil well eng in B; Manchester/Baker, from $50 to..**70.00**
Chief Oshkosh figural H; Towle for Bierly & Sons, from $30 to...**65.00**
CO Gateway to Garden of Gods, emb scenes in B & on H, unmk, $40 to..**75.00**
Cowboy on horse atop Am flag forms H; plain B; Mechanics, $50 to ..**80.00**
Detroit waterfront eng in B; Indian chief figural H; unmk, $75 to .**150.00**
Fair Harvard & building eng on H; eng initials & 1891 on HR....**65.00**

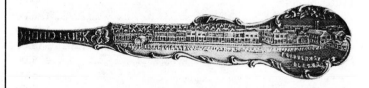

Fairbanks, Alaska, Good Luck on handle, street-scene finial, J.B. Erd, from $125.00 to $175.00.

Faneuil Hall Boston in B; eagle & swords H; Homer, from $50 to...**70.00**
Ft Sumter Charleston SC eng in B; gw, Towle, from $25 to.............**50.00**
Gray's Harbor Salmon eng in B; salmon H; unmk, from $25 to....**50.00**
Halley's Comet & 1910 emb in B; ornate H; Manchester/Baker, $40 to..**60.00**
Hotel Colorado Glenwood Springs CO eng in B; from $25 to......**40.00**
Kewpie finial; enameled Rose O'Neill portrait in B; sterling, $100 to...**150.00**
Knights of Pythias emblem & Souvenir 1897 eng in B; Pairpoint, $30 to....**50.00**
Lawrence KS & windmill eng in B; Lancaster pattern, Gorham, $25 to ..**50.00**
Los Angeles & oranges eng in B; Rose pattern, Wallace, ca 1898, $30 to....**60.00**
Lyons NE Public School eng in B; Violet pattern, Wallace, ca 1905 .**35.00**

Maine & ship eng in B; Wallace, ca 1898, from $30 to **60.00**
Mardi Gras New Orleans pnt B; simple H; from $45 to **70.00**
Natural Bridge Santa Cruz CA & eng scene in B; simple H; unmk, $30 to .**50.00**
Niagara Falls tour boat eng in B; Maid of Mist figural H, $150 to ..**200.00**
Old Spanish Palace Santa Fe NM Built 1590 in B; Versailles pattern...**65.00**
Passaic Falls Paterson NJ eng in B; Chantilly pattern, Gorham **45.00**
Philadelphia PA & House of Betsy Ross on H; Robbins, from $20 to...**40.00**
Pikes Peak CO eng in B; wavy H; Shepard, from $30 to **50.00**
Post Office Jacksonville FL eng in B; bright-cut flower H; $40 to.**60.00**
Presbyterian Church Hastings NE eng in B; Colfax pattern, Gorham ..**25.00**
President Cleveland finial; Nominated 3 Times...Elected Twice, $75 to ..**100.00**
Princess Angeline, Seattle WA eng in B; totem pole H, from $40 to..**60.00**
Rochester IN eng in B; bright-cut flower pattern, Paye & Baker, $30 to..**55.00**
San Diego Expo & CA Building 1915 eng in B; Mayer Bros, from $40 to.**60.00**
San Diego Mission ruins in B; SP, from $10 to..............................**15.00**
Santa Claus figural H; Christmas tree eng in B; Johnston & Co, $100 to .**150.00**
Tijuana eng in B; man roping cow figural H: Anderson Jewelry, $60 to .**100.00**
WBA (Woman's Benefit Assoc) on H; plain B; Gorham, Wood & Hughes..**50.00**

Sporting Goods

Vintage ammunition boxes, duck and goose calls, knives, and fishing gear are just a few of the items that collectors of this type of memorabilia look for today. Also favored are posters, catalogs, and envelopes from well known companies such as Winchester, Remington, Peters, Ithaca, and Dupont.

Duck stamps have been widely collectible in recent years; if you're interested in learning more about the subject, we recommend *Duck Stamps* by L. A. Chappell (Collector Books). See also Fishing Collectibles; Game Calls.

Poster, Ithaca Guns, paper, ca 1913, 15¾x27", G, $600.00.

Award, Trap Shooters...Central Palace, gold on brass, 1915, 1¾"..**300.00**
Book, Colt, Makers of History, 1926, 64-pg, EX **55.00**
Book, Smith & Wesson, Burning Powder, RD Jones, 1931 3rd ed, 64-pg..**155.00**
Book, Weatherby Guide, 12th ed, 1962-63, 144-pg, 8½x11", VG..**115.00**
Booklet, DuPont Trapshooting Hints, 4th ed, 1930s, 16-pg, EX ...**20.00**
Booklet, Federal Cartridge, How To Get Your Duck, 1953, 16-pg..**20.00**
Booklet, Peters Cartridges, From Trigger to Target, 1930, 24-pg, EX..**27.50**
Booklet, Western Silvertip Bullets, opens to form 12x14" poster..**10.00**
Brochure, Ithaca Featherlight Shotguns, ca 1960, opens to 6½x23" ..**20.00**
Brochure, Smith & Wesson, Helpful Hints, prewar, 4-pg, 3x6", VG..**10.00**
Brochure, US Cartridge Co, How To Use Firearms, early, 15-pg, 6x1¾"..**150.00**
Buckle, DuPont Board of Directors Award...1937, silver, 1½" L ...**75.00**
Calendar, US Cartridge Co, grizzly bear/hunter, 1922, 15½x8½"...**475.00**
Cartridge box, UMC 45-85, gr label, blk print, empty, VG+ **100.00**

Cartridge carrier, Huey, leather-covered oak w/brass bindings, 20" L....**400.00**
Catalog, Gun Wise Gun Fitting, Davis Warner Arms, 1920s, 24-pg, VG ..**65.00**
Catalog, Smith & Wesson, 1914, 30-pg w/price list, 7x10" **750.00**
Crate, shipping; US Cartridge 22 Gallery Cartridges, printed wood, EX..**150.00**
Envelope, Remington Guns & Rifles, lady w/rifle, dtd 1903, 3½x6", M ..**350.00**
Envelope, Savage Arms, hand firing gun, 1910, EX **300.00**
Envelope, Shoot DuPont Powders, Perdew, quail scene, unused, G ..**50.00**
Handbook, Colt Target Shooting, 1950s, 44-pg, 4x6", EX **35.00**
Hang tag, Meriden Fire Arms Co Model 15, cb w/string, 5", EX ..**85.00**
Kit bag, Holland Sport, lt gr canvas w/leather sides & strap, 11x13" ..**55.00**
Letter opener, Shoot DuPont Std Loads, 2-color ivory, 1920s, 7½"..**175.00**
Letterhead, Parker, woodcock & High Grade Parker, 1903, 8½x7¼" ..**175.00**
Letterhead, Stevens Arms Co, No 10 Single Shot Target pistol, 1920s...**40.00**
License, hunting; CA 1914, hunters/dogs/birds, 2⅝x4¼", VG **85.00**
License button, MI resident, sm game, 1932, EX **200.00**
Loading tool, Parker, combination shot/powder measure, NP/rosewood.**110.00**
Match holder, Parker, CI, wall mt, Pat 1865 & 1876, 6x4" **150.00**
Medallion, Hercules Powder 50th Anniversary 1912-1962, VG ...**70.00**
Price list, Ithaca, illustrated, 1949, 4-pg, 7x10", VG......................**20.00**
Price list, Parker Guns, illustrated, 1940, 8-pg, 9x11", VG............**75.00**
Price list, Parker Guns, 1939, gray cover, 7-pg, 11x9", VG **65.00**
Price list, parts & rpr; Lefever Arms Co, 1936, 4-pg, 5x8", M.......**15.00**
Price list, parts; Smith & Wesson, 1922, 38-pg, 6x9", VG **35.00**
Price list, Peters Ammunition, illustrated, 1948, 20-pg, 8½x11", VG .**20.00**
Print, Dupont Powder, water fowl scene, LB Hunt, 1927, 13x14½"...**25.00**
Program book, Springfield MA Shooting Club, 1905, 36-pg, EX ..**200.00**
Score book, US Cartridge Co, hardcover, 1908, 55-pg, 5¾x9", EX.**95.00**
Scorecard, Liberty Trap Shooting, unused, 2¾x4½", EX.............**100.00**
Scorecard, trap shooting; DuPont Infallible Smokeless, EX **225.00**
Shot bag, Bailey, Farrell & Co, Pittsburgh, printed cloth, EX **45.00**
Shot bag, Colwell Lead Co, printed cloth, 25-lb, 11½x6¼" **75.00**
Shotshell box, Carlsbad Ammunition 12 Gauge Target Load, empty, M..**15.00**
Shotshell box, Hiawatha ACE 410 Gauge 2½", 1-pc, empty, EX .**35.00**
Shotshell box, Peters Rustless Trap Load Smokeless 12 Ga...Shells, EX.**450.00**
Shotshell box, Peters Rustless Victor, full, 2⅝" L, G **135.00**
Shotshell box, Remington Game Load 12 Gauge, mallard, 1-pc, full, VG...**125.00**
Shotshell box, Remington Kleanbore 16 Gauge, England, full, prewar .**275.00**
Shotshell box, The Gem, Atkin, Grant & Lang 12 gauge, empty, EX.....**75.00**
Shotshell box, US Cartridge 16 Climax Ga, full, VG **125.00**
Shotshell box, WE Ekins Eclipse 410 Gauge, 2-pc box, pk label, EX..**75.00**
Shotshell box, Western Xpert 12 Ga US Property, VG **65.00**
Shotshell box insert, UMC, merger w/Remington, ca 1911, 3¾" sq..**35.00**
Shotshell cartridge puller/extractor, 12 gauge, brass, EX................**35.00**
Snuff box, Parker Guns, NP, hinged top, Pat 1960, ¾x3¼x2" **145.00**
Trade card, Daisy Air Rifle, lady in boat w/boy, 5½x3½", EX.....**275.00**
Trap thrower, hand; Allison & Falkner, usual wear, scarce, VG..**100.00**
Tray, Peters Cartridges, mallards in flight, Hasko, 11x18", EX **85.00**

Sports Collectibles

When sports cards became so widely collectible several years ago, other types of related memorabilia started to interest sports fans. Now they search for baseball uniforms, autographed baseballs, game-used bats and gloves, and all sorts of ephemera. Although baseball is America's all-time favorite, other sports have their own groups of interested collectors. Our advice for this category comes from Paul Longo Americana. Mr. Longo is listed in the Directory under Massachusetts.

To learn more about old golf clubs, we recommend *The Vintage Era of Golf Club Collectibles* by Ronald O. John (Collector Books.) See also Target Balls; Tennis Rackets.

Baseball, Nat'l League, sgn Tom Seaver, 1970s, EX **60.00**
Baseball, Reach, Joe Cronin, Official Am League, cream colored, EX...**125.00**

Baseball, 1930s Philadelphia Athletics, team sgn, EX..............1,000.00
Baseball bat, Hank Greenberg Louisville Slugger, 1940s, 32", EX....165.00
Baseball bat, No 35 Georgia Cracker Hanna Mfg...GA, 3½", EX....100.00
Baseball bat, Safe Hit Lou Gehrig Model, H&B Louisville KY, EX.135.00
Baseball bat, Sears JC Higgins, Rocky Colavito, M.......................65.00
Baseball bat, Ty Cobb Louisville Slugger, 35", VG+....................500.00
Baseball book, Spaulding's Guide, Official National Library, 1909, VG...200.00
Baseball cabinet card, NY Young Ladies...Club, ca 1883, VG+..865.00
Baseball contract, E Collins for White Sox, 1923, player's copy, EX...280.00
Baseball glove, MacGregory #G25, Willie Mays model, early 1950s, VG..100.00
Baseball glove, Metro, buckle-bk/split-finger, 1940s, EX.............145.00
Baseball glove, Pennant, buckle web strap, dk leather, EX..........150.00
Baseball glove, Rawlings, Bill Doak, split-finger, late 1920s, EX...70.00
Baseball glove, Rawlings Mickey Mantel MM5, soft leather, EX..110.00
Baseball glove, Reach, full-web/split-finger, prof model, 1910s, EX.145.00
Baseball glove, Spaulding's Joe Dimaggio, split finger, 1930s, VG.250.00
Baseball jersey shirt, St Louis Cardinals, bl w/red & wht, 1970s, EX.75.00
Baseball Magazine, January 1910, 90 pgs, 9¾x6¾", G+..............200.00
Baseball pennant, Boston Braves, ca 1950s, EX........................200.00
Baseball pennant, Detroit Tigers, 1930s, felt, 34x10", EX...........400.00
Baseball pennant, Milwaukee Braves, mc on bl, 28½", EX...........55.00
Baseball pennant, 1956 National League All Stars, wht on bl, 30", EX..225.00
Baseball press pin, 1957 St Louis Cardinals All Star Game, enamel, EX...250.00
Baseball press pin, 1961 Red Sox All-Star Game, bl star, enamel, EX+..300.00
Baseball program, 1943 World Series, 40 pgs, 9x12", NM...........:200.00
Baseball yearbook, 1955 Brooklyn Dodgers, Williard Bum cover, VG...300.00
Basketball, Hutch Made in USA, leather w/laces, EX...................75.00
Basketball jersey, Boston Celtics #33, Larry Bird, Sand-Knit, EX.60.00
Basketball program, NCAA Eastern Regional..., 1944, EX.........285.00
Basketball shoes, Converse, Chuck Taylor All Star high-tops, canvas, M.125.00
Bowling bag, Brunswick, blk & wht, 1960s-70s, NM....................45.00
Bowling shirt, fuchsia poly rayon, King Louie Creations, 1950s, EX..50.00
Bowling shirt, yel & blk rayon, embr name/sponsor, 1950s, EX....65.00
Football, dk leather w/6 laces, unmk, 1930s, VG.......................135.00
Football, Nat'l League, Wilson, the Duke, early 1960s, EX...........80.00
Football cleats, Rawlings, orig laces, little use, 1920-30s, EX........60.00
Football helmet, MI Wolverines, JC Higgins, 1930s, EX.............700.00
Football helmet, Spaulding, leather, 1930s, EX........................425.00
Football helmet, Wilson, MI-style wing front, leather, 1930s, EX...250.00
Football jersey, TX Longhorns, red & wht, game used, EX.........100.00
Football jersey, USC Trojans, game used, EX..........................125.00
Football pennant, Baltimore Colts, single-bar face mask, 1960s, EX..60.00
Football pennant, Detroit Lions, Briggs Stadium, felt, 1940s, 11x27"...75.00
Football program, Super Bowl VI, 1972, NM............................135.00
Football T-shirt, Philadelphia Eagles Super Bowl, 1981, NM........25.00
Football varsity letter sweater, orange A on bl wool, 1930s, EX....70.00
Golf club, Ben Sayers Rustless putter, 1940s, EX.....................55.00
Golf club, Gibson & Co Skoogee Niblick iron, concave face, 1930, EX..450.00
Golf club, MacGregor Babe Didrikson putter, ca 1935, EX.........125.00
Golf club, MacGregor Duralite Fancy Face, wood w/stainless shaft, 1927..125.00
Golf club, R Forgan Maxmo putter, Forganite, ca 1928, EX........185.00
Golf club, R Forgan Tolley putter, Forganite (compo), ca 1927, EX..350.00
Golf club, R Tug Tyler, rear impact driver, wood shaft, ca 1924, EX......225.00
Golf club, Sid Green Peak Hi driver, wood shaft, ca 1932, EX...635.00
Golf club, Spalding Fancy Face #5 wood, ca 1923, EX.................85.00
Golf club, Wilson Black beauty, metal/wood, ca 1925, EX..........225.00

St. Clair

The St. Clair Glass Company began as a small family-oriented operation in Elwood, Indiana, in 1941. Most famous for their lamps, the family made numerous small items of carnival, pink and caramel slag, and custard glass as well. Later, paperweights became popular production pieces; many command relatively high prices on today's market. Weights are stamped and usually dated, while small production pieces are often unmarked. Lamps are in big demand (prices depend on size and whether or not they are signed) as are items signed by Paul or Ed St. Clair. For further information we recommend *St. Clair Glass Collector's Book, Vol. II*, by our advisor Ted Pruitt. He is listed in the Directory under Indiana.

Animal dish, dolphin, bl, Joe St Clair..175.00
Animal dish, reclining colt, cobalt custard, from $135 to...........160.00
Ashtray, brns, bowl shape w/3 rests, from $85 to......................95.00
Basket, handmade, sm, from $100 to.......................................125.00
Bell, Christmas, from $100 to...125.00
Bell, fruit pattern, bl carnival, from $90 to.............................100.00
Bell, Holly Carillon, cobalt carnival, sgn.................................35.00
Bird, bl & clear, lg, from $75 to..95.00
Bottle, Grape & Gable, w/stopper, bl or red carnival, ea from $125 to..135.00
Bowl, fluted rim, from $225 to..250.00
Bowl, pk slag, ped ft, from $150 to..175.00
Candle holder, sulfide, mc floral, from $75 to...........................85.00
Compote, pk slag, ruffled rim, low ped base, from $150 to..........175.00
Cordial, any color, from $50 to...65.00
Cruet, bl, bulbous w/2 loop hdls, stopper, from $125 to.............150.00

Figurine, Scottie dog, blue carnival, marked R.M. St. Clair, ca 1979, 1½x4x3", from $150.00 to $200.00; same, black (dark amethyst), $700.00 (at auction).

Figurine, Southern Belle, various colors, from $30 to...................40.00
Fruit, blueberry, from $140 to...150.00
Goblet, Hobster, ice bl..25.00
Insulator, handmade, from $100 to...125.00
Lamp, 3-ball, sgn Joe & Bob St Clair....................................1,500.00
Marble, baseball player, Ed St Clair, from $125 to....................150.00
Mug, Holly Band, caramel slag, from $90 to.............................95.00
Paperweight, cameo, windowed, from $250 to...........................300.00
Paperweight, lily, wht, Ed St Clair, from $350 to.......................400.00
Paperweight, pear, bl carnival..100.00
Paperweight, sulfide, Babe Ruth, from $225 to.........................250.00
Paperweight, sulfide, Betsy Ross, Joe St Clair...........................350.00
Paperweight, turtle, from $150 to..175.00
Pen holder, handmade, from $65 to...75.00
Pitcher, Hollyband, caramel slag, from $90 to...........................95.00
Plate, Mt St Helens, from $20 to...25.00
Plate, Reagan - Bush, from $25 to...30.00
Ring holder, clear w/yel flower...50.00
Salt dip, swan, colors other than red or wht, ea from $35 to.........45.00
Salt dip, swan, wht or red, ea from $100 to.............................125.00
Sauce dish, Paneled Grape, ice bl carnival, from $35 to..............40.00
Statue, Kewpie, from $115 to...125.00
Sugar bowl, Hollyband, wht carnival or amber Tiffany, ea from $85 to.100.00
Toothpick holder, fez hat, from $135 to..................................150.00
Toothpick holder, Indian, yel carnival....................................25.00
Toothpick holder, 3 swans, any color, from $35 to.....................45.00
Vase, blown, waisted, from $175 to..200.00

Staffordshire

Scores of potteries sprang up in England's Staffordshire district in the early eighteenth century; several remain to the present time. (See also specific companies.) Figurines and groups were made in great numbers; dogs were favorite subjects. Often they were made in pairs, each a mirror image of the other. They varied in heights from 3" or 4" to the largest, measuring 16" to 18". From 1840 until about 1900, portrait figures were produced to represent specific characters, both real and fictional. As a rule these were never marked.

Historical transferware was made throughout the district; some collectors refer to it as Staffordshire Blue. It was produced as early as 1780, and because much was exported to America, it was very often decorated with transfers depicting scenic views of well-known American landmarks. Early examples were printed in a deep cobalt. By 1830 a softer blue was favored, and within the next decade black, brown, pink, red, and green prints were used. Although sometimes careless about adding their trademark, many companies used their own border designs that were as individual as their names.

This ware should not be confused with the vast amounts of modern china (mostly plates) made from early in the century to the present. These souvenir or commemorative items are usually marketed through gift stores and the like. (See Rowland and Marsellus.)

Our advisor for this category is Jeanne Dunay; she is listed in the Directory under South Carolina. See also specific manufacturers.

Key:
blk — black	l/b — light blue
gr — green	m/b — medium blue
d/b — dark blue	m-d/b — medium dark blue

Figures and Groups

Ram reclining on grassy mound, nineteenth century, 4", $350.00.

Bird & hatchlings in sanded nest, inkwell, wht/yel/pk w/gilt, 2⅝"...**165.00**
Boy, pk/gr attire, feeds wht/gilt swan, 3-color coleslaw, 5"...........**495.00**
Child on dog, mc details, free-standing, 5½"...............................**150.00**
Couple in bower, mc w/coleslaw leaves, flake, 7½"......................**200.00**
Dick Turpin, gray hair, bl coat, w/pistol, on horse, 10¼"............**165.00**
Dog, wht w/red spots, sits on cobalt pillow w/gilt traces, inkwell, 4"...**275.00**
Dogs, red spots, gray paws & muzzle, yel collar, 3¾", pr.............**375.00**
Dogs, wht w/copper lustre & blk decor, sm areas of gr runs, 9¾", pr...**435.00**
Dogs, wht w/red spots, holds flower basket in mouth, 7¼", pr....**550.00**
Dogs (2, w/red & blk spots), run deer in woods, coleslaw, vase, 7", EX...**250.00**
Elephant, mc w/coleslaw grass, chimney vase, sm rpr, 6¾".........**230.00**
Fox head (stirrup cup), red w/blk & wht muzzle, minor wear, 5" L.....**525.00**
Fox head (stirrup cup), red w/blk muzzle, cvd whiskers, gilt, 5", VG...**495.00**
Fox head (stirrup cup), red w/yel eyes & rim, lt wear, 4½" L......**475.00**
Franklin (Benjamin), in bl coat & patterned vest, 14½".............**990.00**
Hound head (stirrup cup), tan w/blk spatter spots, 5"................**775.00**
Lamb, sanded coats, gray ears, gr coleslaw glass, 2¼", pr.............**260.00**

Leopard, yel/blk/gr, 3½x3", EX...**575.00**
Lion, recumbent w/front paws crossed, orange w/gr glass eyes, 10x11"..**350.00**
Lion Slayer, Scotsman in kilt holds lion by paw, rstr, 16½"........**230.00**
Little Eva & Uncle Tom seated, mc, transfer paragraph on base, 7½"...**260.00**
Man & lady in gr w/birds, he leans on anchor, 8", 7⅜", pr.........**385.00**
Man w/bkpack & telescope, pk-striped breeches/orange cape, 8", EX.**145.00**
Napoleon in military dress w/sword & hat, 19th C, 15½"...........**250.00**
Pea hen, wht w/red & gold, on gr base w/coleslaw tufts, 12⅝" ...**400.00**
Poodles (2 on bbl/2nd hiding), cobalt base, 5⅛x5"......................**435.00**
Pr in dk bl coats, she (pk apron) sits by tree (vase), he w/shovel, 7"...**200.00**
Prince Albert, mc, 6¼"..**200.00**
Queen Victoria, mc, 6", NM..**200.00**
Rooster, wht w/red comb & wattle, gold trim, 11½"...............**1,035.00**
Scottish pr, he: bagpipe, red/gr plaid cape; she: basket, on base, 9".**250.00**
Sheep & ram, sanded coats, by tree trunk (vase), coleslaw, rpr, 5", VG...**300.00**
Shepherd & shepherdess w/dog & sheep, chimney vase, 7¾".....**110.00**
Spaniel, blk spots & yel collar, seated, 6", EX...........................**100.00**
Spaniels, blk spots, copper lustre chains & collars, seated, 9", pr.**240.00**
Spaniels, orange spots, copper lustre chains, 12½", pr................**285.00**
Spaniels w/flowers in mouths, HP details, minor rstr, 8", pr........**650.00**
Swan, pk wings/gilt, coleslaw bouquet/red heart, on base, inkwell, 4"...**220.00**
Swans (3), wht w/gilt, tree (vase) w/gold int & lt bl coleslaw, 5"..**275.00**
Welsh shepherds (on base), couple w/sheep at ft, rstr, 14", EX...**385.00**
Woman stands by column, vase of flowers atop, wht w/mc shawl, 9", VG.**145.00**
Zebra, blk stripes/mane/bridle, gr foliage, flake, 6⅛x5½"............**330.00**

Transferware

Basin, Ship of Line in Downs, Am flag, d/b, Wood & Son, 3x12½", NM..**2,900.00**
Basket, landscape, d/b, rtcl body, Davenport, 1840s, 10½" L......**225.00**
Bowl, Blantyre, l/b, oval, ftd, w/lid, Alcock, 7¾x10"..................**225.00**
Bowl, Canova, l/b, oval, w/lid, att Mayer, 6¾x11¼x8½"............**300.00**
Bowl, Centara Bay of Salerno, brn/yel, Wood, 1½x5¾"..............**50.00**
Bowl, fruit; Canova, l/b, rtcl rim/hdls, sq, 4x8½"........................**500.00**
Bowl, Giraffe, d/b, shallow, Ridgway, 7½" **275.00**
Bowl, Pagoda, d/b, oval, Oriental Scenery, Hall, 2½x12x9" **300.00**
Bowl, potato; Italian Buildings, d/b, Hall, 2¼x11½", NM..........**350.00**
Bowl, Ship of the Line in Downs, d/b, oval, w/lid, Wood, 6x10"..**1,380.00**
Bowl, Tuscan Rose, brn, oval, unmk Ridgway, 1½x11¾x9¾".....**200.00**
Coffeepot, classical landscape, d/b, unmk, 11¾"........................**950.00**
Coffeepot, Lafayette at Franklin's Tomb, d/b, rpr, 12¾"...........**2,200.00**
Compote, Arabian (Turkish?) scene, brn, scalloped/ftd, 4¼x10¼".**450.00**
Creamer, Gentlemen's Cabin, brn, Boston Mails Series, Edwards, 5"...**500.00**
Creamer, Lafayette at Franklin's Tomb, d/b, Wood, 6", NM........**450.00**
Cup plate, America & Independence, d/b, partial States border, 4"..**495.00**
Cup plate, America & Independence, d/b, States border, Clews, 4½"...**525.00**
Cup plate, Arms of South Carolina, d/b, unmk Mayer, 4¼".......**850.00**
Cup plate, Arms of US w/eagle & shield, m/b, unmk, 3¾".........**850.00**
Cup plate, Boston State House, m/b, Enoch Wood, 3¾"............**500.00**
Cup plate, Boston State House, m/b, Stevenson & Wms, 4¼"...**650.00**
Cup plate, Broadlands Hampshire, manor house, d/b, Hall, 4" ...**200.00**
Cup plate, Castle Garden Battery NY, d/b, shell border, Wood, 3¾"...**600.00**
Cup plate, Castle Garden Battery NY, d/b, shell border, Wood, 4⅝"...**800.00**
Cup plate, cottage in woods, d/b, trefoil border, Wood & Sons, 3¾"....**195.00**
Cup plate, Customs House Philadelphia, m/b, Ridgway, 3½".......**800.00**
Cup plate, Fakeer's Rock, boat/tower, d/b, Oriental Scenery, Hall, 4"..**200.00**
Cup plate, Ft Edwards, Hudson River, mulberry, unmk Clews, 4⅛", EX.**415.00**
Cup plate, Holiday St Theatre Baltimore, m/b, unmk, 3½"........**600.00**
Cup plate, Hyena, d/b, urn border, Quadrupeds series, Hall, 4" ..**385.00**
Cup plate, Landing of Gen Lafayette, m/b, Clews, 3½"..............**525.00**
Cup plate, Landing of Pilgrims, m/b, Enoch Wood, 4⅝"............**440.00**
Cup plate, Octagon Church, m/b, acorn & oak leaf border, Stevenson, 4".**450.00**
Cup plate, Pittsfield Elm, d/b, floral border vignettes, Clews, 4⅝"..**495.00**
Cup plate, Quebec (so called), m/b, unmk Clews, 3⅞"...............**550.00**

Cup plate, Scudder's American Museum, m/b, Stevenson & Wms, 4¼"...**700.00**

Cup plate, Shirley House Surrey, m/b, Wood, hairline/sm flakes, 3⅝" ..**70.00**

Cup plate, Untitled Broadlands, manor house, d/b, Hall, 4", NM ..**145.00**

Cup plate, Venetian Gardens, purple, unmk, 4"............................**95.00**

Cup plate, Welcome Lafayette the Nation's Guest, m/b, Clews, 4¾"...**650.00**

Cup plate, Woodlands Near Philadelphia, m/b, Stubbs, 3⅛" **450.00**

Drainer, Botanical Beauties, d/b, E&N, 13¾x9¾"....................**450.00**

Drainer, castle, river & mts, m/b, unmk, 14½x10¾"....................**350.00**

Jug, Jardiniere, d/b, Davenport, ca 1805, 7x6" **375.00**

Ladle, Wild Rose, brn, unmk, ca 1820, 11"....................................**225.00**

Mug, Genevese, red, Mintons, 3¼x4½"....................................**200.00**

Pitcher, Abbey Ruins, d/b, Mayer, 10x8½"............................**750.00**

Pitcher, Almshouse Boston/Esplanade &..., d/b, Stevenson, 10", EX ..**2,300.00**

Pitcher, Boston State House/City Hall NY, d/b, unmk Stubbs, 6"....**975.00**

Pitcher, Butterfly & Moth, d/b, ca 1825, 5¼"............................**475.00**

Pitcher, Canova, brn, Thomas Mayer, 1826-35, 8½"....................**650.00**

Pitcher, country vista w/mansion, d/b, States border, Clews, 6¾"..**800.00**

Pitcher, Entrance of Erie Canal/...Bridge at Little Falls, d/b, 5¾"...**1,725.00**

Pitcher, river scene w/bridge, d/b, Clews, rpr, 4¾"......................**385.00**

Pitcher, Victory (ship), brn w/orange trim, pearlware, 6¾" **1,645.00**

Pitcher, View of Erie Canal, d/b, rprs, 6" **715.00**

Pitcher, Welcome Lafayette...Glory, d/b, Clews, 5", NM..........**2,100.00**

Plate, America & Independence, d/b, Clews, rpr, 10½" **260.00**

Plate, America & Independence, d/b, States border, Clews, 10½"..**470.00**

Plate, building/bridge/etc, d/b, French Series, Wood, 10¼" **225.00**

Plate, Cadmus, d/b, shell border, Wood, 10" **585.00**

Plate, Canova, gr, Phillips, 9¼"..**165.00**

Plate, Canova, l/b, scalloped, Mayer, 10½", 4 for **500.00**

Plate, Canova, purple, Mayer, 10½"..**165.00**

Plate, castle & fields, d/b, Adams Warranted, 10¼"....................**275.00**

Plate, Chief Justice Marshall, d/b, shell border, Wood, 8⅜"........**700.00**

Plate, City Hall NY, m/b, Beauties of America, Ridgway, 10"........**375.00**

Plate, Commodore MacDonnough's Victory, d/b, Wood, 6½"....**415.00**

Plate, Commodore MacDonnough's Victory, d/b, Wood, 10⅛"....**440.00**

Plate, Don Quixote & Shepherdesses, d/b, floral border, 10" **275.00**

Plate, Fifteen States, d/b, Am Independence Series, Clews, 10¾"..**450.00**

Plate, Geneves, blk, Mintons, 1822-36, 10¼"............................**175.00**

Plate, Giraffe, d/b, Ridgway, 10¼"..**450.00**

Plate, Hannibal Passing the Alps, red, Knight Elkin & Co, 9" ...**200.00**

Plate, Harvard College, d/b, acorn border, Stevenson, 10¼" **400.00**

Plate, Landing of Fathers at Plymouth, d/b, Wood, 10⅛" **300.00**

Plate, Landing of Gen Lafayette, d/b, Clews, 7¾" **450.00**

Plate, Landing of Gen Lafayette, d/b, Clews, 10", from $450 to .**500.00**

Plate, Landing of Gen Lafayette, d/b, Clews Warranted, 8⅞".....**450.00**

Plate, Landing of Lafayette at Castle Garden..., d/b, Clews, 10¼"...**500.00**

Plate, Lion, d/b, Quadrupeds Series, Hall, 10" **350.00**

Plate, Mogul Scenery, red, Mayer, 10¾"....................................**150.00**

Plate, Picturesque Views Near Fishkill Hudson River, l/b, 10½"..**290.00**

Plate, Pomerania, brn, scalloped, Ridgway, 6¾"............................**80.00**

Plate, Rhode Island Arms of American States, d/b, Mayer, 8¾".**800.00**

Plate, Table Rock Niagara, d/b, shell border, Wood, 10⅛"..........**585.00**

Plate, Valkyries, d/b, E Wood & Sons, 9¼" **275.00**

Plate, View of Greenwich, d/b, Clews, 9"....................................**250.00**

Plate, Vue du Chateau Ermenonville, d/b, Wood & Sons, 10¼"...**275.00**

Plate, Water Works Philadelphia, lt gr, Jackson's Warranted, 9⅛"..**360.00**

Plate, Winter View of Pittsfield MA, d/b, Clews, lt wear, 8½"....**180.00**

Plate, Wm Penn's Treaty, brn, geometric border, 10⅝" **325.00**

Plate, 1st Amendment stated amid 4 medallions, d/b, 9½".........**475.00**

Plate, 3-Story Building & Observatory, d/b, Clews, 10½", NM ..**500.00**

Platter, Battle of Marenro, brn, CJM & Co, 18" L........................**550.00**

Platter, Boston & Bunkers (sic) Hill, d/b, Godwin, 13⅜" **600.00**

Platter, Cape Coast Castle...Gold Coast Africa, d/b, Wood, 16½" ..**2,800.00**

Platter, Dresden Roses, brn, unmk, ca 1850, 15x12"....................**350.00**

Platter, High Bridge, d/b, rtcl rim, Davenport, 1793-1810, 10¼" L..**125.00**

Platter, Lake George State of NY, d/b, shell border, Wood, 16¾"..**1,800.00**

Platter, Niagara From American Side, d/b, shell border, Wood, 15", NM..**2,800.00**

Platter, Oriental Scenery, Musketeer pattern, d/b, Rogers, 17" ...**525.00**

Platter, PA Hospital Philadelphia, d/b, Ridgway, 18½x14⅛"..**1,600.00**

Platter, Pompeii, brn, J&G Alcock, 17¾"....................................**450.00**

Platter, Sandusky & Steamship Henry Clay, d/b, unmk Clews, 16½x13"..**4,625.00**

Platter, Shell, d/b, floral/fruit/urn border, Stubbs & Kent, 21", EX..**2,100.00**

Platter, View of Dublin, d/b, Wood & Sons, 14¾", NM **1,800.00**

Platter, White House, WA, name of 15 states, d/b, Clews, 14¾"..**1,880.00**

Platter, Wild Rose, brn, unmk, ca 1820, 18¼x14¼" **350.00**

Platter, 3-Story Flat-Roof House w/2 Wings, d/b, peaked roof, 16½" .**2,000.00**

Pot, Boston State House, d/b, Rogers, 3¼x5"............................**865.00**

Soup, Boston Octagon Church, d/b, Ridgway, 9¾"....................**385.00**

Soup, Canova, l/b, scalloped, Mayer, 10½", 4 for **500.00**

Soup, Italian Buildings, d/b, Hall, 9¾"......................................**145.00**

Soup, La Capetera Havana.., d/b, 8¾"......................................**600.00**

Soup, William Penn's Treaty, T Goodwin, 10½" **350.00**

Sugar bowl, Lafayette at Franklin's Tomb, d/b, Wood, 5", EX **500.00**

Sugar bowl, mother & child in cottage yard w/dog, m/b, Adams, 6¾"..**300.00**

Sugar bowl, Venus, blk w/mc, Podmore Walker, 8½", EX **125.00**

Tea bowl, Chancellor Livingston, d/b, Wood, stain....................**200.00**

Tea bowl & saucer, Basket & Vase, d/b, Clews, 2½", 5¾"...........**200.00**

Tea bowl & saucer, Florals & Basket, d/b, Stevenson, 2⅜", 6"....**200.00**

Tea bowl & saucer, hunting dogs & floral, d/b, Clews, 2½", 5¾".**325.00**

Tea bowl & saucer, MacDonnough's Victory, d/b, Wood & Sons.**475.00**

Tea bowl & saucer, Tivoli, red, Meigh, 3", 5¾" **100.00**

Teabowl & saucer, Lafayette at Franklin's Tomb, d/b, Wood & Sons ...**300.00**

Teabowl & saucer, Napoleon drives sled in Russia, d/b, Wood ...**250.00**

Teabowl & saucer, WA Standing at Tomb Scroll in Hand, d/b, Wood ..**385.00**

Teapot, Gentlemen's Cabin, brn, Boston Mails Series, Edwards, 9"...**600.00**

Teapot, Lafayette at Franklin's Tomb, d/b, Wood, 9", NM.......**1,400.00**

Teapot, Marino, l/b, Geo Phillips, 9½", EX................................**400.00**

Teapot, Napoleon drives sled in Russia, d/b, Wood & Sons, hairline, 8"....**825.00**

Teapot, Neptune on shell, d/b, unmk Clews, rprs, 8"................**385.00**

Teapot, Venus, blk w/mc details, Podmore Walker, 9½", NM.....**325.00**

Teapot, 3 people by Tudor-style cottages, d/b, Adam's Warranted, 7"...**470.00**

Tureen, Dam & Waterworks at Fair Mount Phila, d/b, Stubbs, w/lid, 16".**3,000.00**

Tureen, sauce; Corinth, l/b, Edwards, 8½x8", +8½" underplate..**450.00**

Tureen, sauce; Italian Flower Garden, brn, Ridgway, +lid/ladle/tray..**650.00**

Tureen, sauce; Oriental Scenery, brn, Mayer, 8½" L, +lid & ladle....**600.00**

Tureen, Wild Rose, brn, w/lid, unmk, ca 1820, 8¼x13" **350.00**

Stained Glass

There are many factors to consider in evaluating a window or panel of stained glass art. Besides the obvious factor of condition, quality of leadwork, intricacy, jeweling, beveling, and the amount of selenium (red, orange, and yellow) present should all be taken into account. Remember, repair work is itself an art and can be very expensive. Our advisor for this category is Carl Heck; he is listed in the Directory under Colorado. See also Tiffany.

Ceiling Lights

10x24", cobalt w/pk & wht dogwood blossoms, VG................**4,800.00**

16", rose/buds, rolled-down umbrella shape, irregular border, crown ..**4,000.00**

18", fleur-de-lis border in 3 colors on lt amber w/sq panels **2,200.00**

20" geometric shade w/geometrics in apron, Duffner/Kimberly.**2,800.00**

20" Prairie School shade, 8 stylized floral panels, 40" overall ..**2,800.00**

22" flower/leaf/butterfly dome shade w/inset medallions, A Hart ..**3,500.00**

24", blade-like-leaves, wide leaf apron w/acorn band, Bent Glass Co...**2,290.00**

24", shouldered form w/grapes & dk latticework on wht, EX...**1,800.00**

24" lattice/panel shade w/very wide stylized floral apron, no mk...**2,500.00**

24" leafy shade w/wide scalloped floral apron, Duffner/Kimberly ..**7,850.00**
28", fishscales w/stylized panels, incurvate/irregular edge, Wilkinson **3,000.00**
30", dome w/petal-shaped pcs, gr w/caramel border **1,400.00**

Table Lamps

16" floral-border shade; simple ftd bronzed base, Unique, 23" .**1,500.00**
16" geometric dome shade; bronzed std, Bigelow & Kennard, 21½" ..**3,250.00**
16" rolled-down shade w/stylized floral border; Duffner/Kimberly, 20" ..**1,850.00**
17" bird (wings wide) shade; swirling std, Gorham, rare, 22" ...**5,500.00**
18" floral & caramel glass shade; hdld urn-form std, 24" **1,250.00**
18" floral & windowpane shade; organic bronzed std, Wilkinson, 26" ...**2,000.00**
18" floral shade w/caramel top; gold-tone organic std, 24" **2,300.00**
18" floral-band shade; bronzed std, 24" **1,400.00**
18" floral-border brickwork shade; emb std/base #537, Wilkinson ..**2,800.00**
18" geometric slag glass shade; emb leaves on std, 27" **1,600.00**
18" rolled-down shade w/stylized floral border; simple std, no mk, 23" ...**840.00**
18" scroll/shell shade w/shaped bottom; organic std, Duffner/Kimberly .**13,000.00**
18" 12-row brickwork shade; simple std, no mk, 23" **850.00**
18" 5-petal flower shade w/shaped border; emb leaf std, Gorham, 22" ...**5,500.00**
20" scroll/shell shade w/shaped bottom; emb/ornate stem/ft, Williamson ..**5,000.00**
21" water lily shade; 4-ftd water lily #525 std, Wilkinson, 31" ...**7,280.00**
22" Louis XIV floral shade; bronze organic std, Wilkinson, rare, 30" .**30,000.00**
23" floral shade w/str bottom; std w/cast rocks/roots, Suess, 23" ...**13,500.00**
23" peonies shade w/leaf border; molded tree trunk std, 27" ..**10,000.00**
27" water lily shade; bronzed tree trunk base, Suess, 22" **15,000.00**
28" geometric shade w/scrolling apron; ornate std, Wilkinson, 28" ...**9,000.00**

Windows

Chevrons in gr & gold on clear w/frosted border, fr, 55x9½", pr ...**1,400.00**
Geometric pattern in style of L Sullivan w/jewels, fr, 35x25" ..**1,400.00**
Irises & rolling hills, 28x24" **2,000.00**
Jewel-fr oval in center, traditional elements, ripple glass, 21x25" **2,900.00**
Lady w/macaw among architectural features/flowers/jewels, fr, 46" sq **14,000.00**
Morning-glory vines in pots (4-color) border clear panel, 37x19", pr ..**1,750.00**
Peacock in landscape, mc jewels, EX workmanship, 55x53" later fr ..**1,925.00**
Peacock w/tail wide, Watson MFG...NY, Pat April 1-25-10, 35x26" ...**5,000.00**
Prairie School, very simple, in orig fr, 30x16", pr **450.00**
Prairie School, 3 stylized flowers, gr on clear field, 38x18", pr **650.00**
Scrolls/fans/ribbons, many jewels, 17x50" **2,500.00**
Windmill on hill & puffy clouds, arched top, unmk, 78½x41" .**3,500.00**

Stanford

The Stanford Pottery Co. was founded in 1945 in Sebring, Ohio. One of the founders was George Stanford, a former manager at Spaulding China (Royal Copley). They continued in operations until the factory was destroyed by a fire about 1961. They produced a Corn line, similar to that of the Shawnee Company, that is today very collectible. Most examples are marked (either Stanford Sebring Ohio or with a paper label), so there should be no difficulty in distinguishing one line from the other.

In addition to their Corn line, they produced planters and figurines, many of which were black trimmed with gold, made to be sold as pairs or sets. Wall pockets and vases were made as well. In 1949 they introduced a line called Tomato Ware, consisting of a cookie jar, grease jar, salt and pepper shakers, creamer and sugar bowl, mustard jar, marmalade jar, etc. These were shaped as bright red tomatoes with green leaves and stems (often used as lid finials), and were marketed under the name 'The Pantry Parade.' Our advisor for this category is Joe Devine; he is listed in the Directory under Iowa.

Ashtray, free-form, orange w/wht 'stucco,' #270-D, mk, 10x7" **12.00**

Corn Line, butter dish **60.00**
Corn Line, casserole, 8" L **50.00**

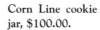

Corn Line cookie jar, $100.00.

Corn Line, creamer & sugar bowl w/lid **60.00**
Corn Line, cup **20.00**
Corn Line, pitcher, 7½" **65.00**
Corn Line, plate, 9" L **35.00**
Corn Line, relish tray **45.00**
Corn Line, shakers, sm, pr **30.00**
Corn Line, shakers, 4", pr **35.00**
Corn Line, snack set, cup & plate w/indent, #709 ....**95.00**
Corn Line, spoon rest **30.00**
Corn Line, teapot **75.00**
Corn Line, tumbler **35.00**
Planter, Dutch boy or girl by tulip, blk w/gold trim, ea **20.00**
Planter, matching drummer, boy or girl, 7", ea **22.00**
Planter, teddy bear, wht w/pk & bl trim, paper label, 7" **35.00**
Tomato Ware, casserole, w/lid, 6x9" **60.00**
Tomato Ware, cookie jar, 8" **90.00**
Tomato Ware, creamer **30.00**
Tomato Ware, grease jar, w/lid **38.00**
Tomato Ware, marmalade jar **35.00**
Tomato Ware, mustard jar **35.00**
Tomato Ware, pitcher, 6½" **65.00**
Tomato Ware, sugar bowl **30.00**
Wall pocket, bird, bl & cobalt w/gold trim, 7", from $40 to **45.00**
Wall pocket, cherry branch, red pie-crust edge, #299, mk, 6¼" **28.00**

Stangl

Stangl Pottery was one of the longest-existing potteries in the United States, having as its beginning in 1814 the Sam Hill Pottery, becoming the Fulper Pottery which gained eminence in the field of art pottery (ca 1860), and then coming under the aegis of Johann Martin Stangl. The German-born Stangl joined Fulper in 1910 as chemical engineer, left for a brief stint at Haeger in Dundee, Illinois, and rejoined Fulper as general manager in 1920. He became president of the firm in 1928. Although Stangl's name was on much of the ware from the late '20s onward, the company's name was not changed officially until 1955. J.M. Stangl died in 1972; the pottery continued under the ownership of Wheaton Industries until 1978, then closed. Stangl is best known for its extensive Birds of American line, styled after Audubon; its brightly colored, hand-carved, hand-painted dinnerware; and its great variety of giftware, including its dry-brushed gold lines. For more information we recommend *Collector's Encyclopedia of Stangl Dinnerware* and *Collector's Encyclopedia of Stangl Artware, Lamps & Birds*, by Robert Runge, Jr. (Collector Books). Another good reference is *Stangl Pottery* by Harvey Duke;

for ordering information refer to the listing for Nancy and Robert Perzel, Popkorn Antiques (our advisors for this category), in the Directory under New Jersey. Also available: *Stangl Pottery, White-Bodied Artware, 1924 – 1942*, by Peter Meissner (Schiffer).

Artware and Novelties

Bowl, Acanthus, turq, deep, #1544, from $40 to **50.00**
Candle holders, blk, scrolled stem, 1930-32, #1360, 10", pr, $175 to ..**190.00**
Candlestick, silver-gr, 2-light, #1191, for Levin, ca 1928, 6", $50 to.**75.00**
Flower box, tangerine w/gr int, for Macy's, #1640, 1933-40, 4x10" ..**60.00**
Flowerpot, Scottie dog figural, apple gr, #1775, 6½x6", $150 to .**175.00**
Flowerpot, sparrow at side, gr matt, #1778, 6½x5" **150.00**
Head vase, lady's head, curls, wht satin/lav, #3419, 6", $195 to ..**235.00**
Jar, tangerine, ribs, 3-hdl, mold cast, 1933-37, 6", from $65 to **80.00**
Jug, water; dog figural, Colonial Blue, #1998, 1935-36, from $250 to ..**300.00**
Sasha gourd cup, bl satin, 1936, from $40 to.................................**50.00**
Shade pull, Chinese, Persian Yellow, #3077, from $100 to **125.00**
Tray, Della-Ware, Festival, #3576, 12" dia, from $150 to **165.00**
Vase, apple gr, ball form, handmade, #1126, 7½", from $75 to **100.00**
Vase, bud; Twist, Blue-of-the-Sky, #1905, 1935-40, 8", from $40 to....**50.00**
Vase, Colonial Blue, dog hdls, #3160, 1938 only, 16", $430 to..**475.00**
Vase, Colonial Blue, tulip form, #3208, mini, from $40 to **50.00**
Vase, copper gr, wide mouth, shouldered, Fulper Faience, #916, 8"..**55.00**
Vase, cornucopia; rust glaze, #1811, mid-1930s, 5½", from $80 to..**100.00**
Vase, gr satin, rim-to-hip hdls, #3104, 1937-39, 7", from $35 to...**45.00**
Vase, Grecian Urn, gr/Caribbean bl sponging, #2041, 1968-70, $35 to...**40.00**
Vase, Madonna in relief, wht satin, #3232, 1938-41, from $95 to....**110.00**
Vase, Mediterranian (bl), triple cylinder, #5106, 10x5", $55 to **65.00**
Vase, Persian Yellow, swirled ball, #1818, mid-1930s, 5½", $85 to...**110.00**
Vase, Scored Rib, tangerine w/gr int, #1906, 1935-38, 7½", $65 to ...**80.00**
Vase, Scroll Horn, wht satin, #2056, 1936-40, 6", from $15 to **18.00**
Vase, tangerine w/turq int, for Macy's, #1571, 1932 only, 7", $90 to..**125.00**
Vase, varigated rust, 3-hdl, handmade, #1710, 1933-35, 9", $100 to .**125.00**
Wall pocket, bird figural, silver-gr, Fulper Faience, #961, $275 to ..**300.00**

Dinnerware

Festival and Laurita cream pitchers, 3¾", $15.00 each.

Amber-Glo #3899, casserole, skillet shape, 6", from $10 to...........**15.00**
Amber-Glo #3899, lazy susan, from $70 to.....................................**85.00**
Amber-Glo #3899, plate, 8", from $5 to **8.00**
Amber-Glo #3899, teapot, from $50 to **65.00**
Americana #2000, ashtray, 4", from $15 to **20.00**
Americana #2000, bowl, oval vegetable; 8", from $15 to **20.00**
Americana #2000, coffeepot, AD; 6-cup, from $75 to.....................**95.00**
Americana #2000, creamer, from $8 to **10.00**
Americana #2000, pitcher, ice lip, 2-qt, from $50 to.....................**70.00**
Americana #2000, platter, oval, 12", from $15 to **25.00**
Americana #2000, teapot, 8-cup, from $95 to **110.00**
Blueberry #3770, bowl, divided vegetable; oval, from $40 to **50.00**

Blueberry #3770, coffeepot, 4-cup; from $100 to **130.00**
Blueberry #3770, cruet, w/stopper, from $40 to **50.00**
Blueberry #3770, plate, 10", from $20 to **30.00**
Blueberry #3770, platter, oval, 11½", from $115 to **130.00**
Blueberry #3770, warmer, from $30 to **40.00**
Colonial #1388, bowl, lug soup; 4½", from $8 to **12.00**
Colonial #1388, bowl, mixing; 9", from $70 to **80.00**
Colonial #1388, cake stand, high, from $25 to **35.00**
Colonial #1388, casserole, w/hdl & lid, ind, from $30 to **35.00**
Colonial #1388, egg cup, from $15 to **20.00**
Colonial #1388, gravy bowl, from $25 to **35.00**
Colonial #1388, pie baker, 11", from $25 to **35.00**
Colonial #1388, plate, 10", from $20 to **25.00**
Colonial #1388, relish, triple, 12", from $25 to **35.00**
Colonial #1388, sugar bowl, bird finial, from $60 to **75.00**
Cosmos #3339, candle holders, scroll shape, #3046, pr, from $20 to.**30.00**
Cosmos #3339, cup, coffee; from $10 to **15.00**
Cosmos #3339, plate, 10", from $25 to **35.00**
Cosmos #3339, sugar bowl, from $15 to **20.00**
Country Garden #3943, cake stand, from $25 to **30.00**
Country Garden #3943, coffeepot, 8-cup, from $90 to **110.00**
Country Garden #3943, plate, 11", from $35 to **45.00**
Country Garden #3943, teapot, from $85 to **100.00**
Daisy #1870, bowl, lug soup; 5", from $15 to **20.00**
Daisy #1870, bowl, salad; 10", from $50 to **65.00**
Daisy #1870, plate, 9", from $20 to **30.00**
Daisy #1870, teapot, from $135 to **175.00**
Floral #3342, ashtray, from $15 to **20.00**
Floral #3342, bowl, salad; 7½", from $25 to **35.00**
Floral #3342, cup, coffee; from $12 to **15.00**
Floral #3342, plate, 10", from $30 to **40.00**
Fruit & Flowers #4030, butter dish, from $60 to **75.00**
Fruit & Flowers #4030, cup & saucer, from $15 to......................**20.00**
Fruit & Flowers #4030, plate, 6", from $8 to **10.00**
Fruit & Flowers #4030, tidbit, 10", from $10 to **15.00**
Fruit #3697, bean pot/cookie jar, from $110 to **125.00**
Fruit #3697, bowl, coupe soup; from $25 to **35.00**
Fruit #3697, bowl, divided; oval, from $35 to **45.00**
Fruit #3697, coffee server, casual; from $175 to **200.00**
Fruit #3697, pickle dish, from $25 to **30.00**
Fruit #3697, pitcher, 1-qt, from $65 to **75.00**
Fruit #3697, plate, 11", from $30 to **35.00**
Garden Flower #3700, candy dish, from $65 to **75.00**
Garden Flower #3700, coaster/ashtray, from $15 to **20.00**
Garden Flower #3700, pitcher, ½-pt, from $25 to **30.00**
Garden Flower #3700, plate, 11", from $40 to **50.00**
Garden Flower #3700, sherbet, from $30 to **35.00**
Golden Harvest #3887, casserole, w/lid, 6", from $20 to **25.00**
Golden Harvest #3887, mug, 2-cup, from $35 to **45.00**
Golden Harvest #3887, pitcher, 2-qt, from $50 to **60.00**
Golden Harvest #3887, plate, 10", from $12 to **15.00**
Golden Harvest #3887, sauce boat, from $25 to **30.00**
Harvest #3341, bowl, salad; 10", from $70 to **80.00**
Harvest #3341, carafe, w/stopper, from #100 to **135.00**
Harvest #3341, plate, chop; 14½", from $90 to **115.00**
Harvest #3341, plate, 8", from $20 to **25.00**
Harvest #3341, shakers, pr, from $20 to **25.00**
Magnolia #3870, bread tray, from $30 to **40.00**
Magnolia #3870, coffee carafe, shape #2000, from $150 to **200.00**
Magnolia #3870, coffeepot, 8-cup, from $50 to **75.00**
Magnolia #3870, mug, coffee; from $20 to **25.00**
Magnolia #3870, plate, 9", from $10 to **12.00**
Magnolia #3870, sugar bowl, ind; from $20 to **25.00**
Norma #3364, bowl lug soup; w/lid, 5", from $25 to....................**35.00**

Norma #3364, plate, chop; 14½", from $100 to............................125.00
Norma #3364, plate, 10", from $35 to 40.00
Norma #3364, shakers, pr, from $20 to..30.00
Orchard Song #5110, cake stand, from $10 to................................15.00
Orchard Song #5110, gravy boat, from $10 to 15.00
Orchard Song #5110, mug, stacking; from $30 to..........................35.00
Orchard Song #5110, relish dish, from $20 to................................25.00
Ranger #3304, bowl, fruit; from $110 to.......................................145.00
Ranger #3304, butter chip, from $40 to..50.00
Ranger #3304, carafe, w/hdl, from $900 to 1,000.00
Ranger #3304, plate, chop; 12½", from $550 to 600.00
Ranger #3304, plate, 9", from $200 to..225.00
Ranger #3304, teapot, from $850 to..950.00
Sculptured Fruit #5179, bowl, fruit; from $8 to..............................10.00
Sculptured Fruit #5179, pitcher, plain, 1-pt, from $20 to 25.00
Sculptured Fruit #5179, plate, 10", from $10 to.............................15.00
Sculptured Fruit #5179, teapot, plain, 4-cup, from $25 to..............30.00
Star Flower #3864, ashtray, rectangular, from $20 to 25.00
Star Flower #3864, butter dish, from $30 to...................................40.00
Star Flower #3864, egg cup, from $10 to 15.00
Star Flower #3864, plate, 11", from $25 to.....................................30.00
Sunflower #3340, bowl, salad; extra deep, 10", from $85 to........100.00
Sunflower #3340, cup & saucer, from $20 to...................................23.00
Sunflower #3340, plate, 9", from $25 to 35.00
Sunflower #3340, teapot, from $120 to 145.00
Tiger Lily #3965, bowl, coupe soup; from $25 to............................30.00
Tiger Lily #3965, creamer, from $15 to...20.00
Tiger Lily #3965, gravy boat, from $25 to.......................................35.00
Tiger Lily #3965, plate, 9", from $20 to..25.00
Tiger Lily #3965, tray for cruets, from $25 to 35.00
Town & Country #5287, baking dish, bl, 7x10", from $75 to 90.00
Town & Country #5287, cake stand/chip & dip, brn, 12½" dia, $50 to..65.00
Town & Country #5287, flowerpot, bl, 5", from $35 to................40.00
Town & Country #5287, mug, stacking; bl, from $50 to 55.00
Town & Country #5287, plate, blk or crimson, 6", from $15 to....20.00
Town & Country #5287, tidbit, blk or crimson, 10⅝", from $20 to...25.00
Town & Country #5287, tray, bl, oval, 8¼", from $25 to.............35.00
Town & Country #5287, vase, honey or yel, #4050, 8", from $25 to...35.00
Town & Country #5287, wall pocket, bl, from $80 to...................95.00
Tulip #3365, plate, chop; 12½", from $85 to 100.00
Tulip #3365, plate, 9", from $25 to 30.00
Tulip #3365, teacup, from $10 to 15.00
Tulip #3365, teapot, from $125 to 150.00
Wild Rose #3929, bowl, vegetable; w/lid, 8", from $75 to 85.00
Wild Rose #3929, coffeepot, 8-cup, from $85 to...........................100.00
Wild Rose #3929, pepper mill, wood top, from $55 to 75.00
Wild Rose #3929, pitcher, 2-qt, from $75 to.................................100.00
Yellow Tulip #3637, casserole, skillet shape, 8", from $30 to.........35.00
Yellow Tulip #3637, gravy boat & underplate, from $35 to...........40.00
Yellow Tulip #3637, pitcher, 1-pt, from $25 to...............................30.00
Yellow Tulip #3637, plate, 8", from $10 to 15.00
Yellow Tulip #3637, tidbit, 10", from $10 to 15.00

Stangl Birds and Animals

The Stangl company introduced their line of ceramic birds in 1940, taking advantage of an import market crippled by the onset of WWII. The figures were an immediate success. Additional employees were hired, and eventually sixty decorators worked at the plant itself, with the overflow contracted out to individuals in private homes. After the war when import trade once again saturated the market, Stangl curtailed their own production but continued to make the birds and animals on a limited basis as late as 1978.

Nearly all the birds were marked. A four-digit number was used to identify the species, and most pieces were signed by the decorator. An 'F' indicates a bird that was decorated at the Flemington plant. Our advisors for this category are Nancy and Robert Perzel, Popkorn Antiques. (See the Directory under New Jersey.) Recommended reference books are listed in the Stangl category.

Animals

#3178F, Percheron, white with black overglaze, 3", $150.00.

#1076, Piggy bank, sponged wht, not cvd, Early American Tulip..100.00
#1076, Piggy bank, Terre Rose, brushed/hand cvd, Early American Tulip...150.00
#3178A Elkhound, wht w/blk overglaze, 3½" 150.00
#3178G, Elephant, wht w/blk overglaze, 2½" 150.00
#3178H, Squirrel, wht w/blk overglaze, 3½" 175.00
#3178J, Gazelle, wht w/blk overglaze, 3½".................................150.00
#3243, Wire-Haired Terrier, 3¼"..350.00
#3244, Draft Horse, 3"..150.00
#3245, Rabbit, 2"..275.00
#3246, Buffalo, 2½"..350.00
#3247, Gazelle, 3¾"...400.00
#3248, Giraffe, 2½"...650.00
#3249, Elephant, Antique Gold, 5" 100.00
#3249, Elephant, 3"...300.00
#3277, Colt, 5"..1,650.00
#3278, Goat, 5"..1,700.00
#3279, Calf, 3½"...900.00
#3280, Dog, sitting, 5¼"..400.00
#3430, Duck, 22"...8,250.00
Burro, blk w/wht overglaze, 3¼"..150.00
Cat, Siamese, Seal Point, sitting, decor, 8½"...............................550.00
Cat, sitting, Granada Gold, 8½"..275.00

Birds

#3250A, Duck, standing, 3¼"..100.00
#3250B, Duck, preening, 3¼" 85.00
#3250D, Duck, grazing, 3¾"...85.00
#3250F, Duck, quacking, 3¼"...85.00
#3273, Rooster, 5¾"...750.00
#3274, Penguin, 6" 500.00
#3275, Turkey, 3½" 475.00
#3276D, Bluebirds (pr), 8½"...160.00
#3281, Duck, mother, 6"..650.00
#3285, Rooster, early, 4½"..120.00
#3286, Hen, late, 3¼"..75.00
#3400, Lovebird, old version, 4"..115.00
#3400, Lovebird, revised, 4"...80.00
#3401, Wren, dk brn, revised, 3½" 50.00
#3401D, Wrens (pr), old version...675.00
#3401D, Wrens (pr), revised version...100.00
#3402, Oriole, beak down, 3½" 125.00

#3402, Oriole, revised, 3¼" 45.00
#3402D, Orioles (pr), revised, w/leaves, 5½" 100.00
#3404D, Lovebirds (pr), kissing, old version, 4½" 400.00
#3405, Cockatoo, 6" 55.00
#3405D, Cockatoos (pr), revised, 9½" 125.00
#3406, Kingfisher, teal, 3½" 90.00
#3406D, Kingfishers (pr), bl, 5" 175.00
#3407, Owl, 5½x2½" 400.00
#3408, Bird of Paradise, 5½" 100.00
#3409D, Redstarts (pr), 9" 165.00
#3431, Duck, standing, grayish wht w/blk spots 1,100.00
#3432, Duck, running, brn 700.00
#3433, Rooster, natural colors, 16", minimum value 8,000.00
#3443, Duck, flying, gray, 9" 250.00
#3443, Duck, flying, teal, 9½x12" 250.00
#3444, Cardinal, female 200.00
#3444, Cardinal, glossy pk, revised, 7" 75.00
#3445, Rooster, gray, 10" 275.00
#3446, Hen, yel, 7" 165.00
#3447, Prothonotary Warbler 60.00
#3448, Blue-Headed Vireo, 4¼" 65.00
#3449, Paroquet, 5½" 175.00
#3450, Passenger Pigeon, 9x18" 1,700.00
#3451, Willow Ptarmigan 3,300.00
#3452, Painted Bunting, 5" 85.00
#3453, Mountain Bluebird, 6⅛" 2,000.00
#3454, Key West Quail Dove, single wing up, 10" 235.00
#3454, Key West Quail Dove, wings up, natural colors ...1,600.00
#3455, Shoveler Duck, 12¼x14" 1,750.00
#3457, Chinese Pheasant, walking, 7¼x15" 3,500.00
#3458, Quail, 7½" 2,000.00
#3459, Fish Hawk 9,300.00
#3491, Hen Pheasant, 6¼x11" 175.00
#3492, Cock Pheasant 185.00
#3518D, White-Crowned Pigeons (pr), bl w/wht heads, 8x14" ..1,050.00
#3580, Cockatoo, med, 8⅞" 140.00
#3580, Cockatoo, wht matt, med 550.00
#3581, Chickadees, brn/wht, group of 3, 5½x8½" 150.00
#3582D, Parakeets (pr), bl, 7" 250.00
#3582D, Parakeets (pr), gr, 7" 235.00
#3583, Parula Warbler, 4¼" 45.00
#3584, Cockatoo, sgn Jacob, lg, 11⅜" 275.00
#3584, Cockatoo, wht matt, lg 1,000.00
#3585, Rufous Hummingbird, 3" 90.00
#3586, Pheasant (Della Ware), natural colors 1,800.00
#3586, Pheasant (Della Ware), Terra Rose, gr 700.00
#3589, Indigo Bunting, 3½" 70.00
#3590, Carolina Wren, 4½" 170.00
#3591, Brewer's Blackbird, 3½" 170.00
#3592, Titmouse, 3" 50.00
#3593, Nuthatch, 2½" 70.00
#3594, Red-Faced Warbler, 3" 100.00
#3595, Bobolink, 4¾" 160.00
#3596, Gray Cardinal, 5" 75.00
#3597, Wilson Warbler, yel & blk, 3" 50.00
#3598, Kentucky Warbler, 3" 45.00
#3599D, Hummingbirds (pr) 300.00
#3626, Broadtail Hummingbird, bl flower 160.00
#3627, Rivoli Hummingbird, pk flower, 6" 160.00
#3628, Rieffer's Hummingbird 150.00
#3629, Broadbill Hummingbird, 4½" 150.00
#3634, Allen Hummingbird, 3½" 100.00
#3635, Gold Finches (group) 185.00
#3715, Blue Jay, w/peanut, Fulper blk/bl glaze 2,100.00

#3715, Blue Jay, w/peanut, 10¼" 700.00
#3716, Blue Jay, w/leaf, 10¼" 650.00
#3717, Blue Jays (pr) 3,500.00
#3746, Canary (right), rose flower, 6¼" 250.00
#3747, Canary (left), bl flower, 6¼" 250.00
#3749, Western Tanager, red matt, 4¾" 425.00
#3750, Scarlet Tanager, 8½" 425.00
#3750D, Western Tanagers (pr), red matt, 8" 550.00
#3751, Red-Headed Woodpecker, glossy pk, 6¼" 350.00
#3751, Red-Headed Woodpecker, red matt, 6¼" 475.00
#3752D, Red-Headed Woodpeckers (pr), glossy pk, 7¼" ...500.00
#3754, White-Wing Crossbill (single) 4,000.00
#3754D, White-Wing Crossbills (pr), glossy pk, 9x8" 500.00
#3755, Audubon Warbler, pk flower, 4¼" 400.00
#3757, Scissor-Tailed Flycatcher, 11" 1,000.00
#3758, Magpie-Jay, 10¾" 1,500.00
#3810, Black-Throated Warbler, 3½" 165.00
#3811, Chestnut Chickadee, 5" 135.00
#3812, Chestnut Warbler, 4½" 150.00
#3813, Crested Goldfinch, 5" 150.00
#3814, Townsend Warbler, 3" 165.00
#3815, Western Bluebird, 7" 450.00
#3848, Golden-Crowned Kinglet, 4¼" 100.00
#3850, Western Warbler, 4" 160.00
#3851, Red-Breasted Nuthatch, 3¾" 100.00
#3852, Cliff Swallow, 3½" 145.00
#3853, Golden-Crowned Kinglets, 5½x5" 750.00
#3868, Summer Tanager, 4" 800.00
#3921, Yellow-Headed Verdin, 4½" 1,350.00
#3922, European Goldfinch 1,300.00
#3923, Vermillion Fly-Catcher, 5¾" 2,450.00
#3924, Yellow Throat, 6" 700.00
#3925, Magnolia Warbler 2,800.00
Stangl Bird dealer sign 1,500.00

Stanley Tools

The Stanley company was founded in Connecticut in 1854, and over the years has absorbed more than a score of tool companies already in existence. By the second decade of the twentieth century, having long since solidified their position as *the* source for tools of the highest grade, the company enjoyed worldwide prestige. Through both World Wars, they were recognized as one of the nation's premier producers of wartime goods. Industrial arts classes introduced baby boomers to Stanley tools and provided yet another impetus to expansion and recognition. Overall, the company's growth and development has kept an easy pace along with the economy of the nation, and it continues today as a leader in the field of tool production.

Three factors to consider when evaluating a tool are these: age, completeness, and condition. One of their earliest trademarks (1854 – 1857) is 'A. Stanley,' found only on rulers. In the early '20s, their now-familiar 'sweetheart' trademark, the letters SW and a heart shape within the confines of a modified rectangle, was adopted. They continued to use this trademark until it was discontinued in 1936. Many other variations were used as well, some of which contain a patent date. A study of these marks will help you determine the age of your tools. Condition is extremely important, and though a light cleaning is acceptable, you should never attempt to 'restore' a tool by sanding, repainting, or replacing parts that may be damaged or missing. Unless noted otherwise in the description lines, our values are for tools in average, 'as found' condition, ranging from very good to excellent. Note: Any common number $20.00 rule with the A. Stanley trademark is easily worth $500.00 plus!

Angle divider, #30, sweetheart logo, ca 1930s, VG **100.00**
Angle divider, #31, rosewood body, EX NP finish, rare, VG **195.00**
Bit extension, #180, 24", EX **25.00**
Brace, #921-10, cocobolo head & hdl, ca 1950s, 10" sweep, NM .**95.00**
Brace, #923-10, cocobolo pad & hdl, NM NP, 10" sweep **50.00**
Brace, #945A-10, maroon plastic hdl, NM NP, 10" sweep **20.00**
Catalog, #34, April 1939, NM **75.00**
Catalog, #134, 1934, EX+ **295.00**
Catalog, pocket; 1927, 55-pg, G **15.00**
Chisel, bevel edge butt; #161, 1½", partial decal on hdl, VG **65.00**
Chisel, bevel edge butt; #750, mk...Made in USA, 9¼", EX.......**35.00**
Chisel, bevel edge firmer; #720, long hdl, 13¼", G+.....................**45.00**
Chisel, bevel edge firmer; #720, shorter hdl, 10¾", VG..............**35.00**
Chisel #60, Stanloid hdl, set of 7, G+ **115.00**
Cutting iron, #8, 2⅝x8", unused...**55.00**
Doweling jig, #59, 6 guides, MIB **50.00**
Drill, breast; #743, Universal chuck, steel fr w/built-in level, VG..**65.00**
Gauge, marking & mortising; #161, brass plate, VG...................**65.00**
Gauge, marking; #61, beech, sweetheart logo, 1930s, EX............**15.00**
Gauge, marking; #1291 Defiance, beech, 1950s, EX+ **15.00**
Gauge, panel; #85½, rosewood, scuffed, EX..........................**125.00**
Gauge; butt; #94, sweetheart logo, EX NP, EX.........................**22.00**
Hammer, claw; bell face, no number (like #203), 7-oz, VG **25.00**
Hammer, tack; #601, decal, 5-oz, NM **40.00**
Hammer, upholsterer's magnetic; #602, 7-oz, EX **40.00**
Hand beader, #66, NM NP, ca 1920, NMIB..............................**175.00**
Jointer gauge (fence); #386, welded, 75% nickel, rpl screw, G- **75.00**
Level, oil burner; #38, Made in USA trademark, 6", EX **35.00**
Plane, #3, rosewood hdl, corrugated bottom, 1930s type, VG.....**135.00**
Plane, #4C, dk patina, NM japanning, corrugated bottom, 1970s, VG........**50.00**
Plane, #40, rosewood hdl & knob, 85% japanning, G+ **95.00**
Plane, #60½, some pitting, G **50.00**
Plane, #112, rnf/rstr pnt, rpl blade, G+ **275.00**
Plane, #140, 70% nickel, usable blade, G **150.00**
Plane, Bedrock #603 type 6, flat top side, rosewood hdl, EX.......**275.00**
Plane, Bedrock #604 type 6, rosewood hdl, ca 1912-22, EX........**245.00**
Plane, Bedrock #604 type 8, rosewood hdl, ca 1930, EX **275.00**
Plane, Bedrock #604½, 1930s, 10".......................................**745.00**
Plane, Bedrock #604½ type 6, rosewood hdl, orig decal, EX+ **575.00**
Plane, Bedrock #605, type 10, rosewood hdl, 95% japanning, late, NM..**150.00**
Plane, block; #62, low angle, 14", EX....................................**495.00**
Plane, bull-nose rabbet; #90, some tarnish, VG **95.00**
Plane, fore; #606 Bedrock, Pat 92, 80% japanning, VG..............**195.00**
Plane, jack; #5¼C, VG japanning...**105.00**
Plane, jack; #5½C, type 11, rpt rosewood, corrugated bottom, G+....**85.00**
Plane, jack; #605 Bedrock type 9, 90% japanning, rosewood knob, EX.**245.00**
Plane, jack; #605C Bedrock type 6, EX patina, 90% japanning, VG ...**225.00**
Plane, jointer; #607 Bedrock, 95% japanning, VG **250.00**
Plane, jointer; #607C Bedrock, 90% japanning, VG...................**295.00**
Plane, jointer; #608C Bedrock, rnd side, 90% japanning, VG....**295.00**

Plumb and level, rosewood, brass bound, ca 1859 – 1879, 20", from $250.00 to $500.00. (Photo courtesy The Tool Merchant)

Plumb & level, #36G, CI, trapezoidal cutouts, grooved, NM japanning...**75.00**
Rule, caliper; #136, boxwood w/brass caliper, Made in USA, 4"...**20.00**
Rule, folding; #62, 4-fold, brass-bound boxwood, VG **25.00**
Scraper, #81, 20% nickel, rpl rosewood & blade, G.....................**80.00**

Screwdriver, offset ratchet; Yankee #3400, 4" overall, EX **25.00**
Screwdriver bit, Stanley #26, Made in USA, 3⁄16", EX **6.00**
Sharpener, dowel; #22, USA logo, up to ¾", EX.......................**30.00**
Spoke shave, #151, adjustable, USA mk on cutter, EX japanning .**40.00**
Spoke shave, #51, 99% japanning, EX **20.00**
Spoke shave, #55, curved hdls, 95% japanning, G+ **55.00**
Spoke shave, #63, USA logo, 80% japanning, G+ **25.00**
Spoke shave, #67 universal, V tradmk, 99% NP, EX+ **190.00**
Spoke shave, dbl; #60, sweetheart logo, VG **55.00**
Square, sliding T bevel, #25, rosewood hdl, sweetheart logo, VG.**85.00**
Square, sliding T bevel, Stanley Defiance, NM finish **22.00**
Square, try; #12, CI, early design, no Pat mk, 6" **35.00**
Square, try; #12 Improved, NP CI, mk hdl, VG..........................**50.00**
Square, Try; #21, NP CI, slot in blade, VG **45.00**
Trammel, #2, brass, X-hatching, med-sz, EX **100.00**

Statue of Liberty

Long before she began greeting immigrants in 1886, the Statue of Liberty was being honored by craftsmen both here and abroad. Her likeness was etched on blades of the finest straight razors from England, captured in finely detailed busts sold as souvenirs to Paris fairgoers in 1878, and presented on colorfully lithographed trade cards (usually satirical) to American shoppers. Perhaps no other object has been represented in more forms or with such frequency as the universal symbol of America. Liberty's keepsakes are also universally accessible. Delightful souvenir models created in 1885 to raise funds for Liberty's pedestal are frequently found at flea markets, while earlier French bronze and terra cotta Liberties have been auctioned for over $100,000.00. Some collectors hunt for the countless forms of nineteenth-century Liberty memorabilia, while many collections were begun in anticipation of the 1986 Centennial with concentration on modern depictions. Our advisor for this category is Mike Brooks; he is listed in the Directory under California.

Belt buckle, cut-out Liberty half dollar w/gold & silver trim, M ...**62.50**
Book, Inauguration of the Statue of Liberty, 1887 ....**60.00**
Booklet, Rays From Liberty's Torch, 1890 ....**30.00**
Bookmark, Bartholdi souvenir & calendar, fabric, 1887 ....**50.00**
Bookmark, 1986 Centennial commemorative, Eaglegraphs...MI, M ..**15.00**
Bottle, seltzer; etched Liberty, A Doeink, Liberty, NY.................**35.00**
Box, Liberty on lid, Limoges, star closure, 3x1½" **65.00**
Brooch, hand holding torch, mk Staret, 1940s (watch for repros) ..**800.00**
Card, admission to inauguration, 1886 ....**70.00**
Cigar box label, Victory Day, WWII..**6.00**
Clock/lamp, figural, flame bulb, copper-tone pot metal, 1940s, 16" ..**165.00**
Container, Yourex Silver Saver, rnd, cb, ca 1930..........................**27.00**
Cup, sterling, Windsor Club, 1907, 2" **22.00**
Doll, Barbie, in red/wht/bl w/crown & torch, FAO Schwarz, 1996, MIB.**125.00**
Flyer, Statue of Liberty steamboat excursions, 1890s **25.00**
Harper's Weekly, various litho prints, 1880s, ea, from $10 to........**25.00**
Invitation to statue's unveiling, 1886, G-....................................**200.00**
Lamp, figural, bronze-tone metal, electric, 11"............................**130.00**
Letter, teen to military father re: parade on Broadway, 1886........**95.00**
Lighter, ST Dupont Statue of Liberty Line 2, ltd ed of 350, MIB..**785.00**
Match safe, silver w/emb Liberty & scrolls, Fr, 2x1½"................**350.00**
Medal, central Valley Nat'l Bank..**18.00**
Napkin holder, sterling..**15.00**
Pennant, felt, 1930s...**25.00**
Pin, enamel, 77th Div, WWI **12.00**
Pipe, glazed clay, 1880s...**90.00**
Plates, various makers, 1980s, ea, from $10 to.............................**20.00**
Pocket watch, Elgin, 1890s **175.00**
Pocket watch, 1986 commemorative limited edition, quartz.........**50.00**

Postcard, real photo w/weight & measurements of monument, 1918 postmk ..35.00
Poster, DeLand, WWI 150.00
Radio speaker stand, wht metal casting, Palcone, 17" 175.00
Reverse painting on glass, in plaster fr w/orig pnt, 25x19", EX 75.00
Runner, damask, ca 1890..85.00
Sampler, Liberty & God Bless America, mc on wht linen, 25x18" in fr..75.00
Scarf, head of Liberty, red/wht/bl, Hermes, 35" sq, NM...............150.00
Scissors, emb metal, Liberty 1 side/Woolworth building on reverse, 6"..55.00
Smoke stand/lamp, Liberty at base, torch lights up, 1940s, 27", EX ..150.00
Smoking stand, figure w/tray on stepped base, patinated metal, 28"..250.00
Snow dome, figural, Atlas Crystal Works, 1920s.............................55.00
Spoon, emb Liberty in hdl, plain bowl, silver, mk Tiffany, 6"........55.00
Statue, Am Committee, gaslight, 1885, extremely rare, 36" 8,000.00
Statue, hand cvd, Mexico, 15" 20.00
Statue, hand-cvd wood (papier-mâché mold), Philippines, 1920s..575.00
Statue, Wenck perfume, 1908..325.00
Statue, 1st commercial status by Follmer, June 18, 1885, 21" ..5,000.00
Studio portrait, Bartholdi, Falk Studio NY, 1880s 200.00
Ticket, Manhattan Day, Columbian Exposition, 1893.....................15.00
Ticket, souvenir of Gauthier et Cie (Liberty foundry), 1883, lg..105.00
Trade card, satirical, A&C Hams, 1880s 70.00
Vase, frosted Liberty hand, Gillinder, 1876 Centennial.................70.00
Vase, Liberty reserve on 7mm WWI shell casing, 13" 190.00

Steamship Collectibles

For centuries, ocean-going vessels with their venturesome officers and crews were the catalyst that changed the unknown aspects of our world to the known. Changing economic conditions, unfortunately, have now placed the North American shipping industry in the same jeopardy as the American passenger train. They are becoming a memory. The surge of interest in railroad collectibles and the railroad-related steamship lines has lead collectors to examine the whole spectrum of steamship collectibles.

Reproduction (sometimes called 'replica') and fantasy dinnerware has been creeping into the steamship dinnerware collecting field. Some of the replica ware is quite well done so one should practice caution and... 'Know Thy Dealer.' Our advisor for this category is Lila Shrader; she is listed in the Directory under California. We recommend *Restaurant China, Volumes 1* and *2*, by Barbara Conroy (Collector Books).

Key:
BS — back stamped
COA — Cetificate of Authenticity
NBS — no back stamp
SM — side logo
SM — side mark
TL — top logo
TM — top mark

Dining Salon

Tray, corn; Great Northern Pacific Steamship, Pacific Coast pattern, top logo, 1916, 10¼", from $85.00 to $135.00. (Photo courtesy Barbara J. Conroy)

Bowl, Eastern SS Lines, Eastern Blue, TL, NBS, 4¼"...................25.00
Bowl, Pure Oil SS Co, cobalt TM logo, Jackson China, 1920s, 4¾"..44.00
Butter pat, Admiral Line, Alexander, TL house flag, Bauscher, 3⅛".56.00
Butter pat, Hamburg Am Line, TL house flag w/HAPAG, 3⅛"....48.00
Carafe, SS United States Lines, Thermos mfg, orig stopper, SL, 9"...135.00
Creamer, Luckenbach SS Co, SM w/swallowtail pennant, no hdl, 2¾"..135.00
Creamer, NordDeutscherLloyd, Bremen, SL SP, 1900s, 4" 68.00
Creamer, US Shipping Board, Granite State, SL, no hdl, 3".........98.00
Cup & saucer, Chinoise, Andrea Doria, Ginori, SL on cup........355.00
Cup & saucer, demi; Wisteria, White Star 650.00
Dish, White Star, Elkington, silver, oval, ornate rim, 9½x13"....412.00
Egg cup, White Star, Wisteria, brn w/gold, 2⅛" 1,515.00
Fork, cocktail; Moore-McCormick, SP by Oneida, TM, 5¾"..........4.00
Glass, liqueur; Holland Am w/dmn NASM SL, 3⅜" 18.00
Glass, wine; RMS Titanic REPLICA w/COA by Stuart, SL, 9½", pr..100.00
Knife, dinner; Cunard, chased holly & berries on blade, TL, 8" ..55.00
Menu, Andrea Doria, cover art by Pollomi, 1954, opens to 9x25" ..45.00
Menu, Matson, SS Lurline, various island scenes, from $20 to 32.00
Pitcher, Allan Line, floral décor, SL, Doulton, 5"......................214.00
Pitcher, Ulster SS Co, company's garter SL w/bl stripe, 4" 25.00
Plate, Goodrich SS Lines, TM w/boxed logo, 6½" 47.00
Plate, Internat'l Mercantile Marine's Panama Pacific w/TL, 9½" .44.00
Plate, White Star Lines, Celtic, TL, NBS, 9" 690.00
Platter, Great Northern Pacific..., Pacific Coast, house flag TM, 9x6" ..138.00
Relish dish, North German Lloyd, wht china w/red TL in wreath, 8½x5" ..46.00
Sugar bowl, Luckenbach SS, SM w/swallowtail pennant, w/lid, 3½" 48.00
Sugar tongs, NordDeutscherLloyd, silver, Wilkins Bremen, TM, 4½" ..25.00

Miscellaneous

Ashtray, Matson w/red M on wht ground, glass, 4½" dia...............30.00
Ashtray w/matchbox holder, Red Star Line, TL, 5¼" dia 298.00
Badge, crewman's; RMS Carpathia, enamel on brass, 1" dia 965.00
Blanket, stateroom; SS United States, wool, TL, 60x84", from $100 to .135.00
Book, Wreck...SS Titanic, US Senate...hearing, 1912, 1,100-pg......2,250.00
Brochure, North German Lloyd Bremen Kronprinzessin Cecile, 1912 ..355.00
Brochure, Peerless Marine Motors, cardstock cover, photos, 16-pg, 6x9"..70.00
Brochure, SS Leviathan, deck plans/fares/etc, 1931, opens to 9x31" ..200.00
Brochure, White Star, Olympic, Homeric & Majestic, 1920s, 24-pg..250.00
Button, Atlantic Refining SS Co, silver-tone w/Xd arrows logo, ⅞" 13.00
Button, Occidental & Oriental, gold-tone w/O/O house flag, 1" ..28.00
Cigarette tin, White Star Line ship litho, striker, 3x4¼", $300 to ..485.00
Clock, Seth Thomas, outside bell, hinged bezel..............................400.00
Framed art, SS United States Lines, circus scene, Koff, 1984, 23x39"..1,200.00
Hat band ribbon, sailor's; NordDeutscherLloyd woven, 1913, 37x1¼"....100.00
Juice machine, Sunkist, SS United States Lines, TM, electric....230.00
Life jacket, Normandie, stenciled on bk: Normandie/LaHavre ...355.00
Luggage label, Hamburg Am SS, shows Bremen & Europa, 2"......10.00
Match holder/striker, Red Star Line, stoneware, SL, conical, 4" dia...165.00
Matchbook, Alaska SS, ea match a mini totem pole, unused..........8.00
Model, builder's; Farrell Line's Austral Endurance, wood, 1/16"=1' ..2,950.00
Pass, annual; Bangor & Aroostook SS Co, Vail, Supt B&ARR, 1897..80.00
Passenger list, United States Lines, Geo Washington, 1925, 20-pg 26.00
Pennant, Canadian Pacific's Empress of France, triangular, 16¼" .46.00
Photo, Lyman T Smith steamer grounded in Great Lakes, 8x10" .40.00
Playing cards, Cunard, 1900s, wide, 52+Joker+1 in orig case......115.00
Playing cards, Moore-McCormick, 1958, dbl deck, w/case 10.00
Postcard, Pacific Steam Navigation, Orizaba on Australian reef, 1905 ..30.00
Postcard, SS Cedric Steamship, woven in silk, ca 1910.................80.00
Poster, French Line, SS Columbie by Edoard Collin, 1940s, 39x21".750.00
Soap, Alaska SS Line printed on wrapper, complementary, 2⅜x1½" 8.00
Souvenir compact, Cunard's RMS Carinthia III scene, enamel on metal...77.00
Souvenir dish, Goodrich SS Lines, Columbus portrait on cobalt..47.00
Souvenir doll, RMS Franconia on sailor doll's cap, Wellings, 12".65.00

Souvenir napkin ring, Laconia, enamel SL on brass, 1920s, 1½"...**180.00**
Souvenir teaspoon, Cleveland & Buffalo Transit, sterling, 5" ...**57.00**
Ticket, Europa, Great Lakes steamer, 1858, complementary **200.00**
Tray, French Line's LaProvence, mc litho on metal, 39x27" **355.00**
View folder, faux leather, Fall River SS, 1890, folds out to 6'........**28.00**

Steins

Steins have been made from pottery, pewter, glass, stoneware, and porcelain, from very small up to the four-liter size. They may be decorated by etching, in-mold relief, decals, and occasionally they may be hand painted. Some porcelain steins have lithophane bases. Collectors often specialize in a particular type — faience, regimental, or figural, for example — while others limit themselves to the products of only one manufacturer. See also Mettlach.

Key:
L — liter   tl — thumb lift
lith — lithophane

Pottery, etched Nach des... (After the day's pains, I praise a cool drink), inlaid lid, repaired thumb lift, J. W. Remy, five-liter, $1,600.00. (Photo courtesy Andre Ammelounx)

Character, alligator, porc, E Bohne & Sohne, .5L **575.00**
Character, artillery shell, porc, custom decor, inlaid lid, .5L **660.00**
Character, Black student, inlaid lid, lith, .5L **485.00**
Character, bull, pottery, pottery lid, #1453, .5L, NM **575.00**
Character, Bustle Lady, stoneware, pewter lid, Hauber & Reuther, .5L ...**800.00**
Character, Chinese man, porc, inlaid lid, Schierholz, rpr, .5L......**575.00**
Character, coffee bag, Kathreiner's Kneiff Malz Kaffee, porc, .5L..**6,325.00**
Character, fireman, stoneware, inlaid lid, .5L **635.00**
Character, hobo, porc, E Bohne & Sohne, .5L **4,000.00**
Character, Munich child, pottery, pottery lid, ⅛-L.....................**285.00**
Character, Nurnberg tower, bl salt glaze, pewter lid, .5L **300.00**
Character, Nurnberg tower, pottery, color, pewter lid, #131, .5L..**430.00**
Character, sailor, pottery, pottery lid, #1821, .5L, NM **465.00**
Character, skull on book, porc, pewter rpr, Schierholz, .5L.........**435.00**
Character, soldier, stoneware, inlaid lid, LB&C, .5L................**1,725.00**
Faience, HP: horse & floral, pewter lid dtd 1811, Bayreuth, 1L..**2,400.00**
Faience, HP: repeating design, 1847 pewter lid, 1L **375.00**
Glass, blown, amber, HP Munich child w/stein, pewter lid, .5L..**400.00**
Glass, blown, amber, silver band w/skull plate/antlers/teeth, 1L..**3,450.00**
Glass, blown, amber w/pewter o/l faces, serpent finial, 1L...........**750.00**
Glass, blown, clear, fluted, ornate pewter lid w/fox, 1L **575.00**
Glass, blown, clear w/bl o/l, cut panels, eng silhouette, .5L.........**660.00**
Glass, blown, clear w/cut design, pewter lid w/fox/duck, .5L.......**750.00**
Glass, blown, clear w/eng instruments, pewter lid, ca 1800, 1L..**1,300.00**
Glass, blown, clear w/HP crest, inlaid lid, ca 1890, .5L..............**200.00**
Glass, blown, clear w/military scene, pewter lid, Ringer, .5L.......**600.00**
Glass, blown, cobalt, pewter lid, ca 1840, .25L **375.00**
Glass, blown, gr w/HP scene of lady w/goblet, inlaid lid, .5L **600.00**

Glass, transfer/HP: auto scene, eng pewter lid, .5L **515.00**
Occupation, coal shoveler, porc, lith, pewter lid, .5L **660.00**
Occupation, relief: miner, pottery, pewter lid, rpr, .5L.................**500.00**
Occupation, transfer/HP: sheepherder, porc, military body, lith, .5L..**450.00**
Occupation, transfer/HP: truck driver, pewter lid, 1939, .5L.......**425.00**
Pewter, relief: 4 ornate scenes, angel ft, pewter lid, 1870s, 1L.....**290.00**
Porc, HP:baseball players, porc inlaid lid w/Latin verse, Delft, .5L ..**3,185.00**
Porc, transfer/HP: Schutzenliesl, pewter lid, .5L **350.00**
Porc, transfer/HP: smoking club, lith, pewter lid, 1903, .5L........**375.00**
Pottery, etch: dwarfs drinking/frog band, Hauber & Reuther #419, .5L..**400.00**
Pottery, etch: fish, pewter lid, Merkelbach & Wicke, .5L...........**350.00**
Pottery, etch: knight caught in cellar, castle body, JWR #954, .5L..**250.00**
Pottery, HP: dbl crest/student society, dtd 1892, pewter lid, .5L..**1,725.00**
Pottery, HP: floral, SP lid w/emb flower, Bonn, .5L **400.00**
Pottery, relief: chicken breeds, Dumler & Brieden #234, .5L **375.00**
Pottery, relief: Germans meeting Romans, pewter lid, #378, .5L.**375.00**
Pottery, relief: Lohengrin opera scene, pewter lid, #390, .5L.......**400.00**
Pottery, relief: monkeys reading books, monkey hdl, #1257, .5L.**460.00**
Pottery, relief: mtns w/hikers, pewter lid, #1264, .5L **375.00**
Pottery, relief: oarsmen/sailboats, buoy inlay lid, #984, .5L **460.00**
Pottery, relief: warriors, Dumier & Breiden #555, 1L...................**350.00**
Regimental, Regt No 121...1904-06, porc, Wurttembert tl, lith, .5L ..**400.00**
Regimental, SM Torpedo...1909-12, eagle tl, stanhope, SP lid, 1L..**1,325.00**
Regimental, SMS Kurfurst...1906-09, porc, eagle tl, .5L **1,495.00**
Regimental, Wurtt Grenadier...Stuttgart 1910-12, porc, roster, .5L...**775.00**
Regimental, 12 CP 4 Magdb...Metz 1903, porc, eagle tl, .5L........**435.00**
Regimental, 3 Komp Kulmer...1910-12, pottery, eagle tl, stanhope, .5L.**700.00**
Regimental, 4 Infantry...Metz 1909-11, porc, roster, lion tl, .5L..**600.00**
Regimental, 5 Battr...Naumburg 1912-14, porc, eagle tl, .5L **600.00**
Regimental, 6 Battr 4 Wurttfeld...1909-11, porc, roster, .5L **575.00**
Regimental, 6 Fahr Battr...Hannover 1911-13, porc, eagle tl, .5L....**835.00**
Regimental, 7 Comp...Morrhingen 1909-11, porc, eagle tl, .5L..**515.00**
Stoneware, etch: wedding scene, inlaid lid, Marzi & Remy #1637, .5L.**350.00**
Stoneware, transfer/HP: boy on toy horse, pewter lid, ⅛-L.........**185.00**
Stoneware, transfer/HP: Munchener Braur Akademie...1900, 1L.**715.00**
Stoneware, transfer/HP: XVI Deutsches...1909, pewter lid, Ringer, .5L..**660.00**
Third Reich, Landes Polizei...1935, pottery, helmet lid, .5L........**550.00**
Third Reich, soldier, stoneware, helmet pewter lid, .5L **700.00**
Third Reich, 16 Batterie..Regt 5 1939, search light, stoneware, .5L ...**1,100.00**
Third Reich, 16 Komp...Sonthofen, machine gun, stoneware, .5L......**700.00**
Third Reich, 17 Komp..., machine gun, stoneware, helmet lid, .5L....**800.00**
Third Reich, 2 Komp...Traunstein 1935/36, machine gun, pottery, .5L..**350.00**

Steuben

Carder Steuben glass was made by the Steuben Glass Works in Corning, New York, while under the direction of Frederick Carder from 1903 to 1932. Perhaps the most popular types of Carder Steuben glass are Gold Aurene which was introduced in 1904 and Blue Aurene, introduced in 1905. Gold and Blue Aurene objects shimmer with the lustrous beauty of their metallic iridescence. Carder also produced other types of 'Aurenes' including red, green, yellow, brown, and decorated, all of which are very rare. Aurene also was cased with Calcite glass. Some pieces had paper labels.

Other types of Carder Steuben include Cluthra, Cintra, Florentia, Rosaline, Ivory, Ivrene, Jades, Verre de Soie; there are many more.

Frederick Carder's leadership of Steuben ended in 1932, and the production of colored glassware soon ceased. Since 1932 the tradition of fine Steuben art glass has been continued in crystal.

In the following listings, examples are signed unless otherwise noted. When no color is mentioned, assume the glass is clear.

Key: ACB — acid cut back

Atomizer, Blue Aurene, intaglio flowers/leaves, unmk, 9¾" **1,050.00**
Basket, Selenium Ruby, silver o/l: vines/lattice/flowers, #455, 15" ..**3,600.00**
Bottle, scent; Blue Aurene, #1414, 7½" **635.00**
Bottle, scent; Blue Aurene, #1455, blk/pk flower stopper, 4¾" .**2,070.00**
Bottle, scent; Bristol Yellow, tall/tapered, pointed stopper, unmk, 8" **525.00**
Bottle, scent; Bristol Yellow w/eng, ped ft, candy-cane stopper, 12" .**2,040.00**
Bottle, scent; Gold Ruby on clear, flame stopper, #1455, squat, 4½" **800.00**
Bottle, scent; Green Jade, pointed alabaster stopper, 4½" **525.00**
Bottle, scent; Green Jade, shouldered, clear twisted stopper, 11¾" ..**345.00**
Bottle, scent; Verre de Soie, belled shape, #2833, 3½" **275.00**
Bowl, ACB Chinese motif, Green Jade on Alabaster, #3103, 4½x13"..**1,700.00**
Bowl, amethyst, folded rim, unmk, 11½" **300.00**
Bowl, Blue Aurene, low, 3-ftd, lt scratches, 10" **425.00**
Bowl, Calcite w/Blue Aurene int, shallow, like #1171, 5" **325.00**
Bowl, Calcite w/Gold Aurene int, ped ft/angle rim, #6170, 2¾x5½" ..**200.00**
Bowl, Calcite w/Gold Aurene int, wide everted rim, #3265, 3x12" **500.00**
Bowl, Gold Aurene, ruffled, #138, 5" **275.00**
Bowl, Gold Aurene, wide/flat rim, like #3074, 1¾x8" **600.00**
Bowl, Gold Aurene on Calcite, F Carder, 2¾x12" **230.00**
Bowl, Gold Aurene/Calcite, #3200, 1910-30s, 3½x10" **265.00**
Bowl, Green Jade, sq, fleur-de-lis mk, 3¾x8" **230.00**
Bowl, Grotesque, dk bl Jade, fan form w/irregular rim, #7535, 6¾" H.**5,250.00**
Bowl, Grotesque, Flemish Blue, #7091, sq, 5x6½" **400.00**
Bowl, Ivory, flared rim, ftd, 3¾x10" **175.00**
Bowl, oval w/6 appl leaves at base, #8091, 6⅛" H......................**325.00**
Bowl, Pomona Green, w/Topaz hdls, fleur-de-lis mk, 15¾" L......**400.00**
Bowl, Verre de Soie, inverted rim, ped ft w/4 in-mold columns, 5x8" ..**350.00**
Candlestick, Aquamarine, vase shape w/hdl, #5146, 4" **375.00**
Candlestick, Blue Aurene, twist stem, saucer base, #686, 8" **925.00**
Candlestick, Cerise Ruby, #5113, 8" **225.00**
Candlesticks, Gold Aurene, twist stem, disk ft, #686, 8", pr **1,850.00**
Candlesticks, Rosaline/Alabaster, twist stems, #686, unmk, 10", pr ..**1,350.00**
Cocktail, cup over air-twist stem, disk base, #7917, 3¾", 12 for .**650.00**
Compote, Amethyst, optic ribs, #6043, 7x7" **225.00**
Compote, Aquamarine, hollow stem, #1331, 4¾x6" **120.00**
Compote, Blue Aurene, swirled bulbous stem, #2604, 6¾x7" .**1,350.00**
Compote, Blue Cintra w/appl blk rim, ped ft, #3179, 6¾" **385.00**
Compote, Gold Aurene, bulbed stem, disk base, #2642, 8" **1,175.00**
Compote, Gold Aurene, shaped bowl w/conforming rim, twist stem, #172..**1,500.00**
Compote, Pomona Green to clear swirls, clear stem, 7x8" **285.00**
Cordial, Gold Aurene w/bl highlights, #2828, 6" **475.00**
Cordial, Oriental Poppy, 5¾x3¼" **635.00**
Creamer & sugar bowl, Topaz w/intaglio flowers, #1759, 3", 4" **200.00**
Donut holder, Green Jade, overturned plate w/twist knob, 5½x9", NM...**460.00**
Figurine, fish, #5501, 2½x4" **150.00**
Figurine, gazell, 6¾" **230.00**
Figurine, rooster, #9074, 10⅛" **350.00**
Goblet, Calcite w/Gold Aurene int, #3116, 6½" **275.00**
Goblet, Celeste Blue bowl & ft, clear stem, F Carder, 6" **180.00**
Goblet, Gold Aurene (strong color), twist stem, #2361, 6".........**600.00**
Goblet, Green Jade, conical w/Alabaster disk ft, #5130, 4⅝" **150.00**
Lamp, ACB Adams pattern, blk on Amethyst, 29", matching faceted finial..**2,000.00**
Lamp, ACB trees/foliage (Honesty), lt/dk Amethyst on Alabaster, 18" .**2,350.00**
Lamp, Purple Moss Agate, multitone swirls, brass mts, #8023, 12"...**3,200.00**
Lamp base, fish w/spiral ribs, Bristol Yellow, on base, 25"...........**325.00**
Luminor, clear sphere w/concentric bubbles, blk light base, 7" ...**350.00**
Mug, Celeste Blue hdl on clear, block-letter mk, 6", NM..............**65.00**
Paperweight, purple flower & bubble set in gr 'pot,' 3½" dia **300.00**
Pear, ivory w/leaf & stem, 3½" **435.00**
Pitcher, water; Green Jade, alabaster hdl, faint ribs, 9¼", EX **240.00**
Plate, clear w/controlled bubbles & red threading, 8¼" **50.00**
Plate, Rouge Flambé #2028, rare, 8½" **7,000.00**

Rose bowl, Verre de Soie, ruffled, #3065, 3½x4" **250.00**
Shakers, Gold Aurene, tall/tapered, unmk, 6¾", pr....................**950.00**
Sherbet, Calcite/Gold Aurene, unmk, 4", +6" undertray **290.00**
Sherbet, Oriental Poppy, pk opal bowl, gr ft & stem, 4¾" **575.00**
Tumbler, Celeste Blue, ribbed, etched fountain scene, 4½", 4 for..**200.00**
Vase, ACB dragons/clouds on blk, 9" **2,150.00**
Vase, ACB flowers/geometrics, Rose Quartz, fleur-de-lis mk, 13" .**2,875.00**
Vase, ACB gazelles on Ivory, Samford pattern, #2683, 10x9" ..**3,250.00**
Vase, ACB overall floral, Rosaline/Alabaster, spherical, unmk, 7"..**1,150.00**
Vase, ACB trees/crane, Mirror Blk on Yellow Jade, aperature, unmk, 10"...**2,200.00**
Vase, Alabaster cylinder on stem, blk dome base, #8388, 9", pr..**765.00**
Vase, Alabaster Green, ribbed, lamp shade form, 5¾"................**525.00**
Vase, Amber, tree-trunk form, fleur-de-lis mk, 6" **230.00**
Vase, Amber w/eng vine band at top, eng clovers at waist, 8¼" .**115.00**
Vase, Amethyst, flared rim, ftd, #938, 5"...................................**200.00**
Vase, Amethyst, slight ribbing, flared top, disk ft, unmk, 9½" **230.00**
Vase, Blue Aurene, bulbous w/raised rim, #2683, 8½" **1,175.00**
Vase, Blue Aurene, flared rim, ribbed, dbl-bulb waist, #7447, 6" ..**1,175.00**
Vase, Blue Aurene, flared rim, swollen w/appl ft, #2776, 6¼".....**475.00**
Vase, Blue Aurene, flared rim, waisted, flared base, #723, 6¼"...**1,295.00**
Vase, Blue Aurene, flared w/swirled ribs, 5½x5¼" **650.00**
Vase, Blue Aurene, gr irid at neck, #1683, 10¾" **1,800.00**
Vase, Blue Aurene, slightly swirled ribs, wide body, unmk, 7".....**725.00**
Vase, Blue Aurene, trumpet form, #2708, 8½" **3,675.00**
Vase, Blue Aurene, 3 appl swirled hdls, squat, ftd, 6" **400.00**
Vase, Blue Aurene, 3 scrolled & scalloped hdls, 10¼x7" **3,200.00**

Vase, Blue Aurene, with hearts and vines decor, decorated neck, 7½", $17,350.00. (Photo courtesy Fontaine's Auctioneers & Appraisers)

Vase, Blue Aurene w/trailing vines, opal int, decor gold neck, 7½" ..**25,875.00**
Vase, Bristol Yellow, Invt T'print, wht threading, 6¼" **90.00**
Vase, Calcite w/Blue Aurene int, ruffled lily form, 6" **3,450.00**
Vase, Celeste Blue, crystal stem, fan form, unmk, 8½" **275.00**
Vase, Celeste Blue, vertical ribs, flared rim, ftd, 6" **175.00**
Vase, Cluthra, Amethyst/wht, bulbous/shouldered, unmk, 8" **800.00**
Vase, Cluthra, gold/ruby/wht, #6862, unmk, 8¼" **1,250.00**
Vase, Cluthra, lt gr/wht, classic form, #2683, 10½" **2,400.00**
Vase, crystal, tree-trunk form, fleur-de-lis mk, 6" **145.00**
Vase, French Blue, 6-sided top w/swirled ribs, 8" **175.00**
Vase, Gold Aurene, cylinder w/thorns, scalloped bl-trim ft, #2741, 8" ...**675.00**
Vase, Gold Aurene, fan form w/4 openings in closed-up rim, #2762, 9"..**1,850.00**
Vase, Gold Aurene, flared rim, shouldered/bulbous, #2683, 8"...**1,175.00**
Vase, Gold Aurene, floriform, #346, 6¼" **750.00**
Vase, Gold Aurene, pk/bl highlights, #2417, broad body, lt wear, 12" ..**1,700.00**
Vase, Gold Aurene, swirling ribs, conical w/disk ft, 12" **1,200.00**
Vase, Gold Aurene, trumpet form w/ruffled rim, #723, Haviland mk, 5"...**750.00**
Vase, Gold Aurene, tube form on disk ft, #2556, 8" **235.00**
Vase, Gold Aurene, 3-stump form, #1744, 6" **780.00**

Vase, Gold Aurene w/red flashes, bl irid ft, 9½" **2,165.00**
Vase, Green Aurene w/Blue Aurene leaves/vines, vasiform neck, #265, 8"....**4,000.00**
Vase, Green Aurene w/lt irid leaves & vines, #550, 3½" **2,950.00**
Vase, Green Cintra w/ACB flowers & trellis, 12" **4,025.00**
Vase, Green Jade, optic ribs, rectangular, #6199, unmk, 9½".......**225.00**
Vase, Green Jade, swirled ribs, fleur-de-lis mk, 6¼" **230.00**
Vase, Green Jade w/ivory M hdls, bulbous w/flared neck, #2939, 12"..**1,850.00**
Vase, Grotesque, gr to clear, ribs, ruffled, clear ft, 11¾" **230.00**
Vase, Grotesque, Ivory, cone form w/pinched corners, label, 9" ..**400.00**
Vase, Grotesque, Ivory, 4 flared ribbed corners, 5⅝x9¼" **260.00**
Vase, Ivrene, optic ribs, flared/ruffled rim, #354, 3¾x6" **125.00**
Vase, pale Amethyst, fan form, 11x9" **230.00**
Vase, Pomona Green, Amethyst stem, fan form w/raised rnd base, 6"...**275.00**
Vase, Pomona Green, swirled, flared ft, 7".........................**85.00**
Vase, Pomona Green, swirled w/Topaz trumpet ft, #6035, 12" **150.00**
Vase, Rosaline, ovoid, 2 appl opal hdls, 7½" **225.00**
Vase, Rosaline w/Alabaster disk ft, tube form, 8¼" **240.00**
Vase, Topaz w/Pomona Green ft, fan form, unmk, 8½" **90.00**
Vase, Tyrian, turq irid w/Blue Aurene hearts/vines, #2785, 5½"...**4,200.00**
Vase, wheel-cut/polished floral on clear, fleur-de-lys mk, bulbous, 5".**90.00**

Stevengraphs

A Stevengraph is a small picture made of woven silk resembling an elaborate ribbon, created by Thomas Stevens in England in the latter half of the 1800s. They were matted and framed by Stevens, usually with his name appearing on the mat or often with the trade announcement on the back of the mat. He also produced silk postcards and bookmarks, all of which have 'Stevens' woven in silk on one of the mitered corners. Anyone wishing to learn more about Stevengraphs is encouraged to contact the Stevengraph Collectors' Association, whose address can be found in the Directory under Clubs, Newsletters, and Catalogs. Unless noted otherwise, assume our values are for examples in excellent condition.

Are You Ready?, EX **300.00**
Called to the Rescue, Heroism at Sea **250.00**
Columbus Leaving Spain, G **225.00**
Coventry, 2 blk & wht scenes, fr, pr **110.00**
Crystal Palace (inside), orig mat, G...........................**385.00**
Death of Nelson, G **195.00**
Declaration of Independence, woven at Columbian Exhibition.**225.00**
Dick Turpin's Last Ride on His Black Bess, Hogarth, VG **150.00**
Finish **150.00**
First Innings, G **325.00**
First Point **80.00**
First Train Built by Geo Stephenson in 1825, 8⅞x11⅝" **150.00**
Full Cry, w/mat **120.00**
God Speed the Plow, G.........................**220.00**
Good Old Days **80.00**
Good Old Days, coach & 4, matted & fr, 7½x10½", M.............**195.00**
Good Old Days, matted & fr, 6⅞x10⅜"................................**140.00**
Grace Darling **200.00**
Kenilworth Castle, orig mat & fr, 15½x22½"......................**175.00**
Lady Godiva Procession **170.00**
Landing of Columbus, NM **250.00**
London & York Mail Coach, 1879 Expo.....................**120.00**
Meet, orig mat, old fr, NM.........................**250.00**
Mersy Tunnel Railway.........................**400.00**
Mrs Cleveland, VG **135.00**
Park in Coventry **75.00**
Present Time, 60 Miles an Hour, from $135 to **160.00**
Queen Victoria Jubilee, 1837-1887, unfr **55.00**
Rescue at Sea, fr, VG **220.00**

Start, matted & fr, 9x12", NM...........................**330.00**
Struggle **80.00**
To the Memory of the Heroic Defenders of Religious Liberty **275.00**
Victoria, Queen of Empire on Which the Sun Never Sets, unfr.**195.00**
Water Jump, fr **225.00**
Wellington & Blugher...........................**300.00**

Miscellaneous

Bookmark, A Wish O May You E'er in Peace Abide..., 11⅜x2⅛" .**50.00**
Bookmark, Behold the Man, blk, fr, G **50.00**
Bookmark, Friend's Blessings **45.00**
Bookmark, Geo Washington, made for Philidelphia Expo, 12x2"..**175.00**
Bookmark, Home Sweet Home **75.00**
Bookmark, Love's Remembrance, VG **75.00**
Bookmark, To My Dear Sister...........................**60.00**
Bookmark, To My Sons, G **40.00**
Postcard, Ann Hathaway's Cottage..........................**40.00**
Postcard, RMS Lusitania, VG **75.00**
Postcard, Shakespeare's Birthday...........................**45.00**

Stevens and Williams

Stevens and Williams glass was produced at the Brierly Hill Glassworks in Stourbridge, England, for nearly a century, beginning in the 1830s. They were credited with being among the first to develop a method of manufacturing a more affordable type of cameo glass. Other lines were also made — silver deposit, alexandrite, and engraved rock crystal, to name but a few. Our advisor for this category is Don Williams; he is listed in the Directory under Missouri.

Cameo

Bottle, scent; allover flowers, umber cut to amber, rnd, 5".......**2,500.00**
Cracker jar, Dolce-Relievo, rose on opal, twist SP hdl/mts, 7" ...**1,000.00**
Vase, grapes/plums, wht on crimson martele, Millward, #6, 1940s, 12"...**2,250.00**
Vase, 4 floral panels, wht on Prussian Blue, stick neck, 10" **6,500.00**

Miscellaneous

Bowl, Osiris, mauve, 5" **1,430.00**
Console bowl, appl cherry/plum branch, opal w/amber ruffle; metal base....**1,150.00**
Decanter, flowers/leaves, gr cut to clear, w/stopper, 10" **2,500.00**
Flask, periwinkle w/intaglio decor, doughnut form, att, 8¼" **650.00**
Lamp base, fine pull-ups, appl sm pk flowers & amber rigaree, 10" ..**800.00**
Nut dish, Swirl, red blends to pk to gold, crimped, bl int, 4", +plate.**1,485.00**
Pitcher, appl floral/leaves, amber/yel/wht on pk/cream, rigaree, 15" ..**2,250.00**
Pitcher, yel/pk opal stripes on clear, ribbed, 6"...........................**225.00**
Plate, Zipper, lt pearl bl, ruffled edge, 7"...........................**75.00**
Rose bowl, Dmn Quilt, deep gr to lt yel MOP, pinched rim, 3" ..**800.00**
Rose bowl, Matsu-no-ke, appl clear branches/ft (3), cased, 4x8"..**785.00**
Vase, MOP Swirl, frost to yel, ovoid w/long concave neck, 7"..**1,150.00**
Vase, Osiris, wht on red-amber, 5½" **1,350.00**
Vase, Peacock Eye (rare), red to wht MOP, pleated incurvate top, 7" **1,600.00**
Vase, rose to pk w/amber cherry-stem hdls & appl fruits & flowers, 20".**2,000.00**

Stickley

Among the leading proponents of the Arts and Crafts Movement, the Stickley brothers — Gustav, Leopold, Charles, Albert, and John George — were at various times and locations separately involved in designing and producing furniture as well as decorative items for the home. (See Arts and Crafts for further information.) The oldest of the five Stickley brothers was Gustav; his work is the most highly regarded of all. He developed the style of furniture referred to as Mission. It was strongly influenced by the type of furnishings found in the Spanish missions of California — utilitarian, squarely built, and simple. It was made most often of oak, and decoration was very limited or non-existent. The work of his brothers display adaptations of many of Gustav's ideas and designs. His factory, the Craftsman Workshop, operated in Eastwood, New York, from the late 1890s until 1915, when he was forced out of business by larger companies who copied his work and sold it at much lower prices. Among his shop marks are the early red decal containing a joiner's compass and the words 'Als Ik Kan,' the branded mark with similar components, and paper labels.

The firm known as Stickley Brothers was located first in Binghamton, New York, and then Grand Rapids, Michigan. Albert and John George made the move to Michigan, leaving Charles in Binghamton (where he and an uncle continued the operation under a different name). After several years John George left the company to rejoin Leopold in New York. (These two later formed their own firm called L. & J.G. Stickley.) The Stickley Brothers Company's early work produced furniture featuring fine inlay work, decorative cutouts, and leaned strongly toward a style of Arts and Crafts with an English influence. It was tagged with a paper label 'Made by Stickley Brothers, Grand Rapids,' or with a brass plate or decal with the words 'Quaint Furniture,' an English term chosen to refer to their product. In addition to furniture, they made metal accessories as well.

The workshops of the L. & J.G. Stickley Company first operated under the name 'Onondaga Shops.' Located in Fayetteville, New York, their designs were often all but copies of Gustav's work. Their products were well made and marketed, and their business was very successful. Their decal labels contained all or a combination of the words 'Handcraft' or 'Onondaga Shops,' along with the brothers' initials and last name. The firm continues in business today. Our advisor for this category is Bruce Austin; he is listed in the Directory under New York. Note: When only one dimension is given for tables, it is length. Cleaning diminishes values; ours are for furniture and metals with excellent original finishes unless noted otherwise. It is also important to mention that collectors are increasingly fussy about condition. Refinishing lowers value from 15% to 30%. Replaced hardware or wood can likewise dramatically and negatively affect value.

For more information see *Stickley Brothers Furniture* by Larry Koon.

Key:

b — brand	hdw — hardware
brd — board	n — no mark
d — red decal	p — paper label
h/cp — hammered copper	t — Quaint metal tag

Charles Stickley

Pitcher, #5, h/cp, can neck, sqd shoulder, tapered body, 17x6" ...**600.00**
Table, trestle; lower shelf, keyed-thru tenons, p, 39x48x30" **800.00**
Wardrobe, 2-panel door, lower drw, drws inside, 71½x35x27".**6,000.00**

Gustav Stickley

Armchair, #330, wide slat ea side/3 across bk, H Ellis design, 40", VG ...**3,750.00**
Armchair, 4-step ladderbk, curved arm, new cushion, n, 38", VG...**3,500.00**
Bed, #912, paneled head/ft brds w/peaked rails, d, rpr, 51x59x70", VG .**4,750.00**
Bed, #924, 12 sq spindles, dbl rails to head/ft brds, b, 50x80x58, VG...**3,750.00**
Bookcase, #700, 3 sm ldgl sqs over long vertical panes, 58x36", VG .**12,000.00**
Bookcase, #715, gallery top, single 12-pane door, V pull, 56x36"...**4,000.00**
Bookcase, #716, 2 8-pane doors, d/p, 56x43x13" **6,500.00**

Bookcase, #718, 2 12-pane doors, slab sides w/keyed tenons, p, 56x57" ..**8,500.00**
Bookcase, 1 16-pane door, mitered mullions, ca 1902-03, 56x31x12" ..**10,000.00**
Bookshelf, #79, 4-shelf, D-shaped hdls, b, 1912-16, 40x14x10" **1,175.00**
Candlesticks, h/cp, tulip cup over sq pan, pyramidal base, 12", pr ...**4,500.00**
Chair, desk; #2578, broad horizontal bk slat, rpl leather, 29", VG ...**750.00**
Chair, desk; #308, H-shape vertical bk slat, b, 40", VG **350.00**
Chair, Morris; #322, flat arms, 5 vertical bk slats, b, no cushion, VG..**9,000.00**
Chair, Morris; #369, slant arm w/5 side slats, rpl leather, d, 36", VG.**12,000.00**
Chair set, #398, low bk w/H-shape slat, new rush seats, 34", VG, 4 for.**3,250.00**
Chair set, 3 vertical slats, leather seat, 6 sides+2 arm, VG **5,500.00**
Chair set, 3-slat bk, leather seat, partial rfn, red d, 36", 5 for ..**2,600.00**
Chest, #625, lg mirror, 2 sm drw over 2, rare hdw, 64x42" **6,500.00**
Chest, #627, 2 sm drw+4, iron hdw, cedar drw bottoms, n, 50x40", VG ..**7,500.00**
Chest, 6 short drw over 3 grad long drw, d, 50½x36x20".........**7,000.00**
China cabinet, #803, 1-pane arched door, glazed sides, n, 60x36", VG ..**8,000.00**
China cabinet, #815, 2 8-pane doors, 8-pane sides, 64, 42", VG ..**9,000.00**
China cabinet, #820, 12-pane door, overhanging top, w/key, d, 63"..**5,500.00**
China cabinet, 12-pane door, h/cp pull, d, 63x36x15" **6,500.00**
Desk, postcard; letter-holder bksplash, 2-drw, d, 36x39½x22", VG .**1,400.00**
Desk, writing; #505, chalet form, paneled drop front, shoe ft, 49", VG..**1,800.00**
Desk set, h/cp, inkwell/letter holder/bookends+6 pcs................**2,950.00**
Dresser, #905, swivel mirror, 2 half & 3 long drw, att, 33x46x22"..**5,000.00**
Footstool, #300, orig leather & tacks, ca 1904, 15x20x16" **1,500.00**
Footstool, #301, rush seat, tapered legs, 17x16x20", VG.............**650.00**
Footstool, #302, chunky flared legs, d, 5x12x12", VG **650.00**
Hall tree, #52, tapered post, 4 shaped ft, rpr/cleaned, 72", VG ...**850.00**
Lamp, floor; mahog buttress base, wicker shade, b, 58" **2,600.00**
Lantern, hammered iron w/amber sq shade, compass mk, 14x9".........**2,900.00**

Lantern, hammered iron with hammered amber glass shade, original patina, 9" square at widest point, 29", VG, $2,600.00. (Photo courtesy Treadway Gallery, Inc.)

Lantern, hammered iron w/cylindrical amber glass shade, n, 12x6" **1,300.00**
Lantern, hammered iron w/rtcl hearts, frosted cylinder shade, 17", VG..**1,500.00**
Magazine stand, 5 open shelves, 1-slat sides, p/b, 47x30x12"...**2,300.00**
Magazine stand, #72, 3-shelf, H Ellis design, rfn, b, 42x22x13", VG ..**2,800.00**
Magazine stand, #79, 4-shelf, extended cut-out slab sides, 40", VG....**1,700.00**
Magazine stand, #514, paneled sides/leather strips, d, 36x14x15".........**5,000.00**
Magazine stand, #548, 4-shelf, paneled sides, beveled top, 44x15", VG ...**4,500.00**
Mirror, #916, peaked top rail w/iron hooks, d, 23x29" **1,800.00**
Mirror fr, overhanging top, arched apron, n, 36x28" **1,000.00**
Rocker, #341, 2 horizontal bk slats, reuphl seat, b, child's, 23" ...**350.00**
Rocker, 3 horizontal bk slats, no arms, p, 32", VG **375.00**
Server, plate rail, 2 drws over 1 long, d, 44x48x21" **3,250.00**
Settee, #165, pyramidal posts, vertical slats, leather seat, rfn...**5,500.00**
Sideboard, #955, 2 short drw, shelf over long drw, 45x60x24" **14,000.00**
Stool, #302, 4 short legs, rush seat, d, 12x4½" **425.00**
Table, dining; #634, split top w/6 leaves, 5-leg, 1904, 54" dia .**19,000.00**
Table, dining; #656, split ped, rfn, 29x60" +2 leaves................**4,500.00**
Table, dining; #656, sq ped w/4 extended ft, vnr loss, p, 54" dia, G.....**3,000.00**
Table, dressing; #914, mirror w/tapered supports, 2-drw, b, 55x18x33" .**4,000.00**

Table, lamp; arched X-stretchers, d, 31x36" dia top 5,500.00
Table, lamp; #436, legs mortised through top, d, 28x23½" dia ...8,000.00
Table, library; #614, 2 drw w/iron pulls, d/p, 30x30x42", VG ..2,900.00
Table, library; #655, 13 thin spindles ea side, p, 29x36x24", VG..3,500.00
Table, lunch; #637, medial shelf, trestle ends, d, 39x48x30"....1,875.00
Table, occasional; #54, cut-corners/shelf/4 post legs, rfn, att, 18"...765.00
Tray, h/cp, riveted twisted wire hdls, unmk, 16x12" 550.00
Vanity, #907, 5-drw, integrated mirror, rprs, d, 55x48x22" 3,750.00
Vase, h/cp, rolled rim, tapered cylinder, circular mk, 10½" 850.00

L. & J.G. Stickley

Armchair, #362, 3 horizonal bk slats, reuphl seat, n, 37", VG 290.00
Armchair, #818, bk w/4 horizontal slats, new leather/rfn, n, 40", VG ...550.00
Bench, piano; #211, overhanging top, slatted sides, label, 40".1,800.00
Bookcase, #46, 4-shelf, 3-side slats, 1916, b, 42x21x12" 1,650.00
Bookcase, #637, 2-door, h/cp pulls, p, 55x36x13¾" 2,900.00
Bookcase, #641 1-door, gallery top, keyed thru-tenons, rfn, n, 55" ..4,000.00
Bookcase, #647, 3 12-pane doors, h/cp hdw, b, 55x72" 18,000.00
Chair, #482, bow-arm, arched apron, gr suede uphl, 39" 2,100.00
Chair, Morris; #412, paddle arm w/corbels, new leather bk/sides, 40"....9,000.00
Chair, Morris; #798, slats to floor, leather uphl, 41x32x36" 4,500.00
Chair, Morris; paddle arms, long corbels, uphl seat, d, 43" 3,750.00
Chair, side; #360, 3-step ladderbk, n, 37", VG............................100.00
Chair, side; #788, 5 vertical bk slats, rpl leather seat, 35" 425.00
Chair, side; curved crest rail over 3 slats, H stretcher, b, 36"........800.00
Chair set, #342, bk w/horizontal slat, 1 38" arm+3 36" sides, VG ..3,250.00
Costumer, cast dbl hooks at top, shoe ft, 67½" 450.00
Desk, postcard; #404, arched kneehole, rpl drw, 35x40¼x23" 900.00
Dresser, #93, 4-drw, mushroom pulls, p, 69¼x48x22¼" 2,300.00
Frame, overhanging top, d, 32x44", VG.....................................750.00
Rocker, open arms, thru tenons at front & rear posts, d, needs reuphl..3,250.00
Settee, like #225, 13-slat bk, shaped top rail, reuphl/rfn, n, 53", VG ..1,400.00
Settle, #232, even arms, 2-slat bk, rpl seat, n, 72" 2,800.00
Settle, #275, even arms, paneled bk/sides, d, reuphl, 84", VG .8,500.00
Sideboard, #732, mirror bk w/columns & shelf, 2 doors/5 drws, n, 61x72"..9,000.00
Stand, magazine; #46, 4-shelf, arched top rails/apron, d, 42x20x12".3,000.00
Table, #558, X-stretchers, overcoated, b, 17x15" dia 750.00
Table, #559, 8-sided, X-stretchers, worn top, d, 20¼x18" 1,200.00
Table, #561, cut corners, arched stretchers, rfn/n, 20x18x18", VG ..450.00
Table, #563, 48" hexagonal top, keyed-tenon X-stretchers, b ..7,500.00
Table, #575, 24" dia top, X-stretchers, sgn 'work of,' VG.........1,000.00
Table, #781, 16" dia top, X-stretchers, att, 18"...........................600.00
Table, dining; #713, 48" dia top, 4 ft w/corbels, +3 leaves, VG ..4,500.00

Stickley Bros.

Armchair, #563½, bent arm, uphl bk/seat, rfn/reuphl, 42", VG..500.00
Armchair, #891½, curved crest, 4 vertical slats, t, 42¾" 325.00
Bookcase, #4762, 2 8-pane doors, copper pulls, 47x36x12" 2,400.00
Chair, Morris; #354, tapered arms, heavy thru-tenons, n, 37x39x34"..2,100.00
Chair, Morris; #412, 5 curved slats, open arms, vinyl pad, 40" ...1,175.00
Chair, slipper; 5-slat bk, seat missing, rfn, 34"..............................200.00
Clock, Secessionst design, h/cp, sq base, att, 11"....................1,400.00
Footstool, #5267, worn leather, cleaned, n, 17x17x12" 170.00
Gong, dinner; #12, slab sides, chimes, striker missing, 11"..........140.00
Magazine stand, 3-shelf, 3 side slats, t, 32x19x12", VG..............950.00
Plant stand, #550, wide apron, splayed legs, rpr to top, 20x18x18"..950.00
Rocker, sewing; #411, notched rail over 3-slat bk, rpl leather seat ..200.00
Rocker, wing-bk; #379-415, 5-slat bk, 3-slat arms, 37" 800.00
Server, #8701, lower shelf, dk finish, 36x36x20", VG 1,000.00
Sideboard, #8902, reverse-taper legs, possible overcoat, 44½x72x25"..6,325.00
Stand, #5671, 3 vertical slats on 4 sides, p, lt cleaning, 24x15", VG 600.00
Table, dining; apron, sq base w/4 ft & corbels, 48" dia+2 leaves...1,100.00

Table, game; #2674, sq top, X-stretcher base, thru tenons, rfn, 30x36"...1,300.00
Table, lunch; #123, appl key tenons to lower stretcher, t, 46x27", VG .1,300.00
Table, lunch; median shelf, thru-tenons, 30x48x27" 1,175.00
Table, 12" sq top, str stretchers, t, 18", VG 230.00
Table, 18" dia top, 4 flared legs, X-stretcher, 28", VG 600.00
Telephone stand, #2886, rectangular, shelf, overcoated, 30x20x18"..300.00
Umbrella stand, #7604, 4 posts w/inset panels, rpl naugahyde, rfn, 25".350.00

Stiegel

Baron Henry Stiegel produced glassware in Pennsylvania as early as 1760, very similar to glass being made concurrently in Germany and England. Without substantiating evidence, it is impossible to positively attribute a specific article to his manufacture. Although he made other types of glass, today the term Stiegel generally refers to any very early ware made in shapes and colors similar to those he is known to have produced — especially that with etched or enameled decoration. It is generally conceded, however, that most glass of this type is of European origin. Our advisor for this category is Mark Vuono; he is listed in the Directory under Connecticut.

Bottle, bright amethyst, 28 ogival pattern, att Flint, 5½" 3,000.00
Bottle, spirits; enameled: bldg, bird w/flag, pewter collar, 8" 240.00
Bottle, spirits; enameled: man w/glass, bk: inscription, 6¾".....1,400.00
Flip, band of repeating floral motifs, 5¾" 240.00
Flip, eng bird/sunburst, 5½" 500.00
Flip, eng sunflower/flowers, dot/bar on conical lid, 10½".........1,700.00
Mug, eng tulip & floral spray, strap hdl, 5⅞" 500.00
Salt cellar, cobalt, 14-dmn, dbl ogee bowl, ftd, 2⅛" 240.00
Sugar bowl, brilliant sapphire, 16-rib, tooled rim, flat ft, 2¼x4".375.00
Sugar bowl, cobalt, ribbed bowl on ribbed ft w/folded rim, open, 3⅜" .700.00
Sugar bowl, dk sapphire bl, 20-dmn, tooled rim, ftd, open, 3x4"..475.00
Tankard, eng bird/sunburst, reed hdl, flared ft, 6¼" 1,400.00
Tankard, eng sunflower/flowers, cylinder w/flared ft, 6½", NM...600.00

Stocks and Bonds

Scripophily (scrip-awfully), the collecting of 'worthless' old stocks and bonds, gained recognition as an area of serious interest around the mid-1970s. Collectors who come from numerous business fields mainly enjoy its hobby aspect, though there are those who consider scripophily an investment. Some collectors like the historical significance that certain certificates have. Others prefer the beauty of older stocks and bonds that were printed in various colors with fancy artwork and ornate engravings. Autograph collectors are found in this field, on the lookout for signed certificates; others collect specific industries.

Many factors help determine the collector value: autograph value, age of the certificate, the industry represented, whether it is issued or not, its attractiveness, condition, and collector demand. Certificates from the mining, energy, and railroad industries are the most popular with collectors. Other industries or special collecting fields include banking, automobiles, aircraft, and territorials. Serious collectors usually prefer only issued certificates that date from before 1930. Unissued certificates are usually worth one-fourth to one-tenth the value of one that has been issued. Inexpensive issued common stocks and bonds dating between the 1940s and 1990s usually retail between $1.00 to $10.00. Those dating between 1890 and 1930 usually sell for $10.00 to $50.00. Those over one hundred years old retail between $25.00 and $100.00 or more, depending on the quantity found and the industry represented. Some stocks are one of a kind while others are found by the hundreds or even thousands, especially railroad certificates. Autographed stocks normally sell anywhere from $50.00 to $1,000.00 or more. A formal collecting organization for scripophilists is known as The Bond and Share Society with an American chapter located in New York City. As is true in any field, potential collectors should take the time to learn the hobby. Prices vary greatly at websites selling old stocks and bonds, sometimes by hundreds of dollars.

Collectors should avoid buying modern certificates being offered for sale at scripophily websites in the $20.00 to $60.00 range, as they have little collector value despite the sales hype. One uncancelled share of some of the modern 'famous name' stocks of the Fortune 500 companies is being offered at two or four times what the stock is currently trading for. These should be avoided, and new collectors who want to buy certificates in modern companies will be better off buying 'one share' stocks in their own name and not someone else's. Take the time to study the market, ask questions, and be patient as a collector. Your collection will be better off. EBay generally serves as a good source for information regarding current values — search under 'Coins.'

Our advisor for this category is Warren Anderson; he is listed in the Directory under Utah. In many of the following listings, two-letter state abbreviations immediately follow company name. Unless noted otherwise, values are for examples in fine condition.

Key:
U — unissued   I/U — issued/uncancelled
I/C — issued/cancelled   vgn — vignette

Agricultural Trust & Savings, PA/1928, eagle vgn, seal, I/U **13.00**
Am Coal Export, NJ/1901, state seal vgn, orange w/gr border, I/U ..**20.00**
Amalgamated Pioche Mines & Smelters, ME/1920, mill vgn, I/U ..**28.00**
Associated Oil, TX/1923, 2 vgns, orange print & seal, I/U **12.00**
Boston & Albany RR, MA/1913, $1,000 bond, panoramic 10" vgn, I/C..**20.00**
Choctaw, OK & Gulf RR, PA, 1904, 2 vgns/ornate title, FBNCo, U..**16.00**
Clear Fork Oil, OH/1901, oilfield vgn, gold seal, I/C **20.00**
Columbia Falls & Southern Railway, MT/19__, eagle vgn, U.......**22.00**
Dugway Consolidated Mining, Ut/1924, eagle vgn, beige seal, I/U..**22.00**
Eastern ID Mining & Water, ID/1883, train vgn, ornate art, U **20.00**
Elk Basin United Oil Co, UT/1927, gusher vgn, fancy border, seal, I/U ...**13.00**
Empire State Oil & Refining Co, SD/1902, train vgn, gold seal, I/U ..**18.00**
Erie Railroad, NY/1942, classical figures/logo vgn, IC **10.00**
Etta May Mining & Milling, 3 vgn, blk/wht w/gold seal, 1920, I/U...**18.00**
First State Savings Bank of W Frankfort, IL/1929, eagle vgn, I/U...**13.00**
Free Coinage Mining..., UT/1906, 3 vgn, blk on wht, gold seal, I/U...**25.00**
Gold Hill & Lee Mountain Mining, MT Territory/1880s, timber vgn, U.**20.00**
Golden West Consolidated Mining, AZ Territory/1910, 3 vgns, I/U...**30.00**
Hancock Gold & Silver Mining, CA/1863, cabin/mtn vgn, U **35.00**
Invader Oil Corp, OK/1921, lg vgn & 2 mythical figures, I/U **20.00**
Isabella Gold Mining, CO/1906, bold title/vgn, orange print, I/C...**28.00**
Jerome Verde Copper Co, AZ/1916, eagle/symbols vgn, I/U **17.00**
Lexington-Concord Mining, AZ/1907, miners vgn, gold seal, I/U .**35.00**
Little Miami RR, OH/1870, 2 train vgns/scene w/farmer & horses, I/C..**28.00**
Lobo Negro Mining..., UT/1956, miners vgn, gr border/seal, I/U..**12.00**
Martin Creek Mining, WA/1897, miners vgn, brn seal/border/print, I/U...**30.00**
Martsolf Fuel Products, PA/1923, eagle vgn, I/U...........................**15.00**
Merrimac Consolidated Mines, CO/1903, miners vgn w/state seal, I/U ..**30.00**
Michigan Central RR, MI/1929, $10,000 bond, lg vgn, ABNCo, U..**20.00**
Middle West Utilities, DE/1931, Miss Liberty vgn, purple print, I/U.**20.00**
Miller Train Control Corp, 1928, 250 shares, I/C.........................**35.00**
Nassau Electric RR, 1894, topless allegorical lady vgn, I/C...........**20.00**
Nat'l Development Co, UT/1918, plain w/no border, blk on wht, I/U...**17.00**
Nat'l Metal Refining & Concentrating, UT/1926, torch vgn, I/U..**17.00**
Nevada Lead & Zinc, NV/1927, miners vgn, gr border/seal, I/U....**22.00**
North Butte Mining, MN/1937, miners vgn, 50 shares, common, I/C...**10.00**
NY Central RR, NY/1966, vgn, brn/blk ink, I/C **10.00**
Ozone Mfg Co, NY/18902, eagle vgn, ornate banner, U **15.00**
PA RR, PA/1966, trains vgn flanked by 2 male figures, I/C...........**14.00**

Park City Mining & Smelting, CO/1922, lg lady vgn, bold title, I/C..**30.00**
Philad'a & West Chester Turnpike, PA/18__, 2 vgns, U **25.00**
Pioche Coalition Mines, NV/1929, miners vgn, gr border, I/U **20.00**
Portland & Boothbay Steamboat Co, ME/18__, 2 steamboats, U.**14.00**
Red Warrior Mining, MN/1923, ornate title, blk on wht, I/U.......**15.00**
Round Mountain Mining, NV/1926, portrait vgn/ornate border, I/C...**25.00**
Salina Coal Co, UT/1927, oval miners vgn, gr border & seal, I/U..**22.00**
Santa Clara Valley Mill & Lumber, CA/1873, bold title, mtn vgn, U..**27.00**
Silver Chief Mining, IL/1880s, miners vgn, nice title, U **23.00**
Texaco Oil & Gas Drilling, 1976, lg refinery vgn, I/C...................**22.50**
Tintic-Ophir Mines, UT/1938, gr border & seal, ornate banner, I/U .**10.00**
Triangle Mining &..., MT/1911, angel/blacksmith/Liberty vgn, I/C ..**20.00**
Triumph Development, UT/1928, miners vgn, I/U........................**14.00**
Uvada Consolidated Mines, UT/1920, miners vgn, gr border/seal, I/U ..**17.00**
Victoria Gold Mining, UT/1916, Liberty vgn, gr print, I/U **25.00**
Wellington Oil Co, CO/1925, gusher by flowing river vgn+2 sm, I/U..**13.00**
West Coast Mining & Smelting, ME/1906, lg eagle vgn, bold title, I/U..**25.00**
White Pine Mining & Smelting of CO, SD/1904, elk vgn, gold seal, I/U..**25.00**
Yerington Malachite Copper Co, NV/1907, title banner, I/U **22.00**

Stoneware

There are three broad periods of time that collectors of American pottery can look to in evaluating and dating the stoneware and earthenware in their collections. Among the first permanent settlers in America were English and German potters who found a great demand for their individually turned wares. The early pottery was produced from red and yellow clays scraped from the ground at surface levels. The earthenware made in these potteries was fragile and coated with lead glazes that periodically created health problems for the people who ate or drank from it. There was little stoneware available for sale until the early 1800s, because the clays used in its production were not readily available in many areas and transportation was prohibitively expensive. The opening of the Erie Canal and improved roads brought about a dramatic increase in the accessibility of stoneware clay, and many new potteries began to open in New York and New England.

Collectors have difficulty today locating earthenware and stoneware jugs produced prior to 1840, because few have survived intact. These ovoid or pear-shaped jugs were designed to be used on a daily basis. When cracked or severely chipped, they were quickly discarded. The value of handcrafted pottery is often determined by the cobalt decoration it carries. Pieces with elaborate scenes (a chicken pecking corn, a bluebird on a branch, a stag standing near a pine tree, a sailing ship, or people) may easily bring $1,000.00 to $12,000.00 at auction.

After the Civil War there was a need and a national demand for stoneware jugs, crocks, canning jars, churns, spittoons, and a wide variety of other pottery items. The competition among the many potteries reached the point where only the largest could survive. To cut costs, most potteries did away with all but the simplest kinds of decoration on their wares. Time-consuming brush-painted birds or flowers quickly gave way to more quickly executed swirls or numbers and stenciled designs. The coming of home refrigeration and Prohibition in 1919 effectively destroyed the American stoneware industry.

Investment possibilities: 1) Early nineteenth-century stoneware with elaborate decorations and a potter's mark is expensive and will continue to rise in price. 2) Late nineteenth-century hand-thrown stoneware with simple cobalt swirls or numbers is still reasonably priced and a good investment. 3) Mass-produced stoneware (ca. 1890 – 1920) is available in large quantities, inexpensive, and slowly increases in price over the years.

Skillfully repaired pieces often surface; their prices should reflect their condition. Look for a slight change in color and texture. The use of a black light is also useful in exposing some repairs. Buyer beware! Hint: Buy only from reputable dealers who will guarantee their merchandise.

In the following listings, 'c/s' means 'cobalt on salt glaze'; all decoration described before this abbreviation is in cobalt. See also Bennington, Stoneware. Assume that values are for examples in near mint condition with only minimal damage unless another condition code is given in the description.

Bank, alarm clock form, Bristol, cobalt Roman Numerals, 1880s, 4" ..**550.00**
Chicken waterer, leaves, c/s, 8", EX..**350.00**
Churn, #1½/flower, c/s, unmk, ca 1860, 12", EX **360.00**
Churn, #2/leaf, c/s, SL Pewtress...Conn, ca 1880, 12", EX **360.00**
Churn, #4/flower wreath & 1866, c/s, Whites Utica, ca 1866, 17", EX ..**825.00**
Churn, #4/Ottman Bros Ft Edward NY, c/s, missing lid, 13" **200.00**
Churn, #5/dbl flower, c/s, J Burger Jr...NY, prof rstr, ca 1885, 18" ..**1,485.00**
Churn, #5/flower basket, c/s, Fort Edward...NY, ca 1870s, 17½" **1,100.00**
Churn, #8/bird on branch, c/s, NA White...Utica NY, 19¼", EX..**4,675.00**
Cooler, #2/dots/squiggles, c/s, 'blind pig' keg, unmk, 1860s, 12" .**465.00**
Cooler, #4/leaf, NY Stoneware...Fort Edward, c/s, bbl shape, ca 1880, EX ..**300.00**
Cream pot, #1/flower (brushed), c/s, unmk, 1860s, 8" **525.00**
Cream pot, drooping flower, c/s, Evan R Jones...PA, ca 1870, 8", VG..**250.00**
Cream pot, flowers in vase, c/s, N Clark...Lyons, ca 1850, 12", EX..**1,075.00**
Crock, #2/bull's eye, c/s, Cowden & Wilcox...PA, 1870s, 7¾"....**575.00**
Crock, #2/crossed plumes, c/s, FB Norton & Co, ca 1870, 9" **525.00**
Crock, #2/drooping flower, EW Farrington...NY, chip, ca 1885, 9"..**600.00**
Crock, #2/flower, c/s, J Burger Jr...NY, ca 1885, 9", EX................**525.00**
Crock, #2/orchid leaf, c/s, White & Wood...NY, line/chip, ca 1885, 9"..**275.00**
Crock, #2/ribbed leaf & flower, c/s, Edmands & Co, 1870s, 9½" .**210.00**
Crock, #3/bird on fence w/1861, c/s, West Troy NY, 10½" **2,975.00**
Crock, #3/drooping orchid, c/s, NA White & Son...NY, ca 1870s, 10" ..**500.00**
Crock, #3/parrot on plume, c/s, FB Norton & Co, ca 1870, 10" .**825.00**
Crock, #4/cabbage flower, c/s, Burger Bros...NY, ca 1869, 11", EX...**330.00**
Crock, #4/dog & ground cover, c/s, Adam Caire...NY, 1880s, 11", EX.**7,700.00**
Crock, #4/stylized leaf, c/s, Geddes NY, ca 1870, crack, 11½" **145.00**
Crock, #4/triple flower, c/s, C Hart Sherburne, line, ca 1870, 11" ...**300.00**
Crock, #6/bird (dotted, lg), c/s, J Burger Jr...NY, ca 1885, 14½"..**4,500.00**
Crock, #6/crested bird on branch (lg), c/s, NA White...Utica, 12¾"..**1,035.00**
Crock, Bread/3 tornadoes, c/s, unmk Midwest, ca 1870, 15"....**1,595.00**
Crock, cake; #2/tulips, c/s, unmk, 1860s, chips, 6¾x14" **550.00**
Crock, cake; drooping tulips at rim, c/s, unmk, 1860s, 11" dia....**635.00**
Inkwell, star, c/s, 1850s, chip, 3¾" dia...**440.00**
Jar, #2/plume, c/s, C Hart...Sherburne, chips, ca 1860, 10½" **385.00**
Jar, #2/poppy (stylized/dotted), c/s, N Wht..., line/stain, 1860s, 11"..**110.00**
Jar, preserve; #½/plumes (brushed), c/s, unmk, 1860s, 9" **250.00**
Jar, preserve; #1/pear, c/s, Pallatine...W VA, ca 1975, 10", EX....**660.00**
Jar, preserve; #2/dbl flower w/tornado, c/s, Cortland, 1860s, 10½"..**360.00**
Jar, preserve; #2/flowers (long stemmed), c/s, unmk, 1850s, 14" .**635.00**
Jar, preserve; #2/grape cluster, c/s, Cowden & Wilcox, 1870s, 11½" .**1,150.00**
Jar, preserve; #4/bird on branch (lg), c/s, W Roberts..., 1860s, 14"..**600.00**
Jar, preserve; #5/flowers (brushed), c/s, unmk, 1850s, 15" **415.00**
Jar, preserve; c/s, John Burger Rochester, ca 1865, 15", EX......**2,200.00**
Jar, storage; #2½/leaf (brushed), c/s, RCR Phila, 1850s, 11½" **220.00**
Jar, swirled leaves at shoulder, c/s, Am, ca 1850s, 8½", EX **230.00**
Jardiniere, #2/repeating flowers, unmk, 1850s, 12½"................**1,485.00**
Jardiniere, #3/allover flowers/squiggles, c/s, unmk, ca 1850, 14" .**850.00**
Jardiniere, #3/repeating leafy flowers, c/s, unmk, ca 1830, 14", EX .**360.00**
Jardiniere, leaves (4 brushed), c/s, RCR Phila, 1850s, 1-qt, 6¼" ...**550.00**
Jug, #1/butterfly, c/s, Smith & Day...Norwalk Con, ca 1845, 10"..**250.00**
Jug, #1/dbl flower (dotted), c/s, Troy NY, ca 1870, 10", EX.........**165.00**
Jug, #1/flower, c/s, C Boynton & Co Troy, stain, ca 1825, 10½"..**440.00**
Jug, #1/paddle-tail bird in pine tree, c/s, NA White & Son, 1870s, EX..**770.00**
Jug, #1/pine tree, c/s, NA White & Son...NY, ca 1870, 11", EX...**250.00**
Jug, #1/plume (brushed), c/s, Lyons, ca 1860, 11" **185.00**
Jug, #1/squat bird (EX art), c/s, Whites Utica, ca 1865, 10", EX.**635.00**
Jug, #1/tulip (brushed), c/s, Cowden & Wilcox...PA, wide mouth, 11" ..**525.00**
Jug, #2/bird on plume, att Edmands, ca 1870s, 13½" **330.00**

Jug, #2/bird on plume, c/s, EW Farrington...NY, ca 1890, 13½" .**965.00**
Jug, #2/bird running/2 scribe lines, Whites Utica, ca 1865, 14", EX..**850.00**
Jug, #2/drooping flower, c/s, AO Whittemore Havana, beehive shape, 12"....**250.00**
Jug, #2/fireworks, c/s, Ballard & Brothers...VT, 1860s, 13", EX..**685.00**
Jug, #2/lovebird, c/s, S Hart Fulton, rpr, ca 1875, 13"................**685.00**
Jug, #2/lyre, c/s, JM Pruden...NJ, ca 1870, 13½", EX..................**275.00**
Jug, #2/ribbed floral, c/s, J Burger Jr...NY, ca 1885, 14" **495.00**
Jug, #2/tic-tac-toe, c/s, West Troy, 1880s, prof rstr, 14" **3,650.00**
Jug, #2/tulip, c/s, N Clark & Co Lyons, ca 1850, 15", EX **1,100.00**
Jug, #2/tulip, c/s, Norton & Son, ovoid w/strap hdl, 13" **435.00**
Jug, #3 w/brushed fr, c/s, J Mantell Penn Yan, ca 1860, sm chip, 15" **330.00**
Jug, #3/dbl flower, c/s, Mantell & Thomas Penn Yan, ca 1854, 15", EX ..**1,100.00**
Jug, #3/long-tailed bird, c/s, Whites Utica, ca 1865, 15½", EX...**525.00**
Jug, #3/stylized leaf, c/s, Brady & Ryan...NY, chips, ca 1885, 15½"..**220.00**

Jug, #3/three buds and ribbed leaves, Clark & Co., Rochester, cobalt on salt glaze, ca 1845, 16", EX, $800.00.

Jug, #3/tulip, c/s, HB Pfaltzgraff York PA, chips, 15¼" **550.00**
Jug, #3/winged eagle w/banner, c/s, WJ Seymour, ca 1855, 15½"..**1,700.00**
Jug, #4/bird (brushed/detailed), c/s, ca 1880s, chip, 17" **855.00**
Jug, #4/floral, c/s, D Weston...NY, prof rstr, ca 1870, 10" **440.00**
Jug, bird (folky/dotted), c/s, unmk, ca 1860, 11".........................**745.00**
Jug, bird on branch, c/s, Fort Edward...Co, ca 1860, 11½", EX+...**1,000.00**
Jug, bird on twig, c/s, W Roberts...NY, ca 1860, 10", EX **1,000.00**
Jug, dots & 1838 at shoulder, c/s, Clark & Fox...NY, ovoid, 10½"...**3,100.00**
Jug, simple flower, c/s, N Clark Jr Athens NY, ca 1850, 12" **250.00**
Jug, 1860 & accents, c/s, Fort Edward...Co, ca 1860, 11", EX+...**825.00**
Milk pan, flower, c/s, Cowden & Wilcox Harrisburg, ca 1870, 11x5½" ...**415.00**
Mug, cobalt bands, Albany slip int, conical, 1850s, 5½".............**350.00**
Pail, batter; plume/flower/etc, c/s, Cowden & Wilcox..., 1870s 8"'...**2,500.00**
Pitcher, #½/snowflake (dotted), c/s, Union Pottery..., 1880s, 8½"...**1,265.00**
Pitcher, #½/swags & leaves (bold)/1859 at rim, c/s, unmk, 10"..**1,925.00**
Pitcher, #½/tulips/swags (allover), unmk, 1860s, 9½"..............**1,425.00**
Pitcher, #1/flower (dbl/brushed), c/s, 1860s, 10½", EX...............**935.00**
Pitcher, #1/flowers (3 draped), c/s, unmk, ca 1860s, 10½" **1,100.00**
Pitcher, #1/swag accents, c/s, AJ Butler...NJ, ca 1870, 10" **415.00**
Pitcher, #1½/dbl floral, c/s, unmk, 1850s, 11½" **1,000.00**
Pitcher, #2, c/s, FT Wright...Mass, wooden lid, ca 1860, 13", EX ..**415.00**
Pitcher, #2/leaves (dotted), unmk NY origin, ca 1870, 12" **685.00**
Pitcher, #2/plumes (2 rows), c/s, WH Lehew...VA, 1880s, 13".**3,200.00**
Pitcher, leaves (3 repeats) & swags, c/s, unmk, 1860s, 7½".........**935.00**
Tenderizer, emb Pat'd Dec 25, 1887, wood hdl, ca 1877, 10", EX..**110.00**

Store

Perhaps more so than any other yesteryear establishment, the country store evokes feelings of nostalgia for folks old enough to remember its charms — barrels for coffee, crackers, and big green pickles; candy in a jar for the grocer to weigh on shiny brass scales; beheaded chickens in the meat case outwardly devoid of nothing but feathers. Today mementos from this segment of Americana are being collected by those who 'lived it' as well as those less fortunate!

Our advisor for this category is Charles Reynolds; he is listed in the Directory under Virginia. For more information we recommend *General Store Collectibles, Vols. I and II,* by David L. Wilson. See also Advertising; Scales.

Bag holder, wooden sq post w/4 attachments to hold bags, 46x10"...**70.00**
Barrel, White House Biscuits stenciled on red tin, 29" **30.00**
Bin, oak, hinged slant front w/glass display window, 28" **125.00**
Bolt cabinet, pine, 18 drws, revolves, 15x30" **2,350.00**
Box, cracker; glass cover, old bl pnt, 8½" **50.00**
Broom holder, heavy wire, 23 loops, hangs, 19th C, 19x16" dia .**180.00**
Butcher's block, maple end stock on trn legs, 32x30" sq **300.00**
Butcher's block, wooden slab on 3 legs, 19th C, 38x28" dia........**800.00**
Cash register, Monitor #1A, wood w/CI sign, 9x13x14", VG **415.00**
Cash register, NCR #3, mahog inlay, deep wood drw, ca 1886, VG .**4,500.00**
Cash register, NCR #7 or #8, detail adder, fleur-de-lis, VG........**850.00**
Cash register, NCR #33, 1903, VG **900.00**
Cash register, NCR #47, oak w/mahog inlay, up to $6, VG **2,250.00**
Cash register, NCR #129-130, bronze, VG **950.00**
Cash register, NCR #130, Art Nouveau cabinet, M................**1,600.00**
Cash register, NCR #226, rare bilingual topsign, VG..............**900.00**
Cash register, NCR #312, #313, or #317, dolphin pattern, VG ..**800.00**
Cash register, NCR #324, rfn...**900.00**
Cash register, NCR #337, dolphin design, M..........................**950.00**
Cash register, NCR #359-G, brass w/marble tray, 1906, EX+......**200.00**
Cash register, NCR #441 or #442, Emp design w/quartered-oak base, M.**1,750.00**
Desk, clerk's; walnut, slant front, 4-drw, attached top, 85" **1,450.00**
Desk, counter; walnut w/scalloped bk, 1830s, 24' L **200.00**
Desk, storekeeper's; roll-top, oak **2,900.00**
Dispenser, spice; AB Davis, litho & HP tin, 8-drw, 21x12x32", EX+...**700.00**
Dispenser, tea; toleware, Oolong & gold stencil, 16x10½x14" ...**195.00**
Display, counter; oak w/tambour front, shelves, 16" H **85.00**
Display, pine fr w/slant front, pigeonholes, 18" H **80.00**
Display case, aluminum w/bent glass, 78x28" dia.......................**1,295.00**
Display case, NP brass w/curved glass front, 1910s, 39x23x21" ..**2,250.00**
Flour bin & sifter, Cream City Flour, ca 1892, 28x13" dia.......**1,200.00**
Jar, Baker's Chocolate, glass w/enameled lettering, 8¾x7" dia **150.00**
Jar, Kis-Me Gum, clear glass, sq, 10½x4⅝" **100.00**
Jar, licorice lozenges, mk Y&S, clear, Am, 1880-1900, 9¼" **50.00**
Lamp, B&H, brass, hangs, electrified, Pat Appl For, 34½" H **250.00**
Paper cutter, blk-enameled metal fr w/wood top, ca 1941, 13x16x22"..**30.00**
Photo, stationery store int scene, ca 1900, 6½x8½" +mat & fr ...**60.00**
Popcorn popper/peanut roaster, Holkum & Hoko, dk oak case ..**2,400.00**
Punch, CI, made to fasten to desk, ca 1904, 6½"...........................**55.00**
Scoop, grain; copper, ca 1900s, lg **65.00**
Scoop, grain; tin, early 19th C, 9½x4½", VG................................**40.00**
Shelf/display, mahog Eastlake style, for notions, 1890s, 31x23".......**245.00**
Spool cabinet, Coats, oak, 22½x16½x15½" on 8" base **625.00**
Spool cabinet, Goff's Best Braid, oak w/tin inserts, 4-drw, 16x14x16"...**550.00**

Stoves

Antique stoves' desirability is based on two criteria: their utility and their decorative merit. It's the latter that adds an 'antique' premium to the basic functional value that could be served just as well by a modern stove. Sheer age is usually irrelevant. Decorative features that enhance desirability include fancy, embossed ornamentation (especially with figures such as cherubs, Old Man Winter, gargoyles, etc.) rather than a solely vegetative motif, nickel-plated trim, mica windows, ceramic tiles, and (in cooking stoves) water reservoirs and high warming closets rather than

mere high shelves. The less sheet metal and the more cast iron, the better. Look for crisp, sharp designs in preference to those made from worn or damaged and repaired foundry patterns. Stoves with a pastel porcelain finish can be very attractive; blue is a favorite, white is least desirable. Chrome trim, rather than nickel, dates a stove to circa 1933 or later and is a good indicator of a post-antique stove. Though purists prefer the earlier models trimmed in nickel rather than chrome, there is now considerable public interest in these post-antique stoves as well, and some people are willing to pay a good price for these appliance-era 'classics.' (Note: Remember, not all bright metal trim is chrome; it is important to learn to distinguish chrome from the earlier, more desirable nickel plate.)

Among stove types, base burners (with self-feeding coal magazines) are the most desirable. Then come the upright, cylindrical 'oak' stoves, kitchen ranges, and wood parlors. Cannon stoves approach the margin of undesirability; laundries and gasoline stoves plunge through it.

There's a thin but continuing stream of desirable antique stoves going to the high-priced Pacific Coast market. Interest in antique stoves is least in the Deep South. Demand for wood/coal stoves is strongest in areas where firewood is affordable and storage of it is practical. Demand for antique gas ranges has become strong, especially in metropolitan markets, and interest in antique electric ranges is slowly dawning. The market for antique stoves is so limited and the variety so bewildering that a consensus on a going price can hardly emerge. They are only worth something to the right individual, and prices realized depend very greatly on who happens to be in the auction crowd. Even an expert's appraisal will usually miss the realized price by a substantial percent.

In judging condition look out for deep rust pits, warped or burnt-out parts, unsound fire bricks, poorly fitting parts, poor repairs, and empty mounting holes indicating missing trim. Search meticulously for cracks in the cast iron. Our listings reflect auction prices of completely restored, safe, and functional stoves, unless indicated otherwise.

Note: Round Oak stoves carrying the words 'Estate of P.D. Beckwith' above the lower door were made prior to 1935. After that date, the company name was changed to Round Oak Company, and the Beckwith reference was no longer used. In our listings, the term 'tea shelf' has been used to describe both drop and swing shelves, as the function of both types was to accommodate teapots and coffeepots.

Key: func — functional

Base Burners

Art Amherst #15, NP trim, tiles, 11" urn, 50x25x28", VG......**2,065.00**
Art Denmark #15, Ransom, Albany NY, tiles/NP/mica, 1897, VG ...**4,950.00**
Art Garland #400, Michigan Stove, gargoyles/NP/mica, 1889, rstr .**10,750.00**
Emerald Jewel #14, Detroit, NPCI, 1909, 54"+15" brass urn ...**1,700.00**
Favorite #30, Piqua OH, ornate CI, mica windows, 52"+14" urn ..**2,200.00**
Glenwood #6, Weir, NP trim, mica windows, 1909, 68" **965.00**
Waverly #12, Thos Caffney, Boston MA, 40x20x22"...............**6,065.00**

Franklin Stoves

Acme Orient #18, 6 tiles, mica windows, fancy, 1890 ....**315.00**
Good Cheer #22, Walker & Pratt, fireplace, 1850s, 32x27x31"..**330.00**
Ideal #3, Magee, CI fireplace, 2 side trivets, 1892, 32x28" **275.00**
Iron Foundry...NH, ornate CI, grate missing, 1820s, 37x26x32" .**220.00**
Kineo #16, Noyes & Nutter, fireplace, 1890s, 32x23x20" **200.00**
Sunny Hearth #2, Southard Robertson, 1880s, 35x20x29½" **315.00**
Villa Franklin, Muzzy & Co, folding doors, 1830s, 30"+4" urn ...**195.00**
Wyer & Noble, CI/brass-trim fireplace, early 1800s.................**2,200.00**

Parlor

The term 'parlor stove' as we use it here is very general and encompasses at least six distinct types recognized by the stove industry: cottage parlor, double-cased airtight, circulator, cylinder, oak, and the fireplace heater.

#1, Tyson, 2 sheet metal columns, swing doors, 36x17x25".........**385.00**
#2, JH Shear, Albany NY, CI, column style, 56".........................**935.00**
#4, Johnson, Geer & Cox, CI, 4-column, 56"......................**1,100.00**
#20, Somersworth, tip-up dome top, 1850s, 39x30x29".............**330.00**
#44, Burdett-Smith, sq, tiles, mica door, 38"+8" urn.................**385.00**
Comfort #23, Bangor Foundry, oval w/dome top, Pat 1875, 33"+10" urn....**200.00**
Ideal Garland #220, wood/coal cottage, missing urn, ca 1893, rstr....**1,300.00**
Ilion #5, ornate CI, ca 1853, 33"+13" 2-pc urn.........................**550.00**
Modern Glenwood Wood Parlor, slide top, 1900s, 45x28x24½".**360.00**
Peerless, Pratt & Wentworth, tip-up dome, 1840s, 37x19x15"...**150.00**
Red Cross #31, Co-Op Foundry Sylvan, tiles, gargoyle legs, Pat 1888-89..**330.00**
Royal Clarion #14, Wood-Bishop, mica door, oven, 1890s, 50", 1856, 28".**275.00**
SH Ransom, ornate CI, rnd air intake, Pat 1846, 26"+14" urn...**300.00**
Temple #5, Vose & Co, CI, Pat 1854, 44"................................**880.00**
Union Airtight, Warnick & Leibrandt, ornate CI, 1851, 26".....**275.00**

Ranges (Gas)

Detroit Jewel, 4-burner, blk/NP, glass oven door, 1918, VG........**550.00**
Insulated Glenwood, Wier, 6-burner/2-oven, wht, 1932, rstr....**4,500.00**
Magic Chef, wht, 6-burner/2-oven, high closet, 1938, rstr, up to..**12,000.00**
Magic Chef, wht, 6-burner/2-oven, high closet, 1938, unrstr ..**1,000.00**
Magic Chef, 6-burner/2-oven, warming closet, 1932, EX.........**2,750.00**
O'Keefe & Merritt, 4-burner, cabinet base, ca 1929, G...............**110.00**
O'Keefe & Merritt, 6-burner, dual oven/broilers, wht porc, EX ..**500.00**
Quick Meal, 4-burner, bl, cabinet style, 1919, G.........................**925.00**
Quick Meal, 4-burner, gray, canopy/high closet, 1924, unrstr.....**375.00**
Quick Meal, 4-burner/1-oven, 1928, unrstr...............................**300.00**
Wedgewood, wht porc, complete w/4 burner covers & lifter, 1930s, EX..**900.00**

Ranges (Wood and Coal)

Ideal Atlantic 8-20, Portland, ornate CI, bk shelf, 1850s.........**1,675.00**
Imperial Clarion #8-20, Wood/Bishop, warming closet, dtd 1898....**1,980.00**
Kineo C, Noyes & Nutter, roll top, water tank, 1900-15 ....**715.00**
Magee 88, 2-oven/8-hole, CI, high closet, no reservoir, 1880, rstr..**5,500.00**
Popular Clarion, Wood/Biship, scrolling, tea shelves, 1890s....**1,150.00**
Quaker Standard #8-20, Taunton Iron Works, NP trim, shelves, 1890s...**945.00**
Queen Atlantic, Portland Stove Foundry, plain w/high shelf, 32x57" L...**685.00**
Village Crawford Royal, Walker & Pratt, tea shelves, 1900s.......**800.00**

Stove Manufacturers' Toy Stoves

Buck's Jr #3, St Louis MO, new body/pnt/recast parts, 26"..........**850.00**
Charter Oak #503, GF Filley, St Louis MO, 14x12x25", EX....**2,050.00**
Dainty, Reading Stove Works, PA, 7x13x8", VG.........................**150.00**
Estate Fresh Air Oven, blk/wht enamel, NP, working gas range, 15"..**2,400.00**
Jersey, Cook & Van Evera, Chicago, ca 1908, 28x15x12", EX..**6,400.00**
Karr Qualified, bl porc w/NP, Belleville IL, 1925, EX **2,500.00**
Karr Qualified Range, aluminum/tin, dial on door, 21½x13", EX...**775.00**
Karr Range, Belleville IL, bl porc, older model, 21½x13x9"....**3,100.00**
Little Eva T Southard, NYC, 8½x14x11", VG w/accessories......**575.00**
Little Fanny, Philadelphia Stove Works, ca 1880, CI, minor rust, EX...**300.00**
Royal American, Bridgeford, Louisville KY, 14x12x10", G.........**950.00**

Toy Manufacturers' Toy Stoves, Cooking

Electric, Empire, Metal Ware Corp, WI, burner+oven, '25, 15x19x7", VG..**50.00**
Electric, Lionel, porc & CI, cream & gr, 4-leg, func, 32x26", EX ..**2,500.00**
Gas, Hotpoint, Arcade, pnt CI range, tan & gr, VG...................**150.00**
Gas, Roper, Arcade, pnt CI range, door opens, 4½", EX...............**70.00**

Wood/coal, Bing, bl steel cookstove, brass trim, Germany, 16½", VG...**600.00**
Wood/coal, Crescent, CI, w/shelves, lids, 5 CI pots, 8", EX........**170.00**
Wood/coal, Crescent, plated CI & steel cookstove, 4-hole, 11½", EX..**230.00**
Wood/coal, Eagle, Hubley, Lancaster PA, NP, recast parts, rstr...**450.00**
Wood/coal, Eagle, Kenton, CI, heavily scrolled, 4-ft, 11½x10", G ..**125.00**
Wood/coal, Eclipse, J&E Stevens, Cromwell CT, CI, EX............**175.00**
Wood/coal, Little Giant, unmk/unidentified, 7½x8½x11", EX orig..**675.00**
Wood/coal, Novelty, Kenton, bl pnt/NP trim, rfn, 13x6½x8½" .**600.00**
Wood/coal, Pet, Adams, CI, cooking, ornate, 1857, 8½" W base...**290.00**
Wood/coal, Rival, J&E Stevens, Cromwell CT, 14x9x16", M, +2 kettles.**1,350.00**
Wood/coal, Rival, no shelves, 12" L, EX....................................**900.00**
Wood/coal, Royal, Kenton, CI/steel, 4-hole/working grates, rpt, 10", G..**50.00**
Wood/coal, Royal, Kenton Hdw, CI & steel, 4-hole, ornate, 10", VG.**100.00**
Wood/coal, Royal, plated CI, stovepipe, shield shape, 16", G.......**85.00**
Wood/coal, Triumph, Kenton OH, 14x8½x19", G.....................**195.00**

Toy Manufacturers' Toy Stoves, Heating

Heater, Spark, Grey Iron...Co, int grate/sliding vents, func, 14", VG...**115.00**
Heater, The Pet, Young & Bro, Albany NY, 10½x6x8½"...........**165.00**

Stretch Glass

Stretch glass, produced from circa 1916 through 1935, was made in an effort to emulate the fine art glass of Tiffany and Carder. The pressed or blown glassware was sprayed with a metallic salts mix while hot, then reshaped, causing a stretch effect in the iridescent finish. Pieces which were not reshaped had the iridized finish without the stretch, as seen on Fenton's #222 lemonade set and #401 guest set. Northwood, Imperial, Fenton, Diamond, Lancaster, Jeannette, Central, Vineland Flint, and the United States Glass Company were the manufacturers of this type of glass.

See also specific companies.

Aquarium bowl, Celeste Blue, Fenton, #604, 6x9¾"......................**95.00**
Basket, gr (rare color), Imperial, #300, 9¾x5¾".........................**150.00**
Bonbon, Ivory (custard), w/lid, Northwood, #643, 6x5⅜"..........**195.00**
Bottle, scent; Dmn Optic, Velva Rose, Fenton, #53, 5"..............**145.00**
Bowl, bl, wide cupped rim, Northwood, #717, 2⅝x12½"............**65.00**
Bowl, Celeste Blue, crimped, 5 rings, Fenton, 2⅛x7½"...............**65.00**
Bowl, Celeste Blue, 12-panel, ftd, Fenton, #550, 5¼x10¼"........**135.00**
Bowl, Egyptian Lustre, cupped, Diamond Glass, 2⅝x5⅝"..........**110.00**
Bowl, gr, flared, US Glass, #310, 2¾x9⅞".................................**80.00**
Bowl, Harding Blue, cupped, Diamond Glass, 1⅞x7"...................**45.00**
Bowl, Jade Blue, blk ft, cupped rim, Northwood, 5¼x10½"........**225.00**
Bowl, lt bl-gr, flared, crimped, Vineland Flint Glass, 3x9¼"...**75.00**
Bowl, marigold, flared, cupped rim, 2¾x7⅛"..............................**35.00**
Bowl, mayonnaise; Persian Pearl (crystal), Fenton, #2005, 5¼"....**45.00**
Bowl, Melon Rib, Tangerine, Fenton, #857, 5⅛x7½"..................**110.00**
Bowl, Melon Rib, topaz, cupped, Fenton, #847, 3⅜x5¾"............**60.00**
Bowl, Optic Swirl, bl, flared rim, Northwood, 3¼x11¾"............**140.00**
Bowl, Pearl Ruby (marigold, art glass), crimped, Imperial, 2¼x8" ..**125.00**
Bowl, ruby, crimped, 3-ftd, Fenton, #603, 5¼x10⅜".................**650.00**
Candlesticks, aquamarine, cornucopia form, Fenton, #950, 6", pr ..**180.00**
Candlesticks, gr, Central, 9¼", pr...**110.00**
Candlesticks, Harding Blue w/wht enameling, Diamond Glass, 9", pr ..**125.00**
Candlesticks, Octagon, pk, #94, US Glass, 1½", pr......................**70.00**
Candlesticks, pk smoke, rolled rim, Imperial, #727, 1⅞", pr.......**175.00**
Candlesticks, Spindle, bl, Northwood, 8¾", pr..........................**150.00**
Candlesticks, Tangerine, ring on stem, Fenton, #316, 3⅜", pr......**80.00**
Candlesticks, topaz, 6-sided base, Fenton, #249, pr..................**120.00**
Candy jar, Adam's Rib, gr, Diamond Glass, 8⅜"........................**110.00**
Candy jar, Persian Pearl, Fenton, #636, 1-lb, 10x4¼"..................**50.00**
Candy jar, topaz, Northwood, #636, 1-lb, 10x4¼"......................**65.00**

Cheese & cracker, Harding Blue, Diamond Glass, 2-pc................90.00
Comport, Adam's Rib, Harding Blue, ftd, Diamond Glass, 6⅜x9½" .95.00
Comport, Celeste Blue, rolled rim, ftd, Fenton, #917, 4x10¼"..140.00
Comport, Cumula, crystal w/gr & wht enamel, US Glass, #179, 6¼x8"...80.00
Comport, dk bl, 8-sided ft w/tree bark, Northwood, 3½x4⅝".......50.00
Comport, Florentine Green, crimped, ftd, Fenton, #9, 4¾x7⅛"...60.00
Comport, gr, Optic Ray stem, 3 raised sides, Diamond Glass, 6x6½"..70.00
Pitcher, Florentine Green, flared cylinder, Fenton, 9¼"............170.00
Plate, Dmn Optic, Velva Rose, Fenton, #1502, 7¾"............65.00
Plate, gr, pressed star base, Diamond Glass, 7⅝"............35.00
Plate, Laurel Leaf, Celeste Blue, Fenton, #757, 7½"............35.00
Plate, Optic, red, 14-panel, Imperial, #656, 14⅜"............425.00
Punch bowl, Harding Blue, Diamond Glass, 6x12"............195.00
Salver, Wisteria (lt purple), ftd, Fenton, #643, 2⅝x6½"............70.00
Sherbet, Optic Panels, Green Ice (bl-gr), Imperial, #599, 3¾"............50.00
Tidbit, Celeste Blue, center hdl, cupped rim, Fenton, #317, 5x9½"..70.00
Tidbit, gr, center hdl, US Glass, #310, 4x10"............65.00
Tidbit, Rose Ice, center hdl, Lancaster, 4¾x11"............90.00
Vase, Blue Ice (bl smoke), Imperial, #693, 10¾x5¾"............95.00
Vase, bud; Celeste Blue, Fenton, #99, 7¼x1⅝"............35.00
Vase, Egyptian Lustre (blk opaque), rolled rim, Diamond Glass, 8⅝"............200.00
Vase, Harding Blue, ribbed stick form, Diamond Glass, 12x2⅜"..50.00
Vase, Pearl, pinched bottle form, Diamond Glass, 9¾"............110.00
Vase, Persian Pearl, crimped rim, Fenton, #106, 3¼x6"............40.00
Vase, Rib Optic, Wisteria (purple), fan form, Fenton, #736, 6"....80.00
Vase, Sweet Pea, Rose Ice (dk marigold), Lancaster, 5½x8¾"............75.00

String Holders

Today, if you want to wrap and secure a package, you have a variety of products to choose from: cellophane tape, staples, etc. But in the 1800s and even well past the advent of Scotch Tape in the early 1930s, string was often the only available binder; thus the string holder, either the hanging or counter type, was a common and practical item found in most homes and businesses. Chalkware and ceramic figurals from the 1930s, 1940s, and 1950s contrast with the cast and wrought-iron examples from the 1800s to make for an interesting collection. Our advisor for this category is Larry G. Pogue (L & J Antiques and Collectibles); he is listed in the Directory under Texas.

See also Advertising.

Apple, pnt chalkware, 7¾" 95.00
Apple & berries, pnt chalkware, 8¼" 75.00
Aunt Jemima, face only, pnt chalkware, 1940s-50s, 7¾"............395.00
Banana bunch, yel chalkware, 1980s, 5¾"............85.00
Betty Boop, face only, pnt chalkware, 1930s-40s, 9x10"............695.00
Betty Boop, head & shoulders, pnt chalkware, 1940s-50s, 7½" ..550.00
Black boy eating melon, pnt chalkware, 1940s, +matching match holder..395.00
Black boy riding alligator, pnt chalkware, Copyright 1948, 9" 345.00
Black girl, blk/red/wht, full figure, Japan, 6½x4" 385.00
Bride w/bouquet, mc ceramic, Japan, 4¼"............135.00
Buster Brown, face only w/Tige, pnt chalkware, Copyright 1938, 7½"..550.00
Carrots, pnt chalkware, 10½" 185.00
Cat holding ball of twine, ceramic, 5½"............95.00
Cat on ball of twine, chalkware, 7"............85.00
Cat w/ball of twine & bow, pnt chalkware, 6½"............105.00
Cat w/lg bow & flower on head, pnt chalkware, 7"............165.00
Cat w/pk bow, ceramic, 7¾"............125.00
Chef, face only, cold-pnt ceramic, Japan, 6", EX............145.00
Chipmunk w/bow, ceramic, 5⅛"............135.00
Conovers chef, pnt chalkware, Conovers Original 1945, 6"........245.00
Dog w/collar scissors holder, Made in England by Arthur Wood, 4½" ..155.00
Drunk man, face only, pnt pottery, mk Elsa, 5½" 210.00

Goldie the Goldfish, chalkware, 1950s, 6¾"............225.00
Grapes in cluster, pnt chalkware, 5½"............100.00
Hippo w/knitting, ceramic, eyeglasses formed by scissors, 6" 75.00
Howdy Doody, face only, pnt chalkware, Copyright 1950, 6½" ..495.00
Indian w/headband, face only, pnt chalkware, 1950s, 10x7¼"....285.00
Jester, face only, pnt chalkware, 7½" 195.00
Little Bo Peep, pnt chalkware, Little Bo Peep Copyright 1942, 9" ..595.00
Little Chef (aka Rice Krispy Guy), pnt chalkware, 1940s-50s, 7" 185.00
Little Monk, head & hand, pnt chalkware, Bello Copyright 1940...275.00
Longshoreman's Mate, lady's head, pnt chalkware, Bello...1940, 9" .295.00
Mammy, bl skirt, pottery, w/scissors holder, 6½"............395.00
Mammy, ceramic w/cloth skirt (covers ball, missing), 4½" 155.00
Mammy, face only, bashful look, pnt chalkware, 1950s, 8½" 395.00
Mammy, wht dress w/brn stripes, ceramic, Made in Japan, 6¼"..235.00
Mammy w/ball of yarn, pnt chalkware, 1940s, 6½"............195.00
Monkey on ball of twine, chalkware, 7½"............245.00
Monkey on bananas, mc chalkware, 1950s, 8¼"............295.00
Mrs Mouse knitting, scissors in nose form glasses, compo, 7" 90.00
Pear & plums, pnt chalkware, 7¾"............85.00
Pumpkin face, winking witch, ceramic, Japan, 5"............180.00
Rose, pnt chalkware, 8"............175.00
Sailor boy, head only, pnt chalkware, Bello, Chicago IL, 8"........265.00
Santa, face only, pnt chalkware, 9¼"............245.00
Senor in wide-brimmed hat, face only, pnt chalkware, 1940s-50s..110.00
Senora, mantilla in hair, head only, pnt chalkware, 1940s-50s ...275.00
Shirley Temple, face only, pnt chalkware, 1940s-50s, 6¾".........395.00
Strawberry w/blossom, pnt chalkware, 6½"............115.00
String Along w/Me on heart, pnt chalkware, 6½"............135.00
Terrier dog, pnt chalkware, 7"............155.00
Westie dog, pnt chalkware, 9"............195.00
Willy the Worm, yel worm on apple 'house,' pnt chalkware, 6½"..110.00
You'll Always Have a Pull w/Me on heart shape, ceramic, Cleminson, 5"..115.00

Sugar Shakers

Sugar shakers (or muffineers, as they were also called) were used during the Victorian era to sprinkle sugar and spice onto breakfast muffins, toast, etc. They were made of art glass, pattern glass, and china. See also specific types and manufacturers (such as Northwood). Our coadvisors for this category are Jeff Bradfield and Dale MacAllister; they are listed in the Directory under Virginia.

Alba, bl opaque, period top, Dithridge, 4¾"............90.00
Beatty Honeycomb, clear opal, AJ Beatty, 4"............160.00
Beatty Rib, bl opal............125.00
Blown Drapery, gr opal............450.00
Blown Twist, vaseline opal............275.00
Bubble Lattice, bl opal............225.00
Bulbous Base Optic, cranberry, 5"............225.00
Challinor's Forget-Me-Not, bl opaque, 3¾"............130.00
Challinor's Forget-Me-Not, pk opaque, 3¾"............170.00
Chrysanthemum Base Swirl, cranberry opal............450.00
Clematis/Flower & Pleat, clear & frosted w/purple & amber stain, 5½"..80.00
Coin Spot, 9-Panel; bl, 4¾"............210.00
Coinspot, cranberry, wide waist, 4½"............325.00
Cone, pk cased, Consolidated, 5¼"............150.00
Cone, pk cased, squatty, Consolidated, 2¾"............170.00
Consolidated Criss-Cross, wht opal............400.00
Corn, wht opaque............140.00
Daisy & Fern, bl opal............275.00
Egg, pk satin opaque, mc pansies (G finish), Mt WA, 4¼".........425.00
Fern, cranberry opal............550.00
Guttate, cranberry, Consolidated (+)............500.00

Hobbs Optic, rubena 230.00
Hobnail (pressed) 60.00
Jewelled Heart, gr opal 475.00
Leaf Mold, cranberry opal 475.00
Leaning Pillars, bl opaque 95.00
Many Lobes, bl opaque, 4¾" 120.00
Netted Oak, wht opaque w/decor, Northwood, 4" 150.00
Nine-Panel, gr, Northwood, 4½" 125.00
Polka Dot, bl opal...650.00
Quilted Phlox, bl, 12-panel, Northwood...........................200.00
Quilted Phlox, gr cased, Northwood 175.00
Quilted Phlox, wht opaque w/bl flowers & gold neck, Northwood .100.00
Reverse Swirl, bl, opal, 4¾" 175.00
Reverse Swirl, vaseline opal, from $150 to.......................200.00
Reverse Swirl, wht opal..175.00
Reverse Swirl (New Albany), bl opal 275.00
Reverse Swirl (New Albany), wht opal 200.00
Ribbed Opal Lattice, bl...250.00
Ribbed Opal Lattice, cranberry...400.00
Ribbed Pillar, frosted cranberry & wht spatter 200.00
Ring Neck, cranberry & wht spatter.................................150.00
Ring Neck Optic, cranberry 200.00
Royal Ivy, frosted rainbow craquelle, Northwood 600.00
Seaweed, bl opal 400.00
Seaweed, cranberry satin...1,000.00
Seaweed, wht opal 225.00
Spanish Lace, wht opal 150.00
Stripe, Wide; bl opal 450.00
Swirl, gr opal..400.00
Twist Blown, bl, wide waist...250.00
Venetian Diamond, cranberry..225.00
Wide Waist, wht opaque w/bl floral, Northwood.............100.00
Windows (Swirled), wht opal 250.00

Sumida Ware

First made outside Kyoto, Japan, about 1870, Sumida Ware is a whimsical yet serious type of art pottery, easily recognized by its painted backgrounds and applied figures. Though most often painted red, examples with green or black backgrounds may be found as well. Vases and mugs are easier to find than other forms, and most are characterized by the human and animal figures that have been attached to their surfaces. Because these figures are in high relief, it is not unsual to find them chipped; it is important to seek a professional if restoration work is needed. It is not uncommon to find examples with the red background paint missing; collectors generally leave such pieces as they find them. Our advisor for this category is Jeffery Person; he is listed in the Directory under Florida.

Ashtray, figure (in gr) hangs on rim, red bowl w/brn border, mk, 5" ...100.00
Ashtray, figure w/arms wide, mouth open, gr/wht pearl, mk/sgn, 4" H...225.00
Ashtray, 4 rats on border (appl), celadon bowl, mk/sgn, oval, 5" .200.00
Biscuit jar, 3 glazed figures appl+1 as finial, red ground, mk/sgn, 7"...350.00
Bowl, boat shape, bsk w/drip glaze, 8" L, man & child on edge, mk/sgn .325.00
Bowl, gr, 3", w/figure (enameled) sitting on edge, mk/sgn 175.00
Bowl, red, oval, 7" L, w/8 appl/enameled figures, mk/sgn 325.00
Bowl, red, 6", 3 figures (enameled/appl) peering into it, mk 175.00
Bowl, 5 scholars, appl/enameled on red ground, ped ft, mk/sgn, 6" H ...350.00
Cr/sug, man on lid, elephant pcs appl on red, trunk hdls, mk/sgn, 4" 325.00
Cup, 2 figures (appl, w/enamel jackets) on red, +plain saucer, mk/sgn..125.00
Figure, male w/dk-glazed clothing holds sm pagoda, mk, 8" 350.00
Figure, man (enameled) holds fishing pole, bsk face/hands, mk, 8" .325.00
Humidor, house shape w/enamel roof, girl as finial, red ground, mk, 6" ..300.00

Humidor, man hugs knees, fly on eye, red ground, boy on lid, mk/sgn, 6"..275.00
Humidor, tigers appl on red ground, enamel border, mk, 6" 250.00
Incense burner, elephant w/pagoda finial, natural colors, mk/sgn, 8" ..300.00
Incense burner, 2 boys on vase/3rd on lid, foo dog ea side on red, ftd.275.00
Incense burner, 2 boys w/ball appl on red, mc border/lid, 3 ft, mk, 5".275.00
Inkwell, dbl; child peers over top, red w/mc, mk/sgn, 5" L...........275.00
Jardiniere, children (mc enamel) bounce balls on red, mk/sgn, 10"......500.00
Jardiniere, elders (bl/wht robed) w/scrolls on red ground, mk/sgn, 14".650.00
Lamp, children (mc enamel) play on bridge, red ground, mk/sgn, 13".500.00
Mug, body: 2 elephants w/trunks as hdls, appl/pnt man w/snail, mk/sgn.175.00
Mug, elephant appl on red w/mc, mk/sgn, 5" 140.00
Mug, man w/egg basket, bl/wht coat, appl on red w/mc drip, mk/sgn, 4"..125.00
Pitcher, dragon hdl (brn), red ground w/drip glaze, mk, 6"..........175.00
Pitcher, leaves/flowers, appl/enameled on red, mk/sgn, 4" 150.00
Pitcher, rooster body w/appl brn wolves in bl/wht jackets, mk/sgn, 13"..350.00
Tankard, 2 lg men w/barrel, appl/enameled on red ground, mk/sgn, 13".450.00
Teapot, boy (full figure) by hut, brn on red, flat style, mk/sgn, 6" 300.00
Teapot, boy/girl blow bubbles, appl on red w/mc at top, mk/sgn, 6" ..250.00
Teapot, 2 children play, appl/enameled on red, flat style, mk/sgn, 8".325.00
Teapot, 2 children play w/shells, brn on red, mk/sgn, 8" L 325.00
Toby jug, hands as spout, red ground, w/lid, mk/sgn, 9"...............300.00
Toothpick holder, seated figure at side, red w/mc top part, mk, 3"...75.00
Vase, medallions w/molded figures (2), clay on brn drip, mk/sgn, 10"..285.00
Vase, monkey & tree, red ground, mk/sgn, 2" 110.00
Vase, monkeys at waterfall (ea side), appl, pilgrim form, mk/sgn, 12"..1,500.00
Vase, wht magnolia/leaves appl, gr ground, sgn/mk, 12" 350.00
Vase, 3 climbing figures in bl/wht robes, mc drip on natural, mk, 9" ..400.00

Vase, 75 monkeys, some in blue and white coats, applied on red ground (paint now missing), marked and signed, 18", $2,200.00. (Photo courtesy Jeffrey Person)

Wall pocket, 4 dressed brn monkeys, appl/enameled on bsk, mk/sgn, 9" W ...325.00
Water jar, 2 dressed monkeys appl on red w/drip border, bail hdl, mk..225.00

Sunderland Lustre

Sunderland lustre was made by various potters in the Sunderland district of England during the eighteenth and nineteenth centuries. It is often characterized by a splashed-on application of the pink lustre, which results in an effect sometimes referred to as the 'cloud' pattern. Some pieces are transfer printed with scenes, ships, florals, or portraits.

Bowl, Ship Caroline blk transfer onw ht w/pk cloud border, 4x10"...435.00
Jar, clipper ship transfer, appl gr hdls, w/lid, 5" 550.00
Jug, May Peace & Plenty on Our Nation..., blk transfer, 9⅜" 650.00

Mug, Christening; Mary Ellen 1854, sailing ship/Iron Bridge **650.00**
Pitcher, 3 oval medallions, blk sailing ship transfer, 7¼" **550.00**
Plaque, clipper ship transfer w/mc, May Peace..., 9½x8½" **400.00**
Plaque, Iron Bridge, blk transfer w/lustre swirls, 1820s, 9x8"......**400.00**
Plaque, Prepare To Meet Thy God, brn transfer w/yel border, 6½"..**500.00**
Plaques, God Is Love/Thou God Seest Me, blk transfer, 7½x8½", pr.**300.00**
Sauce boat, transfer scene in pk, ca 1820, 3¼x5" **110.00**

Surveying Instruments

The practice of surveying offers a wide variety of precision instruments primarily for field use, most of which are associated with the recording of distance and angular measurements. These instruments were primarily made from brass; the larger examples were fitted with tripods and protective cases. These cases also held accessories for the instruments, and these can sometimes play a key part in their evaluation. Instruments in complete condition and showing little use will have much greater values than those that appear to have had moderate or heavy use. Instruments were never polished during use, and those that have been polished as decorator pieces are of little interest to most avid collectors.

Alidade, Gurley, low post explorer model #580, w/cover & case ...**400.00**
Alidade, Gurley explorer's, complete, ca 1915, EX **600.00**
Alidade, W&LE Gurley #584, EXIB **395.00**
Clinometer, Reynolds, Birmingham England, 1767-81, VG........**300.00**
Compass, Alex Mabon & Son, miner's dial, polished brass/wood, ca 1870.**2,000.00**
Compass, Dietzgen Brunton style, aluminum, 1894 to 1926 Pat dates, VG...**105.00**
Compass, Keuffel & Esser #5334, 4" needle, EX, w/ball joint & box ..**225.00**
Compass, Michael Rupp, 5" needle, ca 1860, EX **1,500.00**
Compass, miner's; Keuffell & Esser #5293, dipping needle, EXIB..**175.00**
Compass, solar; WM J Young & Co w/James Foster, 1863, EXIB..**10,000.00**
Compass, W&LE Gurley, 6" needle, mid-1800s, 15" L, G+ in mahog box..**1,795.00**
Compass, Wm J Young, surveyor's venier, 6" needle, 1860s, EXIB...**2,000.00**
Heliotrope, Steinheil; Bausch & Lomb, ca 1910, EX **1,500.00**
Level, combination; AS Aloe, ca 1923, 12", EXIB.....................**450.00**
Level, dumpy; Buff & Buff, ca 1900, 18", EXIB **800.00**
Level, dumpy; Buff & Buff, internal focus, 1920, 15", EXIB........**500.00**
Level, dumpy; Keuffel & Esser, ca 1913, 18", EXIB **500.00**
Level, tier; CL Berger & Sons, ca 1910, EX in maple case.......**1,000.00**
Level, wye; Buff & Buff, ca 1930, 18", EXIB.............................**600.00**
Level, wye; Gurley, aluminum & brass, ca 1948, 18", EXIB **450.00**
Level, wye; Keuffel & Esser, convertible, w/built-in compass, EXIB..**595.00**
Level, wye; Keuffel & Esser architect's #5111, ca 1924, EX.........**450.00**
Level, wye; Stackpole & Bro, removable base, 1870s, 17", VG...**700.00**
Level, wye; W&LE Gurley #376, early 1800s, 20", VG...............**695.00**
Leveling head, plane table; Buff & Buff, ca 1900, EX................**400.00**
Pantograph, Dietzgen model 1893, nickel silver, ca 1930, EXIB..**1,000.00**
Theodolite, FE Brandis & Sons, triangulation w/sliding level, 1906, EX...**3,000.00**
Theodolite, Stackpole & Bro, ca 1870, EX.............................**1,500.00**
Theodolite, T Cooke & Sons, ca 1890, EXIB.........................**2,000.00**
Transit, Berger, for calibrating aircraft compasses, 1;950s, EX **550.00**
Transit, Gurley #52, complete, ca 1929, VG **1,000.00**
Transit, H Heiseley & Son Harrisburg, plated brass, 6¼" dial, 14" ..**1,075.00**
Transit, Heller & Brightly, quick leveling base, ca 1875, EX ...**1,500.00**
Transit, Keuffel & Esser, Y&S #5166 Special Survey, ca 1918, EX ..**695.00**
Transit, Keuffel & Esser #5030, ca 1887, EXIB......................**2,000.00**
Transit, Keuffel & Esser #5077, w/9" scope/compass & full circle, EX...**875.00**
Transit, W&LE Gurley #3B Engineer's, 5" needle, 1890s, EXIB...**1,200.00**
Tripod, Keuffel & Esser, stiff legs, staff mt for compass, early, VG...**275.00**
Tripod, tapered post w/thimble, mid-1700s-1800s, EX...............**500.00**
Tripod, Warren Knight, oak, stiff legs, ca 1920, EX **150.00**
Wading rod set, Gurley's Hydraulic Current Meters #612/621/624, EX..**225.00**

Swastika Keramos

Swastika Keramos was a line of artware made by the Owens China Company of Minerva, Ohio, around 1902 – 1904. It is characterized either by a coralene type of decoration (similar to the Opalesce line made by the J. B. Owens Pottery Company of Zanesville) or by the application of metallic lustres, usually in simple designs. Shapes are often plain and handles squarish and rather thick, suggestive of the Arts and Crafts style. Our advisors for this category are Suzanne Perrault and David Rago; they are listed in the Directory under New Jersey.

Vase, bands of gold swastikas around gray 'stone' panels, 7x5", EX ..**345.00**
Vase, floral on gold, sm rim, shouldered, 8"................................**85.00**
Vase, irises, pk/gold on bronze tone, bulbous, minor wear, 11"....**425.00**
Vase, trees, gold on gold & red, raised medallion, 12x4½", $300 to ..**400.00**
Vase, trees, silver on silver & red, raised medallion, 12x4½", VG ..**150.00**

Syracuse

Syracuse was a line of fine dinnerware and casual ware which was made for nearly a century by the Onondaga Pottery Company of Syracuse, New York. Early patterns were marked O.P. Company. Collectors of American dinnerware are focusing their attention on reassembling some of their many lovely patterns. In 1966 the firm became officially known as the Syracuse China Company in order to better identify with the name of their popular chinaware. Many of the patterns were marked with the shape and color names (Old Ivory, Federal, etc.), not the pattern names. By 1971 dinnerware geared for use in the home was discontinued, and the company turned to the manufacture of hotel, restaurant, and other aspects of commercial tableware.

Accent, plate, dinner; 9¾" **10.00**
Alpine, platter, rnd, 14⅞" **100.00**
Angelica, sugar bowl, w/lid..**65.00**
Apple Blossom, bowl, vegetable; rnd, 8⅞" **75.00**
Apple Blossom, gravy boat, w/attached underplate.........................**90.00**
Arcadia, bowl, vegetable; rnd, 9"..**50.00**
Arcadia, plate, salad; 8", from $17.50 to...**25.00**
Blue Mist, cup & saucer, flat..**15.00**
Bombay, plate, dinner; 10¼" **30.00**
Bracelet, creamer, 3⅛"..**40.00**
Bracelet, cup & saucer, demi; ftd **20.00**
Bracelet, plate, luncheon; 9" **20.00**
Brentwood, gravy boat, w/attached underplate................................**80.00**
Briarcliff, bowl, rim soup; 8" **22.00**
Briarcliff, bowl, vegetable; rnd, w/lid & hdls, 6¾" **110.00**
Briarcliff, plate, chop; rnd, 13⅛"...**90.00**
Burmese, sherbet, 2½" **25.00**
Canterbury, plate, bread & butter; 6¼" **14.00**
Canterbury, ramekin & saucer, 3½"..**30.00**
Caprice, coffeepot, w/lid, 3-cup **120.00**
Carousel, gravy boat, w/attached underplate...................................**100.00**
Carousel, plate, salad; 8⅛"..**14.00**
Cascade, cup & saucer, flat...**14.00**
Cathay (Green Trim), creamer, 2¾"..**55.00**
Cathay (Green Trim), plate, luncheon; 8⅞"......................................**22.00**
Celeste, bowl, vegetable; oval, 10" **80.00**
Celeste, platter, oval, 14⅛"...**70.00**
Charm, relish tray, 8⅛" **35.00**
Charm, sugar bowl, w/lid...**50.00**
China Spring, coffeepot, 4-cup, 6½" **140.00**
China Spring, plate, dinner; 10⅜"...**24.00**

Cliftondale, bowl, cranberry; 5" 45.00
Cliftondale, platter, oval, 14" 80.00
Clover, bowl, cream soup; flat 40.00
Clover, platter, oval, 16¼" 130.00
Concord Rose, celery dish, 12" 30.00
Cornwall, bowl, vegetable; rnd, w/lid 175.00
Cornwall, plate, salad; 8⅛" 17.50
Coronet, gravy boat, w/attached underplate..........70.00
Coronet, teapot, w/lid, 3-cup, 4" 160.00
Dearborn, plate, dinner; 10" 30.00
Dearborn, sugar bowl, w/lid 35.00
Dorian, bowl, cereal; 5¾" 24.00
Dorian, saucer 10.00
Dutchess, cup & saucer, ftd 60.00
Elegance, plate, bread & butter; 6⅜" 10.00
Elegance, platter, oval, 14⅞" 100.00
Elizabeth, bowl, cereal; lug hdl, 6" 20.00
Elizabeth, creamer 30.00
Elizabeth, platter, oval, 11⅞" 70.00
Fairburn, gravy boat, w/attached underplate 90.00
Fairburn, sugar bowl, w/lid 45.00
Festival, bowl, vegetable; rnd, w/lid 210.00
First Love, coffeepot, 4-cup, 8⅜" 140.00
First Love, cup & saucer, ftd 30.00
Floral Fantasy, platter, oval, 13⅜" 80.00
Gardenia, plate, snack 17.50
Gardenia, relish dish, 8" 30.00
Glory, bowl, fruit; 4¾" 20.00
Glory, cup & saucer, flat 30.00
Grace, coffeepot, 4-cup, 8⅜" 190.00
Grace, plate, salad; 8" 17.50
Grace, sugar bowl, w/lid 45.00
Graymont, plate, chop; rnd, 13⅛" 100.00
Graymont, plate, dessert; 7¼" 14.00
Graymont, relish, 8⅞" 35.00
Haddon, bowl, cranberry; 5" 65.00
Jackstraws, bowl, vegetable; divided, oval, 10" 45.00
Jubilee, bowl, vegetable; rnd, 8½" 60.00
Jubilee, cup & saucer, ftd 38.50
Lady Mary, cup, ftd 35.00
Lady Mary, sugar bowl, w/lid 55.00
Largo, bowl, vegetable; rnd, w/lid 80.00
Largo, coffeepot 40.00
Marlene, cup, demi; ftd 25.00
Marlene, cup & saucer, ftd 35.00
Melodie, bowl, cream soup; flat 35.00
Melodie, bowl, vegetable; oval, 10" 60.00
Minuet, plate, dinner; 10¾" 35.00
Minuet, sugar bowl, w/lid 55.00
Nocturne, cigarette holder 25.00
Nocturne, coffeepot, 3-cup, 7⅜" 125.00
Old Colony, bowl, cream soup; flat 20.00
Orchard, gravy boat, w/attached underplate 80.00
Orchard, plate, salad; 8⅛" 20.00
Park Lane, platter, serving; oval, 12½" 40.00
Periwinkle, creamer 45.00
Poppy, plate, dinner; 9¾" 25.00
Raindrop, bowl, soup; rimmed, 8" 25.00
Rhapsody, coffeepot, 4-cup, 6½" 130.00
Rhapsody, plate, dinner; 10⅜" 30.00
Roseleaf, cup & saucer, ftd 35.00
Roseleaf, egg cup, dbl 8.00
Sandra, sugar bowl, w/lid 70.00
Sharon, platter, oval, 12" 55.00

Spring Garden, bowl, vegetable; oval, 9⅞" 80.00
Spring Garden, cup & saucer, ftd 45.00
Stansbury, plate, chop; rnd, 13⅛" 125.00
Surf White, coffeepot, 4-cup, 7¼" 65.00
Viking, gravy boat, w/attached underplate 80.00
Viking, platter, oval, 11⅞" 60.00
Webster, bowl, vegetable; rnd, 9" 80.00
Webster, cup & saucer, ftd 25.00
Windsor, sugar bowl, w/lid, 2¾" 75.00

Syrups

Values are for old, original syrups. Beware of reproductions and watch handle areas for cracks! See also various manufacturers (such as Northwood) and specific types of glass. Our coadvisors are Jeff Bradfield and Dale MacAllister; they are listed in the Directory under Virginia. See also Pattern Glass.

Arabian Nights, canary opal 1,250.00
Beatty Swirl, bl opal 450.00
Blown Twist, bl opal 650.00
Blown Twist, cranberry opal 850.00
Bubble Lattice, cranberry opal 800.00
Bubble Lattice, vaseline opal 650.00
Challinor's #313, bl opaque, Challinor Taylor, 7" 275.00
Challinor's Forget-Me-Not, pk opaque, 5¼" 300.00
Chrysanthemum Base Swirl, bl opal, 7¼", NM 425.00
Chrysanthemum Base Swirl, wht opal 275.00
Coinspot, 9-Panel, gr opal 325.00
Cone, bl cased, squatty, Consolidated, 4¼", EX 375.00
Cone, bl opaque, Consolidated, 6¼" 325.00
Cone, pk cased, Consolidated 325.00
Consolidated Criss-Cross, wht opal 600.00
Daisy & Fern, W VA Optic mold, bl, 6½" 325.00
Daisy & Fern, wht opal 225.00
Diamond Optic, cranberry w/mc floral; Tufts quadruple plate lid & hdl...600.00
Diamond Spearhead, bl opal 650.00
Diamond Spearhead, gr opal, Northwood 900.00
Egg Based, wht opaque w/pansies 175.00
Fern, syrup, wht opal 375.00
Flora, syrup, bl opal 480.00
Gonderman Swirl (Adonis), amber opal 650.00
Guttate, pk cased, Consolidated, 6¾" 375.00
Hobbs Hobnail/No 323 Dew Drop, rubena verde opal............1,000.00
Honeycomb (blown), bl opal 300.00
Inside Ribbing, wht opal 100.00
Invt Baby T'print, vaseline, repro lid 325.00
Invt T'print, amberina, 6" 600.00
Jewelled Heart, gr opal 475.00
Leaf Mold, cased cranberry spatter, NM 625.00
Leaf Mold, vaseline spatter 550.00
Poinsettia, wht opal 275.00
Reverse Swirl, bl, Pat date on lid 350.00
Reverse Swirl, Collared; bl, Model Flint, 6" 450.00
Reverse Swirl, cranberry opal 650.00
Reverse Swirl, pale vaseline opal 400.00
Ribbed Pillar, frosted cranberry & wht spatter, NM ...325.00
Ring Neck, cranberry & wht spatter 350.00
Royal Ivy, cased spatter, Northwood 600.00
Royal Ivy, rubena, Northwood, 6¼", NM 450.00
Seaweed, wht opal 225.00
Spanish Lace, bl opal 375.00
Stripe, Wide; wht opal 225.00

Swirl, cranberry opal 450.00
Swirl, gr opal 375.00
Tokyo, bl opal 250.00
Valencia Waffle, bl, Adams & Co, 8", NM 125.00

Target Balls

Prior to 1880 when the clay pigeon was invented, blown glass target balls were used extensively for shotgun competitions. Approximately 2¾" in diameter, these balls were hand blown into a three-piece mold. All have a ragged hole where the blowpipe was twisted free. Target balls date from approximately 1840 (English) to World War I, although they were most widely used in the 1870 – 1880 period. Common examples are unmarked except for the blower's code — dots, crude numerals, etc. Some balls were embossed in a dot or diamond pattern so they were more likely to shatter when struck by shot, and some have names and/or patent dates. When evaluating condition, bubbles and other minor manufacturing imperfections are acceptable; cracks are not. The prices below are for mint condition examples. Our advisor for this category is C.D. Kilhoffer; he is listed in the Directory under Maryland.

Boers & CR Delft Flesschen Fabriek, lt gr, rare, 2⅝" 500.00
Bogardus' Glass Ball Pat'd Apr 10 1877, amber, hobnails, 2⅝" ..3,250.00
Bogardus' Glass Ball Pat'd April 10 1877, amber, Am, 2¾" 400.00
Bogardus' Glass Ball Pat'd April 10 1877, cobalt, 2¾" 800.00
Bogardus' Glass Ball Pat'd April 10 1877, gr, 4-dot variant 1,600.00
C Newman, Dmn Quilt, amber, rare, 2⅝" 800.00
CTB Co, blk pitch, Pat dates on bottom, Am 200.00
Dmn Quilt w/plain center band, clear, ground top, Am..............150.00
Dmn Quilt w/plain center band, cobalt, 2⅝" 250.00
Dmn Quilt w/shooter emb in 2 panels, clear, English.................300.00
Dmn Quilt w/shooter emb in 2 panels, cobalt, English 700.00
Dmn Quilt w/shooter emb in 2 panels, deep moss gr, English 500.00
Dmn Quilt w/shooter emb in 2 panels, med gr, English 375.00
Emb dmns, dk amber w/hint of red, 2⅝" 325.00
Emb dmns, dk cobalt, 2¾" 550.00
For Hockey's Pat Trap, gr aqua, 2⅜" 900.00
Glashuttenewotte Un Charlottenburg, clear, emb dmns, 2⅝" 700.00
Gurd & Son, London, Ontario, amber, Canadian 500.00
Hockey's Pat Trap, aqua, English, 2½" 900.00
Horizontal bands (7), tobacco amber, 2⅝"...............................200.00
Horizontal ribs (2) intersect w/2 vertical, cobalt, 2⅝"................120.00
Ilmenau (Thur) Sophiehutte, amber, Dmn Quilt, Germany 400.00
Ira Paine's Filled Ball Pat Oct 23 1877, cobalt, w/orig feathers...4,000.00
Man shooting, cobalt, emb dmns, 2⅝" 700.00
Mauritz Widfords, honey amber, 2⅝", EX 600.00
NB Glass Works Perth, pale gr, English...................................100.00
Plain, amber w/mold mks 65.00
Plain, cobalt w/mold mks 150.00
Plain, dk teal gr w/mold mks, 2¾" 300.00
Plain, pk amethyst w/mold mks, 2⅝" 250.00
PMP London, cobalt, chip, 2⅛" 125.00
T Jones, Gunmaker, Blackburn, cobalt, English, 2⅝"................450.00
T Jones, Gunmaker, Blackburn, pale bl, English........................125.00
Van Cutsem A St Quentin, cobalt, 2¾" 100.00

Related Memorabilia

Ball thrower, dbl; old red pnt, ME Card, Pat...78, 79, VG 900.00
Clay birds, Winchester, Pat May 29 1917, 1 flight in box..........100.00
Pitch bird, blk DUVROCK...1.00
Shell, dummy, w/single window, any brand 35.00
Shell, dummy shotgun, Winchester, window w/powder, 6" 125.00

Shell set, dummy, Gamble Stores, 2 window shells, 3 cut out.....125.00
Shell set, dummy, Winchester, 5 window shells 175.00
Shell set, dummy shotgun, Peters, 6 window shells+full box.......175.00
Shotshell loader, rosewood/brass, Parker Bros, Pat 1884.............50.00
Target, Am, sheet metal, rod ends mk Pat Feb 8 '21, set 25.00
Target, blk japanned sheet metal, Bussey Patentee, London.........50.00
Target, BUST-O, blk or wht breakable wafer 20.00
Thrower, oak wood base, heavy steel spring, leather wrap, ca 1900, EX ..1,200.00
Trap, Chamberlain Cartridge...Nov 7th 05...USA, CI, 21½" L, EX ...1,500.00
Trap, DUVROCK, w/blk pitch birds 225.00
Trap, MO-SKEET-O, w/birds 150.00

Taylor, Smith and Taylor

Producers of mainly dinnerware and kitchenware, this company operated in Chester, West Virginia, from about 1900 to 1982. Today collectors enjoy reassembling some of their lovely patterns. Some of their most collectible lines are Lu Ray and Vistosa (see also those categories), but many of their decorated lines are popular as well. Reville Rooster features a large colorful red and orange rooster on simple shapes; Pebble Ford is a plain-colored ware with specks of dark and light blue-green, yellow, gray, and tan sprinkled throughout. There are many others.

They made advertising pieces and souvenir ware as well. If you'd like more information on this type of product, we recommend *Collector's Guide to Souvenir China* by Laurence W. Williams (Collector Books).

Bowl, berry; Boutonniere, 5¼" 5.00
Bowl, Boutonniere, 8" 13.50
Bowl, cereal; Reveille Rooster, 6"...9.00
Bowl, Chateau Buffet, wht w/aqua int, 6"................................8.00
Bowl, Pebble Ford, 5¼" 6.50
Bowl, Reveille Rooster, 9½" L 17.50
Casserole, Boutonniere, w/lid, 10" W 22.00
Casserole, Cathay, w/hdls, 10" W 50.00
Coffeepot, King O'Dell, 8" 50.00
Coffeepot, Pebble Ford, wht 75.00
Creamer, Boutonniere, 4¼" 7.00
Creamer, Empire shape, red/gold leaves on ivory w/red line trim..10.00
Creamer, Iona 42.00
Creamer, Jamaica, Empire shape, gold trim 10.00
Cup, Cathay 4.50
Cup & saucer, Empire shape, pk floral w/wide gr border.............8.00
Cup & saucer, Pebble Ford, 2½", 3¾" 7.50
Gravy boat, Cathay, 4¾" L 28.00
Plate, Azura, 7" 6.00
Plate, Boutonniere, 6¾" 4.50
Plate, Boutonniere, 10"...7.50
Plate, Cathay, 10" 7.00
Plate, Daylily, 10" 15.00
Plate, ear of corn decal, sgn RK Beck, 9½", $55 to....................65.00
Plate, fish decal, sgn RD Beck, 9¾", from $25 to.......................35.00
Plate, Java Key, 6¾" 4.00
Plate, King O'Dell, 8"..10.00
Plate, lady's portrait on yel, sgn Vittori, 9", from $55 to..............65.00
Plate, Music Hath Charms, minstral street scene decal, 8", $25 to..35.00
Plate, Pebble Ford, 10¼"...8.50
Plate, Reveille Rooster, 6¾" 3.00
Plate, roses on shaded brn, ca 1908-15, 9¼", from $40 to 50.00
Platter, Autumn Harvest, 13½" 16.00
Platter, Castle on Lake, red transfer, 10".....................................9.00
Platter, Garland shape, emb leaf border, pk/gray floral, w/gold, 13" ..16.00
Platter, Reveille Rooster, 13½" 22.00
Shakers, Boutonniere, 2", pr...20.00

Shakers, Cathay, w/hdl, 4¼", pr...**42.00**
Shakers, King O'Dell, 3½", pr...**40.00**
Sugar bowl, Vogue shape, pastel florals, silver trim, w/lid.............**15.00**
Tureen, Bridal Flower, w/lid, 9" dia....................................**45.00**

Tea Caddies

Because tea was once regarded as a precious commodity, special boxes called caddies were used to store the tea leaves. They were made from various materials: porcelain, carved and inlaid woods, and metals ranging from painted tin or tole to engraved silver. Our advisor for this category is Tina Carter; she is listed in the Directory under California.

Applewood, apple shape w/silver escutcheon, 4⅛", EX............**1,875.00**
Burl mahog, coffin shape, ball ft, early, 8½x15x8½", EX.........**2,185.00**
Burl vnr w/band inlay, bun ft, compartments, old rfn, 7x15x9" ..**450.00**
Burl vnr w/banded inlay, 8-sided, ivory escutcheon, 5x4½"......**345.00**
Ceramic, bl flower & butterfly transfers, Worcester, 3¾"...........**285.00**
Ironstone, bl & wht bombè form, Stone China, early 19th C, 8"..**485.00**
Mahog vnr w/banded inlay, divided int, 6⅛x12x6", EX.............**315.00**
Mahog vnr w/inlay stringing, dome top, ivory escutcheon, 7" L, EX.**1,400.00**

Mahogany veneer with line and star medallion inlay, three compartments with baffle for mixing bowl, minor repairs, 6x12x5⅛", $1,300.00. (Photo courtesy Garth's Auctions, Inc.)

Mahog vnr w/shell inlay medallions, rprs, 4¼x7½x4½" **800.00**
Mahog w/figured vnr, appl trim, trn ft, hinged lid, 9x14x8"........**575.00**
Metal, coffin shape, fitted int w/brass lids, bracket base, 7x9x5".**260.00**
Oak Wm IV, sarcophagus form, molded lid, Pollard, 6½x10x5½" ..**145.00**

Tea Leaf Ironstone

Tea Leaf Ironstone became popular in the 1880s when middle-class American housewives became bored with the plain white stone china that English potters had been exporting to this country for nearly a century. The original design has been credited to Anthony Shaw of Burslem, who decorated the plain ironstone with a hand-painted copper lustre design of bands and leaves. Originally known as Lustre Band and Sprig, the pattern has since come to be known as Tea Leaf Lustre. It was produced with minor variations by many different firms both in England and the United States. By the early 1900s, it had become so commonplace that it had lost much of its appeal.

Items marked Red Cliff are reproductions made from 1950 until 1980 for this distributing and decorating company of Chicago, Illinois. Hall China provided many of the blanks.

Our advice for this category comes from Home Place Antiques, whose address is listed in the Directory under Illinois.

Baker, Wilkinson, 9½x6¾" **30.00**
Bone dish, scalloped, Meakin...**75.00**
Bone dish, scalloped, Wilkinson **75.00**

Bowl, sq w/scalloped rim, Meakin, ca 1885, 2⅞x8¼x8½", EX......**40.00**
Bowl, vegetable; Cable, w/lid, Burgess...................................**235.00**
Bowl, vegetable; Fish Hook, bracket ft, w/lid, Meakin, 11x7".....**195.00**
Bowl, vegetable; Pagoda, sq, w/lid, Burgess **265.00**
Brush box, Cable, Burgess...**295.00**
Butter dish, Bamboo, Meakin, 4½x6" **165.00**
Butter dish, Fish Hook, Meakin, w/drain **175.00**
Butter pat, Anthony Shaw & Sons, VG..................................**16.00**
Butter pat, Meakin, 2¾" sq..**14.00**
Butter pat, Meakin, 3¼"...**15.00**
Coffeepot, Basketweave, Shaw, 1887....................................**295.00**
Coffeepot, Daisy 'n Chain, Wilkinson, 1890s, 8½" **165.00**
Coffeepot, Lily of the Valley, Shaw, 1860s **425.00**
Coffeepot, Simplicity, Powell & Bishop, 1880s.........................**95.00**
Creamer, Wedgwood, 5¼" **165.00**
Cup & saucer, Adams Microtex..**35.00**
Cup & saucer, Burgess, 2½x3½", 6".....................................**60.00**
Cup & saucer, Pomegranate **85.00**
Cup plate, unmk, 3½" **60.00**
Cup plate, Wilkinson, 3¼"..**60.00**
Egg cup, Boston, wide mouth, ftd **395.00**
Gravy boat, W&E Corn, 8½"..**65.00**
Nappy, Red Cliff, ca 1950-80...**18.00**
Pitcher, milk; Bamboo, Meakin, 7½"....................................**265.00**
Pitcher, Shaw, ca 1860, 5½x4"...**245.00**
Plate, Meakin, 7⅞"...**14.00**
Plate, Morning Glory, 9¾"..**45.00**
Plate, Red Cliff, ca 1950-80, 8¼"...**18.00**
Plate, Teaberry, 8"...**35.00**
Plate, Wedgwood, 8⅝" **20.00**
Platter, Mellor Taylor & Co, 10½x8½".................................**45.00**
Platter, Wedgwood, 14x10¼"...**65.00**
Relish, Lily of the Valley, Shaw **245.00**
Shaving mug, leaf at hdl, Shaw **225.00**
Shaving mug, Meakin, 3¼x3½"...**185.00**
Sugar bowl, Bamboo, Grindley..**95.00**
Sugar bowl, Crystal shape, unmk, 1870s.................................**225.00**
Sugar bowl, low emb ribs, w/lid, Burgess, 6½" **165.00**
Teapot, Fish Hook, Meakin, 8½"..**225.00**
Toothbrush holder, Meakin, 5"..**195.00**
Toothbrush holder, Mellor Taylor **185.00**
Wash bowl & pitcher, Cable, Shaw.......................................**485.00**
Waste bowl, Burgess, 3x5⅜"..**45.00**

Teapots

Teapots have become popular collectibles in recent years with a surge in tea shops featuring tea, teapots, and serving afternoon tea. Collectors should be aware of modern teapots, which imitate older, similar versions. Study the types of pottery, porcelain, and china, as well as the marks. Multicolored, detailed marks over the glaze represent modern pieces. Teapots made in the last thirty years are quite collectible but generally don't demand the same prices as their antique counterparts.

A wide range of teapots can be found by the avid collector. Those from before 1880 are more apt to be found in museums or sold at quality auction houses. Almost every pottery and porcelain manufacturer in Asia, Europe, and America have produced teapots. Some are purely decorative and whimsical, while others are perfect for brewing a pot of tea. Tea drinkers should beware of odd-shaped spouts which sputter and drip. Reproductions to be aware of: majolica styles with modern marks, Blue Willow which has been made continuously for almost two centuries, and those marked Made in China (older teapots have 'chop marks' in Chinese).

Refer to various manufacturers' names for further listings. Our advisor for this category is Tina M. Carter, listed in the Directory under California. Her book, *Teapots*, is available at bookstores or direct from the author.

Aluminum, red hdl & finial, child sz......28.00
Artone (Dickens' character), Toby style, England, mini......25.00
Auto form, silver glaze, Morris Minor, Carlton, 1940s......495.00
Bear holding candy cane, paw spout, Made in Korea, Fitz & Floyd..75.00
Bl lustre w/appl flowers, Made in Germany, mini......25.00
Blue Net, cobalt & gold over wht, Lomonosov, modern......125.00
Bluebird, HP decor, music box base, plays when lifted, Enesco...225.00
Bluebird figural, HP rose vine, rattan hdl, unmk Banko ware, 1930-40s...95.00
Bone china w/HP floral & bl-gr trim, unmk, mini, 3"......25.00
Bonomelli Nice Tea, wht porc, ACF Porzellan mk, ind sz......15.00
Brn & yel mottle, Tundra Canada, 1960s......35.00
Brn coralene w/gold decor, Made in Japan, ca 1950, ind sz......22.00
Carousel horse form, mc ceramic, mk Heritage Mint Ltd, Taiwan.25.00
Charles & Diana reserve on wht, unmk English or German blank..110.00
Cliffs Near Newport Beach transfer w/gold, Made in Germany....35.00
Copper lustre, wht & copper poppies on band, Wade England, 4"..45.00
Coralene floral on blk, hinged lid, Alexandria Pottery...England..150.00
Corn Poppy, Susie Cooper, Wedgwood, 1960s-70s, from $85 to...95.00
Dogwood blossoms on pk lustre, unmk RS Prussia......350.00
Edward VII, 1901-1909; pk lustre w/gold, England......300.00
Elephant w/howdah & rider, metal bail hdl, Japan, 1940s-50s......85.00
Flora Danica, gold trim, Royal Copenhagen, 8-cup......2,800.00
Floral, HP details over transfer on yel matt, Austria, 5"......65.00
Graniteware, HP floral, metal trim, hinged lid, unmk, ca 1898, EX+.225.00
Graniteware, wht enamel souvenir of Oakland, pewter trim, ind sz....500.00
Hadden Hall (floral pattern), no-drip spout, Minton China, 1940s+...125.00
Humpty Dumpty, many colors, Lingard England, ca 1930......125.00
Japan Star, cobalt & red w/gold, tilted finial, Worcester, late 1700s..750.00
John Wesley, mk Wedgwood England, 1950s repro......95.00
June pattern, majolica-like floral, flower finial, Royal Falcon Ware..30.00
Lewis & Clark Expo, Portland OR, scene on cobalt, unmk Germany..40.00
Little Red Riding Hood, shiny tin, USA, modern repro, child sz..22.00
May, scene w/girl, MIE, child sz......65.00
McCormick Tea House, cottage form, 1980s......40.00
Monkey on skates w/candy, decal on wht, Edwin M Knowles USA, child sz...30.00
Orange lustre, sq sides, Crooksville China Co, 1940s......75.00
Oriental garden scene relief w/appl trees & figures, Ardalt..., 8"...50.00
Peking duck on stand, bail hdl, China, mini, 2"......25.00
Persian cat, rose at neck is spout, ribbon hdl, Fitz & Floyd......65.00
Pyrex, rnd w/blown glass hdl, USA mk, 1930s-40s, from $110 to..125.00
Quail, tail hdl, Imari-style decor, Royal Crown Derby, 1988......1,000.00
Rose Chintz, creamware, Johnson Bros for Wedgwood......100.00
Roses HP on wht, loop hdl, HP Japan mk......95.00
SaladaTea, pk or gr, 1930s, ind sz......30.00
Shamrock, Belleek, modern gr mk, 1970s-90s......225.00
Sherlock Holmes, hat removes, Dan Brasier, Hall, 1988, w/pamphlet...250.00
Snowman w/broom & snowball, hat is lid, Made in Korea, Fitz & Floyd...75.00
Tetley Tea, wht porc, figure on lid, Lyons-Tetley Co, modern......75.00
Victorian children playing, heavy wht china, unmk Germany, child sz...45.00
Victorian scene on circular shape, HP & gold decor, unmk Limoges...55.00
Violets w/gold, swirled body, Japan, Enesco, from $45 to......65.00
Voilets decal, Japan Fine China, late 1950s, ind......30.00
Washington DC Capitol transfer w/HP details & gold, Germany.40.00
Watermelon slice form, flower finial, Taiwan, modern......30.00

Teco

Teco artware was made by the American Terra Cotta and Ceramic Company, located near Chicago, Illinois. The firm was established in 1886 and until 1901 produced only brick, sewer tile, and other redware. Their early glaze was inspired by the matt green made popular by Grueby. 'Teco Green' was made for nearly ten years. It was similar to Grueby's, yet with a subtle silver-gray cast. The company was one of the first in the United States to perfect a true crystalline glaze. The only decoration used was through the modeling and glazing techniques; no hand painting was attempted. Favored motifs were naturalistic leaves and flowers. The company broadened their lines to include garden pottery and faience tiles and panels. New matt glazes (browns, yellows, blue, and rose) were added to the green in 1910. By 1922 the artware lines were discontinued; the company was sold in 1930.

Values are dictated by size and shape, with architectural and organic forms being more desirable. Teco is usually marked with a vertical impressed device comprised of a large 'T' to the left of the remaining three letters.

Bowl, gr, emb wreath of leaves & berries, low, 2¼x9"......550.00
Bowl, gr (charcoaled), emb berries/leaves, #136, 2x9½"......1,600.00
Candlestick, terra cotta, cupped cup on slim std, circular hdl, 6".300.00
Chamberstick, lt gr, sqd hdl, rolled saucer edge, 5", NM......210.00
Pitcher, gr, lg curving integral hdl, 3¾"......475.00
Vase, aqua, baluster w/flared neck, buttress hdls, 9⅛"......635.00
Vase, bl, flared stick neck, WD Gates design, 5½"......550.00
Vase, brn, squat w/collar neck, 4"......600.00
Vase, brn, 4 long buttresses, WD Gates design, #A412, 6½"...1,300.00
Vase, cobalt, ovoid, 8¼"......1,000.00
Vase, gr, baluster, 7¾x3"......550.00
Vase, gr, bulbous base, sq open hdls, Gates design, 4"......700.00
Vase, gr, bulbous bottom, sq open hdls, Gates design, 8"......2,600.00
Vase, gr, closed-in rim, 4 triangular buttresses, 8¾", NM......2,100.00
Vase, gr, molded leaves w/openwork, flared, Dodd design, sm rpr, 12".7,000.00
Vase, gr, ovoid w/short neck, 4"......325.00
Vase, gr, sharp shoulder, 4½"......325.00
Vase, gr, spherical, 3"......600.00
Vase, gr, squat w/narrow neck, 5¾x4½"......650.00
Vase, gr, 2 buttressed hdls w/cutouts, WD Gates design, 6"......1,000.00
Vase, gr, 3-lobe/3-leg, 3 pierced quatrefoils, rpr, 9x6¾"......1,400.00
Vase, gr, 4 angular hdls, WD Gates design, sm rpr, 8"......1,900.00
Vase, gr, 4 buttresses, WD Gates design, sm rpr, 10"......5,500.00
Vase, gr, 4-hdld organic form, att F Albert, minor rstr, 15"....34,000.00
Vase, gr, 4-sided, F Albert design, sm rpr, 9¼"......2,800.00
Vase, gr (feathered), ridged & tapered, 4¾"......600.00
Vase, gr speckled, dimpled base, 4-sided neck, #365, 4"......550.00
Vase, gr w/ivory int, V form w/4 buttresses, H Smith, #400, 6x12", EX..4,750.00
Vase, gr w/veining, 4 buttressed hdls, #287, 6½x5½"......3,000.00
Vase, yel-gr, globular, WD Gates design, 4½"......950.00

Teddy Bear Collectibles

The story of Teddy Roosevelt's encounter with the bear cub has been oft recounted with varying degrees of accuracy, so it will suffice to say that it was as a result of this incident in 1902 that the teddy bear got his name. These appealing little creatures are enjoying renewed popularity with collectors today. To one who has not yet succumbed to their obvious charms, one bear seems to look very much like another. How to tell the older ones? Look for long snouts, jointed limbs, large feet and felt paws, long curving arms, and glass or shoe-button eyes. Most old bears have a humped back and are made of mohair stuffed with straw or excelsior. Cute expressions, original clothes, a nice personality, and, of course, good condition add to their value. Early Steiff bears in mint condition may go for a minimum of $150.00 per inch for a small bear up to $300.00 to $350.00 (sometimes even more) per inch for one 20" high or larger. These are easily recognized by the trademark button within the ear. (Please see Toys, Steiff, for specific values.)

Unless noted otherwise, values are for bears in excellent condition. For further information we recommend *Teddy Bear Treasury* by Ken Yenke; and *Teddy Bears, Annalee's & Steiff Animals, Second* and *Third Series,* by Margaret Fox Mandel. All are available from Collector Books. See also Toys, Steiff.

Key: jtd — jointed

Bears

Austria, brn plush, snout/hump/glass eyes, jtd, excelsior stuffed, 15"..225.00
Bing, copper mohair, glass eyes, jtd, excelsior stuffing, 1920s, 18"..8,000.00
Bing, shoe-button eyes, rust-colored nose/claws, ear tag, 12"...4,000.00
Chad Valley, blond mohair, jtd, button eyes, late 1950s, 13"......135.00
Chad Valley, gold mohair, jtd, amber eyes, embr nose, 1940s, 14"..200.00
Enesco, Edmund, Teddy Thompson's series, plush, 1996, 16", M..25.00
England, blond mohair, amber eyes, velvet nose, 1950s, 22".........50.00
England, wht mohair, felt pads, glass eyes, straw stuffed, 1930s, 16"..225.00
Germany, tan mohair, jtd, plastic eyes, late 1970s, 7"................135.00
Germany, tan mohair, jtd, swivel head, straw filled, felt paws, 15" .425.00
Germany, wht mohair, jtd, straw filled, w/crown & ribbon, 8"....375.00
Gund, wht w/velour pads, 9", M in Gotta Getta Gund ltd ed box .90.00
Hermann, blond mohair, inset muzzle, jtd, felt pads, 1930-50, 17" ..235.00
Hermann, brn frosted mohair, growler, jtd, straw stuffed, 1950s, 20" ..265.00
Hermann, chest tag, mini series from 1950, 5", minimum value.200.00
Russia, brn plush, button eyes, jtd, straw stuffed, ca 1930s, 16" ..700.00
Schuco, skater, mohair, key-wind, 1949, 9", minimum value...1,500.00
Schuco, Tricky, golden mohair, tail turns head, glass eyes, 1950, 8" ..950.00
Schuco, yes/no, caramel, glass eyes, 1950s, 5", NM 450.00
Schuco, yes/no, ginger, steel fr w/CI wheels, 1920s, 11½"............375.00
Unknown, brn mohair, jtd, blunt snout, growler, 1930s-40s, 11", VG...275.00
Unknown, brn mohair, MOP eyes, embr nose/mouth (worn), 10", G...225.00
Unknown, cinnamon mohair, embr nose, jtd, 1930s, 16", VG ...275.00
Unknown, gold mohair, jtd, button eyes, embr nose, 18"............425.00
Unknown, gold mohair, jtd, hump, embr nose, rpl pads, 1910s, 19"...275.00
Unknown, long golden mohair, jtd, straw stuffed, felt pads, 21" .375.00
Unknown, red-brn mohair, glass eyes, growler (silent), 18", VG..175.00
Unknown, tan mohair, hump, embr nose, jtd, excelsior stuffed, 14"...175.00
Unknown, tan mohair, jtd, glass eyes, ribbon scarf, 3"..................60.00
Unknown, tan mohair, jtd, growler (silent), 1930s, 21", VG+....550.00
Unknown, wht curly mohair, velveteen pads, 1950s, 17"............265.00

Related Memorabilia

Ad page, Cream of Wheat, teddy by bowl, 1957 Ladies' Home Journal ...6.00
Baby spoon, silver, teddy finial, Rogers Lunt & Bowlen, 3⅞" 85.00
Bedspread, teddy on wht chenille, twin sz, EX............................100.00
Bell, teddy transfer, Morgan Inc, Enesco, 4¼" 12.00
Book, Teddy Bears, Phillippa & Peter Waring, 1984, 128-pg, M...15.00
Bookends, teddy bear, brass, very heavy, 5¼x3½", pr 35.00
Brooch, teddy, Boucher, gold-tone w/pnt blk eyes, 1⅜"................45.00
Brooch, teddy, gold- & silver-tone w/blk crystal eyes....................20.00
Brooch, teddy, gold-tone w/gr faceted glass eyes & belly, 1¾x1¼" ..15.00
Brooch, teddy trio, gold-tone w/rhinestone eyes, ca 1960.............12.00
Cake pan, Wilton Korea #502-3754, aluminum, 1982, 13", EX 7.00
Cake pan, Wilton Microbakes, 1989, 10", M 9.00
Cookie jar, Teddy & I'm Stuffed, Treasure Craft 22.00
Egg cup, teddy figral, HP details, ceramic, unmk, 1940s, 2¼" 45.00
Figurine, girl w/teddy, ceramic w/HP details, Japan, 2½"..............14.00
Hamper, teddy transfer on pk metal, 1940s, child sz 55.00
Paper dolls, Teddy Bear Paper Dolls, Dover Publications, 1983, M uncut..16.00
Pattern, Simplicity Crafts #722, 22" bear & clothes, M 13.00
Photo, Carmen Cartellieri (film star) w/teddy, 1930s, postcard sz....28.00
Photo, girl holding teddy, blk/wht, 1940s, 8½x6½"+fr 35.00

Photo, 3 sisters, youngest w/teddy, ca 1900, 5x3¼".......................17.50
Postcard, Busy Bears series, Tuesday, Wash Day, #429, 1909, EX ..22.50
Postcard, Victorian child kissing bear, Germany, EX 12.00
Tape measure, celluloid figural, cloth tape, Japan, EX 95.00

Telephones

Since Alexander Graham Bell's first successful telephone communication, the phone itself has undergone a complete evolution in style as well as efficiency. Early models, especially those wall types with ornately carved oak boxes, are of special interest to collectors. Also of value are the candlestick phones from the early part of the century and any related memorabilia.

Automatic Electric #40, chrome trim, 1940s, EX orig.................125.00
Automatic Electric #40, no chrome trim, 1930s-50s, working 85.00
Candlestick, blk pnt on brass, no dial, #222A XHL, 11½", G 150.00
Kellogg, candlestick, 5¢ coin box on column, 1910s, rstr...........225.00
Kellogg, cradle style w/rnd base, 1920s, rstr 350.00
Monarch, oak case w/cathedral top, pony receiver, wall style, EX....285.00
Northern Electric, blk Bakelite, desk style, 1930s, VG working .125.00
Pay phone, Am Electric, chrome, 3-slot, EX working.................185.00
Pay phone, chrome, 1950s, working 275.00
Pay phone, rotary dial, chrome trim, 1955, 18x6½x6" 275.00
Stromberg Carlson, lt oak, 2-box wall type, VG orig.................375.00
Stromberg Carlson, metal, 1930s, incoming calls only 95.00
Stromberg Carlson, oak wall style, working, EX rstr..................275.00
Stromberg Carlson, walnut w/nickel trim, 2-box wall style, EX ..375.00
Stromberg Carlson #1058, oak case, wall type, EX orig............195.00
Western Electric, candlestick, #2 dial, rstr................................295.00
Western Electric, metal, wall type, 9x6x4", EX.........................100.00
Western Electric #102, rnd base, #2 dial, 1920s, rstr 250.00
Western Electric #202b1, VG working......................................165.00
Western Electric #302, blk plastic, 1930s-50s 85.00
Western Electric #302, pnt blk metal, 1938-40, VG....................95.00
Western Electric Trimline, clear plastic, rotary dial, 1967, EX....475.00

Novelty Telephones

'57 Chevy, horn ringer, MIB 30.00
Ball resting on bats, 1960s, MIB 40.00
Barbie Solo in the Spotlight, MIB...150.00
Bart Simpson, Columbia, 1990s, MIB..40.00
Bugs Bunny, Warner Exclusive, MIB, from $60 to 70.00
Elvis, sings Jail House rock & dances, 1995, 12", MIB 150.00
Garfield, Tyco, NM..65.00
Kermit (mouth open, holding receiver), EX.................................30.00
Mickey Mouse, AT&T, China, 1990s, 14½", NM 75.00
Mickey Mouse, Synanon, 1988, 10½", NM..................................95.00
Mickey Mouse, Western Electric, 1976, MIB.............................200.00
Power Rangers, MIP...30.00
Snoopy as Joe Cool, 1980s, MIB..50.00
Spider-Man, 1984, MIB..65.00
Tyrannosaurus Rex, 2-pc figural, MIB..95.00
Ziggy, 1989, MIB...75.00
7-Up Spot character, NM...80.00

Blue Bell Paperweights

First issued in the early 1900s, bell-shaped glass paperweights were used as 'give-aways' and/or presented to telephone company executives as tokens of appreciation. The paperweights were used to prevent stacks of papers from blowing off the desks in the days of overhead fans. Over the years they have all but vanished — some taken by retiring employees, others accidentally broken. The weights came to be widely used for advertising by individual telephone companies; and as the smaller companies merged to form larger companies, more and more new paperweights were created. They were widely distributed with the opening of the first transcontinental telephone line in 1915. The bell-shaped paperweight embossed 'Opening of Trans-Pacific Service, Dec. 23, 1931,' in peacock blue glass is very rare, and the price is negotiable. (Weights with 'open' in the price field are also rare and impossible to accurately evaluate.) In 1972 the first Pioneer bell paperweights were made to sell to raise funds for the charities the Pioneers support. This has continued to the present day. These bell paperweights have also become 'collectibles.' For further study we recommend *Blue Bell Paperweights, Telephone Pioneers of America Bells and Other Telephone Related Items, 2003 Revised Edition,* by Jacqueline Linscott Barnes; she is listed in the Directory under Florida.

ABA National Convention, cobalt 150.00
Bell System/Local & Long Distance, peacock 250.00
Bell/Telephone/Manufacturing Co/Anvers Belgique, cobalt ....OPEN
Bell/Telephone/Manufacturing Co/Anvers Belgique, peacock. ....OPEN
New York Telephone Company, ice bl 130.00
Pays 7% Mountain States, peacock 175.00
The Southwestern Telegraph & Telephone Company, cobalt 375.00
Time Is Money/Save It/Don't Go - Don't Write/But..., peacock......OPEN
Western Electric Company, peacock 225.00
Western Electric Company (inkwell), peacock 500.00

Large Telephone Pioneers of America (TPA) Commemoratives

Break-Up of the Bell System, 1984, carnival...............................OPEN
Diamond Jubilee 1911-1986, 1984, dk peacock 70.00
Nevada Bell, blk glass...100.00
Pacific Bell/1984-1994, crystal w/bl swirls 45.00
TPA, 1974, carnival 35.00
TPA, 1994, ruby red 50.00
TPA, 1999, Bell Atlantic, lt bl...25.00
TPA, 2000, Verizon, wht opal..45.00

Small Commemorative Bells

Bell System, The Chesapeake - Potomac, ice bl 425.00
Bell System/Bell System, cobalt 45.00
Bell System/Bell System, ice bl...125.00
Bell System/Bell System, ruby red...60.00
It Pays To Use the Yellow Pages, cobalt......................................95.00
Save Time...Telephone/Save Steps...Telephone, cobalt 125.00
1996 Fall Show Indianapolis IN, cobalt 25.00

Telescopes

Antique telescopes were sold in large quantities to sailors, astronomers, voyeurs, and the military but survive in relatively few numbers because their glass lenses and brass tubes were easily damaged. Even scarcer are antique reflecting telescopes, which use a polished metal mirror to magnify the world. Telescopes used for astronomy give an inverted image, but most old telescopes were used for marine purposes and have more complicated optics that show the world right-side up. Spyglasses are smaller, hand-held telescopes that collapse into their tube and focus by drawing out the tube to the correct length. A more compact instrument, with three or four sections, is also more delicate, and sailors usually preferred a single-draw spyglass. They are almost always of brass, occasionally of nickel silver or silver plate, and usually covered with leather or sometimes a beautiful rosewood veneer. Solid wood barrel spyglasses (with a brass draw tube) tend to be early and rare. Before the mid-

dle of the 1800s, makers put their names in elaborate script on the smallest draw tube, but as 1900 approached, most switched to plain block printing. British instruments from World War I made by a variety of makers are commonly found, sharing a format of a 2" objective, 30" long with three draws extended, a tapered main tube, and sometimes having low- and high-power oculars and beautiful leather cases. U.S. Navy WWII spyglasses are quite common but have outstanding optics and focus by twisting the eyepiece, which makes them weather-proof. The Quartermaster (Q.M.) 16x spyglass is 31" long, with a tapered barrel and a 2½" objective. The Officer of the Deck (O.D.D.) is a 23" cylinder with a 1½" objective. Very massive, short, brass telescopes are usually gun sights or ship equipment and have little interest to most collectors. World War II marked the first widespread use of coated optics, which can be recognized by a colored film on the objective lens. Collectible post-WWII telescopes include early refractors by Unitron or Fecker and reflectors by Cave or Questar. Modern spotting scopes often use a prism to erect the image and are of great interest if made by the best makers, including Nikon and Zeiss. Several modern makers still use lacquered brass, and many replica instruments have been produced.

A telescope with no maker's name is much less interesting than a signed instrument, and 'Made in France' is the most common mark on old spyglasses. Dollond of London made instruments for two hundred years, and this is probably the most common name on antiques; but because of their important technical innovations and very high quality, Dollond telescopes are always valuable. Bardou, Paris, telescopes are also of very high quality. Bardou is another relatively common name, since they were a prolific maker for many years, and their spyglasses were sold by Sears. Alvan Clark and Sons were the most prolific early American makers, in operation from the 1850s to the 1920s, and their astronomical telescopes are of great historical import.

Spyglasses are delicate instruments that were subject to severe use under all weather conditions. Cracked or deeply scratched optics are impossible to repair and lower the value considerably. Most lenses are doublets, two lenses glued together, and deteriorated cement is common. This looks like crazed glaze and is fairly difficult to repair. Dents in the tube and damaged or missing leather covering can usually be fixed. The best test of a telescope is to use it, and the image should be sharp and clear. Any accessories, eyepieces, erecting prisms, or quality cases can add significantly to value. The following descriptions and values assume that the telescope is in very good to fine condition and give the objective lens (obj.) diameter, which is the most important measurement of a telescope.

Our advisor for this category is Peter Abrahams, who studies and collects telescopes and other optics. Please contact him, especially to exchange reference material. (See his comments concerning online auctions under Binoculars; they are applicable to telescopes as well.) Mr. Abrahams is listed in the Directory under Oregon. (Please include SASE with questions.)

Key: obj — objective lens

Adams, George; 2" reflecting, brass cabriole tripod..................3,500.00
Bardou & Son, Paris, 4-draw, 50mm obj, leather, 36"................250.00
Bausch & Lomb, 1-draw, 45mm obj, wrinkled pnt, 17" 90.00
Brashear, 3½" obj, brass, tripod, w/eyepcs..................................4,500.00
Cary, London (script), 2" obj, tripod, w/3 eyepcs 3,000.00
Clark, Alvan; 4" obj, 48", iron mt on wooden legs...................9,000.00
Criterion RV-6 Dynascope, 6" reflector, 1960s............................500.00
Dallmeyer, London (script), 5-draw, 2½" obj, SP, 49" 800.00
Dollond, London (block), 2-draw, 2" obj, leather cover.............290.00
Dollond, London (script), brass, 3" obj, 40", on tripod 2,900.00
Dollond, London (script), 2-draw, 2" obj, leather cover.............450.00
France or Made in France, 3-draw, 30mm obj, lens cap.................80.00
McAlister (script), brass, 3½" obj, 45", tripod.........................3,000.00

Messer, London Day & Night, brass, mahog hand grip, 2-draw, 1860s, EX ..200.00
Mogey, brass, 3" obj, 40", on tripod, w/4 eyepcs 4,000.00
Negretti & Zambra, 2½" obj, equatorial mt, 36", tripod 2,500.00
Plossl, Wein, 2½" obj, Dialytic optics, 24", table-top tripod....4,000.00
Queen & Co (script), 6-draw, 70mm obj, wood vnr, 50" 1,000.00
Questar, reflecting, on astro mt, 1950s, 3½" dia 3,000.00
R&J Beck, 2" obj, 24", table-top tripod w/cabriole legs............2,500.00
Short, James; 3" dia reflecting, brass cabriole tripod.................4,000.00
Student's No 52, altazimuth to equatorial, 36" focal length, w/stand ...125.00
Tel Sct Regt Mk 2 S (many maker's names), UK, WWI 120.00
Unitron, 4" obj, wht, 60", on tripod, many accessories 3,000.00
Unmk, brass, 2" obj, spyglass, leather cover, from $150 to 300.00
Unmk, brass, 2" obj, stand w/cabriole legs 1,200.00
US Military, brass, very heavy, from $100 to............................300.00
US Navy, QM Spyglass, 16X, MK II, in box.............................220.00
Vion, Paris, 40mm obj, 3-draw, 40-power, 21", leather 110.00
Wollensak Mirroscope, 1950s, 12x2" dia, leather case.................300.00
Wood bbl, rnd taper, 1½" obj, sgn, 1800s.................................350.00
Wood bbl, 8-sided, 1½" obj, 1700s, 30" 1,500.00
Zeiss, brass, 60mm obj, w/eyepcs & porro prism, tripod 1,700.00
Zeiss Asiola, 60mm obj, prism spotting scope, pre-WWII 650.00

Televisions

Many early TVs have escalated in value over the last few years. Pre-1943 sets (usually with only one to five channels) are often worth $500.00 to $5,000.00. Unusually styled small-screen wooden 1940s TVs are 'hot'; but most metal, Bakelite, and large-screen sets are still shunned by collectors. Color TVs from the 1950s with 16" or smaller tubes are valuable; larger color sets are not. One of our advisors for this category is Harry Poster, author of *Poster's Radio & Television Price Guide 1920 – 1990, 2nd Edition*; he is listed in the Directory under New Jersey.

Key: t/t — table-top

Airline, #05GSE-3020A, mahog, t/t, 1950, 12" 35.00
Arvin, #3100TB, blond wood, TE-272 chassis, t/t, 1949, 10" 90.00
Capehart-Farnsworth, GV-260, mahog, t/t, 1947, 10" 225.00
Crosley, EU-30, wood console, DuMont RA-119 w/Crosley logo, 1952, 30".750.00

Crosley, #9-420M, 10" mahogany console model, 1949, $75.00.

(Photo courtesy Harry Poster)

Dumont, RA-109-A1, mahog, TV-radio, console, Winslow, 1950, 19"...55.00
Firestone, #13-G-3, mahog, t/t, 1948, 7" 125.00
General Electric, #12C109, mahog console, dbl doors, 1949, 12".45.00
Hallicrafters, T-67, mahog, push-button tuner, t/t, 1949, 10"......100.00
Meck, XB-702, wood t/t, 1948, 7" 175.00

Motorola, #10VK9R, red mahog console, TS-9 chassis, 1949, 10".85.00
National, TV-10T, mahog t/t, 1949, 10" 160.00
Olympic, TV-104, Cruzair, wood t/t, 1948, 10" 80.00
Panasonic, TR-1030C, plastic, portable, w/magnifier, 1984, 1½" .60.00
Philco, #50-T1104, Bakelite t/t, 1950, 10" 85.00
Philco, mahog t/t, #48-1000, 1948, 10" 300.00
RCA, #7T124, mahog console, 1951, 17" 25.00
RCA, #9T246, metal t/t, 1959, 10" 85.00
Regal, #1007, mahog t/t, 1948, 10" 90.00
Sentinel, #412, wood t/t, 1949, 10" 60.00
Sparton, #4952, blond t/t, 1949, 10" 125.00
Stromberg-Carlson, TC10, wood t/t, 1949, 10" 140.00
Sylvania, #120M, mahog t/t, 1-510-1 chassis, Halolight, 1952, 21".90.00
Transvision, #10CL, wood t/t w/built-in magnifier, 1947, 10".....400.00
Westinghouse, H-605T12, wood t/t, 1948, 12" 75.00
Westinghouse, H-611C12, wood consold, dbl doors, 1948, 12" 60.00
Zenith, G2322RZ, mahog t/t, 23G24 chassis, Claridge, 1949, 12"..150.00

Philco Predictas and Related Items

Made in the years between 1958 and 1960, Philco Predictas have become one of the most sought after lines of televisions in the post-war era. Predictas are now over forty-five years old, yet their atom-age styling is just as futuristic today as it was in 1958. Even in the new millennium, the Predicta line will continue to be highly collectible. Philco Predictas feature a swivel or separate enclosed picture tube and radical cabinet designs.

Please note that recently much has been said about sets equipped with the UHF option. Even though few sets were ordered with this option, it in no way makes the set any rarer. Advanced collectors who feel it is important for their collection should not pay more than $50.00 over the price of an equal non-UHF set.

The values given here are for as-found, average, clean, complete, unrestored sets, running or not, that have good picture tubes. Predictas that are missing parts or have damaged viewing screens will have a lower value. Above-average Predictas will have much higher values. Please keep in mind that Predictas that have been completely professionally restored to 'as new' in appearance as well as electronically can easily bring four to five times the stated values.

We need to mention that reproduction Predictas were manufactured in the 1990s. These were color sets (not black and white like the originals) and are currently being sold as 'colorized originals' on the Internet. Buyers need to know that no original Predictas were made in color. If the set is color, it is always a reproduction. Buyer Beware! Our advisor for Predicta televisions is David Weddington; he is listed in the Directory under Tennessee.

G4242 Holiday 21" t/t, wood cabinet, blond finish 475.00
G4242 Holiday 21" t/t, wood cabinet, mahog finish....................425.00
G4654 Barber-Pole 21" console, boomerang front leg, blond......725.00
G4654 Barber-Pole 21" console, boomerang front leg, mahog 650.00
G4710 Tandem 21" separate screeen w/25' cable, mahog finish..650.00
G4720 Stereo Tandem w/matching 1606S phonoamp, mahog...1,200.00
G4720 Stereo Tandem 21" separate screen, 4 brass legs, mahog .900.00
H3406 Motel 17" t/t, metal cabinet, cloth grill, no antenna.......275.00
H3408 Debutante 17" t/t, cloth grill, w/antenna, charcoal 375.00
H3410 Princess 17" t/t, metal grill, plastic tuner window...........400.00
H3410 Princess 17" t/t, orig metal stand, red finish.....................525.00
H3412 Siesta 17" t/t, w/clock-timer above tuner, gold finish 575.00
H4730 Danish Modern 21" console, 4 fin-shaped legs, mahog finish .950.00
H4744 Townhouse 21" room-divider, walnut shelves, brass finish ..1,400.00
17DRP4 picture tube, MIB, replacement for all 17" t/t Predictas.175.00
21EAPR or 21FDP4 picture tube, MIB, replacement for all 21" Predictas..275.00

Tennis Rackets

Early tennis rackets (pre-1940) generally exhibit these characteristics: head shape — may be oval, flat-top, transitional flat-top, triangular (or other); throat wedge — the triangular section of wood at the junction of the head and the handle may be concave, convex, solid, or laminated; handle — most from this era are not covered by leather and are either combed (grooved) or checkered wood, and some may have cork handles or enlargements at the butt end. Values vary, dependent on age, rarity, style, and condition. Brand and model are important, and all identifying decals should be legible and in good condition. Rackets from 1880 to 1940 range in price from $10.00 to $20.00 for the more common examples to hundreds of dollars for rare models such as the Hazel's Streamline.

Our advisor for this category is Donald Jones; he is listed in the Directory under Georgia. In the listings that follow, values apply to examples in excellent condition.

Key:
cx-lam — convex laminated   tran — transitional
cx-s — convex solid

AJ Reach, Driver, concave wedge, combed hdl, oval head, 1920..**75.00**
E Kent, Duchess, concave wedge, bulbous hdl, oval head, 1930 .**120.00**
Hazel's Streamline, branched wedge, leather hdl, oval head, 1935 ..**600.00**
Horsman, Elberton, concave wedge, smooth hdl, flat-top head, 1885..**450.00**
Iver Johnson, Special, cx-s wedge, bulbous hdl, tran head, 1900 ...**175.00**
Magnon, Superior, concave wedge, combed hdl, oval head, 1928.**75.00**
Slazenger, Demon, cx-lam wedge, fishtail hdl, oval head, 1910 ..**250.00**
Spaulding, Park, cx-s wedge, combed hdl, flat-top head, 1895....**450.00**
Wright-Ditson, Hub, cx-s wedge, checkered hdl, oval head, 1890..**175.00**
Wright-Ditson, Octagon, concave head, combed hdl, oval head, 1895..**120.00**
Wright-Ditson, Star, cx-s wedge, combed hdl, oval head, 1904 ..**135.00**

Teplitz

Teplitz, in Bohemia, was an active art pottery center at the turn of the century. The Amphora Pottery Works was only one of the firms that operated there. (See Amphora.) Art Nouveau and Art Deco styles were favored, and much of the ware was hand decorated with the primary emphasis on vases and figurines. Items listed here are marked 'Teplitz' or 'Turn,' a nearby city.

Basket, leaves & berries, mc/textured, cut-out hdl, 10½" **550.00**
Bust, Sappho, mc details, 17" **1,100.00**
Bust of young girl, gold/metallic irid, 16" **1,200.00**
Ewer, lady's profile/vines emb, cream on gr to red, BB 3789, 11⅜" ..**600.00**
Pitcher, flowers/cherries/gold, Stellmacher, elephant hdl, 10½" .**350.00**
Vase, appl roses w/gold on bl-gray, Dachsel, #1202/15, 15¾"...**2,950.00**
Vase, appl roses w/swag accents on bl-gr, Dachsel, #1198/16, 6"..**2,000.00**
Vase, florals, molded mask hdls, 16", pr...**300.00**
Vase, forest silhouette, orchid/wasp band on cobalt, squat, 7".....**275.00**
Vase, fruit & flowers emb on gr matt, gourd w/hdls, rstr, 6¾" **100.00**
Vase, leaves & geometrics, mc, cylindrical, #d, 10", NM **850.00**
Vase, lg hdls w/scrolls/dragons extend to openwork base, HP birds, 20"..**350.00**
Vase, medial band of bees w/decor above, swollen neck, bulbous, 6"..**400.00**
Vase, molded leaf & stem, yel to ivory w/gold rim, 6½", NM **375.00**
Vase, mushrooms & trees, mc, Daschel, shouldered cylinder, 15½"..**2,200.00**
Vase, mushrooms under trees, mc, Daschel, low/wide, 9" **900.00**
Vase, roses, brn/gold/gr/bl on ivory, dbl-gourd, 11" **600.00**
Vase, roses & vines, appl/HP on gourd shape, 19x9", from $900 to...**1,200.00**
Vase, roses on texture, Daschel, hdls/2-opening top, #1172 18, 6½" ...**400.00**
Vase, stylized floral, ivory/gold/brn/gr matt, 4-hdl, 10" **850.00**
Vase, stylized trees, dk gr, Daschel, cylindrical, 8" **1,400.00**

Vase, stylized trees, ivory/gold/brn matt, bulbous bottom, 7½" ...**325.00**
Vase, thistles, wht on gr-bl w/gold, dbl bulb, ca 1900, 4⅝" **400.00**
Vase, trees, ivory/brn tones, textured, gourd shape, 7½" **500.00**
Vase, vines & leaves, bl to gr, Daschel, ornate hdls, 6½" **900.00**
Vase, wheat, mc on texture, hdls, 2-opening top, #1172 18, 6½" **350.00**
Vase, 3-D man leading 2 horses on low ledge, gold/irid, 19"....**1,120.00**

Terra Cotta

Terra cotta is a type of earthenware or clay used for statuary, architectural facings, or domestic articles. It is unglazed, baked to durable hardness, and characterized by the color of the body which may range from brick red to buff.

Bust, lady w/hair in chignon, sq collar, 21"+wooden plinth.....**2,350.00**
Figure, draped nude female, on 8-sided plinth, late 19th C, 33" .**4,400.00**
Figure, lion, 4-color, hand tooling, 5¼x10¼x4½" **100.00**
Urn, Egg & Dart w/grapevines, lion-masks on ped ft, 19th C, 53" ..**3,500.00**
Urn, neoclassical style w/putti hdls & swags, 20th C, 60x31", pr ..**10,575.00**

Thermometers

Few objects man has invented have been so eloquently expressed both functionally and artistically as the ubiquitous thermometer. Developed initially by Galileo in 1593 as a scientific device, thermometers slowly evolved into decorative objet d'art, functional household utensils, and eye-catching advertising specialties. Most American thermometers manufactured early in the twentieth century were produced by Taylor (Tycos), and today their thermometers remain the most plentiful on the market. Decorative thermometers manufactured before 1800 are now ensconced in the permanent collections of approximately a dozen European museums. Because of their fragility, few devices of this era have survived in private collections. Nowadays most antique thermometers find their way to market through estate sales.

Advertising

Many companies have utilitzed thermometers as a means of promoting their products. From gasoline to soda pop, there are scores to choose from. Many were 'button' styles, approximately 12" in diameter with a protective, see-through dome-like cover and a sweep hand. Unless otherwise described, assume that the 12" round examples in our listing are of this design. For more information see *Advertising Thermometers* by Curtis Merritt. Our advisor for this category is Richard T. Porter, who holds the Guinness Book of World Records certificate for his collection of over 4,500 thermometers; he is listed in the Directory under Massachusetts.

B-1 Lemon-Lime, bl/wht strip w/protruding red ball, '50s, 16x5", NMIB ..**185.00**
Carter Inx, wht w/red letters, Pat Mar 16 1915, Ooshocton O, 27x7", VG .**250.00**
Dairy Queen, lg cone/logo, 1960s, 16x6", VG **300.00**
Delco Dry Charge Batteries, bl on wht, TW O'Connell, 12" dia .**175.00**
Double Cola, red w/yel & blk, ca late 1950s, 12" dia **375.00**
Ex-Lax, The Safe Chocolated.... dk bl/yel/wht sign w/temp dial, 36x8"..**425.00**
Grapette, bottle on wht, 1940s, Donaldson Art Sign Co, rectangular, M..**225.00**
Green Spot Soda, hand w/bottle, sign w/temp tube, 1950s, 16x5", NM.**375.00**
M&M Candy, yel w/red & wht behind temps, 1979, EX.............**275.00**
Marathon Oil, stand-up sign pole shape, 1950s, 7x2½" **135.00**
Nu Grape, die-cut tin bottle, 1940s, 17x5", EX **225.00**
Nu Grape Soda, row of bottles, sign w/temp tube, 1930s, 16x6", VG ..**200.00**
Oldsmobile Cutlass, mounts on car door by mirror, MIP............**365.00**
Orange Crush, die-cut tin bottle, 1950s, 28x7½", M...................**325.00**
Pabst Blue Ribbon Beer, wht, bl logo, TM Reg US Pat #2206, 12" dia, EX .**140.00**
Prestone Anti-Freeze, red/cobalt on lt gray enamel, 36x9", NM .**325.00**

Quaker State Motor Oil, gr shamrock/etc on wht, 39x8", EX **195.00**
Royal Crown Cola, bottle & temp tube side by side on wht, 13x6", VG .**185.00**
Schaefer Beer, red on wht, curved glass front, 10" dia **110.00**
Snow White Soda, snowman scene, wht on bl, 1950s, 17x5", EX...**250.00**
Stihl Chain Saws, red w/wht border, 12" dia................................**195.00**
TAB Cola, aluminum band/metal face, 1960s-70s, 12" dia, EX ..**210.00**
Valvoline Oil, can on yel, Pam Co, 1950-60s, 12" dia, VG.........**195.00**

Ornamental

Decorative thermometers run the gamut from plain tin household varieties to the highly ornate creations of Tiffany and Bradley and Hubbard. They have been manufactured from nearly every conceivable material — oak, sterling, brass, and glass being the favorites — and have tested the artistry and technical skills of some of America's finest craftsmen. Ornamental models can be found in free-hanging, wall-mounted, or desk/mantel versions. American-made thermometers available today as collectors' items were made between 1875 and 1940. The golden age of decoratives ended in the early 1940s as modern manufacturing processes and materials robbed them of their natural distinctiveness.

Prices are based on age, ornateness, and whether mercury or alcohol is used as the filler in the tube. A broken or missing tube will cut at least 40% off the value.

Key:
br — brass   Rea — Reaumer
Cen — Centigrade   sc — scale
Fah — Fahrenheit   stl — stainless
mrc — mercury in tube   strl — sterling
pmc — permacolor   VR — very rare
R — rare

Bradley & Hubbard, desk, br fr & Fah sc, mrc, 1895, 13x6" **2,800.00**
Calley, desk, strl inkwell fr, porc Rea sc, mrc, 1899, 5x6" **3,200.00**
Capendium, desk, handmade br/porc fr, Fah/Cen sc, rnd mrc, 4".**850.00**
Carpenter & Westley, desk, ivory w/glass dome mrc, 1880, 6" **950.00**
Casella London, wall, maxi/minimum, 2 units, wood, plastic sc .**430.00**
Chevallier, L'ingre, wall, ivory/mahog, Rea/Cen sc, 1880, 11x3" .**2,350.00**
Clark, desk, ivory ped, crown, mrc, 1904, 7"................................**400.00**
CW Wilder...NH, desk, Deco women, br Fah sc, mrc, R, 8"...**1,300.00**
Desk, cvd walrus tusk, 2-tier disk base, inlay sc, 1860, 9"...........**430.00**
Diamond, wall, br Fah sc on wood, R, 7½x1½"........................**525.00**
Dixie, W (London); desk, gilt/br, Gothic, SP sc, mrc, 8" **790.00**
Dollard London, desk, strl, br sc, mrc, 1908, R, 6" **750.00**
Dollard London, hanging, mahog fr, strl sc, mrc, 1810, 18" **4,600.00**
England, desk, glass obelisk/8-sided, br Fah sc, mrc, 1880........**1,260.00**
England, desk, marble ped fr, Cen, mrc, 1885, 6½" **930.00**
England, wall, br game bag fr, Fah sc, mrc, 1890, 9x5"............**1,650.00**
England, wall, rectangular wood fr, porc Cen sc, mrc, 1905, 5"..**1,350.00**
Farley, travel, walnut base mt, ivory Fah/Cen sc, mrc, 5" **900.00**
Freeborn, desk, bronze w/3 lead decor, br sc, mrc, 8" **180.00**
G Cooper, desk, bell shape w/cupola, strl, dial, 2x3" **400.00**
Gloucenter Scientific, stl case, glass front, pmc, 42" **1,500.00**
Heath & Wing, figural calendar, br w/porc sc, mrc, 1870...........**930.00**
J Waldstein, wall, br Rea sc on wood, mrc, 1900s, VR, 10½" **920.00**
Kendal, desk, strl obelisk, br Fah sc, mrc, 1890, 8", $1,350 to .**1,850.00**
Pairpoint, desk, strl picture fr, mrc, 1907, 5" **650.00**
Pig w/branch of tree, Pairpoint #5604, 5¼"...............................**375.00**
Reau, desk, sq incline base, floral top, mrc, 1895.......................**180.00**
Rowley & Sons, travel, ivory sc, mrc, 1894, 4", +case................**350.00**
Standard, wall, ivory Fah sc on ebony, mrc, 9" **750.00**
Standard..., wall, br fr, enamel dial Fah sc, 1885, 9" dia **650.00**
Taylor, chandelier, 3-side, Fah sc, alcohol, 1887, VR, br, 6"........**400.00**
Taylor, ped, 3-sided, Fah sc, alcohol, 1900, R, 6" **350.00**

Thermindex Switzerland, desk, Bakelite stand, Fah sc, 5"...........**595.00**
Tiffany, desk, strl tetrahedron fr & Fah sc, mrc, 1910, 2x4".....**4,000.00**
Tiffany, gr glass w/pine needles, br sc/mrc, 1902, 8x12" **2,800.00**
Tycos, maxi/minimum, japanned tin/br, mrc, T-5452, 8"............**150.00**
Unknown, cvd wood squirrel, glass Rea sc, mrc, 1905, VR, 10" .**800.00**
Unknown, desk, alabaster w/eagle, Rea/Cen sc, mrc, 1895 ....**875.00**
Unknown, wall, giltwood fr, ivory Fah sc, 1790, 10x3½"........**3,100.00**
W Pratt, desk, wood inlays, ivory sc, mrc, 1900, 6"....................**350.00**
Warren Foundries, wall, umbrella w/dragon hdl, br sc, mrc, 12" .**220.00**
WG Loveday, wall, Clearside, Fah sc, 5" dia **725.00**
Zeradatha, desk, cast metal w/rotate sc, 1926, 7" **140.00**

1000 Faces China

A dinner plate from this pattern, it is said, may have as many as 1,000 hand-painted faces, thus the name. Most of what we see today dates from early in the twentieth century to midway, but some pieces are even older. Though many pieces are unmarked, the majority carries the marks 'Made in Japan' or 'Japan.' 'Kutani,' 'MIOJ,' and other marks are sometimes seen as well.

There are two primary patterns or colors — Gold and Black Face. Gold is just that — most of the pieces are dominated by gold throughout. Black refers to the fact that in this variation the faces are black, usually against a white background. Many rings and bars of colors make up both primary patterns. Variations include 'Men in Robes' and '1000 Geishas.' All patterns usually feature an inner ring of color surrounded by flashes of multiple colors and an outer ring of color with a pattern painted into it.

Gold was the most popular pattern and seems to be the most available today. Examples with Black faces and the variations are scarce and often command higher prices. Only recently two new colors have been discovered — green and blue — leaving us to wonder if there may be still others. These colors are very rare and are demanding a higher value. In the green and blue patterns, the faces are gold and the pattern is the same as the traditional Thousand Faces, but the background colors are in multiple shades of the blue or green. Our advisor for this category is Suzi Hibbard; she is listed in the Directory under California.

Bowl, gold, Royal Satsuma, 9", from $425 to **475.00**
Cup & saucer, coffee; blk, from $15 to.......................................**20.00**
Cup & saucer, coffee; gold, HP Japan, 8", from $120 to **200.00**
Cup & saucer, coffee; Men in Robes, blk, from $45 to **100.00**
Cup & saucer, demi; gold, MIOJ, from $25 to............................**75.00**
Cup & saucer w/pie plate, blk, HP MIJ, from $45 to **75.00**
Cup & saucer w/pie plate, blk, MIJ, from $45 to.........................**75.00**
Ginger jar, gold, MIJ, 3⅞", from $45 to.....................................**55.00**
Incense burner, blk/gold, MIJ, 3½", from $50 to **75.00**
Incense burner, gold, 5", from $35 to..**50.00**
Nappy, blk, MIJ, 5½", from $25 to...**50.00**
Pie plate, gr, from $50 to **75.00**
Pie plates, gold, HP Japan, 7¼", set of 6, from $50 to **100.00**
Plate, blk, MIJ, 7¼", from $15 to...**25.00**
Plate, Men in Robes, red/blk, Kutani, 9½", from $30 to...............**60.00**
Plate, 1000 Conversations variation, 6", from $35 to **45.00**
Platter, gold, Mitsu-Bo Shi, Japan, 9½", from $25 to...................**75.00**
Saucer, Men in Robes, gold, sgn, 5½", from $10 to **20.00**
Snack plate & cup, blk, Kutani, from $40 to **65.00**
Tea set, gold, HP MIJ, teapot+cr/sug w/lid, from $50 to.............**100.00**
Tea set, gold, MIJ, 17-pc, from $150 to **225.00**
Tea set, gold, rattan hdl, sgn, 20-pc, from $175 to......................**250.00**
Tea set, Men in Robes, blk, 24-pc, from $200 to **300.00**
Teapot, 1000 Geishas, gold, sgn, 6x7", from $45 to **85.00**
Vase, gold, 5", from $55 to **70.00**
Vase, Men in Robes, red/blk, sgn, 2⅞", from $75 to....................**125.00**
Vase, Men in Robes variation, mc, from $25 to **50.00**

Tiffany

Louis Comfort Tiffany was born in 1848 to Charles Lewis and Harriet Young Tiffany of New York. By the time he was eighteen, his father's small dry goods and stationery store had grown and developed into the world-renowned Tiffany and Company. Preferring the study of art to joining his father in the family business, Louis spent the next six years under the tutelage of noted artists. He returned to America in 1870 and until 1875 painted canvases that focused on European and North African scenes. Deciding the more lucrative approach was in the application of industrial arts and crafts, he opened a decorating studio called Louis C. Tiffany and Co., Associated Artists. He began seriously experimenting with glass, and eschewing traditionally painted-on details, he instead learned to produce glass with qualities that could suggest natural textures and effects. His experiments broadened, and he soon concentrated his efforts on vases, bowls, etc. that came to be considered the highest achievements of the art. Peacock feathers, leaves and vines, flowers, and abstracts were developed within the plane of the glass as it was blown. Opalescent and metallic lustres were combined with transparent color to produce stunning effects. Tiffany called his glass Favrile, meaning handmade.

In 1900 he established Tiffany Studios and turned his attention full time to producing art glass, leaded-glass lamp shades and windows, and household wares with metal components. He also designed a complete line of jewelry which was sold through his father's store. He became proficiently accomplished in silverwork and produced such articles as hand mirrors embellished with peacock feather designs set with gems and candlesticks with Favrile glass inserts.

Tiffany's work exemplified the Art Nouveau style of design and decoration, and through his own flamboyant personality and business acumen he perpetrated his tastes onto the American market to the extent that his name became a household word. Tiffany Studios continued to prosper until the second decade of this century when due to changing tastes his influence began to diminish. By the early 1930s the company had closed.

Serial numbers were assigned to much of Tiffany's work, and letter prefixes indicated the year of manufacture: A – N for 1896 – 1900, P – Z for 1901 – 1905. After that, the letter followed the numbers with A – N in use from 1906 – 1912; P – Z from 1913 – 1920. O-marked pieces were made especially for friends and relatives; X indicated pieces not made for sale.

Our listings are primarily from the auction houses in the East where Tiffany sells at a premium. All pieces are signed unless noted otherwise.

Glass

Inkwell, blue with silver iridescence, eight-sided bulb form with hinged bronze cap, late nineteenth century, 5½", $8,000.00. (Photo courtesy Skinner, Inc.)

Bottle, gold irid, slim w/chained stopper, #4812, 12½" **4,400.00**
Bowl, aqua irid to opal, flower form, scalloped rim, 1⅞x4⅞" **385.00**
Bowl, finger; gold irid, floriform, 4½" **500.00**
Bowl, gold irid, curved rim, disk base, 1⅞x5⅞" **700.00**
Bowl, gold irid, ribbed, wide flaring rim, 9½" **750.00**
Bowl, gold irid, 10-rib, scalloped, #1104-6619L, 2¼x3⅞" **415.00**

Bowl, gold irid, 10-rib, scalloped, ca 1919, 2¼x4⅛", +6" plate ..**475.00**
Bowl, gold irid w/intaglio leaves & vines, scalloped rim, low, 8"...**1,115.00**
Bowl vase, gold irid, pulled/hooked ribs, 2" **240.00**
Compote, bl irid, stretched rim, dome ft, X, 3x9" **1,650.00**
Compote, gold irid, faint ribs, bulbed stem, disk ft, 3⅝x7¾" **650.00**
Cordial, gold irid, narrow stem, disk base, 4¼", 6 for...............**2,500.00**
Decanter, gold irid, silver mts, #419, ca 1932, 10" **650.00**
Decanter, gold irid, spherical w/4 dimples, stick neck, #414, 10"..**1,300.00**
Goblet, gold irid, shaped top w/open stem, rnd base, 7", 6 for.**4,125.00**
Goblet, gold irid w/horizontal threading, 6 lily pad prunts, 5¼".**475.00**
Inkwell, purple w/yel & bl feathers, tooled bronze cap, 5" **4,750.00**
Plate, Jazz couple dancing, bl/turq, 11"...................................**4,250.00**
Salt, bl irid, ruffled rim, ftd, #X576, 4¼"...................................**550.00**
Salt, gold irid, flat flange rim, sharp shoulder, wide rnd ft, 2¼" ..**245.00**
Salt, gold irid, squat/bulbous w/imp stylized flower, zigzag border...**450.00**
Sherbets, gold irid, 3⅜x4¾", 4 for..**500.00**
Sherbets, Rosaline, 5x4", set of 12 ....**1,400.00**
Vase, Agate design, blk stripes on gr to bl, #R441, 2½" **4,000.00**
Vase, Agate design, stick neck, mini, 3¾" **1,600.00**
Vase, amber & pale yel w/purple hooked/pulled decor, #H4013, 3"..**4,000.00**
Vase, amber w/gr/bl swirls, shouldered, thin, #D233, mini.......**2,400.00**
Vase, bl & purple feathers, low open hdls, #N1983, 4¾".........**6,500.00**
Vase, bl irid, conical, #6286K, 12¼" **1,765.00**
Vase, bl irid, scalloped rim, 10-ribbed/shouldered, #X134, 3½".**1,115.00**
Vase, bl irid to clear opal, disk ft w/opal edge, #1882, 9"...........**535.00**
Vase, bl irid w/bl & gold highlights, prunts/lt ribs, #8392, 3½" ..**800.00**
Vase, blk w/ornate bl & purple pulled decor, #0638, 7½" **2,900.00**
Vase, brn irid (unusual) w/appl purple geometrics, squat, 4½".**4,500.00**
Vase, cameo leaves, dk red frost, 9¼"......................................**6,200.00**
Vase, chocolate brn w/silver & bl feathers, wht opal cased, 4⅜" .**3,000.00**
Vase, cream w/gr & gold pulled decor, bulbed shoulder, 1905, 6½" ..**1,175.00**
Vase, Cypriote, mc swirls, #5366N, 10½" **19,000.00**
Vase, Cypriote w/gold/purple/gr irid, #R1818, 3½" **6,500.00**
Vase, dk bl irid w/lt swirling vines & heart leaves, bulbous, 3" ...**2,150.00**
Vase, floriform; gold, upright top, #1830, 7" **1,900.00**
Vase, floriform; gold irid to wht w/gr feathers, #30a, 11½" **6,000.00**
Vase, floriform; gold irid w/emb ribs, #5922H, 6" **2,400.00**
Vase, floriform; lt amber w/wht swirls, gr ribs, #461V, 19½"..**10,000.00**
Vase, floriform; pk/peach opal petals on opal base, amber stem, 9¾"...**3,175.00**
Vase, floriform; wht w/gr feathers, gold irid ft, #Y6504, 19"...**8,500.00**
Vase, floriform; wht w/gr feathers to base of cup, gr stem, 12" .**6,500.00**
Vase, floriform; wide gr leaves form body, gold irid ruffle, 4½" **2,500.00**
Vase, gold & platinum w/mc peacock feathers, slim, #07466, 12"..**9,000.00**
Vase, gold irid, #6533A, partial label, 2¼" **700.00**
Vase, gold irid, appl buds/tendrils, swollen shoulder, 3½"............**800.00**
Vase, gold irid, emb ribs, stick neck, #1004-7666K, 2¼".............**475.00**
Vase, gold irid, gr/bl/platinum waves at neck, #B1364, 8"........**2,800.00**
Vase, gold irid, hdls, bulbous, #2627B, mini, 2" **550.00**
Vase, gold irid, protrusions at top, #27142, 4"..............................**600.00**
Vase, gold irid, ribbed/twisted decor, #M6725, 3" **550.00**
Vase, gold irid, stretched ruffled rim, #64C, 4¾".......................**1,000.00**
Vase, gold irid, tortured top, #1801A, 2".....................................**475.00**
Vase, gold irid, 10 ribbed panels, #6734, 3½" **415.00**
Vase, gold irid w/gr & brn leaves & vines, #Y8387, ca 1905, 3⅝" .**2,000.00**
Vase, gold irid w/gr feathers, narrow neck, waisted, 3¾"...........**1,500.00**
Vase, gold irid w/gr hearts & vines, bulbous, #999J................**1,500.00**
Vase, gold irid w/gr hearts & vines, cylindrical, 11" **1,800.00**
Vase, gold irid w/gr pulled decor, waisted cone, 14¼" **2,250.00**
Vase, gold irid w/lt gr feathers, water sprinkler form, #M4358...**14,000.00**
Vase, gold irid w/platinum irid, #F8426, 3¼" **600.00**
Vase, gold irid w/platinum irid, gourd form, #U937, 5" **600.00**
Vase, gold irid w/pulled gr threads, trumpet form in gold doré ft, 13" .**1,850.00**
Vase, gold irid w/pulled platinum decor/several prunts, #W389, 3½" **600.00**
Vase, gold w/purple irid, hdls, flattened form, #W9123, 3½" **600.00**

Vase, gold w/rose irid, emb ribs, #W2190, 4½" **600.00**
Vase, gold w/rose irid, organic form w/ribs, #W223, 5" **650.00**
Vase, gold w/rose irid, pinched/tortured, #8063E, 5½" **900.00**
Vase, gr irid w/gold feathers; gold doré acorn mt, #1043, 15" ..**2,700.00**
Vase, gr irid w/silver & gold swirls, gold irid int, #1231C, 2⅜".**1,295.00**
Vase, irid w/peacock feathers, #25KLC, ca 1900, 24"...........**23,000.00**
Vase, irid w/4-peak rim, slim V-shape; in metal ft w/X-cut knop, 15".**1,400.00**
Vase, ivory w/gold feathers, shouldered, #9318M, 6¾" **2,000.00**
Vase, jack-in-pulpit; gold irid, ruffled face, #Y9603, 16" **8,000.00**
Vase, Jack-in-pulpit; gold irid, twisted stem, #3984D, 14" **6,700.00**
Vase, lt yel w/wht swirls, bulbous, #R453, 3½" **1,000.00**
Vase, mc pulled lattice-like decor, ftd, #L6555, 7½" **8,000.00**
Vase, millefiori/trailing lily pads, bl-gr irid on gold, 4x3¾" **3,000.00**
Vase, moonstone w/gold Persian design, gourd shape, #5586B, 5"..**2,600.00**
Vase, multi-tone gr w/rose swirls, wht cased, #406V, 7½" **1,600.00**
Vase, opal w/pk feathers, slim w/wide ft, #1505-4624L, 8".......**1,250.00**
Vase, paperweight; yel flowers w/bl stems & gr leaves in clear, 5¾" ..**4,250.00**
Vase, red w/gold & platinum bl feathers, #7042, 5½" **10,000.00**
Vase, rose w/platinum irid, bottle form, long neck, #3837P, 12" ..**1,300.00**
Vase, wht opal w/pulled/hooked platinum & gold design, #5244, 2½"..**1,700.00**
Vase, wht to rose w/gr feathers, gr stem/gold base, #R9795, 14"....**8,500.00**

Lamps

Lamp prices seem to be getting stronger, especially for leaded lamps with brighter colors (red, blue, purples). Bases that are unusual or rare have brought good prices and added to the value of the more common shades that sold on them. Bases with enamel or glass inserts are very much in demand. Our advisor for Tiffany lamps is Carl Heck; he is listed in the Directory under Colorado.

Key: c-b — counterbalance

Base, bridge; harp std w/3 tall curved legs w/leaf-like pads, 55"..**2,240.00**
Base, floor; Jr, 6-cluster socket, fluted stem, 4-ftd bun base, 61" ...**15,680.00**
Boudoir, Arabian 6½" dia flaring shade/slim std, yel/orange w/dots.**5,000.00**
Bridge, gr damascene 10" shade; plain stem w/3 curved legs, 54" ..**9,000.00**
Candlestick, artichoke feather shade; bronze std, #10050, 17" **4,100.00**
Candlestick, gold irid tulip-form shade; gilt-bronze ft, 11".......**3,000.00**
Ceiling, 6 gold 4½" lily shades; turtle-bk fixture, 11" **22,500.00**
Chandelier, stalactite 12" feather shade; bronze #2048 fixture..**5,500.00**
Desk, damascene 8" shade; gilt-bronze mk std, 14½" **12,950.00**
Desk, damascene 10" dragonfly shade; 4-ply ruffle base, 16"..**15,000.00**
Desk, gold damascene 7" shade; harp base w/Zodiac ft, 13½" ..**6,900.00**
Desk, gr damascene 7" shade w/bl-gr ribbons; c-b base w/EX patina..**10,000.00**
Desk, pulled feather 6x7" bell-shape shade; gold doré std w/rib ft ..**4,750.00**
Desk, turtle-bk insert shade; bronzed base w/jewels, 15" **8,250.00**
Desk, turtle-bk shade; irid glass cabochons in base, 13½"........**9,500.00**
Floor, ldgl 22" apple blossom shade; bronze Spanish-design base, 71".**60,000.00**
Floor, ldgl 22" geometric dome shade; ftd cushion-base std, 66" **34,500.00**
Floor, ldgl 24" geometric/leaf-band shade; 6-ftd ribbed/scrolled std...**84,000.00**
Hanging, ldgl 13x21" 6-sided acorn shape w/long glass strips, rtcl mt..**25,200.00**
Hanging, orange irid stalactite 8" L shade w/milk wht point, 26½" L.**3,165.00**
Lily, 3-light w/gold shades (1 VG); #319 bun base w/emb beading, 13"..**3,165.00**
Lily, 7-light, gold shades; lily pad platform base, #385, 20" **7,650.00**
Lily, 7-light, gold shades; lily-pad bronzed std, mk, 20".........**17,250.00**
Lily, 10-light, amber irid shades (7 sgn/1 rpr); lily pad base ...**14,000.00**
Lily, 10-light, gold irid #381 shades; gold doré base, 21½" **18,000.00**
Lily, 18-light, gold shades (13 sgn); gold doré pond lily base #383.**61,600.00**
Mushroom, bl-gr to gold 6½" shade; stemmed gr & gold base, 12" ..**6,600.00**
Nautilus, shell shade; gold doré base #409 w/emb leaves **5,500.00**
Sconce, bronze fixture w/5 gold irid lily shades, 14x9", pr **14,000.00**
Sconce, bronze 2-arm fixture, decorated glass shades, 8½x14½" ...**10,000.00**
Shade, ldgl w/curtain border, std globe, w/hanging mts, 15x25" **33,000.00**

Table, damascene 7" shade; base #429 w/4 high rtcl legs **5,600.00**
Table, damascene 10" shade w/etched butterflies; #445 3-arm base, 15".**14,000.00**
Table, gold zipper on 2-tone gr shade & base w/appl bands/circles, 14"..**3,750.00**
Table, ldgl 14" gold-mottle acorn-band shade; std #583, 21½"..**14,000.00**
Table, ldgl 14" vine shade; bronze #533 std, 22".....................**8,500.00**
Table, ldgl 16" acorn shade; bronze std w/rnd stepped ft, 21"...**9,000.00**
Table, ldgl 16" acorn shade; squat Grueby base (EX) **15,000.00**
Table, ldgl 16" daffodil shade; 4-ftd floral #28615 std, 21".....**25,000.00**
Table, ldgl 16" mc tulips dome shade; decor library base **55,000.00**
Table, ldgl 16" pomegranate shade; bronze gourd-like std, 19"..**28,175.00**
Table, ldgl 16" pomegranate shade; oil-font base, 25" **8,225.00**
Table, ldgl 16" poppy shade; 4-ftd organic base, 22"..............**72,800.00**
Table, ldgl 16" vine shade; bronze std w/blown-out gr glass, 20" ..**16,000.00**
Table, ldgl 18" geometric #1469 shade w/cap vent; Secessionist shaft...**16,000.00**
Table, ldgl 18" geometric/brickwork shade; 4-leg std w/cat's paw, 29".**25,200.00**
Table, ldgl 20" daffodil #1497 shade; bronze #352S175 base, 25½"..**37,500.00**
Table, ldgl 20" daffodil shade; std #629: cylinder w/emb floral ..**30,800.00**
Table, ldgl 20" geometric shade w/turtle-bk tile band; #532 std..**28,500.00**
Table, ldgl 20" Greek-key shade; twisted-vine gold doré std, 37" ...**43,125.00**
Table, ldgl 20" poppy #8805 shade w/bronze o/l; simple bronze std, 25".**89,500.00**
Table, linenfold 10" 12-panel shade w/abalone inlay; #604 base, 16".**10,650.00**
Table, linenfold 12" 8-panel shade; bronze doré std, 18"..........**4,400.00**
Table, metal o/l 12" 8-sided slag-panel shade; #539 std, 17½"..**15,275.00**
Table, turtle-bk 16" shade; simple 4-ftd stick std, 21" **14,000.00**
Table, 6 upright #496 gold shades on 6 'branches'; bronze std, 15" .**10,575.00**
Tulip, 10-light, 5x2" wht w/gr-feathers shades; lily-pad base ..**47,600.00**

Metal Work

Grapevine and Pine Needle are the most sought-after — dependent, of course, on condition. In the following listings, items are bronze unless otherwise noted.

Ashtray, floor; gold doré artichoke form, ca 1910, 27½"..........**1,800.00**
Ashtray, gold doré, ftd bowl, match holder attached to side, 8" dia...**700.00**
Bookends, Grapevine, slag glass inserts, 6x14", pr...................**2,150.00**
Bowl, emb geometric foliate banding, shallow, 9" **350.00**
Box, cigarette; Grapevine, gr slag inserts, 2x4½x3¼" **600.00**
Box, enameled floral medallion, #138, 2x6x4"...........................**700.00**
Box, gold doré & enamel, 4 ball ft, 4x6½".................................**750.00**
Box, Grapevine, slag glass inserts, 3x8"..................................**2,000.00**
Box, Pine Needle, caramel & wht slag glass inserts, 1½x4" **440.00**
Box, turtle-bk w/10 purple irid inset tiles, rare, 3¾x8⅞" **7,000.00**
Candelabrum, 4 gr glass candle cups, 1904, 15", +snuffer **5,875.00**
Candlestick, organic form w/jewels, EX patina, 17½" **5,500.00**
Candlestick, 2-light, glass jewels, #10076 ....**2,600.00**
Candlesticks, slim stems, gr glass blown into rtcl bobeches, 18", pr ..**4,200.00**
Candlesticks, 2 gr glass cups, 14¼", pr **3,055.00**
Desk set, American Indian, inkwell/pr blotter ends/scissors+3 pcs...**2,070.00**
Desk set, Egyptain-style motif, acid-etch gold, inkwell/scissors+4 pcs ..**2,100.00**
Desk set, Grapevine, mail file/inkwell/clock/calendar/memo pad+6 pcs .**3,700.00**
Desk set, Pine Needle, inkwell/tray/blotter ends/sm fr/vase+2 pcs ...**2,350.00**
Frame, bl enameled Art Nouveau decor, #1611, 12x10" **1,900.00**
Frame, calendar; Venetian, #1648, 6x6½" **785.00**
Frame, Grapevine, bl mottle glass inserts, bifold, 9½x15½" **3,750.00**
Frame, Grapevine, mc glass inserts, #930, 3½x4¾" **900.00**
Frame, Grapevine, slag glass inserts, bifold, 10x16"................**1,900.00**
Frame, Grapevine, slag glass inserts, 9½x7½" **1,750.00**
Frame, Pine Needle, gr/ivory mottle glass inserts, 6½x7½" **1,700.00**
Frame, Zodiac, #942, 8x7", from $800 to **1,000.00**
Frame, Zodiac, #943, 8¼x6¼"...**1,100.00**
Inkwell, Graduate, cobalt glass insert, 2⅝" **325.00**
Inkwell, Grapevine, gr slag glass inserts, #847, 4x6½".................**950.00**
Inkwell, Grapevine, slag glass inserts, #844, 3¾x4" sq **750.00**

Letter opener, Grapevine, bl/ivory glass inserts, 8" **375.00**
Letter rack, Venetian enameling, 6¼x9¾x2¾" **950.00**
Letter rack, Zodiac, gold doré, #1009, 6¼x9½" **500.00**
Mirror, Peacock, 6 feather supports, enameling, rare, 16x17" **25,000.00**
Pen tray, acid-eched gold dorè, emb ferrets/Moorish motif, #1642, 10"...**700.00**
Pen tray, Nautical, oval w/shell & seaweed, 9⅝" **1,115.00**
Planter, inset irid glass tiles, conical, rare, 3¾x11¾" **27,025.00**
Screen, Pine Needle, gold doré, mottled glass inserts, 8x12¾".....**2,700.00**
Tray, enameled leaves ea corner, #370, 13½x11" **765.00**
Vase, gold dorè, enameled base, trumpet form, 13½" **800.00**

Pottery

Vase, gr/bl/pk/yel/cream matt streaks, classic form, 21" **5,750.00**
Vase, gr/gunmetal crystalline, shouldered, 3¼" **750.00**
Vase, mushrooms in relief, cream w/gr int, cylindrical, 3½" **1,725.00**
Vase, narcissus on stems, brn/bl/tan/gray matt, #7, 14½", NM ...**4,000.00**
Vase, yel/chartreuse w/frosted wht accents, classic form, 21x10"..**2,400.00**

Silver

Key: t-oz — troy ounces

Bowl, shaped rim, 3 scalloped ft, 4¼x7¼", 15-t-oz **300.00**
Bowl, trefoil shape w/3 ball ft, 7", 8-t-oz **165.00**
Candelabra, 5-light, detachable branches/nozzles, Tiffany, 15", pr ...**2,000.00**
Cocktail set, shaker+6 goblets+20¾" tray, 78-t-oz **1,500.00**
Coffeepot, Chrysanthemum, 8", 30-t-oz **2,500.00**
Compote, Blackberry, 10x7¼", pr **2,500.00**
Dinner forks, Lap Over Edge, 10 (20-t-oz) for **1,800.00**
Dresser set, emb shells & garlands, 3 brushes+comb+mirror+2 pcs...**800.00**
Mirror, circular w/easel bk, 17" dia **1,100.00**
Pitcher, water; 7¼" **1,300.00**
Platter, well & tree; 20", 77-t-oz **1,300.00**
Presentation cup, 3-hdl, engr inscription, 7", 36-t-oz **1,500.00**
Tazza, Blackberry, 3x7½" **500.00**
Tazza, floral repoussé, ftd, 5½x9", 15-t-oz **850.00**
Trophy bowl, Irish Setter...Dog Show 1936, 4½x8", 26-t-oz **750.00**
Wine cooler, ftd, 8x13½", 58-t-oz **1,800.00**

Windows

Geometric pattern w/rich bl dominating, 58x25" **21,000.00**
Geometric w/center medallion, arched top, 86x25", pr..........**23,575.00**
3 Wise Men (w/gifts), pnt details, 53x36" w/fr **38,000.00**

Tiffin Glass

The Tiffin Glass Company was founded in 1887 in Tiffin, Ohio, one of the many factories composing the U.S. Glass Company. Its early wares consisted of tablewares and decorative items such as lamps and globes. Among the most popular of all Tiffin products was the black satin glass produced there during the 1920s. In 1959 U.S. Glass was sold, and in 1962 the factories closed. The plant was re-opened in 1963 as the Tiffin Art Glass Company. Products from this period were tableware, hand-blown stemware, and other decorative items.

Those interested in learning more about Tiffin glass are encouraged to contact the Tiffin Glass Collectors' Club, whose address can be found in the Directory under Clubs, Newsletters, and Catalogs. See also Black Glass; Glass Animals.

Ashtray, June, rose or bl **55.00**
Ashtray, w/cigarette rest; Flanders, crystal, 2¼x3¾" **55.00**
Basket, Jack Frost, pk, #9574, 6" **150.00**

Basket, Jungle Assortment, #151, 6" **95.00**
Bell, Cherokee Rose, crystal **75.00**
Bell, Fuchsia, crystal, #15083, 5" **75.00**
Bell, June Night, crystal **85.00**
Bitters bottle, Fuchsia, crystal **450.00**
Bonbon, Jungle Assortment, ftd, w/lid, #330, 5½" **60.00**
Bonbon, Psyche **65.00**
Bowl, centerpiece; Psyche, 13" **125.00**
Bowl, cream soup; Cadena, crystal **25.00**
Bowl, finger; Fontaine, amber, gr or pk, #022 ....**45.00**
Bowl, finger; June Night, crystal, 5" **22.00**
Bowl, grapefruit; Cadena, crystal, ftd **50.00**
Bowl, June, crystal, 10" **35.00**
Cake plate, Cherokee Rose, crystal, center hdl, 12½" **55.00**
Candle holder, Jungle Assortment, #330, w/hdl, ea **37.50**
Candlestick, Fontaine, amber, gr or pk, low, #9758, ea **35.00**
Candlestick, June, topaz, 3", ea **30.00**
Candy jar, Flanders, pk, ftd, w/lid **250.00**
Celery, Flanders, yel, 11" **60.00**
Cologne bottle, Jungle Assortment, #5722 ....**125.00**
Comport, Cherokee Rose, crystal, 6" **52.50**
Comport, Flanders, crystal, 6" **65.00**
Creamer, Cadena, pk or yel **30.00**
Creamer, June Night, crystal **30.00**
Creamer, tea; June, rose or bl **80.00**
Creamer & sugar bowl, Kilarney, crystal ft & hdl, #6259 ....**75.00**
Cup, Classic, crystal **65.00**
Decanter & stopper, Jungle Assortment **125.00**
Electric lamp, Fuchsia, crystal **350.00**
Hurricane, Fuchsia, crystal, Chinese style, 12" **250.00**
Icer w/liner, Cherokee Rose, crystal **110.00**
Jug, Julia, amber, ftd, w/lid **325.00**
Mayonnaise, Classic, crystal, ftd **65.00**
Mayonnaise, June Night, crystal, w/liner & ladle **45.00**
Nut cup, Flanders, pk, blown, ftd **80.00**
Pitcher, Cadena, crystal, ftd **225.00**
Pitcher, Classic, pk, 61-oz **495.00**
Pitcher, Flanders, yel, w/lid **295.00**
Pitcher, June Night, crystal **495.00**
Plate, Cadena, pk or yel, 6" **12.00**
Plate, chop; June, crystal, 13" **25.00**
Plate, luncheon; June Night, crystal, 8" **15.00**
Plate, salad; June, topaz, 7½" **13.00**
Relish, Fuchsia, crystal, #5902, 3-part, 6⅜" **25.00**
Rose bowl, Cracquelle, crystal, #17430, rare, 6" **150.00**
Saucer, Cadena, crystal **15.00**
Shakers, Cherokee Rose, crystal, pr **85.00**
Shakers, Flanders, crystal, pr **175.00**
Shakers, Jungle Assortment, gr, ftd, #6205, pr **65.00**
Smoking set, Jungle Assortment, 3 pc, #188 ....**40.00**
Stem, cafe parfait; Fontaine, Twilight, #033 ....**135.00**
Stem, claret, Cherokee Rose, crystal, 4 oz **50.00**
Stem, cocktail, Classic, crystal, 4⅞", 4 oz **27.50**
Stem, cordial, Julia, amber **55.00**
Stem, grapefruit, Psyche, w/liner **85.00**
Stem, oyster cocktail, Flanders, pk, 4½" **55.00**
Stem, saucer champagne, Flanders, yel, 6¼" **20.00**
Stem, sherbet; Psyche **30.00**
Stem, sundae. Fontaine, Twilight, #033 ....**55.00**
Stem, water, Classic, pk, 7¼", 9 oz **60.00**
Stem, water goblet, Psyche **50.00**
Stem, wine, Julia, amber **40.00**
Sugar bowl, Cadena, pk or yel **40.00**
Sugar bowl, Cherokee Rose, crystal **22.00**

Sugar bowl, Julia, amber 40.00
Tumbler, iced tea; Classic, crystal, ftd, 6¹⁄₁₆", 14 oz 30.00
Tumbler, juice; Psyche 40.00
Tumbler, June, rose or bl, ftd, 4½", 5-oz 50.00
Tumbler, tea; Julia, amber, ftd 30.00
Vase, bud; June Night, crystal, 10" 45.00
Vase, Cadena, crystal, 9" 115.00
Vase, Cherokee Rose, crystal, teardrop shape, 8½" 85.00
Vase, cobalt w/opal loops, teardrop shape............................450.00
Vase, crystal, 10-rib optic, #33, sq......................................65.00
Vase, Fontaine, amber, gr or pk, ftd, #2, 8"..........................95.00
Vase, gr w/silver o/l lady & random falling hearts, 8¼" 125.00
Vase, Plum, 10-rib optic, #33, sq..150.00
Vase, sweet pea; cobalt w/opal loops, crystal ball 450.00
Vase, sweet pea; Cracquelle, rare 150.00
Vase, sweet pea; Kilarny, gold etch/laurel band, 6" crystal ft, 6"..200.00
Vase, urn; Kilarny, crystal ft/gold Laurel band, bouquet etch, 10¼"....225.00
Whipped cream, Fuchsia, crystal, 3-ftd, #310................................40.00

Tiles

Revival of the ancient art of tile making dates to mid-nineteenth century England. Following the invention of the dust-pressing process for the manufacturing of buttons, potteries such as Minton and Wedgwood borrowed the technique for mass producing tiles. The Industrial Revolution market thus encouraged replacing the time-consuming medieval encaustic or inlay process for the foolproof press-molding method or the very decorative transfer print.

English tiles adorned American buildings until a good native alternative became available following the Philadelphia Centennial Exposition of 1876. Shortly thereafter, important tile companies sprung up around Boston, Trenton, and East Liverpool, Ohio. By the turn of the century, Victorian aesthetics began to give way to the Arts and Crafts style that was being set forth by John Ruskin and Thomas Carlyle and practiced by William Morris and his Pre-Raphaelite Brotherhood. Tile bodies were once more pressed from wet or faience clay and decorated in bas-relief or in the ancient Spanish techniques of cuenca or cuerda seca. The glazes adorning them became matt and vegetal, reflecting the movement's fondness for medieval and Japanese aesthetics. During the 1920s designs became simpler and more commercialized, but some important artists were still employed by the larger companies (for example, Louis Solon at AETCo), and the California tile industry continued to reflect the love of nature and Spanish Missions well into the 1930s.

Collecting tiles today means purchasing architectural salvage or new old stock. Arts and Crafts pottery and tiles are still extremely collectible. Important and large panels will fetch prices into the six figures. The prices for Victorian tiles have not increased over the last decade, but the value of California tiles, both matt and glossy, has gone through the roof. Catalina pottery and tile collectors are a particularly voracious lot. Larger pieces usually bring more, and condition is paramount. Look for damage and repair, as tiles often will chip or crack during the removal process.

Our advisor for this category is Suzanne Perrault; she is listed in the Directory under New Jersey. See also American Encaustic Tiling Company; California Faience; Cambridge Art Tile Works; Grueby; Newcomb; Rookwood; other specific manufacturers.

Key:
maj — majolica   tp — transfer printed

American

California Art Tile, cottage/bridge/creek, bl & buff, 4"+fr 425.00
California Art Tile, knights dueling at dawn, mc, 5¾x19½"...1,375.00

California Art Tile, Native Am scene, mc, 6", pr 690.00
California Art Tile, pine/river/village, brn engobe, 15½x3¾"+fr..925.00
Claycraft, CA landscape w/mission, mc, 7¾x4"+oak fr.............925.00
Claycraft, mission scene, mc dead matt, 8½x16½"+new fr......1,850.00
Claycraft, mission scene, raised/HP, 7¼x15½"+oak fr, $1,000 to..1,500.00
Flint, sailboat scene, mc cuenca, 6", pr....................................750.00
Franklin, boy fishing w/dog, blk/mustard/lt gr, 9", NM.............915.00
Franklin, lantern lighter, blk on mustard w/turq & red, 9", NM.700.00
Franklin, moose & geese, purple on yel, 13½x9"....................1,500.00
Franklin, sailing ship at sea, mc matt & gloss, 9"....................575.00
Harris Strong, cubist face, mc, 10-tile panel, 32½x14½"+rpl fr..460.00
Harris Strong, medieval minstrels, mc, 12-tile panel, 24½x30½"..1,100.00
Harris Strong, medieval scene, mc, 36-tile panel, 13¾x73¼".5,175.00
Harris Strong, musicians by bridge, mc, 5-tile panel, 36x24"+orig fr ..915.00
Hartford Faience, Eventide, maiden w/flowers mosaic, 13x8"..17,250.00
Isaac Broome, Parthenia, Greek goddess, olive gr gloss, 13x10"+fr..1,150.00
J&JG Low, First Love, old couple, A Osborne, brn, 6", EX.........275.00
Moravian, Autumn, man picking apples, mc mosaic, 1970s, 21" dia..425.00
Moravian, City of God, ivory & bl, 5½", EX 525.00
Mueller, Cancer crab, dk terra cotta w/mustard matt, 7½"..........425.00
Northwestern Terra Cotta, wreath/Co name, terra cotta, 4x5½"....425.00
Pomona, boy (girl) after Velasquez, McCullouch, HP/tp, 12x6", pr..175.00
Sherwin & Cotton, geraniums, purple on gr, maj, 6"...................115.00
Taylor, Native Am brave on horse by canyon, 5-tile panel, 12x18"..2,185.00
Trent, shepherds & flocks, amber maj, 3 6x18" pcs form panel ..1,265.00
Unmk, grape clustre & leaves, mc on curdled beige, 6"+oak fr...635.00
Unmk, rabbit crouching in grasses, mc cuenca, burst bubbles, 4".635.00

Other Countries

De Porceleyne Fles, cat on book, mc cuenca, 8¾x4¾" 1,265.00
De Porceleyne Fles, Christmas 1946, couple in snow, 7¾x5¾"..1,100.00
De Porceleyne Fles, flamingo in marsh, mc cuenca, 13½x5¼", pr .1,725.00
De Porceleyne Fles, goose in marsh, mc cuenca, 4¼x12½", EX .525.00
De Porceleyne Fles, hare & fruit trees, mc cuenca, 4¼x8¼", NM.1,100.00
De Porceleyne Fles, ostriches, mc cuenca on indigo, 8¼x4¼", pr..1,150.00
De Porceleyne Fles, owls by stone wall w/arch, mc, 4¾x9".........700.00
De Porceleyne Fles, peacock, mc cuenca on wht crystalline, 4¾x17".2,365.00
De Porceleyne Fles, peacock/brick wall, mc cuenca, 13½x5½", pr..800.00
De Porceleyne Fles, pelican & young, mc cuenca, 13½x5¼" ..1,725.00
De Porceleyne Fles, rooster, wht cuenca on indigo, 8¼x4¼"......425.00
De Porceleyne Fles, ships flotilla, mc cuenca, 4¼x16½", EX......460.00
De Porceleyne Fles, tall ships on waves, brns/grs, 4¼x8¼".........175.00
De Porceleyne Fles, tiger, mc cuenca, amber tile border, 5¼x13½"..1,265.00
Minton, musicians, after E Hammond, turq on cobalt, 8", EX, pr.425.00
Rozenburg, sheep flock, after A Mauve, sepia tones, 7x15" 1,375.00
Teichert (Meissen), carp & plants, celadon gr, 5¾" facing pr 750.00
Von Schwarz, maiden & poppies, mc cuenca, 10¼x3¾" facing pr ..2,050.00

Tinware

In the American household of the seventeenth and eighteenth centuries, tinware items could be found in abundance, from food containers to foot warmers and mirror frames. Although the first settlers brought much of their tinware with them from Europe, by 1798 sheets of tin plate were being imported from England for use by the growing number of American tinsmiths. Tinwares were often decorated either by piercing or painted designs which were both freehand and stenciled. (See Toleware.) By the early 1900s, many homes had replaced their old tinware with the more attractive aluminum and graniteware.

In the nineteenth century, tenth wedding anniversaries were traditionally celebrated by gifts of tin. Couples gave big parties, dressed in their wedding clothes, and reaffirmed their vows before their friends and families who arrived bearing (and often wearing) tin gifts, most of which were quite humorous. Anniversary tin items may include hats, cradles, slippers and shoes, rolling pins, etc. See also Primitives and Kitchen Collectibles.

Angel food cake pan, center tube, w/lid, early, 6½" H	45.00
Anniversary, bouquet of 8 flowers, 16"	600.00
Anniversary, top hat, lt rust, 8"	525.00
Bathtub, pnt decor, w/seat, foot well, soap holder & splash guard, 44"	260.00
Bunt pan, swirled body, 3x6¾"	35.00
Candlestick, cup on notched shaft, weighted dome base, 11½"	235.00
Coffeepot, punched decor, wire wrigglework, domed lid, rprs, 11"	1,595.00
Coffeepot, punched tulip baskets & twined lines, lt rust, 11"	375.00
Coffeepot, 2 raised decorative bands, brass finial, PA, 10½"	525.00
Colander, handmade, ca 1895, 4x10"	45.00
Egg poacher, 5-cup, Pat App For Buffalo Steam...Poacher, fry-pan shape	25.00
Frying pan, Cold Handle L&G GMf'g Co 53, late 1800s, 9½" dia+hdl	15.00
Lunch pail, oval w/flat bottom, swing hdl, sm, 5¾x5⅝x3¾"	75.00
Mold, bunt cake; scalloped edge w/ears at top, 10¾x11"	195.00
Sconce, oval dish-shaped reflector, crimped rim, 10⅛"	175.00
Sconce, radiating/crimped rnd reflector (wear/corrosion), 14½"	500.00
Scone/muffin pan, 9 swirled cups, late 1800s, 1½x11" sq, VG	12.50
Steamer, ca 1900, 3-pc, 11x10½"	55.00
Strainer, cottage cheese; 4x6⅞"+hdl, EX	35.00
Sugar shaker, ca 1900, 4¾x3"	18.50
Teapot, conical w/hinged lid, ribbon hdl, 7¼x4⅜"	50.00
Tinder box, rnd w/finger loop & soldered candle socket on lid, 2¾"	495.00
Tray, flower transfer, 1950s, 14¼x9", EX	15.00
Vegetable drier, punched circular decorative panels, gr pnt, 9x18x31"	85.00

Tobacciana

Tobacciana is the generally accepted term used to cover a field of collecting that includes smoking pipes, cigar molds, cigarette lighters, humidors — in short, any article having to do with the practice of using tobacco in any form. Perhaps the most valuable variety of pipes is the meerschaum, hand carved from hydrous magnesium, an opaque white-gray or cream-colored mineral of the soapstone family. (Much of this is today mined in Turkey which has the largest meerschaum deposit in the world, though there are other deposits of lesser significance around the globe.) These figural bowls often portray an elaborately carved mythological character, an animal, or a historical scene. Amber is sometimes used for the stem. Other collectible pipes are corn cob (Missouri meerschaum) and Indian peace pipes of clay or catlinite. (See American Indian Art.)

Chosen because it was the Indians who first introduced the white man to smoking, the cigar store Indian was a symbol used to identify tobacco stores in the nineteenth century. The majority of them were hand carved between 1830 and 1900 and are today recognized as some of the finest examples of early wood sculptures. When found they command very high prices.

For further information on lighters, refer to *Collector's Guide to Cigarette Lighters* by James Flanagan. See also Advertising; Snuff Boxes.

Ashtray, blk amethyst, elephant center, Greensburg Glass Works	42.00
Ashtray, cast bronze, sailfish at side, EX patina, 4¼x5½"	30.00
Ashtray, chrome-like dish on ped ft, 3 rests, 4⅜"	8.00
Ashtray, coal scuttle, blk glass, 2 rests, 2¾"	15.00
Ashtray, cobalt glass, oval, Hazel Atlas, 1930s-40s, 5½"	18.00
Ashtray, compo Indian chief beside tray w/glass insert, 5" H	20.00
Ashtray, Daisy & Button, cobalt glass, clover shape, 6¾"	18.00
Ashtray, lady-in-bbl smoker (vent in chest), Handel Ware..., 5½"	65.00
Ashtray, penguin smoker (vent in left eye), Japan, 7"	40.00
Ashtray, SP, center match box, emb scenes, 6¼" dia	50.00
Ashtray, SP, emb drinking scene, European, 5¼"	55.00
Ashtray, windmill scene on fired-on orange, 3 rests, 5¼"	20.00

Cap, Red Dot Cigars, red lettering on wht linen, folds, 1930s, EX	25.00
Cigar/tobacco pouch, gold monogram on leather, 1900s, pocket sz	95.00
Cigarette case, sterling w/emb emblem, mid-1930s, 3½x2¼"	125.00
Cgarette case, sterling w/gold wash & HP harem girl scene, 3¾"	2,000.00
Cigarette case/compact, gold-plated swirls, Evans, 1930s, 5½"	150.00
Cigarette holder/dispenser, elephant w/howdah, CI, EX	95.00
Cigarette lighter, chromium, butane, Colibri (Ireland), 1960s, 3"	75.00
Cigarette lighter, metal boot, lever on bk, ca 1920s, 1¾x2⅝"	125.00
Cigarette lighter, Minerva, floral on porc, Ronson, ca 1953, 3"	50.00
Cigarette lighter, Spirit of St Louis, brass w/rubber tires, table sz	100.00
Cigarette lighter, Tuxedo, chromium/enamel, Ronson, 1930s, 4⅛"	100.00
Cigarette lighter/mechanical pencil, Penciliter, Ronson, 1948, 5⅜"	65.00
Cigarette papers, Top Wheat Straw, RJ Reynolds, 100 in pkg	10.00
Cigarette purse w/attached brass lighter, embr silk, 1950s, 4¼"	70.00
Cutter, CI, Brown's Mule Plug, Enterprise for RJ Reynolds, EX	125.00
Cutter, CI guillotine type, old red pnt, 4x8"	135.00
Cutter, CI table-top style, Arrow, Cupples Co, 17" L	60.00
Humidor, cowboy on box, pnt terra cotta, HM3375, 8x6"	865.00
Humidor, dog w/sled, pnt terra cotta, JM3463, 5½x9½", NM	975.00
Humidor, Indian in warbonnet (head), majolica, EX detail, 8"	400.00
Humidor, man playing guitar on crate, terra cotta, BB8348, 10"	950.00
Humidor, man reading documents, pnt terra cotta, FGW943, 11"	750.00
Humidor, mother & daughter, pnt terra cotta, BB991, 9"	835.00
Humidor, Munich child leaning on bbl, terra cotta, JM3386, 10½"	1,100.00
Humidor, SP w/emb horse & rider, Derby #3404, 7½x9½x5¼"	950.00
Lighter/alarm clock, brass, Phinney-Walker/Evans, 1940s, 5"	125.00
Matchbook, various businesses, ca 1940s, unused, ea from $3 to	10.00
Package, PEP Cigarette Tobacco 5¢, runner on brn, unopened	65.00
Pipe, Billiard Root Briar, Dunhill, 1983, unused, M	220.00
Pipe, Black Forest, bear; EX details, 3⅜x2½x3¼"	115.00
Pipe, Black Forest, dog, trn horn stem & mouthpc, 1900s	175.00
Pipe, meerschaum, gladiator w/shield & sword, EX	195.00
Pipe, meerschaum, male lion walking by tree trunk, ca 1900, 7¼"	210.00
Pipe, meerschaum, nude maiden, slight discoloration, mk WDC, 7x3"	220.00
Pipe, Root Briar, Dunhill, 1953, EX	165.00
Pipe, Tanshell, Dunhill #4032, EX	125.00
Silk, Zira Cigarettes, Little Clarice, 3¼x2⅝", EX	5.00
Silk, Zira Cigarettes, Pretty Polly, 3¼x2⅝"	5.00
Smoke set, brass & Lucite, Evans, 1950s, 3-pc, lighter+box+pen holder	100.00
Smoke set, ceramic w/brass, Stylebuilt, 1950s, tray+lighter+holder	60.00
Smoke set, stag figural, Anchor Silverplate #565	650.00
Tobacco card, Hounds Meeting: Whitehall Near Welwyn, pre-1939, EX	12.00
Tobacco chest, burled/inlaid walnut, fitted int, w/key, 14x17x11", EX	1,125.00
Tobacco flannel, Belgium & horse on gr pennant, early 1900s, 6x3"	15.00
Tobacco flannel, butterflies & flowers, early 1900s, 5¼x8¼"	20.00
Tobacco flannel, Chic Gandil (WA Senators), 1914, EX	75.00
Tobacco flannel, Egyptian flag, Nebo Cigarettes, 3x2½"	8.00
Tobacco flannel, Howard Shankes (baseball player), 19¼", 5¼" sq	25.00
Tobacco flannel, red & wht flag on starry bl ground, 5½x8"	8.00
Tobacco flannel, University of Ohio pennant, early 1900s	15.00
Tobacco flannel, US flag, early 1900s, 5x8½"	19.00
Tobacco rug, geometric w/floral center, early 1900s, 3¾x7"	15.00
Tobacco rug, geometric w/mc border, Factory No 30...NY, 2x3"	9.00
Tobacco silk, raspberries, Nebo Cigarette Co...NJ, 3x2½"	8.00

Toby Jugs

The delightful jug known as the Toby dates back to the eighteenth century, when factories in England produced them for export to the American colonies. Named for the character Toby Philpots in the song *The Little Brown Jug*, the Toby was fashioned in the form of a jolly fellow, usually holding a jug of beer and a glass. The earlier examples were made with strict attention to details such as fingernails and teeth. Originally representing only a non-entity, a trend developed to portray well-known individuals such as George II, Napoleon, and Ben Franklin. Among the most-valued Tobies are those produced by Ralph Wood I in the late 1700s. By the mid-1830s Tobies were being made in America.

When no manufacturer is given, assume the Toby to have been made in Staffordshire, nineteen century; unless otherwise described, because of space restrictions, assume the model is of a seated man.

See also Doulton; Occupied Japan.

Blue Willow jacket, legs crossed, Wm Kent, 5½" **165.00**
Blue Willow jacket/hat, ea hand on decorated jug, w/lid, 7", EX .**325.00**
Bobby (policeman), pour through helmet, Shorter, 7" **125.00**
Edward Prince of Wales in naval uniform, waist up, HP, 6" **265.00**
Elihu Yale Toby (bust), bl, Wedgwood, 1933, 6" **150.00**
Fat man in vest sits/holds pipe, De Vegh, early 20th C, 9".........**375.00**
Gorbachev, by Andrew Moss, Kevin Francis Ceramics, ltd ed **175.00**
Holds mug, wears turban, rpr, 10".....................................**200.00**
Holds stein w/bear paw decor, Pratt, 10" **235.00**
Intarsio, Foley, Wileman & Co, Fenton & Longton, 7" **250.00**
John Bull Churchill astride bulldog, Burleighware, 11½"...........**425.00**
Jug (dotted) on knee, seamed, 4-color wash, sponged stockings, 10", EX...**220.00**
Jug on knee, cobalt coat/yel breeches/blk hat, w/gilt, porc, 8½", VG..**250.00**
Midshipman, playing violin, Beswick #1112, gr label, 5" **150.00**
Nelson stands in bl coat & blk hat, Staffordshire, 20th C, 11"...**175.00**
On keg mk Home Brewed Ale, 11⅜", EX...................................**350.00**
Pitcher (decorated) on knee, legs molded/appl separately, 9"......**275.00**
Punch (EX) (& Judy), standing, Wm Machin, 1890, 10", pr......**600.00**
Romeo on bended knee, Burleigh Ironstone, 5½" **100.00**
Standing, taking pinch of snuff, mc/copper lustre, Allerton's, 9½" ..**85.00**
Toby Ale, brn pitcher on knee, gr coat/red pants, Wade **125.00**
Toby creamer, mc, Allerton's, 1891-1912, 4⅜x4½" **100.00**
Toby Philpott, Beswick #1110, ca 1948-73, 8" **110.00**
Toby sugar bowl, Allerton's, ca 1935, 1¾x3".............................**80.00**
Toby teapot, mc, Allerton's/MIE, ca 1935, 7½x9" **250.00**
Wm McKinley 1896 campaign, Protection/Prosperity, gold coins, 9" ..**675.00**
Ye Old village Innkeeper, jug in ea hand/apron, Wedgwood #762/1, 7" ...**100.00**

Toleware

The term 'toleware' originally came from a French term meaning 'sheet iron.' Today it is used to refer to paint-decorated tin items, most popular from 1800 to 1850s. The craft flourished in Pennsylvania, Connecticut, Maine, and New York state. Early toleware has a very distinctive look. The surface is dull and unvarnished; background colors range from black to cream. Geometrics are quite common, but florals and fruits were also favored. Items made after 1850 were often stenciled, and gold trim was sometimes added.

American toleware is usually found in practical, everyday forms — trays, boxes, and coffeepots are most common — while French examples might include candlesticks, wine coolers, jardinieres, etc. Be sure to note color and design when determining date and value, but condition of the paint is the most important worth-assessing factor. Unless noted otherwise, values are for very good examples with average wear.

Box, deed; flower & fruit, mc on blk, old rpt, 9" **1,700.00**
Box, deed; fruit, mc on blk japanning, 3x4¼x2¾" **635.00**
Box, floral, mc on blk japanning, hinged lid, 4½x5½" dia..........**200.00**
Cabinet, spice; shaped crest, 5 drws w/stenciled names, blk/yel, 14x9"...**420.00**
Candle box, floral, mc on grpt red & yel, cylindrical, 14⅜" **900.00**
Coal scuttle, florals/gold edge, sloped lift lid, English, 1880s, EX...**235.00**
Coffeepot, floral, mc on blk japanning, gooseneck, PA, 10x6" ...**900.00**
Coffeepot, floral, mc on blk japanning, 8½", EX+ **2,100.00**

Coffeepot, floral, mc on brn, lighthouse, lt wear, 10⅜" **935.00**
Coffeepot, floral, red & yel on blk japanning, gooseneck, 11", G **975.00**
Coffeepot, floral & fruit on blk japanning, brass finial, 10", EX+ .**3,135.00**
Creamer, floral on blk japanning, NY, 1850s, 4".....................**175.00**
Sander, starflower, mc on brn japanning, lt wear, 2½" **350.00**
Shaker, floral, mc on blk japanning, cylindrical, 2⅜" **50.00**
Tea caddy, apples & branches on brn japanning, worn, 5x5x3½" ..**350.00**
Tea caddy, floral on dk japanning, 7x4¼" **650.00**
Tea caddy, fruit, mc on dk brn japanning, 4⅛", G **525.00**
Tray, berries & leaves, mc on alligatored red, 9x6" **415.00**
Tray, berries & leaves, mc on blk japanning, rectangular, 13x8".**500.00**
Tray, birds & flowers, mc on blk japanning, 24x18", EX **600.00**
Tray, flower baskets on blk japanning, 2¼x11x10½"..................**300.00**
Tray, roses, mc on lt gr w/gold, Fr, minor crazing, 13½" dia **295.00**

Tools

Before the Civil War, tools for the most part were handmade. Some were primitive to the point of crudeness, while others reflected the skill of those who took pride in their trade. Increasing demand for quality tools and the dawning of the age of industrialization resulted in tools that were mass produced. Factors important in evaluating antique tools are scarcity, usefulness, and portability. Those with a manufacturer's mark are worth more than unmarked items. When no condition is indicated, the items listed here are assumed to be in excellent condition. Our advisor for this category is Jim Calison; he is listed in the Directory under New York. For more information, we recommend *Antique Tools* by Kathryn McNerney (Collector Books). See also Keen Kutter; Stanley; Winchester.

Adz, ship builder's; DR Barton, side lips & poll, 6" W, VG.........**125.00**
Angle divider & bevel, Los Angeles Automatic Tool Co, ca 1900, 10" ...**875.00**
Auger, EC Stearns, adjustable, hollow, Pat Sept 8 68, 5 collars, VG..**95.00**
Auger, James Swan, adjustable, hollow, 2 guides, EX..................**165.00**
Auger ratchet, Millers Falls #4, side hdl, VGIB......................**115.00**
Axe, broad; Powell Tool Co Cleveland O, orig hdl, 26" **195.00**
Axe, ship builder's Campbell's, head only, 6", G+.......................**55.00**
Brace, joist; Millers Falls Co #52, blk metal finish, 19" **165.00**
Brace, Millers Falls #832, rosewood hdl, ca 1900, 10" sweep, VG.**70.00**
Brace, Millers Falls Holdall #733, latest Pat 1910, 8" sweep, EX...**90.00**
Brace, PS&W #1202, Samson Pat chuck dtd 1895, rosewood, VG ..**40.00**
Chisel, bevel-edge socket firmer; Buck Bros, cast steel, 12", G+ ...**30.00**
Chisel, bevel-edge socket firmer; Reliance (early Greenlee), 12"..**30.00**
Chisel, mortise; I&H Sorby, 5/16", VG...................................**35.00**
Chisel, paring; Buck & Hickman, London Pattern, 10" blade, VG ..**75.00**
Chisel, skew; Buck Bros #2, ⅛", VG....................................**30.00**
Chisel, socket firmer; Witherby, 6" blade, 12", VG....................**30.00**
Chisel, socket mortise; Winstead Edge Tool Works, 15½", VG **45.00**
Draw knife, AJ Wilkinson Boston, folding hdls, 8", G+ **80.00**
Draw knife, JS Cantello, folding hdls, Pat 1883, G+ **90.00**
Draw knife, TH Witherby, folding hdls, 8", VG.........................**80.00**
Draw knife, Wilkinson & Co, fruitwood hdls, Pat 1886, 11½" ...**115.00**
Drill, Archimedian, mahog & exotic wood, 2 horns, EX+ **895.00**
Gauge, marking & mortising; Nicholls #17, CI, Pat 1911, VG.....**65.00**
Gauge, roller; Leavitte Mach Co, Pat June 12 18788, VG **25.00**
Gouge, Buck Bros #9, cast steel, brass ferrule, 5", VG **30.00**
Gouge, JB Addis & Sons #7, fruitwood hdl, ⅝", VG **28.00**
Gouge, SJ Addis #7, med sweep, str type, split hdl, VG **45.00**
Hack saw, Disston & Son #240, 22" blade, 24" overall, NM.......**155.00**
Hammer, claw; EL Brown, cast steel, bell face, 10-oz, VG...........**25.00**
Hammer, hoof pick; folding, Stout Pat, ca 1860, EX NP, VG **115.00**
Hammer, saw setting; Simonds, for cross-cuts/etc, VG **45.00**
Hammer, veneer; mk HXC, early, EX patina, 10" **45.00**
Knife, cooper's chamfer; L&IJ White, laminated blade, G+..........**65.00**

Level, CF Richardson, CI, worn japanning, 6", G+ 75.00
Level, Goodel Pratt, CI, 95% japanning, 24", VG.....................85.00
Level, MW Robinson, Davis Pat, CI, EX NP & japanning, 12" .295.00
Level, Standard Tool Co, CI, pitch adjuster, Pat 1897, VG 325.00
Mallet, horse collar; burl head, 7" dia, VG..............................125.00
Plane, block; Sargent #5607, low angle, EXIB 120.00
Plane, buck panel; Spiers mk (made for Buck), closed tote, 13½", G ..565.00
Plane, bull-nose; W Straw & Son, gunmetal & rosewood, EX....200.00
Plane, compass; G Rosebloom Cincinnati, butcher's steel, G........35.00
Plane, grooving; A Smith Rehoboth, skate riveted to body, G ...135.00
Plane, plow; H Chapin Union Factory #239½, applewood, VG.395.00
Plane, smoothing; Norris #13, CI, repolished, 2¼" W, VG.........785.00
Pliers, belting; W Schollhorn, parallel jaws w/punch....................35.00
Pliers, Diamond Handiman DH16, 6½" 40.00
Pliers, Sargent & Co, Bernard's Pat, parallel jaws, EX NP, 5"...25.00
Pliers, Sargent & Co, duck-bill w/parallel jaws 25.00
Pliers, Vacuum Grip, early snap-on type, 4½", VG......................20.00
Plumb bob, Goodell Pratt, 16-oz, VG...40.00
Plumb bob, turnip shape, unmk, 4", VG.....................................30.00
Plumb bob, Warner Tools, NP, w/reel..85.00
Rule, boxwood, folding, ca 1900, 24", EX...................................45.00
Rule, LS Starrett #604R, adjustable hook 1 end, 12", NM...........40.00
Saw, back; WB Cears...NY, cvd beech hdl, VG 80.00
Saw, cross-cut; Henry Disston & Sons #7, 1896-1917 medallion, 26", VG.45.00
Saw, dado; Bishop's Pat, 14", EX+ 250.00
Saw, docking; EC Atkins #590, silver steel, iron hdl, 25"..............60.00
Saw, dvtl; CE Jennings, brass bk, birch hdl, G 60.00
Saw, tenon; Henry Disston & Sons, brass bk, applewood hdl, 10", G...95.00
Saw jointer, Pike Perfect, spring-loaded, NMIB 35.00
Saw set, Disston Triumph #18, adjustable, Pat 1899, VG.............45.00
Saw vise, Disston #1, 9" jaws, VG 50.00
Spoke shave, A Field...NY, boxwood, Marples, 8" 45.00
Spoke shave, AG Batchelder...Mass, cast steel, wood hdls, G+.....40.00
Spoke shave, Millers Falls No 1, rosewood hdls, Pat 1884, 10", G+.65.00
Spoke shave, Phelps Bros...PA, NP brass, flat bottom, 3¾", G......85.00
Square, bevel; CI w/Pat lock on bottom, unmk, 9" 28.00
Square, bevel; Zenith made by Disston, 7", VG 20.00
Square, caliper; Starrett #424, graduated in 32nd & 64th, 5" 25.00
Square, combo; LS Starrett, level bubble & scribe, 12" 40.00
Square, framing; Southing Cutlery Co, 6", VG...........................30.00
Try square, Henry Disston...Philadelphia #1, 8", NM 45.00
Wrench, H&E Wrench Co, dollar slides on hdl, Pat Mar 27 1923, G ...35.00
Wrench, monkey; H&H Balto MD, wedge at bk collar, 6", VG ...85.00
Wrench, pipe; Cook's Pat Jany 28, 1890, self-adjusting, VG.......115.00
Wrench, Universal Pat...1-22-19, crescent type w/pliers action, G 65.00

Toothbrush Holders

Most of the collectible toothbrush holders were made in prewar Japan and were modeled after popular comic strip, Disney, and nursery rhyme characters. Since many were made of bisque and decorated with unfired paint, it's not uncommon to find them in less-than-perfect paint, a factor you must consider when attempting to assess their values. Our advisor for this category is Marilyn Cooper, author of *Pictorial Guide to Toothbrush Holders*; she is listed in the Directory under Texas. Plate numbers in the descriptions that follow refer to her book.

Andy Gump & Min, bsk, plate #221, 4", from $85 to 100.00
Bear, brn w/mc shirt, 2 holes, front tray, Goldcastle, 5½x3x2½" ...155.00
Betty Boop w/toothbrush & cup, KFS, 5", from $85 to 100.00
Big Bird, Taiwan (RCC), plate #263, 4¼", from $80 to 95.00
Cat (Calico), Japan, 5½", from $90 to 110.00
Clown head w/bug on nose, Japan, 5", from $170 to 190.00

Ducky Dandy, Japan, 4", from $150 to 175.00
Indian chief, 2 holes, hangs, tray holds toothpaste, 4½", $250 to ...300.00
Kayo, Japan, plate #116, 5", from $100 to 125.00
Mary Poppins, Japan, plate #119, 6", from $100 to 150.00
Old King Cole, feet hold toothpaste, 1 hole, hangs, Japan, #125, 5".125.00
Old Mother Hubbard, plate #3, from $350 to 425.00
Sailor boy beside sq holder, unmk Japan, 3½", from $45 to 65.00
Snow White, plate #246, 6", from $225 to.................................250.00
Toonerville Trolley, Japan (Fountain Fox), plate #155, 5½" 550.00
Traffic cop, Germany, Don't Forget the Teeth, plate #243, 5", $350 to...375.00

Toothpick Holders

Once common on every table, the toothpick holder was relegated to the china cabinet near the turn of the century. Fortunately, this contributed to their survival. As a result, many are available to collectors today. Because they are small and easily displayed, they are very popular collectibles. They come in a wide range of prices to fit every budget. Many have been reproduced and, unfortunately, are being offered for sale right along with the originals. These 'repros' should be priced in the $10.00 to $30.00 range. Unless you're sure of what you're buying, choose a reputable dealer. In addition to pattern glass, you'll find examples in china, bisque, art glass, and various metals. For further information we recommend *Glass Toothpick Holders, Identification & Values*, by Neila and Tom Bredehoft and Jo and Bob Sanford.

Toothpick holders in the listings that follow are glass unless noted otherwise. See also specific companies (such as Northwood) and types of glassware (such as Burmese, cranberry, etc.).

Basketweave, amber...45.00
Beaded Grape, gr...65.00
Beaded Grape & Leaf, gr w/gold 50.00
Bull's Eye, ruby, ruffled rim..55.00
Coal scuttle, amber..18.00
Colorado, gr w/gold...35.00
Croesus, purple w/gold (+)..120.00
Daisy & Button..18.00
Daisy & Button, amberina, ftd urn form, 2½" 15.00
Daisy & Button, milk glass, Westmoreland 28.00
Darwin (aka Monkey), vaseline..65.00
Diamond & Fan, 2⅝"..18.00
Diamond Quilt, amberina, sq top...275.00
Diamond w/Peg, ruby stain, etched name & 1910......................18.00
Diamond w/Peg, ruby stain, souvenir..45.00
Duncan & Miller's No 58 (aka Clover), ca 1905 ....50.00
Empress, gr..95.00
Famous (Panelled T'print) 30.00
Fine Cut, bl...27.50
Fleur-de-lis (form), milk glass, 3½" 48.00
Holly & Berries, gr...58.00
Imperial #505, Peacock carnival 22.00
Inverted Eye, Riverside, 1902, 2⅝" 45.00
Invt T'print, amberina, ped ft, 2⅞"...150.00
Invt T'print, flared/fluted top..10.00
Iris w/Meander, gr opal..80.00
Ladder w/Diamonds...35.00
Little Lobe, wht satin...200.00
Lower Manhattan, amethyst stain..35.00
Maryland...140.00
Michigan (aka Paneled Jewel), vaseline 45.00
Minnesota, 3-hdl...30.00
Ohio Star, Millersburg, 1910, 2"...125.00
Paneled Sprig, wht opal, Northwood, late 1800s, 2¼"................90.00

Peek-a-Boo, bl, 3¾" 34.00
Peek-a-Boo, McKee, ca 1904 ....56.00
Pennsylvania, clear w/EX gold 60.00
Raindrop, cranberry w/HP forget-me-nots, 2½" 110.00
Reverse Swirl, bl, Buckeye, 2" 60.00
Rexford..55.00
Ribbed, bl opal, AJ Beatty & Sons, 1⅞" 38.00
Ribbed Pillar, cranberry & opal spatter satin, 2¼" ...50.00
Ring Band, custard, floral decor, Heisey, 2¼" 45.00
Scroll w/Cane Band, West Virginia Glass Co, 2¼" ..15.00
Shell & Seaweed, pk cased, Consolidated, 2¼" 110.00
Simplicity Scroll, gr frosted, metal band..........................50.00
Starburst, clear w/gold 10.00
Sunbeam, gr w/gold 80.00
Swan w/open neck, wht opal, 2⅜x2¼" 40.00
Swirl, white opal, 1890, 2⅛" 95.00
Teepee 35.00
Threaded, vaseline threading over cranberry bowl, 2¼"....60.00
Venecia, cranberry, 2½" 60.00
Washington, Knights Templar enameling........................60.00
Windows, wht opal..150.00
Winged Scroll, custard w/gold, Heisey, 2¼" 120.00
Witch's Kettle 15.00
Wreath & Shell, vaseline opal...225.00

Torquay Pottery

Torquay is a unique type of pottery made in the South Devon area of England as early as 1867. At the height of productivity, at least a dozen companies flourished there, producing simple folk pottery from the area's natural red clay. The ware was both wheel-turned and molded and decorated under the glaze with heavy slip resulting in low-relief nature subjects or simple scrollwork. Three of the best known of these potteries were Watcombe (1867 – 1962); Aller Vale (in operation from the mid-1800s, producing domestic ware and architectural products); and Longpark (1890 until 1957). Watcombe and Aller Vale merged in 1901 and operated until 1962 under the name of Royal Aller Vale and Watcombe Art Pottery.

A decline in the popularity of the early classical terra-cotta styles (urns, busts, figures, etc.) lead to the introduction of painted and glazed terra-cotta wares. During the late 1880s, white clay wares, both turned and molded, were decorated with colored glazes (Stapleton ware, grotesque molded figures, ornamental vases, large jardinieres, etc.). By the turn of the century, the market for art pottery was diminishing, so the potteries turned to wares decorated in colored slips (Barbotine, Persian, Scrolls, etc.).

Motto wares were introduced in the late nineteenth century by Aller Vale and taken up in the present century by the other Torquay potteries. This eventually became the 'bread and butter' product of the local industry. This was perhaps the most famous type of ware potted in this area because of the verses, proverbs, and quotations that decorated it. This was achieved by the sgraffito technique — scratching the letters through the slip to expose the red clay underneath. The most popular patterns were Cottage, Black Cockerel, Multi-Cockerel, and a scroll-work design called Scandy. Other popular decorations were Kerswell Daisy, ships, kingfishers, applied bird decorations, Art Deco styles, Egyptian ware, and many others. Aller Vale ware may sometimes be found marked 'H.H. and Company,' a firm who assumed ownership from 1897 to 1901. 'Watcombe Torquay' was an impressed mark used from 1884 to 1927.

Our advisors for this category are Jerry and Gerry Kline; they are listed in the Directory under Ohio. If you're interested in joining a Torquay club, you'll find the address of The North American Torquay Society under Clubs, Newsletters, and Catalogs.

Art Pottery

Biscuit barrel, Apple Blossom, porc, unmk, 6½" 275.00
Biscuit barrel, parrots on branches on bl, wrapped hdl, 6" 125.00
Bottle, scent; rose, pk on bl, att Watcombe, 3" 80.00
Bottle, scent; Scandy, Exeter Art Pottery, crown stopper, 3¼".......85.00
Bowl, Blarney Castle, Watcombe, hdls, ftd, 4½x4¼" 75.00
Candlestick, Persian, Aller Vale, bell form, 9½", ea....................295.00
Candlesticks, Scroll, Aller Vale, ca 1900, 6", pr 100.00
Canoe, Kingfisher, Royal Torquay, 2x9" 88.00
Ginger jar, Apple Blossom, SP lid & hdl, Watcombe, 4" 175.00
Hatpin holder, geometric floral, Longpark, 1890s, 5x3½" 135.00
Jardiniere, Scroll, Aller Vale, early 1900s, 3¾"...........................100.00
Jug, Ruins (Tintern Abbey), Longpark, strap hdl, 5½"................125.00
Tray, dresser; windmill, Aller Vale, no motto, 10½x7" 425.00
Urn, sailing ships, Sepia Ware, Watcombe, 1880s, 12½" 425.00
Vase, Alexandria Rose, twist hdls, 4½" 65.00
Vase, geometric design (resembling tumbling blocks), 9½".........110.00
Vase, windmill scene, Crown Dorset, motto, early 1900s, 4", pr .250.00
Wall pocket, flowers on horn shape, Exeter, 6½x4½" 175.00
Watering can, Scroll, Aller Vale, top & side hdls, 1897-1902, 7" 150.00

Devon Motto Ware

Biscuit jar, Cottage, Watcombe, 'May Your Joys Be...,' 5x6½" 225.00
Bottle, scent; Violets, Esuma, 'Dredges Orig Somerset Violets,' 3" .65.00
Bowl, Cottage, Dartmouth, 'Waste Not Want Not,' 3¾" 42.00
Bowl, Cottage, unmk, 'There Be More in the Larder,' 4½x5½"....58.00
Cheese dish, Cottage, unmk, 'Help Yourself - Don't...,' 6½" 150.00
Coffeepot, Black Cockerel, Watcombe, 'Before You Act...,' 6¾" .125.00
Coffeepot, Black Rooster, 'If You Can't Be Aisy...,' 6½" 175.00
Coffeepot, Cottage, side hdl, 'May You Find That...,' 8" 195.00
Condiment set, Cottage, Watcombe, motto, shakers+mustard+stand..195.00
Creamer, Black Cockerel, 'Elp Yersef Teu Gram,' 2½"..................68.00
Creamer, Scandy, Aller Vale, 'Tak a Little Craim,' mini, 1⅞x2½" ..65.00
Hatpin holder, Colored Cockerel, 'Keep Me on the Dressing...,' 4½" ..200.00
Humidor, Black Cockerel, Longpark, w/motto, 5" 215.00
Inkwell, Colored Cockerel, Aller Vale, 'Good Morning...,' 2¾" dia..95.00
Inkwell & stand, Scandy, Watcombe, 'Send Us a Scrape...,' 2¾x5¼"..120.00
Jardiniere, Cottage, Watcombe, 'Masters Two Will Never...,' 3x4¼" ..95.00
Jug, Black Cat, Aller Vale, 'Oh Where Is My Boy Tonight,' 5x4" ..225.00
Jug, Black Cockerel, 'Good Morning & Fresh...,' 4½" 98.00
Jug, Cottage, Watcombe, 'Don't Worry It May Never...,' 5½" 105.00
Jug, Cottage, Watcombe, 'Stretch Forth Your Hand...,' 1920s, 6" .95.00
Jug, Kerswell Daisy, Aller Vale, 'Earth I Am...,' 8¼x7" 295.00
Jug, Kerswell Daisy, Aller Vale, 'There's a Saying Old...,' 8½" 225.00
Jug, milk; Cockerel, St Mary Church Pottery, motto, 4¼x4" 75.00
Jug, puzzle; Colored Cockerel, 'This Yer Jug Was...,' 3½"............220.00
Jug, puzzle; Cottage, Watcombe, 'Within This Jug...,' 1930s, 4½" .175.00
Jug, Scandy, Longpark, 'Drink Ye Old Heatherdale...,' 5", NM....175.00
Jug, Scroll, 'If Ye Can't Be Aisy...,' 5" 165.00
Match holder, Cottage, Watcombe, 'A Match for Any Man'......100.00
Match striker, Scandy, 2½" 85.00
Mug, Black Cockerel, Longpark, 'For a Good Boy,' 3"................85.00
Mug, Cottage, 'Enough's as Good as a Feast,' 3½x4" 80.00
Mug, Cottage, Watcombe, 'From Rocks & Sands...,' 4½x5½"....100.00
Mug, Cottage, Watcombe, 'Tom Tom the Piper's Son...,' 3x3¼" ..75.00
Mug, Parrots, 'Still Water Runs Deep,' bl bkground, 3½" 60.00
Mug, shaving; Cottage, Watcombe, 'Hair on Head Is Worth...'..125.00
Mug, Thistle, 'There's No Time Like Now,' 3¼"..........................65.00
Plate, Black Cockerel, Longpark, 'Gude Folks Be...,' 7½" 110.00
Salt cellar, Cottage, 'Elp Yerzel...,' 3¼"...65.00
Server, Cottage, Watcombe, 3-compartment (ea w/motto), 8x8½"..150.00
Sugar bowl, Cottage, unmk Devon, 'Sweeten to Your...,' 2x3½"...35.00

Sugar bowl, Scandy, Watcombe, 'Sweeten to Your...,' 2x3½" **35.00**
Teapot, Black Cockerel, Longpart, 'Dauntee Be Fraid...,' 1-cup, 2½" ...**175.00**
Teapot, Colored Cockerel, Longpark, motto, 3½" **175.00**
Toast rack, Cottage, Watcombe, 'Take a Little Toast,' 3x3½" **125.00**
Tray, Black Cockerel, Watcombe, 'There's a Saying...,' 11x7½" .**300.00**
Tray, Cottage, Watcombe, 'Do Not Stain Today's Blue Sky...,' 11" ..**275.00**
Tray, Cottage, Watcombe, 'Full Many a Shaft at Random...,' 11x7½" ..**275.00**
Vase, Cottage, Watcombe, no motto, ca 1910, 10x4½" **195.00**

Tortoise Shell

The outer shell of several species of land turtles, called tortoises, was once commonly used to make brooches, combs, small boxes, and novelty items. It was often used for inlay as well. The material is easily recognized by its mottled brown and yellow coloring. Because some of these turtles are now on the endangered list, such use is prohibited.

Box, deeply cvd w/figures in landscape, China, 1850, 4" dia.......**345.00**
Coffer, sewing; slant lid, divided int, Wm IV, 1830s, 4¼" **1,380.00**
Coffer, Wm IV sargophagus form, hinged lid, 6x7½x4½" **2,185.00**

Tortoise Shell Glass

By combining several shades of glass — brown, clear, and yellow — manufacturers of the nineteenth century were able to produce an art glass that closely resembled the shell of the tortoise. Some of this type of glassware was manufactured in Germany. In America it was made by several firms, the most prominent of which was the Boston and Sandwich Glass Works.

Bottle, scent; bell-like top on bowl-shaped bottom, amber stopper, 4" ..**125.00**
Bowl, sq w/fold-in top, HP florals, att Moser, 3x4¼" **125.00**
Paperweight, pear shape w/gilt leaf, Boston & Sandwich **85.00**
Pitcher, amber hdl, ground pontil, 5x7"..................................**90.00**
Vase, gold bamboo/ferns/birds, pinched & ruffled, 8½" **300.00**
Vase, gold vines, can neck, bulbous w/flared ft, Webb, 8¼x6" **465.00**

Toys

Toys can be classified into at least two categories: early collectible toys with an established history and the newer toys. The antique toys are easier to evaluate. A great deal of research has been done on them, and much data is available. The newer toys are just beginning to be studied; relative information is only now being published, and the lack of production records makes it difficult to know how many may be available. Often warehouse finds of these newer toys can change the market. This has happened with battery-operated toys and to some extent with robots. Review past issues of this guide. You will see the changing trends for the newer toys. All toys become more important as collectibles when a fixed period of manufacture is known. When we know the numbers produced and documentation of the makers is established, the prices become more predictable.

The best way to learn about toys is to attend toy shows and auctions. This will give you the opportunity to compare prices and condition. The more collectors and dealers you meet, the more you will learn. There is no substitute for holding a toy in your hand and seeing for yourself what they are. If you are going to be a serious collector, buy all the books you can find. Read every article you see and study all books that are available. Knowledge is vital to building a good collection. These are some of the most helpful: *Schroeder's Collectible Toys, Antique to Modern,* by Sharon and Bob Huxford; *Cartoon Toys & Collectibles* by David Longest; *G-Men and FBI Toys and Collectibles* by Harry and Jody Whit-

worth; *Breyer Animal Collector's Guide* by Felicia Browell; *Collector's Guide to TV Toys and Memorabilia, 1960s & 1970s, Second Edition,* by Greg Davis and Bill Morgan; *Collector's Guide to Tootsietoys* by David Richter; *Matchbox Toys, 1974 – 1996, Second Edition, Collector's Guide to Diecast Toys and Scale Models,* and *Toy Car Collector's Guide,* by Dana Johnson; *Collector's Guide to Battery Toys, Second Edition,* by Don Hultzman; and *Hot Wheels, The Ultimate Redline Guide, 1968 – 1977, Volume 1* and *2,* by Jack Clark and Robert P. Wicker. All are published by Collector Books. Other informative books are *Collecting Toys, Collecting Toy Soldiers,* and *Collecting Toy Trains, An Identification & Value Guide #3,* by Richard O'Brien. In the listings that follow, toys are listed by manufacturer's name if possible, otherwise by type. Measurements are given when appropriate and available; if only one dimension is noted, it is the greater one — height if the toy is vertical, length if it is horizontal. See also Children's Things; Personalities. For toy stoves, see Stoves.

Key:
b/o — battery operated   NP — nickel plated
cl — celluloid   w/up — wind-up
jtd — jointed

Toys by Various Manufacturers

Keystone, Air Mail Airplane, pressed steel, good paint with overpaint on wings, 23", $468.00 at auction.

Alps, Clown the Magician, b/o, 1950s, 12", MIB **375.00**
Alps, Fido the Xylophone Player, b/o, 1950s, 9", MIB.................**375.00**
Alps, Pipie the Whale, b/o, 1950s, 12", NM............................**325.00**
Alps, Smoking Robot, b/o, 1950s, 12", EXIB.........................**2,200.00**
Alps, Twirly Whirly Rocket Ride, b/o, 1950s, 13", NMIB **1,525.00**
ASC, Monkee-Mobile, b/o, 1967, 12", NMIB **525.00**
ATC, DC Transit GMC Bus, friction, 17", VG **300.00**
Bandai, Hato Bus, diecast, bl & wht, MIP..............................**20.00**
Bandai, Space Patrol Super Cycle, friction, 12", VG+IB **9,900.00**
Bburago, Chevy Corvette (1957), #3024, diecast, MIP **25.00**
Chad Valley, Commer Flat Truck, diecast, MIP **175.00**
Chein, Bass Drummer, w/up, 1930s, 9", NM.............................**400.00**
Chein, Cabin Cruiser, w/up, 15", MIB **700.00**
Chein, Hercules Ice Truck, #600, pressed steel, 20", VG **600.00**
Chein, Playland Whip, #340, w/up, 20" L, NMIB **950.00**
Chein, Popeye Waddler, w/up, 1932, 6½", VG+ **750.00**
Corgi, Batboat & Trailer, #107, MIB....................................**175.00**
Corgi, Batcopter, #925, MIB...**85.00**
Corgi, Hardy Boys' Rolls Royce, #805, MIB.............................**320.00**
Corgi, Holiday Minibus, #508, MIB **125.00**
Corgi, Intercity Minibus, #701, MIB **35.00**
Corgi, Massey-Ferguson 65 Tractor, #50, MIB **125.00**
Corgi, Mercedes Benz 300SL, #304, yel, MIB **450.00**
Corgi, Space Shuttle, #648, MIB **50.00**
Cragstan, Dilly Dalmatian, b/o, 1950s, 10", EX........................**130.00**
Daiya, Astro Racer, b/o, 1960s, 12", NMIB.............................**975.00**
Daiya, Green Caterpillar, b/o, 1950s, 20" L, MIB **250.00**
Dinky, Alfa Romeo 33, #210, MIP..**200.00**
Dinky, Guy Flat Truck w/Tailboard, #513, MIP.........................**400.00**

Dinky, Horse Box Express, #980, MIP 800.00
Dinky, Leyland Comet Cement Lorry, #419, MIP 350.00
Dinky, Pink Panther, #354, MIP 225.00
Dinky, Three-Ton Army Wagon, MIP..200.00
Distler, Mercedes Roadster, w/up, litho tin, 10", NMIB 350.00
Hubley, Mr Magoo Car, b/o, 1961, 8", EXIB...........................225.00
Kingsbury, Stake Truck, #349, w/up, yel, 15½", EX.................7,700.00
Leslie-Henry, Cargo Comet Freight Train Set, diecast, NMIB....125.00
Linemar, Bubble Blowing Popeye, b/o, 1950s, 12", NM 950.00
Linemar, Calypso Joe, b/o, 1950s, 10", EX+ 350.00
Marx, Busy Bridge, 24" L, EX...525.00
Marx, College Jalopy, w/up, 6", EX...250.00
Marx, Joy Rider, w/up, 1929, 8", EX.......................................350.00
Marx, Pinocchio Walker, w/up, WDE, 1939, 9", NMIB.............600.00
Marx, Rocket Racer, w/up, 1930s, 16", EX+ 400.00
SAN, Smoking Bunny, b/o, 1950s, 11", NMIB..........................275.00
Schuco, Electro Hydro Car, b/o, #5720, 10", EX+ 990.00
Steelcraft, Little Jim Dump Truck, 1930s, 23", VG...................450.00
Strauss, Dizzy Lizzy, w/up, NMIB...500.00
Strauss, Ham 'N Sam, w/up, EX..850.00
Strauss, Jolly Pals, w/up, EX 475.00
Structo, Steam Shovel Truck, pressed steel, 1950s, 20", VG.......175.00
TN, Antenna-Car, b/o, 1960s, 15", EXIB.................................225.00
TN, High Jinks at the Circus, b/o, 1950s, MIB.........................375.00
TN, Jolly Popcorn Vendor, b/o, 1950s, 8", MIB........................375.00
TN, Surrey Jeep, b/o, 1960s, 11", M..200.00
Tomiyama, Flying Circus, b/o, 1960s, rare, 17", MIB 1,075.00
Tomiyama, Jaguar E Type, b/o, 12", EXIB................................600.00
Y, Cragstan Mr Atomic, b/o, 1950s, 9", VG+IB......................9,350.00
Y, Willie the Walking Car, b/o, 1960s, 9", MIB........................325.00

Farm Toys

Baler, Case IH, Ertl #274, 1/64 scale, MIB 3.50
Baler, Oliver, Slik #9851, 1952, 10", MIB.................................500.00
Combine, Agco Allis R-52, Ertl #1282, 1/64 scale, MIB.............10.00
Combine, Case IH 1660, Ertl #655, MIB 11.00
Combine, Ford New Holland, Ertl #815, 1/64 scale, MIB.............15.00
Combine, John Deere CTS II, Ertl #5172, 1/64 scale, MIB..........10.00
Crawler, John Deere 430, Ertl #5771, 1/16 scale, MIB................22.00
Disk, New Holland, Ertl #3049, 1/64 scale, MIB...........................4.00
Fertilizer spreader, C&J Systems, Ertl #4433, 1/64 scale, MIB.........5.00
Hay rake, Case IH, Ertl #210, 1/64 scale, MIB 3.00
Planter, Case IH 12-Row 900, Ertl #656, 1/64 scale, MIB.............4.50
Plow, Oliver 2-Bottom, Slik #9850, 1952, 9", MIB...................380.00
Skid cattle loader, Case 090XT, Ertl #4216, 1/64 scale, MIB........25.00
Skid cattle loader, New Holland, Ertl #381, 1/64 scale, MIB..........4.50
Tractor, Farmall 'AV', Ertl #25-TA, MIB..................................35.00
Tractor, Ford 4000, Ertl #3024, 1/64 scale, MIB...........................3.50
Tractor, Fordson Super Major, Ertl #850DO, 1/16 scale, MIB.......30.00
Tractor, International 756 WF, Ertl #2308, 1/16 scale, MIB..........30.00

Guns and Cap Bombs

In years past, virtually every child played with toy guns, and the survival rate of these toys is minimal, at best. The interest in these charming toy guns has increased considerably, especially those with western character examples, as collectors discover their scarcity, quality, and value. Toy gun collectibles encompass the early and the very ornate figural toy guns and bombs through the more realistic ones with recognizable character names, gleaming finishes, faux jewels, dummy bullets, engraving, and colorful grips. This section will cover some of the most popular cast-iron and diecast toy guns from the past one hundred years. Recent market trends have witnessed a decline of interest in the earlier (1900 – 1940) single-

shot cast-iron pistols. The higher collector interest is for known western characters and cap pistols from the 1960 – 1965 era. Generic toy guns such as, Deputy, Pony Boy, Marshal, Ranger, Sheriff, Pirate, Cowboy, Dick, Western, Army, etc., generate only minimal collector interest.

Daisy Model A BB Gun, break action, wood stock, EX...............350.00
Daisy No 105 'Junior Pump Gun,' wood stock, EX 250.00
Halco Texan Double Gun & Holster Set, unused, MIB 350.00
Hubley Colt .45, complete w/6 cap-loading bullets, unused, MIB...300.00
Hubley Double Gun & Holster Set, steer medallions w/ribbons, MIB ..300.00
Ideal Man From UNCLE Napoleon Solo Gun Set, NMIB......1,000.00
Ives Clown on Powder Keg Cap Pistol, ca 1880, 3¾", VG......2,750.00
Ives Sambo Cap Pistol, japanned CI, ca 1883, 5½", EX 4,400.00
J&E Stevens America Revolving Cap Pistol, ca 1880, 8¾", EX.150.00
J&E Stevens Buffalo Bill Repeating Cap Pistol, CI, 8½", VGIB..125.00
J&E Stevens Caps Exploder, japanned, 13" L, EX....................1,850.00
Kenton Lightning Express Cap Pistol, CI, locomotive on bbl, 5", VG..450.00
KO Space Super Jet Gun, litho tin, 9", MIB............................250.00
Leslie-Henry Lone Ranger Carbine Rifle, plastic, 26", NMIB.....450.00
Lockwood Joker Cap Pistol, ca 1880, CI, 4½", EX...................275.00
Marklin Coastal Defense Gun, brass & iron, 6", EX...................225.00
Marx Anti-Aircraft Gun, litho tin, 1930s, NMIB 350.00
Marx Cork Shooting Submarine Gun, 1951, MIB......................250.00
Marx Popeye Pirate Pistol, litho tin, 1930s, NMIB 500.00
Mattel Agent Zero Radio-Rifle, 1960s, NMIB 80.00
Mattel Shootin' Shell Scout Rifle, unused, MIB.........................350.00
MT Automatic Rag Gun, b/o, 18½", EXIB................................300.00
Schmidt Roy Rogers Cap Gun, copper-color metal grips w/red jewel, EX .350.00
Taiyo Space Pilot Jet Ray Gun, 16", NMIB................................60.00

Model Kits

Addar, Planet of the Apes, Cornelius, 1973, MIB (sealed)............90.00
AMT, KISS Custom Chevy Van, 1977, MIB 70.00
Arii, Orguss Flier, MIB..15.00
Aurora, Bride of Frankenstein, 1965, MIB.................................600.00
Aurora, Captain America, 1966, MIB..300.00
Aurora, Creature, 1963, MIB..150.00
Aurora, James Bond 007, 1966, MIB...250.00
Aurora, Mummy's Chariot, 1965, MIB.......................................500.00
Aurora, Spider-Man, 1966, MIB...300.00
Aurora, Spider-Man, 1974, MIB (sealed)...................................150.00
Aurora, Whoosis?, Denty, 1966, MIB..75.00
Aurora, Witch, 1965, MIB..350.00
Bachmann, Animals of the World, Lion, 1959, MIB.....................50.00
Bachmann, Fisher Boy, 1962, MIB...80.00
Bandai, Thunderbird, 1984, MIB...40.00
Billiken, Frankenstein, MIB..150.00
Billiken, She-Creature, 1989, vinyl, MIB....................................65.00
Dark Horse, Mummy, 1995, MIB...150.00
Hawk, Cobra II, 1950s, MIB 75.00
Hawk, Weird-Ohs, Francis the Foul, 1963, MIB..........................50.00
Horizon, Invisible Man, MIB...50.00
Horizon, Mole People, MIB 50.00
Horizon, Robocop, ED-209, 1989, MIB......................................70.00
Hubley, Model A Roadster, metal, MIB 60.00
ITC, Neanderthal Man, 1959, MIB...50.00
Life-Like, Roman Chariot, 1970s, MIB.......................................20.00
Lindberg, Coo Coo Clock, 1965, MIB...40.00
Monogram, Bad Machine, 1970s, MIB..60.00
Monogram, Giraffes, 1961, MIB..50.00
Monogram, Sand Crab, 1969, MIB...50.00
MPC, Hogan's Heroes Jeep, 1968, MIB.....................................125.00
MPC, Spider-Man, 1978, MIB (sealed) 50.00

MPC, Sweathogs Dream Machine, 1976, MIB.............50.00
Palmer, US Navy Vanguard Missile, 1958, MIB 225.00
Pyro, Gladiator Sho Cycle, 1970, MIB.............50.00
Pyro, Peacemaker 45, 1960, MIB (sealed) 100.00
Revell, Moon Ship, 1957, MIB.............225.00
Revell, Peter Pan Pirate Ship, 1960s, MIB (sealed).............125.00
Screamin', Werewolf, MIB.............100.00
Toy Biz, Storm, 1996, MIB (sealed) 30.00
Tsukuda, Mummy, MIB 100.00

Pedal Cars and Ride-On Toys

Allied Van Lines Truck, Buddy L #918, 30", G 9.00
Champion 81 Pioneer, Gendron, 37", EX.............2,300.00
Chrysler Airflow, Skippy, 1937, 46", G.............10,000.00
Dodge, bell on hood, Steelcraft, old rpt, 36" 1,300.00
Fire Chief Car #6, wood fr, Gendron, 42", VG.............2,600.00
Franklin, Steelcraft, 54", EX.............8,000.00
Graham, gear drive, Skippy, 52", VG w/some rstr 8,500.00
Hot Rod, Garton, 35", NM 1,000.00
Ice Truck, w/canvas cover, Buddy L, 1930s, 27", G 1,150.00
Jr Streamliner, Steelcraft, 1930s, 40", G 1,800.00
Lincoln Zephyr, Steelcraft, 1940s, 43", G 1,000.00
Locomotive, Keystone, 1920s, 27", EX.............975.00
Pursuit Army Airplane, Murry, 1949-50, rstr, 45".............2,200.00
Racer, electric lights, pontoon wheel covers, Steelcraft, rstr, 37" ..2,500.00
Speedway Pace Car, Murray, 1960s, rstr, 34" 500.00
Steam Roller, Kenton, #60, 20", EX 450.00
Studebaker, spotlight on running board, Am National, 54", G+ .12,000.00
Woody, Garton, 1930s, rstr, 48".............3,500.00

Penny Toys

Airplane w/pilot, Kellerman, 4½", EX+ 700.00
Boy on rocking horse, Meier, 3¼", EX 825.00
Clowns playing wheelbarrow, Meier, 3', VG+ 2,300.00
Dirigible, Meier, 4½", VG+ 500.00
Express cycle w/driver, Meier, 3" 875.00
Flying Hollander, Meier, 3¼", EX.............875.00
Gnome on egg w/rabbit, Meier, 3", VG+ 1,750.00
Horse-drawn military postal van w/soldier on horse, Meier, 4½", EX...250.00
Luxury coupe, Fischer, 5½", EX 415.00
Meteor launch w/pilot, Meier, 4¾", VG 325.00
Ocean liner, Fischer, 4½", EX.............200.00
Race car w/driver, Distler, 2½", EX 935.00
Removing & Warehousing wagon, Meier, 3½", VG+ 200.00
Stake truck, Fischer, 4", EX.............250.00
Sulky w/ostrich & driver, 3½", VG+ 415.00
Trolley, Kellerman, 3⅛", EX 550.00
Wall telephone, Meier, 4¾", EX.............165.00
Zeppelin in Hangar, Meier, 2¾", VG+.............2,400.00

Pull and Push Toys

Alderney Dairy Milk & Cream Wagon, Schoenhut, EX 2,530.00
Bear, mohair w/muzzle & pull chain, wheels on ft, German, 7x13", NM.350.00
Buffalo on platform, pnt tin, CI spoke wheels, Am, 4½", EX 550.00
Duck, pnt CI, waddles & opens mouth, Hubley, 9", EX.........1,200.00
Girl on duck, pnt pressed steel, friction, Clark, 9", G.............275.00
Goat on platform, wht fur w/glass eyes, baahs, De Camps, EX+ .725.00
Horse & chariot on platform, pnt pressed steel, friction, Clark, G...110.00
Horse-drawn milk wagon, litho tin, Converse, 17½", G 425.00
Horse-drawn streetcar, tin, Am, 11", G.............125.00
Indian riding horse on platform, bell toy, NP CI, 7", VG.............100.00

Jonah & the Whale, bell toy, CI, NH Hill Brass Co, 6", EX ...1,050.00
Locomotive, pnt CI & wood, Walker & Crosby, 11½", VG 1,100.00
Monkey on velocipede, bell toy, CI, J&E Stevens, 7½", EX 3,080.00
Mule-drawn cart w/girl, pnt tin, German, 8¾", EX+ 6,500.00
Puppy Town Fire Dept fire engine, Gong Bell, EX 110.00
Seal w/ball & bear w/bell on platform, litho tin, 10", VG+ 200.00
Sunny Andy Street Railway, litho tin, w/bell, 13", EX 225.00
Woman & duck on platform, pnt pressed steel friction, Clark, 11", G+ .350.00

Robots

Atomic Robot Man, w/up, tin, Japan, 1950s, EXIB 700.00
Busy Cart Robot, b/o, tin/plastic, Japan, 11½", EXIB.............880.00
Change Man Robot (Alien Creature), b/o, tin, Japan, 1960s, 12", EX+ .4,400.00
Change Man Robot (Boy Astronaut), b/o, tin, Japan, 1960s, 14", NM.6,500.00
Cragstan Moon Man, friction, Cobor, 1960s, MOC.............200.00
Cragstan Mr Atomic, b/o, tin/plastic/rubber, Y, 1950s, 9", VG+IB.9,350.00
Dragon Robot, remote control, tin/plastic, Japan, 1960s, EX+IB.2,850.00
Excavator Robot, b/o, tin/plastic, Japan, 1960s, NMIB 275.00
Giant Sonic Robot, b/o, tin, Masudaya, 1950s, 16", VG+ 2,975.00
High Wheel Robot, w/up, tin, KO, 10", EX.............175.00
Krome Dome Robot, b/o, plastic, Japan, 11", EXIB 275.00
Machine Man, b/o, tin, Japan, 1950s, 15", G+ 27,500.00
Mighty Robot, w/up, tin, Japan, 5½", EXIB.............120.00
Mr Mercury Robot, b/o, tin/plastic, Linemar, 1960s, 13", VG.....350.00
Musical Drummer Robot (R-57), b/o, Japan, 1950s, 9", EX+IB.16,500.00
Nonstop Robot (Lavender Robot), b/o, tin, Masudaya, 1950s, 15", G+.1,200.00
Piston Action Robot (Pug Robbie), b/o, tin, Japan, 1950s, 9", EX+IB.1,375.00
Robert Robot, b/o, light on top, Ideal, 1950s, 13", NMIB.............225.00
Rudy the Robot, b/o, plastic, Remco, 1960s, 16", NM.............50.00
Swinging Baby Robot, w/up, tin, Japan, 12", NMIB.............450.00
Walking Robot, w/up, tin, Linemar, 6", VG+ 265.00

Schoenhut

    Our advisor for Schoenhut toys is Keith Kaonis, who has collected these toys for over twenty years. Because of his involvement with the publishing industry (currently *Antique DOLL Collector*, and during the '80s, *Collectors' SHOWCASE*), he has visited collections across the United States, produced several articles on Schoenhut toys, and served a term as president of the Schoenhut Collectors' Club. Keith is listed in the Directory under New York.

    The listings below are for Humpty Dumpty Circus pieces. All values are based on rating conditions of good to very good, i.e., very minor scratches and wear, good original finish, no splits or chips, no excessive paint wear or cracked eyes, and of course completeness and condition of clothes (if dressed figures).

    Clowns with two-part heads (a cast face applied to a wooden head) were made from 1903 to 1912 and are most desirable — condition always is important. There have been nine distinct styles in fourteen different costumes recorded. Only eight costume styles apply to the clowns with two-part heads. The later clowns had one-part heads with features of pressed wood, and the costumes on the later ones, circa 1920+, were no longer tied at the wrists and ankles.

Humpty Dumpty Circus Clowns and Other Personel

Black Dude, reduced sz, from $100 to.............375.00
Black Dude, 1-part head, purple coat, from $250 to 700.00
Black Dude, 2-part head, blk coat, from $400 to 850.00
Chinese Acrobat, 1-part head, from $200 to.............800.00
Chinese Acrobat, 2-part head, rare, from $400 to.............1,400.00
Clown, early, G, from $150 to 600.00
Clown, reduced sz, 1925-53, from $75 to 125.00
Gent Acrobat, bsk head, rare, from $300 to.............750.00
Gent Acrobat, 2-part head, very rare, from $600 to.............1,800.00
Hobo, reduced sz, from $200 to 375.00

Hobo, 1-part head, from $200 to 400.00

Hobo, 2-part head, facet toe ft, from $400 to............................900.00

Hobo, 2-part head, turned-up toes, blk coat, from $500 to 1,200.00

Lady Acrobat, bsk head, from $300 to..750.00

Lady Acrobat, 1-part head, from $150 to 400.00

Lady Rider, bsk head, from $250 to..550.00

Lady Rider, 1-part head, from $150 to 400.00

Lady Rider, 2-part head, very rare, from $500 to.........................800.00

Lion Tamer, bsk head, rare, from $175 to..................................850.00

Lion Tamer, 1-part head, rare, from $150 to 700.00

Lion Tamer, 2-part head, early, very rare, from $700 to...............800.00

Ring Master, bsk, ca 1908-14, from $300 to.............................800.00

Ring Master, 1-part head, from $200 to....................................450.00

Ring Master, 2-part head, blk coat, very rare, from $800 to.....1,800.00

Ring Master, 2-part head, red coat, very rare, from $700 to.....1,600.00

Humpty Dumpty Circus Animals

Humpty Dumpty Circus animals with glass eyes, ca. 1903 – 1914, are more desirable and can demand much higher prices than the later painted-eye versions. As a general rule, a glass-eye version is 30% to 40% more than a painted-eye version. (There are exceptions.) The following list suggests values for both GE (glass-eye) and PE (painted-eye) versions and reflects a **low PE price** to a **high GE price.**

There are other variations and nuances of certain figures: Bulldog — white with black spots or brindle (brown); open- and closed-mouth zebras, camels, and giraffes; ball necks and hemispherical necks on some animals such as the pig, cat, and hippo, to name a few. These points can affect the price and should be judged individually. Condition and rarity affect the price most significantly and the presence of an original box virtually doubles the price.

Alligator, PE/GE, from $250 to..750.00

Arabian Camel, 1 hump, PE/GE, from $250 to 750.00

Bactrain Camel, 2 humps, PE/GE, from $200 to 1,200.00

Brown Bear, PE/GE, from $200 to..800.00

Buffalo, cloth mane, PE/GE, from $300 to 900.00

Buffalo, cvd mane, PE/GE, from $200 to 1,200.00

Bulldog, PE/GE, from $400 to...1,500.00

Burro (farm set), PE/GE, no harness/no belly hole for chariot, $300 to ..800.00

Burro (made to go w/chariot & clown), PE/GE, from $200 to 700.00

Cat, PE/GE, rare, from $500 to...3,000.00

Cow, PE/GE, from $300 to 1,200.00

Deer, PE/GE, from $300 to 1,500.00

Donkey, PE/GE, from $75 to..300.00

Donkey, w/blanket, PE/GE, from $100 to....................................600.00

Elephant, PE/GE, from $75 to 300.00

Elephant, w/blanket, PE/GE, from $200 to 600.00

Gazelle, PE/GE, rare, from $500 to 2,750.00

Giraffe, PE/GE, from $200 to...900.00

Goat, PE/GE, from $150 to..400.00

Goose, PE only, from $200 to 900.00

Gorilla, PE only, from $1,500 to..4,000.00

Hippo, PE/GE, from $200 to..900.00

Horse, brn, saddle & stirrups, PE/GE, from $250 to 500.00

Horse, wht, platform, PE/GE, from $250 to 500.00

Hyena, PE/GE, very rare, from $1,000 to...................................6,000.00

Kangaroo, PE/GE, from $200 to...1,500.00

Lion, cloth mane, GE only, from $500 to 1,200.00

Lion, cvd mane, PE/GE, from $200 to 1,400.00

Monkey, 1-part head, PE only, from $200 to..............................600.00

Monkey, 2-part head, wht face, from $300 to 1,000.00

Ostrich, PE/GE, from $200 to..900.00

Pig, 5 versions, PE/GE, from $200 to..800.00

Polar Bear, PE/GE, from $200 to..2,000.00

Poodle, cloth mane, GE only, from $150 to 450.00

Poodle, PE/GE, from $100 to..300.00

Rabbot, PE/GE, very rare, from $500 to.....................................3,500.00

Rhino, PE/GE, from $250 to..800.00

Sea Lion, PE/GE, from $400 to...1,500.00

Sheep (lamb), w/bell, PE/GE, from $200 to................................700.00

Tiger, PE/GE, from $250 to...1,200.00

Wolf, PE/GE, very rare, from $500 to...5,000.00

Zebra, PE/GE, from $250 to..1,200.00

Zebu, PE/GE, rare, from $500 to..3,000.00

Humpty Dumpty Circus Accessories

There are many accessories: wagons, tents, ladders, chairs, pedestals, tight ropes, weights, and more.

Cage Wagon, ...Greatest Show on Earth, 10" & 12", EX, from $300 to...1,200.00

Menagerie tent, ca 1904, from $1,500 to 3,000.00

Menagerie tent, ca 1914-20, from $1,200 to..............................2,000.00

Oval litho tent, 1926, from $4,000 to..10,000.00

Sideshow panels, 1926, pr, from $2,000 to................................5,000.00

Steiff

Margaret Steiff began making her stuffed felt toys in Germany in the late 1800s. The animals she made were tagged with an elephant in a circle. Her first teddy bear, made in 1903, became such a popular seller that she changed her tag to a bear. Felt stuffing was replaced with excelsior and wool; when it became available, foam was used. In addition to the tag, look for the 'Steiff' ribbon and the button inside the ear.

Early Steiff bears in mint condition may go for a minimum of $150.00 per inch for a small bear up to $300.00 to $350.00 (sometimes even more) per inch for one 20" high or larger. For further information we recommend *Teddy Bears and Steiff Animals*, a full-color identification and value guide by Margaret Fox Mandel, available from Collector Books or your public library.

Bear, blond mohair, dressed in outfit, 1930, EX 350.00

Bear, blond mohair, shoe-button eyes, jtd, rattle, 1910, 5", EX....400.00

Bear, blond mohair, shoe-button eyes, no ID, 1905, 8", VG 700.00

Bear, blond mohair, 1905, no ID, 8", VG...................................700.00

Bear, caramel mohair, jtd, orig bow tie, button/tag, 1980s, 12", EX...115.00

Bear, caramel mohair, jtd, suede paws, button/tag, 3½", NM 65.00

Bear, gold mohair, glass eyes, jtd, excelsior stuffed, 1940s, 11", EX ..275.00

Bear, gold mohair, growler, 1983 repro of 1909 bear, 15", M.......225.00

Bear, honey blond mohair, 1950s, no ID, 3½", VG 100.00

Bear, lt apricot mohair, button eyes/pads, ID, 1905, 12½", VG..1,600.00

Bear, tan mohair, 1930s, no ID, 12", VG+ 500.00

Bear, wht mohair, red, wht & bl neck ribbon w/stop watch, 20", EX ...770.00

Bear on all 4's, cream mohair, 1930s, button/partial tag, 5½", VG..650.00

Berryman Bear, mohair, jtd, 90th Anniversary, M 250.00

Cow on wheels, brn & wht, bell around neck, w/growler, 12", VG..600.00

Dinosaur, T-Rex Tysus, yel & tan mohair, 1960s, no ID, 8", EX .200.00

Horse, gold silky plush/airbrushing, button/tag, 10½", EX............90.00

Horse on wheels, wht mohair w/brn spots, 17x21", VG 250.00

Lion on wheels, w/growler, G..475.00

Petsy, blond woven fur, jtd, squeaker, all ID, 11", EX 165.00

Santa bear, standing upright w/toy bag, 1960s, button/tag, 14", EX...200.00

School kids, boy & girl, stuffed felt w/outfits, 10½", VG....pr....1,600.00

Stork, wht & blk felt/celluloid beak/metal ft, 1950s, 6½", EX 125.00

Toy Soldiers and Accessories

Among the better-known manufacturers of 'Dimestore' soldiers are American Metal Toys, Barclay, and Manoil, all of whom made hollow cast-lead figures; Grey Iron, who used cast iron; and Auburn, who made figures of rubber. They measured about 3" to 3½" tall, and often accessories such as trucks, tents, tanks, and airplanes were designed to add to the enjoyment of staging mock battles, parades, encampments, and wars.

Britains is a very popular line, smaller and usually more detailed than the 'Dimestores.' They've been made in England since 1893, and many of their older boxed sets sell for more than a $100.00.

Some figures are very rare and therefore expensive, but condition is just as important in making a value assessment. Percentages in the description lines refer to the amount of original paint remaining. Our advisors for this category are Stan and Sally Alekna; they are listed in the Directory under Pennsylvania.

American Metal, machine gunner on stump, khaki, scarce, 97%..115.00
American Metal, machine gunner prone, khaki, scarce, 98%.....100.00
American Metal, officer in greatcoat w/pistol, khaki, very scarce, 98%...325.00
American Metal, soldier wounded, prone, khaki, scarce, 97%....125.00
Auburn Rubber, baseball batter, gray w/wht trim, scarce, 99%......70.00
Auburn Rubber, baseball catcher, scarce, NM..................70.00
Auburn Rubber, farmer's wife (milkmaid), 99%...............29.00
Auburn Rubber, football lineman, scarce, 97%.................59.00
Auburn Rubber, marine marching, port arms, bl, 2nd version, 97%..16.00
Auburn Rubber, officer on horse, scarce, 98% 51.00
Auburn Rubber, solder standing by searchlight, 97% 46.00
Auburn Rubber, soldier wounded, prone, 96%.................46.00
Barclay, aviator, 95% 28.00
Barclay, boy skater, M......................................20.00
Barclay, boy train passenger, 99% 17.00
Barclay, bride, 98%...27.00
Barclay, cavalryman, 1930s, 2¼", 95%.......................33.00
Barclay, couple on bench in winter garb, 99% 43.00
Barclay, cowboy w/pistol on horse, 1930s, scarce, 96%.......61.00
Barclay, cowboy w/rifle, 99%................................22.00
Barclay, detective, bl suit, very scarce, 97% 178.00
Barclay, doctor, wht, 80-85%................................14.00
Barclay, fireman w/axe, 98%................................42.00
Barclay, flamethrower, gr, 98%..............................23.00
Barclay, girl in rocker, bl, 95% 20.00
Barclay, groom, 98%..27.00
Barclay, Indian w/spear & knife, 97%........................19.00
Barclay, knight w/sword across chest, 98% 40.00
Barclay, mailman, NM.......................................22.00
Barclay, man on skis, 99%...................................28.00
Barclay, minister holding hat, 98%..........................27.00
Barclay, minister walking, scarce, 97% 80.00
Barclay, newsboy, HO scale, 99%.............................11.00
Barclay, newsboy, M..22.00
Barclay, nurse, blk hair, scarce, 96% 41.00
Barclay, oiler, HO scale, M..................................12.00
Barclay, pirate, red, scarce, 93-95%.........................32.00
Barclay, policeman, HO scale, NM............................12.00
Barclay, sentry in overcoat, 95%............................29.00
Barclay, soldier AA gunner, cast helmet, 99% 34.00
Barclay, soldier at attention, 98%..........................27.00
Barclay, soldier charging, khaki, 99% 19.00
Barclay, soldier crawling w/rifle, 95% 27.00
Barclay, soldier dispatcher w/dog, scarce, 97% 95.00
Barclay, soldier on parade, long stride, 99% 25.00
Barclay, soldier pigeon dispatcher, tin helmet, 98%.........38.00
Barclay, soldier telephone operator, 98%....................30.00
Barclay, train conductor, NM................................21.00
Barclay, train engineer, 86%................................19.00
Barclay, train porter w/whiskbroom, 99%.....................27.00
Barclay, typist w/table & typewriter, scarce, 93%...........99.00

Grey Iron, bandit surrendering, very scarce, 97%.............155.00
Grey Iron, Black cook, scarce, 99%..........................36.00
Grey Iron, Black man digging, scarce, 96%...................32.00
Grey Iron, boy in traveling suit, NM........................18.00
Grey Iron, Boy Scout walking, bl w/red scarf, 99%...........40.00
Grey Iron, boy w/life preserver, very scarce, 97%...........69.00
Grey Iron, cadet, gray jacket & cap, prewar, 95%............32.00
Grey Iron, colonial officer mounted, 96%....................49.00
Grey Iron, cowboy on bucking horse, scarce, 97%.............86.00
Grey Iron, elderly couple on park bench, 3-pc, 97%..........40.00
Grey Iron, Ethiopian tribesman, scarce, 99% 78.00
Grey Iron, girl in riding suit, very scarce, 96%.............68.00
Grey Iron, girl in traveling suit, 99%.......................16.00
Grey Iron, hired hand digging, 98%..........................23.00
Grey Iron, Indian brave shielding eyes, 98%.................39.00
Grey Iron, mailman, 98%....................................16.00
Grey Iron, newsboy, 99%....................................17.00
Grey Iron, pirate w/dagger, bl, 97%.........................39.00
Grey Iron, porter, 98%......................................19.00
Grey Iron, ski trooper, 99%.................................60.00
Grey Iron, soldier w/rifle at attention, 99%................20.00
Grey Iron, train conductor, 99%.............................17.00
Grey Iron, US cavalry officer, 95%..........................49.00
Grey Iron, US doughboy sentry, 90%.........................29.00
Grey Iron, US marine, NM...................................33.00
Grey Iron, woman w/basket, 97%.............................18.00
Jones, cowboy on rearing horse shooting gun while looking bk, NM...325.00
Jones, German charging w/bayonet, 54mm, scarce, NM.............40.00
Jones, soldier wire cutter crawling, NM.....................475.00
Jones, US Infantry Set #5413, 8-pc, M (EX+ box)............250.00
Lincoln Log, cave man (Big Tooth) w/bow, scarce, 96% 68.00
Lincoln Log, cowboy w/lasso, 98%............................18.00
Lincoln Log, farmer, 99%....................................22.00
Lincoln Log, pioneer, 98%...................................19.00
Lincoln Log, redcap, 98%....................................18.00
Manoil, action cannon, camo, later version, 97%.............23.00
Manoil, aviator holding bomb, 97%...........................39.00
Manoil, Black boy eating watermelon, scarce, 95%............100.00
Manoil, boy carrying wood, 94%..............................25.00
Manoil, carpenter sawing lumber, 98%........................28.00
Manoil, doctor, khaki, 98%..................................40.00
Manoil, farmer at water pump, 99%...........................30.00
Manoil, firefighter (Hot Papa), wht, scarce, NM.............155.00
Manoil, hod carrier w/bricks, 98%...........................43.00
Manoil, man chopping wood, 97%..............................28.00
Manoil, sniper camouflaged, 97%.............................37.00
Manoil, soldier bullet feeder, 97%..........................30.00
Manoil, soldier marching w/pack & slung rifle, 99% 38.00
Manoil, soldier wounded, prone, 98%.........................12.00
Manoil, woman laying out wash, 99%..........................30.00
Miller Plaster, soldier flag bearer, 99%....................50.00
Miller Plaster, soldier prone firing, orig rifle, 99% 33.00
Miller Plaster, stretcher bearer, 99%.......................21.00

Trains

Electric trains were produced as early as the late nineteenth century. Names to look for are Lionel, Ives, and American Flyer. Identification numbers given in the listings below actually appear on the item.

Am Flyer, Accessory Kit #35764, EXIB..........................500.00
Am Flyer, Caboose #4011, EXIB...............................1,350.00
Am Flyer, Frontiersman Set #35099, locomotive, tender & 2 cars, EXIB..950.00
Am Flyer, Great Northern Reefer #24422, gr, M................250.00

Am Flyer, Hudson Locomotive & Tender #112, EXIB **525.00**
Am Flyer, NYC Locomotive & Tender #151, MIB (sealed) **400.00**
Am Flyer, Set #501TR, locomotive, tender & 3 cars, NMIB **225.00**
Am Flyer, US Navy Jeep Transport Flatcar, w/2 orig jeeps, EXIB ..**350.00**
Bing, Locomotive, w/up, #1 gauge, 12", G+ **650.00**
Bing, Passenger Car, #2, gr w/yel trim, #1 gauge, VG **100.00**
Bing, Station, 2 canopied platforms flank building w/walkway, 10", EX ...**550.00**
Carette, Locomotive (4-2-0) & Tender, live steam, #3 gauge, VG ..**2,500.00**
Carette, Refrigerator Freight Car, mk LNWR, wht w/blk, G **40.00**
Ives, Locomotive #3217, CI, electric, EX **150.00**
Ives, Set #1071 w/#3236 Engine, 3-pc, EXIB **1,750.00**
Ives, Union Station, w/glass-domed canopy platform, VG **1,430.00**
Lionel, Christmas Car #9400, 1985, MIB **850.00**
Lionel, CSX Set #11779, modern era, MIB **275.00**
Lionel, Ice Station #352, postwar, MIB **850.00**
Lionel, Locomotive #226E & Tender #2226W, postwar, G+ **725.00**
Lionel, LV Hopper #6436, red, VG **150.00**
Lionel, Minuteman Boxcar #3666, postwar, EX **1,000.00**
Lionel, MKT Boxcar #6464-350, postwar, EXIB **500.00**
Lionel, Northern Pacific GP Locomotive #2349, postwar, EX+ ..**700.00**
Lionel, Seaboard Switcher #6250, postwar, VG+ **225.00**
Lionel, Signal Tower #438, prewar, EXIB **1,025.00**
Lionel, Station #116, prewar, EXIB...**3,100.00**
Lionel, Streamliner & Tender #265E, prewar, EX.......................**375.00**
Lionel, Telegraph Set #71, postwar, NMIB **700.00**
Lionel, Tender #2817, red, prewar, NMIB....................................**400.00**
Lionel, Tie Jector #55, postwar, EXIB..**125.00**
Lionel, Track Inspection Car #68, red & wht, postwar, NMIB ...**575.00**
Lionel, Wabash GP Locomotive #2339, EX **400.00**
Lionel, Western Pacific Boxcar #6464-250, postwar, NMIB **300.00**
Lionel, Work Caboose #6429, lt gray, postwar, EXIB...................**150.00**
Marklin, Baggage Car #1728, gr & orange, O gauge, VG **50.00**
Marklin, Good Station #2047, 1906, 15", EX...........................**4,600.00**
Marklin, Passenger Car #1888, hinged roof, VG+ **275.00**
Marklin, Postal Car w/Passenger Compartment #1895, 3 figures, G+..**225.00**
Marklin, Queen Mary Locomotive (4-4-0) w/#E1304 Tender, electric, VG+ .**935.00**
Marx, Empire Express Set, litho tin, w/up, 4-pc, EXIB................**225.00**
Marx, Pacific Stream Liner, litho tin, 6-pc w/12-pc track, w/up, VG .**155.00**
Marx, Santa Fe Passenger Set #44544, 6-pc, VGIB.....................**225.00**
Marx, Western Pacific Passenger #44464, 6-pc, MIB..................**600.00**

Trade Signs

Trade signs were popular during the 1800s. They were usually made in an easily recognizable shape that one could mentally associate with the particular type of business it was to represent, especially appropriate in the days when many customers could not read!

Am Medical Co, pnt wood w/gilt lettering, Am, 19th C, 20x95" ..**700.00**
Apothecary, mortar & pestle w/eagle on sphere, pnt zinc, 32¼"..**500.00**
Barber, Hair Cuts 50¢, rvpt glass oval w/tin bk, 10x15", VG **440.00**
Barber, pnt wrought sheet-iron bowl, 3-D, 1850s, 14x20", G......**175.00**
Blacksmith, cvd/pnt wooden horseshoe, ca 1800, 20x17x2" **3,335.00**
Boarding House/Millinery Shop, 2-sided, pnt wood, 14x60" ...**1,880.00**
Bootmaker, pnt slab w/boot ea end/name of maker, 1800s, 18x61"..**8,200.00**
Brewery, Jacob Hoffman Brewing Co, giltwood & metal, 1890s, 30x69"..**1,495.00**
Cigar mfg, wooden cigar shape w/gr pnt & gold letters, ca 1900, 47"..**700.00**
Cobbler, Boots & Shoes Repaired pnt on wood, 18x32" **1,300.00**
Cobbler, wood boot w/incised details, worn gilt/blk letters, 32x17x3"..**700.00**
Dentist, name on wood panel w/appl strap fr, weathered, 1870s, 12x40"..**700.00**
Fancy Goods & Notions, pnt wood panels, late 19th C, 19x36x½"...**1,000.00**
Fishmonger, Tooms Original..., pnt wood, 2-sided, 19th C, 18x15" ...**1,300.00**
Flower shop, faience mc flowers w/old iron hangers, 20th C, 20"..**625.00**

Fresh Eggs, pnt letters on wht wooden egg cutout on stand, 17".**435.00**
Grocer, wooden panel, blk w/gilt letters, 1890s, 9x66x1".........**2,400.00**
Habidasher, tin top hat, old pnt, 3-D, late 19th C, 20x22x25"..**6,325.00**
Hat, wooden cone w/wide brim, gold lettering, 19th C, 22x25" dia..**4,400.00**
Horse trotting & 2-wheeled sulky on oval, 2-sided, EX pnt, 18x28x35"..**950.00**
Ice Cream Parlor, pnt wood w/appl fr, blk/wht w/red/bl letters, 20x35".**590.00**
Inn, Tingley's Inn, pnt sheet & wrought iron, 19th C, rprs, 36x24"..**2,300.00**
Insurance, Agency for Fire Life..., 2-sided pnt wooden shield, 21x33"..**700.00**
Jeweler, gilt cast metal/pnt tin pocket watch, late 19th C, 17x11x2"..**1,600.00**
Lady's high-heeled shoe, cvd from laminated pine, mc rpt, 27" L......**935.00**
Locksmith, pnt wooden key w/silver/brn traces, 1890s, 15x88x3"....**925.00**
Locksmith, wooden key w/old red & tilt traces, ca 1900, 14x52".**575.00**
Meat packer, cvd steer head w/appl ears/horns, mc pnt, on plaque, 38" ..**865.00**

Optician, Butte Optical Co., two-sided, 30x60", VG, $5,500.00. (Photo courtesy Randy Inman Auctions)

Optician, eyes pnt on wood w/neon glasses fr, early 1900s, 11x29" ...**800.00**
Optician, pnt zinc spectacles w/banner beneath, rpr/breaks, 31" L.**2,000.00**
Pharmacist, molded sheet-metal mortar & pestle, old pnt, 18x18"....**925.00**
Photographer, molded/pnt sheet-iron box camera, ca 1900, 11x7x18" ...**2,500.00**
Saddle shop, horses' heads (zinc/copper) on wooden oval, 19x20x14".**765.00**
Shoemaker, boot, Casper's Shoes, pnt wood w/blk letters, 61" **700.00**
Silversmith, 2-pc cast-metal spoon & fork, late 19th C, 21x4"....**750.00**
Store, White Store...Millinery, brass sheet w/emb blk letters, 30x18".**460.00**
Tailor, wooden scissors, blk w/silver letters, ca 1900, 30" **800.00**
Tavern, pediment & pendant w/lettering, pnt wood, ca 1773, 54x23".**61,650.00**
Tavern, pnt metal w/neon-lit beer glass, early 20th C, 24x14x6" ..**450.00**
Tavern, soldier's silhouette, wrought & sheet iron, 69x19½"...**1,400.00**
Tavern, 2-sided, cvd/trn fr w/iron supports, brn w/yel letters, 41x40".**1,400.00**
Watch, dbl-sided, iron/zinc w/CI ring/winder/bezel, blk name/#s, 23" ...**500.00**
Wool merchant, lettering on blk pnt wood w/strap bracket, 34x84" **550.00**

Tramp Art

'Tramp' is considered a type of folk art. In America it was primarily made from the end of the Civil War through the 1930s, though it employs carving and decorating methods which are much older, originating mostly in Germany and Scandinavia. 'Trampen' probably refers to the itinerant stages of Middle Ages craft apprenticeship. The carving techniques were also used for practice. Tramp art was spread by soldiers in the Civil War and primarily practiced where there was a plentiful and free supply of materials such as cigar boxes and fruit crates. The belief that this work was done by tramps and hobos as payment for room or meals is generally incorrect. The larger pieces especially would have required a lengthy stay in one place.

There is a great variety of tramp art, from boxes and frames which are most common to large pieces of furniture and intricate objects. The most common method of decoration is chip carving with several layers built one on top of another. There are several variations of that form as well as others such as 'Crown of Thorns,' an interlocking method, which are completely different. The most common finishes were lacquer or stain, although paints were also used. The value of tramp art varies according to size, detail, surface, and complexity. The new collector should be aware that tramp art is being made today. While some sell it as new, others are offering it as old. In addition, many people mistakenly use the term as a catchall phrase to refer to other forms of construction — especially things they are uncertain about. This misuse of the term is growing, and makes a difference in the value of pieces. New collectors need to pay attention to how items are described.

For further information we recommend *Tramp Art: A Folk Art Phenomenon* by Helaine Fendelmam, Jonathan Taylor (Photographer)/ Stewart Tabori & Chang; *Hobo & Tramp Art Carving: An Authentic American Folk Tradition* by Adolph Vandertie, Patrick Spielman/Sterling Publications; and *Tramp Art, One Notch at a Time*, by Cornish and Wallach. Our advisors for this category are Matt Lippa and Elizabeth Schaff; they are listed in the Directory under Alabama.

Altar, arched top w/rays & stepped sq finials, drw, mirrors, 19x15" ...**1,500.00**
Ballot box, 2 drw, appl Odd Fellows symbols, 15" L **1,400.00**
Birdcage, house form, bird finials/appl flowers/trees/etc, 19x15x15" ..**3,200.00**
Box, appl pyramidal notched segments, brass tacks, brn pnt, 9x11x8" .**215.00**
Box, chip-cvd, mirrored top, grid sides, 4 mirror-front drws, 17x9x8" ...**350.00**
Box, pyramidal top/sides/ft of stacked sq segments, mirror w/in, 11" **200.00**
Box, sewing; cottage shape over drw, mc pnt, 9x16" **150.00**
Box, stacked chip-cvd moldings, old bl/salmon pnt, 9x16x11" ...**350.00**
Box, stepped dmn motifs/allover star-cut notches, dmn shape, 5x11" L..**585.00**
Bureau w/swivel mirror, appl leaves/crescents, lt/dk wood, 38x23x15" ..**475.00**
Cabinet, notch-cvd, hinged door, dk finish, 22x16x8½" **175.00**
Chest, stained wood w/appl gold-pnt letters/stars/etc, 21x13x9" ...**2,350.00**
Chest of drw, arch mirror fr, 2 short/3 long drw, appl geometrics, 18".**120.00**
Clock, openwork, 5 spirals w/acorn finials, brass bell, ivory #s, 40" **400.00**
Clock case, cruciform finial, peaked crest, stepped ft, 15x9x6" **175.00**
End table, appl chip-cvd geometrics on drw, 20th C, 22x16x14"..**1,500.00**
Floor lamp, sq base w/storage, segmented pole, geometrics, 59" **1,850.00**
Frame, chip-cvd zigzag border w/pinwheels/geometrics, dk stain, 7x5" ..**220.00**
Frame, Crown of Thorns, oval aperture, dk brn pnt, oval, 14¾"..**235.00**
Frame, Crown of Thorns, 3 apertures, inner chip-cvd frs, 33x29"..**250.00**
Frame, Crown of Thorns, 4 apertures w/Xd notched/stacked pcs, 20x19"..**100.00**
Frame, high-relief spool/scroll/geometric devices, 5" W, 39x34" ..**5,400.00**
Frame, notch cvd, appl flowers/leaves/acorns, 30x26", EX **500.00**
Frame, notch-cvd oval w/gilt highlights, 19th C, 16x14" **385.00**
Frame, openwork corner hearts/scroll top/X sides, appl dmns, 32x21"..**400.00**
Frame, pyramidal corner extensions, appl dmns to sides, gilt, 70x70".**5,500.00**
Frame, stacked geometric segments w/mirrored heart opening, 30x30"...**500.00**
Frame, star w/fretwork trim, star at ea point, stars/flowers w/in, 22" **575.00**
Frame, 9 apertures/19 sm fr mirrors, cvd lettering, ornate, 33x35" **2,250.00**
Miniature grand piano, stepped hearts/dmns/triangles, 12" W, +bench.**500.00**
Mirror, heart fr centers crisscrossed anchor/cross, chip-cvd, 15", EX...**2,800.00**
Mirror, stacked chip-cvd pyramidal segments w/beveled glass, 26x32" ..**235.00**
Mirrored fr, 2 apertures, 1918 in top arch, stacked geometrics, 31" L.....**200.00**
Model of church, Gothic arch 'ldgl' windows, gr trim, 15x10x8", VG ..**175.00**
Plant stand, narrow latticed brds, cvd/stacked, 4-leg, pnt, 34x15x15" ..**275.00**
Planter on stand, 3 sq peds, conforming base w/Xd elements, 32x50" W...**2,250.00**
Postcard display cabinet, 2 2-part hinged doors, base drw, top fr, 25" .**3,200.00**
Purse, oval w/upright hdl, inset mirror pcs/velvet strips, 11x10x7" ..**1,650.00**
Rocker, nursing; pierced lyre splat, appl notched molding/buttons......**250.00**
Sewing table, lid cvd Mother, serpentine legs, lower shelf, 34x32x18" ..**2,350.00**
Stacked boxes (3), ped ft/stacked dmns/appl balls to corners, 14x11x8" .**275.00**
Stand, shelf above 2 side stands w/lower tiers, mirrors/abalone, 39" **600.00**
Table, knotch-cvd stepped segments, drw, cvd sq ped, 31x25" sq.**150.00**
Tables, 20" sq tops/peds, assembled from puzzle-like cvd pcs, 30", pr..**3,300.00**
Wall pocket, arched crest w/dmn-shaped mirror, lt & dk wood, 36x16".**235.00**
Wall pocket, cvd 2-tone stacked heart/disk/wavy line elements, 14x7" .**585.00**
Wall rack, chip-cvd stars/stacked dmn ea w/MOP button, bl trim, 12x15" ..**470.00**

Traps

Though of interest to collectors for many years, trap collecting has gained in popularity over the past thirty years in particular, and prices

have appreciated. Traps are usually marked on the pan as to manufacturer, and the condition of these trademarks are important when determining their value. Grading is as follows:

Good: one-half of pan legible.
Very Good: legible in entirety, but light.
Fine: legible in entirety, with strong lettering.
Mint: in like-new, shiny condition.
Our advisor for this category is Boyd Nedry; he is listed in the Directory under Michigan. Prices listed here are for traps in fine condition.

Alligator #2..**200.00**
Anti Cat, automatic mouse trap....................................**65.00**
Arouze, wire cage mouse trap......................................**65.00**
Bigelow Trap, 7½"..**20.00**
Black Hole, plastic gopher trap.......................................**6.00**
Blake & Lamb 'Hercules' #1½, dog legs.........................**45.00**
Blake & Lamb #0 Jump...**25.00**
Blake & Lamb #44, dbl long spring..............................**35.00**
Briddell 'Escape Proof,' single hole pan........................**20.00**
Briddell Champion #0, single long spring......................**180.00**
Camp, glass minnow trap...**80.00**
Canadian snare thrower...**15.00**
Cooks Quick Catch, rattrap...**30.00**
Cooper Barrel Trap #2..**25.00**
Courtland #0, single long spring...................................**250.00**
Dahlgren 'Killer,' 12"...**15.00**
Dahlgren Sure Catch..**10.00**
Death Clutch, gopher trap..**5.00**
Diamond #15..**80.00**
Diamond #21½, single long spring................................**10.00**
Diamond #32, dbl jaw, coil spring.................................**28.00**
E-Z Trip, mole trap..**23.00**
Elgin, metal snap rattrap...**20.00**
EPP, chain loop...**1,000.00**
Executing, metal mouse trap...**180.00**
Fairy, mouse trap w/exercise wheel...............................**100.00**
Flip Trap, metal snap mouse trap...................................**30.00**
Funsten, float trap...**1,000.00**
Gabriel, fish trap...**500.00**
Game Keeper #0, Australian rabbit trap...........................**80.00**
Gibbs, US Standard #3, dbl long spring..........................**80.00**
Gurney's, gopher trap...**18.00**
Hales Perfect, mole trap, Pat 1881.................................**70.00**
Hedas Spiral, gopher trap, Pat 1899..............................**600.00**
Helfrich #45, coil spring...**35.00**
Herters Hudson Bay #0, sq pan....................................**150.00**
Hotchkiss & Son #0, single long spring..........................**200.00**
Ideal, claw type gopher trap..**725.00**
Jack Frost, w/brass trigger...**15.00**
JF Rittenhouse, mole trap...**17.50**
Joe Cook Better, gopher trap..**50.00**
Ketch-Em Tile Trap, 10" L..**35.00**
Ketch-Em Tile Trap, 3" single under spring......................**25.00**
Knap #1½, coil spring..**10.00**
Kompakt #1½, jump..**22.00**
Kricks Dandy, CI..**325.00**
Lastperch, bird trap..**45.00**
Little Throttler, wire killer...**75.00**
Lovell Sure Catch, mouse trap..**3.00**
McWhirter, fish trap..**500.00**
Mirror Decoy, rattrap..**130.00**
Montgomery #1½, coil...**30.00**
Montgomery #2, w/butterfly pan.....................................**80.00**
MWG (Michigan Wire Goods), mole trap...........................**6.00**

Nash Mole Trap, Vicksburg, MI 11.00
Nebraska Trail Trap 800.00
Nelson Killer, Pat 1901 ....225.00
Nesco, fly trap 45.00
Newhouse #50, dbl long spring, bear trap 525.00
Oneida, Jump #12, w/teeth, dbl under spring 70.00
Oneida, Newhouse #4, dbl long spring 35.00
Oneida, Victor #1½ Jump 5.00
Pemco, metal box mouse trap 240.00
Pioneer #1½, single long spring 15.00
Pioneer #4, dbl long spring 35.00
PS&W #100, Rev-O-Noc, single long spring..............................195.00
Queen Bee, wood & screen live bee trap 8.00
Quigle, wood snap mouse trap..22.00
Rival, Joliet IL, wood snap mouse trap 22.00
Roy, mole trap...20.00
Runway, tin mouse trap 45.00
Sabo, den trap 85.00
Sensible, CI 1,200.00
Star, metal snap rattrap 80.00
Sure Hold, wood cone, sm...90.00
Surprise Self-Setting, rattrap 100.00
Teeter, mole trap 35.00
TH Taylor Killer, coil spring 25.00
The Never Fail, brass gopher gun 125.00
The Victor #1, single long spring 10.00
Triumph #0, single long spring..100.00
Triumph #34X, w/clutches, dbl long spring 395.00
Triumph #115X, triple clutch, single long spring 10.00
Triumph #415, high grip, dbl long spring 450.00
Unique, glass fly trap 85.00
Veto, wood snap rattrap, Britain 22.00
Victor #0, cast jaws, single long spring 30.00
Victor #1, long spring 2.00
Victor #2, dbl long spring..40.00
Webley #4, dbl long spring..25.00
Western Exterminator, wood mouse trap.....................................18.00
White House, wood snap mouse trap...20.00
Winona, metal snap mouse trap 15.00
Woods & Waters Killer 14.00
X-Terminator, plastic, live mouse trap 12.00
Ymir, metal mink & martin trap, Canada 20.00
Zip, metal mouse trap, Sears & Roebuck Co................................40.00

Trenton

Trenton, New Jersey, was an area that supported several pottery companies from the mid-1800s until the late 1960s. A consolidation of several smaller companies that occurred in the 1890s was called Trenton Potteries Company. Each company produced their own types of wares independent of the others.

Vase, bl matt, flared rim, bulbed base, elongated hdls, 7½" 75.00

Trevaise

In 1907 the vacant Sandwich glasshouse was purchased and refurbished by the Alton Manufacturing Company. They specialized in lighting and fixtures, but under the direction of an ex-Tiffany glassblower and former Sandwich resident James H. Grady, they also produced a line of iridescent art glass called Trevasise, examples of which are very rare today. It was often decorated with pulled feathers, whorls, leaves, and vines similar to the glassware produced by Tiffany, Quezal, and Durand. Examples that surface on today's market range in price from $1,500.00 to $2,000.00 and up. Trevaise was made for less than one year. Due to financial problems, the company closed in 1908. Our advisor for this category is Frank W. Ford; he is listed in the Directory under Massachusetts.

Vase, gr & opal w/pulled & hooked decor, 1907......................3,500.00

Trivets

Although strictly a decorative item today, the original purpose of the trivet was much more practical. They were used to protect table tops from hot serving dishes, and irons heated on the kitchen range were placed on trivets during use to protect work surfaces. The first patent date was 1869; many of the earliest trivets bore portraits of famous people or patriotic designs. Florals, birds, animals, and fruit were other favored motifs. Watch for remakes of early original designs. Some of these are marked Wilton, Emig, Wright, Iron Art, and V.M. for Virginia Metalcrafters. However, many of these reproductions are becoming collectible. Expect to pay considerably less for these than for the originals, since they are abundant. For more information we recommend *The A – Z Guide to Collecting Trivets* by Margaret Lynn Rosack.

Brass

Heart, Give Your Heart To God Now in cut-out design, 9¼x5⅛"...75.00
Lyre shape w/pierced design, 3-ftd, trn ebonized hdl, 5x6x13" 100.00
Octagonal w/pierced floral, 4 pierced cabriole legs, ca 1860, 4x7½" ..65.00
Queen Victoria 60 Years of HM Reign, 1x5¼x8¾"......................110.00
Squirrel w/leaves & berries, pierced, 3-ftd, 7½x7¾" dia...............45.00
Tiger figure, pierced, paw ft, 4x10x5½" 375.00
William & Mary cypher, W over M, mk CW10-11, 1950, 5½x8"...40.00

Cast Iron

Dutch man center w/I Speak English Yet around border, iron shape, 4x6" ..25.00
Heart shape, 3-ftd, 1¼x5" 55.00
Heart w/pinwheels, old red pnt, 9½" 100.00
Hourglass in center sq fr, 4-ftd, 3¼x11x11" 135.00
Peerelss Iron Co, Cleveland OH mk on top, iron shape, 3-ftd 35.00
President James Garfield in horseshoe, 4-ftd, 5x4½" 200.00
Star center w/rnd border, 3 scroll ft, 10" dia..............................20.00
Turtle shape, openwork bk, 3x4½" 20.00

Wrought Iron

Heart shape, simple trim design, old red pnt, 9" 120.00
Heart shape on 3 rnd legs, 1x4¾x6¼"..75.00
Heart shape w/3 ft, 9⅝" 295.00

Twin Winton

Twin brothers Don and Ross Winton started this California-based company during the mid-1930s while still in high school. In the mid-1940s they shut it down while in the armed forces and started up again in the late 1940s, when older brother Bruce Winton joined them and bought them out in the early 1950s. The company became a major producer of cookie jars, kitchenware, and household items that were sold nationally until it closed its San Juan Capistrano, location in 1977.

Beside their extensive line of very collectible cookie jars, they're also well known for their Hillbilly line — mugs, pitchers, bowls, lamps, ashtrays, and decanters. Many others novelty items were produced as well. From the 1940s through the early 1970s, a variety of decorating methods continued to be developed. Don Winton was the only designer for Twin Winton and created literally thousands of designs for them and hundreds of other companies. He is still sculpting in Corona del Mar, California, and collectors and dealers are continuing to find and document new pieces daily. To learn more about this subject, we recommend *Collector's Guide to Don Winton Designs* by our advisor, Mike Ellis; he is listed in the Directory under California.

Ashtray, elf, TW-205, 8x8"	100.00
Bank, Dobbin, TW-410, 8"	40.00
Bank, Dutch Girl, TW-418, 8"	50.00
Bank, Friar Tuck (Monk), TW-407, 8"	40.00
Bank, kitten, TW-415, 8"	50.00
Bank, owl, TW-420, 8"	65.00
Bank, pig, TW-401, 8"	50.00
Bank, poodle, TW-419, 8"	65.00
Candle holder, El Greco, short, TW-500S, 6 4½", ea	12.00
Candle holder, Strauss, short, TW-502S, 6x4½", ea	12.00
Candy jar, nut, TW-353, 9x8"	75.00
Candy jar, Sailor Elephant, TW-356, 9x6"	65.00
Candy jar, shoe, TW-352, 10x10"	75.00
Canister, Coffee Coop, Canister Farm, TW-113, 6x4"	40.00
Canister, Flour House, Canisterville, TW-101, 11x7"	125.00
Canister, Flour Stable, Canister Farm, TW-111, 10x6"	65.00
Canister, Tea House, Canisterville, TW-104, 7x3"	50.00
Cookie jar, Apple, TW-35, 11x8"	180.00
Cookie jar, Baker, TW-67, 11x7"	400.00
Cookie jar, Bambi, squirrel finial, TW-54, 10x8"	175.00
Cookie jar, Cookie Barn, mc, TW-241, 12x8"	175.00
Cookie jar, Cookie Guard, TW-96, 12x7"	400.00
Cookie jar, Cookie Nut, TW-83, 10x9"	65.00
Cookie jar, Cookie Tepee, TW-96, 11x8"	325.00
Cookie jar, Cookie Time, clock w/mouse finial, TW-81, 14x7½"	45.00
Cookie jar, Cow, TW-69, 8½x13½"	75.00
Cookie jar, Donkey, mc, TW-288, 13x8"	175.00
Cookie jar, Duckling, TW-93, 11x8"	250.00
Cookie jar, Dutch Girl, mc, TW-247, 12x8½"	225.00
Cookie jar, Fire Engine, TW-56, 7x12"	85.00
Cookie jar, Friar Tuck, TW-85, 12x7"	65.00
Cookie jar, Gunfighter Rabbit, mc, TW-287, 13x8"	200.00
Cookie jar, Happy Bull (Ferdinand), TW-95, 12x8½"	85.00
Cookie jar, Mopsy, mc, TW-242, 12x7"	350.00
Cookie jar, Owl, mc, TW-291, 12x6½"	125.00
Cookie jar, Raccoon, blk mask, TW-92, 11½x8"	50.00
Cookie jar, Ranger Bear, mc, TW-284, 12x7"	125.00
Cookie jar, Rooster, mc, TW-268, 12x10"	125.00
Cookie jar, Sailor Elephant, TW-86, 12x9½"	40.00
Cookie jar, Sheriff, TW-55, 11x8"	75.00
Cookie jar, snail w/elf finial, TW-37, 12x7½"	175.00
Cookie jar, squirrel, eating cookie, TW-74, 10½x6"	45.00
Creamer & sugar bowl, rooster, TW-221	200.00
Figurine, Asian boy holding frog, T-15, 5½"	150.00
Figurine, beaver lying down, #315, 1x2½"	8.00
Figurine, blind mouse, #208,¾"	6.00
Figurine, Boo Boo Bear by stump, made for Idea Inc, 4"	75.00
Figurine, boy wearing Mickey Mouse hat, w/plane & hot dog, T-1, 5½"	150.00
Figurine, cat holding paw up in the air, 3"	30.00
Figurine, cowboy on stick horse, 5¼"	200.00
Figurine, duck, #304, lg, 2¼"	10.00
Figurine, football player & girl, 5x6"	275.00
Figurine, girl playing dress-up, T-19, 5½"	200.00
Figurine, Mickey the Apprentice, bsk, 7"	75.00
Figurine, quarterback w/gr jersey, 4½"	175.00

Figurine, rabbit sitting, #301, 2"	9.00
Figurine, skunk sitting, #203,¾"	5.00
Figurine, squirrel, folded hands, 2½x4"	30.00
Figurine, squirrel holding stomach, 2½x4"	30.00
Figurine, Wally Gator, bsk, 6"	80.00
Figurine, Yogi Bear sitting on stump, 5"	150.00
Figurine, zebra, 5"	45.00
Lamp, monkey, TW-259, 13"	175.00
Lamp, Sailor Bear, TW-250, 12"	175.00
Lamp, squirrel on stump, TW-255, 12"	175.00
Men of the Mountain, candy dish, 5¼" dia	75.00
Men of the Mountain, cigarette box, outhouse, H-109, 7"	75.00
Men of the Mountain, ice bucket, suspenders, TW-30, 14x7½"	250.00
Men of the Mountain, ice bucket, w/jug, TW-33, 14x7½"	350.00
Men of the Mountain, mug, H-102, 5"	30.00
Men of the Mountain, pitcher, H-101, 7½"	75.00
Men of the Mountain, pouring spout, H-104, 6½"	25.00
Men of the Mountain, punch cup, #H-111, 3"	15.00
Mug, coffee; Bergie, 5½"	40.00
Mug, elephant head, pk, 3½x5"	125.00
Mug, kitten face, TW-503, 3¼"	85.00
Mug, squirrel hdl, 5"	100.00
Mug, Wood Grain line, rope & spur hdl, 4"	40.00
Napkin holder, Dobbin, TW-487, 7x5"	65.00
Napkin holder, Dutch girl, TW-471, 8½x5½"	75.00
Napkin holder, elf, TW-476, 8x5"	85.00
Napkin holder, Hotei, TW-475, 8x6"	85.00
Napkin holder, Persian cat, TW-470, 5½x7"	75.00
Napkin holder, Porky Pig, TW-473, 8x5"	75.00
Napkin holder, rooster, TW-483, 7x6"	75.00
Napkin holder, Sailor Bear, TW-478, 9x4"	75.00
Planter, box; Merry Xmas, 4x15"	40.00
Planter, cat, w/boat on waves, TW-328, 8"	50.00
Planter, high-heel shoe shape, made for M'Goos Restaurant, 4"	15.00
Planter, pipe, 5"	50.00
Planter, Sailor Bear, TW-324, 8"	50.00
Plate, dinner; Wood Grain line, 10"	40.00
Plate, Santa face, 14"	50.00
Shakers, Artist Palette line, 3½", pr	65.00
Shakers, bucket, TW-65, pr	30.00
Shakers, cable car, TW-198, pr	50.00
Shakers, churn, TW-172, pr	40.00
Shakers, cookie pot, TW-158, pr	30.00
Shakers, cop, TW-149, pr	40.00
Shakers, donkey, TW-188, pr	40.00
Shakers, duck, TW-179, pr	75.00
Shakers, duckling, TW-193, pr	75.00
Shakers, Friar Tuck (Monk), TW-185, pr	35.00
Shakers, garlic head, 3", pr	40.00
Shakers, Happy Bull (Ferdinand), TW-195, pr	40.00
Shakers, lamb, TW-166, pr	30.00
Shakers, lion, TW-190, pr	45.00
Shakers, Pirate Fox, TW-146, pr	45.00
Shakers, Ranger Bear, TW-184, pr	40.00
Spoon rest, Dutch Girl, TW-19, 10x5"	40.00
Spoon rest, Sailor Bear, TW-12, 10x5"	40.00
Spoon rest, Sailor Elephant, TW-13, 10x5"	40.00
Spoon rest, turtle, TW-22, 10x5"	40.00
Stein, Bamboo line, 8"	35.00
Sugar bowl, Artist Palette line, 4" dia	40.00
Teapot, rooster, 10"	125.00
Toothpick dispenser, pig w/floral decor, hind quarters up, 5"	60.00
Vase, bud; snoopy bear, 3x4"	65.00
Wall planter, puppy head, TW-303, 5½"	100.00

Typewriters

The first commercially successful typewriter was the Sholes and Glidden, introduced in 1874. By 1882 other models appeared, and by the 1890s dozens were on the market. At the time of the First World War, the ranks of typewriter-makers thinned, and by the 1920s only a few survived.

Collectors informally divide typewriter history into the pioneering period, up to about 1890; the classic period, from 1890 to 1920; and the modern period, since 1920. There are two broad classifications of early typewriters: (1) Keyboard machines, in which depression of a key prints a character and via a shift key prints up to three different characters per key; (2) Index machines, in which a chart of all the characters appears on the typewriter; the character is selected by a pointer or dial and is printed by operation of a lever or other device. Even though index typewriters were simpler and more primitive than keyboard machines, they were none-the-less a later development, designed to provide a cheaper alternative to the standard keyboard models that were selling for upwards of $100.00. Eventually second-hand keyboard typewriters supplied the low-price customer, and index typewriters vanished except as toys. Both classes of typewriters appeared in a great many designs.

It is difficult, if not impossible, to assign standard market prices to early typewriters. Over the past decade, competition from a handful of wealthy overseas collectors drastically affected the American market, but now Americans are among the top bidders. This surge in interest has resulted in much higher prices on the rarer models. Some auction-realized prices have been astronomical. We have updated values to reflect current market activity. Bear in mind that condition is a very important factor, and typewriters can vary infinitely in condition. Another factor to consider is that an early typewriter achieves its value mainly through the skill, effort, and patience of the collector who restores it to its original condition, in which case its purchase price is insignificant. Some unusual-looking early typewriters are not at all rare or valuable, while some very ordinary-looking ones are scarce and could be quite valuable. No general rules apply.

For further information we recommend *Antique Typewriters & Office Collectibles* by Darryl Rehr (Collector Books). See Clubs, Newsletters, and Catalogs in the Directory for information on the Early Typewriter Collectors Association. When no condition is indicated, the items listed below are assumed to be in excellent, unrestored condition. Our advisor for this category is Mike Brooks; he is listed in the Directory under California.

Adler #8, removable-type basket 100.00
Allen 3-row, frontstrike, nickel...150.00
American Visible, any model...125.00
Automatic, brass w/wood jacket, ca 1881, minimum value......5,000.00
Bennett, silver, 3-row, type wheel, ca 1910 ....60.00
Blickenderfer #8, 3-row, type wheel...100.00
Brooks, 4-row, backstrike, ca 1895, minimum value.................5,000.00
Cash, 4-row, downstrike, flat platen, ca 1887, minimum value ..1,000.00
Columbia Bar-Lock #8, dbl keyboard, downstrike, plain front 100.00
Commercial Visible #6, wht, 3-row, type wheel...........................650.00
Daugherty, 4-row, frontstrike, elongated profile 350.00
Duplex, NP, ca 1892, minimum value..5,000.00
Edison Mimeograph #1, circular index, ca 1892, minimum value..1,000.00
English, curved keyboard, downstrike, Pat 1890, minimum value..3,000.00
Fox Portable #1, 3-row, frontstrike, folding.................................150.00
Gourland, 4-row, frontstrike, ca 1920-25.....................................50.00
Hall, 1st index typewriter, any model...500.00
Hammond #2, str keyboard, 3-row, type shuttle.............................75.00
Hartford, shift key, 4-row, upstrike...200.00
Ingersoll, type-slug index...500.00
Manhattan A, 4-row, upstrike..75.00
McCool #2, 3-row, type wheel, pre-1910.....................................850.00
Morris, rectangular index, wht rubber platen, ca 1886.............3,000.00

Pearl (Searing), circular index, unpnt base, ca 1891 ....1,000.00
Rapid, 4-row, thrust action, caps only, minimum value............1,000.00
Remington Noiseless #5, dbl shift, 3-row, thrust action.................75.00
Remington Portable #3B, 3½-row, frontstrike, ca 1935-36............20.00
Salter #6, str keyboard & pillars, 3-row, downstrike 350.00
Simplex #1, circular index, Pat Applied For (pre-1892)................75.00
Standard Folding #2, 3-row, frontstrike, ca 1908........................57.00
Underwood #1, 4-row, frontstrike 50.00
Universal Crandal #3, 3-row, type sleeve, minimum value 1,000.00
Wellington Empire #2, 3-row, thrust action 75.00
Yankee, type wheel cover dbls as circular index..........................100.00

Uhl Pottery

Founded in Evansville, Indiana, in 1849 by German immigrants, the Uhl Pottery was moved to Huntingburg, Indiana, in 1908 because of the more suitable clay available there. They produced stoneware — Acorn Ware jugs, crocks, and bowls — that was marked with the acorn logo and 'Uhl Pottery.' They also made mugs, pitchers, and vases in simple shapes and solid glazes marked with a circular ink stamp containing the name of the pottery and 'Huntingburg, Indiana.' The pottery closed in the mid-1940s. Those seeking additional information about Uhl pottery are encouraged to contact the Uhl Collectors' Society, whose address is listed in the Directory under Clubs, Newsletters, and Catalogs. For more information, we recommend *Uhl Pottery* by Anna Mary Feldmeyer and Kara Holtzman (Collector Books).

Bean baker, Prairie Green on yellowware, 4¾x9" 25.00
Bowl, Reverse Picket Fence, bl, 5¾x11¾" 115.00
Churn, #2, Acorn Ware, 12x9"..135.00
Crock, #6, Acorn Ware, cobalt on wht, 13"..................................110.00
Jug, bl, ball shape, 6" 90.00
Jug, Christmas, 1933, mini...425.00
Jug, Meier's Wine label on rose, 3½" 60.00
Jug, Ring (donut form), brn gloss, #14, 3½x3"...............................165.00
Jug, shoulder; Albany slip top, Acorn Ware in cobalt on wht, 10½"...75.00
Novelty, child's shoe w/tongue out, rose, 3⅛x5⅛", pr 90.00
Pitcher, Grape, bl w/wht int, 5½x7"...90.00
Planter, cat w/humped bk, lt bl, 2⅞x4⅛x1¾"................................70.00
Roaster, rose, w/lid, 6½x11½" 110.00
Shakers, Aster on red ball, made for Ransburg Pottery, pr............30.00
Spittoon, dk bl, 4¼x7¼"...100.00
Syrup, bl w/wht int, orig bl lid, NM 165.00
Vase, rose, flared neck, shouldered, 5¾"......................................65.00
Vase, rose, waisted cylinder, 1940s, 8¼".....................................60.00
Vase, teal, ped ft, sq top, #155-4, 4¾x3⅞"..................................95.00

Unger Brothers

Art Nouveau silver items of the highest quality were produced by Unger Brothers, who operated in Newark, New Jersey, from the early 1880s until 1919. In addition to tableware, they also made brushes, mirrors, powder boxes, and the like for milady's dressing table as well as jewelry and small personal accessories such as match safes and flasks. They often marked their products with a circle seal containing an intertwined 'UB' and '925 fine sterling.' Some Unger pieces contain a patent date near the mark. In addition to sterling, a very limited amount of gold was also used. Note: This company made no pewter items; Unger designs may occasionally be found in pewter, but these are copies. Items with English hallmarks or signed 'Birmingham' are English (not Unger).

Ashtray, golf scene in center w/4 devil faces in border, 1912, 5" dia ...420.00
Brooch, lady w/flowing hair, ca 1904, ⅞" dia.............................125.00

Buckle, mermaid & sea creature, 1⅜x1½" 285.00
Dresser set, Art Nouveau, 9" mirror+2 brushes+buffer+file+nail cleaner .700.00
Jar, dresser; Love's Dream, 3½x3¾" 350.00
Match safe, Nouveau lady, 2¾x1⅝" 145.00
Pen holder, Nouveau filigree & eng name, hinged, w/pen, 4½" L.140.00
Pendant, whistle; #2663, 1⅝" 60.00
Picture fr, filigree border, ornate stand, 4x3" 100.00

Universal

Universal Potteries Incorporated operated in Cambridge, Ohio, from 1934 to 1956. Many lines of dinnerware and kitchen items were produced in both earthenware and semiporcelain. In 1956 the emphasis was shifted to the manufacture of floor and wall tiles, and the name was changed to the Oxford Tile Company, Division of Universal Potteries. The plant closed in 1976. Our advisor for this category is Ted Haun; he is listed in the Directory under Indiana.

Ballerina, cup & saucer 12.00
Ballerina, plate, dinner 10.00
Ballerina, platter, tab hdls, 12" 20.00
Ballerina (Mist), bowl, vegetable; rnd, open 25.00
Ballerina (Mist), cup & saucer 17.00
Ballerina (Mist), plate, serving; tab hdls, 10" 12.00
Ballerina (Mist), sugar bowl, w/lid, from $15 to 20.00
Bittersweet, bowl, mixing; lg 20.00
Bittersweet, bowl, vegetable; rnd, open 20.00
Bittersweet, bowl, 10¼" 25.00
Bittersweet, casserole, w/lid, 5x9" 35.00
Bittersweet, jar, w/lid, 2" 35.00
Bittersweet, platter, oval, 13½" 30.00
Bittersweet, salt crock, flat bk 30.00
Bittersweet, shaker, pepper; range style 30.00
Bittersweet, shakers, 3½", pr 25.00
Calico Fruit, bowl, dessert 10.00
Calico Fruit, bowl, fish shape, 6x6½" 30.00
Calico Fruit, cup & saucer 20.00
Calico Fruit, pitcher, utility; 6⅜" 35.00
Calico Fruit, plate, bread & butter 8.00
Calico Fruit, plate, salad 9.00
Calico Fruit, plate, 9" 22.50
Calico Fruit, teapot, w/lid, 1-cup 65.00
Cattail, bowl, mixing; 6" 17.50
Cattail, bowl, mixing; 7" 20.00
Cattail, bowl, mixing; 8" 25.00
Cattail, bowl, soup; flat rim, 7¾" 15.00
Cattail, bowl, vegetable; oval 30.00
Cattail, coffeepot, 3-pc 70.00
Cattail, jug, batter; 6" 75.00
Cattail, jug, w/lid, 5¼" 20.00
Cattail, pie plate 30.00
Cattail, plate, luncheon; 9" 35.00
Cattail, platter, 11½", from $15 to 20.00
Cattail, sugar bowl, w/lid, from $20 to 25.00
Cattail, tumbler, glass, 4¾" 25.00
Cherry Blossom, sauce boat 15.00
Circus, platter, 13½" 25.00
Circus, shakers, range style, 4½", pr 22.50
Harvest, plate, dinner 18.00
Highland, gravy boat 35.00
Highland, plate, salad 10.00
Highland, sugar bowl, w/lid 15.00
Iris, butter dish, w/lid, 4x7½" 30.00

Iris, cake plate, tab hdls, 13" 25.00
Kitchen Bouquet, pitcher, water; 7" 40.00
Moss Rose, plate, rnd 30.00
Moss Rose, teapot, w/lid 70.00
Orange Poppy, ball jug, 8" 55.00
Orange Poppy, refrigerator jug, w/spout lid 55.00
Rambler Rose, bowl, fruit 17.00
Rambler Rose, bowl, mixing; 3¾x7½" 30.00
Rambler Rose, creamer 25.00
Rambler Rose, cup & saucer 20.00
Rambler Rose, plate, dinner; 10" 20.00
Rambler Rose, plate, luncheon; 7¼" 18.00
Woodvine, bowl, serving; 3½x9¾" 25.00
Woodvine, cup & saucer 15.00
Woodvine, jar, utility; w/lid 25.00
Woodvine, pitcher, milk; 6½" 35.00
Woodvine, plate, dinner; 10" 12.00
Woodvine, platter, tab hdls, 13¼" 22.50

Val St. Lambert

Since its inception in Belgium at the turn of the nineteenth century, the Val St. Lambert Cristalleries has been involved in the production of high-quality glass, producing some cameo. The factory is still in production.

Bottle, scent; cameo floral, gr on clear, faceted stopper, 7" 300.00
Bottle, scent; cameo garlands/florals, cranberry on frost, 7¾" 250.00
Goblet, cranberry cut to clear, clear stem, 6" 50.00
Shade, overall etching w/HP apple blossoms, scalloped top, 6½" ..100.00

Valentines

Looking for Valentines is an every day pursuit for the avid collector. If you are thinking of collecting, keep in mind that condition is very important. Creases, rough edges, or missing parts are flaws that degrade not only charm but value. As you become more knowledgeable, you'll notice that some cards are more common than others; with study, you'll learn to know which cards are scarce and therefore more valuable. Artist signatures, manufacturer, age, size, and genre are other worth-assessing factors. Our advisor for this category is Katherine Kreider, author of *Valentines With Values, One Hundred Years of Valentines,* and *Valentines for the Eclectic Collector.* She is listed in the Directory under Pennsylvania.

Note: Dimensions in the listings that follow include background space.

Key:
dim — dimension/dimensional   PIG — printed/published in Germany
HCPP — honeycomb paper puff

Collie attached to doghouse with original chain, Made in Germany, 6¾x6x1½", EX, $50.00.

(Photo courtesy Katherine Kreider)

Dim, airplane w/lobster, PIG, 1930s, 10½x8¾x9" **50.00**
Dim, cherub peering from daffodils, 2D, PIG, early 1900s, 6¼x4x¾".**35.00**
Dim, Cupid w/oil lamp, PIG, 2D, early 1900s, 8¾x4½x3" **50.00**
Dim, harp w/HCPP base, PIG, early 1900s, 8x4x2½" **50.00**
Dim, house greeting card, by Hallmark, ca 1950s, 7½x9x2" **35.00**
Dim, Loveland Train Station, USA, 1940s, 3¾x7x10½" **50.00**
Dim, motorcycle, 2D, PIG, 1920s, 7½x6½x3", EX **65.00**
Dim, pk sailboat, 4D, PIG, 1930s, 12x11x3½"............................**75.00**
Dim, steam locomotive, 3D, PIG, early 1900s, 7x8x5" **75.00**
Diorama, Cupid Air Line Co, USA, 1940s, 4¾x5¾x2¾" **20.00**
Diorama, D Cupid's Circus, USA, 1940s, 4¾x5¾x2¾" **20.00**
Flat, African-American flapper, hand-colored, unmk, 1920s, 5x3¾"...**25.00**
Flat, Bingo Valentine, A-meri-card, 1940s, 3½x2½" **8.00**
Flat, children selling hearts, easel bk, PIG, ca 1900s, 6¾x5½" **25.00**
Flat, Daisy, To My Valentine, Nister, Bavaria, early 1900s, 2½x3".**25.00**
Flat, Leap Year Valentine, unmk, 1920s, 4x5" **15.00**
Flat, Look Like a Jay, Newton, Campbell Art Co, 1920s, 6½x3½"...**25.00**
Flat, stick people playing tennis, USA, 1940s, 5½x4" **20.00**
Flat diecut, Cherub Cart, filled w/hearts, easel bk, PIG, 6x6¾" **50.00**
Folded flat, Army Wack, USA, 1940s, 6½x5" **25.00**
Folded flat, Asian children give valentines, USA, 1930s, 4x3½" .**25.00**
Folded flat, heart, hand-colored, w/ribbon, ca 1850, 3½" sq folded .**125.00**
Greeting card, Civil War soldier, hand-colored, 1860s, 7½x6" ...**450.00**
Greeting card, diecut heart opens/reveals lady, PIG, 1900s, 4x4"..**25.00**
Greeting card, Love Token, emb chromolitho, PIG, early 1900s, 7x5" ..**25.00**
Greeting card, To My Valentine, emb litho, Whitney, ca 1900s, 9x6½"..**35.00**
Hanging flat, Buster Brown, Outcault, Tuck & Sons, ca 1900s, 8x8"..**125.00**
Hanging flat, cherubs w/cobweb, PIG, early 1900s, 10x3¼" **65.00**
Hanging flat, Dutch boy & girl, Tuck, PIG, early 1900s, 7¾x7"...**75.00**
Hanging flat, Love's Message, Nister, Bavaria, early 1900s, 5x6½"...**45.00**
Hanging flat, train car, Tuck, PIG, early 1900s, 8x8" folded **125.00**
HCPP, basket filled w/hearts, USA, 1920s, 9x8x6" **50.00**
HCPP, clown, unknown maker, 1920s, 6¾x6x2" **25.00**
HCPP, Miss Muffet, Beistle, USA, 1920s, 9½x7x4" **35.00**
HCPP, Wheel of Fortune, Beistle, USA, 1920s, 9½x6½x3" **45.00**
Mechanical flat, cherub climbing, chromolitho, PIG, ca 1883, 5x3"...**50.00**
Mechanical flat, cobweb, English, 1840s, 8x8" folded **350.00**
Mechanical flat, German children, maker unknown, late 1800s, 4x2½" ..**50.00**
Novelty, celluloid ping-pong paddle, hand-colored, 1900s, 14x7x1".**500.00**
Novelty, Cinderella coach, HCPP center, Hallmark, 11½x11½x10"..**75.00**
Novelty, music box, hand crank, Barker, 1920s, 5½x3½" **25.00**
Novelty, Rosen lollipop card, Mary Contrary, 1940s, 6x5" **8.00**
Novelty, Victorian valentine tag, Nister, early 1900s, 6x4" **25.00**
Penny dreadful, golfer, 1940s, 10½x7½" **15.00**
Penny dreadful, Juggler of Hearts, 1920s, oversz: 13x9¾" **15.00**
Penny dreadful, Miss Extravagant, USA, 1920s, 10¾x7½"...........**10.00**
Penny dreadful, Miss Neatum, hand-colored, ca 1800s, 9x7¼" **95.00**
Penny dreadful, Powder Puff Polly, 1920s, 10½x7½"...................**25.00**
Penny dreadful, railway porter, hand-colored, ca 1800s, 8½x6½".**95.00**

Van Briggle

The Van Briggle Pottery of Colorado Springs, Colorado, was established in 1901 by Artus Van Briggle, whose early career had been shaped by such notables as Karl Langenbeck and Maria Nichols Storer. His quest for several years had been to perfect a completely flat matt glaze, and upon accomplishing his goal, he opened his pottery. His wife, Anne, worked with him, and they, along with George Young, were responsible for the modeling of the wares. Their work typified the flow and form of the Art Nouveau movement, and the shapes they designed played as important a part in their success as their glazes. Some of their most famous pieces were Despondency, Lorelei, and Toast Cup. Increasing demand for their work soon made it necessary to add to their quarters as well as their staff.

Although much of the ware was eventually made from molds, each piece was carefully trimmed and refined before the glaze was sprayed on. Their most popular colors were Persian Rose, Ming Blue, and Mustard Yellow.

Van Briggle died in 1904, but the work was continued by his wife. New facilities were built; and by 1908, in addition to their artware, tiles, gardenware, and commercial lines were added. By the '20s the emphasis had shifted from art pottery to novelties and commercial wares. Reproductions of some of the early designs continue to be made. The double AA mark has always been in use, but after 1920 the dates and/or shape numbers were dropped. Mention should be made here as well that the Anna Van Briggle glaze is a later line which was made between 1956 and 1968. Our advisor for this category is Michelle Ross; she is listed in the Directory under Michigan. For more information, we recommend *Collector's Encyclopedia of Van Briggle Art Pottery* by Richard Sasicki and Josie Fania (Collector Books).

Bookends, bison, turq, AA Walker, late, 6x8½" **300.00**
Bowl, arrowfoot motif, gr, #689, ca 1920s, 6½".........................**250.00**
Bowl, dragonflies, Persian Rose, 8½", +frog flower frog...............**150.00**
Bowl, dragonflies (4) at rim, mulberry, USA, 1920s, 2¾x8¾"....**345.00**
Bowl, floral, tobacco w/blk specks, ca 1907-12, 4"......................**475.00**
Bowl, leaves, lime gr/purple, low/incurvate, 1908-12, 5½".........**375.00**
Bowl, leaves, maroon multi, ca 1920, 4"..................................**200.00**
Bowl, leaves on comma-like stems, turq bl, ca 1925, 3¾" H.......**150.00**
Bowl, pine cones/needles, brn, ca 1913, 10", NM.......................**850.00**
Bowl, Siren of the Sea, maroon & bl, 14x13x9", +flower frog **500.00**
Bowl, Siren of the Sea, mottled brn & gr, 14x13x9", +flower frog ..**475.00**
Bowl vase, leaves, wide/cvd, bl-gr, 1907-12, 3" dia **325.00**
Bowl vase, spade leaves, maroon w/bl overspray, ca 1920, 6½" dia ..**145.00**
Candlestick, gr gloss, 4-petal socket, 4" **50.00**
Candlesticks, Mountain Craig Brown, 8-sided bases, no #/date, 10", pr ...**375.00**
Chamberstick, leaves & buds, gr matt, ca 1908, 3½" dia **300.00**
Console set, Persian Rose, 14¼" bowl+acorn frog+2 chambersticks...**175.00**
Figurine, Colonial peasant, Persian Rose, 8½", pr **150.00**
Figurine, donkey, turq bl, sgn SE, no #/date, 3⅜" **90.00**
Figurine, Viking ship, maroon, post 1920, 4½" H......................**100.00**
Lamp, leaves, bl & turq, butterfly/weed shade, 27x11"................**225.00**
Night light, owl, glass eyes, bl & gr, 7¼"..................................**275.00**
Pitcher, feathered rose, 1904, rstr hdl, 5½".................................**150.00**
Pitcher, gray matt, #452, 1906, 4¾"..**450.00**
Plate, grapes & leaves, bl/red, 1907-12, 9½"..............................**700.00**
Plate, leafy device centers spokes, bl tones, 1907-12, 6"...............**240.00**
Vase, bears at rim (2, 3-dimensional), Persian Rose, 1920s, 15x4½"..**1,900.00**
Vase, bl, leaves, 1907-12, 5"..**700.00**
Vase, bl & gr, short urn form w/incised linear decor, 6½"...........**235.00**
Vase, blossoms, lav to chartreuse, 1908-11, hairline, 3¾"...........**200.00**
Vase, bud; daisies, sheer gr matt, ovoid, 1908-11, 4"...................**600.00**
Vase, bud; mustard w/gray-gr at base, 1918, slender....................**200.00**
Vase, bud; trillium, turq matt, hdls, rstr, ca 1907, 5"...................**125.00**
Vase, buds & wide leaves, red & gr suspended matt, bulbous, 1905, 5".**4,250.00**
Vase, butterflies, Persian Rose, squat, 4" **70.00**
Vase, chartreuse w/red accent, ovoid w/2 sm rim hdls, 1903, 8x3½"...**950.00**
Vase, clover w/whiplash leaves, bl matt w/red highlights, 1906, 5½" ...**1,800.00**
Vase, crocus w/upright stems, lt bl multi, shouldered, 1903, 3½".........**525.00**
Vase, daffodils, leathery gr w/purple, 1906, #367, 9¼x4¼" **2,000.00**
Vase, daffodils w/curving stems, bl multi, brn clay exposed, 1916, 9"...**850.00**
Vase, Dos Cabezas, bl/tan matt, 1918, 7¾".............................**3,750.00**
Vase, dragonfly, brn/gr, ca 1920-30, 7¼".................................**350.00**
Vase, floral, bl/turq, ca 1920, 7⅜"...**160.00**
Vase, floral, brn matt, 1913, 3"...**425.00**
Vase, floral, brn w/gr overspray, #833, ca 1920, 5½".................**230.00**
Vase, floral, deep rose matt, hdls, 1903, 10"...........................**3,500.00**
Vase, floral, gr, sloping hdls, 1904, 12"..................................**6,500.00**
Vase, floral, maroon w/bl overspray, #645, ca 1920, 4".............**115.00**
Vase, floral, red/gr mottle, 1907, 5"......................................**1,700.00**

Vase, floral (shoulder), bl/gr matt, 1906, 8½" 1,400.00
Vase, floral stem/curving leaves, dk purple/cobalt, 1907-11, 3x3"...275.00
Vase, flowerhead (lg w/short stem), bl multi, 1918, 2½" 325.00
Vase, flowerhead (lg/on 2-leaf stem, 4X), brn, bulbous, 1913, 3" .425.00
Vase, flowerheads at shoulder, long stems, dk bl, 1916, 7"...........600.00
Vase, flowerheads at swollen rim, gr crystalline w/exposed clay, 5" .1,000.00
Vase, flowers & vines, maroon w/bl highlights, 1905, 6"............950.00
Vase, gr, cylindrical w/low hdls, 1907-1912, 4¾ "......................500.00
Vase, Indian heads (3), brn & gr, 11" 375.00
Vase, iris, lav/pale gr w/exposed buff clay, 1906/140, 13½x5½" ..2,800.00
Vase, Lady of the Lily, maroon & bl, rpr, 11½"..........................300.00
Vase, leathery gr matt, baluster, 1905, 9"..............................800.00
Vase, leaves, bl to maroon, post-1930s, 4½" 100.00
Vase, leaves, Mountain Craig Brown, squat, 1930s, 4¼x5"...........150.00
Vase, leaves, rose matt w/lt gr highlights, 1904, 13½"..............3,500.00
Vase, leaves, wide/upright, dk bl/gr mottle, incurvate, ca 1907-12, 7"..650.00
Vase, leaves (heart shape/stemmed), pk/bl, ca 1907-12, 2½" 300.00
Vase, leaves (overlapping), olive gr, spherical, 1916, 3¾" 500.00
Vase, leaves (spade shaped), feathery gr, 1908-11, 7¼"..............700.00
Vase, leaves (stylized), multi-tone gr, bulbous, 1904, 5½" W...4,500.00
Vase, leaves (swirling), Cerulean Blue to aqua mottle, 7¼x3"....360.00
Vase, leaves (swirling), gr-gray, flared sides, ca 1907-12, 5"......650.00
Vase, leaves (wide/upright), bl multi, slim cylinder, 1918, 8" 400.00
Vase, leaves & arched stems, Mountain Craig Brown, no #/date, 4" ..120.00
Vase, leaves on wide bottom/buds on tall neck, raspberry/gr, 1913, 9" ..800.00
Vase, leaves/flowers (heart shape/long stems), gray/wht, 4x4½" .250.00
Vase, Lorelei, shaded bl & turq, 10¼"..................................700.00
Vase, mistletoe at rim, frothy sky bl, '07-11, label, 2½x2½" 450.00
Vase, organic waisted design, multi-tone gr matt, 1907-12, 6".1,100.00
Vase, oval panels, gr w/exposed brn clay, dtd ca '06, 4½"............650.00
Vase, poppies, gr matt, tapered cylinder, 1904, 10"...................3,250.00
Vase, poppies on whiplash stems, gr/brn/tobacco, 1918, 8", EX 475.00
Vase, poppy pods on long stems, 2-tone bl, no #/date, 6¾".........375.00
Vase, shell form, gr gloss, post-1930s, 13" L...........................50.00
Vase, stems/leaves (swirling), bl, barbell shape, #666, Co Springs, 8"...650.00
Vase, stylized decor, gr/raspberry mottle, bbl shape, 1908-11, 4¾" 800.00
Vase, triangle-leaf band, mulberry, flared sides, no shape #/date, 9" .600.00
Vase, tulips at shoulder (3X), dk to lt bl, 1918, 2¾x2½" 200.00
Vase, upright stems, red/bl, 1908-12, 2½" 375.00
Vase, yel & lt gr matt, flat shoulder, 1908-11, 4" 300.00

Van Erp, Dirk

Dirk van Erp was a Leeuwarden, Holland, coppersmith who emigrated to the United States in 1886 and began making decorative objects from artillery shell casings in the San Francisco shipyards. He opened a shop in 1908 in Oakland and in 1910 formed a brief (one-year) partnership with D'Arcy Gaw. Apprentices at the studio included his daughter Agatha and Harry Dixon, who was later to open his own shop in San Francisco. Gaw has been assigned design credit for many of the now-famous hammered copper and mica lamps. So popular were the lamps that other San Francisco craftspeople, Lillian Palmer, Fred Brosi, Hans Jauchen, and Old Mission Kopperkraft among them, began producing similar forms. In addition to lamps, he manufactured a broad range of objects including vases, bowls, desk sets, and smoking accessories. Van Erp's work is typically finely hammered with a deep red-brown patina and of good proportions. On rare occasions, van Erp created pieces in a 'warty' finish: an irregular, indeed lumpy surface with a much redder appearance. Van Erp died in 1933. In 1929 the shop was taken over by his son, William, who produced hammered goods in both brass and copper. Many feature Art Deco-style designs and are of considerably lower value than his father's work. The van Erp mark is prominent and takes the form of a windmill above a rectangle that includes his name, sometimes D'Arcy Gaw's name, and sometimes San Francisco.

Please note: Cleaning or scrubbing original patinas diminishes the value of the object. Our prices are for examples with excellent original patina unless noted. Our advisor for this and related Arts and Crafts objects is Bruce Austin, he is listed in the Directory under New York.

Bookends, h/cp, shield shape w/pine needle texture, 6x5" 300.00
Bowl, console; h/cp, red-brn patina, after 1940, oblong, 19¼" L ..1,175.00
Bowl, h/cp, flared/flat rim, 12", VG................................350.00
Box, h/cp, monogram, 3½" W 300.00
Coal, bucket, h/cp, riveted brass bands, flame finial, 17x10" ...4,000.00
Jardiniere, h/cp, early 20th C, 5½"...............................3,000.00
Jardiniere, h/cp, lg broad shape warty, 6x10"....................4,500.00
Lamp, h/cp, 16½" mica shade, red-brn patina, 17¼" 14,000.00
Lamp, h/cp, 20½" mica shade, red-brn patina, 16"............23,500.00
Match holder, h/cp w/cutout of Dutch girl & cat, wall mt, 6½" .375.00
Vase, h/c, wide flared rim, 6½".......................................1,200.00
Vase, h/cp, incurvate rim, 5".......................................1,000.00
Vase, h/cp, warty, open box mk, 8½" 5,500.00
Vase, h/cp, warty cylinder, red-brn patina, after 1915, 15x10" .21,150.00

Vance/Avon Faience

Although pottery had been made in Tiltonville, Ohio, since about 1880, the ware manufactured there was of little significance until after the turn of the century when the Vance Faience Company was organized for the purpose of producing quality artware. By 1902 the name had been changed to the Avon Faience Company, and late in the same year it and three other West Virginia potteries incorporated to form the Wheeling Potteries Company. The Avon branch operated in Tiltonville until 1905 when production was moved to Wheeling. Art pottery was discontinued.

From the beginning, only skilled craftsmen and trained engineers were hired. Wm. P. Jervis and Fredrick Hurten Rhead were among the notable artists responsible for designing some of the early artware. Some of the ware was slip decorated under glaze, while other pieces were molded with high-relief designs. Examples with squeeze-bag decoration by Rhead are obviously forerunners of the Jap Birdimal line he later developed 'for Weller. Ware was marked 'Vance F. Co.'; 'Avon F. Co., Tiltonville'; or 'Avon W. Pts. Co.'

Vase, landscape, in manner of WP Jervis, Avon R166, 5⅞"........550.00
Vase, nude maid in swirling water w/sea life, brn/tan, bulbous, #118..875.00
Vase, stylized flowers/leaves, squeeze-bag, 3-sided, Avon, rstr, 9x3" 750.00
Vase, 4 short necks on shoulder, appl twisted vines, tan/gr, #120, 9" ..600.00

Vaseline

Vaseline, a greenish-yellow colored glass produced by adding uranium oxide to the batch, was produced during the Victorian era. It was made in smaller quantities than other colors and lost much of its popularity with the advent of the electric light. It was used for pressed tablewares, vases, whimsies, souvenir items, oil lamps, perfume bottles, drawer pulls, and doorknobs. Pieces have been reproduced, and some factories still make it today in small batches. Vaseline glass will fluoresce under an ultraviolet light.

Ashtray, oval, 2 rests, 1x4x2¾".....................................25.00
Banana boat, ftd, 1⅞x4⅛x6⅛".....................................75.00
Bottle, scent; pressed pattern, cylindrical, ball stopper, 6" 75.00
Bowl, berry; Invt T'print, 3-ftd, King Glass, 1880s, 2x3¾" 30.00
Bowl, etched flowers & leaves, scalloped, 4-ftd, 3¼x9".................20.00
Cake plate, Daisy & Button, ftd, 5x9½"..................................50.00
Candlesticks, shaped stem on rnd base, 1870s, 8¾x4⅛", pr........350.00

Candy dish, in chrome fr mk H Lerner...NY, 6" dia......................65.00
Compote, tall stem, flared ft, thin & delicate, ca 1910, 6¼x6¾" ..245.00
Cordial, etched floral, ftd,..80.00
Dish, Daisy & Button, low, 6¼" sq 65.00
Goblet, Basketweave, 1880s, 5½"...40.00
Hat, Daisy & Button, 2½"..57.00
Kettle (ring holder), 3-ftd, 2¼x2⅜"...38.00
Pitcher, Fluted Scrolls, ftd, Northwood, 5" 115.00
Sherbet & underplate, 4x4", 6"..20.00
Spoon holder, Dmn Quilt, ftd..78.00
Swan candy bowl, 6¼x9x5"..45.00
Tumbler, Wildflower, Adams, 1880s..65.00
Vase, appl flowers, leaves & vine hdls, ruffled rim, 5½" 225.00
Vase, limousine; pressed pattern, McKee................................125.00
Vase, tricorner w/craquelle finish, cranberry int, squat, 3¼" 450.00

Verlys

Verlys art glass, produced in France after 1931 by the Holophane Company of Verlys, was made in crystal with acid-finished relief work in the Art Deco style. Colored and opalescent glass was also used. In 1935 an American branch was opened in Newark, Ohio, where very similar wares were produced until the factory ceased production in 1951. French Verlys was signed with one of three mold-impressed script signatures, all containing the company name and country of origin. The American-made glassware was signed 'Verlys' only, either scratched with a diamond-tipped pen or impressed in the mold. There is very little if any difference in value between items produced in France and America. Though some seem to feel that the French should be higher priced (assuming it to be scarce), many prefer the American-made product.

In June of 1955, about sixteen Verlys molds were leased to the A.H. Heisey Company. Heisey's versions were not signed with the Verlys name, so if an item is unsigned it is almost certainly a Heisey piece. The molds were returned to Verlys of America in July 1957. Fenton now owns all Verlys molds, but all issues are marked Fenton. Our advisor for this category is Don Frost; he is listed in the Directory under Washington.

Bookends, lady kneels beside deer, clear & frosted, 7", pr 400.00
Bowl, birds & fishes, bl, 13½" dia 1,500.00
Bowl, birds w/wings wide on 4 sides, frosted, 6x10" L..............225.00
Bowl, centerpc; Butterflies, clear & frosted, 2¾x13¾"...............250.00
Bowl, Chrysanthemums, 6x10" L..295.00
Bowl, Cupid, clear & frosted, 2x6" 60.00
Bowl, Dragonfly, 3x13½" L 175.00
Bowl, Pine Cone, frosted, 1¾x6¼" 100.00
Bowl, Pine Cone, smoky topaz, 1¾x6¼"..................................225.00
Bowl, Poppy, frosted, ftd, 2½x13¾" 125.00
Charger, Birds & Bees, clear & frosted, 11¾" 225.00
Charger, Wild Duck, frosted, 13½" 175.00
Vase, Alpine Thistle, amber, ca 1930s, 9¾" 400.00
Vase, Butterflies, frosted, globular, 5" 110.00
Vase, Pansy, frosted, 5⅝x5¼" 225.00
Vase, Seasons, frosted, 8x5" 200.00

Vernon Kilns

Vernon Potteries Ltd. was established by Faye G. Bennison in Vernon, California, in 1931. The name was later changed to Vernon Kilns; until it closed in 1958, dinnerware, specialty plates, artware, and figurines were their primary products. Among its wares most sought after by collectors today are items designed by such famous artists as Rockwell Kent, Walt Disney, Don Blanding, Jane Bennison,

and May and Vieve Hamilton. Our advisor is Maxine Nelson, author of *Collectible Vernon Kilns, Second Edition*; she is listed in the Directory under Arizona.

Chatelaine Shape

This designer pattern by Sharon Merrill was made in four color combinations: Topaz, Bronze, decorated Platinum, and Jade.

Bowl, chowder; decorated Platinum or Jade, 6", from $15 to 20.00
Bowl, chowder; 6", Topaz or Bronze, from $12 to...........................15.00
Creamer, decorated Platinum or Jade, from $30 to 35.00
Creamer, Topaz or Bronze, from $20 to 25.00
Teapot, decorated Platinum or Jade, from $250 to.......................295.00
Teapot, Topaz or Bronze, from $150 to.......................................195.00

Melinda Shape

Patterns found on this shape are Arcadia, Beverly, Blossom Time, Chintz, Cosmos, Dolores, Fruitdale, Hawaii (Lei Lani on Melinda is two and a half times base value), May Flower, Monterey, Native California, and Philodendron. Two patterns, Rosedale and Wheat, were made for Sears, Roebuck & Co. and marked with Sears Harmony House backstamp. The more elaborate the pattern, the higher the value.

Bowl, 9", from $18 to...25.00
Butter dish, ¼-lb, from $35 to 75.00
Casserole, w/lid, 8", from $45 to 75.00
Coffeepot, demi; 2-cup, from $65 to 75.00
Egg cup, from $18 to...25.00
Plate, 9½", from $12 to 15.00
Platter, 14", from $35 to...50.00
Relish, 1-leaf, 12", from $25 to 30.00
Sauce boat, from $20 to..30.00

Montecito Shape (and Coronado)

This was one of the company's most utilized shapes — well over two hundred patterns have been documented. Among the most popular are the solid colors, plaids, florals, Westernware, and the Bird and Turnbull series. Bird, Turnbull, and Winchester 73 (Frontier Days) are two to four times base values. Disney hollow ware is seven to eight times base values. Plaids (except Tweed and Calico), solid colors, and Brown-eyed Susan are represented by the lower range.

Bowl, fruit; 5½", from $6 to 12.00
Bowl, mixing; 5", from $18 to...20.00
Bowl, rim soup; 1½x8¼", from $12 to...20.00
Bowl, serving; 2¼x8½", from $18 to 25.00
Casserole, Hot; w/metal stand, from $65 to..................................85.00
Coffee carafe, 10-cup, w/stopper, from $40 to 75.00
Jam jar, notched lid, 5", from $65 to...95.00
Pitcher, disk; plain or decorated, 2-qt, from $65 to........................100.00
Plate, 10½", from $15 to 25.00
Platter, 12", from $20 to...30.00
Sauce boat, fast stand, dbl spout, from $35 to 50.00
Sugar bowl, reg, open, from $10 to 15.00
Teapot, angular or rnd, from $45 to...95.00

San Clemente (Anytime) Shape

Patterns you will find on this shape include Tickled Pink, Heavenly Days, Anytime, Imperial, Sherwood, Frolic, Young in Heart, Rose-A-Day, and Dis 'N Dot.

Bowl, divided, 9", from $15 to 22.00
Casserole, w/lid, 8", from $30 to 50.00
Creamer, from $8 to...12.00
Cruets, oil & vinegar, on 6" oval tray w/ring hdls, from $100 to.125.00
Mug, 12-oz, from $15 to 25.00
Pitcher, 2-qt, tall, 9⅞", from $22 to 35.00
Plate, 10", from $9 to...15.00
Platter, 11", from $12 to 20.00
Shakers, pr, from $12 to 20.00
Tumbler, 14-oz, from $15 to 25.00

San Fernando Shape

Known patterns for this shape are Desert Bloom, Early Days, Hibiscus, R.F.D., Vernon's 1860, and Vernon Rose.

Bowl, fruit; 5½", from $6 to 10.00
Bowl, lug chowder; 5", from $12 to 18.00
Bowl, mixing; 7", from $22 to 29.00
Cup & saucer, demi; from $15 to 20.00
Olive dish, oval, 10", from $20 to 35.00
Plate, chop; 14", from $35 to 50.00
Shakers, pr, from $15 to 25.00
Sugar bowl, w/lid, from $15 to 20.00
Teapot, 6-cup, from $45 to 85.00

San Marino Shape

Known patterns for this shape are Barkwood, Bel Air, California Originals, Casual California, Gayety, Hawaiian Coral, Heyday, Lei Lani (2½ times base values), Mexicana, Pan American Lei (2½ times base values), Raffia, Seven Seas, Shadow Leaf, Shantung, Sun Garden, and Trade Winds. The Mojave pattern was produced for Montgomery Ward, Wheat Rose for Belmar China Co.

Ashtray, 5½", from $12 to...................................20.00
Bowl, coupe soup; 8½", from $10 to 15.00
Casserole, w/lid, 8" dia, from $35 to 60.00
Creamer, reg, from $10 to 12.00
Egg cup, dbl, from $15 to 22.00
Mug, 9-oz, from $12 to 25.00
Pitcher, 2-qt, from $30 to 40.00
Platter, 9½", from $12 to 18.00
Platter, 11", from $15 to 20.00
Shakers, gourd shape, pr, from $15 to 20.00
Sugar bowl, w/lid, from $12 to 17.00
Tumbler, 14-oz, from $20 to 25.00

Transitional (Year 'Round) Shape

Patterns on this shape include Country Cousin, Lollipop Tree, Blueberry Hill, and Year 'Round.

Bowl, 9", from $12 to......................................17.00
Coffeepot, 6-cup, from $25 to 45.00
Cup & saucer, from $8 to 12.00
Mug, 12-oz, from $12 to 20.00
Platter, 11", from $12 to 20.00
Shakers, pr, from $12 to 15.00
Teapot, from $25 to 50.00

Ultra Shape

More than fifty patterns were issued on this shape. Nearly all the artist-designed lines (Rockwell, Kent, Don Blanding, and Disney) utilized Ultra. The shape was developed by Gale Turnbull, and many of the elaborate flower and fruit patterns can be credited to him as well; use the high end of our range as a minimum value for his work. For Frederick Lunning, use the mid range. For other artist patterns, use these formulae based on the high end: Blanding, 3X (Aquarium, 5X); Disney, 5 – 7X; Kent — Moby Dick, 2 – 4X; Our America, 3 – 5X; and Salamina, 5 – 7X.

Bowl, cereal; 6", from $10 to 15.00
Bowl, salad; 11", from $45 to 85.00
Butter dish, ¼-lb, from $35 to 75.00
Cup & saucer, from $12 to 20.00
Pitcher, 1-pt, 4½", from $35 to 50.00
Plate, 6½", from $6 to 10.00
Plate, 10½", from $12 to 20.00
Shakers, pr, from $20 to 30.00
Tumbler, 5", from $25 to 40.00

Fantasia and Disney Figures

Black Unicorn, #13, gray or blk, from $300 to.............350.00
Donkey Unicorn, #16, from $600 to 700.00
Dumbo, #40, from $75 to 150.00
Dumbo, #41, from $75 to 150.00
Hop Low, #35 or #36, ea from $50 to 75.00
Ostrich, #29, from $1,000 to 1,200.00
Pegasus, #21, from $200 to 300.00
Sprite, #8, hard to find, from $300 to 400.00
Sprite (any except #8), from $250 to 300.00
Winged Pegasus vase, #127, hand decorated, 7½x12", from $1,000 to ...1,400.00
Winged Pegasus vase, #127, solid color, 7½x12", from $500 to ..700.00

Specialty Ware

Ashtray, Frontier Days or Winchester '73, ea..............35.00
Ashtray, map of South Carolina, from $15 to 20.00
Ashtray, Mississippi, red transfer, 5½", from $15 to 20.00
Cup & saucer, race horse..................................35.00
Mai Tai tumbler, relief Hawaiian nude/foliage, mc, from $95 to .125.00
Plate, Chicago, Marshall Field Clock, bl transfer, from $20 to......30.00
Plate, Colorful San Francisco, mc, 10½"..................45.00
Plate, Curtiss-Wright, WWII military pursuit planes in combat, $65 to..95.00
Plate, Eisenhower & Nixon, Our President & Vice President, from $50 to.75.00
Plate, El Camino Real, shows 21 missions, artist: Honeywell, 14"..50.00
Plate, Franklin Roosevelt, Little White House, red transfer, $20 to .45.00
Plate, Frederick Chopin, Music Masters, from $18 to....................25.00
Plate, Grand Chapter of Texas, Order of Eastern Star, from $20 to..35.00
Plate, Ohio State University, red transfer, from $25 to.................35.00
Plate, Santa Claus, mc, 10½", from $35 to................55.00
Plate, US in Action, artist: Goode, hand-tinted WWII transfer ...75.00
Plate, Ye Old Times, mc, 10½", from $35 to 45.00

Villeroy and Boch

The firm of Villeroy and Boch, located in Mettlach, Germany, was brought into being by the 1841 merger of three German factories — the Wallerfangen factory, founded by Nicholas Villeroy in 1787; and Boch's father's factory in Septfontaines, established in 1767. Villeroy and Boch produced many varieties of wares, including earthenware with printed under-glaze designs which carried the well-known castle mark with the name 'Mettlach.' See also Mettlach.

Bowl, rimmed soup; Summer Dreams, 9⅜" 30.00

Bowl, serving; Amapola, 1⅞x12½" 80.00
Bowl, vegetable; Amapola, w/lid, 7¼x7¼" 100.00
Clock, Basket, #1748, 10½" 110.00
Creamer, Geranium, 2x2¾" 45.00
Cruets, oil & vinegar; Amapola, 7¼x2½" dia, pr 150.00
Cruets, oil & vinegar; Fr countryside scene on ea side, 6½", pr ...115.00
Gravy boat, Amapola, 4¾x8½", w/8¼x6¼" underplate 110.00
Jam jar, Amapola, notched lid, 4¼x3½" dia 110.00
Napkin ring, Vieux Luxembourg, bl floral on wht, 1⅝", set of 4 ...150.00
Pitcher, Amapola, mc floral on wht, 6¼x4¼" 130.00
Pitcher, India, flow bl, scalloped rim, 5¾" 240.00
Plate, cake; Dresden Floral, bl on wht, ped ft, 4½x10" 115.00
Plate, Intarsia, #1748, 11⅞" 70.00
Plate, stylized poppies on wht, 11" 110.00
Plate, Winter #4, Four Seasons series, 9" 75.00
Platter, meat; Amapola, tab hdls, 11x17" 115.00
Sugar bowl, Le Balloon, w/lid, 2½x3½" 95.00
Teakettle, Amapola, wood hdl on wire fr, enameled steel, 2-qt.....90.00
Teapot, India, flow bl, 7½" 525.00
Tile, carp & water lily, gr tones, 2-part, 5¾x11½" 925.00
Tile, Nouveau flower, cuenca w/HP, 5¾"", EX 185.00
Tray, serving; Artemis, brn transferware, 6¾x12¾" 80.00
Tureen, vegetable; Amapola, notched lid, hdls, 1½-qt, 8¼x10½"..115.00
Vase, exotic birds & geometrics on bl, #298, ca 1935, 11¼"........200.00
Vase, mottled red crystalline, bulbous, #136, 10x10½"................465.00

Vistosa

Vistosa was produced from about 1938 through the early 1940s. It was Taylor, Smith, and Taylor's answer to the very successful Fiesta line of their nearby competitor, Homer Laughlin. Vistosa was made in four solid colors: mango red, cobalt blue, light green, and deep yellow. 'Pie crust' edges and a dainty five-petal flower molded into handles and lid finials made for a very attractive yet nevertheless commercially unsuccessful product. Our advisor for this category is Ted Haun; he is listed in the Directory under Indiana.

Bowl, cream soup 20.00
Bowl, fruit 10.00
Bowl, nappy; from $40 to 50.00
Bowl, salad; ftd, 12", from $200 to..225.00
Bowl, soup; lug hdl, from $25 to 30.00
Chop plate, 12", from $40 to..50.00
Chop plate, 15", from $50 to..60.00
Coffee cup, AD; from $40 to..50.00
Coffee saucer, AD; from $10 to..15.00
Creamer, from $20 to..25.00
Egg cup, ftd, from $50 to 70.00
Jug, water; 2-qt, from $120 to 150.00
Plate, 6" 10.00
Plate, 7" 12.00
Plate, 9" 15.00
Plate, 10", from $35 to..45.00
Platter, 13", from $40 to 50.00
Sauce boat, from $175 to 200.00
Shakers, pr 32.00
Sugar bowl, w/lid 25.00
Teacup & saucer, from $20 to..30.00
Teapot, 6-cup, from $190 to..225.00

Volkmar

Charles Volkmar established a workshop in Tremont, New York, in 1882. He produced artware decorated under the glaze in the manner of the early barbotine work done at the Haviland factory in Limoges, France. He relocated in 1888 in Menlo Park, New Jersey, and together with J.T. Smith established the Menlo Park Ceramic Company for the production of art tile. The partnership was dissolved in 1893. From 1895 until 1902, Volkmar located in Corona, New York, first under the name Volkmar Ceramic Company, later as Volkmar and Cory, and for the final six years as Crown Point. During the latter period he made art tile, blue under-glaze Delft-type wares, colorful polychrome vases, etc. The Volkmar Kilns were established in 1903 in Metuchen, New Jersey, by Volkmar and his son. Wares were marked with various devices consisting of the Volkmar name, initials, or 'Crown Point Ware.' Our advisors for this category are Suzanne Perrault and David Rago; they are listed in the Directory under New Jersey.

Oil on board, farming scene, 7x12"+gilt-metal fr 1,400.00
Vase, cucumber gr w/charcoling, oatmeal int, 5½x6" 465.00
Vase, dk gr mottled matt, bulbous, rstr rim chips, 10½" 200.00
Vase, horse & cart/farmer, HP underglaze, tub hdls, sgn, 11x11½"....2,200.00
Watercolor, geese in landscape, 8x11½"+oak fr........................600.00

Vontury

Located in New Jersey, F.J. Von Tury is primarily a designer of architectural artware, tile, and murals in particular, but he also produces a line of vases, bowls, and other decorative items. These are signed 'Vontury' in script. Impressionistic florals are favored.

Bowl, brn/tan, no decor, 4½x9½" 38.00
Tray, long-stem tulip w/2 leaves, 7x14" 100.00
Vase, abstract flowers, stepped shoulder, 7x4¾" 125.00
Vase, classical European motif, umber on indigo/ivory/brn, CD, 15x5"...1,600.00

Wade

The Wade Potteries was established in 1867 by George Wade and his partner, a man by the name of Myatt. It was located in Burslem, England, the center of that country's pottery industry. In 1882 George Wade bought out his partner, and the name of the pottery was changed to Wade and Sons. In 1919 the pottery underwent yet another name change and became known as George Wade & Son Ltd. The year 1891 saw the establishment of another Wade Pottery — J & W Wade & Co., which in turn changed its name to A.J. Wade & Co. in 1927. At this time (1927) Wade Heath & Co. Ltd. was also formed.

The three potteries plus a new Irish pottery named Wade (Ireland) Ltd. were incorporated into one company in 1958 and given the name The Wade Group of Potteries. In 1990 the group was taken over by Beauford PLC. and became Wade Ceramics Ltd. It sold again in early 1999 to Wade Management and is now a private company.

For those interested in learning more about Wade pottery, we recommend *The World of Wade, The World of Wade Book 2*, and *The World of Wade — Figurines and Miniatures*, all by Ian Warner and Mike Posgay; Mr. Warner is listed in the Directory under Canada.

Animal, Lion Cub, paw up, underglaze finish, 1935-39, 5¼" 550.00
Animal, Panther, underglaze finish, 1935-39, 8x5" 1,050.00
Animal, Penny (penguin), late 1940s-late 1950s, 2" 230.00
Bird, Goldfinch, wings open, underglaze finish, 1930s-mid 1950s, 4" .620.00
Canadian Red Rose Tea, Fawn, 1967-73 ....5.00
Canadian Red Rose Tea, Fox, 1967-73 ....6.00
Disney, Big Mama, 1981-87, 1¾"..68.00
Disney, Salty the Seal, 6¼" 450.00

Disney, Sgt Tibbs, 1960-64, 2" 145.00
Disney Blow-Up, Si, 1961-65, 5½x5" 250.00
Dog model, Dalmatian, cellulose finish, 1927-early 1930s, 7x8".225.00
Dog model, Setter, cellulose finish, 1927-early 1930s, 6x9¾" 225.00
Drum Box series, Clara, 1956-59, 2" 100.00
Drum Box series, Jem, 1956-59, 2" 100.00
Figurine, Daisette, cellulose finish, 1927-late 1930s, 10" 850.00
Figurine, Queenie, cellulose finish, 1927-late 1930s, 4" 265.00
Flower, Anemone, Ajax bowl, earthenware 200.00
Flower, Anemones, 1930-39, 6" 60.00
Flower, Posy Basket, 1930-39, 3½" 35.00
Nursery Favourite, Boy Blue, 1972-81, 2⅞" 52.00
Nursery Favourite, Miss Muffet, 1972-81, 2⅝" 55.00
Nursery Favourite, Three Bears, 1972-81, 2⅞" 65.00
Nursery Rhyme series, Butcher, 1949-58, 3¼" 360.00
Nursery Rhyme series, Tinker, 1959-58, 2½" 265.00
Souvenir dish, City of London, 4½x4" 48.00
Souvenir dish, Tower Bridge, ca 1957, 1½x4x3" 48.00
Souvenir vase, Nova Scotia, 4½" 16.00
USA Red Rose Tea, Koala bear, 1985, 1⅜" 6.00
USA Red Rose Tea, Langur, 1985, 1⅜" 6.00
USA Red Rose Tea, Orangutan, 1985, 1¼" 5.00
Whimsey-on-Why Village Set, Butcher Shop, 1985, 1⅝" 30.00
Whimsey-on-Why Village Set, Greengrocer's Shop, 1981, 1½" ...15.00
Whimsey-on-Why Village Set, Morgan's the Chemist, 1980, 1¾" ..24.00
Whimsies, Beagle, 1956, ¾x1" 78.00
Whimsies, Bison, 1979, 1⅜x1¾" 15.00
Whimsies, Duck, 1972, 1¼x1½" 8.00
Whimsies, Giant Panda, 1953-59, 1¼" 48.00
Whimsies, Kitten, 1953-59, 1⅜x1¾" 55.00
Whimsies, Shetland Pony, 1955, 1⅜x2" 38.00
Whimsies, Shire Horse, 1953-59, 2" 235.00
Whimsies, Spaniel, 1953, 2x2¾" 46.00
World of Dogs, Poodle, 1990-91, 1½" 16.00
World of Dogs, West Highland Terrier, 1990-91, 1½" 10.00
World of Survival series, African Elephant, 1978-82, 6x10" 500.00
World of Survival series, Harp Seal & Pup, 1978-82, 3¾x9" 600.00

Wallace China

Dinnerware with a Western theme was produced by the Wallace China Company, who operated in California from 1931 until 1964. Artist Till Goodan designed three lines, Rodeo, Pioneer Trails, and Boots and Saddle, which they marketed under the package name Westward Ho. When dinnerware with a western theme became so popular just a few years ago, Rodeo was reproduced, but the new trademark includes neither 'California' or 'Wallace China.'

This ware is very heavy and not prone to chips, but be sure to examine it under a strong light to look for knife scratches, which will lessen its value to a considerable extent when excessive. Our advisor for this category is Marv Fogleman; he is listed in the Directory under California. If you'd like to learn more about this company, we recommend *The Collector's Encyclopedia of California Pottery* by Jack Chipman.

Boots & Saddle, bowl, cereal; 5¾" 70.00
Boots & Saddle, bowl, fruit; 4⅞" 50.00
Boots & Saddle, cup, flat 75.00
Boots & Saddle, plate, bread & butter; 7⅛" 60.00
Boots & Saddle, platter, oval, 15¼" 225.00
Chuck Wagon, bowl, fruit; 5" 70.00
Chuck Wagon, creamer, 2-oz, 2½" 95.00
Chuck Wagon, plate, dinner; 9½" 95.00
Chuck Wagon, platter, oval, 9x13" 110.00

Dahlia, platter, serving; oval, 11½" 40.00
El Rancho, cup & saucer 80.00
El Rancho, plate, bread & butter; 6½" 50.00
El Rancho, plate, Olmus Club, 11⅛" 45.00
El Rancho, plate, salad; 8¼" 45.00
El Rancho, platter, serving; oval, 13½" 175.00
El Rancho, sugar bowl, open 75.00
Longhorn, bowl, mixing; 3x6" 295.00
Longhorn, plate, bread & butter; 7" 75.00
Longhorn, plate, dinner; 10½" 125.00
Pioneer Trails, bowl, vegetable; open, 12" 240.00
Pioneer Trails, cup, flat 80.00
Pioneer Trails, plate, chop; 13½" 270.00
Pioneer Trails, plate, dinner; 9" 100.00
Rodeo, bowl, vegetable; oval, 11⅞" 220.00
Rodeo, creamer, from $100 to 120.00
Rodeo, cup & saucer 70.00
Rodeo, cup & saucer, oversz, 3⅝" 80.00
Rodeo, pitcher, water; sgn Till Goodan, 72-oz 280.00
Rodeo, plate, bread & butter; w/center design, 7⅛" 60.00
Rodeo, plate, dinner; 10¾" 110.00
Rodeo, platter, oval, 15⅛" 300.00
Rodeo, shakers, oversz, 4⅞", pr 140.00
Rodeo, sugar bowl, w/lid, 4½" 125.00
Shadowleaf, cup 70.00
Shadowleaf, plate, bread & butter; 7⅛" 30.00
Shadowleaf, plate, 11¼" 50.00
Ye Olde Mill, plate, dinner; 10⅝" 20.00
49ers, bowl, serving; 8" dia 120.00

Walley

The Walley Pottery operated in West Sterling, Massachusetts, from 1898 to 1919. Never more than a one-man operation, Walley himself handcrafted all his wares from local clay. The majority of his pottery was simple and unadorned and usually glazed in matt green. On occasion, however, you may find high- and semi-gloss green, as well as matt glazes in blue, cream, brown, and red. The rarest and most desirable examples of his work are those with applied or relief-carved decorations. Some pieces are marked 'WJW.' Our advisors for this category are Suzanne Perrault and David Rago; they are listed in the Directory under New Jersey.

Flower holder, brn/gr matt textured, spherical, WJW mk, 2¾x5" ...470.00
Vase, brn shaded w/gr speckling, ftd paneled ovoid, 8x3½" 425.00
Vase, cucumber gr, WJW mk, 5½x5", EX 470.00
Vase, gr matt, 4 appl hdls, mk, 8x4" 2,500.00
Vase, mirrored blk, baluster, 7½x3½" 500.00

Vase, tooled and applied leaves, feathered turquoise semimatt with exposed red clay, WJW, restoration, grinding chips, 5¾x6", $1,380.00. (Photo courtesy David Rago Auctions)

Walrath

Frederick E. Walrath learned his craft as a student of Charles Fergus Binns at Alfred University (1900 – 1904). Walrath worked first, and briefly, at Grueby Faience Company in Boston and then, from 1908 to 1918, as an instructor at the Mechanics Institute in Rochester, New York. He was chief ceramist at Newcomb Pottery (New Orleans) until his death in 1921. A studio potter, Walrath's work bears stylistic similarity to that of Marblehead Pottery, whose founder, Arthur Baggs, was also a student of Binns's. Vases featuring matt glazes of stylized natural motifs (especially florals) are most sought after; sculptural and figural forms (center bowls, flower frogs, various animals) are less desirable. Typically his work is signed with an incised circular signature: Walrath Pottery with conjoined M and I at the center. Our advisor for this and related Arts & Crafts subjects is Bruce A. Austin; he is listed in the Directory under New York.

Bowl, bl-gray, low, 8¾" 175.00
Bowl, gr mottle matt/terra cotta, w/3-D kneeling nude, 6x7", NM ..950.00
Lemonade pitcher, lemons, yel/gr/brn matt, +6 (VG/EX) goblets.3,000.00
Mug, brn w/band of bl berries & gr leaves, 4" 300.00
Scarab, bl matt, 3½", EX..170.00
Vase, Arts & Crafts floral device w/4 stems, brn/gr on olive, 7½" ..3,750.00
Vase, floral (stylized), bl on gray, shouldered, 8", NM 2,200.00
Vase, geometrics w/stylized foliage, peach on bl, 7" 850.00
Vase, stylized trees, gr on red brn, sm neck, bulbous, 4" 3,500.00

Walter, A.

Almaric Walter was employed from 1904 through 1914 at Verreries Artistiques des Freres Daum in Nancy, France. After 1919 he opened his own business where he continued to make the same type of quality objets d'art in pate-de-verre glass as he had earlier. His pieces are signed A. Walter, Nancy H. Berge Sc.

Box, beetle, blk & brn on gr & yel, 2½x4½" dia 5,000.00
Paperweight, lobster figural on base, 3" L 1,050.00
Paperweight, moth, bl/brn/gr/yel, 4½" 2,500.00
Pendant, bug, orange/blk/yel on clear, 1¾"..............................1,100.00
Pendant, iris, purple/yel on clear, 2" dia 850.00
Tray, bee, brn/blk/gr on clear to yel, 4" L 900.00
Vase, beetles on brn/frost mottle, chalice form, 6¼" 5,500.00
Vase, floral, pk/orange on turq, ovoid, 4½" 900.00
Vase, vertical leaves, yel to purple, flaring ftd form, 6½" 2,500.00

Wannopee

The Wannopee Pottery, established in 1892, developed from the reorganization of the financially insecure New Milford Pottery Company of New Milford, Connecticut. They produced a line of mottled-glazed pottery called 'Duchess' and a similar line in porcelain. Both were marked with the impressed sunburst 'W' with 'porcelain' added to indicate that particular body type.

In 1895 semiporcelain pitchers in three sizes were decorated with relief medallion cameos of Beethoven, Mozart, and Napoleon. Lettuce-leaf ware was first produced in 1901 and used actual leaves in the modeling. Scarabronze, made in 1895, was their finest artware. It featured simple Egyptian shapes with a coppery glaze. It was marked with a scarab, either impressed or applied. Production ceased in 1903.

Chamberstick, brn, twisted cylinder w/flared ft, 13¼x8¾" 450.00
Dish, lettuce-leaf shape, 7½" 250.00
Umbrella stand, Duchess, mc mottle, 24" 525.00
Vase, bl/gr/yel drip, high curved hdls, bulbous, 10" 1,100.00

Warwick

The Warwick China Company operated in Wheeling, West Virginia, from 1887 until 1951. They produced both hand-painted and decaled plates, vases, teapots, coffeepots, pitchers, bowls, and jardinieres featuring lovely florals or portraits of beautiful ladies done in luscious colors. Backgrounds were usually blendings of brown and beige, but ivory was also used as well as greens and pinks. Various marks were employed, all of which incorporate the Warwick name. For a more thorough study of the subject, we recommend *Warwick, A to W*, a supplement to *Why Not Warwick* by our advisor, Donald C. Hoffmann, Sr.; his address can be found in the Directory under Illinois. In an effort to inform the collector/dealer, Mr. Hoffmann now has a video available that identifies the company's decals and their variations by number.

Tankard, bl gloss, paternal order, sq hdl, 10", +4 4¼" mugs 900.00
Tankard, bl matt, paternal order, 10", +4 4¼" mugs 1,000.00
Tankard, brn, Christy girl portrait, ring hdl, 13", +4 5" mugs 900.00
Tankard, brn, Christy girl portrait, ring hdl, 15", +4 5¼" mugs..1,100.00
Tankard, brn, Dickens' characters, crossbar hdl, 10", +4¼" mugs..825.00
Tankard, brn, Dickens' characters, ring hdl, 15", +4 5¼" mugs ..950.00
Tankard, brn, fisherman, sq hdl w/bar, 10", +6 4¼" mugs 950.00
Tankard, brn, FOE (newer style), 15", +6 5¼" steins 900.00
Tankard, brn, FOE (old style), 15", +6 5¼" steins....................1,100.00
Tankard, brn, friar, ring hdl, 13", +4 5" mugs, from $900 to 1,000.00
Tankard, brn, fruit, ring hdl, 13", +4 5" mugs 1,200.00
Tankard, brn, Indian w/headdress, 15", +4 5¼" mugs 1,250.00
Tankard, brn, monk in red cap, sq hdl, 10", +4 4¼" mugs 750.00
Tankard, brn, opera decor, ring hdl, 13", +4 5" mugs 1,450.00
Tankard, red, fisherman, sq hdl w/bar, 10" 500.00
Unnamed ewer, brn, Madame LeBrun portrait, A-17, 9¼" 400.00
Unnamed ewer, brn w/floral decor, A-27, 9¼" 450.00
Unnamed ewer, charcoal w/floral decor, C-6, 9¼" 425.00
Unnamed ewer, pk, Aunt Hilda-type portrait, H-1, 9¼"...............680.00
Unnamed funnel type, brn w/floral decor, A-16, 11½" 400.00
Unnamed funnel type, brn w/floral decor, A-20, 11½" 460.00
Unnamed funnel type, yel to gr, portrait, K-1, 11½" 700.00
Violet vase, brn w/floral decor, A-06, 4" 125.00
Violet vase, brn w/floral decor, A-22, 4" 140.00
Violet vase, charcoal w/floral decor, C-5, 4" 160.00
Violet vase, charcoal w/floral decor, C-6, 4" 155.00
Violet vase, red overglaze w/floral decor, E-2, 4" 140.00
Virginia vase, brn, Madame LeBrun portrait, A-17, 10" 275.00
Virginia vase, brn, Madame Recamier portrait, A-17, 10"...........260.00
Virginia vase, brn w/floral decor, A-6, 10" 225.00
Virginia vase, pk, Christy girl portrait, H-10, 10" 650.00
Warwick vase, brn w/floral decor, A-40, 10" 425.00
Warwick vase, pk, Aunt Hilda-type portrait (peony in hair, H-1, 10"...625.00
Warwick vase, pk, Aunt Hilda-type portrait (w/boa), H-1, 10" ..650.00
Warwick vase, pk to bl, Aunt Hilda-type portrait, H-1, 10" 625.00
Windsor vase, brn, Anna Potacka portrait, A-17, 9¼"................450.00
Windsor vase, brn w/floral decor, A-40, 9¼" 460.00
Windsor vase, pk, Christy girl portrait, H-1, 9¼" 680.00

Wash Sets

Before the days of running water, bedrooms were standardly equipped with a wash bowl and pitcher as a matter of necessity. A 'toilet set' was comprised of the pitcher and bowl, toothbrush holder, shaving mug, covered chamber pot, soap dish, and toothbrush holder. Some sets were even more elaborate. Through everyday usage, the smaller items were often broken, and today it is unusual to find a complete set.

Porcelain sets decorated with florals, fruits, or scenics were produced abroad by Limoges in France; some were imported from Germany and England. During the last quarter of the 1800s and until after the turn of the century, American-made toilet sets were manufactured in abundance. Tin and graniteware sets were also made.

Key:
b — bowl
c — chamber pot
cp — cup
l — lid
p — pitcher
s — spittoon
t — toothbrush holder
v — vase

Devon Fieldings, tan w/wht rose reserves & gold, 14" p+16" b+open c..**535.00**
Furnivals, Lily, p+b+c+cp+v+s, 6 pcs **400.00**
Grindley, Windsor #293696 (flow bl), 11x8" p+15½" b..............**500.00**
HH&G, Maida, yel w/blk & wht check rose-reserve band, metal, 12" p+b.**165.00**
Illegible mk, lilies transfer on wht ironstone, ca 1880, 11" p+b, EX..**115.00**
Ironstone England, rose spray on emb wht, 13" p+16" b **120.00**
Ironstone USA, bl to wht w/floral transfer & emb, 11" p+16" (EX) b..**140.00**
Royal Porcelain J Mason, Psyche, floral/gold on wht, 12" p+17" b ..**160.00**
Unknown, #3 on bottom, flow bl w/nude ladies, 11" p+5x15" b.**390.00**
Unknown, bl sponging on yel, emb rim band, 10" p (EX)+15" bowl...**375.00**
Unknown, bl/wht stoneware, Memphis, bulbous p+b, mfg flaw..**365.00**
Unknown, creamware w/HP floral & vine bands, 1800s, 10" p+b..**500.00**

Watch Fobs

Watch fobs have been popular since the last quarter of the nineteenth century. They were often made by retail companies to feature their products. Souvenir, commemorative, and political fobs were also produced. Of special interest today are those with advertising, heavy equipment in particular. Some of the more pricey fobs are listed here, but most of those currently available were produced in such quantities that they are relatively common and should fall within a price range of $3.00 to $10.00. When no material is mentioned in the description, assume the fob is made of metal.

Abraham Fur Co St Louis USA, fox center, EX **250.00**
Advance Threshers, Banner Boy logo, mc on celluloid, EX w/strap..**315.00**
Arrowhead shape w/emb Indan & bowl, brass **40.00**
Brotherhood of Locomotive, Fireman & Engineers, enameled....**200.00**
Cyrus McCormick, brass...**45.00**
Dead Shot, game bird emb on sterling silver, 1¼" dia, M **100.00**
Dodge Bros Motor Vehicles, bl/wht/blk enamel **75.00**
Heinz, brass plated, 57 on 1 side, factory on reverse, 1½x1¾" **50.00**
Hunter Trader Trapper, bear & guns, brass/bronze **110.00**
John Deere, deer & lg D on brass, EX patina **160.00**
Link Belt Speeder, Speeder Mfg Corp, Robbins, 1¾x1¾" **90.00**
Nat'l Sportsman's Magazine, gold-tone metal, emb game, 1⅝x1½"..**75.00**
Pueblo Saddle Co, RT Frazier, saddle form....................................**90.00**
Punty Brand Salt...Milwaukee, enameled, 1900s **120.00**
Savage Arms, Indian Chief emb on bronze, 1⅝" **400.00**
Waterloo Boy, boy & tractor...**435.00**
Winchester, man on horse, brass..**90.00**

Watch Stands

Watch stands were decorative articles designed with a hook from which to hang a watch. Some displayed the watch as the face of a grandfather clock or as part of an interior scene with figures in period costumes and contemporary furnishings. They were popular products of Staffordshire potters and silver companies as well.

Burlwood w/brass fittings, hanger in center of arch, Victorian, 5½"....**200.00**
Ebonized wood w/hinged glass dome, ca 1890, 6x4½" dia..........**135.00**
Glass, gold floral, cylindrical, brass mts, hinged lid, ca 1880 ....**95.00**
Mahog, cvd rectangular box w/peaked bk, hinged door, Swiss, 8½" ..**470.00**
Silver, logs on campfire, watch hangs from branch, Tufts #2623, 1900s ...**265.00**
Spelter, golfer figural, hook for watch on flag stick, ca 1915, 3½"....**625.00**
Tall case clock, cvd mahog & ivory, ca 1800, 14⅜" **3,300.00**
Tall case clock, cvd wood w/inlay, ca 1790, 10¼", VG...............**950.00**
Tall case clock, mahog w/inlay, sailor made, 19th C, 16⅜"......**3,300.00**

Watches

First made in the 1500s in Germany, early watches were actually small clocks, suspended from the neck or belt. By 1700 they had become the approximate shape and size we know today. The first watches produced in America were made in 1810. The well-known Waltham Watch Company was established in 1850. Later, Waterbury produced inexpensive watches which they sold by the thousands.

Open-face and hunting-case watches of the 1890s were often solid gold or gold-filled and were often elaborately decorated in several colors of gold. Gold watches became a status symbol in this decade and were worn by both men and women on chains with fobs or jeweled slides. Ladies sometimes fastened them to their clothing with pins often set with jewels. The chatelaine watch was worn at the waist, only one of several items such as scissors, coin purses, or needle cases, each attached by small chains.

Most turn-of-the-century watch cases were gold-filled; these are plentiful today. Sterling cases, though interest in them is on the increase, are not in great demand. For more information we recommend *Complete Price Guide to Watches, No. 24,* by Cooksey Shugart, Tom Engle, and Richard E. Gilbert (Collector Books).

Our advice for this category comes from Maundy International Watches, Antiquarian Horologists, price consultants and researchers for many watch reference guides and books on Horology. Their firm is a leading purveyor of antique watches of all kinds. They are listed in the Directory under Kansas. For character-related watches, see Personalities.

Key:
adj — adjusted
brg — bridge plate design
d/s — double sunk dial
fbd — finger bridge design
g/f — gold-filled
g/j/s — gold jewel setting
h/c — hunter case
HCI#P — heat, cold,
  isochronism & position
  adjusted
j — jewel
k — karat
k/s — key set
k/w — key wind
l/s — lever set
mvt — movement
o/f — open face
p/s — pendant set
r/g/p — rolled gold plate
s — size
s/s — single sunk dial
s/w — stem wind
w/g/f — white gold-filled
y/g/f — yellow gold-filled

Am Watch Co, 0s, 7j, #1891, 14k, h/c, Am Watch Co, M **500.00**
Am Watch Co, 6s, 7j, #1873, y/g/f, h/c, Am Watch Co, M **250.00**
Am Watch Co, 12s, 17j, #1894, 14k, o/f, Royal, M....................**475.00**
Am Watch Co, 12s, 21j, #1894, 14k, h/c, M **900.00**
Am Watch Co, 16s, 11j, #1872, p/s, silver h/c, Park Road, M **400.00**
Am Watch Co, 16s, 15j, #1899, y/g/f, h/c, M **450.00**
Am Watch Co, 16s, 16j, #1884, 5-min, 14k, Repeater, M.......**6,900.00**
Am Watch Co, 16s, 17j, #1888, Railroader, M.........................**1,725.00**
Am Watch Co, 16s, 19j, #1872, 14k, h/c, Am Watch Woerd's Pat, M..**9,300.00**
Am Watch Co, 16s, 21j, #1888, h/c, 14k, Riverside Maximus, M...**1,700.00**
Am Watch Co, 16s, 21j, #1899, y/g/f, l/s, o/f, Crescent St, M.....**300.00**
Am Watch Co, 16s, 21j, #1908, y/g/f, o/f, Grade #645, M **385.00**
Am Watch Co, 16s, 23j, #1908, o/f, 18k, Premier Maximus, MIB..**15,000.00**

Am Watch Co, 16s, 23j, #1908, y/g/f, o/f, adj, RR, Vanguard, M ..550.00
Am Watch Co, 16s, 23j, #1908, y/g/f, o/f, Vanguard Up/Down, EX ..950.00
Am Watch Co, 18s, #1857, silver h/c, Samuel Curtiss k/w, M ..4,000.00
Am Watch Co, 18s, 7j, #1857, silver case, k/w, CT Parker, M ..4,500.00
Am Watch Co, 18s, 11j, #1857, k/w, 1st run, PS Barlett, M 7,000.00
Am Watch Co, 18s, 11j, #1857, silver h/c, k/w, DH&D, EX ...2,195.00
Am Watch Co, 18s, 11j, #1857, silver h/c, k/w, s/s, Wm Ellery, EX ..125.00
Am Watch Co, 18s, 15j, #1877, k/w, RE Robbins, M 575.00
Am Watch Co, 18s, 15j, #1883, y/g/f, 2-tone, Railroad King, EX ...585.00
Am Watch Co, 18s, 17j, #1883, y/g/f, o/f, Crescent Street, M 275.00
Am Watch Co, 18s, 17j, #1892, HC, Canadian Pacific Railway, M ..1,975.00
Am Watch Co, 18s, 17j, #1892, y/g/f, o/f, Sidereal, rare, M 3,850.00
Am Watch Co, 18s, 17j, 25-yr, y/g/f, o/f, s/s, PS Bartlett, M 295.00
Am Watch Co, 18s, 21j, #1892, y/g/f, o/f, d/s, Crescent St, M....495.00
Am Watch Co, 18s, 21j, #1892, y/g/f, o/f, Grade #845, EX 265.00
Am Watch Co, 18s, 21j, #1892, y/g/f, o/f, Pennsylvania Special, M ..5,750.00
Auburndale Watch Co, 18s, 7j, k/w, l/s, Lincoln, M 2,950.00
Aurora Watch Co, 18s, 11j, k/w, silver h/c, M 475.00
Aurora Watch Co, 18s, 15 ruby j, y/g/f, s/w, 5th pinion, M 1,495.00
Ball (Elgin), 18s, 17j, o/f, silver, Official RR Standard, M 595.00
Ball (Hamilton), 16s, 21j, #999, g/f, o/f, l/s, M 950.00
Ball (Hamilton), 16s, 23j, #998, y/g/f, o/f, Elinvar, M 3,500.00
Ball (Hamilton), 18s, 17j, #999, g/f, o/f, l/s, EX 450.00
Ball (Hampden), 18s, 17j, o/f, adj, RR, Superior Grade, M 3,000.00
Ball (Illinois), 12s, 19j, w/g/f, o/f, M 375.00
Ball (Waltham), 16s, 17j, y/g/f, o/f, RR, Commercial Std, M....650.00
Ball (Waltham), 16s, 21j, o/f, Official RR Standard, M 875.00
Columbus, 6s, 11j, y/g/f hc, M 250.00
Columbus, 18s, 11-15j, k/w, k/s, M 650.00
Columbus, 18s, 15j, o/f, l/s, M 250.00
Columbus, 18s, 15j, y/g/f, o/f, Jay Gould on dial, M 2,400.00
Columbus, 18s, 21j, y/g/f, h/c, train on dial, Railway King, M.1,350.00
Columbus, 18s, 23j, y/g/f, h/c, Columbus King, M...................2,450.00
Cornell, 18s, 15j, s/w, JC Adams, EX 350.00
Cornell, 18s, 15j, silver h/c, k/w, John Evans, EX 375.00
Dudley, 12s, #1, 14k, o/f, flip-bk case, Masonic, G 2,800.00
Elgin, 6s, 11j, 14k, h/c, M 425.00
Elgin, 6s, 15j, 20-yr, y/g/f, h/c, s/s, EX 80.00
Elgin, 10s, 18k, h/c, k/w, k/s, s/s, Gail Borden, M 700.00
Elgin, 12s, 15j, 14k, h/c, EX 325.00
Elgin, 12s, 17j, 14k, h/c, GM Wheeler, M 525.00
Elgin, 16s, 15j, doctor's, 4th model, 18k, 2nd sweep hand, h/c, M ..2,400.00
Elgin, 16s, 15j, 14k, h/c, EX 650.00
Elgin, 16s, 21j, y/g/f, g/j/s, o/f, BW Raymond, EX 265.00
Elgin, 16s, 21j, y/g/f, g/j/s, 3 fbd, h/c, M 925.00
Elgin, 16s, 21j, y/g/f, o/f, l/s, RR, Father Time, M 485.00
Elgin, 16s, 21j, 14k, 3 fbd, grade #91, scarce, M 4,000.00
Elgin, 16s, 23j, up/down indicator, BW Raymond, EX 1,500.00
Elgin, 17s, 7j, k/w, orig silver case, Leader, M 250.00
Elgin, 18s, 11j, silver, h/c, k/w, gilded, MG Odgen, M................295.00
Elgin, 18s, 15j, o/f, d/s, k/w, silver, RR, BW Raymond 1st run, M ..1,795.00
Elgin, 18s, 15j, silver, k/w, k/s, h/c, HL Culver, M 400.00
Elgin, 18s, 15j, silver h/c, Penn RR dial, BW Raymond k/w mvt, M .6,150.00
Elgin, 18s, 17j, silveroid h/c, BW Raymond, M 395.00
Elgin, 18s, 21j, y/g/f, o/f, Father Time, G 225.00
Elgin, 18s, 23j, y/g/f, o/f, 5-position, RR, Veritas, M 795.00
Fredonia, 18s, 11j, y/g/f, h/c, k/w, M 475.00
Hamilton, #4992B, 16s, 22j, o/f, steel case, G 250.00
Hamilton, #910, 12s, 17j, 20-yr, y/g/f, o/f, s/s, EX 100.00
Hamilton, #912, 12s, 17j, y/g/f, o/f, adj, EX 100.00
Hamilton, #920, 12s, 23j, 14k, o/f, M 700.00
Hamilton, #922MP, 12s, 18k case, Masterpiece (sgn), M.........1,500.00
Hamilton, #925, 18s, 17j, y/g/f, h/c, s/s, l/s, M 395.00
Hamilton, #928, 18s, 15j, y/g/f, o/f, s/s, EX 300.00

Hamilton, #933, 18s, 16j, h/c, nickel plate, low serial #, M......1,575.00
Hamilton, #938, 18s, 17j, y/g/f, adj, M...................................1,095.00
Hamilton, #940, 18s, 21j, nickel plate, coin silver, o/f, M...........450.00
Hamilton, #946, 18s, 23j, y/g/f, o/f, g/j/s, M...........................1,275.00
Hamilton, #947 (mk), 18s, 23j, 14k, h/c, orig/sgn, EX 6,000.00
Hamilton, #950, 16s, 23j, y/g/f, o/f, l/s, sgn d/s, M 1,700.00
Hamilton, #965, 16s, 17j, 14k, p/s, h/c, brg, scarce, M 1,695.00
Hamilton, #972, 16s, 17j, y/g/f, g/j/s, o/f, d/s, l/s, adj, EX 195.00
Hamilton, #974, 16s, 17j, 20-yr, y/g/f, o/f, s/s, EX 165.00
Hamilton, #992, 16s, 21j, y/g/f, o/f, adj, d/s, dbl roller, M...........425.00
Hamilton, #992B, 16s, 21j, y/g/f, o/f, l/s, Bar/Crown, M 550.00
Hampden, 12s, 17j, w/g/f, o/f, thin model, Aviator, M 265.00
Hampden, 16s, 17j, o/f, adj, EX..70.00
Hampden, 16s, 17j, y/g/f, h/c, s/w, M 285.00
Hampden, 16s, 21j, g/j/s, y/g/f, NP, h/c, Dueber, ¾-mvt, M.........345.00
Hampden, 16s, 23j, o/f, adj, dbl roller, Special Railway, M 675.00
Hampden, 16s, 7j, gilded, nickel plate, o/f, ¾-mvt, EX.................65.00
Hampden, 18s, 15j, k/w, mk on mvt, Railway, M 1,595.00
Hampden, 18s, 15j, s/w, gilded, JC Perry, M.............................200.00
Hampden, 18s, 15j, silver, k/w, h/c, Hayward, M 345.00
Hampden, 18s, 15j, y/g/f, damascened, h/c, Dueber, M 195.00
Hampden, 18s, 21j, y/g/f, g/j/s, h/c, New Railway, M 495.00
Hampden, 18s, 21j, y/g/f, o/f, d/s, l/s, N Am Railway, M 525.00
Hampden, 18s, 23j, y/g/f, o/f, d/s, adj, New Railway, M.............550.00
Hampden, 18s, 23j, 14k, h/c, Special Railway, M 1,295.00
Hampden, 18s, 7-11j, k/w, gilded, Springfield Mass, EX 150.00
Howard, E; 6s, 15j, s/w, 18k h/c, Series VIII, G sz, M...............1,675.00
Howard, E; 16s, 15j, s/w, 14k h/c, L sz, M..............................1,995.00
Howard, E; 18s, 15j, h/c, silver case, k/w, Series I, N sz, M......4,950.00
Howard, E; 18s, 15j, 18k h/c, k/w, Series II, N sz, M...............5,950.00
Howard, E; 18s, 17j, 25-yr, y/g/f, o/f, orig case, split plate, M...2,385.00
Howard (Keystone), 12s, 23j, 14k, h/c, brg, Series 8, M............795.00
Howard (Keystone), 16s, 17j, y/g/f, o/f, Series 9, M.................345.00
Howard (Keystone), 16s, 21j, y/g/f, o/f, RR Chronometer II, M .775.00
Howard (Keystone), 16s, 23j, y/g/f, o/f, Series 0, jeweled bbl, M..1,395.00
Illinois, 0s, 7j, 14k, l/s, h/c, EX 350.00
Illinois, 8s, 13j, ¾-mvt, Rose LeLand, scarce, M 525.00
Illinois, 12s, 17j, y/g/f, o/f, d/s dial, EX...................................65.00
Illinois, 16s, 17j, y/g/f, o/f, d/s, Bunn, EX 250.00
Illinois, 16s, 21j, g/j/s, h/c, Burlington, M 385.00
Illinois, 16s, 21j, o/f, d/s, Santa Fe Special, M 925.00
Illinois, 16s, 21j, y/g/f, o/f, d/s, Bunn Special, M 595.00
Illinois, 16s, 23j, y/g/f, o/f, d/s, 60-hr, Sangamo Special, mk, M...3,750.00
Illinois, 16s, 23j, y/g/f, stiff bow, o/f, Sangamo Special, EX 1,100.00
Illinois, 18s, 11j, #1, silver, k/w, Alleghany, EX 150.00
Illinois, 18s, 11j, #3, o/f, s/w, l/s, Comet, G 90.00
Illinois, 18s, 11j, Forest City, G 110.00
Illinois, 18s, 15j, #1, adj, y/g/f, k/w, h/c, gilt, Bunn, M 995.00
Illinois, 18s, 15j, #1, k/w, k/s, silver hunter, Stuart, M 1,250.00
Illinois, 18s, 15j, k/w, k/s, gilt, Railway Regulator, M...............1,100.00
Illinois, 18s, 15j, s/w, silveroid, G..65.00
Illinois, 18s, 17j, g/j/s, adj, B&O RR Special (Hunter), h/c, M ..2,895.00
Illinois, 18s, 17j, h/c, s/w, nickel plate, coin silver, Bunn, M.......585.00
Illinois, 18s, 17j, o/f, d/s, adj, silveroid case, Lakeshore, G 95.00
Illinois, 18s, 17j, o/f, s/w, 5th pinion, Miller, EX.......................190.00
Illinois, 18s, 21j, g/j/s, g/f, o/f, A Lincoln, M..........................550.00
Illinois, 18s, 21j, g/j/s, o/f, adj, B&O RR Special, EX...............1,995.00
Illinois, 18s, 21j, 14k, g/j/s, h/c, Bunn Special, M....................1,695.00
Illinois, 18s, 23j, g/j/s, Bunn Special, EX................................900.00
Illinois, 18s, 24j, g/j/s, adj, o/f, Chesapeake & Ohio, M...........5,500.00
Illinois, 18s, 24j, g/j/s, o/f, Bunn Special, EX..........................1,100.00
Illinois, 18s, 26j, g/j/s, o/f, Ben Franklin USA, G 4,750.00
Illinois, 18s, 26j, 14k, Penn Special, M.................................11,000.00
Illinois, 18s, 7j, #3, o/f, Interior, G...85.00

Illinois, 18s, 7j, #3, silveroid, America, G 95.00
Illinois, 18s, 9-11j, o/f, k/w, s/s, silveroid case, Hoyt, M..............265.00
Ingersoll, 16s, 7j, wht base metal, Reliance, G 35.00
Lancaster, 18s, 7j, o/f, k/w, k/s, eng silver case, EX 175.00
Marion US, 18s, h/c, k/w, k/s, ¾-plate, Asa Fuller, M 550.00
Marion US, 18s, 15j, nickel plate, h/c, s/w, Henry Randel, M 525.00
Melrose Watch Co, 18s, 7j, k/w, k/s, G 290.00
New York Watch Co, 18s, 7j, silver, h/c, k/w, Geo Sam Rice, EX...245.00
New York Watch Co, 19j, low sz #, wolf's teeth wind, M 1,800.00
Patek Philippe, 12s, 18j, 18k, o/f, EX 2,100.00
Patek Philippe, 16s, 20j, 18k, h/c, M 3,500.00
Rockford, 16s, 17j, y/g/f, h/c, brg, dbl roller, EX.......................95.00
Rockford, 16s, 21j, #515, y/g/f, M 775.00
Rockford, 16s, 21j, g/j/s, o/f, grade #537, rare, M 1,800.00
Rockford, 16s, 23j, 14k, o/f, mk Doll on dial/mvt, M..............3,400.00
Rockford, 18s, 15j, o/f, k/w, silver case, EX 250.00
Rockford, 18s, 17j, silveroid, 2-tone, M 400.00
Rockford, 18s, 17j, y/g/f, o/f, Winnebago, M 500.00
Rockford, 18s, 21j, o/f, King Edward, M 595.00
Seth Thomas, 18s, 17j, #2, g/j/s, adj, Henry Molineux, EX 675.00
Seth Thomas, 18s, 17j, Edgemere, G 55.00
Seth Thomas, 18s, 25j, g/j/s, g/f, Maiden Lane, EX 2,395.00
Seth Thomas, 18s, 7j, ¾-mvt, bk: eagle/Liberty model, M..........325.00
South Bend, 12s, 21j, dbl roller, Grade #431, M....................275.00
South Bend, 12s, 21j, orig o/f, d/s, Studebaker, M 425.00
South Bend, 18s, 21j, g/j/s, h/c, Studebaker, M 1,495.00
South Bend, 18s, 21j, 14k, h/c, M 1,325.00
Swiss, 18s, 18k, h/c, 1-min, Repeater, High Grade, M 5,500.00

Watt Pottery

The Watt Pottery Company was established in Crooksville, Ohio, on July 5, 1922. From approximately 1922 until 1935, they manufactured hand-turned stone containers — jars, jugs, milk pans, preserve jars, and various sizes of mixing bowls, usually marked with a cobalt blue acorn stamp. In 1936 production of these items was discontinued, and the company began to produce kitchen utility ware and ovenware such as mixing bowls, spaghetti bowls and plates, canister sets, covered casseroles, salt and pepper shakers, cookie jars, ice buckets, pitchers, bean pots, and salad and dinnerware sets. Most Watt ware is individually hand painted with bold brush strokes of red, green, or blue contrasting with the natural buff color of the glazed body. Several patterns were produced: Apple, Autumn Foliage, Cherry, Dutch Tulip, Morning Glory, Rio Rose, Rooster, Tear Drop, Starflower, and Tulip, to name a few. Much of the ware was made for advertising premiums and is often found stamped with the name of the retail company.

Tragedy struck the Watt Pottery Company on October 4, 1965, when fire completely destroyed the factory and warehouse. Production never resumed, but the ware they made has withstood many years of service in American kitchens and is today highly regarded and prized by collectors. The vivid colors and folk art-like execution of each cheerful pattern create a homespun ambiance that will make Watt pottery a treasure for years to come.

For further study we recommend *Watt Pottery, An Identification and Price Guide,* by Susan Morris-Snyder and Dave Morris (Collector Books). Susan is our advisor for this category; she is listed in the Directory under Washington. For the address of the *Matt's News* newsletter, see the the section on Clubs, Newsletters, and Catalogs.

Apple, bowl, #106, ftd, 3½x10¾" dia..350.00
Apple, bowl, cereal; #52, 2¼x6½" dia...50.00
Apple, bowl, mixing; #04, 2x4" dia...65.00
Apple, bowl, mixing; #5, ribbed, 2¾x5" dia.................................65.00
Apple, bowl, mixing; #9, ribbed, 5x9" 85.00

Apple, bowl, mixing; #64, 5x7½" dia...60.00
Apple, canister, #72, lg, 9½x7" dia..500.00
Apple, casserole, #18, French hdl, 4x8" 225.00
Apple, coffeepot, #115, 9¼" 3,000.00
Apple, creamer, #62, 4¼x4½" 90.00
Apple, cruets, oil & vinegar; #126, w/lid, rare, 7", pr.............1,800.00
Apple, grease jar, #01, w/lid, 5½x5¼" 375.00
Apple, mug, #121, 3¾x3" 185.00
Apple, mug, #61, 3x3¾" 500.00
Apple, pitcher, #17, no ice lip, 8" 300.00
Apple, pitcher, refrigerator; squared shape, #69, 8"................550.00
Apple, plate, dinner; unmk bottom, 9½" 450.00
Apple, plate, divided; sm leaves, 10½" 2,000.00
Apple, platter, #31, 15" dia..350.00
Apple, shakers, hourglass shape, 4½", pr................................250.00
Apple, teapot, #112, 6" 1,500.00
Apple, tumbler, #56, 4½" 1,000.00
Autumn Foliage, bowl, #106, 3½x10¾" dia.................................85.00
Autumn Foliage, sugar bowl, #98, w/lid, 4½"............................300.00
Blue/White Banded, casserole, 4½x8¾" dia.................................45.00
Blue/White Banded, pitcher, 7x7¾"..95.00
Brown-Banded, platter, #31, 15" dia..100.00
Butterfly, ice bucket, w/lid, 7¼"...800.00
Cherry, pitcher, #17, 8x8½" 275.00
Cherry, platter, #31, 15" dia..145.00
Cut Leaf Pansy, creamer & sugar bowl, open.............................175.00
Cut-Leaf Pansy, casserole, stick hdl, w/lid, 3¾x7½"...................125.00
Cut-Leaf Pansy, Dutch oven, w/lid, 7x10½" dia.........................175.00
Cut-Leaf Pansy, pie plate, 1½x9" dia......................................150.00
Cut-Leaf Pansy, plate, spaghetti; 8½"......................................40.00
Cut-Leaf Pansy, platter, bull's-eye pattern, 15" dia....................110.00
Dutch Tulip, cheese crock, #80, w/lid, 8x8½" dia.......................475.00
Kitch-N-Queen, bowl, mixing; ribbed, #9, 5x9" dia......................50.00
Kitch-N-Queen, cookie jar, w/lid, #503, 8¼x8¼" 225.00
Kitch-N-Queen, pitcher, ice-lip; #17, 8x8½" 200.00
Morning Glory, cookie jar, #95, w/lid, 10¾x7½" dia..................400.00
Old Pansy, bowl, spaghetti; #39, no blk band, 3x13" dia 80.00
Old Pansy, casserole, #3/19, w/lid, 5x9" dia...............................75.00
Old Pansy, cookie jar, cross-hatch pansy pattern, w/lid, 7½" 275.00
Old Pansy, pitcher, #17, 8x8½" 225.00
Old Pansy, platter, #49, 12" dia...85.00
Old Pansy, platter, cross-hatch pansy pattern, 15" dia 175.00
Raised Pansy, pitcher, 7x7¾"..225.00
Rooster, bowl, #05, w/lid, 4x5" dia..190.00
Rooster, bowl, spaghetti; 3x13" dia......................................3,500.00
Starflower, bowl, berry; 1½x5¾" dia..35.00
Starflower, ice bucket, w/lid, 7¼x7½" 185.00
Starflower, tumbler, #56, rnd sides, 4x3½" 275.00
Starflower (Green-on-Brown), cookie jar, #21, w/lid, 7½"..........125.00
Starflower (Pink-on-Black), casserole, w/lid, 4½x8¾" 125.00
Starlower, bowl, mixing; #04, ribbed, 2x4" dia............................65.00
Tear Drop, casserole, #18, French hdl, w/lid, 4x8" 250.00
Tear Drop, shakers, barrel shape, 4x2½" dia, pr.........................350.00
White Banded, bowl, 4½x6" dia...25.00
White Banded, pitcher, 7x7¾"..85.00
Woodgrain, plate, salad; #102, 7½" dia......................................25.00

Wave Crest

Wave Crest is a line of decorated opal ware (milk glass) patented in 1892 by the C.F. Monroe Co. of Meriden, Connecticut. They made a full line of items for every room of the house, but they are probably best known for their boxes and vases. Most items were hand painted with various levels of decoration, but more transfers were used in the later years prior to the company's demise in 1916. Floral themes are common; items with the scenics and portraits are rarer and more highly prized. Many pieces have ornately scrolled ormolu and brass handles, feet, and rims. Early pieces were unsigned (though they may have had paper labels); later, about 1898, a red banner mark was used. The black mark is probably from about 1902 to 1903. However, the glass is quite distinctive and has not been reproduced, so even unmarked items are easy to recognize. Our advisors for this category are Dolli and Wilfred Cohen; they are listed in the Directory under California. Note: There is no premium for signatures on Wave Crest. Values are given for hand-decorated pieces (unless noted 'transfer') that are *not* worn.

Ash receiver, roses on dk gr, 2½x6½" at hdls 385.00
Box, Baroque Shell, pointillism motif on pale pk, 7" dia.............515.00
Box, cuffs; floral/Collars & Cuffs, blown-out scrolls, 7½x7" dia .850.00
Box, Egg Crate, day lilies, orig metal hdw, sq, 6½x6½"...............795.00
Box, emb flowers, mill scene on lid, 4" dia.....................260.00
Box, glove; chrysanthemums, blown-out mold, scarce, 9¾x4¼x5½" ..2,750.00
Box, gondolas & canal street, 4¾" W 495.00
Box, lg robin on lid, sq, 5¾x6½" 3,500.00
Box, pansies on dk gr, 2⅜x4" 550.00
Box, Puffy w/Swirl base, florals, ftd, 5½x7"......................1,650.00
Box, Scroll, daisies on gr, 7x4x5" 1,250.00
Box, Scroll, floral on wht, 6x7¼" dia 1,000.00
Box, Swirl, blackberries on opal & lt turq w/gold, 5" 500.00
Box, Swirl, daisies w/leaves & branches, 4x7" dia......................400.00
Box, Swirl, floral on wht, 4x7" dia..............................400.00
Box, Swirl, lilacs, orig metal mts, 4½x6"......................600.00
Box, Swirl, lilacs w/gold & brn traceries, 4½x6" dia...................750.00
Box, Swirl, lily of the valley, mc on wht, unmk, 4½x6" dia 595.00
Broom holder, pansies w/wht beads on ivory, 10½x7".............2,100.00
Clock, floral molded scrolls, gilt fr, Pat Jan 13 1891, easel bk, 7"...2,500.00
Creamer & sugar bowl, Swirl, floral, SP mts, w/lid 500.00
Ferner, Puffy, floral on ivory, 4 lion-emb ft, +liner, 6¾" dia........515.00
Humidor, Swirl, daisies on pk to yel, souvenir, 7"..................850.00
Ice bucket, wild roses on bl, ornate lid & hdl, 6¼" dia 1,020.00
Lamp, boudoir; forget-me-nots on bl to wht, socket base, 7".......500.00
Letter holder, Puffy, silver/gold fern fronds on wht, ormolu rim, 6" L...495.00
Match holder, floral w/beading, 4 gold ft........................375.00
Pickle castor, Swirl, toadstools & flowers, SP fr......................550.00
Plaque, nasturtiums & buds on pk to wht, 10x8", +fr 4,250.00
Shakers, lav/bl swirls w/wht & bl stemmed daisies, pr, in Wilcox fr, 7x6"..275.00
Sugar shaker, Swirl, floral/rococo swags, 3x3¼" 585.00
Tray, floral, mc on bl to wht, mirror top, 4½x4" dia 675.00
Tray, pin; Egg Craft, floral on bl, 2-hdl ormolu rim, 2x3" 150.00
Tray, pin; floral, metal collar, 4".......................................100.00
Vase, roses on cylinder w/blown-out scrolls, 6¼" 250.00
Vase, Scroll, floral, metal hdls & base, 6".............................250.00
Vase, Scroll w/dainty flowers, 9½", NM......................................500.00

Weapons

Among the varied areas of specialization within the broad category of weapons, guns are by far the most popular. Muskets are among the earliest firearms; they were large-bore shoulder arms, usually firing black powder with separate loading of powder and shot. Some ignited the charge by flintlock or caplock, while later types used a firing pin with a metallic cartridge. Side arms, referred to as such because they were worn at the side, include pistols and revolvers. Pistols range from early single-shot and multiple barrels to modern types with cartridges held in the handle. Revolvers were supplied with a cylinder that turned to feed a fresh round in front of the barrel breech. Other firearms include shotguns, which fired round or

conical bullets and had a smooth inner barrel surface, and rifles, so named because the interior of the barrel contained spiral grooves (rifling) which increased accuracy. For further study we recommend *Modern Guns, Fifteenth Edition*, by Russell Quertermous and Steve Quertermous, available at your local bookstore. Our advisor for this category is Steve Howard; he is listed the Directory under California. Unless noted otherwise, our values are for examples in excellent condition. See also Militaria.

Key:
bbl — barrel	mod — modified
cal — caliber	oct — octagon
conv — conversion	O/U — over/under
cyl — cylinder	p/b — patch box
f/l — flintlock	perc — percussion
ga — gauge	/s — stock
hdw — hardware	Spec O — Special Order
mag — magazine	

Carbines

Burnside Civil War, 54 cal, 21" bbl, military sights, G 775.00
Gallager's Pat perc, 22" rnd bbl, walnut/s, p/b.............................990.00
Saganor Model M-1 by Inland, 30 cal, 18" bbl, military sights, G ...400.00
Sharps 1853, 52 cal perc, slanting breech, 21½" rnd bbl, EX ..1,875.00
Sharps 1853 John Brown, 52 cal, 21½" bbl, military sights, G...1,350.00
Spencer Civil War, 52 cal, 22" bbl, military sights, VG working ..1,800.00
Spencer Model 1865, walnut/s, steel hdw w/saddle ring, 20" bbl ..1,100.00
Winchester Model 54, 30/06 cal, pistol-grip/s, 30" bbl, VG........425.00
Winchester Model 92, 32 cal, walnut/s, G 550.00
Winchester Model 1894 Saddle Ring, 32/40 cal, 20" bbl, full mag, VG...650.00

Muskets

Buell Model 1808 f/l, 69 cal, 42" rnd bbl, poor reconv, G-...........700.00
European fl, 70 cal, 42¾" bbl, full military/s, ramrod, VG.......1,200.00
Harper's Ferry Model 1816 type III conv, 42" rnd bbl, 1837 on lock, EX .1,265.00
Maubeuge f/l, 70 cal, 44¾" bbl, full-length/s, ca 1763-66, G...1,800.00
Middletown f/l, walnut/s, eng silver thumbpc inlay, 42" rnd bbl, 58"..2,100.00
Pottsdam, perc, 75 cal, 41" rnd bbl, inspectors mks, 56¾"..........440.00
Starr US Model 1816 f/l, 69 cal, 42" rnd bbl, 1831 on lock, EX..1,925.00
T Franch f/l, 59 cal, 42" bbl, full military/s, rpl ramrod, G 500.00
US Bridesburg 1861 f/l, 58 cal, 40" bbl, full mlitary/s, G.............850.00
US Model 1816 conv by Remington Arms dtd 1857, 69 cal, 42" bbl, G...600.00
US Philadelphia 1861 perc, walnut/s, eagle on lock, 3A 30 on bbl, 56".....575.00
US Springfield Model 1817 re-conv f/l, 69 cal, 42" bbl, G..........500.00

Pistols

A Waters Model 1837 f/l, 54 cal, 8½" bbl, ⅔/s, G 1,100.00
Amers Model 1814 Navy perc dtd 1845, 54 cal, 6" bbl, full/s, G...650.00
Colt Mk IV Series 80, 45 ACP cal, 5" bbl, rampant Colt on grips, M.475.00
Colt Model 1908 Pocket, 25 ACP cal, 2" bbl, hard rubber grips, VG..325.00
Colt Super 38, 38 Super cal, 5" bbl, wood grips........................1,650.00
Derringer perc, walnut/s, NP hdw, 1½" bbl, 4¾".....................2,975.00
H Aston & Co perc, brass hdw, lock dtd 1851, 14½", EX..........575.00
Mauser Made Colt 1911, 45 cal, 11.25MM, 5" bbl, wood grips, M...7,000.00
S North 1819 f/l (reconv), 54 cal, 10" bbl, full length/s, VG......750.00
Sharpe f/l, 54 cal, 9" mk brass bbl, full/s w/ramrod, VG 375.00
Smith & Wesson 1913, 35ACP cal, wood grips, 3½" bbl...............325.00
Smith & Wesson 2nd Single Shot, 22LR cal, smooth wood grips, 8" bbl, G...425.00
Stevens Diamond #43 Single Shot, 22 cal, 6" bbl, wood grips....375.00
T Ketland KY f/1, curly maple/s, steel hdw, 5½" oct bbl, 10", G ...600.00
Tower Military f/l, 69 cal, 9" bbl, full/s w/ramrod, VG.................900.00
US H Aston 1843 perc, 54 cal, 8½" bbl, ⅔/s w/brass hdw, G 350.00

Revolvers

Colt Bisley Model, 44/40 cal, 5½" bbl, Colt rubber grips, G ...**1,450.00**
Colt Buntline Special, 45 LC cal, 10" bbl, wood grips, G **800.00**
Colt frontier 6-Shooter, 44/40 cal, 7½" bbl, wood grips, G- **2,000.00**
Colt Model 1860 Civilian Perc, 44 cal, 8" bbl, wood grips, G.**1,100.00**
Colt New Service Target, 44 Russian cal, 7½" bbl, cvd grips, VG...**1,600.00**
Colt 1849 Pocket, 31 cal, eng cyl/5" oct bbl, brass guard, EX..**2,200.00**
Colt 1849 Pocket, 31 cal, faint cyl scene, 5" oct bbl, 10", EX.....**660.00**
Colt 1860 Army, 44 cal, eng cyl scene, 8" bbl, 14", EX..............**825.00**
Colt 1860 Army, 44 cal, eng naval scene, 8" bbl, 14⅜", EX....**1,750.00**
Colt 1860 Army, 44 cal, 8" bbl, smooth wood grips, G **975.00**
Colt 1861 Navy, 36 cal, 7½" bbl, smooth wood grips, rstr NP....**950.00**
Colt 1862 Police, 26 cal, 5⅜" bbl, brass hdw, walnut grips, EX ..**715.00**
Colt 1862 Police, 36 cal, fluted cyl, 4½" bbl, 9½"......................**600.00**
Remington New Model Army, 44 cal, old gold-filled eng on 8" oct bbl...**715.00**
Savage Revolving Firearms, 36 cal perc, 7⅛" oct bbl, 6-shooter, EX....**600.00**
Smith & Wesson #2 Army (Civil War era), 32 rimfire cal, 6" bbl, G-..**500.00**
Smith & Wesson 2nd Double-Action, 44 Russian cal, 5" bbl, G.**450.00**
Smith & Wesson 2nd Model 38 Single-Action, 38 S&W cal, 3¼" bbl, VG.**225.00**
Smith & Wesson 2nd Schofield Single Action, 45 cal, 7" bbl.**2,600.00**
Smith & Wesson 3rd Safety, 38 S&W cal, pearl grips, 3¼" bbl, G..**175.00**

Rifles

Ashmore KY, curly maple/s w/silver inlay, eagle cheek pc, 55" oct bbl..**2,750.00**
Bedford Co f/l att J Stoudenour, curly maple/s, eng pb, 55" **1,350.00**
Colt Burgess, 44-40 cal, lever action/full magazine, 26" oct bbl, 43" ..**4,675.00**
Colt Lightning, 44-40 cal, slide action, full mag, 26" oct bbl ..**2,750.00**
DB Buck Walter long perc, curly maple/s, 39" oct bbl, 54" **600.00**
Femington Fieldmaster Model 121, 22 cal, pump action, 26" bbl..**275.00**
G Honaker perc, curly maple/s, brass hdw, p/b, 36¾" oct bbl, 52".**1,450.00**
HM Quackenbush, 22 cal single shot, later chrome-plating, 33".**220.00**
J Vincent & Son OH half/s perc, silver mts, cap box, 36 oct bbl, EX..**5,750.00**
Manton on lock plate, curly maple half/s, 34" oct bbl, 50½", EX..**600.00**
Mauser Model 1898 Military, 8 mm cal, 24" bbl, full-length/s **675.00**
MRJ Culle f/l military, curly maple/s, 44¾" rnd bbl, 60" **550.00**
New England f/l fowler, cherry/s, brass hdw, 53½" rnd bbl, 70" ..**990.00**
OH perc, curly maple half/s, eng p/b, 37¼" oct bbl, 53", G **500.00**
Remington Model 8, 32 cal, ramp-front sight w/bead, 22" bbl, G...**150.00**
Remington Model 14, 32 cal, pistol-grip/s, 22" bbl, G.................**125.00**
Remington Model 1917 Military by Eddystone, 30/06 cal, 26" bbl.**425.00**
Russian Moisin-Nagant Military, 7.62 Russian cal, full/s, 29" bbl.**260.00**
Snaphaunce, shaped pistol grip/s, wrought iron mechanism, 49" bbl..**330.00**
Springfield Allin Conv Model 1866, 50 cal center fire, 32⅝" bbl, G.**550.00**
Springfield M-1 Garand, 30/06 cal, 24" bbl, military sights **500.00**
T Kentland long f/l, cherry/s, brass hdw, 43½" oct bbl, 59" **1,450.00**
TN long style, 37 cal perc, curly maple/s, cap box, 41" oct bbl, 58" ...**1,650.00**
Winchester Model 52 Target, 22 LR cal, 28" med weight bbl, G ..**300.00**
Winchester Model 1895 Deluxe Take-Down, 30/03 cal, 24" bbl, XXX wood/s..**3,700.00**
Winchester 70 Post-64 Sporting, 375 H&H magnum cal, 24" bbl, NM.**475.00**

Shotguns

Browning A-5 Magnum, 12 ga, 32" ventilated ribbed bbl, full choke, G...**600.00**
Browning BT 99 Single-Bbl, 12 ga, 32" ventilated ribbed bbl, M...**525.00**
Browning Citori Grade VI Lightning Field w/eng, O/U, 45" ..**1,850.00**
H Scherping Dbl-Bbl, 16 ga, 30" fluid-steel bbls, cyl choke, G ..**1,000.00**
Hopkins & Allen Dbl-Bbl, 12 ga, 30" fluid-steel bbls, full choke.**300.00**
Ithaca Grade 4 Dbl-Bbl, 12 ga, 30" Damascus bbls, str-grip/s, G.**725.00**
Remington Model 870, 16 ga, 28" bbl, mod choke, G **150.00**
Remington Model 1100, 12 ga, 26" ventilated ribbed bbl, skeet choke ..**250.00**
Remington Model 1900 Dbl Bbl, 12 ga, field grade, 30" bbls, VG **315.00**
Rex Belgium-Made Dbl-Bbl Hammer, 16 ga, 29½" fluid-steel bbls, G..**200.00**

Stevens Model 18, 410 ga, 24" bbl, full choke, pistol-grip/s **100.00**
W&C Scott Dbl-Bbl, 12 ga, 30" bbls, full/mod chokes, pistol-grip/s, G ..**1,000.00**
Winchester Model 12, 16 ga, 28" plain bbl, mod choke, G.........**200.00**
Winchester Model 1400, 12 ga, 28" ventilated ribbed bbl **150.00**

Swords

All swords listed below are priced 'with scabbard,' unless otherwise noted.

Ames NCO US M1840, dk blade, faint inspector's mks, EX.......**175.00**
Civil War US M1850 foot officer, red patina on brass, EX.........**345.00**
Collins, bright blade, brass hdl, ca 1861, 28½", EX....................**275.00**
European foot artillery, unmk, 19th, EX....................................**260.00**
Imperial Navy Landing Force officer's, 34⅝" blade.....................**430.00**
US M1860 Cavalry, unmk, inspector's mks.................................**230.00**
US NCO M1850 Militia, ivory grips, etched blade, 37", EX.......**150.00**
US Staff & Field Officer's M 1860, single counter guard, no wire, VG.**150.00**

Miscellaneous

Cartridge box, leather w/brass US oval plate on front, 1860s, 8x7"...**600.00**
Flintlock powder tester, walnut grip w/eng, 1860s, 5¾" **450.00**

Weather Vanes

The earliest weather vanes were of handmade wrought iron and were generally simple angular silhouettes with a small hole suggesting an eye. Later, copper, zinc, and polychromed wood with features in relief were fashioned into more realistic forms. Ships, horses, fish, Indians, roosters, and angels were popular motifs. In the nineteenth century, silhouettes were often made from sheet metal. Wooden figures became highly carved and were painted in vivid colors. E.G. Washburne and Company in New York was one of the most prominent manufacturers of weather vanes during the last half of the century. Two-dimensional sheet metal weather vanes are increasing in value due to the already heady prices of the full-bodied variety. Originality, strength of line, and patina help to determine value. When no condition is indicated, the items listed below are assumed to be in excellent condition.

Key: f/fb — flattened full body

Arrow, iron w/gr rpt on tip & feathers, new base, 39" L **935.00**
Banner, copper w/zinc arrow point, att J Howard & Co, 7¾x34"...**3,175.00**
Banner, gilt copper, pierced initial C, w/stand, 25x39" **3,750.00**
Banner, spire & ball finial, sheet copper, verdigris, 21x48"......**2,400.00**
Banner, zinc & sheet copper, verdigris w/gilt traces, 22x40"......**2,200.00**
Bannerette arrow, cut sheet copper, verdigris/gilt traces, 17x24".**635.00**
Bannerette w/scrolled & circular elements, CI, on stand, 79x51".**1,175.00**
Blackhawk horse, att J Harris & Son Boston, worn gilt, 26x19"..**3,500.00**
Blackhawk sulky w/directionals, J Nield 90, EX patina, 20x32" ..**1,000.00**
Bull, molded copper w/verdigris, 19th C, 18x30", VG...........**11,000.00**
Cow, copper full body w/cast zinc head, gilt traces, 25x43" ...**14,100.00**
Cow, copper w/gold traces & EX patina, rstr bullet holes, 15x28"+base.**10,450.00**
Cow, copper/zinc, realistically molded, 12" H, on iron rod **5,000.00**
Dog, sheet copper silhouette, verdigris, w/directionals, 26".........**700.00**
Eagle, copper w/cast zinc head, wings wide, CI directionals, 20" H...**1,525.00**
Eagle, gilt copper, full body, wings wide, on sphere, 19x18"....**1,265.00**
Eagle, sheet iron silhouette w/strap reinforcements, 35x38"....**2,250.00**
Fire wagon w/driver & 2 horses, pnt copper, Cushing, 29x40".......**15,275.00**
Fox, sheet copper w/molded zinc head, gilt traces, w/stand, 15x29".**4,700.00**
Horse, cast zinc/copper, dk patina/verdigris, att J Howard, 20x25"..**17,625.00**

Horse, CI, full body, sheet-iron tail, Rochester Ironworks, 25½" L .25,850.00
Horse, Hackney; copper/zinc, full body, old pnt/verdigris, 22x32" ..5,000.00
Horse & rider, sheet copper, verdigris, att AL Jewell, 38x28" .19,550.00
Horse & rider, sheet iron w/riveted patch, bullet holes, 14x33"..880.00
Horse running, copper, f/fb, EX patina, 18x31" 2,350.00
Horse running, copper, full body, gilt traces, 17x30" 3,400.00
Horse running, copper, full body, verdigris, 23x42" 5,000.00
Horse running, copper & zinc, full body, silver/gilt traces, 19x33"..2,500.00
Horse running, copper full body, zinc head, verdigris, 19x26" .2,300.00
Horse running, copper w/cast zinc head, verdigris, rprs, 30" L .1,000.00
Horse running, copper w/verdigris, att Harris, 19x32½"+stand.3,000.00
Horse running, copper/zinc, Ethan Allen, AJ Harris, 20x30", EX ..5,000.00
Horse running, zinc w/verdigris, old layered pnt, hollow, 16x23" .935.00
Horse-drawn fire wagon, copper w/brushed verdigris, 20th C, 43" L...770.00
Quill pen, iron & copper, regilded/rpr, att LW Cushing & Sons, 34x37"..2,500.00
Rooster, copper, f/fb, verdigris/gilt, att Cushing, 28" 25,850.00
Rooster, copper, full body w/molded sheet details, verdigris, 22x16"...865.00
Rooster, copper & zinc w/gilt, full body, EX details, 37x26" 5,250.00
Rooster, copper w/verdigris & gilt traces, bullet holes, 21x23"..2,875.00
Rooster, pine w/3-color pnt, feather cvg, naturalistic, 1875, 27"..2,100.00
Rooster, sheet iron, weathered pnt/rust, 22x21"..........................800.00
Rooster, sheet metal, gilded, 1860 pierced in arrow feathers, 26"..2,350.00
Rooster, zinc body, copper tail & ft, verdigris w/gilt, 13x12" .11,750.00
Rooster, zinc/copper, att Howard, f/fb, verdigris w/red pnt trim, 30"..16,450.00
Rooster crowing, sheet metal, old silver rpt, OH, 21"+stand 475.00
Rooster crowing on arrow, sheet iron, red pnt, pitting, 20x34"...600.00
Sailing ship w/19 sails, copper w/verdigris, sgn Felix, 1950s, 60x67"..1,150.00
Soldier & cannon, flat metal w/mc pnt, brd base, 21x14", VG .6,325.00
Stag, copper w/cast head & antlers, att Washburne, EX patina, 24"..5,700.00
Stag leaping, molded copper, old regilting, 18x22"...................5,300.00
Sword, molded copper, spire finial, verdigris, 23", +stand........2,500.00

Weaving

Early Americans used a variety of tools and a great amount of time to produce the material from which their clothing was made. Soaked and dried flax was broken on a flax brake to remove waste material. It was then tapped and stroked with a scutching knife. Hackles further removed waste and separated the short fibers from the longer ones. Unspun fibers were placed on the distaff on the spinning wheel for processing into yarn. The yarn was then wound around a reel for measuring. Three tools used for this purpose were the niddy-noddy, the reel yarn winder, and the click reel. After it was washed and dyed, the yarn was transferred to a barrel-cage or squirrel-cage swift and fed onto a bobbin winder.

Today flax wheels are more plentiful than the large wool wheels since they were small and could be more easily stored and preserved. The distaff, an often-discarded or misplaced part of the wheel, is very scarce. French spinners from the Quebec area painted their wheels. Many have been stripped and refinished by those unaware of this fact. Wheels may be very simple or have a great amount of detail, depending upon the owner's ethnic background and the maker's skill.

Distaff, cvd wood w/mc floral, Norwegian, dtd 1909, 34"............175.00
Flax break, Scandanavian ceremonial pc w/tulips, 24" 85.00
Hatchel, wooden base w/old orange-red, bands mk JD IC 1915, 5x15x3" .140.00
Loom, walnut table-top type, old dry finish, 12¼x16x15", VG.....85.00
Swift, walnut/maple, trn base, oak screw, rpr, 19½" 220.00
Wheel, child's treadle w/wrought-iron hdw, orig pnt, 23" 330.00
Wheel, mixed hardwoods, missing spindle, dtd 1833 on side, 37x29"...150.00
Wheel, mixed hardwoods, orig red wash, dbl ft pedals, 55".........550.00
Wheel, trn maple & oak w/wrought hdw, complete, 37".............235.00
Yarn winder, cvd wooden yoke & red milk pnt, 27" 85.00
Yarn winder, maple, 4 arms on shaft w/counter, 19th C, 41".........70.00

Webb

Thomas Webb and Sons have been glassmakers in Stourbridge, England, since 1837. Besides their fine cameo glass, they have also made enameled ware and pieces heavily decorated with applied glass ornaments. The butterfly is a motif that has been so often featured that it tends to suggest Webb as the manufacturer. Our advisor for this category is Don Williams; he is listed in the Directory under Missouri. See also specific types of glass such as Alexandrite, Burmese, Mother of Pearl, and Peachblow.

Cameo

Bowl, floral, wht on Prussian Blue, 2½x5" 650.00
Bowl, morning glories & vines, red on frost, 2½x6" 400.00
Perfume, flowers & butterflies, red & wht on citron, ball form, 6" ..2,700.00
Perfume, fuchsia, wht/red/citron, ball form, 6" 4,600.00
Perfume, Ivory, 2 cloverleaf panels w/flowers, ball form, 4½" .1,050.00
Perfume, lay down; swan head, wht to citron, #1109, 5¾" L .5,000.00
Perfume, lay down; vines w/root system/butterfly, wht on citron, 11" L...2,200.00
Perfume, lay down; water lilies, wht on red, teardrop shape, 3½" L.4,200.00
Perfume, lily of the valley, wht on red, ball shape, 5"...............3,800.00

Rose bowl, floral with large butterfly in flight, white on bright cranberry, 4½x5", $800.00. (Photo courtesy Julia's Auction Company, Fairfield, Maine)

Rose bowl, roses, wht on pk, spherical, 1⅜" 1,100.00
Vase, allover floral/fruit, 4-layer, Tiffany/Paris 1889 mk, 9" ...20,500.00
Vase, allover Persian motif, yel/wht/bl on raisin, 4½" 3,750.00
Vase, Asiatic lilies, wht on sapphire bl, shouldered, ped ft, 5½" .750.00
Vase, branches/leaves, rainbow tones on wht w/citron, dbl gourd, 6"..1,400.00
Vase, cabbage roses, wht on red satin, 10" 1,900.00
Vase, floral, wht on citron, ovoid w/flared neck, 5" 400.00
Vase, floral, wht on yel shaded to salmon, 4¾"............................525.00
Vase, hawthorne, red/wht on citron, bulbous w/slim neck, 5"..2,500.00
Vase, intricate floral, bk: 2 bees/butterfly, wht on bl, 8"...........1,500.00
Vase, Ivory, florals, elephant head hdls at neck, wide base, 6x6" ..2,250.00
Vase, Ivory, simple floral/leaf decor, ruffled cupped rim, 3¾" 625.00
Vase, passion flowers/butterfly, 2 colors on citron, ped ft, 6".......800.00
Vase, roses/leaves, wht/red/citron, sgn Tiffany & Co 1889, 7½"...3,300.00

Miscellaneous

Compote, ruby w/clear stem, threaded ft/ruffled, Pat, 5½x8½"...600.00
Jam jar, Dmn Quilt MOP, cased raspberry, cylindrical, to hdl: 6"....400.00
Pitcher, yel/pk opal vertical stripes on clear, bulb w/can neck, 6" ...225.00
Sweetmeat, heavy gold florals on aqua, SP lid/etc, 5x3⅜" 300.00
Vase, bl mirror irid (Webb Bronze), shouldered, 6½" 275.00
Vase, gray-brn to dk brn w/wht int, gold foliage cascade, bulbous, 7"...400.00
Vase, rainbow (red/yel/bl) w/diagonal ribs, gold branch/butterfly, 14"..400.00
Vase, Swirl, pk/rose/yel stripes on frost, rnd w/stick neck, 7½x5".425.00
Vase, yel to lt yel satin, elongated teardrop shape, long neck, 11" ..285.00

Wedgwood

Josiah Wedgwood established his pottery in Burslem, England, in

1759. He produced only molded utilitarian earthenwares until 1770 when new facilities were opened at Etruria for the production of ornamental wares. It was there he introduced his famous Basalt and Jasperware. Jasperware, an unglazed fine stoneware decorated with classic figures in white relief, was usually produced in blues, but it was also made in ground colors of green, lilac, yellow, black, or white. Occasionally three or more colors were used in combination. It has been in continuous production to the present day and is the most easily recognized of all the Wedgwood lines. Jasper-dip is a ware with a solid-color body or a white body that has been dipped in an overlay color. It was introduced in the late 1700s and is the type most often encountered on today's market.

Though Wedgwood's Jasperware was highly acclaimed, on a more practical basis his improved creamware was his greatest success, due to the ease with which it could be potted and because its lighter weight significantly reduced transportation expenses. Wedgwood was able to offer 'chinaware' at affordable prices. Queen Charlotte was so pleased with the ware that she allowed it to be called 'Queen's Ware.' Most creamware was marked simply 'WEDGWOOD.' ('Wedgwood & Co.' and 'Wedgewood' are marks of other potters.) From 1769 to 1780, Wedgwood was in partnership with Thomas Bentley; artwares of the highest quality may bear the 'Wedgwood & Bentley' mark indicating this partnership. Moonlight Lustre, an allover splashed-on effect of pink intermingling with gray, brown, or yellow, was made from 1805 to 1815. Porcelain was made, though not to any great extent, from 1812 to 1822. Bone china was produced before 1822 and after 1872. These types of wares were marked 'WEDGWOOD' (with a printed 'Portland Vase' mark after 1872). Stone china and Pearlware were made from about 1820 to 1875. Examples of either may be found with a printed or impressed mark to indicate their body type. During the late 1800s, Wedgwood produced some fine parian and majolica. Creamware, hand painted by Emile Lessore, was sold from about 1860 to 1875. From the twentieth century, several lines of lustre wares — Butterfly, Dragon, and Fairyland (designed by Daisy Makeig-Jones) — have attracted the collector and, as their prices suggest, are highly sought after and admired.

Nearly all of Wedgwood's wares are clearly marked. 'WEDGWOOD' was used before 1891, after which time 'ENGLAND' was added. Most examples marked 'MADE IN ENGLAND' were made after 1905. A detailed study of all marks is recommended for accurate dating. See also Majolica.

Key:
WW — WEDGWOOD   WWMIE — WEDGWOOD Made in England
WWE — WEDGWOOD England

Bidet, Queen's Ware, no decor, shaped w/flat rim, early 19th C, 18" ...120.00
Biscuit jar, Jasper, crimson, oak leaves, acorn finial, ca 1920, 8" ...2,250.00
Biscuit jar, Jasper, dk bl, berries/birds, SP rim, WWE, 5¼" 635.00
Bottle, barber; Basalt, florals/rams' heads, w/lid, WW, 10⅛"....1,000.00
Bough pot, Jasper, dk bl, flowering pots, w/lid, WW, 6⅛"........1,100.00
Bough pot, Queen's Qare, brn slip floret band on yel, w/lid, WW, 5"..2,115.00
Bowl, Basalt, arabesque florals, hdls, oval, WW, 6¾"..............1,175.00
Bowl, Basalt, Etruscan & laurel bands, WW, rstr, 12" 4,700.00
Bowl, Basalt, Keith Murray, ca 1940, 6½" 1,000.00
Bowl, Basalt, palmette band, Rosso Antico loop hdls, WW, 9¼", NM..600.00
Bowl, Caneware, appl grapevines, wht on smear glaze, WW, 10⅞"....500.00
Bowl, Drabware, leaf mold, ca 1820, 7"..................................650.00
Bowl, Dragon Lustre, MOP int, ca 1920, wear, 5½"..................300.00
Bowl, Dragon Lustre, MOP int, Z4829, ca 1920, 9½"................650.00
Bowl, Dragon Lustre, MOP int, 3 Jewel design, ca 1920, 7"....1,400.00
Bowl, Dragon Lustre, octagonal, WWMIE, Z4829, 2¾" H.........200.00
Bowl, Fairyland Lustre, elves, MOP int, Z4968, ca 1920, 4½".4,400.00
Bowl, Jasper, Dancing Hours, lav, 1961, 8"...................................265.00
Bowl, Jasper, lt bl, bacchanalian boys, ftd, ca 1785, 8⅞" 7,000.00
Bowl, Lahore Lustre, animals & riders, ca 1920, 8".................3,300.00
Bowl, Queen's Ware, HP figures in landscape, ftd, ca 1865, 4⅛"...415.00

Bowl, Queen's Ware, no decor, central bail hdl, WW, 13" 700.00
Brooch, Jasper, dk bl, Poor Maria, cut steel mts, ca 1800, 3".......585.00
Bust, Basalt, Aristotle, rstr, WW, 7¾" 585.00
Bust, Basalt, Socrates, WW, rstr, 7¾" 585.00
Bust, Carrara, Byron, EW Wyon, ca 1855, 15½" 880.00
Bust, Carrara, Lord Zetland, ca 1868, rpr, 19¾" 1,000.00
Butter tub, Jasper, lt bl, foliate borders, w/lid, WW, 3¼" ...1,000.00
Candle vases, Variegated Agate, foliate hdl/swags, ca 1775, 9½", pr..2,235.00
Candlesticks, Basalt, Juno & Ceres figural w/gilt & bronze, 1880s, pr.2,350.00
Candlesticks, Basalt, sphinx form, WW, rstr, 10⅛", pr...........2,950.00
Candlesticks, Basalt, Triton male w/cornucopia sconce, WW, 11", pr...3,800.00
Candlesticks, Drabware, gold trim, ca 1840, 8", EX, pr 400.00
Candlesticks, Queen's Ware, acanthus leaf border, WW, 10¾", pr ..385.00
Canister, tea; Jasper, crimson, florets, ca 1920, 6½" 1,750.00
Chamberstick, Jasper, crimson, ca 1920, 2¾", EX 2,000.00
Chess figure, Jasper, bl, pawn as warrior, WW, 2⅜", EX 300.00
Coffee biggin, Drabware, floral, wht on smear glaze, 2 inserts, WW, 7".585.00
Coffee can & saucer, Jasper, lilac, foliate relief, WW, 4⅝" dia.1,300.00
Coffee can & saucer, Jasper, 3-color, medallions, WW, 5¼" dia ..1,400.00
Coffee can & saucer, Rosso Antico, blk Basalt hieroglyphs, WW, 5¼"...700.00
Coffee cup & saucer, Caneware, boys at play, WW, 5" dia.........475.00
Coffee set, Basalt, Robert Minkin, Design 63 group, ca 1964, 3-pc.....250.00
Coffeepot, Queen's Ware, emb shells w/gold, floral knop, WW, 9¼" 1,295.00
Coffeepot, Queen's Ware, Tea Party/Shepherd blk transfers, WW, 9½" ...700.00
Compote, Drabware, HP bird & flowers w/gilt, loop hdls, 1830s, 10¼"...385.00
Compote, Hummingbird Lustre, mottled orange int, ca 1920, 10¾"..2,115.00
Compote, Queen's Ware, ivy borders, WW, 5½", pr 1,115.00
Crocus pot, Agate, lid w/4 bulb reservoirs, WW, 6½", NM 1,880.00
Crocus pot, Basalt, hedgehog oval shape, WW, 9", +10" stand ..1,650.00
Custard cup, Jasper, bl, lattice relief, w/lid, WW, rstr, 2½".........350.00
Ewer, Basalt, foliage & laurel band, ca 1770s, rstr, 14½".........2,700.00
Figure, Basalt, King Charles I, ca 1910, 6⅜"...........................475.00
Figure, fallow deer, cream, Skeaping, 20th C, 7¼" 445.00
Figure, Interpretation, Joseph Before Pharoah, Carrara, ca 1860, 19"..3,500.00
Figure, Jasper, wht, Cupid, on bl Jasper drum base, WW, rstr, 7"..1,875.00
Figure, Jasper, wht, Hebe on bl jasper drum base, WW, rstr, 7" ..3,300.00
Figure, Kangaroo, cane color, Skeaping, 20th C, 8¾" 765.00
Figure, lion-form sphinx on plinth, rstr, WW, 7⅝", pr.............6,500.00
Figure, Queen's Ware, girl by basket vase, pk enamel, ca 1875, 6¾".265.00
Hot water pot, Caneware, hieroglyphs on brn band, WW, 8½"....3,800.00
Incense burner, Diceware, Jasper, 3-color, paw ft, WW, 5¼".....9,400.00
Ink pot, Caneware, globular, loop hdls, WW, 2⅛" 825.00
Inkstandish, Drabware, leaf tray w/3 pots, gold trim, WW, 9¼" L..700.00
Jug, Basalt, allover decor, satyr mask at hdl, WW, 7½" 1,650.00
Jug, Basalt, bacchanalian boys, Sybil finial, WW, 9¼".............2,115.00
Jug, Caneware, Domestic Employment scenes, missing lid, WW, 7"..1,000.00
Jug, Queen's Ware, emb feather edge, pear shape, WW, 7½"......825.00
Jug, Rosso Antiquo, blk/red/wht sphinx ea side, ca 1854, 8" ...1,750.00
Jug, tall; Jasper, crimson, grapes on vine, ca 1920, 4" 1,000.00
Jug, water; Caneware, vertical fluting, ca 1800, rstr, 6½" 475.00
Mantel plaque, Jasper, gr, acanthus leaves, key border, WW, 7x18" ...25,850.00
Medallion, Basalt, Philip of Macedon, oval, ca 1790, 4½"..........825.00
Medallion, Jasper, bl, Benjamin Franklin, ca 1775, 3¼"+gilt fr ...4,250.00
Medallion, Jasper, bl, Fame, ca 1775, 3¼", EX..........................500.00
Medallion, Jasper, bl, Geo Washington, oval, ca 1779, 4" 2,450.00
Medallion, Jasper, bl, Io Kissed by Jupiter..., ca 1780, 3¼".......1,175.00
Medallion, Jasper, bl, Wm Shakespeare, ca 1779, 4" 1,050.00
Medallion, Jasper, dk bl, classical relief, polished edge, WW, 2⅛"...265.00
Medallion, Jasper, lt bl, Sir Wm Hamilton, ca 1780, 4⅛"........3,800.00
Medallion, Jasper, 4-color, classical relief, WW, 2⅝".................700.00
Medallion, Jasper, 5-color, classical relief, 8-sided, WW, 2⅝".....880.00
Mug, Caneware, appl gray-gr fern & star, WW, 3⅜"................880.00
Mug, Caneware, boys at play, bbl form, WW, 3½"...................1,525.00
Pie dish, Caneware, crust decor, ca 1800, 8½".............................700.00

Plaque, Basalt, Claudius, self-fr, WW, 6¼" 1,750.00
Plaque, Basalt, Elizabeth I, self-fr, oval, ca 1779, 6⅝" 3,650.00
Plaque, Basalt, King Tutt, ca 1977, ltd ed, 8½x15⅜" 765.00
Plaque, Basalt, Vesputian, self-fr, WW, 6¼" 1,300.00
Plaque, Fairyland Lustre, Picnic by River, ca 1930, 4¾x10⅝" .7,650.00
Plaque, Jasper, lt bl, Eve, A Zinkeisen, ca 1924, 7¼"+modern fr..1,175.00
Plaque, Jasper, lt bl, Fall of Phaeton, ca 1977, 11¼x19¼", EX ...950.00
Plate, Caneware, Greek Key border, bl on wht, ca 1800, 8⅛" .1,650.00
Plate, Dog & Shadow, E Lessore, ca 1865, 9¼" 765.00
Plate, Rosso Antico, Basalt heiroglyphs, WW, 9¼" 700.00
Platter, Queen's Ware, exotic birds, WW, 15¼", NM 1,750.00
Platter, Queen's Ware, Japonica, ca 1880, 18½" 120.00
Rum kettle, Basalt, Antique pattern, Sybil finial, ca 1800, 10½" ..9,700.00
Rum pot, Basalt, bacchanalian boys, w/lid, rstr, WW, 8⅜" 1,525.00
Sardine box, Queen's Ware, floral transfer, fish finial, WW, 8¼" ..500.00
Sconce, peonies on pearlware w/gilt brass mts, 12-arm, 9th C, 7¾"..700.00
Tankard, Basalt, Bringing Home the Game, silver mts, WW, 5" ..2,250.00
Tankard, Basalt, oak leaves band, ca 1778, 4¼" 1,750.00
Tankard, Basalt, oak leaves band, silver mts, WW, 4⅞" 1,100.00
Tankard, Pearlware, blk floral transfer w/gold, WW, 5" 250.00
Tea bowl & saucer, Jasper, lilac, foliate relief, WW, 5¼" dia ...1,300.00
Tea tray, Jasper, bl, acanthus leaves, WW, 17½" 2,000.00
Tea tray, Jasper, bl, arabesque floral/sunflower center, WW, 13¾" ..600.00
Teapot, Caneware, classical females in reserves, WW, 5⅜", EX..585.00
Teapot, Drabware, bl fern & star relief, 1830s, 5⅛" 650.00
Teapot, floral sprays on pearlware, 18th C, 5½", EX 350.00
Teapot, Queen's Ware, Oriental decor, globular, ca 1770, 4¾" .1,175.00
Teapot, Rosso Antico, appl wht prunus, stick hdl, rstr, WW, 4⅝"..1,400.00
Teapot, Rosso Antico, Basalt hieroglyphs, crocodile finial, WW, 9"..1,000.00
Toast rack, Queen's Ware, gr linear decor, rectangular, WW, 7¼" ..265.00
Tureen, Japan pattern, scroll hdls, floral finial, ca 1882, 13"+tray..525.00
Tureen, Queen's Ware, scroll hdls, WW, +lid, stand & ladle 585.00
Tureen, sauce; Stoneware, wht smear glaze, shell finial, WW, 5¼".415.00
Vase, Basalt, central medallion, sphinx-head hdls, ca 1775, 13"..1,000.00
Vase, Basalt, laurel band, lions'-head hdls, ca 1775, 16½" 5,875.00
Vase, Basalt, male figure w/lyre, sphinx-head hdls, ca 1775, 13½"..2,235.00
Vase, Caneware, 4 bamboo canes form w/decor, WW, 10", NM..7,950.00
Vase, Diceware, Jasper, 3-color, classical relief, WW, rstr, 11½" ..1,400.00
Vase, Diceware, Jasper, 3-color, Dancing Hours, WW, 8¾" 2,000.00
Vase, Dragon Lustre, ca 1920, 10⅞"..9,400.00
Vase, Fairyland Lustre, Argus Pheasant, ca 1920, 9" 7,000.00
Vase, Fairyland Lustre, Candlemas, ca 1920, 7½" 9,400.00
Vase, Fairyland Lustre, Pillar design, Z4968, ca 1920, 13⅝"..11,165.00
Vase, Fairyland Lustre, Sycamore Tree, #2410, w/lid, 10" 5,250.00
Vase, Fish Lustre w/gold, Z4920, ca 1920, 8⅞" 1,850.00
Vase, Jasper, gr, classical relief, w/lid, WW, 13" 1,175.00
Vase, Jasper, lt bl, floral festoons/female masks, WW, 5½", EX...585.00
Vase, Marsden Art Ware, flowers & vines, bottle form, ca 1885, 13"...950.00
Vase, Marsden Art Ware, oranges on branches on lt bl, 1890s, 10½"..1,650.00
Vase, Portland, Jasper, blk, classical relief, ca 1900, 8" 450.00
Vase, Portland, Jasper, dk bl, classical figures, WW, 10¼" 1,100.00
Vase, potpourri; Terra Cotta, red slip borders on wht, WW, 4", NM ..1,650.00
Vase, Queen's Ware, floral swags, pierced trumpet form, WWE, 10¼"..950.00
Vase, Queen's Ware, game birds/flowers, loop hdls, ca 1862, 12", pr...3,525.00
Vase, Rosso Antico, Greek Key borders on blk, WW, 5⅞" 950.00
Vase, Terra Cotta, red slip borders on wht, rstr, WW, 6" 700.00
Vase, Victoria Ware, trophies w/in floral festoons, 1880s, 10⅛" ..2,250.00
Wall pocket, Moonlight Lustre, shell form, ca 1810, 9¾", EX 825.00

Weil Ware

Max Weil came to the United States in the 1940s, settling in California. There he began manufacturing dinnerware, figurines, cookie jars, and wall pockets. American clays were used, and the dinnerware was all hand decorated. Weil died in 1954; the company closed two years later. The last backstamp to be used was the outline of a burro with the words 'Weil Ware — Made in California.' Many unmarked pieces found today originally carried a silver foil label; but you'll often find a four-digit handwritten number series, especially on figurines. For further study we recommend *The Collector's Encyclopedia of California Pottery* by Jack Chipman (Collector Books).

Bowl, gr, leaf shape, 8x14"...30.00
Bowl, lug soup; Yellow Rose, 5⅛x6", set of 6 ....90.00
Bowl, vegetable; Malay Bambu, divided, oval, 10½" 40.00
Creamer, Malay Blossom, sq..15.00
Creamer, Mango 14.00
Cup & saucer, Brentwood 12.00
Cup & saucer, Malay Blossom, sq 12.00
Dish, Malay Blossom, divided, #29, 9½x5¾" 30.00
Figurine, lady in lt gr dress w/matching cap, holding flowers, 11½"..70.00
Figurine, lady in yel dress w/wht ribbons & bl bow, matching hat, 8" ...65.00
Flower holder, lady ice skater holding basket, 10"..........................65.00
Flower holder, lady in cream w/2 planters behind, #4051, 12" 70.00
Flower holder, lady in pk w/bl floral decor, lg bl hat, 9¼" 55.00
Flower holder, lady in purple floral dress, yel shawl, 11"..............115.00
Flower holder, lady in yel dress seated between 2 planters, #4028, 9"..65.00
Flower holder, lady in yel dress w/hands in muff, #4031, 10¼" 70.00
Flower holder, lady pushing cart, 8½"...35.00
Pitcher, Malay Bambu, 10", from $90 to 110.00
Planter, donkey w/cart, 8x11"...65.00
Plate, bread & butter; Malay Blossom, sq, 6".....................................8.00
Plate, Malay Blossom, sq, 9¾", from $18 to 21.00
Plate, salad; Brentwood, 8"..8.00
Plate, salad; Malay Blossom, sq, 7¾" 10.00
Saucer, Mango..3.50
Sugar bowl, Malay Blossom, w/lid...20.00
Teapot, Maylay Bambu, 5"..70.00
Tray, Malay Blossom, 13x9"..25.00
Tumbler, water; Malay Bambu, from $18 to 22.00
Vase, Malay Bambu, pinched rim, #1206, 10"................................60.00
Vase, Ming Tree, cylindrical w/slanted top, 11" 45.00
Vase, Ming Tree, sq, #966, 5¾"..40.00
Wall pocket, Oriental girl in bl seated w/flowered pot on ea side, 10" ..35.00

Weller

The Weller Pottery Company was established in Zanesville, Ohio, in 1882, the outgrowth of a small one-kiln log cabin works Sam Weller had operated in Fultonham. Through an association with Wm. Long, he entered the art pottery field in 1895, producing the Lonhuda Ware Long had perfected in Steubenville six years earlier. His famous Louwelsa line was merely a continuation of Lonhuda and was made in at least five hundred different shapes. Many fine lines of artware followed under the direction of Charles Babcock Upjohn, art director from 1895 to 1904: Dickens Ware (1st Line), under-glaze slip decorations on dark backgrounds; Turada, featuring applied ivory bands of delicate openwork on solid dark brown backgrounds; and Aurelian, similar to Louwelsa, but with a brushed-on rather than blended ground. One of their most famous lines was 2nd Line Dickens, introduced in 1900. Backgrounds, characteristically caramel shading to turquoise matt, were decorated by sgraffito with animals, golfers, monks, Indians, and scenes from Dickens novels. The work is often artist signed. Sicardo, 1902, was a metallic lustre line in tones of blue, green, or purple with flowing Art Nouveau patterns developed within the glaze.

Frederick Hurten Rhead, who worked for Weller from 1903 to mid-1904, created the prestigious Jap Birdimal line decorated with geisha girls, landscapes, storks, etc., accomplished through application of heavy slip forced through the tiny nozzle of a squeeze bag. Other lines to his credit are L'Art Nouveau, produced in both high-gloss brown and matt pastels, and 3rd Line Dickens, often decorated with Cruikshank's illustrations in relief. Other early artware lines were Eocean, Floretta, Hunter, Perfecto, Dresden, Etched Matt, and Etna.

In 1920 John Lessel was hired as art director, and under his supervision several new lines were created. LaSa, LaMar, Marengo, and Besline attest to his expertise with metallic lustres. The last of the artware lines and one of the most sought after by collectors today is Hudson, first made during the early 1920s. Hudson, a semimatt glazed ware, was beautifully artist decorated on shaded backgrounds with florals, animals, birds, and scenics. Notable artists often signed their work, among them Hester Pillsbury, Dorothy England Laughead, Ruth Axline, Claude Leffler, Sarah Reid McLaughlin, E.L. Pickens, and Mae Timberlake.

During the late 1920s, Weller produced a line of gardenware and naturalistic life-sized and larger figures of frogs, dogs, cats, swans, ducks, geese, rabbits, squirrels, and playful gnomes, most of which were sold at the Weller store in Zanesville due to the fragile nature of their designs. The Depression brought a slow, steady decline in sales, and by 1948 the pottery was closed.

Note: Several factors come in to play when evaluating a piece of Hudson. Subject matter, artist signature, and size are all important. Artist-signed florals from 5" to 7" range from $395.00 to $895.00; scenics and bud vases from 6" to 8" range from $2,500.00 to $5,000.00, with fine artwork from superior artists at the upper end of the scale. Pieces bearing the signatures of Mae Timberlake or Hester Pillsbury bring top prices.

Our advisor for this category is Mike Nickel; he is listed in the Directory under Michigan.

Alvin, dbl-bud vase, 6" 95.00
Ardsley, console set, bowl w/Iris frog 600.00
Ardsley, fan vase, 8" 200.00
Baldin, vase, apples, bl, 7x6" 400.00
Barcelona, vase, hdls, 14½" 700.00
Barcelona, vase, ogee form w/lg hdls, 6" 225.00
Besline, vase, 11" 600.00
Blossom, dbl vase, G-24, 12½" 200.00
Blue Drapery, candlestick/lamp base, 9½" 175.00
Blue Drapery, jardiniere & pedestal, 33½" 1,500.00
Blue Ware, jardiniere, 2 angels, 8½" H 400.00
Blue Ware, vase, 8½" 300.00
Bonito, vase, foliate spray, artist sgn NC, 10" 400.00
Bouquet, vase, 12" 400.00
Brighton, pheasant, 11½" L 800.00
Burntwood, vase, chickens, 9" 600.00
Cactus, series of figures, ea from $100 to 125.00
Cameo, basket, bl, 7½" 85.00
Cameo Jewel, umbrella stand, 22", from $1,250 to 1,500.00
Chengtu, vase, 12" 225.00
Claremont, candle holder, w/hdls, 8" 225.00
Claywood, bowl, floral, 2x3½" 65.00
Coppertone, pitcher, fish hdl, 7½" 2,500.00
Coppertone, trumpet vase, 4 frog heads at base, 12" 3,500.00
Coppertone, vase, cone shape, 8½" 400.00
Coppertone, vase, frog hdls, 8" 2,250.00
Cornish, vase, 10" 250.00
Darsie, vase, 9½" 100.00
Dickens II, vase, Chief Hollowhorn Bear, sgn AD, 13" 3,500.00
Dickens II, vase, hunting dog, sgn EL Pickens, 9" 2,500.00
Dickens III, vase, inscribed Bailey, 3 rim-to-shoulder hdls, slim, 9" ...1,050.00
Dickens III, vase, inscribed Carter, Dombey & Son, #12, 13" .1,250.00
Eocean (Late Line), vase, floral, sgn MT, 10½" 450.00

Etched Matt, vase, roses on thorn stems, 4-sided, 10½" 450.00
Ethel, vase, 9½" 300.00
Fairfield, vase, cherub band/fluted bottom, 8" 115.00
Flemish, jardiniere & pedestal, paneled w/floral band, 29½" 950.00
Flemish, tub, hdls, 4½" 115.00
Flemish, umbrella stand, stylized apple tree, 22" 1,750.00
Fleron, vase, 9" 200.00
Florala, wall pocket, 10" 225.00
Florenzo, vase, 7" 150.00
Floretta, vase, emb grapes on gray to wht, 5½" 250.00
Forest, basket, strong color & mold, 8½" 500.00
Forest, jardiniere, 8½" 450.00
Forest, vase, 13½" 400.00
Fruitone, vase, 6-panel, 8" 150.00
Glendale, dbl-bud vase, 7" 550.00
Glendale, vase, bird pr, eggs in nest, bulbous, 9" 2,000.00
Glendale, vase, lovebirds on branch, 8½" 950.00
Glendale, wall pocket, cornucopia form, 12½" 450.00
Gloria, ewer, G-12, 9" 150.00
Greora, strawberry pot, 8½" 350.00
Hobart, bowl, 2½x9", +2-nudes flower frog, 7½" 550.00
Ivory (Clinton Ivory), vase, leafy panels, 10" 85.00
Jap Birdimal, vase, geisha girl, sgn VMH, 13" 3,500.00
Jap Birdimal, vase, trees/etc, bl on gray, 13" 1,500.00
Jewel, vase, slim, 9" 500.00
Knifewood, jardiniere, allover daisies, 4-color, 8" 1,250.00
Knifewood, vase, peacock/trees, incurvate cylinder, 9" 1,250.00
L'art Nouveau, ewer, 14½" 600.00
L'art Nouveau, vase, ear of corn, 4½" 300.00
La Sa, vase, no scratches, 6" 375.00
Lamar, vase, no scratches, 8½" 450.00
Lavonia, figurine, girl w/skirt held wide, 7½" 300.00
Lorbeek, vase, 8" 200.00
Louella, vase, 9½" 115.00
Louwelsa, vase, floral branch, artist sgn, 11", from $300 to 350.00
Louwelsa, vase, man's portrait, sgn TTH, pillow form, 8", $1,250 to..1,500.00
Malverne, vase, 5½" 115.00
Mammy, teapot, figural Black lady, 8" 1,500.00
Manhattan, vase, 5½" 80.00
Marbleized, vase, 10½" 200.00
Marengo, vase, 8" 350.00
Marvo, pitcher, 8" 175.00
Melrose, basket, 10" 250.00
Mi-Flo, vase, M-8, 7" 150.00
Mirror Black, vase, 12" 200.00
Muskota, elephant, 7½x12½" 2,500.00
Muskota, nude on rock flower frog, 8" 700.00
Noval, bowl, 3½x8" 85.00
Paragon, vase, red, bulbous w/short collar neck, 7½" 450.00
Patricia, bowl, 3 duck heads at rim, wht, 3x7" 175.00
Pearl, bowl, 3x6" 140.00
Pearl, wall pocket, 8" 350.00
Pop-Eye dog, 4" (beware of forgeries) 500.00
Pop-Eye dog, 9½" 6,000.00
Pumila, vase, 9" 85.00
Ragenda, vase, red, spherical, 9" 395.00
Roba, vase, 13" 300.00
Roma, candlestick, 11½" 130.00
Roma, comport, 11" 150.00
Roma, console bowl, scalloped rim, appl roses, 4 sm ft, 4½x10½"..250.00
Roma, jardiniere, flower basket, 10½" H 325.00
Roma, wall pocket, floral on wht w/stripes, cornucopia form, 8½" ..200.00
Rosemont, vase, bluebird/flowering branch, ogee sides, 10" 600.00
Sabrinian, vase, sea horse hdls, 12" 550.00

Sabrinian, wall pocket, 8½" 700.00
Sabrinian, window box, 3½x9" 375.00
Senic, vase, S-8, 9½" 150.00
Silvertone, vase, butterflies, hdls, 12" 850.00
Suevo, vase, 3-color Indian design, flaring top, 8" 225.00
Turada, mug, #562/7, 6" 225.00
Tutone, vase, 15" 300.00
Velva, vase, 7½" 275.00
Voile, fan vase, 8x9" 200.00
Warwick, vase, 12" 250.00
White & Decorated, vase, floral shoulder, 9½" 250.00
Woodcraft, dbl-bud vase, 8" 150.00
Woodcraft, tankard, foxes, 12½" 1,500.00
Woodcraft, wall pocket, forking branch w/appl cherry cluster, 8" ...300.00
Woodcraft, wall pocket, open branches w/flowers & 2 birds, 14½x13" ...300.00
Zona, pitcher, red apples on ivory gloss, 6" 125.00

Western Americana

The collecting of Western Americana encompasses a broad spectrum of memorabilia. Examples of various areas within the mainstream would include the following fields: weapons, bottles, photographs, mining/railroad artifacts, cowboy paraphernalia, farm and ranch implements, maps, barbed wire, tokens, Indian relics, saloon/gambling items, and branding irons. Some of these areas have their own separate listings in this book. Western Americana is not only a collecting field but is also a collecting era with specific boundries. Depending upon which field the collector decides to specialize in, prices can start at a few dollars and run into the thousands.

Our advisor for this category is Bill Mackin, author of *Cowboy and Gunfighter Collectibles* (order from the author); he is listed in the Directory under Colorado.

Bit, nude lady, chased silver o/l..175.00
Bit, silver o/l w/lg silver rosettes, much eng, 1940s style, 9" 70.00
Blanket, Hudson Bay, 4-point Indian trade, orig tag, 1930s, 86x70" 130.00
Branding iron, hand-wrought iron, short style (carried on saddle), EX....50.00
Bridle, hitched horsehair & braided horse hide w/horsehair reins, 1930..1,900.00
Buggy seat, orig olive gr pnt w/gold & blk striping, 1880s, 14x41x20" ..300.00
Chaps, leather, traditional style w/brass studs, ca 1955, 39" 250.00
Cinch, horsehair, Whitman-Melbach, US Cavalry, 1917.............85.00
Holster, Heiser, tooled leather, dbl loop, early 1900s, VG+ 375.00
Horse skull, orig teeth, brn patina, excavated, 1900s, 23" 60.00
Quirt, blk & orange horsehair, finely hitched, 1920s, EX............550.00
Saddle, child's, Red Ranger tooled leather, padded seat, 1960, NM ..400.00
Saddle, SC Gallup Saddlery Co, ca 1900, EX 865.00
Saddle bags, leather w/buckles & straps, 1950s, 15½x8x2" 50.00

Western Pottery Manufacturing Company

This pottery was originally founded as the Denver China and Pottery Company; William Long was the owner. The company's assets were sold to a group who in 1905 formed the Western Pottery Manufacturing Company, located at 16th Street and Alcott in Denver, Colorado. By 1926, 186 different items were being produced, including crocks, flowerpots, kitchen items, and other stoneware. The company dissolved in 1936.

Seven various marks were used during the years, and values may be higher for items that carry a rare mark. Numbers within the descriptions refer to specific marks, see the line drawings. Prices may vary depending on demand and locale. Our advisors for this category are Cathy Segelke and Pat James; they are listed in the Directory under Colorado.

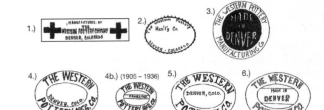

Churn, #2, hdl, 4-gal, M...75.00
Churn, #2, hdl, 5-gal, M...65.00
Churn, #2, no lid, 5-gal, G...80.00
Crock, #4, bail lip, 4-gal, G..55.00
Crock, #4, hdl, no lid, 8-gal, M.......................................90.00
Crock, #4, ice water; bl/wht sponge pnt, 3-gal, NM 30.00
Crock, #4, 6-gal, EX..72.00
Crock, #4b, 20-gal, M...200.00
Crock, #4b, 22x17½", 15-gal, NM.................................150.00
Crock, #5, bail lip, 1½-gal, M..45.00
Crock, #5, no lid, 6-gal, M..70.00
Crock, #6, wire hdl, 10-gal, NM....................................100.00
Crock, #6, 3-gal, M..40.00
Crock, #6, 4-gal, M..50.00
Crock, #6, 5-gal, NM..60.00
Foot warmer, #6, M...60.00
Jug, #6, brn/wht, 1-gal, EX...25.00
Jug, #6, brn/wht, 5-gal, M...75.00
Rabbit feeder, #1, EX...25.00
Rabbit waterer, #1, M...25.00

Western Stoneware Co.

The Western Stoneware Co., Monmouth, Illinois, was formed in 1906 as a merger of seven potteries: Monmouth Pottery Co., Monmouth, IL; Weir Pottery Co., Monmouth, IL; Macomb Pottery Co. and Macomb Stoneware Co., Macomb, IL; D. Culbertson Stoneware Co., Whitehall, IL; Clinton Stoneware Co., Clinton, MO; and Fort Dodge Stoneware Co., Fort Dodge, IA.

Western Stoneware Co. manufactured stoneware, gardenware, flowerpots, artware, and dinnerware. Some early crocks, jugs, and churns are found with a plant number in the Maple Leaf logo. Plants 1 through 7 turn up. In 1926 an artware line was introduced as the Monmouth Pottery Artware. One by one each branch of the operation closed, and today one branch remains. Western Stoneware Co. is still in operation in Monmouth, Illinois, on the site of the Weir Pottery Co. Our advisor for this category is Jim Martin; he is listed in the Directory under Illinois. See also Old Sleepy Eye.

Beehive jug, brn & wht, 1-gal.......................................100.00
Birdbath, burnt wood finish...200.00
Bowl, bl banded, w/advertising..85.00
Chicken waterer, 1-gal..125.00
Churn, flowers on side, 3-gal...200.00
Churn, Maple Leaf (plant 6) mk, 6-gal..........................250.00
Churn, Maple Leaf mk, mini......................................1,000.00
Churn, Maple Leaf mk, oval, 2-gal...............................175.00
Churn, Maple Leaf mk, 1-gal....................................1,200.00
Churn, Maple Leaf mk, 2-gal...200.00
Combinet, w/lid & hdl, mini..700.00
Crock, Maple Leaf mk, mini...700.00
Crock, Maple Leaf mk, 5-gal...60.00
Crock, Maple Leaf mk, 20-gal.......................................125.00
Crock, Maple Leaf mk, 60-gal....................................1,500.00
Custard cup, Colonial...350.00

Flowerpot/ashtray, Cardinal, red flowerpot clay, no glaze 150.00
Hot water bottle, pig, bl tint...225.00
Ice water cooler, bl sponge, w/lid & spigot, 4-gal..................1,500.00
Jar, Maple Leaf & oval mk, 2-gal 50.00
Jardiniere, Egret pattern, brushed gr 75.00
Jardiniere, Egyptian motif, brn-glazed int, 7" 75.00
Jug, Monmouth advertising, 1-qt...125.00
Lard jar, bl tint, w/lid 200.00
Monkey jug, brn & wht, 1-gal 200.00
Paperweight, Maple Leaf, gr & brn 55.00
Pitcher, Cattail, bl & wht, 1-qt..150.00
Shakers, 2nd Nat'l Bank, pr 30.00
Sugar jar, bl tint, w/lid..250.00
Vase, cvd/pnt leaves, bl matt, 16", EX 150.00
Vase, Etruscan pattern, gr & wht 45.00
Wall pocket, Egyptian, Burntwood, #312 ....60.00
Water cooler, Cupid, bl & wht..1,000.00
Water cooler, Egyptian motif, 9¼x11" 450.00
Water cooler, emb maple leaves, bl & wht, w/lid & spigot, 4-gal...2,000.00
Water cooler, Maple Leaf mk, no lid or spigot, 2-gal 400.00

Westmoreland

Originally titled the Specialty Glass Company, Westmoreland began operations in East Liverpool, Ohio, producing utility items as well as tableware in milk glass and crystal. When the company moved to Grapeville, Pennsylvania, in 1890, lamps, vases, covered animal dishes, and decorative plates were introduced. Prior to 1920 Westmoreland was a major manufacturer of carnival glass and soon thereafter added a line of lovely reproduction art glass items. High-quality milk glass became their speciality, accounting for about 90% of their production. Black glass was introduced in the 1940s, and later in the decade ruby-stained pieces and items decorated in the Mary Gregory style became fashionable. By the 1960s colored glassware was being produced, examples of which are very popular with collectors today. Early pieces were marked with a paper label; by the 1960s the ware was embossed with a superimposed 'WG.' The last mark was a circle containing 'Westmoreland' around the perimeter and a large 'W' in the center. The company closed in 1985, and on February 28, 1996, the factory burned to the ground.

Note: Though you may find pieces very similar to Westmoreland's, their Della Robbia has no bananas among the fruits relief. In the descriptions that follow, items in this pattern described as 'crystal with trim' refers to those pieces with the colored lustre stains.

For more information we recommend *Westmoreland Glass, the Popular Years*, by Lorraine Kovar (Collector Books). Our advisor for this category is Philip Rosso, Jr. He is listed in the Directory under Pennsylvania. See also Animal Dishes with Covers; Carnival Glass; Glass Animals.

Basket, English Hobnail/#555, crystal or milk glass, 9"................30.00
Basket, Pansy/#757, milk glass, split hdl.................................20.00
Bottle, oil; Paneled Grape, milk glass 30.00
Bowl, cranberry; English Hobnail, pk, 3"..............................12.50
Bowl, Doric, milk glass, ftd, crimped, 10½"...........................30.00
Bowl, Lotus/#1921, blk, rnd, lg 35.00
Bowl, nappy, Della Robbia, crystal w/appl color, 1-hdl, 6½" 35.00
Bowl, nappy, English Hobnail, pk, cupped, 8".........................30.00
Bowl, Paneled Grape/#1881, milk glass, plate-like, 10" 130.00
Bowl, relish; Old Quilt, milk glass, rnd, 3-part.........................35.00
Bowl, Wakefield, crystal w/red stain, flat, crimped, 12" 75.00
Bowl, wedding; milk glass w/any HP decor, lg 75.00
Box, chocolate; milk glass w/Roses & Bows, heart shape 325.00
Butter dish, English Hobnail, milk glass, w/lid, ¼-lb 25.00
Butter/cheese dish, Old Quilt, milk glass, rnd 45.00

Cake salver, Doric, milk glass, ftd, 11"...................................30.00
Candelabra, Lotus/#1921, any Mist color, 3-light, pr...................50.00
Candle holders, Paneled Grape/#1881, milk glass, 4", pr.............18.00
Candy container, mantel clock, Brandywine Blue, hollow, no mk...35.00
Candy dish, Beaded Grape/#1884, Brandywine Blue, w/lid, 3½" ..20.00
Compote, Della Robbia, crystal w/trim, flanged, 13" 135.00
Compote, sweetmeat; English Hobnail, pk, ball stem, 8" 35.00
Creamer, Beaded Edge, red trim, ftd 13.00
Cup & saucer, English Hobnail, milk glass or crystal 15.00
Decanter, Swirl & Ball, crystal...80.00
Dresser set, milk glass w/Roses & Bows, 4-pc 200.00
Egg tray, Paneled Grape/#1881, milk glass, w/center hdl, 12".......90.00
Goblet, water; Old Quilt/#500, Brandywine Blue or Golden Sunset, 8-oz...15.00
Ice tub, English Hobnail, amber or crystal, 5½" 40.00
Lamp, candle; Cameo, any color w/Beaded Bouquet, w/shade, mini ...50.00
Lamp, candle; Cameo, Crystal Mist w/Roses & Bows, w/shade, mini .55.00
Lamp, candle; Starlite, mc or ruby stained, 2-pc geometric shape.40.00
Lamp, electric; Dolphin 125.00
Lamp, fairy; Irish Waterford, any Mist w/HP flowers, low ft, 2-pc.50.00
Mayonnaise, Paneled Grape, milk glass, ftd, 4" 27.50
Novelty, butterfly, purple, caramel or green marbled, lg 50.00
Novelty, cardinal, ruby or any Mist color, solid.........................25.00
Novelty, egg on gold stand, blk glass (plain/blown/hollow)...........40.00
Novelty, egg trinket box, dk Blue Mist, w/wht cameo, w/lid 35.00
Novelty, Grandma's slipper, any Mist color 25.00
Novelty, owl toothpick holder, aqua, milk glass or pk, 3".............20.00
Novelty, robin, solid, 3¼" 15.00
Novelty, wren, pk or Smoke, 2½" 15.00
Pitcher, Paneled Grape, milk glass, 32-oz 35.00
Plate, Contrary Mule, Brandywine Blue opal, 7".......................42.50
Plate, dinner; Beaded Edge, milk glass w/red trim, 10½" 25.00
Plate, English Hobnail, pk, 8½"..15.00
Plate, Hearts, heart shape/#HP-1, any color w/Anniversary, 8"......20.00
Plate, Lattice Edge/#1890, dk Blue Mist, Mary Gregory style, 11" 65.00
Plate, salad; Della Robbia, crystal 15.00
Plate, wicker border, milk glass w/Christmas bouquet, 9" 50.00
Platter, Della Robbia, crystal w/trim, oval, 14".........................195.00
Punch bowl, Paneled Grape/#1881, milk glass, +base, ladle & 12 cups..400.00
Shakers, Paneled Grape, milk glass, ftd, sm, 4¼", pr 15.00
Sherbet, Della Robbia, crystal w/appl colors, low ft, 5-oz 22.00
Sugar bowl, Beaded Edge, milk glass, plain w/lid, #108 ....12.00
Tray, tidbit; Dolphin, Crystal Mist, center hdl 35.00
Tray, tidbit; English Hobnail, amber or crystal, 2-tier 22.50
Tray, tidbit; Paneled Grape/#1881, any Mist color w/daisies..........35.00
Tumbler, ginger ale; Della Robbia, crystal w/appl colors, 5-oz 25.00
Tumbler, iced tea; English Hobnail, crystal, sq ft, 11-oz...............15.00
Tumbler, Paneled Grape, milk glass, 8-oz 22.50
Vase, English Hobnail, amber or crystal, sq ft, 8".......................40.00
Wine, Della Robbia, crystal w/appl colors, 3-oz 30.00

Wheatley, T. J.

In 1880 after a brief association with the Coultry Works, Thomas J. Wheatley opened his own studio in Cincinnati, Ohio, claiming to have been the first to discover the secret of under-glaze slip decoration on an unbaked clay vessel. He applied for and was granted a patent for his process. Demand for his ware increased to the point that several artists were hired to decorate the ware. The company incorporated in 1880 as the Cincinnati Art Pottery, but until 1882 it continued to operate under Wheatley's name. Ware from this period is marked 'T.J. Wheatley' or 'T.J.W. and Co.,' and it may be dated.

Matt green pieces dominate today's marketplace and will bring much more than the decorated pieces. The matt green pieces are seldom, if ever, marked or dated.

Pitcher, gr gloss, dotted leaves among vertical rows of beads, 8", EX...**165.00**
Tile, flower frieze, mc cuenca on gray, #1135, 4¼x8¼"..............**285.00**
Vase, barbotine pnt rose branches on cobalt, rstr, 1879, 29".......**400.00**
Vase, floral on dmn shape, bl/sage/gr/yel on red & gray streaks, 7" ..**220.00**
Vase, gr matt, cvd wild roses, short neck, 11¼x9"......................**715.00**
Vase, gr matt, lg leaves alternate w/berries, WP/#630, drilled, 14"..**1,400.00**
Vase, oatmeal matt, veined leaves/buds, 4 bud-like ft, #604, 12x9" .**2,000.00**

Wicker

Wicker is the basket-like material used in many types of furniture and accessories. It may be made from bamboo cane, rattan, reed, or artificial fibers. It is airy, lightweight, and very popular in hot regions. Imported from the Orient in the eighteenth century, it was first manufactured in the United States in about 1850. The elaborate, closely woven Victorian designs belong to the mid- to late 1800s, and the simple styles with coarse reedings usually indicate a post-1900 production. Art Deco styles followed in the '20s and '30s. The most important consideration in buying wicker is condition — it can be restored, but only by a professional. Age is an important factor, but be aware that 'Victorian-style' furniture is being manufactured today.

Key:
HB — Heywood Bros.   H/W — Heywood Wakefield

Armchair, circular bk, serpentine arms, splint seat, cushion, 42" **150.00**
Armchair, posing; ornate bk, Aladdin fr, HB, 1890s, 35x20"...**1,650.00**
Cabinet, open top over dbl doors, tight weave, old pk pnt, sm **35.00**
Cabinet, sewing; tight weave & curlicue at legs/sides, 27x17x13"....**900.00**
Chair, corner; dmn shapes, spindles, curved front leg, H/W, 34".....**385.00**
Chair, tight weave, continuous arms, apron, wht pnt, minor rpr **135.00**
Chaise lounge, continuous arms, apron, rpl uphl seat & bk, 32x60x32"...**650.00**
Chaise lounge, overall lattice & braid, skirted, 1920s, 40x67".**1,650.00**
Cradle, swinging, beehive trns, HB, ca 1880, 55x44x23", EX..**1,295.00**
Day bed/porch glider, worn uphl, Loyd Loom, 1920s-30s, 82" L..**1,250.00**
Desk, slant front, latticed gallery/panels, 1920s, +matching chair.....**1,750.00**
Desk, tight weave, apron, cut-out sides, oak drw, wht pnt, 1910s, sm ..**300.00**
Desk, wood top & drw, rope-like trim, wht pnt, 35x28x18", +chair.....**425.00**
Lamp, Eifell Tower-like base w/open-weave dome shade, ca 1920, 68".**250.00**
Loveseat, rolled arms, scrolls & curliques, natural, 38½x47x17" ..**865.00**
Loveseat, rolled-bk str crestrail, curlicue arms/legs/apron, 3-color.**1,800.00**
Magazine rack, 4 ball finials, curliques, ca 1920, 30x19x15", NM....**325.00**
Magazine stand, tight weave, wht pnt, 12½x6½x9" **17.50**
Rocker, bk curves to arms, allover open weave, Arts & Crafts, VG ..**325.00**
Rocker, peacock fan openwork, heavy shaped bk/arms, ornate ...**800.00**
Rocker, platform; rolled arms w/curlicues on fr & base, 1900s, EX .**1,250.00**
Rocker, platform; w/arms, ornate bk, serpentine roll, 1890s, 45" .**1,650.00**
Rocker, uphl seat & bk, tight-weave arms, old rpt, H/W, 36" **115.00**
Rocker, w/arms, shaped top, fancy intricate bk, 41", EX.............**450.00**
Screen/divider, Louis XV style, gold decor, 3 uphl panels, 73x62" ..**3,000.00**
Settee, curlicue crest/sunburst medallion, 1890s, 40x44" **2,650.00**
Settee, latticework/braiding, Bar Harbor, ca 1915, 37x49".......**1,000.00**
Settee, serpentine bk, beadwork/curlicues, cane seat, HB, 1890s, 42"..**2,250.00**
Sewing basket, 2-tier, scrolled brackets, H/W **340.00**
Shelf, 4-tier, open frwork w/lg ball atop, wht pnt, 1880s, 58x19" sq....**1,750.00**
Sofa, tight weave w/dmns, skirt, fancy ft, 1920s, 71x26"..........**1,450.00**
Stool, w/4 legs, handmade in 1930s, 19x15" dia **80.00**
Stroller, curls & curliques, CI fr, late 1800s, doll sz, 26" L...........**235.00**
Table, console; tight weave, 3 curved legs, sm shelf, 33x21x10" .**125.00**
Table, oak base w/wicker top, orig pnt trim, 1920s, 29x29x19"...**215.00**
Table, quarter-sawn oak top w/low shelf, wicker posts/skirt, 72" ..**1,435.00**
Table, wood top, birdcage & curliques, shelf, 31x25" dia.............**550.00**
Tea cart, glass top, 2 storage baskets, cane-wrapped hdl, 1900s, 40" L.**1,250.00**
Wastebasket, oak base, cylindrical, H/W, 16x12"........................**500.00**

Will-George

After years of working in the family garage, William and George Climes founded the Will-George company in Los Angeles, California, in 1934. They manufactured high-quality novelty ware, utilizing both porcelain and earthenware clays. Both brothers, motivated by their love of art pottery, had extensive education and training in manufacturing processes as well as decoration. In 1940 actor Edgar Bergen, a collector of pottery, developed a relationship with the brothers and invested in their business. With this new influx of funds, the company relocated to Pasadena. There they produced an extensive line of art pottery, but they excelled in their creation of bird and animal figurines. In addition, they molded a large line of human figurines similar to Royal Doulton. The brothers, now employing a staff of decorators, precisely molded their pieces with great care and strong emphasis on originality and detail, creating high-quality works of art that were only carried by exclusive gift stores.

In the late 1940s after a split with Bergen, the company moved to San Gabriel to a larger, more modern location and renamed themselves The Claysmiths. Their business flourished and they were able to successfully mass produce many items; but due to the abundance of cheap, postwar imports from Italy and Japan that were then flooding the market, they liquidated the business in 1956. Our advisor for this category is Marty Webster. He is listed in the Directory under Michigan.

Bird figurine, cardinal, red, on branch, 4x4" **20.00**
Bird figurine, cardinal on forked branch (w/openings), 12x9".....**150.00**
Bird figurine, flamingo, head bk, wings closed, 8"........................**160.00**
Bird figurine, flamingo, head bk, wings closed, 10" **200.00**
Bird figurine, flamingo, head down, wings closed, 4½".................**100.00**
Bird figurine, flamingo, head down, wings closed, 6½"..................**115.00**
Bird figurine, flamingo, head up, wings closed, 5¾"......................**120.00**
Bird figurine, flamingo, head up, wings closed, 7¼"......................**175.00**
Bird figurine, flamingo, head up, wings closed, 10".......................**200.00**
Bird figurine, flamingo, head up, wings closed, 11¼".....................**225.00**
Bird figurine, flamingo, head up, wings closed, 12"......................**235.00**
Bird figurine, flamingo, head up, wings up, 7½" **195.00**
Bird figurine, flamingo, head up, wings up, 10½"..........................**300.00**
Bird figurine, flamingo, head up, wings up, 15½"..........................**495.00**
Bird figurine, parrot on branch, 14"...**200.00**
Bird figurine, pheasant, mc, 6x14"..**250.00**
Bird figurine, robin, 3"...**40.00**
Bird figurine, rooster, mc, 4¼"..**50.00**
Boat, 20" L, separate 8½" Oriental man w/oar will attach, NM....**75.00**
Bowl, flamingo pond, 14x9"..**50.00**
Figurine, girl w/hands on hips, wht headscarf, rnd base, 5¼" **75.00**
Figurine, Oriental man w/paddle in hand, 8½"..............................**55.00**
Figurine, spaniel, #204G, 7x9½x3½" **80.00**
Figurine, 2 children sit talking on bench, snake at corner, 7x4x8", EX ..**75.00**
Figurines, giraffes, 14½", 13", pr **260.00**
Martini glass, rooster stem, 5", set of 6 ....**180.00**
Planter, flamingo, seated, head up, 3½x5¼"..................................**235.00**
Platter, onion, 12x10½" **40.00**
Tureen, onion, w/lid, ladle & underplate, lg.................................**70.00**

Willets

The Willets Manufacturing Company of Trenton, New Jersey, produced a type of belleek porcelain during the late 1880s and 1890s. Examples were often marked with a coiled snake that formed a 'W' with 'Willets' below and 'Belleek' above. Not all Willets is factory decorated. Items painted by amateurs outside the factory are worth considerably less. High prices usually equate with fine artwork. In the listings below, all items are belleek unless noted otherwise. Our advisor for this category is Mary Frank Gaston; she is listed in the Directory under Texas.

Compote, floral border w/gold, CB Hatton, ftd, 4½x8½"+hdls ..**165.00**
Cup & saucer, shiny wht ruffled form w/twig hdl, 2½x3½", 6" **78.00**
Mug, lion portrait, 1889-1906 mk, 4½", pr **465.00**
Tankard, chrysanthemums, lizard hdl, Northwind spout, 11¼"...**995.00**
Tankard, lovers portrait/roses on bk, E Matty, 1889-1906, 14x6⅝"..**800.00**
Vases, roses pk on shaded gr, sgn Shufelt, baluster, snake mk, 15¾"..**435.00**

Winchester

The Winchester Repeating Arms Company lost their important government contract after WWI and of necessity turned to the manufacture of sporting goods, hardware items, tools, etc., to augment their gun production. Between 1920 and 1931, over 7,500 different items, each marked 'Winchester Trademark U.S.A.,' were offered for sale by thousands of Winchester Hardware stores throughout the country. After 1931 the firm became Winchester-Western. Collectors prefer the prewar items, and the majority of our listings are from this era.

Concerning current collecting trends: Oil cans that a short time ago could be purchased for $2.00 to $5.00 now often sell for $25.00, some over $50.00, and demand is high. Good examples of advertising posters and calendars seem to have no upper limits and are difficult to find. Winchester fishing lures are strong, and the presence of original boxes increases values by 25% to 40%. Another current trend concerns the price of 'diecuts' (cardboard stand-ups, signs, or hanging signs). These are out-pricing many other items. A short time ago the average value of a 'diecut' ranged from $25.00 to $45.00. Current values for most are in the $200.00 to $800.00 range, with some approaching $2,500.00.

Our advisor for this category is James Anderson; he is listed in the Directory under Minnesota. See also Knives.

Banner, Western...Shoot for Fun!, mc oilcloth, 1940s, 49x57", NM...**850.00**
Battery, lantern; #4802, 6-volt, 1930s, VG+ **150.00**
Battery, 3-cell, tubular, rare, VG...**125.00**
Booklet, Shot Guns & Loaded Shells, 12 bi-fold pgs, 1920s, 4x6"..**250.00**
Box insert, Winchester 22 Cleaning Preparations, 1903, 2¼" sq ..**35.00**
Brochure, Model 12, 1950s, opens to 12½x21", M **35.00**
Calendar, eagle & mtn sheep, 1915, minor rstr, 30x15¼", VG ..**2,500.00**
Calendar, eagle & mtn sheep, 1915, 30x15¼", EX, from $4,500 to ..**5,500.00**
Cannon, breech loading, Model 98, G **350.00**
Catalog, #74, March 1908, EX...**165.00**
Catalog, all models pictured, #2137, 1954, 34-pg, 5x7", G............**30.00**
Catalog, deluxe hardbound, #82, 1919, 208-pg, 9x11", VG **275.00**
Catalog, introduces model 1900, #66, 1900, 164-pg, 5¾x8¾", EX..**225.00**
Cold chisel, #W12, G- **25.00**
Diecut, letter W w/pronghorn sheep, 12x9¼", EX+.................**1,250.00**
Diecut, Super Speed Shotshell, mc cb, 1952, 6x6½", EX **35.00**
Diecut, trapper w/gun, Rifles & Cartridges, 28x20", VG **2,500.00**
Drill, breast; #W44, EX...**130.00**
Emblem, bicycle; convex shape, brass w/3-color enamel, 1920s, 2¼" ...**125.00**
Fishing line, braided silk, EX...**75.00**
Fishing spoon, brass, #9569, VG **85.00**
Flashlight, Mapreader, mk Uses Bulb No 13, 1½x8", EX...............**45.00**
Food chopper, #W12, EX, from $60 to **75.00**
Golf club, VG, from $135 to..**145.00**
Hand trap, VG..**75.00**
Hang tag, Model 37, 410 Gauge, full choke, 28" bbl, EX **55.00**
Hang tag, Model 59, Automatic Shotgun, 12 gauge, 28" bbl, full choke...**40.00**
Hatchet, mk Winchester Special, EX **95.00**
Head lamp, United States Forest Service, complete & orig, EX, $65 to..**75.00**
Headlight, Twin Service, blk metal battery box, complete, EX...**175.00**
Level, #W3, 2 bubble vials, 28", VG+......................................**40.00**

Lock, brass, no key, G, from $70 to..**80.00**
Meat fork, riveted wood hdl, 13", EX **45.00**
Paperweight, 2½" bullet on base, 5½", EX................................**80.00**
Pin-bk button, Always Shoot...Cartridges, bull's-eye, ¾" dia, EX .**40.00**
Pipe wrench, #1022, wood hdl, 10", EX...................................**80.00**
Pipe wrench, #1031, all metal, mk Pat 3-14-23, 8", EX................**50.00**
Plane, #3015, 18", EX..**70.00**
Plane, fore; #3015, 18", EX **40.00**
Playing cards, 1929 store calendar scene on bks, 52 no jokers, EXIB..**525.00**
Pliers, #2489-10, 10", EX..**50.00**
Pocketknife, #3992, VG+, from $125 to **140.00**
Punch, EX...**85.00**
Reel, dbl action, #2442, G+..**130.00**
Reel, single action, #1218, VG **110.00**
Saw, 1-man crosscut; Winchester Trade Mark, Made in USA, EX....**440.00**
Scale, family; #15, VG, from $85 to **110.00**
Screwdriver, July Special, wood hdl w/steel ferrule, 3½", EX **45.00**
Shotshell box, Leader 12-Gauge, full box of 10, 3½" L, G-...........**45.00**
Spatula, #7646, G, from $35 to..**45.00**
Straw hat, lady's, G...**275.00**

Windmill Weights

Windmill weights made of cast iron were used to protect the windmill's plunger rod from damage during high winds by adding weight that slowed down the speed of the blades.

Boss Bull (mk), CI w/old red pnt, 2-pc/bolted, Dempster, 13x13½x4"....**2,500.00**
Bull, Fairbury (unmk), old silver pnt, flat, 19½x24½"+base **635.00**
Bull, Fairbury (unmk), wht w/blk spots, gr base, rpr/pnt wear, 13x14"..**1,500.00**
Crescent moon, Eclipse, Fairbanks Morse, 10½x7½", VG..........**460.00**
Horse, bob tail; CI, Dempster, #58C, 16½x17", EX....................**400.00**
Horse, long tail; CI, gold pnt, att Dempster, 15¾x16½", VG .**1,035.00**
Rooster, CI, Elgin Wind Power, orig pnt, 16x17", NM................**925.00**
Rooster, CI, Elgin wind Power, orig pnt, 18½x19", EX **2,000.00**
Rooster, Hummer # 184, Elgin Wind Power, red traces, 7x10" ...**750.00**
Rooster, Hummer E 184 on tail, old mc pnt, 8½"......................**935.00**
Squirrel, Elgin (att), old pnt traces, 15½x13½" **1,950.00**
W, CI, Althouse-Wheeler, 10x16", G.......................................**400.00**

Wire Ware

Very primitive wire was first made by cutting sheet metal into strips which were shaped with mallet and file. By the late thirteenth century, craftsmen in Europe had developed a method of pulling these strips through progressively smaller holes until the desired gauge was obtained. During the Industrial Revolution of the late 1800s, machinery was developed that could produce wire cheaply and easily; and it became a popular commercial commodity. It was used to produce large items such as garden benches and fencing as well as innumerable small pieces for use in the kitchen or on the farm. Beware of reproductions.

Basket, mc geometric majolica 5¾" plate in bottom, hdls, 8" dia..**165.00**
Compote, crimped, old dk surface, ca 1900, 7x9" **295.00**
Compote, simple openwork weave, trn-down rim, cone ft, G- pnt, 8x14"..**45.00**
Egg basket, top open like flower, ftd, 7½x4" **60.00**
Hanging basket, collapsible, fine chain-woven wire, 10" dia.........**18.00**
Plant stand, 2 lattice shelves w/scroll braces, wht pnt, 44x37"....**325.00**
Rolling pin holder, heavy wire, hangs vertically, rare **65.00**
Soap saver, oblong screenwire soap container w/wire & wood hdl .**25.00**
Tea ball, egg shape, ½" tin band ea side, 2¾" **28.00**
Whisk, fancy twisted stem, target-shaped base, 1870s, 11½".........**70.00**

Wood, Beatrice

A multitalented artist, Beatrice Wood is especially well known for her ceramics which are displayed in the Smithsonian and the Metropolitan Museum of Art as well as several other museums around the world. She was also famous for her work in other mediums, especially painting and photography. She studied drama in Europe at the age of 18, returning to America where she became involved in the revolutionary Dada art movement in New York. She moved to California in the late 1920s and in 1937 opened her own studio. Nicknamed Bea or Beato, she developed wonderful lustre glazes for which she is highly acclaimed. Her style is modernistic, and her work ranges from sedate teapots and vases to whimsical sculptures. She died in 1998 at the age of 105. Her fascinating experiences led her to write her autobiography which so captured the attention of Titanic director James Cameron that he fashioned the role of Rose around her.

Bowl, centerpc; copper/lav/gr/gold lustre, 3¾x17"..................**4,000.00**
Bowl, raspberry & lt gr lustre, str walls, ftd, BW564C, 5¼x5" **950.00**
Bowl, thick multi-tone bl w/dk red clay exposed, Beato, 7½" **850.00**
Bowl, turq (volcanic), conical ped ft, sgn Beato, 4¾x8" **1,175.00**
Bowl, yel & brn flambé on redware, Beato, 3x10", NM **650.00**
Jug, blk volcanic glaze, ball shape, sm opening, 7½x6¾"..........**3,000.00**
Sculpture, eel, gr lustre w/coffee-bean eyes, 2x14", NM...........**1,600.00**
Sculpture, 3 stylized figures (2 ladies/1 man) on rock, matt, 7x9½".**4,000.00**
Vase, gr volcanic w/brn clay showing through, oval, Beato, 9" W .**1,100.00**
Vase, multi-tone bl w/irid, conical ft, Beato, 5½".....................**1,000.00**
Vase, orange volcanic over gr, ped ft, Beato, 4" **1,200.00**
Vase, shaded brn w/irid, pine cone stem, hdls, Beato, 8"..........**1,200.00**
Vase, textured bl gloss, flared, Beato, 4" **700.00**

Wood Carvings

Wood sculptures represent an important section of American folk art. Wood carvings were made not only by skilled woodworkers such as cabinetmakers, carpenters, etc., but by amateur 'whittlers' as well. They take the form of circus-wagon figures, carousel animals, decoys, busts, figurines, and cigar store Indians. Oriental artists show themselves to have been as proficient with the medium of wood as they were with ivory or hardstone. See also Carousel Animals; Decoys; Tobacciana.

Barn owl, John Hyatt, blk pnt/glass eyes, on stand, 20th C, 16", VG...**3,000.00**
Bird on perch, mc pnt, brass tack eyes, Canfield/Ravenna, 27½"..**315.00**
Bust of saint, bearded/cloaked/supported by clouds, German, 1700s, 28" ..**2,250.00**
Cat, crouching on plank base, 10% wht pnt on pine, 1800s, 31" L..**10,575.00**
E Indian girl seated, detailed cvg, mc pnt, old rstr, 16½" **195.00**
Eagle, giltwood, 1 wing up, 2nd half-spread, Am, 19th C, 43x28"...**575.00**
Eagle, wings wide, mc pnt, gr base, sgn D&BS 80 PA, 12x16" **220.00**
Eagle on post, cvd from 1 pc, weathered, 1800s, 46" **2,100.00**
Eagle perched on ball, raised cvd feathers, mc pnt, 70" on tall base ...**1,100.00**
Eagle w/wings wide, EX detail, PA type, EX patina, 19th C, 13x25"..**1,150.00**
Eagle w/wings wide, wht pnt, Am, 19th C, 18½x31x29".........**3,525.00**
Egret, articulated wings, tack eyes, wht pnt, metal stand, 26" **765.00**
Lady Liberty w/raised arm & torch, wht w/gold crown, 38" **1,295.00**
Man w/handlebar mustache, short coat/pantaloons, mc pnt, 24"...**475.00**
Oxen, 2 pr pull sleigh w/logs & driver, missing harness, 27" L....**220.00**
Parrot, mc pnt, mtd on graduated platform base, 20th C, 22" .**4,400.00**
Pointer, mc, resting on natural cedar base, 20th C, 17" L **135.00**
Shotgun Wedding, couple/preacher/father w/gun, mtd on root, 20th C, 17".**250.00**
Spoon, cvd facial features, pnt highlights, ca 1900, 9⅜x6¼" ..**1,650.00**
St George w/arm raised, walnut, Continental, 1750s, 48"........**5,285.00**
Tucan pr mtd on driftwood tree, pnt, 21¼" **495.00**
Woman in flowing robes, allegorical, mc, Continental, 18th C, 42" ..**3,800.00**
2-horse team/driver/bbl wagon, on wood base, leather ears, mc, 17" L..**300.00**

Woodenware

Woodenware (or treenware, as it is sometimes called) generally refers to those wooden items such as spoons, bowls, food molds, etc., that were used in the preparation of food. Common during the eighteenth and nineteenth centuries, these wares were designed from a strictly functional viewpoint and were used on a day-to-day basis. With the advent of the Industrial Revolution which brought with it new materials and products, much of the old woodenware was simply discarded. Today original handcrafted American woodenwares are extremely difficult to find. See also Primitives.

Basin, trn, flat extended rim, dk red pnt, 19th C, 6½x27¼" **500.00**
Bin, flour; poplar, slant top, early 19th C, 27½x36x20" **975.00**
Bowl, ash burl, Am, 19th C, age crack, 6¼x19½" **350.00**
Bowl, ash burl w/EX figure, brn stain, 3¼x10½" **880.00**
Bowl, ash burl w/EX figure, cut-out hdls, 6x19½" **2,750.00**
Bowl, ash burl w/EX figure, scrubbed, trn ring, 4x15".................**935.00**
Bowl, ash burl w/EX figure, scrubbed int, crack, 3¼x9⅛"..........**495.00**
Bowl, ash burl w/VG figure, old mellow brn rfn, 4¾x11¾".....**1,100.00**
Bowl, ash burl w/VG figure, shallow trn ft, raised rim, 5x12"..**1,450.00**
Bowl, ash burl w/VG figure, thinly trn, raised ft, 4¼x13½".....**1,045.00**
Bowl, ash burl w/VG figure & patina, trn ft, splits, 2⅜x5⅝" **415.00**
Bowl, burl w/good figure, hand hewn, scrubbed surface, 5¼x16x13"..**750.00**
Bowl, dough; rectangular w/sloping ends, 4x26x11" **250.00**
Bowl, maple w/old red pnt, scrubbed int, raised rim, 6x19"........**985.00**
Bowl, mixing; trn, bl pnt, 6½x19"...**1,800.00**

Bowl, turned burl with shaped rim and incised band near base, nineteenth century, 6⅛x13", with 10" carved scoop with hook on handle end, $2,645.00. (Photo courtesy Skinner, Inc.)

Bowl, trn, mustard & brn grpt, PA, early 1800s, rpr, 9x10"......**3,335.00**
Bowl, trn, old bl pnt, 19th C, 7x20" **1,600.00**
Bowl, trn, red wash, 3x15" **300.00**
Bowl, trn maple, raised rim, old natural finish, 4½x16" **100.00**
Bowl, trn w/bl rpt (old red w/wavy lines orig), scrubbed int, 3x13"..**250.00**
Butter paddle, bird's-eye maple, simple cvg, EX patina, 10" **165.00**
Butter paddle, burl, bird-head hooked hdl, 10¾x6¼" **880.00**
Butter paddle, curly maple, sea horse hdl, EX patina, 8" **275.00**
Butter paddle, full-body bird hdl terminal, 4¾x8½" **2,200.00**
Cake board, cvd horse-drawn coach, bk: Colonial man w/cart, 11x7" .**600.00**
Canteen, staved interlocking bands, EX patina, 6¾x9½" dia, VG......**125.00**
Cheese press, pine/hickory, sq nails, bj ends, old red pnt, 44x19x12" ...**350.00**
Cookie board, ash w/well cvd/detailed snail on leaf, 3⅛x4⅜" **575.00**
Cookie board, dbl-sided, eagle w/shield/lion, 4½x7" **330.00**
Cookie board, dbl-sided, flowers & birds/Am Indian w/tomahawk, 5x6"...**575.00**
Cookie board, dbl-sided, lady in long dresss/man in waistcoat, 8x20"...**220.00**
Cookie board, medieval rider on horse, red traces, 13x10¼" **165.00**
Cup, Lehnware, mc flowers on salmon w/blk & red trim, yel int, ftd, 5" .**1,500.00**
Firkin, bl pnt, staved wooden bands w/copper tacks, bail hdl, 7"...**475.00**
Firkin, staved, gray over earlier gr, minor chips, 11¼" w/hdl **330.00**
Firkin, staved, red pnt, copper tacks/pegs in lid, wire bail, 8"......**550.00**
Jar, ash burl, EX patina & figure, red traces, urn shape, 6".......**7,700.00**
Jar, Lehnware, HP pansies on peach, strawberries on lid, 4½".**2,200.00**

Jar, saffron; Lehnware, mc strawberries on salmon, urn shape, 4¾"...**1,850.00**
Ladle, deep cvd oval bowl, tapered hdl secured w/iron nail, 19" ...**90.00**
Mallet, ash burl w/sq head, cvd hdl, 13", EX.................................**50.00**
Masher, trn tiger maple pestle type, 9¼x2¼" dia.........................**65.00**
Masher/grinder, burl maple w/spoke-cut design on working end, EX.....**65.00**
Measure, bentwood, lapped seam, old dk gr pnt, iron nails, 5x9" ..**195.00**
Noggin, maple, paneled sides, curved spout, cut-out hdl, 5½" **55.00**
Pastry stamp, walnut, pineapple cvg, 12"....................................**250.00**
Piggin, hollowed-out log w/metal bands, 18th C, 7½" +hdl........**250.00**
Rolling pin, curly maple w/good figure & patina, 19".................**275.00**
Rolling pin, trn walnut, rnd hdl ea end, 29½", EX.....................**135.00**
Slaw board, walnut w/steel blade, iron screws, heart cutout, 17x6"..**90.00**
Spoon, long hdl w/varied cutouts & red pnt decor, rpr, 15½" **85.00**
Trencher, cvd from section of log, 2 hdls, typical wear, 7x18x32" ..**165.00**
Trencher, hand hewn, canted sides, pierced hdl, rprs, 5½x38x15" .**110.00**
Trencher, hand-planed sides, old bl pnt, 5½x1¼x21½" **440.00**

Woodworking Machinery

    Vintage cast-iron woodworking machines are monuments to the highly skilled engineers, foundrymen, and machinists who devised them, thus making possible the mass production of items ranging from clothespins, boxes, and barrels to decorative moldings and furniture. Though attractive from a nostalgic viewpoint, many of these machines are bought by the hobbyist and professional alike, to be put into actual use — at far less cost than new equipment. Many worth-assessing factors must be considered; but as a general rule, a machine in good condition is worth about 65¢ a pound (excluding motors). A machine needing a lot of restoration is not worth more than 35¢ a pound, while one professionally rebuilt and with a warranty can be calculated at $1.10 a pound. Modern, new machinery averages over $3.00 a pound. Two of the best sources of information on purchasing or selling such machines are *Vintage Machines — Searching for the Cast Iron Classics* by Tom Howell, and *Used Machines and Abused Buyers* by Chuck Seidel from *Fine Woodworking*, November/December 1984. Prices quoted are for machines in good condition, less motors and accessories. Our advisor for this category is Mr. Dana Martin Batory, author of *Vintage Woodworking Machinery, An Illustrated Guide to Four Manufacturers*, and *Volume II, An Illustrated Guide to Four More Manufacturers*. See his listing in the Directory under Ohio for further information. No phone calls, please.

American Saw Mill Machinery Company, 1931

Jointer, Monarch Line, #XII, ball-bearing, 16" **1,200.00**
Planer, Monarch Line, single surface, 30" **2,600.00**
Table saw, Monarch Line, #X24, tilting arbor, 16".....................**425.00**

Blue Star Products, 1939

Band saw, #1200, 12" floor model **85.00**
Lathe, #1001, 72" bed, 12" swing...**60.00**
Table saw, #800, 8" **95.00**

Boice-Crane Power Tools, 1937

Band saw, #800, 14"..**100.00**
Drill press, #1600, 15" **75.00**
Lathe, #1100, gap bed..**50.00**
Scroll saw, #900, 24"..**75.00**

Buss Machine Works, ca 1950

Planer, #4-L, 30" **3,120.00**
Planer, #44, 30"...**4,225.00**

Planer, #55, dbl surface, 30"..**6,175.00**
Planer, #66, 30"..**4,865.00**

Defiance Machine Works, 1910

Band saw, 28"...**520.00**
Table saw, #2, hand feed, 20"...**650.00**
Table saw, #2, power feed, 20"..**1,100.00**

Delta Manufacturing Company, 1939

Band saw, #768, 10"..**50.00**
Disk sander, belt drive, #1425, 12"..**35.00**
Jointer, ball bearing, #390, 4"...**35.00**
Jointer, ball bearing, #654, 6"...**50.00**
Lathe, timken bearing, #930, 11"...**45.00**
Table saw, tilt top, #1180, 10"..**95.00**

F.H. Clement Co., 1896

Band saw, 30"..**555.00**
Boring Machine, Post, #2..**325.00**
Ripsaw, #2, iron fr, 16"...**585.00**
Sand-papering machine, #2, Universal..**585.00**
Sander, #3, dbl spindle **585.00**
Shaper, variety, #3, heavy, dbl spindle.....................................**1,300.00**
Splitting saw, #1, iron fr, wood top, 12" **325.00**

Gallmeyer & Livingston Company, 1927

Band saw, Union, 20"..**390.00**
Jointer, Union, motor on arbor, 8"..**370.00**
Table saw, Union #7, 7"...**210.00**

G.N. Goodspeed Company, 1876

Boring Machine, upright..**225.00**
Planer, New & Improved, Pony, 24"..**900.00**
Table saw, 12"...**200.00**

Greenlee Bros. & Company, 1925

Tenoner, #530, sash, door & cabinet, ball-bearing **1,530.00**

Hoyt & Brother Company, 1888

Cut-off saw, overhung, traversing, 14".......................................**650.00**
Planer, matcher & surfacer, New Combined, #2, 24".............**5,200.00**
Planing & matching machine, #7, 13".......................................**3,250.00**
Scroll saw, #1 ....**300.00**
Table saw, #2, 14"...**800.00**
Tenoning machine, #2..**650.00**

J.A. Fay & Egan Company, 1900

Jointer, New #2, 16"..**1,550.00**
Jointer, New #2, 30"..**1,820.00**
Jointer, New #4, extra heavy, 16"..**1,625.00**
Jointer, New #4, extra heavy, 30"..**2,275.00**
Molder, #1½, 4-sided, 4"...**1,050.00**
Molder, #2, 4-sided, 6"...**1,500.00**
Molder, #2½, 4-sided, 7"..**2,100.00**
Mortiser, #5, dbl hollow chisel, horizontal..............................**1,100.00**
Planer, #2½, dbl-belted surface, med sz, 26"...........................**1,850.00**

Saw, rip; #2, Improved Standard................................1,175.00
Saw, rip; #3, self feed, X-lg....................................2,400.00

J.D. Wallace Company, 1940s

Saw, circular (table saw); Universal, 7" 75.00

L. Power & Co., 1888

Mortiser & borer, #2..780.00
Shaper, single spindle, reversible 585.00
Table saw, self feed, 14"...715.00

Ober Manufacturing Company, 1889

Rip saw, self feed, 14"..725.00
Saw, swing cut-off, 18"...275.00
Shaper, saw & jointer combination 400.00

Oliver Machinery Company, 1922

Band saw, #17, 30"...925.00
Shaper, #483, high speed, dbl spindle 1,300.00
Table saw, #32, Variety, 12"......................................500.00

Parks Ball Bearing Machine Company, 1925

Jointer, H-133, Ideal, 12" 400.00
Sanding machine, H-165, Economy, 24".......................230.00
Saw, H-97, swing cut-off, Alert, 12"............................225.00

P.B. Yates Machine Company, 1917

Planer, #160, dbl surface, 20"................................5,225.00
Saw, #232, swing cut-off, 16"....................................260.00

Powermatic, Inc., 1965

Band saw, #81, 20"..500.00
Lathe, #90, 12" 360.00
Planer, #160, 16"..650.00
Planer, #221, 20"..725.00
Sander, #300-01, 12" disk & 6" belt combination.............95.00
Shaper, #26, single spindle 240.00
Tenoner, #2-A, single end..620.00

Richardson, Meriam & Co., 1865

Band saw, Granite State, 36" 400.00
Mortising & boring machine, lg No 1 ....1,300.00
Planing & matching machine, #5, single cutter head 4,225.00
Re-sawing machine, circular, 40"..............................1,300.00
Scroll saw, Patent, common sz 330.00

S.A. Woods Machine Company, 1876

Circular resawing machine, Joslin's Improved, 50" 2,275.00
Planer, panel; Improved, 20".....................................520.00
Planer, surface; Pat Improved, 30"...........................1,430.00

The Sidney Machine Tool Co., 1916 (Famous Woodworking Machinery)

Bandsaw, 20"..325.00
Jointer, Cyclone, 12" 525.00

Jointer, Cyclone, 16" 585.00
Jointer, 20"..1,220.00
Lathe, pattern maker's, 14".......................................275.00
Lathe, pattern maker's, 20".......................................325.00
Mortiser, hollow chisel, new model 585.00
Mortiser & tenoner, combined 575.00
Planer, dbl-belted, 24x8"......................................1,575.00
Planer, 18" 880.00
Planer, 24" 975.00
Saw, combination; No 5, 16" 525.00
Saw, Variety, No 6, 16"..780.00
Saw, Variety, No 8, 20"..650.00
Saw, Variety, No 16, 20"..750.00
Shaper, single spindle 650.00
Woodworker, portable, hand 485.00
Woodworker, Universal, No 40 ....1,300.00
Woodworker, Universal (5 machines in 1), No 30 or No 31, ea...2,015.00

Sprunger Power Tools, 1950s

Band saw, 14"..60.00
Jigsaw, 20"...40.00
Lathe, gap bed, 10" 50.00
Table saw, tilt arbor, 10¼"..75.00

Worcester Porcelain Company

    The Worcester Porcelain Company was deeded in 1751. During the first or Dr. Wall period (so called for one of its proprietors), porcelain with an Oriental influence was decorated in underglaze blue. Useful tablewares represented the largest portion of production, but figurines and decorative items were also made. Very little of the earliest wares were marked and can only be identified by a study of forms, glazes, and the porcelain body, which tends to transmit a greenish cast when held to light. Late in the '50s, a crescent mark was in general use, and rare examples bear a facsimile of the Meissen crossed swords. The first period ended in 1783, and the company went through several changes in ownership during the next eighty years. The years from 1783 to 1792 are referred to as the Flight period. Marks were a small crescent, a crown with 'Royal,' or an impressed 'Flight.' From 1792 to 1807 the company was known as Flight and Barr and used the trademark 'F&B' or 'B,' with or without a small cross. From 1807 to 1813 the company was under the Barr, Flight, and Barr management; this era is recognized as having produced porcelain with the highest quality of artistic decoration. Their mark was 'B.F.B.' From 1813 to 1840 many marks were used, but the most usual was 'F.B.B.' under a crown to indicate Flight, Barr, and Barr. In 1840 the firm merged with Chamberlain, and in 1852 they were succeeded by Kerr and Binns. The firm became known as Royal Worcester in 1862. The production was then marked with a circle with '51' within and a crown on top. The date of manufacture was incised into the bottom or stamped with a letter of the alphabet, just under the circle. In 1891 Royal Worcester England was added to the circle and crown. From that point on, each piece is dated with a code of dots or other symbols. After 1891 most wares had a blush-color ground. Prior to that date it was ivory. Most shapes were marked with a unique number.

    During the early years they produced considerable ornamental wares with a Persian influence. This gave way to a Japanesque influence. James Hadley is most responsible for the Victorian look. He is considered the 'best ever' designer and modeller. He was joined by the finest porcelain painters. Together they produced pieces with very fine detail and exquisite painting and decoration. Figures, vases, and tableware were produced in great volume and are highly collectible. During the 1890s they allowed the artists to sign some of their work. Pieces signed on the face by the Stintons, Baldwyn, Davis, Raby, Austin, Powell, Sedgley, and Rushton (not a complete list) are in great demand. The company is still in production. There is an outstanding museum on the company grounds in Worcester, England.

Note: Most pieces had lids or tops (if there is a flat area on the top lip, chances are it had one); if missing, deduct 30% to 40%.

Candelabra, boy (girl) between 2 branches, 2-light, 1885, 8⅝", pr..**700.00**
Cup & saucer, panels w/floral relief, mc on wht w/gilt **125.00**
Dish, Dr Wall, fruit/pine cones/flowers, crescent mk, 6¼" **330.00**
Ewer, floral w/gold on ivory, bulbous, 8" **150.00**
Figurine, bacchant w/tambourine, mc w/gold, #1441, 9¾" **385.00**
Figurine, farmer sharpening scythe, mc w/gold, #1292, 8½" **475.00**
Figurine, girl w/tambourine, Hadley, #1032, ca 1887, 8¼" **265.00**
Figurine, Roman lady w/shovel, ivory satin, Hadley, #1606, 1892, 13" ...**880.00**
Figurine, Yellow-Headed Blackbird, Dorothy Doughty, 1951, 11½" **1,900.00**
Figurines, male & female water carriers, mc w/gold, ca 1894, 12", pr..**1,175.00**
Jug, bottle form w/HP florals, bronzed/gilt dragon hdl, ca 1880, 11" ...**550.00**
Jug, dbl-wall w/rtcl body & jewels, ca 1879, 5¼" **2,250.00**
Lamp, oil; ivory stain w/gilt trim & mc foliage, late 1800s, 13" ..**560.00**
Salver, Middle Eastern floral transfer w/gold, ca 1878, 14½" **300.00**
Vase, floral panels w/gold, globular base, #1331, ca 1891, 10½" .**825.00**
Vase, floral w/gold, bottle form w/hdls, #1192, ca 1891, 14½" **765.00**
Vase, floral w/gold, bottle form w/hdls, #942, ca 1883, 13" **385.00**
Vase, highlander cows, H Stinton, gilt paw ft, 4⅜" **600.00**
Vase, landscape, mc lustre, bulbous, ca 1926, 10¼" **500.00**
Vase, Moresque pattern, lacy openwork hdls, late 19th C, 20" ...**1,765.00**
Vase, Persian, flowers & butterflies, bronzed hdls, #684, 13½" ...**440.00**

World's Fairs and Expos

Since 1851 and the Crystal Palace Exhibition in London, World's Fairs and Expositions have taken place at a steady pace. Many of them commemorate historical events. The 1904 Louisiana Purchase Exposition, commonly known as the St. Louis World's Fair, celebrated the 100th anniversary of the Louisiana Purchase agreement between Thomas Jefferson and Napoleon in 1803. The 1893 Columbian Exposition commemorated the 400th anniversary of the discovery of America by Columbus in 1492. (Both of these fairs were held one year later than originally scheduled.) The multitude of souvenirs from these and similar events have become a growing area of interest to collectors in recent years. Many items have a 'crossover' interest into other fields: i.e., collectors of postcards and souvenir spoons eagerly search for those from various fairs and expositions.

Values have fallen somewhat due to eBay sales. Many of the so-called common items have come down in value. However, 1939 World's Fair items are still hot. For additional information collectors may contact World's Fairs Collectors Society (WFCS), whose address is in the Directory under Clubs, Newsletters, and Catalogs, or our advisor, Herbert Rolfes. His address is listed in the Directory under Florida.

Key:
T&P — Trylon & Perisphere   WF — World's Fair

1876 Centennial, Philadelphia

Bank, Liberty Bell, mk Money Bank 1776, CI, 5", EX...................**75.00**
Book, Frank Leslie's Illustrated Register, 320 pgs, VG **100.00**
Butter dish, glass, Liberty Bell on bottom & lid, 4x7½" dia, EX...**35.00**
Cup & saucer, First Centennial...Cincinnati, Glosgow Pottery, EX..**45.00**
Goblet, clear pressed glass, 1876 Centennial emb, 6¼" **45.00**
Handkerchief, Memorial Hall w/buildings in corners, 22x22", EX...**75.00**
Plate, eagle over flag, ...Union For Ever emb, Edge Malkin, 8¼"..**85.00**
Plate, Horticultural Hall in red transferware, emb letters on edge, 6" ..**160.00**
Ticket, $2, Go to the Centennial...Fall River Line bet, EX.........**100.00**

1893 Columbian, Chicago

Book, History of the Empire of Japan, 428 pgs, 9½x6¼" **310.00**
Medal, Buffalo Bill Cody/overview of fair, 1½" dia, minimum value ..**120.00**
Print, Columbus & 1492-1892, printed textile, 17x10", VG+ **50.00**
Spoons, Columbus on hdl w/fair buildings in bowl, set of 6, EX (G box) ...**45.00**

1901 Pan American

Cup, collapsible; insignia on lid, tin, EX **30.00**
Cup, raised gr beaded detail, ceramic, 3¼"...................................**45.00**
Encased cent, 1901 Indian head, EX **35.00**
Fan, fair scenes on both sides, 10x19" (open) **85.00**
Figurine, buffalo, bronze, 1¾x2½"...**27.50**
Letter opener, buffalo on top, bronze, slight break to tip, 6¾" **27.50**
Paperweight, glass w/Electric Tower, 4x2½" **35.00**
Pitcher, ruby flashed w/clear hdl & bottom, mk LLW, 5", EX........**25.00**
Tray, N & S America w/ladies holding hands, flag border, tin, 12" dia..**165.00**
Tray, SP tin, emb roses, 4x4", VG+ **25.00**

1904 St. Louis

Book, World Almanac/Encyclopedia...Louisiana Purchase Expo, VG+..**135.00**
Box, WF St Louis 1904 in wht on blk, hinged, 3⅜x2½", EX........**25.00**
Cup, Cascade Gardens & Union Station eng, mk Royal Zinn, metal, 3¼" ..**40.00**
Cup, Palace of Liberal Arts, ceramic, ornate hdl, 3½"...................**60.00**
Figurine, donkey, seated, bronze, Show Me, I'm From Missouri, 3" ...**50.00**
Letterhead, Simmons Hardware Co, fair map on bk, EX **30.00**
Match safe, brass w/boat scene & Cascade Gardens, 2¾x1¼" **340.00**
Miniature, St Louis Union Station, CI w/gold plating, 1½x4½" ...**175.00**
Official workman's photo ID, ticket book, w/leather holder, EX.**100.00**
Pass, See the Baby Incubator, 4⅞x2¾", VG **55.00**
Piggy bank, porcelain w/gold gilt, Palace of Electricity, 3x4" **175.00**
Pitcher, cream; Machinery Building on wht, ceramic, MIG, 3¾" .**95.00**
Pitcher, Machinery Building on wht, ceramic, gold trim, 7" **200.00**
Plate, Cascade Gardens, ceramic, rtcl edge w/gilt, 7½" **25.00**
Plate, Palace of Electricity on wht, ceramic, 7½" **75.00**
Postcard, hold-to-light; Cascade Gardens & Grand Basin, EX......**25.00**
Shakers, St Louis 1904 World's Fair, pewter, bbl shape, pr **25.00**
Tray, LA Purchase Monument image, aluminum, 4¾x3¼" **65.00**

1905 Lewis and Clark

Cup, Mt Hood, Lewis & Clark, papoose & mother, copper-colored, 3½" ..**55.00**
Napkin ring, Lewis/Clark Centennial... eng, aluminum, 1½x1⅝" ...**25.00**
Postcard, Colonnade Entrance to the Expo, EX...........................**10.00**
Postcard, Entrance Forestry Building, BB Rich, unused, EX..........**12.00**
Postcard, overhead view of Expo, unused, EX **13.50**
Tray, 2 eng flying cranes w/L&C Portland 1905, wood, 2x12" dia **20.00**

1909 Alaska Yukon Pacific

Brochure, Great Northern Railway Alaska...Expo, 33-pg tri-fold, EX ...**55.00**
Plate, various landmarks of Expo, ceramic, Rowland & Marsellus, 10".**60.00**
Postcard/ad, Simonds Saw, man stands beside lg saw blade, EX **22.00**
Tray, Alaska...Expo...1909, copper, eng Expo buildings, 4¼x5¾" .**25.00**

1915 Panama Pacific

Bell, bear atop hdl, brass, 1769 El Camino Real eng, 3⅞".............**70.00**
Book, Official Souvenir View..., R Reid, 40-pg, 9¾x12½", EX.....**15.00**
Plate, Horticultural Building, other views around rolled edge, 10¼" .**50.00**
Spoon, Tower of Jewels w/image eng on hdl, blank bowl, 5½", EX **12.00**
Tickets, admission; sheet of 4, 4½x2¾"..**30.00**

1926 Sesquicentennial

Bell, Liberty; Made...Peking China, eng cast brass, w/hanger, EX.35.00
Book, Philadelphia, Birthplace of Liberty, 32-pg, 8x10", EX 15.00
Coin, ½-dollar, Washington & Coolidge w/Liberty Bell on bk, NM...35.00
Medal, Betsy Ross home w/Liberty Bell on bk, 1¼" dia, VG+ 25.00
Medal, Washington w/stars w/man on winged horse on bk, copper, EX ..20.00

1933 Chicago

Ashtray, enameled metal, red center w/emblem & Estelle '27, 5½" dia...35.00
Ashtray, 3-legged pot sits on cross-stick fr, copper, NM.................30.00
Bank, Travel & Transportation Building, gold-pnt metal, 3¾x5", EX...150.00
Book, Official Pictures of the Century of Progress Expo, EX.........25.00
Book, Salon of Photography in the Graphics Arts Building, EX...65.00
Bookends, 1933-Sky Ride-Century of Progress, copper, 3½x5", EX........25.00
Box, arc shape, blk Bakelite, metal hdl on lid, GE Pavillion, 3x5"..70.00
Bracelet, hammered metal w/Egyptian scrollwork & center emblem, EX...22.50
Cigarette case, metal w/Shooting Star emblem, 3½x2¾", NM.....35.00
Elongated cent, Egyptian Pavillion, EX 42.50
Handkerchief, GE Building, blk & wht embr on wht cotton, 16x16", EX...15.00

Hot plate, embossed fair buildings, etc., on aluminum foil over cloth-covered pad, Century of Progress, 6x8", EX, $15.00. (Photo courtesy Early Americana and Historical Auctions)

Matchbox, reverse acid-etched emblem on brass, 1⅝x½", NM 35.00
Pencil, mechanical; Hall of Science, bullet shape, EX...................25.00
Pencil holder, bulldog figural, pencil fits in mouth, metal, 2", EX..25.00
Photo, panoramic; aerial view, glued to wood backboard, 10x120", EX..100.00
Pin, I Was There, 1933 World's Fair w/logo, Geraghty on bk, ⅝".20.00
Plate, Fort Dearborn, red, Johnson Bros for Marshall Field's, 9", NM ...40.00
Playing cards, Hall of Science Avenue of Flags, MIB......................25.00
Pointer, wooden, pnt red w/porc bulldog head on end, 25", NM ..22.50
Poster, aerial map of Chicago, 23x38", M (NM envelope)............90.00
Print, eng night scene, Gerald K Geerlings, 11¾x9", EX..............25.00
Program, Travel by Trail New York Central Lines, 18 pgs, EX 25.00
Program, 25th Annual...Fly & Bait Casting Tournament, 22 pgs, 9x4", EX..110.00
Stereoview, Golden Pavillon..., Keystone #32951, EX...................20.00
Thermometer, 8-sided w/chrome rim on leather trifold, 3¼x3¼", EX ..45.00
Ticket, Union Station to Fair, Royal Aces Club, EX 50.00
Tie bar, Shooting Comet logo, bl enamel w/gold metal, 2½", EX .20.00
Wooden shoe, pincushion on toe w/spool & thimble holder, EX..20.00

1939 New York

Board game, T&P on bk of cards, Parker Brothers, NM (EX box)....75.00
Booklet, Pictorial Map of NY City WF, Sinclair, NM....................12.00
Booklet, street map, NYWF by Automobile, Hagstrom, 16x21", NM..45.00
Bookmark, T&P, 4", NM..15.00
Bowl set, Planters Peanuts, peanut images in bowl, 1 6", 6 3", EX...40.00
Brochure, Heinz 57, color, fold-out, 20x14", EX 10.00
Coasters, ea w/view of fair, metal, set of 6, EX (G box)................32.50
Compact, T&P on orange trimmed in bl, 2⅛x2¼", NM 75.00

Figurine, terrier, seated, shield on side w/T&P, CI, 3", NM..........35.00
Lamp base, T&P, wht w/gold trim, Royal Art Pottery, 8x5⅝", NM+...100.00
License plate, blk on yel, EX..60.00
Mug, NYWF in bl w/T&P in wht sq on gr, ceramic, mk Japan, 5", NM...52.50
Novelty, T&P, yel T & red P on blk base, Bakelite, 4x2⅛"...........45.00
Pajamas, men's, lt & dk bl, T&P image in wht, MIP.....................230.00
Paperweight, T&P, pnt metal, 3½x1¾", NM................................55.00
Photograph, Dolly & Rolly, 2-headed cow, 3¼x5½", EX 5.00
Platter, 5 parts w/frosted buildings, 12x12", NM..........................75.00
Postcard, city scene w/T&P in bkground, color linen, unused.........5.00
Shakers, T&P in orange on bl base, NM.......................................15.00
Teapot, T&P in bl on wht, Porcelier China, 7½", EX+.................160.00
Tumbler, juice; clear w/bl T&P, 3" 12.00
Writing tablet, T&P on cover, 10x8", EX 20.00

1939 San Francisco

Card table, T&P image on top, 26x30x30", VG 75.00
Tablecloth, various buildings, bl, yel & red on wht, 35x37", EX...75.00

1962 Seattle

Ashtray, fair scene w/Space Needle, mk IA-AC Ceramics, 5" dia, NM ...8.00
Binder, 3-ring; wht w/Century 21 w/emblem & scene in bl, EX....40.00
Book, Northwest Coast Indian Art, 104 pgs, softcover, 9x6¾", NM...15.00
Cane/seat, Kan-O-Seat, Space Needle decal on seat, Johnson, 36", EX ..27.50
Decanter, Space Needle, Jim Beam, 13½", EX..............................25.00
Glass set, colored/frosted w/fair attractions, set of 6, 6¾" 60.00
Magazine, Life, 2/9/62, Space Needle article, NM 10.00
Menu, The Eye of the Needle, Western Hotels, NM (EX mailing envelope)....10.00
Plate, fair overview, bl-gr border w/silver stripe, 10¾"..................16.00
Tumbler, Seattle WF Century 21 Exposition in red, 4¾" 12.00

1964 New York

Badge, maintenance; silver w/Unisphere design in center, 2¼x2", NM..150.00
License plate, Unisphere in center on bl & orange, NM...............50.00

Wright, Frank Lloyd

Born in Richland Center, Wisconsin, in 1869, Wright became a pioneer in architectural expression, developing a style referred to as 'prairie.' From early in the century until he died in 1959, he designed houses with rooms that were open, rather than divided by walls in the traditional manner. They exhibited low, horizontal lines and strongly projecting eaves, and he filled them with furnishings whose radical aesthetics complemented the structures to perfection. Several of his homes have been preserved to the present day, and collectors who admire his ideas and the unique, striking look he achieved treasure the stained glass windows, furniture, chinaware, lamps, and other decorative accessories designed by Wright. Our advisor for this category and related Arts and Crafts subjects is Bruce Austin; he is listed in the Directory under New York.

Key:
H — Heritage Henredon

Armchair, tubular steel, orig pnt & uphl, rpl armrests, 1936, 35" ..47,000.00
Cabinet, H, 1 drw between 2 open shelves, Taliesin border, 26x21", VG....550.00
Cabinet, H, 2-door, Taliesin border, 28x20x22", VG 1,000.00
Chair, side; single slat bk, for Browne's Bookstore, 1907, 40" .10,000.00
Chair, tall vertical-slat bk, for Browne's Bookstore, 1907, rfn, 54"...2,100.00
Desk, 2-drw, sq wood knobs, Meyer May house, 1908, rfn/rstr, 39" W ..10,000.00
Planter, Macquette for Price Tower OK, copper, 1952, 6¾x6¾"......7,650.00

Print, drawing for Heurtley House, FLW monogram, oak fr, 12x22" ...**900.00**
Stool, sq box designed to hold cushion (missing), 14x18" sq, 4 for **4,115.00**
Table, 22" slat top, wide X-form base w/Taliesin edges, 17" ...**2,000.00**
Teapot, SP, designed for Midway Gardens, 5½" **2,400.00**

Wrought Iron

Until the middle of the nineteenth century, almost all the metal hand forged in America was made from a material called wrought iron. When wrought iron rusts it appears grainy, while the mild steel that was used later shows no grain but pits to an orange-peel surface. This is an important aid in determining the age of an ironwork piece. See also Fireplace Implements.

Bracket, scrolled ft, 1 flat end for wall mt, appl iron leaves, 78x59" ..**300.00**
Etegere, loop finial over 5 sq graduated shelves w/glass, 85x20" .**300.00**
Game rack, Gothic window style w/hooks along bottom, 18x13" ...**330.00**
Game rack, 6 hooks, 3 brackets, hangs from ceiling, 31x16" dia ..**180.00**
Lectern, scrolled crest w/sunburst, S-scroll trifid legs, 89x24x26" .**925.00**
Meat hook, crown style w/4 3-prong hooks, 13x10" dia **220.00**
Skewer holder, heart motif bk, 6 sleeves w/6 skewers, 16½" L ...**260.00**
Strap hinges, bird beak design, 10x4", pr............................**285.00**
Strap hinges, tulip form, 30", pr...................................**300.00**
Thumb latch, decorative work w/brass inlay, 28" **515.00**
Utensil rack, fine scrolls, 5 hooks, 7½x21½" **195.00**
Utensil rack, stepped crest, twist details, 5 hooks, 13x21" **495.00**
Utensil rack, stepped crest w/birds & scrolls, 5-hook, 10x4" **250.00**
Window grate, hearts/scrolls/stars, 24x35", pr on wood base, 30x18" ...**120.00**
Window grates, sunburst w/11 arrow points, 19½x26", 3 for.......**200.00**

Yellow Ware

Ranging in color from buff to deep mustard, yellow ware which almost always has a clear glaze can be slip banded, plain, Rockingham decorated, flint enamel glazed, or mocha decorated. Black or red mocha decorated pieces are the most desirable. Although blue mocha decorated pieces are the most common, green decorated pieces command the lowest prices. Pieces having a combination of two colors are the rarest. The majority of pieces are plain and do not bear a manufacture's mark. Primarily produced in the United States, England, and Canada, this utilitarian ware was popular from the mid-nineteenth century until the early twentieth century. Yellow ware was first produced in New York, Pennsylvania, and Vermont. However, the center for yellow ware production was East Liverpool, Ohio, a town which once supported more than thirty potters. Yellow ware is still being produced today in both the United States and England. Because of websites and Internet auctions, prices have tended to become uniform throughout the United States. The use of this pottery as accessories in decorating and its exposure in country magazines has caused prices to rise, especially for the more utilitarian forms such as plates and bowls. Note: Because this is a utilitarian ware, it is often found with damage and heavy wear. Damage does have a negative impact on price, especially for the common forms. For further information we recommend *Collector's Guide to Yellow Ware: An Identification and Value Guide, Book I*, written by our advisor John Michel and Lisa McAllister, and *Collector's Guide to Yellow Ware, Book II and III*, by Lisa McAllister. Mr. Michel's address is in the Directory under New York. See also Rockingham.

Bowl, mixing; dk/lt bl band in center, 11"....................................**185.00**
Bowl, mixing; invt arch & Acanthus leaf, gr accents, 2½x5½" ..**190.00**
Bowl, waste; 2 wht slip bands, 6" **225.00**
Bowl, 4 wht rings at top & bottom, 5" **375.00**

Canning jar, plain yel, 8-sided, 7"...**425.00**
Canning jar, plain yel, cylindrical, 7½"..................................**325.00**
Colander, bl seaweed on wht slip band, 11"...........................**5,000.00**
Colander, plain, 11½" **875.00**
Colander, 8 wht bands, 11¼" **1,200.00**
Custard cup, 3 wht bands..**95.00**
Funnel, plain yel...**425.00**
Milk pan, 15"..**550.00**
Mold, frog, plain yel...**650.00**
Mold, parrot on branch, 8¼x10¼" **500.00**
Mold, pear w/leaves, 8¼" dia...**400.00**
Mug, red seaweed decor, 5"...**1,000.00**
Mustard pot, 6 wht bands, 2¼"...**750.00**
Nappy, heart-shaped ft, 12"..**325.00**
Pepper pot, blk mocha on wht slip band, 5".........................**1,125.00**
Pepper pot, plain yel, 4½"...**850.00**
Pepper pot, red mocha on wht slip band, 4¾" **1,500.00**
Pitcher, blk mocha on wht slip w/3 wht bands at top & bottom, 9½".**1,900.00**
Pitcher, 8 wht slip bands at top & bottom, 7¾" **1,250.00**
Rolling pin, plain yel w/orig hdl...**550.00**
Teapot, plain yel w/basketweave design, Jeffords (Phila)............**550.00**

Zanesville Glass

Glassware was produced in Zanesville, Ohio, from as early as 1815 until 1851. Two companies produced clear and colored hollow ware pieces in five characteristic patterns: 1) diamond faceted, 2) broken swirls, 3) vertical swirls, 4) perpendicular fluting, 5) plain, with scalloped or fluted rims and strap handles. The most readily identified product is perhaps the whiskey bottles made in the vertical swirl pattern, often called globular swirls because of their full, round bodies. Their necks vary in width; some have a ringed rim and some are collared. They were made in several colors; amber, light green, and light aquamarine are the most common.

Our advisor for this category is Mark Vuono; he is listed in the Directory under Connecticut.

Bottle, club; aqua, 24 swirl ribs, 7½" **195.00**
Bottle, demi-john; amber, pot stones, att, 16½" **440.00**
Bottle, globular; aqua, 24 melon ribs, few pot stones, 7⅝" **275.00**
Bottle, globular; dk amber, 24 swirl ribs, appl lip, EX impression, 8" ...**750.00**
Bottle, globular; dk amber, 3" **1,320.00**
Bottle, globular; med amber, 24 right-swirl ribs, rolled rim, 8½"....**575.00**
Creamer, brilliant violet bl, appl hdl, 4½" **2,640.00**
Pan, dk amber, 24-rib, folded-in rim, minor scratches, 1¼x6¼" ...**4,840.00**

Zell

The Georg Schmider United Zell Ceramic Factories has a long and colorful history. Affectionately called 'Zell' by those who are attracted to this charming German-Dutch type tin-glazed earthenware, this type of ware came into production in the latter part of the last century.

While Zell has created some lovely majolica-like examples (which are beginning to attract their own following), it is the German-Dutch scenes that are collected with such enthusiasm. Typical scenes are set against a lush green background with windmills on the distant horizon. Into the scenes appear typically garbed girls (long dresses with long white aprons and low-land bonnet head-gear) being teased or admired by little boys attired in pantaloon-type trousers and short rust-colored jackets, all wearing wooden shoes. There are variations on this theme, and occasionally a collector may find an animal theme or even a Kate Greenaway-like scene.

While Zell produced a wide range of wares and even quite recently (1970s) introduced an entirely hand-painted hen/rooster line, it is this early charming German-Dutch theme pottery that is coveted by increasing numbers of devoted collectors.

A similar ware in both theme, technique, and quality but bearing the mark Haag or Made in Austria is included in this listing. Our advisor for this category is Lila Shrader; she is listed in the Directory under California.

Key:
hdl/RA — handle at right angle to spout
KG — Kate Greenaway style
MIA — Made in Austria

Basket, blk hen/rooster, box w/vertical hdl, post-1970s, 3½" H **32.00**
Bowl, berry; rooster chasing Dutch girl, MIA, 5½" **56.00**
Bowl, berry; various Dutch scenes, Baden, 5½" **26.00**
Bowl, cereal; ped ft, Baden, 3x5½" **56.00**
Bowl, Dutch girl w/basket presents fish to cat, 2½x10" **96.00**
Bowl, girl feeding lamb, oval, Baden, 3½x5½" **210.00**
Bowl, rim soup; typical Dutch scene, Germany, 8¼" **55.00**
Bowls, Dutch scenes, MIA, 3 nesting, 3½x6" up to 10" dia........**305.00**
Cake plate, Dutch girl feeding cats, imp hdls, 9½" **158.00**
Cake stand, majolica-like water lilies, ped ft, Germany, 3½x9½"...**110.00**
Child's feeding dish, str sides, 1⅛x8½", from $55 to **95.00**
Child's tea set, bl & wht Dutch scenes, pot w/lid+2 c/s+cr/sug, tiny .**195.00**
Compote, majolica-like blackberries on lt bl, 3x8½" **50.00**
Creamer, bear w/laundry, hdl/RA, MIA, 3¼" **84.00**
Creamer, boy w/geese, MIA, 3" **40.00**
Creamer, girl pulling rooster by tail feathers, MIA/Haag, 3¼" **46.00**
Cup & saucer, boy & girl, harbor & windmills in bkground..........**29.00**
Cup & saucer, typical Dutch scenes, Baden, mini, 2¼", 3½"........**68.00**
Egg cup, Baden, tiny, 2½" **67.00**
Egg cup, boy presents bouquet to girl, short ped, 3" **105.00**
Mug, girl chasing rooster, str sides, 3¼", from $20 to...................**30.00**
Mug, KG scene w/grandfather toting water buckets, bbl like, 3¾" ..**110.00**
Mug, rabbits in field, str sides, MIA, 3¼" **50.00**
Mug, shore scene w/no children, bl & wht, str sides, MIA, 3¼" ..**35.00**
Pitcher, Dutch girl, rooster & ducks, Haag, 5¼" **105.00**
Pitcher, typical Dutch scene, Germany, 7" **92.00**
Planter, Dutch theme w/Art Nouveau border décor, 5x11x6½" .**230.00**
Plaque, typical Dutch scenes, ½" copper or brass band, 5½" **90.00**
Plate, blk rooster/hen w/swagged gr border, post-1970s, 12½x8"...**28.00**
Plate, boys & girls walking along shore, Baden, 8¼" **45.00**
Plate, majolica-like berries & greenery on basketweave, 9¼" **88.00**
Plate, majolica-like dandelions, fluted edge, 8¾" **62.00**
Plate, majolica-like grapes & leaves, abstract flowers, Germany, 9" ...**88.00**
Plate, majolica-like Oak Leaf w/pk & gr on yel, Baden, 7½" **37.00**
Plate, Puss 'n Boots holding fish followed by kittens, MIA, 9½" ..**132.00**
Plate majolica-like Lily Leaf, gr & yel, Germany, 8½"....................**27.00**
Plateau, Dutch boy teasing birl, oval w/brass rctl 1" band, 10x14"...**325.00**
Shakers, typical Dutch scene, Baden, 3⅝", pr, from $54 to...........**85.00**
Shakers, typical Dutch scene, MIA, Haag, 3¼", pr.......................**62.00**
Stein (like), Dutch boys along shore, recessed base, Baden, 5¾"...**110.00**
Tea tile, typical Dutch scene, Baden, 6¼" dia..............................**58.00**
Tea tile, typical Dutch scene, Germany, 6⅜" dia **46.00**
Vase, boy following girls, cylindrical w/narrow neck, 6½x3¼"......**88.00**
Vase, boy teasing cat w/fish, MIA/Haag, 4½"...............................**62.00**
Wall pocket, typical Dutch scene, ½-bowl form, 5½x3" dia **238.00**

Zsolnay

Only until the past decade has the production of the Zsolnay factory become more correctly understood. In the beginning they produced only cement; industrial and kitchenware manufacture began in the 1850s, and in the early 1870s a line of decorative architectural and art pottery was initiated which has continued to the present time.

The city of Pecs (pronounced Paach) is the major provincial city of southwest Hungary close to the Yugoslav border. The old German name for the city was Funfkirchen, meaning 'Five Churches.' (The 'five-steeple' mark became the factory's logo in 1878.)

Although most Americans only think of Zsolnay in terms of the bizarre, reticulated examples of the 1880s and 1890s and the small 'Eosine' green figures of animals and children that have been produced since the 1920s, the factory went through all the art trends of major international art potteries and produced various types of forms and decorations. The 'golden period,' circa 1895 – 1920, is when its Art Nouveau (Sezession in Austro-Hungarian terms) examples were unequaled. Vilmos Zsolnay was a Renaissance man devoted to innovation, and his children carried on the tradition after his death in 1900. Important sculptors and artists of the day were employed (usually anonymously) and married into the family, creating a dynasty.

Nearly all Zsolnay is marked, either impressed 'Zsolnay Pecs' or with the 'five steeple' stamp. Variations and form numbers can date a piece fairly accurately. For the most part, the earlier ethnic historical-revival pieces do not bring the prices that the later Sezession and second Sezession (Deco) examples do. Our advisor for this category is John Gacher; he is listed in the Directory under Rhode Island.

Bowl vase, encircled by 11 red birds/bushes/etc, mc, 1904-05, 6½x9" ..**15,000.00**
Cachepot, relief: girls dance/encircle stump, mc Labrado glazes, 13"..**1,250.00**
Cachepot, trefoils, lobed t'print-band top, gr/gold Eosin, #5686, 10 W..**5,500.00**
Compote, Trellis, appl flowers, pastel majolica, #3658, 12" L, EX.........**650.00**
Ewer, appl acorns/oak leaves/lg red beetles, #4115, 1893, 15½", NM.**4,500.00**
Figural box, putto w/flower on dome lid, mottled Eosin, #8695, 8¼".**3,000.00**
Figurine, cello player, modern design, red/blk/wht, G Furtos, 8½"..**350.00**
Figurine, Deco cat, gr Eosin, J Nador design, late 1960s, 9¼" **60.00**
Figurine, deer, sleeping/head bk, gr Eosin, 5-steeple mk, 3½" L **85.00**
Figurine, lady w/bowl faces sm child, Eosin, 5-steeple mk, 13" ...**250.00**
Figurine, owl on book, Eosin, 6¾"..**90.00**
Figurine, pr ducks stand by water, gr Eosin, 5-steeple mk, 6½" ...**120.00**
Figurine, vulture, brn irid on porc, 3¼x3½".............................**450.00**
Jug, thistles/butterflies, wine/gr on cream, #962, teardrop body, 11"...**1,450.00**
Lion figures, pyrogranite, 1901, worn pnt/edge flakes, 48" L, pr...**17,500.00**
Mug, animal/foliage, bl pencil on wht crackle, #1514, 1885, 4¾"....**250.00**
Pitcher, bent-over morning glory form w/coiled vine hdl, Eosin, #5517 ..**9,500.00**
Pitcher, Old Ivory, dragon hdl/gargoyle spout, ftd, #2994, rpr, 13" ...**850.00**
Pitcher, red/wht heavy crackle glaze, modern design, Torok, '59, 13" ..**600.00**
Plate, lobster on free-form edge, Eosin, 1968, 1½x7" dia **125.00**
Rooster vase, unusual glaze, Sàndor Apàti Abt, #7993, 8½" ...**4,950.00**
Rose bowl, emb flowers/stems, gr Eosin, 3x3¾" **65.00**
Tile, Nouveau floral, bl, from Pecs, 6", EX................................**200.00**
Vase, appl branch & berries, multiple gr w/red, wafer mk, 7" ..**1,600.00**
Vase, appl mouse & tree limb, yel/gr/rose mottle, prof rstr, 7½"..**3,500.00**
Vase, bird/elaborate foliage (enameled), dbl gourd, 7½" **350.00**
Vase, birds (6) cvg, mc metallic, att Darilek, 10" **6,000.00**
Vase, cactus leaves, gr irid on tan to brn, pinched/tortured, 11"...**5,500.00**
Vase, Egyptian, gold & gr Eosin/red/lt bl crackle design, 17½"...**8,500.00**
Vase, flowers/leaves, gr metallic on bl matt Eosin, #5330, 1900, 6"...**1,750.00**
Vase, Goose Girl, gr/bl/gold Eosin, raised design, #5561, 15¾", EX.**20,000.00**
Vase, landscape, mc on coral pk, Nabis design, #8196, 1909, 9¾"...**1,750.00**
Vase, melon-rib teardrop w/scalloped flared neck, red Eosin, 4¾"..**45.00**
Vase, mythological figures (2) on body, lav-gr irid, 9", NM **3,250.00**
Vase, purple/gold/bl irid, 3 lg indentions at waist, bulb body, 7x4"...**425.00**
Vase, trees/berries on red, Sirkorski, gourd form, 7½" **7,000.00**
Vase, Turkish/Hungarian jewel-like decor, ca 1912, 3⅞", NM.**2,500.00**
Vase, 9 exotic birds/leaves, mc/mottled Eosin w/gold, 1908, 12¼"...**22,500.00**

Advisory Board

The editors and staff take this opportunity to express our sincere gratitude and appreciation to each person who has in any way contributed to the preparation of this guide. We believe the credibility of our book is greatly enhanced through their efforts. See each advisor's Directory listing for information concerning their specific areas of expertise.

You will notice that at the conclusion of some of the narratives the advisor's name is given. This is optional and up to the discretion of each individual. Simply because no name is mentioned does not indicate that we have no advisor for that subject. Our board grows with each issue and now numbers nearly 425; if you care to correspond with any of them or anyone listed in our Directory, you must send a SASE with your letter. If you are seeking an appraisal, first ask about their fee, since many of these people are professionals who must naturally charge for their services. Because of our huge circulation, every person who allows us to publish their name runs the risk of their privacy being invaded by too many phone calls and letters. We are indebted to every advisor and very much regret losing any one of them. By far, the majority of those we lose give that reason. Please help us retain them on our board by observing the simple rules of common courtesy. Take the differences in time zones into consideration; some of our advisors tell us they often get phone calls in the middle of the night. For suggestions that may help you evaluate your holdings, see the Introduction.

Barbara K. and Steve Aaronson
Northridge, California

Peter Abrahams
Lake Oswego, Oregon

Charles and Barbara Adams
South Yarmouth, Massachusetts

Stan and Sally Alekna
Lebanon, Pennsylvania

Beverly L. Ales
Pleasanton, California

Charles Alexander
Indianapolis, Indiana

James Anderson
New Brighton, Minnesota

Michele Anderson
Kalispell, Montana

Suzy McLennan Anderson
Holmdel, New Jersey

Tim Anderson
Provo, Utah

Warren R. Anderson
Cedar City, Utah

Bruce A. Austin
Pittsford, New York

Bobby Babcock
Austin, Texas

Veldon Badders
Hamlin, New York

Rod Baer
Vienna, Virginia

Wayne and Gale Bailey
Dacula, Georgia

Jacqueline Linscott Barnes
Titusville, Florida

Kit Barry
Brattleboro, Vermont

Mark Bassett
Lakewood, Ohio

Dana Martin Batory
Crestline, Ohio

Scott Benjamin
LaGrange, Ohio

Sammie Berry
Melbourne, Florida

Phyllis Bess
Tulsa, Oklahoma

Robert Bettinger
Mt. Dora, Florida

William M. Bilsland III
Cedar Rapids, Iowa

Brenda Blake
York Harbor, Maine

Robert and Stan Block
Trumbull, Connecticut

Clarence H. Bodine, Jr.
New Hope, Pennsylvania

Sandra V. Bondhus
Unionville, Connecticut

Clifford Boram
Monticello, Indiana

Jeff Bradfield
Dayton, Virginia

Shane A. Branchcomb
Ashburn, Virginia

Harold Brandenburg
Wichita, Kansas

Mike Brooks
Oakland, California

Jim Broom
Effingham, Illinois

Dr. Kirby William Brown
Paradise, California

Marcia Brown
White City, Oregon

Rick Brown
Newspaper Collector's Society of America
Lansing, Michigan

Donald A. Bull
Wirtz, Virginia

Ann Burton
Decatur, Michigan

Jim Calison
Wallkill, New York

Tina M. Carter
El Cajon, California

Gene Cataldo
Huntsville, Alabama

Cerebro
East Prospect, Pennsylvania

Mick and Lorna Chase
Cookeville, Tennessee

Pat and Chris Christensen
Costa Mesa, California

Victor J.W. Christie, Ed. D.
Ephrata, Pennsylvania

Lanette Clarke
Antioch, California

John Cobabe
Redondo Beach, California

Debbie and Randy Coe
Hillsboro, Oregon

Wilfred and Dolli Cohen
Santa Ana, California

Marilyn Cooper
Houston, Texas

Ryan Cooper
Yarmouthport, Massachusetts

J.W. Courter
Kevil, Kentucky

Rosalind Cranor
Blacksburg, Virginia

Bob Culver
Northville, Michigan

Ron Damaska
New Brighton, Pennsylvania

John Danis
Rockford, Illinois

Patricia M. Davis
Portland, Oregon

Loretta DeLozier
Lake Placid, Florida

Clive Devenish
Orinda, California

Joe Devine
Council Bluffs, Iowa

David Dilley
Indianapolis, Indiana

Ginny Distel
Tiffin, Ohio

Rod Dockery
Ft. Worth, Texas

L.R. 'Les' Docks
San Antonio, Texas

Rebecca Dodds
Coral Springs, Florida

Brenda Dollen
Avoca, Iowa

Darlene Dommel
Minneapolis, Minnesota

Ron Donnelly
Tuscaloosa, Alabama

Kathy Doub
Columbia, Maryland

Robert A. Doyle, CAI, ISA, CAGA, CES
Pleasant Valley, New York

James Dryden
Hot Springs National Park, Arkansas

Louise Dumont
Leesburg, Florida

Jeanne Dunay
Camden, South Carolina

Ken and Jackie Durham
Washington, DC

William Durham
Belvidere, Illinois

Rita and John Ebner
Columbus, Ohio

Bill Edwards
Madison, Indiana

Kathy Eichert
Ojai, California

Michael L. Ellis
Costa Mesa, California

Dr. Robert Elsner
Boynton Beach, Florida

Barbara Endter
Rochester, New York

Bryce Farnsworth
Fargo, North Dakota

Arthur M. Feldman
Highland Park, Illinois

Linda Fields
Dover, Tennessee

Mary J. Finegan
Black Mountain, North Carolina

Vicki Flanigan
Winchester, Virginia

Gene Florence
Lexington, Kentucky

Marv Fogleman
Santa Ana, California

Frank W. Ford
Shrewsbury, Massachusetts

Madeleine France
Ft. Lauderdale, Florida

Peter Frei
Brimfield, Massachusetts

Wendy and Leo Frese
Dallas, Texas

Tony Freyaldenhoven
Conway, Arkansas

Donald M. Frost
Vancouver, Washington

John Gacher
Newport, Rhode Island

William Galaway
Belvidere, Illinois

Lee Garmon
Springfield, Illinois

Sandi and Jerry Garrett
Kokomo, Indiana

Mary Frank Gaston
Bryan, Texas

William L. Geary
Colorado Springs, Colorado

Dr. Joan M. George
Old Bridge, New Jersey

Tony George
Rancho Santa Margarita, California

Roselyn Gerson
Lynbrook, New York

Carl Gibbs, Jr.
Houston, Texas

Pat Gibson
Newark, California

Steve Gillespie
Village of the Oaks, Missouri

Walter Glenn
Atlanta, Georgia

Kathy Goldsworthy
Bothell, Washington

Bob Gottuso
Cranberry Township, Pennsylvania

Shirley Graff
Brunswick, Ohio

Helen Greguire
Lyman, South Carolina

Bonnie Groves
Elgin, Texas

Tom Guenin
Chardon, Ohio

Candace Gunther
Pasadena, California

John Guthrie
Mount Pleasant, South Carolina

Norman Haas
Quincy, Michigan

Don Haase
Mukilteo, Washington

Richard Haigh
Richmond, Virginia

Doug and Coila Hales
Poinciana, Florida

Doris and Burdell Hall
Morton, Illinois

Kathy and Raymond Hall
Monclova, Ohio

Mary 'Tootsie' Hamburg
Danville, Illinois

Jack and Treva Jo Hamlin
Proctorville, Ohio

Burton Handelsman
White Plains, New York

Don and Barbara Hardisty
Las Cruces, New Mexico

Roger and Claudia Hardy
Clarksburg, West Virginia

Jim and Susan Harran
Neptune, New Jersey

John Harrigan
Minneapolis, Minnesota

Gwynneth M. Harrison
Mira Loma, California

Mary Jane Hastings
Mt. Olive, Illinois

John Hathaway
Bryant Pond, Maine

Ted Haun
Kokomo, Indiana

Carl Heck
Aspen, Colorado

John Hess
Andover, Massachusetts

Jerry Heuring
Scott City, Missouri

Suzi Hibbard
Fairfield, California

James Highfield
South Bend, Indiana

Alma Hillman
Searsport, Maine

Michael C. Hinton
Doylestown, Pennsylvania

Susan and Larry Hirshman
Fort Myers, Florida

Steven Hoefs
Avalon, Georgia

Pat and Don Hoffmann, Sr.
Aurora, Illinois

Walter P. Hogan
Ann Arbor, Michigan

William Holland
West Chester, Pennsylvania

Jane Holt
Derry, New Hampshire

Dee Hooks
Percy, Illinois

Dave Hoover
New Albany, Indiana

Dennis Hopp
Chicago, Illinois

Betty Hornback
Elizabethtown, Kentucky

Cindy Horvath
Portland, Michigan

Lar Hothem
Lancaster, Ohio

Steve Howard
San Ramon, California

Hardy Hudson
Longwood, Florida

Murray Hudson
Halls, Tennessee

Kathy Hughes (Mrs. Paul)
Charlotte, North Carolina

George C. Humphrey
Beltsville, Maryland

Billy Ray and Susan Hussey
Bennett, North Carolina

Dan Iannotti
Bloomfield Hills, Michigan

Dave Irons
Northampton, Pennsylvania

Michael Ivankovich
Doylestown, Pennsylvania

Ralph Jaarsma
Pella, Iowa

Denis C. Jackson
Sequim, Washington

Pat James
Hillrose, Colorado

John R. Joiner
Newnan, Georgia

Donald Jones
Savannah, Georgia

Harriet Joyce
DeBary, Florida

Dorothy Kamm
Port St. Lucie, Florida

Fern Kao
Bowling Green, Ohio

Keith Kaonis
Northport, New York

Laurie and Richard Karman
Springfield, Illinois

Jerome R. Katz, Vice President
International Society of Antique
  Scale Collectors
Frederick, Maryland

William and June Keagy
Bloomfield, Indiana

Don and Anne Kier
Toledo, Ohio

C.D. Kilhoffer
Churchill, Maryland

Grace and James Klender
Pioneer, Ohio

Jerry Kline
Bennington, Vermont

Mr. and Mrs. Jerry and Gerry Kline
Maumee, Ohio

Judy A. Knauer
National Toothpick Holder Collectors
  Society
West Chester, Pennsylvania

Joanne M. Koehn
Eden Prairie, Minnesota

Katherine Kreider
Lancaster, Pennsylvania

Michael Krumme
Los Angeles, California

Rod Krupka
Ortonville, Michigan

Louis Kuritzky
Gainesville, Florida

Paris Langford
Jefferson, Louisiana

Elizabeth Langtree
Santa Ynez, California

Patricia and H. Thomas Laun
Syracuse, New York

Gary Lehrer
Woodbridge, Connecticut

Beverly Leslie
Boonville, Indiana

Anita Levi
Windber, Pennsylvania

Matt Lippa
Mentone, Alabama

Elyce Litts
Morris Planes, New Jersey

Howard J. Lockwood
Fort Lee, New Jersey

Dee Long
Lacon, Illinois

Paul J. Longo
Magnolia, Massachusetts

James Lewis Lowe
Norwood, Pennsylvania

Susan Grindberg Lynn
Las Vegas, Nevada

Dale MacAllister
Singers Glen, Virginia

Bill Mackin
Craig, Colorado

Dale MacLean
Dedham, Massachusetts

Betty and Clarence Maier
The Burmese Cruet
Montgomeryville, Pennsylvania

Lucille Malitz
Scarsdale, New York

Abby and Wlodek Malowanczyk
Dallas, Texas

Bev and Jim Mangus
Louisville, Ohio

William Manns
Santa Fe, New Mexico

Linda K. Marsh
Lansing, Michigan

Jim Martin
Monmouth, Illinois

Richard Mathes
Springfield, Ohio

Gene Matzke
Hancock, Wisconsin

Maundy International
Shawnee Mission, Kansas

Oveda L. Maurer
San Anselmo, California

Michael J. McQuillen
Indianapolis, Indiana

John, Jean and Michael Meadows
Baltimore, Maryland

Edward J. Meschi
Monroeville, New Jersey

Barbara and John Michel
New York, New York

Clark Miller
Minneapolis, Minnesota

Larry Miller
East Peoria, Illinois

Robert Miller
Crawfordsville, Indiana

Tom and Linda Millman
Bethel, Ohio

Randall B. Monsen
Vienna, Virginia

Carolyn Moore
Bowling Green, Ohio

Shirley Suber Moore
Tulsa, Oklahoma

Albert Morin
Dracut, Massachusetts

Thomas G. Morris
Medford, Oregon

Patsy Moyer
Deming, New Mexico

James L. Murphy
Columbus, Ohio

Boyd W. Nedry
Comstock Park, Michigan

Leonard Needham
Bernicia, California

C.L. Nelson
Grapevine, Texas

Maxine Nelson
Scottsdale, Arizona

Scott H. Nelson
Santa Fe, New Mexico

Betty Newbound
Sanford, North Carolina

Mike Nickel
Portland, Michigan

Kenn Norris
Sanderson, Texas

Joan Oates
Marshall, Michigan

The Occupied Japan Club
c/o Florence Archambault
Newport, Rhode Island

Grace Ochsner
Niota, Illinois

Susan Otto
Chesterland, Ohio

Naomi Over
Arvada, Colorado

Dick Pardini
Stockton, California

Jim Pasquali
San Francisco, California

Sharon A. Payne
Mt. Vernon, Washington

Suzanne Perrault
Lambertville, New Jersey

Jeffrey Person
St. Petersburg, Florida

Nancy and Robert Perzel
Flemington, New Jersey

T. Phillips
Des Plaines, Illinois

Louis Picek
West Branch, Iowa

David Pierce
Gambler, Ohio

Larry G. Pogue
Terrell, Texas

Richard T. Porter
Onset, Massachusetts

Judy Posner
Englewood, Florida

Harry Poster
S. Hackensack, New Jersey

Ted Pruitt
Anderson, Indiana

Barb Putratz
Spring Lake Park, Minnesota

David Rago
Lambertville, New Jersey

Glen Rairigh
Sunfield, Michigan

Jim Rash
Egg Harbor Township, New Jersey

Lisa Rastello
St. Charles, Illinois

Debbie Rees
Zanesville, Ohio

Leon Reimert
Coatesville, Pennsylvania

Charles Reynolds
Falls Church, Virginia

Joan and Charles Rhoden
Georgetown, Illinois

Blume Rifken
New York

John F. Rinaldi
Kennebunkport, Maine

Angi and David Ringering
Salem, Oregon

Roy B. Ritchie
Hindman, Kentucky

Brenda Roberts
Dayton, Ohio

Fred and Marilyn Roberts
Lake Montezuma, Arizona

Joanne Rodgers
Stretch Glass Society
Lakewood, Ohio

Martin Roenigk
Eureka Springs, Arkansas

Joyce and Fred Roerig
Walterboro, South Carolina

Herbert Rolfes
Mt. Dora, Florida

Barbara Rosen
Wayne, New Jersey

Kenna Rosen
Dallas, Texas

Michelle Ross
Berrien Center, Michigan

Philip Rosso, Jr.
Port Vue, Pennsylvania

John and Barbara Rudisill
Worton, Maryland

Charlotte Safir
New York, New York

Lisa Sanders
Evansville, Indiana

Martha and Steve Sanford
Campbell, California

R.J. Sayers
Hendersonville, North Carolina

Elizabeth Schaaf
Mentone, Alabama

Roselle Schleifman
Spring Valley, New York

Betty and Larry Schwab
Bloomington, Illinois

Roger R. Scott
Tulsa, Oklahoma

Joyce and Harold Screen
Baltimore, Maryland

Cathy Segelke
Merino, Colorado

Lorne Shields
Toronto, Ontario, Canada

Lila Shrader
Crescent City, California

Brenda and Jerry Siegel
St. Louis, Missouri

Elizabeth Simpson
Freeport, Maine

David Smies
Manhattan, Kansas

Carole and Richard Smyth
Huntington, New York

Susan Snyder
Gig Harbor, Washington

Diane Snyder-Haug
St. Petersburg, Florida

Dick Spencer
O'Fallon, Illinois

Rick Spencer
Salt Lake City, Utah

Greg Spiess
Joliet, Illinois

Nancy Steinbock
Chestnut Hill, Massachusetts

Ron Stewart
Hazard, Kentucky

Craig Stifter
Hinsdale, Illinois

Liz Stillwell
Pico Rivera, California

Pamela and Joseph Tanner
Elk Grove, California

Jenny Tarrant
St. Peters, Missouri

Dr. E.E. Taylor
Indianapolis, Indiana

Terry Taylor
East Bend, North Carolina

Bruce Thalberg
Weston, Connecticut

Sharon Thoerner
Bellflower, California

Darrell Thomas
New London, Wisconsin

Chuck Thompson
Houston, Texas

Don Thornton
Moss Beach, California

Donna and John Thorpe
Sun Prairie, Wisconsin

Rosella Tinsley
Osawatomie, Kansas

Marlena Toohey
Longmont, Colorado

Veronica Trainer
Cleveland, Ohio

Valerie and Richard Tucker
Argyle, Texas

Robert Tuggle
New York, New York

Hobart D. Van Deusen
Lakeville, Connecticut

Jean and Dale Van Kuren
Clarence Center, New York

Joan F. Van Patten
Rexford, New York

Linda L. Vines
Santa Monica, California

Stephen Visakay
West Caldwell, New Jersey

Janice and Richard Vogel
Ocala, Florida

Mark Vuono
Stamford, Connecticut

John W. Waddell
Mineral Wells, Texas

Jim Waite
Farmer City, Illinois

Judith and Robert Walthall
Huntsville, Alabama

Ian Warner
Brampton, Ontario, Canada

Marty Webster
Saline, Michigan

David Weddington
Murfreesboro, Tennessee

Robert Weisblut
Ocean Ridge, Florida

Pastor Frederick S. Weiser
New Oxford, Pennsylvania

Stan and Arlene Weitman
Massapequa, New York

BA Wellman
Westminster, Massachusetts

Lonnie Wells
Doe Run, Missouri

David Wendel
Poplar Bluff, Missouri

Kaye and Jim Whitaker
Lynnwood, Washington

Douglass White
Orlando, Florida

John 'Grandpa' White
Denver, Colorado

Judy White
La Jolla, California

Margaret and Kenn Whitmyer
Gahanna, Ohio

Steven Whysel
Cooper City, Florida

Doug Wiesehan
St. Charles, Missouri

Don Williams
Kirksville, Missouri

Linda Williams
Chicopee, Massachusetts

Ron L. Willis
Matlacha, Florida

Roy M. Willis
Lebanon Junction, Kentucky

Jack D. Wilson
Prescott, Arizona

Ralph Winslow
Camdenton, Missouri

Nancy Winston
Northwood, New Hampshire

Jo Ellen Winther
Arvada, Colorado

Raphael C. Wise
West Palm Beach, Florida

Dannie Woodard
Weatherford, Texas

Virginia Woodbury
Rolling Hills Estates, California

Bill Wright
New Albany, Indiana

Libby Yalom
Silver Spring, Maryland

Darlene Yohe
Stuttgart, Arkansas

Mary Young
Kettering, Ohio

Willy Young
Reno, Nevada

Audrey Zeder
North Bend, Washington

Auction Houses

We wish to thank the following auction houses whose catalogs have been used as sources for pricing information. Many have granted us permission to reproduce their photographs as well.

A-1 Auction Service
2042 N. Rio Grande Ave., Suite 'E,' Orlando, FL 32804; 407-839-0004. Specializing in American antique sales. a-1auction@cfl.rr.com

A&B Auctions, Inc.
17 Sherman St., Marlboro, MA 01752-3314; 508-480-0006 or fax 508-460-6101. Specializing in English ceramics, flow blue, pottery, and Mason's Ironstone

Absolute Auction & Realty, Inc./Absolute Auction Center
Robert Doyle
PO Box 1739, Pleasant Valley, NY 12569. Antique and estate auctions twice a month at Absolute Auction Center; Free calendar of auctions; Specializing in specialty collections. www.AbsoluteAuctionRealty.com

Allard Auctions Inc.
Col. Doug Allard
PO Box 1030, 419 Flathead St., Ste. 4, Ignatiuss, MT 59865; 406-745-0500 or fax 406-745-0502. Specializing in American Indian collectibles.
info@allardauctions.com
allardauctions.com

America West Archives
Anderson, Warren
PO Box 100, Cedar City, UT 84721; 435-586-9497. Related Publishes 26-page illustrated catalog 5 times a year that includes auction section of scarce and historical early western documents, letters, autographs, stock certificates, and other important ephemera, Subscription: $13 per year. warren@americawestarchives.com americawestarchives.com www.oldstockresearch.com

American Bottle Auctions
1507 21st St., Ste. 203, Sacramento, CA 95814; 800-806-7722 or fax 916-443-3199. Specializing in antique bottles. www.americanbottle.com

American Social History and Social Movements
PO Box 203, Tucker, GA 30085; 678-937-1835; fax 678-937-1837.
admin@ashsm.com
www.ashsm.com

Americana Auctions
c/o Glen Rairigh
12633 Sandborn, Sunfield, MI 48890. Specializing in Skookum dolls, art glass, and art auctions

Anderson Auctions/Heritage Antiques & Appraisal Services
Suzy McLennan Anderson
65 E. Main St., Holmdel, NJ 07733; 732-946-8801 or (fax) 732-946-1036. Specializing in American furniture and decorative accessories. www.andersonauctions.net/antiques.htm

Andre Ammelounx
The Stein Auction Company
PO Box 136, Palatine, IL 60078-0136; 847-991-5927 or fax 847-991-5947. Specializing in steins, catalogs available. www.tsaco.com

Aston Macek
2825 Country Club Rd., Endwell, NY 13760-3349; 607-754-1180. Specializing in and appraisers of American folk art, other primitives, furniture Shaker, fine art, porcelain, and china.
astonmacek@stnyrr.com
www.astonmacek.com

The Auction Blocks
10 Twarog Place, PO Box 2321, Shelton, CT 06484; 203-924-2802. Buy & sell marbles in online auctions. www.blocksite.com

Bider's
397 Methuen St., Lawrence, MA 01843; 978-688-0923 or 978-475-8336. Antiques appraised, purchased, and sold on consignment.
bider@netway.com
www.biders-auction.com

Bill Bertoia Auctions
2141 DeMarco Dr., Vineland, NJ 08360; 856-692-1881 or fax 856-692-8697. Specializing in toys, dolls, advertising, and related items.
Bill@bertoiaauctions.com
www.bertoiaauctions.com

Bonhams & Butterfields
220 San Bruno Ave., San Francisco, CA 94103; 415-861-7500 or fax 415-861-8951. Also located at 7601 Sunset Blvd., Los Angeles, CA 90046; 323-850-7500 or fax 323-850-5843. Fine art auctioneers and appraisers since 1865. info@butterfields.com www.butterfields.com

Buffalo Bay Auction Co.
5244 Quam Circle, Rogers, MN 55374; 612-428-8480; or fax 612-428-8879. Specializing in advertising, tins, and country store items.
buffalobay@hotmail.com
buffalobayauction.com

Cerebro
PO Box 327, E. Prospect, PA 17317-0327; 717-252-2400 or 800-69-LABEL; fax: 717-252-3685. Specializing in antique advertising labels, especially cigar box labels, cigar bands, food labels, firecracker labels; Holds semiannual auction on tobacco ephemera; Consignments accepted.
Cerebro@Cerebro.com
www.cerebro.com

Charles E. Kirtley
PO Box 2273, Elizabeth City, NC 27096-2273; 252-335-1262. Specializing in World's Fair, Civil War, political, advertising, and other American collectibles. cekirtley@ckirtley.com www.ckirtley.com

Cincinnati Art Galleries
225 E. Sixth, Cincinnati, OH 45202; 513-381-2128; fax 513-381-7527. Specializing in American art pottery, American and European fine paintings, watercolors.
www.cincinnatiart galleries.com

Collector's Auction Services
R.D. 2, Box 431, Oil City, PA 16301-9426; 814-677-6070. Specializing in advertising, oil and gas, toys, rare museum and investment-quality antiques.
director@caswel.com
www.caswel.com

Craftsman Auctions
1485 W Housatonic (Rt 20); Pittsfield, MA 01201; 413-448-8922. Specializing in Arts & Crafts furniture and accessories as well as American art pottery. Color catalogs available.
www.artsncrafts.com or www.ragoarts.com

Dargate Auction Galleries
214 N. Lexington, Pittsburgh, PA 15208. Specializing in estate auctions featuring fine art, antiques, and collectibles. info@dargate.com www.dargate.com

David Rago
333 N. Main, Lambertville, NJ 08530;
609-397-9374 or fax 609-397-9377.
Specializing in American art pottery and
Arts and Crafts. info@ragoarts.com
www.ragoarts.com

Du Mouchelles
409 E Jefferson Ave., Detroit, MI
48226-4300; 313-963-6255 or fax 313-
963-8199. info@dumouchelle.com
dumouchelle.com

Dunbar's Gallery
Leila and Howard Dunbar
76 Haven St., Milford, MA 01757;
508-634-8697 or fax 508-634-8698.
Dunbars@dunbarsgallery.com
www.dunbarsgallery.com

Early American History Auctions
PO Box 3507, Rancho Santa Fe, CA
92067; 858-759-3290 or fax 858-759-
1439. history@earlyamerican.com
www.earlyamerican.com

Early Auction Co.
123 Main St., Milford, OH 45150-
1121; 513-831-4833 or fax 513-831-
1441. info@EarlyAuctionCo.com
EarlyAuctionCo.com

Flying Deuce Auctions & Antiques
14051 W. Chubbuck Rd., Chubbuck
ID 83202 208-237-2002 or fax 208-
237-4544. flying2@ida.net
www.flying2.com

Fontaine's Auction Gallery
1485 W. Housatonic St., Pittsfield, MA
01201; 413-448-8922 or fax 413-442-
1550. Specializing in fine quality antiques;
important 20th-century lighting, clocks,
art glass. Color catalogs available.
info@fontaine auction.com
www.fontaineauction.com

Garth's Auctions Inc.
2690 Stratford Rd., Box 369,
Delaware, OH 43015; 740-362-4771.
info@garths.com or www.garths.com

Glass-Works Auctions
102 Jefferson, East Greenville, PA
18041-11623; 215-679-5849 or fax 215-
679-3068. America's leading auction
company in early American bottles and
glass and barber shop memorabilia.
glswrk@enter.net
www.glswk-auction.com

Heights Antiques
29 Clubhouse Lane, Boynton Beach,
FL 33436-6056; 561-736-1362. Specializing in antique barometers and
nautical instruments

Henry/Pierce Auctioneers
1456 Carson Court, Homewood, IL
60430-4013; 708-798-7508 or fax 708-
799-3594. Specializing in bank auctions

High Noon
9929 Venice Blvd., Los Angeles, CA
90034-5111; 310-202-9010 or fax 310-
202-9011. Specializing in cowboy and
western collectibles.
highnoon@pacbell.net
www.highnoon.com

History Buff's Auctions
6031 Winterset, Lansing, MI 48911.
Specializing in paper collectibles span-
ning five centuries.
admin@historybuffauction.com
www.historybuffauction.com

Horst Auctioneers
Horst Auction Center
50 Durlach Rd. (corner of Rt. 322 &
Durlach Rd., west of Ephrata), Ephrata,
Lancaster County, PA 17522-9741; 717-
738-3080. sale@horstauction.com
www.horst auction.com

Jackson's, International Auctioneers
& Appraisers of Fine Art and
Antiques
2229 Lincoln St., Cedar Falls, IA
50613; 319-277-2256 or fax 319-277-
1252. Specializing in American and
European art pottery and art glass,
American and European paintings,
Russian works of art, decorative arts,
toys and jewelry.
jacksons@jacksonsauction.com
www.jackson sauction.com

James D. Julia Inc.
PO Box 830, Rt. 201, Skowhegan Rd.,
Fairfield, ME 04937-0830; 207-453-
7125 or fax 207-453-2502.
jjulia@juliaauctions.com
www.julia auctions.com

John Toomey Gallery
818 North Blvd., Oak Park, IL 60301-
1302; 708-383-5234 or fax 708-383-
4828. Specializing in furniture and
decorative arts of the Arts & Crafts,
Art Deco, and Modern Design movements; Modern Design expert:
Richard Wright. arts@oprf.com
www.treadwaygallery.com

Joy Luke Fine Art Brokers & Auctioneers
The Gallery
300 East Grove St., Bloomington, IL
61701-5290; 309-828-5533 or fax 309-
829-2266. robert@joyluke.com
www.joyluke.com

Kit Barry Ephemera Auctions
74 Cotton Mill Hill #A252, VT 0530.
Tradecard and ephemera auctions,
fully illustrated catalogs with prices
realized; Consignment inquiries welcome. kbarry@surfglobal.net
www.tradecards.com/kb

Kurt R. Krueger
The American Numismatic Association Marketplace
160 N. Washington St., PO Box 275,
Iola, WI 54945-0275; 715-445-3845
or fax 715-445-4100

L.R. 'Les' Docks
Box 691035, San Antonio, TX 78269-
1035. Providing occasional mail-order
record auctions, rarely consigned; The
only consignments considered are
exceptionally scarce and unusual
records. docks@texas.net
www.docks.home.texas.net

Lloyd Ralston Gallery, Inc.
350 Long Beach Blvd., Stratfort CT
06615; 203-386-9399; fax 203-386-
9519. lrgallery@aol.com
www.lloydralstontoys.com

Lowe, James Lewis
PO Box 8, Norwood, PA 19074. Specializing in Kate Greenaway, postcards; eBay. JLewisLowe@juno.com

Majolica Auctions
Strawser Auction Group
200 North Main, PO Box 332, Wol-
cottville, IN 46795-0332; 260-854-2859
or fax 260-854-3979. Issues colored catalog; Also specializing in Fiesta ware.
info@strawserauctions.com

Manion's International Auction
House, Inc.
PO Box 12214, Kansas City, KS
66112-0214; 913-299-6692 or fax 913-
299-6792. Specializing in international militaria, particularly the US,
Germany, and Japan. Extensive catalogs in antiques and collectibles,
sports, transportation, political and
advertising memorabilia and vintage
clothing and denim. Publishes 9 catalogs for each of the 5 categories per
year. Request a free sample of past auctions, 1 issue of current auction for
$15. collecting@manions.com
www.manions.com

Maritime Antiques & Auctions
935 US Rt. 1, PO Box 322, York, ME
03909-0322; 207-363-4247 or fax 353-
1416. info@maritiques.com
www.maritiques.com

McMasters Harris Auction Company
PO Box 1755, 5855 Glenn Highway,
Cambridge, OH 43725-8768; 740-432-
4419 or fax 740-432-3191.
info@mcmasters harris.com
mcmastersauctions.com

Michael Ivankovich Antiques &
Auction Company Inc.
PO Box 1536, Doylestown, PA, 18901;
215-345-6094 or fax 215-345-6692.
Specializing in early hand-colored
photography and prints. Auction held
4 times each year, providing opportunity for collectors and dealers to compete for the largest variety of Wallace
Nutting, Wallace Nutting-like pictures, Maxfield Parrish, Bessie Pease
Gutmann, R. Atkinson Fox, Philip
Boileau, Harrison Fisher, etc.
ivankovich@wnutting.com

Michael John Verlangieri
PO Box 844, Cambria, CA 93428-
0844; 805-927-4428. Specializing in
fine California pottery; cataloged auctions (video tapes available).
michael@calpots.com
www.calpots.com

Monsen & Baer, Annual Perfume
Bottle Auction
Monsen, Randall; and Baer, Rod
Box 529, Vienna, VA 22183; 703-938-
2129 or fax 703-242-1357. Cataloged
auctions of perfume bottles; Will purchase, sell, and accept consignments;
Specializing in commercial, Czechoslovakian, Lalique, Baccarat, Victorian, crown top, factices, miniatures

Neal Auction Company
Auctioneers & Appraisers of
Antiques & Fine Art
4038 Magazine St., New Orleans, LA
70115; 504-899-5329; fax 504-897-3803.
customerservice@nealauction.com
nealauction.com

New England Absentee Auctions
16 Sixth St., Stamford, CT 06905-4610;
203-975-9055. Specializing in Quimper
pottery. neaauction@aol.com
www.members.tripod.com/~bondhus

Noel Barrett Antiques & Auctions
PO Box 300, 6183 Carversville Rd.,
Carversville, PA 18913; 215-297-5109 or
fax 215-297-0457. toys@noelbarret.com
www.noelbarrett.com

Norman C. Heckler & Company
79 Bradford Corner Rd., Woodstock
Valley, CT 06282-2002; 860-974-1634
or fax 860-974-2003. Auctioneers and
appraisers specializing in early glass
and bottles.
info@hecklerauction.com
www.hecklerauction.com

Past Tyme Pleasures
Steve & Donna Howard
PMB #204, 2491 San Ramon Blvd.,
#1, San Ramon, CA 94583; 925-484-
4488 or fax 925-484-2551. Offers 2
absentee auction catalogs per year pertaining to old advertising items.
pasttyme1@comcast.net
www.pasttyme1.com

Perrault-Rago Gallery
333 N. Main St., Lambertville, NJ
08530; 609-397-9374. Specializing in
American Art Pottery, Tiles, Arts &
Crafts, Moderns, and Bucks County
Paintings. www.ragoarts.com

Richard Opfer Auctioneering, Inc.
1919 Greenspring Dr., Timonium, MD
21093-4113; 410-252-5035; fax 410-
252-5863. info@opferauction.com
www.opferauction.com

Roan Inc.
3530 Lycoming Creek Rd., Cogan Station, PA 17728; 717-494-0170; 800-
955-ROAN. info@roaninc.com

Samuel T. Freeman & Co. Est. 1805
1808 Chestnut St., Philadelphia, PA
19103; 215-563-9275 or fax 215-563-
8236. info@freemansauction.com
freemansauction.com

Schoolmaster Auctions and Real Estate
Kenn Norris
PO Box 4830; 513 N. 2nd St., Sanderson, TX 79848; 915-345-2640. Specializing in school-related items,
barbed wire and related literature, and
L'il Abner

Skinner, Inc.
Auctioneers & Appraisers of
Antiques and Fine Arts
The Heritage on the Garden, 63 Park
Plaza, Boston, MA 02116-3925; 617-
350-5400 or fax 617-350-5429. Sec-
ond address: 357 Main St., Bolton,
MA 01740; 978-779-6241 or fax 978-
779-5144. www.skinnerinc.com

Smith & Jones, Inc.
12 Clark Lane, Sudbury, MA 01776; 978-443-5517 or fax 978-443-8045. Specializing in Dedham dinnerware, Buffalo china and important American art pottery; Full-color catalogs available. smithandjonesauctions.com

SoldUSA.com
1418 Industrial Dr., Box 11, Matthews, NC 28105; 704-815-1500. Specializing in fine sporting collectibles. support@soldusa.com www.Soldusa.com

Sotheby's
1334 York Ave., New York, NY 10021; 212-606-7000; www.sothebys.com

Stanton's Auctioneers & Realtors
144 S. Main St., PO Box 146, Vermontville, MI 49096-0146; 517-726-0181. Specializing in all types of property, at auction, anywhere. stanton@voyager.net www.stantons-auctions.com

Steffen's Historical Militaria
Major Auction Division
PO Box 280, Newport, KY 41072; 858-431-4499 or fax 859-431-3113. Specializing in quality militaria, military art, rare books, antique firearms. www.steffensmilitaria.com

Superior Galleries
9478 West Olympic Boulevard, Beverly Hills, CA 90212-4246; 310-203-9855 or fax 310-203-0496. Specializing in manuscripts, decorative and fine arts, Hollywood memorabilia, sports memorabilia, stamps, and coins; www.superiorgalleries.com

Swann Galleries, Inc.
104 E. 25th St., New York, NY 10010; 312-254-4710 or fax 212-979-1017. swan@swanngalleries.com www.swanngalleries.com

Three Rivers Collectibles
Wendy and Leo Frese
PO Box 551542, Dallas, TX 75355; 214-341-5165. Annual Red Wing and RumRill pottery and stoneware auctions

Toy Scouts, Inc.
137 Casterton Ave., Akron, OH 44303-1543; 330-836-0668 or fax 330-869-8668. Specializing in baby-boom era collectibles. info@toyscouts.com www.toyscouts.com

Tradewinds Auctions
Henry Taron
PO Box 249, 24 Magnolia Ave., Manchester-By-The-Sea, MA 01944-0249; 508-768-3327; Specializing in antique canes. www.tradewindsantiques.com

Treadway Gallery, Inc.
2029 Madison Rd., Cincinnati, OH 45208-3218; 513-321-6742 or fax 513-871-7722. Specializing in American Art Pottery; American and European art glass; European ceramics; Italian glass; fine American and European paintings and graphics; and furniture and decorative arts of the Arts & Crafts, Art Nouveau, Art Deco, and Modern Design Movements. Modern Design expert: Thierry Lorthioir. Members: National Antique Dealers Association, American Art Pottery Association, International Society of Appraisers, American Ceramic Arts Society, Ohio Decorative Arts Society, Art Gallery Association of Cincinnati. info@treadwaygallery.com www.treadwaygallery.com

Vicki and Bruce Waasdorp
PO Box 434; 10931 Main St.; Clarence, NY 14031; 716-759-2361. Specializing in decorated stoneware. waasdorp@antiques-stoneware.com www.antiques stoneware.com

VintagePostcards.Com
Antique Postcards for Collectors
312 Feather Tree Dr. Clearwater FL 33765; 727-467-0333. quality@vintagepostcards.com www.vintagepostcards.com

Weschler's
Adam A. Weschler & Son
905 E. St. N.W., Washington, DC 20004-2006; 202-628-1281. www.weschlers.com

William Doyle Galleries
Auctioneers & Appraisers
175 East 87th St., New York, NY 10128; 212-427-2730 or fax 212-369-0892. info@DoyleNewYork.com www.doylenewyork. com.

Willis Henry Auctions
22 Main St., Marshfield, MA 02050-2808; 781-834-7774 or fax 781-826-3520. wha@willishenry.com www.willishenry.com

York Town Auction Inc.
1625 Haviland Rd., York, PA 17404; 717-751-0211; fax 717-767-772. Specializing in the sale of antiques, art, collections, fine furnishings, and real estate. info@yorktownauction.com www.yorktownauction.com

Directory of Contributors

When contacting any of the buyers/sellers listed in this part of the Directory by mail, you must include an SASE (stamped, self-addressed envelope) if you expect a reply. Many of these people are professional appraisers, and there may be a fee for their time and service. Find out up front. Include a clear photo if you want an item identified. Most items cannot be described clearly enough to make an identification without a photo.

If you call and get their answering machine, when you leave your number so that they can return your call, tell them to call back collect. And please take the differences in time zones into consideration — 7:00 AM in the Midwest is only 4:00 AM in California! And if you're in California, remember that even 7:00 PM is too late to call the east coast. Most people work and are gone during the daytime. Even some of our antique dealers say they prefer after-work phone calls. Don't assume that a person who deals in a particular field will be able to help you with related items. They may seem related to you when they are not.

Please, we need your help. This book sells in such great numbers that allowing their names to be published can create a potential nightmare for each advisor and contributor. Please do your part to help us minimize this, so that we can retain them on our board and in turn pass their experience and knowledge on to you through our book. Their only obligation is to advise us, not to evaluate your holdings. Many of our people tell us that even with the occasional problem, they feel that the good outweighs the bad and makes all their hard work worthwhile.

Alabama

Cataldo, Gene
C.E. Cataldo
4726 Panorama Dr., S.E., Huntsville, 35801; 256-536-6893. Specializing in classic and used cameras. genecams@aol.com

Donnelly, Ron
Saturday Heroes
6302 Championship Dr., Tuscaloosa, 35405. Specializing in Big Little Books, movie posters, premiums, western heroes, Gone With the Wind, character collectibles, early Disney; Inquiries require SASE; No free appraisals

Lippa, Matt; and Schaaf, Elizabeth
Artisans
PO Box 256, Mentone, 35984; 256-634-4037. Specializing in folk art, quilts, painted and folky furniture, tramp art, whirligigs, windmill weights. artisans@folkartisans.com www.folkartisans.com

Walthall, Judith and Robert
PO Box 4465, Huntsville, 35815; 256-881-9198. Judith founded Peanut Pals in 1978. Robert has served two terms as president of Peanut Pals. Specializing in Planters Peanuts memorabilia; also Old Crow collectibles

Arizona

Nelson, Maxine
7657 E. Hazelwood St., Scottsdale, 85251. Specializing in Vernon Kilns; Author of *Collectible Vernon Kilns, 2nd Edition*. SASE appreciated for inquiries

Roberts, Fred and Marilyn
Bah Humbug Collectibles
PO Box 5733, Lake Montezuma, 86342-5733 or fax 815-425-9394. Specializing in Hummel figurines. bahhumbug@juno.com

Wilson, Jack D.
1514 Eagle Ridge Road, Prescott, 86301-5418; 928-445-5137. Specializing in Phoenix and Consolidated glass; buying Ruba Rombic; author of *Phoenix and Consolidated Art glass: 1926-1980*. jdwilson1@earthlink.net http://home.earthlink.net~jdwilson1/

Arkansas

Dryden, James
Dryden Pottery
PO Box 603, Hot Springs National Park, 71902; 501-627-4201. Specializ-ing in hand-thrown artware vases, mugs, ovenware, etc.

Freyaldenhoven, Tony
29 Timothy Ln. Conway, 72034; 501-730-3027 or 501-932-0352; Specializing in Camark pottery. camarket@cyberback.com

Roenigk, Martin
Mechantiques
Crescent Hotel & Spa
75 Prospect Ave., Eureka Springs, 72632; 800-671-6333. Specializing in mechanical musical instruments, music boxes, band organs, musical clocks and watches, coin pianos, orchestrions, monkey organs, automata, mechanical birds and dolls, etc. mroenigk@aol.com www.mechantiques.com

Yohe, Darlene
Timberview Antiques
1303 S. Prairie St., Stuttgart, 72160-5132; 870-673-3437. Specializing in American pattern glass, historical glass, Victorian pattern glass, carnival glass, and custard glass

California

Aaronson, Barbara and Steve
The Victorian Lady
PO Box 7522, Northridge, 91327; 818-368-6052. Specializing in figural napkin rings, pickle castors, American Victorian silverplate.
bjaaronson@aol.com
TheVictorianLady.com

Ales, Beverly Schell
4046 Graham St., Pleasanton, 94566-5619; 925-846-5297. Specializing in knife rests. Kniferests@sbcglobal.net.

Berg, Paul
PO Box 8895, Newport Beach, 92620. Author of Nineteenth Century Photographica Cases and Wall Frames

Brooks, Mike
7335 Skyline, Oakland, 94611; 510-339-1751 (evenings). Specializing in typewriters, transistor radios, early televisions, Statue of Liberty

Brown, Dr. Kirby William
PO Box 1842, Paradise, 95967; 530-877-2159. Authoring book on history and products of California Faience, California Porcelain, and West Coast Porcelain. Any contribution of information, new pieces, etc., is welcome.

Carter, Tina M.
PMB 449, 603 Seagaze Dr., Oceanside, 92054-3005. Specializing in teapots, tea-related items, tea tins, children's and toy tea sets, plastic cookie cutters, etc.; book on teapots available. Send $16 (includes postage) or $17 for CA residents, Canada: add $5, to above address

Christensen, Pat and Chri
1067 Salvador St., Costa Mesa, 92626. Specializing in open salts

Clarke, Lanette
5021 Toyon Way, Antioch, 94532; 925-776-7784. Co-founder of Haeger Pottery Collectors of America; specializing in Haeger and Royal Hickman.
Lanette_Clarke@msn.com

Cobabe, John
800 So. Pacific Coast Hwy; Suite 8-301; Redondo Beach 90277; 310-465-0752. Specializing in Amphora, Zsolnay, and Massier. johncobabe@aol.com

Cohen, Wilfred and Dolli
Antiques & Art Glass
PO Box 27151, Santa Ana, 92799; 714-545-5673. Specializing in Wave Crest (C.F. Monroe); French cameo glass; Victorian-era art and pattern glass (salt shakers, toothpick holders, syrups, cruets, sugar shakers, tumblers, biscuit jars table and pitcher sets); art glass and cameo glass open salts; custard and ruby-stained glass; burmese, peachblow and amberina glass; pottery by Moorcroft (pre-1935 only); Buffalo (Deldare and Emerald ware); Polia Pillin; Shelley China; Chintz China; Clarice Cliff, and Moser Art Glass of Carlsbad Austria. Please include SASE for reply; a photo is very helpful for identification.
antsandartglass@aol.com

Conroy, Barbara J.
PO Box 2369, Santa Clara, 95055-2369. Specializing in commercial china; author and historian

Cox, Susan N.
800 Murray Drive, El Cajon, 92020; 619-697-5922. Specializing in California pottery and Frankoma.
antiqfever@aol.com

Devenish, Clive
PO Box 907, Orinda, 94563; 925-254-8383. Specializing in still and mechanical banks; Buys and Sells

Eichert, Kathy
1539 Loma Dr., Ojai, 93023. Specializing in Gladding McBean.
kathydel@ojai.net

Ellis, Michael L.
266 Rose Ln., Costa Mesa, 92627; 949-646-7112 or fax 949-645-4919. Author (Collector Books) of Collector's Guide to Don Winton Designs, Identification & Values; specializing in Twin Winton

Fogleman, Marv
Marv's Memories
73 Waterman, Irvine, 92602. Specializing in American and English dinnerware

George, Tony
22431-B160 Antonio Pkwy., #252, Rancho Santa Margarita, 92688; 949-589-6075. Specializing in watch fobs

Gibson, Pat
38280 Guava Dr., Newark, 94560; 510-792-0586. Specializing in R.A. Fox

Gunther, Candace (Candelaine)
Phone: 626-796-4568 or fax 626-796-7172. Specializing in Steiff and Schuco bears and animals; send SASE for list. candelaine@aol.com

Harrison, Gwynne
PO Box 1, Mira Loma, 91752-0001; 951-685-5434. Specializing in Autumn Leaf (Jewel Tea). morgan99@pe.net

Hibbard, Suzi
WanderWares
Specializing in Dragonware and 1000 Faces china, other Orientalia.
Dragon_Ware@hotmail.com
related site: www.Dragonware.com

Howard, Steve
Past Tyme Pleasures
PMB #204, 2491 San Ramon Valley Blvd., #1, San Ramon, 94583; 925-484-4488 or fax 925-484-2551. Specializing in antique American firearms, bowie knives, Western Americana, old advertising, vintage gambling items, barber and saloon items. pasttyme1@comcast.net
www.pasttyme1.com

Krumme, Michael
PO Box 48225, Los Angeles, CA 90048-0225; 323-937-1470. Specializing in Paden City glass.
mkrumme@pacbell.net

Langtree, Elizabeth
PO Box 1616, Santa Ynez, CA 93460. Collector of Borsato figures

Main Street Antique Mall
237 E Main St., El Cajon, 92020; 619-447-0800 or fax 619-447-0815

Maurer, Oveda L.
Oveda Maurer Antiques
34 Greenfield Ave., San Anselmo, 94960; 415-454-6439. Specializing in 18th-century and early 19th-century American furniture, lighting, pewter, hearthware, glass, folk art, and paintings; open by chance and appointment

The Meadows Collection
Mark and Adela Meadows
PO Box 819, Carnelian Bay, 96140; 530-546-5516. Specializing in Gouda and Quimper; lecturers, authors of Quimper Pottery, A Guide to Origins, Styles, and Values, serving on the board of directors of the Associated Antiques Dealers of America; Please include SASE for inquiries.
meadows@meadowscollection.com
www.meadowscollection.com

Needham, Leonard
MacAdam's Antiques
707-748-4286. Specializing in advertising. screensider@sbcglobal.net
www.tias.com/stores/macadams

Pardini, Dick
3107 N. El Dorado St., Dept. SAPG, Stockton, 95204-3412; 209-466-5550 (recorder may answer). Specializing in California Perfume Company items dating from 1886 to 1928 and 'go-with' related companies: buyer and information center. Not interested in items that have Avon, Perfection, or Anniversary Keepsake markings. California Perfume Company offerings must be accompanied by a photo, photo copy, or sketching along with a condition report and, most importantly, price wanted. Inquiries require large SASE and must state what information you are seeking; not necessary if offering items for sale.

Pasquali, Jim
479 Church #4, San Francisco, 94114; 415-861-4184. Author of Sanfords Guide to Garden City Pottery, A Hidden Treasure of Northern California

Sanford, Steve and Martha
230 Harrison Ave., Campbell, 95008; 408-978-8408. Authors of 2 books on Brush-McCoy and Sanfords Guide to McCoy Pottery (available from the authors). www.sanfords.com

Shrader, Lila
Shrader Antiques
2025 Hwy. 199, Crescent City, 95531. Specializing in railroad, steamship, and other transportation memorabilia; Shelley china (and its predecessor, Wileman/Foley China); Buffalo china and Buffalo Pottery including Deldare; Niloak, and Zell (and Haag)

Stillwell, Liz
Our Attic Antiques & Belleek
PO Box 1074, Pico Rivera, 90660; 323-257-3879. Specializing in Irish and American Belleek

Tanner, Joseph and Pamela
Wheeler-Tanner Escapes
6442 Canyon Creek Way, Elk Grove, 95758-5431; 916-684-4006. Specializing in handcuffs, leg shackles, balls and chains, restraints, and padlocks of all kinds (including railroad), locking and non-locking devices; also Houdini memorabilia: autographs, photos, posters, books, letters, etc.

Thoerner, Sharon
15549 Ryon Ave., Bellflower, 90706; 562-866-1555. Specializing in covered animal dishes, powder jars with animal and human figures, slag glass

Thornton, Don
PO Box 57, Moss Beach, 94038; 650-563-9445. Specializing in egg beaters and apple parers; author of The Eggbeater Chronicles, 2nd Edition ($50.45 ppd.); and Apple Parers ($59 ppd.).
dont@thorntonhouse.com

Vines, Linda
2911 4th St., #112, Santa Monica, 90405; 310-314-0402. Specializing in Snow Babies, all holidays (Christmas, Easter, Halloween), dolls, toys, Steiff, and Uncle Sam. lleigh2000@hotmail.com

Webb, Frances Finch
1589 Gretel Lane, Mountain View, 94040. Specializing in Kay Finch ceramics

Woodbury, Virginia; President of American Hatpin Society
20 Montecillo Dr., Rolling Hills Estates, 90274; 310-326-2196. Quarterly meetings and newsletters; Membership: $30 per year; SASE required when requesting information.
HATPINGINIA@aol.com

Canada

Shields, Lorne
Vintage Cycling

PO Box 87588, 300 John St. Post Office, Thornhill, Ontario L3T 7R3; 905-886-6911. Specializing in vintage and antique bicycles and related collectibles. vintage-antique@rogers.com

Warner, Ian
PO Box 93022, 499 Main St. S., Brampton, Ontario, L6Y 4V8; 905-453-9074. Specializing in Wade porcelain, author of *The World of Wade*, *The World of Wade Book 2*, *Wade Price Trends*, *The World of Wade — Figurines and Miniatures*, and *The World of Wade Head Vase Planters*; Co-author: Mike Posgay. idwarner@rogers.com

Colorado

Geary, William L.
Glass Appraiser (American & European Art Glass)
PO Box 2247, Colorado Springs 80901; telephone/fax: 719-527-0810. Specializing in Nordic art glass. nordglass@aol.com

Heck, Carl
Carl Heck Decorative Arts
Box 8416, Aspen, 81612; Phone/fax: 970-925-8011. Specializing in Tiffany lamps, art glass, paintings, windows, and chandeliers; also reverse-painted and leaded-glass table lamps, stained and beveled glass windows, bronzes, paintings, etc.; buy and sell; fee for written appraisals. Please include SASE for reply. carlheck5@aol.com
www.carlheck.com

Mackin, Bill
1137 Washington St., Craig, 81625; 970-824-6717. Author of *Cowboy and Gunfighter Collectibles*; available from author; Paperback, $28 ppd.; Other titles available; Specializing in old and fine spurs, guns, gun leather, cowboy gear, Western Americana (collection in the Museum of Northwest Colorado, Craig)

Over, Naomi L.
8909 Sharon Lane, Arvada, 80002; 303-424-5922. Specializing in ruby glassware, author of *Ruby Glass of the 20th Century, Book I*, autographed copies available from author for $25.00 softbound or $32.50 hardbound, ppd.; Book II available (1999 values) for $32.50 softbound or $42.50 hardbound, ppd. Naomi will attempt to make photo identifications for all who include a SASE with correspondence.

Segelke, Cathy; and James, Pat
970-847-3759 (Pat). Specializing in crocks, Western Pottery Mfg. Co. (Denver, CO)

Toohey, Marlena
703 S. Pratt Pky., Longmont, 80501; 303-678-9726. Specializing in black amethyst and black opaque glass (buy, sell or trade); books available from author: Book 1 (over 600 colored pictures, descriptions, and price guide), $34 ppd. (nearly out of print); Book 2 (over 1,200 colored pictures, descriptions and price guide), $34 ppd. for soft bound ($44 ppd. for hard bound)

White, John 'Grandpa'
Grandpa's Depot
6720 E. Mississippi Ave., Unit B, Denver, 80224; 303-758-8540 or fax 303-321-2889. Specializing in railroad-related items; Catalogs available

Winther, Jo Ellen
8449 W. 75th Way, Arvada, 80005; 800-872-2345 or 303-421-2371. Specializing in Coors

Connecticut

Block, Robert and Stan
Block's Box
PO Box 51, Trumbull, 06611; 203-926-8448. Specializing in marbles. blockship@aol.com

Bondhus, Sandra V.
Box 100, Unionville, 06085; 860-678-1808. Author of *Quimper Pottery: A French Folk Art Faience*; specializing in Quimper pottery

Lehrer, Gary
16 Mulberry Road, Woodbridge, 06525-1717. Specializing in pens and pencils; catalog available. www.gopens.com

MacSorley, Earl
823 Indian Hill Rd., Orange, 06477; 203-387-1793 (after 7:00 p.m.). Specializing in nutcrackers, Bessie Pease Gutmann prints, figural lift-top spittoons

Postcards International
Martin J. Shapiro
2321 Whitney Ave., Suite 102, PO Box 185398, Hamden, 06518; 203-248-6621 or fax 203-248-6628. Specializing in vintage picture postcards. www.vintagepostcards.com

Thalberg, Bruce
Mountain View Dr., Weston, 06883; 203-227-8175. Specializing in canes and walking sticks: novelty, carved, and Black

Van Deusen, Hobart D.
15 Belgo Road, Lakeville, 06039-1001; 860-435-0088. Specializing in Canton, SASE required when requesting information. rtn.hoby@snet.net

Vuono, Mark
16 6th St., Stamford, 06905; 203-357-0892 (10 a.m. to 5:30 p.m. E.S.T.). Specializing in historical flasks, blown 3-mold glass, blown American glass

District of Columbia

Durham, Ken and Jackie (By appt.)
909 26 St. N.W., Suite 502, Washington, DC 20037. Specializing in slot machines, jukeboxes, arcade machines, trade stimulators, vending machines, and service manuals. www.GameRoomAntiques.com

Florida

Barnes, Jacqueline Linscott
Line Jewels
3557 Nicklaus Dr., Titusville, 32780; 321-267-9170. Specializing in glass insulators, bell paperweights, and other telephone items. Author and distributor of 2003 edition of *Bluebell Paperweights, Telephone Pioneers of America Bells, and other Telephone Related Items*; LSASE required for information. bluebellwt@aol.com

Berry, Sammie
1076 Sea Grape Dr., Melbourne 32935; 321-259-8273. Specializing in cat collectibles and Ohio potteries

Bettinger, Robert
PO Box 333, Mt. Dora, 32756; 352-735-3575. General antiques, specializing in American art pottery and glass. rgbett@aol.com; RobertBettinger.com

DeLozier, Loretta
101 Grandville Blvd., Lake Placid, 33852. Author of *Collector's Encyclopedia of Lefton China, Books I, II, and III*, and *Lefton Price Guide*. Specializing in Lefton China; buy, sell, and consign; fee for written appraisals

Dodds, Rebecca
Silver Flute
PO Box 670664, Coral Springs, 33067. Specializing in jewelry

Dumont, Louise
318 Palo Verde Dr., Leesburg 34748. Specializing in cookie jars, Abingdon

Elsner, Dr. Robert
29 Clubhouse Lane, Boynton Beach, 33436; 561-736-1362. Specializing in antique barometers and nautical instruments

France, Madeleine
9 N. Federal Highway, Dania Beach, 33004; 954-921-0022. Specializing in top-quality perfume bottles: Rene Lalique, Steuben, Czechoslovakian, DeVilbiss, Baccarat, Commercials; French doré bronze, and decorative arts

Hales, Doug and Coila
Coila's Antiques 145 Bell Tower Crossing W, Poinciana, 34759. Specializing in Victorian art glass and colored pattern glass

Hirshman, Susan and Larry
Ft. Myers. Specializing in china, glassware, and kitchenware. SHirshman@aol.com

Hudson, Hardy
1896 Wingfield Dr., Longwood, 32779; 407-444-9009. Specializing in majolica, American art pottery (buying one piece or entire collections); also buying Weller (garden ornaments, birds, Hudson, Sicard, Sabrinian, Glendale, or animal related), Roseville, Grueby, Newcomb, Overbeck, Kay Finch, Clewell, Tiffany, etc. todiefor@mindspring.com

Joyce, Harriet
415 Soft Shadow Lane, DeBary, 32713. Specializing in Cracker Jack and Checkers (a competitor) early prizes and Flossie Fisher items

Kamm, Dorothy
PO Box 7460, Port St. Lucie, 34985-7460; 772-465-4008. Specializing in American painted porcelain; author of *American Painted Porcelain: Identification & Value Guide* (Collector Books), *Comprehensive Guide to American Painted Porcelain* (Antique Trader Books), and *Painted Porcelain Jewelry and Buttons: Identification & Value Guide* (Collector Books). dorothykamm@adelphia.net

Kuritzky, Louis
4510 NW 17th Place, Gainesville, 32605; 352-377-3193. Author (Collector Books) of *Collector's Guide to Bookends*

Person, Jeffrey M.
1250 Jungle Ave, St Petersburg, 33710. Specializing in Asian art including Cloisonné, Sumida Ware, fine carved furniture, Art Deco, Art Nouveau, and jewelry; has lectured, written articles, and been doing fine antique shows for 40 years. Person1@tampabay.rr.com

Posner, Judy
PO Box 2194 SC, Englewood, 34295, fax 941-475-2645. Specializing in Disneyana, Black memorabilia, salt and pepper shakers, souvenirs of the USA, character and advertising memorabilia, figural pottery; buy, sell, collect. judyandjef@yahoo.com

Rolfes, Herbert
Yesterday's World
PO Box 398, Mt. Dora, 32756; 352-735-3947. Specializing in World's Fairs and Expositions. NY1939@aol.com

Snyder-Haug, Diane
St. Petersburg, 33731. Specializing in women's clothing, 1850 – 1940

Supnick, Mark
2771 Oakbrook Manor, Ft. Lauderdale, 33332. Author of *Collecting Hull Pottery's Little Red Riding Hood* ($12.95 ppd.). Specializing in American pottery

Vogel, Janice and Richard
8420 SW 92 St., Unit B, Ocala, 34481-9317. Authors of *Victorian Trinket Boxes* and *Conta and Boehme Porcelain*. Specializing in Conta and Boehme German porcelain.
vogels@atlantic.net
http://ContaandBoehme.com

Weisblut, Robert
International Ivory Society
5001 Old Ocean Blvd. #1, Ocean Ridge, 33435; 561-276-5657. Specializing in ivory carvings and utilitarian objects. rweisblut@yahoo.com

White, Douglass
A-1 Auction
2042 N. Rio Grande Ave., Suite E, Orlando, 32804; 407-839-0004. Specializing in Fulper, Arts & Crafts furniture (photos helpful). a1auction@cfl.rr.com

Whysel, Steven
4147 Wilbledon Dr., Cooper City, 33026-1136; 954-885-8277. Specializing in Art Nouveau, 19th- and 20th-century art and estate sales

Willis, Ron L.
PO Box 278, Matlacha, 33993; 941-282-5567. Specializing in military collectibles

Wise, Raphael C.
12018 Suellen Circle, West Palm Beach, 33414; 561-793-0986. Specializing in Wedgwood Jasper Ware, Rosenthal (dogs & cats only), Moorcroft, Buffalo Deldare and Emerald Ware, Heisey, contemporary paperweights, English porcelains

Georgia

Bailey, Wayne and Gale
3152 Fence Rd., Dacula, 30019; 770-963-5736. Specializing in Goebels (Friar Tuck)

Glenn, Walter
3420 Sonata Lane, Alpharetta, 30004-7492; 678-624-1298. Specializing in Frankart

Hoefs, Steven
PO Box 1024, Avalon, 90704; 310-510-2623. Specializing in Catalina Island Pottery; author of book, available from the author

Joiner, John R.
Aviation Collectors
130 Peninsula Circle, Newnan, 30263; 770-502-9565. Specializing in commercial aviation collectibles. propJJ@numail.org

Jones, Donald
107 Rivers Edge Dr., Savannah, 31406; 912-354-2133. Specializing in vintage tennis collectibles; SASE with inquiries please.
Glassman912@comcast.net

Illinois

Broom, Jim
Box 65, Effingham, 62401. Specializing in opalescent pattern glassware

Danis, John
2929 Sunnyside Dr. #D362, Rockford, 61114; 815-978-0647 or fax 815-738-2430. Specializing in R. Lalique and Norse pottery. danis6033@aol.com

Feldman, Arthur M.
Arthur M. Feldman Gallery
1815 St. Johns Ave., Highland Park, 60035; 847-432-8858 or fax 847-266-1199. Specializing in Judaica, fine art, and antiques.
www.JudaicaConnection.com

Garmon, Lee
1529 Whittier St., Springfield, 62704; 217-789-9574. Specializing in Royal Haeger, Royal Hickman, glass animals; co-author (Collector Books) of *Glass Animals and Figural Flower Frogs of the Depression Era*

Hall, Doris and Burdell
210 W. Sassafras Dr., Morton, 61550-1254. Authors of *Morton's Potteries: 99 Years* (Vols. I and II); specializing in Morton pottery, American dinnerware, early American pattern glass, historical items, elegant Depression-era glassware

Mary 'Tootsie' Hamburg
Charlotte's, Queen Ann's, and Among Friends shops
All in Corner Victorian in Danville; 217-446-2323; Specializing in German Pink Pigs, Bakelite jewelry, general line

Hastings, Mary Jane
310 West 1st South, Mt. Olive, 62069; Phone: 217-999-7519. Specializing in Chintz dinnerware

Hoffmann, Pat and Don, Sr.
1291 N. Elmwood Dr., Aurora, 60506-1309; 630-859-3435: Authors of *Warwick, A to W*, a supplement to *Why Not Warwick?*; video regarding Warwick decals currently available. P.C.
warwick@ntsource.com

The Home Place Antiques
Durham, William; Galaway, William
615 S. State St., Belvidiere, 61008; 815-544-0577. Specializing in Tea Leaf ironstone and white ironstone

Hooks, Dee
13050 Blackstump Rd., Percy, 62272; 618-965-3832. Specializing in R.S. Prussia and Royal Bayreuth

Hopp, Dennis Carl
Midcentury
Chicago, 773-935-7872. Specializing in 20th-century design, glass, pottery, metal, art

Karman, Laurie and Richard; Editors of *The Fenton Flyer*
815 S. Douglas Ave., Springfield, 62704; Specializing in Fenton art glass

Long, Dee
112 S. Center, Lacon, 61540. Specializing in reamers

Martin, Jim
1095 215th Ave., Monmouth, 61462; 309-734-2703. Specializing in Old Sleepy Eye, Monmouth pottery, Western Stoneware

Miller, Larry
218 Devron Circle, E. Peoria, 61611-1605. Specializing in German and Czechoslovakian Erphila

Ochsner, Grace
Grace Ochsner Doll House
1636 E. County Rd. 2700, Niota, 62358; 217-755-4362. Specializing in piano babies, bisque German dolls and figurines

Phillips, T.
658 Oakwood Ct., Des Plaines, 60016-6227. Specializing in Hagen-Renaker

Rastello, Lisa
Milkweed Antiques
5N531 Ancient Oak Lane, St. Charles, 60175; 630-377-4612. Specializing in Depression-era collectibles

Rhoden, Joan and Charles
8693 N. 1950 East Rd., Georgetown, 61846-6264; 217-662-8046. Specializing in new reference books on antiques and collectibles (mail-order sales only), Heisey and other Elegant glassware, spice tins, lard tins and Yard-Long Prints. Co-authors of *Those Wonderful Yard-Long Prints and More*, and *More Wonderful Yard-Long Prints, Book II*, and *Yard-Long Prints, Book III*, illustrated value guides.
rhoden@soltec.net

Schwab, Betty and Larry
The Paperweight Shoppe
2507 Newport Dr., Bloomington, 61704; 309-662-1956. Specializing in glass paperweights; now buying quality weights, one piece or a collection.
larry@thepaperweightshoppe.com
www.thepaperweightshoppe.com

Spencer, Dick
Glass and More (Shows only)
1203 N. Yale, O'Fallon, 62269; 618-632-9067. Specializing in Cambridge, Fenton, Fostoria, Heisey, etc.

Spiess, Greg
230 E. Washington, Joliet, 60433; 815-722-5639. Specializing in Odd Fellows lodge items
spiessantq@aol.com

Stifter, Craig
218 S. Adams St., Hinsdale, 60521; 630-789-5780. Specializing in Coca-Cola, Pepsi-Cola, Orange Crush, Dr. Pepper, Hires, and other soda-pop brand collectibles.
cstifter@alumni.uchicago.edu.

TV Guide Specialists
Box 20, Macomb 61455; 309-833-1809

Waite, Jim
Main St., Farmer City, 61842; 800-842-2593. Specializing in Sebastians.
bigjim@farmwagon.com

Yester-Daze Glass
c/o Illinois Antique Center
320 S.W. Commercial St., Peoria, 61604; 309-347-1679. Specializing in glass from the 1920s, '30s, and '40s; Fiesta; Hall; pie birds; sprinkler bottles; and Florence figurines

Indiana

Alexander, Charles
221 E. 34th St., Indianapolis, 46205; 317-924-9665. Specializing in Fiesta, Russel Wright, Eva Zeisel

Boram, Clifford
Antique Stove Information Clearinghouse
Monticello; Free consultation by phone only: 219-583-6465

Dilley, David
6125 Knyghton Rd., Indianapolis, 46220; 317-251-0575. Specializing in Royal Haeger and Royal Hickman.
glazebears@aol.com

Dolly Mama's Museum
211 S. Merrill St., Fortville, 46040. Dolls, toys, ephemera; call 317-485-5339 for an appointment

Edwards, Bill
620 W. 2nd, Madison, 47250. Author (Collector Books) on carnival glass

Freese, Carol and Warner
House With the Lions Antiques
On the Square, Covington, 47932. General line

Garrett, Jerry and Sandi
Jerry's Antiques (Shows only)
1807 W. Madison St., Kokomo, 46901; 765-457-5256. Specializing in Greentown glass, old postcards.
sandpiper@iquest.net

Haun, Ted
2426 N. 700 East, Kokomo, 46901. Specializing in American pottery and china, '50s items, Russel Wright designs. Sam17659@cs.com

Highfield, James
1601 Lincolnway East, South Bend, 46613-3418; 574-288-0300. Specializing in relief-style Capo-di-Monte-style porcelain (Doccia, Ginori, and Royal Naples)

Hoover, Dave
1023 Skyview Dr., New Albany, 47150. Specializing in fishing collectibles; also miniature boats and motors. lurejockey@aol.com

Keagy, William and June
PO Box 106, Bloomfield, 47424; 812-384-3471. Co-authors of *Those Wonderful Yard-Long Prints and More, More Wonderful Yard-Long Prints, Book II,* and *Yard-Long Prints, Book III,* illustrated value guides

Leslie, Beverly
Sec./Treasurer of Uhl Collectors Society
801 Poplar St., Boonville, 47601; 812-897-3681. Contact for newsletter and membership information

McQuillen, Michael J. and Polly
McQuillen's Collectibles
PO Box 50022, Indianapolis, 46250-0022; 317-845-1721. Writer of column, *Political Parade,* which appears monthly in *AntiqueWeek* other newspapers; Specializing in political advertising, pin-back buttons, and sports memorabilia; Buys and sells. michael@politicalparade.com www.politicalparade.com

Miller, Robert
44 Hickory Lane North, Crawfordsville, 47833-7601. Specializing in Dryden pottery

Pruitt, Ted
3350 W. 700 N., Anderson, 46011. *St. Clair Glass Collector's Guide, Vol. 2,* available for $25 each at above address

Ricketts, Vicki
Covington Antiques Company
6431 W US Highway 136; Covington 47932. General line

Sanders, Lisa
8900 Old State Rd., Evansville, 47711. Specializing in MA Hadley. 1dlk@insight.bb.com

Slater, Thomas D.
Slater's Americana
1325 W. 86th St., Indianapolis, 46260; 317-257-0863. Specializing in political and sports memorabilia

Taylor, Dr. E.E.
245 N. Oakland Ave., Indianapolis, 46201-3360; 317-638-1641. Specializing in radios; SASE required for replies to inquiries

Webb's Antique Mall
over 400 Quality Dealers
200 W. Union St., Centerville, 47330; 765-855-2489.
webbsin@antquelandusa.com

Wright, Bill
325 Shady Dr., New Albany, 47150. Specializing in knives: Bowie, hunting, military, and pocketknives

---

Iowa

Bilsland, William M., III
PO Box 2671, Cedar Rapids, 52406-2671; 319-368-0658 or 714-328-7219. Specializing in American art pottery

Devine, Dennis; Norman; and Joe
D & D Antique Mall
1411 3rd St., Council Bluffs, 51503; 712-323-5233 or 712-328-7305. Specializing in furniture, phonographs, collectibles, general line. Joe Devine: Royal Copley and other types of pottery (collector), author of *Collector's Guide to Royal Copley Plus Royal Windsor & Spaulding, Books I and II*

Dollen, Brenda
214 N. Elm, P.O. Box 386, Avoca, 51521. Specializing in Red Wing pottery; Co-author (with R.L. Dollen) of *Red Wing Art Pottery, Books I and II; Collector's Encyclopedia of Red Wing Art Pottery* (all Collector Books)

Jaarsma, Ralph
Red Ribbon Antiques
812 Washington St., c/o Red Ribbon Antique Mall, Pella, 50219. Specializing in Dutch antiques; SASE required when requesting information

Picek, Louis
Main Street Antiques
110 W. Main St., Box 340, West Branch, 52358. Specializing in folk art, country Americana, the unusual

---

Kansas

Brandenburg, Harold
662 Chipper Lane, Wichita, 67212; 316-722-1200 (home). Specializing in Royal Bayreuth; charter member of the Royal Bayreuth Collectors Club; buys, sells, and collects

Maundy International
PO Box 13028-GG, Shawnee Mission, 66282; 1-800-235-2866. Specializing in watches — antique pocket and vintage wristwatches. mitime@hotmail.com

Old World Antiques
4436 State Line Rd., Kansas City, 66103; 913-677-4744 or fax 913-677-4879. Specializing in 18th- and 19th-century furniture, paintings, accessories, clocks, chandeliers, sconces, and much more

Smies, David
Pops Collectibles
Box 522, 315 So. 4th, Manhattan, 66502; 785-776-1433. Specializing in coins, stamps, cards, tokens, Masonic collectibles

---

Street, Patti
Currier & Ives (China) Quarterly Newsletter
PO Box 504, Riverton, 66770; 316-848-3529. Subscription: $12 per year (includes 2 free ads)

Tinsley, Rosella
105 15th St., Osawatomie, 66064; 913-755-3237. Specializing in primitives, kitchen, woodenware, and miscellaneous (phone calls only, no letters please)

Kentucky

Courter, J.W.
3935 Kelley Rd., Kevil, 42053; 270-488-2116. Specializing in Aladdin lamps; author of *Aladdin — The Magic Name in Lamps, Revised Edition,* hard bound, 304 pages; *Aladdin Electric Lamps,* soft bound, 229 pages; and *Angle Lamps Collectors Manual & Price Guide,* soft bound, 48 pages

Florence, Gene
Box 22186, Lexington, 40522. Author (Collector Books) on Depression glass, Occupied Japan; Elegant glass, kitchen glassware, salt and pepper shakers

Hornback, Betty
707 Sunrise Lane, Elizabethtown, 42701. Specializing in Kentucky Derby glasses. Detailed Derby, Preakness, Belmont, Breeder's Cup, and others glass information and pictures available in a booklet for $15 ppd. bettysantiques@kvnet.org

Ritchie, Roy B.
197 Royhill Rd., Hindman, 41822; 606-785-5796. Co-author of *Standard Knife Collector's Guide; Standard Guide to Razors; Cattaraugus Cutlery, Identification and Values;* and *The Big Knife Book;* specializing in razors and knives, all types of cutlery

Stewart, Ron
PO Box 2421, Hazard, 41702; 606-436-5917. Co-author of *Standard Knife Collector's Guide; Standard Guide to Razors; Cattaraugus Cutlery, Identification and Values; The Big Book of Pocket Knives; Remington Knives, Identification and Values;* and *The Standard Guide to Razors;* specializing in razors and knives, all types of cutlery

Willis, Roy M.
Heartland of Kentucky Decanters and Steins
PO Box 428, Lebanon Jct., 40150. Huge selection of limited edition decanters, beer steins, and die-cast collectibles — open showroom; include large self-addressed envelope (2 stamps) with correspondence; fee for appraisals. heartlandky@ka.net www.decantersandsteins.com

---

Louisiana

Langford, Paris
Kollecting Kiddles
415 Dodge Ave., Jefferson, 70121; 504-

733-0667. Specializing in all small vinyl dolls of the '60s and '70s; author of *Liddle Kiddles Identification and Value Guide* (now out of print). Please include SASE when requesting information; contact for information concerning Liddle Kiddle convention. bbean415@aol.com

---

Maine

Blake, Brenda
Box 555, York Harbor, 03911; 207-363-6566. Specializing in egg cups. Eggcentric@aol.com

Hathaway, John
Hathaway's Antiques
3 Mills Rd., Bryant Pond, 04219; 207-665-2214. Specializing in fruit jars; mail order a specialty

Hillman, Alma
Antiques at the Hillman's
362 E. Main St., Searsport, 04974; 207-548-6658. Co-author (Collector Books) of *Collector's Encyclopedia of Old Ivory China, The Mystery Explored, Identification & Values.* Specializing in Old Ivory China. oldivory@acadia.net

Rinaldi, John
Nautical Antiques and Related Items
Box 765, Dock Square, Kennebunkport, 04046; 207-967-3218. Specializing in nautical antiques, scrimshaw, naval items, marine paintings, naval items, etc.; fully illustrated catalog: $5

Simpson, Elizabeth
Elizabeth Simpson Antiques
PO Box 201, Freeport, 04032. Specializing in early glass and Sandwich glass

Zayic, Charles S.
Americana Advertising Art
PO Box 57, Ellsworth, 04605; 207-667-7342. Specializing in early magazines, early advertising art, illustrators

---

Maryland

Doub, Kathy
5359 Iron Pen Place, Columbia, 21044; 410-995-1254. Specializing in Candlewick and Imperial milk glass

Humphrey, George C.
4932 Prince George Ave., Beltsville, 20705; 301-937-7899. Specializing in John Rogers groups

Katz, Jerome R.
Katz Collectibles Antique Station, Frederick, 21702; 301-695-0888. Specializing in technological artifacts; please include SASE when requesting information

Kilhoffer, C.D.
Churchville. Specializing in glass target balls

Meadows, John, Jean and Michael
Meadows House Antiques
919 Stiles St., Baltimore, 21202; 410-837-5427. Specializing in antique

wicker furniture (rustic, twig, and old hickory), quilts, and tramp art

Rudisill's Alt Print Haus
Rudisill, John and Barbara
PO Box 199, Worton, 21678; 410-778-9290. Specializing in Currier & Ives; calls for information will be taken in return for a contribution (honor system) to the American Heart Association; call back if not at home; calls will not be returned.
rudi@dmv.com
chesapeake-bay.com/altprinthaus
For information and to new photos of more than Currier & Ives prints, visit the gallery: freepages.rootsweb.com/~vstern (link available from business site)

Screen, Harold and Joyce
2804 Munster Rd., Baltimore, 21234; 410-661-6765. Specializing in soda fountain 'tools of the trade' and paper: catalogs, 'Soda Fountain' magazines, etc. hscreen@comcast.net

Welsh, Joan
7015 Partridge Pl., Hyattsville, 20782; 301-779-6181. Specializing in Chintz; author of *Chintz Ceramics*

Yalom, Libby
The Shoe Lady
3200 NLW Boulevard #615, Silver Spring, 20906; 301-598-0290. Specializing in glass and china shoes; author of book

---
Massachusetts

Adams, Charles and Barbara
South Yarmouth, 02664; 508-760-3290 or (business) 508-587-5640. Specializing in Bennington (brown only). adams_2340@msn.com

Cooper, Ryan
205 White Rock Rd., Yarmouthport, 02675; 508-362-1604. Specializing in flags of historical significance and exceptional design.
rcmaritime@capecod.net

Dunbar's Gallery
Leila and Howard Dunbar
76 Haven St., Milford, 01757; 508-634-8697 or fax 508-634-8698. Specializing in advertising and toys.
Dunbars@mediaone.net
www.dunbarsgallery.com

Ford, Frank W.
237-26 South Street; Shrewsbury, 01545. Specializing in American iridescent art glass, ca 1900 – 1930

Frei, Peter
PO Box 500, Brimfield, 01010; 413-245-4660. Specializing in sewing machines (pre-1875, non-electric only), adding machines, typewriters, and hand-powered vacuum cleaners; SASE required with correspondence

Hess, John A.
Fine Photographic Americana
PO Box 3062, Andover, 01810. Specializing in 19th-century photography

Longo, Paul J.
Paul Longo Americana
Box 5510, Magnolia, 01930; 978-525-2290. Specializing in political pins, ribbons, banners, autographs, old stocks and bonds, baseball and sports memorabilia of all types

MacLean, Dale
183 Robert Rd., Dedham, 02026; 781-329-1303. Specializing in Dedham and Dorchester pottery.
dedham-dorchester@comcast.net

Morin, Albert
668 Robbins Ave. #23, Dracut, 01826; 978-454-7907. Specializing in miscellaneous Akro Agate and Westite. akroal@comcast.net

Porter, Richard T., Curator
Porter Thermometer Museum
Box 944, Onset, 02558; 508-295-5504. Visits (always open) free, with 3,800+ thermometers to see; appraisals, repairs, and traveling lecture (600 given, ages 8 – 98, all venues). Richard is also vice president of the Thermometer Collectors Club of America.
thermometerman@aol.com

Steinbock, Nancy
Nancy Steinbock Posters
800-438-1577. Specializing in posters: travel, literary, advertising; charter member of the IVPDA (International Vintage Poster Dealers Association)

Wellman, BA
PO Box 673, Westminster, 01473-0673. Specializing in all areas of American ceramics, dinnerware, figurines, and art pottery (willing to assist in identification through e-mail free of charge). BA@dishinitout.com

Williams, Linda
46 Columba St, #4D, Chicopee, 01020. Specializing in glass & china, general line antiques. Sito1845@aol.com

---
Michigan

Brown, Rick
Newspaper Collector's Society of America
Lansing, 517-887-1255. Specializing in newspapers. help@historybuff.com
www.historybuff.com

Burton, Ann
43779 Valley Rd., Decatur, 49045. Specializing in Schramberg

Culver, Bob
Night Light Club
38619 Wakefield Ct., Northville, 48167; 248-473-8575. Specializing in miniature oil lamps

Haas, Norman
252 Clizbe Rd., Quincy 49802; 517-639-8537. Specializing in American art pottery

Hogan & Woodworth
Walter P. Hogan and Wendy L. Woodworth
520 N. State, Ann Arbor, 48104; 313-930-1913. Specializing in Kellogg Studio.
www.emunix.emich.edu/~whogan/kellogg/index.html

Iannotti, Dan
212 W. Hickory Grove Rd., Bloomfield Hills, 48302-1127S. 248-335-5042. Specializing in modern mechanical cast-iron banks; member of The Mechanical Bank Collectors of America. modernbanks@prodigy.net

Krupka, Rod
2641 Echo Lane, Ortonville, 48462; 248-627-6351. Specializing in lightning rod balls. krupka@qix.net

Marsh, Linda K.
1229 Gould Rd., Lansing, 48917. Specializing in Degenhart glass

Nedry, Boyd W.
728 Buth Dr., Comstock Park, 49321; 616-784-1513. Specializing in traps (including mice, rat, and fly traps) and trap-related items; please send postage when requesting information

Nickel, Mike
A Nickel's Worth
PO Box 456, Portland, 48875; 517-647-7646. Specializing in American Art Pottery: Roseville, Weller, Rookwood, Kay Finch, Stangl and Pennsbury birds, Van Briggle, UND/North Dakota School of Mines, Pillin, Newcomb, Fulper porcelain lamps and jars.
mandc@voyager.net

Oates, Joan
1107 Deerfield Lane, Marshall, 49068; 269-781-9791. Specializing in Phoenix Bird chinaware.
koates120@earthlink.net

Rairigh, Glen
Americana Auctions
12633 Sandborn, Sunfield, 48890; 800-919-1950. Specializing in Skookum dolls and antique auctions

Ross, Michelle
PO Box 94, Berrien Center, 49102; 269-925-1604. Specializing in Van Briggle and American pottery.
peartime1@cs.com

Webster, Marty
6943 Suncrest Drive, Saline, 48176; 313-944-1188. Specializing in California porcelain and pottery, Orientalia

---
Minnesota

Anderson, James
Box 120704, New Brighton, 55112;

651-484-3198. Specializing in old fishing lures and reels, also tackle catalogs, posters, calendars, Winchester items

Dommel, Darlene
PO Box 22493, Minneapolis, 55422. Collector Books author of *Collector's Encyclopedia of Howard Pierce Porcelain*, *Collector's Encyclopedia of Dakota Potteries*, and *Collector's Encyclopedia of Rosemeade Pottery*; specializing in Howard Pierce and Dakota potteries

Harrigan, John
1900 Hennepin, Minneapolis, 55403; 612-991-1271 or (in winter) 561-732-0525. Specializing in Battersea (English enamel) boxes, Moorcroft, Royal Doulton character jugs, and Toby jugs

Koehn, Joanne M.
Temple's Antiques
PO Box 46237, Eden Prairie, 55344; 952-941-7641. Specializing in Victorian glass and china

Miller, Clark
4444 Garfield Ave., Minneapolis, 55409-1847; 612-827-6062. Specializing in Anton Lang pottery, American art pottery, Tibet postal history

Putratz, Barb
Spring Lake Park, 763-784-0422. Specializing in Norman Rockwell figurines and plates

Schoneck, Steve
HG Handicraft Guild, Minneapolis
PO Box 56, Newport, 55055; 651-459-2980. Specializing in American art pottery, Arts & Crafts, HG Handicraft Guild Minneapolis

---
Missouri

Gillespie, Steve, Publisher
Goofus Glass Gazette
400 Martin Blvd, Village of the Oaks, 64118; 816-455-5558. Specializing in Goofus glass, curator of Goofus Glass Museum, had 4,000+ piece collection of Goofus glass; buy, sell and collect Goofus for 30+ years; expert contributor to forums on Goofus glass; contributor to website for Goofus glass. stegil@sbcglobal.net

Heuring, Jerry
28450 US Highway 61, Scott City, 63780; 573-264-3947. Specializing in Keen Kutter

Siegel, Brenda and Jerry
Tower Grove Antiques
3308 Meramec, St. Louis, 63118; 314-352-9020. Specializing in Ungemach pottery

Tarrant, Jenny
Holly Daze Antiques
4 Gardenview, St. Peters, 63376. Holiday for sale. Specializing in early holiday items, Halloween, Christmas, Easter, etc.; always buying Halloween collectibles (except masks and costumes) and German holiday candy containers. JennyJOL@aol.com
www.holly-days.com

Wells, Lonnie
Things from the Past
125 Moonlight Dr., Doe Run, 63637.
Specializing in Sasha Brastoff.
www.tias.com/stores/thingsfromthe
past.com

Wendel, David
F.E.I., Inc.
PO Box 1187, Poplar Bluff, 63902-
1187; 573-686-1926. Specializing in
Fraternal Elks collectibles

Wiesehan, Doug
D & R Farm Antiques
4535 Hwy. H, St. Charles, 63301. Specializing in salesman's samples and
patent models, antique toys, farm toys,
metal farm signs

Williams, Don
PO Box 147, Kirksville 63501; 660-
627-8009 (between 8 a.m. and 6 p.m.
only). Specializing in art glass; SASE
required with all correspondence

Winslow, Ralph
PO Box 478, Camdenton, 65020. Specializing in Dryden Pottery

Montana

Anderson, Michele
Home Grown Antiques
PO Box 2686 Kalispell, 59903; 406-
756-7259. Specializing in American
dinnerware, glassware and pottery,
with a special emphasis on California
dinnerware. Co-authors of *Collector's
Compass: 20th Century Dinnerware*
(Martingale Press). Selling on the
Internet since 1997.
info@homegrownantiques.com
www.homegrownantiques.com

Nevada

Lynn, Susan Grindberg
4038 Dustin Ave., Las Vegas, 89120;
702-898-7535. Collector book author
of *Collector's Guide to Porcelier China,
Identification and Values.*
suelynn@lvcm.com

Young, Willy
80 Promontory Pointe, Reno, 89509;
775-746-0922. Specializing in fire
grenades

New Hampshire

Apakarian-Russell, Pamela
Halloween Queen Antiques
PO Box 499, Winchester, 03470. Specializing in Halloween (and other holidays) and postcards

Holt, Jane
Jane's Collectibles
PO Box 115, Derry, 03038. Specializ-
ing in Annalee Mobilitee Dolls

Winston, Nancy
Willow Hollow Antiques
648 1st N.H. Turnpike, Northwood,

03261; 603-942-5739. Specializing in
Shaker smalls, primitives, iron, copper,
stoneware, and baskets

New Jersey

Anderson, Suzy McLennan, ISA
CAPP
Heritage Antiques & Appraisal Services
65 E. Main St., Holmdel, 07733;
908-946-8801 or fax 908-946-1036.
Specializing in American furniture
and decorative accessories; please
include photo and SASE when
requesting information; appraisals
and identification are impossible to
do over the phone

Doorstop Collectors of America
Doorstopper Newsletter
Jeanie Bertoia
2413 Madison Ave., Vineland, 08630;
609-692-4092. Membership: $20 per
year, includes 2 newsletters and convention. Send 2-stamp SASE for sample.

George, Dr. Joan M.
ABC Collector's Circle Newsletter
67 Stevens Ave., Old Bridge, 08857;
fax 732-679-6102. Specializing in educational china (particularly ABC
plates and mugs). drgeorge@nac.net

Harran, Jim and Susan
208 Hemlock Dr., Neptune, 07753; 732-
922-2825. Specializing in English and
Continental porcelains with emphasis
on antique cups and saucers; author of
*Collectible Cups and Saucers, Identifica-
tion and Values, Book I & II* (Collector
Books); available for $20.95 ppd.

Litts, Elyce
Happy Memories Antiques & Collectibles
PO Box 394, Morris Plains, 07950; 973-
361-4087. Specializing in general line with
special focus on Geisha Girl Porcelain, vintage compacts and Goebel figurines.
happy-memories@worldnet.att.net
www.happy-memories.com

Lockwood, Howard J.; Publisher
Vetri: Italian Glass News
Box 191, Fort Lee, 07024; 201-969-
0373. Specializing in Italian glass of
the 20th century

Meschi, Edward J.
129 Pinyard Rd., Monroeville, 08343;
856-358-7293. Specializing in Durand
art glass, Icart etchings, Maxfield Parrish prints, Rookwood pottery, occupational shaving mugs, American
paintings, and other fine arts; author of
Durand — The Man and His Glass,
(Antique Publications) available from
author for $39 ppd. ejmeschi@aol.com

Perrault, Suzanne
Perrault-Rago Gallery
333 N. Main St., Lambertville, 08530;
609-397-9374. Specializing in Arts and
Crafts, art pottery, moderns, and tiles

Perzel, Robert and Nancy
Popkorn
The Main Street Antique Center, 156
Main St., PO Box 1057, Flemington,
08822; 908-782-9631. Specializing in
Stangl dinnerware, birds, and artware;
American pottery and dinnerware

Poster, Harry
Vintage TVs
Box 1883, S. Hackensack, 07606; 201-
794-9606. Writes *Poster's Radio and
Television Price Guide*; specializes in
vintage televisions, vintage radios,
stereo cameras; catalog available on
line. www.harryposter.com

Rago, David
333 N. Main St., Lambertville, 08530;
609-397-6780 or fax 609-397-679.
Specializing in Arts & Crafts, art pottery. ragoarts@ragoarts.com
www.ragoarts.com

Rash, Jim
135 Alder Ave., Egg Harbor Township, 08234. Specializing in advertising dolls

Rosen, Barbara
6 Shoshone Trail, Wayne, 07470. Specializing in figural bottle openers and
antique dollhouses

Visakay, Stephen
Vintage Cocktail Shakers (By
appointment)
PO Box 1517, W. Caldwell, 07007-
1517. Author of book and specializing
in vintage cocktail shakers and bar
ware. SVisakay@aol.com

New Mexico

Hardisty, Don
3020 E. Majestic Ridge, Las Cruces,
88011. For information and questions: 505-522-3721; fax 505-522-
7909. Specializing in Bossons and
Hummels. Don's Collectibles carries a
full line of Bossons and Hummel figurines of all marks. When mail ordering Bossons and Hummels, you may
dial toll free 800-620-8995. Contact
Don for restoration questions and
information concerning fakes and
look-alikes. don@donsbossons.com
Donsbossons.com

Manns, William
PO Box 6459, Santa Fe, 87502; 505-
995-0102. Co-author of *Painted Ponies,*
hardbound (226 pages), available from
author for $47 ppd.; specializing in
carousel art and cowboy antique.
zon@nets.com

Moyer, Patsy
PO Box 311, Deming, 88031; Collector Book author on dolls.
moddoll@yahoo.com

Nelson, Scott H.
PO Box 6081, Santa Fe, 87502-6081.
Specializing in ethnographic art

New York

Austin, Bruce A.
1 Hardwood Hill Rd., Pittsford, 14534;
585-387-9820 (evenings); 585-475-
2879 (week days). Specializing in
clocks and Arts & Crafts furnishings
and accessories including metalware,
pottery, and lighting. baagll@rit.edu

Badders, Veldon
692 Martin Rd., Hamlin, 14464; 716-
964-3360. Author (Collector Books)
of *Collector's Guide to Inkwells, Identification & Values*; specializing in
inkwells

Calison, Jim
Tools of Distinction
Wallkill, 12589; 914-895-8035. Specializing in antique and collectible
tools, buying and selling

Doyle, Robert A., CAI, ISA, CAGA,
CES
Absolute Auction & Realty,
Inc./Absolute Auction Center
PO Box 1739, Pleasant Valley, 12569;
845-635-3169. Antique and estate auctions twice a month at Absolute Auction Center; free calendar of auctions
available; specializing in specialty collections. absoluteauction@hvc.rr.com
www.AbsoluteAuctionRealty.com

Endter, Barbara
29 Sandalwood Dr., Rochester, 14616-
1513; 585-621-1433. Specializing in
Chase Brass & Copper Company

Gerson, Roselyn
PO Box 40, Lynbrook, 11563; 516-
593-8746. Author/collector specializing in unusual, gadgetry, figural
compacts, vanity bags and purses, solid
perfumes, and lipsticks

Handelsman, Burton
18 Hotel Dr., White Plains, 10605;
914-428-4480 (home) and 914-761-
8880 (office). Specializing in occupational shaving mugs, accessories

Kaonis, Keith; Manager
Antique Doll Collector Magazine
6 Woodside Ave., Suite 300, Northport, 11768 or PO Box 344, Center
Port, NY 11721-0344; 631-261-4100
or 631-361-0982 (evenings). Specializing in Schoenhut toys

Little Century
H. Thomas and Patricia Laun
215 Paul Ave., Syracuse, 13206; 315-
437-4156. Summer residence: 35109
Country Rte. 7, Cape Vincent, 13618;
315-654-3244. Specializing in firefighting collectibles. All appraisals are free,
and we will respond only to those who
are considerate enough to include a self-
addressed stamped envelope (photo is
requested for accuracy). We are unable
to return phone calls, keep trying.

Malitz, Lucille
Lucid Antiques
Box KH, Scarsdale, 10583; 914-636-7825. Specializing in lithophanes, kaleidoscopes, stereoscopes, medical and dental antiques

Michel, John and Barbara
Iron Star Antiques
200 E. 78th St., 18E, New York City, 10021; 212-861-6094. Specializing in yellow ware, cast iron, tramp art, shooting gallery targets and blue feather-edge. jlm58@columbia.edu.

Rifken, Blume J.
Author of *Silhouettes in America — 1790 – 1840 — A Collector's Guide*. Specializing in American antique silhouettes from 1790 to 1840

Russ, William A.
Russ Trading Post
23 William St., Addison 14801-1326. Animal lure manufacture; hunting and trapping supplies; catalog $1

Safir, Charlotte F.
1349 Lexington Ave., 9-B, New York City, 10128-1513; 212-534-7933. Specializing in cookbooks, children's books (out-of-print only)

Schleifman, Roselle
Ed's Collectibles/The Rage
16 Vincent Rd., Spring Valley, 10977; 845-356-2121. Specializing in Duncan & Miller, Elegant glass, Depression glass

Smyth, Carole and Richard
Carole Smyth Antiques
PO Box 2068, Huntington, 11743. Authors of *Neptune's Treasures — A Study & Value Guide to Sea Shell Art; Pails by Comparison — A Study & Value guide to Sand Pails & Toys;* and *The Burning Passion — A Study & Value Guide to Antique and Collectible Pyrography*. All available from authors at the above address for $25 each +$4.35 postage.

Tuggle, Robert
105 W. St., New York City, 10023; 212-595-0514. Specializing in John Bennett, Anglo-Japanese china

Van Kuren, Jean and Dale
Ruth's Antiques, Inc.
PO Box 152, Clarence Center, 14032; 716-741-8001. Specializing in chocolate molds, Buffalo pottery, Deldare ware. ruthsantq@aol.com

Van Patten, Joan F.
Box 102, Rexford, 12148. Author (Collector Books) of books on Nippon and Noritake

Weitman, Stan and Arlene
PO Box 1186; 101 Cypress St., N. Massapequa, 11758. Author of book on crackle glass (Collector Books). scrackled@earthlink.net
www.crackleglass.com

North Carolina

Finegan, Mary J.
Marfine Antiques
PO Box 1105, Black Mountain, 28711. marfine@earthlink.net
johnson brothersbook.com

Hughes, Kathy (Mrs. Paul)
Tudor House Galleries
8919 Park Rd., DC #30, Charlotte, 28210-08645. 704-676-4871; fax 704-676-5197. Specializing in relief-molded jugs, 18th- and 19th-century English pottery and 19th-century oil paintings. paulh65304@aol.com
www.tudorhouse.com

Hussey, Billy Ray
Southern Folk Pottery Collector's Society
220 Washington Street, Bennett, 27208; 336-581-4246 or fax 336-581-4247. Specializing in historical research and documentation, education and promotion of the traditional folk potter (past and present) to a modern collecting audience. sfpcs@rtmc.net

Iannantuoni, Jean-Paul
4179 Brownwood Lane, Concord, 28027-4501. Discontinued Dinnerware Shopping Service; send $2 for Royal Doulton list; appraisals $2 each. www.freeyellow.com/members/royal doulton/home.html.

Kirtley, Charles E.
PO Box 2273, Elizabeth City, 27096; 919-335-1262. Specializing in monthly auctions and bid sales dealing with World's Fair, Civil War, political, advertising, and other American collectibles

Newbound, Betty
2206 Nob Hill Dr., Sanford, 27330. Author (Collector Books) on Blue Ridge dinnerware, milk glass, wall pockets, figural planters and vases; specializing in collectible china and glass

Savage, Jeff
Drexel Grapevine Antiques, 2784 US Highway 70 East, Valdese 28690; 828-437-5938. Specializing in pottery, china, antique fishing tackle, and much more. info@drexelantiques.com
www.drexelantiques.com

Sayers, R.J.
Southeastern Antiques & Appraisals
PO Box 629, Brevard, 28712. Specializing in Boy Scout collectibles, Pisgah Forest pottery, primitive American furniture; author of *Guide to Scouting Collectibles, Revised 1996 Edition*, available from author for $32.95 ppd.; member New England Appraisers Assn.

Taylor, Terry
3648 Prides Rd., East Bend, 27018. Co-author of *Collector's Encyclopedia of Salt Glaze Stoneware* (Collector Books). Specializing in salt glaze stoneware

North Dakota

Farnsworth, Bryce
1334 14½ St. South, Fargo, 58103; 701-237-3597. Specializing in Rosemeade pottery; if writing for information, please send a picture if possible, also phone number and best time to call

Ohio

Bassett, Mark
PO Box 771233, Lakewood, 44107; 216-221-6025. Buying and selling Ohio art pottery (including Roseville, Cowan, Weller, Rookwood, others), Cleveland arts and crafts, Art Deco, and other 20th Century design movements; author of *Cowan Pottery and the Cleveland School (1997), Introducing Roseville Pottery (1999), Introducing Roseville Pottery* (revised and expanded 2nd edition, 2001), *Bassett's Roseville Prices (2001), Understanding Roseville Pottery (2002),* and *American Art Pottery Wall Pockets* (2003).
Mark@MarkBassett.com
www.MarkBassett.com

Batory, Mr. Dana Martin
402 E. Bucyrus St., Crestline, 44827. Specializing in antique woodworking machinery, old and new woodworking machinery catalogs; author of *Vintage Woodworking Machinery, An Illustrated Guide to Four Manufacturers*, currently available from Astragal Press, PO Box 239, Mendham, NJ 07945 for $26.45 ppd. (signed copies available from author); coming soon from Astragal Press, *Vintage Woodworking Machinery Volume Two, An Illustrated Guide to Four More Manufacturers*. In order to prepare a definitive history on American manufacturers of woodworking machinery, Dana is interested in acquiring (by loan, gift, or photocopy) catalogs, manuals, photos, personal reminiscences, etc., pertaining to woodworking machinery and/or their manufacturers. Also available for $7.50 money order: 70+ page list of catalogs, owner's manuals, parts lists, company publications, etc. (updated quarterly). No phone calls please.

Benjamin, Scott
PO Box 556, LaGrange, 44050-0556; 440-355-6608. Specializing in gas globes; co-author of *Gas Pump Globes* and several other related books, listing nearly 4,000 gas globes with over 1,800 photos, prices, rarity guide, histories, and reproduction information (currently available from author); also available: *Petroleum Collectibles Monthly* Magazine.
www.oilcollectibles.com
www.gasglobes.com

Blair, Betty
Golden Apple Antiques
216 Bridge St., Jackson, 45640; 614-286-4817. Specializing in art pottery, Watt, cookie jars, chocolate molds, Beanie Babies, general line

China Specialties, Inc.
Box 471, Valley City, 44280. Specializing in high-quality reproductions of Homer Laughlin and Hall china, including Autumn Leaf

Distel, Ginny
Distel's Antiques
4041 S.C.R. 22, Tiffin, 44883; 419-447-5832. Specializing in Tiffin glass

Ebner, Rita and John
Columbus. Specializing in door knockers, cast-iron bottle openers, Griswold

Graff, Shirley
4515 Grafton Rd., Brunswick, 44212. Specializing in Pennsbury pottery

Guenin, Tom
Box 454, Chardon, 44024. Specializing in antique telephones and antique telephone restoration

Hall, Kathy
4417 Weckerly Rd., Monclova, 43542; 419-867-1516. Specializing in Labino art glass. kewpieluvin@msn.com.

Hamlin, Jack and Treva Jo
145 Township Rd. 1088, Proctorville, 45669; 740-886-7644. Specializing in Currier and Ives by Royal China Co. and Homer Laughlin China (especially Virginia Rose dinnerware). JackTrevaJo@zoom internet.net

Hothem, Lar
Hothem House
Box 458, Lancaster, 43130. Author of books on Indians and artifacts

Kao, Fern Larking
PO Box 312, Bowling Green, 43402; 419-352-5928. Specializing in jewelry, sewing implements, ladies' accessories

Kier, Anne and Don
202 Marengo St., Toledo, 43614-4213; 419-385-8211. Specializing in glass, china, autographs, Brownies, Royal Bayreuth, 19th-century antiques, general line. d.a.k.@dorldnet.att.net

Kitchen, Lorrie
Toledo, 419-475-1759. Specializing in Depression-era glass, Hall china, Fiesta, Blue Ridge, Shawnee

Klender, James and Grace
Town & Country Antiques & Collectibles
PO Box 447, Pioneer, 43554; 419-737-2880. Specializing in pattern glass, and general line

Kline, Mr. and Mrs. Jerry and Gerry
Two of the founding members of North American Torquay Society and members of Torquay Pottery Collectors' Society
604 Orchard View Dr., Maumee, 43537; 419-893-1226. Specializing in collecting Torquay pottery

Mangus, Bev and Jim
5147 Broadway NE, Louisville, 44641.

Author (Collector Books) of *Shawnee Pottery, An Identification & Value Guide*; specializing in Shawnee pottery

Mathes, Richard
PO Box 1408, Springfield, 45501-1408; 513-324-6917. Specializing in buttonhooks

Millman, Tom and Linda
231 S. Main St., Bethel, 45106; phone/fax: 513-734-6884 (after 9 p.m.). Specializing in perfume lamps, other antique and unique lighting

Moore, Carolyn
445 N. Prospect, Bowling Green, 43402. Specializing in primitives, yellow ware, graniteware, collecting stoneware

Murphy, James L.
1023 Neil Ave., Columbus, 43201; 614-297-0746; Specializing in American Radford, Vance Avon. jlmruphy@columbus. rr.com

Otto, Susan
12204 Fox Run Dr., Chesterland, 44026; 440-729-2686. Specializing in nutcrackers, not toy soldier (Steinbach) type

Pierce, David
PO Box 205, Gambier, 43022. Specializing in Glidden pottery; fee for appraisals

Rees, Debbie
Zanesville. Specializing in Watt, Roseville juvenile and other Roseville pottery, Zanesville area pottery, cookie jars, and Steiff

Roberts, Brenda
Specializing in Hull pottery and general line. Author of *Collector's Encyclopedia of Hull Pottery, Roberts' Ultimate Encyclopedia of Hull Pottery*, and *The Companion Guide to Roberts' Ultimate Encyclopedia of Hull Pottery*, all with accompanying price guides

Rodgers, Joanne
c/o Stretch Glass Society
Membership: $22 in US ($24 US currency in Canada) per year; quarterly newsletter with colored photos; annual spring convention. http://members.aol.com/stretghgl/

Trainer, Veronica
Bayhouse
Box 40443, Cleveland, 44140; 440-871-8584. Specializing in beaded and enameled mesh purses

Tucker, Dan
Toledo, 419-478-3815. Specializing in Depression-era glass, Hall china, Fiesta, Blue Ridge, Shawnee

Whitmyer, Margaret and Kenn
Box 30806, Gahanna, 43230. Author

(Collector Books) on children's dishes; Specializing in Depression-era collectibles

Wilkins, Juanita
The Bird of Paradise
Wapakoneta. Specializing in R.S. china, Old Ivory china, colored pattern glass, lamps, and jewelry

Young, Mary
Box 9244, Wright Brothers Branch, Dayton, 45409; 937-298-4838. Specializing in paper dolls; author of several books

Oklahoma

Bess, Phyllis
14535 E. 13th St., Tulsa, 74108; 918-437-7776. Author of *Frankoma Treasures*, and *Frankoma and Other Oklahoma Potteries*. Specializing in Frankoma and Oklahoma pottery

Ivers, Terry; Terry's Toys and Nostalgia
114 Whitworth Ave., Ponca City, 74601-3438; 580-767-1122. toylady@cableone.net

Moore, Art and Shirley
4423 E. 31st St., Tulsa, 74135; 918-747-4164 or 918-744-8020. Specializing in Lu Ray Pastels, Depression glass

Scott, Roger R.
4250 S. Oswego, Tulsa, 74135; 918-742-8710 or fax 918-582-8803. Specializing in Victor and RCA Victor trademark items along with Nipper. Roger13@mindspring.com

Oregon

Abrahams, Peter
1948 Mapleleaf Rd., Lake Oswego, 97034; 503-636-2988. Specializing in telescopes, binoculars, microscopes. Peter studies and collects optics: telescopes, binoculars, hand magnifiers, and microscopes, and especially seeks reference material on these subjects, including books, catalogs, repair manuals, and histories. telscope@europa.com www.eruopa.com~telescope/binotele.html

Brown, Marcia 'Sparkles'
PO Box 2314, White City, 97503; 541-826-3039 or fax 541-830-5385. Author of *Unsigned Beauties of Costume Jewelry, Signed Beauties of Costume Jewelry, Signed Beauties of Costume Jewelry, Volume II*, and *Coro Jewelry, A Collector's Guide*. (all Collector Books), Co-author and host of 7 volumes: *Hidden Treasures* videos; specializing in rhinestone jewelry; please include SASE if requesting information

Coe, Debbie and Randy
Coe's Mercantile
2459 SE TV Hwy #321, Hillsboro, 97123. Specializing in Elegant and Depression glass, Fenton glass, Liberty Blue, art pottery

Davis, Patricia Morrison
Antique and personal property appraisals
4326 N.W. Tam-O-Shanter Way, Portland, 97229-8738; 503-645-3084. pam100davis@comcast.net

Foland, Doug
PO Box 66854, Portland, 97290; 503-772-0471. Author of *The Florence Collectibles, an Era of Elegance*, available at your local bookstore or from Schiffer publishers

Main Antique Mall
30 N. Riverside, Medford, 97501. Quality products and services for the serious collector, dealer, or those just browsing. http://mainantiquemall.com

Medford Antique Mall
Jim & Eileen Pearson, Owners
1 West 6th St., Medford 97501; 541-773-4983. medama11@mind.net

Miller, Don and Robbie
541-535-1231. Specializing in milk bottles, TV Siamese cat lamps, seltzer bottles, red cocktail shakers

Morris, Thomas G.
Prize Publishers
PO Box 8307, Medford, 97504. Author of *The Carnival Chalk Prize, Books I and II*, pictorial price guides on carnival chalkware figures with brief histories and values for each. chalkman@cdsnet.net

Ringering, David and Angi
Kay Ring Antiques
1395 59th Ave., S.E., Salem, 97301; 503-364-0464 or pager: 503-588-3747. Specializing in Rowland & Marsellus and other souvenir/historical china with scenes of buildings, parks, and other tourist attractions of the 1890s – 1930s. Feel free to contact David if you have any questions about Rowland and Marsellus or other souvenir china. He will be happy to answer questions about souvenir china. AR1480@aol.com

Pennsylvania

Alekna, Stan and Sally
732 Aspen Lane, Lebanon, 17042-9073; 717-228-2361 or fax 717-228-2362. Specializing in American Dimestore Toy Soldiers. Send SASE for 3 to 4 mail-order lists per year; always buying 1 or 100 top-quality figures. salekna@bellatlantic.net

Barrett, Noel
Rosebud Antiques
PO Box 1001, Carversville, 18913; 215-297-5109. Specializing in toys; appraiser on PBS Antiques Roadshow; active in toy-related auctions

Bodine, Clarence H., Jr., Proprietor
East/West Gallery
41B West Ferry St., New Hope, 18938. Specializing in antique Japanese woodblock prints, netsuke, inro, porcelains

Cerebro
PO Box 327, E. Prospect, 17317-0327; 717-252-2400 or 800-69-LABEL; fax 717-252-3685. Specializing in antique advertising labels, especially cigar box labels, cigar bands, food labels, firecracker labels. Cerebro@Cerebro.com www.cerebro.com

Christie, Dr. Victor J.W.; Author/Appraiser/Broker
1050 West Main St., Ephrata, 17522; 717-738-4032. The family designated biographer of Bessie Pease Gutmann. Specializing in Bessie Pease Gutmann and other Gutmann & Gutmann artists, and authored 5 books on these artists, the latest in 2001: *The Gutmann & Gutmann Artists: A Published Works Catalog, Fourth Edition*, a signed copy available from the author for $20 at the above address. thecheshirecat@onemain.com

Damaska, Ron
738 9th Ave., New Brighton, 15066; 724-843-1393. Specializing in Fry cut glass, match holders; SASE required when requesting information

Gottuso, Bob
Bojo
PO Box 1403, Cranberry Township, 16066-0403; phone/fax: 724-776-0621. Specializing in Beatles, Elvis, KISS, Monkees, licensed rock 'n roll memorabilia. www.bojoonline.com

Hain, Henry F., III
Antiques & Collectibles
2623 N. Second St., Harrisburg, 17110; 717-238-0534. Lists available of items for sale

Hinton, Michael C.
246 W. Ashland St., Doylestown, 18901; 215-345-0892. Owns/operates Bucks County Art & Antiques Company and Chem-Clean Furniture Restoration Company; specializing in quality restorations of a wide range of art and antiques from colonial to contemporary; also owns Trading Post Antiques, 532 Durham Rd., Wrightstown, PA, 18940, a 60-dealer antiques co-op with 15,000 square feet — something for everyone in antiques and collectibles. iscsusn@att.net.

Holland, William
hollandarts.com
1554 Paoli Pike, West Chester, 19380-6123; 610-344-9848 or fax 610-344-0651. Specializing in Louis Icart etchings and oils; Tiffany studios lamps, glass, and desk accessories; Maxfield Parrish; Art Nouveau and Art Deco items. Author of *Louis Icart: The Complete Etchings, The Collectible Maxfield Parrish*, and *Louis Icart Erotica*. bill@hollandarts.com www.hollandarts.com

Irons, Dave
Dave Irons Antiques
223 Covered Bridge Rd., Northampton, 18067; 610-262-9335 or fax 610-262-2853. Author of *Irons By Irons*, *More Irons By Irons*, and *Even More Irons by Irons*, available from author, (each contains pictures of over 1,600 irons, current information and price ranges, collecting hints, news of trends, and information for proper care of irons); specializing in pressing irons, country furniture, primitives, quilts, accessories. www.ironsantiques.com

Ivankovich, Michael
Michael Ivankovich Auctions, Inc.
PO Box 1536, Doylestown, 18901; 215-345-6094. Specializing in 20th-century hand-colored photography and prints; author of *The Collector's Value Guide to Popular Early 20th Century American Prints* (1998), $19.95; *The Collector's Guide to Wallace Nutting Pictures*, $18.95; *The Alphabetical and Numerical Index to Wallace Nutting Pictures*, $14.95; and *The Collector's Guide to Wallace Nutting Furniture*, $19.95. Also available: *Wallace Nutting General Catalog, Supreme Edition* (reprint), $13.95; *Wallace Nutting: A Great American Idea* (reprint), $13.95; and *Wallace Nutting's Windsor's: Correct Windsor Furniture* (reprint), $13.95. All these books are currently available at the above address. Shipping is $4.25 for the first item ordered and $1.50 for each additional item.
ivankovich@wnutting.com
www.wnutting.com

Knauer, Judy A.
National Toothpick Holder Collectors Society
1224 Spring Valley Lane, West Chester, 19380-5112; 610-431-3477. Specializing in toothpick holders and Victorian glass

Kreider, Katherine
Kingsbury Antiques
PO Box 7957, Lancaster, 17604-7957; 717-892-3001. Author of *Valentines With Values*, available for $24.45 ppd. ($25.92 PA residents); *One Hundred Years of Valentines*, available for $29.45 ppd. ($30.96 PA residents); and *Valentines for the Eclectic Collector* ($29.45 ppd. ($30.96 PA residents); no free appraisals. Stop by Booth #315 in Stroudtburg Antique Center (formerly Black Angus), in Adamstown, PA, Sundays only. Kingsbry@aol.com

Levi, Anita
Allegheny Mountain Antique Gallery
5151 Clear Shade Dr., Windber, 15963; 814-467-8539. Specializing in novelty clocks, advertising tins, primitives, holiday decorations, quilts, purses, Black memorabilia, linens, stoneware, Roseville, kitchenware, Art Deco

Lowe, James Lewis
Kate Greenaway Society
PO Box 8, Norwood, 19074. Specializing in Kate Greenaway.
PostcardClassics@juno.com

Maier, Clarence and Betty
Mail order: The Burmese Cruet
Box 432, Montgomeryville, 18936; 215-855-5388. Specializing in Victorian art glass. burmesecruet@erols.com. www.burmesecruet.com

McManus, Joe
PO Box 153, Connellsville, 15425. Editor of *Purinton News & Views*, a newsletter for Purinton pottery enthusiasts; subscription: $16 per year; sample copies available with SASE. Specializing in Blair Ceramics and Purinton Pottery. jmcmanus@hhs.net

Merchants Square Mall
Jim and Annetta Vitez, Managers
1901 S. 12th St., Allentown, 18103; 610-797-7743

Reimert, Leon
121 Highland Dr., Coatesville, 19320; 610-383-9880. Specializing in Boehm porcelain

Rosso, Philip J. and Philip Jr.
Wholesale Glass Dealers
1815 Trimble Ave., Port Vue, 15133; 412-678-7352. Specializing in Westmoreland glass

Weiser, Pastor Frederick S.
55 Kohler School Rd., New Oxford, 17350-9210; 717-624-4106. Specializing in frakturs and other Pennsylvania German documents; SASE required when requesting information; no telephone appraisals; must see original or clear colored photocopy

Rhode Island

Gacher, John
The Drawing Room of Newport
152 Spring St., Newport, 02840; 401-841-5060. Specializing in Zsolnay, Fischer, Amphora, and Austro-Hungarian art pottery. www.drawrm.com

The Occupied Japan Club
c/o Florence Archambault
29 Freeborn St., Newport, 02840-1821. Publishes bimonthly newsletter, *The Upside Down World of an O.J. Collector*; SASE required when requesting information. florence@aiconnect.com

South Carolina

Dunay, Jeanne
Bellflower Antiques
Camden. Specializing in historic and Romantic Staffordshire, 1790 – 1850

Greguire, Helen
Helen's Antiques
79 Lake Lyman Hgts., Lyman, 29365; 864-848-0408. Specializing in graniteware (any color), carnival glass lamps and shades, carnival glass lighting of all kinds; author (Collector Books) of *The Collector's Encyclopedia of Graniteware, Colors, Shapes & Values, Book 1* (out of print); second book on graniteware now available (updated 2003, $33.70 ppd; also available is *Carnival in Lights*, featuring carnival glass, lamps, shades, etc. ($13.45 ppd.); and *Collector's Guide to Toasters and Accessories, Identification & Values*, ($21.95 ppd.); available from author; please include SASE when requesting information; looking for people interested in collecting toasters

Guthrie, John
1524 Plover Ave., Mount Pleasant, 29464; 843-884-1873. Specializing in Santa Barbara Ceramic Design

Roerig, Fred and Joyce
1501 Maple Ridge Rd., Walterboro, 29488; 843-538-2487. Specializing in cookie jars; authors of *Collector's Encyclopedia of Cookie Jars, An Illustrated Value Guide*, (three in the series), publishers of *Cookie Jarrin' with Joyce: The Cookie Jar Newsletter*

Tennessee

Chase, Mick and Lorna
Fiesta Plus
380 Hawkins Crawford Rd., Cookeville, 38501; 931-372-8333. Specializing in Fiesta, Harlequin, Riviera, Franciscan, Metlox, Lu Ray, Bauer, Vernon, other American dinnerware

Fields, Linda
158 Bagsby Hill Lane, Dover, 37058; 931-232-5099 after 6 p.m. Specializing in pie birds. Fpiebird@compu.net.

Grist, Everett
PO Box 91375, Chattanooga, 37412-3955; 423-510-8052. Specializing in covered animal dishes and marbles

Hudson, Murray
Murray Hudson Antiquarian Books, Maps, Prints & Globes
109 S. Church St., Box 163, Halls, 38040; 901-836-9057 or 800-748-9946; fax 731-836-9017. Specializing in antique maps, globes, and books with maps, atlases, explorations, travel guides, geographies, surveys, and historical prints. mapman@ecsis.net. www.murrayhudson.com

Weddington, David
Predicta Sales & Service
2702 Albany Ct., Murfreesboro, 37129; 615-890-7498. Specializing in vintage Philco Predicta TVs

Texas

Babcock, Bobby
Jubilation Antiques
5108 Saddleridge Cove, Austin, 78759; 512-418-9373. Specializing in Maxfield Parrish, Black Americana, and brown Roseville Pine Cone. jubantique@aol.com

Cooper, Marilyn
8408 Lofland Dr., Houston, 77055-4811; 713-465-7773 or summer address: PO Box 755, Douglas, MI 49406. Specializing in figural toothbrush holders, candy containers, Pez

Dockery, Rod
4600 Kemble St., Ft. Worth, 76103; 817-536-2168. Specializing in milk glass; SASE required with correspondence

Docks, L.R. 'Les'
Shellac Shack; Discollector
Box 691035, San Antonio, 78269-1035. Author of *American Premium Record Guide*; specializing in vintage records. docks@texas.net. www.docks.home.texas.net

Frese, Leo and Wendy
Three Rivers Collectibles
Box 551542, Dallas, 75355; 214-341-5165. Specializing in RumRill, Red Wing pottery and stoneware

Gibbs, Carl, Jr.
1716 Westheimer Rd, Houston, 77098. Author of *Collector's Encyclopedia of Metlox Potteries, Second Edition*, autographed copies available from author for $32.95 ppd.; specializing in American ceramic dinnerware

Groves, Bonnie
402 North Ave. A, Elgin, 78621. Specializing in boudoir dolls

Nelson, C.L.
310 S. Park Blvd #610, Grapevine, 76051. Specializing in 18th-, 19th-, and 20th-century English pottery and porcelain, among others: Gaudy Welsh, ABC plate, relief-molded jugs, Staffordshire transfer ware. chlpnw@aol.com

Malowanczyk, Abby and Wlodek
Collage-20th Century Classics
1300 N. Industrial Blvd., Dallas, 75207; Phone/fax: 214-828-9888. Specializing in architect-designed furniture and decorative arts from the modern movement. txcollage@aol.com; www.collageclassics.com

Norris, Kenn
Schoolmaster Auctions and Real Estate
PO Box 4830, 513 N. 2nd St., Sanderson, 79848-4830; 915-345-2640. Specializing in school-related items, barbed wire, related literature, and L'il Abner (antique shop in downtown Sanderson)

Pogue, Larry G.
L&J Antiques & Collectibles
8142 Ivan Court, Terrell, 75161-6921; 972-551-0221. Specializing in string holders and head vases.
LandJAntiques@direcway.com
www.LandJAntiques.com

Rosen, Kenna
9138 Loma Vista, Dallas, 75243; 972-503-1436. Specializing in Bluebird china. ke-rosen@swbell.net.

Tucker, Richard and Valerie
Argyle Antiques
PO Box 262, Argyle, 76226; 940-464-3752. Specializing in windmill weights, shooting gallery targets, figural lawn sprinklers, cast-iron advertising paperweights and other unusual figural cast iron. lead1234@gte.net or rtucker@jw.com

Turner, Danny and Gretchen
Running Rabbit Video Auctions
PO Box 701, Waverly, 37185; 615-296-3600. Specializing in marbles

Waddell, John
2903 Stan Terrace, Mineral Wells, 76067. Specializing in buggy steps

Woodard, Dannie; Publisher
The Aluminist
PO Box 1346; Weatherford, 76086; 817-594-4680. Specializing in aluminum items, books, and newsletters about aluminum

Utah

Anderson, Tim
Box 461, Provo, 84603. Specializing in autographs; buys single items or collections — historical, movie stars, US Presidents, sports figures, and pre-1860 correspondence. Autograph questions? Please include photocopies of your autographs if possible and enclose a SASE for guaranteed reply.
www.AutographsOfAmerica.com

Anderson, Warren R.
America West Archives
PO Box 100, Cedar City, 84721; 435-586-9497. Specializing in old stock certificates and bonds, western documents and books, financial ephemera, autographs, maps, photos; author of *Owning Western History*, with 75+ photos of old documents and recommended reference.
warren@americawestarchives.com

Spencer, Rick
Salt Lake City, 801-973-0805. Specializing in American silverplate and sterling flatware, hollow ware, Shawnee, Van Tellingen, salt and pepper shakers. Appraisals available at reasonable cost.

Vermont

Barry, Kit
74 Cotton Mill Hill #A252, Brattleboro, 05301; 802-254-3634. Author of *Reflections 1* and *Reflections 2*, reference books on ephemera. Specializing in advertising trade cards and ephemera in general.
kbarry@surfglobal.net

Kline, Jerry
Florence Showcase
PO Box 468, Bennington, 05201; 802-442-3336. Specializing in Florence ceramics of California, Rookwood pottery, English china, art glass, period furniture (small), tea caddies, brass and copper (early), and other quality items. sweetpea@sweetpea.net.

Virginia

Bradfield, Jeff
Jeff's Antiques
90 Main St., Dayton, 22821; 540-879-9961. Also located at Rolling Hills Antique Mall, Interstate 81, Exit 247B, Harrisonburg, VA; and the Factory Antique Mall, Interstate 81, Exit 227, Verona, VA. Specializing in candy containers, toys, postcards, sugar shakers, lamps, furniture, pottery, and advertising items

Branchcomb, Shane
20932 Winola Ter., Ashburn, 20147. Specializing in antique coffee mills, send SASE for reply.
acmeman@erols.com

Bull, Donald A.
PO Box 596, Wirtz, 24184; 540-721-1128. Author of *The Ultimate Corkscrew Book, Boxes Full of Corkscrews, Bull's Pocket Guide to Corkscrews, Just for Openers* (with John Stanley); *Boxes of Corkscrews, Anri Woodcarvings* (with Philly Rains); and *Soda Advertising Openers*. Specializing in corkscrews.
corkscrew@bullworks.net
www.corkscrewmuseum.com

Cranor, Rosalind
PO Box 859, Blacksburg, 24063. Specializing in Elvis collectibles; author of *Elvis Collectibles* (out of print) and *Best of Elvis Collectibles*, available from author for $21.70 ppd.

Flanigan, Vicki
Flanigan's Antiques
PO Box 1662, Winchester, 22604. Member: UFDC, NADDA (National Antique Doll Dealers Assn); specializing in antique dolls, hand fans, and teddy bears. Please include SASE with correspondence; fee for appraisals.
flanig@shentel.net.

Haigh, Richard
PO Box 29562, Richmond 23242; 804-741-5770. Specializing in Locke Art, Steuben, Loetz, Fry, Italian; SASE required for reply

MacAllister, Dale
PO Box 46, Singers Glen, 22850; Specializing in sugar shakers and syrups

Monsen, Randall; and Baer, Rod
Monsen & Baer
Box 529, Vienna, 22183; 703-938-2129. Specializing in perfume bottles, Roseville pottery, Art Deco

Reynolds, Charles
Reynolds Toys
2836 Monroe St., Falls Church, 22042; 703-533-1322. Specializing in limited-edition mechanical and still banks, figural bottle openers.
reynoldstoys@erols.com

Washington

Frost, Donald M.
Country Estate Antiques (Appointment only)
14800 N.E. 8th St., Vancouver, 98684; 360-604-8434. Specializing in art glass and earlier 20th-century American glass

Goldsworthy, Kathy
Past Glories
425-488-8871. Specializing in vintage needlecraft accessories and textiles.
www.tias.com/stores/pastglories

Haase, Don (Mr. Spode)
The Spode Shop
D&D Antiques
PO Box 818, Mukilteo, 98275; 425-348-7443. Specializing in Spode-Copeland China. Don@mrspode.com
www.mrspode.com

Jackson, Denis C., Editor
The Illustrator Collector's News
PO Box 1958, Sequim, 98382; 360-452-3810. Copy of recent sample: $3. Specializing in old magazines & illustrations such as Rose O'Neill, Maxfield Parrish, pinups, Marilyn Monroe, Norman Rockwell, etc.
ticn@olypen.com

Morris-Snyder, Susan
PO Box 1231, Gig Harbor, 98355. Specializing in Watt pottery and Purinton pottery; co-author of *Watt Pottery — An Identification and Value Guide*, and *Purinton Pottery — An Identification and Value Guide*

Payne, Sharon A.
Antiquities & Art
Specializing in Cordey
hotel_california94546@yahoo.com

Weldin, Bob
Miner's Quest
W. 3015 Weile, Spokane, WA 99208; 509-327-2897. Specializing in mining antiques and collectibles (mail-order business)

Whitaker, Jim and Kaye
Eclectic Antiques
PO Box 475 Dept. S, Lynnwood, 98046. Specializing in Josef Originals and motion lamps; SASE required.
www.eclecticantiques.com

Zeder, Audrey
1320 S.W. 10th Street #S, North Bend, 98045 (appointment only). Specializing in British Royalty Commemorative souvenirs (mail-order catalog available); author (Wallace Homestead) of *British Royalty Commemoratives*

West Virginia

Fostoria Glass Society of America, Inc.
Box 826, Moundsville, 26041. Specializing in Fostoria glass

Hardy, Roger and Claudia
West End Antiques
10 Bailey St., Clarksburg, 26301; 304-624-7600 (days) or 304-624-4523 (evenings). Authors of *The Complete Line of the Akro Agate Co.*; specializing in Akro Agate

Wisconsin

Helley, Phil
Old Kilbourne Antiques
629 Indiana Ave., Wisconsin Dells, 53965; 608-254-8770. Specializing in premiums, German and Japanese tin toys, Cracker Jack, toothbrush holders, radio premiums, pencil sharpeners, and comic strip toys

Knapper, Mary
Phoneco, Inc.
207 E. Mill Rd., PO Box 70, Galesville, 54630; 608-582-4124. Specializing in telephones, antique to modern

Matzke, Gene
Gene's Badges & Emblems
455 Big Horn Ct., Hancock, 54943; phone/fax: 715-249-5695. Specializing in police badges, leg irons, old police photos, fire badges (old), patches, old handcuffs, and memorabilia.
badgeone@uniontel.net.

Thomas, Darrell
Sugar Shakin Antiques
PO Box 418, New London, 54961. Specializing in art pottery, ceramics, Deco era, Goldscheider, and Keramos.
wwodenclockworks@msn.com

Thorpe, Donna and John
204 North St., Sun Prairie, 53590; 608-837-7674. Specializing in Chase Brass and Copper Co.

Clubs, Newsletters, and Catalogs

ABC Collectors' Circle (16-page newsletter, published 3 times a year)
Dr. Joan M. George
67 Stevens Ave., Old Bridge, NJ 08857; fax 732-679-6102. Specializing in ABC plates and mugs.
drjgeorge@nac.net

Abingdon Pottery Collectors Club
Elaine Westover, Membership and Treasurer
210 Knox Hwy. 5, Abingdon, IL 61410; 309-462-3267. Dues $8 for single, $10 per couple. Specializing in collecting and preservation of Abingdon pottery

Akro Agate Collectors Club and *Clarksburg Crow* quarterly newsletter
Claudia and Roger Hardy
10 Bailey St., Clarksburg, WV 26301-2524; 304-624-4523 (evenings) or West End Antiques, 97 Milford St., Clarksburg, WV 26301; 304-624-7600 (week days). Annual membership fee: $25. www.mkl.com/akro/club/

The Akro Arsenal, quarterly catalog
Larry D. Wells
5411 Joyce Ave., Ft. Wayne, IN 46818; 219-489-5842

The Aluminist
Dannie Woodard, Publisher
PO Box 1346, Weatherford, TX 76086. Subscription: $20 (includes membership)

America West Archives
Anderson, Warren
PO Box 100, Cedar City, UT 84721; 435-586-9497. Illustrated catalogs issued 6 times a year; has both fixed-price and auction sections offering early western documents, letters, stock certificates, autographs, and other important ephemera; subscription: $15 per year.
warren@americawestarchives.com

American Antique Deck Collectors
52 Plus Joker Club
Clear the Decks, quarterly publication
Janice Miller, Membership
670 Carlton Dr., Elgin, IL 60120-4008. Membership: $30 (US and Canada), $40 (foreign). Specializing in antique playing cards. Joker1854@aol.com
www.52plusjoker.org

American Cut Glass Association
Kathy Emmerson, Executive Secretary
PO Box 482, Ramona, CA 92065-0482; 760-789-2715 or fax 760-789-7112. Membership dues (includes subscription to newsletter, *The Hobstar*): $45 (USA bulk mail) or $55 (first class and international).
acgakathy@aol.com; www.cutglass.org

American Hatpin Society
Virginia Woodbury, President
20 Montecillo, Rolling Hills Estates, CA 90274; 310-326-2196. Newsletter published quarterly; meetings also quarterly; membership: $35.
HAT PNGINIA@aol.com
www.collector online.com/AHS/

Antique and Art Glass Salt Shaker Collectors' Society (AAGSSCS)
1775 Lakeview Dr., Zeeland, MI 49464-2018. Membership: $18.
antiques@wmis. net
antiquesaltshakers.com

Antique & Collectors Reproduction News
Antiques Coast to Coast
Mark Chervenka, Editor
PO Box 12130, Des Moines, IA 50312-9403; 515-274-5886 or (subscriptions only) 800-227-5531. 12 monthly issues: $32 (US); $41 (Canada); $59 (foreign).
acrn@repronews.com

Antique Advertising Association of America (AAAA)
PO Box 1121, Morton Grove, IL 60053; 708-466-0904. Publishes *Past Times* Newsletter; subscription: $35 in US. AAAA@bblocksonline.com
www.pastimes.org

Antique Bottle & Glass Collector Magazine
Jim Hagenbuch, Publisher
102 Jefferson St., PO Box 180, East Greenville, PA 18041; 215-679-5849 or fax 215-679-3068. Subscription (12 issues): $25 (US); $28 (Canada).
glswrk@enter.net

Antique Purses Catalog: $4
Bayhouse
PO Box 40443, Cleveland, OH 44140; 216-871-8584. Includes colored photos of beaded and enameled mesh purses

Antique Radio Classified (ARC)
PO Box 2, Carlisle, MA 01741; 978-371-0512. ARC@antiqueradio.com

Antique Stove Association
c/o Caroline Royske
PO Box 2101, Waukesha, WI 53187-2101; 262-542-9190 after 6 p.m.

Antique Telephone Collectors Association
PO Box 1252, McPherson, KS 67460; 620-245-9555. An international organization associated with the Museum of Independent Telephony; membership: $35 (+$5 initiation fee for new membership). office@atcaonline.com
www.atcaonline.com

Antique Trader Weekly
Nancy Crowley, Editor
PO Box 1050, Dubuque, IA 52004-

1050. Featuring news about antiques and collectibles, auctions and events; listing over 165,000 buyers and sellers in every edition; subscription: $35 (US) for 52 issues per year; toll free for subscriptions only: 800-258-0929.
collect@krause.com; www.collect.com

Antique Wireless Association
Ormiston Rd., Breesport, NY 14816

Appraisers National Association
25602 Alicia Parkway, PMB 245, Laguna Hills, CA 92653; 949-349-9179. Founded in 1982, a nonprofit organization dedicated to the professionalism and education of personal property appraisers. All members adhere to a code of ethics and abide by professional standards. ANA also works to develop awareness of the professionalism of appraising, and the service it provides to the public. Free referrals to accredited appraisers for antiques, collectibles, art, jewelry, furniture and residential contents.
info@ana-appraisals.org.
www.ana appraisals.org

Association of Coffee Mill Enthusiasts (ACME)
c/o Lucy Fullinwider, Treasurer
PO Box 5761, Midland, TX 79704. Quarterly newsletter, annual convention; Dues are $40 ($50 outside the continental US and Canada), covers cost of quarterly newsletter and copy of membership roster

Auction Times for the West
Michael F. Shores, Publisher
Jeffrey Hill, Editor/General Manager
2329 Santa Clara Ave., Suite 207, Alamedo, CA 94501. 800-791-8592

Autograph Collector e-mail newsletter
Odyssey Publications
510-AS Corona Mall, Corona, CA 91719-1420; 909-371-713.
DBTOG@aol.com

Autographs of America
Tim Anderson
PO Box 461, Provo, UT 84603; 801-226-1787 (please call in the afternoon).
www.AutographsOfAmerica.com

Autumn Leaf
Bill Swanson, Editor
807 Roaring Springs Dr., Allen, TX 75002-2112; 972-727-5527
Gwynne Harrison, President
PO Box 1, Mira Loma, CA 91752-0001; 951-685-5434; Membership: $20. www.nalcc.org

Avon Times (National Avon collectors' newsletter)
c/o Dwight or Vera Young
PO Box 9868, Dept. P., Kansas City,

MO 64134. Membership: $24 (US) or $26 (Canada). SASE required when requesting information.
AvonTimes@aol.com

Beatlefan
PO Box 33515, Decatur, GA 30033. Subscription: $15 (US) for 6 issues or $19 (Canada and Mexico)

Belleek Collectors International Society
PO Box 1498, Great Falls, VA 22066-8498; 1-800-Belleek; 703-272-6270 (outside the US & Canada). Each new member receives a certificate of membership, a new member/renewal gift, a binder for the Belleek Collectors Society magazines, and the opportunity to purchase exclusive limited edition items; US membership: $43.
info@belleek.com

Blue & White Pottery Club
224 12th St., NW, Cedar Rapids, IA 52405; Membership: $12 ($17 for spouse). www.blueandwhitepottery.org

Bojo
PO Box 1403, Cranberry Township, PA 16066-0403. Send $3 for 38 pages of Beatles, toys, dolls, jewelry, autographs, Yellow Submarine items, etc.
bojoonline.com

Bookend Collector Club
c/o Louis Kuritzky, M.D.
4510 NW 17th Place, Gainesville, FL 32650; 352-377-3193. Quarterly full-color glossy newsletter, $25 per year.
lkuritzky@aol.com

Bossons Briefs, quarterly newsletter
Available through membership in the International Bossons Collectors Society, John J. Cassidy, Executive Director
1317 N. San Fernando Blvd, Suite #325, Burbank, CA 91504.
bossonsman@aol.com

Boyd's Art Glass Collectors Guild
PO Box 52, Hatboro, PA 19040-0052

Boyd's Crystal Art Glass
Jody & Darrell's Glass Collectibles Newsletter
PO Box 180833, Arlington, TX 76096-0833. Publishes 6 times a year. Subscription includes an exclusive glass collectible produced by Boyd's Crystal Art Glass. LSASE for current subscription rates. Sample copy of newsletter: $3

British Royal Commemorative Souvenirs Mail Order Catalog
Audrey Zeder
1320 SW 10th St. #S, North Bend, WA 98045; Catalog issued monthly, $5 each

Buckeye Marble Collectors Club
Brenda Longbrake, Secretary
PO Box 3051, Elida, OH 4580. Membership: $10 (payable to club).
brenda@wcoil.com
www.buckeyemarble.com

The Buttonhook Society
Box 287, White Marsh, MD 21162. Publishes bimonthly newsletter *The Boutonneur*, which promotes collecting of buttonhooks and shares research and information contributed by members

Candy Container Collectors of America
The Candy Gram Newsletter
c/o Jo Baldwin, Box 2971, Anderson, IN 46018-2971. epmac27@comcast.net
or Contact: Jeff Bradfield
90 Main St., Dayton, VA 22821
Membership: $25 per family.
www.candycontainer.org

The Cane Collector's Chronicle
Linda Beeman
15 2nd St. N.E., Washington, D.C. 20002; $30 for 4 issues

Cane Collectors Club
PO Box 1004, Englewood Cliff, NJ 07632; 201-886-8826.
liela@walkingstickworld.com

The Carnival Pump
International Carnival Glass Assoc., Inc.
Lee Markley
Box 306, Mentone, IN 46539; Dues: $20 per family per year in US and Canada or $25 overseas.
www.woodsland.com/icga

The Carousel News & Trader
87 Parke Ave. W., Suite 206, Mansfield, OH 44902. A monthly magazine for the carousel enthusiast. Subscription: $35 per year; sample: $4.
www.carouseltrader.com

The Carousel Shopper Resource Catalog
Box 47, Dept. PC, Millwood, NY 10546; Only $2 (+50¢ postage). A full-color catalog featuring dealers of antique carousel art offering single figures or complete carousels, museums, restoration services, organizations, full-size reproductions, books, cards, posters, auction services, and other hard-to-find items for carousel enthusiasts

A Catalog Collection
Kenneth E. Schneringer
271 Sabrina Ct., Woodstock, GA 30188-4228; 770-926-9383. Specializing in catalogs, promochures, view books, labels, trade cards, special paper needs. trademan68@aol.com
www.old-paper.com

Central Florida Insulator Collectors
3557 Nicklaus Dr., Titusville, FL 32780-5356; 407-267-9170. Dues: $10

per year for single or family membership (checks payable to Jacqueline Barnes); dues cover the cost of *Newsnotes*, the club's monthly newsletter, which informs members of meetings and shows, articles of interest on insulators and other collectibles. Members are invited to use free advertising of items for sale or trade. The club meets quarterly in members' homes and hosts a show each January which is open to the public. For club information send SASE to above address.
bluebellwt@aol.com

Ceramic Arts Studio Collector's Association
PO Box 46, Madison, WI 53701; 608-241-9138. Annual membership: $15; inventory record and price guide available

Chicagoland Antique Amusements Slot Machine & Jukebox Gazette
Ken Durham, Editor
909 26 St., N.W., Suite 502, Washington, DC 20037. 16-page newspaper published twice a year; Subscription: 4 issues for $30; Sample: $10.
www.GameRoomAntiques.com

China Specialties, Inc.
Fiesta Collector's Quarterly Newsletter
PO Box 361280, Strongsville, OH 44316-1280. www.chinaspecialties.com

Chintz Connection Newsletter
PO Box 222, Riverdale, MD 20738. Dedicated to helping collectors share information and find matchings; subscription: 4 issues per year for $25

The Cola Clan
Alice Fisher, Treasurer
2084 Continental Dr., N.E., Atlanta, GA 30345

Collector's Life
The World's Foremost Publication for Steiff Enthusiasts
Beth Savino
PO Box 798; Holland, OH 43528; 1-800-862-TOYS; fax 419-473-3947.
info@toystore.net.
www.toystorenet.com

Collector Glass News
Promotional Glass Collectors Association
Box 308, Slippery Rock, PA 16057; 724-946-2838 or fax 724-946-9012. An international publication providing current news to collectors of cartoon, fast-food, and promotional glassware; subscription: $15 per household. cgn@glassnews.com
www.glassnews.com

Collectors of Findlay Glass
PO Box 256, Findlay, OH 45840. An organization dedicated to the study and recognition of Findlay glass;

newsletter *The Melting Pot*, published quarterly; annual convention; membership: $10 per year ($15 per couple)

Compact Collectors
Roselyn Gerson
PO Box 40, Lynbrook, NY 11563; 516-593-8746 or fax 516-593-0610. Publishes *Powder Puff* Newsletter, which contains articles covering all aspects of powder and solid perfume compact collecting, restoration, vintage ads, patents, history, and articles by members and prominent guest writers; seekers and sellers column offered free to members. compactldy@aol.com

Cookie Crumbs
Cookie Cutter Collectors Club
Ruth Capper, Secretary/Treasurer
PO Box 245, Cannon Falls, MN 55009. Subscription $20 per year (4 issues, payable to CCCC).
www.cookiecuttercollectorsclub.com

Cookie Jarrin' With Joyce: The Cookie Jar Newsletter
1501 Maple Ridge Rd., Walterboro, SC 29488

Cookies
Rosemary Henry
9610 Greenview Lane, Manassas, VA 20109-3320. Subscription: $15 per year (6 issues); payable to Cookies

The Copley Courier
1639 N. Catalina St., Burbank, CA 91505

Cowan Pottery Museum Associates
For information write: CPMA, PO Box 16765, Rocky River, OH 44116 or contact Victoria Naumann Peltz, Curatorial Associate, Cowan Pottery Museum at Rocky River Public Library, 1600 Hampton Rd., Rocky River, OH 44116; 440-333-7610, ext. 214. Membership: $25 ($35 dual) includes subscription to biannual *Cowan Pottery Journal* Newsletter.
www.cowanpottery.org

Cracker Jack® Collector's Assoc.
The Prize Insider Newsletter
Theresa Richter, Membership Chairman
5469 S. Dorchester Ave., Chicago, IL 60615. Subscription/membership: $20 per year (single) or $24 (family).
WaddyTMR@aol.com
www.collectoronline.com/CJCA/

Creamers, quarterly newsletter
PO Box 11, Lake Villa, IL 60046-0011. Subscription: $5 per year

Currier & Ives Catalog
Rudisill's Alt Print Haus
PO Box 199, Worton, MD 21678. Please include LSASE. rudi@dmv.com
chesapeake-bay.com/altprinthaus
Gallery: freepages.rootsweb.com/~vstern

(Currier & Ives) C&I Dinnerware Collector Club
E.R. Aupperle, Treasurer
29470 Saxon Road, Toulton, IL 61483; 309-896-3331 or fax 309-856-6005. Membership: $15. royalchinaclub.com

Custard Glass Collectors Society
Custard Connection quarterly newsletter
Sarah Coulon, Editor
591 SW Duxbury Ave., Port St. Lucie, FL 34983; 561-785-9446. Annual membership: $20 (US) or $25 (Canada and Mexico). Live chat every Saturday night at 9 pm EST.
mrsfoxy@aol.com
See website for link:
www.homestead.com/custardsociety

Czechoslovakian Collectors Guild International
Alan Badia
15006 Meadowlake St., Odessa, FL 33556-3126. Annual membership: $65 in US. ab@czechartglass.com
www.czechartglass.com/ccgi

The Dedham Pottery Collectors Society Newsletter
Jim Kaufman, Publisher
248 Highland St., Dedham, MA 02026-5833; 800-283-8070. $5 per issue. DedhamPottery.com

Docks, L.R. 'Les'
Shellac Shack
Box 691035, San Antonio, TX 78269-1035. Send $2 for an illustrated booklet of 78s that Docks wants to buy, the prices he will pay, and shipping instructions.
docks@texas.net
docks.home.texas.net

Doorstop Collectors of America
Doorstopper Newsletter
Jeanie Bertoia
2413 Madison Ave., Vineland, NJ 08630; 609-692-4092. Membership: $20 per year, includes 2 newsletters and convention; send 2-stamp SASE for sample

Dragonware Club
c/o Suzi Hibbard
849 Vintage Ave., Fairfield, CA 94585. Inquiries must be accompanied with LSASE or they will not be responded to; all contributions are welcome.
Dragon_Ware@hotmail.com
www.Dragonware.com

Drawing Room of Newport
Gacher, John
152 Spring St., Newport, RI 02840; 401-841-5060. Book on Zsolnay available; www.drawrm.com

Early Typewriter Collectors Association
ETCetera newsletter
Chuck Dilts and Rich Cincotta, Co-editors

P.O. Box 286; Southborough, MA 01772; 508-229-2064.
etcetera@writeme.com
www.typewriter.rydia.net/etcetera.html

Ed Taylor Radio Museum
245 N. Oakland Ave., Indianapolis, IN 46201-3360; 317-638-1641

Eggcup Collector's Corner
67 Stevens Ave., Old Bridge, NJ 08857. Issued quarterly; Subscription: $18 per year (payable to Joan George). Sample copy: $5

The Elegance of Old Ivory Newsletter
Box 1004, Wilsonville, OR 97070

Fenton Art Glass Collectors of America, Inc.
Butterfly Net Newsletter
Kay Kenworthy, Editor
PO Box 384, 702 W. 5th St., Williamstown, WV 26187. Dues: $20 per year (full membership +$5 for each associate membership, children under 12 free); kkenworthy@foth.com
www.collectoronline.com/clubFAGCA

The Fenton Flyer
Laurie & Rich Karman, Editors
815 S. Douglas, Springfield, IL 62704; 217-787-8166

Fiesta Collector's Quarterly Newsletter
PO Box 471, Valley City, OH 44280. Subscription: $12 per year.
www.chinaspecialties.com/fiesta.html

Figural Bottle Opener Collectors
Linda Fitzsimmons, 9697 Gwynn Park Dr., Ellicott City, MD 21042; 410-465-9296. Please include SASE when requesting information.

Florence Ceramics Collectors Society
1971 Blue Fox Drive; Lansdale, PA 19446-5505. Newsletter and club membership: $35 per year (6 issues in color). FlorenceCeramics@aol.com

Fostoria Glass Society of America, Inc.
PO Box 826, Moundsville, WV 26041. Membership: $16. www.fostoriaglass.org

Frankoma Family Collectors Association
c/o Nancy Littrell
PO Box 32571, Oklahoma City, OK 73123-0771. Membership dues: $35 (includes newsletters); annual convention

Friends of Degenhart
c/o Degenhart Museum
PO Box 186, Cambridge, OH 43725; 740-432-2626. Membership: $5 ($10 for family) includes *Heartbeat* Newsletter (printed quarterly) and free admission to museum.
www.degenhartmuseum.com

H.C. Fry Society
PO Box 41, Beaver, PA 15009. Founded in 1983 for the sole purpose of learning about Fry glass; publishes *Shards*, quarterly newsletter

Goofus Glass Gazette
Steve Gillespie, Publisher
400 Martin Blvd., Village of the Oaks, MO 64118; 888-455-5558.
stegil @sbcglobal.net

The Gonder Collector
917 Hurl Dr.
Pittsburgh, PA 15236

Grandpa's Depot
John 'Grandpa' White
6720 E. Mississippi Ave., Unit B, Denver, CO 80224; 303-758-8540 or fax 303-321-2889. Publishes catalogs on railroad-related items

Haeger Pottery Collectors of America
Lanette Clarke
5021 Toyon Way, Antioch, CA 94509; 925-776-7784. Newsletter published 6 times per year; Dues: $20.
Lanette-Clarke@msn.com

Hall China Collector's Club Newsletter
Virginia Lee
PO Box 360488, Cleveland, OH 44136; 330-220-7456

The Hatpin Society of Great Britain
Estelle Weiner, Chairman
jake@jemah.co.uk

Hammered Aluminum Collectors Association (HACA)
Dannie Woodard
PO Box 1346, Weatherford, TX 76086; 817-594-46

Head Hunters Newsletter
c/o Maddy Gordon
PO Box 83H, Scarsdale, NY 10583; 914-472-0200. Subscription: $26 yearly (quarterly issues).
cbicom.net/~dlb/heads.htm

Homer Laughlin China Collectors Association (HLCCA)
The Dish magazine (a 16-page quarterly included with membership); PO Box 26021; Crystal City, VA 22215-6021. Membership: $25 (single), $40 (couple/family). www.hlcca.org
info@hlcca.org

Ice Screamers
Thor & Patty Foss
PO Box 776, Ephrata, PA 17522. Membership: $20 per year; Annual convention held in Lancaster, PA
thorpat@ptd.net

Ideal Collectors Club
c/o Judith Izen
PO Box 623, Lexington, MA 02173.

Membership: $20 per year, includes a quarterly newsletter; Subscribers get free wanted/for sale ads in each issue.
jizenres@aol.com

The Illustrator Collector's News (TICN)
Denis C. Jackson, Editor
PO Box 6433, Kingman, AZ 86401. A free use site on the Internet for paper collectors of all kinds, listing paper and magazine-related price guides available for sale only at this site.
www.olypen.com/ticn

Indiana Historical Radio Society
245 N. Oakland Ave., Indianapolis, IN 46201-3360; 317-638-1641. Membership: $15 (US), $19 (overseas) includes *IHRS Bulletin* newsletter.
home.att.net/~indianahistoricalradio

International Association of Calculator Collectors
International Calculator Collector Newsletter
Guy Ball, Co-Editor
PO Box 345, Tustin, CA 92781-0345
mrcalc@usa.net.

International Association of R.S. Prussia, Inc.
Linn or Leslie Schultz
PO Box 185, Lost Nation, IA 52254. Membership: $30 per household; Yearly convention. lschultz@netins.net
www.rsprussia.com

International Club for Collectors of Hatpins and Hatpin Holders (ICC of H&HH)
Audrae Heath, Managing Editor
PO Box 1009, Bonners Ferry, ID 83805-1009; Bimonthly *Points* newsletter and *Pictorial Journal*

International Golliwog Collector Club
Beth Savino
PO Box 798; Holland, OH 43528; 1-800-862-TOYS or fax 419-473-3947.
toystorenet.com

International Ivory Society
Robert Weisblut, Co-Founder
5001 Old Ocean Blvd. #1, Ocean Ridge, FL 33435; 561-276-5657. Free membership

International Match Safe Association
Membership Chairman
PO Box 791; Malaga, NJ 08328; 856-694-4167. Membership: $50; quarterly newsletter and annual convention.
imsaoc@aol.com; www.matchsafe.org

International Nippon Collectors Club (INCC)
c/o Jennifer Cavedo, Membership chairperson
8363 Dusty Lane, Mechanicsville, VA 23116; Publishes newsletter 6 times a

year; holds annual convention; membership: $30.
www.nipponcollectors club.com

International Perfume and Scent Bottle Collectors Association
Randall Monsen
PO Box 529, Vienna, VA 22183 or fax 703-242-1357.
or Coleen Abbot
396 Croton Rd., Wayne, PA 19087-2038. Membership: $45 (USA) or $55 (Foreign); Newsletter published quarterly.
www.perfumebottles.org

International Rose O'Neill Club
Contact Karen Stewart
PO Box 668, Branson, MO 6561. Publishes quarterly newsletter *Kewpiesta Kourier*. Membership: (includes newsletter) $15 (single) or $20 (family). wisteriahs@excite.com
www.kewpieroseoneillclub.com

International Society of Antique Scale Collectors (ISASC)
Jan Macho, Executive Secretary
3616 Noakes St., Los Angeles, CA 90023; 323-263-6878. Publishes *Equilibrium* magazine; quarterly newsletter; annual membership directory and out-of-print scale catalogs; annual convention; Membership: $65; please include SASE when requesting information; please visit the ISASC website to learn more: www.isasc.org

International Vintage Poster Dealers Association (IVPDA)
Nancy Steinbock, Charter Member
800-438-1577. Specializing in posters.
info@ivpda.com; www.ivpda.com

John F. Rinaldi
Nautical Antiques and Related Items
Box 765, Dock Square, Kennebunkport, ME 04046; 207-967-3218; or fax 207-967-2918 (appt. only). Illustrated catalog: $5

Josef Originals Newsletter
Jim and Kaye Whitaker
PO Box 475, Dept. S, Lynnwood, WA 98046. Subscription (4 issues): $10 per year

Kate Greenaway Society
James Lewis Lowe
PO Box 8, Norwood, 19074
PostcardClassics@juno.com

Knife Rests of Yesterday and Today
Beverly L. Ales
4046 Graham St., Pleasanton, CA 94566-5619. Subscription: $20 per year for 6 issues

The Laughlin Eagle
Joan Jasper, Publisher
Richard Racheter, Editor
1270 63rd Terrace S., St. Petersburg,

FL 33705; 813-867-3982. Subscription: $18 (4 issues) per year; Sample: $4

Les Amis de Vieux Quimper (Friends of Old Quimper)
c/o Mark and Adela Meadows
PO Box 819, Carnelian Bay, CA 96140. SASE required for written reply. meadows@oldquimper.com
www.oldquimper.com

Liddle Kiddle Konvention
Paris Langford
415 Dodge Ave. Jefferson, LA 70121. Send SASE for information about upcoming Liddle Kiddle Convention, also send additional SASE for Liddle Kiddle Newsletter information.
bbean415@aol.com
liddlekiddlesnewsletter@yahoo.com; www.vintageland.com/liddle_kiddles_convention.htm

Central Florida Insulator Collectors
Line Jewels, NIA #1380
3557 Nicklaus Dr., Titusville, FL 32780

Majolica International Society
Michael Foley, Membership Chairman
77 Wright St., New Bedford, MA 02740. Membership: $40 per year, includes annual meeting and quarterly newsletter *Majolica Matters*. www. majolicasociety.com

Marble Collectors' Society of America
PO Box 222, Trumbull, CT 06611. Publishes *Marble Mania*; Gathers and disseminates information to further the hobby of marbles and marble collecting; $12 adds your name to the contributor mailing list ($21 covers 2 years).
BlockMCSA@aol.com
www.blocksite.com

Marble Collectors Unlimited
PO Box 206, Northboro, MA 01532

Midwest Open Salt Society
c/o Ed Bowman
2411 W. 500 North, Hartford City, IN 47348. Dues: $10 ($6 for spouse)

Midwest Sad Iron Collector Club
Bruce Baumunk
6903 Singing Wood Lane, St. Louis MO 63129; 314-846-9573. Membership: $30 per year.
bruce.baumunk@gte.net
www.irons.com/msicc.htm

Murray Hudson Antiquarian Books, Maps & Globes
109 S. Church St., Box 163, Halls, TN 38040; 800-748-9946 or 731-836-9057; fax 731-836-9017. Buyer and seller specializing in antique maps, globes, and books with maps: atlases,

explorations, travel guides, geographies, surveys, etc.; largest ever catalog of Civil War maps and graphics; largest selection of wall maps and world globes; contact for catalog. mapman@ecis.com

Mystic Lights of the Aladdin Knights, bimonthly newsletter
c/o J.W. Courter
3935 Kelley Rd., Kevil, KY 40253-9532; 270-488-2116. Information and free 8-page *History of the Aladdin Lamp* requires LSASE.
www.aladdinknights.org

National Association of Avon Collectors
c/o Connie Clark
6100 Walnut, Dept. P, Kansas City, MO 64113. Information requires LSASE.

National Association of Breweriana Advertising (NABA)
Publishes *The Breweriana Collector*; Holds annual convention; membership information and directory available on www.nababrew.org

National Association of Warwick China and Pottery Collectors
Betty June Wymer
28 Bachmann Drive, Wheeling, WV 26003; 304-232-3031. Annual dues $15 (single) or $20 (couple), checks payable to NAWCPA; publishes quarterly newsletter; holds annual convention in Wheeling, West Virginia

National Autumn Leaf Collectors' Club
Bill Swanson, President
807 Roaring Springs Dr., Allen, TX 75002-2112; 972-727-5527 or fax 972-727-2107. bescom@nalcc.org
or Gwynne Harrison
PO Box 1, Mira Loma, CA 91752-0001; 909-685-5434 or fax 909-681-1692. Membership: $20, payable to NALCC, c/o Dianna Kowales, PO Box 900968, Palmdale, CA 93590-0968.
morgan99@pe.net; www.nalcc.org

National Blue Ridge Newsletter
Norma Lilly
144 Highland Dr., Blountville, TN 37617. Subscription: $15 per year (6 issues)

National Cambridge Collectors, Inc.
PO Box 416, Cambridge, OH 43725-0416; 740-432-4245 or fax 740-439-9223. Membership: $20 (Associate member: $3).
NCC-Crystal-Ball@ compuserve.com
www.Cambridgeglass.org

National Cuff Link Society
c/o Eugene R. Klompus
PO Box 5970, Vernon Hills, IL 60061; Phone/fax: 847-816-0035. $30 annual dues includes subscription to *The Link*, a quarterly magazine; write for free

booklet *The Fun of Cuff Link Collecting*.
genek@cufflinksrus.com or
ncls@bellsouth.net; www.cufflink.com;

National Depression Glass Association
PO Box, 8264, Wichita, KS 67208-0264. Publishs *News and Views*; Membership: $20 (individual); $5 (associate). www.ndga.net

National Fenton Glass Society
PO Box 4008, Marietta, OH 45750; 740-374-3345; fax 740-376-9708. Membership: $20, includes *The Fenton Flyer* newsletter

National Graniteware Society
PO Box 9248, Cedar Rapids, IA 52409-9248; Membership: $20.
www.graniteware.org

National Greentown Glass Association
PO Box 107, Greentown, IN 46936; Membership: $20.
www.eastern.k12.in.us/gpl/glassass.htm

National Imperial Glass Collectors' Society, Inc.
PO Box 534, Bellaire, OH 43906. Membership: $18 per year (+$3 for each associate member); quarterly newsletter; convention every June info@nigcs.org; www.imperialglass.org

National Insulator Association
1315 Old Mill Path, Broadview Heights, OH 44147. Membership: $12.
kwjacob@uswest.net; www.nia.org

National Milk Glass Collectors' Society and *Opaque News*, quarterly newsletter
Membership: $18 (payable to club)
Barb Pinkston, Membership Chairman
9238 E. Kenosha Ct., Floral City, FL 34436-2438 (Please include SASE).
membership@nmgsc.org
www.nmgcs.org

National Reamer Collectors Association
c/o Debbie Gillham
47 Midline Ct., Gaithersburg, MD 20878; Membership: $25 per household. reamers@erols.com
www.reamers.org

National Shaving Mug Collectors Association
Anise Alkin, Membership
544 Line Rd., Hazlett, NJ 07739. To stimulate the study, collection, and preservation of shaving mugs and all related barbering items; provides quarterly newsletter, bibliography, and directory; holds 2 meetings per year; dues: $25 per year. info@nsma.org
www.nsmca.org

National Shelley China Club
Rochelle Hart, Secretary/Treasurer
591 West 67th Ave., Anchorage, AK 99518-1555; 907-344-9123. Member-

ship: $35 per year, 4 quarterly newsletters plus many other benefits and publications. imahart@alaska.net.
www.nationalshelleychinaclub.com

National Toothpick Holder Collectors Society
Membership Chairperson
PO Box 852, Archer City, TX 76351. Dues: $20 (single) or $25 (couple); Forein dues: $23 (single) or $28 (couple) in US dollars; Includes 10 *Toothpick Bulletin* newsletters per year; annual convention held in August; exclusive toothpick holder annually.
tpinfo@glass-works.com
www.tias.com/collectoronline/NTHCS

National Valentine Collectors Association
Nancy Rosin
PO Box 1404, Santa Ana, CA 92702; 714-547-1355. Membership: $16; Specializing in Valentines and love tokens

New England Society of Open Salt Collectors
Chuck Keys
21 Overbrook Lane, East Greenwich, RI 02818; Dues: $7 per year

Newspaper Collector's Society of America
Rick Brown
Lansing, MI, 517-887-1255. An extensive, searchable, 300,000-word reference library of American history with an emphasis on newspapers publishing speeches; interactive crossword puzzles; regular auctions of ephemera, historic documents, and newspapers; a mall with over one hundred different online catalogs of paper collectibles; and much, much more!
help@historybuff.com
www.history buff.com

Night Light Club/Newsletter
Culver, Bob
3081 Sand Pebble Cove, Pinckney, MI 48169. Specializing in miniature oil lamps; Membership: $15 per year

NM (Nelson McCoy) Express
Carol Seman, Editor
8934 Brecksville Rd., Suite 406, Brecksville, OH 44141-2318; 440-526-2094 (voice & fax). Membership: $26 per year (12 issues).
McCjs@aol.com
www.members.aol.com/nmXpress/

North American Torquay Society
Jerry and Gerry Kline, 2 of the Founding Members
604 Orchard View Dr., Maumee, OH 43537. Send SASE for information.

North American Trap Collectors' Association
c/o Tom Parr
PO Box 94, Galloway, OH 43119-0094. Dues: $25 per year; Publishes bimonthly newsletter

North Dakota Pottery Collectors Society and Newsletter
c/o Sandy Short, Membership Chairman Box 14, Beach, ND 58621. Membership: $15 (includes spouse); Annual convention in June; Quarterly newsletters. csshortnd@mcn.net www.ndpcs.org

Novelty Salt & Pepper Shakers Club
Louise Davis
PO Box 416, Gladstone, OR 72037-0416. Publishes quarterly newsletter; Holds annual convention; Dues: $30 per year in US, Canada and Mexico ($5 extra for couple). dmac925@yahoo.com

Nutcracker Collectors' Club and Newsletter
Susan Otto, Editor
12204 Fox Run Dr., Chesterland, OH 44026; 440-729-2686;. Membership: $15 ($20 foreign) includes quarterly newsletters, free classifieds. nutsue@core.com

The Occupied Japan Club
c/o Florence Archambault
29 Freeborn St., Newport, RI 02840-1821. Publishes *The Upside Down World of an O.J. Collector*, a bimonthly newsletter. Information requires SASE. florence@aiconnect.com

Old Sleepy Eye Collectors Club of America, Inc.
PO Box 12, Monmouth, IL 6146. Membership: $10 per year with additional $1 for spouse (if joining). oseclub@maplecity.com www.maplecity.com/~MARKoseclub/

Old Stuff
Donna and Ron Miller, Publishers
PO Box 449, McMinnville, OR 97128. Published 6 times annually; Copies by mail: $3.50 each; Annual subscription: $20 ($30 in Canada). millers@oldstuffnews.com www.oldstuffnews.com

On the LIGHTER Side Newsletter (bimonthly publication)
International Lighter Collectors
Judith Sanders, Editor
PO Box 1733, Quitman, TX 75783-1733; 903-763-2795 or fax 903-763-4953. Annual convention held in US; Subscription: $43 (overseas) $38 (US and Canada), $30 (Senior member); $25 (Junior member); please include SASE when requesting information

Open Salt Collectors of the Atlantic Regions (O.S.C.A.R.)
Wilbur Rudisill, Treasurer
1844 York Rd., Gettysburg, PA 17325. Dues: $5 per year

Open Salt Seekers of the West, North-ern California Chapter

Sara Conley
84 Margaret Dr., Walnut Creek, CA 94596; Dues: $7 per year

Open Salt Seekers of the West, Southern California Chapter
Janet Hudson
2525 E. Vassar Court, Visalia, CA 93277. Dues: $5 per year

Pacific Northwest Fenton Association
PO Box 881, Tillamook, OR 97141; 503-842-4815. Newsletter subscription: $23 per year (published quarterly, includes annual piece of glass made only for subscribers). jshirley@oregoncoast.com www.glasscastle.com/pnwfa.htm

Paden City Glass Collectors Guild
Paul Torsiello, Editor
42 Aldine Road, Parsippany, NJ, 07054. Publishes newsletter; for subscription information e-mail: pcguild1@yahoo.com

Paper Collectors' Marketplace
PO Box 128, Scandinavia, WI 54977-0128; 715-467-2379 or fax 715-467-2243. Subscription: $19.95 in US (12 issues). pcmpaper@gglbbs.com www.pcmpaper.com

Paper Pile Quarterly Magazine
Ada Fitzsimmons, Editor
PO Box 337, San Anselmo, CA 94979; 415-454-5552 or fax 415-454-2947. Sales and features magazine for paper buyers and sellers since 1980. Quarterly cataloged sales of paper items, large for-sale and wanted sections, auction results, book reviews, quarterly price guide and show schedule; Subscription: $20 per year (shipped 1st class); sample: $5 (returnable as credit toward subscription or advertising).
apaperpile@aol.com www.papercollectibles.com

Paperweight Collectors' Association, Inc.
PMB 130, 274 Eastchester Dr. #117, High Point, NC 27262. 336-869-2769. Sustaining US membership $55 per year (non-US: $35), includes quarterly *PCA Inc. Annual Bulletin* newsletter; biannual convention. info@paperweight.org

Peanut Pals
Judith Walthall, Founder
PO Box 4465, Huntsville, AL 35815; 205-881-9198. Associated collectors of Planters Peanuts memorabilia, bimonthly newsletter *Peanut Papers*; annual directory sent to members; annual convention and regional conventions; primary membership: $20 per year (associate memberships available); membership information: 246 Old Line

Ave., Laurel, MD 20724, or check w/peanutpals.org; sample newsletter: $2

Pen Collectors of America
Bob Nurin, Treasurer
PO Box 80, Redding Ridge, CT 06876. Quarterly newsletter, *Pennant*; annual membership: $30 in US and Canada (includes newsletter and access to reference library). ship@pencollectors.com www.pencollectors.com

Pepsi-Cola Collectors Club Express
Bob Stoddard, Editor
PO Box 817; Claremont, CA 91711-0817

Perrault-Rago Gallery
333 N. Main St., Lambertville, NJ 08530; 609-397-9374. Specializing in 20th-century decorative arts, particularly art pottery and decorative tiles. ragoarts@aol.com

Petroleum Collectibles Monthly
Scott Benjamin and Wayne Henderson, Publishers
PO Box 556, LaGrange, OH 44050-0556; 440-355-6608. Subscription: $35.95 per year US, Canada $44.50, international $71.95, samples $5; 10th year in publication with 2,000 subscribers. Scott advises Gasoline Globes and is devoted to gas and oil collectibles. www.pcmpublishing.com

Phoenix and Consolidated Glass Collectors' Club
Tom Jiamachello, Secretary
41 River View Drive, Essex Junction, VT 05452; 802-878-2682. Membership: $25 (single), $35 (family) per year. Please make checks payable to club. TOPofVT@aol.com home.earthlink.net/~dwilson1

Phoenix Bird Collectors of America (PBCA)
1107 Deerfield Lane, Marshall, MI 49068; 269-781-9791. Membership: (payable to Joan Oates) $12 per year, includes *Phoenix Bird Discoveries*, published 2 times a year; Also available: 1996 Updated Value Guide to be used in conjunction with Books I – IV; now $4.45 ppd; newly cataloged Phoenix Bird since Book IV of 1989, Book Five, published January, 2002, $17.95 + $1.55 postage, 96 pages (32 in color). koates120@earthlink.net

Pickard Collectors Club, Ltd.
Membership office: 300 E. Grove St., Bloomington, IL 61701; 309-828-5533 or fax 309-829-2266. Membership (includes newsletter): $30 a year (single) or $40 (family). www.pickard collectors.org

Pie Birds Unlimited Club & Newsletter
Kathy LoBello
1039 NW Hwy. 101, Lincoln City, OR 97367

Political Collectors of Indiana Club
Michael McQuillen
PO Box 50022, Indianapolis, IN 46250-0022; 317-845-1721; Official APIC (American Political Items Collectors) Chapter comprised of over 300 collectors of presidential and local political items. michael@politicalparade.com www.political parade.com

Porcelain Collector's Companion
c/o Dorothy Kamm
PO Box 7460, Port St. Lucie, FL 34985-4760; 561-464-4008 or fax 561-460-9050

Posner, Judy and Jeff
Specializing in Disneyana, Black memorabilia, salt and pepper shakers, souvenirs of the USA, character and advertising memorabilia and figural pottery. Visit our store at: www.judyposner.com

Powder Puff Compact Collectors' Chronicle
Roselyn Gerson
PO Box 40, Lynbrook, NY 11563; 516-593-8746 or fax 516-593-0610. Author of six books related to figural compacts, vanity bags/purses, solid perfumes, lipsticks, and related gadgetry. compactlady@aol.com

The Prize Insider Newsletter for Cracker Jack Collectors
Larry White
108 Central St., Rowley, MA 01969; 508-948-8187; larrydw@erols.com or Theresa Richter, membership chairperson 5469 S. Dorchester Ave., Chicago, IL 60615; Club membership: $20 (US), $24 (US family); $25 (Canada) www.collectoronline.com/CJCA

Purinton News & Views
Joe McManus, Editor
PO Box 153, Connellsville, PA 15425. Newsletter for Purinton pottery enthusiasts; subscription: $16 per year

R.A. Fox Collector's Club
c/o Pat Gibson
38280 Guava Dr., Newark, CA, 94560; 510-792-0586

Ribbon Tin News Newsletter (quarterly publication)
Hobart D. Van Deusen, Editor
28 The Green, Watertown, CT 06795; 860-945-3456. $30 per year for 24+ color plates. For collectors of typewriters, typewriter ribbon tins, and go-withs. Indexed subscribers' list and participation in occasional mail/phone auctions. rtn.hoby@world net.att.net

Rose Bowl Collectors
Johanna S. Billings, Co-Founder
P.O. Box 244; Danielsville, PA 18038-
0244; 610-261-4775 or fax 610-261-
4782. Issues quarterly newsletter.
bankie@concentric.net

Rosevilles of the Past Newsletter
Nancy Bomm, Editor
PO Box 656, Clarcona, FL 32710-
0656; 407-294-3980 or fax 407-294-
7836. $19.95 per year for 6 newsletters.
rosepast@worldnet.att.net.

Saint Patrick Notes Newsletter
Chuck Thompson, Editor
10802 Greencreek Dr., Suite 203,
Houston, TX 77070-5365. For everyone interested in the legends, myths,
and lore of this great missionary. This
free publication is also of interest to
collectors of St. Patrick cards and
memorabilia. New issues every March.
Requests filled all year. To receive a
copy, send name and address with 2
postage stamps.

Schoenhut Collectors Club
c/o Pat Girbach, Secretary
1003 W. Huron St., Ann Arbor, MI
48103-4217 for membership information

Shawnee Pottery Collectors' Club
PO Box 713, New Smyrna Beach, FL
32170-0713. Monthly nation-wide
newsletter. SASE (c/o Pamela Curran)
required when requesting information;
$3 for sample of current newsletter

Shot Glass Exchange
PO Box 219, Western Springs, IL
60558; 708-246-1559. Primarily preprohibition glasses. Subscription:
(includes 2 semi-annual issues, available in US only) $13 per year, single
copy $8

Society of Inkwell Collectors
PO Box 324, Missville, IL, 61552. Membership: $35 per year, includes subscrip-
tion to *The Stained Finger*, a quarterly
publication. membership@soic.com
www.soic.com

Southern California Marble Club
18361-1 Strothern St., Reseda, CA
91335

Southern Folk Pottery Collectors Society
quarterly newsletter
Society headquarters: 220 Washington
St., Bennett, NC 27208; 336-581-
4246; fax 336-581-4247 (Wednesday
through Saturday, 10:00 to 5:00). Specializing in historical research and
documentation, education and promotion of the traditional southern folk
potter (past and present) to a modern
collecting audience. Membership dues
includes biannual absentee auction
catalogs (at discounted prices), access

to member pieces, opportunities to
meet potters, participate in events,
newsletter information, various print-
ings, and more. The society auctions
represent three centuries of productions from all of the states of the
American south. The bi-annual absentee auctions are structured in a one of
a kind personalized format of sales that
benefits both the seller and buyer to
the utmost. A fully illustrated catalog
accompanies web sale with extensive
biographies of the potters and regions,
along with rare photographs. For more
information contact the society.
sfpcs@rtmc.net

Southern Oregon Antiques & Collectibles Club
PO Box 508, Talent, OR 97540; 541-
535-1231 or fax 541-535-5109. Meets
1st Wednesday of the month; Promotes
2 shows a year in Medford, OR.
contact@soacc.com; www.soacc.com

Stangl/Fulper Collectors Club
PO Box 538, Flemington, NJ 08822.
Yearly membership: $25 (includes
quarterly newsletter); annual auction
in June; American pottery and dinnerware show and sale in October.
www.stanglfulper.com

Still Bank Collectors Club of America
c/o Larry Egelhoff
4175 Millersville Rd., Indianapolis, IN
46205. Membership: $35.
egelhoffl@juno.com
www.stillbank club.com

Stretch Glass Society
Membership: $22 (US) or $24 (US
currency in Canada); Quarterly
newsletter with color photos; annual
spring convention.
members@aol. com/stretchgl

Style: 1900 and Modernism
David Rago
333 N. Main St., Lambertville, 08530;
609-397-4104

The Tanner Restraints Collection
6442 Canyon Creek Way, Elk Grove,
CA 95758-5431; 916-684-4006. 40-
page catalog of magician/escape artist
equipment from trick and regulation
padlocks, handcuffs, leg shackles and
straight jackets to picks and pick sets;
books on all of the above and much
more; catalog: $3

Tarrant, Jenny
Holly Daze Antiques
4 Gardenview, St. Peters, MO 63376.
Specializing in Halloween, Christmas,
Easter, etc.; buying & selling Halloween and holiday items; antique
holiday for sale; Jennyjol@aol.com
www.holly-days.com

Tea Leaf Club International
Maxine Johnson, Membership Chairman
PO Box 377, Belton, MO 64012. Publishes *Tea Leaf Readings* Newsletter;
Membership: $30 per household (up to
2 members); www.tealeafclub.com

Tea Talk
Tina M. Carter, Teapot Columnist
Diana Rosen/Lucy Roman, Editors
PO Box 860, Sausalito, CA 94966;
415-331-1557. teatalk@ aol.com

The TeaTime Gazette
Linda Ashley Leamer
PO Box 40276, St. Paul, MN 55104.
Subscription: $18 (US), $24 (Cana-
da). info@teatimegazette.com
www.teatimegazette.com

THCKK
The Hardware Companies Kollector's
Klub
For information contact Jerry Heuring,
28450 US Highway 61, Scott City,
MO 63780; 573-264-3947. Member-
ship: $20 per year.
jheuring@charter.net
WWW. THCKK.ORG

Thermometer Collectors' Club of
America
Richard Porter, Vice President
PO Box 944, Onset, MA 02558; 508-
295-4405. Visit the Porter Thermometer Museum (world's only, always
open) free with 3,800+ thermometers
to see. Appraisals, repairs, and traveling lecture (600 given, ages 8 – 98, all
venues)

Thimble Collectors International
Tina Samulka, Membership Chairperson
316 Parkwood Rd., Vestal, NY 13850-
1252: Membership: $25 (US), $30
(International).
www.thimblecollectors. com

Three Rivers Depression Era Glass
Society
Meetings held 1st Monday of each
month at 6:00 p.m. at DeMartino's
Restaurant, Carnegie, PA
For more information call: D. Hennen,
3725 Sylvan Rd., Bethel Park, PA
15102; 412-835-1903.
leasure@pulsenet.com

Tiffin Glass Collectors
PO Box 554, Tiffin, OH 44883. Meetings at Seneca County Museum on
2nd Tuesday of each month; Tiffin
Glass Museum, 25 S. Washington, Tiffin, OH, Wednesday – Sunday from
1:00 p.m. – 5:00 p.m.; Membership:
$15; www.tiffinglass.org

Tins 'n Signs
Box 440101, Aurora, CO 80044. Subscription: $25 per year

Toaster Collector Association
PO Box 485, Redding Ridge, CT
06876. Membership: $30.
www.toastercollector.com

Tops & Bottoms Club (Rene Lalique
perfumes only)
c/o Madeleine France
9 N. Federal Highway, Dania Beach,
FL 33004

Toy Shop
Mark Williams, Publisher
700 E. State St., Iola, WI 54990-0001;
715-445-2214 or fax 715-445-4087.
Subscription $33.98 (26 issues) in US.
www.toyshopmag.com

Trick or Treat Trader
PO Box 499, Winchester, NH 03470;
603-239-8875. Subscription: $15 (4
issues). halloweenqueen@cheshire.net
www.userpages.cheshire/net~
halloween queen/home.htmw

TW List (Typewriters)
Rich Cincotta
PO Box 286, Southboro, MA 01772;
508-229-2064.
typewriters@ writeme.com
www.typewriter.rydia.net/etcetera.htm

Uhl Collectors' Society
3704 W. Old Rd. 64, Huntingburg, IN
47542. Membership: $15 per family
kuglerhome@psci.net
Dave and Donna Swick, Newsletter
506 Martin St., Newton, IL 62488;
618-783-3455; www.uhlcollectors.org

Vaseline Glass Collectors, Inc.
Squeaker Bootsma, Secretary
14560 Schleisman, Corona, CA
92880. An organization whose sole
purpose is to unify vaseline glass collectors; newsletter *Glowing Report* published bimonthly; convention held
annually. Membership: $25.
www. vaselineglass.org

Vetri: Italian Glass News
Howard Lockwood, Publisher
PO Box 191, Fort Lee, NJ 07024; 201-
969-0373. Quarterly newsletter about
20th-century Italian glass

Vintage Fashion & Costume Jewelry
Newsletter/Club
PO Box 265, Glen Oaks, NY 11004;
718-939-3095 or fax 718-939-7988.
Subscription (4 issues): $20 US, $25
Canada, $25 International. Back
issues available at $5 each.
vfck@aol.com; www.lizjewel.com/VF

Vintage TVs
Harry Poster
Box 1883, S. Hackensack, 07606; 201-
794-9606. Specializes in vintage TVs,
vintage radios, stereo cameras; catalog.
www.harryposter.com

The Wade Watch
Wade Watch Ltd.
8199 Pierson Ct., Arvada, CO 80005;
303-421-9655 or 303-424-4401; fax
303-421-0317. Year's subscription (4
issues): $10 (US); $16 (International);
articles and photos welcome, but if to
be returned, enclose SASE.
wadewatch@wadewatch.com
www.wadewatch.com

Walking Stick Notes
Marilyn Vlahos, Editor
2611 Catalpa Ave., Pascagoula, MS
39567-1806. Please write to Marilyn
Vlahos at the above address for information about her publication plans.

The Wallace Nutting Collector's Club
PO Box 22475, Beachwood, OH
44122. Membership: $20; Established
in 1973, holds annual conventions,
usually in the northeastern portion of
the country; generally recognized
national center of Wallace Nutting-
like activity are Michael Ivankovich's
Wallace Nutting & Wallace Nutting-
like Specialty Auctions, held 4 times
each year. These auctions provide the
opportunity for collectors and dealers
to compete for the largest variety of
Wallace Nutting and Wallace Nut-

ting-like pictures available anywhere.
These auctions also give sellers the
opportunity to place their items in
front of the country's leading enthusiasts. When writing for information
please include a close-up photograph
which includes the picture's frame and
a SASE. www.wallacenutting.org
www.wallacenutting.com

Warwick China Collectors Club
Pat and Don Hoffmann, Sr.
1291 N. Elmwood Dr., Aurora, IL
60506-1309; 630-859-3435.
warwick@ntsource.com

Watt Collectors' Association
Watt's News Newsletter, for Watt pottery enthusiasts
1431 4th St., SW, MPB221, Mason City,
IA 50401; Membership includes quarterly newsletter) $20; annual convention

Wave Crest Collectors Club
c/o Whitney Newland
PO Box 2013, Santa Barbara, CA
93120. Membership dues: $25
(includes quarterly newsletter); annual
convention. whntique@gte.net

The Wedgwood Society of New York
5 Dogwood Court, Glen Head, NY

11545; 516-626-3427. Membership:
$30 (single) or $35 (family). Publishes
newsletter (6 times per year) and a
scholarly magazine, *Ars Ceramica*, of
original articles published by the society; 6 meetings per year. www.wsny.org

Westmoreland Glass Collector's Newsletter
PO Box 143, North Liberty, IA 52317.
Subscription: $16 per year. This publica-
tion is dedicated to the purpose of preserving Westmoreland Glass and its history.

Westmoreland Glass Society
Steve Jensen
PO Box PO Box 2883, Iowa City, IA
52240-2883. Membership: $15 (single)
or $25 (household).
www.westmorelandglassclubs.org/
nwgsi_mem.html

The Wheelmen
Membership can be organized from
the link below; 4 newsletters, 2 magazines, membership card & directory
listing are $25 for single applicant.
www.thewheelmen.com

The Whimsey Club
c/o Lon Knickerbocker
PO Box 312, Danville, NY, 14437.
Whimsical Notions, quarterly newslet-

ter with colored photos; dues: $10 per
year; annual get together.
mountainmonster@mountain.net
www.whimsey.org

The White Ironstone China Association, Inc.
Diane Dorman, Membership Chairman
PO Box 855, Fairport, NY 14450-
0855. Newsletter available for: $25
(single) or $30 (2 individuals at same
address); www.whiteironstone.com

Willow Review
PO Box 41312, Nashville, TN 37204.
Send SASE for information.

World's Fair Collectors' Society, Inc.
Fair News Newsletter (bimonthly publication for members)
Michael R. Pender, Editor
PO Box 20806, Sarasota, FL 34276-
3806; 941-923-2590. Dues: $20 (US),
$25 (Canada), $30 (overseas).
wfcs@aol.com

The Zsolnay Store
152 Spring St., Newport, RI 02840;
401-841-5060. Zsolnay book available.
www.drawrm.com

Schroeder's Collectible TOYS Antique to Modern Price Guide

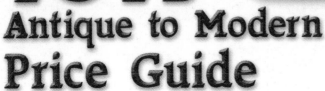

2004

OUR #1 BESTSELLING TOY BOOK NINTH EDITION

#6340 ◆ 8½ x 11 ◆ 496 pgs. ◆ PB ◆ $17.95

OUR #1 BESTSELLING TOY BOOK!

◆ The #1 book the toy field has to offer!
◆ Identification and values of over 20,000 collectible toys of all kinds, from antique to modern.
◆ All-new ninth edition with expanded categories and advisory board.
◆ Features categories including action figures, cast-iron and paper lithographed toys as well as windups, Barbie® dolls, games, character collectibles from the early days of radio and TV, and much more!
◆ Easy-to-use format puts buyers in touch with sellers, magazines, clubs, and newsletters that cover specific fields of collector interest.

Informing Today's Collector

COLLECTOR BOOKS

P.O. Box 3009
Paducah, KY 42002-3009

to place an order or for a
complete listing of our books

1-800-626-5420

7am – 5pm, Mon. – Fri. CT
FAX 1-270-898-8890

www.collectorbooks.com